Official Tournament and Club Word List

2014 Edition

Official Tournament and Club Word List

2014 Edition

Merriam-Webster, Incorporated

Springfield, Massachusetts

Cover designed by Jeremy Hildebrand

ISBN: 978-0-87779-646-6

Made in the United States of America

1st printing Quad Graphics, Fairfield, PA 2014 Jouve

PREFACE

This Official Tournament and Club Word List is derived from *The Official SCRABBLE Players Dictionary, Fifth Edition,* and supplemented with 9- to 15-letter words compiled using similar methods. This word list has been prepared for use solely as a quick reference for competitive play sanctioned by the North American SCRABBLE Players Association.

This list contains words only, no definitions or part-of-speech labels, and includes all inflected forms of up to 15 letters spelled out in full. This list contains words that are excluded from *The Official SCRABBLE Players Dictionary,* such as some usually capitalized trademarks labelled in a standard dictionary as having some lowercase use. No entry in this word list, however, should be regarded as affecting the validity of any trademark or service mark. This list also includes qualified words that are considered offensive, and therefore may be inappropriate for family use.

This book is not intended to replace *The Official SCRABBLE Players Dictionary* or any other dictionary preferred by players as a final reference, but it does represent, as of the date of the copyright, the most up-to-date revisions in *The Official SCRABBLE Players Dictionary.*

North American SCRABBLE Players Association

Every letter counts in SCRABBLE, the classic word game with the iconic gameboard.

And every word that counts is right here in *The Official Tournament and Club Word List* by Merriam-Webster. The SCRABBLE game has always been a case of "your word against mine," and when you go for a challenge, you want to be sure you're not going to be the player to lose their turn!

The game of SCRABBLE might be seen by some as just a little friendly competition, but to win, you've got to choose your words and your spaces very carefully to get those high scores. Look for hooks, shuffle the tiles on your rack and use your letters well. You've come to the right place for an addictive and competitive challenge! May the best words win!

For more information on all things SCRABBLE, go to Hasbro.com/Scrabble.

Consumer contact: Hasbro Games, Consumer Affairs Dept., P.O. Box 200, Pawtucket, RI 02861-1059 USA. Tel: 888-836-7025.

The Official Tournament and Club Word List
is an official publication of the North American
SCRABBLE Players Association (NASPA).

NASPA is a community of tournament, club and avid home players of the SCRABBLE Brand Crossword Game. We foster an atmosphere for people of all skill levels to play their favorite game, improve their abilities and above all, meet people who share a similar love of the game. For more information about our clubs, tournaments and other activities, please find us on Facebook (scrbblplyrs) or Twitter (@NASPA), or contact us at:

NASPA, PO Box 12115
Dallas, TX 75225-0115
info@scrabbleplayers.org
www.scrabbleplayers.org

A

AA
AAH
AAHED
AAHING
AAHS
AAL
AALII
AALIIS
AALS
AARDVARK
AARDVARKS
AARDWOLF
AARDWOLVES
AARGH
AARRGH
AARRGHH
AAS
AASVOGEL
AASVOGELS
AB
ABA
ABACA
ABACAS
ABACI
ABACK
ABACTERIAL
ABACUS
ABACUSES
ABAFT
ABAKA
ABAKAS
ABALONE
ABALONES
ABAMP
ABAMPERE
ABAMPERES
ABAMPS
ABANDON
ABANDONED
ABANDONER
ABANDONERS
ABANDONING
ABANDONMENT
ABANDONMENTS
ABANDONS
ABAPICAL
ABAS
ABASE
ABASED
ABASEDLY
ABASEMENT
ABASEMENTS
ABASER
ABASERS
ABASES
ABASH
ABASHED
ABASHEDLY
ABASHES
ABASHING
ABASHMENT
ABASHMENTS
ABASIA
ABASIAS
ABASING
ABATABLE
ABATE
ABATED
ABATEMENT
ABATEMENTS
ABATER
ABATERS
ABATES
ABATING
ABATIS
ABATISES
ABATOR
ABATORS
ABATTIS
ABATTISES
ABATTOIR
ABATTOIRS
ABAXIAL
ABAXILE
ABAYA
ABAYAS
ABBA
ABBACIES
ABBACY
ABBAS
ABBATIAL
ABBE
ABBES
ABBESS
ABBESSES
ABBEY
ABBEYS
ABBOT
ABBOTCIES
ABBOTCY
ABBOTS
ABBOTSHIP
ABBOTSHIPS
ABBREVIATE
ABBREVIATED
ABBREVIATES
ABBREVIATING
ABBREVIATION
ABBREVIATIONS
ABBREVIATOR
ABBREVIATORS
ABCOULOMB
ABCOULOMBS
ABDICABLE
ABDICATE
ABDICATED
ABDICATES
ABDICATING
ABDICATION
ABDICATIONS
ABDICATOR
ABDICATORS
ABDOMEN
ABDOMENS
ABDOMINA
ABDOMINAL
ABDOMINALLY
ABDOMINALS
ABDUCE
ABDUCED
ABDUCENS
ABDUCENT
ABDUCENTES
ABDUCES
ABDUCING
ABDUCT
ABDUCTED
ABDUCTEE
ABDUCTEES
ABDUCTING
ABDUCTION
ABDUCTIONS
ABDUCTOR
ABDUCTORES
ABDUCTORS
ABDUCTS
ABEAM
ABECEDARIAN
ABECEDARIANS
ABED
ABEGGING
ABELE
ABELES
ABELIA
ABELIAN
ABELIAS
ABELMOSK
ABELMOSKS
ABERRANCE
ABERRANCES
ABERRANCIES
ABERRANCY
ABERRANT
ABERRANTLY
ABERRANTS
ABERRATED
ABERRATION
ABERRATIONAL
ABERRATIONS
ABET
ABETMENT
ABETMENTS
ABETS
ABETTAL
ABETTALS
ABETTED
ABETTER
ABETTERS
ABETTING
ABETTOR
ABETTORS
ABEYANCE
ABEYANCES
ABEYANCIES
ABEYANCY
ABEYANT
ABFARAD
ABFARADS
ABHENRIES
ABHENRY
ABHENRYS
ABHOR
ABHORRED
ABHORRENCE
ABHORRENCES
ABHORRENT
ABHORRENTLY
ABHORRER
ABHORRERS
ABHORRING
ABHORS
ABIDANCE
ABIDANCES
ABIDE
ABIDED
ABIDER
ABIDERS
ABIDES
ABIDING
ABIDINGLY
ABIGAIL
ABIGAILS
ABILITIES
ABILITY
ABIOGENESES
ABIOGENESIS
ABIOGENIC
ABIOGENICALLY
ABIOGENIST
ABIOGENISTS
ABIOLOGICAL
ABIOSES
ABIOSIS
ABIOTIC
ABIOTICALLY
ABJECT
ABJECTION
ABJECTIONS
ABJECTLY
ABJECTNESS
ABJECTNESSES
ABJURATION
ABJURATIONS
ABJURE
ABJURED
ABJURER
ABJURERS
ABJURES
ABJURING
ABLATE
ABLATED
ABLATES
ABLATING
ABLATION
ABLATIONS
ABLATIVE
ABLATIVELY
ABLATIVES
ABLATOR
ABLATORS
ABLAUT
ABLAUTS
ABLAZE
ABLE
ABLED
ABLEGATE
ABLEGATES
ABLEISM
ABLEISMS
ABLEIST

ABLEISTS
ABLER
ABLES
ABLEST
ABLINGS
ABLINS
ABLOOM
ABLUENT
ABLUENTS
ABLUSH
ABLUTED
ABLUTION
ABLUTIONARY
ABLUTIONS
ABLY
ABMHO
ABMHOS
ABNEGATE
ABNEGATED
ABNEGATES
ABNEGATING
ABNEGATION
ABNEGATIONS
ABNEGATOR
ABNEGATORS
ABNORMAL
ABNORMALITIES
ABNORMALITY
ABNORMALLY
ABNORMALS
ABNORMITIES
ABNORMITY
ABO
ABOARD
ABODE
ABODED
ABODES
ABODING
ABOHM
ABOHMS
ABOIDEAU
ABOIDEAUS
ABOIDEAUX
ABOIL
ABOITEAU
ABOITEAUS
ABOITEAUX
ABOLISH
ABOLISHABLE
ABOLISHED
ABOLISHER
ABOLISHERS
ABOLISHES
ABOLISHING
ABOLISHMENT
ABOLISHMENTS
ABOLITION
ABOLITIONARY
ABOLITIONISM
ABOLITIONISMS
ABOLITIONIST
ABOLITIONISTS
ABOLITIONS
ABOLLA
ABOLLAE
ABOMA
ABOMAS
ABOMASA
ABOMASAL
ABOMASI
ABOMASUM
ABOMASUS
ABOMINABLE
ABOMINABLY
ABOMINATE
ABOMINATED
ABOMINATES
ABOMINATING
ABOMINATION
ABOMINATIONS
ABOMINATOR
ABOMINATORS
ABOON
ABORAL
ABORALLY
ABORIGINAL
ABORIGINALLY
ABORIGINALS
ABORIGINE
ABORIGINES
ABORNING
ABORT
ABORTED
ABORTER
ABORTERS
ABORTIFACIENT
ABORTIFACIENTS
ABORTING
ABORTION
ABORTIONIST
ABORTIONISTS
ABORTIONS
ABORTIVE
ABORTIVELY
ABORTIVENESS
ABORTIVENESSES
ABORTS
ABORTUS
ABORTUSES
ABOS
ABOUGHT
ABOULIA
ABOULIAS
ABOULIC
ABOUND
ABOUNDED
ABOUNDING
ABOUNDS
ABOUT
ABOVE
ABOVEBOARD
ABOVEGROUND
ABOVES
ABRACADABRA
ABRACADABRAS
ABRACHIA
ABRACHIAS
ABRADABLE
ABRADANT
ABRADANTS
ABRADE
ABRADED
ABRADER
ABRADERS
ABRADES
ABRADING
ABRASION
ABRASIONS
ABRASIVE
ABRASIVELY
ABRASIVENESS
ABRASIVENESSES
ABRASIVES
ABREACT
ABREACTED
ABREACTING
ABREACTION
ABREACTIONS
ABREACTS
ABREAST
ABRI
ABRIDGE
ABRIDGED
ABRIDGEMENT
ABRIDGEMENTS
ABRIDGER
ABRIDGERS
ABRIDGES
ABRIDGING
ABRIDGMENT
ABRIDGMENTS
ABRIS
ABROACH
ABROAD
ABROGABLE
ABROGATE
ABROGATED
ABROGATES
ABROGATING
ABROGATION
ABROGATIONS
ABROGATOR
ABROGATORS
ABROSIA
ABROSIAS
ABRUPT
ABRUPTER
ABRUPTEST
ABRUPTION
ABRUPTIONS
ABRUPTLY
ABRUPTNESS
ABRUPTNESSES
ABS
ABSCESS
ABSCESSED
ABSCESSES
ABSCESSING
ABSCISE
ABSCISED
ABSCISES
ABSCISIN
ABSCISING
ABSCISINS
ABSCISSA
ABSCISSAE
ABSCISSAS
ABSCISSION
ABSCISSIONS
ABSCOND
ABSCONDED
ABSCONDER
ABSCONDERS
ABSCONDING
ABSCONDS
ABSEIL
ABSEILED
ABSEILER
ABSEILERS
ABSEILING
ABSEILS
ABSENCE
ABSENCES
ABSENT
ABSENTED
ABSENTEE
ABSENTEEISM
ABSENTEEISMS
ABSENTEES
ABSENTER
ABSENTERS
ABSENTING
ABSENTLY
ABSENTMINDED
ABSENTMINDEDLY
ABSENTS
ABSINTH
ABSINTHE
ABSINTHES
ABSINTHS
ABSOLUTE
ABSOLUTELY
ABSOLUTENESS
ABSOLUTENESSES
ABSOLUTER
ABSOLUTES
ABSOLUTEST
ABSOLUTION
ABSOLUTIONS
ABSOLUTISM
ABSOLUTISMS
ABSOLUTIST
ABSOLUTISTIC
ABSOLUTISTS
ABSOLUTIVE
ABSOLUTIZE
ABSOLUTIZED
ABSOLUTIZES
ABSOLUTIZING
ABSOLVE
ABSOLVED
ABSOLVENT
ABSOLVENTS
ABSOLVER
ABSOLVERS
ABSOLVES
ABSOLVING
ABSONANT
ABSORB
ABSORBABILITIES
ABSORBABILITY
ABSORBABLE
ABSORBANCE
ABSORBANCES
ABSORBANCIES

ABSORBANCY
ABSORBANT
ABSORBANTS
ABSORBED
ABSORBENCIES
ABSORBENCY
ABSORBENT
ABSORBENTS
ABSORBER
ABSORBERS
ABSORBING
ABSORBINGLY
ABSORBS
ABSORPTANCE
ABSORPTANCES
ABSORPTIOMETRY
ABSORPTION
ABSORPTIONS
ABSORPTIVE
ABSORPTIVITIES
ABSORPTIVITY
ABSTAIN
ABSTAINED
ABSTAINER
ABSTAINERS
ABSTAINING
ABSTAINS
ABSTEMIOUS
ABSTEMIOUSLY
ABSTEMIOUSNESS
ABSTENTION
ABSTENTIONS
ABSTENTIOUS
ABSTERGE
ABSTERGED
ABSTERGES
ABSTERGING
ABSTINENCE
ABSTINENCES
ABSTINENT
ABSTINENTLY
ABSTRACT
ABSTRACTABLE
ABSTRACTED
ABSTRACTEDLY
ABSTRACTEDNESS
ABSTRACTER
ABSTRACTERS
ABSTRACTEST
ABSTRACTING
ABSTRACTION
ABSTRACTIONAL
ABSTRACTIONISM
ABSTRACTIONISMS
ABSTRACTIONIST
ABSTRACTIONISTS
ABSTRACTIONS
ABSTRACTIVE
ABSTRACTLY
ABSTRACTNESS
ABSTRACTNESSES
ABSTRACTOR
ABSTRACTORS
ABSTRACTS
ABSTRICT
ABSTRICTED
ABSTRICTING
ABSTRICTS
ABSTRUSE
ABSTRUSELY
ABSTRUSENESS
ABSTRUSENESSES
ABSTRUSER
ABSTRUSEST
ABSTRUSITIES
ABSTRUSITY
ABSURD
ABSURDER
ABSURDEST
ABSURDISM
ABSURDISMS
ABSURDIST
ABSURDISTS
ABSURDITIES
ABSURDITY
ABSURDLY
ABSURDNESS
ABSURDNESSES
ABSURDS
ABUBBLE
ABUILDING
ABULIA
ABULIAS
ABULIC
ABUNDANCE
ABUNDANCES
ABUNDANT
ABUNDANTLY
ABUSABLE
ABUSE
ABUSED
ABUSER
ABUSERS
ABUSES
ABUSING
ABUSIVE
ABUSIVELY
ABUSIVENESS
ABUSIVENESSES
ABUT
ABUTILON
ABUTILONS
ABUTMENT
ABUTMENTS
ABUTS
ABUTTAL
ABUTTALS
ABUTTED
ABUTTER
ABUTTERS
ABUTTING
ABUZZ
ABVOLT
ABVOLTS
ABWATT
ABWATTS
ABY
ABYE
ABYES
ABYING
ABYS
ABYSM
ABYSMAL
ABYSMALLY
ABYSMS
ABYSS
ABYSSAL
ABYSSES
ACACIA
ACACIAS
ACADEME
ACADEMES
ACADEMIA
ACADEMIAS
ACADEMIC
ACADEMICAL
ACADEMICALLY
ACADEMICIAN
ACADEMICIANS
ACADEMICISM
ACADEMICISMS
ACADEMICS
ACADEMIES
ACADEMISM
ACADEMISMS
ACADEMY
ACAI
ACAIS
ACAJOU
ACAJOUS
ACALEPH
ACALEPHAE
ACALEPHE
ACALEPHES
ACALEPHS
ACANTHA
ACANTHAE
ACANTHI
ACANTHINE
ACANTHOCEPHALAN
ACANTHOID
ACANTHOUS
ACANTHUS
ACANTHUSES
ACAPNIA
ACAPNIAS
ACARBOSE
ACARBOSES
ACARI
ACARIASES
ACARIASIS
ACARICIDAL
ACARICIDE
ACARICIDES
ACARID
ACARIDAN
ACARIDANS
ACARIDS
ACARINE
ACARINES
ACAROID
ACAROLOGIES
ACAROLOGY
ACARPOUS
ACARUS
ACATALECTIC
ACATALECTICS
ACAUDAL
ACAUDATE
ACAULESCENT
ACAULINE
ACAULOSE
ACAULOUS
ACCEDE
ACCEDED
ACCEDENCE
ACCEDENCES
ACCEDER
ACCEDERS
ACCEDES
ACCEDING
ACCELERANDO
ACCELERANDOS
ACCELERANT
ACCELERANTS
ACCELERATE
ACCELERATED
ACCELERATES
ACCELERATING
ACCELERATINGLY
ACCELERATION
ACCELERATIONS
ACCELERATIVE
ACCELERATOR
ACCELERATORS
ACCELEROMETER
ACCELEROMETERS
ACCENT
ACCENTED
ACCENTING
ACCENTLESS
ACCENTOR
ACCENTORS
ACCENTS
ACCENTUAL
ACCENTUALLY
ACCENTUATE
ACCENTUATED
ACCENTUATES
ACCENTUATING
ACCENTUATION
ACCENTUATIONS
ACCEPT
ACCEPTABILITIES
ACCEPTABILITY
ACCEPTABLE
ACCEPTABLENESS
ACCEPTABLY
ACCEPTANCE
ACCEPTANCES
ACCEPTANT
ACCEPTATION
ACCEPTATIONS
ACCEPTED
ACCEPTEDLY
ACCEPTEE
ACCEPTEES
ACCEPTER
ACCEPTERS
ACCEPTING
ACCEPTINGLY
ACCEPTINGNESS
ACCEPTINGNESSES
ACCEPTIVE
ACCEPTOR

ACCEPTORS
ACCEPTS
ACCESS
ACCESSARIES
ACCESSARY
ACCESSED
ACCESSES
ACCESSIBILITIES
ACCESSIBILITY
ACCESSIBLE
ACCESSIBLENESS
ACCESSIBLY
ACCESSING
ACCESSION
ACCESSIONAL
ACCESSIONED
ACCESSIONING
ACCESSIONS
ACCESSORIAL
ACCESSORIES
ACCESSORISE
ACCESSORISED
ACCESSORISES
ACCESSORISING
ACCESSORIZE
ACCESSORIZED
ACCESSORIZES
ACCESSORIZING
ACCESSORY
ACCIACCATURA
ACCIACCATURAS
ACCIDENCE
ACCIDENCES
ACCIDENT
ACCIDENTAL
ACCIDENTALLY
ACCIDENTALNESS
ACCIDENTALS
ACCIDENTLY
ACCIDENTS
ACCIDIA
ACCIDIAS
ACCIDIE
ACCIDIES
ACCIPITER
ACCIPITERS
ACCIPITRINE
ACCIPITRINES
ACCLAIM
ACCLAIMED
ACCLAIMER
ACCLAIMERS
ACCLAIMING
ACCLAIMS
ACCLAMATION
ACCLAMATIONS
ACCLIMATE
ACCLIMATED
ACCLIMATES
ACCLIMATING
ACCLIMATION
ACCLIMATIONS
ACCLIMATISATION
ACCLIMATISE
ACCLIMATISED
ACCLIMATISES
ACCLIMATISING
ACCLIMATIZATION
ACCLIMATIZE
ACCLIMATIZED
ACCLIMATIZER
ACCLIMATIZERS
ACCLIMATIZES
ACCLIMATIZING
ACCLIVITIES
ACCLIVITY
ACCLIVOUS
ACCOLADE
ACCOLADED
ACCOLADES
ACCOLADING
ACCOMMODATE
ACCOMMODATED
ACCOMMODATES
ACCOMMODATING
ACCOMMODATINGLY
ACCOMMODATION
ACCOMMODATIONAL
ACCOMMODATIONS
ACCOMMODATIVE
ACCOMMODATOR
ACCOMMODATORS
ACCOMPANIED
ACCOMPANIES
ACCOMPANIMENT
ACCOMPANIMENTAL
ACCOMPANIMENTS
ACCOMPANIST
ACCOMPANISTS
ACCOMPANY
ACCOMPANYING
ACCOMPLICE
ACCOMPLICES
ACCOMPLISH
ACCOMPLISHABLE
ACCOMPLISHED
ACCOMPLISHER
ACCOMPLISHERS
ACCOMPLISHES
ACCOMPLISHING
ACCOMPLISHMENT
ACCOMPLISHMENTS
ACCORD
ACCORDANCE
ACCORDANCES
ACCORDANT
ACCORDANTLY
ACCORDED
ACCORDER
ACCORDERS
ACCORDING
ACCORDINGLY
ACCORDION
ACCORDIONIST
ACCORDIONISTS
ACCORDIONS
ACCORDS
ACCOST
ACCOSTED
ACCOSTING
ACCOSTS
ACCOUCHEMENT
ACCOUCHEMENTS
ACCOUCHEUR
ACCOUCHEURS
ACCOUNT
ACCOUNTABILITY
ACCOUNTABLE
ACCOUNTABLENESS
ACCOUNTABLY
ACCOUNTANCIES
ACCOUNTANCY
ACCOUNTANT
ACCOUNTANTS
ACCOUNTANTSHIP
ACCOUNTANTSHIPS
ACCOUNTED
ACCOUNTING
ACCOUNTINGS
ACCOUNTS
ACCOUTER
ACCOUTERED
ACCOUTERING
ACCOUTERMENT
ACCOUTERMENTS
ACCOUTERS
ACCOUTRE
ACCOUTRED
ACCOUTREMENT
ACCOUTREMENTS
ACCOUTRES
ACCOUTRING
ACCREDIT
ACCREDITABLE
ACCREDITATION
ACCREDITATIONS
ACCREDITED
ACCREDITING
ACCREDITS
ACCRETE
ACCRETED
ACCRETES
ACCRETING
ACCRETION
ACCRETIONARY
ACCRETIONS
ACCRETIVE
ACCRUABLE
ACCRUAL
ACCRUALS
ACCRUE
ACCRUED
ACCRUEMENT
ACCRUEMENTS
ACCRUES
ACCRUING
ACCULTURATE
ACCULTURATED
ACCULTURATES
ACCULTURATING
ACCULTURATION
ACCULTURATIONAL
ACCULTURATIONS
ACCULTURATIVE
ACCUMBENT
ACCUMULATE
ACCUMULATED
ACCUMULATES
ACCUMULATING
ACCUMULATION
ACCUMULATIONS
ACCUMULATIVE
ACCUMULATIVELY
ACCUMULATOR
ACCUMULATORS
ACCURACIES
ACCURACY
ACCURATE
ACCURATELY
ACCURATENESS
ACCURATENESSES
ACCURSED
ACCURSEDLY
ACCURSEDNESS
ACCURSEDNESSES
ACCURST
ACCUSABLE
ACCUSABLY
ACCUSAL
ACCUSALS
ACCUSANT
ACCUSANTS
ACCUSATION
ACCUSATIONS
ACCUSATIVE
ACCUSATIVES
ACCUSATORY
ACCUSE
ACCUSED
ACCUSER
ACCUSERS
ACCUSES
ACCUSING
ACCUSINGLY
ACCUSTOM
ACCUSTOMATION
ACCUSTOMATIONS
ACCUSTOMED
ACCUSTOMEDNESS
ACCUSTOMING
ACCUSTOMS
ACE
ACED
ACEDIA
ACEDIAS
ACELDAMA
ACELDAMAS
ACELLULAR
ACENTRIC
ACEPHALIC
ACEPHALOUS
ACEQUIA
ACEQUIAS
ACERATE
ACERATED
ACERB
ACERBATE
ACERBATED
ACERBATES
ACERBATING
ACERBER
ACERBEST
ACERBIC
ACERBICALLY
ACERBITIES

ACERBITY
ACEROLA
ACEROLAS
ACEROSE
ACEROUS
ACERVATE
ACERVULI
ACERVULUS
ACES
ACESCENT
ACESCENTS
ACETA
ACETABULA
ACETABULAR
ACETABULUM
ACETABULUMS
ACETAL
ACETALDEHYDE
ACETALDEHYDES
ACETALS
ACETAMID
ACETAMIDE
ACETAMIDES
ACETAMIDS
ACETAMINOPHEN
ACETAMINOPHENS
ACETANILID
ACETANILIDE
ACETANILIDES
ACETANILIDS
ACETATE
ACETATED
ACETATES
ACETAZOLAMIDE
ACETAZOLAMIDES
ACETIC
ACETIFICATION
ACETIFICATIONS
ACETIFIED
ACETIFIER
ACETIFIERS
ACETIFIES
ACETIFY
ACETIFYING
ACETIN
ACETINS
ACETONE
ACETONES
ACETONIC
ACETONITRILE
ACETONITRILES
ACETOPHENETIDIN
ACETOSE
ACETOUS
ACETOXYL
ACETOXYLS
ACETUM
ACETYL
ACETYLATE
ACETYLATED
ACETYLATES
ACETYLATING
ACETYLATION
ACETYLATIONS
ACETYLATIVE
ACETYLCHOLINE
ACETYLCHOLINES
ACETYLENE
ACETYLENES
ACETYLENIC
ACETYLIC
ACETYLS
ACHALASIA
ACHALASIAS
ACHE
ACHED
ACHENE
ACHENES
ACHENIAL
ACHES
ACHIER
ACHIEST
ACHIEVABLE
ACHIEVE
ACHIEVED
ACHIEVEMENT
ACHIEVEMENTS
ACHIEVER
ACHIEVERS
ACHIEVES
ACHIEVING
ACHILLEA
ACHILLEAS
ACHINESS
ACHINESSES
ACHING
ACHINGLY
ACHIOTE
ACHIOTES
ACHIRAL
ACHLORHYDRIA
ACHLORHYDRIAS
ACHLORHYDRIC
ACHOLIA
ACHOLIAS
ACHONDRITE
ACHONDRITES
ACHONDRITIC
ACHONDROPLASIA
ACHONDROPLASIAS
ACHONDROPLASTIC
ACHOO
ACHROMAT
ACHROMATIC
ACHROMATICALLY
ACHROMATISM
ACHROMATISMS
ACHROMATIZE
ACHROMATIZED
ACHROMATIZES
ACHROMATIZING
ACHROMATS
ACHROMIC
ACHROMOUS
ACHY
ACICULA
ACICULAE
ACICULAR
ACICULAS
ACICULATE
ACICULUM
ACICULUMS
ACID
ACIDEMIA
ACIDEMIAS
ACIDHEAD
ACIDHEADS
ACIDIC
ACIDIFICATION
ACIDIFICATIONS
ACIDIFIED
ACIDIFIER
ACIDIFIERS
ACIDIFIES
ACIDIFY
ACIDIFYING
ACIDIMETER
ACIDIMETERS
ACIDIMETRIC
ACIDIMETRIES
ACIDIMETRY
ACIDITIES
ACIDITY
ACIDLY
ACIDNESS
ACIDNESSES
ACIDOPHIL
ACIDOPHILE
ACIDOPHILES
ACIDOPHILIC
ACIDOPHILS
ACIDOPHILUS
ACIDOSES
ACIDOSIS
ACIDOTIC
ACIDS
ACIDULATE
ACIDULATED
ACIDULATES
ACIDULATING
ACIDULATION
ACIDULATIONS
ACIDULENT
ACIDULOUS
ACIDURIA
ACIDURIAS
ACIDY
ACIERATE
ACIERATED
ACIERATES
ACIERATING
ACIFORM
ACINAR
ACING
ACINI
ACINIC
ACINIFORM
ACINOSE
ACINOUS
ACINUS
ACKEE
ACKEES
ACKNOWLEDGE
ACKNOWLEDGED
ACKNOWLEDGEDLY
ACKNOWLEDGEMENT
ACKNOWLEDGES
ACKNOWLEDGING
ACKNOWLEDGMENT
ACKNOWLEDGMENTS
ACLINIC
ACMATIC
ACME
ACMES
ACMIC
ACNE
ACNED
ACNES
ACNODE
ACNODES
ACOCK
ACOELOMATE
ACOELOMATES
ACOELOUS
ACOLD
ACOLYTE
ACOLYTES
ACONITE
ACONITES
ACONITIC
ACONITUM
ACONITUMS
ACORN
ACORNED
ACORNS
ACOUSTIC
ACOUSTICAL
ACOUSTICALLY
ACOUSTICIAN
ACOUSTICIANS
ACOUSTICS
ACQUAINT
ACQUAINTANCE
ACQUAINTANCES
ACQUAINTED
ACQUAINTING
ACQUAINTS
ACQUEST
ACQUESTS
ACQUIESCE
ACQUIESCED
ACQUIESCENCE
ACQUIESCENCES
ACQUIESCENT
ACQUIESCENTLY
ACQUIESCES
ACQUIESCING
ACQUIRABLE
ACQUIRE
ACQUIRED
ACQUIREE
ACQUIREES
ACQUIREMENT
ACQUIREMENTS
ACQUIRER
ACQUIRERS
ACQUIRES
ACQUIRING
ACQUISITION
ACQUISITIONAL
ACQUISITIONS
ACQUISITIVE
ACQUISITIVELY
ACQUISITIVENESS
ACQUISITOR

ACQUISITORS
ACQUIT
ACQUITS
ACQUITTAL
ACQUITTALS
ACQUITTANCE
ACQUITTANCES
ACQUITTED
ACQUITTER
ACQUITTERS
ACQUITTING
ACRASIA
ACRASIAS
ACRASIN
ACRASINS
ACRATIC
ACRE
ACREAGE
ACREAGES
ACRED
ACRES
ACRID
ACRIDER
ACRIDEST
ACRIDINE
ACRIDINES
ACRIDITIES
ACRIDITY
ACRIDLY
ACRIDNESS
ACRIDNESSES
ACRIFLAVINE
ACRIFLAVINES
ACRIMONIES
ACRIMONIOUS
ACRIMONIOUSLY
ACRIMONIOUSNESS
ACRIMONY
ACRITARCH
ACRITARCHS
ACRITICAL
ACRO
ACROBAT
ACROBATIC
ACROBATICALLY
ACROBATICS
ACROBATS
ACROCENTRIC
ACROCENTRICS
ACRODONT
ACRODONTS
ACROGEN
ACROGENIC
ACROGENS
ACROLECT
ACROLECTS
ACROLEIN
ACROLEINS
ACROLITH
ACROLITHS
ACROMEGALIC
ACROMEGALICS
ACROMEGALIES
ACROMEGALY
ACROMIA
ACROMIAL
ACROMION
ACRONIC
ACRONICAL
ACRONYCAL
ACRONYM
ACRONYMIC
ACRONYMICALLY
ACRONYMS
ACROPETAL
ACROPETALLY
ACROPHOBE
ACROPHOBES
ACROPHOBIA
ACROPHOBIAS
ACROPHOBIC
ACROPOLIS
ACROPOLISES
ACROS
ACROSOMAL
ACROSOME
ACROSOMES
ACROSPIRE
ACROSPIRES
ACROSS
ACROSTIC
ACROSTICAL
ACROSTICALLY
ACROSTICS
ACROTIC
ACROTISM
ACROTISMS
ACRYLAMIDE
ACRYLAMIDES
ACRYLATE
ACRYLATES
ACRYLIC
ACRYLICS
ACRYLONITRILE
ACRYLONITRILES
ACT
ACTA
ACTABILITIES
ACTABILITY
ACTABLE
ACTED
ACTIN
ACTINAL
ACTINALLY
ACTING
ACTINGS
ACTINIA
ACTINIAE
ACTINIAN
ACTINIANS
ACTINIAS
ACTINIC
ACTINICALLY
ACTINIDE
ACTINIDES
ACTINISM
ACTINISMS
ACTINIUM
ACTINIUMS
ACTINOID
ACTINOIDS
ACTINOLITE
ACTINOLITES
ACTINOMETER
ACTINOMETERS
ACTINOMETRIC
ACTINOMETRIES
ACTINOMETRY
ACTINOMORPHIC
ACTINOMORPHIES
ACTINOMORPHY
ACTINOMYCES
ACTINOMYCETE
ACTINOMYCETES
ACTINOMYCETOUS
ACTINOMYCIN
ACTINOMYCINS
ACTINOMYCOSES
ACTINOMYCOSIS
ACTINOMYCOTIC
ACTINON
ACTINONS
ACTINS
ACTION
ACTIONABLE
ACTIONABLY
ACTIONED
ACTIONER
ACTIONERS
ACTIONING
ACTIONLESS
ACTIONS
ACTIVATE
ACTIVATED
ACTIVATES
ACTIVATING
ACTIVATION
ACTIVATIONS
ACTIVATOR
ACTIVATORS
ACTIVE
ACTIVELY
ACTIVENESS
ACTIVENESSES
ACTIVES
ACTIVEWEAR
ACTIVISM
ACTIVISMS
ACTIVIST
ACTIVISTIC
ACTIVISTS
ACTIVITIES
ACTIVITY
ACTIVIZE
ACTIVIZED
ACTIVIZES
ACTIVIZING
ACTOMYOSIN
ACTOMYOSINS
ACTOR
ACTORISH
ACTORLY
ACTORS
ACTRESS
ACTRESSES
ACTRESSY
ACTS
ACTUAL
ACTUALITIES
ACTUALITY
ACTUALIZATION
ACTUALIZATIONS
ACTUALIZE
ACTUALIZED
ACTUALIZES
ACTUALIZING
ACTUALLY
ACTUARIAL
ACTUARIALLY
ACTUARIES
ACTUARY
ACTUATE
ACTUATED
ACTUATES
ACTUATING
ACTUATION
ACTUATIONS
ACTUATOR
ACTUATORS
ACUATE
ACUITIES
ACUITY
ACULEATE
ACULEATED
ACULEATES
ACULEI
ACULEUS
ACUMEN
ACUMENS
ACUMINATE
ACUMINATED
ACUMINATES
ACUMINATING
ACUMINOUS
ACUPRESSURE
ACUPRESSURES
ACUPUNCTURE
ACUPUNCTURES
ACUPUNCTURING
ACUPUNCTURINGS
ACUPUNCTURIST
ACUPUNCTURISTS
ACUTANCE
ACUTANCES
ACUTE
ACUTELY
ACUTENESS
ACUTENESSES
ACUTER
ACUTES
ACUTEST
ACYCLIC
ACYCLOVIR
ACYCLOVIRS
ACYL
ACYLATE
ACYLATED
ACYLATES
ACYLATING
ACYLATION
ACYLATIONS
ACYLOIN
ACYLOINS
ACYLS
AD

ADAGE
ADAGES
ADAGIAL
ADAGIO
ADAGIOS
ADAMANCE
ADAMANCES
ADAMANCIES
ADAMANCY
ADAMANT
ADAMANTINE
ADAMANTLY
ADAMANTS
ADAMSITE
ADAMSITES
ADAPT
ADAPTABILITIES
ADAPTABILITY
ADAPTABLE
ADAPTATION
ADAPTATIONAL
ADAPTATIONALLY
ADAPTATIONIST
ADAPTATIONS
ADAPTED
ADAPTEDNESS
ADAPTEDNESSES
ADAPTER
ADAPTERS
ADAPTING
ADAPTION
ADAPTIONS
ADAPTIVE
ADAPTIVELY
ADAPTIVENESS
ADAPTIVENESSES
ADAPTIVITIES
ADAPTIVITY
ADAPTOGEN
ADAPTOGENIC
ADAPTOGENS
ADAPTOR
ADAPTORS
ADAPTS
ADAXIAL
ADBOT
ADBOTS
ADD
ADDABLE
ADDAX
ADDAXES
ADDED
ADDEDLY
ADDEND
ADDENDA
ADDENDS
ADDENDUM
ADDENDUMS
ADDER
ADDERS
ADDIBLE
ADDICT
ADDICTED
ADDICTING
ADDICTION
ADDICTIONS
ADDICTIVE
ADDICTS
ADDING
ADDITION
ADDITIONAL
ADDITIONALLY
ADDITIONS
ADDITIVE
ADDITIVELY
ADDITIVES
ADDITIVITIES
ADDITIVITY
ADDITORY
ADDLE
ADDLED
ADDLEPATED
ADDLES
ADDLING
ADDRESS
ADDRESSABILITY
ADDRESSABLE
ADDRESSED
ADDRESSEE
ADDRESSEES
ADDRESSER
ADDRESSERS
ADDRESSES
ADDRESSING
ADDRESSOR
ADDRESSORS
ADDREST
ADDS
ADDUCE
ADDUCED
ADDUCENT
ADDUCER
ADDUCERS
ADDUCES
ADDUCIBLE
ADDUCING
ADDUCT
ADDUCTED
ADDUCTING
ADDUCTION
ADDUCTIONS
ADDUCTIVE
ADDUCTOR
ADDUCTORS
ADDUCTS
ADEEM
ADEEMED
ADEEMING
ADEEMS
ADELGID
ADELGIDS
ADEMPTION
ADEMPTIONS
ADENINE
ADENINES
ADENITIS
ADENITISES
ADENOCARCINOMA
ADENOCARCINOMAS
ADENOHYPOPHYSES
ADENOHYPOPHYSIS
ADENOID
ADENOIDAL
ADENOIDS
ADENOMA
ADENOMAS
ADENOMATA
ADENOMATOUS
ADENOSES
ADENOSINE
ADENOSINES
ADENOSIS
ADENOVIRAL
ADENOVIRUS
ADENOVIRUSES
ADENYL
ADENYLS
ADEPT
ADEPTER
ADEPTEST
ADEPTLY
ADEPTNESS
ADEPTNESSES
ADEPTS
ADEQUACIES
ADEQUACY
ADEQUATE
ADEQUATELY
ADEQUATENESS
ADEQUATENESSES
ADHERABLE
ADHERE
ADHERED
ADHERENCE
ADHERENCES
ADHEREND
ADHERENDS
ADHERENT
ADHERENTLY
ADHERENTS
ADHERER
ADHERERS
ADHERES
ADHERING
ADHESION
ADHESIONAL
ADHESIONS
ADHESIVE
ADHESIVELY
ADHESIVENESS
ADHESIVENESSES
ADHESIVES
ADHIBIT
ADHIBITED
ADHIBITING
ADHIBITS
ADIABATIC
ADIABATICALLY
ADIEU
ADIEUS
ADIEUX
ADIOS
ADIOSES
ADIPIC
ADIPOCERE
ADIPOCERES
ADIPOCYTE
ADIPOCYTES
ADIPOSE
ADIPOSES
ADIPOSIS
ADIPOSITIES
ADIPOSITY
ADIPOUS
ADIT
ADITS
ADJACENCE
ADJACENCES
ADJACENCIES
ADJACENCY
ADJACENT
ADJACENTLY
ADJECTIVAL
ADJECTIVALLY
ADJECTIVE
ADJECTIVELY
ADJECTIVES
ADJOIN
ADJOINED
ADJOINING
ADJOINS
ADJOINT
ADJOINTS
ADJOURN
ADJOURNED
ADJOURNING
ADJOURNMENT
ADJOURNMENTS
ADJOURNS
ADJUDGE
ADJUDGED
ADJUDGES
ADJUDGING
ADJUDICATE
ADJUDICATED
ADJUDICATES
ADJUDICATING
ADJUDICATION
ADJUDICATIONS
ADJUDICATIVE
ADJUDICATOR
ADJUDICATORS
ADJUDICATORY
ADJUNCT
ADJUNCTION
ADJUNCTIONS
ADJUNCTIVE
ADJUNCTLY
ADJUNCTS
ADJURATION
ADJURATIONS
ADJURATORY
ADJURE
ADJURED
ADJURER
ADJURERS
ADJURES
ADJURING
ADJUROR
ADJURORS
ADJUST
ADJUSTABILITIES
ADJUSTABILITY
ADJUSTABLE
ADJUSTED

ADJUSTER
ADJUSTERS
ADJUSTING
ADJUSTIVE
ADJUSTMENT
ADJUSTMENTAL
ADJUSTMENTS
ADJUSTOR
ADJUSTORS
ADJUSTS
ADJUTANCIES
ADJUTANCY
ADJUTANT
ADJUTANTS
ADJUVANT
ADJUVANTS
ADLAND
ADLANDS
ADMAN
ADMASS
ADMASSES
ADMEASURE
ADMEASURED
ADMEASUREMENT
ADMEASUREMENTS
ADMEASURES
ADMEASURING
ADMEN
ADMIN
ADMINISTER
ADMINISTERED
ADMINISTERING
ADMINISTERS
ADMINISTRABLE
ADMINISTRANT
ADMINISTRANTS
ADMINISTRATE
ADMINISTRATED
ADMINISTRATES
ADMINISTRATING
ADMINISTRATION
ADMINISTRATIONS
ADMINISTRATIVE
ADMINISTRATOR
ADMINISTRATORS
ADMINISTRATRIX
ADMINS
ADMIRABILITIES
ADMIRABILITY
ADMIRABLE
ADMIRABLENESS
ADMIRABLENESSES
ADMIRABLY
ADMIRAL
ADMIRALS
ADMIRALTIES
ADMIRALTY
ADMIRATION
ADMIRATIONS
ADMIRE
ADMIRED
ADMIRER
ADMIRERS
ADMIRES
ADMIRING
ADMIRINGLY
ADMISSIBILITIES
ADMISSIBILITY
ADMISSIBLE
ADMISSION
ADMISSIONS
ADMISSIVE
ADMIT
ADMITS
ADMITTANCE
ADMITTANCES
ADMITTED
ADMITTEDLY
ADMITTEE
ADMITTEES
ADMITTER
ADMITTERS
ADMITTING
ADMIX
ADMIXED
ADMIXES
ADMIXING
ADMIXT
ADMIXTURE
ADMIXTURES
ADMONISH
ADMONISHED
ADMONISHER
ADMONISHERS
ADMONISHES
ADMONISHING
ADMONISHINGLY
ADMONISHMENT
ADMONISHMENTS
ADMONITION
ADMONITIONS
ADMONITOR
ADMONITORILY
ADMONITORS
ADMONITORY
ADNATE
ADNATION
ADNATIONS
ADNEXA
ADNEXAL
ADNOUN
ADNOUNS
ADO
ADOBE
ADOBELIKE
ADOBES
ADOBO
ADOBOS
ADOLESCENCE
ADOLESCENCES
ADOLESCENT
ADOLESCENTLY
ADOLESCENTS
ADONIS
ADONISES
ADOPT
ADOPTABILITIES
ADOPTABILITY
ADOPTABLE
ADOPTED
ADOPTEE
ADOPTEES
ADOPTER
ADOPTERS
ADOPTIANISM
ADOPTIANISMS
ADOPTING
ADOPTION
ADOPTIONISM
ADOPTIONISMS
ADOPTIONIST
ADOPTIONISTS
ADOPTIONS
ADOPTIVE
ADOPTIVELY
ADOPTS
ADORABILITIES
ADORABILITY
ADORABLE
ADORABLENESS
ADORABLENESSES
ADORABLY
ADORATION
ADORATIONS
ADORE
ADORED
ADORER
ADORERS
ADORES
ADORING
ADORINGLY
ADORN
ADORNED
ADORNER
ADORNERS
ADORNING
ADORNMENT
ADORNMENTS
ADORNS
ADOS
ADOWN
ADOZE
ADRENAL
ADRENALECTOMIES
ADRENALECTOMY
ADRENALIN
ADRENALINE
ADRENALINES
ADRENALINS
ADRENALIZED
ADRENALLY
ADRENALS
ADRENERGIC
ADRENERGICALLY
ADRENOCHROME
ADRENOCHROMES
ADRENOCORTICAL
ADRIFT
ADROIT
ADROITER
ADROITEST
ADROITLY
ADROITNESS
ADROITNESSES
ADS
ADSCITITIOUS
ADSCRIPT
ADSCRIPTS
ADSORB
ADSORBABLE
ADSORBATE
ADSORBATES
ADSORBED
ADSORBENT
ADSORBENTS
ADSORBER
ADSORBERS
ADSORBING
ADSORBS
ADSORPTION
ADSORPTIONS
ADSORPTIVE
ADSUKI
ADSUKIS
ADULARIA
ADULARIAS
ADULATE
ADULATED
ADULATES
ADULATING
ADULATION
ADULATIONS
ADULATOR
ADULATORS
ADULATORY
ADULT
ADULTERANT
ADULTERANTS
ADULTERATE
ADULTERATED
ADULTERATES
ADULTERATING
ADULTERATION
ADULTERATIONS
ADULTERATOR
ADULTERATORS
ADULTERER
ADULTERERS
ADULTERESS
ADULTERESSES
ADULTERIES
ADULTERINE
ADULTEROUS
ADULTEROUSLY
ADULTERY
ADULTHOOD
ADULTHOODS
ADULTLIKE
ADULTLY
ADULTNESS
ADULTNESSES
ADULTRESS
ADULTRESSES
ADULTS
ADUMBRAL
ADUMBRATE
ADUMBRATED
ADUMBRATES
ADUMBRATING
ADUMBRATION
ADUMBRATIONS
ADUMBRATIVE
ADUMBRATIVELY
ADUNC
ADUNCATE

ADUNCOUS
ADUST
ADVANCE
ADVANCED
ADVANCEMENT
ADVANCEMENTS
ADVANCER
ADVANCERS
ADVANCES
ADVANCING
ADVANTAGE
ADVANTAGED
ADVANTAGEOUS
ADVANTAGEOUSLY
ADVANTAGES
ADVANTAGING
ADVECT
ADVECTED
ADVECTING
ADVECTION
ADVECTIONS
ADVECTIVE
ADVECTS
ADVENT
ADVENTITIA
ADVENTITIAL
ADVENTITIAS
ADVENTITIOUS
ADVENTITIOUSLY
ADVENTIVE
ADVENTIVES
ADVENTS
ADVENTURE
ADVENTURED
ADVENTURER
ADVENTURERS
ADVENTURES
ADVENTURESOME
ADVENTURESS
ADVENTURESSES
ADVENTURING
ADVENTURISM
ADVENTURISMS
ADVENTURIST
ADVENTURISTIC
ADVENTURISTS
ADVENTUROUS
ADVENTUROUSLY
ADVENTUROUSNESS
ADVERB
ADVERBIAL
ADVERBIALLY
ADVERBIALS
ADVERBS
ADVERSARIAL
ADVERSARIES
ADVERSARINESS
ADVERSARINESSES
ADVERSARY
ADVERSATIVE
ADVERSATIVELY
ADVERSATIVES
ADVERSE
ADVERSELY
ADVERSENESS
ADVERSENESSES
ADVERSITIES
ADVERSITY
ADVERT
ADVERTED
ADVERTENCE
ADVERTENCES
ADVERTENCIES
ADVERTENCY
ADVERTENT
ADVERTENTLY
ADVERTING
ADVERTISE
ADVERTISED
ADVERTISEMENT
ADVERTISEMENTS
ADVERTISER
ADVERTISERS
ADVERTISES
ADVERTISING
ADVERTISINGS
ADVERTIZE
ADVERTIZED
ADVERTIZEMENT
ADVERTIZEMENTS
ADVERTIZES
ADVERTIZING
ADVERTORIAL
ADVERTORIALS
ADVERTS
ADVICE
ADVICES
ADVISABILITIES
ADVISABILITY
ADVISABLE
ADVISABLENESS
ADVISABLENESSES
ADVISABLY
ADVISE
ADVISED
ADVISEDLY
ADVISEE
ADVISEES
ADVISEMENT
ADVISEMENTS
ADVISER
ADVISERS
ADVISES
ADVISING
ADVISOR
ADVISORIES
ADVISORS
ADVISORY
ADVOCAAT
ADVOCAATS
ADVOCACIES
ADVOCACY
ADVOCATE
ADVOCATED
ADVOCATES
ADVOCATING
ADVOCATION
ADVOCATIONS
ADVOCATIVE
ADVOCATOR
ADVOCATORS
ADVOWSON
ADVOWSONS
ADWARE
ADWARES
ADWOMAN
ADWOMEN
ADYNAMIA
ADYNAMIAS
ADYNAMIC
ADYTA
ADYTUM
ADZ
ADZE
ADZED
ADZES
ADZING
ADZUKI
ADZUKIS
AE
AECIA
AECIAL
AECIDIA
AECIDIAL
AECIDIUM
AECIOSPORE
AECIOSPORES
AECIUM
AEDES
AEDILE
AEDILES
AEDINE
AEGIS
AEGISES
AEGROTAT
AEGROTATS
AENEOUS
AENEUS
AEOLIAN
AEON
AEONIAN
AEONIC
AEONS
AEPYORNIS
AEPYORNISES
AEQUORIN
AEQUORINS
AERADIO
AERADIOS
AERATE
AERATED
AERATES
AERATING
AERATION
AERATIONS
AERATOR
AERATORS
AERENCHYMA
AERENCHYMAS
AERIAL
AERIALIST
AERIALISTS
AERIALLY
AERIALS
AERIE
AERIED
AERIER
AERIES
AERIEST
AERIFIED
AERIFIES
AERIFORM
AERIFY
AERIFYING
AERILY
AERO
AEROBAT
AEROBATIC
AEROBATICS
AEROBATS
AEROBE
AEROBES
AEROBIA
AEROBIC
AEROBICALLY
AEROBICIZE
AEROBICIZED
AEROBICIZES
AEROBICIZING
AEROBICS
AEROBIOLOGICAL
AEROBIOLOGIES
AEROBIOLOGY
AEROBIOSES
AEROBIOSIS
AEROBIUM
AEROBRAKE
AEROBRAKED
AEROBRAKES
AEROBRAKING
AERODROME
AERODROMES
AERODUCT
AERODUCTS
AERODYNAMIC
AERODYNAMICAL
AERODYNAMICALLY
AERODYNAMICIST
AERODYNAMICISTS
AERODYNAMICS
AERODYNE
AERODYNES
AEROELASTIC
AEROELASTICITY
AEROEMBOLISM
AEROEMBOLISMS
AEROFOIL
AEROFOILS
AEROGEL
AEROGELS
AEROGRAM
AEROGRAMME
AEROGRAMMES
AEROGRAMS
AEROLITE
AEROLITES
AEROLITH
AEROLITHS
AEROLITIC
AEROLOGIC
AEROLOGIES
AEROLOGY
AEROMAGNETIC
AEROMECHANICS
AEROMEDICAL

AEROMEDICINE
AEROMEDICINES
AEROMETER
AEROMETERS
AEROMETRIES
AEROMETRY
AERONAUT
AERONAUTIC
AERONAUTICAL
AERONAUTICALLY
AERONAUTICS
AERONAUTS
AERONOMER
AERONOMERS
AERONOMIC
AERONOMICAL
AERONOMIES
AERONOMIST
AERONOMISTS
AERONOMY
AEROPAUSE
AEROPAUSES
AEROPHOBE
AEROPHOBES
AEROPHOBIA
AEROPHOBIAS
AEROPHOBIC
AEROPHORE
AEROPHORES
AEROPHYTE
AEROPHYTES
AEROPLANE
AEROPLANES
AEROPULSE
AEROPULSES
AEROSAT
AEROSATS
AEROSCOPE
AEROSCOPES
AEROSOL
AEROSOLIZATION
AEROSOLIZATIONS
AEROSOLIZE
AEROSOLIZED
AEROSOLIZES
AEROSOLIZING
AEROSOLS
AEROSPACE
AEROSPACES
AEROSTAT
AEROSTATICS
AEROSTATS
AERUGO
AERUGOS
AERY
AESTHESIA
AESTHESIAS
AESTHETE
AESTHETES
AESTHETIC
AESTHETICAL
AESTHETICALLY
AESTHETICIAN
AESTHETICIANS
AESTHETICISM
AESTHETICISMS
AESTHETICIZE
AESTHETICIZED
AESTHETICIZES
AESTHETICIZING
AESTHETICS
AESTIVAL
AESTIVATE
AESTIVATED
AESTIVATES
AESTIVATING
AESTIVATION
AESTIVATIONS
AETATIS
AETHER
AETHEREAL
AETHERIC
AETHERS
AETIOLOGIES
AETIOLOGY
AFAR
AFARS
AFEARD
AFEARED
AFEBRILE
AFF
AFFABILITIES
AFFABILITY
AFFABLE
AFFABLY
AFFAIR
AFFAIRE
AFFAIRES
AFFAIRS
AFFECT
AFFECTABILITIES
AFFECTABILITY
AFFECTABLE
AFFECTATION
AFFECTATIONS
AFFECTED
AFFECTEDLY
AFFECTEDNESS
AFFECTEDNESSES
AFFECTER
AFFECTERS
AFFECTING
AFFECTINGLY
AFFECTION
AFFECTIONAL
AFFECTIONALLY
AFFECTIONATE
AFFECTIONATELY
AFFECTIONED
AFFECTIONLESS
AFFECTIONS
AFFECTIVE
AFFECTIVELY
AFFECTIVITIES
AFFECTIVITY
AFFECTLESS
AFFECTLESSNESS
AFFECTS
AFFENPINSCHER
AFFENPINSCHERS
AFFERENT
AFFERENTLY
AFFERENTS
AFFIANCE
AFFIANCED
AFFIANCES
AFFIANCING
AFFIANT
AFFIANTS
AFFICHE
AFFICHES
AFFICIONADO
AFFICIONADOS
AFFIDAVIT
AFFIDAVITS
AFFILIATE
AFFILIATED
AFFILIATES
AFFILIATING
AFFILIATION
AFFILIATIONS
AFFINAL
AFFINE
AFFINED
AFFINELY
AFFINES
AFFINITIES
AFFINITY
AFFIRM
AFFIRMABLE
AFFIRMANCE
AFFIRMANCES
AFFIRMANT
AFFIRMANTS
AFFIRMATION
AFFIRMATIONS
AFFIRMATIVE
AFFIRMATIVELY
AFFIRMATIVES
AFFIRMED
AFFIRMER
AFFIRMERS
AFFIRMING
AFFIRMS
AFFIX
AFFIXABLE
AFFIXAL
AFFIXATION
AFFIXATIONS
AFFIXED
AFFIXER
AFFIXERS
AFFIXES
AFFIXIAL
AFFIXING
AFFIXMENT
AFFIXMENTS
AFFIXTURE
AFFIXTURES
AFFLATUS
AFFLATUSES
AFFLICT
AFFLICTED
AFFLICTER
AFFLICTERS
AFFLICTING
AFFLICTION
AFFLICTIONS
AFFLICTIVE
AFFLICTIVELY
AFFLICTS
AFFLUENCE
AFFLUENCES
AFFLUENCIES
AFFLUENCY
AFFLUENT
AFFLUENTLY
AFFLUENTS
AFFLUX
AFFLUXES
AFFORD
AFFORDABILITIES
AFFORDABILITY
AFFORDABLE
AFFORDABLY
AFFORDED
AFFORDING
AFFORDS
AFFOREST
AFFORESTATION
AFFORESTATIONS
AFFORESTED
AFFORESTING
AFFORESTS
AFFRAY
AFFRAYED
AFFRAYER
AFFRAYERS
AFFRAYING
AFFRAYS
AFFRICATE
AFFRICATED
AFFRICATES
AFFRICATING
AFFRICATIVE
AFFRICATIVES
AFFRIGHT
AFFRIGHTED
AFFRIGHTING
AFFRIGHTS
AFFRONT
AFFRONTED
AFFRONTING
AFFRONTS
AFFUSION
AFFUSIONS
AFGHAN
AFGHANI
AFGHANIS
AFGHANS
AFICIONADA
AFICIONADAS
AFICIONADO
AFICIONADOS
AFIELD
AFIRE
AFLAME
AFLATOXIN
AFLATOXINS
AFLOAT
AFLUTTER
AFOOT
AFORE
AFOREHAND
AFOREMENTIONED

AFORESAID
AFORETHOUGHT
AFORETIME
AFOUL
AFRAID
AFREET
AFREETS
AFRESH
AFRIT
AFRITS
AFRO
AFROS
AFT
AFTER
AFTERBIRTH
AFTERBIRTHS
AFTERBURNER
AFTERBURNERS
AFTERCARE
AFTERCARES
AFTERCLAP
AFTERCLAPS
AFTERDAMP
AFTERDAMPS
AFTERDECK
AFTERDECKS
AFTEREFFECT
AFTEREFFECTS
AFTERGLOW
AFTERGLOWS
AFTERGUARD
AFTERGUARDS
AFTERIMAGE
AFTERIMAGES
AFTERLIFE
AFTERLIFES
AFTERLIVES
AFTERMARKET
AFTERMARKETS
AFTERMATH
AFTERMATHS
AFTERMOST
AFTERNOON
AFTERNOONS
AFTERPAIN
AFTERPAINS
AFTERPIECE
AFTERPIECES
AFTERS
AFTERSHAVE
AFTERSHAVES
AFTERSHOCK
AFTERSHOCKS
AFTERTASTE
AFTERTASTES
AFTERTAX
AFTERTHOUGHT
AFTERTHOUGHTS
AFTERTIME
AFTERTIMES
AFTERWARD
AFTERWARDS
AFTERWORD
AFTERWORDS
AFTERWORLD
AFTERWORLDS
AFTMOST
AFTOSA
AFTOSAS
AG
AGA
AGAIN
AGAINST
AGALACTIA
AGALACTIAS
AGALLOCH
AGALLOCHS
AGALWOOD
AGALWOODS
AGAMA
AGAMAS
AGAMETE
AGAMETES
AGAMIC
AGAMID
AGAMIDS
AGAMOSPERMIES
AGAMOSPERMY
AGAMOUS
AGAPAE
AGAPAI
AGAPANTHUS
AGAPANTHUSES
AGAPE
AGAPEIC
AGAPES
AGAR
AGARIC
AGARICS
AGAROSE
AGAROSES
AGARS
AGAS
AGATE
AGATES
AGATEWARE
AGATEWARES
AGATIZE
AGATIZED
AGATIZES
AGATIZING
AGATOID
AGAVE
AGAVES
AGAZE
AGE
AGED
AGEDLY
AGEDNESS
AGEDNESSES
AGEE
AGEING
AGEINGS
AGEISM
AGEISMS
AGEIST
AGEISTS
AGELESS
AGELESSLY
AGELESSNESS
AGELESSNESSES
AGELONG
AGEMATE
AGEMATES
AGENCIES
AGENCY
AGENDA
AGENDALESS
AGENDAS
AGENDUM
AGENDUMS
AGENE
AGENES
AGENESES
AGENESIA
AGENESIAS
AGENESIS
AGENETIC
AGENIZE
AGENIZED
AGENIZES
AGENIZING
AGENT
AGENTED
AGENTIAL
AGENTING
AGENTINGS
AGENTIVAL
AGENTIVE
AGENTIVES
AGENTRIES
AGENTRY
AGENTS
AGER
AGERATUM
AGERATUMS
AGERS
AGES
AGGADA
AGGADAH
AGGADAHS
AGGADAS
AGGADIC
AGGADOT
AGGADOTH
AGGER
AGGERS
AGGIE
AGGIES
AGGIORNAMENTO
AGGIORNAMENTOS
AGGLOMERATE
AGGLOMERATED
AGGLOMERATES
AGGLOMERATING
AGGLOMERATION
AGGLOMERATIONS
AGGLOMERATIVE
AGGLUTINABILITY
AGGLUTINABLE
AGGLUTINATE
AGGLUTINATED
AGGLUTINATES
AGGLUTINATING
AGGLUTINATION
AGGLUTINATIONS
AGGLUTINATIVE
AGGLUTININ
AGGLUTININS
AGGLUTINOGEN
AGGLUTINOGENIC
AGGLUTINOGENS
AGGRADATION
AGGRADATIONAL
AGGRADATIONS
AGGRADE
AGGRADED
AGGRADES
AGGRADING
AGGRANDISE
AGGRANDISED
AGGRANDISEMENT
AGGRANDISEMENTS
AGGRANDISES
AGGRANDISING
AGGRANDIZE
AGGRANDIZED
AGGRANDIZEMENT
AGGRANDIZEMENTS
AGGRANDIZER
AGGRANDIZERS
AGGRANDIZES
AGGRANDIZING
AGGRAVATE
AGGRAVATED
AGGRAVATES
AGGRAVATING
AGGRAVATINGLY
AGGRAVATION
AGGRAVATIONS
AGGREGATE
AGGREGATED
AGGREGATELY
AGGREGATENESS
AGGREGATENESSES
AGGREGATES
AGGREGATING
AGGREGATION
AGGREGATIONAL
AGGREGATIONS
AGGREGATIVE
AGGREGATIVELY
AGGRESS
AGGRESSED
AGGRESSES
AGGRESSING
AGGRESSION
AGGRESSIONS
AGGRESSIVE
AGGRESSIVELY
AGGRESSIVENESS
AGGRESSIVITIES
AGGRESSIVITY
AGGRESSOR
AGGRESSORS
AGGRIEVE
AGGRIEVED
AGGRIEVEDLY
AGGRIEVEMENT
AGGRIEVEMENTS
AGGRIEVES
AGGRIEVING
AGGRO
AGGROS
AGHA

AGHAS
AGHAST
AGILE
AGILELY
AGILENESS
AGILENESSES
AGILITIES
AGILITY
AGIN
AGING
AGINGS
AGINNER
AGINNERS
AGIO
AGIOS
AGIOTAGE
AGIOTAGES
AGISM
AGISMS
AGIST
AGISTED
AGISTING
AGISTS
AGITA
AGITABLE
AGITAS
AGITATE
AGITATED
AGITATEDLY
AGITATES
AGITATING
AGITATION
AGITATIONAL
AGITATIONS
AGITATIVE
AGITATO
AGITATOR
AGITATORS
AGITPROP
AGITPROPS
AGLARE
AGLEAM
AGLEE
AGLET
AGLETS
AGLEY
AGLIMMER
AGLITTER
AGLOO
AGLOOS
AGLOW
AGLU
AGLUS
AGLY
AGLYCON
AGLYCONE
AGLYCONES
AGLYCONS
AGMA
AGMAS
AGMINATE
AGNAIL
AGNAILS
AGNATE
AGNATES
AGNATHAN
AGNATHANS
AGNATIC
AGNATICAL
AGNATION
AGNATIONS
AGNIZE
AGNIZED
AGNIZES
AGNIZING
AGNOLOTTI
AGNOLOTTIS
AGNOMEN
AGNOMENS
AGNOMINA
AGNOSIA
AGNOSIAS
AGNOSTIC
AGNOSTICISM
AGNOSTICISMS
AGNOSTICS
AGO
AGOG
AGON
AGONAL
AGONE
AGONES
AGONIC
AGONIES
AGONISE
AGONISED
AGONISES
AGONISING
AGONISINGLY
AGONISM
AGONISMS
AGONIST
AGONISTES
AGONISTIC
AGONISTICALLY
AGONISTS
AGONIZE
AGONIZED
AGONIZES
AGONIZING
AGONIZINGLY
AGONS
AGONY
AGORA
AGORAE
AGORAPHOBE
AGORAPHOBES
AGORAPHOBIA
AGORAPHOBIAS
AGORAPHOBIC
AGORAPHOBICS
AGORAS
AGOROT
AGOROTH
AGOUTI
AGOUTIES
AGOUTIS
AGOUTY
AGRAFE
AGRAFES
AGRAFFE
AGRAFFES
AGRANULOCYTE
AGRANULOCYTES
AGRANULOCYTOSES
AGRANULOCYTOSIS
AGRAPHA
AGRAPHIA
AGRAPHIAS
AGRAPHIC
AGRARIAN
AGRARIANISM
AGRARIANISMS
AGRARIANS
AGRAVIC
AGREE
AGREEABILITIES
AGREEABILITY
AGREEABLE
AGREEABLENESS
AGREEABLENESSES
AGREEABLY
AGREED
AGREEING
AGREEMENT
AGREEMENTS
AGREES
AGRESTAL
AGRESTIC
AGRIA
AGRIAS
AGRIBUSINESS
AGRIBUSINESSES
AGRIBUSINESSMAN
AGRIBUSINESSMEN
AGRICHEMICAL
AGRICHEMICALS
AGRICULTURAL
AGRICULTURALIST
AGRICULTURALLY
AGRICULTURE
AGRICULTURES
AGRICULTURIST
AGRICULTURISTS
AGRIMONIES
AGRIMONY
AGRITOURISM
AGRITOURISMS
AGRO
AGROCHEMICAL
AGROCHEMICALS
AGROECOLOGICAL
AGROECOLOGIES
AGROECOLOGY
AGROFORESTER
AGROFORESTERS
AGROFORESTRIES
AGROFORESTRY
AGROLOGIC
AGROLOGIES
AGROLOGY
AGRONOMIC
AGRONOMICALLY
AGRONOMIES
AGRONOMIST
AGRONOMISTS
AGRONOMY
AGROS
AGROUND
AGRYPNIA
AGRYPNIAS
AGS
AGUACATE
AGUACATES
AGUE
AGUED
AGUELIKE
AGUES
AGUEWEED
AGUEWEEDS
AGUISH
AGUISHLY
AH
AHA
AHCHOO
AHEAD
AHED
AHEM
AHI
AHIMSA
AHIMSAS
AHING
AHIS
AHISTORIC
AHISTORICAL
AHISTORICALLY
AHISTORICISM
AHISTORICISMS
AHISTORICITIES
AHISTORICITY
AHOLD
AHOLDS
AHORSE
AHOY
AHS
AHULL
AI
AIBLINS
AID
AIDE
AIDED
AIDER
AIDERS
AIDES
AIDFUL
AIDING
AIDLESS
AIDMAN
AIDMEN
AIDS
AIGLET
AIGLETS
AIGRET
AIGRETS
AIGRETTE
AIGRETTES
AIGUILLE
AIGUILLES
AIGUILLETTE
AIGUILLETTES
AIKIDO
AIKIDOS
AIL
AILANTHIC
AILANTHUS

AILANTHUSES
AILED
AILERON
AILERONS
AILING
AILMENT
AILMENTS
AILS
AILUROPHILE
AILUROPHILES
AILUROPHOBE
AILUROPHOBES
AIM
AIMED
AIMER
AIMERS
AIMFUL
AIMFULLY
AIMING
AIMLESS
AIMLESSLY
AIMLESSNESS
AIMLESSNESSES
AIMS
AIN
AINS
AINSELL
AINSELLS
AIOLI
AIOLIS
AIR
AIRBAG
AIRBAGS
AIRBASE
AIRBASES
AIRBOAT
AIRBOATS
AIRBORNE
AIRBOUND
AIRBRUSH
AIRBRUSHED
AIRBRUSHES
AIRBRUSHING
AIRBURST
AIRBURSTS
AIRBUS
AIRBUSES
AIRBUSSES
AIRCHECK
AIRCHECKS
AIRCOACH
AIRCOACHES
AIRCRAFT
AIRCREW
AIRCREWS
AIRDATE
AIRDATES
AIRDROME
AIRDROMES
AIRDROP
AIRDROPPED
AIRDROPPING
AIRDROPS
AIRED
AIRER
AIRERS
AIREST
AIRFARE
AIRFARES
AIRFIELD
AIRFIELDS
AIRFLOW
AIRFLOWS
AIRFOIL
AIRFOILS
AIRFRAME
AIRFRAMES
AIRFREIGHT
AIRFREIGHTED
AIRFREIGHTING
AIRFREIGHTS
AIRGLOW
AIRGLOWS
AIRHEAD
AIRHEADED
AIRHEADS
AIRHOLE
AIRHOLES
AIRIER
AIRIEST
AIRILY
AIRINESS
AIRINESSES
AIRING
AIRINGS
AIRLESS
AIRLESSNESS
AIRLESSNESSES
AIRLIFT
AIRLIFTED
AIRLIFTING
AIRLIFTS
AIRLIKE
AIRLINE
AIRLINER
AIRLINERS
AIRLINES
AIRLOCK
AIRLOCKS
AIRMAIL
AIRMAILED
AIRMAILING
AIRMAILS
AIRMAN
AIRMANSHIP
AIRMANSHIPS
AIRMEN
AIRMOBILE
AIRN
AIRNS
AIRPARK
AIRPARKS
AIRPLANE
AIRPLANES
AIRPLAY
AIRPLAYS
AIRPORT
AIRPORTS
AIRPOST
AIRPOSTS
AIRPOWER
AIRPOWERS
AIRPROOF
AIRPROOFED
AIRPROOFING
AIRPROOFS
AIRS
AIRSCAPE
AIRSCAPES
AIRSCREW
AIRSCREWS
AIRSHED
AIRSHEDS
AIRSHIP
AIRSHIPS
AIRSHOT
AIRSHOTS
AIRSHOW
AIRSHOWS
AIRSICK
AIRSICKNESS
AIRSICKNESSES
AIRSIDE
AIRSIDES
AIRSOME
AIRSPACE
AIRSPACES
AIRSPEED
AIRSPEEDS
AIRSTREAM
AIRSTREAMS
AIRSTRIKE
AIRSTRIKES
AIRSTRIP
AIRSTRIPS
AIRT
AIRTED
AIRTH
AIRTHED
AIRTHING
AIRTHS
AIRTIGHT
AIRTIGHTNESS
AIRTIGHTNESSES
AIRTIME
AIRTIMES
AIRTING
AIRTRAM
AIRTRAMS
AIRTS
AIRVAC
AIRVACS
AIRWARD
AIRWAVE
AIRWAVES
AIRWAY
AIRWAYS
AIRWISE
AIRWOMAN
AIRWOMEN
AIRWORTHIER
AIRWORTHIEST
AIRWORTHINESS
AIRWORTHINESSES
AIRWORTHY
AIRY
AIS
AISLE
AISLED
AISLES
AISLEWAY
AISLEWAYS
AIT
AITCH
AITCHBONE
AITCHBONES
AITCHES
AITS
AIVER
AIVERS
AIYEE
AJAR
AJEE
AJI
AJIS
AJIVA
AJIVAS
AJOWAN
AJOWANS
AJUGA
AJUGAS
AKEBIA
AKEBIAS
AKEE
AKEES
AKELA
AKELAS
AKENE
AKENES
AKIMBO
AKIN
AKINESIA
AKINESIAS
AKINETIC
AKRASIA
AKRASIAS
AKRATIC
AKVAVIT
AKVAVITS
AL
ALA
ALABASTER
ALABASTERS
ALABASTRINE
ALACHLOR
ALACHLORS
ALACK
ALACKADAY
ALACRITIES
ALACRITOUS
ALACRITY
ALAE
ALAMEDA
ALAMEDAS
ALAMO
ALAMODE
ALAMODES
ALAMOS
ALAN
ALAND
ALANDS
ALANE
ALANG
ALANIN
ALANINE

ALANINES
ALANINS
ALANS
ALANT
ALANTS
ALANYL
ALANYLS
ALAR
ALARM
ALARMABLE
ALARMED
ALARMEDLY
ALARMING
ALARMINGLY
ALARMISM
ALARMISMS
ALARMIST
ALARMISTS
ALARMS
ALARUM
ALARUMED
ALARUMING
ALARUMS
ALARY
ALAS
ALASKA
ALASKAS
ALASTOR
ALASTORS
ALATE
ALATED
ALATES
ALATION
ALATIONS
ALB
ALBA
ALBACORE
ALBACORES
ALBAS
ALBATA
ALBATAS
ALBATROSS
ALBATROSSES
ALBEDO
ALBEDOES
ALBEDOS
ALBEIT
ALBERTITE
ALBERTITES
ALBESCENT
ALBICORE
ALBICORES
ALBINAL
ALBINIC
ALBINISM
ALBINISMS
ALBINISTIC
ALBINO
ALBINOS
ALBINOTIC
ALBITE
ALBITES
ALBITIC
ALBITICAL
ALBIZIA
ALBIZIAS
ALBIZZIA
ALBIZZIAS
ALBS
ALBUM
ALBUMEN
ALBUMENS
ALBUMIN
ALBUMINOUS
ALBUMINS
ALBUMINURIA
ALBUMINURIAS
ALBUMINURIC
ALBUMOSE
ALBUMOSES
ALBUMS
ALBURNOUS
ALBURNUM
ALBURNUMS
ALBUTEROL
ALBUTEROLS
ALCADE
ALCADES
ALCAHEST
ALCAHESTS
ALCAIC
ALCAICS
ALCAIDE
ALCAIDES
ALCALDE
ALCALDES
ALCAYDE
ALCAYDES
ALCAZAR
ALCAZARS
ALCHEMIC
ALCHEMICAL
ALCHEMICALLY
ALCHEMIES
ALCHEMIST
ALCHEMISTIC
ALCHEMISTICAL
ALCHEMISTS
ALCHEMIZE
ALCHEMIZED
ALCHEMIZES
ALCHEMIZING
ALCHEMY
ALCHYMIES
ALCHYMY
ALCID
ALCIDINE
ALCIDS
ALCOHOL
ALCOHOLIC
ALCOHOLICALLY
ALCOHOLICS
ALCOHOLISM
ALCOHOLISMS
ALCOHOLS
ALCOOL
ALCOOLS
ALCOPOP
ALCOPOPS
ALCOVE
ALCOVED
ALCOVES
ALCYONARIAN
ALCYONARIANS
ALDEHYDE
ALDEHYDES
ALDEHYDIC
ALDER
ALDERFLIES
ALDERFLY
ALDERMAN
ALDERMANIC
ALDERMEN
ALDERS
ALDERWOMAN
ALDERWOMEN
ALDICARB
ALDICARBS
ALDOL
ALDOLASE
ALDOLASES
ALDOLIZATION
ALDOLIZATIONS
ALDOLS
ALDOSE
ALDOSES
ALDOSTERONE
ALDOSTERONES
ALDOSTERONISM
ALDOSTERONISMS
ALDRIN
ALDRINS
ALE
ALEATORIC
ALEATORY
ALEC
ALECITHAL
ALECS
ALEE
ALEF
ALEFS
ALEGAR
ALEGARS
ALEHOUSE
ALEHOUSES
ALEMBIC
ALEMBICS
ALENCON
ALENCONS
ALEPH
ALEPHS
ALERT
ALERTED
ALERTER
ALERTEST
ALERTING
ALERTLY
ALERTNESS
ALERTNESSES
ALERTS
ALES
ALEURON
ALEURONE
ALEURONES
ALEURONIC
ALEURONS
ALEVIN
ALEVINS
ALEWIFE
ALEWIVES
ALEXANDER
ALEXANDERS
ALEXANDRINE
ALEXANDRINES
ALEXANDRITE
ALEXANDRITES
ALEXIA
ALEXIAS
ALEXIC
ALEXIN
ALEXINE
ALEXINES
ALEXINS
ALFA
ALFAKI
ALFAKIS
ALFALFA
ALFALFAS
ALFAQUI
ALFAQUIN
ALFAQUINS
ALFAQUIS
ALFAS
ALFILARIA
ALFILARIAS
ALFILERIA
ALFILERIAS
ALFORJA
ALFORJAS
ALFREDO
ALFRESCO
ALGA
ALGAE
ALGAECIDE
ALGAECIDES
ALGAL
ALGAROBA
ALGAROBAS
ALGARROBA
ALGARROBAS
ALGARROBO
ALGARROBOS
ALGAS
ALGEBRA
ALGEBRAIC
ALGEBRAICALLY
ALGEBRAIST
ALGEBRAISTS
ALGEBRAS
ALGERINE
ALGERINES
ALGICIDAL
ALGICIDE
ALGICIDES
ALGID
ALGIDITIES
ALGIDITY
ALGIDNESS
ALGIDNESSES
ALGIN
ALGINATE
ALGINATES
ALGINS
ALGOID
ALGOLAGNIA

ALGOLAGNIAC
ALGOLAGNIACS
ALGOLAGNIAS
ALGOLOGICAL
ALGOLOGIES
ALGOLOGIST
ALGOLOGISTS
ALGOLOGY
ALGOMETER
ALGOMETERS
ALGOMETRIES
ALGOMETRY
ALGOR
ALGORISM
ALGORISMS
ALGORITHM
ALGORITHMIC
ALGORITHMICALLY
ALGORITHMS
ALGORS
ALGUACIL
ALGUACILS
ALGUAZIL
ALGUAZILS
ALGUM
ALGUMS
ALIAS
ALIASED
ALIASES
ALIASING
ALIASINGS
ALIBI
ALIBIED
ALIBIES
ALIBIING
ALIBIS
ALIBLE
ALICYCLIC
ALIDAD
ALIDADE
ALIDADES
ALIDADS
ALIEN
ALIENABILITIES
ALIENABILITY
ALIENABLE
ALIENAGE
ALIENAGES
ALIENATE
ALIENATED
ALIENATES
ALIENATING
ALIENATION
ALIENATIONS
ALIENATOR
ALIENATORS
ALIENED
ALIENEE
ALIENEES
ALIENER
ALIENERS
ALIENING
ALIENISM
ALIENISMS
ALIENIST
ALIENISTS
ALIENLY
ALIENNESS
ALIENNESSES
ALIENOR
ALIENORS
ALIENS
ALIF
ALIFORM
ALIFS
ALIGHT
ALIGHTED
ALIGHTING
ALIGHTMENT
ALIGHTMENTS
ALIGHTS
ALIGN
ALIGNED
ALIGNER
ALIGNERS
ALIGNING
ALIGNMENT
ALIGNMENTS
ALIGNS
ALIKE
ALIKENESS
ALIKENESSES
ALIMENT
ALIMENTAL
ALIMENTARY
ALIMENTATION
ALIMENTATIONS
ALIMENTED
ALIMENTING
ALIMENTS
ALIMONIED
ALIMONIES
ALIMONY
ALINE
ALINED
ALINEMENT
ALINEMENTS
ALINER
ALINERS
ALINES
ALINING
ALIPED
ALIPEDS
ALIPHATIC
ALIQUANT
ALIQUOT
ALIQUOTS
ALIST
ALIT
ALITERACIES
ALITERACY
ALITERATE
ALITERATES
ALIUNDE
ALIVE
ALIVENESS
ALIVENESSES
ALIYA
ALIYAH
ALIYAHS
ALIYAS
ALIYOS
ALIYOT
ALIYOTH
ALIZARIN
ALIZARINE
ALIZARINES
ALIZARINS
ALKAHEST
ALKAHESTIC
ALKAHESTS
ALKALI
ALKALIC
ALKALIES
ALKALIFIED
ALKALIFIES
ALKALIFY
ALKALIFYING
ALKALIMETER
ALKALIMETERS
ALKALIMETRIES
ALKALIMETRY
ALKALIN
ALKALINE
ALKALINITIES
ALKALINITY
ALKALINIZATION
ALKALINIZATIONS
ALKALINIZE
ALKALINIZED
ALKALINIZES
ALKALINIZING
ALKALIS
ALKALISE
ALKALISED
ALKALISES
ALKALISING
ALKALIZE
ALKALIZED
ALKALIZER
ALKALIZERS
ALKALIZES
ALKALIZING
ALKALOID
ALKALOIDAL
ALKALOIDS
ALKALOSES
ALKALOSIS
ALKALOTIC
ALKANE
ALKANES
ALKANET
ALKANETS
ALKENE
ALKENES
ALKIE
ALKIES
ALKINE
ALKINES
ALKOXIDE
ALKOXIDES
ALKOXY
ALKY
ALKYD
ALKYDS
ALKYL
ALKYLATE
ALKYLATED
ALKYLATES
ALKYLATING
ALKYLATION
ALKYLATIONS
ALKYLIC
ALKYLS
ALKYNE
ALKYNES
ALL
ALLANITE
ALLANITES
ALLANTOIC
ALLANTOID
ALLANTOIDES
ALLANTOIDS
ALLANTOIN
ALLANTOINS
ALLANTOIS
ALLARGANDO
ALLAY
ALLAYED
ALLAYER
ALLAYERS
ALLAYING
ALLAYS
ALLEE
ALLEES
ALLEGATION
ALLEGATIONS
ALLEGE
ALLEGED
ALLEGEDLY
ALLEGER
ALLEGERS
ALLEGES
ALLEGIANCE
ALLEGIANCES
ALLEGIANT
ALLEGIANTS
ALLEGING
ALLEGORIC
ALLEGORICAL
ALLEGORICALLY
ALLEGORICALNESS
ALLEGORIES
ALLEGORISE
ALLEGORISED
ALLEGORISES
ALLEGORISING
ALLEGORIST
ALLEGORISTS
ALLEGORIZATION
ALLEGORIZATIONS
ALLEGORIZE
ALLEGORIZED
ALLEGORIZER
ALLEGORIZERS
ALLEGORIZES
ALLEGORIZING
ALLEGORY
ALLEGRETTO
ALLEGRETTOS
ALLEGRO
ALLEGROS
ALLELE
ALLELES
ALLELIC

ALLELISM
ALLELISMS
ALLELOMORPH
ALLELOMORPHIC
ALLELOMORPHISM
ALLELOMORPHISMS
ALLELOMORPHS
ALLELOPATHIC
ALLELOPATHIES
ALLELOPATHY
ALLELUIA
ALLELUIAS
ALLEMANDE
ALLEMANDES
ALLERGEN
ALLERGENIC
ALLERGENICITIES
ALLERGENICITY
ALLERGENS
ALLERGIC
ALLERGIES
ALLERGIN
ALLERGINS
ALLERGIST
ALLERGISTS
ALLERGY
ALLETHRIN
ALLETHRINS
ALLEVIANT
ALLEVIANTS
ALLEVIATE
ALLEVIATED
ALLEVIATES
ALLEVIATING
ALLEVIATION
ALLEVIATIONS
ALLEVIATOR
ALLEVIATORS
ALLEY
ALLEYS
ALLEYWAY
ALLEYWAYS
ALLHEAL
ALLHEALS
ALLIABLE
ALLIACEOUS
ALLIAK
ALLIAKS
ALLIANCE
ALLIANCES
ALLICIN
ALLICINS
ALLIED

ALLIES
ALLIGATOR
ALLIGATORS
ALLITERATE
ALLITERATED
ALLITERATES
ALLITERATING
ALLITERATION
ALLITERATIONS
ALLITERATIVE
ALLITERATIVELY
ALLIUM
ALLIUMS
ALLOANTIBODIES
ALLOANTIBODY
ALLOANTIGEN
ALLOANTIGENS
ALLOBAR
ALLOBARS
ALLOCABLE
ALLOCATABLE
ALLOCATE
ALLOCATED
ALLOCATES
ALLOCATING
ALLOCATION
ALLOCATIONS
ALLOCATOR
ALLOCATORS
ALLOCUTION
ALLOCUTIONS
ALLOD
ALLODIA
ALLODIAL
ALLODIUM
ALLODS
ALLOGAMIES
ALLOGAMOUS
ALLOGAMY
ALLOGENEIC
ALLOGENIC
ALLOGRAFT
ALLOGRAFTED
ALLOGRAFTING
ALLOGRAFTS
ALLOGRAPH
ALLOGRAPHIC
ALLOGRAPHS
ALLOMETRIC
ALLOMETRIES
ALLOMETRY
ALLOMORPH
ALLOMORPHIC

ALLOMORPHISM
ALLOMORPHISMS
ALLOMORPHS
ALLONGE
ALLONGES
ALLONYM
ALLONYMS
ALLOPATH
ALLOPATHIC
ALLOPATHIES
ALLOPATHS
ALLOPATHY
ALLOPATRIC
ALLOPATRICALLY
ALLOPATRIES
ALLOPATRY
ALLOPHANE
ALLOPHANES
ALLOPHONE
ALLOPHONES
ALLOPHONIC
ALLOPLASM
ALLOPLASMS
ALLOPOLYPLOID
ALLOPOLYPLOIDS
ALLOPOLYPLOIDY
ALLOPURINOL
ALLOPURINOLS
ALLOSAUR
ALLOSAURS
ALLOSAURUS
ALLOSAURUSES
ALLOSTERIC
ALLOSTERICALLY
ALLOSTERIES
ALLOSTERY
ALLOT
ALLOTETRAPLOID
ALLOTETRAPLOIDS
ALLOTETRAPLOIDY
ALLOTMENT
ALLOTMENTS
ALLOTROPE
ALLOTROPES
ALLOTROPIC
ALLOTROPIES
ALLOTROPY
ALLOTS
ALLOTTED
ALLOTTEE
ALLOTTEES
ALLOTTER
ALLOTTERS

ALLOTTING
ALLOTYPE
ALLOTYPES
ALLOTYPIC
ALLOTYPICALLY
ALLOTYPIES
ALLOTYPY
ALLOVER
ALLOVERS
ALLOW
ALLOWABLE
ALLOWABLES
ALLOWABLY
ALLOWANCE
ALLOWANCED
ALLOWANCES
ALLOWANCING
ALLOWED
ALLOWEDLY
ALLOWING
ALLOWS
ALLOXAN
ALLOXANS
ALLOY
ALLOYED
ALLOYING
ALLOYS
ALLS
ALLSEED
ALLSEEDS
ALLSORTS
ALLSPICE
ALLSPICES
ALLUDE
ALLUDED
ALLUDES
ALLUDING
ALLURE
ALLURED
ALLUREMENT
ALLUREMENTS
ALLURER
ALLURERS
ALLURES
ALLURING
ALLURINGLY
ALLUSION
ALLUSIONS
ALLUSIVE
ALLUSIVELY
ALLUSIVENESS
ALLUSIVENESSES
ALLUVIA

ALLUVIAL
ALLUVIALS
ALLUVION
ALLUVIONS
ALLUVIUM
ALLUVIUMS
ALLY
ALLYING
ALLYL
ALLYLIC
ALLYLS
ALMA
ALMAGEST
ALMAGESTS
ALMAH
ALMAHS
ALMANAC
ALMANACK
ALMANACKS
ALMANACS
ALMANDINE
ALMANDINES
ALMANDITE
ALMANDITES
ALMAS
ALME
ALMEH
ALMEHS
ALMEMAR
ALMEMARS
ALMES
ALMIGHTINESS
ALMIGHTINESSES
ALMIGHTY
ALMNER
ALMNERS
ALMOND
ALMONDS
ALMONDY
ALMONER
ALMONERS
ALMONRIES
ALMONRY
ALMOST
ALMS
ALMSGIVER
ALMSGIVERS
ALMSGIVING
ALMSGIVINGS
ALMSHOUSE
ALMSHOUSES
ALMSMAN
ALMSMEN

ALMUCE
ALMUCES
ALMUD
ALMUDE
ALMUDES
ALMUDS
ALMUG
ALMUGS
ALNICO
ALNICOS
ALODIA
ALODIAL
ALODIUM
ALOE
ALOES
ALOETIC
ALOFT
ALOGICAL
ALOGICALLY
ALOHA
ALOHAS
ALOIN
ALOINS
ALONE
ALONENESS
ALONENESSES
ALONG
ALONGSHORE
ALONGSIDE
ALOOF
ALOOFLY
ALOOFNESS
ALOOFNESSES
ALOPECIA
ALOPECIAS
ALOPECIC
ALOUD
ALOW
ALP
ALPACA
ALPACAS
ALPENGLOW
ALPENGLOWS
ALPENHORN
ALPENHORNS
ALPENSTOCK
ALPENSTOCKS
ALPHA
ALPHABET
ALPHABETED
ALPHABETIC
ALPHABETICAL
ALPHABETICALLY
ALPHABETING
ALPHABETISATION
ALPHABETISE
ALPHABETISED
ALPHABETISES
ALPHABETISING
ALPHABETIZATION
ALPHABETIZE
ALPHABETIZED
ALPHABETIZER
ALPHABETIZERS
ALPHABETIZES
ALPHABETIZING
ALPHABETS
ALPHAMERIC
ALPHANUMERIC
ALPHANUMERICAL
ALPHANUMERICS
ALPHAS
ALPHORN
ALPHORNS
ALPHOSIS
ALPHOSISES
ALPHYL
ALPHYLS
ALPINE
ALPINELY
ALPINES
ALPINISM
ALPINISMS
ALPINIST
ALPINISTS
ALPRAZOLAM
ALPRAZOLAMS
ALPROSTADIL
ALPROSTADILS
ALPS
ALREADY
ALRIGHT
ALS
ALSIKE
ALSIKES
ALSO
ALSTROEMERIA
ALSTROEMERIAS
ALT
ALTAR
ALTARPIECE
ALTARPIECES
ALTARS
ALTAZIMUTH
ALTAZIMUTHS
ALTER
ALTERABILITIES
ALTERABILITY
ALTERABLE
ALTERABLY
ALTERANT
ALTERANTS
ALTERATION
ALTERATIONS
ALTERCATE
ALTERCATED
ALTERCATES
ALTERCATING
ALTERCATION
ALTERCATIONS
ALTERED
ALTERER
ALTERERS
ALTERING
ALTERITIES
ALTERITY
ALTERNANT
ALTERNANTS
ALTERNATE
ALTERNATED
ALTERNATELY
ALTERNATES
ALTERNATING
ALTERNATION
ALTERNATIONS
ALTERNATIVE
ALTERNATIVELY
ALTERNATIVENESS
ALTERNATIVES
ALTERNATOR
ALTERNATORS
ALTERS
ALTHAEA
ALTHAEAS
ALTHEA
ALTHEAS
ALTHO
ALTHORN
ALTHORNS
ALTHOUGH
ALTIGRAPH
ALTIGRAPHS
ALTIMETER
ALTIMETERS
ALTIMETRIES
ALTIMETRY
ALTIPLANO
ALTIPLANOS
ALTITUDE
ALTITUDES
ALTITUDINAL
ALTITUDINOUS
ALTO
ALTOCUMULI
ALTOCUMULUS
ALTOGETHER
ALTOGETHERS
ALTOIST
ALTOISTS
ALTOS
ALTOSTRATI
ALTOSTRATUS
ALTRICIAL
ALTRUISM
ALTRUISMS
ALTRUIST
ALTRUISTIC
ALTRUISTICALLY
ALTRUISTS
ALTS
ALUDEL
ALUDELS
ALULA
ALULAE
ALULAR
ALUM
ALUMIN
ALUMINA
ALUMINAS
ALUMINATE
ALUMINATES
ALUMINE
ALUMINES
ALUMINIC
ALUMINIUM
ALUMINIUMS
ALUMINIZE
ALUMINIZED
ALUMINIZES
ALUMINIZING
ALUMINOSILICATE
ALUMINOUS
ALUMINS
ALUMINUM
ALUMINUMS
ALUMNA
ALUMNAE
ALUMNI
ALUMNUS
ALUMROOT
ALUMROOTS
ALUMS
ALUMSTONE
ALUMSTONES
ALUNITE
ALUNITES
ALVAR
ALVARS
ALVEOLAR
ALVEOLARLY
ALVEOLARS
ALVEOLATE
ALVEOLI
ALVEOLUS
ALVINE
ALWAY
ALWAYS
ALYSSUM
ALYSSUMS
AM
AMA
AMADAVAT
AMADAVATS
AMADOU
AMADOUS
AMAH
AMAHS
AMAIN
AMALGAM
AMALGAMATE
AMALGAMATED
AMALGAMATES
AMALGAMATING
AMALGAMATION
AMALGAMATIONS
AMALGAMATOR
AMALGAMATORS
AMALGAMS
AMANDINE
AMANITA
AMANITAS
AMANITIN
AMANITINS
AMANTADINE
AMANTADINES
AMANUENSES
AMANUENSIS
AMARANTH
AMARANTHINE
AMARANTHS
AMARELLE
AMARELLES
AMARETTI
AMARETTO
AMARETTOS

AMARNA
AMARONE
AMARONES
AMARYLLIS
AMARYLLISES
AMAS
AMASS
AMASSABLE
AMASSED
AMASSER
AMASSERS
AMASSES
AMASSING
AMASSMENT
AMASSMENTS
AMATEUR
AMATEURISH
AMATEURISHLY
AMATEURISHNESS
AMATEURISM
AMATEURISMS
AMATEURS
AMATIVE
AMATIVELY
AMATIVENESS
AMATIVENESSES
AMATOL
AMATOLS
AMATORY
AMAUROSES
AMAUROSIS
AMAUROTIC
AMAUTI
AMAUTIK
AMAUTIKS
AMAUTIS
AMAZE
AMAZED
AMAZEDLY
AMAZEMENT
AMAZEMENTS
AMAZES
AMAZING
AMAZINGLY
AMAZON
AMAZONIAN
AMAZONIANS
AMAZONITE
AMAZONITES
AMAZONS
AMAZONSTONE
AMAZONSTONES
AMBAGE
AMBAGES
AMBAGIOUS
AMBARI
AMBARIES
AMBARIS
AMBARY
AMBASSADOR
AMBASSADORIAL
AMBASSADORS
AMBASSADORSHIP
AMBASSADORSHIPS
AMBASSADRESS
AMBASSADRESSES
AMBEER
AMBEERS
AMBER
AMBERGRIS
AMBERGRISES
AMBERIES
AMBERINA
AMBERINAS
AMBERJACK
AMBERJACKS
AMBEROID
AMBEROIDS
AMBERS
AMBERY
AMBIANCE
AMBIANCES
AMBIDEXTERITIES
AMBIDEXTERITY
AMBIDEXTROUS
AMBIDEXTROUSLY
AMBIENCE
AMBIENCES
AMBIENT
AMBIENTS
AMBIGUITIES
AMBIGUITY
AMBIGUOUS
AMBIGUOUSLY
AMBIGUOUSNESS
AMBIGUOUSNESSES
AMBIPOLAR
AMBISEXUAL
AMBISEXUALITIES
AMBISEXUALITY
AMBISEXUALS
AMBIT
AMBITION
AMBITIONED
AMBITIONING
AMBITIONLESS
AMBITIONS
AMBITIOUS
AMBITIOUSLY
AMBITIOUSNESS
AMBITIOUSNESSES
AMBITS
AMBIVALENCE
AMBIVALENCES
AMBIVALENT
AMBIVALENTLY
AMBIVERSION
AMBIVERSIONS
AMBIVERT
AMBIVERTS
AMBLE
AMBLED
AMBLER
AMBLERS
AMBLES
AMBLING
AMBLYGONITE
AMBLYGONITES
AMBLYOPIA
AMBLYOPIAS
AMBLYOPIC
AMBO
AMBOINA
AMBOINAS
AMBONES
AMBOS
AMBOYNA
AMBOYNAS
AMBRIES
AMBROID
AMBROIDS
AMBROSIA
AMBROSIAL
AMBROSIALLY
AMBROSIAN
AMBROSIAS
AMBROTYPE
AMBROTYPES
AMBRY
AMBSACE
AMBSACES
AMBULACRA
AMBULACRAL
AMBULACRUM
AMBULANCE
AMBULANCES
AMBULANT
AMBULATE
AMBULATED
AMBULATES
AMBULATING
AMBULATION
AMBULATIONS
AMBULATOR
AMBULATORIES
AMBULATORILY
AMBULATORS
AMBULATORY
AMBULETTE
AMBULETTES
AMBUSCADE
AMBUSCADED
AMBUSCADER
AMBUSCADERS
AMBUSCADES
AMBUSCADING
AMBUSH
AMBUSHED
AMBUSHER
AMBUSHERS
AMBUSHES
AMBUSHING
AMBUSHMENT
AMBUSHMENTS
AMEBA
AMEBAE
AMEBAN
AMEBAS
AMEBEAN
AMEBIASES
AMEBIASIS
AMEBIC
AMEBOCYTE
AMEBOCYTES
AMEBOID
AMEER
AMEERATE
AMEERATES
AMEERS
AMELCORN
AMELCORNS
AMELIORATE
AMELIORATED
AMELIORATES
AMELIORATING
AMELIORATION
AMELIORATIONS
AMELIORATIVE
AMELIORATOR
AMELIORATORS
AMELIORATORY
AMELOBLAST
AMELOBLASTS
AMEN
AMENABILITIES
AMENABILITY
AMENABLE
AMENABLY
AMEND
AMENDABLE
AMENDATORY
AMENDED
AMENDER
AMENDERS
AMENDING
AMENDMENT
AMENDMENTS
AMENDS
AMENITIES
AMENITY
AMENORRHEA
AMENORRHEAS
AMENORRHEIC
AMENS
AMENT
AMENTA
AMENTIA
AMENTIAS
AMENTIFEROUS
AMENTS
AMENTUM
AMERCE
AMERCED
AMERCEMENT
AMERCEMENTS
AMERCER
AMERCERS
AMERCES
AMERCIABLE
AMERCING
AMERICIUM
AMERICIUMS
AMESACE
AMESACES
AMETHYST
AMETHYSTINE
AMETHYSTS
AMETROPIA
AMETROPIAS
AMETROPIC
AMI
AMIA
AMIABILITIES
AMIABILITY
AMIABLE

AMIABLENESS
AMIABLENESSES
AMIABLY
AMIANTHUS
AMIANTHUSES
AMIANTUS
AMIANTUSES
AMIAS
AMICABILITIES
AMICABILITY
AMICABLE
AMICABLENESS
AMICABLENESSES
AMICABLY
AMICE
AMICES
AMICI
AMICUS
AMID
AMIDASE
AMIDASES
AMIDE
AMIDES
AMIDIC
AMIDIN
AMIDINE
AMIDINES
AMIDINS
AMIDO
AMIDOGEN
AMIDOGENS
AMIDOL
AMIDOLS
AMIDONE
AMIDONES
AMIDS
AMIDSHIP
AMIDSHIPS
AMIDST
AMIE
AMIES
AMIGA
AMIGAS
AMIGO
AMIGOS
AMIN
AMINE
AMINES
AMINIC
AMINITIES
AMINITY
AMINO
AMINOACIDURIA
AMINOACIDURIAS
AMINOPEPTIDASE
AMINOPEPTIDASES
AMINOPHYLLINE
AMINOPHYLLINES
AMINOPTERIN
AMINOPTERINS
AMINOPYRINE
AMINOPYRINES
AMINOS
AMINS
AMIR
AMIRATE
AMIRATES
AMIRS
AMIS
AMISS
AMITIES
AMITOSES
AMITOSIS
AMITOTIC
AMITOTICALLY
AMITRIPTYLINE
AMITRIPTYLINES
AMITROLE
AMITROLES
AMITY
AMMETER
AMMETERS
AMMINE
AMMINES
AMMINO
AMMO
AMMOCETE
AMMOCETES
AMMOLITE
AMMOLITES
AMMONAL
AMMONALS
AMMONIA
AMMONIAC
AMMONIACAL
AMMONIACS
AMMONIAS
AMMONIATE
AMMONIATED
AMMONIATES
AMMONIATING
AMMONIATION
AMMONIATIONS
AMMONIC
AMMONIFICATION
AMMONIFICATIONS
AMMONIFIED
AMMONIFIES
AMMONIFY
AMMONIFYING
AMMONITE
AMMONITES
AMMONITIC
AMMONIUM
AMMONIUMS
AMMONO
AMMONOID
AMMONOIDS
AMMOS
AMMUNITION
AMMUNITIONS
AMNESIA
AMNESIAC
AMNESIACS
AMNESIAS
AMNESIC
AMNESICS
AMNESTIC
AMNESTIED
AMNESTIES
AMNESTY
AMNESTYING
AMNIA
AMNIC
AMNIO
AMNIOCENTESES
AMNIOCENTESIS
AMNION
AMNIONIC
AMNIONS
AMNIOS
AMNIOTE
AMNIOTES
AMNIOTIC
AMOBARBITAL
AMOBARBITALS
AMOEBA
AMOEBAE
AMOEBAEAN
AMOEBAN
AMOEBAS
AMOEBEAN
AMOEBIASES
AMOEBIASIS
AMOEBIC
AMOEBOCYTE
AMOEBOCYTES
AMOEBOID
AMOK
AMOKS
AMOLE
AMOLES
AMONG
AMONGST
AMONTILLADO
AMONTILLADOS
AMORAL
AMORALISM
AMORALISMS
AMORALITIES
AMORALITY
AMORALLY
AMORETTI
AMORETTO
AMORETTOS
AMORINI
AMORINO
AMORIST
AMORISTIC
AMORISTS
AMOROSO
AMOROSOS
AMOROUS
AMOROUSLY
AMOROUSNESS
AMOROUSNESSES
AMORPHISM
AMORPHISMS
AMORPHOUS
AMORPHOUSLY
AMORPHOUSNESS
AMORPHOUSNESSES
AMORT
AMORTISATION
AMORTISATIONS
AMORTISE
AMORTISED
AMORTISES
AMORTISING
AMORTIZABLE
AMORTIZATION
AMORTIZATIONS
AMORTIZE
AMORTIZED
AMORTIZES
AMORTIZING
AMOSITE
AMOSITES
AMOTION
AMOTIONS
AMOUNT
AMOUNTED
AMOUNTING
AMOUNTS
AMOUR
AMOURS
AMOXICILLIN
AMOXICILLINS
AMOXYCILLIN
AMOXYCILLINS
AMP
AMPED
AMPERAGE
AMPERAGES
AMPERE
AMPERES
AMPEROMETRIC
AMPERSAND
AMPERSANDS
AMPHETAMINE
AMPHETAMINES
AMPHIBIA
AMPHIBIAN
AMPHIBIANS
AMPHIBIOUS
AMPHIBIOUSLY
AMPHIBIOUSNESS
AMPHIBOLE
AMPHIBOLES
AMPHIBOLIES
AMPHIBOLITE
AMPHIBOLITES
AMPHIBOLOGIES
AMPHIBOLOGY
AMPHIBOLY
AMPHIBRACH
AMPHIBRACHIC
AMPHIBRACHS
AMPHICTYONIC
AMPHICTYONIES
AMPHICTYONY
AMPHIDIPLOID
AMPHIDIPLOIDIES
AMPHIDIPLOIDS
AMPHIDIPLOIDY
AMPHIGORIES
AMPHIGORY
AMPHIMACER
AMPHIMACERS
AMPHIMIXES
AMPHIMIXIS
AMPHIOXI
AMPHIOXUS
AMPHIOXUSES
AMPHIPATHIC

AMPHIPHILE
AMPHIPHILES
AMPHIPHILIC
AMPHIPLOID
AMPHIPLOIDIES
AMPHIPLOIDS
AMPHIPLOIDY
AMPHIPOD
AMPHIPODS
AMPHIPROSTYLE
AMPHIPROSTYLES
AMPHISBAENA
AMPHISBAENAS
AMPHISBAENIC
AMPHITHEATER
AMPHITHEATERS
AMPHITHEATRE
AMPHITHEATRES
AMPHITHEATRIC
AMPHITHEATRICAL
AMPHORA
AMPHORAE
AMPHORAL
AMPHORAS
AMPHOTERIC
AMPICILLIN
AMPICILLINS
AMPING
AMPLE
AMPLENESS
AMPLENESSES
AMPLER
AMPLEST
AMPLEXUS
AMPLEXUSES
AMPLIDYNE
AMPLIDYNES
AMPLIFICATION
AMPLIFICATIONS
AMPLIFIED
AMPLIFIER
AMPLIFIERS
AMPLIFIES
AMPLIFY
AMPLIFYING
AMPLITUDE
AMPLITUDES
AMPLY
AMPOULE
AMPOULES
AMPS
AMPUL
AMPULE
AMPULES
AMPULLA
AMPULLAE
AMPULLAR
AMPULLARY
AMPULS
AMPUTATE
AMPUTATED
AMPUTATES
AMPUTATING
AMPUTATION
AMPUTATIONS
AMPUTATOR
AMPUTATORS
AMPUTEE
AMPUTEES
AMREETA
AMREETAS
AMRIT
AMRITA
AMRITAS
AMRITS
AMSINCKIA
AMSINCKIAS
AMTRAC
AMTRACK
AMTRACKS
AMTRACS
AMTRAK
AMTRAKS
AMU
AMUCK
AMUCKS
AMULET
AMULETS
AMUS
AMUSABLE
AMUSE
AMUSED
AMUSEDLY
AMUSEMENT
AMUSEMENTS
AMUSER
AMUSERS
AMUSES
AMUSIA
AMUSIAS
AMUSING
AMUSINGLY
AMUSINGNESS
AMUSINGNESSES
AMUSIVE
AMYGDALA
AMYGDALAE
AMYGDALE
AMYGDALES
AMYGDALIN
AMYGDALINS
AMYGDALOID
AMYGDALOIDAL
AMYGDALOIDS
AMYGDULE
AMYGDULES
AMYL
AMYLASE
AMYLASES
AMYLENE
AMYLENES
AMYLIC
AMYLOGEN
AMYLOGENS
AMYLOID
AMYLOIDOSES
AMYLOIDOSIS
AMYLOIDS
AMYLOLYTIC
AMYLOPECTIN
AMYLOPECTINS
AMYLOPLAST
AMYLOPLASTS
AMYLOPSIN
AMYLOPSINS
AMYLOSE
AMYLOSES
AMYLS
AMYLUM
AMYLUMS
AMYOTONIA
AMYOTONIAS
AN
ANA
ANABAENA
ANABAENAS
ANABAPTISM
ANABAPTISMS
ANABAS
ANABASES
ANABASIS
ANABATIC
ANABIOSES
ANABIOSIS
ANABIOTIC
ANABLEPS
ANABLEPSES
ANABOLIC
ANABOLISM
ANABOLISMS
ANABRANCH
ANABRANCHES
ANACHRONIC
ANACHRONISM
ANACHRONISMS
ANACHRONISTIC
ANACHRONOUS
ANACHRONOUSLY
ANACLISES
ANACLISIS
ANACLITIC
ANACOLUTHA
ANACOLUTHIC
ANACOLUTHICALLY
ANACOLUTHON
ANACOLUTHONS
ANACONDA
ANACONDAS
ANACREONTIC
ANACREONTICS
ANACRUSES
ANACRUSIS
ANADEM
ANADEMS
ANADIPLOSES
ANADIPLOSIS
ANADROMOUS
ANAEMIA
ANAEMIAS
ANAEMIC
ANAEMICALLY
ANAEROBE
ANAEROBES
ANAEROBIA
ANAEROBIC
ANAEROBICALLY
ANAEROBIOSES
ANAEROBIOSIS
ANAEROBIUM
ANAESTHESIA
ANAESTHESIAS
ANAESTHESIOLOGY
ANAESTHETIC
ANAESTHETICS
ANAESTHETISE
ANAESTHETISED
ANAESTHETISES
ANAESTHETISING
ANAESTHETIST
ANAESTHETISTS
ANAESTHETIZE
ANAESTHETIZED
ANAESTHETIZES
ANAESTHETIZING
ANAGENESES
ANAGENESIS
ANAGLYPH
ANAGLYPHIC
ANAGLYPHS
ANAGNORISES
ANAGNORISIS
ANAGOGE
ANAGOGES
ANAGOGIC
ANAGOGICAL
ANAGOGICALLY
ANAGOGIES
ANAGOGY
ANAGRAM
ANAGRAMMATIC
ANAGRAMMATICAL
ANAGRAMMATIZE
ANAGRAMMATIZED
ANAGRAMMATIZES
ANAGRAMMATIZING
ANAGRAMMED
ANAGRAMMING
ANAGRAMS
ANAL
ANALCIME
ANALCIMES
ANALCIMIC
ANALCITE
ANALCITES
ANALECTA
ANALECTIC
ANALECTS
ANALEMMA
ANALEMMAS
ANALEMMATA
ANALEMMATIC
ANALEPTIC
ANALEPTICS
ANALGESIA
ANALGESIAS
ANALGESIC
ANALGESICS
ANALGETIC
ANALGETICS
ANALGIA
ANALGIAS
ANALITIES
ANALITY
ANALLY
ANALOG

ANALOGIC
ANALOGICAL
ANALOGICALLY
ANALOGIES
ANALOGISM
ANALOGISMS
ANALOGIST
ANALOGISTS
ANALOGIZE
ANALOGIZED
ANALOGIZES
ANALOGIZING
ANALOGOUS
ANALOGOUSLY
ANALOGOUSNESS
ANALOGOUSNESSES
ANALOGS
ANALOGUE
ANALOGUES
ANALOGY
ANALPHABET
ANALPHABETIC
ANALPHABETICS
ANALPHABETISM
ANALPHABETISMS
ANALPHABETS
ANALYSABLE
ANALYSAND
ANALYSANDS
ANALYSE
ANALYSED
ANALYSER
ANALYSERS
ANALYSES
ANALYSING
ANALYSIS
ANALYST
ANALYSTS
ANALYTE
ANALYTES
ANALYTIC
ANALYTICAL
ANALYTICALLY
ANALYTICITIES
ANALYTICITY
ANALYTICS
ANALYZABILITIES
ANALYZABILITY
ANALYZABLE
ANALYZATION
ANALYZATIONS
ANALYZE
ANALYZED
ANALYZER
ANALYZERS
ANALYZES
ANALYZING
ANAMNESES
ANAMNESIS
ANAMNESTIC
ANAMORPHIC
ANANDA
ANANDAMIDE
ANANDAMIDES
ANANDAS
ANANKE
ANANKES
ANAPAEST
ANAPAESTS
ANAPEST
ANAPESTIC
ANAPESTICS
ANAPESTS
ANAPHASE
ANAPHASES
ANAPHASIC
ANAPHOR
ANAPHORA
ANAPHORAL
ANAPHORAS
ANAPHORIC
ANAPHORICALLY
ANAPHORS
ANAPHRODISIAC
ANAPHRODISIACS
ANAPHYLACTIC
ANAPHYLACTOID
ANAPHYLAXES
ANAPHYLAXIS
ANAPLASIA
ANAPLASIAS
ANAPLASMOSES
ANAPLASMOSIS
ANAPLASTIC
ANAPTYXES
ANAPTYXIS
ANARCH
ANARCHIC
ANARCHICAL
ANARCHICALLY
ANARCHIES
ANARCHISM
ANARCHISMS
ANARCHIST
ANARCHISTIC
ANARCHISTS
ANARCHS
ANARCHY
ANARTHRIA
ANARTHRIAS
ANARTHRIC
ANAS
ANASARCA
ANASARCAS
ANASARCOUS
ANASTIGMAT
ANASTIGMATIC
ANASTIGMATS
ANASTOMOSE
ANASTOMOSED
ANASTOMOSES
ANASTOMOSING
ANASTOMOSIS
ANASTOMOTIC
ANASTROPHE
ANASTROPHES
ANATASE
ANATASES
ANATHEMA
ANATHEMAS
ANATHEMATA
ANATHEMATIZE
ANATHEMATIZED
ANATHEMATIZES
ANATHEMATIZING
ANATOMIC
ANATOMICAL
ANATOMICALLY
ANATOMIES
ANATOMISE
ANATOMISED
ANATOMISES
ANATOMISING
ANATOMIST
ANATOMISTS
ANATOMIZE
ANATOMIZED
ANATOMIZES
ANATOMIZING
ANATOMY
ANATOXIN
ANATOXINS
ANATROPOUS
ANATTO
ANATTOS
ANCESTOR
ANCESTORED
ANCESTORING
ANCESTORS
ANCESTRAL
ANCESTRALLY
ANCESTRESS
ANCESTRESSES
ANCESTRIES
ANCESTRY
ANCHO
ANCHOR
ANCHORAGE
ANCHORAGES
ANCHORED
ANCHORESS
ANCHORESSES
ANCHORET
ANCHORETS
ANCHORING
ANCHORITE
ANCHORITES
ANCHORITIC
ANCHORITICALLY
ANCHORLESS
ANCHORMAN
ANCHORMEN
ANCHORPEOPLE
ANCHORPERSON
ANCHORPERSONS
ANCHORS
ANCHORWOMAN
ANCHORWOMEN
ANCHOS
ANCHOVETA
ANCHOVETAS
ANCHOVETTA
ANCHOVETTAS
ANCHOVIES
ANCHOVY
ANCHUSA
ANCHUSAS
ANCHUSIN
ANCHUSINS
ANCHYLOSE
ANCHYLOSED
ANCHYLOSES
ANCHYLOSING
ANCIENT
ANCIENTER
ANCIENTEST
ANCIENTLY
ANCIENTNESS
ANCIENTNESSES
ANCIENTRIES
ANCIENTRY
ANCIENTS
ANCILLA
ANCILLAE
ANCILLARIES
ANCILLARY
ANCILLAS
ANCIPITAL
ANCON
ANCONAL
ANCONE
ANCONEAL
ANCONES
ANCONOID
ANCRESS
ANCRESSES
ANCYLOSTOMIASES
ANCYLOSTOMIASIS
AND
ANDALUSITE
ANDALUSITES
ANDANTE
ANDANTES
ANDANTINI
ANDANTINO
ANDANTINOS
ANDESITE
ANDESITES
ANDESITIC
ANDESYTE
ANDESYTES
ANDIRON
ANDIRONS
ANDOUILLE
ANDOUILLES
ANDOUILLETTE
ANDOUILLETTES
ANDRADITE
ANDRADITES
ANDRO
ANDROCENTRIC
ANDROCENTRISM
ANDROCENTRISMS
ANDROECIA
ANDROECIUM
ANDROGEN
ANDROGENESES
ANDROGENESIS
ANDROGENETIC
ANDROGENIC
ANDROGENS
ANDROGYNE
ANDROGYNES
ANDROGYNIES
ANDROGYNOUS

ANDROGYNOUSLY
ANDROGYNY
ANDROID
ANDROIDS
ANDROLOGIES
ANDROLOGY
ANDROMEDA
ANDROMEDAS
ANDROPAUSE
ANDROPAUSES
ANDROS
ANDROSTENEDIONE
ANDROSTERONE
ANDROSTERONES
ANDS
ANE
ANEAR
ANEARED
ANEARING
ANEARS
ANECDOTA
ANECDOTAGE
ANECDOTAGES
ANECDOTAL
ANECDOTALISM
ANECDOTALISMS
ANECDOTALIST
ANECDOTALISTS
ANECDOTALLY
ANECDOTE
ANECDOTES
ANECDOTIC
ANECDOTICAL
ANECDOTICALLY
ANECDOTIST
ANECDOTISTS
ANECHOIC
ANELASTIC
ANELASTICITIES
ANELASTICITY
ANELE
ANELED
ANELES
ANELING
ANEMIA
ANEMIAS
ANEMIC
ANEMICALLY
ANEMOGRAPH
ANEMOGRAPHS
ANEMOLOGIES
ANEMOLOGY
ANEMOMETER
ANEMOMETERS
ANEMOMETRIES
ANEMOMETRY
ANEMONE
ANEMONES
ANEMOPHILOUS
ANEMOSES
ANEMOSIS
ANENCEPHALIC
ANENCEPHALIES
ANENCEPHALY
ANENST
ANENT
ANERGIA
ANERGIAS
ANERGIC
ANERGIES
ANERGY
ANEROID
ANEROIDS
ANES
ANESTHESIA
ANESTHESIAS
ANESTHESIOLOGY
ANESTHETIC
ANESTHETICALLY
ANESTHETICS
ANESTHETIST
ANESTHETISTS
ANESTHETIZE
ANESTHETIZED
ANESTHETIZES
ANESTHETIZING
ANESTRI
ANESTROUS
ANESTRUS
ANETHOL
ANETHOLE
ANETHOLES
ANETHOLS
ANEUPLOID
ANEUPLOIDIES
ANEUPLOIDS
ANEUPLOIDY
ANEURIN
ANEURINS
ANEURISM
ANEURISMS
ANEURYSM
ANEURYSMAL
ANEURYSMS
ANEW
ANFRACTUOSITIES
ANFRACTUOSITY
ANFRACTUOUS
ANGA
ANGAKOK
ANGAKOKS
ANGARIA
ANGARIAS
ANGARIES
ANGARY
ANGAS
ANGEL
ANGELED
ANGELFISH
ANGELFISHES
ANGELIC
ANGELICA
ANGELICAL
ANGELICALLY
ANGELICAS
ANGELING
ANGELOLOGIES
ANGELOLOGIST
ANGELOLOGISTS
ANGELOLOGY
ANGELS
ANGELUS
ANGELUSES
ANGER
ANGERED
ANGERING
ANGERLESS
ANGERLY
ANGERS
ANGINA
ANGINAL
ANGINAS
ANGINOSE
ANGINOUS
ANGIOGENESES
ANGIOGENESIS
ANGIOGENIC
ANGIOGRAM
ANGIOGRAMS
ANGIOGRAPHIC
ANGIOGRAPHIES
ANGIOGRAPHY
ANGIOLOGIES
ANGIOLOGY
ANGIOMA
ANGIOMAS
ANGIOMATA
ANGIOMATOUS
ANGIOPLASTIES
ANGIOPLASTY
ANGIOSPERM
ANGIOSPERMOUS
ANGIOSPERMS
ANGIOTENSIN
ANGIOTENSINS
ANGLE
ANGLED
ANGLEPOD
ANGLEPODS
ANGLER
ANGLERFISH
ANGLERFISHES
ANGLERS
ANGLES
ANGLESITE
ANGLESITES
ANGLEWORM
ANGLEWORMS
ANGLICE
ANGLICISATION
ANGLICISATIONS
ANGLICISE
ANGLICISED
ANGLICISES
ANGLICISING
ANGLICISM
ANGLICISMS
ANGLICIZATION
ANGLICIZATIONS
ANGLICIZE
ANGLICIZED
ANGLICIZES
ANGLICIZING
ANGLING
ANGLINGS
ANGLO
ANGLOPHONE
ANGLOPHONES
ANGLOS
ANGORA
ANGORAS
ANGOSTURA
ANGOSTURAS
ANGRIER
ANGRIEST
ANGRILY
ANGRINESS
ANGRINESSES
ANGRY
ANGST
ANGSTIER
ANGSTIEST
ANGSTROM
ANGSTROMS
ANGSTS
ANGSTY
ANGUINE
ANGUISH
ANGUISHED
ANGUISHES
ANGUISHING
ANGULAR
ANGULARITIES
ANGULARITY
ANGULARLY
ANGULATE
ANGULATED
ANGULATES
ANGULATING
ANGULATION
ANGULATIONS
ANGULOSE
ANGULOUS
ANHEDONIA
ANHEDONIAS
ANHEDONIC
ANHEDRAL
ANHEDRALS
ANHINGA
ANHINGAS
ANHYDRIDE
ANHYDRIDES
ANHYDRITE
ANHYDRITES
ANHYDROUS
ANI
ANIL
ANILE
ANILIN
ANILINCTUS
ANILINCTUSES
ANILINE
ANILINES
ANILINGUS
ANILINGUSES
ANILINS
ANILITIES
ANILITY
ANILS
ANIMA
ANIMACIES
ANIMACY
ANIMADVERSION
ANIMADVERSIONS
ANIMADVERT

ANIMADVERTED
ANIMADVERTING
ANIMADVERTS
ANIMAL
ANIMALCULA
ANIMALCULE
ANIMALCULES
ANIMALCULUM
ANIMALIAN
ANIMALIC
ANIMALIER
ANIMALIERS
ANIMALISM
ANIMALISMS
ANIMALIST
ANIMALISTIC
ANIMALISTS
ANIMALITIES
ANIMALITY
ANIMALIZATION
ANIMALIZATIONS
ANIMALIZE
ANIMALIZED
ANIMALIZES
ANIMALIZING
ANIMALLIKE
ANIMALLY
ANIMALS
ANIMAS
ANIMATE
ANIMATED
ANIMATEDLY
ANIMATELY
ANIMATENESS
ANIMATENESSES
ANIMATER
ANIMATERS
ANIMATES
ANIMATI
ANIMATING
ANIMATION
ANIMATIONS
ANIMATISM
ANIMATISMS
ANIMATIST
ANIMATISTS
ANIMATO
ANIMATOR
ANIMATORS
ANIMATOS
ANIMATRONIC
ANIMATRONICALLY
ANIMATRONICS
ANIME
ANIMES
ANIMI
ANIMIS
ANIMISM
ANIMISMS
ANIMIST
ANIMISTIC
ANIMISTS
ANIMOSITIES
ANIMOSITY
ANIMUS
ANIMUSES
ANION
ANIONIC
ANIONS
ANIS
ANISE
ANISEED
ANISEEDS
ANISEIKONIA
ANISEIKONIAS
ANISEIKONIC
ANISES
ANISETTE
ANISETTES
ANISIC
ANISOGAMIES
ANISOGAMOUS
ANISOGAMY
ANISOLE
ANISOLES
ANISOMETROPIA
ANISOMETROPIAS
ANISOMETROPIC
ANISOTROPIC
ANISOTROPICALLY
ANISOTROPIES
ANISOTROPISM
ANISOTROPISMS
ANISOTROPY
ANKERITE
ANKERITES
ANKH
ANKHS
ANKLE
ANKLEBONE
ANKLEBONES
ANKLED
ANKLES
ANKLET
ANKLETS
ANKLING
ANKUS
ANKUSES
ANKUSH
ANKUSHES
ANKYLOSAUR
ANKYLOSAURS
ANKYLOSAURUS
ANKYLOSAURUSES
ANKYLOSE
ANKYLOSED
ANKYLOSES
ANKYLOSING
ANKYLOSIS
ANKYLOSTOMIASES
ANKYLOSTOMIASIS
ANKYLOTIC
ANLACE
ANLACES
ANLAGE
ANLAGEN
ANLAGES
ANLAS
ANLASES
ANNA
ANNAL
ANNALIST
ANNALISTIC
ANNALISTS
ANNALS
ANNAS
ANNATES
ANNATTO
ANNATTOS
ANNEAL
ANNEALED
ANNEALER
ANNEALERS
ANNEALING
ANNEALS
ANNELID
ANNELIDAN
ANNELIDANS
ANNELIDS
ANNEX
ANNEXATION
ANNEXATIONAL
ANNEXATIONIST
ANNEXATIONISTS
ANNEXATIONS
ANNEXE
ANNEXED
ANNEXES
ANNEXING
ANNIHILATE
ANNIHILATED
ANNIHILATES
ANNIHILATING
ANNIHILATION
ANNIHILATIONS
ANNIHILATOR
ANNIHILATORS
ANNIHILATORY
ANNIVERSARIES
ANNIVERSARY
ANNONA
ANNONAS
ANNOTATE
ANNOTATED
ANNOTATES
ANNOTATING
ANNOTATION
ANNOTATIONS
ANNOTATIVE
ANNOTATOR
ANNOTATORS
ANNOUNCE
ANNOUNCED
ANNOUNCEMENT
ANNOUNCEMENTS
ANNOUNCER
ANNOUNCERS
ANNOUNCES
ANNOUNCING
ANNOY
ANNOYANCE
ANNOYANCES
ANNOYED
ANNOYER
ANNOYERS
ANNOYING
ANNOYINGLY
ANNOYS
ANNUAL
ANNUALIZE
ANNUALIZED
ANNUALIZES
ANNUALIZING
ANNUALLY
ANNUALS
ANNUITANT
ANNUITANTS
ANNUITIES
ANNUITY
ANNUL
ANNULAR
ANNULARLY
ANNULATE
ANNULATED
ANNULATION
ANNULATIONS
ANNULET
ANNULETS
ANNULI
ANNULLED
ANNULLING
ANNULMENT
ANNULMENTS
ANNULOSE
ANNULS
ANNULUS
ANNULUSES
ANNUNCIATE
ANNUNCIATED
ANNUNCIATES
ANNUNCIATING
ANNUNCIATION
ANNUNCIATIONS
ANNUNCIATOR
ANNUNCIATORS
ANNUNCIATORY
ANOA
ANOAS
ANODAL
ANODALLY
ANODE
ANODES
ANODIC
ANODICALLY
ANODISE
ANODISED
ANODISER
ANODISERS
ANODISES
ANODISING
ANODIZATION
ANODIZATIONS
ANODIZE
ANODIZED
ANODIZER
ANODIZERS
ANODIZES
ANODIZING
ANODYNE
ANODYNES
ANODYNIC
ANOINT
ANOINTED
ANOINTER
ANOINTERS

ANOINTING
ANOINTMENT
ANOINTMENTS
ANOINTS
ANOLE
ANOLES
ANOLYTE
ANOLYTES
ANOMALIES
ANOMALOUS
ANOMALOUSLY
ANOMALOUSNESS
ANOMALOUSNESSES
ANOMALY
ANOMIC
ANOMIE
ANOMIES
ANOMY
ANON
ANONYM
ANONYMITIES
ANONYMITY
ANONYMOUS
ANONYMOUSLY
ANONYMOUSNESS
ANONYMOUSNESSES
ANONYMS
ANOOPSIA
ANOOPSIAS
ANOPHELES
ANOPHELINE
ANOPHELINES
ANOPIA
ANOPIAS
ANOPSIA
ANOPSIAS
ANORAK
ANORAKS
ANORECTIC
ANORECTICS
ANORETIC
ANORETICS
ANOREXIA
ANOREXIAS
ANOREXIC
ANOREXICS
ANOREXIES
ANOREXIGENIC
ANOREXY
ANORTHIC
ANORTHITE
ANORTHITES
ANORTHITIC
ANORTHOSITE
ANORTHOSITES
ANORTHOSITIC
ANOSMATIC
ANOSMIA
ANOSMIAS
ANOSMIC
ANOTHER
ANOVULANT
ANOVULANTS
ANOVULAR
ANOVULATORY
ANOXEMIA
ANOXEMIAS
ANOXEMIC
ANOXIA
ANOXIAS
ANOXIC
ANSA
ANSAE
ANSATE
ANSATED
ANSERINE
ANSERINES
ANSEROUS
ANSWER
ANSWERABILITIES
ANSWERABILITY
ANSWERABLE
ANSWERED
ANSWERER
ANSWERERS
ANSWERING
ANSWERPHONE
ANSWERPHONES
ANSWERS
ANT
ANTA
ANTACID
ANTACIDS
ANTAE
ANTAGONISE
ANTAGONISED
ANTAGONISES
ANTAGONISING
ANTAGONISM
ANTAGONISMS
ANTAGONIST
ANTAGONISTIC
ANTAGONISTS
ANTAGONIZE
ANTAGONIZED
ANTAGONIZES
ANTAGONIZING
ANTALGIC
ANTALGICS
ANTALKALI
ANTALKALIES
ANTALKALIS
ANTARCTIC
ANTAS
ANTBEAR
ANTBEARS
ANTE
ANTEATER
ANTEATERS
ANTEBELLUM
ANTECEDE
ANTECEDED
ANTECEDENCE
ANTECEDENCES
ANTECEDENT
ANTECEDENTLY
ANTECEDENTS
ANTECEDES
ANTECEDING
ANTECESSOR
ANTECESSORS
ANTECHAMBER
ANTECHAMBERS
ANTECHAPEL
ANTECHAPELS
ANTECHOIR
ANTECHOIRS
ANTED
ANTEDATE
ANTEDATED
ANTEDATES
ANTEDATING
ANTEDATINGS
ANTEDILUVIAN
ANTEDILUVIANS
ANTEED
ANTEFIX
ANTEFIXA
ANTEFIXAE
ANTEFIXAL
ANTEFIXES
ANTEING
ANTELOPE
ANTELOPES
ANTEMORTEM
ANTENATAL
ANTENATALLY
ANTENNA
ANTENNAE
ANTENNAL
ANTENNAS
ANTENNULAR
ANTENNULE
ANTENNULES
ANTENUPTIAL
ANTEPAST
ANTEPASTS
ANTEPENDIA
ANTEPENDIUM
ANTEPENDIUMS
ANTEPENULT
ANTEPENULTIMA
ANTEPENULTIMAS
ANTEPENULTIMATE
ANTEPENULTS
ANTERIOR
ANTERIORLY
ANTEROGRADE
ANTEROOM
ANTEROOMS
ANTES
ANTETYPE
ANTETYPES
ANTEVERT
ANTEVERTED
ANTEVERTING
ANTEVERTS
ANTHELIA
ANTHELICES
ANTHELION
ANTHELIONS
ANTHELIX
ANTHELIXES
ANTHELMINTIC
ANTHELMINTICS
ANTHEM
ANTHEMED
ANTHEMIA
ANTHEMIC
ANTHEMING
ANTHEMION
ANTHEMS
ANTHER
ANTHERAL
ANTHERID
ANTHERIDIA
ANTHERIDIAL
ANTHERIDIUM
ANTHERIDS
ANTHERS
ANTHESES
ANTHESIS
ANTHILL
ANTHILLS
ANTHOCYAN
ANTHOCYANIN
ANTHOCYANINS
ANTHOCYANS
ANTHODIA
ANTHODIUM
ANTHOID
ANTHOLOGICAL
ANTHOLOGIES
ANTHOLOGIST
ANTHOLOGISTS
ANTHOLOGIZE
ANTHOLOGIZED
ANTHOLOGIZER
ANTHOLOGIZERS
ANTHOLOGIZES
ANTHOLOGIZING
ANTHOLOGY
ANTHOPHILOUS
ANTHOPHYLLITE
ANTHOPHYLLITES
ANTHOZOAN
ANTHOZOANS
ANTHOZOIC
ANTHRACENE
ANTHRACENES
ANTHRACES
ANTHRACITE
ANTHRACITES
ANTHRACITIC
ANTHRACNOSE
ANTHRACNOSES
ANTHRANILATE
ANTHRANILATES
ANTHRAQUINONE
ANTHRAQUINONES
ANTHRAX
ANTHRAXES
ANTHRO
ANTHROPIC
ANTHROPICAL
ANTHROPOCENTRIC
ANTHROPOGENIC
ANTHROPOID
ANTHROPOIDS
ANTHROPOLOGICAL
ANTHROPOLOGIES
ANTHROPOLOGIST
ANTHROPOLOGISTS
ANTHROPOLOGY
ANTHROPOMETRIC

ANTHROPOMETRIES
ANTHROPOMETRY
ANTHROPOMORPH
ANTHROPOMORPHIC
ANTHROPOMORPHS
ANTHROPOPATHISM
ANTHROPOPHAGI
ANTHROPOPHAGIES
ANTHROPOPHAGOUS
ANTHROPOPHAGUS
ANTHROPOPHAGY
ANTHROPOSOPHIES
ANTHROPOSOPHIST
ANTHROPOSOPHY
ANTHROS
ANTHURIUM
ANTHURIUMS
ANTI
ANTIABORTION
ANTIABORTIONIST
ANTIABUSE
ANTIACADEMIC
ANTIACNE
ANTIAGGRESSION
ANTIAGGRESSIONS
ANTIAGING
ANTIAIR
ANTIAIRCRAFT
ANTIAIRCRAFTS
ANTIALCOHOL
ANTIALCOHOLISM
ANTIALCOHOLISMS
ANTIALIASING
ANTIALIASINGS
ANTIALIEN
ANTIALLERGENIC
ANTIALLERGY
ANTIANEMIA
ANTIANXIETY
ANTIAPARTHEID
ANTIAPHRODISIAC
ANTIAR
ANTIARIN
ANTIARINS
ANTIARMOR
ANTIARRHYTHMIC
ANTIARS
ANTIARTHRITIC
ANTIARTHRITICS
ANTIARTHRITIS
ANTIASTHMA
ANTIATOM
ANTIATOMS
ANTIAUTHORITY
ANTIAUXIN
ANTIAUXINS
ANTIBACKLASH
ANTIBACTERIAL
ANTIBACTERIALS
ANTIBIAS
ANTIBILLBOARD
ANTIBIOSES
ANTIBIOSIS
ANTIBIOTIC
ANTIBIOTICALLY
ANTIBIOTICS
ANTIBLACK
ANTIBLACKISM
ANTIBLACKISMS
ANTIBODIES
ANTIBODY
ANTIBONDING
ANTIBOSS
ANTIBOURGEOIS
ANTIBOYCOTT
ANTIBUG
ANTIBURGLAR
ANTIBURGLARY
ANTIBUSER
ANTIBUSERS
ANTIBUSINESS
ANTIBUSING
ANTIC
ANTICAKING
ANTICALLY
ANTICANCER
ANTICAPITALISM
ANTICAPITALISMS
ANTICAPITALIST
ANTICAPITALISTS
ANTICAR
ANTICARCINOGEN
ANTICARCINOGENS
ANTICARIES
ANTICELLULITE
ANTICENSORSHIP
ANTICHLOR
ANTICHLORS
ANTICHOICE
ANTICHOICER
ANTICHOICERS
ANTICHOLESTEROL
ANTICHOLINERGIC
ANTICHURCH
ANTICIGARETTE
ANTICIPANT
ANTICIPANTS
ANTICIPATABLE
ANTICIPATE
ANTICIPATED
ANTICIPATES
ANTICIPATING
ANTICIPATION
ANTICIPATIONS
ANTICIPATOR
ANTICIPATORS
ANTICIPATORY
ANTICITY
ANTICIVIC
ANTICK
ANTICKED
ANTICKING
ANTICKS
ANTICLASSICAL
ANTICLERICAL
ANTICLERICALISM
ANTICLERICALS
ANTICLIMACTIC
ANTICLIMACTICAL
ANTICLIMAX
ANTICLIMAXES
ANTICLINAL
ANTICLINE
ANTICLINES
ANTICLING
ANTICLOCKWISE
ANTICLOTTING
ANTICLY
ANTICOAGULANT
ANTICOAGULANTS
ANTICODON
ANTICODONS
ANTICOLD
ANTICOLLISION
ANTICOLONIAL
ANTICOLONIALISM
ANTICOLONIALIST
ANTICOLONIALS
ANTICOMMERCIAL
ANTICOMMUNISM
ANTICOMMUNISMS
ANTICOMMUNIST
ANTICOMMUNISTS
ANTICOMPETITIVE
ANTICONSUMER
ANTICONVULSANT
ANTICONVULSANTS
ANTICONVULSIVE
ANTICONVULSIVES
ANTICORPORATE
ANTICORROSION
ANTICORROSIVE
ANTICORROSIVES
ANTICORRUPTION
ANTICRACK
ANTICREATIVE
ANTICRIME
ANTICRUELTY
ANTICS
ANTICULT
ANTICULTS
ANTICULTURAL
ANTICYCLONE
ANTICYCLONES
ANTICYCLONIC
ANTIDANDRUFF
ANTIDEFAMATION
ANTIDEMOCRATIC
ANTIDEPRESSANT
ANTIDEPRESSANTS
ANTIDEPRESSION
ANTIDERIVATIVE
ANTIDERIVATIVES
ANTIDESICCANT
ANTIDESICCANTS
ANTIDEVELOPMENT
ANTIDIABETIC
ANTIDIARRHEAL
ANTIDIARRHEALS
ANTIDILUTION
ANTIDOGMATIC
ANTIDORA
ANTIDOTAL
ANTIDOTALLY
ANTIDOTE
ANTIDOTED
ANTIDOTES
ANTIDOTING
ANTIDRAFT
ANTIDROMIC
ANTIDROMICALLY
ANTIDRUG
ANTIDUMPING
ANTIECONOMIC
ANTIEDUCATIONAL
ANTIEGALITARIAN
ANTIELECTRON
ANTIELECTRONS
ANTIELITE
ANTIELITES
ANTIELITISM
ANTIELITISMS
ANTIELITIST
ANTIELITISTS
ANTIEMETIC
ANTIEMETICS
ANTIENTROPIC
ANTIEPILEPSY
ANTIEPILEPTIC
ANTIEPILEPTICS
ANTIEROTIC
ANTIESTROGEN
ANTIESTROGENS
ANTIEVOLUTION
ANTIFAMILY
ANTIFASCISM
ANTIFASCISMS
ANTIFASCIST
ANTIFASCISTS
ANTIFASHION
ANTIFASHIONABLE
ANTIFASHIONS
ANTIFAT
ANTIFATIGUE
ANTIFEMALE
ANTIFEMININE
ANTIFEMINISM
ANTIFEMINISMS
ANTIFEMINIST
ANTIFEMINISTS
ANTIFERROMAGNET
ANTIFERTILITY
ANTIFILIBUSTER
ANTIFLU
ANTIFOAM
ANTIFOAMING
ANTIFOG
ANTIFOGGING
ANTIFORECLOSURE
ANTIFOREIGN
ANTIFOREIGNER
ANTIFOREIGNERS
ANTIFORMALIST
ANTIFORMALISTS
ANTIFOULING
ANTIFRAUD
ANTIFREEZE
ANTIFREEZES
ANTIFRICTION
ANTIFUNGAL
ANTIFUNGALS
ANTIFUR
ANTIGAMBLING
ANTIGANG
ANTIGAY

ANTIGEN
ANTIGENE
ANTIGENES
ANTIGENIC
ANTIGENICALLY
ANTIGENICITIES
ANTIGENICITY
ANTIGENS
ANTIGLARE
ANTIGLOBULIN
ANTIGLOBULINS
ANTIGOVERNMENT
ANTIGRAFT
ANTIGRAVITIES
ANTIGRAVITY
ANTIGROWTH
ANTIGUERRILLA
ANTIGUERRILLAS
ANTIGUN
ANTIHARASSMENT
ANTIHELICES
ANTIHELIX
ANTIHELIXES
ANTIHERO
ANTIHEROES
ANTIHEROIC
ANTIHEROINE
ANTIHEROINES
ANTIHERPES
ANTIHIJACK
ANTIHIJACKING
ANTIHISTAMINE
ANTIHISTAMINES
ANTIHISTAMINIC
ANTIHISTAMINICS
ANTIHISTORICAL
ANTIHOMOSEXUAL
ANTIHORMONE
ANTIHORMONES
ANTIHUMAN
ANTIHUMANISM
ANTIHUMANISMS
ANTIHUMANIST
ANTIHUMANISTIC
ANTIHUMANISTS
ANTIHUNGER
ANTIHUNTER
ANTIHUNTING
ANTIHYSTERIC
ANTIHYSTERICS
ANTIJAM
ANTIJAMMING
ANTIKICKBACK
ANTIKING
ANTIKINGS
ANTIKNOCK
ANTIKNOCKS
ANTILABOR
ANTILEAK
ANTILEFT
ANTILEPROSY
ANTILEUKEMIC
ANTILIBERAL
ANTILIBERALISM
ANTILIBERALISMS
ANTILIBERALS
ANTILIBERTARIAN
ANTILIFE
ANTILIFER
ANTILIFERS
ANTILITERARY
ANTILITERATE
ANTILITTER
ANTILITTERING
ANTILOCK
ANTILOG
ANTILOGARITHM
ANTILOGARITHMS
ANTILOGICAL
ANTILOGIES
ANTILOGS
ANTILOGY
ANTILYNCHING
ANTIMACASSAR
ANTIMACASSARS
ANTIMACHO
ANTIMAGNETIC
ANTIMALARIA
ANTIMALARIAL
ANTIMALARIALS
ANTIMALE
ANTIMAN
ANTIMANAGEMENT
ANTIMARIJUANA
ANTIMARKET
ANTIMARKETS
ANTIMASK
ANTIMASKS
ANTIMATERIALISM
ANTIMATERIALIST
ANTIMATTER
ANTIMATTERS
ANTIMECHANIST
ANTIMECHANISTS
ANTIMERE
ANTIMERES
ANTIMERGER
ANTIMERIC
ANTIMETABOLIC
ANTIMETABOLITE
ANTIMETABOLITES
ANTIMICROBIAL
ANTIMICROBIALS
ANTIMILITARISM
ANTIMILITARISMS
ANTIMILITARIST
ANTIMILITARISTS
ANTIMILITARY
ANTIMINE
ANTIMISSILE
ANTIMISSILES
ANTIMITOTIC
ANTIMITOTICS
ANTIMODERN
ANTIMODERNISM
ANTIMODERNIST
ANTIMODERNISTS
ANTIMONARCHICAL
ANTIMONARCHIST
ANTIMONARCHISTS
ANTIMONIAL
ANTIMONIALS
ANTIMONIC
ANTIMONIDE
ANTIMONIDES
ANTIMONIES
ANTIMONOPOLIES
ANTIMONOPOLIST
ANTIMONOPOLISTS
ANTIMONOPOLY
ANTIMONY
ANTIMONYL
ANTIMONYLS
ANTIMOSQUITO
ANTIMUSIC
ANTIMUSICAL
ANTIMUSICS
ANTIMYCIN
ANTIMYCINS
ANTINARCOTICS
ANTINARRATIVE
ANTINARRATIVES
ANTINATIONAL
ANTINATIONALIST
ANTINATIONALS
ANTINATURAL
ANTINATURE
ANTINAUSEA
ANTINEOPLASTIC
ANTINEPOTISM
ANTINEUTRINO
ANTINEUTRINOS
ANTINEUTRON
ANTINEUTRONS
ANTING
ANTINGS
ANTINODAL
ANTINODE
ANTINODES
ANTINOISE
ANTINOME
ANTINOMES
ANTINOMIAN
ANTINOMIANISM
ANTINOMIANISMS
ANTINOMIANS
ANTINOMIC
ANTINOMIES
ANTINOMY
ANTINOVEL
ANTINOVELIST
ANTINOVELISTS
ANTINOVELS
ANTINUCLEAR
ANTINUCLEON
ANTINUCLEONS
ANTINUKE
ANTINUKER
ANTINUKERS
ANTINUKES
ANTIOBESITY
ANTIOBSCENITY
ANTIOXIDANT
ANTIOXIDANTS
ANTIOZONANT
ANTIOZONANTS
ANTIPAPAL
ANTIPARALLEL
ANTIPARASITIC
ANTIPARASITICS
ANTIPARTICLE
ANTIPARTICLES
ANTIPARTIES
ANTIPARTY
ANTIPASTI
ANTIPASTO
ANTIPASTOS
ANTIPATHETIC
ANTIPATHIES
ANTIPATHY
ANTIPERSONNEL
ANTIPERSPIRANT
ANTIPERSPIRANTS
ANTIPESTICIDE
ANTIPHLOGISTIC
ANTIPHON
ANTIPHONAL
ANTIPHONALLY
ANTIPHONALS
ANTIPHONARIES
ANTIPHONARY
ANTIPHONIES
ANTIPHONS
ANTIPHONY
ANTIPHRASES
ANTIPHRASIS
ANTIPILL
ANTIPIRACY
ANTIPLAGUE
ANTIPLAQUE
ANTIPLATELET
ANTIPLATELETS
ANTIPLEASURE
ANTIPOACHING
ANTIPODAL
ANTIPODALS
ANTIPODE
ANTIPODEAN
ANTIPODEANS
ANTIPODES
ANTIPOETIC
ANTIPOLAR
ANTIPOLE
ANTIPOLES
ANTIPOLICE
ANTIPOLITICAL
ANTIPOLITICS
ANTIPOLLUTION
ANTIPOLLUTIONS
ANTIPOPE
ANTIPOPES
ANTIPOPULAR
ANTIPORN
ANTIPORNOGRAPHY
ANTIPOT
ANTIPOVERTY
ANTIPREDATOR
ANTIPRESS
ANTIPROGRESSIVE
ANTIPROTON
ANTIPROTONS
ANTIPRURITIC
ANTIPRURITICS
ANTIPSYCHOTIC
ANTIPSYCHOTICS

ANTIPYIC
ANTIPYICS
ANTIPYRETIC
ANTIPYRETICS
ANTIPYRINE
ANTIPYRINES
ANTIQUARIAN
ANTIQUARIANISM
ANTIQUARIANISMS
ANTIQUARIANS
ANTIQUARIES
ANTIQUARK
ANTIQUARKS
ANTIQUARY
ANTIQUATE
ANTIQUATED
ANTIQUATES
ANTIQUATING
ANTIQUATION
ANTIQUATIONS
ANTIQUE
ANTIQUED
ANTIQUELY
ANTIQUER
ANTIQUERS
ANTIQUES
ANTIQUING
ANTIQUITIES
ANTIQUITY
ANTIRABIES
ANTIRACHITIC
ANTIRACISM
ANTIRACISMS
ANTIRACIST
ANTIRACISTS
ANTIRADAR
ANTIRADARS
ANTIRADICAL
ANTIRADICALISM
ANTIRADICALISMS
ANTIRAPE
ANTIRATIONAL
ANTIRATIONALISM
ANTIRATIONALIST
ANTIRATIONALITY
ANTIREALISM
ANTIREALISMS
ANTIREALIST
ANTIREALISTS
ANTIRECESSION
ANTIRED
ANTIREFLECTION
ANTIREFLECTIVE
ANTIREFORM
ANTIREGULATORY
ANTIREJECTION
ANTIRELIGION
ANTIRELIGIOUS
ANTIREPUBLICAN
ANTIREPUBLICANS
ANTIRETROVIRAL
ANTIRETROVIRALS
ANTIRHEUMATIC
ANTIRHEUMATICS
ANTIRIOT
ANTIRITUALISM
ANTIRITUALISMS
ANTIROCK
ANTIROLL
ANTIROMANTIC
ANTIROMANTICISM
ANTIROMANTICS
ANTIROYAL
ANTIROYALIST
ANTIROYALISTS
ANTIRRHINUM
ANTIRRHINUMS
ANTIRUST
ANTIRUSTS
ANTIS
ANTISAG
ANTISATELLITE
ANTISCIENCE
ANTISCIENCES
ANTISCIENTIFIC
ANTISCORBUTIC
ANTISCORBUTICS
ANTISECRECY
ANTISEGREGATION
ANTISEIZURE
ANTISENSE
ANTISENTIMENTAL
ANTISEPARATIST
ANTISEPARATISTS
ANTISEPSES
ANTISEPSIS
ANTISEPTIC
ANTISEPTICALLY
ANTISEPTICS
ANTISERA
ANTISERUM
ANTISERUMS
ANTISEX
ANTISEXIST
ANTISEXISTS
ANTISEXUAL
ANTISEXUALITIES
ANTISEXUALITY
ANTISHARK
ANTISHIP
ANTISHOCK
ANTISHOCKS
ANTISHOPLIFTING
ANTISKID
ANTISLAVERY
ANTISLEEP
ANTISLIP
ANTISMOG
ANTISMOKE
ANTISMOKER
ANTISMOKERS
ANTISMOKING
ANTISMUGGLING
ANTISMUT
ANTISNOB
ANTISNOBS
ANTISOCIAL
ANTISOCIALIST
ANTISOCIALISTS
ANTISOCIALLY
ANTISOCIALS
ANTISODOMY
ANTISOLAR
ANTISPAM
ANTISPASMODIC
ANTISPASMODICS
ANTISPECULATION
ANTISPECULATIVE
ANTISPENDING
ANTISTAT
ANTISTATE
ANTISTATIC
ANTISTATIST
ANTISTATISTS
ANTISTATS
ANTISTICK
ANTISTORIES
ANTISTORY
ANTISTRESS
ANTISTRIKE
ANTISTROPHE
ANTISTROPHES
ANTISTROPHIC
ANTISTUDENT
ANTISTYLE
ANTISTYLES
ANTISUBMARINE
ANTISUBSIDY
ANTISUBVERSION
ANTISUBVERSIVE
ANTISUICIDE
ANTISYMMETRIC
ANTISYPHILITIC
ANTISYPHILITICS
ANTITAKEOVER
ANTITANK
ANTITARNISH
ANTITAX
ANTITECHNOLOGY
ANTITERRORISM
ANTITERRORISMS
ANTITERRORIST
ANTITERRORISTS
ANTITHEFT
ANTITHEORETICAL
ANTITHESES
ANTITHESIS
ANTITHETIC
ANTITHETICAL
ANTITHETICALLY
ANTITHROMBIN
ANTITHROMBINS
ANTITHYROID
ANTITOBACCO
ANTITOXIC
ANTITOXIN
ANTITOXINS
ANTITRADE
ANTITRADES
ANTITRADITIONAL
ANTITRAGI
ANTITRAGUS
ANTITRUST
ANTITRUSTER
ANTITRUSTERS
ANTITUBERCULAR
ANTITUBERCULARS
ANTITUBERCULOUS
ANTITUMOR
ANTITUMORAL
ANTITUMORS
ANTITUSSIVE
ANTITUSSIVES
ANTITYPE
ANTITYPES
ANTITYPHOID
ANTITYPIC
ANTIULCER
ANTIUNION
ANTIUNIVERSITY
ANTIURBAN
ANTIVENIN
ANTIVENINS
ANTIVENOM
ANTIVENOMS
ANTIVIOLENCE
ANTIVIRAL
ANTIVIRUS
ANTIVIRUSES
ANTIVITAMIN
ANTIVITAMINS
ANTIVIVISECTION
ANTIWAR
ANTIWEAR
ANTIWEED
ANTIWELFARE
ANTIWHALING
ANTIWHITE
ANTIWOMAN
ANTIWRINKLE
ANTLER
ANTLERED
ANTLERLESS
ANTLERS
ANTLIKE
ANTLION
ANTLIONS
ANTONOMASIA
ANTONOMASIAS
ANTONYM
ANTONYMIC
ANTONYMIES
ANTONYMOUS
ANTONYMS
ANTONYMY
ANTRA
ANTRAL
ANTRE
ANTRES
ANTRORSE
ANTRUM
ANTRUMS
ANTS
ANTSIER
ANTSIEST
ANTSINESS
ANTSINESSES
ANTSY
ANURA
ANURAL
ANURAN
ANURANS
ANURESES
ANURESIS
ANURETIC

ANURIA
ANURIAS
ANURIC
ANUROUS
ANUS
ANUSES
ANVIL
ANVILED
ANVILING
ANVILLED
ANVILLING
ANVILS
ANVILTOP
ANVILTOPS
ANXIETIES
ANXIETY
ANXIOLYTIC
ANXIOLYTICS
ANXIOUS
ANXIOUSLY
ANXIOUSNESS
ANXIOUSNESSES
ANY
ANYBODIES
ANYBODY
ANYHOW
ANYMORE
ANYON
ANYONE
ANYONS
ANYPLACE
ANYTHING
ANYTHINGS
ANYTIME
ANYWAY
ANYWAYS
ANYWHERE
ANYWHERES
ANYWISE
AORIST
AORISTIC
AORISTICALLY
AORISTS
AORTA
AORTAE
AORTAL
AORTAS
AORTIC
AORTOGRAPHIC
AORTOGRAPHIES
AORTOGRAPHY
AOUDAD
AOUDADS
APACE
APACHE
APACHES
APAGOGE
APAGOGES
APAGOGIC
APANAGE
APANAGES
APAREJO
APAREJOS
APART
APARTHEID
APARTHEIDS
APARTMENT
APARTMENTAL
APARTMENTS
APARTNESS
APARTNESSES
APATETIC
APATHETIC
APATHETICALLY
APATHIES
APATHY
APATITE
APATITES
APATOSAUR
APATOSAURS
APATOSAURUS
APATOSAURUSES
APE
APEAK
APED
APEEK
APELIKE
APEMAN
APEMEN
APER
APERCU
APERCUS
APERIENT
APERIENTS
APERIES
APERIODIC
APERIODICALLY
APERIODICITIES
APERIODICITY
APERITIF
APERITIFS
APERS
APERTURAL
APERTURE
APERTURED
APERTURES
APERY
APES
APETALIES
APETALOUS
APETALY
APEX
APEXES
APHAERESES
APHAERESIS
APHAERETIC
APHAGIA
APHAGIAS
APHANITE
APHANITES
APHANITIC
APHASIA
APHASIAC
APHASIACS
APHASIAS
APHASIC
APHASICS
APHELIA
APHELIAN
APHELION
APHELIONS
APHERESES
APHERESIS
APHERETIC
APHESES
APHESIS
APHETIC
APHETICALLY
APHID
APHIDES
APHIDIAN
APHIDIANS
APHIDS
APHIS
APHOLATE
APHOLATES
APHONIA
APHONIAS
APHONIC
APHONICS
APHONIES
APHONY
APHORISE
APHORISED
APHORISES
APHORISING
APHORISM
APHORISMS
APHORIST
APHORISTIC
APHORISTICALLY
APHORISTS
APHORIZE
APHORIZED
APHORIZER
APHORIZERS
APHORIZES
APHORIZING
APHOTIC
APHRODISIAC
APHRODISIACAL
APHRODISIACS
APHRODITE
APHRODITES
APHTHA
APHTHAE
APHTHOUS
APHYLLIES
APHYLLOUS
APHYLLY
APIACEOUS
APIAN
APIARIAN
APIARIANS
APIARIES
APIARIST
APIARISTS
APIARY
APICAL
APICALLY
APICALS
APICES
APICULATE
APICULI
APICULTURAL
APICULTURE
APICULTURES
APICULTURIST
APICULTURISTS
APICULUS
APIECE
APIMANIA
APIMANIAS
APING
APIOLOGIES
APIOLOGY
APISH
APISHLY
APISHNESS
APISHNESSES
APIVOROUS
APLANAT
APLANATIC
APLANATS
APLASIA
APLASIAS
APLASTIC
APLENTY
APLITE
APLITES
APLITIC
APLOMB
APLOMBS
APNEA
APNEAL
APNEAS
APNEIC
APNOEA
APNOEAL
APNOEAS
APNOEIC
APO
APOAPSES
APOAPSIDES
APOAPSIS
APOCALYPSE
APOCALYPSES
APOCALYPTIC
APOCALYPTICAL
APOCALYPTICALLY
APOCALYPTICISM
APOCALYPTICISMS
APOCALYPTISM
APOCALYPTISMS
APOCALYPTIST
APOCALYPTISTS
APOCARP
APOCARPIES
APOCARPS
APOCARPY
APOCHROMATIC
APOCOPATE
APOCOPATED
APOCOPATES
APOCOPATING
APOCOPE
APOCOPES
APOCOPIC
APOCRINE
APOCRYPHA
APOCRYPHAL
APOCRYPHALLY
APOCRYPHALNESS
APOD
APODAL

APODEICTIC
APODICTIC
APODICTICALLY
APODOSES
APODOSIS
APODOUS
APODS
APOENZYME
APOENZYMES
APOGAMIC
APOGAMIES
APOGAMOUS
APOGAMY
APOGEAL
APOGEAN
APOGEE
APOGEES
APOGEIC
APOLIPOPROTEIN
APOLIPOPROTEINS
APOLITICAL
APOLITICALLY
APOLITICISM
APOLITICISMS
APOLLO
APOLLOS
APOLOG
APOLOGAL
APOLOGETIC
APOLOGETICALLY
APOLOGETICS
APOLOGIA
APOLOGIAE
APOLOGIAS
APOLOGIES
APOLOGISE
APOLOGISED
APOLOGISES
APOLOGISING
APOLOGIST
APOLOGISTS
APOLOGIZE
APOLOGIZED
APOLOGIZER
APOLOGIZERS
APOLOGIZES
APOLOGIZING
APOLOGS
APOLOGUE
APOLOGUES
APOLOGY
APOLUNE
APOLUNES
APOMICT
APOMICTIC
APOMICTICALLY
APOMICTS
APOMIXES
APOMIXIS
APOMORPHINE
APOMORPHINES
APONEUROSES
APONEUROSIS
APONEUROTIC
APOPHASES
APOPHASIS
APOPHONIES
APOPHONY
APOPHTHEGM
APOPHTHEGMS
APOPHYGE
APOPHYGES
APOPHYLLITE
APOPHYLLITES
APOPHYSEAL
APOPHYSES
APOPHYSIS
APOPLECTIC
APOPLECTICALLY
APOPLEXIES
APOPLEXY
APOPTOSES
APOPTOSIS
APOPTOTIC
APORIA
APORIAS
APORT
APOS
APOSEMATIC
APOSEMATICALLY
APOSIOPESES
APOSIOPESIS
APOSIOPETIC
APOSPORIC
APOSPORIES
APOSPOROUS
APOSPORY
APOSTACIES
APOSTACY
APOSTASIES
APOSTASY
APOSTATE
APOSTATES
APOSTATISE
APOSTATISED
APOSTATISES
APOSTATISING
APOSTATIZE
APOSTATIZED
APOSTATIZES
APOSTATIZING
APOSTIL
APOSTILLE
APOSTILLES
APOSTILS
APOSTLE
APOSTLES
APOSTLESHIP
APOSTLESHIPS
APOSTOLATE
APOSTOLATES
APOSTOLIC
APOSTOLICITIES
APOSTOLICITY
APOSTROPHE
APOSTROPHES
APOSTROPHIC
APOSTROPHISE
APOSTROPHISED
APOSTROPHISES
APOSTROPHISING
APOSTROPHIZE
APOSTROPHIZED
APOSTROPHIZES
APOSTROPHIZING
APOTHECARIES
APOTHECARY
APOTHECE
APOTHECES
APOTHECIA
APOTHECIAL
APOTHECIUM
APOTHEGM
APOTHEGMATIC
APOTHEGMS
APOTHEM
APOTHEMS
APOTHEOSES
APOTHEOSIS
APOTHEOSIZE
APOTHEOSIZED
APOTHEOSIZES
APOTHEOSIZING
APOTROPAIC
APOTROPAICALLY
APP
APPAL
APPALL
APPALLED
APPALLING
APPALLINGLY
APPALLS
APPALOOSA
APPALOOSAS
APPALS
APPANAGE
APPANAGES
APPARAT
APPARATCHIK
APPARATCHIKI
APPARATCHIKS
APPARATS
APPARATUS
APPARATUSES
APPAREL
APPARELED
APPARELING
APPARELLED
APPARELLING
APPARELS
APPARENT
APPARENTLY
APPARENTNESS
APPARENTNESSES
APPARITION
APPARITIONAL
APPARITIONS
APPARITOR
APPARITORS
APPEAL
APPEALABILITIES
APPEALABILITY
APPEALABLE
APPEALED
APPEALER
APPEALERS
APPEALING
APPEALINGLY
APPEALS
APPEAR
APPEARANCE
APPEARANCES
APPEARED
APPEARING
APPEARS
APPEASABLE
APPEASE
APPEASED
APPEASEMENT
APPEASEMENTS
APPEASER
APPEASERS
APPEASES
APPEASING
APPEL
APPELLANT
APPELLANTS
APPELLATE
APPELLATION
APPELLATIONS
APPELLATIVE
APPELLATIVELY
APPELLATIVES
APPELLEE
APPELLEES
APPELLOR
APPELLORS
APPELS
APPEND
APPENDAGE
APPENDAGES
APPENDANT
APPENDANTS
APPENDECTOMIES
APPENDECTOMY
APPENDED
APPENDENT
APPENDENTS
APPENDICECTOMY
APPENDICES
APPENDICITIS
APPENDICITISES
APPENDICULAR
APPENDING
APPENDIX
APPENDIXES
APPENDS
APPERCEIVE
APPERCEIVED
APPERCEIVES
APPERCEIVING
APPERCEPTION
APPERCEPTIONS
APPERCEPTIVE
APPERTAIN
APPERTAINED
APPERTAINING
APPERTAINS
APPESTAT
APPESTATS
APPETENCE
APPETENCES
APPETENCIES
APPETENCY
APPETENT

APPETISER
APPETISERS
APPETISING
APPETISINGLY
APPETITE
APPETITES
APPETITIVE
APPETIZER
APPETIZERS
APPETIZING
APPETIZINGLY
APPLAUD
APPLAUDABLE
APPLAUDABLY
APPLAUDED
APPLAUDER
APPLAUDERS
APPLAUDING
APPLAUDS
APPLAUSE
APPLAUSES
APPLE
APPLECART
APPLECARTS
APPLEJACK
APPLEJACKS
APPLES
APPLESAUCE
APPLESAUCES
APPLET
APPLETS
APPLEY
APPLIABLE
APPLIANCE
APPLIANCES
APPLICABILITIES
APPLICABILITY
APPLICABLE
APPLICANT
APPLICANTS
APPLICATION
APPLICATIONS
APPLICATIVE
APPLICATIVELY
APPLICATOR
APPLICATORS
APPLICATORY
APPLIED
APPLIER
APPLIERS
APPLIES
APPLIEST
APPLIQUE
APPLIQUED
APPLIQUEING
APPLIQUES
APPLY
APPLYING
APPOGGIATURA
APPOGGIATURAS
APPOINT
APPOINTED
APPOINTEE
APPOINTEES
APPOINTER
APPOINTERS
APPOINTING
APPOINTIVE
APPOINTMENT
APPOINTMENTS
APPOINTOR
APPOINTORS
APPOINTS
APPORTION
APPORTIONABLE
APPORTIONED
APPORTIONING
APPORTIONMENT
APPORTIONMENTS
APPORTIONS
APPOSABLE
APPOSE
APPOSED
APPOSER
APPOSERS
APPOSES
APPOSING
APPOSITE
APPOSITELY
APPOSITENESS
APPOSITENESSES
APPOSITION
APPOSITIONAL
APPOSITIONS
APPOSITIVE
APPOSITIVELY
APPOSITIVES
APPRAISAL
APPRAISALS
APPRAISE
APPRAISED
APPRAISEE
APPRAISEES
APPRAISEMENT
APPRAISEMENTS
APPRAISER
APPRAISERS
APPRAISES
APPRAISING
APPRAISINGLY
APPRAISIVE
APPRECIABLE
APPRECIABLY
APPRECIATE
APPRECIATED
APPRECIATES
APPRECIATING
APPRECIATION
APPRECIATIONS
APPRECIATIVE
APPRECIATIVELY
APPRECIATOR
APPRECIATORS
APPRECIATORY
APPREHEND
APPREHENDED
APPREHENDING
APPREHENDS
APPREHENSIBLE
APPREHENSIBLY
APPREHENSION
APPREHENSIONS
APPREHENSIVE
APPREHENSIVELY
APPRENTICE
APPRENTICED
APPRENTICES
APPRENTICESHIP
APPRENTICESHIPS
APPRENTICING
APPRESS
APPRESSED
APPRESSES
APPRESSING
APPRESSORIA
APPRESSORIUM
APPRISE
APPRISED
APPRISER
APPRISERS
APPRISES
APPRISING
APPRIZE
APPRIZED
APPRIZER
APPRIZERS
APPRIZES
APPRIZING
APPROACH
APPROACHABILITY
APPROACHABLE
APPROACHED
APPROACHES
APPROACHING
APPROBATE
APPROBATED
APPROBATES
APPROBATING
APPROBATION
APPROBATIONS
APPROBATORY
APPROPRIABLE
APPROPRIATE
APPROPRIATED
APPROPRIATELY
APPROPRIATENESS
APPROPRIATES
APPROPRIATING
APPROPRIATION
APPROPRIATIONS
APPROPRIATIVE
APPROPRIATOR
APPROPRIATORS
APPROVABLE
APPROVABLY
APPROVAL
APPROVALS
APPROVE
APPROVED
APPROVER
APPROVERS
APPROVES
APPROVING
APPROVINGLY
APPROXIMATE
APPROXIMATED
APPROXIMATELY
APPROXIMATES
APPROXIMATING
APPROXIMATION
APPROXIMATIONS
APPROXIMATIVE
APPS
APPULSE
APPULSES
APPURTENANCE
APPURTENANCES
APPURTENANT
APPURTENANTS
APRACTIC
APRAXIA
APRAXIAS
APRAXIC
APRES
APRICOT
APRICOTS
APRIORITIES
APRIORITY
APRON
APRONED
APRONING
APRONLIKE
APRONS
APROPOS
APROTIC
APSE
APSES
APSIDAL
APSIDES
APSIS
APT
APTER
APTERAL
APTERIA
APTERIUM
APTEROUS
APTERYX
APTERYXES
APTEST
APTITUDE
APTITUDES
APTITUDINAL
APTITUDINALLY
APTLY
APTNESS
APTNESSES
APYRASE
APYRASES
APYRETIC
AQUA
AQUACADE
AQUACADES
AQUACULTURAL
AQUACULTURE
AQUACULTURES
AQUACULTURIST
AQUACULTURISTS
AQUAE
AQUAFARM
AQUAFARMED
AQUAFARMING
AQUAFARMS
AQUAFIT
AQUAFITS
AQUALUNG

AQUALUNGS
AQUAMARINE
AQUAMARINES
AQUANAUT
AQUANAUTS
AQUAPLANE
AQUAPLANED
AQUAPLANER
AQUAPLANERS
AQUAPLANES
AQUAPLANING
AQUAPONICS
AQUARELLE
AQUARELLES
AQUARELLIST
AQUARELLISTS
AQUARIA
AQUARIAL
AQUARIAN
AQUARIANS
AQUARIST
AQUARISTS
AQUARIUM
AQUARIUMS
AQUAS
AQUASCAPE
AQUATIC
AQUATICALLY
AQUATICS
AQUATINT
AQUATINTED
AQUATINTER
AQUATINTERS
AQUATINTING
AQUATINTIST
AQUATINTISTS
AQUATINTS
AQUATONE
AQUATONES
AQUAVIT
AQUAVITS
AQUEDUCT
AQUEDUCTS
AQUEOUS
AQUEOUSLY
AQUICULTURE
AQUICULTURES
AQUIFER
AQUIFEROUS
AQUIFERS
AQUILEGIA
AQUILEGIAS
AQUILINE
AQUILINITIES
AQUILINITY
AQUIVER
AR
ARABESK
ARABESKS
ARABESQUE
ARABESQUES
ARABIC
ARABICA
ARABICAS
ARABICIZATION
ARABICIZATIONS
ARABICIZE
ARABICIZED
ARABICIZES
ARABICIZING
ARABILITIES
ARABILITY
ARABINOSE
ARABINOSES
ARABINOSIDE
ARABINOSIDES
ARABIS
ARABISES
ARABIZE
ARABIZED
ARABIZES
ARABIZING
ARABLE
ARABLES
ARACEOUS
ARACHNID
ARACHNIDS
ARACHNOID
ARACHNOIDS
ARACHNOLOGICAL
ARACHNOLOGIES
ARACHNOLOGIST
ARACHNOLOGISTS
ARACHNOLOGY
ARACHNOPHOBE
ARACHNOPHOBES
ARACHNOPHOBIA
ARACHNOPHOBIAS
ARACHNOPHOBIC
ARACHNOPHOBICS
ARAGONITE
ARAGONITES
ARAGONITIC
ARAK
ARAKS
ARAME
ARAMES
ARAMID
ARAMIDS
ARANEID
ARANEIDAN
ARANEIDS
ARAPAIMA
ARAPAIMAS
ARAROBA
ARAROBAS
ARAUCARIA
ARAUCARIAN
ARAUCARIAS
ARB
ARBALEST
ARBALESTS
ARBALIST
ARBALISTS
ARBELEST
ARBELESTS
ARBITER
ARBITERS
ARBITRABLE
ARBITRAGE
ARBITRAGED
ARBITRAGER
ARBITRAGERS
ARBITRAGES
ARBITRAGEUR
ARBITRAGEURS
ARBITRAGING
ARBITRAL
ARBITRAMENT
ARBITRAMENTS
ARBITRARILY
ARBITRARINESS
ARBITRARINESSES
ARBITRARY
ARBITRATE
ARBITRATED
ARBITRATES
ARBITRATING
ARBITRATION
ARBITRATIONAL
ARBITRATIONS
ARBITRATIVE
ARBITRATOR
ARBITRATORS
ARBITRESS
ARBITRESSES
ARBOR
ARBOREAL
ARBOREALLY
ARBORED
ARBOREOUS
ARBORES
ARBORESCENCE
ARBORESCENCES
ARBORESCENT
ARBORETA
ARBORETUM
ARBORETUMS
ARBORICULTURAL
ARBORICULTURE
ARBORICULTURES
ARBORIST
ARBORISTS
ARBORIZATION
ARBORIZATIONS
ARBORIZE
ARBORIZED
ARBORIZES
ARBORIZING
ARBOROUS
ARBORS
ARBORVITAE
ARBORVITAES
ARBOUR
ARBOURED
ARBOURS
ARBOVIRAL
ARBOVIRUS
ARBOVIRUSES
ARBS
ARBUSCLE
ARBUSCLES
ARBUTE
ARBUTEAN
ARBUTES
ARBUTUS
ARBUTUSES
ARC
ARCADE
ARCADED
ARCADES
ARCADIA
ARCADIAN
ARCADIANS
ARCADIAS
ARCADING
ARCADINGS
ARCANA
ARCANE
ARCANELY
ARCANUM
ARCANUMS
ARCATURE
ARCATURES
ARCCOSINE
ARCCOSINES
ARCED
ARCH
ARCHAEA
ARCHAEAL
ARCHAEAN
ARCHAEANS
ARCHAEBACTERIA
ARCHAEBACTERIUM
ARCHAEOLOGICAL
ARCHAEOLOGIES
ARCHAEOLOGIST
ARCHAEOLOGISTS
ARCHAEOLOGY
ARCHAEON
ARCHAEOPTERYX
ARCHAEOPTERYXES
ARCHAIC
ARCHAICAL
ARCHAICALLY
ARCHAISE
ARCHAISED
ARCHAISES
ARCHAISING
ARCHAISM
ARCHAISMS
ARCHAIST
ARCHAISTIC
ARCHAISTS
ARCHAIZE
ARCHAIZED
ARCHAIZER
ARCHAIZERS
ARCHAIZES
ARCHAIZING
ARCHANGEL
ARCHANGELIC
ARCHANGELS
ARCHBISHOP
ARCHBISHOPRIC
ARCHBISHOPRICS
ARCHBISHOPS
ARCHDEACON
ARCHDEACONRIES
ARCHDEACONRY
ARCHDEACONS
ARCHDIOCESAN
ARCHDIOCESE
ARCHDIOCESES
ARCHDUCAL

ARCHDUCHESS
ARCHDUCHESSES
ARCHDUCHIES
ARCHDUCHY
ARCHDUKE
ARCHDUKEDOM
ARCHDUKEDOMS
ARCHDUKES
ARCHEAN
ARCHED
ARCHEGONIA
ARCHEGONIAL
ARCHEGONIATE
ARCHEGONIATES
ARCHEGONIUM
ARCHENEMIES
ARCHENEMY
ARCHENTERON
ARCHENTERONS
ARCHEOLOGICAL
ARCHEOLOGICALLY
ARCHEOLOGIES
ARCHEOLOGIST
ARCHEOLOGISTS
ARCHEOLOGY
ARCHER
ARCHERFISH
ARCHERFISHES
ARCHERIES
ARCHERS
ARCHERY
ARCHES
ARCHESPORIA
ARCHESPORIAL
ARCHESPORIUM
ARCHETYPAL
ARCHETYPALLY
ARCHETYPE
ARCHETYPES
ARCHETYPICAL
ARCHETYPICALLY
ARCHFIEND
ARCHFIENDS
ARCHFOE
ARCHFOES
ARCHI
ARCHICARP
ARCHICARPS
ARCHIDIACONAL
ARCHIEPISCOPAL
ARCHIEPISCOPATE
ARCHIL
ARCHILS
ARCHIMANDRITE
ARCHIMANDRITES
ARCHINE
ARCHINES
ARCHING
ARCHINGS
ARCHIPELAGIC
ARCHIPELAGO
ARCHIPELAGOES
ARCHIPELAGOS
ARCHITECT
ARCHITECTONIC
ARCHITECTONICS
ARCHITECTS
ARCHITECTURAL
ARCHITECTURALLY
ARCHITECTURE
ARCHITECTURES
ARCHITRAVE
ARCHITRAVES
ARCHIVAL
ARCHIVALLY
ARCHIVE
ARCHIVED
ARCHIVES
ARCHIVING
ARCHIVIST
ARCHIVISTS
ARCHIVOLT
ARCHIVOLTS
ARCHLY
ARCHNESS
ARCHNESSES
ARCHON
ARCHONS
ARCHOSAUR
ARCHOSAURIAN
ARCHOSAURIANS
ARCHOSAURS
ARCHPRIEST
ARCHPRIESTS
ARCHRIVAL
ARCHRIVALS
ARCHWAY
ARCHWAYS
ARCIFORM
ARCING
ARCINGS
ARCKED
ARCKING
ARCO
ARCS
ARCSINE
ARCSINES
ARCTANGENT
ARCTANGENTS
ARCTIC
ARCTICALLY
ARCTICS
ARCUATE
ARCUATED
ARCUATELY
ARCUATION
ARCUATIONS
ARCUS
ARCUSES
ARDEB
ARDEBS
ARDENCIES
ARDENCY
ARDENT
ARDENTLY
ARDOR
ARDORS
ARDOUR
ARDOURS
ARDUOUS
ARDUOUSLY
ARDUOUSNESS
ARDUOUSNESSES
ARE
AREA
AREAE
AREAL
AREALLY
AREAS
AREAWAY
AREAWAYS
ARECA
ARECAS
ARECOLINE
ARECOLINES
AREG
AREIC
ARENA
ARENACEOUS
ARENAS
ARENAVIRUS
ARENAVIRUSES
ARENE
ARENES
ARENICOLOUS
ARENITE
ARENITES
ARENOSE
ARENOUS
AREOCENTRIC
AREOLA
AREOLAE
AREOLAR
AREOLAS
AREOLATE
AREOLATED
AREOLE
AREOLES
AREOLOGIES
AREOLOGY
AREPA
AREPAS
ARES
ARETE
ARETES
ARETHUSA
ARETHUSAS
ARF
ARFS
ARGAL
ARGALA
ARGALAS
ARGALI
ARGALIS
ARGALS
ARGENT
ARGENTAL
ARGENTIC
ARGENTIFEROUS
ARGENTINE
ARGENTINES
ARGENTITE
ARGENTITES
ARGENTOUS
ARGENTS
ARGENTUM
ARGENTUMS
ARGH
ARGIL
ARGILLACEOUS
ARGILLITE
ARGILLITES
ARGILS
ARGINASE
ARGINASES
ARGININE
ARGININES
ARGLE
ARGLED
ARGLES
ARGLING
ARGOL
ARGOLS
ARGON
ARGONAUT
ARGONAUTS
ARGONS
ARGOSIES
ARGOSY
ARGOT
ARGOTIC
ARGOTS
ARGUABLE
ARGUABLY
ARGUE
ARGUED
ARGUER
ARGUERS
ARGUES
ARGUFIED
ARGUFIER
ARGUFIERS
ARGUFIES
ARGUFY
ARGUFYING
ARGUING
ARGUMENT
ARGUMENTA
ARGUMENTATION
ARGUMENTATIONS
ARGUMENTATIVE
ARGUMENTATIVELY
ARGUMENTIVE
ARGUMENTS
ARGUMENTUM
ARGUS
ARGUSES
ARGYLE
ARGYLES
ARGYLL
ARGYLLS
ARHAT
ARHATS
ARHATSHIP
ARHATSHIPS
ARIA
ARIARY
ARIAS
ARIBOFLAVINOSES
ARIBOFLAVINOSIS
ARID
ARIDER
ARIDEST
ARIDITIES
ARIDITY

ARIDLY
ARIDNESS
ARIDNESSES
ARIEL
ARIELS
ARIETTA
ARIETTAS
ARIETTE
ARIETTES
ARIGHT
ARIL
ARILED
ARILLATE
ARILLODE
ARILLODES
ARILLOID
ARILS
ARIOSE
ARIOSI
ARIOSO
ARIOSOS
ARISE
ARISEN
ARISES
ARISING
ARISTA
ARISTAE
ARISTAS
ARISTATE
ARISTO
ARISTOCRACIES
ARISTOCRACY
ARISTOCRAT
ARISTOCRATIC
ARISTOCRATS
ARISTOS
ARITHMETIC
ARITHMETICAL
ARITHMETICALLY
ARITHMETICIAN
ARITHMETICIANS
ARITHMETICS
ARK
ARKOSE
ARKOSES
ARKOSIC
ARKS
ARLES
ARM
ARMADA
ARMADAS
ARMADILLO
ARMADILLOS
ARMAGNAC
ARMAGNACS
ARMAMENT
ARMAMENTARIA
ARMAMENTARIUM
ARMAMENTS
ARMATURE
ARMATURED
ARMATURES
ARMATURING
ARMBAND
ARMBANDS
ARMCHAIR
ARMCHAIRS
ARMED
ARMER
ARMERS
ARMET
ARMETS
ARMFUL
ARMFULS
ARMGUARD
ARMGUARDS
ARMHOLE
ARMHOLES
ARMIES
ARMIGER
ARMIGERAL
ARMIGERO
ARMIGEROS
ARMIGEROUS
ARMIGERS
ARMILLA
ARMILLAE
ARMILLARY
ARMILLAS
ARMING
ARMINGS
ARMISTICE
ARMISTICES
ARMLESS
ARMLET
ARMLETS
ARMLIKE
ARMLOAD
ARMLOADS
ARMLOCK
ARMLOCKS
ARMOIRE
ARMOIRES
ARMONICA
ARMONICAS
ARMOR
ARMORED
ARMORER
ARMORERS
ARMORIAL
ARMORIALLY
ARMORIALS
ARMORIES
ARMORING
ARMORLESS
ARMORS
ARMORY
ARMOUR
ARMOURED
ARMOURER
ARMOURERS
ARMOURIES
ARMOURING
ARMOURS
ARMOURY
ARMPIT
ARMPITS
ARMREST
ARMRESTS
ARMS
ARMSFUL
ARMURE
ARMURES
ARMY
ARMYWORM
ARMYWORMS
ARNATTO
ARNATTOS
ARNICA
ARNICAS
ARNOTTO
ARNOTTOS
AROID
AROIDS
AROINT
AROINTED
AROINTING
AROINTS
AROMA
AROMAS
AROMATASE
AROMATASES
AROMATHERAPIES
AROMATHERAPIST
AROMATHERAPISTS
AROMATHERAPY
AROMATIC
AROMATICALLY
AROMATICITIES
AROMATICITY
AROMATICS
AROMATIZATION
AROMATIZATIONS
AROMATIZE
AROMATIZED
AROMATIZES
AROMATIZING
AROSE
AROUND
AROUSABLE
AROUSAL
AROUSALS
AROUSE
AROUSED
AROUSER
AROUSERS
AROUSES
AROUSING
AROYNT
AROYNTED
AROYNTING
AROYNTS
ARPEGGIATE
ARPEGGIATED
ARPEGGIATES
ARPEGGIATING
ARPEGGIO
ARPEGGIOS
ARPEN
ARPENS
ARPENT
ARPENTS
ARQUEBUS
ARQUEBUSES
ARRACK
ARRACKS
ARRAIGN
ARRAIGNED
ARRAIGNER
ARRAIGNERS
ARRAIGNING
ARRAIGNMENT
ARRAIGNMENTS
ARRAIGNS
ARRANGE
ARRANGED
ARRANGEMENT
ARRANGEMENTS
ARRANGER
ARRANGERS
ARRANGES
ARRANGING
ARRANT
ARRANTLY
ARRAS
ARRASED
ARRASES
ARRAY
ARRAYAL
ARRAYALS
ARRAYED
ARRAYER
ARRAYERS
ARRAYING
ARRAYS
ARREAR
ARREARAGE
ARREARAGES
ARREARS
ARREST
ARRESTANT
ARRESTANTS
ARRESTED
ARRESTEE
ARRESTEES
ARRESTER
ARRESTERS
ARRESTING
ARRESTINGLY
ARRESTIVE
ARRESTMENT
ARRESTMENTS
ARRESTOR
ARRESTORS
ARRESTS
ARRHIZAL
ARRHYTHMIA
ARRHYTHMIAS
ARRHYTHMIC
ARRIBA
ARRIS
ARRISES
ARRIVAL
ARRIVALS
ARRIVE
ARRIVED
ARRIVER
ARRIVERS
ARRIVES
ARRIVING
ARRIVISTE
ARRIVISTES
ARROBA
ARROBAS
ARROCES

ARROGANCE
ARROGANCES
ARROGANCIES
ARROGANCY
ARROGANT
ARROGANTLY
ARROGATE
ARROGATED
ARROGATES
ARROGATING
ARROGATION
ARROGATIONS
ARROGATOR
ARROGATORS
ARRONDISSEMENT
ARRONDISSEMENTS
ARROW
ARROWED
ARROWHEAD
ARROWHEADS
ARROWING
ARROWLESS
ARROWLIKE
ARROWROOT
ARROWROOTS
ARROWS
ARROWWOOD
ARROWWOODS
ARROWWORM
ARROWWORMS
ARROWY
ARROYO
ARROYOS
ARROZ
ARROZES
ARS
ARSE
ARSEHOLE
ARSEHOLES
ARSENAL
ARSENALS
ARSENATE
ARSENATES
ARSENIC
ARSENICAL
ARSENICALS
ARSENICS
ARSENIDE
ARSENIDES
ARSENIOUS
ARSENITE
ARSENITES
ARSENO
ARSENOPYRITE
ARSENOPYRITES
ARSENOUS
ARSES
ARSHIN
ARSHINS
ARSINE
ARSINES
ARSINO
ARSIS
ARSON
ARSONIST
ARSONISTS
ARSONOUS
ARSONS
ARSPHENAMINE
ARSPHENAMINES
ART
ARTAL
ARTEFACT
ARTEFACTS
ARTEL
ARTELS
ARTEMISIA
ARTEMISIAS
ARTERIAL
ARTERIALLY
ARTERIALS
ARTERIES
ARTERIOGRAM
ARTERIOGRAMS
ARTERIOGRAPHIC
ARTERIOGRAPHIES
ARTERIOGRAPHY
ARTERIOLAR
ARTERIOLE
ARTERIOLES
ARTERIOVENOUS
ARTERITIDES
ARTERITIS
ARTERY
ARTESIAN
ARTFUL
ARTFULLY
ARTFULNESS
ARTFULNESSES
ARTHRALGIA
ARTHRALGIAS
ARTHRALGIC
ARTHRITIC
ARTHRITICALLY
ARTHRITICS
ARTHRITIDES
ARTHRITIS
ARTHRODESES
ARTHRODESIS
ARTHROPATHIES
ARTHROPATHY
ARTHROPOD
ARTHROPODAN
ARTHROPODS
ARTHROSCOPE
ARTHROSCOPES
ARTHROSCOPIC
ARTHROSCOPIES
ARTHROSCOPY
ARTHROSES
ARTHROSIS
ARTHROSPORE
ARTHROSPORES
ARTICHOKE
ARTICHOKES
ARTICLE
ARTICLED
ARTICLES
ARTICLING
ARTICULABLE
ARTICULACIES
ARTICULACY
ARTICULAR
ARTICULATE
ARTICULATED
ARTICULATELY
ARTICULATENESS
ARTICULATES
ARTICULATING
ARTICULATION
ARTICULATIONS
ARTICULATIVE
ARTICULATOR
ARTICULATORS
ARTICULATORY
ARTIER
ARTIEST
ARTIFACT
ARTIFACTS
ARTIFACTUAL
ARTIFICE
ARTIFICER
ARTIFICERS
ARTIFICES
ARTIFICIAL
ARTIFICIALITIES
ARTIFICIALITY
ARTIFICIALLY
ARTIFICIALNESS
ARTIGI
ARTIGIS
ARTILLERIES
ARTILLERIST
ARTILLERISTS
ARTILLERY
ARTILLERYMAN
ARTILLERYMEN
ARTILY
ARTINESS
ARTINESSES
ARTIODACTYL
ARTIODACTYLS
ARTISAN
ARTISANAL
ARTISANS
ARTISANSHIP
ARTISANSHIPS
ARTIST
ARTISTE
ARTISTES
ARTISTIC
ARTISTICALLY
ARTISTRIES
ARTISTRY
ARTISTS
ARTLESS
ARTLESSLY
ARTLESSNESS
ARTLESSNESSES
ARTMAKER
ARTMAKERS
ARTS
ARTSIE
ARTSIER
ARTSIES
ARTSIEST
ARTSINESS
ARTSINESSES
ARTSY
ARTWORK
ARTWORKS
ARTY
ARUGOLA
ARUGOLAS
ARUGULA
ARUGULAS
ARUM
ARUMS
ARUSPEX
ARUSPICES
ARVAL
ARVO
ARVOS
ARYL
ARYLS
ARYTENOID
ARYTENOIDS
ARYTHMIA
ARYTHMIAS
ARYTHMIC
AS
ASAFETIDA
ASAFETIDAS
ASAFOETIDA
ASAFOETIDAS
ASANA
ASANAS
ASARUM
ASARUMS
ASBESTIC
ASBESTINE
ASBESTOS
ASBESTOSES
ASBESTOSIS
ASBESTOUS
ASBESTUS
ASBESTUSES
ASCARED
ASCARIASES
ASCARIASIS
ASCARID
ASCARIDES
ASCARIDS
ASCARIS
ASCARISES
ASCEND
ASCENDABLE
ASCENDANCE
ASCENDANCES
ASCENDANCIES
ASCENDANCY
ASCENDANT
ASCENDANTLY
ASCENDANTS
ASCENDED
ASCENDENCE
ASCENDENCES
ASCENDENCIES
ASCENDENCY
ASCENDENT
ASCENDENTS
ASCENDER
ASCENDERS
ASCENDIBLE
ASCENDING

ASCENDS
ASCENSION
ASCENSIONAL
ASCENSIONS
ASCENSIVE
ASCENT
ASCENTS
ASCERTAIN
ASCERTAINABLE
ASCERTAINED
ASCERTAINING
ASCERTAINMENT
ASCERTAINMENTS
ASCERTAINS
ASCESES
ASCESIS
ASCETIC
ASCETICAL
ASCETICALLY
ASCETICISM
ASCETICISMS
ASCETICS
ASCI
ASCIDIA
ASCIDIAN
ASCIDIANS
ASCIDIATE
ASCIDIUM
ASCITES
ASCITIC
ASCLEPIAD
ASCLEPIADS
ASCOCARP
ASCOCARPIC
ASCOCARPS
ASCOGONIA
ASCOGONIUM
ASCOMYCETE
ASCOMYCETES
ASCOMYCETOUS
ASCON
ASCONOID
ASCONS
ASCORBATE
ASCORBATES
ASCORBIC
ASCOSPORE
ASCOSPORES
ASCOSPORIC
ASCOT
ASCOTS
ASCRIBABLE
ASCRIBE
ASCRIBED
ASCRIBES
ASCRIBING
ASCRIPTION
ASCRIPTIONS
ASCRIPTIVE
ASCUS
ASDIC
ASDICS
ASEA
ASEISMIC
ASEPSES
ASEPSIS
ASEPTIC
ASEPTICALLY
ASEXUAL
ASEXUALITIES
ASEXUALITY
ASEXUALLY
ASH
ASHAMED
ASHAMEDLY
ASHCAKE
ASHCAKES
ASHCAN
ASHCANS
ASHED
ASHEN
ASHES
ASHFALL
ASHFALLS
ASHIER
ASHIEST
ASHINE
ASHINESS
ASHINESSES
ASHING
ASHLAR
ASHLARED
ASHLARING
ASHLARS
ASHLER
ASHLERED
ASHLERING
ASHLERS
ASHLESS
ASHMAN
ASHMEN
ASHORE
ASHPAN
ASHPANS
ASHPLANT
ASHPLANTS
ASHRAM
ASHRAMA
ASHRAMAS
ASHRAMS
ASHTANGA
ASHTANGAS
ASHTRAY
ASHTRAYS
ASHY
ASIDE
ASIDES
ASININE
ASININELY
ASININITIES
ASININITY
ASK
ASKANCE
ASKANT
ASKARI
ASKARIS
ASKED
ASKER
ASKERS
ASKESES
ASKESIS
ASKEW
ASKEWNESS
ASKEWNESSES
ASKING
ASKINGS
ASKOI
ASKOS
ASKS
ASLANT
ASLEEP
ASLOPE
ASLOSH
ASOCIAL
ASOCIALS
ASP
ASPARAGINE
ASPARAGINES
ASPARAGUS
ASPARAGUSES
ASPARKLE
ASPARTAME
ASPARTAMES
ASPARTATE
ASPARTATES
ASPECT
ASPECTS
ASPECTUAL
ASPEN
ASPENS
ASPER
ASPERATE
ASPERATED
ASPERATES
ASPERATING
ASPERGES
ASPERGILL
ASPERGILLA
ASPERGILLI
ASPERGILLOSES
ASPERGILLOSIS
ASPERGILLS
ASPERGILLUM
ASPERGILLUMS
ASPERGILLUS
ASPERITIES
ASPERITY
ASPERS
ASPERSE
ASPERSED
ASPERSER
ASPERSERS
ASPERSES
ASPERSING
ASPERSION
ASPERSIONS
ASPERSIVE
ASPERSOR
ASPERSORS
ASPHALT
ASPHALTED
ASPHALTIC
ASPHALTING
ASPHALTITE
ASPHALTITES
ASPHALTS
ASPHALTUM
ASPHALTUMS
ASPHERIC
ASPHERICAL
ASPHODEL
ASPHODELS
ASPHYXIA
ASPHYXIAL
ASPHYXIAS
ASPHYXIATE
ASPHYXIATED
ASPHYXIATES
ASPHYXIATING
ASPHYXIATION
ASPHYXIATIONS
ASPHYXIES
ASPHYXY
ASPIC
ASPICS
ASPIDISTRA
ASPIDISTRAS
ASPIRANT
ASPIRANTS
ASPIRATA
ASPIRATAE
ASPIRATE
ASPIRATED
ASPIRATES
ASPIRATING
ASPIRATION
ASPIRATIONAL
ASPIRATIONALLY
ASPIRATIONS
ASPIRATOR
ASPIRATORS
ASPIRE
ASPIRED
ASPIRER
ASPIRERS
ASPIRES
ASPIRIN
ASPIRING
ASPIRINS
ASPIS
ASPISES
ASPISH
ASPRAWL
ASPS
ASQUINT
ASRAMA
ASRAMAS
ASS
ASSAGAI
ASSAGAIED
ASSAGAIING
ASSAGAIS
ASSAI
ASSAIL
ASSAILABLE
ASSAILANT
ASSAILANTS
ASSAILED
ASSAILER
ASSAILERS
ASSAILING
ASSAILS
ASSAIS
ASSASSIN
ASSASSINATE

ASSASSINATED
ASSASSINATES
ASSASSINATING
ASSASSINATION
ASSASSINATIONS
ASSASSINATOR
ASSASSINATORS
ASSASSINS
ASSAULT
ASSAULTED
ASSAULTER
ASSAULTERS
ASSAULTING
ASSAULTIVE
ASSAULTIVELY
ASSAULTIVENESS
ASSAULTS
ASSAY
ASSAYABLE
ASSAYED
ASSAYER
ASSAYERS
ASSAYING
ASSAYS
ASSEGAI
ASSEGAIED
ASSEGAIING
ASSEGAIS
ASSEMBLAGE
ASSEMBLAGES
ASSEMBLAGIST
ASSEMBLAGISTS
ASSEMBLE
ASSEMBLED
ASSEMBLER
ASSEMBLERS
ASSEMBLES
ASSEMBLIES
ASSEMBLING
ASSEMBLY
ASSEMBLYMAN
ASSEMBLYMEN
ASSEMBLYWOMAN
ASSEMBLYWOMEN
ASSENT
ASSENTATION
ASSENTATIONS
ASSENTED
ASSENTER
ASSENTERS
ASSENTING
ASSENTIVE
ASSENTOR
ASSENTORS
ASSENTS
ASSERT
ASSERTED
ASSERTEDLY
ASSERTER
ASSERTERS
ASSERTING
ASSERTION
ASSERTIONS
ASSERTIVE
ASSERTIVELY
ASSERTIVENESS
ASSERTIVENESSES
ASSERTOR
ASSERTORS
ASSERTS
ASSES
ASSESS
ASSESSABLE
ASSESSED
ASSESSES
ASSESSING
ASSESSMENT
ASSESSMENTS
ASSESSOR
ASSESSORS
ASSET
ASSETLESS
ASSETS
ASSEVERATE
ASSEVERATED
ASSEVERATES
ASSEVERATING
ASSEVERATION
ASSEVERATIONS
ASSEVERATIVE
ASSHOLE
ASSHOLES
ASSIDUITIES
ASSIDUITY
ASSIDUOUS
ASSIDUOUSLY
ASSIDUOUSNESS
ASSIDUOUSNESSES
ASSIGN
ASSIGNABILITIES
ASSIGNABILITY
ASSIGNABLE
ASSIGNAT
ASSIGNATION
ASSIGNATIONS
ASSIGNATS
ASSIGNED
ASSIGNEE
ASSIGNEES
ASSIGNER
ASSIGNERS
ASSIGNING
ASSIGNMENT
ASSIGNMENTS
ASSIGNOR
ASSIGNORS
ASSIGNS
ASSIMILABILITY
ASSIMILABLE
ASSIMILATE
ASSIMILATED
ASSIMILATES
ASSIMILATING
ASSIMILATION
ASSIMILATIONISM
ASSIMILATIONIST
ASSIMILATIONS
ASSIMILATIVE
ASSIMILATOR
ASSIMILATORS
ASSIMILATORY
ASSIST
ASSISTANCE
ASSISTANCES
ASSISTANT
ASSISTANTS
ASSISTANTSHIP
ASSISTANTSHIPS
ASSISTED
ASSISTER
ASSISTERS
ASSISTING
ASSISTIVE
ASSISTOR
ASSISTORS
ASSISTS
ASSIZE
ASSIZES
ASSLIKE
ASSOCIATE
ASSOCIATED
ASSOCIATES
ASSOCIATESHIP
ASSOCIATESHIPS
ASSOCIATING
ASSOCIATION
ASSOCIATIONAL
ASSOCIATIONISM
ASSOCIATIONISMS
ASSOCIATIONIST
ASSOCIATIONISTS
ASSOCIATIONS
ASSOCIATIVE
ASSOCIATIVELY
ASSOCIATIVITIES
ASSOCIATIVITY
ASSOIL
ASSOILED
ASSOILING
ASSOILMENT
ASSOILMENTS
ASSOILS
ASSONANCE
ASSONANCES
ASSONANT
ASSONANTAL
ASSONANTS
ASSONATE
ASSONATED
ASSONATES
ASSONATING
ASSORT
ASSORTATIVE
ASSORTATIVELY
ASSORTED
ASSORTER
ASSORTERS
ASSORTING
ASSORTMENT
ASSORTMENTS
ASSORTS
ASSUAGE
ASSUAGED
ASSUAGEMENT
ASSUAGEMENTS
ASSUAGER
ASSUAGERS
ASSUAGES
ASSUAGING
ASSUASIVE
ASSUMABILITIES
ASSUMABILITY
ASSUMABLE
ASSUMABLY
ASSUME
ASSUMED
ASSUMEDLY
ASSUMER
ASSUMERS
ASSUMES
ASSUMING
ASSUMPSIT
ASSUMPSITS
ASSUMPTION
ASSUMPTIONS
ASSUMPTIVE
ASSURABLE
ASSURANCE
ASSURANCES
ASSURE
ASSURED
ASSUREDLY
ASSUREDNESS
ASSUREDNESSES
ASSUREDS
ASSURER
ASSURERS
ASSURES
ASSURGENT
ASSURING
ASSUROR
ASSURORS
ASSWAGE
ASSWAGED
ASSWAGES
ASSWAGING
ASTANGA
ASTANGAS
ASTARBOARD
ASTASIA
ASTASIAS
ASTATIC
ASTATINE
ASTATINES
ASTER
ASTERIA
ASTERIAS
ASTERIATED
ASTERISK
ASTERISKED
ASTERISKING
ASTERISKLESS
ASTERISKS
ASTERISM
ASTERISMS
ASTERN
ASTERNAL
ASTEROID
ASTEROIDAL
ASTEROIDS
ASTERS
ASTHANGA
ASTHANGAS
ASTHENIA
ASTHENIAS

ASTHENIC
ASTHENICS
ASTHENIES
ASTHENOSPHERE
ASTHENOSPHERES
ASTHENOSPHERIC
ASTHENY
ASTHMA
ASTHMAS
ASTHMATIC
ASTHMATICALLY
ASTHMATICS
ASTIGMATIC
ASTIGMATICS
ASTIGMATISM
ASTIGMATISMS
ASTIGMIA
ASTIGMIAS
ASTILBE
ASTILBES
ASTIR
ASTOMATAL
ASTOMOUS
ASTONIED
ASTONIES
ASTONISH
ASTONISHED
ASTONISHES
ASTONISHING
ASTONISHINGLY
ASTONISHMENT
ASTONISHMENTS
ASTONY
ASTONYING
ASTOUND
ASTOUNDED
ASTOUNDING
ASTOUNDINGLY
ASTOUNDS
ASTRACHAN
ASTRACHANS
ASTRADDLE
ASTRAGAL
ASTRAGALI
ASTRAGALS
ASTRAGALUS
ASTRAKHAN
ASTRAKHANS
ASTRAL
ASTRALLY
ASTRALS
ASTRAY
ASTRICT
ASTRICTED
ASTRICTING
ASTRICTS
ASTRIDE
ASTRINGE
ASTRINGED
ASTRINGENCIES
ASTRINGENCY
ASTRINGENT
ASTRINGENTLY
ASTRINGENTS
ASTRINGES
ASTRINGING
ASTROBIOLOGIES
ASTROBIOLOGIST
ASTROBIOLOGISTS
ASTROBIOLOGY
ASTROCYTE
ASTROCYTES
ASTROCYTIC
ASTROCYTOMA
ASTROCYTOMAS
ASTROCYTOMATA
ASTRODOME
ASTRODOMES
ASTROLABE
ASTROLABES
ASTROLOGER
ASTROLOGERS
ASTROLOGICAL
ASTROLOGICALLY
ASTROLOGIES
ASTROLOGY
ASTROMETRIC
ASTROMETRIES
ASTROMETRY
ASTRONAUT
ASTRONAUTIC
ASTRONAUTICAL
ASTRONAUTICALLY
ASTRONAUTICS
ASTRONAUTS
ASTRONOMER
ASTRONOMERS
ASTRONOMIC
ASTRONOMICAL
ASTRONOMICALLY
ASTRONOMIES
ASTRONOMY
ASTROPHOTOGRAPH
ASTROPHYSICAL
ASTROPHYSICALLY
ASTROPHYSICIST
ASTROPHYSICISTS
ASTROPHYSICS
ASTUTE
ASTUTELY
ASTUTENESS
ASTUTENESSES
ASTYLAR
ASUNDER
ASURA
ASURAS
ASWARM
ASWIM
ASWIRL
ASWOON
ASYLA
ASYLLABIC
ASYLUM
ASYLUMS
ASYMMETRIC
ASYMMETRICAL
ASYMMETRICALLY
ASYMMETRIES
ASYMMETRY
ASYMPTOMATIC
ASYMPTOTE
ASYMPTOTES
ASYMPTOTIC
ASYMPTOTICALLY
ASYNAPSES
ASYNAPSIS
ASYNCHRONIES
ASYNCHRONISM
ASYNCHRONISMS
ASYNCHRONOUS
ASYNCHRONOUSLY
ASYNCHRONY
ASYNDETA
ASYNDETIC
ASYNDETICALLY
ASYNDETON
ASYNDETONS
AT
ATABAL
ATABALS
ATABRINE
ATABRINES
ATACTIC
ATAGHAN
ATAGHANS
ATALAYA
ATALAYAS
ATAMAN
ATAMANS
ATAMASCO
ATAMASCOS
ATAP
ATAPS
ATARACTIC
ATARACTICS
ATARAXIA
ATARAXIAS
ATARAXIC
ATARAXICS
ATARAXIES
ATARAXY
ATAVIC
ATAVISM
ATAVISMS
ATAVIST
ATAVISTIC
ATAVISTICALLY
ATAVISTS
ATAXIA
ATAXIAS
ATAXIC
ATAXICS
ATAXIES
ATAXY
ATE
ATECHNIC
ATELECTASES
ATELECTASIS
ATELIC
ATELIER
ATELIERS
ATEMOYA
ATEMOYAS
ATEMPORAL
ATENOLOL
ATENOLOLS
ATES
ATHANASIES
ATHANASY
ATHEISM
ATHEISMS
ATHEIST
ATHEISTIC
ATHEISTICAL
ATHEISTICALLY
ATHEISTS
ATHELING
ATHELINGS
ATHENAEUM
ATHENAEUMS
ATHENEUM
ATHENEUMS
ATHEORETICAL
ATHEROGENESES
ATHEROGENESIS
ATHEROGENIC
ATHEROMA
ATHEROMAS
ATHEROMATA
ATHEROMATOUS
ATHEROSCLEROSES
ATHEROSCLEROSIS
ATHEROSCLEROTIC
ATHETOID
ATHETOSES
ATHETOSIS
ATHETOTIC
ATHIRST
ATHLETE
ATHLETES
ATHLETIC
ATHLETICALLY
ATHLETICISM
ATHLETICISMS
ATHLETICS
ATHODYD
ATHODYDS
ATHROCYTE
ATHROCYTES
ATHWART
ATHWARTSHIP
ATHWARTSHIPS
ATIGI
ATIGIS
ATILT
ATINGLE
ATISHOO
ATLANTES
ATLAS
ATLASES
ATLATL
ATLATLS
ATMA
ATMAN
ATMANS
ATMAS
ATMOMETER
ATMOMETERS
ATMOSPHERE
ATMOSPHERED
ATMOSPHERES
ATMOSPHERIC
ATMOSPHERICALLY
ATMOSPHERICS
ATOLL

ATOLLS
ATOM
ATOMIC
ATOMICAL
ATOMICALLY
ATOMICITIES
ATOMICITY
ATOMICS
ATOMIES
ATOMISE
ATOMISED
ATOMISER
ATOMISERS
ATOMISES
ATOMISING
ATOMISM
ATOMISMS
ATOMIST
ATOMISTIC
ATOMISTICALLY
ATOMISTS
ATOMIZATION
ATOMIZATIONS
ATOMIZE
ATOMIZED
ATOMIZER
ATOMIZERS
ATOMIZES
ATOMIZING
ATOMS
ATOMY
ATONABLE
ATONAL
ATONALISM
ATONALISMS
ATONALIST
ATONALISTS
ATONALITIES
ATONALITY
ATONALLY
ATONE
ATONEABLE
ATONED
ATONEMENT
ATONEMENTS
ATONER
ATONERS
ATONES
ATONIA
ATONIAS
ATONIC
ATONICITIES
ATONICITY
ATONICS
ATONIES
ATONING
ATONINGLY
ATONY
ATOP
ATOPIC
ATOPIES
ATOPY
ATORVASTATIN
ATORVASTATINS
ATRABILIOUS
ATRABILIOUSNESS
ATRAZINE
ATRAZINES
ATREMBLE
ATRESIA
ATRESIAS
ATRESIC
ATRETIC
ATRIA
ATRIAL
ATRIP
ATRIUM
ATRIUMS
ATROCIOUS
ATROCIOUSLY
ATROCIOUSNESS
ATROCIOUSNESSES
ATROCITIES
ATROCITY
ATROPHIA
ATROPHIAS
ATROPHIC
ATROPHIED
ATROPHIES
ATROPHY
ATROPHYING
ATROPIN
ATROPINE
ATROPINES
ATROPINS
ATROPISM
ATROPISMS
ATT
ATTABOY
ATTABOYS
ATTACH
ATTACHABLE
ATTACHE
ATTACHED
ATTACHER
ATTACHERS
ATTACHES
ATTACHING
ATTACHMENT
ATTACHMENTS
ATTACK
ATTACKED
ATTACKER
ATTACKERS
ATTACKING
ATTACKMAN
ATTACKMEN
ATTACKS
ATTAGIRL
ATTAIN
ATTAINABILITIES
ATTAINABILITY
ATTAINABLE
ATTAINDER
ATTAINDERS
ATTAINED
ATTAINER
ATTAINERS
ATTAINING
ATTAINMENT
ATTAINMENTS
ATTAINS
ATTAINT
ATTAINTED
ATTAINTING
ATTAINTS
ATTAR
ATTARS
ATTEMPER
ATTEMPERED
ATTEMPERING
ATTEMPERS
ATTEMPT
ATTEMPTABLE
ATTEMPTED
ATTEMPTER
ATTEMPTERS
ATTEMPTING
ATTEMPTS
ATTEND
ATTENDANCE
ATTENDANCES
ATTENDANT
ATTENDANTS
ATTENDED
ATTENDEE
ATTENDEES
ATTENDER
ATTENDERS
ATTENDING
ATTENDINGS
ATTENDS
ATTENT
ATTENTION
ATTENTIONAL
ATTENTIONS
ATTENTIVE
ATTENTIVELY
ATTENTIVENESS
ATTENTIVENESSES
ATTENUATE
ATTENUATED
ATTENUATES
ATTENUATING
ATTENUATION
ATTENUATIONS
ATTENUATOR
ATTENUATORS
ATTEST
ATTESTANT
ATTESTANTS
ATTESTATION
ATTESTATIONS
ATTESTED
ATTESTER
ATTESTERS
ATTESTING
ATTESTOR
ATTESTORS
ATTESTS
ATTIC
ATTICISM
ATTICISMS
ATTICIST
ATTICISTS
ATTICIZE
ATTICIZED
ATTICIZES
ATTICIZING
ATTICS
ATTIRE
ATTIRED
ATTIRES
ATTIRING
ATTITUDE
ATTITUDES
ATTITUDINAL
ATTITUDINALLY
ATTITUDINISE
ATTITUDINISED
ATTITUDINISES
ATTITUDINISING
ATTITUDINIZE
ATTITUDINIZED
ATTITUDINIZES
ATTITUDINIZING
ATTORN
ATTORNED
ATTORNEY
ATTORNEYS
ATTORNEYSHIP
ATTORNEYSHIPS
ATTORNING
ATTORNMENT
ATTORNMENTS
ATTORNS
ATTRACT
ATTRACTANCE
ATTRACTANCES
ATTRACTANCIES
ATTRACTANCY
ATTRACTANT
ATTRACTANTS
ATTRACTED
ATTRACTER
ATTRACTERS
ATTRACTING
ATTRACTION
ATTRACTIONS
ATTRACTIVE
ATTRACTIVELY
ATTRACTIVENESS
ATTRACTOR
ATTRACTORS
ATTRACTS
ATTRIBUTABLE
ATTRIBUTE
ATTRIBUTED
ATTRIBUTES
ATTRIBUTING
ATTRIBUTION
ATTRIBUTIONAL
ATTRIBUTIONS
ATTRIBUTIVE
ATTRIBUTIVELY
ATTRIBUTIVES
ATTRIT
ATTRITE
ATTRITED
ATTRITES
ATTRITING
ATTRITION
ATTRITIONAL
ATTRITIONS
ATTRITIVE

ATTRITS
ATTRITTED
ATTRITTING
ATTUNE
ATTUNED
ATTUNEMENT
ATTUNEMENTS
ATTUNES
ATTUNING
ATWAIN
ATWEEN
ATWITTER
ATYPIC
ATYPICAL
ATYPICALITIES
ATYPICALITY
ATYPICALLY
AUBADE
AUBADES
AUBERGE
AUBERGES
AUBERGINE
AUBERGINES
AUBRETIA
AUBRETIAS
AUBRIETA
AUBRIETAS
AUBRIETIA
AUBRIETIAS
AUBURN
AUBURNS
AUCTION
AUCTIONED
AUCTIONEER
AUCTIONEERS
AUCTIONING
AUCTIONS
AUCTORIAL
AUCUBA
AUCUBAS
AUDACIOUS
AUDACIOUSLY
AUDACIOUSNESS
AUDACIOUSNESSES
AUDACITIES
AUDACITY
AUDAD
AUDADS
AUDIAL
AUDIBILITIES
AUDIBILITY
AUDIBILIZE
AUDIBILIZED
AUDIBILIZES
AUDIBILIZING
AUDIBLE
AUDIBLED
AUDIBLES
AUDIBLING
AUDIBLY
AUDIENCE
AUDIENCES
AUDIENT
AUDIENTS
AUDILE
AUDILES
AUDING
AUDINGS
AUDIO
AUDIOBOOK
AUDIOBOOKS
AUDIOCASSETTE
AUDIOCASSETTES
AUDIOGENIC
AUDIOGRAM
AUDIOGRAMS
AUDIOLOGIC
AUDIOLOGICAL
AUDIOLOGIES
AUDIOLOGIST
AUDIOLOGISTS
AUDIOLOGY
AUDIOMETER
AUDIOMETERS
AUDIOMETRIC
AUDIOMETRIES
AUDIOMETRY
AUDIOPHILE
AUDIOPHILES
AUDIOS
AUDIOTAPE
AUDIOTAPED
AUDIOTAPES
AUDIOTAPING
AUDIOVISUAL
AUDIOVISUALS
AUDIPHONE
AUDIPHONES
AUDIT
AUDITABILITIES
AUDITABILITY
AUDITABLE
AUDITED
AUDITEE
AUDITEES
AUDITING
AUDITION
AUDITIONED
AUDITIONING
AUDITIONS
AUDITIVE
AUDITIVES
AUDITOR
AUDITORIA
AUDITORIES
AUDITORILY
AUDITORIUM
AUDITORIUMS
AUDITORS
AUDITORY
AUDITS
AUGEND
AUGENDS
AUGER
AUGERS
AUGH
AUGHT
AUGHTS
AUGITE
AUGITES
AUGITIC
AUGMENT
AUGMENTATION
AUGMENTATIONS
AUGMENTATIVE
AUGMENTATIVES
AUGMENTED
AUGMENTER
AUGMENTERS
AUGMENTING
AUGMENTOR
AUGMENTORS
AUGMENTS
AUGUR
AUGURAL
AUGURED
AUGURER
AUGURERS
AUGURIES
AUGURING
AUGURS
AUGURY
AUGUST
AUGUSTER
AUGUSTEST
AUGUSTLY
AUGUSTNESS
AUGUSTNESSES
AUK
AUKLET
AUKLETS
AUKS
AULD
AULDER
AULDEST
AULIC
AUMBRIES
AUMBRY
AUNT
AUNTHOOD
AUNTHOODS
AUNTIE
AUNTIES
AUNTLIER
AUNTLIEST
AUNTLIKE
AUNTLY
AUNTS
AUNTY
AURA
AURAE
AURAL
AURALITIES
AURALITY
AURALLY
AURAR
AURAS
AURATE
AURATED
AUREATE
AUREATELY
AUREI
AUREOLA
AUREOLAE
AUREOLAS
AUREOLE
AUREOLED
AUREOLES
AUREOLING
AURES
AUREUS
AURIC
AURICLE
AURICLED
AURICLES
AURICULA
AURICULAE
AURICULAR
AURICULARS
AURICULAS
AURICULATE
AURIFEROUS
AURIFORM
AURIS
AURIST
AURISTS
AUROCHS
AUROCHSES
AURORA
AURORAE
AURORAL
AURORALLY
AURORAS
AUROREAN
AUROUS
AURUM
AURUMS
AUSCULTATE
AUSCULTATED
AUSCULTATES
AUSCULTATING
AUSCULTATION
AUSCULTATIONS
AUSCULTATORY
AUSFORM
AUSFORMED
AUSFORMING
AUSFORMS
AUSLANDER
AUSLANDERS
AUSPEX
AUSPICATE
AUSPICATED
AUSPICATES
AUSPICATING
AUSPICE
AUSPICES
AUSPICIOUS
AUSPICIOUSLY
AUSPICIOUSNESS
AUSTENITE
AUSTENITES
AUSTENITIC
AUSTERE
AUSTERELY
AUSTERENESS
AUSTERENESSES
AUSTERER
AUSTEREST
AUSTERITIES
AUSTERITY
AUSTRAL
AUSTRALES
AUSTRALS
AUSUBO

AUSUBOS
AUTACOID
AUTACOIDS
AUTARCH
AUTARCHIC
AUTARCHICAL
AUTARCHIES
AUTARCHS
AUTARCHY
AUTARKIC
AUTARKICAL
AUTARKIES
AUTARKIST
AUTARKISTS
AUTARKY
AUTECIOUS
AUTECISM
AUTECISMS
AUTECOLOGICAL
AUTECOLOGIES
AUTECOLOGY
AUTEUR
AUTEURISM
AUTEURISMS
AUTEURIST
AUTEURISTS
AUTEURS
AUTHENTIC
AUTHENTICALLY
AUTHENTICATE
AUTHENTICATED
AUTHENTICATES
AUTHENTICATING
AUTHENTICATION
AUTHENTICATIONS
AUTHENTICATOR
AUTHENTICATORS
AUTHENTICITIES
AUTHENTICITY
AUTHOR
AUTHORED
AUTHORESS
AUTHORESSES
AUTHORIAL
AUTHORING
AUTHORINGS
AUTHORISATION
AUTHORISATIONS
AUTHORISE
AUTHORISED
AUTHORISES
AUTHORISING
AUTHORITARIAN
AUTHORITARIANS
AUTHORITATIVE
AUTHORITATIVELY
AUTHORITIES
AUTHORITY
AUTHORIZATION
AUTHORIZATIONS
AUTHORIZE
AUTHORIZED
AUTHORIZER
AUTHORIZERS
AUTHORIZES
AUTHORIZING
AUTHORS
AUTHORSHIP
AUTHORSHIPS
AUTISM
AUTISMS
AUTIST
AUTISTIC
AUTISTICALLY
AUTISTICS
AUTISTS
AUTO
AUTOANTIBODIES
AUTOANTIBODY
AUTOBAHN
AUTOBAHNEN
AUTOBAHNS
AUTOBIOGRAPHER
AUTOBIOGRAPHERS
AUTOBIOGRAPHIC
AUTOBIOGRAPHIES
AUTOBIOGRAPHY
AUTOBODIES
AUTOBODY
AUTOBUS
AUTOBUSES
AUTOBUSSES
AUTOCADE
AUTOCADES
AUTOCATALYSES
AUTOCATALYSIS
AUTOCATALYTIC
AUTOCEPHALIES
AUTOCEPHALOUS
AUTOCEPHALY
AUTOCHTHON
AUTOCHTHONES
AUTOCHTHONOUS
AUTOCHTHONOUSLY
AUTOCHTHONS
AUTOCLAVE
AUTOCLAVED
AUTOCLAVES
AUTOCLAVING
AUTOCOID
AUTOCOIDS
AUTOCORRELATION
AUTOCRACIES
AUTOCRACY
AUTOCRAT
AUTOCRATIC
AUTOCRATICAL
AUTOCRATICALLY
AUTOCRATS
AUTOCRINE
AUTOCROSS
AUTOCROSSES
AUTODIAL
AUTODIALED
AUTODIALING
AUTODIALLED
AUTODIALLING
AUTODIALS
AUTODIDACT
AUTODIDACTIC
AUTODIDACTS
AUTODYNE
AUTODYNES
AUTOECIOUS
AUTOECIOUSLY
AUTOECISM
AUTOECISMS
AUTOED
AUTOEROTIC
AUTOEROTICISM
AUTOEROTICISMS
AUTOEROTISM
AUTOEROTISMS
AUTOEXPOSURE
AUTOEXPOSURES
AUTOFOCUS
AUTOFOCUSES
AUTOGAMIC
AUTOGAMIES
AUTOGAMOUS
AUTOGAMY
AUTOGENIC
AUTOGENIES
AUTOGENOUS
AUTOGENOUSLY
AUTOGENY
AUTOGIRO
AUTOGIROS
AUTOGRAFT
AUTOGRAFTED
AUTOGRAFTING
AUTOGRAFTS
AUTOGRAPH
AUTOGRAPHED
AUTOGRAPHIC
AUTOGRAPHICALLY
AUTOGRAPHIES
AUTOGRAPHING
AUTOGRAPHS
AUTOGRAPHY
AUTOGYRO
AUTOGYROS
AUTOHARP
AUTOHARPS
AUTOHYPNOSES
AUTOHYPNOSIS
AUTOHYPNOTIC
AUTOIMMUNE
AUTOIMMUNITIES
AUTOIMMUNITY
AUTOINFECTION
AUTOINFECTIONS
AUTOING
AUTOLOAD
AUTOLOADING
AUTOLOGOUS
AUTOLYSATE
AUTOLYSATES
AUTOLYSE
AUTOLYSED
AUTOLYSES
AUTOLYSIN
AUTOLYSING
AUTOLYSINS
AUTOLYSIS
AUTOLYTIC
AUTOLYZATE
AUTOLYZATES
AUTOLYZE
AUTOLYZED
AUTOLYZES
AUTOLYZING
AUTOMAKER
AUTOMAKERS
AUTOMAN
AUTOMAT
AUTOMATA
AUTOMATABLE
AUTOMATE
AUTOMATED
AUTOMATES
AUTOMATIC
AUTOMATICALLY
AUTOMATICITIES
AUTOMATICITY
AUTOMATICS
AUTOMATING
AUTOMATION
AUTOMATIONS
AUTOMATISM
AUTOMATISMS
AUTOMATIST
AUTOMATISTS
AUTOMATIZATION
AUTOMATIZATIONS
AUTOMATIZE
AUTOMATIZED
AUTOMATIZES
AUTOMATIZING
AUTOMATON
AUTOMATONS
AUTOMATS
AUTOMEN
AUTOMOBILE
AUTOMOBILED
AUTOMOBILES
AUTOMOBILING
AUTOMOBILIST
AUTOMOBILISTS
AUTOMOBILITIES
AUTOMOBILITY
AUTOMORPHISM
AUTOMORPHISMS
AUTOMOTIVE
AUTONOMIC
AUTONOMICALLY
AUTONOMIES
AUTONOMIST
AUTONOMISTS
AUTONOMOUS
AUTONOMOUSLY
AUTONOMY
AUTONYM
AUTONYMS
AUTOPEN
AUTOPENS
AUTOPHAGIES
AUTOPHAGY
AUTOPHYTE
AUTOPHYTES
AUTOPILOT
AUTOPILOTS
AUTOPOLYPLOID
AUTOPOLYPLOIDS
AUTOPOLYPLOIDY

AUTOPSIC
AUTOPSIED
AUTOPSIES
AUTOPSIST
AUTOPSISTS
AUTOPSY
AUTOPSYING
AUTORADIOGRAM
AUTORADIOGRAMS
AUTORADIOGRAPH
AUTORADIOGRAPHS
AUTORADIOGRAPHY
AUTOROTATE
AUTOROTATED
AUTOROTATES
AUTOROTATING
AUTOROTATION
AUTOROTATIONS
AUTOROUTE
AUTOROUTES
AUTOS
AUTOSEXING
AUTOSOMAL
AUTOSOMALLY
AUTOSOME
AUTOSOMES
AUTOSTRADA
AUTOSTRADAS
AUTOSTRADE
AUTOSUGGEST
AUTOSUGGESTED
AUTOSUGGESTING
AUTOSUGGESTION
AUTOSUGGESTIONS
AUTOSUGGESTS
AUTOTELIC
AUTOTETRAPLOID
AUTOTETRAPLOIDS
AUTOTETRAPLOIDY
AUTOTOMIC
AUTOTOMIES
AUTOTOMIZE
AUTOTOMIZED
AUTOTOMIZES
AUTOTOMIZING
AUTOTOMOUS
AUTOTOMY
AUTOTOXIC
AUTOTOXIN
AUTOTOXINS
AUTOTRANSFORMER
AUTOTRANSFUSION
AUTOTROPH
AUTOTROPHIC
AUTOTROPHICALLY
AUTOTROPHIES
AUTOTROPHS
AUTOTROPHY
AUTOTYPE
AUTOTYPES
AUTOTYPIES
AUTOTYPY
AUTOWORKER
AUTOWORKERS
AUTOXIDATION
AUTOXIDATIONS
AUTUMN
AUTUMNAL
AUTUMNALLY
AUTUMNS
AUTUNITE
AUTUNITES
AUXESES
AUXESIS
AUXETIC
AUXETICS
AUXILIARIES
AUXILIARY
AUXIN
AUXINIC
AUXINS
AUXOTROPH
AUXOTROPHIC
AUXOTROPHIES
AUXOTROPHS
AUXOTROPHY
AVA
AVADAVAT
AVADAVATS
AVAIL
AVAILABILITIES
AVAILABILITY
AVAILABLE
AVAILABLENESS
AVAILABLENESSES
AVAILABLY
AVAILED
AVAILING
AVAILS
AVALANCHE
AVALANCHED
AVALANCHES
AVALANCHING
AVANT
AVARICE
AVARICES
AVARICIOUS
AVARICIOUSLY
AVARICIOUSNESS
AVASCULAR
AVASCULARITIES
AVASCULARITY
AVAST
AVATAR
AVATARS
AVAUNT
AVE
AVELLAN
AVELLANE
AVENGE
AVENGED
AVENGEFUL
AVENGER
AVENGERS
AVENGES
AVENGING
AVENS
AVENSES
AVENTAIL
AVENTAILS
AVENTURIN
AVENTURINE
AVENTURINES
AVENTURINS
AVENUE
AVENUES
AVER
AVERAGE
AVERAGED
AVERAGELY
AVERAGENESS
AVERAGENESSES
AVERAGES
AVERAGING
AVERMENT
AVERMENTS
AVERRABLE
AVERRED
AVERRING
AVERS
AVERSE
AVERSELY
AVERSENESS
AVERSENESSES
AVERSION
AVERSIONS
AVERSIVE
AVERSIVELY
AVERSIVENESS
AVERSIVENESSES
AVERSIVES
AVERT
AVERTABLE
AVERTED
AVERTER
AVERTERS
AVERTIBLE
AVERTING
AVERTS
AVES
AVGAS
AVGASES
AVGASSES
AVGOLEMONO
AVGOLEMONOS
AVIAN
AVIANIZE
AVIANIZED
AVIANIZES
AVIANIZING
AVIANS
AVIARIES
AVIARIST
AVIARISTS
AVIARY
AVIATE
AVIATED
AVIATES
AVIATIC
AVIATING
AVIATION
AVIATIONS
AVIATOR
AVIATORS
AVIATRESS
AVIATRESSES
AVIATRICE
AVIATRICES
AVIATRIX
AVIATRIXES
AVICULAR
AVICULTURE
AVICULTURES
AVICULTURIST
AVICULTURISTS
AVID
AVIDIN
AVIDINS
AVIDITIES
AVIDITY
AVIDLY
AVIDNESS
AVIDNESSES
AVIFAUNA
AVIFAUNAE
AVIFAUNAL
AVIFAUNAS
AVIGATOR
AVIGATORS
AVION
AVIONIC
AVIONICS
AVIONS
AVIRULENT
AVISO
AVISOS
AVITAMINOSES
AVITAMINOSIS
AVITAMINOTIC
AVO
AVOCADO
AVOCADOES
AVOCADOS
AVOCATION
AVOCATIONAL
AVOCATIONALLY
AVOCATIONS
AVOCET
AVOCETS
AVODIRE
AVODIRES
AVOID
AVOIDABLE
AVOIDABLY
AVOIDANCE
AVOIDANCES
AVOIDED
AVOIDER
AVOIDERS
AVOIDING
AVOIDS
AVOIRDUPOIS
AVOS
AVOSET
AVOSETS
AVOUCH
AVOUCHED
AVOUCHER
AVOUCHERS
AVOUCHES
AVOUCHING
AVOUCHMENT
AVOUCHMENTS
AVOW
AVOWABLE

AVOWABLY
AVOWAL
AVOWALS
AVOWED
AVOWEDLY
AVOWER
AVOWERS
AVOWING
AVOWS
AVULSE
AVULSED
AVULSES
AVULSING
AVULSION
AVULSIONS
AVUNCULAR
AVUNCULARITIES
AVUNCULARITY
AVUNCULARLY
AW
AWA
AWAIT
AWAITED
AWAITER
AWAITERS
AWAITING
AWAITS
AWAKE
AWAKED
AWAKEN
AWAKENED
AWAKENER
AWAKENERS
AWAKENING
AWAKENINGS
AWAKENS
AWAKES
AWAKING
AWARD
AWARDABLE
AWARDED
AWARDEE
AWARDEES
AWARDER
AWARDERS
AWARDING
AWARDS
AWARE
AWARENESS
AWARENESSES
AWASH
AWAY
AWAYNESS
AWAYNESSES
AWE
AWEARY
AWEATHER
AWED
AWEE
AWEIGH
AWEING
AWELESS
AWES
AWESOME
AWESOMELY
AWESOMENESS
AWESOMENESSES
AWESTRICKEN
AWESTRUCK
AWFUL
AWFULLER
AWFULLEST
AWFULLY
AWFULNESS
AWFULNESSES
AWHILE
AWHIRL
AWING
AWKWARD
AWKWARDER
AWKWARDEST
AWKWARDLY
AWKWARDNESS
AWKWARDNESSES
AWL
AWLESS
AWLS
AWLWORT
AWLWORTS
AWMOUS
AWN
AWNED
AWNING
AWNINGED
AWNINGS
AWNLESS
AWNS
AWNY
AWOKE
AWOKEN
AWOL
AWOLS
AWRY
AX
AXAL
AXE
AXED
AXEL
AXELS
AXEMAN
AXEMEN
AXENIC
AXENICALLY
AXES
AXIAL
AXIALITIES
AXIALITY
AXIALLY
AXIL
AXILE
AXILLA
AXILLAE
AXILLAR
AXILLARIES
AXILLARS
AXILLARY
AXILLAS
AXILS
AXING
AXIOLOGICAL
AXIOLOGICALLY
AXIOLOGIES
AXIOLOGY
AXIOM
AXIOMATIC
AXIOMATICALLY
AXIOMATISATION
AXIOMATISATIONS
AXIOMATIZATION
AXIOMATIZATIONS
AXIOMATIZE
AXIOMATIZED
AXIOMATIZES
AXIOMATIZING
AXIOMS
AXION
AXIONS
AXIS
AXISED
AXISES
AXISYMMETRIC
AXISYMMETRICAL
AXISYMMETRIES
AXISYMMETRY
AXITE
AXITES
AXLE
AXLED
AXLES
AXLETREE
AXLETREES
AXLIKE
AXMAN
AXMEN
AXOLOTL
AXOLOTLS
AXON
AXONAL
AXONE
AXONEMAL
AXONEME
AXONEMES
AXONES
AXONIC
AXONOMETRIC
AXONS
AXOPLASM
AXOPLASMIC
AXOPLASMS
AXSEED
AXSEEDS
AY
AYAH
AYAHS
AYAHUASCA
AYAHUASCAS
AYATOLLAH
AYATOLLAHS
AYAYA
AYAYAS
AYE
AYES
AYIN
AYINS
AYS
AYURVEDA
AYURVEDAS
AYURVEDIC
AYURVEDICS
AZALEA
AZALEAS
AZAN
AZANS
AZATHIOPRINE
AZATHIOPRINES
AZEDARACH
AZEDARACHS
AZEOTROPE
AZEOTROPES
AZEOTROPIES
AZEOTROPY
AZIDE
AZIDES
AZIDO
AZIDOTHYMIDINE
AZIDOTHYMIDINES
AZIMUTH
AZIMUTHAL
AZIMUTHALLY
AZIMUTHS
AZINE
AZINES
AZLON
AZLONS
AZO
AZOIC
AZOLE
AZOLES
AZON
AZONAL
AZONIC
AZONS
AZOOSPERMIA
AZOOSPERMIAS
AZOTE
AZOTED
AZOTEMIA
AZOTEMIAS
AZOTEMIC
AZOTES
AZOTH
AZOTHS
AZOTIC
AZOTISE
AZOTISED
AZOTISES
AZOTISING
AZOTIZE
AZOTIZED
AZOTIZES
AZOTIZING
AZOTOBACTER
AZOTOBACTERS
AZOTURIA
AZOTURIAS
AZUKI
AZUKIS
AZULEJO
AZULEJOS
AZURE
AZURES
AZURITE
AZURITES
AZYGOS
AZYGOSES
AZYGOUS

B

BA
BAA
BAAED
BAAING
BAAL
BAALIM
BAALISM
BAALISMS
BAALS
BAAS
BAASES
BAASKAAP
BAASKAAPS
BAASKAP
BAASKAPS
BAASSKAP
BAASSKAPS
BABA
BABACU
BABACUS
BABAS
BABASSU
BABASSUS
BABBITRIES
BABBITRY
BABBITT
BABBITTED
BABBITTING
BABBITTRIES
BABBITTRY
BABBITTS
BABBLE
BABBLED
BABBLEMENT
BABBLEMENTS
BABBLER
BABBLERS
BABBLES
BABBLING
BABBLINGS
BABE
BABEL
BABELS
BABES
BABESIA
BABESIAS
BABESIOSES
BABESIOSIS
BABICHE
BABICHES
BABIED
BABIER
BABIES
BABIEST
BABIRUSA
BABIRUSAS
BABIRUSSA
BABIRUSSAS
BABKA
BABKAS
BABOO
BABOOL
BABOOLS
BABOON
BABOONERIES
BABOONERY
BABOONISH
BABOONS
BABOOS
BABOUCHE
BABOUCHES
BABU
BABUL
BABULS
BABUS
BABUSHKA
BABUSHKAS
BABY
BABYDOLL
BABYDOLLS
BABYHOOD
BABYHOODS
BABYING
BABYISH
BABYISHLY
BABYLIKE
BABYPROOF
BABYPROOFED
BABYPROOFING
BABYPROOFS
BABYSAT
BABYSIT
BABYSITS
BABYSITTER
BABYSITTERS
BABYSITTING
BABYSITTINGS
BACALAO
BACALAOS
BACALHAU
BACALHAUS
BACCA
BACCAE
BACCALA
BACCALAS
BACCALAUREATE
BACCALAUREATES
BACCARA
BACCARAS
BACCARAT
BACCARATS
BACCATE
BACCATED
BACCHANAL
BACCHANALIA
BACCHANALIAN
BACCHANALIANS
BACCHANALIAS
BACCHANALS
BACCHANT
BACCHANTE
BACCHANTES
BACCHANTS
BACCHIC
BACCHII
BACCHIUS
BACCIES
BACCIFORM
BACCY
BACH
BACHED
BACHELOR
BACHELORDOM
BACHELORDOMS
BACHELORETTE
BACHELORETTES
BACHELORHOOD
BACHELORHOODS
BACHELORS
BACHES
BACHING
BACILLAR
BACILLARY
BACILLI
BACILLUS
BACITRACIN
BACITRACINS
BACK
BACKACHE
BACKACHES
BACKBAR
BACKBARS
BACKBEAT
BACKBEATS
BACKBENCH
BACKBENCHER
BACKBENCHERS
BACKBENCHES
BACKBEND
BACKBENDS
BACKBIT
BACKBITE
BACKBITER
BACKBITERS
BACKBITES
BACKBITING
BACKBITINGS
BACKBITTEN
BACKBLOCK
BACKBLOCKS
BACKBOARD
BACKBOARDS
BACKBONE
BACKBONED
BACKBONES
BACKBREAKER
BACKBREAKERS
BACKBREAKING
BACKCAST
BACKCASTS
BACKCHAT
BACKCHATS
BACKCHECK
BACKCHECKED
BACKCHECKING
BACKCHECKS
BACKCLOTH
BACKCLOTHS
BACKCOMB
BACKCOMBED
BACKCOMBING
BACKCOMBS
BACKCOUNTRIES
BACKCOUNTRY
BACKCOURT
BACKCOURTMAN
BACKCOURTMEN
BACKCOURTS
BACKCROSS
BACKCROSSED
BACKCROSSES
BACKCROSSING
BACKDATE
BACKDATED
BACKDATES
BACKDATING
BACKDOOR
BACKDOWN
BACKDOWNS
BACKDRAFT
BACKDRAFTS
BACKDROP
BACKDROPPED
BACKDROPPING
BACKDROPS
BACKDROPT
BACKED
BACKER
BACKERS
BACKFAT
BACKFATS
BACKFIELD
BACKFIELDS
BACKFILL
BACKFILLED
BACKFILLING
BACKFILLS
BACKFIRE
BACKFIRED
BACKFIRES
BACKFIRING
BACKFIT
BACKFITS
BACKFITTED
BACKFITTING
BACKFLIP
BACKFLIPPED
BACKFLIPPING
BACKFLIPS
BACKFLOW
BACKFLOWS
BACKGAMMON
BACKGAMMONS
BACKGROUND
BACKGROUNDED
BACKGROUNDER
BACKGROUNDERS
BACKGROUNDING
BACKGROUNDS
BACKHAND
BACKHANDED
BACKHANDEDLY
BACKHANDER
BACKHANDERS
BACKHANDING
BACKHANDS
BACKHAUL
BACKHAULED
BACKHAULING
BACKHAULS

BACKHOE
BACKHOED
BACKHOEING
BACKHOES
BACKHOUSE
BACKHOUSES
BACKING
BACKINGS
BACKLAND
BACKLANDS
BACKLASH
BACKLASHED
BACKLASHER
BACKLASHERS
BACKLASHES
BACKLASHING
BACKLESS
BACKLIGHT
BACKLIGHTED
BACKLIGHTING
BACKLIGHTS
BACKLIST
BACKLISTED
BACKLISTING
BACKLISTS
BACKLIT
BACKLOAD
BACKLOADED
BACKLOADING
BACKLOADS
BACKLOG
BACKLOGGED
BACKLOGGING
BACKLOGS
BACKLOT
BACKLOTS
BACKMOST
BACKOUT
BACKOUTS
BACKPACK
BACKPACKED
BACKPACKER
BACKPACKERS
BACKPACKING
BACKPACKINGS
BACKPACKS
BACKPEDAL
BACKPEDALED
BACKPEDALING
BACKPEDALLED
BACKPEDALLING
BACKPEDALS
BACKREST
BACKRESTS
BACKROOM
BACKROOMS
BACKRUSH
BACKRUSHES
BACKS
BACKSAW
BACKSAWS
BACKSCATTER
BACKSCATTERED
BACKSCATTERING
BACKSCATTERINGS
BACKSCATTERS
BACKSEAT
BACKSEATS
BACKSET
BACKSETS
BACKSHORE
BACKSHORES
BACKSIDE
BACKSIDES
BACKSLAP
BACKSLAPPED
BACKSLAPPER
BACKSLAPPERS
BACKSLAPPING
BACKSLAPPINGS
BACKSLAPS
BACKSLASH
BACKSLASHES
BACKSLID
BACKSLIDDEN
BACKSLIDE
BACKSLIDER
BACKSLIDERS
BACKSLIDES
BACKSLIDING
BACKSPACE
BACKSPACED
BACKSPACES
BACKSPACING
BACKSPIN
BACKSPINS
BACKSPLASH
BACKSPLASHES
BACKSTAB
BACKSTABBED
BACKSTABBER
BACKSTABBERS
BACKSTABBING
BACKSTABBINGS
BACKSTABS
BACKSTAGE
BACKSTAGES
BACKSTAIR
BACKSTAIRS
BACKSTAMP
BACKSTAMPED
BACKSTAMPING
BACKSTAMPS
BACKSTAY
BACKSTAYS
BACKSTITCH
BACKSTITCHED
BACKSTITCHES
BACKSTITCHING
BACKSTOP
BACKSTOPPED
BACKSTOPPING
BACKSTOPS
BACKSTORIES
BACKSTORY
BACKSTRAIGHT
BACKSTRAIGHTS
BACKSTREET
BACKSTREETS
BACKSTRETCH
BACKSTRETCHES
BACKSTROKE
BACKSTROKER
BACKSTROKERS
BACKSTROKES
BACKSWEPT
BACKSWIMMER
BACKSWIMMERS
BACKSWING
BACKSWINGS
BACKSWORD
BACKSWORDS
BACKTALK
BACKTALKS
BACKTRACK
BACKTRACKED
BACKTRACKING
BACKTRACKS
BACKUP
BACKUPS
BACKWARD
BACKWARDLY
BACKWARDNESS
BACKWARDNESSES
BACKWARDS
BACKWASH
BACKWASHED
BACKWASHES
BACKWASHING
BACKWATER
BACKWATERS
BACKWIND
BACKWINDED
BACKWINDING
BACKWINDS
BACKWOOD
BACKWOODS
BACKWOODSIER
BACKWOODSIEST
BACKWOODSMAN
BACKWOODSMEN
BACKWOODSY
BACKWRAP
BACKWRAPS
BACKYARD
BACKYARDS
BACLOFEN
BACLOFENS
BACON
BACONS
BACTEREMIA
BACTEREMIAS
BACTEREMIC
BACTERIA
BACTERIAL
BACTERIALLY
BACTERIALS
BACTERIAS
BACTERICIDAL
BACTERICIDALLY
BACTERICIDE
BACTERICIDES
BACTERIN
BACTERINS
BACTERIOCIDAL
BACTERIOCIDE
BACTERIOCIDES
BACTERIOCIN
BACTERIOCINS
BACTERIOLOGIC
BACTERIOLOGICAL
BACTERIOLOGIES
BACTERIOLOGIST
BACTERIOLOGISTS
BACTERIOLOGY
BACTERIOLYSES
BACTERIOLYSIS
BACTERIOLYTIC
BACTERIOPHAGE
BACTERIOPHAGES
BACTERIOPHAGIES
BACTERIOPHAGY
BACTERIOSTASES
BACTERIOSTASIS
BACTERIOSTAT
BACTERIOSTATIC
BACTERIOSTATS
BACTERIUM
BACTERIURIA
BACTERIURIAS
BACTERIZATION
BACTERIZATIONS
BACTERIZE
BACTERIZED
BACTERIZES
BACTERIZING
BACTEROID
BACTEROIDS
BACULA
BACULINE
BACULUM
BACULUMS
BAD
BADASS
BADASSED
BADASSES
BADDER
BADDEST
BADDIE
BADDIES
BADDISH
BADDY
BADE
BADGE
BADGED
BADGELESS
BADGER
BADGERED
BADGERING
BADGERLY
BADGERS
BADGES
BADGING
BADINAGE
BADINAGED
BADINAGES
BADINAGING
BADLAND
BADLANDS
BADLY
BADMAN
BADMEN
BADMINTON
BADMINTONS
BADMOUTH

BADMOUTHED
BADMOUTHING
BADMOUTHS
BADNESS
BADNESSES
BADS
BAFF
BAFFED
BAFFIES
BAFFING
BAFFLE
BAFFLED
BAFFLEGAB
BAFFLEGABS
BAFFLEMENT
BAFFLEMENTS
BAFFLER
BAFFLERS
BAFFLES
BAFFLING
BAFFLINGLY
BAFFS
BAFFY
BAG
BAGASS
BAGASSE
BAGASSES
BAGATELLE
BAGATELLES
BAGEL
BAGELS
BAGFUL
BAGFULS
BAGGAGE
BAGGAGES
BAGGED
BAGGER
BAGGERS
BAGGIE
BAGGIER
BAGGIES
BAGGIEST
BAGGILY
BAGGINESS
BAGGINESSES
BAGGING
BAGGINGS
BAGGY
BAGHOUSE
BAGHOUSES
BAGLIKE
BAGMAN
BAGMEN
BAGNIO
BAGNIOS
BAGPIPE
BAGPIPED
BAGPIPER
BAGPIPERS
BAGPIPES
BAGPIPING
BAGS
BAGSFUL
BAGUET
BAGUETS
BAGUETTE
BAGUETTES
BAGWIG
BAGWIGS
BAGWORM
BAGWORMS
BAH
BAHADUR
BAHADURS
BAHT
BAHTS
BAHUVRIHI
BAHUVRIHIS
BAIDAR
BAIDARKA
BAIDARKAS
BAIDARS
BAIL
BAILABLE
BAILED
BAILEE
BAILEES
BAILER
BAILERS
BAILEY
BAILEYS
BAILIE
BAILIES
BAILIFF
BAILIFFS
BAILIFFSHIP
BAILIFFSHIPS
BAILING
BAILIWICK
BAILIWICKS
BAILMENT
BAILMENTS
BAILOR
BAILORS
BAILOUT
BAILOUTS
BAILS
BAILSMAN
BAILSMEN
BAIRN
BAIRNISH
BAIRNLIER
BAIRNLIEST
BAIRNLY
BAIRNS
BAIT
BAITED
BAITER
BAITERS
BAITFISH
BAITFISHES
BAITH
BAITING
BAITS
BAIZA
BAIZAS
BAIZE
BAIZES
BAKE
BAKEAPPLE
BAKEAPPLES
BAKED
BAKEHOUSE
BAKEHOUSES
BAKELITE
BAKELITES
BAKEMEAT
BAKEMEATS
BAKER
BAKERIES
BAKERS
BAKERY
BAKES
BAKESHOP
BAKESHOPS
BAKEWARE
BAKEWARES
BAKING
BAKINGS
BAKLAVA
BAKLAVAS
BAKLAWA
BAKLAWAS
BAKSHEESH
BAKSHEESHES
BAKSHISH
BAKSHISHED
BAKSHISHES
BAKSHISHING
BAL
BALACLAVA
BALACLAVAS
BALAFON
BALAFONS
BALALAIKA
BALALAIKAS
BALANCE
BALANCED
BALANCER
BALANCERS
BALANCES
BALANCING
BALAS
BALASES
BALATA
BALATAS
BALBOA
BALBOAS
BALBRIGGAN
BALBRIGGANS
BALCONIED
BALCONIES
BALCONY
BALD
BALDACHIN
BALDACHINO
BALDACHINOS
BALDACHINS
BALDAQUIN
BALDAQUINS
BALDED
BALDER
BALDERDASH
BALDERDASHES
BALDEST
BALDFACED
BALDHEAD
BALDHEADS
BALDIE
BALDIES
BALDING
BALDISH
BALDLY
BALDNESS
BALDNESSES
BALDPATE
BALDPATED
BALDPATES
BALDRIC
BALDRICK
BALDRICKS
BALDRICS
BALDS
BALDY
BALE
BALED
BALEEN
BALEENS
BALEFIRE
BALEFIRES
BALEFUL
BALEFULLY
BALEFULNESS
BALEFULNESSES
BALER
BALERS
BALES
BALING
BALINGS
BALISAUR
BALISAURS
BALK
BALKANIZATION
BALKANIZATIONS
BALKANIZE
BALKANIZED
BALKANIZES
BALKANIZING
BALKED
BALKER
BALKERS
BALKIER
BALKIEST
BALKILY
BALKINESS
BALKINESSES
BALKING
BALKLINE
BALKLINES
BALKS
BALKY
BALL
BALLAD
BALLADE
BALLADEER
BALLADEERS
BALLADES
BALLADIC
BALLADIST
BALLADISTS
BALLADRIES
BALLADRY
BALLADS
BALLAST
BALLASTED

BALLASTER
BALLASTERS
BALLASTING
BALLASTS
BALLBOY
BALLBOYS
BALLBUSTER
BALLBUSTERS
BALLCARRIER
BALLCARRIERS
BALLCOCK
BALLCOCKS
BALLED
BALLER
BALLERINA
BALLERINAS
BALLERS
BALLET
BALLETIC
BALLETOMANE
BALLETOMANES
BALLETOMANIA
BALLETOMANIAS
BALLETS
BALLGAME
BALLGAMES
BALLGIRL
BALLGIRLS
BALLHANDLING
BALLHANDLINGS
BALLHAWK
BALLHAWKS
BALLIER
BALLIES
BALLIEST
BALLING
BALLISTA
BALLISTAE
BALLISTAS
BALLISTIC
BALLISTICALLY
BALLISTICS
BALLOCKS
BALLON
BALLONET
BALLONETS
BALLONNE
BALLONNES
BALLONS
BALLOON
BALLOONED
BALLOONING
BALLOONINGS
BALLOONIST
BALLOONISTS
BALLOONS
BALLOT
BALLOTED
BALLOTER
BALLOTERS
BALLOTING
BALLOTS
BALLPARK
BALLPARKS
BALLPLAYER
BALLPLAYERS
BALLPOINT
BALLPOINTS
BALLROOM
BALLROOMS
BALLS
BALLSED
BALLSES
BALLSIER
BALLSIEST
BALLSINESS
BALLSINESSES
BALLSING
BALLSY
BALLUTE
BALLUTES
BALLY
BALLYARD
BALLYARDS
BALLYHOO
BALLYHOOED
BALLYHOOING
BALLYHOOS
BALLYRAG
BALLYRAGGED
BALLYRAGGING
BALLYRAGS
BALM
BALMACAAN
BALMACAANS
BALMIER
BALMIEST
BALMILY
BALMINESS
BALMINESSES
BALMLIKE
BALMORAL
BALMORALS
BALMS
BALMY
BALNEAL
BALNEOLOGIES
BALNEOLOGY
BALONEY
BALONEYS
BALS
BALSA
BALSAM
BALSAMED
BALSAMIC
BALSAMING
BALSAMS
BALSAS
BALTI
BALTIS
BALUSTER
BALUSTERS
BALUSTRADE
BALUSTRADED
BALUSTRADES
BAM
BAMBINI
BAMBINO
BAMBINOS
BAMBOO
BAMBOOS
BAMBOOZLE
BAMBOOZLED
BAMBOOZLEMENT
BAMBOOZLEMENTS
BAMBOOZLES
BAMBOOZLING
BAMMED
BAMMING
BAMS
BAN
BANAL
BANALITIES
BANALITY
BANALIZE
BANALIZED
BANALIZES
BANALIZING
BANALLY
BANANA
BANANAS
BANAUSIC
BANC
BANCO
BANCOS
BANCS
BAND
BANDA
BANDAGE
BANDAGED
BANDAGER
BANDAGERS
BANDAGES
BANDAGING
BANDAGINGS
BANDAID
BANDANA
BANDANAS
BANDANNA
BANDANNAS
BANDAS
BANDBOX
BANDBOXES
BANDEAU
BANDEAUS
BANDEAUX
BANDED
BANDER
BANDERILLA
BANDERILLAS
BANDERILLERO
BANDERILLEROS
BANDEROL
BANDEROLE
BANDEROLES
BANDEROLS
BANDERS
BANDICOOT
BANDICOOTS
BANDIED
BANDIER
BANDIES
BANDIEST
BANDINESS
BANDINESSES
BANDING
BANDINGS
BANDIT
BANDITO
BANDITOS
BANDITRIES
BANDITRY
BANDITS
BANDITTI
BANDLEADER
BANDLEADERS
BANDMASTER
BANDMASTERS
BANDMATE
BANDMATES
BANDOG
BANDOGS
BANDOLEER
BANDOLEERS
BANDOLIER
BANDOLIERS
BANDONEON
BANDONEONS
BANDORA
BANDORAS
BANDORE
BANDORES
BANDPASS
BANDPASSES
BANDS
BANDSAW
BANDSAWS
BANDSHELL
BANDSHELLS
BANDSMAN
BANDSMEN
BANDSTAND
BANDSTANDS
BANDURA
BANDURAS
BANDWAGON
BANDWAGONS
BANDWIDTH
BANDWIDTHS
BANDY
BANDYING
BANE
BANEBERRIES
BANEBERRY
BANED
BANEFUL
BANEFULLY
BANES
BANG
BANGED
BANGER
BANGERS
BANGING
BANGKOK
BANGKOKS
BANGLE
BANGLES
BANGS
BANGTAIL
BANGTAILS
BANI
BANIAN
BANIANS
BANING
BANISH

BANISHED
BANISHER
BANISHERS
BANISHES
BANISHING
BANISHMENT
BANISHMENTS
BANISTER
BANISTERED
BANISTERS
BANJAX
BANJAXED
BANJAXES
BANJAXING
BANJO
BANJOES
BANJOIST
BANJOISTS
BANJOS
BANK
BANKABILITIES
BANKABILITY
BANKABLE
BANKBOOK
BANKBOOKS
BANKCARD
BANKCARDS
BANKED
BANKER
BANKERLY
BANKERS
BANKING
BANKINGS
BANKIT
BANKITS
BANKNOTE
BANKNOTES
BANKROLL
BANKROLLED
BANKROLLER
BANKROLLERS
BANKROLLING
BANKROLLS
BANKRUPT
BANKRUPTCIES
BANKRUPTCY
BANKRUPTED
BANKRUPTING
BANKRUPTS
BANKS
BANKSIA
BANKSIAS
BANKSIDE
BANKSIDES
BANNABLE
BANNED
BANNER
BANNERED
BANNERET
BANNERETS
BANNERETTE
BANNERETTES
BANNERING
BANNEROL
BANNEROLS
BANNERS
BANNET
BANNETS
BANNING
BANNISTER
BANNISTERS
BANNOCK
BANNOCKS
BANNS
BANQUET
BANQUETED
BANQUETER
BANQUETERS
BANQUETING
BANQUETS
BANQUETTE
BANQUETTES
BANS
BANSHEE
BANSHEES
BANSHIE
BANSHIES
BANTAM
BANTAMS
BANTAMWEIGHT
BANTAMWEIGHTS
BANTENG
BANTENGS
BANTER
BANTERED
BANTERER
BANTERERS
BANTERING
BANTERINGLY
BANTERS
BANTIES
BANTLING
BANTLINGS
BANTY
BANYAN
BANYANS
BANZAI
BANZAIS
BAOBAB
BAOBABS
BAP
BAPS
BAPTISE
BAPTISED
BAPTISES
BAPTISIA
BAPTISIAS
BAPTISING
BAPTISM
BAPTISMAL
BAPTISMALLY
BAPTISMS
BAPTIST
BAPTISTERIES
BAPTISTERY
BAPTISTRIES
BAPTISTRY
BAPTISTS
BAPTIZE
BAPTIZED
BAPTIZER
BAPTIZERS
BAPTIZES
BAPTIZING
BAR
BARATHEA
BARATHEAS
BARB
BARBAL
BARBARIAN
BARBARIANISM
BARBARIANISMS
BARBARIANS
BARBARIC
BARBARICALLY
BARBARISM
BARBARISMS
BARBARITIES
BARBARITY
BARBARIZATION
BARBARIZATIONS
BARBARIZE
BARBARIZED
BARBARIZES
BARBARIZING
BARBAROUS
BARBAROUSLY
BARBAROUSNESS
BARBAROUSNESSES
BARBASCO
BARBASCOES
BARBASCOS
BARBATE
BARBE
BARBECUE
BARBECUED
BARBECUER
BARBECUERS
BARBECUES
BARBECUING
BARBED
BARBEL
BARBELL
BARBELLS
BARBELS
BARBEQUE
BARBEQUED
BARBEQUES
BARBEQUING
BARBER
BARBERED
BARBERING
BARBERRIES
BARBERRY
BARBERS
BARBERSHOP
BARBERSHOPS
BARBES
BARBET
BARBETS
BARBETTE
BARBETTES
BARBICAN
BARBICANS
BARBICEL
BARBICELS
BARBIE
BARBIES
BARBING
BARBITAL
BARBITALS
BARBITONE
BARBITONES
BARBITURATE
BARBITURATES
BARBLESS
BARBOT
BARBOTS
BARBOTTE
BARBOTTES
BARBS
BARBULE
BARBULES
BARBUT
BARBUTS
BARBWIRE
BARBWIRES
BARCA
BARCAROLE
BARCAROLES
BARCAROLLE
BARCAROLLES
BARCAS
BARCHAN
BARCHANS
BARD
BARDE
BARDED
BARDES
BARDIC
BARDING
BARDOLATER
BARDOLATERS
BARDOLATRIES
BARDOLATRY
BARDS
BARE
BAREBACK
BAREBACKED
BAREBOAT
BAREBOATING
BAREBOATINGS
BAREBOATS
BAREBONED
BARED
BAREFACED
BAREFACEDLY
BAREFACEDNESS
BAREFACEDNESSES
BAREFIT
BAREFOOT
BAREFOOTED
BAREGE
BAREGES
BAREHAND
BAREHANDED
BAREHANDING
BAREHANDS
BAREHEAD
BAREHEADED
BARELY
BARENESS
BARENESSES
BARER
BARES

BARESARK
BARESARKS
BAREST
BARF
BARFED
BARFI
BARFING
BARFIS
BARFLIES
BARFLY
BARFS
BARGAIN
BARGAINED
BARGAINER
BARGAINERS
BARGAINING
BARGAININGS
BARGAINS
BARGE
BARGEBOARD
BARGEBOARDS
BARGED
BARGEE
BARGEES
BARGELLO
BARGELLOS
BARGEMAN
BARGEMEN
BARGEPOLE
BARGEPOLES
BARGES
BARGHEST
BARGHESTS
BARGING
BARGOON
BARGOONS
BARGUEST
BARGUESTS
BARHOP
BARHOPPED
BARHOPPING
BARHOPS
BARIATRIC
BARIC
BARILLA
BARILLAS
BARING
BARISTA
BARISTAS
BARITE
BARITES
BARITONAL
BARITONE
BARITONES
BARIUM
BARIUMS
BARK
BARKED
BARKEEP
BARKEEPER
BARKEEPERS
BARKEEPS
BARKENTINE
BARKENTINES
BARKER
BARKERS
BARKIER
BARKIEST
BARKING
BARKLESS
BARKS
BARKY
BARLEDUC
BARLEDUCS
BARLESS
BARLEY
BARLEYCORN
BARLEYCORNS
BARLEYS
BARLOW
BARLOWS
BARM
BARMAID
BARMAIDS
BARMAN
BARMEN
BARMIE
BARMIER
BARMIEST
BARMILY
BARMINESS
BARMINESSES
BARMS
BARMY
BARN
BARNACLE
BARNACLED
BARNACLES
BARNED
BARNEY
BARNEYS
BARNIER
BARNIEST
BARNING
BARNLIKE
BARNS
BARNSTORM
BARNSTORMED
BARNSTORMER
BARNSTORMERS
BARNSTORMING
BARNSTORMS
BARNWOOD
BARNWOODS
BARNY
BARNYARD
BARNYARDS
BAROCEPTOR
BAROCEPTORS
BAROGRAM
BAROGRAMS
BAROGRAPH
BAROGRAPHIC
BAROGRAPHS
BAROMETER
BAROMETERS
BAROMETRIC
BAROMETRICALLY
BAROMETRIES
BAROMETRY
BARON
BARONAGE
BARONAGES
BARONESS
BARONESSES
BARONET
BARONETAGE
BARONETAGES
BARONETCIES
BARONETCY
BARONETS
BARONG
BARONGS
BARONIAL
BARONIES
BARONNE
BARONNES
BARONS
BARONY
BAROQUE
BAROQUELY
BAROQUES
BARORECEPTOR
BARORECEPTORS
BAROSAUR
BAROSAURS
BAROSCOPE
BAROSCOPES
BAROTRAUMA
BAROTRAUMAS
BAROUCHE
BAROUCHES
BARQUE
BARQUENTINE
BARQUENTINES
BARQUES
BARQUETTE
BARQUETTES
BARRABLE
BARRACK
BARRACKED
BARRACKER
BARRACKERS
BARRACKING
BARRACKINGS
BARRACKS
BARRACOON
BARRACOONS
BARRACOUTA
BARRACOUTAS
BARRACUDA
BARRACUDAS
BARRAGE
BARRAGED
BARRAGES
BARRAGING
BARRAMUNDA
BARRAMUNDAS
BARRAMUNDI
BARRAMUNDIS
BARRANCA
BARRANCAS
BARRANCO
BARRANCOS
BARRATER
BARRATERS
BARRATOR
BARRATORS
BARRATRIES
BARRATRY
BARRE
BARRED
BARREL
BARRELAGE
BARRELAGES
BARRELED
BARRELFUL
BARRELFULS
BARRELHEAD
BARRELHEADS
BARRELHOUSE
BARRELHOUSES
BARRELING
BARRELLED
BARRELLING
BARRELS
BARRELSFUL
BARREN
BARRENER
BARRENEST
BARRENLY
BARRENNESS
BARRENNESSES
BARRENS
BARRES
BARRET
BARRETOR
BARRETORS
BARRETRIES
BARRETRY
BARRETS
BARRETTE
BARRETTES
BARRICADE
BARRICADED
BARRICADES
BARRICADING
BARRICADO
BARRICADOED
BARRICADOES
BARRICADOING
BARRICADOS
BARRIER
BARRIERS
BARRING
BARRIO
BARRIOS
BARRIQUE
BARRIQUES
BARRISTER
BARRISTERS
BARROOM
BARROOMS
BARROW
BARROWS
BARRY
BARS
BARSTOOL
BARSTOOLS
BARTEND
BARTENDED
BARTENDER
BARTENDERS
BARTENDING
BARTENDS

BARTER
BARTERED
BARTERER
BARTERERS
BARTERING
BARTERS
BARTISAN
BARTISANS
BARTIZAN
BARTIZANS
BARWARE
BARWARES
BARYE
BARYES
BARYON
BARYONIC
BARYONS
BARYTA
BARYTAS
BARYTE
BARYTES
BARYTIC
BARYTON
BARYTONE
BARYTONES
BARYTONS
BAS
BASAL
BASALLY
BASALT
BASALTES
BASALTIC
BASALTINE
BASALTS
BASCINET
BASCINETS
BASCULE
BASCULES
BASE
BASEBALL
BASEBALLS
BASEBOARD
BASEBOARDS
BASEBORN
BASED
BASEHEAD
BASEHEADS
BASELESS
BASELINE
BASELINER
BASELINERS
BASELINES
BASELOAD
BASELOADS
BASELY
BASEMAN
BASEMEN
BASEMENT
BASEMENTLESS
BASEMENTS
BASENESS
BASENESSES
BASENJI
BASENJIS
BASEPATH
BASEPATHS
BASEPLATE
BASEPLATES
BASER
BASERUNNING
BASERUNNINGS
BASES
BASEST
BASH
BASHAW
BASHAWS
BASHED
BASHER
BASHERS
BASHES
BASHFUL
BASHFULLER
BASHFULLEST
BASHFULLY
BASHFULNESS
BASHFULNESSES
BASHING
BASHINGS
BASHLYK
BASHLYKS
BASIC
BASICALLY
BASICITIES
BASICITY
BASICS
BASIDIA
BASIDIAL
BASIDIOMYCETE
BASIDIOMYCETES
BASIDIOMYCETOUS
BASIDIOSPORE
BASIDIOSPORES
BASIDIUM
BASIFICATION
BASIFICATIONS
BASIFIED
BASIFIER
BASIFIERS
BASIFIES
BASIFIXED
BASIFY
BASIFYING
BASIL
BASILAR
BASILARY
BASILECT
BASILECTS
BASILIC
BASILICA
BASILICAE
BASILICAL
BASILICAN
BASILICAS
BASILISK
BASILISKS
BASILS
BASIN
BASINAL
BASINED
BASINET
BASINETS
BASINFUL
BASINFULS
BASING
BASINLIKE
BASINS
BASION
BASIONS
BASIPETAL
BASIPETALLY
BASIS
BASK
BASKED
BASKET
BASKETBALL
BASKETBALLER
BASKETBALLERS
BASKETBALLS
BASKETFUL
BASKETFULS
BASKETLIKE
BASKETRIES
BASKETRY
BASKETS
BASKETSFUL
BASKETWORK
BASKETWORKS
BASKING
BASKS
BASMATI
BASMATIS
BASOPHIL
BASOPHILE
BASOPHILES
BASOPHILIA
BASOPHILIAS
BASOPHILIC
BASOPHILS
BASQUE
BASQUES
BASS
BASSER
BASSES
BASSEST
BASSET
BASSETED
BASSETING
BASSETS
BASSETT
BASSETTED
BASSETTING
BASSETTS
BASSI
BASSINET
BASSINETS
BASSIST
BASSISTS
BASSLY
BASSNESS
BASSNESSES
BASSO
BASSOON
BASSOONIST
BASSOONISTS
BASSOONS
BASSOS
BASSWOOD
BASSWOODS
BASSY
BAST
BASTARD
BASTARDIES
BASTARDISE
BASTARDISED
BASTARDISES
BASTARDISING
BASTARDIZATION
BASTARDIZATIONS
BASTARDIZE
BASTARDIZED
BASTARDIZES
BASTARDIZING
BASTARDLY
BASTARDS
BASTARDY
BASTE
BASTED
BASTER
BASTERS
BASTES
BASTILE
BASTILES
BASTILLE
BASTILLES
BASTINADE
BASTINADED
BASTINADES
BASTINADING
BASTINADO
BASTINADOED
BASTINADOES
BASTINADOING
BASTING
BASTINGS
BASTION
BASTIONED
BASTIONS
BASTS
BAT
BATARD
BATARDS
BATATA
BATATAS
BATBOY
BATBOYS
BATCH
BATCHED
BATCHER
BATCHERS
BATCHES
BATCHING
BATE
BATEAU
BATEAUX
BATED
BATES
BATFISH
BATFISHES
BATFOWL
BATFOWLED
BATFOWLER
BATFOWLERS
BATFOWLING
BATFOWLS
BATGIRL

BATGIRLS
BATH
BATHE
BATHED
BATHER
BATHERS
BATHES
BATHETIC
BATHETICALLY
BATHHOUSE
BATHHOUSES
BATHING
BATHINGS
BATHLESS
BATHMAT
BATHMATS
BATHOLITH
BATHOLITHIC
BATHOLITHS
BATHOS
BATHOSES
BATHROBE
BATHROBES
BATHROOM
BATHROOMS
BATHS
BATHTUB
BATHTUBS
BATHWATER
BATHWATERS
BATHYAL
BATHYMETRIC
BATHYMETRICAL
BATHYMETRICALLY
BATHYMETRIES
BATHYMETRY
BATHYPELAGIC
BATHYSCAPH
BATHYSCAPHE
BATHYSCAPHES
BATHYSCAPHS
BATHYSPHERE
BATHYSPHERES
BATIK
BATIKED
BATIKING
BATIKS
BATING
BATISTE
BATISTES
BATLIKE
BATMAN
BATMEN
BATON
BATONS
BATRACHIAN
BATRACHIANS
BATS
BATSHIT
BATSMAN
BATSMEN
BATT
BATTAILOUS
BATTALIA
BATTALIAS
BATTALION
BATTALIONS
BATTEAU
BATTEAUX
BATTED
BATTEMENT
BATTEMENTS
BATTEN
BATTENED
BATTENER
BATTENERS
BATTENING
BATTENINGS
BATTENS
BATTER
BATTERED
BATTERER
BATTERERS
BATTERIE
BATTERIES
BATTERING
BATTERINGS
BATTERS
BATTERY
BATTIER
BATTIEST
BATTIK
BATTIKS
BATTILY
BATTINESS
BATTINESSES
BATTING
BATTINGS
BATTLE
BATTLED
BATTLEFIELD
BATTLEFIELDS
BATTLEFRONT
BATTLEFRONTS
BATTLEGROUND
BATTLEGROUNDS
BATTLEMENT
BATTLEMENTED
BATTLEMENTS
BATTLER
BATTLERS
BATTLES
BATTLESHIP
BATTLESHIPS
BATTLEWAGON
BATTLEWAGONS
BATTLING
BATTS
BATTU
BATTUE
BATTUES
BATTY
BATWING
BAUBEE
BAUBEES
BAUBLE
BAUBLES
BAUD
BAUDEKIN
BAUDEKINS
BAUDRONS
BAUDRONSES
BAUDS
BAUHINIA
BAUHINIAS
BAULK
BAULKED
BAULKER
BAULKERS
BAULKIER
BAULKIEST
BAULKING
BAULKS
BAULKY
BAUSOND
BAUXITE
BAUXITES
BAUXITIC
BAWBEE
BAWBEES
BAWCOCK
BAWCOCKS
BAWD
BAWDIER
BAWDIES
BAWDIEST
BAWDILY
BAWDINESS
BAWDINESSES
BAWDRIC
BAWDRICS
BAWDRIES
BAWDRY
BAWDS
BAWDY
BAWK
BAWKS
BAWL
BAWLED
BAWLER
BAWLERS
BAWLING
BAWLS
BAWN
BAWNS
BAWSUNT
BAWTIE
BAWTIES
BAWTY
BAY
BAYADEER
BAYADEERS
BAYADERE
BAYADERES
BAYAMO
BAYAMOS
BAYARD
BAYARDS
BAYBERRIES
BAYBERRY
BAYED
BAYER
BAYEST
BAYFRONT
BAYFRONTS
BAYING
BAYMAN
BAYMEN
BAYNODDIES
BAYNODDY
BAYONET
BAYONETED
BAYONETING
BAYONETS
BAYONETTED
BAYONETTING
BAYOU
BAYOUS
BAYS
BAYSIDE
BAYSIDES
BAYWOOD
BAYWOODS
BAYWOP
BAYWOPS
BAZAAR
BAZAARS
BAZAR
BAZARS
BAZILLION
BAZILLIONS
BAZOO
BAZOOKA
BAZOOKAS
BAZOOM
BAZOOMS
BAZOOS
BAZZ
BAZZED
BAZZES
BAZZING
BDELLIUM
BDELLIUMS
BE
BEACH
BEACHBALL
BEACHBALLS
BEACHBOY
BEACHBOYS
BEACHCOMB
BEACHCOMBED
BEACHCOMBER
BEACHCOMBERS
BEACHCOMBING
BEACHCOMBS
BEACHED
BEACHES
BEACHFRONT
BEACHFRONTS
BEACHGOER
BEACHGOERS
BEACHHEAD
BEACHHEADS
BEACHIER
BEACHIEST
BEACHING
BEACHSIDE
BEACHWEAR
BEACHY
BEACON
BEACONED
BEACONING
BEACONS
BEAD
BEADED

BEADER
BEADERS
BEADHOUSE
BEADHOUSES
BEADIER
BEADIEST
BEADILY
BEADINESS
BEADINESSES
BEADING
BEADINGS
BEADLE
BEADLEDOM
BEADLEDOMS
BEADLES
BEADLIKE
BEADMAN
BEADMEN
BEADROLL
BEADROLLS
BEADS
BEADSMAN
BEADSMEN
BEADWORK
BEADWORKS
BEADY
BEAGLE
BEAGLED
BEAGLER
BEAGLERS
BEAGLES
BEAGLING
BEAGLINGS
BEAK
BEAKED
BEAKER
BEAKERS
BEAKIER
BEAKIEST
BEAKLESS
BEAKLIKE
BEAKS
BEAKY
BEAL
BEALING
BEALINGS
BEALS
BEAM
BEAMED
BEAMIER
BEAMIEST
BEAMILY
BEAMING
BEAMINGLY
BEAMISH
BEAMISHLY
BEAMLESS
BEAMLIKE
BEAMS
BEAMY
BEAN
BEANBAG
BEANBAGS
BEANBALL
BEANBALLS
BEANED
BEANERIES
BEANERY
BEANIE
BEANIES
BEANING
BEANLIKE
BEANO
BEANOS
BEANPOLE
BEANPOLES
BEANS
BEANSTALK
BEANSTALKS
BEAR
BEARABILITIES
BEARABILITY
BEARABLE
BEARABLY
BEARBAITING
BEARBAITINGS
BEARBERRIES
BEARBERRY
BEARCAT
BEARCATS
BEARD
BEARDED
BEARDEDNESS
BEARDEDNESSES
BEARDING
BEARDLESS
BEARDS
BEARDTONGUE
BEARDTONGUES
BEARER
BEARERS
BEARGRASS
BEARGRASSES
BEARHUG
BEARHUGS
BEARING
BEARINGS
BEARISH
BEARISHLY
BEARISHNESS
BEARISHNESSES
BEARLIKE
BEARPAW
BEARPAWS
BEARS
BEARSKIN
BEARSKINS
BEARWOOD
BEARWOODS
BEAST
BEASTIE
BEASTIES
BEASTINGS
BEASTLIER
BEASTLIEST
BEASTLINESS
BEASTLINESSES
BEASTLY
BEASTS
BEAT
BEATABLE
BEATBOX
BEATBOXED
BEATBOXES
BEATBOXING
BEATEN
BEATER
BEATERS
BEATIFIC
BEATIFICALLY
BEATIFICATION
BEATIFICATIONS
BEATIFIED
BEATIFIES
BEATIFY
BEATIFYING
BEATING
BEATINGS
BEATITUDE
BEATITUDES
BEATLESS
BEATNIK
BEATNIKS
BEATS
BEAU
BEAUCOUP
BEAUCOUPS
BEAUISH
BEAUS
BEAUT
BEAUTEOUS
BEAUTEOUSLY
BEAUTEOUSNESS
BEAUTEOUSNESSES
BEAUTER
BEAUTEST
BEAUTICIAN
BEAUTICIANS
BEAUTIES
BEAUTIFICATION
BEAUTIFICATIONS
BEAUTIFIED
BEAUTIFIER
BEAUTIFIERS
BEAUTIFIES
BEAUTIFUL
BEAUTIFULLER
BEAUTIFULLEST
BEAUTIFULLY
BEAUTIFULNESS
BEAUTIFULNESSES
BEAUTIFY
BEAUTIFYING
BEAUTS
BEAUTY
BEAUTYBERRIES
BEAUTYBERRY
BEAUX
BEAVER
BEAVERBOARD
BEAVERBOARDS
BEAVERED
BEAVERING
BEAVERS
BEAVERTAIL
BEAVERTAILS
BEBEERINE
BEBEERINES
BEBEERU
BEBEERUS
BEBLOOD
BEBLOODED
BEBLOODING
BEBLOODS
BEBOP
BEBOPPER
BEBOPPERS
BEBOPS
BECALM
BECALMED
BECALMING
BECALMS
BECAME
BECAP
BECAPPED
BECAPPING
BECAPS
BECARPET
BECARPETED
BECARPETING
BECARPETS
BECAUSE
BECCAFICO
BECCAFICOS
BECHALK
BECHALKED
BECHALKING
BECHALKS
BECHAMEL
BECHAMELS
BECHANCE
BECHANCED
BECHANCES
BECHANCING
BECHARM
BECHARMED
BECHARMING
BECHARMS
BECK
BECKED
BECKET
BECKETS
BECKING
BECKON
BECKONED
BECKONER
BECKONERS
BECKONING
BECKONINGLY
BECKONS
BECKS
BECLAMOR
BECLAMORED
BECLAMORING
BECLAMORS
BECLASP
BECLASPED
BECLASPING
BECLASPS
BECLOAK
BECLOAKED
BECLOAKING
BECLOAKS
BECLOG
BECLOGGED

BECLOGGING
BECLOGS
BECLOTHE
BECLOTHED
BECLOTHES
BECLOTHING
BECLOUD
BECLOUDED
BECLOUDING
BECLOUDS
BECLOWN
BECLOWNED
BECLOWNING
BECLOWNS
BECOME
BECOMES
BECOMING
BECOMINGLY
BECOMINGS
BECOWARD
BECOWARDED
BECOWARDING
BECOWARDS
BECQUEREL
BECQUERELS
BECRAWL
BECRAWLED
BECRAWLING
BECRAWLS
BECRIME
BECRIMED
BECRIMES
BECRIMING
BECROWD
BECROWDED
BECROWDING
BECROWDS
BECRUST
BECRUSTED
BECRUSTING
BECRUSTS
BECUDGEL
BECUDGELED
BECUDGELING
BECUDGELLED
BECUDGELLING
BECUDGELS
BECURSE
BECURSED
BECURSES
BECURSING
BECURST
BED
BEDABBLE
BEDABBLED
BEDABBLES
BEDABBLING
BEDAD
BEDAMN
BEDAMNED
BEDAMNING
BEDAMNS
BEDARKEN
BEDARKENED
BEDARKENING
BEDARKENS
BEDAUB
BEDAUBED
BEDAUBING
BEDAUBS
BEDAZZLE
BEDAZZLED
BEDAZZLEMENT
BEDAZZLEMENTS
BEDAZZLES
BEDAZZLING
BEDBOARD
BEDBOARDS
BEDBUG
BEDBUGS
BEDCHAIR
BEDCHAIRS
BEDCHAMBER
BEDCHAMBERS
BEDCLOTHES
BEDCOVER
BEDCOVERING
BEDCOVERINGS
BEDCOVERS
BEDDABLE
BEDDED
BEDDER
BEDDERS
BEDDING
BEDDINGS
BEDEAFEN
BEDEAFENED
BEDEAFENING
BEDEAFENS
BEDECK
BEDECKED
BEDECKING
BEDECKS
BEDEHOUSE
BEDEHOUSES
BEDEL
BEDELL
BEDELLS
BEDELS
BEDEMAN
BEDEMEN
BEDESMAN
BEDESMEN
BEDEVIL
BEDEVILED
BEDEVILING
BEDEVILLED
BEDEVILLING
BEDEVILMENT
BEDEVILMENTS
BEDEVILS
BEDEW
BEDEWED
BEDEWING
BEDEWS
BEDFAST
BEDFELLOW
BEDFELLOWS
BEDFRAME
BEDFRAMES
BEDGOWN
BEDGOWNS
BEDHEAD
BEDHEADS
BEDIAPER
BEDIAPERED
BEDIAPERING
BEDIAPERS
BEDIGHT
BEDIGHTED
BEDIGHTING
BEDIGHTS
BEDIM
BEDIMMED
BEDIMMING
BEDIMPLE
BEDIMPLED
BEDIMPLES
BEDIMPLING
BEDIMS
BEDIRTIED
BEDIRTIES
BEDIRTY
BEDIRTYING
BEDIZEN
BEDIZENED
BEDIZENING
BEDIZENMENT
BEDIZENMENTS
BEDIZENS
BEDLAM
BEDLAMER
BEDLAMERS
BEDLAMITE
BEDLAMITES
BEDLAMP
BEDLAMPS
BEDLAMS
BEDLESS
BEDLIKE
BEDLINER
BEDLINERS
BEDMAKER
BEDMAKERS
BEDMATE
BEDMATES
BEDOTTED
BEDOUIN
BEDOUINS
BEDPAN
BEDPANS
BEDPLATE
BEDPLATES
BEDPOST
BEDPOSTS
BEDQUILT
BEDQUILTS
BEDRAGGLE
BEDRAGGLED
BEDRAGGLES
BEDRAGGLING
BEDRAIL
BEDRAILS
BEDRAPE
BEDRAPED
BEDRAPES
BEDRAPING
BEDRENCH
BEDRENCHED
BEDRENCHES
BEDRENCHING
BEDREST
BEDRESTS
BEDRID
BEDRIDDEN
BEDRIVEL
BEDRIVELED
BEDRIVELING
BEDRIVELLED
BEDRIVELLING
BEDRIVELS
BEDROCK
BEDROCKS
BEDROLL
BEDROLLS
BEDROOM
BEDROOMED
BEDROOMS
BEDRUG
BEDRUGGED
BEDRUGGING
BEDRUGS
BEDS
BEDSHEET
BEDSHEETS
BEDSIDE
BEDSIDES
BEDSIT
BEDSITS
BEDSKIRT
BEDSKIRTS
BEDSOCK
BEDSOCKS
BEDSONIA
BEDSONIAS
BEDSORE
BEDSORES
BEDSPREAD
BEDSPREADS
BEDSPRING
BEDSPRINGS
BEDSTAND
BEDSTANDS
BEDSTEAD
BEDSTEADS
BEDSTRAW
BEDSTRAWS
BEDTICK
BEDTICKS
BEDTIME
BEDTIMES
BEDU
BEDUIN
BEDUINS
BEDUMB
BEDUMBED
BEDUMBING
BEDUMBS
BEDUNCE
BEDUNCED
BEDUNCES
BEDUNCING
BEDWARD
BEDWARDS
BEDWARF

BEDWARFED
BEDWARFING
BEDWARFS
BEDWARMER
BEDWARMERS
BEDWETTER
BEDWETTERS
BEE
BEEBEE
BEEBEES
BEEBREAD
BEEBREADS
BEECH
BEECHDROPS
BEECHEN
BEECHES
BEECHIER
BEECHIEST
BEECHMAST
BEECHMASTS
BEECHNUT
BEECHNUTS
BEECHWOOD
BEECHWOODS
BEECHY
BEEDI
BEEDIES
BEEF
BEEFALO
BEEFALOES
BEEFALOS
BEEFBURGER
BEEFBURGERS
BEEFCAKE
BEEFCAKES
BEEFEATER
BEEFEATERS
BEEFED
BEEFIER
BEEFIEST
BEEFILY
BEEFINESS
BEEFINESSES
BEEFING
BEEFLESS
BEEFS
BEEFSTEAK
BEEFSTEAKS
BEEFWOOD
BEEFWOODS
BEEFY
BEEHIVE
BEEHIVED
BEEHIVES
BEEKEEPER
BEEKEEPERS
BEEKEEPING
BEEKEEPINGS
BEELIKE
BEELINE
BEELINED
BEELINES
BEELINING
BEEN
BEEP
BEEPED
BEEPER
BEEPERS
BEEPING
BEEPS
BEER
BEERIER
BEERIEST
BEERILY
BEERINESS
BEERINESSES
BEERNUT
BEERNUTS
BEERS
BEERY
BEES
BEESTINGS
BEESWAX
BEESWAXED
BEESWAXES
BEESWAXING
BEESWING
BEESWINGS
BEET
BEETLE
BEETLED
BEETLER
BEETLERS
BEETLES
BEETLING
BEETROOT
BEETROOTS
BEETS
BEEVES
BEEYARD
BEEYARDS
BEEZER
BEEZERS
BEFALL
BEFALLEN
BEFALLING
BEFALLS
BEFELL
BEFINGER
BEFINGERED
BEFINGERING
BEFINGERS
BEFIT
BEFITS
BEFITTED
BEFITTING
BEFITTINGLY
BEFLAG
BEFLAGGED
BEFLAGGING
BEFLAGS
BEFLEA
BEFLEAED
BEFLEAING
BEFLEAS
BEFLECK
BEFLECKED
BEFLECKING
BEFLECKS
BEFLOWER
BEFLOWERED
BEFLOWERING
BEFLOWERS
BEFOG
BEFOGGED
BEFOGGING
BEFOGS
BEFOOL
BEFOOLED
BEFOOLING
BEFOOLS
BEFORE
BEFOREHAND
BEFORETIME
BEFOUL
BEFOULED
BEFOULER
BEFOULERS
BEFOULING
BEFOULS
BEFRET
BEFRETS
BEFRETTED
BEFRETTING
BEFRIEND
BEFRIENDED
BEFRIENDING
BEFRIENDS
BEFRINGE
BEFRINGED
BEFRINGES
BEFRINGING
BEFUDDLE
BEFUDDLED
BEFUDDLEMENT
BEFUDDLEMENTS
BEFUDDLES
BEFUDDLING
BEG
BEGAD
BEGALL
BEGALLED
BEGALLING
BEGALLS
BEGAN
BEGAT
BEGAZE
BEGAZED
BEGAZES
BEGAZING
BEGEM
BEGEMMED
BEGEMMING
BEGEMS
BEGET
BEGETS
BEGETTER
BEGETTERS
BEGETTING
BEGGAR
BEGGARDOM
BEGGARDOMS
BEGGARED
BEGGARIES
BEGGARING
BEGGARLINESS
BEGGARLINESSES
BEGGARLY
BEGGARS
BEGGARWEED
BEGGARWEEDS
BEGGARY
BEGGED
BEGGING
BEGIN
BEGINNER
BEGINNERS
BEGINNING
BEGINNINGS
BEGINS
BEGIRD
BEGIRDED
BEGIRDING
BEGIRDLE
BEGIRDLED
BEGIRDLES
BEGIRDLING
BEGIRDS
BEGIRT
BEGLAD
BEGLADDED
BEGLADDING
BEGLADS
BEGLAMOR
BEGLAMORED
BEGLAMORING
BEGLAMORS
BEGLAMOUR
BEGLAMOURED
BEGLAMOURING
BEGLAMOURS
BEGLOOM
BEGLOOMED
BEGLOOMING
BEGLOOMS
BEGOGGLED
BEGONE
BEGONIA
BEGONIAS
BEGORAH
BEGORRA
BEGORRAH
BEGOT
BEGOTTEN
BEGRIM
BEGRIME
BEGRIMED
BEGRIMES
BEGRIMING
BEGRIMMED
BEGRIMMING
BEGRIMS
BEGROAN
BEGROANED
BEGROANING
BEGROANS
BEGRUDGE
BEGRUDGED
BEGRUDGER
BEGRUDGERS
BEGRUDGES
BEGRUDGING
BEGRUDGINGLY
BEGS
BEGUILE

BEGUILED
BEGUILEMENT
BEGUILEMENTS
BEGUILER
BEGUILERS
BEGUILES
BEGUILING
BEGUILINGLY
BEGUINE
BEGUINES
BEGULF
BEGULFED
BEGULFING
BEGULFS
BEGUM
BEGUMS
BEGUN
BEHALF
BEHALVES
BEHAVE
BEHAVED
BEHAVER
BEHAVERS
BEHAVES
BEHAVING
BEHAVIOR
BEHAVIORAL
BEHAVIORALLY
BEHAVIORISM
BEHAVIORISMS
BEHAVIORIST
BEHAVIORISTIC
BEHAVIORISTS
BEHAVIORS
BEHAVIOUR
BEHAVIOURAL
BEHAVIOURISM
BEHAVIOURISMS
BEHAVIOURIST
BEHAVIOURISTS
BEHAVIOURS
BEHEAD
BEHEADAL
BEHEADALS
BEHEADED
BEHEADER
BEHEADERS
BEHEADING
BEHEADINGS
BEHEADS
BEHELD
BEHEMOTH
BEHEMOTHS
BEHEST
BEHESTS
BEHIND
BEHINDHAND
BEHINDS
BEHOLD
BEHOLDEN
BEHOLDER
BEHOLDERS
BEHOLDING
BEHOLDS
BEHOOF
BEHOOFS
BEHOOVE
BEHOOVED
BEHOOVES
BEHOOVING
BEHOVE
BEHOVED
BEHOVES
BEHOVING
BEHOWL
BEHOWLED
BEHOWLING
BEHOWLS
BEIGE
BEIGER
BEIGES
BEIGEST
BEIGNE
BEIGNES
BEIGNET
BEIGNETS
BEIGY
BEING
BEINGS
BEJABBERS
BEJABERS
BEJABERSES
BEJASUS
BEJASUSES
BEJEEBERS
BEJEEZUS
BEJEEZUSES
BEJESUS
BEJESUSES
BEJEWEL
BEJEWELED
BEJEWELING
BEJEWELLED
BEJEWELLING
BEJEWELS
BEJUMBLE
BEJUMBLED
BEJUMBLES
BEJUMBLING
BEKISS
BEKISSED
BEKISSES
BEKISSING
BEKNIGHT
BEKNIGHTED
BEKNIGHTING
BEKNIGHTS
BEKNOT
BEKNOTS
BEKNOTTED
BEKNOTTING
BEL
BELABOR
BELABORED
BELABORING
BELABORS
BELABOUR
BELABOURED
BELABOURING
BELABOURS
BELACED
BELADIED
BELADIES
BELADY
BELADYING
BELATED
BELATEDLY
BELATEDNESS
BELATEDNESSES
BELAUD
BELAUDED
BELAUDING
BELAUDS
BELAY
BELAYED
BELAYER
BELAYERS
BELAYING
BELAYS
BELCH
BELCHED
BELCHER
BELCHERS
BELCHES
BELCHING
BELDAM
BELDAME
BELDAMES
BELDAMS
BELEAGUER
BELEAGUERED
BELEAGUERING
BELEAGUERMENT
BELEAGUERMENTS
BELEAGUERS
BELEAP
BELEAPED
BELEAPING
BELEAPS
BELEAPT
BELEMNITE
BELEMNITES
BELFRIED
BELFRIES
BELFRY
BELGA
BELGAS
BELIE
BELIED
BELIEF
BELIEFS
BELIER
BELIERS
BELIES
BELIEVABILITIES
BELIEVABILITY
BELIEVABLE
BELIEVABLY
BELIEVE
BELIEVED
BELIEVER
BELIEVERS
BELIEVES
BELIEVING
BELIKE
BELIQUOR
BELIQUORED
BELIQUORING
BELIQUORS
BELITTLE
BELITTLED
BELITTLEMENT
BELITTLEMENTS
BELITTLER
BELITTLERS
BELITTLES
BELITTLING
BELIVE
BELL
BELLADONNA
BELLADONNAS
BELLBIRD
BELLBIRDS
BELLBOY
BELLBOYS
BELLBUOY
BELLBUOYS
BELLCAST
BELLE
BELLED
BELLEEK
BELLEEKS
BELLES
BELLETRIST
BELLETRISTIC
BELLETRISTS
BELLFLOWER
BELLFLOWERS
BELLHOP
BELLHOPS
BELLICOSE
BELLICOSITIES
BELLICOSITY
BELLIED
BELLIES
BELLIGERENCE
BELLIGERENCES
BELLIGERENCIES
BELLIGERENCY
BELLIGERENT
BELLIGERENTLY
BELLIGERENTS
BELLING
BELLINGS
BELLMAN
BELLMEN
BELLOW
BELLOWED
BELLOWER
BELLOWERS
BELLOWING
BELLOWINGS
BELLOWS
BELLPULL
BELLPULLS
BELLS
BELLWETHER
BELLWETHERS
BELLWORT
BELLWORTS
BELLY
BELLYACHE
BELLYACHED
BELLYACHER
BELLYACHERS

BELLYACHES
BELLYACHING
BELLYBAND
BELLYBANDS
BELLYFUL
BELLYFULS
BELLYING
BELLYLIKE
BELON
BELONG
BELONGED
BELONGING
BELONGINGNESS
BELONGINGNESSES
BELONGINGS
BELONGS
BELONS
BELOVED
BELOVEDS
BELOW
BELOWDECKS
BELOWGROUND
BELOWS
BELS
BELT
BELTED
BELTER
BELTERS
BELTING
BELTINGS
BELTLESS
BELTLINE
BELTLINES
BELTS
BELTWAY
BELTWAYS
BELUGA
BELUGAS
BELVEDERE
BELVEDERES
BELYING
BEMA
BEMADAM
BEMADAMED
BEMADAMING
BEMADAMS
BEMADDEN
BEMADDENED
BEMADDENING
BEMADDENS
BEMAS
BEMATA
BEMEAN
BEMEANED
BEMEANING
BEMEANS
BEMEDALED
BEMEDALLED
BEMINGLE
BEMINGLED
BEMINGLES
BEMINGLING
BEMIRE
BEMIRED
BEMIRES
BEMIRING
BEMIST
BEMISTED
BEMISTING
BEMISTS
BEMIX
BEMIXED
BEMIXES
BEMIXING
BEMIXT
BEMOAN
BEMOANED
BEMOANING
BEMOANS
BEMOCK
BEMOCKED
BEMOCKING
BEMOCKS
BEMUDDLE
BEMUDDLED
BEMUDDLES
BEMUDDLING
BEMURMUR
BEMURMURED
BEMURMURING
BEMURMURS
BEMUSE
BEMUSED
BEMUSEDLY
BEMUSEMENT
BEMUSEMENTS
BEMUSES
BEMUSING
BEMUZZLE
BEMUZZLED
BEMUZZLES
BEMUZZLING
BEN
BENADRYL
BENADRYLS
BENAME
BENAMED
BENAMES
BENAMING
BENCH
BENCHED
BENCHER
BENCHERS
BENCHES
BENCHING
BENCHLAND
BENCHLANDS
BENCHLESS
BENCHMARK
BENCHMARKED
BENCHMARKING
BENCHMARKINGS
BENCHMARKS
BENCHTOP
BENCHWARMER
BENCHWARMERS
BEND
BENDABLE
BENDAY
BENDAYED
BENDAYING
BENDAYS
BENDED
BENDEE
BENDEES
BENDER
BENDERS
BENDIER
BENDIEST
BENDING
BENDS
BENDWAYS
BENDWISE
BENDY
BENDYS
BENE
BENEATH
BENEDICK
BENEDICKS
BENEDICT
BENEDICTION
BENEDICTIONS
BENEDICTORY
BENEDICTS
BENEFACTION
BENEFACTIONS
BENEFACTOR
BENEFACTORS
BENEFACTRESS
BENEFACTRESSES
BENEFIC
BENEFICE
BENEFICED
BENEFICENCE
BENEFICENCES
BENEFICENT
BENEFICENTLY
BENEFICES
BENEFICIAL
BENEFICIALLY
BENEFICIALNESS
BENEFICIALS
BENEFICIARIES
BENEFICIARY
BENEFICIATE
BENEFICIATED
BENEFICIATES
BENEFICIATING
BENEFICIATION
BENEFICIATIONS
BENEFICING
BENEFIT
BENEFITED
BENEFITER
BENEFITERS
BENEFITING
BENEFITS
BENEFITTED
BENEFITTING
BENEMPT
BENEMPTED
BENES
BENEVOLENCE
BENEVOLENCES
BENEVOLENT
BENEVOLENTLY
BENEVOLENTNESS
BENGALINE
BENGALINES
BENIGHTED
BENIGHTEDLY
BENIGHTEDNESS
BENIGHTEDNESSES
BENIGN
BENIGNANCIES
BENIGNANCY
BENIGNANT
BENIGNANTLY
BENIGNITIES
BENIGNITY
BENIGNLY
BENISON
BENISONS
BENJAMIN
BENJAMINS
BENNE
BENNES
BENNET
BENNETS
BENNI
BENNIES
BENNIS
BENNY
BENOMYL
BENOMYLS
BENS
BENT
BENTGRASS
BENTGRASSES
BENTHAL
BENTHIC
BENTHON
BENTHONIC
BENTHONS
BENTHOS
BENTHOSES
BENTO
BENTONITE
BENTONITES
BENTONITIC
BENTOS
BENTS
BENTWOOD
BENTWOODS
BENUMB
BENUMBED
BENUMBING
BENUMBS
BENZAL
BENZALDEHYDE
BENZALDEHYDES
BENZANTHRACENE
BENZANTHRACENES
BENZENE
BENZENES
BENZENOID
BENZENOIDS
BENZIDIN
BENZIDINE
BENZIDINES
BENZIDINS
BENZIMIDAZOLE
BENZIMIDAZOLES
BENZIN
BENZINE

BENZINES
BENZINS
BENZOAPYRENE
BENZOAPYRENES
BENZOATE
BENZOATES
BENZOCAINE
BENZOCAINES
BENZODIAZEPINE
BENZODIAZEPINES
BENZOFURAN
BENZOFURANS
BENZOIC
BENZOIN
BENZOINS
BENZOL
BENZOLE
BENZOLES
BENZOLS
BENZOPHENONE
BENZOPHENONES
BENZOPYRENE
BENZOPYRENES
BENZOQUINONE
BENZOQUINONES
BENZOYL
BENZOYLS
BENZYL
BENZYLIC
BENZYLS
BEPAINT
BEPAINTED
BEPAINTING
BEPAINTS
BEPIMPLE
BEPIMPLED
BEPIMPLES
BEPIMPLING
BEQUEATH
BEQUEATHAL
BEQUEATHALS
BEQUEATHED
BEQUEATHING
BEQUEATHS
BEQUEST
BEQUESTS
BERAKE
BERAKED
BERAKES
BERAKING
BERASCAL
BERASCALED
BERASCALING
BERASCALS
BERATE
BERATED
BERATES
BERATING
BERBER
BERBERIN
BERBERINE
BERBERINES
BERBERINS
BERBERIS
BERBERISES
BERBERS
BERCEUSE
BERCEUSES
BERDACHE
BERDACHES
BERDASH
BERDASHES
BEREAVE
BEREAVED
BEREAVEMENT
BEREAVEMENTS
BEREAVER
BEREAVERS
BEREAVES
BEREAVING
BEREFT
BERET
BERETS
BERETTA
BERETTAS
BERG
BERGAMOT
BERGAMOTS
BERGENIA
BERGENIAS
BERGERE
BERGERES
BERGS
BERHYME
BERHYMED
BERHYMES
BERHYMING
BERIBBONED
BERIBERI
BERIBERIS
BERIMBAU
BERIMBAUS
BERIME
BERIMED
BERIMES
BERIMING
BERINGED
BERK
BERKELIUM
BERKELIUMS
BERKS
BERLIN
BERLINE
BERLINES
BERLINS
BERM
BERME
BERMED
BERMES
BERMING
BERMS
BERMUDAS
BERNICLE
BERNICLES
BEROBED
BEROUGED
BERRETTA
BERRETTAS
BERRIED
BERRIES
BERRY
BERRYING
BERRYINGS
BERRYLESS
BERRYLIKE
BERSEEM
BERSEEMS
BERSERK
BERSERKER
BERSERKERS
BERSERKLY
BERSERKS
BERTH
BERTHA
BERTHAS
BERTHED
BERTHING
BERTHINGS
BERTHS
BERYL
BERYLINE
BERYLLIUM
BERYLLIUMS
BERYLS
BES
BESCORCH
BESCORCHED
BESCORCHES
BESCORCHING
BESCOUR
BESCOURED
BESCOURING
BESCOURS
BESCREEN
BESCREENED
BESCREENING
BESCREENS
BESEECH
BESEECHED
BESEECHER
BESEECHERS
BESEECHES
BESEECHING
BESEECHINGLY
BESEEM
BESEEMED
BESEEMING
BESEEMS
BESES
BESET
BESETMENT
BESETMENTS
BESETS
BESETTER
BESETTERS
BESETTING
BESHADOW
BESHADOWED
BESHADOWING
BESHADOWS
BESHAME
BESHAMED
BESHAMES
BESHAMING
BESHIVER
BESHIVERED
BESHIVERING
BESHIVERS
BESHOUT
BESHOUTED
BESHOUTING
BESHOUTS
BESHREW
BESHREWED
BESHREWING
BESHREWS
BESHROUD
BESHROUDED
BESHROUDING
BESHROUDS
BESIDE
BESIDES
BESIEGE
BESIEGED
BESIEGER
BESIEGERS
BESIEGES
BESIEGING
BESLAVED
BESLIME
BESLIMED
BESLIMES
BESLIMING
BESMEAR
BESMEARED
BESMEARER
BESMEARERS
BESMEARING
BESMEARS
BESMILE
BESMILED
BESMILES
BESMILING
BESMIRCH
BESMIRCHED
BESMIRCHES
BESMIRCHING
BESMOKE
BESMOKED
BESMOKES
BESMOKING
BESMOOTH
BESMOOTHED
BESMOOTHING
BESMOOTHS
BESMUDGE
BESMUDGED
BESMUDGES
BESMUDGING
BESMUT
BESMUTS
BESMUTTED
BESMUTTING
BESNOW
BESNOWED
BESNOWING
BESNOWS
BESOM
BESOMS
BESOOTHE
BESOOTHED
BESOOTHES
BESOOTHING
BESOT
BESOTS

BESOTTED
BESOTTEDLY
BESOTTING
BESOUGHT
BESPAKE
BESPANGLE
BESPANGLED
BESPANGLES
BESPANGLING
BESPATTER
BESPATTERED
BESPATTERING
BESPATTERS
BESPEAK
BESPEAKING
BESPEAKS
BESPECTACLED
BESPOKE
BESPOKEN
BESPOUSE
BESPOUSED
BESPOUSES
BESPOUSING
BESPREAD
BESPREADING
BESPREADS
BESPRENT
BESPRINKLE
BESPRINKLED
BESPRINKLES
BESPRINKLING
BEST
BESTEAD
BESTEADED
BESTEADING
BESTEADS
BESTED
BESTIAL
BESTIALITIES
BESTIALITY
BESTIALIZE
BESTIALIZED
BESTIALIZES
BESTIALIZING
BESTIALLY
BESTIARIES
BESTIARY
BESTING
BESTIR
BESTIRRED
BESTIRRING
BESTIRS
BESTOW
BESTOWAL
BESTOWALS
BESTOWED
BESTOWER
BESTOWERS
BESTOWING
BESTOWS
BESTREW
BESTREWED
BESTREWING
BESTREWN
BESTREWS
BESTRID
BESTRIDDEN
BESTRIDE
BESTRIDES
BESTRIDING
BESTRODE
BESTROW
BESTROWED
BESTROWING
BESTROWN
BESTROWS
BESTS
BESTSELLERDOM
BESTSELLERDOMS
BESTUD
BESTUDDED
BESTUDDING
BESTUDS
BESUITED
BESWARM
BESWARMED
BESWARMING
BESWARMS
BET
BETA
BETAINE
BETAINES
BETAKE
BETAKEN
BETAKES
BETAKING
BETAS
BETATRON
BETATRONS
BETATTER
BETATTERED
BETATTERING
BETATTERS
BETAXED
BETCHA
BETEL
BETELNUT
BETELNUTS
BETELS
BETH
BETHANK
BETHANKED
BETHANKING
BETHANKS
BETHEL
BETHELS
BETHESDA
BETHESDAS
BETHINK
BETHINKING
BETHINKS
BETHORN
BETHORNED
BETHORNING
BETHORNS
BETHOUGHT
BETHS
BETHUMP
BETHUMPED
BETHUMPING
BETHUMPS
BETIDE
BETIDED
BETIDES
BETIDING
BETIME
BETIMES
BETISE
BETISES
BETOKEN
BETOKENED
BETOKENING
BETOKENS
BETON
BETONIES
BETONS
BETONY
BETOOK
BETRAY
BETRAYAL
BETRAYALS
BETRAYED
BETRAYER
BETRAYERS
BETRAYING
BETRAYS
BETROTH
BETROTHAL
BETROTHALS
BETROTHED
BETROTHEDS
BETROTHING
BETROTHS
BETS
BETTA
BETTAS
BETTED
BETTER
BETTERED
BETTERING
BETTERMENT
BETTERMENTS
BETTERS
BETTING
BETTINGS
BETTOR
BETTORS
BETWEEN
BETWEENBRAIN
BETWEENBRAINS
BETWEENNESS
BETWEENNESSES
BETWEENTIMES
BETWEENWHILES
BETWIXT
BEUNCLED
BEVATRON
BEVATRONS
BEVEL
BEVELED
BEVELER
BEVELERS
BEVELING
BEVELLED
BEVELLER
BEVELLERS
BEVELLING
BEVELS
BEVERAGE
BEVERAGES
BEVIES
BEVOMIT
BEVOMITED
BEVOMITING
BEVOMITS
BEVOR
BEVORS
BEVVIES
BEVVY
BEVY
BEWAIL
BEWAILED
BEWAILER
BEWAILERS
BEWAILING
BEWAILS
BEWARE
BEWARED
BEWARES
BEWARING
BEWEARIED
BEWEARIES
BEWEARY
BEWEARYING
BEWEEP
BEWEEPING
BEWEEPS
BEWEPT
BEWHISKERED
BEWIG
BEWIGGED
BEWIGGING
BEWIGS
BEWILDER
BEWILDERED
BEWILDEREDLY
BEWILDEREDNESS
BEWILDERING
BEWILDERINGLY
BEWILDERMENT
BEWILDERMENTS
BEWILDERS
BEWINGED
BEWITCH
BEWITCHED
BEWITCHER
BEWITCHERIES
BEWITCHERS
BEWITCHERY
BEWITCHES
BEWITCHING
BEWITCHINGLY
BEWITCHMENT
BEWITCHMENTS
BEWORM
BEWORMED
BEWORMING
BEWORMS
BEWORRIED
BEWORRIES
BEWORRY
BEWORRYING
BEWRAP
BEWRAPPED
BEWRAPPING

BEWRAPS
BEWRAPT
BEWRAY
BEWRAYED
BEWRAYER
BEWRAYERS
BEWRAYING
BEWRAYS
BEY
BEYLIC
BEYLICS
BEYLIK
BEYLIKS
BEYOND
BEYONDS
BEYS
BEZANT
BEZANTS
BEZAZZ
BEZAZZES
BEZEL
BEZELS
BEZIL
BEZILS
BEZIQUE
BEZIQUES
BEZOAR
BEZOARS
BEZZANT
BEZZANTS
BHAJI
BHAJIS
BHAKTA
BHAKTAS
BHAKTI
BHAKTIS
BHANG
BHANGRA
BHANGRAS
BHANGS
BHARAL
BHARALS
BHEESTIE
BHEESTIES
BHEESTY
BHELPURI
BHELPURIS
BHISTIE
BHISTIES
BHOOT
BHOOTS
BHUT
BHUTS
BI
BIACETYL
BIACETYLS
BIALI
BIALIES
BIALIS
BIALY
BIALYS
BIANNUAL
BIANNUALLY
BIAS
BIASED
BIASEDLY
BIASES
BIASING
BIASNESS
BIASNESSES
BIASSED
BIASSEDLY
BIASSES
BIASSING
BIATHLETE
BIATHLETES
BIATHLON
BIATHLONS
BIAXAL
BIAXIAL
BIAXIALLY
BIB
BIBASIC
BIBB
BIBBED
BIBBER
BIBBERIES
BIBBERS
BIBBERY
BIBBING
BIBBINGS
BIBBS
BIBCOCK
BIBCOCKS
BIBE
BIBELOT
BIBELOTS
BIBES
BIBLE
BIBLES
BIBLESS
BIBLICAL
BIBLICALLY
BIBLICISM
BIBLICISMS
BIBLICIST
BIBLICISTS
BIBLIKE
BIBLIOGRAPHER
BIBLIOGRAPHERS
BIBLIOGRAPHIC
BIBLIOGRAPHICAL
BIBLIOGRAPHIES
BIBLIOGRAPHY
BIBLIOLATER
BIBLIOLATERS
BIBLIOLATRIES
BIBLIOLATROUS
BIBLIOLATRY
BIBLIOLOGIES
BIBLIOLOGY
BIBLIOMANIA
BIBLIOMANIAC
BIBLIOMANIACAL
BIBLIOMANIACS
BIBLIOMANIAS
BIBLIOPEGIC
BIBLIOPEGIES
BIBLIOPEGIST
BIBLIOPEGISTS
BIBLIOPEGY
BIBLIOPHILE
BIBLIOPHILES
BIBLIOPHILIC
BIBLIOPHILIES
BIBLIOPHILISM
BIBLIOPHILISMS
BIBLIOPHILY
BIBLIOPOLE
BIBLIOPOLES
BIBLIOPOLIST
BIBLIOPOLISTS
BIBLIOTHECA
BIBLIOTHECAE
BIBLIOTHECAL
BIBLIOTHECAS
BIBLIOTHERAPIES
BIBLIOTHERAPY
BIBLIOTIC
BIBLIOTICS
BIBLIOTIST
BIBLIOTISTS
BIBLIST
BIBLISTS
BIBS
BIBULOUS
BIBULOUSLY
BIBULOUSNESS
BIBULOUSNESSES
BICAMERAL
BICAMERALISM
BICAMERALISMS
BICARB
BICARBONATE
BICARBONATES
BICARBS
BICAUDAL
BICE
BICENTENARIES
BICENTENARY
BICENTENNIAL
BICENTENNIALS
BICENTRIC
BICEP
BICEPS
BICEPSES
BICES
BICHROMATE
BICHROMATED
BICHROMATES
BICHROME
BICIPITAL
BICKER
BICKERED
BICKERER
BICKERERS
BICKERING
BICKERINGS
BICKERS
BICOASTAL
BICOLOR
BICOLORED
BICOLORS
BICOLOUR
BICOLOURS
BICOMPONENT
BICOMPONENTS
BICONCAVE
BICONCAVITIES
BICONCAVITY
BICONDITIONAL
BICONDITIONALS
BICONVEX
BICONVEXITIES
BICONVEXITY
BICORN
BICORNE
BICORNES
BICORNS
BICRON
BICRONS
BICULTURAL
BICULTURALISM
BICULTURALISMS
BICUSPID
BICUSPIDS
BICYCLE
BICYCLED
BICYCLER
BICYCLERS
BICYCLES
BICYCLIC
BICYCLING
BICYCLIST
BICYCLISTS
BID
BIDARKA
BIDARKAS
BIDARKEE
BIDARKEES
BIDDABILITIES
BIDDABILITY
BIDDABLE
BIDDABLY
BIDDEN
BIDDER
BIDDERS
BIDDIES
BIDDING
BIDDINGS
BIDDY
BIDE
BIDED
BIDENTAL
BIDENTATE
BIDER
BIDERS
BIDES
BIDET
BIDETS
BIDI
BIDIALECTAL
BIDIALECTALISM
BIDIALECTALISMS
BIDING
BIDIRECTIONAL
BIDIRECTIONALLY
BIDIS
BIDONVILLE
BIDONVILLES
BIDS
BIELD
BIELDED
BIELDING
BIELDS

BIENNALE
BIENNALES
BIENNIA
BIENNIAL
BIENNIALLY
BIENNIALS
BIENNIUM
BIENNIUMS
BIER
BIERS
BIESTINGS
BIFACE
BIFACES
BIFACIAL
BIFACIALLY
BIFARIOUS
BIFF
BIFFED
BIFFIES
BIFFIN
BIFFING
BIFFINS
BIFFS
BIFFY
BIFID
BIFIDA
BIFIDITIES
BIFIDITY
BIFIDLY
BIFIDUM
BIFIDUMS
BIFILAR
BIFILARLY
BIFLAGELLATE
BIFLEX
BIFOCAL
BIFOCALED
BIFOCALS
BIFOLD
BIFOLDS
BIFOLIATE
BIFORATE
BIFORKED
BIFORM
BIFORMED
BIFUNCTIONAL
BIFURCATE
BIFURCATED
BIFURCATES
BIFURCATING
BIFURCATION
BIFURCATIONS
BIG
BIGAMIES
BIGAMIST
BIGAMISTS
BIGAMOUS
BIGAMOUSLY
BIGAMY
BIGARADE
BIGARADES
BIGAROON
BIGAROONS
BIGARREAU
BIGARREAUS
BIGEMINAL
BIGEMINIES
BIGEMINY
BIGENERIC
BIGEYE
BIGEYES
BIGFEET
BIGFOOT
BIGFOOTED
BIGFOOTING
BIGFOOTS
BIGGER
BIGGEST
BIGGETY
BIGGIE
BIGGIES
BIGGIN
BIGGING
BIGGINGS
BIGGINS
BIGGISH
BIGGITY
BIGGY
BIGHEAD
BIGHEADED
BIGHEADS
BIGHEARTED
BIGHEARTEDLY
BIGHEARTEDNESS
BIGHORN
BIGHORNS
BIGHT
BIGHTED
BIGHTING
BIGHTS
BIGLY
BIGMOUTH
BIGMOUTHED
BIGMOUTHS
BIGNESS
BIGNESSES
BIGNONIA
BIGNONIAS
BIGOS
BIGOSES
BIGOT
BIGOTED
BIGOTEDLY
BIGOTRIES
BIGOTRY
BIGOTS
BIGS
BIGSTICK
BIGTIME
BIGUINE
BIGUINES
BIGWIG
BIGWIGS
BIHOURLY
BIJECTION
BIJECTIONS
BIJECTIVE
BIJOU
BIJOUS
BIJOUTERIE
BIJOUTERIES
BIJOUX
BIJUGATE
BIJUGOUS
BIJURAL
BIKE
BIKED
BIKER
BIKERS
BIKES
BIKEWAY
BIKEWAYS
BIKIE
BIKIES
BIKING
BIKINI
BIKINIED
BIKINIS
BILABIAL
BILABIALS
BILABIATE
BILANDER
BILANDERS
BILATERAL
BILATERALISM
BILATERALISMS
BILATERALLY
BILAYER
BILAYERS
BILBERRIES
BILBERRY
BILBIES
BILBO
BILBOA
BILBOAS
BILBOES
BILBOS
BILBY
BILDUNGSROMAN
BILDUNGSROMANS
BILE
BILECTION
BILECTIONS
BILES
BILEVEL
BILEVELS
BILGE
BILGED
BILGES
BILGEWATER
BILGEWATERS
BILGIER
BILGIEST
BILGING
BILGY
BILHARZIA
BILHARZIAL
BILHARZIAS
BILHARZIASES
BILHARZIASIS
BILIARY
BILINEAR
BILINGUAL
BILINGUALISM
BILINGUALISMS
BILINGUALITIES
BILINGUALITY
BILINGUALLY
BILINGUALS
BILIOUS
BILIOUSLY
BILIOUSNESS
BILIOUSNESSES
BILIRUBIN
BILIRUBINS
BILIVERDIN
BILIVERDINS
BILK
BILKED
BILKER
BILKERS
BILKING
BILKS
BILL
BILLABLE
BILLABONG
BILLABONGS
BILLBOARD
BILLBOARDED
BILLBOARDING
BILLBOARDS
BILLBUG
BILLBUGS
BILLED
BILLER
BILLERS
BILLET
BILLETED
BILLETEE
BILLETEES
BILLETER
BILLETERS
BILLETING
BILLETS
BILLFISH
BILLFISHES
BILLFOLD
BILLFOLDS
BILLHEAD
BILLHEADS
BILLHOOK
BILLHOOKS
BILLIARD
BILLIARDS
BILLIE
BILLIES
BILLING
BILLINGS
BILLINGSGATE
BILLINGSGATES
BILLION
BILLIONAIRE
BILLIONAIRES
BILLIONS
BILLIONTH
BILLIONTHS
BILLON
BILLONS
BILLOW
BILLOWED
BILLOWIER
BILLOWIEST
BILLOWING
BILLOWS
BILLOWY

BILLS
BILLY
BILLYCAN
BILLYCANS
BILLYCOCK
BILLYCOCKS
BILOBATE
BILOBATED
BILOBED
BILOBULAR
BILOCATION
BILOCATIONS
BILOCULAR
BILSTED
BILSTEDS
BILTONG
BILTONGS
BIMA
BIMAH
BIMAHS
BIMANOUS
BIMANUAL
BIMANUALLY
BIMAS
BIMBETTE
BIMBETTES
BIMBO
BIMBOES
BIMBOS
BIMENSAL
BIMESTER
BIMESTERS
BIMETAL
BIMETALLIC
BIMETALLICS
BIMETALLISM
BIMETALLISMS
BIMETALLIST
BIMETALLISTIC
BIMETALLISTS
BIMETALS
BIMETHYL
BIMETHYLS
BIMILLENARIES
BIMILLENARY
BIMILLENNIAL
BIMILLENNIALS
BIMINI
BIMINIS
BIMODAL
BIMODALITIES
BIMODALITY
BIMOLECULAR
BIMOLECULARLY
BIMONTHLIES
BIMONTHLY
BIMORPH
BIMORPHEMIC
BIMORPHS
BIN
BINAL
BINARIES
BINARISM
BINARISMS
BINARY
BINATE
BINATELY
BINATIONAL
BINAURAL
BINAURALLY
BIND
BINDABLE
BINDER
BINDERIES
BINDERS
BINDERY
BINDI
BINDING
BINDINGLY
BINDINGNESS
BINDINGNESSES
BINDINGS
BINDIS
BINDLE
BINDLES
BINDS
BINDWEED
BINDWEEDS
BINE
BINER
BINERS
BINES
BING
BINGE
BINGED
BINGEING
BINGEINGS
BINGER
BINGERS
BINGES
BINGING
BINGINGS
BINGO
BINGOES
BINGOS
BINIT
BINITS
BINMAN
BINMEN
BINNACLE
BINNACLES
BINNED
BINNING
BINOCLE
BINOCLES
BINOCS
BINOCULAR
BINOCULARITIES
BINOCULARITY
BINOCULARLY
BINOCULARS
BINOMIAL
BINOMIALLY
BINOMIALS
BINS
BINT
BINTS
BINTURONG
BINTURONGS
BINUCLEAR
BINUCLEATE
BINUCLEATED
BIO
BIOACOUSTICIAN
BIOACOUSTICIANS
BIOACOUSTICS
BIOACTIVE
BIOACTIVITIES
BIOACTIVITY
BIOASSAY
BIOASSAYED
BIOASSAYING
BIOASSAYS
BIOAVAILABILITY
BIOAVAILABLE
BIOBEHAVIORAL
BIOCATALYSES
BIOCATALYSIS
BIOCATALYST
BIOCATALYSTS
BIOCATALYTIC
BIOCENOSE
BIOCENOSES
BIOCENOSIS
BIOCENTRIC
BIOCENTRISM
BIOCENTRISMS
BIOCHEMIC
BIOCHEMICAL
BIOCHEMICALLY
BIOCHEMICALS
BIOCHEMIST
BIOCHEMISTRIES
BIOCHEMISTRY
BIOCHEMISTS
BIOCHIP
BIOCHIPS
BIOCIDAL
BIOCIDE
BIOCIDES
BIOCLEAN
BIOCLIMATIC
BIOCOENOSES
BIOCOENOSIS
BIOCOMPATIBLE
BIOCONTAINMENT
BIOCONTAINMENTS
BIOCONTROL
BIOCONTROLS
BIOCONVERSION
BIOCONVERSIONS
BIOCYCLE
BIOCYCLES
BIODEFENSE
BIODEFENSES
BIODEGRADABLE
BIODEGRADABLES
BIODEGRADATION
BIODEGRADATIONS
BIODEGRADE
BIODEGRADED
BIODEGRADES
BIODEGRADING
BIODIESEL
BIODIESELS
BIODIVERSE
BIODIVERSITIES
BIODIVERSITY
BIODYNAMIC
BIODYNAMICS
BIOELECTRIC
BIOELECTRICAL
BIOELECTRICITY
BIOENERGETIC
BIOENERGETICS
BIOENGINEER
BIOENGINEERED
BIOENGINEERING
BIOENGINEERINGS
BIOENGINEERS
BIOEQUIVALENCE
BIOEQUIVALENCES
BIOEQUIVALENT
BIOETHIC
BIOETHICAL
BIOETHICIST
BIOETHICISTS
BIOETHICS
BIOFEEDBACK
BIOFEEDBACKS
BIOFILM
BIOFILMS
BIOFLAVONOID
BIOFLAVONOIDS
BIOFOULER
BIOFOULERS
BIOFOULING
BIOFOULINGS
BIOFUEL
BIOFUELED
BIOFUELS
BIOG
BIOGAS
BIOGASES
BIOGASSES
BIOGEN
BIOGENESES
BIOGENESIS
BIOGENETIC
BIOGENETICALLY
BIOGENIC
BIOGENIES
BIOGENOUS
BIOGENS
BIOGENY
BIOGEOCHEMICAL
BIOGEOCHEMICALS
BIOGEOCHEMISTRY
BIOGEOGRAPHER
BIOGEOGRAPHERS
BIOGEOGRAPHIC
BIOGEOGRAPHICAL
BIOGEOGRAPHIES
BIOGEOGRAPHY
BIOGRAPHEE
BIOGRAPHEES
BIOGRAPHER
BIOGRAPHERS
BIOGRAPHIC
BIOGRAPHICAL
BIOGRAPHICALLY
BIOGRAPHIES
BIOGRAPHY
BIOGS
BIOHAZARD

BIOHAZARDOUS
BIOHAZARDS
BIOHERM
BIOHERMS
BIOIDENTICAL
BIOINFORMATIC
BIOINFORMATICS
BIOLOGIC
BIOLOGICAL
BIOLOGICALLY
BIOLOGICALS
BIOLOGICS
BIOLOGIES
BIOLOGISM
BIOLOGISMS
BIOLOGIST
BIOLOGISTIC
BIOLOGISTS
BIOLOGY
BIOLUMINESCENCE
BIOLUMINESCENT
BIOLYSES
BIOLYSIS
BIOLYTIC
BIOMARKER
BIOMARKERS
BIOMASS
BIOMASSES
BIOMATERIAL
BIOMATERIALS
BIOMATHEMATICAL
BIOMATHEMATICS
BIOME
BIOMECHANICAL
BIOMECHANICALLY
BIOMECHANICS
BIOMEDICAL
BIOMEDICINE
BIOMEDICINES
BIOMES
BIOMETEOROLOGY
BIOMETER
BIOMETERS
BIOMETRIC
BIOMETRICAL
BIOMETRICIAN
BIOMETRICIANS
BIOMETRICS
BIOMETRIES
BIOMETRY
BIOMIMETIC
BIOMIMETICS
BIOMINERAL
BIOMINERALS
BIOMOLECULAR
BIOMOLECULE
BIOMOLECULES
BIOMORPH
BIOMORPHIC
BIOMORPHS
BIONIC
BIONICS
BIONOMIC
BIONOMICS
BIONOMIES
BIONOMIST
BIONOMISTS
BIONOMY
BIONT
BIONTIC
BIONTS
BIOPESTICIDE
BIOPESTICIDES
BIOPHILIA
BIOPHILIAS
BIOPHYSICAL
BIOPHYSICIST
BIOPHYSICISTS
BIOPHYSICS
BIOPIC
BIOPICS
BIOPIRACIES
BIOPIRACY
BIOPIRATE
BIOPIRATES
BIOPLASM
BIOPLASMS
BIOPOLYMER
BIOPOLYMERS
BIOPROSPECT
BIOPROSPECTED
BIOPROSPECTING
BIOPROSPECTOR
BIOPROSPECTORS
BIOPROSPECTS
BIOPSIC
BIOPSIED
BIOPSIES
BIOPSY
BIOPSYCHOLOGIES
BIOPSYCHOLOGIST
BIOPSYCHOLOGY
BIOPSYING
BIOPTIC
BIOREACTOR
BIOREACTORS
BIOREGION
BIOREGIONAL
BIOREGIONALISM
BIOREGIONALISMS
BIOREGIONALIST
BIOREGIONALISTS
BIOREGIONS
BIOREMEDIATION
BIOREMEDIATIONS
BIORHYTHM
BIORHYTHMIC
BIORHYTHMS
BIOS
BIOSAFETIES
BIOSAFETY
BIOSCIENCE
BIOSCIENCES
BIOSCIENTIFIC
BIOSCIENTIST
BIOSCIENTISTS
BIOSCOPE
BIOSCOPES
BIOSCOPIES
BIOSCOPY
BIOSECURITIES
BIOSECURITY
BIOSENSOR
BIOSENSORS
BIOSOCIAL
BIOSOCIALLY
BIOSOLID
BIOSOLIDS
BIOSPHERE
BIOSPHERES
BIOSPHERIC
BIOSTATISTICAL
BIOSTATISTICIAN
BIOSTATISTICS
BIOSTRATIGRAPHY
BIOSTROME
BIOSTROMES
BIOSYNTHESES
BIOSYNTHESIS
BIOSYNTHETIC
BIOSYSTEMATIC
BIOSYSTEMATICS
BIOSYSTEMATIST
BIOSYSTEMATISTS
BIOTA
BIOTAS
BIOTECH
BIOTECHNICAL
BIOTECHNOLOGIES
BIOTECHNOLOGIST
BIOTECHNOLOGY
BIOTECHS
BIOTELEMETRIC
BIOTELEMETRIES
BIOTELEMETRY
BIOTERROR
BIOTERRORISM
BIOTERRORISMS
BIOTERRORIST
BIOTERRORISTS
BIOTERRORS
BIOTIC
BIOTICAL
BIOTICS
BIOTIN
BIOTINS
BIOTITE
BIOTITES
BIOTITIC
BIOTOPE
BIOTOPES
BIOTOXIN
BIOTOXINS
BIOTRON
BIOTRONS
BIOTURBATED
BIOTURBATION
BIOTURBATIONS
BIOTURBED
BIOTYPE
BIOTYPES
BIOTYPIC
BIOVULAR
BIOWARFARE
BIOWARFARES
BIOWASTE
BIOWASTES
BIOWEAPON
BIOWEAPONS
BIPACK
BIPACKS
BIPARENTAL
BIPARENTALLY
BIPAROUS
BIPARTED
BIPARTISAN
BIPARTISANISM
BIPARTISANISMS
BIPARTISANS
BIPARTISANSHIP
BIPARTISANSHIPS
BIPARTITE
BIPARTITELY
BIPARTITION
BIPARTITIONS
BIPARTY
BIPED
BIPEDAL
BIPEDALISM
BIPEDALISMS
BIPEDALITIES
BIPEDALITY
BIPEDALLY
BIPEDS
BIPHASIC
BIPHENYL
BIPHENYLS
BIPINNATE
BIPINNATELY
BIPLANE
BIPLANES
BIPOD
BIPODS
BIPOLAR
BIPOLARITIES
BIPOLARITY
BIPOLARIZATION
BIPOLARIZATIONS
BIPOLARIZE
BIPOLARIZED
BIPOLARIZES
BIPOLARIZING
BIPROPELLANT
BIPROPELLANTS
BIPYRAMID
BIPYRAMIDAL
BIPYRAMIDS
BIQUADRATIC
BIQUADRATICS
BIRACIAL
BIRACIALISM
BIRACIALISMS
BIRADIAL
BIRADICAL
BIRADICALS
BIRAMOSE
BIRAMOUS
BIRCH
BIRCHED
BIRCHEN
BIRCHES
BIRCHING
BIRD
BIRDBATH
BIRDBATHS

BIRDBRAIN
BIRDBRAINED
BIRDBRAINS
BIRDCAGE
BIRDCAGES
BIRDCALL
BIRDCALLS
BIRDDOG
BIRDDOGGED
BIRDDOGGING
BIRDDOGS
BIRDED
BIRDER
BIRDERS
BIRDFARM
BIRDFARMS
BIRDFEED
BIRDFEEDS
BIRDHOUSE
BIRDHOUSES
BIRDIE
BIRDIED
BIRDIEING
BIRDIES
BIRDING
BIRDINGS
BIRDLIFE
BIRDLIFES
BIRDLIKE
BIRDLIME
BIRDLIMED
BIRDLIMES
BIRDLIMING
BIRDMAN
BIRDMEN
BIRDS
BIRDSEED
BIRDSEEDS
BIRDSEYE
BIRDSEYES
BIRDSHOT
BIRDSHOTS
BIRDSONG
BIRDSONGS
BIRDWATCH
BIRDWATCHED
BIRDWATCHES
BIRDWATCHING
BIREFRINGENCE
BIREFRINGENCES
BIREFRINGENT
BIREME
BIREMES
BIRETTA
BIRETTAS
BIRIANI
BIRIANIS
BIRK
BIRKIE
BIRKIES
BIRKS
BIRL
BIRLE
BIRLED
BIRLER
BIRLERS
BIRLES
BIRLING
BIRLINGS
BIRLS
BIRO
BIROS
BIRR
BIRRED
BIRRETTA
BIRRETTAS
BIRRING
BIRROTCH
BIRRS
BIRSE
BIRSES
BIRTH
BIRTHDAY
BIRTHDAYS
BIRTHED
BIRTHING
BIRTHINGS
BIRTHMARK
BIRTHMARKS
BIRTHNAME
BIRTHNAMES
BIRTHPLACE
BIRTHPLACES
BIRTHRATE
BIRTHRATES
BIRTHRIGHT
BIRTHRIGHTS
BIRTHROOT
BIRTHROOTS
BIRTHS
BIRTHSTONE
BIRTHSTONES
BIRTHWORT
BIRTHWORTS
BIRYANI
BIRYANIS
BIS
BISCOTTI
BISCOTTO
BISCUIT
BISCUITS
BISCUITY
BISE
BISECT
BISECTED
BISECTING
BISECTION
BISECTIONAL
BISECTIONALLY
BISECTIONS
BISECTOR
BISECTORS
BISECTRICES
BISECTRIX
BISECTS
BISERIATE
BISERRATE
BISES
BISEXUAL
BISEXUALITIES
BISEXUALITY
BISEXUALLY
BISEXUALS
BISH
BISHES
BISHOP
BISHOPED
BISHOPING
BISHOPRIC
BISHOPRICS
BISHOPS
BISK
BISKS
BISMARCK
BISMARCKS
BISMUTH
BISMUTHAL
BISMUTHIC
BISMUTHS
BISNAGA
BISNAGAS
BISON
BISONS
BISONTINE
BISPHOSPHONATE
BISPHOSPHONATES
BISQUE
BISQUES
BISTABLE
BISTABLES
BISTATE
BISTER
BISTERED
BISTERS
BISTORT
BISTORTS
BISTOURIES
BISTOURY
BISTRE
BISTRED
BISTRES
BISTRO
BISTROIC
BISTROS
BISULCATE
BISULFATE
BISULFATES
BISULFIDE
BISULFIDES
BISULFITE
BISULFITES
BIT
BITABLE
BITARTRATE
BITARTRATES
BITCH
BITCHED
BITCHEN
BITCHERIES
BITCHERY
BITCHES
BITCHIER
BITCHIEST
BITCHILY
BITCHINESS
BITCHINESSES
BITCHING
BITCHY
BITE
BITEABLE
BITEPLATE
BITEPLATES
BITER
BITERS
BITES
BITEWING
BITEWINGS
BITING
BITINGLY
BITMAP
BITMAPPED
BITMAPPING
BITMAPS
BITS
BITSIER
BITSIEST
BITSTOCK
BITSTOCKS
BITSTREAM
BITSTREAMS
BITSY
BITT
BITTED
BITTEN
BITTER
BITTERBRUSH
BITTERBRUSHES
BITTERED
BITTERER
BITTEREST
BITTERING
BITTERISH
BITTERLY
BITTERN
BITTERNESS
BITTERNESSES
BITTERNS
BITTERNUT
BITTERNUTS
BITTERROOT
BITTERROOTS
BITTERS
BITTERSWEET
BITTERSWEETLY
BITTERSWEETNESS
BITTERSWEETS
BITTERWEED
BITTERWEEDS
BITTIER
BITTIEST
BITTILY
BITTINESS
BITTINESSES
BITTING
BITTINGS
BITTOCK
BITTOCKS
BITTS
BITTY
BITUMEN
BITUMENS
BITUMINIZATION
BITUMINIZATIONS
BITUMINIZE
BITUMINIZED

BITUMINIZES
BITUMINIZING
BITUMINOUS
BITWISE
BIUNIQUE
BIUNIQUENESS
BIUNIQUENESSES
BIVALENCE
BIVALENCES
BIVALENCIES
BIVALENCY
BIVALENT
BIVALENTS
BIVALVE
BIVALVED
BIVALVES
BIVARIATE
BIVINYL
BIVINYLS
BIVOUAC
BIVOUACKED
BIVOUACKING
BIVOUACKS
BIVOUACS
BIWEEKLIES
BIWEEKLY
BIYEARLY
BIZ
BIZARRE
BIZARRELY
BIZARRENESS
BIZARRENESSES
BIZARRERIE
BIZARRERIES
BIZARRES
BIZARRO
BIZARROS
BIZE
BIZES
BIZNAGA
BIZNAGAS
BIZONAL
BIZONE
BIZONES
BIZZES
BLAB
BLABBED
BLABBER
BLABBERED
BLABBERING
BLABBERMOUTH
BLABBERMOUTHS
BLABBERS
BLABBIER
BLABBIEST
BLABBING
BLABBY
BLABS
BLACK
BLACKAMOOR
BLACKAMOORS
BLACKBALL
BLACKBALLED
BLACKBALLING
BLACKBALLS
BLACKBERRIES
BLACKBERRY
BLACKBIRD
BLACKBIRDED
BLACKBIRDER
BLACKBIRDERS
BLACKBIRDING
BLACKBIRDS
BLACKBOARD
BLACKBOARDS
BLACKBODIES
BLACKBODY
BLACKBOY
BLACKBOYS
BLACKBUCK
BLACKBUCKS
BLACKCAP
BLACKCAPS
BLACKCOCK
BLACKCOCKS
BLACKDAMP
BLACKDAMPS
BLACKED
BLACKEN
BLACKENED
BLACKENER
BLACKENERS
BLACKENING
BLACKENINGS
BLACKENS
BLACKER
BLACKEST
BLACKFACE
BLACKFACES
BLACKFIN
BLACKFINS
BLACKFISH
BLACKFISHES
BLACKFLIES
BLACKFLY
BLACKGUARD
BLACKGUARDED
BLACKGUARDING
BLACKGUARDISM
BLACKGUARDISMS
BLACKGUARDLY
BLACKGUARDS
BLACKGUM
BLACKGUMS
BLACKHANDER
BLACKHANDERS
BLACKHEAD
BLACKHEADS
BLACKHEART
BLACKHEARTS
BLACKING
BLACKINGS
BLACKISH
BLACKJACK
BLACKJACKED
BLACKJACKING
BLACKJACKS
BLACKLAND
BLACKLANDS
BLACKLEAD
BLACKLEADS
BLACKLEG
BLACKLEGGED
BLACKLEGGING
BLACKLEGS
BLACKLIST
BLACKLISTED
BLACKLISTER
BLACKLISTERS
BLACKLISTING
BLACKLISTS
BLACKLY
BLACKMAIL
BLACKMAILED
BLACKMAILER
BLACKMAILERS
BLACKMAILING
BLACKMAILS
BLACKNESS
BLACKNESSES
BLACKOUT
BLACKOUTS
BLACKPOLL
BLACKPOLLS
BLACKS
BLACKSMITH
BLACKSMITHING
BLACKSMITHINGS
BLACKSMITHS
BLACKSNAKE
BLACKSNAKES
BLACKTAIL
BLACKTAILS
BLACKTHORN
BLACKTHORNS
BLACKTOP
BLACKTOPPED
BLACKTOPPING
BLACKTOPS
BLACKWATER
BLACKWATERS
BLACKWOOD
BLACKWOODS
BLADDER
BLADDERLIKE
BLADDERNUT
BLADDERNUTS
BLADDERS
BLADDERWORT
BLADDERWORTS
BLADDERY
BLADE
BLADED
BLADELESS
BLADELIKE
BLADER
BLADERS
BLADES
BLADING
BLADINGS
BLAE
BLAEBERRIES
BLAEBERRY
BLAFF
BLAFFS
BLAG
BLAGGED
BLAGGER
BLAGGERS
BLAGGING
BLAGGINGS
BLAGS
BLAGUE
BLAGUES
BLAH
BLAHER
BLAHEST
BLAHS
BLAIN
BLAINS
BLAM
BLAMABLE
BLAMABLY
BLAME
BLAMEABLE
BLAMED
BLAMEFUL
BLAMEFULLY
BLAMELESS
BLAMELESSLY
BLAMELESSNESS
BLAMELESSNESSES
BLAMER
BLAMERS
BLAMES
BLAMEWORTHINESS
BLAMEWORTHY
BLAMING
BLAMMED
BLAMMING
BLAMS
BLANCH
BLANCHED
BLANCHER
BLANCHERS
BLANCHES
BLANCHING
BLANCMANGE
BLANCMANGES
BLAND
BLANDER
BLANDEST
BLANDISH
BLANDISHED
BLANDISHER
BLANDISHERS
BLANDISHES
BLANDISHING
BLANDISHMENT
BLANDISHMENTS
BLANDLY
BLANDNESS
BLANDNESSES
BLANK
BLANKED
BLANKER
BLANKEST
BLANKET
BLANKETED
BLANKETFLOWER
BLANKETFLOWERS
BLANKETIES
BLANKETING
BLANKETINGS
BLANKETLIKE

BLANKETS
BLANKETY
BLANKIE
BLANKIES
BLANKING
BLANKLY
BLANKNESS
BLANKNESSES
BLANKS
BLANQUETTE
BLANQUETTES
BLARE
BLARED
BLARES
BLARING
BLARNEY
BLARNEYED
BLARNEYING
BLARNEYS
BLASE
BLASPHEME
BLASPHEMED
BLASPHEMER
BLASPHEMERS
BLASPHEMES
BLASPHEMIES
BLASPHEMING
BLASPHEMOUS
BLASPHEMOUSLY
BLASPHEMOUSNESS
BLASPHEMY
BLAST
BLASTED
BLASTEMA
BLASTEMAL
BLASTEMAS
BLASTEMATA
BLASTEMATIC
BLASTEMIC
BLASTER
BLASTERS
BLASTIE
BLASTIER
BLASTIES
BLASTIEST
BLASTING
BLASTINGS
BLASTMENT
BLASTMENTS
BLASTOCOEL
BLASTOCOELE
BLASTOCOELES
BLASTOCOELIC
BLASTOCOELS
BLASTOCYST
BLASTOCYSTS
BLASTODERM
BLASTODERMS
BLASTODISC
BLASTODISCS
BLASTOFF
BLASTOFFS
BLASTOMA
BLASTOMAS
BLASTOMATA
BLASTOMERE
BLASTOMERES
BLASTOMYCOSES
BLASTOMYCOSIS
BLASTOPORE
BLASTOPORES
BLASTOPORIC
BLASTOSPORE
BLASTOSPORES
BLASTS
BLASTULA
BLASTULAE
BLASTULAR
BLASTULAS
BLASTULATION
BLASTULATIONS
BLASTY
BLAT
BLATANCIES
BLATANCY
BLATANT
BLATANTLY
BLATE
BLATHER
BLATHERED
BLATHERER
BLATHERERS
BLATHERING
BLATHERINGS
BLATHERS
BLATHERSKITE
BLATHERSKITES
BLATS
BLATTED
BLATTER
BLATTERED
BLATTERING
BLATTERS
BLATTING
BLAUBOK
BLAUBOKS
BLAW
BLAWED
BLAWING
BLAWN
BLAWS
BLAXPLOITATION
BLAXPLOITATIONS
BLAZE
BLAZED
BLAZER
BLAZERED
BLAZERS
BLAZES
BLAZING
BLAZINGLY
BLAZON
BLAZONED
BLAZONER
BLAZONERS
BLAZONING
BLAZONINGS
BLAZONRIES
BLAZONRY
BLAZONS
BLEACH
BLEACHABLE
BLEACHED
BLEACHER
BLEACHERITE
BLEACHERITES
BLEACHERS
BLEACHES
BLEACHING
BLEAK
BLEAKER
BLEAKEST
BLEAKISH
BLEAKLY
BLEAKNESS
BLEAKNESSES
BLEAKS
BLEAR
BLEARED
BLEARER
BLEAREST
BLEAREYED
BLEARIER
BLEARIEST
BLEARILY
BLEARINESS
BLEARINESSES
BLEARING
BLEARS
BLEARY
BLEAT
BLEATED
BLEATER
BLEATERS
BLEATING
BLEATS
BLEB
BLEBBING
BLEBBINGS
BLEBBY
BLEBS
BLECH
BLED
BLEED
BLEEDER
BLEEDERS
BLEEDING
BLEEDINGS
BLEEDS
BLEEP
BLEEPED
BLEEPER
BLEEPERS
BLEEPING
BLEEPS
BLELLUM
BLELLUMS
BLEMISH
BLEMISHED
BLEMISHER
BLEMISHERS
BLEMISHES
BLEMISHING
BLENCH
BLENCHED
BLENCHER
BLENCHERS
BLENCHES
BLENCHING
BLEND
BLENDE
BLENDED
BLENDER
BLENDERS
BLENDES
BLENDING
BLENDINGS
BLENDS
BLENNIES
BLENNIOID
BLENNY
BLENT
BLEPHAROPLAST
BLEPHAROPLASTS
BLEPHAROPLASTY
BLEPHAROSPASM
BLEPHAROSPASMS
BLESBOK
BLESBOKS
BLESBUCK
BLESBUCKS
BLESS
BLESSED
BLESSEDER
BLESSEDEST
BLESSEDLY
BLESSEDNESS
BLESSEDNESSES
BLESSER
BLESSERS
BLESSES
BLESSING
BLESSINGS
BLEST
BLET
BLETHER
BLETHERED
BLETHERING
BLETHERS
BLETS
BLEW
BLEWIT
BLEWITS
BLEWITSES
BLIGHT
BLIGHTED
BLIGHTER
BLIGHTERS
BLIGHTIES
BLIGHTING
BLIGHTS
BLIGHTY
BLIMEY
BLIMP
BLIMPERIES
BLIMPERY
BLIMPISH
BLIMPISHLY
BLIMPISHNESS
BLIMPISHNESSES
BLIMPS
BLIMY
BLIN
BLIND
BLINDAGE

BLINDAGES
BLINDED
BLINDER
BLINDERS
BLINDEST
BLINDFISH
BLINDFISHES
BLINDFOLD
BLINDFOLDED
BLINDFOLDING
BLINDFOLDS
BLINDGUT
BLINDGUTS
BLINDING
BLINDINGLY
BLINDINGS
BLINDLY
BLINDNESS
BLINDNESSES
BLINDS
BLINDSIDE
BLINDSIDED
BLINDSIDES
BLINDSIDING
BLINDWORM
BLINDWORMS
BLING
BLINGED
BLINGING
BLINGS
BLINI
BLINIS
BLINK
BLINKARD
BLINKARDS
BLINKED
BLINKER
BLINKERED
BLINKERING
BLINKERS
BLINKING
BLINKS
BLINTZ
BLINTZE
BLINTZES
BLINY
BLIP
BLIPPED
BLIPPING
BLIPS
BLISS
BLISSED
BLISSES
BLISSFUL
BLISSFULLY
BLISSFULNESS
BLISSFULNESSES
BLISSING
BLISSLESS
BLISTER
BLISTERED
BLISTERING
BLISTERINGLY
BLISTERS
BLISTERY
BLITE
BLITES
BLITHE
BLITHEFUL
BLITHELY
BLITHER
BLITHERED
BLITHERING
BLITHERINGLY
BLITHERS
BLITHESOME
BLITHESOMELY
BLITHEST
BLITZ
BLITZED
BLITZER
BLITZERS
BLITZES
BLITZING
BLITZKRIEG
BLITZKRIEGS
BLIZZARD
BLIZZARDED
BLIZZARDING
BLIZZARDLY
BLIZZARDS
BLIZZARDY
BLOAT
BLOATED
BLOATEDNESS
BLOATEDNESSES
BLOATER
BLOATERS
BLOATING
BLOATINGS
BLOATS
BLOATWARE
BLOATWARES
BLOB
BLOBBED
BLOBBIER
BLOBBIEST
BLOBBING
BLOBBY
BLOBS
BLOC
BLOCK
BLOCKABLE
BLOCKADE
BLOCKADED
BLOCKADER
BLOCKADERS
BLOCKADES
BLOCKADING
BLOCKAGE
BLOCKAGES
BLOCKBUST
BLOCKBUSTED
BLOCKBUSTER
BLOCKBUSTERS
BLOCKBUSTING
BLOCKBUSTINGS
BLOCKBUSTS
BLOCKED
BLOCKER
BLOCKERS
BLOCKHEAD
BLOCKHEADS
BLOCKHOUSE
BLOCKHOUSES
BLOCKIER
BLOCKIEST
BLOCKING
BLOCKINGS
BLOCKISH
BLOCKS
BLOCKY
BLOCS
BLOG
BLOGGED
BLOGGER
BLOGGERS
BLOGGING
BLOGGINGS
BLOGOSPHERE
BLOGOSPHERES
BLOGS
BLOKE
BLOKEISH
BLOKES
BLOKEY
BLOKIER
BLOKIEST
BLOND
BLONDE
BLONDER
BLONDES
BLONDEST
BLONDINE
BLONDINED
BLONDINES
BLONDINING
BLONDISH
BLONDNESS
BLONDNESSES
BLONDS
BLOOD
BLOODBATH
BLOODBATHS
BLOODCURDLING
BLOODED
BLOODFIN
BLOODFINS
BLOODGUILT
BLOODGUILTINESS
BLOODGUILTS
BLOODGUILTY
BLOODHOUND
BLOODHOUNDS
BLOODIED
BLOODIER
BLOODIES
BLOODIEST
BLOODILY
BLOODINESS
BLOODINESSES
BLOODING
BLOODINGS
BLOODLESS
BLOODLESSLY
BLOODLESSNESS
BLOODLESSNESSES
BLOODLETTING
BLOODLETTINGS
BLOODLIKE
BLOODLINE
BLOODLINES
BLOODLUST
BLOODLUSTS
BLOODMOBILE
BLOODMOBILES
BLOODRED
BLOODROOT
BLOODROOTS
BLOODS
BLOODSHED
BLOODSHEDS
BLOODSHOT
BLOODSTAIN
BLOODSTAINED
BLOODSTAINS
BLOODSTOCK
BLOODSTOCKS
BLOODSTONE
BLOODSTONES
BLOODSTREAM
BLOODSTREAMS
BLOODSUCKER
BLOODSUCKERS
BLOODSUCKING
BLOODTHIRSTIER
BLOODTHIRSTIEST
BLOODTHIRSTILY
BLOODTHIRSTY
BLOODWORM
BLOODWORMS
BLOODWORT
BLOODWORTS
BLOODY
BLOODYING
BLOOEY
BLOOIE
BLOOM
BLOOMED
BLOOMER
BLOOMERIES
BLOOMERS
BLOOMERY
BLOOMIER
BLOOMIEST
BLOOMING
BLOOMINGS
BLOOMLESS
BLOOMS
BLOOMY
BLOOP
BLOOPED
BLOOPER
BLOOPERS
BLOOPIER
BLOOPIEST
BLOOPING
BLOOPS
BLOOPY
BLOSSOM
BLOSSOMED
BLOSSOMING
BLOSSOMINGS
BLOSSOMS
BLOSSOMY

BLOT
BLOTCH
BLOTCHED
BLOTCHES
BLOTCHIER
BLOTCHIEST
BLOTCHILY
BLOTCHING
BLOTCHY
BLOTLESS
BLOTS
BLOTTED
BLOTTER
BLOTTERS
BLOTTIER
BLOTTIEST
BLOTTING
BLOTTO
BLOTTY
BLOUSE
BLOUSED
BLOUSES
BLOUSIER
BLOUSIEST
BLOUSILY
BLOUSING
BLOUSON
BLOUSONS
BLOUSY
BLOVIATE
BLOVIATED
BLOVIATES
BLOVIATING
BLOVIATION
BLOVIATIONS
BLOW
BLOWBACK
BLOWBACKS
BLOWBALL
BLOWBALLS
BLOWBY
BLOWBYS
BLOWDART
BLOWDARTS
BLOWDOWN
BLOWDOWNS
BLOWED
BLOWER
BLOWERS
BLOWFISH
BLOWFISHES
BLOWFLIES
BLOWFLY
BLOWGUN
BLOWGUNS
BLOWHARD
BLOWHARDS
BLOWHOLE
BLOWHOLES
BLOWIER
BLOWIEST
BLOWINESS
BLOWINESSES
BLOWING
BLOWJOB
BLOWJOBS
BLOWLAMP
BLOWLAMPS
BLOWN
BLOWOFF
BLOWOFFS
BLOWOUT
BLOWOUTS
BLOWPIPE
BLOWPIPES
BLOWS
BLOWSED
BLOWSIER
BLOWSIEST
BLOWSILY
BLOWSY
BLOWTORCH
BLOWTORCHED
BLOWTORCHES
BLOWTORCHING
BLOWTUBE
BLOWTUBES
BLOWUP
BLOWUPS
BLOWY
BLOWZED
BLOWZIER
BLOWZIEST
BLOWZILY
BLOWZY
BLUB
BLUBBED
BLUBBER
BLUBBERED
BLUBBERER
BLUBBERERS
BLUBBERING
BLUBBERS
BLUBBERY
BLUBBING
BLUBS
BLUCHER
BLUCHERS
BLUDGE
BLUDGED
BLUDGEON
BLUDGEONED
BLUDGEONING
BLUDGEONS
BLUDGER
BLUDGERS
BLUDGES
BLUDGING
BLUE
BLUEBACK
BLUEBACKS
BLUEBALL
BLUEBALLS
BLUEBEARD
BLUEBEARDS
BLUEBEAT
BLUEBEATS
BLUEBELL
BLUEBELLS
BLUEBERRIES
BLUEBERRY
BLUEBILL
BLUEBILLS
BLUEBIRD
BLUEBIRDS
BLUEBLOOD
BLUEBLOODS
BLUEBONNET
BLUEBONNETS
BLUEBOOK
BLUEBOOKS
BLUEBOTTLE
BLUEBOTTLES
BLUECAP
BLUECAPS
BLUECOAT
BLUECOATS
BLUECURLS
BLUED
BLUEFIN
BLUEFINS
BLUEFISH
BLUEFISHES
BLUEGILL
BLUEGILLS
BLUEGRASS
BLUEGRASSES
BLUEGUM
BLUEGUMS
BLUEHEAD
BLUEHEADS
BLUEING
BLUEINGS
BLUEISH
BLUEJACK
BLUEJACKET
BLUEJACKETS
BLUEJACKS
BLUEJAY
BLUEJAYS
BLUEJEANS
BLUELINE
BLUELINER
BLUELINERS
BLUELINES
BLUELY
BLUENESS
BLUENESSES
BLUENOSE
BLUENOSED
BLUENOSES
BLUEPOINT
BLUEPOINTS
BLUEPRINT
BLUEPRINTED
BLUEPRINTING
BLUEPRINTS
BLUER
BLUES
BLUESHIFT
BLUESHIFTED
BLUESHIFTS
BLUESIER
BLUESIEST
BLUESMAN
BLUESMEN
BLUEST
BLUESTEM
BLUESTEMS
BLUESTOCKING
BLUESTOCKINGS
BLUESTONE
BLUESTONES
BLUESY
BLUET
BLUETICK
BLUETICKS
BLUETONGUE
BLUETONGUES
BLUETS
BLUEWEED
BLUEWEEDS
BLUEWOOD
BLUEWOODS
BLUEY
BLUEYS
BLUFF
BLUFFABLE
BLUFFED
BLUFFER
BLUFFERS
BLUFFEST
BLUFFING
BLUFFLY
BLUFFNESS
BLUFFNESSES
BLUFFS
BLUING
BLUINGS
BLUISH
BLUISHNESS
BLUISHNESSES
BLUME
BLUMED
BLUMES
BLUMING
BLUNDER
BLUNDERBUSS
BLUNDERBUSSES
BLUNDERED
BLUNDERER
BLUNDERERS
BLUNDERING
BLUNDERINGLY
BLUNDERS
BLUNGE
BLUNGED
BLUNGER
BLUNGERS
BLUNGES
BLUNGING
BLUNT
BLUNTED
BLUNTER
BLUNTEST
BLUNTING
BLUNTLY
BLUNTNESS
BLUNTNESSES
BLUNTS
BLUR
BLURB
BLURBED
BLURBING
BLURBIST

BLURBISTS
BLURBS
BLURRED
BLURREDLY
BLURRIER
BLURRIEST
BLURRILY
BLURRINESS
BLURRINESSES
BLURRING
BLURRINGLY
BLURRY
BLURS
BLURT
BLURTED
BLURTER
BLURTERS
BLURTING
BLURTS
BLUSH
BLUSHED
BLUSHER
BLUSHERS
BLUSHES
BLUSHFUL
BLUSHING
BLUSHINGLY
BLUSTER
BLUSTERED
BLUSTERER
BLUSTERERS
BLUSTERING
BLUSTERINGLY
BLUSTEROUS
BLUSTERS
BLUSTERY
BLYPE
BLYPES
BO
BOA
BOAR
BOARD
BOARDABLE
BOARDED
BOARDER
BOARDERS
BOARDING
BOARDINGHOUSE
BOARDINGHOUSES
BOARDINGS
BOARDLIKE
BOARDMAN
BOARDMEN
BOARDROOM
BOARDROOMS
BOARDS
BOARDSAILING
BOARDSAILINGS
BOARDSAILOR
BOARDSAILORS
BOARDWALK
BOARDWALKS
BOARFISH
BOARFISHES
BOARHOUND
BOARHOUNDS
BOARISH
BOARS
BOART
BOARTS
BOAS
BOAST
BOASTED
BOASTER
BOASTERS
BOASTFUL
BOASTFULLY
BOASTFULNESS
BOASTFULNESSES
BOASTING
BOASTS
BOAT
BOATABLE
BOATBILL
BOATBILLS
BOATBUILDER
BOATBUILDERS
BOATBUILDING
BOATBUILDINGS
BOATED
BOATEL
BOATELS
BOATER
BOATERS
BOATFUL
BOATFULS
BOATHOOK
BOATHOOKS
BOATHOUSE
BOATHOUSES
BOATING
BOATINGS
BOATLIFT
BOATLIFTED
BOATLIFTING
BOATLIFTS
BOATLIKE
BOATLOAD
BOATLOADS
BOATMAN
BOATMEN
BOATNECK
BOATNECKS
BOATPORT
BOATPORTS
BOATS
BOATSMAN
BOATSMEN
BOATSWAIN
BOATSWAINS
BOATYARD
BOATYARDS
BOB
BOBBED
BOBBER
BOBBERIES
BOBBERS
BOBBERY
BOBBIES
BOBBIN
BOBBINET
BOBBINETS
BOBBING
BOBBINS
BOBBLE
BOBBLED
BOBBLES
BOBBLIER
BOBBLIEST
BOBBLING
BOBBLY
BOBBY
BOBBYSOX
BOBCAT
BOBCATS
BOBECHE
BOBECHES
BOBO
BOBOLINK
BOBOLINKS
BOBOS
BOBS
BOBSKATE
BOBSKATES
BOBSLED
BOBSLEDDED
BOBSLEDDER
BOBSLEDDERS
BOBSLEDDING
BOBSLEDDINGS
BOBSLEDS
BOBSLEIGH
BOBSLEIGHER
BOBSLEIGHERS
BOBSLEIGHING
BOBSLEIGHS
BOBSTAY
BOBSTAYS
BOBTAIL
BOBTAILED
BOBTAILING
BOBTAILS
BOBWHITE
BOBWHITES
BOCACCIO
BOCACCIOS
BOCCE
BOCCES
BOCCI
BOCCIA
BOCCIAS
BOCCIE
BOCCIES
BOCCIS
BOCHE
BOCHES
BOCK
BOCKS
BOD
BODACIOUS
BODACIOUSLY
BODDHISATTVA
BODDHISATTVAS
BODE
BODED
BODEGA
BODEGAS
BODEMENT
BODEMENTS
BODES
BODHISATTVA
BODHISATTVAS
BODHRAN
BODHRANS
BODICE
BODICES
BODIED
BODIES
BODILESS
BODILY
BODING
BODINGLY
BODINGS
BODKIN
BODKINS
BODS
BODY
BODYBOARD
BODYBOARDED
BODYBOARDER
BODYBOARDERS
BODYBOARDING
BODYBOARDS
BODYBUILDER
BODYBUILDERS
BODYBUILDING
BODYBUILDINGS
BODYCHECK
BODYCHECKED
BODYCHECKING
BODYCHECKS
BODYGUARD
BODYGUARDED
BODYGUARDING
BODYGUARDS
BODYING
BODYMAN
BODYMEN
BODYSIDE
BODYSIDES
BODYSUIT
BODYSUITS
BODYSURF
BODYSURFED
BODYSURFER
BODYSURFERS
BODYSURFING
BODYSURFINGS
BODYSURFS
BODYWASH
BODYWASHES
BODYWORK
BODYWORKER
BODYWORKERS
BODYWORKS
BOEHMITE
BOEHMITES
BOEUF
BOEUFS
BOFF
BOFFED
BOFFIN
BOFFING
BOFFINS
BOFFINY

BOFFO
BOFFOLA
BOFFOLAS
BOFFOS
BOFFS
BOG
BOGAN
BOGANS
BOGART
BOGARTED
BOGARTING
BOGARTS
BOGBEAN
BOGBEANS
BOGEY
BOGEYED
BOGEYING
BOGEYMAN
BOGEYMEN
BOGEYS
BOGGED
BOGGIER
BOGGIEST
BOGGINESS
BOGGINESSES
BOGGING
BOGGISH
BOGGLE
BOGGLED
BOGGLER
BOGGLERS
BOGGLES
BOGGLING
BOGGY
BOGHOLE
BOGHOLES
BOGIE
BOGIES
BOGLAND
BOGLANDS
BOGLE
BOGLES
BOGS
BOGUS
BOGUSLY
BOGUSNESS
BOGUSNESSES
BOGWOOD
BOGWOODS
BOGY
BOGYISM
BOGYISMS
BOGYMAN
BOGYMEN
BOHEA
BOHEAS
BOHEMIA
BOHEMIAN
BOHEMIANISM
BOHEMIANISMS
BOHEMIANS
BOHEMIAS
BOHO
BOHOS
BOHRIUM
BOHRIUMS
BOHUNK
BOHUNKS
BOIL
BOILABLE
BOILED
BOILER
BOILERMAKER
BOILERMAKERS
BOILERPLATE
BOILERPLATES
BOILERS
BOILERSUIT
BOILERSUITS
BOILING
BOILINGLY
BOILOFF
BOILOFFS
BOILOVER
BOILOVERS
BOILS
BOING
BOINGED
BOINGING
BOINGS
BOINK
BOINKED
BOINKING
BOINKS
BOISERIE
BOISERIES
BOISTEROUS
BOISTEROUSLY
BOISTEROUSNESS
BOITE
BOITES
BOKKEN
BOKKENS
BOLA
BOLAR
BOLAS
BOLASES
BOLD
BOLDED
BOLDER
BOLDEST
BOLDFACE
BOLDFACED
BOLDFACES
BOLDFACING
BOLDING
BOLDLY
BOLDNESS
BOLDNESSES
BOLDS
BOLE
BOLECTION
BOLECTIONS
BOLERO
BOLEROS
BOLES
BOLETE
BOLETES
BOLETI
BOLETUS
BOLETUSES
BOLIDE
BOLIDES
BOLIVAR
BOLIVARES
BOLIVARS
BOLIVIA
BOLIVIANO
BOLIVIANOS
BOLIVIAS
BOLL
BOLLARD
BOLLARDS
BOLLED
BOLLING
BOLLIX
BOLLIXED
BOLLIXES
BOLLIXING
BOLLOCKING
BOLLOCKINGS
BOLLOCKS
BOLLOX
BOLLOXED
BOLLOXES
BOLLOXING
BOLLS
BOLLWORM
BOLLWORMS
BOLO
BOLOGNA
BOLOGNAS
BOLOGRAPH
BOLOGRAPHS
BOLOMETER
BOLOMETERS
BOLOMETRIC
BOLOMETRICALLY
BOLONEY
BOLONEYS
BOLOS
BOLSHEVIK
BOLSHEVIKI
BOLSHEVIKS
BOLSHEVISM
BOLSHEVISMS
BOLSHEVIZE
BOLSHEVIZED
BOLSHEVIZES
BOLSHEVIZING
BOLSHIE
BOLSHIES
BOLSHY
BOLSON
BOLSONS
BOLSTER
BOLSTERED
BOLSTERER
BOLSTERERS
BOLSTERING
BOLSTERS
BOLT
BOLTED
BOLTER
BOLTERS
BOLTHEAD
BOLTHEADS
BOLTHOLE
BOLTHOLES
BOLTING
BOLTLESS
BOLTLIKE
BOLTONIA
BOLTONIAS
BOLTROPE
BOLTROPES
BOLTS
BOLUS
BOLUSES
BOMB
BOMBABLE
BOMBARD
BOMBARDE
BOMBARDED
BOMBARDER
BOMBARDERS
BOMBARDES
BOMBARDIER
BOMBARDIERS
BOMBARDING
BOMBARDMENT
BOMBARDMENTS
BOMBARDON
BOMBARDONS
BOMBARDS
BOMBAST
BOMBASTER
BOMBASTERS
BOMBASTIC
BOMBASTICALLY
BOMBASTS
BOMBAX
BOMBAZINE
BOMBAZINES
BOMBE
BOMBED
BOMBER
BOMBERS
BOMBES
BOMBESIN
BOMBESINS
BOMBINATE
BOMBINATED
BOMBINATES
BOMBINATING
BOMBINATION
BOMBINATIONS
BOMBING
BOMBINGS
BOMBLET
BOMBLETS
BOMBLOAD
BOMBLOADS
BOMBORA
BOMBORAS
BOMBPROOF
BOMBPROOFED
BOMBPROOFING
BOMBPROOFS
BOMBS
BOMBSHELL
BOMBSHELLS
BOMBSIGHT
BOMBSIGHTS
BOMBYCID

BOMBYCIDS
BOMBYCOID
BOMBYX
BOMBYXES
BONACI
BONACIS
BONANZA
BONANZAS
BONBON
BONBONS
BONCE
BONCES
BOND
BONDABLE
BONDAGE
BONDAGES
BONDED
BONDER
BONDERS
BONDHOLDER
BONDHOLDERS
BONDING
BONDINGS
BONDLESS
BONDMAID
BONDMAIDS
BONDMAN
BONDMEN
BONDS
BONDSMAN
BONDSMEN
BONDSTONE
BONDSTONES
BONDSWOMAN
BONDSWOMEN
BONDUC
BONDUCS
BONDWOMAN
BONDWOMEN
BONE
BONEBED
BONEBEDS
BONEBLACK
BONEBLACKS
BONED
BONEFISH
BONEFISHES
BONEFISHING
BONEFISHINGS
BONEHEAD
BONEHEADED
BONEHEADEDNESS
BONEHEADS
BONELESS
BONEMEAL
BONEMEALS
BONER
BONERS
BONES
BONESET
BONESETS
BONESETTER
BONESETTERS
BONEY
BONEYARD
BONEYARDS
BONEYER
BONEYEST
BONFIRE
BONFIRES
BONG
BONGED
BONGING
BONGO
BONGOES
BONGOIST
BONGOISTS
BONGOS
BONGS
BONHOMIE
BONHOMIES
BONHOMOUS
BONIATO
BONIATOS
BONIER
BONIEST
BONIFACE
BONIFACES
BONINESS
BONINESSES
BONING
BONITA
BONITAS
BONITO
BONITOES
BONITOS
BONK
BONKED
BONKERS
BONKING
BONKS
BONNE
BONNES
BONNET
BONNETED
BONNETING
BONNETS
BONNIE
BONNIER
BONNIES
BONNIEST
BONNILY
BONNINESS
BONNINESSES
BONNOCK
BONNOCKS
BONNY
BONNYCLABBER
BONNYCLABBERS
BONOBO
BONOBOS
BONSAI
BONSPELL
BONSPELLS
BONSPIEL
BONSPIELS
BONTBOK
BONTBOKS
BONTEBOK
BONTEBOKS
BONUS
BONUSES
BONUSING
BONUSINGS
BONY
BONZE
BONZER
BONZES
BOO
BOOB
BOOBED
BOOBIE
BOOBIES
BOOBING
BOOBIRD
BOOBIRDS
BOOBISH
BOOBOISIE
BOOBOISIES
BOOBOO
BOOBOOS
BOOBS
BOOBY
BOOCOO
BOOCOOS
BOODIES
BOODLE
BOODLED
BOODLER
BOODLERS
BOODLES
BOODLING
BOODY
BOOED
BOOGALOO
BOOGALOOED
BOOGALOOING
BOOGALOOS
BOOGER
BOOGERMAN
BOOGERMEN
BOOGERS
BOOGEY
BOOGEYED
BOOGEYING
BOOGEYMAN
BOOGEYMEN
BOOGEYS
BOOGIE
BOOGIED
BOOGIEING
BOOGIEMAN
BOOGIEMEN
BOOGIES
BOOGY
BOOGYING
BOOGYMAN
BOOGYMEN
BOOHOO
BOOHOOED
BOOHOOING
BOOHOOS
BOOING
BOOJUM
BOOJUMS
BOOK
BOOKABLE
BOOKBAG
BOOKBAGS
BOOKBINDER
BOOKBINDERIES
BOOKBINDERS
BOOKBINDERY
BOOKBINDING
BOOKBINDINGS
BOOKCASE
BOOKCASES
BOOKED
BOOKEND
BOOKENDED
BOOKENDING
BOOKENDS
BOOKER
BOOKERS
BOOKFUL
BOOKFULS
BOOKIE
BOOKIES
BOOKING
BOOKINGS
BOOKISH
BOOKISHLY
BOOKISHNESS
BOOKISHNESSES
BOOKKEEPER
BOOKKEEPERS
BOOKKEEPING
BOOKKEEPINGS
BOOKLET
BOOKLETS
BOOKLICE
BOOKLORE
BOOKLORES
BOOKLOUSE
BOOKMAKER
BOOKMAKERS
BOOKMAKING
BOOKMAKINGS
BOOKMAN
BOOKMARK
BOOKMARKED
BOOKMARKER
BOOKMARKERS
BOOKMARKING
BOOKMARKS
BOOKMEN
BOOKMOBILE
BOOKMOBILES
BOOKOO
BOOKOOS
BOOKPLATE
BOOKPLATES
BOOKRACK
BOOKRACKS
BOOKREST
BOOKRESTS
BOOKS
BOOKSELLER
BOOKSELLERS
BOOKSELLING
BOOKSELLINGS
BOOKSHELF
BOOKSHELVES
BOOKSHOP
BOOKSHOPS

BOOKSTALL
BOOKSTALLS
BOOKSTAND
BOOKSTANDS
BOOKSTORE
BOOKSTORES
BOOKWORK
BOOKWORKS
BOOKWORM
BOOKWORMS
BOOM
BOOMBOX
BOOMBOXES
BOOMED
BOOMER
BOOMERANG
BOOMERANGED
BOOMERANGING
BOOMERANGS
BOOMERS
BOOMIER
BOOMIEST
BOOMING
BOOMINGLY
BOOMKIN
BOOMKINS
BOOMLET
BOOMLETS
BOOMS
BOOMTOWN
BOOMTOWNS
BOOMY
BOON
BOONDOCK
BOONDOCKS
BOONDOGGLE
BOONDOGGLED
BOONDOGGLER
BOONDOGGLERS
BOONDOGGLES
BOONDOGGLING
BOONER
BOONEST
BOONIES
BOONLESS
BOONS
BOOR
BOORISH
BOORISHLY
BOORISHNESS
BOORISHNESSES
BOORS
BOOS
BOOST
BOOSTED
BOOSTER
BOOSTERISM
BOOSTERISMS
BOOSTERS
BOOSTING
BOOSTS
BOOT
BOOTABLE
BOOTBLACK
BOOTBLACKS
BOOTED
BOOTEE
BOOTEES
BOOTERIES
BOOTERY
BOOTH
BOOTHS
BOOTIE
BOOTIES
BOOTING
BOOTJACK
BOOTJACKS
BOOTLACE
BOOTLACES
BOOTLEG
BOOTLEGGED
BOOTLEGGER
BOOTLEGGERS
BOOTLEGGING
BOOTLEGGINGS
BOOTLEGS
BOOTLESS
BOOTLESSLY
BOOTLESSNESS
BOOTLESSNESSES
BOOTLICK
BOOTLICKED
BOOTLICKER
BOOTLICKERS
BOOTLICKING
BOOTLICKINGS
BOOTLICKS
BOOTS
BOOTSTRAP
BOOTSTRAPPED
BOOTSTRAPPER
BOOTSTRAPPERS
BOOTSTRAPPING
BOOTSTRAPS
BOOTY
BOOZE
BOOZED
BOOZEHOUND
BOOZEHOUNDS
BOOZER
BOOZERS
BOOZES
BOOZIER
BOOZIEST
BOOZILY
BOOZINESS
BOOZINESSES
BOOZING
BOOZINGS
BOOZY
BOP
BOPEEP
BOPEEPS
BOPPED
BOPPER
BOPPERS
BOPPIER
BOPPIEST
BOPPING
BOPPISH
BOPPY
BOPS
BORA
BORACES
BORACIC
BORACITE
BORACITES
BORAGE
BORAGES
BORAL
BORALS
BORANE
BORANES
BORAS
BORATE
BORATED
BORATES
BORATING
BORAX
BORAXES
BORAZON
BORAZONS
BORBORYGMI
BORBORYGMUS
BORDEAUX
BORDEL
BORDELLO
BORDELLOS
BORDELS
BORDER
BORDEREAU
BORDEREAUX
BORDERED
BORDERER
BORDERERS
BORDERING
BORDERLAND
BORDERLANDS
BORDERLINE
BORDERLINES
BORDERS
BORDURE
BORDURES
BORE
BOREAL
BOREAS
BOREASES
BORECOLE
BORECOLES
BORED
BOREDOM
BOREDOMS
BOREEN
BOREENS
BOREHOLE
BOREHOLES
BORER
BORERS
BORES
BORESCOPE
BORESCOPES
BORESOME
BORIC
BORIDE
BORIDES
BORING
BORINGLY
BORINGNESS
BORINGNESSES
BORINGS
BORK
BORKED
BORKING
BORKINGS
BORKS
BORN
BORNE
BORNEOL
BORNEOLS
BORNITE
BORNITES
BORNITIC
BOROHYDRIDE
BOROHYDRIDES
BORON
BORONIA
BORONIAS
BORONIC
BORONS
BOROSILICATE
BOROSILICATES
BOROUGH
BOROUGHS
BORRELIA
BORRELIAS
BORROW
BORROWED
BORROWER
BORROWERS
BORROWING
BORROWINGS
BORROWS
BORSCH
BORSCHES
BORSCHT
BORSCHTS
BORSHT
BORSHTS
BORSTAL
BORSTALS
BORT
BORTS
BORTY
BORTZ
BORTZES
BORZOI
BORZOIS
BOS
BOSCAGE
BOSCAGES
BOSCHBOK
BOSCHBOKS
BOSCHVARK
BOSCHVARKS
BOSH
BOSHBOK
BOSHBOKS
BOSHES
BOSHVARK
BOSHVARKS
BOSK
BOSKAGE
BOSKAGES
BOSKER
BOSKET

BOSKETS
BOSKIER
BOSKIEST
BOSKINESS
BOSKINESSES
BOSKS
BOSKY
BOSOM
BOSOMED
BOSOMING
BOSOMS
BOSOMY
BOSON
BOSONIC
BOSONS
BOSQUE
BOSQUES
BOSQUET
BOSQUETS
BOSS
BOSSDOM
BOSSDOMS
BOSSED
BOSSER
BOSSES
BOSSEST
BOSSIER
BOSSIES
BOSSIEST
BOSSILY
BOSSINESS
BOSSINESSES
BOSSING
BOSSISM
BOSSISMS
BOSSY
BOSTON
BOSTONS
BOSUN
BOSUNS
BOT
BOTA
BOTANIC
BOTANICA
BOTANICAL
BOTANICALLY
BOTANICALS
BOTANICAS
BOTANIES
BOTANISE
BOTANISED
BOTANISES
BOTANISING
BOTANIST
BOTANISTS
BOTANIZE
BOTANIZED
BOTANIZER
BOTANIZERS
BOTANIZES
BOTANIZING
BOTANY
BOTAS
BOTCH
BOTCHED
BOTCHEDLY
BOTCHER
BOTCHERIES
BOTCHERS
BOTCHERY
BOTCHES
BOTCHIER
BOTCHIEST
BOTCHILY
BOTCHING
BOTCHY
BOTEL
BOTELS
BOTFLIES
BOTFLY
BOTH
BOTHER
BOTHERATION
BOTHERATIONS
BOTHERED
BOTHERING
BOTHERS
BOTHERSOME
BOTHIE
BOTHIES
BOTHRIA
BOTHRIUM
BOTHRIUMS
BOTHY
BOTONEE
BOTONNEE
BOTRYOID
BOTRYOIDAL
BOTRYOSE
BOTRYTIS
BOTRYTISES
BOTS
BOTT
BOTTLE
BOTTLEBRUSH
BOTTLEBRUSHES
BOTTLED
BOTTLEFUL
BOTTLEFULS
BOTTLENECK
BOTTLENECKED
BOTTLENECKING
BOTTLENECKS
BOTTLER
BOTTLERS
BOTTLES
BOTTLING
BOTTLINGS
BOTTOM
BOTTOMED
BOTTOMER
BOTTOMERS
BOTTOMING
BOTTOMLAND
BOTTOMLANDS
BOTTOMLESS
BOTTOMLESSLY
BOTTOMLESSNESS
BOTTOMMOST
BOTTOMRIES
BOTTOMRY
BOTTOMS
BOTTS
BOTULIN
BOTULINAL
BOTULINS
BOTULINUM
BOTULINUMS
BOTULINUS
BOTULINUSES
BOTULISM
BOTULISMS
BOUBOU
BOUBOUS
BOUCHEE
BOUCHEES
BOUCLE
BOUCLES
BOUDIN
BOUDINS
BOUDOIR
BOUDOIRS
BOUFFANT
BOUFFANTS
BOUFFE
BOUFFES
BOUGAINVILLAEA
BOUGAINVILLAEAS
BOUGAINVILLEA
BOUGAINVILLEAS
BOUGH
BOUGHED
BOUGHLESS
BOUGHPOT
BOUGHPOTS
BOUGHS
BOUGHT
BOUGHTEN
BOUGIE
BOUGIES
BOUILLABAISSE
BOUILLABAISSES
BOUILLON
BOUILLONS
BOULDER
BOULDERED
BOULDERER
BOULDERERS
BOULDERING
BOULDERS
BOULDERY
BOULE
BOULES
BOULESES
BOULEVARD
BOULEVARDIER
BOULEVARDIERS
BOULEVARDS
BOULEVERSEMENT
BOULEVERSEMENTS
BOULLE
BOULLES
BOULT
BOULTED
BOULTING
BOULTS
BOUNCE
BOUNCED
BOUNCER
BOUNCERS
BOUNCES
BOUNCIER
BOUNCIEST
BOUNCILY
BOUNCINESS
BOUNCINESSES
BOUNCING
BOUNCINGLY
BOUNCY
BOUND
BOUNDABLE
BOUNDARIES
BOUNDARY
BOUNDARYLESS
BOUNDED
BOUNDEDNESS
BOUNDEDNESSES
BOUNDEN
BOUNDER
BOUNDERISH
BOUNDERS
BOUNDING
BOUNDLESS
BOUNDLESSLY
BOUNDLESSNESS
BOUNDLESSNESSES
BOUNDNESS
BOUNDNESSES
BOUNDS
BOUNTEOUS
BOUNTEOUSLY
BOUNTEOUSNESS
BOUNTEOUSNESSES
BOUNTIED
BOUNTIES
BOUNTIFUL
BOUNTIFULLY
BOUNTIFULNESS
BOUNTIFULNESSES
BOUNTY
BOUQUET
BOUQUETS
BOURBON
BOURBONISM
BOURBONISMS
BOURBONS
BOURDON
BOURDONS
BOURG
BOURGEOIS
BOURGEOISE
BOURGEOISES
BOURGEOISIE
BOURGEOISIES
BOURGEOISIFIED
BOURGEOISIFIES
BOURGEOISIFY
BOURGEOISIFYING
BOURGEON
BOURGEONED
BOURGEONING
BOURGEONS
BOURGS
BOURGUIGNON
BOURGUIGNONNE

BOURN
BOURNE
BOURNES
BOURNS
BOURREE
BOURREES
BOURRIDE
BOURRIDES
BOURSE
BOURSES
BOURSIN
BOURSINS
BOURTREE
BOURTREES
BOUSE
BOUSED
BOUSES
BOUSING
BOUSOUKI
BOUSOUKIA
BOUSOUKIS
BOUSTROPHEDON
BOUSTROPHEDONIC
BOUSTROPHEDONS
BOUSY
BOUT
BOUTADE
BOUTADES
BOUTIQUE
BOUTIQUES
BOUTIQUEY
BOUTON
BOUTONNIERE
BOUTONNIERES
BOUTONS
BOUTS
BOUVARDIA
BOUVARDIAS
BOUVIER
BOUVIERS
BOUZOUKI
BOUZOUKIA
BOUZOUKIS
BOVID
BOVIDS
BOVINE
BOVINELY
BOVINES
BOVINITIES
BOVINITY
BOVVER
BOVVERS
BOW
BOWDLERISE
BOWDLERISED
BOWDLERISES
BOWDLERISING
BOWDLERIZATION
BOWDLERIZATIONS
BOWDLERIZE
BOWDLERIZED
BOWDLERIZER
BOWDLERIZERS
BOWDLERIZES
BOWDLERIZING
BOWED
BOWEL
BOWELED
BOWELING
BOWELLED
BOWELLESS
BOWELLING
BOWELS
BOWER
BOWERBIRD
BOWERBIRDS
BOWERED
BOWERIES
BOWERING
BOWERS
BOWERY
BOWFIN
BOWFINS
BOWFRONT
BOWHEAD
BOWHEADS
BOWHUNT
BOWHUNTED
BOWHUNTER
BOWHUNTERS
BOWHUNTING
BOWHUNTINGS
BOWHUNTS
BOWING
BOWINGLY
BOWINGS
BOWKNOT
BOWKNOTS
BOWL
BOWLDER
BOWLDERS
BOWLED
BOWLEG
BOWLEGGED
BOWLEGS
BOWLER
BOWLERS
BOWLESS
BOWLFUL
BOWLFULS
BOWLIKE
BOWLINE
BOWLINES
BOWLING
BOWLINGS
BOWLLIKE
BOWLS
BOWMAN
BOWMEN
BOWPOT
BOWPOTS
BOWS
BOWSAW
BOWSAWS
BOWSE
BOWSED
BOWSER
BOWSERS
BOWSES
BOWSHOT
BOWSHOTS
BOWSING
BOWSMAN
BOWSMEN
BOWSPRIT
BOWSPRITS
BOWSTRING
BOWSTRINGED
BOWSTRINGING
BOWSTRINGS
BOWSTRUNG
BOWWOOD
BOWWOODS
BOWWOW
BOWWOWED
BOWWOWING
BOWWOWS
BOWYER
BOWYERS
BOX
BOXBALL
BOXBALLS
BOXBERRIES
BOXBERRY
BOXBOARD
BOXBOARDS
BOXCAR
BOXCARS
BOXED
BOXER
BOXERS
BOXES
BOXFISH
BOXFISHES
BOXFUL
BOXFULS
BOXHAUL
BOXHAULED
BOXHAULING
BOXHAULS
BOXIER
BOXIEST
BOXILY
BOXINESS
BOXINESSES
BOXING
BOXINGS
BOXLA
BOXLAS
BOXLIKE
BOXTHORN
BOXTHORNS
BOXWOOD
BOXWOODS
BOXY
BOY
BOYAR
BOYARD
BOYARDS
BOYARISM
BOYARISMS
BOYARS
BOYCHICK
BOYCHICKS
BOYCHIK
BOYCHIKS
BOYCOTT
BOYCOTTED
BOYCOTTER
BOYCOTTERS
BOYCOTTING
BOYCOTTS
BOYFRIEND
BOYFRIENDS
BOYHOOD
BOYHOODS
BOYISH
BOYISHLY
BOYISHNESS
BOYISHNESSES
BOYLA
BOYLAS
BOYO
BOYOS
BOYS
BOYSENBERRIES
BOYSENBERRY
BOZO
BOZOS
BRA
BRABBLE
BRABBLED
BRABBLER
BRABBLERS
BRABBLES
BRABBLING
BRACE
BRACED
BRACELET
BRACELETS
BRACER
BRACERO
BRACEROS
BRACERS
BRACES
BRACH
BRACHES
BRACHET
BRACHETS
BRACHIA
BRACHIAL
BRACHIALS
BRACHIATE
BRACHIATED
BRACHIATES
BRACHIATING
BRACHIATION
BRACHIATIONS
BRACHIATOR
BRACHIATORS
BRACHIOPOD
BRACHIOPODS
BRACHIOSAUR
BRACHIOSAURS
BRACHIUM
BRACHIUMS
BRACHS
BRACHYCEPHALIC
BRACHYCEPHALIES
BRACHYCEPHALY
BRACHYPTEROUS
BRACHYTHERAPIES
BRACHYTHERAPY
BRACING
BRACINGLY

BRACINGS
BRACIOLA
BRACIOLAS
BRACIOLE
BRACIOLES
BRACKEN
BRACKENS
BRACKET
BRACKETED
BRACKETING
BRACKETS
BRACKISH
BRACKISHNESS
BRACKISHNESSES
BRACONID
BRACONIDS
BRACT
BRACTEAL
BRACTEATE
BRACTED
BRACTEOLE
BRACTEOLES
BRACTLESS
BRACTLET
BRACTLETS
BRACTS
BRAD
BRADAWL
BRADAWLS
BRADDED
BRADDING
BRADOON
BRADOONS
BRADS
BRADYCARDIA
BRADYCARDIAS
BRADYKININ
BRADYKININS
BRAE
BRAES
BRAG
BRAGGADOCIO
BRAGGADOCIOS
BRAGGART
BRAGGARTS
BRAGGED
BRAGGER
BRAGGERS
BRAGGEST
BRAGGIER
BRAGGIEST
BRAGGING
BRAGGY
BRAGS
BRAHMA
BRAHMAN
BRAHMANS
BRAHMAS
BRAID
BRAIDED
BRAIDER
BRAIDERS
BRAIDING
BRAIDINGS
BRAIDS
BRAIL
BRAILED
BRAILING
BRAILLE
BRAILLED
BRAILLER
BRAILLERS
BRAILLES
BRAILLEWRITER
BRAILLEWRITERS
BRAILLING
BRAILLIST
BRAILLISTS
BRAILS
BRAIN
BRAINCASE
BRAINCASES
BRAINCHILD
BRAINCHILDREN
BRAINED
BRAINIAC
BRAINIACS
BRAINIER
BRAINIEST
BRAINILY
BRAININESS
BRAININESSES
BRAINING
BRAINISH
BRAINLESS
BRAINLESSLY
BRAINLESSNESS
BRAINLESSNESSES
BRAINPAN
BRAINPANS
BRAINPOWER
BRAINPOWERS
BRAINS
BRAINSICK
BRAINSICKLY
BRAINSTEM
BRAINSTEMS
BRAINSTORM
BRAINSTORMED
BRAINSTORMER
BRAINSTORMERS
BRAINSTORMING
BRAINSTORMINGS
BRAINSTORMS
BRAINTEASER
BRAINTEASERS
BRAINWASH
BRAINWASHED
BRAINWASHER
BRAINWASHERS
BRAINWASHES
BRAINWASHING
BRAINWASHINGS
BRAINY
BRAISE
BRAISED
BRAISES
BRAISING
BRAIZE
BRAIZES
BRAKE
BRAKEAGE
BRAKEAGES
BRAKED
BRAKELESS
BRAKEMAN
BRAKEMEN
BRAKES
BRAKIER
BRAKIEST
BRAKING
BRAKY
BRALESS
BRAMBLE
BRAMBLED
BRAMBLES
BRAMBLIER
BRAMBLIEST
BRAMBLING
BRAMBLINGS
BRAMBLY
BRAN
BRANCH
BRANCHED
BRANCHES
BRANCHIA
BRANCHIAE
BRANCHIAL
BRANCHIER
BRANCHIEST
BRANCHING
BRANCHIOPOD
BRANCHIOPODS
BRANCHLESS
BRANCHLET
BRANCHLETS
BRANCHLINE
BRANCHLINES
BRANCHY
BRAND
BRANDADE
BRANDADES
BRANDED
BRANDER
BRANDERS
BRANDIED
BRANDIES
BRANDING
BRANDINGS
BRANDISH
BRANDISHED
BRANDISHES
BRANDISHING
BRANDLESS
BRANDLING
BRANDLINGS
BRANDS
BRANDY
BRANDYING
BRANK
BRANKS
BRANNED
BRANNER
BRANNERS
BRANNIER
BRANNIEST
BRANNIGAN
BRANNIGANS
BRANNING
BRANNY
BRANS
BRANT
BRANTAIL
BRANTAILS
BRANTS
BRAS
BRASH
BRASHER
BRASHES
BRASHEST
BRASHIER
BRASHIEST
BRASHLY
BRASHNESS
BRASHNESSES
BRASHY
BRASIER
BRASIERS
BRASIL
BRASILEIN
BRASILEINS
BRASILIN
BRASILINS
BRASILS
BRASS
BRASSAGE
BRASSAGES
BRASSARD
BRASSARDS
BRASSART
BRASSARTS
BRASSBOUND
BRASSED
BRASSERIE
BRASSERIES
BRASSES
BRASSICA
BRASSICAS
BRASSIE
BRASSIER
BRASSIERE
BRASSIERES
BRASSIES
BRASSIEST
BRASSILY
BRASSINESS
BRASSINESSES
BRASSING
BRASSISH
BRASSWARE
BRASSWARES
BRASSY
BRAT
BRATS
BRATTICE
BRATTICED
BRATTICES
BRATTICING
BRATTIER
BRATTIEST
BRATTINESS
BRATTINESSES
BRATTISH
BRATTLE
BRATTLED

BRATTLES
BRATTLING
BRATTY
BRATWURST
BRATWURSTS
BRAUNITE
BRAUNITES
BRAUNSCHWEIGER
BRAUNSCHWEIGERS
BRAVA
BRAVADO
BRAVADOES
BRAVADOS
BRAVAS
BRAVE
BRAVED
BRAVELY
BRAVENESS
BRAVENESSES
BRAVER
BRAVERIES
BRAVERS
BRAVERY
BRAVES
BRAVEST
BRAVI
BRAVING
BRAVO
BRAVOED
BRAVOES
BRAVOING
BRAVOS
BRAVURA
BRAVURAS
BRAVURE
BRAW
BRAWER
BRAWEST
BRAWL
BRAWLED
BRAWLER
BRAWLERS
BRAWLIE
BRAWLIER
BRAWLIEST
BRAWLING
BRAWLS
BRAWLY
BRAWN
BRAWNIER
BRAWNIEST
BRAWNILY
BRAWNINESS
BRAWNINESSES
BRAWNS
BRAWNY
BRAWS
BRAXIES
BRAXY
BRAY
BRAYED
BRAYER
BRAYERS
BRAYING
BRAYS
BRAZA
BRAZAS
BRAZE
BRAZED
BRAZEN
BRAZENED
BRAZENING
BRAZENLY
BRAZENNESS
BRAZENNESSES
BRAZENS
BRAZER
BRAZERS
BRAZES
BRAZIER
BRAZIERS
BRAZIL
BRAZILEIN
BRAZILEINS
BRAZILIN
BRAZILINS
BRAZILS
BRAZILWOOD
BRAZILWOODS
BRAZING
BREACH
BREACHED
BREACHER
BREACHERS
BREACHES
BREACHING
BREAD
BREADBASKET
BREADBASKETS
BREADBOARD
BREADBOARDED
BREADBOARDING
BREADBOARDS
BREADBOX
BREADBOXES
BREADED
BREADFRUIT
BREADFRUITS
BREADING
BREADLESS
BREADLINE
BREADLINES
BREADNUT
BREADNUTS
BREADROOT
BREADROOTS
BREADS
BREADSTUFF
BREADSTUFFS
BREADTH
BREADTHS
BREADTHWISE
BREADWINNER
BREADWINNERS
BREADWINNING
BREADWINNINGS
BREADY
BREAK
BREAKABLE
BREAKABLES
BREAKAGE
BREAKAGES
BREAKAWAY
BREAKAWAYS
BREAKDOWN
BREAKDOWNS
BREAKER
BREAKERS
BREAKEVEN
BREAKEVENS
BREAKFAST
BREAKFASTED
BREAKFASTER
BREAKFASTERS
BREAKFASTING
BREAKFASTS
BREAKFRONT
BREAKFRONTS
BREAKING
BREAKINGS
BREAKNECK
BREAKOUT
BREAKOUTS
BREAKS
BREAKTHROUGH
BREAKTHROUGHS
BREAKUP
BREAKUPS
BREAKWALL
BREAKWALLS
BREAKWATER
BREAKWATERS
BREAM
BREAMED
BREAMING
BREAMS
BREAST
BREASTBONE
BREASTBONES
BREASTED
BREASTFED
BREASTFEED
BREASTFEEDING
BREASTFEEDS
BREASTING
BREASTPIN
BREASTPINS
BREASTPLATE
BREASTPLATES
BREASTS
BREASTSTROKE
BREASTSTROKER
BREASTSTROKERS
BREASTSTROKES
BREASTWORK
BREASTWORKS
BREATH
BREATHABILITIES
BREATHABILITY
BREATHABLE
BREATHE
BREATHED
BREATHER
BREATHERS
BREATHES
BREATHIER
BREATHIEST
BREATHILY
BREATHINESS
BREATHINESSES
BREATHING
BREATHINGS
BREATHLESS
BREATHLESSLY
BREATHLESSNESS
BREATHS
BREATHTAKING
BREATHTAKINGLY
BREATHY
BRECCIA
BRECCIAL
BRECCIAS
BRECCIATE
BRECCIATED
BRECCIATES
BRECCIATING
BRECCIATION
BRECCIATIONS
BRECHAM
BRECHAMS
BRECHAN
BRECHANS
BRED
BREDE
BREDES
BREE
BREECH
BREECHBLOCK
BREECHBLOCKS
BREECHCLOTH
BREECHCLOTHS
BREECHCLOUT
BREECHCLOUTS
BREECHED
BREECHES
BREECHING
BREECHINGS
BREECHLOADER
BREECHLOADERS
BREED
BREEDER
BREEDERS
BREEDING
BREEDINGS
BREEDS
BREEKS
BREES
BREEZE
BREEZED
BREEZELESS
BREEZES
BREEZEWAY
BREEZEWAYS
BREEZIER
BREEZIEST
BREEZILY
BREEZINESS
BREEZINESSES
BREEZING
BREEZY
BREGMA
BREGMAS
BREGMATA
BREGMATE
BREGMATIC

BREKKIE
BREKKIES
BREMSSTRAHLUNG
BREMSSTRAHLUNGS
BREN
BRENS
BRENT
BRENTS
BRESAOLA
BRESAOLAS
BRETHREN
BREVE
BREVES
BREVET
BREVETCIES
BREVETCY
BREVETED
BREVETING
BREVETS
BREVETTED
BREVETTING
BREVIARIES
BREVIARY
BREVIER
BREVIERS
BREVITIES
BREVITY
BREW
BREWAGE
BREWAGES
BREWED
BREWER
BREWERIES
BREWERS
BREWERY
BREWING
BREWINGS
BREWIS
BREWISES
BREWMASTER
BREWMASTERS
BREWPUB
BREWPUBS
BREWS
BREWSKI
BREWSKIES
BREWSKIS
BRIAR
BRIARD
BRIARDS
BRIARROOT
BRIARROOTS
BRIARS
BRIARWOOD
BRIARWOODS
BRIARY
BRIBABLE
BRIBE
BRIBED
BRIBEE
BRIBEES
BRIBER
BRIBERIES
BRIBERS
BRIBERY
BRIBES
BRIBING
BRICK
BRICKBAT
BRICKBATS
BRICKED
BRICKFIELD
BRICKFIELDS
BRICKIER
BRICKIEST
BRICKING
BRICKKILN
BRICKKILNS
BRICKLAYER
BRICKLAYERS
BRICKLAYING
BRICKLAYINGS
BRICKLE
BRICKLES
BRICKLIKE
BRICKS
BRICKWORK
BRICKWORKS
BRICKY
BRICKYARD
BRICKYARDS
BRICOLAGE
BRICOLAGES
BRICOLE
BRICOLES
BRICOLEUR
BRICOLEURS
BRIDAL
BRIDALLY
BRIDALS
BRIDE
BRIDEGROOM
BRIDEGROOMS
BRIDES
BRIDESMAID
BRIDESMAIDS
BRIDEWELL
BRIDEWELLS
BRIDGE
BRIDGEABLE
BRIDGED
BRIDGEHEAD
BRIDGEHEADS
BRIDGELESS
BRIDGES
BRIDGEWORK
BRIDGEWORKS
BRIDGING
BRIDGINGS
BRIDIE
BRIDIES
BRIDLE
BRIDLED
BRIDLER
BRIDLERS
BRIDLES
BRIDLING
BRIDOON
BRIDOONS
BRIE
BRIEF
BRIEFCASE
BRIEFCASES
BRIEFED
BRIEFER
BRIEFERS
BRIEFEST
BRIEFING
BRIEFINGS
BRIEFLESS
BRIEFLY
BRIEFNESS
BRIEFNESSES
BRIEFS
BRIER
BRIERROOT
BRIERROOTS
BRIERS
BRIERWOOD
BRIERWOODS
BRIERY
BRIES
BRIG
BRIGADE
BRIGADED
BRIGADES
BRIGADIER
BRIGADIERS
BRIGADING
BRIGAND
BRIGANDAGE
BRIGANDAGES
BRIGANDINE
BRIGANDINES
BRIGANDS
BRIGANTINE
BRIGANTINES
BRIGHT
BRIGHTEN
BRIGHTENED
BRIGHTENER
BRIGHTENERS
BRIGHTENING
BRIGHTENS
BRIGHTER
BRIGHTEST
BRIGHTISH
BRIGHTLY
BRIGHTNESS
BRIGHTNESSES
BRIGHTS
BRIGHTWORK
BRIGHTWORKS
BRIGS
BRILL
BRILLER
BRILLEST
BRILLIANCE
BRILLIANCES
BRILLIANCIES
BRILLIANCY
BRILLIANT
BRILLIANTINE
BRILLIANTINES
BRILLIANTLY
BRILLIANTS
BRILLO
BRILLOS
BRILLS
BRIM
BRIMFUL
BRIMFULL
BRIMFULLY
BRIMLESS
BRIMMED
BRIMMER
BRIMMERS
BRIMMING
BRIMS
BRIMSTONE
BRIMSTONES
BRIMSTONY
BRIN
BRINDED
BRINDLE
BRINDLED
BRINDLES
BRINE
BRINED
BRINELESS
BRINER
BRINERS
BRINES
BRING
BRINGDOWN
BRINGDOWNS
BRINGER
BRINGERS
BRINGING
BRINGS
BRINIER
BRINIES
BRINIEST
BRININESS
BRININESSES
BRINING
BRINISH
BRINK
BRINKMANSHIP
BRINKMANSHIPS
BRINKS
BRINKSMANSHIP
BRINKSMANSHIPS
BRINS
BRINY
BRIO
BRIOCHE
BRIOCHES
BRIOLETTE
BRIOLETTES
BRIONIES
BRIONY
BRIOS
BRIQUET
BRIQUETS
BRIQUETTE
BRIQUETTED
BRIQUETTES
BRIQUETTING
BRIS
BRISANCE
BRISANCES
BRISANT
BRISES
BRISK

BRISKED
BRISKER
BRISKEST
BRISKET
BRISKETS
BRISKING
BRISKLY
BRISKNESS
BRISKNESSES
BRISKS
BRISLING
BRISLINGS
BRISS
BRISSES
BRISTLE
BRISTLED
BRISTLELIKE
BRISTLES
BRISTLETAIL
BRISTLETAILS
BRISTLIER
BRISTLIEST
BRISTLING
BRISTLY
BRISTOL
BRISTOLS
BRIT
BRITANNIA
BRITANNIAS
BRITCHES
BRITH
BRITHS
BRITS
BRITSKA
BRITSKAS
BRITT
BRITTANIA
BRITTANIAS
BRITTLE
BRITTLEBUSH
BRITTLEBUSHES
BRITTLED
BRITTLELY
BRITTLENESS
BRITTLENESSES
BRITTLER
BRITTLES
BRITTLEST
BRITTLING
BRITTLY
BRITTS
BRITZKA
BRITZKAS
BRITZSKA
BRITZSKAS
BRO
BROACH
BROACHED
BROACHER
BROACHERS
BROACHES
BROACHING
BROAD
BROADAX
BROADAXE
BROADAXES
BROADBAND
BROADBANDS
BROADBEAN
BROADBEANS
BROADBILL
BROADBILLS
BROADCAST
BROADCASTED
BROADCASTER
BROADCASTERS
BROADCASTING
BROADCASTS
BROADCLOTH
BROADCLOTHS
BROADEN
BROADENED
BROADENER
BROADENERS
BROADENING
BROADENS
BROADER
BROADEST
BROADISH
BROADLEAF
BROADLEAVES
BROADLOOM
BROADLOOMS
BROADLY
BROADNESS
BROADNESSES
BROADS
BROADSCALE
BROADSHEET
BROADSHEETS
BROADSIDE
BROADSIDED
BROADSIDES
BROADSIDING
BROADSWORD
BROADSWORDS
BROADTAIL
BROADTAILS
BROADWAY
BROADWAYS
BROAST
BROASTED
BROASTING
BROASTS
BROCADE
BROCADED
BROCADES
BROCADING
BROCATEL
BROCATELLE
BROCATELLES
BROCATELS
BROCCOLI
BROCCOLIS
BROCH
BROCHE
BROCHETTE
BROCHETTES
BROCHS
BROCHURE
BROCHURES
BROCK
BROCKAGE
BROCKAGES
BROCKET
BROCKETS
BROCKS
BROCOLI
BROCOLIS
BROGAN
BROGANS
BROGUE
BROGUERIES
BROGUERY
BROGUES
BROGUISH
BROIDER
BROIDERED
BROIDERER
BROIDERERS
BROIDERIES
BROIDERING
BROIDERS
BROIDERY
BROIL
BROILED
BROILER
BROILERS
BROILING
BROILS
BROKAGE
BROKAGES
BROKE
BROKEN
BROKENHEARTED
BROKENLY
BROKENNESS
BROKENNESSES
BROKER
BROKERAGE
BROKERAGES
BROKERED
BROKERING
BROKERINGS
BROKERS
BROKING
BROKINGS
BROLGA
BROLGAS
BROLLIES
BROLLY
BROMAL
BROMALS
BROMANCE
BROMANCES
BROMANTIC
BROMATE
BROMATED
BROMATES
BROMATING
BROME
BROMEGRASS
BROMEGRASSES
BROMELAIN
BROMELAINS
BROMELIA
BROMELIAD
BROMELIADS
BROMELIAS
BROMELIN
BROMELINS
BROMES
BROMIC
BROMID
BROMIDE
BROMIDES
BROMIDIC
BROMIDS
BROMIN
BROMINATE
BROMINATED
BROMINATES
BROMINATING
BROMINATION
BROMINATIONS
BROMINE
BROMINES
BROMINISM
BROMINISMS
BROMINS
BROMISM
BROMISMS
BROMIZE
BROMIZED
BROMIZES
BROMIZING
BROMO
BROMOCRIPTINE
BROMOCRIPTINES
BROMOS
BROMOURACIL
BROMOURACILS
BRONC
BRONCHI
BRONCHIA
BRONCHIAL
BRONCHIALLY
BRONCHIECTASES
BRONCHIECTASIS
BRONCHIOLAR
BRONCHIOLE
BRONCHIOLES
BRONCHIOLITES
BRONCHIOLITIS
BRONCHITIC
BRONCHITIS
BRONCHITISES
BRONCHIUM
BRONCHO
BRONCHODILATOR
BRONCHODILATORS
BRONCHOGENIC
BRONCHOS
BRONCHOSCOPE
BRONCHOSCOPES
BRONCHOSCOPIC
BRONCHOSCOPIES
BRONCHOSCOPIST
BRONCHOSCOPISTS
BRONCHOSCOPY
BRONCHOSPASM
BRONCHOSPASMS
BRONCHOSPASTIC
BRONCHUS
BRONCO

BRONCOBUSTER
BRONCOBUSTERS
BRONCOS
BRONCS
BRONTOSAUR
BRONTOSAURS
BRONTOSAURUS
BRONTOSAURUSES
BRONZE
BRONZED
BRONZER
BRONZERS
BRONZES
BRONZIER
BRONZIEST
BRONZING
BRONZINGS
BRONZY
BROO
BROOCH
BROOCHES
BROOD
BROODED
BROODER
BROODERS
BROODIER
BROODIEST
BROODILY
BROODINESS
BROODINESSES
BROODING
BROODINGLY
BROODLESS
BROODMARE
BROODMARES
BROODS
BROODY
BROOK
BROOKED
BROOKIE
BROOKIES
BROOKING
BROOKITE
BROOKITES
BROOKLET
BROOKLETS
BROOKLIKE
BROOKLIME
BROOKLIMES
BROOKS
BROOM
BROOMBALL
BROOMBALLER
BROOMBALLERS
BROOMBALLS
BROOMCORN
BROOMCORNS
BROOMED
BROOMIER
BROOMIEST
BROOMING
BROOMRAPE
BROOMRAPES
BROOMS
BROOMSTICK
BROOMSTICKS
BROOMY
BROOS
BROS
BROSE
BROSES
BROSY
BROTH
BROTHEL
BROTHELS
BROTHER
BROTHERED
BROTHERHOOD
BROTHERHOODS
BROTHERING
BROTHERLINESS
BROTHERLINESSES
BROTHERLY
BROTHERS
BROTHS
BROTHY
BROUGHAM
BROUGHAMS
BROUGHT
BROUHAHA
BROUHAHAS
BROW
BROWALLIA
BROWALLIAS
BROWBAND
BROWBANDS
BROWBEAT
BROWBEATEN
BROWBEATING
BROWBEATS
BROWBONE
BROWBONES
BROWED
BROWLESS
BROWN
BROWNED
BROWNER
BROWNERS
BROWNEST
BROWNFIELD
BROWNFIELDS
BROWNIE
BROWNIER
BROWNIES
BROWNIEST
BROWNING
BROWNINGS
BROWNISH
BROWNNESS
BROWNNESSES
BROWNNOSE
BROWNNOSED
BROWNNOSER
BROWNNOSERS
BROWNNOSES
BROWNNOSING
BROWNOUT
BROWNOUTS
BROWNS
BROWNSHIRT
BROWNSHIRTS
BROWNSTONE
BROWNSTONES
BROWNY
BROWRIDGE
BROWRIDGES
BROWS
BROWSABLE
BROWSABLES
BROWSE
BROWSED
BROWSER
BROWSERS
BROWSES
BROWSING
BRR
BRRR
BRUCELLA
BRUCELLAE
BRUCELLAS
BRUCELLOSES
BRUCELLOSIS
BRUCIN
BRUCINE
BRUCINES
BRUCINS
BRUCITE
BRUCITES
BRUGH
BRUGHS
BRUIN
BRUINS
BRUISE
BRUISED
BRUISER
BRUISERS
BRUISES
BRUISING
BRUISINGS
BRUIT
BRUITED
BRUITER
BRUITERS
BRUITING
BRUITS
BRULOT
BRULOTS
BRULYIE
BRULYIES
BRULZIE
BRULZIES
BRUMAL
BRUMBIES
BRUMBY
BRUME
BRUMES
BRUMMAGEM
BRUMMAGEMS
BRUMOUS
BRUNCH
BRUNCHED
BRUNCHER
BRUNCHERS
BRUNCHES
BRUNCHING
BRUNET
BRUNETS
BRUNETTE
BRUNETTES
BRUNG
BRUNIZEM
BRUNIZEMS
BRUNT
BRUNTS
BRUSCHETTA
BRUSCHETTAS
BRUSH
BRUSHABILITIES
BRUSHABILITY
BRUSHBACK
BRUSHBACKS
BRUSHED
BRUSHER
BRUSHERS
BRUSHES
BRUSHFIRE
BRUSHFIRES
BRUSHIER
BRUSHIEST
BRUSHING
BRUSHLAND
BRUSHLANDS
BRUSHLESS
BRUSHOFF
BRUSHOFFS
BRUSHSTROKE
BRUSHSTROKES
BRUSHUP
BRUSHUPS
BRUSHWOOD
BRUSHWOODS
BRUSHWORK
BRUSHWORKS
BRUSHY
BRUSK
BRUSKER
BRUSKEST
BRUSQUE
BRUSQUELY
BRUSQUENESS
BRUSQUENESSES
BRUSQUER
BRUSQUERIE
BRUSQUERIES
BRUSQUEST
BRUT
BRUTAL
BRUTALISATION
BRUTALISATIONS
BRUTALISE
BRUTALISED
BRUTALISES
BRUTALISING
BRUTALITIES
BRUTALITY
BRUTALIZATION
BRUTALIZATIONS
BRUTALIZE
BRUTALIZED
BRUTALIZES
BRUTALIZING
BRUTALLY
BRUTE
BRUTED
BRUTELY

BRUTER
BRUTES
BRUTEST
BRUTIFIED
BRUTIFIES
BRUTIFY
BRUTIFYING
BRUTING
BRUTISH
BRUTISHLY
BRUTISHNESS
BRUTISHNESSES
BRUTISM
BRUTISMS
BRUTS
BRUX
BRUXED
BRUXES
BRUXING
BRUXISM
BRUXISMS
BRYOLOGICAL
BRYOLOGIES
BRYOLOGIST
BRYOLOGISTS
BRYOLOGY
BRYONIES
BRYONY
BRYOPHYLLUM
BRYOPHYLLUMS
BRYOPHYTE
BRYOPHYTES
BRYOPHYTIC
BRYOZOAN
BRYOZOANS
BUB
BUBAL
BUBALE
BUBALES
BUBALINE
BUBALIS
BUBALISES
BUBALS
BUBBA
BUBBAS
BUBBE
BUBBES
BUBBIE
BUBBIES
BUBBLE
BUBBLED
BUBBLEGUM
BUBBLEGUMS
BUBBLEHEAD
BUBBLEHEADED
BUBBLEHEADS
BUBBLER
BUBBLERS
BUBBLES
BUBBLIER
BUBBLIES
BUBBLIEST
BUBBLING
BUBBLY
BUBBY
BUBINGA
BUBINGAS
BUBKES
BUBO
BUBOED
BUBOES
BUBONIC
BUBS
BUBU
BUBUS
BUCCAL
BUCCALLY
BUCCANEER
BUCCANEERED
BUCCANEERING
BUCCANEERISH
BUCCANEERS
BUCCINATOR
BUCCINATORS
BUCK
BUCKAROO
BUCKAROOS
BUCKAYRO
BUCKAYROS
BUCKBEAN
BUCKBEANS
BUCKBOARD
BUCKBOARDS
BUCKBRUSH
BUCKBRUSHES
BUCKED
BUCKEEN
BUCKEENS
BUCKER
BUCKEROO
BUCKEROOS
BUCKERS
BUCKET
BUCKETED
BUCKETFUL
BUCKETFULS
BUCKETING
BUCKETS
BUCKETSFUL
BUCKEYE
BUCKEYES
BUCKHOUND
BUCKHOUNDS
BUCKING
BUCKISH
BUCKLE
BUCKLED
BUCKLER
BUCKLERED
BUCKLERING
BUCKLERS
BUCKLES
BUCKLING
BUCKO
BUCKOES
BUCKOS
BUCKRA
BUCKRAM
BUCKRAMED
BUCKRAMING
BUCKRAMS
BUCKRAS
BUCKS
BUCKSAW
BUCKSAWS
BUCKSHEE
BUCKSHEES
BUCKSHOT
BUCKSHOTS
BUCKSKIN
BUCKSKINNED
BUCKSKINS
BUCKTAIL
BUCKTAILS
BUCKTEETH
BUCKTHORN
BUCKTHORNS
BUCKTOOTH
BUCKTOOTHED
BUCKWHEAT
BUCKWHEATS
BUCKYBALL
BUCKYBALLS
BUCKYTUBE
BUCKYTUBES
BUCOLIC
BUCOLICALLY
BUCOLICS
BUD
BUDDED
BUDDER
BUDDERS
BUDDHA
BUDDHAS
BUDDIED
BUDDIES
BUDDING
BUDDINGS
BUDDLE
BUDDLEIA
BUDDLEIAS
BUDDLES
BUDDY
BUDDYING
BUDGE
BUDGED
BUDGER
BUDGERIGAR
BUDGERIGARS
BUDGERS
BUDGES
BUDGET
BUDGETARY
BUDGETED
BUDGETEER
BUDGETEERS
BUDGETER
BUDGETERS
BUDGETING
BUDGETINGS
BUDGETS
BUDGIE
BUDGIES
BUDGING
BUDLESS
BUDLIKE
BUDS
BUDWOOD
BUDWOODS
BUDWORM
BUDWORMS
BUFF
BUFFABLE
BUFFALO
BUFFALOBERRIES
BUFFALOBERRY
BUFFALOED
BUFFALOES
BUFFALOFISH
BUFFALOFISHES
BUFFALOING
BUFFALOS
BUFFED
BUFFER
BUFFERED
BUFFERING
BUFFERS
BUFFEST
BUFFET
BUFFETED
BUFFETER
BUFFETERS
BUFFETING
BUFFETINGS
BUFFETS
BUFFI
BUFFIER
BUFFIEST
BUFFING
BUFFLEHEAD
BUFFLEHEADS
BUFFO
BUFFOON
BUFFOONERIES
BUFFOONERY
BUFFOONISH
BUFFOONS
BUFFOS
BUFFS
BUFFY
BUG
BUGABOO
BUGABOOS
BUGBANE
BUGBANES
BUGBEAR
BUGBEARS
BUGEYE
BUGEYES
BUGGED
BUGGER
BUGGERED
BUGGERIES
BUGGERING
BUGGERS
BUGGERY
BUGGIER
BUGGIES
BUGGIEST
BUGGINESS
BUGGINESSES
BUGGING
BUGGY
BUGHOUSE
BUGHOUSES

BUGLE
BUGLED
BUGLER
BUGLERS
BUGLES
BUGLEWEED
BUGLEWEEDS
BUGLING
BUGLOSS
BUGLOSSES
BUGOUT
BUGOUTS
BUGS
BUGSEED
BUGSEEDS
BUGSHA
BUGSHAS
BUHL
BUHLS
BUHLWORK
BUHLWORKS
BUHR
BUHRS
BUHRSTONE
BUHRSTONES
BUILD
BUILDABLE
BUILDDOWN
BUILDDOWNS
BUILDED
BUILDER
BUILDERS
BUILDING
BUILDINGS
BUILDS
BUILDUP
BUILDUPS
BUILT
BUIRDLY
BULB
BULBAR
BULBED
BULBEL
BULBELS
BULBIL
BULBILS
BULBLET
BULBLETS
BULBOUS
BULBOUSLY
BULBS
BULBUL
BULBULS
BULGAR
BULGARS
BULGE
BULGED
BULGER
BULGERS
BULGES
BULGHUR
BULGHURS
BULGIER
BULGIEST
BULGINESS
BULGINESSES
BULGING
BULGINGLY
BULGUR
BULGURS
BULGY
BULIMIA
BULIMIAC
BULIMIAS
BULIMIC
BULIMICS
BULK
BULKAGE
BULKAGES
BULKED
BULKER
BULKERS
BULKHEAD
BULKHEADS
BULKIER
BULKIEST
BULKILY
BULKINESS
BULKINESSES
BULKING
BULKS
BULKY
BULL
BULLA
BULLACE
BULLACES
BULLAE
BULLATE
BULLBAITING
BULLBAITINGS
BULLBAT
BULLBATS
BULLBRIER
BULLBRIERS
BULLCOOK
BULLCOOKS
BULLDIKE
BULLDIKES
BULLDOG
BULLDOGGED
BULLDOGGER
BULLDOGGERS
BULLDOGGING
BULLDOGGINGS
BULLDOGS
BULLDOZE
BULLDOZED
BULLDOZER
BULLDOZERS
BULLDOZES
BULLDOZING
BULLDYKE
BULLDYKES
BULLED
BULLET
BULLETED
BULLETIN
BULLETINED
BULLETING
BULLETINING
BULLETINS
BULLETPROOF
BULLETS
BULLEY
BULLEYS
BULLFIGHT
BULLFIGHTER
BULLFIGHTERS
BULLFIGHTING
BULLFIGHTINGS
BULLFIGHTS
BULLFINCH
BULLFINCHES
BULLFROG
BULLFROGS
BULLHEAD
BULLHEADED
BULLHEADEDLY
BULLHEADEDNESS
BULLHEADS
BULLHORN
BULLHORNS
BULLIED
BULLIER
BULLIES
BULLIEST
BULLING
BULLION
BULLIONS
BULLISH
BULLISHLY
BULLISHNESS
BULLISHNESSES
BULLMASTIFF
BULLMASTIFFS
BULLNECK
BULLNECKED
BULLNECKS
BULLNOSE
BULLNOSED
BULLNOSES
BULLOCK
BULLOCKS
BULLOCKY
BULLOUS
BULLPEN
BULLPENS
BULLPOUT
BULLPOUTS
BULLRING
BULLRINGS
BULLRUSH
BULLRUSHES
BULLS
BULLSEYE
BULLSEYES
BULLSHAT
BULLSHIT
BULLSHITS
BULLSHITTED
BULLSHITTER
BULLSHITTERS
BULLSHITTING
BULLSHOT
BULLSHOTS
BULLSNAKE
BULLSNAKES
BULLTERRIER
BULLTERRIERS
BULLWEED
BULLWEEDS
BULLWHIP
BULLWHIPPED
BULLWHIPPING
BULLWHIPS
BULLY
BULLYBOY
BULLYBOYS
BULLYING
BULLYRAG
BULLYRAGGED
BULLYRAGGING
BULLYRAGS
BULRUSH
BULRUSHES
BULWARK
BULWARKED
BULWARKING
BULWARKS
BUM
BUMBAG
BUMBAGS
BUMBERSHOOT
BUMBERSHOOTS
BUMBLE
BUMBLEBEE
BUMBLEBEES
BUMBLED
BUMBLER
BUMBLERS
BUMBLES
BUMBLING
BUMBLINGLY
BUMBLINGS
BUMBOAT
BUMBOATS
BUMBOY
BUMBOYS
BUMELIA
BUMELIAS
BUMF
BUMFS
BUMFUZZLE
BUMFUZZLED
BUMFUZZLES
BUMFUZZLING
BUMKIN
BUMKINS
BUMMALO
BUMMALOS
BUMMED
BUMMER
BUMMERS
BUMMEST
BUMMING
BUMP
BUMPED
BUMPER
BUMPERED
BUMPERING
BUMPERS
BUMPH
BUMPHS
BUMPIER
BUMPIEST

BUMPILY
BUMPINESS
BUMPINESSES
BUMPING
BUMPKIN
BUMPKINISH
BUMPKINLY
BUMPKINS
BUMPS
BUMPTIOUS
BUMPTIOUSLY
BUMPTIOUSNESS
BUMPTIOUSNESSES
BUMPY
BUMS
BUMWAD
BUMWADS
BUN
BUNA
BUNAS
BUNCH
BUNCHBERRIES
BUNCHBERRY
BUNCHED
BUNCHER
BUNCHERS
BUNCHES
BUNCHGRASS
BUNCHGRASSES
BUNCHIER
BUNCHIEST
BUNCHILY
BUNCHING
BUNCHY
BUNCO
BUNCOED
BUNCOES
BUNCOING
BUNCOMBE
BUNCOMBES
BUNCOS
BUND
BUNDIST
BUNDISTS
BUNDLE
BUNDLED
BUNDLER
BUNDLERS
BUNDLES
BUNDLING
BUNDLINGS
BUNDS
BUNDT
BUNDTS
BUNFIGHT
BUNFIGHTS
BUNG
BUNGALOW
BUNGALOWS
BUNGED
BUNGEE
BUNGEES
BUNGHOLE
BUNGHOLES
BUNGING
BUNGLE
BUNGLED
BUNGLER
BUNGLERS
BUNGLES
BUNGLESOME
BUNGLING
BUNGLINGLY
BUNGLINGS
BUNGS
BUNHEAD
BUNHEADS
BUNION
BUNIONS
BUNK
BUNKED
BUNKER
BUNKERED
BUNKERING
BUNKERS
BUNKHOUSE
BUNKHOUSES
BUNKIE
BUNKIES
BUNKING
BUNKMATE
BUNKMATES
BUNKO
BUNKOED
BUNKOING
BUNKOS
BUNKS
BUNKUM
BUNKUMS
BUNN
BUNNIES
BUNNS
BUNNY
BUNRAKU
BUNRAKUS
BUNS
BUNT
BUNTED
BUNTER
BUNTERS
BUNTING
BUNTINGS
BUNTLINE
BUNTLINES
BUNTS
BUNYA
BUNYAS
BUNYAVIRUS
BUNYAVIRUSES
BUNYIP
BUNYIPS
BUOY
BUOYAGE
BUOYAGES
BUOYANCE
BUOYANCES
BUOYANCIES
BUOYANCY
BUOYANT
BUOYANTLY
BUOYED
BUOYING
BUOYS
BUPKES
BUPKIS
BUPKUS
BUPPIE
BUPPIES
BUPPY
BUPRESTID
BUPRESTIDS
BUQSHA
BUQSHAS
BUR
BURA
BURAN
BURANS
BURAS
BURB
BURBLE
BURBLED
BURBLER
BURBLERS
BURBLES
BURBLIER
BURBLIEST
BURBLING
BURBLINGS
BURBLY
BURBOT
BURBOTS
BURBS
BURD
BURDEN
BURDENED
BURDENER
BURDENERS
BURDENING
BURDENS
BURDENSOME
BURDIE
BURDIES
BURDOCK
BURDOCKS
BURDS
BUREAU
BUREAUCRACIES
BUREAUCRACY
BUREAUCRAT
BUREAUCRATESE
BUREAUCRATESES
BUREAUCRATIC
BUREAUCRATISE
BUREAUCRATISED
BUREAUCRATISES
BUREAUCRATISING
BUREAUCRATISM
BUREAUCRATISMS
BUREAUCRATIZE
BUREAUCRATIZED
BUREAUCRATIZES
BUREAUCRATIZING
BUREAUCRATS
BUREAUS
BUREAUX
BURET
BURETS
BURETTE
BURETTES
BURFI
BURFIS
BURG
BURGAGE
BURGAGES
BURGEE
BURGEES
BURGEON
BURGEONED
BURGEONING
BURGEONS
BURGER
BURGERS
BURGESS
BURGESSES
BURGH
BURGHAL
BURGHER
BURGHERS
BURGHS
BURGLAR
BURGLARIES
BURGLARIOUS
BURGLARIOUSLY
BURGLARIZE
BURGLARIZED
BURGLARIZES
BURGLARIZING
BURGLARPROOF
BURGLARS
BURGLARY
BURGLE
BURGLED
BURGLES
BURGLING
BURGOMASTER
BURGOMASTERS
BURGONET
BURGONETS
BURGOO
BURGOOS
BURGOUT
BURGOUTS
BURGRAVE
BURGRAVES
BURGS
BURGUNDIES
BURGUNDY
BURIAL
BURIALS
BURIED
BURIER
BURIERS
BURIES
BURIN
BURINS
BURK
BURKA
BURKAS
BURKE
BURKED
BURKER
BURKERS
BURKES
BURKHA
BURKHAS

BURKING
BURKITE
BURKITES
BURKS
BURL
BURLADERO
BURLADEROS
BURLAP
BURLAPS
BURLED
BURLER
BURLERS
BURLESK
BURLESKS
BURLESQUE
BURLESQUED
BURLESQUELY
BURLESQUER
BURLESQUERS
BURLESQUES
BURLESQUING
BURLEY
BURLEYS
BURLIER
BURLIEST
BURLILY
BURLINESS
BURLINESSES
BURLING
BURLS
BURLY
BURN
BURNABLE
BURNABLES
BURNED
BURNER
BURNERS
BURNET
BURNETS
BURNIE
BURNIES
BURNING
BURNINGLY
BURNINGS
BURNISH
BURNISHED
BURNISHER
BURNISHERS
BURNISHES
BURNISHING
BURNISHINGS
BURNOOSE
BURNOOSED
BURNOOSES
BURNOUS
BURNOUSES
BURNOUT
BURNOUTS
BURNS
BURNSIDE
BURNSIDES
BURNT
BURP
BURPED
BURPEE
BURPEES
BURPING
BURPS
BURQA
BURQAS
BURR
BURRED
BURRER
BURRERS
BURRFISH
BURRFISHES
BURRIER
BURRIEST
BURRING
BURRITO
BURRITOS
BURRO
BURROS
BURROW
BURROWED
BURROWER
BURROWERS
BURROWING
BURROWS
BURRS
BURRSTONE
BURRSTONES
BURRY
BURS
BURSA
BURSAE
BURSAL
BURSAR
BURSARIAL
BURSARIES
BURSARS
BURSARY
BURSAS
BURSATE
BURSE
BURSEED
BURSEEDS
BURSERA
BURSES
BURSIFORM
BURSITIS
BURSITISES
BURST
BURSTED
BURSTER
BURSTERS
BURSTIER
BURSTIEST
BURSTING
BURSTONE
BURSTONES
BURSTS
BURSTY
BURTHEN
BURTHENED
BURTHENING
BURTHENS
BURTON
BURTONS
BURWEED
BURWEEDS
BURY
BURYING
BUS
BUSBAR
BUSBARS
BUSBIES
BUSBOY
BUSBOYS
BUSBY
BUSED
BUSES
BUSGIRL
BUSGIRLS
BUSH
BUSHBABIES
BUSHBABY
BUSHBUCK
BUSHBUCKS
BUSHED
BUSHEL
BUSHELED
BUSHELER
BUSHELERS
BUSHELING
BUSHELLED
BUSHELLER
BUSHELLERS
BUSHELLING
BUSHELMAN
BUSHELMEN
BUSHELS
BUSHER
BUSHERS
BUSHES
BUSHFIRE
BUSHFIRES
BUSHGOAT
BUSHGOATS
BUSHIDO
BUSHIDOS
BUSHIER
BUSHIES
BUSHIEST
BUSHILY
BUSHINESS
BUSHINESSES
BUSHING
BUSHINGS
BUSHLAND
BUSHLANDS
BUSHLESS
BUSHLIKE
BUSHLOT
BUSHLOTS
BUSHMAN
BUSHMASTER
BUSHMASTERS
BUSHMEN
BUSHPIG
BUSHPIGS
BUSHRANGER
BUSHRANGERS
BUSHRANGING
BUSHRANGINGS
BUSHTIT
BUSHTITS
BUSHVELD
BUSHVELDS
BUSHWA
BUSHWAH
BUSHWAHS
BUSHWAS
BUSHWHACK
BUSHWHACKED
BUSHWHACKER
BUSHWHACKERS
BUSHWHACKING
BUSHWHACKS
BUSHY
BUSIED
BUSIER
BUSIES
BUSIEST
BUSILY
BUSINESS
BUSINESSES
BUSINESSLIKE
BUSINESSMAN
BUSINESSMEN
BUSINESSPEOPLE
BUSINESSPERSON
BUSINESSPERSONS
BUSINESSWOMAN
BUSINESSWOMEN
BUSING
BUSINGS
BUSK
BUSKED
BUSKER
BUSKERS
BUSKIN
BUSKINED
BUSKING
BUSKINGS
BUSKINS
BUSKS
BUSLOAD
BUSLOADS
BUSMAN
BUSMEN
BUSS
BUSSED
BUSSES
BUSSING
BUSSINGS
BUST
BUSTARD
BUSTARDS
BUSTED
BUSTEE
BUSTEES
BUSTER
BUSTERS
BUSTIC
BUSTICATE
BUSTICATED
BUSTICATES
BUSTICATING
BUSTICS
BUSTIER
BUSTIERS
BUSTIEST
BUSTINESS
BUSTINESSES

BUSTING
BUSTLE
BUSTLED
BUSTLER
BUSTLERS
BUSTLES
BUSTLINE
BUSTLINES
BUSTLING
BUSTLINGLY
BUSTS
BUSTY
BUSULFAN
BUSULFANS
BUSY
BUSYBODIES
BUSYBODY
BUSYING
BUSYNESS
BUSYNESSES
BUSYWORK
BUSYWORKS
BUT
BUTADIENE
BUTADIENES
BUTANE
BUTANES
BUTANOL
BUTANOLS
BUTANONE
BUTANONES
BUTCH
BUTCHER
BUTCHERED
BUTCHERER
BUTCHERERS
BUTCHERIES
BUTCHERING
BUTCHERLY
BUTCHERS
BUTCHERY
BUTCHES
BUTCHEST
BUTCHNESS
BUTCHNESSES
BUTE
BUTENE
BUTENES
BUTEO
BUTEONINE
BUTEONINES
BUTEOS
BUTES
BUTLE
BUTLED
BUTLER
BUTLERIES
BUTLERS
BUTLERY
BUTLES
BUTLING
BUTOH
BUTOHS
BUTS
BUTT
BUTTALS
BUTTE
BUTTED
BUTTER
BUTTERBALL
BUTTERBALLS
BUTTERBUR
BUTTERBURS
BUTTERCREAM
BUTTERCREAMS
BUTTERCUP
BUTTERCUPS
BUTTERED
BUTTERFAT
BUTTERFATS
BUTTERFINGERED
BUTTERFINGERS
BUTTERFISH
BUTTERFISHES
BUTTERFLIED
BUTTERFLIES
BUTTERFLY
BUTTERFLYER
BUTTERFLYERS
BUTTERFLYING
BUTTERHEAD
BUTTERHEADS
BUTTERIER
BUTTERIES
BUTTERIEST
BUTTERING
BUTTERLESS
BUTTERMILK
BUTTERMILKS
BUTTERNUT
BUTTERNUTS
BUTTERS
BUTTERSCOTCH
BUTTERSCOTCHES
BUTTERWEED
BUTTERWEEDS
BUTTERWORT
BUTTERWORTS
BUTTERY
BUTTES
BUTTHEAD
BUTTHEADS
BUTTIES
BUTTING
BUTTINSKI
BUTTINSKIES
BUTTINSKIS
BUTTINSKY
BUTTLE
BUTTLED
BUTTLES
BUTTLING
BUTTOCK
BUTTOCKS
BUTTON
BUTTONBALL
BUTTONBALLS
BUTTONBUSH
BUTTONBUSHES
BUTTONED
BUTTONER
BUTTONERS
BUTTONHOLE
BUTTONHOLED
BUTTONHOLER
BUTTONHOLERS
BUTTONHOLES
BUTTONHOLING
BUTTONHOOK
BUTTONHOOKED
BUTTONHOOKING
BUTTONHOOKS
BUTTONING
BUTTONLESS
BUTTONS
BUTTONWOOD
BUTTONWOODS
BUTTONY
BUTTRESS
BUTTRESSED
BUTTRESSES
BUTTRESSING
BUTTS
BUTTSTOCK
BUTTSTOCKS
BUTTY
BUTUT
BUTUTS
BUTYL
BUTYLATE
BUTYLATED
BUTYLATES
BUTYLATING
BUTYLATION
BUTYLATIONS
BUTYLENE
BUTYLENES
BUTYLS
BUTYRAL
BUTYRALDEHYDE
BUTYRALDEHYDES
BUTYRALS
BUTYRATE
BUTYRATES
BUTYRIC
BUTYRIN
BUTYRINS
BUTYROPHENONE
BUTYROPHENONES
BUTYROUS
BUTYRYL
BUTYRYLS
BUXOM
BUXOMER
BUXOMEST
BUXOMLY
BUXOMNESS
BUXOMNESSES
BUY
BUYABLE
BUYBACK
BUYBACKS
BUYER
BUYERS
BUYING
BUYOFF
BUYOFFS
BUYOUT
BUYOUTS
BUYS
BUZUKI
BUZUKIA
BUZUKIS
BUZZ
BUZZARD
BUZZARDS
BUZZBAIT
BUZZBAITS
BUZZCUT
BUZZCUTS
BUZZED
BUZZER
BUZZERS
BUZZES
BUZZIER
BUZZIEST
BUZZING
BUZZINGLY
BUZZINGS
BUZZKILL
BUZZKILLS
BUZZWIG
BUZZWIGS
BUZZWORD
BUZZWORDS
BUZZY
BWANA
BWANAS
BY
BYCATCH
BYCATCHES
BYE
BYELAW
BYELAWS
BYES
BYGONE
BYGONES
BYLAW
BYLAWS
BYLINE
BYLINED
BYLINER
BYLINERS
BYLINES
BYLINING
BYNAME
BYNAMES
BYPASS
BYPASSED
BYPASSES
BYPASSING
BYPAST
BYPATH
BYPATHS
BYPLAY
BYPLAYS
BYPRODUCT
BYPRODUCTS
BYRE
BYRES
BYRL
BYRLED
BYRLING
BYRLS
BYRNIE

BYRNIES
BYROAD
BYROADS
BYS
BYSSAL
BYSSI
BYSSINOSES
BYSSINOSIS
BYSSUS
BYSSUSES
BYSTANDER
BYSTANDERS
BYSTREET
BYSTREETS
BYTALK
BYTALKS
BYTE
BYTES
BYWAY
BYWAYS
BYWORD
BYWORDS
BYWORK
BYWORKS
BYZANT
BYZANTINE
BYZANTS

C

CAB
CABAL
CABALA
CABALAS
CABALETTA
CABALETTAS
CABALETTE
CABALISM
CABALISMS
CABALIST
CABALISTIC
CABALISTS
CABALLED
CABALLERO
CABALLEROS
CABALLING
CABALS
CABANA
CABANAS
CABARET
CABARETS
CABBAGE
CABBAGED
CABBAGES
CABBAGEWORM
CABBAGEWORMS
CABBAGEY
CABBAGING
CABBAGY
CABBALA
CABBALAH
CABBALAHS
CABBALAS
CABBALISM
CABBALISMS
CABBALIST
CABBALISTS
CABBED
CABBIE
CABBIES
CABBING
CABBY
CABDRIVER
CABDRIVERS
CABER
CABERNET
CABERNETS
CABERS
CABESTRO
CABESTROS
CABEZON
CABEZONE
CABEZONES
CABEZONS
CABILDO
CABILDOS
CABIN
CABINED
CABINET
CABINETMAKER
CABINETMAKERS
CABINETMAKING
CABINETMAKINGS
CABINETRIES
CABINETRY
CABINETS
CABINETWORK
CABINETWORKS
CABINING
CABINMATE
CABINMATES
CABINS
CABLE
CABLECAST
CABLECASTED
CABLECASTING
CABLECASTS
CABLED
CABLEGRAM
CABLEGRAMS
CABLER
CABLERS
CABLES
CABLET
CABLETS
CABLEWAY
CABLEWAYS
CABLING
CABLINGS
CABMAN
CABMEN
CABOB
CABOBS
CABOCHED
CABOCHON
CABOCHONS
CABOMBA
CABOMBAS
CABOODLE
CABOODLES
CABOOSE
CABOOSES
CABOSHED
CABOTAGE
CABOTAGES
CABOVER
CABOVERS
CABRESTA
CABRESTAS
CABRESTO
CABRESTOS
CABRETTA
CABRETTAS
CABRILLA
CABRILLAS
CABRIOLE
CABRIOLES
CABRIOLET
CABRIOLETS
CABS
CABSTAND
CABSTANDS
CACA
CACAO
CACAOS
CACAS
CACCIATORE
CACHACA
CACHACAS
CACHALOT
CACHALOTS
CACHE
CACHECTIC
CACHED
CACHEPOT
CACHEPOTS
CACHES
CACHET
CACHETED
CACHETING
CACHETS
CACHEXIA
CACHEXIAS
CACHEXIC
CACHEXIES
CACHEXY
CACHING
CACHINNATE
CACHINNATED
CACHINNATES
CACHINNATING
CACHINNATION
CACHINNATIONS
CACHOU
CACHOUS
CACHUCHA
CACHUCHAS
CACIQUE
CACIQUES
CACIQUISM
CACIQUISMS
CACKLE
CACKLED
CACKLER
CACKLERS
CACKLES
CACKLING
CACODEMON
CACODEMONIC
CACODEMONS
CACODYL
CACODYLIC
CACODYLS
CACOETHES
CACOGRAPHICAL
CACOGRAPHIES
CACOGRAPHY
CACOMISTLE
CACOMISTLES
CACOMIXL
CACOMIXLE
CACOMIXLES
CACOMIXLS
CACONYM
CACONYMIES

CACONYMS
CACONYMY
CACOPHONIES
CACOPHONOUS
CACOPHONOUSLY
CACOPHONY
CACTI
CACTOID
CACTUS
CACTUSES
CACUMINAL
CACUMINALS
CAD
CADASTER
CADASTERS
CADASTRAL
CADASTRALLY
CADASTRE
CADASTRES
CADAVER
CADAVERIC
CADAVERINE
CADAVERINES
CADAVEROUS
CADAVEROUSLY
CADAVERS
CADDICE
CADDICES
CADDIE
CADDIED
CADDIES
CADDIS
CADDISED
CADDISES
CADDISFLIES
CADDISFLY
CADDISH
CADDISHLY
CADDISHNESS
CADDISHNESSES
CADDISWORM
CADDISWORMS
CADDY
CADDYING
CADE
CADELLE
CADELLES
CADENCE
CADENCED
CADENCES
CADENCIES
CADENCING
CADENCY
CADENT
CADENTIAL
CADENZA
CADENZAS
CADES
CADET
CADETS
CADETSHIP
CADETSHIPS
CADGE
CADGED
CADGER
CADGERS
CADGES
CADGING
CADGY
CADI
CADIS
CADMIC
CADMIUM
CADMIUMS
CADRE
CADRES
CADS
CADUCEAN
CADUCEI
CADUCEUS
CADUCITIES
CADUCITY
CADUCOUS
CAECA
CAECAL
CAECALLY
CAECILIAN
CAECILIANS
CAECUM
CAEOMA
CAEOMAS
CAESAR
CAESAREAN
CAESAREANS
CAESARIAN
CAESARIANS
CAESARISM
CAESARISMS
CAESARS
CAESIOUS
CAESIUM
CAESIUMS
CAESPITOSE
CAESTUS
CAESTUSES
CAESURA
CAESURAE
CAESURAL
CAESURAS
CAESURIC
CAF
CAFARD
CAFARDS
CAFE
CAFES
CAFETERIA
CAFETERIAS
CAFETORIA
CAFETORIUM
CAFETORIUMS
CAFF
CAFFEIN
CAFFEINATED
CAFFEINE
CAFFEINES
CAFFEINIC
CAFFEINS
CAFFS
CAFS
CAFTAN
CAFTANED
CAFTANS
CAGE
CAGED
CAGEFUL
CAGEFULS
CAGELIKE
CAGELING
CAGELINGS
CAGER
CAGERS
CAGES
CAGEY
CAGEYNESS
CAGEYNESSES
CAGIER
CAGIEST
CAGILY
CAGINESS
CAGINESSES
CAGING
CAGOULE
CAGOULES
CAGY
CAHIER
CAHIERS
CAHOOT
CAHOOTS
CAHOUN
CAHOUNS
CAHOW
CAHOWS
CAID
CAIDS
CAIMAN
CAIMANS
CAIN
CAINS
CAIPIRINHA
CAIPIRINHAS
CAIQUE
CAIQUES
CAIRD
CAIRDS
CAIRN
CAIRNED
CAIRNGORM
CAIRNGORMS
CAIRNS
CAIRNY
CAISSON
CAISSONS
CAITIFF
CAITIFFS
CAJAPUT
CAJAPUTS
CAJEPUT
CAJEPUTS
CAJOLE
CAJOLED
CAJOLEMENT
CAJOLEMENTS
CAJOLER
CAJOLERIES
CAJOLERS
CAJOLERY
CAJOLES
CAJOLING
CAJON
CAJONES
CAJUPUT
CAJUPUTS
CAKE
CAKEBOX
CAKEBOXES
CAKED
CAKEHOLE
CAKEHOLES
CAKES
CAKEWALK
CAKEWALKED
CAKEWALKER
CAKEWALKERS
CAKEWALKING
CAKEWALKS
CAKEY
CAKIER
CAKIEST
CAKINESS
CAKINESSES
CAKING
CAKY
CAL
CALABASH
CALABASHES
CALABAZA
CALABAZAS
CALABOOSE
CALABOOSES
CALADIUM
CALADIUMS
CALAMANCO
CALAMANCOES
CALAMANCOS
CALAMANDER
CALAMANDERS
CALAMAR
CALAMARI
CALAMARIES
CALAMARIS
CALAMARS
CALAMARY
CALAMATA
CALAMATAS
CALAMI
CALAMINE
CALAMINED
CALAMINES
CALAMINING
CALAMINT
CALAMINTS
CALAMITE
CALAMITES
CALAMITIES
CALAMITOUS
CALAMITOUSLY
CALAMITY
CALAMONDIN
CALAMONDINS
CALAMUS
CALAMUSES
CALANDO
CALASH
CALASHES
CALATHEA

CALATHEAS
CALATHI
CALATHOS
CALATHUS
CALCANEA
CALCANEAL
CALCANEI
CALCANEUM
CALCANEUS
CALCAR
CALCARATE
CALCAREOUS
CALCAREOUSLY
CALCARIA
CALCARS
CALCEATE
CALCEDONIES
CALCEDONY
CALCES
CALCIC
CALCICOLE
CALCICOLES
CALCICOLOUS
CALCIFEROL
CALCIFEROLS
CALCIFEROUS
CALCIFIC
CALCIFICATION
CALCIFICATIONS
CALCIFIED
CALCIFIES
CALCIFUGE
CALCIFUGES
CALCIFUGOUS
CALCIFY
CALCIFYING
CALCIMINE
CALCIMINED
CALCIMINES
CALCIMINING
CALCINATION
CALCINATIONS
CALCINE
CALCINED
CALCINES
CALCINING
CALCINOSES
CALCINOSIS
CALCITE
CALCITES
CALCITIC
CALCITONIN
CALCITONINS
CALCIUM
CALCIUMS
CALCRETE
CALCRETES
CALCSPAR
CALCSPARS
CALCTUFA
CALCTUFAS
CALCTUFF
CALCTUFFS
CALCULABLE
CALCULATE
CALCULATED
CALCULATEDLY
CALCULATEDNESS
CALCULATES
CALCULATING
CALCULATINGLY
CALCULATION
CALCULATIONAL
CALCULATIONS
CALCULATOR
CALCULATORS
CALCULI
CALCULOUS
CALCULUS
CALCULUSES
CALDARIA
CALDARIUM
CALDERA
CALDERAS
CALDRON
CALDRONS
CALECHE
CALECHES
CALEFACTORIES
CALEFACTORY
CALENDAL
CALENDAR
CALENDARED
CALENDARING
CALENDARS
CALENDER
CALENDERED
CALENDERER
CALENDERERS
CALENDERING
CALENDERS
CALENDRIC
CALENDRICAL
CALENDS
CALENDULA
CALENDULAS
CALENTURE
CALENTURES
CALESA
CALESAS
CALESCENT
CALF
CALFHOOD
CALFHOODS
CALFLIKE
CALFS
CALFSKIN
CALFSKINS
CALIBER
CALIBERED
CALIBERS
CALIBRATE
CALIBRATED
CALIBRATES
CALIBRATING
CALIBRATION
CALIBRATIONS
CALIBRATOR
CALIBRATORS
CALIBRE
CALIBRED
CALIBRES
CALICES
CALICHE
CALICHES
CALICLE
CALICLES
CALICO
CALICOES
CALICOS
CALIF
CALIFATE
CALIFATES
CALIFORNIUM
CALIFORNIUMS
CALIFS
CALIGINOUS
CALIPASH
CALIPASHES
CALIPEE
CALIPEES
CALIPER
CALIPERED
CALIPERING
CALIPERS
CALIPH
CALIPHAL
CALIPHATE
CALIPHATES
CALIPHS
CALISAYA
CALISAYAS
CALISTHENIC
CALISTHENICS
CALIX
CALIXES
CALK
CALKED
CALKER
CALKERS
CALKIN
CALKING
CALKINGS
CALKINS
CALKS
CALL
CALLA
CALLABLE
CALLALOO
CALLALOOS
CALLALOU
CALLALOUS
CALLAN
CALLANS
CALLANT
CALLANTS
CALLAS
CALLBACK
CALLBACKS
CALLBOARD
CALLBOARDS
CALLBOY
CALLBOYS
CALLED
CALLEE
CALLEES
CALLER
CALLERS
CALLET
CALLETS
CALLIGRAPHED
CALLIGRAPHER
CALLIGRAPHERS
CALLIGRAPHIC
CALLIGRAPHIES
CALLIGRAPHIST
CALLIGRAPHISTS
CALLIGRAPHY
CALLING
CALLINGS
CALLIOPE
CALLIOPES
CALLIPEE
CALLIPEES
CALLIPER
CALLIPERED
CALLIPERING
CALLIPERS
CALLIPYGIAN
CALLIPYGOUS
CALLISTHENIC
CALLISTHENICS
CALLITHUMP
CALLITHUMPIAN
CALLITHUMPS
CALLOSE
CALLOSES
CALLOSITIES
CALLOSITY
CALLOUS
CALLOUSED
CALLOUSES
CALLOUSING
CALLOUSLY
CALLOUSNESS
CALLOUSNESSES
CALLOUT
CALLOUTS
CALLOW
CALLOWER
CALLOWEST
CALLOWLY
CALLOWNESS
CALLOWNESSES
CALLS
CALLUNA
CALLUNAS
CALLUS
CALLUSED
CALLUSES
CALLUSING
CALM
CALMATIVE
CALMATIVES
CALMED
CALMER
CALMEST
CALMING
CALMINGLY
CALMLY
CALMNESS
CALMNESSES
CALMODULIN
CALMODULINS
CALMS

CALO
CALOMEL
CALOMELS
CALORIC
CALORICALLY
CALORICS
CALORIE
CALORIES
CALORIFIC
CALORIMETER
CALORIMETERS
CALORIMETRIC
CALORIMETRIES
CALORIMETRY
CALORIZE
CALORIZED
CALORIZES
CALORIZING
CALORY
CALOS
CALOTTE
CALOTTES
CALOTYPE
CALOTYPES
CALOYER
CALOYERS
CALPAC
CALPACK
CALPACKS
CALPACS
CALPAIN
CALPAINS
CALQUE
CALQUED
CALQUES
CALQUING
CALS
CALTHROP
CALTHROPS
CALTRAP
CALTRAPS
CALTROP
CALTROPS
CALUMET
CALUMETS
CALUMNIATE
CALUMNIATED
CALUMNIATES
CALUMNIATING
CALUMNIATION
CALUMNIATIONS
CALUMNIATOR
CALUMNIATORS
CALUMNIED
CALUMNIES
CALUMNIOUS
CALUMNIOUSLY
CALUMNY
CALUMNYING
CALUTRON
CALUTRONS
CALVADOS
CALVADOSES
CALVARIA
CALVARIAL
CALVARIAN
CALVARIAS
CALVARIES
CALVARIUM
CALVARIUMS
CALVARY
CALVE
CALVED
CALVES
CALVING
CALVITIES
CALX
CALXES
CALYCATE
CALYCEAL
CALYCES
CALYCINAL
CALYCINE
CALYCLE
CALYCLES
CALYCULAR
CALYCULI
CALYCULUS
CALYPSO
CALYPSOES
CALYPSONIAN
CALYPSONIANS
CALYPSOS
CALYPTER
CALYPTERS
CALYPTRA
CALYPTRAS
CALYX
CALYXES
CALZONE
CALZONES
CALZONI
CAM
CAMAIL
CAMAILED
CAMAILS
CAMARADERIE
CAMARADERIES
CAMARILLA
CAMARILLAS
CAMAS
CAMASES
CAMASS
CAMASSES
CAMBER
CAMBERED
CAMBERING
CAMBERS
CAMBIA
CAMBIAL
CAMBISM
CAMBISMS
CAMBIST
CAMBISTS
CAMBIUM
CAMBIUMS
CAMBOGIA
CAMBOGIAS
CAMBOOSE
CAMBOOSES
CAMBRIC
CAMBRICS
CAMCORD
CAMCORDED
CAMCORDER
CAMCORDERS
CAMCORDING
CAMCORDS
CAME
CAMEL
CAMELBACK
CAMELBACKS
CAMELEER
CAMELEERS
CAMELHAIR
CAMELHAIRS
CAMELIA
CAMELIAS
CAMELID
CAMELIDS
CAMELLIA
CAMELLIAS
CAMELLIKE
CAMELOPARD
CAMELOPARDS
CAMELS
CAMEO
CAMEOED
CAMEOING
CAMEOS
CAMERA
CAMERAE
CAMERAL
CAMERAMAN
CAMERAMEN
CAMERAPERSON
CAMERAPERSONS
CAMERAS
CAMERAWOMAN
CAMERAWOMEN
CAMERLENGO
CAMERLENGOS
CAMES
CAMI
CAMION
CAMIONS
CAMIS
CAMISA
CAMISADE
CAMISADES
CAMISADO
CAMISADOES
CAMISADOS
CAMISAS
CAMISE
CAMISES
CAMISIA
CAMISIAS
CAMISOLE
CAMISOLES
CAMLET
CAMLETS
CAMMIE
CAMMIES
CAMO
CAMOMILE
CAMOMILES
CAMORRA
CAMORRAS
CAMORRIST
CAMORRISTA
CAMORRISTAS
CAMORRISTI
CAMORRISTS
CAMOS
CAMOUFLAGE
CAMOUFLAGEABLE
CAMOUFLAGED
CAMOUFLAGES
CAMOUFLAGIC
CAMOUFLAGING
CAMP
CAMPAGNA
CAMPAGNE
CAMPAIGN
CAMPAIGNED
CAMPAIGNER
CAMPAIGNERS
CAMPAIGNING
CAMPAIGNS
CAMPANILE
CAMPANILES
CAMPANILI
CAMPANOLOGIES
CAMPANOLOGIST
CAMPANOLOGISTS
CAMPANOLOGY
CAMPANULA
CAMPANULAS
CAMPANULATE
CAMPCRAFT
CAMPCRAFTS
CAMPED
CAMPER
CAMPERS
CAMPESINO
CAMPESINOS
CAMPESTRAL
CAMPFIRE
CAMPFIRES
CAMPGROUND
CAMPGROUNDS
CAMPHENE
CAMPHENES
CAMPHINE
CAMPHINES
CAMPHIRE
CAMPHIRES
CAMPHOL
CAMPHOLS
CAMPHOR
CAMPHORACEOUS
CAMPHORATE
CAMPHORATED
CAMPHORATES
CAMPHORATING
CAMPHORIC
CAMPHORS
CAMPI
CAMPIER
CAMPIEST
CAMPILY
CAMPINESS
CAMPINESSES
CAMPING

CAMPINGS
CAMPION
CAMPIONS
CAMPO
CAMPONG
CAMPONGS
CAMPOREE
CAMPOREES
CAMPOS
CAMPOUT
CAMPOUTS
CAMPS
CAMPSHIRT
CAMPSHIRTS
CAMPSITE
CAMPSITES
CAMPSTOOL
CAMPSTOOLS
CAMPUS
CAMPUSED
CAMPUSES
CAMPUSING
CAMPY
CAMPYLOBACTER
CAMPYLOBACTERS
CAMPYLOTROPOUS
CAMS
CAMSHAFT
CAMSHAFTS
CAMWOOD
CAMWOODS
CAN
CANAILLE
CANAILLES
CANAKIN
CANAKINS
CANAL
CANALBOAT
CANALBOATS
CANALED
CANALICULAR
CANALICULI
CANALICULUS
CANALING
CANALISE
CANALISED
CANALISES
CANALISING
CANALIZATION
CANALIZATIONS
CANALIZE
CANALIZED
CANALIZES
CANALIZING
CANALLED
CANALLER
CANALLERS
CANALLING
CANALS
CANAPE
CANAPES
CANARD
CANARDS
CANARIES
CANARY
CANASTA
CANASTAS
CANCAN
CANCANS
CANCEL
CANCELABLE
CANCELATION
CANCELATIONS
CANCELED
CANCELER
CANCELERS
CANCELING
CANCELLABLE
CANCELLATION
CANCELLATIONS
CANCELLED
CANCELLER
CANCELLERS
CANCELLING
CANCELLOUS
CANCELS
CANCER
CANCERED
CANCEROUS
CANCEROUSLY
CANCERS
CANCHA
CANCHAS
CANCROID
CANCROIDS
CANDELA
CANDELABRA
CANDELABRAS
CANDELABRUM
CANDELABRUMS
CANDELAS
CANDENT
CANDESCENCE
CANDESCENCES
CANDESCENT
CANDID
CANDIDA
CANDIDACIES
CANDIDACY
CANDIDAL
CANDIDAS
CANDIDATE
CANDIDATES
CANDIDATURE
CANDIDATURES
CANDIDER
CANDIDEST
CANDIDIASES
CANDIDIASIS
CANDIDLY
CANDIDNESS
CANDIDNESSES
CANDIDS
CANDIED
CANDIES
CANDLE
CANDLEBERRIES
CANDLEBERRY
CANDLED
CANDLEFISH
CANDLEFISHES
CANDLEHOLDER
CANDLEHOLDERS
CANDLELIGHT
CANDLELIGHTED
CANDLELIGHTER
CANDLELIGHTERS
CANDLELIGHTS
CANDLELIT
CANDLENUT
CANDLENUTS
CANDLEPIN
CANDLEPINS
CANDLEPOWER
CANDLEPOWERS
CANDLER
CANDLERS
CANDLES
CANDLESNUFFER
CANDLESNUFFERS
CANDLESTICK
CANDLESTICKS
CANDLEWICK
CANDLEWICKS
CANDLEWOOD
CANDLEWOODS
CANDLING
CANDOR
CANDORS
CANDOUR
CANDOURS
CANDY
CANDYFLOSS
CANDYFLOSSES
CANDYGRAM
CANDYGRAMS
CANDYING
CANDYMAN
CANDYMEN
CANDYTUFT
CANDYTUFTS
CANE
CANEBRAKE
CANEBRAKES
CANED
CANELLA
CANELLAS
CANEPHOR
CANEPHORS
CANER
CANERS
CANES
CANESCENT
CANEWARE
CANEWARES
CANFIELD
CANFIELDS
CANFUL
CANFULS
CANGUE
CANGUES
CANICULAR
CANID
CANIDS
CANIKIN
CANIKINS
CANINE
CANINES
CANING
CANINGS
CANINITIES
CANINITY
CANISTEL
CANISTELS
CANISTER
CANISTERS
CANITIES
CANKER
CANKERED
CANKERING
CANKEROUS
CANKERS
CANKERWORM
CANKERWORMS
CANNA
CANNABIC
CANNABIN
CANNABINOID
CANNABINOIDS
CANNABINOL
CANNABINOLS
CANNABINS
CANNABIS
CANNABISES
CANNAS
CANNED
CANNEL
CANNELLONI
CANNELON
CANNELONS
CANNELS
CANNER
CANNERIES
CANNERS
CANNERY
CANNIBAL
CANNIBALISE
CANNIBALISED
CANNIBALISES
CANNIBALISING
CANNIBALISM
CANNIBALISMS
CANNIBALISTIC
CANNIBALIZATION
CANNIBALIZE
CANNIBALIZED
CANNIBALIZES
CANNIBALIZING
CANNIBALS
CANNIE
CANNIER
CANNIEST
CANNIKIN
CANNIKINS
CANNILY
CANNINESS
CANNINESSES
CANNING
CANNINGS
CANNISTER
CANNISTERS
CANNOLI
CANNOLIS
CANNON
CANNONADE

CANNONADED
CANNONADES
CANNONADING
CANNONBALL
CANNONBALLED
CANNONBALLING
CANNONBALLS
CANNONED
CANNONEER
CANNONEERS
CANNONING
CANNONRIES
CANNONRY
CANNONS
CANNOT
CANNULA
CANNULAE
CANNULAR
CANNULAS
CANNULATE
CANNULATED
CANNULATES
CANNULATING
CANNULATION
CANNULATIONS
CANNY
CANOE
CANOEABLE
CANOED
CANOEING
CANOEINGS
CANOEIST
CANOEISTS
CANOEMAN
CANOEMEN
CANOER
CANOERS
CANOES
CANOLA
CANOLAS
CANON
CANONESS
CANONESSES
CANONIC
CANONICAL
CANONICALLY
CANONICALS
CANONICITIES
CANONICITY
CANONISATION
CANONISATIONS
CANONISE
CANONISED
CANONISES
CANONISING
CANONIST
CANONISTS
CANONIZATION
CANONIZATIONS
CANONIZE
CANONIZED
CANONIZER
CANONIZERS
CANONIZES
CANONIZING
CANONRIES
CANONRY
CANONS
CANOODLE
CANOODLED
CANOODLES
CANOODLING
CANOPIC
CANOPIED
CANOPIES
CANOPY
CANOPYING
CANOROUS
CANOROUSLY
CANOROUSNESS
CANOROUSNESSES
CANS
CANSFUL
CANSO
CANSOS
CANST
CANT
CANTABILE
CANTABILES
CANTAL
CANTALA
CANTALAS
CANTALOUP
CANTALOUPE
CANTALOUPES
CANTALOUPS
CANTALS
CANTANKEROUS
CANTANKEROUSLY
CANTATA
CANTATAS
CANTATRICE
CANTATRICES
CANTATRICI
CANTDOG
CANTDOGS
CANTED
CANTEEN
CANTEENS
CANTER
CANTERED
CANTERING
CANTERS
CANTHAL
CANTHARI
CANTHARIDES
CANTHARIDIN
CANTHARIDINS
CANTHARIS
CANTHAXANTHIN
CANTHAXANTHINS
CANTHI
CANTHIC
CANTHITIS
CANTHITISES
CANTHUS
CANTIC
CANTICLE
CANTICLES
CANTILENA
CANTILENAS
CANTILEVER
CANTILEVERED
CANTILEVERING
CANTILEVERS
CANTILLATE
CANTILLATED
CANTILLATES
CANTILLATING
CANTILLATION
CANTILLATIONS
CANTINA
CANTINAS
CANTING
CANTLE
CANTLES
CANTO
CANTON
CANTONAL
CANTONED
CANTONING
CANTONMENT
CANTONMENTS
CANTONS
CANTOR
CANTORIAL
CANTORIS
CANTORS
CANTOS
CANTRAIP
CANTRAIPS
CANTRAP
CANTRAPS
CANTRIP
CANTRIPS
CANTS
CANTUS
CANTUSES
CANTY
CANULA
CANULAE
CANULAR
CANULAS
CANULATE
CANULATED
CANULATES
CANULATING
CANVAS
CANVASBACK
CANVASBACKS
CANVASED
CANVASER
CANVASERS
CANVASES
CANVASING
CANVASLIKE
CANVASS
CANVASSED
CANVASSER
CANVASSERS
CANVASSES
CANVASSING
CANYON
CANYONEER
CANYONEERING
CANYONEERINGS
CANYONEERS
CANYONING
CANYONINGS
CANYONS
CANZONA
CANZONAS
CANZONE
CANZONES
CANZONET
CANZONETS
CANZONI
CAOUTCHOUC
CAOUTCHOUCS
CAP
CAPABILITIES
CAPABILITY
CAPABLE
CAPABLENESS
CAPABLENESSES
CAPABLER
CAPABLEST
CAPABLY
CAPACIOUS
CAPACIOUSLY
CAPACIOUSNESS
CAPACIOUSNESSES
CAPACITANCE
CAPACITANCES
CAPACITATE
CAPACITATED
CAPACITATES
CAPACITATING
CAPACITATION
CAPACITATIONS
CAPACITIES
CAPACITIVE
CAPACITIVELY
CAPACITOR
CAPACITORS
CAPACITY
CAPARISON
CAPARISONED
CAPARISONING
CAPARISONS
CAPE
CAPED
CAPEESH
CAPELAN
CAPELANS
CAPELET
CAPELETS
CAPELIN
CAPELINS
CAPELLINI
CAPER
CAPERCAILLIE
CAPERCAILLIES
CAPERCAILZIE
CAPERCAILZIES
CAPERED
CAPERER
CAPERERS
CAPERING
CAPERS
CAPES
CAPESKIN
CAPESKINS
CAPEWORK
CAPEWORKS

CAPFUL
CAPFULS
CAPH
CAPHS
CAPIAS
CAPIASES
CAPILLARIES
CAPILLARITIES
CAPILLARITY
CAPILLARY
CAPING
CAPISCE
CAPITA
CAPITAL
CAPITALISATION
CAPITALISATIONS
CAPITALISE
CAPITALISED
CAPITALISES
CAPITALISING
CAPITALISM
CAPITALISMS
CAPITALIST
CAPITALISTIC
CAPITALISTS
CAPITALIZATION
CAPITALIZATIONS
CAPITALIZE
CAPITALIZED
CAPITALIZES
CAPITALIZING
CAPITALLY
CAPITALS
CAPITATE
CAPITATED
CAPITATES
CAPITATION
CAPITATIONS
CAPITELLA
CAPITELLUM
CAPITOL
CAPITOLS
CAPITULA
CAPITULAR
CAPITULARIES
CAPITULARY
CAPITULATE
CAPITULATED
CAPITULATES
CAPITULATING
CAPITULATION
CAPITULATIONS
CAPITULUM
CAPIZ
CAPIZES
CAPLESS
CAPLET
CAPLETS
CAPLIN
CAPLINS
CAPMAKER
CAPMAKERS
CAPO
CAPOEIRA
CAPOEIRAS
CAPON
CAPONATA
CAPONATAS
CAPONIER
CAPONIERS
CAPONISE
CAPONISED
CAPONISES
CAPONISING
CAPONIZE
CAPONIZED
CAPONIZES
CAPONIZING
CAPONS
CAPORAL
CAPORALS
CAPOS
CAPOT
CAPOTE
CAPOTES
CAPOTS
CAPOUCH
CAPOUCHES
CAPPED
CAPPELLETTI
CAPPER
CAPPERS
CAPPING
CAPPINGS
CAPPUCCINO
CAPPUCCINOS
CAPRESE
CAPRESES
CAPRI
CAPRIC
CAPRICCI
CAPRICCIO
CAPRICCIOS
CAPRICE
CAPRICES
CAPRICIOUS
CAPRICIOUSLY
CAPRICIOUSNESS
CAPRIFICATION
CAPRIFICATIONS
CAPRIFIG
CAPRIFIGS
CAPRINE
CAPRIOLE
CAPRIOLED
CAPRIOLES
CAPRIOLING
CAPRIS
CAPROCK
CAPROCKS
CAPROLACTAM
CAPROLACTAMS
CAPS
CAPSAICIN
CAPSAICINS
CAPSICIN
CAPSICINS
CAPSICUM
CAPSICUMS
CAPSID
CAPSIDAL
CAPSIDS
CAPSIZE
CAPSIZED
CAPSIZES
CAPSIZING
CAPSOMER
CAPSOMERE
CAPSOMERES
CAPSOMERS
CAPSTAN
CAPSTANS
CAPSTONE
CAPSTONES
CAPSULAR
CAPSULATE
CAPSULATED
CAPSULE
CAPSULED
CAPSULES
CAPSULING
CAPSULIZE
CAPSULIZED
CAPSULIZES
CAPSULIZING
CAPTAIN
CAPTAINCIES
CAPTAINCY
CAPTAINED
CAPTAINING
CAPTAINS
CAPTAINSHIP
CAPTAINSHIPS
CAPTAN
CAPTANS
CAPTION
CAPTIONED
CAPTIONING
CAPTIONLESS
CAPTIONS
CAPTIOUS
CAPTIOUSLY
CAPTIOUSNESS
CAPTIOUSNESSES
CAPTIVATE
CAPTIVATED
CAPTIVATES
CAPTIVATING
CAPTIVATION
CAPTIVATIONS
CAPTIVATOR
CAPTIVATORS
CAPTIVE
CAPTIVES
CAPTIVITIES
CAPTIVITY
CAPTOPRIL
CAPTOPRILS
CAPTOR
CAPTORS
CAPTURE
CAPTURED
CAPTURER
CAPTURERS
CAPTURES
CAPTURING
CAPUCHE
CAPUCHED
CAPUCHES
CAPUCHIN
CAPUCHINS
CAPUT
CAPYBARA
CAPYBARAS
CAR
CARABAO
CARABAOS
CARABID
CARABIDS
CARABIN
CARABINE
CARABINEER
CARABINEERS
CARABINER
CARABINERO
CARABINEROS
CARABINERS
CARABINES
CARABINIER
CARABINIERE
CARABINIERI
CARABINIERS
CARABINS
CARACAL
CARACALS
CARACARA
CARACARAS
CARACK
CARACKS
CARACOL
CARACOLE
CARACOLED
CARACOLER
CARACOLERS
CARACOLES
CARACOLING
CARACOLLED
CARACOLLING
CARACOLS
CARACUL
CARACULS
CARAFE
CARAFES
CARAGANA
CARAGANAS
CARAGEEN
CARAGEENS
CARAMBA
CARAMBOLA
CARAMBOLAS
CARAMEL
CARAMELISE
CARAMELISED
CARAMELISES
CARAMELISING
CARAMELIZE
CARAMELIZED
CARAMELIZES
CARAMELIZING
CARAMELS
CARANGID
CARANGIDS
CARANGOID
CARAPACE
CARAPACED

CARAPACES
CARAPAX
CARAPAXES
CARASSOW
CARASSOWS
CARAT
CARATE
CARATES
CARATS
CARAVAN
CARAVANED
CARAVANER
CARAVANERS
CARAVANING
CARAVANNED
CARAVANNER
CARAVANNERS
CARAVANNING
CARAVANS
CARAVANSARIES
CARAVANSARY
CARAVANSERAI
CARAVANSERAIS
CARAVEL
CARAVELLE
CARAVELLES
CARAVELS
CARAWAY
CARAWAYS
CARB
CARBACHOL
CARBACHOLS
CARBAMATE
CARBAMATES
CARBAMAZEPINE
CARBAMAZEPINES
CARBAMIC
CARBAMIDE
CARBAMIDES
CARBAMINO
CARBAMOYL
CARBAMOYLS
CARBAMYL
CARBAMYLS
CARBANION
CARBANIONS
CARBARN
CARBARNS
CARBARYL
CARBARYLS
CARBAZOLE
CARBAZOLES
CARBIDE
CARBIDES
CARBINE
CARBINEER
CARBINEERS
CARBINES
CARBINOL
CARBINOLS
CARBO
CARBOCYCLIC
CARBOHYDRASE
CARBOHYDRASES
CARBOHYDRATE
CARBOHYDRATES
CARBOLIC
CARBOLICS
CARBOLIZE
CARBOLIZED
CARBOLIZES
CARBOLIZING
CARBON
CARBONACEOUS
CARBONADE
CARBONADES
CARBONADO
CARBONADOED
CARBONADOES
CARBONADOING
CARBONADOS
CARBONARA
CARBONARAS
CARBONATE
CARBONATED
CARBONATES
CARBONATING
CARBONATION
CARBONATIONS
CARBONIC
CARBONIFEROUS
CARBONIUM
CARBONIUMS
CARBONIZATION
CARBONIZATIONS
CARBONIZE
CARBONIZED
CARBONIZES
CARBONIZING
CARBONLESS
CARBONNADE
CARBONNADES
CARBONOUS
CARBONS
CARBONYL
CARBONYLATION
CARBONYLATIONS
CARBONYLIC
CARBONYLS
CARBORA
CARBORAS
CARBOS
CARBOXYL
CARBOXYLASE
CARBOXYLASES
CARBOXYLATE
CARBOXYLATED
CARBOXYLATES
CARBOXYLATING
CARBOXYLATION
CARBOXYLATIONS
CARBOXYLIC
CARBOXYLS
CARBOY
CARBOYED
CARBOYS
CARBS
CARBUNCLE
CARBUNCLED
CARBUNCLES
CARBUNCULAR
CARBURET
CARBURETED
CARBURETING
CARBURETION
CARBURETIONS
CARBURETOR
CARBURETORS
CARBURETS
CARBURETTED
CARBURETTER
CARBURETTERS
CARBURETTING
CARBURETTOR
CARBURETTORS
CARBURISE
CARBURISED
CARBURISES
CARBURISING
CARBURIZATION
CARBURIZATIONS
CARBURIZE
CARBURIZED
CARBURIZES
CARBURIZING
CARCAJOU
CARCAJOUS
CARCANET
CARCANETS
CARCASE
CARCASES
CARCASS
CARCASSES
CARCEL
CARCELS
CARCERAL
CARCINOGEN
CARCINOGENESES
CARCINOGENESIS
CARCINOGENIC
CARCINOGENICITY
CARCINOGENS
CARCINOID
CARCINOIDS
CARCINOMA
CARCINOMAS
CARCINOMATA
CARCINOMATOSES
CARCINOMATOSIS
CARCINOMATOUS
CARCINOSARCOMA
CARCINOSARCOMAS
CARD
CARDAMOM
CARDAMOMS
CARDAMON
CARDAMONS
CARDAMUM
CARDAMUMS
CARDBOARD
CARDBOARDS
CARDBOARDY
CARDCASE
CARDCASES
CARDED
CARDER
CARDERS
CARDHOLDER
CARDHOLDERS
CARDIA
CARDIAC
CARDIACS
CARDIAE
CARDIAS
CARDIGAN
CARDIGANS
CARDINAL
CARDINALATE
CARDINALATES
CARDINALITIES
CARDINALITY
CARDINALLY
CARDINALS
CARDINALSHIP
CARDINALSHIPS
CARDING
CARDINGS
CARDIO
CARDIOGENIC
CARDIOGRAM
CARDIOGRAMS
CARDIOGRAPH
CARDIOGRAPHIC
CARDIOGRAPHIES
CARDIOGRAPHS
CARDIOGRAPHY
CARDIOID
CARDIOIDS
CARDIOLOGICAL
CARDIOLOGIES
CARDIOLOGIST
CARDIOLOGISTS
CARDIOLOGY
CARDIOMYOPATHY
CARDIOPATHIES
CARDIOPATHY
CARDIOPULMONARY
CARDIOS
CARDIOTHORACIC
CARDIOTONIC
CARDIOTONICS
CARDIOVASCULAR
CARDIOVERSION
CARDIOVERSIONS
CARDITIC
CARDITIS
CARDITISES
CARDON
CARDONS
CARDOON
CARDOONS
CARDPLAYER
CARDPLAYERS
CARDS
CARDSHARP
CARDSHARPER
CARDSHARPERS
CARDSHARPS
CARE
CARED
CAREEN
CAREENED
CAREENER
CAREENERS
CAREENING

CAREENS
CAREER
CAREERED
CAREERER
CAREERERS
CAREERING
CAREERISM
CAREERISMS
CAREERIST
CAREERISTS
CAREERS
CAREFREE
CAREFUL
CAREFULLER
CAREFULLEST
CAREFULLY
CAREFULNESS
CAREFULNESSES
CAREGIVER
CAREGIVERS
CAREGIVING
CAREGIVINGS
CARELESS
CARELESSLY
CARELESSNESS
CARELESSNESSES
CARER
CARERS
CARES
CARESS
CARESSED
CARESSER
CARESSERS
CARESSES
CARESSING
CARESSINGLY
CARESSIVE
CARESSIVELY
CARET
CARETAKE
CARETAKEN
CARETAKER
CARETAKERS
CARETAKES
CARETAKING
CARETAKINGS
CARETOOK
CARETS
CAREWORN
CAREX
CARFARE
CARFARES
CARFUL
CARFULS
CARGO
CARGOES
CARGOS
CARHOP
CARHOPPED
CARHOPPING
CARHOPS
CARIBE
CARIBES
CARIBOO
CARIBOOS
CARIBOU
CARIBOUS
CARICATURAL
CARICATURE
CARICATURED
CARICATURES
CARICATURING
CARICATURIST
CARICATURISTS
CARICES
CARIED
CARIES
CARILLON
CARILLONNED
CARILLONNEUR
CARILLONNEURS
CARILLONNING
CARILLONS
CARINA
CARINAE
CARINAL
CARINAS
CARINATE
CARINATED
CARING
CARINGLY
CARINGS
CARIOCA
CARIOCAS
CARIOGENIC
CARIOLE
CARIOLES
CARIOSITIES
CARIOSITY
CARIOUS
CARITAS
CARITASES
CARJACK
CARJACKED
CARJACKER
CARJACKERS
CARJACKING
CARJACKINGS
CARJACKS
CARK
CARKED
CARKING
CARKS
CARL
CARLE
CARLES
CARLESS
CARLIN
CARLINE
CARLINES
CARLING
CARLINGS
CARLINS
CARLISH
CARLOAD
CARLOADS
CARLS
CARMAGNOLE
CARMAGNOLES
CARMAKER
CARMAKERS
CARMAN
CARMEN
CARMINATIVE
CARMINATIVES
CARMINE
CARMINES
CARN
CARNAGE
CARNAGES
CARNAL
CARNALITIES
CARNALITY
CARNALLITE
CARNALLITES
CARNALLY
CARNASSIAL
CARNASSIALS
CARNATION
CARNATIONS
CARNAUBA
CARNAUBAS
CARNELIAN
CARNELIANS
CARNET
CARNETS
CARNEY
CARNEYS
CARNIE
CARNIES
CARNIFIED
CARNIFIES
CARNIFY
CARNIFYING
CARNITINE
CARNITINES
CARNIVAL
CARNIVALESQUE
CARNIVALS
CARNIVORA
CARNIVORE
CARNIVORES
CARNIVORIES
CARNIVOROUS
CARNIVOROUSLY
CARNIVOROUSNESS
CARNIVORY
CARNOSAUR
CARNOSAURS
CARNOTITE
CARNOTITES
CARNS
CARNY
CAROACH
CAROACHES
CAROB
CAROBS
CAROCH
CAROCHE
CAROCHES
CAROL
CAROLED
CAROLER
CAROLERS
CAROLI
CAROLING
CAROLINGS
CAROLLED
CAROLLER
CAROLLERS
CAROLLING
CAROLS
CAROLUS
CAROLUSES
CAROM
CAROMED
CAROMING
CAROMS
CAROTENE
CAROTENES
CAROTENOID
CAROTENOIDS
CAROTID
CAROTIDAL
CAROTIDS
CAROTIN
CAROTINOID
CAROTINOIDS
CAROTINS
CAROUSAL
CAROUSALS
CAROUSE
CAROUSED
CAROUSEL
CAROUSELS
CAROUSER
CAROUSERS
CAROUSES
CAROUSING
CARP
CARPACCIO
CARPACCIOS
CARPAL
CARPALE
CARPALIA
CARPALS
CARPED
CARPEL
CARPELLARY
CARPELLATE
CARPELS
CARPENTER
CARPENTERED
CARPENTERING
CARPENTERS
CARPENTRIES
CARPENTRY
CARPER
CARPERS
CARPET
CARPETBAG
CARPETBAGGED
CARPETBAGGER
CARPETBAGGERIES
CARPETBAGGERS
CARPETBAGGERY
CARPETBAGGING
CARPETBAGS
CARPETED
CARPETING
CARPETINGS
CARPETS
CARPETWEED
CARPETWEEDS
CARPI

CARPING
CARPINGLY
CARPINGS
CARPOGONIA
CARPOGONIAL
CARPOGONIUM
CARPOLOGIES
CARPOLOGY
CARPOOL
CARPOOLED
CARPOOLER
CARPOOLERS
CARPOOLING
CARPOOLS
CARPOPHORE
CARPOPHORES
CARPORT
CARPORTS
CARPOSPORE
CARPOSPORES
CARPS
CARPUS
CARR
CARRACK
CARRACKS
CARRAGEEN
CARRAGEENAN
CARRAGEENANS
CARRAGEENIN
CARRAGEENINS
CARRAGEENS
CARRAGHEEN
CARRAGHEENS
CARREFOUR
CARREFOURS
CARREL
CARRELL
CARRELLS
CARRELS
CARRIAGE
CARRIAGES
CARRIAGEWAY
CARRIAGEWAYS
CARRIED
CARRIER
CARRIERS
CARRIES
CARRIOLE
CARRIOLES
CARRION
CARRIONS
CARRITCH
CARRITCHES
CARROCH
CARROCHES
CARROM
CARROMED
CARROMING
CARROMS
CARRONADE
CARRONADES
CARROT
CARROTIER
CARROTIEST
CARROTIN
CARROTINS
CARROTS
CARROTTOP
CARROTTOPPED
CARROTTOPS
CARROTY
CARROUSEL
CARROUSELS
CARRS
CARRY
CARRYALL
CARRYALLS
CARRYBACK
CARRYBACKS
CARRYCOT
CARRYCOTS
CARRYFORWARD
CARRYFORWARDS
CARRYING
CARRYON
CARRYONS
CARRYOUT
CARRYOUTS
CARRYOVER
CARRYOVERS
CARS
CARSE
CARSES
CARSICK
CARSICKNESS
CARSICKNESSES
CARSPIEL
CARSPIELS
CART
CARTABLE
CARTAGE
CARTAGES
CARTE
CARTED
CARTEL
CARTELISE
CARTELISED
CARTELISES
CARTELISING
CARTELIZATION
CARTELIZATIONS
CARTELIZE
CARTELIZED
CARTELIZES
CARTELIZING
CARTELS
CARTER
CARTERS
CARTES
CARTFUL
CARTFULS
CARTHORSE
CARTHORSES
CARTILAGE
CARTILAGES
CARTILAGINOUS
CARTING
CARTLOAD
CARTLOADS
CARTOGRAM
CARTOGRAMS
CARTOGRAPHER
CARTOGRAPHERS
CARTOGRAPHIC
CARTOGRAPHICAL
CARTOGRAPHIES
CARTOGRAPHY
CARTON
CARTONED
CARTONING
CARTONS
CARTOON
CARTOONED
CARTOONIER
CARTOONIEST
CARTOONING
CARTOONINGS
CARTOONISH
CARTOONISHLY
CARTOONIST
CARTOONISTS
CARTOONLIKE
CARTOONS
CARTOONY
CARTOP
CARTOPPER
CARTOPPERS
CARTOUCH
CARTOUCHE
CARTOUCHES
CARTRIDGE
CARTRIDGES
CARTS
CARTULARIES
CARTULARY
CARTWHEEL
CARTWHEELED
CARTWHEELER
CARTWHEELERS
CARTWHEELING
CARTWHEELS
CARUNCLE
CARUNCLES
CARVACROL
CARVACROLS
CARVE
CARVED
CARVEL
CARVELS
CARVEN
CARVER
CARVERIES
CARVERS
CARVERY
CARVES
CARVING
CARVINGS
CARWASH
CARWASHES
CARYATIC
CARYATID
CARYATIDES
CARYATIDS
CARYOPSES
CARYOPSIDES
CARYOPSIS
CARYOTIN
CARYOTINS
CASA
CASABA
CASABAS
CASAS
CASAVA
CASAVAS
CASBAH
CASBAHS
CASCABEL
CASCABELS
CASCABLE
CASCABLES
CASCADE
CASCADED
CASCADES
CASCADING
CASCARA
CASCARAS
CASCARILLA
CASCARILLAS
CASE
CASEASE
CASEASES
CASEATE
CASEATED
CASEATES
CASEATING
CASEATION
CASEATIONS
CASEBEARER
CASEBEARERS
CASEBOOK
CASEBOOKS
CASED
CASEFIED
CASEFIES
CASEFY
CASEFYING
CASEIC
CASEIN
CASEINATE
CASEINATES
CASEINS
CASELAW
CASELAWS
CASELOAD
CASELOADS
CASEMATE
CASEMATED
CASEMATES
CASEMENT
CASEMENTS
CASEOSE
CASEOSES
CASEOUS
CASERN
CASERNE
CASERNES
CASERNS
CASES
CASETTE
CASETTES
CASEWORK
CASEWORKER
CASEWORKERS
CASEWORKS
CASEWORM

CASEWORMS
CASH
CASHABLE
CASHAW
CASHAWS
CASHBACK
CASHBACKS
CASHBOOK
CASHBOOKS
CASHBOX
CASHBOXES
CASHED
CASHES
CASHEW
CASHEWS
CASHIER
CASHIERED
CASHIERING
CASHIERS
CASHING
CASHLESS
CASHMERE
CASHMERES
CASHOO
CASHOOS
CASHPOINT
CASHPOINTS
CASIMERE
CASIMERES
CASIMIRE
CASIMIRES
CASING
CASINGS
CASINI
CASINO
CASINOS
CASITA
CASITAS
CASK
CASKED
CASKET
CASKETED
CASKETING
CASKETS
CASKING
CASKS
CASKY
CASQUE
CASQUED
CASQUES
CASSABA
CASSABAS
CASSATA
CASSATAS
CASSATION
CASSATIONS
CASSAVA
CASSAVAS
CASSENA
CASSENAS
CASSENE
CASSENES
CASSEROLE
CASSEROLES
CASSETTE
CASSETTES
CASSIA
CASSIAS
CASSIMERE
CASSIMERES
CASSINA
CASSINAS
CASSINE
CASSINES
CASSINGLE
CASSINGLES
CASSINO
CASSINOS
CASSIOPE
CASSIOPES
CASSIS
CASSISES
CASSITERITE
CASSITERITES
CASSOCK
CASSOCKED
CASSOCKS
CASSOULET
CASSOULETS
CASSOWARIES
CASSOWARY
CAST
CASTABILITIES
CASTABILITY
CASTABLE
CASTANET
CASTANETS
CASTAWAY
CASTAWAYS
CASTE
CASTEISM
CASTEISMS
CASTELLAN
CASTELLANS
CASTELLATED
CASTER
CASTERED
CASTERS
CASTES
CASTIGATE
CASTIGATED
CASTIGATES
CASTIGATING
CASTIGATION
CASTIGATIONS
CASTIGATOR
CASTIGATORS
CASTING
CASTINGS
CASTLE
CASTLED
CASTLES
CASTLING
CASTLINGS
CASTOFF
CASTOFFS
CASTOR
CASTOREUM
CASTOREUMS
CASTORS
CASTRATE
CASTRATED
CASTRATER
CASTRATERS
CASTRATES
CASTRATI
CASTRATING
CASTRATION
CASTRATIONS
CASTRATO
CASTRATOR
CASTRATORS
CASTRATORY
CASTRATOS
CASTS
CASUAL
CASUALLY
CASUALNESS
CASUALNESSES
CASUALS
CASUALTIES
CASUALTY
CASUARINA
CASUARINAS
CASUIST
CASUISTIC
CASUISTICAL
CASUISTRIES
CASUISTRY
CASUISTS
CASUS
CAT
CATABOLIC
CATABOLICALLY
CATABOLISM
CATABOLISMS
CATABOLITE
CATABOLITES
CATABOLIZE
CATABOLIZED
CATABOLIZES
CATABOLIZING
CATACHRESES
CATACHRESIS
CATACHRESTIC
CATACHRESTICAL
CATACLYSM
CATACLYSMAL
CATACLYSMIC
CATACLYSMICALLY
CATACLYSMS
CATACOMB
CATACOMBS
CATADIOPTRIC
CATADROMOUS
CATAFALQUE
CATAFALQUES
CATALASE
CATALASES
CATALATIC
CATALECTIC
CATALECTICS
CATALEPSIES
CATALEPSY
CATALEPTIC
CATALEPTICALLY
CATALEPTICS
CATALESE
CATALEXES
CATALEXIS
CATALO
CATALOES
CATALOG
CATALOGED
CATALOGER
CATALOGERS
CATALOGIC
CATALOGING
CATALOGS
CATALOGUE
CATALOGUED
CATALOGUER
CATALOGUERS
CATALOGUES
CATALOGUING
CATALOS
CATALPA
CATALPAS
CATALYSE
CATALYSED
CATALYSES
CATALYSING
CATALYSIS
CATALYST
CATALYSTS
CATALYTIC
CATALYTICALLY
CATALYZE
CATALYZED
CATALYZER
CATALYZERS
CATALYZES
CATALYZING
CATAMARAN
CATAMARANS
CATAMENIA
CATAMENIAL
CATAMITE
CATAMITES
CATAMOUNT
CATAMOUNTS
CATAPHORA
CATAPHORAS
CATAPHORESES
CATAPHORESIS
CATAPHORETIC
CATAPHORIC
CATAPHYLL
CATAPHYLLS
CATAPLASM
CATAPLASMS
CATAPLEXIES
CATAPLEXY
CATAPULT
CATAPULTED
CATAPULTING
CATAPULTS
CATARACT
CATARACTOUS
CATARACTS
CATARRH
CATARRHAL
CATARRHALLY
CATARRHINE
CATARRHINES

CATARRHS
CATASTROPHE
CATASTROPHES
CATASTROPHIC
CATASTROPHISM
CATASTROPHISMS
CATASTROPHIST
CATASTROPHISTS
CATATONIA
CATATONIAS
CATATONIC
CATATONICALLY
CATATONICS
CATAWBA
CATAWBAS
CATBIRD
CATBIRDS
CATBOAT
CATBOATS
CATBRIAR
CATBRIARS
CATBRIER
CATBRIERS
CATCALL
CATCALLED
CATCALLER
CATCALLERS
CATCALLING
CATCALLS
CATCH
CATCHABLE
CATCHALL
CATCHALLS
CATCHER
CATCHERS
CATCHES
CATCHFLIES
CATCHFLY
CATCHIER
CATCHIEST
CATCHILY
CATCHING
CATCHMENT
CATCHMENTS
CATCHPENNY
CATCHPHRASE
CATCHPHRASES
CATCHPOLE
CATCHPOLES
CATCHPOLL
CATCHPOLLS
CATCHUP
CATCHUPS
CATCHWORD
CATCHWORDS
CATCHY
CATCLAW
CATCLAWS
CATE
CATECHESES
CATECHESIS
CATECHETICAL
CATECHIN
CATECHINS
CATECHISE
CATECHISED
CATECHISES
CATECHISING
CATECHISM
CATECHISMAL
CATECHISMS
CATECHIST
CATECHISTIC
CATECHISTS
CATECHIZATION
CATECHIZATIONS
CATECHIZE
CATECHIZED
CATECHIZER
CATECHIZERS
CATECHIZES
CATECHIZING
CATECHOL
CATECHOLAMINE
CATECHOLAMINES
CATECHOLS
CATECHU
CATECHUMEN
CATECHUMENS
CATECHUS
CATEGORIC
CATEGORICAL
CATEGORICALLY
CATEGORIES
CATEGORISATION
CATEGORISATIONS
CATEGORISE
CATEGORISED
CATEGORISES
CATEGORISING
CATEGORIZATION
CATEGORIZATIONS
CATEGORIZE
CATEGORIZED
CATEGORIZES
CATEGORIZING
CATEGORY
CATENA
CATENAE
CATENARIES
CATENARY
CATENAS
CATENATE
CATENATED
CATENATES
CATENATING
CATENATION
CATENATIONS
CATENOID
CATENOIDS
CATER
CATERAN
CATERANS
CATERCORNER
CATERCORNERED
CATERED
CATERER
CATERERS
CATERESS
CATERESSES
CATERING
CATERINGS
CATERPILLAR
CATERPILLARS
CATERS
CATERWAUL
CATERWAULED
CATERWAULING
CATERWAULS
CATES
CATFACE
CATFACES
CATFACING
CATFACINGS
CATFALL
CATFALLS
CATFIGHT
CATFIGHTS
CATFISH
CATFISHES
CATGUT
CATGUTS
CATHARSES
CATHARSIS
CATHARTIC
CATHARTICALLY
CATHARTICS
CATHEAD
CATHEADS
CATHECT
CATHECTED
CATHECTIC
CATHECTING
CATHECTS
CATHEDRA
CATHEDRAE
CATHEDRAL
CATHEDRALS
CATHEDRAS
CATHEPSIN
CATHEPSINS
CATHEPTIC
CATHETER
CATHETERISATION
CATHETERIZATION
CATHETERIZE
CATHETERIZED
CATHETERIZES
CATHETERIZING
CATHETERS
CATHEXES
CATHEXIS
CATHODAL
CATHODALLY
CATHODE
CATHODES
CATHODIC
CATHODICALLY
CATHOLIC
CATHOLICALLY
CATHOLICATE
CATHOLICATES
CATHOLICITIES
CATHOLICITY
CATHOLICIZE
CATHOLICIZED
CATHOLICIZES
CATHOLICIZING
CATHOLICOI
CATHOLICON
CATHOLICONS
CATHOLICOS
CATHOLICOSES
CATHOLICS
CATHOUSE
CATHOUSES
CATION
CATIONIC
CATIONICALLY
CATIONS
CATJANG
CATJANGS
CATKIN
CATKINATE
CATKINS
CATLIKE
CATLIN
CATLING
CATLINGS
CATLINS
CATMINT
CATMINTS
CATNAP
CATNAPER
CATNAPERS
CATNAPPED
CATNAPPER
CATNAPPERS
CATNAPPING
CATNAPS
CATNIP
CATNIPS
CATOPTRIC
CATRIGGED
CATS
CATSPAW
CATSPAWS
CATSUIT
CATSUITS
CATSUP
CATSUPS
CATTAIL
CATTAILS
CATTALO
CATTALOES
CATTALOS
CATTED
CATTERIES
CATTERY
CATTIE
CATTIER
CATTIES
CATTIEST
CATTILY
CATTINESS
CATTINESSES
CATTING
CATTISH
CATTISHLY
CATTLE
CATTLEMAN
CATTLEMEN
CATTLEYA
CATTLEYAS
CATTY

CATWALK
CATWALKS
CAUCUS
CAUCUSED
CAUCUSES
CAUCUSING
CAUCUSSED
CAUCUSSES
CAUCUSSING
CAUDAD
CAUDAL
CAUDALLY
CAUDATE
CAUDATED
CAUDATES
CAUDATION
CAUDATIONS
CAUDEX
CAUDEXES
CAUDICES
CAUDILLISMO
CAUDILLISMOS
CAUDILLO
CAUDILLOS
CAUDLE
CAUDLES
CAUGHT
CAUL
CAULD
CAULDRON
CAULDRONS
CAULDS
CAULES
CAULICLE
CAULICLES
CAULIFLOWER
CAULIFLOWERET
CAULIFLOWERETS
CAULIFLOWERS
CAULINE
CAULIS
CAULK
CAULKED
CAULKER
CAULKERS
CAULKING
CAULKINGS
CAULKS
CAULS
CAURI
CAURIS
CAUSABLE
CAUSAL
CAUSALGIA
CAUSALGIAS
CAUSALGIC
CAUSALITIES
CAUSALITY
CAUSALLY
CAUSALS
CAUSATION
CAUSATIONS
CAUSATIVE
CAUSATIVELY
CAUSATIVES
CAUSE
CAUSED
CAUSELESS
CAUSER
CAUSERIE
CAUSERIES
CAUSERS
CAUSES
CAUSEWAY
CAUSEWAYED
CAUSEWAYING
CAUSEWAYS
CAUSEY
CAUSEYS
CAUSING
CAUSTIC
CAUSTICALLY
CAUSTICITIES
CAUSTICITY
CAUSTICS
CAUTERANT
CAUTERANTS
CAUTERIES
CAUTERISATION
CAUTERISATIONS
CAUTERISE
CAUTERIZATION
CAUTERIZATIONS
CAUTERIZE
CAUTERIZED
CAUTERIZES
CAUTERIZING
CAUTERY
CAUTION
CAUTIONARY
CAUTIONED
CAUTIONER
CAUTIONERS
CAUTIONING
CAUTIONS
CAUTIOUS
CAUTIOUSLY
CAUTIOUSNESS
CAUTIOUSNESSES
CAVA
CAVALCADE
CAVALCADES
CAVALERO
CAVALEROS
CAVALETTI
CAVALIER
CAVALIERED
CAVALIERING
CAVALIERISM
CAVALIERISMS
CAVALIERLY
CAVALIERS
CAVALLA
CAVALLAS
CAVALLETTI
CAVALLIES
CAVALLY
CAVALRIES
CAVALRY
CAVALRYMAN
CAVALRYMEN
CAVAS
CAVATINA
CAVATINAS
CAVATINE
CAVE
CAVEAT
CAVEATED
CAVEATING
CAVEATOR
CAVEATORS
CAVEATS
CAVED
CAVEFISH
CAVEFISHES
CAVELIKE
CAVEMAN
CAVEMEN
CAVENDISH
CAVENDISHES
CAVER
CAVERN
CAVERNED
CAVERNICOLOUS
CAVERNING
CAVERNOUS
CAVERNOUSLY
CAVERNS
CAVERS
CAVES
CAVETTI
CAVETTO
CAVETTOS
CAVIAR
CAVIARE
CAVIARES
CAVIARS
CAVICORN
CAVIE
CAVIES
CAVIL
CAVILED
CAVILER
CAVILERS
CAVILING
CAVILLED
CAVILLER
CAVILLERS
CAVILLING
CAVILS
CAVING
CAVINGS
CAVITARY
CAVITATE
CAVITATED
CAVITATES
CAVITATING
CAVITATION
CAVITATIONS
CAVITIED
CAVITIES
CAVITY
CAVORT
CAVORTED
CAVORTER
CAVORTERS
CAVORTING
CAVORTS
CAVY
CAW
CAWED
CAWING
CAWS
CAY
CAYENNE
CAYENNED
CAYENNES
CAYMAN
CAYMANS
CAYS
CAYUSE
CAYUSES
CAZH
CAZHER
CAZHEST
CAZIQUE
CAZIQUES
CEANOTHUS
CEANOTHUSES
CEASE
CEASED
CEASEFIRE
CEASEFIRES
CEASELESS
CEASELESSLY
CEASELESSNESS
CEASELESSNESSES
CEASES
CEASING
CEBID
CEBIDS
CEBOID
CEBOIDS
CECA
CECAL
CECALLY
CECITIES
CECITY
CECROPIA
CECROPIAS
CECUM
CEDAR
CEDARBIRD
CEDARBIRDS
CEDARIER
CEDARIEST
CEDARN
CEDARS
CEDARWOOD
CEDARWOODS
CEDARY
CEDE
CEDED
CEDER
CEDERS
CEDES
CEDI
CEDILLA
CEDILLAS
CEDING
CEDIS
CEDULA
CEDULAS
CEE
CEES

CEFTRIAXONE
CEFTRIAXONES
CEIBA
CEIBAS
CEIL
CEILED
CEILER
CEILERS
CEILI
CEILIDH
CEILIDHS
CEILING
CEILINGED
CEILINGS
CEILIS
CEILOMETER
CEILOMETERS
CEILS
CEINTURE
CEINTURES
CEL
CELADON
CELADONS
CELANDINE
CELANDINES
CELEB
CELEBRANT
CELEBRANTS
CELEBRATE
CELEBRATED
CELEBRATEDNESS
CELEBRATES
CELEBRATING
CELEBRATION
CELEBRATIONS
CELEBRATIVE
CELEBRATOR
CELEBRATORS
CELEBRATORY
CELEBRITIES
CELEBRITY
CELEBS
CELEBUTANTE
CELEBUTANTES
CELERIAC
CELERIACS
CELERIES
CELERITIES
CELERITY
CELERY
CELESTA
CELESTAS
CELESTE
CELESTES
CELESTIAL
CELESTIALLY
CELESTIALS
CELESTINE
CELESTINES
CELESTITE
CELESTITES
CELIAC
CELIACS
CELIBACIES
CELIBACY
CELIBATE
CELIBATES
CELIBATIC
CELL
CELLA
CELLAE
CELLAR
CELLARAGE
CELLARAGES
CELLARED
CELLARER
CELLARERS
CELLARET
CELLARETS
CELLARETTE
CELLARETTES
CELLARING
CELLARS
CELLARWAY
CELLARWAYS
CELLBLOCK
CELLBLOCKS
CELLED
CELLI
CELLING
CELLIST
CELLISTS
CELLMATE
CELLMATES
CELLO
CELLOBIOSE
CELLOBIOSES
CELLOIDIN
CELLOIDINS
CELLOPHANE
CELLOPHANES
CELLOS
CELLPHONE
CELLPHONES
CELLS
CELLULAR
CELLULARITIES
CELLULARITY
CELLULARS
CELLULASE
CELLULASES
CELLULE
CELLULES
CELLULITE
CELLULITES
CELLULITIS
CELLULITISES
CELLULOID
CELLULOIDS
CELLULOLYTIC
CELLULOSE
CELLULOSES
CELLULOSIC
CELLULOSICS
CELLULOUS
CELOM
CELOMATA
CELOMS
CELOSIA
CELOSIAS
CELOTEX
CELOTEXES
CELS
CELT
CELTS
CEMBALI
CEMBALIST
CEMBALISTS
CEMBALO
CEMBALOS
CEMENT
CEMENTA
CEMENTATION
CEMENTATIONS
CEMENTED
CEMENTER
CEMENTERS
CEMENTING
CEMENTITE
CEMENTITES
CEMENTITIOUS
CEMENTS
CEMENTUM
CEMENTUMS
CEMETERIES
CEMETERY
CENACLE
CENACLES
CENOBITE
CENOBITES
CENOBITIC
CENOSPECIES
CENOTAPH
CENOTAPHS
CENOTE
CENOTES
CENOZOIC
CENSE
CENSED
CENSER
CENSERS
CENSES
CENSING
CENSOR
CENSORED
CENSORIAL
CENSORING
CENSORIOUS
CENSORIOUSLY
CENSORIOUSNESS
CENSORS
CENSORSHIP
CENSORSHIPS
CENSUAL
CENSURABLE
CENSURE
CENSURED
CENSURER
CENSURERS
CENSURES
CENSURING
CENSUS
CENSUSED
CENSUSES
CENSUSING
CENT
CENTAI
CENTAL
CENTALS
CENTARE
CENTARES
CENTAS
CENTAUR
CENTAUREA
CENTAUREAS
CENTAURIC
CENTAURIES
CENTAURS
CENTAURY
CENTAVO
CENTAVOS
CENTENARIAN
CENTENARIANS
CENTENARIES
CENTENARY
CENTENNIAL
CENTENNIALLY
CENTENNIALS
CENTER
CENTERBOARD
CENTERBOARDS
CENTERED
CENTEREDNESS
CENTEREDNESSES
CENTERFOLD
CENTERFOLDS
CENTERING
CENTERINGS
CENTERLESS
CENTERLINE
CENTERLINES
CENTERPIECE
CENTERPIECES
CENTERS
CENTESES
CENTESIMAL
CENTESIMI
CENTESIMO
CENTESIMOS
CENTESIS
CENTIARE
CENTIARES
CENTIGRADE
CENTIGRAM
CENTIGRAMS
CENTILE
CENTILES
CENTILITER
CENTILITERS
CENTILITRE
CENTILITRES
CENTILLION
CENTILLIONS
CENTIME
CENTIMES
CENTIMETER
CENTIMETERS
CENTIMETRE
CENTIMETRES
CENTIMO
CENTIMORGAN
CENTIMORGANS
CENTIMOS
CENTIPEDE
CENTIPEDES

CENTNER
CENTNERS
CENTO
CENTONES
CENTOS
CENTRA
CENTRAL
CENTRALER
CENTRALEST
CENTRALISATION
CENTRALISATIONS
CENTRALISE
CENTRALISED
CENTRALISES
CENTRALISING
CENTRALISM
CENTRALISMS
CENTRALIST
CENTRALISTIC
CENTRALISTS
CENTRALITIES
CENTRALITY
CENTRALIZATION
CENTRALIZATIONS
CENTRALIZE
CENTRALIZED
CENTRALIZER
CENTRALIZERS
CENTRALIZES
CENTRALIZING
CENTRALLY
CENTRALS
CENTRE
CENTRED
CENTREFOLD
CENTREFOLDS
CENTREPIECE
CENTREPIECES
CENTRES
CENTRIC
CENTRICAL
CENTRICALLY
CENTRICITIES
CENTRICITY
CENTRIFUGAL
CENTRIFUGALLY
CENTRIFUGALS
CENTRIFUGATION
CENTRIFUGATIONS
CENTRIFUGE
CENTRIFUGED
CENTRIFUGES
CENTRIFUGING
CENTRING
CENTRINGS
CENTRIOLE
CENTRIOLES
CENTRIPETAL
CENTRIPETALLY
CENTRISM
CENTRISMS
CENTRIST
CENTRISTS
CENTROID
CENTROIDS
CENTROMERE
CENTROMERES
CENTROMERIC
CENTROSOME
CENTROSOMES
CENTROSYMMETRIC
CENTRUM
CENTRUMS
CENTS
CENTU
CENTUM
CENTUMS
CENTUPLE
CENTUPLED
CENTUPLES
CENTUPLING
CENTURIAL
CENTURIES
CENTURION
CENTURIONS
CENTURY
CEORL
CEORLISH
CEORLS
CEP
CEPE
CEPES
CEPHALAD
CEPHALEXIN
CEPHALEXINS
CEPHALIC
CEPHALICALLY
CEPHALIN
CEPHALINS
CEPHALIZATION
CEPHALIZATIONS
CEPHALOMETRIC
CEPHALOMETRIES
CEPHALOMETRY
CEPHALOPOD
CEPHALOPODS
CEPHALORIDINE
CEPHALORIDINES
CEPHALOSPORIN
CEPHALOSPORINS
CEPHALOTHIN
CEPHALOTHINS
CEPHALOTHORACES
CEPHALOTHORAX
CEPHALOTHORAXES
CEPHALOUS
CEPHEID
CEPHEIDS
CEPS
CERACEOUS
CERAMAL
CERAMALS
CERAMIC
CERAMICIST
CERAMICISTS
CERAMICS
CERAMIDE
CERAMIDES
CERAMIST
CERAMISTS
CERASTES
CERATE
CERATED
CERATES
CERATIN
CERATINS
CERATODUS
CERATODUSES
CERATOID
CERATOPSIAN
CERATOPSIANS
CERCAL
CERCARIA
CERCARIAE
CERCARIAL
CERCARIAN
CERCARIANS
CERCARIAS
CERCI
CERCIS
CERCISES
CERCUS
CERE
CEREAL
CEREALS
CEREBELLA
CEREBELLAR
CEREBELLUM
CEREBELLUMS
CEREBRA
CEREBRAL
CEREBRALLY
CEREBRALS
CEREBRATE
CEREBRATED
CEREBRATES
CEREBRATING
CEREBRATION
CEREBRATIONS
CEREBRIC
CEREBROSIDE
CEREBROSIDES
CEREBROSPINAL
CEREBROVASCULAR
CEREBRUM
CEREBRUMS
CERECLOTH
CERECLOTHS
CERED
CEREMENT
CEREMENTS
CEREMONIAL
CEREMONIALISM
CEREMONIALISMS
CEREMONIALIST
CEREMONIALISTS
CEREMONIALLY
CEREMONIALS
CEREMONIES
CEREMONIOUS
CEREMONIOUSLY
CEREMONIOUSNESS
CEREMONY
CERES
CERESIN
CERESINS
CEREUS
CEREUSES
CERIA
CERIAS
CERIC
CERING
CERIPH
CERIPHS
CERISE
CERISES
CERITE
CERITES
CERIUM
CERIUMS
CERMET
CERMETS
CERNUOUS
CERO
CEROS
CEROTIC
CEROTYPE
CEROTYPES
CEROUS
CERT
CERTAIN
CERTAINER
CERTAINEST
CERTAINLY
CERTAINTIES
CERTAINTY
CERTES
CERTIFIABLE
CERTIFIABLY
CERTIFICATE
CERTIFICATED
CERTIFICATES
CERTIFICATING
CERTIFICATION
CERTIFICATIONS
CERTIFICATORY
CERTIFIED
CERTIFIER
CERTIFIERS
CERTIFIES
CERTIFY
CERTIFYING
CERTIORARI
CERTIORARIS
CERTITUDE
CERTITUDES
CERTS
CERULEAN
CERULEANS
CERULOPLASMIN
CERULOPLASMINS
CERUMEN
CERUMENS
CERUMINOUS
CERUSE
CERUSES
CERUSITE
CERUSITES
CERUSSITE
CERUSSITES
CERVELAS
CERVELASES
CERVELAT
CERVELATS
CERVEZA

CERVEZAS
CERVICAL
CERVICES
CERVICITIS
CERVICITISES
CERVID
CERVIDS
CERVINE
CERVIX
CERVIXES
CESAREAN
CESAREANS
CESARIAN
CESARIANS
CESIUM
CESIUMS
CESPITOSE
CESS
CESSATION
CESSATIONS
CESSED
CESSES
CESSING
CESSION
CESSIONS
CESSPIT
CESSPITS
CESSPOOL
CESSPOOLS
CESTA
CESTAS
CESTI
CESTODE
CESTODES
CESTOI
CESTOID
CESTOIDS
CESTOS
CESTUS
CESTUSES
CESURA
CESURAE
CESURAS
CETACEAN
CETACEANS
CETACEOUS
CETANE
CETANES
CETE
CETES
CETOLOGIES
CETOLOGIST
CETOLOGISTS
CETOLOGY
CEVICHE
CEVICHES
CHABAZITE
CHABAZITES
CHABLIS
CHABOUK
CHABOUKS
CHABUK
CHABUKS
CHACHKA
CHACHKAS
CHACMA
CHACMAS
CHACONNE
CHACONNES
CHAD
CHADAR
CHADARIM
CHADARS
CHADLESS
CHADOR
CHADORS
CHADRI
CHADS
CHAEBOL
CHAEBOLS
CHAETA
CHAETAE
CHAETAL
CHAETOGNATH
CHAETOGNATHS
CHAETOPOD
CHAETOPODS
CHAFE
CHAFED
CHAFER
CHAFERS
CHAFES
CHAFF
CHAFFED
CHAFFER
CHAFFERED
CHAFFERER
CHAFFERERS
CHAFFERING
CHAFFERS
CHAFFIER
CHAFFIEST
CHAFFINCH
CHAFFINCHES
CHAFFING
CHAFFS
CHAFFY
CHAFING
CHAGRIN
CHAGRINED
CHAGRINING
CHAGRINNED
CHAGRINNING
CHAGRINS
CHAI
CHAIN
CHAINE
CHAINED
CHAINER
CHAINERS
CHAINES
CHAINFALL
CHAINFALLS
CHAINING
CHAINMAN
CHAINMEN
CHAINS
CHAINSAW
CHAINSAWED
CHAINSAWING
CHAINSAWS
CHAINWHEEL
CHAINWHEELS
CHAIR
CHAIRED
CHAIRING
CHAIRLIFT
CHAIRLIFTS
CHAIRMAN
CHAIRMANED
CHAIRMANING
CHAIRMANNED
CHAIRMANNING
CHAIRMANS
CHAIRMANSHIP
CHAIRMANSHIPS
CHAIRMEN
CHAIRPERSON
CHAIRPERSONS
CHAIRS
CHAIRWOMAN
CHAIRWOMEN
CHAIS
CHAISE
CHAISES
CHAKRA
CHAKRAS
CHALAH
CHALAHS
CHALAZA
CHALAZAE
CHALAZAL
CHALAZAS
CHALAZIA
CHALAZION
CHALAZIONS
CHALCEDONIC
CHALCEDONIES
CHALCEDONY
CHALCID
CHALCIDS
CHALCOCITE
CHALCOCITES
CHALCOGEN
CHALCOGENIDE
CHALCOGENIDES
CHALCOGENS
CHALCOPYRITE
CHALCOPYRITES
CHALDRON
CHALDRONS
CHALEH
CHALEHS
CHALET
CHALETS
CHALICE
CHALICED
CHALICES
CHALK
CHALKBOARD
CHALKBOARDS
CHALKED
CHALKIER
CHALKIEST
CHALKING
CHALKS
CHALKY
CHALLA
CHALLAH
CHALLAHS
CHALLAS
CHALLENGE
CHALLENGED
CHALLENGER
CHALLENGERS
CHALLENGES
CHALLENGING
CHALLENGINGLY
CHALLIE
CHALLIES
CHALLIS
CHALLISES
CHALLOT
CHALLOTH
CHALLY
CHALONE
CHALONES
CHALOT
CHALOTH
CHALUMEAU
CHALUMEAUS
CHALUPA
CHALUPAS
CHALUTZ
CHALUTZIM
CHALYBEATE
CHALYBEATES
CHAM
CHAMADE
CHAMADES
CHAMAEPHYTE
CHAMAEPHYTES
CHAMBER
CHAMBERED
CHAMBERING
CHAMBERLAIN
CHAMBERLAINS
CHAMBERMAID
CHAMBERMAIDS
CHAMBERS
CHAMBRAY
CHAMBRAYS
CHAMBRE
CHAMBRES
CHAMELEON
CHAMELEONIC
CHAMELEONLIKE
CHAMELEONS
CHAMFER
CHAMFERED
CHAMFERER
CHAMFERERS
CHAMFERING
CHAMFERS
CHAMFRAIN
CHAMFRAINS
CHAMFRON
CHAMFRONS
CHAMISA
CHAMISAS
CHAMISE
CHAMISES
CHAMISO
CHAMISOS
CHAMMIED

CHAMMIES
CHAMMY
CHAMMYING
CHAMOIS
CHAMOISED
CHAMOISES
CHAMOISING
CHAMOIX
CHAMOMILE
CHAMOMILES
CHAMP
CHAMPAC
CHAMPACA
CHAMPACAS
CHAMPACS
CHAMPAGNE
CHAMPAGNES
CHAMPAIGN
CHAMPAIGNS
CHAMPAK
CHAMPAKS
CHAMPED
CHAMPER
CHAMPERS
CHAMPERTIES
CHAMPERTOUS
CHAMPERTY
CHAMPIGNON
CHAMPIGNONS
CHAMPING
CHAMPION
CHAMPIONED
CHAMPIONING
CHAMPIONS
CHAMPIONSHIP
CHAMPIONSHIPS
CHAMPLEVE
CHAMPLEVES
CHAMPS
CHAMPY
CHAMS
CHANA
CHANAS
CHANCE
CHANCED
CHANCEFUL
CHANCEL
CHANCELLERIES
CHANCELLERY
CHANCELLOR
CHANCELLORIES
CHANCELLORS
CHANCELLORSHIP
CHANCELLORSHIPS
CHANCELLORY
CHANCELS
CHANCER
CHANCERIES
CHANCERS
CHANCERY
CHANCES
CHANCIER
CHANCIEST
CHANCILY
CHANCINESS
CHANCINESSES
CHANCING
CHANCRE
CHANCRES
CHANCROID
CHANCROIDAL
CHANCROIDS
CHANCROUS
CHANCY
CHANDELIER
CHANDELIERED
CHANDELIERS
CHANDELLE
CHANDELLED
CHANDELLES
CHANDELLING
CHANDLER
CHANDLERIES
CHANDLERS
CHANDLERY
CHANFRON
CHANFRONS
CHANG
CHANGE
CHANGEABILITIES
CHANGEABILITY
CHANGEABLE
CHANGEABLENESS
CHANGEABLY
CHANGED
CHANGEFUL
CHANGEFULLY
CHANGEFULNESS
CHANGEFULNESSES
CHANGELESS
CHANGELESSLY
CHANGELESSNESS
CHANGELING
CHANGELINGS
CHANGEOVER
CHANGEOVERS
CHANGER
CHANGERS
CHANGES
CHANGEUP
CHANGEUPS
CHANGING
CHANGS
CHANNEL
CHANNELED
CHANNELER
CHANNELERS
CHANNELING
CHANNELIZATION
CHANNELIZATIONS
CHANNELIZE
CHANNELIZED
CHANNELIZES
CHANNELIZING
CHANNELLED
CHANNELLING
CHANNELS
CHANOYU
CHANOYUS
CHANSON
CHANSONNIER
CHANSONNIERS
CHANSONS
CHANT
CHANTABLE
CHANTAGE
CHANTAGES
CHANTED
CHANTER
CHANTERELLE
CHANTERELLES
CHANTERS
CHANTEUSE
CHANTEUSES
CHANTEY
CHANTEYS
CHANTICLEER
CHANTICLEERS
CHANTIES
CHANTING
CHANTOR
CHANTORS
CHANTRIES
CHANTRY
CHANTS
CHANTY
CHAO
CHAOS
CHAOSES
CHAOTIC
CHAOTICALLY
CHAP
CHAPARAJOS
CHAPAREJOS
CHAPARRAL
CHAPARRALS
CHAPATI
CHAPATIS
CHAPATTI
CHAPATTIS
CHAPBOOK
CHAPBOOKS
CHAPE
CHAPEAU
CHAPEAUS
CHAPEAUX
CHAPEL
CHAPELS
CHAPERON
CHAPERONAGE
CHAPERONAGES
CHAPERONE
CHAPERONED
CHAPERONES
CHAPERONING
CHAPERONS
CHAPES
CHAPFALLEN
CHAPITER
CHAPITERS
CHAPLAIN
CHAPLAINCIES
CHAPLAINCY
CHAPLAINS
CHAPLET
CHAPLETED
CHAPLETS
CHAPMAN
CHAPMEN
CHAPPAL
CHAPPALS
CHAPPATI
CHAPPATIS
CHAPPED
CHAPPIE
CHAPPIES
CHAPPING
CHAPS
CHAPT
CHAPTER
CHAPTERAL
CHAPTERED
CHAPTERING
CHAPTERS
CHAQUETA
CHAQUETAS
CHAR
CHARABANC
CHARABANCS
CHARACID
CHARACIDS
CHARACIN
CHARACINS
CHARACTER
CHARACTERED
CHARACTERFUL
CHARACTERIES
CHARACTERING
CHARACTERISE
CHARACTERISED
CHARACTERISES
CHARACTERISING
CHARACTERISTIC
CHARACTERISTICS
CHARACTERIZE
CHARACTERIZED
CHARACTERIZES
CHARACTERIZING
CHARACTERLESS
CHARACTERS
CHARACTERY
CHARADE
CHARADES
CHARAS
CHARASES
CHARBROIL
CHARBROILED
CHARBROILER
CHARBROILERS
CHARBROILING
CHARBROILS
CHARCOAL
CHARCOALED
CHARCOALING
CHARCOALS
CHARCOALY
CHARCUTERIE
CHARCUTERIES
CHARD
CHARDONNAY
CHARDONNAYS
CHARDS
CHARE
CHARED
CHARES

CHARETTE
CHARETTES
CHARGE
CHARGEABLE
CHARGED
CHARGEHAND
CHARGEHANDS
CHARGER
CHARGERS
CHARGES
CHARGING
CHARGINGS
CHARGRILL
CHARGRILLED
CHARGRILLING
CHARGRILLS
CHARIER
CHARIEST
CHARILY
CHARINESS
CHARINESSES
CHARING
CHARIOT
CHARIOTED
CHARIOTEER
CHARIOTEERS
CHARIOTING
CHARIOTS
CHARISM
CHARISMA
CHARISMAS
CHARISMATA
CHARISMATIC
CHARISMATICS
CHARISMS
CHARITABLE
CHARITABLENESS
CHARITABLY
CHARITIES
CHARITY
CHARIVARI
CHARIVARIED
CHARIVARIING
CHARIVARIS
CHARK
CHARKA
CHARKAS
CHARKED
CHARKHA
CHARKHAS
CHARKING
CHARKS
CHARLADIES
CHARLADY
CHARLATAN
CHARLATANISM
CHARLATANISMS
CHARLATANRIES
CHARLATANRY
CHARLATANS
CHARLEY
CHARLEYS
CHARLIE
CHARLIES
CHARLOCK
CHARLOCKS
CHARLOTTE
CHARLOTTES
CHARM
CHARMED
CHARMER
CHARMERS
CHARMEUSE
CHARMEUSES
CHARMING
CHARMINGER
CHARMINGEST
CHARMINGLY
CHARMLESS
CHARMS
CHARNEL
CHARNELS
CHARPAI
CHARPAIS
CHARPOY
CHARPOYS
CHARQUI
CHARQUID
CHARQUIS
CHARR
CHARRED
CHARRIER
CHARRIEST
CHARRING
CHARRO
CHARROS
CHARRS
CHARRY
CHARS
CHART
CHARTABLE
CHARTED
CHARTER
CHARTERED
CHARTERER
CHARTERERS
CHARTERING
CHARTERS
CHARTING
CHARTISM
CHARTISMS
CHARTIST
CHARTISTS
CHARTLESS
CHARTREUSE
CHARTREUSES
CHARTS
CHARTULARIES
CHARTULARY
CHARWOMAN
CHARWOMEN
CHARY
CHASE
CHASEABLE
CHASED
CHASER
CHASERS
CHASES
CHASING
CHASINGS
CHASM
CHASMAL
CHASMED
CHASMIC
CHASMS
CHASMY
CHASSE
CHASSED
CHASSEING
CHASSEPOT
CHASSEPOTS
CHASSES
CHASSEUR
CHASSEURS
CHASSIS
CHASTE
CHASTELY
CHASTEN
CHASTENED
CHASTENER
CHASTENERS
CHASTENESS
CHASTENESSES
CHASTENING
CHASTENS
CHASTER
CHASTEST
CHASTISE
CHASTISED
CHASTISEMENT
CHASTISEMENTS
CHASTISER
CHASTISERS
CHASTISES
CHASTISING
CHASTITIES
CHASTITY
CHASUBLE
CHASUBLES
CHAT
CHATCHKA
CHATCHKAS
CHATCHKE
CHATCHKES
CHATEAU
CHATEAUBRIAND
CHATEAUBRIANDS
CHATEAUS
CHATEAUX
CHATELAIN
CHATELAINE
CHATELAINES
CHATELAINS
CHATLINE
CHATLINES
CHATOYANCE
CHATOYANCES
CHATOYANCIES
CHATOYANCY
CHATOYANT
CHATOYANTS
CHATROOM
CHATROOMS
CHATS
CHATTED
CHATTEL
CHATTELS
CHATTER
CHATTERBOX
CHATTERBOXES
CHATTERED
CHATTERER
CHATTERERS
CHATTERING
CHATTERS
CHATTERY
CHATTIER
CHATTIEST
CHATTILY
CHATTINESS
CHATTINESSES
CHATTING
CHATTY
CHAUFER
CHAUFERS
CHAUFFER
CHAUFFERS
CHAUFFEUR
CHAUFFEURED
CHAUFFEURING
CHAUFFEURS
CHAULMOOGRA
CHAULMOOGRAS
CHAUNT
CHAUNTED
CHAUNTER
CHAUNTERS
CHAUNTING
CHAUNTS
CHAUSSES
CHAUSSURE
CHAUSSURES
CHAUTAUQUA
CHAUTAUQUAS
CHAUVINISM
CHAUVINISMS
CHAUVINIST
CHAUVINISTIC
CHAUVINISTS
CHAW
CHAWBACON
CHAWBACONS
CHAWED
CHAWER
CHAWERS
CHAWING
CHAWS
CHAY
CHAYOTE
CHAYOTES
CHAYS
CHAZAN
CHAZANIM
CHAZANS
CHAZZAN
CHAZZANIM
CHAZZANS
CHAZZEN
CHAZZENIM
CHAZZENS
CHEAP
CHEAPEN
CHEAPENED
CHEAPENER
CHEAPENERS

CHEAPENING
CHEAPENS
CHEAPER
CHEAPEST
CHEAPIE
CHEAPIES
CHEAPISH
CHEAPISHLY
CHEAPJACK
CHEAPJACKS
CHEAPLY
CHEAPNESS
CHEAPNESSES
CHEAPO
CHEAPOS
CHEAPS
CHEAPSKATE
CHEAPSKATES
CHEAT
CHEATABLE
CHEATED
CHEATER
CHEATERS
CHEATGRASS
CHEATGRASSES
CHEATING
CHEATS
CHEBEC
CHEBECS
CHECHAKO
CHECHAKOS
CHECK
CHECKABLE
CHECKBOOK
CHECKBOOKS
CHECKBOX
CHECKBOXES
CHECKED
CHECKER
CHECKERBERRIES
CHECKERBERRY
CHECKERBOARD
CHECKERBOARDS
CHECKERED
CHECKERING
CHECKERS
CHECKING
CHECKLESS
CHECKLIST
CHECKLISTED
CHECKLISTING
CHECKLISTS
CHECKMARK
CHECKMARKED
CHECKMARKING
CHECKMARKS
CHECKMATE
CHECKMATED
CHECKMATES
CHECKMATING
CHECKOFF
CHECKOFFS
CHECKOUT
CHECKOUTS
CHECKPOINT
CHECKPOINTS
CHECKREIN
CHECKREINS
CHECKROOM
CHECKROOMS
CHECKROW
CHECKROWED
CHECKROWING
CHECKROWS
CHECKS
CHECKSUM
CHECKSUMS
CHECKUP
CHECKUPS
CHEDARIM
CHEDDAR
CHEDDARS
CHEDDARY
CHEDDITE
CHEDDITES
CHEDER
CHEDERS
CHEDITE
CHEDITES
CHEECHAKO
CHEECHAKOS
CHEEK
CHEEKBONE
CHEEKBONES
CHEEKED
CHEEKFUL
CHEEKFULS
CHEEKIER
CHEEKIEST
CHEEKILY
CHEEKINESS
CHEEKINESSES
CHEEKING
CHEEKLESS
CHEEKS
CHEEKY
CHEEP
CHEEPED
CHEEPER
CHEEPERS
CHEEPING
CHEEPS
CHEER
CHEERED
CHEERER
CHEERERS
CHEERFUL
CHEERFULLER
CHEERFULLEST
CHEERFULLY
CHEERFULNESS
CHEERFULNESSES
CHEERIER
CHEERIEST
CHEERILY
CHEERINESS
CHEERINESSES
CHEERING
CHEERIO
CHEERIOS
CHEERLEAD
CHEERLEADER
CHEERLEADERS
CHEERLEADING
CHEERLEADS
CHEERLED
CHEERLESS
CHEERLESSLY
CHEERLESSNESS
CHEERLESSNESSES
CHEERLY
CHEERO
CHEEROS
CHEERS
CHEERY
CHEESE
CHEESEBURGER
CHEESEBURGERS
CHEESECAKE
CHEESECAKES
CHEESECLOTH
CHEESECLOTHS
CHEESED
CHEESEPARING
CHEESEPARINGS
CHEESES
CHEESESTEAK
CHEESESTEAKS
CHEESIER
CHEESIEST
CHEESILY
CHEESINESS
CHEESINESSES
CHEESING
CHEESY
CHEETAH
CHEETAHS
CHEF
CHEFDOM
CHEFDOMS
CHEFED
CHEFFED
CHEFFING
CHEFING
CHEFS
CHEGOE
CHEGOES
CHELA
CHELAE
CHELAS
CHELASHIP
CHELASHIPS
CHELATABLE
CHELATE
CHELATED
CHELATES
CHELATING
CHELATION
CHELATIONS
CHELATOR
CHELATORS
CHELICERA
CHELICERAE
CHELICERAL
CHELIFORM
CHELIPED
CHELIPEDS
CHELOID
CHELOIDS
CHELONIAN
CHELONIANS
CHEM
CHEMIC
CHEMICAL
CHEMICALLY
CHEMICALS
CHEMICS
CHEMIOSMOTIC
CHEMISE
CHEMISES
CHEMISETTE
CHEMISETTES
CHEMISM
CHEMISMS
CHEMISORB
CHEMISORBED
CHEMISORBING
CHEMISORBS
CHEMISORPTION
CHEMISORPTIONS
CHEMIST
CHEMISTRIES
CHEMISTRY
CHEMISTS
CHEMO
CHEMOAUTOTROPHY
CHEMOKINE
CHEMOKINES
CHEMOPREVENTION
CHEMOPREVENTIVE
CHEMORECEPTION
CHEMORECEPTIONS
CHEMORECEPTIVE
CHEMORECEPTOR
CHEMORECEPTORS
CHEMOS
CHEMOSORB
CHEMOSORBED
CHEMOSORBING
CHEMOSORBS
CHEMOSTAT
CHEMOSTATS
CHEMOSURGERIES
CHEMOSURGERY
CHEMOSURGICAL
CHEMOSYNTHESES
CHEMOSYNTHESIS
CHEMOSYNTHETIC
CHEMOTACTIC
CHEMOTACTICALLY
CHEMOTAXES
CHEMOTAXIS
CHEMOTAXONOMIC
CHEMOTAXONOMIES
CHEMOTAXONOMIST
CHEMOTAXONOMY
CHEMOTHERAPIES
CHEMOTHERAPIST
CHEMOTHERAPISTS
CHEMOTHERAPY
CHEMOTROPISM
CHEMOTROPISMS
CHEMS
CHEMURGIC
CHEMURGIES

CHEMURGY
CHENILLE
CHENILLES
CHENOPOD
CHENOPODS
CHEONGSAM
CHEONGSAMS
CHEQUE
CHEQUEBOOK
CHEQUEBOOKS
CHEQUER
CHEQUERED
CHEQUERING
CHEQUERS
CHEQUES
CHERIMOYA
CHERIMOYAS
CHERISH
CHERISHABLE
CHERISHED
CHERISHER
CHERISHERS
CHERISHES
CHERISHING
CHERNOZEM
CHERNOZEMIC
CHERNOZEMS
CHEROOT
CHEROOTS
CHERRIER
CHERRIES
CHERRIEST
CHERRY
CHERRYLIKE
CHERRYSTONE
CHERRYSTONES
CHERRYWOOD
CHERRYWOODS
CHERT
CHERTIER
CHERTIEST
CHERTS
CHERTY
CHERUB
CHERUBIC
CHERUBICALLY
CHERUBIM
CHERUBIMS
CHERUBLIKE
CHERUBS
CHERVIL
CHERVILS
CHESHIRE
CHESHIRES
CHESS
CHESSBOARD
CHESSBOARDS
CHESSES
CHESSMAN
CHESSMEN
CHEST
CHESTED
CHESTERFIELD
CHESTERFIELDS
CHESTFUL
CHESTFULS
CHESTIER
CHESTIEST
CHESTILY
CHESTNUT
CHESTNUTS
CHESTS
CHESTY
CHETAH
CHETAHS
CHETH
CHETHS
CHETRUM
CHETRUMS
CHEVALET
CHEVALETS
CHEVALIER
CHEVALIERS
CHEVELURE
CHEVELURES
CHEVERON
CHEVERONS
CHEVET
CHEVETS
CHEVIED
CHEVIES
CHEVIOT
CHEVIOTS
CHEVRE
CHEVRES
CHEVRET
CHEVRETS
CHEVRON
CHEVRONS
CHEVY
CHEVYING
CHEVYS
CHEW
CHEWABLE
CHEWED
CHEWER
CHEWERS
CHEWIER
CHEWIEST
CHEWINESS
CHEWINESSES
CHEWING
CHEWINK
CHEWINKS
CHEWS
CHEWY
CHEZ
CHI
CHIA
CHIANTI
CHIANTIS
CHIAO
CHIAROSCURIST
CHIAROSCURISTS
CHIAROSCURO
CHIAROSCUROS
CHIAS
CHIASM
CHIASMA
CHIASMAL
CHIASMAS
CHIASMATA
CHIASMATIC
CHIASMI
CHIASMIC
CHIASMS
CHIASMUS
CHIASTIC
CHIAUS
CHIAUSES
CHIBOUK
CHIBOUKS
CHIBOUQUE
CHIBOUQUES
CHIC
CHICA
CHICALOTE
CHICALOTES
CHICANE
CHICANED
CHICANER
CHICANERIES
CHICANERS
CHICANERY
CHICANES
CHICANING
CHICANO
CHICANOS
CHICAS
CHICCORIES
CHICCORY
CHICER
CHICEST
CHICHI
CHICHIER
CHICHIEST
CHICHIS
CHICK
CHICKADEE
CHICKADEES
CHICKAREE
CHICKAREES
CHICKEE
CHICKEES
CHICKEN
CHICKENED
CHICKENHEARTED
CHICKENING
CHICKENS
CHICKENSHIT
CHICKENSHITS
CHICKORIES
CHICKORY
CHICKPEA
CHICKPEAS
CHICKS
CHICKWEED
CHICKWEEDS
CHICLE
CHICLES
CHICLY
CHICNESS
CHICNESSES
CHICO
CHICORIES
CHICORY
CHICOS
CHICOT
CHICOTS
CHICS
CHID
CHIDDEN
CHIDE
CHIDED
CHIDER
CHIDERS
CHIDES
CHIDING
CHIDINGLY
CHIEF
CHIEFDOM
CHIEFDOMS
CHIEFER
CHIEFEST
CHIEFLY
CHIEFS
CHIEFSHIP
CHIEFSHIPS
CHIEFTAIN
CHIEFTAINCIES
CHIEFTAINCY
CHIEFTAINS
CHIEFTAINSHIP
CHIEFTAINSHIPS
CHIEL
CHIELD
CHIELDS
CHIELS
CHIFFCHAFF
CHIFFCHAFFS
CHIFFON
CHIFFONADE
CHIFFONADES
CHIFFONIER
CHIFFONIERS
CHIFFONS
CHIFFOROBE
CHIFFOROBES
CHIGETAI
CHIGETAIS
CHIGGER
CHIGGERS
CHIGNON
CHIGNONED
CHIGNONS
CHIGOE
CHIGOES
CHILBLAIN
CHILBLAINS
CHILD
CHILDBEARING
CHILDBEARINGS
CHILDBED
CHILDBEDS
CHILDBIRTH
CHILDBIRTHS
CHILDCARE
CHILDCARES
CHILDE
CHILDES
CHILDHOOD
CHILDHOODS
CHILDING
CHILDISH
CHILDISHLY

CHILDISHNESS
CHILDISHNESSES
CHILDLESS
CHILDLESSNESS
CHILDLESSNESSES
CHILDLIER
CHILDLIEST
CHILDLIKE
CHILDLIKENESS
CHILDLIKENESSES
CHILDLY
CHILDMINDER
CHILDMINDERS
CHILDPROOF
CHILDREN
CHILE
CHILES
CHILI
CHILIAD
CHILIADAL
CHILIADIC
CHILIADS
CHILIARCH
CHILIARCHS
CHILIASM
CHILIASMS
CHILIAST
CHILIASTIC
CHILIASTS
CHILIDOG
CHILIDOGS
CHILIES
CHILIS
CHILL
CHILLAX
CHILLAXED
CHILLAXES
CHILLAXING
CHILLED
CHILLER
CHILLERS
CHILLEST
CHILLI
CHILLIER
CHILLIES
CHILLIEST
CHILLILY
CHILLINESS
CHILLINESSES
CHILLING
CHILLINGLY
CHILLIS
CHILLNESS
CHILLNESSES
CHILLS
CHILLUM
CHILLUMS
CHILLY
CHILOPOD
CHILOPODS
CHILTEPIN
CHILTEPINE
CHILTEPINES
CHILTEPINS
CHIMAERA
CHIMAERAS
CHIMAERIC
CHIMAERISM
CHIMAERISMS
CHIMAR
CHIMARS
CHIMB
CHIMBLEY
CHIMBLEYS
CHIMBLIES
CHIMBLY
CHIMBS
CHIME
CHIMED
CHIMENEA
CHIMENEAS
CHIMER
CHIMERA
CHIMERAS
CHIMERE
CHIMERES
CHIMERIC
CHIMERICAL
CHIMERICALLY
CHIMERISM
CHIMERISMS
CHIMERS
CHIMES
CHIMICHANGA
CHIMICHANGAS
CHIMINEA
CHIMINEAS
CHIMING
CHIMLA
CHIMLAS
CHIMLEY
CHIMLEYS
CHIMNEY
CHIMNEYLIKE
CHIMNEYPIECE
CHIMNEYPIECES
CHIMNEYS
CHIMP
CHIMPANZEE
CHIMPANZEES
CHIMPS
CHIN
CHINA
CHINABERRIES
CHINABERRY
CHINAS
CHINAWARE
CHINAWARES
CHINBONE
CHINBONES
CHINCAPIN
CHINCAPINS
CHINCH
CHINCHED
CHINCHERINCHEE
CHINCHERINCHEES
CHINCHES
CHINCHIER
CHINCHIEST
CHINCHILLA
CHINCHILLAS
CHINCHING
CHINCHY
CHINE
CHINED
CHINES
CHING
CHINGS
CHINING
CHINK
CHINKAPIN
CHINKAPINS
CHINKED
CHINKIER
CHINKIEST
CHINKING
CHINKS
CHINKY
CHINLESS
CHINNED
CHINNING
CHINO
CHINOIS
CHINOISERIE
CHINOISERIES
CHINOISES
CHINONE
CHINONES
CHINOOK
CHINOOKS
CHINOS
CHINQUAPIN
CHINQUAPINS
CHINS
CHINSE
CHINSED
CHINSES
CHINSING
CHINSTRAP
CHINSTRAPS
CHINTS
CHINTSES
CHINTZ
CHINTZES
CHINTZIER
CHINTZIEST
CHINTZINESS
CHINTZINESSES
CHINTZY
CHINWAG
CHINWAGGED
CHINWAGGING
CHINWAGS
CHIONODOXA
CHIONODOXAS
CHIP
CHIPBOARD
CHIPBOARDS
CHIPMUCK
CHIPMUCKS
CHIPMUNK
CHIPMUNKS
CHIPOLATA
CHIPOLATAS
CHIPOTLE
CHIPOTLES
CHIPPABLE
CHIPPED
CHIPPER
CHIPPERED
CHIPPERING
CHIPPERS
CHIPPIE
CHIPPIER
CHIPPIES
CHIPPIEST
CHIPPING
CHIPPY
CHIPS
CHIPSET
CHIPSETS
CHIRAL
CHIRALITIES
CHIRALITY
CHIRIMOYA
CHIRIMOYAS
CHIRK
CHIRKED
CHIRKER
CHIRKEST
CHIRKING
CHIRKS
CHIRM
CHIRMED
CHIRMING
CHIRMS
CHIRO
CHIROGRAPHER
CHIROGRAPHERS
CHIROGRAPHIC
CHIROGRAPHICAL
CHIROGRAPHIES
CHIROGRAPHY
CHIROMANCER
CHIROMANCERS
CHIROMANCIES
CHIROMANCY
CHIRONOMID
CHIRONOMIDS
CHIROPODIES
CHIROPODIST
CHIROPODISTS
CHIROPODY
CHIROPRACTIC
CHIROPRACTICS
CHIROPRACTOR
CHIROPRACTORS
CHIROPTER
CHIROPTERAN
CHIROPTERANS
CHIROPTERS
CHIROS
CHIRP
CHIRPED
CHIRPER
CHIRPERS
CHIRPIER
CHIRPIEST
CHIRPILY
CHIRPINESS
CHIRPINESSES
CHIRPING
CHIRPS
CHIRPY
CHIRR

CHIRRE
CHIRRED
CHIRREN
CHIRRES
CHIRRING
CHIRRS
CHIRRUP
CHIRRUPED
CHIRRUPING
CHIRRUPS
CHIRRUPY
CHIRU
CHIRURGEON
CHIRURGEONS
CHIRUS
CHIS
CHISEL
CHISELED
CHISELER
CHISELERS
CHISELING
CHISELLED
CHISELLER
CHISELLERS
CHISELLING
CHISELS
CHIT
CHITAL
CHITALS
CHITCHAT
CHITCHATS
CHITCHATTED
CHITCHATTING
CHITIN
CHITINOID
CHITINOUS
CHITINS
CHITLIN
CHITLING
CHITLINGS
CHITLINS
CHITON
CHITONS
CHITOSAN
CHITOSANS
CHITS
CHITTER
CHITTERED
CHITTERING
CHITTERLINGS
CHITTERS
CHITTIES
CHITTY
CHIVALRIC
CHIVALRIES
CHIVALROUS
CHIVALROUSLY
CHIVALROUSNESS
CHIVALRY
CHIVAREE
CHIVAREED
CHIVAREEING
CHIVAREES
CHIVARI
CHIVARIED
CHIVARIES
CHIVARIING
CHIVE
CHIVES
CHIVIED
CHIVIES
CHIVVIED
CHIVVIES
CHIVVY
CHIVVYING
CHIVY
CHIVYING
CHLAMYDES
CHLAMYDIA
CHLAMYDIAE
CHLAMYDIAL
CHLAMYDOSPORE
CHLAMYDOSPORES
CHLAMYS
CHLAMYSES
CHLOASMA
CHLOASMAS
CHLOASMATA
CHLORACNE
CHLORACNES
CHLORAL
CHLORALOSE
CHLORALOSED
CHLORALOSES
CHLORALS
CHLORAMINE
CHLORAMINES
CHLORAMPHENICOL
CHLORATE
CHLORATES
CHLORDAN
CHLORDANE
CHLORDANES
CHLORDANS
CHLORELLA
CHLORELLAS
CHLORENCHYMA
CHLORENCHYMAS
CHLORHEXIDINE
CHLORHEXIDINES
CHLORIC
CHLORID
CHLORIDE
CHLORIDES
CHLORIDIC
CHLORIDS
CHLORIN
CHLORINATE
CHLORINATED
CHLORINATES
CHLORINATING
CHLORINATION
CHLORINATIONS
CHLORINATOR
CHLORINATORS
CHLORINE
CHLORINES
CHLORINITIES
CHLORINITY
CHLORINS
CHLORITE
CHLORITES
CHLORITIC
CHLOROBENZENE
CHLOROBENZENES
CHLOROFORM
CHLOROFORMED
CHLOROFORMING
CHLOROFORMS
CHLOROHYDRIN
CHLOROHYDRINS
CHLOROPHYLL
CHLOROPHYLLOUS
CHLOROPHYLLS
CHLOROPICRIN
CHLOROPICRINS
CHLOROPLAST
CHLOROPLASTIC
CHLOROPLASTS
CHLOROPRENE
CHLOROPRENES
CHLOROQUINE
CHLOROQUINES
CHLOROSES
CHLOROSIS
CHLOROTHIAZIDE
CHLOROTHIAZIDES
CHLOROTIC
CHLOROUS
CHLORPROMAZINE
CHLORPROMAZINES
CHLORPROPAMIDE
CHLORPROPAMIDES
CHLORPYRIFOS
CHLORPYRIFOSES
CHOANA
CHOANAE
CHOANOCYTE
CHOANOCYTES
CHOC
CHOCAHOLIC
CHOCAHOLICS
CHOCK
CHOCKABLOCK
CHOCKED
CHOCKFUL
CHOCKFULL
CHOCKING
CHOCKS
CHOCOHOLIC
CHOCOHOLICS
CHOCOLATE
CHOCOLATES
CHOCOLATEY
CHOCOLATIER
CHOCOLATIERS
CHOCOLATIEST
CHOCOLATY
CHOCS
CHOICE
CHOICELY
CHOICENESS
CHOICENESSES
CHOICER
CHOICES
CHOICEST
CHOIL
CHOILS
CHOIR
CHOIRBOY
CHOIRBOYS
CHOIRED
CHOIRGIRL
CHOIRGIRLS
CHOIRING
CHOIRMASTER
CHOIRMASTERS
CHOIRS
CHOKE
CHOKEABLE
CHOKEBERRIES
CHOKEBERRY
CHOKEBORE
CHOKEBORES
CHOKECHERRIES
CHOKECHERRY
CHOKED
CHOKEDAMP
CHOKEDAMPS
CHOKEHOLD
CHOKEHOLDS
CHOKER
CHOKERS
CHOKES
CHOKEY
CHOKEYS
CHOKIER
CHOKIES
CHOKIEST
CHOKING
CHOKINGLY
CHOKY
CHOLA
CHOLANGIOGRAM
CHOLANGIOGRAMS
CHOLANGIOGRAPHY
CHOLAS
CHOLATE
CHOLATES
CHOLECALCIFEROL
CHOLECYST
CHOLECYSTECTOMY
CHOLECYSTITIDES
CHOLECYSTITIS
CHOLECYSTITISES
CHOLECYSTOKININ
CHOLECYSTS
CHOLELITHIASES
CHOLELITHIASIS
CHOLENT
CHOLENTS
CHOLER
CHOLERA
CHOLERAIC
CHOLERAS
CHOLERIC
CHOLERICALLY
CHOLEROID
CHOLERS
CHOLESTASES
CHOLESTASIS
CHOLESTATIC
CHOLESTERIC
CHOLESTEROL
CHOLESTEROLS

CHOLESTYRAMINE
CHOLESTYRAMINES
CHOLI
CHOLIAMB
CHOLIAMBS
CHOLINE
CHOLINERGIC
CHOLINERGICALLY
CHOLINES
CHOLINESTERASE
CHOLINESTERASES
CHOLIS
CHOLLA
CHOLLAS
CHOLO
CHOLOS
CHOMP
CHOMPED
CHOMPER
CHOMPERS
CHOMPING
CHOMPS
CHON
CHONDRIOSOME
CHONDRIOSOMES
CHONDRITE
CHONDRITES
CHONDRITIC
CHONDROCRANIA
CHONDROCRANIUM
CHONDROCRANIUMS
CHONDROCYTE
CHONDROCYTES
CHONDROITIN
CHONDROITINS
CHONDROMA
CHONDROMAS
CHONDROMATA
CHONDRULE
CHONDRULES
CHONS
CHOOK
CHOOKS
CHOOSE
CHOOSER
CHOOSERS
CHOOSES
CHOOSEY
CHOOSIER
CHOOSIEST
CHOOSILY
CHOOSING
CHOOSY
CHOP
CHOPFALLEN
CHOPHOUSE
CHOPHOUSES
CHOPIN
CHOPINE
CHOPINES
CHOPINS
CHOPLOGIC
CHOPLOGICS
CHOPPED
CHOPPER
CHOPPERED
CHOPPERING
CHOPPERS
CHOPPIER
CHOPPIEST
CHOPPILY
CHOPPINESS
CHOPPINESSES
CHOPPING
CHOPPY
CHOPS
CHOPSOCKIES
CHOPSOCKY
CHOPSTICK
CHOPSTICKS
CHORAGI
CHORAGIC
CHORAGUS
CHORAGUSES
CHORAL
CHORALE
CHORALES
CHORALLY
CHORALS
CHORD
CHORDAL
CHORDAMESODERM
CHORDAMESODERMS
CHORDATE
CHORDATES
CHORDED
CHORDING
CHORDINGS
CHORDS
CHORE
CHOREA
CHOREAL
CHOREAS
CHOREATIC
CHOREBOY
CHOREBOYS
CHORED
CHOREGI
CHOREGUS
CHOREGUSES
CHOREIC
CHOREIFORM
CHOREMAN
CHOREMEN
CHOREOGRAPH
CHOREOGRAPHED
CHOREOGRAPHER
CHOREOGRAPHERS
CHOREOGRAPHIC
CHOREOGRAPHIES
CHOREOGRAPHING
CHOREOGRAPHS
CHOREOGRAPHY
CHOREOID
CHORES
CHORIAL
CHORIAMB
CHORIAMBI
CHORIAMBS
CHORIC
CHORINE
CHORINES
CHORING
CHORIOALLANTOIC
CHORIOALLANTOIS
CHORIOCARCINOMA
CHORIOID
CHORIOIDS
CHORION
CHORIONIC
CHORIONS
CHORISTER
CHORISTERS
CHORIZO
CHORIZOS
CHOROGRAPHER
CHOROGRAPHERS
CHOROGRAPHIC
CHOROGRAPHIES
CHOROGRAPHY
CHOROID
CHOROIDAL
CHOROIDS
CHORTEN
CHORTENS
CHORTLE
CHORTLED
CHORTLER
CHORTLERS
CHORTLES
CHORTLING
CHORUS
CHORUSED
CHORUSES
CHORUSING
CHORUSSED
CHORUSSES
CHORUSSING
CHOSE
CHOSEN
CHOSES
CHOTT
CHOTTS
CHOUCROUTE
CHOUCROUTES
CHOUGH
CHOUGHS
CHOUSE
CHOUSED
CHOUSER
CHOUSERS
CHOUSES
CHOUSH
CHOUSHES
CHOUSING
CHOW
CHOWCHOW
CHOWCHOWS
CHOWDER
CHOWDERED
CHOWDERHEAD
CHOWDERHEADED
CHOWDERHEADS
CHOWDERING
CHOWDERS
CHOWED
CHOWHOUND
CHOWHOUNDS
CHOWING
CHOWS
CHOWSE
CHOWSED
CHOWSES
CHOWSING
CHOWTIME
CHOWTIMES
CHRESARD
CHRESARDS
CHRESTOMATHIES
CHRESTOMATHY
CHRISM
CHRISMA
CHRISMAL
CHRISMATION
CHRISMATIONS
CHRISMON
CHRISMONS
CHRISMS
CHRISOM
CHRISOMS
CHRISTEN
CHRISTENED
CHRISTENING
CHRISTENINGS
CHRISTENS
CHRISTIANIA
CHRISTIANIAS
CHRISTIE
CHRISTIES
CHRISTOPHENE
CHRISTOPHENES
CHRISTOPHINE
CHRISTOPHINES
CHRISTY
CHROMA
CHROMAFFIN
CHROMAFFINS
CHROMAS
CHROMATE
CHROMATES
CHROMATIC
CHROMATICALLY
CHROMATICISM
CHROMATICISMS
CHROMATICITIES
CHROMATICITY
CHROMATICS
CHROMATID
CHROMATIDS
CHROMATIN
CHROMATINIC
CHROMATINS
CHROMATOGRAM
CHROMATOGRAMS
CHROMATOGRAPH
CHROMATOGRAPHED
CHROMATOGRAPHER
CHROMATOGRAPHIC
CHROMATOGRAPHS
CHROMATOGRAPHY
CHROMATOLYSES
CHROMATOLYSIS
CHROMATOLYTIC
CHROMATOPHORE
CHROMATOPHORES

CHROME
CHROMED
CHROMES
CHROMIC
CHROMIDE
CHROMIDES
CHROMIER
CHROMIEST
CHROMINANCE
CHROMINANCES
CHROMING
CHROMINGS
CHROMITE
CHROMITES
CHROMIUM
CHROMIUMS
CHROMIZE
CHROMIZED
CHROMIZES
CHROMIZING
CHROMO
CHROMOCENTER
CHROMOCENTERS
CHROMODYNAMICS
CHROMOGEN
CHROMOGENIC
CHROMOGENS
CHROMOLIES
CHROMOLY
CHROMOMERE
CHROMOMERES
CHROMOMERIC
CHROMONEMA
CHROMONEMATA
CHROMONEMATIC
CHROMOPHIL
CHROMOPHOBE
CHROMOPHOBES
CHROMOPHORE
CHROMOPHORES
CHROMOPHORIC
CHROMOPLAST
CHROMOPLASTS
CHROMOPROTEIN
CHROMOPROTEINS
CHROMOS
CHROMOSOMAL
CHROMOSOMALLY
CHROMOSOME
CHROMOSOMES
CHROMOSPHERE
CHROMOSPHERES
CHROMOSPHERIC
CHROMOUS
CHROMY
CHROMYL
CHROMYLS
CHRONAXIE
CHRONAXIES
CHRONAXY
CHRONIC
CHRONICALLY
CHRONICITIES
CHRONICITY
CHRONICLE
CHRONICLED
CHRONICLER
CHRONICLERS
CHRONICLES
CHRONICLING
CHRONICS
CHRONOBIOLOGIC
CHRONOBIOLOGIES
CHRONOBIOLOGIST
CHRONOBIOLOGY
CHRONOGRAM
CHRONOGRAMS
CHRONOGRAPH
CHRONOGRAPHIC
CHRONOGRAPHIES
CHRONOGRAPHS
CHRONOGRAPHY
CHRONOLOGER
CHRONOLOGERS
CHRONOLOGIC
CHRONOLOGICAL
CHRONOLOGICALLY
CHRONOLOGIES
CHRONOLOGIST
CHRONOLOGISTS
CHRONOLOGY
CHRONOMETER
CHRONOMETERS
CHRONOMETRIC
CHRONOMETRICAL
CHRONOMETRIES
CHRONOMETRY
CHRONON
CHRONONS
CHRONOTHERAPIES
CHRONOTHERAPY
CHRYSALID
CHRYSALIDES
CHRYSALIDS
CHRYSALIS
CHRYSALISES
CHRYSANTHEMUM
CHRYSANTHEMUMS
CHRYSAROBIN
CHRYSAROBINS
CHRYSOBERYL
CHRYSOBERYLS
CHRYSOLITE
CHRYSOLITES
CHRYSOMELID
CHRYSOMELIDS
CHRYSOPHYTE
CHRYSOPHYTES
CHRYSOPRASE
CHRYSOPRASES
CHRYSOTILE
CHRYSOTILES
CHTHONIAN
CHTHONIC
CHUB
CHUBASCO
CHUBASCOS
CHUBBIER
CHUBBIEST
CHUBBILY
CHUBBINESS
CHUBBINESSES
CHUBBY
CHUBS
CHUCK
CHUCKAWALLA
CHUCKAWALLAS
CHUCKED
CHUCKER
CHUCKERS
CHUCKHOLE
CHUCKHOLES
CHUCKIES
CHUCKING
CHUCKLE
CHUCKLED
CHUCKLEHEAD
CHUCKLEHEADED
CHUCKLEHEADS
CHUCKLER
CHUCKLERS
CHUCKLES
CHUCKLESOME
CHUCKLING
CHUCKLINGLY
CHUCKS
CHUCKWAGON
CHUCKWAGONS
CHUCKWALLA
CHUCKWALLAS
CHUCKY
CHUDDAH
CHUDDAHS
CHUDDAR
CHUDDARS
CHUDDER
CHUDDERS
CHUFA
CHUFAS
CHUFF
CHUFFED
CHUFFER
CHUFFEST
CHUFFIER
CHUFFIEST
CHUFFING
CHUFFS
CHUFFY
CHUG
CHUGALUG
CHUGALUGGED
CHUGALUGGING
CHUGALUGS
CHUGGED
CHUGGER
CHUGGERS
CHUGGING
CHUGS
CHUKAR
CHUKARS
CHUKKA
CHUKKAR
CHUKKARS
CHUKKAS
CHUKKER
CHUKKERS
CHUM
CHUMMED
CHUMMIER
CHUMMIES
CHUMMIEST
CHUMMILY
CHUMMINESS
CHUMMINESSES
CHUMMING
CHUMMY
CHUMP
CHUMPED
CHUMPING
CHUMPS
CHUMS
CHUMSHIP
CHUMSHIPS
CHUNDER
CHUNDERED
CHUNDERING
CHUNDERS
CHUNK
CHUNKED
CHUNKIER
CHUNKIEST
CHUNKILY
CHUNKING
CHUNKS
CHUNKY
CHUNNEL
CHUNNELS
CHUNTER
CHUNTERED
CHUNTERING
CHUNTERS
CHUPPA
CHUPPAH
CHUPPAHS
CHUPPAS
CHUPPOT
CHURCH
CHURCHED
CHURCHES
CHURCHGOER
CHURCHGOERS
CHURCHGOING
CHURCHGOINGS
CHURCHIANITIES
CHURCHIANITY
CHURCHIER
CHURCHIEST
CHURCHING
CHURCHINGS
CHURCHLESS
CHURCHLIER
CHURCHLIEST
CHURCHLINESS
CHURCHLINESSES
CHURCHLY
CHURCHMAN
CHURCHMANSHIP
CHURCHMANSHIPS
CHURCHMEN
CHURCHWARDEN
CHURCHWARDENS
CHURCHWOMAN
CHURCHWOMEN
CHURCHY
CHURCHYARD

CHURCHYARDS
CHURINGA
CHURINGAS
CHURL
CHURLISH
CHURLISHLY
CHURLISHNESS
CHURLISHNESSES
CHURLS
CHURN
CHURNED
CHURNER
CHURNERS
CHURNING
CHURNINGS
CHURNS
CHURR
CHURRED
CHURRIGUERESQUE
CHURRING
CHURRO
CHURROS
CHURRS
CHUSE
CHUSED
CHUSES
CHUSING
CHUTE
CHUTED
CHUTES
CHUTING
CHUTIST
CHUTISTS
CHUTNEE
CHUTNEES
CHUTNEY
CHUTNEYS
CHUTZPA
CHUTZPAH
CHUTZPAHS
CHUTZPAS
CHYLE
CHYLES
CHYLOMICRON
CHYLOMICRONS
CHYLOUS
CHYME
CHYMES
CHYMIC
CHYMICS
CHYMIST
CHYMISTS
CHYMOSIN
CHYMOSINS
CHYMOTRYPSIN
CHYMOTRYPSINS
CHYMOTRYPTIC
CHYMOUS
CHYTRID
CHYTRIDS
CIABATTA
CIABATTAS
CIAO
CIBOL
CIBOLS
CIBORIA
CIBORIUM
CIBOULE
CIBOULES
CICADA
CICADAE
CICADAS
CICALA
CICALAS
CICALE
CICATRICE
CICATRICES
CICATRICIAL
CICATRIX
CICATRIXES
CICATRIZATION
CICATRIZATIONS
CICATRIZE
CICATRIZED
CICATRIZES
CICATRIZING
CICELIES
CICELY
CICERO
CICERONE
CICERONES
CICERONI
CICEROS
CICHLID
CICHLIDAE
CICHLIDS
CICISBEI
CICISBEISM
CICISBEISMS
CICISBEO
CICISBEOS
CICOREE
CICOREES
CIDER
CIDERS
CIG
CIGAR
CIGARET
CIGARETS
CIGARETTE
CIGARETTES
CIGARILLO
CIGARILLOS
CIGARLIKE
CIGARS
CIGGIE
CIGGIES
CIGGY
CIGS
CIGUATERA
CIGUATERAS
CILANTRO
CILANTROS
CILIA
CILIARY
CILIATE
CILIATED
CILIATELY
CILIATES
CILIATION
CILIATIONS
CILICE
CILICES
CILIOLATE
CILIUM
CIMBALOM
CIMBALOMS
CIMETIDINE
CIMETIDINES
CIMEX
CIMICES
CINCH
CINCHED
CINCHES
CINCHING
CINCHONA
CINCHONAS
CINCHONIC
CINCHONINE
CINCHONINES
CINCHONISM
CINCHONISMS
CINCTURE
CINCTURED
CINCTURES
CINCTURING
CINDER
CINDERED
CINDERING
CINDEROUS
CINDERS
CINDERY
CINE
CINEAST
CINEASTE
CINEASTES
CINEASTS
CINEMA
CINEMAGOER
CINEMAGOERS
CINEMAS
CINEMATHEQUE
CINEMATHEQUES
CINEMATIC
CINEMATICALLY
CINEMATIZE
CINEMATIZED
CINEMATIZES
CINEMATIZING
CINEMATOGRAPH
CINEMATOGRAPHER
CINEMATOGRAPHIC
CINEMATOGRAPHS
CINEMATOGRAPHY
CINEOL
CINEOLE
CINEOLES
CINEOLS
CINEPHILE
CINEPHILES
CINEPLEX
CINEPLEXES
CINERARIA
CINERARIAS
CINERARIUM
CINERARY
CINEREOUS
CINERIN
CINERINS
CINES
CINGULA
CINGULAR
CINGULATE
CINGULUM
CINNABAR
CINNABARINE
CINNABARS
CINNAMIC
CINNAMON
CINNAMONS
CINNAMONY
CINNAMYL
CINNAMYLS
CINQ
CINQS
CINQUAIN
CINQUAINS
CINQUE
CINQUECENTIST
CINQUECENTISTS
CINQUECENTO
CINQUECENTOS
CINQUEFOIL
CINQUEFOILS
CINQUES
CION
CIONS
CIOPPINO
CIOPPINOS
CIPAILLE
CIPAILLES
CIPHER
CIPHERED
CIPHERER
CIPHERERS
CIPHERING
CIPHERS
CIPHERTEXT
CIPHERTEXTS
CIPHONIES
CIPHONY
CIPOLIN
CIPOLINS
CIPOLLINO
CIPOLLINOS
CIPROFLOXACIN
CIPROFLOXACINS
CIRCA
CIRCADIAN
CIRCINATE
CIRCINATELY
CIRCLE
CIRCLED
CIRCLER
CIRCLERS
CIRCLES
CIRCLET
CIRCLETS
CIRCLING
CIRCS
CIRCUIT
CIRCUITAL
CIRCUITED
CIRCUITIES
CIRCUITING

CIRCUITOUS
CIRCUITOUSLY
CIRCUITOUSNESS
CIRCUITRIES
CIRCUITRY
CIRCUITS
CIRCUITY
CIRCULAR
CIRCULARISE
CIRCULARISED
CIRCULARISES
CIRCULARISING
CIRCULARITIES
CIRCULARITY
CIRCULARIZATION
CIRCULARIZE
CIRCULARIZED
CIRCULARIZES
CIRCULARIZING
CIRCULARLY
CIRCULARNESS
CIRCULARNESSES
CIRCULARS
CIRCULATABLE
CIRCULATE
CIRCULATED
CIRCULATES
CIRCULATING
CIRCULATION
CIRCULATIONS
CIRCULATIVE
CIRCULATOR
CIRCULATORS
CIRCULATORY
CIRCUMAMBIENT
CIRCUMAMBIENTLY
CIRCUMAMBULATE
CIRCUMAMBULATED
CIRCUMAMBULATES
CIRCUMCENTER
CIRCUMCENTERS
CIRCUMCIRCLE
CIRCUMCIRCLES
CIRCUMCISE
CIRCUMCISED
CIRCUMCISER
CIRCUMCISERS
CIRCUMCISES
CIRCUMCISING
CIRCUMCISION
CIRCUMCISIONS
CIRCUMFERENCE
CIRCUMFERENCES
CIRCUMFERENTIAL
CIRCUMFLEX
CIRCUMFLEXES
CIRCUMFLUENT
CIRCUMFLUOUS
CIRCUMFUSE
CIRCUMFUSED
CIRCUMFUSES
CIRCUMFUSING
CIRCUMFUSION
CIRCUMFUSIONS
CIRCUMJACENT
CIRCUMLOCUTION
CIRCUMLOCUTIONS
CIRCUMLOCUTORY
CIRCUMLUNAR
CIRCUMNAVIGATE
CIRCUMNAVIGATED
CIRCUMNAVIGATES
CIRCUMNAVIGATOR
CIRCUMPOLAR
CIRCUMSCISSILE
CIRCUMSCRIBE
CIRCUMSCRIBED
CIRCUMSCRIBES
CIRCUMSCRIBING
CIRCUMSCRIPTION
CIRCUMSPECT
CIRCUMSPECTION
CIRCUMSPECTIONS
CIRCUMSPECTLY
CIRCUMSTANCE
CIRCUMSTANCED
CIRCUMSTANCES
CIRCUMSTANTIAL
CIRCUMSTANTIATE
CIRCUMSTELLAR
CIRCUMVALLATE
CIRCUMVALLATED
CIRCUMVALLATES
CIRCUMVALLATING
CIRCUMVALLATION
CIRCUMVENT
CIRCUMVENTED
CIRCUMVENTING
CIRCUMVENTION
CIRCUMVENTIONS
CIRCUMVENTS
CIRCUMVOLUTION
CIRCUMVOLUTIONS
CIRCUS
CIRCUSES
CIRCUSY
CIRE
CIRES
CIRQUE
CIRQUES
CIRRATE
CIRRHOSED
CIRRHOSES
CIRRHOSIS
CIRRHOTIC
CIRRHOTICS
CIRRI
CIRRIFORM
CIRRIPED
CIRRIPEDE
CIRRIPEDES
CIRRIPEDS
CIRROCUMULI
CIRROCUMULUS
CIRROSE
CIRROSTRATI
CIRROSTRATUS
CIRROUS
CIRRUS
CIRRUSES
CIRSOID
CIS
CISALPINE
CISATLANTIC
CISCO
CISCOES
CISCOS
CISLUNAR
CISPLATIN
CISPLATINS
CISSIES
CISSOID
CISSOIDS
CISSY
CIST
CISTED
CISTERN
CISTERNA
CISTERNAE
CISTERNAL
CISTERNS
CISTRON
CISTRONIC
CISTRONS
CISTS
CISTUS
CISTUSES
CITABLE
CITADEL
CITADELS
CITATION
CITATIONAL
CITATIONS
CITATOR
CITATORS
CITATORY
CITE
CITEABLE
CITED
CITER
CITERS
CITES
CITHARA
CITHARAS
CITHER
CITHERN
CITHERNS
CITHERS
CITHREN
CITHRENS
CITIED
CITIES
CITIFICATION
CITIFICATIONS
CITIFIED
CITIFIES
CITIFY
CITIFYING
CITING
CITIZEN
CITIZENESS
CITIZENESSES
CITIZENLY
CITIZENRIES
CITIZENRY
CITIZENS
CITIZENSHIP
CITIZENSHIPS
CITOLA
CITOLAS
CITOLE
CITOLES
CITRAL
CITRALS
CITRATE
CITRATED
CITRATES
CITREOUS
CITRIC
CITRICULTURE
CITRICULTURES
CITRICULTURIST
CITRICULTURISTS
CITRIN
CITRINE
CITRINES
CITRININ
CITRININS
CITRINS
CITRON
CITRONELLA
CITRONELLAL
CITRONELLALS
CITRONELLAS
CITRONELLOL
CITRONELLOLS
CITRONS
CITROUS
CITRULLINE
CITRULLINES
CITRUS
CITRUSES
CITRUSY
CITTERN
CITTERNS
CITY
CITYFIED
CITYSCAPE
CITYSCAPES
CITYWARD
CITYWIDE
CIVET
CIVETLIKE
CIVETS
CIVIC
CIVICALLY
CIVICISM
CIVICISMS
CIVICS
CIVIE
CIVIES
CIVIL
CIVILIAN
CIVILIANIZATION
CIVILIANIZE
CIVILIANIZED
CIVILIANIZES
CIVILIANIZING
CIVILIANS
CIVILISATION
CIVILISATIONS
CIVILISE
CIVILISED
CIVILISES
CIVILISING

CIVILITIES
CIVILITY
CIVILIZATION
CIVILIZATIONAL
CIVILIZATIONS
CIVILIZE
CIVILIZED
CIVILIZER
CIVILIZERS
CIVILIZES
CIVILIZING
CIVILLY
CIVILNESS
CIVILNESSES
CIVISM
CIVISMS
CIVVIES
CIVVY
CLABBER
CLABBERED
CLABBERING
CLABBERS
CLACH
CLACHAN
CLACHANS
CLACHS
CLACK
CLACKED
CLACKER
CLACKERS
CLACKING
CLACKS
CLAD
CLADDAGH
CLADDAGHS
CLADDED
CLADDING
CLADDINGS
CLADE
CLADES
CLADISM
CLADISMS
CLADIST
CLADISTIC
CLADISTICALLY
CLADISTICS
CLADISTS
CLADOCERAN
CLADOCERANS
CLADODE
CLADODES
CLADODIAL
CLADOGENESES
CLADOGENESIS
CLADOGENETIC
CLADOGRAM
CLADOGRAMS
CLADOPHYLL
CLADOPHYLLS
CLADS
CLAFOUTI
CLAFOUTIS
CLAG
CLAGGED
CLAGGING
CLAGS
CLAIM
CLAIMABLE
CLAIMANT
CLAIMANTS
CLAIMED
CLAIMER
CLAIMERS
CLAIMING
CLAIMS
CLAIRAUDIENCE
CLAIRAUDIENCES
CLAIRAUDIENT
CLAIRAUDIENTLY
CLAIRVOYANCE
CLAIRVOYANCES
CLAIRVOYANT
CLAIRVOYANTLY
CLAIRVOYANTS
CLAM
CLAMANT
CLAMANTLY
CLAMBAKE
CLAMBAKES
CLAMBER
CLAMBERED
CLAMBERER
CLAMBERERS
CLAMBERING
CLAMBERS
CLAMLIKE
CLAMMED
CLAMMER
CLAMMERS
CLAMMIER
CLAMMIEST
CLAMMILY
CLAMMINESS
CLAMMINESSES
CLAMMING
CLAMMY
CLAMOR
CLAMORED
CLAMORER
CLAMORERS
CLAMORING
CLAMOROUS
CLAMOROUSLY
CLAMOROUSNESS
CLAMOROUSNESSES
CLAMORS
CLAMOUR
CLAMOURED
CLAMOURING
CLAMOURS
CLAMP
CLAMPDOWN
CLAMPDOWNS
CLAMPED
CLAMPER
CLAMPERS
CLAMPING
CLAMPS
CLAMS
CLAMSHELL
CLAMSHELLS
CLAMWORM
CLAMWORMS
CLAN
CLANDESTINE
CLANDESTINELY
CLANDESTINENESS
CLANDESTINITIES
CLANDESTINITY
CLANG
CLANGED
CLANGER
CLANGERS
CLANGING
CLANGOR
CLANGORED
CLANGORING
CLANGOROUS
CLANGOROUSLY
CLANGORS
CLANGOUR
CLANGOURED
CLANGOURING
CLANGOURS
CLANGS
CLANK
CLANKED
CLANKIER
CLANKIEST
CLANKING
CLANKINGLY
CLANKS
CLANKY
CLANNISH
CLANNISHLY
CLANNISHNESS
CLANNISHNESSES
CLANS
CLANSMAN
CLANSMEN
CLANSWOMAN
CLANSWOMEN
CLAP
CLAPBOARD
CLAPBOARDED
CLAPBOARDING
CLAPBOARDS
CLAPPED
CLAPPER
CLAPPERCLAW
CLAPPERCLAWED
CLAPPERCLAWING
CLAPPERCLAWS
CLAPPERS
CLAPPING
CLAPS
CLAPT
CLAPTRAP
CLAPTRAPS
CLAQUE
CLAQUER
CLAQUERS
CLAQUES
CLAQUEUR
CLAQUEURS
CLARENCE
CLARENCES
CLARET
CLARETS
CLARIES
CLARIFICATION
CLARIFICATIONS
CLARIFIED
CLARIFIER
CLARIFIERS
CLARIFIES
CLARIFY
CLARIFYING
CLARINET
CLARINETIST
CLARINETISTS
CLARINETS
CLARINETTIST
CLARINETTISTS
CLARION
CLARIONED
CLARIONET
CLARIONETS
CLARIONING
CLARIONS
CLARITIES
CLARITY
CLARKIA
CLARKIAS
CLARO
CLAROES
CLAROS
CLARY
CLASH
CLASHED
CLASHER
CLASHERS
CLASHES
CLASHING
CLASP
CLASPED
CLASPER
CLASPERS
CLASPING
CLASPS
CLASPT
CLASS
CLASSABLE
CLASSED
CLASSER
CLASSERS
CLASSES
CLASSIC
CLASSICAL
CLASSICALITIES
CLASSICALITY
CLASSICALLY
CLASSICALS
CLASSICISM
CLASSICISMS
CLASSICIST
CLASSICISTIC
CLASSICISTS
CLASSICIZE
CLASSICIZED
CLASSICIZES
CLASSICIZING
CLASSICO
CLASSICS
CLASSIER

CLASSIEST
CLASSIFIABLE
CLASSIFICATION
CLASSIFICATIONS
CLASSIFICATORY
CLASSIFIED
CLASSIFIER
CLASSIFIERS
CLASSIFIES
CLASSIFY
CLASSIFYING
CLASSILY
CLASSINESS
CLASSINESSES
CLASSING
CLASSIS
CLASSISM
CLASSISMS
CLASSIST
CLASSISTS
CLASSLESS
CLASSLESSNESS
CLASSLESSNESSES
CLASSMATE
CLASSMATES
CLASSON
CLASSONS
CLASSROOM
CLASSROOMS
CLASSWORK
CLASSWORKS
CLASSY
CLAST
CLASTIC
CLASTICS
CLASTS
CLATHRATE
CLATHRATES
CLATTER
CLATTERED
CLATTERER
CLATTERERS
CLATTERING
CLATTERINGLY
CLATTERS
CLATTERY
CLAUCHT
CLAUDICATION
CLAUDICATIONS
CLAUGHT
CLAUGHTED
CLAUGHTING
CLAUGHTS
CLAUSAL
CLAUSE
CLAUSES
CLAUSTRA
CLAUSTRAL
CLAUSTROPHOBE
CLAUSTROPHOBES
CLAUSTROPHOBIA
CLAUSTROPHOBIAS
CLAUSTROPHOBIC
CLAUSTRUM
CLAVATE
CLAVATELY
CLAVATION
CLAVATIONS
CLAVE
CLAVER
CLAVERED
CLAVERING
CLAVERS
CLAVES
CLAVI
CLAVICHORD
CLAVICHORDIST
CLAVICHORDISTS
CLAVICHORDS
CLAVICLE
CLAVICLES
CLAVICORN
CLAVICULAR
CLAVIER
CLAVIERIST
CLAVIERISTIC
CLAVIERISTS
CLAVIERS
CLAVIFORM
CLAVUS
CLAW
CLAWBACK
CLAWBACKS
CLAWED
CLAWER
CLAWERS
CLAWHAMMER
CLAWHAMMERS
CLAWING
CLAWLESS
CLAWLIKE
CLAWS
CLAXON
CLAXONS
CLAY
CLAYBANK
CLAYBANKS
CLAYED
CLAYEY
CLAYIER
CLAYIEST
CLAYING
CLAYISH
CLAYLIKE
CLAYMORE
CLAYMORES
CLAYPAN
CLAYPANS
CLAYS
CLAYSTONE
CLAYSTONES
CLAYTONIA
CLAYTONIAS
CLAYWARE
CLAYWARES
CLEAN
CLEANABILITIES
CLEANABILITY
CLEANABLE
CLEANED
CLEANER
CLEANERS
CLEANEST
CLEANHANDED
CLEANING
CLEANINGS
CLEANISH
CLEANLIER
CLEANLIEST
CLEANLINESS
CLEANLINESSES
CLEANLY
CLEANNESS
CLEANNESSES
CLEANOUT
CLEANOUTS
CLEANS
CLEANSE
CLEANSED
CLEANSER
CLEANSERS
CLEANSES
CLEANSING
CLEANUP
CLEANUPS
CLEAR
CLEARABLE
CLEARANCE
CLEARANCES
CLEARCUT
CLEARCUTS
CLEARCUTTING
CLEARED
CLEARER
CLEARERS
CLEAREST
CLEAREYED
CLEARHEADED
CLEARHEADEDLY
CLEARHEADEDNESS
CLEARING
CLEARINGHOUSE
CLEARINGHOUSES
CLEARINGS
CLEARLY
CLEARNESS
CLEARNESSES
CLEAROUT
CLEAROUTS
CLEARS
CLEARSTORIES
CLEARSTORY
CLEARWAY
CLEARWAYS
CLEARWEED
CLEARWEEDS
CLEARWING
CLEARWINGS
CLEAT
CLEATED
CLEATING
CLEATS
CLEAVABLE
CLEAVAGE
CLEAVAGES
CLEAVE
CLEAVED
CLEAVER
CLEAVERS
CLEAVES
CLEAVING
CLEEK
CLEEKED
CLEEKING
CLEEKS
CLEF
CLEFS
CLEFT
CLEFTED
CLEFTING
CLEFTS
CLEG
CLEGS
CLEIDOIC
CLEISTOGAMIC
CLEISTOGAMIES
CLEISTOGAMOUS
CLEISTOGAMOUSLY
CLEISTOGAMY
CLEMATIS
CLEMATISES
CLEMENCIES
CLEMENCY
CLEMENT
CLEMENTINE
CLEMENTINES
CLEMENTLY
CLENCH
CLENCHED
CLENCHER
CLENCHERS
CLENCHES
CLENCHING
CLEOME
CLEOMES
CLEPE
CLEPED
CLEPES
CLEPING
CLEPSYDRA
CLEPSYDRAE
CLEPSYDRAS
CLEPT
CLERESTORIES
CLERESTORY
CLERGIES
CLERGY
CLERGYMAN
CLERGYMEN
CLERGYPERSON
CLERGYPERSONS
CLERGYWOMAN
CLERGYWOMEN
CLERIC
CLERICAL
CLERICALISM
CLERICALISMS
CLERICALIST
CLERICALISTS
CLERICALLY
CLERICALS
CLERICS
CLERID
CLERIDS
CLERIHEW

CLERIHEWS
CLERISIES
CLERISY
CLERK
CLERKDOM
CLERKDOMS
CLERKED
CLERKING
CLERKISH
CLERKLIER
CLERKLIEST
CLERKLY
CLERKS
CLERKSHIP
CLERKSHIPS
CLEVEITE
CLEVEITES
CLEVER
CLEVERER
CLEVEREST
CLEVERISH
CLEVERLY
CLEVERNESS
CLEVERNESSES
CLEVIS
CLEVISES
CLEW
CLEWED
CLEWING
CLEWS
CLICHE
CLICHED
CLICHES
CLICK
CLICKABLE
CLICKED
CLICKER
CLICKERS
CLICKING
CLICKLESS
CLICKS
CLICKWRAP
CLIENT
CLIENTAGE
CLIENTAGES
CLIENTAL
CLIENTELE
CLIENTELES
CLIENTLESS
CLIENTS
CLIFF
CLIFFIER
CLIFFIEST
CLIFFLIKE
CLIFFS
CLIFFSIDE
CLIFFSIDES
CLIFFTOP
CLIFFTOPS
CLIFFY
CLIFT
CLIFTS
CLIMACTERIC
CLIMACTERICS
CLIMACTIC
CLIMACTICALLY
CLIMATAL
CLIMATE
CLIMATES
CLIMATIC
CLIMATICALLY
CLIMATIZE
CLIMATIZED
CLIMATIZES
CLIMATIZING
CLIMATOLOGICAL
CLIMATOLOGIES
CLIMATOLOGIST
CLIMATOLOGISTS
CLIMATOLOGY
CLIMAX
CLIMAXED
CLIMAXES
CLIMAXING
CLIMAXLESS
CLIMB
CLIMBABLE
CLIMBDOWN
CLIMBDOWNS
CLIMBED
CLIMBER
CLIMBERS
CLIMBING
CLIMBINGS
CLIMBS
CLIME
CLIMES
CLINAL
CLINALLY
CLINCH
CLINCHED
CLINCHER
CLINCHERS
CLINCHES
CLINCHING
CLINCHINGLY
CLINE
CLINES
CLING
CLINGED
CLINGER
CLINGERS
CLINGFISH
CLINGFISHES
CLINGIER
CLINGIEST
CLINGING
CLINGS
CLINGSTONE
CLINGSTONES
CLINGY
CLINIC
CLINICAL
CLINICALLY
CLINICIAN
CLINICIANS
CLINICS
CLINK
CLINKED
CLINKER
CLINKERED
CLINKERING
CLINKERS
CLINKING
CLINKS
CLINOMETER
CLINOMETERS
CLINQUANT
CLINQUANTS
CLINTONIA
CLINTONIAS
CLIOMETRIC
CLIOMETRICIAN
CLIOMETRICIANS
CLIOMETRICS
CLIP
CLIPBOARD
CLIPBOARDS
CLIPPABLE
CLIPPED
CLIPPER
CLIPPERS
CLIPPING
CLIPPINGS
CLIPS
CLIPSHEET
CLIPSHEETS
CLIPT
CLIQUE
CLIQUED
CLIQUES
CLIQUEY
CLIQUIER
CLIQUIEST
CLIQUING
CLIQUISH
CLIQUISHLY
CLIQUISHNESS
CLIQUISHNESSES
CLIQUY
CLIT
CLITELLA
CLITELLUM
CLITIC
CLITICIZE
CLITICIZED
CLITICIZES
CLITICIZING
CLITICS
CLITORAL
CLITORECTOMIES
CLITORECTOMY
CLITORIC
CLITORIDECTOMY
CLITORIDES
CLITORIS
CLITORISES
CLITS
CLITTER
CLITTERED
CLITTERING
CLITTERS
CLIVERS
CLIVIA
CLIVIAS
CLOACA
CLOACAE
CLOACAL
CLOACAS
CLOAK
CLOAKED
CLOAKING
CLOAKROOM
CLOAKROOMS
CLOAKS
CLOBBER
CLOBBERED
CLOBBERING
CLOBBERS
CLOCHARD
CLOCHARDS
CLOCHE
CLOCHES
CLOCK
CLOCKED
CLOCKER
CLOCKERS
CLOCKING
CLOCKLIKE
CLOCKS
CLOCKWISE
CLOCKWORK
CLOCKWORKS
CLOD
CLODDIER
CLODDIEST
CLODDISH
CLODDISHNESS
CLODDISHNESSES
CLODDY
CLODHOPPER
CLODHOPPERS
CLODHOPPING
CLODPATE
CLODPATES
CLODPOLE
CLODPOLES
CLODPOLL
CLODPOLLS
CLODS
CLOFIBRATE
CLOFIBRATES
CLOG
CLOGGED
CLOGGER
CLOGGERS
CLOGGIER
CLOGGIEST
CLOGGILY
CLOGGING
CLOGGINGS
CLOGGY
CLOGS
CLOISONNE
CLOISONNES
CLOISTER
CLOISTERED
CLOISTERING
CLOISTERS
CLOISTRAL
CLOISTRESS
CLOISTRESSES
CLOMB
CLOMIPHENE
CLOMIPHENES

CLOMIPRAMINE
CLOMIPRAMINES
CLOMP
CLOMPED
CLOMPING
CLOMPS
CLON
CLONAL
CLONALLY
CLONAZEPAM
CLONAZEPAMS
CLONE
CLONED
CLONER
CLONERS
CLONES
CLONIC
CLONICITIES
CLONICITY
CLONIDINE
CLONIDINES
CLONING
CLONINGS
CLONISM
CLONISMS
CLONK
CLONKED
CLONKIER
CLONKIEST
CLONKING
CLONKS
CLONKY
CLONS
CLONUS
CLONUSES
CLOOT
CLOOTS
CLOP
CLOPPED
CLOPPING
CLOPS
CLOQUE
CLOQUES
CLOSABLE
CLOSE
CLOSEABLE
CLOSED
CLOSEDOWN
CLOSEDOWNS
CLOSEFISTED
CLOSELY
CLOSEMOUTHED
CLOSENESS
CLOSENESSES
CLOSEOUT
CLOSEOUTS
CLOSER
CLOSERS
CLOSES
CLOSEST
CLOSESTOOL
CLOSESTOOLS
CLOSET
CLOSETED
CLOSETFUL
CLOSETFULS
CLOSETING
CLOSETS
CLOSEUP
CLOSEUPS
CLOSING
CLOSINGS
CLOSTRIDIA
CLOSTRIDIAL
CLOSTRIDIUM
CLOSURE
CLOSURED
CLOSURES
CLOSURING
CLOT
CLOTBUR
CLOTBURS
CLOTH
CLOTHBOUND
CLOTHE
CLOTHED
CLOTHES
CLOTHESHORSE
CLOTHESHORSES
CLOTHESLINE
CLOTHESLINED
CLOTHESLINES
CLOTHESLINING
CLOTHESPIN
CLOTHESPINS
CLOTHESPRESS
CLOTHESPRESSES
CLOTHIER
CLOTHIERS
CLOTHING
CLOTHINGS
CLOTHLIKE
CLOTHS
CLOTRIMAZOLE
CLOTRIMAZOLES
CLOTS
CLOTTED
CLOTTING
CLOTTY
CLOTURE
CLOTURED
CLOTURES
CLOTURING
CLOUD
CLOUDBERRIES
CLOUDBERRY
CLOUDBURST
CLOUDBURSTS
CLOUDED
CLOUDIER
CLOUDIEST
CLOUDILY
CLOUDINESS
CLOUDINESSES
CLOUDING
CLOUDLAND
CLOUDLANDS
CLOUDLESS
CLOUDLESSLY
CLOUDLESSNESS
CLOUDLESSNESSES
CLOUDLET
CLOUDLETS
CLOUDLIKE
CLOUDS
CLOUDSCAPE
CLOUDSCAPES
CLOUDY
CLOUGH
CLOUGHS
CLOUR
CLOURED
CLOURING
CLOURS
CLOUT
CLOUTED
CLOUTER
CLOUTERS
CLOUTING
CLOUTS
CLOVE
CLOVEN
CLOVER
CLOVERED
CLOVERLEAF
CLOVERLEAFS
CLOVERLEAVES
CLOVERS
CLOVERY
CLOVES
CLOWDER
CLOWDERS
CLOWN
CLOWNED
CLOWNERIES
CLOWNERY
CLOWNING
CLOWNISH
CLOWNISHLY
CLOWNISHNESS
CLOWNISHNESSES
CLOWNS
CLOXACILLIN
CLOXACILLINS
CLOY
CLOYED
CLOYING
CLOYINGLY
CLOYS
CLOZAPINE
CLOZAPINES
CLOZE
CLOZES
CLUB
CLUBABLE
CLUBBABILITIES
CLUBBABILITY
CLUBBABLE
CLUBBED
CLUBBER
CLUBBERS
CLUBBIER
CLUBBIEST
CLUBBINESS
CLUBBINESSES
CLUBBING
CLUBBINGS
CLUBBISH
CLUBBY
CLUBFACE
CLUBFACES
CLUBFEET
CLUBFOOT
CLUBFOOTED
CLUBHAND
CLUBHANDS
CLUBHAUL
CLUBHAULED
CLUBHAULING
CLUBHAULS
CLUBHEAD
CLUBHEADS
CLUBHOUSE
CLUBHOUSES
CLUBLAND
CLUBLANDS
CLUBMAN
CLUBMATE
CLUBMATES
CLUBMEN
CLUBMOSS
CLUBMOSSES
CLUBROOM
CLUBROOMS
CLUBROOT
CLUBROOTS
CLUBS
CLUBWOMAN
CLUBWOMEN
CLUCK
CLUCKED
CLUCKER
CLUCKERS
CLUCKING
CLUCKS
CLUE
CLUED
CLUEING
CLUELESS
CLUES
CLUING
CLUMBER
CLUMBERS
CLUMP
CLUMPED
CLUMPER
CLUMPERS
CLUMPET
CLUMPETS
CLUMPIER
CLUMPIEST
CLUMPING
CLUMPISH
CLUMPLIKE
CLUMPS
CLUMPY
CLUMSIER
CLUMSIEST
CLUMSILY
CLUMSINESS
CLUMSINESSES
CLUMSY
CLUNG
CLUNK
CLUNKED

CLUNKER
CLUNKERS
CLUNKIER
CLUNKIEST
CLUNKING
CLUNKS
CLUNKY
CLUPEID
CLUPEIDS
CLUPEOID
CLUPEOIDS
CLUSTER
CLUSTERED
CLUSTERING
CLUSTERS
CLUSTERY
CLUTCH
CLUTCHED
CLUTCHES
CLUTCHING
CLUTCHY
CLUTTER
CLUTTERED
CLUTTERING
CLUTTERS
CLUTTERY
CLYPEAL
CLYPEATE
CLYPEI
CLYPEUS
CLYSTER
CLYSTERS
CNIDA
CNIDAE
CNIDARIAN
CNIDARIANS
COACERVATE
COACERVATES
COACERVATION
COACERVATIONS
COACH
COACHABLE
COACHED
COACHER
COACHERS
COACHES
COACHING
COACHINGS
COACHLOAD
COACHLOADS
COACHMAN
COACHMEN
COACHWORK
COACHWORKS
COACT
COACTED
COACTING
COACTION
COACTIONS
COACTIVE
COACTOR
COACTORS
COACTS
COADAPTATION
COADAPTATIONS
COADAPTED
COADIES
COADJUTOR
COADJUTORS
COADJUTRICES
COADJUTRIX
COADMIRE
COADMIRED
COADMIRES
COADMIRING
COADMIT
COADMITS
COADMITTED
COADMITTING
COADUNATE
COADY
COADYS
COAEVAL
COAEVALS
COAGENCIES
COAGENCY
COAGENT
COAGENTS
COAGULA
COAGULABILITIES
COAGULABILITY
COAGULABLE
COAGULANT
COAGULANTS
COAGULASE
COAGULASES
COAGULATE
COAGULATED
COAGULATES
COAGULATING
COAGULATION
COAGULATIONS
COAGULUM
COAGULUMS
COAL
COALA
COALAS
COALBIN
COALBINS
COALBOX
COALBOXES
COALED
COALER
COALERS
COALESCE
COALESCED
COALESCENCE
COALESCENCES
COALESCENT
COALESCES
COALESCING
COALFACE
COALFACES
COALFIELD
COALFIELDS
COALFISH
COALFISHES
COALHOLE
COALHOLES
COALIER
COALIEST
COALIFICATION
COALIFICATIONS
COALIFIED
COALIFIES
COALIFY
COALIFYING
COALING
COALITION
COALITIONIST
COALITIONISTS
COALITIONS
COALLESS
COALPIT
COALPITS
COALS
COALSACK
COALSACKS
COALSHED
COALSHEDS
COALY
COALYARD
COALYARDS
COAMING
COAMINGS
COANCHOR
COANCHORED
COANCHORING
COANCHORS
COANNEX
COANNEXED
COANNEXES
COANNEXING
COAPPEAR
COAPPEARED
COAPPEARING
COAPPEARS
COAPT
COAPTATION
COAPTATIONS
COAPTED
COAPTING
COAPTS
COARCTATE
COARCTATION
COARCTATIONS
COARSE
COARSELY
COARSEN
COARSENED
COARSENESS
COARSENESSES
COARSENING
COARSENS
COARSER
COARSEST
COARSISH
COASSIST
COASSISTED
COASSISTING
COASSISTS
COASSUME
COASSUMED
COASSUMES
COASSUMING
COAST
COASTAL
COASTALLY
COASTED
COASTER
COASTERS
COASTGUARD
COASTGUARDMAN
COASTGUARDMEN
COASTGUARDS
COASTGUARDSMAN
COASTGUARDSMEN
COASTING
COASTINGS
COASTLAND
COASTLANDS
COASTLINE
COASTLINES
COASTS
COASTWARD
COASTWARDS
COASTWISE
COAT
COATDRESS
COATDRESSES
COATED
COATEE
COATEES
COATER
COATERS
COATI
COATIMUNDI
COATIMUNDIS
COATING
COATINGS
COATIS
COATLESS
COATRACK
COATRACKS
COATROOM
COATROOMS
COATS
COATTAIL
COATTAILS
COATTEND
COATTENDED
COATTENDING
COATTENDS
COATTEST
COATTESTED
COATTESTING
COATTESTS
COAUTHOR
COAUTHORED
COAUTHORING
COAUTHORS
COAUTHORSHIP
COAUTHORSHIPS
COAX
COAXAL
COAXED
COAXER
COAXERS
COAXES
COAXIAL
COAXIALLY
COAXING
COAXINGLY
COAXINGS
COB

COBALAMIN
COBALAMINS
COBALT
COBALTIC
COBALTINE
COBALTINES
COBALTITE
COBALTITES
COBALTOUS
COBALTS
COBB
COBBER
COBBERS
COBBIER
COBBIEST
COBBLE
COBBLED
COBBLER
COBBLERS
COBBLES
COBBLESTONE
COBBLESTONED
COBBLESTONES
COBBLING
COBBS
COBBY
COBELLIGERENT
COBELLIGERENTS
COBIA
COBIAS
COBLE
COBLES
COBNUT
COBNUTS
COBRA
COBRAS
COBS
COBWEB
COBWEBBED
COBWEBBIER
COBWEBBIEST
COBWEBBING
COBWEBBY
COBWEBS
COCA
COCAIN
COCAINE
COCAINES
COCAINISM
COCAINISMS
COCAINIZATION
COCAINIZATIONS
COCAINIZE
COCAINIZED
COCAINIZES
COCAINIZING
COCAINS
COCAPTAIN
COCAPTAINED
COCAPTAINING
COCAPTAINS
COCARBOXYLASE
COCARBOXYLASES
COCARCINOGEN
COCARCINOGENIC
COCARCINOGENS
COCAS
COCATALYST
COCATALYSTS
COCCAL
COCCI
COCCIC
COCCID
COCCIDIA
COCCIDIOSES
COCCIDIOSIS
COCCIDIUM
COCCIDS
COCCOID
COCCOIDAL
COCCOIDS
COCCOLITH
COCCOLITHS
COCCOUS
COCCUS
COCCYGEAL
COCCYGES
COCCYX
COCCYXES
COCHAIR
COCHAIRED
COCHAIRING
COCHAIRMAN
COCHAIRMEN
COCHAIRPERSON
COCHAIRPERSONS
COCHAIRS
COCHAIRWOMAN
COCHAIRWOMEN
COCHAMPION
COCHAMPIONS
COCHIN
COCHINEAL
COCHINEALS
COCHINS
COCHLEA
COCHLEAE
COCHLEAR
COCHLEAS
COCHLEATE
COCINERA
COCINERAS
COCK
COCKADE
COCKADED
COCKADES
COCKALORUM
COCKALORUMS
COCKAMAMIE
COCKAMAMY
COCKAPOO
COCKAPOOS
COCKATEEL
COCKATEELS
COCKATIEL
COCKATIELS
COCKATOO
COCKATOOS
COCKATRICE
COCKATRICES
COCKBILL
COCKBILLED
COCKBILLING
COCKBILLS
COCKBOAT
COCKBOATS
COCKCHAFER
COCKCHAFERS
COCKCROW
COCKCROWS
COCKED
COCKER
COCKERED
COCKEREL
COCKERELS
COCKERING
COCKERS
COCKEYE
COCKEYED
COCKEYEDLY
COCKEYEDNESS
COCKEYEDNESSES
COCKEYES
COCKFIGHT
COCKFIGHTING
COCKFIGHTINGS
COCKFIGHTS
COCKHORSE
COCKHORSES
COCKIER
COCKIES
COCKIEST
COCKILY
COCKINESS
COCKINESSES
COCKING
COCKISH
COCKLE
COCKLEBUR
COCKLEBURS
COCKLED
COCKLES
COCKLESHELL
COCKLESHELLS
COCKLIKE
COCKLING
COCKLOFT
COCKLOFTS
COCKNEY
COCKNEYFIED
COCKNEYFIES
COCKNEYFY
COCKNEYFYING
COCKNEYISH
COCKNEYISM
COCKNEYISMS
COCKNEYS
COCKPIT
COCKPITS
COCKROACH
COCKROACHES
COCKS
COCKSCOMB
COCKSCOMBS
COCKSFOOT
COCKSFOOTS
COCKSHIES
COCKSHUT
COCKSHUTS
COCKSHY
COCKSMAN
COCKSMEN
COCKSPUR
COCKSPURS
COCKSUCKER
COCKSUCKERS
COCKSURE
COCKSURELY
COCKSURENESS
COCKSURENESSES
COCKSWAIN
COCKSWAINS
COCKTAIL
COCKTAILED
COCKTAILING
COCKTAILS
COCKUP
COCKUPS
COCKY
COCO
COCOA
COCOANUT
COCOANUTS
COCOAS
COCOBOLA
COCOBOLAS
COCOBOLO
COCOBOLOS
COCOMAT
COCOMATS
COCOMPOSER
COCOMPOSERS
COCONSPIRATOR
COCONSPIRATORS
COCONUT
COCONUTS
COCOON
COCOONED
COCOONER
COCOONERS
COCOONING
COCOONINGS
COCOONS
COCOPLUM
COCOPLUMS
COCOS
COCOTTE
COCOTTES
COCOUNSEL
COCOUNSELED
COCOUNSELING
COCOUNSELLED
COCOUNSELLING
COCOUNSELS
COCOYAM
COCOYAMS
COCOZELLE
COCOZELLES
COCREATE
COCREATED
COCREATES
COCREATING
COCREATOR
COCREATORS
COCULTIVATE

COCULTIVATED
COCULTIVATES
COCULTIVATING
COCULTIVATION
COCULTIVATIONS
COCULTURE
COCULTURED
COCULTURES
COCULTURING
COCURATOR
COCURATORS
COCURRICULAR
COD
CODA
CODABLE
CODAS
CODDED
CODDER
CODDERS
CODDING
CODDLE
CODDLED
CODDLER
CODDLERS
CODDLES
CODDLING
CODE
CODEBOOK
CODEBOOKS
CODEBTOR
CODEBTORS
CODEC
CODECS
CODED
CODEFENDANT
CODEFENDANTS
CODEIA
CODEIAS
CODEIN
CODEINA
CODEINAS
CODEINE
CODEINES
CODEINS
CODELESS
CODEN
CODENS
CODEPENDENCE
CODEPENDENCES
CODEPENDENCIES
CODEPENDENCY
CODEPENDENT
CODEPENDENTS
CODER
CODERIVE
CODERIVED
CODERIVES
CODERIVING
CODERS
CODES
CODESIGN
CODESIGNED
CODESIGNING
CODESIGNS
CODETERMINATION
CODEVELOP
CODEVELOPED
CODEVELOPER
CODEVELOPERS
CODEVELOPING
CODEVELOPS
CODEX
CODEXES
CODFISH
CODFISHES
CODGER
CODGERS
CODICES
CODICIL
CODICILLARY
CODICILS
CODICOLOGICAL
CODICOLOGIES
CODICOLOGY
CODIFIABILITIES
CODIFIABILITY
CODIFICATION
CODIFICATIONS
CODIFIED
CODIFIER
CODIFIERS
CODIFIES
CODIFY
CODIFYING
CODING
CODINGS
CODIRECT
CODIRECTED
CODIRECTING
CODIRECTION
CODIRECTIONS
CODIRECTOR
CODIRECTORS
CODIRECTS
CODISCOVER
CODISCOVERED
CODISCOVERER
CODISCOVERERS
CODISCOVERING
CODISCOVERS
CODLIN
CODLING
CODLINGS
CODLINS
CODOMAIN
CODOMAINS
CODOMINANT
CODOMINANTS
CODON
CODONS
CODPIECE
CODPIECES
CODRIVE
CODRIVEN
CODRIVER
CODRIVERS
CODRIVES
CODRIVING
CODROVE
CODS
CODSWALLOP
CODSWALLOPS
COED
COEDIT
COEDITED
COEDITING
COEDITOR
COEDITORS
COEDITS
COEDS
COEDUCATION
COEDUCATIONAL
COEDUCATIONALLY
COEDUCATIONS
COEFFECT
COEFFECTS
COEFFICIENT
COEFFICIENTS
COELACANTH
COELACANTHS
COELENTERA
COELENTERATE
COELENTERATES
COELENTERON
COELENTERONS
COELIAC
COELIACS
COELOM
COELOMATA
COELOMATE
COELOMATES
COELOME
COELOMES
COELOMIC
COELOMS
COELOSTAT
COELOSTATS
COEMBODIED
COEMBODIES
COEMBODY
COEMBODYING
COEMPLOY
COEMPLOYED
COEMPLOYING
COEMPLOYS
COEMPT
COEMPTED
COEMPTING
COEMPTS
COENACT
COENACTED
COENACTING
COENACTS
COENAMOR
COENAMORED
COENAMORING
COENAMORS
COENDURE
COENDURED
COENDURES
COENDURING
COENOBITE
COENOBITES
COENOCYTE
COENOCYTES
COENOCYTIC
COENOSARC
COENOSARCS
COENURE
COENURES
COENURI
COENURUS
COENZYMATIC
COENZYMATICALLY
COENZYME
COENZYMES
COEQUAL
COEQUALITIES
COEQUALITY
COEQUALLY
COEQUALS
COEQUATE
COEQUATED
COEQUATES
COEQUATING
COERCE
COERCED
COERCER
COERCERS
COERCES
COERCIBLE
COERCIBLY
COERCING
COERCION
COERCIONS
COERCIVE
COERCIVELY
COERCIVENESS
COERCIVENESSES
COERCIVITIES
COERCIVITY
COERECT
COERECTED
COERECTING
COERECTS
COESITE
COESITES
COETANEOUS
COETERNAL
COEVAL
COEVALITIES
COEVALITY
COEVALLY
COEVALS
COEVOLUTION
COEVOLUTIONARY
COEVOLUTIONS
COEVOLVE
COEVOLVED
COEVOLVES
COEVOLVING
COEXECUTOR
COEXECUTORS
COEXERT
COEXERTED
COEXERTING
COEXERTS
COEXIST
COEXISTED
COEXISTENCE
COEXISTENCES
COEXISTENT
COEXISTING
COEXISTS
COEXTEND

COEXTENDED
COEXTENDING
COEXTENDS
COEXTENSIVE
COEXTENSIVELY
COFACTOR
COFACTORS
COFAVORITE
COFAVORITES
COFEATURE
COFEATURED
COFEATURES
COFEATURING
COFF
COFFEE
COFFEEHOUSE
COFFEEHOUSES
COFFEEMAKER
COFFEEMAKERS
COFFEEPOT
COFFEEPOTS
COFFEES
COFFER
COFFERDAM
COFFERDAMS
COFFERED
COFFERING
COFFERS
COFFIN
COFFINED
COFFING
COFFINING
COFFINS
COFFLE
COFFLED
COFFLES
COFFLING
COFFRET
COFFRETS
COFFS
COFINANCE
COFINANCED
COFINANCES
COFINANCING
COFOUND
COFOUNDED
COFOUNDER
COFOUNDERS
COFOUNDING
COFOUNDS
COFT
COFUNCTION
COFUNCTIONS
COG
COGENCIES
COGENCY
COGENERATION
COGENERATIONS
COGENERATOR
COGENERATORS
COGENT
COGENTLY
COGGED
COGGING
COGITABLE
COGITATE
COGITATED
COGITATES
COGITATING
COGITATION
COGITATIONS
COGITATIVE
COGITATOR
COGITATORS
COGITO
COGITOS
COGNAC
COGNACS
COGNATE
COGNATELY
COGNATES
COGNATION
COGNATIONS
COGNISANCE
COGNISANCES
COGNISANT
COGNISE
COGNISED
COGNISES
COGNISING
COGNITION
COGNITIONAL
COGNITIONS
COGNITIVE
COGNITIVELY
COGNIZABLE
COGNIZABLY
COGNIZANCE
COGNIZANCES
COGNIZANT
COGNIZE
COGNIZED
COGNIZER
COGNIZERS
COGNIZES
COGNIZING
COGNOMEN
COGNOMENS
COGNOMINA
COGNOMINAL
COGNOSCENTE
COGNOSCENTI
COGNOSCIBLE
COGNOVIT
COGNOVITS
COGON
COGONS
COGS
COGWAY
COGWAYS
COGWHEEL
COGWHEELS
COHABIT
COHABITANT
COHABITANTS
COHABITATION
COHABITATIONS
COHABITED
COHABITER
COHABITERS
COHABITING
COHABITS
COHEAD
COHEADED
COHEADING
COHEADS
COHEIR
COHEIRESS
COHEIRESSES
COHEIRS
COHERE
COHERED
COHERENCE
COHERENCES
COHERENCIES
COHERENCY
COHERENT
COHERENTLY
COHERER
COHERERS
COHERES
COHERING
COHESION
COHESIONLESS
COHESIONS
COHESIVE
COHESIVELY
COHESIVENESS
COHESIVENESSES
COHO
COHOBATE
COHOBATED
COHOBATES
COHOBATING
COHOE
COHOES
COHOG
COHOGS
COHOLDER
COHOLDERS
COHOMOLOGICAL
COHOMOLOGIES
COHOMOLOGY
COHORT
COHORTS
COHOS
COHOSH
COHOSHES
COHOST
COHOSTED
COHOSTESS
COHOSTESSED
COHOSTESSES
COHOSTESSING
COHOSTING
COHOSTS
COHOUSING
COHOUSINGS
COHUNE
COHUNES
COIF
COIFED
COIFFE
COIFFED
COIFFES
COIFFEUR
COIFFEURS
COIFFEUSE
COIFFEUSES
COIFFING
COIFFURE
COIFFURED
COIFFURES
COIFFURING
COIFING
COIFS
COIGN
COIGNE
COIGNED
COIGNES
COIGNING
COIGNS
COIL
COILABILITIES
COILABILITY
COILED
COILER
COILERS
COILING
COILS
COIN
COINABLE
COINAGE
COINAGES
COINCIDE
COINCIDED
COINCIDENCE
COINCIDENCES
COINCIDENT
COINCIDENTAL
COINCIDENTALLY
COINCIDENTLY
COINCIDES
COINCIDING
COINED
COINER
COINERS
COINFECT
COINFECTED
COINFECTING
COINFECTION
COINFECTIONS
COINFECTS
COINFER
COINFERRED
COINFERRING
COINFERS
COINHERE
COINHERED
COINHERES
COINHERING
COINING
COINMATE
COINMATES
COINS
COINSURANCE
COINSURANCES
COINSURE
COINSURED
COINSURER
COINSURERS
COINSURES
COINSURING
COINTER
COINTERRED

COINTERRING
COINTERS
COINTREAU
COINTREAUS
COINVENT
COINVENTED
COINVENTING
COINVENTOR
COINVENTORS
COINVENTS
COINVESTIGATOR
COINVESTIGATORS
COINVESTOR
COINVESTORS
COIR
COIRS
COISTREL
COISTRELS
COISTRIL
COISTRILS
COITAL
COITALLY
COITION
COITIONAL
COITIONS
COITUS
COITUSES
COJOIN
COJOINED
COJOINING
COJOINS
COJONES
COKE
COKED
COKEHEAD
COKEHEADS
COKELIKE
COKES
COKING
COKINGS
COKY
COL
COLA
COLANDER
COLANDERS
COLAS
COLATITUDE
COLATITUDES
COLBIES
COLBY
COLBYS
COLCANNON
COLCANNONS
COLCHICINE
COLCHICINES
COLCHICUM
COLCHICUMS
COLCOTHAR
COLCOTHARS
COLD
COLDBLOOD
COLDCOCK
COLDCOCKED
COLDCOCKING
COLDCOCKS
COLDER
COLDEST
COLDHEARTED
COLDHEARTEDLY
COLDHEARTEDNESS
COLDISH
COLDLY
COLDNESS
COLDNESSES
COLDS
COLE
COLEAD
COLEADER
COLEADERS
COLEADING
COLEADS
COLECTOMIES
COLECTOMY
COLED
COLEMANITE
COLEMANITES
COLEOPTERA
COLEOPTERAN
COLEOPTERANS
COLEOPTERIST
COLEOPTERISTS
COLEOPTEROUS
COLEOPTILE
COLEOPTILES
COLEORHIZA
COLEORHIZAE
COLES
COLESEED
COLESEEDS
COLESLAW
COLESLAWS
COLESSEE
COLESSEES
COLESSOR
COLESSORS
COLEUS
COLEUSES
COLEWORT
COLEWORTS
COLIC
COLICIN
COLICINE
COLICINES
COLICINS
COLICKIER
COLICKIEST
COLICKY
COLICROOT
COLICROOTS
COLICS
COLICWEED
COLICWEEDS
COLIES
COLIFORM
COLIFORMS
COLIN
COLINEAR
COLINEARITIES
COLINEARITY
COLINS
COLIPHAGE
COLIPHAGES
COLISEUM
COLISEUMS
COLISTIN
COLISTINS
COLITIC
COLITIS
COLITISES
COLLABORATE
COLLABORATED
COLLABORATES
COLLABORATING
COLLABORATION
COLLABORATIONS
COLLABORATIVE
COLLABORATIVELY
COLLABORATIVES
COLLABORATOR
COLLABORATORS
COLLAGE
COLLAGED
COLLAGEN
COLLAGENASE
COLLAGENASES
COLLAGENOUS
COLLAGENS
COLLAGES
COLLAGING
COLLAGIST
COLLAGISTS
COLLAPSE
COLLAPSED
COLLAPSES
COLLAPSIBILITY
COLLAPSIBLE
COLLAPSING
COLLAR
COLLARBONE
COLLARBONES
COLLARD
COLLARDS
COLLARED
COLLARET
COLLARETS
COLLARING
COLLARLESS
COLLARS
COLLATE
COLLATED
COLLATERAL
COLLATERALITIES
COLLATERALITY
COLLATERALIZE
COLLATERALIZED
COLLATERALIZES
COLLATERALIZING
COLLATERALLY
COLLATERALS
COLLATES
COLLATING
COLLATION
COLLATIONS
COLLATOR
COLLATORS
COLLEAGUE
COLLEAGUES
COLLEAGUESHIP
COLLEAGUESHIPS
COLLECT
COLLECTABILITY
COLLECTABLE
COLLECTABLES
COLLECTANEA
COLLECTED
COLLECTEDLY
COLLECTEDNESS
COLLECTEDNESSES
COLLECTIBILITY
COLLECTIBLE
COLLECTIBLES
COLLECTING
COLLECTION
COLLECTIONS
COLLECTIVE
COLLECTIVELY
COLLECTIVES
COLLECTIVISE
COLLECTIVISED
COLLECTIVISES
COLLECTIVISING
COLLECTIVISM
COLLECTIVISMS
COLLECTIVIST
COLLECTIVISTIC
COLLECTIVISTS
COLLECTIVITIES
COLLECTIVITY
COLLECTIVIZE
COLLECTIVIZED
COLLECTIVIZES
COLLECTIVIZING
COLLECTOR
COLLECTORS
COLLECTORSHIP
COLLECTORSHIPS
COLLECTS
COLLEEN
COLLEENS
COLLEGE
COLLEGER
COLLEGERS
COLLEGES
COLLEGIA
COLLEGIAL
COLLEGIALITIES
COLLEGIALITY
COLLEGIALLY
COLLEGIAN
COLLEGIANS
COLLEGIATE
COLLEGIATELY
COLLEGIUM
COLLEGIUMS
COLLEMBOLAN
COLLEMBOLANS
COLLEMBOLOUS
COLLENCHYMA
COLLENCHYMAS
COLLENCHYMATOUS
COLLET
COLLETED
COLLETING
COLLETS
COLLIDE

COLLIDED
COLLIDER
COLLIDERS
COLLIDES
COLLIDING
COLLIE
COLLIED
COLLIER
COLLIERIES
COLLIERS
COLLIERY
COLLIES
COLLIESHANGIE
COLLIESHANGIES
COLLIGATE
COLLIGATED
COLLIGATES
COLLIGATING
COLLIGATION
COLLIGATIONS
COLLIGATIVE
COLLIMATE
COLLIMATED
COLLIMATES
COLLIMATING
COLLIMATION
COLLIMATIONS
COLLIMATOR
COLLIMATORS
COLLINEAR
COLLINEARITIES
COLLINEARITY
COLLINS
COLLINSES
COLLINSIA
COLLINSIAS
COLLISION
COLLISIONAL
COLLISIONALLY
COLLISIONS
COLLOCATE
COLLOCATED
COLLOCATES
COLLOCATING
COLLOCATION
COLLOCATIONAL
COLLOCATIONS
COLLODION
COLLODIONS
COLLOGUE
COLLOGUED
COLLOGUES
COLLOGUING
COLLOID
COLLOIDAL
COLLOIDALLY
COLLOIDS
COLLOP
COLLOPS
COLLOQUIA
COLLOQUIAL
COLLOQUIALISM
COLLOQUIALISMS
COLLOQUIALITIES
COLLOQUIALITY
COLLOQUIALLY
COLLOQUIALS
COLLOQUIES
COLLOQUIST
COLLOQUISTS
COLLOQUIUM
COLLOQUIUMS
COLLOQUY
COLLOTYPE
COLLOTYPES
COLLOTYPIES
COLLOTYPY
COLLUDE
COLLUDED
COLLUDER
COLLUDERS
COLLUDES
COLLUDING
COLLUSION
COLLUSIONS
COLLUSIVE
COLLUSIVELY
COLLUVIA
COLLUVIAL
COLLUVIUM
COLLUVIUMS
COLLY
COLLYING
COLLYRIA
COLLYRIUM
COLLYRIUMS
COLLYWOBBLES
COLOBI
COLOBOMA
COLOBOMAS
COLOBOMATA
COLOBUS
COLOBUSES
COLOCATE
COLOCATED
COLOCATES
COLOCATING
COLOCYNTH
COLOCYNTHS
COLOG
COLOGARITHM
COLOGARITHMS
COLOGNE
COLOGNED
COLOGNES
COLOGS
COLOMBARD
COLOMBARDS
COLON
COLONE
COLONEL
COLONELCIES
COLONELCY
COLONELS
COLONES
COLONI
COLONIAL
COLONIALISM
COLONIALISMS
COLONIALIST
COLONIALISTIC
COLONIALISTS
COLONIALIZE
COLONIALIZED
COLONIALIZES
COLONIALIZING
COLONIALLY
COLONIALNESS
COLONIALNESSES
COLONIALS
COLONIC
COLONICS
COLONIES
COLONISATION
COLONISATIONS
COLONISE
COLONISED
COLONISER
COLONISERS
COLONISES
COLONISING
COLONIST
COLONISTS
COLONITIS
COLONITISES
COLONIZATION
COLONIZATIONIST
COLONIZATIONS
COLONIZE
COLONIZED
COLONIZER
COLONIZERS
COLONIZES
COLONIZING
COLONNADE
COLONNADED
COLONNADES
COLONOGRAPHIES
COLONOGRAPHY
COLONOSCOPE
COLONOSCOPES
COLONOSCOPIES
COLONOSCOPY
COLONS
COLONUS
COLONY
COLOPHON
COLOPHONIES
COLOPHONS
COLOPHONY
COLOR
COLORABLE
COLORABLY
COLORADO
COLORANT
COLORANTS
COLORATION
COLORATIONS
COLORATURA
COLORATURAS
COLORBRED
COLORBREED
COLORBREEDING
COLORBREEDS
COLORCAST
COLORCASTED
COLORCASTING
COLORCASTS
COLORECTAL
COLORED
COLOREDS
COLORER
COLORERS
COLORFAST
COLORFASTNESS
COLORFASTNESSES
COLORFUL
COLORFULLY
COLORFULNESS
COLORFULNESSES
COLORIFIC
COLORIMETER
COLORIMETERS
COLORIMETRIC
COLORIMETRIES
COLORIMETRY
COLORING
COLORINGS
COLORISE
COLORISED
COLORISES
COLORISING
COLORISM
COLORISMS
COLORIST
COLORISTIC
COLORISTICALLY
COLORISTS
COLORIZATION
COLORIZATIONS
COLORIZE
COLORIZED
COLORIZER
COLORIZERS
COLORIZES
COLORIZING
COLORLESS
COLORLESSLY
COLORLESSNESS
COLORLESSNESSES
COLORMAN
COLORMEN
COLORPOINT
COLORPOINTS
COLORS
COLORWAY
COLORWAYS
COLOSSAL
COLOSSALLY
COLOSSEUM
COLOSSEUMS
COLOSSI
COLOSSUS
COLOSSUSES
COLOSTOMIES
COLOSTOMY
COLOSTRAL
COLOSTRUM
COLOSTRUMS
COLOTOMIES
COLOTOMY
COLOUR
COLOURANT
COLOURANTS
COLOURATION

COLOURATIONS
COLOURED
COLOURER
COLOURERS
COLOURFAST
COLOURFUL
COLOURFULLY
COLOURING
COLOURINGS
COLOURIST
COLOURISTS
COLOURLESS
COLOURS
COLPITIS
COLPITISES
COLPORTAGE
COLPORTAGES
COLPORTEUR
COLPORTEURS
COLPOSCOPE
COLPOSCOPES
COLPOSCOPIES
COLPOSCOPY
COLS
COLT
COLTAN
COLTANS
COLTER
COLTERS
COLTHOOD
COLTHOODS
COLTISH
COLTISHLY
COLTISHNESS
COLTISHNESSES
COLTS
COLTSFOOT
COLTSFOOTS
COLUBRID
COLUBRIDS
COLUBRINE
COLUGO
COLUGOS
COLUMBARIA
COLUMBARIES
COLUMBARIUM
COLUMBARY
COLUMBIC
COLUMBINE
COLUMBINES
COLUMBITE
COLUMBITES
COLUMBIUM
COLUMBIUMS
COLUMEL
COLUMELLA
COLUMELLAE
COLUMELLAR
COLUMELS
COLUMN
COLUMNAL
COLUMNAR
COLUMNEA
COLUMNEAS
COLUMNED
COLUMNIATION
COLUMNIATIONS
COLUMNIST
COLUMNISTIC
COLUMNISTS
COLUMNS
COLURE
COLURES
COLY
COLZA
COLZAS
COMA
COMADE
COMAE
COMAKE
COMAKER
COMAKERS
COMAKES
COMAKING
COMAL
COMANAGE
COMANAGED
COMANAGEMENT
COMANAGEMENTS
COMANAGER
COMANAGERS
COMANAGES
COMANAGING
COMAS
COMATE
COMATES
COMATIC
COMATIK
COMATIKS
COMATOSE
COMATULA
COMATULAE
COMATULID
COMATULIDS
COMB
COMBAT
COMBATANT
COMBATANTS
COMBATED
COMBATER
COMBATERS
COMBATING
COMBATIVE
COMBATIVELY
COMBATIVENESS
COMBATIVENESSES
COMBATS
COMBATTED
COMBATTING
COMBE
COMBED
COMBER
COMBERS
COMBES
COMBI
COMBINABLE
COMBINATION
COMBINATIONAL
COMBINATIONS
COMBINATIVE
COMBINATORIAL
COMBINATORIALLY
COMBINATORICS
COMBINATORY
COMBINE
COMBINED
COMBINEDS
COMBINER
COMBINERS
COMBINES
COMBING
COMBINGS
COMBINING
COMBIS
COMBLIKE
COMBO
COMBOS
COMBOVER
COMBOVERS
COMBS
COMBUST
COMBUSTED
COMBUSTIBILITY
COMBUSTIBLE
COMBUSTIBLES
COMBUSTIBLY
COMBUSTING
COMBUSTION
COMBUSTIONS
COMBUSTIVE
COMBUSTOR
COMBUSTORS
COMBUSTS
COME
COMEBACK
COMEBACKER
COMEBACKERS
COMEBACKS
COMEDIAN
COMEDIANS
COMEDIC
COMEDICALLY
COMEDIENNE
COMEDIENNES
COMEDIES
COMEDIST
COMEDISTS
COMEDO
COMEDONES
COMEDOS
COMEDOWN
COMEDOWNS
COMEDY
COMELIER
COMELIEST
COMELILY
COMELINESS
COMELINESSES
COMELY
COMEMBER
COMEMBERS
COMER
COMERS
COMES
COMESTIBLE
COMESTIBLES
COMET
COMETARY
COMETH
COMETHER
COMETHERS
COMETIC
COMETS
COMEUPPANCE
COMEUPPANCES
COMFIER
COMFIEST
COMFILY
COMFINESS
COMFINESSES
COMFIT
COMFITS
COMFORT
COMFORTABLE
COMFORTABLENESS
COMFORTABLY
COMFORTED
COMFORTER
COMFORTERS
COMFORTING
COMFORTINGLY
COMFORTLESS
COMFORTS
COMFREY
COMFREYS
COMFY
COMIC
COMICAL
COMICALITIES
COMICALITY
COMICALLY
COMICS
COMING
COMINGLE
COMINGLED
COMINGLES
COMINGLING
COMINGS
COMITIA
COMITIAL
COMITIES
COMITY
COMIX
COMM
COMMA
COMMAND
COMMANDABLE
COMMANDANT
COMMANDANTS
COMMANDED
COMMANDEER
COMMANDEERED
COMMANDEERING
COMMANDEERS
COMMANDER
COMMANDERIES
COMMANDERS
COMMANDERSHIP
COMMANDERSHIPS
COMMANDERY
COMMANDING
COMMANDINGLY
COMMANDMENT
COMMANDMENTS
COMMANDO

COMMANDOES
COMMANDOS
COMMANDS
COMMAS
COMMATA
COMMEMORATE
COMMEMORATED
COMMEMORATES
COMMEMORATING
COMMEMORATION
COMMEMORATIONS
COMMEMORATIVE
COMMEMORATIVELY
COMMEMORATIVES
COMMEMORATOR
COMMEMORATORS
COMMENCE
COMMENCED
COMMENCEMENT
COMMENCEMENTS
COMMENCER
COMMENCERS
COMMENCES
COMMENCING
COMMEND
COMMENDABLE
COMMENDABLY
COMMENDAM
COMMENDAMS
COMMENDATION
COMMENDATIONS
COMMENDATORY
COMMENDED
COMMENDER
COMMENDERS
COMMENDING
COMMENDS
COMMENSAL
COMMENSALISM
COMMENSALISMS
COMMENSALLY
COMMENSALS
COMMENSURABLE
COMMENSURABLY
COMMENSURATE
COMMENSURATELY
COMMENSURATION
COMMENSURATIONS
COMMENT
COMMENTARIAT
COMMENTARIATS
COMMENTARIES
COMMENTARY
COMMENTATE
COMMENTATED
COMMENTATES
COMMENTATING
COMMENTATOR
COMMENTATORS
COMMENTED
COMMENTER
COMMENTERS
COMMENTING
COMMENTS
COMMERCE
COMMERCED
COMMERCES
COMMERCIAL
COMMERCIALISE
COMMERCIALISED
COMMERCIALISES
COMMERCIALISING
COMMERCIALISM
COMMERCIALISMS
COMMERCIALIST
COMMERCIALISTIC
COMMERCIALISTS
COMMERCIALITIES
COMMERCIALITY
COMMERCIALIZE
COMMERCIALIZED
COMMERCIALIZES
COMMERCIALIZING
COMMERCIALLY
COMMERCIALS
COMMERCING
COMMIE
COMMIES
COMMINATION
COMMINATIONS
COMMINATORY
COMMINGLE
COMMINGLED
COMMINGLES
COMMINGLING
COMMINUTE
COMMINUTED
COMMINUTES
COMMINUTING
COMMINUTION
COMMINUTIONS
COMMIS
COMMISERATE
COMMISERATED
COMMISERATES
COMMISERATING
COMMISERATINGLY
COMMISERATION
COMMISERATIONS
COMMISERATIVE
COMMISH
COMMISHES
COMMISSAR
COMMISSARIAL
COMMISSARIAT
COMMISSARIATS
COMMISSARIES
COMMISSARS
COMMISSARY
COMMISSION
COMMISSIONAIRE
COMMISSIONAIRES
COMMISSIONED
COMMISSIONER
COMMISSIONERS
COMMISSIONING
COMMISSIONS
COMMISSURAL
COMMISSURE
COMMISSURES
COMMIT
COMMITMENT
COMMITMENTS
COMMITS
COMMITTABLE
COMMITTAL
COMMITTALS
COMMITTED
COMMITTEE
COMMITTEEMAN
COMMITTEEMEN
COMMITTEES
COMMITTEEWOMAN
COMMITTEEWOMEN
COMMITTING
COMMIX
COMMIXED
COMMIXES
COMMIXING
COMMIXT
COMMIXTURE
COMMIXTURES
COMMO
COMMODE
COMMODES
COMMODIFICATION
COMMODIFIED
COMMODIFIES
COMMODIFY
COMMODIFYING
COMMODIOUS
COMMODIOUSLY
COMMODIOUSNESS
COMMODITIES
COMMODITIZATION
COMMODITIZE
COMMODITIZED
COMMODITIZES
COMMODITIZING
COMMODITY
COMMODORE
COMMODORES
COMMON
COMMONAGE
COMMONAGES
COMMONALITIES
COMMONALITY
COMMONALTIES
COMMONALTY
COMMONER
COMMONERS
COMMONEST
COMMONLY
COMMONNESS
COMMONNESSES
COMMONPLACE
COMMONPLACENESS
COMMONPLACES
COMMONS
COMMONSENSE
COMMONSENSIBLE
COMMONSENSICAL
COMMONWEAL
COMMONWEALS
COMMONWEALTH
COMMONWEALTHS
COMMOS
COMMOTION
COMMOTIONS
COMMOVE
COMMOVED
COMMOVES
COMMOVING
COMMS
COMMUNAL
COMMUNALISM
COMMUNALISMS
COMMUNALIST
COMMUNALISTS
COMMUNALITIES
COMMUNALITY
COMMUNALIZE
COMMUNALIZED
COMMUNALIZES
COMMUNALIZING
COMMUNALLY
COMMUNARD
COMMUNARDS
COMMUNE
COMMUNED
COMMUNER
COMMUNERS
COMMUNES
COMMUNICABILITY
COMMUNICABLE
COMMUNICABLY
COMMUNICANT
COMMUNICANTS
COMMUNICATE
COMMUNICATED
COMMUNICATEE
COMMUNICATEES
COMMUNICATES
COMMUNICATING
COMMUNICATION
COMMUNICATIONAL
COMMUNICATIONS
COMMUNICATIVE
COMMUNICATIVELY
COMMUNICATOR
COMMUNICATORS
COMMUNICATORY
COMMUNING
COMMUNION
COMMUNIONS
COMMUNIQUE
COMMUNIQUES
COMMUNISE
COMMUNISED
COMMUNISES
COMMUNISING
COMMUNISM
COMMUNISMS
COMMUNIST
COMMUNISTIC
COMMUNISTICALLY
COMMUNISTS
COMMUNITARIAN
COMMUNITARIANS
COMMUNITIES
COMMUNITY
COMMUNIZATION
COMMUNIZATIONS
COMMUNIZE
COMMUNIZED

COMMUNIZES
COMMUNIZING
COMMUTABLE
COMMUTATE
COMMUTATED
COMMUTATES
COMMUTATING
COMMUTATION
COMMUTATIONS
COMMUTATIVE
COMMUTATIVITIES
COMMUTATIVITY
COMMUTATOR
COMMUTATORS
COMMUTE
COMMUTED
COMMUTER
COMMUTERS
COMMUTES
COMMUTING
COMMY
COMONOMER
COMONOMERS
COMORBID
COMORBIDITIES
COMORBIDITY
COMOSE
COMOUS
COMP
COMPACT
COMPACTED
COMPACTER
COMPACTERS
COMPACTEST
COMPACTIBLE
COMPACTING
COMPACTION
COMPACTIONS
COMPACTLY
COMPACTNESS
COMPACTNESSES
COMPACTOR
COMPACTORS
COMPACTS
COMPADRE
COMPADRES
COMPANIED
COMPANIES
COMPANION
COMPANIONABLE
COMPANIONABLY
COMPANIONATE
COMPANIONED
COMPANIONING
COMPANIONS
COMPANIONSHIP
COMPANIONSHIPS
COMPANIONWAY
COMPANIONWAYS
COMPANY
COMPANYING
COMPARABILITIES
COMPARABILITY
COMPARABLE
COMPARABLENESS
COMPARABLY
COMPARATIST
COMPARATISTS
COMPARATIVE
COMPARATIVELY
COMPARATIVENESS
COMPARATIVES
COMPARATIVIST
COMPARATIVISTS
COMPARATOR
COMPARATORS
COMPARE
COMPARED
COMPARER
COMPARERS
COMPARES
COMPARING
COMPARISON
COMPARISONS
COMPART
COMPARTED
COMPARTING
COMPARTMENT
COMPARTMENTAL
COMPARTMENTED
COMPARTMENTING
COMPARTMENTS
COMPARTS
COMPAS
COMPASS
COMPASSABLE
COMPASSED
COMPASSES
COMPASSING
COMPASSION
COMPASSIONATE
COMPASSIONATED
COMPASSIONATELY
COMPASSIONATES
COMPASSIONATING
COMPASSIONLESS
COMPASSIONS
COMPATIBILITIES
COMPATIBILITY
COMPATIBLE
COMPATIBLENESS
COMPATIBLES
COMPATIBLY
COMPATRIOT
COMPATRIOTIC
COMPATRIOTS
COMPED
COMPEER
COMPEERED
COMPEERING
COMPEERS
COMPEL
COMPELLABLE
COMPELLATION
COMPELLATIONS
COMPELLED
COMPELLER
COMPELLERS
COMPELLING
COMPELLINGLY
COMPELS
COMPEND
COMPENDIA
COMPENDIOUS
COMPENDIOUSLY
COMPENDIOUSNESS
COMPENDIUM
COMPENDIUMS
COMPENDS
COMPENSABILITY
COMPENSABLE
COMPENSATE
COMPENSATED
COMPENSATES
COMPENSATING
COMPENSATION
COMPENSATIONAL
COMPENSATIONS
COMPENSATIVE
COMPENSATOR
COMPENSATORS
COMPENSATORY
COMPERE
COMPERED
COMPERES
COMPERING
COMPETE
COMPETED
COMPETENCE
COMPETENCES
COMPETENCIES
COMPETENCY
COMPETENT
COMPETENTLY
COMPETES
COMPETING
COMPETITION
COMPETITIONS
COMPETITIVE
COMPETITIVELY
COMPETITIVENESS
COMPETITOR
COMPETITORS
COMPILATION
COMPILATIONS
COMPILE
COMPILED
COMPILER
COMPILERS
COMPILES
COMPILING
COMPING
COMPINGS
COMPLACENCE
COMPLACENCES
COMPLACENCIES
COMPLACENCY
COMPLACENT
COMPLACENTLY
COMPLAIN
COMPLAINANT
COMPLAINANTS
COMPLAINED
COMPLAINER
COMPLAINERS
COMPLAINING
COMPLAININGLY
COMPLAINS
COMPLAINT
COMPLAINTS
COMPLAISANCE
COMPLAISANCES
COMPLAISANT
COMPLAISANTLY
COMPLEAT
COMPLEATED
COMPLEATING
COMPLEATS
COMPLECT
COMPLECTED
COMPLECTING
COMPLECTS
COMPLEMENT
COMPLEMENTAL
COMPLEMENTARIES
COMPLEMENTARILY
COMPLEMENTARITY
COMPLEMENTARY
COMPLEMENTATION
COMPLEMENTED
COMPLEMENTING
COMPLEMENTIZER
COMPLEMENTIZERS
COMPLEMENTS
COMPLETE
COMPLETED
COMPLETELY
COMPLETENESS
COMPLETENESSES
COMPLETER
COMPLETERS
COMPLETES
COMPLETEST
COMPLETING
COMPLETION
COMPLETIONS
COMPLETIST
COMPLETISTS
COMPLETIVE
COMPLEX
COMPLEXATION
COMPLEXATIONS
COMPLEXED
COMPLEXER
COMPLEXES
COMPLEXEST
COMPLEXIFIED
COMPLEXIFIES
COMPLEXIFY
COMPLEXIFYING
COMPLEXING
COMPLEXION
COMPLEXIONAL
COMPLEXIONED
COMPLEXIONS
COMPLEXITIES
COMPLEXITY
COMPLEXLY
COMPLEXNESS
COMPLEXNESSES
COMPLIANCE
COMPLIANCES
COMPLIANCIES
COMPLIANCY
COMPLIANT

COMPLIANTLY
COMPLICACIES
COMPLICACY
COMPLICATE
COMPLICATED
COMPLICATEDLY
COMPLICATEDNESS
COMPLICATES
COMPLICATING
COMPLICATION
COMPLICATIONS
COMPLICE
COMPLICES
COMPLICIT
COMPLICITIES
COMPLICITOUS
COMPLICITY
COMPLIED
COMPLIER
COMPLIERS
COMPLIES
COMPLIMENT
COMPLIMENTARILY
COMPLIMENTARY
COMPLIMENTED
COMPLIMENTING
COMPLIMENTS
COMPLIN
COMPLINE
COMPLINES
COMPLINS
COMPLOT
COMPLOTS
COMPLOTTED
COMPLOTTING
COMPLY
COMPLYING
COMPO
COMPONE
COMPONENT
COMPONENTIAL
COMPONENTS
COMPONY
COMPORT
COMPORTED
COMPORTING
COMPORTMENT
COMPORTMENTS
COMPORTS
COMPOS
COMPOSE
COMPOSED
COMPOSEDLY
COMPOSEDNESS
COMPOSEDNESSES
COMPOSER
COMPOSERS
COMPOSES
COMPOSING
COMPOSITE
COMPOSITED
COMPOSITELY
COMPOSITES
COMPOSITING
COMPOSITION
COMPOSITIONAL
COMPOSITIONALLY
COMPOSITIONIST
COMPOSITIONISTS
COMPOSITIONS
COMPOSITOR
COMPOSITORS
COMPOST
COMPOSTABLE
COMPOSTED
COMPOSTER
COMPOSTERS
COMPOSTING
COMPOSTS
COMPOSURE
COMPOSURES
COMPOTE
COMPOTES
COMPOUND
COMPOUNDABLE
COMPOUNDED
COMPOUNDER
COMPOUNDERS
COMPOUNDING
COMPOUNDS
COMPRADOR
COMPRADORE
COMPRADORES
COMPRADORS
COMPREHEND
COMPREHENDED
COMPREHENDIBLE
COMPREHENDING
COMPREHENDS
COMPREHENSIBLE
COMPREHENSIBLY
COMPREHENSION
COMPREHENSIONS
COMPREHENSIVE
COMPREHENSIVELY
COMPRESS
COMPRESSED
COMPRESSEDLY
COMPRESSES
COMPRESSIBILITY
COMPRESSIBLE
COMPRESSING
COMPRESSION
COMPRESSIONAL
COMPRESSIONS
COMPRESSIVE
COMPRESSIVELY
COMPRESSOR
COMPRESSORS
COMPRISAL
COMPRISALS
COMPRISE
COMPRISED
COMPRISES
COMPRISING
COMPRIZE
COMPRIZED
COMPRIZES
COMPRIZING
COMPROMISE
COMPROMISED
COMPROMISER
COMPROMISERS
COMPROMISES
COMPROMISING
COMPS
COMPT
COMPTED
COMPTING
COMPTROLLER
COMPTROLLERS
COMPTROLLERSHIP
COMPTS
COMPULSION
COMPULSIONS
COMPULSIVE
COMPULSIVELY
COMPULSIVENESS
COMPULSIVITIES
COMPULSIVITY
COMPULSORILY
COMPULSORY
COMPUNCTION
COMPUNCTIONS
COMPUNCTIOUS
COMPURGATION
COMPURGATIONS
COMPURGATOR
COMPURGATORS
COMPUTABILITIES
COMPUTABILITY
COMPUTABLE
COMPUTATION
COMPUTATIONAL
COMPUTATIONALLY
COMPUTATIONS
COMPUTE
COMPUTED
COMPUTER
COMPUTERDOM
COMPUTERDOMS
COMPUTERESE
COMPUTERESES
COMPUTERISATION
COMPUTERISE
COMPUTERISED
COMPUTERISES
COMPUTERISING
COMPUTERIST
COMPUTERISTS
COMPUTERIZABLE
COMPUTERIZATION
COMPUTERIZE
COMPUTERIZED
COMPUTERIZES
COMPUTERIZING
COMPUTERLESS
COMPUTERLIKE
COMPUTERNIK
COMPUTERNIKS
COMPUTERPHOBE
COMPUTERPHOBES
COMPUTERPHOBIA
COMPUTERPHOBIAS
COMPUTERPHOBIC
COMPUTERS
COMPUTES
COMPUTING
COMPUTINGS
COMPUTIST
COMPUTISTS
COMRADE
COMRADELINESS
COMRADELINESSES
COMRADELY
COMRADERIES
COMRADERY
COMRADES
COMRADESHIP
COMRADESHIPS
COMSAT
COMSATS
COMSYMP
COMSYMPS
COMTE
COMTES
CON
CONALBUMIN
CONALBUMINS
CONATION
CONATIONS
CONATIVE
CONATUS
CONCANAVALIN
CONCANAVALINS
CONCATENATE
CONCATENATED
CONCATENATES
CONCATENATING
CONCATENATION
CONCATENATIONS
CONCAVE
CONCAVED
CONCAVELY
CONCAVES
CONCAVING
CONCAVITIES
CONCAVITY
CONCEAL
CONCEALABLE
CONCEALED
CONCEALER
CONCEALERS
CONCEALING
CONCEALINGLY
CONCEALMENT
CONCEALMENTS
CONCEALS
CONCEDE
CONCEDED
CONCEDEDLY
CONCEDER
CONCEDERS
CONCEDES
CONCEDING
CONCEIT
CONCEITED
CONCEITEDLY
CONCEITEDNESS
CONCEITEDNESSES
CONCEITING
CONCEITS
CONCEIVABILITY
CONCEIVABLE
CONCEIVABLENESS

CONCEIVABLY
CONCEIVE
CONCEIVED
CONCEIVER
CONCEIVERS
CONCEIVES
CONCEIVING
CONCELEBRANT
CONCELEBRANTS
CONCELEBRATE
CONCELEBRATED
CONCELEBRATES
CONCELEBRATING
CONCELEBRATION
CONCELEBRATIONS
CONCENT
CONCENTER
CONCENTERED
CONCENTERING
CONCENTERS
CONCENTRATE
CONCENTRATED
CONCENTRATEDLY
CONCENTRATES
CONCENTRATING
CONCENTRATION
CONCENTRATIONS
CONCENTRATIVE
CONCENTRATOR
CONCENTRATORS
CONCENTRIC
CONCENTRICALLY
CONCENTRICITIES
CONCENTRICITY
CONCENTS
CONCEPT
CONCEPTACLE
CONCEPTACLES
CONCEPTI
CONCEPTION
CONCEPTIONAL
CONCEPTIONS
CONCEPTIVE
CONCEPTS
CONCEPTUAL
CONCEPTUALISE
CONCEPTUALISED
CONCEPTUALISES
CONCEPTUALISING
CONCEPTUALISM
CONCEPTUALISMS
CONCEPTUALIST
CONCEPTUALISTIC
CONCEPTUALISTS
CONCEPTUALITIES
CONCEPTUALITY
CONCEPTUALIZE
CONCEPTUALIZED
CONCEPTUALIZER
CONCEPTUALIZERS
CONCEPTUALIZES
CONCEPTUALIZING
CONCEPTUALLY
CONCEPTUS
CONCEPTUSES
CONCERN
CONCERNED
CONCERNING
CONCERNMENT
CONCERNMENTS
CONCERNS
CONCERT
CONCERTED
CONCERTEDLY
CONCERTEDNESS
CONCERTEDNESSES
CONCERTGOER
CONCERTGOERS
CONCERTGOING
CONCERTGOINGS
CONCERTI
CONCERTINA
CONCERTINAS
CONCERTING
CONCERTINO
CONCERTINOS
CONCERTIZE
CONCERTIZED
CONCERTIZES
CONCERTIZING
CONCERTMASTER
CONCERTMASTERS
CONCERTMEISTER
CONCERTMEISTERS
CONCERTO
CONCERTOS
CONCERTS
CONCESSION
CONCESSIONAIRE
CONCESSIONAIRES
CONCESSIONAL
CONCESSIONARY
CONCESSIONER
CONCESSIONERS
CONCESSIONS
CONCESSIVE
CONCESSIVELY
CONCH
CONCHA
CONCHAE
CONCHAL
CONCHAS
CONCHES
CONCHIE
CONCHIES
CONCHO
CONCHOID
CONCHOIDAL
CONCHOIDALLY
CONCHOIDS
CONCHOLOGICAL
CONCHOLOGIES
CONCHOLOGIST
CONCHOLOGISTS
CONCHOLOGY
CONCHOS
CONCHS
CONCHY
CONCIERGE
CONCIERGES
CONCILIAR
CONCILIARLY
CONCILIATE
CONCILIATED
CONCILIATES
CONCILIATING
CONCILIATION
CONCILIATIONS
CONCILIATIVE
CONCILIATOR
CONCILIATORS
CONCILIATORY
CONCINNITIES
CONCINNITY
CONCISE
CONCISELY
CONCISENESS
CONCISENESSES
CONCISER
CONCISEST
CONCISION
CONCISIONS
CONCLAVE
CONCLAVES
CONCLUDE
CONCLUDED
CONCLUDER
CONCLUDERS
CONCLUDES
CONCLUDING
CONCLUSION
CONCLUSIONARY
CONCLUSIONS
CONCLUSIVE
CONCLUSIVELY
CONCLUSIVENESS
CONCLUSORY
CONCOCT
CONCOCTED
CONCOCTER
CONCOCTERS
CONCOCTING
CONCOCTION
CONCOCTIONS
CONCOCTIVE
CONCOCTOR
CONCOCTORS
CONCOCTS
CONCOMITANCE
CONCOMITANCES
CONCOMITANT
CONCOMITANTLY
CONCOMITANTS
CONCORD
CONCORDAL
CONCORDANCE
CONCORDANCES
CONCORDANT
CONCORDANTLY
CONCORDAT
CONCORDATS
CONCORDS
CONCOURS
CONCOURSE
CONCOURSES
CONCRESCENCE
CONCRESCENCES
CONCRESCENT
CONCRETE
CONCRETED
CONCRETELY
CONCRETENESS
CONCRETENESSES
CONCRETES
CONCRETING
CONCRETION
CONCRETIONARY
CONCRETIONS
CONCRETISM
CONCRETISMS
CONCRETIST
CONCRETISTS
CONCRETIZATION
CONCRETIZATIONS
CONCRETIZE
CONCRETIZED
CONCRETIZES
CONCRETIZING
CONCUBINAGE
CONCUBINAGES
CONCUBINE
CONCUBINES
CONCUPISCENCE
CONCUPISCENCES
CONCUPISCENT
CONCUPISCIBLE
CONCUR
CONCURRED
CONCURRENCE
CONCURRENCES
CONCURRENCIES
CONCURRENCY
CONCURRENT
CONCURRENTLY
CONCURRENTS
CONCURRING
CONCURS
CONCUSS
CONCUSSED
CONCUSSES
CONCUSSING
CONCUSSION
CONCUSSIONS
CONCUSSIVE
CONDEMN
CONDEMNABLE
CONDEMNATION
CONDEMNATIONS
CONDEMNATORY
CONDEMNED
CONDEMNER
CONDEMNERS
CONDEMNING
CONDEMNOR
CONDEMNORS
CONDEMNS
CONDENSABLE
CONDENSATE
CONDENSATES
CONDENSATION
CONDENSATIONAL
CONDENSATIONS
CONDENSE
CONDENSED
CONDENSER

CONDENSERS
CONDENSES
CONDENSIBLE
CONDENSING
CONDESCEND
CONDESCENDED
CONDESCENDENCE
CONDESCENDENCES
CONDESCENDING
CONDESCENDINGLY
CONDESCENDS
CONDESCENSION
CONDESCENSIONS
CONDIGN
CONDIGNLY
CONDIMENT
CONDIMENTAL
CONDIMENTS
CONDITION
CONDITIONABLE
CONDITIONAL
CONDITIONALITY
CONDITIONALLY
CONDITIONALS
CONDITIONED
CONDITIONER
CONDITIONERS
CONDITIONING
CONDITIONS
CONDO
CONDOES
CONDOLATORY
CONDOLE
CONDOLED
CONDOLENCE
CONDOLENCES
CONDOLENT
CONDOLER
CONDOLERS
CONDOLES
CONDOLING
CONDOM
CONDOMINIA
CONDOMINIUM
CONDOMINIUMS
CONDOMS
CONDONABLE
CONDONATION
CONDONATIONS
CONDONE
CONDONED
CONDONER
CONDONERS
CONDONES
CONDONING
CONDOR
CONDORES
CONDORS
CONDOS
CONDOTTIERE
CONDOTTIERI
CONDUCE
CONDUCED
CONDUCER
CONDUCERS
CONDUCES
CONDUCING
CONDUCIVE
CONDUCIVENESS
CONDUCIVENESSES
CONDUCT
CONDUCTANCE
CONDUCTANCES
CONDUCTED
CONDUCTIBILITY
CONDUCTIBLE
CONDUCTIMETRIC
CONDUCTING
CONDUCTION
CONDUCTIONS
CONDUCTIVE
CONDUCTIVITIES
CONDUCTIVITY
CONDUCTOMETRIC
CONDUCTOR
CONDUCTORIAL
CONDUCTORS
CONDUCTRESS
CONDUCTRESSES
CONDUCTS
CONDUIT
CONDUITS
CONDUPLICATE
CONDYLAR
CONDYLE
CONDYLES
CONDYLOID
CONDYLOMA
CONDYLOMAS
CONDYLOMATA
CONDYLOMATOUS
CONE
CONED
CONEFLOWER
CONEFLOWERS
CONELRAD
CONELRADS
CONENOSE
CONENOSES
CONEPATE
CONEPATES
CONEPATL
CONEPATLS
CONES
CONEY
CONEYS
CONFAB
CONFABBED
CONFABBING
CONFABS
CONFABULATE
CONFABULATED
CONFABULATES
CONFABULATING
CONFABULATION
CONFABULATIONS
CONFABULATOR
CONFABULATORS
CONFABULATORY
CONFECT
CONFECTED
CONFECTING
CONFECTION
CONFECTIONARIES
CONFECTIONARY
CONFECTIONER
CONFECTIONERIES
CONFECTIONERS
CONFECTIONERY
CONFECTIONS
CONFECTS
CONFEDERACIES
CONFEDERACY
CONFEDERAL
CONFEDERATE
CONFEDERATED
CONFEDERATES
CONFEDERATING
CONFEDERATION
CONFEDERATIONS
CONFEDERATIVE
CONFER
CONFEREE
CONFEREES
CONFERENCE
CONFERENCES
CONFERENCING
CONFERENCINGS
CONFERENTIAL
CONFERMENT
CONFERMENTS
CONFERRABLE
CONFERRAL
CONFERRALS
CONFERRED
CONFERREE
CONFERREES
CONFERRENCE
CONFERRENCES
CONFERRER
CONFERRERS
CONFERRING
CONFERS
CONFERVA
CONFERVAE
CONFERVAL
CONFERVAS
CONFESS
CONFESSABLE
CONFESSED
CONFESSEDLY
CONFESSES
CONFESSING
CONFESSION
CONFESSIONAL
CONFESSIONALISM
CONFESSIONALIST
CONFESSIONALLY
CONFESSIONALS
CONFESSIONS
CONFESSOR
CONFESSORS
CONFETTI
CONFETTO
CONFIDANT
CONFIDANTE
CONFIDANTES
CONFIDANTS
CONFIDE
CONFIDED
CONFIDENCE
CONFIDENCES
CONFIDENT
CONFIDENTIAL
CONFIDENTIALITY
CONFIDENTIALLY
CONFIDENTLY
CONFIDER
CONFIDERS
CONFIDES
CONFIDING
CONFIDINGLY
CONFIDINGNESS
CONFIDINGNESSES
CONFIGURATION
CONFIGURATIONAL
CONFIGURATIONS
CONFIGURATIVE
CONFIGURE
CONFIGURED
CONFIGURES
CONFIGURING
CONFINE
CONFINED
CONFINEMENT
CONFINEMENTS
CONFINER
CONFINERS
CONFINES
CONFINING
CONFIRM
CONFIRMABILITY
CONFIRMABLE
CONFIRMAND
CONFIRMANDS
CONFIRMATION
CONFIRMATIONAL
CONFIRMATIONS
CONFIRMATORY
CONFIRMED
CONFIRMEDLY
CONFIRMEDNESS
CONFIRMEDNESSES
CONFIRMER
CONFIRMERS
CONFIRMING
CONFIRMS
CONFISCABLE
CONFISCATABLE
CONFISCATE
CONFISCATED
CONFISCATES
CONFISCATING
CONFISCATION
CONFISCATIONS
CONFISCATOR
CONFISCATORS
CONFISCATORY
CONFIT
CONFITEOR
CONFITEORS
CONFITS
CONFITURE
CONFITURES
CONFLAGRANT

CONFLAGRATION
CONFLAGRATIONS
CONFLATE
CONFLATED
CONFLATES
CONFLATING
CONFLATION
CONFLATIONS
CONFLICT
CONFLICTED
CONFLICTFUL
CONFLICTING
CONFLICTINGLY
CONFLICTION
CONFLICTIONS
CONFLICTIVE
CONFLICTS
CONFLICTUAL
CONFLUENCE
CONFLUENCES
CONFLUENT
CONFLUENTS
CONFLUX
CONFLUXES
CONFOCAL
CONFOCALLY
CONFORM
CONFORMABLE
CONFORMABLY
CONFORMAL
CONFORMANCE
CONFORMANCES
CONFORMATION
CONFORMATIONAL
CONFORMATIONS
CONFORMED
CONFORMER
CONFORMERS
CONFORMING
CONFORMISM
CONFORMISMS
CONFORMIST
CONFORMISTS
CONFORMITIES
CONFORMITY
CONFORMS
CONFOUND
CONFOUNDED
CONFOUNDEDLY
CONFOUNDER
CONFOUNDERS
CONFOUNDING
CONFOUNDINGLY
CONFOUNDS
CONFRATERNITIES
CONFRATERNITY
CONFRERE
CONFRERES
CONFRONT
CONFRONTAL
CONFRONTALS
CONFRONTATION
CONFRONTATIONAL
CONFRONTATIONS
CONFRONTED
CONFRONTER
CONFRONTERS
CONFRONTING
CONFRONTS
CONFUSE
CONFUSED
CONFUSEDLY
CONFUSEDNESS
CONFUSEDNESSES
CONFUSES
CONFUSING
CONFUSINGLY
CONFUSION
CONFUSIONAL
CONFUSIONS
CONFUTATION
CONFUTATIONS
CONFUTATIVE
CONFUTE
CONFUTED
CONFUTER
CONFUTERS
CONFUTES
CONFUTING
CONGA
CONGAED
CONGAING
CONGAS
CONGE
CONGEAL
CONGEALED
CONGEALER
CONGEALERS
CONGEALING
CONGEALMENT
CONGEALMENTS
CONGEALS
CONGEE
CONGEED
CONGEEING
CONGEES
CONGELATION
CONGELATIONS
CONGENER
CONGENERIC
CONGENEROUS
CONGENERS
CONGENIAL
CONGENIALITIES
CONGENIALITY
CONGENIALLY
CONGENITAL
CONGENITALLY
CONGER
CONGERIES
CONGERS
CONGES
CONGEST
CONGESTED
CONGESTING
CONGESTION
CONGESTIONS
CONGESTIVE
CONGESTS
CONGII
CONGIUS
CONGLOBATE
CONGLOBATED
CONGLOBATES
CONGLOBATING
CONGLOBATION
CONGLOBATIONS
CONGLOBE
CONGLOBED
CONGLOBES
CONGLOBING
CONGLOMERATE
CONGLOMERATED
CONGLOMERATES
CONGLOMERATEUR
CONGLOMERATEURS
CONGLOMERATIC
CONGLOMERATING
CONGLOMERATION
CONGLOMERATIONS
CONGLOMERATIVE
CONGLOMERATOR
CONGLOMERATORS
CONGLUTINATE
CONGLUTINATED
CONGLUTINATES
CONGLUTINATING
CONGLUTINATION
CONGLUTINATIONS
CONGO
CONGOES
CONGOS
CONGOU
CONGOUS
CONGRATS
CONGRATULATE
CONGRATULATED
CONGRATULATES
CONGRATULATING
CONGRATULATION
CONGRATULATIONS
CONGRATULATOR
CONGRATULATORS
CONGRATULATORY
CONGREGANT
CONGREGANTS
CONGREGATE
CONGREGATED
CONGREGATES
CONGREGATING
CONGREGATION
CONGREGATIONAL
CONGREGATIONS
CONGREGATOR
CONGREGATORS
CONGRESS
CONGRESSED
CONGRESSES
CONGRESSING
CONGRESSIONAL
CONGRESSIONALLY
CONGRESSMAN
CONGRESSMEN
CONGRESSPEOPLE
CONGRESSPERSON
CONGRESSPERSONS
CONGRESSWOMAN
CONGRESSWOMEN
CONGRUENCE
CONGRUENCES
CONGRUENCIES
CONGRUENCY
CONGRUENT
CONGRUENTLY
CONGRUITIES
CONGRUITY
CONGRUOUS
CONGRUOUSLY
CONGRUOUSNESS
CONGRUOUSNESSES
CONI
CONIC
CONICAL
CONICALLY
CONICITIES
CONICITY
CONICS
CONIDIA
CONIDIAL
CONIDIAN
CONIDIOPHORE
CONIDIOPHORES
CONIDIUM
CONIES
CONIFER
CONIFEROUS
CONIFERS
CONIINE
CONIINES
CONIN
CONINE
CONINES
CONING
CONINS
CONIOSES
CONIOSIS
CONIUM
CONIUMS
CONJECTURAL
CONJECTURALLY
CONJECTURE
CONJECTURED
CONJECTURER
CONJECTURERS
CONJECTURES
CONJECTURING
CONJOIN
CONJOINED
CONJOINER
CONJOINERS
CONJOINING
CONJOINS
CONJOINT
CONJOINTLY
CONJUGAL
CONJUGALITIES
CONJUGALITY
CONJUGALLY
CONJUGANT
CONJUGANTS
CONJUGATE
CONJUGATED
CONJUGATELY
CONJUGATENESS
CONJUGATENESSES

CONJUGATES
CONJUGATING
CONJUGATION
CONJUGATIONAL
CONJUGATIONALLY
CONJUGATIONS
CONJUNCT
CONJUNCTION
CONJUNCTIONAL
CONJUNCTIONALLY
CONJUNCTIONS
CONJUNCTIVA
CONJUNCTIVAE
CONJUNCTIVAL
CONJUNCTIVAS
CONJUNCTIVE
CONJUNCTIVELY
CONJUNCTIVES
CONJUNCTIVITIS
CONJUNCTS
CONJUNCTURE
CONJUNCTURES
CONJUNTO
CONJUNTOS
CONJURATION
CONJURATIONS
CONJURE
CONJURED
CONJURER
CONJURERS
CONJURES
CONJURING
CONJURINGS
CONJUROR
CONJURORS
CONK
CONKED
CONKER
CONKERS
CONKING
CONKS
CONKY
CONN
CONNATE
CONNATELY
CONNATION
CONNATIONS
CONNATURAL
CONNATURALITIES
CONNATURALITY
CONNATURALLY
CONNECT
CONNECTABLE
CONNECTED
CONNECTEDLY
CONNECTEDNESS
CONNECTEDNESSES
CONNECTER
CONNECTERS
CONNECTIBLE
CONNECTING
CONNECTION
CONNECTIONAL
CONNECTIONISM
CONNECTIONISMS
CONNECTIONIST
CONNECTIONISTS
CONNECTIONS
CONNECTIVE
CONNECTIVELY
CONNECTIVES
CONNECTIVITIES
CONNECTIVITY
CONNECTOR
CONNECTORS
CONNECTS
CONNED
CONNER
CONNERS
CONNEXION
CONNEXIONS
CONNING
CONNIPTION
CONNIPTIONS
CONNIVANCE
CONNIVANCES
CONNIVE
CONNIVED
CONNIVENT
CONNIVER
CONNIVERIES
CONNIVERS
CONNIVERY
CONNIVES
CONNIVING
CONNOISSEUR
CONNOISSEURS
CONNOISSEURSHIP
CONNOR
CONNORS
CONNOTATION
CONNOTATIONAL
CONNOTATIONS
CONNOTATIVE
CONNOTATIVELY
CONNOTE
CONNOTED
CONNOTES
CONNOTING
CONNS
CONNUBIAL
CONNUBIALISM
CONNUBIALISMS
CONNUBIALITIES
CONNUBIALITY
CONNUBIALLY
CONODONT
CONODONTS
CONOID
CONOIDAL
CONOIDS
CONOMINEE
CONOMINEES
CONQUER
CONQUERED
CONQUERER
CONQUERERS
CONQUERING
CONQUEROR
CONQUERORS
CONQUERS
CONQUEST
CONQUESTS
CONQUIAN
CONQUIANS
CONQUISTADOR
CONQUISTADORES
CONQUISTADORS
CONS
CONSANGUINE
CONSANGUINEOUS
CONSANGUINITIES
CONSANGUINITY
CONSCIENCE
CONSCIENCELESS
CONSCIENCES
CONSCIENTIOUS
CONSCIENTIOUSLY
CONSCIONABLE
CONSCIOUS
CONSCIOUSES
CONSCIOUSLY
CONSCIOUSNESS
CONSCIOUSNESSES
CONSCRIBE
CONSCRIBED
CONSCRIBES
CONSCRIBING
CONSCRIPT
CONSCRIPTED
CONSCRIPTING
CONSCRIPTION
CONSCRIPTIONS
CONSCRIPTS
CONSECRATE
CONSECRATED
CONSECRATES
CONSECRATING
CONSECRATION
CONSECRATIONS
CONSECRATIVE
CONSECRATOR
CONSECRATORS
CONSECRATORY
CONSECUTION
CONSECUTIONS
CONSECUTIVE
CONSECUTIVELY
CONSECUTIVENESS
CONSENSUAL
CONSENSUALLY
CONSENSUS
CONSENSUSES
CONSENT
CONSENTANEOUS
CONSENTANEOUSLY
CONSENTED
CONSENTER
CONSENTERS
CONSENTING
CONSENTINGLY
CONSENTS
CONSEQUENCE
CONSEQUENCES
CONSEQUENT
CONSEQUENTIAL
CONSEQUENTIALLY
CONSEQUENTLY
CONSEQUENTS
CONSERVANCIES
CONSERVANCY
CONSERVATION
CONSERVATIONAL
CONSERVATIONIST
CONSERVATIONS
CONSERVATISM
CONSERVATISMS
CONSERVATIVE
CONSERVATIVELY
CONSERVATIVES
CONSERVATIZE
CONSERVATIZED
CONSERVATIZES
CONSERVATIZING
CONSERVATOIRE
CONSERVATOIRES
CONSERVATOR
CONSERVATORIAL
CONSERVATORIES
CONSERVATORS
CONSERVATORSHIP
CONSERVATORY
CONSERVE
CONSERVED
CONSERVER
CONSERVERS
CONSERVES
CONSERVING
CONSIDER
CONSIDERABLE
CONSIDERABLES
CONSIDERABLY
CONSIDERATE
CONSIDERATELY
CONSIDERATENESS
CONSIDERATION
CONSIDERATIONS
CONSIDERED
CONSIDERING
CONSIDERS
CONSIGLIERE
CONSIGLIERES
CONSIGLIERI
CONSIGN
CONSIGNABLE
CONSIGNATION
CONSIGNATIONS
CONSIGNED
CONSIGNEE
CONSIGNEES
CONSIGNER
CONSIGNERS
CONSIGNING
CONSIGNMENT
CONSIGNMENTS
CONSIGNOR
CONSIGNORS
CONSIGNS
CONSILIENCE
CONSILIENCES
CONSIST
CONSISTED
CONSISTENCE
CONSISTENCES
CONSISTENCIES

CONSISTENCY
CONSISTENT
CONSISTENTLY
CONSISTING
CONSISTORIAL
CONSISTORIES
CONSISTORY
CONSISTS
CONSOCIATE
CONSOCIATED
CONSOCIATES
CONSOCIATING
CONSOCIATION
CONSOCIATIONAL
CONSOCIATIONS
CONSOL
CONSOLABLE
CONSOLATION
CONSOLATIONS
CONSOLATORY
CONSOLE
CONSOLED
CONSOLER
CONSOLERS
CONSOLES
CONSOLIDATE
CONSOLIDATED
CONSOLIDATES
CONSOLIDATING
CONSOLIDATION
CONSOLIDATIONS
CONSOLIDATOR
CONSOLIDATORS
CONSOLING
CONSOLINGLY
CONSOLS
CONSOMME
CONSOMMES
CONSONANCE
CONSONANCES
CONSONANCIES
CONSONANCY
CONSONANT
CONSONANTAL
CONSONANTLY
CONSONANTS
CONSORT
CONSORTED
CONSORTIA
CONSORTING
CONSORTIUM
CONSORTIUMS
CONSORTS
CONSPECIFIC
CONSPECIFICS
CONSPECTUS
CONSPECTUSES
CONSPICUITIES
CONSPICUITY
CONSPICUOUS
CONSPICUOUSLY
CONSPICUOUSNESS
CONSPIRACIES
CONSPIRACIST
CONSPIRACISTS
CONSPIRACY
CONSPIRATION
CONSPIRATIONAL
CONSPIRATIONS
CONSPIRATOR
CONSPIRATORIAL
CONSPIRATORS
CONSPIRE
CONSPIRED
CONSPIRER
CONSPIRERS
CONSPIRES
CONSPIRING
CONSTABLE
CONSTABLES
CONSTABULARIES
CONSTABULARY
CONSTANCIES
CONSTANCY
CONSTANT
CONSTANTAN
CONSTANTANS
CONSTANTLY
CONSTANTS
CONSTATIVE
CONSTATIVES
CONSTELLATE
CONSTELLATED
CONSTELLATES
CONSTELLATING
CONSTELLATION
CONSTELLATIONS
CONSTELLATORY
CONSTERNATE
CONSTERNATED
CONSTERNATES
CONSTERNATING
CONSTERNATION
CONSTERNATIONS
CONSTIPATE
CONSTIPATED
CONSTIPATES
CONSTIPATING
CONSTIPATION
CONSTIPATIONS
CONSTITUENCIES
CONSTITUENCY
CONSTITUENT
CONSTITUENTLY
CONSTITUENTS
CONSTITUTE
CONSTITUTED
CONSTITUTES
CONSTITUTING
CONSTITUTION
CONSTITUTIONAL
CONSTITUTIONALS
CONSTITUTIONS
CONSTITUTIVE
CONSTITUTIVELY
CONSTRAIN
CONSTRAINED
CONSTRAINEDLY
CONSTRAINING
CONSTRAINS
CONSTRAINT
CONSTRAINTS
CONSTRICT
CONSTRICTED
CONSTRICTING
CONSTRICTION
CONSTRICTIONS
CONSTRICTIVE
CONSTRICTOR
CONSTRICTORS
CONSTRICTS
CONSTRINGE
CONSTRINGED
CONSTRINGENT
CONSTRINGES
CONSTRINGING
CONSTRUABLE
CONSTRUAL
CONSTRUALS
CONSTRUCT
CONSTRUCTABLE
CONSTRUCTED
CONSTRUCTIBLE
CONSTRUCTING
CONSTRUCTION
CONSTRUCTIONAL
CONSTRUCTIONIST
CONSTRUCTIONS
CONSTRUCTIVE
CONSTRUCTIVELY
CONSTRUCTIVISM
CONSTRUCTIVISMS
CONSTRUCTIVIST
CONSTRUCTIVISTS
CONSTRUCTOR
CONSTRUCTORS
CONSTRUCTS
CONSTRUE
CONSTRUED
CONSTRUER
CONSTRUERS
CONSTRUES
CONSTRUING
CONSUBSTANTIAL
CONSUETUDE
CONSUETUDES
CONSUETUDINARY
CONSUL
CONSULAR
CONSULATE
CONSULATES
CONSULS
CONSULSHIP
CONSULSHIPS
CONSULT
CONSULTANCIES
CONSULTANCY
CONSULTANT
CONSULTANTS
CONSULTANTSHIP
CONSULTANTSHIPS
CONSULTATION
CONSULTATIONS
CONSULTATIVE
CONSULTED
CONSULTER
CONSULTERS
CONSULTING
CONSULTINGS
CONSULTIVE
CONSULTOR
CONSULTORS
CONSULTS
CONSUMABLE
CONSUMABLES
CONSUME
CONSUMED
CONSUMEDLY
CONSUMER
CONSUMERISM
CONSUMERISMS
CONSUMERIST
CONSUMERISTIC
CONSUMERISTS
CONSUMERS
CONSUMERSHIP
CONSUMERSHIPS
CONSUMES
CONSUMING
CONSUMMATE
CONSUMMATED
CONSUMMATELY
CONSUMMATES
CONSUMMATING
CONSUMMATION
CONSUMMATIONS
CONSUMMATIVE
CONSUMMATOR
CONSUMMATORS
CONSUMMATORY
CONSUMPTION
CONSUMPTIONS
CONSUMPTIVE
CONSUMPTIVELY
CONSUMPTIVES
CONTACT
CONTACTED
CONTACTEE
CONTACTEES
CONTACTING
CONTACTOR
CONTACTORS
CONTACTS
CONTAGIA
CONTAGION
CONTAGIONS
CONTAGIOUS
CONTAGIOUSLY
CONTAGIOUSNESS
CONTAGIUM
CONTAIN
CONTAINABLE
CONTAINED
CONTAINER
CONTAINERBOARD
CONTAINERBOARDS
CONTAINERISE
CONTAINERISED
CONTAINERISES
CONTAINERISING
CONTAINERIZE
CONTAINERIZED
CONTAINERIZES
CONTAINERIZING
CONTAINERLESS

CONTAINERPORT
CONTAINERPORTS
CONTAINERS
CONTAINERSHIP
CONTAINERSHIPS
CONTAINING
CONTAINMENT
CONTAINMENTS
CONTAINS
CONTAMINANT
CONTAMINANTS
CONTAMINATE
CONTAMINATED
CONTAMINATES
CONTAMINATING
CONTAMINATION
CONTAMINATIONS
CONTAMINATIVE
CONTAMINATOR
CONTAMINATORS
CONTANGO
CONTANGOS
CONTE
CONTEMN
CONTEMNED
CONTEMNER
CONTEMNERS
CONTEMNING
CONTEMNOR
CONTEMNORS
CONTEMNS
CONTEMPLATE
CONTEMPLATED
CONTEMPLATES
CONTEMPLATING
CONTEMPLATION
CONTEMPLATIONS
CONTEMPLATIVE
CONTEMPLATIVELY
CONTEMPLATIVES
CONTEMPLATOR
CONTEMPLATORS
CONTEMPO
CONTEMPORANEITY
CONTEMPORANEOUS
CONTEMPORARIES
CONTEMPORARILY
CONTEMPORARY
CONTEMPORIZE
CONTEMPORIZED
CONTEMPORIZES
CONTEMPORIZING
CONTEMPT
CONTEMPTIBILITY
CONTEMPTIBLE
CONTEMPTIBLY
CONTEMPTS
CONTEMPTUOUS
CONTEMPTUOUSLY
CONTEND
CONTENDED
CONTENDER
CONTENDERS
CONTENDING
CONTENDS
CONTENT
CONTENTED
CONTENTEDLY
CONTENTEDNESS
CONTENTEDNESSES
CONTENTING
CONTENTION
CONTENTIONS
CONTENTIOUS
CONTENTIOUSLY
CONTENTIOUSNESS
CONTENTMENT
CONTENTMENTS
CONTENTS
CONTERMINOUS
CONTERMINOUSLY
CONTES
CONTESSA
CONTESSAS
CONTEST
CONTESTABLE
CONTESTANT
CONTESTANTS
CONTESTATION
CONTESTATIONS
CONTESTED
CONTESTER
CONTESTERS
CONTESTING
CONTESTS
CONTEXT
CONTEXTLESS
CONTEXTS
CONTEXTUAL
CONTEXTUALISE
CONTEXTUALISED
CONTEXTUALISES
CONTEXTUALISING
CONTEXTUALIZE
CONTEXTUALIZED
CONTEXTUALIZES
CONTEXTUALIZING
CONTEXTUALLY
CONTEXTURE
CONTEXTURES
CONTIGUITIES
CONTIGUITY
CONTIGUOUS
CONTIGUOUSLY
CONTIGUOUSNESS
CONTINENCE
CONTINENCES
CONTINENT
CONTINENTAL
CONTINENTALLY
CONTINENTALS
CONTINENTLY
CONTINENTS
CONTINGENCE
CONTINGENCES
CONTINGENCIES
CONTINGENCY
CONTINGENT
CONTINGENTLY
CONTINGENTS
CONTINUA
CONTINUAL
CONTINUALLY
CONTINUANCE
CONTINUANCES
CONTINUANT
CONTINUANTS
CONTINUATE
CONTINUATION
CONTINUATIONS
CONTINUATIVE
CONTINUATOR
CONTINUATORS
CONTINUE
CONTINUED
CONTINUER
CONTINUERS
CONTINUES
CONTINUING
CONTINUINGLY
CONTINUITIES
CONTINUITY
CONTINUO
CONTINUOS
CONTINUOUS
CONTINUOUSLY
CONTINUOUSNESS
CONTINUUM
CONTINUUMS
CONTO
CONTORT
CONTORTED
CONTORTING
CONTORTION
CONTORTIONIST
CONTORTIONISTIC
CONTORTIONISTS
CONTORTIONS
CONTORTIVE
CONTORTS
CONTOS
CONTOUR
CONTOURED
CONTOURING
CONTOURS
CONTRA
CONTRABAND
CONTRABANDIST
CONTRABANDISTS
CONTRABANDS
CONTRABASS
CONTRABASSES
CONTRABASSIST
CONTRABASSISTS
CONTRABASSOON
CONTRABASSOONS
CONTRACEPTION
CONTRACEPTIONS
CONTRACEPTIVE
CONTRACEPTIVES
CONTRACT
CONTRACTED
CONTRACTIBILITY
CONTRACTIBLE
CONTRACTILE
CONTRACTILITIES
CONTRACTILITY
CONTRACTING
CONTRACTION
CONTRACTIONAL
CONTRACTIONARY
CONTRACTIONS
CONTRACTIVE
CONTRACTOR
CONTRACTORS
CONTRACTS
CONTRACTUAL
CONTRACTUALLY
CONTRACTURE
CONTRACTURES
CONTRADICT
CONTRADICTABLE
CONTRADICTED
CONTRADICTING
CONTRADICTION
CONTRADICTIONS
CONTRADICTIOUS
CONTRADICTOR
CONTRADICTORIES
CONTRADICTORILY
CONTRADICTORS
CONTRADICTORY
CONTRADICTS
CONTRAIL
CONTRAILS
CONTRAINDICATE
CONTRAINDICATED
CONTRAINDICATES
CONTRALATERAL
CONTRALTI
CONTRALTO
CONTRALTOS
CONTRAOCTAVE
CONTRAOCTAVES
CONTRAPOSITION
CONTRAPOSITIONS
CONTRAPOSITIVE
CONTRAPOSITIVES
CONTRAPTION
CONTRAPTIONS
CONTRAPUNTAL
CONTRAPUNTALLY
CONTRAPUNTIST
CONTRAPUNTISTS
CONTRARIAN
CONTRARIANISM
CONTRARIANISMS
CONTRARIANS
CONTRARIES
CONTRARIETIES
CONTRARIETY
CONTRARILY
CONTRARINESS
CONTRARINESSES
CONTRARIOUS
CONTRARIWISE
CONTRARY
CONTRAS
CONTRAST
CONTRASTABLE
CONTRASTED
CONTRASTING
CONTRASTINGLY
CONTRASTIVE
CONTRASTIVELY

CONTRASTS
CONTRASTY
CONTRAVENE
CONTRAVENED
CONTRAVENER
CONTRAVENERS
CONTRAVENES
CONTRAVENING
CONTRAVENTION
CONTRAVENTIONS
CONTREDANSE
CONTREDANSES
CONTRETEMPS
CONTRIBUTE
CONTRIBUTED
CONTRIBUTES
CONTRIBUTING
CONTRIBUTION
CONTRIBUTIONS
CONTRIBUTIVE
CONTRIBUTIVELY
CONTRIBUTOR
CONTRIBUTORS
CONTRIBUTORY
CONTRITE
CONTRITELY
CONTRITENESS
CONTRITENESSES
CONTRITION
CONTRITIONS
CONTRIVANCE
CONTRIVANCES
CONTRIVE
CONTRIVED
CONTRIVER
CONTRIVERS
CONTRIVES
CONTRIVING
CONTROL
CONTROLLABILITY
CONTROLLABLE
CONTROLLED
CONTROLLER
CONTROLLERS
CONTROLLERSHIP
CONTROLLERSHIPS
CONTROLLING
CONTROLMENT
CONTROLMENTS
CONTROLS
CONTROVERSIAL
CONTROVERSIALLY
CONTROVERSIES
CONTROVERSY
CONTROVERT
CONTROVERTED
CONTROVERTER
CONTROVERTERS
CONTROVERTIBLE
CONTROVERTING
CONTROVERTS
CONTUMACIES
CONTUMACIOUS
CONTUMACIOUSLY
CONTUMACY
CONTUMELIES
CONTUMELIOUS
CONTUMELIOUSLY
CONTUMELY
CONTUSE
CONTUSED
CONTUSES
CONTUSING
CONTUSION
CONTUSIONS
CONTUSIVE
CONUNDRUM
CONUNDRUMS
CONURBATION
CONURBATIONS
CONURE
CONURES
CONUS
CONVALESCE
CONVALESCED
CONVALESCENCE
CONVALESCENCES
CONVALESCENT
CONVALESCENTS
CONVALESCES
CONVALESCING
CONVECT
CONVECTED
CONVECTING
CONVECTION
CONVECTIONAL
CONVECTIONS
CONVECTIVE
CONVECTOR
CONVECTORS
CONVECTS
CONVENE
CONVENED
CONVENER
CONVENERS
CONVENES
CONVENIENCE
CONVENIENCES
CONVENIENCIES
CONVENIENCY
CONVENIENT
CONVENIENTLY
CONVENING
CONVENOR
CONVENORS
CONVENT
CONVENTED
CONVENTICLE
CONVENTICLER
CONVENTICLERS
CONVENTICLES
CONVENTING
CONVENTION
CONVENTIONAL
CONVENTIONALISM
CONVENTIONALIST
CONVENTIONALITY
CONVENTIONALIZE
CONVENTIONALLY
CONVENTIONEER
CONVENTIONEERS
CONVENTIONS
CONVENTS
CONVENTUAL
CONVENTUALLY
CONVENTUALS
CONVERGE
CONVERGED
CONVERGENCE
CONVERGENCES
CONVERGENCIES
CONVERGENCY
CONVERGENT
CONVERGES
CONVERGING
CONVERSABLE
CONVERSANCE
CONVERSANCES
CONVERSANCIES
CONVERSANCY
CONVERSANT
CONVERSATE
CONVERSATED
CONVERSATES
CONVERSATING
CONVERSATION
CONVERSATIONAL
CONVERSATIONS
CONVERSAZIONE
CONVERSAZIONES
CONVERSAZIONI
CONVERSE
CONVERSED
CONVERSELY
CONVERSER
CONVERSERS
CONVERSES
CONVERSING
CONVERSION
CONVERSIONAL
CONVERSIONS
CONVERSO
CONVERSOS
CONVERT
CONVERTAPLANE
CONVERTAPLANES
CONVERTED
CONVERTER
CONVERTERS
CONVERTIBILITY
CONVERTIBLE
CONVERTIBLENESS
CONVERTIBLES
CONVERTIBLY
CONVERTING
CONVERTIPLANE
CONVERTIPLANES
CONVERTOR
CONVERTORS
CONVERTS
CONVEX
CONVEXES
CONVEXITIES
CONVEXITY
CONVEXLY
CONVEY
CONVEYANCE
CONVEYANCER
CONVEYANCERS
CONVEYANCES
CONVEYANCING
CONVEYANCINGS
CONVEYED
CONVEYER
CONVEYERS
CONVEYING
CONVEYOR
CONVEYORISE
CONVEYORISED
CONVEYORISES
CONVEYORISING
CONVEYORIZATION
CONVEYORIZE
CONVEYORIZED
CONVEYORIZES
CONVEYORIZING
CONVEYORS
CONVEYS
CONVICT
CONVICTED
CONVICTING
CONVICTION
CONVICTIONS
CONVICTS
CONVINCE
CONVINCED
CONVINCER
CONVINCERS
CONVINCES
CONVINCING
CONVINCINGLY
CONVINCINGNESS
CONVIVIAL
CONVIVIALITIES
CONVIVIALITY
CONVIVIALLY
CONVOCATION
CONVOCATIONAL
CONVOCATIONS
CONVOKE
CONVOKED
CONVOKER
CONVOKERS
CONVOKES
CONVOKING
CONVOLUTE
CONVOLUTED
CONVOLUTES
CONVOLUTING
CONVOLUTION
CONVOLUTIONS
CONVOLVE
CONVOLVED
CONVOLVES
CONVOLVING
CONVOLVULI
CONVOLVULUS
CONVOLVULUSES
CONVOY
CONVOYED
CONVOYING
CONVOYS
CONVULSANT
CONVULSANTS
CONVULSE

CONVULSED
CONVULSES
CONVULSING
CONVULSION
CONVULSIONARY
CONVULSIONS
CONVULSIVE
CONVULSIVELY
CONVULSIVENESS
CONY
CONYS
COO
COOCH
COOCHES
COOCOO
COOED
COOEE
COOEED
COOEEING
COOEES
COOER
COOERS
COOEY
COOEYED
COOEYING
COOEYS
COOF
COOFS
COOING
COOINGLY
COOK
COOKABLE
COOKABLES
COOKBOOK
COOKBOOKS
COOKED
COOKER
COOKERIES
COOKERS
COOKERY
COOKEY
COOKEYS
COOKHOUSE
COOKHOUSES
COOKIE
COOKIES
COOKING
COOKINGS
COOKLESS
COOKOFF
COOKOFFS
COOKOUT
COOKOUTS
COOKS
COOKSHACK
COOKSHACKS
COOKSHOP
COOKSHOPS
COOKSTOVE
COOKSTOVES
COOKTOP
COOKTOPS
COOKWARE
COOKWARES
COOKY
COOL
COOLABAH
COOLABAHS
COOLANT
COOLANTS
COOLDOWN
COOLDOWNS
COOLED
COOLER
COOLERS
COOLEST
COOLHEADED
COOLIBAH
COOLIBAHS
COOLIE
COOLIES
COOLING
COOLISH
COOLLY
COOLNESS
COOLNESSES
COOLS
COOLTH
COOLTHS
COOLY
COOMB
COOMBE
COOMBES
COOMBS
COON
COONCAN
COONCANS
COONHOUND
COONHOUNDS
COONS
COONSHIT
COONSHITS
COONSKIN
COONSKINS
COONTIE
COONTIES
COOP
COOPED
COOPER
COOPERAGE
COOPERAGES
COOPERATE
COOPERATED
COOPERATES
COOPERATING
COOPERATION
COOPERATIONIST
COOPERATIONISTS
COOPERATIONS
COOPERATIVE
COOPERATIVELY
COOPERATIVENESS
COOPERATIVES
COOPERATOR
COOPERATORS
COOPERED
COOPERIES
COOPERING
COOPERS
COOPERY
COOPING
COOPS
COOPT
COOPTED
COOPTING
COOPTION
COOPTIONS
COOPTS
COORDINATE
COORDINATED
COORDINATELY
COORDINATENESS
COORDINATES
COORDINATING
COORDINATION
COORDINATIONS
COORDINATIVE
COORDINATOR
COORDINATORS
COOS
COOT
COOTER
COOTERS
COOTIE
COOTIES
COOTS
COP
COPACETIC
COPAIBA
COPAIBAS
COPAL
COPALM
COPALMS
COPALS
COPARCENARIES
COPARCENARY
COPARCENER
COPARCENERS
COPARENT
COPARENTED
COPARENTING
COPARENTS
COPARTNER
COPARTNERED
COPARTNERING
COPARTNERS
COPARTNERSHIP
COPARTNERSHIPS
COPASETIC
COPASTOR
COPASTORS
COPATRON
COPATRONS
COPAY
COPAYMENT
COPAYMENTS
COPAYS
COPE
COPECK
COPECKS
COPED
COPEMATE
COPEMATES
COPEN
COPENS
COPEPOD
COPEPODS
COPER
COPERNICIUM
COPERNICIUMS
COPERS
COPES
COPESETIC
COPESTONE
COPESTONES
COPIABLE
COPIED
COPIER
COPIERS
COPIES
COPIHUE
COPIHUES
COPILOT
COPILOTED
COPILOTING
COPILOTS
COPING
COPINGS
COPINGSTONE
COPINGSTONES
COPIOUS
COPIOUSLY
COPIOUSNESS
COPIOUSNESSES
COPLANAR
COPLANARITIES
COPLANARITY
COPLOT
COPLOTS
COPLOTTED
COPLOTTING
COPOLYMER
COPOLYMERIC
COPOLYMERIZE
COPOLYMERIZED
COPOLYMERIZES
COPOLYMERIZING
COPOLYMERS
COPOUT
COPOUTS
COPPED
COPPER
COPPERAH
COPPERAHS
COPPERAS
COPPERASES
COPPERED
COPPERHEAD
COPPERHEADS
COPPERIER
COPPERIEST
COPPERING
COPPERPLATE
COPPERPLATES
COPPERS
COPPERSMITH
COPPERSMITHS
COPPERY
COPPICE
COPPICED
COPPICES
COPPICING
COPPING
COPPRA
COPPRAS

COPRA
COPRAH
COPRAHS
COPRAS
COPREMIA
COPREMIAS
COPREMIC
COPRESENT
COPRESENTED
COPRESENTING
COPRESENTS
COPRESIDENT
COPRESIDENTS
COPRINCE
COPRINCES
COPRINCIPAL
COPRINCIPALS
COPRISONER
COPRISONERS
COPROCESSING
COPROCESSOR
COPROCESSORS
COPRODUCE
COPRODUCED
COPRODUCER
COPRODUCERS
COPRODUCES
COPRODUCING
COPRODUCT
COPRODUCTION
COPRODUCTIONS
COPRODUCTS
COPROLALIA
COPROLALIAS
COPROLITE
COPROLITES
COPROLITIC
COPROLOGIES
COPROLOGY
COPROMOTER
COPROMOTERS
COPROPHAGIES
COPROPHAGOUS
COPROPHAGY
COPROPHILIA
COPROPHILIAC
COPROPHILIACS
COPROPHILIAS
COPROPHILOUS
COPROPRIETOR
COPROPRIETORS
COPROSPERITIES
COPROSPERITY
COPS
COPSE
COPSES
COPSY
COPTER
COPTERS
COPUBLISH
COPUBLISHED
COPUBLISHER
COPUBLISHERS
COPUBLISHES
COPUBLISHING
COPULA
COPULAE
COPULAR
COPULAS
COPULATE
COPULATED
COPULATES
COPULATING
COPULATION
COPULATIONS
COPULATIVE
COPULATIVES
COPULATORY
COPURIFIED
COPURIFIES
COPURIFY
COPURIFYING
COPY
COPYABLE
COPYBOOK
COPYBOOKS
COPYBOY
COPYBOYS
COPYCAT
COPYCATS
COPYCATTED
COPYCATTING
COPYDESK
COPYDESKS
COPYEDIT
COPYEDITED
COPYEDITING
COPYEDITS
COPYGIRL
COPYGIRLS
COPYHOLD
COPYHOLDER
COPYHOLDERS
COPYHOLDS
COPYING
COPYIST
COPYISTS
COPYLEFT
COPYLEFTS
COPYREAD
COPYREADER
COPYREADERS
COPYREADING
COPYREADS
COPYRIGHT
COPYRIGHTABLE
COPYRIGHTED
COPYRIGHTING
COPYRIGHTS
COPYWRITER
COPYWRITERS
COQUET
COQUETRIES
COQUETRY
COQUETS
COQUETTE
COQUETTED
COQUETTES
COQUETTING
COQUETTISH
COQUETTISHLY
COQUETTISHNESS
COQUI
COQUILLE
COQUILLES
COQUINA
COQUINAS
COQUIS
COQUITO
COQUITOS
COR
CORACLE
CORACLES
CORACOID
CORACOIDS
CORAL
CORALBELLS
CORALBERRIES
CORALBERRY
CORALLINE
CORALLINES
CORALLOID
CORALROOT
CORALROOTS
CORALS
CORANTO
CORANTOES
CORANTOS
CORBAN
CORBANS
CORBEIL
CORBEILLE
CORBEILLES
CORBEILS
CORBEL
CORBELED
CORBELING
CORBELINGS
CORBELLED
CORBELLING
CORBELS
CORBICULA
CORBICULAE
CORBIE
CORBIES
CORBINA
CORBINAS
CORBY
CORD
CORDAGE
CORDAGES
CORDATE
CORDATELY
CORDED
CORDELLE
CORDELLED
CORDELLES
CORDELLING
CORDER
CORDERS
CORDGRASS
CORDGRASSES
CORDIAL
CORDIALITIES
CORDIALITY
CORDIALLY
CORDIALNESS
CORDIALNESSES
CORDIALS
CORDIERITE
CORDIERITES
CORDIFORM
CORDILLERA
CORDILLERAN
CORDILLERAS
CORDING
CORDINGS
CORDITE
CORDITES
CORDLESS
CORDLESSES
CORDLIKE
CORDOBA
CORDOBAS
CORDON
CORDONED
CORDONING
CORDONNET
CORDONNETS
CORDONS
CORDOVAN
CORDOVANS
CORDS
CORDUROY
CORDUROYED
CORDUROYING
CORDUROYS
CORDWAIN
CORDWAINER
CORDWAINERIES
CORDWAINERS
CORDWAINERY
CORDWAINS
CORDWOOD
CORDWOODS
CORE
CORECIPIENT
CORECIPIENTS
CORED
COREDEEM
COREDEEMED
COREDEEMING
COREDEEMS
COREIGN
COREIGNS
CORELATE
CORELATED
CORELATES
CORELATING
CORELESS
CORELIGIONIST
CORELIGIONISTS
CORELLA
CORELLAS
COREMIA
COREMIUM
COREOPSIS
COREPRESSOR
COREPRESSORS
COREQUISITE
COREQUISITES
CORER
CORERS
CORES
CORESEARCHER

CORESEARCHERS
CORESIDENT
CORESIDENTIAL
CORESIDENTS
CORESPONDENT
CORESPONDENTS
CORF
CORGI
CORGIS
CORIA
CORIACEOUS
CORIANDER
CORIANDERS
CORING
CORIUM
CORIUMS
CORK
CORKAGE
CORKAGES
CORKBOARD
CORKBOARDS
CORKED
CORKER
CORKERS
CORKIER
CORKIEST
CORKINESS
CORKINESSES
CORKING
CORKLIKE
CORKS
CORKSCREW
CORKSCREWED
CORKSCREWING
CORKSCREWS
CORKWOOD
CORKWOODS
CORKY
CORM
CORMEL
CORMELS
CORMLET
CORMLETS
CORMLIKE
CORMOID
CORMORANT
CORMORANTS
CORMOUS
CORMS
CORN
CORNBALL
CORNBALLS
CORNBRAID
CORNBRAIDED
CORNBRAIDING
CORNBRAIDS
CORNBREAD
CORNBREADS
CORNCAKE
CORNCAKES
CORNCOB
CORNCOBS
CORNCRAKE
CORNCRAKES
CORNCRIB
CORNCRIBS
CORNEA
CORNEAL
CORNEAS
CORNED
CORNEITIS
CORNEITISES
CORNEL
CORNELIAN
CORNELIANS
CORNELS
CORNEOUS
CORNER
CORNERBACK
CORNERBACKS
CORNERED
CORNERING
CORNERMAN
CORNERMEN
CORNERS
CORNERSTONE
CORNERSTONES
CORNERWAYS
CORNERWISE
CORNET
CORNETCIES
CORNETCY
CORNETIST
CORNETISTS
CORNETS
CORNETT
CORNETTI
CORNETTIST
CORNETTISTS
CORNETTO
CORNETTOS
CORNETTS
CORNFED
CORNFIELD
CORNFIELDS
CORNFLAKES
CORNFLOWER
CORNFLOWERS
CORNHUSK
CORNHUSKING
CORNHUSKINGS
CORNHUSKS
CORNICE
CORNICED
CORNICES
CORNICHE
CORNICHES
CORNICHON
CORNICHONS
CORNICING
CORNICINGS
CORNICLE
CORNICLES
CORNIER
CORNIEST
CORNIFICATION
CORNIFICATIONS
CORNIFIED
CORNIFIES
CORNIFY
CORNIFYING
CORNILY
CORNINESS
CORNINESSES
CORNING
CORNMEAL
CORNMEALS
CORNPONE
CORNPONES
CORNROW
CORNROWED
CORNROWING
CORNROWS
CORNS
CORNSILK
CORNSILKS
CORNSTALK
CORNSTALKS
CORNSTARCH
CORNSTARCHES
CORNU
CORNUA
CORNUAL
CORNUCOPIA
CORNUCOPIAN
CORNUCOPIAS
CORNUS
CORNUSES
CORNUTE
CORNUTED
CORNUTO
CORNUTOS
CORNY
CORODIES
CORODY
COROLLA
COROLLARIES
COROLLARY
COROLLAS
COROLLATE
COROMANDEL
COROMANDELS
CORONA
CORONACH
CORONACHS
CORONAE
CORONAGRAPH
CORONAGRAPHS
CORONAL
CORONALLY
CORONALS
CORONARIES
CORONARY
CORONAS
CORONATE
CORONATED
CORONATES
CORONATING
CORONATION
CORONATIONS
CORONAVIRUS
CORONAVIRUSES
CORONEL
CORONELS
CORONER
CORONERS
CORONET
CORONETED
CORONETS
CORONOGRAPH
CORONOGRAPHS
CORONOID
COROTATE
COROTATED
COROTATES
COROTATING
COROTATION
COROTATIONS
COROZO
COROZOS
CORPORA
CORPORAL
CORPORALITIES
CORPORALITY
CORPORALLY
CORPORALS
CORPORATE
CORPORATELY
CORPORATES
CORPORATION
CORPORATIONS
CORPORATISM
CORPORATISMS
CORPORATIST
CORPORATISTS
CORPORATIVE
CORPORATIVISM
CORPORATIVISMS
CORPORATIZATION
CORPORATIZE
CORPORATIZED
CORPORATIZES
CORPORATIZING
CORPORATOR
CORPORATORS
CORPOREAL
CORPOREALITIES
CORPOREALITY
CORPOREALLY
CORPOREALNESS
CORPOREALNESSES
CORPOREITIES
CORPOREITY
CORPOSANT
CORPOSANTS
CORPS
CORPSE
CORPSES
CORPSMAN
CORPSMEN
CORPULENCE
CORPULENCES
CORPULENCIES
CORPULENCY
CORPULENT
CORPULENTLY
CORPUS
CORPUSCLE
CORPUSCLES
CORPUSCULAR
CORPUSES
CORRADE
CORRADED
CORRADES
CORRADING

CORRAL
CORRALLED
CORRALLING
CORRALS
CORRASION
CORRASIONS
CORRASIVE
CORRECT
CORRECTABLE
CORRECTED
CORRECTER
CORRECTEST
CORRECTING
CORRECTION
CORRECTIONAL
CORRECTIONS
CORRECTITUDE
CORRECTITUDES
CORRECTIVE
CORRECTIVELY
CORRECTIVES
CORRECTLY
CORRECTNESS
CORRECTNESSES
CORRECTOR
CORRECTORS
CORRECTS
CORRELATABLE
CORRELATE
CORRELATED
CORRELATES
CORRELATING
CORRELATION
CORRELATIONAL
CORRELATIONS
CORRELATIVE
CORRELATIVELY
CORRELATIVES
CORRELATOR
CORRELATORS
CORRESPOND
CORRESPONDED
CORRESPONDENCE
CORRESPONDENCES
CORRESPONDENCY
CORRESPONDENT
CORRESPONDENTS
CORRESPONDING
CORRESPONDINGLY
CORRESPONDS
CORRESPONSIVE
CORRETTO
CORRETTOS
CORRIDA
CORRIDAS
CORRIDOR
CORRIDORS
CORRIE
CORRIES
CORRIGENDA
CORRIGENDUM
CORRIGIBILITIES
CORRIGIBILITY
CORRIGIBLE
CORRIVAL
CORRIVALS
CORROBORANT
CORROBORATE
CORROBORATED
CORROBORATES
CORROBORATING
CORROBORATION
CORROBORATIONS
CORROBORATIVE
CORROBORATOR
CORROBORATORS
CORROBORATORY
CORROBOREE
CORROBOREES
CORRODE
CORRODED
CORRODES
CORRODIBLE
CORRODIES
CORRODING
CORRODY
CORROSION
CORROSIONS
CORROSIVE
CORROSIVELY
CORROSIVENESS
CORROSIVENESSES
CORROSIVES
CORRUGATE
CORRUGATED
CORRUGATES
CORRUGATING
CORRUGATION
CORRUGATIONS
CORRUPT
CORRUPTED
CORRUPTER
CORRUPTERS
CORRUPTEST
CORRUPTIBILITY
CORRUPTIBLE
CORRUPTIBLY
CORRUPTING
CORRUPTION
CORRUPTIONIST
CORRUPTIONISTS
CORRUPTIONS
CORRUPTIVE
CORRUPTIVELY
CORRUPTLY
CORRUPTNESS
CORRUPTNESSES
CORRUPTOR
CORRUPTORS
CORRUPTS
CORS
CORSAC
CORSACS
CORSAGE
CORSAGES
CORSAIR
CORSAIRS
CORSE
CORSELET
CORSELETS
CORSELETTE
CORSELETTES
CORSES
CORSET
CORSETED
CORSETIERE
CORSETIERES
CORSETING
CORSETRIES
CORSETRY
CORSETS
CORSLET
CORSLETS
CORTEGE
CORTEGES
CORTEX
CORTEXES
CORTICAL
CORTICALLY
CORTICATE
CORTICES
CORTICOID
CORTICOIDS
CORTICOSE
CORTICOSTEROID
CORTICOSTEROIDS
CORTICOSTERONE
CORTICOSTERONES
CORTICOTROPHIN
CORTICOTROPHINS
CORTICOTROPIN
CORTICOTROPINS
CORTIN
CORTINA
CORTINAS
CORTINS
CORTISOL
CORTISOLS
CORTISONE
CORTISONES
CORULER
CORULERS
CORUNDUM
CORUNDUMS
CORUSCANT
CORUSCATE
CORUSCATED
CORUSCATES
CORUSCATING
CORUSCATION
CORUSCATIONS
CORVEE
CORVEES
CORVES
CORVET
CORVETS
CORVETTE
CORVETTES
CORVID
CORVIDS
CORVINA
CORVINAS
CORVINE
CORY
CORYBANT
CORYBANTES
CORYBANTIC
CORYBANTS
CORYDALIS
CORYDALISES
CORYMB
CORYMBED
CORYMBOSE
CORYMBOSELY
CORYMBOUS
CORYMBS
CORYNEBACTERIA
CORYNEBACTERIAL
CORYNEBACTERIUM
CORYNEFORM
CORYPHAEI
CORYPHAEUS
CORYPHEE
CORYPHEES
CORYZA
CORYZAL
CORYZAS
COS
COSCENARIST
COSCENARISTS
COSCRIPT
COSCRIPTED
COSCRIPTING
COSCRIPTS
COSEC
COSECANT
COSECANTS
COSECS
COSEISMAL
COSEISMALS
COSEISMIC
COSEISMICS
COSES
COSET
COSETS
COSEY
COSEYS
COSH
COSHED
COSHER
COSHERED
COSHERING
COSHERS
COSHES
COSHING
COSIE
COSIED
COSIER
COSIES
COSIEST
COSIGN
COSIGNATORIES
COSIGNATORY
COSIGNED
COSIGNER
COSIGNERS
COSIGNING
COSIGNS
COSILY
COSINE
COSINES
COSINESS
COSINESSES
COSMECEUTICAL
COSMECEUTICALS

COSMETIC
COSMETICALLY
COSMETICIAN
COSMETICIANS
COSMETICIZE
COSMETICIZED
COSMETICIZES
COSMETICIZING
COSMETICS
COSMETOLOGIES
COSMETOLOGIST
COSMETOLOGISTS
COSMETOLOGY
COSMIC
COSMICAL
COSMICALLY
COSMID
COSMIDS
COSMISM
COSMISMS
COSMIST
COSMISTS
COSMOCHEMICAL
COSMOCHEMIST
COSMOCHEMISTRY
COSMOCHEMISTS
COSMOGENIC
COSMOGONIC
COSMOGONICAL
COSMOGONIES
COSMOGONIST
COSMOGONISTS
COSMOGONY
COSMOGRAPHER
COSMOGRAPHERS
COSMOGRAPHIC
COSMOGRAPHICAL
COSMOGRAPHIES
COSMOGRAPHY
COSMOLINE
COSMOLINED
COSMOLINES
COSMOLINING
COSMOLOGICAL
COSMOLOGICALLY
COSMOLOGIES
COSMOLOGIST
COSMOLOGISTS
COSMOLOGY
COSMONAUT
COSMONAUTS
COSMOPOLIS
COSMOPOLISES
COSMOPOLITAN
COSMOPOLITANISM
COSMOPOLITANS
COSMOPOLITE
COSMOPOLITES
COSMOPOLITISM
COSMOPOLITISMS
COSMOS
COSMOSES
COSMOTRON
COSMOTRONS
COSPONSOR
COSPONSORED
COSPONSORING
COSPONSORS
COSPONSORSHIP
COSPONSORSHIPS
COSS
COSSACK
COSSACKS
COSSET
COSSETED
COSSETING
COSSETS
COST
COSTA
COSTAE
COSTAL
COSTALLY
COSTAR
COSTARD
COSTARDS
COSTARRED
COSTARRING
COSTARS
COSTATE
COSTED
COSTER
COSTERMONGER
COSTERMONGERS
COSTERS
COSTING
COSTINGS
COSTIVE
COSTIVELY
COSTIVENESS
COSTIVENESSES
COSTLESS
COSTLESSLY
COSTLIER
COSTLIEST
COSTLINESS
COSTLINESSES
COSTLY
COSTMARIES
COSTMARY
COSTREL
COSTRELS
COSTS
COSTUME
COSTUMED
COSTUMER
COSTUMERIES
COSTUMERS
COSTUMERY
COSTUMES
COSTUMEY
COSTUMIER
COSTUMIERS
COSTUMING
COSURFACTANT
COSURFACTANTS
COSY
COSYING
COT
COTAN
COTANGENT
COTANGENTS
COTANS
COTE
COTEAU
COTEAUS
COTEAUX
COTED
COTENANCIES
COTENANCY
COTENANT
COTENANTS
COTERIE
COTERIES
COTERMINOUS
COTERMINOUSLY
COTES
COTHURN
COTHURNAL
COTHURNI
COTHURNS
COTHURNUS
COTIDAL
COTILLION
COTILLIONS
COTILLON
COTILLONS
COTING
COTINGA
COTINGAS
COTININE
COTININES
COTONEASTER
COTONEASTERS
COTQUEAN
COTQUEANS
COTRANSDUCE
COTRANSDUCED
COTRANSDUCES
COTRANSDUCING
COTRANSDUCTION
COTRANSDUCTIONS
COTRANSFER
COTRANSFERRED
COTRANSFERRING
COTRANSFERS
COTRANSPORT
COTRANSPORTED
COTRANSPORTING
COTRANSPORTS
COTRUSTEE
COTRUSTEES
COTS
COTTA
COTTAE
COTTAGE
COTTAGED
COTTAGER
COTTAGERS
COTTAGES
COTTAGEY
COTTAGING
COTTAR
COTTARS
COTTAS
COTTER
COTTERED
COTTERLESS
COTTERS
COTTIER
COTTIERS
COTTON
COTTONED
COTTONING
COTTONMOUTH
COTTONMOUTHS
COTTONS
COTTONSEED
COTTONSEEDS
COTTONTAIL
COTTONTAILS
COTTONWEED
COTTONWEEDS
COTTONWOOD
COTTONWOODS
COTTONY
COTURNIX
COTURNIXES
COTYLEDON
COTYLEDONARY
COTYLEDONS
COTYLOID
COTYLOSAUR
COTYLOSAURS
COTYPE
COTYPES
COUCH
COUCHANT
COUCHED
COUCHER
COUCHERS
COUCHES
COUCHETTE
COUCHETTES
COUCHING
COUCHINGS
COUDE
COUDES
COUGAR
COUGARS
COUGH
COUGHED
COUGHER
COUGHERS
COUGHING
COUGHS
COULD
COULDEST
COULDST
COULEE
COULEES
COULIBIAC
COULIBIACS
COULIS
COULISSE
COULISSES
COULOIR
COULOIRS
COULOMB
COULOMBIC
COULOMBS
COULOMETER
COULOMETERS
COULOMETRIC
COULOMETRICALLY
COULOMETRIES

COULOMETRY
COULTER
COULTERS
COUMARIC
COUMARIN
COUMARINS
COUMARONE
COUMARONES
COUMAROU
COUMAROUS
COUNCIL
COUNCILLOR
COUNCILLORS
COUNCILLORSHIP
COUNCILLORSHIPS
COUNCILMAN
COUNCILMANIC
COUNCILMEN
COUNCILOR
COUNCILORS
COUNCILS
COUNCILWOMAN
COUNCILWOMEN
COUNSEL
COUNSELED
COUNSELEE
COUNSELEES
COUNSELING
COUNSELINGS
COUNSELLED
COUNSELLING
COUNSELLINGS
COUNSELLOR
COUNSELLORS
COUNSELLORSHIP
COUNSELLORSHIPS
COUNSELOR
COUNSELORS
COUNSELORSHIP
COUNSELORSHIPS
COUNSELS
COUNT
COUNTABILITIES
COUNTABILITY
COUNTABLE
COUNTABLY
COUNTDOWN
COUNTDOWNS
COUNTED
COUNTENANCE
COUNTENANCED
COUNTENANCER
COUNTENANCERS
COUNTENANCES
COUNTENANCING
COUNTER
COUNTERACT
COUNTERACTED
COUNTERACTING
COUNTERACTION
COUNTERACTIONS
COUNTERACTIVE
COUNTERACTS
COUNTERAGENT
COUNTERAGENTS
COUNTERARGUE
COUNTERARGUED
COUNTERARGUES
COUNTERARGUING
COUNTERARGUMENT
COUNTERASSAULT
COUNTERASSAULTS
COUNTERATTACK
COUNTERATTACKED
COUNTERATTACKER
COUNTERATTACKS
COUNTERBALANCE
COUNTERBALANCED
COUNTERBALANCES
COUNTERBID
COUNTERBIDDING
COUNTERBIDS
COUNTERBLAST
COUNTERBLASTS
COUNTERBLOCKADE
COUNTERBLOW
COUNTERBLOWS
COUNTERCAMPAIGN
COUNTERCHANGE
COUNTERCHANGED
COUNTERCHANGES
COUNTERCHANGING
COUNTERCHARGE
COUNTERCHARGED
COUNTERCHARGES
COUNTERCHARGING
COUNTERCHECK
COUNTERCHECKED
COUNTERCHECKING
COUNTERCHECKS
COUNTERCLAIM
COUNTERCLAIMED
COUNTERCLAIMING
COUNTERCLAIMS
COUNTERCOUP
COUNTERCOUPS
COUNTERCRIES
COUNTERCRY
COUNTERCULTURAL
COUNTERCULTURE
COUNTERCULTURES
COUNTERCURRENT
COUNTERCURRENTS
COUNTERCYCLICAL
COUNTERDEMAND
COUNTERDEMANDS
COUNTERED
COUNTEREFFORT
COUNTEREFFORTS
COUNTEREVIDENCE
COUNTEREXAMPLE
COUNTEREXAMPLES
COUNTERFACTUAL
COUNTERFEIT
COUNTERFEITED
COUNTERFEITER
COUNTERFEITERS
COUNTERFEITING
COUNTERFEITS
COUNTERFIRE
COUNTERFIRED
COUNTERFIRES
COUNTERFIRING
COUNTERFLOW
COUNTERFLOWS
COUNTERFOIL
COUNTERFOILS
COUNTERFORCE
COUNTERFORCES
COUNTERGUERILLA
COUNTERIMAGE
COUNTERIMAGES
COUNTERING
COUNTERINSTANCE
COUNTERINVASION
COUNTERION
COUNTERIONS
COUNTERIRRITANT
COUNTERMAN
COUNTERMAND
COUNTERMANDED
COUNTERMANDING
COUNTERMANDS
COUNTERMARCH
COUNTERMARCHED
COUNTERMARCHES
COUNTERMARCHING
COUNTERMEASURE
COUNTERMEASURES
COUNTERMELODIES
COUNTERMELODY
COUNTERMEMO
COUNTERMEMOS
COUNTERMEN
COUNTERMINE
COUNTERMINES
COUNTERMOVE
COUNTERMOVED
COUNTERMOVEMENT
COUNTERMOVES
COUNTERMOVING
COUNTERMYTH
COUNTERMYTHS
COUNTEROFFER
COUNTEROFFERS
COUNTERORDER
COUNTERORDERED
COUNTERORDERING
COUNTERORDERS
COUNTERPANE
COUNTERPANES
COUNTERPART
COUNTERPARTIES
COUNTERPARTS
COUNTERPARTY
COUNTERPETITION
COUNTERPICKET
COUNTERPICKETED
COUNTERPICKETS
COUNTERPLAN
COUNTERPLANS
COUNTERPLAY
COUNTERPLAYED
COUNTERPLAYER
COUNTERPLAYERS
COUNTERPLAYING
COUNTERPLAYS
COUNTERPLEA
COUNTERPLEAS
COUNTERPLOT
COUNTERPLOTS
COUNTERPLOTTED
COUNTERPLOTTING
COUNTERPLOY
COUNTERPLOYS
COUNTERPOINT
COUNTERPOINTED
COUNTERPOINTING
COUNTERPOINTS
COUNTERPOISE
COUNTERPOISED
COUNTERPOISES
COUNTERPOISING
COUNTERPOSE
COUNTERPOSED
COUNTERPOSES
COUNTERPOSING
COUNTERPOWER
COUNTERPOWERS
COUNTERPRESSURE
COUNTERPROJECT
COUNTERPROJECTS
COUNTERPROPOSAL
COUNTERPROTEST
COUNTERPROTESTS
COUNTERPUNCH
COUNTERPUNCHED
COUNTERPUNCHER
COUNTERPUNCHERS
COUNTERPUNCHES
COUNTERPUNCHING
COUNTERQUESTION
COUNTERRAID
COUNTERRAIDED
COUNTERRAIDING
COUNTERRAIDS
COUNTERRALLIED
COUNTERRALLIES
COUNTERRALLY
COUNTERRALLYING
COUNTERREACTION
COUNTERREFORM
COUNTERREFORMER
COUNTERREFORMS
COUNTERRESPONSE
COUNTERS
COUNTERSHADING
COUNTERSHADINGS
COUNTERSHOT
COUNTERSHOTS
COUNTERSIGN
COUNTERSIGNED
COUNTERSIGNING
COUNTERSIGNS
COUNTERSINK
COUNTERSINKING
COUNTERSINKS
COUNTERSNIPER
COUNTERSNIPERS
COUNTERSPELL
COUNTERSPELLS
COUNTERSPIES
COUNTERSPY
COUNTERSTAIN
COUNTERSTAINED

COUNTERSTAINING
COUNTERSTAINS
COUNTERSTATE
COUNTERSTATED
COUNTERSTATES
COUNTERSTATING
COUNTERSTEP
COUNTERSTEPS
COUNTERSTRATEGY
COUNTERSTREAM
COUNTERSTREAMS
COUNTERSTRICKEN
COUNTERSTRIKE
COUNTERSTRIKES
COUNTERSTRIKING
COUNTERSTROKE
COUNTERSTROKES
COUNTERSTRUCK
COUNTERSTYLE
COUNTERSTYLES
COUNTERSUE
COUNTERSUED
COUNTERSUES
COUNTERSUING
COUNTERSUIT
COUNTERSUITS
COUNTERSUNK
COUNTERTACTIC
COUNTERTACTICS
COUNTERTENDENCY
COUNTERTENOR
COUNTERTENORS
COUNTERTERROR
COUNTERTERRORS
COUNTERTHREAT
COUNTERTHREATS
COUNTERTHRUST
COUNTERTHRUSTS
COUNTERTOP
COUNTERTOPS
COUNTERTRADE
COUNTERTRADES
COUNTERTREND
COUNTERTRENDS
COUNTERVAIL
COUNTERVAILED
COUNTERVAILING
COUNTERVAILS
COUNTERVIEW
COUNTERVIEWS
COUNTERVIOLENCE
COUNTERWEIGHT
COUNTERWEIGHTED
COUNTERWEIGHTS
COUNTERWORLD
COUNTERWORLDS
COUNTESS
COUNTESSES
COUNTIAN
COUNTIANS
COUNTIER
COUNTIES
COUNTING
COUNTINGHOUSE
COUNTINGHOUSES
COUNTLESS
COUNTLESSLY
COUNTRIES
COUNTRIFIED
COUNTRY
COUNTRYFIED
COUNTRYISH
COUNTRYMAN
COUNTRYMEN
COUNTRYSEAT
COUNTRYSEATS
COUNTRYSIDE
COUNTRYSIDES
COUNTRYWIDE
COUNTRYWOMAN
COUNTRYWOMEN
COUNTS
COUNTY
COUP
COUPE
COUPED
COUPES
COUPING
COUPLE
COUPLED
COUPLEDOM
COUPLEDOMS
COUPLEMENT
COUPLEMENTS
COUPLER
COUPLERS
COUPLES
COUPLET
COUPLETS
COUPLING
COUPLINGS
COUPON
COUPONING
COUPONINGS
COUPONS
COUPS
COURAGE
COURAGEOUS
COURAGEOUSLY
COURAGEOUSNESS
COURAGES
COURANT
COURANTE
COURANTES
COURANTO
COURANTOES
COURANTOS
COURANTS
COURGETTE
COURGETTES
COURIER
COURIERED
COURIERING
COURIERS
COURLAN
COURLANS
COURSE
COURSED
COURSER
COURSERS
COURSES
COURSEWARE
COURSEWARES
COURSING
COURSINGS
COURT
COURTED
COURTEOUS
COURTEOUSLY
COURTEOUSNESS
COURTEOUSNESSES
COURTER
COURTERS
COURTESAN
COURTESANS
COURTESIED
COURTESIES
COURTESY
COURTESYING
COURTEZAN
COURTEZANS
COURTHOUSE
COURTHOUSES
COURTIER
COURTIERS
COURTING
COURTLIER
COURTLIEST
COURTLINESS
COURTLINESSES
COURTLY
COURTROOM
COURTROOMS
COURTS
COURTSHIP
COURTSHIPS
COURTSIDE
COURTSIDES
COURTYARD
COURTYARDS
COUSCOUS
COUSCOUSES
COUSIN
COUSINAGE
COUSINAGES
COUSINHOOD
COUSINHOODS
COUSINLY
COUSINRIES
COUSINRY
COUSINS
COUSINSHIP
COUSINSHIPS
COUTEAU
COUTEAUX
COUTER
COUTERS
COUTH
COUTHER
COUTHEST
COUTHIE
COUTHIER
COUTHIEST
COUTHS
COUTURE
COUTURES
COUTURIER
COUTURIERE
COUTURIERES
COUTURIERS
COUVADE
COUVADES
COVALENCE
COVALENCES
COVALENCIES
COVALENCY
COVALENT
COVALENTLY
COVARIANCE
COVARIANCES
COVARIANT
COVARIATE
COVARIATES
COVARIATION
COVARIATIONS
COVARIED
COVARIES
COVARY
COVARYING
COVE
COVED
COVELLINE
COVELLINES
COVELLITE
COVELLITES
COVEN
COVENANT
COVENANTAL
COVENANTED
COVENANTEE
COVENANTEES
COVENANTER
COVENANTERS
COVENANTING
COVENANTOR
COVENANTORS
COVENANTS
COVENS
COVER
COVERABLE
COVERAGE
COVERAGES
COVERALL
COVERALLED
COVERALLS
COVERED
COVERER
COVERERS
COVERING
COVERINGS
COVERLESS
COVERLET
COVERLETS
COVERLID
COVERLIDS
COVERS
COVERSINE
COVERSINES
COVERSLIP
COVERSLIPS
COVERT
COVERTER
COVERTEST
COVERTLY
COVERTNESS

COVERTNESSES
COVERTS
COVERTURE
COVERTURES
COVERUP
COVERUPS
COVES
COVET
COVETABLE
COVETED
COVETER
COVETERS
COVETING
COVETINGLY
COVETOUS
COVETOUSLY
COVETOUSNESS
COVETOUSNESSES
COVETS
COVEY
COVEYS
COVIN
COVINE
COVINES
COVING
COVINGS
COVINS
COW
COWAGE
COWAGES
COWARD
COWARDICE
COWARDICES
COWARDLINESS
COWARDLINESSES
COWARDLY
COWARDS
COWBANE
COWBANES
COWBELL
COWBELLS
COWBERRIES
COWBERRY
COWBIND
COWBINDS
COWBIRD
COWBIRDS
COWBOY
COWBOYED
COWBOYING
COWBOYS
COWCATCHER
COWCATCHERS
COWED
COWEDLY
COWER
COWERED
COWERING
COWERS
COWFISH
COWFISHES
COWFLAP
COWFLAPS
COWFLOP
COWFLOPS
COWGIRL
COWGIRLS
COWHAGE
COWHAGES
COWHAND
COWHANDS
COWHERB
COWHERBS
COWHERD
COWHERDS
COWHIDE
COWHIDED
COWHIDES
COWHIDING
COWIER
COWIEST
COWING
COWINNER
COWINNERS
COWL
COWLED
COWLICK
COWLICKS
COWLIKE
COWLING
COWLINGS
COWLS
COWLSTAFF
COWLSTAFFS
COWLSTAVES
COWMAN
COWMEN
COWORKER
COWORKERS
COWPAT
COWPATS
COWPEA
COWPEAS
COWPIE
COWPIES
COWPLOP
COWPLOPS
COWPOKE
COWPOKES
COWPOX
COWPOXES
COWPUNCHER
COWPUNCHERS
COWPUNK
COWPUNKS
COWRIE
COWRIES
COWRITE
COWRITER
COWRITERS
COWRITES
COWRITING
COWRITTEN
COWROTE
COWRY
COWS
COWSHED
COWSHEDS
COWSKIN
COWSKINS
COWSLIP
COWSLIPS
COWTOWN
COWTOWNS
COWY
COX
COXA
COXAE
COXAL
COXALGIA
COXALGIAS
COXALGIC
COXALGIES
COXALGY
COXCOMB
COXCOMBIC
COXCOMBICAL
COXCOMBRIES
COXCOMBRY
COXCOMBS
COXED
COXES
COXING
COXITIDES
COXITIS
COXLESS
COXSWAIN
COXSWAINED
COXSWAINING
COXSWAINS
COY
COYAU
COYAUS
COYDOG
COYDOGS
COYED
COYER
COYEST
COYING
COYISH
COYLY
COYNESS
COYNESSES
COYOTE
COYOTES
COYOTILLO
COYOTILLOS
COYPOU
COYPOUS
COYPU
COYPUS
COYS
COZ
COZEN
COZENAGE
COZENAGES
COZENED
COZENER
COZENERS
COZENING
COZENS
COZES
COZEY
COZEYS
COZIE
COZIED
COZIER
COZIES
COZIEST
COZILY
COZINESS
COZINESSES
COZY
COZYING
COZZES
CRAAL
CRAALED
CRAALING
CRAALS
CRAB
CRABAPPLE
CRABAPPLES
CRABBED
CRABBEDLY
CRABBEDNESS
CRABBEDNESSES
CRABBER
CRABBERS
CRABBIER
CRABBIEST
CRABBILY
CRABBING
CRABBY
CRABEATER
CRABEATERS
CRABGRASS
CRABGRASSES
CRABLIKE
CRABMEAT
CRABMEATS
CRABS
CRABSTICK
CRABSTICKS
CRABWISE
CRACK
CRACKAJACK
CRACKAJACKS
CRACKBACK
CRACKBACKS
CRACKBRAIN
CRACKBRAINED
CRACKBRAINS
CRACKDOWN
CRACKDOWNS
CRACKED
CRACKER
CRACKERJACK
CRACKERJACKS
CRACKERS
CRACKHEAD
CRACKHEADS
CRACKIE
CRACKIER
CRACKIES
CRACKIEST
CRACKING
CRACKINGS
CRACKLE
CRACKLED
CRACKLES
CRACKLEWARE
CRACKLEWARES
CRACKLIER
CRACKLIEST
CRACKLING

CRACKLINGLY
CRACKLINGS
CRACKLY
CRACKNEL
CRACKNELS
CRACKPOT
CRACKPOTS
CRACKS
CRACKSMAN
CRACKSMEN
CRACKUP
CRACKUPS
CRACKY
CRADLE
CRADLED
CRADLER
CRADLERS
CRADLES
CRADLESONG
CRADLESONGS
CRADLING
CRADLINGS
CRAFT
CRAFTED
CRAFTER
CRAFTERS
CRAFTIER
CRAFTIEST
CRAFTILY
CRAFTINESS
CRAFTINESSES
CRAFTING
CRAFTS
CRAFTSMAN
CRAFTSMANLIKE
CRAFTSMANLY
CRAFTSMANSHIP
CRAFTSMANSHIPS
CRAFTSMEN
CRAFTSPEOPLE
CRAFTSPERSON
CRAFTSPERSONS
CRAFTSWOMAN
CRAFTSWOMEN
CRAFTWORK
CRAFTWORKS
CRAFTY
CRAG
CRAGGED
CRAGGIER
CRAGGIEST
CRAGGILY
CRAGGINESS
CRAGGINESSES
CRAGGY
CRAGS
CRAGSMAN
CRAGSMEN
CRAKE
CRAKES
CRAM
CRAMBE
CRAMBES
CRAMBO
CRAMBOES
CRAMBOS
CRAMMED
CRAMMER
CRAMMERS
CRAMMING
CRAMMINGS
CRAMOISIE
CRAMOISIES
CRAMOISY
CRAMP
CRAMPED
CRAMPFISH
CRAMPFISHES
CRAMPIER
CRAMPIEST
CRAMPING
CRAMPIT
CRAMPITS
CRAMPON
CRAMPONS
CRAMPOON
CRAMPOONS
CRAMPS
CRAMPY
CRAMS
CRANBERRIES
CRANBERRY
CRANCH
CRANCHED
CRANCHES
CRANCHING
CRANE
CRANED
CRANES
CRANESBILL
CRANESBILLS
CRANIA
CRANIAL
CRANIALLY
CRANIATE
CRANIATES
CRANING
CRANIOCEREBRAL
CRANIOFACIAL
CRANIOLOGIES
CRANIOLOGY
CRANIOMETRIES
CRANIOMETRY
CRANIOSACRAL
CRANIOTOMIES
CRANIOTOMY
CRANIUM
CRANIUMS
CRANK
CRANKCASE
CRANKCASES
CRANKED
CRANKER
CRANKEST
CRANKIER
CRANKIEST
CRANKILY
CRANKINESS
CRANKINESSES
CRANKING
CRANKISH
CRANKLE
CRANKLED
CRANKLES
CRANKLING
CRANKLY
CRANKOUS
CRANKPIN
CRANKPINS
CRANKS
CRANKSHAFT
CRANKSHAFTS
CRANKY
CRANNIED
CRANNIES
CRANNOG
CRANNOGE
CRANNOGES
CRANNOGS
CRANNY
CRANREUCH
CRANREUCHS
CRAP
CRAPE
CRAPED
CRAPELIKE
CRAPES
CRAPING
CRAPOLA
CRAPOLAS
CRAPPED
CRAPPER
CRAPPERS
CRAPPIE
CRAPPIER
CRAPPIES
CRAPPIEST
CRAPPING
CRAPPY
CRAPS
CRAPSHOOT
CRAPSHOOTER
CRAPSHOOTERS
CRAPSHOOTS
CRAPULENT
CRAPULOUS
CRASES
CRASH
CRASHED
CRASHER
CRASHERS
CRASHES
CRASHING
CRASHINGLY
CRASHWORTHINESS
CRASHWORTHY
CRASIS
CRASS
CRASSER
CRASSEST
CRASSITUDE
CRASSITUDES
CRASSLY
CRASSNESS
CRASSNESSES
CRATCH
CRATCHES
CRATE
CRATED
CRATEFUL
CRATEFULS
CRATER
CRATERED
CRATERING
CRATERINGS
CRATERLET
CRATERLETS
CRATERLIKE
CRATERS
CRATES
CRATING
CRATON
CRATONIC
CRATONS
CRAUNCH
CRAUNCHED
CRAUNCHES
CRAUNCHING
CRAVAT
CRAVATS
CRAVATTED
CRAVE
CRAVED
CRAVEN
CRAVENED
CRAVENER
CRAVENEST
CRAVENING
CRAVENLY
CRAVENNESS
CRAVENNESSES
CRAVENS
CRAVER
CRAVERS
CRAVES
CRAVING
CRAVINGS
CRAW
CRAWDAD
CRAWDADDIES
CRAWDADDY
CRAWDADS
CRAWFISH
CRAWFISHED
CRAWFISHES
CRAWFISHING
CRAWL
CRAWLED
CRAWLER
CRAWLERS
CRAWLIER
CRAWLIEST
CRAWLING
CRAWLS
CRAWLWAY
CRAWLWAYS
CRAWLY
CRAWS
CRAYFISH
CRAYFISHES
CRAYON
CRAYONED
CRAYONER
CRAYONERS
CRAYONING

CRAYONIST
CRAYONISTS
CRAYONS
CRAZE
CRAZED
CRAZES
CRAZIER
CRAZIES
CRAZIEST
CRAZILY
CRAZINESS
CRAZINESSES
CRAZING
CRAZINGS
CRAZY
CRAZYWEED
CRAZYWEEDS
CREAK
CREAKED
CREAKIER
CREAKIEST
CREAKILY
CREAKINESS
CREAKINESSES
CREAKING
CREAKS
CREAKY
CREAM
CREAMCUPS
CREAMED
CREAMER
CREAMERIES
CREAMERS
CREAMERY
CREAMIER
CREAMIEST
CREAMILY
CREAMINESS
CREAMINESSES
CREAMING
CREAMPUFF
CREAMPUFFS
CREAMS
CREAMWARE
CREAMWARES
CREAMY
CREASE
CREASED
CREASELESS
CREASER
CREASERS
CREASES
CREASIER
CREASIEST
CREASING
CREASY
CREATABLE
CREATE
CREATED
CREATES
CREATIN
CREATINE
CREATINES
CREATING
CREATININE
CREATININES
CREATINS
CREATION
CREATIONISM
CREATIONISMS
CREATIONIST
CREATIONISTS
CREATIONS
CREATIVE
CREATIVELY
CREATIVENESS
CREATIVENESSES
CREATIVES
CREATIVITIES
CREATIVITY
CREATOR
CREATORS
CREATURAL
CREATURE
CREATUREHOOD
CREATUREHOODS
CREATURELINESS
CREATURELY
CREATURES
CRECHE
CRECHES
CRED
CREDAL
CREDENCE
CREDENCES
CREDENDA
CREDENDUM
CREDENT
CREDENTIAL
CREDENTIALED
CREDENTIALING
CREDENTIALISM
CREDENTIALISMS
CREDENTIALLED
CREDENTIALLING
CREDENTIALS
CREDENZA
CREDENZAS
CREDIBILITIES
CREDIBILITY
CREDIBLE
CREDIBLY
CREDIT
CREDITABILITIES
CREDITABILITY
CREDITABLE
CREDITABLENESS
CREDITABLY
CREDITED
CREDITING
CREDITOR
CREDITORS
CREDITS
CREDITWORTHIER
CREDITWORTHIEST
CREDITWORTHY
CREDO
CREDOS
CREDS
CREDULITIES
CREDULITY
CREDULOUS
CREDULOUSLY
CREDULOUSNESS
CREDULOUSNESSES
CREED
CREEDAL
CREEDS
CREEK
CREEKS
CREEKSIDE
CREEKSIDES
CREEL
CREELED
CREELING
CREELS
CREEP
CREEPAGE
CREEPAGES
CREEPED
CREEPER
CREEPERS
CREEPIE
CREEPIER
CREEPIES
CREEPIEST
CREEPILY
CREEPINESS
CREEPINESSES
CREEPING
CREEPS
CREEPY
CREESE
CREESES
CREESH
CREESHED
CREESHES
CREESHING
CREMAINS
CREMATE
CREMATED
CREMATES
CREMATING
CREMATION
CREMATIONS
CREMATOR
CREMATORIA
CREMATORIES
CREMATORIUM
CREMATORIUMS
CREMATORS
CREMATORY
CREME
CREMES
CREMINI
CREMINIS
CRENATE
CRENATED
CRENATELY
CRENATION
CRENATIONS
CRENATURE
CRENATURES
CRENEL
CRENELATE
CRENELATED
CRENELATES
CRENELATING
CRENELATION
CRENELATIONS
CRENELED
CRENELING
CRENELLATED
CRENELLATION
CRENELLATIONS
CRENELLE
CRENELLED
CRENELLES
CRENELLING
CRENELS
CRENSHAW
CRENSHAWS
CRENULATE
CRENULATED
CRENULATION
CRENULATIONS
CREODONT
CREODONTS
CREOLE
CREOLES
CREOLISE
CREOLISED
CREOLISES
CREOLISING
CREOLIZATION
CREOLIZATIONS
CREOLIZE
CREOLIZED
CREOLIZES
CREOLIZING
CREOSOL
CREOSOLS
CREOSOTE
CREOSOTED
CREOSOTES
CREOSOTIC
CREOSOTING
CREPE
CREPED
CREPERIE
CREPERIES
CREPES
CREPEY
CREPIER
CREPIEST
CREPING
CREPITANT
CREPITATE
CREPITATED
CREPITATES
CREPITATING
CREPITATION
CREPITATIONS
CREPITUS
CREPON
CREPONS
CREPT
CREPUSCLE
CREPUSCLES
CREPUSCULAR
CREPUSCULE
CREPUSCULES
CREPY
CRESCENDI
CRESCENDO

CRESCENDOED
CRESCENDOES
CRESCENDOING
CRESCENDOS
CRESCENT
CRESCENTIC
CRESCENTS
CRESCIVE
CRESCIVELY
CRESOL
CRESOLS
CRESS
CRESSES
CRESSET
CRESSETS
CRESSY
CREST
CRESTAL
CRESTED
CRESTFALLEN
CRESTFALLENLY
CRESTFALLENNESS
CRESTING
CRESTINGS
CRESTLESS
CRESTS
CRESYL
CRESYLIC
CRESYLS
CRETIC
CRETICS
CRETIN
CRETINISM
CRETINISMS
CRETINOID
CRETINOUS
CRETINS
CRETONNE
CRETONNES
CRETONS
CREVALLE
CREVALLES
CREVASSE
CREVASSED
CREVASSES
CREVASSING
CREVICE
CREVICED
CREVICES
CREW
CREWCUT
CREWCUTS
CREWED
CREWEL
CREWELS
CREWELWORK
CREWELWORKS
CREWING
CREWLESS
CREWMAN
CREWMATE
CREWMATES
CREWMEN
CREWNECK
CREWNECKS
CREWS
CRIB
CRIBBAGE
CRIBBAGES
CRIBBED
CRIBBER
CRIBBERS
CRIBBING
CRIBBINGS
CRIBBLED
CRIBRIFORM
CRIBROUS
CRIBS
CRIBWORK
CRIBWORKS
CRICETID
CRICETIDS
CRICK
CRICKED
CRICKET
CRICKETED
CRICKETER
CRICKETERS
CRICKETING
CRICKETS
CRICKEY
CRICKING
CRICKS
CRICOID
CRICOIDS
CRIED
CRIER
CRIERS
CRIES
CRIKEY
CRIME
CRIMELESS
CRIMES
CRIMINAL
CRIMINALISATION
CRIMINALISE
CRIMINALISED
CRIMINALISES
CRIMINALISING
CRIMINALIST
CRIMINALISTICS
CRIMINALISTS
CRIMINALITIES
CRIMINALITY
CRIMINALIZATION
CRIMINALIZE
CRIMINALIZED
CRIMINALIZES
CRIMINALIZING
CRIMINALLY
CRIMINALS
CRIMINATE
CRIMINATED
CRIMINATES
CRIMINATING
CRIMINATION
CRIMINATIONS
CRIMINE
CRIMINI
CRIMINIS
CRIMINOLOGICAL
CRIMINOLOGIES
CRIMINOLOGIST
CRIMINOLOGISTS
CRIMINOLOGY
CRIMINOUS
CRIMINY
CRIMMER
CRIMMERS
CRIMP
CRIMPED
CRIMPER
CRIMPERS
CRIMPIER
CRIMPIEST
CRIMPING
CRIMPLE
CRIMPLED
CRIMPLES
CRIMPLING
CRIMPS
CRIMPY
CRIMSON
CRIMSONED
CRIMSONING
CRIMSONS
CRINGE
CRINGED
CRINGER
CRINGERS
CRINGES
CRINGEWORTHIER
CRINGEWORTHIEST
CRINGEWORTHY
CRINGING
CRINGLE
CRINGLES
CRINITE
CRINITES
CRINKLE
CRINKLED
CRINKLES
CRINKLIER
CRINKLIEST
CRINKLING
CRINKLY
CRINOID
CRINOIDAL
CRINOIDS
CRINOLINE
CRINOLINED
CRINOLINES
CRINUM
CRINUMS
CRIOLLO
CRIOLLOS
CRIP
CRIPE
CRIPES
CRIPPLE
CRIPPLED
CRIPPLER
CRIPPLERS
CRIPPLES
CRIPPLING
CRIPPLINGLY
CRIPS
CRIS
CRISES
CRISIC
CRISIS
CRISP
CRISPATE
CRISPATED
CRISPBREAD
CRISPBREADS
CRISPED
CRISPEN
CRISPENED
CRISPENING
CRISPENS
CRISPER
CRISPERS
CRISPEST
CRISPHEAD
CRISPHEADS
CRISPIER
CRISPIEST
CRISPILY
CRISPINESS
CRISPINESSES
CRISPING
CRISPLY
CRISPNESS
CRISPNESSES
CRISPS
CRISPY
CRISSA
CRISSAL
CRISSCROSS
CRISSCROSSED
CRISSCROSSES
CRISSCROSSING
CRISSUM
CRISTA
CRISTAE
CRISTATE
CRISTATED
CRIT
CRITERIA
CRITERIAL
CRITERION
CRITERIONS
CRITERIUM
CRITERIUMS
CRITIC
CRITICAL
CRITICALITIES
CRITICALITY
CRITICALLY
CRITICALNESS
CRITICALNESSES
CRITICASTER
CRITICASTERS
CRITICISE
CRITICISED
CRITICISES
CRITICISING
CRITICISM
CRITICISMS
CRITICIZABLE
CRITICIZE
CRITICIZED
CRITICIZER
CRITICIZERS

CRITICIZES
CRITICIZING
CRITICS
CRITIQUE
CRITIQUED
CRITIQUES
CRITIQUING
CRITS
CRITTER
CRITTERS
CRITTUR
CRITTURS
CROAK
CROAKED
CROAKER
CROAKERS
CROAKIER
CROAKIEST
CROAKILY
CROAKING
CROAKS
CROAKY
CROC
CROCEIN
CROCEINE
CROCEINES
CROCEINS
CROCHET
CROCHETED
CROCHETER
CROCHETERS
CROCHETING
CROCHETS
CROCI
CROCIDOLITE
CROCIDOLITES
CROCINE
CROCK
CROCKED
CROCKERIES
CROCKERY
CROCKET
CROCKETED
CROCKETS
CROCKING
CROCKPOT
CROCKPOTS
CROCKS
CROCODILE
CROCODILES
CROCODILIAN
CROCODILIANS
CROCOITE
CROCOITES
CROCS
CROCUS
CROCUSES
CROFT
CROFTED
CROFTER
CROFTERS
CROFTING
CROFTS
CROISSANT
CROISSANTS
CROJIK
CROJIKS
CROMLECH
CROMLECHS
CRONE
CRONES
CRONIES
CRONISH
CRONY
CRONYISM
CRONYISMS
CROOK
CROOKBACK
CROOKBACKED
CROOKBACKS
CROOKED
CROOKEDER
CROOKEDEST
CROOKEDLY
CROOKEDNESS
CROOKEDNESSES
CROOKER
CROOKERIES
CROOKERY
CROOKEST
CROOKING
CROOKNECK
CROOKNECKS
CROOKS
CROON
CROONED
CROONER
CROONERS
CROONIER
CROONIEST
CROONING
CROONS
CROONY
CROP
CROPLAND
CROPLANDS
CROPLESS
CROPPED
CROPPER
CROPPERS
CROPPIE
CROPPIES
CROPPING
CROPS
CROQUET
CROQUETED
CROQUETING
CROQUETS
CROQUETTE
CROQUETTES
CROQUIGNOLE
CROQUIGNOLES
CROQUIS
CRORE
CRORES
CROSIER
CROSIERS
CROSS
CROSSABILITIES
CROSSABILITY
CROSSABLE
CROSSARM
CROSSARMS
CROSSBANDED
CROSSBANDING
CROSSBANDINGS
CROSSBAR
CROSSBARRED
CROSSBARRING
CROSSBARS
CROSSBEAM
CROSSBEAMS
CROSSBEARER
CROSSBEARERS
CROSSBILL
CROSSBILLS
CROSSBONES
CROSSBOW
CROSSBOWMAN
CROSSBOWMEN
CROSSBOWS
CROSSBRED
CROSSBREDS
CROSSBREED
CROSSBREEDING
CROSSBREEDS
CROSSBUCK
CROSSBUCKS
CROSSCOURT
CROSSCURRENT
CROSSCURRENTS
CROSSCUT
CROSSCUTS
CROSSCUTTING
CROSSCUTTINGS
CROSSE
CROSSED
CROSSER
CROSSERS
CROSSES
CROSSEST
CROSSFIRE
CROSSFIRES
CROSSHAIR
CROSSHAIRS
CROSSHATCH
CROSSHATCHED
CROSSHATCHES
CROSSHATCHING
CROSSHEAD
CROSSHEADS
CROSSING
CROSSINGS
CROSSJACK
CROSSJACKS
CROSSLET
CROSSLETS
CROSSLINGUISTIC
CROSSLY
CROSSNESS
CROSSNESSES
CROSSOPTERYGIAN
CROSSOVER
CROSSOVERS
CROSSPATCH
CROSSPATCHES
CROSSPIECE
CROSSPIECES
CROSSPLY
CROSSROAD
CROSSROADS
CROSSRUFF
CROSSRUFFED
CROSSRUFFING
CROSSRUFFS
CROSSTALK
CROSSTALKS
CROSSTIE
CROSSTIED
CROSSTIES
CROSSTOWN
CROSSTREE
CROSSTREES
CROSSWALK
CROSSWALKS
CROSSWAY
CROSSWAYS
CROSSWIND
CROSSWINDS
CROSSWISE
CROSSWORD
CROSSWORDS
CROSTATA
CROSTATAS
CROSTINI
CROSTINO
CROTALE
CROTALES
CROTCH
CROTCHED
CROTCHES
CROTCHET
CROTCHETINESS
CROTCHETINESSES
CROTCHETS
CROTCHETY
CROTON
CROTONBUG
CROTONBUGS
CROTONS
CROUCH
CROUCHED
CROUCHES
CROUCHING
CROUP
CROUPE
CROUPES
CROUPIER
CROUPIERS
CROUPIEST
CROUPILY
CROUPOUS
CROUPS
CROUPY
CROUSE
CROUSELY
CROUSTADE
CROUSTADES
CROUTE
CROUTES
CROUTON
CROUTONS
CROW
CROWBAIT
CROWBAITS

CROWBAR
CROWBARRED
CROWBARRING
CROWBARS
CROWBERRIES
CROWBERRY
CROWD
CROWDED
CROWDEDLY
CROWDEDNESS
CROWDEDNESSES
CROWDER
CROWDERS
CROWDFUNDING
CROWDFUNDINGS
CROWDIE
CROWDIES
CROWDING
CROWDS
CROWDSOURCING
CROWDSOURCINGS
CROWDY
CROWED
CROWER
CROWERS
CROWFEET
CROWFOOT
CROWFOOTS
CROWING
CROWKEEPER
CROWKEEPERS
CROWN
CROWNED
CROWNER
CROWNERS
CROWNET
CROWNETS
CROWNING
CROWNLESS
CROWNS
CROWS
CROWSFEET
CROWSFOOT
CROWSTEP
CROWSTEPPED
CROWSTEPS
CROZE
CROZER
CROZERS
CROZES
CROZIER
CROZIERS
CRU
CRUCES
CRUCIAL
CRUCIALLY
CRUCIAN
CRUCIANS
CRUCIATE
CRUCIBLE
CRUCIBLES
CRUCIFER
CRUCIFEROUS
CRUCIFERS
CRUCIFIED
CRUCIFIER
CRUCIFIERS
CRUCIFIES
CRUCIFIX
CRUCIFIXES
CRUCIFIXION
CRUCIFIXIONS
CRUCIFORM
CRUCIFORMS
CRUCIFY
CRUCIFYING
CRUCK
CRUCKS
CRUD
CRUDDED
CRUDDIER
CRUDDIEST
CRUDDING
CRUDDY
CRUDE
CRUDELY
CRUDENESS
CRUDENESSES
CRUDER
CRUDES
CRUDEST
CRUDITES
CRUDITIES
CRUDITY
CRUDO
CRUDOS
CRUDS
CRUEL
CRUELER
CRUELEST
CRUELLER
CRUELLEST
CRUELLY
CRUELNESS
CRUELNESSES
CRUELTIES
CRUELTY
CRUET
CRUETS
CRUFT
CRUFTS
CRUISE
CRUISED
CRUISER
CRUISERS
CRUISERWEIGHT
CRUISERWEIGHTS
CRUISES
CRUISEY
CRUISIER
CRUISIEST
CRUISING
CRUISINGS
CRUISY
CRULLER
CRULLERS
CRUMB
CRUMBED
CRUMBER
CRUMBERS
CRUMBIER
CRUMBIEST
CRUMBING
CRUMBLE
CRUMBLED
CRUMBLES
CRUMBLIER
CRUMBLIES
CRUMBLIEST
CRUMBLINESS
CRUMBLINESSES
CRUMBLING
CRUMBLINGS
CRUMBLY
CRUMBS
CRUMBUM
CRUMBUMS
CRUMBY
CRUMHORN
CRUMHORNS
CRUMMIE
CRUMMIER
CRUMMIES
CRUMMIEST
CRUMMILY
CRUMMINESS
CRUMMINESSES
CRUMMY
CRUMP
CRUMPED
CRUMPET
CRUMPETS
CRUMPING
CRUMPLE
CRUMPLED
CRUMPLES
CRUMPLIER
CRUMPLIEST
CRUMPLING
CRUMPLY
CRUMPS
CRUNCH
CRUNCHABLE
CRUNCHED
CRUNCHER
CRUNCHERS
CRUNCHES
CRUNCHIER
CRUNCHIES
CRUNCHIEST
CRUNCHILY
CRUNCHINESS
CRUNCHINESSES
CRUNCHING
CRUNCHY
CRUNK
CRUNKS
CRUNODAL
CRUNODE
CRUNODES
CRUOR
CRUORS
CRUPPER
CRUPPERS
CRURA
CRURAL
CRUS
CRUSADE
CRUSADED
CRUSADER
CRUSADERS
CRUSADES
CRUSADING
CRUSADO
CRUSADOES
CRUSADOS
CRUSE
CRUSES
CRUSET
CRUSETS
CRUSH
CRUSHABLE
CRUSHED
CRUSHER
CRUSHERS
CRUSHES
CRUSHING
CRUSHINGLY
CRUSHPROOF
CRUSILY
CRUST
CRUSTACEA
CRUSTACEAN
CRUSTACEANS
CRUSTACEOUS
CRUSTAL
CRUSTED
CRUSTIER
CRUSTIEST
CRUSTILY
CRUSTINESS
CRUSTINESSES
CRUSTING
CRUSTLESS
CRUSTOSE
CRUSTS
CRUSTY
CRUTCH
CRUTCHED
CRUTCHES
CRUTCHING
CRUX
CRUXES
CRUZADO
CRUZADOES
CRUZADOS
CRUZEIRO
CRUZEIROS
CRWTH
CRWTHS
CRY
CRYBABIES
CRYBABY
CRYER
CRYERS
CRYING
CRYINGLY
CRYOBANK
CRYOBANKS
CRYOBIOLOGICAL
CRYOBIOLOGIES
CRYOBIOLOGIST
CRYOBIOLOGISTS
CRYOBIOLOGY
CRYOGEN

CRYOGENIC
CRYOGENICALLY
CRYOGENICS
CRYOGENIES
CRYOGENS
CRYOGENY
CRYOLITE
CRYOLITES
CRYOMETER
CRYOMETERS
CRYONIC
CRYONICS
CRYOPHILIC
CRYOPHYTE
CRYOPHYTES
CRYOPRESERVE
CRYOPRESERVED
CRYOPRESERVES
CRYOPRESERVING
CRYOPROBE
CRYOPROBES
CRYOPROTECTANT
CRYOPROTECTANTS
CRYOPROTECTIVE
CRYOSCOPE
CRYOSCOPES
CRYOSCOPIC
CRYOSCOPIES
CRYOSCOPY
CRYOSTAT
CRYOSTATIC
CRYOSTATS
CRYOSURGEON
CRYOSURGEONS
CRYOSURGERIES
CRYOSURGERY
CRYOSURGICAL
CRYOTHERAPIES
CRYOTHERAPY
CRYOTRON
CRYOTRONS
CRYPT
CRYPTAL
CRYPTANALYSES
CRYPTANALYSIS
CRYPTANALYST
CRYPTANALYSTS
CRYPTANALYTIC
CRYPTANALYTICAL
CRYPTARITHM
CRYPTARITHMS
CRYPTIC
CRYPTICAL
CRYPTICALLY
CRYPTO
CRYPTOCOCCAL
CRYPTOCOCCI
CRYPTOCOCCOSES
CRYPTOCOCCOSIS
CRYPTOCOCCUS
CRYPTOGAM
CRYPTOGAMIC
CRYPTOGAMOUS
CRYPTOGAMS
CRYPTOGENIC
CRYPTOGRAM
CRYPTOGRAMS
CRYPTOGRAPH
CRYPTOGRAPHER
CRYPTOGRAPHERS
CRYPTOGRAPHIC
CRYPTOGRAPHIES
CRYPTOGRAPHS
CRYPTOGRAPHY
CRYPTOLOGIC
CRYPTOLOGICAL
CRYPTOLOGIES
CRYPTOLOGIST
CRYPTOLOGISTS
CRYPTOLOGY
CRYPTOMERIA
CRYPTOMERIAS
CRYPTONYM
CRYPTONYMS
CRYPTORCHID
CRYPTORCHIDISM
CRYPTORCHIDISMS
CRYPTORCHIDS
CRYPTORCHISM
CRYPTORCHISMS
CRYPTOS
CRYPTOSPORIDIA
CRYPTOSPORIDIUM
CRYPTOSYSTEM
CRYPTOSYSTEMS
CRYPTOZOOLOGIES
CRYPTOZOOLOGIST
CRYPTOZOOLOGY
CRYPTS
CRYSTAL
CRYSTALIZE
CRYSTALIZED
CRYSTALIZES
CRYSTALIZING
CRYSTALLINE
CRYSTALLINITIES
CRYSTALLINITY
CRYSTALLISATION
CRYSTALLISE
CRYSTALLISED
CRYSTALLISES
CRYSTALLISING
CRYSTALLITE
CRYSTALLITES
CRYSTALLIZABLE
CRYSTALLIZATION
CRYSTALLIZE
CRYSTALLIZED
CRYSTALLIZER
CRYSTALLIZERS
CRYSTALLIZES
CRYSTALLIZING
CRYSTALLOGRAPHY
CRYSTALLOID
CRYSTALLOIDAL
CRYSTALLOIDS
CRYSTALS
CSARDAS
CSARDASES
CTENIDIA
CTENIDIUM
CTENOID
CTENOPHORAN
CTENOPHORANS
CTENOPHORE
CTENOPHORES
CUADRILLA
CUADRILLAS
CUATRO
CUATROS
CUB
CUBAGE
CUBAGES
CUBANELLE
CUBANELLES
CUBATURE
CUBATURES
CUBBED
CUBBIES
CUBBING
CUBBISH
CUBBY
CUBBYHOLE
CUBBYHOLES
CUBE
CUBEB
CUBEBS
CUBED
CUBER
CUBERS
CUBES
CUBIC
CUBICAL
CUBICALLY
CUBICITIES
CUBICITY
CUBICLE
CUBICLES
CUBICLY
CUBICS
CUBICULA
CUBICULUM
CUBIFORM
CUBING
CUBISM
CUBISMS
CUBIST
CUBISTIC
CUBISTS
CUBIT
CUBITAL
CUBITI
CUBITS
CUBITUS
CUBITUSES
CUBOID
CUBOIDAL
CUBOIDS
CUBS
CUCKOLD
CUCKOLDED
CUCKOLDING
CUCKOLDRIES
CUCKOLDRY
CUCKOLDS
CUCKOO
CUCKOOED
CUCKOOFLOWER
CUCKOOFLOWERS
CUCKOOING
CUCKOOPINT
CUCKOOPINTS
CUCKOOS
CUCULLATE
CUCUMBER
CUCUMBERS
CUCURBIT
CUCURBITS
CUD
CUDBEAR
CUDBEARS
CUDDIE
CUDDIES
CUDDLE
CUDDLED
CUDDLER
CUDDLERS
CUDDLES
CUDDLESOME
CUDDLIER
CUDDLIEST
CUDDLING
CUDDLY
CUDDY
CUDGEL
CUDGELED
CUDGELER
CUDGELERS
CUDGELING
CUDGELLED
CUDGELLING
CUDGELS
CUDS
CUDWEED
CUDWEEDS
CUE
CUED
CUEING
CUEIST
CUEISTS
CUES
CUESTA
CUESTAS
CUFF
CUFFABLE
CUFFED
CUFFING
CUFFLESS
CUFFLINK
CUFFLINKS
CUFFS
CUIF
CUIFS
CUING
CUIRASS
CUIRASSED
CUIRASSES
CUIRASSIER
CUIRASSIERS
CUIRASSING
CUISH
CUISHES
CUISINART
CUISINARTS
CUISINE

CUISINES
CUISSE
CUISSES
CUITTLE
CUITTLED
CUITTLES
CUITTLING
CUKE
CUKES
CULCH
CULCHES
CULCHIE
CULCHIER
CULCHIES
CULCHIEST
CULET
CULETS
CULEX
CULEXES
CULICES
CULICID
CULICIDS
CULICINE
CULICINES
CULINARIAN
CULINARIANS
CULINARILY
CULINARY
CULL
CULLAY
CULLAYS
CULLED
CULLENDER
CULLENDERS
CULLER
CULLERS
CULLET
CULLETS
CULLIED
CULLIES
CULLING
CULLION
CULLIONS
CULLIS
CULLISES
CULLS
CULLY
CULLYING
CULM
CULMED
CULMEN
CULMINA
CULMINANT
CULMINATE
CULMINATED
CULMINATES
CULMINATING
CULMINATION
CULMINATIONS
CULMING
CULMS
CULOTTE
CULOTTES
CULPA
CULPABILITIES
CULPABILITY
CULPABLE
CULPABLENESS
CULPABLENESSES
CULPABLY
CULPAE
CULPRIT
CULPRITS
CULSHIE
CULSHIER
CULSHIES
CULSHIEST
CULT
CULTCH
CULTCHES
CULTI
CULTIC
CULTIGEN
CULTIGENS
CULTISH
CULTISHLY
CULTISHNESS
CULTISHNESSES
CULTISM
CULTISMS
CULTIST
CULTISTS
CULTIVABILITIES
CULTIVABILITY
CULTIVABLE
CULTIVAR
CULTIVARS
CULTIVATABLE
CULTIVATE
CULTIVATED
CULTIVATES
CULTIVATING
CULTIVATION
CULTIVATIONS
CULTIVATOR
CULTIVATORS
CULTLIKE
CULTRATE
CULTRATED
CULTS
CULTURAL
CULTURALLY
CULTURATI
CULTURE
CULTURED
CULTURES
CULTURING
CULTURIST
CULTURISTS
CULTUS
CULTUSES
CULVER
CULVERIN
CULVERINS
CULVERS
CULVERT
CULVERTED
CULVERTING
CULVERTS
CUM
CUMARIN
CUMARINS
CUMBER
CUMBERBUND
CUMBERBUNDS
CUMBERED
CUMBERER
CUMBERERS
CUMBERING
CUMBERS
CUMBERSOME
CUMBERSOMELY
CUMBERSOMENESS
CUMBIA
CUMBIAS
CUMBRANCE
CUMBRANCES
CUMBROUS
CUMBROUSLY
CUMBROUSNESS
CUMBROUSNESSES
CUMIN
CUMINS
CUMMER
CUMMERBUND
CUMMERBUNDS
CUMMERS
CUMMIN
CUMMING
CUMMINS
CUMQUAT
CUMQUATS
CUMS
CUMSHAW
CUMSHAWS
CUMULATE
CUMULATED
CUMULATES
CUMULATING
CUMULATION
CUMULATIONS
CUMULATIVE
CUMULATIVELY
CUMULATIVENESS
CUMULI
CUMULIFORM
CUMULONIMBI
CUMULONIMBUS
CUMULONIMBUSES
CUMULOUS
CUMULUS
CUMULUSES
CUNCTATION
CUNCTATIONS
CUNCTATIVE
CUNCTATOR
CUNCTATORS
CUNDUM
CUNDUMS
CUNEAL
CUNEATE
CUNEATED
CUNEATELY
CUNEATIC
CUNEIFORM
CUNEIFORMS
CUNIFORM
CUNIFORMS
CUNIT
CUNITS
CUNNER
CUNNERS
CUNNILINCTUS
CUNNILINCTUSES
CUNNILINGUS
CUNNILINGUSES
CUNNING
CUNNINGER
CUNNINGEST
CUNNINGLY
CUNNINGNESS
CUNNINGNESSES
CUNNINGS
CUNT
CUNTS
CUP
CUPBEARER
CUPBEARERS
CUPBOARD
CUPBOARDS
CUPCAKE
CUPCAKES
CUPEL
CUPELED
CUPELER
CUPELERS
CUPELING
CUPELLATION
CUPELLATIONS
CUPELLED
CUPELLER
CUPELLERS
CUPELLING
CUPELS
CUPFERRON
CUPFERRONS
CUPFUL
CUPFULS
CUPID
CUPIDITIES
CUPIDITY
CUPIDS
CUPLIKE
CUPOLA
CUPOLAED
CUPOLAING
CUPOLAS
CUPPA
CUPPAS
CUPPED
CUPPER
CUPPERS
CUPPIER
CUPPIEST
CUPPING
CUPPINGS
CUPPY
CUPREOUS
CUPRIC
CUPRIFEROUS
CUPRITE
CUPRITES
CUPRONICKEL
CUPRONICKELS
CUPROUS

CUPRUM
CUPRUMS
CUPS
CUPSFUL
CUPULA
CUPULAE
CUPULAR
CUPULATE
CUPULE
CUPULES
CUR
CURABILITIES
CURABILITY
CURABLE
CURABLENESS
CURABLENESSES
CURABLY
CURACAO
CURACAOS
CURACIES
CURACOA
CURACOAS
CURACY
CURAGH
CURAGHS
CURANDERA
CURANDERAS
CURANDERO
CURANDEROS
CURARA
CURARAS
CURARE
CURARES
CURARI
CURARINE
CURARINES
CURARIS
CURARIZATION
CURARIZATIONS
CURARIZE
CURARIZED
CURARIZES
CURARIZING
CURASSOW
CURASSOWS
CURATE
CURATED
CURATES
CURATING
CURATION
CURATIONS
CURATIVE
CURATIVELY
CURATIVES
CURATOR
CURATORIAL
CURATORS
CURATORSHIP
CURATORSHIPS
CURB
CURBABLE
CURBED
CURBER
CURBERS
CURBING
CURBINGS
CURBS
CURBSIDE
CURBSIDES
CURBSTONE
CURBSTONES
CURCH
CURCHES
CURCULIO
CURCULIOS
CURCUMA
CURCUMAS
CURCUMIN
CURCUMINS
CURD
CURDED
CURDIER
CURDIEST
CURDING
CURDLE
CURDLED
CURDLER
CURDLERS
CURDLES
CURDLING
CURDS
CURDY
CURE
CURED
CURELESS
CURER
CURERS
CURES
CURET
CURETS
CURETTAGE
CURETTAGES
CURETTE
CURETTED
CURETTEMENT
CURETTEMENTS
CURETTES
CURETTING
CURF
CURFEW
CURFEWS
CURFS
CURIA
CURIAE
CURIAL
CURIE
CURIES
CURING
CURIO
CURIOS
CURIOSA
CURIOSITIES
CURIOSITY
CURIOUS
CURIOUSER
CURIOUSEST
CURIOUSLY
CURIOUSNESS
CURIOUSNESSES
CURITE
CURITES
CURIUM
CURIUMS
CURL
CURLED
CURLER
CURLERS
CURLEW
CURLEWS
CURLICUE
CURLICUED
CURLICUES
CURLICUING
CURLIER
CURLIEST
CURLILY
CURLINESS
CURLINESSES
CURLING
CURLINGS
CURLPAPER
CURLPAPERS
CURLS
CURLY
CURLYCUE
CURLYCUES
CURMUDGEON
CURMUDGEONLY
CURMUDGEONS
CURN
CURNS
CURR
CURRACH
CURRACHS
CURRAGH
CURRAGHS
CURRAJONG
CURRAJONGS
CURRAN
CURRANS
CURRANT
CURRANTS
CURRED
CURREJONG
CURREJONGS
CURRENCIES
CURRENCY
CURRENT
CURRENTLY
CURRENTNESS
CURRENTNESSES
CURRENTS
CURRICLE
CURRICLES
CURRICULA
CURRICULAR
CURRICULUM
CURRICULUMS
CURRIE
CURRIED
CURRIER
CURRIERIES
CURRIERS
CURRIERY
CURRIES
CURRIJONG
CURRIJONGS
CURRING
CURRISH
CURRISHLY
CURRS
CURRY
CURRYCOMB
CURRYCOMBED
CURRYCOMBING
CURRYCOMBS
CURRYING
CURS
CURSE
CURSED
CURSEDER
CURSEDEST
CURSEDLY
CURSEDNESS
CURSEDNESSES
CURSER
CURSERS
CURSES
CURSILLO
CURSILLOS
CURSING
CURSIVE
CURSIVELY
CURSIVENESS
CURSIVENESSES
CURSIVES
CURSOR
CURSORIAL
CURSORILY
CURSORINESS
CURSORINESSES
CURSORS
CURSORY
CURST
CURT
CURTAIL
CURTAILED
CURTAILER
CURTAILERS
CURTAILING
CURTAILMENT
CURTAILMENTS
CURTAILS
CURTAIN
CURTAINED
CURTAINING
CURTAINLESS
CURTAINS
CURTAL
CURTALAX
CURTALAXES
CURTALS
CURTANA
CURTANAS
CURTATE
CURTER
CURTESIES
CURTEST
CURTESY
CURTILAGE
CURTILAGES
CURTLY
CURTNESS
CURTNESSES
CURTSEY

CURTSEYED
CURTSEYING
CURTSEYS
CURTSIED
CURTSIES
CURTSY
CURTSYING
CURULE
CURVACEOUS
CURVACIOUS
CURVATURE
CURVATURES
CURVE
CURVEBALL
CURVEBALLED
CURVEBALLING
CURVEBALLS
CURVED
CURVEDLY
CURVES
CURVET
CURVETED
CURVETING
CURVETS
CURVETTED
CURVETTING
CURVEY
CURVIER
CURVIEST
CURVILINEAR
CURVILINEARITY
CURVING
CURVY
CUSCUS
CUSCUSES
CUSEC
CUSECS
CUSHAT
CUSHATS
CUSHAW
CUSHAWS
CUSHIER
CUSHIEST
CUSHILY
CUSHINESS
CUSHINESSES
CUSHION
CUSHIONED
CUSHIONING
CUSHIONLESS
CUSHIONS
CUSHIONY
CUSHY
CUSK
CUSKS
CUSP
CUSPAL
CUSPATE
CUSPATED
CUSPED
CUSPID
CUSPIDAL
CUSPIDATE
CUSPIDATION
CUSPIDATIONS
CUSPIDES
CUSPIDOR
CUSPIDORS
CUSPIDS
CUSPIS
CUSPS
CUSS
CUSSED
CUSSEDLY
CUSSEDNESS
CUSSEDNESSES
CUSSER
CUSSERS
CUSSES
CUSSING
CUSSO
CUSSOS
CUSSWORD
CUSSWORDS
CUSTARD
CUSTARDIER
CUSTARDIEST
CUSTARDS
CUSTARDY
CUSTODES
CUSTODIAL
CUSTODIAN
CUSTODIANS
CUSTODIANSHIP
CUSTODIANSHIPS
CUSTODIES
CUSTODY
CUSTOM
CUSTOMARIES
CUSTOMARILY
CUSTOMARINESS
CUSTOMARINESSES
CUSTOMARY
CUSTOMER
CUSTOMERS
CUSTOMHOUSE
CUSTOMHOUSES
CUSTOMISABLE
CUSTOMISATION
CUSTOMISATIONS
CUSTOMISE
CUSTOMISED
CUSTOMISES
CUSTOMISING
CUSTOMIZABLE
CUSTOMIZATION
CUSTOMIZATIONS
CUSTOMIZE
CUSTOMIZED
CUSTOMIZER
CUSTOMIZERS
CUSTOMIZES
CUSTOMIZING
CUSTOMS
CUSTOMSHOUSE
CUSTOMSHOUSES
CUSTOS
CUSTUMAL
CUSTUMALS
CUT
CUTABILITIES
CUTABILITY
CUTANEOUS
CUTANEOUSLY
CUTAWAY
CUTAWAYS
CUTBACK
CUTBACKS
CUTBANK
CUTBANKS
CUTBLOCK
CUTBLOCKS
CUTCH
CUTCHERIES
CUTCHERY
CUTCHES
CUTDOWN
CUTDOWNS
CUTE
CUTELY
CUTENESS
CUTENESSES
CUTER
CUTES
CUTESIE
CUTESIER
CUTESIEST
CUTESINESS
CUTESINESSES
CUTEST
CUTESY
CUTEY
CUTEYS
CUTGRASS
CUTGRASSES
CUTICLE
CUTICLES
CUTICULA
CUTICULAE
CUTICULAR
CUTIE
CUTIES
CUTIN
CUTINISE
CUTINISED
CUTINISES
CUTINISING
CUTINIZE
CUTINIZED
CUTINIZES
CUTINIZING
CUTINS
CUTIS
CUTISES
CUTLAS
CUTLASES
CUTLASS
CUTLASSES
CUTLER
CUTLERIES
CUTLERS
CUTLERY
CUTLET
CUTLETS
CUTLETTE
CUTLETTES
CUTLINE
CUTLINES
CUTOFF
CUTOFFS
CUTOUT
CUTOUTS
CUTOVER
CUTOVERS
CUTPURSE
CUTPURSES
CUTS
CUTSCENE
CUTSCENES
CUTTABLE
CUTTAGE
CUTTAGES
CUTTER
CUTTERS
CUTTHROAT
CUTTHROATS
CUTTIES
CUTTING
CUTTINGLY
CUTTINGS
CUTTLE
CUTTLEBONE
CUTTLEBONES
CUTTLED
CUTTLEFISH
CUTTLEFISHES
CUTTLES
CUTTLING
CUTTY
CUTUP
CUTUPS
CUTWATER
CUTWATERS
CUTWORK
CUTWORKS
CUTWORM
CUTWORMS
CUVEE
CUVEES
CUVETTE
CUVETTES
CUZ
CUZES
CUZZES
CWM
CWMS
CYAN
CYANAMID
CYANAMIDE
CYANAMIDES
CYANAMIDS
CYANATE
CYANATES
CYANIC
CYANID
CYANIDE
CYANIDED
CYANIDES
CYANIDING
CYANIDS
CYANIN
CYANINE
CYANINES
CYANINS
CYANITE

CYANITES
CYANITIC
CYANO
CYANOACRYLATE
CYANOACRYLATES
CYANOBACTERIA
CYANOBACTERIUM
CYANOCOBALAMIN
CYANOCOBALAMINE
CYANOCOBALAMINS
CYANOETHYLATE
CYANOETHYLATED
CYANOETHYLATES
CYANOETHYLATING
CYANOETHYLATION
CYANOGEN
CYANOGENESES
CYANOGENESIS
CYANOGENETIC
CYANOGENIC
CYANOGENS
CYANOHYDRIN
CYANOHYDRINS
CYANOSED
CYANOSES
CYANOSIS
CYANOTIC
CYANOTYPE
CYANOTYPES
CYANS
CYANTHIA
CYANURATE
CYANURATES
CYATHIA
CYATHIUM
CYBER
CYBERBULLIES
CYBERBULLY
CYBERBULLYING
CYBERBULLYINGS
CYBERCAFE
CYBERCAFES
CYBERCAST
CYBERCASTS
CYBERCITIZEN
CYBERCITIZENS
CYBERNATE
CYBERNATED
CYBERNATES
CYBERNATING
CYBERNATION
CYBERNATIONS
CYBERNAUT

CYBERNAUTS
CYBERNETIC
CYBERNETICAL
CYBERNETICALLY
CYBERNETICIAN
CYBERNETICIANS
CYBERNETICIST
CYBERNETICISTS
CYBERNETICS
CYBERPORN
CYBERPORNS
CYBERPUNK
CYBERPUNKS
CYBERSECURITIES
CYBERSECURITY
CYBERSEX
CYBERSEXES
CYBERSPACE
CYBERSPACES
CYBERSPEAK
CYBERSPEAKS
CYBERSURFER
CYBERSURFERS
CYBERTERRORISM
CYBERTERRORISMS
CYBERWAR
CYBERWARS
CYBORG
CYBORGS
CYBRARIAN
CYBRARIANS
CYCAD
CYCADEOID
CYCADEOIDS
CYCADOPHYTE
CYCADOPHYTES
CYCADS
CYCAS
CYCASES
CYCASIN
CYCASINS
CYCLAMATE
CYCLAMATES
CYCLAMEN
CYCLAMENS
CYCLASE
CYCLASES
CYCLAZOCINE
CYCLAZOCINES
CYCLE
CYCLECAR
CYCLECARS
CYCLED

CYCLER
CYCLERIES
CYCLERS
CYCLERY
CYCLES
CYCLEWAY
CYCLEWAYS
CYCLIC
CYCLICAL
CYCLICALITIES
CYCLICALITY
CYCLICALLY
CYCLICALS
CYCLICITIES
CYCLICITY
CYCLICLY
CYCLIN
CYCLING
CYCLINGS
CYCLINS
CYCLIST
CYCLISTS
CYCLITOL
CYCLITOLS
CYCLIZATION
CYCLIZATIONS
CYCLIZE
CYCLIZED
CYCLIZES
CYCLIZINE
CYCLIZINES
CYCLIZING
CYCLO
CYCLOADDITION
CYCLOADDITIONS
CYCLOALIPHATIC
CYCLODEXTRIN
CYCLODEXTRINS
CYCLODIENE
CYCLODIENES
CYCLOGENESES
CYCLOGENESIS
CYCLOHEXANE
CYCLOHEXANES
CYCLOHEXANONE
CYCLOHEXANONES
CYCLOHEXIMIDE
CYCLOHEXIMIDES
CYCLOHEXYLAMINE
CYCLOID
CYCLOIDAL
CYCLOIDS
CYCLOMETER

CYCLOMETERS
CYCLONAL
CYCLONE
CYCLONES
CYCLONIC
CYCLONICALLY
CYCLONITE
CYCLONITES
CYCLOOLEFIN
CYCLOOLEFINIC
CYCLOOLEFINS
CYCLOOXYGENASE
CYCLOOXYGENASES
CYCLOPAEDIA
CYCLOPAEDIAS
CYCLOPARAFFIN
CYCLOPARAFFINS
CYCLOPEAN
CYCLOPEDIA
CYCLOPEDIAS
CYCLOPEDIC
CYCLOPES
CYCLOPROPANE
CYCLOPROPANES
CYCLOPS
CYCLORAMA
CYCLORAMAS
CYCLORAMIC
CYCLOS
CYCLOSERINE
CYCLOSERINES
CYCLOSES
CYCLOSIS
CYCLOSPORA
CYCLOSPORAS
CYCLOSPORIN
CYCLOSPORINE
CYCLOSPORINES
CYCLOSPORINS
CYCLOSTOME
CYCLOSTOMES
CYCLOSTYLE
CYCLOSTYLED
CYCLOSTYLES
CYCLOSTYLING
CYCLOTHYMIA
CYCLOTHYMIAS
CYCLOTHYMIC
CYCLOTOMIC
CYCLOTRON
CYCLOTRONS
CYDER
CYDERS

CYESES
CYESIS
CYGNET
CYGNETS
CYLICES
CYLINDER
CYLINDERED
CYLINDERING
CYLINDERS
CYLINDRIC
CYLINDRICAL
CYLINDRICALLY
CYLIX
CYMA
CYMAE
CYMAR
CYMARS
CYMAS
CYMATIA
CYMATIUM
CYMBAL
CYMBALEER
CYMBALEERS
CYMBALER
CYMBALERS
CYMBALIST
CYMBALISTS
CYMBALOM
CYMBALOMS
CYMBALS
CYMBIDIA
CYMBIDIUM
CYMBIDIUMS
CYMBLING
CYMBLINGS
CYME
CYMENE
CYMENES
CYMES
CYMLIN
CYMLING
CYMLINGS
CYMLINS
CYMOGENE
CYMOGENES
CYMOGRAPH
CYMOGRAPHS
CYMOID
CYMOL
CYMOLS
CYMOPHANE
CYMOPHANES
CYMOSE

CYMOSELY
CYMOUS
CYNIC
CYNICAL
CYNICALLY
CYNICISM
CYNICISMS
CYNICS
CYNODONT
CYNODONTS
CYNOSURAL
CYNOSURE
CYNOSURES
CYPHER
CYPHERED
CYPHERING
CYPHERS
CYPRES
CYPRESES
CYPRESS
CYPRESSES
CYPRIAN
CYPRIANS
CYPRINID
CYPRINIDS
CYPRINOID
CYPRINOIDS
CYPRIPEDIUM
CYPRIPEDIUMS
CYPROHEPTADINE
CYPROHEPTADINES
CYPROTERONE
CYPROTERONES
CYPRUS
CYPRUSES
CYPSELA
CYPSELAE
CYST
CYSTEAMINE
CYSTEAMINES
CYSTEIN
CYSTEINE
CYSTEINES
CYSTEINIC
CYSTEINS
CYSTIC
CYSTICERCI
CYSTICERCOID
CYSTICERCOIDS
CYSTICERCOSES
CYSTICERCOSIS
CYSTICERCUS
CYSTINE
CYSTINES
CYSTINURIA
CYSTINURIAS
CYSTITIDES
CYSTITIS
CYSTITISES
CYSTOCARP
CYSTOCARPS
CYSTOCELE
CYSTOCELES
CYSTOID
CYSTOIDS
CYSTOLITH
CYSTOLITHS
CYSTOSCOPE
CYSTOSCOPES
CYSTOSCOPIC
CYSTOSCOPIES
CYSTOSCOPY
CYSTOTOMIES
CYSTOTOMY
CYSTS
CYTASTER
CYTASTERS
CYTIDINE
CYTIDINES
CYTOCHALASIN
CYTOCHALASINS
CYTOCHEMICAL
CYTOCHEMISTRIES
CYTOCHEMISTRY
CYTOCHROME
CYTOCHROMES
CYTOGENETIC
CYTOGENETICAL
CYTOGENETICALLY
CYTOGENETICIST
CYTOGENETICISTS
CYTOGENETICS
CYTOGENIES
CYTOGENY
CYTOKINE
CYTOKINES
CYTOKINESES
CYTOKINESIS
CYTOKINETIC
CYTOKININ
CYTOKININS
CYTOLOGIC
CYTOLOGICAL
CYTOLOGICALLY
CYTOLOGIES
CYTOLOGIST
CYTOLOGISTS
CYTOLOGY
CYTOLYSES
CYTOLYSIN
CYTOLYSINS
CYTOLYSIS
CYTOLYTIC
CYTOMEGALIC
CYTOMEGALOVIRUS
CYTOMEMBRANE
CYTOMEMBRANES
CYTON
CYTONS
CYTOPATHIC
CYTOPATHOGENIC
CYTOPATHOLOGIES
CYTOPATHOLOGIST
CYTOPATHOLOGY
CYTOPHILIC
CYTOPHOTOMETRIC
CYTOPHOTOMETRY
CYTOPLASM
CYTOPLASMIC
CYTOPLASMICALLY
CYTOPLASMS
CYTOPLAST
CYTOPLASTS
CYTOSINE
CYTOSINES
CYTOSKELETAL
CYTOSKELETON
CYTOSKELETONS
CYTOSOL
CYTOSOLIC
CYTOSOLS
CYTOSTATIC
CYTOSTATICALLY
CYTOSTATICS
CYTOTAXONOMIC
CYTOTAXONOMIES
CYTOTAXONOMY
CYTOTECHNOLOGY
CYTOTOXIC
CYTOTOXICITIES
CYTOTOXICITY
CYTOTOXIN
CYTOTOXINS
CZAR
CZARDAS
CZARDASES
CZARDOM
CZARDOMS
CZAREVITCH
CZAREVITCHES
CZAREVNA
CZAREVNAS
CZARINA
CZARINAS
CZARISM
CZARISMS
CZARIST
CZARISTS
CZARITZA
CZARITZAS
CZARS

D

DA
DAB
DABBED
DABBER
DABBERS
DABBING
DABBLE
DABBLED
DABBLER
DABBLERS
DABBLES
DABBLING
DABBLINGS
DABCHICK
DABCHICKS
DABS
DABSTER
DABSTERS
DACE
DACES
DACHA
DACHAS
DACHSHUND
DACHSHUNDS
DACITE
DACITES
DACKER
DACKERED
DACKERING
DACKERS
DACOIT
DACOITIES
DACOITS
DACOITY
DACQUOISE
DACQUOISES
DACRON
DACRONS
DACTYL
DACTYLI

DACTYLIC
DACTYLICS
DACTYLOLOGIES
DACTYLOLOGY
DACTYLS
DACTYLUS
DAD
DADA
DADAISM
DADAISMS
DADAIST
DADAISTIC
DADAISTS
DADAS
DADDIES
DADDLE
DADDLED
DADDLES
DADDLING
DADDY
DADGUM
DADO
DADOED
DADOES
DADOING
DADOS
DADS
DAEDAL
DAEDALEAN
DAEDALIAN
DAEMON
DAEMONES
DAEMONIC
DAEMONS
DAFF
DAFFED
DAFFIER
DAFFIEST
DAFFILY
DAFFINESS
DAFFINESSES
DAFFING
DAFFODIL
DAFFODILS
DAFFS
DAFFY
DAFT
DAFTER
DAFTEST
DAFTLY
DAFTNESS
DAFTNESSES
DAG
DAGGA
DAGGAS
DAGGER
DAGGERBOARD
DAGGERBOARDS
DAGGERED
DAGGERING
DAGGERLIKE
DAGGERS
DAGGLE
DAGGLED
DAGGLES
DAGGLING
DAGLOCK
DAGLOCKS
DAGO
DAGOBA
DAGOBAS
DAGOES
DAGOS
DAGS
DAGUERREOTYPE
DAGUERREOTYPED
DAGUERREOTYPES
DAGUERREOTYPIES
DAGUERREOTYPING
DAGUERREOTYPIST
DAGUERREOTYPY
DAGWOOD
DAGWOODS
DAH
DAHABEAH
DAHABEAHS
DAHABIAH
DAHABIAHS
DAHABIEH
DAHABIEHS
DAHABIYA
DAHABIYAS
DAHL
DAHLIA
DAHLIAS
DAHLS
DAHOON
DAHOONS
DAHS
DAIDZEIN
DAIDZEINS
DAIKER
DAIKERED
DAIKERING
DAIKERS
DAIKON
DAIKONS
DAILIES
DAILINESS
DAILINESSES
DAILY
DAILYNESS
DAILYNESSES
DAIMEN
DAIMIO
DAIMIOS
DAIMON
DAIMONES
DAIMONIC
DAIMONS
DAIMYO
DAIMYOS
DAINTIER
DAINTIES
DAINTIEST
DAINTILY
DAINTINESS
DAINTINESSES
DAINTY
DAIQUIRI
DAIQUIRIS
DAIRIES
DAIRY
DAIRYING
DAIRYINGS
DAIRYMAID
DAIRYMAIDS
DAIRYMAN
DAIRYMEN
DAIS
DAISES
DAISHIKI
DAISHIKIS
DAISIED
DAISIES
DAISY
DAK
DAKERHEN
DAKERHENS
DAKOIT
DAKOITIES
DAKOITS
DAKOITY
DAKS
DAL
DALAPON
DALAPONS
DALASI
DALASIS
DALE
DALEDH
DALEDHS
DALES
DALESMAN
DALESMEN
DALETH
DALETHS
DALLES
DALLIANCE
DALLIANCES
DALLIED
DALLIER
DALLIERS
DALLIES
DALLY
DALLYING
DALMATIAN
DALMATIANS
DALMATIC
DALMATICS
DALS
DALTON
DALTONIAN
DALTONIC
DALTONISM
DALTONISMS
DALTONS
DAM
DAMAGE
DAMAGEABILITIES
DAMAGEABILITY
DAMAGED
DAMAGER
DAMAGERS
DAMAGES
DAMAGING
DAMAGINGLY
DAMAN
DAMANS
DAMAR
DAMARS
DAMASCENE
DAMASCENED
DAMASCENES
DAMASCENING
DAMASK
DAMASKED
DAMASKEEN
DAMASKEENED
DAMASKEENING
DAMASKEENS
DAMASKING
DAMASKS
DAME
DAMES
DAMEWORT
DAMEWORTS
DAMFOOL
DAMFOOLS
DAMIANA
DAMIANAS
DAMMAR
DAMMARS
DAMMED
DAMMER
DAMMERS
DAMMING
DAMMIT
DAMN
DAMNABLE
DAMNABLENESS
DAMNABLENESSES
DAMNABLY
DAMNATION
DAMNATIONS
DAMNATORY
DAMNDEST
DAMNDESTS
DAMNED
DAMNEDER
DAMNEDEST
DAMNEDESTS
DAMNER
DAMNERS
DAMNEST
DAMNESTS
DAMNIFIED
DAMNIFIES
DAMNIFY
DAMNIFYING
DAMNING
DAMNINGLY
DAMNS
DAMOSEL
DAMOSELS
DAMOZEL
DAMOZELS
DAMP
DAMPED
DAMPEN
DAMPENED
DAMPENER
DAMPENERS
DAMPENING
DAMPENS

DAMPER
DAMPERS
DAMPEST
DAMPING
DAMPINGS
DAMPISH
DAMPLY
DAMPNESS
DAMPNESSES
DAMPS
DAMS
DAMSEL
DAMSELFISH
DAMSELFISHES
DAMSELFLIES
DAMSELFLY
DAMSELS
DAMSON
DAMSONS
DAN
DANAZOL
DANAZOLS
DANCE
DANCEABLE
DANCED
DANCER
DANCERS
DANCES
DANCEY
DANCIER
DANCIEST
DANCING
DANDELION
DANDELIONS
DANDER
DANDERED
DANDERING
DANDERS
DANDIACAL
DANDIER
DANDIES
DANDIEST
DANDIFICATION
DANDIFICATIONS
DANDIFIED
DANDIFIES
DANDIFY
DANDIFYING
DANDILY
DANDLE
DANDLED
DANDLER
DANDLERS
DANDLES
DANDLING
DANDRIFF
DANDRIFFS
DANDRUFF
DANDRUFFS
DANDRUFFY
DANDY
DANDYISH
DANDYISHLY
DANDYISM
DANDYISMS
DANEGELD
DANEGELDS
DANEGELT
DANEGELTS
DANEWEED
DANEWEEDS
DANEWORT
DANEWORTS
DANG
DANGED
DANGER
DANGERED
DANGERING
DANGEROUS
DANGEROUSLY
DANGEROUSNESS
DANGEROUSNESSES
DANGERS
DANGEST
DANGING
DANGLE
DANGLED
DANGLER
DANGLERS
DANGLES
DANGLIER
DANGLIEST
DANGLING
DANGLY
DANGS
DANIO
DANIOS
DANISH
DANISHES
DANK
DANKER
DANKEST
DANKLY
DANKNESS
DANKNESSES
DANS
DANSAK
DANSAKS
DANSEUR
DANSEURS
DANSEUSE
DANSEUSES
DAP
DAPHNE
DAPHNES
DAPHNIA
DAPHNIAS
DAPPED
DAPPER
DAPPERER
DAPPEREST
DAPPERLY
DAPPERNESS
DAPPERNESSES
DAPPING
DAPPLE
DAPPLED
DAPPLES
DAPPLING
DAPS
DAPSONE
DAPSONES
DARB
DARBAR
DARBARS
DARBIES
DARBS
DARE
DARED
DAREDEVIL
DAREDEVILRIES
DAREDEVILRY
DAREDEVILS
DAREDEVILTRIES
DAREDEVILTRY
DAREFUL
DARER
DARERS
DARES
DARESAY
DARIC
DARICS
DARING
DARINGLY
DARINGNESS
DARINGNESSES
DARINGS
DARIOLE
DARIOLES
DARK
DARKED
DARKEN
DARKENED
DARKENER
DARKENERS
DARKENING
DARKENS
DARKER
DARKEST
DARKEY
DARKEYS
DARKIE
DARKIES
DARKING
DARKISH
DARKLE
DARKLED
DARKLES
DARKLIER
DARKLIEST
DARKLING
DARKLINGS
DARKLY
DARKNESS
DARKNESSES
DARKROOM
DARKROOMS
DARKS
DARKSOME
DARKY
DARLING
DARLINGLY
DARLINGNESS
DARLINGNESSES
DARLINGS
DARMSTADTIUM
DARMSTADTIUMS
DARN
DARNATION
DARNATIONS
DARNDEST
DARNDESTS
DARNED
DARNEDER
DARNEDEST
DARNEDESTS
DARNEL
DARNELS
DARNER
DARNERS
DARNEST
DARNESTS
DARNING
DARNINGS
DARNS
DARSHAN
DARSHANS
DART
DARTBOARD
DARTBOARDS
DARTED
DARTER
DARTERS
DARTING
DARTINGLY
DARTLE
DARTLED
DARTLES
DARTLING
DARTS
DAS
DASH
DASHBOARD
DASHBOARDS
DASHED
DASHEEN
DASHEENS
DASHER
DASHERS
DASHES
DASHI
DASHIER
DASHIEST
DASHIKI
DASHIKIS
DASHING
DASHINGLY
DASHIS
DASHPOT
DASHPOTS
DASHY
DASSIE
DASSIES
DASTARD
DASTARDLINESS
DASTARDLINESSES
DASTARDLY
DASTARDS
DASYMETER
DASYMETERS
DASYURE
DASYURES
DATA
DATABANK
DATABANKS

DATABASE
DATABASED
DATABASES
DATABASING
DATABLE
DATARIES
DATARY
DATCHA
DATCHAS
DATE
DATEABLE
DATEBOOK
DATEBOOKS
DATED
DATEDLY
DATEDNESS
DATEDNESSES
DATELESS
DATELINE
DATELINED
DATELINES
DATELINING
DATER
DATERS
DATES
DATING
DATINGS
DATIVAL
DATIVE
DATIVELY
DATIVES
DATO
DATOS
DATTO
DATTOS
DATUM
DATUMS
DATURA
DATURAS
DATURIC
DAUB
DAUBE
DAUBED
DAUBER
DAUBERIES
DAUBERS
DAUBERY
DAUBES
DAUBIER
DAUBIEST
DAUBING
DAUBINGLY
DAUBRIES
DAUBRY
DAUBS
DAUBY
DAUGHTER
DAUGHTERLESS
DAUGHTERLY
DAUGHTERS
DAUNDER
DAUNDERED
DAUNDERING
DAUNDERS
DAUNOMYCIN
DAUNOMYCINS
DAUNORUBICIN
DAUNORUBICINS
DAUNT
DAUNTED
DAUNTER
DAUNTERS
DAUNTING
DAUNTINGLY
DAUNTLESS
DAUNTLESSLY
DAUNTLESSNESS
DAUNTLESSNESSES
DAUNTS
DAUPHIN
DAUPHINE
DAUPHINES
DAUPHINS
DAUT
DAUTED
DAUTIE
DAUTIES
DAUTING
DAUTS
DAVEN
DAVENED
DAVENING
DAVENPORT
DAVENPORTS
DAVENS
DAVIES
DAVIT
DAVITS
DAVY
DAW
DAWDLE
DAWDLED
DAWDLER
DAWDLERS
DAWDLES
DAWDLING
DAWED
DAWEN
DAWING
DAWK
DAWKS
DAWN
DAWNED
DAWNING
DAWNINGS
DAWNLIKE
DAWNS
DAWS
DAWSONITE
DAWSONITES
DAWT
DAWTED
DAWTIE
DAWTIES
DAWTING
DAWTS
DAY
DAYBED
DAYBEDS
DAYBOOK
DAYBOOKS
DAYBREAK
DAYBREAKS
DAYCARE
DAYCARES
DAYDREAM
DAYDREAMED
DAYDREAMER
DAYDREAMERS
DAYDREAMING
DAYDREAMLIKE
DAYDREAMS
DAYDREAMT
DAYDREAMY
DAYFLIES
DAYFLOWER
DAYFLOWERS
DAYFLY
DAYGLOW
DAYGLOWS
DAYLIGHT
DAYLIGHTED
DAYLIGHTING
DAYLIGHTINGS
DAYLIGHTS
DAYLILIES
DAYLILY
DAYLIT
DAYLONG
DAYMARE
DAYMARES
DAYPACK
DAYPACKS
DAYROOM
DAYROOMS
DAYS
DAYSAIL
DAYSAILED
DAYSAILING
DAYSAILS
DAYSIDE
DAYSIDES
DAYSMAN
DAYSMEN
DAYSPRING
DAYSPRINGS
DAYSTAR
DAYSTARS
DAYTIME
DAYTIMES
DAYWEAR
DAYWORK
DAYWORKER
DAYWORKERS
DAYWORKS
DAZE
DAZED
DAZEDLY
DAZEDNESS
DAZEDNESSES
DAZES
DAZING
DAZZLE
DAZZLED
DAZZLER
DAZZLERS
DAZZLES
DAZZLING
DAZZLINGLY
DE
DEACCESSION
DEACCESSIONS
DEACIDIFICATION
DEACIDIFIED
DEACIDIFIES
DEACIDIFY
DEACIDIFYING
DEACON
DEACONED
DEACONESS
DEACONESSES
DEACONING
DEACONRIES
DEACONRY
DEACONS
DEACTIVATE
DEACTIVATED
DEACTIVATES
DEACTIVATING
DEACTIVATION
DEACTIVATIONS
DEACTIVATOR
DEACTIVATORS
DEAD
DEADBEAT
DEADBEATS
DEADBOLT
DEADBOLTS
DEADEN
DEADENED
DEADENER
DEADENERS
DEADENING
DEADENINGLY
DEADENINGS
DEADENS
DEADER
DEADEST
DEADEYE
DEADEYES
DEADFALL
DEADFALLS
DEADHEAD
DEADHEADED
DEADHEADING
DEADHEADS
DEADLIER
DEADLIEST
DEADLIFT
DEADLIFTED
DEADLIFTING
DEADLIFTS
DEADLIGHT
DEADLIGHTS
DEADLINE
DEADLINED
DEADLINES
DEADLINESS
DEADLINESSES
DEADLINING
DEADLOCK
DEADLOCKED
DEADLOCKING
DEADLOCKS
DEADLY

DEADMAN
DEADMEN
DEADNESS
DEADNESSES
DEADPAN
DEADPANNED
DEADPANNER
DEADPANNERS
DEADPANNING
DEADPANS
DEADS
DEADWEIGHT
DEADWEIGHTS
DEADWOOD
DEADWOODS
DEAERATE
DEAERATED
DEAERATES
DEAERATING
DEAERATION
DEAERATIONS
DEAERATOR
DEAERATORS
DEAF
DEAFEN
DEAFENED
DEAFENING
DEAFENINGLY
DEAFENINGS
DEAFENS
DEAFER
DEAFEST
DEAFISH
DEAFLY
DEAFNESS
DEAFNESSES
DEAIR
DEAIRED
DEAIRING
DEAIRS
DEAL
DEALATE
DEALATED
DEALATES
DEALATION
DEALATIONS
DEALER
DEALERS
DEALERSHIP
DEALERSHIPS
DEALFISH
DEALFISHES
DEALIGN
DEALIGNED
DEALIGNING
DEALIGNS
DEALING
DEALINGS
DEALS
DEALT
DEAMINASE
DEAMINASES
DEAMINATE
DEAMINATED
DEAMINATES
DEAMINATING
DEAMINATION
DEAMINATIONS
DEAMINIZE
DEAMINIZED
DEAMINIZES
DEAMINIZING
DEAN
DEANED
DEANERIES
DEANERY
DEANING
DEANS
DEANSHIP
DEANSHIPS
DEAR
DEARER
DEAREST
DEARESTS
DEARIE
DEARIES
DEARLY
DEARNESS
DEARNESSES
DEARS
DEARTH
DEARTHS
DEARY
DEASH
DEASHED
DEASHES
DEASHING
DEASIL
DEATH
DEATHBED
DEATHBEDS
DEATHBLOW
DEATHBLOWS
DEATHCARE
DEATHCARES
DEATHCUP
DEATHCUPS
DEATHFUL
DEATHLESS
DEATHLESSLY
DEATHLESSNESS
DEATHLESSNESSES
DEATHLIER
DEATHLIEST
DEATHLIKE
DEATHLY
DEATHS
DEATHSMAN
DEATHSMEN
DEATHTRAP
DEATHTRAPS
DEATHWATCH
DEATHWATCHES
DEATHY
DEAVE
DEAVED
DEAVES
DEAVING
DEB
DEBACLE
DEBACLES
DEBAG
DEBAGGED
DEBAGGING
DEBAGS
DEBAR
DEBARK
DEBARKATION
DEBARKATIONS
DEBARKED
DEBARKER
DEBARKERS
DEBARKING
DEBARKS
DEBARMENT
DEBARMENTS
DEBARRED
DEBARRING
DEBARS
DEBASE
DEBASED
DEBASEMENT
DEBASEMENTS
DEBASER
DEBASERS
DEBASES
DEBASING
DEBATABLE
DEBATABLY
DEBATE
DEBATED
DEBATEMENT
DEBATEMENTS
DEBATER
DEBATERS
DEBATES
DEBATING
DEBAUCH
DEBAUCHED
DEBAUCHEE
DEBAUCHEES
DEBAUCHER
DEBAUCHERIES
DEBAUCHERS
DEBAUCHERY
DEBAUCHES
DEBAUCHING
DEBEAK
DEBEAKED
DEBEAKING
DEBEAKS
DEBEARD
DEBEARDED
DEBEARDING
DEBEARDS
DEBENTURE
DEBENTURES
DEBILITATE
DEBILITATED
DEBILITATES
DEBILITATING
DEBILITATION
DEBILITATIONS
DEBILITIES
DEBILITY
DEBIT
DEBITED
DEBITING
DEBITS
DEBONAIR
DEBONAIRE
DEBONAIRLY
DEBONAIRNESS
DEBONAIRNESSES
DEBONE
DEBONED
DEBONER
DEBONERS
DEBONES
DEBONING
DEBOUCH
DEBOUCHE
DEBOUCHED
DEBOUCHES
DEBOUCHING
DEBOUCHMENT
DEBOUCHMENTS
DEBRIDE
DEBRIDED
DEBRIDEMENT
DEBRIDEMENTS
DEBRIDES
DEBRIDING
DEBRIEF
DEBRIEFED
DEBRIEFER
DEBRIEFERS
DEBRIEFING
DEBRIEFS
DEBRIS
DEBRUISE
DEBRUISED
DEBRUISES
DEBRUISING
DEBS
DEBT
DEBTLESS
DEBTOR
DEBTORS
DEBTS
DEBUG
DEBUGGED
DEBUGGER
DEBUGGERS
DEBUGGING
DEBUGS
DEBUNK
DEBUNKED
DEBUNKER
DEBUNKERS
DEBUNKING
DEBUNKS
DEBUR
DEBURR
DEBURRED
DEBURRING
DEBURRS
DEBURS
DEBUT
DEBUTANT
DEBUTANTE
DEBUTANTES
DEBUTANTS
DEBUTED
DEBUTING

DEBUTS
DEBYE
DEBYES
DECADAL
DECADE
DECADELONG
DECADENCE
DECADENCES
DECADENCIES
DECADENCY
DECADENT
DECADENTLY
DECADENTS
DECADES
DECAF
DECAFFEINATED
DECAFS
DECAGON
DECAGONAL
DECAGONS
DECAGRAM
DECAGRAMS
DECAHEDRA
DECAHEDRON
DECAHEDRONS
DECAL
DECALCIFICATION
DECALCIFIED
DECALCIFIES
DECALCIFY
DECALCIFYING
DECALCOMANIA
DECALCOMANIAS
DECALITER
DECALITERS
DECALOG
DECALOGS
DECALOGUE
DECALOGUES
DECALS
DECAMETER
DECAMETERS
DECAMETHONIUM
DECAMETHONIUMS
DECAMETRIC
DECAMP
DECAMPED
DECAMPING
DECAMPMENT
DECAMPMENTS
DECAMPS
DECAN
DECANAI
DECANAL
DECANE
DECANES
DECANI
DECANS
DECANT
DECANTATION
DECANTATIONS
DECANTED
DECANTER
DECANTERS
DECANTING
DECANTS
DECAPITATE
DECAPITATED
DECAPITATES
DECAPITATING
DECAPITATION
DECAPITATIONS
DECAPITATOR
DECAPITATORS
DECAPOD
DECAPODAL
DECAPODAN
DECAPODANS
DECAPODOUS
DECAPODS
DECARBONATE
DECARBONATED
DECARBONATES
DECARBONATING
DECARBONATION
DECARBONATIONS
DECARBONIZE
DECARBONIZED
DECARBONIZER
DECARBONIZERS
DECARBONIZES
DECARBONIZING
DECARBOXYLASE
DECARBOXYLASES
DECARBOXYLATE
DECARBOXYLATED
DECARBOXYLATES
DECARBOXYLATING
DECARBOXYLATION
DECARBURIZATION
DECARBURIZE
DECARBURIZED
DECARBURIZES
DECARBURIZING
DECARE
DECARES
DECASUALIZATION
DECASYLLABIC
DECASYLLABICS
DECASYLLABLE
DECASYLLABLES
DECATHLETE
DECATHLETES
DECATHLON
DECATHLONS
DECAY
DECAYABLE
DECAYED
DECAYER
DECAYERS
DECAYING
DECAYLESS
DECAYS
DECEASE
DECEASED
DECEASEDS
DECEASES
DECEASING
DECEDENT
DECEDENTS
DECEIT
DECEITFUL
DECEITFULLY
DECEITFULNESS
DECEITFULNESSES
DECEITS
DECEIVABLE
DECEIVE
DECEIVED
DECEIVER
DECEIVERS
DECEIVES
DECEIVING
DECEIVINGLY
DECELERATE
DECELERATED
DECELERATES
DECELERATING
DECELERATION
DECELERATIONS
DECELERATOR
DECELERATORS
DECELERON
DECELERONS
DECEMVIR
DECEMVIRAL
DECEMVIRATE
DECEMVIRATES
DECEMVIRI
DECEMVIRS
DECENARIES
DECENARY
DECENCIES
DECENCY
DECENNARIES
DECENNARY
DECENNIA
DECENNIAL
DECENNIALLY
DECENNIALS
DECENNIUM
DECENNIUMS
DECENT
DECENTER
DECENTERED
DECENTERING
DECENTERINGS
DECENTERS
DECENTEST
DECENTLY
DECENTRALISE
DECENTRALISED
DECENTRALISES
DECENTRALISING
DECENTRALIZE
DECENTRALIZED
DECENTRALIZES
DECENTRALIZING
DECENTRE
DECENTRED
DECENTRES
DECENTRING
DECEPTION
DECEPTIONAL
DECEPTIONS
DECEPTIVE
DECEPTIVELY
DECEPTIVENESS
DECEPTIVENESSES
DECEREBRATE
DECEREBRATED
DECEREBRATES
DECEREBRATING
DECEREBRATION
DECEREBRATIONS
DECERN
DECERNED
DECERNING
DECERNS
DECERTIFICATION
DECERTIFIED
DECERTIFIES
DECERTIFY
DECERTIFYING
DECHLORINATE
DECHLORINATED
DECHLORINATES
DECHLORINATING
DECHLORINATION
DECHLORINATIONS
DECIARE
DECIARES
DECIBEL
DECIBELS
DECIDABILITIES
DECIDABILITY
DECIDABLE
DECIDE
DECIDED
DECIDEDLY
DECIDEDNESS
DECIDEDNESSES
DECIDER
DECIDERS
DECIDES
DECIDING
DECIDUA
DECIDUAE
DECIDUAL
DECIDUAS
DECIDUATE
DECIDUOUS
DECIDUOUSNESS
DECIDUOUSNESSES
DECIGRAM
DECIGRAMS
DECILE
DECILES
DECILITER
DECILITERS
DECILITRE
DECILITRES
DECILLION
DECILLIONS
DECIMAL
DECIMALISATION
DECIMALISATIONS
DECIMALIZATION
DECIMALIZATIONS
DECIMALIZE
DECIMALIZED
DECIMALIZES
DECIMALIZING
DECIMALLY
DECIMALS

DECIMATE
DECIMATED
DECIMATES
DECIMATING
DECIMATION
DECIMATIONS
DECIMATOR
DECIMATORS
DECIMETER
DECIMETERS
DECIMETRE
DECIMETRES
DECIPHER
DECIPHERABLE
DECIPHERED
DECIPHERER
DECIPHERERS
DECIPHERING
DECIPHERMENT
DECIPHERMENTS
DECIPHERS
DECISION
DECISIONAL
DECISIONED
DECISIONING
DECISIONS
DECISIVE
DECISIVELY
DECISIVENESS
DECISIVENESSES
DECK
DECKED
DECKEL
DECKELS
DECKER
DECKERS
DECKHAND
DECKHANDS
DECKHOUSE
DECKHOUSES
DECKING
DECKINGS
DECKLE
DECKLES
DECKLESS
DECKS
DECLAIM
DECLAIMED
DECLAIMER
DECLAIMERS
DECLAIMING
DECLAIMS
DECLAMATION
DECLAMATIONS
DECLAMATORY
DECLARABLE
DECLARANT
DECLARANTS
DECLARATION
DECLARATIONS
DECLARATIVE
DECLARATIVELY
DECLARATORY
DECLARE
DECLARED
DECLARER
DECLARERS
DECLARES
DECLARING
DECLASS
DECLASSE
DECLASSED
DECLASSES
DECLASSIFIED
DECLASSIFIES
DECLASSIFY
DECLASSIFYING
DECLASSING
DECLAW
DECLAWED
DECLAWING
DECLAWS
DECLENSION
DECLENSIONAL
DECLENSIONS
DECLINABLE
DECLINATION
DECLINATIONAL
DECLINATIONS
DECLINE
DECLINED
DECLINER
DECLINERS
DECLINES
DECLINING
DECLINIST
DECLINISTS
DECLIVITIES
DECLIVITOUS
DECLIVITY
DECLUTCH
DECLUTCHED
DECLUTCHES
DECLUTCHING
DECO
DECOCT
DECOCTED
DECOCTING
DECOCTION
DECOCTIONS
DECOCTIVE
DECOCTS
DECODE
DECODED
DECODER
DECODERS
DECODES
DECODING
DECOLLATE
DECOLLATED
DECOLLATES
DECOLLATING
DECOLLATION
DECOLLATIONS
DECOLLETAGE
DECOLLETAGES
DECOLLETE
DECOLLETES
DECOLONISATION
DECOLONISATIONS
DECOLONIZATION
DECOLONIZATIONS
DECOLONIZE
DECOLONIZED
DECOLONIZES
DECOLONIZING
DECOLOR
DECOLORED
DECOLORING
DECOLORIZATION
DECOLORIZATIONS
DECOLORIZE
DECOLORIZED
DECOLORIZER
DECOLORIZERS
DECOLORIZES
DECOLORIZING
DECOLORS
DECOLOUR
DECOLOURED
DECOLOURING
DECOLOURS
DECOMMISSION
DECOMMISSIONED
DECOMMISSIONING
DECOMMISSIONS
DECOMPENSATE
DECOMPENSATED
DECOMPENSATES
DECOMPENSATING
DECOMPENSATION
DECOMPENSATIONS
DECOMPOSABILITY
DECOMPOSABLE
DECOMPOSE
DECOMPOSED
DECOMPOSER
DECOMPOSERS
DECOMPOSES
DECOMPOSING
DECOMPOSITION
DECOMPOSITIONS
DECOMPOUND
DECOMPRESS
DECOMPRESSED
DECOMPRESSES
DECOMPRESSING
DECOMPRESSION
DECOMPRESSIONS
DECONCENTRATE
DECONCENTRATED
DECONCENTRATES
DECONCENTRATING
DECONCENTRATION
DECONDITION
DECONDITIONED
DECONDITIONING
DECONDITIONS
DECONGEST
DECONGESTANT
DECONGESTANTS
DECONGESTED
DECONGESTING
DECONGESTION
DECONGESTIONS
DECONGESTIVE
DECONGESTS
DECONSECRATE
DECONSECRATED
DECONSECRATES
DECONSECRATING
DECONSECRATION
DECONSECRATIONS
DECONSTRUCT
DECONSTRUCTED
DECONSTRUCTING
DECONSTRUCTION
DECONSTRUCTIONS
DECONSTRUCTIVE
DECONSTRUCTOR
DECONSTRUCTORS
DECONSTRUCTS
DECONTAMINATE
DECONTAMINATED
DECONTAMINATES
DECONTAMINATING
DECONTAMINATION
DECONTAMINATOR
DECONTAMINATORS
DECONTEXTUALIZE
DECONTROL
DECONTROLLED
DECONTROLLING
DECONTROLS
DECOR
DECORATE
DECORATED
DECORATES
DECORATING
DECORATION
DECORATIONS
DECORATIVE
DECORATIVELY
DECORATIVENESS
DECORATOR
DECORATORS
DECOROUS
DECOROUSLY
DECOROUSNESS
DECOROUSNESSES
DECORS
DECORTICATE
DECORTICATED
DECORTICATES
DECORTICATING
DECORTICATION
DECORTICATIONS
DECORTICATOR
DECORTICATORS
DECORUM
DECORUMS
DECOS
DECOUPAGE
DECOUPAGED
DECOUPAGES
DECOUPAGING
DECOUPLE
DECOUPLED
DECOUPLER
DECOUPLERS
DECOUPLES
DECOUPLING
DECOY
DECOYED
DECOYER

DECOYERS
DECOYING
DECOYS
DECREASE
DECREASED
DECREASES
DECREASING
DECREASINGLY
DECREE
DECREED
DECREEING
DECREER
DECREERS
DECREES
DECREMENT
DECREMENTAL
DECREMENTS
DECREPIT
DECREPITATE
DECREPITATED
DECREPITATES
DECREPITATING
DECREPITATION
DECREPITATIONS
DECREPITLY
DECREPITUDE
DECREPITUDES
DECRESCENDO
DECRESCENDOS
DECRESCENT
DECRETAL
DECRETALS
DECRETIVE
DECRETORY
DECRIAL
DECRIALS
DECRIED
DECRIER
DECRIERS
DECRIES
DECRIMINALISE
DECRIMINALISED
DECRIMINALISES
DECRIMINALISING
DECRIMINALIZE
DECRIMINALIZED
DECRIMINALIZES
DECRIMINALIZING
DECROWN
DECROWNED
DECROWNING
DECROWNS
DECRY
DECRYING
DECRYPT
DECRYPTED
DECRYPTING
DECRYPTION
DECRYPTIONS
DECRYPTS
DECUMAN
DECUMBENT
DECUPLE
DECUPLED
DECUPLES
DECUPLING
DECURIES
DECURION
DECURIONS
DECURRENT
DECURVE
DECURVED
DECURVES
DECURVING
DECURY
DECUSSATE
DECUSSATED
DECUSSATES
DECUSSATING
DECUSSATION
DECUSSATIONS
DEDAL
DEDANS
DEDENDA
DEDENDUM
DEDENDUMS
DEDICATE
DEDICATED
DEDICATEDLY
DEDICATEE
DEDICATEES
DEDICATES
DEDICATING
DEDICATION
DEDICATIONS
DEDICATOR
DEDICATORS
DEDICATORY
DEDIFFERENTIATE
DEDUCE
DEDUCED
DEDUCES
DEDUCIBLE
DEDUCIBLY
DEDUCING
DEDUCT
DEDUCTED
DEDUCTIBILITIES
DEDUCTIBILITY
DEDUCTIBLE
DEDUCTIBLES
DEDUCTING
DEDUCTION
DEDUCTIONS
DEDUCTIVE
DEDUCTIVELY
DEDUCTS
DEE
DEED
DEEDED
DEEDIER
DEEDIEST
DEEDING
DEEDLESS
DEEDS
DEEDY
DEEJAY
DEEJAYED
DEEJAYING
DEEJAYS
DEEM
DEEMED
DEEMING
DEEMS
DEEMSTER
DEEMSTERS
DEEP
DEEPEN
DEEPENED
DEEPENER
DEEPENERS
DEEPENING
DEEPENS
DEEPER
DEEPEST
DEEPFREEZE
DEEPFREEZES
DEEPFREEZING
DEEPFROZE
DEEPFROZEN
DEEPLY
DEEPNESS
DEEPNESSES
DEEPS
DEEPWATER
DEER
DEERBERRIES
DEERBERRY
DEERFLIES
DEERFLY
DEERHOUND
DEERHOUNDS
DEERLIKE
DEERS
DEERSKIN
DEERSKINS
DEERSTALKER
DEERSTALKERS
DEERWEED
DEERWEEDS
DEERYARD
DEERYARDS
DEES
DEET
DEETS
DEEWAN
DEEWANS
DEF
DEFACE
DEFACED
DEFACEMENT
DEFACEMENTS
DEFACER
DEFACERS
DEFACES
DEFACING
DEFALCATE
DEFALCATED
DEFALCATES
DEFALCATING
DEFALCATION
DEFALCATIONS
DEFALCATOR
DEFALCATORS
DEFAMATION
DEFAMATIONS
DEFAMATORY
DEFAME
DEFAMED
DEFAMER
DEFAMERS
DEFAMES
DEFAMILIARIZE
DEFAMILIARIZED
DEFAMILIARIZES
DEFAMILIARIZING
DEFAMING
DEFANG
DEFANGED
DEFANGING
DEFANGS
DEFAT
DEFATS
DEFATTED
DEFATTING
DEFAULT
DEFAULTED
DEFAULTER
DEFAULTERS
DEFAULTING
DEFAULTS
DEFEASANCE
DEFEASANCES
DEFEASIBILITIES
DEFEASIBILITY
DEFEASIBLE
DEFEAT
DEFEATABLE
DEFEATED
DEFEATER
DEFEATERS
DEFEATING
DEFEATISM
DEFEATISMS
DEFEATIST
DEFEATISTS
DEFEATS
DEFEATURE
DEFEATURES
DEFECATE
DEFECATED
DEFECATES
DEFECATING
DEFECATION
DEFECATIONS
DEFECATOR
DEFECATORS
DEFECT
DEFECTED
DEFECTING
DEFECTION
DEFECTIONS
DEFECTIVE
DEFECTIVELY
DEFECTIVENESS
DEFECTIVENESSES
DEFECTIVES
DEFECTOR
DEFECTORS
DEFECTS
DEFEMINIZATION
DEFEMINIZATIONS
DEFEMINIZE
DEFEMINIZED
DEFEMINIZES

DEFEMINIZING
DEFENCE
DEFENCED
DEFENCELESS
DEFENCEMAN
DEFENCEMEN
DEFENCES
DEFENCING
DEFEND
DEFENDABLE
DEFENDANT
DEFENDANTS
DEFENDED
DEFENDER
DEFENDERS
DEFENDING
DEFENDS
DEFENESTRATE
DEFENESTRATED
DEFENESTRATES
DEFENESTRATING
DEFENESTRATION
DEFENESTRATIONS
DEFENSE
DEFENSED
DEFENSELESS
DEFENSELESSLY
DEFENSELESSNESS
DEFENSEMAN
DEFENSEMEN
DEFENSES
DEFENSIBILITIES
DEFENSIBILITY
DEFENSIBLE
DEFENSIBLY
DEFENSING
DEFENSIVE
DEFENSIVELY
DEFENSIVENESS
DEFENSIVENESSES
DEFENSIVES
DEFER
DEFERENCE
DEFERENCES
DEFERENT
DEFERENTIAL
DEFERENTIALLY
DEFERENTS
DEFERMENT
DEFERMENTS
DEFERRABLE
DEFERRABLES
DEFERRAL
DEFERRALS
DEFERRED
DEFERRER
DEFERRERS
DEFERRING
DEFERS
DEFERVESCENCE
DEFERVESCENCES
DEFFER
DEFFEST
DEFI
DEFIANCE
DEFIANCES
DEFIANT
DEFIANTLY
DEFIBRILLATE
DEFIBRILLATED
DEFIBRILLATES
DEFIBRILLATING
DEFIBRILLATION
DEFIBRILLATIONS
DEFIBRILLATOR
DEFIBRILLATORS
DEFIBRINATE
DEFIBRINATED
DEFIBRINATES
DEFIBRINATING
DEFIBRINATION
DEFIBRINATIONS
DEFICIENCIES
DEFICIENCY
DEFICIENT
DEFICIENTLY
DEFICIENTS
DEFICIT
DEFICITS
DEFIED
DEFIER
DEFIERS
DEFIES
DEFILADE
DEFILADED
DEFILADES
DEFILADING
DEFILE
DEFILED
DEFILEMENT
DEFILEMENTS
DEFILER
DEFILERS
DEFILES
DEFILING
DEFINABLE
DEFINABLY
DEFINE
DEFINED
DEFINEMENT
DEFINEMENTS
DEFINER
DEFINERS
DEFINES
DEFINIENDA
DEFINIENDUM
DEFINIENS
DEFINIENTIA
DEFINING
DEFINITE
DEFINITELY
DEFINITENESS
DEFINITENESSES
DEFINITES
DEFINITION
DEFINITIONAL
DEFINITIONS
DEFINITIVE
DEFINITIVELY
DEFINITIVENESS
DEFINITIVES
DEFINITIZE
DEFINITIZED
DEFINITIZES
DEFINITIZING
DEFINITUDE
DEFINITUDES
DEFIS
DEFLAGRATE
DEFLAGRATED
DEFLAGRATES
DEFLAGRATING
DEFLAGRATION
DEFLAGRATIONS
DEFLATE
DEFLATED
DEFLATER
DEFLATERS
DEFLATES
DEFLATING
DEFLATION
DEFLATIONARY
DEFLATIONS
DEFLATOR
DEFLATORS
DEFLEA
DEFLEAED
DEFLEAING
DEFLEAS
DEFLECT
DEFLECTABLE
DEFLECTED
DEFLECTING
DEFLECTION
DEFLECTIONS
DEFLECTIVE
DEFLECTOR
DEFLECTORS
DEFLECTS
DEFLEXED
DEFLEXION
DEFLEXIONS
DEFLORATION
DEFLORATIONS
DEFLOWER
DEFLOWERED
DEFLOWERER
DEFLOWERERS
DEFLOWERING
DEFLOWERS
DEFOAM
DEFOAMED
DEFOAMER
DEFOAMERS
DEFOAMING
DEFOAMS
DEFOCUS
DEFOCUSED
DEFOCUSES
DEFOCUSING
DEFOCUSSED
DEFOCUSSES
DEFOCUSSING
DEFOG
DEFOGGED
DEFOGGER
DEFOGGERS
DEFOGGING
DEFOGS
DEFOLIANT
DEFOLIANTS
DEFOLIATE
DEFOLIATED
DEFOLIATES
DEFOLIATING
DEFOLIATION
DEFOLIATIONS
DEFOLIATOR
DEFOLIATORS
DEFORCE
DEFORCED
DEFORCEMENT
DEFORCEMENTS
DEFORCER
DEFORCERS
DEFORCES
DEFORCING
DEFOREST
DEFORESTATION
DEFORESTATIONS
DEFORESTED
DEFORESTING
DEFORESTS
DEFORM
DEFORMABLE
DEFORMALIZE
DEFORMALIZED
DEFORMALIZES
DEFORMALIZING
DEFORMATION
DEFORMATIONAL
DEFORMATIONS
DEFORMATIVE
DEFORMED
DEFORMER
DEFORMERS
DEFORMING
DEFORMITIES
DEFORMITY
DEFORMS
DEFRAG
DEFRAGGED
DEFRAGGER
DEFRAGGERS
DEFRAGGING
DEFRAGMENT
DEFRAGMENTATION
DEFRAGMENTED
DEFRAGMENTER
DEFRAGMENTERS
DEFRAGMENTING
DEFRAGMENTS
DEFRAGS
DEFRAUD
DEFRAUDED
DEFRAUDER
DEFRAUDERS
DEFRAUDING
DEFRAUDS
DEFRAY
DEFRAYABLE
DEFRAYAL
DEFRAYALS
DEFRAYED
DEFRAYER

DEFRAYERS
DEFRAYING
DEFRAYS
DEFRIEND
DEFRIENDED
DEFRIENDING
DEFRIENDS
DEFROCK
DEFROCKED
DEFROCKING
DEFROCKS
DEFROST
DEFROSTED
DEFROSTER
DEFROSTERS
DEFROSTING
DEFROSTS
DEFT
DEFTER
DEFTEST
DEFTLY
DEFTNESS
DEFTNESSES
DEFUEL
DEFUELED
DEFUELING
DEFUELLED
DEFUELLING
DEFUELS
DEFUNCT
DEFUND
DEFUNDED
DEFUNDING
DEFUNDS
DEFUSE
DEFUSED
DEFUSER
DEFUSERS
DEFUSES
DEFUSING
DEFUZE
DEFUZED
DEFUZES
DEFUZING
DEFY
DEFYING
DEGAGE
DEGAME
DEGAMES
DEGAMI
DEGAMIS
DEGAS
DEGASES
DEGASSED
DEGASSER
DEGASSERS
DEGASSES
DEGASSING
DEGAUSS
DEGAUSSED
DEGAUSSER
DEGAUSSERS
DEGAUSSES
DEGAUSSING
DEGAUSSINGS
DEGENDER
DEGENDERED
DEGENDERING
DEGENDERIZE
DEGENDERIZED
DEGENDERIZES
DEGENDERIZING
DEGENDERS
DEGENERACIES
DEGENERACY
DEGENERATE
DEGENERATED
DEGENERATELY
DEGENERATENESS
DEGENERATES
DEGENERATING
DEGENERATION
DEGENERATIONS
DEGENERATIVE
DEGERM
DEGERMED
DEGERMING
DEGERMS
DEGLACIATED
DEGLACIATION
DEGLACIATIONS
DEGLAMORIZATION
DEGLAMORIZE
DEGLAMORIZED
DEGLAMORIZES
DEGLAMORIZING
DEGLAZE
DEGLAZED
DEGLAZES
DEGLAZING
DEGLUTITION
DEGLUTITIONS
DEGRADABILITIES
DEGRADABILITY
DEGRADABLE
DEGRADATION
DEGRADATIONS
DEGRADATIVE
DEGRADE
DEGRADED
DEGRADEDLY
DEGRADER
DEGRADERS
DEGRADES
DEGRADING
DEGRADINGLY
DEGRANULATION
DEGRANULATIONS
DEGREASE
DEGREASED
DEGREASER
DEGREASERS
DEGREASES
DEGREASING
DEGREASINGS
DEGREE
DEGREED
DEGREES
DEGRESSIVE
DEGRESSIVELY
DEGRINGOLADE
DEGRINGOLADES
DEGUM
DEGUMMED
DEGUMMING
DEGUMS
DEGUST
DEGUSTATION
DEGUSTATIONS
DEGUSTED
DEGUSTING
DEGUSTS
DEHAIR
DEHAIRED
DEHAIRING
DEHAIRS
DEHISCE
DEHISCED
DEHISCENCE
DEHISCENCES
DEHISCENT
DEHISCES
DEHISCING
DEHORN
DEHORNED
DEHORNER
DEHORNERS
DEHORNING
DEHORNS
DEHORS
DEHORT
DEHORTED
DEHORTING
DEHORTS
DEHUMANISATION
DEHUMANISATIONS
DEHUMANISE
DEHUMANISED
DEHUMANISES
DEHUMANISING
DEHUMANIZATION
DEHUMANIZATIONS
DEHUMANIZE
DEHUMANIZED
DEHUMANIZES
DEHUMANIZING
DEHUMIDIFIED
DEHUMIDIFIER
DEHUMIDIFIERS
DEHUMIDIFIES
DEHUMIDIFY
DEHUMIDIFYING
DEHYDRATE
DEHYDRATED
DEHYDRATES
DEHYDRATING
DEHYDRATION
DEHYDRATIONS
DEHYDRATOR
DEHYDRATORS
DEHYDROGENASE
DEHYDROGENASES
DEHYDROGENATE
DEHYDROGENATED
DEHYDROGENATES
DEHYDROGENATING
DEHYDROGENATION
DEICE
DEICED
DEICER
DEICERS
DEICES
DEICIDAL
DEICIDE
DEICIDES
DEICING
DEICTIC
DEICTICS
DEIFIC
DEIFICAL
DEIFICATION
DEIFICATIONS
DEIFIED
DEIFIER
DEIFIERS
DEIFIES
DEIFORM
DEIFY
DEIFYING
DEIGN
DEIGNED
DEIGNING
DEIGNS
DEIL
DEILS
DEINDUSTRIALIZE
DEINONYCHUS
DEINONYCHUSES
DEIONISE
DEIONISED
DEIONISER
DEIONISERS
DEIONISES
DEIONISING
DEIONIZATION
DEIONIZATIONS
DEIONIZE
DEIONIZED
DEIONIZER
DEIONIZERS
DEIONIZES
DEIONIZING
DEISM
DEISMS
DEIST
DEISTIC
DEISTICAL
DEISTICALLY
DEISTS
DEITIES
DEITY
DEIXIS
DEIXISES
DEJECT
DEJECTA
DEJECTED
DEJECTEDLY
DEJECTEDNESS
DEJECTEDNESSES
DEJECTING
DEJECTION
DEJECTIONS
DEJECTS
DEJEUNER
DEJEUNERS

DEKAGRAM
DEKAGRAMS
DEKALITER
DEKALITERS
DEKALITRE
DEKALITRES
DEKAMETER
DEKAMETERS
DEKAMETRE
DEKAMETRES
DEKAMETRIC
DEKARE
DEKARES
DEKE
DEKED
DEKEING
DEKES
DEKING
DEKKO
DEKKOS
DEL
DELAINE
DELAINES
DELAMINATE
DELAMINATED
DELAMINATES
DELAMINATING
DELAMINATION
DELAMINATIONS
DELATE
DELATED
DELATES
DELATING
DELATION
DELATIONS
DELATOR
DELATORS
DELAY
DELAYABLE
DELAYED
DELAYER
DELAYERS
DELAYING
DELAYS
DELE
DELEAD
DELEADED
DELEADING
DELEADS
DELEAVE
DELEAVED
DELEAVES
DELEAVING
DELECTABILITIES
DELECTABILITY
DELECTABLE
DELECTABLES
DELECTABLY
DELECTATE
DELECTATED
DELECTATES
DELECTATING
DELECTATION
DELECTATIONS
DELED
DELEGABLE
DELEGACIES
DELEGACY
DELEGATE
DELEGATED
DELEGATEE
DELEGATEES
DELEGATES
DELEGATING
DELEGATION
DELEGATIONS
DELEGATOR
DELEGATORS
DELEGITIMATE
DELEGITIMATED
DELEGITIMATES
DELEGITIMATING
DELEGITIMATION
DELEGITIMATIONS
DELEGITIMIZE
DELEGITIMIZED
DELEGITIMIZES
DELEGITIMIZING
DELEING
DELES
DELETABLE
DELETE
DELETED
DELETERIOUS
DELETERIOUSLY
DELETERIOUSNESS
DELETES
DELETING
DELETION
DELETIONS
DELF
DELFS
DELFT
DELFTS
DELFTWARE
DELFTWARES
DELI
DELIBERATE
DELIBERATED
DELIBERATELY
DELIBERATENESS
DELIBERATES
DELIBERATING
DELIBERATION
DELIBERATIONS
DELIBERATIVE
DELIBERATIVELY
DELICACIES
DELICACY
DELICATE
DELICATELY
DELICATES
DELICATESSEN
DELICATESSENS
DELICIOUS
DELICIOUSLY
DELICIOUSNESS
DELICIOUSNESSES
DELICT
DELICTS
DELIGHT
DELIGHTED
DELIGHTEDLY
DELIGHTEDNESS
DELIGHTEDNESSES
DELIGHTER
DELIGHTERS
DELIGHTFUL
DELIGHTFULLY
DELIGHTFULNESS
DELIGHTING
DELIGHTS
DELIGHTSOME
DELIME
DELIMED
DELIMES
DELIMING
DELIMIT
DELIMITATION
DELIMITATIONS
DELIMITED
DELIMITER
DELIMITERS
DELIMITING
DELIMITS
DELINEATE
DELINEATED
DELINEATES
DELINEATING
DELINEATION
DELINEATIONS
DELINEATIVE
DELINEATOR
DELINEATORS
DELINK
DELINKED
DELINKING
DELINKS
DELINQUENCIES
DELINQUENCY
DELINQUENT
DELINQUENTLY
DELINQUENTS
DELIQUESCE
DELIQUESCED
DELIQUESCENCE
DELIQUESCENCES
DELIQUESCENT
DELIQUESCES
DELIQUESCING
DELIRIA
DELIRIOUS
DELIRIOUSLY
DELIRIOUSNESS
DELIRIOUSNESSES
DELIRIUM
DELIRIUMS
DELIS
DELISH
DELIST
DELISTED
DELISTING
DELISTS
DELIVER
DELIVERABILITY
DELIVERABLE
DELIVERANCE
DELIVERANCES
DELIVERED
DELIVERER
DELIVERERS
DELIVERIES
DELIVERING
DELIVERS
DELIVERY
DELIVERYMAN
DELIVERYMEN
DELL
DELLIES
DELLS
DELLY
DELOCALIZATION
DELOCALIZATIONS
DELOCALIZE
DELOCALIZED
DELOCALIZES
DELOCALIZING
DELOUSE
DELOUSED
DELOUSER
DELOUSERS
DELOUSES
DELOUSING
DELPHIC
DELPHICALLY
DELPHINIA
DELPHINIUM
DELPHINIUMS
DELS
DELT
DELTA
DELTAIC
DELTAS
DELTIC
DELTOID
DELTOIDEI
DELTOIDEUS
DELTOIDS
DELTS
DELUDE
DELUDED
DELUDER
DELUDERS
DELUDES
DELUDING
DELUGE
DELUGED
DELUGES
DELUGING
DELUSION
DELUSIONAL
DELUSIONARY
DELUSIONS
DELUSIVE
DELUSIVELY
DELUSIVENESS
DELUSIVENESSES
DELUSORY
DELUSTER
DELUSTERED
DELUSTERING
DELUSTERS
DELUXE
DELVE
DELVED

DELVER
DELVERS
DELVES
DELVING
DEMAGNETIZATION
DEMAGNETIZE
DEMAGNETIZED
DEMAGNETIZER
DEMAGNETIZERS
DEMAGNETIZES
DEMAGNETIZING
DEMAGOG
DEMAGOGED
DEMAGOGIC
DEMAGOGICALLY
DEMAGOGIES
DEMAGOGING
DEMAGOGS
DEMAGOGUE
DEMAGOGUED
DEMAGOGUERIES
DEMAGOGUERY
DEMAGOGUES
DEMAGOGUING
DEMAGOGY
DEMAND
DEMANDABLE
DEMANDANT
DEMANDANTS
DEMANDED
DEMANDER
DEMANDERS
DEMANDING
DEMANDINGLY
DEMANDINGNESS
DEMANDINGNESSES
DEMANDS
DEMANTOID
DEMANTOIDS
DEMARCATE
DEMARCATED
DEMARCATES
DEMARCATING
DEMARCATION
DEMARCATIONS
DEMARCHE
DEMARCHES
DEMARK
DEMARKED
DEMARKING
DEMARKS
DEMAST
DEMASTED
DEMASTING
DEMASTS
DEMATERIALIZE
DEMATERIALIZED
DEMATERIALIZES
DEMATERIALIZING
DEME
DEMEAN
DEMEANED
DEMEANING
DEMEANOR
DEMEANORS
DEMEANOUR
DEMEANOURS
DEMEANS
DEMENT
DEMENTED
DEMENTEDLY
DEMENTEDNESS
DEMENTEDNESSES
DEMENTI
DEMENTIA
DEMENTIAL
DEMENTIAS
DEMENTING
DEMENTIS
DEMENTS
DEMERARA
DEMERARAN
DEMERARAS
DEMERGE
DEMERGED
DEMERGER
DEMERGERED
DEMERGERING
DEMERGERS
DEMERGES
DEMERGING
DEMERIT
DEMERITED
DEMERITING
DEMERITS
DEMERSAL
DEMES
DEMESNE
DEMESNES
DEMETHYLATE
DEMETHYLATED
DEMETHYLATES
DEMETHYLATING
DEMETHYLATION
DEMETHYLATIONS
DEMETON
DEMETONS
DEMIC
DEMIES
DEMIGOD
DEMIGODDESS
DEMIGODDESSES
DEMIGODS
DEMIJOHN
DEMIJOHNS
DEMILITARISE
DEMILITARISED
DEMILITARISES
DEMILITARISING
DEMILITARIZE
DEMILITARIZED
DEMILITARIZES
DEMILITARIZING
DEMILUNE
DEMILUNES
DEMIMONDAINE
DEMIMONDAINES
DEMIMONDE
DEMIMONDES
DEMINER
DEMINERALIZE
DEMINERALIZED
DEMINERALIZER
DEMINERALIZERS
DEMINERALIZES
DEMINERALIZING
DEMINERS
DEMINING
DEMININGS
DEMIREP
DEMIREPS
DEMISABLE
DEMISE
DEMISED
DEMISEMIQUAVER
DEMISEMIQUAVERS
DEMISES
DEMISING
DEMISSION
DEMISSIONS
DEMIST
DEMISTED
DEMISTER
DEMISTERS
DEMISTING
DEMISTS
DEMIT
DEMITASSE
DEMITASSES
DEMITS
DEMITTED
DEMITTING
DEMIURGE
DEMIURGES
DEMIURGIC
DEMIURGICAL
DEMIVOLT
DEMIVOLTE
DEMIVOLTES
DEMIVOLTS
DEMIWORLD
DEMIWORLDS
DEMO
DEMOB
DEMOBBED
DEMOBBING
DEMOBILISATION
DEMOBILISATIONS
DEMOBILISE
DEMOBILISED
DEMOBILISES
DEMOBILISING
DEMOBILIZATION
DEMOBILIZATIONS
DEMOBILIZE
DEMOBILIZED
DEMOBILIZER
DEMOBILIZERS
DEMOBILIZES
DEMOBILIZING
DEMOBS
DEMOCRACIES
DEMOCRACY
DEMOCRAT
DEMOCRATIC
DEMOCRATICALLY
DEMOCRATISATION
DEMOCRATISE
DEMOCRATISED
DEMOCRATISES
DEMOCRATISING
DEMOCRATIZATION
DEMOCRATIZE
DEMOCRATIZED
DEMOCRATIZER
DEMOCRATIZERS
DEMOCRATIZES
DEMOCRATIZING
DEMOCRATS
DEMODE
DEMODED
DEMODULATE
DEMODULATED
DEMODULATES
DEMODULATING
DEMODULATION
DEMODULATIONS
DEMODULATOR
DEMODULATORS
DEMOED
DEMOGRAPHER
DEMOGRAPHERS
DEMOGRAPHIC
DEMOGRAPHICAL
DEMOGRAPHICALLY
DEMOGRAPHICS
DEMOGRAPHIES
DEMOGRAPHY
DEMOI
DEMOING
DEMOISELLE
DEMOISELLES
DEMOLISH
DEMOLISHED
DEMOLISHER
DEMOLISHERS
DEMOLISHES
DEMOLISHING
DEMOLISHMENT
DEMOLISHMENTS
DEMOLITION
DEMOLITIONIST
DEMOLITIONISTS
DEMOLITIONS
DEMON
DEMONESS
DEMONESSES
DEMONETIZATION
DEMONETIZATIONS
DEMONETIZE
DEMONETIZED
DEMONETIZES
DEMONETIZING
DEMONIAC
DEMONIACAL
DEMONIACALLY
DEMONIACS
DEMONIAN
DEMONIC
DEMONICAL
DEMONICALLY
DEMONISE
DEMONISED
DEMONISES
DEMONISING

DEMONISM
DEMONISMS
DEMONIST
DEMONISTS
DEMONIZATION
DEMONIZATIONS
DEMONIZE
DEMONIZED
DEMONIZES
DEMONIZING
DEMONOLOGICAL
DEMONOLOGIES
DEMONOLOGIST
DEMONOLOGISTS
DEMONOLOGY
DEMONS
DEMONSTRABILITY
DEMONSTRABLE
DEMONSTRABLY
DEMONSTRATE
DEMONSTRATED
DEMONSTRATES
DEMONSTRATING
DEMONSTRATION
DEMONSTRATIONAL
DEMONSTRATIONS
DEMONSTRATIVE
DEMONSTRATIVELY
DEMONSTRATIVES
DEMONSTRATOR
DEMONSTRATORS
DEMORALISE
DEMORALISED
DEMORALISES
DEMORALISING
DEMORALIZATION
DEMORALIZATIONS
DEMORALIZE
DEMORALIZED
DEMORALIZER
DEMORALIZERS
DEMORALIZES
DEMORALIZING
DEMORALIZINGLY
DEMOS
DEMOSES
DEMOTE
DEMOTED
DEMOTES
DEMOTIC
DEMOTICS
DEMOTING
DEMOTION
DEMOTIONS
DEMOTIST
DEMOTISTS
DEMOUNT
DEMOUNTABLE
DEMOUNTED
DEMOUNTING
DEMOUNTS
DEMPSTER
DEMPSTERS
DEMULCENT
DEMULCENTS
DEMULSIFIED
DEMULSIFIES
DEMULSIFY
DEMULSIFYING
DEMULTIPLEXER
DEMULTIPLEXERS
DEMUR
DEMURE
DEMURELY
DEMURENESS
DEMURENESSES
DEMURER
DEMUREST
DEMURRAGE
DEMURRAGES
DEMURRAL
DEMURRALS
DEMURRED
DEMURRER
DEMURRERS
DEMURRING
DEMURS
DEMY
DEMYELINATING
DEMYELINATION
DEMYELINATIONS
DEMYSTIFICATION
DEMYSTIFIED
DEMYSTIFIES
DEMYSTIFY
DEMYSTIFYING
DEMYTHOLOGIZE
DEMYTHOLOGIZED
DEMYTHOLOGIZER
DEMYTHOLOGIZERS
DEMYTHOLOGIZES
DEMYTHOLOGIZING
DEN
DENAR
DENARI
DENARII
DENARIUS
DENARS
DENARY
DENATIONALISE
DENATIONALISED
DENATIONALISES
DENATIONALISING
DENATIONALIZE
DENATIONALIZED
DENATIONALIZES
DENATIONALIZING
DENATURALIZE
DENATURALIZED
DENATURALIZES
DENATURALIZING
DENATURANT
DENATURANTS
DENATURATION
DENATURATIONS
DENATURE
DENATURED
DENATURES
DENATURING
DENAZIFICATION
DENAZIFICATIONS
DENAZIFIED
DENAZIFIES
DENAZIFY
DENAZIFYING
DENDRIFORM
DENDRIMER
DENDRIMERS
DENDRITE
DENDRITES
DENDRITIC
DENDROGRAM
DENDROGRAMS
DENDROID
DENDROIDS
DENDROLOGIC
DENDROLOGICAL
DENDROLOGIES
DENDROLOGIST
DENDROLOGISTS
DENDROLOGY
DENDRON
DENDRONS
DENE
DENEGATION
DENEGATIONS
DENERVATE
DENERVATED
DENERVATES
DENERVATING
DENERVATION
DENERVATIONS
DENES
DENGUE
DENGUES
DENI
DENIABILITIES
DENIABILITY
DENIABLE
DENIABLY
DENIAL
DENIALS
DENIED
DENIER
DENIERS
DENIES
DENIGRATE
DENIGRATED
DENIGRATES
DENIGRATING
DENIGRATION
DENIGRATIONS
DENIGRATIVE
DENIGRATOR
DENIGRATORS
DENIGRATORY
DENIM
DENIMED
DENIMS
DENITRATE
DENITRATED
DENITRATES
DENITRATING
DENITRIFICATION
DENITRIFIED
DENITRIFIER
DENITRIFIERS
DENITRIFIES
DENITRIFY
DENITRIFYING
DENIZEN
DENIZENED
DENIZENING
DENIZENS
DENNED
DENNING
DENOMINAL
DENOMINATE
DENOMINATED
DENOMINATES
DENOMINATING
DENOMINATION
DENOMINATIONAL
DENOMINATIONS
DENOMINATIVE
DENOMINATIVES
DENOMINATOR
DENOMINATORS
DENOTABLE
DENOTATION
DENOTATIONS
DENOTATIVE
DENOTE
DENOTED
DENOTEMENT
DENOTEMENTS
DENOTES
DENOTING
DENOTIVE
DENOUEMENT
DENOUEMENTS
DENOUNCE
DENOUNCED
DENOUNCEMENT
DENOUNCEMENTS
DENOUNCER
DENOUNCERS
DENOUNCES
DENOUNCING
DENS
DENSE
DENSELY
DENSENESS
DENSENESSES
DENSER
DENSEST
DENSIFICATION
DENSIFICATIONS
DENSIFIED
DENSIFIES
DENSIFY
DENSIFYING
DENSITIES
DENSITOMETER
DENSITOMETERS
DENSITOMETRIC
DENSITOMETRIES
DENSITOMETRY
DENSITY
DENT
DENTAL
DENTALIA
DENTALITIES
DENTALITY
DENTALIUM

DENTALIUMS
DENTALLY
DENTALS
DENTARIES
DENTARY
DENTATE
DENTATED
DENTATELY
DENTATION
DENTATIONS
DENTED
DENTELLE
DENTELLES
DENTICLE
DENTICLES
DENTICULATE
DENTICULATED
DENTICULATION
DENTICULATIONS
DENTIFORM
DENTIFRICE
DENTIFRICES
DENTIL
DENTILED
DENTILS
DENTIN
DENTINAL
DENTINE
DENTINES
DENTING
DENTINS
DENTIST
DENTISTRIES
DENTISTRY
DENTISTS
DENTITION
DENTITIONS
DENTOID
DENTS
DENTULOUS
DENTURAL
DENTURE
DENTURES
DENTURIST
DENTURISTS
DENUCLEARIZE
DENUCLEARIZED
DENUCLEARIZES
DENUCLEARIZING
DENUDATE
DENUDATED
DENUDATES
DENUDATING
DENUDATION
DENUDATIONS
DENUDE
DENUDED
DENUDEMENT
DENUDEMENTS
DENUDER
DENUDERS
DENUDES
DENUDING
DENUMERABILITY
DENUMERABLE
DENUMERABLY
DENUNCIATION
DENUNCIATIONS
DENUNCIATIVE
DENUNCIATORY
DENY
DENYING
DENYINGLY
DEODAND
DEODANDS
DEODAR
DEODARA
DEODARAS
DEODARS
DEODORANT
DEODORANTS
DEODORISE
DEODORISER
DEODORISERS
DEODORIZATION
DEODORIZATIONS
DEODORIZE
DEODORIZED
DEODORIZER
DEODORIZERS
DEODORIZES
DEODORIZING
DEONTIC
DEONTOLOGICAL
DEONTOLOGIES
DEONTOLOGIST
DEONTOLOGISTS
DEONTOLOGY
DEORBIT
DEORBITED
DEORBITING
DEORBITS
DEOXIDATION
DEOXIDATIONS
DEOXIDIZE
DEOXIDIZED
DEOXIDIZER
DEOXIDIZERS
DEOXIDIZES
DEOXIDIZING
DEOXY
DEOXYGENATE
DEOXYGENATED
DEOXYGENATES
DEOXYGENATING
DEOXYGENATION
DEOXYGENATIONS
DEOXYRIBOSE
DEOXYRIBOSES
DEP
DEPAINT
DEPAINTED
DEPAINTING
DEPAINTS
DEPART
DEPARTED
DEPARTEDS
DEPARTEE
DEPARTEES
DEPARTING
DEPARTMENT
DEPARTMENTAL
DEPARTMENTALISE
DEPARTMENTALIZE
DEPARTMENTALLY
DEPARTMENTS
DEPARTS
DEPARTURE
DEPARTURES
DEPAUPERATE
DEPAUPERATED
DEPAUPERATES
DEPAUPERATING
DEPEND
DEPENDABILITIES
DEPENDABILITY
DEPENDABLE
DEPENDABLENESS
DEPENDABLY
DEPENDANCE
DEPENDANCES
DEPENDANT
DEPENDANTS
DEPENDED
DEPENDENCE
DEPENDENCES
DEPENDENCIES
DEPENDENCY
DEPENDENT
DEPENDENTLY
DEPENDENTS
DEPENDING
DEPENDS
DEPEOPLE
DEPEOPLED
DEPEOPLES
DEPEOPLING
DEPERM
DEPERMED
DEPERMING
DEPERMS
DEPERSONALIZE
DEPERSONALIZED
DEPERSONALIZES
DEPERSONALIZING
DEPHOSPHORYLATE
DEPICT
DEPICTED
DEPICTER
DEPICTERS
DEPICTING
DEPICTION
DEPICTIONS
DEPICTOR
DEPICTORS
DEPICTS
DEPIGMENTATION
DEPIGMENTATIONS
DEPILATE
DEPILATED
DEPILATES
DEPILATING
DEPILATION
DEPILATIONS
DEPILATOR
DEPILATORIES
DEPILATORS
DEPILATORY
DEPLANE
DEPLANED
DEPLANES
DEPLANING
DEPLETABLE
DEPLETE
DEPLETED
DEPLETER
DEPLETERS
DEPLETES
DEPLETING
DEPLETION
DEPLETIONS
DEPLETIVE
DEPLORABLE
DEPLORABLENESS
DEPLORABLY
DEPLORE
DEPLORED
DEPLORER
DEPLORERS
DEPLORES
DEPLORING
DEPLORINGLY
DEPLOY
DEPLOYABLE
DEPLOYED
DEPLOYER
DEPLOYERS
DEPLOYING
DEPLOYMENT
DEPLOYMENTS
DEPLOYS
DEPLUME
DEPLUMED
DEPLUMES
DEPLUMING
DEPOLARIZATION
DEPOLARIZATIONS
DEPOLARIZE
DEPOLARIZED
DEPOLARIZER
DEPOLARIZERS
DEPOLARIZES
DEPOLARIZING
DEPOLISH
DEPOLISHED
DEPOLISHES
DEPOLISHING
DEPOLITICISE
DEPOLITICISED
DEPOLITICISES
DEPOLITICISING
DEPOLITICIZE
DEPOLITICIZED
DEPOLITICIZES
DEPOLITICIZING
DEPOLYMERIZE
DEPOLYMERIZED
DEPOLYMERIZES
DEPOLYMERIZING
DEPONE
DEPONED
DEPONENT
DEPONENTS
DEPONES
DEPONING

DEPOPULATE
DEPOPULATED
DEPOPULATES
DEPOPULATING
DEPOPULATION
DEPOPULATIONS
DEPORT
DEPORTABLE
DEPORTATION
DEPORTATIONS
DEPORTED
DEPORTEE
DEPORTEES
DEPORTER
DEPORTERS
DEPORTING
DEPORTMENT
DEPORTMENTS
DEPORTS
DEPOSABLE
DEPOSAL
DEPOSALS
DEPOSE
DEPOSED
DEPOSER
DEPOSERS
DEPOSES
DEPOSING
DEPOSIT
DEPOSITARIES
DEPOSITARY
DEPOSITED
DEPOSITING
DEPOSITION
DEPOSITIONAL
DEPOSITIONS
DEPOSITOR
DEPOSITORIES
DEPOSITORS
DEPOSITORY
DEPOSITS
DEPOT
DEPOTS
DEPRAVATION
DEPRAVATIONS
DEPRAVE
DEPRAVED
DEPRAVEDLY
DEPRAVEDNESS
DEPRAVEDNESSES
DEPRAVEMENT
DEPRAVEMENTS
DEPRAVER
DEPRAVERS
DEPRAVES
DEPRAVING
DEPRAVITIES
DEPRAVITY
DEPRECATE
DEPRECATED
DEPRECATES
DEPRECATING
DEPRECATINGLY
DEPRECATION
DEPRECATIONS
DEPRECATORILY
DEPRECATORY
DEPRECIABLE
DEPRECIATE
DEPRECIATED
DEPRECIATES
DEPRECIATING
DEPRECIATINGLY
DEPRECIATION
DEPRECIATIONS
DEPRECIATIVE
DEPRECIATOR
DEPRECIATORS
DEPRECIATORY
DEPREDATE
DEPREDATED
DEPREDATES
DEPREDATING
DEPREDATION
DEPREDATIONS
DEPREDATOR
DEPREDATORS
DEPREDATORY
DEPRENYL
DEPRENYLS
DEPRESS
DEPRESSANT
DEPRESSANTS
DEPRESSED
DEPRESSES
DEPRESSIBLE
DEPRESSING
DEPRESSINGLY
DEPRESSION
DEPRESSIONS
DEPRESSIVE
DEPRESSIVELY
DEPRESSIVES
DEPRESSOR
DEPRESSORS
DEPRESSURIZE
DEPRESSURIZED
DEPRESSURIZES
DEPRESSURIZING
DEPRIVAL
DEPRIVALS
DEPRIVATION
DEPRIVATIONS
DEPRIVE
DEPRIVED
DEPRIVER
DEPRIVERS
DEPRIVES
DEPRIVING
DEPROGRAM
DEPROGRAMED
DEPROGRAMING
DEPROGRAMMED
DEPROGRAMMER
DEPROGRAMMERS
DEPROGRAMMING
DEPROGRAMS
DEPS
DEPSIDE
DEPSIDES
DEPTH
DEPTHLESS
DEPTHS
DEPURATE
DEPURATED
DEPURATES
DEPURATING
DEPURATOR
DEPURATORS
DEPUTABLE
DEPUTATION
DEPUTATIONS
DEPUTE
DEPUTED
DEPUTES
DEPUTIES
DEPUTING
DEPUTISE
DEPUTISED
DEPUTISES
DEPUTISING
DEPUTIZATION
DEPUTIZATIONS
DEPUTIZE
DEPUTIZED
DEPUTIZES
DEPUTIZING
DEPUTY
DERACINATE
DERACINATED
DERACINATES
DERACINATING
DERACINATION
DERACINATIONS
DERACINE
DERACINES
DERAIGN
DERAIGNED
DERAIGNING
DERAIGNS
DERAIL
DERAILED
DERAILING
DERAILLEUR
DERAILLEURS
DERAILMENT
DERAILMENTS
DERAILS
DERANGE
DERANGED
DERANGEMENT
DERANGEMENTS
DERANGER
DERANGERS
DERANGES
DERANGING
DERAT
DERATE
DERATED
DERATES
DERATING
DERATION
DERATIONED
DERATIONING
DERATIONS
DERATS
DERATTED
DERATTING
DERAY
DERAYS
DERBIES
DERBY
DERE
DEREALIZATION
DEREALIZATIONS
DERECHO
DERECHOS
DEREGULATE
DEREGULATED
DEREGULATES
DEREGULATING
DEREGULATION
DEREGULATIONS
DERELICT
DERELICTION
DERELICTIONS
DERELICTS
DEREPRESS
DEREPRESSED
DEREPRESSES
DEREPRESSING
DEREPRESSION
DEREPRESSIONS
DERIDE
DERIDED
DERIDER
DERIDERS
DERIDES
DERIDING
DERIDINGLY
DERINGER
DERINGERS
DERISIBLE
DERISION
DERISIONS
DERISIVE
DERISIVELY
DERISIVENESS
DERISIVENESSES
DERISORY
DERIVABLE
DERIVATE
DERIVATES
DERIVATION
DERIVATIONAL
DERIVATIONS
DERIVATIVE
DERIVATIVELY
DERIVATIVENESS
DERIVATIVES
DERIVATIZATION
DERIVATIZATIONS
DERIVATIZE
DERIVATIZED
DERIVATIZES
DERIVATIZING
DERIVE
DERIVED
DERIVER
DERIVERS
DERIVES
DERIVING
DERM
DERMA
DERMABRASION

DERMABRASIONS
DERMAL
DERMAS
DERMATITIDES
DERMATITIS
DERMATITISES
DERMATOGEN
DERMATOGENS
DERMATOGLYPHIC
DERMATOGLYPHICS
DERMATOID
DERMATOLOGIC
DERMATOLOGICAL
DERMATOLOGIES
DERMATOLOGIST
DERMATOLOGISTS
DERMATOLOGY
DERMATOMAL
DERMATOME
DERMATOMES
DERMATOMYOSITIS
DERMATOPHYTE
DERMATOPHYTES
DERMATOSES
DERMATOSIS
DERMESTID
DERMESTIDS
DERMIC
DERMIS
DERMISES
DERMOID
DERMOIDS
DERMS
DERNIER
DEROGATE
DEROGATED
DEROGATES
DEROGATING
DEROGATION
DEROGATIONS
DEROGATIVE
DEROGATORILY
DEROGATORY
DERRICK
DERRICKS
DERRIERE
DERRIERES
DERRIES
DERRINGER
DERRINGERS
DERRIS
DERRISES
DERRY
DERVISH
DERVISHES
DESACRALIZATION
DESACRALIZE
DESACRALIZED
DESACRALIZES
DESACRALIZING
DESALINATE
DESALINATED
DESALINATES
DESALINATING
DESALINATION
DESALINATIONS
DESALINATOR
DESALINATORS
DESALINIZATION
DESALINIZATIONS
DESALINIZE
DESALINIZED
DESALINIZES
DESALINIZING
DESALT
DESALTED
DESALTER
DESALTERS
DESALTING
DESALTS
DESANCTIFIED
DESANCTIFIES
DESANCTIFY
DESANCTIFYING
DESAND
DESANDED
DESANDING
DESANDS
DESCALE
DESCALED
DESCALES
DESCALING
DESCANT
DESCANTED
DESCANTER
DESCANTERS
DESCANTING
DESCANTS
DESCEND
DESCENDANT
DESCENDANTS
DESCENDED
DESCENDENT
DESCENDENTS
DESCENDER
DESCENDERS
DESCENDIBLE
DESCENDING
DESCENDS
DESCENSION
DESCENSIONS
DESCENT
DESCENTS
DESCRAMBLE
DESCRAMBLED
DESCRAMBLER
DESCRAMBLERS
DESCRAMBLES
DESCRAMBLING
DESCRIBABLE
DESCRIBE
DESCRIBED
DESCRIBER
DESCRIBERS
DESCRIBES
DESCRIBING
DESCRIED
DESCRIER
DESCRIERS
DESCRIES
DESCRIPTION
DESCRIPTIONS
DESCRIPTIVE
DESCRIPTIVELY
DESCRIPTIVENESS
DESCRIPTOR
DESCRIPTORS
DESCRY
DESCRYING
DESECRATE
DESECRATED
DESECRATER
DESECRATERS
DESECRATES
DESECRATING
DESECRATION
DESECRATIONS
DESECRATOR
DESECRATORS
DESEED
DESEEDED
DESEEDER
DESEEDERS
DESEEDING
DESEEDS
DESEGREGATE
DESEGREGATED
DESEGREGATES
DESEGREGATING
DESEGREGATION
DESEGREGATIONS
DESELECT
DESELECTED
DESELECTING
DESELECTION
DESELECTIONS
DESELECTS
DESENSITISATION
DESENSITISE
DESENSITISED
DESENSITISES
DESENSITISING
DESENSITIZATION
DESENSITIZE
DESENSITIZED
DESENSITIZER
DESENSITIZERS
DESENSITIZES
DESENSITIZING
DESERT
DESERTED
DESERTER
DESERTERS
DESERTIC
DESERTIFICATION
DESERTIFIED
DESERTIFIES
DESERTIFY
DESERTIFYING
DESERTING
DESERTION
DESERTIONS
DESERTLIKE
DESERTS
DESERVE
DESERVED
DESERVEDLY
DESERVEDNESS
DESERVEDNESSES
DESERVER
DESERVERS
DESERVES
DESERVING
DESERVINGS
DESEX
DESEXED
DESEXES
DESEXING
DESEXUALIZATION
DESEXUALIZE
DESEXUALIZED
DESEXUALIZES
DESEXUALIZING
DESHABILLE
DESHABILLES
DESHI
DESHIS
DESI
DESICCANT
DESICCANTS
DESICCATE
DESICCATED
DESICCATES
DESICCATING
DESICCATION
DESICCATIONS
DESICCATIVE
DESICCATOR
DESICCATORS
DESIDERATA
DESIDERATE
DESIDERATED
DESIDERATES
DESIDERATING
DESIDERATION
DESIDERATIONS
DESIDERATIVE
DESIDERATUM
DESIGN
DESIGNATE
DESIGNATED
DESIGNATES
DESIGNATING
DESIGNATION
DESIGNATIONS
DESIGNATIVE
DESIGNATOR
DESIGNATORS
DESIGNATORY
DESIGNED
DESIGNEDLY
DESIGNEE
DESIGNEES
DESIGNER
DESIGNERS
DESIGNING
DESIGNINGS
DESIGNMENT
DESIGNMENTS
DESIGNS
DESILVER
DESILVERED
DESILVERING
DESILVERS
DESINENCE

DESINENCES
DESINENT
DESIPRAMINE
DESIPRAMINES
DESIRABILITIES
DESIRABILITY
DESIRABLE
DESIRABLENESS
DESIRABLENESSES
DESIRABLES
DESIRABLY
DESIRE
DESIRED
DESIRER
DESIRERS
DESIRES
DESIRING
DESIROUS
DESIROUSLY
DESIROUSNESS
DESIROUSNESSES
DESIS
DESIST
DESISTANCE
DESISTANCES
DESISTED
DESISTING
DESISTS
DESK
DESKBOUND
DESKILL
DESKILLED
DESKILLING
DESKILLS
DESKMAN
DESKMEN
DESKS
DESKTOP
DESKTOPS
DESMAN
DESMANS
DESMID
DESMIDIAN
DESMIDS
DESMOID
DESMOIDS
DESMOSOMAL
DESMOSOME
DESMOSOMES
DESOLATE
DESOLATED
DESOLATELY
DESOLATENESS
DESOLATENESSES
DESOLATER
DESOLATERS
DESOLATES
DESOLATING
DESOLATINGLY
DESOLATION
DESOLATIONS
DESOLATOR
DESOLATORS
DESORB
DESORBED
DESORBER
DESORBERS
DESORBING
DESORBS
DESORPTION
DESORPTIONS
DESOXY
DESPAIR
DESPAIRED
DESPAIRER
DESPAIRERS
DESPAIRING
DESPAIRINGLY
DESPAIRS
DESPATCH
DESPATCHED
DESPATCHES
DESPATCHING
DESPERADO
DESPERADOES
DESPERADOS
DESPERATE
DESPERATELY
DESPERATENESS
DESPERATENESSES
DESPERATION
DESPERATIONS
DESPICABLE
DESPICABLENESS
DESPICABLY
DESPIRITUALIZE
DESPIRITUALIZED
DESPIRITUALIZES
DESPISAL
DESPISALS
DESPISE
DESPISED
DESPISEMENT
DESPISEMENTS
DESPISER
DESPISERS
DESPISES
DESPISING
DESPITE
DESPITED
DESPITEFUL
DESPITEFULLY
DESPITEFULNESS
DESPITEOUS
DESPITEOUSLY
DESPITES
DESPITING
DESPOIL
DESPOILED
DESPOILER
DESPOILERS
DESPOILING
DESPOILMENT
DESPOILMENTS
DESPOILS
DESPOLIATION
DESPOLIATIONS
DESPOND
DESPONDED
DESPONDENCE
DESPONDENCES
DESPONDENCIES
DESPONDENCY
DESPONDENT
DESPONDENTLY
DESPONDING
DESPONDS
DESPOT
DESPOTIC
DESPOTICALLY
DESPOTISM
DESPOTISMS
DESPOTS
DESPUMATE
DESPUMATED
DESPUMATES
DESPUMATING
DESQUAMATE
DESQUAMATED
DESQUAMATES
DESQUAMATING
DESQUAMATION
DESQUAMATIONS
DESSERT
DESSERTS
DESSERTSPOON
DESSERTSPOONFUL
DESSERTSPOONS
DESTABILISATION
DESTABILISE
DESTABILISED
DESTABILISES
DESTABILISING
DESTABILIZATION
DESTABILIZE
DESTABILIZED
DESTABILIZES
DESTABILIZING
DESTAIN
DESTAINED
DESTAINING
DESTAINS
DESTIGMATIZE
DESTIGMATIZED
DESTIGMATIZES
DESTIGMATIZING
DESTINATION
DESTINATIONS
DESTINE
DESTINED
DESTINES
DESTINIES
DESTINING
DESTINY
DESTITUTE
DESTITUTED
DESTITUTENESS
DESTITUTENESSES
DESTITUTES
DESTITUTING
DESTITUTION
DESTITUTIONS
DESTREAM
DESTREAMED
DESTREAMING
DESTREAMS
DESTRESS
DESTRESSED
DESTRESSES
DESTRESSING
DESTRIER
DESTRIERS
DESTROY
DESTROYED
DESTROYER
DESTROYERS
DESTROYING
DESTROYS
DESTRUCT
DESTRUCTED
DESTRUCTIBILITY
DESTRUCTIBLE
DESTRUCTING
DESTRUCTION
DESTRUCTIONIST
DESTRUCTIONISTS
DESTRUCTIONS
DESTRUCTIVE
DESTRUCTIVELY
DESTRUCTIVENESS
DESTRUCTIVITIES
DESTRUCTIVITY
DESTRUCTS
DESUETUDE
DESUETUDES
DESUGAR
DESUGARED
DESUGARING
DESUGARS
DESULFUR
DESULFURED
DESULFURING
DESULFURIZATION
DESULFURIZE
DESULFURIZED
DESULFURIZES
DESULFURIZING
DESULFURS
DESULTORILY
DESULTORINESS
DESULTORINESSES
DESULTORY
DETACH
DETACHABILITIES
DETACHABILITY
DETACHABLE
DETACHABLY
DETACHED
DETACHEDLY
DETACHEDNESS
DETACHEDNESSES
DETACHER
DETACHERS
DETACHES
DETACHING
DETACHMENT
DETACHMENTS
DETAIL
DETAILED
DETAILEDLY
DETAILEDNESS
DETAILEDNESSES
DETAILER
DETAILERS
DETAILING

DETAILINGS
DETAILS
DETAIN
DETAINED
DETAINEE
DETAINEES
DETAINER
DETAINERS
DETAINING
DETAINMENT
DETAINMENTS
DETAINS
DETANGLE
DETANGLED
DETANGLER
DETANGLERS
DETANGLES
DETANGLING
DETASSEL
DETASSELED
DETASSELING
DETASSELLED
DETASSELLING
DETASSELS
DETECT
DETECTABILITIES
DETECTABILITY
DETECTABLE
DETECTED
DETECTER
DETECTERS
DETECTING
DETECTION
DETECTIONS
DETECTIVE
DETECTIVELIKE
DETECTIVES
DETECTOR
DETECTORS
DETECTS
DETENT
DETENTE
DETENTES
DETENTION
DETENTIONS
DETENTIST
DETENTISTS
DETENTS
DETER
DETERGE
DETERGED
DETERGENCIES
DETERGENCY
DETERGENT
DETERGENTS
DETERGER
DETERGERS
DETERGES
DETERGING
DETERIORATE
DETERIORATED
DETERIORATES
DETERIORATING
DETERIORATION
DETERIORATIONS
DETERIORATIVE
DETERMENT
DETERMENTS
DETERMINABLE
DETERMINABLY
DETERMINACIES
DETERMINACY
DETERMINANT
DETERMINANTAL
DETERMINANTS
DETERMINATE
DETERMINATED
DETERMINATELY
DETERMINATENESS
DETERMINATES
DETERMINATING
DETERMINATION
DETERMINATIONS
DETERMINATIVE
DETERMINATIVES
DETERMINATOR
DETERMINATORS
DETERMINE
DETERMINED
DETERMINEDLY
DETERMINEDNESS
DETERMINER
DETERMINERS
DETERMINES
DETERMINING
DETERMINISM
DETERMINISMS
DETERMINIST
DETERMINISTIC
DETERMINISTS
DETERRABILITIES
DETERRABILITY
DETERRABLE
DETERRED
DETERRENCE
DETERRENCES
DETERRENT
DETERRENTLY
DETERRENTS
DETERRER
DETERRERS
DETERRING
DETERS
DETERSIVE
DETERSIVES
DETEST
DETESTABLE
DETESTABLENESS
DETESTABLY
DETESTATION
DETESTATIONS
DETESTED
DETESTER
DETESTERS
DETESTING
DETESTS
DETHATCH
DETHATCHED
DETHATCHES
DETHATCHING
DETHRONE
DETHRONED
DETHRONEMENT
DETHRONEMENTS
DETHRONER
DETHRONERS
DETHRONES
DETHRONING
DETICK
DETICKED
DETICKER
DETICKERS
DETICKING
DETICKS
DETINUE
DETINUES
DETONABILITIES
DETONABILITY
DETONABLE
DETONATABLE
DETONATE
DETONATED
DETONATES
DETONATING
DETONATION
DETONATIONS
DETONATIVE
DETONATOR
DETONATORS
DETOUR
DETOURED
DETOURING
DETOURS
DETOX
DETOXED
DETOXES
DETOXICANT
DETOXICANTS
DETOXICATE
DETOXICATED
DETOXICATES
DETOXICATING
DETOXICATION
DETOXICATIONS
DETOXIFICATION
DETOXIFICATIONS
DETOXIFIED
DETOXIFIES
DETOXIFY
DETOXIFYING
DETOXING
DETRACT
DETRACTED
DETRACTING
DETRACTION
DETRACTIONS
DETRACTIVE
DETRACTIVELY
DETRACTOR
DETRACTORS
DETRACTS
DETRAIN
DETRAINED
DETRAINING
DETRAINMENT
DETRAINMENTS
DETRAINS
DETRIBALIZATION
DETRIBALIZE
DETRIBALIZED
DETRIBALIZES
DETRIBALIZING
DETRIMENT
DETRIMENTAL
DETRIMENTALLY
DETRIMENTALS
DETRIMENTS
DETRITAL
DETRITION
DETRITIONS
DETRITIVORE
DETRITIVORES
DETRITUS
DETRUDE
DETRUDED
DETRUDES
DETRUDING
DETRUSION
DETRUSIONS
DETUMESCENCE
DETUMESCENCES
DETUMESCENT
DETUNE
DETUNED
DETUNES
DETUNING
DEUCE
DEUCED
DEUCEDLY
DEUCES
DEUCING
DEUTERAGONIST
DEUTERAGONISTS
DEUTERANOMALIES
DEUTERANOMALOUS
DEUTERANOMALY
DEUTERANOPE
DEUTERANOPES
DEUTERANOPIA
DEUTERANOPIAS
DEUTERANOPIC
DEUTERATE
DEUTERATED
DEUTERATES
DEUTERATING
DEUTERATION
DEUTERATIONS
DEUTERIC
DEUTERIDE
DEUTERIDES
DEUTERIUM
DEUTERIUMS
DEUTERON
DEUTERONS
DEUTEROSTOME
DEUTEROSTOMES
DEUTOPLASM
DEUTOPLASMS
DEUTSCHMARK
DEUTSCHMARKS
DEUTZIA
DEUTZIAS
DEV
DEVA
DEVALUATE

DEVALUATED
DEVALUATES
DEVALUATING
DEVALUATION
DEVALUATIONS
DEVALUE
DEVALUED
DEVALUES
DEVALUING
DEVAS
DEVASTATE
DEVASTATED
DEVASTATES
DEVASTATING
DEVASTATINGLY
DEVASTATION
DEVASTATIONS
DEVASTATIVE
DEVASTATOR
DEVASTATORS
DEVEIN
DEVEINED
DEVEINING
DEVEINS
DEVEL
DEVELED
DEVELING
DEVELOP
DEVELOPABLE
DEVELOPE
DEVELOPED
DEVELOPER
DEVELOPERS
DEVELOPES
DEVELOPING
DEVELOPMENT
DEVELOPMENTAL
DEVELOPMENTALLY
DEVELOPMENTS
DEVELOPPE
DEVELOPPES
DEVELOPS
DEVELS
DEVERBAL
DEVERBALS
DEVERBATIVE
DEVERBATIVES
DEVEST
DEVESTED
DEVESTING
DEVESTS
DEVI
DEVIANCE
DEVIANCES
DEVIANCIES
DEVIANCY
DEVIANT
DEVIANTS
DEVIATE
DEVIATED
DEVIATES
DEVIATING
DEVIATION
DEVIATIONISM
DEVIATIONISMS
DEVIATIONIST
DEVIATIONISTS
DEVIATIONS
DEVIATIVE
DEVIATOR
DEVIATORS
DEVIATORY
DEVICE
DEVICES
DEVIL
DEVILED
DEVILFISH
DEVILFISHES
DEVILING
DEVILISH
DEVILISHLY
DEVILISHNESS
DEVILISHNESSES
DEVILKIN
DEVILKINS
DEVILLED
DEVILLING
DEVILMENT
DEVILMENTS
DEVILRIES
DEVILRY
DEVILS
DEVILTRIES
DEVILTRY
DEVILWOOD
DEVILWOODS
DEVIOUS
DEVIOUSLY
DEVIOUSNESS
DEVIOUSNESSES
DEVIS
DEVISABLE
DEVISAL
DEVISALS
DEVISE
DEVISED
DEVISEE
DEVISEES
DEVISER
DEVISERS
DEVISES
DEVISING
DEVISOR
DEVISORS
DEVITALIZATION
DEVITALIZATIONS
DEVITALIZE
DEVITALIZED
DEVITALIZES
DEVITALIZING
DEVITRIFICATION
DEVITRIFIED
DEVITRIFIES
DEVITRIFY
DEVITRIFYING
DEVOCALIZE
DEVOCALIZED
DEVOCALIZES
DEVOCALIZING
DEVOICE
DEVOICED
DEVOICES
DEVOICING
DEVOID
DEVOIR
DEVOIRS
DEVOLUTION
DEVOLUTIONARY
DEVOLUTIONIST
DEVOLUTIONISTS
DEVOLUTIONS
DEVOLVE
DEVOLVED
DEVOLVES
DEVOLVING
DEVON
DEVONIAN
DEVONS
DEVOTE
DEVOTED
DEVOTEDLY
DEVOTEDNESS
DEVOTEDNESSES
DEVOTEE
DEVOTEES
DEVOTEMENT
DEVOTEMENTS
DEVOTES
DEVOTING
DEVOTION
DEVOTIONAL
DEVOTIONALLY
DEVOTIONALS
DEVOTIONS
DEVOUR
DEVOURED
DEVOURER
DEVOURERS
DEVOURING
DEVOURS
DEVOUT
DEVOUTER
DEVOUTEST
DEVOUTLY
DEVOUTNESS
DEVOUTNESSES
DEVS
DEW
DEWAN
DEWANS
DEWAR
DEWARS
DEWATER
DEWATERED
DEWATERER
DEWATERERS
DEWATERING
DEWATERS
DEWAX
DEWAXED
DEWAXES
DEWAXING
DEWBERRIES
DEWBERRY
DEWCLAW
DEWCLAWED
DEWCLAWS
DEWDROP
DEWDROPS
DEWED
DEWFALL
DEWFALLS
DEWIER
DEWIEST
DEWILY
DEWINESS
DEWINESSES
DEWING
DEWLAP
DEWLAPPED
DEWLAPS
DEWLESS
DEWOOL
DEWOOLED
DEWOOLING
DEWOOLS
DEWORM
DEWORMED
DEWORMER
DEWORMERS
DEWORMING
DEWORMS
DEWS
DEWY
DEX
DEXAMETHASONE
DEXAMETHASONES
DEXES
DEXFENFLURAMINE
DEXIE
DEXIES
DEXTER
DEXTERITIES
DEXTERITY
DEXTEROUS
DEXTEROUSLY
DEXTEROUSNESS
DEXTEROUSNESSES
DEXTERS
DEXTRAL
DEXTRALLY
DEXTRALS
DEXTRAN
DEXTRANASE
DEXTRANASES
DEXTRANS
DEXTRIN
DEXTRINE
DEXTRINES
DEXTRINS
DEXTRO
DEXTROROTARY
DEXTROROTATORY
DEXTRORSE
DEXTROSE
DEXTROSES
DEXTROUS
DEXTROUSLY
DEXY
DEY
DEYS
DEZINC
DEZINCED
DEZINCING
DEZINCKED

DEZINCKING
DEZINCS
DHAK
DHAKS
DHAL
DHALS
DHANSAK
DHANSAKS
DHARMA
DHARMAS
DHARMIC
DHARNA
DHARNAS
DHIKR
DHIKRS
DHOBI
DHOBIS
DHOLAK
DHOLAKS
DHOLE
DHOLES
DHOOLIES
DHOOLY
DHOORA
DHOORAS
DHOOTI
DHOOTIE
DHOOTIES
DHOOTIS
DHOTI
DHOTIS
DHOURRA
DHOURRAS
DHOW
DHOWS
DHURNA
DHURNAS
DHURRA
DHURRAS
DHURRIE
DHURRIES
DHUTI
DHUTIS
DHYANA
DHYANAS
DIABASE
DIABASES
DIABASIC
DIABETES
DIABETIC
DIABETICS
DIABETOGENIC
DIABETOLOGIST

DIABETOLOGISTS
DIABLERIE
DIABLERIES
DIABLERY
DIABOLIC
DIABOLICAL
DIABOLICALLY
DIABOLICALNESS
DIABOLISM
DIABOLISMS
DIABOLIST
DIABOLISTS
DIABOLIZE
DIABOLIZED
DIABOLIZES
DIABOLIZING
DIABOLO
DIABOLOS
DIACETYL
DIACETYLS
DIACHRONIC
DIACHRONICALLY
DIACHRONIES
DIACHRONY
DIACID
DIACIDIC
DIACIDS
DIACONAL
DIACONATE
DIACONATES
DIACRITIC
DIACRITICAL
DIACRITICS
DIACTINIC
DIADELPHOUS
DIADEM
DIADEMED
DIADEMING
DIADEMS
DIADROMOUS
DIAERESES
DIAERESIS
DIAERETIC
DIAGENESES
DIAGENESIS
DIAGENETIC
DIAGENETICALLY
DIAGEOTROPIC
DIAGNOSABLE
DIAGNOSE
DIAGNOSEABLE
DIAGNOSED
DIAGNOSES

DIAGNOSING
DIAGNOSIS
DIAGNOSTIC
DIAGNOSTICAL
DIAGNOSTICALLY
DIAGNOSTICIAN
DIAGNOSTICIANS
DIAGNOSTICS
DIAGONAL
DIAGONALIZABLE
DIAGONALIZATION
DIAGONALIZE
DIAGONALIZED
DIAGONALIZES
DIAGONALIZING
DIAGONALLY
DIAGONALS
DIAGRAM
DIAGRAMED
DIAGRAMING
DIAGRAMMABLE
DIAGRAMMATIC
DIAGRAMMATICAL
DIAGRAMMED
DIAGRAMMING
DIAGRAMS
DIAGRAPH
DIAGRAPHS
DIAKINESES
DIAKINESIS
DIAL
DIALECT
DIALECTAL
DIALECTALLY
DIALECTIC
DIALECTICAL
DIALECTICALLY
DIALECTICIAN
DIALECTICIANS
DIALECTICS
DIALECTOLOGICAL
DIALECTOLOGIES
DIALECTOLOGIST
DIALECTOLOGISTS
DIALECTOLOGY
DIALECTS
DIALED
DIALER
DIALERS
DIALING
DIALINGS
DIALIST
DIALISTS

DIALLAGE
DIALLAGES
DIALLED
DIALLEL
DIALLER
DIALLERS
DIALLING
DIALLINGS
DIALLIST
DIALLISTS
DIALOG
DIALOGED
DIALOGER
DIALOGERS
DIALOGIC
DIALOGICAL
DIALOGICALLY
DIALOGING
DIALOGIST
DIALOGISTIC
DIALOGISTS
DIALOGS
DIALOGUE
DIALOGUED
DIALOGUER
DIALOGUERS
DIALOGUES
DIALOGUING
DIALS
DIALYSATE
DIALYSATES
DIALYSE
DIALYSED
DIALYSER
DIALYSERS
DIALYSES
DIALYSING
DIALYSIS
DIALYTIC
DIALYZABLE
DIALYZATE
DIALYZATES
DIALYZE
DIALYZED
DIALYZER
DIALYZERS
DIALYZES
DIALYZING
DIAMAGNET
DIAMAGNETIC
DIAMAGNETISM
DIAMAGNETISMS
DIAMAGNETS

DIAMANTE
DIAMANTES
DIAMETER
DIAMETERS
DIAMETRAL
DIAMETRIC
DIAMETRICAL
DIAMETRICALLY
DIAMIDE
DIAMIDES
DIAMIN
DIAMINE
DIAMINES
DIAMINS
DIAMOND
DIAMONDBACK
DIAMONDBACKS
DIAMONDED
DIAMONDIFEROUS
DIAMONDING
DIAMONDS
DIANDROUS
DIANTHUS
DIANTHUSES
DIAPASON
DIAPASONS
DIAPAUSE
DIAPAUSED
DIAPAUSES
DIAPAUSING
DIAPEDESES
DIAPEDESIS
DIAPER
DIAPERED
DIAPERING
DIAPERS
DIAPHANEITIES
DIAPHANEITY
DIAPHANOUS
DIAPHANOUSLY
DIAPHANOUSNESS
DIAPHONE
DIAPHONES
DIAPHONIES
DIAPHONY
DIAPHORASE
DIAPHORASES
DIAPHORESES
DIAPHORESIS
DIAPHORETIC
DIAPHORETICS
DIAPHRAGM
DIAPHRAGMATIC

DIAPHRAGMED
DIAPHRAGMING
DIAPHRAGMS
DIAPHYSEAL
DIAPHYSES
DIAPHYSIAL
DIAPHYSIS
DIAPIR
DIAPIRIC
DIAPIRS
DIAPOSITIVE
DIAPOSITIVES
DIAPSID
DIAPSIDS
DIARCHAL
DIARCHIC
DIARCHIES
DIARCHY
DIARIES
DIARIST
DIARISTIC
DIARISTS
DIARRHEA
DIARRHEAL
DIARRHEAS
DIARRHEIC
DIARRHETIC
DIARRHOEA
DIARRHOEAS
DIARTHROSES
DIARTHROSIS
DIARY
DIASPORA
DIASPORAS
DIASPORE
DIASPORES
DIASPORIC
DIASTASE
DIASTASES
DIASTASIC
DIASTATIC
DIASTEM
DIASTEMA
DIASTEMAS
DIASTEMATA
DIASTEMS
DIASTER
DIASTEREOISOMER
DIASTEREOMER
DIASTEREOMERIC
DIASTEREOMERS
DIASTERS
DIASTOLE
DIASTOLES
DIASTOLIC
DIASTRAL
DIASTROPHIC
DIASTROPHICALLY
DIASTROPHISM
DIASTROPHISMS
DIATESSARON
DIATESSARONS
DIATHERMANOUS
DIATHERMIC
DIATHERMIES
DIATHERMY
DIATHESES
DIATHESIS
DIATHETIC
DIATOM
DIATOMACEOUS
DIATOMIC
DIATOMITE
DIATOMITES
DIATOMS
DIATONIC
DIATONICALLY
DIATREME
DIATREMES
DIATRIBE
DIATRIBES
DIATRON
DIATRONS
DIATROPIC
DIAZEPAM
DIAZEPAMS
DIAZIN
DIAZINE
DIAZINES
DIAZINON
DIAZINONS
DIAZINS
DIAZO
DIAZOLE
DIAZOLES
DIAZONIUM
DIAZONIUMS
DIAZOS
DIAZOTIZATION
DIAZOTIZATIONS
DIAZOTIZE
DIAZOTIZED
DIAZOTIZES
DIAZOTIZING
DIB
DIBASIC
DIBBED
DIBBER
DIBBERS
DIBBING
DIBBLE
DIBBLED
DIBBLER
DIBBLERS
DIBBLES
DIBBLING
DIBBUK
DIBBUKIM
DIBBUKS
DIBENZOFURAN
DIBENZOFURANS
DIBROMIDE
DIBROMIDES
DIBS
DICAMBA
DICAMBAS
DICARBOXYLIC
DICAST
DICASTIC
DICASTS
DICE
DICED
DICENTRA
DICENTRAS
DICENTRIC
DICENTRICS
DICER
DICERS
DICES
DICEY
DICHASIA
DICHASIAL
DICHASIUM
DICHLOROBENZENE
DICHLOROETHANE
DICHLOROETHANES
DICHLORVOS
DICHLORVOSES
DICHOGAMIES
DICHOGAMOUS
DICHOGAMY
DICHONDRA
DICHONDRAS
DICHOTIC
DICHOTICALLY
DICHOTOMIES
DICHOTOMIST
DICHOTOMISTS
DICHOTOMIZATION
DICHOTOMIZE
DICHOTOMIZED
DICHOTOMIZES
DICHOTOMIZING
DICHOTOMOUS
DICHOTOMOUSLY
DICHOTOMOUSNESS
DICHOTOMY
DICHROIC
DICHROISM
DICHROISMS
DICHROITE
DICHROITES
DICHROMAT
DICHROMATE
DICHROMATES
DICHROMATIC
DICHROMATISM
DICHROMATISMS
DICHROMATS
DICHROMIC
DICHROSCOPE
DICHROSCOPES
DICIER
DICIEST
DICING
DICK
DICKCISSEL
DICKCISSELS
DICKED
DICKENS
DICKENSES
DICKER
DICKERED
DICKERER
DICKERERS
DICKERING
DICKERS
DICKEY
DICKEYS
DICKHEAD
DICKHEADS
DICKIE
DICKIER
DICKIES
DICKIEST
DICKING
DICKS
DICKY
DICLINIES
DICLINISM
DICLINISMS
DICLINOUS
DICLINY
DICOT
DICOTS
DICOTYL
DICOTYLEDON
DICOTYLEDONOUS
DICOTYLEDONS
DICOTYLS
DICOUMARIN
DICOUMARINS
DICOUMAROL
DICOUMAROLS
DICROTAL
DICROTIC
DICROTISM
DICROTISMS
DICTA
DICTATE
DICTATED
DICTATES
DICTATING
DICTATION
DICTATIONS
DICTATOR
DICTATORIAL
DICTATORIALLY
DICTATORIALNESS
DICTATORS
DICTATORSHIP
DICTATORSHIPS
DICTIER
DICTIEST
DICTION
DICTIONAL
DICTIONALLY
DICTIONARIES
DICTIONARY
DICTIONS
DICTUM
DICTUMS
DICTY
DICTYOSOME
DICTYOSOMES
DICTYOSTELE
DICTYOSTELES
DICUMAROL
DICUMAROLS
DICYCLIC
DICYCLIES
DICYCLY
DICYNODONT
DICYNODONTS
DID

DIDACT
DIDACTIC
DIDACTICAL
DIDACTICALLY
DIDACTICISM
DIDACTICISMS
DIDACTICS
DIDACTS
DIDACTYL
DIDANOSINE
DIDANOSINES
DIDAPPER
DIDAPPERS
DIDDLE
DIDDLED
DIDDLER
DIDDLERS
DIDDLES
DIDDLEY
DIDDLEYS
DIDDLIES
DIDDLING
DIDDLY
DIDDUMS
DIDGERIDOO
DIDGERIDOOS
DIDIE
DIDIES
DIDJERIDOO
DIDJERIDOOS
DIDJERIDU
DIDJERIDUS
DIDO
DIDOES
DIDOS
DIDST
DIDY
DIDYMIUM
DIDYMIUMS
DIDYMOUS
DIDYNAMIES
DIDYNAMY
DIE
DIEBACK
DIEBACKS
DIECIOUS
DIED
DIEFFENBACHIA
DIEFFENBACHIAS
DIEHARD
DIEHARDS
DIEING
DIEL
DIELDRIN
DIELDRINS
DIELECTRIC
DIELECTRICS
DIEMAKER
DIEMAKERS
DIENCEPHALA
DIENCEPHALIC
DIENCEPHALON
DIENCEPHALONS
DIENE
DIENES
DIEOFF
DIEOFFS
DIERESES
DIERESIS
DIERETIC
DIES
DIESEL
DIESELED
DIESELING
DIESELINGS
DIESELIZATION
DIESELIZATIONS
DIESELIZE
DIESELIZED
DIESELIZES
DIESELIZING
DIESELLING
DIESELLINGS
DIESELS
DIESES
DIESINKER
DIESINKERS
DIESIS
DIESTER
DIESTERS
DIESTOCK
DIESTOCKS
DIESTROUS
DIESTRUM
DIESTRUMS
DIESTRUS
DIESTRUSES
DIET
DIETARIES
DIETARILY
DIETARY
DIETED
DIETER
DIETERS
DIETETIC
DIETETICALLY
DIETETICS
DIETHER
DIETHERS
DIETICIAN
DIETICIANS
DIETING
DIETITIAN
DIETITIANS
DIETS
DIF
DIFF
DIFFER
DIFFERED
DIFFERENCE
DIFFERENCED
DIFFERENCES
DIFFERENCING
DIFFERENT
DIFFERENTIA
DIFFERENTIABLE
DIFFERENTIAE
DIFFERENTIAL
DIFFERENTIALLY
DIFFERENTIALS
DIFFERENTIATE
DIFFERENTIATED
DIFFERENTIATES
DIFFERENTIATING
DIFFERENTIATION
DIFFERENTLY
DIFFERENTNESS
DIFFERENTNESSES
DIFFERING
DIFFERS
DIFFICILE
DIFFICULT
DIFFICULTIES
DIFFICULTLY
DIFFICULTY
DIFFIDENCE
DIFFIDENCES
DIFFIDENT
DIFFIDENTLY
DIFFRACT
DIFFRACTED
DIFFRACTING
DIFFRACTION
DIFFRACTIONS
DIFFRACTOMETER
DIFFRACTOMETERS
DIFFRACTOMETRIC
DIFFRACTOMETRY
DIFFRACTS
DIFFS
DIFFUSE
DIFFUSED
DIFFUSELY
DIFFUSENESS
DIFFUSENESSES
DIFFUSER
DIFFUSERS
DIFFUSES
DIFFUSIBLE
DIFFUSING
DIFFUSION
DIFFUSIONAL
DIFFUSIONISM
DIFFUSIONISMS
DIFFUSIONIST
DIFFUSIONISTS
DIFFUSIONS
DIFFUSIVE
DIFFUSIVELY
DIFFUSIVENESS
DIFFUSIVENESSES
DIFFUSIVITIES
DIFFUSIVITY
DIFFUSOR
DIFFUSORS
DIFS
DIFUNCTIONAL
DIG
DIGAMIES
DIGAMIST
DIGAMISTS
DIGAMMA
DIGAMMAS
DIGAMOUS
DIGAMY
DIGASTRIC
DIGASTRICS
DIGENESES
DIGENESIS
DIGENETIC
DIGERATI
DIGEST
DIGESTED
DIGESTER
DIGESTERS
DIGESTIBILITIES
DIGESTIBILITY
DIGESTIBLE
DIGESTIF
DIGESTIFS
DIGESTING
DIGESTION
DIGESTIONS
DIGESTIVE
DIGESTIVELY
DIGESTIVES
DIGESTOR
DIGESTORS
DIGESTS
DIGGED
DIGGER
DIGGERS
DIGGING
DIGGINGS
DIGHT
DIGHTED
DIGHTING
DIGHTS
DIGICAM
DIGICAMS
DIGIT
DIGITAL
DIGITALIN
DIGITALINS
DIGITALIS
DIGITALISES
DIGITALIZATION
DIGITALIZATIONS
DIGITALIZE
DIGITALIZED
DIGITALIZES
DIGITALIZING
DIGITALLY
DIGITALS
DIGITATE
DIGITATED
DIGITATELY
DIGITIGRADE
DIGITISE
DIGITISED
DIGITISES
DIGITISING
DIGITIZATION
DIGITIZATIONS
DIGITIZE
DIGITIZED
DIGITIZER
DIGITIZERS
DIGITIZES
DIGITIZING
DIGITONIN
DIGITONINS
DIGITOXIGENIN
DIGITOXIGENINS
DIGITOXIN

DIGITOXINS
DIGITS
DIGLOSSIA
DIGLOSSIAS
DIGLOSSIC
DIGLOT
DIGLOTS
DIGLYCERIDE
DIGLYCERIDES
DIGNIFIED
DIGNIFIES
DIGNIFY
DIGNIFYING
DIGNITARIES
DIGNITARY
DIGNITIES
DIGNITY
DIGOXIN
DIGOXINS
DIGRAPH
DIGRAPHIC
DIGRAPHICALLY
DIGRAPHS
DIGRESS
DIGRESSED
DIGRESSES
DIGRESSING
DIGRESSION
DIGRESSIONAL
DIGRESSIONARY
DIGRESSIONS
DIGRESSIVE
DIGRESSIVELY
DIGRESSIVENESS
DIGS
DIHEDRAL
DIHEDRALS
DIHEDRON
DIHEDRONS
DIHYBRID
DIHYBRIDS
DIHYDRIC
DIKDIK
DIKDIKS
DIKE
DIKED
DIKER
DIKERS
DIKES
DIKEY
DIKING
DIKTAT
DIKTATS
DILAPIDATE
DILAPIDATED
DILAPIDATES
DILAPIDATING
DILAPIDATION
DILAPIDATIONS
DILATABILITIES
DILATABILITY
DILATABLE
DILATABLY
DILATANCIES
DILATANCY
DILATANT
DILATANTS
DILATATE
DILATATION
DILATATIONAL
DILATATIONS
DILATATOR
DILATATORS
DILATE
DILATED
DILATER
DILATERS
DILATES
DILATING
DILATION
DILATIONS
DILATIVE
DILATOMETER
DILATOMETERS
DILATOMETRIC
DILATOMETRIES
DILATOMETRY
DILATOR
DILATORILY
DILATORINESS
DILATORINESSES
DILATORS
DILATORY
DILDO
DILDOE
DILDOES
DILDOS
DILEMMA
DILEMMAS
DILEMMATIC
DILEMMIC
DILETTANTE
DILETTANTES
DILETTANTI
DILETTANTISH
DILETTANTISM
DILETTANTISMS
DILIGENCE
DILIGENCES
DILIGENT
DILIGENTLY
DILL
DILLED
DILLIES
DILLS
DILLWEED
DILLWEEDS
DILLY
DILLYDALLIED
DILLYDALLIES
DILLYDALLY
DILLYDALLYING
DILTIAZEM
DILTIAZEMS
DILUENT
DILUENTS
DILUTE
DILUTED
DILUTENESS
DILUTENESSES
DILUTER
DILUTERS
DILUTES
DILUTING
DILUTION
DILUTIONS
DILUTIVE
DILUTOR
DILUTORS
DILUVIA
DILUVIAL
DILUVIAN
DILUVION
DILUVIONS
DILUVIUM
DILUVIUMS
DIM
DIME
DIMENHYDRINATE
DIMENHYDRINATES
DIMENSION
DIMENSIONAL
DIMENSIONALITY
DIMENSIONALLY
DIMENSIONED
DIMENSIONING
DIMENSIONLESS
DIMENSIONS
DIMER
DIMERCAPROL
DIMERCAPROLS
DIMERIC
DIMERISM
DIMERISMS
DIMERIZATION
DIMERIZATIONS
DIMERIZE
DIMERIZED
DIMERIZES
DIMERIZING
DIMEROUS
DIMERS
DIMES
DIMETER
DIMETERS
DIMETHOATE
DIMETHOATES
DIMETHYL
DIMETHYLS
DIMETRIC
DIMIDIATE
DIMIDIATED
DIMIDIATES
DIMIDIATING
DIMINISH
DIMINISHABLE
DIMINISHED
DIMINISHES
DIMINISHING
DIMINISHMENT
DIMINISHMENTS
DIMINUENDO
DIMINUENDOS
DIMINUTION
DIMINUTIONS
DIMINUTIVE
DIMINUTIVELY
DIMINUTIVENESS
DIMINUTIVES
DIMITIES
DIMITY
DIMLY
DIMMABLE
DIMMED
DIMMER
DIMMERS
DIMMEST
DIMMING
DIMMISH
DIMNESS
DIMNESSES
DIMORPH
DIMORPHIC
DIMORPHISM
DIMORPHISMS
DIMORPHOUS
DIMORPHS
DIMOUT
DIMOUTS
DIMPLE
DIMPLED
DIMPLES
DIMPLIER
DIMPLIEST
DIMPLING
DIMPLY
DIMS
DIMWIT
DIMWITS
DIMWITTED
DIN
DINAR
DINARS
DINDLE
DINDLED
DINDLES
DINDLING
DINE
DINED
DINER
DINERIC
DINERO
DINEROS
DINERS
DINES
DINETTE
DINETTES
DING
DINGBAT
DINGBATS
DINGDONG
DINGDONGED
DINGDONGING
DINGDONGS
DINGE
DINGED
DINGER
DINGERS
DINGES
DINGEY
DINGEYS
DINGHIES
DINGHY
DINGIER
DINGIES

DINGIEST
DINGILY
DINGINESS
DINGINESSES
DINGING
DINGLE
DINGLEBERRIES
DINGLEBERRY
DINGLES
DINGO
DINGOES
DINGOS
DINGS
DINGUS
DINGUSES
DINGY
DINING
DININGS
DINITRO
DINITROBENZENE
DINITROBENZENES
DINITROPHENOL
DINITROPHENOLS
DINK
DINKED
DINKEY
DINKEYS
DINKIER
DINKIES
DINKIEST
DINKING
DINKLY
DINKS
DINKUM
DINKUMS
DINKY
DINNED
DINNER
DINNERLESS
DINNERS
DINNERTIME
DINNERTIMES
DINNERWARE
DINNERWARES
DINNING
DINO
DINOFLAGELLATE
DINOFLAGELLATES
DINOS
DINOSAUR
DINOSAURIAN
DINOSAURIC
DINOSAURS
DINOTHERE
DINOTHERES
DINS
DINT
DINTED
DINTING
DINTS
DINUCLEOTIDE
DINUCLEOTIDES
DIOBOL
DIOBOLON
DIOBOLONS
DIOBOLS
DIOCESAN
DIOCESANS
DIOCESE
DIOCESES
DIODE
DIODES
DIOECIES
DIOECIOUS
DIOECISM
DIOECISMS
DIOECY
DIOESTRUS
DIOESTRUSES
DIOICOUS
DIOL
DIOLEFIN
DIOLEFINS
DIOLS
DIONYSIAC
DIONYSIAN
DIOPSIDE
DIOPSIDES
DIOPSIDIC
DIOPTASE
DIOPTASES
DIOPTER
DIOPTERS
DIOPTRAL
DIOPTRE
DIOPTRES
DIOPTRIC
DIOPTRICS
DIORAMA
DIORAMAS
DIORAMIC
DIORITE
DIORITES
DIORITIC
DIOSGENIN
DIOSGENINS
DIOXAN
DIOXANE
DIOXANES
DIOXANS
DIOXID
DIOXIDE
DIOXIDES
DIOXIDS
DIOXIN
DIOXINS
DIP
DIPEPTIDASE
DIPEPTIDASES
DIPEPTIDE
DIPEPTIDES
DIPHASE
DIPHASIC
DIPHENHYDRAMINE
DIPHENYL
DIPHENYLAMINE
DIPHENYLAMINES
DIPHENYLS
DIPHOSGENE
DIPHOSGENES
DIPHOSPHATE
DIPHOSPHATES
DIPHTHERIA
DIPHTHERIAL
DIPHTHERIAS
DIPHTHERITIC
DIPHTHEROID
DIPHTHEROIDS
DIPHTHONG
DIPHTHONGAL
DIPHTHONGED
DIPHTHONGING
DIPHTHONGIZE
DIPHTHONGIZED
DIPHTHONGIZES
DIPHTHONGIZING
DIPHTHONGS
DIPHYLETIC
DIPHYODONT
DIPHYODONTS
DIPLEGIA
DIPLEGIAS
DIPLEGIC
DIPLEX
DIPLEXER
DIPLEXERS
DIPLOBLASTIC
DIPLOCOCCI
DIPLOCOCCUS
DIPLODOCUS
DIPLODOCUSES
DIPLOE
DIPLOES
DIPLOIC
DIPLOID
DIPLOIDIC
DIPLOIDIES
DIPLOIDS
DIPLOIDY
DIPLOMA
DIPLOMACIES
DIPLOMACY
DIPLOMAED
DIPLOMAING
DIPLOMAS
DIPLOMAT
DIPLOMATA
DIPLOMATE
DIPLOMATES
DIPLOMATIC
DIPLOMATICALLY
DIPLOMATIST
DIPLOMATISTS
DIPLOMATS
DIPLONT
DIPLONTIC
DIPLONTS
DIPLOPHASE
DIPLOPHASES
DIPLOPIA
DIPLOPIAS
DIPLOPIC
DIPLOPOD
DIPLOPODS
DIPLOSES
DIPLOSIS
DIPLOTENE
DIPLOTENES
DIPNET
DIPNETS
DIPNETTED
DIPNETTING
DIPNOAN
DIPNOANS
DIPODIC
DIPODIES
DIPODY
DIPOLAR
DIPOLE
DIPOLES
DIPPABLE
DIPPED
DIPPER
DIPPERFUL
DIPPERFULS
DIPPERS
DIPPIER
DIPPIEST
DIPPINESS
DIPPINESSES
DIPPING
DIPPY
DIPROTIC
DIPS
DIPSADES
DIPSAS
DIPSHIT
DIPSHITS
DIPSO
DIPSOMANIA
DIPSOMANIAC
DIPSOMANIACAL
DIPSOMANIACS
DIPSOMANIAS
DIPSOS
DIPSTICK
DIPSTICKS
DIPT
DIPTERA
DIPTERAL
DIPTERAN
DIPTERANS
DIPTEROCARP
DIPTEROCARPS
DIPTERON
DIPTEROUS
DIPTYCA
DIPTYCAS
DIPTYCH
DIPTYCHS
DIQUAT
DIQUATS
DIRAM
DIRAMS
DIRDUM
DIRDUMS
DIRE
DIRECT
DIRECTED
DIRECTEDNESS
DIRECTEDNESSES
DIRECTER
DIRECTEST
DIRECTING
DIRECTION

DIRECTIONAL
DIRECTIONALITY
DIRECTIONLESS
DIRECTIONS
DIRECTIVE
DIRECTIVES
DIRECTIVITIES
DIRECTIVITY
DIRECTLY
DIRECTNESS
DIRECTNESSES
DIRECTOR
DIRECTORATE
DIRECTORATES
DIRECTORIAL
DIRECTORIES
DIRECTORS
DIRECTORSHIP
DIRECTORSHIPS
DIRECTORY
DIRECTRESS
DIRECTRESSES
DIRECTRICE
DIRECTRICES
DIRECTRIX
DIRECTRIXES
DIRECTS
DIREFUL
DIREFULLY
DIRELY
DIRENESS
DIRENESSES
DIRER
DIREST
DIRGE
DIRGEFUL
DIRGELIKE
DIRGES
DIRHAM
DIRHAMS
DIRIGIBLE
DIRIGIBLES
DIRIGISME
DIRIGISMES
DIRIGISTE
DIRIMENT
DIRK
DIRKED
DIRKING
DIRKS
DIRL
DIRLED
DIRLING
DIRLS
DIRNDL
DIRNDLS
DIRT
DIRTBAG
DIRTBAGS
DIRTBALL
DIRTBALLS
DIRTIED
DIRTIER
DIRTIES
DIRTIEST
DIRTILY
DIRTINESS
DIRTINESSES
DIRTS
DIRTY
DIRTYING
DIS
DISABILITIES
DISABILITY
DISABLE
DISABLED
DISABLEMENT
DISABLEMENTS
DISABLER
DISABLERS
DISABLES
DISABLING
DISABUSAL
DISABUSALS
DISABUSE
DISABUSED
DISABUSES
DISABUSING
DISACCHARIDASE
DISACCHARIDASES
DISACCHARIDE
DISACCHARIDES
DISACCORD
DISACCORDED
DISACCORDING
DISACCORDS
DISACCUSTOM
DISACCUSTOMED
DISACCUSTOMING
DISACCUSTOMS
DISADVANTAGE
DISADVANTAGED
DISADVANTAGEOUS
DISADVANTAGES
DISADVANTAGING
DISAFFECT
DISAFFECTED
DISAFFECTING
DISAFFECTION
DISAFFECTIONS
DISAFFECTS
DISAFFILIATE
DISAFFILIATED
DISAFFILIATES
DISAFFILIATING
DISAFFILIATION
DISAFFILIATIONS
DISAFFIRM
DISAFFIRMANCE
DISAFFIRMANCES
DISAFFIRMED
DISAFFIRMING
DISAFFIRMS
DISAGGREGATE
DISAGGREGATED
DISAGGREGATES
DISAGGREGATING
DISAGGREGATION
DISAGGREGATIONS
DISAGGREGATIVE
DISAGREE
DISAGREEABLE
DISAGREEABLY
DISAGREED
DISAGREEING
DISAGREEMENT
DISAGREEMENTS
DISAGREES
DISALLOW
DISALLOWANCE
DISALLOWANCES
DISALLOWED
DISALLOWING
DISALLOWS
DISAMBIGUATE
DISAMBIGUATED
DISAMBIGUATES
DISAMBIGUATING
DISAMBIGUATION
DISAMBIGUATIONS
DISANNUL
DISANNULLED
DISANNULLING
DISANNULS
DISAPPEAR
DISAPPEARANCE
DISAPPEARANCES
DISAPPEARED
DISAPPEARING
DISAPPEARS
DISAPPOINT
DISAPPOINTED
DISAPPOINTEDLY
DISAPPOINTING
DISAPPOINTINGLY
DISAPPOINTMENT
DISAPPOINTMENTS
DISAPPOINTS
DISAPPROBATION
DISAPPROBATIONS
DISAPPROVAL
DISAPPROVALS
DISAPPROVE
DISAPPROVED
DISAPPROVER
DISAPPROVERS
DISAPPROVES
DISAPPROVING
DISAPPROVINGLY
DISARM
DISARMAMENT
DISARMAMENTS
DISARMED
DISARMER
DISARMERS
DISARMING
DISARMINGLY
DISARMS
DISARRANGE
DISARRANGED
DISARRANGEMENT
DISARRANGEMENTS
DISARRANGES
DISARRANGING
DISARRAY
DISARRAYED
DISARRAYING
DISARRAYS
DISARTICULATE
DISARTICULATED
DISARTICULATES
DISARTICULATING
DISARTICULATION
DISASSEMBLE
DISASSEMBLED
DISASSEMBLES
DISASSEMBLIES
DISASSEMBLING
DISASSEMBLY
DISASSOCIATE
DISASSOCIATED
DISASSOCIATES
DISASSOCIATING
DISASSOCIATION
DISASSOCIATIONS
DISASTER
DISASTERS
DISASTROUS
DISASTROUSLY
DISAVOW
DISAVOWABLE
DISAVOWAL
DISAVOWALS
DISAVOWED
DISAVOWER
DISAVOWERS
DISAVOWING
DISAVOWS
DISBAND
DISBANDED
DISBANDING
DISBANDMENT
DISBANDMENTS
DISBANDS
DISBAR
DISBARMENT
DISBARMENTS
DISBARRED
DISBARRING
DISBARS
DISBELIEF
DISBELIEFS
DISBELIEVE
DISBELIEVED
DISBELIEVER
DISBELIEVERS
DISBELIEVES
DISBELIEVING
DISBENEFIT
DISBENEFITS
DISBOSOM
DISBOSOMED
DISBOSOMING
DISBOSOMS
DISBOUND
DISBOWEL
DISBOWELED
DISBOWELING
DISBOWELLED
DISBOWELLING
DISBOWELS
DISBRANCH
DISBRANCHED
DISBRANCHES
DISBRANCHING

DISBUD
DISBUDDED
DISBUDDING
DISBUDS
DISBURDEN
DISBURDENED
DISBURDENING
DISBURDENMENT
DISBURDENMENTS
DISBURDENS
DISBURSAL
DISBURSALS
DISBURSE
DISBURSED
DISBURSEMENT
DISBURSEMENTS
DISBURSER
DISBURSERS
DISBURSES
DISBURSING
DISC
DISCALCED
DISCANT
DISCANTED
DISCANTING
DISCANTS
DISCARD
DISCARDABLE
DISCARDED
DISCARDER
DISCARDERS
DISCARDING
DISCARDS
DISCARNATE
DISCASE
DISCASED
DISCASES
DISCASING
DISCED
DISCEPT
DISCEPTED
DISCEPTING
DISCEPTS
DISCERN
DISCERNABLE
DISCERNED
DISCERNER
DISCERNERS
DISCERNIBLE
DISCERNIBLY
DISCERNING
DISCERNINGLY
DISCERNMENT
DISCERNMENTS
DISCERNS
DISCHARGE
DISCHARGEABLE
DISCHARGED
DISCHARGEE
DISCHARGEES
DISCHARGER
DISCHARGERS
DISCHARGES
DISCHARGING
DISCI
DISCIFORM
DISCING
DISCIPLE
DISCIPLED
DISCIPLES
DISCIPLESHIP
DISCIPLESHIPS
DISCIPLINABLE
DISCIPLINAL
DISCIPLINARIAN
DISCIPLINARIANS
DISCIPLINARILY
DISCIPLINARITY
DISCIPLINARY
DISCIPLINE
DISCIPLINED
DISCIPLINER
DISCIPLINERS
DISCIPLINES
DISCIPLING
DISCIPLINING
DISCLAIM
DISCLAIMED
DISCLAIMER
DISCLAIMERS
DISCLAIMING
DISCLAIMS
DISCLAMATION
DISCLAMATIONS
DISCLESS
DISCLIKE
DISCLIMAX
DISCLIMAXES
DISCLOSE
DISCLOSED
DISCLOSER
DISCLOSERS
DISCLOSES
DISCLOSING
DISCLOSURE
DISCLOSURES
DISCO
DISCOED
DISCOES
DISCOGRAPHER
DISCOGRAPHERS
DISCOGRAPHIC
DISCOGRAPHICAL
DISCOGRAPHIES
DISCOGRAPHY
DISCOID
DISCOIDAL
DISCOIDS
DISCOING
DISCOLOR
DISCOLORATION
DISCOLORATIONS
DISCOLORED
DISCOLORING
DISCOLORS
DISCOLOUR
DISCOLOURED
DISCOLOURING
DISCOLOURS
DISCOMBOBULATE
DISCOMBOBULATED
DISCOMBOBULATES
DISCOMFIT
DISCOMFITED
DISCOMFITING
DISCOMFITINGLY
DISCOMFITS
DISCOMFITURE
DISCOMFITURES
DISCOMFORT
DISCOMFORTABLE
DISCOMFORTED
DISCOMFORTING
DISCOMFORTS
DISCOMMEND
DISCOMMENDED
DISCOMMENDING
DISCOMMENDS
DISCOMMODE
DISCOMMODED
DISCOMMODES
DISCOMMODING
DISCOMPOSE
DISCOMPOSED
DISCOMPOSES
DISCOMPOSING
DISCOMPOSURE
DISCOMPOSURES
DISCONCERT
DISCONCERTED
DISCONCERTING
DISCONCERTINGLY
DISCONCERTMENT
DISCONCERTMENTS
DISCONCERTS
DISCONFIRM
DISCONFIRMATION
DISCONFIRMED
DISCONFIRMING
DISCONFIRMS
DISCONFORMITIES
DISCONFORMITY
DISCONNECT
DISCONNECTED
DISCONNECTEDLY
DISCONNECTING
DISCONNECTION
DISCONNECTIONS
DISCONNECTS
DISCONSOLATE
DISCONSOLATELY
DISCONSOLATION
DISCONSOLATIONS
DISCONTENT
DISCONTENTED
DISCONTENTEDLY
DISCONTENTING
DISCONTENTMENT
DISCONTENTMENTS
DISCONTENTS
DISCONTINUANCE
DISCONTINUANCES
DISCONTINUATION
DISCONTINUE
DISCONTINUED
DISCONTINUES
DISCONTINUING
DISCONTINUITIES
DISCONTINUITY
DISCONTINUOUS
DISCONTINUOUSLY
DISCOPHILE
DISCOPHILES
DISCORD
DISCORDANCE
DISCORDANCES
DISCORDANCIES
DISCORDANCY
DISCORDANT
DISCORDANTLY
DISCORDED
DISCORDING
DISCORDS
DISCOS
DISCOTHEQUE
DISCOTHEQUES
DISCOUNT
DISCOUNTABLE
DISCOUNTED
DISCOUNTENANCE
DISCOUNTENANCED
DISCOUNTENANCES
DISCOUNTER
DISCOUNTERS
DISCOUNTING
DISCOUNTS
DISCOURAGE
DISCOURAGEABLE
DISCOURAGED
DISCOURAGEMENT
DISCOURAGEMENTS
DISCOURAGER
DISCOURAGERS
DISCOURAGES
DISCOURAGING
DISCOURAGINGLY
DISCOURSE
DISCOURSED
DISCOURSER
DISCOURSERS
DISCOURSES
DISCOURSING
DISCOURTEOUS
DISCOURTEOUSLY
DISCOURTESIES
DISCOURTESY
DISCOVER
DISCOVERABLE
DISCOVERED
DISCOVERER
DISCOVERERS
DISCOVERIES
DISCOVERING
DISCOVERS
DISCOVERT
DISCOVERY
DISCREDIT
DISCREDITABLE
DISCREDITABLY
DISCREDITED
DISCREDITING
DISCREDITS
DISCREET
DISCREETER
DISCREETEST

DISCREETLY
DISCREETNESS
DISCREETNESSES
DISCREPANCIES
DISCREPANCY
DISCREPANT
DISCREPANTLY
DISCRETE
DISCRETELY
DISCRETENESS
DISCRETENESSES
DISCRETION
DISCRETIONARY
DISCRETIONS
DISCRIMINABLE
DISCRIMINABLY
DISCRIMINANT
DISCRIMINANTS
DISCRIMINATE
DISCRIMINATED
DISCRIMINATES
DISCRIMINATING
DISCRIMINATION
DISCRIMINATIONS
DISCRIMINATIVE
DISCRIMINATOR
DISCRIMINATORS
DISCRIMINATORY
DISCROWN
DISCROWNED
DISCROWNING
DISCROWNS
DISCS
DISCURSIVE
DISCURSIVELY
DISCURSIVENESS
DISCUS
DISCUSES
DISCUSS
DISCUSSABLE
DISCUSSANT
DISCUSSANTS
DISCUSSED
DISCUSSER
DISCUSSERS
DISCUSSES
DISCUSSIBLE
DISCUSSING
DISCUSSION
DISCUSSIONS
DISDAIN
DISDAINED
DISDAINFUL
DISDAINFULLY
DISDAINFULNESS
DISDAINING
DISDAINS
DISEASE
DISEASED
DISEASES
DISEASING
DISECONOMIES
DISECONOMY
DISEMBARK
DISEMBARKATION
DISEMBARKATIONS
DISEMBARKED
DISEMBARKING
DISEMBARKS
DISEMBARRASS
DISEMBARRASSED
DISEMBARRASSES
DISEMBARRASSING
DISEMBODIED
DISEMBODIES
DISEMBODY
DISEMBODYING
DISEMBOGUE
DISEMBOGUED
DISEMBOGUES
DISEMBOGUING
DISEMBOWEL
DISEMBOWELED
DISEMBOWELING
DISEMBOWELLED
DISEMBOWELLING
DISEMBOWELMENT
DISEMBOWELMENTS
DISEMBOWELS
DISEMPLOY
DISEMPLOYED
DISEMPLOYING
DISEMPLOYS
DISEMPOWER
DISEMPOWERED
DISEMPOWERING
DISEMPOWERMENT
DISEMPOWERMENTS
DISEMPOWERS
DISENABLE
DISENABLED
DISENABLES
DISENABLING
DISENCHANT
DISENCHANTED
DISENCHANTER
DISENCHANTERS
DISENCHANTING
DISENCHANTINGLY
DISENCHANTMENT
DISENCHANTMENTS
DISENCHANTS
DISENCUMBER
DISENCUMBERED
DISENCUMBERING
DISENCUMBERS
DISENDOW
DISENDOWED
DISENDOWER
DISENDOWERS
DISENDOWING
DISENDOWMENT
DISENDOWMENTS
DISENDOWS
DISENFRANCHISE
DISENFRANCHISED
DISENFRANCHISES
DISENGAGE
DISENGAGED
DISENGAGEMENT
DISENGAGEMENTS
DISENGAGES
DISENGAGING
DISENTAIL
DISENTAILED
DISENTAILING
DISENTAILS
DISENTANGLE
DISENTANGLED
DISENTANGLEMENT
DISENTANGLES
DISENTANGLING
DISENTHRAL
DISENTHRALL
DISENTHRALLED
DISENTHRALLING
DISENTHRALLS
DISENTHRALS
DISENTITLE
DISENTITLED
DISENTITLES
DISENTITLING
DISEQUILIBRATE
DISEQUILIBRATED
DISEQUILIBRATES
DISEQUILIBRIA
DISEQUILIBRIUM
DISEQUILIBRIUMS
DISESTABLISH
DISESTABLISHED
DISESTABLISHES
DISESTABLISHING
DISESTEEM
DISESTEEMED
DISESTEEMING
DISESTEEMS
DISEUR
DISEURS
DISEUSE
DISEUSES
DISFAVOR
DISFAVORED
DISFAVORING
DISFAVORS
DISFAVOUR
DISFAVOURED
DISFAVOURING
DISFAVOURS
DISFIGURE
DISFIGURED
DISFIGUREMENT
DISFIGUREMENTS
DISFIGURES
DISFIGURING
DISFRANCHISE
DISFRANCHISED
DISFRANCHISES
DISFRANCHISING
DISFROCK
DISFROCKED
DISFROCKING
DISFROCKS
DISFUNCTION
DISFUNCTIONS
DISFURNISH
DISFURNISHED
DISFURNISHES
DISFURNISHING
DISFURNISHMENT
DISFURNISHMENTS
DISGORGE
DISGORGED
DISGORGES
DISGORGING
DISGRACE
DISGRACED
DISGRACEFUL
DISGRACEFULLY
DISGRACEFULNESS
DISGRACER
DISGRACERS
DISGRACES
DISGRACING
DISGRUNTLE
DISGRUNTLED
DISGRUNTLEMENT
DISGRUNTLEMENTS
DISGRUNTLES
DISGRUNTLING
DISGUISE
DISGUISED
DISGUISEDLY
DISGUISEMENT
DISGUISEMENTS
DISGUISER
DISGUISERS
DISGUISES
DISGUISING
DISGUST
DISGUSTED
DISGUSTEDLY
DISGUSTFUL
DISGUSTFULLY
DISGUSTING
DISGUSTINGLY
DISGUSTS
DISH
DISHABILLE
DISHABILLES
DISHARMONIC
DISHARMONIES
DISHARMONIOUS
DISHARMONIZE
DISHARMONIZED
DISHARMONIZES
DISHARMONIZING
DISHARMONY
DISHCLOTH
DISHCLOTHS
DISHCLOUT
DISHCLOUTS
DISHDASHA
DISHDASHAS
DISHEARTEN
DISHEARTENED
DISHEARTENING
DISHEARTENINGLY
DISHEARTENMENT
DISHEARTENMENTS
DISHEARTENS
DISHED
DISHELM
DISHELMED
DISHELMING
DISHELMS

DISHERIT
DISHERITED
DISHERITING
DISHERITS
DISHES
DISHEVEL
DISHEVELED
DISHEVELING
DISHEVELLED
DISHEVELLING
DISHEVELMENT
DISHEVELMENTS
DISHEVELS
DISHFUL
DISHFULS
DISHIER
DISHIEST
DISHING
DISHLIKE
DISHONEST
DISHONESTIES
DISHONESTLY
DISHONESTY
DISHONOR
DISHONORABLE
DISHONORABLY
DISHONORED
DISHONORER
DISHONORERS
DISHONORING
DISHONORS
DISHONOUR
DISHONOURABLE
DISHONOURABLY
DISHONOURED
DISHONOURING
DISHONOURS
DISHPAN
DISHPANS
DISHRAG
DISHRAGS
DISHTOWEL
DISHTOWELS
DISHWARE
DISHWARES
DISHWASHER
DISHWASHERS
DISHWASHING
DISHWASHINGS
DISHWATER
DISHWATERS
DISHY
DISILLUSION
DISILLUSIONED
DISILLUSIONING
DISILLUSIONMENT
DISILLUSIONS
DISINCENTIVE
DISINCENTIVES
DISINCLINATION
DISINCLINATIONS
DISINCLINE
DISINCLINED
DISINCLINES
DISINCLINING
DISINFECT
DISINFECTANT
DISINFECTANTS
DISINFECTED
DISINFECTING
DISINFECTION
DISINFECTIONS
DISINFECTS
DISINFEST
DISINFESTANT
DISINFESTANTS
DISINFESTATION
DISINFESTATIONS
DISINFESTED
DISINFESTING
DISINFESTS
DISINFLATION
DISINFLATIONARY
DISINFLATIONS
DISINFORM
DISINFORMATION
DISINFORMATIONS
DISINFORMED
DISINFORMING
DISINFORMS
DISINGENUOUS
DISINGENUOUSLY
DISINHERIT
DISINHERITANCE
DISINHERITANCES
DISINHERITED
DISINHERITING
DISINHERITS
DISINHIBIT
DISINHIBITED
DISINHIBITING
DISINHIBITION
DISINHIBITIONS
DISINHIBITOR
DISINHIBITORS
DISINHIBITS
DISINTEGRATE
DISINTEGRATED
DISINTEGRATES
DISINTEGRATING
DISINTEGRATION
DISINTEGRATIONS
DISINTEGRATIVE
DISINTEGRATOR
DISINTEGRATORS
DISINTER
DISINTEREST
DISINTERESTED
DISINTERESTEDLY
DISINTERESTING
DISINTERESTS
DISINTERMEDIATE
DISINTERMENT
DISINTERMENTS
DISINTERRED
DISINTERRING
DISINTERS
DISINTOXICATE
DISINTOXICATED
DISINTOXICATES
DISINTOXICATING
DISINTOXICATION
DISINVEST
DISINVESTED
DISINVESTING
DISINVESTMENT
DISINVESTMENTS
DISINVESTS
DISINVITE
DISINVITED
DISINVITES
DISINVITING
DISJECT
DISJECTED
DISJECTING
DISJECTS
DISJOIN
DISJOINED
DISJOINING
DISJOINS
DISJOINT
DISJOINTED
DISJOINTEDLY
DISJOINTEDNESS
DISJOINTING
DISJOINTS
DISJUNCT
DISJUNCTION
DISJUNCTIONS
DISJUNCTIVE
DISJUNCTIVELY
DISJUNCTIVES
DISJUNCTS
DISJUNCTURE
DISJUNCTURES
DISK
DISKED
DISKER
DISKERS
DISKETTE
DISKETTES
DISKING
DISKLESS
DISKLIKE
DISKS
DISLIKABLE
DISLIKE
DISLIKEABLE
DISLIKED
DISLIKER
DISLIKERS
DISLIKES
DISLIKING
DISLIMN
DISLIMNED
DISLIMNING
DISLIMNS
DISLOCATE
DISLOCATED
DISLOCATES
DISLOCATING
DISLOCATION
DISLOCATIONS
DISLODGE
DISLODGED
DISLODGEMENT
DISLODGEMENTS
DISLODGES
DISLODGING
DISLODGMENT
DISLODGMENTS
DISLOYAL
DISLOYALLY
DISLOYALTIES
DISLOYALTY
DISMAL
DISMALER
DISMALEST
DISMALLY
DISMALNESS
DISMALNESSES
DISMALS
DISMANTLE
DISMANTLED
DISMANTLEMENT
DISMANTLEMENTS
DISMANTLES
DISMANTLING
DISMAST
DISMASTED
DISMASTING
DISMASTS
DISMAY
DISMAYED
DISMAYING
DISMAYINGLY
DISMAYS
DISME
DISMEMBER
DISMEMBERED
DISMEMBERING
DISMEMBERMENT
DISMEMBERMENTS
DISMEMBERS
DISMES
DISMISS
DISMISSAL
DISMISSALS
DISMISSED
DISMISSES
DISMISSING
DISMISSION
DISMISSIONS
DISMISSIVE
DISMISSIVELY
DISMOUNT
DISMOUNTED
DISMOUNTING
DISMOUNTS
DISOBEDIENCE
DISOBEDIENCES
DISOBEDIENT
DISOBEDIENTLY
DISOBEY
DISOBEYED
DISOBEYER
DISOBEYERS
DISOBEYING
DISOBEYS
DISOBLIGE
DISOBLIGED
DISOBLIGES
DISOBLIGING
DISOMIC
DISOMIES

DISOMY
DISORDER
DISORDERED
DISORDEREDLY
DISORDEREDNESS
DISORDERING
DISORDERLINESS
DISORDERLY
DISORDERS
DISORGANISATION
DISORGANISED
DISORGANIZATION
DISORGANIZE
DISORGANIZED
DISORGANIZES
DISORGANIZING
DISORIENT
DISORIENTATE
DISORIENTATED
DISORIENTATES
DISORIENTATING
DISORIENTATION
DISORIENTATIONS
DISORIENTED
DISORIENTING
DISORIENTS
DISOWN
DISOWNED
DISOWNER
DISOWNERS
DISOWNING
DISOWNMENT
DISOWNMENTS
DISOWNS
DISPARAGE
DISPARAGED
DISPARAGEMENT
DISPARAGEMENTS
DISPARAGER
DISPARAGERS
DISPARAGES
DISPARAGING
DISPARAGINGLY
DISPARATE
DISPARATELY
DISPARATENESS
DISPARATENESSES
DISPARITIES
DISPARITY
DISPART
DISPARTED
DISPARTING
DISPARTS
DISPASSION
DISPASSIONATE
DISPASSIONATELY
DISPASSIONS
DISPATCH
DISPATCHED
DISPATCHER
DISPATCHERS
DISPATCHES
DISPATCHING
DISPEL
DISPELLED
DISPELLER
DISPELLERS
DISPELLING
DISPELS
DISPEND
DISPENDED
DISPENDING
DISPENDS
DISPENSABILITY
DISPENSABLE
DISPENSARIES
DISPENSARY
DISPENSATION
DISPENSATIONAL
DISPENSATIONS
DISPENSATORIES
DISPENSATORY
DISPENSE
DISPENSED
DISPENSER
DISPENSERS
DISPENSES
DISPENSING
DISPEOPLE
DISPEOPLED
DISPEOPLES
DISPEOPLING
DISPERSAL
DISPERSALS
DISPERSANT
DISPERSANTS
DISPERSE
DISPERSED
DISPERSEDLY
DISPERSER
DISPERSERS
DISPERSES
DISPERSIBLE
DISPERSING
DISPERSION
DISPERSIONS
DISPERSIVE
DISPERSIVELY
DISPERSIVENESS
DISPERSOID
DISPERSOIDS
DISPIRIT
DISPIRITED
DISPIRITEDLY
DISPIRITEDNESS
DISPIRITING
DISPIRITS
DISPITEOUS
DISPLACE
DISPLACEABLE
DISPLACED
DISPLACEMENT
DISPLACEMENTS
DISPLACER
DISPLACERS
DISPLACES
DISPLACING
DISPLANT
DISPLANTED
DISPLANTING
DISPLANTS
DISPLAY
DISPLAYABLE
DISPLAYED
DISPLAYER
DISPLAYERS
DISPLAYING
DISPLAYS
DISPLEASE
DISPLEASED
DISPLEASES
DISPLEASING
DISPLEASURE
DISPLEASURES
DISPLODE
DISPLODED
DISPLODES
DISPLODING
DISPLOSION
DISPLOSIONS
DISPLUME
DISPLUMED
DISPLUMES
DISPLUMING
DISPORT
DISPORTED
DISPORTING
DISPORTMENT
DISPORTMENTS
DISPORTS
DISPOSABILITIES
DISPOSABILITY
DISPOSABLE
DISPOSABLES
DISPOSAL
DISPOSALS
DISPOSE
DISPOSED
DISPOSER
DISPOSERS
DISPOSES
DISPOSING
DISPOSITION
DISPOSITIONAL
DISPOSITIONS
DISPOSITIVE
DISPOSSESS
DISPOSSESSED
DISPOSSESSES
DISPOSSESSING
DISPOSSESSION
DISPOSSESSIONS
DISPOSSESSOR
DISPOSSESSORS
DISPOSURE
DISPOSURES
DISPRAISE
DISPRAISED
DISPRAISER
DISPRAISERS
DISPRAISES
DISPRAISING
DISPRAISINGLY
DISPREAD
DISPREADING
DISPREADS
DISPRIZE
DISPRIZED
DISPRIZES
DISPRIZING
DISPROOF
DISPROOFS
DISPROPORTION
DISPROPORTIONAL
DISPROPORTIONED
DISPROPORTIONS
DISPROVABLE
DISPROVAL
DISPROVALS
DISPROVE
DISPROVED
DISPROVEN
DISPROVER
DISPROVERS
DISPROVES
DISPROVING
DISPUTABLE
DISPUTABLY
DISPUTANT
DISPUTANTS
DISPUTATION
DISPUTATIONS
DISPUTATIOUS
DISPUTATIOUSLY
DISPUTE
DISPUTED
DISPUTER
DISPUTERS
DISPUTES
DISPUTING
DISQUALIFIED
DISQUALIFIES
DISQUALIFY
DISQUALIFYING
DISQUANTITIED
DISQUANTITIES
DISQUANTITY
DISQUANTITYING
DISQUIET
DISQUIETED
DISQUIETING
DISQUIETINGLY
DISQUIETLY
DISQUIETS
DISQUIETUDE
DISQUIETUDES
DISQUISITION
DISQUISITIONS
DISRATE
DISRATED
DISRATES
DISRATING
DISREGARD
DISREGARDED
DISREGARDFUL
DISREGARDING
DISREGARDS
DISRELATED
DISRELATION
DISRELATIONS
DISRELISH
DISRELISHED
DISRELISHES
DISRELISHING
DISREMEMBER

DISREMEMBERED
DISREMEMBERING
DISREMEMBERS
DISREPAIR
DISREPAIRS
DISREPECTING
DISREPECTS
DISREPUTABILITY
DISREPUTABLE
DISREPUTABLY
DISREPUTE
DISREPUTES
DISRESPECT
DISRESPECTABLE
DISRESPECTED
DISRESPECTFUL
DISRESPECTFULLY
DISRESPECTING
DISRESPECTS
DISROBE
DISROBED
DISROBER
DISROBERS
DISROBES
DISROBING
DISROOT
DISROOTED
DISROOTING
DISROOTS
DISRUPT
DISRUPTED
DISRUPTER
DISRUPTERS
DISRUPTING
DISRUPTION
DISRUPTIONS
DISRUPTIVE
DISRUPTIVELY
DISRUPTIVENESS
DISRUPTOR
DISRUPTORS
DISRUPTS
DISS
DISSATISFACTION
DISSATISFACTORY
DISSATISFIED
DISSATISFIES
DISSATISFY
DISSATISFYING
DISSAVE
DISSAVED
DISSAVER
DISSAVERS

DISSAVES
DISSAVING
DISSAVINGS
DISSEAT
DISSEATED
DISSEATING
DISSEATS
DISSECT
DISSECTED
DISSECTING
DISSECTION
DISSECTIONS
DISSECTOR
DISSECTORS
DISSECTS
DISSED
DISSEISE
DISSEISED
DISSEISEE
DISSEISEES
DISSEISES
DISSEISIN
DISSEISING
DISSEISINS
DISSEISOR
DISSEISORS
DISSEIZE
DISSEIZED
DISSEIZEE
DISSEIZEES
DISSEIZES
DISSEIZIN
DISSEIZING
DISSEIZINS
DISSEIZOR
DISSEIZORS
DISSEMBLE
DISSEMBLED
DISSEMBLER
DISSEMBLERS
DISSEMBLES
DISSEMBLING
DISSEMINATE
DISSEMINATED
DISSEMINATES
DISSEMINATING
DISSEMINATION
DISSEMINATIONS
DISSEMINATOR
DISSEMINATORS
DISSEMINULE
DISSEMINULES
DISSENSION

DISSENSIONS
DISSENSUS
DISSENSUSES
DISSENT
DISSENTED
DISSENTER
DISSENTERS
DISSENTIENT
DISSENTIENTS
DISSENTING
DISSENTION
DISSENTIONS
DISSENTIOUS
DISSENTS
DISSEPIMENT
DISSEPIMENTS
DISSERT
DISSERTATE
DISSERTATED
DISSERTATES
DISSERTATING
DISSERTATION
DISSERTATIONAL
DISSERTATIONS
DISSERTATOR
DISSERTATORS
DISSERTED
DISSERTING
DISSERTS
DISSERVE
DISSERVED
DISSERVES
DISSERVICE
DISSERVICEABLE
DISSERVICES
DISSERVING
DISSES
DISSEVER
DISSEVERANCE
DISSEVERANCES
DISSEVERED
DISSEVERING
DISSEVERMENT
DISSEVERMENTS
DISSEVERS
DISSIDENCE
DISSIDENCES
DISSIDENT
DISSIDENTS
DISSIMILAR
DISSIMILARITIES
DISSIMILARITY
DISSIMILARLY

DISSIMILARS
DISSIMILATE
DISSIMILATED
DISSIMILATES
DISSIMILATING
DISSIMILATION
DISSIMILATIONS
DISSIMILATORY
DISSIMILITUDE
DISSIMILITUDES
DISSIMULATE
DISSIMULATED
DISSIMULATES
DISSIMULATING
DISSIMULATION
DISSIMULATIONS
DISSIMULATOR
DISSIMULATORS
DISSING
DISSIPATE
DISSIPATED
DISSIPATEDLY
DISSIPATEDNESS
DISSIPATER
DISSIPATERS
DISSIPATES
DISSIPATING
DISSIPATION
DISSIPATIONS
DISSIPATIVE
DISSOCIABILITY
DISSOCIABLE
DISSOCIAL
DISSOCIATE
DISSOCIATED
DISSOCIATES
DISSOCIATING
DISSOCIATION
DISSOCIATIONS
DISSOCIATIVE
DISSOLUBLE
DISSOLUTE
DISSOLUTELY
DISSOLUTENESS
DISSOLUTENESSES
DISSOLUTION
DISSOLUTIONS
DISSOLVABLE
DISSOLVE
DISSOLVED
DISSOLVENT
DISSOLVENTS
DISSOLVER

DISSOLVERS
DISSOLVES
DISSOLVING
DISSONANCE
DISSONANCES
DISSONANT
DISSONANTLY
DISSUADE
DISSUADED
DISSUADER
DISSUADERS
DISSUADES
DISSUADING
DISSUASION
DISSUASIONS
DISSUASIVE
DISSUASIVELY
DISSUASIVENESS
DISSYLLABLE
DISSYLLABLES
DISSYMMETRIC
DISSYMMETRIES
DISSYMMETRY
DISTAFF
DISTAFFS
DISTAIN
DISTAINED
DISTAINING
DISTAINS
DISTAL
DISTALLY
DISTANCE
DISTANCED
DISTANCES
DISTANCING
DISTANT
DISTANTLY
DISTANTNESS
DISTANTNESSES
DISTASTE
DISTASTED
DISTASTEFUL
DISTASTEFULLY
DISTASTEFULNESS
DISTASTES
DISTASTING
DISTAVES
DISTELFINK
DISTELFINKS
DISTEMPER
DISTEMPERATE
DISTEMPERATURE
DISTEMPERATURES

DISTEMPERED
DISTEMPERING
DISTEMPERS
DISTEND
DISTENDED
DISTENDER
DISTENDERS
DISTENDING
DISTENDS
DISTENSIBILITY
DISTENSIBLE
DISTENSION
DISTENSIONS
DISTENT
DISTENTION
DISTENTIONS
DISTICH
DISTICHAL
DISTICHOUS
DISTICHS
DISTIL
DISTILL
DISTILLATE
DISTILLATES
DISTILLATION
DISTILLATIONS
DISTILLED
DISTILLER
DISTILLERIES
DISTILLERS
DISTILLERY
DISTILLING
DISTILLS
DISTILS
DISTINCT
DISTINCTER
DISTINCTEST
DISTINCTION
DISTINCTIONS
DISTINCTIVE
DISTINCTIVELY
DISTINCTIVENESS
DISTINCTLY
DISTINCTNESS
DISTINCTNESSES
DISTINGUE
DISTINGUISH
DISTINGUISHABLE
DISTINGUISHABLY
DISTINGUISHED
DISTINGUISHES
DISTINGUISHING
DISTOME
DISTOMES
DISTORT
DISTORTED
DISTORTER
DISTORTERS
DISTORTING
DISTORTION
DISTORTIONAL
DISTORTIONS
DISTORTS
DISTRACT
DISTRACTABLE
DISTRACTED
DISTRACTEDLY
DISTRACTIBILITY
DISTRACTIBLE
DISTRACTING
DISTRACTINGLY
DISTRACTION
DISTRACTIONS
DISTRACTIVE
DISTRACTS
DISTRAIN
DISTRAINABLE
DISTRAINED
DISTRAINER
DISTRAINERS
DISTRAINING
DISTRAINOR
DISTRAINORS
DISTRAINS
DISTRAINT
DISTRAINTS
DISTRAIT
DISTRAITE
DISTRAUGHT
DISTRAUGHTLY
DISTRESS
DISTRESSED
DISTRESSES
DISTRESSFUL
DISTRESSFULLY
DISTRESSFULNESS
DISTRESSING
DISTRESSINGLY
DISTRIBUTARIES
DISTRIBUTARY
DISTRIBUTE
DISTRIBUTED
DISTRIBUTEE
DISTRIBUTEES
DISTRIBUTES
DISTRIBUTING
DISTRIBUTION
DISTRIBUTIONAL
DISTRIBUTIONS
DISTRIBUTIVE
DISTRIBUTIVELY
DISTRIBUTIVITY
DISTRIBUTOR
DISTRIBUTORS
DISTRICT
DISTRICTED
DISTRICTING
DISTRICTS
DISTRUST
DISTRUSTED
DISTRUSTFUL
DISTRUSTFULLY
DISTRUSTFULNESS
DISTRUSTING
DISTRUSTS
DISTURB
DISTURBANCE
DISTURBANCES
DISTURBED
DISTURBER
DISTURBERS
DISTURBING
DISTURBINGLY
DISTURBS
DISUBSTITUTED
DISULFATE
DISULFATES
DISULFID
DISULFIDE
DISULFIDES
DISULFIDS
DISULFIRAM
DISULFIRAMS
DISULFOTON
DISULFOTONS
DISUNION
DISUNIONIST
DISUNIONISTS
DISUNIONS
DISUNITE
DISUNITED
DISUNITER
DISUNITERS
DISUNITES
DISUNITIES
DISUNITING
DISUNITY
DISUSE
DISUSED
DISUSES
DISUSING
DISUTILITIES
DISUTILITY
DISVALUE
DISVALUED
DISVALUES
DISVALUING
DISYLLABIC
DISYLLABLE
DISYLLABLES
DISYOKE
DISYOKED
DISYOKES
DISYOKING
DIT
DITA
DITAS
DITCH
DITCHDIGGER
DITCHDIGGERS
DITCHED
DITCHER
DITCHERS
DITCHES
DITCHING
DITCHWATER
DITCHWATERS
DITE
DITES
DITHEISM
DITHEISMS
DITHEIST
DITHEISTS
DITHER
DITHERED
DITHERER
DITHERERS
DITHERING
DITHERS
DITHERY
DITHIOCARBAMATE
DITHIOL
DITHYRAMB
DITHYRAMBIC
DITHYRAMBICALLY
DITHYRAMBS
DITRANSITIVE
DITRANSITIVES
DITS
DITSIER
DITSIEST
DITSINESS
DITSINESSES
DITSY
DITTANIES
DITTANY
DITTIES
DITTO
DITTOED
DITTOING
DITTOS
DITTY
DITZ
DITZES
DITZIER
DITZIEST
DITZINESS
DITZINESSES
DITZY
DIURESES
DIURESIS
DIURETIC
DIURETICALLY
DIURETICS
DIURNAL
DIURNALLY
DIURNALS
DIURON
DIURONS
DIVA
DIVAGATE
DIVAGATED
DIVAGATES
DIVAGATING
DIVAGATION
DIVAGATIONS
DIVALENCE
DIVALENCES
DIVALENT
DIVAN
DIVANS
DIVARICATE
DIVARICATED
DIVARICATES
DIVARICATING
DIVARICATION
DIVARICATIONS
DIVAS
DIVE
DIVEBOMB
DIVEBOMBED
DIVEBOMBING
DIVEBOMBS
DIVED
DIVER

DIVERGE
DIVERGED
DIVERGENCE
DIVERGENCES
DIVERGENCIES
DIVERGENCY
DIVERGENT
DIVERGENTLY
DIVERGES
DIVERGING
DIVERS
DIVERSE
DIVERSELY
DIVERSENESS
DIVERSENESSES
DIVERSIFICATION
DIVERSIFIED
DIVERSIFIER
DIVERSIFIERS
DIVERSIFIES
DIVERSIFY
DIVERSIFYING
DIVERSION
DIVERSIONARY
DIVERSIONIST
DIVERSIONISTS
DIVERSIONS
DIVERSITIES
DIVERSITY
DIVERT
DIVERTED
DIVERTER
DIVERTERS
DIVERTICULA
DIVERTICULAR
DIVERTICULITIS
DIVERTICULOSES
DIVERTICULOSIS
DIVERTICULUM
DIVERTIMENTI
DIVERTIMENTO
DIVERTIMENTOS
DIVERTING
DIVERTINGLY
DIVERTISSEMENT
DIVERTISSEMENTS
DIVERTS
DIVES
DIVEST
DIVESTED
DIVESTING
DIVESTITURE
DIVESTITURES
DIVESTMENT
DIVESTMENTS
DIVESTS
DIVESTURE
DIVESTURES
DIVIDABLE
DIVIDE
DIVIDED
DIVIDEDLY
DIVIDEDNESS
DIVIDEDNESSES
DIVIDEND
DIVIDENDLESS
DIVIDENDS
DIVIDER
DIVIDERS
DIVIDES
DIVIDING
DIVIDUAL
DIVINATION
DIVINATIONS
DIVINATORY
DIVINE
DIVINED
DIVINELY
DIVINER
DIVINERS
DIVINES
DIVINEST
DIVING
DIVINGS
DIVINING
DIVINISE
DIVINISED
DIVINISES
DIVINISING
DIVINITIES
DIVINITY
DIVINIZE
DIVINIZED
DIVINIZES
DIVINIZING
DIVISIBILITIES
DIVISIBILITY
DIVISIBLE
DIVISIBLY
DIVISION
DIVISIONAL
DIVISIONISM
DIVISIONISMS
DIVISIONIST
DIVISIONISTS
DIVISIONS
DIVISIVE
DIVISIVELY
DIVISIVENESS
DIVISIVENESSES
DIVISOR
DIVISORS
DIVORCE
DIVORCED
DIVORCEE
DIVORCEES
DIVORCEMENT
DIVORCEMENTS
DIVORCER
DIVORCERS
DIVORCES
DIVORCING
DIVORCIVE
DIVOT
DIVOTS
DIVULGATE
DIVULGATED
DIVULGATES
DIVULGATING
DIVULGE
DIVULGED
DIVULGENCE
DIVULGENCES
DIVULGER
DIVULGERS
DIVULGES
DIVULGING
DIVULSE
DIVULSED
DIVULSES
DIVULSING
DIVULSION
DIVULSIONS
DIVULSIVE
DIVVIED
DIVVIES
DIVVY
DIVVYING
DIWAN
DIWANS
DIXIT
DIXITS
DIZEN
DIZENED
DIZENING
DIZENMENT
DIZENMENTS
DIZENS
DIZYGOTIC
DIZYGOUS
DIZZIED
DIZZIER
DIZZIES
DIZZIEST
DIZZILY
DIZZINESS
DIZZINESSES
DIZZY
DIZZYING
DIZZYINGLY
DJEBEL
DJEBELS
DJELLABA
DJELLABAH
DJELLABAHS
DJELLABAS
DJEMBE
DJEMBES
DJIBBA
DJIBBAH
DJIBBAHS
DJIBBAS
DJIN
DJINN
DJINNI
DJINNS
DJINNY
DJINS
DO
DOABLE
DOAT
DOATED
DOATING
DOATS
DOBBER
DOBBERS
DOBBIES
DOBBIN
DOBBINS
DOBBY
DOBE
DOBES
DOBIE
DOBIES
DOBLA
DOBLAS
DOBLON
DOBLONES
DOBLONS
DOBRA
DOBRAS
DOBRO
DOBROS
DOBSON
DOBSONFLIES
DOBSONFLY
DOBSONS
DOBY
DOC
DOCENT
DOCENTS
DOCETIC
DOCILE
DOCILELY
DOCILITIES
DOCILITY
DOCK
DOCKAGE
DOCKAGES
DOCKED
DOCKER
DOCKERS
DOCKET
DOCKETED
DOCKETING
DOCKETS
DOCKHAND
DOCKHANDS
DOCKING
DOCKLAND
DOCKLANDS
DOCKMASTER
DOCKMASTERS
DOCKS
DOCKSIDE
DOCKSIDES
DOCKWORKER
DOCKWORKERS
DOCKYARD
DOCKYARDS
DOCS
DOCTOR
DOCTORAL
DOCTORATE
DOCTORATES
DOCTORED
DOCTORIAL
DOCTORING
DOCTORINGS
DOCTORLESS
DOCTORLY
DOCTORS
DOCTORSHIP
DOCTORSHIPS
DOCTRINAIRE

DOCTRINAIRES
DOCTRINAIRISM
DOCTRINAIRISMS
DOCTRINAL
DOCTRINALLY
DOCTRINE
DOCTRINES
DOCUDRAMA
DOCUDRAMAS
DOCUMENT
DOCUMENTABLE
DOCUMENTAL
DOCUMENTALIST
DOCUMENTALISTS
DOCUMENTARIAN
DOCUMENTARIANS
DOCUMENTARIES
DOCUMENTARILY
DOCUMENTARIST
DOCUMENTARISTS
DOCUMENTARY
DOCUMENTATION
DOCUMENTATIONAL
DOCUMENTATIONS
DOCUMENTED
DOCUMENTER
DOCUMENTERS
DOCUMENTING
DOCUMENTS
DOCUSERIES
DOCUSOAP
DOCUSOAPS
DODDER
DODDERED
DODDERER
DODDERERS
DODDERING
DODDERS
DODDERY
DODDLE
DODDLES
DODECAGON
DODECAGONS
DODECAHEDRA
DODECAHEDRAL
DODECAHEDRON
DODECAHEDRONS
DODECAPHONIC
DODECAPHONIES
DODECAPHONIST
DODECAPHONISTS
DODECAPHONY
DODGE
DODGEBALL
DODGEBALLS
DODGED
DODGEM
DODGEMS
DODGER
DODGERIES
DODGERS
DODGERY
DODGES
DODGIER
DODGIEST
DODGINESS
DODGINESSES
DODGING
DODGY
DODO
DODOES
DODOISM
DODOISMS
DODOS
DOE
DOER
DOERS
DOES
DOESKIN
DOESKINS
DOEST
DOETH
DOFF
DOFFED
DOFFER
DOFFERS
DOFFING
DOFFS
DOG
DOGAN
DOGANS
DOGBANE
DOGBANES
DOGBERRIES
DOGBERRY
DOGCART
DOGCARTS
DOGCATCHER
DOGCATCHERS
DOGDOM
DOGDOMS
DOGE
DOGEAR
DOGEARED
DOGEARING
DOGEARS
DOGEDOM
DOGEDOMS
DOGES
DOGESHIP
DOGESHIPS
DOGEY
DOGEYS
DOGFACE
DOGFACES
DOGFIGHT
DOGFIGHTER
DOGFIGHTERS
DOGFIGHTING
DOGFIGHTS
DOGFISH
DOGFISHES
DOGFOUGHT
DOGGED
DOGGEDLY
DOGGEDNESS
DOGGEDNESSES
DOGGER
DOGGEREL
DOGGERELS
DOGGERIES
DOGGERS
DOGGERY
DOGGIE
DOGGIER
DOGGIES
DOGGIEST
DOGGING
DOGGISH
DOGGISHLY
DOGGISHNESS
DOGGISHNESSES
DOGGO
DOGGONE
DOGGONED
DOGGONEDER
DOGGONEDEST
DOGGONER
DOGGONES
DOGGONEST
DOGGONING
DOGGREL
DOGGRELS
DOGGY
DOGHANGED
DOGHOUSE
DOGHOUSES
DOGIE
DOGIES
DOGLEG
DOGLEGGED
DOGLEGGING
DOGLEGS
DOGLIKE
DOGMA
DOGMAS
DOGMATA
DOGMATIC
DOGMATICAL
DOGMATICALLY
DOGMATICALNESS
DOGMATICS
DOGMATISM
DOGMATISMS
DOGMATIST
DOGMATISTS
DOGMATIZATION
DOGMATIZATIONS
DOGMATIZE
DOGMATIZED
DOGMATIZER
DOGMATIZERS
DOGMATIZES
DOGMATIZING
DOGNAP
DOGNAPED
DOGNAPER
DOGNAPERS
DOGNAPING
DOGNAPPED
DOGNAPPER
DOGNAPPERS
DOGNAPPING
DOGNAPS
DOGROBBER
DOGROBBERS
DOGS
DOGSBODIES
DOGSBODY
DOGSBODYING
DOGSBODYINGS
DOGSKIN
DOGSKINS
DOGSLED
DOGSLEDDED
DOGSLEDDER
DOGSLEDDERS
DOGSLEDDING
DOGSLEDDINGS
DOGSLEDS
DOGSTAIL
DOGSTAILS
DOGTAIL
DOGTAILS
DOGTEETH
DOGTOOTH
DOGTROT
DOGTROTS
DOGTROTTED
DOGTROTTING
DOGVANE
DOGVANES
DOGWATCH
DOGWATCHES
DOGWOOD
DOGWOODS
DOGY
DOH
DOHS
DOILED
DOILIED
DOILIES
DOILY
DOING
DOINGS
DOIT
DOITED
DOITS
DOJO
DOJOS
DOL
DOLABRATE
DOLCE
DOLCETTO
DOLCETTOS
DOLCI
DOLDRUMS
DOLE
DOLED
DOLEFUL
DOLEFULLER
DOLEFULLEST
DOLEFULLY
DOLEFULNESS
DOLEFULNESSES
DOLERITE
DOLERITES
DOLERITIC
DOLES
DOLESOME
DOLICHOCEPHALIC
DOLICHOCEPHALY
DOLING
DOLL
DOLLAR

DOLLARIZATION
DOLLARIZATIONS
DOLLARIZE
DOLLARIZED
DOLLARIZES
DOLLARIZING
DOLLARS
DOLLED
DOLLHOUSE
DOLLHOUSES
DOLLIED
DOLLIES
DOLLING
DOLLISH
DOLLISHLY
DOLLISHNESS
DOLLISHNESSES
DOLLOP
DOLLOPED
DOLLOPING
DOLLOPS
DOLLS
DOLLY
DOLLYBIRD
DOLLYBIRDS
DOLLYING
DOLMA
DOLMADES
DOLMAN
DOLMANS
DOLMAS
DOLMEN
DOLMENIC
DOLMENS
DOLOMITE
DOLOMITES
DOLOMITIC
DOLOMITIZATION
DOLOMITIZATIONS
DOLOMITIZE
DOLOMITIZED
DOLOMITIZES
DOLOMITIZING
DOLOR
DOLOROSO
DOLOROUS
DOLOROUSLY
DOLOROUSNESS
DOLOROUSNESSES
DOLORS
DOLOUR
DOLOURS
DOLPHIN
DOLPHINFISH
DOLPHINFISHES
DOLPHINS
DOLS
DOLT
DOLTISH
DOLTISHLY
DOLTISHNESS
DOLTISHNESSES
DOLTS
DOM
DOMAIN
DOMAINE
DOMAINES
DOMAINS
DOMAL
DOME
DOMED
DOMELIKE
DOMES
DOMESDAY
DOMESDAYS
DOMESTIC
DOMESTICALLY
DOMESTICATE
DOMESTICATED
DOMESTICATES
DOMESTICATING
DOMESTICATION
DOMESTICATIONS
DOMESTICITIES
DOMESTICITY
DOMESTICS
DOMIC
DOMICAL
DOMICALLY
DOMICIL
DOMICILE
DOMICILED
DOMICILES
DOMICILIARY
DOMICILIATE
DOMICILIATED
DOMICILIATES
DOMICILIATING
DOMICILIATION
DOMICILIATIONS
DOMICILING
DOMICILS
DOMINANCE
DOMINANCES
DOMINANCIES
DOMINANCY
DOMINANT
DOMINANTLY
DOMINANTS
DOMINATE
DOMINATED
DOMINATES
DOMINATING
DOMINATION
DOMINATIONS
DOMINATIVE
DOMINATOR
DOMINATORS
DOMINATRICES
DOMINATRIX
DOMINE
DOMINEER
DOMINEERED
DOMINEERING
DOMINEERINGLY
DOMINEERINGNESS
DOMINEERS
DOMINES
DOMING
DOMINICAL
DOMINICK
DOMINICKER
DOMINICKERS
DOMINICKS
DOMINIE
DOMINIES
DOMINION
DOMINIONS
DOMINIQUE
DOMINIQUES
DOMINIUM
DOMINIUMS
DOMINO
DOMINOES
DOMINOS
DOMS
DON
DONA
DONAIR
DONAIRS
DONAS
DONATE
DONATED
DONATES
DONATING
DONATION
DONATIONS
DONATIVE
DONATIVES
DONATOR
DONATORS
DONE
DONEE
DONEES
DONEGAL
DONEGALS
DONENESS
DONENESSES
DONG
DONGA
DONGAS
DONGED
DONGING
DONGLE
DONGLES
DONGOLA
DONGOLAS
DONGS
DONJON
DONJONS
DONKEY
DONKEYS
DONKEYWORK
DONKEYWORKS
DONNA
DONNAS
DONNE
DONNED
DONNEE
DONNEES
DONNERD
DONNERED
DONNERT
DONNICKER
DONNICKERS
DONNIKER
DONNIKERS
DONNING
DONNISH
DONNISHLY
DONNISHNESS
DONNISHNESSES
DONNYBROOK
DONNYBROOKS
DONOR
DONORS
DONORSHIP
DONORSHIPS
DONS
DONSHIP
DONSHIPS
DONSIE
DONSY
DONUT
DONUTS
DONZEL
DONZELS
DOOB
DOOBIE
DOOBIES
DOOBS
DOODAD
DOODADS
DOODAH
DOODAHS
DOODIES
DOODLE
DOODLEBUG
DOODLEBUGS
DOODLED
DOODLER
DOODLERS
DOODLES
DOODLING
DOODOO
DOODOOS
DOODY
DOOFUS
DOOFUSES
DOOHICKEY
DOOHICKEYS
DOOHICKIES
DOOLEE
DOOLEES
DOOLIE
DOOLIES
DOOLY
DOOM
DOOMED
DOOMFUL
DOOMFULLY
DOOMIER
DOOMIEST
DOOMILY
DOOMING
DOOMS
DOOMSAYER
DOOMSAYERS
DOOMSAYING
DOOMSAYINGS
DOOMSDAY
DOOMSDAYER
DOOMSDAYERS
DOOMSDAYS
DOOMSTER

DOOMSTERS
DOOMY
DOOR
DOORBELL
DOORBELLS
DOORCASE
DOORCASES
DOORED
DOORFRAME
DOORFRAMES
DOORJAMB
DOORJAMBS
DOORKEEPER
DOORKEEPERS
DOORKNOB
DOORKNOBS
DOORLESS
DOORMAN
DOORMAT
DOORMATS
DOORMEN
DOORNAIL
DOORNAILS
DOORPLATE
DOORPLATES
DOORPOST
DOORPOSTS
DOORS
DOORSILL
DOORSILLS
DOORSTEP
DOORSTEPS
DOORSTOP
DOORSTOPS
DOORWAY
DOORWAYS
DOORWOMAN
DOORWOMEN
DOORYARD
DOORYARDS
DOOWOP
DOOWOPS
DOOZER
DOOZERS
DOOZIE
DOOZIES
DOOZY
DOPA
DOPAMINE
DOPAMINERGIC
DOPAMINES
DOPANT
DOPANTS
DOPAS
DOPE
DOPED
DOPEHEAD
DOPEHEADS
DOPER
DOPERS
DOPES
DOPESHEET
DOPESHEETS
DOPEST
DOPESTER
DOPESTERS
DOPEY
DOPEYNESS
DOPEYNESSES
DOPIER
DOPIEST
DOPILY
DOPINESS
DOPINESSES
DOPING
DOPINGS
DOPPELGANGER
DOPPELGANGERS
DOPY
DOR
DORADO
DORADOS
DORBEETLE
DORBEETLES
DORBUG
DORBUGS
DORE
DORES
DORHAWK
DORHAWKS
DORIES
DORK
DORKIER
DORKIEST
DORKINESS
DORKINESSES
DORKS
DORKY
DORM
DORMANCIES
DORMANCY
DORMANT
DORMER
DORMERED
DORMERS
DORMICE
DORMIE
DORMIENT
DORMIN
DORMINS
DORMITORIES
DORMITORY
DORMOUSE
DORMS
DORMY
DORNECK
DORNECKS
DORNICK
DORNICKS
DORNOCK
DORNOCKS
DORONICUM
DORONICUMS
DORP
DORPER
DORPERS
DORPS
DORR
DORRS
DORS
DORSA
DORSAD
DORSAL
DORSALLY
DORSALS
DORSEL
DORSELS
DORSER
DORSERS
DORSIVENTRAL
DORSIVENTRALITY
DORSIVENTRALLY
DORSOLATERAL
DORSOVENTRAL
DORSOVENTRALITY
DORSOVENTRALLY
DORSUM
DORTY
DORY
DORYMAN
DORYMEN
DOS
DOSA
DOSAGE
DOSAGES
DOSAI
DOSAS
DOSE
DOSED
DOSER
DOSERS
DOSES
DOSH
DOSHA
DOSHAS
DOSHES
DOSIMETER
DOSIMETERS
DOSIMETRIC
DOSIMETRIES
DOSIMETRY
DOSING
DOSS
DOSSAL
DOSSALS
DOSSED
DOSSEL
DOSSELS
DOSSER
DOSSERET
DOSSERETS
DOSSERS
DOSSES
DOSSHOUSE
DOSSHOUSES
DOSSIER
DOSSIERS
DOSSIL
DOSSILS
DOSSING
DOST
DOT
DOTAGE
DOTAGES
DOTAL
DOTARD
DOTARDLY
DOTARDS
DOTATION
DOTATIONS
DOTE
DOTED
DOTER
DOTERS
DOTES
DOTH
DOTIER
DOTIEST
DOTING
DOTINGLY
DOTS
DOTTED
DOTTEL
DOTTELS
DOTTER
DOTTEREL
DOTTERELS
DOTTERS
DOTTIE
DOTTIER
DOTTIES
DOTTIEST
DOTTILY
DOTTINESS
DOTTINESSES
DOTTING
DOTTLE
DOTTLES
DOTTREL
DOTTRELS
DOTTY
DOTY
DOUBLE
DOUBLED
DOUBLEHANDED
DOUBLEHEADER
DOUBLEHEADERS
DOUBLENESS
DOUBLENESSES
DOUBLER
DOUBLERS
DOUBLES
DOUBLESPEAK
DOUBLESPEAKER
DOUBLESPEAKERS
DOUBLESPEAKS
DOUBLET
DOUBLETHINK
DOUBLETHINKS
DOUBLETON
DOUBLETONS
DOUBLETS
DOUBLING
DOUBLOON
DOUBLOONS
DOUBLURE
DOUBLURES
DOUBLY
DOUBT
DOUBTABLE
DOUBTED
DOUBTER
DOUBTERS
DOUBTFUL
DOUBTFULLY

DOUBTFULNESS
DOUBTFULNESSES
DOUBTING
DOUBTINGLY
DOUBTLESS
DOUBTLESSLY
DOUBTLESSNESS
DOUBTLESSNESSES
DOUBTS
DOUCE
DOUCELY
DOUCER
DOUCEST
DOUCEUR
DOUCEURS
DOUCHE
DOUCHEBAG
DOUCHEBAGS
DOUCHED
DOUCHES
DOUCHING
DOUCHINGS
DOUGH
DOUGHBOY
DOUGHBOYS
DOUGHFACE
DOUGHFACES
DOUGHIER
DOUGHIEST
DOUGHLIKE
DOUGHNUT
DOUGHNUTLIKE
DOUGHNUTS
DOUGHS
DOUGHT
DOUGHTIER
DOUGHTIEST
DOUGHTILY
DOUGHTINESS
DOUGHTINESSES
DOUGHTY
DOUGHY
DOULA
DOULAS
DOUM
DOUMA
DOUMAS
DOUMS
DOUPIONI
DOUPIONIS
DOUPPIONI
DOUPPIONIS
DOUR
DOURA
DOURAH
DOURAHS
DOURAS
DOURER
DOUREST
DOURINE
DOURINES
DOURLY
DOURNESS
DOURNESSES
DOUROUCOULI
DOUROUCOULIS
DOUSE
DOUSED
DOUSER
DOUSERS
DOUSES
DOUSING
DOUT
DOUTED
DOUTING
DOUTS
DOUX
DOUZEPER
DOUZEPERS
DOVE
DOVECOT
DOVECOTE
DOVECOTES
DOVECOTS
DOVEKEY
DOVEKEYS
DOVEKIE
DOVEKIES
DOVELIKE
DOVEN
DOVENED
DOVENING
DOVENS
DOVES
DOVETAIL
DOVETAILED
DOVETAILING
DOVETAILS
DOVISH
DOVISHNESS
DOVISHNESSES
DOW
DOWABLE
DOWAGER
DOWAGERS
DOWDIER
DOWDIES
DOWDIEST
DOWDILY
DOWDINESS
DOWDINESSES
DOWDY
DOWDYISH
DOWED
DOWEL
DOWELED
DOWELING
DOWELINGS
DOWELLED
DOWELLING
DOWELS
DOWER
DOWERED
DOWERIES
DOWERING
DOWERLESS
DOWERS
DOWERY
DOWIE
DOWING
DOWITCHER
DOWITCHERS
DOWN
DOWNBEAT
DOWNBEATS
DOWNBOW
DOWNBOWS
DOWNBURST
DOWNBURSTS
DOWNCAST
DOWNCASTS
DOWNCOME
DOWNCOMES
DOWNCOURT
DOWNDRAFT
DOWNDRAFTS
DOWNED
DOWNER
DOWNERS
DOWNFALL
DOWNFALLEN
DOWNFALLS
DOWNFIELD
DOWNFORCE
DOWNFORCES
DOWNGRADE
DOWNGRADED
DOWNGRADES
DOWNGRADING
DOWNHAUL
DOWNHAULS
DOWNHEARTED
DOWNHEARTEDLY
DOWNHEARTEDNESS
DOWNHILL
DOWNHILLER
DOWNHILLERS
DOWNHILLS
DOWNHOLE
DOWNIER
DOWNIEST
DOWNILY
DOWNINESS
DOWNINESSES
DOWNING
DOWNLAND
DOWNLANDS
DOWNLESS
DOWNLIGHT
DOWNLIGHTS
DOWNLIKE
DOWNLINK
DOWNLINKED
DOWNLINKING
DOWNLINKS
DOWNLOAD
DOWNLOADABLE
DOWNLOADED
DOWNLOADING
DOWNLOADS
DOWNPIPE
DOWNPIPES
DOWNPLAY
DOWNPLAYED
DOWNPLAYING
DOWNPLAYS
DOWNPOUR
DOWNPOURS
DOWNRANGE
DOWNRATE
DOWNRATED
DOWNRATES
DOWNRATING
DOWNRIGHT
DOWNRIGHTLY
DOWNRIGHTNESS
DOWNRIGHTNESSES
DOWNRIVER
DOWNS
DOWNSCALE
DOWNSCALED
DOWNSCALES
DOWNSCALING
DOWNSHIFT
DOWNSHIFTED
DOWNSHIFTING
DOWNSHIFTS
DOWNSIDE
DOWNSIDES
DOWNSIZE
DOWNSIZED
DOWNSIZES
DOWNSIZING
DOWNSLIDE
DOWNSLIDES
DOWNSLOPE
DOWNSPIN
DOWNSPINS
DOWNSPOUT
DOWNSPOUTS
DOWNSTAGE
DOWNSTAGES
DOWNSTAIR
DOWNSTAIRS
DOWNSTATE
DOWNSTATER
DOWNSTATERS
DOWNSTATES
DOWNSTREAM
DOWNSTROKE
DOWNSTROKES
DOWNSWING
DOWNSWINGS
DOWNTHROW
DOWNTHROWS
DOWNTICK
DOWNTICKS
DOWNTIME
DOWNTIMES
DOWNTOWN
DOWNTOWNER
DOWNTOWNERS
DOWNTOWNS
DOWNTREND
DOWNTRENDED
DOWNTRENDING
DOWNTRENDS
DOWNTROD
DOWNTRODDEN
DOWNTURN
DOWNTURNS
DOWNWARD
DOWNWARDLY
DOWNWARDNESS
DOWNWARDNESSES

DOWNWARDS
DOWNWARP
DOWNWARPS
DOWNWASH
DOWNWASHES
DOWNWIND
DOWNY
DOWNZONE
DOWNZONED
DOWNZONES
DOWNZONING
DOWRIES
DOWRY
DOWS
DOWSABEL
DOWSABELS
DOWSE
DOWSED
DOWSER
DOWSERS
DOWSES
DOWSING
DOWSINGS
DOXIE
DOXIES
DOXOLOGIES
DOXOLOGY
DOXORUBICIN
DOXORUBICINS
DOXY
DOXYCYCLINE
DOXYCYCLINES
DOYEN
DOYENNE
DOYENNES
DOYENS
DOYLEY
DOYLEYS
DOYLIES
DOYLY
DOZE
DOZED
DOZEN
DOZENED
DOZENING
DOZENS
DOZENTH
DOZENTHS
DOZER
DOZERS
DOZES
DOZIER
DOZIEST
DOZILY
DOZINESS
DOZINESSES
DOZING
DOZY
DRAB
DRABBED
DRABBER
DRABBEST
DRABBET
DRABBETS
DRABBING
DRABBLE
DRABBLED
DRABBLES
DRABBLING
DRABLY
DRABNESS
DRABNESSES
DRABS
DRACAENA
DRACAENAS
DRACENA
DRACENAS
DRACHM
DRACHMA
DRACHMAE
DRACHMAI
DRACHMAS
DRACHMS
DRACONIAN
DRACONIC
DRACUNCULIASES
DRACUNCULIASIS
DRAFF
DRAFFIER
DRAFFIEST
DRAFFISH
DRAFFS
DRAFFY
DRAFT
DRAFTABLE
DRAFTED
DRAFTEE
DRAFTEES
DRAFTER
DRAFTERS
DRAFTIER
DRAFTIEST
DRAFTILY
DRAFTINESS
DRAFTINESSES
DRAFTING
DRAFTINGS
DRAFTS
DRAFTSMAN
DRAFTSMANLY
DRAFTSMANSHIP
DRAFTSMANSHIPS
DRAFTSMEN
DRAFTSPEOPLE
DRAFTSPERSON
DRAFTSPERSONS
DRAFTY
DRAG
DRAGEE
DRAGEES
DRAGGED
DRAGGER
DRAGGERS
DRAGGIER
DRAGGIEST
DRAGGING
DRAGGINGLY
DRAGGLE
DRAGGLED
DRAGGLES
DRAGGLING
DRAGGY
DRAGLINE
DRAGLINES
DRAGNET
DRAGNETS
DRAGOMAN
DRAGOMANS
DRAGOMEN
DRAGON
DRAGONET
DRAGONETS
DRAGONFLIES
DRAGONFLY
DRAGONHEAD
DRAGONHEADS
DRAGONISH
DRAGONS
DRAGOON
DRAGOONED
DRAGOONING
DRAGOONS
DRAGROPE
DRAGROPES
DRAGS
DRAGSTER
DRAGSTERS
DRAGSTRIP
DRAGSTRIPS
DRAIL
DRAILS
DRAIN
DRAINABLE
DRAINAGE
DRAINAGES
DRAINBOARD
DRAINBOARDS
DRAINED
DRAINER
DRAINERS
DRAINING
DRAINPIPE
DRAINPIPES
DRAINS
DRAKE
DRAKES
DRAM
DRAMA
DRAMADIES
DRAMADY
DRAMAS
DRAMATIC
DRAMATICALLY
DRAMATICS
DRAMATISATION
DRAMATISATIONS
DRAMATISE
DRAMATISED
DRAMATISES
DRAMATISING
DRAMATIST
DRAMATISTS
DRAMATIZABLE
DRAMATIZATION
DRAMATIZATIONS
DRAMATIZE
DRAMATIZED
DRAMATIZES
DRAMATIZING
DRAMATURG
DRAMATURGE
DRAMATURGES
DRAMATURGIC
DRAMATURGICAL
DRAMATURGICALLY
DRAMATURGIES
DRAMATURGY
DRAMEDIES
DRAMEDY
DRAMMED
DRAMMING
DRAMMOCK
DRAMMOCKS
DRAMS
DRAMSHOP
DRAMSHOPS
DRANK
DRAPABILITIES
DRAPABILITY
DRAPABLE
DRAPE
DRAPEABILITIES
DRAPEABILITY
DRAPEABLE
DRAPED
DRAPER
DRAPERIED
DRAPERIES
DRAPERS
DRAPERY
DRAPES
DRAPEY
DRAPING
DRASTIC
DRASTICALLY
DRAT
DRATS
DRATTED
DRATTING
DRAUGHT
DRAUGHTBOARD
DRAUGHTBOARDS
DRAUGHTED
DRAUGHTIER
DRAUGHTIEST
DRAUGHTINESS
DRAUGHTINESSES
DRAUGHTING
DRAUGHTS
DRAUGHTSMAN
DRAUGHTSMANSHIP
DRAUGHTSMEN
DRAUGHTSPERSON
DRAUGHTSPERSONS
DRAUGHTY
DRAVE
DRAW
DRAWABLE
DRAWBACK
DRAWBACKS
DRAWBAR
DRAWBARS
DRAWBORE
DRAWBORES
DRAWBRIDGE

DRAWBRIDGES
DRAWCORD
DRAWCORDS
DRAWDOWN
DRAWDOWNS
DRAWEE
DRAWEES
DRAWER
DRAWERFUL
DRAWERFULS
DRAWERS
DRAWING
DRAWINGS
DRAWKNIFE
DRAWKNIVES
DRAWL
DRAWLED
DRAWLER
DRAWLERS
DRAWLIER
DRAWLIEST
DRAWLING
DRAWLINGLY
DRAWLS
DRAWLY
DRAWN
DRAWNWORK
DRAWNWORKS
DRAWPLATE
DRAWPLATES
DRAWS
DRAWSHAVE
DRAWSHAVES
DRAWSTRING
DRAWSTRINGS
DRAWTUBE
DRAWTUBES
DRAY
DRAYAGE
DRAYAGES
DRAYED
DRAYING
DRAYMAN
DRAYMEN
DRAYS
DREAD
DREADED
DREADER
DREADEST
DREADFUL
DREADFULLY
DREADFULNESS
DREADFULNESSES
DREADFULS
DREADING
DREADLOCK
DREADLOCKED
DREADLOCKS
DREADNOUGHT
DREADNOUGHTS
DREADS
DREAM
DREAMBOAT
DREAMBOATS
DREAMED
DREAMER
DREAMERS
DREAMFUL
DREAMFULLY
DREAMFULNESS
DREAMFULNESSES
DREAMIER
DREAMIEST
DREAMILY
DREAMINESS
DREAMINESSES
DREAMING
DREAMLAND
DREAMLANDS
DREAMLESS
DREAMLESSLY
DREAMLESSNESS
DREAMLESSNESSES
DREAMLIKE
DREAMS
DREAMSCAPE
DREAMSCAPES
DREAMT
DREAMTIME
DREAMTIMES
DREAMWORLD
DREAMWORLDS
DREAMY
DREAR
DREARER
DREAREST
DREARIER
DREARIES
DREARIEST
DREARILY
DREARINESS
DREARINESSES
DREARS
DREARY
DRECK
DRECKIER
DRECKIEST
DRECKISH
DRECKS
DRECKY
DREDGE
DREDGED
DREDGER
DREDGERS
DREDGES
DREDGING
DREDGINGS
DREE
DREED
DREEING
DREES
DREG
DREGGIER
DREGGIEST
DREGGISH
DREGGY
DREGS
DREICH
DREIDEL
DREIDELS
DREIDL
DREIDLS
DREIGH
DREK
DREKKIER
DREKKIEST
DREKKISH
DREKKY
DREKS
DRENCH
DRENCHED
DRENCHER
DRENCHERS
DRENCHES
DRENCHING
DRENCHINGS
DRESS
DRESSAGE
DRESSAGES
DRESSED
DRESSER
DRESSERS
DRESSES
DRESSIER
DRESSIEST
DRESSILY
DRESSINESS
DRESSINESSES
DRESSING
DRESSINGS
DRESSMAKER
DRESSMAKERS
DRESSMAKING
DRESSMAKINGS
DRESSY
DREST
DREW
DRIB
DRIBBED
DRIBBING
DRIBBLE
DRIBBLED
DRIBBLER
DRIBBLERS
DRIBBLES
DRIBBLET
DRIBBLETS
DRIBBLING
DRIBBLY
DRIBLET
DRIBLETS
DRIBS
DRIED
DRIEGH
DRIER
DRIERS
DRIES
DRIEST
DRIFT
DRIFTAGE
DRIFTAGES
DRIFTED
DRIFTER
DRIFTERS
DRIFTIER
DRIFTIEST
DRIFTING
DRIFTINGLY
DRIFTNET
DRIFTNETS
DRIFTPIN
DRIFTPINS
DRIFTS
DRIFTWOOD
DRIFTWOODS
DRIFTY
DRILL
DRILLABILITIES
DRILLABILITY
DRILLABLE
DRILLED
DRILLER
DRILLERS
DRILLING
DRILLINGS
DRILLMASTER
DRILLMASTERS
DRILLS
DRILY
DRINK
DRINKABILITIES
DRINKABILITY
DRINKABLE
DRINKABLES
DRINKABLY
DRINKER
DRINKERS
DRINKING
DRINKINGS
DRINKS
DRIP
DRIPLESS
DRIPPED
DRIPPER
DRIPPERS
DRIPPIER
DRIPPIEST
DRIPPILY
DRIPPING
DRIPPINGS
DRIPPY
DRIPS
DRIPSTONE
DRIPSTONES
DRIPT
DRIVABILITIES
DRIVABILITY
DRIVABLE
DRIVE
DRIVEABILITIES
DRIVEABILITY
DRIVEABLE
DRIVEL
DRIVELED
DRIVELER
DRIVELERS
DRIVELINE
DRIVELINES
DRIVELING
DRIVELLED
DRIVELLER
DRIVELLERS
DRIVELLING
DRIVELS
DRIVEN

DRIVENNESS
DRIVENNESSES
DRIVER
DRIVERLESS
DRIVERS
DRIVES
DRIVESHAFT
DRIVESHAFTS
DRIVETRAIN
DRIVETRAINS
DRIVEWAY
DRIVEWAYS
DRIVING
DRIVINGLY
DRIVINGS
DRIZZLE
DRIZZLED
DRIZZLES
DRIZZLIER
DRIZZLIEST
DRIZZLING
DRIZZLINGLY
DRIZZLY
DROGUE
DROGUES
DROID
DROIDS
DROIT
DROITS
DROKE
DROKES
DROLL
DROLLED
DROLLER
DROLLERIES
DROLLERY
DROLLEST
DROLLING
DROLLNESS
DROLLNESSES
DROLLS
DROLLY
DROMEDARIES
DROMEDARY
DROMON
DROMOND
DROMONDS
DROMONS
DRONE
DRONED
DRONER
DRONERS
DRONES
DRONGO
DRONGOES
DRONGOS
DRONING
DRONINGLY
DRONISH
DROOL
DROOLED
DROOLIER
DROOLIEST
DROOLING
DROOLS
DROOLY
DROOP
DROOPED
DROOPIER
DROOPIEST
DROOPILY
DROOPING
DROOPINGLY
DROOPS
DROOPY
DROP
DROPCLOTH
DROPCLOTHS
DROPFORGE
DROPFORGED
DROPFORGES
DROPFORGING
DROPHEAD
DROPHEADS
DROPKICK
DROPKICKER
DROPKICKERS
DROPKICKS
DROPLET
DROPLETS
DROPLIGHT
DROPLIGHTS
DROPOUT
DROPOUTS
DROPPABLE
DROPPED
DROPPER
DROPPERFUL
DROPPERFULS
DROPPERS
DROPPERSFUL
DROPPING
DROPPINGS
DROPS
DROPSEED
DROPSEEDS
DROPSHOT
DROPSHOTS
DROPSICAL
DROPSIED
DROPSIES
DROPSONDE
DROPSONDES
DROPSY
DROPT
DROPTOP
DROPTOPS
DROPWORT
DROPWORTS
DROSERA
DROSERAS
DROSHKIES
DROSHKY
DROSKIES
DROSKY
DROSOPHILA
DROSOPHILAS
DROSS
DROSSES
DROSSIER
DROSSIEST
DROSSY
DROUGHT
DROUGHTIER
DROUGHTIEST
DROUGHTINESS
DROUGHTINESSES
DROUGHTS
DROUGHTY
DROUK
DROUKED
DROUKING
DROUKS
DROUTH
DROUTHIER
DROUTHIEST
DROUTHS
DROUTHY
DROVE
DROVED
DROVER
DROVERS
DROVES
DROVING
DROVINGS
DROWN
DROWND
DROWNDED
DROWNDING
DROWNDS
DROWNED
DROWNER
DROWNERS
DROWNING
DROWNS
DROWSE
DROWSED
DROWSES
DROWSIER
DROWSIEST
DROWSILY
DROWSINESS
DROWSINESSES
DROWSING
DROWSY
DRUB
DRUBBED
DRUBBER
DRUBBERS
DRUBBING
DRUBBINGS
DRUBS
DRUDGE
DRUDGED
DRUDGER
DRUDGERIES
DRUDGERS
DRUDGERY
DRUDGES
DRUDGING
DRUDGINGLY
DRUG
DRUGGED
DRUGGET
DRUGGETS
DRUGGIE
DRUGGIER
DRUGGIES
DRUGGIEST
DRUGGING
DRUGGIST
DRUGGISTS
DRUGGY
DRUGLESS
DRUGMAKER
DRUGMAKERS
DRUGS
DRUGSTORE
DRUGSTORES
DRUID
DRUIDESS
DRUIDESSES
DRUIDIC
DRUIDICAL
DRUIDISM
DRUIDISMS
DRUIDS
DRUM
DRUMBEAT
DRUMBEATER
DRUMBEATERS
DRUMBEATING
DRUMBEATINGS
DRUMBEATS
DRUMBLE
DRUMBLED
DRUMBLES
DRUMBLING
DRUMFIRE
DRUMFIRES
DRUMFISH
DRUMFISHES
DRUMHEAD
DRUMHEADS
DRUMLIER
DRUMLIEST
DRUMLIKE
DRUMLIN
DRUMLINS
DRUMLY
DRUMMED
DRUMMER
DRUMMERS
DRUMMING
DRUMMINGS
DRUMROLL
DRUMROLLS
DRUMS
DRUMSTICK
DRUMSTICKS
DRUNK
DRUNKARD
DRUNKARDS
DRUNKEN
DRUNKENLY
DRUNKENNESS
DRUNKENNESSES
DRUNKER
DRUNKEST
DRUNKISH
DRUNKS
DRUPACEOUS
DRUPE
DRUPEL
DRUPELET

DRUPELETS
DRUPELS
DRUPES
DRUSE
DRUSES
DRUTHER
DRUTHERS
DRY
DRYABLE
DRYAD
DRYADES
DRYADIC
DRYADS
DRYAS
DRYASDUST
DRYASDUSTS
DRYER
DRYERS
DRYEST
DRYING
DRYISH
DRYLAND
DRYLANDS
DRYLOT
DRYLOTS
DRYLY
DRYNESS
DRYNESSES
DRYOPITHECINE
DRYOPITHECINES
DRYPOINT
DRYPOINTS
DRYS
DRYSALTER
DRYSALTERIES
DRYSALTERS
DRYSALTERY
DRYSTONE
DRYSUIT
DRYSUITS
DRYWALL
DRYWALLED
DRYWALLING
DRYWALLS
DRYWELL
DRYWELLS
DUAD
DUADS
DUAL
DUALISE
DUALISED
DUALISES
DUALISING
DUALISM
DUALISMS
DUALIST
DUALISTIC
DUALISTICALLY
DUALISTS
DUALITIES
DUALITY
DUALIZE
DUALIZED
DUALIZES
DUALIZING
DUALLIE
DUALLIES
DUALLY
DUALS
DUATHLETE
DUATHLETES
DUATHLON
DUATHLONS
DUB
DUBBED
DUBBER
DUBBERS
DUBBIN
DUBBINED
DUBBING
DUBBINGS
DUBBINING
DUBBINS
DUBIETIES
DUBIETY
DUBIOSITIES
DUBIOSITY
DUBIOUS
DUBIOUSLY
DUBIOUSNESS
DUBIOUSNESSES
DUBITABLE
DUBITABLY
DUBITATION
DUBITATIONS
DUBNIUM
DUBNIUMS
DUBONNET
DUBONNETS
DUBS
DUBSTEP
DUBSTEPS
DUCAL
DUCALLY
DUCAT
DUCATS
DUCE
DUCES
DUCHESS
DUCHESSES
DUCHIES
DUCHY
DUCI
DUCK
DUCKBILL
DUCKBILLS
DUCKBOARD
DUCKBOARDS
DUCKED
DUCKER
DUCKERS
DUCKIE
DUCKIER
DUCKIES
DUCKIEST
DUCKING
DUCKISH
DUCKISHES
DUCKLING
DUCKLINGS
DUCKPIN
DUCKPINS
DUCKS
DUCKTAIL
DUCKTAILS
DUCKWALK
DUCKWALKED
DUCKWALKING
DUCKWALKS
DUCKWEED
DUCKWEEDS
DUCKY
DUCT
DUCTAL
DUCTED
DUCTILE
DUCTILELY
DUCTILITIES
DUCTILITY
DUCTING
DUCTINGS
DUCTLESS
DUCTS
DUCTULE
DUCTULES
DUCTWORK
DUCTWORKS
DUD
DUDDIE
DUDDY
DUDE
DUDED
DUDEEN
DUDEENS
DUDENESS
DUDENESSES
DUDES
DUDETTE
DUDETTES
DUDGEON
DUDGEONS
DUDING
DUDISH
DUDISHLY
DUDS
DUE
DUECENTO
DUECENTOS
DUEL
DUELED
DUELER
DUELERS
DUELING
DUELINGS
DUELIST
DUELISTS
DUELLED
DUELLER
DUELLERS
DUELLI
DUELLING
DUELLINGS
DUELLIST
DUELLISTS
DUELLO
DUELLOS
DUELS
DUENDE
DUENDES
DUENESS
DUENESSES
DUENNA
DUENNAS
DUENNASHIP
DUENNASHIPS
DUES
DUET
DUETED
DUETING
DUETS
DUETTED
DUETTING
DUETTIST
DUETTISTS
DUFF
DUFFED
DUFFEL
DUFFELS
DUFFER
DUFFERS
DUFFEST
DUFFING
DUFFLE
DUFFLES
DUFFS
DUFUS
DUFUSES
DUG
DUGONG
DUGONGS
DUGOUT
DUGOUTS
DUGS
DUH
DUI
DUIKER
DUIKERS
DUIT
DUITS
DUKE
DUKED
DUKEDOM
DUKEDOMS
DUKES
DUKING
DULCE
DULCES
DULCET
DULCETLY
DULCETS
DULCIAN
DULCIANA
DULCIANAS
DULCIANS
DULCIFIED
DULCIFIES
DULCIFY
DULCIFYING
DULCIMER
DULCIMERS
DULCIMORE
DULCIMORES
DULCINEA
DULCINEAS
DULIA

DULIAS
DULL
DULLARD
DULLARDS
DULLED
DULLER
DULLEST
DULLING
DULLISH
DULLISHLY
DULLNESS
DULLNESSES
DULLS
DULLSVILLE
DULLSVILLES
DULLY
DULNESS
DULNESSES
DULSE
DULSES
DULY
DUM
DUMA
DUMAS
DUMB
DUMBBELL
DUMBBELLS
DUMBCANE
DUMBCANES
DUMBED
DUMBER
DUMBEST
DUMBFOUND
DUMBFOUNDED
DUMBFOUNDER
DUMBFOUNDERED
DUMBFOUNDERING
DUMBFOUNDERS
DUMBFOUNDING
DUMBFOUNDINGLY
DUMBFOUNDS
DUMBHEAD
DUMBHEADS
DUMBING
DUMBLY
DUMBNESS
DUMBNESSES
DUMBO
DUMBOS
DUMBS
DUMBSHOW
DUMBSHOWS
DUMBSIZE
DUMBSIZED
DUMBSIZES
DUMBSIZING
DUMBSTRUCK
DUMBWAITER
DUMBWAITERS
DUMDUM
DUMDUMS
DUMFOUND
DUMFOUNDED
DUMFOUNDING
DUMFOUNDS
DUMKA
DUMKAS
DUMKY
DUMMIED
DUMMIES
DUMMKOPF
DUMMKOPFS
DUMMY
DUMMYING
DUMORTIERITE
DUMORTIERITES
DUMP
DUMPCART
DUMPCARTS
DUMPED
DUMPER
DUMPERS
DUMPIER
DUMPIEST
DUMPILY
DUMPINESS
DUMPINESSES
DUMPING
DUMPINGS
DUMPISH
DUMPLING
DUMPLINGS
DUMPS
DUMPSITE
DUMPSITES
DUMPSTER
DUMPSTERS
DUMPTRUCK
DUMPTRUCKS
DUMPY
DUN
DUNAM
DUNAMS
DUNCE
DUNCES
DUNCH
DUNCHES
DUNCICAL
DUNCISH
DUNCISHLY
DUNDERHEAD
DUNDERHEADED
DUNDERHEADS
DUNDREARIES
DUNE
DUNELAND
DUNELANDS
DUNELIKE
DUNES
DUNG
DUNGAREE
DUNGAREED
DUNGAREES
DUNGED
DUNGEON
DUNGEONED
DUNGEONING
DUNGEONS
DUNGHEAP
DUNGHEAPS
DUNGHILL
DUNGHILLS
DUNGIER
DUNGIEST
DUNGING
DUNGS
DUNGY
DUNITE
DUNITES
DUNITIC
DUNK
DUNKED
DUNKER
DUNKERS
DUNKING
DUNKINGS
DUNKS
DUNLIN
DUNLINS
DUNNAGE
DUNNAGES
DUNNED
DUNNER
DUNNESS
DUNNESSES
DUNNEST
DUNNING
DUNNITE
DUNNITES
DUNNO
DUNS
DUNT
DUNTED
DUNTING
DUNTS
DUO
DUODECILLION
DUODECILLIONS
DUODECIMAL
DUODECIMALS
DUODECIMO
DUODECIMOS
DUODENA
DUODENAL
DUODENUM
DUODENUMS
DUOLOG
DUOLOGS
DUOLOGUE
DUOLOGUES
DUOMI
DUOMO
DUOMOS
DUOPOLIES
DUOPOLISTIC
DUOPOLY
DUOPSONIES
DUOPSONY
DUOS
DUOTONE
DUOTONES
DUP
DUPABLE
DUPATTA
DUPATTAS
DUPE
DUPED
DUPER
DUPERIES
DUPERS
DUPERY
DUPES
DUPING
DUPINGS
DUPION
DUPIONS
DUPLE
DUPLET
DUPLETS
DUPLEX
DUPLEXED
DUPLEXER
DUPLEXERS
DUPLEXES
DUPLEXING
DUPLEXITIES
DUPLEXITY
DUPLICATE
DUPLICATED
DUPLICATES
DUPLICATING
DUPLICATION
DUPLICATIONS
DUPLICATIVE
DUPLICATOR
DUPLICATORS
DUPLICITIES
DUPLICITOUS
DUPLICITOUSLY
DUPLICITY
DUPPED
DUPPING
DUPS
DURA
DURABILITIES
DURABILITY
DURABLE
DURABLENESS
DURABLENESSES
DURABLES
DURABLY
DURAL
DURALUMIN
DURALUMINS
DURAMEN
DURAMENS
DURANCE
DURANCES
DURAS
DURATION
DURATIONS
DURATIVE
DURATIVES
DURBAR
DURBARS
DURE
DURED
DURES
DURESS
DURESSES
DURIAN
DURIANS
DURING
DURION
DURIONS

DURMAST
DURMASTS
DURN
DURNDEST
DURNED
DURNEDER
DURNEDEST
DURNING
DURNS
DURO
DUROC
DUROCS
DUROMETER
DUROMETERS
DUROS
DURR
DURRA
DURRAS
DURRIE
DURRIES
DURRS
DURST
DURUM
DURUMS
DUSK
DUSKED
DUSKIER
DUSKIEST
DUSKILY
DUSKINESS
DUSKINESSES
DUSKING
DUSKISH
DUSKS
DUSKY
DUST
DUSTBALL
DUSTBALLS
DUSTBIN
DUSTBINS
DUSTCART
DUSTCARTS
DUSTCOVER
DUSTCOVERS
DUSTED
DUSTER
DUSTERS
DUSTHEAP
DUSTHEAPS
DUSTIER
DUSTIEST
DUSTILY
DUSTINESS
DUSTINESSES
DUSTING
DUSTINGS
DUSTLESS
DUSTLIKE
DUSTMAN
DUSTMEN
DUSTOFF
DUSTOFFS
DUSTPAN
DUSTPANS
DUSTPROOF
DUSTRAG
DUSTRAGS
DUSTS
DUSTSTORM
DUSTSTORMS
DUSTUP
DUSTUPS
DUSTY
DUTCH
DUTCHMAN
DUTCHMEN
DUTEOUS
DUTEOUSLY
DUTIABLE
DUTIES
DUTIFUL
DUTIFULLY
DUTIFULNESS
DUTIFULNESSES
DUTY
DUUMVIR
DUUMVIRATE
DUUMVIRATES
DUUMVIRI
DUUMVIRS
DUVET
DUVETINE
DUVETINES
DUVETS
DUVETYN
DUVETYNE
DUVETYNES
DUVETYNS
DUXELLES
DUYKER
DUYKERS
DWALE
DWALES
DWARF
DWARFED
DWARFER
DWARFEST
DWARFING
DWARFISH
DWARFISHLY
DWARFISHNESS
DWARFISHNESSES
DWARFISM
DWARFISMS
DWARFLIKE
DWARFNESS
DWARFNESSES
DWARFS
DWARVES
DWEEB
DWEEBIER
DWEEBIEST
DWEEBISH
DWEEBS
DWEEBY
DWELL
DWELLED
DWELLER
DWELLERS
DWELLING
DWELLINGS
DWELLS
DWELT
DWINDLE
DWINDLED
DWINDLES
DWINDLING
DWINE
DWINED
DWINES
DWINING
DYABLE
DYAD
DYADIC
DYADICALLY
DYADICS
DYADS
DYARCHAL
DYARCHIC
DYARCHIES
DYARCHY
DYBBUK
DYBBUKIM
DYBBUKS
DYE
DYEABILITIES
DYEABILITY
DYEABLE
DYED
DYEING
DYEINGS
DYER
DYERS
DYES
DYESTUFF
DYESTUFFS
DYEWEED
DYEWEEDS
DYEWOOD
DYEWOODS
DYING
DYINGS
DYKE
DYKED
DYKES
DYKEY
DYKING
DYNAMETER
DYNAMETERS
DYNAMIC
DYNAMICAL
DYNAMICALLY
DYNAMICS
DYNAMISM
DYNAMISMS
DYNAMIST
DYNAMISTIC
DYNAMISTS
DYNAMITE
DYNAMITED
DYNAMITER
DYNAMITERS
DYNAMITES
DYNAMITIC
DYNAMITING
DYNAMO
DYNAMOMETER
DYNAMOMETERS
DYNAMOMETRIC
DYNAMOMETRIES
DYNAMOMETRY
DYNAMOS
DYNAMOTOR
DYNAMOTORS
DYNAST
DYNASTIC
DYNASTICALLY
DYNASTIES
DYNASTS
DYNASTY
DYNATRON
DYNATRONS
DYNE
DYNEIN
DYNEINS
DYNEL
DYNELS
DYNES
DYNODE
DYNODES
DYNORPHIN
DYNORPHINS
DYSARTHRIA
DYSARTHRIAS
DYSCRASIA
DYSCRASIAS
DYSCRASIC
DYSCRATIC
DYSENTERIC
DYSENTERIES
DYSENTERY
DYSFUNCTION
DYSFUNCTIONAL
DYSFUNCTIONS
DYSGENESES
DYSGENESIS
DYSGENIC
DYSGENICS
DYSKINESIA
DYSKINESIAS
DYSKINETIC
DYSLALIA
DYSLALIAS
DYSLECTIC
DYSLECTICS
DYSLEXIA
DYSLEXIAS
DYSLEXIC
DYSLEXICS
DYSLOGISTIC
DYSLOGISTICALLY
DYSMENORRHEA
DYSMENORRHEAS
DYSMENORRHEIC
DYSMENORRHOEA
DYSMENORRHOEAS
DYSMORPHIC
DYSPEPSIA
DYSPEPSIAS
DYSPEPSIES
DYSPEPSY
DYSPEPTIC
DYSPEPTICALLY
DYSPEPTICS
DYSPHAGIA

DYSPHAGIAS
DYSPHAGIC
DYSPHASIA
DYSPHASIAS
DYSPHASIC
DYSPHASICS
DYSPHEMISM
DYSPHEMISMS
DYSPHEMISTIC
DYSPHONIA
DYSPHONIAS
DYSPHONIC
DYSPHORIA
DYSPHORIAS
DYSPHORIC
DYSPLASIA
DYSPLASIAS
DYSPLASTIC
DYSPNEA
DYSPNEAL
DYSPNEAS
DYSPNEIC
DYSPNOEA
DYSPNOEAS
DYSPNOIC
DYSPROSIUM
DYSPROSIUMS
DYSRHYTHMIA
DYSRHYTHMIAS
DYSRHYTHMIC
DYSTAXIA
DYSTAXIAS
DYSTHYMIA
DYSTHYMIAS
DYSTHYMIC
DYSTHYMICS
DYSTOCIA
DYSTOCIAS
DYSTONIA
DYSTONIAS
DYSTONIC
DYSTOPIA
DYSTOPIAN
DYSTOPIAS
DYSTROPHIC
DYSTROPHIES
DYSTROPHIN
DYSTROPHINS
DYSTROPHY
DYSURIA
DYSURIAS
DYSURIC
DYVOUR
DYVOURS

E

EACH
EAGER
EAGERER
EAGEREST
EAGERLY
EAGERNESS
EAGERNESSES
EAGERS
EAGLE
EAGLED
EAGLES
EAGLET
EAGLETS
EAGLEWOOD
EAGLEWOODS
EAGLING
EAGRE
EAGRES
EALDORMAN
EALDORMEN
EANLING
EANLINGS
EAR
EARACHE
EARACHES
EARBUD
EARBUDS
EARDROP
EARDROPS
EARDRUM
EARDRUMS
EARED
EARFLAP
EARFLAPS
EARFUL
EARFULS
EARHOLE
EARHOLES
EARING
EARINGS
EARL
EARLAP
EARLAPS
EARLDOM
EARLDOMS
EARLESS
EARLIER
EARLIEST
EARLINESS
EARLINESSES
EARLOBE
EARLOBES
EARLOCK
EARLOCKS
EARLS
EARLSHIP
EARLSHIPS
EARLY
EARLYWOOD
EARLYWOODS
EARMARK
EARMARKED
EARMARKING
EARMARKS
EARMUFF
EARMUFFS
EARN
EARNED
EARNER
EARNERS
EARNEST
EARNESTLY
EARNESTNESS
EARNESTNESSES
EARNESTS
EARNING
EARNINGS
EARNS
EARPHONE
EARPHONES
EARPIECE
EARPIECES
EARPLUG
EARPLUGS
EARRING
EARRINGED
EARRINGS
EARS
EARSHOT
EARSHOTS
EARSPLITTING
EARSTONE
EARSTONES
EARTH
EARTHBORN
EARTHBOUND
EARTHED
EARTHEN
EARTHENWARE
EARTHENWARES
EARTHIER
EARTHIEST
EARTHILY
EARTHINESS
EARTHINESSES
EARTHING
EARTHLIER
EARTHLIEST
EARTHLIGHT
EARTHLIGHTS
EARTHLIKE
EARTHLINESS
EARTHLINESSES
EARTHLING
EARTHLINGS
EARTHLY
EARTHMAN
EARTHMEN
EARTHMOVER
EARTHMOVERS
EARTHMOVING
EARTHMOVINGS
EARTHNUT
EARTHNUTS
EARTHPEA
EARTHPEAS
EARTHQUAKE
EARTHQUAKES
EARTHRISE
EARTHRISES
EARTHS
EARTHSET
EARTHSETS
EARTHSHAKER
EARTHSHAKERS
EARTHSHAKING
EARTHSHAKINGLY
EARTHSHATTERING
EARTHSHINE
EARTHSHINES
EARTHSTAR
EARTHSTARS
EARTHWARD
EARTHWARDS
EARTHWORK
EARTHWORKS
EARTHWORM
EARTHWORMS
EARTHY
EARWAX
EARWAXES
EARWIG
EARWIGGED
EARWIGGING
EARWIGS
EARWITNESS
EARWITNESSES
EARWORM
EARWORMS
EASE

EASED
EASEFUL
EASEFULLY
EASEL
EASELED
EASELS
EASEMENT
EASEMENTS
EASER
EASERS
EASES
EASIER
EASIES
EASIEST
EASILY
EASINESS
EASINESSES
EASING
EAST
EASTBOUND
EASTER
EASTERLIES
EASTERLY
EASTERN
EASTERNER
EASTERNERS
EASTERNMOST
EASTERS
EASTING
EASTINGS
EASTS
EASTWARD
EASTWARDS
EASY
EASYGOING
EASYGOINGNESS
EASYGOINGNESSES
EAT
EATABLE
EATABLES
EATEN
EATER
EATERIES
EATERS
EATERY
EATH
EATING
EATINGS
EATS
EAU
EAUX
EAVE
EAVED
EAVES
EAVESDROP
EAVESDROPPED
EAVESDROPPER
EAVESDROPPERS
EAVESDROPPING
EAVESDROPS
EBB
EBBED
EBBET
EBBETS
EBBING
EBBS
EBON
EBONICS
EBONIES
EBONISE
EBONISED
EBONISES
EBONISING
EBONITE
EBONITES
EBONIZE
EBONIZED
EBONIZES
EBONIZING
EBONS
EBONY
EBOOK
EBOOKS
EBULLIENCE
EBULLIENCES
EBULLIENCIES
EBULLIENCY
EBULLIENT
EBULLIENTLY
EBULLITION
EBULLITIONS
ECARTE
ECARTES
ECAUDATE
ECBOLIC
ECBOLICS
ECCENTRIC
ECCENTRICALLY
ECCENTRICITIES
ECCENTRICITY
ECCENTRICS
ECCHYMOSES
ECCHYMOSIS
ECCHYMOTIC
ECCLESIA
ECCLESIAE
ECCLESIAL
ECCLESIASTIC
ECCLESIASTICAL
ECCLESIASTICISM
ECCLESIASTICS
ECCLESIOLOGICAL
ECCLESIOLOGIES
ECCLESIOLOGIST
ECCLESIOLOGISTS
ECCLESIOLOGY
ECCRINE
ECDYSES
ECDYSIAL
ECDYSIAST
ECDYSIASTS
ECDYSIS
ECDYSISES
ECDYSON
ECDYSONE
ECDYSONES
ECDYSONS
ECESIC
ECESIS
ECESISES
ECHAPPE
ECHARD
ECHARDS
ECHE
ECHED
ECHELLE
ECHELLES
ECHELON
ECHELONED
ECHELONING
ECHELONS
ECHES
ECHEVERIA
ECHEVERIAS
ECHIDNA
ECHIDNAE
ECHIDNAS
ECHINACEA
ECHINACEAS
ECHINATE
ECHINATED
ECHING
ECHINI
ECHINOCOCCI
ECHINOCOCCOSES
ECHINOCOCCOSIS
ECHINOCOCCUS
ECHINODERM
ECHINODERMATOUS
ECHINODERMS
ECHINOID
ECHINOIDS
ECHINUS
ECHINUSES
ECHIUROID
ECHIUROIDS
ECHO
ECHOCARDIOGRAM
ECHOCARDIOGRAMS
ECHOED
ECHOER
ECHOERS
ECHOES
ECHOEY
ECHOGRAM
ECHOGRAMS
ECHOIC
ECHOING
ECHOISM
ECHOISMS
ECHOLALIA
ECHOLALIAS
ECHOLALIC
ECHOLESS
ECHOLOCATION
ECHOLOCATIONS
ECHOS
ECHOVIRUS
ECHOVIRUSES
ECHT
ECLAIR
ECLAIRCISSEMENT
ECLAIRS
ECLAMPSIA
ECLAMPSIAS
ECLAMPTIC
ECLAT
ECLATS
ECLECTIC
ECLECTICALLY
ECLECTICISM
ECLECTICISMS
ECLECTICS
ECLIPSE
ECLIPSED
ECLIPSER
ECLIPSERS
ECLIPSES
ECLIPSING
ECLIPSIS
ECLIPSISES
ECLIPTIC
ECLIPTICS
ECLOGITE
ECLOGITES
ECLOGUE
ECLOGUES
ECLOSE
ECLOSED
ECLOSES
ECLOSING
ECLOSION
ECLOSIONS
ECO
ECOCATASTROPHE
ECOCATASTROPHES
ECOCIDAL
ECOCIDE
ECOCIDES
ECOFEMINISM
ECOFEMINISMS
ECOFEMINIST
ECOFEMINISTS
ECOFREAK
ECOFREAKS
ECOGIFT
ECOGIFTS
ECOLOGIC
ECOLOGICAL
ECOLOGICALLY
ECOLOGIES
ECOLOGIST
ECOLOGISTS
ECOLOGY
ECONOBOX
ECONOBOXES
ECONOMETRIC
ECONOMETRICALLY
ECONOMETRICIAN
ECONOMETRICIANS
ECONOMETRICS
ECONOMETRIST
ECONOMETRISTS
ECONOMIC
ECONOMICAL
ECONOMICALLY
ECONOMICS
ECONOMIES
ECONOMISE
ECONOMISED
ECONOMISES
ECONOMISING
ECONOMIST
ECONOMISTS
ECONOMIZE

ECONOMIZED
ECONOMIZER
ECONOMIZERS
ECONOMIZES
ECONOMIZING
ECONOMY
ECOPHYSIOLOGIES
ECOPHYSIOLOGY
ECORCHE
ECORCHES
ECOS
ECOSPECIES
ECOSPHERE
ECOSPHERES
ECOSYSTEM
ECOSYSTEMS
ECOTAGE
ECOTAGES
ECOTERRORISM
ECOTERRORISMS
ECOTERRORIST
ECOTERRORISTS
ECOTONAL
ECOTONE
ECOTONES
ECOTOPIA
ECOTOPIAS
ECOTOUR
ECOTOURED
ECOTOURING
ECOTOURISM
ECOTOURISMS
ECOTOURIST
ECOTOURISTS
ECOTOURS
ECOTOXICOLOGIES
ECOTOXICOLOGIST
ECOTOXICOLOGY
ECOTYPE
ECOTYPES
ECOTYPIC
ECOZONE
ECOZONES
ECPHRASES
ECPHRASIS
ECRASEUR
ECRASEURS
ECRU
ECRUS
ECSTASIES
ECSTASY
ECSTATIC
ECSTATICALLY
ECSTATICS
ECTASES
ECTASIS
ECTATIC
ECTHYMA
ECTHYMATA
ECTOBLAST
ECTOBLASTS
ECTODERM
ECTODERMAL
ECTODERMS
ECTOGENE
ECTOGENES
ECTOGENIC
ECTOMERE
ECTOMERES
ECTOMERIC
ECTOMORPH
ECTOMORPHIC
ECTOMORPHS
ECTOPARASITE
ECTOPARASITES
ECTOPARASITIC
ECTOPIA
ECTOPIAS
ECTOPIC
ECTOPICALLY
ECTOPLASM
ECTOPLASMIC
ECTOPLASMS
ECTOPROCT
ECTOPROCTS
ECTOSARC
ECTOSARCS
ECTOTHERM
ECTOTHERMIC
ECTOTHERMS
ECTOTROPHIC
ECTOZOA
ECTOZOAN
ECTOZOANS
ECTOZOON
ECTYPAL
ECTYPE
ECTYPES
ECU
ECUMENE
ECUMENES
ECUMENIC
ECUMENICAL
ECUMENICALISM
ECUMENICALISMS
ECUMENICALLY
ECUMENICISM
ECUMENICISMS
ECUMENICIST
ECUMENICISTS
ECUMENICITIES
ECUMENICITY
ECUMENICS
ECUMENISM
ECUMENISMS
ECUMENIST
ECUMENISTS
ECUS
ECZEMA
ECZEMAS
ECZEMATOUS
ED
EDACIOUS
EDACITIES
EDACITY
EDAMAME
EDAMAMES
EDAPHIC
EDAPHICALLY
EDDIED
EDDIES
EDDO
EDDOES
EDDY
EDDYING
EDELWEISS
EDELWEISSES
EDEMA
EDEMAS
EDEMATA
EDEMATOSE
EDEMATOUS
EDENIC
EDENTATE
EDENTATES
EDENTULOUS
EDGE
EDGED
EDGELESS
EDGER
EDGERS
EDGES
EDGEWAYS
EDGEWISE
EDGIER
EDGIEST
EDGILY
EDGINESS
EDGINESSES
EDGING
EDGINGS
EDGY
EDH
EDHS
EDIBILITIES
EDIBILITY
EDIBLE
EDIBLENESS
EDIBLENESSES
EDIBLES
EDICT
EDICTAL
EDICTALLY
EDICTS
EDIFICATION
EDIFICATIONS
EDIFICE
EDIFICES
EDIFICIAL
EDIFIED
EDIFIER
EDIFIERS
EDIFIES
EDIFY
EDIFYING
EDILE
EDILES
EDIT
EDITABLE
EDITED
EDITING
EDITION
EDITIONS
EDITOR
EDITORIAL
EDITORIALIST
EDITORIALISTS
EDITORIALIZE
EDITORIALIZED
EDITORIALIZER
EDITORIALIZERS
EDITORIALIZES
EDITORIALIZING
EDITORIALLY
EDITORIALS
EDITORS
EDITORSHIP
EDITORSHIPS
EDITRESS
EDITRESSES
EDITRICES
EDITRIX
EDITRIXES
EDITS
EDS
EDUCABILITIES
EDUCABILITY
EDUCABLE
EDUCABLES
EDUCATE
EDUCATED
EDUCATEDNESS
EDUCATEDNESSES
EDUCATES
EDUCATING
EDUCATION
EDUCATIONAL
EDUCATIONALIST
EDUCATIONALISTS
EDUCATIONALLY
EDUCATIONESE
EDUCATIONESES
EDUCATIONIST
EDUCATIONISTS
EDUCATIONS
EDUCATIVE
EDUCATOR
EDUCATORS
EDUCATORY
EDUCE
EDUCED
EDUCES
EDUCIBLE
EDUCING
EDUCT
EDUCTION
EDUCTIONS
EDUCTIVE
EDUCTOR
EDUCTORS
EDUCTS
EDULCORATE
EDULCORATED
EDULCORATES
EDULCORATING
EDUTAINMENT
EDUTAINMENTS
EEEW
EEJIT
EEJITS
EEK
EEL
EELGRASS
EELGRASSES
EELIER

EELIEST
EELLIKE
EELPOUT
EELPOUTS
EELS
EELWORM
EELWORMS
EELY
EENSIER
EENSIEST
EENSY
EERIE
EERIER
EERIEST
EERILY
EERINESS
EERINESSES
EERY
EEW
EF
EFF
EFFABLE
EFFACE
EFFACEABLE
EFFACED
EFFACEMENT
EFFACEMENTS
EFFACER
EFFACERS
EFFACES
EFFACING
EFFECT
EFFECTED
EFFECTER
EFFECTERS
EFFECTING
EFFECTIVE
EFFECTIVELY
EFFECTIVENESS
EFFECTIVENESSES
EFFECTIVES
EFFECTIVITIES
EFFECTIVITY
EFFECTOR
EFFECTORS
EFFECTS
EFFECTUAL
EFFECTUALITIES
EFFECTUALITY
EFFECTUALLY
EFFECTUALNESS
EFFECTUALNESSES
EFFECTUATE
EFFECTUATED
EFFECTUATES
EFFECTUATING
EFFECTUATION
EFFECTUATIONS
EFFEMINACIES
EFFEMINACY
EFFEMINATE
EFFEMINATELY
EFFEMINATES
EFFENDI
EFFENDIS
EFFERENT
EFFERENTLY
EFFERENTS
EFFERVESCE
EFFERVESCED
EFFERVESCENCE
EFFERVESCENCES
EFFERVESCENT
EFFERVESCENTLY
EFFERVESCES
EFFERVESCING
EFFETE
EFFETELY
EFFETENESS
EFFETENESSES
EFFICACIES
EFFICACIOUS
EFFICACIOUSLY
EFFICACIOUSNESS
EFFICACITIES
EFFICACITY
EFFICACY
EFFICIENCIES
EFFICIENCY
EFFICIENT
EFFICIENTLY
EFFIGIAL
EFFIGIES
EFFIGY
EFFING
EFFLORESCE
EFFLORESCED
EFFLORESCENCE
EFFLORESCENCES
EFFLORESCENT
EFFLORESCES
EFFLORESCING
EFFLUENCE
EFFLUENCES
EFFLUENT
EFFLUENTS
EFFLUVIA
EFFLUVIAL
EFFLUVIUM
EFFLUVIUMS
EFFLUX
EFFLUXES
EFFLUXION
EFFLUXIONS
EFFORT
EFFORTFUL
EFFORTFULLY
EFFORTFULNESS
EFFORTFULNESSES
EFFORTLESS
EFFORTLESSLY
EFFORTLESSNESS
EFFORTS
EFFRONTERIES
EFFRONTERY
EFFS
EFFULGE
EFFULGED
EFFULGENCE
EFFULGENCES
EFFULGENT
EFFULGES
EFFULGING
EFFUSE
EFFUSED
EFFUSES
EFFUSING
EFFUSION
EFFUSIONS
EFFUSIVE
EFFUSIVELY
EFFUSIVENESS
EFFUSIVENESSES
EFS
EFT
EFTS
EFTSOON
EFTSOONS
EGAD
EGADS
EGAL
EGALITARIAN
EGALITARIANISM
EGALITARIANISMS
EGALITARIANS
EGALITE
EGALITES
EGER
EGERS
EGEST
EGESTA
EGESTED
EGESTING
EGESTION
EGESTIONS
EGESTIVE
EGESTS
EGG
EGGAR
EGGARS
EGGBEATER
EGGBEATERS
EGGCUP
EGGCUPS
EGGED
EGGER
EGGERS
EGGFRUIT
EGGFRUITS
EGGHEAD
EGGHEADED
EGGHEADEDNESS
EGGHEADEDNESSES
EGGHEADS
EGGIER
EGGIEST
EGGING
EGGLESS
EGGNOG
EGGNOGS
EGGPLANT
EGGPLANTS
EGGS
EGGSHELL
EGGSHELLS
EGGY
EGIS
EGISES
EGLANTINE
EGLANTINES
EGLATERE
EGLATERES
EGLOMISE
EGO
EGOCENTRIC
EGOCENTRICALLY
EGOCENTRICITIES
EGOCENTRICITY
EGOCENTRICS
EGOCENTRISM
EGOCENTRISMS
EGOISM
EGOISMS
EGOIST
EGOISTIC
EGOISTICAL
EGOISTICALLY
EGOISTS
EGOLESS
EGOMANIA
EGOMANIAC
EGOMANIACAL
EGOMANIACALLY
EGOMANIACS
EGOMANIAS
EGOS
EGOTISM
EGOTISMS
EGOTIST
EGOTISTIC
EGOTISTICAL
EGOTISTICALLY
EGOTISTS
EGOTIZE
EGOTIZED
EGOTIZES
EGOTIZING
EGREGIOUS
EGREGIOUSLY
EGREGIOUSNESS
EGREGIOUSNESSES
EGRESS
EGRESSED
EGRESSES
EGRESSING
EGRESSION
EGRESSIONS
EGRET
EGRETS
EGYPTIAN
EGYPTIANS
EH
EHRLICHIOSES
EHRLICHIOSIS
EICOSANOID
EICOSANOIDS
EIDE
EIDER
EIDERDOWN
EIDERDOWNS
EIDERS
EIDETIC
EIDETICALLY
EIDETICS
EIDOLA

EIDOLIC
EIDOLON
EIDOLONS
EIDOS
EIGENMODE
EIGENMODES
EIGENVALUE
EIGENVALUES
EIGENVECTOR
EIGENVECTORS
EIGHT
EIGHTBALL
EIGHTBALLS
EIGHTEEN
EIGHTEENS
EIGHTEENTH
EIGHTEENTHS
EIGHTFOLD
EIGHTH
EIGHTHLY
EIGHTHS
EIGHTIES
EIGHTIETH
EIGHTIETHS
EIGHTS
EIGHTVO
EIGHTVOS
EIGHTY
EIKON
EIKONES
EIKONS
EINKORN
EINKORNS
EINSTEIN
EINSTEINIUM
EINSTEINIUMS
EINSTEINS
EIRENIC
EIRENICAL
EIRENICS
EISEGESES
EISEGESIS
EISTEDDFOD
EISTEDDFODAU
EISTEDDFODIC
EISTEDDFODS
EISWEIN
EISWEINS
EITHER
EJACULATE
EJACULATED
EJACULATES
EJACULATING
EJACULATION
EJACULATIONS
EJACULATOR
EJACULATORS
EJACULATORY
EJECT
EJECTA
EJECTABLE
EJECTED
EJECTING
EJECTION
EJECTIONS
EJECTIVE
EJECTIVES
EJECTMENT
EJECTMENTS
EJECTOR
EJECTORS
EJECTS
EJIDO
EJIDOS
EKE
EKED
EKES
EKING
EKISTIC
EKISTICAL
EKISTICS
EKKA
EKKAS
EKPHRASES
EKPHRASIS
EKPWELE
EKPWELES
EKTEXINE
EKTEXINES
EKUELE
EL
ELABORATE
ELABORATED
ELABORATELY
ELABORATENESS
ELABORATENESSES
ELABORATES
ELABORATING
ELABORATION
ELABORATIONS
ELABORATIVE
ELAIN
ELAINS
ELAN
ELAND
ELANDS
ELANS
ELAPHINE
ELAPID
ELAPIDS
ELAPINE
ELAPSE
ELAPSED
ELAPSES
ELAPSING
ELASMOBRANCH
ELASMOBRANCHS
ELASTANE
ELASTANES
ELASTASE
ELASTASES
ELASTIC
ELASTICALLY
ELASTICATED
ELASTICITIES
ELASTICITY
ELASTICIZED
ELASTICS
ELASTIN
ELASTINS
ELASTOMER
ELASTOMERIC
ELASTOMERS
ELATE
ELATED
ELATEDLY
ELATEDNESS
ELATEDNESSES
ELATER
ELATERID
ELATERIDS
ELATERIN
ELATERINS
ELATERITE
ELATERITES
ELATERIUM
ELATERIUMS
ELATERS
ELATES
ELATING
ELATION
ELATIONS
ELATIVE
ELATIVES
ELBOW
ELBOWED
ELBOWING
ELBOWINGS
ELBOWROOM
ELBOWROOMS
ELBOWS
ELD
ELDER
ELDERBERRIES
ELDERBERRY
ELDERCARE
ELDERCARES
ELDERLIES
ELDERLINESS
ELDERLINESSES
ELDERLY
ELDERS
ELDERSHIP
ELDERSHIPS
ELDEST
ELDESTS
ELDORADO
ELDORADOS
ELDRESS
ELDRESSES
ELDRICH
ELDRITCH
ELDS
ELECAMPANE
ELECAMPANES
ELECT
ELECTABILITIES
ELECTABILITY
ELECTABLE
ELECTED
ELECTEE
ELECTEES
ELECTING
ELECTION
ELECTIONEER
ELECTIONEERED
ELECTIONEERER
ELECTIONEERERS
ELECTIONEERING
ELECTIONEERS
ELECTIONS
ELECTIVE
ELECTIVELY
ELECTIVENESS
ELECTIVENESSES
ELECTIVES
ELECTOR
ELECTORAL
ELECTORALLY
ELECTORATE
ELECTORATES
ELECTORS
ELECTRESS
ELECTRESSES
ELECTRET
ELECTRETS
ELECTRIC
ELECTRICAL
ELECTRICALLY
ELECTRICIAN
ELECTRICIANS
ELECTRICITIES
ELECTRICITY
ELECTRICS
ELECTRIFICATION
ELECTRIFIED
ELECTRIFIES
ELECTRIFY
ELECTRIFYING
ELECTRO
ELECTROACOUSTIC
ELECTROANALYSES
ELECTROANALYSIS
ELECTROCAUTERY
ELECTROCHEMICAL
ELECTROCHEMIST
ELECTROCHEMISTS
ELECTROCUTE
ELECTROCUTED
ELECTROCUTES
ELECTROCUTING
ELECTROCUTION
ELECTROCUTIONS
ELECTRODE
ELECTRODEPOSIT
ELECTRODEPOSITS
ELECTRODERMAL
ELECTRODES
ELECTRODIALYSES
ELECTRODIALYSIS
ELECTRODIALYTIC
ELECTRODYNAMIC
ELECTRODYNAMICS
ELECTROED
ELECTROFISHING
ELECTROFISHINGS
ELECTROFORM
ELECTROFORMED
ELECTROFORMING
ELECTROFORMS
ELECTROGENESES
ELECTROGENESIS
ELECTROGENIC
ELECTROGRAM
ELECTROGRAMS

ELECTROING
ELECTROJET
ELECTROJETS
ELECTROKINETIC
ELECTROKINETICS
ELECTROLESS
ELECTROLOGIES
ELECTROLOGIST
ELECTROLOGISTS
ELECTROLOGY
ELECTROLYSES
ELECTROLYSIS
ELECTROLYTE
ELECTROLYTES
ELECTROLYTIC
ELECTROLYZE
ELECTROLYZED
ELECTROLYZES
ELECTROLYZING
ELECTROMAGNET
ELECTROMAGNETIC
ELECTROMAGNETS
ELECTROMETER
ELECTROMETERS
ELECTROMYOGRAM
ELECTROMYOGRAMS
ELECTROMYOGRAPH
ELECTRON
ELECTRONEGATIVE
ELECTRONIC
ELECTRONICA
ELECTRONICALLY
ELECTRONICAS
ELECTRONICS
ELECTRONS
ELECTROOSMOSES
ELECTROOSMOSIS
ELECTROOSMOTIC
ELECTROPHILE
ELECTROPHILES
ELECTROPHILIC
ELECTROPHORESE
ELECTROPHORESED
ELECTROPHORESES
ELECTROPHORESIS
ELECTROPHORETIC
ELECTROPHORI
ELECTROPHORUS
ELECTROPLATE
ELECTROPLATED
ELECTROPLATES
ELECTROPLATING
ELECTROPORATION
ELECTROPOSITIVE
ELECTRORECEPTOR
ELECTROS
ELECTROSCOPE
ELECTROSCOPES
ELECTROSHOCK
ELECTROSHOCKS
ELECTROSTATIC
ELECTROSTATICS
ELECTROSURGERY
ELECTROSURGICAL
ELECTROTHERAPY
ELECTROTHERMAL
ELECTROTONIC
ELECTROTONUS
ELECTROTONUSES
ELECTROTYPE
ELECTROTYPED
ELECTROTYPER
ELECTROTYPERS
ELECTROTYPES
ELECTROTYPING
ELECTROWEAK
ELECTROWINNING
ELECTROWINNINGS
ELECTRUM
ELECTRUMS
ELECTS
ELECTUARIES
ELECTUARY
ELEDOISIN
ELEDOISINS
ELEEMOSYNARY
ELEGANCE
ELEGANCES
ELEGANCIES
ELEGANCY
ELEGANT
ELEGANTLY
ELEGIAC
ELEGIACAL
ELEGIACALLY
ELEGIACS
ELEGIES
ELEGISE
ELEGISED
ELEGISES
ELEGISING
ELEGIST
ELEGISTS
ELEGIT
ELEGITS
ELEGIZE
ELEGIZED
ELEGIZES
ELEGIZING
ELEGY
ELEMENT
ELEMENTAL
ELEMENTALLY
ELEMENTALS
ELEMENTARILY
ELEMENTARINESS
ELEMENTARY
ELEMENTS
ELEMI
ELEMIS
ELENCHI
ELENCHIC
ELENCHTIC
ELENCHUS
ELENCTIC
ELEOPTENE
ELEOPTENES
ELEPHANT
ELEPHANTIASES
ELEPHANTIASIS
ELEPHANTINE
ELEPHANTS
ELEVATE
ELEVATED
ELEVATEDS
ELEVATES
ELEVATING
ELEVATION
ELEVATIONS
ELEVATOR
ELEVATORS
ELEVEN
ELEVENS
ELEVENSES
ELEVENTH
ELEVENTHS
ELEVON
ELEVONS
ELF
ELFIN
ELFINS
ELFISH
ELFISHLY
ELFLIKE
ELFLOCK
ELFLOCKS
ELHI
ELICIT
ELICITATION
ELICITATIONS
ELICITED
ELICITING
ELICITOR
ELICITORS
ELICITS
ELIDE
ELIDED
ELIDES
ELIDIBLE
ELIDING
ELIGIBILITIES
ELIGIBILITY
ELIGIBLE
ELIGIBLES
ELIGIBLY
ELIMINATE
ELIMINATED
ELIMINATES
ELIMINATING
ELIMINATION
ELIMINATIONS
ELIMINATIVE
ELIMINATOR
ELIMINATORS
ELINT
ELINTS
ELISION
ELISIONS
ELITE
ELITES
ELITISM
ELITISMS
ELITIST
ELITISTS
ELIXIR
ELIXIRS
ELK
ELKHOUND
ELKHOUNDS
ELKS
ELL
ELLIPSE
ELLIPSES
ELLIPSIS
ELLIPSOID
ELLIPSOIDAL
ELLIPSOIDS
ELLIPTIC
ELLIPTICAL
ELLIPTICALLY
ELLIPTICALS
ELLIPTICITIES
ELLIPTICITY
ELLS
ELM
ELMIER
ELMIEST
ELMS
ELMWOOD
ELMWOODS
ELMY
ELOCUTION
ELOCUTIONARY
ELOCUTIONIST
ELOCUTIONISTS
ELOCUTIONS
ELODEA
ELODEAS
ELOIGN
ELOIGNED
ELOIGNER
ELOIGNERS
ELOIGNING
ELOIGNS
ELOIN
ELOINED
ELOINER
ELOINERS
ELOINING
ELOINMENT
ELOINMENTS
ELOINS
ELONGATE
ELONGATED
ELONGATES
ELONGATING
ELONGATION
ELONGATIONS
ELOPE
ELOPED
ELOPEMENT
ELOPEMENTS
ELOPER
ELOPERS
ELOPES
ELOPING
ELOQUENCE
ELOQUENCES
ELOQUENT
ELOQUENTLY
ELS
ELSE
ELSEWHERE
ELUANT
ELUANTS

ELUATE
ELUATES
ELUCIDATE
ELUCIDATED
ELUCIDATES
ELUCIDATING
ELUCIDATION
ELUCIDATIONS
ELUCIDATIVE
ELUCIDATOR
ELUCIDATORS
ELUCUBRATE
ELUCUBRATED
ELUCUBRATES
ELUCUBRATING
ELUCUBRATION
ELUCUBRATIONS
ELUDE
ELUDED
ELUDER
ELUDERS
ELUDES
ELUDING
ELUENT
ELUENTS
ELUSION
ELUSIONS
ELUSIVE
ELUSIVELY
ELUSIVENESS
ELUSIVENESSES
ELUSORY
ELUTE
ELUTED
ELUTES
ELUTING
ELUTION
ELUTIONS
ELUTRIATE
ELUTRIATED
ELUTRIATES
ELUTRIATING
ELUTRIATION
ELUTRIATIONS
ELUTRIATOR
ELUTRIATORS
ELUVIA
ELUVIAL
ELUVIATE
ELUVIATED
ELUVIATES
ELUVIATING
ELUVIATION
ELUVIATIONS
ELUVIUM
ELUVIUMS
ELVEN
ELVER
ELVERS
ELVES
ELVISH
ELVISHLY
ELYSIAN
ELYTRA
ELYTROID
ELYTRON
ELYTROUS
ELYTRUM
EM
EMACIATE
EMACIATED
EMACIATES
EMACIATING
EMACIATION
EMACIATIONS
EMAIL
EMAILED
EMAILING
EMAILS
EMALANGENI
EMANANT
EMANATE
EMANATED
EMANATES
EMANATING
EMANATION
EMANATIONS
EMANATIVE
EMANATOR
EMANATORS
EMANCIPATE
EMANCIPATED
EMANCIPATES
EMANCIPATING
EMANCIPATION
EMANCIPATIONIST
EMANCIPATIONS
EMANCIPATOR
EMANCIPATORS
EMANCIPATORY
EMARGINATE
EMARGINATION
EMARGINATIONS
EMASCULATE
EMASCULATED
EMASCULATES
EMASCULATING
EMASCULATION
EMASCULATIONS
EMASCULATOR
EMASCULATORS
EMBALM
EMBALMED
EMBALMER
EMBALMERS
EMBALMING
EMBALMINGS
EMBALMMENT
EMBALMMENTS
EMBALMS
EMBANK
EMBANKED
EMBANKING
EMBANKMENT
EMBANKMENTS
EMBANKS
EMBAR
EMBARCADERO
EMBARCADEROS
EMBARGO
EMBARGOED
EMBARGOES
EMBARGOING
EMBARK
EMBARKATION
EMBARKATIONS
EMBARKED
EMBARKING
EMBARKMENT
EMBARKMENTS
EMBARKS
EMBARRASS
EMBARRASSABLE
EMBARRASSED
EMBARRASSEDLY
EMBARRASSES
EMBARRASSING
EMBARRASSINGLY
EMBARRASSMENT
EMBARRASSMENTS
EMBARRED
EMBARRING
EMBARS
EMBASSAGE
EMBASSAGES
EMBASSIES
EMBASSY
EMBATTLE
EMBATTLED
EMBATTLEMENT
EMBATTLEMENTS
EMBATTLES
EMBATTLING
EMBAY
EMBAYED
EMBAYING
EMBAYMENT
EMBAYMENTS
EMBAYS
EMBED
EMBEDDED
EMBEDDING
EMBEDDINGS
EMBEDMENT
EMBEDMENTS
EMBEDS
EMBELLISH
EMBELLISHED
EMBELLISHER
EMBELLISHERS
EMBELLISHES
EMBELLISHING
EMBELLISHMENT
EMBELLISHMENTS
EMBER
EMBERS
EMBEZZLE
EMBEZZLED
EMBEZZLEMENT
EMBEZZLEMENTS
EMBEZZLER
EMBEZZLERS
EMBEZZLES
EMBEZZLING
EMBITTER
EMBITTERED
EMBITTERING
EMBITTERMENT
EMBITTERMENTS
EMBITTERS
EMBLAZE
EMBLAZED
EMBLAZER
EMBLAZERS
EMBLAZES
EMBLAZING
EMBLAZON
EMBLAZONED
EMBLAZONER
EMBLAZONERS
EMBLAZONING
EMBLAZONMENT
EMBLAZONMENTS
EMBLAZONRIES
EMBLAZONRY
EMBLAZONS
EMBLEM
EMBLEMATIC
EMBLEMATICAL
EMBLEMATICALLY
EMBLEMATIZE
EMBLEMATIZED
EMBLEMATIZES
EMBLEMATIZING
EMBLEMED
EMBLEMENTS
EMBLEMING
EMBLEMIZE
EMBLEMIZED
EMBLEMIZES
EMBLEMIZING
EMBLEMS
EMBODIED
EMBODIER
EMBODIERS
EMBODIES
EMBODIMENT
EMBODIMENTS
EMBODY
EMBODYING
EMBOLDEN
EMBOLDENED
EMBOLDENING
EMBOLDENS
EMBOLECTOMIES
EMBOLECTOMY
EMBOLI
EMBOLIC
EMBOLIES
EMBOLISATION
EMBOLISATIONS
EMBOLISM
EMBOLISMIC
EMBOLISMS
EMBOLIZATION
EMBOLIZATIONS
EMBOLUS
EMBOLY
EMBONPOINT
EMBONPOINTS
EMBORDER
EMBORDERED
EMBORDERING
EMBORDERS
EMBOSK

EMBOSKED
EMBOSKING
EMBOSKS
EMBOSOM
EMBOSOMED
EMBOSOMING
EMBOSOMS
EMBOSS
EMBOSSABLE
EMBOSSED
EMBOSSER
EMBOSSERS
EMBOSSES
EMBOSSING
EMBOSSMENT
EMBOSSMENTS
EMBOUCHURE
EMBOUCHURES
EMBOW
EMBOWED
EMBOWEL
EMBOWELED
EMBOWELING
EMBOWELLED
EMBOWELLING
EMBOWELS
EMBOWER
EMBOWERED
EMBOWERING
EMBOWERS
EMBOWING
EMBOWS
EMBRACE
EMBRACEABLE
EMBRACED
EMBRACEMENT
EMBRACEMENTS
EMBRACEOR
EMBRACEORS
EMBRACER
EMBRACERIES
EMBRACERS
EMBRACERY
EMBRACES
EMBRACING
EMBRACINGLY
EMBRACIVE
EMBRANGLE
EMBRANGLED
EMBRANGLEMENT
EMBRANGLEMENTS
EMBRANGLES
EMBRANGLING
EMBRASURE
EMBRASURES
EMBRITTLE
EMBRITTLED
EMBRITTLEMENT
EMBRITTLEMENTS
EMBRITTLES
EMBRITTLING
EMBROCATE
EMBROCATED
EMBROCATES
EMBROCATING
EMBROCATION
EMBROCATIONS
EMBROGLIO
EMBROGLIOS
EMBROIDER
EMBROIDERED
EMBROIDERER
EMBROIDERERS
EMBROIDERIES
EMBROIDERING
EMBROIDERS
EMBROIDERY
EMBROIL
EMBROILED
EMBROILER
EMBROILERS
EMBROILING
EMBROILMENT
EMBROILMENTS
EMBROILS
EMBROWN
EMBROWNED
EMBROWNING
EMBROWNS
EMBRUE
EMBRUED
EMBRUES
EMBRUING
EMBRUTE
EMBRUTED
EMBRUTES
EMBRUTING
EMBRYO
EMBRYOGENESES
EMBRYOGENESIS
EMBRYOGENETIC
EMBRYOGENIC
EMBRYOGENIES
EMBRYOGENY
EMBRYOID
EMBRYOIDS
EMBRYOLOGICAL
EMBRYOLOGICALLY
EMBRYOLOGIES
EMBRYOLOGIST
EMBRYOLOGISTS
EMBRYOLOGY
EMBRYON
EMBRYONAL
EMBRYONATED
EMBRYONIC
EMBRYONICALLY
EMBRYONS
EMBRYOPHYTE
EMBRYOPHYTES
EMBRYOS
EMBRYOTIC
EMCEE
EMCEED
EMCEEING
EMCEES
EMDASH
EMDASHES
EME
EMEER
EMEERATE
EMEERATES
EMEERS
EMEND
EMENDABLE
EMENDATE
EMENDATED
EMENDATES
EMENDATING
EMENDATION
EMENDATIONS
EMENDATOR
EMENDATORS
EMENDED
EMENDER
EMENDERS
EMENDING
EMENDS
EMERALD
EMERALDS
EMERG
EMERGE
EMERGED
EMERGENCE
EMERGENCES
EMERGENCIES
EMERGENCY
EMERGENT
EMERGENTS
EMERGES
EMERGING
EMERGS
EMERIES
EMERITA
EMERITAE
EMERITAS
EMERITI
EMERITUS
EMEROD
EMERODS
EMEROID
EMEROIDS
EMERSE
EMERSED
EMERSION
EMERSIONS
EMERY
EMES
EMESES
EMESIS
EMESISES
EMETIC
EMETICALLY
EMETICS
EMETIN
EMETINE
EMETINES
EMETINS
EMEU
EMEUS
EMEUTE
EMEUTES
EMIC
EMICS
EMIGRANT
EMIGRANTS
EMIGRATE
EMIGRATED
EMIGRATES
EMIGRATING
EMIGRATION
EMIGRATIONS
EMIGRE
EMIGRES
EMINENCE
EMINENCES
EMINENCIES
EMINENCY
EMINENT
EMINENTLY
EMIR
EMIRATE
EMIRATES
EMIRS
EMISSARIES
EMISSARY
EMISSION
EMISSIONS
EMISSIVE
EMISSIVITIES
EMISSIVITY
EMIT
EMITS
EMITTANCE
EMITTANCES
EMITTED
EMITTER
EMITTERS
EMITTING
EMMENAGOGUE
EMMENAGOGUES
EMMER
EMMERS
EMMET
EMMETROPE
EMMETROPES
EMMETS
EMMY
EMMYS
EMO
EMOCORE
EMOCORES
EMODIN
EMODINS
EMOLLIENT
EMOLLIENTS
EMOLUMENT
EMOLUMENTS
EMOS
EMOTE
EMOTED
EMOTER
EMOTERS
EMOTES
EMOTICON
EMOTICONS
EMOTING
EMOTION
EMOTIONAL
EMOTIONALISM
EMOTIONALISMS
EMOTIONALIST
EMOTIONALISTIC
EMOTIONALISTS
EMOTIONALITIES

EMOTIONALITY
EMOTIONALIZE
EMOTIONALIZED
EMOTIONALIZES
EMOTIONALIZING
EMOTIONALLY
EMOTIONLESS
EMOTIONLESSLY
EMOTIONLESSNESS
EMOTIONS
EMOTIVE
EMOTIVELY
EMOTIVITIES
EMOTIVITY
EMPALE
EMPALED
EMPALER
EMPALERS
EMPALES
EMPALING
EMPANADA
EMPANADAS
EMPANEL
EMPANELED
EMPANELING
EMPANELLED
EMPANELLING
EMPANELS
EMPATHETIC
EMPATHETICALLY
EMPATHIC
EMPATHICALLY
EMPATHIES
EMPATHISE
EMPATHISED
EMPATHISES
EMPATHISING
EMPATHIZE
EMPATHIZED
EMPATHIZER
EMPATHIZERS
EMPATHIZES
EMPATHIZING
EMPATHY
EMPENNAGE
EMPENNAGES
EMPERIES
EMPEROR
EMPERORS
EMPERORSHIP
EMPERORSHIPS
EMPERY
EMPHASES
EMPHASIS
EMPHASISE
EMPHASISED
EMPHASISES
EMPHASISING
EMPHASIZE
EMPHASIZED
EMPHASIZES
EMPHASIZING
EMPHATIC
EMPHATICALLY
EMPHYSEMA
EMPHYSEMAS
EMPHYSEMATOUS
EMPHYSEMIC
EMPIRE
EMPIRES
EMPIRIC
EMPIRICAL
EMPIRICALLY
EMPIRICISM
EMPIRICISMS
EMPIRICIST
EMPIRICISTS
EMPIRICS
EMPLACE
EMPLACED
EMPLACEMENT
EMPLACEMENTS
EMPLACES
EMPLACING
EMPLANE
EMPLANED
EMPLANES
EMPLANING
EMPLOY
EMPLOYABILITIES
EMPLOYABILITY
EMPLOYABLE
EMPLOYABLES
EMPLOYE
EMPLOYED
EMPLOYEE
EMPLOYEES
EMPLOYER
EMPLOYERS
EMPLOYES
EMPLOYING
EMPLOYMENT
EMPLOYMENTS
EMPLOYS
EMPOISON
EMPOISONED
EMPOISONING
EMPOISONMENT
EMPOISONMENTS
EMPOISONS
EMPORIA
EMPORIUM
EMPORIUMS
EMPOWER
EMPOWERED
EMPOWERING
EMPOWERMENT
EMPOWERMENTS
EMPOWERS
EMPRESS
EMPRESSEMENT
EMPRESSEMENTS
EMPRESSES
EMPRISE
EMPRISES
EMPRIZE
EMPRIZES
EMPTIABLE
EMPTIED
EMPTIER
EMPTIERS
EMPTIES
EMPTIEST
EMPTILY
EMPTINESS
EMPTINESSES
EMPTINGS
EMPTINS
EMPTY
EMPTYING
EMPURPLE
EMPURPLED
EMPURPLES
EMPURPLING
EMPYEMA
EMPYEMAS
EMPYEMATA
EMPYEMIC
EMPYREAL
EMPYREAN
EMPYREANS
EMS
EMU
EMULATE
EMULATED
EMULATES
EMULATING
EMULATION
EMULATIONS
EMULATIVE
EMULATIVELY
EMULATOR
EMULATORS
EMULOUS
EMULOUSLY
EMULOUSNESS
EMULOUSNESSES
EMULSIBLE
EMULSIFIABLE
EMULSIFICATION
EMULSIFICATIONS
EMULSIFIED
EMULSIFIER
EMULSIFIERS
EMULSIFIES
EMULSIFY
EMULSIFYING
EMULSION
EMULSIONS
EMULSIVE
EMULSOID
EMULSOIDAL
EMULSOIDS
EMUNCTORIES
EMUNCTORY
EMUS
EMYD
EMYDE
EMYDES
EMYDS
EN
ENABLE
ENABLED
ENABLER
ENABLERS
ENABLES
ENABLING
ENACT
ENACTABLE
ENACTED
ENACTING
ENACTION
ENACTIONS
ENACTIVE
ENACTMENT
ENACTMENTS
ENACTOR
ENACTORS
ENACTORY
ENACTS
ENALAPRIL
ENALAPRILS
ENAMEL
ENAMELED
ENAMELER
ENAMELERS
ENAMELING
ENAMELIST
ENAMELISTS
ENAMELLED
ENAMELLER
ENAMELLERS
ENAMELLING
ENAMELS
ENAMELWARE
ENAMELWARES
ENAMINE
ENAMINES
ENAMOR
ENAMORED
ENAMORING
ENAMORS
ENAMOUR
ENAMOURED
ENAMOURING
ENAMOURS
ENANTIOMER
ENANTIOMERIC
ENANTIOMERS
ENANTIOMORPH
ENANTIOMORPHIC
ENANTIOMORPHISM
ENANTIOMORPHOUS
ENANTIOMORPHS
ENATE
ENATES
ENATIC
ENATION
ENATIONS
ENCAENIA
ENCAGE
ENCAGED
ENCAGES
ENCAGING
ENCAMP
ENCAMPED
ENCAMPING
ENCAMPMENT
ENCAMPMENTS
ENCAMPS
ENCAPSULATE
ENCAPSULATED
ENCAPSULATES
ENCAPSULATING
ENCAPSULATION

ENCAPSULATIONS
ENCAPSULE
ENCAPSULED
ENCAPSULES
ENCAPSULING
ENCASE
ENCASED
ENCASEMENT
ENCASEMENTS
ENCASES
ENCASH
ENCASHABLE
ENCASHED
ENCASHES
ENCASHING
ENCASHMENT
ENCASHMENTS
ENCASING
ENCAUSTIC
ENCAUSTICS
ENCEINTE
ENCEINTES
ENCEPHALA
ENCEPHALITIC
ENCEPHALITIDES
ENCEPHALITIS
ENCEPHALITOGEN
ENCEPHALITOGENS
ENCEPHALOGRAM
ENCEPHALOGRAMS
ENCEPHALOGRAPH
ENCEPHALOGRAPHS
ENCEPHALOGRAPHY
ENCEPHALON
ENCEPHALOPATHIC
ENCEPHALOPATHY
ENCHAIN
ENCHAINED
ENCHAINING
ENCHAINMENT
ENCHAINMENTS
ENCHAINS
ENCHANT
ENCHANTED
ENCHANTER
ENCHANTERS
ENCHANTING
ENCHANTINGLY
ENCHANTMENT
ENCHANTMENTS
ENCHANTRESS
ENCHANTRESSES
ENCHANTS
ENCHASE
ENCHASED
ENCHASER
ENCHASERS
ENCHASES
ENCHASING
ENCHILADA
ENCHILADAS
ENCHIRIDIA
ENCHIRIDION
ENCHORIAL
ENCHORIC
ENCINA
ENCINAL
ENCINAS
ENCIPHER
ENCIPHERED
ENCIPHERER
ENCIPHERERS
ENCIPHERING
ENCIPHERMENT
ENCIPHERMENTS
ENCIPHERS
ENCIRCLE
ENCIRCLED
ENCIRCLEMENT
ENCIRCLEMENTS
ENCIRCLES
ENCIRCLING
ENCLASP
ENCLASPED
ENCLASPING
ENCLASPS
ENCLAVE
ENCLAVED
ENCLAVES
ENCLAVING
ENCLITIC
ENCLITICS
ENCLOSE
ENCLOSED
ENCLOSER
ENCLOSERS
ENCLOSES
ENCLOSING
ENCLOSURE
ENCLOSURES
ENCODABLE
ENCODE
ENCODED
ENCODER
ENCODERS
ENCODES
ENCODING
ENCOMIA
ENCOMIAST
ENCOMIASTIC
ENCOMIASTS
ENCOMIUM
ENCOMIUMS
ENCOMPASS
ENCOMPASSED
ENCOMPASSES
ENCOMPASSING
ENCOMPASSMENT
ENCOMPASSMENTS
ENCORE
ENCORED
ENCORES
ENCORING
ENCOUNTER
ENCOUNTERED
ENCOUNTERING
ENCOUNTERS
ENCOURAGE
ENCOURAGED
ENCOURAGEMENT
ENCOURAGEMENTS
ENCOURAGER
ENCOURAGERS
ENCOURAGES
ENCOURAGING
ENCOURAGINGLY
ENCRIMSON
ENCRIMSONED
ENCRIMSONING
ENCRIMSONS
ENCRINITE
ENCRINITES
ENCROACH
ENCROACHED
ENCROACHER
ENCROACHERS
ENCROACHES
ENCROACHING
ENCROACHMENT
ENCROACHMENTS
ENCRUST
ENCRUSTATION
ENCRUSTATIONS
ENCRUSTED
ENCRUSTING
ENCRUSTS
ENCRYPT
ENCRYPTED
ENCRYPTING
ENCRYPTION
ENCRYPTIONS
ENCRYPTS
ENCULTURATE
ENCULTURATED
ENCULTURATES
ENCULTURATING
ENCULTURATION
ENCULTURATIONS
ENCUMBER
ENCUMBERED
ENCUMBERING
ENCUMBERS
ENCUMBRANCE
ENCUMBRANCER
ENCUMBRANCERS
ENCUMBRANCES
ENCYCLIC
ENCYCLICAL
ENCYCLICALS
ENCYCLICS
ENCYCLOPAEDIA
ENCYCLOPAEDIAS
ENCYCLOPAEDIC
ENCYCLOPEDIA
ENCYCLOPEDIAS
ENCYCLOPEDIC
ENCYCLOPEDISM
ENCYCLOPEDISMS
ENCYCLOPEDIST
ENCYCLOPEDISTS
ENCYST
ENCYSTED
ENCYSTING
ENCYSTMENT
ENCYSTMENTS
ENCYSTS
END
ENDAMAGE
ENDAMAGED
ENDAMAGES
ENDAMAGING
ENDAMEBA
ENDAMEBAE
ENDAMEBAS
ENDAMEBIC
ENDAMOEBA
ENDAMOEBAE
ENDAMOEBAS
ENDANGER
ENDANGERED
ENDANGERING
ENDANGERMENT
ENDANGERMENTS
ENDANGERS
ENDARCH
ENDARCHIES
ENDARCHY
ENDARTERECTOMY
ENDASH
ENDASHES
ENDBRAIN
ENDBRAINS
ENDCAP
ENDCAPS
ENDEAR
ENDEARED
ENDEARING
ENDEARINGLY
ENDEARMENT
ENDEARMENTS
ENDEARS
ENDEAVOR
ENDEAVORED
ENDEAVORING
ENDEAVORS
ENDEAVOUR
ENDEAVOURED
ENDEAVOURING
ENDEAVOURS
ENDED
ENDEMIAL
ENDEMIC
ENDEMICAL
ENDEMICALLY
ENDEMICITIES
ENDEMICITY
ENDEMICS
ENDEMISM
ENDEMISMS
ENDER
ENDERGONIC
ENDERMIC
ENDERS
ENDEXINE
ENDEXINES
ENDGAME
ENDGAMES
ENDING
ENDINGS
ENDITE
ENDITED
ENDITES
ENDITING
ENDIVE
ENDIVES

ENDLEAF
ENDLEAFS
ENDLEAVES
ENDLESS
ENDLESSLY
ENDLESSNESS
ENDLESSNESSES
ENDLONG
ENDMOST
ENDNOTE
ENDNOTES
ENDOBIOTIC
ENDOBLAST
ENDOBLASTS
ENDOCARDIA
ENDOCARDIAL
ENDOCARDITIDES
ENDOCARDITIS
ENDOCARDITISES
ENDOCARDIUM
ENDOCARP
ENDOCARPS
ENDOCAST
ENDOCASTS
ENDOCHONDRAL
ENDOCRINE
ENDOCRINES
ENDOCRINOLOGIC
ENDOCRINOLOGIES
ENDOCRINOLOGIST
ENDOCRINOLOGY
ENDOCYTIC
ENDOCYTOSES
ENDOCYTOSIS
ENDOCYTOTIC
ENDODERM
ENDODERMAL
ENDODERMIS
ENDODERMISES
ENDODERMS
ENDODONTIC
ENDODONTICALLY
ENDODONTICS
ENDODONTIST
ENDODONTISTS
ENDOENZYME
ENDOENZYMES
ENDOERGIC
ENDOGAMIC
ENDOGAMIES
ENDOGAMOUS
ENDOGAMY
ENDOGEN
ENDOGENIC
ENDOGENIES
ENDOGENOUS
ENDOGENOUSLY
ENDOGENS
ENDOGENY
ENDOLITHIC
ENDOLYMPH
ENDOLYMPHATIC
ENDOLYMPHS
ENDOMETRIA
ENDOMETRIAL
ENDOMETRIOSES
ENDOMETRIOSIS
ENDOMETRITIS
ENDOMETRITISES
ENDOMETRIUM
ENDOMITOSES
ENDOMITOSIS
ENDOMITOTIC
ENDOMIXIS
ENDOMIXISES
ENDOMORPH
ENDOMORPHIC
ENDOMORPHIES
ENDOMORPHISM
ENDOMORPHISMS
ENDOMORPHS
ENDOMORPHY
ENDONUCLEASE
ENDONUCLEASES
ENDONUCLEOLYTIC
ENDOPARASITE
ENDOPARASITES
ENDOPARASITIC
ENDOPARASITISM
ENDOPARASITISMS
ENDOPEPTIDASE
ENDOPEPTIDASES
ENDOPEROXIDE
ENDOPEROXIDES
ENDOPHYTE
ENDOPHYTES
ENDOPHYTIC
ENDOPLASM
ENDOPLASMIC
ENDOPLASMS
ENDOPOD
ENDOPODITE
ENDOPODITES
ENDOPODS
ENDOPOLYPLOID
ENDOPOLYPLOIDY
ENDOPROCT
ENDOPROCTS
ENDORPHIN
ENDORPHINS
ENDORSABLE
ENDORSE
ENDORSED
ENDORSEE
ENDORSEES
ENDORSEMENT
ENDORSEMENTS
ENDORSER
ENDORSERS
ENDORSES
ENDORSING
ENDORSIVE
ENDORSOR
ENDORSORS
ENDOSARC
ENDOSARCS
ENDOSCOPE
ENDOSCOPES
ENDOSCOPIC
ENDOSCOPICALLY
ENDOSCOPIES
ENDOSCOPY
ENDOSKELETAL
ENDOSKELETON
ENDOSKELETONS
ENDOSMOS
ENDOSMOSES
ENDOSOME
ENDOSOMES
ENDOSPERM
ENDOSPERMS
ENDOSPORE
ENDOSPORES
ENDOSTEA
ENDOSTEAL
ENDOSTEALLY
ENDOSTEUM
ENDOSTYLE
ENDOSTYLES
ENDOSULFAN
ENDOSULFANS
ENDOSYMBIONT
ENDOSYMBIONTS
ENDOSYMBIOSES
ENDOSYMBIOSIS
ENDOSYMBIOTIC
ENDOTHECIA
ENDOTHECIUM
ENDOTHELIA
ENDOTHELIAL
ENDOTHELIOMA
ENDOTHELIOMAS
ENDOTHELIOMATA
ENDOTHELIUM
ENDOTHERM
ENDOTHERMIC
ENDOTHERMIES
ENDOTHERMS
ENDOTHERMY
ENDOTOXIC
ENDOTOXIN
ENDOTOXINS
ENDOTRACHEAL
ENDOTROPHIC
ENDOW
ENDOWED
ENDOWER
ENDOWERS
ENDOWING
ENDOWMENT
ENDOWMENTS
ENDOWS
ENDOZOIC
ENDPAPER
ENDPAPERS
ENDPLATE
ENDPLATES
ENDPLAY
ENDPLAYED
ENDPLAYING
ENDPLAYS
ENDPOINT
ENDPOINTS
ENDRIN
ENDRINS
ENDS
ENDUE
ENDUED
ENDUES
ENDUING
ENDURABLE
ENDURABLY
ENDURANCE
ENDURANCES
ENDURE
ENDURED
ENDURER
ENDURERS
ENDURES
ENDURING
ENDURINGLY
ENDURINGNESS
ENDURINGNESSES
ENDURO
ENDUROS
ENDWAYS
ENDWISE
ENEMA
ENEMAS
ENEMATA
ENEMIES
ENEMY
ENERGETIC
ENERGETICALLY
ENERGETICS
ENERGID
ENERGIDS
ENERGIES
ENERGISE
ENERGISED
ENERGISER
ENERGISERS
ENERGISES
ENERGISING
ENERGIZATION
ENERGIZATIONS
ENERGIZE
ENERGIZED
ENERGIZER
ENERGIZERS
ENERGIZES
ENERGIZING
ENERGUMEN
ENERGUMENS
ENERGY
ENERVATE
ENERVATED
ENERVATES
ENERVATING
ENERVATINGLY
ENERVATION
ENERVATIONS
ENERVATOR
ENERVATORS
ENFACE
ENFACED
ENFACES
ENFACING
ENFEEBLE
ENFEEBLED
ENFEEBLEMENT
ENFEEBLEMENTS
ENFEEBLER
ENFEEBLERS
ENFEEBLES

ENFEEBLING
ENFEOFF
ENFEOFFED
ENFEOFFING
ENFEOFFMENT
ENFEOFFMENTS
ENFEOFFS
ENFETTER
ENFETTERED
ENFETTERING
ENFETTERS
ENFEVER
ENFEVERED
ENFEVERING
ENFEVERS
ENFILADE
ENFILADED
ENFILADES
ENFILADING
ENFLAME
ENFLAMED
ENFLAMES
ENFLAMING
ENFLEURAGE
ENFLEURAGES
ENFOLD
ENFOLDED
ENFOLDER
ENFOLDERS
ENFOLDING
ENFOLDS
ENFORCE
ENFORCEABILITY
ENFORCEABLE
ENFORCED
ENFORCEMENT
ENFORCEMENTS
ENFORCER
ENFORCERS
ENFORCES
ENFORCING
ENFRAME
ENFRAMED
ENFRAMEMENT
ENFRAMEMENTS
ENFRAMES
ENFRAMING
ENFRANCHISE
ENFRANCHISED
ENFRANCHISEMENT
ENFRANCHISES
ENFRANCHISING
ENG
ENGAGE
ENGAGED
ENGAGEDLY
ENGAGEMENT
ENGAGEMENTS
ENGAGER
ENGAGERS
ENGAGES
ENGAGING
ENGAGINGLY
ENGARLAND
ENGARLANDED
ENGARLANDING
ENGARLANDS
ENGENDER
ENGENDERED
ENGENDERING
ENGENDERS
ENGILD
ENGILDED
ENGILDING
ENGILDS
ENGINE
ENGINED
ENGINEER
ENGINEERED
ENGINEERING
ENGINEERINGS
ENGINEERS
ENGINELESS
ENGINERIES
ENGINERY
ENGINES
ENGINING
ENGINOUS
ENGIRD
ENGIRDED
ENGIRDING
ENGIRDLE
ENGIRDLED
ENGIRDLES
ENGIRDLING
ENGIRDS
ENGIRT
ENGLACIAL
ENGLISH
ENGLISHED
ENGLISHES
ENGLISHING
ENGLUT
ENGLUTS
ENGLUTTED
ENGLUTTING
ENGORGE
ENGORGED
ENGORGEMENT
ENGORGEMENTS
ENGORGES
ENGORGING
ENGRAFT
ENGRAFTED
ENGRAFTING
ENGRAFTMENT
ENGRAFTMENTS
ENGRAFTS
ENGRAIL
ENGRAILED
ENGRAILING
ENGRAILS
ENGRAIN
ENGRAINED
ENGRAINEDLY
ENGRAINING
ENGRAINS
ENGRAM
ENGRAMME
ENGRAMMES
ENGRAMMIC
ENGRAMS
ENGRAVE
ENGRAVED
ENGRAVER
ENGRAVERS
ENGRAVES
ENGRAVING
ENGRAVINGS
ENGROSS
ENGROSSED
ENGROSSER
ENGROSSERS
ENGROSSES
ENGROSSING
ENGROSSINGLY
ENGROSSMENT
ENGROSSMENTS
ENGS
ENGULF
ENGULFED
ENGULFING
ENGULFMENT
ENGULFMENTS
ENGULFS
ENHALO
ENHALOED
ENHALOES
ENHALOING
ENHALOS
ENHANCE
ENHANCED
ENHANCEMENT
ENHANCEMENTS
ENHANCER
ENHANCERS
ENHANCES
ENHANCING
ENHANCIVE
ENHARMONIC
ENHARMONICALLY
ENIGMA
ENIGMAS
ENIGMATA
ENIGMATIC
ENIGMATICAL
ENIGMATICALLY
ENISLE
ENISLED
ENISLES
ENISLING
ENJAMB
ENJAMBED
ENJAMBEMENT
ENJAMBEMENTS
ENJAMBING
ENJAMBMENT
ENJAMBMENTS
ENJAMBS
ENJOIN
ENJOINDER
ENJOINDERS
ENJOINED
ENJOINER
ENJOINERS
ENJOINING
ENJOINS
ENJOY
ENJOYABLE
ENJOYABLENESS
ENJOYABLENESSES
ENJOYABLY
ENJOYED
ENJOYER
ENJOYERS
ENJOYING
ENJOYMENT
ENJOYMENTS
ENJOYS
ENKEPHALIN
ENKEPHALINS
ENKINDLE
ENKINDLED
ENKINDLER
ENKINDLERS
ENKINDLES
ENKINDLING
ENLACE
ENLACED
ENLACEMENT
ENLACEMENTS
ENLACES
ENLACING
ENLARGE
ENLARGEABLE
ENLARGED
ENLARGEMENT
ENLARGEMENTS
ENLARGER
ENLARGERS
ENLARGES
ENLARGING
ENLIGHTEN
ENLIGHTENED
ENLIGHTENING
ENLIGHTENMENT
ENLIGHTENMENTS
ENLIGHTENS
ENLIST
ENLISTED
ENLISTEE
ENLISTEES
ENLISTER
ENLISTERS
ENLISTING
ENLISTMENT
ENLISTMENTS
ENLISTS
ENLIVEN
ENLIVENED
ENLIVENER
ENLIVENERS
ENLIVENING
ENLIVENS
ENMESH
ENMESHED
ENMESHES
ENMESHING
ENMESHMENT
ENMESHMENTS
ENMITIES
ENMITY
ENNEAD
ENNEADIC
ENNEADS

ENNEAGON
ENNEAGONS
ENNOBLE
ENNOBLED
ENNOBLEMENT
ENNOBLEMENTS
ENNOBLER
ENNOBLERS
ENNOBLES
ENNOBLING
ENNUI
ENNUIS
ENNUYE
ENNUYEE
ENOKI
ENOKIDAKE
ENOKIDAKES
ENOKIS
ENOKITAKE
ENOKITAKES
ENOL
ENOLASE
ENOLASES
ENOLIC
ENOLOGICAL
ENOLOGIES
ENOLOGIST
ENOLOGISTS
ENOLOGY
ENOLS
ENOPHILE
ENOPHILES
ENORM
ENORMITIES
ENORMITY
ENORMOUS
ENORMOUSLY
ENORMOUSNESS
ENORMOUSNESSES
ENOSIS
ENOSISES
ENOUGH
ENOUGHS
ENOUNCE
ENOUNCED
ENOUNCES
ENOUNCING
ENOW
ENOWS
ENPLANE
ENPLANED
ENPLANES
ENPLANING
ENQUIRE
ENQUIRED
ENQUIRER
ENQUIRERS
ENQUIRES
ENQUIRIES
ENQUIRING
ENQUIRY
ENRAGE
ENRAGED
ENRAGEDLY
ENRAGES
ENRAGING
ENRAPT
ENRAPTURE
ENRAPTURED
ENRAPTURES
ENRAPTURING
ENRAVISH
ENRAVISHED
ENRAVISHES
ENRAVISHING
ENREGISTER
ENREGISTERED
ENREGISTERING
ENREGISTERS
ENRICH
ENRICHED
ENRICHER
ENRICHERS
ENRICHES
ENRICHING
ENRICHMENT
ENRICHMENTS
ENROBE
ENROBED
ENROBER
ENROBERS
ENROBES
ENROBING
ENROL
ENROLL
ENROLLED
ENROLLEE
ENROLLEES
ENROLLER
ENROLLERS
ENROLLING
ENROLLMENT
ENROLLMENTS
ENROLLS
ENROLMENT
ENROLMENTS
ENROLS
ENROOT
ENROOTED
ENROOTING
ENROOTS
ENS
ENSAMPLE
ENSAMPLES
ENSANGUINE
ENSANGUINED
ENSANGUINES
ENSANGUINING
ENSCONCE
ENSCONCED
ENSCONCES
ENSCONCING
ENSCROLL
ENSCROLLED
ENSCROLLING
ENSCROLLS
ENSEMBLE
ENSEMBLES
ENSERF
ENSERFED
ENSERFING
ENSERFMENT
ENSERFMENTS
ENSERFS
ENSHEATH
ENSHEATHE
ENSHEATHED
ENSHEATHES
ENSHEATHING
ENSHEATHS
ENSHRINE
ENSHRINED
ENSHRINEE
ENSHRINEES
ENSHRINEMENT
ENSHRINEMENTS
ENSHRINES
ENSHRINING
ENSHROUD
ENSHROUDED
ENSHROUDING
ENSHROUDS
ENSIFORM
ENSIGN
ENSIGNCIES
ENSIGNCY
ENSIGNS
ENSILAGE
ENSILAGED
ENSILAGES
ENSILAGING
ENSILE
ENSILED
ENSILES
ENSILING
ENSKIED
ENSKIES
ENSKY
ENSKYED
ENSKYING
ENSLAVE
ENSLAVED
ENSLAVEMENT
ENSLAVEMENTS
ENSLAVER
ENSLAVERS
ENSLAVES
ENSLAVING
ENSNARE
ENSNARED
ENSNARER
ENSNARERS
ENSNARES
ENSNARING
ENSNARL
ENSNARLED
ENSNARLING
ENSNARLS
ENSORCEL
ENSORCELED
ENSORCELING
ENSORCELL
ENSORCELLED
ENSORCELLING
ENSORCELLMENT
ENSORCELLMENTS
ENSORCELLS
ENSORCELS
ENSOUL
ENSOULED
ENSOULING
ENSOULMENT
ENSOULMENTS
ENSOULS
ENSPHERE
ENSPHERED
ENSPHERES
ENSPHERING
ENSTATITE
ENSTATITES
ENSUE
ENSUED
ENSUES
ENSUING
ENSUITE
ENSUITES
ENSURE
ENSURED
ENSURER
ENSURERS
ENSURES
ENSURING
ENSWATHE
ENSWATHED
ENSWATHES
ENSWATHING
ENTABLATURE
ENTABLATURES
ENTAIL
ENTAILED
ENTAILER
ENTAILERS
ENTAILING
ENTAILMENT
ENTAILMENTS
ENTAILS
ENTAMEBA
ENTAMEBAE
ENTAMEBAS
ENTAMOEBA
ENTAMOEBAE
ENTAMOEBAS
ENTANGLE
ENTANGLED
ENTANGLEMENT
ENTANGLEMENTS
ENTANGLER
ENTANGLERS
ENTANGLES
ENTANGLING
ENTASES
ENTASIA
ENTASIAS
ENTASIS
ENTASTIC
ENTELECHIES
ENTELECHY
ENTELLUS
ENTELLUSES
ENTENTE
ENTENTES
ENTER
ENTERA
ENTERABLE
ENTERAL

ENTERALLY
ENTERED
ENTERER
ENTERERS
ENTERIC
ENTERICS
ENTERING
ENTERITIDES
ENTERITIS
ENTERITISES
ENTEROBACTERIA
ENTEROBACTERIAL
ENTEROBACTERIUM
ENTEROBIASES
ENTEROBIASIS
ENTEROCOCCAL
ENTEROCOCCI
ENTEROCOCCUS
ENTEROCOEL
ENTEROCOELE
ENTEROCOELES
ENTEROCOELIC
ENTEROCOELOUS
ENTEROCOELS
ENTEROCOLITIDES
ENTEROCOLITIS
ENTEROCOLITISES
ENTEROGASTRONE
ENTEROGASTRONES
ENTEROKINASE
ENTEROKINASES
ENTERON
ENTERONS
ENTEROPATHIES
ENTEROPATHY
ENTEROSTOMAL
ENTEROSTOMIES
ENTEROSTOMY
ENTEROTOXIGENIC
ENTEROTOXIN
ENTEROTOXINS
ENTEROVIRAL
ENTEROVIRUS
ENTEROVIRUSES
ENTERPRISE
ENTERPRISER
ENTERPRISERS
ENTERPRISES
ENTERPRISING
ENTERS
ENTERTAIN
ENTERTAINED
ENTERTAINER
ENTERTAINERS
ENTERTAINING
ENTERTAININGLY
ENTERTAINMENT
ENTERTAINMENTS
ENTERTAINS
ENTHALPIES
ENTHALPY
ENTHETIC
ENTHRAL
ENTHRALL
ENTHRALLED
ENTHRALLING
ENTHRALLMENT
ENTHRALLMENTS
ENTHRALLS
ENTHRALS
ENTHRONE
ENTHRONED
ENTHRONEMENT
ENTHRONEMENTS
ENTHRONES
ENTHRONING
ENTHUSE
ENTHUSED
ENTHUSES
ENTHUSIASM
ENTHUSIASMS
ENTHUSIAST
ENTHUSIASTIC
ENTHUSIASTS
ENTHUSING
ENTHYMEME
ENTHYMEMES
ENTIA
ENTICE
ENTICED
ENTICEMENT
ENTICEMENTS
ENTICER
ENTICERS
ENTICES
ENTICING
ENTICINGLY
ENTIRE
ENTIRELY
ENTIRENESS
ENTIRENESSES
ENTIRES
ENTIRETIES
ENTIRETY
ENTITIES
ENTITLE
ENTITLED
ENTITLEMENT
ENTITLEMENTS
ENTITLES
ENTITLING
ENTITY
ENTOBLAST
ENTOBLASTS
ENTODERM
ENTODERMAL
ENTODERMIC
ENTODERMS
ENTOIL
ENTOILED
ENTOILING
ENTOILS
ENTOMB
ENTOMBED
ENTOMBING
ENTOMBMENT
ENTOMBMENTS
ENTOMBS
ENTOMOFAUNA
ENTOMOFAUNAE
ENTOMOFAUNAS
ENTOMOLOGICAL
ENTOMOLOGICALLY
ENTOMOLOGIES
ENTOMOLOGIST
ENTOMOLOGISTS
ENTOMOLOGY
ENTOMOPHAGIES
ENTOMOPHAGOUS
ENTOMOPHAGY
ENTOMOPHILIES
ENTOMOPHILOUS
ENTOMOPHILY
ENTOPHYTE
ENTOPHYTES
ENTOPIC
ENTOPROCT
ENTOPROCTS
ENTORHINAL
ENTOURAGE
ENTOURAGES
ENTOZOA
ENTOZOAL
ENTOZOAN
ENTOZOANS
ENTOZOIC
ENTOZOON
ENTRAILS
ENTRAIN
ENTRAINED
ENTRAINER
ENTRAINERS
ENTRAINING
ENTRAINMENT
ENTRAINMENTS
ENTRAINS
ENTRANCE
ENTRANCED
ENTRANCEMENT
ENTRANCEMENTS
ENTRANCES
ENTRANCEWAY
ENTRANCEWAYS
ENTRANCING
ENTRANT
ENTRANTS
ENTRAP
ENTRAPMENT
ENTRAPMENTS
ENTRAPPED
ENTRAPPER
ENTRAPPERS
ENTRAPPING
ENTRAPS
ENTREAT
ENTREATED
ENTREATIES
ENTREATING
ENTREATINGLY
ENTREATMENT
ENTREATMENTS
ENTREATS
ENTREATY
ENTRECHAT
ENTRECHATS
ENTRECOTE
ENTRECOTES
ENTREE
ENTREES
ENTREMETS
ENTRENCH
ENTRENCHED
ENTRENCHES
ENTRENCHING
ENTRENCHMENT
ENTRENCHMENTS
ENTREPOT
ENTREPOTS
ENTREPRENEUR
ENTREPRENEURIAL
ENTREPRENEURS
ENTRESOL
ENTRESOLS
ENTRIES
ENTROPIC
ENTROPICALLY
ENTROPIES
ENTROPION
ENTROPIONS
ENTROPY
ENTRUST
ENTRUSTED
ENTRUSTING
ENTRUSTMENT
ENTRUSTMENTS
ENTRUSTS
ENTRY
ENTRYWAY
ENTRYWAYS
ENTWINE
ENTWINED
ENTWINES
ENTWINING
ENTWIST
ENTWISTED
ENTWISTING
ENTWISTS
ENUCLEATE
ENUCLEATED
ENUCLEATES
ENUCLEATING
ENUCLEATION
ENUCLEATIONS
ENUF
ENUMERABILITIES
ENUMERABILITY
ENUMERABLE
ENUMERATE
ENUMERATED
ENUMERATES
ENUMERATING
ENUMERATION
ENUMERATIONS
ENUMERATIVE
ENUMERATOR
ENUMERATORS
ENUNCIABLE
ENUNCIATE
ENUNCIATED
ENUNCIATES
ENUNCIATING
ENUNCIATION
ENUNCIATIONS
ENUNCIATOR
ENUNCIATORS

ENURE
ENURED
ENURES
ENURESES
ENURESIS
ENURESISES
ENURETIC
ENURETICS
ENURING
ENVELOP
ENVELOPE
ENVELOPED
ENVELOPER
ENVELOPERS
ENVELOPES
ENVELOPING
ENVELOPMENT
ENVELOPMENTS
ENVELOPS
ENVENOM
ENVENOMATE
ENVENOMATED
ENVENOMATES
ENVENOMATING
ENVENOMATION
ENVENOMATIONS
ENVENOMED
ENVENOMING
ENVENOMIZATION
ENVENOMIZATIONS
ENVENOMS
ENVIABLE
ENVIABLENESS
ENVIABLENESSES
ENVIABLY
ENVIED
ENVIER
ENVIERS
ENVIES
ENVIOUS
ENVIOUSLY
ENVIOUSNESS
ENVIOUSNESSES
ENVIRO
ENVIRON
ENVIRONED
ENVIRONING
ENVIRONMENT
ENVIRONMENTAL
ENVIRONMENTALLY
ENVIRONMENTS
ENVIRONS
ENVIROS
ENVISAGE
ENVISAGED
ENVISAGES
ENVISAGING
ENVISION
ENVISIONED
ENVISIONING
ENVISIONS
ENVOI
ENVOIS
ENVOY
ENVOYS
ENVY
ENVYING
ENVYINGLY
ENWHEEL
ENWHEELED
ENWHEELING
ENWHEELS
ENWIND
ENWINDING
ENWINDS
ENWOMB
ENWOMBED
ENWOMBING
ENWOMBS
ENWOUND
ENWRAP
ENWRAPPED
ENWRAPPING
ENWRAPS
ENWREATHE
ENWREATHED
ENWREATHES
ENWREATHING
ENZOOTIC
ENZOOTICS
ENZYM
ENZYMATIC
ENZYMATICALLY
ENZYME
ENZYMES
ENZYMIC
ENZYMICALLY
ENZYMOLOGIES
ENZYMOLOGIST
ENZYMOLOGISTS
ENZYMOLOGY
ENZYMS
EOBIONT
EOBIONTS
EOCENE
EOHIPPUS
EOHIPPUSES
EOLIAN
EOLIPILE
EOLIPILES
EOLITH
EOLITHIC
EOLITHS
EOLOPILE
EOLOPILES
EON
EONIAN
EONISM
EONISMS
EONS
EOSIN
EOSINE
EOSINES
EOSINIC
EOSINOPHIL
EOSINOPHILIA
EOSINOPHILIAS
EOSINOPHILIC
EOSINOPHILS
EOSINS
EPACT
EPACTS
EPARCH
EPARCHIAL
EPARCHIES
EPARCHS
EPARCHY
EPATER
EPATERED
EPATERING
EPATERS
EPAULET
EPAULETS
EPAULETTE
EPAULETTED
EPAULETTES
EPAZOTE
EPAZOTES
EPEE
EPEEIST
EPEEISTS
EPEES
EPEIRIC
EPEIROGENIC
EPEIROGENICALLY
EPEIROGENIES
EPEIROGENY
EPENDYMA
EPENDYMAS
EPENTHESES
EPENTHESIS
EPENTHETIC
EPERGNE
EPERGNES
EPEXEGESES
EPEXEGESIS
EPEXEGETIC
EPEXEGETICAL
EPEXEGETICALLY
EPHA
EPHAH
EPHAHS
EPHAS
EPHEBE
EPHEBES
EPHEBI
EPHEBIC
EPHEBOI
EPHEBOS
EPHEBUS
EPHEDRA
EPHEDRAS
EPHEDRIN
EPHEDRINE
EPHEDRINES
EPHEDRINS
EPHEMERA
EPHEMERAE
EPHEMERAL
EPHEMERALITIES
EPHEMERALITY
EPHEMERALLY
EPHEMERALS
EPHEMERAS
EPHEMERID
EPHEMERIDES
EPHEMERIDS
EPHEMERIS
EPHEMERON
EPHEMERONS
EPHOD
EPHODS
EPHOR
EPHORAL
EPHORATE
EPHORATES
EPHORI
EPHORS
EPIBLAST
EPIBLASTIC
EPIBLASTS
EPIBOLIC
EPIBOLIES
EPIBOLY
EPIC
EPICAL
EPICALLY
EPICALYCES
EPICALYX
EPICALYXES
EPICANTHI
EPICANTHUS
EPICARDIA
EPICARDIAL
EPICARDIUM
EPICARP
EPICARPS
EPICEDIA
EPICEDIUM
EPICENE
EPICENES
EPICENISM
EPICENISMS
EPICENTER
EPICENTERS
EPICENTRA
EPICENTRAL
EPICENTRE
EPICENTRUM
EPICHLOROHYDRIN
EPICLIKE
EPICONTINENTAL
EPICOTYL
EPICOTYLS
EPICRANIA
EPICRANIUM
EPICRITIC
EPICS
EPICURE
EPICUREAN
EPICUREANISM
EPICUREANISMS
EPICUREANS
EPICURES
EPICURISM
EPICURISMS
EPICUTICLE
EPICUTICLES
EPICUTICULAR
EPICYCLE
EPICYCLES
EPICYCLIC
EPICYCLOID
EPICYCLOIDAL
EPICYCLOIDS

EPIDEMIC
EPIDEMICAL
EPIDEMICALLY
EPIDEMICITIES
EPIDEMICITY
EPIDEMICS
EPIDEMIOLOGIC
EPIDEMIOLOGICAL
EPIDEMIOLOGIES
EPIDEMIOLOGIST
EPIDEMIOLOGISTS
EPIDEMIOLOGY
EPIDENDRUM
EPIDENDRUMS
EPIDERM
EPIDERMAL
EPIDERMIC
EPIDERMIS
EPIDERMISES
EPIDERMOID
EPIDERMS
EPIDIASCOPE
EPIDIASCOPES
EPIDIDYMAL
EPIDIDYMIDES
EPIDIDYMIS
EPIDIDYMITIS
EPIDIDYMITISES
EPIDOTE
EPIDOTES
EPIDOTIC
EPIDURAL
EPIDURALS
EPIFAUNA
EPIFAUNAE
EPIFAUNAL
EPIFAUNAS
EPIFOCAL
EPIGASTRIC
EPIGEAL
EPIGEAN
EPIGEIC
EPIGENE
EPIGENESES
EPIGENESIS
EPIGENETIC
EPIGENETICALLY
EPIGENETICS
EPIGENIC
EPIGENIST
EPIGENISTS
EPIGENOUS
EPIGEOUS
EPIGLOTTAL
EPIGLOTTIC
EPIGLOTTIDES
EPIGLOTTIS
EPIGLOTTISES
EPIGON
EPIGONE
EPIGONES
EPIGONI
EPIGONIC
EPIGONISM
EPIGONISMS
EPIGONOUS
EPIGONS
EPIGONUS
EPIGRAM
EPIGRAMMATIC
EPIGRAMMATISM
EPIGRAMMATISMS
EPIGRAMMATIST
EPIGRAMMATISTS
EPIGRAMMATIZE
EPIGRAMMATIZED
EPIGRAMMATIZER
EPIGRAMMATIZERS
EPIGRAMMATIZES
EPIGRAMMATIZING
EPIGRAMS
EPIGRAPH
EPIGRAPHER
EPIGRAPHERS
EPIGRAPHIC
EPIGRAPHICAL
EPIGRAPHICALLY
EPIGRAPHIES
EPIGRAPHIST
EPIGRAPHISTS
EPIGRAPHS
EPIGRAPHY
EPIGYNIES
EPIGYNOUS
EPIGYNY
EPILATE
EPILATED
EPILATES
EPILATING
EPILATION
EPILATIONS
EPILATOR
EPILATORS
EPILEPSIES
EPILEPSY
EPILEPTIC
EPILEPTICALLY
EPILEPTICS
EPILEPTIFORM
EPILEPTOGENIC
EPILEPTOID
EPILIMNIA
EPILIMNION
EPILIMNIONS
EPILOG
EPILOGS
EPILOGUE
EPILOGUED
EPILOGUES
EPILOGUING
EPIMER
EPIMERASE
EPIMERASES
EPIMERE
EPIMERES
EPIMERIC
EPIMERS
EPIMYSIA
EPIMYSIUM
EPINAOI
EPINAOS
EPINASTIC
EPINASTIES
EPINASTY
EPINEPHRIN
EPINEPHRINE
EPINEPHRINES
EPINEPHRINS
EPINEURIA
EPINEURIUM
EPINEURIUMS
EPIPELAGIC
EPIPHANIC
EPIPHANIES
EPIPHANOUS
EPIPHANY
EPIPHENOMENA
EPIPHENOMENAL
EPIPHENOMENALLY
EPIPHENOMENON
EPIPHRAGM
EPIPHRAGMS
EPIPHYSEAL
EPIPHYSES
EPIPHYSIAL
EPIPHYSIS
EPIPHYTE
EPIPHYTES
EPIPHYTIC
EPIPHYTICALLY
EPIPHYTISM
EPIPHYTISMS
EPIPHYTOLOGIES
EPIPHYTOLOGY
EPIPHYTOTIC
EPIPHYTOTICS
EPIROGENIES
EPIROGENY
EPISCIA
EPISCIAS
EPISCOPACIES
EPISCOPACY
EPISCOPAL
EPISCOPALLY
EPISCOPATE
EPISCOPATES
EPISCOPE
EPISCOPES
EPISIOTOMIES
EPISIOTOMY
EPISODE
EPISODES
EPISODIC
EPISODICAL
EPISODICALLY
EPISOMAL
EPISOMALLY
EPISOME
EPISOMES
EPISTASES
EPISTASIES
EPISTASIS
EPISTASY
EPISTATIC
EPISTAXES
EPISTAXIS
EPISTEMIC
EPISTEMICALLY
EPISTEMOLOGICAL
EPISTEMOLOGIES
EPISTEMOLOGIST
EPISTEMOLOGISTS
EPISTEMOLOGY
EPISTERNA
EPISTERNUM
EPISTLE
EPISTLER
EPISTLERS
EPISTLES
EPISTOLARIES
EPISTOLARY
EPISTOLER
EPISTOLERS
EPISTOME
EPISTOMES
EPISTROPHE
EPISTROPHES
EPISTYLE
EPISTYLES
EPITAPH
EPITAPHIAL
EPITAPHIC
EPITAPHS
EPITASES
EPITASIS
EPITAXIAL
EPITAXIALLY
EPITAXIC
EPITAXIES
EPITAXY
EPITHALAMIA
EPITHALAMIC
EPITHALAMION
EPITHALAMIUM
EPITHALAMIUMS
EPITHELIA
EPITHELIAL
EPITHELIALIZE
EPITHELIALIZED
EPITHELIALIZES
EPITHELIALIZING
EPITHELIOID
EPITHELIOMA
EPITHELIOMAS
EPITHELIOMATA
EPITHELIOMATOUS
EPITHELIUM
EPITHELIUMS
EPITHELIZATION
EPITHELIZATIONS
EPITHELIZE
EPITHELIZED
EPITHELIZES
EPITHELIZING
EPITHET
EPITHETIC
EPITHETICAL
EPITHETS
EPITOME
EPITOMES
EPITOMIC
EPITOMICAL
EPITOMISE
EPITOMISED
EPITOMISES

EPITOMISING
EPITOMIZE
EPITOMIZED
EPITOMIZES
EPITOMIZING
EPITOPE
EPITOPES
EPIZOA
EPIZOIC
EPIZOISM
EPIZOISMS
EPIZOITE
EPIZOITES
EPIZOON
EPIZOOTIC
EPIZOOTICS
EPIZOOTIES
EPIZOOTIOLOGIC
EPIZOOTIOLOGIES
EPIZOOTIOLOGY
EPIZOOTY
EPOCH
EPOCHAL
EPOCHALLY
EPOCHS
EPODE
EPODES
EPONYM
EPONYMIC
EPONYMIES
EPONYMOUS
EPONYMS
EPONYMY
EPOPEE
EPOPEES
EPOPOEIA
EPOPOEIAS
EPOS
EPOSES
EPOXIDATION
EPOXIDATIONS
EPOXIDE
EPOXIDES
EPOXIDIZE
EPOXIDIZED
EPOXIDIZES
EPOXIDIZING
EPOXIED
EPOXIES
EPOXY
EPOXYED
EPOXYING
EPSILON
EPSILONIC
EPSILONS
EQUABILITIES
EQUABILITY
EQUABLE
EQUABLENESS
EQUABLENESSES
EQUABLY
EQUAL
EQUALED
EQUALING
EQUALISATION
EQUALISATIONS
EQUALISE
EQUALISED
EQUALISER
EQUALISERS
EQUALISES
EQUALISING
EQUALITARIAN
EQUALITARIANISM
EQUALITARIANS
EQUALITIES
EQUALITY
EQUALIZATION
EQUALIZATIONS
EQUALIZE
EQUALIZED
EQUALIZER
EQUALIZERS
EQUALIZES
EQUALIZING
EQUALLED
EQUALLING
EQUALLY
EQUALS
EQUANIMITIES
EQUANIMITY
EQUATABLE
EQUATE
EQUATED
EQUATES
EQUATING
EQUATION
EQUATIONAL
EQUATIONALLY
EQUATIONS
EQUATIVE
EQUATOR
EQUATORIAL
EQUATORS
EQUATORWARD
EQUERRIES
EQUERRY
EQUES
EQUESTRIAN
EQUESTRIANS
EQUESTRIENNE
EQUESTRIENNES
EQUIANGULAR
EQUICALORIC
EQUID
EQUIDISTANT
EQUIDISTANTLY
EQUIDS
EQUILATERAL
EQUILIBRANT
EQUILIBRANTS
EQUILIBRATE
EQUILIBRATED
EQUILIBRATES
EQUILIBRATING
EQUILIBRATION
EQUILIBRATIONS
EQUILIBRATOR
EQUILIBRATORS
EQUILIBRATORY
EQUILIBRIA
EQUILIBRIST
EQUILIBRISTIC
EQUILIBRISTS
EQUILIBRIUM
EQUILIBRIUMS
EQUIMOLAL
EQUIMOLAR
EQUINE
EQUINELY
EQUINES
EQUINITIES
EQUINITY
EQUINOCTIAL
EQUINOCTIALS
EQUINOX
EQUINOXES
EQUIP
EQUIPAGE
EQUIPAGES
EQUIPMENT
EQUIPMENTS
EQUIPOISE
EQUIPOISED
EQUIPOISES
EQUIPOISING
EQUIPOLLENCE
EQUIPOLLENCES
EQUIPOLLENT
EQUIPOLLENTLY
EQUIPOLLENTS
EQUIPONDERANT
EQUIPOTENTIAL
EQUIPPED
EQUIPPER
EQUIPPERS
EQUIPPING
EQUIPROBABLE
EQUIPS
EQUISETA
EQUISETIC
EQUISETUM
EQUISETUMS
EQUITABILITIES
EQUITABILITY
EQUITABLE
EQUITABLENESS
EQUITABLENESSES
EQUITABLY
EQUITANT
EQUITATION
EQUITATIONS
EQUITES
EQUITIES
EQUITY
EQUIVALENCE
EQUIVALENCES
EQUIVALENCIES
EQUIVALENCY
EQUIVALENT
EQUIVALENTLY
EQUIVALENTS
EQUIVOCAL
EQUIVOCALITIES
EQUIVOCALITY
EQUIVOCALLY
EQUIVOCALNESS
EQUIVOCALNESSES
EQUIVOCATE
EQUIVOCATED
EQUIVOCATES
EQUIVOCATING
EQUIVOCATION
EQUIVOCATIONS
EQUIVOCATOR
EQUIVOCATORS
EQUIVOKE
EQUIVOKES
EQUIVOQUE
EQUIVOQUES
ER
ERA
ERADIATE
ERADIATED
ERADIATES
ERADIATING
ERADICABLE
ERADICANT
ERADICANTS
ERADICATE
ERADICATED
ERADICATES
ERADICATING
ERADICATION
ERADICATIONS
ERADICATOR
ERADICATORS
ERAS
ERASABILITIES
ERASABILITY
ERASABLE
ERASE
ERASED
ERASER
ERASERS
ERASES
ERASING
ERASION
ERASIONS
ERASURE
ERASURES
ERBIUM
ERBIUMS
ERE
ERECT
ERECTABLE
ERECTED
ERECTER
ERECTERS
ERECTILE
ERECTILITIES
ERECTILITY
ERECTING
ERECTION
ERECTIONS
ERECTIVE
ERECTLY
ERECTNESS
ERECTNESSES
ERECTOR
ERECTORS
ERECTS
ERELONG
EREMITE
EREMITES

EREMITIC
EREMITICAL
EREMITISH
EREMITISM
EREMITISMS
EREMURI
EREMURUS
EREMURUSES
ERENOW
EREPSIN
EREPSINS
ERETHIC
ERETHISM
ERETHISMS
ERETHITIC
EREWHILE
EREWHILES
ERG
ERGASTIC
ERGASTOPLASM
ERGASTOPLASMIC
ERGASTOPLASMS
ERGATE
ERGATES
ERGATIVE
ERGATIVES
ERGO
ERGODIC
ERGODICITIES
ERGODICITY
ERGOGENIC
ERGOGRAPH
ERGOGRAPHS
ERGOMETER
ERGOMETERS
ERGOMETRIC
ERGOMETRIES
ERGOMETRY
ERGONOMIC
ERGONOMICALLY
ERGONOMICS
ERGONOMIST
ERGONOMISTS
ERGONOVINE
ERGONOVINES
ERGOSTEROL
ERGOSTEROLS
ERGOT
ERGOTAMINE
ERGOTAMINES
ERGOTIC
ERGOTISM
ERGOTISMS
ERGOTIZED
ERGOTS
ERGS
ERICA
ERICACEOUS
ERICAS
ERICOID
ERIGERON
ERIGERONS
ERINGO
ERINGOES
ERINGOS
ERIOPHYID
ERIOPHYIDS
ERISTIC
ERISTICAL
ERISTICALLY
ERISTICS
ERLKING
ERLKINGS
ERMINE
ERMINED
ERMINES
ERN
ERNE
ERNES
ERNS
ERODABLE
ERODE
ERODED
ERODENT
ERODES
ERODIBILITIES
ERODIBILITY
ERODIBLE
ERODING
EROGENIC
EROGENOUS
EROS
EROSE
EROSELY
EROSES
EROSIBLE
EROSION
EROSIONAL
EROSIONALLY
EROSIONS
EROSIVE
EROSIVENESS
EROSIVENESSES
EROSIVITIES
EROSIVITY
EROTIC
EROTICA
EROTICAL
EROTICALLY
EROTICAS
EROTICISM
EROTICISMS
EROTICIST
EROTICISTS
EROTICIZATION
EROTICIZATIONS
EROTICIZE
EROTICIZED
EROTICIZES
EROTICIZING
EROTICS
EROTISM
EROTISMS
EROTIZATION
EROTIZATIONS
EROTIZE
EROTIZED
EROTIZES
EROTIZING
EROTOGENIC
EROTOMANIA
EROTOMANIAC
EROTOMANIACS
EROTOMANIAS
ERR
ERRABLE
ERRANCIES
ERRANCY
ERRAND
ERRANDS
ERRANT
ERRANTLY
ERRANTRIES
ERRANTRY
ERRANTS
ERRATA
ERRATAS
ERRATIC
ERRATICAL
ERRATICALLY
ERRATICISM
ERRATICISMS
ERRATICS
ERRATUM
ERRED
ERRHINE
ERRHINES
ERRING
ERRINGLY
ERRONEOUS
ERRONEOUSLY
ERRONEOUSNESS
ERRONEOUSNESSES
ERROR
ERRORLESS
ERRORS
ERRS
ERS
ERSATZ
ERSATZES
ERSES
ERST
ERSTWHILE
ERUCT
ERUCTATE
ERUCTATED
ERUCTATES
ERUCTATING
ERUCTATION
ERUCTATIONS
ERUCTED
ERUCTING
ERUCTS
ERUDITE
ERUDITELY
ERUDITION
ERUDITIONS
ERUGO
ERUGOS
ERUMPENT
ERUPT
ERUPTED
ERUPTIBLE
ERUPTING
ERUPTION
ERUPTIONS
ERUPTIVE
ERUPTIVELY
ERUPTIVES
ERUPTS
ERUV
ERUVIM
ERUVS
ERVIL
ERVILS
ERYNGIUM
ERYNGIUMS
ERYNGO
ERYNGOES
ERYNGOS
ERYSIPELAS
ERYSIPELASES
ERYTHEMA
ERYTHEMAS
ERYTHEMATOUS
ERYTHEMIC
ERYTHORBATE
ERYTHORBATES
ERYTHREMIA
ERYTHREMIAS
ERYTHRISM
ERYTHRISMAL
ERYTHRISMS
ERYTHRISTIC
ERYTHRITE
ERYTHRITES
ERYTHROBLAST
ERYTHROBLASTIC
ERYTHROBLASTS
ERYTHROCYTE
ERYTHROCYTES
ERYTHROCYTIC
ERYTHROID
ERYTHROMYCIN
ERYTHROMYCINS
ERYTHRON
ERYTHRONS
ERYTHROPOIESES
ERYTHROPOIESIS
ERYTHROPOIETIC
ERYTHROPOIETIN
ERYTHROPOIETINS
ERYTHROSIN
ERYTHROSINE
ERYTHROSINES
ERYTHROSINS
ES
ESCADRILLE
ESCADRILLES
ESCALADE
ESCALADED
ESCALADER
ESCALADERS
ESCALADES
ESCALADING
ESCALATE
ESCALATED
ESCALATES
ESCALATING
ESCALATION
ESCALATIONS
ESCALATOR
ESCALATORS
ESCALATORY
ESCALLOP

ESCALLOPED
ESCALLOPING
ESCALLOPS
ESCALOP
ESCALOPE
ESCALOPED
ESCALOPES
ESCALOPING
ESCALOPS
ESCAPABLE
ESCAPADE
ESCAPADES
ESCAPE
ESCAPED
ESCAPEE
ESCAPEES
ESCAPEMENT
ESCAPEMENTS
ESCAPER
ESCAPERS
ESCAPES
ESCAPING
ESCAPISM
ESCAPISMS
ESCAPIST
ESCAPISTS
ESCAPOLOGIES
ESCAPOLOGIST
ESCAPOLOGISTS
ESCAPOLOGY
ESCAR
ESCARGOT
ESCARGOTS
ESCAROLE
ESCAROLES
ESCARP
ESCARPED
ESCARPING
ESCARPMENT
ESCARPMENTS
ESCARPS
ESCARS
ESCHALOT
ESCHALOTS
ESCHAR
ESCHAROTIC
ESCHAROTICS
ESCHARS
ESCHATOLOGICAL
ESCHATOLOGIES
ESCHATOLOGY
ESCHEAT
ESCHEATABLE

ESCHEATED
ESCHEATING
ESCHEATOR
ESCHEATORS
ESCHEATS
ESCHEW
ESCHEWAL
ESCHEWALS
ESCHEWED
ESCHEWER
ESCHEWERS
ESCHEWING
ESCHEWS
ESCOLAR
ESCOLARS
ESCORT
ESCORTED
ESCORTING
ESCORTS
ESCOT
ESCOTED
ESCOTING
ESCOTS
ESCRITOIRE
ESCRITOIRES
ESCROW
ESCROWED
ESCROWING
ESCROWS
ESCUAGE
ESCUAGES
ESCUDO
ESCUDOS
ESCULENT
ESCULENTS
ESCUTCHEON
ESCUTCHEONS
ESEMPLASTIC
ESERINE
ESERINES
ESES
ESKAR
ESKARS
ESKER
ESKERS
ESNE
ESNES
ESOPHAGEAL
ESOPHAGI
ESOPHAGITIDES
ESOPHAGITIS
ESOPHAGUS
ESOTERIC

ESOTERICA
ESOTERICALLY
ESOTERICISM
ESOTERICISMS
ESOTROPIA
ESOTROPIAS
ESOTROPIC
ESPADRILLE
ESPADRILLES
ESPALIER
ESPALIERED
ESPALIERING
ESPALIERS
ESPANOL
ESPANOLES
ESPARTO
ESPARTOS
ESPECIAL
ESPECIALLY
ESPERANCE
ESPERANCES
ESPIAL
ESPIALS
ESPIED
ESPIEGLE
ESPIEGLERIE
ESPIEGLERIES
ESPIES
ESPIONAGE
ESPIONAGES
ESPLANADE
ESPLANADES
ESPOIR
ESPOIRS
ESPOUSAL
ESPOUSALS
ESPOUSE
ESPOUSED
ESPOUSER
ESPOUSERS
ESPOUSES
ESPOUSING
ESPRESSO
ESPRESSOS
ESPRIT
ESPRITS
ESPY
ESPYING
ESQUIRE
ESQUIRED
ESQUIRES
ESQUIRING
ESS

ESSAY
ESSAYED
ESSAYER
ESSAYERS
ESSAYING
ESSAYIST
ESSAYISTIC
ESSAYISTS
ESSAYS
ESSE
ESSENCE
ESSENCES
ESSENTIAL
ESSENTIALISM
ESSENTIALISMS
ESSENTIALIST
ESSENTIALISTS
ESSENTIALITIES
ESSENTIALITY
ESSENTIALIZE
ESSENTIALIZED
ESSENTIALIZES
ESSENTIALIZING
ESSENTIALLY
ESSENTIALNESS
ESSENTIALNESSES
ESSENTIALS
ESSES
ESSOIN
ESSOINS
ESSONITE
ESSONITES
EST
ESTABLISH
ESTABLISHABLE
ESTABLISHED
ESTABLISHER
ESTABLISHERS
ESTABLISHES
ESTABLISHING
ESTABLISHMENT
ESTABLISHMENTS
ESTAMINET
ESTAMINETS
ESTANCIA
ESTANCIAS
ESTATE
ESTATED
ESTATES
ESTATING
ESTEEM
ESTEEMED
ESTEEMING

ESTEEMS
ESTER
ESTERASE
ESTERASES
ESTERIFICATION
ESTERIFICATIONS
ESTERIFIED
ESTERIFIES
ESTERIFY
ESTERIFYING
ESTERS
ESTHESES
ESTHESIA
ESTHESIAS
ESTHESIS
ESTHESISES
ESTHETE
ESTHETES
ESTHETIC
ESTHETICAL
ESTHETICALLY
ESTHETICIAN
ESTHETICIANS
ESTHETICISM
ESTHETICISMS
ESTHETICIZE
ESTHETICIZED
ESTHETICIZES
ESTHETICIZING
ESTHETICS
ESTIMABLE
ESTIMABLENESS
ESTIMABLENESSES
ESTIMABLY
ESTIMATE
ESTIMATED
ESTIMATES
ESTIMATING
ESTIMATION
ESTIMATIONS
ESTIMATIVE
ESTIMATOR
ESTIMATORS
ESTIVAL
ESTIVATE
ESTIVATED
ESTIVATES
ESTIVATING
ESTIVATION
ESTIVATIONS
ESTIVATOR
ESTIVATORS
ESTOP

ESTOPPAGE
ESTOPPAGES
ESTOPPED
ESTOPPEL
ESTOPPELS
ESTOPPING
ESTOPS
ESTOVERS
ESTRADIOL
ESTRADIOLS
ESTRAGON
ESTRAGONS
ESTRAL
ESTRANGE
ESTRANGED
ESTRANGEMENT
ESTRANGEMENTS
ESTRANGER
ESTRANGERS
ESTRANGES
ESTRANGING
ESTRAY
ESTRAYED
ESTRAYING
ESTRAYS
ESTREAT
ESTREATED
ESTREATING
ESTREATS
ESTRIN
ESTRINS
ESTRIOL
ESTRIOLS
ESTROGEN
ESTROGENIC
ESTROGENICALLY
ESTROGENS
ESTRONE
ESTRONES
ESTROUS
ESTRUAL
ESTRUM
ESTRUMS
ESTRUS
ESTRUSES
ESTS
ESTUARIAL
ESTUARIES
ESTUARINE
ESTUARY
ESURIENCE
ESURIENCES
ESURIENCIES
ESURIENCY
ESURIENT
ESURIENTLY
ET
ETA
ETAGERE
ETAGERES
ETALON
ETALONS
ETAMIN
ETAMINE
ETAMINES
ETAMINS
ETAPE
ETAPES
ETAS
ETATISM
ETATISMS
ETATIST
ETCETERA
ETCETERAS
ETCH
ETCHANT
ETCHANTS
ETCHED
ETCHER
ETCHERS
ETCHES
ETCHING
ETCHINGS
ETERNAL
ETERNALIZE
ETERNALIZED
ETERNALIZES
ETERNALIZING
ETERNALLY
ETERNALNESS
ETERNALNESSES
ETERNALS
ETERNE
ETERNISE
ETERNISED
ETERNISES
ETERNISING
ETERNITIES
ETERNITY
ETERNIZATION
ETERNIZATIONS
ETERNIZE
ETERNIZED
ETERNIZES
ETERNIZING
ETESIAN
ETESIANS
ETH
ETHAMBUTOL
ETHAMBUTOLS
ETHANAL
ETHANALS
ETHANE
ETHANES
ETHANOL
ETHANOLAMINE
ETHANOLAMINES
ETHANOLS
ETHENE
ETHENES
ETHEPHON
ETHEPHONS
ETHER
ETHEREAL
ETHEREALITIES
ETHEREALITY
ETHEREALIZATION
ETHEREALIZE
ETHEREALIZED
ETHEREALIZES
ETHEREALIZING
ETHEREALLY
ETHEREALNESS
ETHEREALNESSES
ETHERIC
ETHERIFIED
ETHERIFIES
ETHERIFY
ETHERIFYING
ETHERISE
ETHERISED
ETHERISES
ETHERISH
ETHERISING
ETHERIZATION
ETHERIZATIONS
ETHERIZE
ETHERIZED
ETHERIZER
ETHERIZERS
ETHERIZES
ETHERIZING
ETHERS
ETHIC
ETHICAL
ETHICALITIES
ETHICALITY
ETHICALLY
ETHICALNESS
ETHICALNESSES
ETHICALS
ETHICIAN
ETHICIANS
ETHICIST
ETHICISTS
ETHICIZE
ETHICIZED
ETHICIZES
ETHICIZING
ETHICS
ETHINYL
ETHINYLS
ETHION
ETHIONAMID
ETHIONAMIDE
ETHIONAMIDES
ETHIONAMIDS
ETHIONINE
ETHIONINES
ETHIONS
ETHMOID
ETHMOIDAL
ETHMOIDS
ETHNARCH
ETHNARCHIES
ETHNARCHS
ETHNARCHY
ETHNIC
ETHNICAL
ETHNICALLY
ETHNICITIES
ETHNICITY
ETHNICS
ETHNOBIOLOGICAL
ETHNOBIOLOGIES
ETHNOBIOLOGIST
ETHNOBIOLOGISTS
ETHNOBIOLOGY
ETHNOBOTANICAL
ETHNOBOTANIES
ETHNOBOTANIST
ETHNOBOTANISTS
ETHNOBOTANY
ETHNOCENTRIC
ETHNOCENTRICITY
ETHNOCENTRISM
ETHNOCENTRISMS
ETHNOGRAPHER
ETHNOGRAPHERS
ETHNOGRAPHIC
ETHNOGRAPHICAL
ETHNOGRAPHIES
ETHNOGRAPHY
ETHNOHISTORIAN
ETHNOHISTORIANS
ETHNOHISTORIC
ETHNOHISTORICAL
ETHNOHISTORIES
ETHNOHISTORY
ETHNOLOGIC
ETHNOLOGICAL
ETHNOLOGIES
ETHNOLOGIST
ETHNOLOGISTS
ETHNOLOGY
ETHNOMEDICAL
ETHNOMEDICINE
ETHNOMEDICINES
ETHNOMUSICOLOGY
ETHNONYM
ETHNONYMS
ETHNOS
ETHNOSCIENCE
ETHNOSCIENCES
ETHNOSES
ETHOGRAM
ETHOGRAMS
ETHOLOGICAL
ETHOLOGIES
ETHOLOGIST
ETHOLOGISTS
ETHOLOGY
ETHOS
ETHOSES
ETHOXIES
ETHOXY
ETHOXYL
ETHOXYLS
ETHS
ETHYL
ETHYLATE
ETHYLATED
ETHYLATES
ETHYLATING
ETHYLBENZENE
ETHYLBENZENES
ETHYLENE
ETHYLENES
ETHYLENIC
ETHYLIC
ETHYLS
ETHYNE
ETHYNES
ETHYNYL
ETHYNYLS

ETIC
ETICS
ETIDRONATE
ETIDRONATES
ETIOLATE
ETIOLATED
ETIOLATES
ETIOLATING
ETIOLATION
ETIOLATIONS
ETIOLOGIC
ETIOLOGICAL
ETIOLOGICALLY
ETIOLOGIES
ETIOLOGY
ETIQUETTE
ETIQUETTES
ETNA
ETNAS
ETOILE
ETOILES
ETOUFFEE
ETOUFFEES
ETRIER
ETRIERS
ETUDE
ETUDES
ETUI
ETUIS
ETWEE
ETWEES
ETYMA
ETYMOLOGICAL
ETYMOLOGICALLY
ETYMOLOGIES
ETYMOLOGISE
ETYMOLOGISED
ETYMOLOGISES
ETYMOLOGISING
ETYMOLOGIST
ETYMOLOGISTS
ETYMOLOGIZE
ETYMOLOGIZED
ETYMOLOGIZES
ETYMOLOGIZING
ETYMOLOGY
ETYMON
ETYMONS
EUBACTERIA
EUBACTERIAL
EUBACTERIUM
EUCAINE
EUCAINES
EUCALYPT
EUCALYPTI
EUCALYPTOL
EUCALYPTOLE
EUCALYPTOLES
EUCALYPTOLS
EUCALYPTS
EUCALYPTUS
EUCALYPTUSES
EUCARYOTE
EUCARYOTES
EUCHARIS
EUCHARISES
EUCHARISTIC
EUCHRE
EUCHRED
EUCHRES
EUCHRING
EUCHROMATIC
EUCHROMATIN
EUCHROMATINS
EUCLASE
EUCLASES
EUCLIDEAN
EUCLIDIAN
EUCRITE
EUCRITES
EUCRITIC
EUDAEMON
EUDAEMONISM
EUDAEMONISMS
EUDAEMONIST
EUDAEMONISTIC
EUDAEMONISTS
EUDAEMONS
EUDAIMON
EUDAIMONISM
EUDAIMONISMS
EUDAIMONIST
EUDAIMONISTIC
EUDAIMONISTS
EUDAIMONS
EUDEMON
EUDEMONIA
EUDEMONIAS
EUDEMONS
EUDIOMETER
EUDIOMETERS
EUDIOMETRIC
EUDIOMETRICALLY
EUGENIA
EUGENIAS
EUGENIC
EUGENICAL
EUGENICALLY
EUGENICIST
EUGENICISTS
EUGENICS
EUGENIST
EUGENISTS
EUGENOL
EUGENOLS
EUGEOSYNCLINAL
EUGEOSYNCLINE
EUGEOSYNCLINES
EUGLENA
EUGLENAS
EUGLENID
EUGLENIDS
EUGLENOID
EUGLENOIDS
EUGLOBULIN
EUGLOBULINS
EUHEMERISM
EUHEMERISMS
EUHEMERIST
EUHEMERISTIC
EUHEMERISTS
EUKARYOTE
EUKARYOTES
EUKARYOTIC
EULACHAN
EULACHANS
EULACHON
EULACHONS
EULOGIA
EULOGIAE
EULOGIAS
EULOGIES
EULOGISE
EULOGISED
EULOGISES
EULOGISING
EULOGIST
EULOGISTIC
EULOGISTICALLY
EULOGISTS
EULOGIUM
EULOGIUMS
EULOGIZE
EULOGIZED
EULOGIZER
EULOGIZERS
EULOGIZES
EULOGIZING
EULOGY
EUNUCH
EUNUCHISM
EUNUCHISMS
EUNUCHOID
EUNUCHOIDS
EUNUCHS
EUONYMUS
EUONYMUSES
EUPATRID
EUPATRIDAE
EUPATRIDS
EUPEPSIA
EUPEPSIAS
EUPEPSIES
EUPEPSY
EUPEPTIC
EUPHAUSID
EUPHAUSIDS
EUPHAUSIID
EUPHAUSIIDS
EUPHEMISE
EUPHEMISED
EUPHEMISES
EUPHEMISING
EUPHEMISM
EUPHEMISMS
EUPHEMIST
EUPHEMISTIC
EUPHEMISTICALLY
EUPHEMISTS
EUPHEMIZE
EUPHEMIZED
EUPHEMIZER
EUPHEMIZERS
EUPHEMIZES
EUPHEMIZING
EUPHENIC
EUPHENICS
EUPHONIC
EUPHONICALLY
EUPHONIES
EUPHONIOUS
EUPHONIOUSLY
EUPHONIOUSNESS
EUPHONIUM
EUPHONIUMS
EUPHONIZE
EUPHONIZED
EUPHONIZES
EUPHONIZING
EUPHONY
EUPHORBIA
EUPHORBIAS
EUPHORIA
EUPHORIANT
EUPHORIANTS
EUPHORIAS
EUPHORIC
EUPHORICALLY
EUPHOTIC
EUPHRASIES
EUPHRASY
EUPHROE
EUPHROES
EUPHUISM
EUPHUISMS
EUPHUIST
EUPHUISTIC
EUPHUISTICALLY
EUPHUISTS
EUPLASTIC
EUPLASTICS
EUPLOID
EUPLOIDIES
EUPLOIDS
EUPLOIDY
EUPNEA
EUPNEAS
EUPNEIC
EUPNOEA
EUPNOEAS
EUPNOEIC
EUREKA
EUREKAS
EURHYTHMIC
EURHYTHMICS
EURHYTHMIES
EURHYTHMY
EURIPI
EURIPUS
EURO
EUROKIES
EUROKOUS
EUROKY
EUROLAND
EUROLANDS
EUROPIUM
EUROPIUMS
EUROS
EUROZONE
EUROZONES
EURYBATH
EURYBATHIC
EURYBATHS
EURYHALINE
EURYOKIES

EURYOKOUS
EURYOKY
EURYPTERID
EURYPTERIDS
EURYTHERM
EURYTHERMAL
EURYTHERMIC
EURYTHERMOUS
EURYTHERMS
EURYTHMIC
EURYTHMICS
EURYTHMIES
EURYTHMY
EURYTOPIC
EUSOCIAL
EUSOCIALITIES
EUSOCIALITY
EUSTACIES
EUSTACY
EUSTASIES
EUSTASY
EUSTATIC
EUSTELE
EUSTELES
EUTAXIES
EUTAXY
EUTECTIC
EUTECTICS
EUTECTOID
EUTECTOIDS
EUTHANASIA
EUTHANASIAS
EUTHANASIC
EUTHANATIZE
EUTHANATIZED
EUTHANATIZES
EUTHANATIZING
EUTHANIZE
EUTHANIZED
EUTHANIZES
EUTHANIZING
EUTHENICS
EUTHENIST
EUTHENISTS
EUTHERIAN
EUTHERIANS
EUTHYROID
EUTHYROIDS
EUTROPHIC
EUTROPHICATION
EUTROPHICATIONS
EUTROPHIES
EUTROPHY
EUXENITE
EUXENITES
EVACUANT
EVACUANTS
EVACUATE
EVACUATED
EVACUATES
EVACUATING
EVACUATION
EVACUATIONS
EVACUATIVE
EVACUATOR
EVACUATORS
EVACUEE
EVACUEES
EVADABLE
EVADE
EVADED
EVADER
EVADERS
EVADES
EVADIBLE
EVADING
EVADINGLY
EVAGINATE
EVAGINATED
EVAGINATES
EVAGINATING
EVAGINATION
EVAGINATIONS
EVALUABLE
EVALUATE
EVALUATED
EVALUATES
EVALUATING
EVALUATION
EVALUATIONS
EVALUATIVE
EVALUATOR
EVALUATORS
EVANESCE
EVANESCED
EVANESCENCE
EVANESCENCES
EVANESCENT
EVANESCES
EVANESCING
EVANGEL
EVANGELIC
EVANGELICAL
EVANGELICALLY
EVANGELISATION
EVANGELISATIONS
EVANGELISE
EVANGELISED
EVANGELISES
EVANGELISING
EVANGELISM
EVANGELISMS
EVANGELIST
EVANGELISTIC
EVANGELISTS
EVANGELIZATION
EVANGELIZATIONS
EVANGELIZE
EVANGELIZED
EVANGELIZES
EVANGELIZING
EVANGELS
EVANISH
EVANISHED
EVANISHES
EVANISHING
EVAPORATE
EVAPORATED
EVAPORATES
EVAPORATING
EVAPORATION
EVAPORATIONS
EVAPORATIVE
EVAPORATOR
EVAPORATORS
EVAPORITE
EVAPORITES
EVAPORITIC
EVASION
EVASIONAL
EVASIONS
EVASIVE
EVASIVELY
EVASIVENESS
EVASIVENESSES
EVE
EVECTION
EVECTIONS
EVEN
EVENED
EVENER
EVENERS
EVENEST
EVENFALL
EVENFALLS
EVENHANDED
EVENHANDEDLY
EVENHANDEDNESS
EVENING
EVENINGS
EVENLY
EVENNESS
EVENNESSES
EVENS
EVENSONG
EVENSONGS
EVENT
EVENTER
EVENTERS
EVENTFUL
EVENTFULLY
EVENTFULNESS
EVENTFULNESSES
EVENTIDE
EVENTIDES
EVENTING
EVENTINGS
EVENTIVE
EVENTLESS
EVENTS
EVENTUAL
EVENTUALITIES
EVENTUALITY
EVENTUALLY
EVENTUATE
EVENTUATED
EVENTUATES
EVENTUATING
EVER
EVERBLOOMING
EVERDURING
EVERGLADE
EVERGLADES
EVERGREEN
EVERGREENS
EVERLASTING
EVERLASTINGLY
EVERLASTINGNESS
EVERLASTINGS
EVERMORE
EVERSIBLE
EVERSION
EVERSIONS
EVERT
EVERTED
EVERTING
EVERTOR
EVERTORS
EVERTS
EVERWHERE
EVERWHICH
EVERY
EVERYBODY
EVERYDAY
EVERYDAYNESS
EVERYDAYNESSES
EVERYDAYS
EVERYMAN
EVERYMEN
EVERYONE
EVERYPLACE
EVERYTHING
EVERYWAY
EVERYWHERE
EVERYWOMAN
EVERYWOMEN
EVES
EVICT
EVICTED
EVICTEE
EVICTEES
EVICTING
EVICTION
EVICTIONS
EVICTOR
EVICTORS
EVICTS
EVIDENCE
EVIDENCED
EVIDENCES
EVIDENCING
EVIDENT
EVIDENTIAL
EVIDENTIALLY
EVIDENTIARY
EVIDENTLY
EVIL
EVILDOER
EVILDOERS
EVILDOING
EVILDOINGS
EVILER
EVILEST
EVILLER
EVILLEST
EVILLY
EVILNESS
EVILNESSES
EVILS
EVINCE
EVINCED
EVINCES
EVINCIBLE
EVINCING
EVINCIVE

EVISCERATE
EVISCERATED
EVISCERATES
EVISCERATING
EVISCERATION
EVISCERATIONS
EVITABLE
EVITE
EVITED
EVITES
EVITING
EVOCABLE
EVOCATION
EVOCATIONS
EVOCATIVE
EVOCATIVELY
EVOCATIVENESS
EVOCATIVENESSES
EVOCATOR
EVOCATORS
EVOKE
EVOKED
EVOKER
EVOKERS
EVOKES
EVOKING
EVOLUTE
EVOLUTES
EVOLUTION
EVOLUTIONARILY
EVOLUTIONARY
EVOLUTIONISM
EVOLUTIONISMS
EVOLUTIONIST
EVOLUTIONISTS
EVOLUTIONS
EVOLVABLE
EVOLVE
EVOLVED
EVOLVEMENT
EVOLVEMENTS
EVOLVER
EVOLVERS
EVOLVES
EVOLVING
EVONYMUS
EVONYMUSES
EVULSE
EVULSED
EVULSES
EVULSING
EVULSION
EVULSIONS
EVZONE
EVZONES
EWE
EWER
EWERS
EWES
EX
EXABYTE
EXABYTES
EXACERBATE
EXACERBATED
EXACERBATES
EXACERBATING
EXACERBATION
EXACERBATIONS
EXACT
EXACTA
EXACTABLE
EXACTAS
EXACTED
EXACTER
EXACTERS
EXACTEST
EXACTING
EXACTINGLY
EXACTINGNESS
EXACTINGNESSES
EXACTION
EXACTIONS
EXACTITUDE
EXACTITUDES
EXACTLY
EXACTNESS
EXACTNESSES
EXACTOR
EXACTORS
EXACTS
EXAGGERATE
EXAGGERATED
EXAGGERATEDLY
EXAGGERATEDNESS
EXAGGERATES
EXAGGERATING
EXAGGERATION
EXAGGERATIONS
EXAGGERATIVE
EXAGGERATOR
EXAGGERATORS
EXAGGERATORY
EXAHERTZ
EXAHERTZES
EXALT
EXALTATION
EXALTATIONS
EXALTED
EXALTEDLY
EXALTER
EXALTERS
EXALTING
EXALTS
EXAM
EXAMEN
EXAMENS
EXAMINABLE
EXAMINANT
EXAMINANTS
EXAMINATION
EXAMINATIONAL
EXAMINATIONS
EXAMINE
EXAMINED
EXAMINEE
EXAMINEES
EXAMINER
EXAMINERS
EXAMINES
EXAMINING
EXAMPLE
EXAMPLED
EXAMPLES
EXAMPLING
EXAMS
EXANIMATE
EXANTHEM
EXANTHEMA
EXANTHEMAS
EXANTHEMATA
EXANTHEMATIC
EXANTHEMATOUS
EXANTHEMS
EXAPTATION
EXAPTATIONS
EXAPTED
EXAPTIVE
EXARCH
EXARCHAL
EXARCHATE
EXARCHATES
EXARCHIES
EXARCHS
EXARCHY
EXASPERATE
EXASPERATED
EXASPERATEDLY
EXASPERATES
EXASPERATING
EXASPERATINGLY
EXASPERATION
EXASPERATIONS
EXCAUDATE
EXCAVATE
EXCAVATED
EXCAVATES
EXCAVATING
EXCAVATION
EXCAVATIONAL
EXCAVATIONS
EXCAVATOR
EXCAVATORS
EXCEED
EXCEEDANCE
EXCEEDANCES
EXCEEDED
EXCEEDENCE
EXCEEDENCES
EXCEEDER
EXCEEDERS
EXCEEDING
EXCEEDINGLY
EXCEEDS
EXCEL
EXCELLED
EXCELLENCE
EXCELLENCES
EXCELLENCIES
EXCELLENCY
EXCELLENT
EXCELLENTLY
EXCELLING
EXCELS
EXCELSIOR
EXCELSIORS
EXCEPT
EXCEPTED
EXCEPTING
EXCEPTION
EXCEPTIONABLE
EXCEPTIONABLY
EXCEPTIONAL
EXCEPTIONALISM
EXCEPTIONALISMS
EXCEPTIONALIST
EXCEPTIONALISTS
EXCEPTIONALITY
EXCEPTIONALLY
EXCEPTIONALNESS
EXCEPTIONS
EXCEPTIVE
EXCEPTS
EXCERPT
EXCERPTED
EXCERPTER
EXCERPTERS
EXCERPTING
EXCERPTION
EXCERPTIONS
EXCERPTOR
EXCERPTORS
EXCERPTS
EXCESS
EXCESSED
EXCESSES
EXCESSING
EXCESSIVE
EXCESSIVELY
EXCESSIVENESS
EXCESSIVENESSES
EXCHANGE
EXCHANGEABILITY
EXCHANGEABLE
EXCHANGED
EXCHANGER
EXCHANGERS
EXCHANGES
EXCHANGING
EXCHEQUER
EXCHEQUERS
EXCIDE
EXCIDED
EXCIDES
EXCIDING
EXCIMER
EXCIMERS
EXCIPIENT
EXCIPIENTS
EXCIPLE
EXCIPLES
EXCISABLE
EXCISE
EXCISED
EXCISEMAN
EXCISEMEN
EXCISES
EXCISING
EXCISION
EXCISIONAL
EXCISIONS
EXCITABILITIES
EXCITABILITY
EXCITABLE
EXCITABLENESS
EXCITABLENESSES

EXCITABLY
EXCITANT
EXCITANTS
EXCITATION
EXCITATIONS
EXCITATIVE
EXCITATORY
EXCITE
EXCITED
EXCITEDLY
EXCITEMENT
EXCITEMENTS
EXCITER
EXCITERS
EXCITES
EXCITING
EXCITINGLY
EXCITON
EXCITONIC
EXCITONS
EXCITOR
EXCITORS
EXCLAIM
EXCLAIMED
EXCLAIMER
EXCLAIMERS
EXCLAIMING
EXCLAIMS
EXCLAMATION
EXCLAMATIONS
EXCLAMATORY
EXCLAVE
EXCLAVES
EXCLOSURE
EXCLOSURES
EXCLUDABILITIES
EXCLUDABILITY
EXCLUDABLE
EXCLUDE
EXCLUDED
EXCLUDER
EXCLUDERS
EXCLUDES
EXCLUDIBLE
EXCLUDING
EXCLUSION
EXCLUSIONARY
EXCLUSIONIST
EXCLUSIONISTS
EXCLUSIONS
EXCLUSIVE
EXCLUSIVELY
EXCLUSIVENESS
EXCLUSIVENESSES
EXCLUSIVES
EXCLUSIVISM
EXCLUSIVISMS
EXCLUSIVIST
EXCLUSIVISTS
EXCLUSIVITIES
EXCLUSIVITY
EXCLUSORY
EXCOGITATE
EXCOGITATED
EXCOGITATES
EXCOGITATING
EXCOGITATION
EXCOGITATIONS
EXCOGITATIVE
EXCOMMUNICATE
EXCOMMUNICATED
EXCOMMUNICATES
EXCOMMUNICATING
EXCOMMUNICATION
EXCOMMUNICATIVE
EXCOMMUNICATOR
EXCOMMUNICATORS
EXCORIATE
EXCORIATED
EXCORIATES
EXCORIATING
EXCORIATION
EXCORIATIONS
EXCREMENT
EXCREMENTAL
EXCREMENTITIOUS
EXCREMENTS
EXCRESCENCE
EXCRESCENCES
EXCRESCENCIES
EXCRESCENCY
EXCRESCENT
EXCRESCENTLY
EXCRETA
EXCRETAL
EXCRETE
EXCRETED
EXCRETER
EXCRETERS
EXCRETES
EXCRETING
EXCRETION
EXCRETIONS
EXCRETIVE
EXCRETORIES
EXCRETORY
EXCRUCIATE
EXCRUCIATED
EXCRUCIATES
EXCRUCIATING
EXCRUCIATINGLY
EXCRUCIATION
EXCRUCIATIONS
EXCULPATE
EXCULPATED
EXCULPATES
EXCULPATING
EXCULPATION
EXCULPATIONS
EXCULPATORY
EXCURRENT
EXCURSION
EXCURSIONIST
EXCURSIONISTS
EXCURSIONS
EXCURSIVE
EXCURSIVELY
EXCURSIVENESS
EXCURSIVENESSES
EXCURSUS
EXCURSUSES
EXCUSABLE
EXCUSABLENESS
EXCUSABLENESSES
EXCUSABLY
EXCUSATORY
EXCUSE
EXCUSED
EXCUSER
EXCUSERS
EXCUSES
EXCUSING
EXEC
EXECRABLE
EXECRABLENESS
EXECRABLENESSES
EXECRABLY
EXECRATE
EXECRATED
EXECRATES
EXECRATING
EXECRATION
EXECRATIONS
EXECRATIVE
EXECRATOR
EXECRATORS
EXECS
EXECUTABLE
EXECUTANT
EXECUTANTS
EXECUTE
EXECUTED
EXECUTER
EXECUTERS
EXECUTES
EXECUTING
EXECUTION
EXECUTIONER
EXECUTIONERS
EXECUTIONS
EXECUTIVE
EXECUTIVES
EXECUTOR
EXECUTORIAL
EXECUTORS
EXECUTORY
EXECUTRICES
EXECUTRIX
EXECUTRIXES
EXED
EXEDRA
EXEDRAE
EXEDRAS
EXEGESES
EXEGESIS
EXEGETE
EXEGETES
EXEGETIC
EXEGETICAL
EXEGETICS
EXEGETIST
EXEGETISTS
EXEMPLA
EXEMPLAR
EXEMPLARILY
EXEMPLARINESS
EXEMPLARINESSES
EXEMPLARITIES
EXEMPLARITY
EXEMPLARS
EXEMPLARY
EXEMPLIFICATION
EXEMPLIFIED
EXEMPLIFIES
EXEMPLIFY
EXEMPLIFYING
EXEMPLUM
EXEMPT
EXEMPTED
EXEMPTING
EXEMPTION
EXEMPTIONS
EXEMPTIVE
EXEMPTS
EXENTERATE
EXENTERATED
EXENTERATES
EXENTERATING
EXENTERATION
EXENTERATIONS
EXEQUATUR
EXEQUATURS
EXEQUIAL
EXEQUIES
EXEQUY
EXERCISABLE
EXERCISE
EXERCISED
EXERCISER
EXERCISERS
EXERCISES
EXERCISING
EXERCITATION
EXERCITATIONS
EXERCYCLE
EXERCYCLES
EXERGONIC
EXERGUAL
EXERGUE
EXERGUES
EXERT
EXERTED
EXERTING
EXERTION
EXERTIONAL
EXERTIONS
EXERTIVE
EXERTS
EXES
EXEUNT
EXFILTRATE
EXFILTRATED
EXFILTRATES
EXFILTRATING
EXFILTRATION
EXFILTRATIONS
EXFOLIANT
EXFOLIANTS
EXFOLIATE
EXFOLIATED
EXFOLIATES
EXFOLIATING
EXFOLIATION
EXFOLIATIONS
EXFOLIATIVE

EXFOLIATOR
EXFOLIATORS
EXHALANT
EXHALANTS
EXHALATION
EXHALATIONS
EXHALE
EXHALED
EXHALENT
EXHALENTS
EXHALES
EXHALING
EXHAUST
EXHAUSTED
EXHAUSTER
EXHAUSTERS
EXHAUSTIBILITY
EXHAUSTIBLE
EXHAUSTING
EXHAUSTINGLY
EXHAUSTION
EXHAUSTIONS
EXHAUSTIVE
EXHAUSTIVELY
EXHAUSTIVENESS
EXHAUSTIVITIES
EXHAUSTIVITY
EXHAUSTLESS
EXHAUSTLESSLY
EXHAUSTLESSNESS
EXHAUSTS
EXHEDRA
EXHEDRAE
EXHIBIT
EXHIBITED
EXHIBITER
EXHIBITERS
EXHIBITING
EXHIBITION
EXHIBITIONER
EXHIBITIONERS
EXHIBITIONISM
EXHIBITIONISMS
EXHIBITIONIST
EXHIBITIONISTIC
EXHIBITIONISTS
EXHIBITIONS
EXHIBITIVE
EXHIBITOR
EXHIBITORS
EXHIBITORY
EXHIBITS
EXHILARATE
EXHILARATED
EXHILARATES
EXHILARATING
EXHILARATINGLY
EXHILARATION
EXHILARATIONS
EXHILARATIVE
EXHORT
EXHORTATION
EXHORTATIONS
EXHORTATIVE
EXHORTATORY
EXHORTED
EXHORTER
EXHORTERS
EXHORTING
EXHORTS
EXHUMATION
EXHUMATIONS
EXHUME
EXHUMED
EXHUMER
EXHUMERS
EXHUMES
EXHUMING
EXIGENCE
EXIGENCES
EXIGENCIES
EXIGENCY
EXIGENT
EXIGENTLY
EXIGIBLE
EXIGUITIES
EXIGUITY
EXIGUOUS
EXIGUOUSLY
EXIGUOUSNESS
EXIGUOUSNESSES
EXILABLE
EXILE
EXILED
EXILER
EXILERS
EXILES
EXILIAN
EXILIC
EXILING
EXIMIOUS
EXINE
EXINES
EXING
EXIST
EXISTED
EXISTENCE
EXISTENCES
EXISTENT
EXISTENTIAL
EXISTENTIALISM
EXISTENTIALISMS
EXISTENTIALIST
EXISTENTIALISTS
EXISTENTIALLY
EXISTENTS
EXISTING
EXISTS
EXIT
EXITED
EXITING
EXITLESS
EXITS
EXOBIOLOGICAL
EXOBIOLOGIES
EXOBIOLOGIST
EXOBIOLOGISTS
EXOBIOLOGY
EXOCARP
EXOCARPS
EXOCRINE
EXOCRINES
EXOCYCLIC
EXOCYTIC
EXOCYTOSE
EXOCYTOSED
EXOCYTOSES
EXOCYTOSING
EXOCYTOSIS
EXOCYTOTIC
EXODERM
EXODERMIS
EXODERMISES
EXODERMS
EXODOI
EXODONTIA
EXODONTIAS
EXODONTIST
EXODONTISTS
EXODOS
EXODUS
EXODUSES
EXOENZYME
EXOENZYMES
EXOERGIC
EXOERYTHROCYTIC
EXOGAMIC
EXOGAMIES
EXOGAMOUS
EXOGAMY
EXOGEN
EXOGENIC
EXOGENISM
EXOGENISMS
EXOGENOUS
EXOGENOUSLY
EXOGENS
EXON
EXONERATE
EXONERATED
EXONERATES
EXONERATING
EXONERATION
EXONERATIONS
EXONERATIVE
EXONIC
EXONS
EXONUCLEASE
EXONUCLEASES
EXONUMIA
EXONUMIST
EXONUMISTS
EXONYM
EXONYMS
EXOPEPTIDASE
EXOPEPTIDASES
EXOPHTHALMIC
EXOPHTHALMOS
EXOPHTHALMOSES
EXOPHTHALMUS
EXOPHTHALMUSES
EXOPLANET
EXOPLANETS
EXORABLE
EXORBITANCE
EXORBITANCES
EXORBITANT
EXORBITANTLY
EXORCISE
EXORCISED
EXORCISER
EXORCISERS
EXORCISES
EXORCISING
EXORCISM
EXORCISMS
EXORCIST
EXORCISTIC
EXORCISTICAL
EXORCISTS
EXORCIZE
EXORCIZED
EXORCIZES
EXORCIZING
EXORDIA
EXORDIAL
EXORDIUM
EXORDIUMS
EXOSKELETAL
EXOSKELETON
EXOSKELETONS
EXOSMIC
EXOSMOSE
EXOSMOSES
EXOSMOSIS
EXOSMOTIC
EXOSPHERE
EXOSPHERES
EXOSPHERIC
EXOSPORE
EXOSPORES
EXOSPORIA
EXOSPORIUM
EXOSTOSES
EXOSTOSIS
EXOTERIC
EXOTERICALLY
EXOTHERMAL
EXOTHERMALLY
EXOTHERMIC
EXOTHERMICALLY
EXOTHERMICITIES
EXOTHERMICITY
EXOTIC
EXOTICA
EXOTICALLY
EXOTICISM
EXOTICISMS
EXOTICIST
EXOTICISTS
EXOTICNESS
EXOTICNESSES
EXOTICS
EXOTISM
EXOTISMS
EXOTOXIC
EXOTOXIN
EXOTOXINS
EXOTROPIA
EXOTROPIAS
EXOTROPIC
EXPAND
EXPANDABILITIES
EXPANDABILITY
EXPANDABLE

EXPANDED
EXPANDER
EXPANDERS
EXPANDING
EXPANDOR
EXPANDORS
EXPANDS
EXPANSE
EXPANSES
EXPANSIBILITIES
EXPANSIBILITY
EXPANSIBLE
EXPANSILE
EXPANSION
EXPANSIONAL
EXPANSIONARY
EXPANSIONISM
EXPANSIONISMS
EXPANSIONIST
EXPANSIONISTIC
EXPANSIONISTS
EXPANSIONS
EXPANSIVE
EXPANSIVELY
EXPANSIVENESS
EXPANSIVENESSES
EXPANSIVITIES
EXPANSIVITY
EXPAT
EXPATIATE
EXPATIATED
EXPATIATES
EXPATIATING
EXPATIATION
EXPATIATIONS
EXPATRIATE
EXPATRIATED
EXPATRIATES
EXPATRIATING
EXPATRIATION
EXPATRIATIONS
EXPATRIATISM
EXPATRIATISMS
EXPATS
EXPECT
EXPECTABLE
EXPECTABLY
EXPECTANCE
EXPECTANCES
EXPECTANCIES
EXPECTANCY
EXPECTANT
EXPECTANTLY
EXPECTANTS
EXPECTATION
EXPECTATIONAL
EXPECTATIONS
EXPECTATIVE
EXPECTED
EXPECTEDLY
EXPECTEDNESS
EXPECTEDNESSES
EXPECTER
EXPECTERS
EXPECTING
EXPECTORANT
EXPECTORANTS
EXPECTORATE
EXPECTORATED
EXPECTORATES
EXPECTORATING
EXPECTORATION
EXPECTORATIONS
EXPECTS
EXPEDIENCE
EXPEDIENCES
EXPEDIENCIES
EXPEDIENCY
EXPEDIENT
EXPEDIENTIAL
EXPEDIENTLY
EXPEDIENTS
EXPEDITE
EXPEDITED
EXPEDITER
EXPEDITERS
EXPEDITES
EXPEDITING
EXPEDITION
EXPEDITIONARY
EXPEDITIONER
EXPEDITIONERS
EXPEDITIONS
EXPEDITIOUS
EXPEDITIOUSLY
EXPEDITIOUSNESS
EXPEDITOR
EXPEDITORS
EXPEL
EXPELLABLE
EXPELLANT
EXPELLANTS
EXPELLED
EXPELLEE
EXPELLEES
EXPELLENT
EXPELLENTS
EXPELLER
EXPELLERS
EXPELLING
EXPELS
EXPEND
EXPENDABILITIES
EXPENDABILITY
EXPENDABLE
EXPENDABLES
EXPENDED
EXPENDER
EXPENDERS
EXPENDING
EXPENDITURE
EXPENDITURES
EXPENDS
EXPENSE
EXPENSED
EXPENSES
EXPENSING
EXPENSIVE
EXPENSIVELY
EXPENSIVENESS
EXPENSIVENESSES
EXPERIENCE
EXPERIENCED
EXPERIENCES
EXPERIENCING
EXPERIENTIAL
EXPERIENTIALLY
EXPERIMENT
EXPERIMENTAL
EXPERIMENTALISM
EXPERIMENTALIST
EXPERIMENTALLY
EXPERIMENTATION
EXPERIMENTED
EXPERIMENTER
EXPERIMENTERS
EXPERIMENTING
EXPERIMENTS
EXPERT
EXPERTED
EXPERTING
EXPERTISE
EXPERTISES
EXPERTISM
EXPERTISMS
EXPERTIZE
EXPERTIZED
EXPERTIZES
EXPERTIZING
EXPERTLY
EXPERTNESS
EXPERTNESSES
EXPERTS
EXPIABLE
EXPIATE
EXPIATED
EXPIATES
EXPIATING
EXPIATION
EXPIATIONS
EXPIATOR
EXPIATORS
EXPIATORY
EXPIRATION
EXPIRATIONS
EXPIRATORY
EXPIRE
EXPIRED
EXPIRER
EXPIRERS
EXPIRES
EXPIRIES
EXPIRING
EXPIRY
EXPLAIN
EXPLAINABLE
EXPLAINED
EXPLAINER
EXPLAINERS
EXPLAINING
EXPLAINS
EXPLANATION
EXPLANATIONS
EXPLANATIVE
EXPLANATIVELY
EXPLANATORILY
EXPLANATORY
EXPLANT
EXPLANTATION
EXPLANTATIONS
EXPLANTED
EXPLANTING
EXPLANTS
EXPLETIVE
EXPLETIVES
EXPLETORY
EXPLICABLE
EXPLICABLY
EXPLICATE
EXPLICATED
EXPLICATES
EXPLICATING
EXPLICATION
EXPLICATIONS
EXPLICATIVE
EXPLICATIVELY
EXPLICATOR
EXPLICATORS
EXPLICATORY
EXPLICIT
EXPLICITLY
EXPLICITNESS
EXPLICITNESSES
EXPLICITS
EXPLODE
EXPLODED
EXPLODER
EXPLODERS
EXPLODES
EXPLODING
EXPLOIT
EXPLOITABILITY
EXPLOITABLE
EXPLOITATION
EXPLOITATIONS
EXPLOITATIVE
EXPLOITATIVELY
EXPLOITED
EXPLOITER
EXPLOITERS
EXPLOITING
EXPLOITIVE
EXPLOITS
EXPLORATION
EXPLORATIONAL
EXPLORATIONS
EXPLORATIVE
EXPLORATIVELY
EXPLORATORY
EXPLORE
EXPLORED
EXPLORER
EXPLORERS
EXPLORES
EXPLORING
EXPLOSION
EXPLOSIONS
EXPLOSIVE
EXPLOSIVELY
EXPLOSIVENESS
EXPLOSIVENESSES
EXPLOSIVES
EXPO
EXPONENT
EXPONENTIAL

EXPONENTIALLY
EXPONENTIALS
EXPONENTIATION
EXPONENTIATIONS
EXPONENTS
EXPORT
EXPORTABILITIES
EXPORTABILITY
EXPORTABLE
EXPORTATION
EXPORTATIONS
EXPORTED
EXPORTER
EXPORTERS
EXPORTING
EXPORTS
EXPOS
EXPOSABLE
EXPOSAL
EXPOSALS
EXPOSE
EXPOSED
EXPOSER
EXPOSERS
EXPOSES
EXPOSING
EXPOSIT
EXPOSITED
EXPOSITING
EXPOSITION
EXPOSITIONAL
EXPOSITIONS
EXPOSITIVE
EXPOSITOR
EXPOSITORS
EXPOSITORY
EXPOSITS
EXPOSTULATE
EXPOSTULATED
EXPOSTULATES
EXPOSTULATING
EXPOSTULATION
EXPOSTULATIONS
EXPOSTULATORY
EXPOSURE
EXPOSURES
EXPOUND
EXPOUNDED
EXPOUNDER
EXPOUNDERS
EXPOUNDING
EXPOUNDS
EXPRESS
EXPRESSAGE
EXPRESSAGES
EXPRESSED
EXPRESSER
EXPRESSERS
EXPRESSES
EXPRESSIBLE
EXPRESSING
EXPRESSION
EXPRESSIONAL
EXPRESSIONISM
EXPRESSIONISMS
EXPRESSIONIST
EXPRESSIONISTIC
EXPRESSIONISTS
EXPRESSIONLESS
EXPRESSIONS
EXPRESSIVE
EXPRESSIVELY
EXPRESSIVENESS
EXPRESSIVITIES
EXPRESSIVITY
EXPRESSLY
EXPRESSMAN
EXPRESSMEN
EXPRESSO
EXPRESSOS
EXPRESSWAY
EXPRESSWAYS
EXPROPRIATE
EXPROPRIATED
EXPROPRIATES
EXPROPRIATING
EXPROPRIATION
EXPROPRIATIONS
EXPROPRIATOR
EXPROPRIATORS
EXPULSE
EXPULSED
EXPULSES
EXPULSING
EXPULSION
EXPULSIONS
EXPULSIVE
EXPUNCTION
EXPUNCTIONS
EXPUNGE
EXPUNGED
EXPUNGER
EXPUNGERS
EXPUNGES
EXPUNGING
EXPURGATE
EXPURGATED
EXPURGATES
EXPURGATING
EXPURGATION
EXPURGATIONS
EXPURGATOR
EXPURGATORIAL
EXPURGATORS
EXPURGATORY
EXQUISITE
EXQUISITELY
EXQUISITENESS
EXQUISITENESSES
EXQUISITES
EXSANGUINATE
EXSANGUINATED
EXSANGUINATES
EXSANGUINATING
EXSANGUINATION
EXSANGUINATIONS
EXSCIND
EXSCINDED
EXSCINDING
EXSCINDS
EXSECANT
EXSECANTS
EXSECT
EXSECTED
EXSECTING
EXSECTION
EXSECTIONS
EXSECTS
EXSERT
EXSERTED
EXSERTILE
EXSERTING
EXSERTION
EXSERTIONS
EXSERTS
EXSICCATE
EXSICCATED
EXSICCATES
EXSICCATING
EXSICCATION
EXSICCATIONS
EXSOLUTION
EXSOLUTIONS
EXSTROPHIES
EXSTROPHY
EXTANT
EXTEMPORAL
EXTEMPORALLY
EXTEMPORANEITY
EXTEMPORANEOUS
EXTEMPORARILY
EXTEMPORARY
EXTEMPORE
EXTEMPORISATION
EXTEMPORISE
EXTEMPORISED
EXTEMPORISES
EXTEMPORISING
EXTEMPORIZATION
EXTEMPORIZE
EXTEMPORIZED
EXTEMPORIZER
EXTEMPORIZERS
EXTEMPORIZES
EXTEMPORIZING
EXTEND
EXTENDABILITIES
EXTENDABILITY
EXTENDABLE
EXTENDED
EXTENDEDLY
EXTENDEDNESS
EXTENDEDNESSES
EXTENDER
EXTENDERS
EXTENDIBILITIES
EXTENDIBILITY
EXTENDIBLE
EXTENDING
EXTENDS
EXTENSIBILITIES
EXTENSIBILITY
EXTENSIBLE
EXTENSILE
EXTENSION
EXTENSIONAL
EXTENSIONALITY
EXTENSIONALLY
EXTENSIONS
EXTENSITIES
EXTENSITY
EXTENSIVE
EXTENSIVELY
EXTENSIVENESS
EXTENSIVENESSES
EXTENSOMETER
EXTENSOMETERS
EXTENSOR
EXTENSORS
EXTENT
EXTENTS
EXTENUATE
EXTENUATED
EXTENUATES
EXTENUATING
EXTENUATION
EXTENUATIONS
EXTENUATOR
EXTENUATORS
EXTENUATORY
EXTERIOR
EXTERIORISE
EXTERIORISED
EXTERIORISES
EXTERIORISING
EXTERIORITIES
EXTERIORITY
EXTERIORIZATION
EXTERIORIZE
EXTERIORIZED
EXTERIORIZES
EXTERIORIZING
EXTERIORLY
EXTERIORS
EXTERMINATE
EXTERMINATED
EXTERMINATES
EXTERMINATING
EXTERMINATION
EXTERMINATIONS
EXTERMINATOR
EXTERMINATORS
EXTERMINATORY
EXTERMINE
EXTERMINED
EXTERMINES
EXTERMINING
EXTERN
EXTERNAL
EXTERNALISATION
EXTERNALISE
EXTERNALISED
EXTERNALISES
EXTERNALISING
EXTERNALISM
EXTERNALISMS
EXTERNALITIES
EXTERNALITY
EXTERNALIZATION
EXTERNALIZE
EXTERNALIZED
EXTERNALIZES
EXTERNALIZING
EXTERNALLY
EXTERNALS

EXTERNE
EXTERNES
EXTERNS
EXTERNSHIP
EXTERNSHIPS
EXTEROCEPTIVE
EXTEROCEPTOR
EXTEROCEPTORS
EXTERRITORIAL
EXTINCT
EXTINCTED
EXTINCTING
EXTINCTION
EXTINCTIONS
EXTINCTIVE
EXTINCTS
EXTINGUISH
EXTINGUISHABLE
EXTINGUISHED
EXTINGUISHER
EXTINGUISHERS
EXTINGUISHES
EXTINGUISHING
EXTINGUISHMENT
EXTINGUISHMENTS
EXTIRPATE
EXTIRPATED
EXTIRPATES
EXTIRPATING
EXTIRPATION
EXTIRPATIONS
EXTIRPATOR
EXTIRPATORS
EXTOL
EXTOLL
EXTOLLED
EXTOLLER
EXTOLLERS
EXTOLLING
EXTOLLS
EXTOLMENT
EXTOLMENTS
EXTOLS
EXTORT
EXTORTED
EXTORTER
EXTORTERS
EXTORTING
EXTORTION
EXTORTIONARY
EXTORTIONATE
EXTORTIONATELY
EXTORTIONER
EXTORTIONERS
EXTORTIONIST
EXTORTIONISTS
EXTORTIONS
EXTORTIVE
EXTORTS
EXTRA
EXTRABOLD
EXTRABOLDS
EXTRACELLULAR
EXTRACELLULARLY
EXTRACORPOREAL
EXTRACRANIAL
EXTRACT
EXTRACTABILITY
EXTRACTABLE
EXTRACTED
EXTRACTING
EXTRACTION
EXTRACTIONS
EXTRACTIVE
EXTRACTIVELY
EXTRACTIVES
EXTRACTOR
EXTRACTORS
EXTRACTS
EXTRACURRICULAR
EXTRADITABLE
EXTRADITE
EXTRADITED
EXTRADITES
EXTRADITING
EXTRADITION
EXTRADITIONS
EXTRADOS
EXTRADOSES
EXTRAEMBRYONIC
EXTRAGALACTIC
EXTRAHEPATIC
EXTRAJUDICIAL
EXTRAJUDICIALLY
EXTRALEGAL
EXTRALEGALLY
EXTRALIMITAL
EXTRALINGUISTIC
EXTRALITERARY
EXTRALITIES
EXTRALITY
EXTRALOGICAL
EXTRAMARITAL
EXTRAMUNDANE
EXTRAMURAL
EXTRAMURALLY
EXTRAMUSICAL
EXTRANEOUS
EXTRANEOUSLY
EXTRANEOUSNESS
EXTRANET
EXTRANETS
EXTRANUCLEAR
EXTRAORDINAIRE
EXTRAORDINARILY
EXTRAORDINARY
EXTRAPOLATE
EXTRAPOLATED
EXTRAPOLATES
EXTRAPOLATING
EXTRAPOLATION
EXTRAPOLATIONS
EXTRAPOLATIVE
EXTRAPOLATOR
EXTRAPOLATORS
EXTRAPYRAMIDAL
EXTRAS
EXTRASENSORY
EXTRASOLAR
EXTRASYSTOLE
EXTRASYSTOLES
EXTRATEXTUAL
EXTRAUTERINE
EXTRAVAGANCE
EXTRAVAGANCES
EXTRAVAGANCIES
EXTRAVAGANCY
EXTRAVAGANT
EXTRAVAGANTLY
EXTRAVAGANZA
EXTRAVAGANZAS
EXTRAVAGATE
EXTRAVAGATED
EXTRAVAGATES
EXTRAVAGATING
EXTRAVASATE
EXTRAVASATED
EXTRAVASATES
EXTRAVASATING
EXTRAVASATION
EXTRAVASATIONS
EXTRAVASCULAR
EXTRAVEHICULAR
EXTRAVERSION
EXTRAVERSIONS
EXTRAVERT
EXTRAVERTED
EXTRAVERTS
EXTREMA
EXTREME
EXTREMELY
EXTREMENESS
EXTREMENESSES
EXTREMER
EXTREMES
EXTREMEST
EXTREMISM
EXTREMISMS
EXTREMIST
EXTREMISTS
EXTREMITIES
EXTREMITY
EXTREMOPHILE
EXTREMOPHILES
EXTREMUM
EXTREMUMS
EXTRICABLE
EXTRICATE
EXTRICATED
EXTRICATES
EXTRICATING
EXTRICATION
EXTRICATIONS
EXTRINSIC
EXTRINSICALLY
EXTROPIES
EXTROPY
EXTRORSE
EXTROVERSION
EXTROVERSIONS
EXTROVERT
EXTROVERTED
EXTROVERTS
EXTRUDABILITIES
EXTRUDABILITY
EXTRUDABLE
EXTRUDE
EXTRUDED
EXTRUDER
EXTRUDERS
EXTRUDES
EXTRUDING
EXTRUSION
EXTRUSIONS
EXTRUSIVE
EXTUBATE
EXTUBATED
EXTUBATES
EXTUBATING
EXUBERANCE
EXUBERANCES
EXUBERANT
EXUBERANTLY
EXUBERATE
EXUBERATED
EXUBERATES
EXUBERATING
EXUDATE
EXUDATES
EXUDATION
EXUDATIONS
EXUDATIVE
EXUDE
EXUDED
EXUDES
EXUDING
EXULT
EXULTANCE
EXULTANCES
EXULTANCIES
EXULTANCY
EXULTANT
EXULTANTLY
EXULTATION
EXULTATIONS
EXULTED
EXULTING
EXULTINGLY
EXULTS
EXURB
EXURBAN
EXURBANITE
EXURBANITES
EXURBIA
EXURBIAS
EXURBS
EXUVIA
EXUVIAE
EXUVIAL
EXUVIATE
EXUVIATED
EXUVIATES
EXUVIATING
EXUVIATION
EXUVIATIONS
EXUVIUM
EYAS
EYASES
EYASS
EYASSES
EYE
EYEABLE
EYEBALL
EYEBALLED
EYEBALLING

EYEBALLS
EYEBAR
EYEBARS
EYEBEAM
EYEBEAMS
EYEBLACK
EYEBLACKS
EYEBLINK
EYEBLINKS
EYEBOLT
EYEBOLTS
EYEBRIGHT
EYEBRIGHTS
EYEBROW
EYEBROWS
EYECUP
EYECUPS
EYED
EYEDNESS
EYEDNESSES
EYEDROPPER
EYEDROPPERS
EYEDROPS
EYEFOLD
EYEFOLDS
EYEFUL
EYEFULS
EYEGLASS
EYEGLASSES
EYEHOLE
EYEHOLES
EYEHOOK
EYEHOOKS
EYEING
EYELASH
EYELASHES
EYELESS
EYELET
EYELETED
EYELETING
EYELETS
EYELETTED
EYELETTING
EYELID
EYELIDS
EYELIFT
EYELIFTS
EYELIKE
EYELINER
EYELINERS
EYEN
EYEOPENER
EYEOPENERS
EYEPATCH
EYEPATCHES
EYEPIECE
EYEPIECES
EYEPOINT
EYEPOINTS
EYEPOPPER
EYEPOPPERS
EYER
EYERS
EYES
EYESHADE
EYESHADES
EYESHINE
EYESHINES
EYESHOT
EYESHOTS
EYESIGHT
EYESIGHTS
EYESOME
EYESORE
EYESORES
EYESPOT
EYESPOTS
EYESTALK
EYESTALKS
EYESTONE
EYESTONES
EYESTRAIN
EYESTRAINS
EYESTRINGS
EYETEETH
EYETOOTH
EYEWASH
EYEWASHES
EYEWATER
EYEWATERS
EYEWEAR
EYEWINK
EYEWINKS
EYEWITNESS
EYEWITNESSES
EYING
EYNE
EYRA
EYRAS
EYRE
EYRES
EYRIE
EYRIES
EYRIR
EYRY

F

FA
FAB
FABACEOUS
FABBER
FABBEST
FABLE
FABLED
FABLER
FABLERS
FABLES
FABLIAU
FABLIAUX
FABLING
FABRIC
FABRICANT
FABRICANTS
FABRICATE
FABRICATED
FABRICATES
FABRICATING
FABRICATION
FABRICATIONS
FABRICATOR
FABRICATORS
FABRICS
FABRIQUE
FABRIQUES
FABS
FABULAR
FABULATE
FABULATED
FABULATES
FABULATING
FABULATOR
FABULATORS
FABULISM
FABULISMS
FABULIST
FABULISTIC
FABULISTS
FABULOUS
FABULOUSLY
FABULOUSNESS
FABULOUSNESSES
FACADE
FACADES
FACE
FACEABLE
FACECLOTH
FACECLOTHS
FACED
FACEDOWN
FACEDOWNS
FACELESS
FACELESSNESS
FACELESSNESSES
FACELIFT
FACELIFTED
FACELIFTING
FACELIFTS
FACEMASK
FACEMASKS
FACEOFF
FACEOFFS
FACEPLATE
FACEPLATES
FACER
FACERS
FACES
FACET
FACETE
FACETED
FACETELY
FACETIAE
FACETING
FACETINGS
FACETIOUS
FACETIOUSLY
FACETIOUSNESS
FACETIOUSNESSES
FACETS
FACETTED
FACETTING
FACEUP
FACIA
FACIAE
FACIAL
FACIALLY
FACIALS
FACIAS
FACIEND
FACIENDS
FACIES
FACILE
FACILELY
FACILENESS
FACILENESSES
FACILITATE
FACILITATED
FACILITATES
FACILITATING
FACILITATION
FACILITATIONS
FACILITATIVE
FACILITATOR
FACILITATORS
FACILITATORY
FACILITIES
FACILITY
FACING

FACINGS
FACSIMILE
FACSIMILED
FACSIMILEING
FACSIMILES
FACT
FACTA
FACTFUL
FACTICE
FACTICES
FACTICITIES
FACTICITY
FACTION
FACTIONAL
FACTIONALISM
FACTIONALISMS
FACTIONALLY
FACTIONS
FACTIOUS
FACTIOUSLY
FACTIOUSNESS
FACTIOUSNESSES
FACTITIOUS
FACTITIOUSLY
FACTITIOUSNESS
FACTITIVE
FACTITIVELY
FACTOID
FACTOIDAL
FACTOIDS
FACTOR
FACTORABLE
FACTORAGE
FACTORAGES
FACTORED
FACTORIAL
FACTORIALS
FACTORIES
FACTORING
FACTORIZATION
FACTORIZATIONS
FACTORIZE
FACTORIZED
FACTORIZES
FACTORIZING
FACTORS
FACTORSHIP
FACTORSHIPS
FACTORY
FACTORYLIKE
FACTOTUM
FACTOTUMS
FACTS
FACTUAL
FACTUALISM
FACTUALISMS
FACTUALIST
FACTUALISTS
FACTUALITIES
FACTUALITY
FACTUALLY
FACTUALNESS
FACTUALNESSES
FACTUM
FACTUMS
FACTURE
FACTURES
FACULA
FACULAE
FACULAR
FACULTATIVE
FACULTATIVELY
FACULTIES
FACULTY
FAD
FADABLE
FADDIER
FADDIEST
FADDISH
FADDISHLY
FADDISHNESS
FADDISHNESSES
FADDISM
FADDISMS
FADDIST
FADDISTS
FADDY
FADE
FADEAWAY
FADEAWAYS
FADED
FADEDLY
FADEDNESS
FADEDNESSES
FADEIN
FADEINS
FADELESS
FADEOUT
FADEOUTS
FADER
FADERS
FADES
FADGE
FADGED
FADGES
FADGING
FADING
FADINGS
FADLIKE
FADO
FADOS
FADS
FAECAL
FAECES
FAENA
FAENAS
FAERIE
FAERIES
FAERY
FAFF
FAFFED
FAFFING
FAFFS
FAG
FAGGED
FAGGIER
FAGGIEST
FAGGING
FAGGOT
FAGGOTED
FAGGOTING
FAGGOTINGS
FAGGOTRIES
FAGGOTRY
FAGGOTS
FAGGOTY
FAGGY
FAGIN
FAGINS
FAGOT
FAGOTED
FAGOTER
FAGOTERS
FAGOTING
FAGOTINGS
FAGOTS
FAGS
FAH
FAHLBAND
FAHLBANDS
FAHS
FAIENCE
FAIENCES
FAIL
FAILED
FAILING
FAILINGLY
FAILINGS
FAILLE
FAILLES
FAILS
FAILURE
FAILURES
FAIN
FAINEANCE
FAINEANCES
FAINEANT
FAINEANTS
FAINER
FAINEST
FAINT
FAINTED
FAINTER
FAINTERS
FAINTEST
FAINTHEARTED
FAINTHEARTEDLY
FAINTING
FAINTISH
FAINTISHNESS
FAINTISHNESSES
FAINTLY
FAINTNESS
FAINTNESSES
FAINTS
FAIR
FAIRED
FAIRER
FAIREST
FAIRGOER
FAIRGOERS
FAIRGROUND
FAIRGROUNDS
FAIRIER
FAIRIES
FAIRIEST
FAIRING
FAIRINGS
FAIRISH
FAIRISHLY
FAIRLEAD
FAIRLEADER
FAIRLEADERS
FAIRLEADS
FAIRLY
FAIRNESS
FAIRNESSES
FAIRS
FAIRWAY
FAIRWAYS
FAIRY
FAIRYHOOD
FAIRYHOODS
FAIRYISM
FAIRYISMS
FAIRYLAND
FAIRYLANDS
FAIRYLIKE
FAITH
FAITHED
FAITHFUL
FAITHFULLY
FAITHFULNESS
FAITHFULNESSES
FAITHFULS
FAITHING
FAITHLESS
FAITHLESSLY
FAITHLESSNESS
FAITHLESSNESSES
FAITHS
FAITOUR
FAITOURS
FAJITA
FAJITAS
FAKE
FAKED
FAKEER
FAKEERS
FAKER
FAKERIES
FAKERS
FAKERY
FAKES
FAKEY
FAKIE
FAKIES
FAKING
FAKIR
FAKIRS
FALAFEL
FALAFELS
FALBALA
FALBALAS
FALCATE
FALCATED
FALCES
FALCHION
FALCHIONS
FALCIFORM
FALCON
FALCONER
FALCONERS
FALCONET
FALCONETS

FALCONINE
FALCONOID
FALCONRIES
FALCONRY
FALCONS
FALDERAL
FALDERALS
FALDEROL
FALDEROLS
FALDSTOOL
FALDSTOOLS
FALL
FALLACIES
FALLACIOUS
FALLACIOUSLY
FALLACIOUSNESS
FALLACY
FALLAL
FALLALERIES
FALLALERY
FALLALS
FALLAWAY
FALLAWAYS
FALLBACK
FALLBACKS
FALLBOARD
FALLBOARDS
FALLEN
FALLER
FALLERS
FALLFISH
FALLFISHES
FALLIBILITIES
FALLIBILITY
FALLIBLE
FALLIBLY
FALLING
FALLINGS
FALLOFF
FALLOFFS
FALLOUT
FALLOUTS
FALLOW
FALLOWED
FALLOWING
FALLOWNESS
FALLOWNESSES
FALLOWS
FALLS
FALSE
FALSEFACE
FALSEFACES
FALSEHOOD
FALSEHOODS
FALSELY
FALSENESS
FALSENESSES
FALSER
FALSEST
FALSETTO
FALSETTOS
FALSEWORK
FALSEWORKS
FALSIE
FALSIES
FALSIFIABILITY
FALSIFIABLE
FALSIFICATION
FALSIFICATIONS
FALSIFIED
FALSIFIER
FALSIFIERS
FALSIFIES
FALSIFY
FALSIFYING
FALSITIES
FALSITY
FALTBOAT
FALTBOATS
FALTER
FALTERED
FALTERER
FALTERERS
FALTERING
FALTERINGLY
FALTERS
FALX
FAME
FAMED
FAMELESS
FAMES
FAMILIAL
FAMILIAR
FAMILIARISATION
FAMILIARISE
FAMILIARISED
FAMILIARISES
FAMILIARISING
FAMILIARITIES
FAMILIARITY
FAMILIARIZATION
FAMILIARIZE
FAMILIARIZED
FAMILIARIZES
FAMILIARIZING
FAMILIARLY
FAMILIARNESS
FAMILIARNESSES
FAMILIARS
FAMILIES
FAMILISM
FAMILISMS
FAMILIST
FAMILISTIC
FAMILY
FAMILYHOOD
FAMILYHOODS
FAMINE
FAMINES
FAMING
FAMISH
FAMISHED
FAMISHES
FAMISHING
FAMISHMENT
FAMISHMENTS
FAMOUS
FAMOUSLY
FAMOUSNESS
FAMOUSNESSES
FAMULI
FAMULUS
FAN
FANATIC
FANATICAL
FANATICALLY
FANATICALNESS
FANATICALNESSES
FANATICISM
FANATICISMS
FANATICIZE
FANATICIZED
FANATICIZES
FANATICIZING
FANATICS
FANBOY
FANBOYS
FANCIED
FANCIER
FANCIERS
FANCIES
FANCIEST
FANCIFIED
FANCIFIES
FANCIFUL
FANCIFULLY
FANCIFULNESS
FANCIFULNESSES
FANCIFY
FANCIFYING
FANCILESS
FANCILY
FANCINESS
FANCINESSES
FANCY
FANCYING
FANCYWORK
FANCYWORKS
FANDANGO
FANDANGOES
FANDANGOS
FANDOM
FANDOMS
FANE
FANEGA
FANEGADA
FANEGADAS
FANEGAS
FANES
FANFARE
FANFARES
FANFARON
FANFARONADE
FANFARONADES
FANFARONS
FANFIC
FANFICS
FANFOLD
FANFOLDED
FANFOLDING
FANFOLDS
FANG
FANGA
FANGAS
FANGED
FANGIRL
FANGIRLS
FANGLESS
FANGLIKE
FANGS
FANION
FANIONS
FANJET
FANJETS
FANLIGHT
FANLIGHTS
FANLIKE
FANNED
FANNER
FANNERS
FANNIES
FANNING
FANNY
FANO
FANON
FANONS
FANOS
FANS
FANTABULOUS
FANTAIL
FANTAILED
FANTAILS
FANTASIA
FANTASIAS
FANTASIE
FANTASIED
FANTASIES
FANTASISE
FANTASISED
FANTASISES
FANTASISING
FANTASIST
FANTASISTS
FANTASIZE
FANTASIZED
FANTASIZER
FANTASIZERS
FANTASIZES
FANTASIZING
FANTASM
FANTASMS
FANTAST
FANTASTIC
FANTASTICAL
FANTASTICALITY
FANTASTICALLY
FANTASTICALNESS
FANTASTICATE
FANTASTICATED
FANTASTICATES
FANTASTICATING
FANTASTICATION
FANTASTICATIONS
FANTASTICO
FANTASTICOES
FANTASTICS
FANTASTS
FANTASY
FANTASYING
FANTASYLAND
FANTASYLANDS
FANTOCCINI
FANTOD
FANTODS
FANTOM

FANTOMS
FANUM
FANUMS
FANWISE
FANWORT
FANWORTS
FANZINE
FANZINES
FAQIR
FAQIRS
FAQUIR
FAQUIRS
FAR
FARAD
FARADAIC
FARADAY
FARADAYS
FARADIC
FARADISE
FARADISED
FARADISES
FARADISING
FARADISM
FARADISMS
FARADIZE
FARADIZED
FARADIZER
FARADIZERS
FARADIZES
FARADIZING
FARADS
FARANDOLE
FARANDOLES
FARAWAY
FARCE
FARCED
FARCER
FARCERS
FARCES
FARCEUR
FARCEURS
FARCI
FARCICAL
FARCICALITIES
FARCICALITY
FARCICALLY
FARCIE
FARCIES
FARCING
FARCY
FARD
FARDED
FARDEL
FARDELS
FARDING
FARDS
FARE
FAREBOX
FAREBOXES
FARED
FARER
FARERS
FARES
FAREWELL
FAREWELLED
FAREWELLING
FAREWELLS
FARFAL
FARFALLE
FARFALLES
FARFALS
FARFEL
FARFELS
FARFETCHEDNESS
FARINA
FARINACEOUS
FARINAS
FARING
FARINHA
FARINHAS
FARINOSE
FARKLEBERRIES
FARKLEBERRY
FARL
FARLE
FARLES
FARLS
FARM
FARMABLE
FARMED
FARMER
FARMERETTE
FARMERETTES
FARMERS
FARMHAND
FARMHANDS
FARMHOUSE
FARMHOUSES
FARMING
FARMINGS
FARMLAND
FARMLANDS
FARMS
FARMSTEAD
FARMSTEADS
FARMWIFE
FARMWIVES
FARMWORK
FARMWORKER
FARMWORKERS
FARMWORKS
FARMYARD
FARMYARDS
FARNESOL
FARNESOLS
FARNESS
FARNESSES
FARO
FAROLITO
FAROLITOS
FAROS
FAROUCHE
FARRAGINOUS
FARRAGO
FARRAGOES
FARRAGOS
FARRIER
FARRIERIES
FARRIERS
FARRIERY
FARROW
FARROWED
FARROWING
FARROWS
FARSEEING
FARSIDE
FARSIDES
FARSIGHTED
FARSIGHTEDLY
FARSIGHTEDNESS
FART
FARTED
FARTHER
FARTHERMOST
FARTHEST
FARTHING
FARTHINGALE
FARTHINGALES
FARTHINGS
FARTING
FARTLEK
FARTLEKS
FARTS
FAS
FASCES
FASCIA
FASCIAE
FASCIAL
FASCIAS
FASCIATE
FASCIATED
FASCIATION
FASCIATIONS
FASCICLE
FASCICLED
FASCICLES
FASCICULAR
FASCICULARLY
FASCICULATE
FASCICULATED
FASCICULATION
FASCICULATIONS
FASCICULE
FASCICULES
FASCICULI
FASCICULUS
FASCIITIS
FASCIITISES
FASCINATE
FASCINATED
FASCINATES
FASCINATING
FASCINATINGLY
FASCINATION
FASCINATIONS
FASCINATOR
FASCINATORS
FASCINE
FASCINES
FASCIOLIASES
FASCIOLIASIS
FASCISM
FASCISMS
FASCIST
FASCISTIC
FASCISTICALLY
FASCISTS
FASCITIS
FASCITISES
FASH
FASHED
FASHES
FASHING
FASHION
FASHIONABILITY
FASHIONABLE
FASHIONABLENESS
FASHIONABLES
FASHIONABLY
FASHIONED
FASHIONER
FASHIONERS
FASHIONING
FASHIONISTA
FASHIONISTAS
FASHIONMONGER
FASHIONMONGERS
FASHIONS
FASHIONY
FASHIOUS
FAST
FASTBACK
FASTBACKS
FASTBALL
FASTBALLER
FASTBALLERS
FASTBALLS
FASTED
FASTEN
FASTENED
FASTENER
FASTENERS
FASTENING
FASTENINGS
FASTENS
FASTER
FASTEST
FASTIDIOUS
FASTIDIOUSLY
FASTIDIOUSNESS
FASTIGIATE
FASTIGIUM
FASTIGIUMS
FASTING
FASTINGS
FASTNESS
FASTNESSES
FASTS
FASTUOUS
FAT
FATAL
FATALISM
FATALISMS
FATALIST
FATALISTIC
FATALISTICALLY
FATALISTS
FATALITIES
FATALITY
FATALLY
FATALNESS
FATALNESSES
FATBACK
FATBACKS
FATBIRD

FATBIRDS
FATE
FATED
FATEFUL
FATEFULLY
FATEFULNESS
FATEFULNESSES
FATES
FATHEAD
FATHEADED
FATHEADEDLY
FATHEADEDNESS
FATHEADEDNESSES
FATHEADS
FATHER
FATHERED
FATHERHOOD
FATHERHOODS
FATHERING
FATHERINGS
FATHERLAND
FATHERLANDS
FATHERLESS
FATHERLIKE
FATHERLINESS
FATHERLINESSES
FATHERLY
FATHERS
FATHOM
FATHOMABLE
FATHOMED
FATHOMER
FATHOMERS
FATHOMING
FATHOMLESS
FATHOMLESSLY
FATHOMLESSNESS
FATHOMS
FATIDIC
FATIDICAL
FATIGABILITIES
FATIGABILITY
FATIGABLE
FATIGUE
FATIGUED
FATIGUES
FATIGUING
FATIGUINGLY
FATING
FATLESS
FATLIKE
FATLING
FATLINGS
FATLY
FATNESS
FATNESSES
FATS
FATSHEDERA
FATSHEDERAS
FATSO
FATSOES
FATSOS
FATSTOCK
FATSTOCKS
FATTED
FATTEN
FATTENED
FATTENER
FATTENERS
FATTENING
FATTENS
FATTER
FATTEST
FATTIER
FATTIES
FATTIEST
FATTILY
FATTINESS
FATTINESSES
FATTING
FATTISH
FATTY
FATUITIES
FATUITY
FATUOUS
FATUOUSLY
FATUOUSNESS
FATUOUSNESSES
FATWA
FATWAS
FATWOOD
FATWOODS
FAUBOURG
FAUBOURGS
FAUCAL
FAUCALS
FAUCES
FAUCET
FAUCETRIES
FAUCETRY
FAUCETS
FAUCIAL
FAUGH
FAULD
FAULDS
FAULT
FAULTED
FAULTFINDER
FAULTFINDERS
FAULTFINDING
FAULTFINDINGS
FAULTIER
FAULTIEST
FAULTILY
FAULTINESS
FAULTINESSES
FAULTING
FAULTLESS
FAULTLESSLY
FAULTLESSNESS
FAULTLESSNESSES
FAULTS
FAULTY
FAUN
FAUNA
FAUNAE
FAUNAL
FAUNALLY
FAUNAS
FAUNIST
FAUNISTIC
FAUNISTICALLY
FAUNISTS
FAUNLIKE
FAUNS
FAUTEUIL
FAUTEUILS
FAUVE
FAUVES
FAUVISM
FAUVISMS
FAUVIST
FAUVISTS
FAUX
FAVA
FAVAS
FAVE
FAVELA
FAVELAS
FAVELLA
FAVELLAS
FAVEOLATE
FAVES
FAVISM
FAVISMS
FAVONIAN
FAVOR
FAVORABILITIES
FAVORABILITY
FAVORABLE
FAVORABLENESS
FAVORABLENESSES
FAVORABLY
FAVORED
FAVORER
FAVORERS
FAVORING
FAVORITE
FAVORITES
FAVORITISM
FAVORITISMS
FAVORS
FAVOUR
FAVOURABLE
FAVOURABLY
FAVOURED
FAVOURER
FAVOURERS
FAVOURING
FAVOURITE
FAVOURITES
FAVOURITISM
FAVOURITISMS
FAVOURS
FAVUS
FAVUSES
FAWN
FAWNED
FAWNER
FAWNERS
FAWNIER
FAWNIEST
FAWNING
FAWNINGLY
FAWNLIKE
FAWNS
FAWNY
FAX
FAXABLE
FAXED
FAXES
FAXING
FAY
FAYALITE
FAYALITES
FAYED
FAYING
FAYS
FAZE
FAZED
FAZENDA
FAZENDAS
FAZES
FAZING
FE
FEAL
FEALTIES
FEALTY
FEAR
FEARED
FEARER
FEARERS
FEARFUL
FEARFULLER
FEARFULLEST
FEARFULLY
FEARFULNESS
FEARFULNESSES
FEARING
FEARLESS
FEARLESSLY
FEARLESSNESS
FEARLESSNESSES
FEARMONGER
FEARMONGERING
FEARMONGERS
FEARS
FEARSOME
FEARSOMELY
FEARSOMENESS
FEARSOMENESSES
FEASANCE
FEASANCES
FEASE
FEASED
FEASES
FEASIBILITIES
FEASIBILITY
FEASIBLE
FEASIBLY
FEASING
FEAST
FEASTED
FEASTER
FEASTERS
FEASTFUL
FEASTING
FEASTLESS
FEASTS
FEAT
FEATER
FEATEST
FEATHER
FEATHERBED
FEATHERBEDDED

FEATHERBEDDING
FEATHERBEDDINGS
FEATHERBEDS
FEATHERBRAIN
FEATHERBRAINED
FEATHERBRAINS
FEATHERED
FEATHEREDGE
FEATHEREDGED
FEATHEREDGES
FEATHEREDGING
FEATHERHEAD
FEATHERHEADED
FEATHERHEADS
FEATHERIER
FEATHERIEST
FEATHERING
FEATHERINGS
FEATHERLESS
FEATHERLIGHT
FEATHERS
FEATHERSTITCH
FEATHERSTITCHED
FEATHERSTITCHES
FEATHERWEIGHT
FEATHERWEIGHTS
FEATHERY
FEATLIER
FEATLIEST
FEATLY
FEATS
FEATURE
FEATURED
FEATURELESS
FEATURES
FEATURETTE
FEATURETTES
FEATURING
FEAZE
FEAZED
FEAZES
FEAZING
FEBRICITIES
FEBRICITY
FEBRIFIC
FEBRIFUGE
FEBRIFUGES
FEBRILE
FEBRILITIES
FEBRILITY
FECAL
FECES
FECIAL
FECIALS
FECK
FECKLESS
FECKLESSLY
FECKLESSNESS
FECKLESSNESSES
FECKLY
FECKS
FECULA
FECULAE
FECULENCE
FECULENCES
FECULENT
FECUND
FECUNDATE
FECUNDATED
FECUNDATES
FECUNDATING
FECUNDATION
FECUNDATIONS
FECUNDITIES
FECUNDITY
FED
FEDAYEE
FEDAYEEN
FEDERACIES
FEDERACY
FEDERAL
FEDERALESE
FEDERALESES
FEDERALISATION
FEDERALISATIONS
FEDERALISE
FEDERALISED
FEDERALISES
FEDERALISING
FEDERALISM
FEDERALISMS
FEDERALIST
FEDERALISTS
FEDERALIZATION
FEDERALIZATIONS
FEDERALIZE
FEDERALIZED
FEDERALIZES
FEDERALIZING
FEDERALLY
FEDERALS
FEDERATE
FEDERATED
FEDERATES
FEDERATING
FEDERATION
FEDERATIONS
FEDERATIVE
FEDERATIVELY
FEDERATOR
FEDERATORS
FEDEX
FEDEXED
FEDEXES
FEDEXING
FEDORA
FEDORAS
FEDS
FEE
FEEB
FEEBLE
FEEBLEMINDED
FEEBLEMINDEDLY
FEEBLENESS
FEEBLENESSES
FEEBLER
FEEBLEST
FEEBLISH
FEEBLY
FEEBS
FEED
FEEDABLE
FEEDBACK
FEEDBACKS
FEEDBAG
FEEDBAGS
FEEDBOX
FEEDBOXES
FEEDER
FEEDERS
FEEDGRAIN
FEEDGRAINS
FEEDHOLE
FEEDHOLES
FEEDING
FEEDINGS
FEEDLOT
FEEDLOTS
FEEDS
FEEDSTOCK
FEEDSTOCKS
FEEDSTUFF
FEEDSTUFFS
FEEDYARD
FEEDYARDS
FEEING
FEEL
FEELER
FEELERS
FEELESS
FEELING
FEELINGLY
FEELINGNESS
FEELINGNESSES
FEELINGS
FEELS
FEES
FEET
FEETFIRST
FEETLESS
FEEZE
FEEZED
FEEZES
FEEZING
FEH
FEHS
FEIGN
FEIGNED
FEIGNEDLY
FEIGNER
FEIGNERS
FEIGNING
FEIGNS
FEIJOA
FEIJOAS
FEINT
FEINTED
FEINTING
FEINTS
FEIRIE
FEIST
FEISTIER
FEISTIEST
FEISTILY
FEISTINESS
FEISTINESSES
FEISTS
FEISTY
FELAFEL
FELAFELS
FELDSCHER
FELDSCHERS
FELDSHER
FELDSHERS
FELDSPAR
FELDSPARS
FELDSPATHIC
FELICIFIC
FELICITATE
FELICITATED
FELICITATES
FELICITATING
FELICITATION
FELICITATIONS
FELICITATOR
FELICITATORS
FELICITIES
FELICITOUS
FELICITOUSLY
FELICITOUSNESS
FELICITY
FELID
FELIDS
FELINE
FELINELY
FELINES
FELINITIES
FELINITY
FELL
FELLA
FELLABLE
FELLAH
FELLAHEEN
FELLAHIN
FELLAHS
FELLAS
FELLATE
FELLATED
FELLATES
FELLATING
FELLATIO
FELLATION
FELLATIONS
FELLATIOS
FELLATOR
FELLATORS
FELLATRICES
FELLATRIX
FELLATRIXES
FELLED
FELLER
FELLERS
FELLEST
FELLIES
FELLING
FELLMONGER
FELLMONGERED
FELLMONGERIES
FELLMONGERING
FELLMONGERINGS
FELLMONGERS
FELLMONGERY
FELLNESS
FELLNESSES
FELLOE

FELLOES
FELLOW
FELLOWED
FELLOWING
FELLOWLY
FELLOWMAN
FELLOWMEN
FELLOWS
FELLOWSHIP
FELLOWSHIPED
FELLOWSHIPING
FELLOWSHIPPED
FELLOWSHIPPING
FELLOWSHIPS
FELLS
FELLY
FELON
FELONIES
FELONIOUS
FELONIOUSLY
FELONIOUSNESS
FELONIOUSNESSES
FELONRIES
FELONRY
FELONS
FELONY
FELSIC
FELSITE
FELSITES
FELSITIC
FELSPAR
FELSPARS
FELSTONE
FELSTONES
FELT
FELTED
FELTIER
FELTIEST
FELTING
FELTINGS
FELTLIKE
FELTS
FELTY
FELUCCA
FELUCCAS
FELWORT
FELWORTS
FEM
FEMALE
FEMALENESS
FEMALENESSES
FEMALES
FEME
FEMES
FEMINACIES
FEMINACY
FEMINAZI
FEMINAZIS
FEMINIE
FEMININE
FEMININELY
FEMININENESS
FEMININENESSES
FEMININES
FEMININITIES
FEMININITY
FEMINISE
FEMINISED
FEMINISES
FEMINISING
FEMINISM
FEMINISMS
FEMINIST
FEMINISTIC
FEMINISTS
FEMINITIES
FEMINITY
FEMINIZATION
FEMINIZATIONS
FEMINIZE
FEMINIZED
FEMINIZES
FEMINIZING
FEMME
FEMMES
FEMORA
FEMORAL
FEMS
FEMTOSECOND
FEMTOSECONDS
FEMUR
FEMURS
FEN
FENAGLE
FENAGLED
FENAGLES
FENAGLING
FENCE
FENCED
FENCELESS
FENCELESSNESS
FENCELESSNESSES
FENCER
FENCEROW
FENCEROWS
FENCERS
FENCES
FENCIBLE
FENCIBLES
FENCING
FENCINGS
FEND
FENDED
FENDER
FENDERED
FENDERLESS
FENDERS
FENDING
FENDS
FENESTRA
FENESTRAE
FENESTRAL
FENESTRATE
FENESTRATED
FENESTRATES
FENESTRATING
FENESTRATION
FENESTRATIONS
FENFLURAMINE
FENFLURAMINES
FENING
FENINGS
FENLAND
FENLANDS
FENNEC
FENNECS
FENNEL
FENNELS
FENNIER
FENNIEST
FENNING
FENNY
FENS
FENTANYL
FENTANYLS
FENTHION
FENTHIONS
FENUGREEK
FENUGREEKS
FENURON
FENURONS
FEOD
FEODARIES
FEODARY
FEODS
FEOFF
FEOFFED
FEOFFEE
FEOFFEES
FEOFFER
FEOFFERS
FEOFFING
FEOFFMENT
FEOFFMENTS
FEOFFOR
FEOFFORS
FEOFFS
FER
FERACITIES
FERACITY
FERAL
FERALS
FERBAM
FERBAMS
FERE
FERES
FERETORIES
FERETORY
FERIA
FERIAE
FERIAL
FERIAS
FERINE
FERITIES
FERITY
FERLIE
FERLIES
FERLY
FERMATA
FERMATAS
FERMATE
FERMENT
FERMENTABLE
FERMENTATION
FERMENTATIONS
FERMENTATIVE
FERMENTED
FERMENTER
FERMENTERS
FERMENTING
FERMENTOR
FERMENTORS
FERMENTS
FERMI
FERMION
FERMIONIC
FERMIONS
FERMIS
FERMIUM
FERMIUMS
FERN
FERNERIES
FERNERY
FERNIER
FERNIEST
FERNINST
FERNLESS
FERNLIKE
FERNS
FERNY
FEROCIOUS
FEROCIOUSLY
FEROCIOUSNESS
FEROCIOUSNESSES
FEROCITIES
FEROCITY
FERRATE
FERRATES
FERREDOXIN
FERREDOXINS
FERREL
FERRELED
FERRELING
FERRELLED
FERRELLING
FERRELS
FERREOUS
FERRET
FERRETED
FERRETER
FERRETERS
FERRETING
FERRETINGS
FERRETS
FERRETY
FERRIAGE
FERRIAGES
FERRIC
FERRICYANIDE
FERRICYANIDES
FERRIED
FERRIES
FERRIFEROUS
FERRIMAGNET
FERRIMAGNETIC
FERRIMAGNETISM
FERRIMAGNETISMS
FERRIMAGNETS
FERRITE
FERRITES
FERRITIC
FERRITIN
FERRITINS
FERROCENE
FERROCENES

FERROCONCRETE
FERROCONCRETES
FERROCYANIDE
FERROCYANIDES
FERROELECTRIC
FERROELECTRICS
FERROMAGNESIAN
FERROMAGNET
FERROMAGNETIC
FERROMAGNETISM
FERROMAGNETISMS
FERROMAGNETS
FERROMANGANESE
FERROMANGANESES
FERROSILICON
FERROSILICONS
FERROTYPE
FERROTYPED
FERROTYPES
FERROTYPING
FERROUS
FERRUGINOUS
FERRULE
FERRULED
FERRULES
FERRULING
FERRUM
FERRUMS
FERRY
FERRYBOAT
FERRYBOATS
FERRYING
FERRYMAN
FERRYMEN
FERTILE
FERTILELY
FERTILENESS
FERTILENESSES
FERTILISATION
FERTILISATIONS
FERTILISE
FERTILISED
FERTILISER
FERTILISERS
FERTILISES
FERTILISING
FERTILITIES
FERTILITY
FERTILIZABLE
FERTILIZATION
FERTILIZATIONS
FERTILIZE
FERTILIZED
FERTILIZER
FERTILIZERS
FERTILIZES
FERTILIZING
FERULA
FERULAE
FERULAS
FERULE
FERULED
FERULES
FERULING
FERVENCIES
FERVENCY
FERVENT
FERVENTLY
FERVID
FERVIDITIES
FERVIDITY
FERVIDLY
FERVIDNESS
FERVIDNESSES
FERVOR
FERVORS
FERVOUR
FERVOURS
FES
FESCENNINE
FESCUE
FESCUES
FESS
FESSE
FESSED
FESSES
FESSING
FESSWISE
FEST
FESTA
FESTAL
FESTALLY
FESTAS
FESTER
FESTERED
FESTERING
FESTERS
FESTINATE
FESTINATED
FESTINATELY
FESTINATES
FESTINATING
FESTIVAL
FESTIVALGOER
FESTIVALGOERS
FESTIVALS
FESTIVE
FESTIVELY
FESTIVENESS
FESTIVENESSES
FESTIVITIES
FESTIVITY
FESTOON
FESTOONED
FESTOONERIES
FESTOONERY
FESTOONING
FESTOONS
FESTS
FET
FETA
FETAL
FETAS
FETATION
FETATIONS
FETCH
FETCHED
FETCHER
FETCHERS
FETCHES
FETCHING
FETCHINGLY
FETE
FETED
FETERITA
FETERITAS
FETES
FETIAL
FETIALES
FETIALIS
FETIALS
FETICH
FETICHES
FETICHISM
FETICHISMS
FETICIDAL
FETICIDE
FETICIDES
FETID
FETIDITIES
FETIDITY
FETIDLY
FETIDNESS
FETIDNESSES
FETING
FETISH
FETISHES
FETISHISM
FETISHISMS
FETISHIST
FETISHISTIC
FETISHISTICALLY
FETISHISTS
FETISHIZE
FETISHIZED
FETISHIZES
FETISHIZING
FETLOCK
FETLOCKS
FETOLOGIES
FETOLOGIST
FETOLOGISTS
FETOLOGY
FETOPROTEIN
FETOPROTEINS
FETOR
FETORS
FETOSCOPE
FETOSCOPES
FETOSCOPIES
FETOSCOPY
FETS
FETTED
FETTER
FETTERED
FETTERER
FETTERERS
FETTERING
FETTERS
FETTING
FETTLE
FETTLED
FETTLER
FETTLERS
FETTLES
FETTLING
FETTLINGS
FETTUCCINE
FETTUCCINI
FETTUCINE
FETTUCINI
FETUS
FETUSES
FEU
FEUAR
FEUARS
FEUD
FEUDAL
FEUDALISM
FEUDALISMS
FEUDALIST
FEUDALISTIC
FEUDALISTS
FEUDALITIES
FEUDALITY
FEUDALIZATION
FEUDALIZATIONS
FEUDALIZE
FEUDALIZED
FEUDALIZES
FEUDALIZING
FEUDALLY
FEUDARIES
FEUDARY
FEUDATORIES
FEUDATORY
FEUDED
FEUDING
FEUDIST
FEUDISTS
FEUDS
FEUED
FEUILLETON
FEUILLETONISM
FEUILLETONISMS
FEUILLETONIST
FEUILLETONISTS
FEUILLETONS
FEUING
FEUS
FEVER
FEVERED
FEVERFEW
FEVERFEWS
FEVERING
FEVERISH
FEVERISHLY
FEVERISHNESS
FEVERISHNESSES
FEVEROUS
FEVERROOT
FEVERROOTS
FEVERS
FEVERWEED
FEVERWEEDS
FEVERWORT
FEVERWORTS
FEW
FEWER
FEWEST
FEWNESS
FEWNESSES
FEWTRILS
FEY
FEYER

FEYEST
FEYLY
FEYNESS
FEYNESSES
FEZ
FEZES
FEZZED
FEZZES
FEZZY
FIACRE
FIACRES
FIANCE
FIANCEE
FIANCEES
FIANCES
FIANCHETTO
FIANCHETTOED
FIANCHETTOES
FIANCHETTOING
FIANCHETTOS
FIAR
FIARS
FIASCHI
FIASCO
FIASCOES
FIASCOS
FIAT
FIATS
FIB
FIBBED
FIBBER
FIBBERS
FIBBING
FIBER
FIBERBOARD
FIBERBOARDS
FIBERED
FIBERFILL
FIBERFILLS
FIBERGLASS
FIBERGLASSED
FIBERGLASSES
FIBERGLASSING
FIBERIZATION
FIBERIZATIONS
FIBERIZE
FIBERIZED
FIBERIZES
FIBERIZING
FIBERLESS
FIBERLIKE
FIBERS
FIBERSCOPE
FIBERSCOPES
FIBRANNE
FIBRANNES
FIBRE
FIBREBOARD
FIBREBOARDS
FIBRED
FIBREFILL
FIBREFILLS
FIBREGLASS
FIBREGLASSED
FIBREGLASSES
FIBREGLASSING
FIBRES
FIBRIL
FIBRILLA
FIBRILLAE
FIBRILLAR
FIBRILLATE
FIBRILLATED
FIBRILLATES
FIBRILLATING
FIBRILLATION
FIBRILLATIONS
FIBRILS
FIBRIN
FIBRINOGEN
FIBRINOGENS
FIBRINOID
FIBRINOIDS
FIBRINOLYSES
FIBRINOLYSIN
FIBRINOLYSINS
FIBRINOLYSIS
FIBRINOLYTIC
FIBRINOPEPTIDE
FIBRINOPEPTIDES
FIBRINOUS
FIBRINS
FIBROBLAST
FIBROBLASTIC
FIBROBLASTS
FIBROCYSTIC
FIBROID
FIBROIDS
FIBROIN
FIBROINS
FIBROMA
FIBROMAS
FIBROMATA
FIBROMATOUS
FIBROMYALGIA
FIBROMYALGIAS
FIBRONECTIN
FIBRONECTINS
FIBROSARCOMA
FIBROSARCOMAS
FIBROSARCOMATA
FIBROSES
FIBROSIS
FIBROSITIS
FIBROSITISES
FIBROTIC
FIBROUS
FIBROUSLY
FIBROVASCULAR
FIBS
FIBSTER
FIBSTERS
FIBULA
FIBULAE
FIBULAR
FIBULAS
FICE
FICES
FICHE
FICHES
FICHU
FICHUS
FICIN
FICINS
FICKLE
FICKLENESS
FICKLENESSES
FICKLER
FICKLEST
FICKLY
FICO
FICOES
FICTILE
FICTION
FICTIONAL
FICTIONALISE
FICTIONALISED
FICTIONALISES
FICTIONALISING
FICTIONALITIES
FICTIONALITY
FICTIONALIZE
FICTIONALIZED
FICTIONALIZES
FICTIONALIZING
FICTIONALLY
FICTIONEER
FICTIONEERING
FICTIONEERINGS
FICTIONEERS
FICTIONIST
FICTIONISTS
FICTIONIZATION
FICTIONIZATIONS
FICTIONIZE
FICTIONIZED
FICTIONIZES
FICTIONIZING
FICTIONS
FICTITIOUS
FICTITIOUSLY
FICTITIOUSNESS
FICTIVE
FICTIVELY
FICTIVENESS
FICTIVENESSES
FICUS
FICUSES
FID
FIDDLE
FIDDLEBACK
FIDDLEBACKS
FIDDLED
FIDDLEHEAD
FIDDLEHEADS
FIDDLER
FIDDLERS
FIDDLES
FIDDLESTICK
FIDDLESTICKS
FIDDLIER
FIDDLIEST
FIDDLING
FIDDLINGS
FIDDLY
FIDEISM
FIDEISMS
FIDEIST
FIDEISTIC
FIDEISTS
FIDELISMO
FIDELISMOS
FIDELISTA
FIDELISTAS
FIDELITIES
FIDELITY
FIDGE
FIDGED
FIDGES
FIDGET
FIDGETED
FIDGETER
FIDGETERS
FIDGETINESS
FIDGETINESSES
FIDGETING
FIDGETS
FIDGETY
FIDGING
FIDO
FIDOS
FIDS
FIDUCIAL
FIDUCIALLY
FIDUCIARIES
FIDUCIARY
FIE
FIEF
FIEFDOM
FIEFDOMS
FIEFS
FIELD
FIELDED
FIELDER
FIELDERS
FIELDFARE
FIELDFARES
FIELDING
FIELDPIECE
FIELDPIECES
FIELDS
FIELDSMAN
FIELDSMEN
FIELDSTONE
FIELDSTONES
FIELDSTRIP
FIELDSTRIPPED
FIELDSTRIPPING
FIELDSTRIPS
FIELDWORK
FIELDWORKS
FIEND
FIENDISH
FIENDISHLY
FIENDISHNESS
FIENDISHNESSES
FIENDS
FIERCE
FIERCELY
FIERCENESS
FIERCENESSES
FIERCER
FIERCEST
FIERIER
FIERIEST

FIERILY
FIERINESS
FIERINESSES
FIERY
FIESTA
FIESTAS
FIFE
FIFED
FIFER
FIFERS
FIFES
FIFING
FIFTEEN
FIFTEENS
FIFTEENTH
FIFTEENTHS
FIFTH
FIFTHLY
FIFTHS
FIFTIES
FIFTIETH
FIFTIETHS
FIFTY
FIFTYISH
FIG
FIGEATER
FIGEATERS
FIGGED
FIGGING
FIGHT
FIGHTABLE
FIGHTBACK
FIGHTER
FIGHTERS
FIGHTING
FIGHTINGS
FIGHTS
FIGMENT
FIGMENTS
FIGS
FIGTREE
FIGTREES
FIGULINE
FIGULINES
FIGURABLE
FIGURAL
FIGURALLY
FIGURANT
FIGURANTS
FIGURATE
FIGURATION
FIGURATIONS
FIGURATIVE
FIGURATIVELY
FIGURATIVENESS
FIGURE
FIGURED
FIGUREDLY
FIGUREHEAD
FIGUREHEADS
FIGURER
FIGURERS
FIGURES
FIGURINE
FIGURINES
FIGURING
FIGWORT
FIGWORTS
FIL
FILA
FILAGREE
FILAGREED
FILAGREEING
FILAGREES
FILAMENT
FILAMENTARY
FILAMENTOUS
FILAMENTS
FILAR
FILAREE
FILAREES
FILARIA
FILARIAE
FILARIAL
FILARIAN
FILARIASES
FILARIASIS
FILARIID
FILARIIDS
FILATURE
FILATURES
FILBERT
FILBERTS
FILCH
FILCHED
FILCHER
FILCHERS
FILCHES
FILCHING
FILE
FILEABLE
FILED
FILEFISH
FILEFISHES
FILEMOT
FILENAME
FILENAMES
FILER
FILERS
FILES
FILET
FILETED
FILETING
FILETS
FILIAL
FILIALLY
FILIATE
FILIATED
FILIATES
FILIATING
FILIATION
FILIATIONS
FILIBEG
FILIBEGS
FILIBUSTER
FILIBUSTERED
FILIBUSTERER
FILIBUSTERERS
FILIBUSTERING
FILIBUSTERS
FILICIDE
FILICIDES
FILIFORM
FILIGREE
FILIGREED
FILIGREEING
FILIGREES
FILING
FILINGS
FILIOPIETISM
FILIOPIETISMS
FILIOPIETISTIC
FILISTER
FILISTERS
FILK
FILKS
FILL
FILLABLE
FILLAGREE
FILLAGREED
FILLAGREEING
FILLAGREES
FILLE
FILLED
FILLER
FILLERS
FILLES
FILLET
FILLETED
FILLETER
FILLETERS
FILLETING
FILLETS
FILLIES
FILLING
FILLINGS
FILLIP
FILLIPED
FILLIPING
FILLIPS
FILLISTER
FILLISTERS
FILLO
FILLOS
FILLS
FILLY
FILM
FILMABLE
FILMCARD
FILMCARDS
FILMDOM
FILMDOMS
FILMED
FILMER
FILMERS
FILMFEST
FILMFESTS
FILMGOER
FILMGOERS
FILMGOING
FILMGOINGS
FILMI
FILMIC
FILMICALLY
FILMIER
FILMIEST
FILMILY
FILMINESS
FILMINESSES
FILMING
FILMIS
FILMLAND
FILMLANDS
FILMLESS
FILMLIKE
FILMMAKER
FILMMAKERS
FILMMAKING
FILMMAKINGS
FILMOGRAPHIES
FILMOGRAPHY
FILMS
FILMSET
FILMSETS
FILMSETTER
FILMSETTERS
FILMSETTING
FILMSETTINGS
FILMSTRIP
FILMSTRIPS
FILMY
FILO
FILOPLUME
FILOPLUMES
FILOPODIA
FILOPODIUM
FILOS
FILOSE
FILOVIRUS
FILOVIRUSES
FILS
FILTER
FILTERABILITIES
FILTERABILITY
FILTERABLE
FILTERED
FILTERER
FILTERERS
FILTERING
FILTERS
FILTH
FILTHIER
FILTHIEST
FILTHILY
FILTHINESS
FILTHINESSES
FILTHS
FILTHY
FILTRABLE
FILTRATE
FILTRATED
FILTRATES
FILTRATING
FILTRATION
FILTRATIONS
FILUM
FIMBLE
FIMBLES
FIMBRIA
FIMBRIAE
FIMBRIAL
FIMBRIATE
FIMBRIATED
FIMBRIATION
FIMBRIATIONS

FIN
FINABLE
FINAGLE
FINAGLED
FINAGLER
FINAGLERS
FINAGLES
FINAGLING
FINAL
FINALE
FINALES
FINALIS
FINALISATION
FINALISATIONS
FINALISE
FINALISED
FINALISES
FINALISING
FINALISM
FINALISMS
FINALIST
FINALISTS
FINALITIES
FINALITY
FINALIZATION
FINALIZATIONS
FINALIZE
FINALIZED
FINALIZER
FINALIZERS
FINALIZES
FINALIZING
FINALLY
FINALS
FINANCE
FINANCED
FINANCES
FINANCIAL
FINANCIALLY
FINANCIALS
FINANCIER
FINANCIERED
FINANCIERING
FINANCIERS
FINANCING
FINANCINGS
FINASTERIDE
FINASTERIDES
FINBACK
FINBACKS
FINCA
FINCAS
FINCH
FINCHES
FIND
FINDABLE
FINDER
FINDERS
FINDING
FINDINGS
FINDS
FINE
FINEABLE
FINED
FINELY
FINENESS
FINENESSES
FINER
FINERIES
FINERY
FINES
FINESPUN
FINESSE
FINESSED
FINESSES
FINESSING
FINEST
FINESTS
FINFISH
FINFISHES
FINFOOT
FINFOOTS
FINGER
FINGERBOARD
FINGERBOARDS
FINGERED
FINGERER
FINGERERS
FINGERHOLD
FINGERHOLDS
FINGERING
FINGERINGS
FINGERLIKE
FINGERLING
FINGERLINGS
FINGERNAIL
FINGERNAILS
FINGERPICK
FINGERPICKED
FINGERPICKING
FINGERPICKINGS
FINGERPICKS
FINGERPOST
FINGERPOSTS
FINGERPRINT
FINGERPRINTED
FINGERPRINTING
FINGERPRINTINGS
FINGERPRINTS
FINGERS
FINGERTIP
FINGERTIPS
FINIAL
FINIALED
FINIALS
FINICAL
FINICALLY
FINICALNESS
FINICALNESSES
FINICKIER
FINICKIEST
FINICKIN
FINICKINESS
FINICKINESSES
FINICKING
FINICKY
FINIKIN
FINIKING
FINING
FININGS
FINIS
FINISES
FINISH
FINISHED
FINISHER
FINISHERS
FINISHES
FINISHING
FINITE
FINITELY
FINITENESS
FINITENESSES
FINITES
FINITISM
FINITISMS
FINITIST
FINITISTS
FINITO
FINITUDE
FINITUDES
FINK
FINKED
FINKING
FINKS
FINLESS
FINLIKE
FINMARK
FINMARKS
FINNAN
FINNANS
FINNED
FINNICKIER
FINNICKIEST
FINNICKY
FINNIER
FINNIEST
FINNING
FINNMARK
FINNMARKS
FINNY
FINO
FINOCCHIO
FINOCCHIOS
FINOCHIO
FINOCHIOS
FINOS
FINS
FIORATURA
FIORATURAE
FIORD
FIORDS
FIORITURA
FIORITURE
FIPPLE
FIPPLES
FIQUE
FIQUES
FIR
FIRE
FIREABLE
FIREARM
FIREARMED
FIREARMS
FIREBACK
FIREBACKS
FIREBALL
FIREBALLER
FIREBALLERS
FIREBALLING
FIREBALLS
FIREBASE
FIREBASES
FIREBIRD
FIREBIRDS
FIREBOARD
FIREBOARDS
FIREBOAT
FIREBOATS
FIREBOMB
FIREBOMBED
FIREBOMBING
FIREBOMBS
FIREBOX
FIREBOXES
FIREBRAND
FIREBRANDS
FIREBRAT
FIREBRATS
FIREBREAK
FIREBREAKS
FIREBRICK
FIREBRICKS
FIREBUG
FIREBUGS
FIRECLAY
FIRECLAYS
FIRECRACKER
FIRECRACKERS
FIRED
FIREDAMP
FIREDAMPS
FIREDOG
FIREDOGS
FIREDRAKE
FIREDRAKES
FIREFANG
FIREFANGED
FIREFANGING
FIREFANGS
FIREFIGHT
FIREFIGHTER
FIREFIGHTERS
FIREFIGHTING
FIREFIGHTINGS
FIREFIGHTS
FIREFLIES
FIREFLOOD
FIREFLOODS
FIREFLY
FIREGUARD
FIREGUARDS
FIREHALL
FIREHALLS
FIREHOSE
FIREHOSES
FIREHOUSE
FIREHOUSES
FIRELESS
FIRELIGHT
FIRELIGHTS
FIRELIT
FIRELOCK
FIRELOCKS
FIREMAN
FIREMANIC

FIREMEN
FIREPAN
FIREPANS
FIREPINK
FIREPINKS
FIREPIT
FIREPITS
FIREPLACE
FIREPLACED
FIREPLACES
FIREPLUG
FIREPLUGS
FIREPOT
FIREPOTS
FIREPOWER
FIREPOWERS
FIREPROOF
FIREPROOFED
FIREPROOFING
FIREPROOFS
FIRER
FIREREEL
FIREREELS
FIREROOM
FIREROOMS
FIRERS
FIRES
FIRESHIP
FIRESHIPS
FIRESIDE
FIRESIDES
FIRESTONE
FIRESTONES
FIRESTORM
FIRESTORMS
FIRETHORN
FIRETHORNS
FIRETRAP
FIRETRAPS
FIRETRUCK
FIRETRUCKS
FIREWALL
FIREWALLS
FIREWATER
FIREWATERS
FIREWEED
FIREWEEDS
FIREWOOD
FIREWOODS
FIREWORK
FIREWORKS
FIREWORM
FIREWORMS

FIRING
FIRINGS
FIRKIN
FIRKINS
FIRM
FIRMAMENT
FIRMAMENTAL
FIRMAMENTS
FIRMAN
FIRMANS
FIRMED
FIRMER
FIRMERS
FIRMEST
FIRMING
FIRMLY
FIRMNESS
FIRMNESSES
FIRMS
FIRMWARE
FIRMWARES
FIRN
FIRNS
FIRRIER
FIRRIEST
FIRRY
FIRS
FIRST
FIRSTBORN
FIRSTBORNS
FIRSTFRUITS
FIRSTHAND
FIRSTLING
FIRSTLINGS
FIRSTLY
FIRSTNESS
FIRSTNESSES
FIRSTS
FIRTH
FIRTHS
FISC
FISCAL
FISCALIST
FISCALISTS
FISCALLY
FISCALS
FISCS
FISH
FISHABILITIES
FISHABILITY
FISHABLE
FISHBOAT
FISHBOATS

FISHBOLT
FISHBOLTS
FISHBONE
FISHBONES
FISHBOWL
FISHBOWLS
FISHED
FISHER
FISHERFOLK
FISHERIES
FISHERMAN
FISHERMEN
FISHERS
FISHERWOMAN
FISHERWOMEN
FISHERY
FISHES
FISHEYE
FISHEYES
FISHGIG
FISHGIGS
FISHHOOK
FISHHOOKS
FISHIER
FISHIEST
FISHILY
FISHINESS
FISHINESSES
FISHING
FISHINGS
FISHKILL
FISHKILLS
FISHLESS
FISHLIKE
FISHLINE
FISHLINES
FISHMEAL
FISHMEALS
FISHMONGER
FISHMONGERS
FISHNET
FISHNETS
FISHPLATE
FISHPLATES
FISHPOLE
FISHPOLES
FISHPOND
FISHPONDS
FISHTAIL
FISHTAILED
FISHTAILING
FISHTAILS
FISHWAY

FISHWAYS
FISHWIFE
FISHWIVES
FISHWORM
FISHWORMS
FISHY
FISSATE
FISSILE
FISSILITIES
FISSILITY
FISSION
FISSIONABILITY
FISSIONABLE
FISSIONABLES
FISSIONAL
FISSIONED
FISSIONING
FISSIONS
FISSIPAROUS
FISSIPAROUSNESS
FISSIPED
FISSIPEDS
FISSURAL
FISSURE
FISSURED
FISSURES
FISSURING
FIST
FISTED
FISTFIGHT
FISTFIGHTS
FISTFUL
FISTFULS
FISTIC
FISTICUFF
FISTICUFFS
FISTING
FISTINGS
FISTNOTE
FISTNOTES
FISTS
FISTULA
FISTULAE
FISTULAR
FISTULAS
FISTULATE
FISTULOUS
FIT
FITCH
FITCHEE
FITCHES
FITCHET
FITCHETS

FITCHEW
FITCHEWS
FITCHY
FITFUL
FITFULLY
FITFULNESS
FITFULNESSES
FITLY
FITMENT
FITMENTS
FITNESS
FITNESSES
FITS
FITTABLE
FITTED
FITTER
FITTERS
FITTEST
FITTING
FITTINGLY
FITTINGNESS
FITTINGNESSES
FITTINGS
FIVE
FIVEFOLD
FIVEPINS
FIVER
FIVERS
FIVES
FIX
FIXABLE
FIXATE
FIXATED
FIXATES
FIXATIF
FIXATIFS
FIXATING
FIXATION
FIXATIONS
FIXATIVE
FIXATIVES
FIXED
FIXEDLY
FIXEDNESS
FIXEDNESSES
FIXER
FIXERS
FIXES
FIXING
FIXINGS
FIXIT
FIXITIES
FIXITS

FIXITY
FIXT
FIXTURE
FIXTURES
FIXURE
FIXURES
FIZ
FIZGIG
FIZGIGS
FIZZ
FIZZED
FIZZER
FIZZERS
FIZZES
FIZZIER
FIZZIEST
FIZZILY
FIZZING
FIZZLE
FIZZLED
FIZZLES
FIZZLING
FIZZY
FJELD
FJELDS
FJORD
FJORDIC
FJORDS
FLAB
FLABBERGAST
FLABBERGASTED
FLABBERGASTING
FLABBERGASTS
FLABBIER
FLABBIEST
FLABBILY
FLABBINESS
FLABBINESSES
FLABBY
FLABELLA
FLABELLATE
FLABELLIFORM
FLABELLUM
FLABS
FLACCID
FLACCIDITIES
FLACCIDITY
FLACCIDLY
FLACK
FLACKED
FLACKERIES
FLACKERY
FLACKING
FLACKS
FLACON
FLACONS
FLAG
FLAGELLA
FLAGELLANT
FLAGELLANTISM
FLAGELLANTISMS
FLAGELLANTS
FLAGELLAR
FLAGELLATE
FLAGELLATED
FLAGELLATES
FLAGELLATING
FLAGELLATION
FLAGELLATIONS
FLAGELLIN
FLAGELLINS
FLAGELLUM
FLAGELLUMS
FLAGEOLET
FLAGEOLETS
FLAGGED
FLAGGER
FLAGGERS
FLAGGIER
FLAGGIEST
FLAGGING
FLAGGINGLY
FLAGGINGS
FLAGGY
FLAGITIOUS
FLAGITIOUSLY
FLAGITIOUSNESS
FLAGLESS
FLAGMAN
FLAGMEN
FLAGON
FLAGONS
FLAGPOLE
FLAGPOLES
FLAGRANCE
FLAGRANCES
FLAGRANCIES
FLAGRANCY
FLAGRANT
FLAGRANTLY
FLAGS
FLAGSHIP
FLAGSHIPS
FLAGSTAFF
FLAGSTAFFS
FLAGSTAVES
FLAGSTICK
FLAGSTICKS
FLAGSTONE
FLAGSTONES
FLAIL
FLAILED
FLAILING
FLAILS
FLAIR
FLAIRS
FLAK
FLAKE
FLAKED
FLAKER
FLAKERS
FLAKES
FLAKEY
FLAKIER
FLAKIEST
FLAKILY
FLAKINESS
FLAKINESSES
FLAKING
FLAKS
FLAKY
FLAM
FLAMBE
FLAMBEAU
FLAMBEAUS
FLAMBEAUX
FLAMBEE
FLAMBEED
FLAMBEING
FLAMBES
FLAMBOYANCE
FLAMBOYANCES
FLAMBOYANCIES
FLAMBOYANCY
FLAMBOYANT
FLAMBOYANTLY
FLAMBOYANTS
FLAME
FLAMED
FLAMELESS
FLAMELIKE
FLAMEN
FLAMENCO
FLAMENCOS
FLAMENS
FLAMEOUT
FLAMEOUTS
FLAMEPROOF
FLAMEPROOFED
FLAMEPROOFER
FLAMEPROOFERS
FLAMEPROOFING
FLAMEPROOFS
FLAMER
FLAMERS
FLAMES
FLAMETHROWER
FLAMETHROWERS
FLAMIER
FLAMIEST
FLAMINES
FLAMING
FLAMINGLY
FLAMINGO
FLAMINGOES
FLAMINGOS
FLAMMABILITIES
FLAMMABILITY
FLAMMABLE
FLAMMABLES
FLAMMED
FLAMMING
FLAMS
FLAMY
FLAN
FLANCARD
FLANCARDS
FLANERIE
FLANERIES
FLANES
FLANEUR
FLANEURS
FLANGE
FLANGED
FLANGER
FLANGERS
FLANGES
FLANGING
FLANGINGS
FLANK
FLANKED
FLANKEN
FLANKER
FLANKERS
FLANKING
FLANKS
FLANNEL
FLANNELED
FLANNELET
FLANNELETS
FLANNELETTE
FLANNELETTES
FLANNELING
FLANNELLED
FLANNELLING
FLANNELLY
FLANNELMOUTHED
FLANNELS
FLANS
FLAP
FLAPDOODLE
FLAPDOODLES
FLAPERON
FLAPERONS
FLAPJACK
FLAPJACKS
FLAPLESS
FLAPPABLE
FLAPPED
FLAPPER
FLAPPERS
FLAPPIER
FLAPPIEST
FLAPPING
FLAPPY
FLAPS
FLARE
FLAREBACK
FLAREBACKS
FLARED
FLARES
FLAREUP
FLAREUPS
FLARING
FLARINGLY
FLASH
FLASHBACK
FLASHBACKS
FLASHBOARD
FLASHBOARDS
FLASHBULB
FLASHBULBS
FLASHCARD
FLASHCARDS
FLASHCUBE
FLASHCUBES
FLASHED
FLASHER
FLASHERS
FLASHES
FLASHGUN
FLASHGUNS
FLASHIER
FLASHIEST
FLASHILY

FLASHINESS
FLASHINESSES
FLASHING
FLASHINGS
FLASHLAMP
FLASHLAMPS
FLASHLIGHT
FLASHLIGHTS
FLASHOVER
FLASHOVERS
FLASHTUBE
FLASHTUBES
FLASHY
FLASK
FLASKET
FLASKETS
FLASKS
FLAT
FLATBED
FLATBEDS
FLATBOAT
FLATBOATS
FLATBREAD
FLATBREADS
FLATCAP
FLATCAPS
FLATCAR
FLATCARS
FLATFEET
FLATFISH
FLATFISHES
FLATFOOT
FLATFOOTED
FLATFOOTING
FLATFOOTS
FLATHEAD
FLATHEADS
FLATIRON
FLATIRONS
FLATLAND
FLATLANDER
FLATLANDERS
FLATLANDS
FLATLET
FLATLETS
FLATLINE
FLATLINED
FLATLINER
FLATLINERS
FLATLINES
FLATLING
FLATLINGS
FLATLINING
FLATLONG
FLATLY
FLATMATE
FLATMATES
FLATNESS
FLATNESSES
FLATPACK
FLATPACKS
FLATS
FLATTED
FLATTEN
FLATTENED
FLATTENER
FLATTENERS
FLATTENING
FLATTENS
FLATTER
FLATTERED
FLATTERER
FLATTERERS
FLATTERIES
FLATTERING
FLATTERINGLY
FLATTERS
FLATTERY
FLATTEST
FLATTIE
FLATTIES
FLATTING
FLATTISH
FLATTOP
FLATTOPS
FLATULENCE
FLATULENCES
FLATULENCIES
FLATULENCY
FLATULENT
FLATULENTLY
FLATUS
FLATUSES
FLATWARE
FLATWARES
FLATWASH
FLATWASHES
FLATWAYS
FLATWISE
FLATWORK
FLATWORKS
FLATWORM
FLATWORMS
FLAUNT
FLAUNTED
FLAUNTER
FLAUNTERS
FLAUNTIER
FLAUNTIEST
FLAUNTILY
FLAUNTING
FLAUNTINGLY
FLAUNTS
FLAUNTY
FLAUTA
FLAUTAS
FLAUTIST
FLAUTISTS
FLAVA
FLAVANOL
FLAVANOLS
FLAVANONE
FLAVANONES
FLAVAS
FLAVIN
FLAVINE
FLAVINES
FLAVINS
FLAVIVIRUS
FLAVIVIRUSES
FLAVONE
FLAVONES
FLAVONOID
FLAVONOIDS
FLAVONOL
FLAVONOLS
FLAVOPROTEIN
FLAVOPROTEINS
FLAVOR
FLAVORED
FLAVORER
FLAVORERS
FLAVORFUL
FLAVORFULLY
FLAVORING
FLAVORINGS
FLAVORIST
FLAVORISTS
FLAVORLESS
FLAVOROUS
FLAVORS
FLAVORSOME
FLAVORY
FLAVOUR
FLAVOURED
FLAVOURFUL
FLAVOURING
FLAVOURINGS
FLAVOURLESS
FLAVOURS
FLAVOURSOME
FLAVOURY
FLAW
FLAWED
FLAWIER
FLAWIEST
FLAWING
FLAWLESS
FLAWLESSLY
FLAWLESSNESS
FLAWLESSNESSES
FLAWS
FLAWY
FLAX
FLAXEN
FLAXES
FLAXIER
FLAXIEST
FLAXSEED
FLAXSEEDS
FLAXY
FLAY
FLAYED
FLAYER
FLAYERS
FLAYING
FLAYS
FLEA
FLEABAG
FLEABAGS
FLEABANE
FLEABANES
FLEABITE
FLEABITES
FLEAHOPPER
FLEAHOPPERS
FLEAM
FLEAMS
FLEAPIT
FLEAPITS
FLEAS
FLEAWORT
FLEAWORTS
FLECHE
FLECHES
FLECHETTE
FLECHETTES
FLECK
FLECKED
FLECKING
FLECKLESS
FLECKS
FLECKY
FLECTION
FLECTIONS
FLED
FLEDGE
FLEDGED
FLEDGES
FLEDGIER
FLEDGIEST
FLEDGING
FLEDGLING
FLEDGLINGS
FLEDGY
FLEE
FLEECE
FLEECED
FLEECER
FLEECERS
FLEECES
FLEECH
FLEECHED
FLEECHES
FLEECHING
FLEECIER
FLEECIEST
FLEECILY
FLEECING
FLEECY
FLEEING
FLEER
FLEERED
FLEERING
FLEERINGLY
FLEERS
FLEES
FLEET
FLEETED
FLEETER
FLEETEST
FLEETING
FLEETINGLY
FLEETINGNESS
FLEETINGNESSES
FLEETLY
FLEETNESS
FLEETNESSES
FLEETS
FLEHMEN
FLEHMENED
FLEHMENING
FLEHMENS
FLEISHIG
FLEMISH

FLEMISHED
FLEMISHES
FLEMISHING
FLENCH
FLENCHED
FLENCHES
FLENCHING
FLENSE
FLENSED
FLENSER
FLENSERS
FLENSES
FLENSING
FLESH
FLESHED
FLESHER
FLESHERS
FLESHES
FLESHIER
FLESHIEST
FLESHILY
FLESHINESS
FLESHINESSES
FLESHING
FLESHINGS
FLESHLESS
FLESHLIER
FLESHLIEST
FLESHLY
FLESHMENT
FLESHMENTS
FLESHPOT
FLESHPOTS
FLESHY
FLETCH
FLETCHED
FLETCHER
FLETCHERS
FLETCHES
FLETCHING
FLETCHINGS
FLEURON
FLEURONS
FLEURY
FLEW
FLEWS
FLEX
FLEXAGON
FLEXAGONS
FLEXED
FLEXES
FLEXIBILITIES
FLEXIBILITY
FLEXIBLE
FLEXIBLY
FLEXILE
FLEXING
FLEXION
FLEXIONAL
FLEXIONS
FLEXITARIAN
FLEXITARIANS
FLEXITIME
FLEXITIMES
FLEXOGRAPHIC
FLEXOGRAPHIES
FLEXOGRAPHY
FLEXOR
FLEXORS
FLEXTIME
FLEXTIMER
FLEXTIMERS
FLEXTIMES
FLEXUOSE
FLEXUOUS
FLEXURAL
FLEXURE
FLEXURES
FLEXWING
FLEXWINGS
FLEY
FLEYED
FLEYING
FLEYS
FLIBBERTIGIBBET
FLIC
FLICHTER
FLICHTERED
FLICHTERING
FLICHTERS
FLICK
FLICKABLE
FLICKED
FLICKER
FLICKERED
FLICKERIER
FLICKERIEST
FLICKERING
FLICKERINGLY
FLICKERS
FLICKERY
FLICKING
FLICKS
FLICS
FLIED
FLIER
FLIERS
FLIES
FLIEST
FLIGHT
FLIGHTED
FLIGHTIER
FLIGHTIEST
FLIGHTILY
FLIGHTINESS
FLIGHTINESSES
FLIGHTING
FLIGHTLESS
FLIGHTS
FLIGHTY
FLIMFLAM
FLIMFLAMMED
FLIMFLAMMER
FLIMFLAMMERIES
FLIMFLAMMERS
FLIMFLAMMERY
FLIMFLAMMING
FLIMFLAMS
FLIMSIER
FLIMSIES
FLIMSIEST
FLIMSILY
FLIMSINESS
FLIMSINESSES
FLIMSY
FLINCH
FLINCHED
FLINCHER
FLINCHERS
FLINCHES
FLINCHING
FLINDER
FLINDERS
FLING
FLINGER
FLINGERS
FLINGING
FLINGS
FLINKITE
FLINKITES
FLINT
FLINTED
FLINTHEAD
FLINTHEADS
FLINTIER
FLINTIEST
FLINTILY
FLINTINESS
FLINTINESSES
FLINTING
FLINTLIKE
FLINTLOCK
FLINTLOCKS
FLINTS
FLINTY
FLIP
FLIPBOOK
FLIPBOOKS
FLIPFLOP
FLIPFLOPPED
FLIPFLOPPING
FLIPFLOPS
FLIPPANCIES
FLIPPANCY
FLIPPANT
FLIPPANTLY
FLIPPED
FLIPPER
FLIPPERS
FLIPPEST
FLIPPIER
FLIPPIEST
FLIPPING
FLIPPY
FLIPS
FLIR
FLIRS
FLIRT
FLIRTATION
FLIRTATIONS
FLIRTATIOUS
FLIRTATIOUSLY
FLIRTATIOUSNESS
FLIRTED
FLIRTER
FLIRTERS
FLIRTIER
FLIRTIEST
FLIRTING
FLIRTS
FLIRTY
FLIT
FLITCH
FLITCHED
FLITCHES
FLITCHING
FLITE
FLITED
FLITES
FLITING
FLITS
FLITTED
FLITTER
FLITTERED
FLITTERING
FLITTERS
FLITTING
FLIVVER
FLIVVERS
FLIXWEED
FLIXWEEDS
FLOAT
FLOATABLE
FLOATAGE
FLOATAGES
FLOATATION
FLOATATIONS
FLOATED
FLOATEL
FLOATELS
FLOATER
FLOATERS
FLOATIER
FLOATIEST
FLOATING
FLOATPLANE
FLOATPLANES
FLOATS
FLOATY
FLOC
FLOCCED
FLOCCI
FLOCCING
FLOCCOSE
FLOCCULANT
FLOCCULANTS
FLOCCULATE
FLOCCULATED
FLOCCULATES
FLOCCULATING
FLOCCULATION
FLOCCULATIONS
FLOCCULATOR
FLOCCULATORS
FLOCCULE
FLOCCULENT
FLOCCULES
FLOCCULI
FLOCCULUS
FLOCCUS
FLOCK
FLOCKED
FLOCKIER
FLOCKIEST
FLOCKING

FLOCKINGS
FLOCKLESS
FLOCKS
FLOCKY
FLOCS
FLOE
FLOES
FLOG
FLOGGABLE
FLOGGED
FLOGGER
FLOGGERS
FLOGGING
FLOGGINGS
FLOGS
FLOKATI
FLOKATIS
FLONG
FLONGS
FLOOD
FLOODABLE
FLOODED
FLOODER
FLOODERS
FLOODGATE
FLOODGATES
FLOODING
FLOODINGS
FLOODLIGHT
FLOODLIGHTED
FLOODLIGHTING
FLOODLIGHTS
FLOODLIT
FLOODPLAIN
FLOODPLAINS
FLOODS
FLOODTIDE
FLOODTIDES
FLOODWALL
FLOODWALLS
FLOODWATER
FLOODWATERS
FLOODWAY
FLOODWAYS
FLOOEY
FLOOIE
FLOOR
FLOORAGE
FLOORAGES
FLOORBOARD
FLOORBOARDS
FLOORCLOTH
FLOORCLOTHS
FLOORED
FLOORER
FLOORERS
FLOORING
FLOORINGS
FLOORLESS
FLOORPAN
FLOORPANS
FLOORS
FLOORSHOW
FLOORSHOWS
FLOORWALKER
FLOORWALKERS
FLOOSIE
FLOOSIES
FLOOSY
FLOOZIE
FLOOZIES
FLOOZY
FLOP
FLOPHOUSE
FLOPHOUSES
FLOPOVER
FLOPOVERS
FLOPPED
FLOPPER
FLOPPERS
FLOPPIER
FLOPPIES
FLOPPIEST
FLOPPILY
FLOPPINESS
FLOPPINESSES
FLOPPING
FLOPPY
FLOPS
FLORA
FLORAE
FLORAL
FLORALLY
FLORALS
FLORAS
FLOREAT
FLOREATED
FLOREATING
FLOREATS
FLORENCE
FLORENCES
FLORESCENCE
FLORESCENCES
FLORESCENT
FLORET
FLORETS
FLORIATED
FLORIATION
FLORIATIONS
FLORIBUNDA
FLORIBUNDAS
FLORICANE
FLORICANES
FLORICULTURAL
FLORICULTURE
FLORICULTURES
FLORICULTURIST
FLORICULTURISTS
FLORID
FLORIDITIES
FLORIDITY
FLORIDLY
FLORIDNESS
FLORIDNESSES
FLORIFEROUS
FLORIFEROUSNESS
FLORIGEN
FLORIGENIC
FLORIGENS
FLORILEGIA
FLORILEGIUM
FLORIN
FLORINS
FLORIST
FLORISTIC
FLORISTICALLY
FLORISTRIES
FLORISTRY
FLORISTS
FLORUIT
FLORUITED
FLORUITING
FLORUITS
FLOSS
FLOSSED
FLOSSER
FLOSSERS
FLOSSES
FLOSSIE
FLOSSIER
FLOSSIES
FLOSSIEST
FLOSSILY
FLOSSING
FLOSSINGS
FLOSSY
FLOTA
FLOTAGE
FLOTAGES
FLOTAS
FLOTATION
FLOTATIONS
FLOTEL
FLOTELS
FLOTILLA
FLOTILLAS
FLOTSAM
FLOTSAMS
FLOUNCE
FLOUNCED
FLOUNCES
FLOUNCIER
FLOUNCIEST
FLOUNCING
FLOUNCINGS
FLOUNCY
FLOUNDER
FLOUNDERED
FLOUNDERING
FLOUNDERS
FLOUR
FLOURED
FLOURIER
FLOURIEST
FLOURING
FLOURISH
FLOURISHED
FLOURISHER
FLOURISHERS
FLOURISHES
FLOURISHING
FLOURISHINGLY
FLOURLESS
FLOURS
FLOURY
FLOUT
FLOUTED
FLOUTER
FLOUTERS
FLOUTING
FLOUTS
FLOW
FLOWABLE
FLOWAGE
FLOWAGES
FLOWCHART
FLOWCHARTING
FLOWCHARTINGS
FLOWCHARTS
FLOWED
FLOWER
FLOWERAGE
FLOWERAGES
FLOWERED
FLOWERER
FLOWERERS
FLOWERET
FLOWERETS
FLOWERETTE
FLOWERETTES
FLOWERFUL
FLOWERIER
FLOWERIEST
FLOWERILY
FLOWERINESS
FLOWERINESSES
FLOWERING
FLOWERLESS
FLOWERLIKE
FLOWERPOT
FLOWERPOTS
FLOWERS
FLOWERY
FLOWING
FLOWINGLY
FLOWMETER
FLOWMETERS
FLOWN
FLOWS
FLOWSTONE
FLOWSTONES
FLU
FLUB
FLUBBED
FLUBBER
FLUBBERS
FLUBBING
FLUBDUB
FLUBDUBS
FLUBS
FLUCONAZOLE
FLUCONAZOLES
FLUCTUANT
FLUCTUATE
FLUCTUATED
FLUCTUATES
FLUCTUATING
FLUCTUATION
FLUCTUATIONAL
FLUCTUATIONS
FLUE
FLUED
FLUEGELHORN
FLUEGELHORNS
FLUENCIES

FLUENCY
FLUENT
FLUENTLY
FLUERIC
FLUERICS
FLUES
FLUFF
FLUFFED
FLUFFER
FLUFFERS
FLUFFIER
FLUFFIEST
FLUFFILY
FLUFFINESS
FLUFFINESSES
FLUFFING
FLUFFS
FLUFFY
FLUGELHORN
FLUGELHORNIST
FLUGELHORNISTS
FLUGELHORNS
FLUID
FLUIDAL
FLUIDALLY
FLUIDEXTRACT
FLUIDEXTRACTS
FLUIDIC
FLUIDICS
FLUIDISE
FLUIDISED
FLUIDISES
FLUIDISING
FLUIDITIES
FLUIDITY
FLUIDIZATION
FLUIDIZATIONS
FLUIDIZE
FLUIDIZED
FLUIDIZER
FLUIDIZERS
FLUIDIZES
FLUIDIZING
FLUIDLIKE
FLUIDLY
FLUIDNESS
FLUIDNESSES
FLUIDRAM
FLUIDRAMS
FLUIDS
FLUISH
FLUKE
FLUKED
FLUKES
FLUKEY
FLUKIER
FLUKIEST
FLUKILY
FLUKINESS
FLUKINESSES
FLUKING
FLUKY
FLUME
FLUMED
FLUMES
FLUMING
FLUMMERIES
FLUMMERY
FLUMMOX
FLUMMOXED
FLUMMOXES
FLUMMOXING
FLUMP
FLUMPED
FLUMPING
FLUMPS
FLUNG
FLUNK
FLUNKED
FLUNKER
FLUNKERS
FLUNKEY
FLUNKEYS
FLUNKIE
FLUNKIES
FLUNKING
FLUNKS
FLUNKY
FLUNKYISM
FLUNKYISMS
FLUOR
FLUORENE
FLUORENES
FLUORESCE
FLUORESCED
FLUORESCEIN
FLUORESCEINS
FLUORESCENCE
FLUORESCENCES
FLUORESCENT
FLUORESCENTLY
FLUORESCENTS
FLUORESCER
FLUORESCERS
FLUORESCES
FLUORESCING
FLUORIC
FLUORID
FLUORIDATE
FLUORIDATED
FLUORIDATES
FLUORIDATING
FLUORIDATION
FLUORIDATIONS
FLUORIDE
FLUORIDES
FLUORIDS
FLUORIMETER
FLUORIMETERS
FLUORIMETRIC
FLUORIMETRIES
FLUORIMETRY
FLUORIN
FLUORINATE
FLUORINATED
FLUORINATES
FLUORINATING
FLUORINATION
FLUORINATIONS
FLUORINE
FLUORINES
FLUORINS
FLUORITE
FLUORITES
FLUOROCARBON
FLUOROCARBONS
FLUOROCHROME
FLUOROCHROMES
FLUOROGRAPHIC
FLUOROGRAPHIES
FLUOROGRAPHY
FLUOROMETER
FLUOROMETERS
FLUOROMETRIC
FLUOROMETRIES
FLUOROMETRY
FLUOROQUINOLONE
FLUOROSCOPE
FLUOROSCOPED
FLUOROSCOPES
FLUOROSCOPIC
FLUOROSCOPIES
FLUOROSCOPING
FLUOROSCOPIST
FLUOROSCOPISTS
FLUOROSCOPY
FLUOROSES
FLUOROSIS
FLUOROTIC
FLUOROURACIL
FLUOROURACILS
FLUORS
FLUORSPAR
FLUORSPARS
FLUOXETINE
FLUOXETINES
FLUPHENAZINE
FLUPHENAZINES
FLURRIED
FLURRIES
FLURRY
FLURRYING
FLUS
FLUSH
FLUSHABLE
FLUSHED
FLUSHER
FLUSHERS
FLUSHES
FLUSHEST
FLUSHING
FLUSHINGS
FLUSHNESS
FLUSHNESSES
FLUSTER
FLUSTERED
FLUSTEREDLY
FLUSTERING
FLUSTERS
FLUTE
FLUTED
FLUTELIKE
FLUTER
FLUTERS
FLUTES
FLUTEY
FLUTEYER
FLUTEYEST
FLUTIER
FLUTIEST
FLUTING
FLUTINGS
FLUTIST
FLUTISTS
FLUTTER
FLUTTERBOARD
FLUTTERBOARDS
FLUTTERED
FLUTTERER
FLUTTERERS
FLUTTERIER
FLUTTERIEST
FLUTTERING
FLUTTERS
FLUTTERY
FLUTY
FLUVIAL
FLUVIATILE
FLUX
FLUXED
FLUXES
FLUXGATE
FLUXGATES
FLUXING
FLUXION
FLUXIONAL
FLUXIONS
FLUYT
FLUYTS
FLY
FLYABLE
FLYAWAY
FLYAWAYS
FLYBELT
FLYBELTS
FLYBLEW
FLYBLOW
FLYBLOWING
FLYBLOWN
FLYBLOWS
FLYBOAT
FLYBOATS
FLYBOY
FLYBOYS
FLYBRIDGE
FLYBRIDGES
FLYBY
FLYBYS
FLYCATCHER
FLYCATCHERS
FLYER
FLYERS
FLYING
FLYINGS
FLYLEAF
FLYLEAVES
FLYLESS
FLYLINE
FLYLINES
FLYMAN
FLYMEN
FLYOFF
FLYOFFS
FLYOVER
FLYOVERS

FLYPAPER
FLYPAPERS
FLYPAST
FLYPASTS
FLYRODDER
FLYRODDERS
FLYSCH
FLYSCHES
FLYSHEET
FLYSHEETS
FLYSPECK
FLYSPECKED
FLYSPECKING
FLYSPECKS
FLYSWATTER
FLYSWATTERS
FLYTE
FLYTED
FLYTES
FLYTIER
FLYTIERS
FLYTING
FLYTINGS
FLYTRAP
FLYTRAPS
FLYWAY
FLYWAYS
FLYWEIGHT
FLYWEIGHTS
FLYWHEEL
FLYWHEELS
FOAL
FOALED
FOALING
FOALINGS
FOALS
FOAM
FOAMABLE
FOAMED
FOAMER
FOAMERS
FOAMFLOWER
FOAMFLOWERS
FOAMIER
FOAMIEST
FOAMILY
FOAMINESS
FOAMINESSES
FOAMING
FOAMLESS
FOAMLIKE
FOAMS
FOAMY
FOB
FOBBED
FOBBING
FOBS
FOCACCIA
FOCACCIAS
FOCAL
FOCALISE
FOCALISED
FOCALISES
FOCALISING
FOCALIZATION
FOCALIZATIONS
FOCALIZE
FOCALIZED
FOCALIZES
FOCALIZING
FOCALLY
FOCI
FOCUS
FOCUSABLE
FOCUSED
FOCUSER
FOCUSERS
FOCUSES
FOCUSING
FOCUSLESS
FOCUSSED
FOCUSSES
FOCUSSING
FODDER
FODDERED
FODDERING
FODDERS
FODGEL
FOE
FOEHN
FOEHNS
FOEMAN
FOEMEN
FOES
FOETAL
FOETID
FOETIDLY
FOETOR
FOETORS
FOETUS
FOETUSES
FOG
FOGBOUND
FOGBOW
FOGBOWS
FOGDOG
FOGDOGS
FOGEY
FOGEYDOM
FOGEYDOMS
FOGEYISH
FOGEYISM
FOGEYISMS
FOGEYS
FOGFRUIT
FOGFRUITS
FOGGAGE
FOGGAGES
FOGGED
FOGGER
FOGGERS
FOGGIER
FOGGIEST
FOGGILY
FOGGINESS
FOGGINESSES
FOGGING
FOGGINGS
FOGGY
FOGHORN
FOGHORNS
FOGIE
FOGIES
FOGLESS
FOGLIGHT
FOGLIGHTS
FOGS
FOGY
FOGYDOM
FOGYDOMS
FOGYISH
FOGYISM
FOGYISMS
FOH
FOHN
FOHNS
FOIBLE
FOIBLES
FOIL
FOILABLE
FOILED
FOILING
FOILIST
FOILISTS
FOILS
FOILSMAN
FOILSMEN
FOIN
FOINED
FOINING
FOINS
FOISON
FOISONS
FOIST
FOISTED
FOISTING
FOISTS
FOLACIN
FOLACINS
FOLATE
FOLATES
FOLD
FOLDABLE
FOLDAWAY
FOLDAWAYS
FOLDBOAT
FOLDBOATS
FOLDED
FOLDER
FOLDEROL
FOLDEROLS
FOLDERS
FOLDING
FOLDOUT
FOLDOUTS
FOLDS
FOLDUP
FOLDUPS
FOLEY
FOLEYS
FOLIA
FOLIACEOUS
FOLIAGE
FOLIAGED
FOLIAGES
FOLIAR
FOLIATE
FOLIATED
FOLIATES
FOLIATING
FOLIATION
FOLIATIONS
FOLIC
FOLIO
FOLIOED
FOLIOING
FOLIOLATE
FOLIOS
FOLIOSE
FOLIOUS
FOLIUM
FOLIUMS
FOLK
FOLKIE
FOLKIER
FOLKIES
FOLKIEST
FOLKISH
FOLKISHNESS
FOLKISHNESSES
FOLKLIFE
FOLKLIFES
FOLKLIKE
FOLKLIVES
FOLKLORE
FOLKLORES
FOLKLORIC
FOLKLORISH
FOLKLORIST
FOLKLORISTIC
FOLKLORISTS
FOLKMOOT
FOLKMOOTS
FOLKMOT
FOLKMOTE
FOLKMOTES
FOLKMOTS
FOLKS
FOLKSIER
FOLKSIEST
FOLKSILY
FOLKSINESS
FOLKSINESSES
FOLKSINGER
FOLKSINGERS
FOLKSINGING
FOLKSINGINGS
FOLKSONG
FOLKSONGS
FOLKSY
FOLKTALE
FOLKTALES
FOLKWAY
FOLKWAYS
FOLKY
FOLLES
FOLLICLE
FOLLICLES
FOLLICULAR
FOLLICULITIS
FOLLICULITISES
FOLLIES
FOLLIS
FOLLOW
FOLLOWED

FOLLOWER
FOLLOWERS
FOLLOWERSHIP
FOLLOWERSHIPS
FOLLOWING
FOLLOWINGS
FOLLOWS
FOLLOWUP
FOLLOWUPS
FOLLY
FOMENT
FOMENTATION
FOMENTATIONS
FOMENTED
FOMENTER
FOMENTERS
FOMENTING
FOMENTS
FOMITE
FOMITES
FON
FOND
FONDANT
FONDANTS
FONDED
FONDER
FONDEST
FONDING
FONDLE
FONDLED
FONDLER
FONDLERS
FONDLES
FONDLING
FONDLINGS
FONDLY
FONDNESS
FONDNESSES
FONDS
FONDU
FONDUE
FONDUED
FONDUEING
FONDUES
FONDUING
FONDUS
FONS
FONT
FONTAL
FONTANEL
FONTANELLE
FONTANELLES
FONTANELS
FONTINA
FONTINAS
FONTS
FOO
FOOD
FOODERIES
FOODERY
FOODIE
FOODIES
FOODLAND
FOODLANDS
FOODLESS
FOODLESSNESS
FOODLESSNESSES
FOODS
FOODSTUFF
FOODSTUFFS
FOODWAYS
FOOFARAW
FOOFARAWS
FOOL
FOOLED
FOOLERIES
FOOLERY
FOOLFISH
FOOLFISHES
FOOLHARDIER
FOOLHARDIEST
FOOLHARDILY
FOOLHARDINESS
FOOLHARDINESSES
FOOLHARDY
FOOLING
FOOLISH
FOOLISHER
FOOLISHEST
FOOLISHLY
FOOLISHNESS
FOOLISHNESSES
FOOLPROOF
FOOLS
FOOLSCAP
FOOLSCAPS
FOOS
FOOSBALL
FOOSBALLS
FOOT
FOOTAGE
FOOTAGES
FOOTBAG
FOOTBAGS
FOOTBALL
FOOTBALLER
FOOTBALLERS
FOOTBALLING
FOOTBALLS
FOOTBATH
FOOTBATHS
FOOTBED
FOOTBEDS
FOOTBOARD
FOOTBOARDS
FOOTBOY
FOOTBOYS
FOOTBRIDGE
FOOTBRIDGES
FOOTCLOTH
FOOTCLOTHS
FOOTDRAGGER
FOOTDRAGGERS
FOOTED
FOOTER
FOOTERS
FOOTFALL
FOOTFALLS
FOOTFAULT
FOOTFAULTED
FOOTFAULTING
FOOTFAULTS
FOOTGEAR
FOOTGEARS
FOOTHILL
FOOTHILLS
FOOTHOLD
FOOTHOLDS
FOOTIE
FOOTIER
FOOTIES
FOOTIEST
FOOTING
FOOTINGS
FOOTLAMBERT
FOOTLAMBERTS
FOOTLE
FOOTLED
FOOTLER
FOOTLERS
FOOTLES
FOOTLESS
FOOTLESSLY
FOOTLESSNESS
FOOTLESSNESSES
FOOTLIGHT
FOOTLIGHTS
FOOTLIKE
FOOTLING
FOOTLOCKER
FOOTLOCKERS
FOOTLONG
FOOTLONGS
FOOTLOOSE
FOOTMAN
FOOTMARK
FOOTMARKS
FOOTMEN
FOOTNOTE
FOOTNOTED
FOOTNOTES
FOOTNOTING
FOOTPACE
FOOTPACES
FOOTPAD
FOOTPADS
FOOTPATH
FOOTPATHS
FOOTPRINT
FOOTPRINTS
FOOTRACE
FOOTRACES
FOOTREST
FOOTRESTS
FOOTROPE
FOOTROPES
FOOTS
FOOTSIE
FOOTSIES
FOOTSLOG
FOOTSLOGGED
FOOTSLOGGER
FOOTSLOGGERS
FOOTSLOGGING
FOOTSLOGS
FOOTSORE
FOOTSORENESS
FOOTSORENESSES
FOOTSTALK
FOOTSTALKS
FOOTSTALL
FOOTSTALLS
FOOTSTEP
FOOTSTEPS
FOOTSTOCK
FOOTSTOCKS
FOOTSTONE
FOOTSTONES
FOOTSTOOL
FOOTSTOOLS
FOOTSY
FOOTWALL
FOOTWALLS
FOOTWAY
FOOTWAYS
FOOTWEAR
FOOTWELL
FOOTWELLS
FOOTWORK
FOOTWORKS
FOOTWORN
FOOTY
FOOZLE
FOOZLED
FOOZLER
FOOZLERS
FOOZLES
FOOZLING
FOP
FOPPED
FOPPERIES
FOPPERY
FOPPING
FOPPISH
FOPPISHLY
FOPPISHNESS
FOPPISHNESSES
FOPS
FOR
FORA
FORAGE
FORAGED
FORAGER
FORAGERS
FORAGES
FORAGING
FORAM
FORAMEN
FORAMENS
FORAMINA
FORAMINAL
FORAMINIFER
FORAMINIFERA
FORAMINIFERAL
FORAMINIFERAN
FORAMINIFERANS
FORAMINIFERS
FORAMINOUS
FORAMS
FORASMUCH
FORAY
FORAYED
FORAYER
FORAYERS
FORAYING

FORAYS
FORB
FORBAD
FORBADE
FORBARE
FORBEAR
FORBEARANCE
FORBEARANCES
FORBEARER
FORBEARERS
FORBEARING
FORBEARS
FORBID
FORBIDAL
FORBIDALS
FORBIDDANCE
FORBIDDANCES
FORBIDDEN
FORBIDDER
FORBIDDERS
FORBIDDING
FORBIDDINGLY
FORBIDS
FORBODE
FORBODED
FORBODES
FORBODING
FORBORE
FORBORNE
FORBS
FORBY
FORBYE
FORCE
FORCEABLE
FORCED
FORCEDLY
FORCEFUL
FORCEFULLY
FORCEFULNESS
FORCEFULNESSES
FORCELESS
FORCEMEAT
FORCEMEATS
FORCEOUT
FORCEOUTS
FORCEPS
FORCEPSLIKE
FORCER
FORCERS
FORCES
FORCIBLE
FORCIBLENESS
FORCIBLENESSES
FORCIBLY
FORCING
FORCIPES
FORD
FORDABLE
FORDED
FORDID
FORDING
FORDLESS
FORDO
FORDOES
FORDOING
FORDONE
FORDS
FORE
FOREARM
FOREARMED
FOREARMING
FOREARMS
FOREBAY
FOREBAYS
FOREBEAR
FOREBEARER
FOREBEARERS
FOREBEARS
FOREBODE
FOREBODED
FOREBODER
FOREBODERS
FOREBODES
FOREBODIES
FOREBODING
FOREBODINGLY
FOREBODINGNESS
FOREBODINGS
FOREBODY
FOREBOOM
FOREBOOMS
FOREBRAIN
FOREBRAINS
FOREBY
FOREBYE
FORECADDIE
FORECADDIES
FORECAST
FORECASTABLE
FORECASTED
FORECASTER
FORECASTERS
FORECASTING
FORECASTLE
FORECASTLES
FORECASTS
FORECHECK
FORECHECKED
FORECHECKER
FORECHECKERS
FORECHECKING
FORECHECKS
FORECLOSE
FORECLOSED
FORECLOSES
FORECLOSING
FORECLOSURE
FORECLOSURES
FORECOURT
FORECOURTS
FOREDATE
FOREDATED
FOREDATES
FOREDATING
FOREDECK
FOREDECKS
FOREDID
FOREDO
FOREDOES
FOREDOING
FOREDONE
FOREDOOM
FOREDOOMED
FOREDOOMING
FOREDOOMS
FOREFACE
FOREFACES
FOREFATHER
FOREFATHERS
FOREFEEL
FOREFEELING
FOREFEELS
FOREFEET
FOREFELT
FOREFEND
FOREFENDED
FOREFENDING
FOREFENDS
FOREFINGER
FOREFINGERS
FOREFOOT
FOREFRONT
FOREFRONTS
FOREGATHER
FOREGATHERED
FOREGATHERING
FOREGATHERS
FOREGO
FOREGOER
FOREGOERS
FOREGOES
FOREGOING
FOREGONE
FOREGROUND
FOREGROUNDED
FOREGROUNDING
FOREGROUNDS
FOREGUT
FOREGUTS
FOREHAND
FOREHANDED
FOREHANDEDLY
FOREHANDEDNESS
FOREHANDS
FOREHEAD
FOREHEADS
FOREHOOF
FOREHOOFS
FOREHOOVES
FOREIGN
FOREIGNER
FOREIGNERS
FOREIGNISM
FOREIGNISMS
FOREIGNNESS
FOREIGNNESSES
FOREJUDGE
FOREJUDGED
FOREJUDGES
FOREJUDGING
FOREKNEW
FOREKNOW
FOREKNOWING
FOREKNOWLEDGE
FOREKNOWLEDGES
FOREKNOWN
FOREKNOWS
FORELADIES
FORELADY
FORELAND
FORELANDS
FORELEG
FORELEGS
FORELIMB
FORELIMBS
FORELOCK
FORELOCKED
FORELOCKING
FORELOCKS
FOREMAN
FOREMANSHIP
FOREMANSHIPS
FOREMAST
FOREMASTS
FOREMEN
FOREMILK
FOREMILKS
FOREMOST
FOREMOTHER
FOREMOTHERS
FORENAME
FORENAMED
FORENAMES
FORENOON
FORENOONS
FORENSIC
FORENSICALLY
FORENSICS
FOREORDAIN
FOREORDAINED
FOREORDAINING
FOREORDAINS
FOREORDINATION
FOREORDINATIONS
FOREPART
FOREPARTS
FOREPASSED
FOREPAST
FOREPAW
FOREPAWS
FOREPEAK
FOREPEAKS
FOREPLAY
FOREPLAYS
FOREQUARTER
FOREQUARTERS
FORERAN
FORERANK
FORERANKS
FOREREACH
FOREREACHED
FOREREACHES
FOREREACHING
FORERUN
FORERUNNER
FORERUNNERS
FORERUNNING
FORERUNS
FORES
FORESAID
FORESAIL
FORESAILS
FORESAW
FORESEE
FORESEEABILITY

FORESEEABLE
FORESEEING
FORESEEN
FORESEER
FORESEERS
FORESEES
FORESHADOW
FORESHADOWED
FORESHADOWER
FORESHADOWERS
FORESHADOWING
FORESHADOWS
FORESHANK
FORESHANKS
FORESHEET
FORESHEETS
FORESHOCK
FORESHOCKS
FORESHORE
FORESHORES
FORESHORTEN
FORESHORTENED
FORESHORTENING
FORESHORTENS
FORESHOW
FORESHOWED
FORESHOWING
FORESHOWN
FORESHOWS
FORESIDE
FORESIDES
FORESIGHT
FORESIGHTED
FORESIGHTEDLY
FORESIGHTEDNESS
FORESIGHTFUL
FORESIGHTS
FORESKIN
FORESKINS
FORESPAKE
FORESPEAK
FORESPEAKING
FORESPEAKS
FORESPOKE
FORESPOKEN
FOREST
FORESTAGE
FORESTAGES
FORESTAL
FORESTALL
FORESTALLED
FORESTALLER
FORESTALLERS
FORESTALLING
FORESTALLMENT
FORESTALLMENTS
FORESTALLS
FORESTATION
FORESTATIONS
FORESTAY
FORESTAYS
FORESTAYSAIL
FORESTAYSAILS
FORESTED
FORESTER
FORESTERS
FORESTIAL
FORESTING
FORESTLAND
FORESTLANDS
FORESTRIES
FORESTRY
FORESTS
FORESWEAR
FORESWEARING
FORESWEARS
FORESWORE
FORESWORN
FORETASTE
FORETASTED
FORETASTES
FORETASTING
FORETEETH
FORETELL
FORETELLER
FORETELLERS
FORETELLING
FORETELLS
FORETHOUGHT
FORETHOUGHTFUL
FORETHOUGHTS
FORETIME
FORETIMES
FORETOKEN
FORETOKENED
FORETOKENING
FORETOKENS
FORETOLD
FORETOOTH
FORETOP
FORETOPMAN
FORETOPMEN
FORETOPS
FOREVER
FOREVERMORE
FOREVERNESS
FOREVERNESSES
FOREVERS
FOREWARN
FOREWARNED
FOREWARNING
FOREWARNS
FOREWENT
FOREWING
FOREWINGS
FOREWOMAN
FOREWOMEN
FOREWORD
FOREWORDS
FOREWORN
FOREX
FOREXES
FOREYARD
FOREYARDS
FORFEIT
FORFEITABLE
FORFEITED
FORFEITER
FORFEITERS
FORFEITING
FORFEITS
FORFEITURE
FORFEITURES
FORFEND
FORFENDED
FORFENDING
FORFENDS
FORFICATE
FORGAT
FORGATHER
FORGATHERED
FORGATHERING
FORGATHERS
FORGAVE
FORGE
FORGEABILITIES
FORGEABILITY
FORGEABLE
FORGED
FORGER
FORGERIES
FORGERS
FORGERY
FORGES
FORGET
FORGETFUL
FORGETFULLY
FORGETFULNESS
FORGETFULNESSES
FORGETIVE
FORGETS
FORGETTABLE
FORGETTER
FORGETTERS
FORGETTING
FORGING
FORGINGS
FORGIVABLE
FORGIVABLY
FORGIVE
FORGIVEN
FORGIVENESS
FORGIVENESSES
FORGIVER
FORGIVERS
FORGIVES
FORGIVING
FORGIVINGLY
FORGIVINGNESS
FORGIVINGNESSES
FORGO
FORGOER
FORGOERS
FORGOES
FORGOING
FORGONE
FORGOT
FORGOTTEN
FORINT
FORINTS
FORJUDGE
FORJUDGED
FORJUDGES
FORJUDGING
FORK
FORKBALL
FORKBALLS
FORKED
FORKEDLY
FORKER
FORKERS
FORKFUL
FORKFULS
FORKIER
FORKIEST
FORKINESS
FORKINESSES
FORKING
FORKLESS
FORKLIFT
FORKLIFTED
FORKLIFTING
FORKLIFTS
FORKLIKE
FORKS
FORKSFUL
FORKY
FORLORN
FORLORNER
FORLORNEST
FORLORNLY
FORLORNNESS
FORLORNNESSES
FORM
FORMABILITIES
FORMABILITY
FORMABLE
FORMABLY
FORMAL
FORMALDEHYDE
FORMALDEHYDES
FORMALIN
FORMALINS
FORMALISATION
FORMALISATIONS
FORMALISE
FORMALISED
FORMALISES
FORMALISING
FORMALISM
FORMALISMS
FORMALIST
FORMALISTIC
FORMALISTS
FORMALITIES
FORMALITY
FORMALIZABLE
FORMALIZATION
FORMALIZATIONS
FORMALIZE
FORMALIZED
FORMALIZER
FORMALIZERS
FORMALIZES
FORMALIZING
FORMALLY
FORMALNESS
FORMALNESSES
FORMALS
FORMAMIDE
FORMAMIDES
FORMANT
FORMANTS
FORMAT
FORMATE

FORMATES
FORMATION
FORMATIONS
FORMATIVE
FORMATIVELY
FORMATIVES
FORMATS
FORMATTED
FORMATTER
FORMATTERS
FORMATTING
FORME
FORMED
FORMEE
FORMER
FORMERLY
FORMERS
FORMES
FORMFITTING
FORMFUL
FORMIC
FORMICA
FORMICARIES
FORMICARY
FORMICAS
FORMIDABILITIES
FORMIDABILITY
FORMIDABLE
FORMIDABLENESS
FORMIDABLY
FORMING
FORMLESS
FORMLESSLY
FORMLESSNESS
FORMLESSNESSES
FORMOL
FORMOLS
FORMS
FORMULA
FORMULAE
FORMULAIC
FORMULAICALLY
FORMULARIES
FORMULARIZATION
FORMULARIZE
FORMULARIZED
FORMULARIZER
FORMULARIZERS
FORMULARIZES
FORMULARIZING
FORMULARY
FORMULAS
FORMULATE
FORMULATED
FORMULATES
FORMULATING
FORMULATION
FORMULATIONS
FORMULATOR
FORMULATORS
FORMULISM
FORMULISMS
FORMULIST
FORMULISTS
FORMULIZE
FORMULIZED
FORMULIZES
FORMULIZING
FORMWORK
FORMWORKS
FORMYL
FORMYLS
FORNENT
FORNICAL
FORNICATE
FORNICATED
FORNICATES
FORNICATING
FORNICATION
FORNICATIONS
FORNICATOR
FORNICATORS
FORNICES
FORNIX
FORRADER
FORRARDER
FORRIT
FORSAKE
FORSAKEN
FORSAKER
FORSAKERS
FORSAKES
FORSAKING
FORSOOK
FORSOOTH
FORSPENT
FORSWEAR
FORSWEARING
FORSWEARS
FORSWORE
FORSWORN
FORSYTHIA
FORSYTHIAS
FORT
FORTALICE
FORTALICES
FORTE
FORTEPIANO
FORTEPIANOS
FORTES
FORTH
FORTHCOMING
FORTHRIGHT
FORTHRIGHTLY
FORTHRIGHTNESS
FORTHRIGHTS
FORTHWITH
FORTIES
FORTIETH
FORTIETHS
FORTIFICATION
FORTIFICATIONS
FORTIFIED
FORTIFIER
FORTIFIERS
FORTIFIES
FORTIFY
FORTIFYING
FORTIS
FORTISSIMI
FORTISSIMO
FORTISSIMOS
FORTITUDE
FORTITUDES
FORTNIGHT
FORTNIGHTLIES
FORTNIGHTLY
FORTNIGHTS
FORTRESS
FORTRESSED
FORTRESSES
FORTRESSING
FORTRESSLIKE
FORTS
FORTUITIES
FORTUITOUS
FORTUITOUSLY
FORTUITOUSNESS
FORTUITY
FORTUNATE
FORTUNATELY
FORTUNATENESS
FORTUNATENESSES
FORTUNATES
FORTUNE
FORTUNED
FORTUNES
FORTUNING
FORTY
FORTYISH
FORUM
FORUMS
FORWARD
FORWARDED
FORWARDER
FORWARDERS
FORWARDEST
FORWARDING
FORWARDLY
FORWARDNESS
FORWARDNESSES
FORWARDS
FORWENT
FORWHY
FORWORN
FORZANDI
FORZANDO
FORZANDOS
FOSCARNET
FOSCARNETS
FOSS
FOSSA
FOSSAE
FOSSAS
FOSSATE
FOSSE
FOSSES
FOSSETTE
FOSSETTES
FOSSICK
FOSSICKED
FOSSICKER
FOSSICKERS
FOSSICKING
FOSSICKS
FOSSIL
FOSSILIFEROUS
FOSSILISATION
FOSSILISATIONS
FOSSILISE
FOSSILISED
FOSSILISES
FOSSILISING
FOSSILIZATION
FOSSILIZATIONS
FOSSILIZE
FOSSILIZED
FOSSILIZES
FOSSILIZING
FOSSILS
FOSSORIAL
FOSTER
FOSTERAGE
FOSTERAGES
FOSTERED
FOSTERER
FOSTERERS
FOSTERING
FOSTERLING
FOSTERLINGS
FOSTERS
FOU
FOUETTE
FOUETTES
FOUGHT
FOUGHTEN
FOUL
FOULARD
FOULARDS
FOULBROOD
FOULBROODS
FOULED
FOULER
FOULEST
FOULING
FOULINGS
FOULLY
FOULMOUTHED
FOULNESS
FOULNESSES
FOULS
FOUND
FOUNDATION
FOUNDATIONAL
FOUNDATIONALLY
FOUNDATIONLESS
FOUNDATIONS
FOUNDED
FOUNDER
FOUNDERED
FOUNDERING
FOUNDERS
FOUNDING
FOUNDLING
FOUNDLINGS
FOUNDRIES
FOUNDRY
FOUNDS
FOUNT
FOUNTAIN
FOUNTAINED
FOUNTAINHEAD
FOUNTAINHEADS
FOUNTAINING
FOUNTAINS

FOUNTS
FOUR
FOURCHEE
FOURDRINIER
FOURDRINIERS
FOUREYED
FOURFOLD
FOURGON
FOURGONS
FOURPENCE
FOURPENCES
FOURPENNIES
FOURPENNY
FOURPLEX
FOURPLEXES
FOURRAGERE
FOURRAGERES
FOURS
FOURSCORE
FOURSOME
FOURSOMES
FOURSQUARE
FOURTEEN
FOURTEENER
FOURTEENERS
FOURTEENS
FOURTEENTH
FOURTEENTHS
FOURTH
FOURTHLY
FOURTHS
FOUSTIER
FOUSTIEST
FOUSTY
FOVEA
FOVEAE
FOVEAL
FOVEAS
FOVEATE
FOVEATED
FOVEIFORM
FOVEOLA
FOVEOLAE
FOVEOLAR
FOVEOLAS
FOVEOLATE
FOVEOLE
FOVEOLES
FOVEOLET
FOVEOLETS
FOWL
FOWLED
FOWLER

FOWLERS
FOWLING
FOWLINGS
FOWLPOX
FOWLPOXES
FOWLS
FOX
FOXBERRIES
FOXBERRY
FOXED
FOXES
FOXFIRE
FOXFIRES
FOXFISH
FOXFISHES
FOXGLOVE
FOXGLOVES
FOXHOLE
FOXHOLES
FOXHOUND
FOXHOUNDS
FOXHUNT
FOXHUNTED
FOXHUNTER
FOXHUNTERS
FOXHUNTING
FOXHUNTINGS
FOXHUNTS
FOXIER
FOXIEST
FOXILY
FOXINESS
FOXINESSES
FOXING
FOXINGS
FOXLIKE
FOXSKIN
FOXSKINS
FOXTAIL
FOXTAILS
FOXTROT
FOXTROTS
FOXTROTTED
FOXTROTTING
FOXY
FOY
FOYER
FOYERS
FOYS
FOZIER
FOZIEST
FOZINESS
FOZINESSES

FOZY
FRABJOUS
FRACAS
FRACASES
FRACK
FRACKED
FRACKING
FRACKINGS
FRACKS
FRACTAL
FRACTALS
FRACTED
FRACTI
FRACTION
FRACTIONAL
FRACTIONALIZE
FRACTIONALIZED
FRACTIONALIZES
FRACTIONALIZING
FRACTIONALLY
FRACTIONATE
FRACTIONATED
FRACTIONATES
FRACTIONATING
FRACTIONATION
FRACTIONATIONS
FRACTIONATOR
FRACTIONATORS
FRACTIONED
FRACTIONING
FRACTIONS
FRACTIOUS
FRACTIOUSLY
FRACTIOUSNESS
FRACTIOUSNESSES
FRACTUR
FRACTURAL
FRACTURE
FRACTURED
FRACTURER
FRACTURERS
FRACTURES
FRACTURING
FRACTURS
FRACTUS
FRAE
FRAENA
FRAENUM
FRAENUMS
FRAG
FRAGGED
FRAGGING
FRAGGINGS

FRAGILE
FRAGILELY
FRAGILITIES
FRAGILITY
FRAGMENT
FRAGMENTAL
FRAGMENTALLY
FRAGMENTARILY
FRAGMENTARINESS
FRAGMENTARY
FRAGMENTATE
FRAGMENTATED
FRAGMENTATES
FRAGMENTATING
FRAGMENTATION
FRAGMENTATIONS
FRAGMENTED
FRAGMENTING
FRAGMENTIZE
FRAGMENTIZED
FRAGMENTIZES
FRAGMENTIZING
FRAGMENTS
FRAGRANCE
FRAGRANCES
FRAGRANCIES
FRAGRANCY
FRAGRANT
FRAGRANTLY
FRAGS
FRAIL
FRAILER
FRAILEST
FRAILLY
FRAILNESS
FRAILNESSES
FRAILS
FRAILTIES
FRAILTY
FRAISE
FRAISES
FRAKTUR
FRAKTURS
FRAMABLE
FRAMBESIA
FRAMBESIAS
FRAMBOISE
FRAMBOISES
FRAME
FRAMEABLE
FRAMED
FRAMELESS
FRAMER

FRAMERS
FRAMES
FRAMESHIFT
FRAMESHIFTS
FRAMEWORK
FRAMEWORKS
FRAMING
FRAMINGS
FRANC
FRANCHISE
FRANCHISED
FRANCHISEE
FRANCHISEES
FRANCHISER
FRANCHISERS
FRANCHISES
FRANCHISING
FRANCHISOR
FRANCHISORS
FRANCISE
FRANCISED
FRANCISES
FRANCISING
FRANCIUM
FRANCIUMS
FRANCIZE
FRANCIZED
FRANCIZES
FRANCIZING
FRANCOLIN
FRANCOLINS
FRANCOPHONE
FRANCOPHONES
FRANCS
FRANGIBILITIES
FRANGIBILITY
FRANGIBLE
FRANGIPANE
FRANGIPANES
FRANGIPANI
FRANGIPANNI
FRANGLAIS
FRANK
FRANKABLE
FRANKED
FRANKER
FRANKERS
FRANKEST
FRANKFORT
FRANKFORTS
FRANKFURT
FRANKFURTER
FRANKFURTERS

FRANKFURTS
FRANKINCENSE
FRANKINCENSES
FRANKING
FRANKLIN
FRANKLINITE
FRANKLINITES
FRANKLINS
FRANKLY
FRANKNESS
FRANKNESSES
FRANKPLEDGE
FRANKPLEDGES
FRANKS
FRANKUM
FRANKUMS
FRANSERIA
FRANSERIAS
FRANTIC
FRANTICALLY
FRANTICLY
FRANTICNESS
FRANTICNESSES
FRAP
FRAPPE
FRAPPED
FRAPPES
FRAPPING
FRAPS
FRASCATI
FRASCATIS
FRASS
FRASSES
FRAT
FRATER
FRATERNAL
FRATERNALISM
FRATERNALISMS
FRATERNALLY
FRATERNISATION
FRATERNISATIONS
FRATERNISE
FRATERNISED
FRATERNISER
FRATERNISERS
FRATERNISES
FRATERNISING
FRATERNITIES
FRATERNITY
FRATERNIZATION
FRATERNIZATIONS
FRATERNIZE
FRATERNIZED
FRATERNIZER
FRATERNIZERS
FRATERNIZES
FRATERNIZING
FRATERS
FRATRICIDAL
FRATRICIDE
FRATRICIDES
FRATS
FRAUD
FRAUDS
FRAUDSTER
FRAUDSTERS
FRAUDULENCE
FRAUDULENCES
FRAUDULENT
FRAUDULENTLY
FRAUDULENTNESS
FRAUGHT
FRAUGHTED
FRAUGHTING
FRAUGHTS
FRAULEIN
FRAULEINS
FRAXINELLA
FRAXINELLAS
FRAY
FRAYED
FRAYING
FRAYINGS
FRAYS
FRAZIL
FRAZILS
FRAZZLE
FRAZZLED
FRAZZLES
FRAZZLING
FREAK
FREAKED
FREAKIER
FREAKIEST
FREAKILY
FREAKINESS
FREAKINESSES
FREAKING
FREAKISH
FREAKISHLY
FREAKISHNESS
FREAKISHNESSES
FREAKOUT
FREAKOUTS
FREAKS
FREAKY
FRECKLE
FRECKLED
FRECKLES
FRECKLIER
FRECKLIEST
FRECKLING
FRECKLY
FREE
FREEBASE
FREEBASED
FREEBASER
FREEBASERS
FREEBASES
FREEBASING
FREEBEE
FREEBEES
FREEBIE
FREEBIES
FREEBOARD
FREEBOARDS
FREEBOOT
FREEBOOTED
FREEBOOTER
FREEBOOTERS
FREEBOOTING
FREEBOOTS
FREEBORN
FREED
FREEDMAN
FREEDMEN
FREEDOM
FREEDOMS
FREEDWOMAN
FREEDWOMEN
FREEFORM
FREEGAN
FREEGANISM
FREEGANISMS
FREEGANS
FREEHAND
FREEHANDED
FREEHANDEDLY
FREEHANDEDNESS
FREEHEARTED
FREEHEARTEDLY
FREEHOLD
FREEHOLDER
FREEHOLDERS
FREEHOLDS
FREEING
FREELANCE
FREELANCED
FREELANCER
FREELANCERS
FREELANCES
FREELANCING
FREELOAD
FREELOADED
FREELOADER
FREELOADERS
FREELOADING
FREELOADS
FREELY
FREEMAN
FREEMARTIN
FREEMARTINS
FREEMASON
FREEMASONRIES
FREEMASONRY
FREEMASONS
FREEMEN
FREENESS
FREENESSES
FREER
FREERIDE
FREERIDES
FREERS
FREES
FREESIA
FREESIAS
FREEST
FREESTANDING
FREESTONE
FREESTONES
FREESTYLE
FREESTYLER
FREESTYLERS
FREESTYLES
FREETHINKER
FREETHINKERS
FREETHINKING
FREETHINKINGS
FREEWARE
FREEWARES
FREEWAY
FREEWAYS
FREEWHEEL
FREEWHEELED
FREEWHEELER
FREEWHEELERS
FREEWHEELING
FREEWHEELINGLY
FREEWHEELS
FREEWILL
FREEWRITE
FREEWRITES
FREEWRITING
FREEWRITINGS
FREEWRITTEN
FREEWROTE
FREEZABLE
FREEZE
FREEZER
FREEZERS
FREEZES
FREEZING
FREEZINGLY
FREEZINGS
FREIGHT
FREIGHTAGE
FREIGHTAGES
FREIGHTED
FREIGHTER
FREIGHTERS
FREIGHTING
FREIGHTS
FREMD
FREMITUS
FREMITUSES
FRENA
FRENCH
FRENCHED
FRENCHES
FRENCHIFICATION
FRENCHIFIED
FRENCHIFIES
FRENCHIFY
FRENCHIFYING
FRENCHING
FRENEMIES
FRENEMY
FRENETIC
FRENETICALLY
FRENETICISM
FRENETICISMS
FRENETICS
FRENULA
FRENULAR
FRENULUM
FRENULUMS
FRENUM
FRENUMS
FRENZIED
FRENZIEDLY
FRENZIES
FRENZILY
FRENZY
FRENZYING
FREON

FREONS
FREQUENCE
FREQUENCES
FREQUENCIES
FREQUENCY
FREQUENT
FREQUENTATION
FREQUENTATIONS
FREQUENTATIVE
FREQUENTATIVES
FREQUENTED
FREQUENTER
FREQUENTERS
FREQUENTEST
FREQUENTING
FREQUENTLY
FREQUENTNESS
FREQUENTNESSES
FREQUENTS
FRERE
FRERES
FRESCO
FRESCOED
FRESCOER
FRESCOERS
FRESCOES
FRESCOING
FRESCOIST
FRESCOISTS
FRESCOS
FRESH
FRESHED
FRESHEN
FRESHENED
FRESHENER
FRESHENERS
FRESHENING
FRESHENS
FRESHER
FRESHERS
FRESHES
FRESHEST
FRESHET
FRESHETS
FRESHING
FRESHLY
FRESHMAN
FRESHMEN
FRESHNESS
FRESHNESSES
FRESHWATER
FRESHWATERS
FRESNEL
FRESNELS
FRET
FRETBOARD
FRETBOARDS
FRETFUL
FRETFULLY
FRETFULNESS
FRETFULNESSES
FRETLESS
FRETS
FRETSAW
FRETSAWS
FRETSOME
FRETTED
FRETTER
FRETTERS
FRETTIER
FRETTIEST
FRETTING
FRETTY
FRETWORK
FRETWORKS
FRIABILITIES
FRIABILITY
FRIABLE
FRIAR
FRIARBIRD
FRIARBIRDS
FRIARIES
FRIARLY
FRIARS
FRIARY
FRIBBLE
FRIBBLED
FRIBBLER
FRIBBLERS
FRIBBLES
FRIBBLING
FRICANDEAU
FRICANDEAUS
FRICANDO
FRICANDOES
FRICASSEE
FRICASSEED
FRICASSEEING
FRICASSEES
FRICATIVE
FRICATIVES
FRICOT
FRICOTS
FRICTION
FRICTIONAL
FRICTIONALLY
FRICTIONLESS
FRICTIONLESSLY
FRICTIONS
FRIDGE
FRIDGES
FRIED
FRIEDCAKE
FRIEDCAKES
FRIEND
FRIENDED
FRIENDING
FRIENDLESS
FRIENDLESSNESS
FRIENDLIER
FRIENDLIES
FRIENDLIEST
FRIENDLILY
FRIENDLINESS
FRIENDLINESSES
FRIENDLY
FRIENDS
FRIENDSHIP
FRIENDSHIPS
FRIER
FRIERS
FRIES
FRIEZE
FRIEZELIKE
FRIEZES
FRIG
FRIGATE
FRIGATES
FRIGES
FRIGGED
FRIGGING
FRIGHT
FRIGHTED
FRIGHTEN
FRIGHTENED
FRIGHTENING
FRIGHTENINGLY
FRIGHTENS
FRIGHTFUL
FRIGHTFULLY
FRIGHTFULNESS
FRIGHTFULNESSES
FRIGHTING
FRIGHTS
FRIGID
FRIGIDITIES
FRIGIDITY
FRIGIDLY
FRIGIDNESS
FRIGIDNESSES
FRIGORIFIC
FRIGS
FRIJOL
FRIJOLE
FRIJOLES
FRILL
FRILLED
FRILLER
FRILLERIES
FRILLERS
FRILLERY
FRILLIER
FRILLIES
FRILLIEST
FRILLING
FRILLINGS
FRILLS
FRILLY
FRINGE
FRINGED
FRINGES
FRINGIER
FRINGIEST
FRINGING
FRINGINGS
FRINGY
FRIPPERIES
FRIPPERY
FRISBEE
FRISBEES
FRISE
FRISEE
FRISEES
FRISES
FRISETTE
FRISETTES
FRISEUR
FRISEURS
FRISK
FRISKED
FRISKER
FRISKERS
FRISKET
FRISKETS
FRISKIER
FRISKIEST
FRISKILY
FRISKINESS
FRISKINESSES
FRISKING
FRISKS
FRISKY
FRISSON
FRISSONS
FRIT
FRITES
FRITH
FRITHS
FRITILLARIA
FRITILLARIAS
FRITILLARIES
FRITILLARY
FRITS
FRITT
FRITTATA
FRITTATAS
FRITTED
FRITTER
FRITTERED
FRITTERER
FRITTERERS
FRITTERING
FRITTERS
FRITTING
FRITTS
FRITZ
FRITZES
FRIULANO
FRIULANOS
FRIVOL
FRIVOLED
FRIVOLER
FRIVOLERS
FRIVOLING
FRIVOLITIES
FRIVOLITY
FRIVOLLED
FRIVOLLER
FRIVOLLERS
FRIVOLLING
FRIVOLOUS
FRIVOLOUSLY
FRIVOLOUSNESS
FRIVOLOUSNESSES
FRIVOLS
FRIZ
FRIZED
FRIZER
FRIZERS
FRIZES
FRIZETTE
FRIZETTES
FRIZING
FRIZZ
FRIZZED

FRIZZER
FRIZZERS
FRIZZES
FRIZZIER
FRIZZIES
FRIZZIEST
FRIZZILY
FRIZZINESS
FRIZZINESSES
FRIZZING
FRIZZLE
FRIZZLED
FRIZZLER
FRIZZLERS
FRIZZLES
FRIZZLIER
FRIZZLIEST
FRIZZLING
FRIZZLY
FRIZZY
FRO
FROCK
FROCKED
FROCKING
FROCKLESS
FROCKS
FROE
FROES
FROG
FROGEYE
FROGEYED
FROGEYES
FROGFISH
FROGFISHES
FROGGED
FROGGIER
FROGGIEST
FROGGING
FROGGINGS
FROGGY
FROGHOPPER
FROGHOPPERS
FROGLET
FROGLETS
FROGLIKE
FROGMAN
FROGMARCH
FROGMARCHED
FROGMARCHES
FROGMARCHING
FROGMEN
FROGS
FROLIC
FROLICKED
FROLICKER
FROLICKERS
FROLICKING
FROLICKY
FROLICS
FROLICSOME
FROM
FROMAGE
FROMAGES
FROMENTIES
FROMENTY
FROND
FRONDED
FRONDEUR
FRONDEURS
FRONDOSE
FRONDS
FRONS
FRONT
FRONTAGE
FRONTAGES
FRONTAL
FRONTALITIES
FRONTALITY
FRONTALLY
FRONTALS
FRONTCOURT
FRONTCOURTS
FRONTED
FRONTENIS
FRONTENISES
FRONTER
FRONTES
FRONTEST
FRONTIER
FRONTIERS
FRONTIERSMAN
FRONTIERSMEN
FRONTING
FRONTISPIECE
FRONTISPIECES
FRONTLESS
FRONTLET
FRONTLETS
FRONTLINE
FRONTLINES
FRONTLIST
FRONTLISTS
FRONTMAN
FRONTMEN
FRONTOGENESES
FRONTOGENESIS
FRONTOLYSES
FRONTOLYSIS
FRONTON
FRONTONS
FRONTPAGE
FRONTPAGED
FRONTPAGES
FRONTPAGING
FRONTS
FRONTWARD
FRONTWARDS
FRORE
FROSH
FROSHES
FROST
FROSTBIT
FROSTBITE
FROSTBITES
FROSTBITING
FROSTBITINGS
FROSTBITTEN
FROSTED
FROSTEDS
FROSTFISH
FROSTFISHES
FROSTIER
FROSTIEST
FROSTILY
FROSTINESS
FROSTINESSES
FROSTING
FROSTINGS
FROSTLESS
FROSTLINE
FROSTLINES
FROSTNIP
FROSTNIPS
FROSTS
FROSTWORK
FROSTWORKS
FROSTY
FROTH
FROTHED
FROTHER
FROTHERS
FROTHIER
FROTHIEST
FROTHILY
FROTHINESS
FROTHINESSES
FROTHING
FROTHINGS
FROTHS
FROTHY
FROTTAGE
FROTTAGES
FROTTEUR
FROTTEURS
FROUFROU
FROUFROUS
FROUNCE
FROUNCED
FROUNCES
FROUNCING
FROUZIER
FROUZIEST
FROUZY
FROW
FROWARD
FROWARDLY
FROWARDNESS
FROWARDNESSES
FROWN
FROWNED
FROWNER
FROWNERS
FROWNING
FROWNINGLY
FROWNS
FROWS
FROWSIER
FROWSIEST
FROWST
FROWSTED
FROWSTIER
FROWSTIEST
FROWSTING
FROWSTS
FROWSTY
FROWSY
FROWZIER
FROWZIEST
FROWZILY
FROWZY
FROZE
FROZEN
FROZENLY
FROZENNESS
FROZENNESSES
FRUCTIFICATION
FRUCTIFICATIONS
FRUCTIFIED
FRUCTIFIES
FRUCTIFY
FRUCTIFYING
FRUCTOSE
FRUCTOSES
FRUCTUOUS
FRUG
FRUGAL
FRUGALITIES
FRUGALITY
FRUGALLY
FRUGGED
FRUGGING
FRUGIVORE
FRUGIVORES
FRUGIVOROUS
FRUGS
FRUIT
FRUITAGE
FRUITAGES
FRUITARIAN
FRUITARIANS
FRUITCAKE
FRUITCAKES
FRUITED
FRUITER
FRUITERER
FRUITERERS
FRUITERS
FRUITFUL
FRUITFULLER
FRUITFULLEST
FRUITFULLY
FRUITFULNESS
FRUITFULNESSES
FRUITIER
FRUITIEST
FRUITILY
FRUITINESS
FRUITINESSES
FRUITING
FRUITINGS
FRUITION
FRUITIONS
FRUITLESS
FRUITLESSLY
FRUITLESSNESS
FRUITLESSNESSES
FRUITLET
FRUITLETS
FRUITLIKE
FRUITS
FRUITWOOD
FRUITWOODS
FRUITY
FRUMENTIES
FRUMENTY

FRUMP
FRUMPIER
FRUMPIEST
FRUMPILY
FRUMPISH
FRUMPS
FRUMPY
FRUSTA
FRUSTRATE
FRUSTRATED
FRUSTRATES
FRUSTRATING
FRUSTRATINGLY
FRUSTRATION
FRUSTRATIONS
FRUSTULE
FRUSTULES
FRUSTUM
FRUSTUMS
FRUTESCENT
FRUTICOSE
FRY
FRYABLE
FRYBREAD
FRYBREADS
FRYER
FRYERS
FRYING
FRYPAN
FRYPANS
FUB
FUBAR
FUBBED
FUBBING
FUBS
FUBSIER
FUBSIEST
FUBSY
FUCHSIA
FUCHSIAS
FUCHSIN
FUCHSINE
FUCHSINES
FUCHSINS
FUCI
FUCK
FUCKED
FUCKER
FUCKERS
FUCKFACE
FUCKFACES
FUCKHEAD
FUCKHEADS
FUCKING
FUCKOFF
FUCKOFFS
FUCKS
FUCKUP
FUCKUPS
FUCKWIT
FUCKWITS
FUCOID
FUCOIDAL
FUCOIDS
FUCOSE
FUCOSES
FUCOUS
FUCOXANTHIN
FUCOXANTHINS
FUCUS
FUCUSES
FUD
FUDDIES
FUDDLE
FUDDLED
FUDDLES
FUDDLING
FUDDY
FUDGE
FUDGED
FUDGES
FUDGIER
FUDGIEST
FUDGING
FUDGY
FUDS
FUEHRER
FUEHRERS
FUEL
FUELED
FUELER
FUELERS
FUELING
FUELLED
FUELLER
FUELLERS
FUELLING
FUELS
FUELWOOD
FUELWOODS
FUG
FUGACIOUS
FUGACITIES
FUGACITY
FUGAL
FUGALLY
FUGATO
FUGATOS
FUGGED
FUGGIER
FUGGIEST
FUGGILY
FUGGING
FUGGY
FUGIO
FUGIOS
FUGITIVE
FUGITIVELY
FUGITIVENESS
FUGITIVENESSES
FUGITIVES
FUGLE
FUGLED
FUGLEMAN
FUGLEMEN
FUGLES
FUGLING
FUGS
FUGU
FUGUE
FUGUED
FUGUELIKE
FUGUES
FUGUING
FUGUIST
FUGUISTS
FUGUS
FUHRER
FUHRERS
FUJI
FUJIS
FULCRA
FULCRUM
FULCRUMS
FULFIL
FULFILL
FULFILLED
FULFILLER
FULFILLERS
FULFILLING
FULFILLMENT
FULFILLMENTS
FULFILLS
FULFILMENT
FULFILMENTS
FULFILS
FULGENT
FULGENTLY
FULGID
FULGURANT
FULGURATE
FULGURATED
FULGURATES
FULGURATING
FULGURATION
FULGURATIONS
FULGURITE
FULGURITES
FULGUROUS
FULHAM
FULHAMS
FULIGINOUS
FULIGINOUSLY
FULL
FULLAM
FULLAMS
FULLBACK
FULLBACKS
FULLBLOOD
FULLBLOODS
FULLED
FULLER
FULLERED
FULLERENE
FULLERENES
FULLERIES
FULLERING
FULLERS
FULLERY
FULLEST
FULLFACE
FULLFACES
FULLING
FULLMOUTHED
FULLNESS
FULLNESSES
FULLS
FULLY
FULMAR
FULMARS
FULMINANT
FULMINATE
FULMINATED
FULMINATES
FULMINATING
FULMINATION
FULMINATIONS
FULMINE
FULMINED
FULMINES
FULMINIC
FULMINING
FULNESS
FULNESSES
FULSOME
FULSOMELY
FULSOMENESS
FULSOMENESSES
FULVOUS
FUMARASE
FUMARASES
FUMARATE
FUMARATES
FUMARIC
FUMAROLE
FUMAROLES
FUMAROLIC
FUMATORIES
FUMATORY
FUMBLE
FUMBLED
FUMBLER
FUMBLERS
FUMBLES
FUMBLING
FUMBLINGLY
FUME
FUMED
FUMELESS
FUMELIKE
FUMER
FUMERS
FUMES
FUMET
FUMETS
FUMETTE
FUMETTES
FUMIER
FUMIEST
FUMIGANT
FUMIGANTS
FUMIGATE
FUMIGATED
FUMIGATES
FUMIGATING
FUMIGATION
FUMIGATIONS
FUMIGATOR
FUMIGATORS
FUMING
FUMINGLY
FUMITORIES
FUMITORY
FUMULI
FUMULUS

FUMY
FUN
FUNAMBULISM
FUNAMBULISMS
FUNAMBULIST
FUNAMBULISTS
FUNCTION
FUNCTIONAL
FUNCTIONALISM
FUNCTIONALISMS
FUNCTIONALIST
FUNCTIONALISTIC
FUNCTIONALISTS
FUNCTIONALITIES
FUNCTIONALITY
FUNCTIONALLY
FUNCTIONARIES
FUNCTIONARY
FUNCTIONED
FUNCTIONING
FUNCTIONLESS
FUNCTIONS
FUNCTOR
FUNCTORS
FUND
FUNDABLE
FUNDAMENT
FUNDAMENTAL
FUNDAMENTALISM
FUNDAMENTALISMS
FUNDAMENTALIST
FUNDAMENTALISTS
FUNDAMENTALLY
FUNDAMENTALS
FUNDAMENTS
FUNDED
FUNDER
FUNDERS
FUNDI
FUNDIC
FUNDING
FUNDINGS
FUNDRAISE
FUNDRAISED
FUNDRAISES
FUNDRAISING
FUNDS
FUNDUS
FUNERAL
FUNERALS
FUNERARY
FUNEREAL
FUNEREALLY
FUNEST
FUNFAIR
FUNFAIRS
FUNFEST
FUNFESTS
FUNGAL
FUNGALS
FUNGI
FUNGIBILITIES
FUNGIBILITY
FUNGIBLE
FUNGIBLES
FUNGIC
FUNGICIDAL
FUNGICIDALLY
FUNGICIDE
FUNGICIDES
FUNGIFORM
FUNGISTAT
FUNGISTATIC
FUNGISTATS
FUNGO
FUNGOES
FUNGOID
FUNGOIDS
FUNGOS
FUNGOUS
FUNGUS
FUNGUSES
FUNHOUSE
FUNHOUSES
FUNICLE
FUNICLES
FUNICULAR
FUNICULARS
FUNICULI
FUNICULUS
FUNK
FUNKED
FUNKER
FUNKERS
FUNKIA
FUNKIAS
FUNKIER
FUNKIEST
FUNKILY
FUNKINESS
FUNKINESSES
FUNKING
FUNKS
FUNKSTER
FUNKSTERS
FUNKY
FUNNED
FUNNEL
FUNNELED
FUNNELFORM
FUNNELING
FUNNELLED
FUNNELLING
FUNNELS
FUNNER
FUNNEST
FUNNIER
FUNNIES
FUNNIEST
FUNNILY
FUNNINESS
FUNNINESSES
FUNNING
FUNNY
FUNNYMAN
FUNNYMEN
FUNPLEX
FUNPLEXES
FUNS
FUNSTER
FUNSTERS
FUR
FURAN
FURANE
FURANES
FURANOSE
FURANOSES
FURANOSIDE
FURANOSIDES
FURANS
FURAZOLIDONE
FURAZOLIDONES
FURBALL
FURBALLS
FURBEARER
FURBEARERS
FURBELOW
FURBELOWED
FURBELOWING
FURBELOWS
FURBISH
FURBISHED
FURBISHER
FURBISHERS
FURBISHES
FURBISHING
FURCATE
FURCATED
FURCATELY
FURCATES
FURCATING
FURCATION
FURCATIONS
FURCRAEA
FURCRAEAS
FURCULA
FURCULAE
FURCULAR
FURCULUM
FURFUR
FURFURAL
FURFURALS
FURFURAN
FURFURANS
FURFURES
FURIBUND
FURIES
FURIOSO
FURIOUS
FURIOUSLY
FURL
FURLABLE
FURLED
FURLER
FURLERS
FURLESS
FURLING
FURLONG
FURLONGS
FURLOUGH
FURLOUGHED
FURLOUGHING
FURLOUGHS
FURLS
FURMENTIES
FURMENTY
FURMETIES
FURMETY
FURMITIES
FURMITY
FURNACE
FURNACED
FURNACES
FURNACING
FURNISH
FURNISHED
FURNISHER
FURNISHERS
FURNISHES
FURNISHING
FURNISHINGS
FURNITURE
FURNITURES
FUROR
FURORE
FURORES
FURORS
FUROSEMIDE
FUROSEMIDES
FURPIECE
FURPIECES
FURRED
FURRIER
FURRIERIES
FURRIERS
FURRIERY
FURRIEST
FURRILY
FURRINER
FURRINERS
FURRINESS
FURRINESSES
FURRING
FURRINGS
FURROW
FURROWED
FURROWER
FURROWERS
FURROWING
FURROWS
FURROWY
FURRY
FURS
FURTHER
FURTHERANCE
FURTHERANCES
FURTHERED
FURTHERER
FURTHERERS
FURTHERING
FURTHERMORE
FURTHERMOST
FURTHERS
FURTHEST
FURTIVE
FURTIVELY
FURTIVENESS
FURTIVENESSES
FURUNCLE
FURUNCLES
FURUNCULOSES
FURUNCULOSIS
FURY
FURZE
FURZES

FURZIER
FURZIEST
FURZY
FUSAIN
FUSAINS
FUSARIA
FUSARIUM
FUSARIUMS
FUSCOUS
FUSE
FUSED
FUSEE
FUSEES
FUSEL
FUSELAGE
FUSELAGES
FUSELESS
FUSELIKE
FUSELS
FUSES
FUSIBILITIES
FUSIBILITY
FUSIBLE
FUSIBLY
FUSIFORM
FUSIL
FUSILE
FUSILEER
FUSILEERS
FUSILIER
FUSILIERS
FUSILLADE
FUSILLADED
FUSILLADES
FUSILLADING
FUSILLI
FUSILLIS
FUSILS
FUSING
FUSION
FUSIONAL
FUSIONISM
FUSIONISMS
FUSIONIST
FUSIONISTS
FUSIONS
FUSS
FUSSBUDGET
FUSSBUDGETS
FUSSBUDGETY
FUSSED
FUSSER
FUSSERS
FUSSES
FUSSIER
FUSSIEST
FUSSILY
FUSSINESS
FUSSINESSES
FUSSING
FUSSPOT
FUSSPOTS
FUSSY
FUSTIAN
FUSTIANS
FUSTIC
FUSTICS
FUSTIER
FUSTIEST
FUSTIGATE
FUSTIGATED
FUSTIGATES
FUSTIGATING
FUSTIGATION
FUSTIGATIONS
FUSTILY
FUSTINESS
FUSTINESSES
FUSTY
FUSULINID
FUSULINIDS
FUSUMA
FUTHARC
FUTHARCS
FUTHARK
FUTHARKS
FUTHORC
FUTHORCS
FUTHORK
FUTHORKS
FUTILE
FUTILELY
FUTILENESS
FUTILENESSES
FUTILITARIAN
FUTILITARIANISM
FUTILITARIANS
FUTILITIES
FUTILITY
FUTON
FUTONS
FUTTOCK
FUTTOCKS
FUTURAL
FUTURE
FUTURELESS
FUTURELESSNESS
FUTURES
FUTURISM
FUTURISMS
FUTURIST
FUTURISTIC
FUTURISTICALLY
FUTURISTICS
FUTURISTS
FUTURITIES
FUTURITY
FUTUROLOGICAL
FUTUROLOGIES
FUTUROLOGIST
FUTUROLOGISTS
FUTUROLOGY
FUTZ
FUTZED
FUTZES
FUTZING
FUZE
FUZED
FUZEE
FUZEES
FUZELESS
FUZES
FUZIL
FUZILS
FUZING
FUZZ
FUZZBALL
FUZZBALLS
FUZZED
FUZZES
FUZZIER
FUZZIEST
FUZZILY
FUZZINESS
FUZZINESSES
FUZZING
FUZZTONE
FUZZTONES
FUZZY
FYCE
FYCES
FYKE
FYKES
FYLFOT
FYLFOTS
FYNBOS
FYTTE
FYTTES

G

GAB
GABARDINE
GABARDINES
GABBA
GABBARD
GABBARDS
GABBART
GABBARTS
GABBAS
GABBED
GABBER
GABBERS
GABBIER
GABBIEST
GABBINESS
GABBINESSES
GABBING
GABBLE
GABBLED
GABBLER
GABBLERS
GABBLES
GABBLING
GABBRO
GABBROIC
GABBROID
GABBROS
GABBY
GABELLE
GABELLED
GABELLES
GABERDINE
GABERDINES
GABFEST
GABFESTS
GABIES
GABION
GABIONS
GABLE
GABLED
GABLELIKE
GABLES
GABLING
GABOON
GABOONS
GABS
GABY
GACH
GACHED
GACHER
GACHERS
GACHES
GACHING
GAD
GADABOUT

GADABOUTS
GADARENE
GADDED
GADDER
GADDERS
GADDI
GADDING
GADDIS
GADFLIES
GADFLY
GADGET
GADGETEER
GADGETEERS
GADGETIER
GADGETIEST
GADGETRIES
GADGETRY
GADGETS
GADGETY
GADI
GADID
GADIDS
GADIS
GADJE
GADJO
GADOID
GADOIDS
GADOLINITE
GADOLINITES
GADOLINIUM
GADOLINIUMS
GADROON
GADROONED
GADROONING
GADROONINGS
GADROONS
GADS
GADWALL
GADWALLS
GADZOOKERIES
GADZOOKERY
GADZOOKS
GAE
GAED
GAEING
GAEN
GAES
GAFF
GAFFE
GAFFED
GAFFER
GAFFERS
GAFFES
GAFFING
GAFFS
GAG
GAGA
GAGAKU
GAGAKUS
GAGE
GAGEABLE
GAGED
GAGER
GAGERS
GAGES
GAGGED
GAGGER
GAGGERS
GAGGING
GAGGLE
GAGGLED
GAGGLES
GAGGLING
GAGING
GAGMAN
GAGMEN
GAGS
GAGSTER
GAGSTERS
GAHNITE
GAHNITES
GAIETIES
GAIETY
GAIJIN
GAILLARDIA
GAILLARDIAS
GAILY
GAIN
GAINABLE
GAINED
GAINER
GAINERS
GAINFUL
GAINFULLY
GAINFULNESS
GAINFULNESSES
GAINGIVING
GAINGIVINGS
GAINING
GAINLESS
GAINLIER
GAINLIEST
GAINLY
GAINS
GAINSAID
GAINSAY
GAINSAYER
GAINSAYERS
GAINSAYING
GAINSAYS
GAINST
GAIT
GAITED
GAITER
GAITERED
GAITERS
GAITING
GAITS
GAL
GALA
GALABIA
GALABIAS
GALABIEH
GALABIEHS
GALABIYA
GALABIYAH
GALABIYAHS
GALABIYAS
GALACTIC
GALACTORRHEA
GALACTORRHEAS
GALACTOSAMINE
GALACTOSAMINES
GALACTOSE
GALACTOSEMIA
GALACTOSEMIAS
GALACTOSEMIC
GALACTOSES
GALACTOSIDASE
GALACTOSIDASES
GALACTOSIDE
GALACTOSIDES
GALACTOSYL
GALACTOSYLS
GALAGO
GALAGOS
GALAH
GALAHS
GALANGA
GALANGAL
GALANGALS
GALANGAS
GALANTINE
GALANTINES
GALAS
GALATEA
GALATEAS
GALAVANT
GALAVANTED
GALAVANTING
GALAVANTS
GALAX
GALAXES
GALAXIES
GALAXY
GALBANUM
GALBANUMS
GALE
GALEA
GALEAE
GALEAS
GALEATE
GALEATED
GALED
GALENA
GALENAS
GALENIC
GALENICAL
GALENICALS
GALENITE
GALENITES
GALERE
GALERES
GALES
GALETTE
GALETTES
GALILEE
GALILEES
GALING
GALINGALE
GALINGALES
GALIOT
GALIOTS
GALIPOT
GALIPOTS
GALIVANT
GALIVANTED
GALIVANTING
GALIVANTS
GALL
GALLAMINE
GALLAMINES
GALLANT
GALLANTED
GALLANTING
GALLANTLY
GALLANTRIES
GALLANTRY
GALLANTS
GALLATE
GALLATES
GALLBLADDER
GALLBLADDERS
GALLEASS
GALLEASSES
GALLED
GALLEIN
GALLEINS
GALLEON
GALLEONS
GALLERIA
GALLERIAS
GALLERIED
GALLERIES
GALLERY
GALLERYGOER
GALLERYGOERS
GALLERYING
GALLERYITE
GALLERYITES
GALLET
GALLETA
GALLETAS
GALLETED
GALLETING
GALLETS
GALLEY
GALLEYS
GALLFLIES
GALLFLY
GALLIARD
GALLIARDS
GALLIASS
GALLIASSES
GALLIC
GALLICA
GALLICAN
GALLICAS
GALLICISM
GALLICISMS
GALLICIZATION
GALLICIZATIONS
GALLICIZE
GALLICIZED
GALLICIZES
GALLICIZING
GALLIED
GALLIES
GALLIGASKINS
GALLIMAUFRIES
GALLIMAUFRY
GALLINACEOUS
GALLING
GALLINGLY
GALLINIPPER

GALLINIPPERS
GALLINULE
GALLINULES
GALLIOT
GALLIOTS
GALLIPOT
GALLIPOTS
GALLIUM
GALLIUMS
GALLIVANT
GALLIVANTED
GALLIVANTING
GALLIVANTS
GALLIWASP
GALLIWASPS
GALLNUT
GALLNUTS
GALLON
GALLONAGE
GALLONAGES
GALLONS
GALLOON
GALLOONED
GALLOONS
GALLOOT
GALLOOTS
GALLOP
GALLOPADE
GALLOPADES
GALLOPED
GALLOPER
GALLOPERS
GALLOPING
GALLOPS
GALLOUS
GALLOWAY
GALLOWAYS
GALLOWGLASS
GALLOWGLASSES
GALLOWS
GALLOWSES
GALLS
GALLSTONE
GALLSTONES
GALLUS
GALLUSED
GALLUSES
GALLY
GALLYING
GALOOT
GALOOTS
GALOP
GALOPADE
GALOPADES
GALOPED
GALOPING
GALOPS
GALORE
GALORES
GALOSH
GALOSHE
GALOSHED
GALOSHES
GALS
GALUMPH
GALUMPHED
GALUMPHING
GALUMPHS
GALVANIC
GALVANICALLY
GALVANISE
GALVANISED
GALVANISES
GALVANISING
GALVANISM
GALVANISMS
GALVANIZATION
GALVANIZATIONS
GALVANIZE
GALVANIZED
GALVANIZER
GALVANIZERS
GALVANIZES
GALVANIZING
GALVANOMETER
GALVANOMETERS
GALVANOMETRIC
GALVANOSCOPE
GALVANOSCOPES
GALYAC
GALYACS
GALYAK
GALYAKS
GAM
GAMA
GAMAS
GAMASHES
GAMAY
GAMAYS
GAMB
GAMBA
GAMBADE
GAMBADES
GAMBADO
GAMBADOES
GAMBADOS
GAMBAS
GAMBE
GAMBES
GAMBESON
GAMBESONS
GAMBIA
GAMBIAS
GAMBIER
GAMBIERS
GAMBIR
GAMBIRS
GAMBIT
GAMBITS
GAMBLE
GAMBLED
GAMBLER
GAMBLERS
GAMBLES
GAMBLING
GAMBOGE
GAMBOGES
GAMBOGIAN
GAMBOL
GAMBOLED
GAMBOLING
GAMBOLLED
GAMBOLLING
GAMBOLS
GAMBREL
GAMBRELS
GAMBS
GAMBUSIA
GAMBUSIAS
GAME
GAMEBOOK
GAMEBOOKS
GAMECOCK
GAMECOCKS
GAMED
GAMEFISH
GAMEFISHES
GAMEFOWL
GAMEFOWLS
GAMEKEEPER
GAMEKEEPERS
GAMELAN
GAMELANS
GAMELIKE
GAMELY
GAMENESS
GAMENESSES
GAMEPLAY
GAMEPLAYS
GAMER
GAMERS
GAMES
GAMESMAN
GAMESMANSHIP
GAMESMANSHIPS
GAMESMEN
GAMESOME
GAMESOMELY
GAMESOMENESS
GAMESOMENESSES
GAMEST
GAMESTER
GAMESTERS
GAMETAL
GAMETANGIA
GAMETANGIUM
GAMETE
GAMETES
GAMETIC
GAMETICALLY
GAMETOCYTE
GAMETOCYTES
GAMETOGENESES
GAMETOGENESIS
GAMETOGENIC
GAMETOGENOUS
GAMETOPHORE
GAMETOPHORES
GAMETOPHYTE
GAMETOPHYTES
GAMETOPHYTIC
GAMEY
GAMIC
GAMIER
GAMIEST
GAMIFICATION
GAMIFICATIONS
GAMILY
GAMIN
GAMINE
GAMINES
GAMINESS
GAMINESSES
GAMING
GAMINGS
GAMINS
GAMMA
GAMMADIA
GAMMADION
GAMMAS
GAMMED
GAMMER
GAMMERS
GAMMIER
GAMMIEST
GAMMING
GAMMON
GAMMONED
GAMMONER
GAMMONERS
GAMMONING
GAMMONS
GAMMY
GAMODEME
GAMODEMES
GAMOPETALOUS
GAMP
GAMPS
GAMS
GAMUT
GAMUTS
GAMY
GAN
GANACHE
GANACHES
GANCICLOVIR
GANCICLOVIRS
GANDER
GANDERED
GANDERING
GANDERS
GANE
GANEF
GANEFS
GANEV
GANEVS
GANG
GANGBANG
GANGBANGED
GANGBANGER
GANGBANGERS
GANGBANGING
GANGBANGS
GANGBUSTER
GANGBUSTERS
GANGED
GANGER
GANGERS
GANGING
GANGLAND
GANGLANDS
GANGLE
GANGLED
GANGLES
GANGLIA

GANGLIAL
GANGLIAR
GANGLIATE
GANGLIER
GANGLIEST
GANGLING
GANGLION
GANGLIONATED
GANGLIONIC
GANGLIONS
GANGLIOSIDE
GANGLIOSIDES
GANGLY
GANGPLANK
GANGPLANKS
GANGPLOW
GANGPLOWS
GANGREL
GANGRELS
GANGRENE
GANGRENED
GANGRENES
GANGRENING
GANGRENOUS
GANGS
GANGSTA
GANGSTAS
GANGSTER
GANGSTERDOM
GANGSTERDOMS
GANGSTERISH
GANGSTERISM
GANGSTERISMS
GANGSTERS
GANGUE
GANGUES
GANGWAY
GANGWAYS
GANISTER
GANISTERS
GANJA
GANJAH
GANJAHS
GANJAS
GANNET
GANNETRIES
GANNETRY
GANNETS
GANNISTER
GANNISTERS
GANOF
GANOFS
GANOID
GANOIDS
GANTELOPE
GANTELOPES
GANTLET
GANTLETED
GANTLETING
GANTLETS
GANTLINE
GANTLINES
GANTLOPE
GANTLOPES
GANTRIES
GANTRY
GANYMEDE
GANYMEDES
GANZFELD
GANZFELDS
GAOL
GAOLBIRD
GAOLBIRDS
GAOLBREAK
GAOLBREAKS
GAOLED
GAOLER
GAOLERS
GAOLING
GAOLS
GAP
GAPE
GAPED
GAPER
GAPERS
GAPES
GAPESEED
GAPESEEDS
GAPEWORM
GAPEWORMS
GAPING
GAPINGLY
GAPLESS
GAPOSIS
GAPOSISES
GAPPED
GAPPIER
GAPPIEST
GAPPING
GAPPY
GAPS
GAPY
GAR
GARAGE
GARAGED
GARAGEMAN
GARAGEMEN
GARAGES
GARAGING
GARB
GARBAGE
GARBAGEMAN
GARBAGEMEN
GARBAGES
GARBAGEY
GARBAGY
GARBANZO
GARBANZOS
GARBED
GARBING
GARBLE
GARBLED
GARBLER
GARBLERS
GARBLES
GARBLESS
GARBLING
GARBOARD
GARBOARDS
GARBOIL
GARBOILS
GARBOLOGIES
GARBOLOGIST
GARBOLOGISTS
GARBOLOGY
GARBS
GARCON
GARCONS
GARDA
GARDAI
GARDANT
GARDEN
GARDENED
GARDENER
GARDENERS
GARDENFUL
GARDENFULS
GARDENIA
GARDENIAS
GARDENING
GARDENINGS
GARDENS
GARDEROBE
GARDEROBES
GARDYLOO
GARFISH
GARFISHES
GARGANEY
GARGANEYS
GARGANTUA
GARGANTUAN
GARGANTUAS
GARGET
GARGETS
GARGETY
GARGLE
GARGLED
GARGLER
GARGLERS
GARGLES
GARGLING
GARGOYLE
GARGOYLED
GARGOYLES
GARIBALDI
GARIBALDIS
GARIGUE
GARIGUES
GARISH
GARISHLY
GARISHNESS
GARISHNESSES
GARLAND
GARLANDED
GARLANDING
GARLANDS
GARLIC
GARLICKED
GARLICKIER
GARLICKIEST
GARLICKING
GARLICKY
GARLICS
GARMENT
GARMENTED
GARMENTING
GARMENTS
GARNER
GARNERED
GARNERING
GARNERS
GARNET
GARNETIFEROUS
GARNETS
GARNI
GARNIERITE
GARNIERITES
GARNISH
GARNISHED
GARNISHEE
GARNISHEED
GARNISHEEING
GARNISHEES
GARNISHER
GARNISHERS
GARNISHES
GARNISHING
GARNISHMENT
GARNISHMENTS
GARNITURE
GARNITURES
GAROTE
GAROTED
GAROTES
GAROTING
GAROTTE
GAROTTED
GAROTTER
GAROTTERS
GAROTTES
GAROTTING
GARPIKE
GARPIKES
GARRED
GARRET
GARRETED
GARRETS
GARRING
GARRISON
GARRISONED
GARRISONING
GARRISONS
GARRON
GARRONS
GARROTE
GARROTED
GARROTER
GARROTERS
GARROTES
GARROTING
GARROTTE
GARROTTED
GARROTTES
GARROTTING
GARRULITIES
GARRULITY
GARRULOUS
GARRULOUSLY
GARRULOUSNESS
GARRULOUSNESSES
GARS
GARTER
GARTERED
GARTERING
GARTERS

GARTH
GARTHS
GARVEY
GARVEYS
GAS
GASALIER
GASALIERS
GASBAG
GASBAGS
GASCON
GASCONADE
GASCONADED
GASCONADER
GASCONADERS
GASCONADES
GASCONADING
GASCONS
GASEITIES
GASEITY
GASELIER
GASELIERS
GASEOUS
GASEOUSNESS
GASEOUSNESSES
GASES
GASH
GASHED
GASHER
GASHES
GASHEST
GASHING
GASHOLDER
GASHOLDERS
GASHOUSE
GASHOUSES
GASIFICATION
GASIFICATIONS
GASIFIED
GASIFIER
GASIFIERS
GASIFIES
GASIFORM
GASIFY
GASIFYING
GASKET
GASKETED
GASKETS
GASKIN
GASKING
GASKINGS
GASKINS
GASLESS
GASLIGHT
GASLIGHTS
GASLIT
GASMAN
GASMEN
GASOGENE
GASOGENES
GASOHOL
GASOHOLS
GASOLENE
GASOLENES
GASOLIER
GASOLIERS
GASOLINE
GASOLINES
GASOLINIC
GASOMETER
GASOMETERS
GASP
GASPED
GASPER
GASPEREAU
GASPEREAUX
GASPERS
GASPING
GASPINGLY
GASPS
GASSED
GASSER
GASSERS
GASSES
GASSIER
GASSIEST
GASSILY
GASSINESS
GASSINESSES
GASSING
GASSINGS
GASSY
GAST
GASTED
GASTER
GASTERS
GASTHAUS
GASTHAUSER
GASTHAUSES
GASTIGHT
GASTIGHTNESS
GASTIGHTNESSES
GASTING
GASTNESS
GASTNESSES
GASTRAEA
GASTRAEAS
GASTRAL
GASTREA
GASTREAS
GASTRECTOMIES
GASTRECTOMY
GASTRIC
GASTRIN
GASTRINS
GASTRITIC
GASTRITIDES
GASTRITIS
GASTRITISES
GASTROCNEMII
GASTROCNEMIUS
GASTRODUODENAL
GASTROENTERITIS
GASTROLITH
GASTROLITHS
GASTRONOME
GASTRONOMES
GASTRONOMIC
GASTRONOMICAL
GASTRONOMICALLY
GASTRONOMIES
GASTRONOMIST
GASTRONOMISTS
GASTRONOMY
GASTROPOD
GASTROPODS
GASTROPUB
GASTROPUBS
GASTROSCOPE
GASTROSCOPES
GASTROSCOPIC
GASTROSCOPIES
GASTROSCOPIST
GASTROSCOPISTS
GASTROSCOPY
GASTROTRICH
GASTROTRICHS
GASTROVASCULAR
GASTRULA
GASTRULAE
GASTRULAR
GASTRULAS
GASTRULATE
GASTRULATED
GASTRULATES
GASTRULATING
GASTRULATION
GASTRULATIONS
GASTS
GASWORKS
GAT
GATCH
GATCHED
GATCHER
GATCHERS
GATCHES
GATCHING
GATE
GATEAU
GATEAUS
GATEAUX
GATECRASH
GATECRASHED
GATECRASHES
GATECRASHING
GATED
GATEFOLD
GATEFOLDS
GATEHOUSE
GATEHOUSES
GATEKEEPER
GATEKEEPERS
GATEKEEPING
GATELEG
GATELEGS
GATELESS
GATELIKE
GATEMAN
GATEMEN
GATEPOST
GATEPOSTS
GATER
GATERS
GATES
GATEWAY
GATEWAYS
GATHER
GATHERED
GATHERER
GATHERERS
GATHERING
GATHERINGS
GATHERS
GATING
GATINGS
GATOR
GATORS
GATS
GAUCH
GAUCHE
GAUCHED
GAUCHELY
GAUCHENESS
GAUCHENESSES
GAUCHER
GAUCHERIE
GAUCHERIES
GAUCHERS
GAUCHES
GAUCHEST
GAUCHING
GAUCHO
GAUCHOS
GAUD
GAUDERIES
GAUDERY
GAUDIER
GAUDIES
GAUDIEST
GAUDILY
GAUDINESS
GAUDINESSES
GAUDS
GAUDY
GAUFFER
GAUFFERED
GAUFFERING
GAUFFERS
GAUGE
GAUGEABLE
GAUGED
GAUGER
GAUGERS
GAUGES
GAUGING
GAULEITER
GAULEITERS
GAULT
GAULTS
GAUM
GAUMED
GAUMING
GAUMS
GAUN
GAUNCH
GAUNCHES
GAUNT
GAUNTER
GAUNTEST
GAUNTLET
GAUNTLETED
GAUNTLETING
GAUNTLETS
GAUNTLY
GAUNTNESS
GAUNTNESSES

GAUNTRIES
GAUNTRY
GAUR
GAURS
GAUSS
GAUSSES
GAUZE
GAUZELIKE
GAUZES
GAUZIER
GAUZIEST
GAUZILY
GAUZINESS
GAUZINESSES
GAUZY
GAVAGE
GAVAGES
GAVE
GAVEL
GAVELED
GAVELING
GAVELKIND
GAVELKINDS
GAVELLED
GAVELLING
GAVELOCK
GAVELOCKS
GAVELS
GAVIAL
GAVIALOID
GAVIALS
GAVOT
GAVOTS
GAVOTTE
GAVOTTED
GAVOTTES
GAVOTTING
GAWK
GAWKED
GAWKER
GAWKERS
GAWKIER
GAWKIES
GAWKIEST
GAWKILY
GAWKINESS
GAWKINESSES
GAWKING
GAWKISH
GAWKISHLY
GAWKISHNESS
GAWKISHNESSES
GAWKS
GAWKY
GAWMOGE
GAWMOGES
GAWP
GAWPED
GAWPER
GAWPERS
GAWPING
GAWPS
GAWSIE
GAWSY
GAY
GAYAL
GAYALS
GAYDAR
GAYDARS
GAYER
GAYEST
GAYETIES
GAYETY
GAYLY
GAYNESS
GAYNESSES
GAYS
GAYWINGS
GAZABO
GAZABOES
GAZABOS
GAZANIA
GAZANIAS
GAZAR
GAZARS
GAZE
GAZEBO
GAZEBOES
GAZEBOS
GAZED
GAZEHOUND
GAZEHOUNDS
GAZELLE
GAZELLES
GAZER
GAZERS
GAZES
GAZETTE
GAZETTED
GAZETTEER
GAZETTEERS
GAZETTES
GAZETTING
GAZILLION
GAZILLIONAIRE
GAZILLIONAIRES
GAZILLIONS
GAZILLIONTH
GAZING
GAZOGENE
GAZOGENES
GAZOO
GAZOOS
GAZPACHO
GAZPACHOS
GAZUMP
GAZUMPED
GAZUMPER
GAZUMPERS
GAZUMPING
GAZUMPS
GAZUNDER
GAZUNDERED
GAZUNDERING
GAZUNDERS
GEAN
GEANS
GEANTICLINE
GEANTICLINES
GEAR
GEARBOX
GEARBOXES
GEARCASE
GEARCASES
GEARCHANGE
GEARCHANGES
GEARED
GEARHEAD
GEARHEADS
GEARING
GEARINGS
GEARLESS
GEARS
GEARSHIFT
GEARSHIFTS
GEARSTICK
GEARSTICKS
GEARWHEEL
GEARWHEELS
GECK
GECKED
GECKING
GECKO
GECKOES
GECKOS
GECKS
GED
GEDS
GEE
GEED
GEEGAW
GEEGAWS
GEEING
GEEK
GEEKDOM
GEEKDOMS
GEEKED
GEEKIER
GEEKIEST
GEEKINESS
GEEKINESSES
GEEKISH
GEEKS
GEEKY
GEEPOUND
GEEPOUNDS
GEES
GEESE
GEEST
GEESTS
GEEZ
GEEZER
GEEZERHOOD
GEEZERHOODS
GEEZERS
GEGENSCHEIN
GEGENSCHEINS
GEISHA
GEISHAS
GEL
GELABLE
GELADA
GELADAS
GELANDESPRUNG
GELANDESPRUNGS
GELANT
GELANTS
GELATE
GELATED
GELATES
GELATI
GELATIN
GELATINE
GELATINES
GELATING
GELATINIZATION
GELATINIZATIONS
GELATINIZE
GELATINIZED
GELATINIZES
GELATINIZING
GELATINOUS
GELATINOUSLY
GELATINOUSNESS
GELATINS
GELATION
GELATIONS
GELATIS
GELATO
GELATOS
GELCAP
GELCAPS
GELCOAT
GELCOATS
GELD
GELDED
GELDER
GELDERS
GELDING
GELDINGS
GELDS
GELEE
GELEES
GELID
GELIDITIES
GELIDITY
GELIDLY
GELIDNESS
GELIDNESSES
GELIGNITE
GELIGNITES
GELLANT
GELLANTS
GELLED
GELLIES
GELLING
GELLY
GELS
GELSEMIA
GELSEMIUM
GELSEMIUMS
GELT
GELTS
GEM
GEMATRIA
GEMATRIAS
GEMEINSCHAFT
GEMEINSCHAFTS
GEMFIBROZIL
GEMFIBROZILS
GEMINAL
GEMINALLY
GEMINATE
GEMINATED
GEMINATES

GEMINATING
GEMINATION
GEMINATIONS
GEMLIKE
GEMMA
GEMMAE
GEMMATE
GEMMATED
GEMMATES
GEMMATING
GEMMATION
GEMMATIONS
GEMMED
GEMMIER
GEMMIEST
GEMMILY
GEMMINESS
GEMMINESSES
GEMMING
GEMMOLOGIES
GEMMOLOGIST
GEMMOLOGISTS
GEMMOLOGY
GEMMULE
GEMMULES
GEMMY
GEMOLOGICAL
GEMOLOGIES
GEMOLOGIST
GEMOLOGISTS
GEMOLOGY
GEMOT
GEMOTE
GEMOTES
GEMOTS
GEMS
GEMSBOK
GEMSBOKS
GEMSBUCK
GEMSBUCKS
GEMSTONE
GEMSTONES
GEMUTLICH
GEMUTLICHKEIT
GEMUTLICHKEITS
GEN
GENDARME
GENDARMERIE
GENDARMERIES
GENDARMERY
GENDARMES
GENDER
GENDERED
GENDERING
GENDERIZE
GENDERIZED
GENDERIZES
GENDERIZING
GENDERLESS
GENDERLESSNESS
GENDERS
GENE
GENEALOGICAL
GENEALOGICALLY
GENEALOGIES
GENEALOGIST
GENEALOGISTS
GENEALOGY
GENERA
GENERABLE
GENERAL
GENERALCIES
GENERALCY
GENERALISATION
GENERALISATIONS
GENERALISE
GENERALISED
GENERALISES
GENERALISING
GENERALISSIMO
GENERALISSIMOS
GENERALIST
GENERALISTS
GENERALITIES
GENERALITY
GENERALIZABLE
GENERALIZATION
GENERALIZATIONS
GENERALIZE
GENERALIZED
GENERALIZER
GENERALIZERS
GENERALIZES
GENERALIZING
GENERALLY
GENERALS
GENERALSHIP
GENERALSHIPS
GENERATE
GENERATED
GENERATES
GENERATING
GENERATION
GENERATIONAL
GENERATIONALLY
GENERATIONS
GENERATIVE
GENERATOR
GENERATORS
GENERATRICES
GENERATRIX
GENERIC
GENERICAL
GENERICALLY
GENERICNESS
GENERICNESSES
GENERICS
GENEROSITIES
GENEROSITY
GENEROUS
GENEROUSLY
GENEROUSNESS
GENEROUSNESSES
GENES
GENESES
GENESIS
GENET
GENETIC
GENETICAL
GENETICALLY
GENETICIST
GENETICISTS
GENETICS
GENETS
GENETTE
GENETTES
GENEVA
GENEVAS
GENIAL
GENIALITIES
GENIALITY
GENIALLY
GENIC
GENICALLY
GENICULATE
GENICULATED
GENIE
GENIES
GENII
GENIP
GENIPAP
GENIPAPO
GENIPAPOS
GENIPAPS
GENIPS
GENISTA
GENISTAS
GENISTEIN
GENISTEINS
GENITAL
GENITALIA
GENITALIC
GENITALLY
GENITALS
GENITIVAL
GENITIVALLY
GENITIVE
GENITIVES
GENITOR
GENITORS
GENITOURINARY
GENITURE
GENITURES
GENIUS
GENIUSES
GENLOCK
GENLOCKED
GENLOCKING
GENLOCKS
GENNAKER
GENNAKERS
GENNED
GENNING
GENOA
GENOAS
GENOCIDAL
GENOCIDE
GENOCIDES
GENOGRAM
GENOGRAMS
GENOISE
GENOISES
GENOM
GENOME
GENOMES
GENOMIC
GENOMICS
GENOMS
GENOTYPE
GENOTYPES
GENOTYPIC
GENOTYPICAL
GENOTYPICALLY
GENRE
GENRES
GENRO
GENROS
GENS
GENSENG
GENSENGS
GENT
GENTAMICIN
GENTAMICINS
GENTEEL
GENTEELER
GENTEELEST
GENTEELISM
GENTEELISMS
GENTEELLY
GENTEELNESS
GENTEELNESSES
GENTES
GENTIAN
GENTIANS
GENTIL
GENTILE
GENTILES
GENTILESSE
GENTILESSES
GENTILITIES
GENTILITY
GENTLE
GENTLED
GENTLEFOLK
GENTLEFOLKS
GENTLEMAN
GENTLEMANLIKE
GENTLEMANLINESS
GENTLEMANLY
GENTLEMEN
GENTLENESS
GENTLENESSES
GENTLEPERSON
GENTLEPERSONS
GENTLER
GENTLES
GENTLEST
GENTLEWOMAN
GENTLEWOMEN
GENTLING
GENTLY
GENTOO
GENTOOS
GENTRICE
GENTRICES
GENTRIES
GENTRIFICATION
GENTRIFICATIONS
GENTRIFIED
GENTRIFIER
GENTRIFIERS
GENTRIFIES
GENTRIFY
GENTRIFYING
GENTRY

GENTS
GENU
GENUA
GENUFLECT
GENUFLECTED
GENUFLECTING
GENUFLECTION
GENUFLECTIONS
GENUFLECTS
GENUFLEXION
GENUFLEXIONS
GENUINE
GENUINELY
GENUINENESS
GENUINENESSES
GENUS
GENUSES
GEOBOTANIC
GEOBOTANICAL
GEOBOTANIES
GEOBOTANIST
GEOBOTANISTS
GEOBOTANY
GEOCACHE
GEOCACHED
GEOCACHER
GEOCACHERS
GEOCACHES
GEOCACHING
GEOCENTRIC
GEOCENTRICALLY
GEOCHEMICAL
GEOCHEMICALLY
GEOCHEMIST
GEOCHEMISTRIES
GEOCHEMISTRY
GEOCHEMISTS
GEOCHRONOLOGIC
GEOCHRONOLOGIES
GEOCHRONOLOGIST
GEOCHRONOLOGY
GEOCORONA
GEOCORONAE
GEOCORONAS
GEODE
GEODES
GEODESIC
GEODESICS
GEODESIES
GEODESIST
GEODESISTS
GEODESY
GEODETIC
GEODETICAL
GEODETICS
GEODIC
GEODUCK
GEODUCKS
GEOECONOMIC
GEOECONOMICS
GEOGNOSIES
GEOGNOSY
GEOGRAPHER
GEOGRAPHERS
GEOGRAPHIC
GEOGRAPHICAL
GEOGRAPHICALLY
GEOGRAPHIES
GEOGRAPHY
GEOHYDROLOGIC
GEOHYDROLOGIES
GEOHYDROLOGIST
GEOHYDROLOGISTS
GEOHYDROLOGY
GEOID
GEOIDAL
GEOIDS
GEOLOGER
GEOLOGERS
GEOLOGIC
GEOLOGICAL
GEOLOGICALLY
GEOLOGIES
GEOLOGIST
GEOLOGISTS
GEOLOGIZE
GEOLOGIZED
GEOLOGIZES
GEOLOGIZING
GEOLOGY
GEOMAGNETIC
GEOMAGNETICALLY
GEOMAGNETISM
GEOMAGNETISMS
GEOMANCER
GEOMANCERS
GEOMANCIES
GEOMANCY
GEOMANTIC
GEOMETER
GEOMETERS
GEOMETRIC
GEOMETRICAL
GEOMETRICALLY
GEOMETRICIAN
GEOMETRICIANS
GEOMETRICS
GEOMETRID
GEOMETRIDS
GEOMETRIES
GEOMETRISE
GEOMETRISED
GEOMETRISES
GEOMETRISING
GEOMETRIZATION
GEOMETRIZATIONS
GEOMETRIZE
GEOMETRIZED
GEOMETRIZES
GEOMETRIZING
GEOMETRY
GEOMORPHIC
GEOMORPHOLOGIES
GEOMORPHOLOGIST
GEOMORPHOLOGY
GEOPHAGIA
GEOPHAGIAS
GEOPHAGIES
GEOPHAGY
GEOPHONE
GEOPHONES
GEOPHYSICAL
GEOPHYSICALLY
GEOPHYSICIST
GEOPHYSICISTS
GEOPHYSICS
GEOPHYTE
GEOPHYTES
GEOPHYTIC
GEOPOLITICAL
GEOPOLITICALLY
GEOPOLITICIAN
GEOPOLITICIANS
GEOPOLITICS
GEOPONIC
GEOPONICS
GEOPRESSURED
GEOPROBE
GEOPROBES
GEORGETTE
GEORGETTES
GEORGIC
GEORGICAL
GEORGICS
GEOSCIENCE
GEOSCIENCES
GEOSCIENTIST
GEOSCIENTISTS
GEOSTATIONARY
GEOSTRATEGIC
GEOSTRATEGIES
GEOSTRATEGIST
GEOSTRATEGISTS
GEOSTRATEGY
GEOSTROPHIC
GEOSTROPHICALLY
GEOSYNCHRONOUS
GEOSYNCLINAL
GEOSYNCLINE
GEOSYNCLINES
GEOTACTIC
GEOTAXES
GEOTAXIS
GEOTECHNICAL
GEOTECTONIC
GEOTECTONICALLY
GEOTHERMAL
GEOTHERMALLY
GEOTROPIC
GEOTROPICALLY
GEOTROPISM
GEOTROPISMS
GERAH
GERAHS
GERANIAL
GERANIALS
GERANIOL
GERANIOLS
GERANIUM
GERANIUMS
GERARDIA
GERARDIAS
GERBERA
GERBERAS
GERBIL
GERBILLE
GERBILLES
GERBILS
GERENT
GERENTS
GERENUK
GERENUKS
GERFALCON
GERFALCONS
GERIATRIC
GERIATRICIAN
GERIATRICIANS
GERIATRICS
GERM
GERMAN
GERMANDER
GERMANDERS
GERMANE
GERMANELY
GERMANIC
GERMANIUM
GERMANIUMS
GERMANIZATION
GERMANIZATIONS
GERMANIZE
GERMANIZED
GERMANIZES
GERMANIZING
GERMANS
GERMEN
GERMENS
GERMFREE
GERMICIDAL
GERMICIDE
GERMICIDES
GERMIER
GERMIEST
GERMINA
GERMINABILITIES
GERMINABILITY
GERMINAL
GERMINALLY
GERMINANT
GERMINATE
GERMINATED
GERMINATES
GERMINATING
GERMINATION
GERMINATIONS
GERMINATIVE
GERMINESS
GERMINESSES
GERMLIKE
GERMOPHOBE
GERMOPHOBES
GERMOPHOBIC
GERMPLASM
GERMPLASMS
GERMPROOF
GERMS
GERMY
GERONTIC
GERONTOCRACIES
GERONTOCRACY
GERONTOCRAT
GERONTOCRATIC
GERONTOCRATS
GERONTOLOGIC
GERONTOLOGICAL
GERONTOLOGIES

GERONTOLOGIST
GERONTOLOGISTS
GERONTOLOGY
GERONTOMORPHIC
GERRYMANDER
GERRYMANDERED
GERRYMANDERING
GERRYMANDERS
GERUND
GERUNDIAL
GERUNDIVE
GERUNDIVES
GERUNDS
GESELLSCHAFT
GESELLSCHAFTS
GESNERIA
GESNERIAD
GESNERIADS
GESSO
GESSOED
GESSOES
GEST
GESTALT
GESTALTEN
GESTALTIST
GESTALTISTS
GESTALTS
GESTAPO
GESTAPOS
GESTATE
GESTATED
GESTATES
GESTATING
GESTATION
GESTATIONAL
GESTATIONS
GESTATIVE
GESTATORY
GESTE
GESTES
GESTIC
GESTICAL
GESTICULANT
GESTICULATE
GESTICULATED
GESTICULATES
GESTICULATING
GESTICULATION
GESTICULATIONS
GESTICULATIVE
GESTICULATOR
GESTICULATORS
GESTICULATORY
GESTS
GESTURAL
GESTURALLY
GESTURE
GESTURED
GESTURER
GESTURERS
GESTURES
GESTURING
GESUNDHEIT
GESUNDHEITS
GET
GETA
GETABLE
GETAS
GETATABLE
GETAWAY
GETAWAYS
GETOUT
GETOUTS
GETS
GETTABLE
GETTER
GETTERED
GETTERING
GETTERS
GETTING
GETUP
GETUPS
GEUM
GEUMS
GEWGAW
GEWGAWED
GEWGAWS
GEWURZTRAMINER
GEWURZTRAMINERS
GEY
GEYSER
GEYSERED
GEYSERING
GEYSERITE
GEYSERITES
GEYSERS
GHARIAL
GHARIALS
GHARRI
GHARRIES
GHARRIS
GHARRY
GHAST
GHASTFUL
GHASTFULLY
GHASTLIER
GHASTLIEST
GHASTLINESS
GHASTLINESSES
GHASTLY
GHAT
GHATS
GHAUT
GHAUTS
GHAZAL
GHAZALS
GHAZI
GHAZIES
GHAZIS
GHEE
GHEES
GHERAO
GHERAOED
GHERAOES
GHERAOING
GHERAOS
GHERKIN
GHERKINS
GHETTO
GHETTOED
GHETTOES
GHETTOING
GHETTOISE
GHETTOISED
GHETTOISES
GHETTOISING
GHETTOIZATION
GHETTOIZATIONS
GHETTOIZE
GHETTOIZED
GHETTOIZES
GHETTOIZING
GHETTOS
GHI
GHIBLI
GHIBLIS
GHILLIE
GHILLIES
GHIS
GHOST
GHOSTED
GHOSTIER
GHOSTIEST
GHOSTING
GHOSTINGS
GHOSTLIER
GHOSTLIEST
GHOSTLIKE
GHOSTLINESS
GHOSTLINESSES
GHOSTLY
GHOSTS
GHOSTWRITE
GHOSTWRITER
GHOSTWRITERS
GHOSTWRITES
GHOSTWRITING
GHOSTWRITTEN
GHOSTWROTE
GHOSTY
GHOUL
GHOULIE
GHOULIES
GHOULISH
GHOULISHLY
GHOULISHNESS
GHOULISHNESSES
GHOULS
GHYLL
GHYLLS
GI
GIANT
GIANTESS
GIANTESSES
GIANTISM
GIANTISMS
GIANTLIKE
GIANTS
GIAOUR
GIAOURS
GIARDIA
GIARDIAS
GIARDIASES
GIARDIASIS
GIB
GIBBED
GIBBER
GIBBERED
GIBBERELLIN
GIBBERELLINS
GIBBERING
GIBBERISH
GIBBERISHES
GIBBERS
GIBBET
GIBBETED
GIBBETING
GIBBETS
GIBBETTED
GIBBETTING
GIBBING
GIBBON
GIBBONS
GIBBOSE
GIBBOSITIES
GIBBOSITY
GIBBOUS
GIBBOUSLY
GIBBSITE
GIBBSITES
GIBE
GIBED
GIBER
GIBERS
GIBES
GIBING
GIBINGLY
GIBLET
GIBLETS
GIBS
GIBSON
GIBSONS
GID
GIDDAP
GIDDIED
GIDDIER
GIDDIES
GIDDIEST
GIDDILY
GIDDINESS
GIDDINESSES
GIDDY
GIDDYAP
GIDDYING
GIDDYUP
GIDS
GIE
GIED
GIEING
GIEN
GIES
GIF
GIFS
GIFT
GIFTABLE
GIFTABLES
GIFTED
GIFTEDLY
GIFTEDNESS
GIFTEDNESSES
GIFTEE
GIFTEES
GIFTING
GIFTINGS
GIFTLESS

GIFTS
GIFTWARE
GIFTWARES
GIFTWRAP
GIFTWRAPPED
GIFTWRAPPING
GIFTWRAPS
GIG
GIGA
GIGABIT
GIGABITS
GIGABYTE
GIGABYTES
GIGACYCLE
GIGACYCLES
GIGAFLOP
GIGAFLOPS
GIGAHERTZ
GIGAHERTZES
GIGANTEAN
GIGANTESQUE
GIGANTIC
GIGANTICALLY
GIGANTISM
GIGANTISMS
GIGAS
GIGATON
GIGATONS
GIGAWATT
GIGAWATTS
GIGGED
GIGGING
GIGGLE
GIGGLED
GIGGLER
GIGGLERS
GIGGLES
GIGGLIER
GIGGLIEST
GIGGLING
GIGGLINGLY
GIGGLY
GIGHE
GIGLET
GIGLETS
GIGLOT
GIGLOTS
GIGOLO
GIGOLOS
GIGOT
GIGOTS
GIGS
GIGUE
GIGUES
GILBERT
GILBERTS
GILD
GILDED
GILDER
GILDERS
GILDHALL
GILDHALLS
GILDING
GILDINGS
GILDS
GILL
GILLED
GILLER
GILLERS
GILLIE
GILLIED
GILLIES
GILLING
GILLNET
GILLNETS
GILLNETTED
GILLNETTER
GILLNETTERS
GILLNETTING
GILLS
GILLY
GILLYFLOWER
GILLYFLOWERS
GILLYING
GILT
GILTHEAD
GILTHEADS
GILTS
GIMBAL
GIMBALED
GIMBALING
GIMBALLED
GIMBALLING
GIMBALS
GIMCRACK
GIMCRACKERIES
GIMCRACKERY
GIMCRACKS
GIMEL
GIMELS
GIMLET
GIMLETED
GIMLETING
GIMLETS
GIMMAL
GIMMALS
GIMME
GIMMES
GIMMICK
GIMMICKED
GIMMICKIER
GIMMICKIEST
GIMMICKING
GIMMICKRIES
GIMMICKRY
GIMMICKS
GIMMICKY
GIMMIE
GIMMIES
GIMP
GIMPED
GIMPIER
GIMPIEST
GIMPING
GIMPS
GIMPY
GIN
GINCH
GINCHES
GINGAL
GINGALL
GINGALLS
GINGALS
GINGELEY
GINGELEYS
GINGELI
GINGELIES
GINGELIS
GINGELLI
GINGELLIES
GINGELLIS
GINGELLY
GINGELY
GINGER
GINGERBREAD
GINGERBREADED
GINGERBREADS
GINGERBREADY
GINGERED
GINGERIER
GINGERIEST
GINGERING
GINGERLIER
GINGERLIEST
GINGERLINESS
GINGERLINESSES
GINGERLY
GINGERROOT
GINGERROOTS
GINGERS
GINGERSNAP
GINGERSNAPS
GINGERY
GINGHAM
GINGHAMS
GINGILI
GINGILIS
GINGILLI
GINGILLIS
GINGIVA
GINGIVAE
GINGIVAL
GINGIVECTOMIES
GINGIVECTOMY
GINGIVITIS
GINGIVITISES
GINGKO
GINGKOES
GINGKOS
GINK
GINKGO
GINKGOES
GINKGOS
GINKS
GINNED
GINNER
GINNERS
GINNIER
GINNIEST
GINNING
GINNINGS
GINNY
GINORMOUS
GINS
GINSENG
GINSENGS
GINZO
GINZOES
GIP
GIPON
GIPONS
GIPPED
GIPPER
GIPPERS
GIPPING
GIPS
GIPSIED
GIPSIES
GIPSY
GIPSYDOM
GIPSYDOMS
GIPSYING
GIPSYISH
GIPSYISM
GIPSYISMS
GIRAFFE
GIRAFFES
GIRAFFISH
GIRANDOLA
GIRANDOLAS
GIRANDOLE
GIRANDOLES
GIRASOL
GIRASOLE
GIRASOLES
GIRASOLS
GIRD
GIRDED
GIRDER
GIRDERS
GIRDING
GIRDINGLY
GIRDLE
GIRDLED
GIRDLER
GIRDLERS
GIRDLES
GIRDLING
GIRDS
GIRL
GIRLFRIEND
GIRLFRIENDS
GIRLHOOD
GIRLHOODS
GIRLIE
GIRLIER
GIRLIES
GIRLIEST
GIRLISH
GIRLISHLY
GIRLISHNESS
GIRLISHNESSES
GIRLS
GIRLY
GIRN
GIRNED
GIRNING
GIRNS
GIRO
GIROLLE
GIROLLES
GIRON
GIRONS
GIROS
GIROSOL

GIROSOLS
GIRSH
GIRSHES
GIRT
GIRTED
GIRTH
GIRTHED
GIRTHING
GIRTHS
GIRTING
GIRTS
GIS
GISARME
GISARMES
GISMO
GISMOS
GIST
GISTS
GIT
GITANO
GITANOS
GITCH
GITCHES
GITE
GITES
GITS
GITTED
GITTERN
GITTERNS
GITTIN
GITTING
GIVE
GIVEABLE
GIVEAWAY
GIVEAWAYS
GIVEBACK
GIVEBACKS
GIVEN
GIVENS
GIVER
GIVERS
GIVES
GIVING
GIZMO
GIZMOS
GIZZARD
GIZZARDS
GJETOST
GJETOSTS
GLABELLA
GLABELLAE
GLABELLAR
GLABRATE
GLABRESCENT
GLABROUS
GLACE
GLACED
GLACEED
GLACEING
GLACES
GLACIAL
GLACIALLY
GLACIATE
GLACIATED
GLACIATES
GLACIATING
GLACIATION
GLACIATIONS
GLACIER
GLACIERED
GLACIERS
GLACIOLOGICAL
GLACIOLOGIES
GLACIOLOGIST
GLACIOLOGISTS
GLACIOLOGY
GLACIS
GLACISES
GLAD
GLADDED
GLADDEN
GLADDENED
GLADDENER
GLADDENERS
GLADDENING
GLADDENS
GLADDER
GLADDEST
GLADDING
GLADE
GLADELIKE
GLADES
GLADIATE
GLADIATOR
GLADIATORIAL
GLADIATORS
GLADIER
GLADIEST
GLADIOLA
GLADIOLAR
GLADIOLAS
GLADIOLI
GLADIOLUS
GLADIOLUSES
GLADLIER
GLADLIEST
GLADLY
GLADNESS
GLADNESSES
GLADS
GLADSOME
GLADSOMELY
GLADSOMENESS
GLADSOMENESSES
GLADSOMER
GLADSOMEST
GLADSTONE
GLADSTONES
GLADY
GLAIKET
GLAIKIT
GLAIR
GLAIRE
GLAIRED
GLAIRES
GLAIRIER
GLAIRIEST
GLAIRING
GLAIRS
GLAIRY
GLAIVE
GLAIVED
GLAIVES
GLAM
GLAMMED
GLAMMER
GLAMMEST
GLAMMIER
GLAMMIEST
GLAMMING
GLAMMY
GLAMOR
GLAMORISE
GLAMORISED
GLAMORISES
GLAMORISING
GLAMORIZATION
GLAMORIZATIONS
GLAMORIZE
GLAMORIZED
GLAMORIZER
GLAMORIZERS
GLAMORIZES
GLAMORIZING
GLAMOROUS
GLAMOROUSLY
GLAMOROUSNESS
GLAMOROUSNESSES
GLAMORS
GLAMOUR
GLAMOURED
GLAMOURING
GLAMOURIZE
GLAMOURIZED
GLAMOURIZES
GLAMOURIZING
GLAMOURLESS
GLAMOUROUS
GLAMOURS
GLAMS
GLANCE
GLANCED
GLANCER
GLANCERS
GLANCES
GLANCING
GLANCINGLY
GLAND
GLANDERED
GLANDERS
GLANDES
GLANDLESS
GLANDS
GLANDULAR
GLANDULARLY
GLANDULE
GLANDULES
GLANS
GLARE
GLARED
GLARES
GLARIER
GLARIEST
GLARINESS
GLARINESSES
GLARING
GLARINGLY
GLARINGNESS
GLARINGNESSES
GLARY
GLASNOST
GLASNOSTS
GLASS
GLASSBLOWER
GLASSBLOWERS
GLASSBLOWING
GLASSBLOWINGS
GLASSED
GLASSES
GLASSFUL
GLASSFULS
GLASSHOUSE
GLASSHOUSES
GLASSIE
GLASSIER
GLASSIES
GLASSIEST
GLASSILY
GLASSINE
GLASSINES
GLASSINESS
GLASSINESSES
GLASSING
GLASSLESS
GLASSMAKER
GLASSMAKERS
GLASSMAKING
GLASSMAKINGS
GLASSMAN
GLASSMEN
GLASSPAPER
GLASSPAPERED
GLASSPAPERING
GLASSPAPERS
GLASSWARE
GLASSWARES
GLASSWORK
GLASSWORKER
GLASSWORKERS
GLASSWORKS
GLASSWORM
GLASSWORMS
GLASSWORT
GLASSWORTS
GLASSY
GLAUCOMA
GLAUCOMAS
GLAUCONITE
GLAUCONITES
GLAUCONITIC
GLAUCOUS
GLAUCOUSNESS
GLAUCOUSNESSES
GLAZE
GLAZED
GLAZER
GLAZERS
GLAZES
GLAZIER
GLAZIERIES
GLAZIERS
GLAZIERY
GLAZIEST
GLAZILY
GLAZINESS

GLAZINESSES
GLAZING
GLAZINGS
GLAZY
GLEAM
GLEAMED
GLEAMER
GLEAMERS
GLEAMIER
GLEAMIEST
GLEAMING
GLEAMS
GLEAMY
GLEAN
GLEANABLE
GLEANED
GLEANER
GLEANERS
GLEANING
GLEANINGS
GLEANS
GLEBA
GLEBAE
GLEBE
GLEBELESS
GLEBES
GLED
GLEDE
GLEDES
GLEDS
GLEE
GLEED
GLEEDS
GLEEFUL
GLEEFULLY
GLEEFULNESS
GLEEFULNESSES
GLEEK
GLEEKED
GLEEKING
GLEEKS
GLEEMAN
GLEEMEN
GLEES
GLEESOME
GLEET
GLEETED
GLEETIER
GLEETIEST
GLEETING
GLEETS
GLEETY
GLEG
GLEGLY
GLEGNESS
GLEGNESSES
GLEIZATION
GLEIZATIONS
GLEN
GLENGARRIES
GLENGARRY
GLENLIKE
GLENOID
GLENS
GLEY
GLEYED
GLEYING
GLEYINGS
GLEYS
GLIA
GLIADIN
GLIADINE
GLIADINES
GLIADINS
GLIAL
GLIAS
GLIB
GLIBBER
GLIBBEST
GLIBLY
GLIBNESS
GLIBNESSES
GLIDE
GLIDED
GLIDEPATH
GLIDEPATHS
GLIDER
GLIDERS
GLIDES
GLIDING
GLIFF
GLIFFS
GLIM
GLIME
GLIMED
GLIMES
GLIMING
GLIMMER
GLIMMERED
GLIMMERING
GLIMMERINGS
GLIMMERS
GLIMPSE
GLIMPSED
GLIMPSER
GLIMPSERS
GLIMPSES
GLIMPSING
GLIMS
GLINT
GLINTED
GLINTIER
GLINTIEST
GLINTING
GLINTS
GLINTY
GLIOBLASTOMA
GLIOBLASTOMAS
GLIOBLASTOMATA
GLIOMA
GLIOMAS
GLIOMATA
GLIOSES
GLIOSIS
GLISSADE
GLISSADED
GLISSADER
GLISSADERS
GLISSADES
GLISSADING
GLISSANDI
GLISSANDO
GLISSANDOS
GLISSE
GLISSES
GLISTEN
GLISTENED
GLISTENING
GLISTENS
GLISTER
GLISTERED
GLISTERING
GLISTERS
GLITCH
GLITCHES
GLITCHIER
GLITCHIEST
GLITCHY
GLITTER
GLITTERATI
GLITTERED
GLITTERIER
GLITTERIEST
GLITTERING
GLITTERINGLY
GLITTERS
GLITTERY
GLITZ
GLITZED
GLITZES
GLITZIER
GLITZIEST
GLITZILY
GLITZINESS
GLITZINESSES
GLITZING
GLITZY
GLOAM
GLOAMING
GLOAMINGS
GLOAMS
GLOAT
GLOATED
GLOATER
GLOATERS
GLOATING
GLOATINGLY
GLOATS
GLOB
GLOBAL
GLOBALISATION
GLOBALISATIONS
GLOBALISE
GLOBALISED
GLOBALISES
GLOBALISING
GLOBALISM
GLOBALISMS
GLOBALIST
GLOBALISTS
GLOBALIZATION
GLOBALIZATIONS
GLOBALIZE
GLOBALIZED
GLOBALIZES
GLOBALIZING
GLOBALLY
GLOBATE
GLOBATED
GLOBBIER
GLOBBIEST
GLOBBY
GLOBE
GLOBED
GLOBEFISH
GLOBEFISHES
GLOBEFLOWER
GLOBEFLOWERS
GLOBELIKE
GLOBES
GLOBETROT
GLOBETROTS
GLOBETROTTED
GLOBETROTTING
GLOBIN
GLOBING
GLOBINS
GLOBOID
GLOBOIDS
GLOBOSE
GLOBOSELY
GLOBOSITIES
GLOBOSITY
GLOBOUS
GLOBS
GLOBULAR
GLOBULARS
GLOBULE
GLOBULES
GLOBULIN
GLOBULINS
GLOCHID
GLOCHIDIA
GLOCHIDIUM
GLOCHIDS
GLOCKENSPIEL
GLOCKENSPIELS
GLOGG
GLOGGS
GLOM
GLOMERA
GLOMERATE
GLOMERULAR
GLOMERULE
GLOMERULES
GLOMERULI
GLOMERULUS
GLOMMED
GLOMMING
GLOMS
GLOMUS
GLONOIN
GLONOINS
GLOOM
GLOOMED
GLOOMFUL
GLOOMIER
GLOOMIEST
GLOOMILY
GLOOMINESS
GLOOMINESSES
GLOOMING
GLOOMINGS
GLOOMS
GLOOMY

GLOOP
GLOOPIER
GLOOPIEST
GLOOPS
GLOOPY
GLOP
GLOPPED
GLOPPIER
GLOPPIEST
GLOPPING
GLOPPY
GLOPS
GLORIA
GLORIAS
GLORIED
GLORIES
GLORIFICATION
GLORIFICATIONS
GLORIFIED
GLORIFIER
GLORIFIERS
GLORIFIES
GLORIFY
GLORIFYING
GLORIOLE
GLORIOLES
GLORIOUS
GLORIOUSLY
GLORIOUSNESS
GLORIOUSNESSES
GLORY
GLORYING
GLOSS
GLOSSA
GLOSSAE
GLOSSAL
GLOSSARIAL
GLOSSARIES
GLOSSARIST
GLOSSARISTS
GLOSSARY
GLOSSAS
GLOSSATOR
GLOSSATORS
GLOSSED
GLOSSEME
GLOSSEMES
GLOSSER
GLOSSERS
GLOSSES
GLOSSIER
GLOSSIES
GLOSSIEST
GLOSSILY
GLOSSINA
GLOSSINAS
GLOSSINESS
GLOSSINESSES
GLOSSING
GLOSSITIC
GLOSSITIS
GLOSSITISES
GLOSSOGRAPHER
GLOSSOGRAPHERS
GLOSSOLALIA
GLOSSOLALIAS
GLOSSOLALIST
GLOSSOLALISTS
GLOSSY
GLOST
GLOSTS
GLOTTAL
GLOTTIC
GLOTTIDES
GLOTTIS
GLOTTISES
GLOUT
GLOUTED
GLOUTING
GLOUTS
GLOVE
GLOVEBOX
GLOVEBOXES
GLOVED
GLOVER
GLOVERS
GLOVES
GLOVING
GLOW
GLOWED
GLOWER
GLOWERED
GLOWERING
GLOWERS
GLOWFLIES
GLOWFLY
GLOWING
GLOWINGLY
GLOWS
GLOWWORM
GLOWWORMS
GLOXINIA
GLOXINIAS
GLOZE
GLOZED
GLOZES
GLOZING
GLUCAGON
GLUCAGONS
GLUCAN
GLUCANS
GLUCINIC
GLUCINUM
GLUCINUMS
GLUCOCORTICOID
GLUCOCORTICOIDS
GLUCOKINASE
GLUCOKINASES
GLUCONATE
GLUCONATES
GLUCONEOGENESES
GLUCONEOGENESIS
GLUCOSAMINE
GLUCOSAMINES
GLUCOSE
GLUCOSES
GLUCOSIC
GLUCOSIDASE
GLUCOSIDASES
GLUCOSIDE
GLUCOSIDES
GLUCOSIDIC
GLUCURONIDASE
GLUCURONIDASES
GLUCURONIDE
GLUCURONIDES
GLUE
GLUED
GLUEING
GLUELIKE
GLUEPOT
GLUEPOTS
GLUER
GLUERS
GLUES
GLUEY
GLUEYNESS
GLUEYNESSES
GLUG
GLUGGED
GLUGGING
GLUGS
GLUHWEIN
GLUHWEINS
GLUIER
GLUIEST
GLUILY
GLUINESS
GLUINESSES
GLUING
GLUM
GLUME
GLUMES
GLUMLY
GLUMMER
GLUMMEST
GLUMNESS
GLUMNESSES
GLUMPIER
GLUMPIEST
GLUMPILY
GLUMPY
GLUMS
GLUNCH
GLUNCHED
GLUNCHES
GLUNCHING
GLUON
GLUONS
GLUT
GLUTAMATE
GLUTAMATES
GLUTAMINASE
GLUTAMINASES
GLUTAMINE
GLUTAMINES
GLUTARALDEHYDE
GLUTARALDEHYDES
GLUTATHIONE
GLUTATHIONES
GLUTCH
GLUTCHED
GLUTCHES
GLUTCHING
GLUTE
GLUTEAL
GLUTEI
GLUTELIN
GLUTELINS
GLUTEN
GLUTENIN
GLUTENINS
GLUTENOUS
GLUTENS
GLUTES
GLUTETHIMIDE
GLUTETHIMIDES
GLUTEUS
GLUTINOUS
GLUTINOUSLY
GLUTS
GLUTTED
GLUTTING
GLUTTON
GLUTTONIES
GLUTTONOUS
GLUTTONOUSLY
GLUTTONOUSNESS
GLUTTONS
GLUTTONY
GLYCAN
GLYCANS
GLYCEMIA
GLYCEMIAS
GLYCEMIC
GLYCERALDEHYDE
GLYCERALDEHYDES
GLYCERIC
GLYCERIDE
GLYCERIDES
GLYCERIDIC
GLYCERIN
GLYCERINATE
GLYCERINATED
GLYCERINATES
GLYCERINATING
GLYCERINE
GLYCERINES
GLYCERINS
GLYCEROL
GLYCEROLS
GLYCERYL
GLYCERYLS
GLYCIN
GLYCINE
GLYCINES
GLYCINS
GLYCOALKALOID
GLYCOALKALOIDS
GLYCOGEN
GLYCOGENESES
GLYCOGENESIS
GLYCOGENOLYSES
GLYCOGENOLYSIS
GLYCOGENOLYTIC
GLYCOGENS
GLYCOL
GLYCOLIC
GLYCOLIPID
GLYCOLIPIDS
GLYCOLS
GLYCOLYSES
GLYCOLYSIS
GLYCOLYTIC
GLYCONIC

GLYCONICS
GLYCOPEPTIDE
GLYCOPEPTIDES
GLYCOPROTEIN
GLYCOPROTEINS
GLYCOSIDASE
GLYCOSIDASES
GLYCOSIDE
GLYCOSIDES
GLYCOSIDIC
GLYCOSIDICALLY
GLYCOSURIA
GLYCOSURIAS
GLYCOSYL
GLYCOSYLATE
GLYCOSYLATED
GLYCOSYLATES
GLYCOSYLATING
GLYCOSYLATION
GLYCOSYLATIONS
GLYCOSYLS
GLYCYL
GLYCYLS
GLYPH
GLYPHIC
GLYPHOSATE
GLYPHOSATES
GLYPHS
GLYPTIC
GLYPTICS
GNAR
GNARL
GNARLED
GNARLIER
GNARLIEST
GNARLING
GNARLS
GNARLY
GNARR
GNARRED
GNARRING
GNARRS
GNARS
GNASH
GNASHED
GNASHES
GNASHING
GNAT
GNATCATCHER
GNATCATCHERS
GNATHAL
GNATHIC
GNATHION
GNATHIONS
GNATHITE
GNATHITES
GNATHONIC
GNATLIKE
GNATS
GNATTIER
GNATTIEST
GNATTY
GNAW
GNAWABLE
GNAWED
GNAWER
GNAWERS
GNAWING
GNAWINGLY
GNAWINGS
GNAWN
GNAWS
GNEISS
GNEISSES
GNEISSIC
GNEISSOID
GNEISSOSE
GNOCCHI
GNOME
GNOMELIKE
GNOMES
GNOMIC
GNOMICAL
GNOMISH
GNOMIST
GNOMISTS
GNOMON
GNOMONIC
GNOMONS
GNOSES
GNOSIS
GNOSTIC
GNOSTICAL
GNOSTICISM
GNOSTICISMS
GNOSTICS
GNOTOBIOTIC
GNOTOBIOTICALLY
GNU
GNUS
GO
GOA
GOAD
GOADED
GOADING
GOADLIKE
GOADS
GOAL
GOALBALL
GOALBALLS
GOALED
GOALIE
GOALIES
GOALING
GOALKEEPER
GOALKEEPERS
GOALKEEPING
GOALKEEPINGS
GOALLESS
GOALMOUTH
GOALMOUTHS
GOALPOST
GOALPOSTS
GOALS
GOALTENDER
GOALTENDERS
GOALTENDING
GOALTENDINGS
GOALWARD
GOANNA
GOANNAS
GOAS
GOAT
GOATEE
GOATEED
GOATEES
GOATFISH
GOATFISHES
GOATHERD
GOATHERDS
GOATIER
GOATIEST
GOATISH
GOATISHLY
GOATLIKE
GOATS
GOATSKIN
GOATSKINS
GOATSUCKER
GOATSUCKERS
GOATY
GOB
GOBAN
GOBANG
GOBANGS
GOBANS
GOBBED
GOBBET
GOBBETS
GOBBING
GOBBLE
GOBBLED
GOBBLEDEGOOK
GOBBLEDEGOOKS
GOBBLEDYGOOK
GOBBLEDYGOOKS
GOBBLER
GOBBLERS
GOBBLES
GOBBLING
GOBIES
GOBIOID
GOBIOIDS
GOBLET
GOBLETS
GOBLIN
GOBLINS
GOBO
GOBOES
GOBONEE
GOBONY
GOBOS
GOBS
GOBSHITE
GOBSHITES
GOBSMACKED
GOBY
GOD
GODAMNDEST
GODAWFUL
GODCHILD
GODCHILDREN
GODDAM
GODDAMMED
GODDAMMING
GODDAMN
GODDAMNDEST
GODDAMNED
GODDAMNEDEST
GODDAMNING
GODDAMNS
GODDAMS
GODDAUGHTER
GODDAUGHTERS
GODDED
GODDESS
GODDESSES
GODDING
GODET
GODETIA
GODETIAS
GODETS
GODFATHER
GODFATHERED
GODFATHERING
GODFATHERS
GODFORSAKEN
GODHEAD
GODHEADS
GODHOOD
GODHOODS
GODLESS
GODLESSLY
GODLESSNESS
GODLESSNESSES
GODLIER
GODLIEST
GODLIKE
GODLIKENESS
GODLIKENESSES
GODLILY
GODLINESS
GODLINESSES
GODLING
GODLINGS
GODLY
GODMOTHER
GODMOTHERED
GODMOTHERING
GODMOTHERS
GODOWN
GODOWNS
GODPARENT
GODPARENTS
GODROON
GODROONS
GODS
GODSEND
GODSENDS
GODSHIP
GODSHIPS
GODSON
GODSONS
GODWARD
GODWARDS
GODWIT
GODWITS
GOER
GOERS
GOES
GOEST
GOETH
GOETHITE
GOETHITES
GOFER

GOFERS
GOFFER
GOFFERED
GOFFERING
GOFFERINGS
GOFFERS
GOGGLE
GOGGLED
GOGGLER
GOGGLERS
GOGGLES
GOGGLIER
GOGGLIEST
GOGGLING
GOGGLY
GOGLET
GOGLETS
GOGO
GOGOS
GOING
GOINGS
GOITER
GOITERED
GOITERS
GOITRE
GOITRED
GOITRES
GOITROGEN
GOITROGENIC
GOITROGENICITY
GOITROGENS
GOITROUS
GOJI
GOJIS
GOLCONDA
GOLCONDAS
GOLD
GOLDARN
GOLDARNED
GOLDARNING
GOLDARNS
GOLDBRICK
GOLDBRICKED
GOLDBRICKING
GOLDBRICKS
GOLDBUG
GOLDBUGS
GOLDEN
GOLDENER
GOLDENEST
GOLDENEYE
GOLDENEYES
GOLDENLY
GOLDENNESS
GOLDENNESSES
GOLDENROD
GOLDENRODS
GOLDENSEAL
GOLDENSEALS
GOLDER
GOLDEST
GOLDEYE
GOLDEYES
GOLDFIELD
GOLDFIELDS
GOLDFINCH
GOLDFINCHES
GOLDFISH
GOLDFISHES
GOLDS
GOLDSMITH
GOLDSMITHS
GOLDSTONE
GOLDSTONES
GOLDTONE
GOLDURN
GOLDURNS
GOLEM
GOLEMS
GOLF
GOLFED
GOLFER
GOLFERS
GOLFING
GOLFINGS
GOLFS
GOLGOTHA
GOLGOTHAS
GOLIARD
GOLIARDIC
GOLIARDS
GOLIATH
GOLIATHS
GOLLIWOG
GOLLIWOGG
GOLLIWOGGS
GOLLIWOGS
GOLLY
GOLLYWOG
GOLLYWOGS
GOLOSH
GOLOSHE
GOLOSHES
GOMBEEN
GOMBEENS
GOMBO
GOMBOS
GOMBROON
GOMBROONS
GOMER
GOMERAL
GOMERALS
GOMEREL
GOMERELS
GOMERIL
GOMERILS
GOMERS
GOMPHOSES
GOMPHOSIS
GOMUTI
GOMUTIS
GONAD
GONADAL
GONADECTOMIES
GONADECTOMIZED
GONADECTOMY
GONADIAL
GONADIC
GONADOTROPHIC
GONADOTROPHIN
GONADOTROPHINS
GONADOTROPIC
GONADOTROPIN
GONADOTROPINS
GONADS
GONCH
GONCHES
GONDOLA
GONDOLAS
GONDOLIER
GONDOLIERS
GONE
GONEF
GONEFS
GONENESS
GONENESSES
GONER
GONERS
GONFALON
GONFALONS
GONFANON
GONFANONS
GONG
GONGED
GONGING
GONGLIKE
GONGORISTIC
GONGS
GONIA
GONIDIA
GONIDIAL
GONIDIC
GONIDIUM
GONIF
GONIFF
GONIFFS
GONIFS
GONIOMETER
GONIOMETERS
GONIOMETRIC
GONIOMETRIES
GONIOMETRY
GONION
GONIUM
GONOCOCCAL
GONOCOCCI
GONOCOCCUS
GONOCYTE
GONOCYTES
GONOF
GONOFS
GONOPH
GONOPHORE
GONOPHORES
GONOPHS
GONOPORE
GONOPORES
GONORRHEA
GONORRHEAL
GONORRHEAS
GONORRHOEA
GONORRHOEAS
GONZO
GOO
GOOBER
GOOBERS
GOOD
GOODBY
GOODBYE
GOODBYES
GOODBYS
GOODIE
GOODIES
GOODISH
GOODLIER
GOODLIEST
GOODLY
GOODMAN
GOODMEN
GOODNESS
GOODNESSES
GOODS
GOODWIFE
GOODWILL
GOODWILLED
GOODWILLS
GOODWIVES
GOODY
GOOEY
GOOEYNESS
GOOEYNESSES
GOOF
GOOFBALL
GOOFBALLS
GOOFED
GOOFIER
GOOFIEST
GOOFILY
GOOFINESS
GOOFINESSES
GOOFING
GOOFS
GOOFUS
GOOFUSES
GOOFY
GOOGLE
GOOGLED
GOOGLES
GOOGLIES
GOOGLING
GOOGLY
GOOGOL
GOOGOLPLEX
GOOGOLPLEXES
GOOGOLS
GOOIER
GOOIEST
GOOK
GOOKS
GOOKY
GOOLIE
GOOLIES
GOOLY
GOOMBAH
GOOMBAHS
GOOMBAY
GOOMBAYS
GOON
GOONDA
GOONDAS
GOONERIES
GOONERY
GOONEY
GOONEYS
GOONIE

GOONIER
GOONIES
GOONIEST
GOONS
GOONY
GOOP
GOOPIER
GOOPIEST
GOOPS
GOOPY
GOORAL
GOORALS
GOOS
GOOSANDER
GOOSANDERS
GOOSE
GOOSEBERRIES
GOOSEBERRY
GOOSED
GOOSEFISH
GOOSEFISHES
GOOSEFLESH
GOOSEFLESHES
GOOSEFOOT
GOOSEFOOTS
GOOSEGRASS
GOOSEGRASSES
GOOSEHERD
GOOSEHERDS
GOOSENECK
GOOSENECKED
GOOSENECKS
GOOSES
GOOSEY
GOOSIER
GOOSIEST
GOOSING
GOOSY
GOPHER
GOPHERS
GOPIK
GOPIKS
GOR
GORAL
GORALS
GORBELLIES
GORBELLY
GORBLIMY
GORCOCK
GORCOCKS
GORDITA
GORDITAS
GORE
GORED
GOREFEST
GOREFESTS
GORES
GORGE
GORGED
GORGEDLY
GORGEOUS
GORGEOUSLY
GORGEOUSNESS
GORGEOUSNESSES
GORGER
GORGERIN
GORGERINS
GORGERS
GORGES
GORGET
GORGETED
GORGETS
GORGING
GORGON
GORGONIAN
GORGONIANS
GORGONIZE
GORGONIZED
GORGONIZES
GORGONIZING
GORGONS
GORHEN
GORHENS
GORIER
GORIEST
GORILLA
GORILLAS
GORILY
GORINESS
GORINESSES
GORING
GORM
GORMAND
GORMANDISE
GORMANDISED
GORMANDISES
GORMANDISING
GORMANDIZE
GORMANDIZED
GORMANDIZER
GORMANDIZERS
GORMANDIZES
GORMANDIZING
GORMANDS
GORMED
GORMING
GORMLESS
GORMLESSNESS
GORMLESSNESSES
GORMS
GORP
GORPS
GORSE
GORSES
GORSIER
GORSIEST
GORSY
GORY
GOS
GOSH
GOSHAWK
GOSHAWKS
GOSLING
GOSLINGS
GOSPEL
GOSPELER
GOSPELERS
GOSPELLER
GOSPELLERS
GOSPELLY
GOSPELS
GOSPORT
GOSPORTS
GOSSAMER
GOSSAMERS
GOSSAMERY
GOSSAN
GOSSANS
GOSSIP
GOSSIPED
GOSSIPER
GOSSIPERS
GOSSIPIER
GOSSIPIEST
GOSSIPING
GOSSIPMONGER
GOSSIPMONGERS
GOSSIPPED
GOSSIPPER
GOSSIPPERS
GOSSIPPING
GOSSIPRIES
GOSSIPRY
GOSSIPS
GOSSIPY
GOSSOON
GOSSOONS
GOSSYPOL
GOSSYPOLS
GOT
GOTCH
GOTCHA
GOTCHAS
GOTCHES
GOTCHIES
GOTH
GOTHIC
GOTHICALLY
GOTHICISM
GOTHICISMS
GOTHICIZE
GOTHICIZED
GOTHICIZES
GOTHICIZING
GOTHICS
GOTHITE
GOTHITES
GOTHS
GOTTEN
GOUACHE
GOUACHES
GOUGE
GOUGED
GOUGER
GOUGERS
GOUGES
GOUGING
GOULASH
GOULASHES
GOURAMI
GOURAMIES
GOURAMIS
GOURD
GOURDE
GOURDES
GOURDFUL
GOURDFULS
GOURDLIKE
GOURDS
GOURMAND
GOURMANDISE
GOURMANDISED
GOURMANDISES
GOURMANDISING
GOURMANDISM
GOURMANDISMS
GOURMANDIZE
GOURMANDIZED
GOURMANDIZES
GOURMANDIZING
GOURMANDS
GOURMET
GOURMETS
GOUT
GOUTIER
GOUTIEST
GOUTILY
GOUTINESS
GOUTINESSES
GOUTS
GOUTWEED
GOUTWEEDS
GOUTY
GOVERN
GOVERNABLE
GOVERNANCE
GOVERNANCES
GOVERNED
GOVERNESS
GOVERNESSES
GOVERNESSY
GOVERNING
GOVERNMENT
GOVERNMENTAL
GOVERNMENTALISM
GOVERNMENTALIST
GOVERNMENTALIZE
GOVERNMENTALLY
GOVERNMENTESE
GOVERNMENTESES
GOVERNMENTS
GOVERNOR
GOVERNORATE
GOVERNORATES
GOVERNORS
GOVERNORSHIP
GOVERNORSHIPS
GOVERNS
GOWAN
GOWANED
GOWANS
GOWANY
GOWD
GOWDS
GOWK
GOWKS
GOWN
GOWNED
GOWNING
GOWNS
GOWNSMAN
GOWNSMEN
GOX
GOXES
GOY

GOYIM
GOYISH
GOYISHE
GOYS
GRAAL
GRAALS
GRAB
GRABBABLE
GRABBED
GRABBER
GRABBERS
GRABBIER
GRABBIEST
GRABBING
GRABBLE
GRABBLED
GRABBLER
GRABBLERS
GRABBLES
GRABBLING
GRABBY
GRABEN
GRABENS
GRABS
GRACE
GRACED
GRACEFUL
GRACEFULLER
GRACEFULLEST
GRACEFULLY
GRACEFULNESS
GRACEFULNESSES
GRACELESS
GRACELESSLY
GRACELESSNESS
GRACELESSNESSES
GRACES
GRACILE
GRACILENESS
GRACILENESSES
GRACILES
GRACILIS
GRACILITIES
GRACILITY
GRACING
GRACIOSO
GRACIOSOS
GRACIOUS
GRACIOUSLY
GRACIOUSNESS
GRACIOUSNESSES
GRACKLE
GRACKLES
GRAD
GRADABLE
GRADATE
GRADATED
GRADATES
GRADATING
GRADATION
GRADATIONAL
GRADATIONALLY
GRADATIONS
GRADE
GRADED
GRADELESS
GRADER
GRADERS
GRADES
GRADIENT
GRADIENTS
GRADIN
GRADINE
GRADINES
GRADING
GRADINS
GRADIOMETER
GRADIOMETERS
GRADS
GRADUAL
GRADUALISM
GRADUALISMS
GRADUALIST
GRADUALISTIC
GRADUALISTS
GRADUALLY
GRADUALNESS
GRADUALNESSES
GRADUALS
GRADUAND
GRADUANDS
GRADUATE
GRADUATED
GRADUATES
GRADUATING
GRADUATION
GRADUATIONS
GRADUATOR
GRADUATORS
GRADUS
GRADUSES
GRAECIZE
GRAECIZED
GRAECIZES
GRAECIZING
GRAFFITI
GRAFFITIED
GRAFFITIING
GRAFFITING
GRAFFITIS
GRAFFITIST
GRAFFITISTS
GRAFFITO
GRAFT
GRAFTAGE
GRAFTAGES
GRAFTED
GRAFTER
GRAFTERS
GRAFTING
GRAFTS
GRAHAM
GRAHAMS
GRAIL
GRAILS
GRAIN
GRAINED
GRAINER
GRAINERS
GRAINFIELD
GRAINFIELDS
GRAINIER
GRAINIEST
GRAININESS
GRAININESSES
GRAINING
GRAINLESS
GRAINS
GRAINY
GRAM
GRAMA
GRAMARIES
GRAMARY
GRAMARYE
GRAMARYES
GRAMAS
GRAMERCIES
GRAMERCY
GRAMICIDIN
GRAMICIDINS
GRAMINEOUS
GRAMINIVOROUS
GRAMMA
GRAMMAR
GRAMMARIAN
GRAMMARIANS
GRAMMARS
GRAMMAS
GRAMMATICAL
GRAMMATICALITY
GRAMMATICALLY
GRAMMATICALNESS
GRAMME
GRAMMES
GRAMOPHONE
GRAMOPHONES
GRAMP
GRAMPA
GRAMPAS
GRAMPIES
GRAMPS
GRAMPUS
GRAMPUSES
GRAMPY
GRAMS
GRAN
GRANA
GRANADILLA
GRANADILLAS
GRANARIES
GRANARY
GRAND
GRANDAD
GRANDADDIES
GRANDADDY
GRANDADS
GRANDAM
GRANDAME
GRANDAMES
GRANDAMS
GRANDAUNT
GRANDAUNTS
GRANDBABIES
GRANDBABY
GRANDCHILD
GRANDCHILDREN
GRANDDAD
GRANDDADDIES
GRANDDADDY
GRANDDADS
GRANDDAM
GRANDDAMS
GRANDDAUGHTER
GRANDDAUGHTERS
GRANDEE
GRANDEES
GRANDER
GRANDEST
GRANDEUR
GRANDEURS
GRANDFATHER
GRANDFATHERED
GRANDFATHERING
GRANDFATHERLY
GRANDFATHERS
GRANDIFLORA
GRANDIFLORAS
GRANDILOQUENCE
GRANDILOQUENCES
GRANDILOQUENT
GRANDILOQUENTLY
GRANDIOSE
GRANDIOSELY
GRANDIOSENESS
GRANDIOSENESSES
GRANDIOSITIES
GRANDIOSITY
GRANDIOSO
GRANDKID
GRANDKIDS
GRANDLY
GRANDMA
GRANDMAMA
GRANDMAMAS
GRANDMAS
GRANDMOTHER
GRANDMOTHERLY
GRANDMOTHERS
GRANDNEPHEW
GRANDNEPHEWS
GRANDNESS
GRANDNESSES
GRANDNIECE
GRANDNIECES
GRANDPA
GRANDPAPA
GRANDPAPAS
GRANDPARENT
GRANDPARENTAL
GRANDPARENTHOOD
GRANDPARENTS
GRANDPAS
GRANDS
GRANDSIR
GRANDSIRE
GRANDSIRES
GRANDSIRS
GRANDSON
GRANDSONS
GRANDSTAND
GRANDSTANDED
GRANDSTANDER
GRANDSTANDERS
GRANDSTANDING
GRANDSTANDS

GRANDUNCLE
GRANDUNCLES
GRANGE
GRANGER
GRANGERISM
GRANGERISMS
GRANGERS
GRANGES
GRANITA
GRANITAS
GRANITE
GRANITELIKE
GRANITES
GRANITEWARE
GRANITEWARES
GRANITIC
GRANITOID
GRANIVOROUS
GRANNIE
GRANNIES
GRANNY
GRANODIORITE
GRANODIORITES
GRANODIORITIC
GRANOLA
GRANOLAS
GRANOLITH
GRANOLITHIC
GRANOLITHS
GRANOPHYRE
GRANOPHYRES
GRANOPHYRIC
GRANS
GRANT
GRANTABLE
GRANTED
GRANTEE
GRANTEES
GRANTER
GRANTERS
GRANTING
GRANTOR
GRANTORS
GRANTS
GRANTSMAN
GRANTSMANSHIP
GRANTSMANSHIPS
GRANTSMEN
GRANULAR
GRANULARITIES
GRANULARITY
GRANULATE
GRANULATED
GRANULATES
GRANULATING
GRANULATION
GRANULATIONS
GRANULATOR
GRANULATORS
GRANULE
GRANULES
GRANULITE
GRANULITES
GRANULITIC
GRANULOCYTE
GRANULOCYTES
GRANULOCYTIC
GRANULOMA
GRANULOMAS
GRANULOMATA
GRANULOMATOUS
GRANULOSE
GRANULOSES
GRANULOSIS
GRANUM
GRAPE
GRAPEFRUIT
GRAPEFRUITS
GRAPELIKE
GRAPERIES
GRAPERY
GRAPES
GRAPESHOT
GRAPEVINE
GRAPEVINES
GRAPEY
GRAPH
GRAPHED
GRAPHEME
GRAPHEMES
GRAPHEMIC
GRAPHEMICALLY
GRAPHEMICS
GRAPHIC
GRAPHICACIES
GRAPHICACY
GRAPHICAL
GRAPHICALLY
GRAPHICNESS
GRAPHICNESSES
GRAPHICS
GRAPHING
GRAPHITE
GRAPHITES
GRAPHITIC
GRAPHITIZABLE
GRAPHITIZATION
GRAPHITIZATIONS
GRAPHITIZE
GRAPHITIZED
GRAPHITIZES
GRAPHITIZING
GRAPHOLECT
GRAPHOLECTS
GRAPHOLOGICAL
GRAPHOLOGIES
GRAPHOLOGIST
GRAPHOLOGISTS
GRAPHOLOGY
GRAPHS
GRAPIER
GRAPIEST
GRAPINESS
GRAPINESSES
GRAPLE
GRAPLES
GRAPLIN
GRAPLINE
GRAPLINES
GRAPLINS
GRAPNEL
GRAPNELS
GRAPPA
GRAPPAS
GRAPPLE
GRAPPLED
GRAPPLER
GRAPPLERS
GRAPPLES
GRAPPLING
GRAPPLINGS
GRAPTOLITE
GRAPTOLITES
GRAPY
GRASP
GRASPABLE
GRASPED
GRASPER
GRASPERS
GRASPING
GRASPINGLY
GRASPINGNESS
GRASPINGNESSES
GRASPS
GRASS
GRASSED
GRASSES
GRASSHOPPER
GRASSHOPPERS
GRASSIER
GRASSIEST
GRASSILY
GRASSING
GRASSLAND
GRASSLANDS
GRASSLESS
GRASSLIKE
GRASSPLOT
GRASSPLOTS
GRASSROOT
GRASSROOTS
GRASSY
GRAT
GRATE
GRATED
GRATEFUL
GRATEFULLER
GRATEFULLEST
GRATEFULLY
GRATEFULNESS
GRATEFULNESSES
GRATELESS
GRATER
GRATERS
GRATES
GRATICULE
GRATICULES
GRATIFICATION
GRATIFICATIONS
GRATIFIED
GRATIFIER
GRATIFIERS
GRATIFIES
GRATIFY
GRATIFYING
GRATIFYINGLY
GRATIN
GRATINE
GRATINEE
GRATINEED
GRATINEEING
GRATINEES
GRATING
GRATINGLY
GRATINGS
GRATINS
GRATIS
GRATITUDE
GRATITUDES
GRATUITIES
GRATUITOUS
GRATUITOUSLY
GRATUITOUSNESS
GRATUITY
GRATULATE
GRATULATED
GRATULATES
GRATULATING
GRATULATION
GRATULATIONS
GRATULATORY
GRAUPEL
GRAUPELS
GRAVAMEN
GRAVAMENS
GRAVAMINA
GRAVE
GRAVED
GRAVEDIGGER
GRAVEDIGGERS
GRAVEL
GRAVELED
GRAVELESS
GRAVELIKE
GRAVELING
GRAVELLED
GRAVELLIER
GRAVELLIEST
GRAVELLING
GRAVELLY
GRAVELS
GRAVELY
GRAVEN
GRAVENESS
GRAVENESSES
GRAVER
GRAVERS
GRAVES
GRAVESIDE
GRAVESIDES
GRAVESITE
GRAVESITES
GRAVEST
GRAVESTONE
GRAVESTONES
GRAVEWARD
GRAVEYARD
GRAVEYARDS
GRAVID
GRAVIDA
GRAVIDAE
GRAVIDAS
GRAVIDITIES
GRAVIDITY
GRAVIDLY

GRAVIES
GRAVIMETER
GRAVIMETERS
GRAVIMETRIC
GRAVIMETRICALLY
GRAVIMETRIES
GRAVIMETRY
GRAVING
GRAVITAS
GRAVITASES
GRAVITATE
GRAVITATED
GRAVITATES
GRAVITATING
GRAVITATION
GRAVITATIONAL
GRAVITATIONALLY
GRAVITATIONS
GRAVITATIVE
GRAVITIES
GRAVITINO
GRAVITINOS
GRAVITON
GRAVITONS
GRAVITY
GRAVLAKS
GRAVLAX
GRAVLAXES
GRAVURE
GRAVURES
GRAVY
GRAY
GRAYBACK
GRAYBACKS
GRAYBEARD
GRAYBEARDS
GRAYED
GRAYER
GRAYEST
GRAYFISH
GRAYFISHES
GRAYHOUND
GRAYHOUNDS
GRAYING
GRAYISH
GRAYLAG
GRAYLAGS
GRAYLING
GRAYLINGS
GRAYLY
GRAYMAIL
GRAYMAILS
GRAYNESS
GRAYNESSES
GRAYOUT
GRAYOUTS
GRAYS
GRAYSCALE
GRAYWACKE
GRAYWACKES
GRAYWATER
GRAYWATERS
GRAZABLE
GRAZE
GRAZEABLE
GRAZED
GRAZER
GRAZERS
GRAZES
GRAZIER
GRAZIERS
GRAZING
GRAZINGLY
GRAZINGS
GRAZIOSO
GREASE
GREASEBALL
GREASEBALLS
GREASED
GREASELESS
GREASEPAINT
GREASEPAINTS
GREASEPROOF
GREASEPROOFS
GREASER
GREASERS
GREASES
GREASEWOOD
GREASEWOODS
GREASIER
GREASIEST
GREASILY
GREASINESS
GREASINESSES
GREASING
GREASY
GREAT
GREATCOAT
GREATCOATS
GREATEN
GREATENED
GREATENING
GREATENS
GREATER
GREATEST
GREATHEARTED
GREATHEARTEDLY
GREATLY
GREATNESS
GREATNESSES
GREATS
GREAVE
GREAVED
GREAVES
GREBE
GREBES
GRECIANIZE
GRECIANIZED
GRECIANIZES
GRECIANIZING
GRECIZE
GRECIZED
GRECIZES
GRECIZING
GREE
GREED
GREEDIER
GREEDIEST
GREEDILY
GREEDINESS
GREEDINESSES
GREEDLESS
GREEDS
GREEDSOME
GREEDY
GREEGREE
GREEGREES
GREEING
GREEK
GREEN
GREENBACK
GREENBACKER
GREENBACKERS
GREENBACKISM
GREENBACKISMS
GREENBACKS
GREENBELT
GREENBELTS
GREENBRIER
GREENBRIERS
GREENBUG
GREENBUGS
GREENED
GREENER
GREENERIES
GREENERY
GREENEST
GREENFIELD
GREENFIELDS
GREENFINCH
GREENFINCHES
GREENFLIES
GREENFLY
GREENGAGE
GREENGAGES
GREENGROCER
GREENGROCERIES
GREENGROCERS
GREENGROCERY
GREENHEAD
GREENHEADS
GREENHEART
GREENHEARTS
GREENHORN
GREENHORNS
GREENHOUSE
GREENHOUSES
GREENIE
GREENIER
GREENIES
GREENIEST
GREENING
GREENINGS
GREENISH
GREENISHNESS
GREENISHNESSES
GREENKEEPER
GREENKEEPERS
GREENLET
GREENLETS
GREENLIGHT
GREENLIGHTED
GREENLIGHTING
GREENLIGHTS
GREENLING
GREENLINGS
GREENLIT
GREENLY
GREENMAIL
GREENMAILED
GREENMAILER
GREENMAILERS
GREENMAILING
GREENMAILS
GREENNESS
GREENNESSES
GREENOCKITE
GREENOCKITES
GREENROOM
GREENROOMS
GREENS
GREENSAND
GREENSANDS
GREENSHANK
GREENSHANKS
GREENSICK
GREENSICKNESS
GREENSICKNESSES
GREENSKEEPER
GREENSKEEPERS
GREENSTONE
GREENSTONES
GREENSTUFF
GREENSTUFFS
GREENSWARD
GREENSWARDS
GREENTH
GREENTHS
GREENWASH
GREENWASHES
GREENWASHING
GREENWASHINGS
GREENWAY
GREENWAYS
GREENWING
GREENWINGS
GREENWOOD
GREENWOODS
GREENY
GREES
GREET
GREETED
GREETER
GREETERS
GREETING
GREETINGS
GREETS
GREGARINE
GREGARINES
GREGARIOUS
GREGARIOUSLY
GREGARIOUSNESS
GREGO
GREGOS
GREIGE
GREIGES
GREISEN
GREISENS
GREMIAL
GREMIALS
GREMLIN
GREMLINS
GREMMIE
GREMMIES
GREMMY

GRENADE
GRENADES
GRENADIER
GRENADIERS
GRENADINE
GRENADINES
GREW
GREWSOME
GREWSOMER
GREWSOMEST
GREY
GREYED
GREYER
GREYEST
GREYHEN
GREYHENS
GREYHOUND
GREYHOUNDS
GREYING
GREYISH
GREYLAG
GREYLAGS
GREYLY
GREYNESS
GREYNESSES
GREYS
GRIBBLE
GRIBBLES
GRID
GRIDDED
GRIDDER
GRIDDERS
GRIDDING
GRIDDLE
GRIDDLED
GRIDDLES
GRIDDLING
GRIDE
GRIDED
GRIDES
GRIDING
GRIDIRON
GRIDIRONED
GRIDIRONING
GRIDIRONS
GRIDLOCK
GRIDLOCKED
GRIDLOCKING
GRIDLOCKS
GRIDS
GRIEF
GRIEFS
GRIEVANCE
GRIEVANCES
GRIEVANT
GRIEVANTS
GRIEVE
GRIEVED
GRIEVER
GRIEVERS
GRIEVES
GRIEVING
GRIEVOUS
GRIEVOUSLY
GRIEVOUSNESS
GRIEVOUSNESSES
GRIFF
GRIFFE
GRIFFES
GRIFFIN
GRIFFINS
GRIFFON
GRIFFONS
GRIFFS
GRIFT
GRIFTED
GRIFTER
GRIFTERS
GRIFTING
GRIFTS
GRIG
GRIGRI
GRIGRIS
GRIGS
GRILL
GRILLADE
GRILLADES
GRILLAGE
GRILLAGES
GRILLE
GRILLED
GRILLER
GRILLERIES
GRILLERS
GRILLERY
GRILLES
GRILLING
GRILLROOM
GRILLROOMS
GRILLS
GRILLWORK
GRILLWORKS
GRILSE
GRILSES
GRIM
GRIMACE
GRIMACED
GRIMACER
GRIMACERS
GRIMACES
GRIMACING
GRIMALKIN
GRIMALKINS
GRIME
GRIMED
GRIMES
GRIMIER
GRIMIEST
GRIMILY
GRIMINESS
GRIMINESSES
GRIMING
GRIMLY
GRIMMER
GRIMMEST
GRIMNESS
GRIMNESSES
GRIMOIRE
GRIMOIRES
GRIMY
GRIN
GRINCH
GRINCHES
GRIND
GRINDED
GRINDELIA
GRINDELIAS
GRINDER
GRINDERIES
GRINDERS
GRINDERY
GRINDING
GRINDINGLY
GRINDS
GRINDSTONE
GRINDSTONES
GRINGA
GRINGAS
GRINGO
GRINGOS
GRINNED
GRINNER
GRINNERS
GRINNING
GRINNINGLY
GRINS
GRIOT
GRIOTS
GRIP
GRIPE
GRIPED
GRIPER
GRIPERS
GRIPES
GRIPEY
GRIPIER
GRIPIEST
GRIPING
GRIPINGLY
GRIPMAN
GRIPMEN
GRIPPE
GRIPPED
GRIPPER
GRIPPERS
GRIPPES
GRIPPIER
GRIPPIEST
GRIPPING
GRIPPINGLY
GRIPPLE
GRIPPY
GRIPS
GRIPSACK
GRIPSACKS
GRIPT
GRIPY
GRISAILLE
GRISAILLES
GRISEOFULVIN
GRISEOFULVINS
GRISEOUS
GRISETTE
GRISETTES
GRISKIN
GRISKINS
GRISLIER
GRISLIEST
GRISLINESS
GRISLINESSES
GRISLY
GRISON
GRISONS
GRIST
GRISTER
GRISTERS
GRISTLE
GRISTLES
GRISTLIER
GRISTLIEST
GRISTLINESS
GRISTLINESSES
GRISTLY
GRISTMILL
GRISTMILLS
GRISTS
GRIT
GRITH
GRITHS
GRITS
GRITTED
GRITTER
GRITTERS
GRITTIER
GRITTIEST
GRITTILY
GRITTINESS
GRITTINESSES
GRITTING
GRITTY
GRIVET
GRIVETS
GRIZ
GRIZES
GRIZZLE
GRIZZLED
GRIZZLER
GRIZZLERS
GRIZZLES
GRIZZLIER
GRIZZLIES
GRIZZLIEST
GRIZZLING
GRIZZLY
GROAN
GROANED
GROANER
GROANERS
GROANING
GROANS
GROAT
GROATS
GROCER
GROCERIES
GROCERS
GROCERY
GRODIER
GRODIEST
GRODY
GROG
GROGGERIES
GROGGERY
GROGGIER
GROGGIEST
GROGGILY

GROGGINESS
GROGGINESSES
GROGGY
GROGRAM
GROGRAMS
GROGS
GROGSHOP
GROGSHOPS
GROIN
GROINED
GROINING
GROINS
GROK
GROKKED
GROKKING
GROKS
GROMMET
GROMMETED
GROMMETING
GROMMETS
GROMWELL
GROMWELLS
GROOM
GROOMED
GROOMER
GROOMERS
GROOMING
GROOMS
GROOMSMAN
GROOMSMEN
GROOVE
GROOVED
GROOVER
GROOVERS
GROOVES
GROOVIER
GROOVIEST
GROOVILY
GROOVING
GROOVY
GROPE
GROPED
GROPER
GROPERS
GROPES
GROPING
GROPINGLY
GROSBEAK
GROSBEAKS
GROSCHEN
GROSGRAIN
GROSGRAINS
GROSS
GROSSED
GROSSER
GROSSERS
GROSSES
GROSSEST
GROSSING
GROSSLY
GROSSNESS
GROSSNESSES
GROSSULAR
GROSSULARITE
GROSSULARITES
GROSSULARS
GROSZ
GROSZE
GROSZY
GROT
GROTESQUE
GROTESQUELY
GROTESQUENESS
GROTESQUENESSES
GROTESQUERIE
GROTESQUERIES
GROTESQUERY
GROTESQUES
GROTS
GROTTIER
GROTTIEST
GROTTO
GROTTOED
GROTTOES
GROTTOS
GROTTY
GROUCH
GROUCHED
GROUCHES
GROUCHIER
GROUCHIEST
GROUCHILY
GROUCHINESS
GROUCHINESSES
GROUCHING
GROUCHY
GROUND
GROUNDBREAKER
GROUNDBREAKERS
GROUNDBREAKING
GROUNDBURST
GROUNDBURSTS
GROUNDED
GROUNDER
GROUNDERS
GROUNDFISH
GROUNDFISHES
GROUNDHOG
GROUNDHOGS
GROUNDING
GROUNDINGS
GROUNDLESS
GROUNDLESSLY
GROUNDLESSNESS
GROUNDLING
GROUNDLINGS
GROUNDMASS
GROUNDMASSES
GROUNDNUT
GROUNDNUTS
GROUNDOUT
GROUNDOUTS
GROUNDS
GROUNDSEL
GROUNDSELS
GROUNDSHEET
GROUNDSHEETS
GROUNDSKEEPER
GROUNDSKEEPERS
GROUNDSMAN
GROUNDSMEN
GROUNDSWELL
GROUNDSWELLS
GROUNDWATER
GROUNDWATERS
GROUNDWOOD
GROUNDWOODS
GROUNDWORK
GROUNDWORKS
GROUP
GROUPABLE
GROUPAGE
GROUPAGES
GROUPED
GROUPER
GROUPERS
GROUPIE
GROUPIES
GROUPING
GROUPINGS
GROUPOID
GROUPOIDS
GROUPS
GROUPTHINK
GROUPTHINKS
GROUPUSCULE
GROUPUSCULES
GROUPWARE
GROUPWARES
GROUSE
GROUSED
GROUSER
GROUSERS
GROUSES
GROUSING
GROUT
GROUTED
GROUTER
GROUTERS
GROUTIER
GROUTIEST
GROUTING
GROUTS
GROUTY
GROVE
GROVED
GROVEL
GROVELED
GROVELER
GROVELERS
GROVELESS
GROVELING
GROVELINGLY
GROVELLED
GROVELLER
GROVELLERS
GROVELLING
GROVELS
GROVES
GROVIER
GROVIEST
GROVY
GROW
GROWABLE
GROWER
GROWERS
GROWING
GROWINGLY
GROWL
GROWLED
GROWLER
GROWLERS
GROWLIER
GROWLIEST
GROWLINESS
GROWLINESSES
GROWLING
GROWLINGLY
GROWLS
GROWLY
GROWN
GROWNUP
GROWNUPS
GROWS
GROWTH
GROWTHIER
GROWTHIEST
GROWTHINESS
GROWTHINESSES
GROWTHS
GROWTHY
GROYNE
GROYNES
GRR
GRRRL
GRRRLS
GRUB
GRUBBED
GRUBBER
GRUBBERS
GRUBBIER
GRUBBIEST
GRUBBILY
GRUBBINESS
GRUBBINESSES
GRUBBING
GRUBBY
GRUBS
GRUBSTAKE
GRUBSTAKED
GRUBSTAKER
GRUBSTAKERS
GRUBSTAKES
GRUBSTAKING
GRUBWORM
GRUBWORMS
GRUDGE
GRUDGED
GRUDGER
GRUDGERS
GRUDGES
GRUDGING
GRUDGINGLY
GRUE
GRUEL
GRUELED
GRUELER
GRUELERS
GRUELING
GRUELINGLY
GRUELINGS
GRUELLED
GRUELLER
GRUELLERS
GRUELLING

GRUELLINGS
GRUELS
GRUES
GRUESOME
GRUESOMELY
GRUESOMENESS
GRUESOMENESSES
GRUESOMER
GRUESOMEST
GRUFF
GRUFFED
GRUFFER
GRUFFEST
GRUFFIER
GRUFFIEST
GRUFFILY
GRUFFING
GRUFFISH
GRUFFLY
GRUFFNESS
GRUFFNESSES
GRUFFS
GRUFFY
GRUGRU
GRUGRUS
GRUIFORM
GRUM
GRUMBLE
GRUMBLED
GRUMBLER
GRUMBLERS
GRUMBLES
GRUMBLIER
GRUMBLIEST
GRUMBLING
GRUMBLINGLY
GRUMBLY
GRUME
GRUMES
GRUMMER
GRUMMEST
GRUMMET
GRUMMETED
GRUMMETING
GRUMMETS
GRUMOSE
GRUMOUS
GRUMP
GRUMPED
GRUMPHIE
GRUMPHIES
GRUMPHY
GRUMPIER
GRUMPIEST
GRUMPILY
GRUMPINESS
GRUMPINESSES
GRUMPING
GRUMPISH
GRUMPS
GRUMPY
GRUNGE
GRUNGER
GRUNGERS
GRUNGES
GRUNGIER
GRUNGIEST
GRUNGY
GRUNION
GRUNIONS
GRUNT
GRUNTED
GRUNTER
GRUNTERS
GRUNTING
GRUNTLE
GRUNTLED
GRUNTLES
GRUNTLING
GRUNTS
GRUSHIE
GRUTCH
GRUTCHED
GRUTCHES
GRUTCHING
GRUTTEN
GRUYERE
GRUYERES
GRYPHON
GRYPHONS
GUACAMOLE
GUACAMOLES
GUACHARO
GUACHAROES
GUACHAROS
GUACO
GUACOS
GUAIAC
GUAIACOL
GUAIACOLS
GUAIACS
GUAIACUM
GUAIACUMS
GUAIOCUM
GUAIOCUMS
GUAN
GUANABANA
GUANABANAS
GUANACO
GUANACOS
GUANASE
GUANASES
GUANAY
GUANAYS
GUANETHIDINE
GUANETHIDINES
GUANIDIN
GUANIDINE
GUANIDINES
GUANIDINS
GUANIN
GUANINE
GUANINES
GUANINS
GUANO
GUANOS
GUANOSINE
GUANOSINES
GUANS
GUAR
GUARACHE
GUARACHES
GUARANA
GUARANAS
GUARANI
GUARANIES
GUARANIS
GUARANTEE
GUARANTEED
GUARANTEEING
GUARANTEES
GUARANTIED
GUARANTIES
GUARANTOR
GUARANTORS
GUARANTY
GUARANTYING
GUARD
GUARDANT
GUARDANTS
GUARDDOG
GUARDDOGS
GUARDED
GUARDEDLY
GUARDEDNESS
GUARDEDNESSES
GUARDER
GUARDERS
GUARDHOUSE
GUARDHOUSES
GUARDIAN
GUARDIANS
GUARDIANSHIP
GUARDIANSHIPS
GUARDING
GUARDRAIL
GUARDRAILS
GUARDROOM
GUARDROOMS
GUARDS
GUARDSMAN
GUARDSMEN
GUARS
GUAVA
GUAVAS
GUAYABERA
GUAYABERAS
GUAYULE
GUAYULES
GUBBINS
GUBBINSES
GUBERNATORIAL
GUCK
GUCKS
GUDE
GUDES
GUDGEON
GUDGEONED
GUDGEONING
GUDGEONS
GUENON
GUENONS
GUERDON
GUERDONED
GUERDONING
GUERDONS
GUERIDON
GUERIDONS
GUERILLA
GUERILLAS
GUERNSEY
GUERNSEYS
GUERRILLA
GUERRILLAS
GUESS
GUESSABLE
GUESSED
GUESSER
GUESSERS
GUESSES
GUESSING
GUESSTIMATE
GUESSTIMATED
GUESSTIMATES
GUESSTIMATING
GUESSWORK
GUESSWORKS
GUEST
GUESTED
GUESTHOUSE
GUESTHOUSES
GUESTING
GUESTS
GUFF
GUFFAW
GUFFAWED
GUFFAWING
GUFFAWS
GUFFS
GUGGLE
GUGGLED
GUGGLES
GUGGLING
GUGLET
GUGLETS
GUID
GUIDABLE
GUIDANCE
GUIDANCES
GUIDE
GUIDEBOOK
GUIDEBOOKS
GUIDED
GUIDELESS
GUIDELINE
GUIDELINES
GUIDEPOST
GUIDEPOSTS
GUIDER
GUIDERS
GUIDES
GUIDEWAY
GUIDEWAYS
GUIDEWORD
GUIDEWORDS
GUIDING
GUIDON
GUIDONS
GUIDS
GUIDWILLIE
GUILD
GUILDER
GUILDERS
GUILDHALL
GUILDHALLS

GUILDS
GUILDSHIP
GUILDSHIPS
GUILDSMAN
GUILDSMEN
GUILE
GUILED
GUILEFUL
GUILEFULLY
GUILEFULNESS
GUILEFULNESSES
GUILELESS
GUILELESSLY
GUILELESSNESS
GUILELESSNESSES
GUILES
GUILING
GUILLEMET
GUILLEMETS
GUILLEMOT
GUILLEMOTS
GUILLOCHE
GUILLOCHES
GUILLOTINE
GUILLOTINED
GUILLOTINES
GUILLOTINING
GUILT
GUILTED
GUILTIER
GUILTIEST
GUILTILY
GUILTINESS
GUILTINESSES
GUILTING
GUILTLESS
GUILTLESSLY
GUILTLESSNESS
GUILTLESSNESSES
GUILTS
GUILTY
GUIMPE
GUIMPES
GUINEA
GUINEAS
GUINEP
GUINEPS
GUIPURE
GUIPURES
GUIRO
GUIROS
GUISARD
GUISARDS
GUISE
GUISED
GUISES
GUISING
GUITAR
GUITARFISH
GUITARFISHES
GUITARIST
GUITARISTS
GUITARS
GUITGUIT
GUITGUITS
GUL
GULAG
GULAGS
GULAR
GULARS
GULCH
GULCHES
GULDEN
GULDENS
GULES
GULESES
GULF
GULFED
GULFIER
GULFIEST
GULFING
GULFLIKE
GULFS
GULFWEED
GULFWEEDS
GULFY
GULL
GULLABLE
GULLABLY
GULLED
GULLERIES
GULLERY
GULLET
GULLETS
GULLEY
GULLEYS
GULLIBILITIES
GULLIBILITY
GULLIBLE
GULLIBLY
GULLIED
GULLIES
GULLING
GULLS
GULLWING
GULLY
GULLYING
GULOSITIES
GULOSITY
GULP
GULPED
GULPER
GULPERS
GULPIER
GULPIEST
GULPING
GULPINGLY
GULPS
GULPY
GULS
GUM
GUMBALL
GUMBALLS
GUMBO
GUMBOIL
GUMBOILS
GUMBOOT
GUMBOOTS
GUMBOS
GUMBOTIL
GUMBOTILS
GUMDROP
GUMDROPS
GUMLESS
GUMLIKE
GUMLINE
GUMLINES
GUMMA
GUMMAS
GUMMATA
GUMMATOUS
GUMMED
GUMMER
GUMMERS
GUMMI
GUMMIER
GUMMIEST
GUMMILY
GUMMINESS
GUMMINESSES
GUMMING
GUMMIS
GUMMITE
GUMMITES
GUMMOSE
GUMMOSES
GUMMOSIS
GUMMOUS
GUMMY
GUMPTION
GUMPTIONS
GUMPTIOUS
GUMS
GUMSHOE
GUMSHOED
GUMSHOEING
GUMSHOES
GUMTREE
GUMTREES
GUMWEED
GUMWEEDS
GUMWOOD
GUMWOODS
GUN
GUNBOAT
GUNBOATS
GUNCOTTON
GUNCOTTONS
GUNDOG
GUNDOGS
GUNFIGHT
GUNFIGHTER
GUNFIGHTERS
GUNFIGHTING
GUNFIGHTS
GUNFIRE
GUNFIRES
GUNFLINT
GUNFLINTS
GUNFOUGHT
GUNGE
GUNGED
GUNGES
GUNGIER
GUNGIEST
GUNGING
GUNGY
GUNITE
GUNITES
GUNK
GUNKED
GUNKHOLE
GUNKHOLED
GUNKHOLES
GUNKHOLING
GUNKIER
GUNKIEST
GUNKING
GUNKS
GUNKY
GUNLESS
GUNLOCK
GUNLOCKS
GUNMAN
GUNMEN
GUNMETAL
GUNMETALS
GUNNED
GUNNEL
GUNNELS
GUNNEN
GUNNER
GUNNERA
GUNNERAS
GUNNERIES
GUNNERS
GUNNERY
GUNNIES
GUNNING
GUNNINGS
GUNNY
GUNNYBAG
GUNNYBAGS
GUNNYSACK
GUNNYSACKS
GUNPAPER
GUNPAPERS
GUNPLAY
GUNPLAYS
GUNPOINT
GUNPOINTS
GUNPORT
GUNPORTS
GUNPOWDER
GUNPOWDERS
GUNROOM
GUNROOMS
GUNRUNNER
GUNRUNNERS
GUNRUNNING
GUNRUNNINGS
GUNS
GUNSEL
GUNSELS
GUNSHIP
GUNSHIPS
GUNSHOT
GUNSHOTS
GUNSIGHT
GUNSIGHTS
GUNSLINGER
GUNSLINGERS
GUNSLINGING
GUNSLINGINGS
GUNSMITH

GUNSMITHING
GUNSMITHINGS
GUNSMITHS
GUNSTOCK
GUNSTOCKS
GUNTER
GUNTERS
GUNWALE
GUNWALES
GUPPIES
GUPPY
GURDIES
GURDWARA
GURDWARAS
GURDY
GURGE
GURGED
GURGES
GURGING
GURGLE
GURGLED
GURGLES
GURGLET
GURGLETS
GURGLIER
GURGLIEST
GURGLING
GURGLY
GURNARD
GURNARDS
GURNET
GURNETS
GURNEY
GURNEYS
GURRIES
GURRY
GURSH
GURSHES
GURU
GURUS
GURUSHIP
GURUSHIPS
GUSH
GUSHED
GUSHER
GUSHERS
GUSHES
GUSHIER
GUSHIEST
GUSHILY
GUSHINESS
GUSHINESSES
GUSHING
GUSHINGLY
GUSHY
GUSSET
GUSSETED
GUSSETING
GUSSETS
GUSSIE
GUSSIED
GUSSIES
GUSSY
GUSSYING
GUST
GUSTABLE
GUSTABLES
GUSTATION
GUSTATIONS
GUSTATIVE
GUSTATORILY
GUSTATORY
GUSTED
GUSTIER
GUSTIEST
GUSTILY
GUSTINESS
GUSTINESSES
GUSTING
GUSTLESS
GUSTO
GUSTOES
GUSTOS
GUSTS
GUSTY
GUT
GUTBUCKET
GUTBUCKETS
GUTFUL
GUTFULS
GUTLESS
GUTLESSNESS
GUTLESSNESSES
GUTLIKE
GUTS
GUTSIER
GUTSIEST
GUTSILY
GUTSINESS
GUTSINESSES
GUTSY
GUTTA
GUTTAE
GUTTATE
GUTTATED
GUTTATION
GUTTATIONS
GUTTED
GUTTER
GUTTERED
GUTTERING
GUTTERINGS
GUTTERS
GUTTERSNIPE
GUTTERSNIPES
GUTTERSNIPISH
GUTTERY
GUTTIER
GUTTIEST
GUTTING
GUTTLE
GUTTLED
GUTTLER
GUTTLERS
GUTTLES
GUTTLING
GUTTURAL
GUTTURALISM
GUTTURALISMS
GUTTURALLY
GUTTURALS
GUTTY
GUV
GUVS
GUY
GUYED
GUYING
GUYLINE
GUYLINES
GUYOT
GUYOTS
GUYS
GUZZLE
GUZZLED
GUZZLER
GUZZLERS
GUZZLES
GUZZLING
GWEDUC
GWEDUCK
GWEDUCKS
GWEDUCS
GWINE
GYBE
GYBED
GYBES
GYBING
GYM
GYMKHANA
GYMKHANAS
GYMNASIA
GYMNASIAL
GYMNASIUM
GYMNASIUMS
GYMNAST
GYMNASTIC
GYMNASTICALLY
GYMNASTICS
GYMNASTS
GYMNOSOPHIST
GYMNOSOPHISTS
GYMNOSPERM
GYMNOSPERMIES
GYMNOSPERMOUS
GYMNOSPERMS
GYMNOSPERMY
GYMS
GYMSLIP
GYMSLIPS
GYNAECEA
GYNAECEUM
GYNAECIA
GYNAECIUM
GYNAECOLOGICAL
GYNAECOLOGIES
GYNAECOLOGIST
GYNAECOLOGISTS
GYNAECOLOGY
GYNANDRIES
GYNANDROMORPH
GYNANDROMORPHIC
GYNANDROMORPHS
GYNANDROMORPHY
GYNANDROUS
GYNANDRY
GYNARCHIC
GYNARCHIES
GYNARCHY
GYNECIA
GYNECIC
GYNECIUM
GYNECOCRACIES
GYNECOCRACY
GYNECOCRATIC
GYNECOID
GYNECOLOGIC
GYNECOLOGICAL
GYNECOLOGIES
GYNECOLOGIST
GYNECOLOGISTS
GYNECOLOGY
GYNECOMASTIA
GYNECOMASTIAS
GYNIATRIES
GYNIATRY
GYNIE
GYNIES
GYNO
GYNOCENTRIC
GYNOECIA
GYNOECIUM
GYNOGENESES
GYNOGENESIS
GYNOGENETIC
GYNOPHOBE
GYNOPHOBES
GYNOPHORE
GYNOPHORES
GYNOS
GYOZA
GYOZAS
GYP
GYPLURE
GYPLURES
GYPO
GYPOS
GYPPED
GYPPER
GYPPERS
GYPPING
GYPPO
GYPPOS
GYPS
GYPSEIAN
GYPSEOUS
GYPSIED
GYPSIES
GYPSIFEROUS
GYPSOPHILA
GYPSOPHILAS
GYPSTER
GYPSTERS
GYPSUM
GYPSUMS
GYPSY
GYPSYDOM
GYPSYDOMS
GYPSYING
GYPSYISH
GYPSYISM
GYPSYISMS
GYRAL
GYRALLY
GYRASE
GYRASES

GYRATE
GYRATED
GYRATES
GYRATING
GYRATION
GYRATIONAL
GYRATIONS
GYRATOR
GYRATORS
GYRATORY
GYRE
GYRED
GYRENE
GYRENES
GYRES
GYRFALCON
GYRFALCONS
GYRI
GYRING
GYRO
GYROCOMPASS
GYROCOMPASSES
GYROFREQUENCIES
GYROFREQUENCY
GYROIDAL
GYROMAGNETIC
GYRON
GYRONS
GYROPILOT
GYROPILOTS
GYROPLANE
GYROPLANES
GYROS
GYROSCOPE
GYROSCOPES
GYROSCOPIC
GYROSCOPICALLY
GYROSE
GYROSTABILIZER
GYROSTABILIZERS
GYROSTAT
GYROSTATS
GYRUS
GYTTJA
GYTTJAS
GYVE
GYVED
GYVES
GYVING

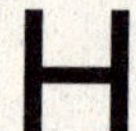

HA
HAAF
HAAFS
HAAR
HAARS
HABANERA
HABANERAS
HABANERO
HABANEROS
HABDALAH
HABDALAHS
HABENDUM
HABENDUMS
HABERDASHER
HABERDASHERIES
HABERDASHERS
HABERDASHERY
HABERGEON
HABERGEONS
HABILE
HABILIMENT
HABILIMENTS
HABILITATE
HABILITATED
HABILITATES
HABILITATING
HABILITATION
HABILITATIONS
HABIT
HABITABILITIES
HABITABILITY
HABITABLE
HABITABLENESS
HABITABLENESSES
HABITABLY
HABITAN
HABITANS
HABITANT
HABITANTS
HABITAT
HABITATION
HABITATIONS
HABITATS
HABITED
HABITING
HABITS
HABITUAL
HABITUALLY
HABITUALNESS
HABITUALNESSES
HABITUATE
HABITUATED
HABITUATES
HABITUATING
HABITUATION
HABITUATIONS
HABITUDE
HABITUDES
HABITUE
HABITUES
HABITUS
HABITUSES
HABOOB
HABOOBS
HABU
HABUS
HACEK
HACEKS
HACENDADO
HACENDADOS
HACHURE
HACHURED
HACHURES
HACHURING
HACIENDA
HACIENDADO
HACIENDADOS
HACIENDAS
HACK
HACKABLE
HACKAMORE
HACKAMORES
HACKBERRIES
HACKBERRY
HACKBUT
HACKBUTS
HACKED
HACKEE
HACKEES
HACKER
HACKERIES
HACKERS
HACKERY
HACKIE
HACKIES
HACKING
HACKINGS
HACKLE
HACKLED
HACKLER
HACKLERS
HACKLES
HACKLIER
HACKLIEST
HACKLING
HACKLY
HACKMAN
HACKMATACK
HACKMATACKS
HACKMEN
HACKNEY
HACKNEYED
HACKNEYING
HACKNEYS
HACKS
HACKSAW
HACKSAWED
HACKSAWING
HACKSAWN
HACKSAWS
HACKWORK
HACKWORKS
HAD
HADAL
HADARIM
HADDEST
HADDOCK
HADDOCKS
HADE
HADED
HADES
HADING
HADITH
HADITHS
HADJ
HADJEE
HADJEES
HADJES
HADJI
HADJIS
HADRON
HADRONIC
HADRONS
HADROSAUR
HADROSAURS
HADST
HAE
HAECCEITIES
HAECCEITY
HAED
HAEING
HAEM
HAEMAL
HAEMATAL
HAEMATIC
HAEMATICS
HAEMATIN
HAEMATINS
HAEMATITE
HAEMATITES
HAEMIC
HAEMIN
HAEMINS
HAEMOGLOBIN
HAEMOGLOBINS

HAEMOID
HAEMOPHILIA
HAEMOPHILIAC
HAEMOPHILIACS
HAEMOPHILIAS
HAEMORRHAGE
HAEMORRHAGED
HAEMORRHAGES
HAEMORRHAGIC
HAEMORRHAGING
HAEMORRHOID
HAEMORRHOIDS
HAEMS
HAEN
HAEREDES
HAERES
HAES
HAET
HAETS
HAFFET
HAFFETS
HAFFIT
HAFFITS
HAFIZ
HAFIZES
HAFNIUM
HAFNIUMS
HAFT
HAFTARA
HAFTARAH
HAFTARAHS
HAFTARAS
HAFTAROS
HAFTAROT
HAFTAROTH
HAFTED
HAFTER
HAFTERS
HAFTING
HAFTORAH
HAFTORAHS
HAFTOROS
HAFTOROT
HAFTOROTH
HAFTS
HAG
HAGADIC
HAGADIST
HAGADISTS
HAGBERRIES
HAGBERRY
HAGBORN
HAGBUSH
HAGBUSHES
HAGBUT
HAGBUTS
HAGDON
HAGDONS
HAGFISH
HAGFISHES
HAGGADA
HAGGADAH
HAGGADAHS
HAGGADAS
HAGGADIC
HAGGADIST
HAGGADISTIC
HAGGADISTS
HAGGADOT
HAGGADOTH
HAGGARD
HAGGARDLY
HAGGARDNESS
HAGGARDNESSES
HAGGARDS
HAGGED
HAGGING
HAGGIS
HAGGISES
HAGGISH
HAGGISHLY
HAGGLE
HAGGLED
HAGGLER
HAGGLERS
HAGGLES
HAGGLING
HAGGLINGS
HAGIARCHIES
HAGIARCHY
HAGIOGRAPHER
HAGIOGRAPHERS
HAGIOGRAPHIC
HAGIOGRAPHICAL
HAGIOGRAPHIES
HAGIOGRAPHY
HAGIOLOGIC
HAGIOLOGICAL
HAGIOLOGIES
HAGIOLOGY
HAGIOSCOPE
HAGIOSCOPES
HAGIOSCOPIC
HAGRIDDEN
HAGRIDE
HAGRIDER
HAGRIDERS
HAGRIDES
HAGRIDING
HAGRODE
HAGS
HAH
HAHA
HAHAS
HAHNIUM
HAHNIUMS
HAHS
HAICK
HAICKS
HAIK
HAIKA
HAIKS
HAIKU
HAIKUS
HAIL
HAILED
HAILER
HAILERS
HAILING
HAILS
HAILSTONE
HAILSTONES
HAILSTORM
HAILSTORMS
HAIMISH
HAINT
HAINTS
HAIR
HAIRBALL
HAIRBALLS
HAIRBAND
HAIRBANDS
HAIRBREADTH
HAIRBREADTHS
HAIRBRUSH
HAIRBRUSHES
HAIRCAP
HAIRCAPS
HAIRCLOTH
HAIRCLOTHS
HAIRCUT
HAIRCUTS
HAIRCUTTER
HAIRCUTTERS
HAIRCUTTING
HAIRCUTTINGS
HAIRDO
HAIRDOS
HAIRDRESSER
HAIRDRESSERS
HAIRDRESSING
HAIRDRESSINGS
HAIRED
HAIRGRIP
HAIRGRIPS
HAIRIER
HAIRIEST
HAIRILY
HAIRINESS
HAIRINESSES
HAIRLESS
HAIRLESSNESS
HAIRLESSNESSES
HAIRLIKE
HAIRLINE
HAIRLINES
HAIRLOCK
HAIRLOCKS
HAIRNET
HAIRNETS
HAIRPIECE
HAIRPIECES
HAIRPIN
HAIRPINS
HAIRS
HAIRSBREADTH
HAIRSBREADTHS
HAIRSPLITTER
HAIRSPLITTERS
HAIRSPLITTING
HAIRSPLITTINGS
HAIRSPRAY
HAIRSPRAYS
HAIRSPRING
HAIRSPRINGS
HAIRSTREAK
HAIRSTREAKS
HAIRSTYLE
HAIRSTYLES
HAIRSTYLING
HAIRSTYLINGS
HAIRSTYLIST
HAIRSTYLISTS
HAIRWING
HAIRWINGS
HAIRWORK
HAIRWORKS
HAIRWORM
HAIRWORMS
HAIRY
HAJ
HAJES
HAJI
HAJIS
HAJJ
HAJJES
HAJJI
HAJJIS
HAKE
HAKEEM
HAKEEMS
HAKES
HAKIM
HAKIMS
HAKU
HAKUS
HALACHA
HALACHAS
HALACHIC
HALACHIST
HALACHISTS
HALACHOT
HALACHOTH
HALAKAH
HALAKAHS
HALAKHA
HALAKHAH
HALAKHAHS
HALAKHAS
HALAKHIC
HALAKHIST
HALAKHISTS
HALAKHOT
HALAKHOTH
HALAKIC
HALAKIST
HALAKISTS
HALAKOTH
HALAL
HALALA
HALALAH
HALALAHS
HALALAS
HALALLED
HALALLING
HALALS
HALATION
HALATIONS
HALAVAH
HALAVAHS
HALAZONE
HALAZONES
HALBERD
HALBERDS
HALBERT

HALBERTS
HALCYON
HALCYONS
HALE
HALED
HALENESS
HALENESSES
HALER
HALERS
HALERU
HALES
HALEST
HALF
HALFBACK
HALFBACKS
HALFBEAK
HALFBEAKS
HALFHEARTED
HALFHEARTEDLY
HALFHEARTEDNESS
HALFLIFE
HALFLIVES
HALFNESS
HALFNESSES
HALFPENCE
HALFPENNIES
HALFPENNY
HALFPIPE
HALFPIPES
HALFTIME
HALFTIMES
HALFTONE
HALFTONES
HALFTRACK
HALFTRACKS
HALFWAY
HALFWIT
HALFWITS
HALIBUT
HALIBUTS
HALID
HALIDE
HALIDES
HALIDOM
HALIDOME
HALIDOMES
HALIDOMS
HALIDS
HALIER
HALIEROV
HALIERS
HALING
HALIOTES
HALIOTIS
HALIOTISES
HALITE
HALITES
HALITOSES
HALITOSIS
HALITUS
HALITUSES
HALL
HALLAH
HALLAHS
HALLAL
HALLALLED
HALLALLING
HALLALS
HALLEL
HALLELS
HALLELUJAH
HALLELUJAHS
HALLIARD
HALLIARDS
HALLMARK
HALLMARKED
HALLMARKING
HALLMARKS
HALLO
HALLOA
HALLOAED
HALLOAING
HALLOAS
HALLOED
HALLOES
HALLOING
HALLOO
HALLOOED
HALLOOING
HALLOOS
HALLOS
HALLOT
HALLOTH
HALLOW
HALLOWED
HALLOWER
HALLOWERS
HALLOWING
HALLOWS
HALLS
HALLUCAL
HALLUCES
HALLUCINATE
HALLUCINATED
HALLUCINATES
HALLUCINATING
HALLUCINATION
HALLUCINATIONS
HALLUCINATOR
HALLUCINATORS
HALLUCINATORY
HALLUCINOGEN
HALLUCINOGENIC
HALLUCINOGENICS
HALLUCINOGENS
HALLUCINOSES
HALLUCINOSIS
HALLUX
HALLWAY
HALLWAYS
HALM
HALMA
HALMAS
HALMS
HALO
HALOBIONT
HALOBIONTS
HALOCARBON
HALOCARBONS
HALOCLINE
HALOCLINES
HALOED
HALOES
HALOGEN
HALOGENATE
HALOGENATED
HALOGENATES
HALOGENATING
HALOGENATION
HALOGENATIONS
HALOGENOUS
HALOGENS
HALOGETON
HALOGETONS
HALOID
HALOIDS
HALOING
HALOLIKE
HALOMORPHIC
HALON
HALONS
HALOPERIDOL
HALOPERIDOLS
HALOPHILE
HALOPHILES
HALOPHILIC
HALOPHYTE
HALOPHYTES
HALOPHYTIC
HALOS
HALOTHANE
HALOTHANES
HALT
HALTED
HALTER
HALTERBREAK
HALTERBREAKING
HALTERBREAKS
HALTERBROKE
HALTERBROKEN
HALTERE
HALTERED
HALTERES
HALTERING
HALTERS
HALTING
HALTINGLY
HALTLESS
HALTS
HALUTZ
HALUTZIM
HALVA
HALVAH
HALVAHS
HALVAS
HALVE
HALVED
HALVERS
HALVES
HALVING
HALVINGS
HALWA
HALWAS
HALYARD
HALYARDS
HAM
HAMADA
HAMADAS
HAMADRYAD
HAMADRYADES
HAMADRYADS
HAMADRYAS
HAMADRYASES
HAMAL
HAMALS
HAMANTASCH
HAMANTASCHEN
HAMARTIA
HAMARTIAS
HAMATE
HAMATES
HAMATSA
HAMATSAS
HAMAUL
HAMAULS
HAMBONE
HAMBONED
HAMBONES
HAMBONING
HAMBURG
HAMBURGER
HAMBURGERS
HAMBURGS
HAME
HAMES
HAMFAT
HAMFATS
HAMLET
HAMLETS
HAMMADA
HAMMADAS
HAMMAL
HAMMALS
HAMMAM
HAMMAMS
HAMMED
HAMMER
HAMMERED
HAMMERER
HAMMERERS
HAMMERHEAD
HAMMERHEADS
HAMMERING
HAMMERINGS
HAMMERKOP
HAMMERKOPS
HAMMERLESS
HAMMERLOCK
HAMMERLOCKS
HAMMERS
HAMMERSTONE
HAMMERSTONES
HAMMERTOE
HAMMERTOES
HAMMIER
HAMMIEST
HAMMILY
HAMMINESS
HAMMINESSES
HAMMING
HAMMOCK
HAMMOCKS
HAMMY
HAMPER
HAMPERED

HAMPERER
HAMPERERS
HAMPERING
HAMPERS
HAMS
HAMSTER
HAMSTERS
HAMSTRING
HAMSTRINGING
HAMSTRINGS
HAMSTRUNG
HAMULAR
HAMULATE
HAMULI
HAMULOSE
HAMULOUS
HAMULUS
HAMZA
HAMZAH
HAMZAHS
HAMZAS
HANAPER
HANAPERS
HANCE
HANCES
HAND
HANDAX
HANDAXES
HANDBAG
HANDBAGS
HANDBALL
HANDBALLS
HANDBARROW
HANDBARROWS
HANDBASKET
HANDBASKETS
HANDBELL
HANDBELLS
HANDBILL
HANDBILLS
HANDBLOWN
HANDBOOK
HANDBOOKS
HANDBREADTH
HANDBREADTHS
HANDCAR
HANDCARS
HANDCART
HANDCARTS
HANDCLAP
HANDCLAPS
HANDCLASP
HANDCLASPS
HANDCRAFT
HANDCRAFTED
HANDCRAFTING
HANDCRAFTS
HANDCRAFTSMAN
HANDCRAFTSMEN
HANDCUFF
HANDCUFFED
HANDCUFFING
HANDCUFFS
HANDED
HANDEDNESS
HANDEDNESSES
HANDER
HANDERS
HANDFAST
HANDFASTED
HANDFASTING
HANDFASTS
HANDFUL
HANDFULS
HANDGRIP
HANDGRIPS
HANDGUN
HANDGUNS
HANDHELD
HANDHELDS
HANDHOLD
HANDHOLDS
HANDICAP
HANDICAPPED
HANDICAPPER
HANDICAPPERS
HANDICAPPING
HANDICAPS
HANDICRAFT
HANDICRAFTER
HANDICRAFTERS
HANDICRAFTS
HANDICRAFTSMAN
HANDICRAFTSMEN
HANDIER
HANDIEST
HANDILY
HANDINESS
HANDINESSES
HANDING
HANDIWORK
HANDIWORKS
HANDKERCHIEF
HANDKERCHIEFS
HANDKERCHIEVES
HANDLE
HANDLEABLE
HANDLEBAR
HANDLEBARS
HANDLED
HANDLELESS
HANDLER
HANDLERS
HANDLES
HANDLESS
HANDLIKE
HANDLINE
HANDLINES
HANDLING
HANDLINGS
HANDLIST
HANDLISTS
HANDLOOM
HANDLOOMS
HANDMADE
HANDMAID
HANDMAIDEN
HANDMAIDENS
HANDMAIDS
HANDOFF
HANDOFFS
HANDOUT
HANDOUTS
HANDOVER
HANDOVERS
HANDPICK
HANDPICKED
HANDPICKING
HANDPICKS
HANDPRESS
HANDPRESSES
HANDPRINT
HANDPRINTS
HANDRAIL
HANDRAILS
HANDS
HANDSAW
HANDSAWS
HANDSBREADTH
HANDSBREADTHS
HANDSEL
HANDSELED
HANDSELING
HANDSELLED
HANDSELLING
HANDSELS
HANDSET
HANDSETS
HANDSEWN
HANDSFUL
HANDSHAKE
HANDSHAKES
HANDSOME
HANDSOMELY
HANDSOMENESS
HANDSOMENESSES
HANDSOMER
HANDSOMEST
HANDSPIKE
HANDSPIKES
HANDSPRING
HANDSPRINGS
HANDSTAMP
HANDSTAMPED
HANDSTAMPING
HANDSTAMPS
HANDSTAND
HANDSTANDS
HANDWHEEL
HANDWHEELS
HANDWORK
HANDWORKER
HANDWORKERS
HANDWORKS
HANDWOVEN
HANDWRINGER
HANDWRINGERS
HANDWRIT
HANDWRITE
HANDWRITES
HANDWRITING
HANDWRITINGS
HANDWRITTEN
HANDWROTE
HANDWROUGHT
HANDY
HANDYMAN
HANDYMEN
HANDYPERSON
HANDYPERSONS
HANG
HANGABLE
HANGAR
HANGARED
HANGARING
HANGARS
HANGBIRD
HANGBIRDS
HANGDOG
HANGDOGS
HANGED
HANGER
HANGERS
HANGFIRE
HANGFIRES
HANGING
HANGINGS
HANGMAN
HANGMEN
HANGNAIL
HANGNAILS
HANGNEST
HANGNESTS
HANGOUT
HANGOUTS
HANGOVER
HANGOVERS
HANGS
HANGTAG
HANGTAGS
HANGUL
HANGUP
HANGUPS
HANIWA
HANK
HANKED
HANKER
HANKERED
HANKERER
HANKERERS
HANKERING
HANKERINGS
HANKERS
HANKIE
HANKIES
HANKING
HANKS
HANKY
HANSA
HANSAS
HANSE
HANSEATIC
HANSEL
HANSELED
HANSELING
HANSELLED
HANSELLING
HANSELS
HANSES
HANSOM
HANSOMS
HANT
HANTAVIRUS
HANTAVIRUSES
HANTED

HANTING
HANTLE
HANTLES
HANTS
HANUMAN
HANUMANS
HAO
HAOLE
HAOLES
HAP
HAPAX
HAPAXES
HAPHAZARD
HAPHAZARDLY
HAPHAZARDNESS
HAPHAZARDNESSES
HAPHAZARDRIES
HAPHAZARDRY
HAPHAZARDS
HAPHTARA
HAPHTARAH
HAPHTARAHS
HAPHTARAS
HAPHTAROT
HAPHTAROTH
HAPKIDO
HAPKIDOS
HAPLESS
HAPLESSLY
HAPLESSNESS
HAPLESSNESSES
HAPLITE
HAPLITES
HAPLOID
HAPLOIDIC
HAPLOIDIES
HAPLOIDS
HAPLOIDY
HAPLOLOGIES
HAPLOLOGY
HAPLONT
HAPLONTIC
HAPLONTS
HAPLOPIA
HAPLOPIAS
HAPLOSES
HAPLOSIS
HAPLOTYPE
HAPLOTYPES
HAPLY
HAPPED
HAPPEN
HAPPENCHANCE
HAPPENCHANCES
HAPPENED
HAPPENING
HAPPENINGS
HAPPENS
HAPPENSTANCE
HAPPENSTANCES
HAPPI
HAPPIER
HAPPIEST
HAPPILY
HAPPINESS
HAPPINESSES
HAPPING
HAPPIS
HAPPY
HAPS
HAPTEN
HAPTENE
HAPTENES
HAPTENIC
HAPTENS
HAPTIC
HAPTICAL
HAPTOGLOBIN
HAPTOGLOBINS
HARAM
HARANGUE
HARANGUED
HARANGUER
HARANGUERS
HARANGUES
HARANGUING
HARASS
HARASSED
HARASSER
HARASSERS
HARASSES
HARASSING
HARASSMENT
HARASSMENTS
HARBINGER
HARBINGERED
HARBINGERING
HARBINGERS
HARBOR
HARBORAGE
HARBORAGES
HARBORED
HARBORER
HARBORERS
HARBORFUL
HARBORFULS
HARBORING
HARBORLESS
HARBORMASTER
HARBORMASTERS
HARBOROUS
HARBORS
HARBORSIDE
HARBOUR
HARBOURED
HARBOURING
HARBOURS
HARD
HARDASS
HARDASSES
HARDBACK
HARDBACKS
HARDBALL
HARDBALLS
HARDBOARD
HARDBOARDS
HARDBODIES
HARDBODY
HARDBOOT
HARDBOOTS
HARDBOUND
HARDBOUNDS
HARDCASE
HARDCASES
HARDCORE
HARDCORES
HARDCOURT
HARDCOVER
HARDCOVERS
HARDEDGE
HARDEDGES
HARDEN
HARDENED
HARDENER
HARDENERS
HARDENING
HARDENINGS
HARDENS
HARDER
HARDEST
HARDFISTED
HARDGOODS
HARDHACK
HARDHACKS
HARDHANDED
HARDHANDEDNESS
HARDHAT
HARDHATS
HARDHEAD
HARDHEADED
HARDHEADEDLY
HARDHEADEDNESS
HARDHEADS
HARDIER
HARDIES
HARDIEST
HARDIHOOD
HARDIHOODS
HARDILY
HARDIMENT
HARDIMENTS
HARDINESS
HARDINESSES
HARDINGGRASS
HARDINGGRASSES
HARDISH
HARDLINE
HARDLY
HARDMOUTHED
HARDNESS
HARDNESSES
HARDNOSE
HARDNOSES
HARDPACK
HARDPACKS
HARDPAN
HARDPANS
HARDS
HARDSCAPE
HARDSCAPES
HARDSCRABBLE
HARDSET
HARDSHIP
HARDSHIPS
HARDSTAND
HARDSTANDING
HARDSTANDINGS
HARDSTANDS
HARDTACK
HARDTACKS
HARDTOP
HARDTOPS
HARDWARE
HARDWARES
HARDWIRE
HARDWIRED
HARDWIRES
HARDWIRING
HARDWOOD
HARDWOODS
HARDWORKING
HARDY
HARE
HAREBELL
HAREBELLS
HAREBRAINED
HARED
HAREEM
HAREEMS
HARELIKE
HARELIP
HARELIPS
HAREM
HAREMS
HARES
HAREWOOD
HAREWOODS
HARIANA
HARIANAS
HARICOT
HARICOTS
HARIJAN
HARIJANS
HARING
HARISSA
HARISSAS
HARK
HARKED
HARKEN
HARKENED
HARKENER
HARKENERS
HARKENING
HARKENS
HARKING
HARKS
HARL
HARLEQUIN
HARLEQUINADE
HARLEQUINADES
HARLEQUINS
HARLOT
HARLOTRIES
HARLOTRY
HARLOTS
HARLS
HARM
HARMATTAN
HARMATTANS
HARMED
HARMER
HARMERS
HARMFUL
HARMFULLY
HARMFULNESS

HARMFULNESSES
HARMIN
HARMINE
HARMINES
HARMING
HARMINS
HARMLESS
HARMLESSLY
HARMLESSNESS
HARMLESSNESSES
HARMONIC
HARMONICA
HARMONICALLY
HARMONICAS
HARMONICIST
HARMONICISTS
HARMONICS
HARMONIES
HARMONIOUS
HARMONIOUSLY
HARMONIOUSNESS
HARMONISATION
HARMONISATIONS
HARMONISE
HARMONISED
HARMONISES
HARMONISING
HARMONIST
HARMONISTS
HARMONIUM
HARMONIUMS
HARMONIZATION
HARMONIZATIONS
HARMONIZE
HARMONIZED
HARMONIZER
HARMONIZERS
HARMONIZES
HARMONIZING
HARMONY
HARMS
HARNESS
HARNESSED
HARNESSES
HARNESSING
HARP
HARPED
HARPER
HARPERS
HARPIES
HARPIN
HARPING
HARPINGS
HARPINS
HARPIST
HARPISTS
HARPOON
HARPOONED
HARPOONER
HARPOONERS
HARPOONING
HARPOONS
HARPS
HARPSICHORD
HARPSICHORDIST
HARPSICHORDISTS
HARPSICHORDS
HARPY
HARPYLIKE
HARQUEBUS
HARQUEBUSES
HARQUEBUSIER
HARQUEBUSIERS
HARRIDAN
HARRIDANS
HARRIED
HARRIER
HARRIERS
HARRIES
HARROW
HARROWED
HARROWER
HARROWERS
HARROWING
HARROWINGLY
HARROWS
HARRUMPH
HARRUMPHED
HARRUMPHING
HARRUMPHS
HARRY
HARRYING
HARSH
HARSHEN
HARSHENED
HARSHENING
HARSHENS
HARSHER
HARSHEST
HARSHLY
HARSHNESS
HARSHNESSES
HARSLET
HARSLETS
HART
HARTAL
HARTALS
HARTEBEEST
HARTEBEESTS
HARTS
HARTSHORN
HARTSHORNS
HARUMPH
HARUMPHED
HARUMPHING
HARUMPHS
HARUSPEX
HARUSPICATION
HARUSPICATIONS
HARUSPICES
HARVEST
HARVESTABLE
HARVESTED
HARVESTER
HARVESTERS
HARVESTING
HARVESTMAN
HARVESTMEN
HARVESTS
HARVESTTIME
HARVESTTIMES
HAS
HASENPFEFFER
HASENPFEFFERS
HASH
HASHED
HASHEESH
HASHEESHES
HASHES
HASHHEAD
HASHHEADS
HASHING
HASHISH
HASHISHES
HASHTAG
HASHTAGS
HASLET
HASLETS
HASP
HASPED
HASPING
HASPS
HASSEL
HASSELS
HASSIUM
HASSIUMS
HASSLE
HASSLED
HASSLES
HASSLING
HASSOCK
HASSOCKS
HAST
HASTATE
HASTATELY
HASTE
HASTED
HASTEFUL
HASTEN
HASTENED
HASTENER
HASTENERS
HASTENING
HASTENS
HASTES
HASTIER
HASTIEST
HASTILY
HASTINESS
HASTINESSES
HASTING
HASTY
HAT
HATABLE
HATBAND
HATBANDS
HATBOX
HATBOXES
HATCH
HATCHABILITIES
HATCHABILITY
HATCHABLE
HATCHBACK
HATCHBACKS
HATCHECK
HATCHECKS
HATCHED
HATCHEL
HATCHELED
HATCHELING
HATCHELLED
HATCHELLING
HATCHELS
HATCHER
HATCHERIES
HATCHERS
HATCHERY
HATCHES
HATCHET
HATCHETS
HATCHING
HATCHINGS
HATCHLING
HATCHLINGS
HATCHMENT
HATCHMENTS
HATCHWAY
HATCHWAYS
HATE
HATEABLE
HATED
HATEFUL
HATEFULLY
HATEFULNESS
HATEFULNESSES
HATER
HATERS
HATES
HATFUL
HATFULS
HATH
HATING
HATLESS
HATLIKE
HATMAKER
HATMAKERS
HATPIN
HATPINS
HATRACK
HATRACKS
HATRED
HATREDS
HATS
HATSFUL
HATTED
HATTER
HATTERIA
HATTERIAS
HATTERS
HATTING
HAUBERK
HAUBERKS
HAUGH
HAUGHS
HAUGHTIER
HAUGHTIEST
HAUGHTILY
HAUGHTINESS
HAUGHTINESSES
HAUGHTY
HAUL
HAULAGE
HAULAGES
HAULBACK
HAULBACKS

HAULED
HAULER
HAULERS
HAULIER
HAULIERS
HAULING
HAULINGS
HAULM
HAULMIER
HAULMIEST
HAULMS
HAULMY
HAULOUT
HAULOUTS
HAULS
HAULYARD
HAULYARDS
HAUNCH
HAUNCHED
HAUNCHES
HAUNT
HAUNTED
HAUNTER
HAUNTERS
HAUNTING
HAUNTINGLY
HAUNTINGS
HAUNTS
HAUSEN
HAUSENS
HAUSFRAU
HAUSFRAUEN
HAUSFRAUS
HAUSTELLA
HAUSTELLUM
HAUSTORIA
HAUSTORIAL
HAUSTORIUM
HAUT
HAUTBOIS
HAUTBOY
HAUTBOYS
HAUTE
HAUTER
HAUTEST
HAUTEUR
HAUTEURS
HAVARTI
HAVARTIS
HAVDALAH
HAVDALAHS
HAVE
HAVELOCK
HAVELOCKS
HAVEN
HAVENED
HAVENING
HAVENS
HAVER
HAVERED
HAVEREL
HAVERELS
HAVERING
HAVERS
HAVERSACK
HAVERSACKS
HAVES
HAVING
HAVIOR
HAVIORS
HAVIOUR
HAVIOURS
HAVOC
HAVOCKED
HAVOCKER
HAVOCKERS
HAVOCKING
HAVOCS
HAW
HAWALA
HAWALAS
HAWEATER
HAWEATERS
HAWED
HAWFINCH
HAWFINCHES
HAWING
HAWK
HAWKBILL
HAWKBILLS
HAWKED
HAWKER
HAWKERS
HAWKEY
HAWKEYED
HAWKEYS
HAWKIE
HAWKIES
HAWKING
HAWKINGS
HAWKISH
HAWKISHLY
HAWKISHNESS
HAWKISHNESSES
HAWKLIKE
HAWKMOTH
HAWKMOTHS
HAWKNOSE
HAWKNOSES
HAWKS
HAWKSBILL
HAWKSBILLS
HAWKSHAW
HAWKSHAWS
HAWKWEED
HAWKWEEDS
HAWS
HAWSE
HAWSEHOLE
HAWSEHOLES
HAWSEPIPE
HAWSEPIPES
HAWSER
HAWSERS
HAWSES
HAWTHORN
HAWTHORNS
HAWTHORNY
HAY
HAYCOCK
HAYCOCKS
HAYED
HAYER
HAYERS
HAYEY
HAYFIELD
HAYFIELDS
HAYFORK
HAYFORKS
HAYING
HAYINGS
HAYLAGE
HAYLAGES
HAYLOFT
HAYLOFTS
HAYMAKER
HAYMAKERS
HAYMOW
HAYMOWS
HAYRACK
HAYRACKS
HAYRICK
HAYRICKS
HAYRIDE
HAYRIDES
HAYS
HAYSEED
HAYSEEDS
HAYSTACK
HAYSTACKS
HAYWARD
HAYWARDS
HAYWIRE
HAYWIRES
HAZAN
HAZANIM
HAZANS
HAZARD
HAZARDED
HAZARDER
HAZARDERS
HAZARDING
HAZARDOUS
HAZARDOUSLY
HAZARDOUSNESS
HAZARDOUSNESSES
HAZARDS
HAZE
HAZED
HAZEL
HAZELHEN
HAZELHENS
HAZELLY
HAZELNUT
HAZELNUTS
HAZELS
HAZER
HAZERS
HAZES
HAZIER
HAZIEST
HAZILY
HAZINESS
HAZINESSES
HAZING
HAZINGS
HAZMAT
HAZMATS
HAZY
HAZZAN
HAZZANIM
HAZZANS
HE
HEAD
HEADACHE
HEADACHES
HEADACHEY
HEADACHIER
HEADACHIEST
HEADACHY
HEADBAND
HEADBANDS
HEADBANGER
HEADBANGERS
HEADBOARD
HEADBOARDS
HEADCHEESE
HEADCHEESES
HEADCOUNT
HEADCOUNTS
HEADDRESS
HEADDRESSES
HEADED
HEADEND
HEADENDS
HEADER
HEADERS
HEADFIRST
HEADFISH
HEADFISHES
HEADFOREMOST
HEADFUL
HEADFULS
HEADGATE
HEADGATES
HEADGEAR
HEADGEARS
HEADHUNT
HEADHUNTED
HEADHUNTER
HEADHUNTERS
HEADHUNTING
HEADHUNTINGS
HEADHUNTS
HEADIER
HEADIEST
HEADILY
HEADINESS
HEADINESSES
HEADING
HEADINGS
HEADLAMP
HEADLAMPS
HEADLAND
HEADLANDS
HEADLESS
HEADLESSNESS
HEADLESSNESSES
HEADLIGHT
HEADLIGHTS
HEADLINE
HEADLINED
HEADLINER
HEADLINERS
HEADLINES

HEADLINING
HEADLOCK
HEADLOCKS
HEADLONG
HEADMAN
HEADMASTER
HEADMASTERLY
HEADMASTERS
HEADMASTERSHIP
HEADMASTERSHIPS
HEADMEN
HEADMISTRESS
HEADMISTRESSES
HEADMOST
HEADNOTE
HEADNOTES
HEADPHONE
HEADPHONES
HEADPIECE
HEADPIECES
HEADPIN
HEADPINS
HEADPOND
HEADPONDS
HEADQUARTER
HEADQUARTERED
HEADQUARTERING
HEADQUARTERS
HEADRACE
HEADRACES
HEADRAIL
HEADRAILS
HEADREST
HEADRESTS
HEADROOM
HEADROOMS
HEADS
HEADSAIL
HEADSAILS
HEADSCARF
HEADSCARVES
HEADSET
HEADSETS
HEADSHIP
HEADSHIPS
HEADSHOT
HEADSHOTS
HEADSHRINKER
HEADSHRINKERS
HEADSMAN
HEADSMEN
HEADSPACE
HEADSPACES
HEADSPRING
HEADSPRINGS
HEADSTALL
HEADSTALLS
HEADSTAND
HEADSTANDS
HEADSTAY
HEADSTAYS
HEADSTOCK
HEADSTOCKS
HEADSTONE
HEADSTONES
HEADSTREAM
HEADSTREAMS
HEADSTRONG
HEADWAITER
HEADWAITERS
HEADWARD
HEADWARDS
HEADWATER
HEADWATERS
HEADWAY
HEADWAYS
HEADWIND
HEADWINDS
HEADWORD
HEADWORDS
HEADWORK
HEADWORKS
HEADY
HEAL
HEALABLE
HEALED
HEALER
HEALERS
HEALING
HEALINGS
HEALS
HEALTH
HEALTHFUL
HEALTHFULLY
HEALTHFULNESS
HEALTHFULNESSES
HEALTHIER
HEALTHIEST
HEALTHILY
HEALTHINESS
HEALTHINESSES
HEALTHS
HEALTHY
HEAP
HEAPED
HEAPER
HEAPERS
HEAPING
HEAPS
HEAPY
HEAR
HEARABLE
HEARD
HEARER
HEARERS
HEARING
HEARINGS
HEARKEN
HEARKENED
HEARKENER
HEARKENERS
HEARKENING
HEARKENS
HEARS
HEARSAY
HEARSAYS
HEARSE
HEARSED
HEARSES
HEARSING
HEART
HEARTACHE
HEARTACHES
HEARTBEAT
HEARTBEATS
HEARTBREAK
HEARTBREAKER
HEARTBREAKERS
HEARTBREAKING
HEARTBREAKINGLY
HEARTBREAKS
HEARTBROKEN
HEARTBURN
HEARTBURNING
HEARTBURNINGS
HEARTBURNS
HEARTED
HEARTEN
HEARTENED
HEARTENER
HEARTENERS
HEARTENING
HEARTENINGLY
HEARTENS
HEARTFELT
HEARTFREE
HEARTH
HEARTHRUG
HEARTHRUGS
HEARTHS
HEARTHSTONE
HEARTHSTONES
HEARTIER
HEARTIES
HEARTIEST
HEARTILY
HEARTINESS
HEARTINESSES
HEARTING
HEARTLAND
HEARTLANDS
HEARTLESS
HEARTLESSLY
HEARTLESSNESS
HEARTLESSNESSES
HEARTRENDING
HEARTRENDINGLY
HEARTS
HEARTSEASE
HEARTSEASES
HEARTSICK
HEARTSICKNESS
HEARTSICKNESSES
HEARTSOME
HEARTSOMELY
HEARTSORE
HEARTSTRING
HEARTSTRINGS
HEARTTHROB
HEARTTHROBS
HEARTWARMING
HEARTWOOD
HEARTWOODS
HEARTWORM
HEARTWORMS
HEARTY
HEAT
HEATABLE
HEATED
HEATEDLY
HEATER
HEATERS
HEATH
HEATHBIRD
HEATHBIRDS
HEATHEN
HEATHENDOM
HEATHENDOMS
HEATHENISH
HEATHENISHLY
HEATHENISM
HEATHENISMS
HEATHENIZE
HEATHENIZED
HEATHENIZES
HEATHENIZING
HEATHENRIES
HEATHENRY
HEATHENS
HEATHER
HEATHERED
HEATHERIER
HEATHERIEST
HEATHERS
HEATHERY
HEATHIER
HEATHIEST
HEATHLAND
HEATHLANDS
HEATHLESS
HEATHLIKE
HEATHS
HEATHY
HEATING
HEATINGS
HEATLESS
HEATPROOF
HEATS
HEATSTROKE
HEATSTROKES
HEAUME
HEAUMES
HEAVE
HEAVED
HEAVEN
HEAVENLIER
HEAVENLIEST
HEAVENLINESS
HEAVENLINESSES
HEAVENLY
HEAVENS
HEAVENWARD
HEAVENWARDS
HEAVER
HEAVERS
HEAVES
HEAVIER
HEAVIES
HEAVIEST
HEAVILY
HEAVINESS
HEAVINESSES
HEAVING
HEAVY
HEAVYHEARTED

HEAVYHEARTEDLY
HEAVYISH
HEAVYSET
HEAVYWEIGHT
HEAVYWEIGHTS
HEBDOMAD
HEBDOMADAL
HEBDOMADALLY
HEBDOMADS
HEBE
HEBEPHRENIA
HEBEPHRENIAS
HEBEPHRENIC
HEBEPHRENICS
HEBES
HEBETATE
HEBETATED
HEBETATES
HEBETATING
HEBETATION
HEBETATIONS
HEBETIC
HEBETUDE
HEBETUDES
HEBETUDINOUS
HEBRAIZATION
HEBRAIZATIONS
HEBRAIZE
HEBRAIZED
HEBRAIZES
HEBRAIZING
HECATOMB
HECATOMBS
HECK
HECKLE
HECKLED
HECKLER
HECKLERS
HECKLES
HECKLING
HECKS
HECKUVA
HECTARE
HECTARES
HECTIC
HECTICAL
HECTICALLY
HECTICLY
HECTICS
HECTOGRAM
HECTOGRAMS
HECTOGRAPH
HECTOGRAPHED
HECTOGRAPHING
HECTOGRAPHS
HECTOLITER
HECTOLITERS
HECTOMETER
HECTOMETERS
HECTOR
HECTORED
HECTORING
HECTORINGLY
HECTORS
HEDARIM
HEDDLE
HEDDLES
HEDER
HEDERS
HEDGE
HEDGED
HEDGEHOG
HEDGEHOGS
HEDGEHOP
HEDGEHOPPED
HEDGEHOPPER
HEDGEHOPPERS
HEDGEHOPPING
HEDGEHOPS
HEDGEPIG
HEDGEPIGS
HEDGER
HEDGEROW
HEDGEROWS
HEDGERS
HEDGES
HEDGIER
HEDGIEST
HEDGING
HEDGINGLY
HEDGY
HEDONIC
HEDONICALLY
HEDONICS
HEDONISM
HEDONISMS
HEDONIST
HEDONISTIC
HEDONISTICALLY
HEDONISTS
HEED
HEEDED
HEEDER
HEEDERS
HEEDFUL
HEEDFULLY
HEEDFULNESS
HEEDFULNESSES
HEEDING
HEEDLESS
HEEDLESSLY
HEEDLESSNESS
HEEDLESSNESSES
HEEDS
HEEHAW
HEEHAWED
HEEHAWING
HEEHAWS
HEEL
HEELBALL
HEELBALLS
HEELED
HEELER
HEELERS
HEELING
HEELINGS
HEELLESS
HEELPIECE
HEELPIECES
HEELPLATE
HEELPLATES
HEELPOST
HEELPOSTS
HEELS
HEELTAP
HEELTAPS
HEEZE
HEEZED
HEEZES
HEEZING
HEFT
HEFTED
HEFTER
HEFTERS
HEFTIER
HEFTIEST
HEFTILY
HEFTINESS
HEFTINESSES
HEFTING
HEFTS
HEFTY
HEGARI
HEGARIS
HEGEMON
HEGEMONIC
HEGEMONIES
HEGEMONS
HEGEMONY
HEGIRA
HEGIRAS
HEGUMEN
HEGUMENE
HEGUMENES
HEGUMENIES
HEGUMENOS
HEGUMENOSES
HEGUMENS
HEGUMENY
HEH
HEHS
HEIFER
HEIFERS
HEIGH
HEIGHT
HEIGHTEN
HEIGHTENED
HEIGHTENING
HEIGHTENS
HEIGHTH
HEIGHTHS
HEIGHTISM
HEIGHTISMS
HEIGHTS
HEIL
HEILED
HEILING
HEILS
HEIMISH
HEINIE
HEINIES
HEINOUS
HEINOUSLY
HEINOUSNESS
HEINOUSNESSES
HEIR
HEIRDOM
HEIRDOMS
HEIRED
HEIRESS
HEIRESSES
HEIRING
HEIRLESS
HEIRLOOM
HEIRLOOMS
HEIRS
HEIRSHIP
HEIRSHIPS
HEISHI
HEIST
HEISTED
HEISTER
HEISTERS
HEISTING
HEISTS
HEJIRA
HEJIRAS
HEKTARE
HEKTARES
HEKTOGRAM
HEKTOGRAMS
HELD
HELDENTENOR
HELDENTENORS
HELENIUM
HELENIUMS
HELIAC
HELIACAL
HELIACALLY
HELIAST
HELIASTS
HELICAL
HELICALLY
HELICES
HELICITIES
HELICITY
HELICLINE
HELICLINES
HELICOID
HELICOIDAL
HELICOIDS
HELICON
HELICONIA
HELICONIAS
HELICONS
HELICOPT
HELICOPTED
HELICOPTER
HELICOPTERED
HELICOPTERING
HELICOPTERS
HELICOPTING
HELICOPTS
HELICTITE
HELICTITES
HELILIFT
HELILIFTED
HELILIFTING
HELILIFTS
HELIO
HELIOCENTRIC
HELIOGRAM
HELIOGRAMS
HELIOGRAPH
HELIOGRAPHED

HELIOGRAPHIC
HELIOGRAPHING
HELIOGRAPHS
HELIOLATRIES
HELIOLATROUS
HELIOLATRY
HELIOMETER
HELIOMETERS
HELIOMETRIC
HELIOMETRICALLY
HELIOS
HELIOSPHERE
HELIOSPHERES
HELIOSPHERIC
HELIOSTAT
HELIOSTATS
HELIOTROPE
HELIOTROPES
HELIOTROPIC
HELIOTROPISM
HELIOTROPISMS
HELIOTYPE
HELIOTYPED
HELIOTYPES
HELIOTYPIES
HELIOTYPING
HELIOTYPY
HELIOZOAN
HELIOZOANS
HELIOZOIC
HELIPAD
HELIPADS
HELIPORT
HELIPORTS
HELISKI
HELISKIED
HELISKIING
HELISKIINGS
HELISKIS
HELISTOP
HELISTOPS
HELITACK
HELITACKS
HELIUM
HELIUMS
HELIX
HELIXES
HELL
HELLACIOUS
HELLACIOUSLY
HELLBENDER
HELLBENDERS
HELLBENT
HELLBOX
HELLBOXES
HELLBROTH
HELLBROTHS
HELLCAT
HELLCATS
HELLDIVER
HELLDIVERS
HELLEBORE
HELLEBORES
HELLED
HELLENIZATION
HELLENIZATIONS
HELLENIZE
HELLENIZED
HELLENIZES
HELLENIZING
HELLER
HELLERI
HELLERIES
HELLERIS
HELLERS
HELLERY
HELLFIRE
HELLFIRES
HELLGRAMMITE
HELLGRAMMITES
HELLHOLE
HELLHOLES
HELLHOUND
HELLHOUNDS
HELLING
HELLION
HELLIONS
HELLISH
HELLISHLY
HELLISHNESS
HELLISHNESSES
HELLKITE
HELLKITES
HELLO
HELLOED
HELLOES
HELLOING
HELLOS
HELLS
HELLUVA
HELLWARD
HELM
HELMED
HELMET
HELMETED
HELMETING
HELMETLIKE
HELMETS
HELMING
HELMINTH
HELMINTHIASES
HELMINTHIASIS
HELMINTHIC
HELMINTHOLOGIES
HELMINTHOLOGY
HELMINTHS
HELMLESS
HELMS
HELMSMAN
HELMSMANSHIP
HELMSMANSHIPS
HELMSMEN
HELMSPERSON
HELMSPERSONS
HELO
HELOS
HELOT
HELOTAGE
HELOTAGES
HELOTISM
HELOTISMS
HELOTRIES
HELOTRY
HELOTS
HELP
HELPABLE
HELPDESK
HELPDESKS
HELPED
HELPER
HELPERS
HELPFUL
HELPFULLY
HELPFULNESS
HELPFULNESSES
HELPING
HELPINGS
HELPLESS
HELPLESSLY
HELPLESSNESS
HELPLESSNESSES
HELPLINE
HELPLINES
HELPMATE
HELPMATES
HELPMEET
HELPMEETS
HELPS
HELVE
HELVED
HELVES
HELVING
HEM
HEMACYTOMETER
HEMACYTOMETERS
HEMAGGLUTINATE
HEMAGGLUTINATED
HEMAGGLUTINATES
HEMAGGLUTININ
HEMAGGLUTININS
HEMAGOG
HEMAGOGS
HEMAL
HEMANGIOMA
HEMANGIOMAS
HEMANGIOMATA
HEMATAL
HEMATEIN
HEMATEINS
HEMATIC
HEMATICS
HEMATIN
HEMATINE
HEMATINES
HEMATINIC
HEMATINICS
HEMATINS
HEMATITE
HEMATITES
HEMATITIC
HEMATOCRIT
HEMATOCRITS
HEMATOGENOUS
HEMATOID
HEMATOLOGIC
HEMATOLOGICAL
HEMATOLOGIES
HEMATOLOGIST
HEMATOLOGISTS
HEMATOLOGY
HEMATOMA
HEMATOMAS
HEMATOMATA
HEMATOPHAGOUS
HEMATOPOIESES
HEMATOPOIESIS
HEMATOPOIETIC
HEMATOPORPHYRIN
HEMATOSES
HEMATOSIS
HEMATOXYLIN
HEMATOXYLINS
HEMATOZOA
HEMATOZOON
HEMATURIA
HEMATURIAS
HEMATURIC
HEME
HEMELYTRA
HEMELYTRON
HEMELYTRUM
HEMEROCALLIS
HEMEROCALLISES
HEMERYTHRIN
HEMERYTHRINS
HEMES
HEMIACETAL
HEMIACETALS
HEMIALGIA
HEMIALGIAS
HEMIC
HEMICELLULOSE
HEMICELLULOSES
HEMICHORDATE
HEMICHORDATES
HEMICYCLE
HEMICYCLES
HEMIHEDRAL
HEMIHYDRATE
HEMIHYDRATED
HEMIHYDRATES
HEMIMETABOLOUS
HEMIMORPHIC
HEMIMORPHISM
HEMIMORPHISMS
HEMIN
HEMINS
HEMIOLA
HEMIOLAS
HEMIOLIA
HEMIOLIAS
HEMIPLEGIA
HEMIPLEGIAS
HEMIPLEGIC
HEMIPLEGICS
HEMIPTER
HEMIPTERAN
HEMIPTERANS
HEMIPTEROUS
HEMIPTERS
HEMISPHERE
HEMISPHERECTOMY
HEMISPHERES
HEMISPHERIC
HEMISPHERICAL

HEMISTICH
HEMISTICHS
HEMITROPE
HEMITROPES
HEMIZYGOUS
HEMLINE
HEMLINES
HEMLOCK
HEMLOCKS
HEMMED
HEMMER
HEMMERS
HEMMING
HEMOCHROMATOSES
HEMOCHROMATOSIS
HEMOCOEL
HEMOCOELS
HEMOCYANIN
HEMOCYANINS
HEMOCYTE
HEMOCYTES
HEMOCYTOMETER
HEMOCYTOMETERS
HEMODIALYSES
HEMODIALYSIS
HEMODILUTION
HEMODILUTIONS
HEMODYNAMIC
HEMODYNAMICALLY
HEMODYNAMICS
HEMOFLAGELLATE
HEMOFLAGELLATES
HEMOGLOBIN
HEMOGLOBINS
HEMOGLOBINURIA
HEMOGLOBINURIAS
HEMOGLOBINURIC
HEMOID
HEMOLYMPH
HEMOLYMPHS
HEMOLYSES
HEMOLYSIN
HEMOLYSINS
HEMOLYSIS
HEMOLYTIC
HEMOLYZE
HEMOLYZED
HEMOLYZES
HEMOLYZING
HEMOPHILE
HEMOPHILES
HEMOPHILIA
HEMOPHILIAC
HEMOPHILIACS
HEMOPHILIAS
HEMOPHILIC
HEMOPHILICS
HEMOPOIESES
HEMOPOIESIS
HEMOPOIETIC
HEMOPROTEIN
HEMOPROTEINS
HEMOPTYSES
HEMOPTYSIS
HEMORRHAGE
HEMORRHAGED
HEMORRHAGES
HEMORRHAGIC
HEMORRHAGING
HEMORRHOID
HEMORRHOIDAL
HEMORRHOIDALS
HEMORRHOIDS
HEMOSIDERIN
HEMOSIDERINS
HEMOSTASES
HEMOSTASIS
HEMOSTAT
HEMOSTATIC
HEMOSTATICS
HEMOSTATS
HEMOTOXIC
HEMOTOXIN
HEMOTOXINS
HEMP
HEMPEN
HEMPIE
HEMPIER
HEMPIEST
HEMPLIKE
HEMPS
HEMPSEED
HEMPSEEDS
HEMPWEED
HEMPWEEDS
HEMPY
HEMS
HEMSTITCH
HEMSTITCHED
HEMSTITCHER
HEMSTITCHERS
HEMSTITCHES
HEMSTITCHING
HEN
HENBANE
HENBANES
HENBIT
HENBITS
HENCE
HENCEFORTH
HENCEFORWARD
HENCHMAN
HENCHMEN
HENCOOP
HENCOOPS
HENDECASYLLABIC
HENDECASYLLABLE
HENDIADYS
HENDIADYSES
HENEQUEN
HENEQUENS
HENEQUIN
HENEQUINS
HENGE
HENGES
HENHOUSE
HENHOUSES
HENIQUEN
HENIQUENS
HENLEY
HENLEYS
HENLIKE
HENNA
HENNAED
HENNAING
HENNAS
HENNERIES
HENNERY
HENNISH
HENNISHLY
HENOTHEISM
HENOTHEISMS
HENOTHEIST
HENOTHEISTIC
HENOTHEISTS
HENPECK
HENPECKED
HENPECKING
HENPECKS
HENRIES
HENRY
HENRYS
HENS
HENT
HENTED
HENTING
HENTS
HEP
HEPARIN
HEPARINISATION
HEPARINISATIONS
HEPARINISE
HEPARINISED
HEPARINISES
HEPARINISING
HEPARINIZATION
HEPARINIZATIONS
HEPARINIZE
HEPARINIZED
HEPARINIZES
HEPARINIZING
HEPARINS
HEPATECTOMIES
HEPATECTOMIZED
HEPATECTOMY
HEPATIC
HEPATICA
HEPATICAE
HEPATICAS
HEPATICS
HEPATITIDES
HEPATITIS
HEPATITISES
HEPATIZE
HEPATIZED
HEPATIZES
HEPATIZING
HEPATOCELLULAR
HEPATOCYTE
HEPATOCYTES
HEPATOMA
HEPATOMAS
HEPATOMATA
HEPATOMEGALIES
HEPATOMEGALY
HEPATOPANCREAS
HEPATOTOXIC
HEPATOTOXICITY
HEPCAT
HEPCATS
HEPPER
HEPPEST
HEPS
HEPTACHLOR
HEPTACHLORS
HEPTAD
HEPTADS
HEPTAGON
HEPTAGONAL
HEPTAGONS
HEPTAMETER
HEPTAMETERS
HEPTANE
HEPTANES
HEPTARCH
HEPTARCHIES
HEPTARCHS
HEPTARCHY
HEPTATHLETE
HEPTATHLETES
HEPTATHLON
HEPTATHLONS
HEPTOSE
HEPTOSES
HER
HERALD
HERALDED
HERALDIC
HERALDICALLY
HERALDING
HERALDIST
HERALDISTS
HERALDRIES
HERALDRY
HERALDS
HERB
HERBACEOUS
HERBAGE
HERBAGED
HERBAGES
HERBAL
HERBALISM
HERBALISMS
HERBALIST
HERBALISTS
HERBALS
HERBARIA
HERBARIAL
HERBARIUM
HERBARIUMS
HERBED
HERBICIDAL
HERBICIDALLY
HERBICIDE
HERBICIDES
HERBIER
HERBIEST
HERBIVORE
HERBIVORES
HERBIVORIES
HERBIVOROUS
HERBIVORY
HERBLESS
HERBLIKE
HERBOLOGIES

HERBOLOGY
HERBS
HERBY
HERCULEAN
HERCULES
HERCULESES
HERD
HERDED
HERDER
HERDERS
HERDIC
HERDICS
HERDING
HERDINGS
HERDLIKE
HERDMAN
HERDMEN
HERDS
HERDSMAN
HERDSMEN
HERE
HEREABOUT
HEREABOUTS
HEREAFTER
HEREAFTERS
HEREAT
HEREAWAY
HEREAWAYS
HEREBY
HEREDES
HEREDITAMENT
HEREDITAMENTS
HEREDITARIAN
HEREDITARIANS
HEREDITARILY
HEREDITARY
HEREDITIES
HEREDITY
HEREIN
HEREINABOVE
HEREINAFTER
HEREINBEFORE
HEREINBELOW
HEREINTO
HEREOF
HEREON
HERES
HERESIARCH
HERESIARCHS
HERESIES
HERESY
HERETIC
HERETICAL
HERETICALLY
HERETICS
HERETO
HERETOFORE
HERETRICES
HERETRIX
HERETRIXES
HEREUNDER
HEREUNTO
HEREUPON
HEREWITH
HERIOT
HERIOTS
HERITABILITIES
HERITABILITY
HERITABLE
HERITABLY
HERITAGE
HERITAGES
HERITOR
HERITORS
HERITRICES
HERITRIX
HERITRIXES
HERL
HERLS
HERM
HERMA
HERMAE
HERMAEAN
HERMAI
HERMAPHRODITE
HERMAPHRODITES
HERMAPHRODITIC
HERMAPHRODITISM
HERMATYPIC
HERMENEUTIC
HERMENEUTICAL
HERMENEUTICALLY
HERMENEUTICS
HERMETIC
HERMETICAL
HERMETICALLY
HERMETICISM
HERMETICISMS
HERMETISM
HERMETISMS
HERMETIST
HERMETISTS
HERMIT
HERMITAGE
HERMITAGES
HERMITIC
HERMITISM
HERMITISMS
HERMITRIES
HERMITRY
HERMITS
HERMS
HERN
HERNIA
HERNIAE
HERNIAL
HERNIAS
HERNIATE
HERNIATED
HERNIATES
HERNIATING
HERNIATION
HERNIATIONS
HERNS
HERO
HEROES
HEROIC
HEROICAL
HEROICALLY
HEROICIZE
HEROICIZED
HEROICIZES
HEROICIZING
HEROICOMIC
HEROICOMICAL
HEROICS
HEROIN
HEROINE
HEROINES
HEROINISM
HEROINISMS
HEROINS
HEROISM
HEROISMS
HEROIZE
HEROIZED
HEROIZES
HEROIZING
HERON
HERONRIES
HERONRY
HERONS
HEROS
HERPES
HERPESES
HERPESVIRUS
HERPESVIRUSES
HERPETIC
HERPETOLOGICAL
HERPETOLOGIES
HERPETOLOGIST
HERPETOLOGISTS
HERPETOLOGY
HERRENVOLK
HERRENVOLKS
HERRIED
HERRIES
HERRING
HERRINGBONE
HERRINGBONED
HERRINGBONES
HERRINGBONING
HERRINGS
HERRY
HERRYING
HERS
HERSELF
HERSTORIES
HERSTORY
HERTZ
HERTZES
HES
HESITANCE
HESITANCES
HESITANCIES
HESITANCY
HESITANT
HESITANTLY
HESITATE
HESITATED
HESITATER
HESITATERS
HESITATES
HESITATING
HESITATINGLY
HESITATION
HESITATIONS
HESITATOR
HESITATORS
HESPERIDIA
HESPERIDIN
HESPERIDINS
HESPERIDIUM
HESSIAN
HESSIANS
HESSITE
HESSITES
HESSONITE
HESSONITES
HEST
HESTS
HET
HETAERA
HETAERAE
HETAERAS
HETAERIC
HETAERISM
HETAERISMS
HETAIRA
HETAIRAI
HETAIRAS
HETAIRISM
HETAIRISMS
HETERO
HETEROATOM
HETEROATOMS
HETEROAUXIN
HETEROAUXINS
HETEROCERCAL
HETEROCHROMATIC
HETEROCHROMATIN
HETEROCLITE
HETEROCLITES
HETEROCYCLE
HETEROCYCLES
HETEROCYCLIC
HETEROCYCLICS
HETEROCYST
HETEROCYSTOUS
HETEROCYSTS
HETERODOX
HETERODOXIES
HETERODOXY
HETERODUPLEX
HETERODUPLEXES
HETERODYNE
HETERODYNED
HETERODYNES
HETERODYNING
HETEROECIOUS
HETEROECISM
HETEROECISMS
HETEROGAMETE
HETEROGAMETES
HETEROGAMETIC
HETEROGAMETIES
HETEROGAMETY
HETEROGAMIES
HETEROGAMOUS
HETEROGAMY
HETEROGENEITIES
HETEROGENEITY
HETEROGENEOUS
HETEROGENEOUSLY
HETEROGENIES

HETEROGENOUS
HETEROGENY
HETEROGLOSSIA
HETEROGLOSSIAS
HETEROGONIC
HETEROGONIES
HETEROGONY
HETEROGRAFT
HETEROGRAFTS
HETEROKARYON
HETEROKARYONS
HETEROKARYOSES
HETEROKARYOSIS
HETEROKARYOTIC
HETEROLOGOUS
HETEROLOGOUSLY
HETEROLYSES
HETEROLYSIS
HETEROLYTIC
HETEROMORPHIC
HETEROMORPHISM
HETEROMORPHISMS
HETERONOMIES
HETERONOMOUS
HETERONOMY
HETERONORMATIVE
HETERONYM
HETERONYMS
HETEROPHIL
HETEROPHILE
HETEROPHONIES
HETEROPHONY
HETEROPHYLLIES
HETEROPHYLLOUS
HETEROPHYLLY
HETEROPLOID
HETEROPLOIDIES
HETEROPLOIDS
HETEROPLOIDY
HETEROPTEROUS
HETEROS
HETEROSES
HETEROSEXISM
HETEROSEXISMS
HETEROSEXIST
HETEROSEXISTS
HETEROSEXUAL
HETEROSEXUALITY
HETEROSEXUALLY
HETEROSEXUALS
HETEROSIS
HETEROSOCIAL
HETEROSPORIES
HETEROSPOROUS
HETEROSPORY
HETEROTHALLIC
HETEROTHALLISM
HETEROTHALLISMS
HETEROTIC
HETEROTOPIC
HETEROTROPH
HETEROTROPHIC
HETEROTROPHIES
HETEROTROPHS
HETEROTROPHY
HETEROTYPIC
HETEROZYGOSES
HETEROZYGOSIS
HETEROZYGOSITY
HETEROZYGOTE
HETEROZYGOTES
HETEROZYGOUS
HETH
HETHS
HETMAN
HETMANS
HETMEN
HETS
HEUCH
HEUCHERA
HEUCHERAS
HEUCHS
HEUGH
HEUGHS
HEULANDITE
HEULANDITES
HEURISTIC
HEURISTICALLY
HEURISTICS
HEVEA
HEVEAS
HEW
HEWABLE
HEWED
HEWER
HEWERS
HEWING
HEWN
HEWS
HEX
HEXACHLORETHANE
HEXACHLOROPHENE
HEXACHORD
HEXACHORDS
HEXAD
HEXADE
HEXADECIMAL
HEXADECIMALS
HEXADES
HEXADIC
HEXADS
HEXAGON
HEXAGONAL
HEXAGONALLY
HEXAGONS
HEXAGRAM
HEXAGRAMS
HEXAHEDRA
HEXAHEDRON
HEXAHEDRONS
HEXAHYDRATE
HEXAHYDRATES
HEXAMETER
HEXAMETERS
HEXAMETHONIUM
HEXAMETHONIUMS
HEXAMINE
HEXAMINES
HEXANE
HEXANES
HEXAPLA
HEXAPLAR
HEXAPLAS
HEXAPLOID
HEXAPLOIDIES
HEXAPLOIDS
HEXAPLOIDY
HEXAPOD
HEXAPODIES
HEXAPODS
HEXAPODY
HEXARCHIES
HEXARCHY
HEXASTICH
HEXASTICHS
HEXED
HEXER
HEXEREI
HEXEREIS
HEXERS
HEXES
HEXING
HEXOBARBITAL
HEXOBARBITALS
HEXOKINASE
HEXOKINASES
HEXONE
HEXONES
HEXOSAMINIDASE
HEXOSAMINIDASES
HEXOSAN
HEXOSANS
HEXOSE
HEXOSES
HEXYL
HEXYLIC
HEXYLRESORCINOL
HEXYLS
HEY
HEYDAY
HEYDAYS
HEYDEY
HEYDEYS
HI
HIATAL
HIATUS
HIATUSES
HIBACHI
HIBACHIS
HIBAKUSHA
HIBERNACULA
HIBERNACULUM
HIBERNAL
HIBERNATE
HIBERNATED
HIBERNATES
HIBERNATING
HIBERNATION
HIBERNATIONS
HIBERNATOR
HIBERNATORS
HIBISCUS
HIBISCUSES
HIC
HICCOUGH
HICCOUGHED
HICCOUGHING
HICCOUGHS
HICCUP
HICCUPED
HICCUPIER
HICCUPIEST
HICCUPING
HICCUPPED
HICCUPPING
HICCUPS
HICCUPY
HICK
HICKER
HICKEST
HICKEY
HICKEYS
HICKIE
HICKIES
HICKISH
HICKORIES
HICKORY
HICKS
HID
HIDABLE
HIDALGO
HIDALGOS
HIDDEN
HIDDENITE
HIDDENITES
HIDDENLY
HIDDENNESS
HIDDENNESSES
HIDE
HIDEAWAY
HIDEAWAYS
HIDEBOUND
HIDED
HIDELESS
HIDEOSITIES
HIDEOSITY
HIDEOUS
HIDEOUSLY
HIDEOUSNESS
HIDEOUSNESSES
HIDEOUT
HIDEOUTS
HIDER
HIDERS
HIDES
HIDING
HIDINGS
HIDROSES
HIDROSIS
HIDROTIC
HIDROTICS
HIE
HIED
HIEING
HIEMAL
HIERARCH
HIERARCHAL
HIERARCHIC
HIERARCHICAL
HIERARCHICALLY
HIERARCHIES
HIERARCHIZATION
HIERARCHIZE
HIERARCHIZED
HIERARCHIZES

HIERARCHIZING
HIERARCHS
HIERARCHY
HIERATIC
HIERATICALLY
HIERODULE
HIERODULES
HIEROGLYPH
HIEROGLYPHIC
HIEROGLYPHICAL
HIEROGLYPHICS
HIEROGLYPHS
HIEROLOGIES
HIEROLOGY
HIEROPHANT
HIEROPHANTIC
HIEROPHANTS
HIERURGIES
HIERURGY
HIES
HIFALUTIN
HIGGLE
HIGGLED
HIGGLER
HIGGLERS
HIGGLES
HIGGLING
HIGH
HIGHBALL
HIGHBALLED
HIGHBALLING
HIGHBALLS
HIGHBINDER
HIGHBINDERS
HIGHBORN
HIGHBOY
HIGHBOYS
HIGHBRED
HIGHBROW
HIGHBROWED
HIGHBROWISM
HIGHBROWISMS
HIGHBROWS
HIGHBUSH
HIGHBUSHES
HIGHCHAIR
HIGHCHAIRS
HIGHER
HIGHEST
HIGHFALUTIN
HIGHFLIER
HIGHFLIERS
HIGHFLYER
HIGHFLYERS
HIGHJACK
HIGHJACKED
HIGHJACKING
HIGHJACKS
HIGHLAND
HIGHLANDER
HIGHLANDERS
HIGHLANDS
HIGHLIFE
HIGHLIFES
HIGHLIGHT
HIGHLIGHTED
HIGHLIGHTER
HIGHLIGHTERS
HIGHLIGHTING
HIGHLIGHTS
HIGHLY
HIGHNESS
HIGHNESSES
HIGHRISE
HIGHRISES
HIGHROAD
HIGHROADS
HIGHS
HIGHSPOT
HIGHSPOTS
HIGHT
HIGHTAIL
HIGHTAILED
HIGHTAILING
HIGHTAILS
HIGHTED
HIGHTH
HIGHTHS
HIGHTING
HIGHTOP
HIGHTOPS
HIGHTS
HIGHWAY
HIGHWAYMAN
HIGHWAYMEN
HIGHWAYS
HIJAB
HIJABS
HIJACK
HIJACKED
HIJACKER
HIJACKERS
HIJACKING
HIJACKS
HIJINKS
HIJRA
HIJRAH
HIJRAHS
HIJRAS
HIKE
HIKED
HIKER
HIKERS
HIKES
HIKING
HILA
HILAR
HILARIOUS
HILARIOUSLY
HILARIOUSNESS
HILARIOUSNESSES
HILARITIES
HILARITY
HILDING
HILDINGS
HILI
HILL
HILLBILLIES
HILLBILLY
HILLCREST
HILLCRESTS
HILLED
HILLER
HILLERS
HILLIER
HILLIEST
HILLINESS
HILLINESSES
HILLING
HILLO
HILLOA
HILLOAED
HILLOAING
HILLOAS
HILLOCK
HILLOCKED
HILLOCKS
HILLOCKY
HILLOED
HILLOES
HILLOING
HILLOS
HILLS
HILLSIDE
HILLSIDES
HILLSLOPE
HILLSLOPES
HILLTOP
HILLTOPS
HILLY
HILT
HILTED
HILTING
HILTLESS
HILTS
HILUM
HILUS
HIM
HIMATIA
HIMATION
HIMATIONS
HIMBO
HIMBOS
HIMS
HIMSELF
HIN
HIND
HINDBRAIN
HINDBRAINS
HINDER
HINDERED
HINDERER
HINDERERS
HINDERING
HINDERS
HINDGUT
HINDGUTS
HINDMILK
HINDMILKS
HINDMOST
HINDQUARTER
HINDQUARTERS
HINDRANCE
HINDRANCES
HINDS
HINDSHANK
HINDSHANKS
HINDSIGHT
HINDSIGHTS
HINDWING
HINDWINGS
HINGE
HINGED
HINGER
HINGERS
HINGES
HINGING
HINKIER
HINKIEST
HINKY
HINNIE
HINNIED
HINNIES
HINNY
HINNYING
HINS
HINT
HINTED
HINTER
HINTERLAND
HINTERLANDS
HINTERS
HINTING
HINTS
HIP
HIPBONE
HIPBONES
HIPHUGGER
HIPLESS
HIPLIKE
HIPLINE
HIPLINES
HIPLY
HIPNESS
HIPNESSES
HIPPARCH
HIPPARCHS
HIPPED
HIPPER
HIPPEST
HIPPIE
HIPPIEDOM
HIPPIEDOMS
HIPPIEISH
HIPPIENESS
HIPPIENESSES
HIPPIER
HIPPIES
HIPPIEST
HIPPINESS
HIPPINESSES
HIPPING
HIPPISH
HIPPO
HIPPOCAMPAL
HIPPOCAMPI
HIPPOCAMPUS
HIPPOCRAS
HIPPOCRASES
HIPPODROME
HIPPODROMES
HIPPOGRIFF
HIPPOGRIFFS
HIPPOPOTAMI
HIPPOPOTAMUS

HIPPOPOTAMUSES
HIPPOS
HIPPY
HIPPYISH
HIPS
HIPSHOT
HIPSTER
HIPSTERISM
HIPSTERISMS
HIPSTERS
HIRABLE
HIRAGANA
HIRAGANAS
HIRCINE
HIRE
HIREABLE
HIRED
HIREE
HIREES
HIRELING
HIRELINGS
HIRER
HIRERS
HIRES
HIRING
HIRPLE
HIRPLED
HIRPLES
HIRPLING
HIRSEL
HIRSELED
HIRSELING
HIRSELLED
HIRSELLING
HIRSELS
HIRSLE
HIRSLED
HIRSLES
HIRSLING
HIRSUTE
HIRSUTENESS
HIRSUTENESSES
HIRSUTISM
HIRSUTISMS
HIRUDIN
HIRUDINS
HIS
HISN
HISPANIDAD
HISPANIDADS
HISPANISM
HISPANISMS
HISPID
HISPIDITIES
HISPIDITY
HISS
HISSED
HISSELF
HISSER
HISSERS
HISSES
HISSIER
HISSIES
HISSIEST
HISSING
HISSINGS
HISSY
HIST
HISTAMIN
HISTAMINASE
HISTAMINASES
HISTAMINE
HISTAMINERGIC
HISTAMINES
HISTAMINS
HISTED
HISTIDIN
HISTIDINE
HISTIDINES
HISTIDINS
HISTING
HISTIOCYTE
HISTIOCYTES
HISTIOCYTIC
HISTOCHEMICAL
HISTOCHEMICALLY
HISTOCHEMISTRY
HISTOGEN
HISTOGENESES
HISTOGENESIS
HISTOGENETIC
HISTOGENS
HISTOGRAM
HISTOGRAMS
HISTOID
HISTOLOGIC
HISTOLOGICAL
HISTOLOGICALLY
HISTOLOGIES
HISTOLOGIST
HISTOLOGISTS
HISTOLOGY
HISTOLYSES
HISTOLYSIS
HISTONE
HISTONES
HISTOPATHOLOGIC
HISTOPATHOLOGY
HISTOPHYSIOLOGY
HISTOPLASMOSES
HISTOPLASMOSIS
HISTORIAN
HISTORIANS
HISTORIC
HISTORICAL
HISTORICALLY
HISTORICALNESS
HISTORICISM
HISTORICISMS
HISTORICIST
HISTORICISTS
HISTORICITIES
HISTORICITY
HISTORICIZE
HISTORICIZED
HISTORICIZES
HISTORIÇIZING
HISTORIED
HISTORIES
HISTORIOGRAPHER
HISTORIOGRAPHIC
HISTORIOGRAPHY
HISTORY
HISTRIONIC
HISTRIONICALLY
HISTRIONICS
HISTS
HIT
HITCH
HITCHED
HITCHER
HITCHERS
HITCHES
HITCHHIKE
HITCHHIKED
HITCHHIKER
HITCHHIKERS
HITCHHIKES
HITCHHIKING
HITCHING
HITHER
HITHERMOST
HITHERTO
HITHERWARD
HITLESS
HITMAKER
HITMAKERS
HITMAN
HITMEN
HITS
HITTABLE
HITTER
HITTERS
HITTING
HIVE
HIVED
HIVELESS
HIVES
HIVING
HIYA
HIZZONER
HIZZONERS
HM
HMM
HMMM
HO
HOACTZIN
HOACTZINES
HOACTZINS
HOAGIE
HOAGIES
HOAGY
HOAR
HOARD
HOARDED
HOARDER
HOARDERS
HOARDING
HOARDINGS
HOARDS
HOARFROST
HOARFROSTS
HOARIER
HOARIEST
HOARILY
HOARINESS
HOARINESSES
HOARS
HOARSE
HOARSELY
HOARSEN
HOARSENED
HOARSENESS
HOARSENESSES
HOARSENING
HOARSENS
HOARSER
HOARSEST
HOARY
HOATZIN
HOATZINES
HOATZINS
HOAX
HOAXED
HOAXER
HOAXERS
HOAXES
HOAXING
HOB
HOBBED
HOBBER
HOBBERS
HOBBIES
HOBBING
HOBBIT
HOBBITS
HOBBLE
HOBBLEBUSH
HOBBLEBUSHES
HOBBLED
HOBBLEDEHOY
HOBBLEDEHOYS
HOBBLER
HOBBLERS
HOBBLES
HOBBLING
HOBBY
HOBBYHORSE
HOBBYHORSES
HOBBYIST
HOBBYISTS
HOBGOBLIN
HOBGOBLINS
HOBLIKE
HOBNAIL
HOBNAILED
HOBNAILING
HOBNAILS
HOBNOB
HOBNOBBED
HOBNOBBER
HOBNOBBERS
HOBNOBBING
HOBNOBS
HOBO
HOBOED
HOBOES
HOBOING
HOBOISM
HOBOISMS
HOBOS
HOBS
HOCK
HOCKED
HOCKER

HOCKERS
HOCKEY
HOCKEYS
HOCKING
HOCKS
HOCKSHOP
HOCKSHOPS
HOCUS
HOCUSED
HOCUSES
HOCUSING
HOCUSSED
HOCUSSES
HOCUSSING
HOD
HODAD
HODADDIES
HODADDY
HODADS
HODDEN
HODDENS
HODDIN
HODDINS
HODGEPODGE
HODGEPODGES
HODOSCOPE
HODOSCOPES
HODS
HOE
HOECAKE
HOECAKES
HOED
HOEDOWN
HOEDOWNS
HOEING
HOELIKE
HOER
HOERS
HOES
HOG
HOGAN
HOGANS
HOGBACK
HOGBACKS
HOGFISH
HOGFISHES
HOGG
HOGGED
HOGGER
HOGGERIES
HOGGERS
HOGGERY
HOGGET
HOGGETS
HOGGING
HOGGISH
HOGGISHLY
HOGGISHNESS
HOGGISHNESSES
HOGGS
HOGLIKE
HOGMANAY
HOGMANAYS
HOGMANE
HOGMANES
HOGMENAY
HOGMENAYS
HOGNOSE
HOGNOSES
HOGNUT
HOGNUTS
HOGS
HOGSHEAD
HOGSHEADS
HOGTIE
HOGTIED
HOGTIEING
HOGTIES
HOGTYING
HOGWASH
HOGWASHES
HOGWEED
HOGWEEDS
HOICK
HOICKED
HOICKING
HOICKS
HOIDEN
HOIDENED
HOIDENING
HOIDENS
HOISE
HOISED
HOISES
HOISIN
HOISING
HOISINS
HOIST
HOISTED
HOISTER
HOISTERS
HOISTING
HOISTS
HOKE
HOKED
HOKES
HOKEY
HOKEYNESS
HOKEYNESSES
HOKEYPOKEY
HOKEYPOKEYS
HOKIER
HOKIEST
HOKILY
HOKINESS
HOKINESSES
HOKING
HOKKU
HOKUM
HOKUMS
HOKYPOKIES
HOKYPOKY
HOLANDRIC
HOLARD
HOLARDS
HOLD
HOLDABLE
HOLDALL
HOLDALLS
HOLDBACK
HOLDBACKS
HOLDDOWN
HOLDDOWNS
HOLDEN
HOLDER
HOLDERS
HOLDFAST
HOLDFASTS
HOLDING
HOLDINGS
HOLDOUT
HOLDOUTS
HOLDOVER
HOLDOVERS
HOLDS
HOLDUP
HOLDUPS
HOLE
HOLED
HOLELESS
HOLES
HOLEY
HOLIBUT
HOLIBUTS
HOLIDAY
HOLIDAYED
HOLIDAYER
HOLIDAYERS
HOLIDAYING
HOLIDAYMAKER
HOLIDAYMAKERS
HOLIDAYS
HOLIER
HOLIES
HOLIEST
HOLILY
HOLINESS
HOLINESSES
HOLING
HOLISM
HOLISMS
HOLIST
HOLISTIC
HOLISTICALLY
HOLISTS
HOLK
HOLKED
HOLKING
HOLKS
HOLLA
HOLLAED
HOLLAING
HOLLAND
HOLLANDAISE
HOLLANDAISES
HOLLANDS
HOLLAS
HOLLER
HOLLERED
HOLLERING
HOLLERS
HOLLIES
HOLLO
HOLLOA
HOLLOAED
HOLLOAING
HOLLOAS
HOLLOED
HOLLOES
HOLLOING
HOLLOO
HOLLOOED
HOLLOOING
HOLLOOS
HOLLOS
HOLLOW
HOLLOWARE
HOLLOWARES
HOLLOWED
HOLLOWER
HOLLOWEST
HOLLOWING
HOLLOWLY
HOLLOWNESS
HOLLOWNESSES
HOLLOWS
HOLLOWWARE
HOLLOWWARES
HOLLY
HOLLYHOCK
HOLLYHOCKS
HOLM
HOLME
HOLMES
HOLMIC
HOLMIUM
HOLMIUMS
HOLMS
HOLO
HOLOBLASTIC
HOLOCAUST
HOLOCAUSTS
HOLOCENE
HOLOCRINE
HOLOENZYME
HOLOENZYMES
HOLOGAMIES
HOLOGAMY
HOLOGRAM
HOLOGRAMS
HOLOGRAPH
HOLOGRAPHED
HOLOGRAPHER
HOLOGRAPHERS
HOLOGRAPHIC
HOLOGRAPHICALLY
HOLOGRAPHIES
HOLOGRAPHING
HOLOGRAPHS
HOLOGRAPHY
HOLOGYNIC
HOLOGYNIES
HOLOGYNY
HOLOHEDRAL
HOLOMETABOLISM
HOLOMETABOLISMS
HOLOMETABOLOUS
HOLOPHRASTIC
HOLOPHYTE
HOLOPHYTES
HOLOPHYTIC
HOLOS
HOLOTHURIAN
HOLOTHURIANS
HOLOTYPE

HOLOTYPES
HOLOTYPIC
HOLOZOIC
HOLP
HOLPEN
HOLS
HOLSTEIN
HOLSTEINS
HOLSTER
HOLSTERED
HOLSTERING
HOLSTERS
HOLT
HOLTS
HOLUBTSI
HOLY
HOLYDAY
HOLYDAYS
HOLYSTONE
HOLYSTONED
HOLYSTONES
HOLYSTONING
HOLYTIDE
HOLYTIDES
HOM
HOMA
HOMAGE
HOMAGED
HOMAGER
HOMAGERS
HOMAGES
HOMAGING
HOMAS
HOMBRE
HOMBRES
HOMBURG
HOMBURGS
HOME
HOMEBODIES
HOMEBODY
HOMEBOUND
HOMEBOY
HOMEBOYS
HOMEBRED
HOMEBREDS
HOMEBREW
HOMEBREWS
HOMEBUILT
HOMEBUYER
HOMEBUYERS
HOMECOMER
HOMECOMERS
HOMECOMING
HOMECOMINGS
HOMED
HOMEGIRL
HOMEGIRLS
HOMEGROWN
HOMELAND
HOMELANDS
HOMELESS
HOMELESSNESS
HOMELESSNESSES
HOMELIER
HOMELIEST
HOMELIKE
HOMELINESS
HOMELINESSES
HOMELY
HOMEMADE
HOMEMAKER
HOMEMAKERS
HOMEMAKING
HOMEMAKINGS
HOMEOBOX
HOMEOBOXES
HOMEOMORPHIC
HOMEOMORPHISM
HOMEOMORPHISMS
HOMEOPATH
HOMEOPATHIC
HOMEOPATHICALLY
HOMEOPATHIES
HOMEOPATHS
HOMEOPATHY
HOMEOSTASES
HOMEOSTASIS
HOMEOSTATIC
HOMEOTHERM
HOMEOTHERMIC
HOMEOTHERMIES
HOMEOTHERMS
HOMEOTHERMY
HOMEOTIC
HOMEOWNER
HOMEOWNERS
HOMEPAGE
HOMEPAGES
HOMEPLACE
HOMEPLACES
HOMEPORT
HOMEPORTED
HOMEPORTING
HOMEPORTS
HOMER
HOMERED
HOMERIC
HOMERING
HOMEROOM
HOMEROOMS
HOMERS
HOMES
HOMESCHOOL
HOMESCHOOLED
HOMESCHOOLER
HOMESCHOOLERS
HOMESCHOOLING
HOMESCHOOLS
HOMESICK
HOMESICKNESS
HOMESICKNESSES
HOMESITE
HOMESITES
HOMESPUN
HOMESPUNS
HOMESTAND
HOMESTANDS
HOMESTAY
HOMESTAYS
HOMESTEAD
HOMESTEADED
HOMESTEADER
HOMESTEADERS
HOMESTEADING
HOMESTEADS
HOMESTRETCH
HOMESTRETCHES
HOMETOWN
HOMETOWNS
HOMEWARD
HOMEWARDS
HOMEWORK
HOMEWORKS
HOMEY
HOMEYNESS
HOMEYNESSES
HOMEYS
HOMICIDAL
HOMICIDALLY
HOMICIDE
HOMICIDES
HOMIE
HOMIER
HOMIES
HOMIEST
HOMILETIC
HOMILETICAL
HOMILETICS
HOMILIES
HOMILIST
HOMILISTS
HOMILY
HOMINES
HOMINESS
HOMINESSES
HOMING
HOMINIAN
HOMINIANS
HOMINID
HOMINIDS
HOMINIES
HOMININ
HOMININE
HOMININS
HOMINIZATION
HOMINIZATIONS
HOMINIZE
HOMINIZED
HOMINIZES
HOMINIZING
HOMINOID
HOMINOIDS
HOMINY
HOMMOCK
HOMMOCKS
HOMMOS
HOMMOSES
HOMO
HOMOCERCAL
HOMOCERCIES
HOMOCERCY
HOMOCYSTEINE
HOMOCYSTEINES
HOMOEOPATH
HOMOEOPATHIC
HOMOEOPATHIES
HOMOEOPATHS
HOMOEOPATHY
HOMOEROTIC
HOMOEROTICISM
HOMOEROTICISMS
HOMOGAMETIC
HOMOGAMIES
HOMOGAMOUS
HOMOGAMY
HOMOGENATE
HOMOGENATES
HOMOGENEITIES
HOMOGENEITY
HOMOGENEOUS
HOMOGENEOUSLY
HOMOGENEOUSNESS
HOMOGENIES
HOMOGENISATION
HOMOGENISATIONS
HOMOGENISE
HOMOGENISED
HOMOGENISES
HOMOGENISING
HOMOGENIZATION
HOMOGENIZATIONS
HOMOGENIZE
HOMOGENIZED
HOMOGENIZER
HOMOGENIZERS
HOMOGENIZES
HOMOGENIZING
HOMOGENOUS
HOMOGENY
HOMOGONIES
HOMOGONY
HOMOGRAFT
HOMOGRAFTS
HOMOGRAPH
HOMOGRAPHIC
HOMOGRAPHS
HOMOIOTHERM
HOMOIOTHERMIC
HOMOIOTHERMIES
HOMOIOTHERMS
HOMOIOTHERMY
HOMOIOUSIAN
HOMOIOUSIANS
HOMOLOG
HOMOLOGATE
HOMOLOGATED
HOMOLOGATES
HOMOLOGATING
HOMOLOGATION
HOMOLOGATIONS
HOMOLOGIC
HOMOLOGICAL
HOMOLOGICALLY
HOMOLOGIES
HOMOLOGIZE
HOMOLOGIZED
HOMOLOGIZER
HOMOLOGIZERS
HOMOLOGIZES
HOMOLOGIZING
HOMOLOGOUS
HOMOLOGS
HOMOLOGUE
HOMOLOGUES
HOMOLOGY

HOMOLYSES
HOMOLYSIS
HOMOLYTIC
HOMOMORPHIC
HOMOMORPHISM
HOMOMORPHISMS
HOMONUCLEAR
HOMONYM
HOMONYMIC
HOMONYMIES
HOMONYMOUS
HOMONYMOUSLY
HOMONYMS
HOMONYMY
HOMOOUSIAN
HOMOOUSIANS
HOMOPHILE
HOMOPHILES
HOMOPHOBE
HOMOPHOBES
HOMOPHOBIA
HOMOPHOBIAS
HOMOPHOBIC
HOMOPHONE
HOMOPHONES
HOMOPHONIC
HOMOPHONIES
HOMOPHONOUS
HOMOPHONY
HOMOPHYLIES
HOMOPHYLY
HOMOPLASIES
HOMOPLASTIC
HOMOPLASY
HOMOPOLAR
HOMOPOLYMER
HOMOPOLYMERIC
HOMOPOLYMERS
HOMOPTERAN
HOMOPTERANS
HOMOPTEROUS
HOMOS
HOMOSCEDASTIC
HOMOSEX
HOMOSEXES
HOMOSEXUAL
HOMOSEXUALITIES
HOMOSEXUALITY
HOMOSEXUALLY
HOMOSEXUALS
HOMOSOCIAL
HOMOSOCIALITIES
HOMOSOCIALITY
HOMOSPORIES
HOMOSPOROUS
HOMOSPORY
HOMOSTYLIES
HOMOSTYLY
HOMOTAXES
HOMOTAXIS
HOMOTHALLIC
HOMOTHALLISM
HOMOTHALLISMS
HOMOTRANSPLANT
HOMOTRANSPLANTS
HOMOZYGOSES
HOMOZYGOSIS
HOMOZYGOSITIES
HOMOZYGOSITY
HOMOZYGOTE
HOMOZYGOTES
HOMOZYGOUS
HOMOZYGOUSLY
HOMS
HOMUNCULI
HOMUNCULUS
HOMY
HON
HONAN
HONANS
HONCHO
HONCHOED
HONCHOES
HONCHOING
HONCHOS
HONDA
HONDAS
HONDLE
HONDLED
HONDLES
HONDLING
HONE
HONED
HONER
HONERS
HONES
HONEST
HONESTER
HONESTEST
HONESTIES
HONESTLY
HONESTY
HONEWORT
HONEWORTS
HONEY
HONEYBEE
HONEYBEES
HONEYBUN
HONEYBUNS
HONEYCOMB
HONEYCOMBED
HONEYCOMBING
HONEYCOMBS
HONEYCREEPER
HONEYCREEPERS
HONEYDEW
HONEYDEWS
HONEYEATER
HONEYEATERS
HONEYED
HONEYFUL
HONEYGUIDE
HONEYGUIDES
HONEYING
HONEYMOON
HONEYMOONED
HONEYMOONER
HONEYMOONERS
HONEYMOONING
HONEYMOONS
HONEYPOT
HONEYPOTS
HONEYS
HONEYSUCKLE
HONEYSUCKLES
HONG
HONGI
HONGIED
HONGIES
HONGIING
HONGS
HONIED
HONING
HONK
HONKED
HONKER
HONKERS
HONKEY
HONKEYS
HONKIE
HONKIES
HONKING
HONKS
HONKY
HONOR
HONORABILITIES
HONORABILITY
HONORABLE
HONORABLENESS
HONORABLENESSES
HONORABLY
HONORAND
HONORANDS
HONORARIA
HONORARIES
HONORARILY
HONORARIUM
HONORARIUMS
HONORARY
HONORED
HONOREE
HONOREES
HONORER
HONORERS
HONORIFIC
HONORIFICALLY
HONORIFICS
HONORING
HONORS
HONOUR
HONOURABLE
HONOURABLY
HONOURARY
HONOURED
HONOUREE
HONOUREES
HONOURER
HONOURERS
HONOURING
HONOURS
HONS
HOO
HOOCH
HOOCHES
HOOCHIE
HOOCHIES
HOOD
HOODED
HOODEDNESS
HOODEDNESSES
HOODIE
HOODIER
HOODIES
HOODIEST
HOODING
HOODLESS
HOODLIKE
HOODLUM
HOODLUMISH
HOODLUMISM
HOODLUMISMS
HOODLUMS
HOODMOLD
HOODMOLDS
HOODOO
HOODOOED
HOODOOING
HOODOOISM
HOODOOISMS
HOODOOS
HOODS
HOODWINK
HOODWINKED
HOODWINKER
HOODWINKERS
HOODWINKING
HOODWINKS
HOODY
HOOEY
HOOEYS
HOOF
HOOFBEAT
HOOFBEATS
HOOFBOUND
HOOFED
HOOFER
HOOFERS
HOOFING
HOOFLESS
HOOFLIKE
HOOFPRINT
HOOFPRINTS
HOOFS
HOOK
HOOKA
HOOKAH
HOOKAHS
HOOKAS
HOOKED
HOOKER
HOOKERS
HOOKEY
HOOKEYS
HOOKIER
HOOKIES
HOOKIEST
HOOKING
HOOKINGS
HOOKLESS
HOOKLET
HOOKLETS
HOOKLIKE
HOOKNOSE
HOOKNOSED
HOOKNOSES

HOOKS
HOOKUP
HOOKUPS
HOOKWORM
HOOKWORMS
HOOKY
HOOLIE
HOOLIGAN
HOOLIGANISM
HOOLIGANISMS
HOOLIGANS
HOOLY
HOOP
HOOPED
HOOPER
HOOPERS
HOOPING
HOOPLA
HOOPLAS
HOOPLESS
HOOPLIKE
HOOPOE
HOOPOES
HOOPOO
HOOPOOS
HOOPS
HOOPSKIRT
HOOPSKIRTS
HOOPSTER
HOOPSTERS
HOORAH
HOORAHED
HOORAHING
HOORAHS
HOORAY
HOORAYED
HOORAYING
HOORAYS
HOOSEGOW
HOOSEGOWS
HOOSGOW
HOOSGOWS
HOOT
HOOTCH
HOOTCHES
HOOTED
HOOTENANNIES
HOOTENANNY
HOOTER
HOOTERS
HOOTIER
HOOTIEST
HOOTING
HOOTS
HOOTY
HOOVED
HOOVER
HOOVERED
HOOVERING
HOOVERS
HOOVES
HOP
HOPAK
HOPAKS
HOPE
HOPED
HOPEFUL
HOPEFULLY
HOPEFULNESS
HOPEFULNESSES
HOPEFULS
HOPELESS
HOPELESSLY
HOPELESSNESS
HOPELESSNESSES
HOPER
HOPERS
HOPES
HOPHEAD
HOPHEADS
HOPING
HOPINGLY
HOPLITE
HOPLITES
HOPLITIC
HOPPED
HOPPER
HOPPERS
HOPPIER
HOPPIEST
HOPPING
HOPPINGS
HOPPLE
HOPPLED
HOPPLES
HOPPLING
HOPPY
HOPS
HOPSACK
HOPSACKING
HOPSACKINGS
HOPSACKS
HOPSCOTCH
HOPSCOTCHED
HOPSCOTCHES
HOPSCOTCHING
HOPTOAD
HOPTOADS
HORA
HORAH
HORAHS
HORAL
HORARY
HORAS
HORDE
HORDED
HORDEIN
HORDEINS
HORDEOLA
HORDEOLUM
HORDES
HORDING
HOREHOUND
HOREHOUNDS
HORIZON
HORIZONAL
HORIZONLESS
HORIZONS
HORIZONTAL
HORIZONTALITIES
HORIZONTALITY
HORIZONTALLY
HORIZONTALS
HORK
HORKED
HORKING
HORKS
HORMOGONIA
HORMOGONIUM
HORMONAL
HORMONALLY
HORMONE
HORMONELIKE
HORMONES
HORMONIC
HORN
HORNBEAM
HORNBEAMS
HORNBILL
HORNBILLS
HORNBLENDE
HORNBLENDES
HORNBLENDIC
HORNBOOK
HORNBOOKS
HORNDOG
HORNDOGS
HORNED
HORNEDNESS
HORNEDNESSES
HORNET
HORNETS
HORNFELS
HORNFELSES
HORNIER
HORNIEST
HORNILY
HORNINESS
HORNINESSES
HORNING
HORNINGS
HORNIST
HORNISTS
HORNITO
HORNITOS
HORNLESS
HORNLESSNESS
HORNLESSNESSES
HORNLIKE
HORNPIPE
HORNPIPES
HORNPOUT
HORNPOUTS
HORNS
HORNSTONE
HORNSTONES
HORNSWOGGLE
HORNSWOGGLED
HORNSWOGGLES
HORNSWOGGLING
HORNTAIL
HORNTAILS
HORNWORM
HORNWORMS
HORNWORT
HORNWORTS
HORNY
HOROLOGE
HOROLOGER
HOROLOGERS
HOROLOGES
HOROLOGIC
HOROLOGICAL
HOROLOGIES
HOROLOGIST
HOROLOGISTS
HOROLOGY
HOROSCOPE
HOROSCOPES
HOROSCOPIES
HOROSCOPY
HORRENDOUS
HORRENDOUSLY
HORRENT
HORRIBLE
HORRIBLENESS
HORRIBLENESSES
HORRIBLES
HORRIBLY
HORRID
HORRIDER
HORRIDEST
HORRIDLY
HORRIDNESS
HORRIDNESSES
HORRIFIC
HORRIFICALLY
HORRIFIED
HORRIFIES
HORRIFY
HORRIFYING
HORRIFYINGLY
HORROR
HORRORS
HORSE
HORSEBACK
HORSEBACKS
HORSEBEAN
HORSEBEANS
HORSEBOX
HORSEBOXES
HORSECAR
HORSECARS
HORSED
HORSEFEATHERS
HORSEFLESH
HORSEFLESHES
HORSEFLIES
HORSEFLY
HORSEHAIR
HORSEHAIRS
HORSEHIDE
HORSEHIDES
HORSELAUGH
HORSELAUGHS
HORSELESS
HORSELIKE
HORSEMAN
HORSEMANSHIP
HORSEMANSHIPS
HORSEMEN
HORSEMINT
HORSEMINTS
HORSEPLAY
HORSEPLAYER

HORSEPLAYERS
HORSEPLAYS
HORSEPOWER
HORSEPOWERS
HORSEPOX
HORSEPOXES
HORSERACE
HORSERACES
HORSERACING
HORSERACINGS
HORSERADISH
HORSERADISHES
HORSES
HORSESHIT
HORSESHITS
HORSESHOD
HORSESHOE
HORSESHOED
HORSESHOEING
HORSESHOER
HORSESHOERS
HORSESHOES
HORSETAIL
HORSETAILS
HORSEWEED
HORSEWEEDS
HORSEWHIP
HORSEWHIPPED
HORSEWHIPPER
HORSEWHIPPERS
HORSEWHIPPING
HORSEWHIPS
HORSEWOMAN
HORSEWOMEN
HORSEY
HORSIE
HORSIER
HORSIES
HORSIEST
HORSILY
HORSINESS
HORSINESSES
HORSING
HORST
HORSTE
HORSTES
HORSTS
HORSY
HORTATIVE
HORTATIVELY
HORTATORY
HORTICULTURAL
HORTICULTURALLY
HORTICULTURE
HORTICULTURES
HORTICULTURIST
HORTICULTURISTS
HOS
HOSANNA
HOSANNAED
HOSANNAH
HOSANNAHS
HOSANNAING
HOSANNAS
HOSE
HOSED
HOSEL
HOSELIKE
HOSELS
HOSEN
HOSEPIPE
HOSEPIPES
HOSER
HOSERS
HOSES
HOSEY
HOSEYED
HOSEYING
HOSEYS
HOSIER
HOSIERIES
HOSIERS
HOSIERY
HOSING
HOSPICE
HOSPICES
HOSPITABLE
HOSPITABLY
HOSPITAL
HOSPITALISATION
HOSPITALISE
HOSPITALISED
HOSPITALISES
HOSPITALISING
HOSPITALIST
HOSPITALISTS
HOSPITALITIES
HOSPITALITY
HOSPITALIZATION
HOSPITALIZE
HOSPITALIZED
HOSPITALIZES
HOSPITALIZING
HOSPITALS
HOSPITIA
HOSPITIUM
HOSPODAR
HOSPODARS
HOST
HOSTA
HOSTAGE
HOSTAGES
HOSTAS
HOSTED
HOSTEL
HOSTELED
HOSTELER
HOSTELERS
HOSTELING
HOSTELLED
HOSTELLER
HOSTELLERS
HOSTELLING
HOSTELRIES
HOSTELRY
HOSTELS
HOSTESS
HOSTESSED
HOSTESSES
HOSTESSING
HOSTILE
HOSTILELY
HOSTILES
HOSTILITIES
HOSTILITY
HOSTING
HOSTLER
HOSTLERS
HOSTLY
HOSTS
HOT
HOTBED
HOTBEDS
HOTBLOOD
HOTBLOODS
HOTBOX
HOTBOXES
HOTCAKE
HOTCAKES
HOTCH
HOTCHED
HOTCHES
HOTCHING
HOTCHPOT
HOTCHPOTCH
HOTCHPOTCHES
HOTCHPOTS
HOTDOG
HOTDOGGED
HOTDOGGER
HOTDOGGERS
HOTDOGGING
HOTDOGS
HOTEL
HOTELDOM
HOTELDOMS
HOTELIER
HOTELIERS
HOTELMAN
HOTELMEN
HOTELS
HOTFOOT
HOTFOOTED
HOTFOOTING
HOTFOOTS
HOTHEAD
HOTHEADED
HOTHEADEDLY
HOTHEADEDNESS
HOTHEADEDNESSES
HOTHEADS
HOTHOUSE
HOTHOUSED
HOTHOUSES
HOTHOUSING
HOTLINE
HOTLINER
HOTLINERS
HOTLINES
HOTLINK
HOTLINKS
HOTLY
HOTNESS
HOTNESSES
HOTPOT
HOTPOTS
HOTPRESS
HOTPRESSED
HOTPRESSES
HOTPRESSING
HOTROD
HOTRODS
HOTS
HOTSHOT
HOTSHOTS
HOTSPOT
HOTSPOTS
HOTSPUR
HOTSPURS
HOTTED
HOTTER
HOTTEST
HOTTIE
HOTTIES
HOTTING
HOTTISH
HOTTY
HOUDAH
HOUDAHS
HOUMMOS
HOUMMOSES
HOUND
HOUNDED
HOUNDER
HOUNDERS
HOUNDING
HOUNDS
HOUNDSTOOTH
HOUNDSTOOTHS
HOUNGAN
HOUNGANS
HOUR
HOURGLASS
HOURGLASSES
HOURI
HOURIS
HOURLIES
HOURLONG
HOURLY
HOURS
HOUSE
HOUSEBOAT
HOUSEBOATER
HOUSEBOATERS
HOUSEBOATS
HOUSEBOUND
HOUSEBOY
HOUSEBOYS
HOUSEBREAK
HOUSEBREAKER
HOUSEBREAKERS
HOUSEBREAKING
HOUSEBREAKINGS
HOUSEBREAKS
HOUSEBROKE
HOUSEBROKEN
HOUSECARL
HOUSECARLS
HOUSECLEAN
HOUSECLEANED
HOUSECLEANING
HOUSECLEANINGS
HOUSECLEANS
HOUSECOAT
HOUSECOATS

HOUSED
HOUSEDRESS
HOUSEDRESSES
HOUSEFATHER
HOUSEFATHERS
HOUSEFLIES
HOUSEFLY
HOUSEFRONT
HOUSEFRONTS
HOUSEFUL
HOUSEFULS
HOUSEGUEST
HOUSEGUESTS
HOUSEHOLD
HOUSEHOLDER
HOUSEHOLDERS
HOUSEHOLDS
HOUSEHUSBAND
HOUSEHUSBANDS
HOUSEKEEP
HOUSEKEEPER
HOUSEKEEPERS
HOUSEKEEPING
HOUSEKEEPINGS
HOUSEKEEPS
HOUSEKEPT
HOUSEL
HOUSELED
HOUSELEEK
HOUSELEEKS
HOUSELESS
HOUSELESSNESS
HOUSELESSNESSES
HOUSELIGHTS
HOUSELING
HOUSELLED
HOUSELLING
HOUSELS
HOUSEMAID
HOUSEMAIDS
HOUSEMAN
HOUSEMASTER
HOUSEMASTERS
HOUSEMATE
HOUSEMATES
HOUSEMEN
HOUSEMOTHER
HOUSEMOTHERS
HOUSEPAINTER
HOUSEPAINTERS
HOUSEPARENT
HOUSEPARENTS
HOUSEPERSON
HOUSEPERSONS
HOUSEPLANT
HOUSEPLANTS
HOUSER
HOUSEROOM
HOUSEROOMS
HOUSERS
HOUSES
HOUSESAT
HOUSESIT
HOUSESITS
HOUSESITTER
HOUSESITTERS
HOUSESITTING
HOUSETOP
HOUSETOPS
HOUSEWARES
HOUSEWARMING
HOUSEWARMINGS
HOUSEWIFE
HOUSEWIFELINESS
HOUSEWIFELY
HOUSEWIFERIES
HOUSEWIFERY
HOUSEWIFEY
HOUSEWIVES
HOUSEWORK
HOUSEWORKS
HOUSEY
HOUSIER
HOUSIEST
HOUSING
HOUSINGS
HOUSTONIA
HOUSTONIAS
HOVE
HOVEL
HOVELED
HOVELING
HOVELLED
HOVELLING
HOVELS
HOVER
HOVERCRAFT
HOVERCRAFTS
HOVERED
HOVERER
HOVERERS
HOVERFLIES
HOVERFLY
HOVERING
HOVERS
HOW
HOWBEIT
HOWDAH
HOWDAHS
HOWDIE
HOWDIED
HOWDIES
HOWDY
HOWDYING
HOWE
HOWES
HOWEVER
HOWF
HOWFF
HOWFFS
HOWFS
HOWITZER
HOWITZERS
HOWK
HOWKED
HOWKING
HOWKS
HOWL
HOWLED
HOWLER
HOWLERS
HOWLET
HOWLETS
HOWLING
HOWLINGLY
HOWLS
HOWS
HOWSOEVER
HOY
HOYA
HOYAS
HOYDEN
HOYDENED
HOYDENING
HOYDENISH
HOYDENS
HOYLE
HOYLES
HOYS
HRYVNA
HRYVNAS
HRYVNIA
HRYVNIAS
HRYVNYA
HRYVNYAS
HUARACHE
HUARACHES
HUARACHO
HUARACHOS
HUB
HUBBIES
HUBBLY
HUBBUB
HUBBUBS
HUBBY
HUBCAP
HUBCAPS
HUBLESS
HUBRIS
HUBRISES
HUBRISTIC
HUBS
HUCK
HUCKABACK
HUCKABACKS
HUCKLE
HUCKLEBERRIES
HUCKLEBERRY
HUCKLES
HUCKS
HUCKSTER
HUCKSTERED
HUCKSTERING
HUCKSTERISM
HUCKSTERISMS
HUCKSTERS
HUDDLE
HUDDLED
HUDDLER
HUDDLERS
HUDDLES
HUDDLING
HUE
HUED
HUELESS
HUES
HUFF
HUFFED
HUFFIER
HUFFIEST
HUFFILY
HUFFINESS
HUFFINESSES
HUFFING
HUFFISH
HUFFISHLY
HUFFS
HUFFY
HUG
HUGE
HUGELY
HUGENESS
HUGENESSES
HUGEOUS
HUGEOUSLY
HUGER
HUGEST
HUGGABLE
HUGGED
HUGGER
HUGGERS
HUGGIER
HUGGIEST
HUGGING
HUGGY
HUGS
HUH
HUIC
HUIPIL
HUIPILES
HUIPILS
HUISACHE
HUISACHES
HULA
HULAS
HULK
HULKED
HULKIER
HULKIEST
HULKING
HULKS
HULKY
HULL
HULLABALOO
HULLABALOOS
HULLED
HULLER
HULLERS
HULLING
HULLO
HULLOA
HULLOAED
HULLOAING
HULLOAS
HULLOED
HULLOES
HULLOING
HULLOO
HULLOOED
HULLOOING
HULLOOS
HULLOS
HULLS
HUM
HUMAN

HUMANE
HUMANELY
HUMANENESS
HUMANENESSES
HUMANER
HUMANEST
HUMANHOOD
HUMANHOODS
HUMANISE
HUMANISED
HUMANISES
HUMANISING
HUMANISM
HUMANISMS
HUMANIST
HUMANISTIC
HUMANISTICALLY
HUMANISTS
HUMANITARIAN
HUMANITARIANISM
HUMANITARIANS
HUMANITIES
HUMANITY
HUMANIZATION
HUMANIZATIONS
HUMANIZE
HUMANIZED
HUMANIZER
HUMANIZERS
HUMANIZES
HUMANIZING
HUMANKIND
HUMANLIKE
HUMANLY
HUMANNESS
HUMANNESSES
HUMANOID
HUMANOIDS
HUMANS
HUMATE
HUMATES
HUMBLE
HUMBLEBEE
HUMBLEBEES
HUMBLED
HUMBLENESS
HUMBLENESSES
HUMBLER
HUMBLERS
HUMBLES
HUMBLEST
HUMBLING
HUMBLINGLY
HUMBLY
HUMBUG
HUMBUGGED
HUMBUGGER
HUMBUGGERIES
HUMBUGGERS
HUMBUGGERY
HUMBUGGING
HUMBUGS
HUMDINGER
HUMDINGERS
HUMDRUM
HUMDRUMS
HUMECTANT
HUMECTANTS
HUMERAL
HUMERALS
HUMERI
HUMERUS
HUMIC
HUMID
HUMIDEX
HUMIDEXES
HUMIDIFICATION
HUMIDIFICATIONS
HUMIDIFIED
HUMIDIFIER
HUMIDIFIERS
HUMIDIFIES
HUMIDIFY
HUMIDIFYING
HUMIDISTAT
HUMIDISTATS
HUMIDITIES
HUMIDITY
HUMIDLY
HUMIDNESS
HUMIDNESSES
HUMIDOR
HUMIDORS
HUMIFICATION
HUMIFICATIONS
HUMIFIED
HUMILIATE
HUMILIATED
HUMILIATES
HUMILIATING
HUMILIATINGLY
HUMILIATION
HUMILIATIONS
HUMILITIES
HUMILITY
HUMINT
HUMINTS
HUMITURE
HUMITURES
HUMMABLE
HUMMED
HUMMER
HUMMERS
HUMMING
HUMMINGBIRD
HUMMINGBIRDS
HUMMOCK
HUMMOCKED
HUMMOCKING
HUMMOCKS
HUMMOCKY
HUMMUS
HUMMUSES
HUMONGOUS
HUMOR
HUMORAL
HUMORED
HUMORESQUE
HUMORESQUES
HUMORFUL
HUMORING
HUMORIST
HUMORISTIC
HUMORISTS
HUMORLESS
HUMORLESSLY
HUMORLESSNESS
HUMORLESSNESSES
HUMOROUS
HUMOROUSLY
HUMOROUSNESS
HUMOROUSNESSES
HUMORS
HUMOUR
HUMOURED
HUMOURING
HUMOURLESS
HUMOURS
HUMOUS
HUMOUSES
HUMP
HUMPBACK
HUMPBACKED
HUMPBACKS
HUMPED
HUMPER
HUMPERS
HUMPH
HUMPHED
HUMPHING
HUMPHS
HUMPIER
HUMPIES
HUMPIEST
HUMPINESS
HUMPINESSES
HUMPING
HUMPLESS
HUMPS
HUMPY
HUMS
HUMUNGOUS
HUMUS
HUMUSES
HUMUSIER
HUMUSIEST
HUMUSY
HUMVEE
HUMVEES
HUN
HUNCH
HUNCHBACK
HUNCHBACKED
HUNCHBACKS
HUNCHED
HUNCHES
HUNCHING
HUNDRED
HUNDREDFOLD
HUNDREDS
HUNDREDTH
HUNDREDTHS
HUNDREDWEIGHT
HUNDREDWEIGHTS
HUNG
HUNGER
HUNGERED
HUNGERING
HUNGERS
HUNGOVER
HUNGRIER
HUNGRIEST
HUNGRILY
HUNGRINESS
HUNGRINESSES
HUNGRY
HUNH
HUNK
HUNKER
HUNKERED
HUNKERING
HUNKERS
HUNKEY
HUNKEYS
HUNKIE
HUNKIER
HUNKIES
HUNKIEST
HUNKS
HUNKY
HUNNISH
HUNS
HUNT
HUNTABLE
HUNTED
HUNTEDLY
HUNTER
HUNTERS
HUNTING
HUNTINGS
HUNTRESS
HUNTRESSES
HUNTS
HUNTSMAN
HUNTSMEN
HUP
HUPPAH
HUPPAHS
HURDIES
HURDLE
HURDLED
HURDLER
HURDLERS
HURDLES
HURDLING
HURDS
HURL
HURLED
HURLER
HURLERS
HURLEY
HURLEYS
HURLIES
HURLING
HURLINGS
HURLS
HURLY
HURRAH
HURRAHED
HURRAHING
HURRAHS
HURRAY
HURRAYED
HURRAYING
HURRAYS

HURRICANE
HURRICANES
HURRIED
HURRIEDLY
HURRIEDNESS
HURRIEDNESSES
HURRIER
HURRIERS
HURRIES
HURRY
HURRYING
HURST
HURSTS
HURT
HURTER
HURTERS
HURTFUL
HURTFULLY
HURTFULNESS
HURTFULNESSES
HURTING
HURTLE
HURTLED
HURTLES
HURTLESS
HURTLING
HURTS
HUSBAND
HUSBANDED
HUSBANDER
HUSBANDERS
HUSBANDING
HUSBANDLY
HUSBANDMAN
HUSBANDMEN
HUSBANDRIES
HUSBANDRY
HUSBANDS
HUSH
HUSHABY
HUSHABYE
HUSHED
HUSHEDLY
HUSHES
HUSHFUL
HUSHING
HUSHPUPPIES
HUSHPUPPY
HUSK
HUSKED
HUSKER
HUSKERS
HUSKIER
HUSKIES
HUSKIEST
HUSKILY
HUSKINESS
HUSKINESSES
HUSKING
HUSKINGS
HUSKLIKE
HUSKS
HUSKY
HUSSAR
HUSSARS
HUSSIES
HUSSY
HUSTINGS
HUSTLE
HUSTLED
HUSTLER
HUSTLERS
HUSTLES
HUSTLING
HUSWIFE
HUSWIFES
HUSWIVES
HUT
HUTCH
HUTCHED
HUTCHES
HUTCHING
HUTLIKE
HUTMENT
HUTMENTS
HUTS
HUTTED
HUTTING
HUTZPA
HUTZPAH
HUTZPAHS
HUTZPAS
HUZZA
HUZZAED
HUZZAH
HUZZAHED
HUZZAHING
HUZZAHS
HUZZAING
HUZZAS
HWAN
HWYL
HWYLS
HYACINTH
HYACINTHINE
HYACINTHS
HYAENA
HYAENAS
HYAENIC
HYALIN
HYALINE
HYALINES
HYALINS
HYALITE
HYALITES
HYALOGEN
HYALOGENS
HYALOID
HYALOIDS
HYALOPLASM
HYALOPLASMS
HYALURONIDASE
HYALURONIDASES
HYBRID
HYBRIDISM
HYBRIDISMS
HYBRIDIST
HYBRIDISTS
HYBRIDITIES
HYBRIDITY
HYBRIDIZATION
HYBRIDIZATIONS
HYBRIDIZE
HYBRIDIZED
HYBRIDIZER
HYBRIDIZERS
HYBRIDIZES
HYBRIDIZING
HYBRIDOMA
HYBRIDOMAS
HYBRIDS
HYBRIS
HYBRISES
HYBRISTIC
HYDATHODE
HYDATHODES
HYDATID
HYDATIDS
HYDRA
HYDRACID
HYDRACIDS
HYDRAE
HYDRAGOG
HYDRAGOGS
HYDRALAZINE
HYDRALAZINES
HYDRANGEA
HYDRANGEAS
HYDRANT
HYDRANTH
HYDRANTHS
HYDRANTS
HYDRAS
HYDRASE
HYDRASES
HYDRASTIS
HYDRASTISES
HYDRATE
HYDRATED
HYDRATES
HYDRATING
HYDRATION
HYDRATIONS
HYDRATOR
HYDRATORS
HYDRAULIC
HYDRAULICALLY
HYDRAULICS
HYDRAZIDE
HYDRAZIDES
HYDRAZINE
HYDRAZINES
HYDRIA
HYDRIAE
HYDRIC
HYDRID
HYDRIDE
HYDRIDES
HYDRIDS
HYDRILLA
HYDRILLAS
HYDRO
HYDROBIOLOGICAL
HYDROBIOLOGIES
HYDROBIOLOGIST
HYDROBIOLOGISTS
HYDROBIOLOGY
HYDROCARBON
HYDROCARBONS
HYDROCAST
HYDROCASTS
HYDROCELE
HYDROCELES
HYDROCEPHALI
HYDROCEPHALIC
HYDROCEPHALICS
HYDROCEPHALIES
HYDROCEPHALUS
HYDROCEPHALUSES
HYDROCEPHALY
HYDROCHLORIDE
HYDROCHLORIDES
HYDROCOLLOID
HYDROCOLLOIDAL
HYDROCOLLOIDS
HYDROCORTISONE
HYDROCORTISONES
HYDROCRACK
HYDROCRACKED
HYDROCRACKER
HYDROCRACKERS
HYDROCRACKING
HYDROCRACKINGS
HYDROCRACKS
HYDRODYNAMIC
HYDRODYNAMICAL
HYDRODYNAMICIST
HYDRODYNAMICS
HYDROELECTRIC
HYDROFOIL
HYDROFOILS
HYDROGEL
HYDROGELS
HYDROGEN
HYDROGENASE
HYDROGENASES
HYDROGENATE
HYDROGENATED
HYDROGENATES
HYDROGENATING
HYDROGENATION
HYDROGENATIONS
HYDROGENOUS
HYDROGENS
HYDROGEOLOGIES
HYDROGEOLOGIST
HYDROGEOLOGISTS
HYDROGEOLOGY
HYDROGRAPHER
HYDROGRAPHERS
HYDROGRAPHIC
HYDROGRAPHIES
HYDROGRAPHY
HYDROID
HYDROIDS
HYDROKINETIC
HYDROLASE
HYDROLASES
HYDROLOGIC
HYDROLOGICAL
HYDROLOGICALLY
HYDROLOGIES
HYDROLOGIST
HYDROLOGISTS
HYDROLOGY

HYDROLYSATE
HYDROLYSATES
HYDROLYSES
HYDROLYSIS
HYDROLYTE
HYDROLYTES
HYDROLYTIC
HYDROLYTICALLY
HYDROLYZABLE
HYDROLYZATE
HYDROLYZATES
HYDROLYZE
HYDROLYZED
HYDROLYZES
HYDROLYZING
HYDROMAGNETIC
HYDROMANCIES
HYDROMANCY
HYDROMASSAGE
HYDROMASSAGES
HYDROMECHANICAL
HYDROMECHANICS
HYDROMEDUSA
HYDROMEDUSAE
HYDROMEL
HYDROMELS
HYDROMETALLURGY
HYDROMETEOR
HYDROMETEORS
HYDROMETER
HYDROMETERS
HYDROMETRIC
HYDROMORPHIC
HYDRONIC
HYDRONICALLY
HYDRONIUM
HYDRONIUMS
HYDROPATH
HYDROPATHIC
HYDROPATHIES
HYDROPATHS
HYDROPATHY
HYDROPEROXIDE
HYDROPEROXIDES
HYDROPHANE
HYDROPHANES
HYDROPHILIC
HYDROPHILICITY
HYDROPHOBIA
HYDROPHOBIAS
HYDROPHOBIC
HYDROPHOBICITY
HYDROPHONE
HYDROPHONES
HYDROPHYTE
HYDROPHYTES
HYDROPHYTIC
HYDROPIC
HYDROPLANE
HYDROPLANED
HYDROPLANES
HYDROPLANING
HYDROPONIC
HYDROPONICALLY
HYDROPONICS
HYDROPOWER
HYDROPOWERS
HYDROPS
HYDROPSES
HYDROPSIES
HYDROPSY
HYDROQUINONE
HYDROQUINONES
HYDROS
HYDROSERE
HYDROSERES
HYDROSKI
HYDROSKIS
HYDROSOL
HYDROSOLIC
HYDROSOLS
HYDROSPACE
HYDROSPACES
HYDROSPHERE
HYDROSPHERES
HYDROSPHERIC
HYDROSTAT
HYDROSTATIC
HYDROSTATICALLY
HYDROSTATICS
HYDROSTATS
HYDROTHERAPIES
HYDROTHERAPY
HYDROTHERMAL
HYDROTHERMALLY
HYDROTHORACES
HYDROTHORAX
HYDROTHORAXES
HYDROTROPIC
HYDROTROPISM
HYDROTROPISMS
HYDROUS
HYDROXIDE
HYDROXIDES
HYDROXY
HYDROXYAPATITE
HYDROXYAPATITES
HYDROXYL
HYDROXYLAMINE
HYDROXYLAMINES
HYDROXYLAPATITE
HYDROXYLASE
HYDROXYLASES
HYDROXYLATE
HYDROXYLATED
HYDROXYLATES
HYDROXYLATING
HYDROXYLATION
HYDROXYLATIONS
HYDROXYLIC
HYDROXYLS
HYDROXYPROLINE
HYDROXYPROLINES
HYDROXYUREA
HYDROXYUREAS
HYDROXYZINE
HYDROXYZINES
HYDROZOAN
HYDROZOANS
HYENA
HYENAS
HYENIC
HYENINE
HYENOID
HYETAL
HYGEIST
HYGEISTS
HYGIEIST
HYGIEISTS
HYGIENE
HYGIENES
HYGIENIC
HYGIENICALLY
HYGIENICS
HYGIENIST
HYGIENISTS
HYGROGRAPH
HYGROGRAPHS
HYGROMETER
HYGROMETERS
HYGROMETRIC
HYGROPHILOUS
HYGROPHYTE
HYGROPHYTES
HYGROPHYTIC
HYGROSCOPIC
HYGROSCOPICITY
HYGROSTAT
HYGROSTATS
HYING
HYLA
HYLAS
HYLOZOIC
HYLOZOISM
HYLOZOISMS
HYLOZOIST
HYLOZOISTIC
HYLOZOISTS
HYMEN
HYMENAL
HYMENEAL
HYMENEALLY
HYMENEALS
HYMENIA
HYMENIAL
HYMENIUM
HYMENIUMS
HYMENOPTERA
HYMENOPTERAN
HYMENOPTERANS
HYMENOPTERON
HYMENOPTERONS
HYMENOPTEROUS
HYMENS
HYMN
HYMNAL
HYMNALS
HYMNARIES
HYMNARY
HYMNBOOK
HYMNBOOKS
HYMNED
HYMNIC
HYMNING
HYMNIST
HYMNISTS
HYMNLESS
HYMNLIKE
HYMNODIES
HYMNODIST
HYMNODISTS
HYMNODY
HYMNOLOGIES
HYMNOLOGY
HYMNS
HYOID
HYOIDAL
HYOIDEAN
HYOIDS
HYOSCINE
HYOSCINES
HYOSCYAMINE
HYOSCYAMINES
HYP
HYPABYSSAL
HYPABYSSALLY
HYPAETHRAL
HYPALLAGE
HYPALLAGES
HYPANTHIA
HYPANTHIUM
HYPE
HYPED
HYPER
HYPERACID
HYPERACIDITIES
HYPERACIDITY
HYPERACTIVE
HYPERACTIVES
HYPERACTIVITIES
HYPERACTIVITY
HYPERACUITIES
HYPERACUITY
HYPERACUTE
HYPERAESTHESIA
HYPERAESTHESIAS
HYPERAESTHETIC
HYPERAGGRESSIVE
HYPERALERT
HYPERARID
HYPERAROUSAL
HYPERAROUSALS
HYPERAWARE
HYPERAWARENESS
HYPERBARIC
HYPERBARICALLY
HYPERBOLA
HYPERBOLAE
HYPERBOLAS
HYPERBOLE
HYPERBOLES
HYPERBOLIC
HYPERBOLICAL
HYPERBOLICALLY
HYPERBOLIST
HYPERBOLISTS
HYPERBOLIZE
HYPERBOLIZED
HYPERBOLIZES
HYPERBOLIZING
HYPERBOLOID
HYPERBOLOIDAL
HYPERBOLOIDS
HYPERBOREAN
HYPERBOREANS

HYPERCALCEMIA
HYPERCALCEMIAS
HYPERCALCEMIC
HYPERCAPNIA
HYPERCAPNIAS
HYPERCAPNIC
HYPERCATABOLISM
HYPERCATALECTIC
HYPERCATALEXES
HYPERCATALEXIS
HYPERCAUTIOUS
HYPERCHARGE
HYPERCHARGED
HYPERCHARGES
HYPERCIVILIZED
HYPERCOAGULABLE
HYPERCOMPLEX
HYPERCONSCIOUS
HYPERCORRECT
HYPERCORRECTION
HYPERCORRECTLY
HYPERCRITIC
HYPERCRITICAL
HYPERCRITICALLY
HYPERCRITICISM
HYPERCRITICISMS
HYPERCRITICS
HYPERCUBE
HYPERCUBES
HYPERDRIVE
HYPERDRIVES
HYPEREFFICIENT
HYPEREMIA
HYPEREMIAS
HYPEREMIC
HYPEREMOTIONAL
HYPERENDEMIC
HYPERENERGETIC
HYPERER
HYPEREST
HYPERESTHESIA
HYPERESTHESIAS
HYPERESTHETIC
HYPEREUTECTIC
HYPEREUTECTOID
HYPEREXCITABLE
HYPEREXCITED
HYPEREXCITEMENT
HYPEREXCRETION
HYPEREXCRETIONS
HYPEREXTEND
HYPEREXTENDED
HYPEREXTENDING
HYPEREXTENDS
HYPEREXTENSION
HYPEREXTENSIONS
HYPERFASTIDIOUS
HYPERFINE
HYPERFUNCTION
HYPERFUNCTIONAL
HYPERFUNCTIONS
HYPERGAMIES
HYPERGAMY
HYPERGLYCEMIA
HYPERGLYCEMIAS
HYPERGLYCEMIC
HYPERGOL
HYPERGOLIC
HYPERGOLICALLY
HYPERGOLS
HYPERHIDROSES
HYPERHIDROSIS
HYPERHYDROSIS
HYPERHYDROSISES
HYPERIMMUNE
HYPERIMMUNIZE
HYPERIMMUNIZED
HYPERIMMUNIZES
HYPERIMMUNIZING
HYPERINFLATED
HYPERINFLATION
HYPERINFLATIONS
HYPERINSULINISM
HYPERINTENSE
HYPERINVOLUTION
HYPERIRRITABLE
HYPERKERATOSES
HYPERKERATOSIS
HYPERKERATOTIC
HYPERKINESES
HYPERKINESIA
HYPERKINESIAS
HYPERKINESIS
HYPERKINETIC
HYPERLINK
HYPERLINKED
HYPERLINKING
HYPERLINKS
HYPERLIPEMIA
HYPERLIPEMIAS
HYPERLIPEMIC
HYPERLIPIDEMIA
HYPERLIPIDEMIAS
HYPERMANIA
HYPERMANIAS
HYPERMANIC
HYPERMARKET
HYPERMARKETS
HYPERMASCULINE
HYPERMEDIA
HYPERMEDIAS
HYPERMETABOLIC
HYPERMETABOLISM
HYPERMETER
HYPERMETERS
HYPERMETRIC
HYPERMETRICAL
HYPERMETROPIA
HYPERMETROPIAS
HYPERMETROPIC
HYPERMILER
HYPERMILERS
HYPERMILING
HYPERMILINGS
HYPERMNESIA
HYPERMNESIAS
HYPERMNESIC
HYPERMOBILITIES
HYPERMOBILITY
HYPERMODERN
HYPERMODERNIST
HYPERMODERNISTS
HYPERMUTABILITY
HYPERMUTABLE
HYPERNYM
HYPERNYMS
HYPERON
HYPERONS
HYPEROPE
HYPEROPES
HYPEROPIA
HYPEROPIAS
HYPEROPIC
HYPEROSTOSES
HYPEROSTOSIS
HYPEROSTOSISES
HYPEROSTOTIC
HYPERPARASITE
HYPERPARASITES
HYPERPARASITIC
HYPERPARASITISM
HYPERPHAGIA
HYPERPHAGIAS
HYPERPHAGIC
HYPERPHYSICAL
HYPERPIGMENTED
HYPERPITUITARY
HYPERPLANE
HYPERPLANES
HYPERPLASIA
HYPERPLASIAS
HYPERPLASTIC
HYPERPLOID
HYPERPLOIDIES
HYPERPLOIDS
HYPERPLOIDY
HYPERPNEA
HYPERPNEAS
HYPERPNEIC
HYPERPOLARIZE
HYPERPOLARIZED
HYPERPOLARIZES
HYPERPOLARIZING
HYPERPRODUCER
HYPERPRODUCERS
HYPERPRODUCTION
HYPERPURE
HYPERPYREXIA
HYPERPYREXIAS
HYPERRATIONAL
HYPERREACTIVE
HYPERREACTIVITY
HYPERREACTOR
HYPERREACTORS
HYPERREALISM
HYPERREALISMS
HYPERREALIST
HYPERREALISTIC
HYPERRESPONSIVE
HYPERROMANTIC
HYPERROMANTICS
HYPERS
HYPERSALINE
HYPERSALINITIES
HYPERSALINITY
HYPERSALIVATION
HYPERSECRETION
HYPERSECRETIONS
HYPERSENSITIVE
HYPERSENSITIZE
HYPERSENSITIZED
HYPERSENSITIZES
HYPERSEXUAL
HYPERSEXUALITY
HYPERSOMNOLENCE
HYPERSONIC
HYPERSONICALLY
HYPERSPACE
HYPERSPACES
HYPERSTATIC
HYPERSTHENE
HYPERSTHENES
HYPERSTHENIC
HYPERSTIMULATE
HYPERSTIMULATED
HYPERSTIMULATES
HYPERSURFACE
HYPERSURFACES
HYPERTENSE
HYPERTENSION
HYPERTENSIONS
HYPERTENSIVE
HYPERTENSIVES
HYPERTEXT
HYPERTEXTS
HYPERTEXTUAL
HYPERTHERMIA
HYPERTHERMIAS
HYPERTHERMIC
HYPERTHYROID
HYPERTHYROIDISM
HYPERTONIA
HYPERTONIAS
HYPERTONIC
HYPERTONICITIES
HYPERTONICITY
HYPERTROPHIC
HYPERTROPHIED
HYPERTROPHIES
HYPERTROPHY
HYPERTROPHYING
HYPERTYPICAL
HYPERURBANISM
HYPERURBANISMS
HYPERURICEMIA
HYPERURICEMIAS
HYPERVARIABLE
HYPERVELOCITIES
HYPERVELOCITY
HYPERVENTILATE
HYPERVENTILATED
HYPERVENTILATES
HYPERVIGILANCE
HYPERVIGILANCES
HYPERVIGILANT
HYPERVIRULENT
HYPERVISCOSITY
HYPES
HYPETHRAL
HYPHA
HYPHAE
HYPHAL
HYPHEMIA
HYPHEMIAS
HYPHEN

HYPHENATE
HYPHENATED
HYPHENATES
HYPHENATING
HYPHENATION
HYPHENATIONS
HYPHENED
HYPHENIC
HYPHENING
HYPHENLESS
HYPHENS
HYPING
HYPNAGOGIC
HYPNIC
HYPNOGOGIC
HYPNOID
HYPNOIDAL
HYPNOLOGIES
HYPNOLOGY
HYPNOPOMPIC
HYPNOSES
HYPNOSIS
HYPNOTHERAPIES
HYPNOTHERAPIST
HYPNOTHERAPISTS
HYPNOTHERAPY
HYPNOTIC
HYPNOTICALLY
HYPNOTICS
HYPNOTISE
HYPNOTISED
HYPNOTISES
HYPNOTISING
HYPNOTISM
HYPNOTISMS
HYPNOTIST
HYPNOTISTS
HYPNOTIZABILITY
HYPNOTIZABLE
HYPNOTIZE
HYPNOTIZED
HYPNOTIZES
HYPNOTIZING
HYPO
HYPOACID
HYPOALLERGENIC
HYPOBARIC
HYPOBLAST
HYPOBLASTS
HYPOCALCEMIA
HYPOCALCEMIAS
HYPOCALCEMIC
HYPOCAUST
HYPOCAUSTS
HYPOCENTER
HYPOCENTERS
HYPOCENTRAL
HYPOCHLORITE
HYPOCHLORITES
HYPOCHONDRIA
HYPOCHONDRIAC
HYPOCHONDRIACAL
HYPOCHONDRIACS
HYPOCHONDRIAS
HYPOCHONDRIASES
HYPOCHONDRIASIS
HYPOCHROMIC
HYPOCORISM
HYPOCORISMS
HYPOCORISTIC
HYPOCORISTICAL
HYPOCOTYL
HYPOCOTYLS
HYPOCRISIES
HYPOCRISY
HYPOCRITE
HYPOCRITES
HYPOCRITICAL
HYPOCRITICALLY
HYPOCYCLOID
HYPOCYCLOIDS
HYPODERM
HYPODERMA
HYPODERMAL
HYPODERMAS
HYPODERMIC
HYPODERMICALLY
HYPODERMICS
HYPODERMIS
HYPODERMISES
HYPODERMS
HYPODIPLOID
HYPODIPLOIDIES
HYPODIPLOIDY
HYPOED
HYPOEUTECTOID
HYPOGASTRIC
HYPOGEA
HYPOGEAL
HYPOGEAN
HYPOGENE
HYPOGEOUS
HYPOGEUM
HYPOGLOSSAL
HYPOGLOSSALS
HYPOGLYCEMIA
HYPOGLYCEMIAS
HYPOGLYCEMIC
HYPOGLYCEMICS
HYPOGYNIES
HYPOGYNOUS
HYPOGYNY
HYPOID
HYPOIDS
HYPOING
HYPOKALEMIA
HYPOKALEMIAS
HYPOKALEMIC
HYPOLIMNIA
HYPOLIMNION
HYPOMAGNESEMIA
HYPOMAGNESEMIAS
HYPOMANIA
HYPOMANIAS
HYPOMANIC
HYPOMANICS
HYPOMORPH
HYPOMORPHIC
HYPOMORPHS
HYPONASTIES
HYPONASTY
HYPONEA
HYPONEAS
HYPONOIA
HYPONOIAS
HYPONYM
HYPONYMIES
HYPONYMS
HYPONYMY
HYPOPHARYNGES
HYPOPHARYNX
HYPOPHARYNXES
HYPOPHYSEAL
HYPOPHYSECTOMY
HYPOPHYSES
HYPOPHYSIAL
HYPOPHYSIS
HYPOPITUITARISM
HYPOPITUITARY
HYPOPLASIA
HYPOPLASIAS
HYPOPLASTIC
HYPOPLOID
HYPOPLOIDS
HYPOPNEA
HYPOPNEAS
HYPOPNEIC
HYPOPYON
HYPOPYONS
HYPOS
HYPOSENSITIZE
HYPOSENSITIZED
HYPOSENSITIZES
HYPOSENSITIZING
HYPOSPADIAS
HYPOSPADIASES
HYPOSTASES
HYPOSTASIS
HYPOSTATIC
HYPOSTATICALLY
HYPOSTATIZATION
HYPOSTATIZE
HYPOSTATIZED
HYPOSTATIZES
HYPOSTATIZING
HYPOSTOME
HYPOSTOMES
HYPOSTYLE
HYPOSTYLES
HYPOTACTIC
HYPOTAXES
HYPOTAXIS
HYPOTENSION
HYPOTENSIONS
HYPOTENSIVE
HYPOTENSIVES
HYPOTENUSE
HYPOTENUSES
HYPOTHALAMI
HYPOTHALAMIC
HYPOTHALAMUS
HYPOTHEC
HYPOTHECATE
HYPOTHECATED
HYPOTHECATES
HYPOTHECATING
HYPOTHECATION
HYPOTHECATIONS
HYPOTHECATOR
HYPOTHECATORS
HYPOTHECS
HYPOTHENUSE
HYPOTHENUSES
HYPOTHERMAL
HYPOTHERMIA
HYPOTHERMIAS
HYPOTHERMIC
HYPOTHESES
HYPOTHESIS
HYPOTHESISE
HYPOTHESISED
HYPOTHESISES
HYPOTHESISING
HYPOTHESIZE
HYPOTHESIZED
HYPOTHESIZES
HYPOTHESIZING
HYPOTHETICAL
HYPOTHETICALLY
HYPOTHYROID
HYPOTHYROIDISM
HYPOTHYROIDISMS
HYPOTONIA
HYPOTONIAS
HYPOTONIC
HYPOTONICITIES
HYPOTONICITY
HYPOXANTHINE
HYPOXANTHINES
HYPOXEMIA
HYPOXEMIAS
HYPOXEMIC
HYPOXIA
HYPOXIAS
HYPOXIC
HYPS
HYPSOMETER
HYPSOMETERS
HYPSOMETRIC
HYRACES
HYRACOID
HYRACOIDS
HYRAX
HYRAXES
HYSON
HYSONS
HYSSOP
HYSSOPS
HYSTERECTOMIES
HYSTERECTOMIZED
HYSTERECTOMY
HYSTERESES
HYSTERESIS
HYSTERETIC
HYSTERIA
HYSTERIAS
HYSTERIC
HYSTERICAL
HYSTERICALLY
HYSTERICS
HYSTEROID
HYSTEROSCOPE
HYSTEROSCOPES
HYSTEROSCOPIC
HYSTEROSCOPIES
HYSTEROSCOPY
HYSTEROTOMIES
HYSTEROTOMY
HYTE

I

IAMB
IAMBI
IAMBIC
IAMBICS
IAMBS
IAMBUS
IAMBUSES
IATRIC
IATRICAL
IATROGENESES
IATROGENESIS
IATROGENIC
IATROGENICALLY
IBEX
IBEXES
IBICES
IBIDEM
IBIS
IBISES
IBOGAINE
IBOGAINES
IBUPROFEN
IBUPROFENS
ICE
ICEBERG
ICEBERGS
ICEBLINK
ICEBLINKS
ICEBOAT
ICEBOATED
ICEBOATER
ICEBOATERS
ICEBOATING
ICEBOATINGS
ICEBOATS
ICEBOUND
ICEBOX
ICEBOXES
ICEBREAKER
ICEBREAKERS
ICECAP
ICECAPPED
ICECAPS
ICED
ICEFALL
ICEFALLS
ICEFIELD
ICEFIELDS
ICEFISH
ICEFISHED
ICEFISHES
ICEFISHING
ICEHOUSE
ICEHOUSES
ICEKHANA
ICEKHANAS
ICELESS
ICELIKE
ICEMAKER
ICEMAKERS
ICEMAN
ICEMEN
ICES
ICESCAPE
ICESCAPES
ICEWINE
ICEWINES
ICEWORM
ICEWORMS
ICH
ICHNEUMON
ICHNEUMONS
ICHNITE
ICHNITES
ICHNOLITE
ICHNOLITES
ICHNOLOGIES
ICHNOLOGY
ICHOR
ICHOROUS
ICHORS
ICHS
ICHTHYIC
ICHTHYOFAUNA
ICHTHYOFAUNAE
ICHTHYOFAUNAL
ICHTHYOFAUNAS
ICHTHYOID
ICHTHYOIDS
ICHTHYOLOGICAL
ICHTHYOLOGIES
ICHTHYOLOGIST
ICHTHYOLOGISTS
ICHTHYOLOGY
ICHTHYOPHAGOUS
ICHTHYOSAUR
ICHTHYOSAURIAN
ICHTHYOSAURIANS
ICHTHYOSAURS
ICICLE
ICICLED
ICICLES
ICIER
ICIEST
ICILY
ICINESS
ICINESSES
ICING
ICINGS
ICK
ICKER
ICKERS
ICKIER
ICKIEST
ICKILY
ICKINESS
ICKINESSES
ICKS
ICKY
ICON
ICONES
ICONIC
ICONICAL
ICONICALLY
ICONICITIES
ICONICITY
ICONOCLASM
ICONOCLASMS
ICONOCLAST
ICONOCLASTIC
ICONOCLASTS
ICONOGRAPHER
ICONOGRAPHERS
ICONOGRAPHIC
ICONOGRAPHICAL
ICONOGRAPHIES
ICONOGRAPHY
ICONOLATRIES
ICONOLATRY
ICONOLOGICAL
ICONOLOGIES
ICONOLOGY
ICONOSCOPE
ICONOSCOPES
ICONOSTASES
ICONOSTASIS
ICONS
ICOSAHEDRA
ICOSAHEDRAL
ICOSAHEDRON
ICOSAHEDRONS
ICTERIC
ICTERICAL
ICTERICS
ICTERUS
ICTERUSES
ICTIC
ICTUS
ICTUSES
ICY
ID
IDEA
IDEAL
IDEALESS
IDEALISATION
IDEALISATIONS
IDEALISE
IDEALISED
IDEALISES
IDEALISING
IDEALISM
IDEALISMS
IDEALIST
IDEALISTIC
IDEALISTICALLY
IDEALISTS
IDEALITIES
IDEALITY
IDEALIZATION
IDEALIZATIONS
IDEALIZE
IDEALIZED
IDEALIZER
IDEALIZERS
IDEALIZES
IDEALIZING
IDEALLESS
IDEALLY
IDEALOGIES
IDEALOGUE
IDEALOGUES
IDEALOGY
IDEALS
IDEAS
IDEATE
IDEATED
IDEATES
IDEATING
IDEATION
IDEATIONAL
IDEATIONALLY
IDEATIONS
IDEATIVE
IDEM
IDEMPOTENT
IDEMPOTENTS
IDENT
IDENTIC
IDENTICAL
IDENTICALLY
IDENTICALNESS
IDENTICALNESSES
IDENTIFIABLE
IDENTIFIABLY
IDENTIFICATION
IDENTIFICATIONS
IDENTIFIED
IDENTIFIER
IDENTIFIERS
IDENTIFIES
IDENTIFY
IDENTIFYING
IDENTIKIT
IDENTITIES
IDENTITY
IDENTS
IDEOGRAM
IDEOGRAMIC
IDEOGRAMMATIC
IDEOGRAMMIC
IDEOGRAMS
IDEOGRAPH
IDEOGRAPHIC
IDEOGRAPHICALLY
IDEOGRAPHIES
IDEOGRAPHS
IDEOGRAPHY
IDEOLOGIC
IDEOLOGICAL
IDEOLOGICALLY
IDEOLOGIES
IDEOLOGIST
IDEOLOGISTS
IDEOLOGIZE
IDEOLOGIZED
IDEOLOGIZES
IDEOLOGIZING
IDEOLOGUE
IDEOLOGUES
IDEOLOGY
IDEOMOTOR
IDEOPHONE
IDEOPHONES
IDES
IDIOBLAST
IDIOBLASTIC
IDIOBLASTS
IDIOCIES
IDIOCY
IDIOGRAPHIC

IDIOLECT
IDIOLECTAL
IDIOLECTS
IDIOM
IDIOMATIC
IDIOMATICALLY
IDIOMATICNESS
IDIOMATICNESSES
IDIOMORPHIC
IDIOMS
IDIOPATHIC
IDIOPATHICALLY
IDIOPATHIES
IDIOPATHY
IDIOPLASM
IDIOPLASMS
IDIOSYNCRASIES
IDIOSYNCRASY
IDIOSYNCRATIC
IDIOT
IDIOTIC
IDIOTICAL
IDIOTICALLY
IDIOTISM
IDIOTISMS
IDIOTPROOF
IDIOTS
IDIOTYPE
IDIOTYPES
IDIOTYPIC
IDLE
IDLED
IDLENESS
IDLENESSES
IDLER
IDLERS
IDLES
IDLESSE
IDLESSES
IDLEST
IDLING
IDLY
IDOCRASE
IDOCRASES
IDOL
IDOLATER
IDOLATERS
IDOLATOR
IDOLATORS
IDOLATRIES
IDOLATROUS
IDOLATROUSLY
IDOLATROUSNESS
IDOLATRY
IDOLISATION
IDOLISATIONS
IDOLISE
IDOLISED
IDOLISER
IDOLISERS
IDOLISES
IDOLISING
IDOLISM
IDOLISMS
IDOLIZATION
IDOLIZATIONS
IDOLIZE
IDOLIZED
IDOLIZER
IDOLIZERS
IDOLIZES
IDOLIZING
IDOLS
IDONEITIES
IDONEITY
IDONEOUS
IDS
IDYL
IDYLIST
IDYLISTS
IDYLL
IDYLLIC
IDYLLICALLY
IDYLLIST
IDYLLISTS
IDYLLS
IDYLS
IF
IFF
IFFIER
IFFIEST
IFFILY
IFFINESS
IFFINESSES
IFFY
IFS
IGG
IGGED
IGGING
IGGS
IGLOO
IGLOOS
IGLU
IGLUS
IGNATIA
IGNATIAS
IGNEOUS
IGNESCENT
IGNESCENTS
IGNIFIED
IGNIFIES
IGNIFY
IGNIFYING
IGNIMBRITE
IGNIMBRITES
IGNITABILITIES
IGNITABILITY
IGNITABLE
IGNITE
IGNITED
IGNITER
IGNITERS
IGNITES
IGNITIBLE
IGNITING
IGNITION
IGNITIONS
IGNITOR
IGNITORS
IGNITRON
IGNITRONS
IGNOBILITIES
IGNOBILITY
IGNOBLE
IGNOBLENESS
IGNOBLENESSES
IGNOBLER
IGNOBLEST
IGNOBLY
IGNOMINIES
IGNOMINIOUS
IGNOMINIOUSLY
IGNOMINIOUSNESS
IGNOMINY
IGNORABLE
IGNORAMI
IGNORAMUS
IGNORAMUSES
IGNORANCE
IGNORANCES
IGNORANT
IGNORANTLY
IGNORANTNESS
IGNORANTNESSES
IGNORE
IGNORED
IGNORER
IGNORERS
IGNORES
IGNORING
IGUANA
IGUANAS
IGUANIAN
IGUANIANS
IGUANID
IGUANIDS
IGUANODON
IGUANODONS
IHRAM
IHRAMS
IKAT
IKATS
IKEBANA
IKEBANAS
IKON
IKONS
ILEA
ILEAC
ILEAL
ILEITIDES
ILEITIS
ILEITISES
ILEOSTOMIES
ILEOSTOMY
ILEUM
ILEUS
ILEUSES
ILEX
ILEXES
ILIA
ILIAC
ILIAD
ILIADS
ILIAL
ILIUM
ILK
ILKA
ILKS
ILL
ILLATION
ILLATIONS
ILLATIVE
ILLATIVELY
ILLATIVES
ILLAUDABLE
ILLAUDABLY
ILLEGAL
ILLEGALITIES
ILLEGALITY
ILLEGALIZATION
ILLEGALIZATIONS
ILLEGALIZE
ILLEGALIZED
ILLEGALIZES
ILLEGALIZING
ILLEGALLY
ILLEGALS
ILLEGIBILITIES
ILLEGIBILITY
ILLEGIBLE
ILLEGIBLY
ILLEGITIMACIES
ILLEGITIMACY
ILLEGITIMATE
ILLEGITIMATELY
ILLER
ILLEST
ILLIBERAL
ILLIBERALISM
ILLIBERALISMS
ILLIBERALITIES
ILLIBERALITY
ILLIBERALLY
ILLIBERALNESS
ILLIBERALNESSES
ILLICIT
ILLICITLY
ILLIMITABILITY
ILLIMITABLE
ILLIMITABLENESS
ILLIMITABLY
ILLINIUM
ILLINIUMS
ILLIQUID
ILLIQUIDITIES
ILLIQUIDITY
ILLITE
ILLITERACIES
ILLITERACY
ILLITERATE
ILLITERATELY
ILLITERATENESS
ILLITERATES
ILLITES
ILLITIC
ILLNESS
ILLNESSES
ILLOCUTIONARY
ILLOGIC
ILLOGICAL
ILLOGICALITIES
ILLOGICALITY
ILLOGICALLY
ILLOGICALNESS
ILLOGICALNESSES

ILLOGICS
ILLS
ILLUDE
ILLUDED
ILLUDES
ILLUDING
ILLUME
ILLUMED
ILLUMES
ILLUMINABLE
ILLUMINANCE
ILLUMINANCES
ILLUMINANT
ILLUMINANTS
ILLUMINATE
ILLUMINATED
ILLUMINATES
ILLUMINATI
ILLUMINATING
ILLUMINATINGLY
ILLUMINATION
ILLUMINATIONS
ILLUMINATIVE
ILLUMINATOR
ILLUMINATORS
ILLUMINE
ILLUMINED
ILLUMINES
ILLUMING
ILLUMINING
ILLUMINISM
ILLUMINISMS
ILLUMINIST
ILLUMINISTS
ILLUSION
ILLUSIONAL
ILLUSIONARY
ILLUSIONISM
ILLUSIONISMS
ILLUSIONIST
ILLUSIONISTIC
ILLUSIONISTS
ILLUSIONS
ILLUSIVE
ILLUSIVELY
ILLUSIVENESS
ILLUSIVENESSES
ILLUSORILY
ILLUSORINESS
ILLUSORINESSES
ILLUSORY
ILLUSTRATE
ILLUSTRATED
ILLUSTRATES
ILLUSTRATING
ILLUSTRATION
ILLUSTRATIONAL
ILLUSTRATIONS
ILLUSTRATIVE
ILLUSTRATIVELY
ILLUSTRATOR
ILLUSTRATORS
ILLUSTRIOUS
ILLUSTRIOUSLY
ILLUSTRIOUSNESS
ILLUVIA
ILLUVIAL
ILLUVIATE
ILLUVIATED
ILLUVIATES
ILLUVIATING
ILLUVIATION
ILLUVIATIONS
ILLUVIUM
ILLUVIUMS
ILLY
ILMENITE
ILMENITES
IMAGE
IMAGEABLE
IMAGED
IMAGER
IMAGERIES
IMAGERS
IMAGERY
IMAGES
IMAGINABLE
IMAGINABLENESS
IMAGINABLY
IMAGINAL
IMAGINARIES
IMAGINARILY
IMAGINARINESS
IMAGINARINESSES
IMAGINARY
IMAGINATION
IMAGINATIONS
IMAGINATIVE
IMAGINATIVELY
IMAGINATIVENESS
IMAGINE
IMAGINED
IMAGINER
IMAGINERS
IMAGINES
IMAGING
IMAGINGS
IMAGINING
IMAGININGS
IMAGISM
IMAGISMS
IMAGIST
IMAGISTIC
IMAGISTICALLY
IMAGISTS
IMAGO
IMAGOES
IMAGOS
IMAM
IMAMATE
IMAMATES
IMAMS
IMARET
IMARETS
IMAUM
IMAUMS
IMBALANCE
IMBALANCED
IMBALANCES
IMBALM
IMBALMED
IMBALMER
IMBALMERS
IMBALMING
IMBALMS
IMBARK
IMBARKED
IMBARKING
IMBARKS
IMBECILE
IMBECILES
IMBECILIC
IMBECILITIES
IMBECILITY
IMBED
IMBEDDED
IMBEDDING
IMBEDS
IMBIBE
IMBIBED
IMBIBER
IMBIBERS
IMBIBES
IMBIBING
IMBIBITION
IMBIBITIONAL
IMBIBITIONS
IMBITTER
IMBITTERED
IMBITTERING
IMBITTERS
IMBLAZE
IMBLAZED
IMBLAZES
IMBLAZING
IMBODIED
IMBODIES
IMBODY
IMBODYING
IMBOLDEN
IMBOLDENED
IMBOLDENING
IMBOLDENS
IMBOSOM
IMBOSOMED
IMBOSOMING
IMBOSOMS
IMBOWER
IMBOWERED
IMBOWERING
IMBOWERS
IMBRICATE
IMBRICATED
IMBRICATES
IMBRICATING
IMBRICATION
IMBRICATIONS
IMBROGLIO
IMBROGLIOS
IMBROWN
IMBROWNED
IMBROWNING
IMBROWNS
IMBRUE
IMBRUED
IMBRUES
IMBRUING
IMBRUTE
IMBRUTED
IMBRUTES
IMBRUTING
IMBUE
IMBUED
IMBUEMENT
IMBUEMENTS
IMBUES
IMBUING
IMID
IMIDAZOLE
IMIDAZOLES
IMIDE
IMIDES
IMIDIC
IMIDO
IMIDS
IMINE
IMINES
IMINO
IMIPRAMINE
IMIPRAMINES
IMITABLE
IMITATE
IMITATED
IMITATES
IMITATING
IMITATION
IMITATIONS
IMITATIVE
IMITATIVELY
IMITATIVENESS
IMITATIVENESSES
IMITATOR
IMITATORS
IMMACULACIES
IMMACULACY
IMMACULATE
IMMACULATELY
IMMANE
IMMANENCE
IMMANENCES
IMMANENCIES
IMMANENCY
IMMANENT
IMMANENTISM
IMMANENTISMS
IMMANENTIST
IMMANENTISTIC
IMMANENTISTS
IMMANENTLY
IMMATERIAL
IMMATERIALISM
IMMATERIALISMS
IMMATERIALIST
IMMATERIALISTS
IMMATERIALITIES
IMMATERIALITY
IMMATERIALIZE
IMMATERIALIZED
IMMATERIALIZES
IMMATERIALIZING
IMMATURE
IMMATURELY
IMMATURER
IMMATURES
IMMATUREST

IMMATURITIES
IMMATURITY
IMMEASURABLE
IMMEASURABLY
IMMEDIACIES
IMMEDIACY
IMMEDIATE
IMMEDIATELY
IMMEDIATENESS
IMMEDIATENESSES
IMMEDICABLE
IMMEDICABLY
IMMEMORIAL
IMMEMORIALLY
IMMENSE
IMMENSELY
IMMENSENESS
IMMENSENESSES
IMMENSER
IMMENSEST
IMMENSITIES
IMMENSITY
IMMENSURABLE
IMMERGE
IMMERGED
IMMERGES
IMMERGING
IMMERSE
IMMERSED
IMMERSES
IMMERSIBLE
IMMERSING
IMMERSION
IMMERSIONS
IMMESH
IMMESHED
IMMESHES
IMMESHING
IMMETHODICAL
IMMETHODICALLY
IMMIES
IMMIGRANT
IMMIGRANTS
IMMIGRATE
IMMIGRATED
IMMIGRATES
IMMIGRATING
IMMIGRATION
IMMIGRATIONAL
IMMIGRATIONS
IMMINENCE
IMMINENCES
IMMINENCIES
IMMINENCY
IMMINENT
IMMINENTLY
IMMINGLE
IMMINGLED
IMMINGLES
IMMINGLING
IMMISCIBILITIES
IMMISCIBILITY
IMMISCIBLE
IMMISERATION
IMMISERATIONS
IMMITIGABLE
IMMITIGABLY
IMMITTANCE
IMMITTANCES
IMMIX
IMMIXED
IMMIXES
IMMIXING
IMMIXTURE
IMMIXTURES
IMMOBILE
IMMOBILISATION
IMMOBILISATIONS
IMMOBILISE
IMMOBILISED
IMMOBILISER
IMMOBILISERS
IMMOBILISES
IMMOBILISING
IMMOBILISM
IMMOBILISMS
IMMOBILITIES
IMMOBILITY
IMMOBILIZATION
IMMOBILIZATIONS
IMMOBILIZE
IMMOBILIZED
IMMOBILIZER
IMMOBILIZERS
IMMOBILIZES
IMMOBILIZING
IMMODERACIES
IMMODERACY
IMMODERATE
IMMODERATELY
IMMODERATENESS
IMMODERATION
IMMODERATIONS
IMMODEST
IMMODESTER
IMMODESTEST
IMMODESTIES
IMMODESTLY
IMMODESTY
IMMOLATE
IMMOLATED
IMMOLATES
IMMOLATING
IMMOLATION
IMMOLATIONS
IMMOLATOR
IMMOLATORS
IMMORAL
IMMORALISM
IMMORALISMS
IMMORALIST
IMMORALISTS
IMMORALITIES
IMMORALITY
IMMORALLY
IMMORTAL
IMMORTALISE
IMMORTALISED
IMMORTALISES
IMMORTALISING
IMMORTALITIES
IMMORTALITY
IMMORTALIZATION
IMMORTALIZE
IMMORTALIZED
IMMORTALIZER
IMMORTALIZERS
IMMORTALIZES
IMMORTALIZING
IMMORTALLY
IMMORTALS
IMMORTELLE
IMMORTELLES
IMMOTILE
IMMOVABILITIES
IMMOVABILITY
IMMOVABLE
IMMOVABLENESS
IMMOVABLENESSES
IMMOVABLES
IMMOVABLY
IMMUNE
IMMUNER
IMMUNES
IMMUNEST
IMMUNISATION
IMMUNISATIONS
IMMUNISE
IMMUNISED
IMMUNISES
IMMUNISING
IMMUNITIES
IMMUNITY
IMMUNIZATION
IMMUNIZATIONS
IMMUNIZE
IMMUNIZED
IMMUNIZER
IMMUNIZERS
IMMUNIZES
IMMUNIZING
IMMUNOASSAY
IMMUNOASSAYABLE
IMMUNOASSAYS
IMMUNOBLOT
IMMUNOBLOTS
IMMUNOBLOTTING
IMMUNOBLOTTINGS
IMMUNOCHEMICAL
IMMUNOCHEMIST
IMMUNOCHEMISTRY
IMMUNOCHEMISTS
IMMUNOCOMPETENT
IMMUNODEFICIENT
IMMUNODIAGNOSES
IMMUNODIAGNOSIS
IMMUNODIFFUSION
IMMUNOGEN
IMMUNOGENESES
IMMUNOGENESIS
IMMUNOGENETIC
IMMUNOGENETICS
IMMUNOGENIC
IMMUNOGENICITY
IMMUNOGENS
IMMUNOGLOBULIN
IMMUNOGLOBULINS
IMMUNOLOGIC
IMMUNOLOGICAL
IMMUNOLOGICALLY
IMMUNOLOGIES
IMMUNOLOGIST
IMMUNOLOGISTS
IMMUNOLOGY
IMMUNOMODULATOR
IMMUNOPATHOLOGY
IMMUNOREACTIVE
IMMUNOSORBENT
IMMUNOSORBENTS
IMMUNOSUPPRESS
IMMUNOTHERAPIES
IMMUNOTHERAPY
IMMURE
IMMURED
IMMUREMENT
IMMUREMENTS
IMMURES
IMMURING
IMMUTABILITIES
IMMUTABILITY
IMMUTABLE
IMMUTABLENESS
IMMUTABLENESSES
IMMUTABLY
IMMY
IMP
IMPACT
IMPACTED
IMPACTER
IMPACTERS
IMPACTFUL
IMPACTING
IMPACTION
IMPACTIONS
IMPACTIVE
IMPACTOR
IMPACTORS
IMPACTS
IMPAINT
IMPAINTED
IMPAINTING
IMPAINTS
IMPAIR
IMPAIRED
IMPAIRER
IMPAIRERS
IMPAIRING
IMPAIRMENT
IMPAIRMENTS
IMPAIRS
IMPALA
IMPALAS
IMPALE
IMPALED
IMPALEMENT
IMPALEMENTS
IMPALER
IMPALERS
IMPALES
IMPALING
IMPALPABILITIES
IMPALPABILITY
IMPALPABLE
IMPALPABLY
IMPANEL

IMPANELED
IMPANELING
IMPANELLED
IMPANELLING
IMPANELS
IMPARADISE
IMPARADISED
IMPARADISES
IMPARADISING
IMPARITIES
IMPARITY
IMPARK
IMPARKED
IMPARKING
IMPARKS
IMPART
IMPARTATION
IMPARTATIONS
IMPARTED
IMPARTER
IMPARTERS
IMPARTIAL
IMPARTIALITIES
IMPARTIALITY
IMPARTIALLY
IMPARTIBLE
IMPARTIBLY
IMPARTING
IMPARTMENT
IMPARTMENTS
IMPARTS
IMPASSABILITIES
IMPASSABILITY
IMPASSABLE
IMPASSABLENESS
IMPASSABLY
IMPASSE
IMPASSES
IMPASSIBILITIES
IMPASSIBILITY
IMPASSIBLE
IMPASSIBLY
IMPASSION
IMPASSIONED
IMPASSIONING
IMPASSIONS
IMPASSIVE
IMPASSIVELY
IMPASSIVENESS
IMPASSIVENESSES
IMPASSIVITIES
IMPASSIVITY
IMPASTE
IMPASTED
IMPASTES
IMPASTING
IMPASTO
IMPASTOED
IMPASTOS
IMPATIENCE
IMPATIENCES
IMPATIENS
IMPATIENT
IMPATIENTLY
IMPAVID
IMPAWN
IMPAWNED
IMPAWNING
IMPAWNS
IMPEACH
IMPEACHABLE
IMPEACHED
IMPEACHER
IMPEACHERS
IMPEACHES
IMPEACHING
IMPEACHMENT
IMPEACHMENTS
IMPEARL
IMPEARLED
IMPEARLING
IMPEARLS
IMPECCABILITIES
IMPECCABILITY
IMPECCABLE
IMPECCABLY
IMPECCANT
IMPECUNIOSITIES
IMPECUNIOSITY
IMPECUNIOUS
IMPECUNIOUSLY
IMPECUNIOUSNESS
IMPED
IMPEDANCE
IMPEDANCES
IMPEDE
IMPEDED
IMPEDER
IMPEDERS
IMPEDES
IMPEDIMENT
IMPEDIMENTA
IMPEDIMENTS
IMPEDING
IMPEL
IMPELLED
IMPELLENT
IMPELLENTS
IMPELLER
IMPELLERS
IMPELLING
IMPELLOR
IMPELLORS
IMPELS
IMPEND
IMPENDED
IMPENDENT
IMPENDING
IMPENDS
IMPENETRABILITY
IMPENETRABLE
IMPENETRABLY
IMPENITENCE
IMPENITENCES
IMPENITENT
IMPENITENTLY
IMPERATIVE
IMPERATIVELY
IMPERATIVENESS
IMPERATIVES
IMPERATOR
IMPERATORIAL
IMPERATORS
IMPERCEIVABLE
IMPERCEPTIBLE
IMPERCEPTIBLY
IMPERCEPTIVE
IMPERCIPIENCE
IMPERCIPIENCES
IMPERCIPIENT
IMPERFECT
IMPERFECTER
IMPERFECTEST
IMPERFECTION
IMPERFECTIONS
IMPERFECTIVE
IMPERFECTIVES
IMPERFECTLY
IMPERFECTNESS
IMPERFECTNESSES
IMPERFECTS
IMPERFORATE
IMPERIA
IMPERIAL
IMPERIALISM
IMPERIALISMS
IMPERIALIST
IMPERIALISTIC
IMPERIALISTS
IMPERIALLY
IMPERIALS
IMPERIL
IMPERILED
IMPERILING
IMPERILLED
IMPERILLING
IMPERILMENT
IMPERILMENTS
IMPERILS
IMPERIOUS
IMPERIOUSLY
IMPERIOUSNESS
IMPERIOUSNESSES
IMPERISHABILITY
IMPERISHABLE
IMPERISHABLES
IMPERISHABLY
IMPERIUM
IMPERIUMS
IMPERMANENCE
IMPERMANENCES
IMPERMANENCIES
IMPERMANENCY
IMPERMANENT
IMPERMANENTLY
IMPERMEABILITY
IMPERMEABLE
IMPERMISSIBLE
IMPERMISSIBLY
IMPERSONAL
IMPERSONALITIES
IMPERSONALITY
IMPERSONALIZE
IMPERSONALIZED
IMPERSONALIZES
IMPERSONALIZING
IMPERSONALLY
IMPERSONATE
IMPERSONATED
IMPERSONATES
IMPERSONATING
IMPERSONATION
IMPERSONATIONS
IMPERSONATOR
IMPERSONATORS
IMPERTINENCE
IMPERTINENCES
IMPERTINENCIES
IMPERTINENCY
IMPERTINENT
IMPERTINENTLY
IMPERTURBABLE
IMPERTURBABLY
IMPERVIOUS
IMPERVIOUSLY
IMPERVIOUSNESS
IMPETIGINOUS
IMPETIGO
IMPETIGOS
IMPETRATE
IMPETRATED
IMPETRATES
IMPETRATING
IMPETRATION
IMPETRATIONS
IMPETUOSITIES
IMPETUOSITY
IMPETUOUS
IMPETUOUSLY
IMPETUOUSNESS
IMPETUOUSNESSES
IMPETUS
IMPETUSES
IMPHEE
IMPHEES
IMPI
IMPIETIES
IMPIETY
IMPING
IMPINGE
IMPINGED
IMPINGEMENT
IMPINGEMENTS
IMPINGER
IMPINGERS
IMPINGES
IMPINGING
IMPINGS
IMPIOUS
IMPIOUSLY
IMPIS
IMPISH
IMPISHLY
IMPISHNESS
IMPISHNESSES
IMPLACABILITIES
IMPLACABILITY
IMPLACABLE
IMPLACABLY
IMPLANT
IMPLANTABLE
IMPLANTATION
IMPLANTATIONS
IMPLANTED
IMPLANTER

IMPLANTERS
IMPLANTING
IMPLANTS
IMPLAUSIBILITY
IMPLAUSIBLE
IMPLAUSIBLY
IMPLEAD
IMPLEADED
IMPLEADER
IMPLEADERS
IMPLEADING
IMPLEADS
IMPLED
IMPLEDGE
IMPLEDGED
IMPLEDGES
IMPLEDGING
IMPLEMENT
IMPLEMENTATION
IMPLEMENTATIONS
IMPLEMENTED
IMPLEMENTER
IMPLEMENTERS
IMPLEMENTING
IMPLEMENTOR
IMPLEMENTORS
IMPLEMENTS
IMPLETION
IMPLETIONS
IMPLICATE
IMPLICATED
IMPLICATES
IMPLICATING
IMPLICATION
IMPLICATIONS
IMPLICATIVE
IMPLICATIVELY
IMPLICATIVENESS
IMPLICIT
IMPLICITLY
IMPLICITNESS
IMPLICITNESSES
IMPLIED
IMPLIES
IMPLODE
IMPLODED
IMPLODES
IMPLODING
IMPLORE
IMPLORED
IMPLORER
IMPLORERS
IMPLORES
IMPLORING
IMPLORINGLY
IMPLOSION
IMPLOSIONS
IMPLOSIVE
IMPLOSIVES
IMPLY
IMPLYING
IMPOLICIES
IMPOLICY
IMPOLITE
IMPOLITELY
IMPOLITENESS
IMPOLITENESSES
IMPOLITER
IMPOLITEST
IMPOLITIC
IMPOLITICAL
IMPOLITICALLY
IMPOLITICLY
IMPONDERABILITY
IMPONDERABLE
IMPONDERABLES
IMPONDERABLY
IMPONE
IMPONED
IMPONES
IMPONING
IMPOROUS
IMPORT
IMPORTABLE
IMPORTANCE
IMPORTANCES
IMPORTANCIES
IMPORTANCY
IMPORTANT
IMPORTANTLY
IMPORTATION
IMPORTATIONS
IMPORTED
IMPORTER
IMPORTERS
IMPORTING
IMPORTS
IMPORTUNATE
IMPORTUNATELY
IMPORTUNATENESS
IMPORTUNE
IMPORTUNED
IMPORTUNELY
IMPORTUNER
IMPORTUNERS
IMPORTUNES
IMPORTUNING
IMPORTUNITIES
IMPORTUNITY
IMPOSABLE
IMPOSE
IMPOSED
IMPOSER
IMPOSERS
IMPOSES
IMPOSING
IMPOSINGLY
IMPOSITION
IMPOSITIONS
IMPOSSIBILITIES
IMPOSSIBILITY
IMPOSSIBLE
IMPOSSIBLENESS
IMPOSSIBLY
IMPOST
IMPOSTED
IMPOSTER
IMPOSTERS
IMPOSTHUME
IMPOSTHUMES
IMPOSTING
IMPOSTOR
IMPOSTORS
IMPOSTS
IMPOSTUME
IMPOSTUMES
IMPOSTURE
IMPOSTURES
IMPOTENCE
IMPOTENCES
IMPOTENCIES
IMPOTENCY
IMPOTENT
IMPOTENTLY
IMPOTENTS
IMPOUND
IMPOUNDED
IMPOUNDER
IMPOUNDERS
IMPOUNDING
IMPOUNDMENT
IMPOUNDMENTS
IMPOUNDS
IMPOVERISH
IMPOVERISHED
IMPOVERISHER
IMPOVERISHERS
IMPOVERISHES
IMPOVERISHING
IMPOVERISHMENT
IMPOVERISHMENTS
IMPOWER
IMPOWERED
IMPOWERING
IMPOWERS
IMPRACTICABLE
IMPRACTICABLY
IMPRACTICAL
IMPRACTICALITY
IMPRACTICALLY
IMPRECATE
IMPRECATED
IMPRECATES
IMPRECATING
IMPRECATION
IMPRECATIONS
IMPRECATORY
IMPRECISE
IMPRECISELY
IMPRECISENESS
IMPRECISENESSES
IMPRECISION
IMPRECISIONS
IMPREGN
IMPREGNABILITY
IMPREGNABLE
IMPREGNABLENESS
IMPREGNABLY
IMPREGNANT
IMPREGNANTS
IMPREGNATE
IMPREGNATED
IMPREGNATES
IMPREGNATING
IMPREGNATION
IMPREGNATIONS
IMPREGNATOR
IMPREGNATORS
IMPREGNED
IMPREGNING
IMPREGNS
IMPRESA
IMPRESARIO
IMPRESARIOS
IMPRESAS
IMPRESE
IMPRESES
IMPRESS
IMPRESSARIOS
IMPRESSED
IMPRESSES
IMPRESSIBILITY
IMPRESSIBLE
IMPRESSING
IMPRESSION
IMPRESSIONABLE
IMPRESSIONISM
IMPRESSIONISMS
IMPRESSIONIST
IMPRESSIONISTIC
IMPRESSIONISTS
IMPRESSIONS
IMPRESSIVE
IMPRESSIVELY
IMPRESSIVENESS
IMPRESSMENT
IMPRESSMENTS
IMPRESSURE
IMPRESSURES
IMPREST
IMPRESTS
IMPRIMATUR
IMPRIMATURS
IMPRIMIS
IMPRINT
IMPRINTED
IMPRINTER
IMPRINTERS
IMPRINTING
IMPRINTINGS
IMPRINTS
IMPRISON
IMPRISONED
IMPRISONING
IMPRISONMENT
IMPRISONMENTS
IMPRISONS
IMPRO
IMPROBABILITIES
IMPROBABILITY
IMPROBABLE
IMPROBABLY
IMPROBITIES
IMPROBITY
IMPROMPTU
IMPROMPTUS
IMPROPER
IMPROPERER
IMPROPEREST
IMPROPERLY
IMPROPERNESS
IMPROPERNESSES
IMPROPRIETIES
IMPROPRIETY
IMPROS

IMPROV
IMPROVABILITIES
IMPROVABILITY
IMPROVABLE
IMPROVE
IMPROVED
IMPROVEMENT
IMPROVEMENTS
IMPROVER
IMPROVERS
IMPROVES
IMPROVIDENCE
IMPROVIDENCES
IMPROVIDENT
IMPROVIDENTLY
IMPROVING
IMPROVISATION
IMPROVISATIONAL
IMPROVISATIONS
IMPROVISATOR
IMPROVISATORE
IMPROVISATORES
IMPROVISATORI
IMPROVISATORIAL
IMPROVISATORS
IMPROVISATORY
IMPROVISE
IMPROVISED
IMPROVISER
IMPROVISERS
IMPROVISES
IMPROVISING
IMPROVISOR
IMPROVISORS
IMPROVS
IMPRUDENCE
IMPRUDENCES
IMPRUDENT
IMPRUDENTLY
IMPS
IMPUDENCE
IMPUDENCES
IMPUDENCIES
IMPUDENCY
IMPUDENT
IMPUDENTLY
IMPUDICITIES
IMPUDICITY
IMPUGN
IMPUGNABLE
IMPUGNED
IMPUGNER
IMPUGNERS
IMPUGNING
IMPUGNS
IMPUISSANCE
IMPUISSANCES
IMPUISSANT
IMPULSE
IMPULSED
IMPULSES
IMPULSING
IMPULSION
IMPULSIONS
IMPULSIVE
IMPULSIVELY
IMPULSIVENESS
IMPULSIVENESSES
IMPULSIVITIES
IMPULSIVITY
IMPUNITIES
IMPUNITY
IMPURE
IMPURELY
IMPURENESS
IMPURENESSES
IMPURER
IMPUREST
IMPURITIES
IMPURITY
IMPUTABILITIES
IMPUTABILITY
IMPUTABLE
IMPUTABLY
IMPUTATION
IMPUTATIONS
IMPUTATIVE
IMPUTATIVELY
IMPUTE
IMPUTED
IMPUTER
IMPUTERS
IMPUTES
IMPUTING
IN
INABILITIES
INABILITY
INACCESSIBILITY
INACCESSIBLE
INACCESSIBLY
INACCURACIES
INACCURACY
INACCURATE
INACCURATELY
INACTION
INACTIONS
INACTIVATE
INACTIVATED
INACTIVATES
INACTIVATING
INACTIVATION
INACTIVATIONS
INACTIVE
INACTIVELY
INACTIVITIES
INACTIVITY
INADEQUACIES
INADEQUACY
INADEQUATE
INADEQUATELY
INADEQUATENESS
INADMISSIBILITY
INADMISSIBLE
INADMISSIBLY
INADVERTENCE
INADVERTENCES
INADVERTENCIES
INADVERTENCY
INADVERTENT
INADVERTENTLY
INADVISABILITY
INADVISABLE
INALIENABILITY
INALIENABLE
INALIENABLY
INALTERABILITY
INALTERABLE
INALTERABLENESS
INALTERABLY
INAMORATA
INAMORATAS
INAMORATO
INAMORATOS
INANE
INANELY
INANENESS
INANENESSES
INANER
INANES
INANEST
INANIMATE
INANIMATELY
INANIMATENESS
INANIMATENESSES
INANITIES
INANITION
INANITIONS
INANITY
INAPPARENT
INAPPARENTLY
INAPPEASABLE
INAPPETENCE
INAPPETENCES
INAPPLICABILITY
INAPPLICABLE
INAPPLICABLY
INAPPOSITE
INAPPOSITELY
INAPPOSITENESS
INAPPRECIABLE
INAPPRECIABLY
INAPPRECIATIVE
INAPPROACHABLE
INAPPROPRIATE
INAPPROPRIATELY
INAPT
INAPTER
INAPTEST
INAPTITUDE
INAPTITUDES
INAPTLY
INAPTNESS
INAPTNESSES
INARABLE
INARCH
INARCHED
INARCHES
INARCHING
INARGUABLE
INARGUABLY
INARM
INARMED
INARMING
INARMS
INARTICULACIES
INARTICULACY
INARTICULATE
INARTICULATELY
INARTICULATES
INARTISTIC
INARTISTICALLY
INASMUCH
INATTENTION
INATTENTIONS
INATTENTIVE
INATTENTIVELY
INATTENTIVENESS
INAUDIBILITIES
INAUDIBILITY
INAUDIBLE
INAUDIBLY
INAUGURAL
INAUGURALS
INAUGURATE
INAUGURATED
INAUGURATES
INAUGURATING
INAUGURATION
INAUGURATIONS
INAUGURATOR
INAUGURATORS
INAUSPICIOUS
INAUSPICIOUSLY
INAUTHENTIC
INAUTHENTICITY
INBEING
INBEINGS
INBOARD
INBOARDS
INBORN
INBOUND
INBOUNDED
INBOUNDING
INBOUNDS
INBOX
INBOXES
INBREATHE
INBREATHED
INBREATHES
INBREATHING
INBRED
INBREDS
INBREED
INBREEDER
INBREEDERS
INBREEDING
INBREEDINGS
INBREEDS
INBUILT
INBURST
INBURSTS
INBY
INBYE
INCAGE
INCAGED
INCAGES
INCAGING
INCALCULABILITY
INCALCULABLE
INCALCULABLY
INCALESCENCE
INCALESCENCES
INCALESCENT
INCANDESCE
INCANDESCED

INCANDESCENCE
INCANDESCENCES
INCANDESCENT
INCANDESCENTLY
INCANDESCENTS
INCANDESCES
INCANDESCING
INCANT
INCANTATION
INCANTATIONAL
INCANTATIONS
INCANTATORY
INCANTED
INCANTING
INCANTS
INCAPABILITIES
INCAPABILITY
INCAPABLE
INCAPABLENESS
INCAPABLENESSES
INCAPABLY
INCAPACITATE
INCAPACITATED
INCAPACITATES
INCAPACITATING
INCAPACITATION
INCAPACITATIONS
INCAPACITIES
INCAPACITY
INCARCERATE
INCARCERATED
INCARCERATES
INCARCERATING
INCARCERATION
INCARCERATIONS
INCARDINATION
INCARDINATIONS
INCARNADINE
INCARNADINED
INCARNADINES
INCARNADINING
INCARNATE
INCARNATED
INCARNATES
INCARNATING
INCARNATION
INCARNATIONAL
INCARNATIONS
INCASE
INCASED
INCASES
INCASING
INCAUTION
INCAUTIONS
INCAUTIOUS
INCAUTIOUSLY
INCAUTIOUSNESS
INCENDIARIES
INCENDIARISM
INCENDIARISMS
INCENDIARY
INCENSE
INCENSED
INCENSES
INCENSING
INCENT
INCENTED
INCENTER
INCENTERS
INCENTING
INCENTIVE
INCENTIVES
INCENTIVIZE
INCENTIVIZED
INCENTIVIZES
INCENTIVIZING
INCENTS
INCEPT
INCEPTED
INCEPTING
INCEPTION
INCEPTIONS
INCEPTIVE
INCEPTIVELY
INCEPTIVES
INCEPTOR
INCEPTORS
INCEPTS
INCERTITUDE
INCERTITUDES
INCESSANCIES
INCESSANCY
INCESSANT
INCESSANTLY
INCEST
INCESTS
INCESTUOUS
INCESTUOUSLY
INCESTUOUSNESS
INCH
INCHED
INCHER
INCHERS
INCHES
INCHING
INCHMEAL
INCHOATE
INCHOATELY
INCHOATENESS
INCHOATENESSES
INCHOATIVE
INCHOATIVELY
INCHOATIVES
INCHWORM
INCHWORMS
INCIDENCE
INCIDENCES
INCIDENT
INCIDENTAL
INCIDENTALLY
INCIDENTALS
INCIDENTS
INCINERATE
INCINERATED
INCINERATES
INCINERATING
INCINERATION
INCINERATIONS
INCINERATOR
INCINERATORS
INCIPIENCE
INCIPIENCES
INCIPIENCIES
INCIPIENCY
INCIPIENT
INCIPIENTLY
INCIPIT
INCIPITS
INCISAL
INCISE
INCISED
INCISES
INCISING
INCISION
INCISIONS
INCISIVE
INCISIVELY
INCISIVENESS
INCISIVENESSES
INCISOR
INCISORS
INCISORY
INCISURE
INCISURES
INCITABLE
INCITANT
INCITANTS
INCITATION
INCITATIONS
INCITE
INCITED
INCITEMENT
INCITEMENTS
INCITER
INCITERS
INCITES
INCITING
INCIVIL
INCIVILITIES
INCIVILITY
INCLASP
INCLASPED
INCLASPING
INCLASPS
INCLEMENCIES
INCLEMENCY
INCLEMENT
INCLEMENTLY
INCLINABLE
INCLINATION
INCLINATIONAL
INCLINATIONS
INCLINE
INCLINED
INCLINER
INCLINERS
INCLINES
INCLINING
INCLININGS
INCLINOMETER
INCLINOMETERS
INCLIP
INCLIPPED
INCLIPPING
INCLIPS
INCLOSE
INCLOSED
INCLOSER
INCLOSERS
INCLOSES
INCLOSING
INCLOSURE
INCLOSURES
INCLUDABLE
INCLUDE
INCLUDED
INCLUDES
INCLUDIBLE
INCLUDING
INCLUSION
INCLUSIONARY
INCLUSIONS
INCLUSIVE
INCLUSIVELY
INCLUSIVENESS
INCLUSIVENESSES
INCLUSIVITIES
INCLUSIVITY
INCOERCIBLE
INCOG
INCOGITANT
INCOGNITA
INCOGNITAS
INCOGNITO
INCOGNITOS
INCOGNIZANCE
INCOGNIZANCES
INCOGNIZANT
INCOGS
INCOHERENCE
INCOHERENCES
INCOHERENT
INCOHERENTLY
INCOMBUSTIBLE
INCOMBUSTIBLES
INCOME
INCOMER
INCOMERS
INCOMES
INCOMING
INCOMINGS
INCOMMENSURABLE
INCOMMENSURABLY
INCOMMENSURATE
INCOMMODE
INCOMMODED
INCOMMODES
INCOMMODING
INCOMMODIOUS
INCOMMODIOUSLY
INCOMMODITIES
INCOMMODITY
INCOMMUNICABLE
INCOMMUNICABLY
INCOMMUNICADO
INCOMMUNICATIVE
INCOMMUTABLE
INCOMMUTABLY
INCOMPACT
INCOMPARABILITY
INCOMPARABLE
INCOMPARABLY
INCOMPATIBILITY
INCOMPATIBLE
INCOMPATIBLES

INCOMPATIBLY
INCOMPETENCE
INCOMPETENCES
INCOMPETENCIES
INCOMPETENCY
INCOMPETENT
INCOMPETENTLY
INCOMPETENTS
INCOMPLETE
INCOMPLETELY
INCOMPLETENESS
INCOMPLIANT
INCOMPREHENSION
INCOMPRESSIBLE
INCOMPUTABLE
INCOMPUTABLY
INCONCEIVABLE
INCONCEIVABLY
INCONCINNITIES
INCONCINNITY
INCONCLUSIVE
INCONCLUSIVELY
INCONDITE
INCONFORMITIES
INCONFORMITY
INCONGRUENCE
INCONGRUENCES
INCONGRUENT
INCONGRUENTLY
INCONGRUITIES
INCONGRUITY
INCONGRUOUS
INCONGRUOUSLY
INCONGRUOUSNESS
INCONNU
INCONNUS
INCONSCIENT
INCONSECUTIVE
INCONSEQUENCE
INCONSEQUENCES
INCONSEQUENT
INCONSEQUENTIAL
INCONSEQUENTLY
INCONSIDERABLE
INCONSIDERABLY
INCONSIDERATE
INCONSIDERATELY
INCONSIDERATION
INCONSISTENCE
INCONSISTENCES
INCONSISTENCIES
INCONSISTENCY
INCONSISTENT
INCONSISTENTLY
INCONSOLABLE
INCONSOLABLY
INCONSONANCE
INCONSONANCES
INCONSONANT
INCONSPICUOUS
INCONSPICUOUSLY
INCONSTANCIES
INCONSTANCY
INCONSTANT
INCONSTANTLY
INCONSUMABLE
INCONSUMABLY
INCONTESTABLE
INCONTESTABLY
INCONTINENCE
INCONTINENCES
INCONTINENCIES
INCONTINENCY
INCONTINENT
INCONTINENTLY
INCONTROLLABLE
INCONVENIENCE
INCONVENIENCED
INCONVENIENCES
INCONVENIENCIES
INCONVENIENCING
INCONVENIENCY
INCONVENIENT
INCONVENIENTLY
INCONVERTIBLE
INCONVERTIBLY
INCONVINCIBLE
INCONY
INCOORDINATION
INCOORDINATIONS
INCORPORABLE
INCORPORATE
INCORPORATED
INCORPORATES
INCORPORATING
INCORPORATION
INCORPORATIONS
INCORPORATIVE
INCORPORATOR
INCORPORATORS
INCORPOREAL
INCORPOREALLY
INCORPOREITIES
INCORPOREITY
INCORPSE
INCORPSED
INCORPSES
INCORPSING
INCORRECT
INCORRECTLY
INCORRECTNESS
INCORRECTNESSES
INCORRIGIBILITY
INCORRIGIBLE
INCORRIGIBLES
INCORRIGIBLY
INCORRUPT
INCORRUPTED
INCORRUPTIBLE
INCORRUPTIBLES
INCORRUPTIBLY
INCORRUPTION
INCORRUPTIONS
INCORRUPTLY
INCORRUPTNESS
INCORRUPTNESSES
INCREASABLE
INCREASE
INCREASED
INCREASER
INCREASERS
INCREASES
INCREASING
INCREASINGLY
INCREATE
INCREDIBILITIES
INCREDIBILITY
INCREDIBLE
INCREDIBLENESS
INCREDIBLY
INCREDULITIES
INCREDULITY
INCREDULOUS
INCREDULOUSLY
INCREMENT
INCREMENTAL
INCREMENTALISM
INCREMENTALISMS
INCREMENTALIST
INCREMENTALISTS
INCREMENTALLY
INCREMENTS
INCRESCENT
INCRETION
INCRETIONS
INCRIMINATE
INCRIMINATED
INCRIMINATES
INCRIMINATING
INCRIMINATION
INCRIMINATIONS
INCRIMINATORY
INCROSS
INCROSSED
INCROSSES
INCROSSING
INCRUST
INCRUSTATION
INCRUSTATIONS
INCRUSTED
INCRUSTING
INCRUSTS
INCUBATE
INCUBATED
INCUBATES
INCUBATING
INCUBATION
INCUBATIONS
INCUBATIVE
INCUBATOR
INCUBATORS
INCUBATORY
INCUBI
INCUBUS
INCUBUSES
INCUDAL
INCUDATE
INCUDES
INCULCATE
INCULCATED
INCULCATES
INCULCATING
INCULCATION
INCULCATIONS
INCULCATOR
INCULCATORS
INCULPABLE
INCULPATE
INCULPATED
INCULPATES
INCULPATING
INCULPATION
INCULPATIONS
INCULPATORY
INCULT
INCUMBENCIES
INCUMBENCY
INCUMBENT
INCUMBENTS
INCUMBER
INCUMBERED
INCUMBERING
INCUMBERS
INCUNABLE
INCUNABLES
INCUNABULA
INCUNABULUM
INCUR
INCURABLE
INCURABLES
INCURABLY
INCURIOSITIES
INCURIOSITY
INCURIOUS
INCURIOUSLY
INCURIOUSNESS
INCURIOUSNESSES
INCURRED
INCURRENCE
INCURRENCES
INCURRENT
INCURRING
INCURS
INCURSION
INCURSIONS
INCURSIVE
INCURVATE
INCURVATED
INCURVATES
INCURVATING
INCURVATION
INCURVATIONS
INCURVATURE
INCURVATURES
INCURVE
INCURVED
INCURVES
INCURVING
INCUS
INCUSE
INCUSED
INCUSES
INCUSING
INDABA
INDABAS
INDAGATE
INDAGATED
INDAGATES
INDAGATING
INDAGATION
INDAGATIONS
INDAGATOR
INDAGATORS
INDAMIN
INDAMINE

INDAMINES
INDAMINS
INDEBTED
INDEBTEDNESS
INDEBTEDNESSES
INDECENCIES
INDECENCY
INDECENT
INDECENTER
INDECENTEST
INDECENTLY
INDECIPHERABLE
INDECISION
INDECISIONS
INDECISIVE
INDECISIVELY
INDECISIVENESS
INDECLINABLE
INDECOMPOSABLE
INDECOROUS
INDECOROUSLY
INDECOROUSNESS
INDECORUM
INDECORUMS
INDEED
INDEEDY
INDEFATIGABLE
INDEFATIGABLY
INDEFEASIBILITY
INDEFEASIBLE
INDEFEASIBLY
INDEFECTIBILITY
INDEFECTIBLE
INDEFECTIBLY
INDEFENSIBILITY
INDEFENSIBLE
INDEFENSIBLY
INDEFINABILITY
INDEFINABLE
INDEFINABLENESS
INDEFINABLES
INDEFINABLY
INDEFINITE
INDEFINITELY
INDEFINITENESS
INDEFINITES
INDEHISCENCE
INDEHISCENCES
INDEHISCENT
INDELIBILITIES
INDELIBILITY
INDELIBLE
INDELIBLY
INDELICACIES
INDELICACY
INDELICATE
INDELICATELY
INDELICATENESS
INDEMNIFICATION
INDEMNIFIED
INDEMNIFIER
INDEMNIFIERS
INDEMNIFIES
INDEMNIFY
INDEMNIFYING
INDEMNITIES
INDEMNITY
INDEMONSTRABLE
INDEMONSTRABLY
INDENE
INDENES
INDENT
INDENTATION
INDENTATIONS
INDENTED
INDENTER
INDENTERS
INDENTING
INDENTION
INDENTIONS
INDENTOR
INDENTORS
INDENTS
INDENTURE
INDENTURED
INDENTURES
INDENTURING
INDEPENDENCE
INDEPENDENCES
INDEPENDENCIES
INDEPENDENCY
INDEPENDENT
INDEPENDENTLY
INDEPENDENTS
INDESCRIBABLE
INDESCRIBABLY
INDESTRUCTIBLE
INDESTRUCTIBLY
INDETERMINABLE
INDETERMINABLY
INDETERMINACIES
INDETERMINACY
INDETERMINATE
INDETERMINATELY
INDETERMINATION
INDETERMINISM
INDETERMINISMS
INDETERMINIST
INDETERMINISTIC
INDETERMINISTS
INDEVOUT
INDEX
INDEXABLE
INDEXATION
INDEXATIONS
INDEXED
INDEXER
INDEXERS
INDEXES
INDEXICAL
INDEXICALS
INDEXING
INDEXINGS
INDICAN
INDICANS
INDICANT
INDICANTS
INDICATE
INDICATED
INDICATES
INDICATING
INDICATION
INDICATIONAL
INDICATIONS
INDICATIVE
INDICATIVELY
INDICATIVES
INDICATOR
INDICATORS
INDICATORY
INDICES
INDICIA
INDICIAS
INDICIUM
INDICIUMS
INDICT
INDICTABLE
INDICTED
INDICTEE
INDICTEES
INDICTER
INDICTERS
INDICTING
INDICTION
INDICTIONS
INDICTMENT
INDICTMENTS
INDICTOR
INDICTORS
INDICTS
INDIE
INDIES
INDIFFERENCE
INDIFFERENCES
INDIFFERENCIES
INDIFFERENCY
INDIFFERENT
INDIFFERENTISM
INDIFFERENTISMS
INDIFFERENTIST
INDIFFERENTISTS
INDIFFERENTLY
INDIGEN
INDIGENCE
INDIGENCES
INDIGENCIES
INDIGENCY
INDIGENE
INDIGENES
INDIGENIZATION
INDIGENIZATIONS
INDIGENIZE
INDIGENIZED
INDIGENIZES
INDIGENIZING
INDIGENOUS
INDIGENOUSLY
INDIGENOUSNESS
INDIGENS
INDIGENT
INDIGENTS
INDIGESTABILITY
INDIGESTED
INDIGESTIBILITY
INDIGESTIBLE
INDIGESTIBLES
INDIGESTION
INDIGESTIONS
INDIGN
INDIGNANT
INDIGNANTLY
INDIGNATION
INDIGNATIONS
INDIGNITIES
INDIGNITY
INDIGNLY
INDIGO
INDIGOES
INDIGOID
INDIGOIDS
INDIGOS
INDIGOTIN
INDIGOTINS
INDINAVIR
INDINAVIRS
INDIRECT
INDIRECTION
INDIRECTIONS
INDIRECTLY
INDIRECTNESS
INDIRECTNESSES
INDISCERNIBLE
INDISCIPLINABLE
INDISCIPLINE
INDISCIPLINED
INDISCIPLINES
INDISCOVERABLE
INDISCREET
INDISCREETER
INDISCREETEST
INDISCREETLY
INDISCREETNESS
INDISCRETION
INDISCRETIONS
INDISCRIMINATE
INDISPENSABLE
INDISPENSABLES
INDISPENSABLY
INDISPOSE
INDISPOSED
INDISPOSES
INDISPOSING
INDISPOSITION
INDISPOSITIONS
INDISPUTABLE
INDISPUTABLY
INDISSOCIABLE
INDISSOCIABLY
INDISSOLUBILITY
INDISSOLUBLE
INDISSOLUBLY
INDISTINCT
INDISTINCTIVE
INDISTINCTLY
INDISTINCTNESS
INDITE
INDITED
INDITER
INDITERS
INDITES
INDITING
INDIUM
INDIUMS
INDIVIDUAL
INDIVIDUALISE

INDIVIDUALISED
INDIVIDUALISES
INDIVIDUALISING
INDIVIDUALISM
INDIVIDUALISMS
INDIVIDUALIST
INDIVIDUALISTIC
INDIVIDUALISTS
INDIVIDUALITIES
INDIVIDUALITY
INDIVIDUALIZE
INDIVIDUALIZED
INDIVIDUALIZES
INDIVIDUALIZING
INDIVIDUALLY
INDIVIDUALS
INDIVIDUATE
INDIVIDUATED
INDIVIDUATES
INDIVIDUATING
INDIVIDUATION
INDIVIDUATIONS
INDIVISIBILITY
INDIVISIBLE
INDIVISIBLES
INDIVISIBLY
INDOCILE
INDOCILITIES
INDOCILITY
INDOCTRINATE
INDOCTRINATED
INDOCTRINATES
INDOCTRINATING
INDOCTRINATION
INDOCTRINATIONS
INDOCTRINATOR
INDOCTRINATORS
INDOL
INDOLE
INDOLENCE
INDOLENCES
INDOLENT
INDOLENTLY
INDOLES
INDOLS
INDOMETHACIN
INDOMETHACINS
INDOMITABILITY
INDOMITABLE
INDOMITABLENESS
INDOMITABLY
INDOOR
INDOORS
INDOPHENOL
INDOPHENOLS
INDORSE
INDORSED
INDORSEE
INDORSEES
INDORSEMENT
INDORSEMENTS
INDORSER
INDORSERS
INDORSES
INDORSING
INDORSOR
INDORSORS
INDOW
INDOWED
INDOWING
INDOWS
INDOXYL
INDOXYLS
INDRAFT
INDRAFTS
INDRAUGHT
INDRAUGHTS
INDRAWN
INDRI
INDRIS
INDUBITABILITY
INDUBITABLE
INDUBITABLENESS
INDUBITABLY
INDUCE
INDUCED
INDUCEMENT
INDUCEMENTS
INDUCER
INDUCERS
INDUCES
INDUCIBILITIES
INDUCIBILITY
INDUCIBLE
INDUCING
INDUCT
INDUCTANCE
INDUCTANCES
INDUCTED
INDUCTEE
INDUCTEES
INDUCTILE
INDUCTING
INDUCTION
INDUCTIONS
INDUCTIVE
INDUCTIVELY
INDUCTOR
INDUCTORS
INDUCTS
INDUE
INDUED
INDUES
INDUING
INDULGE
INDULGED
INDULGENCE
INDULGENCES
INDULGENT
INDULGENTLY
INDULGER
INDULGERS
INDULGES
INDULGING
INDULIN
INDULINE
INDULINES
INDULINS
INDULT
INDULTS
INDUNA
INDUNAS
INDURATE
INDURATED
INDURATES
INDURATING
INDURATION
INDURATIONS
INDURATIVE
INDUSIA
INDUSIAL
INDUSIATE
INDUSIUM
INDUSTRIAL
INDUSTRIALISE
INDUSTRIALISED
INDUSTRIALISES
INDUSTRIALISING
INDUSTRIALISM
INDUSTRIALISMS
INDUSTRIALIST
INDUSTRIALISTS
INDUSTRIALIZE
INDUSTRIALIZED
INDUSTRIALIZES
INDUSTRIALIZING
INDUSTRIALLY
INDUSTRIALS
INDUSTRIES
INDUSTRIOUS
INDUSTRIOUSLY
INDUSTRIOUSNESS
INDUSTRY
INDWELL
INDWELLER
INDWELLERS
INDWELLING
INDWELLS
INDWELT
INEARTH
INEARTHED
INEARTHING
INEARTHS
INEBRIANT
INEBRIANTS
INEBRIATE
INEBRIATED
INEBRIATES
INEBRIATING
INEBRIATION
INEBRIATIONS
INEBRIETIES
INEBRIETY
INEDIBLE
INEDIBLY
INEDITA
INEDITED
INEDUCABILITIES
INEDUCABILITY
INEDUCABLE
INEFFABILITIES
INEFFABILITY
INEFFABLE
INEFFABLENESS
INEFFABLENESSES
INEFFABLY
INEFFACEABILITY
INEFFACEABLE
INEFFACEABLY
INEFFECTIVE
INEFFECTIVELY
INEFFECTIVENESS
INEFFECTUAL
INEFFECTUALITY
INEFFECTUALLY
INEFFECTUALNESS
INEFFICACIES
INEFFICACIOUS
INEFFICACIOUSLY
INEFFICACY
INEFFICIENCIES
INEFFICIENCY
INEFFICIENT
INEFFICIENTLY
INEFFICIENTS
INEGALITARIAN
INELASTIC
INELASTICITIES
INELASTICITY
INELEGANCE
INELEGANCES
INELEGANT
INELEGANTLY
INELIGIBILITIES
INELIGIBILITY
INELIGIBLE
INELIGIBLES
INELOQUENT
INELOQUENTLY
INELUCTABILITY
INELUCTABLE
INELUCTABLY
INELUDIBLE
INENARRABLE
INEPT
INEPTER
INEPTEST
INEPTITUDE
INEPTITUDES
INEPTLY
INEPTNESS
INEPTNESSES
INEQUALITIES
INEQUALITY
INEQUITABLE
INEQUITABLY
INEQUITIES
INEQUITY
INEQUIVALVE
INEQUIVALVED
INERADICABILITY
INERADICABLE
INERADICABLY
INERRABLE
INERRANCIES
INERRANCY
INERRANT
INERT
INERTIA
INERTIAE
INERTIAL
INERTIALLY
INERTIAS
INERTLY
INERTNESS

INERTNESSES
INERTS
INESCAPABLE
INESCAPABLY
INESSENTIAL
INESSENTIALS
INESTIMABLE
INESTIMABLY
INEVITABILITIES
INEVITABILITY
INEVITABLE
INEVITABLENESS
INEVITABLY
INEXACT
INEXACTITUDE
INEXACTITUDES
INEXACTLY
INEXACTNESS
INEXACTNESSES
INEXCUSABLE
INEXCUSABLENESS
INEXCUSABLY
INEXHAUSTIBLE
INEXHAUSTIBLY
INEXISTENCE
INEXISTENCES
INEXISTENT
INEXORABILITIES
INEXORABILITY
INEXORABLE
INEXORABLENESS
INEXORABLY
INEXPEDIENCE
INEXPEDIENCES
INEXPEDIENCIES
INEXPEDIENCY
INEXPEDIENT
INEXPEDIENTLY
INEXPENSIVE
INEXPENSIVELY
INEXPENSIVENESS
INEXPERIENCE
INEXPERIENCED
INEXPERIENCES
INEXPERT
INEXPERTLY
INEXPERTNESS
INEXPERTNESSES
INEXPERTS
INEXPIABLE
INEXPIABLY
INEXPLAINABLE
INEXPLICABILITY
INEXPLICABLE
INEXPLICABLY
INEXPLICIT
INEXPRESSIBLE
INEXPRESSIBLY
INEXPRESSIVE
INEXPRESSIVELY
INEXPUGNABLE
INEXPUGNABLY
INEXPUNGIBLE
INEXTRICABILITY
INEXTRICABLE
INEXTRICABLY
INFALL
INFALLIBILITIES
INFALLIBILITY
INFALLIBLE
INFALLIBLY
INFALLING
INFALLS
INFAMIES
INFAMOUS
INFAMOUSLY
INFAMY
INFANCIES
INFANCY
INFANT
INFANTA
INFANTAS
INFANTE
INFANTES
INFANTICIDAL
INFANTICIDE
INFANTICIDES
INFANTILE
INFANTILISM
INFANTILISMS
INFANTILITIES
INFANTILITY
INFANTILIZATION
INFANTILIZE
INFANTILIZED
INFANTILIZES
INFANTILIZING
INFANTINE
INFANTRIES
INFANTRY
INFANTRYMAN
INFANTRYMEN
INFANTS
INFARCT
INFARCTED
INFARCTION
INFARCTIONS
INFARCTS
INFARE
INFARES
INFATUATE
INFATUATED
INFATUATES
INFATUATING
INFATUATION
INFATUATIONS
INFAUNA
INFAUNAE
INFAUNAL
INFAUNAS
INFEASIBILITIES
INFEASIBILITY
INFEASIBLE
INFECT
INFECTANT
INFECTED
INFECTER
INFECTERS
INFECTING
INFECTION
INFECTIONS
INFECTIOUS
INFECTIOUSLY
INFECTIOUSNESS
INFECTIVE
INFECTIVITIES
INFECTIVITY
INFECTOR
INFECTORS
INFECTS
INFECUND
INFEED
INFEEDS
INFELICITIES
INFELICITOUS
INFELICITOUSLY
INFELICITY
INFEOFF
INFEOFFED
INFEOFFING
INFEOFFS
INFER
INFERABLE
INFERABLY
INFERENCE
INFERENCES
INFERENTIAL
INFERENTIALLY
INFERIOR
INFERIORITIES
INFERIORITY
INFERIORLY
INFERIORS
INFERNAL
INFERNALLY
INFERNO
INFERNOS
INFERRED
INFERRER
INFERRERS
INFERRIBLE
INFERRING
INFERS
INFERTILE
INFERTILITIES
INFERTILITY
INFEST
INFESTANT
INFESTANTS
INFESTATION
INFESTATIONS
INFESTED
INFESTER
INFESTERS
INFESTING
INFESTS
INFIBULATION
INFIBULATIONS
INFIDEL
INFIDELIC
INFIDELITIES
INFIDELITY
INFIDELS
INFIELD
INFIELDER
INFIELDERS
INFIELDS
INFIGHT
INFIGHTER
INFIGHTERS
INFIGHTING
INFIGHTINGS
INFIGHTS
INFILL
INFILLED
INFILLING
INFILLS
INFILTRATE
INFILTRATED
INFILTRATES
INFILTRATING
INFILTRATION
INFILTRATIONS
INFILTRATIVE
INFILTRATOR
INFILTRATORS
INFINITE
INFINITELY
INFINITENESS
INFINITENESSES
INFINITES
INFINITESIMAL
INFINITESIMALLY
INFINITESIMALS
INFINITIES
INFINITIVAL
INFINITIVE
INFINITIVELY
INFINITIVES
INFINITUDE
INFINITUDES
INFINITY
INFIRM
INFIRMARIES
INFIRMARY
INFIRMED
INFIRMING
INFIRMITIES
INFIRMITY
INFIRMLY
INFIRMS
INFIX
INFIXATION
INFIXATIONS
INFIXED
INFIXES
INFIXING
INFIXION
INFIXIONS
INFLAME
INFLAMED
INFLAMER
INFLAMERS
INFLAMES
INFLAMING
INFLAMMABILITY
INFLAMMABLE
INFLAMMABLENESS
INFLAMMABLES
INFLAMMABLY
INFLAMMATION
INFLAMMATIONS
INFLAMMATORILY
INFLAMMATORY
INFLATABLE

INFLATABLES
INFLATE
INFLATED
INFLATER
INFLATERS
INFLATES
INFLATING
INFLATION
INFLATIONARY
INFLATIONISM
INFLATIONISMS
INFLATIONIST
INFLATIONISTS
INFLATIONS
INFLATOR
INFLATORS
INFLECT
INFLECTABLE
INFLECTED
INFLECTING
INFLECTION
INFLECTIONAL
INFLECTIONALLY
INFLECTIONS
INFLECTIVE
INFLECTOR
INFLECTORS
INFLECTS
INFLEXED
INFLEXIBILITIES
INFLEXIBILITY
INFLEXIBLE
INFLEXIBLENESS
INFLEXIBLY
INFLEXION
INFLEXIONAL
INFLEXIONS
INFLICT
INFLICTED
INFLICTER
INFLICTERS
INFLICTING
INFLICTION
INFLICTIONS
INFLICTIVE
INFLICTOR
INFLICTORS
INFLICTS
INFLIGHT
INFLORESCENCE
INFLORESCENCES
INFLOW
INFLOWING
INFLOWINGS
INFLOWS
INFLUENCE
INFLUENCEABLE
INFLUENCED
INFLUENCES
INFLUENCING
INFLUENT
INFLUENTIAL
INFLUENTIALLY
INFLUENTIALS
INFLUENTS
INFLUENZA
INFLUENZAL
INFLUENZAS
INFLUX
INFLUXES
INFO
INFOBAHN
INFOBAHNS
INFOLD
INFOLDED
INFOLDER
INFOLDERS
INFOLDING
INFOLDS
INFOMERCIAL
INFOMERCIALS
INFORM
INFORMAL
INFORMALITIES
INFORMALITY
INFORMALLY
INFORMANT
INFORMANTS
INFORMATICS
INFORMATION
INFORMATIONAL
INFORMATIONALLY
INFORMATIONS
INFORMATIVE
INFORMATIVELY
INFORMATIVENESS
INFORMATORILY
INFORMATORY
INFORMED
INFORMEDLY
INFORMER
INFORMERS
INFORMING
INFORMS
INFOS
INFOTAINMENT
INFOTAINMENTS
INFOTECH
INFOTECHS
INFOUGHT
INFRA
INFRACT
INFRACTED
INFRACTING
INFRACTION
INFRACTIONS
INFRACTOR
INFRACTORS
INFRACTS
INFRAHUMAN
INFRAHUMANS
INFRANGIBILITY
INFRANGIBLE
INFRANGIBLY
INFRAORDER
INFRAORDERS
INFRARED
INFRAREDS
INFRASONIC
INFRASPECIFIC
INFRASTRUCTURAL
INFRASTRUCTURE
INFRASTRUCTURES
INFREQUENCE
INFREQUENCES
INFREQUENCIES
INFREQUENCY
INFREQUENT
INFREQUENTLY
INFRINGE
INFRINGED
INFRINGEMENT
INFRINGEMENTS
INFRINGER
INFRINGERS
INFRINGES
INFRINGING
INFRUGAL
INFULA
INFULAE
INFUNDIBULA
INFUNDIBULAR
INFUNDIBULIFORM
INFUNDIBULUM
INFURIATE
INFURIATED
INFURIATES
INFURIATING
INFURIATINGLY
INFURIATION
INFURIATIONS
INFUSCATE
INFUSE
INFUSED
INFUSER
INFUSERS
INFUSES
INFUSIBILITIES
INFUSIBILITY
INFUSIBLE
INFUSIBLENESS
INFUSIBLENESSES
INFUSING
INFUSION
INFUSIONS
INFUSIVE
INFUSORIAN
INFUSORIANS
INGATE
INGATES
INGATHER
INGATHERED
INGATHERING
INGATHERINGS
INGATHERS
INGENIOUS
INGENIOUSLY
INGENIOUSNESS
INGENIOUSNESSES
INGENUE
INGENUES
INGENUITIES
INGENUITY
INGENUOUS
INGENUOUSLY
INGENUOUSNESS
INGENUOUSNESSES
INGEST
INGESTA
INGESTED
INGESTIBLE
INGESTING
INGESTION
INGESTIONS
INGESTIVE
INGESTS
INGLE
INGLENOOK
INGLENOOKS
INGLES
INGLORIOUS
INGLORIOUSLY
INGLORIOUSNESS
INGOING
INGOT
INGOTED
INGOTING
INGOTS
INGRAFT
INGRAFTED
INGRAFTING
INGRAFTS
INGRAIN
INGRAINED
INGRAINEDLY
INGRAINING
INGRAINS
INGRATE
INGRATES
INGRATIATE
INGRATIATED
INGRATIATES
INGRATIATING
INGRATIATINGLY
INGRATIATION
INGRATIATIONS
INGRATIATORY
INGRATITUDE
INGRATITUDES
INGREDIENT
INGREDIENTS
INGRESS
INGRESSES
INGRESSION
INGRESSIONS
INGRESSIVE
INGRESSIVENESS
INGRESSIVES
INGROUND
INGROUP
INGROUPS
INGROWING
INGROWN
INGROWNNESS
INGROWNNESSES
INGROWTH
INGROWTHS
INGUINAL
INGULF
INGULFED
INGULFING
INGULFS
INGURGITATE
INGURGITATED
INGURGITATES

INGURGITATING
INGURGITATION
INGURGITATIONS
INHABIT
INHABITABLE
INHABITANCIES
INHABITANCY
INHABITANT
INHABITANTS
INHABITATION
INHABITATIONS
INHABITED
INHABITER
INHABITERS
INHABITING
INHABITS
INHALANT
INHALANTS
INHALATION
INHALATIONAL
INHALATIONS
INHALATOR
INHALATORS
INHALE
INHALED
INHALER
INHALERS
INHALES
INHALING
INHARMONIC
INHARMONIES
INHARMONIOUS
INHARMONIOUSLY
INHARMONY
INHAUL
INHAULER
INHAULERS
INHAULS
INHERE
INHERED
INHERENCE
INHERENCES
INHERENCIES
INHERENCY
INHERENT
INHERENTLY
INHERES
INHERING
INHERIT
INHERITABILITY
INHERITABLE
INHERITABLENESS
INHERITANCE
INHERITANCES
INHERITED
INHERITING
INHERITOR
INHERITORS
INHERITRESS
INHERITRESSES
INHERITRICES
INHERITRIX
INHERITRIXES
INHERITS
INHESION
INHESIONS
INHIBIN
INHIBINS
INHIBIT
INHIBITED
INHIBITER
INHIBITERS
INHIBITING
INHIBITION
INHIBITIONS
INHIBITIVE
INHIBITOR
INHIBITORS
INHIBITORY
INHIBITS
INHOLDER
INHOLDERS
INHOLDING
INHOLDINGS
INHOMOGENEITIES
INHOMOGENEITY
INHOMOGENEOUS
INHOSPITABLE
INHOSPITABLY
INHOSPITALITIES
INHOSPITALITY
INHUMAN
INHUMANE
INHUMANELY
INHUMANER
INHUMANEST
INHUMANITIES
INHUMANITY
INHUMANLY
INHUMANNESS
INHUMANNESSES
INHUMATION
INHUMATIONS
INHUME
INHUMED
INHUMER
INHUMERS
INHUMES
INHUMING
INIA
INIMICAL
INIMICALLY
INIMITABLE
INIMITABLENESS
INIMITABLY
INION
INIONS
INIQUITIES
INIQUITOUS
INIQUITOUSLY
INIQUITOUSNESS
INIQUITY
INITIAL
INITIALED
INITIALER
INITIALERS
INITIALING
INITIALISM
INITIALISMS
INITIALIZATION
INITIALIZATIONS
INITIALIZE
INITIALIZED
INITIALIZES
INITIALIZING
INITIALLED
INITIALLING
INITIALLY
INITIALNESS
INITIALNESSES
INITIALS
INITIATE
INITIATED
INITIATES
INITIATING
INITIATION
INITIATIONS
INITIATIVE
INITIATIVES
INITIATOR
INITIATORS
INITIATORY
INJECT
INJECTABLE
INJECTABLES
INJECTANT
INJECTANTS
INJECTED
INJECTING
INJECTION
INJECTIONS
INJECTIVE
INJECTOR
INJECTORS
INJECTS
INJERA
INJERAS
INJUDICIOUS
INJUDICIOUSLY
INJUDICIOUSNESS
INJUNCTION
INJUNCTIONS
INJUNCTIVE
INJURABLE
INJURE
INJURED
INJURER
INJURERS
INJURES
INJURIES
INJURING
INJURIOUS
INJURIOUSLY
INJURIOUSNESS
INJURIOUSNESSES
INJURY
INJUSTICE
INJUSTICES
INK
INKBERRIES
INKBERRY
INKBLOT
INKBLOTS
INKED
INKER
INKERS
INKHORN
INKHORNS
INKIER
INKIEST
INKINESS
INKINESSES
INKING
INKJET
INKJETS
INKLE
INKLES
INKLESS
INKLIKE
INKLING
INKLINGS
INKPOT
INKPOTS
INKS
INKSTAND
INKSTANDS
INKSTONE
INKSTONES
INKWELL
INKWELLS
INKWOOD
INKWOODS
INKY
INLACE
INLACED
INLACES
INLACING
INLAID
INLAND
INLANDER
INLANDERS
INLANDS
INLAY
INLAYER
INLAYERS
INLAYING
INLAYS
INLET
INLETS
INLETTING
INLIER
INLIERS
INLY
INLYING
INMATE
INMATES
INMESH
INMESHED
INMESHES
INMESHING
INMOST
INN
INNAGE
INNAGES
INNARDS
INNATE
INNATELY
INNATENESS
INNATENESSES
INNED
INNER
INNERLY
INNERMOST
INNERMOSTS
INNERNESS

INNERNESSES
INNERS
INNERSOLE
INNERSOLES
INNERSPRING
INNERSPRINGS
INNERVATE
INNERVATED
INNERVATES
INNERVATING
INNERVATION
INNERVATIONS
INNERVE
INNERVED
INNERVES
INNERVING
INNING
INNINGS
INNINGSES
INNKEEPER
INNKEEPERS
INNLESS
INNOCENCE
INNOCENCES
INNOCENCIES
INNOCENCY
INNOCENT
INNOCENTER
INNOCENTEST
INNOCENTLY
INNOCENTS
INNOCUOUS
INNOCUOUSLY
INNOCUOUSNESS
INNOCUOUSNESSES
INNOMINATE
INNOVATE
INNOVATED
INNOVATES
INNOVATING
INNOVATION
INNOVATIONAL
INNOVATIONS
INNOVATIVE
INNOVATIVELY
INNOVATIVENESS
INNOVATOR
INNOVATORS
INNOVATORY
INNOXIOUS
INNS
INNUENDO
INNUENDOED
INNUENDOES
INNUENDOING
INNUENDOS
INNUMERABLE
INNUMERABLY
INNUMERACIES
INNUMERACY
INNUMERATE
INNUMERATES
INNUMEROUS
INOBSERVANCE
INOBSERVANCES
INOBSERVANT
INOCULA
INOCULANT
INOCULANTS
INOCULATE
INOCULATED
INOCULATES
INOCULATING
INOCULATION
INOCULATIONS
INOCULATIVE
INOCULATOR
INOCULATORS
INOCULUM
INOCULUMS
INODOROUS
INOFFENSIVE
INOFFENSIVELY
INOFFENSIVENESS
INOPERABLE
INOPERATIVE
INOPERATIVENESS
INOPERCULATE
INOPERCULATES
INOPPORTUNE
INOPPORTUNELY
INOPPORTUNENESS
INORDINATE
INORDINATELY
INORDINATENESS
INORGANIC
INORGANICALLY
INOSCULATE
INOSCULATED
INOSCULATES
INOSCULATING
INOSCULATION
INOSCULATIONS
INOSINE
INOSINES
INOSITE
INOSITES
INOSITOL
INOSITOLS
INOTROPE
INOTROPES
INOTROPIC
INPATIENT
INPATIENTS
INPHASE
INPOUR
INPOURED
INPOURING
INPOURINGS
INPOURS
INPUT
INPUTS
INPUTTED
INPUTTER
INPUTTERS
INPUTTING
INQUEST
INQUESTS
INQUIET
INQUIETED
INQUIETING
INQUIETS
INQUIETUDE
INQUIETUDES
INQUILINE
INQUILINES
INQUIRE
INQUIRED
INQUIRER
INQUIRERS
INQUIRES
INQUIRIES
INQUIRING
INQUIRINGLY
INQUIRY
INQUISITION
INQUISITIONAL
INQUISITIONS
INQUISITIVE
INQUISITIVELY
INQUISITIVENESS
INQUISITOR
INQUISITORIAL
INQUISITORIALLY
INQUISITORS
INRO
INROAD
INROADS
INRUN
INRUNS
INRUSH
INRUSHES
INRUSHING
INRUSHINGS
INS
INSALUBRIOUS
INSALUBRITIES
INSALUBRITY
INSANE
INSANELY
INSANENESS
INSANENESSES
INSANER
INSANEST
INSANITARY
INSANITATION
INSANITATIONS
INSANITIES
INSANITY
INSATIABILITIES
INSATIABILITY
INSATIABLE
INSATIABLENESS
INSATIABLY
INSATIATE
INSATIATELY
INSATIATENESS
INSATIATENESSES
INSCAPE
INSCAPES
INSCRIBE
INSCRIBED
INSCRIBER
INSCRIBERS
INSCRIBES
INSCRIBING
INSCRIPTION
INSCRIPTIONAL
INSCRIPTIONS
INSCRIPTIVE
INSCRIPTIVELY
INSCROLL
INSCROLLED
INSCROLLING
INSCROLLS
INSCRUTABILITY
INSCRUTABLE
INSCRUTABLENESS
INSCRUTABLY
INSCULP
INSCULPED
INSCULPING
INSCULPS
INSEAM
INSEAMS
INSECT
INSECTAN
INSECTARIES
INSECTARY
INSECTICIDAL
INSECTICIDALLY
INSECTICIDE
INSECTICIDES
INSECTILE
INSECTIVORE
INSECTIVORES
INSECTIVOROUS
INSECTS
INSECURE
INSECURELY
INSECURENESS
INSECURENESSES
INSECURER
INSECUREST
INSECURITIES
INSECURITY
INSELBERG
INSELBERGE
INSELBERGS
INSEMINATE
INSEMINATED
INSEMINATES
INSEMINATING
INSEMINATION
INSEMINATIONS
INSEMINATOR
INSEMINATORS
INSENSATE
INSENSATELY
INSENSIBILITIES
INSENSIBILITY
INSENSIBLE
INSENSIBLENESS
INSENSIBLY
INSENSITIVE
INSENSITIVELY
INSENSITIVENESS
INSENSITIVITIES
INSENSITIVITY
INSENTIENCE
INSENTIENCES
INSENTIENT
INSEPARABILITY
INSEPARABLE
INSEPARABLENESS

INSEPARABLES
INSEPARABLY
INSERT
INSERTED
INSERTER
INSERTERS
INSERTING
INSERTION
INSERTIONAL
INSERTIONS
INSERTS
INSET
INSETS
NSETTED
INSETTER
NSETTERS
INSETTING
NSHEATH
NSHEATHE
NSHEATHED
NSHEATHES
NSHEATHING
NSHEATHS
NSHORE
NSHRINE
NSHRINED
NSHRINES
NSHRINING
NSIDE
NSIDER
NSIDERS
NSIDES
NSIDIOUS
NSIDIOUSLY
NSIDIOUSNESS
NSIDIOUSNESSES
NSIGHT
NSIGHTFUL
NSIGHTFULLY
NSIGHTFULNESS
NSIGHTS
NSIGNE
NSIGNIA
NSIGNIAS
NSIGNIFICANCE
NSIGNIFICANCES
SIGNIFICANCY
SIGNIFICANT
NSIGNIFICANTLY
SINCERE
SINCERELY
SINCERER
SINCEREST
INSINCERITIES
INSINCERITY
INSINUATE
INSINUATED
INSINUATES
INSINUATING
INSINUATINGLY
INSINUATION
INSINUATIONS
INSINUATIVE
INSINUATOR
INSINUATORS
INSIPID
INSIPIDER
INSIPIDEST
INSIPIDITIES
INSIPIDITY
INSIPIDLY
INSIST
INSISTED
INSISTENCE
INSISTENCES
INSISTENCIES
INSISTENCY
INSISTENT
INSISTENTLY
INSISTER
INSISTERS
INSISTING
INSISTS
INSNARE
INSNARED
INSNARER
INSNARERS
INSNARES
INSNARING
INSOBRIETIES
INSOBRIETY
INSOCIABILITIES
INSOCIABILITY
INSOCIABLE
INSOCIABLY
INSOFAR
INSOLATE
INSOLATED
INSOLATES
INSOLATING
INSOLATION
INSOLATIONS
INSOLE
INSOLENCE
INSOLENCES
INSOLENT
INSOLENTLY
INSOLENTS
INSOLES
INSOLUBILITIES
INSOLUBILITY
INSOLUBILIZE
INSOLUBILIZED
INSOLUBILIZES
INSOLUBILIZING
INSOLUBLE
INSOLUBLENESS
INSOLUBLENESSES
INSOLUBLES
INSOLUBLY
INSOLVABLE
INSOLVABLY
INSOLVENCIES
INSOLVENCY
INSOLVENT
INSOLVENTS
INSOMNIA
INSOMNIAC
INSOMNIACS
INSOMNIAS
INSOMUCH
INSOUCIANCE
INSOUCIANCES
INSOUCIANT
INSOUCIANTLY
INSOUL
INSOULED
INSOULING
INSOULS
INSOURCE
INSOURCED
INSOURCES
INSOURCING
INSPAN
INSPANNED
INSPANNING
INSPANS
INSPECT
INSPECTED
INSPECTING
INSPECTION
INSPECTIONS
INSPECTIVE
INSPECTOR
INSPECTORATE
INSPECTORATES
INSPECTORS
INSPECTORSHIP
INSPECTORSHIPS
INSPECTS
INSPHERE
INSPHERED
INSPHERES
INSPHERING
INSPIRATION
INSPIRATIONAL
INSPIRATIONALLY
INSPIRATIONS
INSPIRATOR
INSPIRATORS
INSPIRATORY
INSPIRE
INSPIRED
INSPIRER
INSPIRERS
INSPIRES
INSPIRING
INSPIRINGLY
INSPIRIT
INSPIRITED
INSPIRITING
INSPIRITINGLY
INSPIRITS
INSPISSATE
INSPISSATED
INSPISSATES
INSPISSATING
INSPISSATION
INSPISSATIONS
INSPISSATOR
INSPISSATORS
INSTABILITIES
INSTABILITY
INSTABLE
INSTAL
INSTALL
INSTALLATION
INSTALLATIONS
INSTALLED
INSTALLER
INSTALLERS
INSTALLING
INSTALLMENT
INSTALLMENTS
INSTALLS
INSTALMENT
INSTALMENTS
INSTALS
INSTANCE
INSTANCED
INSTANCES
INSTANCIES
INSTANCING
INSTANCY
INSTANT
INSTANTANEITIES
INSTANTANEITY
INSTANTANEOUS
INSTANTANEOUSLY
INSTANTER
INSTANTIATE
INSTANTIATED
INSTANTIATES
INSTANTIATING
INSTANTIATION
INSTANTIATIONS
INSTANTLY
INSTANTNESS
INSTANTNESSES
INSTANTS
INSTAR
INSTARRED
INSTARRING
INSTARS
INSTATE
INSTATED
INSTATES
INSTATING
INSTAURATION
INSTAURATIONS
INSTEAD
INSTEP
INSTEPS
INSTIGATE
INSTIGATED
INSTIGATES
INSTIGATING
INSTIGATION
INSTIGATIONS
INSTIGATIVE
INSTIGATOR
INSTIGATORS
INSTIL
INSTILL
INSTILLATION
INSTILLATIONS
INSTILLED
INSTILLER
INSTILLERS
INSTILLING
INSTILLMENT
INSTILLMENTS
INSTILLS
INSTILS
INSTINCT

INSTINCTIVE
INSTINCTIVELY
INSTINCTS
INSTINCTUAL
INSTINCTUALLY
INSTITUTE
INSTITUTED
INSTITUTER
INSTITUTERS
INSTITUTES
INSTITUTING
INSTITUTION
INSTITUTIONAL
INSTITUTIONALLY
INSTITUTIONS
INSTITUTOR
INSTITUTORS
INSTROKE
INSTROKES
INSTRUCT
INSTRUCTED
INSTRUCTING
INSTRUCTION
INSTRUCTIONAL
INSTRUCTIONS
INSTRUCTIVE
INSTRUCTIVELY
INSTRUCTIVENESS
INSTRUCTOR
INSTRUCTORS
INSTRUCTORSHIP
INSTRUCTORSHIPS
INSTRUCTRESS
INSTRUCTRESSES
INSTRUCTS
INSTRUMENT
INSTRUMENTAL
INSTRUMENTALISM
INSTRUMENTALIST
INSTRUMENTALITY
INSTRUMENTALLY
INSTRUMENTALS
INSTRUMENTATION
INSTRUMENTED
INSTRUMENTING
INSTRUMENTS
INSUBORDINATE
INSUBORDINATELY
INSUBORDINATES
INSUBORDINATION
INSUBSTANTIAL
INSUFFERABLE
INSUFFERABLY

INSUFFICIENCIES
INSUFFICIENCY
INSUFFICIENT
INSUFFICIENTLY
INSUFFLATE
INSUFFLATED
INSUFFLATES
INSUFFLATING
INSUFFLATION
INSUFFLATIONS
INSUFFLATOR
INSUFFLATORS
INSULA
INSULAE
INSULANT
INSULANTS
INSULAR
INSULARISM
INSULARISMS
INSULARITIES
INSULARITY
INSULARLY
INSULARS
INSULATE
INSULATED
INSULATES
INSULATING
INSULATION
INSULATIONS
INSULATOR
INSULATORS
INSULIN
INSULINS
INSULT
INSULTED
INSULTER
INSULTERS
INSULTING
INSULTINGLY
INSULTS
INSUPERABLE
INSUPERABLY
INSUPPORTABLE
INSUPPORTABLY
INSUPPRESSIBLE
INSURABILITIES
INSURABILITY
INSURABLE
INSURANCE
INSURANCES
INSURANT
INSURANTS
INSURE

INSURED
INSUREDS
INSURER
INSURERS
INSURES
INSURGENCE
INSURGENCES
INSURGENCIES
INSURGENCY
INSURGENT
INSURGENTLY
INSURGENTS
INSURING
INSURMOUNTABLE
INSURMOUNTABLY
INSURRECTION
INSURRECTIONAL
INSURRECTIONARY
INSURRECTIONIST
INSURRECTIONS
INSUSCEPTIBLE
INSUSCEPTIBLY
INSWATHE
INSWATHED
INSWATHES
INSWATHING
INSWEPT
INTACT
INTACTLY
INTACTNESS
INTACTNESSES
INTAGLI
INTAGLIO
INTAGLIOED
INTAGLIOES
INTAGLIOING
INTAGLIOS
INTAKE
INTAKES
INTANGIBILITIES
INTANGIBILITY
INTANGIBLE
INTANGIBLENESS
INTANGIBLES
INTANGIBLY
INTARSIA
INTARSIAS
INTEGER
INTEGERS
INTEGRABILITIES
INTEGRABILITY
INTEGRABLE
INTEGRAL

INTEGRALITIES
INTEGRALITY
INTEGRALLY
INTEGRALS
INTEGRAND
INTEGRANDS
INTEGRANT
INTEGRANTS
INTEGRATE
INTEGRATED
INTEGRATES
INTEGRATING
INTEGRATION
INTEGRATIONIST
INTEGRATIONISTS
INTEGRATIONS
INTEGRATIVE
INTEGRATOR
INTEGRATORS
INTEGRIN
INTEGRINS
INTEGRITIES
INTEGRITY
INTEGUMENT
INTEGUMENTARY
INTEGUMENTS
INTELLECT
INTELLECTION
INTELLECTIONS
INTELLECTIVE
INTELLECTIVELY
INTELLECTS
INTELLECTUAL
INTELLECTUALISM
INTELLECTUALIST
INTELLECTUALITY
INTELLECTUALIZE
INTELLECTUALLY
INTELLECTUALS
INTELLIGENCE
INTELLIGENCER
INTELLIGENCERS
INTELLIGENCES
INTELLIGENT
INTELLIGENTIAL
INTELLIGENTLY
INTELLIGENTSIA
INTELLIGENTSIAS
INTELLIGIBILITY
INTELLIGIBLE
INTELLIGIBLY
INTEMPERANCE
INTEMPERANCES

INTEMPERATE
INTEMPERATELY
INTEMPERATENESS
INTEND
INTENDANCE
INTENDANCES
INTENDANT
INTENDANTS
INTENDED
INTENDEDLY
INTENDEDS
INTENDER
INTENDERS
INTENDING
INTENDMENT
INTENDMENTS
INTENDS
INTENERATE
INTENERATED
INTENERATES
INTENERATING
INTENERATION
INTENERATIONS
INTENSE
INTENSELY
INTENSENESS
INTENSENESSES
INTENSER
INTENSEST
INTENSIFICATION
INTENSIFIED
INTENSIFIER
INTENSIFIERS
INTENSIFIES
INTENSIFY
INTENSIFYING
INTENSION
INTENSIONAL
INTENSIONALITY
INTENSIONALLY
INTENSIONS
INTENSITIES
INTENSITY
INTENSIVE
INTENSIVELY
INTENSIVENESS
INTENSIVENESSES
INTENSIVES
INTENT
INTENTION
INTENTIONAL
INTENTIONALITY
INTENTIONALLY

INTENTIONS
INTENTLY
INTENTNESS
INTENTNESSES
INTENTS
INTER
INTERABANG
INTERABANGS
INTERACT
INTERACTANT
INTERACTANTS
INTERACTED
INTERACTING
INTERACTION
INTERACTIONAL
INTERACTIONS
INTERACTIVE
INTERACTIVELY
INTERACTIVITIES
INTERACTIVITY
INTERACTS
INTERAGE
INTERAGENCIES
INTERAGENCY
INTERALLELIC
INTERALLIED
INTERANIMATION
INTERANIMATIONS
INTERANNUAL
INTERARCH
INTERARCHED
INTERARCHES
INTERARCHING
INTERATOMIC
INTERBANK
INTERBASIN
INTERBASINS
INTERBED
INTERBEDDED
INTERBEDDING
INTERBEDS
INTERBEHAVIOR
INTERBEHAVIORAL
INTERBEHAVIORS
INTERBOROUGH
INTERBOROUGHS
INTERBRANCH
INTERBRANCHES
INTERBRED
INTERBREED
INTERBREEDING
INTERBREEDS
INTERCALARIES
INTERCALARY
INTERCALATE
INTERCALATED
INTERCALATES
INTERCALATING
INTERCALATION
INTERCALATIONS
INTERCAMPUS
INTERCASTE
INTERCASTES
INTERCEDE
INTERCEDED
INTERCEDER
INTERCEDERS
INTERCEDES
INTERCEDING
INTERCELL
INTERCELLULAR
INTERCENSAL
INTERCEPT
INTERCEPTED
INTERCEPTER
INTERCEPTERS
INTERCEPTING
INTERCEPTION
INTERCEPTIONS
INTERCEPTOR
INTERCEPTORS
INTERCEPTS
INTERCESSION
INTERCESSIONAL
INTERCESSIONS
INTERCESSOR
INTERCESSORS
INTERCESSORY
INTERCHAIN
INTERCHAINS
INTERCHANGE
INTERCHANGEABLE
INTERCHANGEABLY
INTERCHANGED
INTERCHANGER
INTERCHANGERS
INTERCHANGES
INTERCHANGING
INTERCHANNEL
INTERCHANNELS
INTERCHURCH
INTERCITY
INTERCLAN
INTERCLASS
INTERCLASSES
INTERCLUB
INTERCLUSTER
INTERCLUSTERS
INTERCOASTAL
INTERCOLLEGIATE
INTERCOLONIAL
INTERCOM
INTERCOMMUNAL
INTERCOMMUNION
INTERCOMMUNIONS
INTERCOMMUNITY
INTERCOMPANIES
INTERCOMPANY
INTERCOMPARE
INTERCOMPARED
INTERCOMPARES
INTERCOMPARING
INTERCOMPARISON
INTERCOMS
INTERCONNECT
INTERCONNECTED
INTERCONNECTING
INTERCONNECTION
INTERCONNECTS
INTERCONVERSION
INTERCONVERT
INTERCONVERTED
INTERCONVERTING
INTERCONVERTS
INTERCOOLER
INTERCOOLERS
INTERCORPORATE
INTERCORRELATE
INTERCORRELATED
INTERCORRELATES
INTERCORTICAL
INTERCOSTAL
INTERCOSTALS
INTERCOUNTIES
INTERCOUNTRIES
INTERCOUNTRY
INTERCOUNTY
INTERCOUPLE
INTERCOUPLED
INTERCOUPLES
INTERCOUPLING
INTERCOURSE
INTERCOURSES
INTERCRATER
INTERCROP
INTERCROPPED
INTERCROPPING
INTERCROPS
INTERCROSS
INTERCROSSED
INTERCROSSES
INTERCROSSING
INTERCULTURAL
INTERCULTURALLY
INTERCULTURE
INTERCULTURES
INTERCURRENT
INTERCURRENTS
INTERCUT
INTERCUTS
INTERCUTTING
INTERDEALER
INTERDEALERS
INTERDENTAL
INTERDENTALLY
INTERDEPEND
INTERDEPENDED
INTERDEPENDENCE
INTERDEPENDENCY
INTERDEPENDENT
INTERDEPENDENTS
INTERDEPENDING
INTERDEPENDS
INTERDIALECTAL
INTERDICT
INTERDICTED
INTERDICTING
INTERDICTION
INTERDICTIONS
INTERDICTIVE
INTERDICTOR
INTERDICTORS
INTERDICTORY
INTERDICTS
INTERDIFFUSE
INTERDIFFUSED
INTERDIFFUSES
INTERDIFFUSING
INTERDIFFUSION
INTERDIFFUSIONS
INTERDIGITATE
INTERDIGITATED
INTERDIGITATES
INTERDIGITATING
INTERDIGITATION
INTERDISTRICT
INTERDISTRICTS
INTERDIVISIONAL
INTERDOMINION
INTERELECTRODE
INTERELECTRON
INTERELECTRONIC
INTEREPIDEMIC
INTEREST
INTERESTED
INTERESTEDLY
INTERESTING
INTERESTINGLY
INTERESTINGNESS
INTERESTS
INTERETHNIC
INTERETHNICS
INTERFACE
INTERFACED
INTERFACES
INTERFACIAL
INTERFACING
INTERFACINGS
INTERFACULTY
INTERFAITH
INTERFAMILIAL
INTERFAMILY
INTERFERE
INTERFERED
INTERFERENCE
INTERFERENCES
INTERFERENTIAL
INTERFERER
INTERFERERS
INTERFERES
INTERFERING
INTERFEROGRAM
INTERFEROGRAMS
INTERFEROMETER
INTERFEROMETERS
INTERFEROMETRIC
INTERFEROMETRY
INTERFERON
INTERFERONS
INTERFERTILE
INTERFERTILITY
INTERFIBER
INTERFIBERS
INTERFILE
INTERFILED
INTERFILES
INTERFILING
INTERFIRM
INTERFLOW
INTERFLOWED
INTERFLOWING
INTERFLOWS
INTERFLUVE
INTERFLUVES
INTERFLUVIAL

INTERFOLD
INTERFOLDED
INTERFOLDING
INTERFOLDS
INTERFRATERNITY
INTERFUSE
INTERFUSED
INTERFUSES
INTERFUSING
INTERFUSION
INTERFUSIONS
INTERGALACTIC
INTERGANG
INTERGENERATION
INTERGENERIC
INTERGLACIAL
INTERGLACIALS
INTERGRADATION
INTERGRADATIONS
INTERGRADE
INTERGRADED
INTERGRADES
INTERGRADING
INTERGRAFT
INTERGRAFTED
INTERGRAFTING
INTERGRAFTS
INTERGRANULAR
INTERGROUP
INTERGROUPS
INTERGROWTH
INTERGROWTHS
INTERHOSPITAL
INTERIM
INTERIMS
INTERINDIVIDUAL
INTERINDUSTRY
INTERINFLUENCE
INTERINFLUENCED
INTERINFLUENCES
INTERINVOLVE
INTERINVOLVED
INTERINVOLVES
INTERINVOLVING
INTERIONIC
INTERIOR
INTERIORISE
INTERIORISED
INTERIORISES
INTERIORISING
INTERIORITIES
INTERIORITY
INTERIORIZATION
INTERIORIZE
INTERIORIZED
INTERIORIZES
INTERIORIZING
INTERIORLY
INTERIORS
INTERISLAND
INTERJECT
INTERJECTED
INTERJECTING
INTERJECTION
INTERJECTIONAL
INTERJECTIONS
INTERJECTOR
INTERJECTORS
INTERJECTORY
INTERJECTS
INTERJOIN
INTERJOINED
INTERJOINING
INTERJOINS
INTERKNIT
INTERKNITS
INTERKNITTED
INTERKNITTING
INTERKNOT
INTERKNOTS
INTERKNOTTED
INTERKNOTTING
INTERLACE
INTERLACED
INTERLACEMENT
INTERLACEMENTS
INTERLACES
INTERLACING
INTERLACUSTRINE
INTERLAID
INTERLAMINAR
INTERLAP
INTERLAPPED
INTERLAPPING
INTERLAPS
INTERLARD
INTERLARDED
INTERLARDING
INTERLARDS
INTERLAY
INTERLAYER
INTERLAYERED
INTERLAYERING
INTERLAYERS
INTERLAYING
INTERLAYS
INTERLEAF
INTERLEAGUE
INTERLEAGUES
INTERLEAVE
INTERLEAVED
INTERLEAVES
INTERLEAVING
INTERLEND
INTERLENDING
INTERLENDS
INTERLENT
INTERLEUKIN
INTERLEUKINS
INTERLIBRARY
INTERLINE
INTERLINEAR
INTERLINEARLY
INTERLINEARS
INTERLINEATION
INTERLINEATIONS
INTERLINED
INTERLINER
INTERLINERS
INTERLINES
INTERLINGUAL
INTERLINING
INTERLININGS
INTERLINK
INTERLINKED
INTERLINKING
INTERLINKS
INTERLOAN
INTERLOANS
INTERLOBULAR
INTERLOCAL
INTERLOCALS
INTERLOCK
INTERLOCKED
INTERLOCKING
INTERLOCKS
INTERLOCUTOR
INTERLOCUTORS
INTERLOCUTORY
INTERLOOP
INTERLOOPED
INTERLOOPING
INTERLOOPS
INTERLOPE
INTERLOPED
INTERLOPER
INTERLOPERS
INTERLOPES
INTERLOPING
INTERLUDE
INTERLUDES
INTERLUNAR
INTERLUNARY
INTERMALE
INTERMARGINAL
INTERMARRIAGE
INTERMARRIAGES
INTERMARRIED
INTERMARRIES
INTERMARRY
INTERMARRYING
INTERMAT
INTERMATS
INTERMATTED
INTERMATTING
INTERMEDDLE
INTERMEDDLED
INTERMEDDLER
INTERMEDDLERS
INTERMEDDLES
INTERMEDDLING
INTERMEDIACIES
INTERMEDIACY
INTERMEDIARIES
INTERMEDIARY
INTERMEDIATE
INTERMEDIATED
INTERMEDIATELY
INTERMEDIATES
INTERMEDIATING
INTERMEDIATION
INTERMEDIATIONS
INTERMEDIN
INTERMEDINS
INTERMEMBRANE
INTERMEMBRANES
INTERMENSTRUAL
INTERMENT
INTERMENTS
INTERMESH
INTERMESHED
INTERMESHES
INTERMESHING
INTERMETALLIC
INTERMETALLICS
INTERMEZZI
INTERMEZZO
INTERMEZZOS
INTERMINABLE
INTERMINABLY
INTERMINGLE
INTERMINGLED
INTERMINGLES
INTERMINGLING
INTERMISSION
INTERMISSIONS
INTERMIT
INTERMITOTIC
INTERMITS
INTERMITTED
INTERMITTENCE
INTERMITTENCES
INTERMITTENCIES
INTERMITTENCY
INTERMITTENT
INTERMITTENTLY
INTERMITTER
INTERMITTERS
INTERMITTING
INTERMIX
INTERMIXED
INTERMIXES
INTERMIXING
INTERMIXTURE
INTERMIXTURES
INTERMODAL
INTERMODULATION
INTERMOLECULAR
INTERMONT
INTERMONTANE
INTERMOUNTAIN
INTERN
INTERNAL
INTERNALISATION
INTERNALISE
INTERNALISED
INTERNALISES
INTERNALISING
INTERNALITIES
INTERNALITY
INTERNALIZATION
INTERNALIZE
INTERNALIZED
INTERNALIZES
INTERNALIZING
INTERNALLY
INTERNALS
INTERNATIONAL
INTERNATIONALLY
INTERNATIONALS
INTERNE
INTERNECINE
INTERNED
INTERNEE
INTERNEES

INTERNES
INTERNEURON
INTERNEURONAL
INTERNEURONS
INTERNING
INTERNIST
INTERNISTS
INTERNMENT
INTERNMENTS
INTERNODAL
INTERNODE
INTERNODES
INTERNS
INTERNSHIP
INTERNSHIPS
INTERNUCLEAR
INTERNUCLEON
INTERNUCLEONIC
INTERNUCLEOTIDE
INTERNUNCIAL
INTERNUNCIO
INTERNUNCIOS
INTEROBSERVER
INTEROBSERVERS
INTEROCEAN
INTEROCEANIC
INTEROCEPTIVE
INTEROCEPTOR
INTEROCEPTORS
INTEROFFICE
INTEROFFICES
INTEROPERABLE
INTEROPERATE
INTEROPERATED
INTEROPERATES
INTEROPERATING
INTEROPERATIVE
INTERORBITAL
INTERORBITALS
INTERORGAN
INTERPANDEMIC
INTERPARISH
INTERPAROCHIAL
INTERPAROXYSMAL
INTERPARTICLE
INTERPARTIES
INTERPARTY
INTERPELLATE
INTERPELLATED
INTERPELLATES
INTERPELLATING
INTERPELLATION
INTERPELLATIONS
INTERPELLATOR
INTERPELLATORS
INTERPENETRATE
INTERPENETRATED
INTERPENETRATES
INTERPERCEPTUAL
INTERPERMEATE
INTERPERMEATED
INTERPERMEATES
INTERPERMEATING
INTERPERSONAL
INTERPERSONALLY
INTERPHALANGEAL
INTERPHASE
INTERPHASES
INTERPLANETARY
INTERPLANT
INTERPLANTED
INTERPLANTING
INTERPLANTS
INTERPLAY
INTERPLAYED
INTERPLAYING
INTERPLAYS
INTERPLEAD
INTERPLEADED
INTERPLEADER
INTERPLEADERS
INTERPLEADING
INTERPLEADS
INTERPLED
INTERPLUVIAL
INTERPOINT
INTERPOLATE
INTERPOLATED
INTERPOLATES
INTERPOLATING
INTERPOLATION
INTERPOLATIONS
INTERPOLATIVE
INTERPOLATOR
INTERPOLATORS
INTERPOPULATION
INTERPOSE
INTERPOSED
INTERPOSER
INTERPOSERS
INTERPOSES
INTERPOSING
INTERPOSITION
INTERPOSITIONS
INTERPRET
INTERPRETABLE
INTERPRETATION
INTERPRETATIONS
INTERPRETATIVE
INTERPRETED
INTERPRETER
INTERPRETERS
INTERPRETING
INTERPRETIVE
INTERPRETIVELY
INTERPRETS
INTERPROVINCIAL
INTERPROXIMAL
INTERPSYCHIC
INTERPUPILLARY
INTERRACE
INTERRACIAL
INTERRACIALLY
INTERRACIALS
INTERRED
INTERREGES
INTERREGIONAL
INTERREGIONALS
INTERREGNA
INTERREGNUM
INTERREGNUMS
INTERRELATE
INTERRELATED
INTERRELATEDLY
INTERRELATES
INTERRELATING
INTERRELATION
INTERRELATIONS
INTERRELIGIOUS
INTERRENAL
INTERREX
INTERRING
INTERROBANG
INTERROBANGS
INTERROGATE
INTERROGATED
INTERROGATEE
INTERROGATEES
INTERROGATES
INTERROGATING
INTERROGATION
INTERROGATIONAL
INTERROGATIONS
INTERROGATIVE
INTERROGATIVELY
INTERROGATIVES
INTERROGATOR
INTERROGATORIES
INTERROGATORS
INTERROGATORY
INTERROGEE
INTERROGEES
INTERROW
INTERRUPT
INTERRUPTED
INTERRUPTER
INTERRUPTERS
INTERRUPTIBLE
INTERRUPTING
INTERRUPTION
INTERRUPTIONS
INTERRUPTIVE
INTERRUPTOR
INTERRUPTORS
INTERRUPTS
INTERS
INTERSCHOLASTIC
INTERSCHOOL
INTERSECT
INTERSECTED
INTERSECTING
INTERSECTION
INTERSECTIONAL
INTERSECTIONALS
INTERSECTIONS
INTERSECTS
INTERSEGMENT
INTERSEGMENTAL
INTERSEGMENTS
INTERSENSORY
INTERSERVICE
INTERSERVICES
INTERSESSION
INTERSESSIONS
INTERSEX
INTERSEXES
INTERSEXUAL
INTERSEXUALITY
INTERSEXUALLY
INTERSEXUALS
INTERSOCIETAL
INTERSOCIETY
INTERSPACE
INTERSPACED
INTERSPACES
INTERSPACING
INTERSPECIES
INTERSPECIFIC
INTERSPERSE
INTERSPERSED
INTERSPERSES
INTERSPERSING
INTERSPERSION
INTERSPERSIONS
INTERSTADIAL
INTERSTADIALS
INTERSTAGE
INTERSTAGES
INTERSTATE
INTERSTATES
INTERSTATION
INTERSTATIONS
INTERSTELLAR
INTERSTERILE
INTERSTERILITY
INTERSTICE
INTERSTICES
INTERSTIMULI
INTERSTIMULUS
INTERSTITIAL
INTERSTITIALLY
INTERSTRAIN
INTERSTRAINS
INTERSTRAND
INTERSTRANDS
INTERSTRATIFIED
INTERSTRATIFIES
INTERSTRATIFY
INTERSUBJECTIVE
INTERSYSTEM
INTERSYSTEMS
INTERTERM
INTERTERMINAL
INTERTERMINALS
INTERTEXTUAL
INTERTEXTUALITY
INTERTEXTUALLY
INTERTIDAL
INTERTIDALLY
INTERTIE
INTERTIES
INTERTILL
INTERTILLAGE
INTERTILLAGES
INTERTILLED
INTERTILLING
INTERTILLS
INTERTRIAL
INTERTRIBAL
INTERTROOP
INTERTROPICAL
INTERTWINE
INTERTWINED
INTERTWINEMENT
INTERTWINEMENTS

INTERTWINES
INTERTWINING
INTERTWIST
INTERTWISTED
INTERTWISTING
INTERTWISTS
INTERUNION
INTERUNIONS
INTERUNIT
INTERUNIVERSITY
INTERURBAN
INTERVAL
INTERVALE
INTERVALES
INTERVALLEY
INTERVALLIC
INTERVALOMETER
INTERVALOMETERS
INTERVALS
INTERVENE
INTERVENED
INTERVENER
INTERVENERS
INTERVENES
INTERVENING
INTERVENOR
INTERVENORS
INTERVENTION
INTERVENTIONAL
INTERVENTIONISM
INTERVENTIONIST
INTERVENTIONS
INTERVERTEBRAL
INTERVIEW
INTERVIEWED
INTERVIEWEE
INTERVIEWEES
INTERVIEWER
INTERVIEWERS
INTERVIEWING
INTERVIEWS
INTERVILLAGE
INTERVISIBILITY
INTERVISIBLE
INTERVISITATION
INTERVOCALIC
INTERWAR
INTERWEAVE
INTERWEAVED
INTERWEAVES
INTERWEAVING
INTERWORK
INTERWORKED
INTERWORKING
INTERWORKINGS
INTERWORKS
INTERWOVE
INTERWOVEN
INTERZONAL
INTERZONE
INTESTACIES
INTESTACY
INTESTATE
INTESTATES
INTESTINAL
INTESTINALLY
INTESTINE
INTESTINES
INTHRAL
INTHRALL
INTHRALLED
INTHRALLING
INTHRALLS
INTHRALS
INTHRONE
INTHRONED
INTHRONES
INTHRONING
INTI
INTIFADA
INTIFADAH
INTIFADAHS
INTIFADAS
INTIFADEH
INTIFADEHS
INTIMA
INTIMACIES
INTIMACY
INTIMAE
INTIMAL
INTIMAS
INTIMATE
INTIMATED
INTIMATELY
INTIMATENESS
INTIMATENESSES
INTIMATER
INTIMATERS
INTIMATES
INTIMATING
INTIMATION
INTIMATIONS
INTIME
INTIMIDATE
INTIMIDATED
INTIMIDATES
INTIMIDATING
INTIMIDATINGLY
INTIMIDATION
INTIMIDATIONS
INTIMIDATOR
INTIMIDATORS
INTIMIDATORY
INTIMIST
INTIMISTS
INTINCTION
INTINCTIONS
INTINE
INTINES
INTIS
INTITLE
INTITLED
INTITLES
INTITLING
INTITULE
INTITULED
INTITULES
INTITULING
INTO
INTOLERABILITY
INTOLERABLE
INTOLERABLENESS
INTOLERABLY
INTOLERANCE
INTOLERANCES
INTOLERANT
INTOLERANTLY
INTOLERANTNESS
INTOMB
INTOMBED
INTOMBING
INTOMBS
INTONATE
INTONATED
INTONATES
INTONATING
INTONATION
INTONATIONAL
INTONATIONS
INTONE
INTONED
INTONER
INTONERS
INTONES
INTONING
INTORT
INTORTED
INTORTING
INTORTS
INTOWN
INTOXICANT
INTOXICANTS
INTOXICATE
INTOXICATED
INTOXICATEDLY
INTOXICATES
INTOXICATING
INTOXICATION
INTOXICATIONS
INTRACARDIAC
INTRACARDIAL
INTRACARDIALLY
INTRACELLULAR
INTRACELLULARLY
INTRACEREBRAL
INTRACEREBRALLY
INTRACITY
INTRACOMPANY
INTRACRANIAL
INTRACRANIALLY
INTRACTABILITY
INTRACTABLE
INTRACTABLY
INTRACUTANEOUS
INTRADAY
INTRADERMAL
INTRADERMALLY
INTRADOS
INTRADOSES
INTRAFALLOPIAN
INTRAGALACTIC
INTRAGENIC
INTRAMOLECULAR
INTRAMURAL
INTRAMURALLY
INTRAMUSCULAR
INTRAMUSCULARLY
INTRANASAL
INTRANASALLY
INTRANET
INTRANETS
INTRANSIGEANCE
INTRANSIGEANCES
INTRANSIGEANT
INTRANSIGEANTLY
INTRANSIGEANTS
INTRANSIGENCE
INTRANSIGENCES
INTRANSIGENT
INTRANSIGENTLY
INTRANSIGENTS
INTRANSITIVE
INTRANSITIVELY
INTRANSITIVITY
INTRANT
INTRANTS
INTRAOCULAR
INTRAOCULARLY
INTRAPERITONEAL
INTRAPERSONAL
INTRAPLATE
INTRAPOPULATION
INTRAPRENEUR
INTRAPRENEURIAL
INTRAPRENEURS
INTRAPSYCHIC
INTRASPECIES
INTRASPECIFIC
INTRASTATE
INTRATHECAL
INTRATHECALLY
INTRATHORACIC
INTRAUTERINE
INTRAVASCULAR
INTRAVASCULARLY
INTRAVENOUS
INTRAVENOUSLY
INTRAVITAL
INTRAVITALLY
INTRAVITAM
INTRAZONAL
INTREAT
INTREATED
INTREATING
INTREATS
INTRENCH
INTRENCHED
INTRENCHES
INTRENCHING
INTREPID
INTREPIDITIES
INTREPIDITY
INTREPIDLY
INTREPIDNESS
INTREPIDNESSES
INTRICACIES
INTRICACY
INTRICATE
INTRICATELY
INTRICATENESS
INTRICATENESSES
INTRIGANT
INTRIGANTS
INTRIGUANT
INTRIGUANTS

INTRIGUE
INTRIGUED
INTRIGUER
INTRIGUERS
INTRIGUES
INTRIGUING
INTRIGUINGLY
INTRINSIC
INTRINSICAL
INTRINSICALLY
INTRO
INTRODUCE
INTRODUCED
INTRODUCER
INTRODUCERS
INTRODUCES
INTRODUCING
INTRODUCTION
INTRODUCTIONS
INTRODUCTORILY
INTRODUCTORY
INTROFIED
INTROFIES
INTROFY
INTROFYING
INTROGRESSANT
INTROGRESSANTS
INTROGRESSION
INTROGRESSIONS
INTROGRESSIVE
INTROIT
INTROITS
INTROJECT
INTROJECTED
INTROJECTING
INTROJECTION
INTROJECTIONS
INTROJECTS
INTROMISSION
INTROMISSIONS
INTROMIT
INTROMITS
INTROMITTED
INTROMITTENT
INTROMITTER
INTROMITTERS
INTROMITTING
INTRON
INTRONIC
INTRONS
INTRORSE
INTROS
INTROSPECT
INTROSPECTED
INTROSPECTING
INTROSPECTION
INTROSPECTIONAL
INTROSPECTIONS
INTROSPECTIVE
INTROSPECTIVELY
INTROSPECTS
INTROVERSION
INTROVERSIONS
INTROVERSIVE
INTROVERSIVELY
INTROVERT
INTROVERTED
INTROVERTING
INTROVERTS
INTRUDE
INTRUDED
INTRUDER
INTRUDERS
INTRUDES
INTRUDING
INTRUSION
INTRUSIONS
INTRUSIVE
INTRUSIVELY
INTRUSIVENESS
INTRUSIVENESSES
INTRUSIVES
INTRUST
INTRUSTED
INTRUSTING
INTRUSTS
INTUBATE
INTUBATED
INTUBATES
INTUBATING
INTUBATION
INTUBATIONS
INTUIT
INTUITABLE
INTUITED
INTUITING
INTUITION
INTUITIONAL
INTUITIONISM
INTUITIONISMS
INTUITIONIST
INTUITIONISTS
INTUITIONS
INTUITIVE
INTUITIVELY
INTUITIVENESS
INTUITIVENESSES
INTUITS
INTUMESCE
INTUMESCED
INTUMESCENCE
INTUMESCENCES
INTUMESCENT
INTUMESCES
INTUMESCING
INTURN
INTURNED
INTURNS
INTUSSUSCEPT
INTUSSUSCEPTED
INTUSSUSCEPTING
INTUSSUSCEPTION
INTUSSUSCEPTIVE
INTUSSUSCEPTS
INTWINE
INTWINED
INTWINES
INTWINING
INTWIST
INTWISTED
INTWISTING
INTWISTS
INUKSHUK
INUKSHUKS
INUKSUIT
INUKSUK
INUKSUKS
INULASE
INULASES
INULIN
INULINS
INUNCTION
INUNCTIONS
INUNDANT
INUNDATE
INUNDATED
INUNDATES
INUNDATING
INUNDATION
INUNDATIONS
INUNDATOR
INUNDATORS
INUNDATORY
INURBANE
INURE
INURED
INUREMENT
INUREMENTS
INURES
INURING
INURN
INURNED
INURNING
INURNMENT
INURNMENTS
INURNS
INUTILE
INUTILELY
INUTILITIES
INUTILITY
INVADE
INVADED
INVADER
INVADERS
INVADES
INVADING
INVAGINATE
INVAGINATED
INVAGINATES
INVAGINATING
INVAGINATION
INVAGINATIONS
INVALID
INVALIDATE
INVALIDATED
INVALIDATES
INVALIDATING
INVALIDATION
INVALIDATIONS
INVALIDATOR
INVALIDATORS
INVALIDED
INVALIDER
INVALIDEST
INVALIDING
INVALIDISM
INVALIDISMS
INVALIDITIES
INVALIDITY
INVALIDLY
INVALIDS
INVALUABLE
INVALUABLENESS
INVALUABLY
INVAR
INVARIABILITIES
INVARIABILITY
INVARIABLE
INVARIABLES
INVARIABLY
INVARIANCE
INVARIANCES
INVARIANT
INVARIANTS
INVARS
INVASION
INVASIONS
INVASIVE
INVASIVENESS
INVASIVENESSES
INVECTED
INVECTIVE
INVECTIVELY
INVECTIVENESS
INVECTIVENESSES
INVECTIVES
INVEIGH
INVEIGHED
INVEIGHER
INVEIGHERS
INVEIGHING
INVEIGHS
INVEIGLE
INVEIGLED
INVEIGLEMENT
INVEIGLEMENTS
INVEIGLER
INVEIGLERS
INVEIGLES
INVEIGLING
INVENT
INVENTED
INVENTER
INVENTERS
INVENTING
INVENTION
INVENTIONS
INVENTIVE
INVENTIVELY
INVENTIVENESS
INVENTIVENESSES
INVENTOR
INVENTORIAL
INVENTORIALLY
INVENTORIED
INVENTORIES
INVENTORS
INVENTORY
INVENTORYING
INVENTRESS
INVENTRESSES
INVENTS
INVERITIES
INVERITY
INVERNESS

INVERNESSES
INVERSE
INVERSED
INVERSELY
INVERSES
INVERSING
INVERSION
INVERSIONS
INVERSIVE
INVERT
INVERTASE
INVERTASES
INVERTEBRATE
INVERTEBRATES
INVERTED
INVERTER
INVERTERS
INVERTIBLE
INVERTIN
INVERTING
INVERTINS
INVERTOR
INVERTORS
INVERTS
INVEST
INVESTABLE
INVESTED
INVESTIGATE
INVESTIGATED
INVESTIGATES
INVESTIGATING
INVESTIGATION
INVESTIGATIONAL
INVESTIGATIONS
INVESTIGATIVE
INVESTIGATOR
INVESTIGATORS
INVESTIGATORY
INVESTING
INVESTITURE
INVESTITURES
INVESTMENT
INVESTMENTS
INVESTOR
INVESTORS
INVESTS
INVETERACIES
INVETERACY
INVETERATE
INVETERATELY
INVIABILITIES
INVIABILITY
INVIABLE
INVIABLY
INVIDIOUS
INVIDIOUSLY
INVIDIOUSNESS
INVIDIOUSNESSES
INVIGILATE
INVIGILATED
INVIGILATES
INVIGILATING
INVIGILATION
INVIGILATIONS
INVIGILATOR
INVIGILATORS
INVIGORATE
INVIGORATED
INVIGORATES
INVIGORATING
INVIGORATINGLY
INVIGORATION
INVIGORATIONS
INVIGORATOR
INVIGORATORS
INVINCIBILITIES
INVINCIBILITY
INVINCIBLE
INVINCIBLENESS
INVINCIBLY
INVIOLABILITIES
INVIOLABILITY
INVIOLABLE
INVIOLABLENESS
INVIOLABLY
INVIOLACIES
INVIOLACY
INVIOLATE
INVIOLATELY
INVIOLATENESS
INVIOLATENESSES
INVIRILE
INVISCID
INVISIBILITIES
INVISIBILITY
INVISIBLE
INVISIBLENESS
INVISIBLENESSES
INVISIBLES
INVISIBLY
INVITAL
INVITATION
INVITATIONAL
INVITATIONALS
INVITATIONS
INVITATORIES
INVITATORY
INVITE
INVITED
INVITEE
INVITEES
INVITER
INVITERS
INVITES
INVITING
INVITINGLY
INVOCATE
INVOCATED
INVOCATES
INVOCATING
INVOCATION
INVOCATIONAL
INVOCATIONS
INVOCATORY
INVOICE
INVOICED
INVOICES
INVOICING
INVOKE
INVOKED
INVOKER
INVOKERS
INVOKES
INVOKING
INVOLUCEL
INVOLUCELS
INVOLUCRA
INVOLUCRAL
INVOLUCRATE
INVOLUCRE
INVOLUCRES
INVOLUCRUM
INVOLUNTARILY
INVOLUNTARINESS
INVOLUNTARY
INVOLUTE
INVOLUTED
INVOLUTES
INVOLUTING
INVOLUTION
INVOLUTIONAL
INVOLUTIONS
INVOLVE
INVOLVED
INVOLVEDLY
INVOLVEMENT
INVOLVEMENTS
INVOLVER
INVOLVERS
INVOLVES
INVOLVING
INVULNERABILITY
INVULNERABLE
INVULNERABLY
INWALL
INWALLED
INWALLING
INWALLS
INWARD
INWARDLY
INWARDNESS
INWARDNESSES
INWARDS
INWEAVE
INWEAVED
INWEAVES
INWEAVING
INWIND
INWINDING
INWINDS
INWOUND
INWOVE
INWOVEN
INWRAP
INWRAPPED
INWRAPPING
INWRAPS
INWROUGHT
IODATE
IODATED
IODATES
IODATING
IODATION
IODATIONS
IODIC
IODID
IODIDE
IODIDES
IODIDS
IODIN
IODINATE
IODINATED
IODINATES
IODINATING
IODINATION
IODINATIONS
IODINE
IODINES
IODINS
IODISE
IODISED
IODISES
IODISING
IODISM
IODISMS
IODIZE
IODIZED
IODIZER
IODIZERS
IODIZES
IODIZING
IODOFORM
IODOFORMS
IODOMETRIES
IODOMETRY
IODOPHOR
IODOPHORS
IODOPSIN
IODOPSINS
IODOUS
IOLITE
IOLITES
ION
IONIC
IONICITIES
IONICITY
IONICS
IONISE
IONISED
IONISER
IONISERS
IONISES
IONISING
IONIUM
IONIUMS
IONIZABLE
IONIZATION
IONIZATIONS
IONIZE
IONIZED
IONIZER
IONIZERS
IONIZES
IONIZING
IONOGEN
IONOGENIC
IONOGENS
IONOMER
IONOMERS
IONONE
IONONES
IONOPHORE
IONOPHORES
IONOSONDE
IONOSONDES

IONOSPHERE
IONOSPHERES
IONOSPHERIC
IONOSPHERICALLY
IONS
IONTOPHORESES
IONTOPHORESIS
IONTOPHORETIC
IOTA
IOTACISM
IOTACISMS
IOTAS
IPECAC
IPECACS
IPECACUANHA
IPECACUANHAS
IPOMOEA
IPOMOEAS
IPRONIAZID
IPRONIAZIDS
IPSILATERAL
IPSILATERALLY
IRACUND
IRADE
IRADES
IRAIMBILANJA
RASCIBILITIES
IRASCIBILITY
IRASCIBLE
RASCIBLENESS
IRASCIBLENESSES
RASCIBLY
IRATE
RATELY
RATENESS
IRATENESSES
IRATER
RATEST
RE
RED
REFUL
IREFULLY
RELESS
RENIC
RENICAL
RENICALLY
RENICS
RES
RID
RIDES
RIDESCENCE
RIDESCENCES
RIDESCENT
IRIDESCENTLY
IRIDIC
IRIDIUM
IRIDIUMS
IRIDOLOGIES
IRIDOLOGIST
IRIDOLOGISTS
IRIDOLOGY
IRIDOSMINE
IRIDOSMINES
IRIDS
IRING
IRIS
IRISED
IRISES
IRISING
IRITIC
IRITIS
IRITISES
IRK
IRKED
IRKING
IRKS
IRKSOME
IRKSOMELY
IRKSOMENESS
IRKSOMENESSES
IROKO
IROKOS
IRON
IRONBARK
IRONBARKS
IRONBOUND
IRONCLAD
IRONCLADS
IRONE
IRONED
IRONER
IRONERS
IRONES
IRONFISTED
IRONHANDED
IRONHEARTED
IRONIC
IRONICAL
IRONICALLY
IRONICALNESS
IRONICALNESSES
IRONIER
IRONIES
IRONIEST
IRONING
IRONINGS
IRONISE
IRONISED
IRONISES
IRONISING
IRONIST
IRONISTS
IRONIZE
IRONIZED
IRONIZES
IRONIZING
IRONLESS
IRONLIKE
IRONMAN
IRONMASTER
IRONMASTERS
IRONMEN
IRONMONGER
IRONMONGERIES
IRONMONGERS
IRONMONGERY
IRONNESS
IRONNESSES
IRONS
IRONSIDE
IRONSIDES
IRONSMITH
IRONSMITHS
IRONSTONE
IRONSTONES
IRONWARE
IRONWARES
IRONWEED
IRONWEEDS
IRONWOMAN
IRONWOMEN
IRONWOOD
IRONWOODS
IRONWORK
IRONWORKER
IRONWORKERS
IRONWORKS
IRONY
IRRADIANCE
IRRADIANCES
IRRADIANT
IRRADIATE
IRRADIATED
IRRADIATES
IRRADIATING
IRRADIATION
IRRADIATIONS
IRRADIATIVE
IRRADIATOR
IRRADIATORS
IRRADICABLE
IRRADICABLY
IRRATIONAL
IRRATIONALISM
IRRATIONALISMS
IRRATIONALIST
IRRATIONALISTIC
IRRATIONALISTS
IRRATIONALITIES
IRRATIONALITY
IRRATIONALLY
IRRATIONALS
IRREAL
IRREALITIES
IRREALITY
IRRECLAIMABLE
IRRECLAIMABLY
IRRECONCILABLE
IRRECONCILABLES
IRRECONCILABLY
IRRECOVERABLE
IRRECOVERABLY
IRRECUSABLE
IRRECUSABLY
IRREDEEMABLE
IRREDEEMABLY
IRREDENTA
IRREDENTAS
IRREDENTISM
IRREDENTISMS
IRREDENTIST
IRREDENTISTS
IRREDUCIBILITY
IRREDUCIBLE
IRREDUCIBLY
IRREFLEXIVE
IRREFORMABILITY
IRREFORMABLE
IRREFRAGABILITY
IRREFRAGABLE
IRREFRAGABLY
IRREFUTABILITY
IRREFUTABLE
IRREFUTABLY
IRREGARDLESS
IRREGULAR
IRREGULARITIES
IRREGULARITY
IRREGULARLY
IRREGULARS
IRRELATIVE
IRRELATIVELY
IRRELEVANCE
IRRELEVANCES
IRRELEVANCIES
IRRELEVANCY
IRRELEVANT
IRRELEVANTLY
IRRELIGION
IRRELIGIONIST
IRRELIGIONISTS
IRRELIGIONS
IRRELIGIOUS
IRRELIGIOUSLY
IRREMEABLE
IRREMEDIABLE
IRREMEDIABLY
IRREMOVABILITY
IRREMOVABLE
IRREMOVABLY
IRREPARABLE
IRREPARABLENESS
IRREPARABLY
IRREPEALABILITY
IRREPEALABLE
IRREPLACEABLE
IRREPLACEABLY
IRREPRESSIBLE
IRREPRESSIBLY
IRREPROACHABLE
IRREPROACHABLY
IRREPRODUCIBLE
IRRESISTABILITY
IRRESISTABLE
IRRESISTABLY
IRRESISTIBILITY
IRRESISTIBLE
IRRESISTIBLY
IRRESOLUBLE
IRRESOLUTE
IRRESOLUTELY
IRRESOLUTENESS
IRRESOLUTION
IRRESOLUTIONS
IRRESOLVABLE
IRRESPONSIBLE
IRRESPONSIBLES
IRRESPONSIBLY
IRRESPONSIVE
IRRETRIEVABLE
IRRETRIEVABLY
IRREVERENCE
IRREVERENCES
IRREVERENT
IRREVERENTLY

IRREVERSIBILITY
IRREVERSIBLE
IRREVERSIBLY
IRREVOCABILITY
IRREVOCABLE
IRREVOCABLENESS
IRREVOCABLY
IRRIDENTA
IRRIDENTAS
IRRIGABLE
IRRIGABLY
IRRIGATE
IRRIGATED
IRRIGATES
IRRIGATING
IRRIGATION
IRRIGATIONS
IRRIGATOR
IRRIGATORS
IRRIGUOUS
IRRITABILITIES
IRRITABILITY
IRRITABLE
IRRITABLENESS
IRRITABLENESSES
IRRITABLY
IRRITANCIES
IRRITANCY
IRRITANT
IRRITANTS
IRRITATE
IRRITATED
IRRITATES
IRRITATING
IRRITATINGLY
IRRITATION
IRRITATIONS
IRRITATIVE
IRRITATOR
IRRITATORS
IRROTATIONAL
IRRUPT
IRRUPTED
IRRUPTING
IRRUPTION
IRRUPTIONS
IRRUPTIVE
IRRUPTIVELY
IRRUPTS
IS
ISAGOGE
ISAGOGES
ISAGOGIC
ISAGOGICS
ISALLOBAR
ISALLOBARIC
ISALLOBARS
ISARITHM
ISARITHMS
ISATIN
ISATINE
ISATINES
ISATINIC
ISATINS
ISBA
ISBAS
ISCHAEMIA
ISCHAEMIAS
ISCHEMIA
ISCHEMIAS
ISCHEMIC
ISCHIA
ISCHIADIC
ISCHIAL
ISCHIATIC
ISCHIUM
ISEIKONIA
ISEIKONIAS
ISEIKONIC
ISENTROPIC
ISENTROPICALLY
ISINGLASS
ISINGLASSES
ISLAND
ISLANDED
ISLANDER
ISLANDERS
ISLANDING
ISLANDS
ISLE
ISLED
ISLELESS
ISLES
ISLET
ISLETED
ISLETS
ISLING
ISM
ISMS
ISOAGGLUTININ
ISOAGGLUTININS
ISOALLOXAZINE
ISOALLOXAZINES
ISOANTIBODIES
ISOANTIBODY
ISOANTIGEN
ISOANTIGENIC
ISOANTIGENS
ISOBAR
ISOBARE
ISOBARES
ISOBARIC
ISOBARISM
ISOBARISMS
ISOBARS
ISOBATH
ISOBATHIC
ISOBATHS
ISOBUTANE
ISOBUTANES
ISOBUTENE
ISOBUTENES
ISOBUTYL
ISOBUTYLENE
ISOBUTYLENES
ISOBUTYLS
ISOCALORIC
ISOCARBOXAZID
ISOCARBOXAZIDS
ISOCHEIM
ISOCHEIMS
ISOCHIME
ISOCHIMES
ISOCHOR
ISOCHORE
ISOCHORES
ISOCHORIC
ISOCHORS
ISOCHROMOSOME
ISOCHROMOSOMES
ISOCHRON
ISOCHRONAL
ISOCHRONALLY
ISOCHRONE
ISOCHRONES
ISOCHRONISM
ISOCHRONISMS
ISOCHRONOUS
ISOCHRONOUSLY
ISOCHRONS
ISOCLINAL
ISOCLINALS
ISOCLINE
ISOCLINES
ISOCLINIC
ISOCLINICS
ISOCRACIES
ISOCRACY
ISOCYANATE
ISOCYANATES
ISOCYCLIC
ISODIAMETRIC
ISODOSE
ISOELECTRIC
ISOELECTRONIC
ISOENZYMATIC
ISOENZYME
ISOENZYMES
ISOENZYMIC
ISOFLAVONE
ISOFLAVONES
ISOFORM
ISOFORMS
ISOGAMETE
ISOGAMETES
ISOGAMETIC
ISOGAMIES
ISOGAMOUS
ISOGAMY
ISOGENEIC
ISOGENIC
ISOGENIES
ISOGENOUS
ISOGENY
ISOGLOSS
ISOGLOSSAL
ISOGLOSSES
ISOGLOSSIC
ISOGON
ISOGONAL
ISOGONALS
ISOGONE
ISOGONES
ISOGONIC
ISOGONICS
ISOGONIES
ISOGONS
ISOGONY
ISOGRAFT
ISOGRAFTED
ISOGRAFTING
ISOGRAFTS
ISOGRAM
ISOGRAMS
ISOGRAPH
ISOGRAPHS
ISOGRIV
ISOGRIVS
ISOHEL
ISOHELS
ISOHYET
ISOHYETAL
ISOHYETS
ISOLABLE
ISOLATABLE
ISOLATE
ISOLATED
ISOLATES
ISOLATING
ISOLATION
ISOLATIONISM
ISOLATIONISMS
ISOLATIONIST
ISOLATIONISTS
ISOLATIONS
ISOLATOR
ISOLATORS
ISOLEAD
ISOLEADS
ISOLEUCINE
ISOLEUCINES
ISOLINE
ISOLINES
ISOLOG
ISOLOGOUS
ISOLOGS
ISOLOGUE
ISOLOGUES
ISOMER
ISOMERASE
ISOMERASES
ISOMERIC
ISOMERISM
ISOMERISMS
ISOMERIZATION
ISOMERIZATIONS
ISOMERIZE
ISOMERIZED
ISOMERIZES
ISOMERIZING
ISOMEROUS
ISOMERS
ISOMETRIC
ISOMETRICALLY
ISOMETRICS
ISOMETRIES
ISOMETRY
ISOMORPH
ISOMORPHIC
ISOMORPHICALLY
ISOMORPHISM
ISOMORPHISMS
ISOMORPHOUS
ISOMORPHS
ISONIAZID

ISONIAZIDS
ISONOMIC
ISONOMIES
ISONOMY
ISOOCTANE
ISOOCTANES
ISOPACH
ISOPACHS
ISOPHOTAL
ISOPHOTE
ISOPHOTES
ISOPIESTIC
ISOPLETH
ISOPLETHIC
ISOPLETHS
ISOPOD
ISOPODAN
ISOPODANS
ISOPODS
ISOPRENALINE
ISOPRENALINES
ISOPRENE
ISOPRENES
ISOPRENOID
ISOPRENOIDS
ISOPROPYL
ISOPROPYLS
ISOPROTERENOL
ISOPROTERENOLS
ISOPYCNIC
ISOSCELES
ISOSMOTIC
ISOSMOTICALLY
ISOSPIN
ISOSPINS
ISOSPORIES
ISOSPORY
ISOSTACIES
ISOSTACY
ISOSTASIES
ISOSTASY
ISOSTATIC
ISOSTATICALLY
ISOSTERIC
ISOTACH
ISOTACHS
ISOTACTIC
ISOTHERAL
ISOTHERE
ISOTHERES
ISOTHERM
ISOTHERMAL
ISOTHERMALLY
ISOTHERMS
ISOTHIOCYANATE
ISOTHIOCYANATES
ISOTONE
ISOTONES
ISOTONIC
ISOTONICALLY
ISOTONICITIES
ISOTONICITY
ISOTOPE
ISOTOPES
ISOTOPIC
ISOTOPICALLY
ISOTOPIES
ISOTOPY
ISOTRETINOIN
ISOTRETINOINS
ISOTROPIC
ISOTROPIES
ISOTROPY
ISOTYPE
ISOTYPES
ISOTYPIC
ISOZYME
ISOZYMES
ISOZYMIC
ISSEI
ISSEIS
ISSUABLE
ISSUABLY
ISSUANCE
ISSUANCES
ISSUANT
ISSUE
ISSUED
ISSUELESS
ISSUER
ISSUERS
ISSUES
ISSUING
ISTHMI
ISTHMIAN
ISTHMIANS
ISTHMIC
ISTHMOID
ISTHMUS
ISTHMUSES
ISTLE
ISTLES
IT
ITALIANATE
ITALIANATED
ITALIANATES
ITALIANATING
ITALIANISE
ITALIANISED
ITALIANISES
ITALIANISING
ITALIANIZE
ITALIANIZED
ITALIANIZES
ITALIANIZING
ITALIC
ITALICISE
ITALICISED
ITALICISES
ITALICISING
ITALICIZATION
ITALICIZATIONS
ITALICIZE
ITALICIZED
ITALICIZES
ITALICIZING
ITALICS
ITCH
ITCHED
ITCHES
ITCHIER
ITCHIEST
ITCHILY
ITCHINESS
ITCHINESSES
ITCHING
ITCHINGS
ITCHY
ITEM
ITEMED
ITEMING
ITEMISE
ITEMISED
ITEMISER
ITEMISERS
ITEMISES
ITEMISING
ITEMIZATION
ITEMIZATIONS
ITEMIZE
ITEMIZED
ITEMIZER
ITEMIZERS
ITEMIZES
ITEMIZING
ITEMS
ITERANCE
ITERANCES
ITERANT
ITERATE
ITERATED
ITERATES
ITERATING
ITERATION
ITERATIONS
ITERATIVE
ITERATIVELY
ITERUM
ITHER
ITHYPHALLIC
ITINERACIES
ITINERACY
ITINERANCIES
ITINERANCY
ITINERANT
ITINERANTLY
ITINERANTS
ITINERARIES
ITINERARY
ITINERATE
ITINERATED
ITINERATES
ITINERATING
ITINERATION
ITINERATIONS
ITS
ITSELF
IVERMECTIN
IVERMECTINS
IVIED
IVIES
IVORIED
IVORIER
IVORIES
IVORIEST
IVORY
IVORYBILL
IVORYBILLS
IVORYLIKE
IVY
IVYLIKE
IWIS
IXIA
IXIAS
IXNAY
IXODID
IXODIDS
IXORA
IXORAS
IXTLE
IXTLES
IZAR
IZARD
IZARDS
IZARS
IZZARD
IZZARDS

J

JAB
JABBED
JABBER
JABBERED
JABBERER
JABBERERS
JABBERING
JABBERS
JABBERWOCKIES
JABBERWOCKY
JABBING
JABIRU
JABIRUS
JABORANDI
JABORANDIS
JABOT
JABOTICABA
JABOTICABAS
JABOTS
JABS
JACAL
JACALES
JACALS
JACAMAR
JACAMARS
JACANA
JACANAS
JACARANDA
JACARANDAS
JACINTH
JACINTHE
JACINTHES
JACINTHS
JACK
JACKAL
JACKALS
JACKANAPES
JACKANAPESES
JACKAROO
JACKAROOS
JACKASS
JACKASSERIES
JACKASSERY
JACKASSES
JACKBOOT
JACKBOOTED
JACKBOOTS
JACKDAW
JACKDAWS
JACKED
JACKER
JACKEROO
JACKEROOS
JACKERS
JACKET
JACKETED
JACKETING
JACKETLESS
JACKETS
JACKFISH
JACKFISHES
JACKFRUIT
JACKFRUITS
JACKHAMMER
JACKHAMMERED
JACKHAMMERING
JACKHAMMERS
JACKIES
JACKING
JACKKNIFE
JACKKNIFED
JACKKNIFES
JACKKNIFING
JACKKNIVES
JACKLEG
JACKLEGS
JACKLIGHT
JACKLIGHTED
JACKLIGHTING
JACKLIGHTS
JACKPLANE
JACKPLANES
JACKPOT
JACKPOTS
JACKRABBIT
JACKRABBITS
JACKROLL
JACKROLLED
JACKROLLING
JACKROLLS
JACKS
JACKSCREW
JACKSCREWS
JACKSHAFT
JACKSHAFTS
JACKSMELT
JACKSMELTS
JACKSNIPE
JACKSNIPES
JACKSTAY
JACKSTAYS
JACKSTONE
JACKSTONES
JACKSTRAW
JACKSTRAWS
JACKY
JACOBIN
JACOBINS
JACOBUS
JACOBUSES
JACONET
JACONETS
JACQUARD
JACQUARDS
JACQUERIE
JACQUERIES
JACTATION
JACTATIONS
JACTITATION
JACTITATIONS
JACULATE
JACULATED
JACULATES
JACULATING
JACUZZI
JACUZZIS
JADE
JADED
JADEDLY
JADEDNESS
JADEDNESSES
JADEITE
JADEITES
JADELIKE
JADES
JADING
JADISH
JADISHLY
JADITIC
JAEGER
JAEGERS
JAG
JAGER
JAGERS
JAGG
JAGGARIES
JAGGARY
JAGGED
JAGGEDER
JAGGEDEST
JAGGEDLY
JAGGEDNESS
JAGGEDNESSES
JAGGER
JAGGERIES
JAGGERS
JAGGERY
JAGGHERIES
JAGGHERY
JAGGIER
JAGGIES
JAGGIEST
JAGGING
JAGGS
JAGGY
JAGLESS
JAGRA
JAGRAS
JAGS
JAGUAR
JAGUARONDI
JAGUARONDIS
JAGUARS
JAGUARUNDI
JAGUARUNDIS
JAIL
JAILABLE
JAILBAIT
JAILBAITS
JAILBIRD
JAILBIRDS
JAILBREAK
JAILBREAKS
JAILED
JAILER
JAILERS
JAILHOUSE
JAILHOUSES
JAILING
JAILOR
JAILORS
JAILS
JAKE
JAKER
JAKES
JAKESES
JAKEST
JALAP
JALAPENO
JALAPENOS
JALAPIC
JALAPIN
JALAPINS
JALAPS
JALOP
JALOPIES
JALOPPIES
JALOPPY
JALOPS
JALOPY
JALOUSIE
JALOUSIED
JALOUSIES
JAM
JAMB
JAMBALAYA
JAMBALAYAS
JAMBE
JAMBEAU
JAMBEAUS
JAMBEAUX
JAMBED
JAMBES
JAMBING
JAMBOREE
JAMBOREES
JAMBS
JAMLIKE
JAMMABLE
JAMMED
JAMMER
JAMMERS
JAMMIER
JAMMIES
JAMMIEST
JAMMING
JAMMY
JAMPACKED
JAMS
JANE
JANES
JANGLE
JANGLED
JANGLER
JANGLERS
JANGLES
JANGLIER
JANGLIEST
JANGLING
JANGLY
JANIFORM
JANISARIES
JANISARY
JANISSARIES
JANISSARY
JANITOR
JANITORIAL
JANITORS
JANIZARIES
JANIZARY

JANNEY
JANNEYED
JANNEYING
JANNEYS
JANNIED
JANNIES
JANNY
JANNYING
JANNYINGS
JANTY
JAPAN
JAPANIZE
JAPANIZED
JAPANIZES
JAPANIZING
JAPANNED
JAPANNER
JAPANNERS
JAPANNING
JAPANS
JAPE
JAPED
JAPER
JAPERIES
JAPERS
JAPERY
JAPES
JAPING
JAPINGLY
JAPONAISERIE
JAPONAISERIES
JAPONICA
JAPONICAS
JAR
JARDINIERE
JARDINIERES
JARFUL
JARFULS
JARGON
JARGONED
JARGONEER
JARGONEERS
JARGONEL
JARGONELS
JARGONIER
JARGONIEST
JARGONING
JARGONISH
JARGONIST
JARGONISTIC
JARGONISTS
JARGONIZE
JARGONIZED
JARGONIZES
JARGONIZING
JARGONS
JARGONY
JARGOON
JARGOONS
JARHEAD
JARHEADS
JARINA
JARINAS
JARL
JARLDOM
JARLDOMS
JARLS
JARLSBERG
JARLSBERGS
JAROSITE
JAROSITES
JAROVIZE
JAROVIZED
JAROVIZES
JAROVIZING
JARRAH
JARRAHS
JARRED
JARRING
JARRINGLY
JARS
JARSFUL
JARVEY
JARVEYS
JASMIN
JASMINE
JASMINES
JASMINS
JASPER
JASPERS
JASPERWARE
JASPERWARES
JASPERY
JASPILITE
JASPILITES
JASSID
JASSIDS
JATO
JATOS
JAUK
JAUKED
JAUKING
JAUKS
JAUNCE
JAUNCED
JAUNCES
JAUNCING
JAUNDICE
JAUNDICED
JAUNDICES
JAUNDICING
JAUNT
JAUNTED
JAUNTIER
JAUNTIEST
JAUNTILY
JAUNTINESS
JAUNTINESSES
JAUNTING
JAUNTS
JAUNTY
JAUP
JAUPED
JAUPING
JAUPS
JAVA
JAVAS
JAVELIN
JAVELINA
JAVELINAS
JAVELINED
JAVELINING
JAVELINS
JAW
JAWAN
JAWANS
JAWBONE
JAWBONED
JAWBONER
JAWBONERS
JAWBONES
JAWBONING
JAWBONINGS
JAWBREAKER
JAWBREAKERS
JAWED
JAWING
JAWLESS
JAWLIKE
JAWLINE
JAWLINES
JAWS
JAY
JAYBIRD
JAYBIRDS
JAYGEE
JAYGEES
JAYHAWKER
JAYHAWKERS
JAYS
JAYVEE
JAYVEES
JAYWALK
JAYWALKED
JAYWALKER
JAYWALKERS
JAYWALKING
JAYWALKS
JAZZ
JAZZBO
JAZZBOS
JAZZED
JAZZER
JAZZERS
JAZZES
JAZZIER
JAZZIEST
JAZZILY
JAZZINESS
JAZZINESSES
JAZZING
JAZZLIKE
JAZZMAN
JAZZMEN
JAZZY
JEALOUS
JEALOUSER
JEALOUSEST
JEALOUSIES
JEALOUSLY
JEALOUSNESS
JEALOUSNESSES
JEALOUSY
JEAN
JEANED
JEANS
JEBEL
JEBELS
JEE
JEED
JEEING
JEEP
JEEPED
JEEPERS
JEEPING
JEEPNEY
JEEPNEYS
JEEPS
JEER
JEERED
JEERER
JEERERS
JEERING
JEERINGLY
JEERS
JEES
JEESLIER
JEESLIEST
JEESLY
JEEZ
JEEZE
JEEZELIER
JEEZELIEST
JEEZELY
JEEZLIER
JEEZLIEST
JEEZLY
JEFE
JEFES
JEHAD
JEHADI
JEHADIS
JEHADIST
JEHADISTS
JEHADS
JEHU
JEHUS
JEJUNA
JEJUNAL
JEJUNE
JEJUNELY
JEJUNENESS
JEJUNENESSES
JEJUNITIES
JEJUNITY
JEJUNUM
JEJUNUMS
JELL
JELLABA
JELLABAS
JELLED
JELLIED
JELLIES
JELLIFIED
JELLIFIES
JELLIFY
JELLIFYING
JELLING
JELLO
JELLOS
JELLS
JELLY
JELLYBEAN
JELLYBEANS
JELLYFISH

JELLYFISHES
JELLYING
JELLYLIKE
JELLYROLL
JELLYROLLS
JELUTONG
JELUTONGS
JEMADAR
JEMADARS
JEMIDAR
JEMIDARS
JEMMIED
JEMMIES
JEMMY
JEMMYING
JENNET
JENNETS
JENNIES
JENNY
JEON
JEOPARD
JEOPARDED
JEOPARDIES
JEOPARDING
JEOPARDISE
JEOPARDISED
JEOPARDISES
JEOPARDISING
JEOPARDIZE
JEOPARDIZED
JEOPARDIZES
JEOPARDIZING
JEOPARDS
JEOPARDY
JEQUIRITIES
JEQUIRITY
JERBOA
JERBOAS
JEREED
JEREEDS
JEREMIAD
JEREMIADS
JERID
JERIDS
JERK
JERKED
JERKER
JERKERS
JERKIER
JERKIES
JERKIEST
JERKILY
JERKIN
JERKINESS
JERKINESSES
JERKING
JERKINGLY
JERKINS
JERKS
JERKWATER
JERKWATERS
JERKY
JEROBOAM
JEROBOAMS
JERREED
JERREEDS
JERRICAN
JERRICANS
JERRID
JERRIDS
JERRIES
JERRY
JERRYCAN
JERRYCANS
JERSEY
JERSEYED
JERSEYS
JESS
JESSAMINE
JESSAMINES
JESSANT
JESSE
JESSED
JESSES
JESSING
JEST
JESTED
JESTER
JESTERS
JESTFUL
JESTING
JESTINGLY
JESTINGS
JESTS
JESUIT
JESUITIC
JESUITICAL
JESUITICALLY
JESUITISM
JESUITISMS
JESUITRIES
JESUITRY
JESUITS
JET
JETBEAD
JETBEADS
JETE
JETES
JETFOIL
JETFOILS
JETLAG
JETLAGS
JETLIKE
JETLINER
JETLINERS
JETON
JETONS
JETPACK
JETPACKS
JETPORT
JETPORTS
JETS
JETSAM
JETSAMS
JETSOM
JETSOMS
JETSTREAM
JETSTREAMS
JETTED
JETTIED
JETTIER
JETTIES
JETTIEST
JETTINESS
JETTINESSES
JETTING
JETTISON
JETTISONABLE
JETTISONED
JETTISONING
JETTISONS
JETTON
JETTONS
JETTY
JETTYING
JETWAY
JETWAYS
JEU
JEUX
JEW
JEWED
JEWEL
JEWELED
JEWELER
JEWELERS
JEWELFISH
JEWELFISHES
JEWELING
JEWELLED
JEWELLER
JEWELLERIES
JEWELLERS
JEWELLERY
JEWELLIKE
JEWELLING
JEWELRIES
JEWELRY
JEWELS
JEWELWEED
JEWELWEEDS
JEWFISH
JEWFISHES
JEWING
JEWS
JEZAIL
JEZAILS
JEZEBEL
JEZEBELS
JIAO
JIB
JIBB
JIBBA
JIBBAH
JIBBAHS
JIBBAS
JIBBED
JIBBER
JIBBERS
JIBBING
JIBBOOM
JIBBOOMS
JIBBS
JIBE
JIBED
JIBER
JIBERS
JIBES
JIBING
JIBINGLY
JIBS
JICAMA
JICAMAS
JIFF
JIFFIES
JIFFS
JIFFY
JIG
JIGABOO
JIGABOOS
JIGGED
JIGGER
JIGGERED
JIGGERING
JIGGERS
JIGGIER
JIGGIEST
JIGGING
JIGGISH
JIGGLE
JIGGLED
JIGGLES
JIGGLIER
JIGGLIEST
JIGGLING
JIGGLY
JIGGY
JIGLIKE
JIGS
JIGSAW
JIGSAWED
JIGSAWING
JIGSAWN
JIGSAWS
JIHAD
JIHADI
JIHADIS
JIHADIST
JIHADISTS
JIHADS
JILL
JILLION
JILLIONS
JILLS
JILT
JILTED
JILTER
JILTERS
JILTING
JILTS
JIMINY
JIMJAMS
JIMMIE
JIMMIED
JIMMIES
JIMMINY
JIMMY
JIMMYING
JIMP
JIMPER
JIMPEST
JIMPLY
JIMPY
JIMSON
JIMSONS
JIMSONWEED

JIMSONWEEDS
JIN
JINGAL
JINGALL
JINGALLS
JINGALS
JINGKO
JINGKOES
JINGLE
JINGLED
JINGLER
JINGLERS
JINGLES
JINGLIER
JINGLIEST
JINGLING
JINGLY
JINGO
JINGOES
JINGOISH
JINGOISM
JINGOISMS
JINGOIST
JINGOISTIC
JINGOISTICALLY
JINGOISTS
JINK
JINKED
JINKER
JINKERS
JINKING
JINKS
JINN
JINNEE
JINNI
JINNIS
JINNS
JINRICKSHA
JINRICKSHAS
JINRIKISHA
JINRIKISHAS
JINRIKSHA
JINRIKSHAS
JINS
JINX
JINXED
JINXES
JINXING
JIPIJAPA
JIPIJAPAS
JIRD
JIRDS
JISM
JISMS
JITNEY
JITNEYS
JITTER
JITTERBUG
JITTERBUGGED
JITTERBUGGING
JITTERBUGS
JITTERED
JITTERIER
JITTERIEST
JITTERINESS
JITTERINESSES
JITTERING
JITTERS
JITTERY
JIUJITSU
JIUJITSUS
JIUJUTSU
JIUJUTSUS
JIVE
JIVEASS
JIVED
JIVER
JIVERS
JIVES
JIVEST
JIVEY
JIVIER
JIVIEST
JIVING
JIVY
JIZZ
JIZZES
JNANA
JNANAS
JO
JOANNES
JOB
JOBBED
JOBBER
JOBBERIES
JOBBERS
JOBBERY
JOBBIE
JOBBIES
JOBBING
JOBHOLDER
JOBHOLDERS
JOBLESS
JOBLESSNESS
JOBLESSNESSES
JOBNAME
JOBNAMES
JOBS
JOCK
JOCKDOM
JOCKDOMS
JOCKETTE
JOCKETTES
JOCKEY
JOCKEYED
JOCKEYING
JOCKEYISH
JOCKEYS
JOCKIER
JOCKIEST
JOCKISH
JOCKO
JOCKOS
JOCKS
JOCKSTRAP
JOCKSTRAPS
JOCKY
JOCOSE
JOCOSELY
JOCOSENESS
JOCOSENESSES
JOCOSER
JOCOSEST
JOCOSITIES
JOCOSITY
JOCULAR
JOCULARITIES
JOCULARITY
JOCULARLY
JOCUND
JOCUNDER
JOCUNDEST
JOCUNDITIES
JOCUNDITY
JOCUNDLY
JODHPUR
JODHPURS
JOE
JOES
JOEY
JOEYS
JOG
JOGGED
JOGGER
JOGGERS
JOGGING
JOGGINGS
JOGGLE
JOGGLED
JOGGLER
JOGGLERS
JOGGLES
JOGGLING
JOGS
JOGTROT
JOGTROTS
JOGTROTTED
JOGTROTTING
JOHANNES
JOHN
JOHNBOAT
JOHNBOATS
JOHNNIE
JOHNNIES
JOHNNY
JOHNNYCAKE
JOHNNYCAKES
JOHNS
JOHNSON
JOHNSONGRASS
JOHNSONGRASSES
JOHNSONS
JOIN
JOINABLE
JOINDER
JOINDERS
JOINED
JOINER
JOINERIES
JOINERS
JOINERY
JOINING
JOININGS
JOINS
JOINT
JOINTED
JOINTEDLY
JOINTEDNESS
JOINTEDNESSES
JOINTER
JOINTERS
JOINTING
JOINTLESS
JOINTLY
JOINTRESS
JOINTRESSES
JOINTS
JOINTURE
JOINTURED
JOINTURES
JOINTURING
JOINTWEED
JOINTWEEDS
JOINTWORM
JOINTWORMS
JOIST
JOISTED
JOISTING
JOISTS
JOJOBA
JOJOBAS
JOKE
JOKED
JOKER
JOKERS
JOKES
JOKESTER
JOKESTERS
JOKEY
JOKIER
JOKIEST
JOKILY
JOKINESS
JOKINESSES
JOKING
JOKINGLY
JOKY
JOLE
JOLES
JOLLIED
JOLLIER
JOLLIERS
JOLLIES
JOLLIEST
JOLLIFICATION
JOLLIFICATIONS
JOLLIFIED
JOLLIFIES
JOLLIFY
JOLLIFYING
JOLLILY
JOLLINESS
JOLLINESSES
JOLLITIES
JOLLITY
JOLLY
JOLLYBOAT
JOLLYBOATS
JOLLYING
JOLT
JOLTED
JOLTER
JOLTERS
JOLTIER
JOLTIEST

JOLTILY
JOLTING
JOLTINGLY
JOLTS
JOLTY
JOMON
JONES
JONESED
JONESES
JONESING
JONGLEUR
JONGLEURS
JONNYCAKE
JONNYCAKES
JONQUIL
JONQUILS
JOOK
JOOKS
JORAM
JORAMS
JORDAN
JORDANS
JORUM
JORUMS
JOSEPH
JOSEPHS
JOSH
JOSHED
JOSHER
JOSHERS
JOSHES
JOSHING
JOSHINGLY
JOSHINGS
JOSS
JOSSES
JOSTLE
JOSTLED
JOSTLER
JOSTLERS
JOSTLES
JOSTLING
JOT
JOTA
JOTAS
JOTS
JOTTED
JOTTER
JOTTERS
JOTTING
JOTTINGS
JOTTY
JOUAL
JOUALS
JOUK
JOUKED
JOUKING
JOUKS
JOULE
JOULES
JOUNCE
JOUNCED
JOUNCES
JOUNCIER
JOUNCIEST
JOUNCING
JOUNCY
JOURNAL
JOURNALED
JOURNALESE
JOURNALESES
JOURNALING
JOURNALISM
JOURNALISMS
JOURNALIST
JOURNALISTIC
JOURNALISTS
JOURNALIZE
JOURNALIZED
JOURNALIZER
JOURNALIZERS
JOURNALIZES
JOURNALIZING
JOURNALS
JOURNEY
JOURNEYED
JOURNEYER
JOURNEYERS
JOURNEYING
JOURNEYMAN
JOURNEYMEN
JOURNEYS
JOURNEYWORK
JOURNEYWORKS
JOURNO
JOURNOS
JOUST
JOUSTED
JOUSTER
JOUSTERS
JOUSTING
JOUSTINGS
JOUSTS
JOVIAL
JOVIALITIES
JOVIALITY
JOVIALLY
JOVIALTIES
JOVIALTY
JOW
JOWAR
JOWARS
JOWED
JOWING
JOWL
JOWLED
JOWLIER
JOWLIEST
JOWLINESS
JOWLINESSES
JOWLS
JOWLY
JOWS
JOY
JOYANCE
JOYANCES
JOYED
JOYFUL
JOYFULLER
JOYFULLEST
JOYFULLY
JOYFULNESS
JOYFULNESSES
JOYING
JOYLESS
JOYLESSLY
JOYLESSNESS
JOYLESSNESSES
JOYOUS
JOYOUSLY
JOYOUSNESS
JOYOUSNESSES
JOYPAD
JOYPADS
JOYPOP
JOYPOPPED
JOYPOPPER
JOYPOPPERS
JOYPOPPING
JOYPOPS
JOYRIDDEN
JOYRIDE
JOYRIDER
JOYRIDERS
JOYRIDES
JOYRIDING
JOYRIDINGS
JOYRODE
JOYS
JOYSTICK
JOYSTICKS
JUBA
JUBAS
JUBBAH
JUBBAHS
JUBE
JUBES
JUBHAH
JUBHAHS
JUBILANCE
JUBILANCES
JUBILANT
JUBILANTLY
JUBILARIAN
JUBILARIANS
JUBILATE
JUBILATED
JUBILATES
JUBILATING
JUBILATION
JUBILATIONS
JUBILE
JUBILEE
JUBILEES
JUBILES
JUCO
JUCOS
JUDAS
JUDASES
JUDDER
JUDDERED
JUDDERIER
JUDDERIEST
JUDDERING
JUDDERS
JUDDERY
JUDGE
JUDGED
JUDGEMENT
JUDGEMENTAL
JUDGEMENTS
JUDGER
JUDGERS
JUDGES
JUDGESHIP
JUDGESHIPS
JUDGING
JUDGMATIC
JUDGMATICAL
JUDGMATICALLY
JUDGMENT
JUDGMENTAL
JUDGMENTALLY
JUDGMENTS
JUDICABLE
JUDICARE
JUDICARES
JUDICATORIES
JUDICATORY
JUDICATURE
JUDICATURES
JUDICIAL
JUDICIALLY
JUDICIARIES
JUDICIARY
JUDICIOUS
JUDICIOUSLY
JUDICIOUSNESS
JUDICIOUSNESSES
JUDIES
JUDO
JUDOIST
JUDOISTS
JUDOKA
JUDOKAS
JUDOS
JUDY
JUG
JUGA
JUGAL
JUGATE
JUGFUL
JUGFULS
JUGGED
JUGGERNAUT
JUGGERNAUTS
JUGGING
JUGGLE
JUGGLED
JUGGLER
JUGGLERIES
JUGGLERS
JUGGLERY
JUGGLES
JUGGLING
JUGGLINGS
JUGHEAD
JUGHEADS
JUGS
JUGSFUL
JUGULA
JUGULAR
JUGULARS
JUGULATE
JUGULATED

JUGULATES
JUGULATING
JUGULUM
JUGUM
JUGUMS
JUICE
JUICED
JUICEHEAD
JUICEHEADS
JUICELESS
JUICER
JUICERS
JUICES
JUICIER
JUICIEST
JUICILY
JUICINESS
JUICINESSES
JUICING
JUICY
JUJITSU
JUJITSUS
JUJU
JUJUBE
JUJUBES
JUJUISM
JUJUISMS
JUJUIST
JUJUISTS
JUJUS
JUJUTSU
JUJUTSUS
JUKE
JUKEBOX
JUKEBOXES
JUKED
JUKES
JUKING
JUKU
JUKUS
JULEP
JULEPS
JULIENNE
JULIENNED
JULIENNES
JULIENNING
JUMAR
JUMARED
JUMARING
JUMARRED
JUMARRING
JUMARS
JUMBAL
JUMBALS
JUMBIE
JUMBIES
JUMBLE
JUMBLED
JUMBLER
JUMBLERS
JUMBLES
JUMBLING
JUMBO
JUMBOS
JUMBUCK
JUMBUCKS
JUMP
JUMPABLE
JUMPED
JUMPER
JUMPERS
JUMPIER
JUMPIEST
JUMPILY
JUMPINESS
JUMPINESSES
JUMPING
JUMPINGLY
JUMPINGS
JUMPMASTER
JUMPMASTERS
JUMPOFF
JUMPOFFS
JUMPROPE
JUMPROPES
JUMPS
JUMPSHOT
JUMPSHOTS
JUMPSIES
JUMPSUIT
JUMPSUITS
JUMPY
JUN
JUNCO
JUNCOES
JUNCOS
JUNCTION
JUNCTIONAL
JUNCTIONS
JUNCTURAL
JUNCTURE
JUNCTURES
JUNGLE
JUNGLED
JUNGLEGYM
JUNGLEGYMS
JUNGLELIKE
JUNGLES
JUNGLIER
JUNGLIEST
JUNGLIST
JUNGLISTS
JUNGLY
JUNIOR
JUNIORATE
JUNIORATES
JUNIORED
JUNIORING
JUNIORITIES
JUNIORITY
JUNIORS
JUNIPER
JUNIPERS
JUNK
JUNKED
JUNKER
JUNKERS
JUNKET
JUNKETED
JUNKETEER
JUNKETEERED
JUNKETEERING
JUNKETEERS
JUNKETER
JUNKETERS
JUNKETING
JUNKETINGS
JUNKETS
JUNKIE
JUNKIER
JUNKIES
JUNKIEST
JUNKING
JUNKMAN
JUNKMEN
JUNKS
JUNKY
JUNKYARD
JUNKYARDS
JUNTA
JUNTAS
JUNTO
JUNTOS
JUPE
JUPES
JUPON
JUPONS
JURA
JURAL
JURALLY
JURANT
JURANTS
JURASSIC
JURAT
JURATORY
JURATS
JUREL
JURELS
JURIDIC
JURIDICAL
JURIDICALLY
JURIED
JURIES
JURISCONSULT
JURISCONSULTS
JURISDICTION
JURISDICTIONAL
JURISDICTIONS
JURISPRUDENCE
JURISPRUDENCES
JURISPRUDENT
JURISPRUDENTIAL
JURISPRUDENTS
JURIST
JURISTIC
JURISTICALLY
JURISTS
JUROR
JURORS
JURY
JURYING
JURYLESS
JURYMAN
JURYMEN
JURYWOMAN
JURYWOMEN
JUS
JUSES
JUSSIVE
JUSSIVES
JUST
JUSTED
JUSTER
JUSTERS
JUSTEST
JUSTICE
JUSTICES
JUSTICIABILITY
JUSTICIABLE
JUSTICIAR
JUSTICIARS
JUSTIFIABILITY
JUSTIFIABLE
JUSTIFIABLY
JUSTIFICATION
JUSTIFICATIONS
JUSTIFICATIVE
JUSTIFICATORY
JUSTIFIED
JUSTIFIER
JUSTIFIERS
JUSTIFIES
JUSTIFY
JUSTIFYING
JUSTING
JUSTLE
JUSTLED
JUSTLES
JUSTLING
JUSTLY
JUSTNESS
JUSTNESSES
JUSTS
JUT
JUTE
JUTELIKE
JUTES
JUTS
JUTTED
JUTTIED
JUTTIES
JUTTING
JUTTINGLY
JUTTY
JUTTYING
JUVENAL
JUVENALS
JUVENESCENCE
JUVENESCENCES
JUVENESCENT
JUVENILE
JUVENILES
JUVENILIA
JUVENILITIES
JUVENILITY
JUVIE
JUVIES
JUXTAPOSE
JUXTAPOSED
JUXTAPOSES
JUXTAPOSING
JUXTAPOSITION
JUXTAPOSITIONAL
JUXTAPOSITIONS

KA
KAAS
KAB
KABAB
KABABS
KABADDI
KABADDIS
KABAKA
KABAKAS
KABALA
KABALAS
KABALISM
KABALISMS
KABALIST
KABALISTS
KABAR
KABARS
KABAYA
KABAYAS
KABBALA
KABBALAH
KABBALAHS
KABBALAS
KABBALISM
KABBALISMS
KABBALIST
KABBALISTIC
KABBALISTS
KABELJOU
KABELJOUS
KABIKI
KABIKIS
KABLOOEY
KABLOOIE
KABLOONA
KABLOONAS
KABLOONAT
KABOB
KABOBS
KABOCHA
KABOCHAS
KABOODLE
KABOODLES
KABOOM
KABOOMS
KABS
KABUKI
KABUKIS
KACHINA
KACHINAS
KADDISH
KADDISHES
KADDISHIM
KADI
KADIS
KAE
KAES
KAF
KAFFEEKLATSCH
KAFFEEKLATSCHES
KAFFIR
KAFFIRS
KAFFIYAH
KAFFIYAHS
KAFFIYEH
KAFFIYEHS
KAFIR
KAFIRS
KAFS
KAFTAN
KAFTANS
KAFUFFLE
KAFUFFLES
KAGU
KAGUS
KAHUNA
KAHUNAS
KAIAK
KAIAKS
KAIF
KAIFS
KAIL
KAILS
KAILYARD
KAILYARDS
KAIN
KAINIT
KAINITE
KAINITES
KAINITS
KAINS
KAIROMONE
KAIROMONES
KAISER
KAISERDOM
KAISERDOMS
KAISERIN
KAISERINS
KAISERISM
KAISERISMS
KAISERS
KAIZEN
KAIZENS
KAJEPUT
KAJEPUTS
KAKA
KAKAPO
KAKAPOS
KAKAS
KAKEMONO
KAKEMONOS
KAKI
KAKIEMON
KAKIEMONS
KAKIS
KAKIVAK
KAKIVAKS
KALAM
KALAMATA
KALAMATAS
KALAMS
KALANCHOE
KALANCHOES
KALE
KALEIDOSCOPE
KALEIDOSCOPES
KALEIDOSCOPIC
KALENDS
KALES
KALEWIFE
KALEWIVES
KALEYARD
KALEYARDS
KALIAN
KALIANS
KALIF
KALIFATE
KALIFATES
KALIFS
KALIMBA
KALIMBAS
KALIPH
KALIPHATE
KALIPHATES
KALIPHS
KALIUM
KALIUMS
KALLIDIN
KALLIDINS
KALLIKREIN
KALLIKREINS
KALMIA
KALMIAS
KALONG
KALONGS
KALPA
KALPAC
KALPACS
KALPAK
KALPAKS
KALPAS
KALSOMINE
KALSOMINED
KALSOMINES
KALSOMINING
KALYPTRA
KALYPTRAS
KAMAAINA
KAMAAINAS
KAMACITE
KAMACITES
KAMALA
KAMALAS
KAME
KAMEEZ
KAMEEZES
KAMES
KAMI
KAMIK
KAMIKAZE
KAMIKAZES
KAMIKS
KAMOTIK
KAMOTIKS
KAMOTIQ
KAMOTIQS
KAMPONG
KAMPONGS
KAMSEEN
KAMSEENS
KAMSIN
KAMSINS
KANA
KANAKA
KANAKAS
KANAMYCIN
KANAMYCINS
KANAS
KANBAN
KANBANS
KANE
KANES
KANGAROO
KANGAROOS
KANJI
KANJIS
KANTAR
KANTARS
KANTELE
KANTELES
KANZU
KANZUS
KAOLIANG
KAOLIANGS
KAOLIN
KAOLINE
KAOLINES
KAOLINIC
KAOLINITE
KAOLINITES
KAOLINITIC
KAOLINS
KAON
KAONIC
KAONS
KAPA
KAPAS
KAPEEK
KAPELLMEISTER
KAPELLMEISTERS
KAPEYKA
KAPH
KAPHS
KAPOK
KAPOKS
KAPOW
KAPOWS
KAPPA
KAPPAS
KAPU
KAPUS
KAPUT
KAPUTT
KARABINER
KARABINERS
KARAHI
KARAHIS
KARAKUL
KARAKULS
KARAOKE
KARAOKES
KARAT
KARATE
KARATEIST
KARATEISTS
KARATES
KARATS
KARMA
KARMAS
KARMIC

KARN
KARNS
KAROO
KAROOS
KAROSS
KAROSSES
KARRI
KARRIS
KARROO
KARROOS
KARST
KARSTIC
KARSTS
KART
KARTING
KARTINGS
KARTS
KARYOGAMIES
KARYOGAMY
KARYOKINESES
KARYOKINESIS
KARYOKINETIC
KARYOLOGIC
KARYOLOGICAL
KARYOLOGIES
KARYOLOGY
KARYOLYMPH
KARYOLYMPHS
KARYOSOME
KARYOSOMES
KARYOTIN
KARYOTINS
KARYOTYPE
KARYOTYPED
KARYOTYPES
KARYOTYPIC
KARYOTYPICALLY
KARYOTYPING
KAS
KASBAH
KASBAHS
KASHA
KASHAS
KASHER
KASHERED
KASHERING
KASHERS
KASHMIR
KASHMIRS
KASHRUT
KASHRUTH
KASHRUTHS
KASHRUTS
KAT
KATA
KATABATIC
KATAKANA
KATAKANAS
KATANA
KATANAS
KATAS
KATCHINA
KATCHINAS
KATCINA
KATCINAS
KATHARSES
KATHARSIS
KATHODAL
KATHODE
KATHODES
KATHODIC
KATHUMP
KATHUMPS
KATION
KATIONS
KATS
KATSINA
KATSINAM
KATSINAS
KATSURA
KATSURAS
KATYDID
KATYDIDS
KATZENJAMMER
KATZENJAMMERS
KAURI
KAURIES
KAURIS
KAURY
KAVA
KAVAKAVA
KAVAKAVAS
KAVAS
KAVASS
KAVASSES
KAY
KAYAK
KAYAKED
KAYAKER
KAYAKERS
KAYAKING
KAYAKINGS
KAYAKS
KAYLES
KAYO
KAYOED
KAYOES
KAYOING
KAYOS
KAYS
KAZACHKI
KAZACHOC
KAZACHOCS
KAZACHOK
KAZATSKI
KAZATSKIES
KAZATSKY
KAZILLION
KAZILLIONS
KAZOO
KAZOOS
KBAR
KBARS
KEA
KEAS
KEBAB
KEBABS
KEBAR
KEBARS
KEBBIE
KEBBIES
KEBBOCK
KEBBOCKS
KEBBUCK
KEBBUCKS
KEBLAH
KEBLAHS
KEBOB
KEBOBS
KECK
KECKED
KECKING
KECKLE
KECKLED
KECKLES
KECKLING
KECKS
KEDDAH
KEDDAHS
KEDGE
KEDGED
KEDGEREE
KEDGEREES
KEDGES
KEDGING
KEEF
KEEFS
KEEK
KEEKED
KEEKING
KEEKS
KEEL
KEELAGE
KEELAGES
KEELBOAT
KEELBOATS
KEELED
KEELHALE
KEELHALED
KEELHALES
KEELHALING
KEELHAUL
KEELHAULED
KEELHAULING
KEELHAULS
KEELING
KEELLESS
KEELS
KEELSON
KEELSONS
KEEN
KEENED
KEENER
KEENERS
KEENEST
KEENING
KEENINGS
KEENLY
KEENNESS
KEENNESSES
KEENS
KEEP
KEEPABLE
KEEPER
KEEPERS
KEEPING
KEEPINGS
KEEPS
KEEPSAKE
KEEPSAKES
KEESHOND
KEESHONDEN
KEESHONDS
KEESTER
KEESTERS
KEET
KEETS
KEEVE
KEEVES
KEF
KEFFIYAH
KEFFIYAHS
KEFFIYEH
KEFFIYEHS
KEFIR
KEFIRS
KEFS
KEG
KEGELER
KEGELERS
KEGGED
KEGGER
KEGGERS
KEGGING
KEGLER
KEGLERS
KEGLING
KEGLINGS
KEGS
KEIR
KEIRETSU
KEIRETSUS
KEIRS
KEISTER
KEISTERS
KEITLOA
KEITLOAS
KELEP
KELEPS
KELIM
KELIMS
KELLIES
KELLY
KELOID
KELOIDAL
KELOIDS
KELP
KELPED
KELPFISH
KELPFISHES
KELPIE
KELPIES
KELPING
KELPS
KELPY
KELSON
KELSONS
KELT
KELTER
KELTERS
KELTS
KELVIN
KELVINS
KEMP
KEMPIER

KEMPIEST
KEMPS
KEMPT
KEMPY
KEN
KENAF
KENAFS
KENCH
KENCHES
KENDO
KENDOIST
KENDOISTS
KENDOS
KENNED
KENNEL
KENNELED
KENNELING
KENNELLED
KENNELLING
KENNELS
KENNING
KENNINGS
KENO
KENOS
KENOSIS
KENOSISES
KENOTIC
KENOTRON
KENOTRONS
KENS
KENSPECKLE
KENT
KENTE
KENTES
KENTLEDGE
KENTLEDGES
KEP
KEPHALIN
KEPHALINS
KEPI
KEPIS
KEPPED
KEPPEN
KEPPING
KEPS
KEPT
KERAMIC
KERAMICS
KERATECTOMIES
KERATECTOMY
KERATIN
KERATINIZATION
KERATINIZATIONS
KERATINIZE
KERATINIZED
KERATINIZES
KERATINIZING
KERATINOPHILIC
KERATINOUS
KERATINS
KERATITIDES
KERATITIS
KERATITISES
KERATOID
KERATOMA
KERATOMAS
KERATOMATA
KERATOMILEUSES
KERATOMILEUSIS
KERATOPLASTIES
KERATOPLASTY
KERATOSE
KERATOSES
KERATOSIC
KERATOSIS
KERATOTIC
KERB
KERBED
KERBING
KERBS
KERBSIDE
KERBSIDES
KERCHIEF
KERCHIEFED
KERCHIEFS
KERCHIEVES
KERCHOO
KERF
KERFED
KERFING
KERFLOOEY
KERFS
KERFUFFLE
KERFUFFLES
KERMES
KERMESES
KERMESS
KERMESSE
KERMESSES
KERMIS
KERMISES
KERMODE
KERMODES
KERN
KERNE
KERNED
KERNEL
KERNELED
KERNELING
KERNELLED
KERNELLING
KERNELLY
KERNELS
KERNES
KERNING
KERNINGS
KERNITE
KERNITES
KERNS
KEROGEN
KEROGENS
KEROSENE
KEROSENES
KEROSINE
KEROSINES
KERPLUNK
KERPLUNKED
KERPLUNKING
KERPLUNKS
KERRIA
KERRIAS
KERRIES
KERRY
KERSEY
KERSEYMERE
KERSEYMERES
KERSEYS
KERYGMA
KERYGMAS
KERYGMATA
KERYGMATIC
KESTREL
KESTRELS
KETA
KETAINE
KETAINER
KETAMINE
KETAMINES
KETAS
KETCH
KETCHES
KETCHUP
KETCHUPIER
KETCHUPIEST
KETCHUPS
KETCHUPY
KETENE
KETENES
KETO
KETOCONAZOLE
KETOCONAZOLES
KETOGENESES
KETOGENESIS
KETOGENIC
KETOL
KETOLS
KETONE
KETONEMIA
KETONEMIAS
KETONES
KETONIC
KETONURIA
KETONURIAS
KETOSE
KETOSES
KETOSIS
KETOSTEROID
KETOSTEROIDS
KETOTIC
KETTLE
KETTLEBELL
KETTLEBELLS
KETTLEDRUM
KETTLEDRUMS
KETTLES
KEVEL
KEVELS
KEVIL
KEVILS
KEWPIE
KEWPIES
KEX
KEXES
KEY
KEYBOARD
KEYBOARDED
KEYBOARDER
KEYBOARDERS
KEYBOARDING
KEYBOARDIST
KEYBOARDISTS
KEYBOARDS
KEYBUTTON
KEYBUTTONS
KEYCARD
KEYCARDS
KEYED
KEYER
KEYERS
KEYEST
KEYFRAME
KEYFRAMES
KEYHOLE
KEYHOLES
KEYING
KEYLESS
KEYNOTE
KEYNOTED
KEYNOTER
KEYNOTERS
KEYNOTES
KEYNOTING
KEYPAD
KEYPADS
KEYPAL
KEYPALS
KEYPRESS
KEYPRESSES
KEYPUNCH
KEYPUNCHED
KEYPUNCHER
KEYPUNCHERS
KEYPUNCHES
KEYPUNCHING
KEYS
KEYSET
KEYSETS
KEYSTER
KEYSTERS
KEYSTONE
KEYSTONES
KEYSTROKE
KEYSTROKED
KEYSTROKES
KEYSTROKING
KEYWAY
KEYWAYS
KEYWORD
KEYWORDS
KHADDAR
KHADDARS
KHADI
KHADIS
KHAF
KHAFS
KHAKI
KHAKILIKE
KHAKIS
KHALIF
KHALIFA
KHALIFAS
KHALIFATE
KHALIFATES
KHALIFS
KHAMSEEN

KHAMSEENS
KHAMSIN
KHAMSINS
KHAN
KHANATE
KHANATES
KHANS
KHAPH
KHAPHS
KHAT
KHATS
KHAZEN
KHAZENIM
KHAZENS
KHEDA
KHEDAH
KHEDAHS
KHEDAS
KHEDIVAL
KHEDIVE
KHEDIVES
KHEDIVIAL
KHET
KHETH
KHETHS
KHETS
KHI
KHIRKAH
KHIRKAHS
KHIS
KHOUM
KHOUMS
KI
KIACK
KIACKS
KIANG
KIANGS
KIAUGH
KIAUGHS
KIBBE
KIBBEH
KIBBEHS
KIBBES
KIBBI
KIBBIS
KIBBITZ
KIBBITZED
KIBBITZER
KIBBITZERS
KIBBITZES
KIBBITZING
KIBBLE
KIBBLED
KIBBLES
KIBBLING
KIBBUTZ
KIBBUTZIM
KIBBUTZNIK
KIBBUTZNIKS
KIBE
KIBEI
KIBEIS
KIBES
KIBITKA
KIBITKAS
KIBITZ
KIBITZED
KIBITZER
KIBITZERS
KIBITZES
KIBITZING
KIBLA
KIBLAH
KIBLAHS
KIBLAS
KIBOSH
KIBOSHED
KIBOSHES
KIBOSHING
KICK
KICKABLE
KICKBACK
KICKBACKS
KICKBALL
KICKBALLS
KICKBOARD
KICKBOARDS
KICKBOX
KICKBOXED
KICKBOXER
KICKBOXERS
KICKBOXES
KICKBOXING
KICKBOXINGS
KICKED
KICKER
KICKERS
KICKIER
KICKIEST
KICKING
KICKINGS
KICKOFF
KICKOFFS
KICKS
KICKSHAW
KICKSHAWS
KICKSTAND
KICKSTANDS
KICKSTART
KICKSTARTED
KICKSTARTING
KICKSTARTS
KICKUP
KICKUPS
KICKY
KID
KIDDED
KIDDER
KIDDERS
KIDDIE
KIDDIES
KIDDING
KIDDINGLY
KIDDISH
KIDDO
KIDDOES
KIDDOS
KIDDUSH
KIDDUSHES
KIDDY
KIDLIKE
KIDLIT
KIDLITS
KIDNAP
KIDNAPED
KIDNAPEE
KIDNAPEES
KIDNAPER
KIDNAPERS
KIDNAPING
KIDNAPPED
KIDNAPPEE
KIDNAPPEES
KIDNAPPER
KIDNAPPERS
KIDNAPPING
KIDNAPS
KIDNEY
KIDNEYS
KIDS
KIDSKIN
KIDSKINS
KIDVID
KIDVIDS
KIEF
KIEFS
KIELBASA
KIELBASAS
KIELBASI
KIELBASY
KIER
KIERS
KIESELGUHR
KIESELGUHRS
KIESELGUR
KIESELGURS
KIESERITE
KIESERITES
KIESTER
KIESTERS
KIF
KIFS
KIKE
KIKES
KIKUYU
KIKUYUS
KILDERKIN
KILDERKINS
KILIM
KILIMS
KILL
KILLABLE
KILLDEE
KILLDEER
KILLDEERS
KILLDEES
KILLED
KILLER
KILLERS
KILLICK
KILLICKS
KILLIE
KILLIES
KILLIFISH
KILLIFISHES
KILLING
KILLINGLY
KILLINGS
KILLJOY
KILLJOYS
KILLOCK
KILLOCKS
KILLS
KILN
KILNED
KILNING
KILNS
KILO
KILOBAR
KILOBARS
KILOBASE
KILOBASES
KILOBAUD
KILOBAUDS
KILOBIT
KILOBITS
KILOBYTE
KILOBYTES
KILOCALORIE
KILOCALORIES
KILOCURIE
KILOCURIES
KILOCYCLE
KILOCYCLES
KILOGAUSS
KILOGAUSSES
KILOGRAM
KILOGRAMS
KILOHERTZ
KILOHERTZES
KILOJOULE
KILOJOULES
KILOLITER
KILOLITERS
KILOLITRE
KILOLITRES
KILOMETER
KILOMETERS
KILOMETRE
KILOMETRES
KILOMOLE
KILOMOLES
KILOPARSEC
KILOPARSECS
KILOPASCAL
KILOPASCALS
KILORAD
KILORADS
KILOS
KILOTON
KILOTONS
KILOVOLT
KILOVOLTS
KILOWATT
KILOWATTS
KILT
KILTED
KILTER
KILTERS
KILTIE
KILTIES
KILTING
KILTINGS
KILTLIKE
KILTS

KILTY
KIMBERLITE
KIMBERLITES
KIMCHEE
KIMCHEES
KIMCHI
KIMCHIS
KIMONO
KIMONOED
KIMONOS
KIN
KINA
KINARA
KINARAS
KINAS
KINASE
KINASES
KIND
KINDA
KINDER
KINDERGARTEN
KINDERGARTENER
KINDERGARTENERS
KINDERGARTENS
KINDERGARTNER
KINDERGARTNERS
KINDEST
KINDHEARTED
KINDHEARTEDLY
KINDHEARTEDNESS
KINDLE
KINDLED
KINDLER
KINDLERS
KINDLES
KINDLESS
KINDLESSLY
KINDLIER
KINDLIEST
KINDLINESS
KINDLINESSES
KINDLING
KINDLINGS
KINDLY
KINDNESS
KINDNESSES
KINDRED
KINDREDS
KINDS
KINE
KINEMA
KINEMAS
KINEMATIC
KINEMATICAL
KINEMATICALLY
KINEMATICS
KINES
KINESCOPE
KINESCOPED
KINESCOPES
KINESCOPING
KINESES
KINESIC
KINESICS
KINESIOLOGIES
KINESIOLOGIST
KINESIOLOGISTS
KINESIOLOGY
KINESIS
KINESISES
KINESTHESES
KINESTHESIA
KINESTHESIAS
KINESTHESIS
KINESTHETIC
KINESTHETICALLY
KINETIC
KINETICALLY
KINETICIST
KINETICISTS
KINETICS
KINETIN
KINETINS
KINETOCHORE
KINETOCHORES
KINETOPLAST
KINETOPLASTS
KINETOSCOPE
KINETOSCOPES
KINETOSOME
KINETOSOMES
KINFOLK
KINFOLKS
KING
KINGBIRD
KINGBIRDS
KINGBOLT
KINGBOLTS
KINGCRAFT
KINGCRAFTS
KINGCUP
KINGCUPS
KINGDOM
KINGDOMS
KINGED
KINGFISH
KINGFISHER
KINGFISHERS
KINGFISHES
KINGHOOD
KINGHOODS
KINGING
KINGLESS
KINGLET
KINGLETS
KINGLIER
KINGLIEST
KINGLIKE
KINGLINESS
KINGLINESSES
KINGLY
KINGMAKER
KINGMAKERS
KINGPIN
KINGPINS
KINGPOST
KINGPOSTS
KINGS
KINGSHIP
KINGSHIPS
KINGSIDE
KINGSIDES
KINGSNAKE
KINGSNAKES
KINGWOOD
KINGWOODS
KININ
KININS
KINK
KINKAJOU
KINKAJOUS
KINKED
KINKIER
KINKIEST
KINKILY
KINKINESS
KINKINESSES
KINKING
KINKS
KINKY
KINLESS
KINNIKINNICK
KINNIKINNICKS
KINO
KINOS
KINS
KINSFOLK
KINSHIP
KINSHIPS
KINSMAN
KINSMEN
KINSWOMAN
KINSWOMEN
KIOSK
KIOSKS
KIP
KIPPA
KIPPAH
KIPPAHS
KIPPAS
KIPPED
KIPPEN
KIPPER
KIPPERED
KIPPERER
KIPPERERS
KIPPERING
KIPPERS
KIPPING
KIPS
KIPSKIN
KIPSKINS
KIR
KIRIGAMI
KIRIGAMIS
KIRK
KIRKMAN
KIRKMEN
KIRKS
KIRMESS
KIRMESSES
KIRN
KIRNED
KIRNING
KIRNS
KIRPAN
KIRPANS
KIRS
KIRSCH
KIRSCHES
KIRTLE
KIRTLED
KIRTLES
KIS
KISHKA
KISHKAS
KISHKE
KISHKES
KISKADEE
KISKADEES
KISMAT
KISMATS
KISMET
KISMETIC
KISMETS
KISS
KISSABLE
KISSABLY
KISSED
KISSER
KISSERS
KISSES
KISSIER
KISSIEST
KISSING
KISSY
KIST
KISTFUL
KISTFULS
KISTS
KIT
KITBAG
KITBAGS
KITCHEN
KITCHENET
KITCHENETS
KITCHENETTE
KITCHENETTES
KITCHENS
KITCHENWARE
KITCHENWARES
KITE
KITEBOARDING
KITEBOARDINGS
KITED
KITELIKE
KITER
KITERS
KITES
KITH
KITHARA
KITHARAS
KITHE
KITHED
KITHES
KITHING
KITHS
KITING
KITINGS
KITLING
KITLINGS
KITS
KITSCH
KITSCHES
KITSCHIER

KITSCHIEST
KITSCHIFIED
KITSCHIFIES
KITSCHIFY
KITSCHIFYING
KITSCHY
KITTED
KITTEL
KITTEN
KITTENED
KITTENING
KITTENISH
KITTENISHLY
KITTENISHNESS
KITTENISHNESSES
KITTENS
KITTIES
KITTING
KITTIWAKE
KITTIWAKES
KITTLE
KITTLED
KITTLER
KITTLES
KITTLEST
KITTLING
KITTY
KIVA
KIVAS
KIWI
KIWIFRUIT
KIWIFRUITS
KIWIS
KLATCH
KLATCHES
KLATSCH
KLATSCHES
KLAVERN
KLAVERNS
KLAXON
KLAXONS
KLEAGLE
KLEAGLES
KLEBSIELLA
KLEBSIELLAS
KLEENEX
KLEENEXES
KLEPHT
KLEPHTIC
KLEPHTS
KLEPTO
KLEPTOCRACIES
KLEPTOCRACY
KLEPTOCRAT
KLEPTOCRATIC
KLEPTOCRATS
KLEPTOMANIA
KLEPTOMANIAC
KLEPTOMANIACS
KLEPTOMANIAS
KLEPTOS
KLEZMER
KLEZMERS
KLEZMORIM
KLICK
KLICKS
KLIEG
KLIEGS
KLIK
KLIKS
KLISTER
KLISTERS
KLONDIKE
KLONDIKES
KLONG
KLONGS
KLOOF
KLOOFS
KLUDGE
KLUDGED
KLUDGES
KLUDGEY
KLUDGIER
KLUDGIEST
KLUDGING
KLUDGY
KLUGE
KLUGED
KLUGES
KLUGING
KLUTZ
KLUTZES
KLUTZIER
KLUTZIEST
KLUTZINESS
KLUTZINESSES
KLUTZY
KLYSTRON
KLYSTRONS
KNACK
KNACKED
KNACKER
KNACKERED
KNACKERIES
KNACKERING
KNACKERS
KNACKERY
KNACKING
KNACKS
KNACKWURST
KNACKWURSTS
KNAIDEL
KNAIDELS
KNAIDLACH
KNAP
KNAPPED
KNAPPER
KNAPPERS
KNAPPING
KNAPS
KNAPSACK
KNAPSACKED
KNAPSACKS
KNAPWEED
KNAPWEEDS
KNAR
KNARRED
KNARRY
KNARS
KNAUR
KNAURS
KNAVE
KNAVERIES
KNAVERY
KNAVES
KNAVISH
KNAVISHLY
KNAWE
KNAWEL
KNAWELS
KNAWES
KNEAD
KNEADABLE
KNEADED
KNEADER
KNEADERS
KNEADING
KNEADS
KNEE
KNEECAP
KNEECAPPED
KNEECAPPING
KNEECAPPINGS
KNEECAPS
KNEED
KNEEHOLE
KNEEHOLES
KNEEING
KNEEL
KNEELED
KNEELER
KNEELERS
KNEELING
KNEELS
KNEEPAD
KNEEPADS
KNEEPAN
KNEEPANS
KNEEPIECE
KNEEPIECES
KNEES
KNEESIES
KNEESOCK
KNEESOCKS
KNEIDEL
KNEIDELS
KNEIDLACH
KNELL
KNELLED
KNELLING
KNELLS
KNELT
KNESSET
KNESSETS
KNEW
KNICKERBOCKER
KNICKERBOCKERS
KNICKERS
KNICKKNACK
KNICKKNACKS
KNIFE
KNIFED
KNIFELIKE
KNIFEPOINT
KNIFEPOINTS
KNIFER
KNIFERS
KNIFES
KNIFING
KNIFINGS
KNIGHT
KNIGHTED
KNIGHTHOOD
KNIGHTHOODS
KNIGHTING
KNIGHTLIER
KNIGHTLIEST
KNIGHTLINESS
KNIGHTLINESSES
KNIGHTLY
KNIGHTS
KNISH
KNISHES
KNIT
KNITBONE
KNITBONES
KNITS
KNITTABLE
KNITTED
KNITTER
KNITTERS
KNITTING
KNITTINGS
KNITWEAR
KNIVES
KNOB
KNOBBED
KNOBBIER
KNOBBIEST
KNOBBING
KNOBBLIER
KNOBBLIEST
KNOBBLY
KNOBBY
KNOBKERRIE
KNOBKERRIES
KNOBLIKE
KNOBS
KNOCK
KNOCKABOUT
KNOCKABOUTS
KNOCKBACK
KNOCKBACKS
KNOCKDOWN
KNOCKDOWNS
KNOCKED
KNOCKER
KNOCKERS
KNOCKING
KNOCKLESS
KNOCKOFF
KNOCKOFFS
KNOCKOUT
KNOCKOUTS
KNOCKS
KNOCKWURST
KNOCKWURSTS
KNOLL
KNOLLED
KNOLLER
KNOLLERS
KNOLLING
KNOLLS
KNOLLY
KNOP

KNOPPED
KNOPS
KNOSP
KNOSPS
KNOT
KNOTGRASS
KNOTGRASSES
KNOTHEAD
KNOTHEADS
KNOTHOLE
KNOTHOLES
KNOTLESS
KNOTLIKE
KNOTS
KNOTTED
KNOTTER
KNOTTERS
KNOTTIER
KNOTTIEST
KNOTTILY
KNOTTINESS
KNOTTINESSES
KNOTTING
KNOTTINGS
KNOTTY
KNOTWEED
KNOTWEEDS
KNOUT
KNOUTED
KNOUTING
KNOUTS
KNOW
KNOWABLE
KNOWER
KNOWERS
KNOWING
KNOWINGER
KNOWINGEST
KNOWINGLY
KNOWINGNESS
KNOWINGNESSES
KNOWINGS
KNOWLEDGE
KNOWLEDGEABLE
KNOWLEDGEABLY
KNOWLEDGES
KNOWN
KNOWNS
KNOWS
KNUBBIER
KNUBBIEST
KNUBBY
KNUCKLE
KNUCKLEBALL
KNUCKLEBALLER
KNUCKLEBALLERS
KNUCKLEBALLS
KNUCKLEBONE
KNUCKLEBONES
KNUCKLED
KNUCKLEHEAD
KNUCKLEHEADED
KNUCKLEHEADS
KNUCKLER
KNUCKLERS
KNUCKLES
KNUCKLIER
KNUCKLIEST
KNUCKLING
KNUCKLY
KNUR
KNURL
KNURLED
KNURLIER
KNURLIEST
KNURLING
KNURLS
KNURLY
KNURR
KNURRS
KNURS
KOA
KOALA
KOALAS
KOAN
KOANS
KOAS
KOB
KOBO
KOBOLD
KOBOLDS
KOBOS
KOBS
KOCHIA
KOCHIAS
KOEL
KOELS
KOFTA
KOFTAS
KOHL
KOHLRABI
KOHLRABIES
KOHLS
KOI
KOINE
KOINES
KOIS
KOJI
KOJIS
KOKAM
KOKAMS
KOKANEE
KOKANEES
KOKUM
KOKUMS
KOLA
KOLACKY
KOLAS
KOLBASI
KOLBASIS
KOLBASSA
KOLBASSAS
KOLBASSI
KOLBASSIS
KOLHOZ
KOLHOZES
KOLHOZY
KOLINSKI
KOLINSKIES
KOLINSKY
KOLKHOS
KOLKHOSES
KOLKHOSY
KOLKHOZ
KOLKHOZES
KOLKHOZNIK
KOLKHOZNIKI
KOLKHOZNIKS
KOLKHOZY
KOLKOZ
KOLKOZES
KOLKOZY
KOLO
KOLOS
KOMATIK
KOMATIKS
KOMBU
KOMBUS
KOMONDOR
KOMONDOROCK
KOMONDOROK
KOMONDORS
KONGONI
KONK
KONKED
KONKING
KONKS
KOODOO
KOODOOS
KOOK
KOOKABURRA
KOOKABURRAS
KOOKIE
KOOKIER
KOOKIEST
KOOKILY
KOOKINESS
KOOKINESSES
KOOKS
KOOKUM
KOOKUMS
KOOKY
KOP
KOPECK
KOPECKS
KOPEK
KOPEKS
KOPH
KOPHS
KOPIYKA
KOPIYKAS
KOPJE
KOPJES
KOPPA
KOPPAS
KOPPIE
KOPPIES
KOPS
KOR
KORA
KORAI
KORAS
KORAT
KORATS
KORE
KORMA
KORMAS
KORS
KORUN
KORUNA
KORUNAS
KORUNY
KOS
KOSHER
KOSHERED
KOSHERING
KOSHERS
KOSS
KOTO
KOTOS
KOTOW
KOTOWED
KOTOWER
KOTOWERS
KOTOWING
KOTOWS
KOUMIS
KOUMISES
KOUMISS
KOUMISSES
KOUMYS
KOUMYSES
KOUMYSS
KOUMYSSES
KOUPREY
KOUPREYS
KOUROI
KOUROS
KOUSSO
KOUSSOS
KOWTOW
KOWTOWED
KOWTOWER
KOWTOWERS
KOWTOWING
KOWTOWS
KRAAL
KRAALED
KRAALING
KRAALS
KRAFT
KRAFTS
KRAI
KRAIS
KRAIT
KRAITS
KRAKEN
KRAKENS
KRATER
KRATERS
KRAUT
KRAUTS
KRAY
KRAYS
KREEP
KREEPS
KREMLIN
KREMLINOLOGIES
KREMLINOLOGIST
KREMLINOLOGISTS
KREMLINOLOGY
KREMLINS
KREPLACH
KREPLECH
KREUTZER

KREUTZERS
KREUZER
KREUZERS
KREWE
KREWES
KRILL
KRILLS
KRIMMER
KRIMMERS
KRIS
KRISES
KRONA
KRONE
KRONEN
KRONER
KRONOR
KRONUR
KROON
KROONI
KROONS
KRUBI
KRUBIS
KRUBUT
KRUBUTS
KRULLER
KRULLERS
KRUMHORN
KRUMHORNS
KRUMKAKE
KRUMKAKES
KRUMMHOLZ
KRUMMHORN
KRUMMHORNS
KRYOLITE
KRYOLITES
KRYOLITH
KRYOLITHS
KRYPTON
KRYPTONS
KUBASA
KUBASAS
KUBIE
KUBIES
KUCHEN
KUCHENS
KUDLIK
KUDLIKS
KUDO
KUDOS
KUDOSES
KUDU
KUDUS
KUDZU
KUDZUS
KUE
KUES
KUFI
KUFIS
KUGEL
KUGELS
KUKRI
KUKRIS
KULAK
KULAKI
KULAKS
KULFI
KULFIS
KULTUR
KULTURS
KUMIS
KUMISES
KUMISS
KUMISSES
KUMKUM
KUMKUMS
KUMMEL
KUMMELS
KUMQUAT
KUMQUATS
KUMYS
KUMYSES
KUNA
KUNDALINI
KUNDALINIS
KUNE
KUNZITE
KUNZITES
KURBASH
KURBASHED
KURBASHES
KURBASHING
KURGAN
KURGANS
KURRAJONG
KURRAJONGS
KURTA
KURTAS
KURTOSES
KURTOSIS
KURTOSISES
KURU
KURUS
KURUSH
KURUSHES
KUSSO
KUSSOS
KUVASZ
KUVASZOK
KVAS
KVASES
KVASS
KVASSES
KVELL
KVELLED
KVELLING
KVELLS
KVETCH
KVETCHED
KVETCHER
KVETCHERS
KVETCHES
KVETCHIER
KVETCHIEST
KVETCHING
KVETCHY
KWACHA
KWACHAS
KWANZA
KWANZAS
KWASHIORKOR
KWASHIORKORS
KYACK
KYACKS
KYAK
KYAKS
KYANISE
KYANISED
KYANISES
KYANISING
KYANITE
KYANITES
KYANITIC
KYANIZE
KYANIZED
KYANIZES
KYANIZING
KYAR
KYARS
KYAT
KYATS
KYBOSH
KYBOSHED
KYBOSHES
KYBOSHING
KYE
KYES
KYLIKES
KYLIN
KYLINS
KYLIX
KYLIXES
KYMOGRAM
KYMOGRAMS
KYMOGRAPH
KYMOGRAPHIC
KYMOGRAPHIES
KYMOGRAPHS
KYMOGRAPHY
KYPHOSES
KYPHOSIS
KYPHOTIC
KYRIE
KYRIES
KYTE
KYTES
KYTHE
KYTHED
KYTHES
KYTHING

L

LA
LAAGER
LAAGERED
LAAGERING
LAAGERS
LAARI
LAARIS
LAB
LABANOTATION
LABANOTATIONS
LABARA
LABARUM
LABARUMS
LABDANUM
LABDANUMS
LABEL
LABELABLE
LABELED
LABELER
LABELERS
LABELING
LABELLA
LABELLATE
LABELLED
LABELLER
LABELLERS
LABELLING
LABELLOID
LABELLUM
LABELMATE
LABELMATES
LABELS
LABIA
LABIAL
LABIALITIES

LABIALITY
LABIALIZATION
LABIALIZATIONS
LABIALIZE
LABIALIZED
LABIALIZES
LABIALIZING
LABIALLY
LABIALS
LABIATE
LABIATED
LABIATES
LABILE
LABILITIES
LABILITY
LABIODENTAL
LABIODENTALS
LABIOVELAR
LABIOVELARS
LABIUM
LABOR
LABORATORIES
LABORATORY
LABORED
LABOREDLY
LABORER
LABORERS
LABORING
LABORIOUS
LABORIOUSLY
LABORIOUSNESS
LABORIOUSNESSES
LABORITE
LABORITES
LABORS
LABORSAVING
LABOUR
LABOURED
LABOURER
LABOURERS
LABOURING
LABOURS
LABRA
LABRADOODLE
LABRADOODLES
LABRADOR
LABRADORITE
LABRADORITES
LABRADORS
LABRAL
LABRET
LABRETS
LABROID
LABROIDS
LABRUM
LABRUMS
LABRUSCA
LABRUSCAS
LABS
LABURNUM
LABURNUMS
LABYRINTH
LABYRINTHIAN
LABYRINTHINE
LABYRINTHODONT
LABYRINTHODONTS
LABYRINTHS
LAC
LACCOLITH
LACCOLITHIC
LACCOLITHS
LACE
LACED
LACELESS
LACELIKE
LACER
LACERABLE
LACERATE
LACERATED
LACERATES
LACERATING
LACERATION
LACERATIONS
LACERATIVE
LACERS
LACERTID
LACERTIDS
LACES
LACEWING
LACEWINGS
LACEWOOD
LACEWOODS
LACEWORK
LACEWORKS
LACEY
LACHES
LACHESES
LACHRYMAL
LACHRYMALS
LACHRYMATOR
LACHRYMATORS
LACHRYMOSE
LACHRYMOSELY
LACHRYMOSITIES
LACHRYMOSITY
LACIER
LACIEST
LACILY
LACINESS
LACINESSES
LACING
LACINGS
LACINIATE
LACINIATION
LACINIATIONS
LACK
LACKADAISICAL
LACKADAISICALLY
LACKADAY
LACKED
LACKER
LACKERED
LACKERING
LACKERS
LACKEY
LACKEYED
LACKEYING
LACKEYS
LACKING
LACKLUSTER
LACKLUSTERS
LACKLUSTRE
LACKS
LACONIC
LACONICALLY
LACONISM
LACONISMS
LACQUER
LACQUERED
LACQUERER
LACQUERERS
LACQUERING
LACQUERS
LACQUERWARE
LACQUERWARES
LACQUERWORK
LACQUERWORKS
LACQUEY
LACQUEYED
LACQUEYING
LACQUEYS
LACRIMAL
LACRIMALS
LACRIMATION
LACRIMATIONS
LACRIMATOR
LACRIMATORS
LACROSSE
LACROSSES
LACRYMAL
LACRYMALS
LACS
LACTALBUMIN
LACTALBUMINS
LACTAM
LACTAMS
LACTARY
LACTASE
LACTASES
LACTATE
LACTATED
LACTATES
LACTATING
LACTATION
LACTATIONAL
LACTATIONS
LACTEAL
LACTEALLY
LACTEALS
LACTEAN
LACTEOUS
LACTIC
LACTIFEROUS
LACTITOL
LACTITOLS
LACTOBACILLI
LACTOBACILLUS
LACTOGENIC
LACTOGLOBULIN
LACTOGLOBULINS
LACTONE
LACTONES
LACTONIC
LACTOSE
LACTOSES
LACUNA
LACUNAE
LACUNAL
LACUNAR
LACUNARIA
LACUNARS
LACUNARY
LACUNAS
LACUNATE
LACUNE
LACUNES
LACUNOSE
LACUSTRINE
LACY
LAD
LADANUM
LADANUMS
LADDER
LADDERED
LADDERING
LADDERLIKE
LADDERS
LADDIE
LADDIER
LADDIES
LADDIEST
LADDISH
LADDISHNESS
LADDISHNESSES
LADDISM
LADDISMS
LADDY
LADE
LADED
LADEN
LADENED
LADENING
LADENS
LADER
LADERS
LADES
LADHOOD
LADHOODS
LADIES
LADING
LADINGS
LADINO
LADINOS
LADLE
LADLED
LADLEFUL
LADLEFULS
LADLER
LADLERS
LADLES
LADLING
LADRON
LADRONE
LADRONES
LADRONS
LADS
LADY
LADYBIRD
LADYBIRDS
LADYBUG
LADYBUGS
LADYFINGER
LADYFINGERS
LADYFISH
LADYFISHES

LADYHOOD
LADYHOODS
LADYISH
LADYKIN
LADYKINS
LADYLIKE
LADYLOVE
LADYLOVES
LADYNESS
LADYNESSES
LADYPALM
LADYPALMS
LADYSHIP
LADYSHIPS
LAETRILE
LAETRILES
LAEVO
LAG
LAGAN
LAGANS
LAGEND
LAGENDS
LAGER
LAGERED
LAGERING
LAGERS
LAGGARD
LAGGARDLY
LAGGARDNESS
LAGGARDNESSES
LAGGARDS
LAGGED
LAGGER
LAGGERS
LAGGING
LAGGINGS
LAGNAPPE
LAGNAPPES
LAGNIAPPE
LAGNIAPPES
LAGOMORPH
LAGOMORPHS
LAGOON
LAGOONAL
LAGOONS
LAGS
LAGUNA
LAGUNAS
LAGUNE
LAGUNES
LAH
LAHAL
LAHALS
LAHAR
LAHARS
LAHS
LAIC
LAICAL
LAICALLY
LAICH
LAICHS
LAICISE
LAICISED
LAICISES
LAICISING
LAICISM
LAICISMS
LAICIZATION
LAICIZATIONS
LAICIZE
LAICIZED
LAICIZES
LAICIZING
LAICS
LAID
LAIGH
LAIGHS
LAIN
LAIR
LAIRAGE
LAIRAGES
LAIRD
LAIRDLY
LAIRDS
LAIRDSHIP
LAIRDSHIPS
LAIRED
LAIRIER
LAIRIEST
LAIRING
LAIRS
LAIRY
LAITANCE
LAITANCES
LAITH
LAITHLY
LAITIES
LAITY
LAKE
LAKEBED
LAKEBEDS
LAKED
LAKEFILL
LAKEFILLS
LAKEFRONT
LAKEFRONTS
LAKEHEAD
LAKEHEADS
LAKELAND
LAKELANDS
LAKELIKE
LAKEPORT
LAKEPORTS
LAKER
LAKERS
LAKES
LAKESHORE
LAKESHORES
LAKESIDE
LAKESIDES
LAKEVIEW
LAKEWARD
LAKEWARDS
LAKH
LAKHS
LAKIER
LAKIEST
LAKING
LAKINGS
LAKY
LALIQUE
LALIQUES
LALL
LALLAN
LALLAND
LALLANDS
LALLANS
LALLATION
LALLATIONS
LALLED
LALLING
LALLS
LALLYGAG
LALLYGAGGED
LALLYGAGGER
LALLYGAGGERS
LALLYGAGGING
LALLYGAGS
LAM
LAMA
LAMAS
LAMASERIES
LAMASERY
LAMB
LAMBADA
LAMBADAS
LAMBAST
LAMBASTE
LAMBASTED
LAMBASTES
LAMBASTING
LAMBASTS
LAMBDA
LAMBDAS
LAMBDOID
LAMBED
LAMBENCIES
LAMBENCY
LAMBENT
LAMBENTLY
LAMBER
LAMBERS
LAMBERT
LAMBERTS
LAMBIE
LAMBIER
LAMBIES
LAMBIEST
LAMBING
LAMBINGS
LAMBKILL
LAMBKILLS
LAMBKIN
LAMBKINS
LAMBLIKE
LAMBREQUIN
LAMBREQUINS
LAMBRUSCO
LAMBRUSCOS
LAMBS
LAMBSKIN
LAMBSKINS
LAMBSWOOL
LAMBSWOOLS
LAMBY
LAME
LAMEBRAIN
LAMEBRAINED
LAMEBRAINS
LAMED
LAMEDH
LAMEDHS
LAMEDS
LAMELLA
LAMELLAE
LAMELLAR
LAMELLAS
LAMELLATE
LAMELLATELY
LAMELLIBRANCH
LAMELLIBRANCHS
LAMELLICORN
LAMELLICORNS
LAMELLIFORM
LAMELLOSE
LAMELY
LAMENESS
LAMENESSES
LAMENT
LAMENTABLE
LAMENTABLENESS
LAMENTABLY
LAMENTATION
LAMENTATIONS
LAMENTED
LAMENTEDLY
LAMENTER
LAMENTERS
LAMENTING
LAMENTS
LAMER
LAMES
LAMEST
LAMIA
LAMIAE
LAMIAS
LAMINA
LAMINABLE
LAMINAE
LAMINAL
LAMINALS
LAMINAR
LAMINARIA
LAMINARIAN
LAMINARIANS
LAMINARIAS
LAMINARIN
LAMINARINS
LAMINARY
LAMINAS
LAMINATE
LAMINATED
LAMINATES
LAMINATING
LAMINATION
LAMINATIONS
LAMINATOR
LAMINATORS
LAMING
LAMININ
LAMININS
LAMINITIS
LAMINITISES
LAMINOSE
LAMINOUS

LAMISTER
LAMISTERS
LAMMED
LAMMERGEIER
LAMMERGEIERS
LAMMERGEYER
LAMMERGEYERS
LAMMING
LAMP
LAMPAD
LAMPADS
LAMPAS
LAMPASES
LAMPBLACK
LAMPBLACKS
LAMPED
LAMPERS
LAMPERSES
LAMPING
LAMPION
LAMPIONS
LAMPLESS
LAMPLIGHT
LAMPLIGHTER
LAMPLIGHTERS
LAMPLIGHTS
LAMPLIT
LAMPOON
LAMPOONED
LAMPOONER
LAMPOONERIES
LAMPOONERS
LAMPOONERY
LAMPOONING
LAMPOONS
LAMPPOST
LAMPPOSTS
LAMPREY
LAMPREYS
LAMPS
LAMPSHADE
LAMPSHADES
LAMPSHELL
LAMPSHELLS
LAMPYRID
LAMPYRIDS
LAMS
LAMSTER
LAMSTERS
LANAI
LANAIS
LANATE
LANATED
LANCE
LANCED
LANCELET
LANCELETS
LANCEOLATE
LANCER
LANCERS
LANCES
LANCET
LANCETED
LANCETS
LANCEWOOD
LANCEWOODS
LANCH
LANCHED
LANCHES
LANCHING
LANCIERS
LANCIFORM
LANCINATE
LANCINATED
LANCINATES
LANCINATING
LANCING
LAND
LANDAU
LANDAULET
LANDAULETS
LANDAUS
LANDED
LANDER
LANDERS
LANDFALL
LANDFALLS
LANDFAST
LANDFILL
LANDFILLED
LANDFILLING
LANDFILLS
LANDFORM
LANDFORMS
LANDGRAB
LANDGRABS
LANDGRAVE
LANDGRAVES
LANDHOLDER
LANDHOLDERS
LANDHOLDING
LANDHOLDINGS
LANDING
LANDINGS
LANDLADIES
LANDLADY
LANDLER
LANDLERS
LANDLESS
LANDLESSNESS
LANDLESSNESSES
LANDLINE
LANDLINES
LANDLOCKED
LANDLOPER
LANDLOPERS
LANDLORD
LANDLORDISM
LANDLORDISMS
LANDLORDS
LANDLUBBER
LANDLUBBERLY
LANDLUBBERS
LANDLUBBING
LANDMAN
LANDMARK
LANDMARKED
LANDMARKING
LANDMARKS
LANDMASS
LANDMASSES
LANDMEN
LANDOWNER
LANDOWNERS
LANDOWNERSHIP
LANDOWNERSHIPS
LANDOWNING
LANDOWNINGS
LANDS
LANDSCAPE
LANDSCAPED
LANDSCAPER
LANDSCAPERS
LANDSCAPES
LANDSCAPING
LANDSCAPIST
LANDSCAPISTS
LANDSIDE
LANDSIDES
LANDSKIP
LANDSKIPS
LANDSLEIT
LANDSLID
LANDSLIDDEN
LANDSLIDE
LANDSLIDES
LANDSLIDING
LANDSLIP
LANDSLIPS
LANDSMAN
LANDSMEN
LANDWARD
LANDWARDS
LANDWASH
LANDWASHES
LANE
LANELY
LANES
LANEWAY
LANEWAYS
LANG
LANGBEINITE
LANGBEINITES
LANGLAUF
LANGLAUFER
LANGLAUFERS
LANGLAUFS
LANGLEY
LANGLEYS
LANGOSTINO
LANGOSTINOS
LANGOUSTE
LANGOUSTES
LANGOUSTINE
LANGOUSTINES
LANGRAGE
LANGRAGES
LANGREL
LANGRELS
LANGRIDGE
LANGRIDGES
LANGSHAN
LANGSHANS
LANGSYNE
LANGSYNES
LANGUAGE
LANGUAGES
LANGUE
LANGUED
LANGUES
LANGUET
LANGUETS
LANGUETTE
LANGUETTES
LANGUID
LANGUIDLY
LANGUIDNESS
LANGUIDNESSES
LANGUISH
LANGUISHED
LANGUISHER
LANGUISHERS
LANGUISHES
LANGUISHING
LANGUISHINGLY
LANGUISHMENT
LANGUISHMENTS
LANGUOR
LANGUOROUS
LANGUOROUSLY
LANGUORS
LANGUR
LANGURS
LANIARD
LANIARDS
LANIARIES
LANIARY
LANITAL
LANITALS
LANK
LANKER
LANKEST
LANKIER
LANKIEST
LANKILY
LANKINESS
LANKINESSES
LANKLY
LANKNESS
LANKNESSES
LANKY
LANNER
LANNERET
LANNERETS
LANNERS
LANOLIN
LANOLINE
LANOLINES
LANOLINS
LANOSE
LANOSITIES
LANOSITY
LANTANA
LANTANAS
LANTERN
LANTERNS
LANTHANIDE
LANTHANIDES
LANTHANOID
LANTHANOIDS
LANTHANON
LANTHANONS
LANTHANUM
LANTHANUMS
LANTHORN

LANTHORNS
LANUGINOUS
LANUGO
LANUGOS
LANYARD
LANYARDS
LAOGAI
LAOGAIS
LAP
LAPAROSCOPE
LAPAROSCOPES
LAPAROSCOPIC
LAPAROSCOPIES
LAPAROSCOPIST
LAPAROSCOPISTS
LAPAROSCOPY
LAPAROTOMIES
LAPAROTOMY
LAPBOARD
LAPBOARDS
LAPDOG
LAPDOGS
LAPEL
LAPELED
LAPELLED
LAPELS
LAPFUL
LAPFULS
LAPIDARIAN
LAPIDARIES
LAPIDARY
LAPIDATE
LAPIDATED
LAPIDATES
LAPIDATING
LAPIDES
LAPIDIFIED
LAPIDIFIES
LAPIDIFY
LAPIDIFYING
LAPIDIST
LAPIDISTS
LAPILLI
LAPILLUS
LAPIN
LAPINS
LAPIS
LAPISES
LAPPED
LAPPER
LAPPERED
LAPPERING
LAPPERS
LAPPET
LAPPETED
LAPPETS
LAPPING
LAPS
LAPSABLE
LAPSE
LAPSED
LAPSER
LAPSERS
LAPSES
LAPSIBLE
LAPSING
LAPSTRAKE
LAPSTREAK
LAPSUS
LAPTOP
LAPTOPS
LAPWING
LAPWINGS
LAR
LARBOARD
LARBOARDS
LARCENER
LARCENERS
LARCENIES
LARCENIST
LARCENISTS
LARCENOUS
LARCENOUSLY
LARCENY
LARCH
LARCHEN
LARCHES
LARD
LARDED
LARDER
LARDERS
LARDIER
LARDIEST
LARDING
LARDLIKE
LARDON
LARDONS
LARDOON
LARDOONS
LARDS
LARDY
LAREE
LAREES
LARES
LARGANDO
LARGE
LARGEHEARTED
LARGELY
LARGEMOUTH
LARGEMOUTHS
LARGENESS
LARGENESSES
LARGER
LARGES
LARGESS
LARGESSE
LARGESSES
LARGEST
LARGHETTO
LARGHETTOS
LARGISH
LARGO
LARGOS
LARI
LARIAT
LARIATED
LARIATING
LARIATS
LARIGAN
LARIGANS
LARINE
LARIS
LARK
LARKED
LARKER
LARKERS
LARKIER
LARKIEST
LARKINESS
LARKINESSES
LARKING
LARKISH
LARKS
LARKSOME
LARKSPUR
LARKSPURS
LARKY
LARN
LARNED
LARNING
LARNS
LARNT
LARRIGAN
LARRIGANS
LARRIKIN
LARRIKINS
LARRUP
LARRUPED
LARRUPER
LARRUPERS
LARRUPING
LARRUPS
LARS
LARUM
LARUMS
LARVA
LARVAE
LARVAL
LARVAS
LARVICIDAL
LARVICIDE
LARVICIDES
LARYNGAL
LARYNGALS
LARYNGEAL
LARYNGEALS
LARYNGECTOMEE
LARYNGECTOMEES
LARYNGECTOMIES
LARYNGECTOMIZED
LARYNGECTOMY
LARYNGES
LARYNGITIC
LARYNGITIDES
LARYNGITIS
LARYNGITISES
LARYNGOLOGIES
LARYNGOLOGY
LARYNGOSCOPE
LARYNGOSCOPES
LARYNGOSCOPIES
LARYNGOSCOPY
LARYNX
LARYNXES
LAS
LASAGNA
LASAGNAS
LASAGNE
LASAGNES
LASCAR
LASCARS
LASCIVIOUS
LASCIVIOUSLY
LASCIVIOUSNESS
LASE
LASED
LASER
LASERDISC
LASERDISCS
LASERDISK
LASERDISKS
LASERED
LASERING
LASERS
LASES
LASH
LASHED
LASHER
LASHERS
LASHES
LASHING
LASHINGS
LASHINS
LASHKAR
LASHKARS
LASHLESS
LASING
LASS
LASSES
LASSI
LASSIE
LASSIES
LASSIS
LASSITUDE
LASSITUDES
LASSO
LASSOED
LASSOER
LASSOERS
LASSOES
LASSOING
LASSOS
LASSY
LAST
LASTBORN
LASTBORNS
LASTED
LASTER
LASTERS
LASTING
LASTINGLY
LASTINGNESS
LASTINGNESSES
LASTINGS
LASTLY
LASTS
LAT
LATAKIA
LATAKIAS
LATCH
LATCHED
LATCHES
LATCHET
LATCHETS
LATCHING

LATCHKEY
LATCHKEYS
LATCHSTRING
LATCHSTRINGS
LATE
LATECOMER
LATECOMERS
LATED
LATEEN
LATEENER
LATEENERS
LATEENS
LATELY
LATEN
LATENCIES
LATENCY
LATENED
LATENESS
LATENESSES
LATENING
LATENS
LATENSIFICATION
LATENT
LATENTLY
LATENTS
LATER
LATERAD
LATERAL
LATERALED
LATERALING
LATERALIZATION
LATERALIZATIONS
LATERALIZE
LATERALIZED
LATERALIZES
LATERALIZING
LATERALLED
LATERALLING
LATERALLY
LATERALS
LATERBORN
LATERBORNS
LATERITE
LATERITES
LATERITIC
LATERIZATION
LATERIZATIONS
LATERIZE
LATERIZED
LATERIZES
LATERIZING
LATEST
LATESTS
LATEWOOD
LATEWOODS
LATEX
LATEXES
LATH
LATHE
LATHED
LATHER
LATHERED
LATHERER
LATHERERS
LATHERING
LATHERS
LATHERY
LATHES
LATHI
LATHIER
LATHIEST
LATHING
LATHINGS
LATHIS
LATHS
LATHWORK
LATHWORKS
LATHY
LATHYRISM
LATHYRISMS
LATHYRITIC
LATI
LATICES
LATICIFER
LATICIFERS
LATIFUNDIA
LATIFUNDIO
LATIFUNDIOS
LATIFUNDIUM
LATIFUNDIUMS
LATIGO
LATIGOES
LATIGOS
LATILLA
LATILLAS
LATIMERIA
LATIMERIAS
LATINA
LATINAS
LATINITIES
LATINITY
LATINIZATION
LATINIZATIONS
LATINIZE
LATINIZED
LATINIZES
LATINIZING
LATINO
LATINOS
LATISH
LATITUDE
LATITUDES
LATITUDINAL
LATITUDINALLY
LATITUDINARIAN
LATITUDINARIANS
LATKE
LATKES
LATOSOL
LATOSOLIC
LATOSOLS
LATRIA
LATRIAS
LATRINE
LATRINES
LATS
LATTE
LATTEN
LATTENS
LATTER
LATTERLY
LATTERS
LATTES
LATTICE
LATTICED
LATTICES
LATTICEWORK
LATTICEWORKS
LATTICING
LATTICINGS
LATTIN
LATTINS
LATU
LAUAN
LAUANS
LAUD
LAUDABLE
LAUDABLENESS
LAUDABLENESSES
LAUDABLY
LAUDANUM
LAUDANUMS
LAUDATION
LAUDATIONS
LAUDATIVE
LAUDATOR
LAUDATORS
LAUDATORY
LAUDED
LAUDER
LAUDERS
LAUDING
LAUDS
LAUGH
LAUGHABLE
LAUGHABLENESS
LAUGHABLENESSES
LAUGHABLY
LAUGHED
LAUGHER
LAUGHERS
LAUGHING
LAUGHINGLY
LAUGHINGS
LAUGHINGSTOCK
LAUGHINGSTOCKS
LAUGHLINE
LAUGHLINES
LAUGHS
LAUGHTER
LAUGHTERS
LAUNCE
LAUNCES
LAUNCH
LAUNCHED
LAUNCHER
LAUNCHERS
LAUNCHES
LAUNCHING
LAUNCHPAD
LAUNCHPADS
LAUNDER
LAUNDERED
LAUNDERER
LAUNDERERS
LAUNDERETTE
LAUNDERETTES
LAUNDERING
LAUNDERS
LAUNDRESS
LAUNDRESSES
LAUNDRETTE
LAUNDRETTES
LAUNDRIES
LAUNDRY
LAUNDRYMAN
LAUNDRYMEN
LAURA
LAURAE
LAURAS
LAUREATE
LAUREATED
LAUREATES
LAUREATESHIP
LAUREATESHIPS
LAUREATING
LAUREATION
LAUREATIONS
LAUREL
LAURELED
LAURELING
LAURELLED
LAURELLING
LAURELS
LAUWINE
LAUWINES
LAV
LAVA
LAVABO
LAVABOES
LAVABOS
LAVAGE
LAVAGES
LAVALAVA
LAVALAVAS
LAVALIER
LAVALIERE
LAVALIERES
LAVALIERS
LAVALIKE
LAVALLIERE
LAVALLIERES
LAVAS
LAVASH
LAVASHES
LAVATERA
LAVATERAS
LAVATION
LAVATIONS
LAVATORIES
LAVATORY
LAVE
LAVED
LAVEER
LAVEERED
LAVEERING
LAVEERS
LAVENDER
LAVENDERED
LAVENDERING
LAVENDERS
LAVER
LAVEROCK
LAVEROCKS
LAVERS

LAVES
LAVING
LAVISH
LAVISHED
LAVISHER
LAVISHERS
LAVISHES
LAVISHEST
LAVISHING
LAVISHLY
LAVISHNESS
LAVISHNESSES
LAVROCK
LAVROCKS
LAVS
LAW
LAWBOOK
LAWBOOKS
LAWBREAKER
LAWBREAKERS
LAWBREAKING
LAWBREAKINGS
LAWED
LAWFUL
LAWFULLY
LAWFULNESS
LAWFULNESSES
LAWGIVER
LAWGIVERS
LAWGIVING
LAWGIVINGS
LAWINE
LAWINES
LAWING
LAWINGS
LAWLESS
LAWLESSLY
LAWLESSNESS
LAWLESSNESSES
LAWLIKE
LAWMAKER
LAWMAKERS
LAWMAKING
LAWMAKINGS
LAWMAN
LAWMEN
LAWN
LAWNED
LAWNING
LAWNMOWER
LAWNMOWERS
LAWNS
LAWNY
LAWRENCIUM
LAWRENCIUMS
LAWS
LAWSUIT
LAWSUITS
LAWYER
LAWYERED
LAWYERING
LAWYERINGS
LAWYERLIKE
LAWYERLY
LAWYERS
LAX
LAXATION
LAXATIONS
LAXATIVE
LAXATIVES
LAXER
LAXES
LAXEST
LAXITIES
LAXITY
LAXLY
LAXNESS
LAXNESSES
LAY
LAYABOUT
LAYABOUTS
LAYAWAY
LAYAWAYS
LAYED
LAYER
LAYERAGE
LAYERAGES
LAYERED
LAYERING
LAYERINGS
LAYERS
LAYETTE
LAYETTES
LAYIN
LAYING
LAYINS
LAYMAN
LAYMEN
LAYOFF
LAYOFFS
LAYOUT
LAYOUTS
LAYOVER
LAYOVERS
LAYPEOPLE
LAYPERSON
LAYPERSONS
LAYS
LAYUP
LAYUPS
LAYWOMAN
LAYWOMEN
LAZAR
LAZARET
LAZARETS
LAZARETTE
LAZARETTES
LAZARETTO
LAZARETTOS
LAZARS
LAZE
LAZED
LAZES
LAZIED
LAZIER
LAZIES
LAZIEST
LAZILY
LAZINESS
LAZINESSES
LAZING
LAZULI
LAZULIS
LAZULITE
LAZULITES
LAZURITE
LAZURITES
LAZY
LAZYBONES
LAZYING
LAZYISH
LAZZARONE
LAZZARONI
LEA
LEACH
LEACHABILITIES
LEACHABILITY
LEACHABLE
LEACHATE
LEACHATES
LEACHED
LEACHER
LEACHERS
LEACHES
LEACHIER
LEACHIEST
LEACHING
LEACHY
LEAD
LEADABLE
LEADED
LEADEN
LEADENED
LEADENING
LEADENLY
LEADENNESS
LEADENNESSES
LEADENS
LEADER
LEADERBOARD
LEADERBOARDS
LEADERLESS
LEADERS
LEADERSHIP
LEADERSHIPS
LEADIER
LEADIEST
LEADING
LEADINGS
LEADLESS
LEADMAN
LEADMEN
LEADOFF
LEADOFFS
LEADPLANT
LEADPLANTS
LEADS
LEADSCREW
LEADSCREWS
LEADSMAN
LEADSMEN
LEADWORK
LEADWORKS
LEADWORT
LEADWORTS
LEADY
LEAF
LEAFAGE
LEAFAGES
LEAFED
LEAFHOPPER
LEAFHOPPERS
LEAFIER
LEAFIEST
LEAFINESS
LEAFINESSES
LEAFING
LEAFLESS
LEAFLET
LEAFLETED
LEAFLETEER
LEAFLETEERS
LEAFLETER
LEAFLETERS
LEAFLETING
LEAFLETS
LEAFLETTED
LEAFLETTING
LEAFLIKE
LEAFMOLD
LEAFMOLDS
LEAFROLL
LEAFROLLS
LEAFS
LEAFSTALK
LEAFSTALKS
LEAFWORM
LEAFWORMS
LEAFY
LEAGUE
LEAGUED
LEAGUER
LEAGUERED
LEAGUERING
LEAGUERS
LEAGUES
LEAGUING
LEAK
LEAKAGE
LEAKAGES
LEAKED
LEAKER
LEAKERS
LEAKIER
LEAKIEST
LEAKILY
LEAKINESS
LEAKINESSES
LEAKING
LEAKLESS
LEAKPROOF
LEAKS
LEAKY
LEAL
LEALLY
LEALTIES
LEALTY
LEAN
LEANED
LEANER
LEANERS
LEANEST
LEANING
LEANINGS
LEANLY

LEANNESS
LEANNESSES
LEANS
LEANT
LEAP
LEAPED
LEAPER
LEAPERS
LEAPFROG
LEAPFROGGED
LEAPFROGGING
LEAPFROGS
LEAPING
LEAPS
LEAPT
LEAR
LEARIER
LEARIEST
LEARN
LEARNABLE
LEARNED
LEARNEDLY
LEARNEDNESS
LEARNEDNESSES
LEARNER
LEARNERS
LEARNING
LEARNINGS
LEARNS
LEARNT
LEARS
LEARY
LEAS
LEASABLE
LEASE
LEASEBACK
LEASEBACKS
LEASED
LEASEHOLD
LEASEHOLDER
LEASEHOLDERS
LEASEHOLDS
LEASER
LEASERS
LEASES
LEASH
LEASHED
LEASHES
LEASHING
LEASING
LEASINGS
LEAST
LEASTS
LEASTWAYS
LEASTWISE
LEATHER
LEATHERBACK
LEATHERBACKS
LEATHERED
LEATHERETTE
LEATHERETTES
LEATHERIER
LEATHERIEST
LEATHERING
LEATHERINGS
LEATHERLEAF
LEATHERLEAFS
LEATHERLEAVES
LEATHERLIKE
LEATHERN
LEATHERNECK
LEATHERNECKS
LEATHERS
LEATHERWOOD
LEATHERWOODS
LEATHERWORK
LEATHERWORKS
LEATHERY
LEAVE
LEAVED
LEAVEN
LEAVENED
LEAVENER
LEAVENERS
LEAVENING
LEAVENINGS
LEAVENS
LEAVER
LEAVERS
LEAVES
LEAVIER
LEAVIEST
LEAVING
LEAVINGS
LEAVY
LEBEN
LEBENS
LEBENSRAUM
LEBENSRAUMS
LEBKUCHEN
LECH
LECHAYIM
LECHAYIMS
LECHED
LECHER
LECHERED
LECHERIES
LECHERING
LECHEROUS
LECHEROUSLY
LECHEROUSNESS
LECHEROUSNESSES
LECHERS
LECHERY
LECHES
LECHING
LECHWE
LECHWES
LECITHIN
LECITHINASE
LECITHINASES
LECITHINS
LECTERN
LECTERNS
LECTIN
LECTINS
LECTION
LECTIONARIES
LECTIONARY
LECTIONS
LECTOR
LECTORS
LECTOTYPE
LECTOTYPES
LECTURE
LECTURED
LECTURER
LECTURERS
LECTURES
LECTURESHIP
LECTURESHIPS
LECTURING
LECYTHI
LECYTHIS
LECYTHUS
LED
LEDE
LEDERHOSEN
LEDES
LEDGE
LEDGED
LEDGER
LEDGERS
LEDGES
LEDGIER
LEDGIEST
LEDGY
LEE
LEEBOARD
LEEBOARDS
LEECH
LEECHED
LEECHES
LEECHING
LEECHLIKE
LEEK
LEEKS
LEER
LEERED
LEERIER
LEERIEST
LEERILY
LEERINESS
LEERINESSES
LEERING
LEERINGLY
LEERS
LEERY
LEES
LEET
LEETS
LEEWARD
LEEWARDLY
LEEWARDS
LEEWAY
LEEWAYS
LEFT
LEFTER
LEFTEST
LEFTIE
LEFTIES
LEFTISH
LEFTISM
LEFTISMS
LEFTIST
LEFTISTS
LEFTMOST
LEFTMOSTS
LEFTOVER
LEFTOVERS
LEFTS
LEFTWARD
LEFTWARDS
LEFTWING
LEFTY
LEG
LEGACIES
LEGACY
LEGAL
LEGALESE
LEGALESES
LEGALISATION
LEGALISATIONS
LEGALISE
LEGALISED
LEGALISES
LEGALISING
LEGALISM
LEGALISMS
LEGALIST
LEGALISTIC
LEGALISTICALLY
LEGALISTS
LEGALITIES
LEGALITY
LEGALIZATION
LEGALIZATIONS
LEGALIZE
LEGALIZED
LEGALIZER
LEGALIZERS
LEGALIZES
LEGALIZING
LEGALLY
LEGALS
LEGATE
LEGATED
LEGATEE
LEGATEES
LEGATES
LEGATESHIP
LEGATESHIPS
LEGATINE
LEGATING
LEGATION
LEGATIONS
LEGATO
LEGATOR
LEGATORS
LEGATOS
LEGEND
LEGENDARIES
LEGENDARILY
LEGENDARY
LEGENDIZE
LEGENDIZED
LEGENDIZES
LEGENDIZING
LEGENDRIES
LEGENDRY
LEGENDS
LEGER
LEGERDEMAIN
LEGERDEMAINS
LEGERITIES

LEGERITY
LEGERS
LEGES
LEGGED
LEGGIER
LEGGIERO
LEGGIES
LEGGIEST
LEGGIN
LEGGINESS
LEGGINESSES
LEGGING
LEGGINGS
LEGGINS
LEGGY
LEGHOLD
LEGHOLDS
LEGHORN
LEGHORNS
LEGIBILITIES
LEGIBILITY
LEGIBLE
LEGIBLY
LEGION
LEGIONARIES
LEGIONARY
LEGIONNAIRE
LEGIONNAIRES
LEGIONS
LEGISLATE
LEGISLATED
LEGISLATES
LEGISLATING
LEGISLATION
LEGISLATIONS
LEGISLATIVE
LEGISLATIVELY
LEGISLATIVES
LEGISLATOR
LEGISLATORIAL
LEGISLATORS
LEGISLATORSHIP
LEGISLATORSHIPS
LEGISLATURE
LEGISLATURES
LEGIST
LEGISTS
LEGIT
LEGITIMACIES
LEGITIMACY
LEGITIMATE
LEGITIMATED
LEGITIMATELY
LEGITIMATES
LEGITIMATING
LEGITIMATION
LEGITIMATIONS
LEGITIMATIZE
LEGITIMATIZED
LEGITIMATIZES
LEGITIMATIZING
LEGITIMATOR
LEGITIMATORS
LEGITIMISE
LEGITIMISED
LEGITIMISES
LEGITIMISING
LEGITIMISM
LEGITIMISMS
LEGITIMIST
LEGITIMISTS
LEGITIMIZATION
LEGITIMIZATIONS
LEGITIMIZE
LEGITIMIZED
LEGITIMIZER
LEGITIMIZERS
LEGITIMIZES
LEGITIMIZING
LEGITS
LEGLESS
LEGLIKE
LEGMAN
LEGMEN
LEGONG
LEGONGS
LEGROOM
LEGROOMS
LEGS
LEGUME
LEGUMES
LEGUMIN
LEGUMINOUS
LEGUMINS
LEGWARMER
LEGWARMERS
LEGWORK
LEGWORKS
LEHAYIM
LEHAYIMS
LEHR
LEHRS
LEHUA
LEHUAS
LEI
LEIOMYOMA
LEIOMYOMAS
LEIOMYOMATA
LEIS
LEISHMANIA
LEISHMANIAL
LEISHMANIAS
LEISHMANIASES
LEISHMANIASIS
LEISTER
LEISTERED
LEISTERING
LEISTERS
LEISURE
LEISURED
LEISURELINESS
LEISURELINESSES
LEISURELY
LEISURES
LEITMOTIF
LEITMOTIFS
LEITMOTIV
LEITMOTIVS
LEK
LEKE
LEKKED
LEKKING
LEKS
LEKU
LEKVAR
LEKVARS
LEKYTHI
LEKYTHOI
LEKYTHOS
LEKYTHUS
LEMAN
LEMANS
LEMMA
LEMMAS
LEMMATA
LEMMATIZE
LEMMATIZED
LEMMATIZES
LEMMATIZING
LEMMING
LEMMINGLIKE
LEMMINGS
LEMNISCAL
LEMNISCATE
LEMNISCATES
LEMNISCI
LEMNISCUS
LEMON
LEMONADE
LEMONADES
LEMONGRASS
LEMONGRASSES
LEMONIER
LEMONIEST
LEMONISH
LEMONLIKE
LEMONS
LEMONY
LEMPIRA
LEMPIRAS
LEMUR
LEMURES
LEMURINE
LEMURLIKE
LEMUROID
LEMUROIDS
LEMURS
LEND
LENDABLE
LENDER
LENDERS
LENDING
LENDINGS
LENDS
LENES
LENGTH
LENGTHEN
LENGTHENED
LENGTHENER
LENGTHENERS
LENGTHENING
LENGTHENS
LENGTHIER
LENGTHIEST
LENGTHILY
LENGTHINESS
LENGTHINESSES
LENGTHS
LENGTHWAYS
LENGTHWISE
LENGTHY
LENIENCE
LENIENCES
LENIENCIES
LENIENCY
LENIENT
LENIENTLY
LENIS
LENITE
LENITED
LENITES
LENITIES
LENITING
LENITION
LENITIONS
LENITIVE
LENITIVELY
LENITIVES
LENITY
LENO
LENOS
LENS
LENSE
LENSED
LENSES
LENSING
LENSINGS
LENSLESS
LENSMAN
LENSMEN
LENT
LENTAMENTE
LENTANDO
LENTEN
LENTIC
LENTICEL
LENTICELS
LENTICULAR
LENTICULE
LENTICULES
LENTIGINES
LENTIGO
LENTIL
LENTILS
LENTISK
LENTISKS
LENTISSIMO
LENTIVIRUS
LENTIVIRUSES
LENTO
LENTOID
LENTOIDS
LENTOS
LEONE
LEONES
LEONINE
LEOPARD
LEOPARDESS
LEOPARDESSES
LEOPARDS
LEOTARD
LEOTARDED
LEOTARDS
LEPER
LEPERS

LEPIDOLITE
LEPIDOLITES
LEPIDOPTERA
LEPIDOPTERAN
LEPIDOPTERANS
LEPIDOPTERIST
LEPIDOPTERISTS
LEPIDOPTEROLOGY
LEPIDOPTEROUS
LEPIDOTE
LEPIDOTES
LEPORID
LEPORIDAE
LEPORIDS
LEPORINE
LEPRECHAUN
LEPRECHAUNISH
LEPRECHAUNS
LEPROMATOUS
LEPROSARIA
LEPROSARIUM
LEPROSARIUMS
LEPROSE
LEPROSIES
LEPROSY
LEPROTIC
LEPROUS
LEPROUSLY
LEPT
LEPTA
LEPTIN
LEPTINS
LEPTOCEPHALI
LEPTOCEPHALUS
LEPTON
LEPTONIC
LEPTONS
LEPTOPHOS
LEPTOPHOSES
LEPTOSOME
LEPTOSOMES
LEPTOSPIRAL
LEPTOSPIRE
LEPTOSPIRES
LEPTOSPIROSES
LEPTOSPIROSIS
LEPTOTENE
LEPTOTENES
LES
LESBIAN
LESBIANISM
LESBIANISMS
LESBIANS
LESBIGAY
LESBIGAYS
LESBO
LESBOS
LESES
LESION
LESIONED
LESIONING
LESIONS
LESPEDEZA
LESPEDEZAS
LESS
LESSEE
LESSEES
LESSEN
LESSENED
LESSENING
LESSENS
LESSER
LESSON
LESSONED
LESSONING
LESSONS
LESSOR
LESSORS
LEST
LET
LETCH
LETCHED
LETCHES
LETCHING
LETDOWN
LETDOWNS
LETHAL
LETHALITIES
LETHALITY
LETHALLY
LETHALS
LETHARGIC
LETHARGICALLY
LETHARGIES
LETHARGY
LETHE
LETHEAN
LETHES
LETOUT
LETOUTS
LETS
LETTED
LETTER
LETTERBOX
LETTERBOXED
LETTERBOXES
LETTERBOXING
LETTERBOXINGS
LETTERED
LETTERER
LETTERERS
LETTERFORM
LETTERFORMS
LETTERHEAD
LETTERHEADS
LETTERING
LETTERINGS
LETTERMAN
LETTERMEN
LETTERPRESS
LETTERPRESSES
LETTERS
LETTERSPACING
LETTERSPACINGS
LETTING
LETTUCE
LETTUCES
LETUP
LETUPS
LEU
LEUCEMIA
LEUCEMIAS
LEUCEMIC
LEUCIN
LEUCINE
LEUCINES
LEUCINS
LEUCITE
LEUCITES
LEUCITIC
LEUCOCIDIN
LEUCOCIDINS
LEUCOCYTE
LEUCOCYTES
LEUCOMA
LEUCOMAS
LEUCON
LEUCONS
LEUCOPLAST
LEUCOPLASTS
LEUCOSES
LEUCOSIS
LEUCOTIC
LEUD
LEUDES
LEUDS
LEUKAEMIA
LEUKAEMIAS
LEUKAEMIC
LEUKAEMOGENESES
LEUKAEMOGENESIS
LEUKEMIA
LEUKEMIAS
LEUKEMIC
LEUKEMICS
LEUKEMOGENESES
LEUKEMOGENESIS
LEUKEMOGENIC
LEUKEMOID
LEUKOCYTE
LEUKOCYTES
LEUKOCYTIC
LEUKOCYTOSES
LEUKOCYTOSIS
LEUKODYSTROPHY
LEUKOMA
LEUKOMAS
LEUKON
LEUKONS
LEUKOPENIA
LEUKOPENIAS
LEUKOPENIC
LEUKOPLAKIA
LEUKOPLAKIAS
LEUKOPLAKIC
LEUKOPOIESES
LEUKOPOIESIS
LEUKOPOIETIC
LEUKORRHEA
LEUKORRHEAL
LEUKORRHEAS
LEUKOSES
LEUKOSIS
LEUKOTIC
LEUKOTOMIES
LEUKOTOMY
LEUKOTRIENE
LEUKOTRIENES
LEV
LEVA
LEVAMISOLE
LEVAMISOLES
LEVANT
LEVANTED
LEVANTER
LEVANTERS
LEVANTINE
LEVANTINES
LEVANTING
LEVANTS
LEVAS
LEVATOR
LEVATORES
LEVATORS
LEVEE
LEVEED
LEVEEING
LEVEES
LEVEL
LEVELED
LEVELER
LEVELERS
LEVELHEADED
LEVELHEADEDNESS
LEVELING
LEVELLED
LEVELLER
LEVELLERS
LEVELLING
LEVELLY
LEVELNESS
LEVELNESSES
LEVELS
LEVER
LEVERAGE
LEVERAGED
LEVERAGES
LEVERAGING
LEVERED
LEVERET
LEVERETS
LEVERING
LEVERS
LEVIABLE
LEVIATHAN
LEVIATHANS
LEVIED
LEVIER
LEVIERS
LEVIES
LEVIGATE
LEVIGATED
LEVIGATES
LEVIGATING
LEVIGATION
LEVIGATIONS
LEVIN
LEVINS
LEVIRATE
LEVIRATES
LEVIRATIC
LEVIS
LEVITATE
LEVITATED
LEVITATES

LEVITATING
LEVITATION
LEVITATIONAL
LEVITATIONS
LEVITATOR
LEVITATORS
LEVITIES
LEVITY
LEVO
LEVODOPA
LEVODOPAS
LEVOGYRE
LEVONORGESTREL
LEVONORGESTRELS
LEVOROTARY
LEVOROTATORY
LEVS
LEVULIN
LEVULINS
LEVULOSE
LEVULOSES
LEVY
LEVYING
LEWD
LEWDER
LEWDEST
LEWDLY
LEWDNESS
LEWDNESSES
LEWIS
LEWISES
LEWISITE
LEWISITES
LEWISSON
LEWISSONS
LEX
LEXEME
LEXEMES
LEXEMIC
LEXES
LEXICA
LEXICAL
LEXICALISATION
LEXICALISATIONS
LEXICALITIES
LEXICALITY
LEXICALIZATION
LEXICALIZATIONS
LEXICALIZE
LEXICALIZED
LEXICALIZES
LEXICALIZING
LEXICALLY
LEXICOGRAPHER
LEXICOGRAPHERS
LEXICOGRAPHIC
LEXICOGRAPHICAL
LEXICOGRAPHIES
LEXICOGRAPHY
LEXICOLOGICAL
LEXICOLOGIES
LEXICOLOGIST
LEXICOLOGISTS
LEXICOLOGY
LEXICON
LEXICONS
LEXIGRAM
LEXIGRAMS
LEXIS
LEXISES
LEY
LEYS
LEZ
LEZZES
LEZZIE
LEZZIES
LEZZY
LI
LIABILITIES
LIABILITY
LIABLE
LIAISE
LIAISED
LIAISES
LIAISING
LIAISON
LIAISONS
LIANA
LIANAS
LIANE
LIANES
LIANG
LIANGS
LIANOID
LIAR
LIARD
LIARDS
LIARS
LIAS
LIASES
LIASSIC
LIATRIS
LIATRISES
LIB
LIBATION
LIBATIONARY
LIBATIONS
LIBBER
LIBBERS
LIBECCHIO
LIBECCHIOS
LIBECCIO
LIBECCIOS
LIBEL
LIBELANT
LIBELANTS
LIBELED
LIBELEE
LIBELEES
LIBELER
LIBELERS
LIBELING
LIBELIST
LIBELISTS
LIBELLANT
LIBELLANTS
LIBELLED
LIBELLEE
LIBELLEES
LIBELLER
LIBELLERS
LIBELLING
LIBELLOUS
LIBELOUS
LIBELS
LIBER
LIBERAL
LIBERALISATION
LIBERALISATIONS
LIBERALISE
LIBERALISED
LIBERALISES
LIBERALISING
LIBERALISM
LIBERALISMS
LIBERALIST
LIBERALISTIC
LIBERALISTS
LIBERALITIES
LIBERALITY
LIBERALIZATION
LIBERALIZATIONS
LIBERALIZE
LIBERALIZED
LIBERALIZER
LIBERALIZERS
LIBERALIZES
LIBERALIZING
LIBERALLY
LIBERALNESS
LIBERALNESSES
LIBERALS
LIBERATE
LIBERATED
LIBERATES
LIBERATING
LIBERATION
LIBERATIONIST
LIBERATIONISTS
LIBERATIONS
LIBERATOR
LIBERATORS
LIBERATORY
LIBERS
LIBERTARIAN
LIBERTARIANISM
LIBERTARIANISMS
LIBERTARIANS
LIBERTIES
LIBERTINAGE
LIBERTINAGES
LIBERTINE
LIBERTINES
LIBERTINISM
LIBERTINISMS
LIBERTY
LIBIDINAL
LIBIDINALLY
LIBIDINOUS
LIBIDINOUSLY
LIBIDINOUSNESS
LIBIDO
LIBIDOS
LIBLAB
LIBLABS
LIBRA
LIBRAE
LIBRARIAN
LIBRARIANS
LIBRARIANSHIP
LIBRARIANSHIPS
LIBRARIES
LIBRARY
LIBRAS
LIBRATE
LIBRATED
LIBRATES
LIBRATING
LIBRATION
LIBRATIONAL
LIBRATIONS
LIBRATORY
LIBRETTI
LIBRETTIST
LIBRETTISTS
LIBRETTO
LIBRETTOS
LIBRI
LIBRIFORM
LIBS
LICE
LICENCE
LICENCED
LICENCEE
LICENCEES
LICENCER
LICENCERS
LICENCES
LICENCING
LICENSABLE
LICENSE
LICENSED
LICENSEE
LICENSEES
LICENSER
LICENSERS
LICENSES
LICENSING
LICENSOR
LICENSORS
LICENSURE
LICENSURES
LICENTE
LICENTIATE
LICENTIATES
LICENTIOUS
LICENTIOUSLY
LICENTIOUSNESS
LICH
LICHEE
LICHEES
LICHEN
LICHENED
LICHENIN
LICHENING
LICHENINS
LICHENOLOGICAL
LICHENOLOGIES
LICHENOLOGIST
LICHENOLOGISTS
LICHENOLOGY
LICHENOSE
LICHENOUS
LICHENS
LICHES

LICHGATE
LICHGATES
LICHI
LICHIS
LICHT
LICHTED
LICHTING
LICHTLY
LICHTS
LICIT
LICITLY
LICITNESS
LICITNESSES
LICK
LICKED
LICKER
LICKERISH
LICKERISHLY
LICKERISHNESS
LICKERISHNESSES
LICKERS
LICKING
LICKINGS
LICKS
LICKSPIT
LICKSPITS
LICKSPITTLE
LICKSPITTLES
LICORICE
LICORICES
LICTOR
LICTORIAN
LICTORS
LID
LIDAR
LIDARS
LIDDED
LIDDING
LIDLESS
LIDO
LIDOCAINE
LIDOCAINES
LIDOS
LIDS
LIE
LIEBFRAUMILCH
LIEBFRAUMILCHS
LIED
LIEDER
LIEF
LIEFER
LIEFEST
LIEFLY
LIEGE
LIEGEMAN
LIEGEMEN
LIEGES
LIEN
LIENABLE
LIENAL
LIENS
LIENTERIES
LIENTERY
LIER
LIERNE
LIERNES
LIERS
LIES
LIEU
LIEUS
LIEUTENANCIES
LIEUTENANCY
LIEUTENANT
LIEUTENANTS
LIEVE
LIEVER
LIEVEST
LIFE
LIFEBELT
LIFEBELTS
LIFEBLOOD
LIFEBLOODS
LIFEBOAT
LIFEBOATS
LIFEBUOY
LIFEBUOYS
LIFECARE
LIFECARES
LIFEFUL
LIFEGUARD
LIFEGUARDED
LIFEGUARDING
LIFEGUARDS
LIFELESS
LIFELESSLY
LIFELESSNESS
LIFELESSNESSES
LIFELIKE
LIFELIKENESS
LIFELIKENESSES
LIFELINE
LIFELINES
LIFELONG
LIFEMANSHIP
LIFEMANSHIPS
LIFER
LIFERS
LIFESAVER
LIFESAVERS
LIFESAVING
LIFESAVINGS
LIFESPAN
LIFESPANS
LIFESTYLE
LIFESTYLES
LIFETIME
LIFETIMES
LIFEWAY
LIFEWAYS
LIFEWORK
LIFEWORKS
LIFEWORLD
LIFEWORLDS
LIFT
LIFTABLE
LIFTED
LIFTER
LIFTERS
LIFTGATE
LIFTGATES
LIFTING
LIFTMAN
LIFTMEN
LIFTOFF
LIFTOFFS
LIFTS
LIGAMENT
LIGAMENTOUS
LIGAMENTS
LIGAN
LIGAND
LIGANDS
LIGANS
LIGASE
LIGASES
LIGATE
LIGATED
LIGATES
LIGATING
LIGATION
LIGATIONS
LIGATIVE
LIGATURE
LIGATURED
LIGATURES
LIGATURING
LIGER
LIGERS
LIGHT
LIGHTBULB
LIGHTBULBS
LIGHTED
LIGHTEN
LIGHTENED
LIGHTENER
LIGHTENERS
LIGHTENING
LIGHTENINGS
LIGHTENS
LIGHTER
LIGHTERAGE
LIGHTERAGES
LIGHTERED
LIGHTERING
LIGHTERS
LIGHTEST
LIGHTFACE
LIGHTFACED
LIGHTFACES
LIGHTFAST
LIGHTFASTNESS
LIGHTFASTNESSES
LIGHTFUL
LIGHTHEARTED
LIGHTHEARTEDLY
LIGHTHOUSE
LIGHTHOUSES
LIGHTING
LIGHTINGS
LIGHTISH
LIGHTLESS
LIGHTLY
LIGHTNESS
LIGHTNESSES
LIGHTNING
LIGHTNINGED
LIGHTNINGS
LIGHTPLANE
LIGHTPLANES
LIGHTPROOF
LIGHTS
LIGHTSHIP
LIGHTSHIPS
LIGHTSOME
LIGHTSOMELY
LIGHTSOMENESS
LIGHTSOMENESSES
LIGHTTIGHT
LIGHTWAVE
LIGHTWEIGHT
LIGHTWEIGHTS
LIGHTWOOD
LIGHTWOODS
LIGNALOES
LIGNAN
LIGNANS
LIGNEOUS
LIGNIFICATION
LIGNIFICATIONS
LIGNIFIED
LIGNIFIES
LIGNIFY
LIGNIFYING
LIGNIN
LIGNINS
LIGNITE
LIGNITES
LIGNITIC
LIGNOCELLULOSE
LIGNOCELLULOSES
LIGNOCELLULOSIC
LIGNOSULFONATE
LIGNOSULFONATES
LIGROIN
LIGROINE
LIGROINES
LIGROINS
LIGULA
LIGULAE
LIGULAR
LIGULAS
LIGULATE
LIGULATED
LIGULE
LIGULES
LIGULOID
LIGURE
LIGURES
LIKABILITIES
LIKABILITY
LIKABLE
LIKABLENESS
LIKABLENESSES
LIKABLY
LIKE
LIKEABILITIES
LIKEABILITY
LIKEABLE
LIKEABLY
LIKED
LIKELIER
LIKELIEST
LIKELIHOOD
LIKELIHOODS
LIKELINESS

LIKELINESSES
LIKELY
LIKEN
LIKENED
LIKENESS
LIKENESSES
LIKENING
LIKENS
LIKER
LIKERS
LIKES
LIKEST
LIKEWISE
LIKING
LIKINGS
LIKUTA
LILAC
LILACS
LILANGENI
LILIED
LILIES
LILLIPUT
LILLIPUTIAN
LILLIPUTIANS
LILLIPUTS
LILO
LILOS
LILT
LILTED
LILTING
LILTINGLY
LILTINGNESS
LILTINGNESSES
LILTS
LILY
LILYLIKE
LIMA
LIMACINE
LIMACON
LIMACONS
LIMAN
LIMANS
LIMAS
LIMB
LIMBA
LIMBAS
LIMBATE
LIMBECK
LIMBECKS
LIMBED
LIMBER
LIMBERED
LIMBERER
LIMBEREST
LIMBERING
LIMBERLY
LIMBERNESS
LIMBERNESSES
LIMBERS
LIMBI
LIMBIC
LIMBIER
LIMBIEST
LIMBING
LIMBLESS
LIMBO
LIMBOED
LIMBOES
LIMBOING
LIMBOS
LIMBS
LIMBUS
LIMBUSES
LIMBY
LIME
LIMEADE
LIMEADES
LIMED
LIMEKILN
LIMEKILNS
LIMELESS
LIMELIGHT
LIMELIGHTED
LIMELIGHTING
LIMELIGHTS
LIMEN
LIMENS
LIMERICK
LIMERICKS
LIMES
LIMESTONE
LIMESTONES
LIMEWASH
LIMEWASHES
LIMEWATER
LIMEWATERS
LIMEY
LIMEYS
LIMIER
LIMIEST
LIMINA
LIMINAL
LIMINESS
LIMINESSES
LIMING
LIMIT
LIMITABLE
LIMITARY
LIMITATION
LIMITATIONAL
LIMITATIONS
LIMITATIVE
LIMITED
LIMITEDLY
LIMITEDNESS
LIMITEDNESSES
LIMITEDS
LIMITER
LIMITERS
LIMITES
LIMITING
LIMITINGLY
LIMITLESS
LIMITLESSLY
LIMITLESSNESS
LIMITLESSNESSES
LIMITROPHE
LIMITS
LIMMER
LIMMERS
LIMN
LIMNED
LIMNER
LIMNERS
LIMNETIC
LIMNIC
LIMNING
LIMNOLOGIC
LIMNOLOGICAL
LIMNOLOGIES
LIMNOLOGIST
LIMNOLOGISTS
LIMNOLOGY
LIMNS
LIMO
LIMONENE
LIMONENES
LIMONITE
LIMONITES
LIMONITIC
LIMONIUM
LIMONIUMS
LIMOS
LIMOUSINE
LIMOUSINES
LIMP
LIMPA
LIMPAS
LIMPED
LIMPER
LIMPERS
LIMPEST
LIMPET
LIMPETS
LIMPID
LIMPIDITIES
LIMPIDITY
LIMPIDLY
LIMPIDNESS
LIMPIDNESSES
LIMPING
LIMPINGLY
LIMPKIN
LIMPKINS
LIMPLY
LIMPNESS
LIMPNESSES
LIMPS
LIMPSEY
LIMPSIER
LIMPSIEST
LIMPSY
LIMULI
LIMULOID
LIMULOIDS
LIMULUS
LIMY
LIN
LINABLE
LINAC
LINACS
LINAGE
LINAGES
LINALOL
LINALOLS
LINALOOL
LINALOOLS
LINCHPIN
LINCHPINS
LINCOMYCIN
LINCOMYCINS
LINCTUS
LINCTUSES
LINDANE
LINDANES
LINDEN
LINDENS
LINDIED
LINDIES
LINDY
LINDYING
LINE
LINEABLE
LINEAGE
LINEAGES
LINEAL
LINEALITIES
LINEALITY
LINEALLY
LINEAMENT
LINEAMENTAL
LINEAMENTS
LINEAR
LINEARISE
LINEARISED
LINEARISES
LINEARISING
LINEARITIES
LINEARITY
LINEARIZATION
LINEARIZATIONS
LINEARIZE
LINEARIZED
LINEARIZES
LINEARIZING
LINEARLY
LINEATE
LINEATED
LINEATION
LINEATIONS
LINEBACKER
LINEBACKERS
LINEBACKING
LINEBACKINGS
LINEBRED
LINEBREEDING
LINEBREEDINGS
LINECASTER
LINECASTERS
LINECASTING
LINECASTINGS
LINECUT
LINECUTS
LINED
LINELESS
LINELIKE
LINEMAN
LINEMATE
LINEMATES
LINEMEN
LINEN
LINENS
LINENY
LINEOLATE
LINER

LINERBOARD
LINERBOARDS
LINERLESS
LINERS
LINES
LINESMAN
LINESMEN
LINEUP
LINEUPS
LINEY
LING
LINGA
LINGAM
LINGAMS
LINGAS
LINGBERRIES
LINGBERRY
LINGCOD
LINGCODS
LINGER
LINGERED
LINGERER
LINGERERS
LINGERIE
LINGERIES
LINGERING
LINGERINGLY
LINGERS
LINGIER
LINGIEST
LINGO
LINGOES
LINGONBERRIES
LINGONBERRY
LINGOS
LINGS
LINGUA
LINGUAE
LINGUAL
LINGUALLY
LINGUALS
LINGUICA
LINGUICAS
LINGUINE
LINGUINES
LINGUINI
LINGUINIS
LINGUISA
LINGUISAS
LINGUIST
LINGUISTIC
LINGUISTICAL
LINGUISTICALLY
LINGUISTICIAN
LINGUISTICIANS
LINGUISTICS
LINGUISTS
LINGULA
LINGULAE
LINGULAR
LINGULATE
LINGY
LINHAY
LINHAYS
LINIER
LINIEST
LINIMENT
LINIMENTS
LININ
LINING
LININGS
LININS
LINK
LINKABLE
LINKAGE
LINKAGES
LINKBOY
LINKBOYS
LINKED
LINKER
LINKERS
LINKING
LINKMAN
LINKMEN
LINKS
LINKSLAND
LINKSLANDS
LINKSMAN
LINKSMEN
LINKUP
LINKUPS
LINKWORK
LINKWORKS
LINKY
LINN
LINNET
LINNETS
LINNEY
LINNEYS
LINNIES
LINNS
LINNY
LINO
LINOCUT
LINOCUTS
LINOCUTTING
LINOCUTTINGS
LINOLEATE
LINOLEATES
LINOLEUM
LINOLEUMS
LINOS
LINOTYPE
LINOTYPED
LINOTYPER
LINOTYPERS
LINOTYPES
LINOTYPING
LINS
LINSANG
LINSANGS
LINSEED
LINSEEDS
LINSEY
LINSEYS
LINSTOCK
LINSTOCKS
LINT
LINTED
LINTEL
LINTELED
LINTELLED
LINTELS
LINTER
LINTERS
LINTIER
LINTIEST
LINTING
LINTLESS
LINTOL
LINTOLS
LINTS
LINTWHITE
LINTWHITES
LINTY
LINUM
LINUMS
LINURON
LINURONS
LINY
LION
LIONESS
LIONESSES
LIONFISH
LIONFISHES
LIONHEARTED
LIONISE
LIONISED
LIONISER
LIONISERS
LIONISES
LIONISING
LIONIZATION
LIONIZATIONS
LIONIZE
LIONIZED
LIONIZER
LIONIZERS
LIONIZES
LIONIZING
LIONLIKE
LIONS
LIP
LIPA
LIPAS
LIPASE
LIPASES
LIPE
LIPECTOMIES
LIPECTOMY
LIPGLOSS
LIPGLOSSES
LIPID
LIPIDE
LIPIDES
LIPIDIC
LIPIDS
LIPIN
LIPINS
LIPLESS
LIPLIKE
LIPLINER
LIPLINERS
LIPO
LIPOCYTE
LIPOCYTES
LIPOGENESES
LIPOGENESIS
LIPOGRAM
LIPOGRAMS
LIPOID
LIPOIDAL
LIPOIDS
LIPOLITIC
LIPOLYSES
LIPOLYSIS
LIPOLYTIC
LIPOMA
LIPOMAS
LIPOMATA
LIPOMATOUS
LIPOPHILIC
LIPOPROTEIN
LIPOPROTEINS
LIPOS
LIPOSOMAL
LIPOSOME
LIPOSOMES
LIPOSUCTION
LIPOSUCTIONS
LIPOTROPIC
LIPOTROPIES
LIPOTROPIN
LIPOTROPINS
LIPOTROPY
LIPPED
LIPPEN
LIPPENED
LIPPENING
LIPPENS
LIPPER
LIPPERED
LIPPERING
LIPPERS
LIPPIER
LIPPIEST
LIPPINESS
LIPPINESSES
LIPPING
LIPPINGS
LIPPY
LIPREAD
LIPREADER
LIPREADERS
LIPREADING
LIPREADINGS
LIPREADS
LIPS
LIPSTICK
LIPSTICKED
LIPSTICKS
LIQUATE
LIQUATED
LIQUATES
LIQUATING
LIQUATION
LIQUATIONS
LIQUEFACTION
LIQUEFACTIONS
LIQUEFIED
LIQUEFIER
LIQUEFIERS
LIQUEFIES
LIQUEFY
LIQUEFYING

LIQUESCENT
LIQUEUR
LIQUEURS
LIQUID
LIQUIDAMBAR
LIQUIDAMBARS
LIQUIDATE
LIQUIDATED
LIQUIDATES
LIQUIDATING
LIQUIDATION
LIQUIDATIONS
LIQUIDATOR
LIQUIDATORS
LIQUIDIER
LIQUIDIEST
LIQUIDITIES
LIQUIDITY
LIQUIDIZE
LIQUIDIZED
LIQUIDIZER
LIQUIDIZERS
LIQUIDIZES
LIQUIDIZING
LIQUIDLY
LIQUIDNESS
LIQUIDNESSES
LIQUIDS
LIQUIDY
LIQUIFIED
LIQUIFIES
LIQUIFY
LIQUIFYING
LIQUOR
LIQUORED
LIQUORICE
LIQUORICES
LIQUORING
LIQUORISH
LIQUORS
LIRA
LIRAS
LIRE
LIRI
LIRIOPE
LIRIOPES
LIRIPIPE
LIRIPIPES
LIROT
LIROTH
LIS
LISENTE
LISLE
LISLES
LISP
LISPED
LISPER
LISPERS
LISPING
LISPINGLY
LISPINGS
LISPS
LISSOM
LISSOME
LISSOMELY
LISSOMENESS
LISSOMENESSES
LISSOMLY
LIST
LISTABLE
LISTBOX
LISTBOXES
LISTED
LISTEE
LISTEES
LISTEL
LISTELS
LISTEN
LISTENABLE
LISTENED
LISTENER
LISTENERS
LISTENERSHIP
LISTENERSHIPS
LISTENING
LISTENS
LISTER
LISTERIA
LISTERIAS
LISTERIOSES
LISTERIOSIS
LISTERS
LISTING
LISTINGS
LISTLESS
LISTLESSLY
LISTLESSNESS
LISTLESSNESSES
LISTS
LISTSERV
LISTSERVS
LIT
LITAI
LITANIES
LITANY
LITAS
LITCHI
LITCHIS
LITE
LITENESS
LITENESSES
LITER
LITERACIES
LITERACY
LITERAL
LITERALISM
LITERALISMS
LITERALIST
LITERALISTIC
LITERALISTS
LITERALITIES
LITERALITY
LITERALIZATION
LITERALIZATIONS
LITERALIZE
LITERALIZED
LITERALIZES
LITERALIZING
LITERALLY
LITERALNESS
LITERALNESSES
LITERALS
LITERARILY
LITERARINESS
LITERARINESSES
LITERARY
LITERATE
LITERATELY
LITERATENESS
LITERATENESSES
LITERATES
LITERATI
LITERATIM
LITERATION
LITERATIONS
LITERATOR
LITERATORS
LITERATURE
LITERATURES
LITERATUS
LITERS
LITES
LITEST
LITHARGE
LITHARGES
LITHE
LITHELY
LITHEMIA
LITHEMIAS
LITHEMIC
LITHENESS
LITHENESSES
LITHER
LITHESOME
LITHEST
LITHIA
LITHIAS
LITHIASES
LITHIASIS
LITHIC
LITHIFICATION
LITHIFICATIONS
LITHIFIED
LITHIFIES
LITHIFY
LITHIFYING
LITHIUM
LITHIUMS
LITHO
LITHOED
LITHOES
LITHOGRAPH
LITHOGRAPHED
LITHOGRAPHER
LITHOGRAPHERS
LITHOGRAPHIC
LITHOGRAPHIES
LITHOGRAPHING
LITHOGRAPHS
LITHOGRAPHY
LITHOID
LITHOIDAL
LITHOING
LITHOLOGIC
LITHOLOGICAL
LITHOLOGICALLY
LITHOLOGIES
LITHOLOGY
LITHOPHANE
LITHOPHANES
LITHOPHYTE
LITHOPHYTES
LITHOPONE
LITHOPONES
LITHOPS
LITHOS
LITHOSOL
LITHOSOLS
LITHOSPHERE
LITHOSPHERES
LITHOSPHERIC
LITHOTOMIES
LITHOTOMY
LITHOTRIPSIES
LITHOTRIPSY
LITHOTRIPTER
LITHOTRIPTERS
LITHOTRIPTOR
LITHOTRIPTORS
LITIGABLE
LITIGANT
LITIGANTS
LITIGATE
LITIGATED
LITIGATES
LITIGATING
LITIGATION
LITIGATIONS
LITIGATOR
LITIGATORS
LITIGIOUS
LITIGIOUSLY
LITIGIOUSNESS
LITIGIOUSNESSES
LITMUS
LITMUSES
LITORAL
LITOTES
LITOTIC
LITRE
LITRES
LITS
LITTEN
LITTER
LITTERATEUR
LITTERATEURS
LITTERBAG
LITTERBAGS
LITTERBUG
LITTERBUGS
LITTERED
LITTERER
LITTERERS
LITTERING
LITTERMATE
LITTERMATES
LITTERS
LITTERY
LITTLE
LITTLENECK
LITTLENECKS
LITTLENESS
LITTLENESSES
LITTLER
LITTLES

LITTLEST
LITTLISH
LITTORAL
LITTORALS
LITU
LITURGIC
LITURGICAL
LITURGICALLY
LITURGICS
LITURGIES
LITURGIOLOGIES
LITURGIOLOGIST
LITURGIOLOGISTS
LITURGIOLOGY
LITURGISM
LITURGISMS
LITURGIST
LITURGISTS
LITURGY
LIVABILITIES
LIVABILITY
LIVABLE
LIVABLENESS
LIVABLENESSES
LIVE
LIVEABILITIES
LIVEABILITY
LIVEABLE
LIVED
LIVELIER
LIVELIEST
LIVELIHOOD
LIVELIHOODS
LIVELILY
LIVELINESS
LIVELINESSES
LIVELONG
LIVELY
LIVEN
LIVENED
LIVENER
LIVENERS
LIVENESS
LIVENESSES
LIVENING
LIVENS
LIVER
LIVERED
LIVERIED
LIVERIES
LIVERING
LIVERISH
LIVERISHNESS
LIVERISHNESSES
LIVERLEAF
LIVERLEAVES
LIVERS
LIVERWORT
LIVERWORTS
LIVERWURST
LIVERWURSTS
LIVERY
LIVERYMAN
LIVERYMEN
LIVES
LIVEST
LIVESTOCK
LIVESTOCKS
LIVETRAP
LIVETRAPPED
LIVETRAPPING
LIVETRAPS
LIVEWARE
LIVEWARES
LIVEWELL
LIVEWELLS
LIVEYER
LIVEYERS
LIVID
LIVIDITIES
LIVIDITY
LIVIDLY
LIVIDNESS
LIVIDNESSES
LIVIER
LIVIERS
LIVING
LIVINGLY
LIVINGNESS
LIVINGNESSES
LIVINGS
LIVRE
LIVRES
LIVYER
LIVYERS
LIXIVIA
LIXIVIAL
LIXIVIATE
LIXIVIATED
LIXIVIATES
LIXIVIATING
LIXIVIATION
LIXIVIATIONS
LIXIVIUM
LIXIVIUMS
LIZARD
LIZARDS
LLAMA
LLAMAS
LLANO
LLANOS
LO
LOACH
LOACHES
LOAD
LOADABLE
LOADED
LOADER
LOADERS
LOADING
LOADINGS
LOADMASTER
LOADMASTERS
LOADS
LOADSTAR
LOADSTARS
LOADSTONE
LOADSTONES
LOAF
LOAFED
LOAFER
LOAFERS
LOAFING
LOAFINGS
LOAFS
LOAM
LOAMED
LOAMIER
LOAMIEST
LOAMINESS
LOAMINESSES
LOAMING
LOAMLESS
LOAMS
LOAMY
LOAN
LOANABLE
LOANED
LOANEE
LOANEES
LOANER
LOANERS
LOANING
LOANINGS
LOANS
LOANSHIFT
LOANSHIFTS
LOANWORD
LOANWORDS
LOATH
LOATHE
LOATHED
LOATHER
LOATHERS
LOATHES
LOATHFUL
LOATHING
LOATHINGS
LOATHLY
LOATHNESS
LOATHNESSES
LOATHSOME
LOATHSOMELY
LOATHSOMENESS
LOATHSOMENESSES
LOAVES
LOB
LOBAR
LOBATE
LOBATED
LOBATELY
LOBATION
LOBATIONS
LOBBED
LOBBER
LOBBERS
LOBBIED
LOBBIES
LOBBING
LOBBY
LOBBYER
LOBBYERS
LOBBYGOW
LOBBYGOWS
LOBBYING
LOBBYINGS
LOBBYISM
LOBBYISMS
LOBBYIST
LOBBYISTS
LOBE
LOBECTOMIES
LOBECTOMY
LOBED
LOBEFIN
LOBEFINS
LOBELESS
LOBELIA
LOBELIAS
LOBELINE
LOBELINES
LOBES
LOBLOLLIES
LOBLOLLY
LOBO
LOBOS
LOBOTOMIES
LOBOTOMISE
LOBOTOMISED
LOBOTOMISES
LOBOTOMISING
LOBOTOMIZE
LOBOTOMIZED
LOBOTOMIZES
LOBOTOMIZING
LOBOTOMY
LOBS
LOBSCOUSE
LOBSCOUSES
LOBSTER
LOBSTERED
LOBSTERER
LOBSTERERS
LOBSTERING
LOBSTERINGS
LOBSTERLIKE
LOBSTERMAN
LOBSTERMEN
LOBSTERS
LOBSTICK
LOBSTICKS
LOBTAIL
LOBTAILED
LOBTAILING
LOBTAILINGS
LOBTAILS
LOBULAR
LOBULARLY
LOBULATE
LOBULATED
LOBULATION
LOBULATIONS
LOBULE
LOBULES
LOBULOSE
LOBWORM
LOBWORMS
LOCA
LOCAL
LOCALE
LOCALES
LOCALISATION
LOCALISATIONS
LOCALISE
LOCALISED

LOCALISES
LOCALISING
LOCALISM
LOCALISMS
LOCALIST
LOCALISTS
LOCALITE
LOCALITES
LOCALITIES
LOCALITY
LOCALIZABILITY
LOCALIZABLE
LOCALIZATION
LOCALIZATIONS
LOCALIZE
LOCALIZED
LOCALIZER
LOCALIZERS
LOCALIZES
LOCALIZING
LOCALLY
LOCALNESS
LOCALNESSES
LOCALS
LOCATABLE
LOCATE
LOCATED
LOCATER
LOCATERS
LOCATES
LOCATING
LOCATION
LOCATIONAL
LOCATIONALLY
LOCATIONS
LOCATIVE
LOCATIVES
LOCATOR
LOCATORS
LOCAVORE
LOCAVORES
LOCH
LOCHAN
LOCHANS
LOCHE
LOCHES
LOCHIA
LOCHIAL
LOCHIAS
LOCHS
LOCI
LOCIE
LOCIES
LOCIS
LOCK
LOCKABLE
LOCKAGE
LOCKAGES
LOCKBOX
LOCKBOXES
LOCKDOWN
LOCKDOWNS
LOCKED
LOCKER
LOCKERS
LOCKET
LOCKETS
LOCKING
LOCKJAW
LOCKJAWS
LOCKKEEPER
LOCKKEEPERS
LOCKLESS
LOCKMAKER
LOCKMAKERS
LOCKNUT
LOCKNUTS
LOCKOUT
LOCKOUTS
LOCKRAM
LOCKRAMS
LOCKS
LOCKSET
LOCKSETS
LOCKSMITH
LOCKSMITHING
LOCKSMITHINGS
LOCKSMITHS
LOCKSTEP
LOCKSTEPS
LOCKSTITCH
LOCKSTITCHED
LOCKSTITCHES
LOCKSTITCHING
LOCKUP
LOCKUPS
LOCO
LOCOED
LOCOES
LOCOFOCO
LOCOFOCOS
LOCOING
LOCOISM
LOCOISMS
LOCOMOTE
LOCOMOTED
LOCOMOTES
LOCOMOTING
LOCOMOTION
LOCOMOTIONS
LOCOMOTIVE
LOCOMOTIVES
LOCOMOTOR
LOCOMOTORS
LOCOMOTORY
LOCOS
LOCOWEED
LOCOWEEDS
LOCULAR
LOCULATE
LOCULATED
LOCULE
LOCULED
LOCULES
LOCULI
LOCULICIDAL
LOCULUS
LOCUM
LOCUMS
LOCUS
LOCUST
LOCUSTA
LOCUSTAE
LOCUSTAL
LOCUSTS
LOCUTION
LOCUTIONS
LOCUTORIES
LOCUTORY
LODE
LODEN
LODENS
LODES
LODESTAR
LODESTARS
LODESTONE
LODESTONES
LODGE
LODGED
LODGEMENT
LODGEMENTS
LODGER
LODGERS
LODGES
LODGING
LODGINGS
LODGMENT
LODGMENTS
LODICULE
LODICULES
LOESS
LOESSAL
LOESSES
LOESSIAL
LOESSIC
LOFT
LOFTED
LOFTER
LOFTERS
LOFTIER
LOFTIEST
LOFTILY
LOFTINESS
LOFTINESSES
LOFTING
LOFTLESS
LOFTLIKE
LOFTS
LOFTY
LOG
LOGAN
LOGANBERRIES
LOGANBERRY
LOGANIA
LOGANS
LOGAOEDIC
LOGAOEDICS
LOGARITHM
LOGARITHMIC
LOGARITHMICALLY
LOGARITHMS
LOGBOOK
LOGBOOKS
LOGE
LOGES
LOGGATS
LOGGED
LOGGER
LOGGERHEAD
LOGGERHEADS
LOGGERS
LOGGETS
LOGGIA
LOGGIAS
LOGGIE
LOGGIER
LOGGIEST
LOGGING
LOGGINGS
LOGGISH
LOGGY
LOGIA
LOGIC
LOGICAL
LOGICALITIES
LOGICALITY
LOGICALLY
LOGICALNESS
LOGICALNESSES
LOGICIAN
LOGICIANS
LOGICISE
LOGICISED
LOGICISES
LOGICISING
LOGICIZE
LOGICIZED
LOGICIZES
LOGICIZING
LOGICLESS
LOGICS
LOGIER
LOGIEST
LOGILY
LOGIN
LOGINESS
LOGINESSES
LOGINS
LOGION
LOGIONS
LOGISTIC
LOGISTICAL
LOGISTICALLY
LOGISTICIAN
LOGISTICIANS
LOGISTICS
LOGJAM
LOGJAMMED
LOGJAMMING
LOGJAMS
LOGNORMAL
LOGNORMALITIES
LOGNORMALITY
LOGNORMALLY
LOGO
LOGOCENTRIC
LOGOCENTRISM
LOGOCENTRISMS
LOGOED
LOGOFF
LOGOFFS
LOGOGRAM
LOGOGRAMMATIC
LOGOGRAMS
LOGOGRAPH

LOGOGRAPHIC
LOGOGRAPHICALLY
LOGOGRAPHS
LOGOGRIPH
LOGOGRIPHS
LOGOI
LOGOMACH
LOGOMACHIES
LOGOMACHS
LOGOMACHY
LOGON
LOGONS
LOGOPHILE
LOGOPHILES
LOGORRHEA
LOGORRHEAS
LOGORRHEIC
LOGOS
LOGOTYPE
LOGOTYPES
LOGOTYPIES
LOGOTYPY
LOGOUT
LOGOUTS
LOGROLL
LOGROLLED
LOGROLLER
LOGROLLERS
LOGROLLING
LOGROLLINGS
LOGROLLS
LOGS
LOGWAY
LOGWAYS
LOGWOOD
LOGWOODS
LOGY
LOIASES
LOIASIS
LOIASISES
LOID
LOIDED
LOIDING
LOIDS
LOIN
LOINCLOTH
LOINCLOTHS
LOINS
LOITER
LOITERED
LOITERER
LOITERERS
LOITERING
LOITERS
LOLL
LOLLAPALOOZA
LOLLAPALOOZAS
LOLLED
LOLLER
LOLLERS
LOLLIES
LOLLING
LOLLINGLY
LOLLIPOP
LOLLIPOPS
LOLLOP
LOLLOPED
LOLLOPING
LOLLOPS
LOLLOPY
LOLLS
LOLLY
LOLLYGAG
LOLLYGAGGED
LOLLYGAGGER
LOLLYGAGGERS
LOLLYGAGGING
LOLLYGAGS
LOLLYPOP
LOLLYPOPS
LOMEIN
LOMEINS
LOMENT
LOMENTA
LOMENTS
LOMENTUM
LOMENTUMS
LONE
LONELIER
LONELIEST
LONELILY
LONELINESS
LONELINESSES
LONELY
LONENESS
LONENESSES
LONER
LONERS
LONESOME
LONESOMELY
LONESOMENESS
LONESOMENESSES
LONESOMES
LONG
LONGAN
LONGANIMITIES
LONGANIMITY
LONGANS
LONGBOAT
LONGBOATS
LONGBOW
LONGBOWMAN
LONGBOWMEN
LONGBOWS
LONGCLOTH
LONGCLOTHS
LONGE
LONGED
LONGEING
LONGER
LONGERON
LONGERONS
LONGERS
LONGES
LONGEST
LONGEVITIES
LONGEVITY
LONGEVOUS
LONGHAIR
LONGHAIRED
LONGHAIRS
LONGHAND
LONGHANDS
LONGHEAD
LONGHEADED
LONGHEADEDNESS
LONGHEADS
LONGHORN
LONGHORNS
LONGHOUSE
LONGHOUSES
LONGICORN
LONGICORNS
LONGIES
LONGING
LONGINGLY
LONGINGS
LONGISH
LONGITUDE
LONGITUDES
LONGITUDINAL
LONGITUDINALLY
LONGJUMP
LONGJUMPED
LONGJUMPING
LONGJUMPS
LONGLEAF
LONGLEAVES
LONGLINE
LONGLINES
LONGLY
LONGNECK
LONGNECKS
LONGNESS
LONGNESSES
LONGS
LONGSHIP
LONGSHIPS
LONGSHORE
LONGSHOREMAN
LONGSHOREMEN
LONGSHORING
LONGSHORINGS
LONGSIGHTED
LONGSIGHTEDNESS
LONGSOME
LONGSOMELY
LONGSOMENESS
LONGSOMENESSES
LONGSPUR
LONGSPURS
LONGTIME
LONGUEUR
LONGUEURS
LONGWAYS
LONGWISE
LONICERA
LONICERAS
LOO
LOOBIES
LOOBY
LOOED
LOOEY
LOOEYS
LOOF
LOOFA
LOOFAH
LOOFAHS
LOOFAS
LOOFS
LOOIE
LOOIES
LOOING
LOOK
LOOKALIKE
LOOKALIKES
LOOKDOWN
LOOKDOWNS
LOOKED
LOOKER
LOOKERS
LOOKIE
LOOKING
LOOKISM
LOOKISMS
LOOKIST
LOOKISTS
LOOKIT
LOOKITED
LOOKITING
LOOKITS
LOOKOUT
LOOKOUTS
LOOKS
LOOKSISM
LOOKSISMS
LOOKUP
LOOKUPS
LOOKY
LOOM
LOOMED
LOOMING
LOOMS
LOON
LOONEY
LOONEYS
LOONIE
LOONIER
LOONIES
LOONIEST
LOONILY
LOONINESS
LOONINESSES
LOONS
LOONY
LOOP
LOOPED
LOOPER
LOOPERS
LOOPHOLE
LOOPHOLED
LOOPHOLES
LOOPHOLING
LOOPIER
LOOPIEST
LOOPILY
LOOPINESS
LOOPINESSES
LOOPING
LOOPS
LOOPY
LOOS
LOOSE
LOOSED
LOOSELY

LOOSEN
LOOSENED
LOOSENER
LOOSENERS
LOOSENESS
LOOSENESSES
LOOSENING
LOOSENS
LOOSER
LOOSES
LOOSEST
LOOSESTRIFE
LOOSESTRIFES
LOOSING
LOOT
LOOTED
LOOTER
LOOTERS
LOOTING
LOOTINGS
LOOTS
LOP
LOPE
LOPED
LOPER
LOPERS
LOPES
LOPHOPHORE
LOPHOPHORES
LOPING
LOPINGLY
LOPPED
LOPPER
LOPPERED
LOPPERING
LOPPERS
LOPPET
LOPPETS
LOPPIER
LOPPIEST
LOPPING
LOPPY
LOPS
LOPSIDED
LOPSIDEDLY
LOPSIDEDNESS
LOPSIDEDNESSES
LOPSTICK
LOPSTICKS
LOQUACIOUS
LOQUACIOUSLY
LOQUACIOUSNESS
LOQUACITIES
LOQUACITY
LOQUAT
LOQUATS
LOQUITUR
LOR
LORAL
LORAN
LORANS
LORAZEPAM
LORAZEPAMS
LORD
LORDED
LORDING
LORDINGS
LORDLESS
LORDLIER
LORDLIEST
LORDLIKE
LORDLINESS
LORDLINESSES
LORDLING
LORDLINGS
LORDLY
LORDOMA
LORDOMAS
LORDOSES
LORDOSIS
LORDOTIC
LORDS
LORDSHIP
LORDSHIPS
LORE
LOREAL
LORES
LORGNETTE
LORGNETTES
LORGNON
LORGNONS
LORICA
LORICAE
LORICAS
LORICATE
LORICATED
LORICATES
LORIES
LORIKEET
LORIKEETS
LORIMER
LORIMERS
LORINER
LORINERS
LORIS
LORISES
LORN
LORNER
LORNEST
LORNNESS
LORNNESSES
LORRIES
LORRY
LORY
LOSABLE
LOSABLENESS
LOSABLENESSES
LOSE
LOSEL
LOSELS
LOSER
LOSERS
LOSES
LOSING
LOSINGEST
LOSINGLY
LOSINGS
LOSS
LOSSES
LOSSLESS
LOSSY
LOST
LOSTNESS
LOSTNESSES
LOT
LOTA
LOTAH
LOTAHS
LOTAS
LOTH
LOTHARIO
LOTHARIOS
LOTHSOME
LOTI
LOTIC
LOTION
LOTIONS
LOTO
LOTOS
LOTOSES
LOTS
LOTSA
LOTTA
LOTTE
LOTTED
LOTTER
LOTTERIES
LOTTERS
LOTTERY
LOTTES
LOTTING
LOTTO
LOTTOS
LOTUS
LOTUSES
LOTUSLAND
LOTUSLANDS
LOUCHE
LOUD
LOUDEN
LOUDENED
LOUDENING
LOUDENS
LOUDER
LOUDEST
LOUDHAILER
LOUDHAILERS
LOUDISH
LOUDLIER
LOUDLIEST
LOUDLY
LOUDMOUTH
LOUDMOUTHED
LOUDMOUTHS
LOUDNESS
LOUDNESSES
LOUDSPEAKER
LOUDSPEAKERS
LOUGH
LOUGHS
LOUIE
LOUIES
LOUIS
LOUMA
LOUMAS
LOUNGE
LOUNGED
LOUNGER
LOUNGERS
LOUNGES
LOUNGEWEAR
LOUNGEWEARS
LOUNGEY
LOUNGIER
LOUNGIEST
LOUNGING
LOUNGY
LOUP
LOUPE
LOUPED
LOUPEN
LOUPES
LOUPING
LOUPS
LOUR
LOURED
LOURING
LOURS
LOURY
LOUSE
LOUSED
LOUSES
LOUSEWORT
LOUSEWORTS
LOUSIER
LOUSIEST
LOUSILY
LOUSINESS
LOUSINESSES
LOUSING
LOUSY
LOUT
LOUTED
LOUTING
LOUTISH
LOUTISHLY
LOUTISHNESS
LOUTISHNESSES
LOUTS
LOUVER
LOUVERED
LOUVERS
LOUVRE
LOUVRED
LOUVRES
LOVABILITIES
LOVABILITY
LOVABLE
LOVABLENESS
LOVABLENESSES
LOVABLY
LOVAGE
LOVAGES
LOVASTATIN
LOVASTATINS
LOVAT
LOVATS
LOVE
LOVEABLE
LOVEABLY
LOVEBIRD
LOVEBIRDS
LOVEBUG
LOVEBUGS
LOVED

LOVEFEST
LOVEFESTS
LOVELESS
LOVELESSLY
LOVELESSNESS
LOVELESSNESSES
LOVELIER
LOVELIES
LOVELIEST
LOVELILY
LOVELINESS
LOVELINESSES
LOVELOCK
LOVELOCKS
LOVELORN
LOVELORNNESS
LOVELORNNESSES
LOVELY
LOVEMAKER
LOVEMAKERS
LOVEMAKING
LOVEMAKINGS
LOVER
LOVERLY
LOVERS
LOVES
LOVESEAT
LOVESEATS
LOVESICK
LOVESICKNESS
LOVESICKNESSES
LOVESOME
LOVEVINE
LOVEVINES
LOVEY
LOVEYS
LOVIER
LOVIEST
LOVING
LOVINGLY
LOVINGNESS
LOVINGNESSES
LOVINGS
LOW
LOWBALL
LOWBALLED
LOWBALLING
LOWBALLINGS
LOWBALLS
LOWBORN
LOWBOY
LOWBOYS
LOWBRED
LOWBROW
LOWBROWED
LOWBROWS
LOWBUSH
LOWBUSHES
LOWDOWN
LOWDOWNS
LOWE
LOWED
LOWER
LOWERCASE
LOWERCASED
LOWERCASES
LOWERCASING
LOWERED
LOWERING
LOWERMOST
LOWERS
LOWERY
LOWES
LOWEST
LOWING
LOWINGS
LOWISH
LOWLAND
LOWLANDER
LOWLANDERS
LOWLANDS
LOWLIER
LOWLIEST
LOWLIFE
LOWLIFER
LOWLIFERS
LOWLIFES
LOWLIGHT
LOWLIGHTS
LOWLIHEAD
LOWLIHEADS
LOWLILY
LOWLINESS
LOWLINESSES
LOWLIVES
LOWLY
LOWN
LOWNESS
LOWNESSES
LOWPASS
LOWRIDER
LOWRIDERS
LOWS
LOWSE
LOX
LOXED
LOXES
LOXING
LOXODROME
LOXODROMES
LOYAL
LOYALER
LOYALEST
LOYALISM
LOYALISMS
LOYALIST
LOYALISTS
LOYALLY
LOYALTIES
LOYALTY
LOZENGE
LOZENGES
LUAU
LUAUS
LUBBER
LUBBERLINESS
LUBBERLINESSES
LUBBERLY
LUBBERS
LUBE
LUBED
LUBES
LUBING
LUBRIC
LUBRICAL
LUBRICANT
LUBRICANTS
LUBRICATE
LUBRICATED
LUBRICATES
LUBRICATING
LUBRICATION
LUBRICATIONS
LUBRICATIVE
LUBRICATOR
LUBRICATORS
LUBRICIOUS
LUBRICIOUSLY
LUBRICITIES
LUBRICITY
LUBRICOUS
LUCARNE
LUCARNES
LUCE
LUCENCE
LUCENCES
LUCENCIES
LUCENCY
LUCENT
LUCENTLY
LUCERN
LUCERNE
LUCERNES
LUCERNS
LUCES
LUCID
LUCIDER
LUCIDEST
LUCIDITIES
LUCIDITY
LUCIDLY
LUCIDNESS
LUCIDNESSES
LUCIFER
LUCIFERASE
LUCIFERASES
LUCIFERIN
LUCIFERINS
LUCIFEROUS
LUCIFERS
LUCITE
LUCITES
LUCK
LUCKED
LUCKIE
LUCKIER
LUCKIES
LUCKIEST
LUCKILY
LUCKINESS
LUCKINESSES
LUCKING
LUCKLESS
LUCKS
LUCKY
LUCRATIVE
LUCRATIVELY
LUCRATIVENESS
LUCRATIVENESSES
LUCRE
LUCRES
LUCUBRATE
LUCUBRATED
LUCUBRATES
LUCUBRATING
LUCUBRATION
LUCUBRATIONS
LUCULENT
LUCULENTLY
LUD
LUDE
LUDES
LUDIC
LUDICROUS
LUDICROUSLY
LUDICROUSNESS
LUDICROUSNESSES
LUDO
LUDOS
LUDS
LUES
LUETIC
LUETICS
LUFF
LUFFA
LUFFAS
LUFFED
LUFFING
LUFFS
LUFTMENSCH
LUFTMENSCHEN
LUG
LUGE
LUGED
LUGEING
LUGER
LUGERS
LUGES
LUGGAGE
LUGGAGES
LUGGED
LUGGER
LUGGERS
LUGGIE
LUGGIES
LUGGING
LUGING
LUGS
LUGSAIL
LUGSAILS
LUGUBRIOUS
LUGUBRIOUSLY
LUGUBRIOUSNESS
LUGWORM
LUGWORMS
LUKEWARM
LUKEWARMLY
LUKEWARMNESS
LUKEWARMNESSES
LULL
LULLABIED
LULLABIES
LULLABY
LULLABYING
LULLED

LULLER
LULLERS
LULLING
LULLS
LULU
LULUS
LUM
LUMA
LUMAS
LUMBAGO
LUMBAGOS
LUMBAR
LUMBARS
LUMBER
LUMBERED
LUMBERER
LUMBERERS
LUMBERING
LUMBERINGS
LUMBERJACK
LUMBERJACKS
LUMBERLY
LUMBERMAN
LUMBERMEN
LUMBERS
LUMBERYARD
LUMBERYARDS
LUMBOSACRAL
LUMBRICAL
LUMBRICALS
LUMEN
LUMENAL
LUMENS
LUMINA
LUMINAIRE
LUMINAIRES
LUMINAL
LUMINANCE
LUMINANCES
LUMINARIA
LUMINARIAS
LUMINARIES
LUMINARY
LUMINESCE
LUMINESCED
LUMINESCENCE
LUMINESCENCES
LUMINESCENT
LUMINESCES
LUMINESCING
LUMINIFEROUS
LUMINISM
LUMINISMS
LUMINIST
LUMINISTS
LUMINOSITIES
LUMINOSITY
LUMINOUS
LUMINOUSLY
LUMINOUSNESS
LUMINOUSNESSES
LUMMOX
LUMMOXES
LUMP
LUMPECTOMIES
LUMPECTOMY
LUMPED
LUMPEN
LUMPENS
LUMPER
LUMPERS
LUMPFISH
LUMPFISHES
LUMPIA
LUMPIAS
LUMPIER
LUMPIEST
LUMPILY
LUMPINESS
LUMPINESSES
LUMPING
LUMPINGLY
LUMPISH
LUMPISHLY
LUMPISHNESS
LUMPISHNESSES
LUMPS
LUMPY
LUMS
LUN
LUNA
LUNACIES
LUNACY
LUNAR
LUNARIAN
LUNARIANS
LUNARS
LUNAS
LUNATE
LUNATED
LUNATELY
LUNATES
LUNATIC
LUNATICS
LUNATION
LUNATIONS
LUNCH
LUNCHBOX
LUNCHBOXES
LUNCHED
LUNCHEON
LUNCHEONETTE
LUNCHEONETTES
LUNCHEONS
LUNCHER
LUNCHERS
LUNCHES
LUNCHING
LUNCHMEAT
LUNCHMEATS
LUNCHROOM
LUNCHROOMS
LUNCHTIME
LUNCHTIMES
LUNE
LUNES
LUNET
LUNETS
LUNETTE
LUNETTES
LUNG
LUNGAN
LUNGANS
LUNGE
LUNGED
LUNGEE
LUNGEES
LUNGEING
LUNGER
LUNGERS
LUNGES
LUNGFISH
LUNGFISHES
LUNGFUL
LUNGFULS
LUNGI
LUNGING
LUNGIS
LUNGLESS
LUNGS
LUNGWORM
LUNGWORMS
LUNGWORT
LUNGWORTS
LUNGYI
LUNGYIS
LUNIER
LUNIES
LUNIEST
LUNISOLAR
LUNITIDAL
LUNK
LUNKER
LUNKERS
LUNKHEAD
LUNKHEADED
LUNKHEADS
LUNKS
LUNS
LUNT
LUNTED
LUNTING
LUNTS
LUNULA
LUNULAE
LUNULAR
LUNULATE
LUNULATED
LUNULE
LUNULES
LUNY
LUPANAR
LUPANARS
LUPIN
LUPINE
LUPINES
LUPINS
LUPOID
LUPOUS
LUPULIN
LUPULINS
LUPUS
LUPUSES
LURCH
LURCHED
LURCHER
LURCHERS
LURCHES
LURCHING
LURDAN
LURDANE
LURDANES
LURDANS
LURE
LURED
LURER
LURERS
LURES
LUREX
LUREXES
LURID
LURIDLY
LURIDNESS
LURIDNESSES
LURING
LURINGLY
LURK
LURKED
LURKER
LURKERS
LURKING
LURKINGLY
LURKS
LUSCIOUS
LUSCIOUSLY
LUSCIOUSNESS
LUSCIOUSNESSES
LUSH
LUSHED
LUSHER
LUSHES
LUSHEST
LUSHING
LUSHLY
LUSHNESS
LUSHNESSES
LUST
LUSTED
LUSTER
LUSTERED
LUSTERING
LUSTERLESS
LUSTERS
LUSTERWARE
LUSTERWARES
LUSTFUL
LUSTFULLY
LUSTFULNESS
LUSTFULNESSES
LUSTIER
LUSTIEST
LUSTIHOOD
LUSTIHOODS
LUSTILY
LUSTINESS
LUSTINESSES
LUSTING
LUSTRA
LUSTRAL
LUSTRATE
LUSTRATED
LUSTRATES
LUSTRATING
LUSTRATION
LUSTRATIONS

LUSTRE
LUSTRED
LUSTRELESS
LUSTRES
LUSTRINE
LUSTRINES
LUSTRING
LUSTRINGS
LUSTROUS
LUSTROUSLY
LUSTROUSNESS
LUSTROUSNESSES
LUSTRUM
LUSTRUMS
LUSTS
LUSTY
LUSUS
LUSUSES
LUTANIST
LUTANISTS
LUTE
LUTEA
LUTEAL
LUTECIUM
LUTECIUMS
LUTED
LUTEFISK
LUTEFISKS
LUTEIN
LUTEINIZATION
LUTEINIZATIONS
LUTEINIZE
LUTEINIZED
LUTEINIZES
LUTEINIZING
LUTEINS
LUTENIST
LUTENISTS
LUTEOLIN
LUTEOLINS
LUTEOTROPHIC
LUTEOTROPHIN
LUTEOTROPHINS
LUTEOTROPIC
LUTEOTROPIN
LUTEOTROPINS
LUTEOUS
LUTES
LUTESTRING
LUTESTRINGS
LUTETIUM
LUTETIUMS
LUTEUM
LUTFISK
LUTFISKS
LUTHERN
LUTHERNS
LUTHIER
LUTHIERS
LUTING
LUTINGS
LUTIST
LUTISTS
LUTZ
LUTZES
LUV
LUVED
LUVING
LUVS
LUVVED
LUVVIE
LUVVIES
LUVVING
LUVVY
LUX
LUXATE
LUXATED
LUXATES
LUXATING
LUXATION
LUXATIONS
LUXE
LUXER
LUXES
LUXEST
LUXURIANCE
LUXURIANCES
LUXURIANT
LUXURIANTLY
LUXURIATE
LUXURIATED
LUXURIATES
LUXURIATING
LUXURIES
LUXURIOUS
LUXURIOUSLY
LUXURIOUSNESS
LUXURIOUSNESSES
LUXURY
LWEI
LWEIS
LYARD
LYART
LYASE
LYASES
LYCANTHROPIC
LYCANTHROPIES
LYCANTHROPY
LYCEA
LYCEE
LYCEES
LYCEUM
LYCEUMS
LYCH
LYCHEE
LYCHEES
LYCHES
LYCHGATE
LYCHGATES
LYCHNIS
LYCHNISES
LYCOPENE
LYCOPENES
LYCOPOD
LYCOPODIUM
LYCOPODIUMS
LYCOPODS
LYCOPSID
LYCOPSIDS
LYCRA
LYCRAS
LYDDITE
LYDDITES
LYE
LYES
LYING
LYINGLY
LYINGS
LYMPH
LYMPHADENITIS
LYMPHADENITISES
LYMPHADENOPATHY
LYMPHANGIOGRAM
LYMPHANGIOGRAMS
LYMPHATIC
LYMPHATICALLY
LYMPHATICS
LYMPHEDEMA
LYMPHEDEMAS
LYMPHOBLAST
LYMPHOBLASTIC
LYMPHOBLASTS
LYMPHOCYTE
LYMPHOCYTES
LYMPHOCYTIC
LYMPHOCYTOSES
LYMPHOCYTOSIS
LYMPHOGRAM
LYMPHOGRAMS
LYMPHOGRANULOMA
LYMPHOGRAPHIC
LYMPHOGRAPHIES
LYMPHOGRAPHY
LYMPHOID
LYMPHOKINE
LYMPHOKINES
LYMPHOMA
LYMPHOMAS
LYMPHOMATA
LYMPHOMATOSES
LYMPHOMATOSIS
LYMPHOMATOUS
LYMPHOMITOSES
LYMPHOMITOSIS
LYMPHOSARCOMA
LYMPHOSARCOMAS
LYMPHOSARCOMATA
LYMPHOUS
LYMPHS
LYNCEAN
LYNCH
LYNCHED
LYNCHER
LYNCHERS
LYNCHES
LYNCHING
LYNCHINGS
LYNCHPIN
LYNCHPINS
LYNX
LYNXES
LYONNAISE
LYOPHILE
LYOPHILED
LYOPHILIC
LYOPHILISE
LYOPHILISED
LYOPHILISES
LYOPHILISING
LYOPHILIZATION
LYOPHILIZATIONS
LYOPHILIZE
LYOPHILIZED
LYOPHILIZER
LYOPHILIZERS
LYOPHILIZES
LYOPHILIZING
LYOPHOBIC
LYRATE
LYRATED
LYRATELY
LYRE
LYREBIRD
LYREBIRDS
LYRES
LYRIC
LYRICAL
LYRICALLY
LYRICALNESS
LYRICALNESSES
LYRICISE
LYRICISED
LYRICISES
LYRICISING
LYRICISM
LYRICISMS
LYRICIST
LYRICISTS
LYRICIZE
LYRICIZED
LYRICIZES
LYRICIZING
LYRICON
LYRICONS
LYRICS
LYRIFORM
LYRISM
LYRISMS
LYRIST
LYRISTS
LYSATE
LYSATES
LYSE
LYSED
LYSES
LYSIMETER
LYSIMETERS
LYSIMETRIC
LYSIN
LYSINE
LYSINES
LYSING
LYSINS
LYSIS
LYSOGEN
LYSOGENIC
LYSOGENICITIES
LYSOGENICITY
LYSOGENIES
LYSOGENISE
LYSOGENISED
LYSOGENISES
LYSOGENISING
LYSOGENIZATION
LYSOGENIZATIONS

LYSOGENIZE
LYSOGENIZED
LYSOGENIZES
LYSOGENIZING
LYSOGENS
LYSOGENY
LYSOLECITHIN
LYSOLECITHINS
LYSOSOMAL
LYSOSOME
LYSOSOMES
LYSOZYME
LYSOZYMES
LYSSA
LYSSAS
LYTHRUM
LYTHRUMS
LYTIC
LYTICALLY
LYTTA
LYTTAE
LYTTAS

M

MA
MAAR
MAARS
MABE
MABES
MAC
MACABER
MACABRE
MACABRELY
MACABRER
MACABREST
MACACO
MACACOS
MACADAM
MACADAMED
MACADAMIA
MACADAMIAS
MACADAMIZE
MACADAMIZED
MACADAMIZES
MACADAMIZING
MACADAMS
MACAQUE
MACAQUES
MACARONI
MACARONIC
MACARONICS
MACARONIES
MACARONIS
MACAROON
MACAROONS
MACAW
MACAWS
MACCABAW
MACCABAWS
MACCABOY
MACCABOYS
MACCHIA
MACCHIATO
MACCHIATOS
MACCHIE
MACCOBOY
MACCOBOYS
MACE
MACED
MACEDOINE
MACEDOINES
MACER
MACERATE
MACERATED
MACERATER
MACERATERS
MACERATES
MACERATING
MACERATION
MACERATIONS
MACERATOR
MACERATORS
MACERS
MACES
MACH
MACHACA
MACHACAS
MACHE
MACHER
MACHERS
MACHES
MACHETE
MACHETES
MACHICOLATED
MACHICOLATION
MACHICOLATIONS
MACHINABILITIES
MACHINABILITY
MACHINABLE
MACHINATE
MACHINATED
MACHINATES
MACHINATING
MACHINATION
MACHINATIONS
MACHINATOR
MACHINATORS
MACHINE
MACHINEABILITY
MACHINEABLE
MACHINED
MACHINELIKE
MACHINERIES
MACHINERY
MACHINES
MACHINING
MACHINIST
MACHINISTS
MACHISMO
MACHISMOS
MACHO
MACHOISM
MACHOISMS
MACHOS
MACHREE
MACHREES
MACHS
MACHZOR
MACHZORIM
MACHZORS
MACING
MACINTOSH
MACINTOSHES
MACK
MACKEREL
MACKERELS
MACKINAW
MACKINAWS
MACKINTOSH
MACKINTOSHES
MACKLE
MACKLED
MACKLES
MACKLING
MACKS
MACLE
MACLED
MACLES
MACON
MACONS
MACRAME
MACRAMES
MACRO
MACROAGGREGATE
MACROAGGREGATED
MACROAGGREGATES
MACROBIOTIC
MACROBIOTICS
MACROCOSM
MACROCOSMIC
MACROCOSMICALLY
MACROCOSMS
MACROCYCLIC
MACROCYST
MACROCYSTS
MACROCYTE
MACROCYTES
MACROCYTIC
MACROCYTOSES
MACROCYTOSIS
MACRODONT
MACROECONOMIC
MACROECONOMICS
MACROEVOLUTION
MACROEVOLUTIONS
MACROFOSSIL
MACROFOSSILS
MACROGAMETE
MACROGAMETES
MACROGLOBULIN
MACROGLOBULINS
MACROMERE
MACROMERES
MACROMOLE
MACROMOLECULAR
MACROMOLECULE
MACROMOLECULES
MACROMOLES
MACRON
MACRONS
MACRONUCLEAR
MACRONUCLEI
MACRONUCLEUS
MACRONUCLEUSES
MACRONUTRIENT
MACRONUTRIENTS
MACROPHAGE
MACROPHAGES
MACROPHAGIC
MACROPHOTOGRAPH
MACROPHYTE
MACROPHYTES
MACROPHYTIC
MACROPOD
MACROPODS
MACROPTEROUS
MACROS
MACROSCALE
MACROSCALES
MACROSCOPIC
MACROSCOPICALLY
MACROSTRUCTURAL
MACROSTRUCTURE
MACROSTRUCTURES

MACRURAL
MACRURAN
MACRURANS
MACRUROUS
MACS
MACULA
MACULAE
MACULAR
MACULAS
MACULATE
MACULATED
MACULATES
MACULATING
MACULATION
MACULATIONS
MACULE
MACULED
MACULES
MACULING
MACUMBA
MACUMBAS
MAD
MADAM
MADAME
MADAMES
MADAMS
MADCAP
MADCAPS
MADDED
MADDEN
MADDENED
MADDENING
MADDENINGLY
MADDENS
MADDER
MADDERS
MADDEST
MADDING
MADDISH
MADE
MADEIRA
MADEIRAS
MADELEINE
MADELEINES
MADEMOISELLE
MADEMOISELLES
MADERIZE
MADERIZED
MADERIZES
MADERIZING
MADHOUSE
MADHOUSES
MADLY
MADMAN
MADMEN
MADNESS
MADNESSES
MADONNA
MADONNAS
MADRAS
MADRASA
MADRASAH
MADRASAHS
MADRASAS
MADRASES
MADRASSA
MADRASSAH
MADRASSAHS
MADRASSAS
MADRE
MADREPORE
MADREPORES
MADREPORIAN
MADREPORIANS
MADREPORIC
MADREPORITE
MADREPORITES
MADRES
MADRIGAL
MADRIGALIAN
MADRIGALIST
MADRIGALISTS
MADRIGALS
MADRILENE
MADRILENES
MADRONA
MADRONAS
MADRONE
MADRONES
MADRONO
MADRONOS
MADS
MADTOM
MADTOMS
MADURO
MADUROS
MADWOMAN
MADWOMEN
MADWORT
MADWORTS
MADZOON
MADZOONS
MAE
MAELSTROM
MAELSTROMS
MAENAD
MAENADES
MAENADIC
MAENADISM
MAENADISMS
MAENADS
MAES
MAESTOSO
MAESTOSOS
MAESTRI
MAESTRO
MAESTROS
MAFFIA
MAFFIAS
MAFFICK
MAFFICKED
MAFFICKER
MAFFICKERS
MAFFICKING
MAFFICKS
MAFIA
MAFIAS
MAFIC
MAFIOSI
MAFIOSO
MAFIOSOS
MAFTIR
MAFTIRS
MAG
MAGALOG
MAGALOGS
MAGALOGUE
MAGALOGUES
MAGAZINE
MAGAZINES
MAGAZINIST
MAGAZINISTS
MAGDALEN
MAGDALENE
MAGDALENES
MAGDALENS
MAGE
MAGENTA
MAGENTAS
MAGES
MAGGOT
MAGGOTS
MAGGOTY
MAGI
MAGIAN
MAGIANS
MAGIC
MAGICAL
MAGICALLY
MAGICIAN
MAGICIANS
MAGICKED
MAGICKING
MAGICS
MAGILP
MAGILPS
MAGISTER
MAGISTERIAL
MAGISTERIALLY
MAGISTERIUM
MAGISTERIUMS
MAGISTERS
MAGISTRACIES
MAGISTRACY
MAGISTRAL
MAGISTRALLY
MAGISTRATE
MAGISTRATES
MAGISTRATICAL
MAGISTRATICALLY
MAGISTRATURE
MAGISTRATURES
MAGLEV
MAGLEVS
MAGMA
MAGMAS
MAGMATA
MAGMATIC
MAGNANIMITIES
MAGNANIMITY
MAGNANIMOUS
MAGNANIMOUSLY
MAGNANIMOUSNESS
MAGNATE
MAGNATES
MAGNESIA
MAGNESIAN
MAGNESIAS
MAGNESIC
MAGNESITE
MAGNESITES
MAGNESIUM
MAGNESIUMS
MAGNET
MAGNETIC
MAGNETICALLY
MAGNETICS
MAGNETISABLE
MAGNETISATION
MAGNETISATIONS
MAGNETISE
MAGNETISED
MAGNETISES
MAGNETISING
MAGNETISM
MAGNETISMS
MAGNETITE
MAGNETITES
MAGNETIZABLE
MAGNETIZATION
MAGNETIZATIONS
MAGNETIZE
MAGNETIZED
MAGNETIZER
MAGNETIZERS
MAGNETIZES
MAGNETIZING
MAGNETO
MAGNETOELECTRIC
MAGNETOGRAPH
MAGNETOGRAPHS
MAGNETOMETER
MAGNETOMETERS
MAGNETOMETRIC
MAGNETOMETRIES
MAGNETOMETRY
MAGNETON
MAGNETONS
MAGNETOPAUSE
MAGNETOPAUSES
MAGNETOS
MAGNETOSPHERE
MAGNETOSPHERES
MAGNETOSPHERIC
MAGNETOSTATIC
MAGNETRON
MAGNETRONS
MAGNETS
MAGNIFIC
MAGNIFICAL
MAGNIFICALLY
MAGNIFICAT
MAGNIFICATION
MAGNIFICATIONS
MAGNIFICATS
MAGNIFICENCE
MAGNIFICENCES
MAGNIFICENT
MAGNIFICENTLY
MAGNIFICO
MAGNIFICOES
MAGNIFICOS
MAGNIFIED
MAGNIFIER
MAGNIFIERS

MAGNIFIES
MAGNIFY
MAGNIFYING
MAGNILOQUENCE
MAGNILOQUENCES
MAGNILOQUENT
MAGNILOQUENTLY
MAGNITUDE
MAGNITUDES
MAGNOLIA
MAGNOLIAS
MAGNOX
MAGNOXES
MAGNUM
MAGNUMS
MAGOT
MAGOTS
MAGPIE
MAGPIES
MAGS
MAGUEY
MAGUEYS
MAGUS
MAHANT
MAHANTS
MAHARAJA
MAHARAJAH
MAHARAJAHS
MAHARAJAS
MAHARANEE
MAHARANEES
MAHARANI
MAHARANIS
MAHARISHI
MAHARISHIS
MAHATMA
MAHATMAS
MAHIMAHI
MAHIMAHIS
MAHJONG
MAHJONGG
MAHJONGGS
MAHJONGS
MAHLSTICK
MAHLSTICKS
MAHOE
MAHOES
MAHOGANIES
MAHOGANY
MAHONIA
MAHONIAS
MAHOUT
MAHOUTS
MAHUA
MAHUANG
MAHUANGS
MAHUAS
MAHWA
MAHWAS
MAHZOR
MAHZORIM
MAHZORS
MAIASAUR
MAIASAURA
MAIASAURAS
MAIASAURS
MAID
MAIDAN
MAIDANS
MAIDEN
MAIDENHAIR
MAIDENHAIRS
MAIDENHEAD
MAIDENHEADS
MAIDENHOOD
MAIDENHOODS
MAIDENLINESS
MAIDENLINESSES
MAIDENLY
MAIDENS
MAIDHOOD
MAIDHOODS
MAIDISH
MAIDS
MAIDSERVANT
MAIDSERVANTS
MAIEUTIC
MAIGRE
MAIHEM
MAIHEMS
MAIL
MAILABILITIES
MAILABILITY
MAILABLE
MAILBAG
MAILBAGS
MAILBOX
MAILBOXES
MAILE
MAILED
MAILER
MAILERS
MAILES
MAILGRAM
MAILGRAMS
MAILING
MAILINGS
MAILL
MAILLESS
MAILLOT
MAILLOTS
MAILLS
MAILMAN
MAILMEN
MAILROOM
MAILROOMS
MAILS
MAILSHOT
MAILSHOTS
MAIM
MAIMED
MAIMER
MAIMERS
MAIMING
MAIMS
MAIN
MAINFRAME
MAINFRAMES
MAINLAND
MAINLANDER
MAINLANDERS
MAINLANDS
MAINLINE
MAINLINED
MAINLINER
MAINLINERS
MAINLINES
MAINLINING
MAINLY
MAINMAST
MAINMASTS
MAINS
MAINSAIL
MAINSAILS
MAINSHEET
MAINSHEETS
MAINSPRING
MAINSPRINGS
MAINSTAY
MAINSTAYS
MAINSTREAM
MAINSTREAMED
MAINSTREAMING
MAINSTREAMS
MAINTAIN
MAINTAINABILITY
MAINTAINABLE
MAINTAINED
MAINTAINER
MAINTAINERS
MAINTAINING
MAINTAINS
MAINTENANCE
MAINTENANCES
MAINTOP
MAINTOPS
MAIOLICA
MAIOLICAS
MAIR
MAIRS
MAISONETTE
MAISONETTES
MAIST
MAISTS
MAIZE
MAIZES
MAJAGUA
MAJAGUAS
MAJESTIC
MAJESTICALLY
MAJESTIES
MAJESTY
MAJLIS
MAJLISES
MAJOLICA
MAJOLICAS
MAJOR
MAJORDOMO
MAJORDOMOS
MAJORED
MAJORETTE
MAJORETTES
MAJORING
MAJORITARIAN
MAJORITARIANISM
MAJORITARIANS
MAJORITIES
MAJORITY
MAJORLY
MAJORS
MAJUSCULAR
MAJUSCULE
MAJUSCULES
MAKABLE
MAKAR
MAKARS
MAKE
MAKEABLE
MAKEBATE
MAKEBATES
MAKEFAST
MAKEFASTS
MAKEOVER
MAKEOVERS
MAKER
MAKEREADIES
MAKEREADY
MAKERS
MAKES
MAKESHIFT
MAKESHIFTS
MAKEUP
MAKEUPS
MAKEWEIGHT
MAKEWEIGHTS
MAKI
MAKIMONO
MAKIMONOS
MAKING
MAKINGS
MAKIS
MAKO
MAKOS
MAKUTA
MALABSORPTION
MALABSORPTIONS
MALACCA
MALACCAS
MALACHITE
MALACHITES
MALACOLOGICAL
MALACOLOGIES
MALACOLOGIST
MALACOLOGISTS
MALACOLOGY
MALACOSTRACAN
MALACOSTRACANS
MALADAPTATION
MALADAPTATIONS
MALADAPTED
MALADAPTIVE
MALADIES
MALADJUSTED
MALADJUSTIVE
MALADJUSTMENT
MALADJUSTMENTS
MALADMINISTER
MALADMINISTERED
MALADMINISTERS
MALADROIT
MALADROITLY
MALADROITNESS
MALADROITNESSES
MALADROITS
MALADY

MALAGUENA
MALAGUENAS
MALAISE
MALAISES
MALAMUTE
MALAMUTES
MALANDERS
MALANGA
MALANGAS
MALAPERT
MALAPERTLY
MALAPERTNESS
MALAPERTNESSES
MALAPERTS
MALAPPORTIONED
MALAPROP
MALAPROPIAN
MALAPROPISM
MALAPROPISMS
MALAPROPIST
MALAPROPISTS
MALAPROPOS
MALAPROPS
MALAR
MALARIA
MALARIAL
MALARIAN
MALARIAS
MALARIOLOGIES
MALARIOLOGIST
MALARIOLOGISTS
MALARIOLOGY
MALARIOUS
MALARKEY
MALARKEYS
MALARKIES
MALARKY
MALAROMA
MALAROMAS
MALARS
MALATE
MALATES
MALATHION
MALATHIONS
MALCONTENT
MALCONTENTED
MALCONTENTEDLY
MALCONTENTS
MALDISTRIBUTION
MALE
MALEATE
MALEATES
MALEDICT
MALEDICTED
MALEDICTING
MALEDICTION
MALEDICTIONS
MALEDICTORY
MALEDICTS
MALEFACTION
MALEFACTIONS
MALEFACTOR
MALEFACTORS
MALEFIC
MALEFICENCE
MALEFICENCES
MALEFICENT
MALEMIUT
MALEMIUTS
MALEMUTE
MALEMUTES
MALENESS
MALENESSES
MALES
MALEVOLENCE
MALEVOLENCES
MALEVOLENT
MALEVOLENTLY
MALFEASANCE
MALFEASANCES
MALFED
MALFORMATION
MALFORMATIONS
MALFORMED
MALFUNCTION
MALFUNCTIONED
MALFUNCTIONING
MALFUNCTIONS
MALGRE
MALIC
MALICE
MALICES
MALICIOUS
MALICIOUSLY
MALICIOUSNESS
MALICIOUSNESSES
MALIGN
MALIGNANCE
MALIGNANCES
MALIGNANCIES
MALIGNANCY
MALIGNANT
MALIGNANTLY
MALIGNED
MALIGNER
MALIGNERS
MALIGNING
MALIGNITIES
MALIGNITY
MALIGNLY
MALIGNS
MALIHINI
MALIHINIS
MALINE
MALINES
MALINGER
MALINGERED
MALINGERER
MALINGERERS
MALINGERING
MALINGERS
MALISON
MALISONS
MALKIN
MALKINS
MALL
MALLARD
MALLARDS
MALLEABILITIES
MALLEABILITY
MALLEABLE
MALLEABLY
MALLED
MALLEE
MALLEES
MALLEI
MALLEMUCK
MALLEMUCKS
MALLEOLAR
MALLEOLI
MALLEOLUS
MALLET
MALLETS
MALLEUS
MALLING
MALLINGS
MALLOW
MALLOWS
MALLS
MALM
MALMIER
MALMIEST
MALMS
MALMSEY
MALMSEYS
MALMY
MALNOURISHED
MALNUTRITION
MALNUTRITIONS
MALOCCLUSION
MALOCCLUSIONS
MALODOR
MALODOROUS
MALODOROUSLY
MALODOROUSNESS
MALODORS
MALOLACTIC
MALONATE
MALONATES
MALOTI
MALPIGHIA
MALPOSED
MALPOSITION
MALPOSITIONS
MALPRACTICE
MALPRACTICES
MALPRACTITIONER
MALT
MALTASE
MALTASES
MALTED
MALTEDS
MALTHA
MALTHAS
MALTIER
MALTIEST
MALTINESS
MALTINESSES
MALTING
MALTINGS
MALTODEXTRIN
MALTODEXTRINS
MALTOL
MALTOLS
MALTOSE
MALTOSES
MALTREAT
MALTREATED
MALTREATER
MALTREATERS
MALTREATING
MALTREATMENT
MALTREATMENTS
MALTREATS
MALTS
MALTSTER
MALTSTERS
MALTY
MALVASIA
MALVASIAN
MALVASIAS
MALVERSATION
MALVERSATIONS
MALWARE
MALWARES
MAM
MAMA
MAMALIGA
MAMALIGAS
MAMAS
MAMASAN
MAMASANS
MAMATEEK
MAMATEEKS
MAMBA
MAMBAS
MAMBO
MAMBOED
MAMBOES
MAMBOING
MAMBOS
MAMEE
MAMEES
MAMELUKE
MAMELUKES
MAMEY
MAMEYES
MAMEYS
MAMIE
MAMIES
MAMILLA
MAMILLAE
MAMLUK
MAMLUKS
MAMMA
MAMMAE
MAMMAL
MAMMALIAN
MAMMALIANS
MAMMALITIES
MAMMALITY
MAMMALOGIES
MAMMALOGIST
MAMMALOGISTS
MAMMALOGY
MAMMALS
MAMMARIES
MAMMARY
MAMMAS
MAMMATE
MAMMATI
MAMMATUS
MAMMEE
MAMMEES
MAMMER

MAMMERED
MAMMERING
MAMMERS
MAMMET
MAMMETS
MAMMEY
MAMMEYS
MAMMIE
MAMMIES
MAMMILLA
MAMMILLAE
MAMMILLARY
MAMMILLATED
MAMMITIDES
MAMMITIS
MAMMOCK
MAMMOCKED
MAMMOCKING
MAMMOCKS
MAMMOGRAM
MAMMOGRAMS
MAMMOGRAPHIC
MAMMOGRAPHIES
MAMMOGRAPHY
MAMMON
MAMMONISM
MAMMONISMS
MAMMONIST
MAMMONISTS
MAMMONS
MAMMOTH
MAMMOTHS
MAMMY
MAMS
MAMZER
MAMZERS
MAN
MANA
MANACLE
MANACLED
MANACLES
MANACLING
MANAGE
MANAGEABILITIES
MANAGEABILITY
MANAGEABLE
MANAGEABLENESS
MANAGEABLY
MANAGED
MANAGEMENT
MANAGEMENTAL
MANAGEMENTS
MANAGER
MANAGERESS
MANAGERESSES
MANAGERIAL
MANAGERIALLY
MANAGERS
MANAGERSHIP
MANAGERSHIPS
MANAGES
MANAGING
MANAKIN
MANAKINS
MANANA
MANANAS
MANAS
MANAT
MANATEE
MANATEES
MANATOID
MANATS
MANCHE
MANCHES
MANCHET
MANCHETS
MANCHINEEL
MANCHINEELS
MANCIPLE
MANCIPLES
MANDALA
MANDALAS
MANDALIC
MANDAMUS
MANDAMUSED
MANDAMUSES
MANDAMUSING
MANDARIN
MANDARINATE
MANDARINATES
MANDARINIC
MANDARINISM
MANDARINISMS
MANDARINS
MANDATARIES
MANDATARY
MANDATE
MANDATED
MANDATES
MANDATING
MANDATOR
MANDATORIES
MANDATORILY
MANDATORS
MANDATORY
MANDIBLE
MANDIBLES
MANDIBULAR
MANDIBULATE
MANDIOCA
MANDIOCAS
MANDOLA
MANDOLAS
MANDOLIN
MANDOLINE
MANDOLINES
MANDOLINIST
MANDOLINISTS
MANDOLINS
MANDORA
MANDORAS
MANDORLA
MANDORLAS
MANDRAGORA
MANDRAGORAS
MANDRAKE
MANDRAKES
MANDREL
MANDRELS
MANDRIL
MANDRILL
MANDRILLS
MANDRILS
MANDUCATE
MANDUCATED
MANDUCATES
MANDUCATING
MANE
MANEB
MANEBS
MANED
MANEGE
MANEGES
MANELESS
MANES
MANEUVER
MANEUVERABILITY
MANEUVERABLE
MANEUVERED
MANEUVERER
MANEUVERERS
MANEUVERING
MANEUVERS
MANFUL
MANFULLER
MANFULLEST
MANFULLY
MANFULNESS
MANFULNESSES
MANGA
MANGABEY
MANGABEYS
MANGABIES
MANGABY
MANGANATE
MANGANATES
MANGANESE
MANGANESES
MANGANESIAN
MANGANIC
MANGANIN
MANGANINS
MANGANITE
MANGANITES
MANGANOUS
MANGAS
MANGE
MANGEL
MANGELS
MANGER
MANGERS
MANGES
MANGETOUT
MANGETOUTS
MANGEY
MANGIER
MANGIEST
MANGILY
MANGINESS
MANGINESSES
MANGLE
MANGLED
MANGLER
MANGLERS
MANGLES
MANGLING
MANGO
MANGOES
MANGOLD
MANGOLDS
MANGONEL
MANGONELS
MANGOS
MANGOSTEEN
MANGOSTEENS
MANGROVE
MANGROVES
MANGY
MANHANDLE
MANHANDLED
MANHANDLES
MANHANDLING
MANHATTAN
MANHATTANS
MANHOLE
MANHOLES
MANHOOD
MANHOODS
MANHUNT
MANHUNTS
MANIA
MANIAC
MANIACAL
MANIACALLY
MANIACS
MANIAS
MANIC
MANICALLY
MANICOTTI
MANICOTTIS
MANICS
MANICURE
MANICURED
MANICURES
MANICURING
MANICURIST
MANICURISTS
MANIFEST
MANIFESTANT
MANIFESTANTS
MANIFESTATION
MANIFESTATIONS
MANIFESTED
MANIFESTER
MANIFESTERS
MANIFESTING
MANIFESTLY
MANIFESTO
MANIFESTOED
MANIFESTOES
MANIFESTOING
MANIFESTOS
MANIFESTS
MANIFOLD
MANIFOLDED
MANIFOLDING
MANIFOLDLY
MANIFOLDNESS
MANIFOLDNESSES
MANIFOLDS
MANIHOT
MANIHOTS
MANIKIN
MANIKINS
MANILA

MANILAS
MANILLA
MANILLAS
MANILLE
MANILLES
MANIOC
MANIOCA
MANIOCAS
MANIOCS
MANIPLE
MANIPLES
MANIPULABILITY
MANIPULABLE
MANIPULAR
MANIPULARS
MANIPULATABLE
MANIPULATE
MANIPULATED
MANIPULATES
MANIPULATING
MANIPULATION
MANIPULATIONS
MANIPULATIVE
MANIPULATIVELY
MANIPULATIVES
MANIPULATOR
MANIPULATORS
MANIPULATORY
MANITO
MANITOS
MANITOU
MANITOUS
MANITU
MANITUS
MANKIER
MANKIEST
MANKIND
MANKINDS
MANKY
MANLESS
MANLIER
MANLIEST
MANLIKE
MANLIKELY
MANLILY
MANLINESS
MANLINESSES
MANLY
MANMADE
MANNA
MANNAN
MANNANS
MANNAS
MANNED
MANNEQUIN
MANNEQUINS
MANNER
MANNERED
MANNERISM
MANNERISMS
MANNERIST
MANNERISTIC
MANNERISTS
MANNERLESS
MANNERLINESS
MANNERLINESSES
MANNERLY
MANNERS
MANNIKIN
MANNIKINS
MANNING
MANNISH
MANNISHLY
MANNISHNESS
MANNISHNESSES
MANNITE
MANNITES
MANNITIC
MANNITOL
MANNITOLS
MANNOSE
MANNOSES
MANO
MANOEUVRABILITY
MANOEUVRABLE
MANOEUVRE
MANOEUVRED
MANOEUVRES
MANOEUVRING
MANOMETER
MANOMETERS
MANOMETRIC
MANOMETRICALLY
MANOMETRIES
MANOMETRY
MANOR
MANORIAL
MANORIALISM
MANORIALISMS
MANORS
MANOS
MANPACK
MANPOWER
MANPOWERS
MANQUE
MANROPE
MANROPES
MANS
MANSARD
MANSARDED
MANSARDS
MANSCAPE
MANSCAPED
MANSCAPES
MANSCAPING
MANSE
MANSERVANT
MANSES
MANSION
MANSIONS
MANSLAUGHTER
MANSLAUGHTERS
MANSLAYER
MANSLAYERS
MANSUETUDE
MANSUETUDES
MANTA
MANTAS
MANTEAU
MANTEAUS
MANTEAUX
MANTEL
MANTELET
MANTELETS
MANTELPIECE
MANTELPIECES
MANTELS
MANTELSHELF
MANTELSHELVES
MANTES
MANTIC
MANTICORE
MANTICORES
MANTID
MANTIDS
MANTILLA
MANTILLAS
MANTIS
MANTISES
MANTISSA
MANTISSAS
MANTLE
MANTLED
MANTLES
MANTLET
MANTLETS
MANTLING
MANTLINGS
MANTRA
MANTRAM
MANTRAMS
MANTRAP
MANTRAPS
MANTRAS
MANTRIC
MANTUA
MANTUAS
MANUAL
MANUALLY
MANUALS
MANUARY
MANUBRIA
MANUBRIAL
MANUBRIUM
MANUBRIUMS
MANUCODE
MANUCODES
MANUFACTORIES
MANUFACTORY
MANUFACTURABLE
MANUFACTURE
MANUFACTURED
MANUFACTURER
MANUFACTURERS
MANUFACTURES
MANUFACTURING
MANUFACTURINGS
MANUKA
MANUKAS
MANUMISSION
MANUMISSIONS
MANUMIT
MANUMITS
MANUMITTED
MANUMITTING
MANURE
MANURED
MANURER
MANURERS
MANURES
MANURIAL
MANURING
MANUS
MANUSCRIPT
MANUSCRIPTS
MANWARD
MANWARDS
MANWISE
MANY
MANYFOLD
MANYPLIES
MANZANITA
MANZANITAS
MAP
MAPLE
MAPLELIKE
MAPLES
MAPLESS
MAPLIKE
MAPMAKER
MAPMAKERS
MAPMAKING
MAPMAKINGS
MAPPABLE
MAPPED
MAPPER
MAPPERS
MAPPING
MAPPINGS
MAPS
MAQUETTE
MAQUETTES
MAQUI
MAQUILA
MAQUILADORA
MAQUILADORAS
MAQUILAS
MAQUILLAGE
MAQUILLAGES
MAQUIS
MAR
MARA
MARABOU
MARABOUS
MARABOUT
MARABOUTS
MARACA
MARACAS
MARAKA
MARANATHA
MARANATHAS
MARANTA
MARANTAS
MARAS
MARASCA
MARASCAS
MARASCHINO
MARASCHINOS
MARASMIC
MARASMOID
MARASMUS
MARASMUSES
MARATHON
MARATHONER
MARATHONERS

MARATHONING
MARATHONINGS
MARATHONS
MARAUD
MARAUDED
MARAUDER
MARAUDERS
MARAUDING
MARAUDS
MARAVEDI
MARAVEDIS
MARBELIZE
MARBELIZED
MARBELIZES
MARBELIZING
MARBLE
MARBLED
MARBLEISE
MARBLEISED
MARBLEISES
MARBLEISING
MARBLEIZE
MARBLEIZED
MARBLEIZES
MARBLEIZING
MARBLER
MARBLERS
MARBLES
MARBLIER
MARBLIEST
MARBLING
MARBLINGS
MARBLY
MARC
MARCASITE
MARCASITES
MARCATO
MARCATOS
MARCEL
MARCELLED
MARCELLER
MARCELLERS
MARCELLING
MARCELS
MARCH
MARCHED
MARCHEN
MARCHER
MARCHERS
MARCHES
MARCHESA
MARCHESE
MARCHESI
MARCHING
MARCHIONESS
MARCHIONESSES
MARCHLAND
MARCHLANDS
MARCHLIKE
MARCHPANE
MARCHPANES
MARCONI
MARCONIS
MARCS
MARE
MAREMMA
MAREMME
MARENGO
MARES
MARGARIC
MARGARIN
MARGARINE
MARGARINES
MARGARINS
MARGARITA
MARGARITAS
MARGARITE
MARGARITES
MARGATE
MARGATES
MARGAY
MARGAYS
MARGE
MARGENT
MARGENTED
MARGENTING
MARGENTS
MARGES
MARGIN
MARGINAL
MARGINALIA
MARGINALISATION
MARGINALISE
MARGINALISED
MARGINALISES
MARGINALISING
MARGINALITIES
MARGINALITY
MARGINALIZATION
MARGINALIZE
MARGINALIZED
MARGINALIZES
MARGINALIZING
MARGINALLY
MARGINALS
MARGINATE
MARGINATED
MARGINATES
MARGINATING
MARGINATION
MARGINATIONS
MARGINED
MARGINING
MARGINS
MARGRAVATE
MARGRAVATES
MARGRAVE
MARGRAVES
MARGRAVIAL
MARGRAVIATE
MARGRAVIATES
MARGRAVINE
MARGRAVINES
MARGUERITE
MARGUERITES
MARIA
MARIACHI
MARIACHIS
MARICULTURE
MARICULTURES
MARICULTURIST
MARICULTURISTS
MARIGOLD
MARIGOLDS
MARIHUANA
MARIHUANAS
MARIJUANA
MARIJUANAS
MARIMBA
MARIMBAS
MARIMBIST
MARIMBISTS
MARINA
MARINADE
MARINADED
MARINADES
MARINADING
MARINARA
MARINARAS
MARINAS
MARINATE
MARINATED
MARINATES
MARINATING
MARINATION
MARINATIONS
MARINE
MARINER
MARINERS
MARINES
MARIONBERRIES
MARIONBERRY
MARIONETTE
MARIONETTES
MARIPOSA
MARIPOSAS
MARISH
MARISHES
MARITAL
MARITALLY
MARITIME
MARJORAM
MARJORAMS
MARK
MARKA
MARKAS
MARKDOWN
MARKDOWNS
MARKED
MARKEDLY
MARKEDNESS
MARKEDNESSES
MARKER
MARKERS
MARKET
MARKETABILITIES
MARKETABILITY
MARKETABLE
MARKETED
MARKETEER
MARKETEERS
MARKETER
MARKETERS
MARKETING
MARKETINGS
MARKETIZATION
MARKETIZATIONS
MARKETPLACE
MARKETPLACES
MARKETS
MARKHOOR
MARKHOORS
MARKHOR
MARKHORS
MARKING
MARKINGS
MARKKA
MARKKAA
MARKKAS
MARKS
MARKSMAN
MARKSMANSHIP
MARKSMANSHIPS
MARKSMEN
MARKSWOMAN
MARKSWOMEN
MARKUP
MARKUPS
MARL
MARLED
MARLIER
MARLIEST
MARLIN
MARLINE
MARLINES
MARLINESPIKE
MARLINESPIKES
MARLING
MARLINGS
MARLINS
MARLINSPIKE
MARLINSPIKES
MARLITE
MARLITES
MARLITIC
MARLS
MARLSTONE
MARLSTONES
MARLY
MARMALADE
MARMALADES
MARMITE
MARMITES
MARMOREAL
MARMOREALLY
MARMOREAN
MARMOSET
MARMOSETS
MARMOT
MARMOTS
MAROCAIN
MAROCAINS
MAROON
MAROONED
MAROONING
MAROONS
MARPLOT
MARPLOTS
MARQUE
MARQUEE
MARQUEES
MARQUES
MARQUESS
MARQUESSATE
MARQUESSATES

MARQUESSES
MARQUETERIE
MARQUETERIES
MARQUETRIES
MARQUETRY
MARQUIS
MARQUISATE
MARQUISATES
MARQUISE
MARQUISES
MARQUISETTE
MARQUISETTES
MARRAM
MARRAMS
MARRANO
MARRANOS
MARRED
MARRER
MARRERS
MARRIAGE
MARRIAGEABILITY
MARRIAGEABLE
MARRIAGES
MARRIED
MARRIEDS
MARRIER
MARRIERS
MARRIES
MARRING
MARRON
MARRONS
MARROW
MARROWBONE
MARROWBONES
MARROWED
MARROWFAT
MARROWFATS
MARROWING
MARROWS
MARROWY
MARRY
MARRYING
MARS
MARSALA
MARSALAS
MARSE
MARSEILLE
MARSEILLES
MARSES
MARSH
MARSHAL
MARSHALCIES
MARSHALCY
MARSHALED
MARSHALING
MARSHALL
MARSHALLED
MARSHALLING
MARSHALLS
MARSHALS
MARSHALSHIP
MARSHALSHIPS
MARSHED
MARSHES
MARSHIER
MARSHIEST
MARSHINESS
MARSHINESSES
MARSHLAND
MARSHLANDS
MARSHLIKE
MARSHMALLOW
MARSHMALLOWS
MARSHMALLOWY
MARSHY
MARSUPIA
MARSUPIAL
MARSUPIALS
MARSUPIUM
MART
MARTAGON
MARTAGONS
MARTED
MARTELLO
MARTELLOS
MARTEN
MARTENS
MARTENSITE
MARTENSITES
MARTENSITIC
MARTENSITICALLY
MARTIAL
MARTIALLY
MARTIAN
MARTIANS
MARTIN
MARTINET
MARTINETS
MARTING
MARTINGAL
MARTINGALE
MARTINGALES
MARTINGALS
MARTINI
MARTINIS
MARTINS
MARTLET
MARTLETS
MARTS
MARTYR
MARTYRDOM
MARTYRDOMS
MARTYRED
MARTYRIES
MARTYRING
MARTYRIZATION
MARTYRIZATIONS
MARTYRIZE
MARTYRIZED
MARTYRIZES
MARTYRIZING
MARTYRLY
MARTYROLOGIES
MARTYROLOGIST
MARTYROLOGISTS
MARTYROLOGY
MARTYRS
MARTYRY
MARVEL
MARVELED
MARVELER
MARVELERS
MARVELING
MARVELLED
MARVELLING
MARVELLOUS
MARVELLOUSLY
MARVELOUS
MARVELOUSLY
MARVELOUSNESS
MARVELOUSNESSES
MARVELS
MARVY
MARYJANE
MARYJANES
MARZIPAN
MARZIPANNED
MARZIPANNING
MARZIPANS
MAS
MASA
MASALA
MASALAS
MASAS
MASCARA
MASCARAED
MASCARAING
MASCARAS
MASCARPONE
MASCARPONES
MASCON
MASCONS
MASCOT
MASCOTS
MASCULINE
MASCULINELY
MASCULINES
MASCULINISE
MASCULINISED
MASCULINISES
MASCULINISING
MASCULINIST
MASCULINISTS
MASCULINITIES
MASCULINITY
MASCULINIZATION
MASCULINIZE
MASCULINIZED
MASCULINIZES
MASCULINIZING
MASER
MASERS
MASES
MASH
MASHED
MASHER
MASHERS
MASHES
MASHGIACH
MASHGIAH
MASHGICHIM
MASHGIHIM
MASHIE
MASHIES
MASHING
MASHY
MASJID
MASJIDS
MASK
MASKABLE
MASKED
MASKEG
MASKEGS
MASKER
MASKERS
MASKING
MASKINGS
MASKLIKE
MASKS
MASOCHISM
MASOCHISMS
MASOCHIST
MASOCHISTIC
MASOCHISTICALLY
MASOCHISTS
MASON
MASONED
MASONIC
MASONING
MASONITE
MASONITES
MASONRIES
MASONRY
MASONS
MASQUE
MASQUER
MASQUERADE
MASQUERADED
MASQUERADER
MASQUERADERS
MASQUERADES
MASQUERADING
MASQUERS
MASQUES
MASS
MASSA
MASSACRE
MASSACRED
MASSACRER
MASSACRERS
MASSACRES
MASSACRING
MASSAGE
MASSAGED
MASSAGER
MASSAGERS
MASSAGES
MASSAGING
MASSAS
MASSASAUGA
MASSASAUGAS
MASSCULT
MASSCULTS
MASSE
MASSED
MASSEDLY
MASSES
MASSETER
MASSETERIC
MASSETERS
MASSEUR
MASSEURS
MASSEUSE
MASSEUSES
MASSICOT

MASSICOTS
MASSIER
MASSIEST
MASSIF
MASSIFS
MASSINESS
MASSINESSES
MASSING
MASSIVE
MASSIVELY
MASSIVENESS
MASSIVENESSES
MASSLESS
MASSY
MAST
MASTABA
MASTABAH
MASTABAHS
MASTABAS
MASTECTOMIES
MASTECTOMY
MASTED
MASTER
MASTERDOM
MASTERDOMS
MASTERED
MASTERFUL
MASTERFULLY
MASTERFULNESS
MASTERFULNESSES
MASTERIES
MASTERING
MASTERLINESS
MASTERLINESSES
MASTERLY
MASTERMIND
MASTERMINDED
MASTERMINDING
MASTERMINDS
MASTERPIECE
MASTERPIECES
MASTERS
MASTERSHIP
MASTERSHIPS
MASTERSINGER
MASTERSINGERS
MASTERSTROKE
MASTERSTROKES
MASTERWORK
MASTERWORKS
MASTERY
MASTHEAD
MASTHEADED
MASTHEADING
MASTHEADS
MASTIC
MASTICATE
MASTICATED
MASTICATES
MASTICATING
MASTICATION
MASTICATIONS
MASTICATOR
MASTICATORIES
MASTICATORS
MASTICATORY
MASTICHE
MASTICHES
MASTICS
MASTIFF
MASTIFFS
MASTIGOPHORAN
MASTIGOPHORANS
MASTING
MASTITIC
MASTITIDES
MASTITIS
MASTIX
MASTIXES
MASTLESS
MASTLIKE
MASTODON
MASTODONIC
MASTODONS
MASTODONT
MASTODONTS
MASTOID
MASTOIDECTOMIES
MASTOIDECTOMY
MASTOIDITIDES
MASTOIDITIS
MASTOIDITISES
MASTOIDS
MASTOPEXIES
MASTOPEXY
MASTS
MASTURBATE
MASTURBATED
MASTURBATES
MASTURBATING
MASTURBATION
MASTURBATIONS
MASTURBATOR
MASTURBATORS
MASTURBATORY
MASURIUM
MASURIUMS
MAT
MATADOR
MATADORS
MATAMBALA
MATCH
MATCHABLE
MATCHBOARD
MATCHBOARDS
MATCHBOOK
MATCHBOOKS
MATCHBOX
MATCHBOXES
MATCHED
MATCHER
MATCHERS
MATCHES
MATCHING
MATCHLESS
MATCHLESSLY
MATCHLOCK
MATCHLOCKS
MATCHMADE
MATCHMAKE
MATCHMAKER
MATCHMAKERS
MATCHMAKES
MATCHMAKING
MATCHMAKINGS
MATCHMARK
MATCHMARKED
MATCHMARKING
MATCHMARKS
MATCHSTICK
MATCHSTICKS
MATCHUP
MATCHUPS
MATCHWOOD
MATCHWOODS
MATE
MATED
MATELASSE
MATELASSES
MATELESS
MATELOT
MATELOTE
MATELOTES
MATELOTS
MATER
MATERFAMILIAS
MATERFAMILIASES
MATERIAL
MATERIALISE
MATERIALISED
MATERIALISES
MATERIALISING
MATERIALISM
MATERIALISMS
MATERIALIST
MATERIALISTIC
MATERIALISTS
MATERIALITIES
MATERIALITY
MATERIALIZATION
MATERIALIZE
MATERIALIZED
MATERIALIZER
MATERIALIZERS
MATERIALIZES
MATERIALIZING
MATERIALLY
MATERIALNESS
MATERIALNESSES
MATERIALS
MATERIEL
MATERIELS
MATERNAL
MATERNALLY
MATERNITIES
MATERNITY
MATERS
MATES
MATESHIP
MATESHIPS
MATEY
MATEYNESS
MATEYNESSES
MATEYS
MATH
MATHEMATIC
MATHEMATICAL
MATHEMATICALLY
MATHEMATICIAN
MATHEMATICIANS
MATHEMATICS
MATHEMATIZATION
MATHEMATIZE
MATHEMATIZED
MATHEMATIZES
MATHEMATIZING
MATHS
MATIER
MATIEST
MATILDA
MATILDAS
MATIN
MATINAL
MATINEE
MATINEES
MATINESS
MATINESSES
MATING
MATINGS
MATINS
MATLESS
MATRASS
MATRASSES
MATRES
MATRIARCH
MATRIARCHAL
MATRIARCHATE
MATRIARCHATES
MATRIARCHIES
MATRIARCHS
MATRIARCHY
MATRIC
MATRICES
MATRICIDAL
MATRICIDE
MATRICIDES
MATRICS
MATRICULANT
MATRICULANTS
MATRICULATE
MATRICULATED
MATRICULATES
MATRICULATING
MATRICULATION
MATRICULATIONS
MATRILINEAL
MATRILINEALLY
MATRIMONIAL
MATRIMONIALLY
MATRIMONIES
MATRIMONY
MATRIX
MATRIXES
MATRON
MATRONAL
MATRONIZE
MATRONIZED
MATRONIZES
MATRONIZING
MATRONLY
MATRONS
MATRONYMIC
MATRONYMICS
MATS
MATSAH

MATSAHS
MATSUTAKE
MATSUTAKES
MATT
MATTE
MATTED
MATTEDLY
MATTER
MATTERED
MATTERFUL
MATTERING
MATTERS
MATTERY
MATTES
MATTIN
MATTING
MATTINGS
MATTINS
MATTOCK
MATTOCKS
MATTOID
MATTOIDS
MATTRASS
MATTRASSES
MATTRESS
MATTRESSES
MATTS
MATURATE
MATURATED
MATURATES
MATURATING
MATURATION
MATURATIONAL
MATURATIONS
MATURE
MATURED
MATURELY
MATURER
MATURERS
MATURES
MATUREST
MATURING
MATURITIES
MATURITY
MATUTINAL
MATUTINALLY
MATZA
MATZAH
MATZAHS
MATZAS
MATZO
MATZOH
MATZOHS
MATZOON
MATZOONS
MATZOS
MATZOT
MATZOTH
MAUD
MAUDLIN
MAUDLINLY
MAUDS
MAUGER
MAUGRE
MAUL
MAULED
MAULER
MAULERS
MAULING
MAULINGS
MAULS
MAULSTICK
MAULSTICKS
MAUMET
MAUMETRIES
MAUMETRY
MAUMETS
MAUN
MAUND
MAUNDER
MAUNDERED
MAUNDERER
MAUNDERERS
MAUNDERING
MAUNDERS
MAUNDIES
MAUNDS
MAUNDY
MAUSIER
MAUSIEST
MAUSOLEA
MAUSOLEAN
MAUSOLEUM
MAUSOLEUMS
MAUSY
MAUT
MAUTS
MAUVE
MAUVES
MAUZIER
MAUZIEST
MAUZY
MAVEN
MAVENS
MAVERICK
MAVERICKS
MAVIE
MAVIES
MAVIN
MAVINS
MAVIS
MAVISES
MAVOURNEEN
MAVOURNEENS
MAVOURNIN
MAVOURNINS
MAW
MAWED
MAWING
MAWKISH
MAWKISHLY
MAWKISHNESS
MAWKISHNESSES
MAWN
MAWS
MAX
MAXED
MAXES
MAXI
MAXIBOAT
MAXIBOATS
MAXICOAT
MAXICOATS
MAXILLA
MAXILLAE
MAXILLARIES
MAXILLARY
MAXILLAS
MAXILLIPED
MAXILLIPEDS
MAXILLOFACIAL
MAXIM
MAXIMA
MAXIMAL
MAXIMALIST
MAXIMALISTS
MAXIMALLY
MAXIMALS
MAXIMAND
MAXIMANDS
MAXIMIN
MAXIMINS
MAXIMISATION
MAXIMISATIONS
MAXIMISE
MAXIMISED
MAXIMISES
MAXIMISING
MAXIMITE
MAXIMITES
MAXIMIZATION
MAXIMIZATIONS
MAXIMIZE
MAXIMIZED
MAXIMIZER
MAXIMIZERS
MAXIMIZES
MAXIMIZING
MAXIMS
MAXIMUM
MAXIMUMLY
MAXIMUMS
MAXING
MAXIS
MAXIXE
MAXIXES
MAXWELL
MAXWELLS
MAY
MAYA
MAYAN
MAYAPPLE
MAYAPPLES
MAYAS
MAYBE
MAYBES
MAYBIRD
MAYBIRDS
MAYBUSH
MAYBUSHES
MAYDAY
MAYDAYS
MAYED
MAYEST
MAYFLIES
MAYFLOWER
MAYFLOWERS
MAYFLY
MAYHAP
MAYHAPPEN
MAYHEM
MAYHEMS
MAYING
MAYINGS
MAYO
MAYONNAISE
MAYONNAISES
MAYOR
MAYORAL
MAYORALTIES
MAYORALTY
MAYORESS
MAYORESSES
MAYORS
MAYORSHIP
MAYORSHIPS
MAYOS
MAYPOLE
MAYPOLES
MAYPOP
MAYPOPS
MAYS
MAYST
MAYVIN
MAYVINS
MAYWEED
MAYWEEDS
MAZAEDIA
MAZAEDIUM
MAZARD
MAZARDS
MAZE
MAZED
MAZEDLY
MAZEDNESS
MAZEDNESSES
MAZELIKE
MAZELTOV
MAZER
MAZERS
MAZES
MAZIER
MAZIEST
MAZILY
MAZINESS
MAZINESSES
MAZING
MAZOURKA
MAZOURKAS
MAZUMA
MAZUMAS
MAZURKA
MAZURKAS
MAZY
MAZZARD
MAZZARDS
MBAQANGA
MBAQANGAS
MBIRA
MBIRAS
ME
MEAD
MEADOW
MEADOWFOAM
MEADOWFOAMS

MEADOWLAND
MEADOWLANDS
MEADOWLARK
MEADOWLARKS
MEADOWS
MEADOWSWEET
MEADOWSWEETS
MEADOWY
MEADS
MEAGER
MEAGERER
MEAGEREST
MEAGERLY
MEAGERNESS
MEAGERNESSES
MEAGRE
MEAGRELY
MEAGRER
MEAGREST
MEAL
MEALIE
MEALIER
MEALIES
MEALIEST
MEALINESS
MEALINESSES
MEALLESS
MEALS
MEALTIME
MEALTIMES
MEALWORM
MEALWORMS
MEALY
MEALYBUG
MEALYBUGS
MEALYMOUTHED
MEAN
MEANDER
MEANDERED
MEANDERER
MEANDERERS
MEANDERING
MEANDERS
MEANDROUS
MEANER
MEANERS
MEANEST
MEANIE
MEANIES
MEANING
MEANINGFUL
MEANINGFULLY
MEANINGFULNESS
MEANINGLESS
MEANINGLESSLY
MEANINGLESSNESS
MEANINGLY
MEANINGS
MEANLY
MEANNESS
MEANNESSES
MEANS
MEANT
MEANTIME
MEANTIMES
MEANWHILE
MEANWHILES
MEANY
MEASLE
MEASLED
MEASLES
MEASLIER
MEASLIEST
MEASLY
MEASURABILITIES
MEASURABILITY
MEASURABLE
MEASURABLY
MEASURE
MEASURED
MEASUREDLY
MEASURELESS
MEASUREMENT
MEASUREMENTS
MEASURER
MEASURERS
MEASURES
MEASURING
MEAT
MEATAL
MEATBALL
MEATBALLS
MEATED
MEATHEAD
MEATHEADS
MEATHOOK
MEATHOOKS
MEATIER
MEATIEST
MEATILY
MEATINESS
MEATINESSES
MEATLESS
MEATLOAF
MEATLOAVES
MEATMAN
MEATMEN
MEATPACKING
MEATPACKINGS
MEATS
MEATUS
MEATUSES
MEATY
MECAMYLAMINE
MECAMYLAMINES
MECCA
MECCAS
MECH
MECHANIC
MECHANICAL
MECHANICALLY
MECHANICALS
MECHANICIAN
MECHANICIANS
MECHANICS
MECHANISATION
MECHANISATIONS
MECHANISE
MECHANISED
MECHANISM
MECHANISMS
MECHANIST
MECHANISTIC
MECHANISTICALLY
MECHANISTS
MECHANIZABLE
MECHANIZATION
MECHANIZATIONS
MECHANIZE
MECHANIZED
MECHANIZER
MECHANIZERS
MECHANIZES
MECHANIZING
MECHANOCHEMICAL
MECHANORECEPTOR
MECHITZA
MECHITZAS
MECHITZOT
MECHOUI
MECHOUIS
MECHS
MECLIZINE
MECLIZINES
MECONIUM
MECONIUMS
MED
MEDAILLON
MEDAILLONS
MEDAKA
MEDAKAS
MEDAL
MEDALED
MEDALING
MEDALIST
MEDALISTS
MEDALLED
MEDALLIC
MEDALLING
MEDALLION
MEDALLIONS
MEDALLIST
MEDALLISTS
MEDALS
MEDDLE
MEDDLED
MEDDLER
MEDDLERS
MEDDLES
MEDDLESOME
MEDDLESOMENESS
MEDDLING
MEDEVAC
MEDEVACED
MEDEVACING
MEDEVACKED
MEDEVACKING
MEDEVACS
MEDFLIES
MEDFLY
MEDIA
MEDIACIES
MEDIACY
MEDIAD
MEDIAE
MEDIAEVAL
MEDIAEVALS
MEDIAGENIC
MEDIAL
MEDIALLY
MEDIALS
MEDIAN
MEDIANLY
MEDIANS
MEDIANT
MEDIANTS
MEDIAS
MEDIASCAPE
MEDIASCAPES
MEDIASTINA
MEDIASTINAL
MEDIASTINUM
MEDIATE
MEDIATED
MEDIATELY
MEDIATES
MEDIATING
MEDIATION
MEDIATIONAL
MEDIATIONS
MEDIATIVE
MEDIATIZE
MEDIATIZED
MEDIATIZES
MEDIATIZING
MEDIATOR
MEDIATORS
MEDIATORY
MEDIATRICES
MEDIATRIX
MEDIATRIXES
MEDIC
MEDICABLE
MEDICAID
MEDICAIDS
MEDICAL
MEDICALIZATION
MEDICALIZATIONS
MEDICALIZE
MEDICALIZED
MEDICALIZES
MEDICALIZING
MEDICALLY
MEDICALS
MEDICAMENT
MEDICAMENTOUS
MEDICAMENTS
MEDICANT
MEDICANTS
MEDICARE
MEDICARES
MEDICATE
MEDICATED
MEDICATES
MEDICATING
MEDICATION
MEDICATIONS
MEDICIDE
MEDICIDES
MEDICINABLE
MEDICINAL
MEDICINALLY
MEDICINALS
MEDICINE
MEDICINED

MEDICINES
MEDICINING
MEDICK
MEDICKS
MEDICO
MEDICOLEGAL
MEDICOS
MEDICS
MEDIEVAL
MEDIEVALISM
MEDIEVALISMS
MEDIEVALIST
MEDIEVALISTS
MEDIEVALLY
MEDIEVALS
MEDIGAP
MEDIGAPS
MEDII
MEDINA
MEDINAS
MEDIOCRE
MEDIOCRITIES
MEDIOCRITY
MEDITATE
MEDITATED
MEDITATES
MEDITATING
MEDITATION
MEDITATIONS
MEDITATIVE
MEDITATIVELY
MEDITATIVENESS
MEDITATOR
MEDITATORS
MEDITERRANEAN
MEDIUM
MEDIUMISTIC
MEDIUMS
MEDIUMSHIP
MEDIUMSHIPS
MEDIUS
MEDIVAC
MEDIVACED
MEDIVACING
MEDIVACKED
MEDIVACKING
MEDIVACS
MEDLAR
MEDLARS
MEDLEY
MEDLEYS
MEDRESE
MEDRESES
MEDS
MEDULLA
MEDULLAE
MEDULLAR
MEDULLARY
MEDULLAS
MEDULLATED
MEDULLOBLASTOMA
MEDUSA
MEDUSAE
MEDUSAL
MEDUSAN
MEDUSANS
MEDUSAS
MEDUSOID
MEDUSOIDS
MEED
MEEDS
MEEK
MEEKER
MEEKEST
MEEKLY
MEEKNESS
MEEKNESSES
MEERKAT
MEERKATS
MEERSCHAUM
MEERSCHAUMS
MEET
MEETER
MEETERS
MEETING
MEETINGHOUSE
MEETINGHOUSES
MEETINGS
MEETLY
MEETNESS
MEETNESSES
MEETS
MEFLOQUINE
MEFLOQUINES
MEG
MEGA
MEGABAR
MEGABARS
MEGABIT
MEGABITS
MEGABUCK
MEGABUCKS
MEGABYTE
MEGABYTES
MEGACITIES
MEGACITY
MEGACORPORATION
MEGACYCLE
MEGACYCLES
MEGADEAL
MEGADEALS
MEGADEATH
MEGADEATHS
MEGADOSE
MEGADOSES
MEGADYNE
MEGADYNES
MEGAFAUNA
MEGAFAUNAE
MEGAFAUNAL
MEGAFAUNAS
MEGAFLOP
MEGAFLOPS
MEGAGAMETE
MEGAGAMETES
MEGAGAMETOPHYTE
MEGAHERTZ
MEGAHERTZES
MEGAHIT
MEGAHITS
MEGAKARYOCYTE
MEGAKARYOCYTES
MEGAKARYOCYTIC
MEGALITH
MEGALITHIC
MEGALITHS
MEGALOBLAST
MEGALOBLASTIC
MEGALOBLASTS
MEGALOMANIA
MEGALOMANIAC
MEGALOMANIACAL
MEGALOMANIACS
MEGALOMANIAS
MEGALOMANIC
MEGALOPIC
MEGALOPOLIS
MEGALOPOLISES
MEGALOPOLITAN
MEGALOPOLITANS
MEGALOPS
MEGALOPSES
MEGAMALL
MEGAMALLS
MEGAMERGER
MEGAMERGERS
MEGAPARSEC
MEGAPARSECS
MEGAPHONE
MEGAPHONED
MEGAPHONES
MEGAPHONIC
MEGAPHONING
MEGAPIXEL
MEGAPIXELS
MEGAPLEX
MEGAPLEXES
MEGAPOD
MEGAPODE
MEGAPODES
MEGAPODS
MEGAPROJECT
MEGAPROJECTS
MEGARA
MEGARON
MEGASCOPIC
MEGASCOPICALLY
MEGASPORANGIA
MEGASPORANGIUM
MEGASPORE
MEGASPORES
MEGASPORIC
MEGASPOROPHYLL
MEGASPOROPHYLLS
MEGASS
MEGASSE
MEGASSES
MEGASTAR
MEGASTARDOM
MEGASTARDOMS
MEGASTARS
MEGASTORE
MEGASTORES
MEGATHERE
MEGATHERES
MEGATON
MEGATONNAGE
MEGATONNAGES
MEGATONS
MEGAVITAMIN
MEGAVITAMINS
MEGAVOLT
MEGAVOLTS
MEGAWATT
MEGAWATTS
MEGILLA
MEGILLAH
MEGILLAHS
MEGILLAS
MEGILP
MEGILPH
MEGILPHS
MEGILPS
MEGOHM
MEGOHMS
MEGRIM
MEGRIMS
MEGS
MEH
MEHNDI
MEHNDIS
MEIKLE
MEINIE
MEINIES
MEINY
MEIOSES
MEIOSIS
MEIOTIC
MEIOTICALLY
MEISTER
MEISTERS
MEITNERIUM
MEITNERIUMS
MEL
MELAENA
MELAENAS
MELALEUCA
MELALEUCAS
MELAMDIM
MELAMED
MELAMINE
MELAMINES
MELANCHOLIA
MELANCHOLIAC
MELANCHOLIACS
MELANCHOLIAS
MELANCHOLIC
MELANCHOLICS
MELANCHOLIES
MELANCHOLY
MELANGE
MELANGES
MELANIAN
MELANIC
MELANICS
MELANIN
MELANINS
MELANISM
MELANISMS
MELANIST
MELANISTIC
MELANISTS
MELANITE
MELANITES
MELANITIC

MELANIZATION
MELANIZATIONS
MELANIZE
MELANIZED
MELANIZES
MELANIZING
MELANOBLAST
MELANOBLASTS
MELANOCYTE
MELANOCYTES
MELANOGENESES
MELANOGENESIS
MELANOID
MELANOIDS
MELANOMA
MELANOMAS
MELANOMATA
MELANOPHORE
MELANOPHORES
MELANOSES
MELANOSIS
MELANOSOME
MELANOSOMES
MELANOTIC
MELANOUS
MELAPHYRE
MELAPHYRES
MELASTOME
MELATONIN
MELATONINS
MELD
MELDED
MELDER
MELDERS
MELDING
MELDS
MELEE
MELEES
MELENA
MELENAS
MELIC
MELILITE
MELILITES
MELILOT
MELILOTS
MELINITE
MELINITES
MELIORATE
MELIORATED
MELIORATES
MELIORATING
MELIORATION
MELIORATIONS
MELIORATIVE
MELIORATOR
MELIORATORS
MELIORISM
MELIORISMS
MELIORIST
MELIORISTIC
MELIORISTS
MELISMA
MELISMAS
MELISMATA
MELISMATIC
MELL
MELLED
MELLIFIC
MELLIFLUENT
MELLIFLUENTLY
MELLIFLUOUS
MELLIFLUOUSLY
MELLIFLUOUSNESS
MELLING
MELLOPHONE
MELLOPHONES
MELLOTRON
MELLOTRONS
MELLOW
MELLOWED
MELLOWER
MELLOWEST
MELLOWING
MELLOWLY
MELLOWNESS
MELLOWNESSES
MELLOWS
MELLS
MELODEON
MELODEONS
MELODIA
MELODIAS
MELODIC
MELODICA
MELODICALLY
MELODICAS
MELODIES
MELODION
MELODIONS
MELODIOUS
MELODIOUSLY
MELODIOUSNESS
MELODIOUSNESSES
MELODISE
MELODISED
MELODISES
MELODISING
MELODIST
MELODISTS
MELODIZE
MELODIZED
MELODIZER
MELODIZERS
MELODIZES
MELODIZING
MELODRAMA
MELODRAMAS
MELODRAMATIC
MELODRAMATICS
MELODRAMATISE
MELODRAMATISED
MELODRAMATISES
MELODRAMATISING
MELODRAMATIST
MELODRAMATISTS
MELODRAMATIZE
MELODRAMATIZED
MELODRAMATIZES
MELODRAMATIZING
MELODY
MELOID
MELOIDS
MELON
MELONGENE
MELONGENES
MELONS
MELONY
MELPHALAN
MELPHALANS
MELS
MELT
MELTABILITIES
MELTABILITY
MELTABLE
MELTAGE
MELTAGES
MELTDOWN
MELTDOWNS
MELTED
MELTER
MELTERS
MELTING
MELTINGLY
MELTON
MELTONS
MELTS
MELTWATER
MELTWATERS
MELTY
MEM
MEMBER
MEMBERED
MEMBERS
MEMBERSHIP
MEMBERSHIPS
MEMBRANAL
MEMBRANE
MEMBRANED
MEMBRANES
MEMBRANOUS
MEMBRANOUSLY
MEME
MEMENTO
MEMENTOES
MEMENTOS
MEMES
MEMETIC
MEMETICS
MEMO
MEMOIR
MEMOIRIST
MEMOIRISTS
MEMOIRS
MEMORABILIA
MEMORABILITIES
MEMORABILITY
MEMORABLE
MEMORABLENESS
MEMORABLENESSES
MEMORABLY
MEMORANDA
MEMORANDUM
MEMORANDUMS
MEMORIAL
MEMORIALISE
MEMORIALISED
MEMORIALISES
MEMORIALISING
MEMORIALIST
MEMORIALISTS
MEMORIALIZATION
MEMORIALIZE
MEMORIALIZED
MEMORIALIZES
MEMORIALIZING
MEMORIALLY
MEMORIALS
MEMORIES
MEMORISATION
MEMORISATIONS
MEMORISE
MEMORISED
MEMORISES
MEMORISING
MEMORITER
MEMORIZABLE
MEMORIZATION
MEMORIZATIONS
MEMORIZE
MEMORIZED
MEMORIZER
MEMORIZERS
MEMORIZES
MEMORIZING
MEMORY
MEMOS
MEMS
MEMSAHIB
MEMSAHIBS
MEN
MENACE
MENACED
MENACER
MENACERS
MENACES
MENACING
MENACINGLY
MENAD
MENADIONE
MENADIONES
MENADS
MENAGE
MENAGERIE
MENAGERIES
MENAGES
MENARCHE
MENARCHEAL
MENARCHES
MENAZON
MENAZONS
MEND
MENDABLE
MENDACIOUS
MENDACIOUSLY
MENDACIOUSNESS
MENDACITIES
MENDACITY
MENDED
MENDELEVIUM
MENDELEVIUMS
MENDER
MENDERS
MENDICANCIES
MENDICANCY
MENDICANT

MENDICANTS
MENDICITIES
MENDICITY
MENDIGO
MENDIGOS
MENDING
MENDINGS
MENDS
MENFOLK
MENFOLKS
MENHADEN
MENHADENS
MENHIR
MENHIRS
MENIAL
MENIALLY
MENIALS
MENINGEAL
MENINGES
MENINGIOMA
MENINGIOMAS
MENINGIOMATA
MENINGITIC
MENINGITIDES
MENINGITIS
MENINGOCOCCAL
MENINGOCOCCI
MENINGOCOCCIC
MENINGOCOCCUS
MENINX
MENISCAL
MENISCATE
MENISCI
MENISCOID
MENISCUS
MENISCUSES
MENO
MENOLOGIES
MENOLOGY
MENOPAUSAL
MENOPAUSE
MENOPAUSES
MENORAH
MENORAHS
MENORRHAGIA
MENORRHAGIAS
MENORRHEA
MENORRHEAS
MENSA
MENSAE
MENSAL
MENSAS
MENSCH
MENSCHEN
MENSCHES
MENSCHY
MENSE
MENSED
MENSEFUL
MENSELESS
MENSERVANTS
MENSES
MENSH
MENSHEN
MENSHES
MENSING
MENSTRUA
MENSTRUAL
MENSTRUALLY
MENSTRUATE
MENSTRUATED
MENSTRUATES
MENSTRUATING
MENSTRUATION
MENSTRUATIONS
MENSTRUUM
MENSTRUUMS
MENSURABILITIES
MENSURABILITY
MENSURABLE
MENSURAL
MENSURATION
MENSURATIONS
MENSWEAR
MENTA
MENTAL
MENTALESE
MENTALESES
MENTALISM
MENTALISMS
MENTALIST
MENTALISTIC
MENTALISTS
MENTALITIES
MENTALITY
MENTALLY
MENTATION
MENTATIONS
MENTEE
MENTEES
MENTHENE
MENTHENES
MENTHOL
MENTHOLATED
MENTHOLS
MENTION
MENTIONABLE
MENTIONED
MENTIONER
MENTIONERS
MENTIONING
MENTIONS
MENTO
MENTOR
MENTORED
MENTORING
MENTORS
MENTORSHIP
MENTORSHIPS
MENTOS
MENTUM
MENU
MENUDO
MENUDOS
MENUS
MEOU
MEOUED
MEOUING
MEOUS
MEOW
MEOWED
MEOWING
MEOWS
MEPERIDINE
MEPERIDINES
MEPHITIC
MEPHITIS
MEPHITISES
MEPROBAMATE
MEPROBAMATES
MERBROMIN
MERBROMINS
MERC
MERCADO
MERCADOS
MERCANTILE
MERCANTILISM
MERCANTILISMS
MERCANTILIST
MERCANTILISTIC
MERCANTILISTS
MERCAPTAN
MERCAPTANS
MERCAPTO
MERCAPTOPURINE
MERCAPTOPURINES
MERCENARIES
MERCENARILY
MERCENARINESS
MERCENARINESSES
MERCENARY
MERCER
MERCERIES
MERCERISE
MERCERISED
MERCERISES
MERCERISING
MERCERIZATION
MERCERIZATIONS
MERCERIZE
MERCERIZED
MERCERIZES
MERCERIZING
MERCERS
MERCERY
MERCES
MERCH
MERCHANDISE
MERCHANDISED
MERCHANDISER
MERCHANDISERS
MERCHANDISES
MERCHANDISING
MERCHANDISINGS
MERCHANDIZE
MERCHANDIZED
MERCHANDIZES
MERCHANDIZING
MERCHANDIZINGS
MERCHANT
MERCHANTABILITY
MERCHANTABLE
MERCHANTED
MERCHANTING
MERCHANTMAN
MERCHANTMEN
MERCHANTS
MERCHES
MERCIES
MERCIFUL
MERCIFULLY
MERCIFULNESS
MERCIFULNESSES
MERCILESS
MERCILESSLY
MERCILESSNESS
MERCILESSNESSES
MERCS
MERCURATE
MERCURATED
MERCURATES
MERCURATING
MERCURATION
MERCURATIONS
MERCURIAL
MERCURIALLY
MERCURIALNESS
MERCURIALNESSES
MERCURIALS
MERCURIC
MERCURIES
MERCUROUS
MERCURY
MERCY
MERDE
MERDES
MERE
MERELY
MERENGUE
MERENGUES
MERER
MERES
MEREST
MERETRICIOUS
MERETRICIOUSLY
MERGANSER
MERGANSERS
MERGE
MERGED
MERGEE
MERGEES
MERGENCE
MERGENCES
MERGER
MERGERS
MERGES
MERGING
MERGINGS
MERGUEZ
MERIDIAN
MERIDIANS
MERIDIONAL
MERIDIONALLY
MERIDIONALS
MERINGUE
MERINGUES
MERINO
MERINOS
MERISES
MERISIS
MERISTEM
MERISTEMATIC
MERISTEMS
MERISTIC
MERISTICALLY

MERIT
MERITED
MERITING
MERITLESS
MERITOCRACIES
MERITOCRACY
MERITOCRAT
MERITOCRATIC
MERITOCRATS
MERITORIOUS
MERITORIOUSLY
MERITORIOUSNESS
MERITS
MERK
MERKS
MERL
MERLE
MERLES
MERLIN
MERLINS
MERLON
MERLONS
MERLOT
MERLOTS
MERLS
MERMAID
MERMAIDS
MERMAN
MERMEN
MEROBLASTIC
MEROBLASTICALLY
MEROCRINE
MEROMORPHIC
MEROMYOSIN
MEROMYOSINS
MERONYM
MERONYMIES
MERONYMS
MERONYMY
MEROPIA
MEROPIAS
MEROPIC
MEROZOITE
MEROZOITES
MERRIER
MERRIEST
MERRILY
MERRIMENT
MERRIMENTS
MERRINESS
MERRINESSES
MERRY
MERRYMAKER
MERRYMAKERS
MERRYMAKING
MERRYMAKINGS
MERRYTHOUGHT
MERRYTHOUGHTS
MES
MESA
MESALLIANCE
MESALLIANCES
MESALLY
MESARCH
MESAS
MESCAL
MESCALIN
MESCALINE
MESCALINES
MESCALINS
MESCALS
MESCLUN
MESCLUNS
MESDAMES
MESDEMOISELLES
MESEEMED
MESEEMETH
MESEEMS
MESENCEPHALA
MESENCEPHALIC
MESENCEPHALON
MESENCHYMAL
MESENCHYME
MESENCHYMES
MESENTERA
MESENTERIC
MESENTERIES
MESENTERON
MESENTERY
MESH
MESHED
MESHES
MESHIER
MESHIEST
MESHING
MESHINGS
MESHUGA
MESHUGAAS
MESHUGAH
MESHUGGA
MESHUGGAH
MESHUGGE
MESHUGGENER
MESHUGGENERS
MESHWORK
MESHWORKS
MESHY
MESIAL
MESIALLY
MESIAN
MESIC
MESICALLY
MESMERIC
MESMERICALLY
MESMERISE
MESMERISED
MESMERISES
MESMERISING
MESMERISM
MESMERISMS
MESMERIST
MESMERISTS
MESMERIZE
MESMERIZED
MESMERIZER
MESMERIZERS
MESMERIZES
MESMERIZING
MESNALTIES
MESNALTY
MESNE
MESNES
MESOBLAST
MESOBLASTS
MESOCARP
MESOCARPS
MESOCRANIES
MESOCRANY
MESOCYCLONE
MESOCYCLONES
MESODERM
MESODERMAL
MESODERMS
MESOGLEA
MESOGLEAL
MESOGLEAS
MESOGLOEA
MESOGLOEAS
MESOMERE
MESOMERES
MESOMORPH
MESOMORPHIC
MESOMORPHIES
MESOMORPHS
MESOMORPHY
MESON
MESONEPHRIC
MESONEPHROI
MESONEPHROS
MESONIC
MESONS
MESOPAUSE
MESOPAUSES
MESOPELAGIC
MESOPHYL
MESOPHYLL
MESOPHYLLIC
MESOPHYLLOUS
MESOPHYLLS
MESOPHYLS
MESOPHYTE
MESOPHYTES
MESOPHYTIC
MESOSAUR
MESOSAURS
MESOSCALE
MESOSOME
MESOSOMES
MESOSPHERE
MESOSPHERES
MESOSPHERIC
MESOTHELIA
MESOTHELIAL
MESOTHELIOMA
MESOTHELIOMAS
MESOTHELIOMATA
MESOTHELIUM
MESOTHORACES
MESOTHORACIC
MESOTHORAX
MESOTHORAXES
MESOTRON
MESOTRONS
MESOTROPHIC
MESOZOAN
MESOZOANS
MESOZOIC
MESQUIT
MESQUITE
MESQUITES
MESQUITS
MESS
MESSAGE
MESSAGED
MESSAGES
MESSAGING
MESSAGINGS
MESSALINE
MESSALINES
MESSAN
MESSANS
MESSED
MESSEIGNEURS
MESSENGER
MESSENGERED
MESSENGERING
MESSENGERS
MESSES
MESSIAH
MESSIAHS
MESSIAHSHIP
MESSIAHSHIPS
MESSIANIC
MESSIANISM
MESSIANISMS
MESSIER
MESSIEST
MESSIEURS
MESSILY
MESSINESS
MESSINESSES
MESSING
MESSMAN
MESSMATE
MESSMATES
MESSMEN
MESSUAGE
MESSUAGES
MESSY
MESTEE
MESTEES
MESTESO
MESTESOES
MESTESOS
MESTINO
MESTINOES
MESTINOS
MESTIZA
MESTIZAS
MESTIZO
MESTIZOES
MESTIZOS
MESTRANOL
MESTRANOLS
MET
META
METABOLIC
METABOLICALLY
METABOLISE
METABOLISED
METABOLISES
METABOLISING
METABOLISM
METABOLISMS
METABOLITE

METABOLITES
METABOLIZABLE
METABOLIZE
METABOLIZED
METABOLIZES
METABOLIZING
METACARPAL
METACARPALS
METACARPI
METACARPUS
METACARPUSES
METACENTER
METACENTERS
METACENTRIC
METACENTRICS
METACERCARIA
METACERCARIAE
METACERCARIAL
METACERCARIAS
METACHROMATIC
METACOGNITION
METACOGNITIONS
METADATA
METADATAS
METAETHICAL
METAETHICS
METAFICTION
METAFICTIONAL
METAFICTIONIST
METAFICTIONISTS
METAFICTIONS
METAGALACTIC
METAGALAXIES
METAGALAXY
METAGE
METAGENESES
METAGENESIS
METAGENETIC
METAGENIC
METAGES
METAL
METALANGUAGE
METALANGUAGES
METALDEHYDE
METALDEHYDES
METALED
METALHEAD
METALHEADS
METALING
METALINGUISTIC
METALINGUISTICS
METALISE
METALISED
METALISES
METALISING
METALIST
METALISTS
METALIZE
METALIZED
METALIZES
METALIZING
METALLED
METALLIC
METALLICALLY
METALLICS
METALLIFEROUS
METALLIKE
METALLINE
METALLING
METALLIST
METALLISTS
METALLIZATION
METALLIZATIONS
METALLIZE
METALLIZED
METALLIZES
METALLIZING
METALLOGRAPHER
METALLOGRAPHERS
METALLOGRAPHIC
METALLOGRAPHIES
METALLOGRAPHY
METALLOID
METALLOIDAL
METALLOIDS
METALLOPHONE
METALLOPHONES
METALLURGICAL
METALLURGICALLY
METALLURGIES
METALLURGIST
METALLURGISTS
METALLURGY
METALMARK
METALMARKS
METALS
METALSMITH
METALSMITHS
METALWARE
METALWARES
METALWORK
METALWORKER
METALWORKERS
METALWORKING
METALWORKINGS
METALWORKS
METAMATHEMATICS
METAMER
METAMERE
METAMERES
METAMERIC
METAMERICALLY
METAMERISM
METAMERISMS
METAMERS
METAMORPHIC
METAMORPHICALLY
METAMORPHISM
METAMORPHISMS
METAMORPHOSE
METAMORPHOSED
METAMORPHOSES
METAMORPHOSING
METAMORPHOSIS
METANALYSES
METANALYSIS
METANEPHRIC
METANEPHROI
METANEPHROS
METANOIA
METANOIAS
METAPHASE
METAPHASES
METAPHOR
METAPHORIC
METAPHORICAL
METAPHORICALLY
METAPHORS
METAPHOSPHATE
METAPHOSPHATES
METAPHRASE
METAPHRASES
METAPHYSIC
METAPHYSICAL
METAPHYSICALLY
METAPHYSICIAN
METAPHYSICIANS
METAPHYSICS
METAPLASIA
METAPLASIAS
METAPLASM
METAPLASMS
METAPLASTIC
METAPSYCHOLOGY
METASEQUOIA
METASEQUOIAS
METASOMATIC
METASOMATISM
METASOMATISMS
METASTABILITIES
METASTABILITY
METASTABLE
METASTABLY
METASTASES
METASTASIS
METASTASIZE
METASTASIZED
METASTASIZES
METASTASIZING
METASTATIC
METASTATICALLY
METATAG
METATAGS
METATARSAL
METATARSALS
METATARSI
METATARSUS
METATARSUSES
METATE
METATES
METATHESES
METATHESIS
METATHETIC
METATHETICAL
METATHETICALLY
METATHORACES
METATHORACIC
METATHORAX
METATHORAXES
METAXYLEM
METAXYLEMS
METAZOA
METAZOAL
METAZOAN
METAZOANS
METAZOIC
METAZOON
METE
METED
METEMPSYCHOSES
METEMPSYCHOSIS
METENCEPHALA
METENCEPHALIC
METENCEPHALON
METEOR
METEORIC
METEORICALLY
METEORITE
METEORITES
METEORITIC
METEORITICAL
METEORITICIST
METEORITICISTS
METEORITICS
METEOROID
METEOROIDAL
METEOROIDS
METEOROLOGIC
METEOROLOGICAL
METEOROLOGIES
METEOROLOGIST
METEOROLOGISTS
METEOROLOGY
METEORS
METEPA
METEPAS
METER
METERAGE
METERAGES
METERED
METERING
METERS
METERSTICK
METERSTICKS
METES
METESTRUS
METESTRUSES
METFORMIN
METFORMINS
METH
METHACRYLATE
METHACRYLATES
METHADON
METHADONE
METHADONES
METHADONS
METHAMPHETAMINE
METHANAL
METHANALS
METHANATION
METHANATIONS
METHANE
METHANES
METHANOL
METHANOLS
METHAQUALONE
METHAQUALONES
METHEDRINE
METHEDRINES
METHEGLIN
METHEGLINS
METHEMOGLOBIN
METHEMOGLOBINS
METHENAMINE
METHENAMINES

METHICILLIN
METHICILLINS
METHINKS
METHIONINE
METHIONINES
METHOD
METHODIC
METHODICAL
METHODICALLY
METHODICALNESS
METHODISE
METHODISED
METHODISES
METHODISING
METHODISM
METHODISMS
METHODIST
METHODISTIC
METHODISTS
METHODIZE
METHODIZED
METHODIZES
METHODIZING
METHODOLOGICAL
METHODOLOGIES
METHODOLOGIST
METHODOLOGISTS
METHODOLOGY
METHODS
METHOTREXATE
METHOTREXATES
METHOUGHT
METHOXIDE
METHOXIDES
METHOXY
METHOXYCHLOR
METHOXYCHLORS
METHOXYFLURANE
METHOXYFLURANES
METHOXYL
METHS
METHYL
METHYLAL
METHYLALS
METHYLAMINE
METHYLAMINES
METHYLASE
METHYLASES
METHYLATE
METHYLATED
METHYLATES
METHYLATING
METHYLATION
METHYLATIONS
METHYLATOR
METHYLATORS
METHYLCELLULOSE
METHYLDOPA
METHYLDOPAS
METHYLENE
METHYLENES
METHYLIC
METHYLMERCURIES
METHYLMERCURY
METHYLPHENIDATE
METHYLS
METHYLXANTHINE
METHYLXANTHINES
METHYSERGIDE
METHYSERGIDES
METICAIS
METICAL
METICALS
METICULOSITIES
METICULOSITY
METICULOUS
METICULOUSLY
METICULOUSNESS
METIER
METIERS
METING
METIS
METISSE
METISSES
METOL
METOLS
METONYM
METONYMIC
METONYMICAL
METONYMIES
METONYMS
METONYMY
METOPAE
METOPE
METOPES
METOPIC
METOPON
METOPONS
METOPROLOL
METOPROLOLS
METRALGIA
METRALGIAS
METRAZOL
METRAZOLS
METRE
METRED
METRES
METRIC
METRICAL
METRICALLY
METRICATE
METRICATED
METRICATES
METRICATING
METRICATION
METRICATIONS
METRICISM
METRICISMS
METRICIZE
METRICIZED
METRICIZES
METRICIZING
METRICS
METRIFIED
METRIFIES
METRIFY
METRIFYING
METRING
METRIST
METRISTS
METRITIS
METRITISES
METRO
METROLOGICAL
METROLOGIES
METROLOGIST
METROLOGISTS
METROLOGY
METRONIDAZOLE
METRONIDAZOLES
METRONOME
METRONOMES
METRONOMIC
METRONOMICAL
METRONOMICALLY
METROPLEX
METROPLEXES
METROPOLIS
METROPOLISES
METROPOLITAN
METROPOLITANS
METRORRHAGIA
METRORRHAGIAS
METROS
METROSEXUAL
METROSEXUALITY
METROSEXUALS
METTLE
METTLED
METTLES
METTLESOME
METUMP
METUMPS
MEUNIERE
MEW
MEWED
MEWING
MEWL
MEWLED
MEWLER
MEWLERS
MEWLING
MEWLS
MEWS
MEWSES
MEZCAL
MEZCALS
MEZE
MEZEREON
MEZEREONS
MEZEREUM
MEZEREUMS
MEZES
MEZQUIT
MEZQUITE
MEZQUITES
MEZQUITS
MEZUZA
MEZUZAH
MEZUZAHS
MEZUZAS
MEZUZOT
MEZUZOTH
MEZZALUNA
MEZZALUNAS
MEZZANINE
MEZZANINES
MEZZO
MEZZOS
MEZZOTINT
MEZZOTINTED
MEZZOTINTING
MEZZOTINTS
MHO
MHOS
MI
MIAOU
MIAOUED
MIAOUING
MIAOUS
MIAOW
MIAOWED
MIAOWING
MIAOWS
MIASM
MIASMA
MIASMAL
MIASMAS
MIASMATA
MIASMATIC
MIASMIC
MIASMICALLY
MIASMS
MIAUL
MIAULED
MIAULING
MIAULS
MIB
MIBS
MIC
MICA
MICACEOUS
MICAS
MICAWBER
MICAWBERS
MICE
MICELL
MICELLA
MICELLAE
MICELLAR
MICELLE
MICELLES
MICELLS
MICHE
MICHED
MICHES
MICHING
MICK
MICKEY
MICKEYS
MICKIES
MICKLE
MICKLER
MICKLES
MICKLEST
MICKS
MICKY
MICONAZOLE
MICONAZOLES
MICRA
MICRIFIED
MICRIFIES
MICRIFY
MICRIFYING
MICRO

MICROAMPERE
MICROAMPERES
MICROANALYSES
MICROANALYSIS
MICROANALYST
MICROANALYSTS
MICROANALYTIC
MICROANALYTICAL
MICROANATOMICAL
MICROANATOMIES
MICROANATOMY
MICROARRAY
MICROARRAYS
MICROBALANCE
MICROBALANCES
MICROBAR
MICROBAROGRAPH
MICROBAROGRAPHS
MICROBARS
MICROBE
MICROBEAM
MICROBEAMS
MICROBES
MICROBIAL
MICROBIAN
MICROBIC
MICROBICIDAL
MICROBICIDE
MICROBICIDES
MICROBIOLOGIC
MICROBIOLOGICAL
MICROBIOLOGIES
MICROBIOLOGIST
MICROBIOLOGISTS
MICROBIOLOGY
MICROBLOG
MICROBLOGGING
MICROBLOGGINGS
MICROBREW
MICROBREWED
MICROBREWER
MICROBREWERIES
MICROBREWERS
MICROBREWERY
MICROBREWING
MICROBREWINGS
MICROBREWS
MICROBURST
MICROBURSTS
MICROBUS
MICROBUSES
MICROBUSSES
MICROCAP
MICROCAPSULE
MICROCAPSULES
MICROCAR
MICROCARS
MICROCASSETTE
MICROCASSETTES
MICROCEPHALIC
MICROCEPHALICS
MICROCEPHALIES
MICROCEPHALY
MICROCHIP
MICROCHIPS
MICROCIRCUIT
MICROCIRCUITRY
MICROCIRCUITS
MICROCLIMATE
MICROCLIMATES
MICROCLIMATIC
MICROCLINE
MICROCLINES
MICROCOCCAL
MICROCOCCI
MICROCOCCUS
MICROCODE
MICROCODES
MICROCOMPUTER
MICROCOMPUTERS
MICROCONTROLLER
MICROCOPIES
MICROCOPY
MICROCOSM
MICROCOSMIC
MICROCOSMICALLY
MICROCOSMOS
MICROCOSMOSES
MICROCOSMS
MICROCRYSTAL
MICROCRYSTALS
MICROCULTURAL
MICROCULTURE
MICROCULTURES
MICROCURIE
MICROCURIES
MICROCYTE
MICROCYTES
MICROCYTIC
MICRODISSECTION
MICRODONT
MICRODOT
MICRODOTS
MICROEARTHQUAKE
MICROECONOMIC
MICROECONOMICS
MICROECONOMIST
MICROECONOMISTS
MICROELECTRODE
MICROELECTRODES
MICROELECTRONIC
MICROELEMENT
MICROELEMENTS
MICROENTERPRISE
MICROEVOLUTION
MICROEVOLUTIONS
MICROFARAD
MICROFARADS
MICROFAUNA
MICROFAUNAE
MICROFAUNAL
MICROFAUNAS
MICROFIBER
MICROFIBERS
MICROFIBRIL
MICROFIBRILLAR
MICROFIBRILS
MICROFICHE
MICROFICHES
MICROFILAMENT
MICROFILAMENTS
MICROFILARIA
MICROFILARIAE
MICROFILARIAL
MICROFILARIAS
MICROFILM
MICROFILMABLE
MICROFILMED
MICROFILMER
MICROFILMERS
MICROFILMING
MICROFILMS
MICROFLORA
MICROFLORAE
MICROFLORAL
MICROFLORAS
MICROFORM
MICROFORMS
MICROFOSSIL
MICROFOSSILS
MICROFUNGI
MICROFUNGUS
MICROFUNGUSES
MICROGAMETE
MICROGAMETES
MICROGAMETOCYTE
MICROGRAM
MICROGRAMS
MICROGRAPH
MICROGRAPHED
MICROGRAPHIC
MICROGRAPHICS
MICROGRAPHING
MICROGRAPHS
MICROGRAVITIES
MICROGRAVITY
MICROGREEN
MICROGREENS
MICROGROOVE
MICROGROOVES
MICROHABITAT
MICROHABITATS
MICROHM
MICROHMS
MICROIMAGE
MICROIMAGES
MICROINCH
MICROINCHES
MICROINJECT
MICROINJECTED
MICROINJECTING
MICROINJECTION
MICROINJECTIONS
MICROINJECTS
MICROLITER
MICROLITERS
MICROLITH
MICROLITHIC
MICROLITHS
MICROLOAN
MICROLOANS
MICROLUCES
MICROLUX
MICROLUXES
MICROMANAGE
MICROMANAGED
MICROMANAGEMENT
MICROMANAGER
MICROMANAGERS
MICROMANAGES
MICROMANAGING
MICROMERE
MICROMERES
MICROMETEORITE
MICROMETEORITES
MICROMETEORITIC
MICROMETEOROID
MICROMETEOROIDS
MICROMETER
MICROMETERS
MICROMETHOD
MICROMETHODS
MICROMETRE
MICROMETRES
MICROMHO
MICROMHOS
MICROMINI
MICROMINIATURE
MICROMINIS
MICROMOLAR
MICROMOLE
MICROMOLES
MICROMORPHOLOGY
MICRON
MICRONIZE
MICRONIZED
MICRONIZES
MICRONIZING
MICRONS
MICRONUCLEI
MICRONUCLEUS
MICRONUCLEUSES
MICRONUTRIENT
MICRONUTRIENTS
MICROORGANISM
MICROORGANISMS
MICROPARTICLE
MICROPARTICLES
MICROPHAGE
MICROPHAGES
MICROPHONE
MICROPHONES
MICROPHONIC
MICROPHONICS
MICROPHOTOGRAPH
MICROPHOTOMETER
MICROPHOTOMETRY
MICROPHYLL
MICROPHYLLOUS
MICROPHYLLS
MICROPHYSICAL
MICROPHYSICALLY
MICROPHYSICS
MICROPIPET
MICROPIPETS
MICROPIPETTE
MICROPIPETTES
MICROPLANKTON
MICROPLANKTONS
MICROPOLITAN
MICROPORE
MICROPORES
MICROPOROSITIES
MICROPOROSITY
MICROPOROUS

MICROPRISM
MICROPRISMS
MICROPROBE
MICROPROBES
MICROPROCESSOR
MICROPROCESSORS
MICROPROGRAM
MICROPROGRAMS
MICROPROJECTION
MICROPROJECTOR
MICROPROJECTORS
MICROPUBLISHER
MICROPUBLISHERS
MICROPUBLISHING
MICROPULSATION
MICROPULSATIONS
MICROPUNCTURE
MICROPUNCTURES
MICROPYLAR
MICROPYLE
MICROPYLES
MICROQUAKE
MICROQUAKES
MICRORADIOGRAPH
MICROREADER
MICROREADERS
MICROS
MICROSATELLITE
MICROSATELLITES
MICROSCALE
MICROSCALES
MICROSCOPE
MICROSCOPES
MICROSCOPIC
MICROSCOPICAL
MICROSCOPICALLY
MICROSCOPIES
MICROSCOPIST
MICROSCOPISTS
MICROSCOPY
MICROSECOND
MICROSECONDS
MICROSEISM
MICROSEISMIC
MICROSEISMICITY
MICROSEISMS
MICROSENSOR
MICROSENSORS
MICROSOMAL
MICROSOME
MICROSOMES
MICROSPHERE
MICROSPHERES
MICROSPHERICAL
MICROSPORANGIA
MICROSPORANGIUM
MICROSPORE
MICROSPORES
MICROSPOROCYTE
MICROSPOROCYTES
MICROSPOROPHYLL
MICROSPOROUS
MICROSTATE
MICROSTATES
MICROSTRUCTURAL
MICROSTRUCTURE
MICROSTRUCTURES
MICROSURGERIES
MICROSURGERY
MICROSURGICAL
MICROSWITCH
MICROSWITCHES
MICROTECHNIC
MICROTECHNICS
MICROTECHNIQUE
MICROTECHNIQUES
MICROTECHNOLOGY
MICROTITER
MICROTITERS
MICROTOME
MICROTOMES
MICROTOMIES
MICROTOMY
MICROTONAL
MICROTONALITIES
MICROTONALITY
MICROTONALLY
MICROTONE
MICROTONES
MICROTUBULAR
MICROTUBULE
MICROTUBULES
MICROVASCULAR
MICROVILLAR
MICROVILLI
MICROVILLOUS
MICROVILLUS
MICROVOLT
MICROVOLTS
MICROWATT
MICROWATTS
MICROWAVABLE
MICROWAVE
MICROWAVEABLE
MICROWAVED
MICROWAVES
MICROWAVING
MICROWORLD
MICROWORLDS
MICRURGIES
MICRURGY
MICS
MICTURATE
MICTURATED
MICTURATES
MICTURATING
MICTURITION
MICTURITIONS
MID
MIDAFTERNOON
MIDAFTERNOONS
MIDAIR
MIDAIRS
MIDBRAIN
MIDBRAINS
MIDCAP
MIDCOURSE
MIDCULT
MIDCULTS
MIDDAY
MIDDAYS
MIDDEN
MIDDENS
MIDDIES
MIDDLE
MIDDLEBROW
MIDDLEBROWS
MIDDLED
MIDDLEMAN
MIDDLEMEN
MIDDLER
MIDDLERS
MIDDLES
MIDDLEWEIGHT
MIDDLEWEIGHTS
MIDDLING
MIDDLINGLY
MIDDLINGS
MIDDORSAL
MIDDY
MIDFIELD
MIDFIELDER
MIDFIELDERS
MIDFIELDS
MIDGE
MIDGES
MIDGET
MIDGETS
MIDGUT
MIDGUTS
MIDI
MIDINETTE
MIDINETTES
MIDIRON
MIDIRONS
MIDIS
MIDISKIRT
MIDISKIRTS
MIDLAND
MIDLANDS
MIDLATITUDE
MIDLATITUDES
MIDLEG
MIDLEGS
MIDLIFE
MIDLIFER
MIDLIFERS
MIDLINE
MIDLINES
MIDLIST
MIDLISTS
MIDLIVES
MIDMONTH
MIDMONTHS
MIDMORNING
MIDMORNINGS
MIDMOST
MIDMOSTS
MIDNIGHT
MIDNIGHTLY
MIDNIGHTS
MIDNOON
MIDNOONS
MIDPOINT
MIDPOINTS
MIDRANGE
MIDRANGES
MIDRASH
MIDRASHIC
MIDRASHIM
MIDRASHOT
MIDRASHOTH
MIDRIB
MIDRIBS
MIDRIFF
MIDRIFFS
MIDS
MIDSAGITTAL
MIDSEASON
MIDSECTION
MIDSECTIONS
MIDSHIP
MIDSHIPMAN
MIDSHIPMEN
MIDSHIPS
MIDSHORE
MIDSIZE
MIDSIZED
MIDSOLE
MIDSOLES
MIDSPACE
MIDSPACES
MIDST
MIDSTORIES
MIDSTORY
MIDSTREAM
MIDSTREAMS
MIDSTS
MIDSUMMER
MIDSUMMERS
MIDTERM
MIDTERMS
MIDTOWN
MIDTOWNS
MIDWATCH
MIDWATCHES
MIDWATER
MIDWATERS
MIDWAY
MIDWAYS
MIDWEEK
MIDWEEKLY
MIDWEEKS
MIDWIFE
MIDWIFED
MIDWIFERIES
MIDWIFERY
MIDWIFES
MIDWIFING
MIDWINTER
MIDWINTERS
MIDWIVED
MIDWIVES
MIDWIVING
MIDYEAR
MIDYEARS
MIEN
MIENS
MIFEPRISTONE
MIFEPRISTONES
MIFF
MIFFED
MIFFIER
MIFFIEST
MIFFINESS

MIFFINESSES
MIFFING
MIFFS
MIFFY
MIG
MIGAWD
MIGG
MIGGLE
MIGGLES
MIGGS
MIGHT
MIGHTIER
MIGHTIEST
MIGHTILY
MIGHTINESS
MIGHTINESSES
MIGHTS
MIGHTY
MIGNON
MIGNONETTE
MIGNONETTES
MIGNONNE
MIGNONS
MIGRAINE
MIGRAINES
MIGRAINEUR
MIGRAINEURS
MIGRAINOUS
MIGRANT
MIGRANTS
MIGRATE
MIGRATED
MIGRATES
MIGRATING
MIGRATION
MIGRATIONAL
MIGRATIONS
MIGRATOR
MIGRATORS
MIGRATORY
MIGS
MIHRAB
MIHRABS
MIJNHEER
MIJNHEERS
MIKADO
MIKADOS
MIKE
MIKED
MIKES
MIKING
MIKRA
MIKRON
MIKRONS
MIKVA
MIKVAH
MIKVAHS
MIKVAS
MIKVEH
MIKVEHS
MIKVOS
MIKVOT
MIKVOTH
MIL
MILADI
MILADIES
MILADIS
MILADY
MILAGE
MILAGES
MILCH
MILCHIG
MILD
MILDED
MILDEN
MILDENED
MILDENING
MILDENS
MILDER
MILDEST
MILDEW
MILDEWCIDE
MILDEWCIDES
MILDEWED
MILDEWING
MILDEWS
MILDEWY
MILDING
MILDISH
MILDLY
MILDNESS
MILDNESSES
MILDS
MILE
MILEAGE
MILEAGES
MILEOMETER
MILEOMETERS
MILEPOST
MILEPOSTS
MILER
MILERS
MILES
MILESIAN
MILESIMO
MILESIMOS
MILESTONE
MILESTONES
MILFOIL
MILFOILS
MILIA
MILIARIA
MILIARIAL
MILIARIAS
MILIARY
MILIEU
MILIEUS
MILIEUX
MILING
MILINGS
MILITANCE
MILITANCES
MILITANCIES
MILITANCY
MILITANT
MILITANTLY
MILITANTNESS
MILITANTNESSES
MILITANTS
MILITARIA
MILITARIES
MILITARILY
MILITARISATION
MILITARISATIONS
MILITARISE
MILITARISED
MILITARISES
MILITARISING
MILITARISM
MILITARISMS
MILITARIST
MILITARISTIC
MILITARISTS
MILITARIZATION
MILITARIZATIONS
MILITARIZE
MILITARIZED
MILITARIZES
MILITARIZING
MILITARY
MILITATE
MILITATED
MILITATES
MILITATING
MILITIA
MILITIAMAN
MILITIAMEN
MILITIAS
MILIUM
MILK
MILKED
MILKER
MILKERS
MILKFISH
MILKFISHES
MILKIER
MILKIEST
MILKILY
MILKINESS
MILKINESSES
MILKING
MILKLESS
MILKMAID
MILKMAIDS
MILKMAN
MILKMEN
MILKS
MILKSHAKE
MILKSHAKES
MILKSHED
MILKSHEDS
MILKSOP
MILKSOPPY
MILKSOPS
MILKWEED
MILKWEEDS
MILKWOOD
MILKWOODS
MILKWORT
MILKWORTS
MILKY
MILL
MILLABLE
MILLAGE
MILLAGES
MILLBOARD
MILLBOARDS
MILLCAKE
MILLCAKES
MILLDAM
MILLDAMS
MILLE
MILLED
MILLEFIORI
MILLEFIORIS
MILLEFLEUR
MILLEFLEURS
MILLENARIAN
MILLENARIANISM
MILLENARIANISMS
MILLENARIANS
MILLENARIES
MILLENARY
MILLENNIA
MILLENNIAL
MILLENNIALISM
MILLENNIALISMS
MILLENNIALIST
MILLENNIALISTS
MILLENNIALS
MILLENNIUM
MILLENNIUMS
MILLEPED
MILLEPEDE
MILLEPEDES
MILLEPEDS
MILLEPORE
MILLEPORES
MILLER
MILLERITE
MILLERITES
MILLERS
MILLES
MILLESIMAL
MILLESIMALLY
MILLESIMALS
MILLET
MILLETS
MILLHOUSE
MILLHOUSES
MILLIAMP
MILLIAMPERE
MILLIAMPERES
MILLIAMPS
MILLIARD
MILLIARDS
MILLIARE
MILLIARES
MILLIARIES
MILLIARY
MILLIBAR
MILLIBARS
MILLICURIE
MILLICURIES
MILLIDEGREE
MILLIDEGREES
MILLIEME
MILLIEMES
MILLIER
MILLIERS
MILLIGAL
MILLIGALS
MILLIGAUSS
MILLIGAUSSES
MILLIGRAM

MILLIGRAMME
MILLIGRAMMES
MILLIGRAMS
MILLIHENRIES
MILLIHENRY
MILLIHENRYS
MILLILAMBERT
MILLILAMBERTS
MILLILITER
MILLILITERS
MILLILITRE
MILLILITRES
MILLILUCES
MILLILUX
MILLILUXES
MILLIME
MILLIMES
MILLIMETER
MILLIMETERS
MILLIMETRE
MILLIMETRES
MILLIMHO
MILLIMHOS
MILLIMICRON
MILLIMICRONS
MILLIMOLAR
MILLIMOLE
MILLIMOLES
MILLINE
MILLINER
MILLINERIES
MILLINERS
MILLINERY
MILLINES
MILLING
MILLINGS
MILLIOHM
MILLIOHMS
MILLION
MILLIONAIRE
MILLIONAIRES
MILLIONAIRESS
MILLIONAIRESSES
MILLIONFOLD
MILLIONS
MILLIONTH
MILLIONTHS
MILLIOSMOL
MILLIOSMOLS
MILLIPED
MILLIPEDE
MILLIPEDES
MILLIPEDS
MILLIRADIAN
MILLIRADIANS
MILLIREM
MILLIREMS
MILLIROENTGEN
MILLIROENTGENS
MILLISECOND
MILLISECONDS
MILLIVOLT
MILLIVOLTS
MILLIWATT
MILLIWATTS
MILLPOND
MILLPONDS
MILLRACE
MILLRACES
MILLRUN
MILLRUNS
MILLS
MILLSTONE
MILLSTONES
MILLSTREAM
MILLSTREAMS
MILLWORK
MILLWORKS
MILLWRIGHT
MILLWRIGHTS
MILNEB
MILNEBS
MILO
MILOMETER
MILOMETERS
MILORD
MILORDS
MILOS
MILPA
MILPAS
MILQUETOAST
MILQUETOASTS
MILREIS
MILS
MILT
MILTED
MILTER
MILTERS
MILTIER
MILTIEST
MILTING
MILTS
MILTY
MIM
MIMBAR
MIMBARS
MIME
MIMED
MIMEO
MIMEOED
MIMEOGRAPH
MIMEOGRAPHED
MIMEOGRAPHING
MIMEOGRAPHS
MIMEOING
MIMEOS
MIMER
MIMERS
MIMES
MIMESES
MIMESIS
MIMESISES
MIMETIC
MIMETICALLY
MIMETITE
MIMETITES
MIMIC
MIMICAL
MIMICKED
MIMICKER
MIMICKERS
MIMICKING
MIMICRIES
MIMICRY
MIMICS
MIMING
MIMOSA
MIMOSAS
MIMULUS
MIMULUSES
MINA
MINABLE
MINACIOUS
MINACITIES
MINACITY
MINAE
MINARET
MINARETED
MINARETS
MINAS
MINATORY
MINAUDIERE
MINAUDIERES
MINBAR
MINBARS
MINCE
MINCED
MINCEMEAT
MINCEMEATS
MINCER
MINCERS
MINCES
MINCIER
MINCIEST
MINCING
MINCINGLY
MINCY
MIND
MINDBLOWER
MINDBLOWERS
MINDED
MINDEDLY
MINDEDNESS
MINDEDNESSES
MINDER
MINDERS
MINDFUCK
MINDFUCKS
MINDFUL
MINDFULLY
MINDFULNESS
MINDFULNESSES
MINDING
MINDLESS
MINDLESSLY
MINDLESSNESS
MINDLESSNESSES
MINDS
MINDSET
MINDSETS
MINE
MINEABLE
MINED
MINEFIELD
MINEFIELDS
MINELAYER
MINELAYERS
MINER
MINERAL
MINERALISE
MINERALISED
MINERALISES
MINERALISING
MINERALIZABLE
MINERALIZATION
MINERALIZATIONS
MINERALIZE
MINERALIZED
MINERALIZER
MINERALIZERS
MINERALIZES
MINERALIZING
MINERALOGIC
MINERALOGICAL
MINERALOGICALLY
MINERALOGIES
MINERALOGIST
MINERALOGISTS
MINERALOGY
MINERALS
MINERS
MINES
MINESHAFT
MINESHAFTS
MINESTRONE
MINESTRONES
MINESWEEPER
MINESWEEPERS
MINESWEEPING
MINESWEEPINGS
MINGIER
MINGIEST
MINGILY
MINGINESS
MINGINESSES
MINGLE
MINGLED
MINGLER
MINGLERS
MINGLES
MINGLING
MINGY
MINI
MINIATURE
MINIATURES
MINIATURISATION
MINIATURISE
MINIATURISED
MINIATURISES
MINIATURISING
MINIATURIST
MINIATURISTIC
MINIATURISTS
MINIATURIZATION
MINIATURIZE
MINIATURIZED
MINIATURIZES
MINIATURIZING
MINIBAR
MINIBARS
MINIBIKE
MINIBIKER
MINIBIKERS
MINIBIKES
MINIBUS

MINIBUSES
MINIBUSSES
MINICAB
MINICABS
MINICAM
MINICAMP
MINICAMPS
MINICAMS
MINICAR
MINICARS
MINICOMPUTER
MINICOMPUTERS
MINICOURSE
MINICOURSES
MINIDISC
MINIDISCS
MINIDRESS
MINIDRESSES
MINIFIED
MINIFIES
MINIFY
MINIFYING
MINIGOLF
MINIGOLFS
MINIKIN
MINIKINS
MINILAB
MINILABS
MINIM
MINIMA
MINIMAL
MINIMALISM
MINIMALISMS
MINIMALIST
MINIMALISTS
MINIMALLY
MINIMALS
MINIMAX
MINIMAXES
MINIMILL
MINIMILLS
MINIMISATION
MINIMISATIONS
MINIMISE
MINIMISED
MINIMISES
MINIMISING
MINIMIZATION
MINIMIZATIONS
MINIMIZE
MINIMIZED
MINIMIZER
MINIMIZERS
MINIMIZES
MINIMIZING
MINIMS
MINIMUM
MINIMUMS
MINING
MININGS
MINION
MINIONS
MINIPARK
MINIPARKS
MINIPILL
MINIPILLS
MINIS
MINISCHOOL
MINISCHOOLS
MINISCULE
MINISCULES
MINISERIES
MINISH
MINISHED
MINISHES
MINISHING
MINISKI
MINISKIRT
MINISKIRTED
MINISKIRTS
MINISKIS
MINISTATE
MINISTATES
MINISTER
MINISTERED
MINISTERIAL
MINISTERIALLY
MINISTERING
MINISTERS
MINISTRANT
MINISTRANTS
MINISTRATION
MINISTRATIONS
MINISTRIES
MINISTROKE
MINISTROKES
MINISTRY
MINITOWER
MINITOWERS
MINITRACK
MINITRACKS
MINIUM
MINIUMS
MINIVAN
MINIVANS
MINIVER
MINIVERS
MINK
MINKE
MINKES
MINKS
MINNEOLA
MINNEOLAS
MINNESINGER
MINNESINGERS
MINNIES
MINNOW
MINNOWS
MINNY
MINOR
MINORCA
MINORCAS
MINORED
MINORING
MINORITIES
MINORITY
MINORS
MINOXIDIL
MINOXIDILS
MINSTER
MINSTERS
MINSTREL
MINSTRELS
MINSTRELSIES
MINSTRELSY
MINT
MINTAGE
MINTAGES
MINTED
MINTER
MINTERS
MINTIER
MINTIEST
MINTING
MINTS
MINTY
MINUEND
MINUENDS
MINUET
MINUETED
MINUETING
MINUETS
MINUS
MINUSCULE
MINUSCULES
MINUSES
MINUTE
MINUTED
MINUTELY
MINUTEMAN
MINUTEMEN
MINUTENESS
MINUTENESSES
MINUTER
MINUTES
MINUTEST
MINUTIA
MINUTIAE
MINUTIAL
MINUTING
MINX
MINXES
MINXISH
MINYAN
MINYANIM
MINYANS
MIOCENE
MIOSES
MIOSIS
MIOSISES
MIOTIC
MIOTICS
MIPS
MIQUELET
MIQUELETS
MIR
MIRABELLE
MIRABELLES
MIRACIDIA
MIRACIDIAL
MIRACIDIUM
MIRACLE
MIRACLES
MIRACULOUS
MIRACULOUSLY
MIRACULOUSNESS
MIRADOR
MIRADORS
MIRAGE
MIRAGES
MIRANDIZE
MIRANDIZED
MIRANDIZES
MIRANDIZING
MIRE
MIRED
MIREPOIX
MIRES
MIREX
MIREXES
MIRI
MIRID
MIRIDS
MIRIER
MIRIEST
MIRIN
MIRINESS
MIRINESSES
MIRING
MIRINS
MIRK
MIRKER
MIRKEST
MIRKIER
MIRKIEST
MIRKILY
MIRKS
MIRKY
MIRLITON
MIRLITONS
MIRROR
MIRRORED
MIRRORING
MIRRORINGS
MIRRORLIKE
MIRRORS
MIRS
MIRTH
MIRTHFUL
MIRTHFULLY
MIRTHFULNESS
MIRTHFULNESSES
MIRTHLESS
MIRTHLESSLY
MIRTHS
MIRY
MIRZA
MIRZAS
MIS
MISACT
MISACTED
MISACTING
MISACTS
MISADAPT
MISADAPTED
MISADAPTING
MISADAPTS
MISADD
MISADDED
MISADDING
MISADDRESS
MISADDRESSED
MISADDRESSES
MISADDRESSING
MISADDS

MISADJUST
MISADJUSTED
MISADJUSTING
MISADJUSTS
MISADVENTURE
MISADVENTURES
MISADVICE
MISADVICES
MISADVISE
MISADVISED
MISADVISES
MISADVISING
MISAGENT
MISAGENTS
MISAIM
MISAIMED
MISAIMING
MISAIMS
MISALIGN
MISALIGNED
MISALIGNING
MISALIGNMENT
MISALIGNMENTS
MISALIGNS
MISALLIANCE
MISALLIANCES
MISALLIED
MISALLIES
MISALLOCATE
MISALLOCATED
MISALLOCATES
MISALLOCATING
MISALLOCATION
MISALLOCATIONS
MISALLOT
MISALLOTS
MISALLOTTED
MISALLOTTING
MISALLY
MISALLYING
MISALTER
MISALTERED
MISALTERING
MISALTERS
MISANALYSES
MISANALYSIS
MISANDRIES
MISANDRIST
MISANDRISTS
MISANDRY
MISANTHROPE
MISANTHROPES
MISANTHROPIC
MISANTHROPIES
MISANTHROPY
MISAPPLICATION
MISAPPLICATIONS
MISAPPLIED
MISAPPLIES
MISAPPLY
MISAPPLYING
MISAPPRAISAL
MISAPPRAISALS
MISAPPREHEND
MISAPPREHENDED
MISAPPREHENDING
MISAPPREHENDS
MISAPPREHENSION
MISAPPROPRIATE
MISAPPROPRIATED
MISAPPROPRIATES
MISARTICULATE
MISARTICULATED
MISARTICULATES
MISARTICULATING
MISASSAY
MISASSAYED
MISASSAYING
MISASSAYS
MISASSEMBLE
MISASSEMBLED
MISASSEMBLES
MISASSEMBLING
MISASSIGN
MISASSIGNED
MISASSIGNING
MISASSIGNS
MISASSUMPTION
MISASSUMPTIONS
MISATE
MISATONE
MISATONED
MISATONES
MISATONING
MISATTRIBUTE
MISATTRIBUTED
MISATTRIBUTES
MISATTRIBUTING
MISATTRIBUTION
MISATTRIBUTIONS
MISAVER
MISAVERRED
MISAVERRING
MISAVERS
MISAWARD
MISAWARDED
MISAWARDING
MISAWARDS
MISBALANCE
MISBALANCED
MISBALANCES
MISBALANCING
MISBECAME
MISBECOME
MISBECOMES
MISBECOMING
MISBEGAN
MISBEGIN
MISBEGINNING
MISBEGINS
MISBEGOT
MISBEGOTTEN
MISBEGUN
MISBEHAVE
MISBEHAVED
MISBEHAVER
MISBEHAVERS
MISBEHAVES
MISBEHAVING
MISBEHAVIOR
MISBEHAVIORS
MISBEHAVIOUR
MISBEHAVIOURS
MISBELIEF
MISBELIEFS
MISBELIEVE
MISBELIEVED
MISBELIEVER
MISBELIEVERS
MISBELIEVES
MISBELIEVING
MISBIAS
MISBIASED
MISBIASES
MISBIASING
MISBIASSED
MISBIASSES
MISBIASSING
MISBILL
MISBILLED
MISBILLING
MISBILLS
MISBIND
MISBINDING
MISBINDS
MISBOUND
MISBRAND
MISBRANDED
MISBRANDING
MISBRANDS
MISBUILD
MISBUILDING
MISBUILDS
MISBUILT
MISBUTTON
MISBUTTONED
MISBUTTONING
MISBUTTONS
MISCALCULATE
MISCALCULATED
MISCALCULATES
MISCALCULATING
MISCALCULATION
MISCALCULATIONS
MISCALL
MISCALLED
MISCALLER
MISCALLERS
MISCALLING
MISCALLS
MISCAPTION
MISCAPTIONED
MISCAPTIONING
MISCAPTIONS
MISCARRIAGE
MISCARRIAGES
MISCARRIED
MISCARRIES
MISCARRY
MISCARRYING
MISCAST
MISCASTING
MISCASTS
MISCATALOG
MISCATALOGED
MISCATALOGING
MISCATALOGS
MISCEGENATION
MISCEGENATIONAL
MISCEGENATIONS
MISCELLANEA
MISCELLANEOUS
MISCELLANEOUSLY
MISCELLANIES
MISCELLANIST
MISCELLANISTS
MISCELLANY
MISCHANCE
MISCHANCES
MISCHANNEL
MISCHANNELED
MISCHANNELING
MISCHANNELLED
MISCHANNELLING
MISCHANNELS
MISCHARACTERIZE
MISCHARGE
MISCHARGED
MISCHARGES
MISCHARGING
MISCHIEF
MISCHIEFS
MISCHIEVOUS
MISCHIEVOUSLY
MISCHIEVOUSNESS
MISCHOICE
MISCHOICES
MISCHOOSE
MISCHOOSES
MISCHOOSING
MISCHOSE
MISCHOSEN
MISCIBILITIES
MISCIBILITY
MISCIBLE
MISCITATION
MISCITATIONS
MISCITE
MISCITED
MISCITES
MISCITING
MISCLAIM
MISCLAIMED
MISCLAIMING
MISCLAIMS
MISCLASS
MISCLASSED
MISCLASSES
MISCLASSIFIED
MISCLASSIFIES
MISCLASSIFY
MISCLASSIFYING
MISCLASSING
MISCODE
MISCODED
MISCODES
MISCODING
MISCOIN
MISCOINED
MISCOINING
MISCOINS
MISCOLOR
MISCOLORED
MISCOLORING
MISCOLORS

MISCOMPUTATION
MISCOMPUTATIONS
MISCOMPUTE
MISCOMPUTED
MISCOMPUTES
MISCOMPUTING
MISCONCEIVE
MISCONCEIVED
MISCONCEIVER
MISCONCEIVERS
MISCONCEIVES
MISCONCEIVING
MISCONCEPTION
MISCONCEPTIONS
MISCONDUCT
MISCONDUCTED
MISCONDUCTING
MISCONDUCTS
MISCONNECT
MISCONNECTED
MISCONNECTING
MISCONNECTION
MISCONNECTIONS
MISCONNECTS
MISCONSTRUCTION
MISCONSTRUE
MISCONSTRUED
MISCONSTRUES
MISCONSTRUING
MISCOOK
MISCOOKED
MISCOOKING
MISCOOKS
MISCOPIED
MISCOPIES
MISCOPY
MISCOPYING
MISCORRELATION
MISCORRELATIONS
MISCOUNT
MISCOUNTED
MISCOUNTING
MISCOUNTS
MISCREANT
MISCREANTS
MISCREATE
MISCREATED
MISCREATES
MISCREATING
MISCREATION
MISCREATIONS
MISCUE
MISCUED
MISCUEING
MISCUES
MISCUING
MISCUT
MISCUTS
MISCUTTING
MISDATE
MISDATED
MISDATES
MISDATING
MISDEAL
MISDEALER
MISDEALERS
MISDEALING
MISDEALS
MISDEALT
MISDEED
MISDEEDS
MISDEEM
MISDEEMED
MISDEEMING
MISDEEMS
MISDEFINE
MISDEFINED
MISDEFINES
MISDEFINING
MISDEMEANANT
MISDEMEANANTS
MISDEMEANOR
MISDEMEANORS
MISDEMEANOUR
MISDEMEANOURS
MISDESCRIBE
MISDESCRIBED
MISDESCRIBES
MISDESCRIBING
MISDESCRIPTION
MISDESCRIPTIONS
MISDEVELOP
MISDEVELOPED
MISDEVELOPING
MISDEVELOPS
MISDIAGNOSE
MISDIAGNOSED
MISDIAGNOSES
MISDIAGNOSING
MISDIAGNOSIS
MISDIAL
MISDIALED
MISDIALING
MISDIALLED
MISDIALLING
MISDIALS
MISDID
MISDIRECT
MISDIRECTED
MISDIRECTING
MISDIRECTION
MISDIRECTIONS
MISDIRECTS
MISDISTRIBUTION
MISDIVIDE
MISDIVIDED
MISDIVIDES
MISDIVIDING
MISDIVISION
MISDIVISIONS
MISDO
MISDOER
MISDOERS
MISDOES
MISDOING
MISDOINGS
MISDONE
MISDOUBT
MISDOUBTED
MISDOUBTING
MISDOUBTS
MISDRAW
MISDRAWING
MISDRAWN
MISDRAWS
MISDREW
MISDRIVE
MISDRIVEN
MISDRIVES
MISDRIVING
MISDROVE
MISE
MISEASE
MISEASES
MISEAT
MISEATEN
MISEATING
MISEATS
MISEDIT
MISEDITED
MISEDITING
MISEDITS
MISEDUCATE
MISEDUCATED
MISEDUCATES
MISEDUCATING
MISEDUCATION
MISEDUCATIONS
MISEMPHASES
MISEMPHASIS
MISEMPHASIZE
MISEMPHASIZED
MISEMPHASIZES
MISEMPHASIZING
MISEMPLOY
MISEMPLOYED
MISEMPLOYING
MISEMPLOYMENT
MISEMPLOYMENTS
MISEMPLOYS
MISENROL
MISENROLL
MISENROLLED
MISENROLLING
MISENROLLS
MISENROLS
MISENTER
MISENTERED
MISENTERING
MISENTERS
MISENTRIES
MISENTRY
MISER
MISERABLE
MISERABLENESS
MISERABLENESSES
MISERABLES
MISERABLY
MISERERE
MISERERES
MISERICORD
MISERICORDE
MISERICORDES
MISERICORDS
MISERIES
MISERLINESS
MISERLINESSES
MISERLY
MISERS
MISERY
MISES
MISESTEEM
MISESTEEMED
MISESTEEMING
MISESTEEMS
MISESTIMATE
MISESTIMATED
MISESTIMATES
MISESTIMATING
MISESTIMATION
MISESTIMATIONS
MISEVALUATE
MISEVALUATED
MISEVALUATES
MISEVALUATING
MISEVALUATION
MISEVALUATIONS
MISEVENT
MISEVENTS
MISFAITH
MISFAITHS
MISFEASANCE
MISFEASANCES
MISFEASOR
MISFEASORS
MISFED
MISFEED
MISFEEDING
MISFEEDS
MISFIELD
MISFIELDED
MISFIELDING
MISFIELDS
MISFILE
MISFILED
MISFILES
MISFILING
MISFIRE
MISFIRED
MISFIRES
MISFIRING
MISFIT
MISFITS
MISFITTED
MISFITTING
MISFOCUS
MISFOCUSED
MISFOCUSES
MISFOCUSING
MISFOCUSSED
MISFOCUSSES
MISFOCUSSING
MISFORM
MISFORMED
MISFORMING
MISFORMS
MISFORTUNE
MISFORTUNES
MISFRAME
MISFRAMED
MISFRAMES
MISFRAMING
MISFUNCTION
MISFUNCTIONED
MISFUNCTIONING

MISFUNCTIONS
MISGAUGE
MISGAUGED
MISGAUGES
MISGAUGING
MISGAVE
MISGIVE
MISGIVEN
MISGIVES
MISGIVING
MISGIVINGS
MISGOVERN
MISGOVERNED
MISGOVERNING
MISGOVERNMENT
MISGOVERNMENTS
MISGOVERNS
MISGRADE
MISGRADED
MISGRADES
MISGRADING
MISGRAFT
MISGRAFTED
MISGRAFTING
MISGRAFTS
MISGREW
MISGROW
MISGROWING
MISGROWN
MISGROWS
MISGUESS
MISGUESSED
MISGUESSES
MISGUESSING
MISGUIDANCE
MISGUIDANCES
MISGUIDE
MISGUIDED
MISGUIDEDLY
MISGUIDEDNESS
MISGUIDEDNESSES
MISGUIDER
MISGUIDERS
MISGUIDES
MISGUIDING
MISHANDLE
MISHANDLED
MISHANDLES
MISHANDLING
MISHANTER
MISHANTERS
MISHAP
MISHAPS
MISHEAR
MISHEARD
MISHEARING
MISHEARS
MISHEGAAS
MISHEGOSS
MISHIT
MISHITS
MISHITTING
MISHMASH
MISHMASHES
MISHMOSH
MISHMOSHES
MISHUGAS
MISHUGASES
MISIDENTIFIED
MISIDENTIFIES
MISIDENTIFY
MISIDENTIFYING
MISIMPRESSION
MISIMPRESSIONS
MISINFER
MISINFERRED
MISINFERRING
MISINFERS
MISINFORM
MISINFORMATION
MISINFORMATIONS
MISINFORMED
MISINFORMING
MISINFORMS
MISINTER
MISINTERPRET
MISINTERPRETED
MISINTERPRETING
MISINTERPRETS
MISINTERRED
MISINTERRING
MISINTERS
MISJOIN
MISJOINDER
MISJOINDERS
MISJOINED
MISJOINING
MISJOINS
MISJUDGE
MISJUDGED
MISJUDGEMENT
MISJUDGEMENTS
MISJUDGES
MISJUDGING
MISJUDGMENT
MISJUDGMENTS
MISKAL
MISKALS
MISKEEP
MISKEEPING
MISKEEPS
MISKEPT
MISKEY
MISKEYED
MISKEYING
MISKEYS
MISKICK
MISKICKED
MISKICKING
MISKICKS
MISKNEW
MISKNOW
MISKNOWING
MISKNOWLEDGE
MISKNOWLEDGES
MISKNOWN
MISKNOWS
MISLABEL
MISLABELED
MISLABELING
MISLABELLED
MISLABELLING
MISLABELS
MISLABOR
MISLABORED
MISLABORING
MISLABORS
MISLAID
MISLAIN
MISLAY
MISLAYER
MISLAYERS
MISLAYING
MISLAYS
MISLEAD
MISLEADER
MISLEADERS
MISLEADING
MISLEADINGLY
MISLEADS
MISLEARED
MISLEARN
MISLEARNED
MISLEARNING
MISLEARNS
MISLEARNT
MISLED
MISLIE
MISLIES
MISLIGHT
MISLIGHTED
MISLIGHTING
MISLIGHTS
MISLIKE
MISLIKED
MISLIKER
MISLIKERS
MISLIKES
MISLIKING
MISLIT
MISLIVE
MISLIVED
MISLIVES
MISLIVING
MISLOCATE
MISLOCATED
MISLOCATES
MISLOCATING
MISLOCATION
MISLOCATIONS
MISLODGE
MISLODGED
MISLODGES
MISLODGING
MISLYING
MISMADE
MISMAKE
MISMAKES
MISMAKING
MISMANAGE
MISMANAGED
MISMANAGEMENT
MISMANAGEMENTS
MISMANAGES
MISMANAGING
MISMARK
MISMARKED
MISMARKING
MISMARKS
MISMARRIAGE
MISMARRIAGES
MISMATCH
MISMATCHED
MISMATCHES
MISMATCHING
MISMATE
MISMATED
MISMATES
MISMATING
MISMEASURE
MISMEASURED
MISMEASUREMENT
MISMEASUREMENTS
MISMEASURES
MISMEASURING
MISMEET
MISMEETING
MISMEETS
MISMET
MISMOVE
MISMOVED
MISMOVES
MISMOVING
MISNAME
MISNAMED
MISNAMES
MISNAMING
MISNOMER
MISNOMERED
MISNOMERS
MISNUMBER
MISNUMBERED
MISNUMBERING
MISNUMBERS
MISO
MISOGAMIC
MISOGAMIES
MISOGAMIST
MISOGAMISTS
MISOGAMY
MISOGYNIC
MISOGYNIES
MISOGYNIST
MISOGYNISTIC
MISOGYNISTS
MISOGYNY
MISOLOGIES
MISOLOGY
MISONEISM
MISONEISMS
MISONEIST
MISONEISTS
MISOPROSTOL
MISOPROSTOLS
MISORDER
MISORDERED
MISORDERING
MISORDERS
MISORIENT
MISORIENTATION
MISORIENTATIONS
MISORIENTED
MISORIENTING
MISORIENTS
MISOS

MISPACKAGE
MISPACKAGED
MISPACKAGES
MISPACKAGING
MISPAGE
MISPAGED
MISPAGES
MISPAGING
MISPAINT
MISPAINTED
MISPAINTING
MISPAINTS
MISPARSE
MISPARSED
MISPARSES
MISPARSING
MISPART
MISPARTED
MISPARTING
MISPARTS
MISPATCH
MISPATCHED
MISPATCHES
MISPATCHING
MISPEN
MISPENNED
MISPENNING
MISPENS
MISPERCEIVE
MISPERCEIVED
MISPERCEIVES
MISPERCEIVING
MISPERCEPTION
MISPERCEPTIONS
MISPHRASE
MISPHRASED
MISPHRASES
MISPHRASING
MISPICKEL
MISPICKELS
MISPLACE
MISPLACED
MISPLACEMENT
MISPLACEMENTS
MISPLACES
MISPLACING
MISPLAN
MISPLANNED
MISPLANNING
MISPLANS
MISPLANT
MISPLANTED
MISPLANTING
MISPLANTS
MISPLAY
MISPLAYED
MISPLAYING
MISPLAYS
MISPLEAD
MISPLEADED
MISPLEADING
MISPLEADS
MISPLED
MISPOINT
MISPOINTED
MISPOINTING
MISPOINTS
MISPOISE
MISPOISED
MISPOISES
MISPOISING
MISPOSITION
MISPOSITIONED
MISPOSITIONING
MISPOSITIONS
MISPRICE
MISPRICED
MISPRICES
MISPRICING
MISPRINT
MISPRINTED
MISPRINTING
MISPRINTS
MISPRISION
MISPRISIONS
MISPRIZE
MISPRIZED
MISPRIZER
MISPRIZERS
MISPRIZES
MISPRIZING
MISPROGRAM
MISPROGRAMED
MISPROGRAMING
MISPROGRAMMED
MISPROGRAMMING
MISPROGRAMS
MISPRONOUNCE
MISPRONOUNCED
MISPRONOUNCES
MISPRONOUNCING
MISQUOTATION
MISQUOTATIONS
MISQUOTE
MISQUOTED
MISQUOTER
MISQUOTERS
MISQUOTES
MISQUOTING
MISRAISE
MISRAISED
MISRAISES
MISRAISING
MISRATE
MISRATED
MISRATES
MISRATING
MISREAD
MISREADING
MISREADS
MISRECKON
MISRECKONED
MISRECKONING
MISRECKONS
MISRECOLLECTION
MISRECORD
MISRECORDED
MISRECORDING
MISRECORDS
MISREFER
MISREFERENCE
MISREFERENCED
MISREFERENCES
MISREFERENCING
MISREFERRED
MISREFERRING
MISREFERS
MISREGISTER
MISREGISTERED
MISREGISTERING
MISREGISTERS
MISREGISTRATION
MISRELATE
MISRELATED
MISRELATES
MISRELATING
MISRELIED
MISRELIES
MISRELY
MISRELYING
MISREMEMBER
MISREMEMBERED
MISREMEMBERING
MISREMEMBERS
MISRENDER
MISRENDERED
MISRENDERING
MISRENDERS
MISREPORT
MISREPORTED
MISREPORTING
MISREPORTS
MISREPRESENT
MISREPRESENTED
MISREPRESENTING
MISREPRESENTS
MISRHYMED
MISROUTE
MISROUTED
MISROUTES
MISROUTING
MISRULE
MISRULED
MISRULES
MISRULING
MISS
MISSABLE
MISSAID
MISSAL
MISSALETTE
MISSALETTES
MISSALS
MISSAY
MISSAYING
MISSAYS
MISSEAT
MISSEATED
MISSEATING
MISSEATS
MISSED
MISSEL
MISSELS
MISSEND
MISSENDING
MISSENDS
MISSENSE
MISSENSES
MISSENT
MISSES
MISSET
MISSETS
MISSETTING
MISSHAPE
MISSHAPED
MISSHAPEN
MISSHAPENLY
MISSHAPER
MISSHAPERS
MISSHAPES
MISSHAPING
MISSHOD
MISSIES
MISSILE
MISSILEER
MISSILEERS
MISSILEMAN
MISSILEMEN
MISSILERIES
MISSILERY
MISSILES
MISSILRIES
MISSILRY
MISSING
MISSIOLOGIES
MISSIOLOGY
MISSION
MISSIONAL
MISSIONARIES
MISSIONARY
MISSIONED
MISSIONER
MISSIONERS
MISSIONING
MISSIONIZATION
MISSIONIZATIONS
MISSIONIZE
MISSIONIZED
MISSIONIZER
MISSIONIZERS
MISSIONIZES
MISSIONIZING
MISSIONS
MISSIS
MISSISES
MISSIVE
MISSIVES
MISSORT
MISSORTED
MISSORTING
MISSORTS
MISSOUND
MISSOUNDED
MISSOUNDING
MISSOUNDS
MISSOUT
MISSOUTS
MISSPACE
MISSPACED
MISSPACES
MISSPACING
MISSPEAK
MISSPEAKING
MISSPEAKS
MISSPELL
MISSPELLED

ISSPELLING
ISSPELLINGS
ISSPELLS
ISSPELT
ISSPEND
ISSPENDING
ISSPENDS
ISSPENT
ISSPOKE
ISSPOKEN
ISSTAMP
ISSTAMPED
ISSTAMPING
ISSTAMPS
ISSTART
ISSTARTED
ISSTARTING
ISSTARTS
ISSTATE
ISSTATED
ISSTATEMENT
ISSTATEMENTS
ISSTATES
ISSTATING
ISSTEER
ISSTEERED
ISSTEERING
ISSTEERS
ISSTEP
ISSTEPPED
ISSTEPPING
ISSTEPS
ISSTOP
ISSTOPPED
ISSTOPPING
ISSTOPS
ISSTRICKEN
ISSTRIKE
ISSTRIKES
ISSTRIKING
ISSTRUCK
ISSTYLE
ISSTYLED
ISSTYLES
ISSTYLING
ISSUIT
ISSUITED
ISSUITING
ISSUITS
ISSUS
ISSUSES
ISSY
IST

MISTAKABLE
MISTAKE
MISTAKEN
MISTAKENLY
MISTAKER
MISTAKERS
MISTAKES
MISTAKING
MISTAUGHT
MISTBOW
MISTBOWS
MISTEACH
MISTEACHES
MISTEACHING
MISTED
MISTEND
MISTENDED
MISTENDING
MISTENDS
MISTER
MISTERM
MISTERMED
MISTERMING
MISTERMS
MISTERS
MISTEUK
MISTHINK
MISTHINKING
MISTHINKS
MISTHOUGHT
MISTHREW
MISTHROW
MISTHROWING
MISTHROWN
MISTHROWS
MISTIER
MISTIEST
MISTILY
MISTIME
MISTIMED
MISTIMES
MISTIMING
MISTINESS
MISTINESSES
MISTING
MISTITLE
MISTITLED
MISTITLES
MISTITLING
MISTLETOE
MISTLETOES
MISTOOK
MISTOUCH

MISTOUCHED
MISTOUCHES
MISTOUCHING
MISTRACE
MISTRACED
MISTRACES
MISTRACING
MISTRAIN
MISTRAINED
MISTRAINING
MISTRAINS
MISTRAL
MISTRALS
MISTRANSCRIBE
MISTRANSCRIBED
MISTRANSCRIBES
MISTRANSCRIBING
MISTRANSLATE
MISTRANSLATED
MISTRANSLATES
MISTRANSLATING
MISTRANSLATION
MISTRANSLATIONS
MISTREAT
MISTREATED
MISTREATING
MISTREATMENT
MISTREATMENTS
MISTREATS
MISTRESS
MISTRESSES
MISTRIAL
MISTRIALS
MISTRUST
MISTRUSTED
MISTRUSTFUL
MISTRUSTFULLY
MISTRUSTFULNESS
MISTRUSTING
MISTRUSTS
MISTRUTH
MISTRUTHS
MISTRYST
MISTRYSTED
MISTRYSTING
MISTRYSTS
MISTS
MISTUNE
MISTUNED
MISTUNES
MISTUNING
MISTUTOR
MISTUTORED

MISTUTORING
MISTUTORS
MISTY
MISTYPE
MISTYPED
MISTYPES
MISTYPING
MISUNDERSTAND
MISUNDERSTANDS
MISUNDERSTOOD
MISUNION
MISUNIONS
MISUSAGE
MISUSAGES
MISUSE
MISUSED
MISUSER
MISUSERS
MISUSES
MISUSING
MISUTILIZATION
MISUTILIZATIONS
MISVALUE
MISVALUED
MISVALUES
MISVALUING
MISVOCALIZATION
MISWORD
MISWORDED
MISWORDING
MISWORDS
MISWRIT
MISWRITE
MISWRITES
MISWRITING
MISWRITTEN
MISWROTE
MISYOKE
MISYOKED
MISYOKES
MISYOKING
MITE
MITER
MITERED
MITERER
MITERERS
MITERING
MITERS
MITERWORT
MITERWORTS
MITES
MITHER
MITHERS

MITHRIDATE
MITHRIDATES
MITICIDAL
MITICIDE
MITICIDES
MITIER
MITIEST
MITIGABLE
MITIGANT
MITIGANTS
MITIGATE
MITIGATED
MITIGATES
MITIGATING
MITIGATION
MITIGATIONS
MITIGATIVE
MITIGATOR
MITIGATORS
MITIGATORY
MITIS
MITISES
MITOCHONDRIA
MITOCHONDRIAL
MITOCHONDRION
MITOGEN
MITOGENIC
MITOGENICITIES
MITOGENICITY
MITOGENS
MITOMYCIN
MITOMYCINS
MITOSES
MITOSIS
MITOTIC
MITOTICALLY
MITRAL
MITRE
MITRED
MITRES
MITREWORT
MITREWORTS
MITRING
MITSVAH
MITSVAHS
MITSVOTH
MITT
MITTEN
MITTENED
MITTENS
MITTIMUS
MITTIMUSES
MITTS

MITY
MITZVAH
MITZVAHS
MITZVOTH
MIX
MIXABLE
MIXDOWN
MIXDOWNS
MIXED
MIXEDLY
MIXER
MIXERS
MIXES
MIXIBLE
MIXING
MIXOLOGIES
MIXOLOGIST
MIXOLOGISTS
MIXOLOGY
MIXT
MIXTAPE
MIXTAPES
MIXTURE
MIXTURES
MIXUP
MIXUPS
MIZEN
MIZENMAST
MIZENMASTS
MIZENS
MIZUNA
MIZUNAS
MIZZEN
MIZZENMAST
MIZZENMASTS
MIZZENS
MIZZLE
MIZZLED
MIZZLES
MIZZLIER
MIZZLIEST
MIZZLING
MIZZLY
MM
MMM
MNEMONIC
MNEMONICALLY
MNEMONICS
MO
MOA
MOAN
MOANED
MOANER
MOANERS
MOANFUL
MOANING
MOANINGLY
MOANS
MOAS
MOAT
MOATED
MOATING
MOATLIKE
MOATS
MOB
MOBBED
MOBBER
MOBBERS
MOBBING
MOBBISH
MOBBISHLY
MOBBISM
MOBBISMS
MOBCAP
MOBCAPS
MOBILE
MOBILES
MOBILISATION
MOBILISATIONS
MOBILISE
MOBILISED
MOBILISES
MOBILISING
MOBILITIES
MOBILITY
MOBILIZATION
MOBILIZATIONS
MOBILIZE
MOBILIZED
MOBILIZER
MOBILIZERS
MOBILIZES
MOBILIZING
MOBLED
MOBLOG
MOBLOGGING
MOBLOGGINGS
MOBLOGS
MOBOCRACIES
MOBOCRACY
MOBOCRAT
MOBOCRATIC
MOBOCRATS
MOBS
MOBSTER
MOBSTERS
MOC
MOCCASIN
MOCCASINED
MOCCASINS
MOCHA
MOCHAS
MOCHI
MOCHILA
MOCHILAS
MOCHIS
MOCK
MOCKABLE
MOCKED
MOCKER
MOCKERIES
MOCKERS
MOCKERY
MOCKING
MOCKINGBIRD
MOCKINGBIRDS
MOCKINGLY
MOCKS
MOCKTAIL
MOCKTAILS
MOCKUMENTARIES
MOCKUMENTARY
MOCKUP
MOCKUPS
MOCS
MOD
MODAL
MODALISM
MODALISMS
MODALIST
MODALISTS
MODALITIES
MODALITY
MODALLY
MODALS
MODE
MODEL
MODELED
MODELER
MODELERS
MODELING
MODELINGS
MODELIST
MODELISTS
MODELLED
MODELLER
MODELLERS
MODELLING
MODELLINGS
MODELS
MODEM
MODEMED
MODEMING
MODEMS
MODERATE
MODERATED
MODERATELY
MODERATENESS
MODERATENESSES
MODERATES
MODERATING
MODERATION
MODERATIONS
MODERATO
MODERATOR
MODERATORS
MODERATORSHIP
MODERATORSHIPS
MODERATOS
MODERN
MODERNE
MODERNER
MODERNES
MODERNEST
MODERNISATION
MODERNISATIONS
MODERNISE
MODERNISED
MODERNISES
MODERNISING
MODERNISM
MODERNISMS
MODERNIST
MODERNISTIC
MODERNISTS
MODERNITIES
MODERNITY
MODERNIZATION
MODERNIZATIONS
MODERNIZE
MODERNIZED
MODERNIZER
MODERNIZERS
MODERNIZES
MODERNIZING
MODERNLY
MODERNNESS
MODERNNESSES
MODERNS
MODES
MODEST
MODESTER
MODESTEST
MODESTIES
MODESTLY
MODESTY
MODI
MODICA
MODICUM
MODICUMS
MODIFIABILITIES
MODIFIABILITY
MODIFIABLE
MODIFICATION
MODIFICATIONS
MODIFIED
MODIFIER
MODIFIERS
MODIFIES
MODIFY
MODIFYING
MODILLION
MODILLIONS
MODIOLI
MODIOLUS
MODISH
MODISHLY
MODISHNESS
MODISHNESSES
MODISTE
MODISTES
MODS
MODULABILITIES
MODULABILITY
MODULAR
MODULARITIES
MODULARITY
MODULARIZED
MODULARLY
MODULARS
MODULATE
MODULATED
MODULATES
MODULATING
MODULATION
MODULATIONS
MODULATOR
MODULATORS
MODULATORY
MODULE
MODULES
MODULI
MODULO
MODULUS
MODUS

MOFETTE
MOFETTES
MOFFETTE
MOFFETTES
MOFO
MOFOS
MOG
MOGGED
MOGGIE
MOGGIES
MOGGING
MOGGY
MOGHUL
MOGHULS
MOGS
MOGUL
MOGULED
MOGULS
MOHAIR
MOHAIRS
MOHALIM
MOHAWK
MOHAWKS
MOHEL
MOHELIM
MOHELS
MOHO
MOHOS
MOHUR
MOHURS
MOI
MOIDORE
MOIDORES
MOIETIES
MOIETY
MOIL
MOILED
MOILER
MOILERS
MOILING
MOILINGLY
MOILS
MOIRA
MOIRAI
MOIRE
MOIRES
MOIST
MOISTEN
MOISTENED
MOISTENER
MOISTENERS
MOISTENING
MOISTENS
MOISTER
MOISTEST
MOISTFUL
MOISTLY
MOISTNESS
MOISTNESSES
MOISTURE
MOISTURES
MOISTURISE
MOISTURISED
MOISTURISER
MOISTURISERS
MOISTURISES
MOISTURISING
MOISTURIZE
MOISTURIZED
MOISTURIZER
MOISTURIZERS
MOISTURIZES
MOISTURIZING
MOJARRA
MOJARRAS
MOJITO
MOJITOS
MOJO
MOJOES
MOJOS
MOKE
MOKES
MOKSHA
MOKSHAS
MOL
MOLA
MOLAL
MOLALITIES
MOLALITY
MOLAR
MOLARITIES
MOLARITY
MOLARS
MOLAS
MOLASSES
MOLASSESES
MOLD
MOLDABLE
MOLDBOARD
MOLDBOARDS
MOLDED
MOLDER
MOLDERED
MOLDERING
MOLDERS
MOLDIER
MOLDIEST
MOLDINESS
MOLDINESSES
MOLDING
MOLDINGS
MOLDS
MOLDWARP
MOLDWARPS
MOLDY
MOLE
MOLECULAR
MOLECULARLY
MOLECULE
MOLECULES
MOLEHILL
MOLEHILLS
MOLES
MOLESKIN
MOLESKINS
MOLEST
MOLESTATION
MOLESTATIONS
MOLESTED
MOLESTER
MOLESTERS
MOLESTING
MOLESTS
MOLIES
MOLINE
MOLL
MOLLAH
MOLLAHS
MOLLIE
MOLLIES
MOLLIFICATION
MOLLIFICATIONS
MOLLIFIED
MOLLIFIER
MOLLIFIERS
MOLLIFIES
MOLLIFY
MOLLIFYING
MOLLS
MOLLUSC
MOLLUSCA
MOLLUSCAN
MOLLUSCANS
MOLLUSCICIDAL
MOLLUSCICIDE
MOLLUSCICIDES
MOLLUSCS
MOLLUSCUM
MOLLUSK
MOLLUSKAN
MOLLUSKANS
MOLLUSKS
MOLLY
MOLLYCODDLE
MOLLYCODDLED
MOLLYCODDLER
MOLLYCODDLERS
MOLLYCODDLES
MOLLYCODDLING
MOLLYMAWK
MOLLYMAWKS
MOLOCH
MOLOCHS
MOLS
MOLT
MOLTED
MOLTEN
MOLTENLY
MOLTER
MOLTERS
MOLTING
MOLTO
MOLTS
MOLY
MOLYBDATE
MOLYBDATES
MOLYBDENITE
MOLYBDENITES
MOLYBDENUM
MOLYBDENUMS
MOLYBDIC
MOLYBDOUS
MOLYS
MOM
MOME
MOMENT
MOMENTA
MOMENTARILY
MOMENTARINESS
MOMENTARINESSES
MOMENTARY
MOMENTLY
MOMENTO
MOMENTOES
MOMENTOS
MOMENTOUS
MOMENTOUSLY
MOMENTOUSNESS
MOMENTOUSNESSES
MOMENTS
MOMENTUM
MOMENTUMS
MOMES
MOMI
MOMISM
MOMISMS
MOMMA
MOMMAS
MOMMIES
MOMMY
MOMS
MOMSER
MOMSERS
MOMUS
MOMUSES
MOMZER
MOMZERS
MON
MONACHAL
MONACHISM
MONACHISMS
MONACID
MONACIDIC
MONACIDS
MONAD
MONADAL
MONADELPHOUS
MONADES
MONADIC
MONADICAL
MONADISM
MONADISMS
MONADNOCK
MONADNOCKS
MONADS
MONAMINE
MONAMINES
MONANDRIES
MONANDRY
MONARCH
MONARCHAL
MONARCHIAL
MONARCHIC
MONARCHICAL
MONARCHICALLY
MONARCHIES
MONARCHISM
MONARCHISMS
MONARCHIST
MONARCHISTS
MONARCHS
MONARCHY
MONARDA
MONARDAS
MONAS

MONASTERIES
MONASTERY
MONASTIC
MONASTICALLY
MONASTICISM
MONASTICISMS
MONASTICS
MONATOMIC
MONAURAL
MONAURALLY
MONAXIAL
MONAXON
MONAXONS
MONAZITE
MONAZITES
MONDE
MONDEGREEN
MONDEGREENS
MONDES
MONDO
MONDOS
MONECIAN
MONECIOUS
MONELLIN
MONELLINS
MONERAN
MONERANS
MONESTROUS
MONETARILY
MONETARISM
MONETARISMS
MONETARIST
MONETARISTS
MONETARY
MONETISE
MONETISED
MONETISES
MONETISING
MONETIZABLE
MONETIZATION
MONETIZATIONS
MONETIZE
MONETIZED
MONETIZES
MONETIZING
MONEY
MONEYBAG
MONEYBAGS
MONEYED
MONEYER
MONEYERS
MONEYGRUBBING
MONEYGRUBBINGS
MONEYLENDER
MONEYLENDERS
MONEYLESS
MONEYMAKER
MONEYMAKERS
MONEYMAKING
MONEYMAKINGS
MONEYMAN
MONEYMEN
MONEYS
MONEYWORT
MONEYWORTS
MONGEESE
MONGER
MONGERED
MONGERING
MONGERS
MONGO
MONGOE
MONGOES
MONGOL
MONGOLIAN
MONGOLISM
MONGOLISMS
MONGOLOID
MONGOLOIDS
MONGOLS
MONGOOSE
MONGOOSES
MONGOS
MONGREL
MONGRELIZATION
MONGRELIZATIONS
MONGRELIZE
MONGRELIZED
MONGRELIZES
MONGRELIZING
MONGRELLY
MONGRELS
MONGST
MONIC
MONICKER
MONICKERS
MONIE
MONIED
MONIES
MONIKER
MONIKERED
MONIKERS
MONILIA
MONILIAE
MONILIASES
MONILIASIS
MONILIFORM
MONISH
MONISHED
MONISHES
MONISHING
MONISM
MONISMS
MONIST
MONISTIC
MONISTS
MONITION
MONITIONS
MONITIVE
MONITOR
MONITORED
MONITORIAL
MONITORIES
MONITORING
MONITORS
MONITORSHIP
MONITORSHIPS
MONITORY
MONK
MONKERIES
MONKERY
MONKEY
MONKEYED
MONKEYING
MONKEYISH
MONKEYPOD
MONKEYPODS
MONKEYPOT
MONKEYPOTS
MONKEYPOX
MONKEYPOXES
MONKEYS
MONKEYSHINE
MONKEYSHINES
MONKFISH
MONKFISHES
MONKHOOD
MONKHOODS
MONKISH
MONKISHLY
MONKS
MONKSHOOD
MONKSHOODS
MONO
MONOACID
MONOACIDIC
MONOACIDS
MONOAMINE
MONOAMINERGIC
MONOAMINES
MONOBASIC
MONOBLOC
MONOCARBOXYLIC
MONOCARP
MONOCARPIC
MONOCARPS
MONOCHASIA
MONOCHASIAL
MONOCHASIUM
MONOCHORD
MONOCHORDS
MONOCHROMAT
MONOCHROMATIC
MONOCHROMATISM
MONOCHROMATISMS
MONOCHROMATOR
MONOCHROMATORS
MONOCHROMATS
MONOCHROME
MONOCHROMES
MONOCHROMIC
MONOCHROMIST
MONOCHROMISTS
MONOCLE
MONOCLED
MONOCLES
MONOCLINE
MONOCLINES
MONOCLINIC
MONOCLONAL
MONOCLONALS
MONOCOQUE
MONOCOQUES
MONOCOT
MONOCOTS
MONOCOTYL
MONOCOTYLEDON
MONOCOTYLEDONS
MONOCOTYLS
MONOCRACIES
MONOCRACY
MONOCRAT
MONOCRATIC
MONOCRATS
MONOCROP
MONOCROPPED
MONOCROPPING
MONOCROPS
MONOCRYSTAL
MONOCRYSTALLINE
MONOCRYSTALS
MONOCULAR
MONOCULARLY
MONOCULARS
MONOCULTURAL
MONOCULTURE
MONOCULTURES
MONOCYCLE
MONOCYCLES
MONOCYCLIC
MONOCYTE
MONOCYTES
MONOCYTIC
MONODIC
MONODICAL
MONODICALLY
MONODIES
MONODISPERSE
MONODIST
MONODISTS
MONODRAMA
MONODRAMAS
MONODRAMATIC
MONODY
MONOECIES
MONOECIOUS
MONOECISM
MONOECISMS
MONOECY
MONOESTER
MONOESTERS
MONOFIL
MONOFILAMENT
MONOFILAMENTS
MONOFILS
MONOFUEL
MONOFUELS
MONOGAMIC
MONOGAMIES
MONOGAMIST
MONOGAMISTS
MONOGAMOUS
MONOGAMOUSLY
MONOGAMY
MONOGASTRIC
MONOGENEAN
MONOGENEANS
MONOGENESES
MONOGENESIS
MONOGENETIC
MONOGENIC
MONOGENICALLY
MONOGENIES
MONOGENY
MONOGERM

MONOGLOT
MONOGLOTS
MONOGLYCERIDE
MONOGLYCERIDES
MONOGRAM
MONOGRAMED
MONOGRAMING
MONOGRAMMATIC
MONOGRAMMED
MONOGRAMMER
MONOGRAMMERS
MONOGRAMMING
MONOGRAMS
MONOGRAPH
MONOGRAPHED
MONOGRAPHIC
MONOGRAPHING
MONOGRAPHS
MONOGYNIES
MONOGYNOUS
MONOGYNY
MONOHULL
MONOHULLED
MONOHULLS
MONOHYBRID
MONOHYBRIDS
MONOHYDRIC
MONOHYDROXY
MONOICOUS
MONOKINE
MONOKINES
MONOKINI
MONOKINIS
MONOLAYER
MONOLAYERS
MONOLINGUAL
MONOLINGUALS
MONOLITH
MONOLITHIC
MONOLITHICALLY
MONOLITHS
MONOLOG
MONOLOGGED
MONOLOGGING
MONOLOGIC
MONOLOGIES
MONOLOGIST
MONOLOGISTS
MONOLOGS
MONOLOGUE
MONOLOGUED
MONOLOGUES
MONOLOGUING

MONOLOGUIST
MONOLOGUISTS
MONOLOGY
MONOMANIA
MONOMANIAC
MONOMANIACAL
MONOMANIACALLY
MONOMANIACS
MONOMANIAS
MONOMER
MONOMERIC
MONOMERS
MONOMETALLIC
MONOMETALLISM
MONOMETALLISMS
MONOMETALLIST
MONOMETALLISTS
MONOMETER
MONOMETERS
MONOMIAL
MONOMIALS
MONOMOLECULAR
MONOMOLECULARLY
MONOMORPHEMIC
MONOMORPHIC
MONOMORPHISM
MONOMORPHISMS
MONONUCLEAR
MONONUCLEARS
MONONUCLEATE
MONONUCLEATED
MONONUCLEOSES
MONONUCLEOSIS
MONONUCLEOTIDE
MONONUCLEOTIDES
MONOPHAGIES
MONOPHAGOUS
MONOPHAGY
MONOPHONIC
MONOPHONICALLY
MONOPHONIES
MONOPHONY
MONOPHTHONG
MONOPHTHONGAL
MONOPHTHONGS
MONOPHYLETIC
MONOPHYLIES
MONOPHYLY
MONOPLANE
MONOPLANES
MONOPLOID
MONOPLOIDS
MONOPOD

MONOPODE
MONOPODES
MONOPODIA
MONOPODIAL
MONOPODIALLY
MONOPODIES
MONOPODIUM
MONOPODS
MONOPODY
MONOPOLE
MONOPOLES
MONOPOLIES
MONOPOLISATION
MONOPOLISATIONS
MONOPOLISE
MONOPOLISED
MONOPOLISES
MONOPOLISING
MONOPOLIST
MONOPOLISTIC
MONOPOLISTS
MONOPOLIZATION
MONOPOLIZATIONS
MONOPOLIZE
MONOPOLIZED
MONOPOLIZER
MONOPOLIZERS
MONOPOLIZES
MONOPOLIZING
MONOPOLY
MONOPROPELLANT
MONOPROPELLANTS
MONOPSONIES
MONOPSONISTIC
MONOPSONY
MONORAIL
MONORAILS
MONORCHID
MONORCHIDISM
MONORCHIDISMS
MONORCHIDS
MONORHYME
MONORHYMED
MONORHYMES
MONOS
MONOSACCHARIDE
MONOSACCHARIDES
MONOSKI
MONOSKIING
MONOSKIS
MONOSOME
MONOSOMES
MONOSOMIC

MONOSOMICS
MONOSOMIES
MONOSOMY
MONOSPECIFIC
MONOSPECIFICITY
MONOSTELE
MONOSTELES
MONOSTELIC
MONOSTELIES
MONOSTELY
MONOSTICH
MONOSTICHS
MONOSTOME
MONOSYLLABIC
MONOSYLLABICITY
MONOSYLLABLE
MONOSYLLABLES
MONOSYNAPTIC
MONOTERPENE
MONOTERPENES
MONOTHEISM
MONOTHEISMS
MONOTHEIST
MONOTHEISTIC
MONOTHEISTICAL
MONOTHEISTS
MONOTINT
MONOTINTS
MONOTONE
MONOTONES
MONOTONIC
MONOTONICALLY
MONOTONICITIES
MONOTONICITY
MONOTONIES
MONOTONOUS
MONOTONOUSLY
MONOTONOUSNESS
MONOTONY
MONOTREME
MONOTREMES
MONOTYPE
MONOTYPES
MONOTYPIC
MONOUNSATURATE
MONOUNSATURATED
MONOUNSATURATES
MONOVALENT
MONOVULAR
MONOXIDE
MONOXIDES
MONOZYGOTIC
MONS

MONSEIGNEUR
MONSEIGNEURS
MONSIEUR
MONSIGNOR
MONSIGNORI
MONSIGNORIAL
MONSIGNORS
MONSOON
MONSOONAL
MONSOONS
MONSTER
MONSTERA
MONSTERAS
MONSTERS
MONSTRANCE
MONSTRANCES
MONSTROSITIES
MONSTROSITY
MONSTROUS
MONSTROUSLY
MONSTROUSNESS
MONSTROUSNESSES
MONTADALE
MONTADALES
MONTAGE
MONTAGED
MONTAGES
MONTAGING
MONTAGNARD
MONTAGNARDS
MONTANE
MONTANES
MONTE
MONTEITH
MONTEITHS
MONTERO
MONTEROS
MONTES
MONTH
MONTHLIES
MONTHLONG
MONTHLY
MONTHS
MONTICULE
MONTICULES
MONTIES
MONTMORILLONITE
MONTY
MONUMENT
MONUMENTAL
MONUMENTALITIES
MONUMENTALITY
MONUMENTALIZE

MONUMENTALIZED
MONUMENTALIZES
MONUMENTALIZING
MONUMENTALLY
MONUMENTS
MONURON
MONURONS
MONY
MONZONITE
MONZONITES
MOO
MOOCH
MOOCHED
MOOCHER
MOOCHERS
MOOCHES
MOOCHING
MOOD
MOODIER
MOODIEST
MOODILY
MOODINESS
MOODINESSES
MOODS
MOODY
MOOED
MOOING
MOOK
MOOKS
MOOL
MOOLA
MOOLAH
MOOLAHS
MOOLAS
MOOLEY
MOOLEYS
MOOLS
MOON
MOONBEAM
MOONBEAMS
MOONBLIND
MOONBOW
MOONBOWS
MOONCALF
MOONCALVES
MOONCHILD
MOONCHILDREN
MOONDOG
MOONDOGS
MOONDUST
MOONDUSTS
MOONED
MOONER
MOONERS
MOONEYE
MOONEYES
MOONFACED
MOONFISH
MOONFISHES
MOONFLOWER
MOONFLOWERS
MOONGATE
MOONGATES
MOONIER
MOONIEST
MOONILY
MOONINESS
MOONINESSES
MOONING
MOONISH
MOONISHLY
MOONLESS
MOONLET
MOONLETS
MOONLIGHT
MOONLIGHTED
MOONLIGHTER
MOONLIGHTERS
MOONLIGHTING
MOONLIGHTS
MOONLIKE
MOONLIT
MOONPORT
MOONPORTS
MOONQUAKE
MOONQUAKES
MOONRISE
MOONRISES
MOONROOF
MOONROOFS
MOONS
MOONSAIL
MOONSAILS
MOONSCAPE
MOONSCAPES
MOONSEED
MOONSEEDS
MOONSET
MOONSETS
MOONSHINE
MOONSHINED
MOONSHINER
MOONSHINERS
MOONSHINES
MOONSHINING
MOONSHINY
MOONSHOT
MOONSHOTS
MOONSTONE
MOONSTONES
MOONSTRUCK
MOONWALK
MOONWALKED
MOONWALKING
MOONWALKS
MOONWARD
MOONWARDS
MOONWORT
MOONWORTS
MOONY
MOOR
MOORAGE
MOORAGES
MOORCOCK
MOORCOCKS
MOORED
MOORFOWL
MOORFOWLS
MOORHEN
MOORHENS
MOORIER
MOORIEST
MOORING
MOORINGS
MOORISH
MOORLAND
MOORLANDS
MOORS
MOORWORT
MOORWORTS
MOORY
MOOS
MOOSE
MOOSEBIRD
MOOSEBIRDS
MOOSEWOOD
MOOSEWOODS
MOOT
MOOTED
MOOTER
MOOTERS
MOOTING
MOOTNESS
MOOTNESSES
MOOTS
MOP
MOPBOARD
MOPBOARDS
MOPE
MOPED
MOPEDS
MOPER
MOPERIES
MOPERS
MOPERY
MOPES
MOPEY
MOPHEAD
MOPHEADS
MOPIER
MOPIEST
MOPILY
MOPINESS
MOPINESSES
MOPING
MOPINGLY
MOPISH
MOPISHLY
MOPOKE
MOPOKES
MOPPED
MOPPER
MOPPERS
MOPPET
MOPPETS
MOPPIER
MOPPIEST
MOPPING
MOPPY
MOPS
MOPY
MOQUETTE
MOQUETTES
MOR
MORA
MORAE
MORAINAL
MORAINE
MORAINES
MORAINIC
MORAL
MORALE
MORALES
MORALISE
MORALISED
MORALISER
MORALISES
MORALISING
MORALISM
MORALISMS
MORALIST
MORALISTIC
MORALISTICALLY
MORALISTS
MORALITIES
MORALITY
MORALIZATION
MORALIZATIONS
MORALIZE
MORALIZED
MORALIZER
MORALIZERS
MORALIZES
MORALIZING
MORALLY
MORALS
MORAS
MORASS
MORASSES
MORASSY
MORATORIA
MORATORIUM
MORATORIUMS
MORATORY
MORAY
MORAYS
MORBID
MORBIDITIES
MORBIDITY
MORBIDLY
MORBIDNESS
MORBIDNESSES
MORBIFIC
MORBILLI
MORBILLIVIRUS
MORBILLIVIRUSES
MORCEAU
MORCEAUX
MORDACITIES
MORDACITY
MORDANCIES
MORDANCY
MORDANT
MORDANTED
MORDANTING
MORDANTLY
MORDANTS
MORDENT
MORDENTS
MORE
MOREEN
MOREENS
MOREISH
MOREL
MORELLE

MORELLES
MORELLO
MORELLOS
MORELS
MORENESS
MORENESSES
MOREOVER
MORES
MORESQUE
MORESQUES
MORGAN
MORGANATIC
MORGANATICALLY
MORGANITE
MORGANITES
MORGANS
MORGEN
MORGENS
MORGUE
MORGUES
MORIBUND
MORIBUNDITIES
MORIBUNDITY
MORION
MORIONS
MORISH
MORN
MORNAY
MORNAYS
MORNING
MORNINGS
MORNS
MOROCCO
MOROCCOS
MORON
MORONIC
MORONICALLY
MORONISM
MORONISMS
MORONITIES
MORONITY
MORONS
MOROSE
MOROSELY
MOROSENESS
MOROSENESSES
MOROSITIES
MOROSITY
MORPH
MORPHACTIN
MORPHACTINS
MORPHALLAXES
MORPHALLAXIS
MORPHED
MORPHEME
MORPHEMES
MORPHEMIC
MORPHEMICALLY
MORPHEMICS
MORPHIA
MORPHIAS
MORPHIC
MORPHIN
MORPHINE
MORPHINES
MORPHING
MORPHINGS
MORPHINIC
MORPHINISM
MORPHINISMS
MORPHINS
MORPHO
MORPHOGEN
MORPHOGENESES
MORPHOGENESIS
MORPHOGENETIC
MORPHOGENIC
MORPHOGENS
MORPHOLOGIC
MORPHOLOGICAL
MORPHOLOGICALLY
MORPHOLOGIES
MORPHOLOGIST
MORPHOLOGISTS
MORPHOLOGY
MORPHOMETRIC
MORPHOMETRIES
MORPHOMETRY
MORPHOPHONEMICS
MORPHOS
MORPHOSES
MORPHOSIS
MORPHS
MORRION
MORRIONS
MORRIS
MORRISES
MORRO
MORROS
MORROW
MORROWS
MORS
MORSE
MORSEL
MORSELED
MORSELING
MORSELLED
MORSELLING
MORSELS
MORT
MORTADELLA
MORTADELLAS
MORTAL
MORTALITIES
MORTALITY
MORTALLY
MORTALS
MORTAR
MORTARBOARD
MORTARBOARDS
MORTARED
MORTARING
MORTARLESS
MORTARMAN
MORTARMEN
MORTARS
MORTARY
MORTGAGE
MORTGAGED
MORTGAGEE
MORTGAGEES
MORTGAGER
MORTGAGERS
MORTGAGES
MORTGAGING
MORTGAGOR
MORTGAGORS
MORTICE
MORTICED
MORTICER
MORTICERS
MORTICES
MORTICIAN
MORTICIANS
MORTICING
MORTIFICATION
MORTIFICATIONS
MORTIFIED
MORTIFIER
MORTIFIERS
MORTIFIES
MORTIFY
MORTIFYING
MORTIFYINGLY
MORTISE
MORTISED
MORTISER
MORTISERS
MORTISES
MORTISING
MORTMAIN
MORTMAINS
MORTS
MORTUARIES
MORTUARY
MORULA
MORULAE
MORULAR
MORULAS
MORULATION
MORULATIONS
MOS
MOSAIC
MOSAICALLY
MOSAICISM
MOSAICISMS
MOSAICIST
MOSAICISTS
MOSAICKED
MOSAICKING
MOSAICLIKE
MOSAICS
MOSASAUR
MOSASAURS
MOSCATO
MOSCATOS
MOSCHATE
MOSCHATEL
MOSCHATELS
MOSELLE
MOSELLES
MOSEY
MOSEYED
MOSEYING
MOSEYS
MOSH
MOSHAV
MOSHAVIM
MOSHED
MOSHER
MOSHERS
MOSHES
MOSHING
MOSHINGS
MOSK
MOSKS
MOSQUE
MOSQUES
MOSQUITO
MOSQUITOES
MOSQUITOEY
MOSQUITOS
MOSS
MOSSBACK
MOSSBACKED
MOSSBACKS
MOSSED
MOSSER
MOSSERS
MOSSES
MOSSGROWN
MOSSIER
MOSSIEST
MOSSINESS
MOSSINESSES
MOSSING
MOSSLIKE
MOSSO
MOSSY
MOST
MOSTE
MOSTEST
MOSTESTS
MOSTLY
MOSTS
MOT
MOTE
MOTEL
MOTELS
MOTES
MOTET
MOTETS
MOTEY
MOTH
MOTHBALL
MOTHBALLED
MOTHBALLING
MOTHBALLS
MOTHER
MOTHERBOARD
MOTHERBOARDS
MOTHERED
MOTHERFUCKER
MOTHERFUCKERS
MOTHERFUCKING
MOTHERHOOD
MOTHERHOODS
MOTHERHOUSE
MOTHERHOUSES
MOTHERING
MOTHERINGS
MOTHERLAND
MOTHERLANDS
MOTHERLESS
MOTHERLESSNESS

MOTHERLINESS
MOTHERLINESSES
MOTHERLY
MOTHERS
MOTHERY
MOTHIER
MOTHIEST
MOTHLIKE
MOTHPROOF
MOTHPROOFED
MOTHPROOFER
MOTHPROOFERS
MOTHPROOFING
MOTHPROOFS
MOTHS
MOTHY
MOTIF
MOTIFIC
MOTIFS
MOTILE
MOTILES
MOTILITIES
MOTILITY
MOTION
MOTIONAL
MOTIONED
MOTIONER
MOTIONERS
MOTIONING
MOTIONLESS
MOTIONLESSLY
MOTIONLESSNESS
MOTIONS
MOTIVATE
MOTIVATED
MOTIVATES
MOTIVATING
MOTIVATION
MOTIVATIONAL
MOTIVATIONALLY
MOTIVATIONS
MOTIVATIVE
MOTIVATOR
MOTIVATORS
MOTIVE
MOTIVED
MOTIVELESS
MOTIVELESSLY
MOTIVES
MOTIVIC
MOTIVING
MOTIVITIES
MOTIVITY

MOTLEY
MOTLEYER
MOTLEYEST
MOTLEYS
MOTLIER
MOTLIEST
MOTMOT
MOTMOTS
MOTOCROSS
MOTOCROSSES
MOTONEURON
MOTONEURONAL
MOTONEURONS
MOTOR
MOTORBIKE
MOTORBIKED
MOTORBIKES
MOTORBIKING
MOTORBOAT
MOTORBOATED
MOTORBOATER
MOTORBOATERS
MOTORBOATING
MOTORBOATINGS
MOTORBOATS
MOTORBUS
MOTORBUSES
MOTORBUSSES
MOTORCADE
MOTORCADED
MOTORCADES
MOTORCADING
MOTORCAR
MOTORCARS
MOTORCYCLE
MOTORCYCLED
MOTORCYCLES
MOTORCYCLING
MOTORCYCLIST
MOTORCYCLISTS
MOTORDOM
MOTORDOMS
MOTORED
MOTORIC
MOTORICALLY
MOTORING
MOTORINGS
MOTORISE
MOTORISED
MOTORISES
MOTORISING
MOTORIST
MOTORISTS

MOTORIZATION
MOTORIZATIONS
MOTORIZE
MOTORIZED
MOTORIZES
MOTORIZING
MOTORLESS
MOTORMAN
MOTORMEN
MOTORMOUTH
MOTORMOUTHED
MOTORMOUTHS
MOTORS
MOTORSHIP
MOTORSHIPS
MOTORTRUCK
MOTORTRUCKS
MOTORWAY
MOTORWAYS
MOTS
MOTT
MOTTE
MOTTES
MOTTLE
MOTTLED
MOTTLER
MOTTLERS
MOTTLES
MOTTLING
MOTTLINGS
MOTTO
MOTTOES
MOTTOS
MOTTS
MOUCH
MOUCHED
MOUCHES
MOUCHING
MOUCHOIR
MOUCHOIRS
MOUE
MOUES
MOUFFLON
MOUFFLONS
MOUFLON
MOUFLONS
MOUILLE
MOUJIK
MOUJIKS
MOULAGE
MOULAGES
MOULD
MOULDED

MOULDER
MOULDERED
MOULDERING
MOULDERS
MOULDIER
MOULDIEST
MOULDING
MOULDINGS
MOULDS
MOULDY
MOULIN
MOULINS
MOULT
MOULTED
MOULTER
MOULTERS
MOULTING
MOULTS
MOUND
MOUNDBIRD
MOUNDBIRDS
MOUNDED
MOUNDING
MOUNDS
MOUNT
MOUNTABLE
MOUNTAIN
MOUNTAINEER
MOUNTAINEERING
MOUNTAINEERINGS
MOUNTAINEERS
MOUNTAINOUS
MOUNTAINOUSLY
MOUNTAINOUSNESS
MOUNTAINS
MOUNTAINSIDE
MOUNTAINSIDES
MOUNTAINTOP
MOUNTAINTOPS
MOUNTAINY
MOUNTEBANK
MOUNTEBANKED
MOUNTEBANKERIES
MOUNTEBANKERY
MOUNTEBANKING
MOUNTEBANKS
MOUNTED
MOUNTER
MOUNTERS
MOUNTING
MOUNTINGS
MOUNTS
MOURN

MOURNED
MOURNER
MOURNERS
MOURNFUL
MOURNFULLER
MOURNFULLEST
MOURNFULLY
MOURNFULNESS
MOURNFULNESSES
MOURNING
MOURNINGLY
MOURNINGS
MOURNS
MOUSAKA
MOUSAKAS
MOUSE
MOUSEBIRD
MOUSEBIRDS
MOUSED
MOUSELIKE
MOUSEPAD
MOUSEPADS
MOUSER
MOUSERS
MOUSES
MOUSETAIL
MOUSETAILS
MOUSETRAP
MOUSETRAPPED
MOUSETRAPPING
MOUSETRAPS
MOUSEY
MOUSIER
MOUSIEST
MOUSILY
MOUSINESS
MOUSINESSES
MOUSING
MOUSINGS
MOUSSAKA
MOUSSAKAS
MOUSSE
MOUSSED
MOUSSELINE
MOUSSELINES
MOUSSES
MOUSSEUX
MOUSSING
MOUSTACHE
MOUSTACHED
MOUSTACHES
MOUSTACHIO
MOUSTACHIOED

MOUSTACHIOS
MOUSY
MOUTH
MOUTHBREEDER
MOUTHBREEDERS
MOUTHED
MOUTHER
MOUTHERS
MOUTHFEEL
MOUTHFEELS
MOUTHFUL
MOUTHFULS
MOUTHIER
MOUTHIEST
MOUTHILY
MOUTHING
MOUTHLESS
MOUTHLIKE
MOUTHPART
MOUTHPARTS
MOUTHPIECE
MOUTHPIECES
MOUTHS
MOUTHWASH
MOUTHWASHES
MOUTHWATERING
MOUTHWATERINGLY
MOUTHY
MOUTON
MOUTONNEE
MOUTONS
MOVABILITIES
MOVABILITY
MOVABLE
MOVABLENESS
MOVABLENESSES
MOVABLES
MOVABLY
MOVANT
MOVANTS
MOVE
MOVEABLE
MOVEABLES
MOVEABLY
MOVED
MOVELESS
MOVELESSLY
MOVELESSNESS
MOVELESSNESSES
MOVEMENT
MOVEMENTS
MOVER
MOVERS
MOVES
MOVIE
MOVIEDOM
MOVIEDOMS
MOVIEGOER
MOVIEGOERS
MOVIEGOING
MOVIEGOINGS
MOVIEMAKER
MOVIEMAKERS
MOVIEMAKING
MOVIEMAKINGS
MOVIEOLA
MOVIEOLAS
MOVIES
MOVING
MOVINGLY
MOVIOLA
MOVIOLAS
MOW
MOWED
MOWER
MOWERS
MOWING
MOWINGS
MOWN
MOWS
MOXA
MOXAS
MOXIBUSTION
MOXIBUSTIONS
MOXIE
MOXIES
MOZETTA
MOZETTAS
MOZETTE
MOZO
MOZOS
MOZZARELLA
MOZZARELLAS
MOZZETTA
MOZZETTAS
MOZZETTE
MRIDANGA
MRIDANGAM
MRIDANGAMS
MRIDANGAS
MU
MUCH
MUCHACHA
MUCHACHAS
MUCHACHO
MUCHACHOS
MUCHES
MUCHLY
MUCHNESS
MUCHNESSES
MUCHO
MUCID
MUCIDITIES
MUCIDITY
MUCILAGE
MUCILAGES
MUCILAGINOUS
MUCILAGINOUSLY
MUCIN
MUCINOGEN
MUCINOGENS
MUCINOID
MUCINOUS
MUCINS
MUCK
MUCKAMUCK
MUCKAMUCKS
MUCKED
MUCKER
MUCKERS
MUCKIER
MUCKIEST
MUCKILY
MUCKING
MUCKLE
MUCKLER
MUCKLES
MUCKLEST
MUCKLUCK
MUCKLUCKS
MUCKRAKE
MUCKRAKED
MUCKRAKER
MUCKRAKERS
MUCKRAKES
MUCKRAKING
MUCKRAKINGS
MUCKS
MUCKWORM
MUCKWORMS
MUCKY
MUCLUC
MUCLUCS
MUCOCUTANEOUS
MUCOID
MUCOIDAL
MUCOIDS
MUCOLYTIC
MUCOPEPTIDE
MUCOPEPTIDES
MUCOPROTEIN
MUCOPROTEINS
MUCOR
MUCORS
MUCOSA
MUCOSAE
MUCOSAL
MUCOSAS
MUCOSE
MUCOSITIES
MUCOSITY
MUCOUS
MUCRO
MUCRONATE
MUCRONES
MUCROS
MUCUS
MUCUSES
MUD
MUDBANK
MUDBANKS
MUDBUG
MUDBUGS
MUDCAP
MUDCAPPED
MUDCAPPING
MUDCAPS
MUDCAT
MUDCATS
MUDDED
MUDDER
MUDDERS
MUDDIED
MUDDIER
MUDDIES
MUDDIEST
MUDDILY
MUDDINESS
MUDDINESSES
MUDDING
MUDDLE
MUDDLED
MUDDLEHEADED
MUDDLEHEADEDLY
MUDDLER
MUDDLERS
MUDDLES
MUDDLING
MUDDLY
MUDDY
MUDDYING
MUDFISH
MUDFISHES
MUDFLAP
MUDFLAPS
MUDFLAT
MUDFLATS
MUDFLOW
MUDFLOWS
MUDGUARD
MUDGUARDS
MUDHEN
MUDHENS
MUDHOLE
MUDHOLES
MUDLARK
MUDLARKS
MUDPACK
MUDPACKS
MUDPIE
MUDPIES
MUDPUPPIES
MUDPUPPY
MUDRA
MUDRAS
MUDROCK
MUDROCKS
MUDROOM
MUDROOMS
MUDS
MUDSILL
MUDSILLS
MUDSKIPPER
MUDSKIPPERS
MUDSLIDE
MUDSLIDES
MUDSLING
MUDSLINGER
MUDSLINGERS
MUDSLINGING
MUDSLINGINGS
MUDSLINGS
MUDSLUNG
MUDSTONE
MUDSTONES
MUEDDIN
MUEDDINS
MUENSTER
MUENSTERS
MUESLI
MUESLIS
MUEZZIN
MUEZZINS
MUFF
MUFFALETTA

MUFFALETTAS
MUFFED
MUFFIN
MUFFINEER
MUFFINEERS
MUFFING
MUFFINS
MUFFLE
MUFFLED
MUFFLER
MUFFLERED
MUFFLERS
MUFFLES
MUFFLING
MUFFS
MUFFULETTA
MUFFULETTAS
MUFTI
MUFTIS
MUG
MUGFUL
MUGFULS
MUGG
MUGGAR
MUGGARS
MUGGED
MUGGEE
MUGGEES
MUGGER
MUGGERS
MUGGIER
MUGGIEST
MUGGILY
MUGGINESS
MUGGINESSES
MUGGING
MUGGINGS
MUGGINS
MUGGINSES
MUGGS
MUGGUR
MUGGURS
MUGGY
MUGHAL
MUGHALS
MUGS
MUGSHOT
MUGSHOTS
MUGWORT
MUGWORTS
MUGWUMP
MUGWUMPS
MUHLIES
MUHLY
MUJAHEDEEN
MUJAHEDIN
MUJAHIDEEN
MUJAHIDIN
MUJIK
MUJIKS
MUKHTAR
MUKHTARS
MUKLUK
MUKLUKS
MUKTUK
MUKTUKS
MULATTO
MULATTOES
MULATTOS
MULBERRIES
MULBERRY
MULCH
MULCHED
MULCHES
MULCHING
MULCT
MULCTED
MULCTING
MULCTS
MULE
MULED
MULES
MULETA
MULETAS
MULETEER
MULETEERS
MULEY
MULEYS
MULIE
MULIEBRITIES
MULIEBRITY
MULIES
MULING
MULISH
MULISHLY
MULISHNESS
MULISHNESSES
MULL
MULLA
MULLAH
MULLAHISM
MULLAHISMS
MULLAHS
MULLAS
MULLED
MULLEIN
MULLEINS
MULLEN
MULLENS
MULLER
MULLERS
MULLET
MULLETS
MULLEY
MULLEYS
MULLIGAN
MULLIGANS
MULLIGATAWNIES
MULLIGATAWNY
MULLING
MULLION
MULLIONED
MULLIONING
MULLIONS
MULLITE
MULLITES
MULLOCK
MULLOCKS
MULLOCKY
MULLS
MULTIAGE
MULTIAGENCIES
MULTIAGENCY
MULTIARMED
MULTIATOM
MULTIAUTHOR
MULTIAUTHORED
MULTIAUTHORS
MULTIAXIAL
MULTIBAND
MULTIBANK
MULTIBARREL
MULTIBARRELED
MULTIBARRELS
MULTIBILLION
MULTIBILLIONS
MULTIBLADED
MULTIBRANCHED
MULTIBUILDING
MULTIBUILDINGS
MULTIBUTTON
MULTICAMPUS
MULTICAMPUSES
MULTICANDIDATE
MULTICANDIDATES
MULTICAR
MULTICARBON
MULTICAUSAL
MULTICELL
MULTICELLED
MULTICELLULAR
MULTICENTER
MULTICENTERED
MULTICENTERS
MULTICHAIN
MULTICHAINS
MULTICHAMBERED
MULTICHANNEL
MULTICHANNELS
MULTICHARACTER
MULTICHARACTERS
MULTICITY
MULTICLIENT
MULTICLIENTS
MULTICOATED
MULTICOLOR
MULTICOLORED
MULTICOLORS
MULTICOLOURED
MULTICOLUMN
MULTICOLUMNS
MULTICOMPONENT
MULTICOMPONENTS
MULTICONDUCTOR
MULTICONDUCTORS
MULTICOPY
MULTICOUNTRIES
MULTICOUNTY
MULTICOURSE
MULTICOURSES
MULTICULTI
MULTICULTURAL
MULTICULTURALLY
MULTICURIE
MULTICURRENCIES
MULTICURRENCY
MULTIDAY
MULTIDIALECTAL
MULTIDISC
MULTIDISCIPLINE
MULTIDIVISIONAL
MULTIDOMAIN
MULTIDRUG
MULTIELECTRODE
MULTIELECTRODES
MULTIELEMENT
MULTIELEMENTS
MULTIEMPLOYER
MULTIEMPLOYERS
MULTIENGINE
MULTIENGINES
MULTIENZYME
MULTIENZYMES
MULTIETHNIC
MULTIETHNICITY
MULTIETHNICS
MULTIFACETED
MULTIFACTOR
MULTIFACTORIAL
MULTIFACTORS
MULTIFAMILIES
MULTIFAMILY
MULTIFARIOUS
MULTIFEATURED
MULTIFID
MULTIFILAMENT
MULTIFILAMENTS
MULTIFLASH
MULTIFLASHES
MULTIFOCAL
MULTIFOIL
MULTIFOILS
MULTIFOLD
MULTIFORM
MULTIFORMITIES
MULTIFORMITY
MULTIFREQUENCY
MULTIFRONT
MULTIFRONTS
MULTIFUNCTION
MULTIFUNCTIONAL
MULTIFUNCTIONS
MULTIGENIC
MULTIGERM
MULTIGRADE
MULTIGRADES
MULTIGRAIN
MULTIGRAINS
MULTIGRID
MULTIGROUP
MULTIGROUPS
MULTIHEADED
MULTIHOMER
MULTIHOMERS
MULTIHOSPITAL
MULTIHOSPITALS
MULTIHUED
MULTIHULL
MULTIHULLED
MULTIHULLS
MULTIJET
MULTILANE
MULTILANES
MULTILATERAL
MULTILATERALISM

MULTILATERALIST
MULTILATERALLY
MULTILAYER
MULTILAYERED
MULTILAYERS
MULTILEVEL
MULTILEVELED
MULTILEVELS
MULTILINE
MULTILINGUAL
MULTILINGUALISM
MULTILINGUALLY
MULTILOBE
MULTILOBED
MULTILOBES
MULTILOCATION
MULTILOCATIONS
MULTIMANNED
MULTIMEDIA
MULTIMEDIAS
MULTIMEGATON
MULTIMEGATONS
MULTIMEGAWATT
MULTIMEGAWATTS
MULTIMEMBER
MULTIMETALLIC
MULTIMETER
MULTIMETERS
MULTIMILLENNIAL
MULTIMILLION
MULTIMILLIONS
MULTIMODAL
MULTIMODE
MULTIMODES
MULTIMOLECULAR
MULTINATION
MULTINATIONAL
MULTINATIONALS
MULTINATIONS
MULTINOMIAL
MULTINOMIALS
MULTINUCLEAR
MULTINUCLEATE
MULTINUCLEATED
MULTIORGASMIC
MULTIPACK
MULTIPACKS
MULTIPAGE
MULTIPANED
MULTIPARA
MULTIPARAE
MULTIPARAMETER
MULTIPARAMETERS
MULTIPARAS
MULTIPAROUS
MULTIPART
MULTIPARTICLE
MULTIPARTICLES
MULTIPARTIES
MULTIPARTITE
MULTIPARTY
MULTIPATH
MULTIPED
MULTIPEDE
MULTIPEDES
MULTIPEDS
MULTIPHASE
MULTIPHASES
MULTIPHASIC
MULTIPHOTON
MULTIPHOTONS
MULTIPICTURE
MULTIPICTURES
MULTIPIECE
MULTIPIECES
MULTIPION
MULTIPISTON
MULTIPLANT
MULTIPLANTS
MULTIPLATINUM
MULTIPLATINUMS
MULTIPLAYER
MULTIPLAYERS
MULTIPLE
MULTIPLES
MULTIPLET
MULTIPLETS
MULTIPLEX
MULTIPLEXED
MULTIPLEXER
MULTIPLEXERS
MULTIPLEXES
MULTIPLEXING
MULTIPLEXOR
MULTIPLEXORS
MULTIPLICAND
MULTIPLICANDS
MULTIPLICATION
MULTIPLICATIONS
MULTIPLICATIVE
MULTIPLICITIES
MULTIPLICITY
MULTIPLIED
MULTIPLIER
MULTIPLIERS
MULTIPLIES
MULTIPLY
MULTIPLYING
MULTIPOLAR
MULTIPOLARITIES
MULTIPOLARITY
MULTIPOLE
MULTIPOLES
MULTIPORT
MULTIPOTENTIAL
MULTIPOWER
MULTIPOWERS
MULTIPROBLEM
MULTIPROBLEMS
MULTIPROCESSING
MULTIPROCESSOR
MULTIPROCESSORS
MULTIPRODUCT
MULTIPRODUCTS
MULTIPRONGED
MULTIPURPOSE
MULTIPURPOSES
MULTIRACIAL
MULTIRACIALISM
MULTIRACIALISMS
MULTIRANGE
MULTIRANGES
MULTIREGIONAL
MULTIRELIGIOUS
MULTIROOM
MULTISCREEN
MULTISCREENS
MULTISENSE
MULTISENSES
MULTISENSORY
MULTISERVICE
MULTISERVICES
MULTISIDED
MULTISITE
MULTISIZE
MULTISKILLED
MULTISOURCE
MULTISOURCES
MULTISPECIES
MULTISPECTRAL
MULTISPEED
MULTISPEEDS
MULTISPORT
MULTISPORTS
MULTISTAGE
MULTISTAGES
MULTISTATE
MULTISTATES
MULTISTEMMED
MULTISTEP
MULTISTOREY
MULTISTOREYS
MULTISTORIED
MULTISTORIES
MULTISTORY
MULTISTRANDED
MULTISYLLABIC
MULTISYSTEM
MULTISYSTEMS
MULTITALENTED
MULTITASK
MULTITASKED
MULTITASKER
MULTITASKERS
MULTITASKING
MULTITASKINGS
MULTITASKS
MULTITERMINAL
MULTITERMINALS
MULTITIERED
MULTITON
MULTITONE
MULTITONES
MULTITOWERED
MULTITRACK
MULTITRACKS
MULTITRILLION
MULTITRILLIONS
MULTITUDE
MULTITUDES
MULTITUDINOUS
MULTITUDINOUSLY
MULTIUNION
MULTIUNIONS
MULTIUNIT
MULTIUSE
MULTIUSER
MULTIVALENCE
MULTIVALENCES
MULTIVALENT
MULTIVALENTS
MULTIVALVE
MULTIVALVES
MULTIVARIABLE
MULTIVARIATE
MULTIVERSE
MULTIVERSES
MULTIVERSITIES
MULTIVERSITY
MULTIVITAMIN
MULTIVITAMINS
MULTIVOICED
MULTIVOLTINE
MULTIVOLUME
MULTIVOLUMES
MULTIWALL
MULTIWARHEAD
MULTIWARHEADS
MULTIWAVELENGTH
MULTIWAY
MULTIYEAR
MULTURE
MULTURES
MUM
MUMBLE
MUMBLED
MUMBLER
MUMBLERS
MUMBLES
MUMBLING
MUMBLINGS
MUMBLY
MUMM
MUMMED
MUMMER
MUMMERED
MUMMERIES
MUMMERING
MUMMERINGS
MUMMERS
MUMMERY
MUMMICHOG
MUMMICHOGS
MUMMIED
MUMMIES
MUMMIFICATION
MUMMIFICATIONS
MUMMIFIED
MUMMIFIES
MUMMIFY
MUMMIFYING
MUMMING
MUMMINGS
MUMMS
MUMMY
MUMMYING
MUMP
MUMPED
MUMPER
MUMPERS
MUMPING
MUMPISH
MUMPS
MUMS
MUMSIER

MUMSIES
MUMSIEST
MUMSY
MUMU
MUMUS
MUN
MUNCH
MUNCHABLE
MUNCHABLES
MUNCHED
MUNCHER
MUNCHERS
MUNCHES
MUNCHIE
MUNCHIER
MUNCHIES
MUNCHIEST
MUNCHING
MUNCHKIN
MUNCHKINS
MUNCHY
MUNDANE
MUNDANELY
MUNDANENESS
MUNDANENESSES
MUNDANITIES
MUNDANITY
MUNDUNGO
MUNDUNGOS
MUNDUNGUS
MUNDUNGUSES
MUNG
MUNGO
MUNGOES
MUNGOOSE
MUNGOOSES
MUNGOS
MUNGS
MUNI
MUNICIPAL
MUNICIPALITIES
MUNICIPALITY
MUNICIPALIZE
MUNICIPALIZED
MUNICIPALIZES
MUNICIPALIZING
MUNICIPALLY
MUNICIPALS
MUNIFICENCE
MUNIFICENCES
MUNIFICENT
MUNIFICENTLY
MUNIMENT
MUNIMENTS
MUNIS
MUNITION
MUNITIONED
MUNITIONING
MUNITIONS
MUNNION
MUNNIONS
MUNS
MUNSTER
MUNSTERS
MUNTIN
MUNTINED
MUNTING
MUNTINGS
MUNTINS
MUNTJAC
MUNTJACS
MUNTJAK
MUNTJAKS
MUON
MUONIC
MUONIUM
MUONIUMS
MUONS
MURA
MURAENID
MURAENIDS
MURAGE
MURAGES
MURAL
MURALED
MURALIST
MURALISTS
MURALLED
MURALS
MURAS
MURDER
MURDERED
MURDEREE
MURDEREES
MURDERER
MURDERERS
MURDERESS
MURDERESSES
MURDERING
MURDEROUS
MURDEROUSLY
MURDEROUSNESS
MURDEROUSNESSES
MURDERS
MURE
MURED
MUREIN
MUREINS
MURES
MUREX
MUREXES
MURIATE
MURIATED
MURIATES
MURICATE
MURICATED
MURICES
MURID
MURIDS
MURINE
MURINES
MURING
MURK
MURKER
MURKEST
MURKIER
MURKIEST
MURKILY
MURKINESS
MURKINESSES
MURKLY
MURKS
MURKY
MURMUR
MURMURED
MURMURER
MURMURERS
MURMURING
MURMURINGS
MURMUROUS
MURMUROUSLY
MURMURS
MURPHIES
MURPHY
MURR
MURRA
MURRAIN
MURRAINS
MURRAS
MURRE
MURRELET
MURRELETS
MURRES
MURREY
MURREYS
MURRHA
MURRHAS
MURRHINE
MURRIES
MURRINE
MURRS
MURRY
MURTHER
MURTHERED
MURTHERING
MURTHERS
MUS
MUSCA
MUSCADEL
MUSCADELS
MUSCADET
MUSCADETS
MUSCADINE
MUSCADINES
MUSCAE
MUSCARINE
MUSCARINES
MUSCARINIC
MUSCAT
MUSCATEL
MUSCATELS
MUSCATS
MUSCID
MUSCIDS
MUSCLE
MUSCLED
MUSCLEMAN
MUSCLEMEN
MUSCLES
MUSCLIER
MUSCLIEST
MUSCLING
MUSCLY
MUSCOVADO
MUSCOVADOS
MUSCOVITE
MUSCOVITES
MUSCULAR
MUSCULARITIES
MUSCULARITY
MUSCULARLY
MUSCULATURE
MUSCULATURES
MUSCULOSKELETAL
MUSE
MUSED
MUSEFUL
MUSEOLOGICAL
MUSEOLOGIES
MUSEOLOGIST
MUSEOLOGISTS
MUSEOLOGY
MUSER
MUSERS
MUSES
MUSETTE
MUSETTES
MUSEUM
MUSEUMGOER
MUSEUMGOERS
MUSEUMS
MUSH
MUSHED
MUSHER
MUSHERS
MUSHES
MUSHIER
MUSHIEST
MUSHILY
MUSHINESS
MUSHINESSES
MUSHING
MUSHINGS
MUSHRAT
MUSHRATS
MUSHROOM
MUSHROOMED
MUSHROOMING
MUSHROOMS
MUSHY
MUSIC
MUSICAL
MUSICALE
MUSICALES
MUSICALISE
MUSICALISED
MUSICALISES
MUSICALISING
MUSICALITIES
MUSICALITY
MUSICALIZATION
MUSICALIZATIONS
MUSICALIZE
MUSICALIZED
MUSICALIZES
MUSICALIZING
MUSICALLY
MUSICALS
MUSICIAN
MUSICIANLY
MUSICIANS
MUSICIANSHIP
MUSICIANSHIPS
MUSICK
MUSICKED

MUSICKING
MUSICKS
MUSICLESS
MUSICOLOGICAL
MUSICOLOGIES
MUSICOLOGIST
MUSICOLOGISTS
MUSICOLOGY
MUSICS
MUSING
MUSINGLY
MUSINGS
MUSJID
MUSJIDS
MUSK
MUSKEG
MUSKEGS
MUSKELLUNGE
MUSKET
MUSKETEER
MUSKETEERS
MUSKETRIES
MUSKETRY
MUSKETS
MUSKIE
MUSKIER
MUSKIES
MUSKIEST
MUSKILY
MUSKINESS
MUSKINESSES
MUSKIT
MUSKITS
MUSKMELON
MUSKMELONS
MUSKOX
MUSKOXEN
MUSKRAT
MUSKRATS
MUSKROOT
MUSKROOTS
MUSKS
MUSKY
MUSLIN
MUSLINED
MUSLINS
MUSO
MUSOS
MUSPIKE
MUSPIKES
MUSQUASH
MUSQUASHES
MUSS
MUSSED
MUSSEL
MUSSELS
MUSSES
MUSSIER
MUSSIEST
MUSSILY
MUSSINESS
MUSSINESSES
MUSSING
MUSSY
MUST
MUSTACHE
MUSTACHED
MUSTACHES
MUSTACHIO
MUSTACHIOED
MUSTACHIOS
MUSTANG
MUSTANGS
MUSTARD
MUSTARDS
MUSTARDY
MUSTED
MUSTEE
MUSTEES
MUSTELID
MUSTELIDS
MUSTELINE
MUSTER
MUSTERED
MUSTERING
MUSTERS
MUSTH
MUSTHS
MUSTIER
MUSTIEST
MUSTILY
MUSTINESS
MUSTINESSES
MUSTING
MUSTS
MUSTY
MUT
MUTABILITIES
MUTABILITY
MUTABLE
MUTABLY
MUTAGEN
MUTAGENESES
MUTAGENESIS
MUTAGENIC
MUTAGENICALLY
MUTAGENICITIES
MUTAGENICITY
MUTAGENS
MUTANT
MUTANTS
MUTASE
MUTASES
MUTATE
MUTATED
MUTATES
MUTATING
MUTATION
MUTATIONAL
MUTATIONALLY
MUTATIONS
MUTATIVE
MUTATOR
MUTATORS
MUTCH
MUTCHES
MUTCHKIN
MUTCHKINS
MUTE
MUTED
MUTEDLY
MUTELY
MUTENESS
MUTENESSES
MUTER
MUTES
MUTEST
MUTHA
MUTHAS
MUTICOUS
MUTILATE
MUTILATED
MUTILATES
MUTILATING
MUTILATION
MUTILATIONS
MUTILATOR
MUTILATORS
MUTINE
MUTINED
MUTINEER
MUTINEERED
MUTINEERING
MUTINEERS
MUTINES
MUTING
MUTINIED
MUTINIES
MUTINING
MUTINOUS
MUTINOUSLY
MUTINOUSNESS
MUTINOUSNESSES
MUTINY
MUTINYING
MUTISM
MUTISMS
MUTON
MUTONS
MUTS
MUTT
MUTTER
MUTTERED
MUTTERER
MUTTERERS
MUTTERING
MUTTERS
MUTTON
MUTTONCHOPS
MUTTONFISH
MUTTONFISHES
MUTTONS
MUTTONY
MUTTS
MUTUAL
MUTUALISM
MUTUALISMS
MUTUALIST
MUTUALISTIC
MUTUALISTS
MUTUALITIES
MUTUALITY
MUTUALIZATION
MUTUALIZATIONS
MUTUALIZE
MUTUALIZED
MUTUALIZES
MUTUALIZING
MUTUALLY
MUTUALS
MUTUEL
MUTUELS
MUTULAR
MUTULE
MUTULES
MUUMUU
MUUMUUS
MUX
MUXED
MUXES
MUXING
MUZAK
MUZAKS
MUZHIK
MUZHIKS
MUZJIK
MUZJIKS
MUZZIER
MUZZIEST
MUZZILY
MUZZINESS
MUZZINESSES
MUZZLE
MUZZLED
MUZZLER
MUZZLERS
MUZZLES
MUZZLING
MUZZY
MY
MYALGIA
MYALGIAS
MYALGIC
MYASES
MYASIS
MYASTHENIA
MYASTHENIAS
MYASTHENIC
MYASTHENICS
MYC
MYCELE
MYCELES
MYCELIA
MYCELIAL
MYCELIAN
MYCELIUM
MYCELOID
MYCETOMA
MYCETOMAS
MYCETOMATA
MYCETOMATOUS
MYCETOPHAGOUS
MYCETOZOAN
MYCETOZOANS
MYCOBACTERIA
MYCOBACTERIAL
MYCOBACTERIUM
MYCOFLORA
MYCOFLORAE
MYCOFLORAS
MYCOLOGIC
MYCOLOGICAL
MYCOLOGICALLY
MYCOLOGIES
MYCOLOGIST

MYCOLOGISTS
MYCOLOGY
MYCOPHAGIES
MYCOPHAGIST
MYCOPHAGISTS
MYCOPHAGOUS
MYCOPHAGY
MYCOPHILE
MYCOPHILES
MYCOPLASMA
MYCOPLASMAL
MYCOPLASMAS
MYCOPLASMATA
MYCORHIZA
MYCORHIZAE
MYCORHIZAS
MYCORRHIZA
MYCORRHIZAE
MYCORRHIZAL
MYCORRHIZAS
MYCOSES
MYCOSIS
MYCOTIC
MYCOTOXIN
MYCOTOXINS
MYCOVIRUS
MYCOVIRUSES
MYCS
MYDRIASES
MYDRIASIS
MYDRIATIC
MYDRIATICS
MYELENCEPHALA
MYELENCEPHALIC
MYELENCEPHALON
MYELIN
MYELINATED
MYELINE
MYELINES
MYELINIC
MYELINS
MYELITES
MYELITIDES
MYELITIS
MYELITISES
MYELOBLAST
MYELOBLASTIC
MYELOBLASTS
MYELOCYTE
MYELOCYTES
MYELOCYTIC
MYELOFIBROSES
MYELOFIBROSIS
MYELOFIBROTIC
MYELOGENOUS
MYELOGRAM
MYELOGRAMS
MYELOID
MYELOMA
MYELOMAS
MYELOMATA
MYELOMATOUS
MYELOPATHIC
MYELOPATHIES
MYELOPATHY
MYIASES
MYIASIS
MYLAR
MYLARS
MYLODON
MYLODONS
MYLONITE
MYLONITES
MYNA
MYNAH
MYNAHS
MYNAS
MYNHEER
MYNHEERS
MYOBLAST
MYOBLASTS
MYOCARDIA
MYOCARDIAL
MYOCARDITIS
MYOCARDITISES
MYOCARDIUM
MYOCLONIC
MYOCLONUS
MYOCLONUSES
MYOELECTRIC
MYOELECTRICAL
MYOFIBRIL
MYOFIBRILLAR
MYOFIBRILS
MYOFILAMENT
MYOFILAMENTS
MYOGENIC
MYOGLOBIN
MYOGLOBINS
MYOGRAPH
MYOGRAPHS
MYOID
MYOINOSITOL
MYOINOSITOLS
MYOLOGIC
MYOLOGIES
MYOLOGIST
MYOLOGISTS
MYOLOGY
MYOMA
MYOMAS
MYOMATA
MYOMATOUS
MYOMECTOMIES
MYOMECTOMY
MYOMERE
MYOMERES
MYONEURAL
MYOPATHIC
MYOPATHIES
MYOPATHY
MYOPE
MYOPES
MYOPIA
MYOPIAS
MYOPIC
MYOPICALLY
MYOPIES
MYOPY
MYOSCOPE
MYOSCOPES
MYOSES
MYOSIN
MYOSINS
MYOSIS
MYOSISES
MYOSITIS
MYOSITISES
MYOSOTE
MYOSOTES
MYOSOTIS
MYOSOTISES
MYOTIC
MYOTICS
MYOTOME
MYOTOMES
MYOTONIA
MYOTONIAS
MYOTONIC
MYRIAD
MYRIADS
MYRIAPOD
MYRIAPODS
MYRICA
MYRICAS
MYRIOPOD
MYRIOPODS
MYRMECOLOGICAL
MYRMECOLOGIES
MYRMECOLOGIST
MYRMECOLOGISTS
MYRMECOLOGY
MYRMECOPHILE
MYRMECOPHILES
MYRMECOPHILOUS
MYRMIDON
MYRMIDONES
MYRMIDONS
MYROBALAN
MYROBALANS
MYRRH
MYRRHIC
MYRRHS
MYRRHY
MYRTLE
MYRTLES
MYSELF
MYSID
MYSIDS
MYSOST
MYSOSTS
MYSTAGOG
MYSTAGOGIES
MYSTAGOGS
MYSTAGOGUE
MYSTAGOGUES
MYSTAGOGY
MYSTERIES
MYSTERIOUS
MYSTERIOUSLY
MYSTERIOUSNESS
MYSTERY
MYSTIC
MYSTICAL
MYSTICALLY
MYSTICETE
MYSTICETES
MYSTICISM
MYSTICISMS
MYSTICLY
MYSTICS
MYSTIFICATION
MYSTIFICATIONS
MYSTIFIED
MYSTIFIER
MYSTIFIERS
MYSTIFIES
MYSTIFY
MYSTIFYING
MYSTIFYINGLY
MYSTIQUE
MYSTIQUES
MYTH
MYTHIC
MYTHICAL
MYTHICALLY
MYTHICIZE
MYTHICIZED
MYTHICIZER
MYTHICIZERS
MYTHICIZES
MYTHICIZING
MYTHIER
MYTHIEST
MYTHMAKER
MYTHMAKERS
MYTHMAKING
MYTHMAKINGS
MYTHOGRAPHER
MYTHOGRAPHERS
MYTHOGRAPHIES
MYTHOGRAPHY
MYTHOI
MYTHOLOGER
MYTHOLOGERS
MYTHOLOGIC
MYTHOLOGICAL
MYTHOLOGICALLY
MYTHOLOGIES
MYTHOLOGISE
MYTHOLOGISED
MYTHOLOGISES
MYTHOLOGISING
MYTHOLOGIST
MYTHOLOGISTS
MYTHOLOGIZE
MYTHOLOGIZED
MYTHOLOGIZER
MYTHOLOGIZERS
MYTHOLOGIZES
MYTHOLOGIZING
MYTHOLOGY
MYTHOMANIA
MYTHOMANIAC
MYTHOMANIACS
MYTHOMANIAS
MYTHOPEIC
MYTHOPOEIA
MYTHOPOEIAS
MYTHOPOEIC
MYTHOPOETIC
MYTHOPOETICAL
MYTHOS
MYTHS
MYTHY

MYXAMEBA
MYXAMEBAE
MYXAMEBAS
MYXAMOEBA
MYXAMOEBAE
MYXAMOEBAS
MYXEDEMA
MYXEDEMAS
MYXEDEMATOUS
MYXEDEMIC
MYXOCYTE
MYXOCYTES
MYXOEDEMA
MYXOEDEMAS
MYXOID
MYXOMA
MYXOMAS
MYXOMATA
MYXOMATOSES
MYXOMATOSIS
MYXOMATOUS
MYXOMYCETE
MYXOMYCETES
MYXOVIRAL
MYXOVIRUS
MYXOVIRUSES

N

NA
NAAN
NAANS
NAB
NABBED
NABBER
NABBERS
NABBING
NABE
NABES
NABIS
NABOB
NABOBERIES
NABOBERY
NABOBESS
NABOBESSES
NABOBISH
NABOBISM
NABOBISMS
NABOBS
NABS
NACELLE
NACELLES
NACHAS
NACHES
NACHESES
NACHO
NACHOS
NACRE
NACRED
NACREOUS
NACRES
NADA
NADAS
NADIR
NADIRAL
NADIRS
NAE
NAES
NAETHING
NAETHINGS
NAEVI
NAEVOID
NAEVUS
NAFF
NAFFED
NAFFER
NAFFEST
NAFFING
NAFFNESS
NAFFNESSES
NAFFS
NAG
NAGA
NAGANA
NAGANAS
NAGAS
NAGGED
NAGGER
NAGGERS
NAGGIER
NAGGIEST
NAGGING
NAGGINGLY
NAGGINGS
NAGGY
NAGS
NAGWARE
NAGWARES
NAH
NAIAD
NAIADES
NAIADS
NAIF
NAIFS
NAIL
NAILBITER
NAILBITERS
NAILBRUSH
NAILBRUSHES
NAILED
NAILER
NAILERS
NAILFOLD
NAILFOLDS
NAILHEAD
NAILHEADS
NAILING
NAILLESS
NAILS
NAILSET
NAILSETS
NAINSOOK
NAINSOOKS
NAIRA
NAIRAS
NAIRU
NAIRUS
NAISSANCE
NAISSANCES
NAIVE
NAIVELY
NAIVENESS
NAIVENESSES
NAIVER
NAIVES
NAIVEST
NAIVETE
NAIVETES
NAIVETIES
NAIVETY
NAKED
NAKEDER
NAKEDEST
NAKEDLY
NAKEDNESS
NAKEDNESSES
NAKFA
NAKFAS
NALA
NALAS
NALED
NALEDS
NALORPHINE
NALORPHINES
NALOXONE
NALOXONES
NALTREXONE
NALTREXONES
NAM
NAMABLE
NAMAYCUSH
NAMAYCUSHES
NAME
NAMEABLE
NAMED
NAMELESS
NAMELESSLY
NAMELESSNESS
NAMELESSNESSES
NAMELY
NAMEPLATE
NAMEPLATES
NAMER
NAMERS
NAMES
NAMESAKE
NAMESAKES
NAMETAG
NAMETAGS
NAMETAPE
NAMETAPES
NAMING
NAN
NANA
NANAS
NANCE
NANCES
NANCIER
NANCIES
NANCIEST
NANCIFIED
NANCY
NANDIN
NANDINA
NANDINAS
NANDINS
NANDROLONE
NANDROLONES
NANISM
NANISMS
NANKEEN
NANKEENS
NANKIN
NANKINS
NANNA
NANNAS
NANNIE
NANNIED
NANNIES
NANNOPLANKTON
NANNOPLANKTONS
NANNY
NANNYING
NANNYISH

NANO
NANOBOT
NANOBOTS
NANOCRYSTAL
NANOCRYSTALLINE
NANOCRYSTALS
NANOGRAM
NANOGRAMS
NANOMACHINE
NANOMACHINES
NANOMETER
NANOMETERS
NANOMETRE
NANOMETRES
NANOPARTICLE
NANOPARTICLES
NANOPLANKTON
NANOPLANKTONS
NANOS
NANOSCALE
NANOSECOND
NANOSECONDS
NANOSTRUCTURE
NANOSTRUCTURED
NANOSTRUCTURES
NANOTECH
NANOTECHNOLOGY
NANOTECHS
NANOTESLA
NANOTESLAS
NANOTUBE
NANOTUBES
NANOWATT
NANOWATTS
NANS
NAOI
NAOS
NAP
NAPA
NAPALM
NAPALMED
NAPALMING
NAPALMS
NAPAS
NAPE
NAPERIES
NAPERY
NAPES
NAPHTHA
NAPHTHALENE
NAPHTHALENES
NAPHTHAS
NAPHTHENE
NAPHTHENES
NAPHTHENIC
NAPHTHOL
NAPHTHOLS
NAPHTHOUS
NAPHTHYL
NAPHTHYLAMINE
NAPHTHYLAMINES
NAPHTHYLS
NAPHTOL
NAPHTOLS
NAPIFORM
NAPKIN
NAPKINS
NAPLESS
NAPOLEON
NAPOLEONS
NAPPA
NAPPAS
NAPPE
NAPPED
NAPPER
NAPPERS
NAPPES
NAPPIE
NAPPIER
NAPPIES
NAPPIEST
NAPPINESS
NAPPINESSES
NAPPING
NAPPY
NAPRAPATHIES
NAPRAPATHY
NAPROXEN
NAPROXENS
NAPS
NARC
NARCEIN
NARCEINE
NARCEINES
NARCEINS
NARCISM
NARCISMS
NARCISSI
NARCISSISM
NARCISSISMS
NARCISSIST
NARCISSISTIC
NARCISSISTS
NARCISSUS
NARCISSUSES
NARCIST
NARCISTIC
NARCISTS
NARCO
NARCOLEPSIES
NARCOLEPSY
NARCOLEPTIC
NARCOLEPTICS
NARCOMA
NARCOMAS
NARCOMATA
NARCOS
NARCOSE
NARCOSES
NARCOSIS
NARCOTIC
NARCOTICALLY
NARCOTICS
NARCOTISM
NARCOTISMS
NARCOTIZE
NARCOTIZED
NARCOTIZES
NARCOTIZING
NARCS
NARD
NARDINE
NARDOO
NARDOOS
NARDS
NARES
NARGHILE
NARGHILES
NARGILE
NARGILEH
NARGILEHS
NARGILES
NARIAL
NARIC
NARINE
NARIS
NARK
NARKED
NARKIER
NARKIEST
NARKING
NARKS
NARKY
NARRATE
NARRATED
NARRATER
NARRATERS
NARRATES
NARRATING
NARRATION
NARRATIONAL
NARRATIONS
NARRATIVE
NARRATIVELY
NARRATIVES
NARRATOLOGICAL
NARRATOLOGIES
NARRATOLOGIST
NARRATOLOGISTS
NARRATOLOGY
NARRATOR
NARRATORS
NARROW
NARROWBAND
NARROWCASTING
NARROWCASTINGS
NARROWED
NARROWER
NARROWEST
NARROWING
NARROWISH
NARROWLY
NARROWNESS
NARROWNESSES
NARROWS
NARTHEX
NARTHEXES
NARWAL
NARWALS
NARWHAL
NARWHALE
NARWHALES
NARWHALS
NARY
NASAL
NASALISE
NASALISED
NASALISES
NASALISING
NASALISM
NASALISMS
NASALITIES
NASALITY
NASALIZATION
NASALIZATIONS
NASALIZE
NASALIZED
NASALIZES
NASALIZING
NASALLY
NASALS
NASCENCE
NASCENCES
NASCENCIES
NASCENCY
NASCENT
NASEBERRIES
NASEBERRY
NASIAL
NASION
NASIONS
NASOGASTRIC
NASOPHARYNGEAL
NASOPHARYNGES
NASOPHARYNX
NASOPHARYNXES
NASTIC
NASTIER
NASTIES
NASTIEST
NASTILY
NASTINESS
NASTINESSES
NASTURTIUM
NASTURTIUMS
NASTY
NATAL
NATALITIES
NATALITY
NATANT
NATANTLY
NATATION
NATATIONS
NATATORIA
NATATORIAL
NATATORIUM
NATATORIUMS
NATATORY
NATCH
NATES
NATHELESS
NATHLESS
NATION
NATIONAL
NATIONALISATION
NATIONALISE
NATIONALISED
NATIONALISES
NATIONALISING
NATIONALISM
NATIONALISMS
NATIONALIST
NATIONALISTIC
NATIONALISTS
NATIONALITIES

NATIONALITY
NATIONALIZATION
NATIONALIZE
NATIONALIZED
NATIONALIZER
NATIONALIZERS
NATIONALIZES
NATIONALIZING
NATIONALLY
NATIONALS
NATIONHOOD
NATIONHOODS
NATIONS
NATIONWIDE
NATIVE
NATIVELY
NATIVENESS
NATIVENESSES
NATIVES
NATIVISM
NATIVISMS
NATIVIST
NATIVISTIC
NATIVISTS
NATIVITIES
NATIVITY
NATRIUM
NATRIUMS
NATRIURESES
NATRIURESIS
NATRIURESISES
NATRIURETIC
NATRIURETICS
NATROLITE
NATROLITES
NATRON
NATRONS
NATTER
NATTERED
NATTERER
NATTERERS
NATTERING
NATTERS
NATTIER
NATTIEST
NATTILY
NATTINESS
NATTINESSES
NATTY
NATURAL
NATURALISATION
NATURALISATIONS
NATURALISE
NATURALISED
NATURALISES
NATURALISING
NATURALISM
NATURALISMS
NATURALIST
NATURALISTIC
NATURALISTS
NATURALIZATION
NATURALIZATIONS
NATURALIZE
NATURALIZED
NATURALIZES
NATURALIZING
NATURALLY
NATURALNESS
NATURALNESSES
NATURALS
NATURE
NATURED
NATURES
NATURISM
NATURISMS
NATURIST
NATURISTS
NATUROPATH
NATUROPATHIC
NATUROPATHIES
NATUROPATHS
NATUROPATHY
NAUGAHYDE
NAUGAHYDES
NAUGHT
NAUGHTIER
NAUGHTIES
NAUGHTIEST
NAUGHTILY
NAUGHTINESS
NAUGHTINESSES
NAUGHTS
NAUGHTY
NAUMACHIA
NAUMACHIAE
NAUMACHIAS
NAUMACHIES
NAUMACHY
NAUPLIAL
NAUPLII
NAUPLIUS
NAUSEA
NAUSEANT
NAUSEANTS
NAUSEAS
NAUSEATE
NAUSEATED
NAUSEATES
NAUSEATING
NAUSEATINGLY
NAUSEOUS
NAUSEOUSLY
NAUSEOUSNESS
NAUSEOUSNESSES
NAUTCH
NAUTCHES
NAUTICAL
NAUTICALLY
NAUTILI
NAUTILOID
NAUTILOIDS
NAUTILUS
NAUTILUSES
NAV
NAVAID
NAVAIDS
NAVAL
NAVALLY
NAVAR
NAVARIN
NAVARINS
NAVARS
NAVE
NAVEL
NAVELS
NAVELWORT
NAVELWORTS
NAVES
NAVETTE
NAVETTES
NAVICERT
NAVICERTS
NAVICULAR
NAVICULARS
NAVIES
NAVIGABILITIES
NAVIGABILITY
NAVIGABLE
NAVIGABLY
NAVIGATE
NAVIGATED
NAVIGATES
NAVIGATING
NAVIGATION
NAVIGATIONAL
NAVIGATIONALLY
NAVIGATIONS
NAVIGATOR
NAVIGATORS
NAVS
NAVVIES
NAVVY
NAVY
NAW
NAWAB
NAWABS
NAY
NAYS
NAYSAID
NAYSAY
NAYSAYER
NAYSAYERS
NAYSAYING
NAYSAYINGS
NAYSAYS
NAZI
NAZIFICATION
NAZIFICATIONS
NAZIFIED
NAZIFIES
NAZIFY
NAZIFYING
NAZIS
NE
NEAP
NEAPS
NEAR
NEARBY
NEARED
NEARER
NEAREST
NEARING
NEARISH
NEARLIER
NEARLIEST
NEARLY
NEARNESS
NEARNESSES
NEARS
NEARSHORE
NEARSIDE
NEARSIDES
NEARSIGHTED
NEARSIGHTEDLY
NEARSIGHTEDNESS
NEAT
NEATEN
NEATENED
NEATENING
NEATENS
NEATER
NEATEST
NEATH
NEATHERD
NEATHERDS
NEATLY
NEATNESS
NEATNESSES
NEATNIK
NEATNIKS
NEATS
NEB
NEBBISH
NEBBISHES
NEBBISHY
NEBENKERN
NEBENKERNS
NEBS
NEBULA
NEBULAE
NEBULAR
NEBULAS
NEBULE
NEBULISE
NEBULISED
NEBULISES
NEBULISING
NEBULIZATION
NEBULIZATIONS
NEBULIZE
NEBULIZED
NEBULIZER
NEBULIZERS
NEBULIZES
NEBULIZING
NEBULOSE
NEBULOSITIES
NEBULOSITY
NEBULOUS
NEBULOUSLY
NEBULOUSNESS
NEBULOUSNESSES
NEBULY
NECESSARIES
NECESSARILY
NECESSARY
NECESSITARIAN
NECESSITARIANS
NECESSITATE
NECESSITATED
NECESSITATES
NECESSITATING
NECESSITATION
NECESSITATIONS

NECESSITIES
NECESSITOUS
NECESSITOUSLY
NECESSITOUSNESS
NECESSITY
NECK
NECKBAND
NECKBANDS
NECKCLOTH
NECKCLOTHS
NECKED
NECKER
NECKERCHIEF
NECKERCHIEFS
NECKERCHIEVES
NECKERS
NECKING
NECKINGS
NECKLACE
NECKLACED
NECKLACES
NECKLACING
NECKLESS
NECKLET
NECKLETS
NECKLIKE
NECKLINE
NECKLINES
NECKPIECE
NECKPIECES
NECKS
NECKTIE
NECKTIES
NECKWEAR
NECROLOGICAL
NECROLOGIES
NECROLOGIST
NECROLOGISTS
NECROLOGY
NECROMANCER
NECROMANCERS
NECROMANCIES
NECROMANCY
NECROMANTIC
NECROMANTICALLY
NECROPHAGOUS
NECROPHILIA
NECROPHILIAC
NECROPHILIACS
NECROPHILIAS
NECROPHILIC
NECROPHILISM
NECROPHILISMS
NECROPOLEIS
NECROPOLES
NECROPOLI
NECROPOLIS
NECROPOLISES
NECROPSIED
NECROPSIES
NECROPSY
NECROPSYING
NECROSE
NECROSED
NECROSES
NECROSING
NECROSIS
NECROTIC
NECROTIZE
NECROTIZED
NECROTIZES
NECROTIZING
NECROTOMIES
NECROTOMY
NECTAR
NECTAREAN
NECTARIAL
NECTARIED
NECTARIES
NECTARINE
NECTARINES
NECTAROUS
NECTARS
NECTARY
NEDDIES
NEDDY
NEE
NEED
NEEDED
NEEDER
NEEDERS
NEEDFUL
NEEDFULLY
NEEDFULNESS
NEEDFULNESSES
NEEDFULS
NEEDIER
NEEDIEST
NEEDILY
NEEDINESS
NEEDINESSES
NEEDING
NEEDLE
NEEDLED
NEEDLEFISH
NEEDLEFISHES
NEEDLELIKE
NEEDLEPOINT
NEEDLEPOINTS
NEEDLER
NEEDLERS
NEEDLES
NEEDLESS
NEEDLESSLY
NEEDLESSNESS
NEEDLESSNESSES
NEEDLESTICK
NEEDLESTICKS
NEEDLEWOMAN
NEEDLEWOMEN
NEEDLEWORK
NEEDLEWORKER
NEEDLEWORKERS
NEEDLEWORKS
NEEDLING
NEEDLINGS
NEEDS
NEEDY
NEEM
NEEMS
NEEP
NEEPS
NEFARIOUS
NEFARIOUSLY
NEG
NEGATE
NEGATED
NEGATER
NEGATERS
NEGATES
NEGATING
NEGATION
NEGATIONAL
NEGATIONS
NEGATIVE
NEGATIVED
NEGATIVELY
NEGATIVENESS
NEGATIVENESSES
NEGATIVES
NEGATIVING
NEGATIVISM
NEGATIVISMS
NEGATIVIST
NEGATIVISTIC
NEGATIVISTS
NEGATIVITIES
NEGATIVITY
NEGATON
NEGATONS
NEGATOR
NEGATORS
NEGATORY
NEGATRON
NEGATRONS
NEGLECT
NEGLECTED
NEGLECTER
NEGLECTERS
NEGLECTFUL
NEGLECTFULLY
NEGLECTFULNESS
NEGLECTING
NEGLECTOR
NEGLECTORS
NEGLECTS
NEGLIGE
NEGLIGEE
NEGLIGEES
NEGLIGENCE
NEGLIGENCES
NEGLIGENT
NEGLIGENTLY
NEGLIGES
NEGLIGIBILITIES
NEGLIGIBILITY
NEGLIGIBLE
NEGLIGIBLY
NEGOTIABILITIES
NEGOTIABILITY
NEGOTIABLE
NEGOTIANT
NEGOTIANTS
NEGOTIATE
NEGOTIATED
NEGOTIATES
NEGOTIATING
NEGOTIATION
NEGOTIATIONS
NEGOTIATOR
NEGOTIATORS
NEGOTIATORY
NEGRITUDE
NEGRITUDES
NEGROID
NEGROIDS
NEGRONI
NEGRONIS
NEGROPHIL
NEGROPHILS
NEGROPHOBE
NEGROPHOBES
NEGROPHOBIA
NEGROPHOBIAS
NEGS
NEGUS
NEGUSES
NEIF
NEIFS
NEIGH
NEIGHBOR
NEIGHBORED
NEIGHBORHOOD
NEIGHBORHOODS
NEIGHBORING
NEIGHBORLINESS
NEIGHBORLY
NEIGHBORS
NEIGHBOUR
NEIGHBOURED
NEIGHBOURHOOD
NEIGHBOURHOODS
NEIGHBOURING
NEIGHBOURLY
NEIGHBOURS
NEIGHED
NEIGHING
NEIGHS
NEIST
NEITHER
NEKTON
NEKTONIC
NEKTONS
NELLIE
NELLIES
NELLY
NELSON
NELSONS
NELUMBIUM
NELUMBIUMS
NELUMBO
NELUMBOS
NEMA
NEMAS
NEMATIC
NEMATICIDAL
NEMATICIDE
NEMATICIDES
NEMATICS
NEMATOCIDAL
NEMATOCIDE
NEMATOCIDES
NEMATOCYST
NEMATOCYSTS
NEMATODE

NEMATODES
NEMATOLOGICAL
NEMATOLOGIES
NEMATOLOGIST
NEMATOLOGISTS
NEMATOLOGY
NEMERTEAN
NEMERTEANS
NEMERTINE
NEMERTINES
NEMESES
NEMESIA
NEMESIAS
NEMESIS
NEMOPHILA
NEMOPHILAS
NENE
NENES
NEOCLASSIC
NEOCLASSICAL
NEOCLASSICISM
NEOCLASSICISMS
NEOCLASSICIST
NEOCLASSICISTS
NEOCOLONIAL
NEOCOLONIALISM
NEOCOLONIALISMS
NEOCOLONIALIST
NEOCOLONIALISTS
NEOCON
NEOCONS
NEOCONSERVATISM
NEOCONSERVATIVE
NEOCORTEX
NEOCORTEXES
NEOCORTICAL
NEOCORTICES
NEODYMIUM
NEODYMIUMS
NEOGENE
NEOLIBERAL
NEOLIBERALISM
NEOLIBERALISMS
NEOLIBERALS
NEOLITH
NEOLITHIC
NEOLITHS
NEOLOGIC
NEOLOGIES
NEOLOGISM
NEOLOGISMS
NEOLOGIST
NEOLOGISTIC
NEOLOGISTS
NEOLOGIZE
NEOLOGIZED
NEOLOGIZES
NEOLOGIZING
NEOLOGY
NEOMORPH
NEOMORPHS
NEOMYCIN
NEOMYCINS
NEON
NEONATAL
NEONATALLY
NEONATE
NEONATES
NEONATOLOGIES
NEONATOLOGIST
NEONATOLOGISTS
NEONATOLOGY
NEONED
NEONS
NEOORTHODOX
NEOORTHODOXIES
NEOORTHODOXY
NEOPAGAN
NEOPAGANS
NEOPHILIA
NEOPHILIAC
NEOPHILIACS
NEOPHILIAS
NEOPHYTE
NEOPHYTES
NEOPHYTIC
NEOPLASIA
NEOPLASIAS
NEOPLASM
NEOPLASMS
NEOPLASTIC
NEOPLASTICISM
NEOPLASTICISMS
NEOPLASTICIST
NEOPLASTICISTS
NEOPLASTIES
NEOPLASTY
NEOPRENE
NEOPRENES
NEOREALISM
NEOREALISMS
NEOREALIST
NEOREALISTIC
NEOREALISTS
NEOSCHOLASTIC
NEOSTIGMINE
NEOSTIGMINES
NEOTENIC
NEOTENIES
NEOTENOUS
NEOTENY
NEOTERIC
NEOTERICS
NEOTROPIC
NEOTROPICAL
NEOTROPICS
NEOTYPE
NEOTYPES
NEPENTHE
NEPENTHEAN
NEPENTHES
NEPETA
NEPETAS
NEPHELINE
NEPHELINES
NEPHELINIC
NEPHELINITE
NEPHELINITES
NEPHELINITIC
NEPHELITE
NEPHELITES
NEPHELOMETER
NEPHELOMETERS
NEPHELOMETRIC
NEPHELOMETRIES
NEPHELOMETRY
NEPHEW
NEPHEWS
NEPHOGRAM
NEPHOGRAMS
NEPHOLOGIES
NEPHOLOGY
NEPHOSCOPE
NEPHOSCOPES
NEPHRECTOMIES
NEPHRECTOMIZE
NEPHRECTOMIZED
NEPHRECTOMIZES
NEPHRECTOMIZING
NEPHRECTOMY
NEPHRIC
NEPHRIDIA
NEPHRIDIAL
NEPHRIDIUM
NEPHRISM
NEPHRISMS
NEPHRITE
NEPHRITES
NEPHRITIC
NEPHRITIDES
NEPHRITIS
NEPHRITISES
NEPHROLOGIES
NEPHROLOGIST
NEPHROLOGISTS
NEPHROLOGY
NEPHRON
NEPHRONS
NEPHROPATHIC
NEPHROPATHIES
NEPHROPATHY
NEPHROSES
NEPHROSIS
NEPHROSTOME
NEPHROSTOMES
NEPHROTIC
NEPHROTICS
NEPHROTOXIC
NEPHROTOXICITY
NEPOTIC
NEPOTISM
NEPOTISMS
NEPOTIST
NEPOTISTIC
NEPOTISTS
NEPTUNIUM
NEPTUNIUMS
NERD
NERDIER
NERDIEST
NERDINESS
NERDINESSES
NERDISH
NERDS
NERDY
NEREID
NEREIDES
NEREIDS
NEREIS
NERITIC
NEROL
NEROLI
NEROLIS
NEROLS
NERTS
NERTZ
NERVATE
NERVATION
NERVATIONS
NERVATURE
NERVATURES
NERVE
NERVED
NERVELESS
NERVELESSLY
NERVELESSNESS
NERVELESSNESSES
NERVES
NERVIER
NERVIEST
NERVILY
NERVINE
NERVINES
NERVINESS
NERVINESSES
NERVING
NERVINGS
NERVOSITIES
NERVOSITY
NERVOUS
NERVOUSLY
NERVOUSNESS
NERVOUSNESSES
NERVULE
NERVULES
NERVURE
NERVURES
NERVY
NESCIENCE
NESCIENCES
NESCIENT
NESCIENTS
NESS
NESSES
NEST
NESTABLE
NESTED
NESTER
NESTERS
NESTFUL
NESTFULS
NESTING
NESTLE
NESTLED
NESTLER
NESTLERS
NESTLES
NESTLIKE
NESTLING
NESTLINGS
NESTMATE
NESTMATES
NESTOR
NESTORS
NESTS

NET
NETBALL
NETBALLS
NETBOOK
NETBOOKS
NETFUL
NETFULS
NETHER
NETHERMOST
NETHERWORLD
NETHERWORLDS
NETIQUETTE
NETIQUETTES
NETIZEN
NETIZENS
NETLESS
NETLIKE
NETMINDER
NETMINDERS
NETOP
NETOPS
NETROOTS
NETS
NETSUKE
NETSUKES
NETSURF
NETSURFED
NETSURFING
NETSURFS
NETT
NETTABLE
NETTED
NETTER
NETTERS
NETTIER
NETTIEST
NETTING
NETTINGS
NETTLE
NETTLED
NETTLER
NETTLERS
NETTLES
NETTLESOME
NETTLIER
NETTLIEST
NETTLING
NETTLY
NETTS
NETTY
NETWORK
NETWORKED
NETWORKER
NETWORKERS
NETWORKING
NETWORKINGS
NETWORKS
NEUK
NEUKS
NEUM
NEUMATIC
NEUME
NEUMES
NEUMIC
NEUMS
NEURAL
NEURALGIA
NEURALGIAS
NEURALGIC
NEURALLY
NEURAMINIDASE
NEURAMINIDASES
NEURASTHENIA
NEURASTHENIAS
NEURASTHENIC
NEURASTHENICS
NEURAXON
NEURAXONS
NEURILEMMA
NEURILEMMAL
NEURILEMMAS
NEURINE
NEURINES
NEURITIC
NEURITICS
NEURITIDES
NEURITIS
NEURITISES
NEUROACTIVE
NEUROANATOMIC
NEUROANATOMICAL
NEUROANATOMIES
NEUROANATOMIST
NEUROANATOMISTS
NEUROANATOMY
NEUROBIOLOGICAL
NEUROBIOLOGIES
NEUROBIOLOGIST
NEUROBIOLOGISTS
NEUROBIOLOGY
NEUROBLASTOMA
NEUROBLASTOMAS
NEUROBLASTOMATA
NEUROCHEMICAL
NEUROCHEMICALS
NEUROCHEMIST
NEUROCHEMISTRY
NEUROCHEMISTS
NEUROCOEL
NEUROCOELS
NEUROENDOCRINE
NEUROFIBRIL
NEUROFIBRILLARY
NEUROFIBRILS
NEUROFIBROMA
NEUROFIBROMAS
NEUROFIBROMATA
NEUROGENIC
NEUROGENICALLY
NEUROGLIA
NEUROGLIAL
NEUROGLIAS
NEUROHORMONAL
NEUROHORMONE
NEUROHORMONES
NEUROHUMOR
NEUROHUMORAL
NEUROHUMORS
NEUROHYPOPHYSES
NEUROHYPOPHYSIS
NEUROID
NEUROIMAGING
NEUROIMAGINGS
NEUROLEPTIC
NEUROLEPTICS
NEUROLOGIC
NEUROLOGICAL
NEUROLOGICALLY
NEUROLOGIES
NEUROLOGIST
NEUROLOGISTS
NEUROLOGY
NEUROMA
NEUROMAS
NEUROMAST
NEUROMASTS
NEUROMATA
NEUROMUSCULAR
NEURON
NEURONAL
NEURONE
NEURONES
NEURONIC
NEURONS
NEUROPATH
NEUROPATHIC
NEUROPATHICALLY
NEUROPATHIES
NEUROPATHOLOGIC
NEUROPATHOLOGY
NEUROPATHS
NEUROPATHY
NEUROPEPTIDE
NEUROPEPTIDES
NEUROPHYSIOLOGY
NEUROPLASTICITY
NEUROPROTECTIVE
NEUROPSYCHIATRY
NEUROPSYCHOLOGY
NEUROPTERAN
NEUROPTERANS
NEUROPTEROUS
NEURORADIOLOGY
NEUROSAL
NEUROSCIENCE
NEUROSCIENCES
NEUROSCIENTIFIC
NEUROSCIENTIST
NEUROSCIENTISTS
NEUROSECRETION
NEUROSECRETIONS
NEUROSECRETORY
NEUROSENSORY
NEUROSES
NEUROSIS
NEUROSPORA
NEUROSPORAS
NEUROSURGEON
NEUROSURGEONS
NEUROSURGERIES
NEUROSURGERY
NEUROSURGICAL
NEUROTIC
NEUROTICALLY
NEUROTICISM
NEUROTICISMS
NEUROTICS
NEUROTOMIES
NEUROTOMY
NEUROTOXIC
NEUROTOXICITIES
NEUROTOXICITY
NEUROTOXIN
NEUROTOXINS
NEUROTROPIC
NEURULA
NEURULAE
NEURULAR
NEURULAS
NEURULATION
NEURULATIONS
NEUSTIC
NEUSTON
NEUSTONIC
NEUSTONS
NEUTER
NEUTERED
NEUTERING
NEUTERS
NEUTRAL
NEUTRALISATION
NEUTRALISATIONS
NEUTRALISE
NEUTRALISED
NEUTRALISES
NEUTRALISING
NEUTRALISM
NEUTRALISMS
NEUTRALIST
NEUTRALISTIC
NEUTRALISTS
NEUTRALITIES
NEUTRALITY
NEUTRALIZATION
NEUTRALIZATIONS
NEUTRALIZE
NEUTRALIZED
NEUTRALIZER
NEUTRALIZERS
NEUTRALIZES
NEUTRALIZING
NEUTRALLY
NEUTRALNESS
NEUTRALNESSES
NEUTRALS
NEUTRINO
NEUTRINOLESS
NEUTRINOS
NEUTRON
NEUTRONIC
NEUTRONS
NEUTROPENIA
NEUTROPENIAS
NEUTROPENIC
NEUTROPHIL
NEUTROPHILIC
NEUTROPHILS
NEVE
NEVER
NEVERMIND
NEVERMINDS
NEVERMORE
NEVERTHELESS
NEVES
NEVI

NEVIRAPINE
NEVIRAPINES
NEVOID
NEVUS
NEW
NEWB
NEWBIE
NEWBIES
NEWBORN
NEWBORNS
NEWBS
NEWCOMER
NEWCOMERS
NEWEL
NEWELS
NEWER
NEWEST
NEWFANGLED
NEWFANGLEDNESS
NEWFOUND
NEWIE
NEWIES
NEWISH
NEWLY
NEWLYWED
NEWLYWEDS
NEWMARKET
NEWMARKETS
NEWMOWN
NEWNESS
NEWNESSES
NEWS
NEWSAGENT
NEWSAGENTS
NEWSBEAT
NEWSBEATS
NEWSBOY
NEWSBOYS
NEWSBREAK
NEWSBREAKS
NEWSCAST
NEWSCASTER
NEWSCASTERS
NEWSCASTS
NEWSDEALER
NEWSDEALERS
NEWSDESK
NEWSDESKS
EWSFEED
EWSFEEDS
EWSGIRL
EWSGIRLS
EWSGROUP
NEWSGROUPS
NEWSHAWK
NEWSHAWKS
NEWSHOUND
NEWSHOUNDS
NEWSIE
NEWSIER
NEWSIES
NEWSIEST
NEWSINESS
NEWSINESSES
NEWSLESS
NEWSLETTER
NEWSLETTERS
NEWSMAGAZINE
NEWSMAGAZINES
NEWSMAKER
NEWSMAKERS
NEWSMAN
NEWSMEN
NEWSMONGER
NEWSMONGERS
NEWSPAPER
NEWSPAPERED
NEWSPAPERING
NEWSPAPERMAN
NEWSPAPERMEN
NEWSPAPERS
NEWSPAPERWOMAN
NEWSPAPERWOMEN
NEWSPEAK
NEWSPEAKS
NEWSPEOPLE
NEWSPERSON
NEWSPERSONS
NEWSPRINT
NEWSPRINTS
NEWSREADER
NEWSREADERS
NEWSREEL
NEWSREELS
NEWSROOM
NEWSROOMS
NEWSSTAND
NEWSSTANDS
NEWSWEEKLIES
NEWSWEEKLY
NEWSWIRE
NEWSWIRES
NEWSWOMAN
NEWSWOMEN
NEWSWORTHIER
NEWSWORTHIEST
NEWSWORTHINESS
NEWSWORTHY
NEWSWRITING
NEWSWRITINGS
NEWSY
NEWT
NEWTON
NEWTONS
NEWTS
NEWWAVER
NEWWAVERS
NEXT
NEXTDOOR
NEXTS
NEXUS
NEXUSES
NGULTRUM
NGULTRUMS
NGWEE
NGWEES
NIACIN
NIACINAMIDE
NIACINAMIDES
NIACINS
NIAGARA
NIAGARAS
NIALAMIDE
NIALAMIDES
NIB
NIBBED
NIBBING
NIBBLE
NIBBLED
NIBBLER
NIBBLERS
NIBBLES
NIBBLIES
NIBBLING
NIBBLY
NIBLICK
NIBLICKS
NIBLIKE
NIBS
NICAD
NICADS
NICCOLITE
NICCOLITES
NICE
NICELY
NICENESS
NICENESSES
NICER
NICEST
NICETIES
NICETY
NICHE
NICHED
NICHES
NICHING
NICHROME
NICHROMES
NICK
NICKED
NICKEL
NICKELED
NICKELIC
NICKELIFEROUS
NICKELING
NICKELLED
NICKELLING
NICKELODEON
NICKELODEONS
NICKELOUS
NICKELS
NICKER
NICKERED
NICKERING
NICKERS
NICKING
NICKLE
NICKLED
NICKLES
NICKLING
NICKNACK
NICKNACKS
NICKNAME
NICKNAMED
NICKNAMER
NICKNAMERS
NICKNAMES
NICKNAMING
NICKS
NICOISE
NICOL
NICOLS
NICOTIANA
NICOTIANAS
NICOTIN
NICOTINAMIDE
NICOTINAMIDES
NICOTINE
NICOTINES
NICOTINIC
NICOTINS
NICTATE
NICTATED
NICTATES
NICTATING
NICTATION
NICTATIONS
NICTITANT
NICTITATE
NICTITATED
NICTITATES
NICTITATING
NIDAL
NIDATE
NIDATED
NIDATES
NIDATING
NIDATION
NIDATIONS
NIDDERING
NIDDERINGS
NIDE
NIDED
NIDERING
NIDERINGS
NIDES
NIDGET
NIDGETS
NIDI
NIDICOLOUS
NIDIFICATION
NIDIFICATIONS
NIDIFIED
NIDIFIES
NIDIFUGOUS
NIDIFY
NIDIFYING
NIDING
NIDUS
NIDUSES
NIECE
NIECES
NIELLI
NIELLIST
NIELLISTS
NIELLO
NIELLOED
NIELLOING
NIELLOS
NIENTE
NIEVE
NIEVES
NIFEDIPINE
NIFEDIPINES
NIFF
NIFFED

NIFFER
NIFFERED
NIFFERING
NIFFERS
NIFFIER
NIFFIEST
NIFFING
NIFFS
NIFFY
NIFTIER
NIFTIES
NIFTIEST
NIFTILY
NIFTINESS
NIFTINESSES
NIFTY
NIGELLA
NIGELLAS
NIGGARD
NIGGARDED
NIGGARDING
NIGGARDLINESS
NIGGARDLINESSES
NIGGARDLY
NIGGARDS
NIGGER
NIGGERS
NIGGLE
NIGGLED
NIGGLER
NIGGLERS
NIGGLES
NIGGLIER
NIGGLIEST
NIGGLING
NIGGLINGLY
NIGGLINGS
NIGGLY
NIGH
NIGHED
NIGHER
NIGHEST
NIGHING
NIGHNESS
NIGHNESSES
NIGHS
NIGHT
NIGHTCAP
NIGHTCAPS
NIGHTCLOTHES
NIGHTCLUB
NIGHTCLUBBED
NIGHTCLUBBER
NIGHTCLUBBERS
NIGHTCLUBBING
NIGHTCLUBS
NIGHTDRESS
NIGHTDRESSES
NIGHTFALL
NIGHTFALLS
NIGHTGLOW
NIGHTGLOWS
NIGHTGOWN
NIGHTGOWNS
NIGHTHAWK
NIGHTHAWKS
NIGHTIE
NIGHTIES
NIGHTINGALE
NIGHTINGALES
NIGHTJAR
NIGHTJARS
NIGHTLESS
NIGHTLIFE
NIGHTLIFES
NIGHTLIGHT
NIGHTLIGHTS
NIGHTLIVES
NIGHTLONG
NIGHTLY
NIGHTMARE
NIGHTMARES
NIGHTMARISH
NIGHTMARISHLY
NIGHTS
NIGHTSCOPE
NIGHTSCOPES
NIGHTSHADE
NIGHTSHADES
NIGHTSHIRT
NIGHTSHIRTS
NIGHTSIDE
NIGHTSIDES
NIGHTSPOT
NIGHTSPOTS
NIGHTSTAND
NIGHTSTANDS
NIGHTSTICK
NIGHTSTICKS
NIGHTTIDE
NIGHTTIDES
NIGHTTIME
NIGHTTIMES
NIGHTWALKER
NIGHTWALKERS
NIGHTWEAR
NIGHTY
NIGRIFIED
NIGRIFIES
NIGRIFY
NIGRIFYING
NIGRITUDE
NIGRITUDES
NIGROSIN
NIGROSINE
NIGROSINES
NIGROSINS
NIHIL
NIHILISM
NIHILISMS
NIHILIST
NIHILISTIC
NIHILISTS
NIHILITIES
NIHILITY
NIHILS
NIKAH
NIKAHS
NIL
NILGAI
NILGAIS
NILGAU
NILGAUS
NILGHAI
NILGHAIS
NILGHAU
NILGHAUS
NILL
NILLED
NILLING
NILLS
NILPOTENT
NILPOTENTS
NILS
NIM
NIMBI
NIMBLE
NIMBLENESS
NIMBLENESSES
NIMBLER
NIMBLEST
NIMBLY
NIMBOSTRATI
NIMBOSTRATUS
NIMBUS
NIMBUSED
NIMBUSES
NIMBYNESS
NIMBYNESSES
NIMIETIES
NIMIETY
NIMIOUS
NIMMED
NIMMING
NIMROD
NIMRODS
NIMS
NINCOMPOOP
NINCOMPOOPERIES
NINCOMPOOPERY
NINCOMPOOPS
NINE
NINEBARK
NINEBARKS
NINEFOLD
NINEPIN
NINEPINS
NINER
NINERS
NINES
NINETEEN
NINETEENS
NINETEENTH
NINETEENTHS
NINETIES
NINETIETH
NINETIETHS
NINETY
NINHYDRIN
NINHYDRINS
NINJA
NINJAS
NINJUTSU
NINJUTSUS
NINNIES
NINNY
NINNYHAMMER
NINNYHAMMERS
NINNYISH
NINON
NINONS
NINTH
NINTHLY
NINTHS
NIOBATE
NIOBATES
NIOBIC
NIOBITE
NIOBITES
NIOBIUM
NIOBIUMS
NIOBOUS
NIP
NIPA
NIPAS
NIPPED
NIPPER
NIPPERS
NIPPIER
NIPPIEST
NIPPILY
NIPPINESS
NIPPINESSES
NIPPING
NIPPINGLY
NIPPLE
NIPPLED
NIPPLES
NIPPY
NIPS
NIQAAB
NIQAABS
NIQAB
NIQABS
NIRVANA
NIRVANAS
NIRVANIC
NISEI
NISEIS
NISI
NISUS
NIT
NITCHIE
NITCHIES
NITE
NITER
NITERIE
NITERIES
NITERS
NITERY
NITES
NITID
NITINOL
NITINOLS
NITON
NITONS
NITPICK
NITPICKED
NITPICKER
NITPICKERS
NITPICKIER
NITPICKIEST
NITPICKING
NITPICKS
NITPICKY

NITRATE
NITRATED
NITRATES
NITRATING
NITRATION
NITRATIONS
NITRATOR
NITRATORS
NITRE
NITRES
NITRIC
NITRID
NITRIDE
NITRIDED
NITRIDES
NITRIDING
NITRIDS
NITRIFICATION
NITRIFICATIONS
NITRIFIED
NITRIFIER
NITRIFIERS
NITRIFIES
NITRIFY
NITRIFYING
NITRIL
NITRILE
NITRILES
NITRILS
NITRITE
NITRITES
NITRO
NITROBENZENE
NITROBENZENES
NITROCELLULOSE
NITROCELLULOSES
NITROFURAN
NITROFURANS
NITROGEN
NITROGENASE
NITROGENASES
NITROGENOUS
NITROGENS
NITROGLYCERIN
NITROGLYCERINE
NITROGLYCERINES
NITROGLYCERINS
NITROLIC
NITROMETHANE
NITROMETHANES
NITROPARAFFIN
NITROPARAFFINS
NITROS
NITROSAMINE
NITROSAMINES
NITROSO
NITROSYL
NITROSYLS
NITROUS
NITS
NITTIER
NITTIEST
NITTY
NITWIT
NITWITS
NITWITTED
NIVAL
NIVEOUS
NIX
NIXE
NIXED
NIXES
NIXIE
NIXIES
NIXING
NIXY
NIZAM
NIZAMATE
NIZAMATES
NIZAMS
NO
NOB
NOBBIER
NOBBIEST
NOBBILY
NOBBLE
NOBBLED
NOBBLER
NOBBLERS
NOBBLES
NOBBLING
NOBBY
NOBELIUM
NOBELIUMS
NOBILIARY
NOBILITIES
NOBILITY
NOBLE
NOBLEMAN
NOBLEMEN
NOBLENESS
NOBLENESSES
NOBLER
NOBLES
NOBLESSE
NOBLESSES
NOBLEST
NOBLEWOMAN
NOBLEWOMEN
NOBLY
NOBODIES
NOBODY
NOBS
NOCEBO
NOCEBOS
NOCENT
NOCICEPTIVE
NOCICEPTOR
NOCICEPTORS
NOCK
NOCKED
NOCKING
NOCKS
NOCTAMBULIST
NOCTAMBULISTS
NOCTILUCA
NOCTILUCAS
NOCTUID
NOCTUIDS
NOCTULE
NOCTULES
NOCTUOID
NOCTURN
NOCTURNAL
NOCTURNALLY
NOCTURNE
NOCTURNES
NOCTURNS
NOCUOUS
NOCUOUSLY
NOD
NODAL
NODALITIES
NODALITY
NODALLY
NODDED
NODDER
NODDERS
NODDIES
NODDING
NODDINGLY
NODDLE
NODDLED
NODDLES
NODDLING
NODDY
NODE
NODES
NODI
NODICAL
NODOSE
NODOSITIES
NODOSITY
NODOUS
NODS
NODULAR
NODULATION
NODULATIONS
NODULE
NODULES
NODULOSE
NODULOUS
NODUS
NOEL
NOELS
NOES
NOESIS
NOESISES
NOETIC
NOG
NOGG
NOGGED
NOGGIN
NOGGING
NOGGINGS
NOGGINS
NOGGS
NOGS
NOH
NOHOW
NOIL
NOILS
NOILY
NOIR
NOIRISH
NOIRS
NOISE
NOISED
NOISELESS
NOISELESSLY
NOISEMAKER
NOISEMAKERS
NOISEMAKING
NOISEMAKINGS
NOISES
NOISETTE
NOISETTES
NOISIER
NOISIEST
NOISILY
NOISINESS
NOISINESSES
NOISING
NOISOME
NOISOMELY
NOISOMENESS
NOISOMENESSES
NOISY
NOLO
NOLOS
NOM
NOMA
NOMAD
NOMADIC
NOMADISM
NOMADISMS
NOMADS
NOMARCH
NOMARCHIES
NOMARCHS
NOMARCHY
NOMAS
NOMBLES
NOMBRIL
NOMBRILS
NOME
NOMEN
NOMENCLATOR
NOMENCLATORIAL
NOMENCLATORS
NOMENCLATURAL
NOMENCLATURE
NOMENCLATURES
NOMENS
NOMES
NOMINA
NOMINAL
NOMINALISM
NOMINALISMS
NOMINALIST
NOMINALISTIC
NOMINALISTS
NOMINALLY
NOMINALS
NOMINATABLE
NOMINATE
NOMINATED
NOMINATES
NOMINATING
NOMINATION
NOMINATIONS
NOMINATIVE
NOMINATIVES
NOMINATOR
NOMINATORS

NOMINEE
NOMINEES
NOMISM
NOMISMS
NOMISTIC
NOMOGRAM
NOMOGRAMS
NOMOGRAPH
NOMOGRAPHIC
NOMOGRAPHIES
NOMOGRAPHS
NOMOGRAPHY
NOMOI
NOMOLOGIC
NOMOLOGICAL
NOMOLOGIES
NOMOLOGY
NOMOS
NOMOTHETIC
NOMS
NONA
NONABRASIVE
NONABRASIVES
NONABSORBABLE
NONABSORBENT
NONABSORPTIVE
NONABSTRACT
NONACADEMIC
NONACADEMICS
NONACCEPTANCE
NONACCEPTANCES
NONACCOUNTABLE
NONACCREDITED
NONACCRUAL
NONACCRUALS
NONACHIEVEMENT
NONACHIEVEMENTS
NONACID
NONACIDIC
NONACIDS
NONACQUISITIVE
NONACTING
NONACTION
NONACTIONS
NONACTIVATED
NONACTIVE
NONACTOR
NONACTORS
NONADAPTIVE
NONADDICT
NONADDICTIVE
NONADDICTS
NONADDITIVE
NONADDITIVES
NONADDITIVITIES
NONADDITIVITY
NONADHESIVE
NONADIABATIC
NONADJACENT
NONADMIRER
NONADMIRERS
NONADMISSION
NONADMISSIONS
NONADULT
NONADULTS
NONAEROSOL
NONAEROSOLS
NONAESTHETIC
NONAESTHETICS
NONAFFILIATED
NONAFFLUENT
NONAGE
NONAGENARIAN
NONAGENARIANS
NONAGES
NONAGGRESSION
NONAGGRESSIONS
NONAGGRESSIVE
NONAGON
NONAGONAL
NONAGONS
NONAGRICULTURAL
NONALCOHOLIC
NONALCOHOLICS
NONALIGNED
NONALIGNMENT
NONALIGNMENTS
NONALLELIC
NONALLERGENIC
NONALLERGIC
NONALPHABETIC
NONALUMINUM
NONAMBIGUOUS
NONANALYTIC
NONANALYTICS
NONANATOMIC
NONANE
NONANES
NONANIMAL
NONANSWER
NONANSWERS
NONANTAGONISTIC
NONANTIBIOTIC
NONANTIBIOTICS
NONANTIGENIC
NONAPPEARANCE
NONAPPEARANCES
NONAQUATIC
NONAQUEOUS
NONARABLE
NONARBITRARY
NONARCHITECT
NONARCHITECTS
NONARCHITECTURE
NONARGUMENT
NONARGUMENTS
NONARIES
NONARISTOCRATIC
NONAROMATIC
NONAROMATICS
NONART
NONARTIST
NONARTISTIC
NONARTISTS
NONARTS
NONARY
NONAS
NONASCETIC
NONASPIRIN
NONASSERTIVE
NONASSOCIATED
NONASTRONOMICAL
NONATHLETE
NONATHLETES
NONATHLETIC
NONATHLETICS
NONATOMIC
NONATTACHED
NONATTACHMENT
NONATTACHMENTS
NONATTENDANCE
NONATTENDANCES
NONATTENDER
NONATTENDERS
NONAUDITORY
NONAUTHOR
NONAUTHORS
NONAUTOMATED
NONAUTOMATIC
NONAUTOMOTIVE
NONAUTONOMOUS
NONAVAILABILITY
NONBACTERIAL
NONBANK
NONBANKING
NONBANKS
NONBARBITURATE
NONBARBITURATES
NONBARYONIC
NONBASIC
NONBEARING
NONBEHAVIORAL
NONBEING
NONBEINGS
NONBELIEF
NONBELIEFS
NONBELIEVER
NONBELIEVERS
NONBELLIGERENCY
NONBELLIGERENT
NONBELLIGERENTS
NONBETTING
NONBIBLICAL
NONBINARIES
NONBINARY
NONBINDING
NONBIOGRAPHICAL
NONBIOLOGICAL
NONBIOLOGICALLY
NONBIOLOGIST
NONBIOLOGISTS
NONBITING
NONBLACK
NONBLACKS
NONBODIES
NONBODY
NONBONDED
NONBONDING
NONBOOK
NONBOOKS
NONBOTANIST
NONBOTANISTS
NONBRAND
NONBREAKABLE
NONBREAKABLES
NONBREATHING
NONBREEDER
NONBREEDERS
NONBREEDING
NONBROADCAST
NONBROADCASTS
NONBUILDING
NONBUILDINGS
NONBURNABLE
NONBUSINESS
NONBUSINESSES
NONBUYING
NONCABINET
NONCAKING
NONCALLABLE
NONCALORIC
NONCAMPUS
NONCANCELABLE
NONCANCEROUS
NONCANDIDACIES
NONCANDIDACY
NONCANDIDATE
NONCANDIDATES
NONCANONICAL
NONCAPITAL
NONCAPITALIST
NONCAPITALISTS
NONCAPITALS
NONCARCINOGEN
NONCARCINOGENIC
NONCARCINOGENS
NONCARDIAC
NONCAREER
NONCARRIER
NONCARRIERS
NONCASH
NONCASUAL
NONCAUSAL
NONCE
NONCELEBRATION
NONCELEBRATIONS
NONCELEBRITIES
NONCELEBRITY
NONCELLULAR
NONCELLULOSIC
NONCENTRAL
NONCEREAL
NONCERTIFICATED
NONCERTIFIED
NONCES
NONCHALANCE
NONCHALANCES
NONCHALANT
NONCHALANTLY
NONCHARACTER
NONCHARACTERS
NONCHARISMATIC
NONCHARISMATICS
NONCHAUVINIST
NONCHAUVINISTS
NONCHEMICAL
NONCHEMICALS
NONCHROMOSOMAL
NONCHURCH
NONCHURCHGOER
NONCHURCHGOERS
NONCIRCULAR
NONCIRCULATING
NONCITIZEN
NONCITIZENS

NONCLANDESTINE
NONCLASS
NONCLASSES
NONCLASSICAL
NONCLASSIFIED
NONCLASSIFIEDS
NONCLASSROOM
NONCLASSROOMS
NONCLERICAL
NONCLING
NONCLINICAL
NONCLOGGING
NONCODING
NONCOERCIVE
NONCOGNITIVE
NONCOHERENT
NONCOINCIDENCE
NONCOINCIDENCES
NONCOITAL
NONCOKING
NONCOLA
NONCOLAS
NONCOLLECTOR
NONCOLLECTORS
NONCOLLEGE
NONCOLLEGES
NONCOLLEGIATE
NONCOLLINEAR
NONCOLOR
NONCOLORED
NONCOLOREDS
NONCOLORFAST
NONCOLORS
NONCOM
NONCOMBAT
NONCOMBATANT
NONCOMBATANTS
NONCOMBATIVE
NONCOMBATS
NONCOMBUSTIBLE
NONCOMBUSTIBLES
NONCOMEDOGENIC
NONCOMMERCIAL
NONCOMMISSIONED
NONCOMMITMENT
NONCOMMITMENTS
NONCOMMITTAL
NONCOMMITTALLY
NONCOMMITTALS
NONCOMMITTED
NONCOMMUNIST
NONCOMMUNISTS
NONCOMMUNITIES
NONCOMMUNITY
NONCOMMUTATIVE
NONCOMPARABLE
NONCOMPATIBLE
NONCOMPETITION
NONCOMPETITIONS
NONCOMPETITIVE
NONCOMPETITOR
NONCOMPETITORS
NONCOMPLEX
NONCOMPLIANCE
NONCOMPLIANCES
NONCOMPLIANT
NONCOMPLICATED
NONCOMPLYING
NONCOMPOSER
NONCOMPOSERS
NONCOMPOUND
NONCOMPOUNDS
NONCOMPRESSIBLE
NONCOMPUTER
NONCOMPUTERIZED
NONCOMPUTERS
NONCOMS
NONCONCEPTUAL
NONCONCERN
NONCONCERNS
NONCONCLUSION
NONCONCLUSIONS
NONCONCUR
NONCONCURRED
NONCONCURRENCE
NONCONCURRENCES
NONCONCURRENT
NONCONCURRING
NONCONCURS
NONCONDENSABLE
NONCONDITIONED
NONCONDUCTING
NONCONDUCTION
NONCONDUCTIONS
NONCONDUCTIVE
NONCONDUCTOR
NONCONDUCTORS
NONCONFERENCE
NONCONFERENCES
NONCONFIDENCE
NONCONFIDENCES
NONCONFIDENTIAL
NONCONFLICTING
NONCONFORM
NONCONFORMANCE
NONCONFORMANCES
NONCONFORMED
NONCONFORMER
NONCONFORMERS
NONCONFORMING
NONCONFORMISM
NONCONFORMISMS
NONCONFORMIST
NONCONFORMISTS
NONCONFORMITIES
NONCONFORMITY
NONCONFORMS
NONCONGRUENT
NONCONJUGATED
NONCONNECTION
NONCONNECTIONS
NONCONSCIOUS
NONCONSECUTIVE
NONCONSENSUAL
NONCONSERVATION
NONCONSERVATIVE
NONCONSOLIDATED
NONCONSTANT
NONCONSTANTS
NONCONSTRUCTION
NONCONSTRUCTIVE
NONCONSUMER
NONCONSUMERS
NONCONSUMING
NONCONSUMPTION
NONCONSUMPTIONS
NONCONSUMPTIVE
NONCONTACT
NONCONTACTS
NONCONTAGIOUS
NONCONTEMPORARY
NONCONTIGUOUS
NONCONTINGENT
NONCONTINUOUS
NONCONTRACT
NONCONTRACTS
NONCONTRACTUAL
NONCONTRIBUTORY
NONCONTROLLABLE
NONCONTROLLED
NONCONTROLLING
NONCONVENTIONAL
NONCONVERTIBLE
NONCONVERTIBLES
NONCOOPERATION
NONCOOPERATIONS
NONCOOPERATIVE
NONCOOPERATIVES
NONCOOPERATOR
NONCOOPERATORS
NONCOPLANAR
NONCORE
NONCORPORATE
NONCORRELATION
NONCORRELATIONS
NONCORRODIBLE
NONCORRODING
NONCORROSIVE
NONCORROSIVES
NONCOUNT
NONCOUNTRIES
NONCOUNTRY
NONCOUNTY
NONCOVERAGE
NONCOVERAGES
NONCREATIVE
NONCREATIVITIES
NONCREATIVITY
NONCREDENTIALED
NONCREDIT
NONCRIME
NONCRIMES
NONCRIMINAL
NONCRIMINALS
NONCRISES
NONCRISIS
NONCRITICAL
NONCROSSOVER
NONCROSSOVERS
NONCRUSHABLE
NONCRYSTALLINE
NONCULINARY
NONCULTIVATED
NONCULTIVATION
NONCULTIVATIONS
NONCULTURAL
NONCUMULATIVE
NONCURRENT
NONCURRENTS
NONCUSTODIAL
NONCUSTOMER
NONCUSTOMERS
NONCYCLIC
NONCYCLICAL
NONDAIRY
NONDANCE
NONDANCER
NONDANCERS
NONDANCES
NONDECEPTIVE
NONDECISION
NONDECISIONS
NONDECREASING
NONDEDUCTIBLE
NONDEDUCTIBLES
NONDEDUCTIVE
NONDEFENSE
NONDEFENSES
NONDEFERRABLE
NONDEFORMING
NONDEGENERATE
NONDEGENERATES
NONDEGRADABLE
NONDEGREE
NONDELEGATE
NONDELEGATES
NONDELIBERATE
NONDELINQUENT
NONDELINQUENTS
NONDELIVERIES
NONDELIVERY
NONDEMAND
NONDEMANDING
NONDEMANDS
NONDEMOCRATIC
NONDEPARTMENTAL
NONDEPENDENT
NONDEPENDENTS
NONDEPLETABLE
NONDEPLETING
NONDEPOSITION
NONDEPOSITIONS
NONDEPRESSED
NONDERIVATIVE
NONDERIVATIVES
NONDESCRIPT
NONDESCRIPTIVE
NONDESCRIPTS
NONDESERT
NONDESTRUCTIVE
NONDETACHABLE
NONDEVELOPMENT
NONDEVELOPMENTS
NONDEVIANT
NONDEVIANTS
NONDIABETIC
NONDIABETICS
NONDIALYZABLE
NONDIAPAUSING
NONDIDACTIC
NONDIFFUSIBLE
NONDIMENSIONAL
NONDIPLOMATIC
NONDIRECTED
NONDIRECTIONAL

NONDIRECTIVE
NONDIRECTIVES
NONDISABLED
NONDISCLOSURE
NONDISCLOSURES
NONDISCOUNT
NONDISCOUNTS
NONDISCURSIVE
NONDISJUNCTION
NONDISJUNCTIONS
NONDISPERSIVE
NONDISRUPTIVE
NONDISTINCTIVE
NONDIVERSIFIED
NONDIVIDING
NONDOCTOR
NONDOCTORS
NONDOCTRINAIRE
NONDOCTRINAIRES
NONDOCUMENTARY
NONDOGMATIC
NONDOLLAR
NONDOMESTIC
NONDOMESTICS
NONDOMINANT
NONDORMANT
NONDRAMATIC
NONDRINKER
NONDRINKERS
NONDRINKING
NONDRIP
NONDRIVER
NONDRIVERS
NONDRUG
NONDRYING
NONDURABLE
NONDURABLES
NONE
NONEARNING
NONEARNINGS
NONECONOMIC
NONECONOMIST
NONECONOMISTS
NONEDIBLE
NONEDIBLES
NONEDITORIAL
NONEDITORIALS
NONEDUCATION
NONEDUCATIONAL
NONEDUCATIONS
NONEFFECTIVE
NONEGO
NONEGOS
NONELASTIC
NONELASTICS
NONELECT
NONELECTED
NONELECTION
NONELECTIONS
NONELECTIVE
NONELECTIVES
NONELECTRIC
NONELECTRICAL
NONELECTRICS
NONELECTROLYTE
NONELECTROLYTES
NONELECTRONIC
NONELEMENTARY
NONELITE
NONEMERGENCIES
NONEMERGENCY
NONEMOTIONAL
NONEMPHATIC
NONEMPIRICAL
NONEMPLOYEE
NONEMPLOYEES
NONEMPLOYMENT
NONEMPLOYMENTS
NONEMPTY
NONENCAPSULATED
NONENDING
NONENERGY
NONENFORCEMENT
NONENFORCEMENTS
NONENGAGEMENT
NONENGAGEMENTS
NONENGINEERING
NONENTITIES
NONENTITY
NONENTRIES
NONENTRY
NONENZYMATIC
NONENZYMIC
NONEQUAL
NONEQUALS
NONEQUILIBRIA
NONEQUILIBRIUM
NONEQUILIBRIUMS
NONEQUIVALENCE
NONEQUIVALENCES
NONEQUIVALENT
NONEQUIVALENTS
NONEROTIC
NONES
NONESSENTIAL
NONESSENTIALS
NONESTABLISHED
NONESTERIFIED
NONESUCH
NONESUCHES
NONET
NONETHELESS
NONETHICAL
NONETHNIC
NONETHNICS
NONETS
NONEVALUATIVE
NONEVENT
NONEVENTS
NONEVIDENCE
NONEVIDENCES
NONEXCLUSIVE
NONEXCLUSIVES
NONEXECUTIVE
NONEXECUTIVES
NONEXEMPT
NONEXEMPTS
NONEXISTENCE
NONEXISTENCES
NONEXISTENT
NONEXISTENTIAL
NONEXISTENTS
NONEXOTIC
NONEXPENDABLE
NONEXPENDABLES
NONEXPERIMENTAL
NONEXPERT
NONEXPERTS
NONEXPLANATORY
NONEXPLOITATION
NONEXPLOITATIVE
NONEXPLOITIVE
NONEXPLOSIVE
NONEXPLOSIVES
NONEXPOSED
NONEXTANT
NONFACT
NONFACTOR
NONFACTORS
NONFACTS
NONFACTUAL
NONFACULTIES
NONFACULTY
NONFADING
NONFAMILIAL
NONFAMILIES
NONFAMILY
NONFAN
NONFANS
NONFARM
NONFARMER
NONFARMERS
NONFAT
NONFATAL
NONFATTENING
NONFATTY
NONFEASANCE
NONFEASANCES
NONFEDERAL
NONFEDERATED
NONFEMINIST
NONFEMINISTS
NONFERROUS
NONFEUDAL
NONFICTION
NONFICTIONAL
NONFICTIONS
NONFIGURATIVE
NONFILAMENTOUS
NONFILIAL
NONFILTERABLE
NONFINAL
NONFINANCIAL
NONFINITE
NONFISCAL
NONFISSIONABLE
NONFLAMMABILITY
NONFLAMMABLE
NONFLAMMABLES
NONFLOWERING
NONFLUENCIES
NONFLUENCY
NONFLUID
NONFLUIDS
NONFLUORESCENT
NONFLUORESCENTS
NONFLYING
NONFOCAL
NONFOOD
NONFORFEITABLE
NONFORFEITURE
NONFORFEITURES
NONFORMAL
NONFOSSIL
NONFREEZING
NONFRIVOLOUS
NONFROZEN
NONFUEL
NONFULFILLMENT
NONFULFILLMENTS
NONFUNCTIONAL
NONFUNCTIONING
NONFUNDED
NONGAME
NONGASEOUS
NONGAY
NONGAYS
NONGENETIC
NONGENITAL
NONGEOMETRICAL
NONGHETTO
NONGLAMOROUS
NONGLARE
NONGLARES
NONGLAZED
NONGLOSSY
NONGOLFER
NONGOLFERS
NONGONOCOCCAL
NONGOVERNMENT
NONGOVERNMENTAL
NONGOVERNMENTS
NONGRADED
NONGRADUATE
NONGRADUATES
NONGRAMMATICAL
NONGRANULAR
NONGREASY
NONGREEN
NONGREGARIOUS
NONGROWING
NONGROWTH
NONGROWTHS
NONGUEST
NONGUESTS
NONGUILT
NONGUILTS
NONHALOGENATED
NONHANDICAPPED
NONHAPPENING
NONHAPPENINGS
NONHARDY
NONHARMONIC
NONHAZARDOUS
NONHEME
NONHEMOLYTIC
NONHEREDITARY
NONHERO
NONHEROES
NONHEROIC
NONHETEROSEXUAL
NONHIERARCHICAL
NONHISTONE
NONHISTONES
NONHISTORICAL

NONHOME
NONHOMOGENEOUS
NONHOMOLOGOUS
NONHOMOSEXUAL
NONHOMOSEXUALS
NONHORMONAL
NONHOSPITAL
NONHOSPITALIZED
NONHOSPITALS
NONHOSTILE
NONHOUSING
NONHUMAN
NONHUMANS
NONHUNTER
NONHUNTERS
NONHUNTING
NONHYGROSCOPIC
NONHYSTERICAL
NONIDEAL
NONIDENTICAL
NONIDENTITIES
NONIDENTITY
NONIDEOLOGICAL
NONILLION
NONILLIONS
NONIMAGE
NONIMAGES
NONIMITATIVE
NONIMMIGRANT
NONIMMIGRANTS
NONIMMUNE
NONIMPACT
NONIMPLICATION
NONIMPLICATIONS
NONIMPORTATION
NONIMPORTATIONS
NONINCLUSION
NONINCLUSIONS
NONINCREASING
NONINCUMBENT
NONINCUMBENTS
NONINDEPENDENCE
NONINDIGENOUS
NONINDIVIDUAL
NONINDIVIDUALS
NONINDUCTIVE
NONINDUSTRIAL
NONINDUSTRIALS
NONINDUSTRIES
NONINDUSTRY
NONINERT
NONINFECTED
NONINFECTIOUS
NONINFECTIVE
NONINFESTED
NONINFLAMMABLE
NONINFLAMMABLES
NONINFLAMMATORY
NONINFLATIONARY
NONINFLECTIONAL
NONINFLUENCE
NONINFLUENCES
NONINFORMATION
NONINFORMATIONS
NONINFRINGEMENT
NONINITIAL
NONINITIALS
NONINITIATE
NONINITIATES
NONINJURIES
NONINJURY
NONINSECT
NONINSECTICIDAL
NONINSECTS
NONINSTALLMENT
NONINSTALLMENTS
NONINSTRUMENTAL
NONINSURANCE
NONINSURANCES
NONINSURED
NONINTEGRAL
NONINTEGRALS
NONINTEGRATED
NONINTELLECTUAL
NONINTERACTING
NONINTERACTIVE
NONINTERCOURSE
NONINTERCOURSES
NONINTEREST
NONINTERESTS
NONINTERFERENCE
NONINTERLACED
NONINTERSECTING
NONINTERVENTION
NONINTIMIDATING
NONINTOXICANT
NONINTOXICANTS
NONINTOXICATING
NONINTRUSIVE
NONINTUITIVE
NONINVASIVE
NONINVASIVELY
NONINVOLVED
NONINVOLVEMENT
NONINVOLVEMENTS
NONIONIC
NONIONIZING
NONIRON
NONIRRADIATED
NONIRRIGATED
NONIRRITANT
NONIRRITANTS
NONIRRITATING
NONISSUE
NONISSUES
NONJOINDER
NONJOINDERS
NONJOINER
NONJOINERS
NONJUDGEMENTAL
NONJUDGMENTAL
NONJUDGMENTALLY
NONJUDICIAL
NONJURIES
NONJURING
NONJUROR
NONJURORS
NONJURY
NONJUSTICIABLE
NONKOSHER
NONKOSHERS
NONLABOR
NONLANDOWNER
NONLANDOWNERS
NONLANGUAGE
NONLANGUAGES
NONLAWYER
NONLAWYERS
NONLEADED
NONLEAFY
NONLEAGUE
NONLEGAL
NONLEGUME
NONLEGUMES
NONLEGUMINOUS
NONLETHAL
NONLEVEL
NONLEXICAL
NONLIABLE
NONLIBRARIAN
NONLIBRARIANS
NONLIBRARIES
NONLIBRARY
NONLIFE
NONLINEAL
NONLINEAR
NONLINEARITIES
NONLINEARITY
NONLINGUISTIC
NONLIQUID
NONLIQUIDS
NONLITERAL
NONLITERARY
NONLITERATE
NONLITERATES
NONLIVES
NONLIVING
NONLIVINGS
NONLOCAL
NONLOCALS
NONLOGICAL
NONLOVING
NONLOYAL
NONLUMINOUS
NONLYRIC
NONMAGNETIC
NONMAINSTREAM
NONMAINSTREAMS
NONMAJOR
NONMAJORS
NONMALIGNANT
NONMALLEABLE
NONMAMMALIAN
NONMAMMALIANS
NONMAN
NONMANAGEMENT
NONMANAGEMENTS
NONMANAGERIAL
NONMANUAL
NONMARITAL
NONMARKET
NONMARKETS
NONMATERIAL
NONMATERIALS
NONMATHEMATICAL
NONMATRICULATED
NONMATURE
NONMEANINGFUL
NONMEASURABLE
NONMEAT
NONMECHANICAL
NONMECHANISTIC
NONMEDICAL
NONMEETING
NONMEETINGS
NONMEMBER
NONMEMBERS
NONMEMBERSHIP
NONMEMBERSHIPS
NONMEN
NONMENTAL
NONMERCURIAL
NONMETAL
NONMETALLIC
NONMETALS
NONMETAMERIC
NONMETAPHORICAL
NONMETRIC
NONMETRICAL
NONMETRO
NONMETROPOLITAN
NONMICROBIAL
NONMIGRANT
NONMIGRANTS
NONMIGRATORY
NONMILITANT
NONMILITANTS
NONMILITARIES
NONMILITARY
NONMIMETIC
NONMINORITIES
NONMINORITY
NONMOBILE
NONMODAL
NONMODERN
NONMODERNS
NONMOLECULAR
NONMONETARIST
NONMONETARISTS
NONMONETARY
NONMONEY
NONMONOGAMOUS
NONMORAL
NONMORTAL
NONMORTALS
NONMOTILE
NONMOTILITIES
NONMOTILITY
NONMOTORIZED
NONMOVING
NONMUNICIPAL
NONMUNICIPALS
NONMUSIC
NONMUSICAL
NONMUSICALS
NONMUSICIAN
NONMUSICIANS
NONMUSICS
NONMUTANT
NONMUTANTS
NONMUTUAL
NONMYELINATED
NONMYSTICAL
NONNARRATIVE
NONNARRATIVES

NONNASAL
NONNATIONAL
NONNATIONALS
NONNATIVE
NONNATIVES
NONNATURAL
NONNAVAL
NONNECESSITIES
NONNECESSITY
NONNEGATIVE
NONNEGLIGENT
NONNEGOTIABLE
NONNEGOTIABLES
NONNETWORK
NONNETWORKS
NONNEURAL
NONNEWS
NONNITROGENOUS
NONNOBLE
NONNORMAL
NONNORMATIVE
NONNOVEL
NONNOVELS
NONNUCLEAR
NONNUCLEATED
NONNUMERICAL
NONNUTRITIOUS
NONNUTRITIVE
NONOBESE
NONOBJECTIVE
NONOBJECTIVES
NONOBJECTIVISM
NONOBJECTIVISMS
NONOBJECTIVIST
NONOBJECTIVISTS
NONOBJECTIVITY
NONOBSCENE
NONOBSERVANCE
NONOBSERVANCES
NONOBSERVANT
NONOBVIOUS
NONOCCUPATIONAL
NONOCCURRENCE
NONOCCURRENCES
NONOFFICIAL
NONOFFICIALS
NONOHMIC
NONOILY
NONOPERATIC
NONOPERATING
NONOPERATIONAL
NONOPERATIVE
NONOPTIMAL
NONORAL
NONORALLY
NONORGANIC
NONORGASMIC
NONORTHODOX
NONORTHODOXES
NONOVERLAPPING
NONOWNER
NONOWNERS
NONOXIDIZING
NONPAGAN
NONPAGANS
NONPAID
NONPAPAL
NONPAPIST
NONPAPISTS
NONPAR
NONPARALLEL
NONPARALLELS
NONPARAMETRIC
NONPARASITIC
NONPAREIL
NONPAREILS
NONPARENT
NONPARENTS
NONPARITIES
NONPARITY
NONPARTICIPANT
NONPARTICIPANTS
NONPARTIES
NONPARTISAN
NONPARTISANS
NONPARTISANSHIP
NONPARTY
NONPASSERINE
NONPASSERINES
NONPASSIVE
NONPASSIVES
NONPAST
NONPASTS
NONPATHOGENIC
NONPAYING
NONPAYMENT
NONPAYMENTS
NONPEAK
NONPERFORMANCE
NONPERFORMANCES
NONPERFORMER
NONPERFORMERS
NONPERFORMING
NONPERISHABLE
NONPERISHABLES
NONPERMISSIVE
NONPERSISTENT
NONPERSON
NONPERSONAL
NONPERSONS
NONPETROLEUM
NONPETROLEUMS
NONPHILOSOPHER
NONPHILOSOPHERS
NONPHONEMIC
NONPHONETIC
NONPHOSPHATE
NONPHOSPHATES
NONPHOTOGRAPHIC
NONPHYSICAL
NONPHYSICALS
NONPHYSICIAN
NONPHYSICIANS
NONPLANAR
NONPLASTIC
NONPLASTICS
NONPLAY
NONPLAYER
NONPLAYERS
NONPLAYING
NONPLAYS
NONPLIANT
NONPLUS
NONPLUSED
NONPLUSES
NONPLUSING
NONPLUSSED
NONPLUSSES
NONPLUSSING
NONPOETIC
NONPOINT
NONPOISONOUS
NONPOLAR
NONPOLARIZABLE
NONPOLICE
NONPOLITICAL
NONPOLITICALLY
NONPOLITICIAN
NONPOLITICIANS
NONPOLLUTING
NONPOOR
NONPOROUS
NONPOSSESSION
NONPOSSESSIONS
NONPOSTAL
NONPRACTICAL
NONPRACTICING
NONPREGNANT
NONPRESCRIPTION
NONPRINT
NONPROBLEM
NONPROBLEMS
NONPRODUCING
NONPRODUCTIVE
NONPROFESSIONAL
NONPROFESSORIAL
NONPROFIT
NONPROFITS
NONPROGRAM
NONPROGRAMMER
NONPROGRAMMERS
NONPROGRAMS
NONPROGRESSIVE
NONPROGRESSIVES
NONPROPRIETARY
NONPROS
NONPROSSED
NONPROSSES
NONPROSSING
NONPROTEIN
NONPROTEINS
NONPROVEN
NONPSYCHIATRIC
NONPSYCHIATRIST
NONPSYCHOTIC
NONPSYCHOTICS
NONPUBLIC
NONPUNITIVE
NONPURPOSIVE
NONQUANTIFIABLE
NONQUANTITATIVE
NONQUOTA
NONRACIAL
NONRACIALLY
NONRADIOACTIVE
NONRAILROAD
NONRAILROADS
NONRANDOM
NONRANDOMNESS
NONRANDOMNESSES
NONRATED
NONRATIONAL
NONREACTIVE
NONREACTOR
NONREACTORS
NONREADER
NONREADERS
NONREADING
NONREALISTIC
NONRECEIPT
NONRECEIPTS
NONRECIPROCAL
NONRECIPROCALS
NONRECOGNITION
NONRECOGNITIONS
NONRECOMBINANT
NONRECOMBINANTS
NONRECOURSE
NONRECOURSES
NONRECURRENT
NONRECURRING
NONRECYCLABLE
NONRECYCLABLES
NONREDUCING
NONREDUNDANT
NONREFILLABLE
NONREFLECTING
NONREFUNDABLE
NONREGULATED
NONREGULATION
NONREGULATIONS
NONRELATIVE
NONRELATIVES
NONRELATIVISTIC
NONRELEVANT
NONRELIGIOUS
NONRENEWABLE
NONRENEWABLES
NONRENEWAL
NONRENEWALS
NONREPAYABLE
NONREPRODUCTIVE
NONRESIDENCE
NONRESIDENCES
NONRESIDENCIES
NONRESIDENCY
NONRESIDENT
NONRESIDENTIAL
NONRESIDENTS
NONRESISTANCE
NONRESISTANCES
NONRESISTANT
NONRESISTANTS
NONRESONANT
NONRESONANTS
NONRESPONDENT
NONRESPONDENTS
NONRESPONDER
NONRESPONDERS
NONRESPONSE
NONRESPONSES
NONRESPONSIVE
NONRESTRICTED
NONRESTRICTIVE
NONRESTRICTIVES

NONRETRACTILE
NONRETROACTIVE
NONRETURNABLE
NONRETURNABLES
NONREUSABLE
NONREVERSIBLE
NONREVERSIBLES
NONRHOTIC
NONRIGID
NONRIOTER
NONRIOTERS
NONRIOTING
NONRIVAL
NONRIVALS
NONROTATING
NONROUTINE
NONROUTINES
NONROYAL
NONRUBBER
NONRULING
NONRUMINANT
NONRUMINANTS
NONRURAL
NONSACRED
NONSALABLE
NONSALINE
NONSALINES
NONSAPONIFIABLE
NONSCHEDULED
NONSCHOOL
NONSCIENCE
NONSCIENCES
NONSCIENTIFIC
NONSCIENTIST
NONSCIENTISTS
NONSEASONAL
NONSECRET
NONSECRETOR
NONSECRETORS
NONSECRETORY
NONSECRETS
NONSECTARIAN
NONSECTARIANS
NONSECURE
NONSEDIMENTABLE
NONSEGREGATED
NONSEGREGATION
NONSEGREGATIONS
NONSELECTED
NONSELECTIVE
NONSELF
NONSELVES
NONSENSATIONAL
NONSENSE
NONSENSES
NONSENSICAL
NONSENSICALLY
NONSENSICALNESS
NONSENSITIVE
NONSENSUOUS
NONSENTENCE
NONSENTENCES
NONSEPTATE
NONSEQUENTIAL
NONSEQUENTIALLY
NONSERIAL
NONSERIALS
NONSERIOUS
NONSEXIST
NONSEXUAL
NONSHRINK
NONSHRINKABLE
NONSIGNER
NONSIGNERS
NONSIGNIFICANT
NONSIMULTANEOUS
NONSINKABLE
NONSKATER
NONSKATERS
NONSKED
NONSKEDS
NONSKELETAL
NONSKID
NONSKIER
NONSKIERS
NONSLIP
NONSMOKER
NONSMOKERS
NONSMOKING
NONSOCIAL
NONSOCIALIST
NONSOCIALISTS
NONSOLAR
NONSOLID
NONSOLIDS
NONSOLUTION
NONSOLUTIONS
NONSPATIAL
NONSPEAKER
NONSPEAKERS
NONSPEAKING
NONSPECIALIST
NONSPECIALISTS
NONSPECIFIC
NONSPECIFICALLY
NONSPECIFICS
NONSPECTACULAR
NONSPECTACULARS
NONSPECULATIVE
NONSPEECH
NONSPHERICAL
NONSPORTING
NONSTANDARD
NONSTANDARDS
NONSTAPLE
NONSTAPLES
NONSTARTER
NONSTARTERS
NONSTATIC
NONSTATIONARY
NONSTATISTICAL
NONSTEADY
NONSTEROID
NONSTEROIDAL
NONSTEROIDS
NONSTICK
NONSTICKY
NONSTOP
NONSTOPS
NONSTORIES
NONSTORY
NONSTRATEGIC
NONSTRUCTURAL
NONSTRUCTURED
NONSTUDENT
NONSTUDENTS
NONSTYLE
NONSTYLES
NONSUBJECT
NONSUBJECTIVE
NONSUBJECTS
NONSUBSIDIZED
NONSUCCESS
NONSUCCESSES
NONSUCH
NONSUCHES
NONSUGAR
NONSUGARS
NONSUIT
NONSUITED
NONSUITING
NONSUITS
NONSUPERVISORY
NONSUPPORT
NONSUPPORTS
NONSURGICAL
NONSWIMMER
NONSWIMMERS
NONSYLLABIC
NONSYMBOLIC
NONSYMMETRIC
NONSYMMETRICAL
NONSYNCHRONOUS
NONSYSTEM
NONSYSTEMATIC
NONSYSTEMIC
NONSYSTEMICS
NONSYSTEMS
NONTALKER
NONTALKERS
NONTARGET
NONTARIFF
NONTARIFFS
NONTAX
NONTAXABLE
NONTAXES
NONTEACHING
NONTECHNICAL
NONTEMPORAL
NONTENURED
NONTERMINAL
NONTERMINALS
NONTERMINATING
NONTHEATRICAL
NONTHEATRICALS
NONTHEIST
NONTHEISTIC
NONTHEISTS
NONTHEOLOGICAL
NONTHEORETICAL
NONTHERAPEUTIC
NONTHERMAL
NONTHERMALS
NONTHINKING
NONTHREATENING
NONTIDAL
NONTITLE
NONTOBACCO
NONTOBACCOS
NONTONAL
NONTONIC
NONTOTALITARIAN
NONTOXIC
NONTRADITIONAL
NONTRAGIC
NONTRANSFERABLE
NONTREATMENT
NONTREATMENTS
NONTRIBAL
NONTRIVIAL
NONTROPICAL
NONTRUMP
NONTRUTH
NONTRUTHS
NONTURBULENT
NONTYPICAL
NONUNANIMOUS
NONUNIFORM
NONUNIFORMITIES
NONUNIFORMITY
NONUNIFORMS
NONUNION
NONUNIONIZED
NONUNIONS
NONUNIQUE
NONUNIQUENESS
NONUNIQUENESSES
NONUNIVERSAL
NONUNIVERSALS
NONUNIVERSITIES
NONUNIVERSITY
NONUPLE
NONUPLES
NONURBAN
NONURGENT
NONUSABLE
NONUSE
NONUSER
NONUSERS
NONUSES
NONUSING
NONUTILITARIAN
NONUTILITARIANS
NONUTILITIES
NONUTILITY
NONUTOPIAN
NONUTOPIANS
NONVACANT
NONVALID
NONVALIDITIES
NONVALIDITY
NONVANISHING
NONVASCULAR
NONVECTOR
NONVECTORS
NONVEGETARIAN
NONVEGETARIANS
NONVENOMOUS
NONVENOUS
NONVERBAL
NONVERBALLY
NONVESTED
NONVETERAN
NONVETERANS
NONVIABLE

NONVIEWER
NONVIEWERS
NONVINTAGE
NONVINTAGES
NONVIOLENCE
NONVIOLENCES
NONVIOLENT
NONVIOLENTLY
NONVIRAL
NONVIRGIN
NONVIRGINS
NONVIRILE
NONVISCOUS
NONVISUAL
NONVITAL
NONVOCAL
NONVOCALS
NONVOCATIONAL
NONVOLATILE
NONVOLATILES
NONVOLCANIC
NONVOLUNTARIES
NONVOLUNTARY
NONVOTER
NONVOTERS
NONVOTING
NONWAGE
NONWAR
NONWARS
NONWHITE
NONWHITES
NONWINGED
NONWINNING
NONWOODY
NONWOOL
NONWORD
NONWORDS
NONWORK
NONWORKER
NONWORKERS
NONWORKING
NONWOVEN
NONWOVENS
NONWRITER
NONWRITERS
NONYELLOWING
NONYL
NONYLS
NONZERO
NOO
NOODGE
NOODGED
NOODGES
NOODGING
NOODLE
NOODLED
NOODLES
NOODLING
NOODLINGS
NOOGIE
NOOGIES
NOOK
NOOKIE
NOOKIES
NOOKLIKE
NOOKS
NOOKY
NOON
NOONDAY
NOONDAYS
NOONER
NOONERS
NOONING
NOONINGS
NOONS
NOONTIDE
NOONTIDES
NOONTIME
NOONTIMES
NOOSE
NOOSED
NOOSER
NOOSERS
NOOSES
NOOSING
NOOSPHERE
NOOSPHERES
NOOTROPIC
NOOTROPICS
NOPAL
NOPALES
NOPALITO
NOPALITOS
NOPALS
NOPE
NOPLACE
NOR
NORADRENALIN
NORADRENALINE
NORADRENALINES
NORADRENALINS
NORADRENERGIC
NORDIC
NOREPINEPHRINE
NOREPINEPHRINES
NORETHINDRONE
NORETHINDRONES
NORI
NORIA
NORIAS
NORIS
NORITE
NORITES
NORITIC
NORLAND
NORLANDS
NORM
NORMAL
NORMALCIES
NORMALCY
NORMALISATION
NORMALISATIONS
NORMALISE
NORMALISED
NORMALISES
NORMALISING
NORMALITIES
NORMALITY
NORMALIZABLE
NORMALIZATION
NORMALIZATIONS
NORMALIZE
NORMALIZED
NORMALIZER
NORMALIZERS
NORMALIZES
NORMALIZING
NORMALLY
NORMALS
NORMANDE
NORMATIVE
NORMATIVELY
NORMATIVENESS
NORMATIVENESSES
NORMED
NORMLESS
NORMOTENSIVE
NORMOTENSIVES
NORMOTHERMIA
NORMOTHERMIAS
NORMOTHERMIC
NORMS
NOROVIRUS
NOROVIRUSES
NORTENA
NORTENAS
NORTENO
NORTENOS
NORTH
NORTHBOUND
NORTHEAST
NORTHEASTER
NORTHEASTERLY
NORTHEASTERN
NORTHEASTERNER
NORTHEASTERNERS
NORTHEASTERS
NORTHEASTS
NORTHEASTWARD
NORTHEASTWARDS
NORTHER
NORTHERLIES
NORTHERLY
NORTHERN
NORTHERNER
NORTHERNERS
NORTHERNMOST
NORTHERNS
NORTHERS
NORTHING
NORTHINGS
NORTHLAND
NORTHLANDS
NORTHMOST
NORTHS
NORTHWARD
NORTHWARDS
NORTHWEST
NORTHWESTER
NORTHWESTERLY
NORTHWESTERN
NORTHWESTERNER
NORTHWESTERNERS
NORTHWESTERS
NORTHWESTS
NORTHWESTWARD
NORTHWESTWARDS
NORTRIPTYLINE
NORTRIPTYLINES
NOS
NOSE
NOSEBAG
NOSEBAGS
NOSEBAND
NOSEBANDS
NOSEBLEED
NOSEBLEEDS
NOSED
NOSEDIVE
NOSEDIVED
NOSEDIVES
NOSEDIVING
NOSEDOVE
NOSEGAY
NOSEGAYS
NOSEGUARD
NOSEGUARDS
NOSELESS
NOSELIKE
NOSEPIECE
NOSEPIECES
NOSES
NOSEWHEEL
NOSEWHEELS
NOSEY
NOSH
NOSHED
NOSHER
NOSHERS
NOSHES
NOSHING
NOSIER
NOSIEST
NOSILY
NOSINESS
NOSINESSES
NOSING
NOSINGS
NOSOCOMIAL
NOSOLOGIC
NOSOLOGICAL
NOSOLOGICALLY
NOSOLOGIES
NOSOLOGY
NOSTALGIA
NOSTALGIAS
NOSTALGIC
NOSTALGICALLY
NOSTALGICS
NOSTALGIST
NOSTALGISTS
NOSTOC
NOSTOCS
NOSTOLOGIES
NOSTOLOGY
NOSTRIL
NOSTRILS
NOSTRUM
NOSTRUMS
NOSY
NOT
NOTA
NOTABILIA
NOTABILITIES
NOTABILITY

NOTABLE
NOTABLENESS
NOTABLENESSES
NOTABLES
NOTABLY
NOTAL
NOTARIAL
NOTARIALLY
NOTARIES
NOTARISE
NOTARISED
NOTARISES
NOTARISING
NOTARIZATION
NOTARIZATIONS
NOTARIZE
NOTARIZED
NOTARIZES
NOTARIZING
NOTARY
NOTATE
NOTATED
NOTATES
NOTATING
NOTATION
NOTATIONAL
NOTATIONS
NOTATOR
NOTATORS
NOTCH
NOTCHBACK
NOTCHBACKS
NOTCHED
NOTCHER
NOTCHERS
NOTCHES
NOTCHIER
NOTCHIEST
NOTCHING
NOTCHY
NOTE
NOTEBOOK
NOTEBOOKS
NOTECARD
NOTECARDS
NOTECASE
NOTECASES
NOTED
NOTEDLY
NOTEDNESS
NOTEDNESSES
NOTELESS
NOTELET
NOTELETS
NOTEPAD
NOTEPADS
NOTEPAPER
NOTEPAPERS
NOTER
NOTERS
NOTES
NOTEWORTHIER
NOTEWORTHIEST
NOTEWORTHILY
NOTEWORTHINESS
NOTEWORTHY
NOTHER
NOTHING
NOTHINGNESS
NOTHINGNESSES
NOTHINGS
NOTICE
NOTICEABLE
NOTICEABLY
NOTICEBOARD
NOTICEBOARDS
NOTICED
NOTICER
NOTICERS
NOTICES
NOTICING
NOTIFIABLE
NOTIFICATION
NOTIFICATIONS
NOTIFIED
NOTIFIER
NOTIFIERS
NOTIFIES
NOTIFY
NOTIFYING
NOTING
NOTION
NOTIONAL
NOTIONALITIES
NOTIONALITY
NOTIONALLY
NOTIONS
NOTOCHORD
NOTOCHORDAL
NOTOCHORDS
NOTORIETIES
NOTORIETY
NOTORIOUS
NOTORIOUSLY
NOTORNIS
NOTTURNI
NOTTURNO
NOTUM
NOTWITHSTANDING
NOUGAT
NOUGATS
NOUGHT
NOUGHTS
NOUMENA
NOUMENAL
NOUMENON
NOUN
NOUNAL
NOUNALLY
NOUNLESS
NOUNS
NOURISH
NOURISHED
NOURISHER
NOURISHERS
NOURISHES
NOURISHING
NOURISHMENT
NOURISHMENTS
NOUS
NOUSES
NOUVEAU
NOUVELLE
NOUVELLES
NOVA
NOVACULITE
NOVACULITES
NOVAE
NOVALIKE
NOVAS
NOVATE
NOVATED
NOVATES
NOVATING
NOVATION
NOVATIONS
NOVEL
NOVELETTE
NOVELETTES
NOVELETTISH
NOVELISE
NOVELISED
NOVELISES
NOVELISING
NOVELIST
NOVELISTIC
NOVELISTICALLY
NOVELISTS
NOVELIZATION
NOVELIZATIONS
NOVELIZE
NOVELIZED
NOVELIZER
NOVELIZERS
NOVELIZES
NOVELIZING
NOVELLA
NOVELLAS
NOVELLE
NOVELLY
NOVELS
NOVELTIES
NOVELTY
NOVEMDECILLION
NOVEMDECILLIONS
NOVENA
NOVENAE
NOVENAS
NOVERCAL
NOVICE
NOVICES
NOVICIATE
NOVICIATES
NOVITIATE
NOVITIATES
NOVOBIOCIN
NOVOBIOCINS
NOVOCAINE
NOVOCAINES
NOW
NOWADAYS
NOWAY
NOWAYS
NOWHERE
NOWHERES
NOWHERESVILLE
NOWHERESVILLES
NOWHITHER
NOWISE
NOWNESS
NOWNESSES
NOWS
NOWT
NOWTS
NOXIOUS
NOXIOUSLY
NOXIOUSNESS
NOXIOUSNESSES
NOYADE
NOYADES
NOYAU
NOYAUX
NOZZLE
NOZZLES
NTH
NU
NUANCE
NUANCED
NUANCES
NUANCING
NUB
NUBBIER
NUBBIEST
NUBBIN
NUBBINESS
NUBBINESSES
NUBBINS
NUBBLE
NUBBLES
NUBBLIER
NUBBLIEST
NUBBLY
NUBBY
NUBIA
NUBIAS
NUBILE
NUBILITIES
NUBILITY
NUBILOSE
NUBILOUS
NUBS
NUBUCK
NUBUCKS
NUCELLAR
NUCELLI
NUCELLUS
NUCHA
NUCHAE
NUCHAL
NUCHALS
NUCLEAL
NUCLEAR
NUCLEASE
NUCLEASES
NUCLEATE
NUCLEATED
NUCLEATES
NUCLEATING
NUCLEATION
NUCLEATIONS
NUCLEATOR
NUCLEATORS
NUCLEI
NUCLEIN
NUCLEINIC

NUCLEINS
NUCLEOCAPSID
NUCLEOCAPSIDS
NUCLEOID
NUCLEOIDS
NUCLEOLAR
NUCLEOLE
NUCLEOLES
NUCLEOLI
NUCLEOLUS
NUCLEON
NUCLEONIC
NUCLEONICS
NUCLEONS
NUCLEOPHILE
NUCLEOPHILES
NUCLEOPHILIC
NUCLEOPHILICITY
NUCLEOPLASM
NUCLEOPLASMIC
NUCLEOPLASMS
NUCLEOPROTEIN
NUCLEOPROTEINS
NUCLEOSIDE
NUCLEOSIDES
NUCLEOSOMAL
NUCLEOSOME
NUCLEOSOMES
NUCLEOSYNTHESES
NUCLEOSYNTHESIS
NUCLEOSYNTHETIC
NUCLEOTIDASE
NUCLEOTIDASES
NUCLEOTIDE
NUCLEOTIDES
NUCLEUS
NUCLEUSES
NUCLIDE
NUCLIDES
NUCLIDIC
NUDE
NUDELY
NUDENESS
NUDENESSES
NUDER
NUDES
NUDEST
NUDGE
NUDGED
NUDGER
NUDGERS
NUDGES
NUDGING
NUDIBRANCH
NUDIBRANCHS
NUDICAUL
NUDIE
NUDIES
NUDISM
NUDISMS
NUDIST
NUDISTS
NUDITIES
NUDITY
NUDNICK
NUDNICKS
NUDNIK
NUDNIKS
NUDZH
NUDZHED
NUDZHES
NUDZHING
NUFF
NUFFS
NUG
NUGATORY
NUGGET
NUGGETS
NUGGETY
NUGS
NUISANCE
NUISANCES
NUKE
NUKED
NUKES
NUKING
NULL
NULLAH
NULLAHS
NULLED
NULLIFICATION
NULLIFICATIONS
NULLIFIED
NULLIFIER
NULLIFIERS
NULLIFIES
NULLIFY
NULLIFYING
NULLING
NULLIPARA
NULLIPARAE
NULLIPARAS
NULLIPAROUS
NULLIPORE
NULLIPORES
NULLITIES
NULLITY
NULLS
NUMB
NUMBAT
NUMBATS
NUMBED
NUMBER
NUMBERABLE
NUMBERED
NUMBERER
NUMBERERS
NUMBERING
NUMBERLESS
NUMBERS
NUMBEST
NUMBFISH
NUMBFISHES
NUMBING
NUMBINGLY
NUMBLES
NUMBLY
NUMBNESS
NUMBNESSES
NUMBNUTS
NUMBNUTSES
NUMBS
NUMBSKULL
NUMBSKULLS
NUMCHUCK
NUMCHUCKS
NUMDAH
NUMDAHS
NUMEN
NUMERABLE
NUMERABLY
NUMERACIES
NUMERACY
NUMERAL
NUMERALLY
NUMERALS
NUMERARY
NUMERATE
NUMERATED
NUMERATES
NUMERATING
NUMERATION
NUMERATIONS
NUMERATOR
NUMERATORS
NUMERIC
NUMERICAL
NUMERICALLY
NUMERICS
NUMEROLOGICAL
NUMEROLOGIES
NUMEROLOGIST
NUMEROLOGISTS
NUMEROLOGY
NUMEROUS
NUMEROUSLY
NUMEROUSNESS
NUMEROUSNESSES
NUMINA
NUMINOUS
NUMINOUSNESS
NUMINOUSNESSES
NUMISMATIC
NUMISMATICALLY
NUMISMATICS
NUMISMATIST
NUMISMATISTS
NUMMARY
NUMMIER
NUMMIEST
NUMMULAR
NUMMULITE
NUMMULITES
NUMMY
NUMNAH
NUMNAHS
NUMSKULL
NUMSKULLS
NUN
NUNATAK
NUNATAKS
NUNCHAKU
NUNCHAKUS
NUNCHUK
NUNCHUKS
NUNCIATURE
NUNCIATURES
NUNCIO
NUNCIOS
NUNCLE
NUNCLES
NUNCUPATIVE
NUNLIKE
NUNNATION
NUNNATIONS
NUNNERIES
NUNNERY
NUNNISH
NUNS
NUPTIAL
NUPTIALITIES
NUPTIALITY
NUPTIALLY
NUPTIALS
NURD
NURDS
NURL
NURLED
NURLING
NURLS
NURSE
NURSED
NURSEMAID
NURSEMAIDS
NURSER
NURSERIES
NURSERS
NURSERY
NURSERYMAN
NURSERYMEN
NURSES
NURSING
NURSINGS
NURSLING
NURSLINGS
NURTURAL
NURTURANCE
NURTURANCES
NURTURANT
NURTURE
NURTURED
NURTURER
NURTURERS
NURTURES
NURTURING
NUS
NUT
NUTANT
NUTATE
NUTATED
NUTATES
NUTATING
NUTATION
NUTATIONAL
NUTATIONS
NUTBAR
NUTBARS
NUTBROWN
NUTCASE
NUTCASES
NUTCRACKER
NUTCRACKERS
NUTGALL
NUTGALLS
NUTGRASS

NUTGRASSES
NUTHATCH
NUTHATCHES
NUTHIN
NUTHOUSE
NUTHOUSES
NUTLET
NUTLETS
NUTLIKE
NUTMEAT
NUTMEATS
NUTMEG
NUTMEGGIER
NUTMEGGIEST
NUTMEGGY
NUTMEGS
NUTPICK
NUTPICKS
NUTRACEUTICAL
NUTRACEUTICALS
NUTRIA
NUTRIAS
NUTRICEUTICAL
NUTRICEUTICALS
NUTRIENT
NUTRIENTS
NUTRIMENT
NUTRIMENTS
NUTRITION
NUTRITIONAL
NUTRITIONALLY
NUTRITIONIST
NUTRITIONISTS
NUTRITIONS
NUTRITIOUS
NUTRITIOUSLY
NUTRITIOUSNESS
NUTRITIVE
NUTRITIVELY
NUTRITIVES
NUTS
NUTSEDGE
NUTSEDGES
NUTSHELL
NUTSHELLS
NUTSIER
NUTSIEST
NUTSO
NUTSOS
NUTSY
NUTTED
NUTTER
NUTTERS
NUTTIER
NUTTIEST
NUTTILY
NUTTINESS
NUTTINESSES
NUTTING
NUTTINGS
NUTTY
NUTWOOD
NUTWOODS
NUZZLE
NUZZLED
NUZZLER
NUZZLERS
NUZZLES
NUZZLING
NYAH
NYALA
NYALAS
NYCTALOPIA
NYCTALOPIAS
NYLGHAI
NYLGHAIS
NYLGHAU
NYLGHAUS
NYLON
NYLONED
NYLONS
NYMPH
NYMPHA
NYMPHAE
NYMPHAL
NYMPHALID
NYMPHALIDS
NYMPHEAN
NYMPHED
NYMPHET
NYMPHETIC
NYMPHETS
NYMPHETTE
NYMPHETTES
NYMPHING
NYMPHO
NYMPHOLEPSIES
NYMPHOLEPSY
NYMPHOLEPT
NYMPHOLEPTIC
NYMPHOLEPTS
NYMPHOMANIA
NYMPHOMANIAC
NYMPHOMANIACAL
NYMPHOMANIACS
NYMPHOMANIAS
NYMPHOS
NYMPHS
NYSTAGMIC
NYSTAGMUS
NYSTAGMUSES
NYSTATIN
NYSTATINS

O

OAF
OAFISH
OAFISHLY
OAFISHNESS
OAFISHNESSES
OAFS
OAK
OAKED
OAKEN
OAKIER
OAKIEST
OAKINESS
OAKINESSES
OAKLIKE
OAKMOSS
OAKMOSSES
OAKS
OAKUM
OAKUMS
OAKY
OAR
OARED
OARFISH
OARFISHES
OARING
OARLESS
OARLIKE
OARLOCK
OARLOCKS
OARS
OARSMAN
OARSMANSHIP
OARSMANSHIPS
OARSMEN
OARSWOMAN
OARSWOMEN
OASES
OASIS
OAST
OASTHOUSE
OASTHOUSES
OASTS
OAT
OATCAKE
OATCAKES
OATEN
OATER
OATERS
OATH
OATHS
OATIER
OATIEST
OATLIKE
OATMEAL
OATMEALS
OATS
OATY
OAVES
OBA
OBAS
OBBLIGATI
OBBLIGATO
OBBLIGATOS
OBCONIC
OBCONICAL
OBCORDATE
OBDURACIES
OBDURACY
OBDURATE
OBDURATELY
OBDURATENESS
OBDURATENESSES
OBE
OBEAH
OBEAHISM
OBEAHISMS
OBEAHS
OBEDIENCE
OBEDIENCES
OBEDIENT
OBEDIENTLY
OBEISANCE
OBEISANCES
OBEISANT
OBEISANTLY
OBELI
OBELIA
OBELIAS
OBELISCAL
OBELISE
OBELISED
OBELISES
OBELISING
OBELISK
OBELISKS
OBELISM
OBELISMS
OBELIZE
OBELIZED
OBELIZES

OBELIZING
OBELUS
OBENTO
OBENTOS
OBES
OBESE
OBESELY
OBESENESS
OBESENESSES
OBESITIES
OBESITY
OBESOGENIC
OBEY
OBEYABLE
OBEYED
OBEYER
OBEYERS
OBEYING
OBEYS
OBFUSCATE
OBFUSCATED
OBFUSCATES
OBFUSCATING
OBFUSCATION
OBFUSCATIONS
OBFUSCATORY
OBI
OBIA
OBIAS
OBIISM
OBIISMS
OBIS
OBIT
OBITS
OBITUARIES
OBITUARIST
OBITUARISTS
OBITUARY
OBJECT
OBJECTED
OBJECTIFICATION
OBJECTIFIED
OBJECTIFIES
OBJECTIFY
OBJECTIFYING
OBJECTING
OBJECTION
OBJECTIONABLE
OBJECTIONABLY
OBJECTIONS
OBJECTIVE
OBJECTIVELY
OBJECTIVENESS
OBJECTIVENESSES
OBJECTIVES
OBJECTIVISM
OBJECTIVISMS
OBJECTIVIST
OBJECTIVISTIC
OBJECTIVISTS
OBJECTIVITIES
OBJECTIVITY
OBJECTLESS
OBJECTLESSNESS
OBJECTOR
OBJECTORS
OBJECTS
OBJET
OBJETS
OBJURGATE
OBJURGATED
OBJURGATES
OBJURGATING
OBJURGATION
OBJURGATIONS
OBJURGATORY
OBLANCEOLATE
OBLAST
OBLASTI
OBLASTS
OBLATE
OBLATELY
OBLATENESS
OBLATENESSES
OBLATES
OBLATION
OBLATIONS
OBLATORY
OBLIGABLE
OBLIGATE
OBLIGATED
OBLIGATELY
OBLIGATES
OBLIGATI
OBLIGATING
OBLIGATION
OBLIGATIONS
OBLIGATO
OBLIGATOR
OBLIGATORILY
OBLIGATORS
OBLIGATORY
OBLIGATOS
OBLIGE
OBLIGED
OBLIGEE
OBLIGEES
OBLIGER
OBLIGERS
OBLIGES
OBLIGING
OBLIGINGLY
OBLIGINGNESS
OBLIGINGNESSES
OBLIGOR
OBLIGORS
OBLIQUE
OBLIQUED
OBLIQUELY
OBLIQUENESS
OBLIQUENESSES
OBLIQUES
OBLIQUING
OBLIQUITIES
OBLIQUITY
OBLITERATE
OBLITERATED
OBLITERATES
OBLITERATING
OBLITERATION
OBLITERATIONS
OBLITERATIVE
OBLITERATOR
OBLITERATORS
OBLIVION
OBLIVIONS
OBLIVIOUS
OBLIVIOUSLY
OBLIVIOUSNESS
OBLIVIOUSNESSES
OBLONG
OBLONGLY
OBLONGS
OBLOQUIAL
OBLOQUIES
OBLOQUY
OBNOXIOUS
OBNOXIOUSLY
OBNOXIOUSNESS
OBNOXIOUSNESSES
OBNUBILATE
OBNUBILATED
OBNUBILATES
OBNUBILATING
OBNUBILATION
OBNUBILATIONS
OBOE
OBOES
OBOIST
OBOISTS
OBOL
OBOLE
OBOLES
OBOLI
OBOLS
OBOLUS
OBOVATE
OBOVOID
OBSCENE
OBSCENELY
OBSCENER
OBSCENEST
OBSCENITIES
OBSCENITY
OBSCURANT
OBSCURANTIC
OBSCURANTISM
OBSCURANTISMS
OBSCURANTIST
OBSCURANTISTS
OBSCURANTS
OBSCURATION
OBSCURATIONS
OBSCURE
OBSCURED
OBSCURELY
OBSCURENESS
OBSCURENESSES
OBSCURER
OBSCURES
OBSCUREST
OBSCURING
OBSCURITIES
OBSCURITY
OBSECRATE
OBSECRATED
OBSECRATES
OBSECRATING
OBSEQUIES
OBSEQUIOUS
OBSEQUIOUSLY
OBSEQUIOUSNESS
OBSEQUY
OBSERVABILITIES
OBSERVABILITY
OBSERVABLE
OBSERVABLES
OBSERVABLY
OBSERVANCE
OBSERVANCES
OBSERVANT
OBSERVANTLY
OBSERVANTS
OBSERVATION
OBSERVATIONAL
OBSERVATIONALLY
OBSERVATIONS
OBSERVATORIES
OBSERVATORY
OBSERVE
OBSERVED
OBSERVER
OBSERVERS
OBSERVES
OBSERVING
OBSERVINGLY
OBSESS
OBSESSED
OBSESSES
OBSESSING
OBSESSION
OBSESSIONAL
OBSESSIONALLY
OBSESSIONS
OBSESSIVE
OBSESSIVELY
OBSESSIVENESS
OBSESSIVENESSES
OBSESSIVES
OBSESSOR
OBSESSORS
OBSIDIAN
OBSIDIANS
OBSOLESCE
OBSOLESCED
OBSOLESCENCE
OBSOLESCENCES
OBSOLESCENT
OBSOLESCENTLY
OBSOLESCES
OBSOLESCING
OBSOLETE
OBSOLETED
OBSOLETELY
OBSOLETENESS
OBSOLETENESSES
OBSOLETES
OBSOLETING
OBSTACLE
OBSTACLES
OBSTETRIC
OBSTETRICAL
OBSTETRICALLY
OBSTETRICIAN
OBSTETRICIANS

OBSTETRICS
OBSTINACIES
OBSTINACY
OBSTINATE
OBSTINATELY
OBSTINATENESS
OBSTINATENESSES
OBSTREPEROUS
OBSTREPEROUSLY
OBSTRUCT
OBSTRUCTED
OBSTRUCTING
OBSTRUCTION
OBSTRUCTIONISM
OBSTRUCTIONISMS
OBSTRUCTIONIST
OBSTRUCTIONISTS
OBSTRUCTIONS
OBSTRUCTIVE
OBSTRUCTIVENESS
OBSTRUCTIVES
OBSTRUCTOR
OBSTRUCTORS
OBSTRUCTS
OBSTRUENT
OBSTRUENTS
OBTAIN
OBTAINABILITIES
OBTAINABILITY
OBTAINABLE
OBTAINED
OBTAINER
OBTAINERS
OBTAINING
OBTAINMENT
OBTAINMENTS
OBTAINS
OBTECT
OBTECTED
OBTEST
OBTESTED
OBTESTING
OBTESTS
OBTRUDE
OBTRUDED
OBTRUDER
OBTRUDERS
OBTRUDES
OBTRUDING
OBTRUSION
OBTRUSIONS
OBTRUSIVE
OBTRUSIVELY
OBTRUSIVENESS
OBTRUSIVENESSES
OBTUND
OBTUNDED
OBTUNDENT
OBTUNDENTS
OBTUNDING
OBTUNDITIES
OBTUNDITY
OBTUNDS
OBTURATE
OBTURATED
OBTURATES
OBTURATING
OBTURATION
OBTURATIONS
OBTURATOR
OBTURATORS
OBTUSE
OBTUSELY
OBTUSENESS
OBTUSENESSES
OBTUSER
OBTUSEST
OBTUSITIES
OBTUSITY
OBVERSE
OBVERSELY
OBVERSES
OBVERSION
OBVERSIONS
OBVERT
OBVERTED
OBVERTING
OBVERTS
OBVIABLE
OBVIATE
OBVIATED
OBVIATES
OBVIATING
OBVIATION
OBVIATIONS
OBVIATOR
OBVIATORS
OBVIOUS
OBVIOUSLY
OBVIOUSNESS
OBVIOUSNESSES
OBVOLUTE
OCA
OCARINA
OCARINAS
OCAS
OCCASION
OCCASIONAL
OCCASIONALLY
OCCASIONED
OCCASIONING
OCCASIONS
OCCIDENT
OCCIDENTAL
OCCIDENTALIZE
OCCIDENTALIZED
OCCIDENTALIZES
OCCIDENTALIZING
OCCIDENTALLY
OCCIDENTS
OCCIPITA
OCCIPITAL
OCCIPITALLY
OCCIPITALS
OCCIPUT
OCCIPUTS
OCCLUDE
OCCLUDED
OCCLUDENT
OCCLUDES
OCCLUDING
OCCLUSAL
OCCLUSION
OCCLUSIONS
OCCLUSIVE
OCCLUSIVES
OCCULT
OCCULTATION
OCCULTATIONS
OCCULTED
OCCULTER
OCCULTERS
OCCULTING
OCCULTISM
OCCULTISMS
OCCULTIST
OCCULTISTS
OCCULTLY
OCCULTS
OCCUPANCIES
OCCUPANCY
OCCUPANT
OCCUPANTS
OCCUPATION
OCCUPATIONAL
OCCUPATIONALLY
OCCUPATIONS
OCCUPIED
OCCUPIER
OCCUPIERS
OCCUPIES
OCCUPY
OCCUPYING
OCCUR
OCCURRED
OCCURRENCE
OCCURRENCES
OCCURRENT
OCCURRENTS
OCCURRING
OCCURS
OCEAN
OCEANARIA
OCEANARIUM
OCEANARIUMS
OCEANAUT
OCEANAUTS
OCEANFRONT
OCEANFRONTS
OCEANGOING
OCEANIC
OCEANOGRAPHER
OCEANOGRAPHERS
OCEANOGRAPHIC
OCEANOGRAPHICAL
OCEANOGRAPHIES
OCEANOGRAPHY
OCEANOLOGIES
OCEANOLOGIST
OCEANOLOGISTS
OCEANOLOGY
OCEANS
OCELLAR
OCELLATE
OCELLATED
OCELLI
OCELLUS
OCELOID
OCELOT
OCELOTS
OCH
OCHE
OCHER
OCHERED
OCHERING
OCHERISH
OCHEROID
OCHEROUS
OCHERS
OCHERY
OCHES
OCHLOCRACIES
OCHLOCRACY
OCHLOCRAT
OCHLOCRATIC
OCHLOCRATICAL
OCHLOCRATS
OCHONE
OCHRE
OCHREA
OCHREAE
OCHREAS
OCHRED
OCHREOUS
OCHRES
OCHRING
OCHROID
OCHROUS
OCHRY
OCICAT
OCICATS
OCKER
OCKERS
OCOTILLO
OCOTILLOS
OCREA
OCREAE
OCREAS
OCREATE
OCTACHORD
OCTACHORDS
OCTAD
OCTADIC
OCTADS
OCTAGON
OCTAGONAL
OCTAGONALLY
OCTAGONS
OCTAHEDRA
OCTAHEDRAL
OCTAHEDRALLY
OCTAHEDRON
OCTAHEDRONS
OCTAL
OCTAMETER
OCTAMETERS
OCTAN
OCTANE
OCTANES
OCTANGLE
OCTANGLES
OCTANOL
OCTANOLS
OCTANS
OCTANT

OCTANTAL
OCTANTS
OCTAPEPTIDE
OCTAPEPTIDES
OCTARCHIES
OCTARCHY
OCTAVAL
OCTAVE
OCTAVES
OCTAVO
OCTAVOS
OCTENNIAL
OCTET
OCTETS
OCTETTE
OCTETTES
OCTILLION
OCTILLIONS
OCTODECILLION
OCTODECILLIONS
OCTOGENARIAN
OCTOGENARIANS
OCTONARIES
OCTONARY
OCTOPI
OCTOPLOID
OCTOPLOIDS
OCTOPOD
OCTOPODAN
OCTOPODANS
OCTOPODES
OCTOPODS
OCTOPOID
OCTOPUS
OCTOPUSES
OCTOROON
OCTOROONS
OCTOSYLLABIC
OCTOSYLLABICS
OCTOSYLLABLE
OCTOSYLLABLES
OCTOTHORP
OCTOTHORPE
OCTOTHORPES
OCTOTHORPS
OCTROI
OCTROIS
OCTUPLE
OCTUPLED
OCTUPLES
OCTUPLET
OCTUPLETS
OCTUPLEX
OCTUPLING
OCTUPLY
OCTYL
OCTYLS
OCULAR
OCULARIST
OCULARISTS
OCULARLY
OCULARS
OCULI
OCULIST
OCULISTS
OCULOMOTOR
OCULUS
OD
ODA
ODAH
ODAHS
ODALISK
ODALISKS
ODALISQUE
ODALISQUES
ODAS
ODD
ODDBALL
ODDBALLS
ODDER
ODDEST
ODDISH
ODDITIES
ODDITY
ODDLY
ODDMENT
ODDMENTS
ODDNESS
ODDNESSES
ODDS
ODDSMAKER
ODDSMAKERS
ODE
ODEA
ODEON
ODEONS
ODES
ODEUM
ODEUMS
ODIC
ODIFEROUS
ODIOUS
ODIOUSLY
ODIOUSNESS
ODIOUSNESSES
ODIST
ODISTS
ODIUM
ODIUMS
ODOGRAPH
ODOGRAPHS
ODOMETER
ODOMETERS
ODOMETRIES
ODOMETRY
ODONATA
ODONATE
ODONATES
ODONTOBLAST
ODONTOBLASTIC
ODONTOBLASTS
ODONTOGLOSSUM
ODONTOGLOSSUMS
ODONTOID
ODONTOIDS
ODOR
ODORANT
ODORANTS
ODORED
ODORFUL
ODORIFEROUS
ODORIFEROUSLY
ODORIFEROUSNESS
ODORIZE
ODORIZED
ODORIZER
ODORIZERS
ODORIZES
ODORIZING
ODORLESS
ODOROUS
ODOROUSLY
ODOROUSNESS
ODOROUSNESSES
ODORS
ODOUR
ODOURFUL
ODOURLESS
ODOURS
ODS
ODYL
ODYLE
ODYLES
ODYLS
ODYSSEAN
ODYSSEY
ODYSSEYS
OE
OECOLOGIES
OECOLOGY
OECUMENICAL
OEDEMA
OEDEMAS
OEDEMATA
OEDIPAL
OEDIPALLY
OEDIPEAN
OEILLADE
OEILLADES
OENOLOGICAL
OENOLOGIES
OENOLOGIST
OENOLOGISTS
OENOLOGY
OENOMEL
OENOMELS
OENOPHILE
OENOPHILES
OERSTED
OERSTEDS
OES
OESOPHAGI
OESOPHAGUS
OESTRIN
OESTRINS
OESTRIOL
OESTRIOLS
OESTROGEN
OESTROGENIC
OESTROGENS
OESTRONE
OESTRONES
OESTROUS
OESTRUAL
OESTRUM
OESTRUMS
OESTRUS
OESTRUSES
OEUVRE
OEUVRES
OF
OFAY
OFAYS
OFF
OFFA
OFFAL
OFFALS
OFFBEAT
OFFBEATS
OFFCAST
OFFCASTS
OFFCUT
OFFCUTS
OFFED
OFFENCE
OFFENCES
OFFEND
OFFENDED
OFFENDER
OFFENDERS
OFFENDING
OFFENDS
OFFENSE
OFFENSELESS
OFFENSES
OFFENSIVE
OFFENSIVELY
OFFENSIVENESS
OFFENSIVENESSES
OFFENSIVES
OFFER
OFFERED
OFFEREE
OFFEREES
OFFERER
OFFERERS
OFFERING
OFFERINGS
OFFEROR
OFFERORS
OFFERS
OFFERTORIES
OFFERTORY
OFFHAND
OFFHANDED
OFFHANDEDLY
OFFHANDEDNESS
OFFHANDEDNESSES
OFFICE
OFFICEHOLDER
OFFICEHOLDERS
OFFICER
OFFICERED
OFFICERING
OFFICERS
OFFICES
OFFICIAL
OFFICIALDOM
OFFICIALDOMS
OFFICIALESE
OFFICIALESES
OFFICIALISM
OFFICIALISMS
OFFICIALLY
OFFICIALS

OFFICIANT
OFFICIANTS
OFFICIARIES
OFFICIARY
OFFICIATE
OFFICIATED
OFFICIATES
OFFICIATING
OFFICIATION
OFFICIATIONS
OFFICINAL
OFFICINALS
OFFICIOUS
OFFICIOUSLY
OFFICIOUSNESS
OFFICIOUSNESSES
OFFING
OFFINGS
OFFISH
OFFISHLY
OFFISHNESS
OFFISHNESSES
OFFKEY
OFFLINE
OFFLOAD
OFFLOADED
OFFLOADING
OFFLOADS
OFFPRINT
OFFPRINTED
OFFPRINTING
OFFPRINTS
OFFRAMP
OFFRAMPS
OFFS
OFFSCOURING
OFFSCOURINGS
OFFSCREEN
OFFSET
OFFSETS
OFFSETTING
OFFSHOOT
OFFSHOOTS
OFFSHORE
OFFSHORES
OFFSHORING
OFFSHORINGS
OFFSIDE
OFFSIDES
OFFSPRING
OFFSPRINGS
OFFSTAGE
OFFSTAGES
OFFTRACK
OFT
OFTEN
OFTENER
OFTENEST
OFTENTIMES
OFTER
OFTEST
OFTTIMES
OGAM
OGAMS
OGDOAD
OGDOADS
OGEE
OGEED
OGEES
OGHAM
OGHAMIC
OGHAMIST
OGHAMISTS
OGHAMS
OGIVAL
OGIVE
OGIVES
OGLE
OGLED
OGLER
OGLERS
OGLES
OGLING
OGRE
OGREISH
OGREISHLY
OGREISM
OGREISMS
OGRES
OGRESS
OGRESSES
OGRISH
OGRISHLY
OGRISM
OGRISMS
OH
OHED
OHIA
OHIAS
OHING
OHM
OHMAGE
OHMAGES
OHMIC
OHMICALLY
OHMMETER
OHMMETERS
OHMS
OHO
OHS
OI
OIDIA
OIDIOID
OIDIUM
OIK
OIKS
OIL
OILBIRD
OILBIRDS
OILCAMP
OILCAMPS
OILCAN
OILCANS
OILCLOTH
OILCLOTHS
OILCUP
OILCUPS
OILED
OILER
OILERS
OILFIELD
OILFIELDS
OILHOLE
OILHOLES
OILIER
OILIEST
OILILY
OILINESS
OILINESSES
OILING
OILMAN
OILMEN
OILPAPER
OILPAPERS
OILPROOF
OILS
OILSEED
OILSEEDS
OILSKIN
OILSKINS
OILSTONE
OILSTONES
OILTIGHT
OILWAY
OILWAYS
OILY
OINK
OINKED
OINKING
OINKS
OINOLOGIES
OINOLOGY
OINOMEL
OINOMELS
OINTMENT
OINTMENTS
OITICICA
OITICICAS
OKA
OKAPI
OKAPIS
OKAS
OKAY
OKAYED
OKAYING
OKAYS
OKE
OKEH
OKEHS
OKES
OKEYDOKE
OKEYDOKEY
OKRA
OKRAS
OLALLIEBERRIES
OLALLIEBERRY
OLD
OLDE
OLDEN
OLDER
OLDEST
OLDFANGLED
OLDIE
OLDIES
OLDISH
OLDNESS
OLDNESSES
OLDS
OLDSQUAW
OLDSQUAWS
OLDSTER
OLDSTERS
OLDSTYLE
OLDSTYLES
OLDWIFE
OLDWIVES
OLDY
OLE
OLEA
OLEAGINOUS
OLEAGINOUSLY
OLEAGINOUSNESS
OLEANDER
OLEANDERS
OLEANDOMYCIN
OLEANDOMYCINS
OLEASTER
OLEASTERS
OLEATE
OLEATES
OLECRANAL
OLECRANON
OLECRANONS
OLEFIN
OLEFINE
OLEFINES
OLEFINIC
OLEFINS
OLEIC
OLEIN
OLEINE
OLEINES
OLEINS
OLEO
OLEOGRAPH
OLEOGRAPHS
OLEOMARGARINE
OLEOMARGARINES
OLEORESIN
OLEORESINOUS
OLEORESINS
OLEOS
OLES
OLESTRA
OLESTRAS
OLEUM
OLEUMS
OLFACTION
OLFACTIONS
OLFACTIVE
OLFACTOMETER
OLFACTOMETERS
OLFACTORIES
OLFACTORILY
OLFACTORY
OLIBANUM
OLIBANUMS
OLICOOK
OLICOOKS
OLIGARCH
OLIGARCHIC
OLIGARCHICAL
OLIGARCHIES
OLIGARCHS
OLIGARCHY

OLIGOCENE
OLIGOCHAETE
OLIGOCHAETES
OLIGOCLASE
OLIGOCLASES
OLIGODENDROCYTE
OLIGODENDROGLIA
OLIGOGENE
OLIGOGENES
OLIGOMER
OLIGOMERIC
OLIGOMERIZATION
OLIGOMERS
OLIGONUCLEOTIDE
OLIGOPHAGIES
OLIGOPHAGOUS
OLIGOPHAGY
OLIGOPOLIES
OLIGOPOLIST
OLIGOPOLISTIC
OLIGOPOLISTS
OLIGOPOLY
OLIGOPSONIES
OLIGOPSONISTIC
OLIGOPSONY
OLIGOSACCHARIDE
OLIGOTROPHIC
OLIGURIA
OLIGURIAS
OLIGURIC
OLINGO
OLINGOS
OLIO
OLIOS
OLIVACEOUS
OLIVARY
OLIVE
OLIVENITE
OLIVENITES
OLIVES
OLIVINE
OLIVINES
OLIVINIC
OLIVINITIC
OLLA
OLLAS
OLLIE
OLLIED
OLLIEING
OLLIES
OLOGIES
OLOGIST
OLOGISTS
OLOGY
OLOLIUQUI
OLOLIUQUIS
OLOROSO
OLOROSOS
OLYMPIAD
OLYMPIADS
OM
OMA
OMADHAUN
OMADHAUNS
OMAS
OMASA
OMASUM
OMBER
OMBERS
OMBRE
OMBRES
OMBUDSMAN
OMBUDSMANSHIP
OMBUDSMANSHIPS
OMBUDSMEN
OMBUDSPERSON
OMBUDSPERSONS
OMEGA
OMEGAS
OMELET
OMELETS
OMELETTE
OMELETTES
OMEN
OMENED
OMENING
OMENS
OMENTA
OMENTAL
OMENTUM
OMENTUMS
OMEPRAZOLE
OMEPRAZOLES
OMER
OMERS
OMERTA
OMERTAS
OMICRON
OMICRONS
OMIKRON
OMIKRONS
OMINOUS
OMINOUSLY
OMINOUSNESS
OMINOUSNESSES
OMISSIBLE
OMISSION
OMISSIONS
OMISSIVE
OMIT
OMITS
OMITTED
OMITTER
OMITTERS
OMITTING
OMMATIDIA
OMMATIDIAL
OMMATIDIUM
OMNIARCH
OMNIARCHS
OMNIBUS
OMNIBUSES
OMNIBUSSES
OMNICOMPETENCE
OMNICOMPETENCES
OMNICOMPETENT
OMNIDIRECTIONAL
OMNIFARIOUS
OMNIFIC
OMNIFICENT
OMNIFORM
OMNIMODE
OMNIPOTENCE
OMNIPOTENCES
OMNIPOTENT
OMNIPOTENTLY
OMNIPOTENTS
OMNIPRESENCE
OMNIPRESENCES
OMNIPRESENT
OMNIRANGE
OMNIRANGES
OMNISCIENCE
OMNISCIENCES
OMNISCIENT
OMNISCIENTLY
OMNIVORA
OMNIVORE
OMNIVORES
OMNIVOROUS
OMNIVOROUSLY
OMOPHAGIA
OMOPHAGIAS
OMOPHAGIC
OMOPHAGIES
OMOPHAGY
OMPHALI
OMPHALOI
OMPHALOS
OMPHALOSKEPSES
OMPHALOSKEPSIS
OMS
ON
ONAGER
ONAGERS
ONAGRI
ONANISM
ONANISMS
ONANIST
ONANISTIC
ONANISTS
ONBOARD
ONCE
ONCES
ONCET
ONCHOCERCIASES
ONCHOCERCIASIS
ONCIDIUM
ONCIDIUMS
ONCOGENE
ONCOGENES
ONCOGENESES
ONCOGENESIS
ONCOGENIC
ONCOGENICITIES
ONCOGENICITY
ONCOLOGIC
ONCOLOGICAL
ONCOLOGIES
ONCOLOGIST
ONCOLOGISTS
ONCOLOGY
ONCOMING
ONCOMINGS
ONCORNAVIRUS
ONCORNAVIRUSES
ONCOVIRUS
ONCOVIRUSES
ONDOGRAM
ONDOGRAMS
ONE
ONEFOLD
ONEIRIC
ONEIRICALLY
ONEIROMANCIES
ONEIROMANCY
ONENESS
ONENESSES
ONERIER
ONERIEST
ONEROUS
ONEROUSLY
ONEROUSNESS
ONEROUSNESSES
ONERY
ONES
ONESELF
ONETIME
ONGOING
ONGOINGNESS
ONGOINGNESSES
ONION
ONIONS
ONIONSKIN
ONIONSKINS
ONIONY
ONIUM
ONLAY
ONLAYS
ONLIEST
ONLINE
ONLOAD
ONLOADED
ONLOADING
ONLOADS
ONLOOKER
ONLOOKERS
ONLOOKING
ONLY
ONO
ONOMAST
ONOMASTIC
ONOMASTICALLY
ONOMASTICIAN
ONOMASTICIANS
ONOMASTICS
ONOMASTS
ONOMATOLOGIES
ONOMATOLOGIST
ONOMATOLOGISTS
ONOMATOLOGY
ONOMATOPOEIA
ONOMATOPOEIAS
ONOMATOPOEIC
ONOMATOPOETIC
ONOS
ONRUSH
ONRUSHES
ONRUSHING
ONS
ONSCREEN
ONSET
ONSETS
ONSHORE
ONSIDE

ONSLAUGHT
ONSLAUGHTS
ONSTAGE
ONSTREAM
ONTIC
ONTICALLY
ONTO
ONTOGENESES
ONTOGENESIS
ONTOGENETIC
ONTOGENETICALLY
ONTOGENIC
ONTOGENIES
ONTOGENY
ONTOLOGIC
ONTOLOGICAL
ONTOLOGICALLY
ONTOLOGIES
ONTOLOGIST
ONTOLOGISTS
ONTOLOGY
ONUS
ONUSES
ONWARD
ONWARDS
ONYCHOPHORAN
ONYCHOPHORANS
ONYX
ONYXES
OOCYST
OOCYSTS
OOCYTE
OOCYTES
OODLES
OODLINS
OOF
OOGAMETE
OOGAMETES
OOGAMIES
OOGAMOUS
OOGAMY
OOGENESES
OOGENESIS
OOGENETIC
OOGENIES
OOGENY
OOGONIA
OOGONIAL
OOGONIUM
OOGONIUMS
OOH
OOHED
OOHING
OOHS
OOLACHAN
OOLACHANS
OOLICHAN
OOLICHANS
OOLITE
OOLITES
OOLITH
OOLITHS
OOLITIC
OOLOGIC
OOLOGICAL
OOLOGIES
OOLOGIST
OOLOGISTS
OOLOGY
OOLONG
OOLONGS
OOMIAC
OOMIACK
OOMIACKS
OOMIACS
OOMIAK
OOMIAKS
OOMPAH
OOMPAHED
OOMPAHING
OOMPAHS
OOMPH
OOMPHS
OOPHORECTOMIES
OOPHORECTOMY
OOPHYTE
OOPHYTES
OOPHYTIC
OOPS
OORALI
OORALIS
OORIE
OOSPERM
OOSPERMS
OOSPHERE
OOSPHERES
OOSPORE
OOSPORES
OOSPORIC
OOT
OOTHECA
OOTHECAE
OOTHECAL
OOTID
OOTIDS
OOTS
OOZE
OOZED
OOZES
OOZIER
OOZIEST
OOZILY
OOZINESS
OOZINESSES
OOZING
OOZY
OP
OPA
OPACIFIED
OPACIFIER
OPACIFIERS
OPACIFIES
OPACIFY
OPACIFYING
OPACITIES
OPACITY
OPAH
OPAHS
OPAL
OPALESCE
OPALESCED
OPALESCENCE
OPALESCENCES
OPALESCENT
OPALESCENTLY
OPALESCES
OPALESCING
OPALINE
OPALINES
OPALS
OPAQUE
OPAQUED
OPAQUELY
OPAQUENESS
OPAQUENESSES
OPAQUER
OPAQUES
OPAQUEST
OPAQUING
OPAS
OPE
OPED
OPEN
OPENABILITIES
OPENABILITY
OPENABLE
OPENCAST
OPENED
OPENER
OPENERS
OPENEST
OPENHANDED
OPENHANDEDLY
OPENHANDEDNESS
OPENHEARTED
OPENHEARTEDLY
OPENHEARTEDNESS
OPENING
OPENINGS
OPENLY
OPENMOUTHED
OPENMOUTHEDLY
OPENMOUTHEDNESS
OPENNESS
OPENNESSES
OPENS
OPENWORK
OPENWORKS
OPERA
OPERABILITIES
OPERABILITY
OPERABLE
OPERABLY
OPERAGOER
OPERAGOERS
OPERAGOING
OPERAGOINGS
OPERAND
OPERANDS
OPERANT
OPERANTLY
OPERANTS
OPERAS
OPERATE
OPERATED
OPERATES
OPERATIC
OPERATICALLY
OPERATICS
OPERATING
OPERATION
OPERATIONAL
OPERATIONALISM
OPERATIONALISMS
OPERATIONALIST
OPERATIONALISTS
OPERATIONALLY
OPERATIONISM
OPERATIONISMS
OPERATIONIST
OPERATIONISTS
OPERATIONS
OPERATIVE
OPERATIVELY
OPERATIVENESS
OPERATIVENESSES
OPERATIVES
OPERATOR
OPERATORLESS
OPERATORS
OPERCELE
OPERCELES
OPERCULA
OPERCULAR
OPERCULARS
OPERCULATE
OPERCULATED
OPERCULE
OPERCULES
OPERCULUM
OPERCULUMS
OPERETTA
OPERETTAS
OPERETTIST
OPERETTISTS
OPERON
OPERONS
OPEROSE
OPEROSELY
OPEROSENESS
OPEROSENESSES
OPES
OPHIDIAN
OPHIDIANS
OPHIOLITE
OPHIOLITES
OPHIOLOGIES
OPHIOLOGY
OPHITE
OPHITES
OPHITIC
OPHIUROID
OPHIUROIDS
OPHTHALMIA
OPHTHALMIAS
OPHTHALMIC
OPHTHALMOLOGIC
OPHTHALMOLOGIES
OPHTHALMOLOGIST
OPHTHALMOLOGY
OPHTHALMOSCOPE
OPHTHALMOSCOPES
OPHTHALMOSCOPIC
OPHTHALMOSCOPY
OPIATE

OPIATED
OPIATES
OPIATING
OPINE
OPINED
OPINES
OPING
OPINING
OPINION
OPINIONATED
OPINIONATEDLY
OPINIONATEDNESS
OPINIONATIVE
OPINIONATIVELY
OPINIONED
OPINIONS
OPIOID
OPIOIDS
OPISTHOBRANCH
OPISTHOBRANCHS
OPIUM
OPIUMISM
OPIUMISMS
OPIUMS
OPOPANAX
OPOPANAXES
OPOSSUM
OPOSSUMS
OPPIDAN
OPPIDANS
OPPILANT
OPPILATE
OPPILATED
OPPILATES
OPPILATING
OPPONENCIES
OPPONENCY
OPPONENS
OPPONENT
OPPONENTS
OPPORTUNE
OPPORTUNELY
OPPORTUNENESS
OPPORTUNENESSES
OPPORTUNISM
OPPORTUNISMS
OPPORTUNIST
OPPORTUNISTIC
OPPORTUNISTS
OPPORTUNITIES
OPPORTUNITY
OPPOSABILITIES
OPPOSABILITY
OPPOSABLE
OPPOSE
OPPOSED
OPPOSELESS
OPPOSER
OPPOSERS
OPPOSES
OPPOSING
OPPOSITE
OPPOSITELY
OPPOSITENESS
OPPOSITENESSES
OPPOSITES
OPPOSITION
OPPOSITIONAL
OPPOSITIONIST
OPPOSITIONISTS
OPPOSITIONS
OPPRESS
OPPRESSED
OPPRESSES
OPPRESSING
OPPRESSION
OPPRESSIONS
OPPRESSIVE
OPPRESSIVELY
OPPRESSIVENESS
OPPRESSOR
OPPRESSORS
OPPROBRIOUS
OPPROBRIOUSLY
OPPROBRIOUSNESS
OPPROBRIUM
OPPROBRIUMS
OPPUGN
OPPUGNANT
OPPUGNED
OPPUGNER
OPPUGNERS
OPPUGNING
OPPUGNS
OPS
OPSIMATH
OPSIMATHS
OPSIN
OPSINS
OPSONIC
OPSONIFIED
OPSONIFIES
OPSONIFY
OPSONIFYING
OPSONIN
OPSONINS
OPSONISE
OPSONISED
OPSONISES
OPSONISING
OPSONIZE
OPSONIZED
OPSONIZES
OPSONIZING
OPT
OPTATIVE
OPTATIVELY
OPTATIVES
OPTED
OPTIC
OPTICAL
OPTICALLY
OPTICIAN
OPTICIANS
OPTICIST
OPTICISTS
OPTICS
OPTIMA
OPTIMAL
OPTIMALITIES
OPTIMALITY
OPTIMALLY
OPTIME
OPTIMES
OPTIMISATION
OPTIMISATIONS
OPTIMISE
OPTIMISED
OPTIMISES
OPTIMISING
OPTIMISM
OPTIMISMS
OPTIMIST
OPTIMISTIC
OPTIMISTICALLY
OPTIMISTS
OPTIMIZATION
OPTIMIZATIONS
OPTIMIZE
OPTIMIZED
OPTIMIZER
OPTIMIZERS
OPTIMIZES
OPTIMIZING
OPTIMUM
OPTIMUMS
OPTING
OPTION
OPTIONAL
OPTIONALITIES
OPTIONALITY
OPTIONALLY
OPTIONALS
OPTIONED
OPTIONEE
OPTIONEES
OPTIONING
OPTIONS
OPTOELECTRONIC
OPTOELECTRONICS
OPTOKINETIC
OPTOMETER
OPTOMETERS
OPTOMETRIC
OPTOMETRIES
OPTOMETRIST
OPTOMETRISTS
OPTOMETRY
OPTRONIC
OPTS
OPULENCE
OPULENCES
OPULENCIES
OPULENCY
OPULENT
OPULENTLY
OPUNTIA
OPUNTIAS
OPUS
OPUSCULA
OPUSCULAR
OPUSCULE
OPUSCULES
OPUSCULUM
OPUSES
OQUASSA
OQUASSAS
OR
ORA
ORACH
ORACHE
ORACHES
ORACIES
ORACLE
ORACLES
ORACULAR
ORACULARITIES
ORACULARITY
ORACULARLY
ORACY
ORAD
ORAL
ORALISM
ORALISMS
ORALIST
ORALISTS
ORALITIES
ORALITY
ORALLY
ORALS
ORANG
ORANGE
ORANGEADE
ORANGEADES
ORANGERIE
ORANGERIES
ORANGERY
ORANGES
ORANGEWOOD
ORANGEWOODS
ORANGEY
ORANGIER
ORANGIEST
ORANGISH
ORANGS
ORANGUTAN
ORANGUTANS
ORANGY
ORATE
ORATED
ORATES
ORATING
ORATION
ORATIONS
ORATOR
ORATORICAL
ORATORICALLY
ORATORIES
ORATORIO
ORATORIOS
ORATORS
ORATORY
ORATRESS
ORATRESSES
ORATRICES
ORATRIX
ORATURE
ORATURES
ORB
ORBED
ORBICULAR
ORBICULARLY
ORBICULATE
ORBIER
ORBIEST

ORBING
ORBIT
ORBITAL
ORBITALS
ORBITED
ORBITER
ORBITERS
ORBITING
ORBITS
ORBLESS
ORBS
ORBY
ORC
ORCA
ORCAS
ORCEIN
ORCEINS
ORCHARD
ORCHARDIST
ORCHARDISTS
ORCHARDS
ORCHESTRA
ORCHESTRAL
ORCHESTRALLY
ORCHESTRAS
ORCHESTRATE
ORCHESTRATED
ORCHESTRATER
ORCHESTRATERS
ORCHESTRATES
ORCHESTRATING
ORCHESTRATION
ORCHESTRATIONAL
ORCHESTRATIONS
ORCHESTRATOR
ORCHESTRATORS
ORCHID
ORCHIDACEOUS
ORCHIDLIKE
ORCHIDS
ORCHIECTOMIES
ORCHIECTOMY
ORCHIL
ORCHILLA
ORCHILLAS
ORCHILS
ORCHIS
ORCHISES
ORCHITIC
ORCHITIS
ORCHITISES
ORCIN
ORCINOL
ORCINOLS
ORCINS
ORCS
ORDAIN
ORDAINED
ORDAINER
ORDAINERS
ORDAINING
ORDAINMENT
ORDAINMENTS
ORDAINS
ORDEAL
ORDEALS
ORDER
ORDERABLE
ORDERED
ORDERER
ORDERERS
ORDERING
ORDERLESS
ORDERLIES
ORDERLINESS
ORDERLINESSES
ORDERLY
ORDERS
ORDINAL
ORDINALLY
ORDINALS
ORDINANCE
ORDINANCES
ORDINAND
ORDINANDS
ORDINARIER
ORDINARIES
ORDINARIEST
ORDINARILY
ORDINARINESS
ORDINARINESSES
ORDINARY
ORDINATE
ORDINATES
ORDINATION
ORDINATIONS
ORDINES
ORDNANCE
ORDNANCES
ORDO
ORDONNANCE
ORDONNANCES
ORDOS
ORDURE
ORDURES
ORDUROUS
ORE
OREAD
OREADS
OREBODIES
OREBODY
ORECCHIETTE
ORECTIC
ORECTIVE
OREGANO
OREGANOS
OREIDE
OREIDES
OREODONT
OREODONTS
ORES
ORFRAY
ORFRAYS
ORG
ORGAN
ORGANA
ORGANDIE
ORGANDIES
ORGANDY
ORGANELLE
ORGANELLES
ORGANIC
ORGANICALLY
ORGANICISM
ORGANICISMS
ORGANICIST
ORGANICISTS
ORGANICITIES
ORGANICITY
ORGANICS
ORGANISATION
ORGANISATIONAL
ORGANISATIONS
ORGANISE
ORGANISED
ORGANISER
ORGANISERS
ORGANISES
ORGANISING
ORGANISM
ORGANISMAL
ORGANISMIC
ORGANISMICALLY
ORGANISMS
ORGANIST
ORGANISTS
ORGANIZABLE
ORGANIZATION
ORGANIZATIONAL
ORGANIZATIONS
ORGANIZE
ORGANIZED
ORGANIZER
ORGANIZERS
ORGANIZES
ORGANIZING
ORGANOCHLORINE
ORGANOCHLORINES
ORGANOGENESES
ORGANOGENESIS
ORGANOGENETIC
ORGANOLEPTIC
ORGANOLOGIES
ORGANOLOGY
ORGANOMERCURIAL
ORGANOMETALLIC
ORGANOMETALLICS
ORGANON
ORGANONS
ORGANOPHOSPHATE
ORGANOSOL
ORGANOSOLS
ORGANS
ORGANUM
ORGANUMS
ORGANZA
ORGANZAS
ORGANZINE
ORGANZINES
ORGASM
ORGASMED
ORGASMIC
ORGASMING
ORGASMS
ORGASTIC
ORGEAT
ORGEATS
ORGIAC
ORGIAST
ORGIASTIC
ORGIASTICALLY
ORGIASTS
ORGIC
ORGIES
ORGONE
ORGONES
ORGS
ORGULOUS
ORGY
ORIBATID
ORIBATIDS
ORIBI
ORIBIS
ORICHALC
ORICHALCS
ORIEL
ORIELS
ORIENT
ORIENTAL
ORIENTALISM
ORIENTALISMS
ORIENTALIST
ORIENTALISTS
ORIENTALIZATION
ORIENTALIZE
ORIENTALIZED
ORIENTALIZES
ORIENTALIZING
ORIENTALLY
ORIENTALS
ORIENTATE
ORIENTATED
ORIENTATES
ORIENTATING
ORIENTATION
ORIENTATIONAL
ORIENTATIONALLY
ORIENTATIONS
ORIENTED
ORIENTEER
ORIENTEERING
ORIENTEERINGS
ORIENTEERS
ORIENTER
ORIENTERS
ORIENTING
ORIENTS
ORIFICE
ORIFICES
ORIFICIAL
ORIFLAMME
ORIFLAMMES
ORIGAMI
ORIGAMIS
ORIGAN
ORIGANS
ORIGANUM
ORIGANUMS
ORIGIN
ORIGINAL
ORIGINALITIES
ORIGINALITY
ORIGINALLY
ORIGINALS
ORIGINATE

ORIGINATED
ORIGINATES
ORIGINATING
ORIGINATION
ORIGINATIONS
ORIGINATIVE
ORIGINATIVELY
ORIGINATOR
ORIGINATORS
ORIGINS
ORINASAL
ORINASALS
ORIOLE
ORIOLES
ORISHA
ORISHAS
ORISMOLOGICAL
ORISMOLOGIES
ORISMOLOGY
ORISON
ORISONS
ORLE
ORLES
ORLON
ORLONS
ORLOP
ORLOPS
ORMER
ORMERS
ORMOLU
ORMOLUS
ORNAMENT
ORNAMENTAL
ORNAMENTALLY
ORNAMENTALS
ORNAMENTATION
ORNAMENTATIONS
ORNAMENTED
ORNAMENTING
ORNAMENTS
ORNATE
ORNATELY
ORNATENESS
ORNATENESSES
ORNERIER
ORNERIEST
ORNERINESS
ORNERINESSES
ORNERY
ORNIS
ORNITHES
ORNITHIC
ORNITHINE
ORNITHINES
ORNITHISCHIAN
ORNITHISCHIANS
ORNITHOID
ORNITHOLOGIC
ORNITHOLOGICAL
ORNITHOLOGIES
ORNITHOLOGIST
ORNITHOLOGISTS
ORNITHOLOGY
ORNITHOPOD
ORNITHOPODS
ORNITHOPTER
ORNITHOPTERS
ORNITHOSES
ORNITHOSIS
OROGEN
OROGENESES
OROGENESIS
OROGENETIC
OROGENIC
OROGENIES
OROGENS
OROGENY
OROGRAPHIC
OROGRAPHICAL
OROGRAPHIES
OROGRAPHY
OROIDE
OROIDES
OROLOGIES
OROLOGIST
OROLOGISTS
OROLOGY
OROMETER
OROMETERS
OROPHARYNGEAL
OROPHARYNGES
OROPHARYNX
OROPHARYNXES
OROTUND
OROTUNDITIES
OROTUNDITY
ORPHAN
ORPHANAGE
ORPHANAGES
ORPHANED
ORPHANHOOD
ORPHANHOODS
ORPHANING
ORPHANS
ORPHIC
ORPHICAL
ORPHICALLY
ORPHISM
ORPHISMS
ORPHREY
ORPHREYED
ORPHREYS
ORPIMENT
ORPIMENTS
ORPIN
ORPINE
ORPINES
ORPINS
ORRA
ORRERIES
ORRERY
ORRICE
ORRICES
ORRIS
ORRISES
ORRISROOT
ORRISROOTS
ORS
ORT
ORTHICON
ORTHICONS
ORTHO
ORTHOCENTER
ORTHOCENTERS
ORTHOCHROMATIC
ORTHOCLASE
ORTHOCLASES
ORTHODONTIA
ORTHODONTIAS
ORTHODONTIC
ORTHODONTICALLY
ORTHODONTICS
ORTHODONTIST
ORTHODONTISTS
ORTHODOX
ORTHODOXES
ORTHODOXIES
ORTHODOXLY
ORTHODOXY
ORTHOEPIC
ORTHOEPICALLY
ORTHOEPIES
ORTHOEPIST
ORTHOEPISTS
ORTHOEPY
ORTHOGENESES
ORTHOGENESIS
ORTHOGENETIC
ORTHOGONAL
ORTHOGONALITIES
ORTHOGONALITY
ORTHOGONALIZE
ORTHOGONALIZED
ORTHOGONALIZES
ORTHOGONALIZING
ORTHOGONALLY
ORTHOGRADE
ORTHOGRAPHIC
ORTHOGRAPHICAL
ORTHOGRAPHIES
ORTHOGRAPHY
ORTHOMOLECULAR
ORTHOMYXOVIRUS
ORTHONORMAL
ORTHOPAEDIC
ORTHOPAEDICS
ORTHOPAEDIST
ORTHOPAEDISTS
ORTHOPEDIC
ORTHOPEDICALLY
ORTHOPEDICS
ORTHOPEDIST
ORTHOPEDISTS
ORTHOPHOSPHATE
ORTHOPHOSPHATES
ORTHOPSYCHIATRY
ORTHOPTER
ORTHOPTERA
ORTHOPTERAN
ORTHOPTERANS
ORTHOPTERIST
ORTHOPTERISTS
ORTHOPTEROID
ORTHOPTEROIDS
ORTHOPTERS
ORTHOPTIC
ORTHORHOMBIC
ORTHOSCOPIC
ORTHOSES
ORTHOSIS
ORTHOSTATIC
ORTHOTIC
ORTHOTICS
ORTHOTIST
ORTHOTISTS
ORTHOTROPOUS
ORTOLAN
ORTOLANS
ORTS
ORYX
ORYXES
ORZO
ORZOS
OS
OSAR
OSCAR
OSCARS
OSCILLATE
OSCILLATED
OSCILLATES
OSCILLATING
OSCILLATION
OSCILLATIONAL
OSCILLATIONS
OSCILLATOR
OSCILLATORS
OSCILLATORY
OSCILLOGRAM
OSCILLOGRAMS
OSCILLOGRAPH
OSCILLOGRAPHIC
OSCILLOGRAPHIES
OSCILLOGRAPHS
OSCILLOGRAPHY
OSCILLOSCOPE
OSCILLOSCOPES
OSCILLOSCOPIC
OSCINE
OSCINES
OSCININE
OSCITANCE
OSCITANCES
OSCITANCIES
OSCITANCY
OSCITANT
OSCULA
OSCULANT
OSCULAR
OSCULATE
OSCULATED
OSCULATES
OSCULATING
OSCULATION
OSCULATIONS
OSCULATORY
OSCULE
OSCULES
OSCULUM
OSE
OSES
OSETRA
OSETRAS
OSIER
OSIERED
OSIERS

OSMATIC
OSMETERIA
OSMETERIUM
OSMIC
OSMICALLY
OSMICS
OSMIOUS
OSMIRIDIUM
OSMIRIDIUMS
OSMIUM
OSMIUMS
OSMOL
OSMOLAL
OSMOLALITIES
OSMOLALITY
OSMOLAR
OSMOLARITIES
OSMOLARITY
OSMOLE
OSMOLES
OSMOLS
OSMOMETER
OSMOMETERS
OSMOMETRIC
OSMOMETRIES
OSMOMETRY
OSMOREGULATION
OSMOREGULATIONS
OSMOREGULATORY
OSMOSE
OSMOSED
OSMOSES
OSMOSING
OSMOSIS
OSMOTIC
OSMOTICALLY
OSMOUS
OSMUND
OSMUNDA
OSMUNDAS
OSMUNDINE
OSMUNDINES
OSMUNDS
OSNABURG
OSNABURGS
OSPREY
OSPREYS
OSSA
OSSATURE
OSSATURES
OSSEIN
OSSEINS
OSSEOUS
OSSEOUSLY
OSSETRA
OSSETRAS
OSSIA
OSSICLE
OSSICLES
OSSICULAR
OSSIFIC
OSSIFICATION
OSSIFICATIONS
OSSIFIED
OSSIFIER
OSSIFIERS
OSSIFIES
OSSIFRAGE
OSSIFRAGES
OSSIFY
OSSIFYING
OSSOBUCO
OSSOBUCOS
OSSUARIES
OSSUARY
OSTEAL
OSTEITIC
OSTEITIDES
OSTEITIS
OSTENSIBLE
OSTENSIBLY
OSTENSIVE
OSTENSIVELY
OSTENSORIA
OSTENSORIES
OSTENSORIUM
OSTENSORY
OSTENTATION
OSTENTATIONS
OSTENTATIOUS
OSTENTATIOUSLY
OSTEOARTHRITIC
OSTEOARTHRITIS
OSTEOBLAST
OSTEOBLASTIC
OSTEOBLASTS
OSTEOCLAST
OSTEOCLASTIC
OSTEOCLASTS
OSTEOCYTE
OSTEOCYTES
OSTEOGENESES
OSTEOGENESIS
OSTEOGENIC
OSTEOID
OSTEOIDS
OSTEOLOGICAL
OSTEOLOGIES
OSTEOLOGIST
OSTEOLOGISTS
OSTEOLOGY
OSTEOMA
OSTEOMALACIA
OSTEOMALACIAS
OSTEOMAS
OSTEOMATA
OSTEOMYELITIDES
OSTEOMYELITIS
OSTEOMYELITISES
OSTEOPATH
OSTEOPATHIC
OSTEOPATHICALLY
OSTEOPATHIES
OSTEOPATHS
OSTEOPATHY
OSTEOPHYTE
OSTEOPHYTES
OSTEOPLASTIC
OSTEOPLASTIES
OSTEOPLASTY
OSTEOPOROSES
OSTEOPOROSIS
OSTEOPOROTIC
OSTEOSARCOMA
OSTEOSARCOMAS
OSTEOSARCOMATA
OSTEOSES
OSTEOSIS
OSTEOSISES
OSTEOTOME
OSTEOTOMES
OSTEOTOMIES
OSTEOTOMY
OSTIA
OSTIARIES
OSTIARY
OSTINATI
OSTINATO
OSTINATOS
OSTIOLAR
OSTIOLE
OSTIOLES
OSTIUM
OSTLER
OSTLERS
OSTMARK
OSTMARKS
OSTOMATE
OSTOMATES
OSTOMIES
OSTOMY
OSTOSES
OSTOSIS
OSTOSISES
OSTRACA
OSTRACISE
OSTRACISED
OSTRACISES
OSTRACISING
OSTRACISM
OSTRACISMS
OSTRACIZE
OSTRACIZED
OSTRACIZES
OSTRACIZING
OSTRACOD
OSTRACODE
OSTRACODERM
OSTRACODERMS
OSTRACODES
OSTRACODS
OSTRACON
OSTRAKA
OSTRAKON
OSTRICH
OSTRICHES
OSTRICHLIKE
OTAKU
OTALGIA
OTALGIAS
OTALGIC
OTALGIES
OTALGY
OTHER
OTHERGUESS
OTHERNESS
OTHERNESSES
OTHERS
OTHERWHERE
OTHERWHILE
OTHERWHILES
OTHERWISE
OTHERWORLD
OTHERWORLDLY
OTHERWORLDS
OTIC
OTIOSE
OTIOSELY
OTIOSENESS
OTIOSENESSES
OTIOSITIES
OTIOSITY
OTITIC
OTITIDES
OTITIS
OTITISES
OTOCYST
OTOCYSTIC
OTOCYSTS
OTOLARYNGOLOGY
OTOLITH
OTOLITHIC
OTOLITHS
OTOLOGIC
OTOLOGICAL
OTOLOGIES
OTOLOGIST
OTOLOGISTS
OTOLOGY
OTOPLASTIES
OTOPLASTY
OTOSCLEROSES
OTOSCLEROSIS
OTOSCOPE
OTOSCOPES
OTOSCOPIES
OTOSCOPY
OTOTOXIC
OTOTOXICITIES
OTOTOXICITY
OTTAR
OTTARS
OTTAVA
OTTAVAS
OTTER
OTTERHOUND
OTTERHOUNDS
OTTERS
OTTO
OTTOMAN
OTTOMANS
OTTOS
OUABAIN
OUABAINS
OUBLIETTE
OUBLIETTES
OUCH
OUCHED
OUCHES
OUCHING
OUD
OUDS
OUGHT
OUGHTED
OUGHTING

OUGHTS
OUGIYA
OUGIYAS
OUGUIYA
OUGUIYAS
OUISTITI
OUISTITIS
OUNCE
OUNCES
OUPH
OUPHE
OUPHES
OUPHS
OUR
OURANG
OURANGS
OURARI
OURARIS
OUREBI
OUREBIS
OURIE
OURS
OURSELF
OURSELVES
OUSEL
OUSELS
OUST
OUSTED
OUSTER
OUSTERS
OUSTING
OUSTS
OUT
OUTA
OUTACHIEVE
OUTACHIEVED
OUTACHIEVES
OUTACHIEVING
OUTACT
OUTACTED
OUTACTING
OUTACTS
OUTADD
OUTADDED
OUTADDING
OUTADDS
OUTAGE
OUTAGES
OUTARGUE
OUTARGUED
OUTARGUES
OUTARGUING
OUTASK
OUTASKED
OUTASKING
OUTASKS
OUTATE
OUTBACK
OUTBACKER
OUTBACKERS
OUTBACKS
OUTBAKE
OUTBAKED
OUTBAKES
OUTBAKING
OUTBALANCE
OUTBALANCED
OUTBALANCES
OUTBALANCING
OUTBARGAIN
OUTBARGAINED
OUTBARGAINING
OUTBARGAINS
OUTBARK
OUTBARKED
OUTBARKING
OUTBARKS
OUTBAWL
OUTBAWLED
OUTBAWLING
OUTBAWLS
OUTBEAM
OUTBEAMED
OUTBEAMING
OUTBEAMS
OUTBEG
OUTBEGGED
OUTBEGGING
OUTBEGS
OUTBID
OUTBIDDEN
OUTBIDDER
OUTBIDDERS
OUTBIDDING
OUTBIDS
OUTBITCH
OUTBITCHED
OUTBITCHES
OUTBITCHING
OUTBLAZE
OUTBLAZED
OUTBLAZES
OUTBLAZING
OUTBLEAT
OUTBLEATED
OUTBLEATING
OUTBLEATS
OUTBLESS
OUTBLESSED
OUTBLESSES
OUTBLESSING
OUTBLOOM
OUTBLOOMED
OUTBLOOMING
OUTBLOOMS
OUTBLUFF
OUTBLUFFED
OUTBLUFFING
OUTBLUFFS
OUTBLUSH
OUTBLUSHED
OUTBLUSHES
OUTBLUSHING
OUTBOARD
OUTBOARDS
OUTBOAST
OUTBOASTED
OUTBOASTING
OUTBOASTS
OUTBOUGHT
OUTBOUND
OUTBOX
OUTBOXED
OUTBOXES
OUTBOXING
OUTBRAG
OUTBRAGGED
OUTBRAGGING
OUTBRAGS
OUTBRAVE
OUTBRAVED
OUTBRAVES
OUTBRAVING
OUTBRAWL
OUTBRAWLED
OUTBRAWLING
OUTBRAWLS
OUTBRAZEN
OUTBRAZENED
OUTBRAZENING
OUTBRAZENS
OUTBREAK
OUTBREAKS
OUTBRED
OUTBREED
OUTBREEDING
OUTBREEDINGS
OUTBREEDS
OUTBRIBE
OUTBRIBED
OUTBRIBES
OUTBRIBING
OUTBUILD
OUTBUILDING
OUTBUILDINGS
OUTBUILDS
OUTBUILT
OUTBULGE
OUTBULGED
OUTBULGES
OUTBULGING
OUTBULK
OUTBULKED
OUTBULKING
OUTBULKS
OUTBULLIED
OUTBULLIES
OUTBULLY
OUTBULLYING
OUTBURN
OUTBURNED
OUTBURNING
OUTBURNS
OUTBURNT
OUTBURST
OUTBURSTS
OUTBUY
OUTBUYING
OUTBUYS
OUTBY
OUTBYE
OUTCALL
OUTCALLS
OUTCAPER
OUTCAPERED
OUTCAPERING
OUTCAPERS
OUTCAST
OUTCASTE
OUTCASTED
OUTCASTES
OUTCASTING
OUTCASTS
OUTCATCH
OUTCATCHES
OUTCATCHING
OUTCAUGHT
OUTCAVIL
OUTCAVILED
OUTCAVILING
OUTCAVILLED
OUTCAVILLING
OUTCAVILS
OUTCHARGE
OUTCHARGED
OUTCHARGES
OUTCHARGING
OUTCHARM
OUTCHARMED
OUTCHARMING
OUTCHARMS
OUTCHEAT
OUTCHEATED
OUTCHEATING
OUTCHEATS
OUTCHID
OUTCHIDDEN
OUTCHIDE
OUTCHIDED
OUTCHIDES
OUTCHIDING
OUTCITIES
OUTCITY
OUTCLASS
OUTCLASSED
OUTCLASSES
OUTCLASSING
OUTCLIMB
OUTCLIMBED
OUTCLIMBING
OUTCLIMBS
OUTCLOMB
OUTCOACH
OUTCOACHED
OUTCOACHES
OUTCOACHING
OUTCOME
OUTCOMES
OUTCOMPETE
OUTCOMPETED
OUTCOMPETES
OUTCOMPETING
OUTCOOK
OUTCOOKED
OUTCOOKING
OUTCOOKS
OUTCOUNT
OUTCOUNTED
OUTCOUNTING
OUTCOUNTS
OUTCRAWL
OUTCRAWLED
OUTCRAWLING
OUTCRAWLS
OUTCRIED

OUTCRIES
OUTCROP
OUTCROPPED
OUTCROPPING
OUTCROPPINGS
OUTCROPS
OUTCROSS
OUTCROSSED
OUTCROSSES
OUTCROSSING
OUTCROW
OUTCROWD
OUTCROWDED
OUTCROWDING
OUTCROWDS
OUTCROWED
OUTCROWING
OUTCROWS
OUTCRY
OUTCRYING
OUTCURSE
OUTCURSED
OUTCURSES
OUTCURSING
OUTCURVE
OUTCURVES
OUTDANCE
OUTDANCED
OUTDANCES
OUTDANCING
OUTDARE
OUTDARED
OUTDARES
OUTDARING
OUTDATE
OUTDATED
OUTDATEDLY
OUTDATEDNESS
OUTDATEDNESSES
OUTDATES
OUTDATING
OUTDAZZLE
OUTDAZZLED
OUTDAZZLES
OUTDAZZLING
OUTDEBATE
OUTDEBATED
OUTDEBATES
OUTDEBATING
OUTDELIVER
OUTDELIVERED
OUTDELIVERING
OUTDELIVERS
OUTDESIGN
OUTDESIGNED
OUTDESIGNING
OUTDESIGNS
OUTDID
OUTDISTANCE
OUTDISTANCED
OUTDISTANCES
OUTDISTANCING
OUTDO
OUTDODGE
OUTDODGED
OUTDODGES
OUTDODGING
OUTDOER
OUTDOERS
OUTDOES
OUTDOING
OUTDONE
OUTDOOR
OUTDOORS
OUTDOORSMAN
OUTDOORSMANSHIP
OUTDOORSMEN
OUTDOORSWOMAN
OUTDOORSWOMEN
OUTDOORSY
OUTDRAG
OUTDRAGGED
OUTDRAGGING
OUTDRAGS
OUTDRANK
OUTDRAW
OUTDRAWING
OUTDRAWN
OUTDRAWS
OUTDREAM
OUTDREAMED
OUTDREAMING
OUTDREAMS
OUTDREAMT
OUTDRESS
OUTDRESSED
OUTDRESSES
OUTDRESSING
OUTDREW
OUTDRINK
OUTDRINKING
OUTDRINKS
OUTDRIVE
OUTDRIVEN
OUTDRIVES
OUTDRIVING
OUTDROP
OUTDROPPED
OUTDROPPING
OUTDROPS
OUTDROVE
OUTDRUNK
OUTDUEL
OUTDUELED
OUTDUELING
OUTDUELLED
OUTDUELLING
OUTDUELS
OUTEARN
OUTEARNED
OUTEARNING
OUTEARNS
OUTEAT
OUTEATEN
OUTEATING
OUTEATS
OUTECHO
OUTECHOED
OUTECHOES
OUTECHOING
OUTED
OUTER
OUTERCOAT
OUTERCOATS
OUTERCOURSE
OUTERCOURSES
OUTERMOST
OUTERS
OUTERWEAR
OUTFABLE
OUTFABLED
OUTFABLES
OUTFABLING
OUTFACE
OUTFACED
OUTFACES
OUTFACING
OUTFALL
OUTFALLS
OUTFAST
OUTFASTED
OUTFASTING
OUTFASTS
OUTFAWN
OUTFAWNED
OUTFAWNING
OUTFAWNS
OUTFEAST
OUTFEASTED
OUTFEASTING
OUTFEASTS
OUTFEEL
OUTFEELING
OUTFEELS
OUTFELT
OUTFENCE
OUTFENCED
OUTFENCES
OUTFENCING
OUTFIELD
OUTFIELDER
OUTFIELDERS
OUTFIELDS
OUTFIGHT
OUTFIGHTING
OUTFIGHTS
OUTFIGURE
OUTFIGURED
OUTFIGURES
OUTFIGURING
OUTFIND
OUTFINDING
OUTFINDS
OUTFIRE
OUTFIRED
OUTFIRES
OUTFIRING
OUTFISH
OUTFISHED
OUTFISHES
OUTFISHING
OUTFIT
OUTFITS
OUTFITTED
OUTFITTER
OUTFITTERS
OUTFITTING
OUTFLANK
OUTFLANKED
OUTFLANKING
OUTFLANKS
OUTFLEW
OUTFLIES
OUTFLOAT
OUTFLOATED
OUTFLOATING
OUTFLOATS
OUTFLOW
OUTFLOWED
OUTFLOWING
OUTFLOWN
OUTFLOWS
OUTFLY
OUTFLYING
OUTFOOL
OUTFOOLED
OUTFOOLING
OUTFOOLS
OUTFOOT
OUTFOOTED
OUTFOOTING
OUTFOOTS
OUTFOUGHT
OUTFOUND
OUTFOX
OUTFOXED
OUTFOXES
OUTFOXING
OUTFROWN
OUTFROWNED
OUTFROWNING
OUTFROWNS
OUTFUMBLE
OUTFUMBLED
OUTFUMBLES
OUTFUMBLING
OUTGAIN
OUTGAINED
OUTGAINING
OUTGAINS
OUTGALLOP
OUTGALLOPED
OUTGALLOPING
OUTGALLOPS
OUTGAMBLE
OUTGAMBLED
OUTGAMBLES
OUTGAMBLING
OUTGAS
OUTGASES
OUTGASSED
OUTGASSES
OUTGASSING
OUTGAVE
OUTGAZE
OUTGAZED
OUTGAZES
OUTGAZING
OUTGENERAL
OUTGENERALED
OUTGENERALING
OUTGENERALS
OUTGIVE
OUTGIVEN
OUTGIVES

OUTGIVING
OUTGIVINGS
OUTGLARE
OUTGLARED
OUTGLARES
OUTGLARING
OUTGLEAM
OUTGLEAMED
OUTGLEAMING
OUTGLEAMS
OUTGLITTER
OUTGLITTERED
OUTGLITTERING
OUTGLITTERS
OUTGLOW
OUTGLOWED
OUTGLOWING
OUTGLOWS
OUTGNAW
OUTGNAWED
OUTGNAWING
OUTGNAWN
OUTGNAWS
OUTGO
OUTGOES
OUTGOING
OUTGOINGNESS
OUTGOINGNESSES
OUTGOINGS
OUTGONE
OUTGREW
OUTGRIN
OUTGRINNED
OUTGRINNING
OUTGRINS
OUTGROSS
OUTGROSSED
OUTGROSSES
OUTGROSSING
OUTGROUP
OUTGROUPS
OUTGROW
OUTGROWING
OUTGROWN
OUTGROWS
OUTGROWTH
OUTGROWTHS
OUTGUESS
OUTGUESSED
OUTGUESSES
OUTGUESSING
OUTGUIDE
OUTGUIDED
OUTGUIDES
OUTGUIDING
OUTGUN
OUTGUNNED
OUTGUNNING
OUTGUNS
OUTGUSH
OUTGUSHED
OUTGUSHES
OUTGUSHING
OUTHANDLE
OUTHANDLED
OUTHANDLES
OUTHANDLING
OUTHAUL
OUTHAULS
OUTHEAR
OUTHEARD
OUTHEARING
OUTHEARS
OUTHIT
OUTHITS
OUTHITTING
OUTHOMER
OUTHOMERED
OUTHOMERING
OUTHOMERS
OUTHOUSE
OUTHOUSES
OUTHOWL
OUTHOWLED
OUTHOWLING
OUTHOWLS
OUTHUMOR
OUTHUMORED
OUTHUMORING
OUTHUMORS
OUTHUNT
OUTHUNTED
OUTHUNTING
OUTHUNTS
OUTHUSTLE
OUTHUSTLED
OUTHUSTLES
OUTHUSTLING
OUTING
OUTINGS
OUTINTRIGUE
OUTINTRIGUED
OUTINTRIGUES
OUTINTRIGUING
OUTJINX
OUTJINXED
OUTJINXES
OUTJINXING
OUTJOCKEY
OUTJOCKEYED
OUTJOCKEYING
OUTJOCKEYS
OUTJUGGLE
OUTJUGGLED
OUTJUGGLES
OUTJUGGLING
OUTJUMP
OUTJUMPED
OUTJUMPING
OUTJUMPS
OUTJUT
OUTJUTS
OUTJUTTED
OUTJUTTING
OUTKEEP
OUTKEEPING
OUTKEEPS
OUTKEPT
OUTKICK
OUTKICKED
OUTKICKING
OUTKICKS
OUTKILL
OUTKILLED
OUTKILLING
OUTKILLS
OUTKISS
OUTKISSED
OUTKISSES
OUTKISSING
OUTLAID
OUTLAIN
OUTLAND
OUTLANDER
OUTLANDERS
OUTLANDISH
OUTLANDISHLY
OUTLANDISHNESS
OUTLANDS
OUTLAST
OUTLASTED
OUTLASTING
OUTLASTS
OUTLAUGH
OUTLAUGHED
OUTLAUGHING
OUTLAUGHS
OUTLAW
OUTLAWED
OUTLAWING
OUTLAWRIES
OUTLAWRY
OUTLAWS
OUTLAY
OUTLAYING
OUTLAYS
OUTLEAD
OUTLEADING
OUTLEADS
OUTLEAP
OUTLEAPED
OUTLEAPING
OUTLEAPS
OUTLEAPT
OUTLEARN
OUTLEARNED
OUTLEARNING
OUTLEARNS
OUTLEARNT
OUTLED
OUTLET
OUTLETS
OUTLIE
OUTLIER
OUTLIERS
OUTLIES
OUTLINE
OUTLINED
OUTLINER
OUTLINERS
OUTLINES
OUTLINING
OUTLIVE
OUTLIVED
OUTLIVER
OUTLIVERS
OUTLIVES
OUTLIVING
OUTLOOK
OUTLOOKS
OUTLOVE
OUTLOVED
OUTLOVES
OUTLOVING
OUTLYING
OUTMAN
OUTMANEUVER
OUTMANEUVERED
OUTMANEUVERING
OUTMANEUVERS
OUTMANIPULATE
OUTMANIPULATED
OUTMANIPULATES
OUTMANIPULATING
OUTMANNED
OUTMANNING
OUTMANOEUVRE
OUTMANOEUVRED
OUTMANOEUVRES
OUTMANOEUVRING
OUTMANS
OUTMARCH
OUTMARCHED
OUTMARCHES
OUTMARCHING
OUTMASTER
OUTMASTERED
OUTMASTERING
OUTMASTERS
OUTMATCH
OUTMATCHED
OUTMATCHES
OUTMATCHING
OUTMODE
OUTMODED
OUTMODES
OUTMODING
OUTMOST
OUTMOVE
OUTMOVED
OUTMOVES
OUTMOVING
OUTMUSCLE
OUTMUSCLED
OUTMUSCLES
OUTMUSCLING
OUTNUMBER
OUTNUMBERED
OUTNUMBERING
OUTNUMBERS
OUTOFFICE
OUTOFFICES
OUTORGANIZE
OUTORGANIZED
OUTORGANIZES
OUTORGANIZING
OUTPACE
OUTPACED
OUTPACES
OUTPACING
OUTPAINT
OUTPAINTED
OUTPAINTING
OUTPAINTS
OUTPASS

OUTPASSED
OUTPASSES
OUTPASSING
OUTPATIENT
OUTPATIENTS
OUTPEOPLE
OUTPEOPLED
OUTPEOPLES
OUTPEOPLING
OUTPERFORM
OUTPERFORMED
OUTPERFORMING
OUTPERFORMS
OUTPITCH
OUTPITCHED
OUTPITCHES
OUTPITCHING
OUTPITIED
OUTPITIES
OUTPITY
OUTPITYING
OUTPLACE
OUTPLACED
OUTPLACEMENT
OUTPLACEMENTS
OUTPLACES
OUTPLACING
OUTPLAN
OUTPLANNED
OUTPLANNING
OUTPLANS
OUTPLAY
OUTPLAYED
OUTPLAYING
OUTPLAYS
OUTPLOD
OUTPLODDED
OUTPLODDING
OUTPLODS
OUTPLOT
OUTPLOTS
OUTPLOTTED
OUTPLOTTING
OUTPOINT
OUTPOINTED
OUTPOINTING
OUTPOINTS
OUTPOLITICK
OUTPOLITICKED
OUTPOLITICKING
OUTPOLITICKS
OUTPOLL
OUTPOLLED
OUTPOLLING
OUTPOLLS
OUTPOPULATE
OUTPOPULATED
OUTPOPULATES
OUTPOPULATING
OUTPORT
OUTPORTS
OUTPOST
OUTPOSTS
OUTPOUR
OUTPOURED
OUTPOURER
OUTPOURERS
OUTPOURING
OUTPOURINGS
OUTPOURS
OUTPOWER
OUTPOWERED
OUTPOWERING
OUTPOWERS
OUTPRAY
OUTPRAYED
OUTPRAYING
OUTPRAYS
OUTPREACH
OUTPREACHED
OUTPREACHES
OUTPREACHING
OUTPREEN
OUTPREENED
OUTPREENING
OUTPREENS
OUTPRESS
OUTPRESSED
OUTPRESSES
OUTPRESSING
OUTPRICE
OUTPRICED
OUTPRICES
OUTPRICING
OUTPRODUCE
OUTPRODUCED
OUTPRODUCES
OUTPRODUCING
OUTPROMISE
OUTPROMISED
OUTPROMISES
OUTPROMISING
OUTPSYCH
OUTPSYCHED
OUTPSYCHING
OUTPSYCHS
OUTPULL
OUTPULLED
OUTPULLING
OUTPULLS
OUTPUNCH
OUTPUNCHED
OUTPUNCHES
OUTPUNCHING
OUTPUPIL
OUTPUPILS
OUTPURSUE
OUTPURSUED
OUTPURSUES
OUTPURSUING
OUTPUSH
OUTPUSHED
OUTPUSHES
OUTPUSHING
OUTPUT
OUTPUTS
OUTPUTTED
OUTPUTTING
OUTQUOTE
OUTQUOTED
OUTQUOTES
OUTQUOTING
OUTRACE
OUTRACED
OUTRACES
OUTRACING
OUTRAGE
OUTRAGED
OUTRAGEOUS
OUTRAGEOUSLY
OUTRAGEOUSNESS
OUTRAGES
OUTRAGING
OUTRAISE
OUTRAISED
OUTRAISES
OUTRAISING
OUTRAN
OUTRANCE
OUTRANCES
OUTRANG
OUTRANGE
OUTRANGED
OUTRANGES
OUTRANGING
OUTRANK
OUTRANKED
OUTRANKING
OUTRANKS
OUTRATE
OUTRATED
OUTRATES
OUTRATING
OUTRAVE
OUTRAVED
OUTRAVES
OUTRAVING
OUTRE
OUTREACH
OUTREACHED
OUTREACHES
OUTREACHING
OUTREAD
OUTREADING
OUTREADS
OUTREASON
OUTREASONED
OUTREASONING
OUTREASONS
OUTREBOUND
OUTREBOUNDED
OUTREBOUNDING
OUTREBOUNDS
OUTRECKON
OUTRECKONED
OUTRECKONING
OUTRECKONS
OUTREPRODUCE
OUTREPRODUCED
OUTREPRODUCES
OUTREPRODUCING
OUTRIDDEN
OUTRIDE
OUTRIDER
OUTRIDERS
OUTRIDES
OUTRIDING
OUTRIG
OUTRIGGED
OUTRIGGER
OUTRIGGERS
OUTRIGGING
OUTRIGHT
OUTRIGHTLY
OUTRIGS
OUTRING
OUTRINGING
OUTRINGS
OUTRIVAL
OUTRIVALED
OUTRIVALING
OUTRIVALLED
OUTRIVALLING
OUTRIVALS
OUTRO
OUTROAR
OUTROARED
OUTROARING
OUTROARS
OUTROCK
OUTROCKED
OUTROCKING
OUTROCKS
OUTRODE
OUTROLL
OUTROLLED
OUTROLLING
OUTROLLS
OUTROOT
OUTROOTED
OUTROOTING
OUTROOTS
OUTROS
OUTROW
OUTROWED
OUTROWING
OUTROWS
OUTRUN
OUTRUNG
OUTRUNNER
OUTRUNNERS
OUTRUNNING
OUTRUNS
OUTRUSH
OUTRUSHED
OUTRUSHES
OUTRUSHING
OUTS
OUTSAID
OUTSAIL
OUTSAILED
OUTSAILING
OUTSAILS
OUTSANG
OUTSAT
OUTSAVOR
OUTSAVORED
OUTSAVORING
OUTSAVORS
OUTSAW
OUTSAY
OUTSAYING
OUTSAYS
OUTSCHEME
OUTSCHEMED

OUTSCHEMES
OUTSCHEMING
OUTSCOLD
OUTSCOLDED
OUTSCOLDING
OUTSCOLDS
OUTSCOOP
OUTSCOOPED
OUTSCOOPING
OUTSCOOPS
OUTSCORE
OUTSCORED
OUTSCORES
OUTSCORING
OUTSCORN
OUTSCORNED
OUTSCORNING
OUTSCORNS
OUTSCREAM
OUTSCREAMED
OUTSCREAMING
OUTSCREAMS
OUTSEE
OUTSEEING
OUTSEEN
OUTSEES
OUTSELL
OUTSELLING
OUTSELLS
OUTSERT
OUTSERTS
OUTSERVE
OUTSERVED
OUTSERVES
OUTSERVING
OUTSET
OUTSETS
OUTSHAME
OUTSHAMED
OUTSHAMES
OUTSHAMING
OUTSHINE
OUTSHINED
OUTSHINES
OUTSHINING
OUTSHONE
OUTSHOOT
OUTSHOOTING
OUTSHOOTS
OUTSHOT
OUTSHOUT
OUTSHOUTED
OUTSHOUTING
OUTSHOUTS
OUTSIDE
OUTSIDER
OUTSIDERNESS
OUTSIDERNESSES
OUTSIDERS
OUTSIDES
OUTSIGHT
OUTSIGHTS
OUTSIN
OUTSING
OUTSINGING
OUTSINGS
OUTSINNED
OUTSINNING
OUTSINS
OUTSIT
OUTSITS
OUTSITTING
OUTSIZE
OUTSIZED
OUTSIZES
OUTSKATE
OUTSKATED
OUTSKATES
OUTSKATING
OUTSKIRT
OUTSKIRTS
OUTSLEEP
OUTSLEEPING
OUTSLEEPS
OUTSLEPT
OUTSLICK
OUTSLICKED
OUTSLICKING
OUTSLICKS
OUTSMART
OUTSMARTED
OUTSMARTING
OUTSMARTS
OUTSMELL
OUTSMELLED
OUTSMELLING
OUTSMELLS
OUTSMELT
OUTSMILE
OUTSMILED
OUTSMILES
OUTSMILING
OUTSMOKE
OUTSMOKED
OUTSMOKES
OUTSMOKING
OUTSNORE
OUTSNORED
OUTSNORES
OUTSNORING
OUTSOAR
OUTSOARED
OUTSOARING
OUTSOARS
OUTSOLD
OUTSOLE
OUTSOLES
OUTSOURCE
OUTSOURCED
OUTSOURCES
OUTSOURCING
OUTSOURCINGS
OUTSPAN
OUTSPANNED
OUTSPANNING
OUTSPANS
OUTSPARKLE
OUTSPARKLED
OUTSPARKLES
OUTSPARKLING
OUTSPEAK
OUTSPEAKING
OUTSPEAKS
OUTSPED
OUTSPEED
OUTSPEEDED
OUTSPEEDING
OUTSPEEDS
OUTSPELL
OUTSPELLED
OUTSPELLING
OUTSPELLS
OUTSPELT
OUTSPEND
OUTSPENDING
OUTSPENDS
OUTSPENT
OUTSPOKE
OUTSPOKEN
OUTSPOKENLY
OUTSPOKENNESS
OUTSPOKENNESSES
OUTSPRANG
OUTSPREAD
OUTSPREADING
OUTSPREADS
OUTSPRING
OUTSPRINGING
OUTSPRINGS
OUTSPRINT
OUTSPRINTED
OUTSPRINTING
OUTSPRINTS
OUTSPRUNG
OUTSTAND
OUTSTANDING
OUTSTANDINGLY
OUTSTANDS
OUTSTARE
OUTSTARED
OUTSTARES
OUTSTARING
OUTSTART
OUTSTARTED
OUTSTARTING
OUTSTARTS
OUTSTATE
OUTSTATED
OUTSTATES
OUTSTATING
OUTSTATION
OUTSTATIONS
OUTSTAY
OUTSTAYED
OUTSTAYING
OUTSTAYS
OUTSTEER
OUTSTEERED
OUTSTEERING
OUTSTEERS
OUTSTEP
OUTSTEPPED
OUTSTEPPING
OUTSTEPS
OUTSTOOD
OUTSTRETCH
OUTSTRETCHED
OUTSTRETCHES
OUTSTRETCHING
OUTSTRIDDEN
OUTSTRIDE
OUTSTRIDES
OUTSTRIDING
OUTSTRIP
OUTSTRIPPED
OUTSTRIPPING
OUTSTRIPS
OUTSTRIVE
OUTSTRIVEN
OUTSTRIVES
OUTSTRIVING
OUTSTRODE
OUTSTROKE
OUTSTROKES
OUTSTROVE
OUTSTUDIED
OUTSTUDIES
OUTSTUDY
OUTSTUDYING
OUTSTUNT
OUTSTUNTED
OUTSTUNTING
OUTSTUNTS
OUTSULK
OUTSULKED
OUTSULKING
OUTSULKS
OUTSUNG
OUTSWAM
OUTSWARE
OUTSWEAR
OUTSWEARING
OUTSWEARS
OUTSWEEP
OUTSWEEPING
OUTSWEEPS
OUTSWEPT
OUTSWIM
OUTSWIMMING
OUTSWIMS
OUTSWING
OUTSWINGING
OUTSWINGS
OUTSWORE
OUTSWORN
OUTSWUM
OUTSWUNG
OUTTA
OUTTAKE
OUTTAKES
OUTTALK
OUTTALKED
OUTTALKING
OUTTALKS
OUTTASK
OUTTASKED
OUTTASKING
OUTTASKS
OUTTELL
OUTTELLING
OUTTELLS
OUTTHANK
OUTTHANKED
OUTTHANKING
OUTTHANKS

OUTTHIEVE
OUTTHIEVED
OUTTHIEVES
OUTTHIEVING
OUTTHINK
OUTTHINKING
OUTTHINKS
OUTTHOUGHT
OUTTHREW
OUTTHROB
OUTTHROBBED
OUTTHROBBING
OUTTHROBS
OUTTHROW
OUTTHROWING
OUTTHROWN
OUTTHROWS
OUTTHRUST
OUTTHRUSTED
OUTTHRUSTING
OUTTHRUSTS
OUTTOLD
OUTTOWER
OUTTOWERED
OUTTOWERING
OUTTOWERS
OUTTRADE
OUTTRADED
OUTTRADES
OUTTRADING
OUTTRAVEL
OUTTRAVELED
OUTTRAVELING
OUTTRAVELLED
OUTTRAVELLING
OUTTRAVELS
OUTTRICK
OUTTRICKED
OUTTRICKING
OUTTRICKS
OUTTROT
OUTTROTS
OUTTROTTED
OUTTROTTING
OUTTRUMP
OUTTRUMPED
OUTTRUMPING
OUTTRUMPS
OUTTURN
OUTTURNS
OUTVALUE
OUTVALUED
OUTVALUES
OUTVALUING
OUTVAUNT
OUTVAUNTED
OUTVAUNTING
OUTVAUNTS
OUTVIE
OUTVIED
OUTVIES
OUTVOICE
OUTVOICED
OUTVOICES
OUTVOICING
OUTVOTE
OUTVOTED
OUTVOTES
OUTVOTING
OUTVYING
OUTWAIT
OUTWAITED
OUTWAITING
OUTWAITS
OUTWALK
OUTWALKED
OUTWALKING
OUTWALKS
OUTWAR
OUTWARD
OUTWARDLY
OUTWARDNESS
OUTWARDNESSES
OUTWARDS
OUTWARRED
OUTWARRING
OUTWARS
OUTWASH
OUTWASHES
OUTWASTE
OUTWASTED
OUTWASTES
OUTWASTING
OUTWATCH
OUTWATCHED
OUTWATCHES
OUTWATCHING
OUTWEAR
OUTWEARIED
OUTWEARIES
OUTWEARING
OUTWEARS
OUTWEARY
OUTWEARYING
OUTWEEP
OUTWEEPING
OUTWEEPS
OUTWEIGH
OUTWEIGHED
OUTWEIGHING
OUTWEIGHS
OUTWENT
OUTWEPT
OUTWHIRL
OUTWHIRLED
OUTWHIRLING
OUTWHIRLS
OUTWILE
OUTWILED
OUTWILES
OUTWILING
OUTWILL
OUTWILLED
OUTWILLING
OUTWILLS
OUTWIND
OUTWINDED
OUTWINDING
OUTWINDS
OUTWISH
OUTWISHED
OUTWISHES
OUTWISHING
OUTWIT
OUTWITH
OUTWITS
OUTWITTED
OUTWITTING
OUTWORE
OUTWORK
OUTWORKED
OUTWORKER
OUTWORKERS
OUTWORKING
OUTWORKS
OUTWORN
OUTWRESTLE
OUTWRESTLED
OUTWRESTLES
OUTWRESTLING
OUTWRIT
OUTWRITE
OUTWRITES
OUTWRITING
OUTWRITTEN
OUTWROTE
OUTWROUGHT
OUTYELL
OUTYELLED
OUTYELLING
OUTYELLS
OUTYELP
OUTYELPED
OUTYELPING
OUTYELPS
OUTYIELD
OUTYIELDED
OUTYIELDING
OUTYIELDS
OUZEL
OUZELS
OUZO
OUZOS
OVA
OVAL
OVALBUMIN
OVALBUMINS
OVALITIES
OVALITY
OVALLY
OVALNESS
OVALNESSES
OVALS
OVARIAL
OVARIAN
OVARIECTOMIES
OVARIECTOMIZED
OVARIECTOMY
OVARIES
OVARIOLE
OVARIOLES
OVARIOTOMIES
OVARIOTOMY
OVARITIDES
OVARITIS
OVARY
OVATE
OVATELY
OVATION
OVATIONAL
OVATIONS
OVEN
OVENBIRD
OVENBIRDS
OVENLIKE
OVENPROOF
OVENS
OVENWARE
OVENWARES
OVER
OVERABLE
OVERABSTRACT
OVERABUNDANCE
OVERABUNDANCES
OVERABUNDANT
OVERACCENTUATE
OVERACCENTUATED
OVERACCENTUATES
OVERACHIEVE
OVERACHIEVED
OVERACHIEVEMENT
OVERACHIEVER
OVERACHIEVERS
OVERACHIEVES
OVERACHIEVING
OVERACT
OVERACTED
OVERACTING
OVERACTION
OVERACTIONS
OVERACTIVE
OVERACTIVITIES
OVERACTIVITY
OVERACTS
OVERACUTE
OVERADJUSTMENT
OVERADJUSTMENTS
OVERADVERTISE
OVERADVERTISED
OVERADVERTISES
OVERADVERTISING
OVERAGE
OVERAGED
OVERAGES
OVERAGGRESSIVE
OVERALERT
OVERALL
OVERALLED
OVERALLS
OVERAMBITIOUS
OVERAMPLIFIED
OVERANALYSES
OVERANALYSIS
OVERANALYTICAL
OVERANALYZE
OVERANALYZED
OVERANALYZES
OVERANALYZING
OVERANXIETIES
OVERANXIETY
OVERANXIOUS
OVERAPPLICATION
OVERAPT
OVERARCH
OVERARCHED

OVERARCHES
OVERARCHING
OVERARM
OVERARMED
OVERARMING
OVERARMS
OVERAROUSAL
OVERAROUSALS
OVERARRANGE
OVERARRANGED
OVERARRANGES
OVERARRANGING
OVERARTICULATE
OVERARTICULATED
OVERARTICULATES
OVERASSERT
OVERASSERTED
OVERASSERTING
OVERASSERTION
OVERASSERTIONS
OVERASSERTIVE
OVERASSERTS
OVERASSESSMENT
OVERASSESSMENTS
OVERATE
OVERATTENTION
OVERATTENTIONS
OVERAWE
OVERAWED
OVERAWES
OVERAWING
OVERBAKE
OVERBAKED
OVERBAKES
OVERBAKING
OVERBALANCE
OVERBALANCED
OVERBALANCES
OVERBALANCING
OVERBEAR
OVERBEARING
OVERBEARINGLY
OVERBEARS
OVERBEAT
OVERBEATEN
OVERBEATING
OVERBEATS
OVERBED
OVERBEJEWELED
OVERBET
OVERBETS
OVERBETTED
OVERBETTING
OVERBID
OVERBIDDEN
OVERBIDDING
OVERBIDS
OVERBIG
OVERBILL
OVERBILLED
OVERBILLING
OVERBILLS
OVERBITE
OVERBITES
OVERBLEACH
OVERBLEACHED
OVERBLEACHES
OVERBLEACHING
OVERBLEW
OVERBLOUSE
OVERBLOUSES
OVERBLOW
OVERBLOWING
OVERBLOWINGS
OVERBLOWN
OVERBLOWS
OVERBOARD
OVERBOIL
OVERBOILED
OVERBOILING
OVERBOILS
OVERBOLD
OVERBOOK
OVERBOOKED
OVERBOOKING
OVERBOOKS
OVERBOOT
OVERBOOTS
OVERBORE
OVERBORN
OVERBORNE
OVERBORROW
OVERBORROWED
OVERBORROWING
OVERBORROWS
OVERBOUGHT
OVERBRAKE
OVERBRAKED
OVERBRAKES
OVERBRAKING
OVERBREATHING
OVERBREATHINGS
OVERBRED
OVERBREED
OVERBREEDING
OVERBREEDS
OVERBRIEF
OVERBRIEFED
OVERBRIEFING
OVERBRIEFS
OVERBRIGHT
OVERBROAD
OVERBROWSE
OVERBROWSED
OVERBROWSES
OVERBROWSING
OVERBRUTAL
OVERBUILD
OVERBUILDING
OVERBUILDS
OVERBUILT
OVERBURDEN
OVERBURDENED
OVERBURDENING
OVERBURDENS
OVERBURN
OVERBURNED
OVERBURNING
OVERBURNS
OVERBURNT
OVERBUSY
OVERBUY
OVERBUYING
OVERBUYS
OVERCALL
OVERCALLED
OVERCALLING
OVERCALLS
OVERCAME
OVERCAPACITIES
OVERCAPACITY
OVERCAPITALIZE
OVERCAPITALIZED
OVERCAPITALIZES
OVERCAREFUL
OVERCAST
OVERCASTED
OVERCASTING
OVERCASTINGS
OVERCASTS
OVERCAUTION
OVERCAUTIONS
OVERCAUTIOUS
OVERCENTRALIZE
OVERCENTRALIZED
OVERCENTRALIZES
OVERCHARGE
OVERCHARGED
OVERCHARGES
OVERCHARGING
OVERCHEAP
OVERCHILL
OVERCHILLED
OVERCHILLING
OVERCHILLS
OVERCIVIL
OVERCIVILIZED
OVERCLAIM
OVERCLAIMED
OVERCLAIMING
OVERCLAIMS
OVERCLASS
OVERCLASSES
OVERCLASSIFIED
OVERCLASSIFIES
OVERCLASSIFY
OVERCLASSIFYING
OVERCLEAN
OVERCLEANED
OVERCLEANING
OVERCLEANS
OVERCLEAR
OVERCLEARED
OVERCLEARING
OVERCLEARS
OVERCLOSE
OVERCLOUD
OVERCLOUDED
OVERCLOUDING
OVERCLOUDS
OVERCOACH
OVERCOACHED
OVERCOACHES
OVERCOACHING
OVERCOAT
OVERCOATS
OVERCOLD
OVERCOLOR
OVERCOLORED
OVERCOLORING
OVERCOLORS
OVERCOME
OVERCOMER
OVERCOMERS
OVERCOMES
OVERCOMING
OVERCOMMIT
OVERCOMMITMENT
OVERCOMMITMENTS
OVERCOMMITS
OVERCOMMITTED
OVERCOMMITTING
OVERCOMMUNICATE
OVERCOMPENSATE
OVERCOMPENSATED
OVERCOMPENSATES
OVERCOMPLEX
OVERCOMPLIANCE
OVERCOMPLIANCES
OVERCOMPLICATE
OVERCOMPLICATED
OVERCOMPLICATES
OVERCOMPRESS
OVERCOMPRESSED
OVERCOMPRESSES
OVERCOMPRESSING
OVERCONCERN
OVERCONCERNED
OVERCONCERNING
OVERCONCERNS
OVERCONFIDENCE
OVERCONFIDENCES
OVERCONFIDENT
OVERCONFIDENTLY
OVERCONSCIOUS
OVERCONSTRUCT
OVERCONSTRUCTED
OVERCONSTRUCTS
OVERCONSUME
OVERCONSUMED
OVERCONSUMES
OVERCONSUMING
OVERCONSUMPTION
OVERCONTROL
OVERCONTROLLED
OVERCONTROLLING
OVERCONTROLS
OVERCOOK
OVERCOOKED
OVERCOOKING
OVERCOOKS
OVERCOOL
OVERCOOLED
OVERCOOLING
OVERCOOLS
OVERCORRECT
OVERCORRECTED
OVERCORRECTING
OVERCORRECTS
OVERCOUNT
OVERCOUNTED
OVERCOUNTING
OVERCOUNTS
OVERCOY
OVERCRAM

OVERCRAMMED
OVERCRAMMING
OVERCRAMS
OVERCREDULOUS
OVERCRITICAL
OVERCROP
OVERCROPPED
OVERCROPPING
OVERCROPS
OVERCROWD
OVERCROWDED
OVERCROWDING
OVERCROWDS
OVERCULTIVATION
OVERCURE
OVERCURED
OVERCURES
OVERCURING
OVERCUT
OVERCUTS
OVERCUTTING
OVERDARE
OVERDARED
OVERDARES
OVERDARING
OVERDEAR
OVERDECK
OVERDECKED
OVERDECKING
OVERDECKS
OVERDECORATE
OVERDECORATED
OVERDECORATES
OVERDECORATING
OVERDECORATION
OVERDECORATIONS
OVERDEMANDING
OVERDEPENDENCE
OVERDEPENDENCES
OVERDEPENDENT
OVERDESIGN
OVERDESIGNED
OVERDESIGNING
OVERDESIGNS
OVERDETERMINED
OVERDEVELOP
OVERDEVELOPED
OVERDEVELOPING
OVERDEVELOPMENT
OVERDEVELOPS
OVERDIAGNOSE
OVERDIAGNOSED
OVERDIAGNOSES
OVERDIAGNOSING
OVERDIAGNOSIS
OVERDID
OVERDIRECT
OVERDIRECTED
OVERDIRECTING
OVERDIRECTS
OVERDISCOUNT
OVERDISCOUNTED
OVERDISCOUNTING
OVERDISCOUNTS
OVERDIVERSITIES
OVERDIVERSITY
OVERDO
OVERDOCUMENT
OVERDOCUMENTED
OVERDOCUMENTING
OVERDOCUMENTS
OVERDOER
OVERDOERS
OVERDOES
OVERDOG
OVERDOGS
OVERDOING
OVERDOMINANCE
OVERDOMINANCES
OVERDOMINANT
OVERDONE
OVERDOSAGE
OVERDOSAGES
OVERDOSE
OVERDOSED
OVERDOSES
OVERDOSING
OVERDRAFT
OVERDRAFTS
OVERDRAMATIC
OVERDRAMATIZE
OVERDRAMATIZED
OVERDRAMATIZES
OVERDRAMATIZING
OVERDRANK
OVERDRAW
OVERDRAWING
OVERDRAWN
OVERDRAWS
OVERDRESS
OVERDRESSED
OVERDRESSES
OVERDRESSING
OVERDREW
OVERDRIED
OVERDRIES
OVERDRINK
OVERDRINKING
OVERDRINKS
OVERDRIVE
OVERDRIVEN
OVERDRIVES
OVERDRIVING
OVERDROVE
OVERDRUNK
OVERDRY
OVERDRYING
OVERDUB
OVERDUBBED
OVERDUBBING
OVERDUBS
OVERDUE
OVERDYE
OVERDYED
OVERDYEING
OVERDYER
OVERDYERS
OVERDYES
OVEREAGER
OVEREAGERNESS
OVEREAGERNESSES
OVEREARNEST
OVEREASY
OVEREAT
OVEREATEN
OVEREATER
OVEREATERS
OVEREATING
OVEREATS
OVERED
OVEREDIT
OVEREDITED
OVEREDITING
OVEREDITS
OVEREDUCATE
OVEREDUCATED
OVEREDUCATES
OVEREDUCATING
OVEREDUCATION
OVEREDUCATIONS
OVERELABORATE
OVERELABORATED
OVERELABORATES
OVERELABORATING
OVERELABORATION
OVEREMBELLISH
OVEREMBELLISHED
OVEREMBELLISHES
OVEREMOTE
OVEREMOTED
OVEREMOTES
OVEREMOTING
OVEREMOTIONAL
OVEREMPHASES
OVEREMPHASIS
OVEREMPHASIZE
OVEREMPHASIZED
OVEREMPHASIZES
OVEREMPHASIZING
OVEREMPHATIC
OVERENAMORED
OVERENCOURAGE
OVERENCOURAGED
OVERENCOURAGES
OVERENCOURAGING
OVERENERGETIC
OVERENGINEER
OVERENGINEERED
OVERENGINEERING
OVERENGINEERS
OVERENROLLED
OVERENTERTAINED
OVERENTHUSIASM
OVERENTHUSIASMS
OVEREQUIPPED
OVERESTIMATE
OVERESTIMATED
OVERESTIMATES
OVERESTIMATING
OVERESTIMATION
OVERESTIMATIONS
OVEREVALUATION
OVEREVALUATIONS
OVEREXAGGERATE
OVEREXAGGERATED
OVEREXAGGERATES
OVEREXCITE
OVEREXCITED
OVEREXCITES
OVEREXCITING
OVEREXERCISE
OVEREXERCISED
OVEREXERCISES
OVEREXERCISING
OVEREXERT
OVEREXERTED
OVEREXERTING
OVEREXERTION
OVEREXERTIONS
OVEREXERTS
OVEREXPAND
OVEREXPANDED
OVEREXPANDING
OVEREXPANDS
OVEREXPANSION
OVEREXPANSIONS
OVEREXPECTATION
OVEREXPLAIN
OVEREXPLAINED
OVEREXPLAINING
OVEREXPLAINS
OVEREXPLICIT
OVEREXPLOIT
OVEREXPLOITED
OVEREXPLOITING
OVEREXPLOITS
OVEREXPOSE
OVEREXPOSED
OVEREXPOSES
OVEREXPOSING
OVEREXPOSURE
OVEREXPOSURES
OVEREXTEND
OVEREXTENDED
OVEREXTENDING
OVEREXTENDS
OVEREXTENSION
OVEREXTENSIONS
OVEREXTRACTION
OVEREXTRACTIONS
OVEREXTRAVAGANT
OVEREXUBERANT
OVERFACILE
OVERFAMILIAR
OVERFAMILIARITY
OVERFAR
OVERFAST
OVERFASTIDIOUS
OVERFAT
OVERFATIGUE
OVERFATIGUED
OVERFATIGUES
OVERFATIGUING
OVERFAVOR
OVERFAVORED
OVERFAVORING
OVERFAVORS
OVERFEAR
OVERFEARED
OVERFEARING
OVERFEARS
OVERFED
OVERFEED
OVERFEEDING
OVERFEEDS

OVERFERTILIZE
OVERFERTILIZED
OVERFERTILIZES
OVERFERTILIZING
OVERFILL
OVERFILLED
OVERFILLING
OVERFILLS
OVERFINE
OVERFISH
OVERFISHED
OVERFISHES
OVERFISHING
OVERFIT
OVERFLEW
OVERFLIES
OVERFLIGHT
OVERFLIGHTS
OVERFLOOD
OVERFLOODED
OVERFLOODING
OVERFLOODS
OVERFLOW
OVERFLOWED
OVERFLOWING
OVERFLOWN
OVERFLOWS
OVERFLY
OVERFLYING
OVERFOCUS
OVERFOCUSED
OVERFOCUSES
OVERFOCUSING
OVERFOCUSSED
OVERFOCUSSES
OVERFOCUSSING
OVERFOND
OVERFOUL
OVERFRANK
OVERFREE
OVERFULFILL
OVERFULFILLED
OVERFULFILLING
OVERFULFILLS
OVERFULL
OVERFUND
OVERFUNDED
OVERFUNDING
OVERFUNDS
OVERFUSSY
OVERGARMENT
OVERGARMENTS
OVERGENERALIZE
OVERGENERALIZED
OVERGENERALIZES
OVERGENEROSITY
OVERGENEROUS
OVERGENEROUSLY
OVERGILD
OVERGILDED
OVERGILDING
OVERGILDS
OVERGILT
OVERGIRD
OVERGIRDED
OVERGIRDING
OVERGIRDS
OVERGIRT
OVERGLAD
OVERGLAMORIZE
OVERGLAMORIZED
OVERGLAMORIZES
OVERGLAMORIZING
OVERGLAZE
OVERGLAZED
OVERGLAZES
OVERGLAZING
OVERGOAD
OVERGOADED
OVERGOADING
OVERGOADS
OVERGOVERN
OVERGOVERNED
OVERGOVERNING
OVERGOVERNS
OVERGRADE
OVERGRADED
OVERGRADES
OVERGRADING
OVERGRAZE
OVERGRAZED
OVERGRAZES
OVERGRAZING
OVERGREAT
OVERGREW
OVERGROUND
OVERGROW
OVERGROWING
OVERGROWN
OVERGROWS
OVERGROWTH
OVERGROWTHS
OVERHAND
OVERHANDED
OVERHANDING
OVERHANDLE
OVERHANDLED
OVERHANDLES
OVERHANDLING
OVERHANDS
OVERHANG
OVERHANGING
OVERHANGS
OVERHARD
OVERHARVEST
OVERHARVESTED
OVERHARVESTING
OVERHARVESTS
OVERHASTY
OVERHATE
OVERHATED
OVERHATES
OVERHATING
OVERHAUL
OVERHAULED
OVERHAULING
OVERHAULS
OVERHEAD
OVERHEADS
OVERHEAP
OVERHEAPED
OVERHEAPING
OVERHEAPS
OVERHEAR
OVERHEARD
OVERHEARING
OVERHEARS
OVERHEAT
OVERHEATED
OVERHEATING
OVERHEATS
OVERHELD
OVERHIGH
OVERHOLD
OVERHOLDING
OVERHOLDS
OVERHOLY
OVERHOMOGENIZE
OVERHOMOGENIZED
OVERHOMOGENIZES
OVERHONOR
OVERHONORED
OVERHONORING
OVERHONORS
OVERHOPE
OVERHOPED
OVERHOPES
OVERHOPING
OVERHOT
OVERHUNG
OVERHUNT
OVERHUNTED
OVERHUNTING
OVERHUNTINGS
OVERHUNTS
OVERHYPE
OVERHYPED
OVERHYPES
OVERHYPING
OVERIDEALIZE
OVERIDEALIZED
OVERIDEALIZES
OVERIDEALIZING
OVERIDENTIFIED
OVERIDENTIFIES
OVERIDENTIFY
OVERIDENTIFYING
OVERIDLE
OVERIMAGINATIVE
OVERIMPRESS
OVERIMPRESSED
OVERIMPRESSES
OVERIMPRESSING
OVERINDULGE
OVERINDULGED
OVERINDULGENCE
OVERINDULGENCES
OVERINDULGENT
OVERINDULGES
OVERINDULGING
OVERINFLATE
OVERINFLATED
OVERINFLATES
OVERINFLATING
OVERINFLATION
OVERINFLATIONS
OVERINFORM
OVERINFORMED
OVERINFORMING
OVERINFORMS
OVERING
OVERINGENIOUS
OVERINGENUITIES
OVERINGENUITY
OVERINSISTENT
OVERINTENSE
OVERINTENSITIES
OVERINTENSITY
OVERINVESTMENT
OVERINVESTMENTS
OVERISSUANCE
OVERISSUANCES
OVERISSUE
OVERISSUED
OVERISSUES
OVERISSUING
OVERJOY
OVERJOYED
OVERJOYING
OVERJOYS
OVERJUST
OVERKEEN
OVERKILL
OVERKILLED
OVERKILLING
OVERKILLS
OVERKIND
OVERLABOR
OVERLABORED
OVERLABORING
OVERLABORS
OVERLADE
OVERLADED
OVERLADEN
OVERLADES
OVERLADING
OVERLAID
OVERLAIN
OVERLAND
OVERLANDS
OVERLAP
OVERLAPPED
OVERLAPPING
OVERLAPS
OVERLARGE
OVERLATE
OVERLAVISH
OVERLAVISHED
OVERLAVISHES
OVERLAVISHING
OVERLAX
OVERLAY
OVERLAYING
OVERLAYS
OVERLEAF
OVERLEAP
OVERLEAPED
OVERLEAPING
OVERLEAPS
OVERLEAPT
OVERLEARN
OVERLEARNED
OVERLEARNING
OVERLEARNS
OVERLEARNT

OVERLEND
OVERLENDING
OVERLENDS
OVERLENGTH
OVERLENGTHEN
OVERLENGTHENED
OVERLENGTHENING
OVERLENGTHENS
OVERLENGTHS
OVERLENT
OVERLET
OVERLETS
OVERLETTING
OVERLEWD
OVERLIE
OVERLIES
OVERLIGHT
OVERLIGHTED
OVERLIGHTING
OVERLIGHTS
OVERLIT
OVERLITERAL
OVERLITERARY
OVERLIVE
OVERLIVED
OVERLIVES
OVERLIVING
OVERLOAD
OVERLOADED
OVERLOADING
OVERLOADS
OVERLONG
OVERLOOK
OVERLOOKED
OVERLOOKING
OVERLOOKS
OVERLORD
OVERLORDED
OVERLORDING
OVERLORDS
OVERLORDSHIP
OVERLORDSHIPS
OVERLOUD
OVERLOVE
OVERLOVED
OVERLOVES
OVERLOVING
OVERLUSH
OVERLY
OVERLYING
OVERMAN
OVERMANAGE
OVERMANAGED
OVERMANAGES
OVERMANAGING
OVERMANNED
OVERMANNERED
OVERMANNING
OVERMANS
OVERMANTEL
OVERMANTELS
OVERMANY
OVERMASTER
OVERMASTERED
OVERMASTERING
OVERMASTERS
OVERMATCH
OVERMATCHED
OVERMATCHES
OVERMATCHING
OVERMATURE
OVERMATURITIES
OVERMATURITY
OVERMEDICATE
OVERMEDICATED
OVERMEDICATES
OVERMEDICATING
OVERMEDICATION
OVERMEDICATIONS
OVERMEEK
OVERMELT
OVERMELTED
OVERMELTING
OVERMELTS
OVERMEN
OVERMIGHTY
OVERMILD
OVERMILK
OVERMILKED
OVERMILKING
OVERMILKS
OVERMINE
OVERMINED
OVERMINES
OVERMINING
OVERMIX
OVERMIXED
OVERMIXES
OVERMIXING
OVERMODEST
OVERMODESTLY
OVERMUCH
OVERMUCHES
OVERMUSCLED
OVERNEAR
OVERNEAT
OVERNEW
OVERNICE
OVERNIGHT
OVERNIGHTED
OVERNIGHTER
OVERNIGHTERS
OVERNIGHTING
OVERNIGHTS
OVERNOURISH
OVERNOURISHED
OVERNOURISHES
OVERNOURISHING
OVERNUTRITION
OVERNUTRITIONS
OVEROBVIOUS
OVEROPERATE
OVEROPERATED
OVEROPERATES
OVEROPERATING
OVEROPINIONATED
OVEROPTIMISM
OVEROPTIMISMS
OVEROPTIMIST
OVEROPTIMISTIC
OVEROPTIMISTS
OVERORCHESTRATE
OVERORGANIZE
OVERORGANIZED
OVERORGANIZES
OVERORGANIZING
OVERORNAMENT
OVERORNAMENTED
OVERORNAMENTING
OVERORNAMENTS
OVERPACK
OVERPACKAGE
OVERPACKAGED
OVERPACKAGES
OVERPACKAGING
OVERPACKED
OVERPACKING
OVERPACKS
OVERPAID
OVERPARTICULAR
OVERPASS
OVERPASSED
OVERPASSES
OVERPASSING
OVERPAST
OVERPAY
OVERPAYING
OVERPAYMENT
OVERPAYMENTS
OVERPAYS
OVERPEDAL
OVERPEDALED
OVERPEDALING
OVERPEDALLED
OVERPEDALLING
OVERPEDALS
OVERPEOPLE
OVERPEOPLED
OVERPEOPLES
OVERPEOPLING
OVERPERSUADE
OVERPERSUADED
OVERPERSUADES
OVERPERSUADING
OVERPERSUASION
OVERPERSUASIONS
OVERPERT
OVERPLAID
OVERPLAIDED
OVERPLAIDS
OVERPLAN
OVERPLANNED
OVERPLANNING
OVERPLANS
OVERPLANT
OVERPLANTED
OVERPLANTING
OVERPLANTS
OVERPLAY
OVERPLAYED
OVERPLAYING
OVERPLAYS
OVERPLIED
OVERPLIES
OVERPLOT
OVERPLOTS
OVERPLOTTED
OVERPLOTTING
OVERPLUS
OVERPLUSES
OVERPLY
OVERPLYING
OVERPOPULATE
OVERPOPULATED
OVERPOPULATES
OVERPOPULATING
OVERPOPULATION
OVERPOPULATIONS
OVERPOTENT
OVERPOWER
OVERPOWERED
OVERPOWERING
OVERPOWERINGLY
OVERPOWERS
OVERPRAISE
OVERPRAISED
OVERPRAISES
OVERPRAISING
OVERPRECISE
OVERPREDICT
OVERPREDICTED
OVERPREDICTING
OVERPREDICTION
OVERPREDICTIONS
OVERPREDICTS
OVERPRESCRIBE
OVERPRESCRIBED
OVERPRESCRIBES
OVERPRESCRIBING
OVERPRESSURE
OVERPRESSURED
OVERPRESSURES
OVERPRESSURING
OVERPRICE
OVERPRICED
OVERPRICES
OVERPRICING
OVERPRINT
OVERPRINTED
OVERPRINTING
OVERPRINTS
OVERPRIVILEGED
OVERPRIZE
OVERPRIZED
OVERPRIZES
OVERPRIZING
OVERPROCESS
OVERPROCESSED
OVERPROCESSES
OVERPROCESSING
OVERPRODUCE
OVERPRODUCED
OVERPRODUCES
OVERPRODUCING
OVERPRODUCTION
OVERPRODUCTIONS
OVERPROGRAM
OVERPROGRAMED
OVERPROGRAMING
OVERPROGRAMMED
OVERPROGRAMMING
OVERPROGRAMS
OVERPROMISE
OVERPROMISED
OVERPROMISES

OVERPROMISING
OVERPROMOTE
OVERPROMOTED
OVERPROMOTES
OVERPROMOTING
OVERPROOF
OVERPROPORTION
OVERPROPORTIONS
OVERPROTECT
OVERPROTECTED
OVERPROTECTING
OVERPROTECTION
OVERPROTECTIONS
OVERPROTECTIVE
OVERPROTECTS
OVERPROUD
OVERPUMP
OVERPUMPED
OVERPUMPING
OVERPUMPS
OVERQUALIFIED
OVERQUICK
OVERRAN
OVERRANK
OVERRASH
OVERRATE
OVERRATED
OVERRATES
OVERRATING
OVERREACH
OVERREACHED
OVERREACHER
OVERREACHERS
OVERREACHES
OVERREACHING
OVERREACT
OVERREACTED
OVERREACTING
OVERREACTION
OVERREACTIONS
OVERREACTS
OVERREFINED
OVERREFINEMENT
OVERREFINEMENTS
OVERREGULATE
OVERREGULATED
OVERREGULATES
OVERREGULATING
OVERREGULATION
OVERREGULATIONS
OVERRELIANCE
OVERRELIANCES
OVERREPORT
OVERREPORTED
OVERREPORTING
OVERREPORTS
OVERREPRESENTED
OVERRESPOND
OVERRESPONDED
OVERRESPONDING
OVERRESPONDS
OVERRICH
OVERRIDDEN
OVERRIDE
OVERRIDES
OVERRIDING
OVERRIFE
OVERRIGID
OVERRIPE
OVERROAST
OVERROASTED
OVERROASTING
OVERROASTS
OVERRODE
OVERRUDE
OVERRUFF
OVERRUFFED
OVERRUFFING
OVERRUFFS
OVERRULE
OVERRULED
OVERRULES
OVERRULING
OVERRUN
OVERRUNNING
OVERRUNS
OVERS
OVERSAD
OVERSALE
OVERSALES
OVERSALT
OVERSALTED
OVERSALTING
OVERSALTS
OVERSANGUINE
OVERSATURATE
OVERSATURATED
OVERSATURATES
OVERSATURATING
OVERSATURATION
OVERSATURATIONS
OVERSAUCE
OVERSAUCED
OVERSAUCES
OVERSAUCING
OVERSAVE
OVERSAVED
OVERSAVES
OVERSAVING
OVERSAW
OVERSCALE
OVERSCALED
OVERSCORE
OVERSCORED
OVERSCORES
OVERSCORING
OVERSCRUPULOUS
OVERSEA
OVERSEAS
OVERSECRETION
OVERSECRETIONS
OVERSEE
OVERSEED
OVERSEEDED
OVERSEEDING
OVERSEEDS
OVERSEEING
OVERSEEN
OVERSEER
OVERSEERS
OVERSEES
OVERSELL
OVERSELLING
OVERSELLS
OVERSENSITIVE
OVERSENSITIVITY
OVERSERIOUS
OVERSERIOUSLY
OVERSERVICE
OVERSERVICED
OVERSERVICES
OVERSERVICING
OVERSET
OVERSETS
OVERSETTING
OVERSEW
OVERSEWED
OVERSEWING
OVERSEWN
OVERSEWS
OVERSEXED
OVERSHADE
OVERSHADED
OVERSHADES
OVERSHADING
OVERSHADOW
OVERSHADOWED
OVERSHADOWING
OVERSHADOWS
OVERSHARP
OVERSHIRT
OVERSHIRTS
OVERSHOE
OVERSHOES
OVERSHOOT
OVERSHOOTING
OVERSHOOTS
OVERSHOT
OVERSHOTS
OVERSICK
OVERSIDE
OVERSIDES
OVERSIGHT
OVERSIGHTS
OVERSIMPLE
OVERSIMPLIFIED
OVERSIMPLIFIES
OVERSIMPLIFY
OVERSIMPLIFYING
OVERSIMPLISTIC
OVERSIMPLY
OVERSIZE
OVERSIZED
OVERSIZES
OVERSKIRT
OVERSKIRTS
OVERSLAUGH
OVERSLAUGHED
OVERSLAUGHING
OVERSLAUGHS
OVERSLEEP
OVERSLEEPING
OVERSLEEPS
OVERSLEPT
OVERSLIP
OVERSLIPPED
OVERSLIPPING
OVERSLIPS
OVERSLIPT
OVERSLOW
OVERSMOKE
OVERSMOKED
OVERSMOKES
OVERSMOKING
OVERSOAK
OVERSOAKED
OVERSOAKING
OVERSOAKS
OVERSOFT
OVERSOLD
OVERSOLICITOUS
OVERSOON
OVERSOUL
OVERSOULS
OVERSPECIALIZE
OVERSPECIALIZED
OVERSPECIALIZES
OVERSPECULATE
OVERSPECULATED
OVERSPECULATES
OVERSPECULATING
OVERSPECULATION
OVERSPEND
OVERSPENDER
OVERSPENDERS
OVERSPENDING
OVERSPENDS
OVERSPENT
OVERSPICE
OVERSPICED
OVERSPICES
OVERSPICING
OVERSPILL
OVERSPILLED
OVERSPILLING
OVERSPILLS
OVERSPILT
OVERSPIN
OVERSPINS
OVERSPREAD
OVERSPREADING
OVERSPREADS
OVERSTABILITIES
OVERSTABILITY
OVERSTAFF
OVERSTAFFED
OVERSTAFFING
OVERSTAFFS
OVERSTATE
OVERSTATED
OVERSTATEMENT
OVERSTATEMENTS
OVERSTATES
OVERSTATING
OVERSTAY
OVERSTAYED
OVERSTAYING
OVERSTAYS
OVERSTEER
OVERSTEERED
OVERSTEERING
OVERSTEERS
OVERSTEP
OVERSTEPPED
OVERSTEPPING

OVERSTEPS
OVERSTIMULATE
OVERSTIMULATED
OVERSTIMULATES
OVERSTIMULATING
OVERSTIMULATION
OVERSTIR
OVERSTIRRED
OVERSTIRRING
OVERSTIRS
OVERSTOCK
OVERSTOCKED
OVERSTOCKING
OVERSTOCKS
OVERSTORED
OVERSTORIES
OVERSTORY
OVERSTRAIN
OVERSTRAINED
OVERSTRAINING
OVERSTRAINS
OVERSTRESS
OVERSTRESSED
OVERSTRESSES
OVERSTRESSING
OVERSTRETCH
OVERSTRETCHED
OVERSTRETCHES
OVERSTRETCHING
OVERSTREW
OVERSTREWED
OVERSTREWING
OVERSTREWN
OVERSTREWS
OVERSTRIDDEN
OVERSTRIDE
OVERSTRIDES
OVERSTRIDING
OVERSTRODE
OVERSTRUCTURED
OVERSTRUNG
OVERSTUDIED
OVERSTUDIES
OVERSTUDY
OVERSTUDYING
OVERSTUFF
OVERSTUFFED
OVERSTUFFING
OVERSTUFFS
OVERSUBSCRIBE
OVERSUBSCRIBED
OVERSUBSCRIBES
OVERSUBSCRIBING
OVERSUBTLE
OVERSUDS
OVERSUDSED
OVERSUDSES
OVERSUDSING
OVERSUP
OVERSUPPED
OVERSUPPING
OVERSUPPLIED
OVERSUPPLIES
OVERSUPPLY
OVERSUPPLYING
OVERSUPS
OVERSURE
OVERSUSPICIOUS
OVERSWEET
OVERSWEETEN
OVERSWEETENED
OVERSWEETENING
OVERSWEETENS
OVERSWEETNESS
OVERSWEETNESSES
OVERSWING
OVERSWINGING
OVERSWINGS
OVERSWUNG
OVERT
OVERTAKE
OVERTAKEN
OVERTAKES
OVERTAKING
OVERTALK
OVERTALKATIVE
OVERTALKED
OVERTALKING
OVERTALKS
OVERTAME
OVERTART
OVERTASK
OVERTASKED
OVERTASKING
OVERTASKS
OVERTAUGHT
OVERTAX
OVERTAXATION
OVERTAXATIONS
OVERTAXED
OVERTAXES
OVERTAXING
OVERTEACH
OVERTEACHES
OVERTEACHING
OVERTHICK
OVERTHIN
OVERTHINK
OVERTHINKING
OVERTHINKS
OVERTHOUGHT
OVERTHREW
OVERTHROW
OVERTHROWING
OVERTHROWN
OVERTHROWS
OVERTIGHT
OVERTIGHTEN
OVERTIGHTENED
OVERTIGHTENING
OVERTIGHTENS
OVERTIME
OVERTIMED
OVERTIMES
OVERTIMID
OVERTIMING
OVERTIP
OVERTIPPED
OVERTIPPING
OVERTIPS
OVERTIRE
OVERTIRED
OVERTIRES
OVERTIRING
OVERTLY
OVERTNESS
OVERTNESSES
OVERTOIL
OVERTOILED
OVERTOILING
OVERTOILS
OVERTONE
OVERTONES
OVERTOOK
OVERTOP
OVERTOPPED
OVERTOPPING
OVERTOPS
OVERTRADE
OVERTRADED
OVERTRADES
OVERTRADING
OVERTRAIN
OVERTRAINED
OVERTRAINING
OVERTRAINS
OVERTREAT
OVERTREATED
OVERTREATING
OVERTREATMENT
OVERTREATMENTS
OVERTREATS
OVERTRICK
OVERTRICKS
OVERTRIM
OVERTRIMMED
OVERTRIMMING
OVERTRIMS
OVERTRUMP
OVERTRUMPED
OVERTRUMPING
OVERTRUMPS
OVERTURE
OVERTURED
OVERTURES
OVERTURING
OVERTURN
OVERTURNED
OVERTURNING
OVERTURNS
OVERURGE
OVERURGED
OVERURGES
OVERURGING
OVERUSE
OVERUSED
OVERUSES
OVERUSING
OVERUTILIZATION
OVERUTILIZE
OVERUTILIZED
OVERUTILIZES
OVERUTILIZING
OVERVALUATION
OVERVALUATIONS
OVERVALUE
OVERVALUED
OVERVALUES
OVERVALUING
OVERVIEW
OVERVIEWS
OVERVIOLENT
OVERVIVID
OVERVOLTAGE
OVERVOLTAGES
OVERVOTE
OVERVOTED
OVERVOTES
OVERVOTING
OVERWARM
OVERWARMED
OVERWARMING
OVERWARMS
OVERWARY
OVERWATCH
OVERWATCHED
OVERWATCHES
OVERWATCHING
OVERWATER
OVERWATERED
OVERWATERING
OVERWATERS
OVERWEAK
OVERWEAR
OVERWEARIED
OVERWEARIES
OVERWEARING
OVERWEARS
OVERWEARY
OVERWEARYING
OVERWEEN
OVERWEENED
OVERWEENING
OVERWEENINGLY
OVERWEENS
OVERWEIGH
OVERWEIGHED
OVERWEIGHING
OVERWEIGHS
OVERWEIGHT
OVERWEIGHTED
OVERWEIGHTING
OVERWEIGHTS
OVERWET
OVERWETS
OVERWETTED
OVERWETTING
OVERWHELM
OVERWHELMED
OVERWHELMING
OVERWHELMINGLY
OVERWHELMS
OVERWIDE
OVERWILY
OVERWIND
OVERWINDING
OVERWINDS
OVERWINTER
OVERWINTERED
OVERWINTERING
OVERWINTERS
OVERWISE
OVERWITHHELD
OVERWITHHOLD
OVERWITHHOLDING

OVERWITHHOLDS
OVERWORD
OVERWORDS
OVERWORE
OVERWORK
OVERWORKED
OVERWORKING
OVERWORKS
OVERWORN
OVERWOUND
OVERWRITE
OVERWRITES
OVERWRITING
OVERWRITTEN
OVERWROTE
OVERWROUGHT
OVERZEAL
OVERZEALOUS
OVERZEALOUSLY
OVERZEALOUSNESS
OVERZEALS
OVIBOS
OVICIDAL
OVICIDE
OVICIDES
OVIDUCAL
OVIDUCT
OVIDUCTAL
OVIDUCTS
OVIFEROUS
OVIFORM
OVINE
OVINES
OVIPARA
OVIPARITIES
OVIPARITY
OVIPAROUS
OVIPOSIT
OVIPOSITED
OVIPOSITING
OVIPOSITION
OVIPOSITIONAL
OVIPOSITIONS
OVIPOSITOR
OVIPOSITORS
OVIPOSITS
OVIRAPTOR
OVIRAPTORS
OVISAC
OVISACS
OVOID
OVOIDAL
OVOIDALS
OVOIDS
OVOLI
OVOLO
OVOLOS
OVONIC
OVONICS
OVOTESTES
OVOTESTIS
OVOVIVIPAROUS
OVOVIVIPAROUSLY
OVULAR
OVULARY
OVULATE
OVULATED
OVULATES
OVULATING
OVULATION
OVULATIONS
OVULATORY
OVULE
OVULES
OVUM
OW
OWE
OWED
OWES
OWING
OWL
OWLERIES
OWLERY
OWLET
OWLETS
OWLIER
OWLIEST
OWLISH
OWLISHLY
OWLISHNESS
OWLISHNESSES
OWLLIKE
OWLS
OWLY
OWN
OWNABLE
OWNED
OWNER
OWNERLESS
OWNERS
OWNERSHIP
OWNERSHIPS
OWNING
OWNS
OWSE
OWSEN
OWT
OWTS
OX
OXACILLIN
OXACILLINS
OXALACETATE
OXALACETATES
OXALATE
OXALATED
OXALATES
OXALATING
OXALIC
OXALIS
OXALISES
OXALOACETATE
OXALOACETATES
OXAZEPAM
OXAZEPAMS
OXAZINE
OXAZINES
OXAZOLE
OXAZOLES
OXBLOOD
OXBLOODS
OXBOW
OXBOWS
OXCART
OXCARTS
OXEN
OXER
OXERS
OXES
OXEYE
OXEYES
OXFORD
OXFORDS
OXHEART
OXHEARTS
OXHERD
OXHERDS
OXHIDE
OXHIDES
OXIC
OXID
OXIDABLE
OXIDANT
OXIDANTS
OXIDASE
OXIDASES
OXIDASIC
OXIDATE
OXIDATED
OXIDATES
OXIDATING
OXIDATION
OXIDATIONS
OXIDATIVE
OXIDATIVELY
OXIDE
OXIDES
OXIDIC
OXIDISE
OXIDISED
OXIDISER
OXIDISERS
OXIDISES
OXIDISING
OXIDIZABLE
OXIDIZE
OXIDIZED
OXIDIZER
OXIDIZERS
OXIDIZES
OXIDIZING
OXIDOREDUCTASE
OXIDOREDUCTASES
OXIDS
OXIM
OXIME
OXIMES
OXIMETER
OXIMETERS
OXIMETRIES
OXIMETRY
OXIMS
OXLIKE
OXLIP
OXLIPS
OXO
OXPECKER
OXPECKERS
OXTAIL
OXTAILS
OXTER
OXTERS
OXTONGUE
OXTONGUES
OXY
OXYACETYLENE
OXYACID
OXYACIDS
OXYCODONE
OXYCODONES
OXYGEN
OXYGENASE
OXYGENASES
OXYGENATE
OXYGENATED
OXYGENATES
OXYGENATING
OXYGENATION
OXYGENATIONS
OXYGENATOR
OXYGENATORS
OXYGENIC
OXYGENIZE
OXYGENIZED
OXYGENIZES
OXYGENIZING
OXYGENLESS
OXYGENOUS
OXYGENS
OXYHEMOGLOBIN
OXYHEMOGLOBINS
OXYHYDROGEN
OXYMORA
OXYMORON
OXYMORONIC
OXYMORONICALLY
OXYMORONS
OXYPHENBUTAZONE
OXYPHIL
OXYPHILE
OXYPHILES
OXYPHILIC
OXYPHILS
OXYSALT
OXYSALTS
OXYSOME
OXYSOMES
OXYTETRACYCLINE
OXYTOCIC
OXYTOCICS
OXYTOCIN
OXYTOCINS
OXYTONE
OXYTONES
OXYTROPE
OXYTROPES
OXYURIASES
OXYURIASIS
OY
OYER
OYERS
OYES
OYESSES
OYEZ
OYEZES
OYSTER

YSTERCATCHER
YSTERCATCHERS
YSTERED
YSTERER
YSTERERS
YSTERING
YSTERINGS
YSTERMAN
YSTERMEN
OYSTERS
OZALID
OZALIDS
OZOCERITE
OZOCERITES
OZOKERITE
OZOKERITES
OZONATE
OZONATED
OZONATES
OZONATING
OZONATION
OZONATIONS
OZONE
OZONES
OZONIC
OZONIDE
OZONIDES
OZONISE
OZONISED
OZONISER
OZONISERS
OZONISES
OZONISING
OZONIZATION
OZONIZATIONS
OZONIZE
OZONIZED
OZONIZER
OZONIZERS
OZONIZES
OZONIZING
OZONOSPHERE
OZONOSPHERES
OZONOUS

P

A
AAN
AANS
ABLUM
ABLUMS
ABULAR
ABULUM
ABULUMS
AC
CA
CAS
CE
CED
CEMAKER
CEMAKERS
CEMAKING
CEMAKINGS
CER
CERS
CES
CESETTER
CESETTERS
CESETTING
CEY
CHA
CHADOM
CHADOMS
CHALIC
CHALICS
CHAS
CHINKO
CHINKOS
CHISI
CHISIS
PACHOULI
PACHOULIS
PACHUCO
PACHUCOS
PACHYDERM
PACHYDERMATOUS
PACHYDERMS
PACHYSANDRA
PACHYSANDRAS
PACHYTENE
PACHYTENES
PACIER
PACIEST
PACIFIABLE
PACIFIC
PACIFICAL
PACIFICALLY
PACIFICATION
PACIFICATIONS
PACIFICATOR
PACIFICATORS
PACIFICISM
PACIFICISMS
PACIFICIST
PACIFICISTS
PACIFIED
PACIFIER
PACIFIERS
PACIFIES
PACIFISM
PACIFISMS
PACIFIST
PACIFISTIC
PACIFISTICALLY
PACIFISTS
PACIFY
PACIFYING
PACING
PACINGS
PACK
PACKABILITIES
PACKABILITY
PACKABLE
PACKAGE
PACKAGED
PACKAGER
PACKAGERS
PACKAGES
PACKAGING
PACKAGINGS
PACKBOARD
PACKBOARDS
PACKED
PACKER
PACKERS
PACKET
PACKETED
PACKETING
PACKETS
PACKHORSE
PACKHORSES
PACKING
PACKINGHOUSE
PACKINGHOUSES
PACKINGS
PACKLY
PACKMAN
PACKMEN
PACKNESS
PACKNESSES
PACKS
PACKSACK
PACKSACKS
PACKSADDLE
PACKSADDLES
PACKTHREAD
PACKTHREADS
PACKWAX
PACKWAXES
PACLITAXEL
PACLITAXELS
PACS
PACT
PACTION
PACTIONS
PACTS
PACY
PACZKI
PACZKIS
PAD
PADAUK
PADAUKS
PADDED
PADDER
PADDERS
PADDIES
PADDING
PADDINGS
PADDLE
PADDLEBALL
PADDLEBALLS
PADDLEBOARD
PADDLEBOARDS
PADDLEBOAT
PADDLEBOATS
PADDLED
PADDLEFISH
PADDLEFISHES
PADDLER
PADDLERS
PADDLES
PADDLING
PADDLINGS
PADDOCK
PADDOCKED
PADDOCKING
PADDOCKS
PADDY
PADDYWACK
PADDYWACKED
PADDYWACKING
PADDYWACKS
PADI
PADIS
PADISHAH
PADISHAHS
PADLE
PADLES
PADLOCK
PADLOCKED
PADLOCKING
PADLOCKS
PADNAG
PADNAGS
PADOUK
PADOUKS

PADRE
PADRES
PADRI
PADRONA
PADRONAS
PADRONE
PADRONES
PADRONI
PADRONISM
PADRONISMS
PADS
PADSHAH
PADSHAHS
PADUASOY
PADUASOYS
PAEAN
PAEANISM
PAEANISMS
PAEANS
PAEDIATRIC
PAEDIATRICIAN
PAEDIATRICIANS
PAEDIATRICS
PAEDOGENESES
PAEDOGENESIS
PAEDOGENETIC
PAEDOGENIC
PAEDOMORPHIC
PAEDOMORPHISM
PAEDOMORPHISMS
PAEDOMORPHOSES
PAEDOMORPHOSIS
PAEDOPHILE
PAEDOPHILES
PAEDOPHILIA
PAEDOPHILIAS
PAELLA
PAELLAS
PAEON
PAEONIC
PAEONS
PAESAN
PAESANI
PAESANO
PAESANOS
PAESANS
PAGAN
PAGANDOM
PAGANDOMS
PAGANISE
PAGANISED
PAGANISES
PAGANISH
PAGANISING
PAGANISM
PAGANISMS
PAGANIST
PAGANISTS
PAGANIZE
PAGANIZED
PAGANIZER
PAGANIZERS
PAGANIZES
PAGANIZING
PAGANS
PAGE
PAGEANT
PAGEANTRIES
PAGEANTRY
PAGEANTS
PAGEBOY
PAGEBOYS
PAGED
PAGEFUL
PAGEFULS
PAGER
PAGERS
PAGES
PAGINAL
PAGINATE
PAGINATED
PAGINATES
PAGINATING
PAGINATION
PAGINATIONS
PAGING
PAGINGS
PAGOD
PAGODA
PAGODAS
PAGODS
PAGURIAN
PAGURIANS
PAGURID
PAGURIDS
PAH
PAHLAVI
PAHLAVIS
PAHOEHOE
PAHOEHOES
PAID
PAIK
PAIKED
PAIKING
PAIKS
PAIL
PAILFUL
PAILFULS
PAILLARD
PAILLARDS
PAILLASSE
PAILLASSES
PAILLETTE
PAILLETTES
PAILS
PAILSFUL
PAIN
PAINCH
PAINCHES
PAINED
PAINFUL
PAINFULLER
PAINFULLEST
PAINFULLY
PAINFULNESS
PAINFULNESSES
PAINING
PAINKILLER
PAINKILLERS
PAINKILLING
PAINLESS
PAINLESSLY
PAINLESSNESS
PAINLESSNESSES
PAINS
PAINSTAKING
PAINSTAKINGLY
PAINSTAKINGS
PAINT
PAINTABLE
PAINTBALL
PAINTBALLS
PAINTBOX
PAINTBOXES
PAINTBRUSH
PAINTBRUSHES
PAINTED
PAINTER
PAINTERLINESS
PAINTERLINESSES
PAINTERLY
PAINTERS
PAINTIER
PAINTIEST
PAINTING
PAINTINGS
PAINTS
PAINTWORK
PAINTWORKS
PAINTY
PAIR
PAIRED
PAIRING
PAIRINGS
PAIRS
PAIRWISE
PAISA
PAISAN
PAISANA
PAISANAS
PAISANO
PAISANOS
PAISANS
PAISAS
PAISE
PAISLEY
PAISLEYS
PAJAMA
PAJAMAED
PAJAMAS
PAK
PAKEHA
PAKEHAS
PAKORA
PAKORAS
PAKS
PAL
PALABRA
PALABRAS
PALACE
PALACED
PALACES
PALADIN
PALADINS
PALAEOLITHIC
PALAEONTOLOGIES
PALAEONTOLOGIST
PALAEONTOLOGY
PALAESTRA
PALAESTRAE
PALAESTRAS
PALAIS
PALANKEEN
PALANKEENS
PALANQUIN
PALANQUINS
PALAPA
PALAPAS
PALATABILITIES
PALATABILITY
PALATABLE
PALATABLENESS
PALATABLENESSES
PALATABLY
PALATAL
PALATALIZATION
PALATALIZATIONS
PALATALIZE
PALATALIZED
PALATALIZES
PALATALIZING
PALATALLY
PALATALS
PALATE
PALATES
PALATIAL
PALATIALLY
PALATIALNESS
PALATIALNESSES
PALATINATE
PALATINATES
PALATINE
PALATINES
PALAVER
PALAVERED
PALAVERER
PALAVERERS
PALAVERING
PALAVERS
PALAZZI
PALAZZO
PALAZZOS
PALE
PALEA
PALEAE
PALEAL
PALEATE
PALED
PALEFACE
PALEFACES
PALELY
PALENESS
PALENESSES
PALEOBIOLOGIC
PALEOBIOLOGICAL
PALEOBIOLOGIES
PALEOBIOLOGIST
PALEOBIOLOGISTS
PALEOBIOLOGY
PALEOBOTANIC
PALEOBOTANICAL
PALEOBOTANIES
PALEOBOTANIST
PALEOBOTANISTS
PALEOBOTANY

'ALEOCENE
'ALEOCLIMATIC
'ALEOCON
'ALEOCONS
'ALEOECOLOGIC
'ALEOECOLOGICAL
ALEOECOLOGIES
ALEOECOLOGIST
ALEOECOLOGISTS
ALEOECOLOGY
ALEOGENE
ALEOGEOGRAPHIC
ALEOGEOGRAPHY
ALEOGRAPHER
ALEOGRAPHERS
ALEOGRAPHIC
ALEOGRAPHICAL
ALEOGRAPHIES
ALEOGRAPHY
ALEOLITH
ALEOLITHIC
ALEOLITHS
ALEOLOGIES
ALEOLOGY
ALEOMAGNETIC
ALEOMAGNETISM
ALEOMAGNETISMS
ALEOMAGNETIST
ALEOMAGNETISTS
ALEONTOLOGIC
ALEONTOLOGICAL
ALEONTOLOGIES
ALEONTOLOGIST
ALEONTOLOGISTS
LEONTOLOGY
ALEOPATHOLOGY
LEOSOL
LEOSOLS
LEOZOIC
LEOZOOLOGICAL
LEOZOOLOGIES
LEOZOOLOGIST
LEOZOOLOGISTS
LEOZOOLOGY
LER
LES
LEST
LESTRA
LESTRAE
LESTRAL
LESTRAS
LET
LETOT
PALETOTS
PALETS
PALETTE
PALETTES
PALEWAYS
PALEWISE
PALFREY
PALFREYS
PALI
PALIER
PALIEST
PALIKAR
PALIKARS
PALIMONIES
PALIMONY
PALIMPSEST
PALIMPSESTS
PALINDROME
PALINDROMES
PALINDROMIC
PALINDROMIST
PALINDROMISTS
PALING
PALINGENESES
PALINGENESIS
PALINGENETIC
PALINGS
PALINODE
PALINODES
PALIS
PALISADE
PALISADED
PALISADES
PALISADING
PALISH
PALL
PALLADIA
PALLADIC
PALLADIUM
PALLADIUMS
PALLADOUS
PALLBEARER
PALLBEARERS
PALLED
PALLET
PALLETED
PALLETING
PALLETISE
PALLETISED
PALLETISES
PALLETISING
PALLETIZATION
PALLETIZATIONS
PALLETIZE
PALLETIZED
PALLETIZER
PALLETIZERS
PALLETIZES
PALLETIZING
PALLETS
PALLETTE
PALLETTES
PALLIA
PALLIAL
PALLIASSE
PALLIASSES
PALLIATE
PALLIATED
PALLIATES
PALLIATING
PALLIATION
PALLIATIONS
PALLIATIVE
PALLIATIVELY
PALLIATIVES
PALLIATOR
PALLIATORS
PALLID
PALLIDER
PALLIDEST
PALLIDLY
PALLIDNESS
PALLIDNESSES
PALLIDOTOMIES
PALLIDOTOMY
PALLIER
PALLIEST
PALLING
PALLIUM
PALLIUMS
PALLOR
PALLORS
PALLS
PALLY
PALM
PALMAR
PALMARY
PALMATE
PALMATED
PALMATELY
PALMATION
PALMATIONS
PALMBALL
PALMBALLS
PALMED
PALMER
PALMERS
PALMERWORM
PALMERWORMS
PALMETTE
PALMETTES
PALMETTO
PALMETTOES
PALMETTOS
PALMFUL
PALMFULS
PALMIER
PALMIERS
PALMIEST
PALMING
PALMIST
PALMISTER
PALMISTERS
PALMISTRIES
PALMISTRY
PALMISTS
PALMITATE
PALMITATES
PALMITIN
PALMITINS
PALMLIKE
PALMS
PALMTOP
PALMTOPS
PALMY
PALMYRA
PALMYRAS
PALOMINO
PALOMINOS
PALOOKA
PALOOKAS
PALOVERDE
PALOVERDES
PALP
PALPABILITIES
PALPABILITY
PALPABLE
PALPABLY
PALPAL
PALPATE
PALPATED
PALPATES
PALPATING
PALPATION
PALPATIONS
PALPATOR
PALPATORS
PALPATORY
PALPEBRA
PALPEBRAE
PALPEBRAL
PALPEBRAS
PALPED
PALPI
PALPING
PALPITANT
PALPITATE
PALPITATED
PALPITATES
PALPITATING
PALPITATION
PALPITATIONS
PALPS
PALPUS
PALPUSES
PALS
PALSA
PALSAS
PALSGRAVE
PALSGRAVES
PALSHIP
PALSHIPS
PALSIED
PALSIER
PALSIES
PALSIEST
PALSY
PALSYING
PALSYLIKE
PALTER
PALTERED
PALTERER
PALTERERS
PALTERING
PALTERS
PALTRIER
PALTRIEST
PALTRILY
PALTRINESS
PALTRINESSES
PALTRY
PALUDAL
PALUDISM
PALUDISMS
PALY
PALYNOLOGIC
PALYNOLOGICAL
PALYNOLOGICALLY
PALYNOLOGIES
PALYNOLOGIST
PALYNOLOGISTS
PALYNOLOGY

PAM
PAMPA
PAMPAS
PAMPEAN
PAMPEANS
PAMPER
PAMPERED
PAMPERER
PAMPERERS
PAMPERING
PAMPERO
PAMPEROS
PAMPERS
PAMPHLET
PAMPHLETED
PAMPHLETEER
PAMPHLETEERED
PAMPHLETEERING
PAMPHLETEERS
PAMPHLETING
PAMPHLETS
PAMS
PAN
PANACEA
PANACEAN
PANACEAS
PANACHE
PANACHES
PANADA
PANADAS
PANAMA
PANAMAS
PANATELA
PANATELAS
PANATELLA
PANATELLAS
PANBROIL
PANBROILED
PANBROILING
PANBROILS
PANCAKE
PANCAKED
PANCAKES
PANCAKING
PANCETTA
PANCETTAS
PANCHAX
PANCHAXES
PANCHROMATIC
PANCRATIA
PANCRATIC
PANCRATIUM
PANCRATIUMS
PANCREAS
PANCREASES
PANCREATECTOMY
PANCREATIC
PANCREATIN
PANCREATINS
PANCREATITIDES
PANCREATITIS
PANCREOZYMIN
PANCREOZYMINS
PANCYTOPENIA
PANCYTOPENIAS
PANDA
PANDAN
PANDANI
PANDANS
PANDANUS
PANDANUSES
PANDAS
PANDECT
PANDECTS
PANDEMIC
PANDEMICS
PANDEMONIUM
PANDEMONIUMS
PANDER
PANDERED
PANDERER
PANDERERS
PANDERING
PANDERS
PANDIED
PANDIES
PANDIT
PANDITS
PANDOOR
PANDOORS
PANDORA
PANDORAS
PANDORE
PANDORES
PANDOUR
PANDOURS
PANDOWDIES
PANDOWDY
PANDURA
PANDURAS
PANDURATE
PANDY
PANDYING
PANE
PANED
PANEER
PANEERS
PANEGYRIC
PANEGYRICAL
PANEGYRICALLY
PANEGYRICS
PANEGYRIST
PANEGYRISTS
PANEL
PANELED
PANELESS
PANELING
PANELINGS
PANELIST
PANELISTS
PANELIZED
PANELLED
PANELLING
PANELLINGS
PANELS
PANES
PANETELA
PANETELAS
PANETELLA
PANETELLAS
PANETTONE
PANETTONES
PANETTONI
PANFISH
PANFISHED
PANFISHES
PANFISHING
PANFISHINGS
PANFORTE
PANFORTES
PANFRIED
PANFRIES
PANFRY
PANFRYING
PANFUL
PANFULS
PANG
PANGA
PANGAS
PANGED
PANGEN
PANGENE
PANGENES
PANGENESES
PANGENESIS
PANGENETIC
PANGENS
PANGING
PANGOLIN
PANGOLINS
PANGRAM
PANGRAMS
PANGS
PANHANDLE
PANHANDLED
PANHANDLER
PANHANDLERS
PANHANDLES
PANHANDLING
PANHUMAN
PANIC
PANICALLY
PANICKED
PANICKIER
PANICKIEST
PANICKING
PANICKY
PANICLE
PANICLED
PANICLES
PANICS
PANICULATE
PANICUM
PANICUMS
PANIER
PANIERS
PANINI
PANINIS
PANINO
PANJANDRA
PANJANDRUM
PANJANDRUMS
PANLEUKOPENIA
PANLEUKOPENIAS
PANLIKE
PANMICTIC
PANMIXES
PANMIXIA
PANMIXIAS
PANMIXIS
PANNE
PANNED
PANNER
PANNERS
PANNES
PANNIER
PANNIERED
PANNIERS
PANNIKIN
PANNIKINS
PANNING
PANNIST
PANNISTS
PANOCHA
PANOCHAS
PANOCHE
PANOCHES
PANOPLIED
PANOPLIES
PANOPLY
PANOPTIC
PANORAMA
PANORAMAS
PANORAMIC
PANORAMICALLY
PANPIPE
PANPIPES
PANS
PANSEXUAL
PANSEXUALITIES
PANSEXUALITY
PANSEXUALS
PANSIES
PANSOPHIC
PANSOPHIES
PANSOPHY
PANSY
PANT
PANTALET
PANTALETS
PANTALETTES
PANTALONE
PANTALONES
PANTALOON
PANTALOONS
PANTDRESS
PANTDRESSES
PANTECHNICON
PANTECHNICONS
PANTED
PANTHEISM
PANTHEISMS
PANTHEIST
PANTHEISTIC
PANTHEISTICAL
PANTHEISTICALLY
PANTHEISTS
PANTHEON
PANTHEONS
PANTHER
PANTHERS
PANTIE
PANTIES
PANTIHOSE
PANTILE

ANTILED
ANTILES
ANTING
ANTINGLY
ANTISOCRACIES
ANTISOCRACY
ANTISOCRATIC
ANTISOCRATICAL
ANTISOCRATIST
ANTISOCRATISTS
ANTO
ANTOFFLE
ANTOFFLES
ANTOFLE
ANTOFLES
ANTOGRAPH
ANTOGRAPHIC
ANTOGRAPHS
ANTOMIME
ANTOMIMED
ANTOMIMES
ANTOMIMIC
ANTOMIMING
ANTOMIMIST
ANTOMIMISTS
ANTOS
NTOTHENATE
NTOTHENATES
NTOUM
NTOUMS
NTRIES
NTROPIC
NTROPICAL
NTRY
NTRYMAN
NTRYMEN
NTS
NTSUIT
NTSUITED
NTSUITS
NTY
NTYHOSE
NTYWAIST
NTYWAISTS
NZER
NZERS
P
PA
PACIES
PACY
PADAM
PADAMS
PADOM
PAPADOMS
PAPADUM
PAPADUMS
PAPAIN
PAPAINS
PAPAL
PAPALIST
PAPALISTS
PAPALLY
PAPARAZZI
PAPARAZZO
PAPAS
PAPAVERINE
PAPAVERINES
PAPAW
PAPAWS
PAPAYA
PAPAYAN
PAPAYAS
PAPER
PAPERBACK
PAPERBACKED
PAPERBACKS
PAPERBARK
PAPERBARKS
PAPERBOARD
PAPERBOARDS
PAPERBOUND
PAPERBOUNDS
PAPERBOY
PAPERBOYS
PAPERCLIP
PAPERCLIPS
PAPERED
PAPERER
PAPERERS
PAPERGIRL
PAPERGIRLS
PAPERHANGER
PAPERHANGERS
PAPERHANGING
PAPERHANGINGS
PAPERINESS
PAPERINESSES
PAPERING
PAPERLESS
PAPERMAKER
PAPERMAKERS
PAPERMAKING
PAPERMAKINGS
PAPERS
PAPERWEIGHT
PAPERWEIGHTS
PAPERWHITE
PAPERWHITES
PAPERWORK
PAPERWORKS
PAPERY
PAPETERIE
PAPETERIES
PAPHIAN
PAPHIANS
PAPILIONACEOUS
PAPILLA
PAPILLAE
PAPILLAR
PAPILLARY
PAPILLATE
PAPILLOMA
PAPILLOMAS
PAPILLOMATA
PAPILLOMATOUS
PAPILLOMAVIRUS
PAPILLON
PAPILLONS
PAPILLOSE
PAPILLOTE
PAPILLOTES
PAPISM
PAPISMS
PAPIST
PAPISTIC
PAPISTRIES
PAPISTRY
PAPISTS
PAPOOSE
PAPOOSES
PAPOVAVIRUS
PAPOVAVIRUSES
PAPPADAM
PAPPADAMS
PAPPADUM
PAPPADUMS
PAPPARDELLE
PAPPI
PAPPIER
PAPPIES
PAPPIEST
PAPPOOSE
PAPPOOSES
PAPPOSE
PAPPOUS
PAPPUS
PAPPY
PAPRICA
PAPRICAS
PAPRIKA
PAPRIKAS
PAPS
PAPULA
PAPULAE
PAPULAR
PAPULAS
PAPULE
PAPULES
PAPULOSE
PAPULOUS
PAPYRAL
PAPYRI
PAPYRIAN
PAPYRINE
PAPYROLOGIES
PAPYROLOGIST
PAPYROLOGISTS
PAPYROLOGY
PAPYRUS
PAPYRUSES
PAR
PARA
PARABIOSES
PARABIOSIS
PARABIOTIC
PARABIOTICALLY
PARABLAST
PARABLASTS
PARABLE
PARABLES
PARABOLA
PARABOLAE
PARABOLAS
PARABOLIC
PARABOLICALLY
PARABOLOID
PARABOLOIDAL
PARABOLOIDS
PARACETAMOL
PARACETAMOLS
PARACHOR
PARACHORS
PARACHUTE
PARACHUTED
PARACHUTES
PARACHUTIC
PARACHUTING
PARACHUTIST
PARACHUTISTS
PARACLETE
PARACLETES
PARACRINE
PARADE
PARADED
PARADER
PARADERS
PARADES
PARADIDDLE
PARADIDDLES
PARADIGM
PARADIGMATIC
PARADIGMS
PARADING
PARADISAIC
PARADISAICAL
PARADISAICALLY
PARADISAL
PARADISE
PARADISES
PARADISIAC
PARADISIACAL
PARADISIACALLY
PARADISIAL
PARADISICAL
PARADOR
PARADORES
PARADORS
PARADOS
PARADOSES
PARADOX
PARADOXES
PARADOXICAL
PARADOXICALITY
PARADOXICALLY
PARADOXICALNESS
PARADROP
PARADROPPED
PARADROPPING
PARADROPS
PARAE
PARAESTHESIA
PARAESTHESIAS
PARAFFIN
PARAFFINE
PARAFFINED
PARAFFINES
PARAFFINIC
PARAFFINING
PARAFFINS
PARAFOIL
PARAFOILS
PARAFORM
PARAFORMS
PARAGENESES
PARAGENESIS

PARAGENETIC
PARAGENETICALLY
PARAGLIDE
PARAGLIDED
PARAGLIDER
PARAGLIDERS
PARAGLIDES
PARAGLIDING
PARAGOGE
PARAGOGES
PARAGON
PARAGONED
PARAGONING
PARAGONS
PARAGRAPH
PARAGRAPHED
PARAGRAPHER
PARAGRAPHERS
PARAGRAPHIC
PARAGRAPHING
PARAGRAPHS
PARAINFLUENZA
PARAINFLUENZAS
PARAJOURNALISM
PARAJOURNALISMS
PARAKEET
PARAKEETS
PARAKITE
PARAKITES
PARALANGUAGE
PARALANGUAGES
PARALDEHYDE
PARALDEHYDES
PARALEGAL
PARALEGALS
PARALINGUISTIC
PARALINGUISTICS
PARALLACTIC
PARALLAX
PARALLAXES
PARALLEL
PARALLELED
PARALLELEPIPED
PARALLELEPIPEDS
PARALLELING
PARALLELISM
PARALLELISMS
PARALLELLED
PARALLELLING
PARALLELOGRAM
PARALLELOGRAMS
PARALLELS
PARALOGISM
PARALOGISMS
PARALYSE
PARALYSED
PARALYSES
PARALYSING
PARALYSIS
PARALYTIC
PARALYTICALLY
PARALYTICS
PARALYZATION
PARALYZATIONS
PARALYZE
PARALYZED
PARALYZER
PARALYZERS
PARALYZES
PARALYZING
PARALYZINGLY
PARAMAGNET
PARAMAGNETIC
PARAMAGNETISM
PARAMAGNETISMS
PARAMAGNETS
PARAMATTA
PARAMATTAS
PARAMECIA
PARAMECIUM
PARAMECIUMS
PARAMEDIC
PARAMEDICAL
PARAMEDICALS
PARAMEDICS
PARAMENT
PARAMENTA
PARAMENTS
PARAMETER
PARAMETERIZE
PARAMETERIZED
PARAMETERIZES
PARAMETERIZING
PARAMETERS
PARAMETRIC
PARAMETRICALLY
PARAMETRIZATION
PARAMETRIZE
PARAMETRIZED
PARAMETRIZES
PARAMETRIZING
PARAMILITARIES
PARAMILITARY
PARAMNESIA
PARAMNESIAS
PARAMO
PARAMORPH
PARAMORPHS
PARAMOS
PARAMOUNT
PARAMOUNTCIES
PARAMOUNTCY
PARAMOUNTLY
PARAMOUNTS
PARAMOUR
PARAMOURS
PARAMYLUM
PARAMYLUMS
PARAMYXOVIRUS
PARAMYXOVIRUSES
PARANG
PARANGS
PARANOEA
PARANOEAS
PARANOIA
PARANOIAC
PARANOIACS
PARANOIAS
PARANOIC
PARANOICALLY
PARANOICS
PARANOID
PARANOIDAL
PARANOIDS
PARANORMAL
PARANORMALITIES
PARANORMALITY
PARANORMALLY
PARANORMALS
PARANYMPH
PARANYMPHS
PARAPET
PARAPETED
PARAPETS
PARAPH
PARAPHERNALIA
PARAPHILIA
PARAPHILIAC
PARAPHILIACS
PARAPHILIAS
PARAPHILIC
PARAPHILICS
PARAPHRASABLE
PARAPHRASE
PARAPHRASED
PARAPHRASER
PARAPHRASERS
PARAPHRASES
PARAPHRASING
PARAPHRASTIC
PARAPHS
PARAPHYSES
PARAPHYSIS
PARAPLEGIA
PARAPLEGIAS
PARAPLEGIC
PARAPLEGICS
PARAPODIA
PARAPODIAL
PARAPODIUM
PARAPSYCHOLOGY
PARAQUAT
PARAQUATS
PARAQUET
PARAQUETS
PARARESCUE
PARARESCUEMAN
PARARESCUEMEN
PARARESCUER
PARARESCUERS
PARARESCUES
PARAROSANILINE
PARAROSANILINES
PARAS
PARASAIL
PARASAILED
PARASAILING
PARASAILINGS
PARASAILS
PARASANG
PARASANGS
PARASEXUAL
PARASEXUALITIES
PARASEXUALITY
PARASHAH
PARASHAHS
PARASHIOTH
PARASHOT
PARASHOTH
PARASITE
PARASITES
PARASITIC
PARASITICAL
PARASITICALLY
PARASITICIDAL
PARASITICIDE
PARASITICIDES
PARASITISE
PARASITISED
PARASITISES
PARASITISING
PARASITISM
PARASITISMS
PARASITIZATION
PARASITIZATIONS
PARASITIZE
PARASITIZED
PARASITIZES
PARASITIZING
PARASITOID
PARASITOIDS
PARASITOLOGIC
PARASITOLOGICAL
PARASITOLOGIES
PARASITOLOGIST
PARASITOLOGISTS
PARASITOLOGY
PARASITOSES
PARASITOSIS
PARASOL
PARASOLED
PARASOLS
PARASYMPATHETIC
PARASYNTHESES
PARASYNTHESIS
PARASYNTHETIC
PARATACTIC
PARATACTICAL
PARATACTICALLY
PARATAXES
PARATAXIS
PARATHA
PARATHAS
PARATHION
PARATHIONS
PARATHORMONE
PARATHORMONES
PARATHYROID
PARATHYROIDS
PARATRANSIT
PARATRANSITS
PARATROOP
PARATROOPER
PARATROOPERS
PARATROOPS
PARATYPHOID
PARATYPHOIDS
PARAVANE
PARAVANES
PARAWING
PARAWINGS
PARAZOAN
PARAZOANS
PARBAKE
PARBAKED

ARBAKES
ARBAKING
ARBOIL
ARBOILED
ARBOILING
ARBOILS
ARBUCKLE
ARBUCKLED
ARBUCKLES
ARBUCKLING
ARCEL
ARCELED
ARCELING
ARCELLED
ARCELLING
ARCELS
ARCENARIES
ARCENARY
ARCENER
ARCENERS
ARCH
ARCHED
ARCHEESI
ARCHEESIS
ARCHES
ARCHESI
ARCHESIS
ARCHING
ARCHISI
ARCHISIS
ARCHMENT
ARCHMENTS
ARCLOSE
ARCLOSES
ARD
ARDAH
ARDAHS
ARDEE
ARDI
ARDIE
ARDINE
ARDNER
ARDNERS
ARDON
ARDONABLE
ARDONABLENESS
ARDONABLY
ARDONED
ARDONER
ARDONERS
ARDONING
ARDONS
ARDS
PARDY
PARE
PARECISM
PARECISMS
PARED
PAREGORIC
PAREGORICS
PAREIRA
PAREIRAS
PAREN
PARENCHYMA
PARENCHYMAL
PARENCHYMAS
PARENCHYMATOUS
PARENS
PARENT
PARENTAGE
PARENTAGES
PARENTAL
PARENTALLY
PARENTED
PARENTERAL
PARENTERALLY
PARENTHESES
PARENTHESIS
PARENTHESIZE
PARENTHESIZED
PARENTHESIZES
PARENTHESIZING
PARENTHETIC
PARENTHETICAL
PARENTHETICALLY
PARENTHOOD
PARENTHOODS
PARENTING
PARENTINGS
PARENTLESS
PARENTS
PAREO
PAREOS
PARER
PARERGA
PARERGON
PARERS
PARES
PARESES
PARESIS
PARESTHESIA
PARESTHESIAS
PARESTHETIC
PARETIC
PARETICS
PAREU
PAREUS
PAREVE
PARFAIT
PARFAITS
PARFLECHE
PARFLECHES
PARFLESH
PARFLESHES
PARFOCAL
PARFOCALITIES
PARFOCALITY
PARFOCALIZE
PARFOCALIZED
PARFOCALIZES
PARFOCALIZING
PARGE
PARGED
PARGES
PARGET
PARGETED
PARGETING
PARGETINGS
PARGETS
PARGETTED
PARGETTING
PARGING
PARGINGS
PARGO
PARGOS
PARGYLINE
PARGYLINES
PARHELIA
PARHELIC
PARHELION
PARIAH
PARIAHS
PARIAN
PARIANS
PARIES
PARIETAL
PARIETALS
PARIETES
PARING
PARINGS
PARIS
PARISES
PARISH
PARISHES
PARISHIONER
PARISHIONERS
PARITIES
PARITY
PARK
PARKA
PARKADE
PARKADES
PARKAS
PARKED
PARKER
PARKERS
PARKETTE
PARKETTES
PARKIER
PARKIEST
PARKIN
PARKING
PARKINGS
PARKINS
PARKINSONIAN
PARKINSONIANS
PARKINSONISM
PARKINSONISMS
PARKLAND
PARKLANDS
PARKLIKE
PARKOUR
PARKOURS
PARKS
PARKWAY
PARKWAYS
PARKY
PARLANCE
PARLANCES
PARLANDO
PARLANTE
PARLAY
PARLAYED
PARLAYING
PARLAYS
PARLE
PARLED
PARLES
PARLEY
PARLEYED
PARLEYER
PARLEYERS
PARLEYING
PARLEYS
PARLIAMENT
PARLIAMENTARIAN
PARLIAMENTARY
PARLIAMENTS
PARLING
PARLOR
PARLORS
PARLOUR
PARLOURS
PARLOUS
PARLOUSLY
PARMESAN
PARMESANS
PARMIGIANA
PARMIGIANO
PAROCHIAL
PAROCHIALISM
PAROCHIALISMS
PAROCHIALLY
PARODIC
PARODICAL
PARODIED
PARODIES
PARODIST
PARODISTIC
PARODISTS
PARODOI
PARODOS
PARODY
PARODYING
PAROL
PAROLABLE
PAROLE
PAROLED
PAROLEE
PAROLEES
PAROLES
PAROLING
PAROLS
PARONOMASIA
PARONOMASIAS
PARONOMASTIC
PARONYM
PARONYMIC
PARONYMIES
PARONYMOUS
PARONYMS
PARONYMY
PAROQUET
PAROQUETS
PAROSMIA
PAROSMIAS
PAROTIC
PAROTID
PAROTIDS
PAROTITIC
PAROTITIDES
PAROTITIS
PAROTITISES
PAROTOID
PAROTOIDS

PAROUS
PAROXETINE
PAROXETINES
PAROXYSM
PAROXYSMAL
PAROXYSMS
PARQUET
PARQUETED
PARQUETING
PARQUETRIES
PARQUETRY
PARQUETS
PARR
PARRAKEET
PARRAKEETS
PARRAL
PARRALS
PARRED
PARREL
PARRELS
PARRICIDAL
PARRICIDE
PARRICIDES
PARRIDGE
PARRIDGES
PARRIED
PARRIER
PARRIERS
PARRIES
PARRING
PARRITCH
PARRITCHES
PARROKET
PARROKETS
PARROT
PARROTED
PARROTER
PARROTERS
PARROTING
PARROTS
PARROTY
PARRS
PARRY
PARRYING
PARS
PARSABLE
PARSE
PARSEC
PARSECS
PARSED
PARSER
PARSERS
PARSES
PARSIMONIES
PARSIMONIOUS
PARSIMONIOUSLY
PARSIMONY
PARSING
PARSLEY
PARSLEYED
PARSLEYS
PARSLIED
PARSNIP
PARSNIPS
PARSON
PARSONAGE
PARSONAGES
PARSONIC
PARSONISH
PARSONS
PART
PARTAKE
PARTAKEN
PARTAKER
PARTAKERS
PARTAKES
PARTAKING
PARTAN
PARTANS
PARTED
PARTER
PARTERRE
PARTERRES
PARTERS
PARTHENOCARPIC
PARTHENOCARPIES
PARTHENOCARPY
PARTHENOGENESES
PARTHENOGENESIS
PARTHENOGENETIC
PARTHENOGENIC
PARTIAL
PARTIALITIES
PARTIALITY
PARTIALLY
PARTIALS
PARTIBILITIES
PARTIBILITY
PARTIBLE
PARTICIPANT
PARTICIPANTS
PARTICIPATE
PARTICIPATED
PARTICIPATES
PARTICIPATING
PARTICIPATION
PARTICIPATIONAL
PARTICIPATIONS
PARTICIPATIVE
PARTICIPATOR
PARTICIPATORIES
PARTICIPATORS
PARTICIPATORY
PARTICIPIAL
PARTICIPIALLY
PARTICIPLE
PARTICIPLES
PARTICLE
PARTICLEBOARD
PARTICLEBOARDS
PARTICLES
PARTICULAR
PARTICULARISE
PARTICULARISED
PARTICULARISES
PARTICULARISING
PARTICULARISM
PARTICULARISMS
PARTICULARIST
PARTICULARISTIC
PARTICULARISTS
PARTICULARITIES
PARTICULARITY
PARTICULARIZE
PARTICULARIZED
PARTICULARIZES
PARTICULARIZING
PARTICULARLY
PARTICULARS
PARTICULATE
PARTICULATES
PARTIED
PARTIER
PARTIERS
PARTIES
PARTIEST
PARTING
PARTINGS
PARTISAN
PARTISANLY
PARTISANS
PARTISANSHIP
PARTISANSHIPS
PARTITA
PARTITAS
PARTITE
PARTITION
PARTITIONED
PARTITIONER
PARTITIONERS
PARTITIONING
PARTITIONIST
PARTITIONISTS
PARTITIONS
PARTITIVE
PARTITIVELY
PARTITIVES
PARTIZAN
PARTIZANS
PARTLET
PARTLETS
PARTLY
PARTNER
PARTNERED
PARTNERING
PARTNERLESS
PARTNERS
PARTNERSHIP
PARTNERSHIPS
PARTON
PARTONS
PARTOOK
PARTRIDGE
PARTRIDGEBERRY
PARTRIDGES
PARTS
PARTURIENT
PARTURIENTS
PARTURITION
PARTURITIONS
PARTWAY
PARTY
PARTYER
PARTYERS
PARTYGOER
PARTYGOERS
PARTYING
PARTYINGS
PARURA
PARURAS
PARURE
PARURES
PARVE
PARVENU
PARVENUE
PARVENUES
PARVENUS
PARVIS
PARVISE
PARVISES
PARVO
PARVOLIN
PARVOLINE
PARVOLINES
PARVOLINS
PARVOS
PARVOVIRUS
PARVOVIRUSES
PAS
PASCAL
PASCALS
PASCHAL
PASCHALS
PASE
PASEO
PASEOS
PASES
PASH
PASHA
PASHADOM
PASHADOMS
PASHALIC
PASHALICS
PASHALIK
PASHALIKS
PASHAS
PASHED
PASHES
PASHING
PASHKA
PASHKAS
PASHM
PASHMINA
PASHMINAS
PASHMS
PASKA
PASKAS
PASKHA
PASKHAS
PASODOBLE
PASODOBLES
PASQUEFLOWER
PASQUEFLOWERS
PASQUIL
PASQUILS
PASQUINADE
PASQUINADED
PASQUINADES
PASQUINADING
PASS
PASSABLE
PASSABLY
PASSACAGLIA
PASSACAGLIAS
PASSADE

ASSADES
ASSADO
ASSADOES
ASSADOS
ASSAGE
ASSAGED
ASSAGES
ASSAGEWAY
ASSAGEWAYS
ASSAGEWORK
ASSAGEWORKS
ASSAGING
ASSALONG
ASSALONGS
ASSANT
ASSBAND
ASSBANDS
ASSBOOK
ASSBOOKS
ASSE
ASSED
ASSEE
ASSEL
ASSELS
ASSEMENTERIE
ASSEMENTERIES
ASSENGER
ASSENGERS
ASSEPIED
ASSEPIEDS
ASSER
ASSERBY
ASSERINE
ASSERINES
ASSERS
ASSERSBY
ASSES
ASSIBLE
ASSIM
ASSING
ASSINGLY
ASSINGS
ASSION
ASSIONAL
ASSIONALS
ASSIONATE
ASSIONATELY
ASSIONATENESS
ASSIONFLOWER
ASSIONFLOWERS
ASSIONLESS
ASSIONS
ASSIVATE
PASSIVATED
PASSIVATES
PASSIVATING
PASSIVATION
PASSIVATIONS
PASSIVE
PASSIVELY
PASSIVENESS
PASSIVENESSES
PASSIVES
PASSIVISM
PASSIVISMS
PASSIVIST
PASSIVISTS
PASSIVITIES
PASSIVITY
PASSKEY
PASSKEYS
PASSLESS
PASSOVER
PASSOVERS
PASSPORT
PASSPORTS
PASSUS
PASSUSES
PASSWORD
PASSWORDS
PAST
PASTA
PASTALIKE
PASTAS
PASTE
PASTEBOARD
PASTEBOARDS
PASTED
PASTEDOWN
PASTEDOWNS
PASTEL
PASTELIST
PASTELISTS
PASTELLIST
PASTELLISTS
PASTELS
PASTER
PASTERN
PASTERNS
PASTERS
PASTES
PASTEUP
PASTEUPS
PASTEURISATION
PASTEURISATIONS
PASTEURISE
PASTEURISED
PASTEURISES
PASTEURISING
PASTEURIZATION
PASTEURIZATIONS
PASTEURIZE
PASTEURIZED
PASTEURIZER
PASTEURIZERS
PASTEURIZES
PASTEURIZING
PASTICCI
PASTICCIO
PASTICCIOS
PASTICHE
PASTICHES
PASTICHEUR
PASTICHEURS
PASTIE
PASTIER
PASTIES
PASTIEST
PASTIL
PASTILLE
PASTILLES
PASTILS
PASTILY
PASTIME
PASTIMES
PASTINA
PASTINAS
PASTINESS
PASTINESSES
PASTING
PASTINGS
PASTIS
PASTISES
PASTITSIO
PASTITSIOS
PASTITSO
PASTITSOS
PASTLESS
PASTNESS
PASTNESSES
PASTOR
PASTORAL
PASTORALE
PASTORALES
PASTORALI
PASTORALISM
PASTORALISMS
PASTORALIST
PASTORALISTS
PASTORALLY
PASTORALNESS
PASTORALNESSES
PASTORALS
PASTORATE
PASTORATES
PASTORED
PASTORING
PASTORIUM
PASTORIUMS
PASTORLY
PASTORS
PASTORSHIP
PASTORSHIPS
PASTRAMI
PASTRAMIS
PASTRIES
PASTROMI
PASTROMIS
PASTRY
PASTS
PASTURAGE
PASTURAGES
PASTURAL
PASTURE
PASTURED
PASTURELAND
PASTURELANDS
PASTURER
PASTURERS
PASTURES
PASTURING
PASTY
PAT
PATACA
PATACAS
PATAGIA
PATAGIAL
PATAGIUM
PATAMAR
PATAMARS
PATCH
PATCHABLE
PATCHBOARD
PATCHBOARDS
PATCHED
PATCHER
PATCHERS
PATCHES
PATCHIER
PATCHIEST
PATCHILY
PATCHINESS
PATCHINESSES
PATCHING
PATCHOULI
PATCHOULIES
PATCHOULIS
PATCHOULY
PATCHWORK
PATCHWORKED
PATCHWORKING
PATCHWORKS
PATCHY
PATE
PATED
PATELLA
PATELLAE
PATELLAR
PATELLAS
PATELLATE
PATELLIFORM
PATEN
PATENCIES
PATENCY
PATENS
PATENT
PATENTABILITIES
PATENTABILITY
PATENTABLE
PATENTED
PATENTEE
PATENTEES
PATENTING
PATENTLY
PATENTOR
PATENTORS
PATENTS
PATER
PATERFAMILIAS
PATERNAL
PATERNALISM
PATERNALISMS
PATERNALIST
PATERNALISTIC
PATERNALISTS
PATERNALLY
PATERNITIES
PATERNITY
PATERNOSTER
PATERNOSTERS
PATERS
PATES
PATH
PATHBREAKING
PATHETIC

PATHETICAL
PATHETICALLY
PATHFINDER
PATHFINDERS
PATHFINDING
PATHFINDINGS
PATHLESS
PATHLESSNESS
PATHLESSNESSES
PATHNAME
PATHNAMES
PATHOBIOLOGIES
PATHOBIOLOGY
PATHOGEN
PATHOGENE
PATHOGENES
PATHOGENESES
PATHOGENESIS
PATHOGENETIC
PATHOGENIC
PATHOGENICITIES
PATHOGENICITY
PATHOGENIES
PATHOGENS
PATHOGENY
PATHOGNOMONIC
PATHOGRAPHIES
PATHOGRAPHY
PATHOLOGIC
PATHOLOGICAL
PATHOLOGICALLY
PATHOLOGIES
PATHOLOGIST
PATHOLOGISTS
PATHOLOGIZE
PATHOLOGIZED
PATHOLOGIZES
PATHOLOGIZING
PATHOLOGY
PATHOPHYSIOLOGY
PATHOS
PATHOSES
PATHS
PATHWAY
PATHWAYS
PATIENCE
PATIENCES
PATIENT
PATIENTER
PATIENTEST
PATIENTLY
PATIENTS
PATIN
PATINA
PATINAE
PATINAED
PATINAS
PATINATE
PATINATED
PATINATES
PATINATING
PATINATION
PATINATIONS
PATINE
PATINED
PATINES
PATINING
PATINIZE
PATINIZED
PATINIZES
PATINIZING
PATINS
PATIO
PATIOS
PATISSERIE
PATISSERIES
PATISSIER
PATISSIERS
PATLY
PATNESS
PATNESSES
PATOIS
PATONCE
PATOOT
PATOOTIE
PATOOTIES
PATOOTS
PATRESFAMILIAS
PATRIARCH
PATRIARCHAL
PATRIARCHATE
PATRIARCHATES
PATRIARCHIES
PATRIARCHS
PATRIARCHY
PATRIATE
PATRIATED
PATRIATES
PATRIATING
PATRICIAN
PATRICIANS
PATRICIATE
PATRICIATES
PATRICIDAL
PATRICIDE
PATRICIDES
PATRILINEAL
PATRILINIES
PATRILINY
PATRIMONIAL
PATRIMONIES
PATRIMONY
PATRIOT
PATRIOTIC
PATRIOTICALLY
PATRIOTISM
PATRIOTISMS
PATRIOTS
PATRISTIC
PATRISTICAL
PATRISTICS
PATROL
PATROLLED
PATROLLER
PATROLLERS
PATROLLING
PATROLMAN
PATROLMEN
PATROLS
PATRON
PATRONAGE
PATRONAGES
PATRONAL
PATRONESS
PATRONESSES
PATRONISE
PATRONISED
PATRONISES
PATRONISING
PATRONIZATION
PATRONIZATIONS
PATRONIZE
PATRONIZED
PATRONIZES
PATRONIZING
PATRONIZINGLY
PATRONLY
PATRONS
PATRONYMIC
PATRONYMICS
PATROON
PATROONS
PATS
PATSIES
PATSY
PATTAMAR
PATTAMARS
PATTED
PATTEE
PATTEN
PATTENED
PATTENS
PATTER
PATTERED
PATTERER
PATTERERS
PATTERING
PATTERN
PATTERNED
PATTERNING
PATTERNINGS
PATTERNLESS
PATTERNS
PATTERS
PATTEST
PATTIE
PATTIES
PATTING
PATTY
PATTYPAN
PATTYPANS
PATULENT
PATULOUS
PATY
PATZER
PATZERS
PAUA
PAUAS
PAUCITIES
PAUCITY
PAUGHTY
PAULDRON
PAULDRONS
PAULIN
PAULINS
PAULOWNIA
PAULOWNIAS
PAUNCH
PAUNCHED
PAUNCHES
PAUNCHIER
PAUNCHIEST
PAUNCHINESS
PAUNCHINESSES
PAUNCHY
PAUPER
PAUPERED
PAUPERING
PAUPERISM
PAUPERISMS
PAUPERIZATION
PAUPERIZATIONS
PAUPERIZE
PAUPERIZED
PAUPERIZES
PAUPERIZING
PAUPERS
PAUPIETTE
PAUPIETTES
PAURAQUE
PAURAQUES
PAUROPOD
PAUROPODS
PAUSAL
PAUSE
PAUSED
PAUSER
PAUSERS
PAUSES
PAUSING
PAVAN
PAVANE
PAVANES
PAVANS
PAVE
PAVED
PAVEED
PAVEMENT
PAVEMENTS
PAVER
PAVERS
PAVES
PAVID
PAVILION
PAVILIONED
PAVILIONING
PAVILIONS
PAVILLON
PAVILLONS
PAVIN
PAVING
PAVINGS
PAVINS
PAVIOR
PAVIORS
PAVIOUR
PAVIOURS
PAVIS
PAVISE
PAVISER
PAVISERS
PAVISES
PAVISSE
PAVISSES
PAVLOVA

PAVLOVAS
PAVONINE
PAW
PAWED
PAWER
PAWERS
PAWING
PAWKIER
PAWKIEST
PAWKILY
PAWKINESS
PAWKINESSES
PAWKY
PAWL
PAWLS
PAWN
PAWNABLE
PAWNAGE
PAWNAGES
PAWNBROKER
PAWNBROKERS
PAWNBROKING
PAWNBROKINGS
PAWNED
PAWNEE
PAWNEES
PAWNER
PAWNERS
PAWNING
PAWNOR
PAWNORS
PAWNS
PAWNSHOP
PAWNSHOPS
PAWPAW
PAWPAWS
PAWS
PAX
PAXES
PAXWAX
PAXWAXES
PAY
PAYABLE
PAYABLES
PAYABLY
PAYBACK
PAYBACKS
PAYCHECK
PAYCHECKS
PAYDAY
PAYDAYS
PAYDOWN
PAYDOWNS
PAYED
PAYEE
PAYEES
PAYER
PAYERS
PAYESS
PAYGRADE
PAYGRADES
PAYING
PAYLOAD
PAYLOADS
PAYMASTER
PAYMASTERS
PAYMENT
PAYMENTS
PAYNIM
PAYNIMS
PAYOFF
PAYOFFS
PAYOLA
PAYOLAS
PAYOR
PAYORS
PAYOUT
PAYOUTS
PAYROLL
PAYROLLS
PAYS
PAYSLIP
PAYSLIPS
PAYWALL
PAYWALLS
PAZAZZ
PAZAZZES
PE
PEA
PEABERRIES
PEABERRY
PEABRAIN
PEABRAINS
PEACE
PEACEABLE
PEACEABLENESS
PEACEABLENESSES
PEACEABLY
PEACED
PEACEFUL
PEACEFULLER
PEACEFULLEST
PEACEFULLY
PEACEFULNESS
PEACEFULNESSES
PEACEKEEPER
PEACEKEEPERS
PEACEKEEPING
PEACEKEEPINGS
PEACEMAKER
PEACEMAKERS
PEACEMAKING
PEACEMAKINGS
PEACENIK
PEACENIKS
PEACES
PEACETIME
PEACETIMES
PEACH
PEACHBLOW
PEACHBLOWS
PEACHED
PEACHER
PEACHERS
PEACHES
PEACHICK
PEACHICKS
PEACHIER
PEACHIEST
PEACHING
PEACHY
PEACING
PEACOAT
PEACOATS
PEACOCK
PEACOCKED
PEACOCKIER
PEACOCKIEST
PEACOCKING
PEACOCKISH
PEACOCKS
PEACOCKY
PEAFOWL
PEAFOWLS
PEAG
PEAGE
PEAGES
PEAGS
PEAHEN
PEAHENS
PEAK
PEAKED
PEAKEDNESS
PEAKEDNESSES
PEAKIER
PEAKIEST
PEAKING
PEAKISH
PEAKLESS
PEAKLIKE
PEAKS
PEAKY
PEAL
PEALED
PEALIKE
PEALING
PEALS
PEAN
PEANS
PEANUT
PEANUTS
PEANUTTIER
PEANUTTIEST
PEANUTTY
PEAR
PEARL
PEARLASH
PEARLASHES
PEARLED
PEARLER
PEARLERS
PEARLESCENCE
PEARLESCENCES
PEARLESCENT
PEARLIER
PEARLIES
PEARLIEST
PEARLING
PEARLISED
PEARLITE
PEARLITES
PEARLITIC
PEARLIZED
PEARLS
PEARLY
PEARMAIN
PEARMAINS
PEARS
PEART
PEARTER
PEARTEST
PEARTLY
PEARTNESS
PEARTNESSES
PEARWOOD
PEARWOODS
PEAS
PEASANT
PEASANTRIES
PEASANTRY
PEASANTS
PEASANTY
PEASCOD
PEASCODS
PEASE
PEASECOD
PEASECODS
PEASEN
PEASES
PEASHOOTER
PEASHOOTERS
PEASOUPER
PEASOUPERS
PEAT
PEATIER
PEATIEST
PEATLAND
PEATLANDS
PEATS
PEATY
PEAVEY
PEAVEYS
PEAVIES
PEAVY
PEBBLE
PEBBLED
PEBBLES
PEBBLIER
PEBBLIEST
PEBBLING
PEBBLY
PEC
PECAN
PECANS
PECCABLE
PECCADILLO
PECCADILLOES
PECCADILLOS
PECCANCIES
PECCANCY
PECCANT
PECCANTLY
PECCARIES
PECCARY
PECCAVI
PECCAVIS
PECH
PECHAN
PECHANS
PECHED
PECHING
PECHS
PECK
PECKED
PECKER

PECKERS
PECKERWOOD
PECKERWOODS
PECKIER
PECKIEST
PECKING
PECKISH
PECKISHLY
PECKS
PECKY
PECORINI
PECORINO
PECORINOS
PECS
PECTASE
PECTASES
PECTATE
PECTATES
PECTEN
PECTENS
PECTIC
PECTIN
PECTINACEOUS
PECTINATE
PECTINATION
PECTINATIONS
PECTINES
PECTINESTERASE
PECTINESTERASES
PECTINOUS
PECTINS
PECTIZE
PECTIZED
PECTIZES
PECTIZING
PECTORAL
PECTORALS
PECULATE
PECULATED
PECULATES
PECULATING
PECULATION
PECULATIONS
PECULATOR
PECULATORS
PECULIA
PECULIAR
PECULIARITIES
PECULIARITY
PECULIARLY
PECULIARS
PECULIUM
PECUNIARILY
PECUNIARY
PED
PEDAGOG
PEDAGOGIC
PEDAGOGICAL
PEDAGOGICALLY
PEDAGOGICS
PEDAGOGIES
PEDAGOGS
PEDAGOGUE
PEDAGOGUES
PEDAGOGY
PEDAL
PEDALED
PEDALER
PEDALERS
PEDALFER
PEDALFERS
PEDALIER
PEDALIERS
PEDALING
PEDALLED
PEDALLER
PEDALLERS
PEDALLING
PEDALO
PEDALOS
PEDALS
PEDANT
PEDANTIC
PEDANTICALLY
PEDANTRIES
PEDANTRY
PEDANTS
PEDATE
PEDATELY
PEDDLE
PEDDLED
PEDDLER
PEDDLERIES
PEDDLERS
PEDDLERY
PEDDLES
PEDDLING
PEDERAST
PEDERASTIC
PEDERASTIES
PEDERASTS
PEDERASTY
PEDES
PEDESTAL
PEDESTALED
PEDESTALING
PEDESTALLED
PEDESTALLING
PEDESTALS
PEDESTRIAN
PEDESTRIANISE
PEDESTRIANISED
PEDESTRIANISES
PEDESTRIANISING
PEDESTRIANISM
PEDESTRIANISMS
PEDESTRIANIZE
PEDESTRIANIZED
PEDESTRIANIZES
PEDESTRIANIZING
PEDESTRIANS
PEDIATRIC
PEDIATRICIAN
PEDIATRICIANS
PEDIATRICS
PEDIATRIST
PEDIATRISTS
PEDICAB
PEDICABS
PEDICEL
PEDICELLATE
PEDICELS
PEDICLE
PEDICLED
PEDICLES
PEDICULAR
PEDICULATE
PEDICULATES
PEDICULOSES
PEDICULOSIS
PEDICULOUS
PEDICURE
PEDICURED
PEDICURES
PEDICURING
PEDICURIST
PEDICURISTS
PEDIFORM
PEDIGREE
PEDIGREED
PEDIGREES
PEDIMENT
PEDIMENTAL
PEDIMENTED
PEDIMENTS
PEDIPALP
PEDIPALPS
PEDLAR
PEDLARIES
PEDLARS
PEDLARY
PEDLER
PEDLERIES
PEDLERS
PEDLERY
PEDOCAL
PEDOCALIC
PEDOCALS
PEDOGENESES
PEDOGENESIS
PEDOGENETIC
PEDOGENIC
PEDOLOGIC
PEDOLOGICAL
PEDOLOGIES
PEDOLOGIST
PEDOLOGISTS
PEDOLOGY
PEDOMETER
PEDOMETERS
PEDOPHILE
PEDOPHILES
PEDOPHILIA
PEDOPHILIAC
PEDOPHILIAS
PEDOPHILIC
PEDORTHIC
PEDORTHICS
PEDORTHIST
PEDORTHISTS
PEDRO
PEDROS
PEDS
PEDUNCLE
PEDUNCLED
PEDUNCLES
PEDUNCULAR
PEDUNCULATE
PEDUNCULATED
PEDWAY
PEDWAYS
PEE
PEEBEEN
PEEBEENS
PEED
PEEING
PEEK
PEEKABOO
PEEKABOOS
PEEKAPOO
PEEKAPOOS
PEEKED
PEEKING
PEEKS
PEEL
PEELABLE
PEELED
PEELER
PEELERS
PEELING
PEELINGS
PEELS
PEEN
PEENED
PEENING
PEENINGS
PEENS
PEEP
PEEPBO
PEEPBOS
PEEPED
PEEPER
PEEPERS
PEEPHOLE
PEEPHOLES
PEEPING
PEEPS
PEEPSHOW
PEEPSHOWS
PEEPUL
PEEPULS
PEER
PEERAGE
PEERAGES
PEERED
PEERESS
PEERESSES
PEERIE
PEERIES
PEERING
PEERLESS
PEERS
PEERY
PEES
PEESWEEP
PEESWEEPS
PEETWEET
PEETWEETS
PEEVE
PEEVED
PEEVES
PEEVING
PEEVISH
PEEVISHLY
PEEVISHNESS

PEEVISHNESSES
PEEWEE
PEEWEES
PEEWIT
PEEWITS
PEG
PEGBOARD
PEGBOARDS
PEGBOX
PEGBOXES
PEGGED
PEGGING
PEGLEGGED
PEGLESS
PEGLIKE
PEGMATITE
PEGMATITES
PEGMATITIC
PEGS
PEGTOP
PEGTOPS
PEH
PEHS
PEIGNOIR
PEIGNOIRS
PEIN
PEINED
PEINING
PEINS
PEISE
PEISED
PEISES
PEISING
PEJORATIVE
PEJORATIVELY
PEJORATIVES
PEKAN
PEKANS
PEKE
PEKEPOO
PEKEPOOS
PEKES
PEKIN
PEKINS
PEKOE
PEKOES
PELAGE
PELAGES
PELAGIAL
PELAGIC
PELAGICS
PELARGONIUM
PELARGONIUMS
PELAU
PELAUS
PELE
PELECYPOD
PELECYPODS
PELERINE
PELERINES
PELES
PELF
PELFS
PELHAM
PELHAMS
PELICAN
PELICANS
PELISSE
PELISSES
PELITE
PELITES
PELITIC
PELLAGRA
PELLAGRAS
PELLAGRIN
PELLAGRINS
PELLAGROUS
PELLET
PELLETAL
PELLETED
PELLETING
PELLETISE
PELLETISED
PELLETISES
PELLETISING
PELLETIZATION
PELLETIZATIONS
PELLETIZE
PELLETIZED
PELLETIZER
PELLETIZERS
PELLETIZES
PELLETIZING
PELLETS
PELLICLE
PELLICLES
PELLITORIES
PELLITORY
PELLMELL
PELLMELLS
PELLUCID
PELLUCIDLY
PELMET
PELMETS
PELON
PELORIA
PELORIAN
PELORIAS
PELORIC
PELORUS
PELORUSES
PELOTA
PELOTAS
PELOTON
PELOTONS
PELT
PELTAST
PELTASTS
PELTATE
PELTATELY
PELTATION
PELTATIONS
PELTED
PELTER
PELTERED
PELTERING
PELTERS
PELTING
PELTLESS
PELTRIES
PELTRY
PELTS
PELVES
PELVIC
PELVICS
PELVIS
PELVISES
PELYCOSAUR
PELYCOSAURS
PEMBINA
PEMBINAS
PEMICAN
PEMICANS
PEMMICAN
PEMMICANS
PEMOLINE
PEMOLINES
PEMPHIGI
PEMPHIGUS
PEMPHIGUSES
PEMPHIX
PEMPHIXES
PEN
PENAL
PENALISE
PENALISED
PENALISES
PENALISING
PENALITIES
PENALITY
PENALIZATION
PENALIZATIONS
PENALIZE
PENALIZED
PENALIZES
PENALIZING
PENALLY
PENALTIES
PENALTY
PENANCE
PENANCED
PENANCES
PENANCING
PENANG
PENANGS
PENATES
PENCE
PENCEL
PENCELS
PENCHANT
PENCHANTS
PENCIL
PENCILED
PENCILER
PENCILERS
PENCILING
PENCILINGS
PENCILLED
PENCILLER
PENCILLERS
PENCILLING
PENCILLINGS
PENCILS
PEND
PENDANT
PENDANTLY
PENDANTS
PENDED
PENDENCIES
PENDENCY
PENDENT
PENDENTIVE
PENDENTIVES
PENDENTLY
PENDENTS
PENDING
PENDRAGON
PENDRAGONS
PENDS
PENDULAR
PENDULOUS
PENDULOUSLY
PENDULOUSNESS
PENDULOUSNESSES
PENDULUM
PENDULUMS
PENEPLAIN
PENEPLAINS
PENEPLANE
PENEPLANES
PENES
PENETRABILITIES
PENETRABILITY
PENETRABLE
PENETRALIA
PENETRANCE
PENETRANCES
PENETRANT
PENETRANTS
PENETRATE
PENETRATED
PENETRATES
PENETRATING
PENETRATINGLY
PENETRATION
PENETRATIONS
PENETRATIVE
PENETROMETER
PENETROMETERS
PENGO
PENGOS
PENGUIN
PENGUINS
PENHOLDER
PENHOLDERS
PENIAL
PENICIL
PENICILLAMINE
PENICILLAMINES
PENICILLATE
PENICILLIA
PENICILLIN
PENICILLINASE
PENICILLINASES
PENICILLINS
PENICILLIUM
PENICILS
PENILE
PENINSULA
PENINSULAR
PENINSULAS
PENIS
PENISES
PENITENCE
PENITENCES

PENITENT
PENITENTIAL
PENITENTIALLY
PENITENTIARIES
PENITENTIARY
PENITENTLY
PENITENTS
PENKNIFE
PENKNIVES
PENLIGHT
PENLIGHTS
PENLITE
PENLITES
PENMAN
PENMANSHIP
PENMANSHIPS
PENMEN
PENNA
PENNAE
PENNAME
PENNAMES
PENNANT
PENNANTS
PENNATE
PENNATED
PENNE
PENNED
PENNER
PENNERS
PENNES
PENNI
PENNIA
PENNIES
PENNILESS
PENNINE
PENNINES
PENNING
PENNIS
PENNON
PENNONCEL
PENNONCELS
PENNONED
PENNONS
PENNY
PENNYCRESS
PENNYCRESSES
PENNYROYAL
PENNYROYALS
PENNYWEIGHT
PENNYWEIGHTS
PENNYWHISTLE
PENNYWHISTLES
PENNYWISE
PENNYWORT
PENNYWORTH
PENNYWORTHS
PENNYWORTS
PENOCHE
PENOCHES
PENOLOGICAL
PENOLOGIES
PENOLOGIST
PENOLOGISTS
PENOLOGY
PENONCEL
PENONCELS
PENPOINT
PENPOINTS
PENS
PENSEE
PENSEES
PENSIL
PENSILE
PENSILS
PENSION
PENSIONABLE
PENSIONARIES
PENSIONARY
PENSIONE
PENSIONED
PENSIONER
PENSIONERS
PENSIONES
PENSIONI
PENSIONING
PENSIONLESS
PENSIONS
PENSIVE
PENSIVELY
PENSIVENESS
PENSIVENESSES
PENSTEMON
PENSTEMONS
PENSTER
PENSTERS
PENSTOCK
PENSTOCKS
PENT
PENTACLE
PENTACLES
PENTAD
PENTADS
PENTAGON
PENTAGONAL
PENTAGONALLY
PENTAGONALS
PENTAGONS
PENTAGRAM
PENTAGRAMS
PENTAHEDRA
PENTAHEDRAL
PENTAHEDRON
PENTAHEDRONS
PENTAMERIES
PENTAMEROUS
PENTAMERY
PENTAMETER
PENTAMETERS
PENTAMIDINE
PENTAMIDINES
PENTANE
PENTANES
PENTANGLE
PENTANGLES
PENTANOL
PENTANOLS
PENTAPEPTIDE
PENTAPEPTIDES
PENTAPLOID
PENTAPLOIDIES
PENTAPLOIDS
PENTAPLOIDY
PENTARCH
PENTARCHIES
PENTARCHS
PENTARCHY
PENTATHLETE
PENTATHLETES
PENTATHLON
PENTATHLONS
PENTATONIC
PENTAVALENT
PENTAZOCINE
PENTAZOCINES
PENTENE
PENTENES
PENTHOUSE
PENTHOUSES
PENTIMENTI
PENTIMENTO
PENTLANDITE
PENTLANDITES
PENTOBARBITAL
PENTOBARBITALS
PENTOBARBITONE
PENTOBARBITONES
PENTODE
PENTODES
PENTOMIC
PENTOSAN
PENTOSANS
PENTOSE
PENTOSES
PENTOSIDE
PENTOSIDES
PENTOXIDE
PENTOXIDES
PENTSTEMON
PENTSTEMONS
PENTYL
PENTYLS
PENUCHE
PENUCHES
PENUCHI
PENUCHIS
PENUCHLE
PENUCHLES
PENUCKLE
PENUCKLES
PENULT
PENULTIMA
PENULTIMAS
PENULTIMATE
PENULTIMATELY
PENULTS
PENUMBRA
PENUMBRAE
PENUMBRAL
PENUMBRAS
PENURIES
PENURIOUS
PENURIOUSLY
PENURIOUSNESS
PENURIOUSNESSES
PENURY
PEON
PEONAGE
PEONAGES
PEONES
PEONIES
PEONISM
PEONISMS
PEONS
PEONY
PEOPLE
PEOPLED
PEOPLEHOOD
PEOPLEHOODS
PEOPLELESS
PEOPLER
PEOPLERS
PEOPLES
PEOPLING
PEP
PEPEROMIA
PEPEROMIAS
PEPERONI
PEPERONIS
PEPINO
PEPINOS
PEPITA
PEPITAS
PEPLA
PEPLOS
PEPLOSES
PEPLUM
PEPLUMED
PEPLUMS
PEPLUS
PEPLUSES
PEPO
PEPONIDA
PEPONIDAS
PEPONIUM
PEPONIUMS
PEPOS
PEPPED
PEPPER
PEPPERBOX
PEPPERBOXES
PEPPERCORN
PEPPERCORNS
PEPPERED
PEPPERER
PEPPERERS
PEPPERGRASS
PEPPERGRASSES
PEPPERINESS
PEPPERINESSES
PEPPERING
PEPPERMINT
PEPPERMINTS
PEPPERMINTY
PEPPERONI
PEPPERONIS
PEPPERS
PEPPERTREE
PEPPERTREES
PEPPERY
PEPPIER
PEPPIEST
PEPPILY
PEPPINESS
PEPPINESSES
PEPPING

PEPPY
PEPS
PEPSI
PEPSIN
PEPSINATE
PEPSINATED
PEPSINATES
PEPSINATING
PEPSINE
PEPSINES
PEPSINOGEN
PEPSINOGENS
PEPSINS
PEPSIS
PEPTALK
PEPTALKED
PEPTALKING
PEPTALKS
PEPTIC
PEPTICS
PEPTID
PEPTIDASE
PEPTIDASES
PEPTIDE
PEPTIDES
PEPTIDIC
PEPTIDOGLYCAN
PEPTIDOGLYCANS
PEPTIDS
PEPTIZE
PEPTIZED
PEPTIZER
PEPTIZERS
PEPTIZES
PEPTIZING
PEPTONE
PEPTONES
PEPTONIC
PEPTONIZE
PEPTONIZED
PEPTONIZES
PEPTONIZING
PER
PERACID
PERACIDS
PERADVENTURE
PERADVENTURES
PERAMBULATE
PERAMBULATED
PERAMBULATES
PERAMBULATING
PERAMBULATION
PERAMBULATIONS

PERAMBULATOR
PERAMBULATORS
PERAMBULATORY
PERBORATE
PERBORATES
PERC
PERCALE
PERCALES
PERCALINE
PERCALINES
PERCEIVABLE
PERCEIVABLY
PERCEIVE
PERCEIVED
PERCEIVER
PERCEIVERS
PERCEIVES
PERCEIVING
PERCENT
PERCENTAGE
PERCENTAGES
PERCENTAL
PERCENTILE
PERCENTILES
PERCENTS
PERCEPT
PERCEPTIBILITY
PERCEPTIBLE
PERCEPTIBLY
PERCEPTION
PERCEPTIONAL
PERCEPTIONS
PERCEPTIVE
PERCEPTIVELY
PERCEPTIVENESS
PERCEPTIVITIES
PERCEPTIVITY
PERCEPTS
PERCEPTUAL
PERCEPTUALLY
PERCH
PERCHANCE
PERCHED
PERCHER
PERCHERS
PERCHES
PERCHING
PERCHLORATE
PERCHLORATES
PERCID
PERCIDS
PERCIPIENCE
PERCIPIENCES

PERCIPIENT
PERCIPIENTLY
PERCIPIENTS
PERCOID
PERCOIDS
PERCOLATE
PERCOLATED
PERCOLATES
PERCOLATING
PERCOLATION
PERCOLATIONS
PERCOLATOR
PERCOLATORS
PERCS
PERCUSS
PERCUSSED
PERCUSSES
PERCUSSING
PERCUSSION
PERCUSSIONIST
PERCUSSIONISTS
PERCUSSIONS
PERCUSSIVE
PERCUSSIVELY
PERCUSSIVENESS
PERCUSSOR
PERCUSSORS
PERCUTANEOUS
PERCUTANEOUSLY
PERDIE
PERDITION
PERDITIONS
PERDU
PERDUE
PERDUES
PERDURABILITIES
PERDURABILITY
PERDURABLE
PERDURABLY
PERDURE
PERDURED
PERDURES
PERDURING
PERDUS
PERDY
PERE
PEREA
PEREGRIN
PEREGRINATE
PEREGRINATED
PEREGRINATES
PEREGRINATING
PEREGRINATION

PEREGRINATIONS
PEREGRINE
PEREGRINES
PEREGRINS
PEREIA
PEREION
PEREIONS
PEREIOPOD
PEREIOPODS
PEREMPTORILY
PEREMPTORINESS
PEREMPTORY
PERENNATE
PERENNATED
PERENNATES
PERENNATING
PERENNATION
PERENNATIONS
PERENNIAL
PERENNIALLY
PERENNIALS
PEREON
PEREONS
PEREOPOD
PEREOPODS
PERES
PERESTROIKA
PERESTROIKAS
PERFECT
PERFECTA
PERFECTABILITY
PERFECTAS
PERFECTED
PERFECTER
PERFECTERS
PERFECTEST
PERFECTIBILITY
PERFECTIBLE
PERFECTING
PERFECTION
PERFECTIONISM
PERFECTIONISMS
PERFECTIONIST
PERFECTIONISTIC
PERFECTIONISTS
PERFECTIONS
PERFECTIVE
PERFECTIVELY
PERFECTIVENESS
PERFECTIVES
PERFECTIVITIES
PERFECTIVITY
PERFECTLY

PERFECTNESS
PERFECTNESSES
PERFECTO
PERFECTOS
PERFECTS
PERFERVID
PERFIDIES
PERFIDIOUS
PERFIDIOUSLY
PERFIDIOUSNESS
PERFIDY
PERFLUOROCARBON
PERFOLIATE
PERFORATE
PERFORATED
PERFORATES
PERFORATING
PERFORATION
PERFORATIONS
PERFORATOR
PERFORATORS
PERFORCE
PERFORM
PERFORMABILITY
PERFORMABLE
PERFORMANCE
PERFORMANCES
PERFORMATIVE
PERFORMATIVES
PERFORMATORY
PERFORMED
PERFORMER
PERFORMERS
PERFORMING
PERFORMS
PERFUME
PERFUMED
PERFUMER
PERFUMERIES
PERFUMERS
PERFUMERY
PERFUMES
PERFUMING
PERFUMY
PERFUNCTORILY
PERFUNCTORINESS
PERFUNCTORY
PERFUSATE
PERFUSATES
PERFUSE
PERFUSED
PERFUSES
PERFUSING

PERFUSION
PERFUSIONIST
PERFUSIONISTS
PERFUSIONS
PERFUSIVE
PERGOLA
PERGOLAS
PERHAPS
PERHAPSES
PERI
PERIANTH
PERIANTHS
PERIAPSES
PERIAPSIS
PERIAPT
PERIAPTS
PERIBLEM
PERIBLEMS
PERICARDIA
PERICARDIAL
PERICARDITIDES
PERICARDITIS
PERICARDITISES
PERICARDIUM
PERICARP
PERICARPS
PERICHONDRAL
PERICHONDRIA
PERICHONDRIUM
PERICOPAE
PERICOPAL
PERICOPE
PERICOPES
PERICOPIC
PERICRANIA
PERICRANIAL
PERICRANIUM
PERICYCLE
PERICYCLES
PERICYCLIC
PERIDERM
PERIDERMS
PERIDIA
PERIDIAL
PERIDIUM
PERIDOT
PERIDOTIC
PERIDOTITE
PERIDOTITES
PERIDOTITIC
PERIDOTS
PERIGEAL
PERIGEAN
PERIGEE
PERIGEES
PERIGON
PERIGONS
PERIGYNIES
PERIGYNOUS
PERIGYNY
PERIHELIA
PERIHELIAL
PERIHELION
PERIKARYA
PERIKARYAL
PERIKARYON
PERIL
PERILED
PERILING
PERILLA
PERILLAS
PERILLED
PERILLING
PERILOUS
PERILOUSLY
PERILOUSNESS
PERILOUSNESSES
PERILS
PERILUNE
PERILUNES
PERILYMPH
PERILYMPHS
PERIMENOPAUSAL
PERIMENOPAUSE
PERIMENOPAUSES
PERIMETER
PERIMETERS
PERIMETRIES
PERIMETRY
PERIMORPH
PERIMORPHS
PERIMYSIA
PERIMYSIUM
PERINATAL
PERINATALLY
PERINATOLOGIES
PERINATOLOGIST
PERINATOLOGISTS
PERINATOLOGY
PERINEA
PERINEAL
PERINEUM
PERINEURIA
PERINEURIUM
PERIOD
PERIODATE
PERIODATES
PERIODIC
PERIODICAL
PERIODICALLY
PERIODICALS
PERIODICITIES
PERIODICITY
PERIODID
PERIODIDS
PERIODIZATION
PERIODIZATIONS
PERIODONTAL
PERIODONTALLY
PERIODONTICS
PERIODONTIST
PERIODONTISTS
PERIODONTITIDES
PERIODONTITIS
PERIODONTOLOGY
PERIODS
PERIONYCHIA
PERIONYCHIUM
PERIOPERATIVE
PERIOSTEA
PERIOSTEAL
PERIOSTEUM
PERIOSTITIDES
PERIOSTITIS
PERIOSTITISES
PERIOTIC
PERIPATETIC
PERIPATETICALLY
PERIPATETICS
PERIPATUS
PERIPATUSES
PERIPETEIA
PERIPETEIAS
PERIPETIA
PERIPETIAS
PERIPETIES
PERIPETY
PERIPHERAL
PERIPHERALLY
PERIPHERALS
PERIPHERIES
PERIPHERY
PERIPHRASES
PERIPHRASIS
PERIPHRASTIC
PERIPHYTIC
PERIPHYTON
PERIPHYTONS
PERIPLASM
PERIPLASMIC
PERIPLASMS
PERIPLAST
PERIPLASTS
PERIPTER
PERIPTERS
PERIQUE
PERIQUES
PERIS
PERISARC
PERISARCS
PERISCOPE
PERISCOPES
PERISCOPIC
PERISH
PERISHABILITIES
PERISHABILITY
PERISHABLE
PERISHABLES
PERISHED
PERISHER
PERISHERS
PERISHES
PERISHING
PERISSODACTYL
PERISSODACTYLS
PERISTALSES
PERISTALSIS
PERISTALTIC
PERISTOME
PERISTOMES
PERISTOMIAL
PERISTYLE
PERISTYLES
PERITHECIA
PERITHECIAL
PERITHECIUM
PERITI
PERITONEA
PERITONEAL
PERITONEALLY
PERITONEUM
PERITONEUMS
PERITONITIS
PERITONITISES
PERITRICH
PERITRICHA
PERITRICHOUS
PERITRICHOUSLY
PERITRICHS
PERITUS
PERIWIG
PERIWIGGED
PERIWIGS
PERIWINKLE
PERIWINKLES
PERJURE
PERJURED
PERJURER
PERJURERS
PERJURES
PERJURIES
PERJURING
PERJURIOUS
PERJURIOUSLY
PERJURY
PERK
PERKED
PERKIER
PERKIEST
PERKILY
PERKINESS
PERKINESSES
PERKING
PERKISH
PERKS
PERKY
PERLITE
PERLITES
PERLITIC
PERM
PERMACULTURE
PERMACULTURES
PERMAFROST
PERMAFROSTS
PERMALLOY
PERMALLOYS
PERMANENCE
PERMANENCES
PERMANENCIES
PERMANENCY
PERMANENT
PERMANENTLY
PERMANENTNESS
PERMANENTNESSES
PERMANENTS
PERMANGANATE
PERMANGANATES
PERMEABILITIES
PERMEABILITY
PERMEABLE
PERMEABLY
PERMEANCE
PERMEANCES
PERMEANT
PERMEASE

ERMEASES
ERMEATE
ERMEATED
ERMEATES
ERMEATING
ERMEATION
ERMEATIONS
ERMEATIVE
ERMEATOR
ERMEATORS
ERMED
ERMETHRIN
ERMETHRINS
ERMIAN
ERMILLAGE
ERMILLAGES
ERMING
ERMISSIBILITY
ERMISSIBLE
ERMISSIBLENESS
ERMISSIBLY
ERMISSION
ERMISSIONS
ERMISSIVE
ERMISSIVELY
ERMISSIVENESS
ERMIT
ERMITS
ERMITTED
ERMITTEE
ERMITTEES
ERMITTER
ERMITTERS
ERMITTING
ERMITTIVITIES
ERMITTIVITY
ERMS
ERMUTABLE
ERMUTATION
ERMUTATIONAL
ERMUTATIONS
ERMUTE
ERMUTED
ERMUTES
ERMUTING
ERNICIOUS
ERNICIOUSLY
ERNICIOUSNESS
ERNICKETY
ERNIO
ERNIONES
ERNOD
ERNODS

PEROGI
PEROGIE
PEROGIES
PEROGIS
PEROGY
PERONEAL
PERORAL
PERORALLY
PERORATE
PERORATED
PERORATES
PERORATING
PERORATION
PERORATIONAL
PERORATIONS
PERORATOR
PERORATORS
PEROVSKITE
PEROVSKITES
PEROXID
PEROXIDASE
PEROXIDASES
PEROXIDATION
PEROXIDATIONS
PEROXIDE
PEROXIDED
PEROXIDES
PEROXIDIC
PEROXIDING
PEROXIDS
PEROXISOMAL
PEROXISOME
PEROXISOMES
PEROXY
PERP
PERPEND
PERPENDED
PERPENDICULAR
PERPENDICULARLY
PERPENDICULARS
PERPENDING
PERPENDS
PERPENT
PERPENTS
PERPETRATE
PERPETRATED
PERPETRATES
PERPETRATING
PERPETRATION
PERPETRATIONS
PERPETRATOR
PERPETRATORS
PERPETUAL

PERPETUALLY
PERPETUALS
PERPETUATE
PERPETUATED
PERPETUATES
PERPETUATING
PERPETUATION
PERPETUATIONS
PERPETUATOR
PERPETUATORS
PERPETUITIES
PERPETUITY
PERPHENAZINE
PERPHENAZINES
PERPLEX
PERPLEXED
PERPLEXEDLY
PERPLEXER
PERPLEXERS
PERPLEXES
PERPLEXING
PERPLEXITIES
PERPLEXITY
PERPS
PERQUISITE
PERQUISITES
PERRIES
PERRON
PERRONS
PERRY
PERSALT
PERSALTS
PERSE
PERSECUTE
PERSECUTED
PERSECUTEE
PERSECUTEES
PERSECUTES
PERSECUTING
PERSECUTION
PERSECUTIONS
PERSECUTIVE
PERSECUTOR
PERSECUTORS
PERSECUTORY
PERSES
PERSEVERANCE
PERSEVERANCES
PERSEVERATE
PERSEVERATED
PERSEVERATES
PERSEVERATING
PERSEVERATION

PERSEVERATIONS
PERSEVERATIVE
PERSEVERE
PERSEVERED
PERSEVERES
PERSEVERING
PERSEVERINGLY
PERSIFLAGE
PERSIFLAGES
PERSIMMON
PERSIMMONS
PERSIST
PERSISTED
PERSISTENCE
PERSISTENCES
PERSISTENCIES
PERSISTENCY
PERSISTENT
PERSISTENTLY
PERSISTER
PERSISTERS
PERSISTING
PERSISTS
PERSNICKETINESS
PERSNICKETY
PERSON
PERSONA
PERSONABLE
PERSONABLENESS
PERSONAE
PERSONAGE
PERSONAGES
PERSONAL
PERSONALISE
PERSONALISED
PERSONALISES
PERSONALISING
PERSONALISM
PERSONALISMS
PERSONALIST
PERSONALISTIC
PERSONALISTS
PERSONALITIES
PERSONALITY
PERSONALIZATION
PERSONALIZE
PERSONALIZED
PERSONALIZES
PERSONALIZING
PERSONALLY
PERSONALS
PERSONALTIES
PERSONALTY

PERSONAS
PERSONATE
PERSONATED
PERSONATES
PERSONATING
PERSONATION
PERSONATIONS
PERSONATIVE
PERSONATOR
PERSONATORS
PERSONHOOD
PERSONHOODS
PERSONIFICATION
PERSONIFIED
PERSONIFIER
PERSONIFIERS
PERSONIFIES
PERSONIFY
PERSONIFYING
PERSONNEL
PERSONNELS
PERSONS
PERSPECTIVAL
PERSPECTIVE
PERSPECTIVELY
PERSPECTIVES
PERSPEX
PERSPEXES
PERSPICACIOUS
PERSPICACIOUSLY
PERSPICACITIES
PERSPICACITY
PERSPICUITIES
PERSPICUITY
PERSPICUOUS
PERSPICUOUSLY
PERSPICUOUSNESS
PERSPIRATION
PERSPIRATIONS
PERSPIRATORY
PERSPIRE
PERSPIRED
PERSPIRES
PERSPIRING
PERSPIRY
PERSUADABLE
PERSUADE
PERSUADED
PERSUADER
PERSUADERS
PERSUADES
PERSUADING
PERSUASIBLE

PERSUASION
PERSUASIONS
PERSUASIVE
PERSUASIVELY
PERSUASIVENESS
PERT
PERTAIN
PERTAINED
PERTAINING
PERTAINS
PERTER
PERTEST
PERTINACIOUS
PERTINACIOUSLY
PERTINACITIES
PERTINACITY
PERTINENCE
PERTINENCES
PERTINENCIES
PERTINENCY
PERTINENT
PERTINENTLY
PERTLY
PERTNESS
PERTNESSES
PERTURB
PERTURBABLE
PERTURBATION
PERTURBATIONAL
PERTURBATIONS
PERTURBED
PERTURBER
PERTURBERS
PERTURBING
PERTURBS
PERTUSSAL
PERTUSSES
PERTUSSIS
PERTUSSISES
PERUKE
PERUKED
PERUKES
PERUSABLE
PERUSAL
PERUSALS
PERUSE
PERUSED
PERUSER
PERUSERS
PERUSES
PERUSING
PERV
PERVADE
PERVADED
PERVADER
PERVADERS
PERVADES
PERVADING
PERVASION
PERVASIONS
PERVASIVE
PERVASIVELY
PERVASIVENESS
PERVASIVENESSES
PERVERSE
PERVERSELY
PERVERSENESS
PERVERSENESSES
PERVERSION
PERVERSIONS
PERVERSITIES
PERVERSITY
PERVERSIVE
PERVERT
PERVERTED
PERVERTEDLY
PERVERTEDNESS
PERVERTEDNESSES
PERVERTER
PERVERTERS
PERVERTING
PERVERTS
PERVIER
PERVIEST
PERVIOUS
PERVIOUSNESS
PERVIOUSNESSES
PERVO
PERVOS
PERVS
PERVY
PES
PESADE
PESADES
PESCATARIAN
PESCATARIANS
PESCETARIAN
PESCETARIANS
PESETA
PESETAS
PESEWA
PESEWAS
PESKIER
PESKIEST
PESKILY
PESKINESS
PESKINESSES
PESKY
PESO
PESOS
PESSARIES
PESSARY
PESSIMISM
PESSIMISMS
PESSIMIST
PESSIMISTIC
PESSIMISTICALLY
PESSIMISTS
PEST
PESTER
PESTERED
PESTERER
PESTERERS
PESTERING
PESTERS
PESTHOLE
PESTHOLES
PESTHOUSE
PESTHOUSES
PESTICIDAL
PESTICIDE
PESTICIDES
PESTIER
PESTIEST
PESTIFEROUS
PESTIFEROUSLY
PESTIFEROUSNESS
PESTILENCE
PESTILENCES
PESTILENT
PESTILENTIAL
PESTILENTIALLY
PESTILENTLY
PESTLE
PESTLED
PESTLES
PESTLING
PESTO
PESTOS
PESTS
PESTY
PET
PETABYTE
PETABYTES
PETAHERTZ
PETAHERTZES
PETAL
PETALED
PETALINE
PETALLED
PETALLIKE
PETALODIES
PETALODY
PETALOID
PETALOUS
PETALS
PETANQUE
PETANQUES
PETARD
PETARDS
PETASOS
PETASOSES
PETASUS
PETASUSES
PETCOCK
PETCOCKS
PETECHIA
PETECHIAE
PETECHIAL
PETER
PETERED
PETERING
PETERS
PETIOLAR
PETIOLATE
PETIOLE
PETIOLED
PETIOLES
PETIOLULE
PETIOLULES
PETIT
PETITE
PETITENESS
PETITENESSES
PETITES
PETITION
PETITIONARY
PETITIONED
PETITIONER
PETITIONERS
PETITIONING
PETITIONS
PETNAP
PETNAPER
PETNAPERS
PETNAPING
PETNAPINGS
PETNAPPED
PETNAPPER
PETNAPPERS
PETNAPPING
PETNAPS
PETRALE
PETRALES
PETREL
PETRELS
PETRIFACTION
PETRIFACTIONS
PETRIFICATION
PETRIFICATIONS
PETRIFIED
PETRIFIER
PETRIFIERS
PETRIFIES
PETRIFY
PETRIFYING
PETROCHEMICAL
PETROCHEMICALS
PETROCHEMISTRY
PETRODOLLAR
PETRODOLLARS
PETROGENESES
PETROGENESIS
PETROGENETIC
PETROGENIES
PETROGENY
PETROGLYPH
PETROGLYPHS
PETROGRAPHER
PETROGRAPHERS
PETROGRAPHIC
PETROGRAPHICAL
PETROGRAPHIES
PETROGRAPHY
PETROL
PETROLATUM
PETROLATUMS
PETROLEUM
PETROLEUMS
PETROLIC
PETROLOGIC
PETROLOGICAL
PETROLOGICALLY
PETROLOGIES
PETROLOGIST
PETROLOGISTS
PETROLOGY
PETROLS
PETRONEL
PETRONELS
PETROSAL
PETROSALS
PETROUS
PETS
PETSAI

PETSAIS
PETTABLE
PETTED
PETTEDLY
PETTER
PETTERS
PETTI
PETTICOAT
PETTICOATED
PETTICOATS
PETTIER
PETTIEST
PETTIFOG
PETTIFOGGED
PETTIFOGGER
PETTIFOGGERIES
PETTIFOGGERS
PETTIFOGGERY
PETTIFOGGING
PETTIFOGGINGS
PETTIFOGS
PETTILY
PETTINESS
PETTINESSES
PETTING
PETTINGS
PETTISH
PETTISHLY
PETTISHNESS
PETTISHNESSES
PETTITOES
PETTLE
PETTLED
PETTLES
PETTLING
PETTO
PETTY
PETULANCE
PETULANCES
PETULANCIES
PETULANCY
PETULANT
PETULANTLY
PETUNIA
PETUNIAS
PETUNTSE
PETUNTSES
PETUNTZE
PETUNTZES
PEW
PEWEE
PEWEES
PEWHOLDER
PEWHOLDERS
PEWIT
PEWITS
PEWS
PEWTER
PEWTERER
PEWTERERS
PEWTERIER
PEWTERIEST
PEWTERS
PEWTERY
PEYOTE
PEYOTES
PEYOTISM
PEYOTISMS
PEYOTL
PEYOTLS
PEYTRAL
PEYTRALS
PEYTREL
PEYTRELS
PFENNIG
PFENNIGE
PFENNIGS
PFFT
PFUI
PHAETON
PHAETONS
PHAGE
PHAGEDENA
PHAGEDENAS
PHAGES
PHAGOCYTE
PHAGOCYTES
PHAGOCYTIC
PHAGOCYTIZE
PHAGOCYTIZED
PHAGOCYTIZES
PHAGOCYTIZING
PHAGOCYTOSE
PHAGOCYTOSED
PHAGOCYTOSES
PHAGOCYTOSING
PHAGOCYTOSIS
PHAGOCYTOTIC
PHAGOSOME
PHAGOSOMES
PHALAENOPSES
PHALAENOPSIS
PHALANGAL
PHALANGE
PHALANGEAL
PHALANGER
PHALANGERS
PHALANGES
PHALANSTERIES
PHALANSTERY
PHALANX
PHALANXES
PHALAROPE
PHALAROPES
PHALLI
PHALLIC
PHALLICALLY
PHALLICISM
PHALLICISMS
PHALLISM
PHALLISMS
PHALLIST
PHALLISTS
PHALLOCENTRIC
PHALLOCENTRISM
PHALLOCENTRISMS
PHALLOCRATIC
PHALLUS
PHALLUSES
PHANEROGAM
PHANEROGAMS
PHANEROPHYTE
PHANEROPHYTES
PHANTASIED
PHANTASIES
PHANTASM
PHANTASMA
PHANTASMAGORIA
PHANTASMAGORIAS
PHANTASMAGORIC
PHANTASMAL
PHANTASMATA
PHANTASMIC
PHANTASMS
PHANTAST
PHANTASTS
PHANTASY
PHANTASYING
PHANTOM
PHANTOMLIKE
PHANTOMS
PHARAOH
PHARAOHS
PHARAONIC
PHARISAIC
PHARISAICAL
PHARISAICALLY
PHARISAICALNESS
PHARISAISM
PHARISAISMS
PHARISEE
PHARISEES
PHARMA
PHARMACEUTICAL
PHARMACEUTICALS
PHARMACIES
PHARMACIST
PHARMACISTS
PHARMACODYNAMIC
PHARMACOGENOMIC
PHARMACOGNOSIES
PHARMACOGNOSTIC
PHARMACOGNOSY
PHARMACOKINETIC
PHARMACOLOGIC
PHARMACOLOGICAL
PHARMACOLOGIES
PHARMACOLOGIST
PHARMACOLOGISTS
PHARMACOLOGY
PHARMACOPEIA
PHARMACOPEIAL
PHARMACOPEIAS
PHARMACOPOEIA
PHARMACOPOEIAL
PHARMACOPOEIAS
PHARMACOTHERAPY
PHARMACY
PHARMAS
PHARMER
PHARMERS
PHARMING
PHARMINGS
PHAROS
PHAROSES
PHARYNGAL
PHARYNGALS
PHARYNGEAL
PHARYNGES
PHARYNGITIDES
PHARYNGITIS
PHARYNX
PHARYNXES
PHASE
PHASEAL
PHASED
PHASEDOWN
PHASEDOWNS
PHASEOUT
PHASEOUTS
PHASER
PHASERS
PHASES
PHASIC
PHASING
PHASIS
PHASMID
PHASMIDS
PHAT
PHATIC
PHATICALLY
PHATTER
PHATTEST
PHEASANT
PHEASANTS
PHELLEM
PHELLEMS
PHELLODERM
PHELLODERMS
PHELLOGEN
PHELLOGENS
PHELONIA
PHELONION
PHELONIONS
PHENACAINE
PHENACAINES
PHENACETIN
PHENACETINS
PHENACITE
PHENACITES
PHENAKITE
PHENAKITES
PHENANTHRENE
PHENANTHRENES
PHENATE
PHENATES
PHENAZIN
PHENAZINE
PHENAZINES
PHENAZINS
PHENCYCLIDINE
PHENCYCLIDINES
PHENETIC
PHENETICIST
PHENETICISTS
PHENETICS
PHENETOL
PHENETOLE
PHENETOLES
PHENETOLS
PHENIX
PHENIXES
PHENMETRAZINE
PHENMETRAZINES
PHENOBARBITAL

PHENOBARBITALS
PHENOBARBITONE
PHENOBARBITONES
PHENOCOPIES
PHENOCOPY
PHENOCRYST
PHENOCRYSTIC
PHENOCRYSTS
PHENOL
PHENOLATE
PHENOLATED
PHENOLATES
PHENOLATING
PHENOLIC
PHENOLICS
PHENOLOGICAL
PHENOLOGICALLY
PHENOLOGIES
PHENOLOGY
PHENOLPHTHALEIN
PHENOLS
PHENOM
PHENOMENA
PHENOMENAL
PHENOMENALISM
PHENOMENALISMS
PHENOMENALIST
PHENOMENALISTIC
PHENOMENALISTS
PHENOMENALLY
PHENOMENAS
PHENOMENOLOGIES
PHENOMENOLOGIST
PHENOMENOLOGY
PHENOMENON
PHENOMENONS
PHENOMS
PHENOTHIAZINE
PHENOTHIAZINES
PHENOTYPE
PHENOTYPES
PHENOTYPIC
PHENOTYPICAL
PHENOTYPICALLY
PHENOXIDE
PHENOXIDES
PHENOXY
PHENTERMINE
PHENTERMINES
PHENTOLAMINE
PHENTOLAMINES
PHENYL
PHENYLALANINE
PHENYLALANINES
PHENYLBUTAZONE
PHENYLBUTAZONES
PHENYLENE
PHENYLENES
PHENYLEPHRINE
PHENYLEPHRINES
PHENYLIC
PHENYLKETONURIA
PHENYLKETONURIC
PHENYLS
PHENYLTHIOUREA
PHENYLTHIOUREAS
PHENYTOIN
PHENYTOINS
PHERESES
PHERESIS
PHEROMONAL
PHEROMONE
PHEROMONES
PHEW
PHI
PHIAL
PHIALS
PHILABEG
PHILABEGS
PHILADELPHUS
PHILADELPHUSES
PHILANDER
PHILANDERED
PHILANDERER
PHILANDERERS
PHILANDERING
PHILANDERS
PHILANTHROPIC
PHILANTHROPICAL
PHILANTHROPIES
PHILANTHROPIST
PHILANTHROPISTS
PHILANTHROPOID
PHILANTHROPOIDS
PHILANTHROPY
PHILATELIC
PHILATELICALLY
PHILATELIES
PHILATELIST
PHILATELISTS
PHILATELY
PHILHARMONIC
PHILHARMONICS
PHILHELLENE
PHILHELLENES
PHILHELLENIC
PHILHELLENISM
PHILHELLENISMS
PHILHELLENIST
PHILHELLENISTS
PHILIBEG
PHILIBEGS
PHILIPPIC
PHILIPPICS
PHILISTIA
PHILISTIAS
PHILISTINE
PHILISTINES
PHILISTINISM
PHILISTINISMS
PHILLUMENIST
PHILLUMENISTS
PHILODENDRA
PHILODENDRON
PHILODENDRONS
PHILOGYNIES
PHILOGYNY
PHILOLOGICAL
PHILOLOGICALLY
PHILOLOGIES
PHILOLOGIST
PHILOLOGISTS
PHILOLOGY
PHILOMEL
PHILOMELA
PHILOMELAS
PHILOMELS
PHILOSOPHE
PHILOSOPHER
PHILOSOPHERS
PHILOSOPHES
PHILOSOPHIC
PHILOSOPHICAL
PHILOSOPHICALLY
PHILOSOPHIES
PHILOSOPHISE
PHILOSOPHISED
PHILOSOPHISES
PHILOSOPHISING
PHILOSOPHIZE
PHILOSOPHIZED
PHILOSOPHIZER
PHILOSOPHIZERS
PHILOSOPHIZES
PHILOSOPHIZING
PHILOSOPHY
PHILTER
PHILTERED
PHILTERING
PHILTERS
PHILTRA
PHILTRE
PHILTRED
PHILTRES
PHILTRING
PHILTRUM
PHIMOSES
PHIMOSIS
PHIMOTIC
PHIS
PHISH
PHISHED
PHISHER
PHISHERS
PHISHES
PHISHING
PHISHINGS
PHIZ
PHIZES
PHIZZ
PHIZZES
PHLEBITIC
PHLEBITIDES
PHLEBITIS
PHLEBITISES
PHLEBOGRAM
PHLEBOGRAMS
PHLEBOGRAPHIC
PHLEBOGRAPHIES
PHLEBOGRAPHY
PHLEBOLOGIES
PHLEBOLOGY
PHLEBOTOMIES
PHLEBOTOMIST
PHLEBOTOMISTS
PHLEBOTOMY
PHLEGM
PHLEGMATIC
PHLEGMATICALLY
PHLEGMIER
PHLEGMIEST
PHLEGMS
PHLEGMY
PHLOEM
PHLOEMS
PHLOGISTIC
PHLOGISTON
PHLOGISTONS
PHLOGOPITE
PHLOGOPITES
PHLORIZIN
PHLORIZINS
PHLOX
PHLOXES
PHLYCTENA
PHLYCTENAE
PHO
PHOBIA
PHOBIAS
PHOBIC
PHOBICS
PHOCINE
PHOEBE
PHOEBES
PHOEBUS
PHOEBUSES
PHOENIX
PHOENIXES
PHOENIXLIKE
PHON
PHONAL
PHONATE
PHONATED
PHONATES
PHONATHON
PHONATHONS
PHONATING
PHONATION
PHONATIONS
PHONE
PHONED
PHONEMATIC
PHONEME
PHONEMES
PHONEMIC
PHONEMICALLY
PHONEMICIST
PHONEMICISTS
PHONEMICS
PHONER
PHONERS
PHONES
PHONETIC
PHONETICALLY
PHONETICIAN
PHONETICIANS
PHONETICS
PHONETIST
PHONETISTS
PHONEY
PHONEYED
PHONEYING
PHONEYS
PHONIC
PHONICALLY

PHONICS
PHONIED
PHONIER
PHONIES
PHONIEST
PHONILY
PHONINESS
PHONINESSES
PHONING
PHONO
PHONOCARDIOGRAM
PHONOGRAM
PHONOGRAMIC
PHONOGRAMICALLY
PHONOGRAMMIC
PHONOGRAMS
PHONOGRAPH
PHONOGRAPHER
PHONOGRAPHERS
PHONOGRAPHIC
PHONOGRAPHIES
PHONOGRAPHS
PHONOGRAPHY
PHONOLITE
PHONOLITES
PHONOLOGIC
PHONOLOGICAL
PHONOLOGICALLY
PHONOLOGIES
PHONOLOGIST
PHONOLOGISTS
PHONOLOGY
PHONON
PHONONS
PHONOS
PHONOTACTIC
PHONOTACTICS
PHONOTYPE
PHONOTYPES
PHONOTYPIES
PHONOTYPY
PHONS
PHONY
PHONYING
PHOOEY
PHORATE
PHORATES
PHORESIES
PHORESY
PHORETIC
PHORONID
PHORONIDS
PHOS
PHOSGENE
PHOSGENES
PHOSPHATASE
PHOSPHATASES
PHOSPHATE
PHOSPHATES
PHOSPHATIC
PHOSPHATIDE
PHOSPHATIDES
PHOSPHATIDIC
PHOSPHATIDYL
PHOSPHATIDYLS
PHOSPHATIZATION
PHOSPHATIZE
PHOSPHATIZED
PHOSPHATIZES
PHOSPHATIZING
PHOSPHATURIA
PHOSPHATURIAS
PHOSPHENE
PHOSPHENES
PHOSPHID
PHOSPHIDE
PHOSPHIDES
PHOSPHIDS
PHOSPHIN
PHOSPHINE
PHOSPHINES
PHOSPHINS
PHOSPHITE
PHOSPHITES
PHOSPHOCREATINE
PHOSPHOKINASE
PHOSPHOKINASES
PHOSPHOLIPASE
PHOSPHOLIPASES
PHOSPHOLIPID
PHOSPHOLIPIDS
PHOSPHONIUM
PHOSPHONIUMS
PHOSPHOPROTEIN
PHOSPHOPROTEINS
PHOSPHOR
PHOSPHORE
PHOSPHORES
PHOSPHORESCE
PHOSPHORESCED
PHOSPHORESCENCE
PHOSPHORESCENT
PHOSPHORESCES
PHOSPHORESCING
PHOSPHORI
PHOSPHORIC
PHOSPHORITE
PHOSPHORITES
PHOSPHORITIC
PHOSPHOROLYSES
PHOSPHOROLYSIS
PHOSPHOROLYTIC
PHOSPHOROUS
PHOSPHORS
PHOSPHORUS
PHOSPHORUSES
PHOSPHORYL
PHOSPHORYLASE
PHOSPHORYLASES
PHOSPHORYLATE
PHOSPHORYLATED
PHOSPHORYLATES
PHOSPHORYLATING
PHOSPHORYLATION
PHOSPHORYLATIVE
PHOSPHORYLS
PHOT
PHOTIC
PHOTICALLY
PHOTICS
PHOTINO
PHOTINOS
PHOTO
PHOTOAGING
PHOTOAGINGS
PHOTOAUTOTROPH
PHOTOAUTOTROPHS
PHOTOBIOLOGIC
PHOTOBIOLOGICAL
PHOTOBIOLOGIES
PHOTOBIOLOGIST
PHOTOBIOLOGISTS
PHOTOBIOLOGY
PHOTOCALL
PHOTOCALLS
PHOTOCATHODE
PHOTOCATHODES
PHOTOCELL
PHOTOCELLS
PHOTOCHEMICAL
PHOTOCHEMICALLY
PHOTOCHEMIST
PHOTOCHEMISTRY
PHOTOCHEMISTS
PHOTOCHROMIC
PHOTOCHROMISM
PHOTOCHROMISMS
PHOTOCOMPOSE
PHOTOCOMPOSED
PHOTOCOMPOSER
PHOTOCOMPOSERS
PHOTOCOMPOSES
PHOTOCOMPOSING
PHOTOCONDUCTIVE
PHOTOCOPIED
PHOTOCOPIER
PHOTOCOPIERS
PHOTOCOPIES
PHOTOCOPY
PHOTOCOPYING
PHOTOCURRENT
PHOTOCURRENTS
PHOTODEGRADABLE
PHOTODETECTOR
PHOTODETECTORS
PHOTODIODE
PHOTODIODES
PHOTODISSOCIATE
PHOTODUPLICATE
PHOTODUPLICATED
PHOTODUPLICATES
PHOTODYNAMIC
PHOTOED
PHOTOELECTRIC
PHOTOELECTRON
PHOTOELECTRONIC
PHOTOELECTRONS
PHOTOEMISSION
PHOTOEMISSIONS
PHOTOEMISSIVE
PHOTOENGRAVE
PHOTOENGRAVED
PHOTOENGRAVER
PHOTOENGRAVERS
PHOTOENGRAVES
PHOTOENGRAVING
PHOTOENGRAVINGS
PHOTOEXCITATION
PHOTOEXCITED
PHOTOFINISHER
PHOTOFINISHERS
PHOTOFINISHING
PHOTOFINISHINGS
PHOTOFLASH
PHOTOFLASHES
PHOTOFLOOD
PHOTOFLOODS
PHOTOG
PHOTOGENE
PHOTOGENES
PHOTOGENIC
PHOTOGENICALLY
PHOTOGEOLOGIC
PHOTOGEOLOGICAL
PHOTOGEOLOGIES
PHOTOGEOLOGIST
PHOTOGEOLOGISTS
PHOTOGEOLOGY
PHOTOGRAM
PHOTOGRAMMETRIC
PHOTOGRAMMETRY
PHOTOGRAMS
PHOTOGRAPH
PHOTOGRAPHED
PHOTOGRAPHER
PHOTOGRAPHERS
PHOTOGRAPHIC
PHOTOGRAPHIES
PHOTOGRAPHING
PHOTOGRAPHS
PHOTOGRAPHY
PHOTOGRAVURE
PHOTOGRAVURES
PHOTOGS
PHOTOINDUCED
PHOTOINDUCTION
PHOTOINDUCTIONS
PHOTOINDUCTIVE
PHOTOING
PHOTOIONIZATION
PHOTOIONIZE
PHOTOIONIZED
PHOTOIONIZES
PHOTOIONIZING
PHOTOJOURNALISM
PHOTOJOURNALIST
PHOTOKINESES
PHOTOKINESIS
PHOTOKINETIC
PHOTOLITHOGRAPH
PHOTOLYSES
PHOTOLYSIS
PHOTOLYTIC
PHOTOLYTICALLY
PHOTOLYZABLE
PHOTOLYZE
PHOTOLYZED
PHOTOLYZES
PHOTOLYZING
PHOTOMAP
PHOTOMAPPED
PHOTOMAPPING
PHOTOMAPS
PHOTOMASK
PHOTOMASKS

PHOTOMECHANICAL
PHOTOMETER
PHOTOMETERS
PHOTOMETRIC
PHOTOMETRICALLY
PHOTOMETRIES
PHOTOMETRY
PHOTOMICROGRAPH
PHOTOMONTAGE
PHOTOMONTAGES
PHOTOMOSAIC
PHOTOMOSAICS
PHOTOMULTIPLIER
PHOTOMURAL
PHOTOMURALS
PHOTON
PHOTONEGATIVE
PHOTONIC
PHOTONICS
PHOTONS
PHOTONUCLEAR
PHOTOOXIDATION
PHOTOOXIDATIONS
PHOTOOXIDATIVE
PHOTOOXIDIZE
PHOTOOXIDIZED
PHOTOOXIDIZES
PHOTOOXIDIZING
PHOTOPERIOD
PHOTOPERIODIC
PHOTOPERIODISM
PHOTOPERIODISMS
PHOTOPERIODS
PHOTOPHASE
PHOTOPHASES
PHOTOPHOBIA
PHOTOPHOBIAS
PHOTOPHOBIC
PHOTOPHORE
PHOTOPHORES
PHOTOPIA
PHOTOPIAS
PHOTOPIC
PHOTOPLAY
PHOTOPLAYS
PHOTOPOLYMER
PHOTOPOLYMERS
PHOTOPOSITIVE
PHOTOPRODUCT
PHOTOPRODUCTION
PHOTOPRODUCTS
PHOTOREACTION
PHOTOREACTIONS
PHOTORECEPTION
PHOTORECEPTIONS
PHOTORECEPTIVE
PHOTORECEPTOR
PHOTORECEPTORS
PHOTOREDUCE
PHOTOREDUCED
PHOTOREDUCES
PHOTOREDUCING
PHOTOREDUCTION
PHOTOREDUCTIONS
PHOTORESIST
PHOTORESISTS
PHOTOS
PHOTOSCAN
PHOTOSCANNED
PHOTOSCANNING
PHOTOSCANS
PHOTOSENSITIVE
PHOTOSENSITIZE
PHOTOSENSITIZED
PHOTOSENSITIZER
PHOTOSENSITIZES
PHOTOSET
PHOTOSETS
PHOTOSETTER
PHOTOSETTERS
PHOTOSETTING
PHOTOSHOP
PHOTOSHOPPED
PHOTOSHOPPING
PHOTOSHOPS
PHOTOSPHERE
PHOTOSPHERES
PHOTOSPHERIC
PHOTOSTAT
PHOTOSTATED
PHOTOSTATIC
PHOTOSTATING
PHOTOSTATS
PHOTOSTATTED
PHOTOSTATTING
PHOTOSYNTHATE
PHOTOSYNTHATES
PHOTOSYNTHESES
PHOTOSYNTHESIS
PHOTOSYNTHESIZE
PHOTOSYNTHETIC
PHOTOSYSTEM
PHOTOSYSTEMS
PHOTOTACTIC
PHOTOTACTICALLY
PHOTOTAXES
PHOTOTAXIES
PHOTOTAXIS
PHOTOTAXY
PHOTOTELEGRAPHY
PHOTOTHERAPIES
PHOTOTHERAPY
PHOTOTOXIC
PHOTOTOXICITIES
PHOTOTOXICITY
PHOTOTRANSISTOR
PHOTOTROPIC
PHOTOTROPICALLY
PHOTOTROPISM
PHOTOTROPISMS
PHOTOTUBE
PHOTOTUBES
PHOTOTYPE
PHOTOTYPES
PHOTOTYPESETTER
PHOTOVOLTAIC
PHOTOVOLTAICS
PHOTS
PHPHT
PHRAGMITES
PHRAGMOPLAST
PHRAGMOPLASTS
PHRASAL
PHRASALLY
PHRASE
PHRASED
PHRASEMAKER
PHRASEMAKERS
PHRASEMAKING
PHRASEMAKINGS
PHRASEMONGER
PHRASEMONGERING
PHRASEMONGERS
PHRASEOLOGICAL
PHRASEOLOGIES
PHRASEOLOGIST
PHRASEOLOGISTS
PHRASEOLOGY
PHRASES
PHRASING
PHRASINGS
PHRATRAL
PHRATRIC
PHRATRIES
PHRATRY
PHREAK
PHREAKED
PHREAKER
PHREAKERS
PHREAKING
PHREAKINGS
PHREAKS
PHREATIC
PHREATOPHYTE
PHREATOPHYTES
PHREATOPHYTIC
PHRENETIC
PHRENIC
PHRENITIDES
PHRENITIS
PHRENITISES
PHRENOLOGICAL
PHRENOLOGIES
PHRENOLOGIST
PHRENOLOGISTS
PHRENOLOGY
PHRENSIED
PHRENSIES
PHRENSY
PHRENSYING
PHT
PHTHALATE
PHTHALATES
PHTHALEIN
PHTHALEINS
PHTHALIC
PHTHALIN
PHTHALINS
PHTHALOCYANINE
PHTHALOCYANINES
PHTHISES
PHTHISIC
PHTHISICAL
PHTHISICS
PHTHISIS
PHUT
PHUTS
PHYCOCYANIN
PHYCOCYANINS
PHYCOERYTHRIN
PHYCOERYTHRINS
PHYCOLOGICAL
PHYCOLOGIES
PHYCOLOGIST
PHYCOLOGISTS
PHYCOLOGY
PHYCOMYCETE
PHYCOMYCETES
PHYCOMYCETOUS
PHYLA
PHYLACTERIES
PHYLACTERY
PHYLAE
PHYLAR
PHYLAXIS
PHYLAXISES
PHYLE
PHYLESES
PHYLESIS
PHYLESISES
PHYLETIC
PHYLETICALLY
PHYLETICS
PHYLIC
PHYLLARIES
PHYLLARY
PHYLLITE
PHYLLITES
PHYLLITIC
PHYLLO
PHYLLOCLADE
PHYLLOCLADES
PHYLLODE
PHYLLODES
PHYLLODIA
PHYLLODIUM
PHYLLOID
PHYLLOIDS
PHYLLOME
PHYLLOMES
PHYLLOMIC
PHYLLOPOD
PHYLLOPODS
PHYLLOS
PHYLLOTACTIC
PHYLLOTAXES
PHYLLOTAXIES
PHYLLOTAXIS
PHYLLOTAXY
PHYLLOXERA
PHYLLOXERAS
PHYLOGENETIC
PHYLOGENIES
PHYLOGENY
PHYLON
PHYLUM
PHYSALIS
PHYSALISES
PHYSED
PHYSEDS
PHYSES
PHYSIATRIES
PHYSIATRIST
PHYSIATRISTS
PHYSIATRY

PHYSIC
PHYSICAL
PHYSICALISM
PHYSICALISMS
PHYSICALIST
PHYSICALISTIC
PHYSICALISTS
PHYSICALITIES
PHYSICALITY
PHYSICALIZE
PHYSICALIZED
PHYSICALIZES
PHYSICALIZING
PHYSICALLY
PHYSICALNESS
PHYSICALNESSES
PHYSICALS
PHYSICIAN
PHYSICIANS
PHYSICIST
PHYSICISTS
PHYSICKED
PHYSICKING
PHYSICOCHEMICAL
PHYSICS
PHYSIO
PHYSIOCRAT
PHYSIOCRATIC
PHYSIOCRATS
PHYSIOGNOMIC
PHYSIOGNOMICAL
PHYSIOGNOMIES
PHYSIOGNOMY
PHYSIOGRAPHER
PHYSIOGRAPHERS
PHYSIOGRAPHIC
PHYSIOGRAPHICAL
PHYSIOGRAPHIES
PHYSIOGRAPHY
PHYSIOLOGIC
PHYSIOLOGICAL
PHYSIOLOGICALLY
PHYSIOLOGIES
PHYSIOLOGIST
PHYSIOLOGISTS
PHYSIOLOGY
PHYSIOPATHOLOGY
PHYSIOS
PHYSIOTHERAPIES
PHYSIOTHERAPIST
PHYSIOTHERAPY
PHYSIQUE
PHYSIQUED
PHYSIQUES
PHYSIS
PHYSOSTIGMINE
PHYSOSTIGMINES
PHYTANE
PHYTANES
PHYTIN
PHYTINS
PHYTOALEXIN
PHYTOALEXINS
PHYTOCHEMICAL
PHYTOCHEMICALLY
PHYTOCHEMIST
PHYTOCHEMISTRY
PHYTOCHEMISTS
PHYTOCHROME
PHYTOCHROMES
PHYTOESTROGEN
PHYTOESTROGENS
PHYTOFLAGELLATE
PHYTOGENIES
PHYTOGENY
PHYTOGEOGRAPHER
PHYTOGEOGRAPHIC
PHYTOGEOGRAPHY
PHYTOHORMONE
PHYTOHORMONES
PHYTOID
PHYTOL
PHYTOLITH
PHYTOLITHS
PHYTOLOGIES
PHYTOLOGY
PHYTOLS
PHYTON
PHYTONIC
PHYTONS
PHYTONUTRIENT
PHYTONUTRIENTS
PHYTOPATHOGEN
PHYTOPATHOGENIC
PHYTOPATHOGENS
PHYTOPATHOLOGY
PHYTOPHAGOUS
PHYTOPLANKTER
PHYTOPLANKTERS
PHYTOPLANKTON
PHYTOPLANKTONIC
PHYTOPLANKTONS
PHYTOPLASMA
PHYTOPLASMAS
PHYTOSOCIOLOGY
PHYTOSTEROL
PHYTOSTEROLS
PHYTOTOXIC
PHYTOTOXICITIES
PHYTOTOXICITY
PHYTOTRON
PHYTOTRONS
PI
PIA
PIACULAR
PIAFFE
PIAFFED
PIAFFER
PIAFFERS
PIAFFES
PIAFFING
PIAL
PIAN
PIANI
PIANIC
PIANISM
PIANISMS
PIANISSIMI
PIANISSIMO
PIANISSIMOS
PIANIST
PIANISTIC
PIANISTICALLY
PIANISTS
PIANO
PIANOFORTE
PIANOFORTES
PIANOLA
PIANOLAS
PIANOS
PIANS
PIAS
PIASABA
PIASABAS
PIASAVA
PIASAVAS
PIASSABA
PIASSABAS
PIASSAVA
PIASSAVAS
PIASTER
PIASTERS
PIASTRE
PIASTRES
PIAZZA
PIAZZAS
PIAZZE
PIBAL
PIBALS
PIBROCH
PIBROCHS
PIC
PICA
PICACHO
PICACHOS
PICADILLO
PICADILLOS
PICADOR
PICADORES
PICADORS
PICAL
PICANINNIES
PICANINNY
PICANTE
PICARA
PICARAS
PICARESQUE
PICARESQUES
PICARO
PICAROON
PICAROONED
PICAROONING
PICAROONS
PICAROS
PICAS
PICAYUNE
PICAYUNES
PICAYUNISH
PICCALILLI
PICCALILLIS
PICCATA
PICCATAS
PICCOLO
PICCOLOIST
PICCOLOISTS
PICCOLOS
PICE
PICEOUS
PICHOLINE
PICHOLINES
PICIFORM
PICK
PICKABACK
PICKABACKED
PICKABACKING
PICKABACKS
PICKABLE
PICKADIL
PICKADILS
PICKANINNIES
PICKANINNY
PICKAROON
PICKAROONS
PICKAX
PICKAXE
PICKAXED
PICKAXES
PICKAXING
PICKED
PICKEER
PICKEERED
PICKEERING
PICKEERS
PICKER
PICKEREL
PICKERELS
PICKERELWEED
PICKERELWEEDS
PICKERS
PICKET
PICKETBOAT
PICKETBOATS
PICKETED
PICKETER
PICKETERS
PICKETING
PICKETS
PICKIER
PICKIEST
PICKINESS
PICKINESSES
PICKING
PICKINGS
PICKLE
PICKLED
PICKLER
PICKLERS
PICKLES
PICKLEWEED
PICKLEWEEDS
PICKLING
PICKLOCK
PICKLOCKS
PICKNEY
PICKNEYS
PICKOFF
PICKOFFS
PICKPOCKET
PICKPOCKETS
PICKPROOF
PICKS
PICKTHANK
PICKTHANKS
PICKUP
PICKUPS

PICKWICK
PICKWICKS
PICKY
PICLORAM
PICLORAMS
PICNIC
PICNICKED
PICNICKER
PICNICKERS
PICNICKING
PICNICKY
PICNICS
PICOFARAD
PICOFARADS
PICOGRAM
PICOGRAMS
PICOLIN
PICOLINE
PICOLINES
PICOLINS
PICOMETER
PICOMETERS
PICOMETRE
PICOMETRES
PICOMOLE
PICOMOLES
PICORNAVIRUS
PICORNAVIRUSES
PICOSECOND
PICOSECONDS
PICOT
PICOTED
PICOTEE
PICOTEES
PICOTING
PICOTS
PICOWAVE
PICOWAVED
PICOWAVES
PICOWAVING
PICQUET
PICQUETS
PICRATE
PICRATED
PICRATES
PICRIC
PICRITE
PICRITES
PICRITIC
PICROTOXIN
PICROTOXINS
PICS
PICTOGRAM
PICTOGRAMS
PICTOGRAPH
PICTOGRAPHIC
PICTOGRAPHIES
PICTOGRAPHS
PICTOGRAPHY
PICTORIAL
PICTORIALISM
PICTORIALISMS
PICTORIALIST
PICTORIALISTS
PICTORIALIZE
PICTORIALIZED
PICTORIALIZES
PICTORIALIZING
PICTORIALLY
PICTORIALNESS
PICTORIALNESSES
PICTORIALS
PICTURE
PICTURED
PICTUREPHONE
PICTUREPHONES
PICTURES
PICTURESQUE
PICTURESQUELY
PICTURESQUENESS
PICTURING
PICTURIZATION
PICTURIZATIONS
PICTURIZE
PICTURIZED
PICTURIZES
PICTURIZING
PICUL
PICULS
PIDDLE
PIDDLED
PIDDLER
PIDDLERS
PIDDLES
PIDDLING
PIDDLY
PIDDOCK
PIDDOCKS
PIDGIN
PIDGINIZATION
PIDGINIZATIONS
PIDGINIZE
PIDGINIZED
PIDGINIZES
PIDGINIZING
PIDGINS
PIE
PIEBALD
PIEBALDS
PIECE
PIECED
PIECEMEAL
PIECER
PIECERS
PIECES
PIECEWISE
PIECEWORK
PIECEWORKER
PIECEWORKERS
PIECEWORKS
PIECING
PIECINGS
PIECRUST
PIECRUSTS
PIED
PIEDFORT
PIEDFORTS
PIEDMONT
PIEDMONTS
PIEFORT
PIEFORTS
PIEHOLE
PIEHOLES
PIEING
PIEINGS
PIEPLANT
PIEPLANTS
PIER
PIERCE
PIERCED
PIERCER
PIERCERS
PIERCES
PIERCING
PIERCINGLY
PIERCINGS
PIERIDINE
PIEROGI
PIEROGIES
PIERROT
PIERROTS
PIERS
PIES
PIETA
PIETAS
PIETIES
PIETISM
PIETISMS
PIETIST
PIETISTIC
PIETISTICALLY
PIETISTS
PIETY
PIEZO
PIEZOELECTRIC
PIEZOMETER
PIEZOMETERS
PIEZOMETRIC
PIFFLE
PIFFLED
PIFFLER
PIFFLERS
PIFFLES
PIFFLING
PIG
PIGBOAT
PIGBOATS
PIGEON
PIGEONHOLE
PIGEONHOLED
PIGEONHOLER
PIGEONHOLERS
PIGEONHOLES
PIGEONHOLING
PIGEONITE
PIGEONITES
PIGEONRIES
PIGEONRY
PIGEONS
PIGEONWING
PIGEONWINGS
PIGFISH
PIGFISHES
PIGGED
PIGGERIES
PIGGERY
PIGGIE
PIGGIER
PIGGIES
PIGGIEST
PIGGIN
PIGGINESS
PIGGINESSES
PIGGING
PIGGINS
PIGGISH
PIGGISHLY
PIGGISHNESS
PIGGISHNESSES
PIGGY
PIGGYBACK
PIGGYBACKED
PIGGYBACKING
PIGGYBACKS
PIGHEADED
PIGHEADEDLY
PIGHEADEDNESS
PIGHEADEDNESSES
PIGLET
PIGLETS
PIGLIKE
PIGMENT
PIGMENTARY
PIGMENTATION
PIGMENTATIONS
PIGMENTED
PIGMENTING
PIGMENTS
PIGMIES
PIGMY
PIGNOLI
PIGNOLIA
PIGNOLIAS
PIGNOLIS
PIGNORA
PIGNUS
PIGNUT
PIGNUTS
PIGOUT
PIGOUTS
PIGPEN
PIGPENS
PIGS
PIGSKIN
PIGSKINS
PIGSNEY
PIGSNEYS
PIGSTICK
PIGSTICKED
PIGSTICKER
PIGSTICKERS
PIGSTICKING
PIGSTICKS
PIGSTIES
PIGSTY
PIGTAIL
PIGTAILED
PIGTAILS
PIGWEED
PIGWEEDS
PIING
PIKA
PIKAKE
PIKAKES
PIKAS

PIKE
PIKED
PIKEMAN
PIKEMEN
PIKEMINNOW
PIKEMINNOWS
PIKEPERCH
PIKEPERCHES
PIKER
PIKERS
PIKES
PIKESTAFF
PIKESTAFFS
PIKESTAVES
PIKI
PIKING
PIKIS
PILAF
PILAFF
PILAFFS
PILAFS
PILAR
PILASTER
PILASTERS
PILAU
PILAUS
PILAW
PILAWS
PILCHARD
PILCHARDS
PILE
PILEA
PILEATE
PILEATED
PILED
PILEI
PILELESS
PILEOUS
PILES
PILEUM
PILEUP
PILEUPS
PILEUS
PILEWORT
PILEWORTS
PILFER
PILFERABLE
PILFERAGE
PILFERAGES
PILFERED
PILFERER
PILFERERS
PILFERING
PILFERPROOF
PILFERS
PILGARLIC
PILGARLICS
PILGRIM
PILGRIMAGE
PILGRIMAGED
PILGRIMAGES
PILGRIMAGING
PILGRIMED
PILGRIMING
PILGRIMS
PILI
PILIFORM
PILING
PILINGS
PILIS
PILL
PILLAGE
PILLAGED
PILLAGER
PILLAGERS
PILLAGES
PILLAGING
PILLAR
PILLARED
PILLARING
PILLARLESS
PILLARS
PILLBOX
PILLBOXES
PILLBUG
PILLBUGS
PILLED
PILLING
PILLION
PILLIONS
PILLOCK
PILLOCKS
PILLORIED
PILLORIES
PILLORY
PILLORYING
PILLOW
PILLOWCASE
PILLOWCASES
PILLOWED
PILLOWIER
PILLOWIEST
PILLOWING
PILLOWS
PILLOWSLIP
PILLOWSLIPS
PILLOWY
PILLS
PILOCARPINE
PILOCARPINES
PILONIDAL
PILOSE
PILOSITIES
PILOSITY
PILOT
PILOTAGE
PILOTAGES
PILOTED
PILOTFISH
PILOTFISHES
PILOTHOUSE
PILOTHOUSES
PILOTING
PILOTINGS
PILOTLESS
PILOTS
PILOUS
PILSENER
PILSENERS
PILSNER
PILSNERS
PILULAR
PILULE
PILULES
PILUS
PILY
PIMA
PIMAS
PIMENTO
PIMENTOS
PIMIENTO
PIMIENTOS
PIMP
PIMPED
PIMPERNEL
PIMPERNELS
PIMPING
PIMPINGS
PIMPLE
PIMPLED
PIMPLES
PIMPLIER
PIMPLIEST
PIMPLY
PIMPMOBILE
PIMPMOBILES
PIMPS
PIN
PINA
PINACEOUS
PINAFORE
PINAFORED
PINAFORES
PINANG
PINANGS
PINAS
PINASTER
PINASTERS
PINATA
PINATAS
PINBALL
PINBALLED
PINBALLING
PINBALLS
PINBONE
PINBONES
PINCER
PINCERLIKE
PINCERS
PINCH
PINCHBECK
PINCHBECKS
PINCHBUG
PINCHBUGS
PINCHCOCK
PINCHCOCKS
PINCHECK
PINCHECKS
PINCHED
PINCHER
PINCHERS
PINCHES
PINCHING
PINCHPENNY
PINCURL
PINCURLS
PINCUSHION
PINCUSHIONS
PINDER
PINDERS
PINDLING
PINE
PINEAL
PINEALECTOMIES
PINEALECTOMIZE
PINEALECTOMIZED
PINEALECTOMIZES
PINEALECTOMY
PINEALS
PINEAPPLE
PINEAPPLES
PINECONE
PINECONES
PINED
PINEDROPS
PINELAND
PINELANDS
PINELIKE
PINENE
PINENES
PINERIES
PINERY
PINES
PINESAP
PINESAPS
PINETA
PINETUM
PINEWOOD
PINEWOODS
PINEY
PINFEATHER
PINFEATHERS
PINFISH
PINFISHES
PINFOLD
PINFOLDED
PINFOLDING
PINFOLDS
PING
PINGED
PINGER
PINGERS
PINGING
PINGO
PINGOES
PINGOS
PINGRASS
PINGRASSES
PINGS
PINGUID
PINHEAD
PINHEADED
PINHEADEDNESS
PINHEADEDNESSES
PINHEADS
PINHOLE
PINHOLES
PINIER
PINIEST
PINING
PINION
PINIONED
PINIONING
PINIONS
PINITE

PINITES
PINITOL
PINITOLS
PINK
PINKED
PINKEN
PINKENED
PINKENING
PINKENS
PINKER
PINKERS
PINKEST
PINKEY
PINKEYE
PINKEYES
PINKEYS
PINKIE
PINKIER
PINKIES
PINKIEST
PINKING
PINKINGS
PINKISH
PINKISHNESS
PINKISHNESSES
PINKLY
PINKNESS
PINKNESSES
PINKO
PINKOES
PINKOS
PINKROOT
PINKROOTS
PINKS
PINKY
PINLESS
PINNA
PINNACE
PINNACES
PINNACLE
PINNACLED
PINNACLES
PINNACLING
PINNAE
PINNAL
PINNAS
PINNATE
PINNATED
PINNATELY
PINNATIFID
PINNATION
PINNATIONS
PINNED
PINNER
PINNERS
PINNIES
PINNING
PINNIPED
PINNIPEDS
PINNULA
PINNULAE
PINNULAR
PINNULATE
PINNULE
PINNULES
PINNY
PINOCHLE
PINOCHLES
PINOCLE
PINOCLES
PINOCYTIC
PINOCYTOSES
PINOCYTOSIS
PINOCYTOTIC
PINOCYTOTICALLY
PINOLE
PINOLES
PINON
PINONES
PINONS
PINOT
PINOTAGE
PINOTAGES
PINOTS
PINPOINT
PINPOINTED
PINPOINTING
PINPOINTS
PINPRICK
PINPRICKED
PINPRICKING
PINPRICKS
PINS
PINSCHER
PINSCHERS
PINSETTER
PINSETTERS
PINSPOT
PINSPOTS
PINSPOTTED
PINSPOTTER
PINSPOTTERS
PINSPOTTING
PINSTRIPE
PINSTRIPES
PINT
PINTA
PINTADA
PINTADAS
PINTADO
PINTADOES
PINTADOS
PINTAIL
PINTAILED
PINTAILS
PINTANO
PINTANOS
PINTAS
PINTLE
PINTLES
PINTO
PINTOES
PINTOS
PINTS
PINTSIZE
PINTSIZED
PINTUCK
PINTUCKED
PINTUCKING
PINTUCKINGS
PINTUCKS
PINUP
PINUPS
PINWALE
PINWALES
PINWEED
PINWEEDS
PINWHEEL
PINWHEELED
PINWHEELING
PINWHEELS
PINWORK
PINWORKS
PINWORM
PINWORMS
PINWRENCH
PINWRENCHES
PINY
PINYIN
PINYINS
PINYON
PINYONS
PIOLET
PIOLETS
PION
PIONEER
PIONEERED
PIONEERING
PIONEERS
PIONIC
PIONS
PIOSITIES
PIOSITY
PIOUS
PIOUSLY
PIOUSNESS
PIOUSNESSES
PIP
PIPA
PIPAGE
PIPAGES
PIPAL
PIPALS
PIPAS
PIPE
PIPEAGE
PIPEAGES
PIPECLAY
PIPECLAYED
PIPECLAYING
PIPECLAYS
PIPED
PIPEFISH
PIPEFISHES
PIPEFUL
PIPEFULS
PIPELESS
PIPELIKE
PIPELINE
PIPELINED
PIPELINES
PIPELINING
PIPER
PIPERAZINE
PIPERAZINES
PIPERIDINE
PIPERIDINES
PIPERINE
PIPERINES
PIPERONAL
PIPERONALS
PIPERS
PIPES
PIPESTEM
PIPESTEMS
PIPESTONE
PIPESTONES
PIPET
PIPETS
PIPETTE
PIPETTED
PIPETTES
PIPETTING
PIPEWORK
PIPEWORKS
PIPIER
PIPIEST
PIPINESS
PIPINESSES
PIPING
PIPINGLY
PIPINGS
PIPISTREL
PIPISTRELLE
PIPISTRELLES
PIPISTRELS
PIPIT
PIPITS
PIPKIN
PIPKINS
PIPLESS
PIPPED
PIPPIN
PIPPING
PIPPINS
PIPS
PIPSISSEWA
PIPSISSEWAS
PIPSQUEAK
PIPSQUEAKS
PIPY
PIQUANCE
PIQUANCES
PIQUANCIES
PIQUANCY
PIQUANT
PIQUANTLY
PIQUANTNESS
PIQUANTNESSES
PIQUE
PIQUED
PIQUES
PIQUET
PIQUETS
PIQUING
PIRACETAM
PIRACETAMS
PIRACIES
PIRACY
PIRAGUA
PIRAGUAS
PIRANA
PIRANAS
PIRANHA
PIRANHAS

IRARUCU
IRARUCUS
IRATE
IRATED
IRATES
IRATIC
IRATICAL
IRATICALLY
IRATING
IRAYA
IRAYAS
IRIFORM
IRN
IRNS
IROG
IROGEN
IROGHI
IROGI
IROGIES
IROGUE
IROGUES
IROJKI
IROPLASM
IROPLASMA
IROPLASMATA
IROPLASMS
IROQUE
IROQUES
IROSHKI
IROUETTE
IROUETTED
IROUETTES
IROUETTING
IROZHKI
IROZHOK
IS
ISCARIES
ISCARY
ISCATOR
ISCATORIAL
ISCATORS
ISCATORY
ISCICULTURE
ISCICULTURES
ISCIFORM
ISCINA
ISCINAE
ISCINAL
ISCINAS
ISCINE
ISCIVORE
ISCIVORES
ISCIVOROUS

PISCO
PISCOS
PISH
PISHED
PISHER
PISHERS
PISHES
PISHING
PISHOGE
PISHOGES
PISHOGUE
PISHOGUES
PISIFORM
PISIFORMS
PISMIRE
PISMIRES
PISO
PISOLITE
PISOLITES
PISOLITH
PISOLITHS
PISOLITIC
PISOS
PISS
PISSANT
PISSANTS
PISSED
PISSER
PISSERS
PISSES
PISSHOLE
PISSHOLES
PISSIER
PISSIEST
PISSING
PISSOIR
PISSOIRS
PISSY
PISTACHE
PISTACHES
PISTACHIO
PISTACHIOS
PISTAREEN
PISTAREENS
PISTE
PISTES
PISTIL
PISTILLATE
PISTILS
PISTOL
PISTOLE
PISTOLED
PISTOLEER

PISTOLEERS
PISTOLERO
PISTOLEROS
PISTOLES
PISTOLIER
PISTOLIERS
PISTOLING
PISTOLLED
PISTOLLING
PISTOLS
PISTON
PISTONS
PISTOU
PISTOUS
PIT
PITA
PITAHAYA
PITAHAYAS
PITAPAT
PITAPATS
PITAPATTED
PITAPATTING
PITAS
PITAYA
PITAYAS
PITCH
PITCHBLENDE
PITCHBLENDES
PITCHED
PITCHER
PITCHERFUL
PITCHERFULS
PITCHERS
PITCHERSFUL
PITCHES
PITCHFORK
PITCHFORKED
PITCHFORKING
PITCHFORKS
PITCHIER
PITCHIEST
PITCHILY
PITCHING
PITCHMAN
PITCHMEN
PITCHOUT
PITCHOUTS
PITCHPOLE
PITCHPOLED
PITCHPOLES
PITCHPOLING
PITCHWOMAN
PITCHWOMEN

PITCHY
PITEOUS
PITEOUSLY
PITEOUSNESS
PITEOUSNESSES
PITFALL
PITFALLS
PITH
PITHEAD
PITHEADS
PITHECANTHROPI
PITHECANTHROPUS
PITHECOID
PITHED
PITHIER
PITHIEST
PITHILY
PITHINESS
PITHINESSES
PITHING
PITHLESS
PITHOI
PITHOS
PITHS
PITHY
PITIABLE
PITIABLENESS
PITIABLENESSES
PITIABLY
PITIED
PITIER
PITIERS
PITIES
PITIFUL
PITIFULLER
PITIFULLEST
PITIFULLY
PITIFULNESS
PITIFULNESSES
PITILESS
PITILESSLY
PITILESSNESS
PITILESSNESSES
PITMAN
PITMANS
PITMEN
PITON
PITONS
PITOT
PITOTS
PITS
PITSAW
PITSAWS

PITTA
PITTANCE
PITTANCES
PITTAS
PITTED
PITTING
PITTINGS
PITTOSPORUM
PITTOSPORUMS
PITUITARIES
PITUITARY
PITY
PITYING
PITYINGLY
PITYRIASES
PITYRIASIS
PIU
PIVOT
PIVOTABLE
PIVOTAL
PIVOTALLY
PIVOTED
PIVOTING
PIVOTMAN
PIVOTMEN
PIVOTS
PIX
PIXEL
PIXELATE
PIXELATED
PIXELATES
PIXELATING
PIXELS
PIXES
PIXIE
PIXIEISH
PIXIES
PIXILATE
PIXILATED
PIXILATES
PIXILATING
PIXILATION
PIXILATIONS
PIXILLATED
PIXINESS
PIXINESSES
PIXY
PIXYISH
PIZAZZ
PIZAZZES
PIZAZZY
PIZZA
PIZZALIKE

PIZZAS
PIZZAZ
PIZZAZES
PIZZAZZ
PIZZAZZES
PIZZAZZY
PIZZELLE
PIZZELLES
PIZZERIA
PIZZERIAS
PIZZICATI
PIZZICATO
PIZZLE
PIZZLES
PLACABILITIES
PLACABILITY
PLACABLE
PLACABLY
PLACARD
PLACARDED
PLACARDING
PLACARDS
PLACATE
PLACATED
PLACATER
PLACATERS
PLACATES
PLACATING
PLACATINGLY
PLACATION
PLACATIONS
PLACATIVE
PLACATORY
PLACE
PLACEABLE
PLACEBO
PLACEBOES
PLACEBOS
PLACED
PLACEHOLDER
PLACEHOLDERS
PLACEKICK
PLACEKICKED
PLACEKICKER
PLACEKICKERS
PLACEKICKING
PLACEKICKS
PLACELESS
PLACELESSLY
PLACELESSNESS
PLACELESSNESSES
PLACEMAN
PLACEMAT
PLACEMATS
PLACEMEN
PLACEMENT
PLACEMENTS
PLACENTA
PLACENTAE
PLACENTAL
PLACENTALS
PLACENTAS
PLACENTATION
PLACENTATIONS
PLACER
PLACERS
PLACES
PLACET
PLACETS
PLACID
PLACIDITIES
PLACIDITY
PLACIDLY
PLACIDNESS
PLACIDNESSES
PLACING
PLACINGS
PLACK
PLACKET
PLACKETS
PLACKS
PLACODERM
PLACODERMS
PLACOID
PLACOIDS
PLAFOND
PLAFONDS
PLAGAL
PLAGE
PLAGES
PLAGIARIES
PLAGIARISE
PLAGIARISED
PLAGIARISES
PLAGIARISING
PLAGIARISM
PLAGIARISMS
PLAGIARIST
PLAGIARISTIC
PLAGIARISTS
PLAGIARIZE
PLAGIARIZED
PLAGIARIZER
PLAGIARIZERS
PLAGIARIZES
PLAGIARIZING
PLAGIARY
PLAGIOCLASE
PLAGIOCLASES
PLAGIOTROPIC
PLAGUE
PLAGUED
PLAGUER
PLAGUERS
PLAGUES
PLAGUEY
PLAGUILY
PLAGUING
PLAGUY
PLAICE
PLAICES
PLAID
PLAIDED
PLAIDS
PLAIN
PLAINCHANT
PLAINCHANTS
PLAINCLOTHES
PLAINCLOTHESMAN
PLAINCLOTHESMEN
PLAINED
PLAINER
PLAINEST
PLAINING
PLAINLY
PLAINNESS
PLAINNESSES
PLAINS
PLAINSMAN
PLAINSMEN
PLAINSONG
PLAINSONGS
PLAINSPOKEN
PLAINSPOKENNESS
PLAINT
PLAINTEXT
PLAINTEXTS
PLAINTFUL
PLAINTIFF
PLAINTIFFS
PLAINTIVE
PLAINTIVELY
PLAINTIVENESS
PLAINTIVENESSES
PLAINTS
PLAISTER
PLAISTERED
PLAISTERING
PLAISTERS
PLAIT
PLAITED
PLAITER
PLAITERS
PLAITING
PLAITINGS
PLAITS
PLAN
PLANAR
PLANARIA
PLANARIAN
PLANARIANS
PLANARIAS
PLANARITIES
PLANARITY
PLANATE
PLANATION
PLANATIONS
PLANCH
PLANCHE
PLANCHES
PLANCHET
PLANCHETS
PLANCHETTE
PLANCHETTES
PLANE
PLANED
PLANELOAD
PLANELOADS
PLANENESS
PLANENESSES
PLANER
PLANERS
PLANES
PLANESIDE
PLANESIDES
PLANET
PLANETARIA
PLANETARIES
PLANETARIUM
PLANETARIUMS
PLANETARY
PLANETESIMAL
PLANETESIMALS
PLANETLIKE
PLANETOID
PLANETOIDAL
PLANETOIDS
PLANETOLOGICAL
PLANETOLOGIES
PLANETOLOGIST
PLANETOLOGISTS
PLANETOLOGY
PLANETS
PLANETWIDE
PLANFORM
PLANFORMS
PLANGENCIES
PLANGENCY
PLANGENT
PLANGENTLY
PLANIMETER
PLANIMETERS
PLANIMETRIC
PLANIMETRICALLY
PLANING
PLANISH
PLANISHED
PLANISHER
PLANISHERS
PLANISHES
PLANISHING
PLANISPHERE
PLANISPHERES
PLANISPHERIC
PLANK
PLANKED
PLANKING
PLANKINGS
PLANKS
PLANKTER
PLANKTERS
PLANKTIC
PLANKTON
PLANKTONIC
PLANKTONS
PLANLESS
PLANLESSLY
PLANLESSNESS
PLANLESSNESSES
PLANNED
PLANNER
PLANNERS
PLANNING
PLANNINGS
PLANOGRAM
PLANOGRAMS
PLANOGRAPHIC
PLANOGRAPHIES
PLANOGRAPHY
PLANOSOL
PLANOSOLS
PLANS
PLANT
PLANTABLE
PLANTAIN

LANTAINS
LANTAR
LANTATION
LANTATIONS
LANTED
LANTER
LANTERS
LANTIGRADE
LANTIGRADES
LANTING
LANTINGS
LANTLET
LANTLETS
LANTLIKE
LANTOCRACIES
LANTOCRACY
LANTS
LANTSMAN
LANTSMEN
LANULA
LANULAE
LANULAR
LANULATE
LANULOID
LAQUE
LAQUES
LASH
LASHED
LASHER
LASHERS
LASHES
LASHIER
LASHIEST
LASHING
LASHY
LASM
LASMA
LASMAGEL
LASMAGELS
LASMAGENE
LASMAGENES
LASMALEMMA
LASMALEMMAS
LASMAPHERESES
LASMAPHERESIS
ASMAS
ASMASOL
ASMASOLS
ASMATIC
ASMIC
ASMID
ASMIDS
ASMIN

PLASMINOGEN
PLASMINOGENS
PLASMINS
PLASMODESM
PLASMODESMA
PLASMODESMAS
PLASMODESMATA
PLASMODIA
PLASMODIUM
PLASMOGAMIES
PLASMOGAMY
PLASMOID
PLASMOIDS
PLASMOLYSES
PLASMOLYSIS
PLASMOLYTIC
PLASMOLYZE
PLASMOLYZED
PLASMOLYZES
PLASMOLYZING
PLASMON
PLASMONS
PLASMS
PLASTER
PLASTERBOARD
PLASTERBOARDS
PLASTERED
PLASTERER
PLASTERERS
PLASTERING
PLASTERINGS
PLASTERS
PLASTERWORK
PLASTERWORKS
PLASTERY
PLASTIC
PLASTICALLY
PLASTICENE
PLASTICENES
PLASTICINE
PLASTICINES
PLASTICITIES
PLASTICITY
PLASTICIZATION
PLASTICIZATIONS
PLASTICIZE
PLASTICIZED
PLASTICIZER
PLASTICIZERS
PLASTICIZES
PLASTICIZING
PLASTICKY
PLASTICLY

PLASTICS
PLASTICWARE
PLASTICWARES
PLASTID
PLASTIDIAL
PLASTIDS
PLASTINATION
PLASTINATIONS
PLASTIQUE
PLASTIQUES
PLASTISOL
PLASTISOLS
PLASTOCYANIN
PLASTOCYANINS
PLASTOQUINONE
PLASTOQUINONES
PLASTRAL
PLASTRON
PLASTRONS
PLASTRUM
PLASTRUMS
PLAT
PLATAN
PLATANE
PLATANES
PLATANS
PLATE
PLATEAU
PLATEAUED
PLATEAUING
PLATEAUS
PLATEAUX
PLATED
PLATEFUL
PLATEFULS
PLATEGLASS
PLATELESS
PLATELET
PLATELETS
PLATELIKE
PLATEMAKER
PLATEMAKERS
PLATEMAKING
PLATEMAKINGS
PLATEN
PLATENS
PLATER
PLATERESQUE
PLATERS
PLATES
PLATESFUL
PLATFORM
PLATFORMS

PLATIER
PLATIES
PLATIEST
PLATINA
PLATINAS
PLATING
PLATINGS
PLATINIC
PLATINIZE
PLATINIZED
PLATINIZES
PLATINIZING
PLATINOCYANIDE
PLATINOCYANIDES
PLATINOID
PLATINOIDS
PLATINOUS
PLATINUM
PLATINUMS
PLATITUDE
PLATITUDES
PLATITUDINAL
PLATITUDINARIAN
PLATITUDINIZE
PLATITUDINIZED
PLATITUDINIZES
PLATITUDINIZING
PLATITUDINOUS
PLATITUDINOUSLY
PLATONIC
PLATONICALLY
PLATONISM
PLATONISMS
PLATOON
PLATOONED
PLATOONING
PLATOONS
PLATS
PLATTED
PLATTER
PLATTERFUL
PLATTERFULS
PLATTERS
PLATTERSFUL
PLATTING
PLATY
PLATYFISH
PLATYFISHES
PLATYHELMINTH
PLATYHELMINTHIC
PLATYHELMINTHS
PLATYPI
PLATYPUS

PLATYPUSES
PLATYRRHINE
PLATYRRHINES
PLATYS
PLAUDIT
PLAUDITS
PLAUSIBILITIES
PLAUSIBILITY
PLAUSIBLE
PLAUSIBLENESS
PLAUSIBLENESSES
PLAUSIBLY
PLAUSIVE
PLAY
PLAYA
PLAYABILITIES
PLAYABILITY
PLAYABLE
PLAYACT
PLAYACTED
PLAYACTING
PLAYACTINGS
PLAYACTOR
PLAYACTORS
PLAYACTS
PLAYAS
PLAYBACK
PLAYBACKS
PLAYBILL
PLAYBILLS
PLAYBOOK
PLAYBOOKS
PLAYBOY
PLAYBOYS
PLAYDATE
PLAYDATES
PLAYDAY
PLAYDAYS
PLAYDOWN
PLAYDOWNS
PLAYED
PLAYER
PLAYERS
PLAYFELLOW
PLAYFELLOWS
PLAYFIELD
PLAYFIELDS
PLAYFUL
PLAYFULLY
PLAYFULNESS
PLAYFULNESSES
PLAYGIRL
PLAYGIRLS

PLAYGOER
PLAYGOERS
PLAYGOING
PLAYGOINGS
PLAYGROUND
PLAYGROUNDS
PLAYGROUP
PLAYGROUPS
PLAYHOUSE
PLAYHOUSES
PLAYING
PLAYLAND
PLAYLANDS
PLAYLESS
PLAYLET
PLAYLETS
PLAYLIKE
PLAYLIST
PLAYLISTED
PLAYLISTING
PLAYLISTS
PLAYMAKER
PLAYMAKERS
PLAYMAKING
PLAYMAKINGS
PLAYMATE
PLAYMATES
PLAYOFF
PLAYOFFS
PLAYPEN
PLAYPENS
PLAYROOM
PLAYROOMS
PLAYS
PLAYSET
PLAYSETS
PLAYSUIT
PLAYSUITS
PLAYTHING
PLAYTHINGS
PLAYTIME
PLAYTIMES
PLAYWEAR
PLAYWRIGHT
PLAYWRIGHTING
PLAYWRIGHTINGS
PLAYWRIGHTS
PLAYWRITING
PLAYWRITINGS
PLAZA
PLAZAS
PLEA
PLEACH
PLEACHED
PLEACHES
PLEACHING
PLEAD
PLEADABLE
PLEADED
PLEADER
PLEADERS
PLEADING
PLEADINGLY
PLEADINGS
PLEADS
PLEAS
PLEASANCE
PLEASANCES
PLEASANT
PLEASANTER
PLEASANTEST
PLEASANTLY
PLEASANTNESS
PLEASANTNESSES
PLEASANTRIES
PLEASANTRY
PLEASE
PLEASED
PLEASER
PLEASERS
PLEASES
PLEASING
PLEASINGLY
PLEASINGNESS
PLEASINGNESSES
PLEASURABILITY
PLEASURABLE
PLEASURABLENESS
PLEASURABLY
PLEASURE
PLEASURED
PLEASURELESS
PLEASURES
PLEASURING
PLEAT
PLEATED
PLEATER
PLEATERS
PLEATHER
PLEATHERS
PLEATING
PLEATINGS
PLEATLESS
PLEATS
PLEB
PLEBE
PLEBEIAN
PLEBEIANISM
PLEBEIANISMS
PLEBEIANLY
PLEBEIANS
PLEBES
PLEBISCITARY
PLEBISCITE
PLEBISCITES
PLEBS
PLECOPTERAN
PLECOPTERANS
PLECTRA
PLECTRON
PLECTRONS
PLECTRUM
PLECTRUMS
PLED
PLEDGE
PLEDGED
PLEDGEE
PLEDGEES
PLEDGEOR
PLEDGEORS
PLEDGER
PLEDGERS
PLEDGES
PLEDGET
PLEDGETS
PLEDGING
PLEDGOR
PLEDGORS
PLEIAD
PLEIADES
PLEIADS
PLEINAIRISM
PLEINAIRISMS
PLEINAIRIST
PLEINAIRISTS
PLEIOCENE
PLEIOTAXIES
PLEIOTAXY
PLEIOTROPIC
PLEIOTROPIES
PLEIOTROPY
PLENA
PLENARIES
PLENARILY
PLENARY
PLENCH
PLENCHES
PLENIPOTENT
PLENIPOTENTIARY
PLENISH
PLENISHED
PLENISHES
PLENISHING
PLENISM
PLENISMS
PLENIST
PLENISTS
PLENITUDE
PLENITUDES
PLENITUDINOUS
PLENTEOUS
PLENTEOUSLY
PLENTEOUSNESS
PLENTEOUSNESSES
PLENTIES
PLENTIFUL
PLENTIFULLY
PLENTIFULNESS
PLENTIFULNESSES
PLENTITUDE
PLENTITUDES
PLENTY
PLENUM
PLENUMS
PLEOCHROIC
PLEOCHROISM
PLEOCHROISMS
PLEOMORPHIC
PLEOMORPHISM
PLEOMORPHISMS
PLEON
PLEONAL
PLEONASM
PLEONASMS
PLEONASTIC
PLEONASTICALLY
PLEONIC
PLEONS
PLEOPOD
PLEOPODS
PLEROCERCOID
PLEROCERCOIDS
PLEROMA
PLEROMAS
PLESIOSAUR
PLESIOSAURS
PLESSOR
PLESSORS
PLETHORA
PLETHORAS
PLETHORIC
PLETHYSMOGRAM
PLETHYSMOGRAMS
PLETHYSMOGRAPH
PLETHYSMOGRAPHS
PLETHYSMOGRAPHY
PLEURA
PLEURAE
PLEURAL
PLEURAS
PLEURISIES
PLEURISY
PLEURITIC
PLEURON
PLEUROPNEUMONIA
PLEUSTON
PLEUSTONIC
PLEUSTONS
PLEW
PLEWS
PLEX
PLEXAL
PLEXES
PLEXIFORM
PLEXIGLASS
PLEXIGLASSES
PLEXOR
PLEXORS
PLEXUS
PLEXUSES
PLIABILITIES
PLIABILITY
PLIABLE
PLIABLENESS
PLIABLENESSES
PLIABLY
PLIANCIES
PLIANCY
PLIANT
PLIANTLY
PLIANTNESS
PLIANTNESSES
PLICA
PLICAE
PLICAL
PLICAS
PLICATE
PLICATED
PLICATELY
PLICATION
PLICATIONS
PLICATURE
PLICATURES
PLIE
PLIED

LIER
LIERS
LIES
LIGHT
LIGHTED
LIGHTER
LIGHTERS
LIGHTING
LIGHTS
LIMSOL
LIMSOLE
LIMSOLES
LIMSOLL
LIMSOLLS
LIMSOLS
LINK
LINKED
LINKER
LINKERS
LINKIER
LINKIEST
LINKING
LINKS
LINKY
LINTH
LINTHS
LIOCENE
LIOFILM
LIOFILMS
LIOTRON
LIOTRONS
LISKIE
LISKIES
LISKY
LISSE
LISSES
LOD
LODDED
LODDER
LODDERS
LODDING
LODDINGLY
LODS
LOIDIES
LOIDY
LONK
LONKED
LONKER
LONKERS
LONKING
LONKS
LOP
LOPPED
PLOPPING
PLOPS
PLOSION
PLOSIONS
PLOSIVE
PLOSIVES
PLOT
PLOTLESS
PLOTLESSNESS
PLOTLESSNESSES
PLOTLINE
PLOTLINES
PLOTS
PLOTTAGE
PLOTTAGES
PLOTTED
PLOTTER
PLOTTERS
PLOTTIER
PLOTTIES
PLOTTIEST
PLOTTINESS
PLOTTINESSES
PLOTTING
PLOTTY
PLOTZ
PLOTZED
PLOTZES
PLOTZING
PLOUGH
PLOUGHED
PLOUGHER
PLOUGHERS
PLOUGHING
PLOUGHS
PLOUGHSHARE
PLOUGHSHARES
PLOVER
PLOVERS
PLOW
PLOWABLE
PLOWBACK
PLOWBACKS
PLOWBOY
PLOWBOYS
PLOWED
PLOWER
PLOWERS
PLOWHEAD
PLOWHEADS
PLOWING
PLOWLAND
PLOWLANDS
PLOWMAN
PLOWMEN
PLOWS
PLOWSHARE
PLOWSHARES
PLOY
PLOYE
PLOYED
PLOYES
PLOYING
PLOYS
PLUCK
PLUCKED
PLUCKER
PLUCKERS
PLUCKIER
PLUCKIEST
PLUCKILY
PLUCKINESS
PLUCKINESSES
PLUCKING
PLUCKS
PLUCKY
PLUG
PLUGGED
PLUGGER
PLUGGERS
PLUGGING
PLUGHOLE
PLUGHOLES
PLUGLESS
PLUGOLA
PLUGOLAS
PLUGS
PLUGUGLIES
PLUGUGLY
PLUM
PLUMAGE
PLUMAGED
PLUMAGES
PLUMATE
PLUMB
PLUMBABLE
PLUMBAGO
PLUMBAGOS
PLUMBED
PLUMBEOUS
PLUMBER
PLUMBERIES
PLUMBERS
PLUMBERY
PLUMBIC
PLUMBING
PLUMBINGS
PLUMBISM
PLUMBISMS
PLUMBNESS
PLUMBNESSES
PLUMBOUS
PLUMBS
PLUMBUM
PLUMBUMS
PLUME
PLUMED
PLUMELET
PLUMELETS
PLUMERIA
PLUMERIAS
PLUMERIES
PLUMERY
PLUMES
PLUMIER
PLUMIEST
PLUMING
PLUMIPED
PLUMIPEDS
PLUMLIKE
PLUMMER
PLUMMEST
PLUMMET
PLUMMETED
PLUMMETING
PLUMMETS
PLUMMIER
PLUMMIEST
PLUMMY
PLUMOSE
PLUMOSELY
PLUMOSITIES
PLUMOSITY
PLUMP
PLUMPED
PLUMPEN
PLUMPENED
PLUMPENING
PLUMPENS
PLUMPER
PLUMPERS
PLUMPEST
PLUMPIER
PLUMPIEST
PLUMPING
PLUMPISH
PLUMPLY
PLUMPNESS
PLUMPNESSES
PLUMPS
PLUMPY
PLUMS
PLUMULAR
PLUMULE
PLUMULES
PLUMULOSE
PLUMY
PLUNDER
PLUNDERED
PLUNDERER
PLUNDERERS
PLUNDERING
PLUNDEROUS
PLUNDERS
PLUNGE
PLUNGED
PLUNGER
PLUNGERS
PLUNGES
PLUNGING
PLUNK
PLUNKED
PLUNKER
PLUNKERS
PLUNKIER
PLUNKIEST
PLUNKING
PLUNKS
PLUNKY
PLUOT
PLUOTS
PLUPERFECT
PLUPERFECTS
PLURAL
PLURALISM
PLURALISMS
PLURALIST
PLURALISTIC
PLURALISTICALLY
PLURALISTS
PLURALITIES
PLURALITY
PLURALIZATION
PLURALIZATIONS
PLURALIZE
PLURALIZED
PLURALIZES
PLURALIZING
PLURALLY
PLURALS
PLURIPOTENT
PLUS

PLUSES
PLUSH
PLUSHED
PLUSHER
PLUSHES
PLUSHEST
PLUSHIER
PLUSHIEST
PLUSHILY
PLUSHINESS
PLUSHINESSES
PLUSHLY
PLUSHNESS
PLUSHNESSES
PLUSHY
PLUSSAGE
PLUSSAGES
PLUSSES
PLUTEI
PLUTEUS
PLUTOCRACIES
PLUTOCRACY
PLUTOCRAT
PLUTOCRATIC
PLUTOCRATICALLY
PLUTOCRATS
PLUTON
PLUTONIAN
PLUTONIC
PLUTONISM
PLUTONISMS
PLUTONIUM
PLUTONIUMS
PLUTONS
PLUVIAL
PLUVIALS
PLUVIAN
PLUVIOSE
PLUVIOUS
PLY
PLYER
PLYERS
PLYING
PLYINGLY
PLYOMETRIC
PLYOMETRICS
PLYWOOD
PLYWOODS
PNEUMA
PNEUMAS
PNEUMATIC
PNEUMATICALLY
PNEUMATICITIES
PNEUMATICITY
PNEUMATICS
PNEUMATOLOGIES
PNEUMATOLOGY
PNEUMATOLYTIC
PNEUMATOPHORE
PNEUMATOPHORES
PNEUMOCOCCAL
PNEUMOCOCCI
PNEUMOCOCCUS
PNEUMOCONIOSES
PNEUMOCONIOSIS
PNEUMOGRAPH
PNEUMOGRAPHS
PNEUMONECTOMIES
PNEUMONECTOMY
PNEUMONIA
PNEUMONIAS
PNEUMONIC
PNEUMONITIDES
PNEUMONITIS
PNEUMONITISES
PNEUMOTHORACES
PNEUMOTHORAX
PNEUMOTHORAXES
PO
POACEOUS
POACH
POACHABLE
POACHED
POACHER
POACHERS
POACHES
POACHIER
POACHIEST
POACHING
POACHY
POBLANO
POBLANOS
POBOY
POBOYS
POCHARD
POCHARDS
POCK
POCKED
POCKET
POCKETABLE
POCKETBOOK
POCKETBOOKS
POCKETED
POCKETER
POCKETERS
POCKETFUL
POCKETFULS
POCKETING
POCKETKNIFE
POCKETKNIVES
POCKETS
POCKETSFUL
POCKIER
POCKIEST
POCKILY
POCKING
POCKMARK
POCKMARKED
POCKMARKING
POCKMARKS
POCKS
POCKY
POCO
POCOCURANTE
POCOCURANTISM
POCOCURANTISMS
POCOSEN
POCOSENS
POCOSIN
POCOSINS
POCOSON
POCOSONS
POD
PODAGRA
PODAGRAL
PODAGRAS
PODAGRIC
PODAGROUS
PODCAST
PODCASTED
PODCASTER
PODCASTING
PODCASTINGS
PODCASTS
PODDED
PODDING
PODESTA
PODESTAS
PODGIER
PODGIEST
PODGILY
PODGY
PODIA
PODIATRIC
PODIATRIES
PODIATRIST
PODIATRISTS
PODIATRY
PODITE
PODITES
PODITIC
PODIUM
PODIUMS
PODLIKE
PODOCARP
PODOMERE
PODOMERES
PODOPHYLLI
PODOPHYLLIN
PODOPHYLLINS
PODOPHYLLUM
PODOPHYLLUMS
PODS
PODSOL
PODSOLIC
PODSOLIZATION
PODSOLIZATIONS
PODSOLS
PODUNK
PODUNKS
PODZOL
PODZOLIC
PODZOLIZATION
PODZOLIZATIONS
PODZOLIZE
PODZOLIZED
PODZOLIZES
PODZOLIZING
PODZOLS
POECHORE
POECHORES
POEM
POEMS
POENOLOGIES
POENOLOGY
POESIES
POESY
POET
POETASTER
POETASTERS
POETESS
POETESSES
POETIC
POETICAL
POETICALLY
POETICALNESS
POETICALNESSES
POETICISM
POETICISMS
POETICIZE
POETICIZED
POETICIZES
POETICIZING
POETICS
POETISE
POETISED
POETISER
POETISERS
POETISES
POETISING
POETIZE
POETIZED
POETIZER
POETIZERS
POETIZES
POETIZING
POETLESS
POETLIKE
POETRIES
POETRY
POETS
POGEY
POGEYS
POGIES
POGO
POGOED
POGOES
POGOING
POGONIA
POGONIAS
POGONIP
POGONIPS
POGONOPHORAN
POGONOPHORANS
POGOS
POGROM
POGROMED
POGROMING
POGROMIST
POGROMISTS
POGROMS
POGY
POH
POI
POIGNANCE
POIGNANCES
POIGNANCIES
POIGNANCY
POIGNANT
POIGNANTLY
POIKILOTHERM
POIKILOTHERMIC
POIKILOTHERMS
POILU
POILUS

OINCIANA
OINCIANAS
OIND
OINDED
OINDING
OINDS
OINSETTIA
OINSETTIAS
OINT
OINTABLE
OINTE
OINTED
OINTEDLY
OINTEDNESS
OINTEDNESSES
OINTELLE
OINTELLES
OINTER
OINTERS
OINTES
OINTIER
OINTIEST
OINTILLISM
OINTILLISMS
OINTILLIST
OINTILLISTIC
OINTILLISTS
OINTING
OINTINGS
OINTLESS
OINTLESSLY
OINTLESSNESS
OINTLESSNESSES
OINTMAN
OINTMEN
OINTS
OINTY
IS
ISE
ISED
ISER
ISERS
ISES
ISHA
ISING
ISON
ISONED
ISONER
ISONERS
ISONING
ISONOUS
ISONOUSLY
ISONS
POISONWOOD
POISONWOODS
POITREL
POITRELS
POKABLE
POKE
POKEBERRIES
POKEBERRY
POKED
POKER
POKEROOT
POKEROOTS
POKERS
POKES
POKEWEED
POKEWEEDS
POKEY
POKEYS
POKIER
POKIES
POKIEST
POKILY
POKINESS
POKINESSES
POKING
POKY
POL
POLACK
POLACKS
POLAR
POLARIMETER
POLARIMETERS
POLARIMETRIC
POLARIMETRIES
POLARIMETRY
POLARISATION
POLARISATIONS
POLARISCOPE
POLARISCOPES
POLARISCOPIC
POLARISE
POLARISED
POLARISES
POLARISING
POLARITIES
POLARITY
POLARIZABILITY
POLARIZABLE
POLARIZATION
POLARIZATIONS
POLARIZE
POLARIZED
POLARIZER
POLARIZERS
POLARIZES
POLARIZING
POLAROGRAPHIC
POLAROGRAPHIES
POLAROGRAPHY
POLARON
POLARONS
POLARS
POLDER
POLDERS
POLE
POLEAX
POLEAXE
POLEAXED
POLEAXES
POLEAXING
POLECAT
POLECATS
POLED
POLEIS
POLELESS
POLEMIC
POLEMICAL
POLEMICALLY
POLEMICIST
POLEMICISTS
POLEMICIZE
POLEMICIZED
POLEMICIZES
POLEMICIZING
POLEMICS
POLEMIST
POLEMISTS
POLEMIZE
POLEMIZED
POLEMIZES
POLEMIZING
POLEMONIUM
POLEMONIUMS
POLENTA
POLENTAS
POLER
POLERS
POLES
POLESTAR
POLESTARS
POLEWARD
POLEYN
POLEYNS
POLICE
POLICED
POLICEMAN
POLICEMEN
POLICER
POLICERS
POLICES
POLICEWOMAN
POLICEWOMEN
POLICIER
POLICIERS
POLICIES
POLICING
POLICY
POLICYHOLDER
POLICYHOLDERS
POLIES
POLING
POLIO
POLIOMYELITIDES
POLIOMYELITIS
POLIOS
POLIOVIRUS
POLIOVIRUSES
POLIS
POLISH
POLISHED
POLISHER
POLISHERS
POLISHES
POLISHING
POLITBURO
POLITBUROS
POLITE
POLITELY
POLITENESS
POLITENESSES
POLITER
POLITESSE
POLITESSES
POLITEST
POLITIC
POLITICAL
POLITICALIZE
POLITICALIZED
POLITICALIZES
POLITICALIZING
POLITICALLY
POLITICIAN
POLITICIANS
POLITICISATION
POLITICISATIONS
POLITICISE
POLITICISED
POLITICISES
POLITICISING
POLITICIZATION
POLITICIZATIONS
POLITICIZE
POLITICIZED
POLITICIZES
POLITICIZING
POLITICK
POLITICKED
POLITICKER
POLITICKERS
POLITICKING
POLITICKS
POLITICLY
POLITICO
POLITICOES
POLITICOS
POLITICS
POLITIES
POLITY
POLKA
POLKAED
POLKAING
POLKAS
POLL
POLLACK
POLLACKS
POLLARD
POLLARDED
POLLARDING
POLLARDS
POLLED
POLLEE
POLLEES
POLLEN
POLLENATE
POLLENATED
POLLENATES
POLLENATING
POLLENED
POLLENING
POLLENIZER
POLLENIZERS
POLLENOSES
POLLENOSIS
POLLENS
POLLER
POLLERS
POLLEX
POLLICAL
POLLICES
POLLINATE
POLLINATED
POLLINATES

POLLINATING
POLLINATION
POLLINATIONS
POLLINATOR
POLLINATORS
POLLING
POLLINGS
POLLINIA
POLLINIC
POLLINIUM
POLLINIZE
POLLINIZED
POLLINIZER
POLLINIZERS
POLLINIZES
POLLINIZING
POLLINOSES
POLLINOSIS
POLLIST
POLLISTS
POLLIWOG
POLLIWOGS
POLLOCK
POLLOCKS
POLLS
POLLSTER
POLLSTERS
POLLTAKER
POLLTAKERS
POLLUTANT
POLLUTANTS
POLLUTE
POLLUTED
POLLUTER
POLLUTERS
POLLUTES
POLLUTING
POLLUTION
POLLUTIONS
POLLUTIVE
POLLYWOG
POLLYWOGS
POLO
POLOIST
POLOISTS
POLONAISE
POLONAISES
POLONIUM
POLONIUMS
POLOS
POLS
POLTERGEIST
POLTERGEISTS
POLTROON
POLTROONERIES
POLTROONERY
POLTROONS
POLY
POLYACRYLAMIDE
POLYACRYLAMIDES
POLYADIC
POLYALCOHOL
POLYALCOHOLS
POLYAMIDE
POLYAMIDES
POLYAMINE
POLYAMINES
POLYAMORIES
POLYAMORIST
POLYAMORISTS
POLYAMOROUS
POLYAMORY
POLYANDRIES
POLYANDROUS
POLYANDRY
POLYANTHA
POLYANTHAS
POLYANTHI
POLYANTHUS
POLYANTHUSES
POLYATOMIC
POLYBAG
POLYBAGGED
POLYBAGGING
POLYBAGS
POLYBASIC
POLYBRID
POLYBRIDS
POLYBUTADIENE
POLYBUTADIENES
POLYCARBONATE
POLYCARBONATES
POLYCARPIES
POLYCARPY
POLYCENTRIC
POLYCENTRISM
POLYCENTRISMS
POLYCHAETE
POLYCHAETES
POLYCHETE
POLYCHETES
POLYCHOTOMIES
POLYCHOTOMOUS
POLYCHOTOMY
POLYCHROMATIC
POLYCHROME
POLYCHROMED
POLYCHROMES
POLYCHROMIES
POLYCHROMING
POLYCHROMY
POLYCISTRONIC
POLYCLINIC
POLYCLINICS
POLYCLONAL
POLYCOT
POLYCOTS
POLYCRYSTAL
POLYCRYSTALLINE
POLYCRYSTALS
POLYCYCLIC
POLYCYSTIC
POLYCYTHAEMIA
POLYCYTHAEMIAS
POLYCYTHEMIA
POLYCYTHEMIAS
POLYCYTHEMIC
POLYDACTYL
POLYDACTYLIES
POLYDACTYLY
POLYDIPSIA
POLYDIPSIAS
POLYDIPSIC
POLYDISPERSE
POLYDISPERSITY
POLYDRUG
POLYELECTROLYTE
POLYEMBRYONIC
POLYEMBRYONIES
POLYEMBRYONY
POLYENE
POLYENES
POLYENIC
POLYESTER
POLYESTERS
POLYESTROUS
POLYETHYLENE
POLYETHYLENES
POLYGALA
POLYGALAS
POLYGAMIC
POLYGAMIES
POLYGAMIST
POLYGAMISTS
POLYGAMIZE
POLYGAMIZED
POLYGAMIZES
POLYGAMIZING
POLYGAMOUS
POLYGAMY
POLYGENE
POLYGENES
POLYGENESES
POLYGENESIS
POLYGENETIC
POLYGENIC
POLYGLOT
POLYGLOTISM
POLYGLOTISMS
POLYGLOTS
POLYGLOTTISM
POLYGLOTTISMS
POLYGON
POLYGONAL
POLYGONALLY
POLYGONIES
POLYGONS
POLYGONUM
POLYGONUMS
POLYGONY
POLYGRAPH
POLYGRAPHED
POLYGRAPHER
POLYGRAPHERS
POLYGRAPHIC
POLYGRAPHING
POLYGRAPHIST
POLYGRAPHISTS
POLYGRAPHS
POLYGYNE
POLYGYNIES
POLYGYNOUS
POLYGYNY
POLYHEDRA
POLYHEDRAL
POLYHEDRON
POLYHEDRONS
POLYHEDROSES
POLYHEDROSIS
POLYHISTOR
POLYHISTORIC
POLYHISTORS
POLYHYDROXY
POLYIMIDE
POLYIMIDES
POLYISOPRENE
POLYISOPRENES
POLYKETIDE
POLYKETIDES
POLYLYSINE
POLYLYSINES
POLYMATH
POLYMATHIC
POLYMATHIES
POLYMATHS
POLYMATHY
POLYMER
POLYMERASE
POLYMERASES
POLYMERIC
POLYMERISATION
POLYMERISATIONS
POLYMERISE
POLYMERISED
POLYMERISES
POLYMERISING
POLYMERISM
POLYMERISMS
POLYMERIZATION
POLYMERIZATIONS
POLYMERIZE
POLYMERIZED
POLYMERIZES
POLYMERIZING
POLYMERS
POLYMORPH
POLYMORPHIC
POLYMORPHICALLY
POLYMORPHISM
POLYMORPHISMS
POLYMORPHOUS
POLYMORPHOUSLY
POLYMORPHS
POLYMYOSITIS
POLYMYOSITISES
POLYMYXIN
POLYMYXINS
POLYNEURITIDES
POLYNEURITIS
POLYNEURITISES
POLYNOMIAL
POLYNOMIALS
POLYNUCLEAR
POLYNUCLEOTIDE
POLYNUCLEOTIDES
POLYNYA
POLYNYAS
POLYNYI
POLYOL
POLYOLEFIN
POLYOLEFINS
POLYOLS
POLYOMA
POLYOMAS
POLYOMAVIRUS

OLYOMAVIRUSES
OLYONYMIES
OLYONYMOUS
OLYONYMY
OLYP
OLYPARIA
OLYPARIES
OLYPARIUM
OLYPARY
OLYPED
OLYPEDS
OLYPEPTIDE
OLYPEPTIDES
OLYPEPTIDIC
OLYPETALOUS
OLYPHAGIA
OLYPHAGIAS
OLYPHAGIES
OLYPHAGOUS
OLYPHAGY
OLYPHARMACIES
OLYPHARMACY
OLYPHASE
OLYPHASIC
OLYPHENOL
OLYPHENOLIC
OLYPHENOLS
LYPHONE
LYPHONES
LYPHONIC
LYPHONICALLY
LYPHONIES
LYPHONOUS
LYPHONOUSLY
LYPHONY
LYPHYLETIC
LYPI
LYPIDE
LYPIDES
LYPLOID
LYPLOIDIES
LYPLOIDS
LYPLOIDY
LYPNEA
LYPNEAS
LYPNEIC
LYPOD
LYPODIES
LYPODS
LYPODY
LYPOID
LYPORE
LYPORES
POLYPOUS
POLYPROPYLENE
POLYPROPYLENES
POLYPS
POLYPTYCH
POLYPTYCHS
POLYPUS
POLYPUSES
POLYRHYTHM
POLYRHYTHMIC
POLYRHYTHMS
POLYRIBOSOMAL
POLYRIBOSOME
POLYRIBOSOMES
POLYS
POLYSACCHARIDE
POLYSACCHARIDES
POLYSEMIC
POLYSEMIES
POLYSEMOUS
POLYSEMY
POLYSOME
POLYSOMES
POLYSOMIC
POLYSOMICS
POLYSORBATE
POLYSORBATES
POLYSTICHOUS
POLYSTYRENE
POLYSTYRENES
POLYSULFIDE
POLYSULFIDES
POLYSYLLABIC
POLYSYLLABLE
POLYSYLLABLES
POLYSYNAPTIC
POLYSYNDETON
POLYSYNDETONS
POLYTECHNIC
POLYTECHNICS
POLYTENE
POLYTENIES
POLYTENY
POLYTHEISM
POLYTHEISMS
POLYTHEIST
POLYTHEISTIC
POLYTHEISTICAL
POLYTHEISTS
POLYTHENE
POLYTHENES
POLYTONAL
POLYTONALITIES
POLYTONALITY
POLYTONALLY
POLYTYPE
POLYTYPES
POLYTYPIC
POLYUNSATURATED
POLYURETHANE
POLYURETHANES
POLYURIA
POLYURIAS
POLYURIC
POLYVALENCE
POLYVALENCES
POLYVALENT
POLYVINYL
POLYWATER
POLYWATERS
POLYZOAN
POLYZOANS
POLYZOARIES
POLYZOARY
POLYZOIC
POM
POMACE
POMACEOUS
POMACES
POMADE
POMADED
POMADES
POMADING
POMANDER
POMANDERS
POMATUM
POMATUMS
POMBE
POMBES
POME
POMEGRANATE
POMEGRANATES
POMELO
POMELOS
POMES
POMFRET
POMFRETS
POMMEE
POMMEL
POMMELED
POMMELING
POMMELLED
POMMELLING
POMMELS
POMMIE
POMMIES
POMMY
POMO
POMOLOGICAL
POMOLOGIES
POMOLOGIST
POMOLOGISTS
POMOLOGY
POMOS
POMP
POMPADOUR
POMPADOURED
POMPADOURS
POMPANO
POMPANOS
POMPOM
POMPOMS
POMPON
POMPONS
POMPOSITIES
POMPOSITY
POMPOUS
POMPOUSLY
POMPOUSNESS
POMPOUSNESSES
POMPS
POMS
PONCE
PONCED
PONCES
PONCEY
PONCHO
PONCHOED
PONCHOS
PONCIER
PONCIEST
PONCING
PONCY
POND
PONDED
PONDER
PONDERABLE
PONDERED
PONDERER
PONDERERS
PONDERING
PONDEROSA
PONDEROSAS
PONDEROUS
PONDEROUSLY
PONDEROUSNESS
PONDEROUSNESSES
PONDERS
PONDING
PONDS
PONDWEED
PONDWEEDS
PONE
PONENT
PONES
PONG
PONGAL
PONGALS
PONGED
PONGEE
PONGEES
PONGID
PONGIDS
PONGIER
PONGIEST
PONGING
PONGO
PONGOS
PONGS
PONGY
PONIARD
PONIARDED
PONIARDING
PONIARDS
PONIED
PONIES
PONS
PONTES
PONTIFEX
PONTIFF
PONTIFFS
PONTIFIC
PONTIFICAL
PONTIFICALLY
PONTIFICALS
PONTIFICATE
PONTIFICATED
PONTIFICATES
PONTIFICATING
PONTIFICATION
PONTIFICATIONS
PONTIFICATOR
PONTIFICATORS
PONTIFICES
PONTIL
PONTILS
PONTINE
PONTON
PONTONIER
PONTONIERS
PONTONS
PONTOON

PONTOONED
PONTOONING
PONTOONS
PONY
PONYING
PONYTAIL
PONYTAILED
PONYTAILS
PONZU
PONZUS
POO
POOBAH
POOBAHS
POOCH
POOCHED
POOCHES
POOCHING
POOD
POODLE
POODLES
POODS
POOED
POOF
POOFIER
POOFIEST
POOFS
POOFTAH
POOFTAHS
POOFTER
POOFTERS
POOFY
POOH
POOHED
POOHING
POOHS
POOING
POOJA
POOJAS
POOKA
POOKAS
POOL
POOLED
POOLER
POOLERS
POOLHALL
POOLHALLS
POOLING
POOLROOM
POOLROOMS
POOLS
POOLSIDE
POOLSIDES
POON
POONS
POONTANG
POONTANGS
POOP
POOPED
POOPIER
POOPIEST
POOPING
POOPS
POOPY
POOR
POORER
POOREST
POORHOUSE
POORHOUSES
POORI
POORIS
POORISH
POORLY
POORMOUTH
POORMOUTHED
POORMOUTHING
POORMOUTHS
POORNESS
POORNESSES
POORTITH
POORTITHS
POORWILL
POORWILLS
POOS
POOVE
POOVES
POP
POPCORN
POPCORNS
POPE
POPEDOM
POPEDOMS
POPELESS
POPELIKE
POPERIES
POPERY
POPES
POPEYED
POPGUN
POPGUNS
POPINJAY
POPINJAYS
POPISH
POPISHLY
POPLAR
POPLARS
POPLIN
POPLINS
POPLITEAL
POPLITEI
POPLITEUS
POPLITIC
POPOUT
POPOUTS
POPOVER
POPOVERS
POPPA
POPPADOM
POPPADOMS
POPPADUM
POPPADUMS
POPPAS
POPPED
POPPER
POPPERS
POPPET
POPPETS
POPPIED
POPPIER
POPPIES
POPPIEST
POPPING
POPPLE
POPPLED
POPPLES
POPPLIER
POPPLIEST
POPPLING
POPPLY
POPPY
POPPYCOCK
POPPYCOCKS
POPPYHEAD
POPPYHEADS
POPS
POPSICLE
POPSICLES
POPSIE
POPSIES
POPSTER
POPSTERS
POPSY
POPULACE
POPULACES
POPULAR
POPULARISATION
POPULARISATIONS
POPULARISE
POPULARISED
POPULARISES
POPULARISING
POPULARITIES
POPULARITY
POPULARIZATION
POPULARIZATIONS
POPULARIZE
POPULARIZED
POPULARIZER
POPULARIZERS
POPULARIZES
POPULARIZING
POPULARLY
POPULATE
POPULATED
POPULATES
POPULATING
POPULATION
POPULATIONAL
POPULATIONS
POPULISM
POPULISMS
POPULIST
POPULISTIC
POPULISTS
POPULOUS
POPULOUSLY
POPULOUSNESS
POPULOUSNESSES
PORBEAGLE
PORBEAGLES
PORCELAIN
PORCELAINIZE
PORCELAINIZED
PORCELAINIZES
PORCELAINIZING
PORCELAINLIKE
PORCELAINS
PORCELANEOUS
PORCELLANEOUS
PORCH
PORCHED
PORCHES
PORCINE
PORCINI
PORCINIS
PORCINO
PORCUPINE
PORCUPINES
PORE
PORED
PORES
PORGIES
PORGY
PORIFERAL
PORIFERAN
PORIFERANS
PORIN
PORING
PORINS
PORISM
PORISMS
PORK
PORKED
PORKER
PORKERS
PORKIER
PORKIES
PORKIEST
PORKINESS
PORKINESSES
PORKING
PORKPIE
PORKPIES
PORKS
PORKWOOD
PORKWOODS
PORKY
PORN
PORNIER
PORNIEST
PORNO
PORNOGRAPHER
PORNOGRAPHERS
PORNOGRAPHIC
PORNOGRAPHIES
PORNOGRAPHY
PORNOS
PORNS
PORNY
POROMERIC
POROMERICS
POROSE
POROSITIES
POROSITY
POROUS
POROUSLY
POROUSNESS
POROUSNESSES
PORPHYRIA
PORPHYRIAS
PORPHYRIC
PORPHYRIES
PORPHYRIN
PORPHYRINS
PORPHYRITIC
PORPHYROPSIN

ORPHYROPSINS
ORPHYRY
ORPOISE
ORPOISED
ORPOISES
ORPOISING
ORRECT
ORRIDGE
ORRIDGES
ORRIDGY
ORRINGER
ORRINGERS
ORT
ORTABELLA
ORTABELLAS
ORTABELLO
ORTABELLOS
ORTABILITIES
ORTABILITY
ORTABLE
ORTABLES
ORTABLY
ORTAGE
ORTAGED
ORTAGES
ORTAGING
ORTAL
ORTALED
ORTALS
ORTAMENTI
ORTAMENTO
ORTANCE
ORTANCES
ORTAPACK
ORTAPACKS
ORTAPAK
ORTAPAKS
ORTATIVE
ORTCULLIS
ORTCULLISES
ORTED
ORTEND
ORTENDED
ORTENDING
ORTENDS
ORTENT
RTENTOUS
RTENTOUSLY
RTENTOUSNESS
RTENTS
RTER
RTERAGE
RTERAGES
PORTERED
PORTERESS
PORTERESSES
PORTERHOUSE
PORTERHOUSES
PORTERING
PORTERS
PORTFOLIO
PORTFOLIOS
PORTHOLE
PORTHOLES
PORTICO
PORTICOED
PORTICOES
PORTICOS
PORTIERE
PORTIERES
PORTING
PORTION
PORTIONED
PORTIONER
PORTIONERS
PORTIONING
PORTIONLESS
PORTIONS
PORTLESS
PORTLIER
PORTLIEST
PORTLINESS
PORTLINESSES
PORTLY
PORTMANTEAU
PORTMANTEAUS
PORTMANTEAUX
PORTOBELLO
PORTOBELLOS
PORTOLAN
PORTOLANS
PORTRAIT
PORTRAITIST
PORTRAITISTS
PORTRAITS
PORTRAITURE
PORTRAITURES
PORTRAY
PORTRAYAL
PORTRAYALS
PORTRAYED
PORTRAYER
PORTRAYERS
PORTRAYING
PORTRAYS
PORTRESS
PORTRESSES
PORTS
PORTSIDE
PORTULACA
PORTULACAS
POS
POSABLE
POSADA
POSADAS
POSE
POSEABLE
POSED
POSER
POSERS
POSES
POSEUR
POSEURS
POSEY
POSEYS
POSH
POSHER
POSHEST
POSHLY
POSHNESS
POSHNESSES
POSIER
POSIES
POSIEST
POSING
POSINGLY
POSIT
POSITED
POSITING
POSITION
POSITIONAL
POSITIONALLY
POSITIONED
POSITIONING
POSITIONS
POSITIVE
POSITIVELY
POSITIVENESS
POSITIVENESSES
POSITIVER
POSITIVES
POSITIVEST
POSITIVISM
POSITIVISMS
POSITIVIST
POSITIVISTIC
POSITIVISTS
POSITIVITIES
POSITIVITY
POSITRON
POSITRONIUM
POSITRONIUMS
POSITRONS
POSITS
POSOLE
POSOLES
POSOLOGIC
POSOLOGIES
POSOLOGY
POSSE
POSSES
POSSESS
POSSESSED
POSSESSEDLY
POSSESSEDNESS
POSSESSEDNESSES
POSSESSES
POSSESSING
POSSESSION
POSSESSIONAL
POSSESSIONLESS
POSSESSIONS
POSSESSIVE
POSSESSIVELY
POSSESSIVENESS
POSSESSIVES
POSSESSOR
POSSESSORS
POSSESSORY
POSSET
POSSETS
POSSIBILITIES
POSSIBILITY
POSSIBLE
POSSIBLER
POSSIBLES
POSSIBLEST
POSSIBLY
POSSUM
POSSUMS
POST
POSTABORTION
POSTACCIDENT
POSTADOLESCENT
POSTAGE
POSTAGES
POSTAL
POSTALLY
POSTALS
POSTAMPUTATION
POSTANAL
POSTAPARTHEID
POSTAPOCALYPTIC
POSTARREST
POSTATOMIC
POSTATTACK
POSTAXIAL
POSTBAG
POSTBAGS
POSTBASE
POSTBELLUM
POSTBIBLICAL
POSTBOURGEOIS
POSTBOX
POSTBOXES
POSTBOY
POSTBOYS
POSTBURN
POSTCAPITALIST
POSTCARD
POSTCARDLIKE
POSTCARDS
POSTCAVA
POSTCAVAE
POSTCAVAL
POSTCAVAS
POSTCLASSIC
POSTCLASSICAL
POSTCODE
POSTCODES
POSTCOITAL
POSTCOLLEGE
POSTCOLLEGIATE
POSTCOLONIAL
POSTCOMMUNIST
POSTCONCEPTION
POSTCONCERT
POSTCONQUEST
POSTCONSONANTAL
POSTCONSUMER
POSTCONVENTION
POSTCOPULATORY
POSTCORONARY
POSTCOUP
POSTCRANIAL
POSTCRANIALLY
POSTCRASH
POSTCRISIS
POSTDATE
POSTDATED
POSTDATES
POSTDATING
POSTDEADLINE
POSTDEBATE
POSTDEBUTANTE

POSTDELIVERY
POSTDEPRESSION
POSTDEVALUATION
POSTDILUVIAN
POSTDILUVIANS
POSTDIVE
POSTDIVESTITURE
POSTDIVORCE
POSTDOC
POSTDOCS
POSTDOCTORAL
POSTDOCTORALS
POSTDOCTORATE
POSTDOCTORATES
POSTDRUG
POSTED
POSTEDITING
POSTEEN
POSTEENS
POSTELECTION
POSTEMBRYONAL
POSTEMBRYONIC
POSTEMERGENCE
POSTEMERGENCY
POSTEPILEPTIC
POSTER
POSTERED
POSTERING
POSTERIOR
POSTERIORITIES
POSTERIORITY
POSTERIORLY
POSTERIORS
POSTERITIES
POSTERITY
POSTERN
POSTERNS
POSTEROLATERAL
POSTERS
POSTERUPTIVE
POSTEXERCISE
POSTEXILIC
POSTEXPERIENCE
POSTEXPOSURE
POSTFACE
POSTFACES
POSTFAULT
POSTFEMINIST
POSTFEMINISTS
POSTFIRE
POSTFIX
POSTFIXAL
POSTFIXED
POSTFIXES
POSTFIXING
POSTFLIGHT
POSTFORM
POSTFORMED
POSTFORMING
POSTFORMS
POSTFRACTURE
POSTFREEZE
POSTGAME
POSTGANGLIONIC
POSTGLACIAL
POSTGRAD
POSTGRADS
POSTGRADUATE
POSTGRADUATES
POSTGRADUATION
POSTHARVEST
POSTHASTE
POSTHASTES
POSTHEAT
POSTHEATS
POSTHEMORRHAGIC
POSTHOLE
POSTHOLES
POSTHOLIDAY
POSTHOLOCAUST
POSTHOSPITAL
POSTHUMOUS
POSTHUMOUSLY
POSTHUMOUSNESS
POSTHYPNOTIC
POSTICHE
POSTICHES
POSTIE
POSTIES
POSTILION
POSTILIONS
POSTILLION
POSTILLIONS
POSTIMPACT
POSTIMPERIAL
POSTIN
POSTINAUGURAL
POSTINDUSTRIAL
POSTINFECTION
POSTING
POSTINGS
POSTINJECTION
POSTINOCULATION
POSTINS
POSTIQUE
POSTIQUES
POSTIRRADIATION
POSTISCHEMIC
POSTISOLATION
POSTLANDING
POSTLAPSARIAN
POSTLAPSARIANS
POSTLAUNCH
POSTLIBERATION
POSTLITERATE
POSTLITERATES
POSTLUDE
POSTLUDES
POSTMAN
POSTMARITAL
POSTMARK
POSTMARKED
POSTMARKING
POSTMARKS
POSTMASTECTOMY
POSTMASTER
POSTMASTERS
POSTMASTERSHIP
POSTMASTERSHIPS
POSTMATING
POSTMEDIEVAL
POSTMEN
POSTMENOPAUSAL
POSTMENOPAUSE
POSTMIDNIGHT
POSTMILLENARIAN
POSTMILLENNIAL
POSTMILLENNIALS
POSTMISTRESS
POSTMISTRESSES
POSTMODERN
POSTMODERNISM
POSTMODERNISMS
POSTMODERNIST
POSTMODERNISTS
POSTMODERNITIES
POSTMODERNITY
POSTMODERNS
POSTMORTEM
POSTMORTEMS
POSTNASAL
POSTNATAL
POSTNATALLY
POSTNEONATAL
POSTNUPTIAL
POSTNUPTIALS
POSTOP
POSTOPERATIVE
POSTOPERATIVELY
POSTOPS
POSTORAL
POSTORBITAL
POSTORGASMIC
POSTPAID
POSTPARTUM
POSTPOLLINATION
POSTPONABLE
POSTPONE
POSTPONED
POSTPONEMENT
POSTPONEMENTS
POSTPONER
POSTPONERS
POSTPONES
POSTPONING
POSTPOSE
POSTPOSED
POSTPOSES
POSTPOSING
POSTPOSITION
POSTPOSITIONAL
POSTPOSITIONS
POSTPOSITIVE
POSTPOSITIVELY
POSTPRANDIAL
POSTPRANDIALLY
POSTPRIMARY
POSTPRISON
POSTPRODUCTION
POSTPRODUCTIONS
POSTPUBERTY
POSTPUBESCENT
POSTPUBESCENTS
POSTPUNK
POSTRACE
POSTRECESSION
POSTRETIREMENT
POSTRIDER
POSTRIDERS
POSTRIOT
POSTROMANTIC
POSTROMANTICS
POSTS
POSTSCRIPT
POSTSCRIPTS
POSTSEASON
POSTSEASONS
POSTSECONDARIES
POSTSECONDARY
POSTSHOW
POSTSTIMULATION
POSTSTIMULATORY
POSTSTIMULUS
POSTSTRIKE
POSTSURGICAL
POSTSURGICALLY
POSTSYNAPTIC
POSTSYNC
POSTSYNCED
POSTSYNCING
POSTSYNCS
POSTTAX
POSTTEEN
POSTTEENS
POSTTENSION
POSTTENSIONED
POSTTENSIONING
POSTTENSIONS
POSTTEST
POSTTESTS
POSTTRANSFUSION
POSTTRAUMATIC
POSTTREATMENT
POSTTREATMENTS
POSTTRIAL
POSTULANCIES
POSTULANCY
POSTULANT
POSTULANTS
POSTULATE
POSTULATED
POSTULATES
POSTULATING
POSTULATION
POSTULATIONAL
POSTULATIONS
POSTULATOR
POSTULATORS
POSTURAL
POSTURE
POSTURED
POSTURER
POSTURERS
POSTURES
POSTURING
POSTURIST
POSTURISTS
POSTVACCINAL
POSTVACCINATION
POSTVAGOTOMY
POSTVASECTOMY
POSTVOCALIC
POSTWAR
POSTWEANING
POSTWOMAN

POSTWOMEN
POSTWORKSHOP
POSY
POT
POTABILITIES
POTABILITY
POTABLE
POTABLENESS
POTABLENESSES
POTABLES
POTAGE
POTAGES
POTAMIC
POTASH
POTASHES
POTASSIC
POTASSIUM
POTASSIUMS
POTATION
POTATIONS
POTATO
POTATOBUG
POTATOBUGS
POTATOES
POTATORY
POTBELLIED
POTBELLIES
POTBELLY
POTBOIL
POTBOILED
POTBOILER
POTBOILERS
POTBOILING
POTBOILS
POTBOUND
POTBOY
POTBOYS
POTEEN
POTEENS
POTENCE
POTENCES
POTENCIES
POTENCY
POTENT
POTENTATE
POTENTATES
POTENTIAL
POTENTIALITIES
POTENTIALITY
POTENTIALLY
POTENTIALS
POTENTIATE
POTENTIATED
POTENTIATES
POTENTIATING
POTENTIATION
POTENTIATIONS
POTENTIATOR
POTENTIATORS
POTENTILLA
POTENTILLAS
POTENTIOMETER
POTENTIOMETERS
POTENTIOMETRIC
POTENTLY
POTFUL
POTFULS
POTHEAD
POTHEADS
POTHEEN
POTHEENS
POTHER
POTHERB
POTHERBS
POTHERED
POTHERING
POTHERS
POTHOLDER
POTHOLDERS
POTHOLE
POTHOLED
POTHOLER
POTHOLERS
POTHOLES
POTHOLING
POTHOLINGS
POTHOOK
POTHOOKS
POTHOS
POTHOUSE
POTHOUSES
POTHUNTER
POTHUNTERS
POTHUNTING
POTHUNTINGS
POTICHE
POTICHES
POTION
POTIONS
POTLACH
POTLACHE
POTLACHES
POTLATCH
POTLATCHED
POTLATCHES
POTLATCHING
POTLIKE
POTLINE
POTLINES
POTLUCK
POTLUCKS
POTMAN
POTMEN
POTOMETER
POTOMETERS
POTPIE
POTPIES
POTPOURRI
POTPOURRIS
POTS
POTSHARD
POTSHARDS
POTSHERD
POTSHERDS
POTSHOT
POTSHOTS
POTSHOTTING
POTSIE
POTSIES
POTSTONE
POTSTONES
POTSY
POTTAGE
POTTAGES
POTTED
POTTEEN
POTTEENS
POTTER
POTTERED
POTTERER
POTTERERS
POTTERIES
POTTERING
POTTERINGLY
POTTERS
POTTERY
POTTIER
POTTIES
POTTIEST
POTTINESS
POTTINESSES
POTTING
POTTLE
POTTLES
POTTO
POTTOS
POTTY
POTZER
POTZERS
POUCH
POUCHED
POUCHES
POUCHIER
POUCHIEST
POUCHING
POUCHY
POUF
POUFED
POUFF
POUFFE
POUFFED
POUFFES
POUFFS
POUFFY
POUFS
POULARD
POULARDE
POULARDES
POULARDS
POULT
POULTER
POULTERER
POULTERERS
POULTERS
POULTICE
POULTICED
POULTICES
POULTICING
POULTRIES
POULTRY
POULTRYMAN
POULTRYMEN
POULTS
POUNCE
POUNCED
POUNCER
POUNCERS
POUNCES
POUNCING
POUND
POUNDAGE
POUNDAGES
POUNDAL
POUNDALS
POUNDCAKE
POUNDCAKES
POUNDED
POUNDER
POUNDERS
POUNDING
POUNDS
POUR
POURABLE
POURBOIRE
POURBOIRES
POURED
POURER
POURERS
POURING
POURINGLY
POURPARLER
POURPARLERS
POURPOINT
POURPOINTS
POURS
POUSSETTE
POUSSETTED
POUSSETTES
POUSSETTING
POUSSIE
POUSSIES
POUT
POUTED
POUTER
POUTERS
POUTFUL
POUTIER
POUTIEST
POUTINE
POUTINES
POUTING
POUTINGLY
POUTS
POUTY
POVERTIES
POVERTY
POW
POWDER
POWDERED
POWDERER
POWDERERS
POWDERING
POWDERLESS
POWDERLIKE
POWDERS
POWDERY
POWER
POWERBOAT
POWERBOATER
POWERBOATERS
POWERBOATING
POWERBOATS
POWERED
POWERFUL
POWERFULLY

POWERHOUSE
POWERHOUSES
POWERING
POWERLESS
POWERLESSLY
POWERLESSNESS
POWERLESSNESSES
POWERS
POWS
POWTER
POWTERS
POWWOW
POWWOWED
POWWOWING
POWWOWS
POX
POXED
POXES
POXIER
POXIEST
POXING
POXVIRUS
POXVIRUSES
POXY
POYOU
POYOUS
POZOLE
POZOLES
POZZOLAN
POZZOLANA
POZZOLANAS
POZZOLANIC
POZZOLANS
PRAAM
PRAAMS
PRACTIC
PRACTICABILITY
PRACTICABLE
PRACTICABLENESS
PRACTICABLY
PRACTICAL
PRACTICALITIES
PRACTICALITY
PRACTICALLY
PRACTICALNESS
PRACTICALNESSES
PRACTICALS
PRACTICE
PRACTICED
PRACTICER
PRACTICERS
PRACTICES
PRACTICING
PRACTICUM
PRACTICUMS
PRACTISE
PRACTISED
PRACTISES
PRACTISING
PRACTITIONER
PRACTITIONERS
PRAECIPE
PRAECIPES
PRAEDIAL
PRAEFECT
PRAEFECTS
PRAELECT
PRAELECTED
PRAELECTING
PRAELECTS
PRAEMUNIRE
PRAEMUNIRES
PRAENOMEN
PRAENOMENS
PRAENOMINA
PRAESIDIA
PRAESIDIUM
PRAESIDIUMS
PRAETOR
PRAETORIAL
PRAETORIAN
PRAETORIANS
PRAETORS
PRAETORSHIP
PRAETORSHIPS
PRAGMATIC
PRAGMATICAL
PRAGMATICALLY
PRAGMATICISM
PRAGMATICISMS
PRAGMATICIST
PRAGMATICISTS
PRAGMATICS
PRAGMATISM
PRAGMATISMS
PRAGMATIST
PRAGMATISTIC
PRAGMATISTS
PRAHU
PRAHUS
PRAIRIE
PRAIRIES
PRAISE
PRAISED
PRAISER
PRAISERS
PRAISES
PRAISEWORTHIER
PRAISEWORTHIEST
PRAISEWORTHILY
PRAISEWORTHY
PRAISING
PRAJNA
PRAJNAS
PRALINE
PRALINES
PRALLTRILLER
PRALLTRILLERS
PRAM
PRAMS
PRANA
PRANAS
PRANCE
PRANCED
PRANCER
PRANCERS
PRANCES
PRANCING
PRANDIAL
PRANG
PRANGED
PRANGING
PRANGS
PRANK
PRANKED
PRANKING
PRANKISH
PRANKISHLY
PRANKISHNESS
PRANKISHNESSES
PRANKS
PRANKSTER
PRANKSTERS
PRAO
PRAOS
PRASE
PRASEODYMIUM
PRASEODYMIUMS
PRASES
PRAT
PRATE
PRATED
PRATER
PRATERS
PRATES
PRATFALL
PRATFALLS
PRATIE
PRATIES
PRATINCOLE
PRATINCOLES
PRATING
PRATINGLY
PRATIQUE
PRATIQUES
PRATS
PRATTLE
PRATTLED
PRATTLER
PRATTLERS
PRATTLES
PRATTLING
PRATTLINGLY
PRAU
PRAUS
PRAVASTATIN
PRAVASTATINS
PRAWN
PRAWNED
PRAWNER
PRAWNERS
PRAWNING
PRAWNS
PRAXEOLOGICAL
PRAXEOLOGIES
PRAXEOLOGY
PRAXES
PRAXIS
PRAXISES
PRAY
PRAYED
PRAYER
PRAYERFUL
PRAYERFULLY
PRAYERFULNESS
PRAYERFULNESSES
PRAYERS
PRAYING
PRAYS
PREABSORB
PREABSORBED
PREABSORBING
PREABSORBS
PREACCUSE
PREACCUSED
PREACCUSES
PREACCUSING
PREACH
PREACHED
PREACHER
PREACHERS
PREACHES
PREACHIER
PREACHIEST
PREACHIFIED
PREACHIFIES
PREACHIFY
PREACHIFYING
PREACHILY
PREACHINESS
PREACHINESSES
PREACHING
PREACHINGLY
PREACHMENT
PREACHMENTS
PREACHY
PREACT
PREACTED
PREACTING
PREACTS
PREADAPT
PREADAPTATION
PREADAPTATIONS
PREADAPTED
PREADAPTING
PREADAPTIVE
PREADAPTS
PREADJUST
PREADJUSTED
PREADJUSTING
PREADJUSTS
PREADMISSION
PREADMISSIONS
PREADMIT
PREADMITS
PREADMITTED
PREADMITTING
PREADOLESCENCE
PREADOLESCENCES
PREADOLESCENT
PREADOLESCENTS
PREADOPT
PREADOPTED
PREADOPTING
PREADOPTS
PREADULT
PREADULTS
PREAGED
PREAGRICULTURAL
PREALLOT
PREALLOTS
PREALLOTTED
PREALLOTTING
PREALTER
PREALTERED

PREALTERING
PREALTERS
PREAMBLE
PREAMBLED
PREAMBLES
PREAMP
PREAMPLIFIER
PREAMPLIFIERS
PREAMPS
PREANAL
PREANESTHETIC
PREANNOUNCE
PREANNOUNCED
PREANNOUNCES
PREANNOUNCING
PREAPPLIED
PREAPPLIES
PREAPPLY
PREAPPLYING
PREAPPROVAL
PREAPPROVALS
PREAPPROVE
PREAPPROVED
PREAPPROVES
PREAPPROVING
PREARM
PREARMED
PREARMING
PREARMS
PREARRANGE
PREARRANGED
PREARRANGEMENT
PREARRANGEMENTS
PREARRANGES
PREARRANGING
PREASSEMBLED
PREASSIGN
PREASSIGNED
PREASSIGNING
PREASSIGNS
PREASSURE
PREASSURED
PREASSURES
PREASSURING
PREATOMIC
PREATTUNE
PREATTUNED
PREATTUNES
PREATTUNING
PREAUDIT
PREAUDITS
PREAVER
PREAVERRED

PREAVERRING
PREAVERS
PREAXIAL
PREBADE
PREBAKE
PREBAKED
PREBAKES
PREBAKING
PREBASAL
PREBATTLE
PREBEND
PREBENDAL
PREBENDARIES
PREBENDARY
PREBENDS
PREBIBLICAL
PREBID
PREBIDDEN
PREBIDDING
PREBIDS
PREBILL
PREBILLED
PREBILLING
PREBILLS
PREBIND
PREBINDING
PREBINDS
PREBIOLOGIC
PREBIOLOGICAL
PREBIOTIC
PREBIRTH
PREBIRTHS
PREBLESS
PREBLESSED
PREBLESSES
PREBLESSING
PREBOARD
PREBOARDED
PREBOARDING
PREBOARDS
PREBOIL
PREBOILED
PREBOILING
PREBOILS
PREBOOK
PREBOOKED
PREBOOKING
PREBOOKS
PREBOOM
PREBOUGHT
PREBOUND
PREBREAKFAST
PREBUDGET

PREBUDGETS
PREBUILD
PREBUILDING
PREBUILDS
PREBUILT
PREBUY
PREBUYING
PREBUYS
PRECALCULI
PRECALCULUS
PRECALCULUSES
PRECANCEL
PRECANCELED
PRECANCELING
PRECANCELLATION
PRECANCELLED
PRECANCELLING
PRECANCELS
PRECANCER
PRECANCEROUS
PRECANCERS
PRECAPITALIST
PRECARIOUS
PRECARIOUSLY
PRECARIOUSNESS
PRECAST
PRECASTING
PRECASTS
PRECATIVE
PRECATORY
PRECAUDAL
PRECAUTION
PRECAUTIONARY
PRECAUTIONS
PRECAVA
PRECAVAE
PRECAVAL
PRECEDE
PRECEDED
PRECEDENCE
PRECEDENCES
PRECEDENCIES
PRECEDENCY
PRECEDENT
PRECEDENTS
PRECEDES
PRECEDING
PRECENSOR
PRECENSORED
PRECENSORING
PRECENSORS
PRECENT
PRECENTED

PRECENTING
PRECENTOR
PRECENTORIAL
PRECENTORS
PRECENTORSHIP
PRECENTORSHIPS
PRECENTS
PRECEPT
PRECEPTIVE
PRECEPTOR
PRECEPTORIAL
PRECEPTORIALS
PRECEPTORIES
PRECEPTORS
PRECEPTORSHIP
PRECEPTORSHIPS
PRECEPTORY
PRECEPTS
PRECESS
PRECESSED
PRECESSES
PRECESSING
PRECESSION
PRECESSIONAL
PRECESSIONS
PRECHARGE
PRECHARGED
PRECHARGES
PRECHARGING
PRECHECK
PRECHECKED
PRECHECKING
PRECHECKS
PRECHILL
PRECHILLED
PRECHILLING
PRECHILLS
PRECHOOSE
PRECHOOSES
PRECHOOSING
PRECHOSE
PRECHOSEN
PRECIEUSE
PRECIEUX
PRECINCT
PRECINCTS
PRECIOSITIES
PRECIOSITY
PRECIOUS
PRECIOUSES
PRECIOUSLY
PRECIOUSNESS
PRECIOUSNESSES

PRECIP
PRECIPE
PRECIPES
PRECIPICE
PRECIPICES
PRECIPITABLE
PRECIPITANCE
PRECIPITANCES
PRECIPITANCIES
PRECIPITANCY
PRECIPITANT
PRECIPITANTLY
PRECIPITANTNESS
PRECIPITANTS
PRECIPITATE
PRECIPITATED
PRECIPITATELY
PRECIPITATENESS
PRECIPITATES
PRECIPITATING
PRECIPITATION
PRECIPITATIONS
PRECIPITATIVE
PRECIPITATOR
PRECIPITATORS
PRECIPITIN
PRECIPITINOGEN
PRECIPITINOGENS
PRECIPITINS
PRECIPITOUS
PRECIPITOUSLY
PRECIPITOUSNESS
PRECIPS
PRECIS
PRECISE
PRECISED
PRECISELY
PRECISENESS
PRECISENESSES
PRECISER
PRECISES
PRECISEST
PRECISIAN
PRECISIANS
PRECISING
PRECISION
PRECISIONIST
PRECISIONISTS
PRECISIONS
PRECITED
PRECLEAN
PRECLEANED
PRECLEANING

PRECLEANS
PRECLEAR
PRECLEARANCE
PRECLEARANCES
PRECLEARED
PRECLEARING
PRECLEARS
PRECLINICAL
PRECLUDE
PRECLUDED
PRECLUDES
PRECLUDING
PRECLUSION
PRECLUSIONS
PRECLUSIVE
PRECLUSIVELY
PRECOCIAL
PRECOCIOUS
PRECOCIOUSLY
PRECOCIOUSNESS
PRECOCITIES
PRECOCITY
PRECODE
PRECODED
PRECODES
PRECODING
PRECOGNITION
PRECOGNITIONS
PRECOGNITIVE
PRECOITAL
PRECOLLEGE
PRECOLLEGIATE
PRECOLONIAL
PRECOLONIALS
PRECOMBUSTION
PRECOMBUSTIONS
PRECOMMITMENT
PRECOMMITMENTS
PRECOMPUTE
PRECOMPUTED
PRECOMPUTER
PRECOMPUTERS
PRECOMPUTES
PRECOMPUTING
PRECONCEIVE
PRECONCEIVED
PRECONCEIVES
PRECONCEIVING
PRECONCEPTION
PRECONCEPTIONS
PRECONCERT
PRECONCERTED
PRECONCERTING
PRECONCERTS
PRECONCILIAR
PRECONDITION
PRECONDITIONED
PRECONDITIONING
PRECONDITIONS
PRECONIZE
PRECONIZED
PRECONIZES
PRECONIZING
PRECONQUEST
PRECONSCIOUS
PRECONSCIOUSES
PRECONSCIOUSLY
PRECONSONANTAL
PRECONSTRUCTED
PRECONTACT
PRECONVENTION
PRECONVICTION
PRECONVICTIONS
PRECOOK
PRECOOKED
PRECOOKER
PRECOOKERS
PRECOOKING
PRECOOKS
PRECOOL
PRECOOLED
PRECOOLING
PRECOOLS
PRECOPULATORY
PRECOUP
PRECRASH
PRECREASE
PRECREASED
PRECREASES
PRECREASING
PRECRISIS
PRECRITICAL
PRECURE
PRECURED
PRECURES
PRECURING
PRECURSOR
PRECURSORS
PRECURSORY
PRECUT
PRECUTS
PRECUTTING
PREDACEOUS
PREDACEOUSNESS
PREDACIOUS
PREDACITIES
PREDACITY
PREDATE
PREDATED
PREDATES
PREDATING
PREDATION
PREDATIONS
PREDATISM
PREDATISMS
PREDATOR
PREDATORS
PREDATORY
PREDAWN
PREDAWNS
PREDEATH
PREDEATHS
PREDEBATE
PREDECEASE
PREDECEASED
PREDECEASES
PREDECEASING
PREDECESSOR
PREDECESSORS
PREDEDUCT
PREDEDUCTED
PREDEDUCTING
PREDEDUCTS
PREDEFINE
PREDEFINED
PREDEFINES
PREDEFINING
PREDELIVERIES
PREDELIVERY
PREDELLA
PREDELLAS
PREDEPARTURE
PREDESIGNATE
PREDESIGNATED
PREDESIGNATES
PREDESIGNATING
PREDESTINARIAN
PREDESTINARIANS
PREDESTINATE
PREDESTINATED
PREDESTINATES
PREDESTINATING
PREDESTINATION
PREDESTINATIONS
PREDESTINATOR
PREDESTINATORS
PREDESTINE
PREDESTINED
PREDESTINES
PREDESTINING
PREDETERMINE
PREDETERMINED
PREDETERMINER
PREDETERMINERS
PREDETERMINES
PREDETERMINING
PREDEVALUATION
PREDEVELOPMENT
PREDEVELOPMENTS
PREDIABETES
PREDIABETESES
PREDIABETIC
PREDIABETICS
PREDIAL
PREDICABLE
PREDICABLES
PREDICAMENT
PREDICAMENTS
PREDICANT
PREDICANTS
PREDICATE
PREDICATED
PREDICATES
PREDICATING
PREDICATION
PREDICATIONS
PREDICATIVE
PREDICATIVELY
PREDICATORY
PREDICT
PREDICTABILITY
PREDICTABLE
PREDICTABLY
PREDICTED
PREDICTING
PREDICTION
PREDICTIONS
PREDICTIVE
PREDICTIVELY
PREDICTOR
PREDICTORS
PREDICTS
PREDIGEST
PREDIGESTED
PREDIGESTING
PREDIGESTION
PREDIGESTIONS
PREDIGESTS
PREDILECTION
PREDILECTIONS
PREDINNER
PREDINNERS
PREDISCHARGE
PREDISCOVERIES
PREDISCOVERY
PREDISPOSE
PREDISPOSED
PREDISPOSES
PREDISPOSING
PREDISPOSITION
PREDISPOSITIONS
PREDIVE
PREDNISOLONE
PREDNISOLONES
PREDNISONE
PREDNISONES
PREDOCTORAL
PREDOCTORALS
PREDOMINANCE
PREDOMINANCES
PREDOMINANCIES
PREDOMINANCY
PREDOMINANT
PREDOMINANTLY
PREDOMINATE
PREDOMINATED
PREDOMINATELY
PREDOMINATES
PREDOMINATING
PREDOMINATION
PREDOMINATIONS
PREDRAFT
PREDRIED
PREDRIES
PREDRILL
PREDRILLED
PREDRILLING
PREDRILLS
PREDRY
PREDRYING
PREDUSK
PREDUSKS
PREDYNASTIC
PREE
PREECLAMPSIA
PREECLAMPSIAS
PREECLAMPTIC
PREED
PREEDIT
PREEDITED
PREEDITING
PREEDITS
PREEING
PREELECT
PREELECTED

PREELECTING
PREELECTION
PREELECTRIC
PREELECTRONIC
PREELECTS
PREEMBARGO
PREEMERGENCE
PREEMERGENCES
PREEMERGENT
PREEMIE
PREEMIES
PREEMINENCE
PREEMINENCES
PREEMINENT
PREEMINENTLY
PREEMPLOYMENT
PREEMPT
PREEMPTED
PREEMPTING
PREEMPTION
PREEMPTIONS
PREEMPTIVE
PREEMPTIVELY
PREEMPTOR
PREEMPTORS
PREEMPTS
PREEN
PREENACT
PREENACTED
PREENACTING
PREENACTS
PREENED
PREENER
PREENERS
PREENING
PREENROLLMENT
PREENROLLMENTS
PREENS
PREERECT
PREERECTED
PREERECTING
PREERECTS
PREES
PREESTABLISH
PREESTABLISHED
PREESTABLISHES
PREESTABLISHING
PREETHICAL
PREEXCITE
PREEXCITED
PREEXCITES
PREEXCITING
PREEXEMPT
PREEXEMPTED
PREEXEMPTING
PREEXEMPTS
PREEXILIC
PREEXIST
PREEXISTED
PREEXISTENCE
PREEXISTENCES
PREEXISTENT
PREEXISTING
PREEXISTS
PREEXPERIMENT
PREEXPERIMENTS
PREEXPOSE
PREEXPOSED
PREEXPOSES
PREEXPOSING
PREFAB
PREFABBED
PREFABBING
PREFABRICATE
PREFABRICATED
PREFABRICATES
PREFABRICATING
PREFABRICATION
PREFABRICATIONS
PREFABS
PREFACE
PREFACED
PREFACER
PREFACERS
PREFACES
PREFACING
PREFADE
PREFADED
PREFADES
PREFADING
PREFASCIST
PREFASCISTS
PREFATORY
PREFECT
PREFECTS
PREFECTURAL
PREFECTURE
PREFECTURES
PREFEMINIST
PREFEMINISTS
PREFER
PREFERABILITIES
PREFERABILITY
PREFERABLE
PREFERABLY
PREFERENCE
PREFERENCES
PREFERENTIAL
PREFERENTIALLY
PREFERMENT
PREFERMENTS
PREFERRED
PREFERRER
PREFERRERS
PREFERRING
PREFERS
PREFEUDAL
PREFIGHT
PREFIGURATION
PREFIGURATIONS
PREFIGURATIVE
PREFIGURATIVELY
PREFIGURE
PREFIGURED
PREFIGUREMENT
PREFIGUREMENTS
PREFIGURES
PREFIGURING
PREFILE
PREFILED
PREFILES
PREFILING
PREFILLED
PREFINANCE
PREFINANCED
PREFINANCES
PREFINANCING
PREFIRE
PREFIRED
PREFIRES
PREFIRING
PREFIX
PREFIXAL
PREFIXED
PREFIXES
PREFIXING
PREFIXION
PREFIXIONS
PREFLAME
PREFLIGHT
PREFLIGHTED
PREFLIGHTING
PREFLIGHTS
PREFOCUS
PREFOCUSED
PREFOCUSES
PREFOCUSING
PREFOCUSSED
PREFOCUSSES
PREFOCUSSING
PREFORM
PREFORMAT
PREFORMATION
PREFORMATIONIST
PREFORMATIONS
PREFORMATS
PREFORMATTED
PREFORMATTING
PREFORMED
PREFORMING
PREFORMS
PREFORMULATE
PREFORMULATED
PREFORMULATES
PREFORMULATING
PREFRANK
PREFRANKED
PREFRANKING
PREFRANKS
PREFREEZE
PREFREEZES
PREFREEZING
PREFRESHMAN
PREFRESHMEN
PREFRONTAL
PREFRONTALS
PREFROZE
PREFROZEN
PREFUND
PREFUNDED
PREFUNDING
PREFUNDS
PREGAME
PREGAMES
PREGANGLIONIC
PREGENITAL
PREGENITALS
PREGGERS
PREGNABILITIES
PREGNABILITY
PREGNABLE
PREGNANCIES
PREGNANCY
PREGNANT
PREGNANTLY
PREGNENOLONE
PREGNENOLONES
PREGROWTH
PREGROWTHS
PREGUIDE
PREGUIDED
PREGUIDES
PREGUIDING
PREHANDLE
PREHANDLED
PREHANDLES
PREHANDLING
PREHARDEN
PREHARDENED
PREHARDENING
PREHARDENS
PREHARVEST
PREHARVESTED
PREHARVESTING
PREHARVESTS
PREHEADACHE
PREHEAT
PREHEATED
PREHEATER
PREHEATERS
PREHEATING
PREHEATS
PREHENSILE
PREHENSILITIES
PREHENSILITY
PREHENSION
PREHENSIONS
PREHIRING
PREHISTORIAN
PREHISTORIANS
PREHISTORIC
PREHISTORICAL
PREHISTORICALLY
PREHISTORIES
PREHISTORY
PREHOLIDAY
PREHOLIDAYS
PREHOMINID
PREHOMINIDS
PREHUMAN
PREHUMANS
PREIGNITION
PREIGNITIONS
PREIMPLANTATION
PREIMPOSE
PREIMPOSED
PREIMPOSES
PREIMPOSING
PREINAUGURAL
PREINDUCTION
PREINDUCTIONS
PREINDUSTRIAL
PREINFORM
PREINFORMED
PREINFORMING

PREINFORMS
PREINSERT
PREINSERTED
PREINSERTING
PREINSERTS
PREINSTALL
PREINSTALLATION
PREINSTALLED
PREINSTALLING
PREINSTALLS
PREINTERVIEW
PREINTERVIEWED
PREINTERVIEWING
PREINTERVIEWS
PREINVASION
PREINVITE
PREINVITED
PREINVITES
PREINVITING
PREJUDGE
PREJUDGED
PREJUDGER
PREJUDGERS
PREJUDGES
PREJUDGING
PREJUDGMENT
PREJUDGMENTS
PREJUDICE
PREJUDICED
PREJUDICES
PREJUDICIAL
PREJUDICIALLY
PREJUDICIALNESS
PREJUDICING
PREKINDERGARTEN
PRELACIES
PRELACY
PRELAPSARIAN
PRELAPSARIANS
PRELATE
PRELATES
PRELATIC
PRELATISM
PRELATISMS
PRELATURE
PRELATURES
PRELAUNCH
PRELAUNCHED
PRELAUNCHES
PRELAUNCHING
PRELAW
PRELECT
PRELECTED
PRELECTING
PRELECTION
PRELECTIONS
PRELECTOR
PRELECTORS
PRELECTS
PRELEGAL
PRELIBATION
PRELIBATIONS
PRELIFE
PRELIM
PRELIMINARIES
PRELIMINARILY
PRELIMINARY
PRELIMIT
PRELIMITED
PRELIMITING
PRELIMITS
PRELIMS
PRELITERARY
PRELITERATE
PRELITERATES
PRELIVES
PRELOAD
PRELOADED
PRELOADING
PRELOADS
PRELOCATE
PRELOCATED
PRELOCATES
PRELOCATING
PRELOGICAL
PRELUDE
PRELUDED
PRELUDER
PRELUDERS
PRELUDES
PRELUDIAL
PRELUDING
PRELUNCH
PRELUNCHEON
PRELUSION
PRELUSIONS
PRELUSIVE
PRELUSIVELY
PRELUSORY
PREMADE
PREMALIGNANT
PREMAN
PREMANUFACTURE
PREMANUFACTURED
PREMANUFACTURES
PREMARITAL
PREMARITALLY
PREMARKET
PREMARKETED
PREMARKETING
PREMARKETS
PREMARRIAGE
PREMATURE
PREMATURELY
PREMATURENESS
PREMATURENESSES
PREMATURES
PREMATURITIES
PREMATURITY
PREMAXILLA
PREMAXILLAE
PREMAXILLARIES
PREMAXILLARY
PREMAXILLAS
PREMEAL
PREMEASURE
PREMEASURED
PREMEASURES
PREMEASURING
PREMED
PREMEDIC
PREMEDICAL
PREMEDICS
PREMEDIEVAL
PREMEDITATE
PREMEDITATED
PREMEDITATEDLY
PREMEDITATES
PREMEDITATING
PREMEDITATION
PREMEDITATIONS
PREMEDITATIVE
PREMEDITATOR
PREMEDITATORS
PREMEDS
PREMEET
PREMEIOTIC
PREMEN
PREMENOPAUSAL
PREMENSTRUAL
PREMENSTRUALLY
PREMERGER
PREMIE
PREMIER
PREMIERE
PREMIERED
PREMIERES
PREMIERING
PREMIERS
PREMIERSHIP
PREMIERSHIPS
PREMIES
PREMIGRATION
PREMIGRATIONS
PREMILLENARIAN
PREMILLENARIANS
PREMILLENNIAL
PREMILLENNIALLY
PREMILLENNIALS
PREMISE
PREMISED
PREMISES
PREMISING
PREMISS
PREMISSES
PREMIUM
PREMIUMS
PREMIX
PREMIXED
PREMIXES
PREMIXING
PREMIXT
PREMODERN
PREMODIFICATION
PREMODIFIED
PREMODIFIES
PREMODIFY
PREMODIFYING
PREMOISTEN
PREMOISTENED
PREMOISTENING
PREMOISTENS
PREMOLAR
PREMOLARS
PREMOLD
PREMOLDED
PREMOLDING
PREMOLDS
PREMOLT
PREMONISH
PREMONISHED
PREMONISHES
PREMONISHING
PREMONITION
PREMONITIONS
PREMONITORILY
PREMONITORY
PREMORAL
PREMORSE
PREMOTOR
PREMUNE
PREMUNITION
PREMUNITIONS
PREMYCOTIC
PRENAME
PRENAMES
PRENATAL
PRENATALLY
PRENOMEN
PRENOMENS
PRENOMINA
PRENOMINATE
PRENOMINATED
PRENOMINATES
PRENOMINATING
PRENOMINATION
PRENOMINATIONS
PRENOON
PRENOTIFICATION
PRENOTIFIED
PRENOTIFIES
PRENOTIFY
PRENOTIFYING
PRENOTION
PRENOTIONS
PRENTICE
PRENTICED
PRENTICES
PRENTICING
PRENUMBER
PRENUMBERED
PRENUMBERING
PRENUMBERS
PRENUP
PRENUPS
PRENUPTIAL
PRENUPTIALS
PREOBTAIN
PREOBTAINED
PREOBTAINING
PREOBTAINS
PREOCCUPANCIES
PREOCCUPANCY
PREOCCUPATION
PREOCCUPATIONS
PREOCCUPIED
PREOCCUPIES
PREOCCUPY
PREOCCUPYING
PREOP
PREOPENING
PREOPERATIONAL
PREOPERATIVE
PREOPERATIVELY
PREOPS

PREOPTION
PREOPTIONS
PREORAL
PREORDAIN
PREORDAINED
PREORDAINING
PREORDAINMENT
PREORDAINMENTS
PREORDAINS
PREORDER
PREORDERED
PREORDERING
PREORDERS
PREORDINATION
PREORDINATIONS
PREOVULATORY
PREOWNED
PREP
PREPACK
PREPACKAGE
PREPACKAGED
PREPACKAGES
PREPACKAGING
PREPACKED
PREPACKING
PREPACKS
PREPAID
PREPARATION
PREPARATIONS
PREPARATIVE
PREPARATIVELY
PREPARATIVES
PREPARATOR
PREPARATORILY
PREPARATORS
PREPARATORY
PREPARE
PREPARED
PREPAREDLY
PREPAREDNESS
PREPAREDNESSES
PREPARER
PREPARERS
PREPARES
PREPARING
PREPASTE
PREPASTED
PREPASTES
PREPASTING
PREPAVE
PREPAVED
PREPAVES
PREPAVING
PREPAY
PREPAYING
PREPAYMENT
PREPAYMENTS
PREPAYS
PREPENSE
PREPENSELY
PREPERFORMANCE
PREPERFORMANCES
PREPILL
PREPLACE
PREPLACED
PREPLACES
PREPLACING
PREPLAN
PREPLANNED
PREPLANNING
PREPLANS
PREPLANT
PREPLANTING
PREPONDERANCE
PREPONDERANCES
PREPONDERANCIES
PREPONDERANCY
PREPONDERANT
PREPONDERANTLY
PREPONDERATE
PREPONDERATED
PREPONDERATELY
PREPONDERATES
PREPONDERATING
PREPONDERATION
PREPONDERATIONS
PREPORTION
PREPORTIONED
PREPORTIONING
PREPORTIONS
PREPOSE
PREPOSED
PREPOSES
PREPOSING
PREPOSITION
PREPOSITIONAL
PREPOSITIONALLY
PREPOSITIONS
PREPOSITIVE
PREPOSITIVELY
PREPOSSESS
PREPOSSESSED
PREPOSSESSES
PREPOSSESSING
PREPOSSESSION
PREPOSSESSIONS
PREPOSTEROUS
PREPOSTEROUSLY
PREPOTENCIES
PREPOTENCY
PREPOTENT
PREPOTENTLY
PREPPED
PREPPIE
PREPPIER
PREPPIES
PREPPIEST
PREPPILY
PREPPINESS
PREPPINESSES
PREPPING
PREPPY
PREPRANDIAL
PREPREG
PREPREGS
PREPREPARED
PREPRESIDENTIAL
PREPRESS
PREPRICE
PREPRICED
PREPRICES
PREPRICING
PREPRIMARIES
PREPRIMARY
PREPRINT
PREPRINTED
PREPRINTING
PREPRINTS
PREPROCESS
PREPROCESSED
PREPROCESSES
PREPROCESSING
PREPROCESSOR
PREPROCESSORS
PREPRODUCTION
PREPRODUCTIONS
PREPROFESSIONAL
PREPROGRAM
PREPROGRAMED
PREPROGRAMING
PREPROGRAMMED
PREPROGRAMMING
PREPROGRAMS
PREPS
PREPSYCHEDELIC
PREPUBERAL
PREPUBERTAL
PREPUBERTIES
PREPUBERTY
PREPUBES
PREPUBESCENCE
PREPUBESCENCES
PREPUBESCENT
PREPUBESCENTS
PREPUBIS
PREPUBLICATION
PREPUBLICATIONS
PREPUCE
PREPUCES
PREPUEBLO
PREPUNCH
PREPUNCHED
PREPUNCHES
PREPUNCHING
PREPUPA
PREPUPAE
PREPUPAL
PREPUPAS
PREPURCHASE
PREPURCHASED
PREPURCHASES
PREPURCHASING
PREPUTIAL
PREQUALIFIED
PREQUALIFIES
PREQUALIFY
PREQUALIFYING
PREQUEL
PREQUELS
PRERACE
PRERADIO
PRERECESSION
PRERECORD
PRERECORDED
PRERECORDING
PRERECORDS
PRERECTAL
PREREFORM
PREREGISTER
PREREGISTERED
PREREGISTERING
PREREGISTERS
PREREGISTRATION
PREREHEARSAL
PREREHEARSALS
PRERELEASE
PRERELEASED
PRERELEASES
PRERELEASING
PRERENAL
PREREQUIRE
PREREQUIRED
PREREQUIRES
PREREQUIRING
PREREQUISITE
PREREQUISITES
PRERETIREMENT
PRERETIREMENTS
PRERETURN
PREREVIEW
PREREVISIONIST
PREREVOLUTION
PREREVOLUTIONS
PRERINSE
PRERINSED
PRERINSES
PRERINSING
PRERIOT
PREROCK
PREROGATIVE
PREROGATIVED
PREROGATIVES
PREROMANTIC
PREROMANTICS
PRESA
PRESAGE
PRESAGED
PRESAGEFUL
PRESAGER
PRESAGERS
PRESAGES
PRESAGING
PRESALE
PRESALES
PRESANCTIFIED
PRESBYOPE
PRESBYOPES
PRESBYOPIA
PRESBYOPIAS
PRESBYOPIC
PRESBYOPICS
PRESBYOPTICS
PRESBYTER
PRESBYTERATE
PRESBYTERATES
PRESBYTERIAL
PRESBYTERIALLY
PRESBYTERIALS
PRESBYTERIAN
PRESBYTERIES
PRESBYTERS
PRESBYTERY
PRESCHEDULE
PRESCHEDULED
PRESCHEDULES

PRESCHEDULING
PRESCHOOL
PRESCHOOLER
PRESCHOOLERS
PRESCHOOLS
PRESCIENCE
PRESCIENCES
PRESCIENT
PRESCIENTIFIC
PRESCIENTLY
PRESCIND
PRESCINDED
PRESCINDING
PRESCINDS
PRESCORE
PRESCORED
PRESCORES
PRESCORING
PRESCREEN
PRESCREENED
PRESCREENING
PRESCREENS
PRESCRIBE
PRESCRIBED
PRESCRIBER
PRESCRIBERS
PRESCRIBES
PRESCRIBING
PRESCRIPT
PRESCRIPTION
PRESCRIPTIONS
PRESCRIPTIVE
PRESCRIPTIVELY
PRESCRIPTS
PRESE
PRESEASON
PRESEASONS
PRESELECT
PRESELECTED
PRESELECTING
PRESELECTION
PRESELECTIONS
PRESELECTS
PRESELL
PRESELLING
PRESELLS
PRESENCE
PRESENCES
PRESENT
PRESENTABILITY
PRESENTABLE
PRESENTABLENESS
PRESENTABLY
PRESENTATION
PRESENTATIONAL
PRESENTATIONS
PRESENTATIVE
PRESENTED
PRESENTEE
PRESENTEES
PRESENTENCE
PRESENTENCED
PRESENTENCES
PRESENTENCING
PRESENTER
PRESENTERS
PRESENTIENT
PRESENTIMENT
PRESENTIMENTAL
PRESENTIMENTS
PRESENTING
PRESENTISM
PRESENTISMS
PRESENTIST
PRESENTISTS
PRESENTLY
PRESENTMENT
PRESENTMENTS
PRESENTNESS
PRESENTNESSES
PRESENTS
PRESERVABILITY
PRESERVABLE
PRESERVATION
PRESERVATIONIST
PRESERVATIONS
PRESERVATIVE
PRESERVATIVES
PRESERVE
PRESERVED
PRESERVER
PRESERVERS
PRESERVES
PRESERVICE
PRESERVICED
PRESERVICES
PRESERVICING
PRESERVING
PRESET
PRESETS
PRESETTING
PRESETTLE
PRESETTLED
PRESETTLEMENT
PRESETTLEMENTS
PRESETTLES
PRESETTLING
PRESHAPE
PRESHAPED
PRESHAPES
PRESHAPING
PRESHIP
PRESHIPPED
PRESHIPPING
PRESHIPS
PRESHOW
PRESHOWED
PRESHOWING
PRESHOWN
PRESHOWS
PRESHRANK
PRESHRINK
PRESHRINKING
PRESHRINKS
PRESHRUNK
PRESHRUNKEN
PRESIDE
PRESIDED
PRESIDENCIES
PRESIDENCY
PRESIDENT
PRESIDENTIAL
PRESIDENTIALLY
PRESIDENTS
PRESIDENTSHIP
PRESIDENTSHIPS
PRESIDER
PRESIDERS
PRESIDES
PRESIDIA
PRESIDIAL
PRESIDIARY
PRESIDING
PRESIDIO
PRESIDIOS
PRESIDIUM
PRESIDIUMS
PRESIFT
PRESIFTED
PRESIFTING
PRESIFTS
PRESIGNAL
PRESIGNALED
PRESIGNALING
PRESIGNALLED
PRESIGNALLING
PRESIGNALS
PRESIGNIFIED
PRESIGNIFIES
PRESIGNIFY
PRESIGNIFYING
PRESLAUGHTER
PRESLEEP
PRESLICE
PRESLICED
PRESLICES
PRESLICING
PRESOAK
PRESOAKED
PRESOAKING
PRESOAKS
PRESOLD
PRESOLVE
PRESOLVED
PRESOLVES
PRESOLVING
PRESONG
PRESORT
PRESORTED
PRESORTING
PRESORTS
PRESPECIFIED
PRESPECIFIES
PRESPECIFY
PRESPECIFYING
PRESPLIT
PRESS
PRESSBOARD
PRESSBOARDS
PRESSED
PRESSER
PRESSERS
PRESSES
PRESSGANG
PRESSGANGS
PRESSING
PRESSINGLY
PRESSINGS
PRESSMAN
PRESSMARK
PRESSMARKS
PRESSMEN
PRESSOR
PRESSORS
PRESSROOM
PRESSROOMS
PRESSRUN
PRESSRUNS
PRESSURE
PRESSURED
PRESSURELESS
PRESSURES
PRESSURING
PRESSURISATION
PRESSURISATIONS
PRESSURISE
PRESSURISED
PRESSURISES
PRESSURISING
PRESSURIZATION
PRESSURIZATIONS
PRESSURIZE
PRESSURIZED
PRESSURIZER
PRESSURIZERS
PRESSURIZES
PRESSURIZING
PRESSWORK
PRESSWORKS
PREST
PRESTAMP
PRESTAMPED
PRESTAMPING
PRESTAMPS
PRESTER
PRESTERILIZE
PRESTERILIZED
PRESTERILIZES
PRESTERILIZING
PRESTERNA
PRESTERNUM
PRESTERS
PRESTIDIGITATOR
PRESTIGE
PRESTIGEFUL
PRESTIGES
PRESTIGIOUS
PRESTIGIOUSLY
PRESTIGIOUSNESS
PRESTISSIMO
PRESTO
PRESTORAGE
PRESTORE
PRESTORED
PRESTORES
PRESTORING
PRESTOS
PRESTRESS
PRESTRESSED
PRESTRESSES
PRESTRESSING
PRESTRIKE
PRESTRUCTURE
PRESTRUCTURED
PRESTRUCTURES

RESTRUCTURING
RESTS
RESUMABLE
RESUMABLY
RESUME
RESUMED
RESUMEDLY
RESUMER
RESUMERS
RESUMES
RESUMING
RESUMINGLY
RESUMMIT
RESUMMITS
RESUMPTION
RESUMPTIONS
RESUMPTIVE
RESUMPTIVELY
RESUMPTUOUS
RESUMPTUOUSLY
RESUPPOSE
RESUPPOSED
RESUPPOSES
RESUPPOSING
RESUPPOSITION
RESUPPOSITIONS
RESURGERY
RESURVEY
RESURVEYED
RESURVEYING
RESURVEYS
RESWEETEN
RESWEETENED
RESWEETENING
RESWEETENS
RESYMPTOMATIC
RESYNAPTIC
RESYNAPTICALLY
RETAPE
RETAPED
RETAPES
RETAPING
RETASTE
RETASTED
RETASTES
RETASTING
RETAX
RETEEN
RETEENS
RETELEVISION
RETELL
RETELLING
RETELLS

PRETENCE
PRETENCES
PRETEND
PRETENDED
PRETENDEDLY
PRETENDER
PRETENDERS
PRETENDING
PRETENDS
PRETENSE
PRETENSES
PRETENSION
PRETENSIONED
PRETENSIONING
PRETENSIONLESS
PRETENSIONS
PRETENTIOUS
PRETENTIOUSLY
PRETENTIOUSNESS
PRETERIT
PRETERITE
PRETERITES
PRETERITS
PRETERM
PRETERMINAL
PRETERMINATION
PRETERMINATIONS
PRETERMISSION
PRETERMISSIONS
PRETERMIT
PRETERMITS
PRETERMITTED
PRETERMITTING
PRETERMS
PRETERNATURAL
PRETERNATURALLY
PRETEST
PRETESTED
PRETESTING
PRETESTS
PRETEXT
PRETEXTED
PRETEXTING
PRETEXTS
PRETHEATER
PRETOLD
PRETOR
PRETORIAL
PRETORIAN
PRETORIANS
PRETORS
PRETOURNAMENT
PRETRAIN

PRETRAINED
PRETRAINING
PRETRAINS
PRETRAVEL
PRETREAT
PRETREATED
PRETREATING
PRETREATMENT
PRETREATMENTS
PRETREATS
PRETRIAL
PRETRIALS
PRETRIM
PRETRIMMED
PRETRIMMING
PRETRIMS
PRETTIED
PRETTIER
PRETTIES
PRETTIEST
PRETTIFICATION
PRETTIFICATIONS
PRETTIFIED
PRETTIFIER
PRETTIFIERS
PRETTIFIES
PRETTIFY
PRETTIFYING
PRETTILY
PRETTINESS
PRETTINESSES
PRETTY
PRETTYING
PRETTYISH
PRETYPE
PRETYPED
PRETYPES
PRETYPING
PRETZEL
PRETZELLED
PRETZELLING
PRETZELS
PREUNIFICATION
PREUNION
PREUNIONS
PREUNITE
PREUNITED
PREUNITES
PREUNITING
PREUNIVERSITIES
PREUNIVERSITY
PREVAIL
PREVAILED

PREVAILER
PREVAILERS
PREVAILING
PREVAILS
PREVALENCE
PREVALENCES
PREVALENT
PREVALENTLY
PREVALENTS
PREVALUE
PREVALUED
PREVALUES
PREVALUING
PREVARICATE
PREVARICATED
PREVARICATES
PREVARICATING
PREVARICATION
PREVARICATIONS
PREVARICATOR
PREVARICATORS
PREVENIENT
PREVENIENTLY
PREVENT
PREVENTABILITY
PREVENTABLE
PREVENTATIVE
PREVENTATIVES
PREVENTED
PREVENTER
PREVENTERS
PREVENTIBLE
PREVENTING
PREVENTION
PREVENTIONS
PREVENTIVE
PREVENTIVELY
PREVENTIVENESS
PREVENTIVES
PREVENTS
PREVERB
PREVERBAL
PREVERBS
PREVIABLE
PREVIEW
PREVIEWED
PREVIEWER
PREVIEWERS
PREVIEWING
PREVIEWS
PREVIOUS
PREVIOUSLY
PREVIOUSNESS

PREVIOUSNESSES
PREVISE
PREVISED
PREVISES
PREVISING
PREVISION
PREVISIONAL
PREVISIONARY
PREVISIONED
PREVISIONING
PREVISIONS
PREVISIT
PREVISITED
PREVISITING
PREVISITS
PREVISOR
PREVISORS
PREVOCALIC
PREVOCATIONAL
PREVUE
PREVUED
PREVUES
PREVUING
PREWAR
PREWARM
PREWARMED
PREWARMING
PREWARMS
PREWARN
PREWARNED
PREWARNING
PREWARNS
PREWASH
PREWASHED
PREWASHES
PREWASHING
PREWEANING
PREWEIGH
PREWEIGHED
PREWEIGHING
PREWEIGHS
PREWIRE
PREWIRED
PREWIRES
PREWIRING
PREWORK
PREWORKED
PREWORKING
PREWORKS
PREWORN
PREWRAP
PREWRAPPED
PREWRAPPING

PREWRAPS
PREWRITING
PREWRITINGS
PREX
PREXES
PREXIES
PREXY
PREY
PREYED
PREYER
PREYERS
PREYING
PREYS
PREZ
PREZES
PREZZIE
PREZZIES
PRIAPEAN
PRIAPI
PRIAPIC
PRIAPISM
PRIAPISMS
PRIAPUS
PRIAPUSES
PRICE
PRICEABLE
PRICED
PRICELESS
PRICELESSLY
PRICER
PRICERS
PRICES
PRICEY
PRICIER
PRICIEST
PRICILY
PRICING
PRICK
PRICKED
PRICKER
PRICKERS
PRICKET
PRICKETS
PRICKIER
PRICKIEST
PRICKING
PRICKINGS
PRICKLE
PRICKLED
PRICKLES
PRICKLIER
PRICKLIEST
PRICKLINESS
PRICKLINESSES
PRICKLING
PRICKLY
PRICKS
PRICKY
PRICY
PRIDE
PRIDED
PRIDEFUL
PRIDEFULLY
PRIDEFULNESS
PRIDEFULNESSES
PRIDES
PRIDING
PRIED
PRIEDIEU
PRIEDIEUS
PRIEDIEUX
PRIER
PRIERS
PRIES
PRIEST
PRIESTED
PRIESTESS
PRIESTESSES
PRIESTHOOD
PRIESTHOODS
PRIESTING
PRIESTLIER
PRIESTLIEST
PRIESTLINESS
PRIESTLINESSES
PRIESTLY
PRIESTS
PRIG
PRIGGED
PRIGGERIES
PRIGGERY
PRIGGING
PRIGGISH
PRIGGISHLY
PRIGGISHNESS
PRIGGISHNESSES
PRIGGISM
PRIGGISMS
PRIGS
PRILL
PRILLED
PRILLING
PRILLS
PRIM
PRIMA
PRIMACIES
PRIMACY
PRIMAEVAL
PRIMAGE
PRIMAGES
PRIMAL
PRIMALITIES
PRIMALITY
PRIMALLY
PRIMARIES
PRIMARILY
PRIMARY
PRIMAS
PRIMATAL
PRIMATALS
PRIMATE
PRIMATES
PRIMATESHIP
PRIMATESHIPS
PRIMATIAL
PRIMATIALS
PRIMATOLOGICAL
PRIMATOLOGIES
PRIMATOLOGIST
PRIMATOLOGISTS
PRIMATOLOGY
PRIMAVERA
PRIMAVERAS
PRIME
PRIMED
PRIMELY
PRIMENESS
PRIMENESSES
PRIMER
PRIMERO
PRIMEROS
PRIMERS
PRIMES
PRIMEVAL
PRIMEVALLY
PRIMI
PRIMINE
PRIMINES
PRIMING
PRIMINGS
PRIMIPARA
PRIMIPARAE
PRIMIPARAS
PRIMIPAROUS
PRIMITIVE
PRIMITIVELY
PRIMITIVENESS
PRIMITIVENESSES
PRIMITIVES
PRIMITIVISM
PRIMITIVISMS
PRIMITIVIST
PRIMITIVISTIC
PRIMITIVISTS
PRIMITIVITIES
PRIMITIVITY
PRIMLY
PRIMMED
PRIMMER
PRIMMEST
PRIMMING
PRIMNESS
PRIMNESSES
PRIMO
PRIMOGENITOR
PRIMOGENITORS
PRIMOGENITURE
PRIMOGENITURES
PRIMORDIA
PRIMORDIAL
PRIMORDIALLY
PRIMORDIUM
PRIMOS
PRIMP
PRIMPED
PRIMPING
PRIMPS
PRIMROSE
PRIMROSES
PRIMS
PRIMSIE
PRIMULA
PRIMULAS
PRIMUS
PRIMUSES
PRINCE
PRINCEDOM
PRINCEDOMS
PRINCEKIN
PRINCEKINS
PRINCELET
PRINCELETS
PRINCELIER
PRINCELIEST
PRINCELINESS
PRINCELINESSES
PRINCELING
PRINCELINGS
PRINCELY
PRINCES
PRINCESHIP
PRINCESHIPS
PRINCESS
PRINCESSE
PRINCESSES
PRINCIPAL
PRINCIPALITIES
PRINCIPALITY
PRINCIPALLY
PRINCIPALS
PRINCIPALSHIP
PRINCIPALSHIPS
PRINCIPE
PRINCIPI
PRINCIPIA
PRINCIPIUM
PRINCIPLE
PRINCIPLED
PRINCIPLES
PRINCOCK
PRINCOCKS
PRINCOX
PRINCOXES
PRINK
PRINKED
PRINKER
PRINKERS
PRINKING
PRINKS
PRINT
PRINTABILITIES
PRINTABILITY
PRINTABLE
PRINTED
PRINTER
PRINTERIES
PRINTERS
PRINTERY
PRINTHEAD
PRINTHEADS
PRINTING
PRINTINGS
PRINTLESS
PRINTMAKER
PRINTMAKERS
PRINTMAKING
PRINTMAKINGS
PRINTOUT
PRINTOUTS
PRINTS
PRION
PRIONS
PRIOR
PRIORATE
PRIORATES

PRIORESS
PRIORESSES
PRIORIES
PRIORITIES
PRIORITISE
PRIORITISED
PRIORITISES
PRIORITISING
PRIORITIZATION
PRIORITIZATIONS
PRIORITIZE
PRIORITIZED
PRIORITIZES
PRIORITIZING
PRIORITY
PRIORLY
PRIORS
PRIORSHIP
PRIORSHIPS
PRIORY
PRISE
PRISED
PRISERE
PRISERES
PRISES
PRISING
PRISM
PRISMATIC
PRISMATICALLY
PRISMATOID
PRISMATOIDS
PRISMOID
PRISMOIDAL
PRISMOIDS
PRISMS
PRISON
PRISONED
PRISONER
PRISONERS
PRISONING
PRISONS
PRISS
PRISSED
PRISSES
PRISSIER
PRISSIES
PRISSIEST
PRISSILY
PRISSINESS
PRISSINESSES
PRISSING
PRISSY
PRISTANE
PRISTANES
PRISTINE
PRISTINELY
PRITHEE
PRIVACIES
PRIVACY
PRIVATDOCENT
PRIVATDOCENTS
PRIVATDOZENT
PRIVATDOZENTS
PRIVATE
PRIVATEER
PRIVATEERED
PRIVATEERING
PRIVATEERS
PRIVATELY
PRIVATENESS
PRIVATENESSES
PRIVATER
PRIVATES
PRIVATEST
PRIVATION
PRIVATIONS
PRIVATISATION
PRIVATISATIONS
PRIVATISE
PRIVATISED
PRIVATISES
PRIVATISING
PRIVATISM
PRIVATISMS
PRIVATIST
PRIVATISTS
PRIVATIVE
PRIVATIVELY
PRIVATIVES
PRIVATIZATION
PRIVATIZATIONS
PRIVATIZE
PRIVATIZED
PRIVATIZES
PRIVATIZING
PRIVET
PRIVETS
PRIVIER
PRIVIES
PRIVIEST
PRIVILEGE
PRIVILEGED
PRIVILEGES
PRIVILEGING
PRIVILY
PRIVITIES
PRIVITY
PRIVY
PRIZE
PRIZED
PRIZEFIGHT
PRIZEFIGHTER
PRIZEFIGHTERS
PRIZEFIGHTING
PRIZEFIGHTINGS
PRIZEFIGHTS
PRIZER
PRIZERS
PRIZES
PRIZEWINNER
PRIZEWINNERS
PRIZEWINNING
PRIZING
PRO
PROA
PROABORTION
PROACTION
PROACTIONS
PROACTIVE
PROACTIVELY
PROAS
PROB
PROBABILISM
PROBABILISMS
PROBABILIST
PROBABILISTIC
PROBABILISTS
PROBABILITIES
PROBABILITY
PROBABLE
PROBABLES
PROBABLY
PROBAND
PROBANDS
PROBANG
PROBANGS
PROBATE
PROBATED
PROBATES
PROBATING
PROBATION
PROBATIONAL
PROBATIONALLY
PROBATIONARY
PROBATIONER
PROBATIONERS
PROBATIONS
PROBATIVE
PROBATORY
PROBE
PROBED
PROBENECID
PROBENECIDS
PROBER
PROBERS
PROBES
PROBING
PROBINGLY
PROBIOTIC
PROBIOTICS
PROBIT
PROBITIES
PROBITS
PROBITY
PROBLEM
PROBLEMATIC
PROBLEMATICAL
PROBLEMATICALLY
PROBLEMATICS
PROBLEMATIZE
PROBLEMATIZED
PROBLEMATIZES
PROBLEMATIZING
PROBLEMS
PROBOSCIDEAN
PROBOSCIDEANS
PROBOSCIDES
PROBOSCIDIAN
PROBOSCIDIANS
PROBOSCIS
PROBOSCISES
PROBS
PROCAINE
PROCAINES
PROCAMBIA
PROCAMBIAL
PROCAMBIUM
PROCAMBIUMS
PROCARBAZINE
PROCARBAZINES
PROCARP
PROCARPS
PROCARYOTE
PROCARYOTES
PROCATHEDRAL
PROCATHEDRALS
PROCEDURAL
PROCEDURALLY
PROCEDURALS
PROCEDURE
PROCEDURES
PROCEED
PROCEEDED
PROCEEDER
PROCEEDERS
PROCEEDING
PROCEEDINGS
PROCEEDS
PROCEPHALIC
PROCERCOID
PROCERCOIDS
PROCESS
PROCESSABILITY
PROCESSABLE
PROCESSED
PROCESSER
PROCESSERS
PROCESSES
PROCESSIBILITY
PROCESSIBLE
PROCESSING
PROCESSION
PROCESSIONAL
PROCESSIONALLY
PROCESSIONALS
PROCESSIONED
PROCESSIONING
PROCESSIONS
PROCESSOR
PROCESSORS
PROCHAIN
PROCHEIN
PROCHOICE
PROCHURCH
PROCLAIM
PROCLAIMED
PROCLAIMER
PROCLAIMERS
PROCLAIMING
PROCLAIMS
PROCLAMATION
PROCLAMATIONS
PROCLISES
PROCLISIS
PROCLITIC
PROCLITICS
PROCLIVITIES
PROCLIVITY
PROCONSUL
PROCONSULAR
PROCONSULATE
PROCONSULATES
PROCONSULS
PROCONSULSHIP
PROCONSULSHIPS

PROCRASTINATE
PROCRASTINATED
PROCRASTINATES
PROCRASTINATING
PROCRASTINATION
PROCRASTINATOR
PROCRASTINATORS
PROCREANT
PROCREATE
PROCREATED
PROCREATES
PROCREATING
PROCREATION
PROCREATIONS
PROCREATIVE
PROCREATOR
PROCREATORS
PROCRUSTEAN
PROCRYPTIC
PROCTITIDES
PROCTITIS
PROCTITISES
PROCTODAEA
PROCTODAEUM
PROCTODAEUMS
PROCTODEA
PROCTODEUM
PROCTODEUMS
PROCTOLOGIC
PROCTOLOGICAL
PROCTOLOGIES
PROCTOLOGIST
PROCTOLOGISTS
PROCTOLOGY
PROCTOR
PROCTORED
PROCTORIAL
PROCTORING
PROCTORS
PROCTORSHIP
PROCTORSHIPS
PROCUMBENT
PROCURABLE
PROCURAL
PROCURALS
PROCURATION
PROCURATIONS
PROCURATOR
PROCURATORIAL
PROCURATORS
PROCURE
PROCURED
PROCUREMENT
PROCUREMENTS
PROCURER
PROCURERS
PROCURES
PROCURESS
PROCURESSES
PROCURING
PROD
PRODDED
PRODDER
PRODDERS
PRODDING
PRODIGAL
PRODIGALITIES
PRODIGALITY
PRODIGALLY
PRODIGALS
PRODIGIES
PRODIGIOUS
PRODIGIOUSLY
PRODIGIOUSNESS
PRODIGY
PRODROMAL
PRODROMATA
PRODROME
PRODROMES
PRODROMIC
PRODRUG
PRODRUGS
PRODS
PRODUCE
PRODUCED
PRODUCER
PRODUCERS
PRODUCES
PRODUCIBLE
PRODUCING
PRODUCT
PRODUCTION
PRODUCTIONAL
PRODUCTIONS
PRODUCTIVE
PRODUCTIVELY
PRODUCTIVENESS
PRODUCTIVITIES
PRODUCTIVITY
PRODUCTS
PROEM
PROEMIAL
PROEMS
PROENZYME
PROENZYMES
PROESTRUS
PROESTRUSES
PROETTE
PROETTES
PROF
PROFAMILY
PROFANATION
PROFANATIONS
PROFANATORY
PROFANE
PROFANED
PROFANELY
PROFANENESS
PROFANENESSES
PROFANER
PROFANERS
PROFANES
PROFANING
PROFANITIES
PROFANITY
PROFESS
PROFESSED
PROFESSEDLY
PROFESSES
PROFESSING
PROFESSION
PROFESSIONAL
PROFESSIONALISE
PROFESSIONALISM
PROFESSIONALIZE
PROFESSIONALLY
PROFESSIONALS
PROFESSIONS
PROFESSOR
PROFESSORATE
PROFESSORATES
PROFESSORIAL
PROFESSORIALLY
PROFESSORIAT
PROFESSORIATE
PROFESSORIATES
PROFESSORIATS
PROFESSORS
PROFESSORSHIP
PROFESSORSHIPS
PROFFER
PROFFERED
PROFFERER
PROFFERERS
PROFFERING
PROFFERS
PROFICIENCIES
PROFICIENCY
PROFICIENT
PROFICIENTLY
PROFICIENTS
PROFILE
PROFILED
PROFILER
PROFILERS
PROFILES
PROFILING
PROFILINGS
PROFIT
PROFITABILITIES
PROFITABILITY
PROFITABLE
PROFITABLENESS
PROFITABLY
PROFITED
PROFITEER
PROFITEERED
PROFITEERING
PROFITEERS
PROFITER
PROFITEROLE
PROFITEROLES
PROFITERS
PROFITING
PROFITLESS
PROFITS
PROFITWISE
PROFLIGACIES
PROFLIGACY
PROFLIGATE
PROFLIGATELY
PROFLIGATES
PROFLUENT
PROFORMA
PROFOUND
PROFOUNDER
PROFOUNDEST
PROFOUNDLY
PROFOUNDNESS
PROFOUNDNESSES
PROFOUNDS
PROFS
PROFUNDITIES
PROFUNDITY
PROFUSE
PROFUSELY
PROFUSENESS
PROFUSENESSES
PROFUSION
PROFUSIONS
PROFUSIVE
PROG
PROGENIES
PROGENITOR
PROGENITORS
PROGENY
PROGERIA
PROGERIAS
PROGESTATIONAL
PROGESTERONE
PROGESTERONES
PROGESTIN
PROGESTINS
PROGESTOGEN
PROGESTOGENIC
PROGESTOGENS
PROGGED
PROGGER
PROGGERS
PROGGING
PROGLOTTID
PROGLOTTIDES
PROGLOTTIDS
PROGLOTTIS
PROGNATHIC
PROGNATHISM
PROGNATHISMS
PROGNATHOUS
PROGNOSE
PROGNOSED
PROGNOSES
PROGNOSING
PROGNOSIS
PROGNOSTIC
PROGNOSTICATE
PROGNOSTICATED
PROGNOSTICATES
PROGNOSTICATING
PROGNOSTICATION
PROGNOSTICATIVE
PROGNOSTICATOR
PROGNOSTICATORS
PROGNOSTICS
PROGRADE
PROGRAM
PROGRAMED
PROGRAMER
PROGRAMERS
PROGRAMING
PROGRAMINGS
PROGRAMMABILITY
PROGRAMMABLE
PROGRAMMABLES
PROGRAMMATIC
PROGRAMME

PROGRAMMED
PROGRAMMER
PROGRAMMERS
PROGRAMMES
PROGRAMMING
PROGRAMMINGS
PROGRAMS
PROGRESS
PROGRESSED
PROGRESSES
PROGRESSING
PROGRESSION
PROGRESSIONAL
PROGRESSIONS
PROGRESSIVE
PROGRESSIVELY
PROGRESSIVENESS
PROGRESSIVES
PROGRESSIVISM
PROGRESSIVISMS
PROGRESSIVIST
PROGRESSIVISTIC
PROGRESSIVISTS
PROGRESSIVITIES
PROGRESSIVITY
PROGS
PROGUN
PROHIBIT
PROHIBITED
PROHIBITING
PROHIBITION
PROHIBITIONIST
PROHIBITIONISTS
PROHIBITIONS
PROHIBITIVE
PROHIBITIVELY
PROHIBITIVENESS
PROHIBITORY
PROHIBITS
PROINSULIN
PROINSULINS
PROJECT
PROJECTABLE
PROJECTED
PROJECTILE
PROJECTILES
PROJECTING
PROJECTION
PROJECTIONAL
PROJECTIONIST
PROJECTIONISTS
PROJECTIONS
PROJECTIVE
PROJECTIVELY
PROJECTOR
PROJECTORS
PROJECTS
PROJET
PROJETS
PROKARYOTE
PROKARYOTES
PROKARYOTIC
PROLABOR
PROLACTIN
PROLACTINS
PROLAMIN
PROLAMINE
PROLAMINES
PROLAMINS
PROLAN
PROLANS
PROLAPSE
PROLAPSED
PROLAPSES
PROLAPSING
PROLAPSUS
PROLATE
PROLATELY
PROLE
PROLEG
PROLEGOMENA
PROLEGOMENON
PROLEGOMENOUS
PROLEGS
PROLEPSES
PROLEPSIS
PROLEPTIC
PROLEPTICALLY
PROLES
PROLETARIAN
PROLETARIANISE
PROLETARIANISED
PROLETARIANISES
PROLETARIANIZE
PROLETARIANIZED
PROLETARIANIZES
PROLETARIANS
PROLETARIAT
PROLETARIATS
PROLETARIES
PROLETARY
PROLIFERATE
PROLIFERATED
PROLIFERATES
PROLIFERATING
PROLIFERATION
PROLIFERATIONS
PROLIFERATIVE
PROLIFIC
PROLIFICACIES
PROLIFICACY
PROLIFICALLY
PROLIFICITIES
PROLIFICITY
PROLIFICNESS
PROLIFICNESSES
PROLINE
PROLINES
PROLIX
PROLIXITIES
PROLIXITY
PROLIXLY
PROLOCUTOR
PROLOCUTORS
PROLOG
PROLOGED
PROLOGING
PROLOGIST
PROLOGISTS
PROLOGIZE
PROLOGIZED
PROLOGIZES
PROLOGIZING
PROLOGS
PROLOGUE
PROLOGUED
PROLOGUES
PROLOGUING
PROLOGUIZE
PROLOGUIZED
PROLOGUIZES
PROLOGUIZING
PROLONG
PROLONGATION
PROLONGATIONS
PROLONGE
PROLONGED
PROLONGER
PROLONGERS
PROLONGES
PROLONGING
PROLONGS
PROLUSION
PROLUSIONS
PROLUSORY
PROM
PROMENADE
PROMENADED
PROMENADER
PROMENADERS
PROMENADES
PROMENADING
PROMETHIUM
PROMETHIUMS
PROMETRIC
PROMINE
PROMINENCE
PROMINENCES
PROMINENT
PROMINENTLY
PROMINES
PROMISCUITIES
PROMISCUITY
PROMISCUOUS
PROMISCUOUSLY
PROMISCUOUSNESS
PROMISE
PROMISED
PROMISEE
PROMISEES
PROMISER
PROMISERS
PROMISES
PROMISING
PROMISINGLY
PROMISOR
PROMISORS
PROMISSORY
PROMO
PROMODERN
PROMOED
PROMOING
PROMONTORIES
PROMONTORY
PROMOS
PROMOTABILITIES
PROMOTABILITY
PROMOTABLE
PROMOTE
PROMOTED
PROMOTER
PROMOTERS
PROMOTES
PROMOTING
PROMOTION
PROMOTIONAL
PROMOTIONS
PROMOTIVE
PROMOTIVENESS
PROMOTIVENESSES
PROMOTOR
PROMOTORS
PROMPT
PROMPTBOOK
PROMPTBOOKS
PROMPTED
PROMPTER
PROMPTERS
PROMPTEST
PROMPTING
PROMPTITUDE
PROMPTITUDES
PROMPTLY
PROMPTNESS
PROMPTNESSES
PROMPTS
PROMS
PROMULGATE
PROMULGATED
PROMULGATES
PROMULGATING
PROMULGATION
PROMULGATIONS
PROMULGATOR
PROMULGATORS
PROMULGE
PROMULGED
PROMULGES
PROMULGING
PRONATE
PRONATED
PRONATES
PRONATING
PRONATION
PRONATIONS
PRONATOR
PRONATORES
PRONATORS
PRONE
PRONELY
PRONENESS
PRONENESSES
PRONEPHRA
PRONEPHRIC
PRONEPHROI
PRONEPHROS
PRONEPHROSES
PRONER
PRONEST
PRONG
PRONGED
PRONGHORN
PRONGHORNS
PRONGING
PRONGS

PRONOMINAL
PRONOMINALLY
PRONOTA
PRONOTUM
PRONOUN
PRONOUNCE
PRONOUNCEABLE
PRONOUNCED
PRONOUNCEDLY
PRONOUNCEMENT
PRONOUNCEMENTS
PRONOUNCER
PRONOUNCERS
PRONOUNCES
PRONOUNCING
PRONOUNS
PRONTO
PRONUCLEAR
PRONUCLEI
PRONUCLEUS
PRONUCLEUSES
PRONUNCIAMENTO
PRONUNCIAMENTOS
PRONUNCIATION
PRONUNCIATIONAL
PRONUNCIATIONS
PROOF
PROOFED
PROOFER
PROOFERS
PROOFING
PROOFREAD
PROOFREADER
PROOFREADERS
PROOFREADING
PROOFREADS
PROOFROOM
PROOFROOMS
PROOFS
PROP
PROPAEDEUTIC
PROPAEDEUTICS
PROPAGABLE
PROPAGANDA
PROPAGANDAS
PROPAGANDISE
PROPAGANDISED
PROPAGANDISES
PROPAGANDISING
PROPAGANDIST
PROPAGANDISTIC
PROPAGANDISTS
PROPAGANDIZE
PROPAGANDIZED
PROPAGANDIZER
PROPAGANDIZERS
PROPAGANDIZES
PROPAGANDIZING
PROPAGATE
PROPAGATED
PROPAGATES
PROPAGATING
PROPAGATION
PROPAGATIONS
PROPAGATIVE
PROPAGATOR
PROPAGATORS
PROPAGULE
PROPAGULES
PROPANE
PROPANES
PROPANOL
PROPANOLS
PROPEL
PROPELLANT
PROPELLANTS
PROPELLED
PROPELLENT
PROPELLENTS
PROPELLER
PROPELLERS
PROPELLING
PROPELLOR
PROPELLORS
PROPELS
PROPEND
PROPENDED
PROPENDING
PROPENDS
PROPENE
PROPENES
PROPENOL
PROPENOLS
PROPENSE
PROPENSITIES
PROPENSITY
PROPENYL
PROPER
PROPERDIN
PROPERDINS
PROPERER
PROPEREST
PROPERLY
PROPERNESS
PROPERNESSES
PROPERS
PROPERTIED
PROPERTIES
PROPERTY
PROPERTYLESS
PROPHAGE
PROPHAGES
PROPHASE
PROPHASES
PROPHASIC
PROPHECIES
PROPHECY
PROPHESIED
PROPHESIER
PROPHESIERS
PROPHESIES
PROPHESIZE
PROPHESIZED
PROPHESIZES
PROPHESIZING
PROPHESY
PROPHESYING
PROPHET
PROPHETESS
PROPHETESSES
PROPHETHOOD
PROPHETHOODS
PROPHETIC
PROPHETICAL
PROPHETICALLY
PROPHETS
PROPHYLACTIC
PROPHYLACTICS
PROPHYLAXES
PROPHYLAXIS
PROPINE
PROPINED
PROPINES
PROPINING
PROPINQUITIES
PROPINQUITY
PROPIONATE
PROPIONATES
PROPITIATE
PROPITIATED
PROPITIATES
PROPITIATING
PROPITIATION
PROPITIATIONS
PROPITIATOR
PROPITIATORS
PROPITIATORY
PROPITIOUS
PROPITIOUSLY
PROPITIOUSNESS
PROPJET
PROPJETS
PROPLASTID
PROPLASTIDS
PROPMAN
PROPMEN
PROPOLIS
PROPOLISES
PROPONE
PROPONED
PROPONENT
PROPONENTS
PROPONES
PROPONING
PROPORTION
PROPORTIONABLE
PROPORTIONABLY
PROPORTIONAL
PROPORTIONALITY
PROPORTIONALLY
PROPORTIONALS
PROPORTIONATE
PROPORTIONATED
PROPORTIONATELY
PROPORTIONATES
PROPORTIONATING
PROPORTIONED
PROPORTIONING
PROPORTIONS
PROPOSAL
PROPOSALS
PROPOSE
PROPOSED
PROPOSER
PROPOSERS
PROPOSES
PROPOSING
PROPOSITI
PROPOSITION
PROPOSITIONAL
PROPOSITIONED
PROPOSITIONING
PROPOSITIONS
PROPOSITUS
PROPOUND
PROPOUNDED
PROPOUNDER
PROPOUNDERS
PROPOUNDING
PROPOUNDS
PROPOXYPHENE
PROPOXYPHENES
PROPPED
PROPPING
PROPRAETOR
PROPRAETORS
PROPRANOLOL
PROPRANOLOLS
PROPRETOR
PROPRETORS
PROPRIA
PROPRIETARIES
PROPRIETARY
PROPRIETIES
PROPRIETOR
PROPRIETORIAL
PROPRIETORS
PROPRIETORSHIP
PROPRIETORSHIPS
PROPRIETRESS
PROPRIETRESSES
PROPRIETY
PROPRIOCEPTION
PROPRIOCEPTIONS
PROPRIOCEPTIVE
PROPRIOCEPTOR
PROPRIOCEPTORS
PROPRIUM
PROPS
PROPTOSES
PROPTOSIS
PROPULSION
PROPULSIONS
PROPULSIVE
PROPYL
PROPYLA
PROPYLAEA
PROPYLAEUM
PROPYLENE
PROPYLENES
PROPYLIC
PROPYLITE
PROPYLITES
PROPYLON
PROPYLS
PROPYNE
PROPYNES
PRORATE
PRORATED
PRORATES
PRORATING
PRORATION
PRORATIONS
PROREFORM
PROROGATE

PROROGATED
PROROGATES
PROROGATING
PROROGATION
PROROGATIONS
PROROGUE
PROROGUED
PROROGUES
PROROGUING
PROS
PROSAIC
PROSAICAL
PROSAICALLY
PROSAISM
PROSAISMS
PROSAIST
PROSAISTS
PROSATEUR
PROSATEURS
PROSAUROPOD
PROSAUROPODS
PROSCENIA
PROSCENIUM
PROSCENIUMS
PROSCIUTTI
PROSCIUTTO
PROSCIUTTOS
PROSCRIBE
PROSCRIBED
PROSCRIBER
PROSCRIBERS
PROSCRIBES
PROSCRIBING
PROSCRIPTION
PROSCRIPTIONS
PROSCRIPTIVE
PROSCRIPTIVELY
PROSE
PROSECCO
PROSECCOS
PROSECT
PROSECTED
PROSECTING
PROSECTOR
PROSECTORS
PROSECTS
PROSECUTABLE
PROSECUTE
PROSECUTED
PROSECUTES
PROSECUTING
PROSECUTION
PROSECUTIONS

PROSECUTOR
PROSECUTORIAL
PROSECUTORS
PROSED
PROSELYTE
PROSELYTED
PROSELYTES
PROSELYTING
PROSELYTISE
PROSELYTISED
PROSELYTISES
PROSELYTISING
PROSELYTISM
PROSELYTISMS
PROSELYTIZATION
PROSELYTIZE
PROSELYTIZED
PROSELYTIZER
PROSELYTIZERS
PROSELYTIZES
PROSELYTIZING
PROSEMINAR
PROSEMINARS
PROSENCEPHALA
PROSENCEPHALIC
PROSENCEPHALON
PROSER
PROSERS
PROSES
PROSIER
PROSIEST
PROSIFIED
PROSIFIES
PROSIFY
PROSIFYING
PROSILY
PROSIMIAN
PROSIMIANS
PROSINESS
PROSINESSES
PROSING
PROSIT
PROSO
PROSOBRANCH
PROSOBRANCHS
PROSODIC
PROSODICAL
PROSODICALLY
PROSODIES
PROSODIST
PROSODISTS
PROSODY
PROSOMA

PROSOMAL
PROSOMAS
PROSOMATA
PROSOPOGRAPHIES
PROSOPOGRAPHY
PROSOPOPOEIA
PROSOPOPOEIAS
PROSOS
PROSPECT
PROSPECTED
PROSPECTING
PROSPECTIVE
PROSPECTIVELY
PROSPECTOR
PROSPECTORS
PROSPECTS
PROSPECTUS
PROSPECTUSES
PROSPER
PROSPERED
PROSPERING
PROSPERITIES
PROSPERITY
PROSPEROUS
PROSPEROUSLY
PROSPEROUSNESS
PROSPERS
PROSS
PROSSES
PROSSIE
PROSSIES
PROST
PROSTACYCLIN
PROSTACYCLINS
PROSTAGLANDIN
PROSTAGLANDINS
PROSTATE
PROSTATECTOMIES
PROSTATECTOMY
PROSTATES
PROSTATIC
PROSTATISM
PROSTATISMS
PROSTATITIS
PROSTATITISES
PROSTHESES
PROSTHESIS
PROSTHETIC
PROSTHETICALLY
PROSTHETICS
PROSTHETIST
PROSTHETISTS
PROSTHODONTICS

PROSTHODONTIST
PROSTHODONTISTS
PROSTIE
PROSTIES
PROSTITUTE
PROSTITUTED
PROSTITUTES
PROSTITUTING
PROSTITUTION
PROSTITUTIONS
PROSTITUTOR
PROSTITUTORS
PROSTOMIA
PROSTOMIAL
PROSTOMIUM
PROSTRATE
PROSTRATED
PROSTRATES
PROSTRATING
PROSTRATION
PROSTRATIONS
PROSTYLE
PROSTYLES
PROSUMER
PROSUMERS
PROSY
PROTACTINIUM
PROTACTINIUMS
PROTAGONIST
PROTAGONISTS
PROTAMIN
PROTAMINE
PROTAMINES
PROTAMINS
PROTASES
PROTASIS
PROTATIC
PROTEA
PROTEAN
PROTEANS
PROTEAS
PROTEASE
PROTEASES
PROTECT
PROTECTABLE
PROTECTANT
PROTECTANTS
PROTECTED
PROTECTER
PROTECTERS
PROTECTING
PROTECTION
PROTECTIONISM

PROTECTIONISMS
PROTECTIONIST
PROTECTIONISTS
PROTECTIONS
PROTECTIVE
PROTECTIVELY
PROTECTIVENESS
PROTECTOR
PROTECTORAL
PROTECTORATE
PROTECTORATES
PROTECTORIES
PROTECTORS
PROTECTORSHIP
PROTECTORSHIPS
PROTECTORY
PROTECTRESS
PROTECTRESSES
PROTECTS
PROTEGE
PROTEGEE
PROTEGEES
PROTEGES
PROTEI
PROTEID
PROTEIDE
PROTEIDES
PROTEIDS
PROTEIN
PROTEINACEOUS
PROTEINASE
PROTEINASES
PROTEINIC
PROTEINS
PROTEINURIA
PROTEINURIAS
PROTEND
PROTENDED
PROTENDING
PROTENDS
PROTENSIVE
PROTENSIVELY
PROTEOGLYCAN
PROTEOGLYCANS
PROTEOLYSES
PROTEOLYSIS
PROTEOLYTIC
PROTEOLYTICALLY
PROTEOME
PROTEOMES
PROTEOMIC
PROTEOMICS
PROTEOSE

PROTEOSES
PROTEST
PROTESTANT
PROTESTANTS
PROTESTATION
PROTESTATIONS
PROTESTED
PROTESTER
PROTESTERS
PROTESTING
PROTESTOR
PROTESTORS
PROTESTS
PROTEUS
PROTEUSES
PROTHALAMIA
PROTHALAMION
PROTHALAMIUM
PROTHALLI
PROTHALLIA
PROTHALLIUM
PROTHALLUS
PROTHALLUSES
PROTHESES
PROTHESIS
PROTHETIC
PROTHONOTARIAL
PROTHONOTARIES
PROTHONOTARY
PROTHORACES
PROTHORACIC
PROTHORAX
PROTHORAXES
PROTHROMBIN
PROTHROMBINS
PROTIST
PROTISTAN
PROTISTANS
PROTISTIC
PROTISTS
PROTIUM
PROTIUMS
PROTOCERATOPS
PROTOCERATOPSES
PROTOCOL
PROTOCOLED
PROTOCOLING
PROTOCOLLED
PROTOCOLLING
PROTOCOLS
PROTODERM
PROTODERMS
PROTOGALAXIES
PROTOGALAXY
PROTOHISTORIAN
PROTOHISTORIANS
PROTOHISTORIC
PROTOHISTORIES
PROTOHISTORY
PROTOHUMAN
PROTOHUMANS
PROTOLANGUAGE
PROTOLANGUAGES
PROTOMARTYR
PROTOMARTYRS
PROTON
PROTONATE
PROTONATED
PROTONATES
PROTONATING
PROTONATION
PROTONATIONS
PROTONEMA
PROTONEMAL
PROTONEMATA
PROTONEMATAL
PROTONIC
PROTONOTARIES
PROTONOTARY
PROTONS
PROTOPATHIC
PROTOPHLOEM
PROTOPHLOEMS
PROTOPLANET
PROTOPLANETARY
PROTOPLANETS
PROTOPLASM
PROTOPLASMIC
PROTOPLASMS
PROTOPLAST
PROTOPLASTS
PROTOPOD
PROTOPODS
PROTOPORPHYRIN
PROTOPORPHYRINS
PROTOSTAR
PROTOSTARS
PROTOSTELE
PROTOSTELES
PROTOSTELIC
PROTOSTOME
PROTOSTOMES
PROTOTROPH
PROTOTROPHIC
PROTOTROPHIES
PROTOTROPHS
PROTOTROPHY
PROTOTYPAL
PROTOTYPE
PROTOTYPED
PROTOTYPES
PROTOTYPIC
PROTOTYPICAL
PROTOTYPICALLY
PROTOTYPING
PROTOXID
PROTOXIDE
PROTOXIDES
PROTOXIDS
PROTOXYLEM
PROTOXYLEMS
PROTOZOA
PROTOZOAL
PROTOZOAN
PROTOZOANS
PROTOZOIC
PROTOZOOLOGIES
PROTOZOOLOGIST
PROTOZOOLOGISTS
PROTOZOOLOGY
PROTOZOON
PROTOZOONS
PROTRACT
PROTRACTED
PROTRACTILE
PROTRACTING
PROTRACTION
PROTRACTIONS
PROTRACTIVE
PROTRACTOR
PROTRACTORS
PROTRACTS
PROTRADE
PROTREPTIC
PROTREPTICS
PROTRUDE
PROTRUDED
PROTRUDES
PROTRUDING
PROTRUSIBLE
PROTRUSION
PROTRUSIONS
PROTRUSIVE
PROTRUSIVELY
PROTRUSIVENESS
PROTUBERANCE
PROTUBERANCES
PROTUBERANT
PROTUBERANTLY
PROTURAN
PROTURANS
PROTYL
PROTYLE
PROTYLES
PROTYLS
PROUD
PROUDER
PROUDEST
PROUDFUL
PROUDHEARTED
PROUDLY
PROUDNESS
PROUDNESSES
PROUNION
PROUSTITE
PROUSTITES
PROVABLE
PROVABLENESS
PROVABLENESSES
PROVABLY
PROVASCULAR
PROVE
PROVED
PROVEN
PROVENANCE
PROVENANCES
PROVENDER
PROVENDERS
PROVENIENCE
PROVENIENCES
PROVENLY
PROVENTRICULI
PROVENTRICULUS
PROVER
PROVERB
PROVERBED
PROVERBIAL
PROVERBIALLY
PROVERBING
PROVERBS
PROVERS
PROVES
PROVIDE
PROVIDED
PROVIDENCE
PROVIDENCES
PROVIDENT
PROVIDENTIAL
PROVIDENTIALLY
PROVIDENTLY
PROVIDER
PROVIDERS
PROVIDES
PROVIDING
PROVINCE
PROVINCES
PROVINCIAL
PROVINCIALISM
PROVINCIALISMS
PROVINCIALIST
PROVINCIALISTS
PROVINCIALITIES
PROVINCIALITY
PROVINCIALIZE
PROVINCIALIZED
PROVINCIALIZES
PROVINCIALIZING
PROVINCIALLY
PROVINCIALS
PROVING
PROVIRAL
PROVIRUS
PROVIRUSES
PROVISION
PROVISIONAL
PROVISIONALLY
PROVISIONALS
PROVISIONARY
PROVISIONED
PROVISIONER
PROVISIONERS
PROVISIONING
PROVISIONS
PROVISO
PROVISOES
PROVISORY
PROVISOS
PROVITAMIN
PROVITAMINS
PROVOCATEUR
PROVOCATEURS
PROVOCATION
PROVOCATIONS
PROVOCATIVE
PROVOCATIVELY
PROVOCATIVENESS
PROVOCATIVES
PROVOKE
PROVOKED
PROVOKER
PROVOKERS
PROVOKES
PROVOKING
PROVOKINGLY
PROVOLONE

ROVOLONES
ROVOST
ROVOSTS
ROW
ROWAR
ROWER
ROWESS
ROWESSES
ROWEST
ROWL
ROWLED
ROWLER
ROWLERS
ROWLING
ROWLS
ROWS
ROXEMIC
ROXEMICS
ROXIES
ROXIMAL
ROXIMALLY
ROXIMATE
ROXIMATELY
ROXIMATENESS
ROXIMATENESSES
ROXIMITIES
ROXIMITY
ROXIMO
ROXY
RUDE
RUDENCE
RUDENCES
RUDENT
RUDENTIAL
RUDENTIALLY
RUDENTLY
RUDERIES
RUDERY
RUDES
RUDISH
RUDISHLY
RUDISHNESS
RUDISHNESSES
RUINOSE
RUNABLE
RUNE
RUNED
RUNELLA
RUNELLAS
RUNELLE
RUNELLES
RUNELLO
RUNELLOS
PRUNER
PRUNERS
PRUNES
PRUNEY
PRUNIER
PRUNIEST
PRUNING
PRUNUS
PRUNUSES
PRURIENCE
PRURIENCES
PRURIENCIES
PRURIENCY
PRURIENT
PRURIENTLY
PRURIGO
PRURIGOS
PRURITIC
PRURITUS
PRURITUSES
PRUSSIANISE
PRUSSIANISED
PRUSSIANISES
PRUSSIANISING
PRUSSIANIZATION
PRUSSIANIZE
PRUSSIANIZED
PRUSSIANIZES
PRUSSIANIZING
PRUSSIATE
PRUSSIATES
PRUSSIC
PRUTA
PRUTAH
PRUTOT
PRUTOTH
PRY
PRYER
PRYERS
PRYING
PRYINGLY
PRYTHEE
PSALM
PSALMBOOK
PSALMBOOKS
PSALMED
PSALMIC
PSALMING
PSALMIST
PSALMISTS
PSALMODIC
PSALMODIES
PSALMODY
PSALMS
PSALTER
PSALTERIA
PSALTERIES
PSALTERIUM
PSALTERS
PSALTERY
PSALTRIES
PSALTRY
PSAMMITE
PSAMMITES
PSAMMITIC
PSAMMON
PSAMMONS
PSCHENT
PSCHENTS
PSEPHITE
PSEPHITES
PSEPHITIC
PSEPHOLOGICAL
PSEPHOLOGIES
PSEPHOLOGIST
PSEPHOLOGISTS
PSEPHOLOGY
PSEUD
PSEUDEPIGRAPH
PSEUDEPIGRAPHA
PSEUDEPIGRAPHON
PSEUDEPIGRAPHS
PSEUDEPIGRAPHY
PSEUDO
PSEUDOALLELE
PSEUDOALLELES
PSEUDOCLASSIC
PSEUDOCLASSICS
PSEUDOCOEL
PSEUDOCOELOMATE
PSEUDOCOELS
PSEUDOCYESES
PSEUDOCYESIS
PSEUDOEPHEDRINE
PSEUDOMONAD
PSEUDOMONADES
PSEUDOMONADS
PSEUDOMONAS
PSEUDOMORPH
PSEUDOMORPHIC
PSEUDOMORPHISM
PSEUDOMORPHISMS
PSEUDOMORPHOUS
PSEUDOMORPHS
PSEUDONYM
PSEUDONYMITIES
PSEUDONYMITY
PSEUDONYMOUS
PSEUDONYMOUSLY
PSEUDONYMS
PSEUDOPOD
PSEUDOPODAL
PSEUDOPODIA
PSEUDOPODIAL
PSEUDOPODIUM
PSEUDOPODS
PSEUDOPREGNANCY
PSEUDOPREGNANT
PSEUDORANDOM
PSEUDOS
PSEUDOSCIENCE
PSEUDOSCIENCES
PSEUDOSCIENTIST
PSEUDOSCORPION
PSEUDOSCORPIONS
PSEUDS
PSHAW
PSHAWED
PSHAWING
PSHAWS
PSI
PSILOCIN
PSILOCINS
PSILOCYBIN
PSILOCYBINS
PSILOPHYTE
PSILOPHYTES
PSILOPHYTIC
PSILOSES
PSILOSIS
PSILOTIC
PSIONIC
PSIS
PSITTACINE
PSITTACINES
PSITTACOSES
PSITTACOSIS
PSITTACOTIC
PSOAE
PSOAI
PSOAS
PSOATIC
PSOCID
PSOCIDS
PSORALEA
PSORALEAS
PSORALEN
PSORALENS
PSORIASES
PSORIASIS
PSORIATIC
PSORIATICS
PSST
PST
PSYCH
PSYCHASTHENIA
PSYCHASTHENIAS
PSYCHASTHENIC
PSYCHASTHENICS
PSYCHE
PSYCHED
PSYCHEDELIA
PSYCHEDELIAS
PSYCHEDELIC
PSYCHEDELICALLY
PSYCHEDELICS
PSYCHES
PSYCHIATRIC
PSYCHIATRICALLY
PSYCHIATRIES
PSYCHIATRIST
PSYCHIATRISTS
PSYCHIATRY
PSYCHIC
PSYCHICAL
PSYCHICALLY
PSYCHICS
PSYCHING
PSYCHISM
PSYCHISMS
PSYCHO
PSYCHOACOUSTIC
PSYCHOACOUSTICS
PSYCHOACTIVE
PSYCHOANALYSE
PSYCHOANALYSED
PSYCHOANALYSES
PSYCHOANALYSING
PSYCHOANALYSIS
PSYCHOANALYST
PSYCHOANALYSTS
PSYCHOANALYTIC
PSYCHOANALYZE
PSYCHOANALYZED
PSYCHOANALYZES
PSYCHOANALYZING
PSYCHOBABBLE
PSYCHOBABBLED
PSYCHOBABBLER
PSYCHOBABBLERS
PSYCHOBABBLES
PSYCHOBABBLING

PSYCHOBIOGRAPHY
PSYCHOBIOLOGIC
PSYCHOBIOLOGIES
PSYCHOBIOLOGIST
PSYCHOBIOLOGY
PSYCHOCHEMICAL
PSYCHOCHEMICALS
PSYCHODRAMA
PSYCHODRAMAS
PSYCHODRAMATIC
PSYCHODYNAMIC
PSYCHODYNAMICS
PSYCHOGENESES
PSYCHOGENESIS
PSYCHOGENETIC
PSYCHOGENIC
PSYCHOGENICALLY
PSYCHOGRAPH
PSYCHOGRAPHIC
PSYCHOGRAPHICS
PSYCHOGRAPHS
PSYCHOHISTORIAN
PSYCHOHISTORIES
PSYCHOHISTORY
PSYCHOKINESES
PSYCHOKINESIS
PSYCHOKINETIC
PSYCHOLINGUIST
PSYCHOLINGUISTS
PSYCHOLOGIC
PSYCHOLOGICAL
PSYCHOLOGICALLY
PSYCHOLOGIES
PSYCHOLOGISE
PSYCHOLOGISED
PSYCHOLOGISES
PSYCHOLOGISING
PSYCHOLOGISM
PSYCHOLOGISMS
PSYCHOLOGIST
PSYCHOLOGISTS
PSYCHOLOGIZE
PSYCHOLOGIZED
PSYCHOLOGIZES
PSYCHOLOGIZING
PSYCHOLOGY
PSYCHOMETRIC
PSYCHOMETRICIAN
PSYCHOMETRICS
PSYCHOMETRIES
PSYCHOMETRY
PSYCHOMOTOR
PSYCHONEUROSES
PSYCHONEUROSIS
PSYCHONEUROTIC
PSYCHONEUROTICS
PSYCHOPATH
PSYCHOPATHIC
PSYCHOPATHICS
PSYCHOPATHIES
PSYCHOPATHOLOGY
PSYCHOPATHS
PSYCHOPATHY
PSYCHOPHYSICAL
PSYCHOPHYSICIST
PSYCHOPHYSICS
PSYCHOS
PSYCHOSES
PSYCHOSEXUAL
PSYCHOSEXUALITY
PSYCHOSEXUALLY
PSYCHOSIS
PSYCHOSOCIAL
PSYCHOSOCIALLY
PSYCHOSOMATIC
PSYCHOSOMATICS
PSYCHOSURGEON
PSYCHOSURGEONS
PSYCHOSURGERIES
PSYCHOSURGERY
PSYCHOSURGICAL
PSYCHOSYNTHESES
PSYCHOSYNTHESIS
PSYCHOTHERAPIES
PSYCHOTHERAPIST
PSYCHOTHERAPY
PSYCHOTIC
PSYCHOTICALLY
PSYCHOTICS
PSYCHOTOMIMETIC
PSYCHOTROPIC
PSYCHOTROPICS
PSYCHROMETER
PSYCHROMETERS
PSYCHROMETRIC
PSYCHROMETRIES
PSYCHROMETRY
PSYCHROPHILIC
PSYCHS
PSYLLA
PSYLLAS
PSYLLID
PSYLLIDS
PSYLLIUM
PSYLLIUMS
PSYOPS
PSYWAR
PSYWARS
PTARMIGAN
PTARMIGANS
PTERANODON
PTERANODONS
PTERIDINE
PTERIDINES
PTERIDOLOGICAL
PTERIDOLOGIES
PTERIDOLOGIST
PTERIDOLOGISTS
PTERIDOLOGY
PTERIDOPHYTE
PTERIDOPHYTES
PTERIDOSPERM
PTERIDOSPERMS
PTERIN
PTERINS
PTERODACTYL
PTERODACTYLS
PTEROPOD
PTEROPODS
PTEROSAUR
PTEROSAURS
PTERYGIA
PTERYGIAL
PTERYGIUM
PTERYGIUMS
PTERYGOID
PTERYGOIDS
PTERYLA
PTERYLAE
PTISAN
PTISANS
PTOMAIN
PTOMAINE
PTOMAINES
PTOMAINIC
PTOMAINS
PTOOEY
PTOSES
PTOSIS
PTOTIC
PTUI
PTYALIN
PTYALINS
PTYALISM
PTYALISMS
PUB
PUBBING
PUBBINGS
PUBERAL
PUBERTAL
PUBERTIES
PUBERTY
PUBERULENT
PUBES
PUBESCENCE
PUBESCENCES
PUBESCENT
PUBIC
PUBIS
PUBLIC
PUBLICALLY
PUBLICAN
PUBLICANS
PUBLICATION
PUBLICATIONS
PUBLICISE
PUBLICISED
PUBLICISES
PUBLICISING
PUBLICIST
PUBLICISTS
PUBLICITIES
PUBLICITY
PUBLICIZE
PUBLICIZED
PUBLICIZES
PUBLICIZING
PUBLICLY
PUBLICNESS
PUBLICNESSES
PUBLICS
PUBLISH
PUBLISHABLE
PUBLISHED
PUBLISHER
PUBLISHERS
PUBLISHES
PUBLISHING
PUBLISHINGS
PUBS
PUCCOON
PUCCOONS
PUCE
PUCES
PUCK
PUCKA
PUCKER
PUCKERED
PUCKERER
PUCKERERS
PUCKERIER
PUCKERIEST
PUCKERING
PUCKERS
PUCKERY
PUCKISH
PUCKISHLY
PUCKISHNESS
PUCKISHNESSES
PUCKS
PUCKSTER
PUCKSTERS
PUD
PUDDING
PUDDINGIER
PUDDINGIEST
PUDDINGS
PUDDINGY
PUDDLE
PUDDLED
PUDDLER
PUDDLERS
PUDDLES
PUDDLIER
PUDDLIEST
PUDDLING
PUDDLINGS
PUDDLY
PUDENCIES
PUDENCY
PUDENDA
PUDENDAL
PUDENDUM
PUDEUR
PUDEURS
PUDGE
PUDGES
PUDGIER
PUDGIEST
PUDGILY
PUDGINESS
PUDGINESSES
PUDGY
PUDIBUND
PUDIC
PUDS
PUDU
PUDUS
PUEBLO
PUEBLOS
PUERILE
PUERILELY
PUERILISM
PUERILISMS
PUERILITIES

UERILITY
UERPERA
UERPERAE
UERPERAL
UERPERIA
UERPERIUM
UFF
UFFBACK
UFFBACKS
UFFBALL
UFFBALLS
UFFBIRD
UFFBIRDS
UFFED
UFFER
UFFERIES
UFFERS
UFFERY
UFFIER
UFFIEST
UFFILY
UFFIN
UFFINESS
UFFINESSES
UFFING
UFFINS
UFFS
UFFY
UG
UGAREE
UGAREES
UGGAREE
UGGAREES
UGGED
UGGIER
UGGIEST
UGGINESS
JGGINESSES
UGGING
UGGINGS
UGGISH
JGGREE
UGGREES
UGGRIES
UGGRY
JGGY
JGH
UGILISM
JGILISMS
UGILIST
JGILISTIC
JGILISTS
JGMARK
PUGMARKS
PUGNACIOUS
PUGNACIOUSLY
PUGNACIOUSNESS
PUGNACITIES
PUGNACITY
PUGREE
PUGREES
PUGS
PUISNE
PUISNES
PUISSANCE
PUISSANCES
PUISSANT
PUJA
PUJAH
PUJAHS
PUJAS
PUKE
PUKED
PUKES
PUKEY
PUKIER
PUKIEST
PUKING
PUKKA
PUKKAH
PUL
PULA
PULAO
PULAOS
PULAS
PULCHRITUDE
PULCHRITUDES
PULCHRITUDINOUS
PULE
PULED
PULER
PULERS
PULES
PULI
PULICENE
PULICIDE
PULICIDES
PULIK
PULING
PULINGLY
PULINGS
PULIS
PULK
PULKA
PULKAS
PULKS
PULL
PULLBACK
PULLBACKS
PULLED
PULLER
PULLERS
PULLET
PULLETS
PULLEY
PULLEYED
PULLEYING
PULLEYS
PULLING
PULLMAN
PULLMANS
PULLOUT
PULLOUTS
PULLOVER
PULLOVERS
PULLS
PULLULATE
PULLULATED
PULLULATES
PULLULATING
PULLULATION
PULLULATIONS
PULLUP
PULLUPS
PULMONARY
PULMONATE
PULMONATES
PULMONIC
PULMONOLOGIST
PULMONOLOGISTS
PULMOTOR
PULMOTORS
PULP
PULPAL
PULPALLY
PULPED
PULPER
PULPERS
PULPIER
PULPIEST
PULPILY
PULPINESS
PULPINESSES
PULPING
PULPINGS
PULPIT
PULPITAL
PULPITS
PULPLESS
PULPOUS
PULPS
PULPWOOD
PULPWOODS
PULPY
PULQUE
PULQUES
PULS
PULSANT
PULSAR
PULSARS
PULSATE
PULSATED
PULSATES
PULSATILE
PULSATING
PULSATION
PULSATIONS
PULSATIVE
PULSATOR
PULSATORS
PULSATORY
PULSE
PULSED
PULSEJET
PULSEJETS
PULSER
PULSERS
PULSES
PULSING
PULSION
PULSIONS
PULSOJET
PULSOJETS
PULTRUDE
PULTRUDED
PULTRUDES
PULTRUDING
PULVERABLE
PULVERISE
PULVERISED
PULVERISES
PULVERISING
PULVERIZABLE
PULVERIZATION
PULVERIZATIONS
PULVERIZE
PULVERIZED
PULVERIZER
PULVERIZERS
PULVERIZES
PULVERIZING
PULVERULENT
PULVILLAR
PULVILLI
PULVILLUS
PULVINAR
PULVINATE
PULVINI
PULVINUS
PUMA
PUMAS
PUMELO
PUMELOS
PUMICE
PUMICED
PUMICEOUS
PUMICER
PUMICERS
PUMICES
PUMICING
PUMICITE
PUMICITES
PUMMEL
PUMMELED
PUMMELING
PUMMELLED
PUMMELLING
PUMMELO
PUMMELOS
PUMMELS
PUMP
PUMPABLE
PUMPED
PUMPER
PUMPERNICKEL
PUMPERNICKELS
PUMPERS
PUMPING
PUMPJACK
PUMPJACKS
PUMPKIN
PUMPKINS
PUMPKINSEED
PUMPKINSEEDS
PUMPLESS
PUMPLIKE
PUMPS
PUN
PUNA
PUNAS
PUNCH
PUNCHBALL
PUNCHBALLS
PUNCHBOARD
PUNCHBOARDS

PUNCHED
PUNCHEON
PUNCHEONS
PUNCHER
PUNCHERS
PUNCHES
PUNCHIER
PUNCHIEST
PUNCHILY
PUNCHINELLO
PUNCHINELLOS
PUNCHING
PUNCHLESS
PUNCHOUT
PUNCHOUTS
PUNCHY
PUNCTA
PUNCTATE
PUNCTATED
PUNCTATION
PUNCTATIONS
PUNCTILIO
PUNCTILIOS
PUNCTILIOUS
PUNCTILIOUSLY
PUNCTILIOUSNESS
PUNCTUAL
PUNCTUALITIES
PUNCTUALITY
PUNCTUALLY
PUNCTUATE
PUNCTUATED
PUNCTUATES
PUNCTUATING
PUNCTUATION
PUNCTUATIONS
PUNCTUATOR
PUNCTUATORS
PUNCTUM
PUNCTURE
PUNCTURED
PUNCTURES
PUNCTURING
PUNDIT
PUNDITIC
PUNDITOCRACIES
PUNDITOCRACY
PUNDITRIES
PUNDITRY
PUNDITS
PUNG
PUNGENCIES
PUNGENCY
PUNGENT
PUNGENTLY
PUNGLE
PUNGLED
PUNGLES
PUNGLING
PUNGS
PUNIER
PUNIEST
PUNILY
PUNINESS
PUNINESSES
PUNISH
PUNISHABILITIES
PUNISHABILITY
PUNISHABLE
PUNISHED
PUNISHER
PUNISHERS
PUNISHES
PUNISHING
PUNISHMENT
PUNISHMENTS
PUNITION
PUNITIONS
PUNITIVE
PUNITIVELY
PUNITIVENESS
PUNITIVENESSES
PUNITORY
PUNJI
PUNJIS
PUNK
PUNKA
PUNKAH
PUNKAHS
PUNKAS
PUNKER
PUNKERS
PUNKEST
PUNKETTE
PUNKETTES
PUNKEY
PUNKEYS
PUNKIE
PUNKIER
PUNKIES
PUNKIEST
PUNKIN
PUNKINESS
PUNKINESSES
PUNKINS
PUNKISH
PUNKS
PUNKY
PUNNED
PUNNER
PUNNERS
PUNNET
PUNNETS
PUNNIER
PUNNIEST
PUNNING
PUNNINGLY
PUNNINGS
PUNNY
PUNS
PUNSTER
PUNSTERS
PUNT
PUNTED
PUNTER
PUNTERS
PUNTIES
PUNTING
PUNTO
PUNTOS
PUNTS
PUNTY
PUNY
PUP
PUPA
PUPAE
PUPAL
PUPARIA
PUPARIAL
PUPARIUM
PUPAS
PUPATE
PUPATED
PUPATES
PUPATING
PUPATION
PUPATIONS
PUPFISH
PUPFISHES
PUPIL
PUPILAGE
PUPILAGES
PUPILAR
PUPILARY
PUPILLAGE
PUPILLAGES
PUPILLARY
PUPILS
PUPPED
PUPPET
PUPPETEER
PUPPETEERED
PUPPETEERING
PUPPETEERS
PUPPETLIKE
PUPPETRIES
PUPPETRY
PUPPETS
PUPPIES
PUPPING
PUPPY
PUPPYDOM
PUPPYDOMS
PUPPYHOOD
PUPPYHOODS
PUPPYISH
PUPPYLIKE
PUPS
PUPU
PUPUS
PUR
PURANA
PURANAS
PURANIC
PURBLIND
PURBLINDLY
PURBLINDNESS
PURBLINDNESSES
PURCHASABLE
PURCHASE
PURCHASED
PURCHASER
PURCHASERS
PURCHASES
PURCHASING
PURDA
PURDAH
PURDAHS
PURDAS
PURE
PUREBLOOD
PUREBLOODS
PUREBRED
PUREBREDS
PUREE
PUREED
PUREEING
PUREES
PURELY
PURENESS
PURENESSES
PURER
PUREST
PURFLE
PURFLED
PURFLER
PURFLERS
PURFLES
PURFLING
PURFLINGS
PURGATION
PURGATIONS
PURGATIVE
PURGATIVES
PURGATORIAL
PURGATORIES
PURGATORY
PURGE
PURGEABLE
PURGED
PURGER
PURGERS
PURGES
PURGING
PURGINGS
PURI
PURIFICATION
PURIFICATIONS
PURIFICATOR
PURIFICATORS
PURIFICATORY
PURIFIED
PURIFIER
PURIFIERS
PURIFIES
PURIFY
PURIFYING
PURIN
PURINE
PURINES
PURINS
PURIS
PURISM
PURISMS
PURIST
PURISTIC
PURISTICALLY
PURISTS
PURITAN
PURITANIC
PURITANICAL
PURITANICALLY
PURITANISM
PURITANISMS
PURITANS

URITIES
URITY
URL
URLED
URLIEU
URLIEUS
URLIEUX
URLIN
URLINE
URLINES
URLING
URLINGS
URLINS
URLOIN
URLOINED
URLOINER
URLOINERS
URLOINING
JRLOINS
JRLS
JROMYCIN
JROMYCINS
JRPLE
JRPLED
URPLEHEART
URPLEHEARTS
JRPLER
JRPLES
JRPLEST
JRPLING
JRPLISH
JRPLY
JRPORT
JRPORTED
JRPORTEDLY
JRPORTING
JRPORTS
JRPOSE
JRPOSED
JRPOSEFUL
JRPOSEFULLY
JRPOSEFULNESS
JRPOSELESS
JRPOSELESSLY
JRPOSELESSNESS
JRPOSELY
JRPOSES
JRPOSING
JRPOSIVE
JRPOSIVELY
JRPOSIVENESS
JRPOSIVENESSES
JRPURA
PURPURAS
PURPURE
PURPURES
PURPURIC
PURPURIN
PURPURINS
PURR
PURRED
PURRING
PURRINGLY
PURRS
PURS
PURSE
PURSED
PURSELIKE
PURSER
PURSERS
PURSES
PURSIER
PURSIEST
PURSILY
PURSINESS
PURSINESSES
PURSING
PURSLANE
PURSLANES
PURSUABLE
PURSUANCE
PURSUANCES
PURSUANT
PURSUE
PURSUED
PURSUER
PURSUERS
PURSUES
PURSUING
PURSUIT
PURSUITS
PURSUIVANT
PURSUIVANTS
PURSY
PURTENANCE
PURTENANCES
PURTIER
PURTIEST
PURTY
PURULENCE
PURULENCES
PURULENCIES
PURULENCY
PURULENT
PURVEY
PURVEYANCE
PURVEYANCES
PURVEYED
PURVEYING
PURVEYOR
PURVEYORS
PURVEYS
PURVIEW
PURVIEWS
PUS
PUSES
PUSH
PUSHBACK
PUSHBACKS
PUSHBALL
PUSHBALLS
PUSHCART
PUSHCARTS
PUSHCHAIR
PUSHCHAIRS
PUSHDOWN
PUSHDOWNS
PUSHED
PUSHER
PUSHERS
PUSHES
PUSHFUL
PUSHFULNESS
PUSHFULNESSES
PUSHIER
PUSHIEST
PUSHILY
PUSHINESS
PUSHINESSES
PUSHING
PUSHINGLY
PUSHOVER
PUSHOVERS
PUSHPIN
PUSHPINS
PUSHROD
PUSHRODS
PUSHUP
PUSHUPS
PUSHY
PUSILLANIMITIES
PUSILLANIMITY
PUSILLANIMOUS
PUSILLANIMOUSLY
PUSLEY
PUSLEYS
PUSLIKE
PUSS
PUSSES
PUSSIER
PUSSIES
PUSSIEST
PUSSLEY
PUSSLEYS
PUSSLIES
PUSSLIKE
PUSSLY
PUSSY
PUSSYCAT
PUSSYCATS
PUSSYFOOT
PUSSYFOOTED
PUSSYFOOTER
PUSSYFOOTERS
PUSSYFOOTING
PUSSYFOOTS
PUSSYTOES
PUSTULANT
PUSTULANTS
PUSTULAR
PUSTULATE
PUSTULATED
PUSTULATES
PUSTULATING
PUSTULATION
PUSTULATIONS
PUSTULE
PUSTULED
PUSTULES
PUSTULOUS
PUT
PUTAMEN
PUTAMENS
PUTAMINA
PUTATIVE
PUTATIVELY
PUTDOWN
PUTDOWNS
PUTLOCK
PUTLOCKS
PUTLOG
PUTLOGS
PUTOFF
PUTOFFS
PUTON
PUTONGHUA
PUTONGHUAS
PUTONS
PUTOUT
PUTOUTS
PUTREFACTION
PUTREFACTIONS
PUTREFACTIVE
PUTREFIED
PUTREFIER
PUTREFIERS
PUTREFIES
PUTREFY
PUTREFYING
PUTRESCENCE
PUTRESCENCES
PUTRESCENT
PUTRESCIBLE
PUTRESCINE
PUTRESCINES
PUTRID
PUTRIDITIES
PUTRIDITY
PUTRIDLY
PUTS
PUTSCH
PUTSCHES
PUTSCHIST
PUTSCHISTS
PUTT
PUTTANESCA
PUTTED
PUTTEE
PUTTEES
PUTTER
PUTTERED
PUTTERER
PUTTERERS
PUTTERING
PUTTERS
PUTTI
PUTTIE
PUTTIED
PUTTIER
PUTTIERS
PUTTIES
PUTTING
PUTTO
PUTTS
PUTTY
PUTTYING
PUTTYLESS
PUTTYLIKE
PUTTYROOT
PUTTYROOTS
PUTZ
PUTZED
PUTZES
PUTZING
PUZZLE

PUZZLED
PUZZLEDLY
PUZZLEHEADED
PUZZLEMENT
PUZZLEMENTS
PUZZLER
PUZZLERS
PUZZLES
PUZZLING
PUZZLINGLY
PYA
PYAEMIA
PYAEMIAS
PYAEMIC
PYAS
PYCNIDIA
PYCNIDIAL
PYCNIDIUM
PYCNOGONID
PYCNOGONIDS
PYCNOMETER
PYCNOMETERS
PYCNOSES
PYCNOSIS
PYCNOTIC
PYE
PYELITIC
PYELITIS
PYELITISES
PYELOGRAM
PYELOGRAMS
PYELONEPHRITIC
PYELONEPHRITIS
PYEMIA
PYEMIAS
PYEMIC
PYES
PYGIDIA
PYGIDIAL
PYGIDIUM
PYGMAEAN
PYGMEAN
PYGMIES
PYGMOID
PYGMY
PYGMYISH
PYGMYISM
PYGMYISMS
PYIC
PYIN
PYINS
PYJAMA
PYJAMAS
PYKNIC
PYKNICS
PYKNOSES
PYKNOSIS
PYKNOTIC
PYLON
PYLONS
PYLORI
PYLORIC
PYLORUS
PYLORUSES
PYODERMA
PYODERMAS
PYODERMIC
PYOGENIC
PYOID
PYORRHEA
PYORRHEAL
PYORRHEAS
PYORRHOEA
PYORRHOEAS
PYOSES
PYOSIS
PYRACANTHA
PYRACANTHAS
PYRALID
PYRALIDID
PYRALIDIDS
PYRALIDS
PYRAMID
PYRAMIDAL
PYRAMIDALLY
PYRAMIDED
PYRAMIDIC
PYRAMIDICAL
PYRAMIDING
PYRAMIDOLOGIES
PYRAMIDOLOGIST
PYRAMIDOLOGISTS
PYRAMIDOLOGY
PYRAMIDS
PYRAN
PYRANOID
PYRANOSE
PYRANOSES
PYRANOSIDE
PYRANOSIDES
PYRANS
PYRARGYRITE
PYRARGYRITES
PYRE
PYRENE
PYRENES
PYRENOID
PYRENOIDS
PYRES
PYRETHRIN
PYRETHRINS
PYRETHROID
PYRETHROIDS
PYRETHRUM
PYRETHRUMS
PYRETIC
PYREX
PYREXES
PYREXIA
PYREXIAL
PYREXIAS
PYREXIC
PYRHELIOMETER
PYRHELIOMETERS
PYRHELIOMETRIC
PYRIC
PYRIDIC
PYRIDINE
PYRIDINES
PYRIDOXAL
PYRIDOXALS
PYRIDOXAMINE
PYRIDOXAMINES
PYRIDOXIN
PYRIDOXINE
PYRIDOXINES
PYRIDOXINS
PYRIFORM
PYRIMETHAMINE
PYRIMETHAMINES
PYRIMIDINE
PYRIMIDINES
PYRITE
PYRITES
PYRITIC
PYRITICAL
PYRITISE
PYRITISED
PYRITISES
PYRITISING
PYRITIZE
PYRITIZED
PYRITIZES
PYRITIZING
PYRITOUS
PYRO
PYROCATECHOL
PYROCATECHOLS
PYROCERAM
PYROCERAMS
PYROCLASTIC
PYROELECTRIC
PYROELECTRICITY
PYROGALLOL
PYROGALLOLS
PYROGEN
PYROGENIC
PYROGENICITIES
PYROGENICITY
PYROGENS
PYROGIES
PYROGY
PYROHIES
PYROHY
PYROLA
PYROLAS
PYROLIZE
PYROLIZED
PYROLIZES
PYROLIZING
PYROLOGIES
PYROLOGY
PYROLUSITE
PYROLUSITES
PYROLYSATE
PYROLYSATES
PYROLYSE
PYROLYSED
PYROLYSES
PYROLYSING
PYROLYSIS
PYROLYTIC
PYROLYTICALLY
PYROLYZABLE
PYROLYZATE
PYROLYZATES
PYROLYZE
PYROLYZED
PYROLYZER
PYROLYZERS
PYROLYZES
PYROLYZING
PYROMANCIES
PYROMANCY
PYROMANIA
PYROMANIAC
PYROMANIACAL
PYROMANIACS
PYROMANIAS
PYROMETALLURGY
PYROMETER
PYROMETERS
PYROMETRIC
PYROMETRICALLY
PYROMETRIES
PYROMETRY
PYROMORPHITE
PYROMORPHITES
PYRONE
PYRONES
PYRONINE
PYRONINES
PYRONINOPHILIC
PYROPE
PYROPES
PYROPHORIC
PYROPHOSPHATE
PYROPHOSPHATES
PYROPHYLLITE
PYROPHYLLITES
PYROS
PYROSIS
PYROSISES
PYROSTAT
PYROSTATS
PYROTECHNIC
PYROTECHNICAL
PYROTECHNICALLY
PYROTECHNICIAN
PYROTECHNICIANS
PYROTECHNICS
PYROTECHNIST
PYROTECHNISTS
PYROXENE
PYROXENES
PYROXENIC
PYROXENITE
PYROXENITES
PYROXENITIC
PYROXENOID
PYROXENOIDS
PYROXYLIN
PYROXYLINS
PYRRHIC
PYRRHICS
PYRRHOTITE
PYRRHOTITES
PYRROL
PYRROLE
PYRROLES
PYRROLIC
PYRROLS
PYRUVATE
PYRUVATES
PYSANKA

YSANKY
YTHON
YTHONESS
YTHONESSES
PYTHONIC
PYTHONS
PYURIA
PYURIAS
PYX
PYXES
PYXIDES
PYXIDIA
PYXIDIUM
PYXIE
PYXIES
PYXIS
PZAZZ
PZAZZES

Q

ABALA
ABALAH
ABALAHS
ABALAS
ADI
ADIS
AID
AIDS
AJAQ
AJAQS
AMUTIK
AMUTIKS
ANAT
ANATS
T
TS
WWALI
WWALIS

BLA
BLAS
GONG
GONGS
NDAR
NDARKA
NDARS
NTAR
NTARS
S
VIUT
VIUTS
PH
PHS
JA
JAALUDE
JAALUDES
ACK
ACKED
ACKERIES
QUACKERY
QUACKIER
QUACKIEST
QUACKING
QUACKISH
QUACKISM
QUACKISMS
QUACKS
QUACKSALVER
QUACKSALVERS
QUACKY
QUAD
QUADDED
QUADDING
QUADPLEX
QUADPLEXES
QUADRANGLE
QUADRANGLES
QUADRANGULAR
QUADRANS
QUADRANT
QUADRANTAL
QUADRANTES
QUADRANTS
QUADRAPHONIC
QUADRAPHONICS
QUADRAT
QUADRATE
QUADRATED
QUADRATES
QUADRATI
QUADRATIC
QUADRATICALLY
QUADRATICS
QUADRATING
QUADRATS
QUADRATURE
QUADRATURES
QUADRENNIA
QUADRENNIAL
QUADRENNIALLY
QUADRENNIALS
QUADRENNIUM
QUADRENNIUMS
QUADRIC
QUADRICEP
QUADRICEPS
QUADRICEPSES
QUADRICS
QUADRIFID
QUADRIGA
QUADRIGAE
QUADRILATERAL
QUADRILATERALS
QUADRILLE
QUADRILLES
QUADRILLION
QUADRILLIONS
QUADRILLIONTH
QUADRILLIONTHS
QUADRIPARTITE
QUADRIPHONIC
QUADRIPHONICS
QUADRIPLEGIA
QUADRIPLEGIAS
QUADRIPLEGIC
QUADRIPLEGICS
QUADRIVALENT
QUADRIVALENTS
QUADRIVIA
QUADRIVIAL
QUADRIVIUM
QUADROON
QUADROONS
QUADRUMANOUS
QUADRUMVIR
QUADRUMVIRATE
QUADRUMVIRATES
QUADRUMVIRS
QUADRUPED
QUADRUPEDAL
QUADRUPEDS
QUADRUPLE
QUADRUPLED
QUADRUPLES
QUADRUPLET
QUADRUPLETS
QUADRUPLICATE
QUADRUPLICATED
QUADRUPLICATES
QUADRUPLICATING
QUADRUPLICATION
QUADRUPLICITIES
QUADRUPLICITY
QUADRUPLING
QUADRUPLY
QUADRUPOLE
QUADRUPOLES
QUADS
QUAERE
QUAERES
QUAESTOR
QUAESTORS
QUAFF
QUAFFED
QUAFFER
QUAFFERS
QUAFFING
QUAFFS
QUAG
QUAGGA
QUAGGAS
QUAGGIER
QUAGGIEST
QUAGGY
QUAGMIRE
QUAGMIRES
QUAGMIRIER
QUAGMIRIEST
QUAGMIRY
QUAGS
QUAHAUG
QUAHAUGS
QUAHOG
QUAHOGS
QUAI
QUAICH
QUAICHES
QUAICHS
QUAIGH
QUAIGHS
QUAIL
QUAILED
QUAILING
QUAILS
QUAINT
QUAINTER
QUAINTEST
QUAINTLY
QUAINTNESS
QUAINTNESSES
QUAIS
QUAKE
QUAKED
QUAKER
QUAKERS
QUAKES
QUAKIER
QUAKIEST
QUAKILY
QUAKINESS
QUAKINESSES
QUAKING
QUAKINGLY
QUAKY
QUALE

QUALIA
QUALIFIABLE
QUALIFICATION
QUALIFICATIONS
QUALIFIED
QUALIFIEDLY
QUALIFIER
QUALIFIERS
QUALIFIES
QUALIFY
QUALIFYING
QUALITATIVE
QUALITATIVELY
QUALITIES
QUALITY
QUALM
QUALMIER
QUALMIEST
QUALMISH
QUALMISHLY
QUALMISHNESS
QUALMISHNESSES
QUALMS
QUALMY
QUAMASH
QUAMASHES
QUANDANG
QUANDANGS
QUANDARIES
QUANDARY
QUANDONG
QUANDONGS
QUANGO
QUANGOS
QUANT
QUANTA
QUANTAL
QUANTALLY
QUANTED
QUANTIC
QUANTICS
QUANTIFIABLE
QUANTIFICATION
QUANTIFICATIONS
QUANTIFIED
QUANTIFIER
QUANTIFIERS
QUANTIFIES
QUANTIFY
QUANTIFYING
QUANTILE
QUANTILES
QUANTING
QUANTISE
QUANTISED
QUANTISES
QUANTISING
QUANTITATE
QUANTITATED
QUANTITATES
QUANTITATING
QUANTITATION
QUANTITATIONS
QUANTITATIVE
QUANTITATIVELY
QUANTITIES
QUANTITY
QUANTIZATION
QUANTIZATIONS
QUANTIZE
QUANTIZED
QUANTIZER
QUANTIZERS
QUANTIZES
QUANTIZING
QUANTONG
QUANTONGS
QUANTS
QUANTUM
QUARANTINE
QUARANTINED
QUARANTINES
QUARANTINING
QUARE
QUARK
QUARKS
QUARREL
QUARRELED
QUARRELER
QUARRELERS
QUARRELING
QUARRELLED
QUARRELLER
QUARRELLERS
QUARRELLING
QUARRELS
QUARRELSOME
QUARRELSOMELY
QUARRELSOMENESS
QUARRIED
QUARRIER
QUARRIERS
QUARRIES
QUARRY
QUARRYING
QUARRYINGS
QUARRYMAN
QUARRYMEN
QUART
QUARTAN
QUARTANS
QUARTE
QUARTER
QUARTERAGE
QUARTERAGES
QUARTERBACK
QUARTERBACKED
QUARTERBACKING
QUARTERBACKS
QUARTERDECK
QUARTERDECKS
QUARTERED
QUARTERER
QUARTERERS
QUARTERFINAL
QUARTERFINALIST
QUARTERFINALS
QUARTERING
QUARTERINGS
QUARTERLIES
QUARTERLY
QUARTERMASTER
QUARTERMASTERS
QUARTERN
QUARTERNS
QUARTERS
QUARTERSAWED
QUARTERSAWN
QUARTERSTAFF
QUARTERSTAVES
QUARTES
QUARTET
QUARTETS
QUARTETTE
QUARTETTES
QUARTIC
QUARTICS
QUARTIER
QUARTIERS
QUARTILE
QUARTILES
QUARTO
QUARTOS
QUARTS
QUARTZ
QUARTZES
QUARTZITE
QUARTZITES
QUARTZITIC
QUARTZOSE
QUARTZOUS
QUASAR
QUASARS
QUASH
QUASHED
QUASHER
QUASHERS
QUASHES
QUASHING
QUASI
QUASICRYSTAL
QUASICRYSTALS
QUASIPARTICLE
QUASIPARTICLES
QUASIPERIODIC
QUASS
QUASSES
QUASSIA
QUASSIAS
QUASSIN
QUASSINS
QUATE
QUATERCENTENARY
QUATERNARIES
QUATERNARY
QUATERNION
QUATERNIONS
QUATERNITIES
QUATERNITY
QUATORZE
QUATORZES
QUATRAIN
QUATRAINS
QUATRE
QUATREFOIL
QUATREFOILS
QUATRES
QUATTROCENTO
QUATTROCENTOS
QUAVER
QUAVERED
QUAVERER
QUAVERERS
QUAVERING
QUAVERINGLY
QUAVERS
QUAVERY
QUAY
QUAYAGE
QUAYAGES
QUAYLIKE
QUAYS
QUAYSIDE
QUAYSIDES
QUBIT
QUBITS
QUBYTE
QUBYTES
QUEAN
QUEANS
QUEASIER
QUEASIEST
QUEASILY
QUEASINESS
QUEASINESSES
QUEASY
QUEAZIER
QUEAZIEST
QUEAZY
QUEBRACHO
QUEBRACHOS
QUEEN
QUEENCUP
QUEENCUPS
QUEENDOM
QUEENDOMS
QUEENED
QUEENIER
QUEENIEST
QUEENING
QUEENLIER
QUEENLIEST
QUEENLINESS
QUEENLINESSES
QUEENLY
QUEENS
QUEENSHIP
QUEENSHIPS
QUEENSIDE
QUEENSIDES
QUEENY
QUEER
QUEERED
QUEERER
QUEEREST
QUEERING
QUEERISH
QUEERLY
QUEERNESS
QUEERNESSES
QUEERS
QUELEA
QUELEAS
QUELL
QUELLABLE

UELLED
UELLER
UELLERS
UELLING
UELLS
UENCH
UENCHABLE
UENCHED
UENCHER
UENCHERS
UENCHES
UENCHING
UENCHLESS
UENELLE
UENELLES
UERCETIC
UERCETIN
UERCETINS
UERCINE
UERCITRON
UERCITRONS
UERIDA
UERIDAS
UERIED
UERIER
UERIERS
UERIES
UERIST
UERISTS
UERN
UERNS
UERULOUS
UERULOUSLY
UERULOUSNESS
UERULOUSNESSES
UERY
UERYING
UESADILLA
UESADILLAS
UEST
UESTED
UESTER
UESTERS
UESTING
UESTION
ESTIONABLE
ESTIONABLY
ESTIONARIES
ESTIONARY
ESTIONED
ESTIONER
ESTIONERS
ESTIONING
QUESTIONINGLY
QUESTIONINGS
QUESTIONLESS
QUESTIONNAIRE
QUESTIONNAIRES
QUESTIONS
QUESTOR
QUESTORS
QUESTS
QUETZAL
QUETZALES
QUETZALS
QUEUE
QUEUED
QUEUEING
QUEUER
QUEUERS
QUEUES
QUEUING
QUEY
QUEYS
QUEZAL
QUEZALES
QUEZALS
QUIBBLE
QUIBBLED
QUIBBLER
QUIBBLERS
QUIBBLES
QUIBBLING
QUICHE
QUICHES
QUICK
QUICKEN
QUICKENED
QUICKENER
QUICKENERS
QUICKENING
QUICKENS
QUICKER
QUICKEST
QUICKIE
QUICKIES
QUICKLIME
QUICKLIMES
QUICKLY
QUICKNESS
QUICKNESSES
QUICKS
QUICKSAND
QUICKSANDS
QUICKSET
QUICKSETS
QUICKSILVER
QUICKSILVERS
QUICKSTEP
QUICKSTEPS
QUID
QUIDDITIES
QUIDDITY
QUIDNUNC
QUIDNUNCS
QUIDS
QUIESCENCE
QUIESCENCES
QUIESCENT
QUIESCENTLY
QUIET
QUIETED
QUIETEN
QUIETENED
QUIETENER
QUIETENERS
QUIETENING
QUIETENS
QUIETER
QUIETERS
QUIETEST
QUIETING
QUIETISM
QUIETISMS
QUIETIST
QUIETISTIC
QUIETISTS
QUIETLY
QUIETNESS
QUIETNESSES
QUIETS
QUIETUDE
QUIETUDES
QUIETUS
QUIETUSES
QUIFF
QUIFFED
QUIFFS
QUILL
QUILLAI
QUILLAIA
QUILLAIAS
QUILLAIS
QUILLAJA
QUILLAJAS
QUILLBACK
QUILLBACKS
QUILLED
QUILLET
QUILLETS
QUILLING
QUILLINGS
QUILLOW
QUILLOWS
QUILLS
QUILLWORK
QUILLWORKS
QUILLWORT
QUILLWORTS
QUILT
QUILTED
QUILTER
QUILTERS
QUILTING
QUILTINGS
QUILTS
QUIN
QUINACRINE
QUINACRINES
QUINARIES
QUINARY
QUINATE
QUINCE
QUINCENTENARIES
QUINCENTENARY
QUINCENTENNIAL
QUINCENTENNIALS
QUINCES
QUINCUNCIAL
QUINCUNX
QUINCUNXES
QUINCUNXIAL
QUINDECILLION
QUINDECILLIONS
QUINELA
QUINELAS
QUINELLA
QUINELLAS
QUINIC
QUINIDINE
QUINIDINES
QUINIELA
QUINIELAS
QUININ
QUININA
QUININAS
QUININE
QUININES
QUININS
QUINNAT
QUINNATS
QUINOA
QUINOAS
QUINOID
QUINOIDAL
QUINOIDS
QUINOL
QUINOLIN
QUINOLINE
QUINOLINES
QUINOLINS
QUINOLONE
QUINOLONES
QUINOLS
QUINONE
QUINONES
QUINONOID
QUINQUENNIA
QUINQUENNIAL
QUINQUENNIALLY
QUINQUENNIALS
QUINQUENNIUM
QUINQUENNIUMS
QUINS
QUINSIED
QUINSIES
QUINSY
QUINT
QUINTA
QUINTAIN
QUINTAINS
QUINTAL
QUINTALS
QUINTAN
QUINTANS
QUINTAR
QUINTARS
QUINTAS
QUINTE
QUINTES
QUINTESSENCE
QUINTESSENCES
QUINTESSENTIAL
QUINTET
QUINTETS
QUINTETTE
QUINTETTES
QUINTIC
QUINTICS
QUINTILE
QUINTILES
QUINTILLION
QUINTILLIONS
QUINTILLIONTH
QUINTILLIONTHS

QUINTIN
QUINTINS
QUINTS
QUINTUPLE
QUINTUPLED
QUINTUPLES
QUINTUPLET
QUINTUPLETS
QUINTUPLICATE
QUINTUPLICATED
QUINTUPLICATES
QUINTUPLICATING
QUINTUPLING
QUINTUPLY
QUINZHEE
QUINZHEES
QUINZIE
QUINZIES
QUIP
QUIPPED
QUIPPER
QUIPPERS
QUIPPIER
QUIPPIEST
QUIPPING
QUIPPISH
QUIPPU
QUIPPUS
QUIPPY
QUIPS
QUIPSTER
QUIPSTERS
QUIPU
QUIPUS
QUIRE
QUIRED
QUIRES
QUIRING
QUIRK
QUIRKED
QUIRKIER
QUIRKIEST
QUIRKILY
QUIRKINESS
QUIRKINESSES
QUIRKING
QUIRKISH
QUIRKS
QUIRKY
QUIRT
QUIRTED
QUIRTING
QUIRTS
QUISLING
QUISLINGISM
QUISLINGISMS
QUISLINGS
QUIT
QUITCH
QUITCHES
QUITCLAIM
QUITCLAIMED
QUITCLAIMING
QUITCLAIMS
QUITE
QUITRENT
QUITRENTS
QUITS
QUITTANCE
QUITTANCES
QUITTED
QUITTER
QUITTERS
QUITTING
QUITTOR
QUITTORS
QUIVER
QUIVERED
QUIVERER
QUIVERERS
QUIVERIER
QUIVERIEST
QUIVERING
QUIVERINGLY
QUIVERS
QUIVERY
QUIXOTE
QUIXOTES
QUIXOTIC
QUIXOTICAL
QUIXOTICALLY
QUIXOTISM
QUIXOTISMS
QUIXOTRIES
QUIXOTRY
QUIZ
QUIZMASTER
QUIZMASTERS
QUIZZED
QUIZZER
QUIZZERS
QUIZZES
QUIZZICAL
QUIZZICALITIES
QUIZZICALITY
QUIZZICALLY
QUIZZING
QULLIQ
QULLIQS
QUOD
QUODLIBET
QUODLIBETS
QUODS
QUOHOG
QUOHOGS
QUOIN
QUOINED
QUOINING
QUOININGS
QUOINS
QUOIT
QUOITED
QUOITING
QUOITS
QUOKKA
QUOKKAS
QUOLL
QUOLLS
QUOMODO
QUOMODOS
QUONDAM
QUORUM
QUORUMS
QUOTA
QUOTABILITIES
QUOTABILITY
QUOTABLE
QUOTABLY
QUOTAS
QUOTATION
QUOTATIONS
QUOTATIVE
QUOTATIVES
QUOTE
QUOTED
QUOTER
QUOTERS
QUOTES
QUOTH
QUOTHA
QUOTIDIAN
QUOTIDIANS
QUOTIENT
QUOTIENTS
QUOTING
QURSH
QURSHES
QURUSH
QURUSHES
QWERTY
QWERTYS

R

RABASKA
RABASKAS
RABAT
RABATO
RABATOS
RABATS
RABBET
RABBETED
RABBETING
RABBETS
RABBI
RABBIES
RABBIN
RABBINATE
RABBINATES
RABBINIC
RABBINICAL
RABBINICALLY
RABBINISM
RABBINISMS
RABBINS
RABBIS
RABBIT
RABBITBRUSH
RABBITBRUSHES
RABBITED
RABBITER
RABBITERS
RABBITING
RABBITRIES
RABBITRY
RABBITS
RABBITY
RABBLE
RABBLED
RABBLEMENT
RABBLEMENTS
RABBLER
RABBLERS
RABBLES
RABBLING
RABBONI
RABBONIS
RABIC
RABID
RABIDITIES
RABIDITY
RABIDLY
RABIDNESS
RABIDNESSES

ABIES
ABIESES
ABIETIC
ACCOON
ACCOONS
ACE
ACECOURSE
ACECOURSES
ACED
ACEGOER
ACEGOERS
ACEHORSE
ACEHORSES
ACEMATE
ACEMATES
ACEME
ACEMED
ACEMES
ACEMIC
ACEMISM
CEMISMS
CEMIZATION
CEMIZATIONS
CEMIZE
CEMIZED
CEMIZES
CEMIZING
CEMOID
CEMOSE
CEMOUS
CER
CERS
CES
CETRACK
CETRACKER
CETRACKERS
CETRACKS
CEWALK
CEWALKED
CEWALKER
CEWALKERS
CEWALKING
CEWALKINGS
CEWALKS
CEWAY
CEWAYS
HET
HETED
HETING
HETS
HIAL
HIDES
HILLA
RACHILLAE
RACHIS
RACHISES
RACHITIC
RACHITIDES
RACHITIS
RACHITISES
RACIAL
RACIALISM
RACIALISMS
RACIALIST
RACIALISTIC
RACIALISTS
RACIALIZE
RACIALIZED
RACIALIZES
RACIALIZING
RACIALLY
RACIER
RACIEST
RACILY
RACINESS
RACINESSES
RACING
RACINGS
RACINO
RACINOS
RACISM
RACISMS
RACIST
RACISTS
RACK
RACKED
RACKER
RACKERS
RACKET
RACKETED
RACKETEER
RACKETEERED
RACKETEERING
RACKETEERS
RACKETIER
RACKETIEST
RACKETING
RACKETS
RACKETY
RACKFUL
RACKFULS
RACKING
RACKINGLY
RACKLE
RACKS
RACKWORK
RACKWORKS
RACLETTE
RACLETTES
RACON
RACONS
RACONTEUR
RACONTEURS
RACOON
RACOONS
RACQUET
RACQUETBALL
RACQUETBALLS
RACQUETS
RACY
RAD
RADAR
RADARS
RADARSCOPE
RADARSCOPES
RADDED
RADDER
RADDEST
RADDING
RADDLE
RADDLED
RADDLES
RADDLING
RADIABLE
RADIAL
RADIALE
RADIALIA
RADIALLY
RADIALS
RADIAN
RADIANCE
RADIANCES
RADIANCIES
RADIANCY
RADIANS
RADIANT
RADIANTLY
RADIANTS
RADIATE
RADIATED
RADIATELY
RADIATES
RADIATING
RADIATION
RADIATIONAL
RADIATIONLESS
RADIATIONS
RADIATIVE
RADIATOR
RADIATORS
RADICAL
RADICALISE
RADICALISED
RADICALISES
RADICALISING
RADICALISM
RADICALISMS
RADICALIZATION
RADICALIZATIONS
RADICALIZE
RADICALIZED
RADICALIZES
RADICALIZING
RADICALLY
RADICALNESS
RADICALNESSES
RADICALS
RADICAND
RADICANDS
RADICATE
RADICATED
RADICATES
RADICATING
RADICCHIO
RADICCHIOS
RADICEL
RADICELS
RADICES
RADICLE
RADICLES
RADICULAR
RADICULOPATHIES
RADICULOPATHY
RADII
RADIO
RADIOACTIVE
RADIOACTIVELY
RADIOACTIVITIES
RADIOACTIVITY
RADIOAUTOGRAPH
RADIOAUTOGRAPHS
RADIOAUTOGRAPHY
RADIOBIOLOGIC
RADIOBIOLOGICAL
RADIOBIOLOGIES
RADIOBIOLOGIST
RADIOBIOLOGISTS
RADIOBIOLOGY
RADIOCARBON
RADIOCARBONS
RADIOCHEMICAL
RADIOCHEMICALLY
RADIOCHEMIST
RADIOCHEMISTRY
RADIOCHEMISTS
RADIOECOLOGIES
RADIOECOLOGY
RADIOED
RADIOELEMENT
RADIOELEMENTS
RADIOES
RADIOGENIC
RADIOGRAM
RADIOGRAMS
RADIOGRAPH
RADIOGRAPHED
RADIOGRAPHER
RADIOGRAPHERS
RADIOGRAPHIC
RADIOGRAPHIES
RADIOGRAPHING
RADIOGRAPHS
RADIOGRAPHY
RADIOING
RADIOISOTOPE
RADIOISOTOPES
RADIOISOTOPIC
RADIOLABEL
RADIOLABELED
RADIOLABELING
RADIOLABELLED
RADIOLABELLING
RADIOLABELS
RADIOLARIA
RADIOLARIAN
RADIOLARIANS
RADIOLOGIC
RADIOLOGICAL
RADIOLOGICALLY
RADIOLOGIES
RADIOLOGIST
RADIOLOGISTS
RADIOLOGY
RADIOLUCENCIES
RADIOLUCENCY
RADIOLUCENT
RADIOLYSES
RADIOLYSIS
RADIOLYTIC
RADIOMAN
RADIOMEN
RADIOMETER
RADIOMETERS
RADIOMETRIC
RADIOMETRICALLY

RADIOMETRIES
RADIOMETRY
RADIOMIMETIC
RADIONICS
RADIONUCLIDE
RADIONUCLIDES
RADIOPAQUE
RADIOPHONE
RADIOPHONES
RADIOPHOTO
RADIOPHOTOS
RADIOPROTECTION
RADIOPROTECTIVE
RADIOS
RADIOSENSITIVE
RADIOSONDE
RADIOSONDES
RADIOSTRONTIUM
RADIOSTRONTIUMS
RADIOSURGERIES
RADIOSURGERY
RADIOTELEGRAPH
RADIOTELEGRAPHS
RADIOTELEGRAPHY
RADIOTELEMETRIC
RADIOTELEMETRY
RADIOTELEPHONE
RADIOTELEPHONES
RADIOTELEPHONY
RADIOTHERAPIES
RADIOTHERAPIST
RADIOTHERAPISTS
RADIOTHERAPY
RADIOTHORIUM
RADIOTHORIUMS
RADIOTRACER
RADIOTRACERS
RADISH
RADISHES
RADIUM
RADIUMS
RADIUS
RADIUSED
RADIUSES
RADIUSING
RADIX
RADIXES
RADOME
RADOMES
RADON
RADONS
RADS
RADULA
RADULAE
RADULAR
RADULAS
RADWASTE
RADWASTES
RAFF
RAFFIA
RAFFIAS
RAFFINATE
RAFFINATES
RAFFINOSE
RAFFINOSES
RAFFISH
RAFFISHLY
RAFFISHNESS
RAFFISHNESSES
RAFFLE
RAFFLED
RAFFLER
RAFFLERS
RAFFLES
RAFFLESIA
RAFFLESIAS
RAFFLING
RAFFS
RAFT
RAFTED
RAFTER
RAFTERED
RAFTERS
RAFTING
RAFTINGS
RAFTS
RAFTSMAN
RAFTSMEN
RAG
RAGA
RAGAMUFFIN
RAGAMUFFINS
RAGAS
RAGBAG
RAGBAGS
RAGE
RAGED
RAGEE
RAGEES
RAGEFUL
RAGER
RAGERS
RAGES
RAGG
RAGGA
RAGGAS
RAGGED
RAGGEDER
RAGGEDEST
RAGGEDIER
RAGGEDIEST
RAGGEDLY
RAGGEDNESS
RAGGEDNESSES
RAGGEDY
RAGGEE
RAGGEES
RAGGIES
RAGGING
RAGGINGS
RAGGLE
RAGGLES
RAGGS
RAGGY
RAGHEAD
RAGHEADS
RAGI
RAGING
RAGINGLY
RAGIS
RAGLAN
RAGLANS
RAGMAN
RAGMEN
RAGOUT
RAGOUTED
RAGOUTING
RAGOUTS
RAGPICKER
RAGPICKERS
RAGS
RAGTAG
RAGTAGS
RAGTAIL
RAGTIME
RAGTIMES
RAGTOP
RAGTOPS
RAGWEED
RAGWEEDS
RAGWORM
RAGWORMS
RAGWORT
RAGWORTS
RAH
RAI
RAIA
RAIAS
RAID
RAIDED
RAIDER
RAIDERS
RAIDING
RAIDS
RAIL
RAILBED
RAILBEDS
RAILBIRD
RAILBIRDS
RAILBUS
RAILBUSES
RAILBUSSES
RAILCAR
RAILCARD
RAILCARDS
RAILCARS
RAILED
RAILER
RAILERS
RAILHEAD
RAILHEADS
RAILING
RAILINGS
RAILLERIES
RAILLERY
RAILMAN
RAILMEN
RAILROAD
RAILROADED
RAILROADER
RAILROADERS
RAILROADING
RAILROADINGS
RAILROADS
RAILS
RAILWAY
RAILWAYMAN
RAILWAYMEN
RAILWAYS
RAIMENT
RAIMENTS
RAIN
RAINBAND
RAINBANDS
RAINBIRD
RAINBIRDS
RAINBOW
RAINBOWLIKE
RAINBOWS
RAINCHECK
RAINCHECKS
RAINCOAT
RAINCOATS
RAINDROP
RAINDROPS
RAINED
RAINFALL
RAINFALLS
RAINIER
RAINIEST
RAINILY
RAININESS
RAININESSES
RAINING
RAINLESS
RAINMAKER
RAINMAKERS
RAINMAKING
RAINMAKINGS
RAINOUT
RAINOUTS
RAINPROOF
RAINPROOFED
RAINPROOFING
RAINPROOFS
RAINS
RAINSPOUT
RAINSPOUTS
RAINSQUALL
RAINSQUALLS
RAINSTORM
RAINSTORMS
RAINSUIT
RAINSUITS
RAINWASH
RAINWASHED
RAINWASHES
RAINWASHING
RAINWATER
RAINWATERS
RAINWEAR
RAINY
RAIS
RAISABLE
RAISE
RAISEABLE
RAISED
RAISER
RAISERS
RAISES
RAISIN
RAISING
RAISINGS
RAISINS
RAISINY

AISONNE
AITA
AITAS
AJ
AJA
AJAH
AJAHS
AJAS
AJES
AKE
AKED
AKEE
AKEES
AKEHELL
AKEHELLS
AKEHELLY
AKEOFF
AKEOFFS
AKER
AKERS
AKES
KI
KING
KIS
KISH
KISHLY
KISHNESS
KISHNESSES
KU
KUS
LE
LES
LLENTANDO
LLIED
LLIER
LLIERS
LLIES
LLIFORM
LLINE
LLY
LLYE
LLYES
LYING
LYINGS
LYIST
LYISTS
OXIFENE
OXIFENES
PH
PHED
PHING
PHS
M

RAMADA
RAMADAS
RAMAL
RAMATE
RAMBLA
RAMBLAS
RAMBLE
RAMBLED
RAMBLER
RAMBLERS
RAMBLES
RAMBLING
RAMBLINGLY
RAMBOUILLET
RAMBOUILLETS
RAMBUNCTIOUS
RAMBUNCTIOUSLY
RAMBUTAN
RAMBUTANS
RAMEE
RAMEES
RAMEKIN
RAMEKINS
RAMEN
RAMENTA
RAMENTUM
RAMEQUIN
RAMEQUINS
RAMET
RAMETS
RAMI
RAMIE
RAMIES
RAMIFICATION
RAMIFICATIONS
RAMIFIED
RAMIFIES
RAMIFORM
RAMIFY
RAMIFYING
RAMILIE
RAMILIES
RAMILLIE
RAMILLIES
RAMIN
RAMINS
RAMJET
RAMJETS
RAMMED
RAMMER
RAMMERS
RAMMIER
RAMMIEST

RAMMING
RAMMISH
RAMMY
RAMONA
RAMONAS
RAMOSE
RAMOSELY
RAMOSITIES
RAMOSITY
RAMOUS
RAMP
RAMPAGE
RAMPAGED
RAMPAGEOUS
RAMPAGEOUSLY
RAMPAGEOUSNESS
RAMPAGER
RAMPAGERS
RAMPAGES
RAMPAGING
RAMPANCIES
RAMPANCY
RAMPANT
RAMPANTLY
RAMPART
RAMPARTED
RAMPARTING
RAMPARTS
RAMPED
RAMPIKE
RAMPIKES
RAMPING
RAMPION
RAMPIONS
RAMPOLE
RAMPOLES
RAMPS
RAMROD
RAMRODDED
RAMRODDING
RAMRODS
RAMS
RAMSHACKLE
RAMSHORN
RAMSHORNS
RAMSON
RAMSONS
RAMTIL
RAMTILLA
RAMTILLAS
RAMTILS
RAMULOSE
RAMULOUS

RAMUS
RAN
RANCE
RANCES
RANCH
RANCHED
RANCHER
RANCHERA
RANCHERAS
RANCHERIA
RANCHERIAS
RANCHERO
RANCHEROS
RANCHERS
RANCHES
RANCHING
RANCHINGS
RANCHLESS
RANCHLIKE
RANCHMAN
RANCHMEN
RANCHO
RANCHOS
RANCID
RANCIDER
RANCIDEST
RANCIDITIES
RANCIDITY
RANCIDLY
RANCIDNESS
RANCIDNESSES
RANCOR
RANCORED
RANCOROUS
RANCOROUSLY
RANCORS
RANCOUR
RANCOURED
RANCOUROUS
RANCOURS
RAND
RANDAN
RANDANS
RANDIER
RANDIES
RANDIEST
RANDINESS
RANDINESSES
RANDOM
RANDOMISE
RANDOMISED
RANDOMISES
RANDOMISING

RANDOMIZATION
RANDOMIZATIONS
RANDOMIZE
RANDOMIZED
RANDOMIZER
RANDOMIZERS
RANDOMIZES
RANDOMIZING
RANDOMLY
RANDOMNESS
RANDOMNESSES
RANDOMS
RANDS
RANDY
RANEE
RANEES
RANG
RANGE
RANGED
RANGELAND
RANGELANDS
RANGER
RANGERS
RANGES
RANGIER
RANGIEST
RANGINESS
RANGINESSES
RANGING
RANGS
RANGY
RANI
RANID
RANIDS
RANIS
RANITIDINE
RANITIDINES
RANK
RANKED
RANKER
RANKERS
RANKEST
RANKING
RANKINGS
RANKISH
RANKLE
RANKLED
RANKLES
RANKLESS
RANKLING
RANKLY
RANKNESS
RANKNESSES

RANKS
RANPIKE
RANPIKES
RANSACK
RANSACKED
RANSACKER
RANSACKERS
RANSACKING
RANSACKS
RANSOM
RANSOMED
RANSOMER
RANSOMERS
RANSOMING
RANSOMS
RANT
RANTED
RANTER
RANTERS
RANTING
RANTINGLY
RANTINGS
RANTS
RANULA
RANULAR
RANULAS
RANUNCULI
RANUNCULUS
RANUNCULUSES
RAP
RAPACIOUS
RAPACIOUSLY
RAPACIOUSNESS
RAPACIOUSNESSES
RAPACITIES
RAPACITY
RAPE
RAPED
RAPER
RAPERS
RAPES
RAPESEED
RAPESEEDS
RAPHAE
RAPHE
RAPHES
RAPHIA
RAPHIAS
RAPHIDE
RAPHIDES
RAPHIS
RAPID
RAPIDER
RAPIDEST
RAPIDITIES
RAPIDITY
RAPIDLY
RAPIDNESS
RAPIDNESSES
RAPIDS
RAPIER
RAPIERED
RAPIERS
RAPINE
RAPINES
RAPING
RAPINI
RAPIST
RAPISTS
RAPPAREE
RAPPAREES
RAPPED
RAPPEE
RAPPEES
RAPPEL
RAPPELED
RAPPELING
RAPPELLED
RAPPELLING
RAPPELS
RAPPEN
RAPPER
RAPPERS
RAPPING
RAPPINI
RAPPORT
RAPPORTEUR
RAPPORTEURS
RAPPORTS
RAPPROCHEMENT
RAPPROCHEMENTS
RAPS
RAPSCALLION
RAPSCALLIONS
RAPT
RAPTLY
RAPTNESS
RAPTNESSES
RAPTOR
RAPTORIAL
RAPTORS
RAPTURE
RAPTURED
RAPTURES
RAPTURING
RAPTUROUS
RAPTUROUSLY
RAPTUROUSNESS
RAPTUROUSNESSES
RARE
RAREBIT
RAREBITS
RARED
RAREFACTION
RAREFACTIONAL
RAREFACTIONS
RAREFIED
RAREFIER
RAREFIERS
RAREFIES
RAREFY
RAREFYING
RARELY
RARENESS
RARENESSES
RARER
RARERIPE
RARERIPES
RARES
RAREST
RARIFIED
RARIFIES
RARIFY
RARIFYING
RARING
RARITIES
RARITY
RAS
RASBORA
RASBORAS
RASCAL
RASCALITIES
RASCALITY
RASCALLY
RASCALS
RASE
RASED
RASER
RASERS
RASES
RASH
RASHER
RASHERS
RASHES
RASHEST
RASHLIKE
RASHLY
RASHNESS
RASHNESSES
RASING
RASORIAL
RASP
RASPBERRIES
RASPBERRY
RASPED
RASPER
RASPERS
RASPIER
RASPIEST
RASPINESS
RASPINESSES
RASPING
RASPINGLY
RASPINGS
RASPISH
RASPS
RASPY
RASSLE
RASSLED
RASSLER
RASSLERS
RASSLES
RASSLING
RASTER
RASTERS
RASURE
RASURES
RAT
RATABLE
RATABLES
RATABLY
RATAFEE
RATAFEES
RATAFIA
RATAFIAS
RATAL
RATALS
RATAN
RATANIES
RATANS
RATANY
RATAPLAN
RATAPLANNED
RATAPLANNING
RATAPLANS
RATATAT
RATATATS
RATATOUILLE
RATATOUILLES
RATBAG
RATBAGS
RATCH
RATCHES
RATCHET
RATCHETED
RATCHETING
RATCHETS
RATE
RATEABLE
RATEABLY
RATED
RATEL
RATELS
RATEMETER
RATEMETERS
RATEPAYER
RATEPAYERS
RATER
RATERS
RATES
RATFINK
RATFINKS
RATFISH
RATFISHES
RATH
RATHE
RATHER
RATHOLE
RATHOLES
RATHSKELLER
RATHSKELLERS
RATICIDE
RATICIDES
RATIFICATION
RATIFICATIONS
RATIFIED
RATIFIER
RATIFIERS
RATIFIES
RATIFY
RATIFYING
RATINE
RATINES
RATING
RATINGS
RATIO
RATIOCINATE
RATIOCINATED
RATIOCINATES
RATIOCINATING
RATIOCINATION
RATIOCINATIONS
RATIOCINATIVE
RATIOCINATOR
RATIOCINATORS

ATION
ATIONAL
ATIONALE
ATIONALES
ATIONALISATION
ATIONALISE
ATIONALISED
ATIONALISES
ATIONALISING
ATIONALISM
ATIONALISMS
ATIONALIST
ATIONALISTIC
ATIONALISTS
ATIONALITIES
ATIONALITY
ATIONALIZABLE
ATIONALIZATION
ATIONALIZE
ATIONALIZED
ATIONALIZER
ATIONALIZERS
ATIONALIZES
ATIONALIZING
ATIONALLY
ATIONALNESS
ATIONALNESSES
ATIONALS
TIONED
TIONING
TIONS
TIOS
TITE
TITES
TLIKE
TLIN
TLINE
TLINES
TLINS
TO
TOON
TOONED
TOONER
TOONERS
TOONING
TOONS
TOS
TS
TSBANE
TSBANES
TAIL
TAILED
TAILS
RATTAN
RATTANS
RATTED
RATTEEN
RATTEENS
RATTEN
RATTENED
RATTENER
RATTENERS
RATTENING
RATTENS
RATTER
RATTERS
RATTIER
RATTIEST
RATTILY
RATTING
RATTISH
RATTLE
RATTLEBOX
RATTLEBOXES
RATTLEBRAIN
RATTLEBRAINED
RATTLEBRAINS
RATTLED
RATTLER
RATTLERS
RATTLES
RATTLESNAKE
RATTLESNAKES
RATTLETRAP
RATTLETRAPS
RATTLIER
RATTLIEST
RATTLING
RATTLINGLY
RATTLINGS
RATTLY
RATTON
RATTONS
RATTOON
RATTOONED
RATTOONING
RATTOONS
RATTRAP
RATTRAPS
RATTY
RAUCITIES
RAUCITY
RAUCOUS
RAUCOUSLY
RAUCOUSNESS
RAUCOUSNESSES
RAUNCH
RAUNCHES
RAUNCHIER
RAUNCHIEST
RAUNCHILY
RAUNCHINESS
RAUNCHINESSES
RAUNCHY
RAUWOLFIA
RAUWOLFIAS
RAVAGE
RAVAGED
RAVAGEMENT
RAVAGEMENTS
RAVAGER
RAVAGERS
RAVAGES
RAVAGING
RAVE
RAVED
RAVEL
RAVELED
RAVELER
RAVELERS
RAVELIN
RAVELING
RAVELINGS
RAVELINS
RAVELLED
RAVELLER
RAVELLERS
RAVELLING
RAVELLINGS
RAVELLY
RAVELMENT
RAVELMENTS
RAVELS
RAVEN
RAVENED
RAVENER
RAVENERS
RAVENEST
RAVENING
RAVENINGS
RAVENLIKE
RAVENOUS
RAVENOUSLY
RAVENOUSNESS
RAVENOUSNESSES
RAVENS
RAVER
RAVERS
RAVES
RAVEY
RAVIER
RAVIEST
RAVIGOTE
RAVIGOTES
RAVIGOTTE
RAVIGOTTES
RAVIN
RAVINE
RAVINED
RAVINES
RAVING
RAVINGLY
RAVINGS
RAVINING
RAVINS
RAVIOLI
RAVIOLIS
RAVISH
RAVISHED
RAVISHER
RAVISHERS
RAVISHES
RAVISHING
RAVISHINGLY
RAVISHMENT
RAVISHMENTS
RAW
RAWBONED
RAWER
RAWEST
RAWHIDE
RAWHIDED
RAWHIDES
RAWHIDING
RAWIN
RAWINS
RAWINSONDE
RAWINSONDES
RAWISH
RAWLY
RAWNESS
RAWNESSES
RAWS
RAX
RAXED
RAXES
RAXING
RAY
RAYA
RAYAH
RAYAHS
RAYAS
RAYED
RAYGRASS
RAYGRASSES
RAYING
RAYLESS
RAYLESSNESS
RAYLESSNESSES
RAYLIKE
RAYON
RAYONS
RAYS
RAZE
RAZED
RAZEE
RAZEED
RAZEEING
RAZEES
RAZER
RAZERS
RAZES
RAZING
RAZOR
RAZORBACK
RAZORBACKS
RAZORBILL
RAZORBILLS
RAZORED
RAZORING
RAZORS
RAZZ
RAZZAMATAZZ
RAZZAMATAZZES
RAZZBERRIES
RAZZBERRY
RAZZED
RAZZES
RAZZIA
RAZZIAS
RAZZING
RAZZLE
RAZZLES
RAZZMATAZZ
RAZZMATAZZES
RE
REABSORB
REABSORBED
REABSORBING
REABSORBS
REABSORPTION
REABSORPTIONS
REACCEDE
REACCEDED
REACCEDES

REACCEDING
REACCELERATE
REACCELERATED
REACCELERATES
REACCELERATING
REACCENT
REACCENTED
REACCENTING
REACCENTS
REACCEPT
REACCEPTED
REACCEPTING
REACCEPTS
REACCESSION
REACCESSIONS
REACCLAIM
REACCLAIMED
REACCLAIMING
REACCLAIMS
REACCLIMATIZE
REACCLIMATIZED
REACCLIMATIZES
REACCLIMATIZING
REACCREDIT
REACCREDITATION
REACCREDITED
REACCREDITING
REACCREDITS
REACCUSE
REACCUSED
REACCUSES
REACCUSING
REACH
REACHABLE
REACHED
REACHER
REACHERS
REACHES
REACHING
REACQUAINT
REACQUAINTED
REACQUAINTING
REACQUAINTS
REACQUIRE
REACQUIRED
REACQUIRES
REACQUIRING
REACQUISITION
REACQUISITIONS
REACT
REACTANCE
REACTANCES
REACTANT
REACTANTS
REACTED
REACTING
REACTION
REACTIONARIES
REACTIONARY
REACTIONARYISM
REACTIONARYISMS
REACTIONS
REACTIVATE
REACTIVATED
REACTIVATES
REACTIVATING
REACTIVATION
REACTIVATIONS
REACTIVE
REACTIVELY
REACTIVENESS
REACTIVENESSES
REACTIVITIES
REACTIVITY
REACTOR
REACTORS
REACTS
READ
READABILITIES
READABILITY
READABLE
READABLENESS
READABLENESSES
READABLY
READAPT
READAPTED
READAPTING
READAPTS
READD
READDED
READDICT
READDICTED
READDICTING
READDICTS
READDING
READDRESS
READDRESSED
READDRESSES
READDRESSING
READDS
READER
READERLY
READERS
READERSHIP
READERSHIPS
READIED
READIER
READIES
READIEST
READILY
READINESS
READINESSES
READING
READINGS
READJUST
READJUSTED
READJUSTING
READJUSTMENT
READJUSTMENTS
READJUSTS
READMISSION
READMISSIONS
READMIT
READMITS
READMITTED
READMITTING
READOPT
READOPTED
READOPTING
READOPTS
READORN
READORNED
READORNING
READORNS
READOUT
READOUTS
READS
READY
READYING
READYMADE
READYMADES
REAFFIRM
REAFFIRMATION
REAFFIRMATIONS
REAFFIRMED
REAFFIRMING
REAFFIRMS
REAFFIX
REAFFIXED
REAFFIXES
REAFFIXING
REAFFOREST
REAFFORESTATION
REAFFORESTED
REAFFORESTING
REAFFORESTS
REAGENT
REAGENTS
REAGGREGATE
REAGGREGATED
REAGGREGATES
REAGGREGATING
REAGGREGATION
REAGGREGATIONS
REAGIN
REAGINIC
REAGINS
REAL
REALER
REALES
REALEST
REALGAR
REALGARS
REALIA
REALIGN
REALIGNED
REALIGNING
REALIGNMENT
REALIGNMENTS
REALIGNS
REALISABLE
REALISATION
REALISATIONS
REALISE
REALISED
REALISER
REALISERS
REALISES
REALISING
REALISM
REALISMS
REALIST
REALISTIC
REALISTICALLY
REALISTS
REALITIES
REALITY
REALIZABLE
REALIZATION
REALIZATIONS
REALIZE
REALIZED
REALIZER
REALIZERS
REALIZES
REALIZING
REALLOCATE
REALLOCATED
REALLOCATES
REALLOCATING
REALLOCATION
REALLOCATIONS
REALLOT
REALLOTS
REALLOTTED
REALLOTTING
REALLY
REALM
REALMS
REALNESS
REALNESSES
REALPOLITIK
REALPOLITIKS
REALS
REALTER
REALTERED
REALTERING
REALTERS
REALTIES
REALTOR
REALTORS
REALTY
REAM
REAMED
REAMER
REAMERS
REAMING
REAMS
REANALYSES
REANALYSIS
REANALYZE
REANALYZED
REANALYZES
REANALYZING
REANIMATE
REANIMATED
REANIMATES
REANIMATING
REANIMATION
REANIMATIONS
REANNEX
REANNEXATION
REANNEXATIONS
REANNEXED
REANNEXES
REANNEXING
REANOINT
REANOINTED
REANOINTING
REANOINTS
REAP
REAPABLE
REAPED
REAPER
REAPERS

EAPHOOK
EAPHOOKS
EAPING
EAPPEAR
EAPPEARANCE
EAPPEARANCES
EAPPEARED
EAPPEARING
EAPPEARS
EAPPLICATION
EAPPLICATIONS
EAPPLIED
EAPPLIES
EAPPLY
EAPPLYING
EAPPOINT
EAPPOINTED
EAPPOINTING
EAPPOINTMENT
EAPPOINTMENTS
EAPPOINTS
EAPPORTION
EAPPORTIONED
EAPPORTIONING
EAPPORTIONMENT
EAPPORTIONS
EAPPRAISAL
EAPPRAISALS
EAPPRAISE
EAPPRAISED
EAPPRAISES
EAPPRAISING
EAPPROPRIATE
EAPPROPRIATED
EAPPROPRIATES
EAPPROPRIATING
EAPPROVE
EAPPROVED
EAPPROVES
EAPPROVING
EAPS
EAR
EARED
EARER
EARERS
EARGUARD
EARGUARDS
ARGUE
EARGUED
ARGUES
ARGUING
ARGUMENT
ARGUMENTS

REARING
REARINGS
REARM
REARMAMENT
REARMAMENTS
REARMED
REARMICE
REARMING
REARMOST
REARMOUSE
REARMS
REAROUSAL
REAROUSALS
REAROUSE
REAROUSED
REAROUSES
REAROUSING
REARRANGE
REARRANGED
REARRANGEMENT
REARRANGEMENTS
REARRANGES
REARRANGING
REARREST
REARRESTED
REARRESTING
REARRESTS
REARS
REARTICULATE
REARTICULATED
REARTICULATES
REARTICULATING
REARWARD
REARWARDS
REASCEND
REASCENDED
REASCENDING
REASCENDS
REASCENT
REASCENTS
REASON
REASONABILITIES
REASONABILITY
REASONABLE
REASONABLENESS
REASONABLY
REASONED
REASONER
REASONERS
REASONING
REASONINGS
REASONLESS
REASONLESSLY

REASONS
REASSAIL
REASSAILED
REASSAILING
REASSAILS
REASSEMBLAGE
REASSEMBLAGES
REASSEMBLE
REASSEMBLED
REASSEMBLES
REASSEMBLIES
REASSEMBLING
REASSEMBLY
REASSERT
REASSERTED
REASSERTING
REASSERTION
REASSERTIONS
REASSERTS
REASSESS
REASSESSED
REASSESSES
REASSESSING
REASSESSMENT
REASSESSMENTS
REASSIGN
REASSIGNED
REASSIGNING
REASSIGNMENT
REASSIGNMENTS
REASSIGNS
REASSORT
REASSORTED
REASSORTING
REASSORTS
REASSUME
REASSUMED
REASSUMES
REASSUMING
REASSURANCE
REASSURANCES
REASSURE
REASSURED
REASSURES
REASSURING
REASSURINGLY
REATA
REATAS
REATTACH
REATTACHED
REATTACHES
REATTACHING
REATTACHMENT

REATTACHMENTS
REATTACK
REATTACKED
REATTACKING
REATTACKS
REATTAIN
REATTAINED
REATTAINING
REATTAINS
REATTEMPT
REATTEMPTED
REATTEMPTING
REATTEMPTS
REATTRIBUTE
REATTRIBUTED
REATTRIBUTES
REATTRIBUTING
REATTRIBUTION
REATTRIBUTIONS
REAUTHORIZATION
REAUTHORIZE
REAUTHORIZED
REAUTHORIZES
REAUTHORIZING
REAVAIL
REAVAILED
REAVAILING
REAVAILS
REAVE
REAVED
REAVER
REAVERS
REAVES
REAVING
REAVOW
REAVOWED
REAVOWING
REAVOWS
REAWAKE
REAWAKED
REAWAKEN
REAWAKENED
REAWAKENING
REAWAKENS
REAWAKES
REAWAKING
REAWOKE
REAWOKEN
REB
REBAIT
REBAITED
REBAITING
REBAITS

REBALANCE
REBALANCED
REBALANCES
REBALANCING
REBAPTISM
REBAPTISMS
REBAPTIZE
REBAPTIZED
REBAPTIZES
REBAPTIZING
REBAR
REBARBATIVE
REBARBATIVELY
REBARS
REBASE
REBASED
REBASES
REBASING
REBATE
REBATED
REBATER
REBATERS
REBATES
REBATING
REBATO
REBATOS
REBBE
REBBES
REBBETZIN
REBBETZINS
REBEC
REBECK
REBECKS
REBECS
REBEGAN
REBEGIN
REBEGINNING
REBEGINS
REBEGUN
REBEL
REBELDOM
REBELDOMS
REBELLED
REBELLING
REBELLION
REBELLIONS
REBELLIOUS
REBELLIOUSLY
REBELLIOUSNESS
REBELS
REBID
REBIDDEN
REBIDDING

REBIDS
REBILL
REBILLED
REBILLING
REBILLS
REBIND
REBINDING
REBINDS
REBIRTH
REBIRTHS
REBLEND
REBLENDED
REBLENDING
REBLENDS
REBLENT
REBLOOM
REBLOOMED
REBLOOMING
REBLOOMS
REBOANT
REBOARD
REBOARDED
REBOARDING
REBOARDS
REBODIED
REBODIES
REBODY
REBODYING
REBOIL
REBOILED
REBOILING
REBOILS
REBOOK
REBOOKED
REBOOKING
REBOOKS
REBOOT
REBOOTED
REBOOTING
REBOOTS
REBOP
REBOPS
REBORE
REBORED
REBORES
REBORING
REBORN
REBOTTLE
REBOTTLED
REBOTTLES
REBOTTLING
REBOUGHT
REBOUND
REBOUNDED
REBOUNDER
REBOUNDERS
REBOUNDING
REBOUNDS
REBOZO
REBOZOS
REBRANCH
REBRANCHED
REBRANCHES
REBRANCHING
REBRAND
REBRANDED
REBRANDING
REBRANDINGS
REBRANDS
REBRED
REBREED
REBREEDING
REBREEDS
REBROADCAST
REBROADCASTED
REBROADCASTING
REBROADCASTS
REBS
REBUFF
REBUFFED
REBUFFING
REBUFFS
REBUILD
REBUILDED
REBUILDING
REBUILDS
REBUILT
REBUKE
REBUKED
REBUKER
REBUKERS
REBUKES
REBUKING
REBURIAL
REBURIALS
REBURIED
REBURIES
REBURY
REBURYING
REBUS
REBUSES
REBUT
REBUTS
REBUTTABLE
REBUTTAL
REBUTTALS
REBUTTED
REBUTTER
REBUTTERS
REBUTTING
REBUTTON
REBUTTONED
REBUTTONING
REBUTTONS
REBUY
REBUYING
REBUYS
REC
RECALCITRANCE
RECALCITRANCES
RECALCITRANCIES
RECALCITRANCY
RECALCITRANT
RECALCITRANTS
RECALCULATE
RECALCULATED
RECALCULATES
RECALCULATING
RECALCULATION
RECALCULATIONS
RECALIBRATE
RECALIBRATED
RECALIBRATES
RECALIBRATING
RECALIBRATION
RECALIBRATIONS
RECALL
RECALLABILITIES
RECALLABILITY
RECALLABLE
RECALLED
RECALLER
RECALLERS
RECALLING
RECALLS
RECAMIER
RECAMIERS
RECANALIZATION
RECANALIZATIONS
RECANALIZE
RECANALIZED
RECANALIZES
RECANALIZING
RECANE
RECANED
RECANES
RECANING
RECANT
RECANTATION
RECANTATIONS
RECANTED
RECANTER
RECANTERS
RECANTING
RECANTS
RECAP
RECAPITALIZE
RECAPITALIZED
RECAPITALIZES
RECAPITALIZING
RECAPITULATE
RECAPITULATED
RECAPITULATES
RECAPITULATING
RECAPITULATION
RECAPITULATIONS
RECAPPABLE
RECAPPED
RECAPPING
RECAPS
RECAPTURE
RECAPTURED
RECAPTURES
RECAPTURING
RECARPET
RECARPETED
RECARPETING
RECARPETS
RECARRIED
RECARRIES
RECARRY
RECARRYING
RECAST
RECASTING
RECASTS
RECATALOG
RECATALOGED
RECATALOGING
RECATALOGS
RECATEGORIZE
RECATEGORIZED
RECATEGORIZES
RECATEGORIZING
RECAUTION
RECAUTIONED
RECAUTIONING
RECAUTIONS
RECCE
RECCED
RECCEING
RECCES
RECEDE
RECEDED
RECEDES
RECEDING
RECEIPT
RECEIPTED
RECEIPTING
RECEIPTOR
RECEIPTORS
RECEIPTS
RECEIVABLE
RECEIVABLES
RECEIVE
RECEIVED
RECEIVER
RECEIVERS
RECEIVERSHIP
RECEIVERSHIPS
RECEIVES
RECEIVING
RECEMENT
RECEMENTED
RECEMENTING
RECEMENTS
RECENCIES
RECENCY
RECENSION
RECENSIONS
RECENSOR
RECENSORED
RECENSORING
RECENSORS
RECENT
RECENTER
RECENTEST
RECENTLY
RECENTNESS
RECENTNESSES
RECENTRIFUGE
RECENTRIFUGED
RECENTRIFUGES
RECENTRIFUGING
RECEPT
RECEPTACLE
RECEPTACLES
RECEPTION
RECEPTIONIST
RECEPTIONISTS
RECEPTIONS
RECEPTIVE
RECEPTIVELY
RECEPTIVENESS
RECEPTIVENESSES
RECEPTIVITIES

ECEPTIVITY
ECEPTOR
ECEPTORS
ECEPTS
ECERTIFICATION
ECERTIFIED
ECERTIFIES
ECERTIFY
ECERTIFYING
ECESS
ECESSED
ECESSES
ECESSING
ECESSION
ECESSIONAL
ECESSIONALS
ECESSIONARY
ECESSIONS
ECESSIVE
ECESSIVELY
ECESSIVENESS
ECESSIVENESSES
ECESSIVES
ECHALLENGE
ECHALLENGED
ECHALLENGES
ECHALLENGING
ECHANGE
ECHANGED
ECHANGES
ECHANGING
ECHANNEL
ECHANNELED
ECHANNELING
ECHANNELLED
ECHANNELLING
ECHANNELS
ECHARGE
ECHARGEABLE
ECHARGED
ECHARGER
ECHARGERS
ECHARGES
ECHARGING
ECHART
ECHARTED
ECHARTER
ECHARTERED
ECHARTERING
ECHARTERS
ECHARTING
ECHARTS
ECHAUFFE

RECHAUFFES
RECHEAT
RECHEATS
RECHECK
RECHECKED
RECHECKING
RECHECKS
RECHERCHE
RECHEW
RECHEWED
RECHEWING
RECHEWS
RECHOOSE
RECHOOSES
RECHOOSING
RECHOREOGRAPH
RECHOREOGRAPHED
RECHOREOGRAPHS
RECHOSE
RECHOSEN
RECHRISTEN
RECHRISTENED
RECHRISTENING
RECHRISTENS
RECHROMATOGRAPH
RECIDIVISM
RECIDIVISMS
RECIDIVIST
RECIDIVISTIC
RECIDIVISTS
RECIPE
RECIPES
RECIPIENT
RECIPIENTS
RECIPROCAL
RECIPROCALLY
RECIPROCALS
RECIPROCATE
RECIPROCATED
RECIPROCATES
RECIPROCATING
RECIPROCATION
RECIPROCATIONS
RECIPROCATIVE
RECIPROCATOR
RECIPROCATORS
RECIPROCITIES
RECIPROCITY
RECIRCLE
RECIRCLED
RECIRCLES
RECIRCLING
RECIRCULATE

RECIRCULATED
RECIRCULATES
RECIRCULATING
RECIRCULATION
RECIRCULATIONS
RECISION
RECISIONS
RECIT
RECITAL
RECITALIST
RECITALISTS
RECITALS
RECITATION
RECITATIONS
RECITATIVE
RECITATIVES
RECITATIVI
RECITATIVO
RECITATIVOS
RECITE
RECITED
RECITER
RECITERS
RECITES
RECITING
RECITS
RECK
RECKED
RECKING
RECKLESS
RECKLESSLY
RECKLESSNESS
RECKLESSNESSES
RECKON
RECKONED
RECKONER
RECKONERS
RECKONING
RECKONINGS
RECKONS
RECKS
RECLAD
RECLADDED
RECLADDING
RECLADS
RECLAIM
RECLAIMABLE
RECLAIMED
RECLAIMER
RECLAIMERS
RECLAIMING
RECLAIMS
RECLAMATION

RECLAMATIONS
RECLAME
RECLAMES
RECLASP
RECLASPED
RECLASPING
RECLASPS
RECLASSIFIED
RECLASSIFIES
RECLASSIFY
RECLASSIFYING
RECLEAN
RECLEANED
RECLEANING
RECLEANS
RECLINATE
RECLINE
RECLINED
RECLINER
RECLINERS
RECLINES
RECLINING
RECLOSABLE
RECLOTHE
RECLOTHED
RECLOTHES
RECLOTHING
RECLUSE
RECLUSES
RECLUSION
RECLUSIONS
RECLUSIVE
RECLUSIVELY
RECLUSIVENESS
RECLUSIVENESSES
RECOAL
RECOALED
RECOALING
RECOALS
RECOAT
RECOATED
RECOATING
RECOATS
RECOCK
RECOCKED
RECOCKING
RECOCKS
RECODE
RECODED
RECODES
RECODIFICATION
RECODIFICATIONS
RECODIFIED

RECODIFIES
RECODIFY
RECODIFYING
RECODING
RECOGNISABLE
RECOGNISABLY
RECOGNISE
RECOGNISED
RECOGNISES
RECOGNISING
RECOGNITION
RECOGNITIONS
RECOGNIZABILITY
RECOGNIZABLE
RECOGNIZABLY
RECOGNIZANCE
RECOGNIZANCES
RECOGNIZE
RECOGNIZED
RECOGNIZER
RECOGNIZERS
RECOGNIZES
RECOGNIZING
RECOIL
RECOILED
RECOILER
RECOILERS
RECOILING
RECOILLESS
RECOILS
RECOIN
RECOINAGE
RECOINAGES
RECOINED
RECOINING
RECOINS
RECOLLECT
RECOLLECTED
RECOLLECTING
RECOLLECTION
RECOLLECTIONS
RECOLLECTS
RECOLONIZATION
RECOLONIZATIONS
RECOLONIZE
RECOLONIZED
RECOLONIZES
RECOLONIZING
RECOLOR
RECOLORED
RECOLORING
RECOLORS
RECOLOUR

RECOLOURED
RECOLOURING
RECOLOURS
RECOMB
RECOMBED
RECOMBINANT
RECOMBINANTS
RECOMBINATION
RECOMBINATIONAL
RECOMBINATIONS
RECOMBINE
RECOMBINED
RECOMBINES
RECOMBING
RECOMBINING
RECOMBS
RECOMMENCE
RECOMMENCED
RECOMMENCEMENT
RECOMMENCEMENTS
RECOMMENCES
RECOMMENCING
RECOMMEND
RECOMMENDABLE
RECOMMENDATION
RECOMMENDATIONS
RECOMMENDATORY
RECOMMENDED
RECOMMENDER
RECOMMENDERS
RECOMMENDING
RECOMMENDS
RECOMMISSION
RECOMMISSIONED
RECOMMISSIONING
RECOMMISSIONS
RECOMMIT
RECOMMITMENT
RECOMMITMENTS
RECOMMITS
RECOMMITTAL
RECOMMITTALS
RECOMMITTED
RECOMMITTING
RECOMPENSE
RECOMPENSED
RECOMPENSES
RECOMPENSING
RECOMPILATION
RECOMPILATIONS
RECOMPILE
RECOMPILED
RECOMPILES
RECOMPILING
RECOMPOSE
RECOMPOSED
RECOMPOSES
RECOMPOSING
RECOMPOSITION
RECOMPOSITIONS
RECOMPUTATION
RECOMPUTATIONS
RECOMPUTE
RECOMPUTED
RECOMPUTES
RECOMPUTING
RECON
RECONCEIVE
RECONCEIVED
RECONCEIVES
RECONCEIVING
RECONCENTRATE
RECONCENTRATED
RECONCENTRATES
RECONCENTRATING
RECONCENTRATION
RECONCEPTION
RECONCEPTIONS
RECONCEPTUALIZE
RECONCILABILITY
RECONCILABLE
RECONCILE
RECONCILED
RECONCILEMENT
RECONCILEMENTS
RECONCILER
RECONCILERS
RECONCILES
RECONCILIATION
RECONCILIATIONS
RECONCILIATORY
RECONCILING
RECONDENSE
RECONDENSED
RECONDENSES
RECONDENSING
RECONDITE
RECONDITELY
RECONDITENESS
RECONDITENESSES
RECONDITION
RECONDITIONED
RECONDITIONING
RECONDITIONS
RECONDUCT
RECONDUCTED
RECONDUCTING
RECONDUCTS
RECONFER
RECONFERRED
RECONFERRING
RECONFERS
RECONFIGURATION
RECONFIGURE
RECONFIGURED
RECONFIGURES
RECONFIGURING
RECONFINE
RECONFINED
RECONFINES
RECONFINING
RECONFIRM
RECONFIRMATION
RECONFIRMATIONS
RECONFIRMED
RECONFIRMING
RECONFIRMS
RECONNAISSANCE
RECONNAISSANCES
RECONNECT
RECONNECTED
RECONNECTING
RECONNECTION
RECONNECTIONS
RECONNECTS
RECONNED
RECONNING
RECONNOITER
RECONNOITERED
RECONNOITERING
RECONNOITERS
RECONNOITRE
RECONNOITRED
RECONNOITRES
RECONNOITRING
RECONQUER
RECONQUERED
RECONQUERING
RECONQUERS
RECONQUEST
RECONQUESTS
RECONS
RECONSECRATE
RECONSECRATED
RECONSECRATES
RECONSECRATING
RECONSECRATION
RECONSECRATIONS
RECONSIDER
RECONSIDERATION
RECONSIDERED
RECONSIDERING
RECONSIDERS
RECONSIGN
RECONSIGNED
RECONSIGNING
RECONSIGNS
RECONSOLE
RECONSOLED
RECONSOLES
RECONSOLIDATE
RECONSOLIDATED
RECONSOLIDATES
RECONSOLIDATING
RECONSOLING
RECONSTITUTE
RECONSTITUTED
RECONSTITUTES
RECONSTITUTING
RECONSTITUTION
RECONSTITUTIONS
RECONSTRUCT
RECONSTRUCTED
RECONSTRUCTIBLE
RECONSTRUCTING
RECONSTRUCTION
RECONSTRUCTIONS
RECONSTRUCTIVE
RECONSTRUCTOR
RECONSTRUCTORS
RECONSTRUCTS
RECONSULT
RECONSULTED
RECONSULTING
RECONSULTS
RECONTACT
RECONTACTED
RECONTACTING
RECONTACTS
RECONTAMINATE
RECONTAMINATED
RECONTAMINATES
RECONTAMINATING
RECONTAMINATION
RECONTEXTUALIZE
RECONTOUR
RECONTOURED
RECONTOURING
RECONTOURS
RECONVENE
RECONVENED
RECONVENES
RECONVENING
RECONVERSION
RECONVERSIONS
RECONVERT
RECONVERTED
RECONVERTING
RECONVERTS
RECONVEY
RECONVEYANCE
RECONVEYANCES
RECONVEYED
RECONVEYING
RECONVEYS
RECONVICT
RECONVICTED
RECONVICTING
RECONVICTION
RECONVICTIONS
RECONVICTS
RECONVINCE
RECONVINCED
RECONVINCES
RECONVINCING
RECOOK
RECOOKED
RECOOKING
RECOOKS
RECOPIED
RECOPIES
RECOPY
RECOPYING
RECORD
RECORDABLE
RECORDATION
RECORDATIONS
RECORDED
RECORDER
RECORDERS
RECORDING
RECORDINGS
RECORDIST
RECORDISTS
RECORDS
RECORK
RECORKED
RECORKING
RECORKS
RECOUNT
RECOUNTAL
RECOUNTALS
RECOUNTED
RECOUNTER
RECOUNTERS

RECOUNTING
RECOUNTS
RECOUP
RECOUPABLE
RECOUPE
RECOUPED
RECOUPING
RECOUPLE
RECOUPLED
RECOUPLES
RECOUPLING
RECOUPMENT
RECOUPMENTS
RECOUPS
RECOURSE
RECOURSES
RECOVER
RECOVERABILITY
RECOVERABLE
RECOVERED
RECOVERER
RECOVERERS
RECOVERIES
RECOVERING
RECOVERS
RECOVERY
RECRATE
RECRATED
RECRATES
RECRATING
RECREANCE
RECREANCES
RECREANCIES
RECREANCY
RECREANT
RECREANTS
RECREATE
RECREATED
RECREATES
RECREATING
RECREATION
RECREATIONAL
RECREATIONIST
RECREATIONISTS
RECREATIONS
RECREATIVE
RECREMENT
RECREMENTS
RECRIMINATE
RECRIMINATED
RECRIMINATES
RECRIMINATING
RECRIMINATION
RECRIMINATIONS
RECRIMINATIVE
RECRIMINATORY
RECROSS
RECROSSED
RECROSSES
RECROSSING
RECROWN
RECROWNED
RECROWNING
RECROWNS
RECRUDESCE
RECRUDESCED
RECRUDESCENCE
RECRUDESCENCES
RECRUDESCENT
RECRUDESCES
RECRUDESCING
RECRUIT
RECRUITED
RECRUITER
RECRUITERS
RECRUITING
RECRUITMENT
RECRUITMENTS
RECRUITS
RECRYSTALLIZE
RECRYSTALLIZED
RECRYSTALLIZES
RECRYSTALLIZING
RECS
RECTA
RECTAL
RECTALLY
RECTANGLE
RECTANGLES
RECTANGULAR
RECTANGULARITY
RECTANGULARLY
RECTI
RECTIFIABILITY
RECTIFIABLE
RECTIFICATION
RECTIFICATIONS
RECTIFIED
RECTIFIER
RECTIFIERS
RECTIFIES
RECTIFY
RECTIFYING
RECTILINEAR
RECTILINEARITY
RECTILINEARLY
RECTITUDE
RECTITUDES
RECTITUDINOUS
RECTO
RECTOCELE
RECTOCELES
RECTOR
RECTORATE
RECTORATES
RECTORIAL
RECTORIES
RECTORS
RECTORSHIP
RECTORSHIPS
RECTORY
RECTOS
RECTRICES
RECTRIX
RECTUM
RECTUMS
RECTUS
RECULTIVATE
RECULTIVATED
RECULTIVATES
RECULTIVATING
RECUMBENCIES
RECUMBENCY
RECUMBENT
RECUPERATE
RECUPERATED
RECUPERATES
RECUPERATING
RECUPERATION
RECUPERATIONS
RECUPERATIVE
RECUR
RECURRED
RECURRENCE
RECURRENCES
RECURRENT
RECURRENTLY
RECURRING
RECURS
RECURSION
RECURSIONS
RECURSIVE
RECURSIVELY
RECURSIVENESS
RECURSIVENESSES
RECURVATE
RECURVE
RECURVED
RECURVES
RECURVING
RECUSAL
RECUSALS
RECUSANCIES
RECUSANCY
RECUSANT
RECUSANTS
RECUSE
RECUSED
RECUSES
RECUSING
RECUT
RECUTS
RECUTTING
RECYCLABILITIES
RECYCLABILITY
RECYCLABLE
RECYCLABLES
RECYCLE
RECYCLED
RECYCLER
RECYCLERS
RECYCLES
RECYCLING
RED
REDACT
REDACTED
REDACTING
REDACTION
REDACTIONAL
REDACTIONS
REDACTOR
REDACTORS
REDACTS
REDAMAGE
REDAMAGED
REDAMAGES
REDAMAGING
REDAN
REDANS
REDARGUE
REDARGUED
REDARGUES
REDARGUING
REDATE
REDATED
REDATES
REDATING
REDBAIT
REDBAITED
REDBAITER
REDBAITERS
REDBAITING
REDBAITS
REDBAY
REDBAYS
REDBIRD
REDBIRDS
REDBONE
REDBONES
REDBREAST
REDBREASTS
REDBRICK
REDBRICKS
REDBUD
REDBUDS
REDBUG
REDBUGS
REDCAP
REDCAPS
REDCOAT
REDCOATS
REDD
REDDED
REDDEN
REDDENED
REDDENING
REDDENS
REDDER
REDDERS
REDDEST
REDDIER
REDDIEST
REDDING
REDDISH
REDDISHNESS
REDDISHNESSES
REDDLE
REDDLED
REDDLES
REDDLING
REDDS
REDDY
REDE
REDEAR
REDEARS
REDECIDE
REDECIDED
REDECIDES
REDECIDING
REDECORATE
REDECORATED
REDECORATES
REDECORATING
REDECORATION
REDECORATIONS

REDECORATOR
REDECORATORS
REDED
REDEDICATE
REDEDICATED
REDEDICATES
REDEDICATING
REDEDICATION
REDEDICATIONS
REDEEM
REDEEMABLE
REDEEMED
REDEEMER
REDEEMERS
REDEEMING
REDEEMS
REDEFEAT
REDEFEATED
REDEFEATING
REDEFEATS
REDEFECT
REDEFECTED
REDEFECTING
REDEFECTS
REDEFIED
REDEFIES
REDEFINE
REDEFINED
REDEFINES
REDEFINING
REDEFINITION
REDEFINITIONS
REDEFY
REDEFYING
REDELIVER
REDELIVERED
REDELIVERIES
REDELIVERING
REDELIVERS
REDELIVERY
REDEMAND
REDEMANDED
REDEMANDING
REDEMANDS
REDEMPTION
REDEMPTIONER
REDEMPTIONERS
REDEMPTIONS
REDEMPTIVE
REDEMPTORY
REDENIED
REDENIES
REDENY
REDENYING
REDEPLOY
REDEPLOYED
REDEPLOYING
REDEPLOYMENT
REDEPLOYMENTS
REDEPLOYS
REDEPOSIT
REDEPOSITED
REDEPOSITING
REDEPOSITS
REDES
REDESCEND
REDESCENDED
REDESCENDING
REDESCENDS
REDESCRIBE
REDESCRIBED
REDESCRIBES
REDESCRIBING
REDESCRIPTION
REDESCRIPTIONS
REDESIGN
REDESIGNED
REDESIGNING
REDESIGNS
REDETERMINATION
REDETERMINE
REDETERMINED
REDETERMINES
REDETERMINING
REDEVELOP
REDEVELOPED
REDEVELOPER
REDEVELOPERS
REDEVELOPING
REDEVELOPMENT
REDEVELOPMENTS
REDEVELOPS
REDEYE
REDEYES
REDFIN
REDFINS
REDFISH
REDFISHES
REDHEAD
REDHEADED
REDHEADS
REDHORSE
REDHORSES
REDIA
REDIAE
REDIAL
REDIALED
REDIALING
REDIALLED
REDIALLING
REDIALS
REDIAS
REDICTATE
REDICTATED
REDICTATES
REDICTATING
REDID
REDIGEST
REDIGESTED
REDIGESTING
REDIGESTION
REDIGESTIONS
REDIGESTS
REDIGRESS
REDIGRESSED
REDIGRESSES
REDIGRESSING
REDING
REDINGOTE
REDINGOTES
REDINTEGRATE
REDINTEGRATED
REDINTEGRATES
REDINTEGRATING
REDINTEGRATION
REDINTEGRATIONS
REDINTEGRATIVE
REDIP
REDIPPED
REDIPPING
REDIPS
REDIPT
REDIRECT
REDIRECTED
REDIRECTING
REDIRECTION
REDIRECTIONS
REDIRECTS
REDISCOUNT
REDISCOUNTABLE
REDISCOUNTED
REDISCOUNTING
REDISCOUNTS
REDISCOVER
REDISCOVERED
REDISCOVERIES
REDISCOVERING
REDISCOVERS
REDISCOVERY
REDISCUSS
REDISCUSSED
REDISCUSSES
REDISCUSSING
REDISPLAY
REDISPLAYED
REDISPLAYING
REDISPLAYS
REDISPOSE
REDISPOSED
REDISPOSES
REDISPOSING
REDISPOSITION
REDISPOSITIONS
REDISSOLVE
REDISSOLVED
REDISSOLVES
REDISSOLVING
REDISTILL
REDISTILLATION
REDISTILLATIONS
REDISTILLED
REDISTILLING
REDISTILLS
REDISTRIBUTE
REDISTRIBUTED
REDISTRIBUTES
REDISTRIBUTING
REDISTRIBUTION
REDISTRIBUTIONS
REDISTRIBUTIVE
REDISTRICT
REDISTRICTED
REDISTRICTING
REDISTRICTS
REDIVIDE
REDIVIDED
REDIVIDES
REDIVIDING
REDIVISION
REDIVISIONS
REDIVIVUS
REDIVORCE
REDIVORCED
REDIVORCES
REDIVORCING
REDLEG
REDLEGS
REDLINE
REDLINED
REDLINER
REDLINERS
REDLINES
REDLINING
REDLININGS
REDLY
REDNECK
REDNECKED
REDNECKS
REDNESS
REDNESSES
REDO
REDOCK
REDOCKED
REDOCKING
REDOCKS
REDOES
REDOING
REDOLENCE
REDOLENCES
REDOLENCIES
REDOLENCY
REDOLENT
REDOLENTLY
REDON
REDONE
REDONNED
REDONNING
REDONS
REDOS
REDOUBLE
REDOUBLED
REDOUBLER
REDOUBLERS
REDOUBLES
REDOUBLING
REDOUBT
REDOUBTABLE
REDOUBTABLY
REDOUBTS
REDOUND
REDOUNDED
REDOUNDING
REDOUNDS
REDOUT
REDOUTS
REDOWA
REDOWAS
REDOX
REDOXES
REDPOLL
REDPOLLS
REDRAFT
REDRAFTED
REDRAFTING
REDRAFTS

REDRAW
REDRAWER
REDRAWERS
REDRAWING
REDRAWN
REDRAWS
REDREAM
REDREAMED
REDREAMING
REDREAMS
REDREAMT
REDRESS
REDRESSED
REDRESSER
REDRESSERS
REDRESSES
REDRESSING
REDRESSOR
REDRESSORS
REDREW
REDRIED
REDRIES
REDRILL
REDRILLED
REDRILLING
REDRILLS
REDRIVE
REDRIVEN
REDRIVES
REDRIVING
REDROOT
REDROOTS
REDROVE
REDRY
REDRYING
REDS
REDSHANK
REDSHANKS
REDSHIFT
REDSHIFTED
REDSHIFTS
REDSHIRT
REDSHIRTED
REDSHIRTING
REDSHIRTS
REDSKIN
REDSKINS
REDSTART
REDSTARTS
REDTAIL
REDTAILS
REDTOP
REDTOPS
REDUB
REDUBBED
REDUBBING
REDUBS
REDUCE
REDUCED
REDUCER
REDUCERS
REDUCES
REDUCIBILITIES
REDUCIBILITY
REDUCIBLE
REDUCIBLY
REDUCING
REDUCTANT
REDUCTANTS
REDUCTASE
REDUCTASES
REDUCTION
REDUCTIONAL
REDUCTIONISM
REDUCTIONISMS
REDUCTIONIST
REDUCTIONISTIC
REDUCTIONISTS
REDUCTIONS
REDUCTIVE
REDUCTIVELY
REDUCTIVENESS
REDUCTIVENESSES
REDUCTIVES
REDUCTOR
REDUCTORS
REDUNDANCIES
REDUNDANCY
REDUNDANT
REDUNDANTLY
REDUPLICATE
REDUPLICATED
REDUPLICATES
REDUPLICATING
REDUPLICATION
REDUPLICATIONS
REDUPLICATIVE
REDUPLICATIVELY
REDUVIID
REDUVIIDS
REDUX
REDWARE
REDWARES
REDWATER
REDWATERS
REDWING
REDWINGS
REDWOOD
REDWOODS
REDYE
REDYED
REDYEING
REDYES
REE
REEARN
REEARNED
REEARNING
REEARNS
REEBOK
REEBOKS
REECHIER
REECHIEST
REECHO
REECHOED
REECHOES
REECHOING
REECHY
REED
REEDBIRD
REEDBIRDS
REEDBUCK
REEDBUCKS
REEDED
REEDIER
REEDIEST
REEDIFIED
REEDIFIES
REEDIFY
REEDIFYING
REEDILY
REEDINESS
REEDINESSES
REEDING
REEDINGS
REEDIT
REEDITED
REEDITING
REEDITION
REEDITIONS
REEDITS
REEDLIKE
REEDLING
REEDLINGS
REEDMAN
REEDMEN
REEDS
REEDUCATE
REEDUCATED
REEDUCATES
REEDUCATING
REEDUCATION
REEDUCATIONS
REEDUCATIVE
REEDY
REEF
REEFABLE
REEFED
REEFER
REEFERS
REEFIER
REEFIEST
REEFING
REEFS
REEFY
REEJECT
REEJECTED
REEJECTING
REEJECTS
REEK
REEKED
REEKER
REEKERS
REEKIER
REEKIEST
REEKING
REEKS
REEKY
REEL
REELABLE
REELECT
REELECTED
REELECTING
REELECTION
REELECTIONS
REELECTS
REELED
REELER
REELERS
REELEVATE
REELEVATED
REELEVATES
REELEVATING
REELIGIBILITIES
REELIGIBILITY
REELIGIBLE
REELING
REELINGS
REELS
REEMBARK
REEMBARKED
REEMBARKING
REEMBARKS
REEMBODIED
REEMBODIES
REEMBODY
REEMBODYING
REEMBRACE
REEMBRACED
REEMBRACES
REEMBRACING
REEMBROIDER
REEMBROIDERED
REEMBROIDERING
REEMBROIDERS
REEMERGE
REEMERGED
REEMERGENCE
REEMERGENCES
REEMERGES
REEMERGING
REEMISSION
REEMISSIONS
REEMIT
REEMITS
REEMITTED
REEMITTING
REEMPHASES
REEMPHASIS
REEMPHASIZE
REEMPHASIZED
REEMPHASIZES
REEMPHASIZING
REEMPLOY
REEMPLOYED
REEMPLOYING
REEMPLOYMENT
REEMPLOYMENTS
REEMPLOYS
REENACT
REENACTED
REENACTING
REENACTMENT
REENACTMENTS
REENACTOR
REENACTORS
REENACTS
REENCOUNTER
REENCOUNTERED
REENCOUNTERING
REENCOUNTERS
REENDOW
REENDOWED
REENDOWING
REENDOWS
REENERGIZE

REENERGIZED
REENERGIZES
REENERGIZING
REENFORCE
REENFORCED
REENFORCES
REENFORCING
REENGAGE
REENGAGED
REENGAGEMENT
REENGAGEMENTS
REENGAGES
REENGAGING
REENGINEER
REENGINEERED
REENGINEERING
REENGINEERS
REENGRAVE
REENGRAVED
REENGRAVES
REENGRAVING
REENJOY
REENJOYED
REENJOYING
REENJOYS
REENLARGE
REENLARGED
REENLARGES
REENLARGING
REENLIST
REENLISTED
REENLISTING
REENLISTMENT
REFNLISTMENTS
REENLISTS
REENROLL
REENROLLED
REENROLLING
REENROLLS
REENSLAVE
REENSLAVED
REENSLAVES
REENSLAVING
REENTER
REENTERED
REENTERING
REENTERS
REENTHRONE
REENTHRONED
REENTHRONES
REENTHRONING
REENTRANCE
REENTRANCES
REENTRANT
REENTRANTS
REENTRIES
REENTRY
REENVISION
REENVISIONED
REENVISIONING
REENVISIONS
REEQUIP
REEQUIPMENT
REEQUIPMENTS
REEQUIPPED
REEQUIPPING
REEQUIPS
REERECT
REERECTED
REERECTING
REERECTS
REES
REESCALATE
REESCALATED
REESCALATES
REESCALATING
REESCALATION
REESCALATIONS
REEST
REESTABLISH
REESTABLISHED
REESTABLISHES
REESTABLISHING
REESTABLISHMENT
REESTED
REESTIMATE
REESTIMATED
REESTIMATES
REESTIMATING
REESTING
REESTS
REEVALUATE
REEVALUATED
REEVALUATES
REEVALUATING
REEVALUATION
REEVALUATIONS
REEVE
REEVED
REEVES
REEVING
REEVOKE
REEVOKED
REEVOKES
REEVOKING
REEXAMINATION
REEXAMINATIONS
REEXAMINE
REEXAMINED
REEXAMINES
REEXAMINING
REEXECUTE
REEXECUTED
REEXECUTES
REEXECUTING
REEXHIBIT
REEXHIBITED
REEXHIBITING
REEXHIBITS
REEXPEL
REEXPELLED
REEXPELLING
REEXPELS
REEXPERIENCE
REEXPERIENCED
REEXPERIENCES
REEXPERIENCING
REEXPLAIN
REEXPLAINED
REEXPLAINING
REEXPLAINS
REEXPLORE
REEXPLORED
REEXPLORES
REEXPLORING
REEXPORT
REEXPORTATION
REEXPORTATIONS
REEXPORTED
REEXPORTING
REEXPORTS
REEXPOSE
REEXPOSED
REEXPOSES
REEXPOSING
REEXPOSURE
REEXPOSURES
REEXPRESS
REEXPRESSED
REEXPRESSES
REEXPRESSING
REF
REFACE
REFACED
REFACES
REFACING
REFALL
REFALLEN
REFALLING
REFALLS
REFASHION
REFASHIONED
REFASHIONING
REFASHIONS
REFASTEN
REFASTENED
REFASTENING
REFASTENS
REFECT
REFECTED
REFECTING
REFECTION
REFECTIONS
REFECTIVE
REFECTORIES
REFECTORY
REFECTS
REFED
REFEED
REFEEDING
REFEEDS
REFEEL
REFEELING
REFEELS
REFEL
REFELL
REFELLED
REFELLING
REFELS
REFELT
REFENCE
REFENCED
REFENCES
REFENCING
REFER
REFERABLE
REFEREE
REFEREED
REFEREEING
REFEREES
REFERENCE
REFERENCED
REFERENCES
REFERENCING
REFERENDA
REFERENDUM
REFERENDUMS
REFERENT
REFERENTIAL
REFERENTIALITY
REFERENTIALLY
REFERENTS
REFERRAL
REFERRALS
REFERRED
REFERRER
REFERRERS
REFERRING
REFERS
REFFED
REFFING
REFFINGS
REFIGHT
REFIGHTING
REFIGHTS
REFIGURE
REFIGURED
REFIGURES
REFIGURING
REFILE
REFILED
REFILES
REFILING
REFILL
REFILLABLE
REFILLED
REFILLING
REFILLS
REFILM
REFILMED
REFILMING
REFILMS
REFILTER
REFILTERED
REFILTERING
REFILTERS
REFINABLE
REFINANCE
REFINANCED
REFINANCES
REFINANCING
REFIND
REFINDING
REFINDS
REFINE
REFINED
REFINEMENT
REFINEMENTS
REFINER
REFINERIES
REFINERS
REFINERY
REFINES
REFINING
REFININGS

REFINISH
REFINISHED
REFINISHER
REFINISHERS
REFINISHES
REFINISHING
REFIRE
REFIRED
REFIRES
REFIRING
REFIT
REFITS
REFITTED
REFITTING
REFIX
REFIXED
REFIXES
REFIXING
REFLAG
REFLAGGED
REFLAGGING
REFLAGS
REFLATE
REFLATED
REFLATES
REFLATING
REFLATION
REFLATIONARY
REFLATIONS
REFLECT
REFLECTANCE
REFLECTANCES
REFLECTED
REFLECTING
REFLECTION
REFLECTIONAL
REFLECTIONS
REFLECTIVE
REFLECTIVELY
REFLECTIVENESS
REFLECTIVITIES
REFLECTIVITY
REFLECTOMETER
REFLECTOMETERS
REFLECTOMETRIES
REFLECTOMETRY
REFLECTOR
REFLECTORIZE
REFLECTORIZED
REFLECTORIZES
REFLECTORIZING
REFLECTORS
REFLECTS
REFLET
REFLETS
REFLEW
REFLEX
REFLEXED
REFLEXES
REFLEXING
REFLEXION
REFLEXIONS
REFLEXIVE
REFLEXIVELY
REFLEXIVENESS
REFLEXIVENESSES
REFLEXIVES
REFLEXIVITIES
REFLEXIVITY
REFLEXLY
REFLEXOLOGIES
REFLEXOLOGIST
REFLEXOLOGISTS
REFLEXOLOGY
REFLIES
REFLOAT
REFLOATED
REFLOATING
REFLOATS
REFLOOD
REFLOODED
REFLOODING
REFLOODS
REFLOW
REFLOWED
REFLOWER
REFLOWERED
REFLOWERING
REFLOWERS
REFLOWING
REFLOWN
REFLOWS
REFLUENCE
REFLUENCES
REFLUENT
REFLUX
REFLUXED
REFLUXES
REFLUXING
REFLY
REFLYING
REFOCUS
REFOCUSED
REFOCUSES
REFOCUSING
REFOCUSSED
REFOCUSSES
REFOCUSSING
REFOLD
REFOLDED
REFOLDING
REFOLDS
REFOREST
REFORESTATION
REFORESTATIONS
REFORESTED
REFORESTING
REFORESTS
REFORGE
REFORGED
REFORGES
REFORGING
REFORM
REFORMABILITIES
REFORMABILITY
REFORMABLE
REFORMAT
REFORMATE
REFORMATES
REFORMATION
REFORMATIONAL
REFORMATIONS
REFORMATIVE
REFORMATORIES
REFORMATORY
REFORMATS
REFORMATTED
REFORMATTING
REFORMED
REFORMER
REFORMERS
REFORMING
REFORMISM
REFORMISMS
REFORMIST
REFORMISTS
REFORMS
REFORMULATE
REFORMULATED
REFORMULATES
REFORMULATING
REFORMULATION
REFORMULATIONS
REFORTIFICATION
REFORTIFIED
REFORTIFIES
REFORTIFY
REFORTIFYING
REFOUGHT
REFOUND
REFOUNDATION
REFOUNDATIONS
REFOUNDED
REFOUNDING
REFOUNDS
REFRACT
REFRACTED
REFRACTILE
REFRACTING
REFRACTION
REFRACTIONS
REFRACTIVE
REFRACTIVELY
REFRACTIVENESS
REFRACTIVITIES
REFRACTIVITY
REFRACTOMETER
REFRACTOMETERS
REFRACTOMETRIC
REFRACTOMETRIES
REFRACTOMETRY
REFRACTOR
REFRACTORIES
REFRACTORILY
REFRACTORINESS
REFRACTORS
REFRACTORY
REFRACTS
REFRAIN
REFRAINED
REFRAINER
REFRAINERS
REFRAINING
REFRAINMENT
REFRAINMENTS
REFRAINS
REFRAME
REFRAMED
REFRAMES
REFRAMING
REFRANGIBILITY
REFRANGIBLE
REFRANGIBLENESS
REFREEZE
REFREEZES
REFREEZING
REFRESH
REFRESHED
REFRESHEN
REFRESHENED
REFRESHENING
REFRESHENS
REFRESHER
REFRESHERS
REFRESHES
REFRESHING
REFRESHINGLY
REFRESHMENT
REFRESHMENTS
REFRIED
REFRIES
REFRIGERANT
REFRIGERANTS
REFRIGERATE
REFRIGERATED
REFRIGERATES
REFRIGERATING
REFRIGERATION
REFRIGERATIONS
REFRIGERATOR
REFRIGERATORS
REFRONT
REFRONTED
REFRONTING
REFRONTS
REFROZE
REFROZEN
REFRY
REFRYING
REFS
REFT
REFUEL
REFUELED
REFUELING
REFUELLED
REFUELLING
REFUELS
REFUGE
REFUGED
REFUGEE
REFUGEEISM
REFUGEEISMS
REFUGEES
REFUGES
REFUGIA
REFUGING
REFUGIUM
REFULGENCE
REFULGENCES
REFULGENT
REFUND
REFUNDABILITIES
REFUNDABILITY
REFUNDABLE
REFUNDED

REFUNDER
REFUNDERS
REFUNDING
REFUNDS
REFURBISH
REFURBISHED
REFURBISHER
REFURBISHERS
REFURBISHES
REFURBISHING
REFURBISHMENT
REFURBISHMENTS
REFURNISH
REFURNISHED
REFURNISHES
REFURNISHING
REFUSABLE
REFUSAL
REFUSALS
REFUSE
REFUSED
REFUSENIK
REFUSENIKS
REFUSER
REFUSERS
REFUSES
REFUSING
REFUSNIK
REFUSNIKS
REFUTABLE
REFUTABLY
REFUTAL
REFUTALS
REFUTATION
REFUTATIONS
REFUTE
REFUTED
REFUTER
REFUTERS
REFUTES
REFUTING
REG
REGAIN
REGAINED
REGAINER
REGAINERS
REGAINING
REGAINS
REGAL
REGALE
REGALED
REGALER
REGALERS
REGALES
REGALIA
REGALING
REGALITIES
REGALITY
REGALLY
REGALNESS
REGALNESSES
REGARD
REGARDANT
REGARDED
REGARDFUL
REGARDFULLY
REGARDFULNESS
REGARDFULNESSES
REGARDING
REGARDLESS
REGARDLESSLY
REGARDLESSNESS
REGARDS
REGATHER
REGATHERED
REGATHERING
REGATHERS
REGATTA
REGATTAS
REGAUGE
REGAUGED
REGAUGES
REGAUGING
REGAVE
REGEAR
REGEARED
REGEARING
REGEARS
REGELATE
REGELATED
REGELATES
REGELATING
REGENCIES
REGENCY
REGENERABLE
REGENERACIES
REGENERACY
REGENERATE
REGENERATED
REGENERATELY
REGENERATENESS
REGENERATES
REGENERATING
REGENERATION
REGENERATIONS
REGENERATIVE
REGENERATOR
REGENERATORS
REGENT
REGENTAL
REGENTS
REGES
REGGAE
REGGAES
REGGAETON
REGGAETONS
REGICIDAL
REGICIDE
REGICIDES
REGIE
REGIES
REGIFT
REGIFTED
REGIFTER
REGIFTERS
REGIFTING
REGIFTS
REGILD
REGILDED
REGILDING
REGILDS
REGILT
REGIME
REGIMEN
REGIMENS
REGIMENT
REGIMENTAL
REGIMENTALS
REGIMENTATION
REGIMENTATIONS
REGIMENTED
REGIMENTING
REGIMENTS
REGIMES
REGINA
REGINAE
REGINAL
REGINAS
REGION
REGIONAL
REGIONALISM
REGIONALISMS
REGIONALIST
REGIONALISTIC
REGIONALISTS
REGIONALIZATION
REGIONALIZE
REGIONALIZED
REGIONALIZES
REGIONALIZING
REGIONALLY
REGIONALS
REGIONS
REGISSEUR
REGISSEURS
REGISTER
REGISTERABLE
REGISTERED
REGISTERING
REGISTERS
REGISTRABLE
REGISTRANT
REGISTRANTS
REGISTRAR
REGISTRARS
REGISTRATION
REGISTRATIONS
REGISTRIES
REGISTRY
REGIUS
REGIVE
REGIVEN
REGIVES
REGIVING
REGLAZE
REGLAZED
REGLAZES
REGLAZING
REGLET
REGLETS
REGLORIFIED
REGLORIFIES
REGLORIFY
REGLORIFYING
REGLOSS
REGLOSSED
REGLOSSES
REGLOSSING
REGLOW
REGLOWED
REGLOWING
REGLOWS
REGLUE
REGLUED
REGLUES
REGLUING
REGMA
REGMATA
REGNA
REGNAL
REGNANCIES
REGNANCY
REGNANT
REGNUM
REGOLITH
REGOLITHS
REGORGE
REGORGED
REGORGES
REGORGING
REGOSOL
REGOSOLS
REGRADE
REGRADED
REGRADES
REGRADING
REGRAFT
REGRAFTED
REGRAFTING
REGRAFTS
REGRANT
REGRANTED
REGRANTING
REGRANTS
REGRATE
REGRATED
REGRATES
REGRATING
REGREEN
REGREENED
REGREENING
REGREENS
REGREET
REGREETED
REGREETING
REGREETS
REGRESS
REGRESSED
REGRESSES
REGRESSING
REGRESSION
REGRESSIONS
REGRESSIVE
REGRESSIVELY
REGRESSIVENESS
REGRESSIVITIES
REGRESSIVITY
REGRESSOR
REGRESSORS
REGRET
REGRETFUL
REGRETFULLY
REGRETFULNESS
REGRETFULNESSES
REGRETS

REGRETTABLE
REGRETTABLY
REGRETTED
REGRETTER
REGRETTERS
REGRETTING
REGREW
REGRIND
REGRINDING
REGRINDS
REGROOM
REGROOMED
REGROOMING
REGROOMS
REGROOVE
REGROOVED
REGROOVES
REGROOVING
REGROUND
REGROUP
REGROUPED
REGROUPING
REGROUPS
REGROW
REGROWING
REGROWN
REGROWS
REGROWTH
REGROWTHS
REGS
REGULABLE
REGULAR
REGULARISE
REGULARISED
REGULARISES
REGULARISING
REGULARITIES
REGULARITY
REGULARIZATION
REGULARIZATIONS
REGULARIZE
REGULARIZED
REGULARIZES
REGULARIZING
REGULARLY
REGULARS
REGULATE
REGULATED
REGULATES
REGULATING
REGULATION
REGULATIONS
REGULATIVE
REGULATOR
REGULATORS
REGULATORY
REGULI
REGULINE
REGULUS
REGULUSES
REGURGITATE
REGURGITATED
REGURGITATES
REGURGITATING
REGURGITATION
REGURGITATIONS
REHAB
REHABBED
REHABBER
REHABBERS
REHABBING
REHABILITANT
REHABILITANTS
REHABILITATE
REHABILITATED
REHABILITATES
REHABILITATING
REHABILITATION
REHABILITATIONS
REHABILITATIVE
REHABILITATOR
REHABILITATORS
REHABS
REHAMMER
REHAMMERED
REHAMMERING
REHAMMERS
REHANDLE
REHANDLED
REHANDLES
REHANDLING
REHANG
REHANGED
REHANGING
REHANGS
REHARDEN
REHARDENED
REHARDENING
REHARDENS
REHARMONIZE
REHARMONIZED
REHARMONIZES
REHARMONIZING
REHASH
REHASHED
REHASHES
REHASHING
REHEAR
REHEARD
REHEARING
REHEARINGS
REHEARS
REHEARSAL
REHEARSALS
REHEARSE
REHEARSED
REHEARSER
REHEARSERS
REHEARSES
REHEARSING
REHEAT
REHEATED
REHEATER
REHEATERS
REHEATING
REHEATS
REHEEL
REHEELED
REHEELING
REHEELS
REHEM
REHEMMED
REHEMMING
REHEMS
REHINGE
REHINGED
REHINGES
REHINGING
REHIRE
REHIRED
REHIRES
REHIRING
REHOBOAM
REHOBOAMS
REHOSPITALIZE
REHOSPITALIZED
REHOSPITALIZES
REHOSPITALIZING
REHOUSE
REHOUSED
REHOUSES
REHOUSING
REHUMANIZE
REHUMANIZED
REHUMANIZES
REHUMANIZING
REHUNG
REHYDRATABLE
REHYDRATE
REHYDRATED
REHYDRATES
REHYDRATING
REHYDRATION
REHYDRATIONS
REHYPNOTIZE
REHYPNOTIZED
REHYPNOTIZES
REHYPNOTIZING
REI
REICHSMARK
REICHSMARKS
REIDENTIFIED
REIDENTIFIES
REIDENTIFY
REIDENTIFYING
REIF
REIFICATION
REIFICATIONS
REIFIED
REIFIER
REIFIERS
REIFIES
REIFS
REIFY
REIFYING
REIGN
REIGNED
REIGNING
REIGNITE
REIGNITED
REIGNITES
REIGNITING
REIGNITION
REIGNITIONS
REIGNS
REIKI
REIKIS
REIMAGE
REIMAGED
REIMAGES
REIMAGINE
REIMAGINED
REIMAGINES
REIMAGING
REIMAGINING
REIMBURSABLE
REIMBURSE
REIMBURSED
REIMBURSEMENT
REIMBURSEMENTS
REIMBURSES
REIMBURSING
REIMMERSE
REIMMERSED
REIMMERSES
REIMMERSING
REIMPLANT
REIMPLANTATION
REIMPLANTATIONS
REIMPLANTED
REIMPLANTING
REIMPLANTS
REIMPORT
REIMPORTATION
REIMPORTATIONS
REIMPORTED
REIMPORTING
REIMPORTS
REIMPOSE
REIMPOSED
REIMPOSES
REIMPOSING
REIMPOSITION
REIMPOSITIONS
REIMPRESSION
REIMPRESSIONS
REIN
REINCARNATE
REINCARNATED
REINCARNATES
REINCARNATING
REINCARNATION
REINCARNATIONS
REINCITE
REINCITED
REINCITES
REINCITING
REINCORPORATE
REINCORPORATED
REINCORPORATES
REINCORPORATING
REINCORPORATION
REINCUR
REINCURRED
REINCURRING
REINCURS
REINDEER
REINDEERS
REINDEX
REINDEXED
REINDEXES
REINDEXING
REINDICT
REINDICTED
REINDICTING

REINDICTMENT
REINDICTMENTS
REINDICTS
REINDUCE
REINDUCED
REINDUCES
REINDUCING
REINDUCT
REINDUCTED
REINDUCTING
REINDUCTS
REINDUSTRIALIZE
REINED
REINFECT
REINFECTED
REINFECTING
REINFECTION
REINFECTIONS
REINFECTS
REINFESTATION
REINFESTATIONS
REINFLAME
REINFLAMED
REINFLAMES
REINFLAMING
REINFLATE
REINFLATED
REINFLATES
REINFLATING
REINFLATION
REINFLATIONS
REINFORCE
REINFORCEABLE
REINFORCED
REINFORCEMENT
REINFORCEMENTS
REINFORCER
REINFORCERS
REINFORCES
REINFORCING
REINFORM
REINFORMED
REINFORMING
REINFORMS
REINFUSE
REINFUSED
REINFUSES
REINFUSING
REINFUSION
REINFUSIONS
REINHABIT
REINHABITED
REINHABITING
REINHABITS
REINING
REINITIATE
REINITIATED
REINITIATES
REINITIATING
REINJECT
REINJECTED
REINJECTING
REINJECTION
REINJECTIONS
REINJECTS
REINJURE
REINJURED
REINJURES
REINJURIES
REINJURING
REINJURY
REINK
REINKED
REINKING
REINKS
REINLESS
REINNERVATE
REINNERVATED
REINNERVATES
REINNERVATING
REINNERVATION
REINNERVATIONS
REINOCULATE
REINOCULATED
REINOCULATES
REINOCULATING
REINOCULATION
REINOCULATIONS
REINS
REINSCRIBE
REINSCRIBED
REINSCRIBES
REINSCRIBING
REINSERT
REINSERTED
REINSERTING
REINSERTION
REINSERTIONS
REINSERTS
REINSMAN
REINSMEN
REINSPECT
REINSPECTED
REINSPECTING
REINSPECTION
REINSPECTIONS
REINSPECTS
REINSPIRE
REINSPIRED
REINSPIRES
REINSPIRING
REINSTALL
REINSTALLATION
REINSTALLATIONS
REINSTALLED
REINSTALLING
REINSTALLS
REINSTATE
REINSTATED
REINSTATEMENT
REINSTATEMENTS
REINSTATES
REINSTATING
REINSTITUTE
REINSTITUTED
REINSTITUTES
REINSTITUTING
REINSURANCE
REINSURANCES
REINSURE
REINSURED
REINSURER
REINSURERS
REINSURES
REINSURING
REINTEGRATE
REINTEGRATED
REINTEGRATES
REINTEGRATING
REINTEGRATION
REINTEGRATIONS
REINTEGRATIVE
REINTER
REINTERMENT
REINTERMENTS
REINTERPRET
REINTERPRETED
REINTERPRETING
REINTERPRETS
REINTERRED
REINTERRING
REINTERS
REINTERVIEW
REINTERVIEWED
REINTERVIEWING
REINTERVIEWS
REINTRODUCE
REINTRODUCED
REINTRODUCES
REINTRODUCING
REINTRODUCTION
REINTRODUCTIONS
REINVADE
REINVADED
REINVADES
REINVADING
REINVASION
REINVASIONS
REINVENT
REINVENTED
REINVENTING
REINVENTION
REINVENTIONS
REINVENTS
REINVEST
REINVESTED
REINVESTIGATE
REINVESTIGATED
REINVESTIGATES
REINVESTIGATING
REINVESTIGATION
REINVESTING
REINVESTMENT
REINVESTMENTS
REINVESTS
REINVIGORATE
REINVIGORATED
REINVIGORATES
REINVIGORATING
REINVIGORATION
REINVIGORATIONS
REINVIGORATOR
REINVIGORATORS
REINVITE
REINVITED
REINVITES
REINVITING
REINVOKE
REINVOKED
REINVOKES
REINVOKING
REINVOLVE
REINVOLVED
REINVOLVES
REINVOLVING
REIS
REISHI
REISHIS
REISSUE
REISSUED
REISSUER
REISSUERS
REISSUES
REISSUING
REITBOK
REITBOKS
REITERATE
REITERATED
REITERATES
REITERATING
REITERATION
REITERATIONS
REITERATIVE
REITERATIVELY
REIVE
REIVED
REIVER
REIVERS
REIVES
REIVING
REIVINGS
REJACKET
REJACKETED
REJACKETING
REJACKETS
REJECT
REJECTED
REJECTEE
REJECTEES
REJECTER
REJECTERS
REJECTING
REJECTINGLY
REJECTION
REJECTIONS
REJECTIVE
REJECTOR
REJECTORS
REJECTS
REJIG
REJIGGED
REJIGGER
REJIGGERED
REJIGGERING
REJIGGERS
REJIGGING
REJIGS
REJOICE
REJOICED
REJOICER
REJOICERS
REJOICES
REJOICING
REJOICINGLY
REJOICINGS

REJOIN
REJOINDER
REJOINDERS
REJOINED
REJOINING
REJOINS
REJUDGE
REJUDGED
REJUDGES
REJUDGING
REJUGGLE
REJUGGLED
REJUGGLES
REJUGGLING
REJUSTIFIED
REJUSTIFIES
REJUSTIFY
REJUSTIFYING
REJUVENATE
REJUVENATED
REJUVENATES
REJUVENATING
REJUVENATION
REJUVENATIONS
REJUVENATOR
REJUVENATORS
REJUVENESCENCE
REJUVENESCENCES
REJUVENESCENT
REKEY
REKEYBOARD
REKEYBOARDED
REKEYBOARDING
REKEYBOARDS
REKEYED
REKEYING
REKEYS
REKINDLE
REKINDLED
REKINDLES
REKINDLING
REKINDLINGS
REKNIT
REKNITS
REKNITTED
REKNITTING
REKNOT
REKNOTS
REKNOTTED
REKNOTTING
RELABEL
RELABELED
RELABELING
RELABELLED
RELABELLING
RELABELS
RELACE
RELACED
RELACES
RELACING
RELACQUER
RELACQUERED
RELACQUERING
RELACQUERS
RELAID
RELAND
RELANDED
RELANDING
RELANDS
RELANDSCAPE
RELANDSCAPED
RELANDSCAPES
RELANDSCAPING
RELAPSE
RELAPSED
RELAPSER
RELAPSERS
RELAPSES
RELAPSING
RELATABLE
RELATE
RELATED
RELATEDLY
RELATEDNESS
RELATEDNESSES
RELATER
RELATERS
RELATES
RELATING
RELATION
RELATIONAL
RELATIONALLY
RELATIONS
RELATIONSHIP
RELATIONSHIPS
RELATIVE
RELATIVELY
RELATIVES
RELATIVISM
RELATIVISMS
RELATIVIST
RELATIVISTIC
RELATIVISTS
RELATIVITIES
RELATIVITY
RELATIVIZE
RELATIVIZED
RELATIVIZES
RELATIVIZING
RELATOR
RELATORS
RELAUNCH
RELAUNCHED
RELAUNCHES
RELAUNCHING
RELAUNDER
RELAUNDERED
RELAUNDERING
RELAUNDERS
RELAX
RELAXABLE
RELAXANT
RELAXANTS
RELAXATION
RELAXATIONS
RELAXED
RELAXEDLY
RELAXEDNESS
RELAXEDNESSES
RELAXER
RELAXERS
RELAXES
RELAXIN
RELAXING
RELAXINS
RELAY
RELAYED
RELAYING
RELAYS
RELEARN
RELEARNED
RELEARNING
RELEARNS
RELEARNT
RELEASABLE
RELEASE
RELEASED
RELEASEE
RELEASEES
RELEASER
RELEASERS
RELEASES
RELEASING
RELEASOR
RELEASORS
RELEGABLE
RELEGATE
RELEGATED
RELEGATES
RELEGATING
RELEGATION
RELEGATIONS
RELEGITIMIZE
RELEGITIMIZED
RELEGITIMIZES
RELEGITIMIZING
RELEND
RELENDING
RELENDS
RELENT
RELENTED
RELENTING
RELENTLESS
RELENTLESSLY
RELENTLESSNESS
RELENTS
RELET
RELETS
RELETTER
RELETTERED
RELETTERING
RELETTERS
RELETTING
RELEVANCE
RELEVANCES
RELEVANCIES
RELEVANCY
RELEVANT
RELEVANTLY
RELEVE
RELEVES
RELIABILITIES
RELIABILITY
RELIABLE
RELIABLENESS
RELIABLENESSES
RELIABLES
RELIABLY
RELIANCE
RELIANCES
RELIANT
RELIANTLY
RELIC
RELICENSE
RELICENSED
RELICENSES
RELICENSING
RELICENSURE
RELICENSURES
RELICS
RELICT
RELICTION
RELICTIONS
RELICTS
RELIED
RELIEF
RELIEFS
RELIER
RELIERS
RELIES
RELIEVABLE
RELIEVE
RELIEVED
RELIEVEDLY
RELIEVER
RELIEVERS
RELIEVES
RELIEVING
RELIEVO
RELIEVOS
RELIGHT
RELIGHTED
RELIGHTING
RELIGHTS
RELIGION
RELIGIONIST
RELIGIONISTS
RELIGIONLESS
RELIGIONS
RELIGIOSE
RELIGIOSITIES
RELIGIOSITY
RELIGIOUS
RELIGIOUSLY
RELIGIOUSNESS
RELIGIOUSNESSES
RELINE
RELINED
RELINES
RELINING
RELINK
RELINKED
RELINKING
RELINKS
RELINQUISH
RELINQUISHED
RELINQUISHES
RELINQUISHING
RELINQUISHMENT
RELINQUISHMENTS
RELIQUARIES
RELIQUARY
RELIQUE
RELIQUEFIED
RELIQUEFIES

RELIQUEFY
RELIQUEFYING
RELIQUES
RELIQUIAE
RELISH
RELISHABLE
RELISHED
RELISHES
RELISHING
RELIST
RELISTED
RELISTING
RELISTS
RELIT
RELIVABLE
RELIVE
RELIVED
RELIVES
RELIVING
RELLENO
RELLENOS
RELOAD
RELOADABLE
RELOADED
RELOADER
RELOADERS
RELOADING
RELOADS
RELOAN
RELOANED
RELOANING
RELOANS
RELOCATABLE
RELOCATE
RELOCATED
RELOCATEE
RELOCATEES
RELOCATES
RELOCATING
RELOCATION
RELOCATIONS
RELOCK
RELOCKED
RELOCKING
RELOCKS
RELOOK
RELOOKED
RELOOKING
RELOOKS
RELUBRICATE
RELUBRICATED
RELUBRICATES
RELUBRICATING
RELUBRICATION
RELUBRICATIONS
RELUCENT
RELUCT
RELUCTANCE
RELUCTANCES
RELUCTANCIES
RELUCTANCY
RELUCTANT
RELUCTANTLY
RELUCTATE
RELUCTATED
RELUCTATES
RELUCTATING
RELUCTATION
RELUCTATIONS
RELUCTED
RELUCTING
RELUCTS
RELUME
RELUMED
RELUMES
RELUMINE
RELUMINED
RELUMINES
RELUMING
RELUMINING
RELY
RELYING
REM
REMADE
REMAIL
REMAILED
REMAILER
REMAILERS
REMAILING
REMAILS
REMAIN
REMAINDER
REMAINDERED
REMAINDERING
REMAINDERS
REMAINED
REMAINING
REMAINS
REMAKE
REMAKER
REMAKERS
REMAKES
REMAKING
REMAN
REMAND
REMANDED
REMANDING
REMANDS
REMANENCE
REMANENCES
REMANENT
REMANNED
REMANNING
REMANS
REMANUFACTURE
REMANUFACTURED
REMANUFACTURER
REMANUFACTURERS
REMANUFACTURES
REMANUFACTURING
REMAP
REMAPPED
REMAPPING
REMAPS
REMARK
REMARKABLE
REMARKABLENESS
REMARKABLY
REMARKED
REMARKER
REMARKERS
REMARKET
REMARKETED
REMARKETING
REMARKETS
REMARKING
REMARKS
REMARQUE
REMARQUES
REMARRIAGE
REMARRIAGES
REMARRIED
REMARRIES
REMARRY
REMARRYING
REMASTER
REMASTERED
REMASTERING
REMASTERS
REMATCH
REMATCHED
REMATCHES
REMATCHING
REMATE
REMATED
REMATERIALIZE
REMATERIALIZED
REMATERIALIZES
REMATERIALIZING
REMATES
REMATING
REMEASURE
REMEASURED
REMEASUREMENT
REMEASUREMENTS
REMEASURES
REMEASURING
REMEDIABILITIES
REMEDIABILITY
REMEDIABLE
REMEDIAL
REMEDIALLY
REMEDIATE
REMEDIATED
REMEDIATES
REMEDIATING
REMEDIATION
REMEDIATIONS
REMEDIED
REMEDIES
REMEDILESS
REMEDY
REMEDYING
REMEET
REMEETING
REMEETS
REMELT
REMELTED
REMELTING
REMELTS
REMEMBER
REMEMBERABILITY
REMEMBERABLE
REMEMBERED
REMEMBERER
REMEMBERERS
REMEMBERING
REMEMBERS
REMEMBRANCE
REMEMBRANCER
REMEMBRANCERS
REMEMBRANCES
REMEND
REMENDED
REMENDING
REMENDS
REMERGE
REMERGED
REMERGES
REMERGING
REMET
REMEX
REMIGES
REMIGIAL
REMIGRATE
REMIGRATED
REMIGRATES
REMIGRATING
REMIGRATION
REMIGRATIONS
REMILITARIZE
REMILITARIZED
REMILITARIZES
REMILITARIZING
REMIND
REMINDED
REMINDER
REMINDERS
REMINDFUL
REMINDING
REMINDS
REMINISCE
REMINISCED
REMINISCENCE
REMINISCENCES
REMINISCENT
REMINISCENTIAL
REMINISCENTLY
REMINISCER
REMINISCERS
REMINISCES
REMINISCING
REMINT
REMINTED
REMINTING
REMINTS
REMISE
REMISED
REMISES
REMISING
REMISS
REMISSIBLE
REMISSIBLY
REMISSION
REMISSIONS
REMISSIVE
REMISSLY
REMISSNESS
REMISSNESSES
REMIT
REMITMENT
REMITMENTS
REMITS
REMITTABLE
REMITTAL

REMITTALS
REMITTANCE
REMITTANCES
REMITTED
REMITTENT
REMITTER
REMITTERS
REMITTING
REMITTOR
REMITTORS
REMIX
REMIXED
REMIXER
REMIXERS
REMIXES
REMIXING
REMIXT
REMIXTURE
REMIXTURES
REMNANT
REMNANTAL
REMNANTS
REMOBILIZATION
REMOBILIZATIONS
REMOBILIZE
REMOBILIZED
REMOBILIZES
REMOBILIZING
REMODEL
REMODELED
REMODELER
REMODELERS
REMODELING
REMODELLED
REMODELLING
REMODELS
REMODIFIED
REMODIFIES
REMODIFY
REMODIFYING
REMOISTEN
REMOISTENED
REMOISTENING
REMOISTENS
REMOLADE
REMOLADES
REMOLD
REMOLDED
REMOLDING
REMOLDS
REMONETIZATION
REMONETIZATIONS
REMONETIZE
REMONETIZED
REMONETIZES
REMONETIZING
REMONSTRANCE
REMONSTRANCES
REMONSTRANT
REMONSTRANTLY
REMONSTRANTS
REMONSTRATE
REMONSTRATED
REMONSTRATES
REMONSTRATING
REMONSTRATION
REMONSTRATIONS
REMONSTRATIVE
REMONSTRATIVELY
REMONSTRATOR
REMONSTRATORS
REMONTANT
REMONTANTS
REMORA
REMORAS
REMORID
REMORSE
REMORSEFUL
REMORSEFULLY
REMORSEFULNESS
REMORSELESS
REMORSELESSLY
REMORSELESSNESS
REMORSES
REMORTGAGE
REMORTGAGED
REMORTGAGES
REMORTGAGING
REMOTE
REMOTELY
REMOTENESS
REMOTENESSES
REMOTER
REMOTES
REMOTEST
REMOTION
REMOTIONS
REMOTIVATE
REMOTIVATED
REMOTIVATES
REMOTIVATING
REMOTIVATION
REMOTIVATIONS
REMOULADE
REMOULADES
REMOULD
REMOULDED
REMOULDING
REMOULDS
REMOUNT
REMOUNTED
REMOUNTING
REMOUNTS
REMOVABILITIES
REMOVABILITY
REMOVABLE
REMOVABLENESS
REMOVABLENESSES
REMOVABLY
REMOVAL
REMOVALS
REMOVE
REMOVEABLE
REMOVED
REMOVEDLY
REMOVER
REMOVERS
REMOVES
REMOVING
REMS
REMUDA
REMUDAS
REMUNERATE
REMUNERATED
REMUNERATES
REMUNERATING
REMUNERATION
REMUNERATIONS
REMUNERATIVE
REMUNERATIVELY
REMUNERATOR
REMUNERATORS
REMUNERATORY
REMYTHOLOGIZE
REMYTHOLOGIZED
REMYTHOLOGIZES
REMYTHOLOGIZING
RENAIL
RENAILED
RENAILING
RENAILS
RENAISSANCE
RENAISSANCES
RENAL
RENAME
RENAMED
RENAMES
RENAMING
RENASCENCE
RENASCENCES
RENASCENT
RENATIONALIZE
RENATIONALIZED
RENATIONALIZES
RENATIONALIZING
RENATURATION
RENATURATIONS
RENATURE
RENATURED
RENATURES
RENATURING
RENCONTRE
RENCONTRES
RENCOUNTER
RENCOUNTERED
RENCOUNTERING
RENCOUNTERS
REND
RENDED
RENDER
RENDERABLE
RENDERED
RENDERER
RENDERERS
RENDERING
RENDERINGS
RENDERS
RENDEZVOUS
RENDEZVOUSED
RENDEZVOUSES
RENDEZVOUSING
RENDIBLE
RENDING
RENDITION
RENDITIONS
RENDS
RENDZINA
RENDZINAS
RENEGADE
RENEGADED
RENEGADES
RENEGADING
RENEGADO
RENEGADOES
RENEGADOS
RENEGE
RENEGED
RENEGER
RENEGERS
RENEGES
RENEGING
RENEGOTIABLE
RENEGOTIATE
RENEGOTIATED
RENEGOTIATES
RENEGOTIATING
RENEGOTIATION
RENEGOTIATIONS
RENEGUE
RENEGUED
RENEGUES
RENEGUING
RENEST
RENESTED
RENESTING
RENESTS
RENEW
RENEWABILITIES
RENEWABILITY
RENEWABLE
RENEWABLES
RENEWABLY
RENEWAL
RENEWALS
RENEWED
RENEWEDLY
RENEWER
RENEWERS
RENEWING
RENEWS
RENIFORM
RENIG
RENIGGED
RENIGGING
RENIGS
RENIN
RENINS
RENITENCE
RENITENCES
RENITENCIES
RENITENCY
RENITENT
RENMINBI
RENNASE
RENNASES
RENNET
RENNETS
RENNIN
RENNINS
RENO
RENOGRAM
RENOGRAMS
RENOGRAPHIC
RENOGRAPHIES
RENOGRAPHY

RENOMINATE
RENOMINATED
RENOMINATES
RENOMINATING
RENOMINATION
RENOMINATIONS
RENOS
RENOTIFIED
RENOTIFIES
RENOTIFY
RENOTIFYING
RENOUNCE
RENOUNCED
RENOUNCEMENT
RENOUNCEMENTS
RENOUNCER
RENOUNCERS
RENOUNCES
RENOUNCING
RENOVASCULAR
RENOVATE
RENOVATED
RENOVATES
RENOVATING
RENOVATION
RENOVATIONS
RENOVATIVE
RENOVATOR
RENOVATORS
RENOWN
RENOWNED
RENOWNING
RENOWNS
RENT
RENTABILITIES
RENTABILITY
RENTABLE
RENTAL
RENTALS
RENTE
RENTED
RENTER
RENTERS
RENTES
RENTIER
RENTIERS
RENTING
RENTS
RENUMBER
RENUMBERED
RENUMBERING
RENUMBERS
RENUNCIATION
RENUNCIATIONS
RENUNCIATIVE
RENUNCIATORY
RENVOI
RENVOIS
REOBJECT
REOBJECTED
REOBJECTING
REOBJECTS
REOBSERVE
REOBSERVED
REOBSERVES
REOBSERVING
REOBTAIN
REOBTAINED
REOBTAINING
REOBTAINS
REOCCUPATION
REOCCUPATIONS
REOCCUPIED
REOCCUPIES
REOCCUPY
REOCCUPYING
REOCCUR
REOCCURRED
REOCCURRENCE
REOCCURRENCES
REOCCURRING
REOCCURS
REOFFEND
REOFFENDED
REOFFENDING
REOFFENDS
REOFFER
REOFFERED
REOFFERING
REOFFERS
REOIL
REOILED
REOILING
REOILS
REOPEN
REOPENED
REOPENING
REOPENINGS
REOPENS
REOPERATE
REOPERATED
REOPERATES
REOPERATING
REOPERATION
REOPERATIONS
REOPPOSE
REOPPOSED
REOPPOSES
REOPPOSING
REORCHESTRATE
REORCHESTRATED
REORCHESTRATES
REORCHESTRATING
REORCHESTRATION
REORDAIN
REORDAINED
REORDAINING
REORDAINS
REORDER
REORDERED
REORDERING
REORDERS
REORG
REORGANISATION
REORGANISATIONS
REORGANISE
REORGANISED
REORGANISES
REORGANISING
REORGANIZATION
REORGANIZATIONS
REORGANIZE
REORGANIZED
REORGANIZER
REORGANIZERS
REORGANIZES
REORGANIZING
REORGED
REORGING
REORGS
REORIENT
REORIENTATE
REORIENTATED
REORIENTATES
REORIENTATING
REORIENTATION
REORIENTATIONS
REORIENTED
REORIENTING
REORIENTS
REOUTFIT
REOUTFITS
REOUTFITTED
REOUTFITTING
REOVIRUS
REOVIRUSES
REOXIDATION
REOXIDATIONS
REOXIDIZE
REOXIDIZED
REOXIDIZES
REOXIDIZING
REOXYGENATE
REOXYGENATED
REOXYGENATES
REOXYGENATING
REOXYGENATION
REOXYGENATIONS
REP
REPACIFIED
REPACIFIES
REPACIFY
REPACIFYING
REPACK
REPACKAGE
REPACKAGED
REPACKAGER
REPACKAGERS
REPACKAGES
REPACKAGING
REPACKED
REPACKING
REPACKS
REPAID
REPAINT
REPAINTED
REPAINTING
REPAINTS
REPAIR
REPAIRABILITIES
REPAIRABILITY
REPAIRABLE
REPAIRED
REPAIRER
REPAIRERS
REPAIRING
REPAIRMAN
REPAIRMEN
REPAIRS
REPAND
REPANDLY
REPANEL
REPANELED
REPANELING
REPANELLED
REPANELLING
REPANELS
REPAPER
REPAPERED
REPAPERING
REPAPERS
REPARABLE
REPARABLY
REPARATION
REPARATIONS
REPARATIVE
REPARK
REPARKED
REPARKING
REPARKS
REPARTEE
REPARTEES
REPARTITION
REPARTITIONS
REPASS
REPASSAGE
REPASSAGES
REPASSED
REPASSES
REPASSING
REPAST
REPASTED
REPASTING
REPASTS
REPATCH
REPATCHED
REPATCHES
REPATCHING
REPATRIATE
REPATRIATED
REPATRIATES
REPATRIATING
REPATRIATION
REPATRIATIONS
REPATTERN
REPATTERNED
REPATTERNING
REPATTERNS
REPAVE
REPAVED
REPAVES
REPAVING
REPAY
REPAYABLE
REPAYING
REPAYMENT
REPAYMENTS
REPAYS
REPEAL
REPEALABLE
REPEALED
REPEALER
REPEALERS
REPEALING
REPEALS

EPEAT
EPEATABILITIES
EPEATABILITY
EPEATABLE
EPEATED
EPEATEDLY
EPEATER
EPEATERS
EPEATING
EPEATS
EPECHAGE
EPECHAGES
EPEG
EPEGGED
EPEGGING
EPEGS
EPEL
EPELLANT
EPELLANTS
EPELLED
EPELLENCIES
EPELLENCY
EPELLENT
EPELLENTLY
EPELLENTS
EPELLER
EPELLERS
EPELLING
EPELS
EPENT
EPENTANCE
EPENTANCES
EPENTANT
EPENTANTLY
EPENTED
EPENTER
EPENTERS
EPENTING
EPENTS
EPEOPLE
EPEOPLED
EPEOPLES
EPEOPLING
EPERCUSSION
EPERCUSSIONS
EPERCUSSIVE
EPERFUSION
EPERFUSIONS
EPERK
EPERKED
EPERKING
EPERKS
EPERTOIRE
REPERTOIRES
REPERTORIES
REPERTORY
REPETEND
REPETENDS
REPETITION
REPETITIONAL
REPETITIONS
REPETITIOUS
REPETITIOUSLY
REPETITIOUSNESS
REPETITIVE
REPETITIVELY
REPETITIVENESS
REPHOTOGRAPH
REPHOTOGRAPHED
REPHOTOGRAPHING
REPHOTOGRAPHS
REPHRASE
REPHRASED
REPHRASES
REPHRASING
REPIGMENT
REPIGMENTED
REPIGMENTING
REPIGMENTS
REPIN
REPINE
REPINED
REPINER
REPINERS
REPINES
REPINING
REPINNED
REPINNING
REPINS
REPLACE
REPLACEABLE
REPLACED
REPLACEMENT
REPLACEMENTS
REPLACER
REPLACERS
REPLACES
REPLACING
REPLAN
REPLANNED
REPLANNING
REPLANS
REPLANT
REPLANTATION
REPLANTATIONS
REPLANTED
REPLANTING
REPLANTS
REPLASTER
REPLASTERED
REPLASTERING
REPLASTERS
REPLATE
REPLATED
REPLATES
REPLATING
REPLAY
REPLAYED
REPLAYING
REPLAYS
REPLEAD
REPLEADED
REPLEADER
REPLEADERS
REPLEADING
REPLEADS
REPLED
REPLEDGE
REPLEDGED
REPLEDGES
REPLEDGING
REPLENISH
REPLENISHABLE
REPLENISHED
REPLENISHER
REPLENISHERS
REPLENISHES
REPLENISHING
REPLENISHMENT
REPLENISHMENTS
REPLETE
REPLETELY
REPLETENESS
REPLETENESSES
REPLETES
REPLETION
REPLETIONS
REPLEVIABLE
REPLEVIED
REPLEVIES
REPLEVIN
REPLEVINED
REPLEVINING
REPLEVINS
REPLEVY
REPLEVYING
REPLICA
REPLICABILITIES
REPLICABILITY
REPLICABLE
REPLICAS
REPLICASE
REPLICASES
REPLICATE
REPLICATED
REPLICATES
REPLICATING
REPLICATION
REPLICATIONS
REPLICATIVE
REPLICON
REPLICONS
REPLIED
REPLIER
REPLIERS
REPLIES
REPLOT
REPLOTS
REPLOTTED
REPLOTTING
REPLOW
REPLOWED
REPLOWING
REPLOWS
REPLUMB
REPLUMBED
REPLUMBING
REPLUMBS
REPLUNGE
REPLUNGED
REPLUNGES
REPLUNGING
REPLY
REPLYING
REPO
REPOINT
REPOINTED
REPOINTING
REPOINTS
REPOLARIZATION
REPOLARIZATIONS
REPOLARIZE
REPOLARIZED
REPOLARIZES
REPOLARIZING
REPOLISH
REPOLISHED
REPOLISHES
REPOLISHING
REPOLL
REPOLLED
REPOLLING
REPOLLS
REPOPULARIZE
REPOPULARIZED
REPOPULARIZES
REPOPULARIZING
REPOPULATE
REPOPULATED
REPOPULATES
REPOPULATING
REPOPULATION
REPOPULATIONS
REPORT
REPORTABLE
REPORTAGE
REPORTAGES
REPORTED
REPORTEDLY
REPORTER
REPORTERS
REPORTING
REPORTINGS
REPORTORIAL
REPORTORIALLY
REPORTS
REPOS
REPOSAL
REPOSALS
REPOSE
REPOSED
REPOSEDLY
REPOSEFUL
REPOSEFULLY
REPOSEFULNESS
REPOSEFULNESSES
REPOSER
REPOSERS
REPOSES
REPOSING
REPOSIT
REPOSITED
REPOSITING
REPOSITION
REPOSITIONED
REPOSITIONING
REPOSITIONS
REPOSITORIES
REPOSITORY
REPOSITS
REPOSSESS
REPOSSESSED
REPOSSESSES
REPOSSESSING
REPOSSESSION

REPOSSESSIONS
REPOSSESSOR
REPOSSESSORS
REPOT
REPOTS
REPOTTED
REPOTTING
REPOUR
REPOURED
REPOURING
REPOURS
REPOUSSE
REPOUSSES
REPOWER
REPOWERED
REPOWERING
REPOWERS
REPP
REPPED
REPPING
REPPS
REPREHEND
REPREHENDED
REPREHENDING
REPREHENDS
REPREHENSIBLE
REPREHENSIBLY
REPREHENSION
REPREHENSIONS
REPREHENSIVE
REPRESENT
REPRESENTABLE
REPRESENTATION
REPRESENTATIONS
REPRESENTATIVE
REPRESENTATIVES
REPRESENTED
REPRESENTER
REPRESENTERS
REPRESENTING
REPRESENTS
REPRESS
REPRESSED
REPRESSER
REPRESSERS
REPRESSES
REPRESSIBILITY
REPRESSIBLE
REPRESSING
REPRESSION
REPRESSIONIST
REPRESSIONS
REPRESSIVE
REPRESSIVELY
REPRESSIVENESS
REPRESSOR
REPRESSORS
REPRESSURIZE
REPRESSURIZED
REPRESSURIZES
REPRESSURIZING
REPRICE
REPRICED
REPRICES
REPRICING
REPRIEVAL
REPRIEVALS
REPRIEVE
REPRIEVED
REPRIEVES
REPRIEVING
REPRIMAND
REPRIMANDED
REPRIMANDING
REPRIMANDS
REPRINT
REPRINTED
REPRINTER
REPRINTERS
REPRINTING
REPRINTS
REPRISAL
REPRISALS
REPRISE
REPRISED
REPRISES
REPRISING
REPRISTINATE
REPRISTINATED
REPRISTINATES
REPRISTINATING
REPRISTINATION
REPRISTINATIONS
REPRIVATIZATION
REPRIVATIZE
REPRIVATIZED
REPRIVATIZES
REPRIVATIZING
REPRO
REPROACH
REPROACHABLE
REPROACHED
REPROACHER
REPROACHERS
REPROACHES
REPROACHFUL
REPROACHFULLY
REPROACHFULNESS
REPROACHING
REPROACHINGLY
REPROBANCE
REPROBANCES
REPROBATE
REPROBATED
REPROBATES
REPROBATING
REPROBATION
REPROBATIONS
REPROBATIVE
REPROBATORY
REPROBE
REPROBED
REPROBES
REPROBING
REPROCESS
REPROCESSED
REPROCESSES
REPROCESSING
REPRODUCE
REPRODUCED
REPRODUCER
REPRODUCERS
REPRODUCES
REPRODUCIBILITY
REPRODUCIBLE
REPRODUCIBLES
REPRODUCIBLY
REPRODUCING
REPRODUCTION
REPRODUCTIONS
REPRODUCTIVE
REPRODUCTIVELY
REPRODUCTIVES
REPROGRAM
REPROGRAMED
REPROGRAMING
REPROGRAMMABLE
REPROGRAMMED
REPROGRAMMING
REPROGRAMS
REPROGRAPHER
REPROGRAPHERS
REPROGRAPHIC
REPROGRAPHICS
REPROGRAPHIES
REPROGRAPHY
REPROOF
REPROOFS
REPROS
REPROVAL
REPROVALS
REPROVE
REPROVED
REPROVER
REPROVERS
REPROVES
REPROVING
REPROVINGLY
REPROVISION
REPROVISIONED
REPROVISIONING
REPROVISIONS
REPS
REPTANT
REPTILE
REPTILES
REPTILIA
REPTILIAN
REPTILIANS
REPTILIUM
REPUBLIC
REPUBLICAN
REPUBLICANISM
REPUBLICANISMS
REPUBLICANIZE
REPUBLICANIZED
REPUBLICANIZES
REPUBLICANIZING
REPUBLICANS
REPUBLICATION
REPUBLICATIONS
REPUBLICS
REPUBLISH
REPUBLISHED
REPUBLISHER
REPUBLISHERS
REPUBLISHES
REPUBLISHING
REPUDIATE
REPUDIATED
REPUDIATES
REPUDIATING
REPUDIATION
REPUDIATIONIST
REPUDIATIONISTS
REPUDIATIONS
REPUDIATOR
REPUDIATORS
REPUGN
REPUGNANCE
REPUGNANCES
REPUGNANCIES
REPUGNANCY
REPUGNANT
REPUGNANTLY
REPUGNED
REPUGNING
REPUGNS
REPULSE
REPULSED
REPULSER
REPULSERS
REPULSES
REPULSING
REPULSION
REPULSIONS
REPULSIVE
REPULSIVELY
REPULSIVENESS
REPULSIVENESSES
REPUMP
REPUMPED
REPUMPING
REPUMPS
REPUNCTUATION
REPUNCTUATIONS
REPURCHASE
REPURCHASED
REPURCHASES
REPURCHASING
REPURIFIED
REPURIFIES
REPURIFY
REPURIFYING
REPURPOSE
REPURPOSED
REPURPOSES
REPURPOSING
REPURSUE
REPURSUED
REPURSUES
REPURSUING
REPUTABILITIES
REPUTABILITY
REPUTABLE
REPUTABLY
REPUTATION
REPUTATIONAL
REPUTATIONS
REPUTE
REPUTED
REPUTEDLY
REPUTES
REPUTING
REQUALIFIED

EQUALIFIES
EQUALIFY
EQUALIFYING
EQUEST
EQUESTED
EQUESTER
EQUESTERS
EQUESTING
EQUESTOR
EQUESTORS
EQUESTS
EQUIEM
EQUIEMS
EQUIESCAT
EQUIESCATS
EQUIN
EQUINS
EQUINTO
EQUINTOS
EQUIRE
EQUIRED
EQUIREMENT
EQUIREMENTS
EQUIRER
EQUIRERS
EQUIRES
EQUIRING
EQUISITE
EQUISITENESS
EQUISITENESSES
EQUISITES
EQUISITION
EQUISITIONED
EQUISITIONING
EQUISITIONS
EQUITAL
EQUITALS
EQUITE
EQUITED
EQUITER
EQUITERS
EQUITES
EQUITING
ERACK
ERACKED
ERACKING
ERACKS
ERADIATE
ERADIATED
ERADIATES
ERADIATING
ERADIATION
ERADIATIONS

RERAISE
RERAISED
RERAISES
RERAISING
RERAN
REREAD
REREADING
REREADINGS
REREADS
REREBRACE
REREBRACES
RERECORD
RERECORDED
RERECORDING
RERECORDS
REREDOS
REREDOSES
REREGISTER
REREGISTERED
REREGISTERING
REREGISTERS
REREGISTRATION
REREGISTRATIONS
REREGULATE
REREGULATED
REREGULATES
REREGULATING
REREGULATION
REREGULATIONS
RERELEASE
RERELEASED
RERELEASES
RERELEASING
REREMICE
REREMIND
REREMINDED
REREMINDING
REREMINDS
REREMOUSE
RERENT
RERENTED
RERENTING
RERENTS
REREPEAT
REREPEATED
REREPEATING
REREPEATS
REREVIEW
REREVIEWED
REREVIEWING
REREVIEWS
REREWARD
REREWARDS

RERIG
RERIGGED
RERIGGING
RERIGS
RERISE
RERISEN
RERISES
RERISING
REROLL
REROLLED
REROLLER
REROLLERS
REROLLING
REROLLS
REROOF
REROOFED
REROOFING
REROOFS
REROSE
REROUTE
REROUTED
REROUTES
REROUTING
RERUN
RERUNNING
RERUNS
RES
RESADDLE
RESADDLED
RESADDLES
RESADDLING
RESAID
RESAIL
RESAILED
RESAILING
RESAILS
RESALABLE
RESALE
RESALES
RESALUTE
RESALUTED
RESALUTES
RESALUTING
RESAMPLE
RESAMPLED
RESAMPLES
RESAMPLING
RESAT
RESAW
RESAWED
RESAWING
RESAWN
RESAWS

RESAY
RESAYING
RESAYS
RESCALE
RESCALED
RESCALES
RESCALING
RESCHEDULE
RESCHEDULED
RESCHEDULES
RESCHEDULING
RESCHOOL
RESCHOOLED
RESCHOOLING
RESCHOOLS
RESCIND
RESCINDED
RESCINDER
RESCINDERS
RESCINDING
RESCINDMENT
RESCINDMENTS
RESCINDS
RESCISSION
RESCISSIONS
RESCISSORY
RESCORE
RESCORED
RESCORES
RESCORING
RESCREEN
RESCREENED
RESCREENING
RESCREENS
RESCRIPT
RESCRIPTS
RESCUABLE
RESCUE
RESCUED
RESCUEE
RESCUEES
RESCUER
RESCUERS
RESCUES
RESCUING
RESCULPT
RESCULPTED
RESCULPTING
RESCULPTS
RESEAL
RESEALABLE
RESEALED
RESEALING

RESEALS
RESEARCH
RESEARCHABLE
RESEARCHED
RESEARCHER
RESEARCHERS
RESEARCHES
RESEARCHING
RESEARCHIST
RESEARCHISTS
RESEASON
RESEASONED
RESEASONING
RESEASONS
RESEAT
RESEATED
RESEATING
RESEATS
RESEAU
RESEAUS
RESEAUX
RESECT
RESECTABILITIES
RESECTABILITY
RESECTABLE
RESECTED
RESECTING
RESECTION
RESECTIONS
RESECTS
RESECURE
RESECURED
RESECURES
RESECURING
RESEDA
RESEDAS
RESEE
RESEED
RESEEDED
RESEEDING
RESEEDS
RESEEING
RESEEK
RESEEKING
RESEEKS
RESEEN
RESEES
RESEGREGATE
RESEGREGATED
RESEGREGATES
RESEGREGATING
RESEGREGATION
RESEGREGATIONS

RESEIZE
RESEIZED
RESEIZES
RESEIZING
RESEIZURE
RESEIZURES
RESELECT
RESELECTED
RESELECTING
RESELECTS
RESELL
RESELLER
RESELLERS
RESELLING
RESELLS
RESEMBLANCE
RESEMBLANCES
RESEMBLANT
RESEMBLE
RESEMBLED
RESEMBLER
RESEMBLERS
RESEMBLES
RESEMBLING
RESEND
RESENDING
RESENDS
RESENSITIZE
RESENSITIZED
RESENSITIZES
RESENSITIZING
RESENT
RESENTED
RESENTENCE
RESENTENCED
RESENTENCES
RESENTENCING
RESENTFUL
RESENTFULLY
RESENTFULNESS
RESENTFULNESSES
RESENTING
RESENTIVE
RESENTMENT
RESENTMENTS
RESENTS
RESERPINE
RESERPINES
RESERVABLE
RESERVATION
RESERVATIONIST
RESERVATIONISTS
RESERVATIONS
RESERVE
RESERVED
RESERVEDLY
RESERVEDNESS
RESERVEDNESSES
RESERVER
RESERVERS
RESERVES
RESERVICE
RESERVICED
RESERVICES
RESERVICING
RESERVING
RESERVIST
RESERVISTS
RESERVOIR
RESERVOIRS
RESES
RESET
RESETS
RESETTABLE
RESETTER
RESETTERS
RESETTING
RESETTLE
RESETTLED
RESETTLEMENT
RESETTLEMENTS
RESETTLES
RESETTLING
RESEW
RESEWED
RESEWING
RESEWN
RESEWS
RESH
RESHAPE
RESHAPED
RESHAPER
RESHAPERS
RESHAPES
RESHAPING
RESHARPEN
RESHARPENED
RESHARPENING
RESHARPENS
RESHAVE
RESHAVED
RESHAVEN
RESHAVES
RESHAVING
RESHES
RESHINE
RESHINED
RESHINES
RESHINGLE
RESHINGLED
RESHINGLES
RESHINGLING
RESHINING
RESHIP
RESHIPPED
RESHIPPER
RESHIPPERS
RESHIPPING
RESHIPS
RESHOD
RESHOE
RESHOED
RESHOEING
RESHOES
RESHONE
RESHOOT
RESHOOTING
RESHOOTS
RESHOT
RESHOW
RESHOWED
RESHOWER
RESHOWERED
RESHOWERING
RESHOWERS
RESHOWING
RESHOWN
RESHOWS
RESHUFFLE
RESHUFFLED
RESHUFFLES
RESHUFFLING
RESID
RESIDE
RESIDED
RESIDENCE
RESIDENCES
RESIDENCIES
RESIDENCY
RESIDENT
RESIDENTIAL
RESIDENTIALLY
RESIDENTS
RESIDER
RESIDERS
RESIDES
RESIDING
RESIDS
RESIDUA
RESIDUAL
RESIDUALLY
RESIDUALS
RESIDUARY
RESIDUE
RESIDUES
RESIDUUM
RESIDUUMS
RESIFT
RESIFTED
RESIFTING
RESIFTS
RESIGHT
RESIGHTED
RESIGHTING
RESIGHTS
RESIGN
RESIGNATION
RESIGNATIONS
RESIGNED
RESIGNEDLY
RESIGNEDNESS
RESIGNEDNESSES
RESIGNER
RESIGNERS
RESIGNING
RESIGNS
RESILE
RESILED
RESILES
RESILIENCE
RESILIENCES
RESILIENCIES
RESILIENCY
RESILIENT
RESILIENTLY
RESILIN
RESILING
RESILINS
RESILVER
RESILVERED
RESILVERING
RESILVERS
RESIN
RESINATE
RESINATED
RESINATES
RESINATING
RESINED
RESINIER
RESINIEST
RESINIFIED
RESINIFIES
RESINIFY
RESINIFYING
RESINING
RESINLIKE
RESINOID
RESINOIDS
RESINOUS
RESINS
RESINY
RESIST
RESISTANCE
RESISTANCES
RESISTANT
RESISTANTS
RESISTED
RESISTER
RESISTERS
RESISTIBILITIES
RESISTIBILITY
RESISTIBLE
RESISTING
RESISTIVE
RESISTIVELY
RESISTIVENESS
RESISTIVENESSES
RESISTIVITIES
RESISTIVITY
RESISTLESS
RESISTLESSLY
RESISTLESSNESS
RESISTOR
RESISTORS
RESISTS
RESIT
RESITE
RESITED
RESITES
RESITING
RESITS
RESITTING
RESITTINGS
RESITUATE
RESITUATED
RESITUATES
RESITUATING
RESIZE
RESIZED
RESIZES
RESIZING
RESKETCH
RESKETCHED
RESKETCHES
RESKETCHING

ESKIN
ESKINNED
ESKINNING
ESKINS
ESLATE
ESLATED
ESLATES
ESLATING
ESMELT
ESMELTED
ESMELTING
ESMELTS
ESMETHRIN
ESMETHRINS
ESMOOTH
ESMOOTHED
ESMOOTHING
ESMOOTHS
ESOAK
ESOAKED
ESOAKING
ESOAKS
ESOCIALIZATION
ESOCIALIZE
ESOCIALIZED
ESOCIALIZES
ESOCIALIZING
ESOD
ESODDED
ESODDING
ESODS
ESOFTEN
ESOFTENED
ESOFTENING
ESOFTENS
ESOJET
ESOJETS
ESOLD
ESOLDER
ESOLDERED
ESOLDERING
ESOLDERS
ESOLE
ESOLED
ESOLES
ESOLIDIFIED
ESOLIDIFIES
ESOLIDIFY
ESOLIDIFYING
SOLING
SOLUBLE
SOLUTE
SOLUTELY
RESOLUTENESS
RESOLUTENESSES
RESOLUTER
RESOLUTES
RESOLUTEST
RESOLUTION
RESOLUTIONS
RESOLVABLE
RESOLVE
RESOLVED
RESOLVENT
RESOLVENTS
RESOLVER
RESOLVERS
RESOLVES
RESOLVING
RESONANCE
RESONANCES
RESONANT
RESONANTLY
RESONANTS
RESONATE
RESONATED
RESONATES
RESONATING
RESONATOR
RESONATORS
RESORB
RESORBED
RESORBING
RESORBS
RESORCIN
RESORCINOL
RESORCINOLS
RESORCINS
RESORPTION
RESORPTIONS
RESORPTIVE
RESORT
RESORTED
RESORTER
RESORTERS
RESORTING
RESORTS
RESOUGHT
RESOUND
RESOUNDED
RESOUNDING
RESOUNDINGLY
RESOUNDS
RESOURCE
RESOURCED
RESOURCEFUL
RESOURCEFULLY
RESOURCEFULNESS
RESOURCES
RESOURCING
RESOW
RESOWED
RESOWING
RESOWN
RESOWS
RESPACE
RESPACED
RESPACES
RESPACING
RESPADE
RESPADED
RESPADES
RESPADING
RESPEAK
RESPEAKING
RESPEAKS
RESPECIFIED
RESPECIFIES
RESPECIFY
RESPECIFYING
RESPECT
RESPECTABILITY
RESPECTABLE
RESPECTABLENESS
RESPECTABLES
RESPECTABLY
RESPECTED
RESPECTER
RESPECTERS
RESPECTFUL
RESPECTFULLY
RESPECTFULNESS
RESPECTING
RESPECTIVE
RESPECTIVELY
RESPECTIVENESS
RESPECTS
RESPELL
RESPELLED
RESPELLING
RESPELLINGS
RESPELLS
RESPELT
RESPIRABLE
RESPIRATION
RESPIRATIONS
RESPIRATOR
RESPIRATORS
RESPIRATORY
RESPIRE
RESPIRED
RESPIRES
RESPIRING
RESPIRITUALIZE
RESPIRITUALIZED
RESPIRITUALIZES
RESPIROMETER
RESPIROMETERS
RESPIROMETRIC
RESPIROMETRIES
RESPIROMETRY
RESPITE
RESPITED
RESPITES
RESPITING
RESPLENDENCE
RESPLENDENCES
RESPLENDENCIES
RESPLENDENCY
RESPLENDENT
RESPLENDENTLY
RESPLICE
RESPLICED
RESPLICES
RESPLICING
RESPLIT
RESPLITS
RESPLITTING
RESPOKE
RESPOKEN
RESPOND
RESPONDED
RESPONDENT
RESPONDENTS
RESPONDER
RESPONDERS
RESPONDING
RESPONDS
RESPONSA
RESPONSE
RESPONSES
RESPONSIBILITY
RESPONSIBLE
RESPONSIBLENESS
RESPONSIBLY
RESPONSIONS
RESPONSIVE
RESPONSIVELY
RESPONSIVENESS
RESPONSORIES
RESPONSORY
RESPONSUM
RESPOOL
RESPOOLED
RESPOOLING
RESPOOLS
RESPOT
RESPOTS
RESPOTTED
RESPOTTING
RESPRANG
RESPRAY
RESPRAYED
RESPRAYING
RESPRAYS
RESPREAD
RESPREADING
RESPREADS
RESPRING
RESPRINGING
RESPRINGS
RESPROUT
RESPROUTED
RESPROUTING
RESPROUTS
RESPRUNG
RESSENTIMENT
RESSENTIMENTS
REST
RESTABILIZE
RESTABILIZED
RESTABILIZES
RESTABILIZING
RESTABLE
RESTABLED
RESTABLES
RESTABLING
RESTACK
RESTACKED
RESTACKING
RESTACKS
RESTAFF
RESTAFFED
RESTAFFING
RESTAFFS
RESTAGE
RESTAGED
RESTAGES
RESTAGING
RESTAMP
RESTAMPED
RESTAMPING
RESTAMPS
RESTART
RESTARTABLE

RESTARTED
RESTARTING
RESTARTS
RESTATE
RESTATED
RESTATEMENT
RESTATEMENTS
RESTATES
RESTATING
RESTATION
RESTATIONED
RESTATIONING
RESTATIONS
RESTAURANT
RESTAURANTEUR
RESTAURANTEURS
RESTAURANTS
RESTAURATEUR
RESTAURATEURS
RESTED
RESTENOSES
RESTENOSIS
RESTER
RESTERS
RESTFUL
RESTFULLER
RESTFULLEST
RESTFULLY
RESTFULNESS
RESTFULNESSES
RESTIFORM
RESTIMULATE
RESTIMULATED
RESTIMULATES
RESTIMULATING
RESTIMULATION
RESTIMULATIONS
RESTING
RESTITCH
RESTITCHED
RESTITCHES
RESTITCHING
RESTITUTE
RESTITUTED
RESTITUTES
RESTITUTING
RESTITUTION
RESTITUTIONS
RESTIVE
RESTIVELY
RESTIVENESS
RESTIVENESSES
RESTLESS
RESTLESSLY
RESTLESSNESS
RESTLESSNESSES
RESTOCK
RESTOCKED
RESTOCKING
RESTOCKS
RESTOKE
RESTOKED
RESTOKES
RESTOKING
RESTORABLE
RESTORAL
RESTORALS
RESTORATION
RESTORATIONS
RESTORATIVE
RESTORATIVES
RESTORE
RESTORED
RESTORER
RESTORERS
RESTORES
RESTORING
RESTRAIN
RESTRAINABLE
RESTRAINED
RESTRAINEDLY
RESTRAINER
RESTRAINERS
RESTRAINING
RESTRAINS
RESTRAINT
RESTRAINTS
RESTRENGTHEN
RESTRENGTHENED
RESTRENGTHENING
RESTRENGTHENS
RESTRESS
RESTRESSED
RESTRESSES
RESTRESSING
RESTRETCH
RESTRETCHED
RESTRETCHES
RESTRETCHING
RESTRICKEN
RESTRICT
RESTRICTED
RESTRICTEDLY
RESTRICTING
RESTRICTION
RESTRICTIONISM
RESTRICTIONISMS
RESTRICTIONIST
RESTRICTIONISTS
RESTRICTIONS
RESTRICTIVE
RESTRICTIVELY
RESTRICTIVENESS
RESTRICTIVES
RESTRICTS
RESTRIKE
RESTRIKES
RESTRIKING
RESTRING
RESTRINGING
RESTRINGS
RESTRIVE
RESTRIVEN
RESTRIVES
RESTRIVING
RESTROOM
RESTROOMS
RESTROVE
RESTRUCK
RESTRUCTURE
RESTRUCTURED
RESTRUCTURES
RESTRUCTURING
RESTRUCTURINGS
RESTRUNG
RESTS
RESTUDIED
RESTUDIES
RESTUDY
RESTUDYING
RESTUFF
RESTUFFED
RESTUFFING
RESTUFFS
RESTYLE
RESTYLED
RESTYLES
RESTYLING
RESUBJECT
RESUBJECTED
RESUBJECTING
RESUBJECTS
RESUBMISSION
RESUBMISSIONS
RESUBMIT
RESUBMITS
RESUBMITTED
RESUBMITTING
RESULT
RESULTANT
RESULTANTLY
RESULTANTS
RESULTED
RESULTFUL
RESULTING
RESULTLESS
RESULTS
RESUMABLE
RESUME
RESUMED
RESUMER
RESUMERS
RESUMES
RESUMING
RESUMMON
RESUMMONED
RESUMMONING
RESUMMONS
RESUMPTION
RESUMPTIONS
RESUPINATE
RESUPINE
RESUPPLIED
RESUPPLIES
RESUPPLY
RESUPPLYING
RESURFACE
RESURFACED
RESURFACER
RESURFACERS
RESURFACES
RESURFACING
RESURGE
RESURGED
RESURGENCE
RESURGENCES
RESURGENT
RESURGES
RESURGING
RESURRECT
RESURRECTED
RESURRECTING
RESURRECTION
RESURRECTIONAL
RESURRECTIONIST
RESURRECTIONS
RESURRECTS
RESURVEY
RESURVEYED
RESURVEYING
RESURVEYS
RESUSCITATE
RESUSCITATED
RESUSCITATES
RESUSCITATING
RESUSCITATION
RESUSCITATIONS
RESUSCITATIVE
RESUSCITATOR
RESUSCITATORS
RESUSPEND
RESUSPENDED
RESUSPENDING
RESUSPENDS
RESUSPENSION
RESUSPENSIONS
RESVERATROL
RESVERATROLS
RESWALLOW
RESWALLOWED
RESWALLOWING
RESWALLOWS
RESYNTHESES
RESYNTHESIS
RESYNTHESIZE
RESYNTHESIZED
RESYNTHESIZES
RESYNTHESIZING
RESYSTEMATIZE
RESYSTEMATIZED
RESYSTEMATIZES
RESYSTEMATIZING
RET
RETABLE
RETABLES
RETABLO
RETABLOS
RETACK
RETACKED
RETACKING
RETACKLE
RETACKLED
RETACKLES
RETACKLING
RETACKS
RETAG
RETAGGED
RETAGGING
RETAGS
RETAIL
RETAILED
RETAILER
RETAILERS
RETAILING
RETAILINGS

RETAILOR
RETAILORED
RETAILORING
RETAILORS
RETAILS
RETAIN
RETAINED
RETAINER
RETAINERS
RETAINING
RETAINS
RETAKE
RETAKEN
RETAKER
RETAKERS
RETAKES
RETAKING
RETALIATE
RETALIATED
RETALIATES
RETALIATING
RETALIATION
RETALIATIONS
RETALIATIVE
RETALIATORY
RETALLIED
RETALLIES
RETALLY
RETALLYING
RETAPE
RETAPED
RETAPES
RETAPING
RETARD
RETARDANT
RETARDANTS
RETARDATE
RETARDATES
RETARDATION
RETARDATIONS
RETARDED
RETARDER
RETARDERS
RETARDING
RETARDS
RETARGET
RETARGETED
RETARGETING
RETARGETS
RETASTE
RETASTED
RETASTES
RETASTING
RETAUGHT
RETAX
RETAXED
RETAXES
RETAXING
RETCH
RETCHED
RETCHES
RETCHING
RETCHINGS
RETE
RETEACH
RETEACHES
RETEACHING
RETEAM
RETEAMED
RETEAMING
RETEAMS
RETEAR
RETEARING
RETEARS
RETELL
RETELLER
RETELLERS
RETELLING
RETELLINGS
RETELLS
RETEM
RETEMPER
RETEMPERED
RETEMPERING
RETEMPERS
RETEMS
RETENE
RETENES
RETENTION
RETENTIONS
RETENTIVE
RETENTIVELY
RETENTIVENESS
RETENTIVENESSES
RETENTIVITIES
RETENTIVITY
RETEST
RETESTED
RETESTIFIED
RETESTIFIES
RETESTIFY
RETESTIFYING
RETESTING
RETESTS
RETEXTURE
RETEXTURED
RETEXTURES
RETEXTURING
RETHEORIZATION
RETHEORIZATIONS
RETHEORIZE
RETHEORIZED
RETHEORIZES
RETHEORIZING
RETHINK
RETHINKER
RETHINKERS
RETHINKING
RETHINKINGS
RETHINKS
RETHOUGHT
RETHREAD
RETHREADED
RETHREADING
RETHREADS
RETIA
RETIAL
RETIARII
RETIARIUS
RETIARY
RETICENCE
RETICENCES
RETICENCIES
RETICENCY
RETICENT
RETICENTLY
RETICLE
RETICLES
RETICULA
RETICULAR
RETICULATE
RETICULATED
RETICULATELY
RETICULATES
RETICULATING
RETICULATION
RETICULATIONS
RETICULE
RETICULES
RETICULOCYTE
RETICULOCYTES
RETICULUM
RETICULUMS
RETIE
RETIED
RETIEING
RETIES
RETIFORM
RETIGHTEN
RETIGHTENED
RETIGHTENING
RETIGHTENS
RETILE
RETILED
RETILES
RETILING
RETIME
RETIMED
RETIMES
RETIMING
RETINA
RETINACULA
RETINACULUM
RETINAE
RETINAL
RETINALS
RETINAS
RETINE
RETINENE
RETINENES
RETINES
RETINITE
RETINITES
RETINITIDES
RETINITIS
RETINITISES
RETINOBLASTOMA
RETINOBLASTOMAS
RETINOID
RETINOIDS
RETINOL
RETINOLS
RETINOPATHIES
RETINOPATHY
RETINOSCOPIES
RETINOSCOPY
RETINOTECTAL
RETINT
RETINTED
RETINTING
RETINTS
RETINUE
RETINUED
RETINUES
RETINULA
RETINULAE
RETINULAR
RETINULAS
RETIRANT
RETIRANTS
RETIRE
RETIRED
RETIREDLY
RETIREDNESS
RETIREDNESSES
RETIREE
RETIREES
RETIREMENT
RETIREMENTS
RETIRER
RETIRERS
RETIRES
RETIRING
RETIRINGLY
RETIRINGNESS
RETIRINGNESSES
RETITLE
RETITLED
RETITLES
RETITLING
RETOLD
RETOOK
RETOOL
RETOOLED
RETOOLING
RETOOLS
RETORE
RETORN
RETORSION
RETORSIONS
RETORT
RETORTED
RETORTER
RETORTERS
RETORTING
RETORTION
RETORTIONS
RETORTS
RETOTAL
RETOTALED
RETOTALING
RETOTALLED
RETOTALLING
RETOTALS
RETOUCH
RETOUCHED
RETOUCHER
RETOUCHERS
RETOUCHES
RETOUCHING
RETOUCHINGS
RETRACE
RETRACED
RETRACER
RETRACERS

RETRACES
RETRACING
RETRACK
RETRACKED
RETRACKING
RETRACKS
RETRACT
RETRACTABLE
RETRACTED
RETRACTILE
RETRACTILITIES
RETRACTILITY
RETRACTING
RETRACTION
RETRACTIONS
RETRACTOR
RETRACTORS
RETRACTS
RETRAIN
RETRAINABLE
RETRAINED
RETRAINEE
RETRAINEES
RETRAINING
RETRAINS
RETRAL
RETRALLY
RETRANSFER
RETRANSFERRED
RETRANSFERRING
RETRANSFERS
RETRANSFORM
RETRANSFORMED
RETRANSFORMING
RETRANSFORMS
RETRANSLATE
RETRANSLATED
RETRANSLATES
RETRANSLATING
RETRANSLATION
RETRANSLATIONS
RETRANSMISSION
RETRANSMISSIONS
RETRANSMIT
RETRANSMITS
RETRANSMITTED
RETRANSMITTING
RETREAD
RETREADED
RETREADING
RETREADS
RETREAT
RETREATANT
RETREATANTS
RETREATED
RETREATER
RETREATERS
RETREATING
RETREATS
RETRENCH
RETRENCHED
RETRENCHES
RETRENCHING
RETRENCHMENT
RETRENCHMENTS
RETRIAL
RETRIALS
RETRIBALIZATION
RETRIBUTION
RETRIBUTIONS
RETRIBUTIVE
RETRIBUTIVELY
RETRIBUTORY
RETRIED
RETRIES
RETRIEVABILITY
RETRIEVABLE
RETRIEVAL
RETRIEVALS
RETRIEVE
RETRIEVED
RETRIEVER
RETRIEVERS
RETRIEVES
RETRIEVING
RETRIM
RETRIMMED
RETRIMMING
RETRIMS
RETRO
RETROACT
RETROACTED
RETROACTING
RETROACTION
RETROACTIONS
RETROACTIVE
RETROACTIVELY
RETROACTIVITIES
RETROACTIVITY
RETROACTS
RETROCEDE
RETROCEDED
RETROCEDES
RETROCEDING
RETROCESSION
RETROCESSIONS
RETROD
RETRODDEN
RETRODICT
RETRODICTED
RETRODICTING
RETRODICTION
RETRODICTIONS
RETRODICTIVE
RETRODICTS
RETROFIRE
RETROFIRED
RETROFIRES
RETROFIRING
RETROFIT
RETROFITS
RETROFITTED
RETROFITTING
RETROFLECTION
RETROFLECTIONS
RETROFLEX
RETROFLEXES
RETROFLEXION
RETROFLEXIONS
RETROGRADATION
RETROGRADATIONS
RETROGRADE
RETROGRADED
RETROGRADELY
RETROGRADES
RETROGRADING
RETROGRESS
RETROGRESSED
RETROGRESSES
RETROGRESSING
RETROGRESSION
RETROGRESSIONS
RETROGRESSIVE
RETROGRESSIVELY
RETRONYM
RETRONYMS
RETROPACK
RETROPACKS
RETROPERITONEAL
RETROREFLECTION
RETROREFLECTIVE
RETROREFLECTOR
RETROREFLECTORS
RETRORSE
RETROS
RETROSPECT
RETROSPECTED
RETROSPECTING
RETROSPECTION
RETROSPECTIONS
RETROSPECTIVE
RETROSPECTIVELY
RETROSPECTIVES
RETROSPECTS
RETROUSSE
RETROVERSION
RETROVERSIONS
RETROVIRAL
RETROVIROLOGIES
RETROVIROLOGIST
RETROVIROLOGY
RETROVIRUS
RETROVIRUSES
RETRY
RETRYING
RETS
RETSINA
RETSINAS
RETTED
RETTING
RETUNE
RETUNED
RETUNES
RETUNING
RETURN
RETURNABLE
RETURNABLES
RETURNED
RETURNEE
RETURNEES
RETURNER
RETURNERS
RETURNING
RETURNS
RETUSE
RETWIST
RETWISTED
RETWISTING
RETWISTS
RETYING
RETYPE
RETYPED
RETYPES
RETYPING
REUNIFICATION
REUNIFICATIONS
REUNIFIED
REUNIFIES
REUNIFY
REUNIFYING
REUNION
REUNIONIST
REUNIONISTIC
REUNIONISTS
REUNIONS
REUNITE
REUNITED
REUNITER
REUNITERS
REUNITES
REUNITING
REUPHOLSTER
REUPHOLSTERED
REUPHOLSTERING
REUPHOLSTERS
REUPTAKE
REUPTAKES
REUSABILITIES
REUSABILITY
REUSABLE
REUSABLES
REUSE
REUSED
REUSES
REUSING
REUTILIZATION
REUTILIZATIONS
REUTILIZE
REUTILIZED
REUTILIZES
REUTILIZING
REUTTER
REUTTERED
REUTTERING
REUTTERS
REV
REVACCINATE
REVACCINATED
REVACCINATES
REVACCINATING
REVACCINATION
REVACCINATIONS
REVALIDATE
REVALIDATED
REVALIDATES
REVALIDATING
REVALIDATION
REVALIDATIONS
REVALORIZATION
REVALORIZATIONS
REVALORIZE
REVALORIZED
REVALORIZES
REVALORIZING
REVALUATE

EVALUATED
EVALUATES
EVALUATING
EVALUATION
EVALUATIONS
EVALUE
EVALUED
EVALUES
EVALUING
VAMP
VAMPED
VAMPER
VAMPERS
VAMPING
VAMPINGS
VAMPS
VANCHE
VANCHES
VANCHISM
VANCHISMS
VANCHIST
VANCHISTS
VARNISH
VARNISHED
VARNISHES
VARNISHING
VEAL
VEALABLE
VEALED
VEALER
VEALERS
VEALING
VEALINGLY
VEALMENT
VEALMENTS
VEALS
VEGETATE
VEGETATED
VEGETATES
VEGETATING
VEGETATION
VEGETATIONS
VEHENT
VEILLE
VEILLES
VEL
VELATION
VELATIONS
VELATOR
VELATORS
VELATORY
VELED
VELER

REVELERS
REVELING
REVELLED
REVELLER
REVELLERS
REVELLING
REVELMENT
REVELMENTS
REVELRIES
REVELROUS
REVELRY
REVELS
REVENANT
REVENANTS
REVENGE
REVENGED
REVENGEFUL
REVENGEFULLY
REVENGEFULNESS
REVENGER
REVENGERS
REVENGES
REVENGING
REVENUAL
REVENUE
REVENUED
REVENUER
REVENUERS
REVENUES
REVERABLE
REVERB
REVERBED
REVERBERANT
REVERBERANTLY
REVERBERATE
REVERBERATED
REVERBERATES
REVERBERATING
REVERBERATION
REVERBERATIONS
REVERBERATIVE
REVERBERATORY
REVERBING
REVERBS
REVERE
REVERED
REVERENCE
REVERENCED
REVERENCER
REVERENCERS
REVERENCES
REVERENCING
REVEREND

REVERENDS
REVERENT
REVERENTIAL
REVERENTIALLY
REVERENTLY
REVERER
REVERERS
REVERES
REVERIE
REVERIES
REVERIFIED
REVERIFIES
REVERIFY
REVERIFYING
REVERING
REVERS
REVERSAL
REVERSALS
REVERSE
REVERSED
REVERSELY
REVERSER
REVERSERS
REVERSES
REVERSIBILITIES
REVERSIBILITY
REVERSIBLE
REVERSIBLES
REVERSIBLY
REVERSING
REVERSION
REVERSIONAL
REVERSIONARY
REVERSIONER
REVERSIONERS
REVERSIONS
REVERSO
REVERSOS
REVERT
REVERTANT
REVERTANTS
REVERTED
REVERTER
REVERTERS
REVERTIBLE
REVERTING
REVERTIVE
REVERTS
REVERY
REVEST
REVESTED
REVESTING
REVESTS

REVET
REVETMENT
REVETMENTS
REVETS
REVETTED
REVETTING
REVIBRATE
REVIBRATED
REVIBRATES
REVIBRATING
REVICTIMIZE
REVICTIMIZED
REVICTIMIZES
REVICTIMIZING
REVICTUAL
REVICTUALED
REVICTUALING
REVICTUALLED
REVICTUALLING
REVICTUALS
REVIEW
REVIEWABLE
REVIEWAL
REVIEWALS
REVIEWED
REVIEWER
REVIEWERS
REVIEWING
REVIEWS
REVILE
REVILED
REVILEMENT
REVILEMENTS
REVILER
REVILERS
REVILES
REVILING
REVILINGS
REVIOLATE
REVIOLATED
REVIOLATES
REVIOLATING
REVISABLE
REVISAL
REVISALS
REVISE
REVISED
REVISER
REVISERS
REVISES
REVISING
REVISION
REVISIONARY

REVISIONISM
REVISIONISMS
REVISIONIST
REVISIONISTS
REVISIONS
REVISIT
REVISITED
REVISITING
REVISITS
REVISOR
REVISORS
REVISORY
REVISUALIZATION
REVITALISATION
REVITALISATIONS
REVITALISE
REVITALISED
REVITALISES
REVITALISING
REVITALIZATION
REVITALIZATIONS
REVITALIZE
REVITALIZED
REVITALIZES
REVITALIZING
REVIVABLE
REVIVAL
REVIVALISM
REVIVALISMS
REVIVALIST
REVIVALISTIC
REVIVALISTS
REVIVALS
REVIVE
REVIVED
REVIVER
REVIVERS
REVIVES
REVIVIFICATION
REVIVIFICATIONS
REVIVIFIED
REVIVIFIES
REVIVIFY
REVIVIFYING
REVIVING
REVIVISCENCE
REVIVISCENCES
REVIVISCENT
REVOCABLE
REVOCABLY
REVOCATION
REVOCATIONS
REVOICE

REVOICED
REVOICES
REVOICING
REVOKABLE
REVOKE
REVOKED
REVOKER
REVOKERS
REVOKES
REVOKING
REVOLT
REVOLTED
REVOLTER
REVOLTERS
REVOLTING
REVOLTINGLY
REVOLTS
REVOLUTE
REVOLUTION
REVOLUTIONARIES
REVOLUTIONARILY
REVOLUTIONARY
REVOLUTIONISE
REVOLUTIONISED
REVOLUTIONISES
REVOLUTIONISING
REVOLUTIONIST
REVOLUTIONISTS
REVOLUTIONIZE
REVOLUTIONIZED
REVOLUTIONIZER
REVOLUTIONIZERS
REVOLUTIONIZES
REVOLUTIONIZING
REVOLUTIONS
REVOLVABLE
REVOLVE
REVOLVED
REVOLVER
REVOLVERS
REVOLVES
REVOLVING
REVOTE
REVOTED
REVOTES
REVOTING
REVS
REVUE
REVUES
REVUIST
REVUISTS
REVULSED
REVULSION
REVULSIONS
REVULSIVE
REVVED
REVVING
REWAKE
REWAKED
REWAKEN
REWAKENED
REWAKENING
REWAKENS
REWAKES
REWAKING
REWAN
REWARD
REWARDABLE
REWARDED
REWARDER
REWARDERS
REWARDING
REWARDINGLY
REWARDS
REWARM
REWARMED
REWARMING
REWARMS
REWASH
REWASHED
REWASHES
REWASHING
REWAX
REWAXED
REWAXES
REWAXING
REWEAR
REWEARING
REWEARS
REWEAVE
REWEAVED
REWEAVES
REWEAVING
REWED
REWEDDED
REWEDDING
REWEDS
REWEIGH
REWEIGHED
REWEIGHING
REWEIGHS
REWELD
REWELDED
REWELDING
REWELDS
REWET
REWETS
REWETTED
REWETTING
REWIDEN
REWIDENED
REWIDENING
REWIDENS
REWIN
REWIND
REWINDED
REWINDER
REWINDERS
REWINDING
REWINDS
REWINNING
REWINS
REWIRE
REWIRED
REWIRES
REWIRING
REWOKE
REWOKEN
REWON
REWORD
REWORDED
REWORDING
REWORDS
REWORE
REWORK
REWORKED
REWORKING
REWORKS
REWORN
REWOUND
REWOVE
REWOVEN
REWRAP
REWRAPPED
REWRAPPING
REWRAPS
REWRAPT
REWRITE
REWRITER
REWRITERS
REWRITES
REWRITING
REWRITTEN
REWROTE
REWROUGHT
REX
REXES
REXINE
REXINES
REYNARD
REYNARDS
REZ
REZERO
REZEROED
REZEROES
REZEROING
REZEROS
REZES
REZONE
REZONED
REZONES
REZONING
REZZES
RHABDOCOELE
RHABDOCOELES
RHABDOM
RHABDOMAL
RHABDOMANCER
RHABDOMANCERS
RHABDOMANCIES
RHABDOMANCY
RHABDOME
RHABDOMERE
RHABDOMERES
RHABDOMES
RHABDOMS
RHABDOMYOLYSES
RHABDOMYOLYSIS
RHABDOVIRUS
RHABDOVIRUSES
RHACHIDES
RHACHIS
RHACHISES
RHADAMANTHINE
RHAMNOSE
RHAMNOSES
RHAMNUS
RHAMNUSES
RHAPHAE
RHAPHE
RHAPHES
RHAPSODE
RHAPSODES
RHAPSODIC
RHAPSODICAL
RHAPSODICALLY
RHAPSODIES
RHAPSODISE
RHAPSODISED
RHAPSODISES
RHAPSODISING
RHAPSODIST
RHAPSODISTS
RHAPSODIZE
RHAPSODIZED
RHAPSODIZES
RHAPSODIZING
RHAPSODY
RHATANIES
RHATANY
RHEA
RHEAS
RHEBOK
RHEBOKS
RHEMATIC
RHEME
RHEMES
RHENIUM
RHENIUMS
RHEOBASE
RHEOBASES
RHEOBASIC
RHEOLOGIC
RHEOLOGICAL
RHEOLOGICALLY
RHEOLOGIES
RHEOLOGIST
RHEOLOGISTS
RHEOLOGY
RHEOMETER
RHEOMETERS
RHEOPHIL
RHEOPHILE
RHEOPHILES
RHEOSTAT
RHEOSTATIC
RHEOSTATS
RHEOTAXES
RHEOTAXIS
RHESUS
RHESUSES
RHETOR
RHETORIC
RHETORICAL
RHETORICALLY
RHETORICIAN
RHETORICIANS
RHETORICS
RHETORS
RHEUM
RHEUMATIC
RHEUMATICALLY
RHEUMATICS
RHEUMATISM
RHEUMATISMS

EUMATIZ
EUMATIZES
EUMATOID
EUMATOLOGIC
EUMATOLOGICAL
EUMATOLOGIES
EUMATOLOGIST
EUMATOLOGISTS
EUMATOLOGY
EUMIC
EUMIER
EUMIEST
EUMS
EUMY
IGOLENE
IGOLENES
INAL
INENCEPHALA
INENCEPHALIC
NENCEPHALON
INESTONE
NESTONED
NESTONES
INITIDES
NITIS
NITISES
NO
NOCERI
NOCEROS
NOCEROSES
NOLOGIES
NOLOGY
NOPLASTIES
NOPLASTY
NOS
NOSCOPIES
NOSCOPY
NOVIRUS
NOVIRUSES
ZOBIA
ZOBIAL
ZOBIUM
ZOCTONIA
ZOCTONIAS
ZOID
ZOIDAL
ZOIDS
ZOMA
ZOMATA
ZOMATOUS
ZOME
ZOMES
ZOMIC

RHIZOPI
RHIZOPLANE
RHIZOPLANES
RHIZOPOD
RHIZOPODS
RHIZOPUS
RHIZOPUSES
RHIZOSPHERE
RHIZOSPHERES
RHIZOTOMIES
RHIZOTOMY
RHO
RHODAMIN
RHODAMINE
RHODAMINES
RHODAMINS
RHODIC
RHODIUM
RHODIUMS
RHODOCHROSITE
RHODOCHROSITES
RHODODENDRON
RHODODENDRONS
RHODOLITE
RHODOLITES
RHODOMONTADE
RHODOMONTADES
RHODONITE
RHODONITES
RHODOPSIN
RHODOPSINS
RHODORA
RHODORAS
RHOMB
RHOMBENCEPHALA
RHOMBENCEPHALON
RHOMBI
RHOMBIC
RHOMBICAL
RHOMBOHEDRA
RHOMBOHEDRAL
RHOMBOHEDRON
RHOMBOHEDRONS
RHOMBOID
RHOMBOIDAL
RHOMBOIDEI
RHOMBOIDEUS
RHOMBOIDS
RHOMBS
RHOMBUS
RHOMBUSES
RHONCHAL
RHONCHI

RHONCHIAL
RHONCHUS
RHOS
RHOTACISM
RHOTACISMS
RHOTIC
RHUBARB
RHUBARBS
RHUMB
RHUMBA
RHUMBAED
RHUMBAING
RHUMBAS
RHUMBS
RHUS
RHUSES
RHYME
RHYMED
RHYMELESS
RHYMER
RHYMERS
RHYMES
RHYMESTER
RHYMESTERS
RHYMING
RHYOLITE
RHYOLITES
RHYOLITIC
RHYTA
RHYTHM
RHYTHMIC
RHYTHMICAL
RHYTHMICALLY
RHYTHMICITIES
RHYTHMICITY
RHYTHMICS
RHYTHMIST
RHYTHMISTS
RHYTHMIZATION
RHYTHMIZATIONS
RHYTHMIZE
RHYTHMIZED
RHYTHMIZES
RHYTHMIZING
RHYTHMS
RHYTIDOME
RHYTIDOMES
RHYTON
RHYTONS
RIA
RIAL
RIALS
RIALTO

RIALTOS
RIANT
RIANTLY
RIAS
RIATA
RIATAS
RIB
RIBALD
RIBALDER
RIBALDEST
RIBALDLY
RIBALDRIES
RIBALDRY
RIBALDS
RIBAND
RIBANDS
RIBAVIRIN
RIBAVIRINS
RIBBAND
RIBBANDS
RIBBED
RIBBER
RIBBERS
RIBBIE
RIBBIER
RIBBIES
RIBBIEST
RIBBING
RIBBINGS
RIBBIT
RIBBITS
RIBBON
RIBBONED
RIBBONFISH
RIBBONFISHES
RIBBONING
RIBBONLIKE
RIBBONS
RIBBONY
RIBBY
RIBES
RIBEYE
RIBEYES
RIBGRASS
RIBGRASSES
RIBIER
RIBIERS
RIBLESS
RIBLET
RIBLETS
RIBLIKE
RIBOFLAVIN
RIBOFLAVINS

RIBONUCLEASE
RIBONUCLEASES
RIBONUCLEOSIDE
RIBONUCLEOSIDES
RIBONUCLEOTIDE
RIBONUCLEOTIDES
RIBOSE
RIBOSES
RIBOSOMAL
RIBOSOME
RIBOSOMES
RIBOZYMAL
RIBOZYME
RIBOZYMES
RIBS
RIBULOSE
RIBULOSES
RIBWORT
RIBWORTS
RICE
RICEBIRD
RICEBIRDS
RICED
RICER
RICERCAR
RICERCARE
RICERCARI
RICERCARS
RICERS
RICES
RICH
RICHEN
RICHENED
RICHENING
RICHENS
RICHER
RICHES
RICHEST
RICHLY
RICHNESS
RICHNESSES
RICHWEED
RICHWEEDS
RICIN
RICING
RICINS
RICINUS
RICINUSES
RICK
RICKED
RICKETIER
RICKETIEST
RICKETS

RICKETTSIA
RICKETTSIAE
RICKETTSIAL
RICKETTSIAS
RICKETY
RICKEY
RICKEYS
RICKING
RICKRACK
RICKRACKS
RICKS
RICKSHA
RICKSHAS
RICKSHAW
RICKSHAWS
RICOCHET
RICOCHETED
RICOCHETING
RICOCHETS
RICOCHETTED
RICOCHETTING
RICOTTA
RICOTTAS
RICRAC
RICRACS
RICTAL
RICTUS
RICTUSES
RID
RIDABLE
RIDDANCE
RIDDANCES
RIDDED
RIDDEN
RIDDER
RIDDERS
RIDDING
RIDDLE
RIDDLED
RIDDLER
RIDDLERS
RIDDLES
RIDDLING
RIDE
RIDEABLE
RIDENT
RIDER
RIDERLESS
RIDERS
RIDERSHIP
RIDERSHIPS
RIDES
RIDGE
RIDGEBACK
RIDGEBACKS
RIDGED
RIDGEL
RIDGELINE
RIDGELINES
RIDGELING
RIDGELINGS
RIDGELS
RIDGEPOLE
RIDGEPOLES
RIDGES
RIDGETOP
RIDGETOPS
RIDGEWAY
RIDGEWAYS
RIDGIER
RIDGIEST
RIDGIL
RIDGILS
RIDGING
RIDGLING
RIDGLINGS
RIDGY
RIDICULE
RIDICULED
RIDICULER
RIDICULERS
RIDICULES
RIDICULING
RIDICULOUS
RIDICULOUSLY
RIDICULOUSNESS
RIDING
RIDINGS
RIDLEY
RIDLEYS
RIDOTTO
RIDOTTOS
RIDS
RIEL
RIELS
RIESLING
RIESLINGS
RIEVER
RIEVERS
RIF
RIFAMPICIN
RIFAMPICINS
RIFAMPIN
RIFAMPINS
RIFAMYCIN
RIFAMYCINS
RIFE
RIFELY
RIFENESS
RIFENESSES
RIFER
RIFEST
RIFF
RIFFAGE
RIFFAGES
RIFFED
RIFFING
RIFFLE
RIFFLED
RIFFLER
RIFFLERS
RIFFLES
RIFFLING
RIFFRAFF
RIFFRAFFS
RIFFS
RIFLE
RIFLEBIRD
RIFLEBIRDS
RIFLED
RIFLEMAN
RIFLEMEN
RIFLER
RIFLERIES
RIFLERS
RIFLERY
RIFLES
RIFLING
RIFLINGS
RIFLIP
RIFLIPS
RIFS
RIFT
RIFTED
RIFTING
RIFTLESS
RIFTS
RIG
RIGADOON
RIGADOONS
RIGAMAROLE
RIGAMAROLES
RIGATONI
RIGATONIS
RIGAUDON
RIGAUDONS
RIGGED
RIGGER
RIGGERS
RIGGING
RIGGINGS
RIGHT
RIGHTED
RIGHTEOUS
RIGHTEOUSLY
RIGHTEOUSNESS
RIGHTEOUSNESSES
RIGHTER
RIGHTERS
RIGHTEST
RIGHTFUL
RIGHTFULLY
RIGHTFULNESS
RIGHTFULNESSES
RIGHTIER
RIGHTIES
RIGHTIEST
RIGHTING
RIGHTISH
RIGHTISM
RIGHTISMS
RIGHTIST
RIGHTISTS
RIGHTLY
RIGHTMOST
RIGHTNESS
RIGHTNESSES
RIGHTO
RIGHTS
RIGHTSIZE
RIGHTSIZED
RIGHTSIZES
RIGHTSIZING
RIGHTWARD
RIGHTWARDS
RIGHTY
RIGID
RIGIDER
RIGIDEST
RIGIDIFICATION
RIGIDIFICATIONS
RIGIDIFIED
RIGIDIFIES
RIGIDIFY
RIGIDIFYING
RIGIDITIES
RIGIDITY
RIGIDLY
RIGIDNESS
RIGIDNESSES
RIGMAROLE
RIGMAROLES
RIGOR
RIGORISM
RIGORISMS
RIGORIST
RIGORISTIC
RIGORISTS
RIGOROUS
RIGOROUSLY
RIGOROUSNESS
RIGOROUSNESSES
RIGORS
RIGOUR
RIGOURS
RIGS
RIJSTAFEL
RIJSTAFELS
RIJSTTAFEL
RIJSTTAFELS
RIKISHA
RIKISHAS
RIKISHI
RIKSHAW
RIKSHAWS
RILE
RILED
RILES
RILEY
RILIEVI
RILIEVO
RILING
RILL
RILLE
RILLED
RILLES
RILLET
RILLETS
RILLETTES
RILLING
RILLS
RIM
RIME
RIMED
RIMER
RIMERS
RIMES
RIMESTER
RIMESTERS
RIMFIRE
RIMFIRES
RIMIER
RIMIEST
RIMINESS
RIMINESSES

MING
MLAND
MLANDS
MLESS
MMED
MMER
MMERS
MMING
MOSE
MOSELY
MOSITIES
MOSITY
MOUS
MPLE
MPLED
MPLES
MPLING
MROCK
MROCKS
MS
MSHOT
MSHOTS
Y
I
D
DED
DERPEST
DERPESTS
DING
DLESS
DS
DY
G
GBARK
GBARKED
GBARKING
GBARKS
GBOLT
GBOLTS
GBONE
GBONES
GDOVE
GDOVES
GED
GENT
GER
GERS
GETTE
GETTES
GGIT
GGITS
GHALS
GHALSES

RINGING
RINGINGLY
RINGLEADER
RINGLEADERS
RINGLESS
RINGLET
RINGLETED
RINGLETS
RINGLETY
RINGLIKE
RINGMASTER
RINGMASTERS
RINGNECK
RINGNECKS
RINGS
RINGSIDE
RINGSIDES
RINGSTER
RINGSTERS
RINGSTRAKED
RINGTAIL
RINGTAILS
RINGTAW
RINGTAWS
RINGTONE
RINGTONES
RINGTOSS
RINGTOSSES
RINGWORK
RINGWORKS
RINGWORM
RINGWORMS
RINK
RINKHALS
RINKHALSES
RINKS
RINKSIDE
RINKSIDES
RINNING
RINS
RINSABLE
RINSE
RINSED
RINSER
RINSERS
RINSES
RINSIBLE
RINSING
RINSINGS
RIOJA
RIOJAS
RIOT
RIOTED

RIOTER
RIOTERS
RIOTING
RIOTINGS
RIOTOUS
RIOTOUSLY
RIOTOUSNESS
RIOTOUSNESSES
RIOTS
RIP
RIPARIAN
RIPCORD
RIPCORDS
RIPE
RIPED
RIPELY
RIPEN
RIPENED
RIPENER
RIPENERS
RIPENESS
RIPENESSES
RIPENING
RIPENS
RIPER
RIPES
RIPEST
RIPIENI
RIPIENO
RIPIENOS
RIPING
RIPOFF
RIPOFFS
RIPOST
RIPOSTE
RIPOSTED
RIPOSTES
RIPOSTING
RIPOSTS
RIPPABLE
RIPPED
RIPPER
RIPPERS
RIPPING
RIPPINGLY
RIPPLE
RIPPLED
RIPPLER
RIPPLERS
RIPPLES
RIPPLET
RIPPLETS
RIPPLIER

RIPPLIEST
RIPPLING
RIPPLY
RIPRAP
RIPRAPPED
RIPRAPPING
RIPRAPS
RIPS
RIPSAW
RIPSAWED
RIPSAWING
RIPSAWN
RIPSAWS
RIPSNORTER
RIPSNORTERS
RIPSNORTING
RIPSTOP
RIPSTOPS
RIPTIDE
RIPTIDES
RISE
RISEN
RISER
RISERS
RISES
RISHI
RISHIS
RISIBILITIES
RISIBILITY
RISIBLE
RISIBLES
RISIBLY
RISING
RISINGS
RISK
RISKED
RISKER
RISKERS
RISKIER
RISKIEST
RISKILY
RISKINESS
RISKINESSES
RISKING
RISKLESS
RISKS
RISKY
RISORGIMENTO
RISORGIMENTOS
RISOTTO
RISOTTOS
RISPERIDONE
RISPERIDONES

RISQUE
RISSOLE
RISSOLES
RISTRA
RISTRAS
RISUS
RISUSES
RITARD
RITARDANDO
RITARDANDOS
RITARDS
RITE
RITES
RITONAVIR
RITONAVIRS
RITORNELLI
RITORNELLO
RITORNELLOS
RITTER
RITTERS
RITUAL
RITUALISM
RITUALISMS
RITUALIST
RITUALISTIC
RITUALISTICALLY
RITUALISTS
RITUALIZATION
RITUALIZATIONS
RITUALIZE
RITUALIZED
RITUALIZES
RITUALIZING
RITUALLY
RITUALS
RITZ
RITZES
RITZIER
RITZIEST
RITZILY
RITZINESS
RITZINESSES
RITZY
RIVAGE
RIVAGES
RIVAL
RIVALED
RIVALING
RIVALLED
RIVALLING
RIVALRIES
RIVALROUS
RIVALRY

RIVALS
RIVE
RIVED
RIVEN
RIVER
RIVERBANK
RIVERBANKS
RIVERBED
RIVERBEDS
RIVERBOAT
RIVERBOATS
RIVERFRONT
RIVERFRONTS
RIVERHEAD
RIVERHEADS
RIVERINE
RIVERLESS
RIVERLIKE
RIVERMAN
RIVERMEN
RIVERS
RIVERSIDE
RIVERSIDES
RIVERWARD
RIVERWARDS
RIVERWEED
RIVERWEEDS
RIVES
RIVET
RIVETED
RIVETER
RIVETERS
RIVETING
RIVETINGLY
RIVETS
RIVETTED
RIVETTING
RIVIERA
RIVIERAS
RIVIERE
RIVIERES
RIVING
RIVULET
RIVULETS
RIVULOSE
RIVULUS
RIVULUSES
RIYAL
RIYALS
ROACH
ROACHED
ROACHES
ROACHING
ROAD
ROADABILITIES
ROADABILITY
ROADBED
ROADBEDS
ROADBLOCK
ROADBLOCKED
ROADBLOCKING
ROADBLOCKS
ROADEO
ROADEOS
ROADHOLDING
ROADHOLDINGS
ROADHOUSE
ROADHOUSES
ROADIE
ROADIES
ROADKILL
ROADKILLS
ROADLESS
ROADRUNNER
ROADRUNNERS
ROADS
ROADSHOW
ROADSHOWS
ROADSIDE
ROADSIDES
ROADSTEAD
ROADSTEADS
ROADSTER
ROADSTERS
ROADWAY
ROADWAYS
ROADWORK
ROADWORKS
ROADWORTHINESS
ROADWORTHY
ROAM
ROAMED
ROAMER
ROAMERS
ROAMING
ROAMINGS
ROAMS
ROAN
ROANS
ROAR
ROARED
ROARER
ROARERS
ROARING
ROARINGLY
ROARINGS
ROARS
ROAST
ROASTED
ROASTER
ROASTERS
ROASTING
ROASTINGS
ROASTS
ROB
ROBALO
ROBALOS
ROBAND
ROBANDS
ROBATA
ROBATAS
ROBBED
ROBBER
ROBBERIES
ROBBERS
ROBBERY
ROBBIN
ROBBING
ROBBINS
ROBE
ROBED
ROBES
ROBIN
ROBING
ROBINIA
ROBINIAS
ROBINS
ROBLE
ROBLES
ROBOCALL
ROBOCALLS
ROBORANT
ROBORANTS
ROBOT
ROBOTIC
ROBOTICALLY
ROBOTICIST
ROBOTICISTS
ROBOTICS
ROBOTISE
ROBOTISED
ROBOTISES
ROBOTISING
ROBOTISM
ROBOTISMS
ROBOTIZATION
ROBOTIZATIONS
ROBOTIZE
ROBOTIZED
ROBOTIZES
ROBOTIZING
ROBOTRIES
ROBOTRY
ROBOTS
ROBS
ROBUST
ROBUSTA
ROBUSTAS
ROBUSTER
ROBUSTEST
ROBUSTIOUS
ROBUSTIOUSLY
ROBUSTIOUSNESS
ROBUSTLY
ROBUSTNESS
ROBUSTNESSES
ROC
ROCAILLE
ROCAILLES
ROCAMBOLE
ROCAMBOLES
ROCHET
ROCHETS
ROCK
ROCKABIES
ROCKABILLIES
ROCKABILLY
ROCKABLE
ROCKABY
ROCKABYE
ROCKABYES
ROCKAWAY
ROCKAWAYS
ROCKBOUND
ROCKED
ROCKER
ROCKERIES
ROCKERS
ROCKERY
ROCKET
ROCKETED
ROCKETEER
ROCKETEERS
ROCKETER
ROCKETERS
ROCKETING
ROCKETRIES
ROCKETRY
ROCKETS
ROCKFALL
ROCKFALLS
ROCKFISH
ROCKFISHES
ROCKHOPPER
ROCKHOPPERS
ROCKHOUND
ROCKHOUNDING
ROCKHOUNDINGS
ROCKHOUNDS
ROCKIER
ROCKIEST
ROCKILY
ROCKINESS
ROCKINESSES
ROCKING
ROCKINGLY
ROCKLESS
ROCKLIKE
ROCKLING
ROCKLINGS
ROCKOON
ROCKOONS
ROCKROSE
ROCKROSES
ROCKS
ROCKSHAFT
ROCKSHAFTS
ROCKSLIDE
ROCKSLIDES
ROCKWEED
ROCKWEEDS
ROCKWOOL
ROCKWOOLS
ROCKWORK
ROCKWORKS
ROCKY
ROCOCO
ROCOCOS
ROCS
ROD
RODDED
RODDING
RODE
RODENT
RODENTICIDE
RODENTICIDES
RODENTS
RODEO
RODEOED
RODEOING
RODEOS
RODES
RODLESS
RODLIKE
RODMAN

ODMEN
ODNEY
ODNEYS
ODOMONTADE
ODOMONTADES
ODS
ODSMAN
ODSMEN
OE
OEBUCK
OEBUCKS
OENTGEN
OENTGENIUM
OENTGENIUMS
OENTGENOGRAM
OENTGENOGRAMS
OENTGENOGRAPHY
OENTGENOLOGIC
OENTGENOLOGIES
OENTGENOLOGIST
OENTGENOLOGY
OENTGENS
ES
GATION
GATIONS
GATORY
GER
GERED
GERING
GERS
GUE
GUED
GUEING
GUERIES
GUERY
GUES
GUING
GUISH
GUISHLY
GUISHNESS
GUISHNESSES
IL
LED
LIER
LIEST
LING
LS
LY
STER
STERED
STERER
STERERS
STERING
ROISTEROUS
ROISTEROUSLY
ROISTERS
ROLAMITE
ROLAMITES
ROLE
ROLES
ROLF
ROLFED
ROLFER
ROLFERS
ROLFING
ROLFS
ROLL
ROLLABLE
ROLLAWAY
ROLLAWAYS
ROLLBACK
ROLLBACKS
ROLLED
ROLLER
ROLLERS
ROLLICK
ROLLICKED
ROLLICKING
ROLLICKINGS
ROLLICKS
ROLLICKY
ROLLIE
ROLLIES
ROLLING
ROLLINGS
ROLLMOP
ROLLMOPS
ROLLOUT
ROLLOUTS
ROLLOVER
ROLLOVERS
ROLLS
ROLLTOP
ROLLUP
ROLLUPS
ROLLWAY
ROLLWAYS
ROM
ROMAINE
ROMAINES
ROMAJI
ROMAJIS
ROMAN
ROMANCE
ROMANCED
ROMANCER
ROMANCERS
ROMANCES
ROMANCING
ROMANISE
ROMANISED
ROMANISES
ROMANISING
ROMANIZATION
ROMANIZATIONS
ROMANIZE
ROMANIZED
ROMANIZES
ROMANIZING
ROMANO
ROMANOS
ROMANS
ROMANTIC
ROMANTICALLY
ROMANTICISE
ROMANTICISED
ROMANTICISES
ROMANTICISING
ROMANTICISM
ROMANTICISMS
ROMANTICIST
ROMANTICISTS
ROMANTICIZATION
ROMANTICIZE
ROMANTICIZED
ROMANTICIZES
ROMANTICIZING
ROMANTICS
ROMAUNT
ROMAUNTS
ROMELDALE
ROMELDALES
ROMEO
ROMEOS
ROMP
ROMPED
ROMPER
ROMPERS
ROMPING
ROMPINGLY
ROMPISH
ROMPS
ROMS
RONDE
RONDEAU
RONDEAUX
RONDEL
RONDELET
RONDELETS
RONDELLE
RONDELLES
RONDELS
RONDES
RONDO
RONDOS
RONDURE
RONDURES
RONIN
RONINS
RONION
RONIONS
RONNEL
RONNELS
RONTGEN
RONTGENS
RONYON
RONYONS
ROO
ROOD
ROODS
ROOF
ROOFED
ROOFER
ROOFERS
ROOFIE
ROOFIES
ROOFING
ROOFINGS
ROOFLESS
ROOFLIKE
ROOFLINE
ROOFLINES
ROOFS
ROOFTOP
ROOFTOPS
ROOFTREE
ROOFTREES
ROOIBOS
ROOIBOSES
ROOK
ROOKED
ROOKERIES
ROOKERY
ROOKIE
ROOKIER
ROOKIES
ROOKIEST
ROOKING
ROOKS
ROOKY
ROOM
ROOMED
ROOMER
ROOMERS
ROOMETTE
ROOMETTES
ROOMFUL
ROOMFULS
ROOMIE
ROOMIER
ROOMIES
ROOMIEST
ROOMILY
ROOMINESS
ROOMINESSES
ROOMING
ROOMMATE
ROOMMATES
ROOMS
ROOMSFUL
ROOMY
ROORBACH
ROORBACHS
ROORBACK
ROORBACKS
ROOS
ROOSE
ROOSED
ROOSER
ROOSERS
ROOSES
ROOSING
ROOST
ROOSTED
ROOSTER
ROOSTERS
ROOSTING
ROOSTS
ROOT
ROOTAGE
ROOTAGES
ROOTBALL
ROOTBALLS
ROOTCAP
ROOTCAPS
ROOTED
ROOTEDNESS
ROOTEDNESSES
ROOTER
ROOTERS
ROOTHOLD
ROOTHOLDS
ROOTIER
ROOTIEST
ROOTINESS

ROOTINESSES
ROOTING
ROOTLE
ROOTLED
ROOTLES
ROOTLESS
ROOTLESSNESS
ROOTLESSNESSES
ROOTLET
ROOTLETS
ROOTLIKE
ROOTLING
ROOTS
ROOTSIER
ROOTSIEST
ROOTSTALK
ROOTSTALKS
ROOTSTOCK
ROOTSTOCKS
ROOTSY
ROOTWORM
ROOTWORMS
ROOTY
ROPABLE
ROPE
ROPED
ROPEDANCER
ROPEDANCERS
ROPEDANCING
ROPEDANCINGS
ROPELIKE
ROPER
ROPERIES
ROPERS
ROPERY
ROPES
ROPEWALK
ROPEWALKER
ROPEWALKERS
ROPEWALKING
ROPEWALKINGS
ROPEWALKS
ROPEWAY
ROPEWAYS
ROPEY
ROPIER
ROPIEST
ROPILY
ROPINESS
ROPINESSES
ROPING
ROPINGS
ROPY
ROQUE
ROQUELAURE
ROQUELAURES
ROQUES
ROQUET
ROQUETED
ROQUETING
ROQUETS
ROQUETTE
ROQUETTES
RORQUAL
RORQUALS
ROSACE
ROSACEA
ROSACEAS
ROSACEOUS
ROSACES
ROSANILIN
ROSANILINS
ROSARIA
ROSARIAN
ROSARIANS
ROSARIES
ROSARIUM
ROSARIUMS
ROSARY
ROSCOE
ROSCOES
ROSE
ROSEATE
ROSEATELY
ROSEBAY
ROSEBAYS
ROSEBOWL
ROSEBOWLS
ROSEBUD
ROSEBUDS
ROSEBUSH
ROSEBUSHES
ROSED
ROSEFISH
ROSEFISHES
ROSEHIP
ROSEHIPS
ROSELIKE
ROSELLA
ROSELLAS
ROSELLE
ROSELLES
ROSEMALING
ROSEMALINGS
ROSEMARIES
ROSEMARY
ROSEOLA
ROSEOLAR
ROSEOLAS
ROSERIES
ROSEROOT
ROSEROOTS
ROSERY
ROSES
ROSESLUG
ROSESLUGS
ROSET
ROSETS
ROSETTE
ROSETTED
ROSETTES
ROSEWATER
ROSEWOOD
ROSEWOODS
ROSHI
ROSHIS
ROSIER
ROSIEST
ROSILY
ROSIN
ROSINED
ROSINESS
ROSINESSES
ROSING
ROSINIER
ROSINIEST
ROSINING
ROSINOL
ROSINOLS
ROSINOUS
ROSINS
ROSINWEED
ROSINWEEDS
ROSINY
ROSOLIO
ROSOLIOS
ROSTELLA
ROSTELLAR
ROSTELLUM
ROSTELLUMS
ROSTER
ROSTERED
ROSTERING
ROSTERS
ROSTI
ROSTIS
ROSTRA
ROSTRAL
ROSTRALLY
ROSTRATE
ROSTRUM
ROSTRUMS
ROSULATE
ROSY
ROT
ROTA
ROTAMETER
ROTAMETERS
ROTARIES
ROTARY
ROTAS
ROTATABLE
ROTATE
ROTATED
ROTATES
ROTATING
ROTATION
ROTATIONAL
ROTATIONS
ROTATIVE
ROTATIVELY
ROTATOR
ROTATORES
ROTATORS
ROTATORY
ROTAVIRUS
ROTAVIRUSES
ROTCH
ROTCHE
ROTCHES
ROTE
ROTENONE
ROTENONES
ROTES
ROTGUT
ROTGUTS
ROTI
ROTIFER
ROTIFERAL
ROTIFERAN
ROTIFERANS
ROTIFERS
ROTIFORM
ROTINI
ROTINIS
ROTIS
ROTISSERIE
ROTISSERIES
ROTL
ROTLS
ROTO
ROTOGRAVURE
ROTOGRAVURES
ROTOR
ROTORCRAFT
ROTORCRAFTS
ROTORS
ROTOS
ROTOTILL
ROTOTILLED
ROTOTILLER
ROTOTILLERS
ROTOTILLING
ROTOTILLS
ROTS
ROTTE
ROTTED
ROTTEN
ROTTENER
ROTTENEST
ROTTENLY
ROTTENNESS
ROTTENNESSES
ROTTENSTONE
ROTTENSTONES
ROTTER
ROTTERS
ROTTES
ROTTING
ROTTWEILER
ROTTWEILERS
ROTUND
ROTUNDA
ROTUNDAS
ROTUNDER
ROTUNDEST
ROTUNDITIES
ROTUNDITY
ROTUNDLY
ROTUNDNESS
ROTUNDNESSES
ROTURIER
ROTURIERS
ROUBLE
ROUBLES
ROUCHE
ROUCHES
ROUE
ROUEN
ROUENS
ROUES
ROUGE
ROUGED
ROUGES
ROUGH

OUGHAGE
OUGHAGES
OUGHBACK
OUGHBACKS
OUGHCAST
OUGHCASTING
OUGHCASTS
OUGHDRIED
OUGHDRIES
OUGHDRY
OUGHDRYING
OUGHED
OUGHEN
OUGHENED
OUGHENING
OUGHENS
OUGHER
OUGHERS
OUGHEST
OUGHHEW
OUGHHEWED
OUGHHEWING
OUGHHEWN
OUGHHEWS
OUGHHOUSE
OUGHHOUSED
OUGHHOUSES
OUGHHOUSING
OUGHIES
OUGHING
OUGHINGS
OUGHISH
OUGHLEG
OUGHLEGS
OUGHLY
OUGHNECK
OUGHNECKED
OUGHNECKING
OUGHNECKS
OUGHNESS
OUGHNESSES
OUGHOUT
OUGHOUTS
UGHRIDER
UGHRIDERS
UGHS
UGHSHOD
UGHY
UGING
UILLE
UILLES
ULADE
ULADES
ROULEAU
ROULEAUS
ROULEAUX
ROULETTE
ROULETTED
ROULETTES
ROULETTING
ROUND
ROUNDABOUT
ROUNDABOUTNESS
ROUNDABOUTS
ROUNDBALL
ROUNDBALLS
ROUNDED
ROUNDEDNESS
ROUNDEDNESSES
ROUNDEL
ROUNDELAY
ROUNDELAYS
ROUNDELS
ROUNDER
ROUNDERS
ROUNDEST
ROUNDHEADED
ROUNDHEADEDNESS
ROUNDHEEL
ROUNDHEELS
ROUNDHOUSE
ROUNDHOUSES
ROUNDING
ROUNDISH
ROUNDLET
ROUNDLETS
ROUNDLY
ROUNDNESS
ROUNDNESSES
ROUNDS
ROUNDSMAN
ROUNDSMEN
ROUNDTABLE
ROUNDTABLES
ROUNDTRIP
ROUNDTRIPS
ROUNDUP
ROUNDUPS
ROUNDWOOD
ROUNDWOODS
ROUNDWORM
ROUNDWORMS
ROUP
ROUPED
ROUPET
ROUPIER
ROUPIEST
ROUPILY
ROUPING
ROUPS
ROUPY
ROUSABLE
ROUSE
ROUSEABOUT
ROUSEABOUTS
ROUSED
ROUSEMENT
ROUSEMENTS
ROUSER
ROUSERS
ROUSES
ROUSING
ROUSINGLY
ROUSSEAU
ROUSSEAUS
ROUST
ROUSTABOUT
ROUSTABOUTS
ROUSTED
ROUSTER
ROUSTERS
ROUSTING
ROUSTS
ROUT
ROUTE
ROUTED
ROUTEING
ROUTEMAN
ROUTEMEN
ROUTER
ROUTERS
ROUTES
ROUTEWAY
ROUTEWAYS
ROUTH
ROUTHS
ROUTINE
ROUTINELY
ROUTINES
ROUTING
ROUTINISM
ROUTINISMS
ROUTINIST
ROUTINISTS
ROUTINIZATION
ROUTINIZATIONS
ROUTINIZE
ROUTINIZED
ROUTINIZES
ROUTINIZING
ROUTS
ROUX
ROVE
ROVED
ROVEN
ROVER
ROVERS
ROVES
ROVING
ROVINGLY
ROVINGS
ROW
ROWABLE
ROWAN
ROWANBERRIES
ROWANBERRY
ROWANS
ROWBOAT
ROWBOATS
ROWDIER
ROWDIES
ROWDIEST
ROWDILY
ROWDINESS
ROWDINESSES
ROWDY
ROWDYISH
ROWDYISM
ROWDYISMS
ROWED
ROWEL
ROWELED
ROWELING
ROWELLED
ROWELLING
ROWELS
ROWEN
ROWENS
ROWER
ROWERS
ROWING
ROWINGS
ROWLOCK
ROWLOCKS
ROWS
ROWTH
ROWTHS
ROYAL
ROYALISM
ROYALISMS
ROYALIST
ROYALISTS
ROYALLY
ROYALMAST
ROYALMASTS
ROYALS
ROYALTIES
ROYALTY
ROYSTER
ROYSTERED
ROYSTERING
ROYSTERS
ROZZER
ROZZERS
RUANA
RUANAS
RUB
RUBABOO
RUBABOOS
RUBACE
RUBACES
RUBAIYAT
RUBASSE
RUBASSES
RUBATI
RUBATO
RUBATOS
RUBBABOO
RUBBABOOS
RUBBED
RUBBER
RUBBERED
RUBBERIER
RUBBERIEST
RUBBERING
RUBBERISED
RUBBERIZE
RUBBERIZED
RUBBERIZES
RUBBERIZING
RUBBERLIKE
RUBBERNECK
RUBBERNECKED
RUBBERNECKER
RUBBERNECKERS
RUBBERNECKING
RUBBERNECKS
RUBBERS
RUBBERY
RUBBIES
RUBBING
RUBBINGS
RUBBISH
RUBBISHED
RUBBISHES

RUBBISHING
RUBBISHY
RUBBLE
RUBBLED
RUBBLES
RUBBLIER
RUBBLIEST
RUBBLING
RUBBLY
RUBBOARD
RUBBOARDS
RUBBY
RUBBYDUB
RUBBYDUBS
RUBDOWN
RUBDOWNS
RUBE
RUBEFACIENT
RUBEFACIENTS
RUBEL
RUBELLA
RUBELLAS
RUBELLITE
RUBELLITES
RUBELS
RUBEOLA
RUBEOLAR
RUBEOLAS
RUBES
RUBESCENT
RUBICUND
RUBICUNDITIES
RUBICUNDITY
RUBIDIC
RUBIDIUM
RUBIDIUMS
RUBIED
RUBIER
RUBIES
RUBIEST
RUBIGO
RUBIGOS
RUBIOUS
RUBLE
RUBLES
RUBLI
RUBOFF
RUBOFFS
RUBOUT
RUBOUTS
RUBRIC
RUBRICAL
RUBRICALLY
RUBRICATE
RUBRICATED
RUBRICATES
RUBRICATING
RUBRICATION
RUBRICATIONS
RUBRICATOR
RUBRICATORS
RUBRICIAN
RUBRICIANS
RUBRICS
RUBS
RUBUS
RUBY
RUBYING
RUBYLIKE
RUBYTHROAT
RUBYTHROATS
RUCHE
RUCHED
RUCHES
RUCHING
RUCHINGS
RUCK
RUCKED
RUCKING
RUCKLE
RUCKLED
RUCKLES
RUCKLING
RUCKS
RUCKSACK
RUCKSACKS
RUCKUS
RUCKUSES
RUCOLA
RUCOLAS
RUCTION
RUCTIONS
RUCTIOUS
RUDBECKIA
RUDBECKIAS
RUDD
RUDDER
RUDDERLESS
RUDDERPOST
RUDDERPOSTS
RUDDERS
RUDDIED
RUDDIER
RUDDIES
RUDDIEST
RUDDILY
RUDDINESS
RUDDINESSES
RUDDLE
RUDDLED
RUDDLEMAN
RUDDLEMEN
RUDDLES
RUDDLING
RUDDOCK
RUDDOCKS
RUDDS
RUDDY
RUDDYING
RUDE
RUDELY
RUDENESS
RUDENESSES
RUDER
RUDERAL
RUDERALS
RUDERIES
RUDERY
RUDESBIES
RUDESBY
RUDEST
RUDIMENT
RUDIMENTAL
RUDIMENTARILY
RUDIMENTARINESS
RUDIMENTARY
RUDIMENTS
RUDIST
RUDISTID
RUDISTIDS
RUDISTS
RUE
RUED
RUEFUL
RUEFULLY
RUEFULNESS
RUEFULNESSES
RUEING
RUER
RUERS
RUES
RUFESCENT
RUFF
RUFFE
RUFFED
RUFFES
RUFFIAN
RUFFIANISM
RUFFIANISMS
RUFFIANLY
RUFFIANS
RUFFING
RUFFLE
RUFFLED
RUFFLER
RUFFLERS
RUFFLES
RUFFLIER
RUFFLIEST
RUFFLIKE
RUFFLING
RUFFLY
RUFFS
RUFIYAA
RUFOUS
RUFOUSES
RUG
RUGA
RUGAE
RUGAL
RUGALACH
RUGATE
RUGBIES
RUGBY
RUGELACH
RUGELACHS
RUGGED
RUGGEDER
RUGGEDEST
RUGGEDIZATION
RUGGEDIZATIONS
RUGGEDIZE
RUGGEDIZED
RUGGEDIZES
RUGGEDIZING
RUGGEDLY
RUGGEDNESS
RUGGEDNESSES
RUGGER
RUGGERS
RUGGING
RUGLIKE
RUGOLA
RUGOLAS
RUGOSA
RUGOSAS
RUGOSE
RUGOSELY
RUGOSITIES
RUGOSITY
RUGOUS
RUGRAT
RUGRATS
RUGS
RUGULOSE
RUIN
RUINABLE
RUINATE
RUINATED
RUINATES
RUINATING
RUINATION
RUINATIONS
RUINED
RUINER
RUINERS
RUING
RUINING
RUINOUS
RUINOUSLY
RUINOUSNESS
RUINOUSNESSES
RUINS
RUKH
RUKHS
RULABLE
RULE
RULED
RULELESS
RULER
RULERS
RULERSHIP
RULERSHIPS
RULES
RULIER
RULIEST
RULING
RULINGS
RULY
RUM
RUMAKI
RUMAKIS
RUMBA
RUMBAED
RUMBAING
RUMBAS
RUMBLE
RUMBLED
RUMBLER
RUMBLERS
RUMBLES
RUMBLING
RUMBLINGS
RUMBLY
RUMBUSTIOUS

UMBUSTIOUSLY
UMBUSTIOUSNESS
UMDUM
UMDUMS
UMEN
UMENS
UMINA
UMINAL
UMINANT
UMINANTLY
UMINANTS
UMINATE
UMINATED
UMINATES
UMINATING
UMINATION
UMINATIONS
UMINATIVE
UMINATIVELY
UMINATOR
UMINATORS
UMLY
UMMAGE
UMMAGED
UMMAGER
UMMAGERS
UMMAGES
UMMAGING
UMMER
UMMERS
UMMEST
UMMIER
UMMIES
UMMIEST
UMMY
UMNESS
UMNESSES
MOR
MORED
MORING
MORMONGER
MORMONGERING
MORMONGERINGS
MORMONGERS
MORS
MOUR
MOURED
MOURING
MOURMONGER
MOURMONGERS
MOURS
MP
MPLE
RUMPLED
RUMPLES
RUMPLESS
RUMPLIER
RUMPLIEST
RUMPLING
RUMPLY
RUMPOT
RUMPOTS
RUMPS
RUMPUS
RUMPUSES
RUMRUNNER
RUMRUNNERS
RUMS
RUN
RUNABOUT
RUNABOUTS
RUNAGATE
RUNAGATES
RUNAROUND
RUNAROUNDS
RUNAWAY
RUNAWAYS
RUNBACK
RUNBACKS
RUNCINATE
RUNDLE
RUNDLES
RUNDLET
RUNDLETS
RUNDOWN
RUNDOWNS
RUNE
RUNELIKE
RUNES
RUNG
RUNGED
RUNGLESS
RUNGS
RUNIC
RUNKLE
RUNKLED
RUNKLES
RUNKLING
RUNLESS
RUNLET
RUNLETS
RUNNABLE
RUNNEL
RUNNELS
RUNNER
RUNNERS
RUNNIER
RUNNIEST
RUNNINESS
RUNNINESSES
RUNNING
RUNNINGS
RUNNY
RUNOFF
RUNOFFS
RUNOUT
RUNOUTS
RUNOVER
RUNOVERS
RUNROUND
RUNROUNDS
RUNS
RUNT
RUNTIER
RUNTIEST
RUNTINESS
RUNTINESSES
RUNTISH
RUNTISHLY
RUNTS
RUNTY
RUNWAY
RUNWAYS
RUPEE
RUPEES
RUPIAH
RUPIAHS
RUPTURE
RUPTURED
RUPTURES
RUPTURING
RURAL
RURALISE
RURALISED
RURALISES
RURALISING
RURALISM
RURALISMS
RURALIST
RURALISTS
RURALITE
RURALITES
RURALITIES
RURALITY
RURALIZE
RURALIZED
RURALIZES
RURALIZING
RURALLY
RURBAN
RUSE
RUSES
RUSH
RUSHED
RUSHEE
RUSHEES
RUSHER
RUSHERS
RUSHES
RUSHIER
RUSHIEST
RUSHING
RUSHINGS
RUSHLIGHT
RUSHLIGHTS
RUSHLIKE
RUSHY
RUSINE
RUSK
RUSKS
RUSSET
RUSSETED
RUSSETING
RUSSETINGS
RUSSETS
RUSSETTING
RUSSETTINGS
RUSSETY
RUSSIFIED
RUSSIFIES
RUSSIFY
RUSSIFYING
RUSSULA
RUSSULAS
RUST
RUSTABLE
RUSTED
RUSTIC
RUSTICAL
RUSTICALLY
RUSTICALS
RUSTICATE
RUSTICATED
RUSTICATES
RUSTICATING
RUSTICATION
RUSTICATIONS
RUSTICATOR
RUSTICATORS
RUSTICITIES
RUSTICITY
RUSTICLY
RUSTICS
RUSTIER
RUSTIEST
RUSTILY
RUSTINESS
RUSTINESSES
RUSTING
RUSTLE
RUSTLED
RUSTLER
RUSTLERS
RUSTLES
RUSTLESS
RUSTLING
RUSTPROOF
RUSTPROOFED
RUSTPROOFING
RUSTPROOFS
RUSTS
RUSTY
RUT
RUTABAGA
RUTABAGAS
RUTH
RUTHENIC
RUTHENIUM
RUTHENIUMS
RUTHER
RUTHERFORDIUM
RUTHERFORDIUMS
RUTHFUL
RUTHFULLY
RUTHFULNESS
RUTHFULNESSES
RUTHLESS
RUTHLESSLY
RUTHLESSNESS
RUTHLESSNESSES
RUTHS
RUTILANT
RUTILE
RUTILES
RUTIN
RUTINS
RUTS
RUTTED
RUTTIER
RUTTIEST
RUTTILY
RUTTINESS
RUTTINESSES
RUTTING
RUTTISH

RUTTISHLY
RUTTISHNESS
RUTTISHNESSES
RUTTY
RYA
RYAS
RYE
RYEGRASS
RYEGRASSES
RYES
RYKE
RYKED
RYKES
RYKING
RYND
RYNDS
RYOKAN
RYOKANS
RYOT
RYOTS
RYU
RYUS

S

SAB
SABADILLA
SABADILLAS
SABAL
SABALS
SABATON
SABATONS
SABAYON
SABAYONS
SABBAT
SABBATH
SABBATHS
SABBATIC
SABBATICAL
SABBATICALS
SABBATICS
SABBATS
SABBED
SABBING
SABE
SABED
SABEING
SABER
SABERED
SABERING
SABERLIKE
SABERMETRICIAN
SABERMETRICIANS
SABERMETRICS
SABERS
SABES
SABICU
SABICUS
SABIN
SABINE
SABINES
SABINS
SABIR
SABIRS
SABKHA
SABKHAS
SABLE
SABLEFISH
SABLEFISHES
SABLER
SABLES
SABLEST
SABOT
SABOTAGE
SABOTAGED
SABOTAGES
SABOTAGING
SABOTED
SABOTEUR
SABOTEURS
SABOTS
SABRA
SABRAS
SABRE
SABRED
SABRES
SABRING
SABS
SABULOSE
SABULOUS
SAC
SACAHUISTA
SACAHUISTAS
SACAHUISTE
SACAHUISTES
SACATON
SACATONS
SACBUT
SACBUTS
SACCADE
SACCADES
SACCADIC
SACCATE
SACCHARASE
SACCHARASES
SACCHARIC
SACCHARIDE
SACCHARIDES
SACCHARIFIED
SACCHARIFIES
SACCHARIFY
SACCHARIFYING
SACCHARIMETER
SACCHARIMETERS
SACCHARIN
SACCHARINE
SACCHARINITIES
SACCHARINITY
SACCHARINS
SACCHAROIDAL
SACCHAROMETER
SACCHAROMETERS
SACCHAROMYCES
SACCHAROMYCETES
SACCULAR
SACCULATE
SACCULATED
SACCULATION
SACCULATIONS
SACCULE
SACCULES
SACCULI
SACCULUS
SACERDOTAL
SACERDOTALISM
SACERDOTALISMS
SACERDOTALIST
SACERDOTALISTS
SACERDOTALLY
SACHEM
SACHEMIC
SACHEMS
SACHET
SACHETED
SACHETS
SACK
SACKABLE
SACKBUT
SACKBUTS
SACKCLOTH
SACKCLOTHS
SACKED
SACKER
SACKERS
SACKFUL
SACKFULS
SACKING
SACKINGS
SACKLIKE
SACKS
SACKSFUL
SACLIKE
SACQUE
SACQUES
SACRA
SACRAL
SACRALIZATION
SACRALIZATIONS
SACRALIZE
SACRALIZED
SACRALIZES
SACRALIZING
SACRALS
SACRAMENT
SACRAMENTAL
SACRAMENTALISM
SACRAMENTALISMS
SACRAMENTALIST
SACRAMENTALISTS
SACRAMENTALLY
SACRAMENTALS
SACRAMENTS
SACRARIA
SACRARIAL
SACRARIUM
SACRARIUMS
SACRED
SACREDER
SACREDEST
SACREDLY
SACREDNESS
SACREDNESSES
SACRIFICE
SACRIFICED
SACRIFICER
SACRIFICERS
SACRIFICES
SACRIFICIAL
SACRIFICIALLY
SACRIFICING
SACRILEGE
SACRILEGES
SACRILEGIOUS
SACRILEGIOUSLY
SACRING
SACRINGS
SACRIST
SACRISTAN
SACRISTANS
SACRISTIES
SACRISTS
SACRISTY
SACROILIAC
SACROILIACS
SACROSANCT

ACROSANCTITIES
ACROSANCTITY
ACRUM
ACRUMS
ACS
AD
ADDEN
ADDENED
ADDENING
ADDENS
ADDER
ADDEST
ADDHU
ADDHUS
ADDISH
ADDLE
ADDLEBAG
ADDLEBAGS
ADDLEBOW
ADDLEBOWS
ADDLEBRED
ADDLEBREDS
ADDLECLOTH
ADDLECLOTHS
ADDLED
ADDLELESS
ADDLER
ADDLERIES
ADDLERS
ADDLERY
ADDLES
ADDLETREE
ADDLETREES
ADDLING
ADE
ADES
ADHE
ADHES
ADHU
ADHUS
ADI
ADIRON
ADIRONS
ADIS
DISM
ADISMS
ADIST
DISTIC
DISTICALLY
DISTS
DLY
DNESS
DNESSES
SADOMASOCHISM
SADOMASOCHISMS
SADOMASOCHIST
SADOMASOCHISTIC
SADOMASOCHISTS
SAE
SAFARI
SAFARIED
SAFARIING
SAFARIS
SAFE
SAFECRACKER
SAFECRACKERS
SAFECRACKING
SAFECRACKINGS
SAFEGUARD
SAFEGUARDED
SAFEGUARDING
SAFEGUARDS
SAFEKEEPING
SAFEKEEPINGS
SAFELIGHT
SAFELIGHTS
SAFELY
SAFENESS
SAFENESSES
SAFER
SAFES
SAFEST
SAFETIED
SAFETIES
SAFETY
SAFETYING
SAFETYMAN
SAFETYMEN
SAFFLOWER
SAFFLOWERS
SAFFRON
SAFFRONIER
SAFFRONIEST
SAFFRONS
SAFFRONY
SAFRANIN
SAFRANINE
SAFRANINES
SAFRANINS
SAFROL
SAFROLE
SAFROLES
SAFROLS
SAG
SAGA
SAGACIOUS
SAGACIOUSLY
SAGACIOUSNESS
SAGACIOUSNESSES
SAGACITIES
SAGACITY
SAGAMAN
SAGAMEN
SAGAMORE
SAGAMORES
SAGANASH
SAGANASHES
SAGAS
SAGBUT
SAGBUTS
SAGE
SAGEBRUSH
SAGEBRUSHES
SAGEHOOD
SAGEHOODS
SAGELY
SAGENESS
SAGENESSES
SAGER
SAGES
SAGEST
SAGGAR
SAGGARD
SAGGARDS
SAGGARED
SAGGARING
SAGGARS
SAGGED
SAGGER
SAGGERED
SAGGERING
SAGGERS
SAGGIER
SAGGIEST
SAGGING
SAGGY
SAGIER
SAGIEST
SAGITTAL
SAGITTALLY
SAGITTARIES
SAGITTARY
SAGITTATE
SAGO
SAGOS
SAGS
SAGUARO
SAGUAROS
SAGUM
SAGY
SAHIB
SAHIBS
SAHIWAL
SAHIWALS
SAHUARO
SAHUAROS
SAICE
SAICES
SAID
SAIDS
SAIGA
SAIGAS
SAIL
SAILABLE
SAILBOARD
SAILBOARDED
SAILBOARDER
SAILBOARDERS
SAILBOARDING
SAILBOARDINGS
SAILBOARDS
SAILBOAT
SAILBOATER
SAILBOATERS
SAILBOATING
SAILBOATINGS
SAILBOATS
SAILCLOTH
SAILCLOTHS
SAILED
SAILER
SAILERS
SAILFISH
SAILFISHES
SAILING
SAILINGS
SAILLESS
SAILMAKER
SAILMAKERS
SAILOR
SAILORLY
SAILORS
SAILPAST
SAILPASTS
SAILPLANE
SAILPLANED
SAILPLANER
SAILPLANERS
SAILPLANES
SAILPLANING
SAILS
SAIMIN
SAIMINS
SAIN
SAINED
SAINFOIN
SAINFOINS
SAINING
SAINS
SAINT
SAINTDOM
SAINTDOMS
SAINTED
SAINTHOOD
SAINTHOODS
SAINTING
SAINTLIER
SAINTLIEST
SAINTLIKE
SAINTLINESS
SAINTLINESSES
SAINTLY
SAINTS
SAINTSHIP
SAINTSHIPS
SAITH
SAITHE
SAIYID
SAIYIDS
SAJOU
SAJOUS
SAKE
SAKER
SAKERS
SAKES
SAKI
SAKIS
SAKTI
SAKTIS
SAL
SALAAM
SALAAMED
SALAAMING
SALAAMS
SALABILITIES
SALABILITY
SALABLE
SALABLY
SALACIOUS
SALACIOUSLY
SALACIOUSNESS
SALACIOUSNESSES
SALACITIES
SALACITY
SALAD

SALADANG
SALADANGS
SALADS
SALAL
SALALS
SALAMANDER
SALAMANDERS
SALAMANDRINE
SALAMI
SALAMIS
SALARIAT
SALARIATS
SALARIED
SALARIES
SALARY
SALARYING
SALARYMAN
SALARYMEN
SALAT
SALATS
SALCHOW
SALCHOWS
SALE
SALEABLE
SALEABLY
SALEP
SALEPS
SALERATUS
SALERATUSES
SALEROOM
SALEROOMS
SALES
SALESCLERK
SALESCLERKS
SALESGIRL
SALESGIRLS
SALESLADIES
SALESLADY
SALESMAN
SALESMANSHIP
SALESMANSHIPS
SALESMEN
SALESPEOPLE
SALESPERSON
SALESPERSONS
SALESROOM
SALESROOMS
SALESWOMAN
SALESWOMEN
SALIC
SALICIN
SALICINE
SALICINES
SALICINS
SALICYLATE
SALICYLATES
SALIENCE
SALIENCES
SALIENCIES
SALIENCY
SALIENT
SALIENTLY
SALIENTS
SALIFIED
SALIFIES
SALIFY
SALIFYING
SALIMETER
SALIMETERS
SALIMETRIES
SALIMETRY
SALINA
SALINAS
SALINE
SALINES
SALINITIES
SALINITY
SALINIZATION
SALINIZATIONS
SALINIZE
SALINIZED
SALINIZES
SALINIZING
SALINOMETER
SALINOMETERS
SALIVA
SALIVARY
SALIVAS
SALIVATE
SALIVATED
SALIVATES
SALIVATING
SALIVATION
SALIVATIONS
SALIVATOR
SALIVATORS
SALL
SALLET
SALLETS
SALLIED
SALLIER
SALLIERS
SALLIES
SALLOW
SALLOWED
SALLOWER
SALLOWEST
SALLOWING
SALLOWISH
SALLOWLY
SALLOWNESS
SALLOWNESSES
SALLOWS
SALLOWY
SALLY
SALLYING
SALMAGUNDI
SALMAGUNDIES
SALMAGUNDIS
SALMI
SALMIS
SALMON
SALMONBERRIES
SALMONBERRY
SALMONELLA
SALMONELLAE
SALMONELLAS
SALMONELLOSES
SALMONELLOSIS
SALMONID
SALMONIDS
SALMONOID
SALMONOIDS
SALMONS
SALMONY
SALOL
SALOLS
SALOMETER
SALOMETERS
SALON
SALONS
SALOON
SALOONS
SALOOP
SALOOPS
SALP
SALPA
SALPAE
SALPAS
SALPIAN
SALPIANS
SALPICON
SALPICONS
SALPID
SALPIDS
SALPIFORM
SALPIGLOSSES
SALPIGLOSSIS
SALPIGLOSSISES
SALPINGES
SALPINGITIS
SALPINGITISES
SALPINX
SALPS
SALS
SALSA
SALSAS
SALSIFIES
SALSIFY
SALSILLA
SALSILLAS
SALT
SALTANT
SALTARELLO
SALTARELLOS
SALTATION
SALTATIONS
SALTATORIAL
SALTATORY
SALTBOX
SALTBOXES
SALTBUSH
SALTBUSHES
SALTCELLAR
SALTCELLARS
SALTCHUCK
SALTCHUCKS
SALTED
SALTER
SALTERIES
SALTERN
SALTERNS
SALTERS
SALTERY
SALTEST
SALTIE
SALTIER
SALTIERS
SALTIES
SALTIEST
SALTILY
SALTIMBOCCA
SALTIMBOCCAS
SALTINE
SALTINES
SALTINESS
SALTINESSES
SALTING
SALTINGS
SALTIRE
SALTIRES
SALTISH
SALTLESS
SALTLIKE
SALTNESS
SALTNESSES
SALTPAN
SALTPANS
SALTPETER
SALTPETERS
SALTPETRE
SALTPETRES
SALTS
SALTSHAKER
SALTSHAKERS
SALTWATER
SALTWATERS
SALTWORK
SALTWORKS
SALTWORT
SALTWORTS
SALTY
SALUBRIOUS
SALUBRIOUSLY
SALUBRIOUSNESS
SALUBRITIES
SALUBRITY
SALUKI
SALUKIS
SALURETIC
SALURETICS
SALUT
SALUTARILY
SALUTARINESS
SALUTARINESSES
SALUTARY
SALUTATION
SALUTATIONAL
SALUTATIONS
SALUTATORIAN
SALUTATORIANS
SALUTATORIES
SALUTATORY
SALUTE
SALUTED
SALUTER
SALUTERS
SALUTES
SALUTIFEROUS
SALUTING
SALVABLE
SALVABLY
SALVAGE
SALVAGEABILITY
SALVAGEABLE

ALVAGED
ALVAGEE
ALVAGEES
ALVAGER
ALVAGERS
ALVAGES
ALVAGING
ALVARSAN
ALVARSANS
ALVATION
ALVATIONAL
ALVATIONISM
ALVATIONISMS
ALVATIONIST
ALVATIONISTS
ALVATIONS
ALVE
ALVED
ALVER
ALVERFORM
ALVERS
ALVES
ALVIA
ALVIAS
ALVIFIC
ALVING
ALVO
ALVOED
ALVOES
ALVOING
ALVOR
ALVORS
ALVOS
ALWAR
ALWARS
AMADHI
AMADHIS
AMARA
AMARAS
AMARITAN
AMARITANS
AMARIUM
AMARIUMS
AMARSKITE
AMARSKITES
AMBA
AMBAED
AMBAING
AMBAL
AMBALS
AMBAR
AMBARS
AMBAS
SAMBHAR
SAMBHARS
SAMBHUR
SAMBHURS
SAMBO
SAMBOES
SAMBOS
SAMBUCA
SAMBUCAS
SAMBUKE
SAMBUKES
SAMBUR
SAMBURS
SAME
SAMECH
SAMECHS
SAMEK
SAMEKH
SAMEKHS
SAMEKS
SAMENESS
SAMENESSES
SAMEY
SAMFU
SAMFUS
SAMIEL
SAMIELS
SAMIER
SAMIEST
SAMISEN
SAMISENS
SAMITE
SAMITES
SAMIZDAT
SAMIZDATS
SAMLET
SAMLETS
SAMOSA
SAMOSAS
SAMOVAR
SAMOVARS
SAMOYED
SAMOYEDS
SAMP
SAMPAN
SAMPANS
SAMPHIRE
SAMPHIRES
SAMPLE
SAMPLED
SAMPLER
SAMPLERS
SAMPLES
SAMPLING
SAMPLINGS
SAMPS
SAMSARA
SAMSARAS
SAMSARIC
SAMSHU
SAMSHUS
SAMSKARA
SAMSKARAS
SAMURAI
SAMURAIS
SAN
SANATIVE
SANATORIA
SANATORIUM
SANATORIUMS
SANBENITO
SANBENITOS
SANCTA
SANCTIFICATION
SANCTIFICATIONS
SANCTIFIED
SANCTIFIER
SANCTIFIERS
SANCTIFIES
SANCTIFY
SANCTIFYING
SANCTIMONIES
SANCTIMONIOUS
SANCTIMONIOUSLY
SANCTIMONY
SANCTION
SANCTIONABLE
SANCTIONED
SANCTIONING
SANCTIONINGS
SANCTIONS
SANCTITIES
SANCTITY
SANCTUARIES
SANCTUARY
SANCTUM
SANCTUMS
SAND
SANDABLE
SANDAL
SANDALED
SANDALING
SANDALLED
SANDALLING
SANDALS
SANDALWOOD
SANDALWOODS
SANDARAC
SANDARACS
SANDBAG
SANDBAGGED
SANDBAGGER
SANDBAGGERS
SANDBAGGING
SANDBAGS
SANDBANK
SANDBANKS
SANDBAR
SANDBARS
SANDBLAST
SANDBLASTED
SANDBLASTER
SANDBLASTERS
SANDBLASTING
SANDBLASTS
SANDBOX
SANDBOXES
SANDBUR
SANDBURR
SANDBURRS
SANDBURS
SANDCRACK
SANDCRACKS
SANDDAB
SANDDABS
SANDED
SANDER
SANDERLING
SANDERLINGS
SANDERS
SANDFISH
SANDFISHES
SANDFLIES
SANDFLY
SANDGLASS
SANDGLASSES
SANDGROUSE
SANDGROUSES
SANDHI
SANDHILL
SANDHILLS
SANDHIS
SANDHOG
SANDHOGS
SANDIER
SANDIEST
SANDINESS
SANDINESSES
SANDING
SANDLESS
SANDLIKE
SANDLING
SANDLINGS
SANDLOT
SANDLOTS
SANDLOTTER
SANDLOTTERS
SANDMAN
SANDMEN
SANDPAINTING
SANDPAINTINGS
SANDPAPER
SANDPAPERED
SANDPAPERING
SANDPAPERS
SANDPAPERY
SANDPEEP
SANDPEEPS
SANDPILE
SANDPILES
SANDPIPER
SANDPIPERS
SANDPIT
SANDPITS
SANDS
SANDSHOE
SANDSHOES
SANDSOAP
SANDSOAPS
SANDSPIT
SANDSPITS
SANDSPUR
SANDSPURS
SANDSTONE
SANDSTONES
SANDSTORM
SANDSTORMS
SANDWICH
SANDWICHED
SANDWICHES
SANDWICHING
SANDWORM
SANDWORMS
SANDWORT
SANDWORTS
SANDY
SANDYISH
SANE
SANED
SANELY
SANENESS
SANENESSES

SANER
SANES
SANEST
SANG
SANGA
SANGAR
SANGAREE
SANGAREES
SANGARS
SANGAS
SANGER
SANGERS
SANGFROID
SANGFROIDS
SANGH
SANGHA
SANGHAS
SANGHS
SANGRAIL
SANGRAILS
SANGREAL
SANGREALS
SANGRIA
SANGRIAS
SANGUINARIA
SANGUINARIAS
SANGUINARILY
SANGUINARY
SANGUINE
SANGUINELY
SANGUINENESS
SANGUINENESSES
SANGUINEOUS
SANGUINES
SANGUINITIES
SANGUINITY
SANICLE
SANICLES
SANIDINE
SANIDINES
SANIES
SANING
SANIOUS
SANITARIA
SANITARIAN
SANITARIANS
SANITARIES
SANITARILY
SANITARIUM
SANITARIUMS
SANITARY
SANITATE
SANITATED
SANITATES
SANITATING
SANITATION
SANITATIONS
SANITIES
SANITISE
SANITISED
SANITISES
SANITISING
SANITIZATION
SANITIZATIONS
SANITIZE
SANITIZED
SANITIZER
SANITIZERS
SANITIZES
SANITIZING
SANITORIA
SANITORIUM
SANITORIUMS
SANITY
SANJAK
SANJAKS
SANK
SANNOP
SANNOPS
SANNUP
SANNUPS
SANNYASI
SANNYASIN
SANNYASINS
SANNYASIS
SANS
SANSAR
SANSARS
SANSCULOTTE
SANSCULOTTES
SANSCULOTTIC
SANSCULOTTISH
SANSCULOTTISM
SANSCULOTTISMS
SANSEI
SANSEIS
SANSERIF
SANSERIFS
SANSEVIERIA
SANSEVIERIAS
SANTALIC
SANTALOL
SANTALOLS
SANTERA
SANTERAS
SANTERIA
SANTERIAS
SANTERO
SANTEROS
SANTIM
SANTIMI
SANTIMS
SANTIMU
SANTIR
SANTIRS
SANTO
SANTOL
SANTOLINA
SANTOLINAS
SANTOLS
SANTONICA
SANTONICAS
SANTONIN
SANTONINS
SANTOOR
SANTOORS
SANTOS
SANTOUR
SANTOURS
SANTUR
SANTURS
SANYASI
SANYASIS
SAP
SAPAJOU
SAPAJOUS
SAPANWOOD
SAPANWOODS
SAPELE
SAPELES
SAPHEAD
SAPHEADED
SAPHEADS
SAPHENA
SAPHENAE
SAPHENAS
SAPHENOUS
SAPID
SAPIDER
SAPIDEST
SAPIDITIES
SAPIDITY
SAPIENCE
SAPIENCES
SAPIENCIES
SAPIENCY
SAPIENS
SAPIENT
SAPIENTLY
SAPIENTS
SAPLESS
SAPLESSNESS
SAPLESSNESSES
SAPLING
SAPLINGS
SAPODILLA
SAPODILLAS
SAPOGENIN
SAPOGENINS
SAPONACEOUS
SAPONACEOUSNESS
SAPONATED
SAPONIFIABLE
SAPONIFICATION
SAPONIFICATIONS
SAPONIFIED
SAPONIFIER
SAPONIFIERS
SAPONIFIES
SAPONIFY
SAPONIFYING
SAPONIN
SAPONINE
SAPONINES
SAPONINS
SAPONITE
SAPONITES
SAPOR
SAPORIFIC
SAPOROUS
SAPORS
SAPOTA
SAPOTAS
SAPOTE
SAPOTES
SAPOUR
SAPOURS
SAPPED
SAPPER
SAPPERS
SAPPHIC
SAPPHICS
SAPPHIRE
SAPPHIRES
SAPPHIRINE
SAPPHISM
SAPPHISMS
SAPPHIST
SAPPHISTS
SAPPIER
SAPPIEST
SAPPILY
SAPPINESS
SAPPINESSES
SAPPING
SAPPINGS
SAPPY
SAPRAEMIA
SAPRAEMIAS
SAPREMIA
SAPREMIAS
SAPREMIC
SAPROBE
SAPROBES
SAPROBIAL
SAPROBIC
SAPROGENIC
SAPROGENICITIES
SAPROGENICITY
SAPROLITE
SAPROLITES
SAPROPEL
SAPROPELS
SAPROPHAGOUS
SAPROPHYTE
SAPROPHYTES
SAPROPHYTIC
SAPROPHYTICALLY
SAPROZOIC
SAPS
SAPSAGO
SAPSAGOS
SAPSUCKER
SAPSUCKERS
SAPWOOD
SAPWOODS
SAQUINAVIR
SAQUINAVIRS
SARABAND
SARABANDE
SARABANDES
SARABANDS
SARAN
SARANGI
SARANGIS
SARANS
SARAPE
SARAPES
SARCASM
SARCASMS
SARCASTIC
SARCASTICALLY
SARCENET
SARCENETS
SARCINA

ARCINAE
ARCINAS
ARCOCARP
ARCOCARPS
ARCOID
ARCOIDOSES
ARCOIDOSIS
ARCOIDS
ARCOLEMMA
ARCOLEMMAL
ARCOLEMMAS
ARCOLOGIES
ARCOLOGY
ARCOMA
ARCOMAS
ARCOMATA
ARCOMATOSES
ARCOMATOSIS
ARCOMATOUS
ARCOMERE
ARCOMERES
ARCOPHAGI
ARCOPHAGUS
ARCOPHAGUSES
ARCOPLASM
ARCOPLASMIC
ARCOPLASMS
ARCOSOMAL
ARCOSOME
ARCOSOMES
ARCOUS
ARD
ARDANA
ARDANAS
ARDAR
ARDARS
ARDINE
ARDINED
ARDINES
ARDINING
ARDIUS
ARDIUSES
ARDONIC
ARDONICALLY
ARDONICISM
ARDONICISMS
ARDONYX
ARDONYXES
ARDS
AREE
AREES
ARGASSA
ARGASSO
SARGASSOES
SARGASSOS
SARGASSUM
SARGASSUMS
SARGE
SARGES
SARGO
SARGOS
SARI
SARIN
SARINS
SARIS
SARK
SARKIER
SARKIEST
SARKILY
SARKS
SARKY
SARMENT
SARMENTA
SARMENTS
SARMENTUM
SARNIE
SARNIES
SAROD
SARODE
SARODES
SARODIST
SARODISTS
SARODS
SARONG
SARONGS
SAROS
SAROSES
SARRACENIA
SARRACENIAS
SARSAPARILLA
SARSAPARILLAS
SARSAR
SARSARS
SARSEN
SARSENET
SARSENETS
SARSENS
SARSNET
SARSNETS
SARTOR
SARTORIAL
SARTORIALLY
SARTORII
SARTORIUS
SARTORS
SASANQUA
SASANQUAS
SASH
SASHAY
SASHAYED
SASHAYING
SASHAYS
SASHED
SASHES
SASHIMI
SASHIMIS
SASHING
SASHLESS
SASIN
SASINS
SASKATOON
SASKATOONS
SASQUATCH
SASQUATCHES
SASS
SASSABIES
SASSABY
SASSAFRAS
SASSAFRASES
SASSED
SASSES
SASSIER
SASSIES
SASSIEST
SASSILY
SASSINESS
SASSINESSES
SASSING
SASSWOOD
SASSWOODS
SASSY
SASSYWOOD
SASSYWOODS
SASTRUGA
SASTRUGI
SAT
SATANG
SATANGS
SATANIC
SATANICAL
SATANICALLY
SATANISM
SATANISMS
SATANIST
SATANISTS
SATARA
SATARAS
SATAY
SATAYS
SATCHEL
SATCHELED
SATCHELFUL
SATCHELFULS
SATCHELS
SATCHELSFUL
SATCOM
SATCOMS
SATE
SATED
SATEEN
SATEENS
SATELLITE
SATELLITES
SATEM
SATES
SATI
SATIABLE
SATIABLY
SATIATE
SATIATED
SATIATES
SATIATING
SATIATION
SATIATIONS
SATIETIES
SATIETY
SATIN
SATINED
SATINET
SATINETS
SATINETTE
SATINETTES
SATING
SATINIER
SATINIEST
SATINING
SATINPOD
SATINPODS
SATINS
SATINWOOD
SATINWOODS
SATINY
SATIRE
SATIRES
SATIRIC
SATIRICAL
SATIRICALLY
SATIRISE
SATIRISED
SATIRISES
SATIRISING
SATIRIST
SATIRISTS
SATIRIZABLE
SATIRIZE
SATIRIZED
SATIRIZER
SATIRIZERS
SATIRIZES
SATIRIZING
SATIS
SATISFACTION
SATISFACTIONS
SATISFACTORILY
SATISFACTORY
SATISFIABLE
SATISFICE
SATISFICED
SATISFICES
SATISFICING
SATISFIED
SATISFIER
SATISFIERS
SATISFIES
SATISFY
SATISFYING
SATISFYINGLY
SATORI
SATORIS
SATRAP
SATRAPIES
SATRAPS
SATRAPY
SATSANG
SATSANGS
SATSUMA
SATSUMAS
SATURABLE
SATURANT
SATURANTS
SATURATE
SATURATED
SATURATER
SATURATERS
SATURATES
SATURATING
SATURATION
SATURATIONS
SATURATOR
SATURATORS
SATURNALIA
SATURNALIAN
SATURNALIANLY
SATURNALIAS
SATURNIID

SATURNIIDS
SATURNINE
SATURNISM
SATURNISMS
SATYAGRAHA
SATYAGRAHAS
SATYR
SATYRIASES
SATYRIASIS
SATYRIC
SATYRICAL
SATYRID
SATYRIDS
SATYRLIKE
SATYRS
SAU
SAUCE
SAUCEBOAT
SAUCEBOATS
SAUCEBOX
SAUCEBOXES
SAUCED
SAUCEPAN
SAUCEPANS
SAUCEPOT
SAUCEPOTS
SAUCER
SAUCERLIKE
SAUCERS
SAUCES
SAUCH
SAUCHS
SAUCIER
SAUCIERS
SAUCIEST
SAUCILY
SAUCINESS
SAUCINESSES
SAUCING
SAUCY
SAUERBRATEN
SAUERBRATENS
SAUERKRAUT
SAUERKRAUTS
SAUGER
SAUGERS
SAUGH
SAUGHS
SAUGHY
SAUL
SAULS
SAULT
SAULTS
SAUNA
SAUNAED
SAUNAING
SAUNAS
SAUNTER
SAUNTERED
SAUNTERER
SAUNTERERS
SAUNTERING
SAUNTERS
SAUREL
SAURELS
SAURIAN
SAURIANS
SAURIES
SAURISCHIAN
SAURISCHIANS
SAUROPOD
SAUROPODS
SAURY
SAUSAGE
SAUSAGES
SAUTE
SAUTED
SAUTEED
SAUTEING
SAUTERNE
SAUTERNES
SAUTES
SAUTOIR
SAUTOIRE
SAUTOIRES
SAUTOIRS
SAVABLE
SAVAGE
SAVAGED
SAVAGELY
SAVAGENESS
SAVAGENESSES
SAVAGER
SAVAGERIES
SAVAGERY
SAVAGES
SAVAGEST
SAVAGING
SAVAGISM
SAVAGISMS
SAVANNA
SAVANNAH
SAVANNAHS
SAVANNAS
SAVANT
SAVANTS
SAVARIN
SAVARINS
SAVATE
SAVATES
SAVE
SAVEABLE
SAVED
SAVELOY
SAVELOYS
SAVER
SAVERS
SAVES
SAVIN
SAVINE
SAVINES
SAVING
SAVINGLY
SAVINGS
SAVINS
SAVIOR
SAVIORS
SAVIOUR
SAVIOURS
SAVOR
SAVORED
SAVORER
SAVORERS
SAVORIER
SAVORIES
SAVORIEST
SAVORILY
SAVORINESS
SAVORINESSES
SAVORING
SAVORLESS
SAVOROUS
SAVORS
SAVORY
SAVOUR
SAVOURED
SAVOURER
SAVOURERS
SAVOURIER
SAVOURIES
SAVOURIEST
SAVOURING
SAVOURS
SAVOURY
SAVOY
SAVOYS
SAVVIED
SAVVIER
SAVVIES
SAVVIEST
SAVVILY
SAVVINESS
SAVVINESSES
SAVVY
SAVVYING
SAW
SAWBILL
SAWBILLS
SAWBONES
SAWBONESES
SAWBUCK
SAWBUCKS
SAWDUST
SAWDUSTS
SAWDUSTY
SAWED
SAWER
SAWERS
SAWFISH
SAWFISHES
SAWFLIES
SAWFLY
SAWGRASS
SAWGRASSES
SAWHORSE
SAWHORSES
SAWING
SAWLIKE
SAWLOG
SAWLOGS
SAWMILL
SAWMILLS
SAWN
SAWNEY
SAWNEYS
SAWS
SAWTEETH
SAWTIMBER
SAWTIMBERS
SAWTOOTH
SAWYER
SAWYERS
SAX
SAXATILE
SAXES
SAXHORN
SAXHORNS
SAXICOLOUS
SAXIFRAGE
SAXIFRAGES
SAXIST
SAXISTS
SAXITOXIN
SAXITOXINS
SAXMAN
SAXMEN
SAXONIES
SAXONY
SAXOPHONE
SAXOPHONES
SAXOPHONIC
SAXOPHONIST
SAXOPHONISTS
SAXTUBA
SAXTUBAS
SAY
SAYABLE
SAYED
SAYEDS
SAYER
SAYERS
SAYEST
SAYID
SAYIDS
SAYING
SAYINGS
SAYONARA
SAYONARAS
SAYS
SAYST
SAYYID
SAYYIDS
SCAB
SCABBARD
SCABBARDED
SCABBARDING
SCABBARDS
SCABBED
SCABBIER
SCABBIEST
SCABBILY
SCABBING
SCABBLE
SCABBLED
SCABBLES
SCABBLING
SCABBY
SCABIES
SCABIETIC
SCABIOSA
SCABIOSAS
SCABIOUS
SCABIOUSES
SCABLAND
SCABLANDS

SCABLIKE
SCABROUS
SCABROUSLY
SCABROUSNESS
SCABROUSNESSES
SCABS
SCAD
SCADS
SCAFFOLD
SCAFFOLDED
SCAFFOLDING
SCAFFOLDINGS
SCAFFOLDS
SCAG
SCAGLIOLA
SCAGLIOLAS
SCAGS
SCALABILITIES
SCALABILITY
SCALABLE
SCALABLY
SCALADE
SCALADES
SCALADO
SCALADOS
SCALAGE
SCALAGES
SCALAR
SCALARE
SCALARES
SCALARIFORM
SCALARIFORMLY
SCALARS
SCALATION
SCALATIONS
SCALAWAG
SCALAWAGS
SCALD
SCALDED
SCALDIC
SCALDING
SCALDS
SCALE
SCALED
SCALELESS
SCALELIKE
SCALENE
SCALENES
SCALENI
SCALENUS
SCALEPAN
SCALEPANS
SCALER
SCALERS
SCALES
SCALETAIL
SCALETAILS
SCALEUP
SCALEUPS
SCALIER
SCALIEST
SCALINESS
SCALINESSES
SCALING
SCALINGS
SCALL
SCALLAWAG
SCALLAWAGS
SCALLION
SCALLIONS
SCALLOP
SCALLOPED
SCALLOPER
SCALLOPERS
SCALLOPING
SCALLOPINGS
SCALLOPINI
SCALLOPINIS
SCALLOPS
SCALLS
SCALLYWAG
SCALLYWAGS
SCALOGRAM
SCALOGRAMS
SCALOPPINE
SCALOPPINES
SCALP
SCALPED
SCALPEL
SCALPELS
SCALPER
SCALPERS
SCALPING
SCALPS
SCALY
SCAM
SCAMMED
SCAMMER
SCAMMERS
SCAMMING
SCAMMONIES
SCAMMONY
SCAMP
SCAMPED
SCAMPER
SCAMPERED
SCAMPERER
SCAMPERERS
SCAMPERING
SCAMPERINGS
SCAMPERS
SCAMPI
SCAMPIES
SCAMPING
SCAMPISH
SCAMPS
SCAMS
SCAMSTER
SCAMSTERS
SCAN
SCANDAL
SCANDALED
SCANDALING
SCANDALISE
SCANDALISED
SCANDALISES
SCANDALISING
SCANDALIZE
SCANDALIZED
SCANDALIZES
SCANDALIZING
SCANDALLED
SCANDALLING
SCANDALMONGER
SCANDALMONGERS
SCANDALOUS
SCANDALOUSLY
SCANDALOUSNESS
SCANDALS
SCANDENT
SCANDIA
SCANDIAS
SCANDIC
SCANDIUM
SCANDIUMS
SCANNABLE
SCANNED
SCANNER
SCANNERS
SCANNING
SCANNINGS
SCANS
SCANSION
SCANSIONS
SCANT
SCANTED
SCANTER
SCANTEST
SCANTIER
SCANTIES
SCANTIEST
SCANTILY
SCANTINESS
SCANTINESSES
SCANTING
SCANTLING
SCANTLINGS
SCANTLY
SCANTNESS
SCANTNESSES
SCANTS
SCANTY
SCAPE
SCAPED
SCAPEGOAT
SCAPEGOATED
SCAPEGOATING
SCAPEGOATISM
SCAPEGOATISMS
SCAPEGOATS
SCAPEGRACE
SCAPEGRACES
SCAPES
SCAPHOID
SCAPHOIDS
SCAPHOPOD
SCAPHOPODS
SCAPING
SCAPOLITE
SCAPOLITES
SCAPOSE
SCAPULA
SCAPULAE
SCAPULAR
SCAPULARS
SCAPULARY
SCAPULAS
SCAR
SCARAB
SCARABAEI
SCARABAEUS
SCARABAEUSES
SCARABOID
SCARABS
SCARAMOUCH
SCARAMOUCHE
SCARAMOUCHES
SCARCE
SCARCELY
SCARCENESS
SCARCENESSES
SCARCER
SCARCEST
SCARCITIES
SCARCITY
SCARE
SCARECROW
SCARECROWS
SCARED
SCAREDER
SCAREDEST
SCAREHEAD
SCAREHEADS
SCAREMONGER
SCAREMONGERING
SCAREMONGERS
SCARER
SCARERS
SCARES
SCAREY
SCARF
SCARFED
SCARFER
SCARFERS
SCARFING
SCARFPIN
SCARFPINS
SCARFS
SCARFSKIN
SCARFSKINS
SCARIER
SCARIEST
SCARIFICATION
SCARIFICATIONS
SCARIFIED
SCARIFIER
SCARIFIERS
SCARIFIES
SCARIFY
SCARIFYING
SCARIFYINGLY
SCARILY
SCARINESS
SCARINESSES
SCARING
SCARIOSE
SCARIOUS
SCARLATINA
SCARLATINAL
SCARLATINAS
SCARLESS
SCARLET
SCARLETS
SCARP
SCARPED

SCARPER
SCARPERED
SCARPERING
SCARPERS
SCARPH
SCARPHED
SCARPHING
SCARPHS
SCARPING
SCARPS
SCARRED
SCARRIER
SCARRIEST
SCARRING
SCARRY
SCARS
SCART
SCARTED
SCARTING
SCARTS
SCARVED
SCARVES
SCARY
SCAT
SCATBACK
SCATBACKS
SCATHE
SCATHED
SCATHELESS
SCATHES
SCATHING
SCATHINGLY
SCATOLOGICAL
SCATOLOGIES
SCATOLOGY
SCATS
SCATT
SCATTED
SCATTER
SCATTERATION
SCATTERATIONS
SCATTERBRAIN
SCATTERBRAINED
SCATTERBRAINS
SCATTERED
SCATTERER
SCATTERERS
SCATTERGOOD
SCATTERGOODS
SCATTERGRAM
SCATTERGRAMS
SCATTERGUN
SCATTERGUNS
SCATTERING
SCATTERINGLY
SCATTERINGS
SCATTERS
SCATTERSHOT
SCATTIER
SCATTIEST
SCATTILY
SCATTING
SCATTS
SCATTY
SCAUP
SCAUPER
SCAUPERS
SCAUPS
SCAUR
SCAURS
SCAVENGE
SCAVENGED
SCAVENGER
SCAVENGERS
SCAVENGES
SCAVENGING
SCAVENGINGS
SCENA
SCENARIO
SCENARIOS
SCENARIST
SCENARISTS
SCENAS
SCEND
SCENDED
SCENDING
SCENDS
SCENE
SCENERIES
SCENERY
SCENES
SCENESHIFTER
SCENESHIFTERS
SCENIC
SCENICAL
SCENICALLY
SCENICS
SCENOGRAPHER
SCENOGRAPHERS
SCENOGRAPHIC
SCENOGRAPHIES
SCENOGRAPHY
SCENT
SCENTED
SCENTING
SCENTLESS
SCENTS
SCEPTER
SCEPTERED
SCEPTERING
SCEPTERS
SCEPTIC
SCEPTICAL
SCEPTICALLY
SCEPTICISM
SCEPTICISMS
SCEPTICS
SCEPTRAL
SCEPTRE
SCEPTRED
SCEPTRES
SCEPTRING
SCHADENFREUDE
SCHADENFREUDES
SCHAPPE
SCHAPPES
SCHATCHEN
SCHATCHENS
SCHAV
SCHAVS
SCHEDULAR
SCHEDULE
SCHEDULED
SCHEDULER
SCHEDULERS
SCHEDULES
SCHEDULING
SCHEDULINGS
SCHEELITE
SCHEELITES
SCHEFFLERA
SCHEFFLERAS
SCHEMA
SCHEMAS
SCHEMATA
SCHEMATIC
SCHEMATICALLY
SCHEMATICS
SCHEMATISM
SCHEMATISMS
SCHEMATIZATION
SCHEMATIZATIONS
SCHEMATIZE
SCHEMATIZED
SCHEMATIZES
SCHEMATIZING
SCHEME
SCHEMED
SCHEMER
SCHEMERS
SCHEMES
SCHEMING
SCHEMINGS
SCHERZANDO
SCHERZANDOS
SCHERZI
SCHERZO
SCHERZOS
SCHILLER
SCHILLERS
SCHILLING
SCHILLINGS
SCHIPPERKE
SCHIPPERKES
SCHISM
SCHISMATIC
SCHISMATICAL
SCHISMATICALLY
SCHISMATICS
SCHISMATIZE
SCHISMATIZED
SCHISMATIZES
SCHISMATIZING
SCHISMS
SCHIST
SCHISTOSE
SCHISTOSITIES
SCHISTOSITY
SCHISTOSOMAL
SCHISTOSOME
SCHISTOSOMES
SCHISTOSOMIASES
SCHISTOSOMIASIS
SCHISTOUS
SCHISTS
SCHIZIER
SCHIZIEST
SCHIZO
SCHIZOCARP
SCHIZOCARPS
SCHIZOGONIC
SCHIZOGONIES
SCHIZOGONOUS
SCHIZOGONY
SCHIZOID
SCHIZOIDS
SCHIZONT
SCHIZONTS
SCHIZOPHRENE
SCHIZOPHRENES
SCHIZOPHRENIA
SCHIZOPHRENIAS
SCHIZOPHRENIC
SCHIZOPHRENICS
SCHIZOPOD
SCHIZOPODS
SCHIZOS
SCHIZY
SCHIZZIER
SCHIZZIEST
SCHIZZY
SCHLEMIEL
SCHLEMIELS
SCHLEMIHL
SCHLEMIHLS
SCHLEP
SCHLEPP
SCHLEPPED
SCHLEPPER
SCHLEPPERS
SCHLEPPIER
SCHLEPPIEST
SCHLEPPING
SCHLEPPS
SCHLEPPY
SCHLEPS
SCHLIERE
SCHLIEREN
SCHLIERENS
SCHLIERIC
SCHLOCK
SCHLOCKIER
SCHLOCKIEST
SCHLOCKS
SCHLOCKY
SCHLONG
SCHLONGS
SCHLUB
SCHLUBS
SCHLUMP
SCHLUMPED
SCHLUMPIER
SCHLUMPIEST
SCHLUMPING
SCHLUMPS
SCHLUMPY
SCHMALTZ
SCHMALTZES
SCHMALTZIER
SCHMALTZIEST
SCHMALTZY
SCHMALZ
SCHMALZES
SCHMALZIER
SCHMALZIEST

CHMALZY
CHMATTE
CHMATTES
CHMEAR
CHMEARED
CHMEARING
CHMEARS
CHMEER
CHMEERED
CHMEERING
CHMEERS
CHMELZE
CHMELZES
CHMO
CHMOE
CHMOES
CHMOOS
CHMOOSE
CHMOOSED
CHMOOSES
CHMOOSING
CHMOOZE
CHMOOZED
CHMOOZER
CHMOOZERS
CHMOOZES
CHMOOZIER
CHMOOZIEST
CHMOOZING
CHMOOZY
CHMOS
CHMUCK
CHMUCKED
CHMUCKIER
CHMUCKIEST
CHMUCKING
CHMUCKS
CHMUCKY
CHMUTZ
CHMUTZES
CHNAPPER
CHNAPPERS
CHNAPPS
CHNAPPSES
CHNAPS
CHNAUZER
CHNAUZERS
CHNECKE
CHNECKEN
CHNITZEL
CHNITZELS
CHNOOK
CHNOOKS

SCHNORKEL
SCHNORKELED
SCHNORKELING
SCHNORKELS
SCHNORRER
SCHNORRERS
SCHNOZ
SCHNOZES
SCHNOZZ
SCHNOZZES
SCHNOZZLE
SCHNOZZLES
SCHOLAR
SCHOLARLY
SCHOLARS
SCHOLARSHIP
SCHOLARSHIPS
SCHOLASTIC
SCHOLASTICALLY
SCHOLASTICATE
SCHOLASTICATES
SCHOLASTICISM
SCHOLASTICISMS
SCHOLASTICS
SCHOLIA
SCHOLIAST
SCHOLIASTIC
SCHOLIASTS
SCHOLIUM
SCHOLIUMS
SCHOOL
SCHOOLBAG
SCHOOLBAGS
SCHOOLBOOK
SCHOOLBOOKS
SCHOOLBOY
SCHOOLBOYISH
SCHOOLBOYS
SCHOOLCHILD
SCHOOLCHILDREN
SCHOOLED
SCHOOLER
SCHOOLERS
SCHOOLFELLOW
SCHOOLFELLOWS
SCHOOLGIRL
SCHOOLGIRLS
SCHOOLHOUSE
SCHOOLHOUSES
SCHOOLING
SCHOOLINGS
SCHOOLKID
SCHOOLKIDS

SCHOOLMAN
SCHOOLMARM
SCHOOLMARMISH
SCHOOLMARMS
SCHOOLMASTER
SCHOOLMASTERISH
SCHOOLMASTERLY
SCHOOLMASTERS
SCHOOLMATE
SCHOOLMATES
SCHOOLMEN
SCHOOLMISTRESS
SCHOOLMISTRESSY
SCHOOLROOM
SCHOOLROOMS
SCHOOLS
SCHOOLTEACHER
SCHOOLTEACHERS
SCHOOLTIME
SCHOOLTIMES
SCHOOLWORK
SCHOOLWORKS
SCHOOLYARD
SCHOOLYARDS
SCHOONER
SCHOONERS
SCHORL
SCHORLS
SCHOTTISCHE
SCHOTTISCHES
SCHRIK
SCHRIKS
SCHROD
SCHRODS
SCHTICK
SCHTICKS
SCHTIK
SCHTIKS
SCHTUM
SCHTUP
SCHTUPPED
SCHTUPPING
SCHTUPS
SCHUIT
SCHUITS
SCHUL
SCHULN
SCHULS
SCHUSS
SCHUSSBOOMER
SCHUSSBOOMERS
SCHUSSED
SCHUSSER

SCHUSSERS
SCHUSSES
SCHUSSING
SCHVARTZE
SCHVARTZES
SCHVITZ
SCHVITZED
SCHVITZES
SCHVITZING
SCHWA
SCHWARMEREI
SCHWARMEREIS
SCHWARTZE
SCHWARTZES
SCHWAS
SCIAENID
SCIAENIDS
SCIAENOID
SCIAENOIDS
SCIAMACHIES
SCIAMACHY
SCIATIC
SCIATICA
SCIATICAS
SCIATICS
SCIENCE
SCIENCES
SCIENTIAL
SCIENTIFIC
SCIENTIFICALLY
SCIENTISM
SCIENTISMS
SCIENTIST
SCIENTISTIC
SCIENTISTS
SCIENTIZE
SCIENTIZED
SCIENTIZES
SCIENTIZING
SCILICET
SCILLA
SCILLAS
SCIMETAR
SCIMETARS
SCIMITAR
SCIMITARS
SCIMITER
SCIMITERS
SCINCOID
SCINCOIDS
SCINTIGRAPHIC
SCINTIGRAPHIES
SCINTIGRAPHY

SCINTILLA
SCINTILLAE
SCINTILLANT
SCINTILLANTLY
SCINTILLAS
SCINTILLATE
SCINTILLATED
SCINTILLATES
SCINTILLATING
SCINTILLATION
SCINTILLATIONS
SCINTILLATOR
SCINTILLATORS
SCINTILLOMETER
SCINTILLOMETERS
SCIOLISM
SCIOLISMS
SCIOLIST
SCIOLISTIC
SCIOLISTS
SCION
SCIONS
SCIROCCO
SCIROCCOS
SCIRRHI
SCIRRHOID
SCIRRHOUS
SCIRRHUS
SCIRRHUSES
SCISSILE
SCISSION
SCISSIONS
SCISSOR
SCISSORED
SCISSORING
SCISSORS
SCISSORTAIL
SCISSORTAILS
SCISSURE
SCISSURES
SCIURID
SCIURIDS
SCIURINE
SCIURINES
SCIUROID
SCLAFF
SCLAFFED
SCLAFFER
SCLAFFERS
SCLAFFING
SCLAFFS
SCLERA
SCLERAE

SCLERAL
SCLERAS
SCLEREID
SCLEREIDS
SCLERENCHYMA
SCLERENCHYMAS
SCLERITE
SCLERITES
SCLERITIC
SCLERITIS
SCLERITISES
SCLERODERMA
SCLERODERMAS
SCLERODERMATA
SCLEROID
SCLEROMA
SCLEROMAS
SCLEROMATA
SCLEROMETER
SCLEROMETERS
SCLEROPROTEIN
SCLEROPROTEINS
SCLEROSAL
SCLEROSE
SCLEROSED
SCLEROSES
SCLEROSING
SCLEROSIS
SCLEROTHERAPIES
SCLEROTHERAPY
SCLEROTIA
SCLEROTIAL
SCLEROTIC
SCLEROTICS
SCLEROTIN
SCLEROTINS
SCLEROTIUM
SCLEROTIZATION
SCLEROTIZATIONS
SCLEROTIZED
SCLEROUS
SCOFF
SCOFFED
SCOFFER
SCOFFERS
SCOFFING
SCOFFLAW
SCOFFLAWS
SCOFFS
SCOLD
SCOLDED
SCOLDER
SCOLDERS
SCOLDING
SCOLDINGS
SCOLDS
SCOLECES
SCOLECITE
SCOLECITES
SCOLEX
SCOLICES
SCOLIOMA
SCOLIOMAS
SCOLIOSES
SCOLIOSIS
SCOLIOTIC
SCOLLOP
SCOLLOPED
SCOLLOPING
SCOLLOPS
SCOLOPENDRA
SCOLOPENDRAS
SCOMBRID
SCOMBRIDS
SCOMBROID
SCOMBROIDS
SCONCE
SCONCED
SCONCES
SCONCHEON
SCONCHEONS
SCONCING
SCONE
SCONES
SCOOCH
SCOOCHED
SCOOCHES
SCOOCHING
SCOOP
SCOOPABLE
SCOOPED
SCOOPER
SCOOPERS
SCOOPFUL
SCOOPFULS
SCOOPING
SCOOPS
SCOOPSFUL
SCOOT
SCOOTCH
SCOOTCHED
SCOOTCHES
SCOOTCHING
SCOOTED
SCOOTER
SCOOTERED
SCOOTERING
SCOOTERS
SCOOTING
SCOOTS
SCOP
SCOPA
SCOPAE
SCOPE
SCOPED
SCOPES
SCOPING
SCOPOLAMINE
SCOPOLAMINES
SCOPS
SCOPULA
SCOPULAE
SCOPULAS
SCOPULATE
SCORBUTIC
SCORCH
SCORCHED
SCORCHER
SCORCHERS
SCORCHES
SCORCHING
SCORCHINGLY
SCORE
SCOREBOARD
SCOREBOARDS
SCORECARD
SCORECARDS
SCORED
SCOREKEEPER
SCOREKEEPERS
SCORELESS
SCORELINE
SCORELINES
SCOREPAD
SCOREPADS
SCORER
SCORERS
SCORES
SCORESHEET
SCORESHEETS
SCORIA
SCORIACEOUS
SCORIAE
SCORIFIED
SCORIFIER
SCORIFIERS
SCORIFIES
SCORIFY
SCORIFYING
SCORING
SCORINGS
SCORN
SCORNED
SCORNER
SCORNERS
SCORNFUL
SCORNFULLY
SCORNFULNESS
SCORNFULNESSES
SCORNING
SCORNS
SCORPAENID
SCORPAENIDS
SCORPIOID
SCORPION
SCORPIONS
SCOT
SCOTCH
SCOTCHED
SCOTCHES
SCOTCHING
SCOTER
SCOTERS
SCOTIA
SCOTIAS
SCOTOMA
SCOTOMAS
SCOTOMATA
SCOTOPHIL
SCOTOPIA
SCOTOPIAS
SCOTOPIC
SCOTS
SCOTTIE
SCOTTIES
SCOUNDREL
SCOUNDRELLY
SCOUNDRELS
SCOUR
SCOURED
SCOURER
SCOURERS
SCOURGE
SCOURGED
SCOURGER
SCOURGERS
SCOURGES
SCOURGING
SCOURGINGS
SCOURING
SCOURINGS
SCOURS
SCOUSE
SCOUSES
SCOUT
SCOUTCRAFT
SCOUTCRAFTS
SCOUTED
SCOUTER
SCOUTERS
SCOUTH
SCOUTHER
SCOUTHERED
SCOUTHERING
SCOUTHERS
SCOUTHS
SCOUTING
SCOUTINGS
SCOUTMASTER
SCOUTMASTERS
SCOUTS
SCOW
SCOWDER
SCOWDERED
SCOWDERING
SCOWDERS
SCOWED
SCOWING
SCOWL
SCOWLED
SCOWLER
SCOWLERS
SCOWLING
SCOWLINGLY
SCOWLS
SCOWS
SCRABBLE
SCRABBLED
SCRABBLER
SCRABBLERS
SCRABBLES
SCRABBLIER
SCRABBLIEST
SCRABBLING
SCRABBLINGS
SCRABBLY
SCRAG
SCRAGGED
SCRAGGIER
SCRAGGIEST
SCRAGGILY
SCRAGGING
SCRAGGLIER
SCRAGGLIEST
SCRAGGLY

CRAGGY
CRAGS
CRAICH
CRAICHED
CRAICHING
CRAICHS
CRAIGH
CRAIGHED
CRAIGHING
CRAIGHS
CRAM
CRAMBLE
CRAMBLED
CRAMBLER
CRAMBLERS
CRAMBLES
CRAMBLING
CRAMBLINGS
CRAMJET
CRAMJETS
CRAMMED
CRAMMING
CRAMS
CRAN
CRANNEL
CRANNELS
CRANS
CRAP
CRAPBOOK
CRAPBOOKS
CRAPE
CRAPED
CRAPER
CRAPERS
CRAPES
CRAPHEAP
CRAPHEAPS
CRAPIE
CRAPIES
CRAPING
CRAPINGS
CRAPPAGE
CRAPPAGES
CRAPPED
CRAPPER
CRAPPERS
CRAPPIER
CRAPPIEST
CRAPPILY
CRAPPINESS
CRAPPINESSES
CRAPPING
CRAPPINGS
SCRAPPLE
SCRAPPLES
SCRAPPY
SCRAPS
SCRAPYARD
SCRAPYARDS
SCRATCH
SCRATCHBOARD
SCRATCHBOARDS
SCRATCHED
SCRATCHER
SCRATCHERS
SCRATCHES
SCRATCHIER
SCRATCHIEST
SCRATCHILY
SCRATCHINESS
SCRATCHINESSES
SCRATCHING
SCRATCHINGS
SCRATCHY
SCRAVEL
SCRAVELED
SCRAVELING
SCRAVELLED
SCRAVELLING
SCRAVELS
SCRAWB
SCRAWBED
SCRAWBING
SCRAWBS
SCRAWL
SCRAWLED
SCRAWLER
SCRAWLERS
SCRAWLIER
SCRAWLIEST
SCRAWLING
SCRAWLINGS
SCRAWLS
SCRAWLY
SCRAWNIER
SCRAWNIEST
SCRAWNINESS
SCRAWNINESSES
SCRAWNY
SCREAK
SCREAKED
SCREAKING
SCREAKS
SCREAKY
SCREAM
SCREAMED
SCREAMER
SCREAMERS
SCREAMING
SCREAMINGLY
SCREAMINGS
SCREAMS
SCREE
SCREECH
SCREECHED
SCREECHER
SCREECHERS
SCREECHES
SCREECHIER
SCREECHIEST
SCREECHING
SCREECHY
SCREED
SCREEDED
SCREEDING
SCREEDS
SCREEN
SCREENABLE
SCREENED
SCREENER
SCREENERS
SCREENFUL
SCREENFULS
SCREENING
SCREENINGS
SCREENLAND
SCREENLANDS
SCREENPLAY
SCREENPLAYS
SCREENS
SCREENSHOT
SCREENSHOTS
SCREENWRITER
SCREENWRITERS
SCREES
SCREW
SCREWABLE
SCREWBALL
SCREWBALLS
SCREWBEAN
SCREWBEANS
SCREWDRIVER
SCREWDRIVERS
SCREWED
SCREWER
SCREWERS
SCREWIER
SCREWIEST
SCREWINESS
SCREWINESSES
SCREWING
SCREWLIKE
SCREWS
SCREWUP
SCREWUPS
SCREWWORM
SCREWWORMS
SCREWY
SCRIBAL
SCRIBBLE
SCRIBBLED
SCRIBBLER
SCRIBBLERS
SCRIBBLES
SCRIBBLING
SCRIBBLINGS
SCRIBBLY
SCRIBE
SCRIBED
SCRIBER
SCRIBERS
SCRIBES
SCRIBING
SCRIED
SCRIES
SCRIEVE
SCRIEVED
SCRIEVES
SCRIEVING
SCRIM
SCRIMMAGE
SCRIMMAGED
SCRIMMAGER
SCRIMMAGERS
SCRIMMAGES
SCRIMMAGING
SCRIMP
SCRIMPED
SCRIMPER
SCRIMPERS
SCRIMPIER
SCRIMPIEST
SCRIMPILY
SCRIMPING
SCRIMPINGS
SCRIMPIT
SCRIMPS
SCRIMPY
SCRIMS
SCRIMSHANDER
SCRIMSHANDERS
SCRIMSHAW
SCRIMSHAWED
SCRIMSHAWING
SCRIMSHAWS
SCRIP
SCRIPS
SCRIPT
SCRIPTED
SCRIPTER
SCRIPTERS
SCRIPTING
SCRIPTORIA
SCRIPTORIUM
SCRIPTORIUMS
SCRIPTS
SCRIPTURAL
SCRIPTURALLY
SCRIPTURE
SCRIPTURES
SCRIPTWRITER
SCRIPTWRITERS
SCRITCH
SCRITCHES
SCRIVE
SCRIVED
SCRIVENER
SCRIVENERS
SCRIVES
SCRIVING
SCROB
SCROBBED
SCROBBING
SCROBS
SCROD
SCRODS
SCROFULA
SCROFULAS
SCROFULOUS
SCROGGIER
SCROGGIEST
SCROGGY
SCROLL
SCROLLED
SCROLLER
SCROLLERS
SCROLLING
SCROLLINGS
SCROLLS
SCROLLWORK
SCROLLWORKS
SCROOCH
SCROOCHED
SCROOCHES
SCROOCHING

SCROOGE
SCROOGES
SCROOP
SCROOPED
SCROOPING
SCROOPS
SCROOTCH
SCROOTCHED
SCROOTCHES
SCROOTCHING
SCROTA
SCROTAL
SCROTUM
SCROTUMS
SCROUGE
SCROUGED
SCROUGES
SCROUGING
SCROUNGE
SCROUNGED
SCROUNGER
SCROUNGERS
SCROUNGES
SCROUNGIER
SCROUNGIEST
SCROUNGING
SCROUNGINGS
SCROUNGY
SCRUB
SCRUBBABLE
SCRUBBED
SCRUBBER
SCRUBBERS
SCRUBBIER
SCRUBBIEST
SCRUBBILY
SCRUBBING
SCRUBBINGS
SCRUBBY
SCRUBLAND
SCRUBLANDS
SCRUBS
SCRUBWOMAN
SCRUBWOMEN
SCRUFF
SCRUFFED
SCRUFFIER
SCRUFFIEST
SCRUFFILY
SCRUFFINESS
SCRUFFINESSES
SCRUFFING
SCRUFFS
SCRUFFY
SCRUM
SCRUMMAGE
SCRUMMAGED
SCRUMMAGES
SCRUMMAGING
SCRUMMED
SCRUMMIER
SCRUMMIEST
SCRUMMING
SCRUMMY
SCRUMPIES
SCRUMPLE
SCRUMPLED
SCRUMPLES
SCRUMPLING
SCRUMPTIOUS
SCRUMPTIOUSLY
SCRUMPY
SCRUMS
SCRUNCH
SCRUNCHED
SCRUNCHES
SCRUNCHIE
SCRUNCHIES
SCRUNCHING
SCRUNCHINGS
SCRUNCHY
SCRUPLE
SCRUPLED
SCRUPLES
SCRUPLING
SCRUPULOSITIES
SCRUPULOSITY
SCRUPULOUS
SCRUPULOUSLY
SCRUPULOUSNESS
SCRUTABLE
SCRUTINEER
SCRUTINEERS
SCRUTINIES
SCRUTINISE
SCRUTINISED
SCRUTINISER
SCRUTINISERS
SCRUTINISES
SCRUTINISING
SCRUTINIZE
SCRUTINIZED
SCRUTINIZER
SCRUTINIZERS
SCRUTINIZES
SCRUTINIZING
SCRUTINY
SCRY
SCRYER
SCRYERS
SCRYING
SCUBA
SCUBAED
SCUBAING
SCUBAS
SCUD
SCUDDED
SCUDDING
SCUDI
SCUDO
SCUDS
SCUFF
SCUFFED
SCUFFER
SCUFFERS
SCUFFING
SCUFFLE
SCUFFLED
SCUFFLER
SCUFFLERS
SCUFFLES
SCUFFLING
SCUFFLINGS
SCUFFS
SCULCH
SCULCHES
SCULK
SCULKED
SCULKER
SCULKERS
SCULKING
SCULKS
SCULL
SCULLED
SCULLER
SCULLERIES
SCULLERS
SCULLERY
SCULLING
SCULLION
SCULLIONS
SCULLS
SCULP
SCULPED
SCULPIN
SCULPING
SCULPINS
SCULPS
SCULPT
SCULPTED
SCULPTING
SCULPTOR
SCULPTORS
SCULPTRESS
SCULPTRESSES
SCULPTS
SCULPTURAL
SCULPTURALLY
SCULPTURE
SCULPTURED
SCULPTURES
SCULPTURESQUE
SCULPTURESQUELY
SCULPTURING
SCULTCH
SCULTCHES
SCUM
SCUMBAG
SCUMBAGS
SCUMBALL
SCUMBALLS
SCUMBLE
SCUMBLED
SCUMBLES
SCUMBLING
SCUMLESS
SCUMLIKE
SCUMMED
SCUMMER
SCUMMERS
SCUMMIER
SCUMMIEST
SCUMMILY
SCUMMING
SCUMMY
SCUMS
SCUNCHEON
SCUNCHEONS
SCUNGILE
SCUNGILI
SCUNGILLI
SCUNGILLIS
SCUNNER
SCUNNERED
SCUNNERING
SCUNNERS
SCUP
SCUPPAUG
SCUPPAUGS
SCUPPER
SCUPPERED
SCUPPERING
SCUPPERNONG
SCUPPERNONGS
SCUPPERS
SCUPS
SCURF
SCURFIER
SCURFIEST
SCURFS
SCURFY
SCURRIED
SCURRIES
SCURRIL
SCURRILE
SCURRILITIES
SCURRILITY
SCURRILOUS
SCURRILOUSLY
SCURRILOUSNESS
SCURRY
SCURRYING
SCURVIER
SCURVIES
SCURVIEST
SCURVILY
SCURVINESS
SCURVINESSES
SCURVY
SCUT
SCUTA
SCUTAGE
SCUTAGES
SCUTATE
SCUTCH
SCUTCHED
SCUTCHEON
SCUTCHEONS
SCUTCHER
SCUTCHERS
SCUTCHES
SCUTCHING
SCUTE
SCUTELLA
SCUTELLAR
SCUTELLATE
SCUTELLATED
SCUTELLUM
SCUTES
SCUTIFORM
SCUTS
SCUTTER
SCUTTERED
SCUTTERING
SCUTTERS

CUTTLE
CUTTLEBUTT
CUTTLEBUTTS
CUTTLED
CUTTLES
CUTTLING
CUTTLINGS
CUTUM
CUTWORK
CUTWORKS
CUZZ
CUZZBAG
CUZZBAGS
CUZZBALL
CUZZBALLS
CUZZES
CUZZIER
CUZZIEST
CUZZY
CYPHATE
CYPHI
CYPHISTOMA
CYPHISTOMAE
CYPHISTOMAS
CYPHOZOAN
CYPHOZOANS
CYPHUS
CYTHE
CYTHED
CYTHES
CYTHING
EA
EABAG
EABAGS
EABEACH
EABEACHES
EABED
EABEDS
EABIRD
EABIRDS
EABOARD
EABOARDS
EABOOT
EABOOTS
EABORGIUM
EABORGIUMS
EABORNE
EACOAST
EACOASTS
EACOCK
EACOCKS
EACRAFT
EACRAFTS
SEADOG
SEADOGS
SEADROME
SEADROMES
SEAFARER
SEAFARERS
SEAFARING
SEAFARINGS
SEAFLOOR
SEAFLOORS
SEAFOAM
SEAFOAMS
SEAFOOD
SEAFOODS
SEAFOWL
SEAFOWLS
SEAFRONT
SEAFRONTS
SEAGIRT
SEAGOING
SEAGRASS
SEAGRASSES
SEAGULL
SEAGULLS
SEAHORSE
SEAHORSES
SEAKALE
SEAKALES
SEAL
SEALABLE
SEALANT
SEALANTS
SEALED
SEALER
SEALERIES
SEALERS
SEALERY
SEALIFT
SEALIFTED
SEALIFTING
SEALIFTS
SEALING
SEALINGS
SEALLIKE
SEALS
SEALSKIN
SEALSKINS
SEAM
SEAMAN
SEAMANLIKE
SEAMANLY
SEAMANSHIP
SEAMANSHIPS
SEAMARK
SEAMARKS
SEAMED
SEAMEN
SEAMER
SEAMERS
SEAMIER
SEAMIEST
SEAMINESS
SEAMINESSES
SEAMING
SEAMLESS
SEAMLESSLY
SEAMLESSNESS
SEAMLESSNESSES
SEAMLIKE
SEAMOUNT
SEAMOUNTS
SEAMS
SEAMSTER
SEAMSTERS
SEAMSTRESS
SEAMSTRESSES
SEAMY
SEANCE
SEANCES
SEAPIECE
SEAPIECES
SEAPLANE
SEAPLANES
SEAPORT
SEAPORTS
SEAQUAKE
SEAQUAKES
SEAR
SEARCH
SEARCHABLE
SEARCHED
SEARCHER
SEARCHERS
SEARCHES
SEARCHING
SEARCHINGLY
SEARCHINGS
SEARCHLESS
SEARCHLIGHT
SEARCHLIGHTS
SEARED
SEARER
SEAREST
SEARING
SEARINGLY
SEAROBIN
SEAROBINS
SEARS
SEAS
SEASCAPE
SEASCAPES
SEASCOUT
SEASCOUTS
SEASHELL
SEASHELLS
SEASHORE
SEASHORES
SEASICK
SEASICKNESS
SEASICKNESSES
SEASIDE
SEASIDES
SEASON
SEASONABLE
SEASONABLENESS
SEASONABLY
SEASONAL
SEASONALITIES
SEASONALITY
SEASONALLY
SEASONALS
SEASONED
SEASONER
SEASONERS
SEASONING
SEASONINGS
SEASONLESS
SEASONS
SEASTRAND
SEASTRANDS
SEAT
SEATBACK
SEATBACKS
SEATBELT
SEATBELTS
SEATED
SEATER
SEATERS
SEATING
SEATINGS
SEATLESS
SEATMATE
SEATMATES
SEATRAIN
SEATRAINS
SEATROUT
SEATROUTS
SEATS
SEATWORK
SEATWORKS
SEAWALL
SEAWALLS
SEAWAN
SEAWANS
SEAWANT
SEAWANTS
SEAWARD
SEAWARDS
SEAWARE
SEAWARES
SEAWATER
SEAWATERS
SEAWAY
SEAWAYS
SEAWEED
SEAWEEDIER
SEAWEEDIEST
SEAWEEDS
SEAWEEDY
SEAWORTHIER
SEAWORTHIEST
SEAWORTHINESS
SEAWORTHINESSES
SEAWORTHY
SEBACEOUS
SEBACIC
SEBASIC
SEBORRHEA
SEBORRHEAS
SEBORRHEIC
SEBUM
SEBUMS
SEC
SECALOSE
SECALOSES
SECANT
SECANTLY
SECANTS
SECATEUR
SECATEURS
SECCO
SECCOS
SECEDE
SECEDED
SECEDER
SECEDERS
SECEDES
SECEDING
SECERN
SECERNED
SECERNING
SECERNS

SECESSION
SECESSIONISM
SECESSIONISMS
SECESSIONIST
SECESSIONISTS
SECESSIONS
SECLUDE
SECLUDED
SECLUDEDLY
SECLUDEDNESS
SECLUDEDNESSES
SECLUDES
SECLUDING
SECLUSION
SECLUSIONS
SECLUSIVE
SECLUSIVELY
SECLUSIVENESS
SECLUSIVENESSES
SECOBARBITAL
SECOBARBITALS
SECONAL
SECONALS
SECOND
SECONDARIES
SECONDARILY
SECONDARINESS
SECONDARINESSES
SECONDARY
SECONDE
SECONDED
SECONDEE
SECONDEES
SECONDER
SECONDERS
SECONDES
SECONDHAND
SECONDI
SECONDING
SECONDINGS
SECONDLY
SECONDMENT
SECONDMENTS
SECONDO
SECONDS
SECPAR
SECPARS
SECRECIES
SECRECY
SECRET
SECRETAGOGUE
SECRETAGOGUES
SECRETARIAL
SECRETARIAT
SECRETARIATS
SECRETARIES
SECRETARY
SECRETARYSHIP
SECRETARYSHIPS
SECRETE
SECRETED
SECRETER
SECRETES
SECRETEST
SECRETIN
SECRETING
SECRETINS
SECRETION
SECRETIONARY
SECRETIONS
SECRETIVE
SECRETIVELY
SECRETIVENESS
SECRETIVENESSES
SECRETLY
SECRETOR
SECRETORIES
SECRETORS
SECRETORY
SECRETS
SECS
SECT
SECTARIAN
SECTARIANISM
SECTARIANISMS
SECTARIANIZE
SECTARIANIZED
SECTARIANIZES
SECTARIANIZING
SECTARIANS
SECTARIES
SECTARY
SECTILE
SECTILITIES
SECTILITY
SECTION
SECTIONAL
SECTIONALISM
SECTIONALISMS
SECTIONALLY
SECTIONALS
SECTIONED
SECTIONING
SECTIONS
SECTOR
SECTORAL
SECTORED
SECTORIAL
SECTORIALS
SECTORING
SECTORS
SECTS
SECULAR
SECULARISATION
SECULARISATIONS
SECULARISE
SECULARISED
SECULARISES
SECULARISING
SECULARISM
SECULARISMS
SECULARIST
SECULARISTIC
SECULARISTS
SECULARITIES
SECULARITY
SECULARIZATION
SECULARIZATIONS
SECULARIZE
SECULARIZED
SECULARIZER
SECULARIZERS
SECULARIZES
SECULARIZING
SECULARLY
SECULARS
SECUND
SECUNDLY
SECUNDUM
SECURABLE
SECURANCE
SECURANCES
SECURE
SECURED
SECURELY
SECUREMENT
SECUREMENTS
SECURENESS
SECURENESSES
SECURER
SECURERS
SECURES
SECUREST
SECURING
SECURITIES
SECURITIZATION
SECURITIZATIONS
SECURITIZE
SECURITIZED
SECURITIZES
SECURITIZING
SECURITY
SEDAN
SEDANS
SEDARIM
SEDATE
SEDATED
SEDATELY
SEDATENESS
SEDATENESSES
SEDATER
SEDATES
SEDATEST
SEDATING
SEDATION
SEDATIONS
SEDATIVE
SEDATIVES
SEDENTARY
SEDER
SEDERS
SEDERUNT
SEDERUNTS
SEDGE
SEDGES
SEDGIER
SEDGIEST
SEDGY
SEDILE
SEDILIA
SEDILIUM
SEDIMENT
SEDIMENTABLE
SEDIMENTARY
SEDIMENTATION
SEDIMENTATIONS
SEDIMENTED
SEDIMENTING
SEDIMENTOLOGIC
SEDIMENTOLOGIES
SEDIMENTOLOGIST
SEDIMENTOLOGY
SEDIMENTS
SEDITION
SEDITIONS
SEDITIOUS
SEDITIOUSLY
SEDITIOUSNESS
SEDITIOUSNESSES
SEDUCE
SEDUCED
SEDUCEMENT
SEDUCEMENTS
SEDUCER
SEDUCERS
SEDUCES
SEDUCIBLE
SEDUCING
SEDUCIVE
SEDUCTION
SEDUCTIONS
SEDUCTIVE
SEDUCTIVELY
SEDUCTIVENESS
SEDUCTIVENESSES
SEDUCTRESS
SEDUCTRESSES
SEDULITIES
SEDULITY
SEDULOUS
SEDULOUSLY
SEDULOUSNESS
SEDULOUSNESSES
SEDUM
SEDUMS
SEE
SEEABLE
SEECATCH
SEECATCHIE
SEED
SEEDBED
SEEDBEDS
SEEDCAKE
SEEDCAKES
SEEDCASE
SEEDCASES
SEEDEATER
SEEDEATERS
SEEDED
SEEDER
SEEDERS
SEEDIER
SEEDIEST
SEEDILY
SEEDINESS
SEEDINESSES
SEEDING
SEEDLESS
SEEDLIKE
SEEDLING
SEEDLINGS
SEEDMAN
SEEDMEN
SEEDPOD
SEEDPODS

EEDS
EEDSMAN
EEDSMEN
EEDSTOCK
EEDSTOCKS
EEDTIME
EEDTIMES
EEDY
EEING
EEINGS
EEK
EEKER
EEKERS
EEKING
EEKS
EEL
EELED
EELING
EELS
EELY
EEM
EEMED
EEMER
EEMERS
EEMING
EEMINGLY
EEMINGS
EEMLIER
EEMLIEST
EEMLINESS
EEMLINESSES
EEMLY
EEMS
EEN
EEP
EEPAGE
EEPAGES
EEPED
EEPIER
EEPIEST
EEPING
EEPS
EEPY
EER
ERESS
ERESSES
ERS
ERSUCKER
ERSUCKERS
ES
ESAW
ESAWED
ESAWING
SEESAWS
SEETHE
SEETHED
SEETHES
SEETHING
SEG
SEGETAL
SEGGAR
SEGGARS
SEGMENT
SEGMENTAL
SEGMENTALLY
SEGMENTARY
SEGMENTATION
SEGMENTATIONS
SEGMENTED
SEGMENTING
SEGMENTS
SEGNI
SEGNO
SEGNOS
SEGO
SEGOS
SEGREGANT
SEGREGANTS
SEGREGATE
SEGREGATED
SEGREGATES
SEGREGATING
SEGREGATION
SEGREGATIONIST
SEGREGATIONISTS
SEGREGATIONS
SEGREGATIVE
SEGS
SEGUE
SEGUED
SEGUEING
SEGUES
SEGUIDILLA
SEGUIDILLAS
SEI
SEICENTO
SEICENTOS
SEICHE
SEICHES
SEIDEL
SEIDELS
SEIF
SEIFS
SEIGNEUR
SEIGNEURIAL
SEIGNEURIES
SEIGNEURS
SEIGNEURY
SEIGNIOR
SEIGNIORAGE
SEIGNIORAGES
SEIGNIORIES
SEIGNIORS
SEIGNIORY
SEIGNORAGE
SEIGNORAGES
SEIGNORIAL
SEIGNORIES
SEIGNORY
SEINE
SEINED
SEINER
SEINERS
SEINES
SEINING
SEININGS
SEIS
SEISABLE
SEISE
SEISED
SEISER
SEISERS
SEISES
SEISIN
SEISING
SEISINGS
SEISINS
SEISM
SEISMAL
SEISMIC
SEISMICAL
SEISMICALLY
SEISMICITIES
SEISMICITY
SEISMISM
SEISMISMS
SEISMOGRAM
SEISMOGRAMS
SEISMOGRAPH
SEISMOGRAPHER
SEISMOGRAPHERS
SEISMOGRAPHIC
SEISMOGRAPHIES
SEISMOGRAPHS
SEISMOGRAPHY
SEISMOLOGIC
SEISMOLOGICAL
SEISMOLOGIES
SEISMOLOGIST
SEISMOLOGISTS
SEISMOLOGY
SEISMOMETER
SEISMOMETERS
SEISMOMETRIC
SEISMOMETRIES
SEISMOMETRY
SEISMS
SEISOR
SEISORS
SEISURE
SEISURES
SEITAN
SEITANS
SEIZA
SEIZABLE
SEIZAS
SEIZE
SEIZED
SEIZER
SEIZERS
SEIZES
SEIZIN
SEIZING
SEIZINGS
SEIZINS
SEIZOR
SEIZORS
SEIZURE
SEIZURES
SEJANT
SEJEANT
SEL
SELACHIAN
SELACHIANS
SELADANG
SELADANGS
SELAGINELLA
SELAGINELLAS
SELAH
SELAHS
SELAMLIK
SELAMLIKS
SELCOUTH
SELDOM
SELDOMLY
SELECT
SELECTABLE
SELECTED
SELECTEE
SELECTEES
SELECTING
SELECTION
SELECTIONIST
SELECTIONISTS
SELECTIONS
SELECTIVE
SELECTIVELY
SELECTIVENESS
SELECTIVENESSES
SELECTIVITIES
SELECTIVITY
SELECTLY
SELECTMAN
SELECTMEN
SELECTNESS
SELECTNESSES
SELECTOR
SELECTORS
SELECTS
SELENATE
SELENATES
SELENIC
SELENIDE
SELENIDES
SELENIFEROUS
SELENIOUS
SELENITE
SELENITES
SELENITIC
SELENIUM
SELENIUMS
SELENOCENTRIC
SELENOLOGICAL
SELENOLOGIES
SELENOLOGIST
SELENOLOGISTS
SELENOLOGY
SELENOSES
SELENOSIS
SELENOUS
SELF
SELFDOM
SELFDOMS
SELFED
SELFHEAL
SELFHEALS
SELFHOOD
SELFHOODS
SELFIE
SELFIES
SELFING
SELFISH
SELFISHLY
SELFISHNESS
SELFISHNESSES

SELFLESS
SELFLESSLY
SELFLESSNESS
SELFLESSNESSES
SELFNESS
SELFNESSES
SELFS
SELFSAME
SELFSAMENESS
SELFSAMENESSES
SELFWARD
SELFWARDS
SELKIE
SELKIES
SELL
SELLABLE
SELLE
SELLER
SELLERS
SELLES
SELLING
SELLOFF
SELLOFFS
SELLOTAPE
SELLOTAPED
SELLOTAPES
SELLOTAPING
SELLOUT
SELLOUTS
SELLS
SELS
SELSYN
SELSYNS
SELTZER
SELTZERS
SELVA
SELVAGE
SELVAGED
SELVAGES
SELVAS
SELVEDGE
SELVEDGED
SELVEDGES
SELVES
SEMAINIER
SEMAINIERS
SEMANTEME
SEMANTEMES
SEMANTIC
SEMANTICAL
SEMANTICALLY
SEMANTICIST
SEMANTICISTS
SEMANTICS
SEMAPHORE
SEMAPHORED
SEMAPHORES
SEMAPHORING
SEMASIOLOGICAL
SEMASIOLOGIES
SEMASIOLOGY
SEMATIC
SEMBLABLE
SEMBLABLES
SEMBLABLY
SEMBLANCE
SEMBLANCES
SEME
SEMEE
SEMEIOLOGIES
SEMEIOLOGY
SEMEIOTIC
SEMEIOTICS
SEMELPAROUS
SEMEME
SEMEMES
SEMEMIC
SEMEN
SEMENS
SEMES
SEMESTER
SEMESTERED
SEMESTERING
SEMESTERINGS
SEMESTERS
SEMESTRAL
SEMESTRIAL
SEMI
SEMIABSTRACT
SEMIABSTRACTION
SEMIABSTRACTS
SEMIANGLE
SEMIANGLES
SEMIANNUAL
SEMIANNUALLY
SEMIAQUATIC
SEMIARBOREAL
SEMIARID
SEMIARIDITIES
SEMIARIDITY
SEMIAUTOMATIC
SEMIAUTOMATICS
SEMIAUTONOMOUS
SEMIBALD
SEMIBOLD
SEMIBREVE
SEMIBREVES
SEMICENTENNIAL
SEMICENTENNIALS
SEMICIRCLE
SEMICIRCLED
SEMICIRCLES
SEMICIRCLING
SEMICIRCULAR
SEMICIVILIZED
SEMICLASSIC
SEMICLASSICAL
SEMICLASSICS
SEMICOLON
SEMICOLONIAL
SEMICOLONIALISM
SEMICOLONIES
SEMICOLONS
SEMICOLONY
SEMICOMA
SEMICOMAS
SEMICOMMERCIAL
SEMICONDUCTING
SEMICONDUCTOR
SEMICONDUCTORS
SEMICONSCIOUS
SEMICRYSTALLINE
SEMICURED
SEMICYLINDRICAL
SEMIDARKNESS
SEMIDARKNESSES
SEMIDEAF
SEMIDEIFIED
SEMIDEIFIES
SEMIDEIFY
SEMIDEIFYING
SEMIDESERT
SEMIDESERTS
SEMIDETACHED
SEMIDIAMETER
SEMIDIAMETERS
SEMIDIURNAL
SEMIDIVINE
SEMIDOCUMENTARY
SEMIDOME
SEMIDOMED
SEMIDOMES
SEMIDOMINANT
SEMIDRY
SEMIDRYING
SEMIDWARF
SEMIDWARFS
SEMIDWARVES
SEMIEMPIRICAL
SEMIERECT
SEMIEVERGREEN
SEMIEVERGREENS
SEMIFEUDAL
SEMIFINAL
SEMIFINALIST
SEMIFINALISTS
SEMIFINALS
SEMIFINISHED
SEMIFIT
SEMIFITTED
SEMIFLEXIBLE
SEMIFLUID
SEMIFLUIDS
SEMIFORMAL
SEMIFORMALS
SEMIGALA
SEMIGLOSS
SEMIGLOSSES
SEMIGROUP
SEMIGROUPS
SEMIHARD
SEMIHIGH
SEMIHOBO
SEMIHOBOES
SEMIHOBOS
SEMILEGENDARY
SEMILETHAL
SEMILETHALS
SEMILIQUID
SEMILIQUIDS
SEMILITERATE
SEMILITERATES
SEMILLON
SEMILLONS
SEMILOG
SEMILOGARITHMIC
SEMILUNAR
SEMILUSTROUS
SEMIMAT
SEMIMATT
SEMIMATTE
SEMIMETAL
SEMIMETALLIC
SEMIMETALS
SEMIMICRO
SEMIMILD
SEMIMOIST
SEMIMONASTIC
SEMIMONTHLIES
SEMIMONTHLY
SEMIMUTE
SEMIMYSTICAL
SEMINA
SEMINAL
SEMINALLY
SEMINAR
SEMINARIAN
SEMINARIANS
SEMINARIES
SEMINARIST
SEMINARISTS
SEMINARS
SEMINARY
SEMINATURAL
SEMINIFEROUS
SEMINOMA
SEMINOMAD
SEMINOMADIC
SEMINOMADS
SEMINOMAS
SEMINOMATA
SEMINUDE
SEMINUDITIES
SEMINUDITY
SEMIOFFICIAL
SEMIOFFICIALLY
SEMIOFFICIALS
SEMIOLOGICAL
SEMIOLOGICALLY
SEMIOLOGIES
SEMIOLOGIST
SEMIOLOGISTS
SEMIOLOGY
SEMIOPAQUE
SEMIOPEN
SEMIOSES
SEMIOSIS
SEMIOTIC
SEMIOTICIAN
SEMIOTICIANS
SEMIOTICIST
SEMIOTICISTS
SEMIOTICS
SEMIOVAL
SEMIPALMATED
SEMIPARASITE
SEMIPARASITES
SEMIPARASITIC
SEMIPERMANENT
SEMIPERMEABLE
SEMIPIOUS
SEMIPOLITICAL
SEMIPOPULAR
SEMIPORCELAIN
SEMIPORCELAINS

EMIPORNOGRAPHY
EMIPOSTAL
EMIPOSTALS
EMIPRECIOUS
EMIPRIVATE
EMIPRO
EMIPROS
EMIPUBLIC
EMIQUAVER
EMIQUAVERS
EMIRAW
EMIRELIGIOUS
EMIRETIRED
EMIRETIREMENT
EMIRETIREMENTS
EMIRIGID
EMIROUND
EMIROUNDS
EMIRURAL
EMIS
EMISACRED
EMISECRET
EMISEDENTARY
EMISES
EMISHRUBBY
EMISKILLED
EMISOFT
MISOLID
MISOLIDS
MISTIFF
MISUBMERSIBLE
MISWEET
MISYNTHETIC
MISYNTHETICS
MITERRESTRIAL
MITIST
MITISTS
MITONAL
MITONALLY
MITONE
MITONES
MITONIC
MITONICALLY
MITRAILER
MITRAILERS
MITRANSLUCENT
MITRANSPARENT
MITROPIC
MITROPICAL
MITROPICS
MITRUCK
MITRUCKS
MIURBAN

SEMIVOWEL
SEMIVOWELS
SEMIWEEKLIES
SEMIWEEKLY
SEMIWILD
SEMIWORKS
SEMIYEARLY
SEMOLINA
SEMOLINAS
SEMPERVIVUM
SEMPERVIVUMS
SEMPITERNAL
SEMPITERNALLY
SEMPITERNITIES
SEMPITERNITY
SEMPLE
SEMPLICE
SEMPRE
SEMPSTRESS
SEMPSTRESSES
SEN
SENARII
SENARIUS
SENARY
SENATE
SENATES
SENATOR
SENATORIAL
SENATORIAN
SENATORS
SENATORSHIP
SENATORSHIPS
SEND
SENDABLE
SENDAL
SENDALS
SENDED
SENDER
SENDERS
SENDING
SENDOFF
SENDOFFS
SENDS
SENDUP
SENDUPS
SENE
SENECA
SENECAS
SENECIO
SENECIOS
SENECTITUDE
SENECTITUDES
SENEGA

SENEGAS
SENES
SENESCE
SENESCED
SENESCENCE
SENESCENCES
SENESCENT
SENESCES
SENESCHAL
SENESCHALS
SENESCING
SENGI
SENHOR
SENHORA
SENHORAS
SENHORES
SENHORITA
SENHORITAS
SENHORS
SENILE
SENILELY
SENILES
SENILITIES
SENILITY
SENIOR
SENIORITIES
SENIORITIS
SENIORITISES
SENIORITY
SENIORS
SENITI
SENITIS
SENNA
SENNACHIE
SENNACHIES
SENNAS
SENNET
SENNETS
SENNIGHT
SENNIGHTS
SENNIT
SENNITS
SENOPIA
SENOPIAS
SENOR
SENORA
SENORAS
SENORES
SENORITA
SENORITAS
SENORS
SENRYU
SENSA

SENSATE
SENSATED
SENSATELY
SENSATES
SENSATING
SENSATION
SENSATIONAL
SENSATIONALISE
SENSATIONALISED
SENSATIONALISES
SENSATIONALISM
SENSATIONALISMS
SENSATIONALIST
SENSATIONALISTS
SENSATIONALIZE
SENSATIONALIZED
SENSATIONALIZES
SENSATIONALLY
SENSATIONS
SENSE
SENSED
SENSEFUL
SENSEI
SENSEIS
SENSELESS
SENSELESSLY
SENSELESSNESS
SENSELESSNESSES
SENSES
SENSIBILIA
SENSIBILITIES
SENSIBILITY
SENSIBLE
SENSIBLENESS
SENSIBLENESSES
SENSIBLER
SENSIBLES
SENSIBLEST
SENSIBLY
SENSILLA
SENSILLAE
SENSILLUM
SENSING
SENSITISATION
SENSITISATIONS
SENSITISE
SENSITISED
SENSITISES
SENSITISING
SENSITIVE
SENSITIVELY
SENSITIVENESS
SENSITIVENESSES

SENSITIVES
SENSITIVITIES
SENSITIVITY
SENSITIZATION
SENSITIZATIONS
SENSITIZE
SENSITIZED
SENSITIZER
SENSITIZERS
SENSITIZES
SENSITIZING
SENSITOMETER
SENSITOMETERS
SENSITOMETRIC
SENSITOMETRIES
SENSITOMETRY
SENSOR
SENSORIA
SENSORIAL
SENSORIALLY
SENSORIMOTOR
SENSORINEURAL
SENSORIUM
SENSORIUMS
SENSORS
SENSORY
SENSUAL
SENSUALISM
SENSUALISMS
SENSUALIST
SENSUALISTIC
SENSUALISTS
SENSUALITIES
SENSUALITY
SENSUALIZATION
SENSUALIZATIONS
SENSUALIZE
SENSUALIZED
SENSUALIZES
SENSUALIZING
SENSUALLY
SENSUM
SENSUOSITIES
SENSUOSITY
SENSUOUS
SENSUOUSLY
SENSUOUSNESS
SENSUOUSNESSES
SENT
SENTE
SENTENCE
SENTENCED
SENTENCER

SENTENCERS
SENTENCES
SENTENCING
SENTENTIA
SENTENTIAE
SENTENTIAL
SENTENTIOUS
SENTENTIOUSLY
SENTENTIOUSNESS
SENTI
SENTIENCE
SENTIENCES
SENTIENCIES
SENTIENCY
SENTIENT
SENTIENTLY
SENTIENTS
SENTIMENT
SENTIMENTAL
SENTIMENTALISE
SENTIMENTALISED
SENTIMENTALISES
SENTIMENTALISM
SENTIMENTALISMS
SENTIMENTALIST
SENTIMENTALISTS
SENTIMENTALITY
SENTIMENTALIZE
SENTIMENTALIZED
SENTIMENTALIZES
SENTIMENTALLY
SENTIMENTS
SENTIMO
SENTIMOS
SENTINEL
SENTINELED
SENTINELING
SENTINELLED
SENTINELLING
SENTINELS
SENTRIES
SENTRY
SENTS
SEPAL
SEPALED
SEPALINE
SEPALLED
SEPALOID
SEPALOUS
SEPALS
SEPARABILITIES
SEPARABILITY
SEPARABLE
SEPARABLENESS
SEPARABLENESSES
SEPARABLY
SEPARATE
SEPARATED
SEPARATELY
SEPARATENESS
SEPARATENESSES
SEPARATES
SEPARATING
SEPARATION
SEPARATIONIST
SEPARATIONISTS
SEPARATIONS
SEPARATISM
SEPARATISMS
SEPARATIST
SEPARATISTIC
SEPARATISTS
SEPARATIVE
SEPARATOR
SEPARATORS
SEPIA
SEPIAS
SEPIC
SEPIOLITE
SEPIOLITES
SEPOY
SEPOYS
SEPPUKU
SEPPUKUS
SEPS
SEPSES
SEPSIS
SEPT
SEPTA
SEPTAGE
SEPTAGES
SEPTAL
SEPTARIA
SEPTARIAN
SEPTARIUM
SEPTATE
SEPTENARIES
SEPTENARII
SEPTENARIUS
SEPTENARY
SEPTENDECILLION
SEPTENNIAL
SEPTENNIALLY
SEPTENTRION
SEPTENTRIONAL
SEPTENTRIONS
SEPTET
SEPTETS
SEPTETTE
SEPTETTES
SEPTIC
SEPTICAEMIA
SEPTICAEMIAS
SEPTICAL
SEPTICEMIA
SEPTICEMIAS
SEPTICEMIC
SEPTICIDAL
SEPTICITIES
SEPTICITY
SEPTICS
SEPTILLION
SEPTILLIONS
SEPTIMAL
SEPTIME
SEPTIMES
SEPTORIA
SEPTORIAS
SEPTS
SEPTUAGENARIAN
SEPTUAGENARIANS
SEPTUM
SEPTUMS
SEPTUPLE
SEPTUPLED
SEPTUPLES
SEPTUPLET
SEPTUPLETS
SEPTUPLING
SEPULCHER
SEPULCHERED
SEPULCHERING
SEPULCHERS
SEPULCHRAL
SEPULCHRALLY
SEPULCHRE
SEPULCHRED
SEPULCHRES
SEPULCHRING
SEPULTURE
SEPULTURES
SEQUACIOUS
SEQUACIOUSLY
SEQUACITIES
SEQUACITY
SEQUEL
SEQUELA
SEQUELAE
SEQUELIZE
SEQUELIZED
SEQUELIZES
SEQUELIZING
SEQUELS
SEQUENCE
SEQUENCED
SEQUENCER
SEQUENCERS
SEQUENCES
SEQUENCIES
SEQUENCING
SEQUENCY
SEQUENT
SEQUENTIAL
SEQUENTIALLY
SEQUENTS
SEQUESTER
SEQUESTERED
SEQUESTERES
SEQUESTERING
SEQUESTERS
SEQUESTRA
SEQUESTRATE
SEQUESTRATED
SEQUESTRATES
SEQUESTRATING
SEQUESTRATION
SEQUESTRATIONS
SEQUESTRATOR
SEQUESTRATORS
SEQUESTRUM
SEQUESTRUMS
SEQUIN
SEQUINED
SEQUINING
SEQUINNED
SEQUINS
SEQUITUR
SEQUITURS
SEQUOIA
SEQUOIAS
SER
SERA
SERAC
SERACS
SERAGLIO
SERAGLIOS
SERAI
SERAIL
SERAILS
SERAIS
SERAL
SERAPE
SERAPES
SERAPH
SERAPHIC
SERAPHICALLY
SERAPHIM
SERAPHIMS
SERAPHIN
SERAPHS
SERDAB
SERDABS
SERE
SERED
SEREIN
SEREINS
SERENADE
SERENADED
SERENADER
SERENADERS
SERENADES
SERENADING
SERENATA
SERENATAS
SERENATE
SERENDIPITIES
SERENDIPITOUS
SERENDIPITOUSLY
SERENDIPITY
SERENE
SERENELY
SERENENESS
SERENENESSES
SERENER
SERENES
SERENEST
SERENITIES
SERENITY
SERER
SERES
SEREST
SERF
SERFAGE
SERFAGES
SERFDOM
SERFDOMS
SERFHOOD
SERFHOODS
SERFISH
SERFLIKE
SERFS
SERGE
SERGEANCIES
SERGEANCY
SERGEANT

ERGEANTIES
ERGEANTS
ERGEANTY
ERGED
ERGER
ERGERS
ERGES
ERGING
ERGINGS
ERIAL
ERIALISATION
ERIALISATIONS
ERIALISE
ERIALISED
ERIALISES
ERIALISING
ERIALISM
ERIALISMS
ERIALIST
RIALISTS
RIALIZATION
RIALIZATIONS
RIALIZE
RIALIZED
RIALIZES
RIALIZING
RIALLY
RIALS
RIATE
RIATED
RIATELY
RIATES
RIATIM
RIATING
RIATION
RIATIONS
RICEOUS
RICIN
RICINS
RICULTURAL
RICULTURE
RICULTURES
RICULTURIST
RICULTURISTS
RIEMA
RIEMAS
RIES
RIF
RIFED
RIFFED
RIFS
RIGRAPH
RIGRAPHER

SERIGRAPHERS
SERIGRAPHIES
SERIGRAPHS
SERIGRAPHY
SERIN
SERINE
SERINES
SERING
SERINGA
SERINGAS
SERINS
SERIOCOMIC
SERIOCOMICALLY
SERIOUS
SERIOUSLY
SERIOUSNESS
SERIOUSNESSES
SERJEANT
SERJEANTIES
SERJEANTS
SERJEANTY
SERMON
SERMONETTE
SERMONETTES
SERMONIC
SERMONISE
SERMONISED
SERMONISER
SERMONISERS
SERMONISES
SERMONISING
SERMONIZE
SERMONIZED
SERMONIZER
SERMONIZERS
SERMONIZES
SERMONIZING
SERMONS
SEROCONVERSION
SEROCONVERSIONS
SEROCONVERT
SEROCONVERTED
SEROCONVERTING
SEROCONVERTS
SERODIAGNOSES
SERODIAGNOSIS
SERODIAGNOSTIC
SEROLOGIC
SEROLOGICAL
SEROLOGICALLY
SEROLOGIES
SEROLOGIST
SEROLOGISTS

SEROLOGY
SERONEGATIVE
SERONEGATIVITY
SEROPOSITIVE
SEROPOSITIVITY
SEROPREVALENCE
SEROPREVALENCES
SEROPURULENT
SEROSA
SEROSAE
SEROSAL
SEROSAS
SEROSITIES
SEROSITY
SEROTINAL
SEROTINE
SEROTINES
SEROTINIES
SEROTINOUS
SEROTINY
SEROTONERGIC
SEROTONIN
SEROTONINERGIC
SEROTONINS
SEROTYPE
SEROTYPED
SEROTYPES
SEROTYPING
SEROUS
SEROVAR
SEROVARS
SEROW
SEROWS
SERPENT
SERPENTINE
SERPENTINELY
SERPENTINES
SERPENTS
SERPIGINES
SERPIGINOUS
SERPIGINOUSLY
SERPIGO
SERPIGOES
SERPIGOS
SERRANID
SERRANIDS
SERRANO
SERRANOID
SERRANOS
SERRATE
SERRATED
SERRATES
SERRATING

SERRATION
SERRATIONS
SERRATURE
SERRATURES
SERRIED
SERRIEDLY
SERRIEDNESS
SERRIEDNESSES
SERRIES
SERRULATE
SERRY
SERRYING
SERS
SERTRALINE
SERTRALINES
SERUM
SERUMAL
SERUMS
SERVABLE
SERVAL
SERVALS
SERVANT
SERVANTHOOD
SERVANTHOODS
SERVANTLESS
SERVANTS
SERVE
SERVED
SERVER
SERVERIES
SERVERS
SERVERY
SERVES
SERVICE
SERVICEABILITY
SERVICEABLE
SERVICEABLENESS
SERVICEABLY
SERVICEBERRIES
SERVICEBERRY
SERVICED
SERVICEMAN
SERVICEMEN
SERVICER
SERVICERS
SERVICES
SERVICEWOMAN
SERVICEWOMEN
SERVICING
SERVIETTE
SERVIETTES
SERVILE
SERVILELY

SERVILENESS
SERVILENESSES
SERVILITIES
SERVILITY
SERVING
SERVINGS
SERVITOR
SERVITORS
SERVITUDE
SERVITUDES
SERVO
SERVOMECHANISM
SERVOMECHANISMS
SERVOMOTOR
SERVOMOTORS
SERVOS
SESAME
SESAMES
SESAMOID
SESAMOIDS
SESH
SESHES
SESQUICARBONATE
SESQUICENTENARY
SESQUIPEDALIAN
SESQUITERPENE
SESQUITERPENES
SESSILE
SESSILITIES
SESSILITY
SESSION
SESSIONAL
SESSIONS
SESSPOOL
SESSPOOLS
SESTERCE
SESTERCES
SESTERTIA
SESTERTIUM
SESTET
SESTETS
SESTINA
SESTINAS
SESTINE
SESTINES
SET
SETA
SETACEOUS
SETAE
SETAL
SETBACK
SETBACKS
SETENANT

SETENANTS
SETIFORM
SETLINE
SETLINES
SETOFF
SETOFFS
SETON
SETONS
SETOSE
SETOUS
SETOUT
SETOUTS
SETS
SETSCREW
SETSCREWS
SETT
SETTEE
SETTEES
SETTER
SETTERS
SETTING
SETTINGS
SETTLE
SETTLEABLE
SETTLED
SETTLEMENT
SETTLEMENTS
SETTLER
SETTLERS
SETTLES
SETTLING
SETTLINGS
SETTLOR
SETTLORS
SETTS
SETULOSE
SETULOUS
SETUP
SETUPS
SEV
SEVEN
SEVENFOLD
SEVENS
SEVENTEEN
SEVENTEENS
SEVENTEENTH
SEVENTEENTHS
SEVENTH
SEVENTHLY
SEVENTHS
SEVENTIES
SEVENTIETH
SEVENTIETHS
SEVENTY
SEVER
SEVERABILITIES
SEVERABILITY
SEVERABLE
SEVERAL
SEVERALFOLD
SEVERALLY
SEVERALS
SEVERALTIES
SEVERALTY
SEVERANCE
SEVERANCES
SEVERE
SEVERED
SEVERELY
SEVERENESS
SEVERENESSES
SEVERER
SEVEREST
SEVERIES
SEVERING
SEVERITIES
SEVERITY
SEVERS
SEVERY
SEVICHE
SEVICHES
SEVRUGA
SEVRUGAS
SEVS
SEW
SEWABILITIES
SEWABILITY
SEWABLE
SEWAGE
SEWAGES
SEWAN
SEWANS
SEWAR
SEWARS
SEWED
SEWER
SEWERAGE
SEWERAGES
SEWERED
SEWERING
SEWERLESS
SEWERLIKE
SEWERS
SEWING
SEWINGS
SEWN
SEWS
SEX
SEXAGENARIAN
SEXAGENARIANS
SEXAGESIMAL
SEXAGESIMALS
SEXDECILLION
SEXDECILLIONS
SEXED
SEXENNIAL
SEXENNIALS
SEXER
SEXERS
SEXES
SEXIER
SEXIEST
SEXILY
SEXINESS
SEXINESSES
SEXING
SEXISM
SEXISMS
SEXIST
SEXISTS
SEXLESS
SEXLESSLY
SEXLESSNESS
SEXLESSNESSES
SEXOLOGIC
SEXOLOGIES
SEXOLOGIST
SEXOLOGISTS
SEXOLOGY
SEXPERT
SEXPERTS
SEXPLOITATION
SEXPLOITATIONS
SEXPOT
SEXPOTS
SEXT
SEXTAIN
SEXTAINS
SEXTAN
SEXTANS
SEXTANT
SEXTANTS
SEXTARII
SEXTARIUS
SEXTET
SEXTETS
SEXTETTE
SEXTETTES
SEXTILE
SEXTILES
SEXTILLION
SEXTILLIONS
SEXTING
SEXTINGS
SEXTO
SEXTODECIMO
SEXTODECIMOS
SEXTON
SEXTONS
SEXTOS
SEXTS
SEXTUPLE
SEXTUPLED
SEXTUPLES
SEXTUPLET
SEXTUPLETS
SEXTUPLICATE
SEXTUPLICATED
SEXTUPLICATES
SEXTUPLICATING
SEXTUPLING
SEXTUPLY
SEXUAL
SEXUALITIES
SEXUALITY
SEXUALIZE
SEXUALIZED
SEXUALIZES
SEXUALIZING
SEXUALLY
SEXY
SEZ
SFERICS
SFORZANDI
SFORZANDO
SFORZANDOS
SFORZATO
SFORZATOS
SFUMATO
SFUMATOS
SGRAFFITI
SGRAFFITO
SH
SHA
SHABBATOT
SHABBIER
SHABBIEST
SHABBILY
SHABBINESS
SHABBINESSES
SHABBY
SHACK
SHACKED
SHACKIER
SHACKIEST
SHACKING
SHACKLE
SHACKLEBONE
SHACKLEBONES
SHACKLED
SHACKLER
SHACKLERS
SHACKLES
SHACKLING
SHACKO
SHACKOES
SHACKOS
SHACKS
SHACKY
SHAD
SHADBERRIES
SHADBERRY
SHADBLOW
SHADBLOWS
SHADBUSH
SHADBUSHES
SHADCHAN
SHADCHANIM
SHADCHANS
SHADDOCK
SHADDOCKS
SHADDUP
SHADE
SHADED
SHADELESS
SHADER
SHADERS
SHADES
SHADFLIES
SHADFLY
SHADIER
SHADIEST
SHADILY
SHADINESS
SHADINESSES
SHADING
SHADINGS
SHADKHAN
SHADKHANIM
SHADKHANS
SHADOOF
SHADOOFS
SHADOW
SHADOWBOX
SHADOWBOXED

HADOWBOXES
HADOWBOXING
HADOWED
HADOWER
HADOWERS
HADOWGRAPH
HADOWGRAPHIES
HADOWGRAPHS
HADOWGRAPHY
HADOWIER
HADOWIEST
HADOWILY
HADOWINESS
HADOWINESSES
HADOWING
HADOWLESS
HADOWLIKE
HADOWS
HADOWY
HADRACH
HADRACHS
ADS
ADUF
ADUFS
ADY
AFT
AFTED
AFTING
AFTINGS
AFTS
AG
AGBARK
AGBARKS
AGGED
AGGER
AGGERS
AGGIER
AGGIEST
AGGILY
AGGINESS
AGGINESSES
AGGING
AGGY
AGGYMANE
AGGYMANES
AGREEN
AGREENS
AGS
AH
AHADA
AHADAH
AHADAHS
AHADAS
SHAHDOM
SHAHDOMS
SHAHEED
SHAHEEDS
SHAHID
SHAHIDS
SHAHS
SHAIKH
SHAIKHS
SHAIRD
SHAIRDS
SHAIRN
SHAIRNS
SHAITAN
SHAITANS
SHAKABLE
SHAKE
SHAKEABLE
SHAKEDOWN
SHAKEDOWNS
SHAKEN
SHAKEOUT
SHAKEOUTS
SHAKER
SHAKERS
SHAKES
SHAKEUP
SHAKEUPS
SHAKIER
SHAKIEST
SHAKILY
SHAKINESS
SHAKINESSES
SHAKING
SHAKO
SHAKOES
SHAKOS
SHAKY
SHALE
SHALED
SHALELIKE
SHALES
SHALEY
SHALIER
SHALIEST
SHALL
SHALLOON
SHALLOONS
SHALLOP
SHALLOPS
SHALLOT
SHALLOTS
SHALLOW
SHALLOWED
SHALLOWER
SHALLOWEST
SHALLOWING
SHALLOWLY
SHALLOWNESS
SHALLOWNESSES
SHALLOWS
SHALOM
SHALOMS
SHALT
SHALWAR
SHALWARS
SHALY
SHAM
SHAMABLE
SHAMABLY
SHAMAL
SHAMALS
SHAMAN
SHAMANIC
SHAMANISM
SHAMANISMS
SHAMANIST
SHAMANISTIC
SHAMANISTS
SHAMANS
SHAMAS
SHAMBA
SHAMBAS
SHAMBLE
SHAMBLED
SHAMBLES
SHAMBLING
SHAMBOLIC
SHAME
SHAMEABLE
SHAMEABLY
SHAMED
SHAMEFACED
SHAMEFACEDLY
SHAMEFACEDNESS
SHAMEFAST
SHAMEFUL
SHAMEFULLY
SHAMEFULNESS
SHAMEFULNESSES
SHAMELESS
SHAMELESSLY
SHAMELESSNESS
SHAMELESSNESSES
SHAMES
SHAMIANA
SHAMIANAS
SHAMING
SHAMISEN
SHAMISENS
SHAMMAS
SHAMMASH
SHAMMASHIM
SHAMMASIM
SHAMMED
SHAMMER
SHAMMERS
SHAMMES
SHAMMIED
SHAMMIES
SHAMMING
SHAMMOS
SHAMMOSIM
SHAMMY
SHAMMYING
SHAMOIS
SHAMOS
SHAMOSIM
SHAMOY
SHAMOYED
SHAMOYING
SHAMOYS
SHAMPOO
SHAMPOOED
SHAMPOOER
SHAMPOOERS
SHAMPOOING
SHAMPOOS
SHAMROCK
SHAMROCKS
SHAMS
SHAMUS
SHAMUSES
SHANACHIE
SHANACHIES
SHANDIES
SHANDY
SHANDYGAFF
SHANDYGAFFS
SHANGHAI
SHANGHAIED
SHANGHAIER
SHANGHAIERS
SHANGHAIING
SHANGHAIS
SHANK
SHANKED
SHANKING
SHANKPIECE
SHANKPIECES
SHANKS
SHANNIES
SHANNY
SHANTEY
SHANTEYS
SHANTI
SHANTIES
SHANTIH
SHANTIHS
SHANTIS
SHANTUNG
SHANTUNGS
SHANTY
SHANTYMAN
SHANTYMEN
SHANTYTOWN
SHANTYTOWNS
SHAPABLE
SHAPE
SHAPEABLE
SHAPED
SHAPELESS
SHAPELESSLY
SHAPELESSNESS
SHAPELESSNESSES
SHAPELIER
SHAPELIEST
SHAPELINESS
SHAPELINESSES
SHAPELY
SHAPEN
SHAPER
SHAPERS
SHAPES
SHAPEUP
SHAPEUPS
SHAPEWEAR
SHAPING
SHARABLE
SHARD
SHARDS
SHARE
SHAREABILITIES
SHAREABILITY
SHAREABLE
SHARECROP
SHARECROPPED
SHARECROPPER
SHARECROPPERS
SHARECROPPING
SHARECROPS
SHARED

SHAREHOLDER
SHAREHOLDERS
SHAREHOLDING
SHAREHOLDINGS
SHARER
SHARERS
SHARES
SHAREWARE
SHAREWARES
SHARIA
SHARIAH
SHARIAHS
SHARIAS
SHARIAT
SHARIATS
SHARIF
SHARIFIAN
SHARIFS
SHARING
SHARK
SHARKED
SHARKER
SHARKERS
SHARKING
SHARKISH
SHARKLIKE
SHARKS
SHARKSKIN
SHARKSKINS
SHARN
SHARNS
SHARNY
SHARP
SHARPED
SHARPEN
SHARPENED
SHARPENER
SHARPENERS
SHARPENING
SHARPENS
SHARPER
SHARPERS
SHARPEST
SHARPIE
SHARPIES
SHARPING
SHARPISH
SHARPLY
SHARPNESS
SHARPNESSES
SHARPS
SHARPSHOOTER
SHARPSHOOTERS
SHARPSHOOTING
SHARPSHOOTINGS
SHARPY
SHASHLICK
SHASHLICKS
SHASHLIK
SHASHLIKS
SHASLIK
SHASLIKS
SHASTA
SHASTAS
SHAT
SHATOOSH
SHATOOSHES
SHATTER
SHATTERED
SHATTERER
SHATTERERS
SHATTERING
SHATTERINGLY
SHATTERPROOF
SHATTERS
SHAUGH
SHAUGHS
SHAUL
SHAULED
SHAULING
SHAULS
SHAVABLE
SHAVE
SHAVED
SHAVELING
SHAVELINGS
SHAVEN
SHAVER
SHAVERS
SHAVES
SHAVETAIL
SHAVETAILS
SHAVIE
SHAVIES
SHAVING
SHAVINGS
SHAW
SHAWARMA
SHAWARMAS
SHAWED
SHAWING
SHAWL
SHAWLED
SHAWLING
SHAWLS
SHAWM
SHAWMS
SHAWN
SHAWS
SHAY
SHAYKH
SHAYKHS
SHAYS
SHAZAM
SHE
SHEA
SHEAF
SHEAFED
SHEAFING
SHEAFLIKE
SHEAFS
SHEAL
SHEALING
SHEALINGS
SHEALS
SHEAR
SHEARED
SHEARER
SHEARERS
SHEARING
SHEARINGS
SHEARLEGS
SHEARLING
SHEARLINGS
SHEARS
SHEARWATER
SHEARWATERS
SHEAS
SHEATFISH
SHEATFISHES
SHEATH
SHEATHBILL
SHEATHBILLS
SHEATHE
SHEATHED
SHEATHER
SHEATHERS
SHEATHES
SHEATHING
SHEATHINGS
SHEATHS
SHEAVE
SHEAVED
SHEAVES
SHEAVING
SHEBANG
SHEBANGS
SHEBEAN
SHEBEANS
SHEBEEN
SHEBEENS
SHED
SHEDABLE
SHEDDABLE
SHEDDED
SHEDDER
SHEDDERS
SHEDDING
SHEDLIKE
SHEDS
SHEEN
SHEENED
SHEENEY
SHEENEYS
SHEENFUL
SHEENIE
SHEENIER
SHEENIES
SHEENIEST
SHEENING
SHEENS
SHEENY
SHEEP
SHEEPBERRIES
SHEEPBERRY
SHEEPCOT
SHEEPCOTE
SHEEPCOTES
SHEEPCOTS
SHEEPDOG
SHEEPDOGS
SHEEPFOLD
SHEEPFOLDS
SHEEPHEAD
SHEEPHEADS
SHEEPHERDER
SHEEPHERDERS
SHEEPHERDING
SHEEPHERDINGS
SHEEPISH
SHEEPISHLY
SHEEPISHNESS
SHEEPISHNESSES
SHEEPMAN
SHEEPMEN
SHEEPSHANK
SHEEPSHANKS
SHEEPSHEAD
SHEEPSHEADS
SHEEPSHEARER
SHEEPSHEARERS
SHEEPSHEARING
SHEEPSHEARINGS
SHEEPSKIN
SHEEPSKINS
SHEEPWALK
SHEEPWALKS
SHEER
SHEERED
SHEERER
SHEEREST
SHEERING
SHEERLEGS
SHEERLY
SHEERNESS
SHEERNESSES
SHEERS
SHEESH
SHEET
SHEETED
SHEETER
SHEETERS
SHEETFED
SHEETING
SHEETINGS
SHEETLESS
SHEETLIKE
SHEETROCK
SHEETROCKED
SHEETROCKING
SHEETROCKS
SHEETS
SHEEVE
SHEEVES
SHEGETZ
SHEHNAI
SHEHNAIS
SHEIK
SHEIKDOM
SHEIKDOMS
SHEIKH
SHEIKHDOM
SHEIKHDOMS
SHEIKHS
SHEIKS
SHEILA
SHEILAS
SHEITAN
SHEITANS
SHEITEL
SHEITELS
SHEKALIM
SHEKEL
SHEKELIM
SHEKELS

ELDRAKE
ELDRAKES
ELDUCK
ELDUCKS
ELF
ELFFUL
ELFFULS
ELFLIKE
ELL
ELLAC
ELLACK
ELLACKED
ELLACKING
ELLACKINGS
ELLACKS
ELLACS
ELLBACK
ELLBACKS
ELLBARK
ELLBARKS
ELLCRACKER
ELLCRACKERS
ELLED
ELLER
ELLERS
ELLFIRE
ELLFIRES
ELLFISH
ELLFISHERIES
ELLFISHERY
ELLFISHES
ELLIER
ELLIEST
ELLING
ELLPROOF
ELLS
ELLWORK
ELLWORKS
ELLY
LTA
LTAS
LTER
LTERBELT
LTERBELTS
LTERED
LTERER
LTERERS
LTERING
LTERLESS
LTERS
LTIE
LTIES
LTY
SHELVE
SHELVED
SHELVER
SHELVERS
SHELVES
SHELVIER
SHELVIEST
SHELVING
SHELVINGS
SHELVY
SHEMALE
SHEMALES
SHEN
SHENAI
SHENAIS
SHENANIGAN
SHENANIGANS
SHEND
SHENDING
SHENDS
SHENT
SHEOL
SHEOLS
SHEPHERD
SHEPHERDED
SHEPHERDESS
SHEPHERDESSES
SHEPHERDING
SHEPHERDINGS
SHEPHERDS
SHEQALIM
SHEQEL
SHEQELS
SHERBERT
SHERBERTS
SHERBET
SHERBETS
SHERD
SHERDS
SHEREEF
SHEREEFS
SHERGOTTITE
SHERGOTTITES
SHERIF
SHERIFF
SHERIFFDOM
SHERIFFDOMS
SHERIFFS
SHERIFS
SHERLOCK
SHERLOCKS
SHERO
SHEROES
SHEROOT
SHEROOTS
SHERPA
SHERPAS
SHERRIED
SHERRIES
SHERRIS
SHERRISES
SHERRY
SHERWANI
SHERWANIS
SHES
SHETLAND
SHETLANDS
SHEUCH
SHEUCHS
SHEUGH
SHEUGHS
SHEW
SHEWBREAD
SHEWBREADS
SHEWED
SHEWER
SHEWERS
SHEWING
SHEWN
SHEWS
SHH
SHHH
SHIATSU
SHIATSUS
SHIATZU
SHIATZUS
SHIBAH
SHIBAHS
SHIBBOLETH
SHIBBOLETHS
SHICKER
SHICKERED
SHICKERS
SHICKSA
SHICKSAS
SHIED
SHIEL
SHIELD
SHIELDED
SHIELDER
SHIELDERS
SHIELDING
SHIELDS
SHIELING
SHIELINGS
SHIELS
SHIER
SHIERS
SHIES
SHIEST
SHIFT
SHIFTABLE
SHIFTED
SHIFTER
SHIFTERS
SHIFTIER
SHIFTIEST
SHIFTILY
SHIFTINESS
SHIFTINESSES
SHIFTING
SHIFTINGS
SHIFTLESS
SHIFTLESSLY
SHIFTLESSNESS
SHIFTLESSNESSES
SHIFTS
SHIFTY
SHIGELLA
SHIGELLAE
SHIGELLAS
SHIGELLOSES
SHIGELLOSIS
SHIITAKE
SHIITAKES
SHIKAR
SHIKARA
SHIKARAS
SHIKAREE
SHIKAREES
SHIKARI
SHIKARIS
SHIKARRED
SHIKARRING
SHIKARS
SHIKKER
SHIKKERED
SHIKKERS
SHIKRA
SHIKRAS
SHIKSA
SHIKSAS
SHIKSE
SHIKSEH
SHIKSEHS
SHIKSES
SHILINGI
SHILL
SHILLALA
SHILLALAH
SHILLALAHS
SHILLALAS
SHILLED
SHILLELAGH
SHILLELAGHS
SHILLELAH
SHILLELAHS
SHILLING
SHILLINGS
SHILLS
SHILPIT
SHILY
SHIM
SHIMMED
SHIMMER
SHIMMERED
SHIMMERING
SHIMMERS
SHIMMERY
SHIMMIED
SHIMMIES
SHIMMING
SHIMMY
SHIMMYING
SHIMS
SHIN
SHINBONE
SHINBONES
SHINDIES
SHINDIG
SHINDIGS
SHINDY
SHINDYS
SHINE
SHINED
SHINER
SHINERS
SHINES
SHINGLE
SHINGLED
SHINGLER
SHINGLERS
SHINGLES
SHINGLING
SHINGLY
SHINGUARD
SHINGUARDS
SHINIER
SHINIEST
SHINILY
SHININESS
SHININESSES

SHINING
SHININGLY
SHINLEAF
SHINLEAFS
SHINLEAVES
SHINNED
SHINNERIES
SHINNERY
SHINNEY
SHINNEYED
SHINNEYING
SHINNEYS
SHINNIED
SHINNIES
SHINNING
SHINNY
SHINNYING
SHINOLA
SHINOLAS
SHINPLASTER
SHINPLASTERS
SHINS
SHINSPLINTS
SHINTIES
SHINTY
SHINY
SHIP
SHIPBOARD
SHIPBOARDS
SHIPBORNE
SHIPBUILDER
SHIPBUILDERS
SHIPBUILDING
SHIPBUILDINGS
SHIPFITTER
SHIPFITTERS
SHIPLAP
SHIPLAPPED
SHIPLAPPING
SHIPLAPS
SHIPLESS
SHIPLOAD
SHIPLOADS
SHIPMAN
SHIPMASTER
SHIPMASTERS
SHIPMATE
SHIPMATES
SHIPMEN
SHIPMENT
SHIPMENTS
SHIPOWNER
SHIPOWNERS
SHIPPABLE
SHIPPED
SHIPPEN
SHIPPENS
SHIPPER
SHIPPERS
SHIPPING
SHIPPINGS
SHIPPON
SHIPPONS
SHIPS
SHIPSHAPE
SHIPSIDE
SHIPSIDES
SHIPTIME
SHIPTIMES
SHIPWAY
SHIPWAYS
SHIPWORM
SHIPWORMS
SHIPWRECK
SHIPWRECKED
SHIPWRECKING
SHIPWRECKS
SHIPWRIGHT
SHIPWRIGHTS
SHIPYARD
SHIPYARDS
SHIRAZ
SHIRAZES
SHIRE
SHIRES
SHIRK
SHIRKED
SHIRKER
SHIRKERS
SHIRKING
SHIRKS
SHIRR
SHIRRED
SHIRRING
SHIRRINGS
SHIRRS
SHIRT
SHIRTDRESS
SHIRTDRESSES
SHIRTED
SHIRTFRONT
SHIRTFRONTS
SHIRTIER
SHIRTIEST
SHIRTILY
SHIRTING
SHIRTINGS
SHIRTLESS
SHIRTMAKER
SHIRTMAKERS
SHIRTS
SHIRTSLEEVE
SHIRTSLEEVED
SHIRTSLEEVES
SHIRTTAIL
SHIRTTAILED
SHIRTTAILING
SHIRTTAILS
SHIRTWAIST
SHIRTWAISTS
SHIRTY
SHIST
SHISTS
SHIT
SHITAKE
SHITAKES
SHITBAG
SHITBAGS
SHITCAN
SHITCANNED
SHITCANNING
SHITCANS
SHITE
SHITES
SHITFACE
SHITFACED
SHITFACES
SHITHEAD
SHITHEADS
SHITHEEL
SHITHEELS
SHITHOLE
SHITHOLES
SHITLESS
SHITLIST
SHITLISTS
SHITLOAD
SHITLOADS
SHITS
SHITTAH
SHITTAHS
SHITTED
SHITTER
SHITTERS
SHITTIER
SHITTIEST
SHITTIM
SHITTIMS
SHITTIMWOOD
SHITTIMWOODS
SHITTING
SHITTY
SHITWORK
SHITWORKS
SHIUR
SHIURIM
SHIV
SHIVA
SHIVAH
SHIVAHS
SHIVAREE
SHIVAREED
SHIVAREEING
SHIVAREES
SHIVAS
SHIVE
SHIVER
SHIVERED
SHIVERER
SHIVERERS
SHIVERIER
SHIVERIEST
SHIVERING
SHIVERS
SHIVERY
SHIVES
SHIVITI
SHIVITIS
SHIVS
SHKOTZIM
SHLEMIEHL
SHLEMIEHLS
SHLEMIEL
SHLEMIELS
SHLEP
SHLEPP
SHLEPPED
SHLEPPER
SHLEPPERS
SHLEPPIER
SHLEPPIEST
SHLEPPING
SHLEPPS
SHLEPPY
SHLEPS
SHLIMAZEL
SHLIMAZELS
SHLOCK
SHLOCKIER
SHLOCKIEST
SHLOCKS
SHLOCKY
SHLONG
SHLONGS
SHLUB
SHLUBS
SHLUMP
SHLUMPED
SHLUMPING
SHLUMPS
SHLUMPY
SHMALTZ
SHMALTZES
SHMALTZIER
SHMALTZIEST
SHMALTZY
SHMATTE
SHMATTES
SHMEAR
SHMEARED
SHMEARING
SHMEARS
SHMEER
SHMEERED
SHMEERING
SHMEERS
SHMO
SHMOE
SHMOES
SHMOOZE
SHMOOZED
SHMOOZER
SHMOOZERS
SHMOOZES
SHMOOZIER
SHMOOZIEST
SHMOOZING
SHMOOZY
SHMUCK
SHMUCKIER
SHMUCKIEST
SHMUCKS
SHMUCKY
SHNAPPS
SHNAPS
SHNOOK
SHNOOKS
SHNORRER
SHNORRERS
SHO
SHOAL
SHOALED
SHOALER
SHOALEST
SHOALIER

HOALIEST
HOALING
HOALS
HOALY
HOAT
HOATS
HOCHET
HOCHETIM
HOCHU
HOCHUS
HOCK
OCKABLE
OCKED
OCKER
OCKERS
OCKING
OCKINGLY
OCKPROOF
OCKS
OD
ODDEN
ODDIER
ODDIES
ODDIEST
ODDILY
ODDINESS
ODDINESSES
ODDY
OE
OEBILL
OEBILLS
OEBLACK
OEBLACKS
OEBOX
OEBOXES
OED
OEHORN
OEHORNED
OEHORNING
OEHORNS
OEING
OELACE
OELACES
OELESS
OEMAKER
OEMAKERS
OEMAKING
OEPAC
OEPACK
OEPACKS
OEPACS
OER
OERS
SHOES
SHOESHINE
SHOESHINES
SHOESTRING
SHOESTRINGS
SHOETREE
SHOETREES
SHOFAR
SHOFARS
SHOFROTH
SHOG
SHOGGED
SHOGGING
SHOGI
SHOGIS
SHOGS
SHOGUN
SHOGUNAL
SHOGUNATE
SHOGUNATES
SHOGUNS
SHOJI
SHOJIS
SHOJO
SHOLOM
SHOLOMS
SHONE
SHOO
SHOOED
SHOOFLIES
SHOOFLY
SHOOING
SHOOK
SHOOKS
SHOOL
SHOOLED
SHOOLING
SHOOLS
SHOON
SHOOS
SHOOSH
SHOOSHED
SHOOSHES
SHOOSHING
SHOOT
SHOOTAROUND
SHOOTAROUNDS
SHOOTDOWN
SHOOTDOWNS
SHOOTER
SHOOTERS
SHOOTING
SHOOTINGS
SHOOTIST
SHOOTISTS
SHOOTOUT
SHOOTOUTS
SHOOTS
SHOP
SHOPAHOLIC
SHOPAHOLICS
SHOPBOY
SHOPBOYS
SHOPGIRL
SHOPGIRLS
SHOPHAR
SHOPHARS
SHOPHROTH
SHOPKEEPER
SHOPKEEPERS
SHOPLESS
SHOPLIFT
SHOPLIFTED
SHOPLIFTER
SHOPLIFTERS
SHOPLIFTING
SHOPLIFTINGS
SHOPLIFTS
SHOPMAN
SHOPMEN
SHOPPE
SHOPPED
SHOPPER
SHOPPERS
SHOPPES
SHOPPIER
SHOPPIEST
SHOPPING
SHOPPINGS
SHOPPY
SHOPS
SHOPTALK
SHOPTALKS
SHOPWINDOW
SHOPWINDOWS
SHOPWORN
SHORAN
SHORANS
SHORE
SHOREBIRD
SHOREBIRDS
SHORED
SHOREFRONT
SHOREFRONTS
SHORELESS
SHORELINE
SHORELINES
SHORES
SHORESIDE
SHOREWARD
SHOREWARDS
SHORING
SHORINGS
SHORL
SHORLS
SHORN
SHORT
SHORTAGE
SHORTAGES
SHORTBREAD
SHORTBREADS
SHORTCAKE
SHORTCAKES
SHORTCHANGE
SHORTCHANGED
SHORTCHANGER
SHORTCHANGERS
SHORTCHANGES
SHORTCHANGING
SHORTCOMING
SHORTCOMINGS
SHORTCUT
SHORTCUTS
SHORTCUTTING
SHORTED
SHORTEN
SHORTENED
SHORTENER
SHORTENERS
SHORTENING
SHORTENINGS
SHORTENS
SHORTER
SHORTEST
SHORTFALL
SHORTFALLS
SHORTHAIR
SHORTHAIRED
SHORTHAIRS
SHORTHAND
SHORTHANDED
SHORTHANDS
SHORTHEAD
SHORTHEADS
SHORTHORN
SHORTHORNS
SHORTIA
SHORTIAS
SHORTIE
SHORTIES
SHORTING
SHORTISH
SHORTLIST
SHORTLISTED
SHORTLISTING
SHORTLISTS
SHORTLY
SHORTNESS
SHORTNESSES
SHORTS
SHORTSIGHTED
SHORTSIGHTEDLY
SHORTSTOP
SHORTSTOPS
SHORTWAVE
SHORTWAVED
SHORTWAVES
SHORTWAVING
SHORTY
SHOT
SHOTE
SHOTES
SHOTGUN
SHOTGUNNED
SHOTGUNNER
SHOTGUNNERS
SHOTGUNNING
SHOTGUNS
SHOTHOLE
SHOTHOLES
SHOTS
SHOTT
SHOTTED
SHOTTEN
SHOTTING
SHOTTS
SHOULD
SHOULDER
SHOULDERED
SHOULDERING
SHOULDERS
SHOULDEST
SHOULDST
SHOUT
SHOUTED
SHOUTER
SHOUTERS
SHOUTIER
SHOUTIEST
SHOUTING
SHOUTS
SHOUTY

SHOVE
SHOVED
SHOVEL
SHOVELED
SHOVELER
SHOVELERS
SHOVELFUL
SHOVELFULS
SHOVELING
SHOVELLED
SHOVELLER
SHOVELLERS
SHOVELLING
SHOVELNOSE
SHOVELNOSES
SHOVELS
SHOVELSFUL
SHOVER
SHOVERS
SHOVES
SHOVING
SHOW
SHOWABLE
SHOWBIZ
SHOWBIZZES
SHOWBIZZIER
SHOWBIZZIEST
SHOWBIZZY
SHOWBOAT
SHOWBOATED
SHOWBOATER
SHOWBOATERS
SHOWBOATING
SHOWBOATS
SHOWBREAD
SHOWBREADS
SHOWCASE
SHOWCASED
SHOWCASES
SHOWCASING
SHOWDOWN
SHOWDOWNS
SHOWED
SHOWER
SHOWERED
SHOWERER
SHOWERERS
SHOWERHEAD
SHOWERHEADS
SHOWERING
SHOWERLESS
SHOWERS
SHOWERY
SHOWGIRL
SHOWGIRLS
SHOWGOER
SHOWGOERS
SHOWIER
SHOWIEST
SHOWILY
SHOWINESS
SHOWINESSES
SHOWING
SHOWINGS
SHOWMAN
SHOWMANLY
SHOWMANSHIP
SHOWMANSHIPS
SHOWMEN
SHOWN
SHOWOFF
SHOWOFFS
SHOWPIECE
SHOWPIECES
SHOWPLACE
SHOWPLACES
SHOWRING
SHOWRINGS
SHOWROOM
SHOWROOMS
SHOWS
SHOWSTOPPER
SHOWSTOPPERS
SHOWSTOPPING
SHOWTIME
SHOWTIMES
SHOWY
SHOYU
SHOYUS
SHRANK
SHRAPNEL
SHRAPNELS
SHRED
SHREDDED
SHREDDER
SHREDDERS
SHREDDING
SHREDS
SHREW
SHREWD
SHREWDER
SHREWDEST
SHREWDIE
SHREWDIES
SHREWDLY
SHREWDNESS
SHREWDNESSES
SHREWED
SHREWING
SHREWISH
SHREWISHLY
SHREWISHNESS
SHREWISHNESSES
SHREWLIKE
SHREWMICE
SHREWMOUSE
SHREWS
SHRI
SHRIEK
SHRIEKED
SHRIEKER
SHRIEKERS
SHRIEKIER
SHRIEKIEST
SHRIEKING
SHRIEKS
SHRIEKY
SHRIEVAL
SHRIEVALTIES
SHRIEVALTY
SHRIEVE
SHRIEVED
SHRIEVES
SHRIEVING
SHRIFT
SHRIFTS
SHRIKE
SHRIKES
SHRILL
SHRILLED
SHRILLER
SHRILLEST
SHRILLING
SHRILLNESS
SHRILLNESSES
SHRILLS
SHRILLY
SHRIMP
SHRIMPED
SHRIMPER
SHRIMPERS
SHRIMPIER
SHRIMPIEST
SHRIMPING
SHRIMPLIKE
SHRIMPS
SHRIMPY
SHRINE
SHRINED
SHRINES
SHRINING
SHRINK
SHRINKABLE
SHRINKAGE
SHRINKAGES
SHRINKER
SHRINKERS
SHRINKING
SHRINKS
SHRIS
SHRIVE
SHRIVED
SHRIVEL
SHRIVELED
SHRIVELING
SHRIVELLED
SHRIVELLING
SHRIVELS
SHRIVEN
SHRIVER
SHRIVERS
SHRIVES
SHRIVING
SHROFF
SHROFFED
SHROFFING
SHROFFS
SHROOM
SHROOMER
SHROOMERS
SHROOMS
SHROUD
SHROUDED
SHROUDING
SHROUDS
SHROVE
SHRUB
SHRUBBERIES
SHRUBBERY
SHRUBBIER
SHRUBBIEST
SHRUBBY
SHRUBLAND
SHRUBLANDS
SHRUBLIKE
SHRUBS
SHRUG
SHRUGGED
SHRUGGING
SHRUGS
SHRUNK
SHRUNKEN
SHTETEL
SHTETELS
SHTETL
SHTETLACH
SHTETLS
SHTICK
SHTICKIER
SHTICKIEST
SHTICKS
SHTICKY
SHTIK
SHTIKS
SHTUM
SHTUMMER
SHTUP
SHTUPPED
SHTUPPING
SHTUPS
SHUCK
SHUCKED
SHUCKER
SHUCKERS
SHUCKING
SHUCKINGS
SHUCKS
SHUDDER
SHUDDERED
SHUDDERING
SHUDDERS
SHUDDERY
SHUFFLE
SHUFFLEBOARD
SHUFFLEBOARDS
SHUFFLED
SHUFFLER
SHUFFLERS
SHUFFLES
SHUFFLING
SHUL
SHULN
SHULS
SHUMAI
SHUN
SHUNNABLE
SHUNNED
SHUNNER
SHUNNERS
SHUNNING
SHUNPIKE
SHUNPIKED
SHUNPIKER
SHUNPIKERS
SHUNPIKES

UNPIKING
UNPIKINGS
UNS
UNT
UNTED
UNTER
UNTERS
UNTING
UNTS
URA
URAS
USH
USHED
USHER
USHERS
USHES
USHING
UT
UTDOWN
UTDOWNS
UTE
UTED
UTES
UTEYE
UTEYES
UTING
UTOFF
UTOFFS
UTOUT
UTOUTS
UTS
UTTER
UTTERBUG
UTTERBUGS
UTTERED
UTTERING
UTTERLESS
UTTERS
UTTING
UTTLE
UTTLECOCK
UTTLECOCKED
UTTLECOCKING
UTTLECOCKS
UTTLED
UTTLELESS
UTTLER
UTTLERS
UTTLES
UTTLING
ARTZE
ARTZES
TZ
SHVITZED
SHVITZES
SHVITZING
SHWA
SHWANPAN
SHWANPANS
SHWAS
SHY
SHYER
SHYERS
SHYEST
SHYING
SHYLOCK
SHYLOCKED
SHYLOCKING
SHYLOCKS
SHYLY
SHYNESS
SHYNESSES
SHYSTER
SHYSTERS
SI
SIAL
SIALAGOGUE
SIALAGOGUES
SIALIC
SIALID
SIALIDAN
SIALIDANS
SIALIDS
SIALOID
SIALS
SIAMANG
SIAMANGS
SIAMESE
SIAMESES
SIB
SIBB
SIBBS
SIBILANCE
SIBILANCES
SIBILANCIES
SIBILANCY
SIBILANT
SIBILANTLY
SIBILANTS
SIBILATE
SIBILATED
SIBILATES
SIBILATING
SIBILATION
SIBILATIONS
SIBILATOR
SIBILATORS
SIBLING
SIBLINGS
SIBS
SIBSHIP
SIBSHIPS
SIBYL
SIBYLIC
SIBYLLIC
SIBYLLINE
SIBYLS
SIC
SICCAN
SICCATIVE
SICCATIVES
SICCED
SICCING
SICE
SICES
SICK
SICKBAY
SICKBAYS
SICKBED
SICKBEDS
SICKED
SICKEE
SICKEES
SICKEN
SICKENED
SICKENER
SICKENERS
SICKENING
SICKENINGLY
SICKENS
SICKER
SICKERLY
SICKEST
SICKIE
SICKIES
SICKING
SICKISH
SICKISHLY
SICKISHNESS
SICKISHNESSES
SICKLE
SICKLED
SICKLEMIA
SICKLEMIAS
SICKLEMIC
SICKLES
SICKLIED
SICKLIER
SICKLIES
SICKLIEST
SICKLILY
SICKLINESS
SICKLINESSES
SICKLING
SICKLY
SICKLYING
SICKNESS
SICKNESSES
SICKO
SICKOS
SICKOUT
SICKOUTS
SICKROOM
SICKROOMS
SICKS
SICKY
SICS
SIDALCEA
SIDALCEAS
SIDDHA
SIDDHAS
SIDDHI
SIDDHIS
SIDDUR
SIDDURIM
SIDDURS
SIDE
SIDEARM
SIDEARMED
SIDEARMING
SIDEARMS
SIDEBAND
SIDEBANDS
SIDEBAR
SIDEBARS
SIDEBOARD
SIDEBOARDS
SIDEBURN
SIDEBURNED
SIDEBURNS
SIDECAR
SIDECARS
SIDECHECK
SIDECHECKS
SIDED
SIDEDLY
SIDEDNESS
SIDEDNESSES
SIDEDRESS
SIDEDRESSES
SIDEHILL
SIDEHILLS
SIDEKICK
SIDEKICKS
SIDELESS
SIDELIGHT
SIDELIGHTS
SIDELINE
SIDELINED
SIDELINER
SIDELINERS
SIDELINES
SIDELING
SIDELINING
SIDELOCK
SIDELOCKS
SIDELONG
SIDEMAN
SIDEMEAT
SIDEMEATS
SIDEMEN
SIDEPIECE
SIDEPIECES
SIDEREAL
SIDERITE
SIDERITES
SIDERITIC
SIDEROAD
SIDEROADS
SIDEROLITE
SIDEROLITES
SIDEROSES
SIDEROSIS
SIDEROTIC
SIDES
SIDESADDLE
SIDESADDLES
SIDESHOW
SIDESHOWS
SIDESLIP
SIDESLIPPED
SIDESLIPPING
SIDESLIPS
SIDESMAN
SIDESMEN
SIDESPIN
SIDESPINS
SIDESPLITTING
SIDESPLITTINGLY
SIDESTEP
SIDESTEPPED
SIDESTEPPER
SIDESTEPPERS
SIDESTEPPING
SIDESTEPS

SIDESTREAM
SIDESTROKE
SIDESTROKES
SIDESWIPE
SIDESWIPED
SIDESWIPES
SIDESWIPING
SIDETRACK
SIDETRACKED
SIDETRACKING
SIDETRACKS
SIDEWALK
SIDEWALKS
SIDEWALL
SIDEWALLS
SIDEWARD
SIDEWARDS
SIDEWAY
SIDEWAYS
SIDEWINDER
SIDEWINDERS
SIDEWISE
SIDH
SIDHE
SIDING
SIDINGS
SIDLE
SIDLED
SIDLER
SIDLERS
SIDLES
SIDLING
SIDLINGLY
SIEGE
SIEGED
SIEGES
SIEGING
SIEMENS
SIEMENSES
SIENITE
SIENITES
SIENNA
SIENNAS
SIEROZEM
SIEROZEMS
SIERRA
SIERRAN
SIERRAS
SIESTA
SIESTAS
SIEUR
SIEURS
SIEVE
SIEVED
SIEVERT
SIEVERTS
SIEVES
SIEVING
SIFAKA
SIFAKAS
SIFFLEUR
SIFFLEURS
SIFT
SIFTED
SIFTER
SIFTERS
SIFTING
SIFTINGS
SIFTS
SIG
SIGANID
SIGANIDS
SIGH
SIGHED
SIGHER
SIGHERS
SIGHING
SIGHLESS
SIGHLIKE
SIGHS
SIGHT
SIGHTED
SIGHTER
SIGHTERS
SIGHTING
SIGHTINGS
SIGHTLESS
SIGHTLESSLY
SIGHTLESSNESS
SIGHTLESSNESSES
SIGHTLIER
SIGHTLIEST
SIGHTLINE
SIGHTLINES
SIGHTLINESS
SIGHTLINESSES
SIGHTLY
SIGHTS
SIGHTSAW
SIGHTSEE
SIGHTSEEING
SIGHTSEEINGS
SIGHTSEEN
SIGHTSEER
SIGHTSEERS
SIGHTSEES
SIGIL
SIGILS
SIGLA
SIGLOI
SIGLOS
SIGLUM
SIGMA
SIGMAS
SIGMATE
SIGMOID
SIGMOIDAL
SIGMOIDALLY
SIGMOIDOSCOPE
SIGMOIDOSCOPES
SIGMOIDOSCOPIC
SIGMOIDOSCOPIES
SIGMOIDOSCOPY
SIGMOIDS
SIGN
SIGNA
SIGNAGE
SIGNAGES
SIGNAL
SIGNALED
SIGNALER
SIGNALERS
SIGNALING
SIGNALISE
SIGNALISED
SIGNALISES
SIGNALISING
SIGNALIZATION
SIGNALIZATIONS
SIGNALIZE
SIGNALIZED
SIGNALIZES
SIGNALIZING
SIGNALLED
SIGNALLER
SIGNALLERS
SIGNALLING
SIGNALLY
SIGNALMAN
SIGNALMEN
SIGNALMENT
SIGNALMENTS
SIGNALS
SIGNATORIES
SIGNATORY
SIGNATURE
SIGNATURES
SIGNBOARD
SIGNBOARDS
SIGNED
SIGNEE
SIGNEES
SIGNER
SIGNERS
SIGNET
SIGNETED
SIGNETING
SIGNETS
SIGNIFICANCE
SIGNIFICANCES
SIGNIFICANCIES
SIGNIFICANCY
SIGNIFICANT
SIGNIFICANTLY
SIGNIFICATION
SIGNIFICATIONS
SIGNIFICATIVE
SIGNIFICS
SIGNIFIED
SIGNIFIEDS
SIGNIFIER
SIGNIFIERS
SIGNIFIES
SIGNIFY
SIGNIFYING
SIGNIFYINGS
SIGNING
SIGNINGS
SIGNIOR
SIGNIORI
SIGNIORIES
SIGNIORS
SIGNIORY
SIGNOR
SIGNORA
SIGNORAS
SIGNORE
SIGNORI
SIGNORIES
SIGNORINA
SIGNORINAS
SIGNORINE
SIGNORS
SIGNORY
SIGNPOST
SIGNPOSTED
SIGNPOSTING
SIGNPOSTS
SIGNS
SIGS
SIKA
SIKAS
SIKE
SIKER
SIKES
SIKSIK
SIKSIKS
SILAGE
SILAGES
SILANE
SILANES
SILASTIC
SILASTICS
SILD
SILDENAFIL
SILDENAFILS
SILDS
SILENCE
SILENCED
SILENCER
SILENCERS
SILENCES
SILENCING
SILENI
SILENT
SILENTER
SILENTEST
SILENTLY
SILENTNESS
SILENTNESSES
SILENTS
SILENUS
SILESIA
SILESIAS
SILEX
SILEXES
SILHOUETTE
SILHOUETTED
SILHOUETTES
SILHOUETTING
SILHOUETTIST
SILHOUETTISTS
SILICA
SILICAS
SILICATE
SILICATES
SILICEOUS
SILICIC
SILICIDE
SILICIDES
SILICIFICATION
SILICIFICATIONS
SILICIFIED
SILICIFIES
SILICIFY

LICIFYING
LICIOUS
LICIUM
ICIUMS
ICLE
ICLES
ICON
ICONE
ICONES
ICONIZED
ICONS
ICOSES
ICOSIS
ICOTIC
ICOTICS
ICULA
ICULAE
IQUA
IQUAE
IQUE
IQUES
IQUOSE
IQUOUS
K
KALINE
KALINES
KED
KEN
KIE
KIER
KIES
KIEST
KILY
KINESS
KINESSES
KING
KLIKE
KOLINE
KOLINES
KS
KWEED
KWEEDS
KWORM
KWORMS
KY
L
LABUB
LABUBS
LER
LERS
LIBUB
LIBUBS
LIER

SILLIES
SILLIEST
SILLILY
SILLIMANITE
SILLIMANITES
SILLINESS
SILLINESSES
SILLS
SILLY
SILO
SILOED
SILOING
SILOS
SILOXANE
SILOXANES
SILT
SILTATION
SILTATIONS
SILTED
SILTIER
SILTIEST
SILTING
SILTS
SILTSTONE
SILTSTONES
SILTY
SILURIAN
SILURID
SILURIDS
SILUROID
SILUROIDS
SILVA
SILVAE
SILVAN
SILVANS
SILVAS
SILVER
SILVERBACK
SILVERBACKS
SILVERBERRIES
SILVERBERRY
SILVERED
SILVERER
SILVERERS
SILVERFISH
SILVERFISHES
SILVERIER
SILVERIEST
SILVERINESS
SILVERINESSES
SILVERING
SILVERINGS
SILVERLY

SILVERN
SILVERPOINT
SILVERPOINTS
SILVERS
SILVERSIDE
SILVERSIDES
SILVERSMITH
SILVERSMITHING
SILVERSMITHINGS
SILVERSMITHS
SILVERSWORD
SILVERSWORDS
SILVERTIP
SILVERTIPS
SILVERWARE
SILVERWARES
SILVERWEED
SILVERWEEDS
SILVERY
SILVEX
SILVEXES
SILVICAL
SILVICS
SILVICULTURAL
SILVICULTURALLY
SILVICULTURE
SILVICULTURES
SILVICULTURIST
SILVICULTURISTS
SIM
SIMA
SIMAR
SIMARS
SIMARUBA
SIMARUBAS
SIMAS
SIMAZINE
SIMAZINES
SIMCHA
SIMCHAS
SIMIAN
SIMIANS
SIMILAR
SIMILARITIES
SIMILARITY
SIMILARLY
SIMILE
SIMILES
SIMILITUDE
SIMILITUDES
SIMIOID
SIMIOUS
SIMITAR

SIMITARS
SIMLIN
SIMLINS
SIMMER
SIMMERED
SIMMERING
SIMMERS
SIMNEL
SIMNELS
SIMOLEON
SIMOLEONS
SIMONIAC
SIMONIACAL
SIMONIACALLY
SIMONIACS
SIMONIES
SIMONIST
SIMONISTS
SIMONIZE
SIMONIZED
SIMONIZES
SIMONIZING
SIMONY
SIMOOM
SIMOOMS
SIMOON
SIMOONS
SIMP
SIMPATICO
SIMPER
SIMPERED
SIMPERER
SIMPERERS
SIMPERING
SIMPERS
SIMPLE
SIMPLEMINDED
SIMPLEMINDEDLY
SIMPLENESS
SIMPLENESSES
SIMPLER
SIMPLES
SIMPLEST
SIMPLETON
SIMPLETONS
SIMPLEX
SIMPLEXES
SIMPLICES
SIMPLICIA
SIMPLICIAL
SIMPLICIALLY
SIMPLICITIES
SIMPLICITY

SIMPLIFICATION
SIMPLIFICATIONS
SIMPLIFIED
SIMPLIFIER
SIMPLIFIERS
SIMPLIFIES
SIMPLIFY
SIMPLIFYING
SIMPLISM
SIMPLISMS
SIMPLIST
SIMPLISTIC
SIMPLISTICALLY
SIMPLISTS
SIMPLY
SIMPS
SIMS
SIMULACRA
SIMULACRE
SIMULACRES
SIMULACRUM
SIMULACRUMS
SIMULANT
SIMULANTS
SIMULAR
SIMULARS
SIMULATE
SIMULATED
SIMULATES
SIMULATING
SIMULATION
SIMULATIONS
SIMULATIVE
SIMULATOR
SIMULATORS
SIMULCAST
SIMULCASTED
SIMULCASTING
SIMULCASTS
SIMULTANEITIES
SIMULTANEITY
SIMULTANEOUS
SIMULTANEOUSLY
SIMVASTATIN
SIMVASTATINS
SIN
SINAPISM
SINAPISMS
SINCE
SINCERE
SINCERELY
SINCERENESS
SINCERENESSES

SINCERER
SINCEREST
SINCERITIES
SINCERITY
SINCIPITA
SINCIPITAL
SINCIPUT
SINCIPUTS
SINE
SINECURE
SINECURES
SINES
SINEW
SINEWED
SINEWING
SINEWLESS
SINEWS
SINEWY
SINFONIA
SINFONIAS
SINFONIE
SINFONIETTA
SINFONIETTAS
SINFUL
SINFULLY
SINFULNESS
SINFULNESSES
SING
SINGABLE
SINGALONG
SINGALONGS
SINGE
SINGED
SINGEING
SINGER
SINGERS
SINGES
SINGING
SINGINGS
SINGLE
SINGLED
SINGLENESS
SINGLENESSES
SINGLES
SINGLESTICK
SINGLESTICKS
SINGLET
SINGLETON
SINGLETONS
SINGLETREE
SINGLETREES
SINGLETS
SINGLING
SINGLY
SINGS
SINGSONG
SINGSONGS
SINGSONGY
SINGSPIEL
SINGSPIELS
SINGULAR
SINGULARITIES
SINGULARITY
SINGULARIZE
SINGULARIZED
SINGULARIZES
SINGULARIZING
SINGULARLY
SINGULARS
SINH
SINHS
SINICIZE
SINICIZED
SINICIZES
SINICIZING
SINISTER
SINISTERLY
SINISTERNESS
SINISTERNESSES
SINISTRAL
SINISTROUS
SINK
SINKABLE
SINKAGE
SINKAGES
SINKER
SINKERS
SINKFUL
SINKFULS
SINKHOLE
SINKHOLES
SINKING
SINKS
SINLESS
SINLESSLY
SINLESSNESS
SINLESSNESSES
SINNED
SINNER
SINNERS
SINNET
SINNETS
SINNING
SINOATRIAL
SINOLOGICAL
SINOLOGIES
SINOLOGIST
SINOLOGISTS
SINOLOGUE
SINOLOGUES
SINOLOGY
SINOPIA
SINOPIAS
SINOPIE
SINS
SINSEMILLA
SINSEMILLAS
SINSYNE
SINTER
SINTERABILITIES
SINTERABILITY
SINTERED
SINTERING
SINTERS
SINUATE
SINUATED
SINUATELY
SINUATES
SINUATING
SINUATION
SINUATIONS
SINUOSITIES
SINUOSITY
SINUOUS
SINUOUSLY
SINUOUSNESS
SINUOUSNESSES
SINUS
SINUSES
SINUSITIS
SINUSITISES
SINUSLIKE
SINUSOID
SINUSOIDAL
SINUSOIDALLY
SINUSOIDS
SIP
SIPE
SIPED
SIPES
SIPHON
SIPHONAGE
SIPHONAGES
SIPHONAL
SIPHONED
SIPHONIC
SIPHONING
SIPHONOPHORE
SIPHONOPHORES
SIPHONOSTELE
SIPHONOSTELES
SIPHONS
SIPING
SIPPABLE
SIPPED
SIPPER
SIPPERS
SIPPET
SIPPETS
SIPPING
SIPS
SIR
SIRDAR
SIRDARS
SIRE
SIRED
SIREE
SIREES
SIREN
SIRENIAN
SIRENIANS
SIRENS
SIRES
SIRING
SIRLOIN
SIRLOINS
SIROCCO
SIROCCOS
SIRRA
SIRRAH
SIRRAHS
SIRRAS
SIRREE
SIRREES
SIRS
SIRUP
SIRUPED
SIRUPIER
SIRUPIEST
SIRUPING
SIRUPS
SIRUPY
SIRVENTE
SIRVENTES
SIS
SISAL
SISALS
SISES
SISKIN
SISKINS
SISSES
SISSIER
SISSIES
SISSIEST
SISSIFIED
SISSINESS
SISSINESSES
SISSY
SISSYISH
SISSYNESS
SISSYNESSES
SISTER
SISTERED
SISTERHOOD
SISTERHOODS
SISTERING
SISTERLY
SISTERS
SISTRA
SISTROID
SISTRUM
SISTRUMS
SIT
SITAR
SITARIST
SITARISTS
SITARS
SITCOM
SITCOMS
SITE
SITED
SITES
SITH
SITHENCE
SITHENS
SITING
SITOLOGIES
SITOLOGY
SITOSTEROL
SITOSTEROLS
SITREP
SITREPS
SITS
SITTEN
SITTER
SITTERS
SITTING
SITTINGS
SITU
SITUATE
SITUATED
SITUATES
SITUATING
SITUATION
SITUATIONAL

TUATIONALLY
TUATIONS
TUP
TUPS
TUS
TUSES
TZMARK
TZMARKS
VER
VERS
K
KER
KERS
KES
KFOLD
KMO
KMOS
KPENCE
KPENCES
KPENNY
KTE
KTEEN
KTEENMO
KTEENMOS
KTEENS
KTEENTH
KTEENTHS
KTES
KTH
KTHLY
THS
TIES
TIETH
TIETHS
TY
TYISH
ABLE
ABLENESS
ABLENESSES
ABLY
AR
ARS
ARSHIP
ARSHIPS
E
EABLE
EABLY
ED
ER
ERS
ES
ER
EST
SIZINESS
SIZINESSES
SIZING
SIZINGS
SIZY
SIZZLE
SIZZLED
SIZZLER
SIZZLERS
SIZZLES
SIZZLING
SJAMBOK
SJAMBOKED
SJAMBOKING
SJAMBOKS
SKA
SKAG
SKAGS
SKALD
SKALDIC
SKALDS
SKALDSHIP
SKALDSHIPS
SKANK
SKANKED
SKANKER
SKANKERS
SKANKIER
SKANKIEST
SKANKING
SKANKS
SKANKY
SKAS
SKAT
SKATE
SKATEBOARD
SKATEBOARDED
SKATEBOARDER
SKATEBOARDERS
SKATEBOARDING
SKATEBOARDINGS
SKATEBOARDS
SKATED
SKATER
SKATERS
SKATES
SKATING
SKATINGS
SKATOL
SKATOLE
SKATOLES
SKATOLS
SKATS
SKEAN
SKEANE
SKEANES
SKEANS
SKED
SKEDADDLE
SKEDADDLED
SKEDADDLER
SKEDADDLERS
SKEDADDLES
SKEDADDLING
SKEDDED
SKEDDING
SKEDS
SKEE
SKEED
SKEEING
SKEEN
SKEENS
SKEES
SKEET
SKEETER
SKEETERS
SKEETS
SKEEVIER
SKEEVIEST
SKEEVY
SKEG
SKEGS
SKEIGH
SKEIN
SKEINED
SKEINING
SKEINS
SKELETAL
SKELETALLY
SKELETON
SKELETONIC
SKELETONISE
SKELETONISED
SKELETONISES
SKELETONISING
SKELETONIZE
SKELETONIZED
SKELETONIZER
SKELETONIZERS
SKELETONIZES
SKELETONIZING
SKELETONS
SKELL
SKELLS
SKELLUM
SKELLUMS
SKELM
SKELMS
SKELP
SKELPED
SKELPING
SKELPIT
SKELPS
SKELTER
SKELTERED
SKELTERING
SKELTERS
SKENE
SKENES
SKEP
SKEPS
SKEPSIS
SKEPSISES
SKEPTIC
SKEPTICAL
SKEPTICALLY
SKEPTICISM
SKEPTICISMS
SKEPTICS
SKERRIES
SKERRY
SKETCH
SKETCHBOOK
SKETCHBOOKS
SKETCHED
SKETCHER
SKETCHERS
SKETCHES
SKETCHIER
SKETCHIEST
SKETCHILY
SKETCHINESS
SKETCHINESSES
SKETCHING
SKETCHPAD
SKETCHPADS
SKETCHY
SKEW
SKEWBACK
SKEWBACKS
SKEWBALD
SKEWBALDS
SKEWED
SKEWER
SKEWERED
SKEWERING
SKEWERS
SKEWING
SKEWNESS
SKEWNESSES
SKEWS
SKI
SKIABLE
SKIAGRAM
SKIAGRAMS
SKIAGRAPH
SKIAGRAPHS
SKIASCOPE
SKIASCOPES
SKIASCOPIES
SKIASCOPY
SKIBOB
SKIBOBBED
SKIBOBBER
SKIBOBBERS
SKIBOBBING
SKIBOBBINGS
SKIBOBS
SKID
SKIDDED
SKIDDER
SKIDDERS
SKIDDIER
SKIDDIEST
SKIDDING
SKIDDINGS
SKIDDOO
SKIDDOOED
SKIDDOOING
SKIDDOOS
SKIDDY
SKIDOO
SKIDOOED
SKIDOOER
SKIDOOERS
SKIDOOING
SKIDOOS
SKIDPAD
SKIDPADS
SKIDPROOF
SKIDS
SKIDWAY
SKIDWAYS
SKIED
SKIER
SKIERS
SKIES
SKIEY
SKIFF
SKIFFLE
SKIFFLED
SKIFFLES

SKIFFLESS
SKIFFLING
SKIFFS
SKIING
SKIINGS
SKIJORER
SKIJORERS
SKIJORING
SKIJORINGS
SKILFUL
SKILFULL
SKILFULLY
SKILFULNESS
SKILFULNESSES
SKILL
SKILLED
SKILLESS
SKILLESSNESS
SKILLESSNESSES
SKILLET
SKILLETS
SKILLFUL
SKILLFULLY
SKILLFULNESS
SKILLFULNESSES
SKILLING
SKILLINGS
SKILLS
SKIM
SKIMBOARD
SKIMBOARDS
SKIMMED
SKIMMER
SKIMMERS
SKIMMIA
SKIMMIAS
SKIMMING
SKIMMINGS
SKIMO
SKIMOBILE
SKIMOBILED
SKIMOBILES
SKIMOBILING
SKIMOS
SKIMP
SKIMPED
SKIMPIER
SKIMPIEST
SKIMPILY
SKIMPINESS
SKIMPINESSES
SKIMPING
SKIMPS
SKIMPY
SKIMS
SKIN
SKINFLICK
SKINFLICKS
SKINFLINT
SKINFLINTS
SKINFUL
SKINFULS
SKINHEAD
SKINHEADS
SKINK
SKINKED
SKINKER
SKINKERS
SKINKING
SKINKS
SKINLESS
SKINLIKE
SKINNED
SKINNER
SKINNERS
SKINNIER
SKINNIES
SKINNIEST
SKINNINESS
SKINNINESSES
SKINNING
SKINNY
SKINS
SKINT
SKINTIGHT
SKIORING
SKIORINGS
SKIP
SKIPJACK
SKIPJACKS
SKIPLANE
SKIPLANES
SKIPPABLE
SKIPPED
SKIPPER
SKIPPERED
SKIPPERING
SKIPPERS
SKIPPET
SKIPPETS
SKIPPING
SKIPS
SKIRL
SKIRLED
SKIRLING
SKIRLS
SKIRMISH
SKIRMISHED
SKIRMISHER
SKIRMISHERS
SKIRMISHES
SKIRMISHING
SKIRMISHINGS
SKIRR
SKIRRED
SKIRRET
SKIRRETS
SKIRRING
SKIRRS
SKIRT
SKIRTED
SKIRTER
SKIRTERS
SKIRTING
SKIRTINGS
SKIRTLESS
SKIRTLIKE
SKIRTS
SKIS
SKIT
SKITE
SKITED
SKITES
SKITING
SKITS
SKITTER
SKITTERED
SKITTERIER
SKITTERIEST
SKITTERING
SKITTERS
SKITTERY
SKITTISH
SKITTISHLY
SKITTISHNESS
SKITTISHNESSES
SKITTLE
SKITTLES
SKIVE
SKIVED
SKIVER
SKIVERS
SKIVES
SKIVING
SKIVVIED
SKIVVIES
SKIVVY
SKIVVYING
SKIWEAR
SKLENT
SKLENTED
SKLENTING
SKLENTS
SKOAL
SKOALED
SKOALING
SKOALS
SKOL
SKOLED
SKOLING
SKOLS
SKOOKUM
SKOOKUMS
SKORT
SKORTS
SKOSH
SKOSHES
SKREEGH
SKREEGHED
SKREEGHING
SKREEGHS
SKREIGH
SKREIGHED
SKREIGHING
SKREIGHS
SKRIED
SKRIES
SKRY
SKRYING
SKUA
SKUAS
SKULDUGGERIES
SKULDUGGERY
SKULK
SKULKED
SKULKER
SKULKERS
SKULKING
SKULKS
SKULL
SKULLCAP
SKULLCAPS
SKULLDUGGERIES
SKULLDUGGERY
SKULLED
SKULLING
SKULLS
SKUNK
SKUNKBRUSH
SKUNKBRUSHES
SKUNKED
SKUNKIER
SKUNKIEST
SKUNKING
SKUNKS
SKUNKWEED
SKUNKWEEDS
SKUNKY
SKY
SKYBOARD
SKYBOARDS
SKYBORNE
SKYBOX
SKYBOXES
SKYBRIDGE
SKYBRIDGES
SKYCAP
SKYCAPS
SKYDIVE
SKYDIVED
SKYDIVER
SKYDIVERS
SKYDIVES
SKYDIVING
SKYDIVINGS
SKYDOVE
SKYED
SKYEY
SKYGLOW
SKYGLOWS
SKYHOOK
SKYHOOKS
SKYING
SKYJACK
SKYJACKED
SKYJACKER
SKYJACKERS
SKYJACKING
SKYJACKINGS
SKYJACKS
SKYLARK
SKYLARKED
SKYLARKER
SKYLARKERS
SKYLARKING
SKYLARKS
SKYLESS
SKYLIGHT
SKYLIGHTED
SKYLIGHTS
SKYLIKE
SKYLINE
SKYLINES
SKYLIT
SKYMAN

KYMEN
KYPHOI
KYPHOS
KYROCKET
KYROCKETED
KYROCKETING
KYROCKETS
KYSAIL
KYSAILS
KYSCAPE
KYSCAPES
KYSCRAPER
KYSCRAPERS
KYSCRAPING
KYSURF
KYSURFED
KYSURFER
KYSURFERS
KYSURFING
KYSURFINGS
KYSURFS
KYWALK
KYWALKS
KYWARD
KYWARDS
KYWATCH
KYWATCHED
KYWATCHES
YWATCHING
YWAY
YWAYS
YWRITE
YWRITER
YWRITERS
YWRITES
YWRITING
YWRITINGS
YWRITTEN
YWROTE
AB
ABBED
ABBER
ABBERED
ABBERING
ABBERS
ABBERY
ABBIER
ABBIEST
ABBING
ABBINGS
ABBY
ABLIKE
ABS

SLACK
SLACKED
SLACKEN
SLACKENED
SLACKENER
SLACKENERS
SLACKENING
SLACKENS
SLACKER
SLACKERS
SLACKEST
SLACKING
SLACKLY
SLACKNESS
SLACKNESSES
SLACKS
SLAG
SLAGGED
SLAGGIER
SLAGGIEST
SLAGGING
SLAGGINGS
SLAGGY
SLAGS
SLAHAL
SLAHALS
SLAIN
SLAINTE
SLAKABLE
SLAKE
SLAKED
SLAKER
SLAKERS
SLAKES
SLAKING
SLALOM
SLALOMED
SLALOMER
SLALOMERS
SLALOMING
SLALOMIST
SLALOMISTS
SLALOMS
SLAM
SLAMDANCE
SLAMDANCED
SLAMDANCES
SLAMDANCING
SLAMMED
SLAMMER
SLAMMERS
SLAMMING
SLAMMINGS

SLAMS
SLANDER
SLANDERED
SLANDERER
SLANDERERS
SLANDERING
SLANDEROUS
SLANDEROUSLY
SLANDEROUSNESS
SLANDERS
SLANG
SLANGED
SLANGIER
SLANGIEST
SLANGILY
SLANGINESS
SLANGINESSES
SLANGING
SLANGS
SLANGUAGE
SLANGUAGES
SLANGY
SLANK
SLANT
SLANTED
SLANTIER
SLANTIEST
SLANTING
SLANTINGLY
SLANTLY
SLANTS
SLANTWAYS
SLANTWISE
SLANTY
SLAP
SLAPDASH
SLAPDASHES
SLAPHAPPIER
SLAPHAPPIEST
SLAPHAPPY
SLAPJACK
SLAPJACKS
SLAPPED
SLAPPER
SLAPPERS
SLAPPING
SLAPS
SLAPSHOT
SLAPSHOTS
SLAPSTICK
SLAPSTICKS
SLAPSTICKY
SLASH

SLASHED
SLASHER
SLASHERS
SLASHES
SLASHING
SLASHINGLY
SLASHINGS
SLAT
SLATCH
SLATCHES
SLATE
SLATED
SLATELIKE
SLATER
SLATERS
SLATES
SLATEY
SLATHER
SLATHERED
SLATHERING
SLATHERS
SLATIER
SLATIEST
SLATINESS
SLATINESSES
SLATING
SLATINGS
SLATS
SLATTED
SLATTERN
SLATTERNLINESS
SLATTERNLY
SLATTERNS
SLATTING
SLATTINGS
SLATY
SLAUGHTER
SLAUGHTERED
SLAUGHTERER
SLAUGHTERERS
SLAUGHTERHOUSE
SLAUGHTERHOUSES
SLAUGHTERING
SLAUGHTEROUS
SLAUGHTEROUSLY
SLAUGHTERS
SLAVE
SLAVED
SLAVEHOLDER
SLAVEHOLDERS
SLAVEHOLDING
SLAVEHOLDINGS
SLAVER

SLAVERED
SLAVERER
SLAVERERS
SLAVERIES
SLAVERING
SLAVERS
SLAVERY
SLAVES
SLAVEY
SLAVEYS
SLAVING
SLAVISH
SLAVISHLY
SLAVISHNESS
SLAVISHNESSES
SLAVOCRACIES
SLAVOCRACY
SLAVOCRAT
SLAVOCRATS
SLAW
SLAWS
SLAY
SLAYABLE
SLAYED
SLAYER
SLAYERS
SLAYING
SLAYINGS
SLAYS
SLEAVE
SLEAVED
SLEAVES
SLEAVING
SLEAZE
SLEAZEBAG
SLEAZEBAGS
SLEAZEBALL
SLEAZEBALLS
SLEAZED
SLEAZES
SLEAZIER
SLEAZIEST
SLEAZILY
SLEAZINESS
SLEAZINESSES
SLEAZING
SLEAZO
SLEAZOID
SLEAZOIDS
SLEAZOS
SLEAZY
SLED
SLEDDED

SLEDDER
SLEDDERS
SLEDDING
SLEDDINGS
SLEDGE
SLEDGED
SLEDGEHAMMER
SLEDGEHAMMERED
SLEDGEHAMMERING
SLEDGEHAMMERS
SLEDGES
SLEDGING
SLEDS
SLEEK
SLEEKED
SLEEKEN
SLEEKENED
SLEEKENING
SLEEKENS
SLEEKER
SLEEKERS
SLEEKEST
SLEEKIER
SLEEKIEST
SLEEKING
SLEEKIT
SLEEKLY
SLEEKNESS
SLEEKNESSES
SLEEKS
SLEEKY
SLEEP
SLEEPAWAY
SLEEPER
SLEEPERS
SLEEPIER
SLEEPIEST
SLEEPILY
SLEEPINESS
SLEEPINESSES
SLEEPING
SLEEPINGS
SLEEPLESS
SLEEPLESSLY
SLEEPLESSNESS
SLEEPLESSNESSES
SLEEPLIKE
SLEEPOVER
SLEEPOVERS
SLEEPS
SLEEPWALK
SLEEPWALKED
SLEEPWALKER
SLEEPWALKERS
SLEEPWALKING
SLEEPWALKS
SLEEPWEAR
SLEEPY
SLEEPYHEAD
SLEEPYHEADS
SLEET
SLEETED
SLEETIER
SLEETIEST
SLEETING
SLEETS
SLEETY
SLEEVE
SLEEVED
SLEEVEEN
SLEEVEENS
SLEEVELESS
SLEEVELET
SLEEVELETS
SLEEVES
SLEEVING
SLEEVINGS
SLEIGH
SLEIGHED
SLEIGHER
SLEIGHERS
SLEIGHING
SLEIGHINGS
SLEIGHS
SLEIGHT
SLEIGHTS
SLENDER
SLENDERER
SLENDEREST
SLENDERIZE
SLENDERIZED
SLENDERIZES
SLENDERIZING
SLENDERLY
SLENDERNESS
SLENDERNESSES
SLEPT
SLEUTH
SLEUTHED
SLEUTHHOUND
SLEUTHHOUNDS
SLEUTHING
SLEUTHINGS
SLEUTHS
SLEW
SLEWED
SLEWING
SLEWS
SLICE
SLICEABLE
SLICED
SLICER
SLICERS
SLICES
SLICING
SLICK
SLICKED
SLICKEN
SLICKENED
SLICKENER
SLICKENERS
SLICKENING
SLICKENS
SLICKENSIDE
SLICKENSIDES
SLICKER
SLICKERS
SLICKEST
SLICKING
SLICKLY
SLICKNESS
SLICKNESSES
SLICKROCK
SLICKROCKS
SLICKS
SLICKSTER
SLICKSTERS
SLID
SLIDABLE
SLIDDEN
SLIDE
SLIDER
SLIDERS
SLIDES
SLIDEWAY
SLIDEWAYS
SLIDING
SLIER
SLIEST
SLIEVE
SLIEVES
SLIGHT
SLIGHTED
SLIGHTER
SLIGHTERS
SLIGHTEST
SLIGHTING
SLIGHTINGLY
SLIGHTLY
SLIGHTNESS
SLIGHTNESSES
SLIGHTS
SLILY
SLIM
SLIME
SLIMEBALL
SLIMEBALLS
SLIMED
SLIMES
SLIMIER
SLIMIEST
SLIMILY
SLIMINESS
SLIMINESSES
SLIMING
SLIMLINE
SLIMLY
SLIMMED
SLIMMER
SLIMMERS
SLIMMEST
SLIMMING
SLIMMINGS
SLIMNASTICS
SLIMNESS
SLIMNESSES
SLIMPSIER
SLIMPSIEST
SLIMPSY
SLIMS
SLIMSIER
SLIMSIEST
SLIMSY
SLIMY
SLING
SLINGBACK
SLINGBACKS
SLINGER
SLINGERS
SLINGING
SLINGS
SLINGSHOT
SLINGSHOTS
SLINK
SLINKED
SLINKIER
SLINKIEST
SLINKILY
SLINKINESS
SLINKINESSES
SLINKING
SLINKS
SLINKY
SLIP
SLIPCASE
SLIPCASED
SLIPCASES
SLIPCOVER
SLIPCOVERED
SLIPCOVERING
SLIPCOVERS
SLIPDRESS
SLIPDRESSES
SLIPE
SLIPED
SLIPES
SLIPFORM
SLIPFORMED
SLIPFORMING
SLIPFORMS
SLIPING
SLIPKNOT
SLIPKNOTS
SLIPLESS
SLIPOUT
SLIPOUTS
SLIPOVER
SLIPOVERS
SLIPPAGE
SLIPPAGES
SLIPPED
SLIPPER
SLIPPERED
SLIPPERIER
SLIPPERIEST
SLIPPERINESS
SLIPPERINESSES
SLIPPERS
SLIPPERY
SLIPPIER
SLIPPIEST
SLIPPILY
SLIPPING
SLIPPY
SLIPS
SLIPSHEET
SLIPSHEETED
SLIPSHEETING
SLIPSHEETS
SLIPSHOD
SLIPSLOP
SLIPSLOPS
SLIPSOLE
SLIPSOLES
SLIPSTREAM

LIPSTREAMED
LIPSTREAMING
LIPSTREAMS
LIPT
LIPUP
LIPUPS
LIPWARE
LIPWARES
LIPWAY
LIPWAYS
LIT
LITHER
LITHERED
LITHERIER
LITHERIEST
LITHERING
LITHERS
LITHERY
LITLESS
LITLIKE
LITS
LITTED
LITTER
LITTERS
LITTIER
LITTIEST
LITTING
LITTY
LIVER
LIVERED
LIVERER
LIVERERS
LIVERING
LIVERS
LIVOVIC
LIVOVICES
LIVOVITZ
LIVOVITZES
OB
OBBER
OBBERED
OBBERER
OBBERERS
OBBERIER
OBBERIEST
OBBERING
OBBERS
OBBERY
OBBIER
OBBIEST
OBBISH
OBBY
OBS

SLOE
SLOES
SLOG
SLOGAN
SLOGANED
SLOGANEER
SLOGANEERED
SLOGANEERING
SLOGANEERS
SLOGANIZE
SLOGANIZED
SLOGANIZES
SLOGANIZING
SLOGANS
SLOGGED
SLOGGER
SLOGGERS
SLOGGING
SLOGS
SLOID
SLOIDS
SLOJD
SLOJDS
SLOMO
SLOMOS
SLOOP
SLOOPS
SLOP
SLOPE
SLOPED
SLOPER
SLOPERS
SLOPES
SLOPING
SLOPINGLY
SLOPPED
SLOPPIER
SLOPPIEST
SLOPPILY
SLOPPINESS
SLOPPINESSES
SLOPPING
SLOPPY
SLOPS
SLOPWORK
SLOPWORKS
SLOSH
SLOSHED
SLOSHES
SLOSHIER
SLOSHIEST
SLOSHING
SLOSHY

SLOT
SLOTBACK
SLOTBACKS
SLOTH
SLOTHFUL
SLOTHFULLY
SLOTHFULNESS
SLOTHFULNESSES
SLOTHS
SLOTS
SLOTTED
SLOTTER
SLOTTERS
SLOTTING
SLOUCH
SLOUCHED
SLOUCHER
SLOUCHERS
SLOUCHES
SLOUCHIER
SLOUCHIEST
SLOUCHILY
SLOUCHINESS
SLOUCHINESSES
SLOUCHING
SLOUCHY
SLOUGH
SLOUGHED
SLOUGHIER
SLOUGHIEST
SLOUGHING
SLOUGHS
SLOUGHY
SLOVEN
SLOVENLIER
SLOVENLIEST
SLOVENLINESS
SLOVENLINESSES
SLOVENLY
SLOVENS
SLOW
SLOWCOACH
SLOWCOACHES
SLOWDOWN
SLOWDOWNS
SLOWED
SLOWER
SLOWEST
SLOWING
SLOWISH
SLOWLY
SLOWNESS
SLOWNESSES

SLOWPOKE
SLOWPOKES
SLOWS
SLOWWORM
SLOWWORMS
SLOYD
SLOYDS
SLUB
SLUBBED
SLUBBER
SLUBBERED
SLUBBERING
SLUBBERS
SLUBBEST
SLUBBING
SLUBBINGS
SLUBS
SLUDGE
SLUDGED
SLUDGES
SLUDGIER
SLUDGIEST
SLUDGING
SLUDGY
SLUE
SLUED
SLUES
SLUFF
SLUFFED
SLUFFING
SLUFFS
SLUG
SLUGABED
SLUGABEDS
SLUGFEST
SLUGFESTS
SLUGGARD
SLUGGARDLY
SLUGGARDNESS
SLUGGARDNESSES
SLUGGARDS
SLUGGED
SLUGGER
SLUGGERS
SLUGGING
SLUGGISH
SLUGGISHLY
SLUGGISHNESS
SLUGGISHNESSES
SLUGS
SLUICE
SLUICED
SLUICES

SLUICEWAY
SLUICEWAYS
SLUICING
SLUICY
SLUING
SLUM
SLUMBER
SLUMBERED
SLUMBERER
SLUMBERERS
SLUMBERING
SLUMBEROUS
SLUMBERS
SLUMBERY
SLUMBROUS
SLUMGULLION
SLUMGULLIONS
SLUMGUM
SLUMGUMS
SLUMISM
SLUMISMS
SLUMLORD
SLUMLORDS
SLUMMED
SLUMMER
SLUMMERS
SLUMMIER
SLUMMIEST
SLUMMING
SLUMMY
SLUMP
SLUMPED
SLUMPFLATION
SLUMPFLATIONS
SLUMPIER
SLUMPIEST
SLUMPING
SLUMPS
SLUMPY
SLUMS
SLUNG
SLUNGSHOT
SLUNGSHOTS
SLUNK
SLUR
SLURB
SLURBAN
SLURBS
SLURP
SLURPED
SLURPIER
SLURPIEST
SLURPING

SLURPS
SLURPY
SLURRED
SLURRIED
SLURRIES
SLURRING
SLURRY
SLURRYING
SLURS
SLURVE
SLURVES
SLUSH
SLUSHED
SLUSHES
SLUSHIER
SLUSHIES
SLUSHIEST
SLUSHILY
SLUSHINESS
SLUSHINESSES
SLUSHING
SLUSHY
SLUT
SLUTS
SLUTTIER
SLUTTIEST
SLUTTISH
SLUTTISHLY
SLUTTISHNESS
SLUTTISHNESSES
SLUTTY
SLY
SLYBOOTS
SLYER
SLYEST
SLYLY
SLYNESS
SLYNESSES
SLYPE
SLYPES
SMACK
SMACKDOWN
SMACKDOWNS
SMACKED
SMACKER
SMACKERS
SMACKING
SMACKS
SMALL
SMALLAGE
SMALLAGES
SMALLCLOTHES
SMALLER
SMALLEST
SMALLHOLDER
SMALLHOLDERS
SMALLHOLDING
SMALLHOLDINGS
SMALLISH
SMALLMOUTH
SMALLMOUTHS
SMALLNESS
SMALLNESSES
SMALLPOX
SMALLPOXES
SMALLS
SMALLSWORD
SMALLSWORDS
SMALLTIME
SMALT
SMALTI
SMALTINE
SMALTINES
SMALTITE
SMALTITES
SMALTO
SMALTOS
SMALTS
SMARAGD
SMARAGDE
SMARAGDES
SMARAGDINE
SMARAGDITE
SMARAGDITES
SMARAGDS
SMARM
SMARMED
SMARMIER
SMARMIEST
SMARMILY
SMARMINESS
SMARMINESSES
SMARMING
SMARMS
SMARMY
SMART
SMARTASS
SMARTASSES
SMARTED
SMARTEN
SMARTENED
SMARTENING
SMARTENS
SMARTER
SMARTEST
SMARTIE
SMARTIES
SMARTING
SMARTISH
SMARTLY
SMARTNESS
SMARTNESSES
SMARTPHONE
SMARTPHONES
SMARTS
SMARTWEED
SMARTWEEDS
SMARTY
SMASH
SMASHED
SMASHER
SMASHERS
SMASHES
SMASHING
SMASHINGLY
SMASHMOUTH
SMASHUP
SMASHUPS
SMATTER
SMATTERED
SMATTERER
SMATTERERS
SMATTERING
SMATTERINGS
SMATTERS
SMAZE
SMAZES
SMEAR
SMEARCASE
SMEARCASES
SMEARED
SMEARER
SMEARERS
SMEARIER
SMEARIEST
SMEARING
SMEARS
SMEARY
SMECTIC
SMECTITE
SMECTITES
SMECTITIC
SMEDDUM
SMEDDUMS
SMEEK
SMEEKED
SMEEKING
SMEEKS
SMEGMA
SMEGMAS
SMELL
SMELLED
SMELLER
SMELLERS
SMELLIER
SMELLIEST
SMELLING
SMELLS
SMELLY
SMELT
SMELTED
SMELTER
SMELTERIES
SMELTERS
SMELTERY
SMELTING
SMELTINGS
SMELTS
SMERK
SMERKED
SMERKING
SMERKS
SMEW
SMEWS
SMIDGE
SMIDGEN
SMIDGENS
SMIDGEON
SMIDGEONS
SMIDGES
SMIDGIN
SMIDGINS
SMIERCASE
SMIERCASES
SMILAX
SMILAXES
SMILE
SMILED
SMILELESS
SMILER
SMILERS
SMILES
SMILEY
SMILEYS
SMILIER
SMILIES
SMILIEST
SMILING
SMILINGLY
SMIRCH
SMIRCHED
SMIRCHES
SMIRCHING
SMIRK
SMIRKED
SMIRKER
SMIRKERS
SMIRKIER
SMIRKIEST
SMIRKILY
SMIRKING
SMIRKS
SMIRKY
SMIT
SMITE
SMITER
SMITERS
SMITES
SMITH
SMITHEREENS
SMITHERIES
SMITHERS
SMITHERY
SMITHIES
SMITHING
SMITHINGS
SMITHS
SMITHSONITE
SMITHSONITES
SMITHY
SMITING
SMITTEN
SMOCK
SMOCKED
SMOCKING
SMOCKINGS
SMOCKS
SMOG
SMOGGIER
SMOGGIEST
SMOGGY
SMOGLESS
SMOGS
SMOKABLE
SMOKE
SMOKEABLE
SMOKEBOX
SMOKEBOXES
SMOKED
SMOKEHOUSE
SMOKEHOUSES
SMOKEJACK
SMOKEJACKS
SMOKELESS
SMOKELIKE

MOKEPOT
MOKEPOTS
MOKER
MOKERS
MOKES
MOKESTACK
MOKESTACKS
MOKEY
MOKEYS
MOKIE
MOKIER
MOKIES
MOKIEST
MOKILY
MOKINESS
MOKINESSES
MOKING
MOKINGS
MOKY
MOLDER
MOLDERED
MOLDERING
MOLDERS
MOLT
MOLTS
MOOCH
MOOCHED
MOOCHER
MOOCHERS
MOOCHES
MOOCHIER
MOOCHIEST
MOOCHING
MOOCHY
MOOSH
MOOSHED
MOOSHES
MOOSHING
MOOTH
MOOTHBORE
MOOTHBORES
MOOTHE
MOOTHED
MOOTHEN
MOOTHENED
MOOTHENING
MOOTHENS
MOOTHER
MOOTHERS
MOOTHES
MOOTHEST
MOOTHIE
MOOTHIES
SMOOTHING
SMOOTHLY
SMOOTHNESS
SMOOTHNESSES
SMOOTHS
SMOOTHY
SMORG
SMORGASBORD
SMORGASBORDS
SMORGS
SMOTE
SMOTHER
SMOTHERED
SMOTHERER
SMOTHERERS
SMOTHERING
SMOTHERS
SMOTHERY
SMOULDER
SMOULDERED
SMOULDERING
SMOULDERS
SMRITI
SMRITIS
SMUDGE
SMUDGED
SMUDGES
SMUDGIER
SMUDGIEST
SMUDGILY
SMUDGINESS
SMUDGINESSES
SMUDGING
SMUDGINGS
SMUDGY
SMUG
SMUGGER
SMUGGEST
SMUGGLE
SMUGGLED
SMUGGLER
SMUGGLERS
SMUGGLES
SMUGGLING
SMUGGLINGS
SMUGLY
SMUGNESS
SMUGNESSES
SMUSH
SMUSHED
SMUSHES
SMUSHING
SMUT
SMUTCH
SMUTCHED
SMUTCHES
SMUTCHIER
SMUTCHIEST
SMUTCHING
SMUTCHY
SMUTS
SMUTTED
SMUTTIER
SMUTTIEST
SMUTTILY
SMUTTINESS
SMUTTINESSES
SMUTTING
SMUTTY
SNACK
SNACKED
SNACKER
SNACKERS
SNACKIER
SNACKIEST
SNACKING
SNACKS
SNACKY
SNAFFLE
SNAFFLED
SNAFFLES
SNAFFLING
SNAFU
SNAFUED
SNAFUING
SNAFUS
SNAG
SNAGGED
SNAGGER
SNAGGERS
SNAGGIER
SNAGGIEST
SNAGGING
SNAGGLE
SNAGGLES
SNAGGLETEETH
SNAGGLETOOTH
SNAGGLETOOTHED
SNAGGY
SNAGLIKE
SNAGS
SNAIL
SNAILED
SNAILING
SNAILLIKE
SNAILS
SNAKE
SNAKEBIRD
SNAKEBIRDS
SNAKEBIT
SNAKEBITE
SNAKEBITES
SNAKEBITTEN
SNAKED
SNAKEFISH
SNAKEFISHES
SNAKEHEAD
SNAKEHEADS
SNAKELIKE
SNAKEPIT
SNAKEPITS
SNAKEROOT
SNAKEROOTS
SNAKES
SNAKESKIN
SNAKESKINS
SNAKEWEED
SNAKEWEEDS
SNAKEY
SNAKIER
SNAKIEST
SNAKILY
SNAKINESS
SNAKINESSES
SNAKING
SNAKISH
SNAKY
SNAP
SNAPBACK
SNAPBACKS
SNAPDRAGON
SNAPDRAGONS
SNAPLESS
SNAPPED
SNAPPER
SNAPPERS
SNAPPIER
SNAPPIEST
SNAPPILY
SNAPPINESS
SNAPPINESSES
SNAPPING
SNAPPISH
SNAPPISHLY
SNAPPISHNESS
SNAPPISHNESSES
SNAPPY
SNAPS
SNAPSHOOTER
SNAPSHOOTERS
SNAPSHOT
SNAPSHOTS
SNAPSHOTTED
SNAPSHOTTING
SNAPWEED
SNAPWEEDS
SNARE
SNARED
SNARER
SNARERS
SNARES
SNARF
SNARFED
SNARFING
SNARFLE
SNARFLED
SNARFLES
SNARFLING
SNARFS
SNARING
SNARK
SNARKIER
SNARKIEST
SNARKILY
SNARKS
SNARKY
SNARL
SNARLED
SNARLER
SNARLERS
SNARLIER
SNARLIEST
SNARLING
SNARLS
SNARLY
SNASH
SNASHES
SNATCH
SNATCHED
SNATCHER
SNATCHERS
SNATCHES
SNATCHIER
SNATCHIEST
SNATCHING
SNATCHY
SNATH
SNATHE
SNATHES
SNATHS
SNAW
SNAWED

SNAWING
SNAWS
SNAZZIER
SNAZZIEST
SNAZZILY
SNAZZY
SNEAK
SNEAKBOX
SNEAKBOXES
SNEAKED
SNEAKER
SNEAKERED
SNEAKERS
SNEAKIER
SNEAKIEST
SNEAKILY
SNEAKINESS
SNEAKINESSES
SNEAKING
SNEAKINGLY
SNEAKS
SNEAKY
SNEAP
SNEAPED
SNEAPING
SNEAPS
SNECK
SNECKS
SNED
SNEDDED
SNEDDING
SNEDS
SNEER
SNEERED
SNEERER
SNEERERS
SNEERFUL
SNEERIER
SNEERIEST
SNEERING
SNEERINGLY
SNEERS
SNEERY
SNEESH
SNEESHES
SNEEZE
SNEEZED
SNEEZER
SNEEZERS
SNEEZES
SNEEZEWEED
SNEEZEWEEDS
SNEEZIER
SNEEZIEST
SNEEZING
SNEEZY
SNELL
SNELLED
SNELLER
SNELLEST
SNELLING
SNELLS
SNIB
SNIBBED
SNIBBING
SNIBS
SNICK
SNICKED
SNICKER
SNICKERED
SNICKERER
SNICKERERS
SNICKERING
SNICKERS
SNICKERSNEE
SNICKERSNEES
SNICKERY
SNICKING
SNICKS
SNIDE
SNIDELY
SNIDENESS
SNIDENESSES
SNIDER
SNIDEST
SNIFF
SNIFFABLE
SNIFFED
SNIFFER
SNIFFERS
SNIFFIER
SNIFFIEST
SNIFFILY
SNIFFINESS
SNIFFINESSES
SNIFFING
SNIFFISH
SNIFFISHLY
SNIFFISHNESS
SNIFFISHNESSES
SNIFFLE
SNIFFLED
SNIFFLER
SNIFFLERS
SNIFFLES
SNIFFLIER
SNIFFLIEST
SNIFFLING
SNIFFLY
SNIFFS
SNIFFY
SNIFTER
SNIFTERS
SNIGGER
SNIGGERED
SNIGGERER
SNIGGERERS
SNIGGERING
SNIGGERS
SNIGGLE
SNIGGLED
SNIGGLER
SNIGGLERS
SNIGGLES
SNIGGLING
SNIGLET
SNIGLETS
SNIP
SNIPE
SNIPED
SNIPER
SNIPERS
SNIPERSCOPE
SNIPERSCOPES
SNIPES
SNIPING
SNIPINGS
SNIPPED
SNIPPER
SNIPPERS
SNIPPERSNAPPER
SNIPPERSNAPPERS
SNIPPET
SNIPPETIER
SNIPPETIEST
SNIPPETS
SNIPPETY
SNIPPIER
SNIPPIEST
SNIPPILY
SNIPPING
SNIPPINGS
SNIPPY
SNIPS
SNIT
SNITCH
SNITCHED
SNITCHER
SNITCHERS
SNITCHES
SNITCHING
SNITS
SNITTIER
SNITTIEST
SNITTY
SNIVEL
SNIVELED
SNIVELER
SNIVELERS
SNIVELING
SNIVELLED
SNIVELLER
SNIVELLERS
SNIVELLIER
SNIVELLIEST
SNIVELLING
SNIVELLY
SNIVELS
SNOB
SNOBBERIES
SNOBBERY
SNOBBIER
SNOBBIEST
SNOBBILY
SNOBBISH
SNOBBISHLY
SNOBBISHNESS
SNOBBISHNESSES
SNOBBISM
SNOBBISMS
SNOBBY
SNOBS
SNOCOACH
SNOCOACHES
SNOG
SNOGGED
SNOGGER
SNOGGERS
SNOGGING
SNOGS
SNOLLYGOSTER
SNOLLYGOSTERS
SNOOD
SNOODED
SNOODING
SNOODS
SNOOK
SNOOKED
SNOOKER
SNOOKERED
SNOOKERING
SNOOKERS
SNOOKING
SNOOKS
SNOOL
SNOOLED
SNOOLING
SNOOLS
SNOOP
SNOOPED
SNOOPER
SNOOPERS
SNOOPIER
SNOOPIEST
SNOOPILY
SNOOPING
SNOOPS
SNOOPY
SNOOSE
SNOOSES
SNOOT
SNOOTED
SNOOTFUL
SNOOTFULS
SNOOTIER
SNOOTIEST
SNOOTILY
SNOOTINESS
SNOOTINESSES
SNOOTING
SNOOTS
SNOOTY
SNOOZE
SNOOZED
SNOOZER
SNOOZERS
SNOOZES
SNOOZIER
SNOOZIEST
SNOOZING
SNOOZLE
SNOOZLED
SNOOZLES
SNOOZLING
SNOOZY
SNORE
SNORED
SNORER
SNORERS
SNORES
SNORING
SNORINGS
SNORKEL
SNORKELED
SNORKELER

NORKELERS
NORKELING
NORKELINGS
NORKELLED
NORKELLER
NORKELLERS
NORKELLING
NORKELS
NORT
NORTED
NORTER
NORTERS
NORTING
NORTS
NOT
NOTS
NOTTIER
NOTTIEST
NOTTILY
NOTTINESS
NOTTINESSES
NOTTY
NOUT
NOUTED
NOUTIER
NOUTIEST
NOUTING
NOUTISH
NOUTS
NOUTY
NOW
NOWBALL
NOWBALLED
NOWBALLING
NOWBALLS
NOWBANK
NOWBANKS
NOWBELL
NOWBELLS
NOWBELT
NOWBELTS
NOWBERRIES
NOWBERRY
NOWBIRD
NOWBIRDS
NOWBLINK
NOWBLINKS
NOWBLOWER
NOWBLOWERS
NOWBOARD
NOWBOARDCROSS
NOWBOARDED
NOWBOARDER
SNOWBOARDERS
SNOWBOARDING
SNOWBOARDINGS
SNOWBOARDS
SNOWBOUND
SNOWBRUSH
SNOWBRUSHES
SNOWBUSH
SNOWBUSHES
SNOWCAP
SNOWCAPPED
SNOWCAPS
SNOWCAT
SNOWCATS
SNOWDRIFT
SNOWDRIFTS
SNOWDROP
SNOWDROPS
SNOWED
SNOWFALL
SNOWFALLS
SNOWFIELD
SNOWFIELDS
SNOWFLAKE
SNOWFLAKES
SNOWFLEA
SNOWFLEAS
SNOWIER
SNOWIEST
SNOWILY
SNOWINESS
SNOWINESSES
SNOWING
SNOWLAND
SNOWLANDS
SNOWLESS
SNOWLIKE
SNOWMAKER
SNOWMAKERS
SNOWMAKING
SNOWMAN
SNOWMELT
SNOWMELTS
SNOWMEN
SNOWMOBILE
SNOWMOBILER
SNOWMOBILERS
SNOWMOBILES
SNOWMOBILING
SNOWMOBILINGS
SNOWMOBILIST
SNOWMOBILISTS
SNOWMOLD
SNOWMOLDS
SNOWPACK
SNOWPACKS
SNOWPLOUGH
SNOWPLOUGHED
SNOWPLOUGHING
SNOWPLOUGHS
SNOWPLOW
SNOWPLOWED
SNOWPLOWING
SNOWPLOWS
SNOWS
SNOWSCAPE
SNOWSCAPES
SNOWSHED
SNOWSHEDS
SNOWSHOE
SNOWSHOED
SNOWSHOEING
SNOWSHOEINGS
SNOWSHOER
SNOWSHOERS
SNOWSHOES
SNOWSLIDE
SNOWSLIDES
SNOWSTORM
SNOWSTORMS
SNOWSUIT
SNOWSUITS
SNOWY
SNUB
SNUBBED
SNUBBER
SNUBBERS
SNUBBEST
SNUBBIER
SNUBBIEST
SNUBBINESS
SNUBBINESSES
SNUBBING
SNUBBY
SNUBNESS
SNUBNESSES
SNUBS
SNUCK
SNUFF
SNUFFBOX
SNUFFBOXES
SNUFFED
SNUFFER
SNUFFERS
SNUFFIER
SNUFFIEST
SNUFFILY
SNUFFING
SNUFFLE
SNUFFLED
SNUFFLER
SNUFFLERS
SNUFFLES
SNUFFLIER
SNUFFLIEST
SNUFFLING
SNUFFLY
SNUFFS
SNUFFY
SNUG
SNUGGED
SNUGGER
SNUGGERIE
SNUGGERIES
SNUGGERY
SNUGGEST
SNUGGIES
SNUGGING
SNUGGLE
SNUGGLED
SNUGGLES
SNUGGLIER
SNUGGLIEST
SNUGGLING
SNUGGLY
SNUGLY
SNUGNESS
SNUGNESSES
SNUGS
SNYE
SNYES
SO
SOAK
SOAKAGE
SOAKAGES
SOAKED
SOAKER
SOAKERS
SOAKING
SOAKINGS
SOAKS
SOAP
SOAPBARK
SOAPBARKS
SOAPBERRIES
SOAPBERRY
SOAPBOX
SOAPBOXED
SOAPBOXES
SOAPBOXING
SOAPED
SOAPER
SOAPERS
SOAPFISH
SOAPFISHES
SOAPIER
SOAPIEST
SOAPILY
SOAPINESS
SOAPINESSES
SOAPING
SOAPLESS
SOAPLIKE
SOAPS
SOAPSTONE
SOAPSTONES
SOAPSUDS
SOAPSUDSY
SOAPWORT
SOAPWORTS
SOAPY
SOAR
SOARED
SOARER
SOARERS
SOARING
SOARINGLY
SOARINGS
SOARS
SOAVE
SOAVES
SOB
SOBA
SOBAS
SOBBED
SOBBER
SOBBERS
SOBBING
SOBBINGLY
SOBEIT
SOBER
SOBERED
SOBERER
SOBEREST
SOBERING
SOBERIZE
SOBERIZED
SOBERIZES
SOBERIZING
SOBERLY
SOBERNESS
SOBERNESSES

SOBERS
SOBERSIDED
SOBERSIDEDNESS
SOBERSIDES
SOBFUL
SOBRIETIES
SOBRIETY
SOBRIQUET
SOBRIQUETS
SOBS
SOC
SOCA
SOCAGE
SOCAGER
SOCAGERS
SOCAGES
SOCAS
SOCCAGE
SOCCAGES
SOCCER
SOCCERS
SOCES
SOCIABILITIES
SOCIABILITY
SOCIABLE
SOCIABLENESS
SOCIABLENESSES
SOCIABLES
SOCIABLY
SOCIAL
SOCIALISATION
SOCIALISATIONS
SOCIALISE
SOCIALISED
SOCIALISER
SOCIALISERS
SOCIALISES
SOCIALISING
SOCIALISM
SOCIALISMS
SOCIALIST
SOCIALISTIC
SOCIALISTICALLY
SOCIALISTS
SOCIALITE
SOCIALITES
SOCIALITIES
SOCIALITY
SOCIALIZATION
SOCIALIZATIONS
SOCIALIZE
SOCIALIZED
SOCIALIZER
SOCIALIZERS
SOCIALIZES
SOCIALIZING
SOCIALLY
SOCIALS
SOCIETAL
SOCIETALLY
SOCIETIES
SOCIETY
SOCIOBIOLOGICAL
SOCIOBIOLOGIES
SOCIOBIOLOGIST
SOCIOBIOLOGISTS
SOCIOBIOLOGY
SOCIOCULTURAL
SOCIOCULTURALLY
SOCIOECONOMIC
SOCIOGRAM
SOCIOGRAMS
SOCIOHISTORICAL
SOCIOLECT
SOCIOLECTS
SOCIOLINGUIST
SOCIOLINGUISTIC
SOCIOLINGUISTS
SOCIOLOGESE
SOCIOLOGESES
SOCIOLOGIC
SOCIOLOGICAL
SOCIOLOGICALLY
SOCIOLOGIES
SOCIOLOGIST
SOCIOLOGISTS
SOCIOLOGY
SOCIOMETRIC
SOCIOMETRIES
SOCIOMETRY
SOCIOPATH
SOCIOPATHIC
SOCIOPATHS
SOCIOPOLITICAL
SOCIORELIGIOUS
SOCIOSEXUAL
SOCK
SOCKDOLAGER
SOCKDOLAGERS
SOCKDOLOGER
SOCKDOLOGERS
SOCKED
SOCKET
SOCKETED
SOCKETING
SOCKETS
SOCKETTE
SOCKETTES
SOCKEYE
SOCKEYES
SOCKING
SOCKLESS
SOCKMAN
SOCKMEN
SOCKO
SOCKS
SOCLE
SOCLES
SOCMAN
SOCMEN
SOD
SODA
SODALESS
SODALIST
SODALISTS
SODALITE
SODALITES
SODALITIES
SODALITY
SODAMIDE
SODAMIDES
SODAS
SODBUSTER
SODBUSTERS
SODDED
SODDEN
SODDENED
SODDENING
SODDENLY
SODDENNESS
SODDENNESSES
SODDENS
SODDIE
SODDIES
SODDING
SODDY
SODIC
SODIUM
SODIUMS
SODOM
SODOMIES
SODOMISE
SODOMISED
SODOMISES
SODOMISING
SODOMIST
SODOMISTS
SODOMITE
SODOMITES
SODOMITIC
SODOMITICAL
SODOMIZE
SODOMIZED
SODOMIZES
SODOMIZING
SODOMS
SODOMY
SODS
SOEVER
SOFA
SOFABED
SOFABEDS
SOFAR
SOFARS
SOFAS
SOFFIT
SOFFITS
SOFT
SOFTA
SOFTAS
SOFTBACK
SOFTBACKS
SOFTBALL
SOFTBALLER
SOFTBALLERS
SOFTBALLS
SOFTBOUND
SOFTBOUNDS
SOFTCORE
SOFTCOVER
SOFTCOVERS
SOFTEN
SOFTENED
SOFTENER
SOFTENERS
SOFTENING
SOFTENS
SOFTER
SOFTEST
SOFTGOODS
SOFTHEAD
SOFTHEADED
SOFTHEADEDLY
SOFTHEADEDNESS
SOFTHEADS
SOFTHEARTED
SOFTHEARTEDLY
SOFTHEARTEDNESS
SOFTIE
SOFTIES
SOFTISH
SOFTLY
SOFTNESS
SOFTNESSES
SOFTS
SOFTSCAPE
SOFTSCAPES
SOFTSHELL
SOFTSHELLS
SOFTWARE
SOFTWARES
SOFTWOOD
SOFTWOODS
SOFTY
SOGGED
SOGGIER
SOGGIEST
SOGGILY
SOGGINESS
SOGGINESSES
SOGGY
SOH
SOHS
SOIGNE
SOIGNEE
SOIL
SOILAGE
SOILAGES
SOILBORNE
SOILED
SOILING
SOILLESS
SOILS
SOILURE
SOILURES
SOIREE
SOIREES
SOJA
SOJAS
SOJOURN
SOJOURNED
SOJOURNER
SOJOURNERS
SOJOURNING
SOJOURNS
SOJU
SOJUS
SOKE
SOKEMAN
SOKEMEN
SOKES
SOKOL
SOKOLS
SOL
SOLA

OLACE
OLACED
OLACEMENT
OLACEMENTS
OLACER
OLACERS
OLACES
OLACING
OLAN
OLANACEOUS
OLAND
OLANDER
OLANDERS
OLANDS
OLANIN
OLANINE
OLANINES
OLANINS
OLANO
OLANOS
OLANS
OLANUM
OLANUMS
OLAR
OLARIA
OLARISE
OLARISED
OLARISES
OLARISING
OLARISM
OLARISMS
OLARIUM
OLARIUMS
OLARIZATION
OLARIZATIONS
OLARIZE
OLARIZED
OLARIZES
OLARIZING
OLARS
OLAS
OLATE
OLATED
OLATES
OLATIA
OLATING
OLATION
OLATIONS
OLATIUM
OLD
OLDAN
OLDANS
OLDER
SOLDERABILITIES
SOLDERABILITY
SOLDERED
SOLDERER
SOLDERERS
SOLDERING
SOLDERS
SOLDI
SOLDIER
SOLDIERED
SOLDIERIES
SOLDIERING
SOLDIERINGS
SOLDIERLY
SOLDIERS
SOLDIERSHIP
SOLDIERSHIPS
SOLDIERY
SOLDO
SOLE
SOLECISE
SOLECISED
SOLECISES
SOLECISING
SOLECISM
SOLECISMS
SOLECIST
SOLECISTIC
SOLECISTS
SOLECIZE
SOLECIZED
SOLECIZES
SOLECIZING
SOLED
SOLEI
SOLELESS
SOLELY
SOLEMN
SOLEMNER
SOLEMNEST
SOLEMNIFIED
SOLEMNIFIES
SOLEMNIFY
SOLEMNIFYING
SOLEMNISE
SOLEMNISED
SOLEMNISES
SOLEMNISING
SOLEMNITIES
SOLEMNITY
SOLEMNIZATION
SOLEMNIZATIONS
SOLEMNIZE
SOLEMNIZED
SOLEMNIZES
SOLEMNIZING
SOLEMNLY
SOLEMNNESS
SOLEMNNESSES
SOLENESS
SOLENESSES
SOLENODON
SOLENODONS
SOLENOID
SOLENOIDAL
SOLENOIDS
SOLEPLATE
SOLEPLATES
SOLEPRINT
SOLEPRINTS
SOLERA
SOLERAS
SOLERET
SOLERETS
SOLES
SOLEUS
SOLEUSES
SOLFATARA
SOLFATARAS
SOLFEGE
SOLFEGES
SOLFEGGI
SOLFEGGIO
SOLFEGGIOS
SOLFERINO
SOLFERINOS
SOLGEL
SOLI
SOLICIT
SOLICITANT
SOLICITANTS
SOLICITATION
SOLICITATIONS
SOLICITED
SOLICITING
SOLICITOR
SOLICITORS
SOLICITORSHIP
SOLICITORSHIPS
SOLICITOUS
SOLICITOUSLY
SOLICITOUSNESS
SOLICITS
SOLICITUDE
SOLICITUDES
SOLID
SOLIDAGO
SOLIDAGOS
SOLIDARISM
SOLIDARISMS
SOLIDARIST
SOLIDARISTIC
SOLIDARISTS
SOLIDARITIES
SOLIDARITY
SOLIDARY
SOLIDER
SOLIDEST
SOLIDI
SOLIDIFICATION
SOLIDIFICATIONS
SOLIDIFIED
SOLIDIFIES
SOLIDIFY
SOLIDIFYING
SOLIDITIES
SOLIDITY
SOLIDLY
SOLIDNESS
SOLIDNESSES
SOLIDS
SOLIDUS
SOLIFLUCTION
SOLIFLUCTIONS
SOLILOQUIES
SOLILOQUISE
SOLILOQUISED
SOLILOQUISES
SOLILOQUISING
SOLILOQUIST
SOLILOQUISTS
SOLILOQUIZE
SOLILOQUIZED
SOLILOQUIZER
SOLILOQUIZERS
SOLILOQUIZES
SOLILOQUIZING
SOLILOQUY
SOLING
SOLION
SOLIONS
SOLIPSISM
SOLIPSISMS
SOLIPSIST
SOLIPSISTIC
SOLIPSISTICALLY
SOLIPSISTS
SOLIQUID
SOLIQUIDS
SOLITAIRE
SOLITAIRES
SOLITARIES
SOLITARILY
SOLITARINESS
SOLITARINESSES
SOLITARY
SOLITON
SOLITONS
SOLITUDE
SOLITUDES
SOLITUDINARIAN
SOLITUDINARIANS
SOLLERET
SOLLERETS
SOLMIZATION
SOLMIZATIONS
SOLO
SOLOED
SOLOES
SOLOING
SOLOIST
SOLOISTIC
SOLOISTS
SOLON
SOLONCHAK
SOLONCHAKS
SOLONETS
SOLONETSES
SOLONETZ
SOLONETZES
SOLONETZIC
SOLONS
SOLOS
SOLS
SOLSTICE
SOLSTICES
SOLSTITIAL
SOLUBILISE
SOLUBILISED
SOLUBILISES
SOLUBILISING
SOLUBILITIES
SOLUBILITY
SOLUBILIZATION
SOLUBILIZATIONS
SOLUBILIZE
SOLUBILIZED
SOLUBILIZES
SOLUBILIZING
SOLUBLE
SOLUBLES
SOLUBLY

SOLUM
SOLUMS
SOLUNAR
SOLUS
SOLUTE
SOLUTES
SOLUTION
SOLUTIONS
SOLVABILITIES
SOLVABILITY
SOLVABLE
SOLVATE
SOLVATED
SOLVATES
SOLVATING
SOLVATION
SOLVATIONS
SOLVE
SOLVED
SOLVENCIES
SOLVENCY
SOLVENT
SOLVENTLESS
SOLVENTLY
SOLVENTS
SOLVER
SOLVERS
SOLVES
SOLVING
SOLVOLYSES
SOLVOLYSIS
SOLVOLYTIC
SOM
SOMA
SOMAN
SOMANS
SOMAS
SOMATA
SOMATIC
SOMATICALLY
SOMATIZATION
SOMATIZATIONS
SOMATOLOGICAL
SOMATOLOGIES
SOMATOLOGY
SOMATOMEDIN
SOMATOMEDINS
SOMATOPLEURE
SOMATOPLEURES
SOMATOSENSORY
SOMATOSTATIN
SOMATOSTATINS
SOMATOTROPHIN
SOMATOTROPHINS
SOMATOTROPIN
SOMATOTROPINS
SOMATOTYPE
SOMATOTYPES
SOMBER
SOMBERER
SOMBEREST
SOMBERLY
SOMBERNESS
SOMBERNESSES
SOMBRE
SOMBRELY
SOMBRER
SOMBRERO
SOMBREROS
SOMBREST
SOMBROUS
SOME
SOMEBODIES
SOMEBODY
SOMEDAY
SOMEDEAL
SOMEHOW
SOMEONE
SOMEONES
SOMEPLACE
SOMEPLACES
SOMERSAULT
SOMERSAULTED
SOMERSAULTING
SOMERSAULTS
SOMERSET
SOMERSETED
SOMERSETING
SOMERSETS
SOMERSETTED
SOMERSETTING
SOMETHING
SOMETHINGS
SOMETIME
SOMETIMES
SOMEWAY
SOMEWAYS
SOMEWHAT
SOMEWHATS
SOMEWHEN
SOMEWHERE
SOMEWHERES
SOMEWHITHER
SOMEWISE
SOMITAL
SOMITE
SOMITES
SOMITIC
SOMMELIER
SOMMELIERS
SOMNAMBULANT
SOMNAMBULATE
SOMNAMBULATED
SOMNAMBULATES
SOMNAMBULATING
SOMNAMBULATION
SOMNAMBULATIONS
SOMNAMBULISM
SOMNAMBULISMS
SOMNAMBULIST
SOMNAMBULISTIC
SOMNAMBULISTS
SOMNIFACIENT
SOMNIFACIENTS
SOMNIFEROUS
SOMNOLENCE
SOMNOLENCES
SOMNOLENT
SOMNOLENTLY
SOMONI
SOMONIS
SOMS
SON
SONANCE
SONANCES
SONANT
SONANTAL
SONANTIC
SONANTS
SONAR
SONARMAN
SONARMEN
SONARS
SONATA
SONATAS
SONATINA
SONATINAS
SONATINE
SONDE
SONDER
SONDERS
SONDES
SONE
SONES
SONG
SONGBIRD
SONGBIRDS
SONGBOOK
SONGBOOKS
SONGFEST
SONGFESTS
SONGFUL
SONGFULLY
SONGFULNESS
SONGFULNESSES
SONGLESS
SONGLESSLY
SONGLIKE
SONGS
SONGSMITH
SONGSMITHS
SONGSTER
SONGSTERS
SONGSTRESS
SONGSTRESSES
SONGWRITER
SONGWRITERS
SONGWRITING
SONGWRITINGS
SONHOOD
SONHOODS
SONIC
SONICALLY
SONICATE
SONICATED
SONICATES
SONICATING
SONICATION
SONICATIONS
SONICATOR
SONICATORS
SONICS
SONLESS
SONLIKE
SONLY
SONNET
SONNETED
SONNETEER
SONNETEERING
SONNETEERINGS
SONNETEERS
SONNETING
SONNETIZE
SONNETIZED
SONNETIZES
SONNETIZING
SONNETS
SONNETTED
SONNETTING
SONNIES
SONNY
SONOBUOY
SONOBUOYS
SONOGRAM
SONOGRAMS
SONOGRAPHER
SONOGRAPHERS
SONOGRAPHIC
SONOGRAPHIES
SONOGRAPHY
SONORANT
SONORANTS
SONORITIES
SONORITY
SONOROUS
SONOROUSLY
SONOROUSNESS
SONOROUSNESSES
SONOVOX
SONOVOXES
SONS
SONSHIP
SONSHIPS
SONSIE
SONSIER
SONSIEST
SONSY
SOOCHONG
SOOCHONGS
SOOEY
SOOK
SOOKS
SOON
SOONER
SOONERS
SOONEST
SOONISH
SOOT
SOOTED
SOOTH
SOOTHE
SOOTHED
SOOTHER
SOOTHERS
SOOTHES
SOOTHEST
SOOTHFAST
SOOTHING
SOOTHINGLY
SOOTHINGNESS
SOOTHINGNESSES
SOOTHLY
SOOTHS
SOOTHSAID
SOOTHSAY

OOTHSAYER
OOTHSAYERS
OOTHSAYING
OOTHSAYINGS
OOTHSAYS
OOTIER
OOTIEST
OOTILY
OOTINESS
OOTINESSES
OOTING
OOTS
OOTY
OP
OPAIPILLA
OPAIPILLAS
OPAPILLA
OPAPILLAS
OPH
OPHIES
OPHISM
OPHISMS
OPHIST
OPHISTIC
OPHISTICAL
OPHISTICALLY
OPHISTICATE
OPHISTICATED
OPHISTICATEDLY
OPHISTICATES
OPHISTICATING
OPHISTICATION
OPHISTICATIONS
OPHISTRIES
OPHISTRY
OPHISTS
OPHOMORE
OPHOMORES
OPHOMORIC
OPHS
OPHY
OPITE
OPITED
OPITES
OPITING
OPOR
OPORIFEROUS
OPORIFIC
OPORIFICS
OPORS
OPPED
OPPIER
OPPIEST
SOPPILY
SOPPINESS
SOPPINESSES
SOPPING
SOPPY
SOPRANI
SOPRANINO
SOPRANINOS
SOPRANO
SOPRANOS
SOPS
SORA
SORAS
SORB
SORBABILITIES
SORBABILITY
SORBABLE
SORBATE
SORBATES
SORBED
SORBENT
SORBENTS
SORBET
SORBETS
SORBIC
SORBING
SORBITAN
SORBITANS
SORBITOL
SORBITOLS
SORBOSE
SORBOSES
SORBS
SORCERER
SORCERERS
SORCERESS
SORCERESSES
SORCERIES
SORCEROUS
SORCERY
SORD
SORDID
SORDIDLY
SORDIDNESS
SORDIDNESSES
SORDINE
SORDINES
SORDINI
SORDINO
SORDOR
SORDORS
SORDS
SORE
SORED
SOREHEAD
SOREHEADED
SOREHEADS
SOREL
SORELS
SORELY
SORENESS
SORENESSES
SORER
SORES
SOREST
SORGHO
SORGHOS
SORGHUM
SORGHUMS
SORGO
SORGOS
SORI
SORICINE
SORING
SORINGS
SORITES
SORITIC
SORN
SORNED
SORNER
SORNERS
SORNING
SORNS
SOROCHE
SOROCHES
SORORAL
SORORALLY
SORORATE
SORORATES
SORORITIES
SORORITY
SOROSES
SOROSIS
SOROSISES
SORPTION
SORPTIONS
SORPTIVE
SORREL
SORRELS
SORRIER
SORRIEST
SORRILY
SORRINESS
SORRINESSES
SORROW
SORROWED
SORROWER
SORROWERS
SORROWFUL
SORROWFULLY
SORROWFULNESS
SORROWFULNESSES
SORROWING
SORROWS
SORRY
SORT
SORTA
SORTABLE
SORTABLY
SORTAL
SORTALS
SORTED
SORTER
SORTERS
SORTES
SORTIE
SORTIED
SORTIEING
SORTIES
SORTILEGE
SORTILEGES
SORTING
SORTINGS
SORTITION
SORTITIONS
SORTS
SORUS
SOS
SOSTENUTI
SOSTENUTO
SOSTENUTOS
SOT
SOTERIOLOGICAL
SOTERIOLOGIES
SOTERIOLOGY
SOTH
SOTHS
SOTOL
SOTOLS
SOTS
SOTTED
SOTTEDLY
SOTTISH
SOTTISHLY
SOTTISHNESS
SOTTISHNESSES
SOU
SOUARI
SOUARIS
SOUBISE
SOUBISES
SOUBRETTE
SOUBRETTES
SOUBRIQUET
SOUBRIQUETS
SOUCAR
SOUCARS
SOUCHONG
SOUCHONGS
SOUDAN
SOUDANS
SOUFFLE
SOUFFLED
SOUFFLEED
SOUFFLES
SOUGH
SOUGHED
SOUGHING
SOUGHS
SOUGHT
SOUK
SOUKOUS
SOUKOUSES
SOUKS
SOUL
SOULED
SOULFUL
SOULFULLY
SOULFULNESS
SOULFULNESSES
SOULLESS
SOULLESSLY
SOULLESSNESS
SOULLESSNESSES
SOULLIKE
SOULMATE
SOULMATES
SOULS
SOULSTER
SOULSTERS
SOUND
SOUNDABLE
SOUNDALIKE
SOUNDALIKES
SOUNDBOARD
SOUNDBOARDS
SOUNDBOX
SOUNDBOXES
SOUNDED
SOUNDER
SOUNDERS
SOUNDEST

SOUNDING
SOUNDINGLY
SOUNDINGS
SOUNDLESS
SOUNDLESSLY
SOUNDLY
SOUNDMAN
SOUNDMEN
SOUNDNESS
SOUNDNESSES
SOUNDPROOF
SOUNDPROOFED
SOUNDPROOFING
SOUNDPROOFS
SOUNDS
SOUNDSCAPE
SOUNDSCAPES
SOUNDSTAGE
SOUNDSTAGES
SOUNDTRACK
SOUNDTRACKS
SOUP
SOUPCON
SOUPCONS
SOUPED
SOUPIER
SOUPIEST
SOUPILY
SOUPING
SOUPLESS
SOUPLIKE
SOUPS
SOUPSPOON
SOUPSPOONS
SOUPY
SOUR
SOURBALL
SOURBALLS
SOURCE
SOURCEBOOK
SOURCEBOOKS
SOURCED
SOURCEFUL
SOURCELESS
SOURCES
SOURCING
SOURCINGS
SOURDINE
SOURDINES
SOURDOUGH
SOURDOUGHS
SOURED
SOURER
SOUREST
SOURGUM
SOURGUMS
SOURING
SOURISH
SOURLY
SOURNESS
SOURNESSES
SOURPUSS
SOURPUSSES
SOURS
SOURSOP
SOURSOPS
SOURWOOD
SOURWOODS
SOUS
SOUSAPHONE
SOUSAPHONES
SOUSE
SOUSED
SOUSER
SOUSERS
SOUSES
SOUSING
SOUSLIK
SOUSLIKS
SOUTACHE
SOUTACHES
SOUTANE
SOUTANES
SOUTER
SOUTERS
SOUTH
SOUTHBOUND
SOUTHEAST
SOUTHEASTER
SOUTHEASTERLY
SOUTHEASTERN
SOUTHEASTERNER
SOUTHEASTERNERS
SOUTHEASTERS
SOUTHEASTS
SOUTHEASTWARD
SOUTHEASTWARDS
SOUTHED
SOUTHER
SOUTHERLIES
SOUTHERLY
SOUTHERN
SOUTHERNER
SOUTHERNERS
SOUTHERNMOST
SOUTHERNNESS
SOUTHERNNESSES
SOUTHERNS
SOUTHERNWOOD
SOUTHERNWOODS
SOUTHERS
SOUTHING
SOUTHINGS
SOUTHLAND
SOUTHLANDS
SOUTHPAW
SOUTHPAWS
SOUTHRON
SOUTHRONS
SOUTHS
SOUTHWARD
SOUTHWARDS
SOUTHWEST
SOUTHWESTER
SOUTHWESTERLY
SOUTHWESTERN
SOUTHWESTERNER
SOUTHWESTERNERS
SOUTHWESTERS
SOUTHWESTS
SOUTHWESTWARD
SOUTHWESTWARDS
SOUVENIR
SOUVENIRS
SOUVLAKI
SOUVLAKIA
SOUVLAKIAS
SOUVLAKIS
SOVEREIGN
SOVEREIGNLY
SOVEREIGNS
SOVEREIGNTIES
SOVEREIGNTY
SOVIET
SOVIETISM
SOVIETISMS
SOVIETIZATION
SOVIETIZATIONS
SOVIETIZE
SOVIETIZED
SOVIETIZES
SOVIETIZING
SOVIETS
SOVKHOZ
SOVKHOZES
SOVKHOZY
SOVRAN
SOVRANLY
SOVRANS
SOVRANTIES
SOVRANTY
SOW
SOWABLE
SOWANS
SOWAR
SOWARS
SOWBACK
SOWBACKS
SOWBELLIES
SOWBELLY
SOWBREAD
SOWBREADS
SOWBUG
SOWBUGS
SOWCAR
SOWCARS
SOWED
SOWENS
SOWER
SOWERS
SOWING
SOWINGS
SOWN
SOWS
SOX
SOY
SOYA
SOYAS
SOYBEAN
SOYBEANS
SOYMEAL
SOYMEALS
SOYMILK
SOYMILKS
SOYS
SOYUZ
SOYUZES
SOZIN
SOZINE
SOZINES
SOZINS
SOZZLED
SPA
SPACE
SPACEBAND
SPACEBANDS
SPACECRAFT
SPACECRAFTS
SPACED
SPACEFARING
SPACEFLIGHT
SPACEFLIGHTS
SPACELAB
SPACELABS
SPACELESS
SPACEMAN
SPACEMEN
SPACEPORT
SPACEPORTS
SPACER
SPACERS
SPACES
SPACESHIP
SPACESHIPS
SPACESUIT
SPACESUITS
SPACEWALK
SPACEWALKED
SPACEWALKER
SPACEWALKERS
SPACEWALKING
SPACEWALKS
SPACEWARD
SPACEY
SPACIAL
SPACIALLY
SPACIER
SPACIEST
SPACINESS
SPACINESSES
SPACING
SPACINGS
SPACIOUS
SPACIOUSLY
SPACIOUSNESS
SPACIOUSNESSES
SPACKLE
SPACKLED
SPACKLES
SPACKLING
SPACY
SPADE
SPADED
SPADEFISH
SPADEFISHES
SPADEFUL
SPADEFULS
SPADER
SPADERS
SPADES
SPADEWORK
SPADEWORKS
SPADICES
SPADILLE
SPADILLES

PADING
PADIX
PADIXES
PADO
PADONES
PAE
PAED
PAEING
PAEINGS
PAES
PAETZLE
PAETZLES
PAGHETTI
PAGHETTILIKE
PAGHETTINI
PAGHETTINIS
PAGHETTIS
PAGYRIC
PAGYRICS
PAHEE
PAHEES
PAHI
PAHIS
PAIL
PAILS
PAIT
PAITS
PAKE
PALDEEN
PALDEENS
PALE
PALES
PALL
PALLABLE
PALLATION
PALLATIONS
PALLED
PALLER
PALLERS
PALLING
PALLINGS
PALLS
PALPEEN
PALPEENS
PALTED
PAM
PAMBOT
PAMBOTS
PAMMED
PAMMER
PAMMERS
PAMMING
PAMMINGS
SPAMS
SPAN
SPANAKOPITA
SPANAKOPITAS
SPANCEL
SPANCELED
SPANCELING
SPANCELLED
SPANCELLING
SPANCELS
SPANDEX
SPANDEXED
SPANDEXES
SPANDREL
SPANDRELS
SPANDRIL
SPANDRILS
SPANG
SPANGLE
SPANGLED
SPANGLES
SPANGLIER
SPANGLIEST
SPANGLING
SPANGLY
SPANIEL
SPANIELS
SPANK
SPANKED
SPANKER
SPANKERS
SPANKING
SPANKINGS
SPANKS
SPANLESS
SPANNED
SPANNER
SPANNERS
SPANNING
SPANOKOPITA
SPANOKOPITAS
SPANS
SPANSULE
SPANSULES
SPANWORM
SPANWORMS
SPAR
SPARABLE
SPARABLES
SPARE
SPAREABLE
SPARED
SPARELY
SPARENESS
SPARENESSES
SPARER
SPARERIB
SPARERIBS
SPARERS
SPARES
SPAREST
SPARGE
SPARGED
SPARGER
SPARGERS
SPARGES
SPARGING
SPARID
SPARIDS
SPARING
SPARINGLY
SPARK
SPARKED
SPARKER
SPARKERS
SPARKIER
SPARKIEST
SPARKILY
SPARKING
SPARKISH
SPARKLE
SPARKLED
SPARKLER
SPARKLERS
SPARKLES
SPARKLET
SPARKLETS
SPARKLIER
SPARKLIEST
SPARKLING
SPARKLY
SPARKPLUG
SPARKPLUGGED
SPARKPLUGGING
SPARKPLUGS
SPARKS
SPARKY
SPARLIKE
SPARLING
SPARLINGS
SPAROID
SPAROIDS
SPARRED
SPARRIER
SPARRIEST
SPARRING
SPARROW
SPARROWLIKE
SPARROWS
SPARRY
SPARS
SPARSE
SPARSELY
SPARSENESS
SPARSENESSES
SPARSER
SPARSEST
SPARSITIES
SPARSITY
SPARTAN
SPARTEINE
SPARTEINES
SPARTINA
SPARTINAS
SPAS
SPASM
SPASMED
SPASMING
SPASMODIC
SPASMODICALLY
SPASMOLYTIC
SPASMOLYTICS
SPASMS
SPASTIC
SPASTICALLY
SPASTICITIES
SPASTICITY
SPASTICS
SPAT
SPATE
SPATES
SPATHAL
SPATHE
SPATHED
SPATHES
SPATHIC
SPATHOSE
SPATHULATE
SPATIAL
SPATIALITIES
SPATIALITY
SPATIALLY
SPATIOTEMPORAL
SPATS
SPATTED
SPATTER
SPATTERDOCK
SPATTERDOCKS
SPATTERED
SPATTERING
SPATTERS
SPATTING
SPATULA
SPATULAR
SPATULAS
SPATULATE
SPATZLE
SPATZLES
SPAVIE
SPAVIES
SPAVIET
SPAVIN
SPAVINED
SPAVINS
SPAWN
SPAWNED
SPAWNER
SPAWNERS
SPAWNING
SPAWNS
SPAY
SPAYED
SPAYING
SPAYS
SPAZ
SPAZZ
SPAZZES
SPEAK
SPEAKABLE
SPEAKEASIES
SPEAKEASY
SPEAKER
SPEAKERPHONE
SPEAKERPHONES
SPEAKERS
SPEAKERSHIP
SPEAKERSHIPS
SPEAKING
SPEAKINGS
SPEAKS
SPEAN
SPEANED
SPEANING
SPEANS
SPEAR
SPEARED
SPEARER
SPEARERS
SPEARFISH
SPEARFISHED
SPEARFISHES
SPEARFISHING

SPEARGUN
SPEARGUNS
SPEARHEAD
SPEARHEADED
SPEARHEADING
SPEARHEADS
SPEARING
SPEARINGS
SPEARLIKE
SPEARMAN
SPEARMEN
SPEARMINT
SPEARMINTS
SPEARS
SPEARWORT
SPEARWORTS
SPEC
SPECCED
SPECCING
SPECIAL
SPECIALER
SPECIALEST
SPECIALISATION
SPECIALISATIONS
SPECIALISE
SPECIALISED
SPECIALISES
SPECIALISING
SPECIALISM
SPECIALISMS
SPECIALIST
SPECIALISTIC
SPECIALISTS
SPECIALITIES
SPECIALITY
SPECIALIZATION
SPECIALIZATIONS
SPECIALIZE
SPECIALIZED
SPECIALIZES
SPECIALIZING
SPECIALLY
SPECIALNESS
SPECIALNESSES
SPECIALS
SPECIALTIES
SPECIALTY
SPECIATE
SPECIATED
SPECIATES
SPECIATING
SPECIATION
SPECIATIONAL
SPECIATIONS
SPECIE
SPECIES
SPECIESISM
SPECIESISMS
SPECIFIABLE
SPECIFIC
SPECIFICALLY
SPECIFICATION
SPECIFICATIONS
SPECIFICITIES
SPECIFICITY
SPECIFICS
SPECIFIED
SPECIFIER
SPECIFIERS
SPECIFIES
SPECIFY
SPECIFYING
SPECIMEN
SPECIMENS
SPECIOSITIES
SPECIOSITY
SPECIOUS
SPECIOUSLY
SPECIOUSNESS
SPECIOUSNESSES
SPECK
SPECKED
SPECKIER
SPECKIEST
SPECKING
SPECKLE
SPECKLED
SPECKLES
SPECKLING
SPECKS
SPECKY
SPECS
SPECT
SPECTACLE
SPECTACLED
SPECTACLES
SPECTACULAR
SPECTACULARLY
SPECTACULARS
SPECTATE
SPECTATED
SPECTATES
SPECTATING
SPECTATOR
SPECTATORIAL
SPECTATORS
SPECTATORSHIP
SPECTATORSHIPS
SPECTED
SPECTER
SPECTERS
SPECTING
SPECTINOMYCIN
SPECTINOMYCINS
SPECTRA
SPECTRAL
SPECTRALLY
SPECTRE
SPECTRES
SPECTROGRAM
SPECTROGRAMS
SPECTROGRAPH
SPECTROGRAPHIC
SPECTROGRAPHIES
SPECTROGRAPHS
SPECTROGRAPHY
SPECTROMETER
SPECTROMETERS
SPECTROMETRIC
SPECTROMETRIES
SPECTROMETRY
SPECTROSCOPE
SPECTROSCOPES
SPECTROSCOPIC
SPECTROSCOPIES
SPECTROSCOPIST
SPECTROSCOPISTS
SPECTROSCOPY
SPECTRUM
SPECTRUMS
SPECTS
SPECULA
SPECULAR
SPECULARITIES
SPECULARITY
SPECULARLY
SPECULATE
SPECULATED
SPECULATES
SPECULATING
SPECULATION
SPECULATIONS
SPECULATIVE
SPECULATIVELY
SPECULATOR
SPECULATORS
SPECULUM
SPECULUMS
SPED
SPEECH
SPEECHES
SPEECHIFIED
SPEECHIFIES
SPEECHIFY
SPEECHIFYING
SPEECHLESS
SPEECHLESSLY
SPEECHLESSNESS
SPEECHWRITER
SPEECHWRITERS
SPEED
SPEEDBALL
SPEEDBALLED
SPEEDBALLING
SPEEDBALLS
SPEEDBOAT
SPEEDBOATING
SPEEDBOATINGS
SPEEDBOATS
SPEEDED
SPEEDER
SPEEDERS
SPEEDIER
SPEEDIEST
SPEEDILY
SPEEDINESS
SPEEDINESSES
SPEEDING
SPEEDINGS
SPEEDO
SPEEDOMETER
SPEEDOMETERS
SPEEDOS
SPEEDREAD
SPEEDREADING
SPEEDREADS
SPEEDS
SPEEDSTER
SPEEDSTERS
SPEEDUP
SPEEDUPS
SPEEDWAY
SPEEDWAYS
SPEEDWELL
SPEEDWELLS
SPEEDY
SPEEL
SPEELED
SPEELING
SPEELS
SPEER
SPEERED
SPEERING
SPEERINGS
SPEERS
SPEIL
SPEILED
SPEILING
SPEILS
SPEIR
SPEIRED
SPEIRING
SPEIRS
SPEISE
SPEISES
SPEISS
SPEISSES
SPELAEAN
SPELEAN
SPELEOLOGICAL
SPELEOLOGIES
SPELEOLOGIST
SPELEOLOGISTS
SPELEOLOGY
SPELL
SPELLBIND
SPELLBINDER
SPELLBINDERS
SPELLBINDING
SPELLBINDINGLY
SPELLBINDS
SPELLBOUND
SPELLDOWN
SPELLDOWNS
SPELLED
SPELLER
SPELLERS
SPELLING
SPELLINGS
SPELLS
SPELT
SPELTER
SPELTERS
SPELTS
SPELTZ
SPELTZES
SPELUNK
SPELUNKED
SPELUNKER
SPELUNKERS
SPELUNKING
SPELUNKINGS
SPELUNKS
SPENCE
SPENCER

PENCERS
PENCES
PEND
PENDABLE
PENDER
PENDERS
PENDIER
PENDIEST
PENDING
PENDS
PENDTHRIFT
PENDTHRIFTS
PENDY
PENSE
PENSES
PENT
PERM
PERMACETI
PERMACETIS
PERMAGONIA
PERMAGONIUM
PERMARIES
PERMARY
PERMATHECA
ERMATHECAE
PERMATHECAS
ERMATIA
ERMATIAL
ERMATIC
ERMATID
ERMATIDS
ERMATIUM
ERMATOCYTE
ERMATOCYTES
ERMATOGENESES
ERMATOGENESIS
ERMATOGENIC
ERMATOGONIA
ERMATOGONIAL
ERMATOGONIUM
ERMATOPHORE
ERMATOPHORES
ERMATOPHYTE
ERMATOPHYTES
ERMATOPHYTIC
ERMATOZOA
ERMATOZOAL
ERMATOZOAN
ERMATOZOANS
ERMATOZOID
ERMATOZOIDS
ERMATOZOON
ERMIC
SPERMICIDAL
SPERMICIDE
SPERMICIDES
SPERMINE
SPERMINES
SPERMIOGENESES
SPERMIOGENESIS
SPERMOPHILE
SPERMOPHILES
SPERMOUS
SPERMS
SPERRYLITE
SPERRYLITES
SPESSARTINE
SPESSARTINES
SPESSARTITE
SPESSARTITES
SPEW
SPEWED
SPEWER
SPEWERS
SPEWING
SPEWS
SPHAGNOUS
SPHAGNUM
SPHAGNUMS
SPHALERITE
SPHALERITES
SPHENE
SPHENES
SPHENIC
SPHENODON
SPHENODONS
SPHENODONT
SPHENOID
SPHENOIDAL
SPHENOIDS
SPHENOPSID
SPHENOPSIDS
SPHERAL
SPHERE
SPHERED
SPHERES
SPHERIC
SPHERICAL
SPHERICALLY
SPHERICITIES
SPHERICITY
SPHERICS
SPHERIER
SPHERIEST
SPHERING
SPHEROID
SPHEROIDAL
SPHEROIDALLY
SPHEROIDS
SPHEROMETER
SPHEROMETERS
SPHEROPLAST
SPHEROPLASTS
SPHERULAR
SPHERULE
SPHERULES
SPHERULITE
SPHERULITES
SPHERULITIC
SPHERY
SPHINCTER
SPHINCTERIC
SPHINCTERS
SPHINGES
SPHINGID
SPHINGIDS
SPHINGOSINE
SPHINGOSINES
SPHINX
SPHINXES
SPHINXLIKE
SPHYGMIC
SPHYGMOGRAPH
SPHYGMOGRAPHS
SPHYGMUS
SPHYGMUSES
SPHYNX
SPHYNXES
SPIC
SPICA
SPICAE
SPICAS
SPICATE
SPICATED
SPICCATO
SPICCATOS
SPICE
SPICEBUSH
SPICEBUSHES
SPICED
SPICELESS
SPICER
SPICERIES
SPICERS
SPICERY
SPICES
SPICEY
SPICIER
SPICIEST
SPICILY
SPICINESS
SPICINESSES
SPICING
SPICK
SPICKS
SPICS
SPICULA
SPICULAE
SPICULAR
SPICULATE
SPICULATION
SPICULATIONS
SPICULE
SPICULES
SPICULUM
SPICY
SPIDER
SPIDERED
SPIDERIER
SPIDERIEST
SPIDERING
SPIDERISH
SPIDERLIKE
SPIDERS
SPIDERWEB
SPIDERWEBS
SPIDERWORT
SPIDERWORTS
SPIDERY
SPIED
SPIEGEL
SPIEGELEISEN
SPIEGELEISENS
SPIEGELS
SPIEL
SPIELED
SPIELER
SPIELERS
SPIELING
SPIELS
SPIER
SPIERED
SPIERING
SPIERS
SPIES
SPIFF
SPIFFED
SPIFFIED
SPIFFIER
SPIFFIES
SPIFFIEST
SPIFFILY
SPIFFINESS
SPIFFINESSES
SPIFFING
SPIFFS
SPIFFY
SPIFFYING
SPIGOT
SPIGOTS
SPIK
SPIKE
SPIKED
SPIKELET
SPIKELETS
SPIKELIKE
SPIKENARD
SPIKENARDS
SPIKER
SPIKERS
SPIKES
SPIKEY
SPIKIER
SPIKIEST
SPIKILY
SPIKINESS
SPIKINESSES
SPIKING
SPIKS
SPIKY
SPILE
SPILED
SPILES
SPILIKIN
SPILIKINS
SPILING
SPILINGS
SPILITE
SPILITES
SPILITIC
SPILL
SPILLABLE
SPILLAGE
SPILLAGES
SPILLED
SPILLER
SPILLERS
SPILLIKIN
SPILLIKINS
SPILLING
SPILLOVER
SPILLOVERS
SPILLS
SPILLWAY
SPILLWAYS

SPILT
SPILTH
SPILTHS
SPIN
SPINACH
SPINACHES
SPINACHIER
SPINACHIEST
SPINACHLIKE
SPINACHY
SPINAGE
SPINAGES
SPINAL
SPINALLY
SPINALS
SPINATE
SPINDLE
SPINDLED
SPINDLER
SPINDLERS
SPINDLES
SPINDLIER
SPINDLIEST
SPINDLING
SPINDLY
SPINDRIFT
SPINDRIFTS
SPINE
SPINED
SPINEL
SPINELESS
SPINELESSLY
SPINELESSNESS
SPINELESSNESSES
SPINELIKE
SPINELLE
SPINELLES
SPINELS
SPINES
SPINET
SPINETS
SPINIER
SPINIEST
SPINIFEX
SPINIFEXES
SPININESS
SPININESSES
SPINLESS
SPINMASTER
SPINMASTERS
SPINMEISTER
SPINMEISTERS
SPINNAKER
SPINNAKERS
SPINNER
SPINNERET
SPINNERETS
SPINNERETTE
SPINNERETTES
SPINNERIES
SPINNERS
SPINNERY
SPINNEY
SPINNEYS
SPINNIER
SPINNIES
SPINNIEST
SPINNING
SPINNINGS
SPINNY
SPINOFF
SPINOFFS
SPINOR
SPINORS
SPINOSE
SPINOSELY
SPINOSITIES
SPINOSITY
SPINOUS
SPINOUT
SPINOUTS
SPINS
SPINSTER
SPINSTERHOOD
SPINSTERHOODS
SPINSTERISH
SPINSTERLY
SPINSTERS
SPINTHARISCOPE
SPINTHARISCOPES
SPINTO
SPINTOS
SPINULA
SPINULAE
SPINULE
SPINULES
SPINULOSE
SPINY
SPIRACLE
SPIRACLES
SPIRACULAR
SPIRAEA
SPIRAEAS
SPIRAL
SPIRALED
SPIRALING
SPIRALITIES
SPIRALITY
SPIRALLED
SPIRALLING
SPIRALLY
SPIRALS
SPIRANT
SPIRANTS
SPIRE
SPIREA
SPIREAS
SPIRED
SPIREM
SPIREME
SPIREMES
SPIREMS
SPIRES
SPIRIER
SPIRIEST
SPIRILLA
SPIRILLUM
SPIRING
SPIRIT
SPIRITED
SPIRITEDLY
SPIRITEDNESS
SPIRITEDNESSES
SPIRITING
SPIRITISM
SPIRITISMS
SPIRITIST
SPIRITISTIC
SPIRITISTS
SPIRITLESS
SPIRITLESSLY
SPIRITLESSNESS
SPIRITOSO
SPIRITOUS
SPIRITS
SPIRITUAL
SPIRITUALISM
SPIRITUALISMS
SPIRITUALIST
SPIRITUALISTIC
SPIRITUALISTS
SPIRITUALITIES
SPIRITUALITY
SPIRITUALIZE
SPIRITUALIZED
SPIRITUALIZES
SPIRITUALIZING
SPIRITUALLY
SPIRITUALNESS
SPIRITUALNESSES
SPIRITUALS
SPIRITUALTIES
SPIRITUALTY
SPIRITUEL
SPIRITUELLE
SPIRITUOUS
SPIRITUS
SPIROCHAETE
SPIROCHAETES
SPIROCHETAL
SPIROCHETE
SPIROCHETES
SPIROCHETOSES
SPIROCHETOSIS
SPIROGYRA
SPIROGYRAS
SPIROID
SPIROMETER
SPIROMETERS
SPIROMETRIC
SPIROMETRIES
SPIROMETRY
SPIRT
SPIRTED
SPIRTING
SPIRTS
SPIRULA
SPIRULAE
SPIRULAS
SPIRULINA
SPIRULINAS
SPIRY
SPIT
SPITAL
SPITALS
SPITBALL
SPITBALLED
SPITBALLING
SPITBALLS
SPITE
SPITED
SPITEFUL
SPITEFULLER
SPITEFULLEST
SPITEFULLY
SPITEFULNESS
SPITEFULNESSES
SPITES
SPITFIRE
SPITFIRES
SPITING
SPITS
SPITTED
SPITTER
SPITTERS
SPITTIER
SPITTIEST
SPITTING
SPITTLE
SPITTLEBUG
SPITTLEBUGS
SPITTLES
SPITTLY
SPITTOON
SPITTOONS
SPITTY
SPITZ
SPITZES
SPIV
SPIVS
SPIVVIER
SPIVVIEST
SPIVVISH
SPIVVY
SPLAKE
SPLAKES
SPLANCHNIC
SPLASH
SPLASHBOARD
SPLASHBOARDS
SPLASHDOWN
SPLASHDOWNS
SPLASHED
SPLASHER
SPLASHERS
SPLASHES
SPLASHIER
SPLASHIEST
SPLASHILY
SPLASHINESS
SPLASHINESSES
SPLASHING
SPLASHY
SPLAT
SPLATS
SPLATTED
SPLATTER
SPLATTERED
SPLATTERING
SPLATTERS
SPLATTING
SPLAY
SPLAYED
SPLAYFEET
SPLAYFOOT

PLAYFOOTED
PLAYING
PLAYS
PLEEN
LEENFUL
LEENIER
LEENIEST
LEENISH
LEENS
LEENWORT
LEENWORTS
LEENY
LENDENT
LENDID
LENDIDER
LENDIDEST
LENDIDLY
LENDIDNESS
LENDIDNESSES
LENDIFEROUS
LENDIFEROUSLY
LENDOR
LENDOROUS
LENDORS
LENDOUR
LENDOURS
LENDROUS
LENECTOMIES
LENECTOMIZE
LENECTOMIZED
LENECTOMIZES
LENECTOMIZING
LENECTOMY
LENETIC
LENETICALLY
LENETICS
LENIA
LENIAL
LENIC
LENII
LENIUM
LENIUMS
LENIUS
LENOMEGALIES
LENOMEGALY
LENT
LENTS
LEUCHAN
LEUCHANS
ICE
ICED
ICER
ICERS
SPLICES
SPLICING
SPLIFF
SPLIFFS
SPLINE
SPLINED
SPLINES
SPLINING
SPLINT
SPLINTED
SPLINTER
SPLINTERED
SPLINTERING
SPLINTERS
SPLINTERY
SPLINTING
SPLINTS
SPLIT
SPLITS
SPLITTER
SPLITTERS
SPLITTING
SPLODGE
SPLODGED
SPLODGES
SPLODGIER
SPLODGIEST
SPLODGING
SPLODGY
SPLORE
SPLORES
SPLOSH
SPLOSHED
SPLOSHES
SPLOSHING
SPLOTCH
SPLOTCHED
SPLOTCHES
SPLOTCHIER
SPLOTCHIEST
SPLOTCHING
SPLOTCHY
SPLURGE
SPLURGED
SPLURGER
SPLURGERS
SPLURGES
SPLURGIER
SPLURGIEST
SPLURGING
SPLURGY
SPLURT
SPLURTED
SPLURTING
SPLURTS
SPLUTTER
SPLUTTERED
SPLUTTERER
SPLUTTERERS
SPLUTTERING
SPLUTTERS
SPLUTTERY
SPODE
SPODES
SPODOSOL
SPODOSOLS
SPODUMENE
SPODUMENES
SPOIL
SPOILABLE
SPOILAGE
SPOILAGES
SPOILED
SPOILER
SPOILERS
SPOILING
SPOILS
SPOILSMAN
SPOILSMEN
SPOILSPORT
SPOILSPORTS
SPOILT
SPOKE
SPOKED
SPOKEN
SPOKES
SPOKESHAVE
SPOKESHAVES
SPOKESMAN
SPOKESMANSHIP
SPOKESMANSHIPS
SPOKESMEN
SPOKESMODEL
SPOKESMODELS
SPOKESPEOPLE
SPOKESPERSON
SPOKESPERSONS
SPOKESWOMAN
SPOKESWOMEN
SPOKING
SPOLIATE
SPOLIATED
SPOLIATES
SPOLIATING
SPOLIATION
SPOLIATIONS
SPOLIATOR
SPOLIATORS
SPONDAIC
SPONDAICS
SPONDEE
SPONDEES
SPONDYLITIDES
SPONDYLITIS
SPONDYLITISES
SPONGE
SPONGED
SPONGEING
SPONGELIKE
SPONGER
SPONGERS
SPONGES
SPONGEWARE
SPONGEWARES
SPONGIER
SPONGIEST
SPONGILY
SPONGIN
SPONGINESS
SPONGINESSES
SPONGING
SPONGINS
SPONGY
SPONSAL
SPONSION
SPONSIONS
SPONSON
SPONSONS
SPONSOR
SPONSORED
SPONSORIAL
SPONSORING
SPONSORS
SPONSORSHIP
SPONSORSHIPS
SPONTANEITIES
SPONTANEITY
SPONTANEOUS
SPONTANEOUSLY
SPONTANEOUSNESS
SPONTOON
SPONTOONS
SPOOF
SPOOFED
SPOOFER
SPOOFERIES
SPOOFERS
SPOOFERY
SPOOFING
SPOOFS
SPOOFY
SPOOK
SPOOKED
SPOOKERIES
SPOOKERY
SPOOKIER
SPOOKIEST
SPOOKILY
SPOOKINESS
SPOOKINESSES
SPOOKING
SPOOKISH
SPOOKS
SPOOKY
SPOOL
SPOOLED
SPOOLER
SPOOLERS
SPOOLING
SPOOLINGS
SPOOLS
SPOON
SPOONBILL
SPOONBILLS
SPOONED
SPOONER
SPOONERISM
SPOONERISMS
SPOONERS
SPOONEY
SPOONEYS
SPOONFUL
SPOONFULS
SPOONIER
SPOONIES
SPOONIEST
SPOONILY
SPOONING
SPOONS
SPOONSFUL
SPOONY
SPOOR
SPOORED
SPOORER
SPOORERS
SPOORING
SPOORS
SPORADIC
SPORADICALLY
SPORAL
SPORANGIA
SPORANGIAL

SPORANGIOPHORE
SPORANGIOPHORES
SPORANGIUM
SPORE
SPORED
SPORES
SPORICIDAL
SPORICIDE
SPORICIDES
SPORING
SPOROCARP
SPOROCARPS
SPOROCYST
SPOROCYSTS
SPOROGENESES
SPOROGENESIS
SPOROGENIC
SPOROGENOUS
SPOROGONIA
SPOROGONIC
SPOROGONIES
SPOROGONIUM
SPOROGONY
SPOROID
SPOROPHORE
SPOROPHORES
SPOROPHYL
SPOROPHYLL
SPOROPHYLLS
SPOROPHYLS
SPOROPHYTE
SPOROPHYTES
SPOROPHYTIC
SPOROPOLLENIN
SPOROPOLLENINS
SPOROTRICHOSES
SPOROTRICHOSIS
SPOROZOA
SPOROZOAL
SPOROZOAN
SPOROZOANS
SPOROZOIC
SPOROZOITE
SPOROZOITES
SPOROZOON
SPORRAN
SPORRANS
SPORT
SPORTED
SPORTER
SPORTERS
SPORTFISHERMAN
SPORTFISHERMEN
SPORTFISHING
SPORTFISHINGS
SPORTFUL
SPORTFULLY
SPORTFULNESS
SPORTFULNESSES
SPORTIER
SPORTIEST
SPORTIF
SPORTIFS
SPORTILY
SPORTINESS
SPORTINESSES
SPORTING
SPORTINGLY
SPORTIVE
SPORTIVELY
SPORTIVENESS
SPORTIVENESSES
SPORTS
SPORTSCAST
SPORTSCASTER
SPORTSCASTERS
SPORTSCASTS
SPORTSMAN
SPORTSMANLIKE
SPORTSMANLY
SPORTSMANSHIP
SPORTSMANSHIPS
SPORTSMEN
SPORTSWEAR
SPORTSWEARS
SPORTSWOMAN
SPORTSWOMEN
SPORTSWRITER
SPORTSWRITERS
SPORTSWRITING
SPORTSWRITINGS
SPORTY
SPORULAR
SPORULATE
SPORULATED
SPORULATES
SPORULATING
SPORULATION
SPORULATIONS
SPORULATIVE
SPORULE
SPORULES
SPOT
SPOTLESS
SPOTLESSLY
SPOTLESSNESS
SPOTLESSNESSES
SPOTLIGHT
SPOTLIGHTED
SPOTLIGHTING
SPOTLIGHTS
SPOTLIT
SPOTS
SPOTTABLE
SPOTTED
SPOTTER
SPOTTERS
SPOTTIER
SPOTTIEST
SPOTTILY
SPOTTINESS
SPOTTINESSES
SPOTTING
SPOTTINGS
SPOTTY
SPOUSAL
SPOUSALLY
SPOUSALS
SPOUSE
SPOUSED
SPOUSES
SPOUSING
SPOUT
SPOUTED
SPOUTER
SPOUTERS
SPOUTING
SPOUTINGS
SPOUTLESS
SPOUTS
SPRACHGEFUHL
SPRACHGEFUHLS
SPRADDLE
SPRADDLED
SPRADDLES
SPRADDLING
SPRAG
SPRAGS
SPRAIN
SPRAINED
SPRAINING
SPRAINS
SPRANG
SPRANGS
SPRAT
SPRATS
SPRATTLE
SPRATTLED
SPRATTLES
SPRATTLING
SPRAWL
SPRAWLED
SPRAWLER
SPRAWLERS
SPRAWLIER
SPRAWLIEST
SPRAWLING
SPRAWLS
SPRAWLY
SPRAY
SPRAYED
SPRAYER
SPRAYERS
SPRAYING
SPRAYS
SPREAD
SPREADABILITIES
SPREADABILITY
SPREADABLE
SPREADER
SPREADERS
SPREADING
SPREADS
SPREADSHEET
SPREADSHEETS
SPREE
SPREES
SPRENT
SPRIER
SPRIEST
SPRIG
SPRIGGED
SPRIGGER
SPRIGGERS
SPRIGGIER
SPRIGGIEST
SPRIGGING
SPRIGGY
SPRIGHT
SPRIGHTFUL
SPRIGHTFULLY
SPRIGHTFULNESS
SPRIGHTLIER
SPRIGHTLIEST
SPRIGHTLINESS
SPRIGHTLINESSES
SPRIGHTLY
SPRIGHTS
SPRIGS
SPRIGTAIL
SPRIGTAILS
SPRING
SPRINGAL
SPRINGALD
SPRINGALDS
SPRINGALS
SPRINGBOARD
SPRINGBOARDS
SPRINGBOK
SPRINGBOKS
SPRINGE
SPRINGED
SPRINGEING
SPRINGER
SPRINGERS
SPRINGES
SPRINGHEAD
SPRINGHEADS
SPRINGHOUSE
SPRINGHOUSES
SPRINGIER
SPRINGIEST
SPRINGILY
SPRINGINESS
SPRINGINESSES
SPRINGING
SPRINGINGS
SPRINGLET
SPRINGLETS
SPRINGLIKE
SPRINGS
SPRINGTAIL
SPRINGTAILS
SPRINGTIDE
SPRINGTIDES
SPRINGTIME
SPRINGTIMES
SPRINGWATER
SPRINGWATERS
SPRINGWOOD
SPRINGWOODS
SPRINGY
SPRINKLE
SPRINKLED
SPRINKLER
SPRINKLERED
SPRINKLERING
SPRINKLERS
SPRINKLES
SPRINKLING
SPRINKLINGS
SPRINT
SPRINTED
SPRINTER
SPRINTERS

NTING
NTINGS
NTS
T
TE
TELIER
TELIEST
TELY
TES
TS
TSAIL
TSAILS
TZ
TZED
TZER
TZERS
TZES
TZIER
TZIEST
TZING
TZY
OCKET
OCKETS
OG
OGLET
OGLETS
OGS
OUT
OUTED
OUTING
OUTS
UCE
UCED
UCELY
UCENESS
UCENESSES
UCER
UCES
UCEST
UCIER
UCIEST
UCING
UCY
UE
UES
UG
UGS
UNG
Y
YER
YEST
YLY
YNESS

SPRYNESSES
SPUD
SPUDDED
SPUDDER
SPUDDERS
SPUDDING
SPUDGEL
SPUDGELS
SPUDS
SPUE
SPUED
SPUES
SPUING
SPUMANTE
SPUMANTES
SPUME
SPUMED
SPUMES
SPUMIER
SPUMIEST
SPUMING
SPUMONE
SPUMONES
SPUMONI
SPUMONIS
SPUMOUS
SPUMY
SPUN
SPUNBONDED
SPUNK
SPUNKED
SPUNKIE
SPUNKIER
SPUNKIES
SPUNKIEST
SPUNKILY
SPUNKINESS
SPUNKINESSES
SPUNKING
SPUNKS
SPUNKY
SPUR
SPURGALL
SPURGALLED
SPURGALLING
SPURGALLS
SPURGE
SPURGES
SPURIOUS
SPURIOUSLY
SPURIOUSNESS
SPURIOUSNESSES
SPURLESS

SPURN
SPURNED
SPURNER
SPURNERS
SPURNING
SPURNS
SPURRED
SPURRER
SPURRERS
SPURREY
SPURREYS
SPURRIER
SPURRIERS
SPURRIES
SPURRING
SPURRY
SPURS
SPURT
SPURTED
SPURTER
SPURTERS
SPURTING
SPURTLE
SPURTLES
SPURTS
SPUTA
SPUTNIK
SPUTNIKS
SPUTTER
SPUTTERED
SPUTTERER
SPUTTERERS
SPUTTERING
SPUTTERS
SPUTTERY
SPUTUM
SPY
SPYGLASS
SPYGLASSES
SPYING
SPYMASTER
SPYMASTERS
SPYWARE
SPYWARES
SQUAB
SQUABBIER
SQUABBIEST
SQUABBLE
SQUABBLED
SQUABBLER
SQUABBLERS
SQUABBLES
SQUABBLING

SQUABBY
SQUABS
SQUAD
SQUADDED
SQUADDIE
SQUADDIES
SQUADDING
SQUADDY
SQUADRON
SQUADRONED
SQUADRONING
SQUADRONS
SQUADS
SQUALENE
SQUALENES
SQUALID
SQUALIDER
SQUALIDEST
SQUALIDLY
SQUALIDNESS
SQUALIDNESSES
SQUALL
SQUALLED
SQUALLER
SQUALLERS
SQUALLIER
SQUALLIEST
SQUALLING
SQUALLISH
SQUALLS
SQUALLY
SQUALOR
SQUALORS
SQUAMA
SQUAMAE
SQUAMATE
SQUAMATES
SQUAMATION
SQUAMATIONS
SQUAMOSAL
SQUAMOSALS
SQUAMOSE
SQUAMOUS
SQUAMULOSE
SQUANDER
SQUANDERED
SQUANDERER
SQUANDERERS
SQUANDERING
SQUANDERS
SQUARE
SQUARED
SQUARELY

SQUARENESS
SQUARENESSES
SQUARER
SQUARERS
SQUARES
SQUAREST
SQUARING
SQUARISH
SQUARISHLY
SQUARISHNESS
SQUARISHNESSES
SQUARK
SQUARKS
SQUARROSE
SQUASH
SQUASHED
SQUASHER
SQUASHERS
SQUASHES
SQUASHIER
SQUASHIEST
SQUASHILY
SQUASHINESS
SQUASHINESSES
SQUASHING
SQUASHY
SQUAT
SQUATLY
SQUATNESS
SQUATNESSES
SQUATS
SQUATTED
SQUATTER
SQUATTERED
SQUATTERING
SQUATTERS
SQUATTEST
SQUATTIER
SQUATTIEST
SQUATTILY
SQUATTING
SQUATTY
SQUAW
SQUAWBUSH
SQUAWBUSHES
SQUAWFISH
SQUAWFISHES
SQUAWK
SQUAWKED
SQUAWKER
SQUAWKERS
SQUAWKING
SQUAWKS

SQUAWROOT
SQUAWROOTS
SQUAWS
SQUEAK
SQUEAKED
SQUEAKER
SQUEAKERS
SQUEAKIER
SQUEAKIEST
SQUEAKILY
SQUEAKINESS
SQUEAKINESSES
SQUEAKING
SQUEAKS
SQUEAKY
SQUEAL
SQUEALED
SQUEALER
SQUEALERS
SQUEALING
SQUEALS
SQUEAMISH
SQUEAMISHLY
SQUEAMISHNESS
SQUEAMISHNESSES
SQUEEGEE
SQUEEGEED
SQUEEGEEING
SQUEEGEES
SQUEEZABILITIES
SQUEEZABILITY
SQUEEZABLE
SQUEEZE
SQUEEZED
SQUEEZER
SQUEEZERS
SQUEEZES
SQUEEZING
SQUEG
SQUEGGED
SQUEGGING
SQUEGS
SQUELCH
SQUELCHED
SQUELCHER
SQUELCHERS
SQUELCHES
SQUELCHIER
SQUELCHIEST
SQUELCHING
SQUELCHY
SQUETEAGUE
SQUIB
SQUIBBED
SQUIBBER
SQUIBBERS
SQUIBBING
SQUIBS
SQUID
SQUIDDED
SQUIDDING
SQUIDGIER
SQUIDGIEST
SQUIDGY
SQUIDS
SQUIFFED
SQUIFFIER
SQUIFFIEST
SQUIFFY
SQUIGGLE
SQUIGGLED
SQUIGGLES
SQUIGGLIER
SQUIGGLIEST
SQUIGGLING
SQUIGGLY
SQUILGEE
SQUILGEED
SQUILGEEING
SQUILGEES
SQUILL
SQUILLA
SQUILLAE
SQUILLAS
SQUILLS
SQUINCH
SQUINCHED
SQUINCHES
SQUINCHING
SQUINNIED
SQUINNIER
SQUINNIES
SQUINNIEST
SQUINNY
SQUINNYING
SQUINT
SQUINTED
SQUINTER
SQUINTERS
SQUINTEST
SQUINTIER
SQUINTIEST
SQUINTING
SQUINTINGLY
SQUINTS
SQUINTY
SQUIRARCHIES
SQUIRARCHY
SQUIRE
SQUIREARCHIES
SQUIREARCHY
SQUIRED
SQUIREEN
SQUIREENS
SQUIRELY
SQUIRES
SQUIRING
SQUIRISH
SQUIRL
SQUIRLS
SQUIRM
SQUIRMED
SQUIRMER
SQUIRMERS
SQUIRMIER
SQUIRMIEST
SQUIRMING
SQUIRMS
SQUIRMY
SQUIRREL
SQUIRRELED
SQUIRRELFISH
SQUIRRELFISHES
SQUIRRELING
SQUIRRELLED
SQUIRRELLIER
SQUIRRELLIEST
SQUIRRELLING
SQUIRRELLY
SQUIRRELS
SQUIRRELY
SQUIRT
SQUIRTED
SQUIRTER
SQUIRTERS
SQUIRTING
SQUIRTS
SQUISH
SQUISHED
SQUISHES
SQUISHIER
SQUISHIEST
SQUISHINESS
SQUISHINESSES
SQUISHING
SQUISHY
SQUITTERS
SQUOOSH
SQUOOSHED
SQUOOSHES
SQUOOSHIER
SQUOOSHIEST
SQUOOSHING
SQUOOSHY
SQUUSH
SQUUSHED
SQUUSHES
SQUUSHING
SRADDHA
SRADDHAS
SRADHA
SRADHAS
SRI
SRIS
STAB
STABBED
STABBER
STABBERS
STABBING
STABBINGS
STABILE
STABILES
STABILISATION
STABILISATIONS
STABILISE
STABILISED
STABILISER
STABILISERS
STABILISES
STABILISING
STABILITIES
STABILITY
STABILIZATION
STABILIZATIONS
STABILIZE
STABILIZED
STABILIZER
STABILIZERS
STABILIZES
STABILIZING
STABLE
STABLEBOY
STABLEBOYS
STABLED
STABLEMAN
STABLEMATE
STABLEMATES
STABLEMEN
STABLENESS
STABLENESSES
STABLER
STABLERS
STABLES
STABLEST
STABLING
STABLINGS
STABLISH
STABLISHED
STABLISHES
STABLISHING
STABLISHMENT
STABLISHMENTS
STABLY
STABS
STACCATI
STACCATO
STACCATOS
STACK
STACKABLE
STACKED
STACKER
STACKERS
STACKING
STACKLESS
STACKS
STACKUP
STACKUPS
STACTE
STACTES
STADDLE
STADDLES
STADE
STADES
STADIA
STADIAS
STADIUM
STADIUMS
STADTHOLDER
STADTHOLDERATE
STADTHOLDERATES
STADTHOLDERS
STADTHOLDERSHIP
STAFF
STAFFED
STAFFER
STAFFERS
STAFFING
STAFFINGS
STAFFS
STAG
STAGE
STAGEABLE
STAGECOACH
STAGECOACHES
STAGECRAFT

AGECRAFTS
AGED
AGEFUL
AGEFULS
AGEHAND
AGEHANDS
AGELIKE
AGER
AGERS
AGES
AGESTRUCK
AGETTE
AGETTES
AGEY
AGFLATION
AGFLATIONARY
AGFLATIONS
AGGARD
AGGARDS
AGGART
AGGARTS
AGGED
AGGER
AGGERBUSH
AGGERBUSHES
AGGERED
AGGERER
AGGERERS
AGGERING
GGERINGLY
GGERS
GGERY
GGIE
GGIER
GGIES
GGIEST
GGING
GGY
GHORN
GHORNS
GHOUND
GHOUNDS
GIER
GIEST
GILY
GINESS
GINESSES
GING
GINGS
GNANCE
GNANCES
GNANCIES
GNANCY

STAGNANT
STAGNANTLY
STAGNATE
STAGNATED
STAGNATES
STAGNATING
STAGNATION
STAGNATIONS
STAGS
STAGY
STAID
STAIDER
STAIDEST
STAIDLY
STAIDNESS
STAIDNESSES
STAIG
STAIGS
STAIN
STAINABILITIES
STAINABILITY
STAINABLE
STAINED
STAINER
STAINERS
STAINING
STAINLESS
STAINLESSES
STAINLESSLY
STAINPROOF
STAINS
STAIR
STAIRCASE
STAIRCASES
STAIRHEAD
STAIRHEADS
STAIRLESS
STAIRLIKE
STAIRS
STAIRSTEP
STAIRSTEPPED
STAIRSTEPPING
STAIRSTEPS
STAIRWAY
STAIRWAYS
STAIRWELL
STAIRWELLS
STAITHE
STAITHES
STAKE
STAKED
STAKEHOLDER
STAKEHOLDERS

STAKEHOLDING
STAKEHOLDINGS
STAKEOUT
STAKEOUTS
STAKER
STAKERS
STAKES
STAKING
STALACTITE
STALACTITES
STALACTITIC
STALAG
STALAGMITE
STALAGMITES
STALAGMITIC
STALAGS
STALE
STALED
STALELY
STALEMATE
STALEMATED
STALEMATES
STALEMATING
STALENESS
STALENESSES
STALER
STALES
STALEST
STALING
STALK
STALKED
STALKER
STALKERAZZI
STALKERAZZO
STALKERS
STALKIER
STALKIEST
STALKILY
STALKING
STALKINGS
STALKLESS
STALKLIKE
STALKS
STALKY
STALL
STALLED
STALLHOLDER
STALLHOLDERS
STALLING
STALLION
STALLIONS
STALLS
STALWART

STALWARTLY
STALWARTNESS
STALWARTNESSES
STALWARTS
STALWORTH
STALWORTHS
STAMEN
STAMENED
STAMENS
STAMINA
STAMINAL
STAMINAS
STAMINATE
STAMINEAL
STAMINODE
STAMINODES
STAMINODIA
STAMINODIES
STAMINODIUM
STAMINODY
STAMMEL
STAMMELS
STAMMER
STAMMERED
STAMMERER
STAMMERERS
STAMMERING
STAMMERS
STAMP
STAMPED
STAMPEDE
STAMPEDED
STAMPEDER
STAMPEDERS
STAMPEDES
STAMPEDING
STAMPER
STAMPERS
STAMPING
STAMPLESS
STAMPS
STANCE
STANCES
STANCH
STANCHED
STANCHER
STANCHERS
STANCHES
STANCHEST
STANCHING
STANCHION
STANCHIONED
STANCHIONING

STANCHIONS
STANCHLY
STAND
STANDARD
STANDARDBRED
STANDARDBREDS
STANDARDISATION
STANDARDISE
STANDARDISED
STANDARDISES
STANDARDISING
STANDARDIZATION
STANDARDIZE
STANDARDIZED
STANDARDIZES
STANDARDIZING
STANDARDLESS
STANDARDLY
STANDARDS
STANDAWAY
STANDBY
STANDBYS
STANDDOWN
STANDDOWNS
STANDEE
STANDEES
STANDER
STANDERS
STANDFAST
STANDFASTS
STANDING
STANDINGS
STANDISH
STANDISHES
STANDOFF
STANDOFFISH
STANDOFFISHLY
STANDOFFISHNESS
STANDOFFS
STANDOUT
STANDOUTS
STANDPAT
STANDPATTER
STANDPATTERS
STANDPATTISM
STANDPATTISMS
STANDPIPE
STANDPIPES
STANDPOINT
STANDPOINTS
STANDS
STANDSTILL
STANDSTILLS

STANDUP
STANDUPS
STANE
STANED
STANES
STANG
STANGED
STANGING
STANGS
STANHOPE
STANHOPES
STANINE
STANINES
STANING
STANK
STANKS
STANNARIES
STANNARY
STANNIC
STANNITE
STANNITES
STANNOUS
STANNUM
STANNUMS
STANOL
STANOLS
STANZA
STANZAED
STANZAIC
STANZAS
STAPEDECTOMIES
STAPEDECTOMY
STAPEDES
STAPEDIAL
STAPELIA
STAPELIAS
STAPES
STAPH
STAPHS
STAPHYLINID
STAPHYLINIDAE
STAPHYLINIDS
STAPHYLOCOCCAL
STAPHYLOCOCCI
STAPHYLOCOCCIC
STAPHYLOCOCCUS
STAPLE
STAPLED
STAPLER
STAPLERS
STAPLES
STAPLING
STAR
STARBOARD
STARBOARDED
STARBOARDING
STARBOARDS
STARBURST
STARBURSTS
STARCH
STARCHED
STARCHER
STARCHERS
STARCHES
STARCHIER
STARCHIEST
STARCHILY
STARCHINESS
STARCHINESSES
STARCHING
STARCHY
STARDOM
STARDOMS
STARDUST
STARDUSTS
STARE
STARED
STARER
STARERS
STARES
STARETS
STARFISH
STARFISHES
STARFLOWER
STARFLOWERS
STARFRUIT
STARFRUITS
STARGAZE
STARGAZED
STARGAZER
STARGAZERS
STARGAZES
STARGAZING
STARGAZINGS
STARING
STARINGLY
STARK
STARKER
STARKERS
STARKEST
STARKLY
STARKNESS
STARKNESSES
STARLESS
STARLET
STARLETS
STARLIGHT
STARLIGHTS
STARLIKE
STARLING
STARLINGS
STARLIT
STARNOSE
STARNOSES
STARRED
STARRIER
STARRIEST
STARRILY
STARRING
STARRY
STARS
STARSHIP
STARSHIPS
STARSTRUCK
START
STARTED
STARTER
STARTERS
STARTING
STARTLE
STARTLED
STARTLEMENT
STARTLEMENTS
STARTLER
STARTLERS
STARTLES
STARTLING
STARTLINGLY
STARTS
STARTSY
STARTUP
STARTUPS
STARVATION
STARVATIONS
STARVE
STARVED
STARVELING
STARVELINGS
STARVER
STARVERS
STARVES
STARVING
STARWORT
STARWORTS
STASES
STASH
STASHED
STASHES
STASHING
STASIMA
STASIMON
STASIS
STAT
STATABLE
STATAL
STATANT
STATE
STATEABLE
STATECRAFT
STATECRAFTS
STATED
STATEDLY
STATEHOOD
STATEHOODS
STATEHOUSE
STATEHOUSES
STATELESS
STATELESSNESS
STATELESSNESSES
STATELET
STATELETS
STATELIER
STATELIEST
STATELINESS
STATELINESSES
STATELY
STATEMENT
STATEMENTS
STATER
STATEROOM
STATEROOMS
STATERS
STATES
STATESIDE
STATESMAN
STATESMANLIKE
STATESMANLY
STATESMANSHIP
STATESMANSHIPS
STATESMEN
STATESWOMAN
STATESWOMEN
STATEWIDE
STATIC
STATICAL
STATICALLY
STATICE
STATICES
STATICKY
STATICS
STATIN
STATING
STATINS
STATION
STATIONAL
STATIONARY
STATIONED
STATIONER
STATIONERIES
STATIONERS
STATIONERY
STATIONING
STATIONMASTER
STATIONMASTERS
STATIONS
STATISM
STATISMS
STATIST
STATISTIC
STATISTICAL
STATISTICALLY
STATISTICIAN
STATISTICIANS
STATISTICS
STATISTS
STATIVE
STATIVES
STATOBLAST
STATOBLASTS
STATOCYST
STATOCYSTS
STATOLITH
STATOLITHS
STATOR
STATORS
STATOSCOPE
STATOSCOPES
STATS
STATUARIES
STATUARY
STATUE
STATUED
STATUES
STATUESQUE
STATUESQUELY
STATUETTE
STATUETTES
STATURE
STATURED
STATURES
STATUS
STATUSES
STATUSY
STATUTABLE
STATUTE

ATUTES
ATUTORILY
ATUTORY
AUMREL
AUMRELS
AUNCH
AUNCHED
AUNCHER
AUNCHES
AUNCHEST
AUNCHING
AUNCHLY
AUNCHNESS
AUNCHNESSES
AUROLITE
AUROLITES
AUROLITIC
AVE
AVED
AVES
AVESACRE
AVESACRES
AVING
AVUDINE
AVUDINES
W
Y
YCATION
YCATIONER
YCATIONERS
YCATIONS
YED
YER
YERS
YING
YS
YSAIL
YSAILS
AD
ADED
ADFAST
ADFASTLY
ADFASTNESS
ADFASTNESSES
ADIED
ADIER
ADIERS
ADIES
ADIEST
ADILY
ADINESS
ADINESSES
ADING

STEADINGS
STEADS
STEADY
STEADYING
STEAK
STEAKS
STEAL
STEALABLE
STEALAGE
STEALAGES
STEALER
STEALERS
STEALING
STEALINGS
STEALS
STEALTH
STEALTHIER
STEALTHIEST
STEALTHILY
STEALTHINESS
STEALTHINESSES
STEALTHS
STEALTHY
STEAM
STEAMBOAT
STEAMBOATS
STEAMED
STEAMER
STEAMERED
STEAMERING
STEAMERS
STEAMFITTER
STEAMFITTERS
STEAMIE
STEAMIER
STEAMIES
STEAMIEST
STEAMILY
STEAMINESS
STEAMINESSES
STEAMING
STEAMPUNK
STEAMPUNKS
STEAMROLL
STEAMROLLED
STEAMROLLER
STEAMROLLERED
STEAMROLLERING
STEAMROLLERS
STEAMROLLING
STEAMROLLS
STEAMS
STEAMSHIP

STEAMSHIPS
STEAMY
STEAPSIN
STEAPSINS
STEARATE
STEARATES
STEARIC
STEARIN
STEARINE
STEARINES
STEARINS
STEATITE
STEATITES
STEATITIC
STEATOPYGIA
STEATOPYGIAS
STEATOPYGIC
STEATOPYGOUS
STEATORRHEA
STEATORRHEAS
STEATORRHOEA
STEATORRHOEAS
STEDFAST
STEED
STEEDLIKE
STEEDS
STEEK
STEEKED
STEEKING
STEEKS
STEEL
STEELED
STEELHEAD
STEELHEADS
STEELIE
STEELIER
STEELIES
STEELIEST
STEELINESS
STEELINESSES
STEELING
STEELMAKER
STEELMAKERS
STEELMAKING
STEELMAKINGS
STEELS
STEELWORK
STEELWORKER
STEELWORKERS
STEELWORKS
STEELY
STEELYARD
STEELYARDS

STEENBOK
STEENBOKS
STEENBUCK
STEENBUCKS
STEEP
STEEPED
STEEPEN
STEEPENED
STEEPENING
STEEPENS
STEEPER
STEEPERS
STEEPEST
STEEPING
STEEPISH
STEEPLE
STEEPLEBUSH
STEEPLEBUSHES
STEEPLECHASE
STEEPLECHASER
STEEPLECHASERS
STEEPLECHASES
STEEPLECHASING
STEEPLECHASINGS
STEEPLED
STEEPLEJACK
STEEPLEJACKS
STEEPLES
STEEPLING
STEEPLY
STEEPNESS
STEEPNESSES
STEEPS
STEER
STEERABLE
STEERAGE
STEERAGES
STEERAGEWAY
STEERAGEWAYS
STEERED
STEERER
STEERERS
STEERING
STEERINGS
STEERS
STEERSMAN
STEERSMEN
STEEVE
STEEVED
STEEVES
STEEVING
STEEVINGS
STEGANOGRAPHIC

STEGANOGRAPHIES
STEGANOGRAPHY
STEGODON
STEGODONS
STEGOSAUR
STEGOSAURS
STEGOSAURUS
STEGOSAURUSES
STEIN
STEINBOK
STEINBOKS
STEINS
STELA
STELAE
STELAI
STELAR
STELE
STELENE
STELES
STELIC
STELLA
STELLAR
STELLAS
STELLATE
STELLATED
STELLIFIED
STELLIFIES
STELLIFY
STELLIFYING
STELLITE
STELLITES
STELLULAR
STEM
STEMLESS
STEMLIKE
STEMMA
STEMMAS
STEMMATA
STEMMATIC
STEMMED
STEMMER
STEMMERIES
STEMMERS
STEMMERY
STEMMIER
STEMMIEST
STEMMING
STEMMY
STEMS
STEMSON
STEMSONS
STEMWARE
STEMWARES

STENCH
STENCHES
STENCHFUL
STENCHIER
STENCHIEST
STENCHY
STENCIL
STENCILED
STENCILER
STENCILERS
STENCILING
STENCILINGS
STENCILLED
STENCILLER
STENCILLERS
STENCILLING
STENCILS
STENGAH
STENGAHS
STENO
STENOBATH
STENOBATHIC
STENOBATHS
STENOGRAPHER
STENOGRAPHERS
STENOGRAPHIC
STENOGRAPHIES
STENOGRAPHY
STENOHALINE
STENOKIES
STENOKOUS
STENOKY
STENOS
STENOSED
STENOSES
STENOSING
STENOSIS
STENOTHERM
STENOTHERMAL
STENOTHERMS
STENOTIC
STENOTOPIC
STENOTYPE
STENOTYPED
STENOTYPES
STENOTYPIES
STENOTYPING
STENOTYPIST
STENOTYPISTS
STENOTYPY
STENT
STENTOR
STENTORIAN
STENTORS
STENTS
STEP
STEPBROTHER
STEPBROTHERS
STEPCHILD
STEPCHILDREN
STEPDAD
STEPDADS
STEPDAME
STEPDAMES
STEPDAUGHTER
STEPDAUGHTERS
STEPFAMILIES
STEPFAMILY
STEPFATHER
STEPFATHERS
STEPHANOTIS
STEPHANOTISES
STEPLADDER
STEPLADDERS
STEPLESS
STEPLIKE
STEPMOM
STEPMOMS
STEPMOTHER
STEPMOTHERS
STEPPARENT
STEPPARENTING
STEPPARENTINGS
STEPPARENTS
STEPPE
STEPPED
STEPPER
STEPPERS
STEPPES
STEPPING
STEPS
STEPSISTER
STEPSISTERS
STEPSON
STEPSONS
STEPSTOOL
STEPSTOOLS
STEPWISE
STERADIAN
STERADIANS
STERANE
STERANES
STERCORACEOUS
STERCULIA
STERE
STEREO
STEREOCHEMICAL
STEREOCHEMISTRY
STEREOED
STEREOGRAM
STEREOGRAMS
STEREOGRAPH
STEREOGRAPHED
STEREOGRAPHIC
STEREOGRAPHIES
STEREOGRAPHING
STEREOGRAPHS
STEREOGRAPHY
STEREOING
STEREOISOMER
STEREOISOMERIC
STEREOISOMERISM
STEREOISOMERS
STEREOLOGICAL
STEREOLOGICALLY
STEREOLOGIES
STEREOLOGY
STEREOPHONIC
STEREOPHONIES
STEREOPHONY
STEREOPSES
STEREOPSIS
STEREOPTICON
STEREOPTICONS
STEREOREGULAR
STEREOS
STEREOSCOPE
STEREOSCOPES
STEREOSCOPIC
STEREOSCOPIES
STEREOSCOPY
STEREOSPECIFIC
STEREOTACTIC
STEREOTAXIC
STEREOTAXICALLY
STEREOTYPE
STEREOTYPED
STEREOTYPER
STEREOTYPERS
STEREOTYPES
STEREOTYPIC
STEREOTYPICAL
STEREOTYPICALLY
STEREOTYPIES
STEREOTYPING
STEREOTYPY
STERES
STERIC
STERICAL
STERICALLY
STERIGMA
STERIGMAS
STERIGMATA
STERILANT
STERILANTS
STERILE
STERILELY
STERILISATION
STERILISATIONS
STERILISE
STERILISED
STERILISER
STERILISERS
STERILISES
STERILISING
STERILITIES
STERILITY
STERILIZATION
STERILIZATIONS
STERILIZE
STERILIZED
STERILIZER
STERILIZERS
STERILIZES
STERILIZING
STERLET
STERLETS
STERLING
STERLINGLY
STERLINGNESS
STERLINGNESSES
STERLINGS
STERN
STERNA
STERNAL
STERNED
STERNER
STERNEST
STERNFOREMOST
STERNITE
STERNITES
STERNLY
STERNMOST
STERNNESS
STERNNESSES
STERNOCOSTAL
STERNPOST
STERNPOSTS
STERNS
STERNSON
STERNSONS
STERNUM
STERNUMS
STERNUTATION
STERNUTATIONS
STERNUTATOR
STERNUTATORS
STERNWARD
STERNWARDS
STERNWAY
STERNWAYS
STEROID
STEROIDAL
STEROIDOGENESES
STEROIDOGENESIS
STEROIDOGENIC
STEROIDS
STEROL
STEROLS
STERTOR
STERTOROUS
STERTOROUSLY
STERTORS
STET
STETHOSCOPE
STETHOSCOPES
STETHOSCOPIC
STETS
STETSON
STETSONS
STETTED
STETTING
STEVEDORE
STEVEDORED
STEVEDORES
STEVEDORING
STEVIA
STEVIAS
STEW
STEWABLE
STEWARD
STEWARDED
STEWARDESS
STEWARDESSES
STEWARDING
STEWARDS
STEWARDSHIP
STEWARDSHIPS
STEWBUM
STEWBUMS
STEWED
STEWING
STEWPAN
STEWPANS
STEWPOT

EWPOTS
EWS
EWY
EY
HENIA
HENIAS
HENIC
BIAL
BINE
BINES
BIUM
BIUMS
BNITE
BNITES
CH
CHIC
CHOMYTHIA
CHOMYTHIAS
CHOMYTHIC
CHOMYTHIES
CHOMYTHY
CHS
CK
CKABLE
CKBALL
CKBALLS
CKED
CKER
CKERED
CKERING
CKERS
CKFUL
CKFULS
CKHANDLE
CKHANDLED
CKHANDLER
CKHANDLERS
CKHANDLES
CKHANDLING
CKIE
CKIER
CKIES
CKIEST
CKILY
CKINESS
CKINESSES
CKING
CKIT
KLE
KLEBACK
KLEBACKS
KLED
KLER
STICKLERS
STICKLES
STICKLIKE
STICKLING
STICKMAN
STICKMEN
STICKOUT
STICKOUTS
STICKPIN
STICKPINS
STICKS
STICKSEED
STICKSEEDS
STICKTIGHT
STICKTIGHTS
STICKUM
STICKUMS
STICKUP
STICKUPS
STICKWEED
STICKWEEDS
STICKWORK
STICKWORKS
STICKY
STICTION
STICTIONS
STIED
STIES
STIFF
STIFFED
STIFFEN
STIFFENED
STIFFENER
STIFFENERS
STIFFENING
STIFFENINGS
STIFFENS
STIFFER
STIFFEST
STIFFIE
STIFFIES
STIFFING
STIFFISH
STIFFLY
STIFFNESS
STIFFNESSES
STIFFS
STIFFY
STIFLE
STIFLED
STIFLER
STIFLERS
STIFLES
STIFLING
STIFLINGLY
STIGMA
STIGMAL
STIGMAS
STIGMASTEROL
STIGMASTEROLS
STIGMATA
STIGMATIC
STIGMATICALLY
STIGMATICS
STIGMATISATION
STIGMATISATIONS
STIGMATISE
STIGMATISED
STIGMATISES
STIGMATISING
STIGMATIST
STIGMATISTS
STIGMATIZATION
STIGMATIZATIONS
STIGMATIZE
STIGMATIZED
STIGMATIZES
STIGMATIZING
STILBENE
STILBENES
STILBESTROL
STILBESTROLS
STILBITE
STILBITES
STILE
STILES
STILETTO
STILETTOED
STILETTOES
STILETTOING
STILETTOS
STILL
STILLAGE
STILLAGES
STILLBIRTH
STILLBIRTHS
STILLBORN
STILLBORNS
STILLED
STILLER
STILLEST
STILLIER
STILLIEST
STILLING
STILLMAN
STILLMEN
STILLNESS
STILLNESSES
STILLROOM
STILLROOMS
STILLS
STILLSON
STILLSONS
STILLY
STILT
STILTED
STILTEDLY
STILTEDNESS
STILTEDNESSES
STILTING
STILTS
STIME
STIMES
STIMIED
STIMIES
STIMULANT
STIMULANTS
STIMULATE
STIMULATED
STIMULATES
STIMULATING
STIMULATION
STIMULATIONS
STIMULATIVE
STIMULATOR
STIMULATORS
STIMULATORY
STIMULI
STIMULUS
STIMY
STIMYING
STING
STINGAREE
STINGAREES
STINGE
STINGER
STINGERS
STINGES
STINGIER
STINGIEST
STINGILY
STINGINESS
STINGINESSES
STINGING
STINGINGLY
STINGLESS
STINGO
STINGOS
STINGRAY
STINGRAYS
STINGS
STINGY
STINK
STINKARD
STINKARDS
STINKBUG
STINKBUGS
STINKER
STINKEROO
STINKEROOS
STINKERS
STINKHORN
STINKHORNS
STINKIER
STINKIEST
STINKING
STINKINGLY
STINKO
STINKPOT
STINKPOTS
STINKS
STINKWEED
STINKWEEDS
STINKWOOD
STINKWOODS
STINKY
STINT
STINTED
STINTER
STINTERS
STINTING
STINTS
STIPE
STIPED
STIPEL
STIPELS
STIPEND
STIPENDIARIES
STIPENDIARY
STIPENDS
STIPES
STIPIFORM
STIPITATE
STIPITES
STIPPLE
STIPPLED
STIPPLER
STIPPLERS
STIPPLES
STIPPLING
STIPPLINGS
STIPULAR

STIPULATE
STIPULATED
STIPULATES
STIPULATING
STIPULATION
STIPULATIONS
STIPULATOR
STIPULATORS
STIPULATORY
STIPULE
STIPULED
STIPULES
STIR
STIRABOUT
STIRABOUTS
STIRK
STIRKS
STIRP
STIRPES
STIRPS
STIRRED
STIRRER
STIRRERS
STIRRING
STIRRINGS
STIRRUP
STIRRUPS
STIRS
STITCH
STITCHED
STITCHER
STITCHERIES
STITCHERS
STITCHERY
STITCHES
STITCHING
STITCHINGS
STITCHWORT
STITCHWORTS
STITHIED
STITHIES
STITHY
STITHYING
STIVER
STIVERS
STOA
STOAE
STOAI
STOAS
STOAT
STOATS
STOB
STOBBED
STOBBING
STOBS
STOCCADO
STOCCADOS
STOCCATA
STOCCATAS
STOCHASTIC
STOCHASTICALLY
STOCK
STOCKADE
STOCKADED
STOCKADES
STOCKADING
STOCKAGE
STOCKAGES
STOCKBREEDER
STOCKBREEDERS
STOCKBROKER
STOCKBROKERAGE
STOCKBROKERAGES
STOCKBROKERS
STOCKBROKING
STOCKBROKINGS
STOCKCAR
STOCKCARS
STOCKED
STOCKER
STOCKERS
STOCKFISH
STOCKFISHES
STOCKHOLDER
STOCKHOLDERS
STOCKIER
STOCKIEST
STOCKILY
STOCKINESS
STOCKINESSES
STOCKINET
STOCKINETS
STOCKINETTE
STOCKINETTES
STOCKING
STOCKINGED
STOCKINGS
STOCKISH
STOCKIST
STOCKISTS
STOCKJOBBER
STOCKJOBBERS
STOCKJOBBING
STOCKJOBBINGS
STOCKKEEPER
STOCKKEEPERS
STOCKMAN
STOCKMEN
STOCKPILE
STOCKPILED
STOCKPILER
STOCKPILERS
STOCKPILES
STOCKPILING
STOCKPOT
STOCKPOTS
STOCKROOM
STOCKROOMS
STOCKS
STOCKTAKING
STOCKTAKINGS
STOCKY
STOCKYARD
STOCKYARDS
STODGE
STODGED
STODGES
STODGIER
STODGIEST
STODGILY
STODGINESS
STODGINESSES
STODGING
STODGY
STOGEY
STOGEYS
STOGIE
STOGIES
STOGY
STOIC
STOICAL
STOICALLY
STOICHIOMETRIC
STOICHIOMETRIES
STOICHIOMETRY
STOICISM
STOICISMS
STOICS
STOKE
STOKED
STOKEHOLD
STOKEHOLDS
STOKEHOLE
STOKEHOLES
STOKER
STOKERS
STOKES
STOKESIA
STOKESIAS
STOKING
STOLE
STOLED
STOLEN
STOLES
STOLID
STOLIDER
STOLIDEST
STOLIDITIES
STOLIDITY
STOLIDLY
STOLLEN
STOLLENS
STOLON
STOLONATE
STOLONIC
STOLONIFEROUS
STOLONS
STOLPORT
STOLPORTS
STOMA
STOMACH
STOMACHACHE
STOMACHACHES
STOMACHED
STOMACHER
STOMACHERS
STOMACHIC
STOMACHICS
STOMACHING
STOMACHS
STOMACHY
STOMAL
STOMAS
STOMATA
STOMATAL
STOMATE
STOMATES
STOMATIC
STOMATITIDES
STOMATITIS
STOMATITISES
STOMATOPOD
STOMATOPODS
STOMATOUS
STOMODAEA
STOMODAEAL
STOMODAEUM
STOMODAEUMS
STOMODEA
STOMODEAL
STOMODEUM
STOMODEUMS
STOMP
STOMPED
STOMPER
STOMPERS
STOMPIER
STOMPIEST
STOMPING
STOMPS
STOMPY
STONABLE
STONE
STONEBOAT
STONEBOATS
STONECHAT
STONECHATS
STONECROP
STONECROPS
STONECUT
STONECUTS
STONECUTTER
STONECUTTERS
STONECUTTING
STONECUTTINGS
STONED
STONEFISH
STONEFISHES
STONEFLIES
STONEFLY
STONEMASON
STONEMASONRIES
STONEMASONRY
STONEMASONS
STONER
STONERS
STONES
STONEWALL
STONEWALLED
STONEWALLER
STONEWALLERS
STONEWALLING
STONEWALLS
STONEWARE
STONEWARES
STONEWASH
STONEWASHED
STONEWASHES
STONEWASHING
STONEWORK
STONEWORKER
STONEWORKERS
STONEWORKS
STONEWORT
STONEWORTS

ONEY
ONIER
ONIEST
ONILY
ONINESS
ONINESSES
ONING
ONISH
ONISHED
ONISHES
ONISHING
ONK
ONKED
ONKER
ONKERS
ONKING
ONKS
ONY
ONYHEARTED
OOD
OOGE
OOGED
OOGES
OOGING
OOK
OOKED
OOKER
OOKERS
OOKING
OOKINGS
OOKS
OOL
OOLED
OOLIE
OOLIES
OOLING
OOLS
OOP
OPBALL
OPBALLS
OPED
OPER
OPERS
OPING
OPS
P
PBAND
PBANDS
PBANK
PBANKS
PCOCK
PCOCKS
PE

STOPED
STOPER
STOPERS
STOPES
STOPGAP
STOPGAPS
STOPING
STOPINGS
STOPLIGHT
STOPLIGHTS
STOPOFF
STOPOFFS
STOPOVER
STOPOVERS
STOPPABLE
STOPPAGE
STOPPAGES
STOPPED
STOPPER
STOPPERED
STOPPERING
STOPPERS
STOPPING
STOPPLE
STOPPLED
STOPPLES
STOPPLING
STOPS
STOPT
STOPWATCH
STOPWATCHES
STOPWORD
STOPWORDS
STORABLE
STORABLES
STORAGE
STORAGES
STORAX
STORAXES
STORE
STORED
STOREFRONT
STOREFRONTS
STOREHOUSE
STOREHOUSES
STOREKEEPER
STOREKEEPERS
STOREMAN
STOREMEN
STORER
STOREROOM
STOREROOMS
STORERS

STORES
STORESHIP
STORESHIPS
STOREWIDE
STOREY
STOREYED
STOREYS
STORIED
STORIES
STORING
STORK
STORKS
STORKSBILL
STORKSBILLS
STORM
STORMBOUND
STORMED
STORMIER
STORMIEST
STORMILY
STORMINESS
STORMINESSES
STORMING
STORMS
STORMY
STORY
STORYBOARD
STORYBOARDED
STORYBOARDING
STORYBOARDS
STORYBOOK
STORYBOOKS
STORYING
STORYTELLER
STORYTELLERS
STORYTELLING
STORYTELLINGS
STOSS
STOT
STOTIN
STOTINKA
STOTINKI
STOTINOV
STOTINS
STOTS
STOTT
STOTTED
STOTTING
STOTTS
STOUND
STOUNDED
STOUNDING
STOUNDS

STOUP
STOUPS
STOUR
STOURE
STOURES
STOURIE
STOURS
STOURY
STOUT
STOUTEN
STOUTENED
STOUTENING
STOUTENS
STOUTER
STOUTEST
STOUTHEARTED
STOUTHEARTEDLY
STOUTISH
STOUTLY
STOUTNESS
STOUTNESSES
STOUTS
STOVE
STOVED
STOVEPIPE
STOVEPIPES
STOVER
STOVERS
STOVES
STOVETOP
STOVETOPS
STOVING
STOW
STOWABLE
STOWAGE
STOWAGES
STOWAWAY
STOWAWAYS
STOWED
STOWING
STOWP
STOWPS
STOWS
STRABISMIC
STRABISMUS
STRABISMUSES
STRADDLE
STRADDLED
STRADDLER
STRADDLERS
STRADDLES
STRADDLING
STRAFE

STRAFED
STRAFER
STRAFERS
STRAFES
STRAFING
STRAGGLE
STRAGGLED
STRAGGLER
STRAGGLERS
STRAGGLES
STRAGGLIER
STRAGGLIEST
STRAGGLING
STRAGGLY
STRAIGHT
STRAIGHTAWAY
STRAIGHTAWAYS
STRAIGHTBRED
STRAIGHTBREDS
STRAIGHTED
STRAIGHTEDGE
STRAIGHTEDGES
STRAIGHTEN
STRAIGHTENED
STRAIGHTENER
STRAIGHTENERS
STRAIGHTENING
STRAIGHTENS
STRAIGHTER
STRAIGHTEST
STRAIGHTFORWARD
STRAIGHTING
STRAIGHTISH
STRAIGHTJACKET
STRAIGHTJACKETS
STRAIGHTLACED
STRAIGHTLY
STRAIGHTNESS
STRAIGHTNESSES
STRAIGHTS
STRAIGHTWAY
STRAIN
STRAINED
STRAINER
STRAINERS
STRAINING
STRAINS
STRAIT
STRAITEN
STRAITENED
STRAITENING
STRAITENS
STRAITER

STRAITEST
STRAITJACKET
STRAITJACKETED
STRAITJACKETING
STRAITJACKETS
STRAITLACED
STRAITLACEDLY
STRAITLACEDNESS
STRAITLY
STRAITNESS
STRAITNESSES
STRAITS
STRAKE
STRAKED
STRAKES
STRAMASH
STRAMASHES
STRAMONIES
STRAMONIUM
STRAMONIUMS
STRAMONY
STRAND
STRANDED
STRANDEDNESS
STRANDEDNESSES
STRANDER
STRANDERS
STRANDING
STRANDLINE
STRANDLINES
STRANDS
STRANG
STRANGE
STRANGELY
STRANGENESS
STRANGENESSES
STRANGER
STRANGERED
STRANGERING
STRANGERS
STRANGES
STRANGEST
STRANGLE
STRANGLED
STRANGLEHOLD
STRANGLEHOLDS
STRANGLER
STRANGLERS
STRANGLES
STRANGLING
STRANGULATE
STRANGULATED
STRANGULATES

STRANGULATING
STRANGULATION
STRANGULATIONS
STRANGURIES
STRANGURY
STRAP
STRAPHANG
STRAPHANGED
STRAPHANGER
STRAPHANGERS
STRAPHANGING
STRAPHANGS
STRAPHUNG
STRAPLESS
STRAPLESSES
STRAPPADO
STRAPPADOES
STRAPPADOS
STRAPPED
STRAPPER
STRAPPERS
STRAPPIER
STRAPPIEST
STRAPPING
STRAPPINGS
STRAPPY
STRAPS
STRASS
STRASSES
STRATA
STRATAGEM
STRATAGEMS
STRATAL
STRATAS
STRATEGIC
STRATEGICAL
STRATEGICALLY
STRATEGIES
STRATEGISE
STRATEGISED
STRATEGISES
STRATEGISING
STRATEGIST
STRATEGISTS
STRATEGIZE
STRATEGIZED
STRATEGIZES
STRATEGIZING
STRATEGY
STRATH
STRATHS
STRATHSPEY
STRATHSPEYS

STRATI
STRATIFICATION
STRATIFICATIONS
STRATIFIED
STRATIFIES
STRATIFORM
STRATIFY
STRATIFYING
STRATIGRAPHIC
STRATIGRAPHICAL
STRATIGRAPHIES
STRATIGRAPHY
STRATOCRACIES
STRATOCRACY
STRATOCUMULI
STRATOCUMULUS
STRATOSPHERE
STRATOSPHERES
STRATOSPHERIC
STRATOUS
STRATOVOLCANO
STRATOVOLCANOES
STRATOVOLCANOS
STRATUM
STRATUMS
STRATUS
STRATUSES
STRAVAGE
STRAVAGED
STRAVAGES
STRAVAGING
STRAVAIG
STRAVAIGED
STRAVAIGING
STRAVAIGS
STRAW
STRAWBERRIES
STRAWBERRY
STRAWED
STRAWFLOWER
STRAWFLOWERS
STRAWHAT
STRAWIER
STRAWIEST
STRAWING
STRAWS
STRAWWORM
STRAWWORMS
STRAWY
STRAY
STRAYED
STRAYER
STRAYERS

STRAYING
STRAYS
STREAK
STREAKED
STREAKER
STREAKERS
STREAKIER
STREAKIEST
STREAKILY
STREAKINESS
STREAKINESSES
STREAKING
STREAKINGS
STREAKS
STREAKY
STREAM
STREAMBED
STREAMBEDS
STREAMED
STREAMER
STREAMERS
STREAMIER
STREAMIEST
STREAMING
STREAMINGS
STREAMLET
STREAMLETS
STREAMLINE
STREAMLINED
STREAMLINER
STREAMLINERS
STREAMLINES
STREAMLINING
STREAMS
STREAMSIDE
STREAMSIDES
STREAMY
STREEK
STREEKED
STREEKER
STREEKERS
STREEKING
STREEKS
STREEL
STREELED
STREELING
STREELS
STREET
STREETCAR
STREETCARS
STREETED
STREETLAMP
STREETLAMPS

STREETLIGHT
STREETLIGHTS
STREETS
STREETSCAPE
STREETSCAPES
STREETWALKER
STREETWALKERS
STREETWALKING
STREETWALKINGS
STREETWISE
STRENGTH
STRENGTHEN
STRENGTHENED
STRENGTHENER
STRENGTHENERS
STRENGTHENING
STRENGTHENS
STRENGTHS
STRENUOSITIES
STRENUOSITY
STRENUOUS
STRENUOUSLY
STRENUOUSNESS
STRENUOUSNESSE
STREP
STREPS
STREPTOBACILLI
STREPTOBACILLUS
STREPTOCARPUS
STREPTOCARPUSE
STREPTOCOCCAL
STREPTOCOCCI
STREPTOCOCCIC
STREPTOCOCCUS
STREPTOKINASE
STREPTOKINASES
STREPTOLYSIN
STREPTOLYSINS
STREPTOMYCES
STREPTOMYCETE
STREPTOMYCETES
STREPTOMYCIN
STREPTOMYCINS
STREPTOTHRICIN
STREPTOTHRICINS
STRESS
STRESSED
STRESSES
STRESSFUL
STRESSFULLY
STRESSING
STRESSLESS
STRESSLESSNESS

RESSOR
RESSORS
RETCH
RETCHABILITY
RETCHABLE
RETCHED
RETCHER
RETCHERED
RETCHERING
RETCHERS
RETCHES
RETCHIER
RETCHIEST
RETCHING
RETCHY
RETTA
RETTAS
RETTE
RETTI
RETTO
RETTOS
REUSEL
REUSELS
REW
REWED
REWER
REWERS
REWING
REWMENT
REWMENTS
REWN
REWS
IA
IAE
IATA
IATAL
IATE
IATED
IATES
IATING
IATION
IATIONS
IATUM
ICK
ICKEN
ICKLE
ICKLED
ICKLES
ICKLING
ICKS
ICT
ICTER
ICTEST

STRICTION
STRICTIONS
STRICTLY
STRICTNESS
STRICTNESSES
STRICTURE
STRICTURES
STRIDDEN
STRIDE
STRIDENCE
STRIDENCES
STRIDENCIES
STRIDENCY
STRIDENT
STRIDENTLY
STRIDER
STRIDERS
STRIDES
STRIDING
STRIDOR
STRIDORS
STRIDULATE
STRIDULATED
STRIDULATES
STRIDULATING
STRIDULATION
STRIDULATIONS
STRIDULATORY
STRIDULOUS
STRIDULOUSLY
STRIFE
STRIFEFUL
STRIFELESS
STRIFES
STRIGIL
STRIGILS
STRIGOSE
STRIKE
STRIKEBOUND
STRIKEBREAKER
STRIKEBREAKERS
STRIKEBREAKING
STRIKEBREAKINGS
STRIKEOUT
STRIKEOUTS
STRIKEOVER
STRIKEOVERS
STRIKER
STRIKERS
STRIKES
STRIKING
STRIKINGLY
STRIKINGS

STRINE
STRINES
STRING
STRINGCOURSE
STRINGCOURSES
STRINGED
STRINGENCIES
STRINGENCY
STRINGENDO
STRINGENT
STRINGENTLY
STRINGER
STRINGERS
STRINGHALT
STRINGHALTED
STRINGHALTS
STRINGIER
STRINGIEST
STRINGILY
STRINGINESS
STRINGINESSES
STRINGING
STRINGINGS
STRINGLESS
STRINGPIECE
STRINGPIECES
STRINGS
STRINGY
STRINGYBARK
STRINGYBARKS
STRIP
STRIPE
STRIPED
STRIPELESS
STRIPER
STRIPERS
STRIPES
STRIPEY
STRIPIER
STRIPIEST
STRIPING
STRIPINGS
STRIPLING
STRIPLINGS
STRIPPABLE
STRIPPED
STRIPPER
STRIPPERS
STRIPPING
STRIPS
STRIPT
STRIPTEASE
STRIPTEASER

STRIPTEASERS
STRIPTEASES
STRIPY
STRIVE
STRIVED
STRIVEN
STRIVER
STRIVERS
STRIVES
STRIVING
STROBE
STROBED
STROBES
STROBIC
STROBIL
STROBILA
STROBILAE
STROBILAR
STROBILATION
STROBILATIONS
STROBILE
STROBILES
STROBILI
STROBILS
STROBILUS
STROBING
STROBINGS
STROBOSCOPE
STROBOSCOPES
STROBOSCOPIC
STROBOTRON
STROBOTRONS
STRODE
STROKE
STROKED
STROKER
STROKERS
STROKES
STROKING
STROLL
STROLLED
STROLLER
STROLLERS
STROLLING
STROLLS
STROMA
STROMAL
STROMATA
STROMATIC
STROMATOLITE
STROMATOLITES
STROMATOLITIC
STRONG

STRONGBOX
STRONGBOXES
STRONGER
STRONGEST
STRONGHOLD
STRONGHOLDS
STRONGISH
STRONGLY
STRONGMAN
STRONGMEN
STRONGPOINT
STRONGPOINTS
STRONGYL
STRONGYLE
STRONGYLES
STRONGYLOIDOSES
STRONGYLOIDOSIS
STRONGYLS
STRONTIA
STRONTIAN
STRONTIANITE
STRONTIANITES
STRONTIANS
STRONTIAS
STRONTIC
STRONTIUM
STRONTIUMS
STROOK
STROP
STROPHANTHIN
STROPHANTHINS
STROPHE
STROPHES
STROPHIC
STROPHOID
STROPHOIDS
STROPHULI
STROPHULUS
STROPPED
STROPPER
STROPPERS
STROPPIER
STROPPIEST
STROPPINESS
STROPPINESSES
STROPPING
STROPPY
STROPS
STROUD
STROUDING
STROUDINGS
STROUDS
STROVE

STROW
STROWED
STROWING
STROWN
STROWS
STROY
STROYED
STROYER
STROYERS
STROYING
STROYS
STRUCK
STRUCKEN
STRUCTURAL
STRUCTURALISM
STRUCTURALISMS
STRUCTURALIST
STRUCTURALISTS
STRUCTURALIZE
STRUCTURALIZED
STRUCTURALIZES
STRUCTURALIZING
STRUCTURALLY
STRUCTURATION
STRUCTURATIONS
STRUCTURE
STRUCTURED
STRUCTURELESS
STRUCTURES
STRUCTURING
STRUDEL
STRUDELS
STRUGGLE
STRUGGLED
STRUGGLER
STRUGGLERS
STRUGGLES
STRUGGLING
STRUM
STRUMA
STRUMAE
STRUMAS
STRUMATIC
STRUMMED
STRUMMER
STRUMMERS
STRUMMING
STRUMOSE
STRUMOUS
STRUMPET
STRUMPETS
STRUMS
STRUNG
STRUNT
STRUNTED
STRUNTING
STRUNTS
STRUT
STRUTHIOUS
STRUTS
STRUTTED
STRUTTER
STRUTTERS
STRUTTING
STRYCHNIC
STRYCHNINE
STRYCHNINES
STUB
STUBBED
STUBBIER
STUBBIES
STUBBIEST
STUBBILY
STUBBING
STUBBLE
STUBBLED
STUBBLES
STUBBLIER
STUBBLIEST
STUBBLY
STUBBORN
STUBBORNER
STUBBORNEST
STUBBORNLY
STUBBORNNESS
STUBBORNNESSES
STUBBY
STUBS
STUCCO
STUCCOED
STUCCOER
STUCCOERS
STUCCOES
STUCCOING
STUCCOS
STUCCOWORK
STUCCOWORKS
STUCK
STUD
STUDBOOK
STUDBOOKS
STUDDED
STUDDIE
STUDDIES
STUDDING
STUDDINGS
STUDENT
STUDENTS
STUDENTSHIP
STUDENTSHIPS
STUDFISH
STUDFISHES
STUDHORSE
STUDHORSES
STUDIED
STUDIEDLY
STUDIEDNESS
STUDIEDNESSES
STUDIER
STUDIERS
STUDIES
STUDIO
STUDIOS
STUDIOUS
STUDIOUSLY
STUDIOUSNESS
STUDIOUSNESSES
STUDLIER
STUDLIEST
STUDLY
STUDS
STUDWORK
STUDWORKS
STUDY
STUDYING
STUFF
STUFFED
STUFFER
STUFFERS
STUFFIER
STUFFIEST
STUFFILY
STUFFINESS
STUFFINESSES
STUFFING
STUFFINGS
STUFFLESS
STUFFS
STUFFY
STUIVER
STUIVERS
STULL
STULLS
STULTIFICATION
STULTIFICATIONS
STULTIFIED
STULTIFIES
STULTIFY
STULTIFYING
STUM
STUMBLE
STUMBLEBUM
STUMBLEBUMS
STUMBLED
STUMBLER
STUMBLERS
STUMBLES
STUMBLING
STUMBLINGLY
STUMMED
STUMMING
STUMP
STUMPAGE
STUMPAGES
STUMPED
STUMPER
STUMPERS
STUMPIER
STUMPIEST
STUMPILY
STUMPING
STUMPS
STUMPY
STUMS
STUN
STUNG
STUNK
STUNNED
STUNNER
STUNNERS
STUNNING
STUNNINGLY
STUNS
STUNSAIL
STUNSAILS
STUNT
STUNTED
STUNTEDNESS
STUNTEDNESSES
STUNTING
STUNTMAN
STUNTMEN
STUNTS
STUNTWOMAN
STUNTWOMEN
STUPA
STUPAS
STUPE
STUPEFACTION
STUPEFACTIONS
STUPEFIED
STUPEFIER
STUPEFIERS
STUPEFIES
STUPEFY
STUPEFYING
STUPEFYINGLY
STUPENDOUS
STUPENDOUSLY
STUPENDOUSNESS
STUPES
STUPID
STUPIDER
STUPIDEST
STUPIDITIES
STUPIDITY
STUPIDLY
STUPIDNESS
STUPIDNESSES
STUPIDS
STUPOR
STUPOROUS
STUPORS
STURDIED
STURDIER
STURDIES
STURDIEST
STURDILY
STURDINESS
STURDINESSES
STURDY
STURGEON
STURGEONS
STURT
STURTS
STUTTER
STUTTERED
STUTTERER
STUTTERERS
STUTTERING
STUTTERS
STY
STYE
STYED
STYES
STYGIAN
STYING
STYLAR
STYLATE
STYLE
STYLEBOOK
STYLEBOOKS
STYLED
STYLELESS
STYLELESSNESS

YLELESSNESSES
YLER
YLERS
YLES
YLET
YLETS
YLI
YLIFORM
YLING
YLINGS
YLISE
YLISED
YLISER
YLISERS
YLISES
YLISH
YLISHLY
YLISHNESS
YLISHNESSES
YLISING
YLIST
YLISTIC
YLISTICALLY
YLISTICS
YLISTS
YLITE
YLITES
YLITIC
YLITISM
YLITISMS
YLIZATION
YLIZATIONS
YLIZE
YLIZED
YLIZER
YLIZERS
YLIZES
YLIZING
YLOBATE
LOBATES
YLOGRAPHIES
YLOGRAPHY
YLOID
LOIDS
YLOLITE
LOLITES
LOPID
LOPIDS
LOPODIA
LOPODIUM
LOPS
LUS
LUSES
STYMIE
STYMIED
STYMIEING
STYMIES
STYMY
STYMYING
STYPSIS
STYPSISES
STYPTIC
STYPTICAL
STYPTICS
STYRAX
STYRAXES
STYRENE
STYRENES
STYROFOAM
STYROFOAMS
SUABILITIES
SUABILITY
SUABLE
SUABLY
SUASION
SUASIONS
SUASIVE
SUASIVELY
SUASIVENESS
SUASIVENESSES
SUASORY
SUAVE
SUAVELY
SUAVENESS
SUAVENESSES
SUAVER
SUAVEST
SUAVITIES
SUAVITY
SUB
SUBA
SUBABBOT
SUBABBOTS
SUBACID
SUBACIDLY
SUBACIDNESS
SUBACIDNESSES
SUBACRID
SUBACUTE
SUBACUTELY
SUBADAR
SUBADARS
SUBADOLESCENT
SUBADOLESCENTS
SUBADULT
SUBADULTS
SUBAERIAL
SUBAERIALLY
SUBAGENCIES
SUBAGENCY
SUBAGENT
SUBAGENTS
SUBAH
SUBAHDAR
SUBAHDARS
SUBAHS
SUBALAR
SUBALLOCATION
SUBALLOCATIONS
SUBALPINE
SUBALTERN
SUBALTERNS
SUBANTARCTIC
SUBAPICAL
SUBAQUATIC
SUBAQUEOUS
SUBARACHNOID
SUBARACHNOIDAL
SUBARACHNOIDS
SUBARCTIC
SUBARCTICS
SUBAREA
SUBAREAS
SUBARID
SUBAS
SUBASSEMBLIES
SUBASSEMBLY
SUBASTRAL
SUBATMOSPHERIC
SUBATOM
SUBATOMIC
SUBATOMS
SUBAUDIBLE
SUBAUDITION
SUBAUDITIONS
SUBAURAL
SUBAVERAGE
SUBAXIAL
SUBBASE
SUBBASEMENT
SUBBASEMENTS
SUBBASES
SUBBASIN
SUBBASINS
SUBBASS
SUBBASSES
SUBBED
SUBBING
SUBBINGS
SUBBITUMINOUS
SUBBLOCK
SUBBLOCKS
SUBBRANCH
SUBBRANCHES
SUBBREED
SUBBREEDS
SUBBUREAU
SUBBUREAUS
SUBBUREAUX
SUBCABINET
SUBCABINETS
SUBCAPSULAR
SUBCASTE
SUBCASTES
SUBCATEGORIES
SUBCATEGORIZE
SUBCATEGORIZED
SUBCATEGORIZES
SUBCATEGORIZING
SUBCATEGORY
SUBCAUSE
SUBCAUSES
SUBCAVITIES
SUBCAVITY
SUBCEILING
SUBCEILINGS
SUBCELL
SUBCELLAR
SUBCELLARS
SUBCELLS
SUBCELLULAR
SUBCENTER
SUBCENTERS
SUBCENTRAL
SUBCENTRALLY
SUBCHAPTER
SUBCHAPTERS
SUBCHASER
SUBCHASERS
SUBCHIEF
SUBCHIEFS
SUBCLAIM
SUBCLAIMS
SUBCLAN
SUBCLANS
SUBCLASS
SUBCLASSED
SUBCLASSES
SUBCLASSIFIED
SUBCLASSIFIES
SUBCLASSIFY
SUBCLASSIFYING
SUBCLASSING
SUBCLAUSE
SUBCLAUSES
SUBCLAVIAN
SUBCLAVIANS
SUBCLERK
SUBCLERKS
SUBCLIMAX
SUBCLIMAXES
SUBCLINICAL
SUBCLINICALLY
SUBCLUSTER
SUBCLUSTERED
SUBCLUSTERING
SUBCLUSTERS
SUBCODE
SUBCODES
SUBCOLLECTION
SUBCOLLECTIONS
SUBCOLLEGE
SUBCOLLEGES
SUBCOLLEGIATE
SUBCOLONIES
SUBCOLONY
SUBCOMMISSION
SUBCOMMISSIONED
SUBCOMMISSIONS
SUBCOMMITTEE
SUBCOMMITTEES
SUBCOMMUNITIES
SUBCOMMUNITY
SUBCOMPACT
SUBCOMPACTS
SUBCOMPONENT
SUBCOMPONENTS
SUBCONSCIOUS
SUBCONSCIOUSES
SUBCONSCIOUSLY
SUBCONSUL
SUBCONSULS
SUBCONTINENT
SUBCONTINENTAL
SUBCONTINENTS
SUBCONTRACT
SUBCONTRACTED
SUBCONTRACTING
SUBCONTRACTOR
SUBCONTRACTORS
SUBCONTRACTS
SUBCONTRAOCTAVE
SUBCONTRARIES
SUBCONTRARY
SUBCOOL

SUBCOOLED
SUBCOOLING
SUBCOOLS
SUBCORDATE
SUBCORIACEOUS
SUBCORTEX
SUBCORTEXES
SUBCORTICAL
SUBCORTICES
SUBCOSTAL
SUBCOSTALS
SUBCOUNTIES
SUBCOUNTY
SUBCRITICAL
SUBCRUSTAL
SUBCULT
SUBCULTS
SUBCULTURAL
SUBCULTURALLY
SUBCULTURE
SUBCULTURED
SUBCULTURES
SUBCULTURING
SUBCURATIVE
SUBCUTANEOUS
SUBCUTANEOUSLY
SUBCUTES
SUBCUTIS
SUBCUTISES
SUBDEACON
SUBDEACONS
SUBDEALER
SUBDEALERS
SUBDEAN
SUBDEANS
SUBDEB
SUBDEBS
SUBDEBUTANTE
SUBDEBUTANTES
SUBDECISION
SUBDECISIONS
SUBDEPARTMENT
SUBDEPARTMENTS
SUBDEPOT
SUBDEPOTS
SUBDEPUTIES
SUBDEPUTY
SUBDERMAL
SUBDERMALLY
SUBDEVELOPMENT
SUBDEVELOPMENTS
SUBDIALECT
SUBDIALECTS
SUBDIRECTOR
SUBDIRECTORS
SUBDISCIPLINE
SUBDISCIPLINES
SUBDISTRICT
SUBDISTRICTS
SUBDIVIDABLE
SUBDIVIDE
SUBDIVIDED
SUBDIVIDER
SUBDIVIDERS
SUBDIVIDES
SUBDIVIDING
SUBDIVISION
SUBDIVISIONS
SUBDOMINANT
SUBDOMINANTS
SUBDUABLE
SUBDUABLY
SUBDUAL
SUBDUALS
SUBDUCE
SUBDUCED
SUBDUCES
SUBDUCING
SUBDUCT
SUBDUCTED
SUBDUCTING
SUBDUCTION
SUBDUCTIONS
SUBDUCTS
SUBDUE
SUBDUED
SUBDUEDLY
SUBDUER
SUBDUERS
SUBDUES
SUBDUING
SUBDURAL
SUBDWARF
SUBDWARFS
SUBECHO
SUBECHOES
SUBECONOMIES
SUBECONOMY
SUBEDIT
SUBEDITED
SUBEDITING
SUBEDITOR
SUBEDITORIAL
SUBEDITORS
SUBEDITS
SUBEMPLOYED
SUBEMPLOYMENT
SUBEMPLOYMENTS
SUBENTRIES
SUBENTRY
SUBEPIDERMAL
SUBEPOCH
SUBEPOCHS
SUBER
SUBERECT
SUBERIC
SUBERIN
SUBERINS
SUBERISE
SUBERISED
SUBERISES
SUBERISING
SUBERIZATION
SUBERIZATIONS
SUBERIZE
SUBERIZED
SUBERIZES
SUBERIZING
SUBEROSE
SUBEROUS
SUBERS
SUBFACULTIES
SUBFACULTY
SUBFAMILIES
SUBFAMILY
SUBFIELD
SUBFIELDS
SUBFILE
SUBFILES
SUBFIX
SUBFIXES
SUBFLOOR
SUBFLOORS
SUBFLUID
SUBFOSSIL
SUBFOSSILS
SUBFRAGMENT
SUBFRAGMENTS
SUBFRAME
SUBFRAMES
SUBFREEZING
SUBFUSC
SUBFUSCS
SUBGENERA
SUBGENERATION
SUBGENERATIONS
SUBGENRE
SUBGENRES
SUBGENUS
SUBGENUSES
SUBGLACIAL
SUBGLACIALLY
SUBGOAL
SUBGOALS
SUBGOVERNMENT
SUBGOVERNMENTS
SUBGRADE
SUBGRADES
SUBGRAPH
SUBGRAPHS
SUBGROUP
SUBGROUPED
SUBGROUPING
SUBGROUPS
SUBGUM
SUBGUMS
SUBHEAD
SUBHEADING
SUBHEADINGS
SUBHEADS
SUBHUMAN
SUBHUMANS
SUBHUMID
SUBIDEA
SUBIDEAS
SUBINDEX
SUBINDEXES
SUBINDICES
SUBINDUSTRIES
SUBINDUSTRY
SUBINFEUD
SUBINFEUDATE
SUBINFEUDATED
SUBINFEUDATES
SUBINFEUDATING
SUBINFEUDATION
SUBINFEUDATIONS
SUBINFEUDED
SUBINFEUDING
SUBINFEUDS
SUBINHIBITORY
SUBINTERVAL
SUBINTERVALS
SUBIRRIGATE
SUBIRRIGATED
SUBIRRIGATES
SUBIRRIGATING
SUBIRRIGATION
SUBIRRIGATIONS
SUBITEM
SUBITEMS
SUBITO
SUBJACENCIES
SUBJACENCY
SUBJACENT
SUBJACENTLY
SUBJECT
SUBJECTED
SUBJECTING
SUBJECTION
SUBJECTIONS
SUBJECTIVE
SUBJECTIVELY
SUBJECTIVENESS
SUBJECTIVES
SUBJECTIVISE
SUBJECTIVISED
SUBJECTIVISES
SUBJECTIVISING
SUBJECTIVISM
SUBJECTIVISMS
SUBJECTIVIST
SUBJECTIVISTIC
SUBJECTIVISTS
SUBJECTIVITIES
SUBJECTIVITY
SUBJECTIVIZE
SUBJECTIVIZED
SUBJECTIVIZES
SUBJECTIVIZING
SUBJECTLESS
SUBJECTS
SUBJOIN
SUBJOINED
SUBJOINING
SUBJOINS
SUBJUGATE
SUBJUGATED
SUBJUGATES
SUBJUGATING
SUBJUGATION
SUBJUGATIONS
SUBJUGATOR
SUBJUGATORS
SUBJUNCTION
SUBJUNCTIONS
SUBJUNCTIVE
SUBJUNCTIVES
SUBKINGDOM
SUBKINGDOMS
SUBLANGUAGE
SUBLANGUAGES
SUBLATE
SUBLATED
SUBLATES

JBLATING
JBLATION
JBLATIONS
JBLEASE
JBLEASED
BLEASES
BLEASING
JBLESSEE
JBLESSEES
JBLESSOR
JBLESSORS
JBLET
JBLETHAL
JBLETHALLY
JBLETS
JBLETTING
BLEVEL
BLEVELS
BLIBRARIAN
BLIBRARIANS
BLICENSE
BLICENSED
BLICENSES
BLICENSING
BLIEUTENANT
BLIEUTENANTS
BLIMABLE
BLIMATE
BLIMATED
BLIMATES
BLIMATING
BLIMATION
BLIMATIONS
BLIME
BLIMED
BLIMELY
BLIMENESS
BLIMENESSES
BLIMER
BLIMERS
BLIMES
BLIMEST
BLIMINAL
BLIMINALLY
BLIMING
BLIMIT
BLIMITIES
BLIMITS
BLIMITY
BLINE
BLINES
BLINGUAL
BLITERACIES
SUBLITERACY
SUBLITERARY
SUBLITERATE
SUBLITERATES
SUBLITERATURE
SUBLITERATURES
SUBLITTORAL
SUBLITTORALS
SUBLOT
SUBLOTS
SUBLUNAR
SUBLUNARY
SUBLUXATION
SUBLUXATIONS
SUBMANAGER
SUBMANAGERS
SUBMANDIBULAR
SUBMANDIBULARS
SUBMARGINAL
SUBMARINE
SUBMARINED
SUBMARINER
SUBMARINERS
SUBMARINES
SUBMARINING
SUBMARKET
SUBMARKETS
SUBMAXILLARIES
SUBMAXILLARY
SUBMAXIMAL
SUBMEDIANT
SUBMEDIANTS
SUBMENU
SUBMENUS
SUBMERGE
SUBMERGED
SUBMERGENCE
SUBMERGENCES
SUBMERGES
SUBMERGIBLE
SUBMERGING
SUBMERSE
SUBMERSED
SUBMERSES
SUBMERSIBLE
SUBMERSIBLES
SUBMERSING
SUBMERSION
SUBMERSIONS
SUBMETACENTRIC
SUBMETACENTRICS
SUBMICROGRAM
SUBMICRON
SUBMICROSCOPIC
SUBMILLIMETER
SUBMINIATURE
SUBMINIMAL
SUBMINIMUM
SUBMINIMUMS
SUBMINISTER
SUBMINISTERED
SUBMINISTERING
SUBMINISTERS
SUBMISS
SUBMISSION
SUBMISSIONS
SUBMISSIVE
SUBMISSIVELY
SUBMISSIVENESS
SUBMIT
SUBMITS
SUBMITTAL
SUBMITTALS
SUBMITTED
SUBMITTER
SUBMITTERS
SUBMITTING
SUBMUCOSA
SUBMUCOSAE
SUBMUCOSAL
SUBMUCOSAS
SUBMULTIPLE
SUBMULTIPLES
SUBMUNITION
SUBMUNITIONS
SUBNASAL
SUBNATIONAL
SUBNET
SUBNETS
SUBNETWORK
SUBNETWORKED
SUBNETWORKING
SUBNETWORKS
SUBNICHE
SUBNICHES
SUBNODAL
SUBNORMAL
SUBNORMALITIES
SUBNORMALITY
SUBNORMALLY
SUBNORMALS
SUBNOTEBOOK
SUBNOTEBOOKS
SUBNUCLEAR
SUBNUCLEI
SUBNUCLEUS
SUBNUCLEUSES
SUBOCEAN
SUBOCEANIC
SUBOPTIC
SUBOPTIMAL
SUBOPTIMIZATION
SUBOPTIMIZE
SUBOPTIMIZED
SUBOPTIMIZES
SUBOPTIMIZING
SUBOPTIMUM
SUBOPTIMUMS
SUBORAL
SUBORBICULAR
SUBORBITAL
SUBORDER
SUBORDERS
SUBORDINATE
SUBORDINATED
SUBORDINATELY
SUBORDINATENESS
SUBORDINATES
SUBORDINATING
SUBORDINATION
SUBORDINATIONS
SUBORDINATIVE
SUBORDINATOR
SUBORDINATORS
SUBORGANIZATION
SUBORN
SUBORNATION
SUBORNATIONS
SUBORNED
SUBORNER
SUBORNERS
SUBORNING
SUBORNS
SUBOSCINE
SUBOSCINES
SUBOVAL
SUBOVATE
SUBOXIDE
SUBOXIDES
SUBPANEL
SUBPANELS
SUBPAR
SUBPARAGRAPH
SUBPARAGRAPHS
SUBPARALLEL
SUBPART
SUBPARTS
SUBPENA
SUBPENAED
SUBPENAING
SUBPENAS
SUBPERIOD
SUBPERIODS
SUBPHASE
SUBPHASES
SUBPHYLA
SUBPHYLAR
SUBPHYLUM
SUBPHYLUMS
SUBPLOT
SUBPLOTS
SUBPOENA
SUBPOENAED
SUBPOENAING
SUBPOENAS
SUBPOLAR
SUBPOPULATION
SUBPOPULATIONS
SUBPOTENCIES
SUBPOTENCY
SUBPOTENT
SUBPRIMATE
SUBPRIMATES
SUBPRIME
SUBPRINCIPAL
SUBPRINCIPALS
SUBPROBLEM
SUBPROBLEMS
SUBPROCESS
SUBPROCESSES
SUBPRODUCT
SUBPRODUCTS
SUBPROFESSIONAL
SUBPROGRAM
SUBPROGRAMS
SUBPROJECT
SUBPROJECTS
SUBPROLETARIAT
SUBPROLETARIATS
SUBPUBIC
SUBRACE
SUBRACES
SUBRATIONAL
SUBREGION
SUBREGIONAL
SUBREGIONS
SUBRENT
SUBRENTS
SUBREPTION
SUBREPTIONS
SUBREPTITIOUS
SUBREPTITIOUSLY

SUBRING
SUBRINGS
SUBROGATE
SUBROGATED
SUBROGATES
SUBROGATING
SUBROGATION
SUBROGATIONS
SUBROUTINE
SUBROUTINES
SUBRULE
SUBRULES
SUBS
SUBSALE
SUBSALES
SUBSAMPLE
SUBSAMPLED
SUBSAMPLES
SUBSAMPLING
SUBSATELLITE
SUBSATELLITES
SUBSATURATED
SUBSATURATION
SUBSATURATIONS
SUBSCALE
SUBSCALES
SUBSCIENCE
SUBSCIENCES
SUBSCRIBE
SUBSCRIBED
SUBSCRIBER
SUBSCRIBERS
SUBSCRIBES
SUBSCRIBING
SUBSCRIPT
SUBSCRIPTION
SUBSCRIPTIONS
SUBSCRIPTS
SUBSEA
SUBSECRETARIES
SUBSECRETARY
SUBSECT
SUBSECTION
SUBSECTIONS
SUBSECTOR
SUBSECTORS
SUBSECTS
SUBSEGMENT
SUBSEGMENTS
SUBSEIZURE
SUBSEIZURES
SUBSENSE
SUBSENSES
SUBSENTENCE
SUBSENTENCES
SUBSEQUENCE
SUBSEQUENCES
SUBSEQUENT
SUBSEQUENTLY
SUBSEQUENTS
SUBSERE
SUBSERES
SUBSERIES
SUBSERVE
SUBSERVED
SUBSERVES
SUBSERVIENCE
SUBSERVIENCES
SUBSERVIENCIES
SUBSERVIENCY
SUBSERVIENT
SUBSERVIENTLY
SUBSERVING
SUBSET
SUBSETS
SUBSHAFT
SUBSHAFTS
SUBSHELL
SUBSHELLS
SUBSHRUB
SUBSHRUBS
SUBSIDE
SUBSIDED
SUBSIDENCE
SUBSIDENCES
SUBSIDER
SUBSIDERS
SUBSIDES
SUBSIDIARIES
SUBSIDIARILY
SUBSIDIARITIES
SUBSIDIARITY
SUBSIDIARY
SUBSIDIES
SUBSIDING
SUBSIDISATION
SUBSIDISATIONS
SUBSIDISE
SUBSIDISED
SUBSIDISES
SUBSIDISING
SUBSIDIZATION
SUBSIDIZATIONS
SUBSIDIZE
SUBSIDIZED
SUBSIDIZER
SUBSIDIZERS
SUBSIDIZES
SUBSIDIZING
SUBSIDY
SUBSIST
SUBSISTED
SUBSISTENCE
SUBSISTENCES
SUBSISTENT
SUBSISTER
SUBSISTERS
SUBSISTING
SUBSISTS
SUBSITE
SUBSITES
SUBSKILL
SUBSKILLS
SUBSOCIAL
SUBSOCIETIES
SUBSOCIETY
SUBSOIL
SUBSOILED
SUBSOILER
SUBSOILERS
SUBSOILING
SUBSOILINGS
SUBSOILS
SUBSOLAR
SUBSONIC
SUBSONICALLY
SUBSPACE
SUBSPACES
SUBSPECIALIST
SUBSPECIALISTS
SUBSPECIALIZE
SUBSPECIALIZED
SUBSPECIALIZES
SUBSPECIALIZING
SUBSPECIALTIES
SUBSPECIALTY
SUBSPECIES
SUBSPECIFIC
SUBSTAGE
SUBSTAGES
SUBSTANCE
SUBSTANCELESS
SUBSTANCES
SUBSTANDARD
SUBSTANDARDS
SUBSTANTIAL
SUBSTANTIALITY
SUBSTANTIALLY
SUBSTANTIALNESS
SUBSTANTIALS
SUBSTANTIATE
SUBSTANTIATED
SUBSTANTIATES
SUBSTANTIATING
SUBSTANTIATION
SUBSTANTIATIONS
SUBSTANTIATIVE
SUBSTANTIVAL
SUBSTANTIVALLY
SUBSTANTIVE
SUBSTANTIVELY
SUBSTANTIVENESS
SUBSTANTIVES
SUBSTANTIVIZE
SUBSTANTIVIZED
SUBSTANTIVIZES
SUBSTANTIVIZING
SUBSTATE
SUBSTATES
SUBSTATION
SUBSTATIONS
SUBSTELLAR
SUBSTITUENT
SUBSTITUENTS
SUBSTITUTABLE
SUBSTITUTE
SUBSTITUTED
SUBSTITUTES
SUBSTITUTING
SUBSTITUTION
SUBSTITUTIONAL
SUBSTITUTIONARY
SUBSTITUTIONS
SUBSTITUTIVE
SUBSTITUTIVELY
SUBSTRATA
SUBSTRATE
SUBSTRATES
SUBSTRATUM
SUBSTRATUMS
SUBSTRUCTURAL
SUBSTRUCTURE
SUBSTRUCTURES
SUBSUMABLE
SUBSUME
SUBSUMED
SUBSUMES
SUBSUMING
SUBSUMPTION
SUBSUMPTIONS
SUBSURFACE
SUBSURFACES
SUBSYSTEM
SUBSYSTEMS
SUBTASK
SUBTASKS
SUBTAXA
SUBTAXON
SUBTAXONS
SUBTEEN
SUBTEENS
SUBTEMPERATE
SUBTENANCIES
SUBTENANCY
SUBTENANT
SUBTENANTS
SUBTEND
SUBTENDED
SUBTENDING
SUBTENDS
SUBTERFUGE
SUBTERFUGES
SUBTERMINAL
SUBTERRANEAN
SUBTERRANEANLY
SUBTERRANEOUS
SUBTERRANEOUSLY
SUBTEST
SUBTESTS
SUBTEXT
SUBTEXTS
SUBTEXTUAL
SUBTEXTUALLY
SUBTHEME
SUBTHEMES
SUBTHERAPEUTIC
SUBTHRESHOLD
SUBTILE
SUBTILELY
SUBTILENESS
SUBTILENESSES
SUBTILER
SUBTILEST
SUBTILIN
SUBTILINS
SUBTILISE
SUBTILISED
SUBTILISES
SUBTILISIN
SUBTILISING
SUBTILISINS
SUBTILITIES
SUBTILITY
SUBTILIZATION
SUBTILIZATIONS

JBTILIZE
JBTILIZED
JBTILIZES
JBTILIZING
JBTILTIES
JBTILTY
JBTITLE
JBTITLED
JBTITLES
BTITLING
JBTLE
JBTLENESS
JBTLENESSES
JBTLER
BTLEST
JBTLETIES
JBTLETY
JBTLY
JBTONE
BTONES
BTONIC
BTONICS
BTOPIA
BTOPIAS
BTOPIC
BTOPICS
BTORRID
BTOTAL
BTOTALED
BTOTALING
BTOTALLED
BTOTALLING
BTOTALLY
BTOTALS
BTRACT
BTRACTED
BTRACTER
BTRACTERS
BTRACTING
BTRACTION
BTRACTIONS
BTRACTIVE
BTRACTS
BTRADE
BTRADES
BTRAHEND
BTRAHENDS
BTREASURIES
BTREASURY
BTREND
BTRENDS
BTRIBE
BTRIBES

SUBTROPIC
SUBTROPICAL
SUBTROPICS
SUBTUNIC
SUBTUNICS
SUBTYPE
SUBTYPES
SUBULATE
SUBUMBRELLA
SUBUMBRELLAS
SUBUNIT
SUBUNITS
SUBURB
SUBURBAN
SUBURBANISE
SUBURBANISED
SUBURBANISES
SUBURBANISING
SUBURBANITE
SUBURBANITES
SUBURBANIZATION
SUBURBANIZE
SUBURBANIZED
SUBURBANIZES
SUBURBANIZING
SUBURBANS
SUBURBED
SUBURBIA
SUBURBIAS
SUBURBS
SUBVARIETIES
SUBVARIETY
SUBVASSAL
SUBVASSALS
SUBVENE
SUBVENED
SUBVENES
SUBVENING
SUBVENTION
SUBVENTIONARY
SUBVENTIONS
SUBVERSION
SUBVERSIONARY
SUBVERSIONS
SUBVERSIVE
SUBVERSIVELY
SUBVERSIVENESS
SUBVERSIVES
SUBVERT
SUBVERTED
SUBVERTER
SUBVERTERS
SUBVERTING

SUBVERTS
SUBVICAR
SUBVICARS
SUBVIRAL
SUBVIRUS
SUBVIRUSES
SUBVISIBLE
SUBVISUAL
SUBVOCAL
SUBVOCALIZATION
SUBVOCALIZE
SUBVOCALIZED
SUBVOCALIZES
SUBVOCALIZING
SUBVOCALLY
SUBWAY
SUBWAYED
SUBWAYING
SUBWAYS
SUBWOOFER
SUBWOOFERS
SUBWORLD
SUBWORLDS
SUBWRITER
SUBWRITERS
SUBZERO
SUBZONE
SUBZONES
SUCCAH
SUCCAHS
SUCCEDANEA
SUCCEDANEOUS
SUCCEDANEUM
SUCCEDANEUMS
SUCCEDENT
SUCCEED
SUCCEEDED
SUCCEEDER
SUCCEEDERS
SUCCEEDING
SUCCEEDS
SUCCESS
SUCCESSES
SUCCESSFUL
SUCCESSFULLY
SUCCESSFULNESS
SUCCESSION
SUCCESSIONAL
SUCCESSIONALLY
SUCCESSIONS
SUCCESSIVE
SUCCESSIVELY
SUCCESSIVENESS

SUCCESSOR
SUCCESSORS
SUCCINATE
SUCCINATES
SUCCINCT
SUCCINCTER
SUCCINCTEST
SUCCINCTLY
SUCCINCTNESS
SUCCINCTNESSES
SUCCINIC
SUCCINYL
SUCCINYLCHOLINE
SUCCINYLS
SUCCOR
SUCCORED
SUCCORER
SUCCORERS
SUCCORIES
SUCCORING
SUCCORS
SUCCORY
SUCCOTASH
SUCCOTASHES
SUCCOTH
SUCCOUR
SUCCOURED
SUCCOURING
SUCCOURS
SUCCUBA
SUCCUBAE
SUCCUBAS
SUCCUBI
SUCCUBUS
SUCCUBUSES
SUCCULENCE
SUCCULENCES
SUCCULENT
SUCCULENTLY
SUCCULENTS
SUCCUMB
SUCCUMBED
SUCCUMBING
SUCCUMBS
SUCCUSS
SUCCUSSED
SUCCUSSES
SUCCUSSING
SUCH
SUCHLIKE
SUCHLIKES
SUCHNESS
SUCHNESSES

SUCK
SUCKED
SUCKER
SUCKERED
SUCKERING
SUCKERS
SUCKFISH
SUCKFISHES
SUCKHOLE
SUCKHOLED
SUCKHOLES
SUCKHOLING
SUCKIER
SUCKIEST
SUCKING
SUCKLE
SUCKLED
SUCKLER
SUCKLERS
SUCKLES
SUCKLESS
SUCKLING
SUCKLINGS
SUCKS
SUCKY
SUCRALOSE
SUCRALOSES
SUCRASE
SUCRASES
SUCRE
SUCRES
SUCROSE
SUCROSES
SUCTION
SUCTIONAL
SUCTIONED
SUCTIONING
SUCTIONS
SUCTORIAL
SUCTORIAN
SUCTORIANS
SUDARIA
SUDARIES
SUDARIUM
SUDARY
SUDATION
SUDATIONS
SUDATORIA
SUDATORIES
SUDATORIUM
SUDATORIUMS
SUDATORY
SUDD

SUDDEN
SUDDENLY
SUDDENNESS
SUDDENNESSES
SUDDENS
SUDDS
SUDOKU
SUDOKUS
SUDOR
SUDORAL
SUDORIFEROUS
SUDORIFIC
SUDORIFICS
SUDORS
SUDS
SUDSED
SUDSER
SUDSERS
SUDSES
SUDSIER
SUDSIEST
SUDSING
SUDSLESS
SUDSY
SUE
SUED
SUEDE
SUEDED
SUEDES
SUEDING
SUER
SUERS
SUES
SUET
SUETE
SUETES
SUETIER
SUETIEST
SUETS
SUETY
SUFFARI
SUFFARIS
SUFFER
SUFFERABLE
SUFFERABLENESS
SUFFERABLY
SUFFERANCE
SUFFERANCES
SUFFERED
SUFFERER
SUFFERERS
SUFFERING
SUFFERINGS
SUFFERS
SUFFICE
SUFFICED
SUFFICER
SUFFICERS
SUFFICES
SUFFICIENCIES
SUFFICIENCY
SUFFICIENT
SUFFICIENTLY
SUFFICING
SUFFIX
SUFFIXAL
SUFFIXATION
SUFFIXATIONS
SUFFIXED
SUFFIXES
SUFFIXING
SUFFIXION
SUFFIXIONS
SUFFLATE
SUFFLATED
SUFFLATES
SUFFLATING
SUFFOCATE
SUFFOCATED
SUFFOCATES
SUFFOCATING
SUFFOCATINGLY
SUFFOCATION
SUFFOCATIONS
SUFFOCATIVE
SUFFRAGAN
SUFFRAGANS
SUFFRAGE
SUFFRAGES
SUFFRAGETTE
SUFFRAGETTES
SUFFRAGIST
SUFFRAGISTS
SUFFUSE
SUFFUSED
SUFFUSES
SUFFUSING
SUFFUSION
SUFFUSIONS
SUFFUSIVE
SUGAR
SUGARBERRIES
SUGARBERRY
SUGARBUSH
SUGARBUSHES
SUGARCANE
SUGARCANES
SUGARCOAT
SUGARCOATED
SUGARCOATING
SUGARCOATS
SUGARED
SUGARER
SUGARERS
SUGARHOUSE
SUGARHOUSES
SUGARIER
SUGARIEST
SUGARING
SUGARINGS
SUGARLESS
SUGARLIKE
SUGARLOAF
SUGARLOAVES
SUGARPLUM
SUGARPLUMS
SUGARS
SUGARY
SUGGEST
SUGGESTED
SUGGESTER
SUGGESTERS
SUGGESTIBILITY
SUGGESTIBLE
SUGGESTING
SUGGESTION
SUGGESTIONS
SUGGESTIVE
SUGGESTIVELY
SUGGESTIVENESS
SUGGESTS
SUGH
SUGHED
SUGHING
SUGHS
SUICIDAL
SUICIDALLY
SUICIDE
SUICIDED
SUICIDES
SUICIDING
SUING
SUINT
SUINTS
SUIT
SUITABILITIES
SUITABILITY
SUITABLE
SUITABLENESS
SUITABLENESSES
SUITABLY
SUITCASE
SUITCASES
SUITE
SUITED
SUITER
SUITERS
SUITES
SUITING
SUITINGS
SUITLIKE
SUITOR
SUITORS
SUITS
SUK
SUKH
SUKHS
SUKIYAKI
SUKIYAKIS
SUKKAH
SUKKAHS
SUKKOT
SUKKOTH
SUKS
SULCAL
SULCATE
SULCATED
SULCATION
SULCATIONS
SULCI
SULCUS
SULDAN
SULDANS
SULFA
SULFADIAZINE
SULFADIAZINES
SULFANILAMIDE
SULFANILAMIDES
SULFAS
SULFATASE
SULFATASES
SULFATE
SULFATED
SULFATES
SULFATING
SULFATION
SULFATIONS
SULFHYDRYL
SULFHYDRYLS
SULFID
SULFIDE
SULFIDES
SULFIDS
SULFINPYRAZONE
SULFINPYRAZONES
SULFINYL
SULFINYLS
SULFITE
SULFITES
SULFITIC
SULFO
SULFONAMIDE
SULFONAMIDES
SULFONATE
SULFONATED
SULFONATES
SULFONATING
SULFONATION
SULFONATIONS
SULFONE
SULFONES
SULFONIC
SULFONIUM
SULFONIUMS
SULFONYL
SULFONYLS
SULFONYLUREA
SULFONYLUREAS
SULFORAPHANE
SULFORAPHANES
SULFOXIDE
SULFOXIDES
SULFUR
SULFURATE
SULFURATED
SULFURATES
SULFURATING
SULFURED
SULFURET
SULFURETED
SULFURETING
SULFURETS
SULFURETTED
SULFURETTING
SULFURIC
SULFURING
SULFURIZE
SULFURIZED
SULFURIZES
SULFURIZING
SULFUROUS
SULFUROUSLY
SULFUROUSNESS
SULFUROUSNESSES
SULFURS

LFURY
LFURYL
LFURYLS
LK
LKED
LKER
LKERS
LKIER
LKIES
LKIEST
LKILY
LKINESS
LKINESSES
LKING
LKS
LKY
LLAGE
LLAGES
LLEN
LLENER
LLENEST
LLENLY
LLENNESS
LLENNESSES
LLIABLE
LLIED
LLIES
LLY
LLYING
LPHA
LPHAS
LPHATE
LPHATED
LPHATES
LPHATING
LPHID
LPHIDE
LPHIDES
LPHIDS
LPHITE
LPHITES
LPHONE
LPHONES
LPHUR
LPHURED
LPHUREOUS
LPHURING
LPHURISE
LPHURISED
LPHURISES
LPHURISING
LPHUROUS
LPHURS

SULPHURY
SULTAN
SULTANA
SULTANAS
SULTANATE
SULTANATES
SULTANESS
SULTANESSES
SULTANIC
SULTANS
SULTRIER
SULTRIEST
SULTRILY
SULTRINESS
SULTRINESSES
SULTRY
SULU
SULUS
SUM
SUMAC
SUMACH
SUMACHS
SUMACS
SUMATRIPTAN
SUMATRIPTANS
SUMBITCH
SUMBITCHES
SUMI
SUMIS
SUMLESS
SUMMA
SUMMABILITIES
SUMMABILITY
SUMMABLE
SUMMAE
SUMMAND
SUMMANDS
SUMMARIES
SUMMARILY
SUMMARISATION
SUMMARISATIONS
SUMMARISE
SUMMARISED
SUMMARISES
SUMMARISING
SUMMARIST
SUMMARISTS
SUMMARIZABLE
SUMMARIZATION
SUMMARIZATIONS
SUMMARIZE
SUMMARIZED
SUMMARIZER

SUMMARIZERS
SUMMARIZES
SUMMARIZING
SUMMARY
SUMMAS
SUMMATE
SUMMATED
SUMMATES
SUMMATING
SUMMATION
SUMMATIONAL
SUMMATIONS
SUMMATIVE
SUMMED
SUMMER
SUMMERED
SUMMERHOUSE
SUMMERHOUSES
SUMMERIER
SUMMERIEST
SUMMERING
SUMMERLIKE
SUMMERLONG
SUMMERLY
SUMMERS
SUMMERSAULT
SUMMERSAULTED
SUMMERSAULTING
SUMMERSAULTS
SUMMERSET
SUMMERSETS
SUMMERSETTED
SUMMERSETTING
SUMMERTIME
SUMMERTIMES
SUMMERWOOD
SUMMERWOODS
SUMMERY
SUMMING
SUMMIT
SUMMITAL
SUMMITED
SUMMITEER
SUMMITEERS
SUMMITING
SUMMITRIES
SUMMITRY
SUMMITS
SUMMON
SUMMONABLE
SUMMONED
SUMMONER
SUMMONERS

SUMMONING
SUMMONS
SUMMONSED
SUMMONSES
SUMMONSING
SUMO
SUMOIST
SUMOISTS
SUMOS
SUMP
SUMPS
SUMPTER
SUMPTERS
SUMPTUARY
SUMPTUOUS
SUMPTUOUSLY
SUMPTUOUSNESS
SUMPTUOUSNESSES
SUMPWEED
SUMPWEEDS
SUMS
SUMY
SUN
SUNBACK
SUNBAKED
SUNBATH
SUNBATHE
SUNBATHED
SUNBATHER
SUNBATHERS
SUNBATHES
SUNBATHING
SUNBATHS
SUNBEAM
SUNBEAMS
SUNBEAMY
SUNBED
SUNBEDS
SUNBELT
SUNBELTS
SUNBIRD
SUNBIRDS
SUNBLOCK
SUNBLOCKS
SUNBONNET
SUNBONNETS
SUNBOW
SUNBOWS
SUNBURN
SUNBURNED
SUNBURNING
SUNBURNS
SUNBURNT

SUNBURST
SUNBURSTS
SUNCARE
SUNCARES
SUNCHOKE
SUNCHOKES
SUNDAE
SUNDAES
SUNDECK
SUNDECKS
SUNDER
SUNDERED
SUNDERER
SUNDERERS
SUNDERING
SUNDERS
SUNDEW
SUNDEWS
SUNDIAL
SUNDIALS
SUNDOG
SUNDOGS
SUNDOWN
SUNDOWNED
SUNDOWNER
SUNDOWNERS
SUNDOWNING
SUNDOWNS
SUNDRESS
SUNDRESSES
SUNDRIES
SUNDRILY
SUNDROPS
SUNDRY
SUNFAST
SUNFISH
SUNFISHES
SUNFLOWER
SUNFLOWERS
SUNG
SUNGLASS
SUNGLASSES
SUNGLOW
SUNGLOWS
SUNK
SUNKEN
SUNKER
SUNKERS
SUNKET
SUNKETS
SUNLAMP
SUNLAMPS
SUNLAND

SUNLANDS
SUNLESS
SUNLIGHT
SUNLIGHTS
SUNLIKE
SUNLIT
SUNN
SUNNA
SUNNAH
SUNNAHS
SUNNAS
SUNNED
SUNNIER
SUNNIEST
SUNNILY
SUNNINESS
SUNNINESSES
SUNNING
SUNNS
SUNNY
SUNPORCH
SUNPORCHES
SUNPROOF
SUNRAY
SUNRAYS
SUNRISE
SUNRISES
SUNROOF
SUNROOFS
SUNROOM
SUNROOMS
SUNS
SUNSCALD
SUNSCALDS
SUNSCREEN
SUNSCREENING
SUNSCREENS
SUNSEEKER
SUNSEEKERS
SUNSET
SUNSETS
SUNSHADE
SUNSHADES
SUNSHINE
SUNSHINES
SUNSHINY
SUNSPOT
SUNSPOTS
SUNSTAR
SUNSTARS
SUNSTONE
SUNSTONES
SUNSTROKE
SUNSTROKES
SUNSTRUCK
SUNSUIT
SUNSUITS
SUNTAN
SUNTANNED
SUNTANNING
SUNTANS
SUNTRAP
SUNTRAPS
SUNUP
SUNUPS
SUNWARD
SUNWARDS
SUNWISE
SUP
SUPE
SUPER
SUPERABLE
SUPERABLENESS
SUPERABLENESSES
SUPERABLY
SUPERABOUND
SUPERABOUNDED
SUPERABOUNDING
SUPERABOUNDS
SUPERABSORBENT
SUPERABSORBENTS
SUPERABUNDANCE
SUPERABUNDANCES
SUPERABUNDANT
SUPERABUNDANTLY
SUPERACCURATE
SUPERACHIEVER
SUPERACHIEVERS
SUPERACTIVITIES
SUPERACTIVITY
SUPERADD
SUPERADDED
SUPERADDING
SUPERADDITION
SUPERADDITIONS
SUPERADDS
SUPERAGENCIES
SUPERAGENCY
SUPERAGENT
SUPERAGENTS
SUPERALLOY
SUPERALLOYS
SUPERALTERN
SUPERALTERNS
SUPERAMBITIOUS
SUPERANNUATE
SUPERANNUATED
SUPERANNUATES
SUPERANNUATING
SUPERANNUATION
SUPERANNUATIONS
SUPERATHLETE
SUPERATHLETES
SUPERATOM
SUPERATOMS
SUPERB
SUPERBAD
SUPERBANK
SUPERBANKS
SUPERBER
SUPERBEST
SUPERBITCH
SUPERBITCHES
SUPERBLOCK
SUPERBLOCKS
SUPERBLY
SUPERBNESS
SUPERBNESSES
SUPERBOARD
SUPERBOARDS
SUPERBOMB
SUPERBOMBER
SUPERBOMBERS
SUPERBOMBS
SUPERBRIGHT
SUPERBUG
SUPERBUGS
SUPERBUREAUCRAT
SUPERCABINET
SUPERCABINETS
SUPERCALENDER
SUPERCALENDERED
SUPERCALENDERS
SUPERCAR
SUPERCARGO
SUPERCARGOES
SUPERCARGOS
SUPERCARRIER
SUPERCARRIERS
SUPERCARS
SUPERCAUTIOUS
SUPERCEDE
SUPERCEDED
SUPERCEDES
SUPERCEDING
SUPERCELL
SUPERCELLS
SUPERCENTER
SUPERCENTERS
SUPERCHARGE
SUPERCHARGED
SUPERCHARGER
SUPERCHARGERS
SUPERCHARGES
SUPERCHARGING
SUPERCHEAP
SUPERCHIC
SUPERCHURCH
SUPERCHURCHES
SUPERCILIARY
SUPERCILIOUS
SUPERCILIOUSLY
SUPERCITIES
SUPERCITY
SUPERCIVILIZED
SUPERCLASS
SUPERCLASSES
SUPERCLEAN
SUPERCLUB
SUPERCLUBS
SUPERCLUSTER
SUPERCLUSTERS
SUPERCOIL
SUPERCOILED
SUPERCOILING
SUPERCOILS
SUPERCOLLIDER
SUPERCOLLIDERS
SUPERCOLOSSAL
SUPERCOMPETENT
SUPERCOMPUTER
SUPERCOMPUTERS
SUPERCONDUCT
SUPERCONDUCTED
SUPERCONDUCTING
SUPERCONDUCTIVE
SUPERCONDUCTOR
SUPERCONDUCTORS
SUPERCONDUCTS
SUPERCONFIDENT
SUPERCONTINENT
SUPERCONTINENTS
SUPERCONVENIENT
SUPERCOOL
SUPERCOOLED
SUPERCOOLING
SUPERCOOLS
SUPERCOP
SUPERCOPS
SUPERCRIMINAL
SUPERCRIMINALS
SUPERCRITICAL
SUPERCROSS
SUPERCROSSES
SUPERCURRENT
SUPERCURRENTS
SUPERCUTE
SUPERDELEGATE
SUPERDELEGATES
SUPERDELUXE
SUPERDIPLOMAT
SUPERDIPLOMATS
SUPERED
SUPEREFFECTIVE
SUPEREFFICIENCY
SUPEREFFICIENT
SUPEREGO
SUPEREGOIST
SUPEREGOISTS
SUPEREGOS
SUPERELEVATE
SUPERELEVATED
SUPERELEVATES
SUPERELEVATING
SUPERELEVATION
SUPERELEVATIONS
SUPERELITE
SUPERELITES
SUPEREMINENCE
SUPEREMINENCES
SUPEREMINENT
SUPEREMINENTLY
SUPEREROGATION
SUPEREROGATIONS
SUPEREROGATORY
SUPERETTE
SUPERETTES
SUPEREXPENSIVE
SUPEREXPRESS
SUPEREXPRESSES
SUPERFAMILIES
SUPERFAMILY
SUPERFAN
SUPERFANS
SUPERFARM
SUPERFARMS
SUPERFAST
SUPERFATTED
SUPERFETATION
SUPERFETATIONS
SUPERFICIAL
SUPERFICIALITY
SUPERFICIALLY
SUPERFICIES
SUPERFINE

UPERFIRM
UPERFIRMS
UPERFIX
UPERFIXES
UPERFLACK
UPERFLACKS
UPERFLUID
UPERFLUIDITIES
UPERFLUIDITY
UPERFLUIDS
UPERFLUITIES
UPERFLUITY
UPERFLUOUS
UPERFLUOUSLY
UPERFLUOUSNESS
UPERFLY
UPERFUND
UPERFUNDS
UPERGENE
UPERGENES
UPERGIANT
UPERGIANTS
UPERGLUE
UPERGLUED
UPERGLUEING
UPERGLUES
UPERGLUING
UPERGOOD
UPERGOVERNMENT
UPERGRAPHICS
UPERGRASS
UPERGRASSES
UPERGRAVITIES
UPERGRAVITY
UPERGROUP
UPERGROUPS
UPERGROWTH
UPERGROWTHS
UPERHARDEN
UPERHARDENED
UPERHARDENING
UPERHARDENS
UPERHEAT
UPERHEATED
UPERHEATER
UPERHEATERS
UPERHEATING
UPERHEATS
UPERHEAVIES
UPERHEAVY
UPERHELICAL
UPERHELICES
UPERHELIX

SUPERHELIXES
SUPERHERO
SUPERHEROES
SUPERHEROINE
SUPERHEROINES
SUPERHETERODYNE
SUPERHIGHWAY
SUPERHIGHWAYS
SUPERHIT
SUPERHITS
SUPERHOT
SUPERHUMAN
SUPERHUMANITIES
SUPERHUMANITY
SUPERHUMANLY
SUPERHUMANNESS
SUPERHUMANS
SUPERHYPE
SUPERHYPED
SUPERHYPES
SUPERHYPING
SUPERIMPOSABLE
SUPERIMPOSE
SUPERIMPOSED
SUPERIMPOSES
SUPERIMPOSING
SUPERIMPOSITION
SUPERINCUMBENT
SUPERINDIVIDUAL
SUPERINDUCE
SUPERINDUCED
SUPERINDUCES
SUPERINDUCING
SUPERINDUCTION
SUPERINDUCTIONS
SUPERINFECT
SUPERINFECTED
SUPERINFECTING
SUPERINFECTION
SUPERINFECTIONS
SUPERINFECTS
SUPERING
SUPERINSULATED
SUPERINTEND
SUPERINTENDED
SUPERINTENDENCE
SUPERINTENDENCY
SUPERINTENDENT
SUPERINTENDENTS
SUPERINTENDING
SUPERINTENDS
SUPERINTENSITY
SUPERIOR

SUPERIORITIES
SUPERIORITY
SUPERIORLY
SUPERIORS
SUPERJACENT
SUPERJET
SUPERJETS
SUPERJOCK
SUPERJOCKS
SUPERJUMBO
SUPERJUMBOS
SUPERLAIN
SUPERLARGE
SUPERLATIVE
SUPERLATIVELY
SUPERLATIVENESS
SUPERLATIVES
SUPERLAWYER
SUPERLAWYERS
SUPERLAY
SUPERLIE
SUPERLIES
SUPERLIGHT
SUPERLINER
SUPERLINERS
SUPERLOBBYIST
SUPERLOBBYISTS
SUPERLONG
SUPERLOYALIST
SUPERLOYALISTS
SUPERLUNAR
SUPERLUNARY
SUPERLUXURIES
SUPERLUXURIOUS
SUPERLUXURY
SUPERLYING
SUPERMACHO
SUPERMAJORITIES
SUPERMAJORITY
SUPERMALE
SUPERMALES
SUPERMAN
SUPERMARKET
SUPERMARKETS
SUPERMASCULINE
SUPERMASSIVE
SUPERMEN
SUPERMICRO
SUPERMICROS
SUPERMILITANT
SUPERMILITANTS
SUPERMIND
SUPERMINDS

SUPERMINI
SUPERMINIS
SUPERMINISTER
SUPERMINISTERS
SUPERMODEL
SUPERMODELS
SUPERMODERN
SUPERMOM
SUPERMOMS
SUPERNAL
SUPERNALLY
SUPERNATANT
SUPERNATANTS
SUPERNATE
SUPERNATES
SUPERNATION
SUPERNATIONAL
SUPERNATIONS
SUPERNATURAL
SUPERNATURALISM
SUPERNATURALIST
SUPERNATURALLY
SUPERNATURALS
SUPERNATURE
SUPERNATURES
SUPERNORMAL
SUPERNORMALITY
SUPERNORMALLY
SUPERNOVA
SUPERNOVAE
SUPERNOVAS
SUPERNUMERARIES
SUPERNUMERARY
SUPERNUTRITION
SUPERNUTRITIONS
SUPERORDER
SUPERORDERS
SUPERORDINATE
SUPERORGANIC
SUPERORGANISM
SUPERORGANISMS
SUPERORGASM
SUPERORGASMS
SUPEROVULATE
SUPEROVULATED
SUPEROVULATES
SUPEROVULATING
SUPEROVULATION
SUPEROVULATIONS
SUPEROXIDE
SUPEROXIDES
SUPERPARASITISM
SUPERPATRIOT

SUPERPATRIOTIC
SUPERPATRIOTISM
SUPERPATRIOTS
SUPERPEOPLE
SUPERPERSON
SUPERPERSONAL
SUPERPERSONS
SUPERPHENOMENA
SUPERPHENOMENON
SUPERPHOSPHATE
SUPERPHOSPHATES
SUPERPHYSICAL
SUPERPIMP
SUPERPIMPS
SUPERPLANE
SUPERPLANES
SUPERPLASTIC
SUPERPLASTICITY
SUPERPLAYER
SUPERPLAYERS
SUPERPOLITE
SUPERPORT
SUPERPORTS
SUPERPOSABLE
SUPERPOSE
SUPERPOSED
SUPERPOSES
SUPERPOSING
SUPERPOSITION
SUPERPOSITIONS
SUPERPOWER
SUPERPOWERED
SUPERPOWERFUL
SUPERPOWERS
SUPERPREMIUM
SUPERPREMIUMS
SUPERPRO
SUPERPROFIT
SUPERPROFITS
SUPERPROS
SUPERQUALITIES
SUPERQUALITY
SUPERRACE
SUPERRACES
SUPERREAL
SUPERREALISM
SUPERREALISMS
SUPERREGIONAL
SUPERREGIONALS
SUPERRICH
SUPERROAD
SUPERROADS
SUPERROMANTIC

SUPERS
SUPERSAFE
SUPERSALE
SUPERSALES
SUPERSALESMAN
SUPERSALESMEN
SUPERSATURATE
SUPERSATURATED
SUPERSATURATES
SUPERSATURATING
SUPERSATURATION
SUPERSAUR
SUPERSAURS
SUPERSCALE
SUPERSCALES
SUPERSCHOOL
SUPERSCHOOLS
SUPERSCOUT
SUPERSCOUTS
SUPERSCRIBE
SUPERSCRIBED
SUPERSCRIBES
SUPERSCRIBING
SUPERSCRIPT
SUPERSCRIPTION
SUPERSCRIPTIONS
SUPERSCRIPTS
SUPERSECRECIES
SUPERSECRECY
SUPERSECRET
SUPERSECRETS
SUPERSEDE
SUPERSEDEAS
SUPERSEDED
SUPERSEDER
SUPERSEDERS
SUPERSEDES
SUPERSEDING
SUPERSEDURE
SUPERSEDURES
SUPERSELL
SUPERSELLER
SUPERSELLERS
SUPERSELLING
SUPERSELLS
SUPERSENSIBLE
SUPERSENSITIVE
SUPERSENSORY
SUPERSESSION
SUPERSESSIONS
SUPERSEX
SUPERSEXES
SUPERSEXUALITY
SUPERSHARP
SUPERSHOW
SUPERSHOWS
SUPERSINGER
SUPERSINGERS
SUPERSIZE
SUPERSIZED
SUPERSIZES
SUPERSIZING
SUPERSLEUTH
SUPERSLEUTHS
SUPERSLICK
SUPERSMART
SUPERSMOOTH
SUPERSOFT
SUPERSOLD
SUPERSONIC
SUPERSONICALLY
SUPERSONICS
SUPERSPECIAL
SUPERSPECIALIST
SUPERSPECIALS
SUPERSPECTACLE
SUPERSPECTACLES
SUPERSPIES
SUPERSPY
SUPERSTAR
SUPERSTARDOM
SUPERSTARDOMS
SUPERSTARS
SUPERSTATE
SUPERSTATES
SUPERSTATION
SUPERSTATIONS
SUPERSTIMULATE
SUPERSTIMULATED
SUPERSTIMULATES
SUPERSTITION
SUPERSTITIONS
SUPERSTITIOUS
SUPERSTITIOUSLY
SUPERSTOCK
SUPERSTOCKS
SUPERSTORE
SUPERSTORES
SUPERSTRATA
SUPERSTRATUM
SUPERSTRENGTH
SUPERSTRENGTHS
SUPERSTRIKE
SUPERSTRIKES
SUPERSTRING
SUPERSTRINGS
SUPERSTRONG
SUPERSTRUCTURAL
SUPERSTRUCTURE
SUPERSTRUCTURES
SUPERSTUD
SUPERSTUDS
SUPERSUBTLE
SUPERSUBTLETIES
SUPERSUBTLETY
SUPERSURGEON
SUPERSURGEONS
SUPERSWEET
SUPERSYMMETRIC
SUPERSYMMETRIES
SUPERSYMMETRY
SUPERSYSTEM
SUPERSYSTEMS
SUPERTANKER
SUPERTANKERS
SUPERTAX
SUPERTAXES
SUPERTERRIFIC
SUPERTHICK
SUPERTHIN
SUPERTHRILLER
SUPERTHRILLERS
SUPERTIGHT
SUPERTITLE
SUPERTITLES
SUPERTONIC
SUPERTONICS
SUPERVENE
SUPERVENED
SUPERVENES
SUPERVENIENT
SUPERVENING
SUPERVENTION
SUPERVENTIONS
SUPERVIRILE
SUPERVIRTUOSI
SUPERVIRTUOSO
SUPERVIRTUOSOS
SUPERVISE
SUPERVISED
SUPERVISES
SUPERVISING
SUPERVISION
SUPERVISIONS
SUPERVISOR
SUPERVISORS
SUPERVISORY
SUPERWAVE
SUPERWAVES
SUPERWEAPON
SUPERWEAPONS
SUPERWIDE
SUPERWIDES
SUPERWIFE
SUPERWIVES
SUPERWOMAN
SUPERWOMEN
SUPES
SUPINATE
SUPINATED
SUPINATES
SUPINATING
SUPINATION
SUPINATIONS
SUPINATOR
SUPINATORS
SUPINE
SUPINELY
SUPINENESS
SUPINENESSES
SUPINES
SUPPED
SUPPER
SUPPERS
SUPPERTIME
SUPPERTIMES
SUPPING
SUPPLANT
SUPPLANTATION
SUPPLANTATIONS
SUPPLANTED
SUPPLANTER
SUPPLANTERS
SUPPLANTING
SUPPLANTS
SUPPLE
SUPPLED
SUPPLEJACK
SUPPLEJACKS
SUPPLELY
SUPPLEMENT
SUPPLEMENTAL
SUPPLEMENTALS
SUPPLEMENTARY
SUPPLEMENTATION
SUPPLEMENTED
SUPPLEMENTER
SUPPLEMENTERS
SUPPLEMENTING
SUPPLEMENTS
SUPPLENESS
SUPPLENESSES
SUPPLER
SUPPLES
SUPPLEST
SUPPLETION
SUPPLETIONS
SUPPLETIVE
SUPPLETORY
SUPPLIANCE
SUPPLIANCES
SUPPLIANT
SUPPLIANTLY
SUPPLIANTS
SUPPLICANT
SUPPLICANTS
SUPPLICATE
SUPPLICATED
SUPPLICATES
SUPPLICATING
SUPPLICATION
SUPPLICATIONS
SUPPLICATORY
SUPPLIED
SUPPLIER
SUPPLIERS
SUPPLIES
SUPPLING
SUPPLY
SUPPLYING
SUPPORT
SUPPORTABILITY
SUPPORTABLE
SUPPORTED
SUPPORTER
SUPPORTERS
SUPPORTING
SUPPORTIVE
SUPPORTIVENESS
SUPPORTS
SUPPOSABLE
SUPPOSABLY
SUPPOSAL
SUPPOSALS
SUPPOSE
SUPPOSED
SUPPOSEDLY
SUPPOSER
SUPPOSERS
SUPPOSES
SUPPOSING
SUPPOSITION
SUPPOSITIONAL
SUPPOSITIONS
SUPPOSITIOUS

SUPPOSITITIOUS
SUPPOSITORIES
SUPPOSITORY
SUPPRESS
SUPPRESSANT
SUPPRESSANTS
SUPPRESSED
SUPPRESSES
SUPPRESSIBILITY
SUPPRESSIBLE
SUPPRESSING
SUPPRESSION
SUPPRESSIONS
SUPPRESSIVE
SUPPRESSIVENESS
SUPPRESSOR
SUPPRESSORS
SUPPURATE
SUPPURATED
SUPPURATES
SUPPURATING
SUPPURATION
SUPPURATIONS
SUPPURATIVE
SUPRA
SUPRALIMINAL
SUPRAMOLECULAR
SUPRANATIONAL
SUPRAOPTIC
SUPRAORBITAL
SUPRARATIONAL
SUPRARENAL
SUPRARENALS
SUPRASEGMENTAL
SUPRAVITAL
SUPRAVITALLY
SUPREMACIES
SUPREMACIST
SUPREMACISTS
SUPREMACY
SUPREMATISM
SUPREMATISMS
SUPREMATIST
SUPREMATISTS
SUPREME
SUPREMELY
SUPREMENESS
SUPREMENESSES
SUPREMER
SUPREMES
SUPREMEST
SUPREMO
SUPREMOS
SUPS
SUQ
SUQS
SURA
SURAH
SURAHS
SURAL
SURAS
SURBASE
SURBASED
SURBASES
SURCEASE
SURCEASED
SURCEASES
SURCEASING
SURCHARGE
SURCHARGED
SURCHARGES
SURCHARGING
SURCINGLE
SURCINGLED
SURCINGLES
SURCINGLING
SURCOAT
SURCOATS
SURCULOSE
SURD
SURDS
SURE
SUREFIRE
SUREFOOTED
SUREFOOTEDLY
SUREFOOTEDNESS
SURELY
SURENESS
SURENESSES
SURER
SUREST
SURETIES
SURETY
SURETYSHIP
SURETYSHIPS
SURF
SURFABLE
SURFACE
SURFACED
SURFACER
SURFACERS
SURFACES
SURFACING
SURFACINGS
SURFACTANT
SURFACTANTS
SURFBIRD
SURFBIRDS
SURFBOARD
SURFBOARDED
SURFBOARDER
SURFBOARDERS
SURFBOARDING
SURFBOARDS
SURFBOAT
SURFBOATS
SURFED
SURFEIT
SURFEITED
SURFEITER
SURFEITERS
SURFEITING
SURFEITS
SURFER
SURFERS
SURFFISH
SURFFISHES
SURFICIAL
SURFIER
SURFIEST
SURFING
SURFINGS
SURFLIKE
SURFMAN
SURFMEN
SURFPERCH
SURFPERCHES
SURFS
SURFSIDE
SURFY
SURGE
SURGED
SURGEON
SURGEONFISH
SURGEONFISHES
SURGEONS
SURGER
SURGERIES
SURGERS
SURGERY
SURGES
SURGICAL
SURGICALLY
SURGING
SURGY
SURICATE
SURICATES
SURIMI
SURIMIS
SURJECTION
SURJECTIONS
SURJECTIVE
SURLIER
SURLIEST
SURLILY
SURLINESS
SURLINESSES
SURLY
SURMISE
SURMISED
SURMISER
SURMISERS
SURMISES
SURMISING
SURMOUNT
SURMOUNTABLE
SURMOUNTED
SURMOUNTING
SURMOUNTS
SURMULLET
SURMULLETS
SURNAME
SURNAMED
SURNAMER
SURNAMERS
SURNAMES
SURNAMING
SURPASS
SURPASSABLE
SURPASSED
SURPASSER
SURPASSERS
SURPASSES
SURPASSING
SURPASSINGLY
SURPLICE
SURPLICED
SURPLICES
SURPLUS
SURPLUSAGE
SURPLUSAGES
SURPLUSED
SURPLUSES
SURPLUSING
SURPLUSSED
SURPLUSSES
SURPLUSSING
SURPRINT
SURPRINTED
SURPRINTING
SURPRINTS
SURPRISAL
SURPRISALS
SURPRISE
SURPRISED
SURPRISER
SURPRISERS
SURPRISES
SURPRISING
SURPRISINGLY
SURPRIZE
SURPRIZED
SURPRIZES
SURPRIZING
SURRA
SURRAS
SURREAL
SURREALISM
SURREALISMS
SURREALIST
SURREALISTIC
SURREALISTS
SURREALITIES
SURREALITY
SURREALLY
SURREBUTTER
SURREBUTTERS
SURREJOINDER
SURREJOINDERS
SURRENDER
SURRENDERED
SURRENDERING
SURRENDERS
SURREPTITIOUS
SURREPTITIOUSLY
SURREY
SURREYS
SURROGACIES
SURROGACY
SURROGATE
SURROGATED
SURROGATES
SURROGATING
SURROUND
SURROUNDED
SURROUNDING
SURROUNDINGS
SURROUNDS
SURROYAL
SURROYALS
SURTAX
SURTAXED
SURTAXES
SURTAXING
SURTITLE

SURTITLES
SURTOUT
SURTOUTS
SURVEIL
SURVEILLANCE
SURVEILLANCES
SURVEILLANT
SURVEILLANTS
SURVEILLED
SURVEILLING
SURVEILS
SURVEY
SURVEYED
SURVEYING
SURVEYINGS
SURVEYOR
SURVEYORS
SURVEYS
SURVIVABILITIES
SURVIVABILITY
SURVIVABLE
SURVIVAL
SURVIVALISM
SURVIVALISMS
SURVIVALIST
SURVIVALISTS
SURVIVALS
SURVIVANCE
SURVIVANCES
SURVIVE
SURVIVED
SURVIVER
SURVIVERS
SURVIVES
SURVIVING
SURVIVOR
SURVIVORS
SURVIVORSHIP
SURVIVORSHIPS
SUS
SUSCEPTIBILITY
SUSCEPTIBLE
SUSCEPTIBLENESS
SUSCEPTIBLY
SUSCEPTIVE
SUSCEPTIVENESS
SUSCEPTIVITIES
SUSCEPTIVITY
SUSED
SUSES
SUSHI
SUSHIS
SUSING
SUSLIK
SUSLIKS
SUSPECT
SUSPECTED
SUSPECTING
SUSPECTS
SUSPEND
SUSPENDED
SUSPENDER
SUSPENDERED
SUSPENDERS
SUSPENDING
SUSPENDS
SUSPENSE
SUSPENSEFUL
SUSPENSEFULLY
SUSPENSEFULNESS
SUSPENSELESS
SUSPENSER
SUSPENSERS
SUSPENSES
SUSPENSION
SUSPENSIONS
SUSPENSIVE
SUSPENSIVELY
SUSPENSOR
SUSPENSORIES
SUSPENSORS
SUSPENSORY
SUSPICION
SUSPICIONED
SUSPICIONING
SUSPICIONS
SUSPICIOUS
SUSPICIOUSLY
SUSPICIOUSNESS
SUSPIRATION
SUSPIRATIONS
SUSPIRE
SUSPIRED
SUSPIRES
SUSPIRING
SUSS
SUSSED
SUSSES
SUSSING
SUSTAIN
SUSTAINABILITY
SUSTAINABLE
SUSTAINABLY
SUSTAINED
SUSTAINEDLY
SUSTAINER
SUSTAINERS
SUSTAINING
SUSTAINS
SUSTENANCE
SUSTENANCES
SUSTENTATION
SUSTENTATIONS
SUSTENTATIVE
SUSURRANT
SUSURRATE
SUSURRATED
SUSURRATES
SUSURRATING
SUSURRATION
SUSURRATIONS
SUSURROUS
SUSURRUS
SUSURRUSES
SUTLER
SUTLERS
SUTRA
SUTRAS
SUTTA
SUTTAS
SUTTEE
SUTTEES
SUTURAL
SUTURALLY
SUTURE
SUTURED
SUTURES
SUTURING
SUZERAIN
SUZERAINS
SUZERAINTIES
SUZERAINTY
SVARAJ
SVARAJES
SVEDBERG
SVEDBERGS
SVELTE
SVELTELY
SVELTENESS
SVELTENESSES
SVELTER
SVELTEST
SWAB
SWABBED
SWABBER
SWABBERS
SWABBIE
SWABBIES
SWABBING
SWABBY
SWABS
SWACKED
SWADDLE
SWADDLED
SWADDLES
SWADDLING
SWAG
SWAGE
SWAGED
SWAGER
SWAGERS
SWAGES
SWAGGED
SWAGGER
SWAGGERED
SWAGGERER
SWAGGERERS
SWAGGERING
SWAGGERINGLY
SWAGGERS
SWAGGIE
SWAGGIES
SWAGGING
SWAGING
SWAGMAN
SWAGMEN
SWAGS
SWAIL
SWAILS
SWAIN
SWAINISH
SWAINISHNESS
SWAINISHNESSES
SWAINS
SWALE
SWALES
SWALLOW
SWALLOWABLE
SWALLOWED
SWALLOWER
SWALLOWERS
SWALLOWING
SWALLOWS
SWALLOWTAIL
SWALLOWTAILS
SWAM
SWAMI
SWAMIES
SWAMIS
SWAMP
SWAMPED
SWAMPER
SWAMPERS
SWAMPIER
SWAMPIEST
SWAMPINESS
SWAMPINESSES
SWAMPING
SWAMPISH
SWAMPLAND
SWAMPLANDS
SWAMPS
SWAMPY
SWAMY
SWAN
SWANG
SWANHERD
SWANHERDS
SWANK
SWANKED
SWANKER
SWANKEST
SWANKIER
SWANKIEST
SWANKILY
SWANKINESS
SWANKINESSES
SWANKING
SWANKS
SWANKY
SWANLIKE
SWANNED
SWANNERIES
SWANNERY
SWANNING
SWANNY
SWANPAN
SWANPANS
SWANS
SWANSDOWN
SWANSDOWNS
SWANSKIN
SWANSKINS
SWAP
SWAPFILE
SWAPFILES
SWAPPED
SWAPPER
SWAPPERS
SWAPPING
SWAPS
SWARAJ
SWARAJES
SWARAJISM
SWARAJISMS

WARAJIST
WARAJISTS
WARD
WARDED
WARDING
VARDS
WARE
WARF
WARFS
VARM
WARMED
WARMER
VARMERS
VARMING
WARMINGS
WARMS
VART
VARTH
WARTHIER
VARTHIEST
VARTHILY
VARTHINESS
WARTHINESSES
VARTHS
VARTHY
/ARTNESS
/ARTNESSES
VARTY
VASH
/ASHBUCKLE
VASHBUCKLED
VASHBUCKLER
VASHBUCKLERS
/ASHBUCKLES
VASHBUCKLING
VASHED
/ASHER
VASHERS
VASHES
VASHING
/ASTICA
VASTICAS
VASTIKA
/ASTIKAS
/AT
VATCH
VATCHES
/ATH
VATHE
VATHED
/ATHER
/ATHERS
/ATHES
SWATHING
SWATHS
SWATS
SWATTED
SWATTER
SWATTERS
SWATTING
SWAY
SWAYABLE
SWAYBACK
SWAYBACKED
SWAYBACKS
SWAYED
SWAYER
SWAYERS
SWAYFUL
SWAYING
SWAYS
SWEAR
SWEARER
SWEARERS
SWEARING
SWEARINGS
SWEARS
SWEARWORD
SWEARWORDS
SWEAT
SWEATBAND
SWEATBANDS
SWEATBOX
SWEATBOXES
SWEATED
SWEATER
SWEATERDRESS
SWEATERDRESSES
SWEATERED
SWEATERS
SWEATIER
SWEATIEST
SWEATILY
SWEATINESS
SWEATINESSES
SWEATING
SWEATPANTS
SWEATS
SWEATSHIRT
SWEATSHIRTS
SWEATSHOP
SWEATSHOPS
SWEATSUIT
SWEATSUITS
SWEATY
SWEDE
SWEDES
SWEENEY
SWEENEYS
SWEENIES
SWEENY
SWEEP
SWEEPBACK
SWEEPBACKS
SWEEPER
SWEEPERS
SWEEPIER
SWEEPIEST
SWEEPING
SWEEPINGLY
SWEEPINGNESS
SWEEPINGNESSES
SWEEPINGS
SWEEPS
SWEEPSTAKES
SWEEPY
SWEER
SWEET
SWEETBREAD
SWEETBREADS
SWEETBRIAR
SWEETBRIARS
SWEETBRIER
SWEETBRIERS
SWEETEN
SWEETENED
SWEETENER
SWEETENERS
SWEETENING
SWEETENINGS
SWEETENS
SWEETER
SWEETEST
SWEETGRASS
SWEETGRASSES
SWEETHEART
SWEETHEARTS
SWEETIE
SWEETIES
SWEETING
SWEETINGS
SWEETISH
SWEETISHLY
SWEETLIP
SWEETLIPS
SWEETLY
SWEETMEAT
SWEETMEATS
SWEETNESS
SWEETNESSES
SWEETS
SWEETSHOP
SWEETSHOPS
SWEETSOP
SWEETSOPS
SWELL
SWELLED
SWELLER
SWELLEST
SWELLFISH
SWELLFISHES
SWELLHEAD
SWELLHEADED
SWELLHEADEDNESS
SWELLHEADS
SWELLING
SWELLINGS
SWELLS
SWELTER
SWELTERED
SWELTERING
SWELTERINGLY
SWELTERS
SWELTRIER
SWELTRIEST
SWELTRY
SWEPT
SWEPTBACK
SWEPTWING
SWEPTWINGS
SWERVE
SWERVED
SWERVER
SWERVERS
SWERVES
SWERVING
SWEVEN
SWEVENS
SWIDDEN
SWIDDENS
SWIFT
SWIFTER
SWIFTERS
SWIFTEST
SWIFTIE
SWIFTIES
SWIFTLET
SWIFTLETS
SWIFTLY
SWIFTNESS
SWIFTNESSES
SWIFTS
SWIG
SWIGGED
SWIGGER
SWIGGERS
SWIGGING
SWIGS
SWILE
SWILER
SWILERS
SWILES
SWILING
SWILINGS
SWILL
SWILLED
SWILLER
SWILLERS
SWILLING
SWILLS
SWIM
SWIMMABLE
SWIMMER
SWIMMERET
SWIMMERETS
SWIMMERS
SWIMMIER
SWIMMIEST
SWIMMILY
SWIMMING
SWIMMINGLY
SWIMMINGS
SWIMMY
SWIMS
SWIMSUIT
SWIMSUITS
SWIMWEAR
SWINDLE
SWINDLED
SWINDLER
SWINDLERS
SWINDLES
SWINDLING
SWINE
SWINEHERD
SWINEHERDS
SWINEPOX
SWINEPOXES
SWINES
SWING
SWINGBY
SWINGBYS
SWINGE
SWINGED
SWINGEING

SWINGER
SWINGERS
SWINGES
SWINGIER
SWINGIEST
SWINGING
SWINGINGEST
SWINGINGLY
SWINGINGS
SWINGLE
SWINGLED
SWINGLES
SWINGLETREE
SWINGLETREES
SWINGLING
SWINGMAN
SWINGMEN
SWINGS
SWINGY
SWINISH
SWINISHLY
SWINISHNESS
SWINISHNESSES
SWINK
SWINKED
SWINKING
SWINKS
SWINNEY
SWINNEYS
SWIPE
SWIPED
SWIPER
SWIPERS
SWIPES
SWIPING
SWIPLE
SWIPLES
SWIPPLE
SWIPPLES
SWIRL
SWIRLED
SWIRLIER
SWIRLIEST
SWIRLING
SWIRLINGLY
SWIRLS
SWIRLY
SWISH
SWISHED
SWISHER
SWISHERS
SWISHES
SWISHEST
SWISHIER
SWISHIEST
SWISHING
SWISHINGLY
SWISHY
SWISS
SWISSES
SWITCH
SWITCHABLE
SWITCHBACK
SWITCHBACKED
SWITCHBACKING
SWITCHBACKS
SWITCHBLADE
SWITCHBLADES
SWITCHBOARD
SWITCHBOARDS
SWITCHED
SWITCHEL
SWITCHELS
SWITCHER
SWITCHEROO
SWITCHEROOS
SWITCHERS
SWITCHES
SWITCHGRASS
SWITCHGRASSES
SWITCHING
SWITCHMAN
SWITCHMEN
SWITCHYARD
SWITCHYARDS
SWITH
SWITHE
SWITHER
SWITHERED
SWITHERING
SWITHERS
SWITHLY
SWIVE
SWIVED
SWIVEL
SWIVELED
SWIVELING
SWIVELLED
SWIVELLING
SWIVELS
SWIVES
SWIVET
SWIVETS
SWIVING
SWIZZLE
SWIZZLED
SWIZZLER
SWIZZLERS
SWIZZLES
SWIZZLING
SWOB
SWOBBED
SWOBBER
SWOBBERS
SWOBBING
SWOBS
SWOLLEN
SWOON
SWOONED
SWOONER
SWOONERS
SWOONIER
SWOONIEST
SWOONING
SWOONINGLY
SWOONS
SWOONY
SWOOP
SWOOPED
SWOOPER
SWOOPERS
SWOOPIER
SWOOPIEST
SWOOPING
SWOOPS
SWOOPSTAKE
SWOOPY
SWOOSH
SWOOSHED
SWOOSHES
SWOOSHING
SWOP
SWOPPED
SWOPPER
SWOPPERS
SWOPPING
SWOPS
SWORD
SWORDFISH
SWORDFISHES
SWORDLIKE
SWORDMAN
SWORDMEN
SWORDPLAY
SWORDPLAYER
SWORDPLAYERS
SWORDPLAYS
SWORDS
SWORDSMAN
SWORDSMANSHIP
SWORDSMANSHIPS
SWORDSMEN
SWORDTAIL
SWORDTAILS
SWORE
SWORN
SWOT
SWOTS
SWOTTED
SWOTTER
SWOTTERS
SWOTTING
SWOUN
SWOUND
SWOUNDED
SWOUNDING
SWOUNDS
SWOUNED
SWOUNING
SWOUNS
SWUM
SWUNG
SYBARITE
SYBARITES
SYBARITIC
SYBARITICALLY
SYBARITISM
SYBARITISMS
SYBO
SYBOES
SYCAMINE
SYCAMINES
SYCAMORE
SYCAMORES
SYCE
SYCEE
SYCEES
SYCES
SYCOMORE
SYCOMORES
SYCON
SYCONIA
SYCONIUM
SYCONOID
SYCONS
SYCOPHANCIES
SYCOPHANCY
SYCOPHANT
SYCOPHANTIC
SYCOPHANTICALLY
SYCOPHANTISH
SYCOPHANTISHLY
SYCOPHANTISM
SYCOPHANTISMS
SYCOPHANTLY
SYCOPHANTS
SYCOSES
SYCOSIS
SYENITE
SYENITES
SYENITIC
SYKE
SYKES
SYLI
SYLIS
SYLLABARIES
SYLLABARY
SYLLABI
SYLLABIC
SYLLABICALLY
SYLLABICATE
SYLLABICATED
SYLLABICATES
SYLLABICATING
SYLLABICATION
SYLLABICATIONS
SYLLABICITIES
SYLLABICITY
SYLLABICS
SYLLABIFICATION
SYLLABIFIED
SYLLABIFIES
SYLLABIFY
SYLLABIFYING
SYLLABISM
SYLLABISMS
SYLLABIZE
SYLLABIZED
SYLLABIZES
SYLLABIZING
SYLLABLE
SYLLABLED
SYLLABLES
SYLLABLING
SYLLABUB
SYLLABUBS
SYLLABUS
SYLLABUSES
SYLLEPSES
SYLLEPSIS
SYLLEPTIC
SYLLOGISM
SYLLOGISMS
SYLLOGIST
SYLLOGISTIC

LLOGISTICALLY
LLOGISTS
LLOGIZE
LLOGIZED
LLOGIZES
LLOGIZING
LPH
LPHIC
LPHID
LPHIDS
LPHISH
LPHLIKE
LPHS
LPHY
LVA
LVAE
LVAN
LVANITE
LVANITES
LVANS
LVAS
LVATIC
LVICULTURE
LVICULTURES
LVIN
LVINE
LVINES
LVINITE
LVINITES
LVINS
LVITE
LVITES
MBION
MBIONS
MBIONT
MBIONTS
MBIOSES
MBIOSIS
MBIOT
MBIOTE
MBIOTES
MBIOTIC
MBIOTICALLY
MBIOTS
MBOL
MBOLED
MBOLIC
MBOLICAL
MBOLICALLY
MBOLING
MBOLISE
MBOLISED
MBOLISES

SYMBOLISING
SYMBOLISM
SYMBOLISMS
SYMBOLIST
SYMBOLISTIC
SYMBOLISTS
SYMBOLIZATION
SYMBOLIZATIONS
SYMBOLIZE
SYMBOLIZED
SYMBOLIZER
SYMBOLIZERS
SYMBOLIZES
SYMBOLIZING
SYMBOLLED
SYMBOLLING
SYMBOLOGIES
SYMBOLOGY
SYMBOLS
SYMMETALLISM
SYMMETALLISMS
SYMMETRIC
SYMMETRICAL
SYMMETRICALLY
SYMMETRICALNESS
SYMMETRIES
SYMMETRIZATION
SYMMETRIZATIONS
SYMMETRIZE
SYMMETRIZED
SYMMETRIZES
SYMMETRIZING
SYMMETRY
SYMPATHECTOMIES
SYMPATHECTOMY
SYMPATHETIC
SYMPATHETICALLY
SYMPATHETICS
SYMPATHIES
SYMPATHIN
SYMPATHINS
SYMPATHISE
SYMPATHISED
SYMPATHISER
SYMPATHISERS
SYMPATHISES
SYMPATHISING
SYMPATHIZE
SYMPATHIZED
SYMPATHIZER
SYMPATHIZERS
SYMPATHIZES
SYMPATHIZING

SYMPATHOLYTIC
SYMPATHOLYTICS
SYMPATHOMIMETIC
SYMPATHY
SYMPATICO
SYMPATRIC
SYMPATRICALLY
SYMPATRIES
SYMPATRY
SYMPETALIES
SYMPETALOUS
SYMPETALY
SYMPHONIC
SYMPHONICALLY
SYMPHONIES
SYMPHONIOUS
SYMPHONIOUSLY
SYMPHONIST
SYMPHONISTS
SYMPHONY
SYMPHYSEAL
SYMPHYSES
SYMPHYSIAL
SYMPHYSIS
SYMPODIA
SYMPODIAL
SYMPODIUM
SYMPOSIA
SYMPOSIAC
SYMPOSIACS
SYMPOSIARCH
SYMPOSIARCHS
SYMPOSIAST
SYMPOSIASTS
SYMPOSIUM
SYMPOSIUMS
SYMPTOM
SYMPTOMATIC
SYMPTOMATICALLY
SYMPTOMATOLOGIC
SYMPTOMATOLOGY
SYMPTOMLESS
SYMPTOMS
SYN
SYNAERESES
SYNAERESIS
SYNAESTHESES
SYNAESTHESIA
SYNAESTHESIAS
SYNAESTHESIS
SYNAGOG
SYNAGOGAL
SYNAGOGS

SYNAGOGUE
SYNAGOGUES
SYNALEPHA
SYNALEPHAS
SYNALOEPHA
SYNALOEPHAS
SYNANON
SYNANONS
SYNAPOMORPHIES
SYNAPOMORPHY
SYNAPSE
SYNAPSED
SYNAPSES
SYNAPSID
SYNAPSIDS
SYNAPSING
SYNAPSIS
SYNAPTIC
SYNAPTICALLY
SYNAPTOSOMAL
SYNAPTOSOME
SYNAPTOSOMES
SYNARTHRODIAL
SYNARTHROSES
SYNARTHROSIS
SYNC
SYNCARP
SYNCARPIES
SYNCARPOUS
SYNCARPS
SYNCARPY
SYNCED
SYNCH
SYNCHED
SYNCHING
SYNCHRO
SYNCHROMESH
SYNCHROMESHES
SYNCHRONAL
SYNCHRONEITIES
SYNCHRONEITY
SYNCHRONIC
SYNCHRONICAL
SYNCHRONICALLY
SYNCHRONICITIES
SYNCHRONICITY
SYNCHRONIES
SYNCHRONISATION
SYNCHRONISE
SYNCHRONISED
SYNCHRONISES
SYNCHRONISING
SYNCHRONISM

SYNCHRONISMS
SYNCHRONISTIC
SYNCHRONIZATION
SYNCHRONIZE
SYNCHRONIZED
SYNCHRONIZER
SYNCHRONIZERS
SYNCHRONIZES
SYNCHRONIZING
SYNCHRONOUS
SYNCHRONOUSLY
SYNCHRONOUSNESS
SYNCHRONY
SYNCHROS
SYNCHROSCOPE
SYNCHROSCOPES
SYNCHROTRON
SYNCHROTRONS
SYNCHS
SYNCING
SYNCLINAL
SYNCLINE
SYNCLINES
SYNCOM
SYNCOMS
SYNCOPAL
SYNCOPATE
SYNCOPATED
SYNCOPATES
SYNCOPATING
SYNCOPATION
SYNCOPATIONS
SYNCOPATIVE
SYNCOPATOR
SYNCOPATORS
SYNCOPE
SYNCOPES
SYNCOPIC
SYNCRETIC
SYNCRETISE
SYNCRETISED
SYNCRETISES
SYNCRETISING
SYNCRETISM
SYNCRETISMS
SYNCRETIST
SYNCRETISTIC
SYNCRETISTS
SYNCRETIZE
SYNCRETIZED
SYNCRETIZES
SYNCRETIZING
SYNCS

SYNCYTIA
SYNCYTIAL
SYNCYTIUM
SYNDACTYL
SYNDACTYLIES
SYNDACTYLISM
SYNDACTYLISMS
SYNDACTYLS
SYNDACTYLY
SYNDESES
SYNDESIS
SYNDESISES
SYNDESMOSES
SYNDESMOSIS
SYNDET
SYNDETIC
SYNDETICALLY
SYNDETS
SYNDIC
SYNDICAL
SYNDICALISM
SYNDICALISMS
SYNDICALIST
SYNDICALISTS
SYNDICATE
SYNDICATED
SYNDICATES
SYNDICATING
SYNDICATION
SYNDICATIONS
SYNDICATOR
SYNDICATORS
SYNDICS
SYNDROME
SYNDROMES
SYNDROMIC
SYNE
SYNECDOCHE
SYNECDOCHES
SYNECDOCHIC
SYNECDOCHICAL
SYNECDOCHICALLY
SYNECOLOGICAL
SYNECOLOGIES
SYNECOLOGY
SYNECTIC
SYNERESES
SYNERESIS
SYNERGETIC
SYNERGIA
SYNERGIAS
SYNERGIC
SYNERGICALLY
SYNERGID
SYNERGIDS
SYNERGIES
SYNERGISM
SYNERGISMS
SYNERGIST
SYNERGISTIC
SYNERGISTICALLY
SYNERGISTS
SYNERGY
SYNESIS
SYNESISES
SYNESTHESIA
SYNESTHESIAS
SYNESTHETE
SYNESTHETES
SYNESTHETIC
SYNFUEL
SYNFUELS
SYNGAMIC
SYNGAMIES
SYNGAMOUS
SYNGAMY
SYNGAS
SYNGASES
SYNGASSES
SYNGENEIC
SYNGENIC
SYNIZESES
SYNIZESIS
SYNKARYA
SYNKARYON
SYNKARYONS
SYNOD
SYNODAL
SYNODIC
SYNODICAL
SYNODS
SYNOICOUS
SYNONYM
SYNONYME
SYNONYMES
SYNONYMIC
SYNONYMICAL
SYNONYMIES
SYNONYMIST
SYNONYMISTS
SYNONYMITIES
SYNONYMITY
SYNONYMIZE
SYNONYMIZED
SYNONYMIZES
SYNONYMIZING
SYNONYMOUS
SYNONYMOUSLY
SYNONYMS
SYNONYMY
SYNOPSES
SYNOPSIS
SYNOPSIZE
SYNOPSIZED
SYNOPSIZES
SYNOPSIZING
SYNOPTIC
SYNOPTICAL
SYNOPTICALLY
SYNOSTOSES
SYNOSTOSIS
SYNOVIA
SYNOVIAL
SYNOVIAS
SYNOVITIS
SYNOVITISES
SYNTACTIC
SYNTACTICAL
SYNTACTICALLY
SYNTACTICIAN
SYNTACTICIANS
SYNTACTICS
SYNTAGM
SYNTAGMA
SYNTAGMAS
SYNTAGMATA
SYNTAGMATIC
SYNTAGMS
SYNTAX
SYNTAXES
SYNTH
SYNTHASE
SYNTHASES
SYNTHESES
SYNTHESIS
SYNTHESISE
SYNTHESISED
SYNTHESISER
SYNTHESISERS
SYNTHESISES
SYNTHESISING
SYNTHESIST
SYNTHESISTS
SYNTHESIZE
SYNTHESIZED
SYNTHESIZER
SYNTHESIZERS
SYNTHESIZES
SYNTHESIZING
SYNTHETASE
SYNTHETASES
SYNTHETIC
SYNTHETICALLY
SYNTHETICS
SYNTHPOP
SYNTHPOPS
SYNTHS
SYNTONE
SYNTONES
SYNTONIC
SYNTONIES
SYNTONY
SYNTYPE
SYNTYPES
SYNURA
SYNURAE
SYPH
SYPHER
SYPHERED
SYPHERING
SYPHERS
SYPHILIS
SYPHILISES
SYPHILITIC
SYPHILITICS
SYPHILOID
SYPHON
SYPHONAL
SYPHONED
SYPHONIC
SYPHONING
SYPHONS
SYPHS
SYREN
SYRENS
SYRETTE
SYRETTES
SYRINGA
SYRINGAS
SYRINGE
SYRINGEAL
SYRINGED
SYRINGES
SYRINGING
SYRINGOMYELIA
SYRINGOMYELIAS
SYRINGOMYELIC
SYRINX
SYRINXES
SYRPHIAN
SYRPHIANS
SYRPHID
SYRPHIDS
SYRUP
SYRUPED
SYRUPIER
SYRUPIEST
SYRUPING
SYRUPLIKE
SYRUPS
SYRUPY
SYSADMIN
SYSADMINS
SYSOP
SYSOPS
SYSTALTIC
SYSTEM
SYSTEMATIC
SYSTEMATICALLY
SYSTEMATICNESS
SYSTEMATICS
SYSTEMATISE
SYSTEMATISED
SYSTEMATISES
SYSTEMATISING
SYSTEMATISM
SYSTEMATISMS
SYSTEMATIST
SYSTEMATISTS
SYSTEMATIZATION
SYSTEMATIZE
SYSTEMATIZED
SYSTEMATIZER
SYSTEMATIZERS
SYSTEMATIZES
SYSTEMATIZING
SYSTEMIC
SYSTEMICALLY
SYSTEMICS
SYSTEMIZATION
SYSTEMIZATIONS
SYSTEMIZE
SYSTEMIZED
SYSTEMIZES
SYSTEMIZING
SYSTEMLESS
SYSTEMS
SYSTOLE
SYSTOLES
SYSTOLIC
SYZYGAL
SYZYGETIC
SYZYGIAL
SYZYGIES
SYZYGY

T

B
BANID
BANIDS
BARD
BARDED
BARDS
BARET
BARETS
BBED
BBIED
BBIES
BBING
BBINGS
BBIS
BBISES
BBOULEH
BBOULEHS
BBY
BBYING
BER
BERED
BERING
BERNACLE
BERNACLED
BERNACLES
BERNACLING
BERNACULAR
BERS
BES
BETIC
BETICS
BID
BLA
BLAS
BLATURE
BLATURES
BLE
BLEAU
BLEAUS
BLEAUX
BLECLOTH
BLECLOTHS
BLED
BLEFUL
BLEFULS
BLELAND
BLELANDS
BLELESS
BLEMATE
BLEMATES
BLES

TABLESFUL
TABLESPOON
TABLESPOONFUL
TABLESPOONFULS
TABLESPOONS
TABLESPOONSFUL
TABLET
TABLETED
TABLETING
TABLETOP
TABLETOPS
TABLETS
TABLETTED
TABLETTING
TABLEWARE
TABLEWARES
TABLING
TABLINGS
TABLOID
TABLOIDISM
TABLOIDISMS
TABLOIDS
TABOO
TABOOED
TABOOING
TABOOLEY
TABOOLEYS
TABOOS
TABOR
TABORED
TABORER
TABORERS
TABORET
TABORETS
TABORIN
TABORINE
TABORINES
TABORING
TABORINS
TABORS
TABOULEH
TABOULEHS
TABOULI
TABOULIS
TABOUR
TABOURED
TABOURER
TABOURERS
TABOURET
TABOURETS
TABOURING
TABOURS

TABS
TABU
TABUED
TABUING
TABULABLE
TABULAR
TABULARLY
TABULATE
TABULATED
TABULATES
TABULATING
TABULATION
TABULATIONS
TABULATOR
TABULATORS
TABULI
TABULIS
TABUN
TABUNS
TABUS
TACAMAHAC
TACAMAHACS
TACAN
TACANS
TACE
TACES
TACET
TACH
TACHE
TACHES
TACHINID
TACHINIDS
TACHISM
TACHISME
TACHISMES
TACHISMS
TACHIST
TACHISTE
TACHISTES
TACHISTOSCOPE
TACHISTOSCOPES
TACHISTOSCOPIC
TACHISTS
TACHOGRAPH
TACHOGRAPHS
TACHOMETER
TACHOMETERS
TACHS
TACHYARRHYTHMIA
TACHYCARDIA
TACHYCARDIAS
TACHYLITE

TACHYLITES
TACHYLYTE
TACHYLYTES
TACHYON
TACHYONIC
TACHYONS
TACIT
TACITLY
TACITNESS
TACITNESSES
TACITURN
TACITURNITIES
TACITURNITY
TACK
TACKBOARD
TACKBOARDS
TACKED
TACKER
TACKERS
TACKET
TACKETS
TACKEY
TACKIER
TACKIEST
TACKIFIED
TACKIFIER
TACKIFIERS
TACKIFIES
TACKIFY
TACKIFYING
TACKILY
TACKINESS
TACKINESSES
TACKING
TACKLE
TACKLED
TACKLER
TACKLERS
TACKLES
TACKLESS
TACKLING
TACKLINGS
TACKS
TACKY
TACNODE
TACNODES
TACO
TACONITE
TACONITES
TACOS
TACRINE
TACRINES

TACT
TACTFUL
TACTFULLY
TACTFULNESS
TACTFULNESSES
TACTIC
TACTICAL
TACTICALLY
TACTICIAN
TACTICIANS
TACTICS
TACTILE
TACTILELY
TACTILITIES
TACTILITY
TACTION
TACTIONS
TACTLESS
TACTLESSLY
TACTLESSNESS
TACTLESSNESSES
TACTS
TACTUAL
TACTUALLY
TAD
TADPOLE
TADPOLES
TADS
TAE
TAEKWONDO
TAEKWONDOS
TAEL
TAELS
TAENIA
TAENIAE
TAENIAS
TAENIASES
TAENIASIS
TAENIOID
TAENITE
TAENITES
TAFFAREL
TAFFARELS
TAFFEREL
TAFFERELS
TAFFETA
TAFFETAS
TAFFETIZED
TAFFIA
TAFFIAS
TAFFIES
TAFFRAIL

TAFFRAILS
TAFFY
TAFIA
TAFIAS
TAG
TAGALONG
TAGALONGS
TAGBOARD
TAGBOARDS
TAGETES
TAGGANT
TAGGANTS
TAGGED
TAGGER
TAGGERS
TAGGING
TAGINE
TAGINES
TAGLIATELLE
TAGLIATELLES
TAGLIKE
TAGLINE
TAGLINES
TAGMEME
TAGMEMES
TAGMEMIC
TAGMEMICS
TAGRAG
TAGRAGS
TAGS
TAHINA
TAHINAS
TAHINI
TAHINIS
TAHR
TAHRS
TAHSIL
TAHSILDAR
TAHSILDARS
TAHSILS
TAIGA
TAIGAS
TAIGLACH
TAIKO
TAIKOS
TAIL
TAILBACK
TAILBACKS
TAILBOARD
TAILBOARDS
TAILBONE
TAILBONES
TAILCOAT
TAILCOATED
TAILCOATS
TAILED
TAILENDER
TAILENDERS
TAILER
TAILERS
TAILFAN
TAILFANS
TAILFIN
TAILFINS
TAILGATE
TAILGATED
TAILGATER
TAILGATERS
TAILGATES
TAILGATING
TAILHOOK
TAILHOOKS
TAILING
TAILINGS
TAILLAMP
TAILLAMPS
TAILLE
TAILLES
TAILLESS
TAILLEUR
TAILLEURS
TAILLIGHT
TAILLIGHTS
TAILLIKE
TAILOR
TAILORBIRD
TAILORBIRDS
TAILORED
TAILORING
TAILORINGS
TAILORS
TAILPIECE
TAILPIECES
TAILPIPE
TAILPIPES
TAILPLANE
TAILPLANES
TAILRACE
TAILRACES
TAILS
TAILSKID
TAILSKIDS
TAILSLIDE
TAILSLIDES
TAILSPIN
TAILSPINNED
TAILSPINNING
TAILSPINS
TAILSPUN
TAILSTOCK
TAILSTOCKS
TAILWATER
TAILWATERS
TAILWIND
TAILWINDS
TAIN
TAINS
TAINT
TAINTED
TAINTING
TAINTLESS
TAINTS
TAIPAN
TAIPANS
TAJ
TAJES
TAJINE
TAJINES
TAKA
TAKABLE
TAKAHE
TAKAHES
TAKAS
TAKE
TAKEABLE
TAKEAWAY
TAKEAWAYS
TAKEDOWN
TAKEDOWNS
TAKEN
TAKEOFF
TAKEOFFS
TAKEOUT
TAKEOUTS
TAKEOVER
TAKEOVERS
TAKER
TAKERS
TAKES
TAKEUP
TAKEUPS
TAKIN
TAKING
TAKINGLY
TAKINGS
TAKINS
TALA
TALAPOIN
TALAPOINS
TALAR
TALARIA
TALARS
TALAS
TALBOT
TALBOTS
TALC
TALCED
TALCIER
TALCIEST
TALCING
TALCKED
TALCKING
TALCKY
TALCOSE
TALCOUS
TALCS
TALCUM
TALCUMED
TALCUMING
TALCUMS
TALCY
TALE
TALEBEARER
TALEBEARERS
TALEBEARING
TALEBEARINGS
TALEGGIO
TALEGGIOS
TALENT
TALENTED
TALENTLESS
TALENTS
TALER
TALERS
TALES
TALESMAN
TALESMEN
TALEYSIM
TALI
TALION
TALIONS
TALIPED
TALIPEDS
TALIPES
TALIPOT
TALIPOTS
TALISMAN
TALISMANIC
TALISMANICALLY
TALISMANS
TALK
TALKABLE
TALKATHON
TALKATHONS
TALKATIVE
TALKATIVELY
TALKATIVENESS
TALKATIVENESSES
TALKBACK
TALKBACKS
TALKED
TALKER
TALKERS
TALKFEST
TALKFESTS
TALKIE
TALKIER
TALKIES
TALKIEST
TALKINESS
TALKINESSES
TALKING
TALKINGS
TALKS
TALKY
TALL
TALLAGE
TALLAGED
TALLAGES
TALLAGING
TALLAISIM
TALLBOY
TALLBOYS
TALLER
TALLEST
TALLGRASS
TALLGRASSES
TALLIED
TALLIER
TALLIERS
TALLIES
TALLIS
TALLISES
TALLISH
TALLISIM
TALLIT
TALLITH
TALLITHES
TALLITHIM
TALLITHS
TALLITIM
TALLITOTH
TALLITS
TALLNESS
TALLNESSES

LLOL
LLOLS
LLOW
LLOWED
LLOWIER
LLOWIEST
LLOWING
LLOWS
LLOWY
LLS
LLY
LLYHO
LLYHOED
LLYHOES
LLYHOING
LLYHOS
LLYING
LLYMAN
LLYMEN
MUDIC
MUDISM
MUDISMS
ON
ONED
ONS
OOKA
OOKAS
UK
UKA
UKAS
UKS
US
USES
I
ABLE
AL
ALE
ALES
ALS
ANDU
ANDUA
ANDUAS
ANDUS
ARACK
ARACKS
ARAO
ARAOS
ARAU
ARAUS
ARI
ARILLO
ARILLOS
ARIN
TAMARIND
TAMARINDS
TAMARINS
TAMARIS
TAMARISK
TAMARISKS
TAMASHA
TAMASHAS
TAMBAC
TAMBACS
TAMBAK
TAMBAKS
TAMBALA
TAMBALAS
TAMBOUR
TAMBOURA
TAMBOURAS
TAMBOURED
TAMBOURER
TAMBOURERS
TAMBOURIN
TAMBOURINE
TAMBOURINES
TAMBOURING
TAMBOURINS
TAMBOURS
TAMBUR
TAMBURA
TAMBURAS
TAMBURS
TAME
TAMEABLE
TAMED
TAMEIN
TAMEINS
TAMELESS
TAMELY
TAMENESS
TAMENESSES
TAMER
TAMERS
TAMES
TAMEST
TAMING
TAMIS
TAMISES
TAMMIE
TAMMIES
TAMMY
TAMOXIFEN
TAMOXIFENS
TAMP
TAMPALA
TAMPALAS
TAMPAN
TAMPANS
TAMPED
TAMPER
TAMPERED
TAMPERER
TAMPERERS
TAMPERING
TAMPERPROOF
TAMPERS
TAMPING
TAMPINGS
TAMPION
TAMPIONS
TAMPON
TAMPONED
TAMPONING
TAMPONS
TAMPS
TAMS
TAN
TANAGER
TANAGERS
TANBARK
TANBARKS
TANDEM
TANDEMS
TANDOOR
TANDOORI
TANDOORIS
TANDOORS
TANG
TANGA
TANGAS
TANGED
TANGELO
TANGELOS
TANGENCE
TANGENCES
TANGENCIES
TANGENCY
TANGENT
TANGENTAL
TANGENTIAL
TANGENTIALLY
TANGENTS
TANGERINE
TANGERINES
TANGIBILITIES
TANGIBILITY
TANGIBLE
TANGIBLENESS
TANGIBLENESSES
TANGIBLES
TANGIBLY
TANGIER
TANGIEST
TANGINESS
TANGINESSES
TANGING
TANGLE
TANGLED
TANGLEMENT
TANGLEMENTS
TANGLER
TANGLERS
TANGLES
TANGLIER
TANGLIEST
TANGLING
TANGLY
TANGO
TANGOED
TANGOES
TANGOING
TANGOLIKE
TANGOS
TANGRAM
TANGRAMS
TANGS
TANGY
TANIST
TANISTRIES
TANISTRY
TANISTS
TANK
TANKA
TANKAGE
TANKAGES
TANKARD
TANKARDS
TANKAS
TANKED
TANKER
TANKERS
TANKFUL
TANKFULS
TANKING
TANKINI
TANKINIS
TANKLESS
TANKLIKE
TANKS
TANKSHIP
TANKSHIPS
TANNABLE
TANNAGE
TANNAGES
TANNATE
TANNATES
TANNED
TANNER
TANNERIES
TANNERS
TANNERY
TANNEST
TANNIC
TANNIN
TANNING
TANNINGS
TANNINS
TANNISH
TANNOY
TANNOYS
TANREC
TANRECS
TANS
TANSIES
TANSY
TANTALATE
TANTALATES
TANTALIC
TANTALISE
TANTALISED
TANTALISER
TANTALISERS
TANTALISES
TANTALISING
TANTALISINGLY
TANTALITE
TANTALITES
TANTALIZE
TANTALIZED
TANTALIZER
TANTALIZERS
TANTALIZES
TANTALIZING
TANTALIZINGLY
TANTALOUS
TANTALUM
TANTALUMS
TANTALUS
TANTALUSES
TANTAMOUNT
TANTARA
TANTARAS
TANTIVIES
TANTIVY

TANTO
TANTOS
TANTRA
TANTRAS
TANTRIC
TANTRISM
TANTRISMS
TANTRIST
TANTRISTS
TANTRUM
TANTRUMS
TANUKI
TANUKIS
TANYARD
TANYARDS
TANZANITE
TANZANITES
TAO
TAOS
TAP
TAPA
TAPADERA
TAPADERAS
TAPADERO
TAPADEROS
TAPALO
TAPALOS
TAPAS
TAPE
TAPEABLE
TAPED
TAPELESS
TAPELIKE
TAPELINE
TAPELINES
TAPENADE
TAPENADES
TAPER
TAPERED
TAPERER
TAPERERS
TAPERING
TAPERS
TAPERSTICK
TAPERSTICKS
TAPES
TAPESTRIED
TAPESTRIES
TAPESTRY
TAPESTRYING
TAPETA
TAPETAL
TAPETUM
TAPETUMS
TAPEWORM
TAPEWORMS
TAPHOLE
TAPHOLES
TAPHONOMIC
TAPHONOMIES
TAPHONOMIST
TAPHONOMISTS
TAPHONOMY
TAPHOUSE
TAPHOUSES
TAPING
TAPINGS
TAPIOCA
TAPIOCAS
TAPIR
TAPIROID
TAPIROIDS
TAPIRS
TAPIS
TAPISES
TAPLESS
TAPPABLE
TAPPED
TAPPER
TAPPERS
TAPPET
TAPPETS
TAPPING
TAPPINGS
TAPROOM
TAPROOMS
TAPROOT
TAPROOTS
TAPS
TAPSTER
TAPSTERS
TAQUERIA
TAQUERIAS
TAR
TARABISH
TARABISHES
TARADIDDLE
TARADIDDLES
TARAMA
TARAMAS
TARANTAS
TARANTASES
TARANTELLA
TARANTELLAS
TARANTISM
TARANTISMS
TARANTIST
TARANTISTS
TARANTULA
TARANTULAE
TARANTULAS
TARBOOSH
TARBOOSHES
TARBUSH
TARBUSHES
TARDIER
TARDIES
TARDIEST
TARDIGRADE
TARDIGRADES
TARDILY
TARDINESS
TARDINESSES
TARDIVE
TARDO
TARDY
TARDYON
TARDYONS
TARE
TARED
TARES
TARGA
TARGAS
TARGE
TARGES
TARGET
TARGETABLE
TARGETED
TARGETING
TARGETS
TARIFF
TARIFFED
TARIFFING
TARIFFS
TARING
TARLATAN
TARLATANS
TARLETAN
TARLETANS
TARMAC
TARMACADAM
TARMACADAMS
TARMACKED
TARMACKING
TARMACS
TARN
TARNAL
TARNALLY
TARNATION
TARNATIONS
TARNISH
TARNISHABLE
TARNISHED
TARNISHES
TARNISHING
TARNS
TARO
TAROC
TAROCS
TAROK
TAROKS
TAROS
TAROT
TAROTS
TARP
TARPAN
TARPANS
TARPAPER
TARPAPERS
TARPAULIN
TARPAULINS
TARPON
TARPONS
TARPS
TARRADIDDLE
TARRADIDDLES
TARRAGON
TARRAGONS
TARRE
TARRED
TARRES
TARRIANCE
TARRIANCES
TARRIED
TARRIER
TARRIERS
TARRIES
TARRIEST
TARRINESS
TARRINESSES
TARRING
TARRY
TARRYING
TARS
TARSAL
TARSALS
TARSI
TARSIA
TARSIAS
TARSIER
TARSIERS
TARSOMETATARSI
TARSOMETATARSUS
TARSUS
TART
TARTAN
TARTANA
TARTANAS
TARTANS
TARTAR
TARTARE
TARTARIC
TARTAROUS
TARTARS
TARTED
TARTER
TARTEST
TARTIER
TARTIEST
TARTILY
TARTINESS
TARTINESSES
TARTING
TARTISH
TARTLET
TARTLETS
TARTLY
TARTNESS
TARTNESSES
TARTRATE
TARTRATED
TARTRATES
TARTS
TARTUFE
TARTUFES
TARTUFFE
TARTUFFES
TARTUFI
TARTUFO
TARTUFOS
TARTY
TARWEED
TARWEEDS
TARZAN
TARZANS
TAS
TASE
TASED
TASER
TASERS
TASES
TASING
TASK
TASKBAR
TASKBARS

SKED
SKING
SKMASTER
SKMASTERS
SKMISTRESS
SKMISTRESSES
SKS
SKWORK
SKWORKS
SS
SSE
SSEL
SSELED
SSELING
SSELLED
SSELLING
SSELS
SSES
SSET
SSETS
SSIE
SSIES
SSO
SSOS
TABLE
TE
TEABLE
TED
TEFUL
TEFULLY
TEFULNESS
TEFULNESSES
TELESS
TELESSLY
TELESSNESS
TELESSNESSES
TEMAKER
TEMAKERS
TER
TERS
TES
TIER
TIEST
TILY
TINESS
TINESSES
TING
TINGS
TY
MI
MIS
R

TATARS
TATE
TATER
TATERS
TATES
TATHATA
TATHATAS
TATOUAY
TATOUAYS
TATS
TATSOI
TATSOIS
TATTED
TATTER
TATTERDEMALION
TATTERDEMALIONS
TATTERED
TATTERING
TATTERS
TATTERSALL
TATTERSALLS
TATTIE
TATTIER
TATTIES
TATTIEST
TATTILY
TATTINESS
TATTINESSES
TATTING
TATTINGS
TATTLE
TATTLED
TATTLER
TATTLERS
TATTLES
TATTLETALE
TATTLETALES
TATTLING
TATTOO
TATTOOED
TATTOOER
TATTOOERS
TATTOOING
TATTOOIST
TATTOOISTS
TATTOOS
TATTY
TAU
TAUGHT
TAUNT
TAUNTED
TAUNTER
TAUNTERS

TAUNTING
TAUNTINGLY
TAUNTS
TAUON
TAUONS
TAUPE
TAUPES
TAURINE
TAURINES
TAUS
TAUT
TAUTAUG
TAUTAUGS
TAUTED
TAUTEN
TAUTENED
TAUTENING
TAUTENS
TAUTER
TAUTEST
TAUTING
TAUTLY
TAUTNESS
TAUTNESSES
TAUTOG
TAUTOGS
TAUTOLOGICAL
TAUTOLOGICALLY
TAUTOLOGIES
TAUTOLOGOUS
TAUTOLOGOUSLY
TAUTOLOGY
TAUTOMER
TAUTOMERIC
TAUTOMERISM
TAUTOMERISMS
TAUTOMERS
TAUTONYM
TAUTONYMIES
TAUTONYMS
TAUTONYMY
TAUTS
TAV
TAVERN
TAVERNA
TAVERNAS
TAVERNER
TAVERNERS
TAVERNS
TAVS
TAW
TAWDRIER
TAWDRIES

TAWDRIEST
TAWDRILY
TAWDRINESS
TAWDRINESSES
TAWDRY
TAWED
TAWER
TAWERS
TAWIE
TAWING
TAWNEY
TAWNEYS
TAWNIER
TAWNIES
TAWNIEST
TAWNILY
TAWNINESS
TAWNINESSES
TAWNY
TAWPIE
TAWPIES
TAWS
TAWSE
TAWSED
TAWSES
TAWSING
TAX
TAXA
TAXABLE
TAXABLES
TAXABLY
TAXATION
TAXATIONS
TAXED
TAXEME
TAXEMES
TAXEMIC
TAXER
TAXERS
TAXES
TAXI
TAXICAB
TAXICABS
TAXIDERMIC
TAXIDERMIES
TAXIDERMIST
TAXIDERMISTS
TAXIDERMY
TAXIED
TAXIES
TAXIING
TAXIMAN
TAXIMEN

TAXIMETER
TAXIMETERS
TAXING
TAXINGLY
TAXIS
TAXISES
TAXITE
TAXITES
TAXITIC
TAXIWAY
TAXIWAYS
TAXLESS
TAXMAN
TAXMEN
TAXOL
TAXOLS
TAXON
TAXONOMIC
TAXONOMICAL
TAXONOMICALLY
TAXONOMIES
TAXONOMIST
TAXONOMISTS
TAXONOMY
TAXONS
TAXPAID
TAXPAYER
TAXPAYERS
TAXPAYING
TAXPAYINGS
TAXUS
TAXWISE
TAXYING
TAYBERRIES
TAYBERRY
TAYRA
TAYRAS
TAZZA
TAZZAS
TAZZE
TCHOTCHKE
TCHOTCHKES
TE
TEA
TEABERRIES
TEABERRY
TEABOARD
TEABOARDS
TEABOWL
TEABOWLS
TEABOX
TEABOXES
TEACAKE

TEACAKES
TEACART
TEACARTS
TEACH
TEACHABLE
TEACHABLENESS
TEACHABLENESSES
TEACHABLY
TEACHER
TEACHERLY
TEACHERS
TEACHES
TEACHING
TEACHINGS
TEACUP
TEACUPFUL
TEACUPFULS
TEACUPS
TEACUPSFUL
TEAHOUSE
TEAHOUSES
TEAK
TEAKETTLE
TEAKETTLES
TEAKS
TEAKWOOD
TEAKWOODS
TEAL
TEALIKE
TEALS
TEAM
TEAMAKER
TEAMAKERS
TEAMED
TEAMING
TEAMMATE
TEAMMATES
TEAMS
TEAMSTER
TEAMSTERS
TEAMWORK
TEAMWORKS
TEAPOT
TEAPOTS
TEAPOY
TEAPOYS
TEAR
TEARABLE
TEARAWAY
TEARAWAYS
TEARDOWN
TEARDOWNS
TEARDROP
TEARDROPS
TEARED
TEARER
TEARERS
TEARFUL
TEARFULLY
TEARFULNESS
TEARFULNESSES
TEARGAS
TEARGASES
TEARGASSED
TEARGASSES
TEARGASSING
TEARIER
TEARIEST
TEARILY
TEARINESS
TEARINESSES
TEARING
TEARJERKER
TEARJERKERS
TEARLESS
TEARLIKE
TEAROOM
TEAROOMS
TEARS
TEARSTAIN
TEARSTAINED
TEARSTAINS
TEARSTRIP
TEARSTRIPS
TEARY
TEAS
TEASABLE
TEASE
TEASED
TEASEL
TEASELED
TEASELER
TEASELERS
TEASELING
TEASELLED
TEASELLER
TEASELLERS
TEASELLING
TEASELS
TEASER
TEASERS
TEASES
TEASHOP
TEASHOPS
TEASING
TEASINGLY
TEASPOON
TEASPOONFUL
TEASPOONFULS
TEASPOONS
TEASPOONSFUL
TEAT
TEATASTER
TEATASTERS
TEATED
TEATIME
TEATIMES
TEATS
TEAWARE
TEAWARES
TEAZEL
TEAZELED
TEAZELING
TEAZELLED
TEAZELLING
TEAZELS
TEAZLE
TEAZLED
TEAZLES
TEAZLING
TEC
TECH
TECHED
TECHIE
TECHIER
TECHIES
TECHIEST
TECHILY
TECHNETIUM
TECHNETIUMS
TECHNETRONIC
TECHNIC
TECHNICAL
TECHNICALITIES
TECHNICALITY
TECHNICALIZE
TECHNICALIZED
TECHNICALIZES
TECHNICALIZING
TECHNICALLY
TECHNICALS
TECHNICIAN
TECHNICIANS
TECHNICS
TECHNIQUE
TECHNIQUES
TECHNO
TECHNOBABBLE
TECHNOBABBLES
TECHNOCRACIES
TECHNOCRACY
TECHNOCRAT
TECHNOCRATIC
TECHNOCRATS
TECHNOID
TECHNOIDS
TECHNOLOGIC
TECHNOLOGICAL
TECHNOLOGICALLY
TECHNOLOGIES
TECHNOLOGIST
TECHNOLOGISTS
TECHNOLOGIZE
TECHNOLOGIZED
TECHNOLOGIZES
TECHNOLOGIZING
TECHNOLOGY
TECHNOPHILE
TECHNOPHILES
TECHNOPHILIA
TECHNOPHILIAS
TECHNOPHOBE
TECHNOPHOBES
TECHNOPHOBIA
TECHNOPHOBIAS
TECHNOPHOBIC
TECHNOPOP
TECHNOPOPS
TECHNOPRENEUR
TECHNOPRENEURS
TECHNOS
TECHNOSTRUCTURE
TECHS
TECHY
TECS
TECTA
TECTAL
TECTITE
TECTITES
TECTONIC
TECTONICALLY
TECTONICS
TECTONISM
TECTONISMS
TECTORIAL
TECTRICES
TECTRIX
TECTUM
TECTUMS
TED
TEDDED
TEDDER
TEDDERED
TEDDERING
TEDDERS
TEDDIES
TEDDING
TEDDY
TEDIOUS
TEDIOUSLY
TEDIOUSNESS
TEDIOUSNESSES
TEDIUM
TEDIUMS
TEDS
TEE
TEED
TEEING
TEEL
TEELS
TEEM
TEEMED
TEEMER
TEEMERS
TEEMING
TEEMINGLY
TEEMINGNESS
TEEMINGNESSES
TEEMS
TEEN
TEENAGE
TEENAGED
TEENAGER
TEENAGERS
TEENDOM
TEENDOMS
TEENER
TEENERS
TEENFUL
TEENIER
TEENIEST
TEENS
TEENSIER
TEENSIEST
TEENSPLOITATION
TEENSY
TEENTSIER
TEENTSIEST
TEENTSY
TEENY
TEENYBOP
TEENYBOPPER
TEENYBOPPERS
TEEPEE
TEEPEES

ES
ETER
ETERBOARD
ETERBOARDS
ETERED
ETERING
ETERS
ETH
ETHE
ETHED
ETHER
ETHERS
ETHES
ETHING
ETHINGS
ETHLESS
ETHRIDGE
ETHRIDGES
ETOTAL
ETOTALED
ETOTALER
ETOTALERS
ETOTALING
ETOTALISM
ETOTALISMS
ETOTALIST
ETOTALISTS
ETOTALLED
ETOTALLER
ETOTALLERS
ETOTALLING
ETOTALLY
TOTALS
TOTUM
TOTUMS
VEE
VEES
F
FS
LLIN
LON
LONS
G
GS
MEN
MENTA
MENTAL
MENTUM
MINA
MINAL
S
U

TEGUA
TEGUAS
TEGULA
TEGULAE
TEGULAR
TEGULARLY
TEGULATED
TEGUMEN
TEGUMENT
TEGUMENTS
TEGUMINA
TEGUS
TEIGLACH
TEIID
TEIIDS
TEIN
TEIND
TEINDS
TEINS
TEKKIE
TEKKIES
TEKTITE
TEKTITES
TEKTITIC
TEL
TELA
TELAE
TELAMON
TELAMONES
TELANGIECTASES
TELANGIECTASIA
TELANGIECTASIAS
TELANGIECTASIS
TELANGIECTATIC
TELCO
TELCOS
TELE
TELECAST
TELECASTED
TELECASTER
TELECASTERS
TELECASTING
TELECASTS
TELECINE
TELECINES
TELECOM
TELECOMM
TELECOMMS
TELECOMMUTE
TELECOMMUTED
TELECOMMUTER
TELECOMMUTERS
TELECOMMUTES

TELECOMMUTING
TELECOMS
TELECONFERENCE
TELECONFERENCES
TELECOURSE
TELECOURSES
TELEDU
TELEDUS
TELEFACSIMILE
TELEFACSIMILES
TELEFAX
TELEFAXED
TELEFAXES
TELEFAXING
TELEFILM
TELEFILMS
TELEGA
TELEGAS
TELEGENIC
TELEGONIC
TELEGONIES
TELEGONY
TELEGRAM
TELEGRAMMED
TELEGRAMMING
TELEGRAMS
TELEGRAPH
TELEGRAPHED
TELEGRAPHER
TELEGRAPHERS
TELEGRAPHESE
TELEGRAPHESES
TELEGRAPHIC
TELEGRAPHICALLY
TELEGRAPHIES
TELEGRAPHING
TELEGRAPHIST
TELEGRAPHISTS
TELEGRAPHS
TELEGRAPHY
TELEKINESES
TELEKINESIS
TELEKINETIC
TELEKINETICALLY
TELEMAN
TELEMARK
TELEMARKER
TELEMARKERS
TELEMARKETER
TELEMARKETERS
TELEMARKETING
TELEMARKETINGS
TELEMARKING

TELEMARKS
TELEMEDICINE
TELEMEDICINES
TELEMEN
TELEMETER
TELEMETERED
TELEMETERING
TELEMETERS
TELEMETRIC
TELEMETRICALLY
TELEMETRIES
TELEMETRY
TELENCEPHALA
TELENCEPHALIC
TELENCEPHALON
TELENCEPHALONS
TELENOVELA
TELENOVELAS
TELEOLOGIC
TELEOLOGICAL
TELEOLOGICALLY
TELEOLOGIES
TELEOLOGIST
TELEOLOGISTS
TELEOLOGY
TELEONOMIC
TELEONOMIES
TELEONOMY
TELEOST
TELEOSTEAN
TELEOSTEANS
TELEOSTS
TELEPATH
TELEPATHIC
TELEPATHICALLY
TELEPATHIES
TELEPATHS
TELEPATHY
TELEPHONE
TELEPHONED
TELEPHONER
TELEPHONERS
TELEPHONES
TELEPHONIC
TELEPHONICALLY
TELEPHONIES
TELEPHONING
TELEPHONIST
TELEPHONISTS
TELEPHONY
TELEPHOTO
TELEPHOTOGRAPHY
TELEPHOTOS

TELEPLAY
TELEPLAYS
TELEPORT
TELEPORTATION
TELEPORTATIONS
TELEPORTED
TELEPORTING
TELEPORTS
TELEPRINTER
TELEPRINTERS
TELEPROCESSING
TELEPROCESSINGS
TELEPROMPTER
TELEPROMPTERS
TELERAN
TELERANS
TELES
TELESALES
TELESCOPE
TELESCOPED
TELESCOPES
TELESCOPIC
TELESCOPICALLY
TELESCOPIES
TELESCOPING
TELESCOPY
TELESES
TELESHOP
TELESHOPPED
TELESHOPPING
TELESHOPPINGS
TELESHOPS
TELESIS
TELESTIC
TELESTICH
TELESTICHS
TELESTICS
TELETEXT
TELETEXTS
TELETHON
TELETHONS
TELETYPE
TELETYPED
TELETYPES
TELETYPEWRITER
TELETYPEWRITERS
TELETYPING
TELEUTOSPORE
TELEUTOSPORES
TELEVANGELISM
TELEVANGELISMS
TELEVANGELIST
TELEVANGELISTS

TELEVIEW
TELEVIEWED
TELEVIEWER
TELEVIEWERS
TELEVIEWING
TELEVIEWINGS
TELEVIEWS
TELEVISE
TELEVISED
TELEVISES
TELEVISING
TELEVISION
TELEVISIONS
TELEVISOR
TELEVISORS
TELEVISUAL
TELEWORK
TELEWORKED
TELEWORKER
TELEWORKERS
TELEWORKING
TELEWORKINGS
TELEWORKS
TELEX
TELEXED
TELEXES
TELEXING
TELFER
TELFERED
TELFERING
TELFERS
TELFORD
TELFORDS
TELIA
TELIAL
TELIC
TELICALLY
TELICITIES
TELICITY
TELIOSPORE
TELIOSPORES
TELIUM
TELL
TELLABLE
TELLER
TELLERS
TELLIES
TELLING
TELLINGLY
TELLS
TELLTALE
TELLTALES
TELLURIAN
TELLURIANS
TELLURIC
TELLURIDE
TELLURIDES
TELLURION
TELLURIONS
TELLURITE
TELLURITES
TELLURIUM
TELLURIUMS
TELLURIZE
TELLURIZED
TELLURIZES
TELLURIZING
TELLUROMETER
TELLUROMETERS
TELLUROUS
TELLY
TELLYS
TELNET
TELNETED
TELNETING
TELNETS
TELNETTED
TELNETTING
TELOCENTRIC
TELOCENTRICS
TELOI
TELOME
TELOMERASE
TELOMERASES
TELOMERE
TELOMERES
TELOMES
TELOMIC
TELOPHASE
TELOPHASES
TELOS
TELOSES
TELOTAXES
TELOTAXIS
TELPHER
TELPHERED
TELPHERING
TELPHERS
TELS
TELSON
TELSONIC
TELSONS
TEMBLOR
TEMBLORES
TEMBLORS
TEMERARIOUS
TEMERARIOUSLY
TEMERARIOUSNESS
TEMERITIES
TEMERITY
TEMP
TEMPED
TEMPEH
TEMPEHS
TEMPER
TEMPERA
TEMPERABLE
TEMPERAMENT
TEMPERAMENTAL
TEMPERAMENTALLY
TEMPERAMENTS
TEMPERANCE
TEMPERANCES
TEMPERAS
TEMPERATE
TEMPERATELY
TEMPERATENESS
TEMPERATENESSES
TEMPERATURE
TEMPERATURES
TEMPERED
TEMPERER
TEMPERERS
TEMPERING
TEMPERS
TEMPEST
TEMPESTED
TEMPESTING
TEMPESTS
TEMPESTUOUS
TEMPESTUOUSLY
TEMPESTUOUSNESS
TEMPI
TEMPING
TEMPLAR
TEMPLARS
TEMPLATE
TEMPLATES
TEMPLE
TEMPLED
TEMPLES
TEMPLET
TEMPLETS
TEMPO
TEMPORAL
TEMPORALITIES
TEMPORALITY
TEMPORALIZE
TEMPORALIZED
TEMPORALIZES
TEMPORALIZING
TEMPORALLY
TEMPORALS
TEMPORARIES
TEMPORARILY
TEMPORARINESS
TEMPORARINESSES
TEMPORARY
TEMPORISE
TEMPORISED
TEMPORISES
TEMPORISING
TEMPORIZATION
TEMPORIZATIONS
TEMPORIZE
TEMPORIZED
TEMPORIZER
TEMPORIZERS
TEMPORIZES
TEMPORIZING
TEMPOS
TEMPS
TEMPT
TEMPTABLE
TEMPTATION
TEMPTATIONS
TEMPTED
TEMPTER
TEMPTERS
TEMPTING
TEMPTINGLY
TEMPTRESS
TEMPTRESSES
TEMPTS
TEMPURA
TEMPURAS
TEN
TENABILITIES
TENABILITY
TENABLE
TENABLENESS
TENABLENESSES
TENABLY
TENACE
TENACES
TENACIOUS
TENACIOUSLY
TENACIOUSNESS
TENACIOUSNESSES
TENACITIES
TENACITY
TENACULA
TENACULUM
TENACULUMS
TENAIL
TENAILLE
TENAILLES
TENAILS
TENANCIES
TENANCY
TENANT
TENANTABLE
TENANTED
TENANTING
TENANTLESS
TENANTRIES
TENANTRY
TENANTS
TENCH
TENCHES
TEND
TENDANCE
TENDANCES
TENDED
TENDENCE
TENDENCES
TENDENCIES
TENDENCIOUS
TENDENCY
TENDENTIOUS
TENDENTIOUSLY
TENDENTIOUSNES
TENDER
TENDERED
TENDERER
TENDERERS
TENDEREST
TENDERFEET
TENDERFOOT
TENDERFOOTS
TENDERHEARTED
TENDERHEARTEDI
TENDERING
TENDERISATION
TENDERISATIONS
TENDERISE
TENDERISED
TENDERISER
TENDERISERS
TENDERISES
TENDERISING
TENDERIZATION
TENDERIZATIONS
TENDERIZE
TENDERIZED

NDERIZER
NDERIZERS
NDERIZES
NDERIZING
NDERLOIN
NDERLOINS
NDERLY
NDERNESS
NDERNESSES
NDEROMETER
NDEROMETERS
NDERS
NDING
NDINITIDES
NDINITIS
NDINITISES
NDINOUS
NDON
NDONITIDES
DONITIS
NDONITISES
DONS
DRESSE
DRESSES
DRIL
DRILED
DRILLED
DRILOUS
DRILS
DS
DU
DUS
EBRAE
EBRIFIC
EBRIONID
EBRIONIDS
EBRIOUS
EBRISM
EBRISMS
EBRIST
EBRISTS
EBROUS
EMENT
EMENTS
ESI
ESMIC
ESMUS
ESMUSES
ET
ETS
OLD
OLDS
GE

TENGES
TENIA
TENIAE
TENIAS
TENIASES
TENIASIS
TENNE
TENNER
TENNERS
TENNES
TENNESI
TENNIES
TENNIS
TENNISES
TENNIST
TENNISTS
TENNO
TENNOS
TENNY
TENON
TENONED
TENONER
TENONERS
TENONING
TENONS
TENOR
TENORINI
TENORINO
TENORIST
TENORISTS
TENORITE
TENORITES
TENORMAN
TENORMEN
TENORS
TENOSYNOVITIS
TENOSYNOVITISES
TENOTOMIES
TENOTOMY
TENOUR
TENOURS
TENPENCE
TENPENCES
TENPENNY
TENPIN
TENPINS
TENPOUNDER
TENPOUNDERS
TENREC
TENRECS
TENS
TENSE
TENSED

TENSELY
TENSENESS
TENSENESSES
TENSER
TENSES
TENSEST
TENSIBLE
TENSIBLY
TENSILE
TENSILELY
TENSILITIES
TENSILITY
TENSING
TENSIOMETER
TENSIOMETERS
TENSIOMETRIC
TENSIOMETRIES
TENSIOMETRY
TENSION
TENSIONAL
TENSIONED
TENSIONER
TENSIONERS
TENSIONING
TENSIONLESS
TENSIONS
TENSITIES
TENSITY
TENSIVE
TENSOR
TENSORIAL
TENSORS
TENT
TENTACLE
TENTACLED
TENTACLES
TENTACULAR
TENTAGE
TENTAGES
TENTATIVE
TENTATIVELY
TENTATIVENESS
TENTATIVENESSES
TENTATIVES
TENTED
TENTER
TENTERED
TENTERHOOK
TENTERHOOKS
TENTERING
TENTERS
TENTH
TENTHLY

TENTHS
TENTIE
TENTIER
TENTIEST
TENTING
TENTLESS
TENTLIKE
TENTMAKER
TENTMAKERS
TENTORIA
TENTORIAL
TENTORIUM
TENTPOLE
TENTPOLES
TENTS
TENTY
TENUES
TENUIS
TENUITIES
TENUITY
TENUOUS
TENUOUSLY
TENUOUSNESS
TENUOUSNESSES
TENURABLE
TENURE
TENURED
TENURES
TENURIAL
TENURIALLY
TENURING
TENUTI
TENUTO
TENUTOS
TEOCALLI
TEOCALLIS
TEOPAN
TEOPANS
TEOSINTE
TEOSINTES
TEPA
TEPACHE
TEPACHES
TEPAL
TEPALS
TEPAS
TEPEE
TEPEES
TEPEFIED
TEPEFIES
TEPEFY
TEPEFYING
TEPHRA

TEPHRAS
TEPHRITE
TEPHRITES
TEPHRITIC
TEPID
TEPIDITIES
TEPIDITY
TEPIDLY
TEPIDNESS
TEPIDNESSES
TEPOY
TEPOYS
TEPPANYAKI
TEQUILA
TEQUILAS
TERABYTE
TERABYTES
TERAFLOP
TERAFLOPS
TERAHERTZ
TERAHERTZES
TERAI
TERAIS
TERAOHM
TERAOHMS
TERAPH
TERAPHIM
TERATISM
TERATISMS
TERATOCARCINOMA
TERATOGEN
TERATOGENESES
TERATOGENESIS
TERATOGENIC
TERATOGENICITY
TERATOGENS
TERATOID
TERATOLOGIC
TERATOLOGICAL
TERATOLOGIES
TERATOLOGIST
TERATOLOGISTS
TERATOLOGY
TERATOMA
TERATOMAS
TERATOMATA
TERAWATT
TERAWATTS
TERBIA
TERBIAS
TERBIC
TERBIUM
TERBIUMS

TERBUTALINE
TERBUTALINES
TERCE
TERCEL
TERCELET
TERCELETS
TERCELS
TERCENTENARIES
TERCENTENARY
TERCENTENNIAL
TERCENTENNIALS
TERCES
TERCET
TERCETS
TEREBENE
TEREBENES
TEREBIC
TEREBINTH
TEREBINTHS
TEREDINES
TEREDO
TEREDOS
TEREFAH
TEREPHTHALATE
TEREPHTHALATES
TERES
TERESES
TERETE
TERETES
TERGA
TERGAL
TERGITE
TERGITES
TERGIVERSATE
TERGIVERSATED
TERGIVERSATES
TERGIVERSATING
TERGIVERSATION
TERGIVERSATIONS
TERGIVERSATOR
TERGIVERSATORS
TERGUM
TERIYAKI
TERIYAKIS
TERM
TERMAGANT
TERMAGANTS
TERMED
TERMER
TERMERS
TERMINABLE
TERMINABLENESS
TERMINABLY
TERMINAL
TERMINALLY
TERMINALS
TERMINATE
TERMINATED
TERMINATES
TERMINATING
TERMINATION
TERMINATIONAL
TERMINATIONS
TERMINATIVE
TERMINATIVELY
TERMINATOR
TERMINATORS
TERMINER
TERMINERS
TERMING
TERMINI
TERMINOLOGICAL
TERMINOLOGIES
TERMINOLOGY
TERMINUS
TERMINUSES
TERMITARIA
TERMITARIES
TERMITARIUM
TERMITARIUMS
TERMITARY
TERMITE
TERMITES
TERMITIC
TERMLESS
TERMLY
TERMOR
TERMORS
TERMS
TERMTIME
TERMTIMES
TERN
TERNARIES
TERNARY
TERNATE
TERNATELY
TERNE
TERNEPLATE
TERNEPLATES
TERNES
TERNION
TERNIONS
TERNS
TERPENE
TERPENELESS
TERPENES
TERPENIC
TERPENOID
TERPENOIDS
TERPINEOL
TERPINEOLS
TERPINOL
TERPINOLS
TERPOLYMER
TERPOLYMERS
TERPSICHOREAN
TERRA
TERRACE
TERRACED
TERRACES
TERRACING
TERRAE
TERRAFORM
TERRAFORMED
TERRAFORMING
TERRAFORMS
TERRAIN
TERRAINS
TERRANE
TERRANES
TERRAPIN
TERRAPINS
TERRAQUEOUS
TERRARIA
TERRARIUM
TERRARIUMS
TERRAS
TERRASES
TERRASSE
TERRAZZO
TERRAZZOS
TERREEN
TERREENS
TERRELLA
TERRELLAS
TERRENE
TERRENELY
TERRENES
TERREPLEIN
TERREPLEINS
TERRESTRIAL
TERRESTRIALLY
TERRESTRIALS
TERRET
TERRETS
TERRIBLE
TERRIBLENESS
TERRIBLENESSES
TERRIBLY
TERRICOLOUS
TERRIER
TERRIERS
TERRIES
TERRIFIC
TERRIFICALLY
TERRIFIED
TERRIFIER
TERRIFIERS
TERRIFIES
TERRIFY
TERRIFYING
TERRIFYINGLY
TERRIGENOUS
TERRINE
TERRINES
TERRIT
TERRITORIAL
TERRITORIALISM
TERRITORIALISMS
TERRITORIALIST
TERRITORIALISTS
TERRITORIALITY
TERRITORIALIZE
TERRITORIALIZED
TERRITORIALIZES
TERRITORIALLY
TERRITORIALS
TERRITORIES
TERRITORY
TERRITS
TERROIR
TERROIRS
TERROR
TERRORISE
TERRORISED
TERRORISES
TERRORISING
TERRORISM
TERRORISMS
TERRORIST
TERRORISTIC
TERRORISTS
TERRORIZATION
TERRORIZATIONS
TERRORIZE
TERRORIZED
TERRORIZES
TERRORIZING
TERRORLESS
TERRORS
TERRY
TERSE
TERSELY
TERSENESS
TERSENESSES
TERSER
TERSEST
TERTIAL
TERTIALS
TERTIAN
TERTIANS
TERTIARIES
TERTIARY
TERVALENT
TERYLENE
TERYLENES
TERZETTI
TERZETTO
TERZETTOS
TES
TESLA
TESLAS
TESSELATE
TESSELATED
TESSELATES
TESSELATING
TESSELLATE
TESSELLATED
TESSELLATES
TESSELLATING
TESSELLATION
TESSELLATIONS
TESSERA
TESSERACT
TESSERACTS
TESSERAE
TESSERAL
TESSITURA
TESSITURAS
TESSITURE
TEST
TESTA
TESTABILITIES
TESTABILITY
TESTABLE
TESTACEAN
TESTACEANS
TESTACEOUS
TESTACIES
TESTACY
TESTAE
TESTAMENT
TESTAMENTARY
TESTAMENTS
TESTATE

STATES
STATOR
STATORS
STATRICES
STATRIX
STATRIXES
STCROSS
STCROSSED
STCROSSES
STCROSSING
STED
STEE
STEES
STER
STERS
STES
STICLE
STICLES
STICULAR
TIER
TIEST
TIFIED
TIFIER
TIFIERS
TIFIES
TIFY
TIFYING
TILY
TIMONIAL
TIMONIALS
TIMONIES
TIMONY
TINESS
TINESSES
TING
TINGS
TIS
TON
TONS
TOON
TOONS
OSTERONE
OSTERONES
TS
UDINES
UDO
UDOS
Y
NAL
NIC
NICAL
NICALLY

TETANICS
TETANIES
TETANISE
TETANISED
TETANISES
TETANISING
TETANIZATION
TETANIZATIONS
TETANIZE
TETANIZED
TETANIZES
TETANIZING
TETANOID
TETANUS
TETANUSES
TETANY
TETARTOHEDRAL
TETCHED
TETCHIER
TETCHIEST
TETCHILY
TETCHINESS
TETCHINESSES
TETCHY
TETH
TETHER
TETHERBALL
TETHERBALLS
TETHERED
TETHERING
TETHERS
TETHS
TETOTUM
TETOTUMS
TETRA
TETRACAINE
TETRACAINES
TETRACHLORIDE
TETRACHLORIDES
TETRACHORD
TETRACHORDS
TETRACID
TETRACIDS
TETRACYCLINE
TETRACYCLINES
TETRAD
TETRADIC
TETRADRACHM
TETRADRACHMS
TETRADS
TETRADYNAMOUS
TETRAFLUORIDE
TETRAFLUORIDES

TETRAGON
TETRAGONAL
TETRAGONALLY
TETRAGONS
TETRAGRAM
TETRAGRAMMATON
TETRAGRAMMATONS
TETRAGRAMS
TETRAHEDRA
TETRAHEDRAL
TETRAHEDRALLY
TETRAHEDRITE
TETRAHEDRITES
TETRAHEDRON
TETRAHEDRONS
TETRAHYDROFURAN
TETRAHYMENA
TETRAHYMENAS
TETRALOGIES
TETRALOGY
TETRAMER
TETRAMERIC
TETRAMEROUS
TETRAMERS
TETRAMETER
TETRAMETERS
TETRAMETHYLLEAD
TETRAPLOID
TETRAPLOIDIES
TETRAPLOIDS
TETRAPLOIDY
TETRAPOD
TETRAPODS
TETRAPYRROLE
TETRAPYRROLES
TETRARCH
TETRARCHIC
TETRARCHIES
TETRARCHS
TETRARCHY
TETRAS
TETRASPORE
TETRASPORES
TETRASPORIC
TETRAVALENT
TETRAZOLIUM
TETRAZOLIUMS
TETRAZZINI
TETRI
TETRIS
TETRODE
TETRODES
TETRODOTOXIN

TETRODOTOXINS
TETROSE
TETROSES
TETROXID
TETROXIDE
TETROXIDES
TETROXIDS
TETRYL
TETRYLS
TETS
TETTER
TETTERS
TEUCH
TEUGH
TEUGHLY
TEUTONIZE
TEUTONIZED
TEUTONIZES
TEUTONIZING
TEVATRON
TEVATRONS
TEW
TEWED
TEWING
TEWS
TEXAS
TEXASES
TEXT
TEXTBOOK
TEXTBOOKISH
TEXTBOOKS
TEXTED
TEXTER
TEXTERS
TEXTILE
TEXTILES
TEXTING
TEXTLESS
TEXTS
TEXTUAL
TEXTUALITIES
TEXTUALITY
TEXTUALIZATION
TEXTUALIZATIONS
TEXTUALIZE
TEXTUALIZED
TEXTUALIZES
TEXTUALIZING
TEXTUALLY
TEXTUARIES
TEXTUARY
TEXTURAL
TEXTURALLY

TEXTURE
TEXTURED
TEXTURELESS
TEXTURES
TEXTURING
TEXTURINGS
TEXTURIZE
TEXTURIZED
TEXTURIZES
TEXTURIZING
THACK
THACKED
THACKING
THACKS
THAE
THAIRM
THAIRMS
THALAMI
THALAMIC
THALAMUS
THALASSAEMIA
THALASSAEMIAS
THALASSEMIA
THALASSEMIAS
THALASSEMIC
THALASSEMICS
THALASSIC
THALASSOCRACIES
THALASSOCRACY
THALASSOCRAT
THALASSOCRATS
THALASSOTHERAPY
THALER
THALERS
THALI
THALIDOMIDE
THALIDOMIDES
THALIS
THALLI
THALLIC
THALLIOUS
THALLIUM
THALLIUMS
THALLOID
THALLOPHYTE
THALLOPHYTES
THALLOPHYTIC
THALLOUS
THALLUS
THALLUSES
THALWEG
THALWEGS
THAN

THANAGE
THANAGES
THANATOLOGICAL
THANATOLOGIES
THANATOLOGIST
THANATOLOGISTS
THANATOLOGY
THANATOS
THANATOSES
THANE
THANEDOM
THANEDOMS
THANES
THANESHIP
THANESHIPS
THANG
THANGS
THANK
THANKED
THANKER
THANKERS
THANKFUL
THANKFULLER
THANKFULLEST
THANKFULLY
THANKFULNESS
THANKFULNESSES
THANKING
THANKLESS
THANKLESSLY
THANKLESSNESS
THANKLESSNESSES
THANKS
THANKSGIVING
THANKSGIVINGS
THANKWORTHIER
THANKWORTHIEST
THANKWORTHY
THARM
THARMS
THAT
THATAWAY
THATCH
THATCHED
THATCHER
THATCHERS
THATCHES
THATCHIER
THATCHIEST
THATCHING
THATCHINGS
THATCHY
THAUMATURGE
THAUMATURGES
THAUMATURGIC
THAUMATURGIES
THAUMATURGIST
THAUMATURGISTS
THAUMATURGY
THAW
THAWED
THAWER
THAWERS
THAWING
THAWINGS
THAWLESS
THAWS
THE
THEARCHIES
THEARCHY
THEATER
THEATERGOER
THEATERGOERS
THEATERGOING
THEATERGOINGS
THEATERS
THEATRE
THEATREGOER
THEATREGOERS
THEATRES
THEATRIC
THEATRICAL
THEATRICALISM
THEATRICALISMS
THEATRICALITIES
THEATRICALITY
THEATRICALIZE
THEATRICALIZED
THEATRICALIZES
THEATRICALIZING
THEATRICALLY
THEATRICALS
THEATRICS
THEBAINE
THEBAINES
THEBE
THEBES
THECA
THECAE
THECAL
THECATE
THECODONT
THECODONTS
THEE
THEELIN
THEELINS
THEELOL
THEELOLS
THEFT
THEFTS
THEGN
THEGNLY
THEGNS
THEIN
THEINE
THEINES
THEINS
THEIR
THEIRS
THEIRSELF
THEIRSELVES
THEISM
THEISMS
THEIST
THEISTIC
THEISTICAL
THEISTICALLY
THEISTS
THELITIS
THELITISES
THEM
THEMATIC
THEMATICALLY
THEMATICS
THEME
THEMED
THEMES
THEMING
THEMSELF
THEMSELVES
THEN
THENAGE
THENAGES
THENAL
THENAR
THENARS
THENCE
THENCEFORTH
THENCEFORWARD
THENCEFORWARDS
THENS
THEOBROMINE
THEOBROMINES
THEOCENTRIC
THEOCENTRICITY
THEOCENTRISM
THEOCENTRISMS
THEOCRACIES
THEOCRACY
THEOCRAT
THEOCRATIC
THEOCRATICAL
THEOCRATICALLY
THEOCRATS
THEODICIES
THEODICY
THEODOLITE
THEODOLITES
THEOGONIC
THEOGONIES
THEOGONY
THEOLOG
THEOLOGIAN
THEOLOGIANS
THEOLOGIC
THEOLOGICAL
THEOLOGICALLY
THEOLOGIES
THEOLOGISE
THEOLOGISED
THEOLOGISES
THEOLOGISING
THEOLOGIZE
THEOLOGIZED
THEOLOGIZER
THEOLOGIZERS
THEOLOGIZES
THEOLOGIZING
THEOLOGS
THEOLOGUE
THEOLOGUES
THEOLOGY
THEOMACHIES
THEOMACHY
THEONOMIES
THEONOMOUS
THEONOMY
THEOPHANIC
THEOPHANIES
THEOPHANY
THEOPHYLLINE
THEOPHYLLINES
THEORBO
THEORBOS
THEOREM
THEOREMATIC
THEOREMS
THEORETIC
THEORETICAL
THEORETICALLY
THEORETICIAN
THEORETICIANS
THEORIES
THEORISE
THEORISED
THEORISES
THEORISING
THEORIST
THEORISTS
THEORIZATION
THEORIZATIONS
THEORIZE
THEORIZED
THEORIZER
THEORIZERS
THEORIZES
THEORIZING
THEORY
THEOSOPHICAL
THEOSOPHICALLY
THEOSOPHIES
THEOSOPHIST
THEOSOPHISTS
THEOSOPHY
THERAPEUSES
THERAPEUSIS
THERAPEUTIC
THERAPEUTICALLY
THERAPEUTICS
THERAPIES
THERAPIST
THERAPISTS
THERAPSID
THERAPSIDS
THERAPY
THERE
THEREABOUT
THEREABOUTS
THEREAFTER
THEREAT
THEREBY
THEREFOR
THEREFORE
THEREFROM
THEREIN
THEREINAFTER
THEREINTO
THEREMIN
THEREMINS
THEREOF
THEREON
THEREOUT
THERES
THERETO
THERETOFORE

EREUNDER
EREUNTO
EREUPON
EREWITH
EREWITHAL
ERIAC
ERIACA
ERIACAL
ERIACAS
ERIACS
ERIAN
ERIANS
ERIOMORPHIC
ERM
ERMAE
ERMAL
ERMALIZATION
ERMALIZATIONS
ERMALIZE
ERMALIZED
ERMALIZES
ERMALIZING
ERMALLY
ERMALS
ERME
ERMEL
ERMELS
RMES
RMIC
RMICALLY
RMIDOR
RMIDORS
RMION
RMIONIC
RMIONICS
RMIONS
RMISTOR
RMISTORS
RMIT
RMITE
RMITES
RMITS
RMOCHEMICAL
RMOCHEMIST
RMOCHEMISTRY
RMOCHEMISTS
RMOCLINE
RMOCLINES
RMOCOUPLE
RMOCOUPLES
RMODURIC
RMODYNAMIC
RMODYNAMICAL
THERMODYNAMICS
THERMOELECTRIC
THERMOELEMENT
THERMOELEMENTS
THERMOFORM
THERMOFORMABLE
THERMOFORMED
THERMOFORMING
THERMOFORMS
THERMOGENESES
THERMOGENESIS
THERMOGENIC
THERMOGRAM
THERMOGRAMS
THERMOGRAPH
THERMOGRAPHER
THERMOGRAPHERS
THERMOGRAPHIC
THERMOGRAPHIES
THERMOGRAPHS
THERMOGRAPHY
THERMOHALINE
THERMOJUNCTION
THERMOJUNCTIONS
THERMOLABILE
THERMOLABILITY
THERMOMAGNETIC
THERMOMETER
THERMOMETERS
THERMOMETRIC
THERMOMETRIES
THERMOMETRY
THERMONUCLEAR
THERMOPERIODISM
THERMOPHILE
THERMOPHILES
THERMOPHILIC
THERMOPHILOUS
THERMOPILE
THERMOPILES
THERMOPLASTIC
THERMOPLASTICS
THERMORECEPTOR
THERMORECEPTORS
THERMOREGULATE
THERMOREGULATED
THERMOREGULATES
THERMOREGULATOR
THERMOREMANENCE
THERMOREMANENT
THERMOS
THERMOSCOPE
THERMOSCOPES
THERMOSES
THERMOSET
THERMOSETS
THERMOSETTING
THERMOSPHERE
THERMOSPHERES
THERMOSPHERIC
THERMOSTABILITY
THERMOSTABLE
THERMOSTAT
THERMOSTATED
THERMOSTATIC
THERMOSTATING
THERMOSTATS
THERMOSTATTED
THERMOSTATTING
THERMOTACTIC
THERMOTAXES
THERMOTAXIS
THERMOTROPIC
THERMOTROPISM
THERMOTROPISMS
THERMS
THEROID
THEROPOD
THEROPODS
THESAURAL
THESAURI
THESAURUS
THESAURUSES
THESE
THESES
THESIS
THESP
THESPIAN
THESPIANS
THESPS
THETA
THETAS
THETIC
THETICAL
THETICALLY
THEURGIC
THEURGICAL
THEURGIES
THEURGIST
THEURGISTS
THEURGY
THEW
THEWIER
THEWIEST
THEWLESS
THEWS
THEWY
THEY
THIABENDAZOLE
THIABENDAZOLES
THIAMIN
THIAMINASE
THIAMINASES
THIAMINE
THIAMINES
THIAMINS
THIAZIDE
THIAZIDES
THIAZIN
THIAZINE
THIAZINES
THIAZINS
THIAZOL
THIAZOLE
THIAZOLES
THIAZOLS
THICK
THICKEN
THICKENED
THICKENER
THICKENERS
THICKENING
THICKENINGS
THICKENS
THICKER
THICKEST
THICKET
THICKETED
THICKETS
THICKETY
THICKHEAD
THICKHEADED
THICKHEADS
THICKISH
THICKLY
THICKNESS
THICKNESSES
THICKS
THICKSET
THICKSETS
THIEF
THIEVE
THIEVED
THIEVERIES
THIEVERY
THIEVES
THIEVING
THIEVISH
THIEVISHLY
THIEVISHNESS
THIEVISHNESSES
THIGH
THIGHBONE
THIGHBONES
THIGHED
THIGHS
THIGMOTAXES
THIGMOTAXIS
THIGMOTROPISM
THIGMOTROPISMS
THILL
THILLS
THIMBLE
THIMBLEBERRIES
THIMBLEBERRY
THIMBLEFUL
THIMBLEFULS
THIMBLERIG
THIMBLERIGGED
THIMBLERIGGER
THIMBLERIGGERS
THIMBLERIGGING
THIMBLERIGS
THIMBLES
THIMBLESFUL
THIMBLEWEED
THIMBLEWEEDS
THIMEROSAL
THIMEROSALS
THIN
THINCLAD
THINCLADS
THINDOWN
THINDOWNS
THINE
THING
THINGAMABOB
THINGAMABOBS
THINGAMAJIG
THINGAMAJIGS
THINGIES
THINGNESS
THINGNESSES
THINGS
THINGUMAJIG
THINGUMAJIGS
THINGUMMIES
THINGUMMY
THINGY
THINK
THINKABLE
THINKABLENESS

THINKABLENESSES
THINKABLY
THINKER
THINKERS
THINKING
THINKINGLY
THINKINGNESS
THINKINGNESSES
THINKINGS
THINKS
THINLY
THINNED
THINNER
THINNERS
THINNESS
THINNESSES
THINNEST
THINNING
THINNINGS
THINNISH
THINS
THIO
THIOCYANATE
THIOCYANATES
THIOL
THIOLIC
THIOLS
THIONATE
THIONATES
THIONIC
THIONIN
THIONINE
THIONINES
THIONINS
THIONYL
THIONYLS
THIOPENTAL
THIOPENTALS
THIOPHEN
THIOPHENE
THIOPHENES
THIOPHENS
THIORIDAZINE
THIORIDAZINES
THIOSULFATE
THIOSULFATES
THIOTEPA
THIOTEPAS
THIOURACIL
THIOURACILS
THIOUREA
THIOUREAS
THIR
THIRAM
THIRAMS
THIRD
THIRDHAND
THIRDLY
THIRDS
THIRL
THIRLAGE
THIRLAGES
THIRLED
THIRLING
THIRLS
THIRST
THIRSTED
THIRSTER
THIRSTERS
THIRSTIER
THIRSTIEST
THIRSTILY
THIRSTINESS
THIRSTINESSES
THIRSTING
THIRSTS
THIRSTY
THIRTEEN
THIRTEENS
THIRTEENTH
THIRTEENTHS
THIRTIES
THIRTIETH
THIRTIETHS
THIRTY
THIRTYISH
THIRTYSOMETHING
THIS
THISAWAY
THISTLE
THISTLEDOWN
THISTLEDOWNS
THISTLES
THISTLIER
THISTLIEST
THISTLY
THITHER
THITHERTO
THITHERWARD
THITHERWARDS
THIXOTROPIC
THIXOTROPIES
THIXOTROPY
THO
THOLE
THOLED
THOLEIITE
THOLEIITES
THOLEIITIC
THOLEPIN
THOLEPINS
THOLES
THOLING
THOLOI
THOLOS
THONG
THONGED
THONGIER
THONGIEST
THONGING
THONGS
THONGY
THORACAL
THORACES
THORACIC
THORACICALLY
THORACOTOMIES
THORACOTOMY
THORAX
THORAXES
THORIA
THORIANITE
THORIANITES
THORIAS
THORIC
THORITE
THORITES
THORIUM
THORIUMS
THORN
THORNBACK
THORNBACKS
THORNBUSH
THORNBUSHES
THORNED
THORNIER
THORNIEST
THORNILY
THORNINESS
THORNINESSES
THORNING
THORNLESS
THORNLIKE
THORNS
THORNY
THORO
THORON
THORONS
THOROUGH
THOROUGHBASS
THOROUGHBASSES
THOROUGHBRACE
THOROUGHBRACES
THOROUGHBRED
THOROUGHBREDS
THOROUGHER
THOROUGHEST
THOROUGHFARE
THOROUGHFARES
THOROUGHGOING
THOROUGHGOINGLY
THOROUGHLY
THOROUGHNESS
THOROUGHNESSES
THOROUGHPIN
THOROUGHPINS
THOROUGHWORT
THOROUGHWORTS
THORP
THORPE
THORPES
THORPS
THOSE
THOU
THOUED
THOUGH
THOUGHT
THOUGHTFUL
THOUGHTFULLY
THOUGHTFULNESS
THOUGHTLESS
THOUGHTLESSLY
THOUGHTLESSNESS
THOUGHTS
THOUGHTWAY
THOUGHTWAYS
THOUING
THOUS
THOUSAND
THOUSANDFOLD
THOUSANDS
THOUSANDTH
THOUSANDTHS
THOWLESS
THRALDOM
THRALDOMS
THRALL
THRALLDOM
THRALLDOMS
THRALLED
THRALLING
THRALLS
THRASH
THRASHED
THRASHER
THRASHERS
THRASHES
THRASHIER
THRASHIEST
THRASHING
THRASHINGS
THRASHY
THRASONICAL
THRASONICALLY
THRAVE
THRAVES
THRAW
THRAWART
THRAWED
THRAWING
THRAWN
THRAWNLY
THRAWS
THREAD
THREADBARE
THREADBARENESS
THREADED
THREADER
THREADERS
THREADFIN
THREADFINS
THREADIER
THREADIEST
THREADINESS
THREADINESSES
THREADING
THREADLESS
THREADLIKE
THREADS
THREADWORM
THREADWORMS
THREADY
THREAP
THREAPED
THREAPER
THREAPERS
THREAPING
THREAPS
THREAT
THREATED
THREATEN
THREATENED
THREATENER
THREATENERS
THREATENING

REATENINGLY
REATENS
REATING
REATS
REE
REEFOLD
REEP
REEPED
REEPENCE
REEPENCES
REEPENNY
REEPING
REEPS
REES
REESCORE
REESOME
REESOMES
RENODE
RENODES
RENODIC
RENODIES
RENODIST
RENODISTS
RENODY
REONINE
REONINES
RESH
RESHED
RESHER
RESHERS
RESHES
RESHING
RESHINGS
RESHOLD
RESHOLDS
REW
RICE
RIFT
RIFTIER
RIFTIEST
RIFTILY
RIFTINESS
RIFTINESSES
RIFTLESS
RIFTLESSLY
RIFTLESSNESS
RIFTS
RIFTY
RILL
RILLED
RILLER
RILLERS
RILLING
THRILLINGLY
THRILLS
THRIP
THRIPS
THRIVE
THRIVED
THRIVEN
THRIVER
THRIVERS
THRIVES
THRIVING
THRIVINGLY
THRO
THROAT
THROATED
THROATIER
THROATIEST
THROATILY
THROATINESS
THROATINESSES
THROATING
THROATLATCH
THROATLATCHES
THROATS
THROATY
THROB
THROBBED
THROBBER
THROBBERS
THROBBING
THROBS
THROE
THROES
THROMBI
THROMBIN
THROMBINS
THROMBOCYTE
THROMBOCYTES
THROMBOCYTIC
THROMBOEMBOLIC
THROMBOEMBOLISM
THROMBOKINASE
THROMBOKINASES
THROMBOLYSES
THROMBOLYSIS
THROMBOLYTIC
THROMBOPLASTIC
THROMBOPLASTIN
THROMBOPLASTINS
THROMBOSE
THROMBOSED
THROMBOSES
THROMBOSING
THROMBOSIS
THROMBOTIC
THROMBOXANE
THROMBOXANES
THROMBUS
THRONE
THRONED
THRONES
THRONG
THRONGED
THRONGING
THRONGS
THRONING
THROSTLE
THROSTLES
THROTTLE
THROTTLEABLE
THROTTLED
THROTTLEHOLD
THROTTLEHOLDS
THROTTLER
THROTTLERS
THROTTLES
THROTTLING
THROUGH
THROUGHITHER
THROUGHLY
THROUGHOTHER
THROUGHOUT
THROUGHPUT
THROUGHPUTS
THROUGHWAY
THROUGHWAYS
THROVE
THROW
THROWAWAY
THROWAWAYS
THROWBACK
THROWBACKS
THROWER
THROWERS
THROWING
THROWN
THROWS
THROWSTER
THROWSTERS
THRU
THRUM
THRUMMED
THRUMMER
THRUMMERS
THRUMMIER
THRUMMIEST
THRUMMING
THRUMMY
THRUMS
THRUPUT
THRUPUTS
THRUSH
THRUSHES
THRUST
THRUSTED
THRUSTER
THRUSTERS
THRUSTFUL
THRUSTING
THRUSTINGS
THRUSTOR
THRUSTORS
THRUSTS
THRUWAY
THRUWAYS
THUD
THUDDED
THUDDING
THUDS
THUG
THUGGEE
THUGGEES
THUGGERIES
THUGGERY
THUGGISH
THUGS
THUJA
THUJAS
THULIA
THULIAS
THULIUM
THULIUMS
THUMB
THUMBED
THUMBHOLE
THUMBHOLES
THUMBING
THUMBKIN
THUMBKINS
THUMBLESS
THUMBNAIL
THUMBNAILS
THUMBNUT
THUMBNUTS
THUMBPRINT
THUMBPRINTS
THUMBS
THUMBSCREW
THUMBSCREWS
THUMBTACK
THUMBTACKED
THUMBTACKING
THUMBTACKS
THUMBWHEEL
THUMBWHEELS
THUMP
THUMPED
THUMPER
THUMPERS
THUMPING
THUMPINGLY
THUMPS
THUNDER
THUNDERBIRD
THUNDERBIRDS
THUNDERBOLT
THUNDERBOLTS
THUNDERCLAP
THUNDERCLAPS
THUNDERCLOUD
THUNDERCLOUDS
THUNDERED
THUNDERER
THUNDERERS
THUNDERHEAD
THUNDERHEADS
THUNDERIER
THUNDERIEST
THUNDERING
THUNDERINGLY
THUNDEROUS
THUNDEROUSLY
THUNDERS
THUNDERSHOWER
THUNDERSHOWERS
THUNDERSTONE
THUNDERSTONES
THUNDERSTORM
THUNDERSTORMS
THUNDERSTRICKEN
THUNDERSTRIKE
THUNDERSTRIKES
THUNDERSTRIKING
THUNDERSTROKE
THUNDERSTROKES
THUNDERSTRUCK
THUNDERY
THUNK
THUNKED
THUNKING
THUNKS
THURIBLE

THURIBLES
THURIFER
THURIFERS
THURL
THURLS
THUS
THUSLY
THUYA
THUYAS
THWACK
THWACKED
THWACKER
THWACKERS
THWACKING
THWACKS
THWART
THWARTED
THWARTER
THWARTERS
THWARTING
THWARTLY
THWARTS
THWARTWISE
THY
THYLACINE
THYLACINES
THYLAKOID
THYLAKOIDS
THYME
THYMECTOMIES
THYMECTOMIZE
THYMECTOMIZED
THYMECTOMIZES
THYMECTOMIZING
THYMECTOMY
THYMES
THYMEY
THYMI
THYMIC
THYMIDINE
THYMIDINES
THYMIER
THYMIEST
THYMINE
THYMINES
THYMOCYTE
THYMOCYTES
THYMOL
THYMOLS
THYMOMA
THYMOMAS
THYMOMATA
THYMOSIN
THYMOSINS
THYMUS
THYMUSES
THYMY
THYRATRON
THYRATRONS
THYREOID
THYRISTOR
THYRISTORS
THYROCALCITONIN
THYROGLOBULIN
THYROGLOBULINS
THYROID
THYROIDAL
THYROIDECTOMIES
THYROIDECTOMY
THYROIDITIDES
THYROIDITIS
THYROIDITISES
THYROIDS
THYROTOXICOSES
THYROTOXICOSIS
THYROTROPHIC
THYROTROPHIN
THYROTROPHINS
THYROTROPIC
THYROTROPIN
THYROTROPINS
THYROXIN
THYROXINE
THYROXINES
THYROXINS
THYRSE
THYRSES
THYRSI
THYRSOID
THYRSUS
THYSANURAN
THYSANURANS
THYSELF
TI
TIAN
TIANS
TIARA
TIARAED
TIARAS
TIBIA
TIBIAE
TIBIAL
TIBIALES
TIBIALIS
TIBIAS
TIBIOFIBULA
TIBIOFIBULAE
TIBIOFIBULAS
TIC
TICAL
TICALS
TICCED
TICCING
TICK
TICKED
TICKER
TICKERS
TICKET
TICKETED
TICKETING
TICKETLESS
TICKETS
TICKING
TICKINGS
TICKLACE
TICKLACES
TICKLE
TICKLED
TICKLER
TICKLERS
TICKLES
TICKLIER
TICKLIEST
TICKLING
TICKLISH
TICKLISHLY
TICKLISHNESS
TICKLISHNESSES
TICKLY
TICKS
TICKSEED
TICKSEEDS
TICKTACK
TICKTACKED
TICKTACKING
TICKTACKS
TICKTACKTOE
TICKTACKTOES
TICKTOCK
TICKTOCKED
TICKTOCKING
TICKTOCKS
TICS
TICTAC
TICTACKED
TICTACKING
TICTACS
TICTOC
TICTOCKED
TICTOCKING
TICTOCS
TIDAL
TIDALLY
TIDBIT
TIDBITS
TIDDLEDYWINKS
TIDDLER
TIDDLERS
TIDDLIER
TIDDLIEST
TIDDLY
TIDDLYWINKS
TIDE
TIDED
TIDELAND
TIDELANDS
TIDELESS
TIDELIKE
TIDELINE
TIDELINES
TIDEMARK
TIDEMARKS
TIDERIP
TIDERIPS
TIDES
TIDEWATER
TIDEWATERS
TIDEWAY
TIDEWAYS
TIDIED
TIDIER
TIDIERS
TIDIES
TIDIEST
TIDILY
TIDINESS
TIDINESSES
TIDING
TIDINGS
TIDY
TIDYING
TIDYTIPS
TIE
TIEBACK
TIEBACKS
TIEBREAK
TIEBREAKER
TIEBREAKERS
TIEBREAKS
TIECLASP
TIECLASPS
TIED
TIEING
TIELESS
TIEMANNITE
TIEMANNITES
TIEPIN
TIEPINS
TIER
TIERCE
TIERCED
TIERCEL
TIERCELS
TIERCERON
TIERCERONS
TIERCES
TIERED
TIERING
TIERS
TIES
TIFF
TIFFANIES
TIFFANY
TIFFED
TIFFIN
TIFFINED
TIFFING
TIFFINING
TIFFINS
TIFFS
TIGER
TIGEREYE
TIGEREYES
TIGERISH
TIGERISHLY
TIGERISHNESS
TIGERISHNESSES
TIGERLIKE
TIGERS
TIGHT
TIGHTEN
TIGHTENED
TIGHTENER
TIGHTENERS
TIGHTENING
TIGHTENS
TIGHTER
TIGHTEST
TIGHTFISTED
TIGHTFISTEDNESS
TIGHTKNIT
TIGHTLY
TIGHTNESS
TIGHTNESSES
TIGHTROPE

GHTROPES
GHTS
GHTWAD
GHTWADS
GHTWIRE
GHTWIRES
GLON
GLONS
GNON
GNONS
GON
GONS
GRESS
GRESSES
GRISH
KE
KES
KI
KIS
KKA
KKAS
AK
AKS
APIA
APIAS
BURIES
BURY
DE
DES
E
ED
EFISH
EFISHES
ELIKE
ER
ERS
ES
ING
INGS
L
LABLE
LAGE
LAGES
LANDSIA
LANDSIAS
LED
LER
LERED
LERING
LERMAN
LERMEN
LERS

TILLING
TILLITE
TILLITES
TILLS
TILS
TILT
TILTABLE
TILTED
TILTER
TILTERS
TILTH
TILTHS
TILTING
TILTMETER
TILTMETERS
TILTROTOR
TILTROTORS
TILTS
TILTYARD
TILTYARDS
TIMARAU
TIMARAUS
TIMBAL
TIMBALE
TIMBALES
TIMBALS
TIMBER
TIMBERDOODLE
TIMBERDOODLES
TIMBERED
TIMBERHEAD
TIMBERHEADS
TIMBERING
TIMBERINGS
TIMBERLAND
TIMBERLANDS
TIMBERLINE
TIMBERLINES
TIMBERMAN
TIMBERMEN
TIMBERS
TIMBERWORK
TIMBERWORKS
TIMBERY
TIMBRAL
TIMBRE
TIMBREL
TIMBRELLED
TIMBRELS
TIMBRES
TIME
TIMECARD
TIMECARDS

TIMED
TIMEKEEPER
TIMEKEEPERS
TIMEKEEPING
TIMEKEEPINGS
TIMELESS
TIMELESSLY
TIMELESSNESS
TIMELESSNESSES
TIMELIER
TIMELIEST
TIMELINE
TIMELINES
TIMELINESS
TIMELINESSES
TIMELY
TIMEOUS
TIMEOUSLY
TIMEOUT
TIMEOUTS
TIMEPIECE
TIMEPIECES
TIMEPLEASER
TIMEPLEASERS
TIMER
TIMERS
TIMES
TIMESAVER
TIMESAVERS
TIMESAVING
TIMESCALE
TIMESCALES
TIMESERVER
TIMESERVERS
TIMESERVING
TIMESERVINGS
TIMETABLE
TIMETABLES
TIMEWORK
TIMEWORKER
TIMEWORKERS
TIMEWORKS
TIMEWORN
TIMID
TIMIDER
TIMIDEST
TIMIDITIES
TIMIDITY
TIMIDLY
TIMIDNESS
TIMIDNESSES
TIMING
TIMINGS

TIMOCRACIES
TIMOCRACY
TIMOCRATIC
TIMOCRATICAL
TIMOLOL
TIMOLOLS
TIMOROUS
TIMOROUSLY
TIMOROUSNESS
TIMOROUSNESSES
TIMOTHIES
TIMOTHY
TIMPANA
TIMPANI
TIMPANIST
TIMPANISTS
TIMPANO
TIMPANUM
TIMPANUMS
TIN
TINAMOU
TINAMOUS
TINCAL
TINCALS
TINCT
TINCTED
TINCTING
TINCTORIAL
TINCTORIALLY
TINCTS
TINCTURE
TINCTURED
TINCTURES
TINCTURING
TINDER
TINDERBOX
TINDERBOXES
TINDERIER
TINDERIEST
TINDERS
TINDERY
TINE
TINEA
TINEAL
TINEAS
TINED
TINEID
TINEIDS
TINES
TINFOIL
TINFOILS
TINFUL
TINFULS

TING
TINGE
TINGED
TINGEING
TINGES
TINGING
TINGLE
TINGLED
TINGLER
TINGLERS
TINGLES
TINGLIER
TINGLIEST
TINGLING
TINGLINGLY
TINGLY
TINGS
TINHORN
TINHORNS
TINIER
TINIEST
TINILY
TININESS
TININESSES
TINING
TINKER
TINKERED
TINKERER
TINKERERS
TINKERING
TINKERS
TINKERTOY
TINKERTOYS
TINKLE
TINKLED
TINKLER
TINKLERS
TINKLES
TINKLIER
TINKLIEST
TINKLING
TINKLINGS
TINKLY
TINLIKE
TINMAN
TINMEN
TINNED
TINNER
TINNERS
TINNIER
TINNIEST
TINNILY
TINNINESS

TINNINESSES
TINNING
TINNITUS
TINNITUSES
TINNY
TINPLATE
TINPLATED
TINPLATES
TINPLATING
TINPOT
TINS
TINSEL
TINSELED
TINSELIER
TINSELIEST
TINSELING
TINSELLED
TINSELLING
TINSELLY
TINSELS
TINSELY
TINSMITH
TINSMITHING
TINSMITHINGS
TINSMITHS
TINSNIPS
TINSTONE
TINSTONES
TINT
TINTED
TINTER
TINTERS
TINTING
TINTINGS
TINTINNABULARY
TINTLESS
TINTS
TINTYPE
TINTYPES
TINWARE
TINWARES
TINWORK
TINWORKS
TINY
TIP
TIPCART
TIPCARTS
TIPCAT
TIPCATS
TIPI
TIPIS
TIPLESS
TIPOFF
TIPOFFS
TIPPABLE
TIPPED
TIPPER
TIPPERS
TIPPET
TIPPETS
TIPPIER
TIPPIEST
TIPPING
TIPPLE
TIPPLED
TIPPLER
TIPPLERS
TIPPLES
TIPPLING
TIPPY
TIPPYTOE
TIPPYTOED
TIPPYTOEING
TIPPYTOES
TIPS
TIPSHEET
TIPSHEETS
TIPSIER
TIPSIEST
TIPSILY
TIPSINESS
TIPSINESSES
TIPSTAFF
TIPSTAFFS
TIPSTAVES
TIPSTER
TIPSTERS
TIPSTOCK
TIPSTOCKS
TIPSY
TIPTOE
TIPTOED
TIPTOEING
TIPTOES
TIPTOP
TIPTOPS
TIRADE
TIRADES
TIRAMISU
TIRAMISUS
TIRE
TIRED
TIREDER
TIREDEST
TIREDLY
TIREDNESS
TIREDNESSES
TIRELESS
TIRELESSLY
TIRELESSNESS
TIRELESSNESSES
TIRES
TIRESOME
TIRESOMELY
TIRESOMENESS
TIRESOMENESSES
TIREWOMAN
TIREWOMEN
TIRING
TIRL
TIRLED
TIRLING
TIRLS
TIRO
TIROS
TIRRIVEE
TIRRIVEES
TIS
TISANE
TISANES
TISSUAL
TISSUE
TISSUED
TISSUES
TISSUEY
TISSUING
TISSULAR
TIT
TITAN
TITANATE
TITANATES
TITANESS
TITANESSES
TITANIA
TITANIAS
TITANIC
TITANICALLY
TITANIFEROUS
TITANISM
TITANISMS
TITANITE
TITANITES
TITANIUM
TITANIUMS
TITANOUS
TITANS
TITBIT
TITBITS
TITCH
TITCHES
TITCHIE
TITCHIER
TITCHIEST
TITCHY
TITER
TITERS
TITFER
TITFERS
TITHABLE
TITHE
TITHED
TITHER
TITHERS
TITHES
TITHING
TITHINGS
TITHONIA
TITHONIAS
TITI
TITIAN
TITIANS
TITILLATE
TITILLATED
TITILLATES
TITILLATING
TITILLATINGLY
TITILLATION
TITILLATIONS
TITILLATIVE
TITIS
TITIVATE
TITIVATED
TITIVATES
TITIVATING
TITIVATION
TITIVATIONS
TITLARK
TITLARKS
TITLE
TITLED
TITLEHOLDER
TITLEHOLDERS
TITLES
TITLING
TITLIST
TITLISTS
TITMAN
TITMEN
TITMICE
TITMOUSE
TITRABLE
TITRANT
TITRANTS
TITRATABLE
TITRATE
TITRATED
TITRATES
TITRATING
TITRATION
TITRATIONS
TITRATOR
TITRATORS
TITRE
TITRES
TITRIMETRIC
TITS
TITTER
TITTERED
TITTERER
TITTERERS
TITTERING
TITTERS
TITTIE
TITTIES
TITTIVATE
TITTIVATED
TITTIVATES
TITTIVATING
TITTLE
TITTLES
TITTUP
TITTUPED
TITTUPING
TITTUPPED
TITTUPPING
TITTUPPY
TITTUPS
TITTY
TITUBANT
TITULAR
TITULARIES
TITULARLY
TITULARS
TITULARY
TIVY
TIX
TIYIN
TIYINS
TIYN
TIYNS
TIZ
TIZES
TIZZ
TIZZES
TIZZIES

ZZY
IESES
IESIS

AD
ADEATER
ADEATERS
ADFISH
ADFISHES
ADFLAX
ADFLAXES
ADIED
ADIES
ADISH
ADLESS
ADLET
ADLETS
ADLIKE
ADS
ADSTONE
ADSTONES
ADSTOOL
ADSTOOLS
ADY
ADYING
ADYISH
ADYISM
ADYISMS
AST
ASTED
ASTER
ASTERS
ASTIER
ASTIEST
ASTING
ASTINGS
ASTMASTER
ASTMASTERS
ASTMISTRESS
ASTMISTRESSES
ASTS
ASTY
BACCO
BACCOES
BACCONIST
BACCONISTS
BACCOS
BIES
BOGGAN
BOGGANED
BOGGANER
BOGGANERS
BOGGANING

TOBOGGANINGS
TOBOGGANIST
TOBOGGANISTS
TOBOGGANS
TOBY
TOCCATA
TOCCATAS
TOCCATE
TOCHER
TOCHERED
TOCHERING
TOCHERS
TOCK
TOCKED
TOCKING
TOCKS
TOCO
TOCOLOGIES
TOCOLOGY
TOCOPHEROL
TOCOPHEROLS
TOCOS
TOCSIN
TOCSINS
TOD
TODAY
TODAYS
TODDIES
TODDLE
TODDLED
TODDLER
TODDLERHOOD
TODDLERHOODS
TODDLERS
TODDLES
TODDLING
TODDY
TODIES
TODS
TODY
TOE
TOEA
TOEAS
TOECAP
TOECAPS
TOECLIP
TOECLIPS
TOED
TOEHOLD
TOEHOLDS
TOEING
TOELESS
TOELIKE

TOENAIL
TOENAILED
TOENAILING
TOENAILS
TOEPIECE
TOEPIECES
TOEPLATE
TOEPLATES
TOERAG
TOERAGS
TOES
TOESHOE
TOESHOES
TOFF
TOFFEE
TOFFEES
TOFFIES
TOFFS
TOFFY
TOFT
TOFTS
TOFU
TOFUS
TOFUTTI
TOFUTTIS
TOG
TOGA
TOGAE
TOGAED
TOGAS
TOGATE
TOGATED
TOGAVIRUS
TOGAVIRUSES
TOGETHER
TOGETHERNESS
TOGETHERNESSES
TOGGED
TOGGERIES
TOGGERY
TOGGING
TOGGLE
TOGGLED
TOGGLER
TOGGLERS
TOGGLES
TOGGLING
TOGS
TOGUE
TOGUES
TOIL
TOILE
TOILED

TOILER
TOILERS
TOILES
TOILET
TOILETED
TOILETING
TOILETINGS
TOILETRIES
TOILETRY
TOILETS
TOILETTE
TOILETTES
TOILFUL
TOILFULLY
TOILING
TOILS
TOILSOME
TOILSOMELY
TOILSOMENESS
TOILSOMENESSES
TOILWORN
TOIT
TOITED
TOITING
TOITS
TOKAMAK
TOKAMAKS
TOKAY
TOKAYS
TOKE
TOKED
TOKEN
TOKENED
TOKENING
TOKENISM
TOKENISMS
TOKENS
TOKER
TOKERS
TOKES
TOKING
TOKOLOGIES
TOKOLOGY
TOKOMAK
TOKOMAKS
TOKONOMA
TOKONOMAS
TOLA
TOLAN
TOLANE
TOLANES
TOLANS
TOLAR

TOLARJEV
TOLARS
TOLAS
TOLBOOTH
TOLBOOTHS
TOLBUTAMIDE
TOLBUTAMIDES
TOLD
TOLE
TOLED
TOLEDO
TOLEDOS
TOLERABILITIES
TOLERABILITY
TOLERABLE
TOLERABLY
TOLERANCE
TOLERANCES
TOLERANT
TOLERANTLY
TOLERATE
TOLERATED
TOLERATES
TOLERATING
TOLERATION
TOLERATIONS
TOLERATIVE
TOLERATOR
TOLERATORS
TOLES
TOLEWARE
TOLEWARES
TOLIDIN
TOLIDINE
TOLIDINES
TOLIDINS
TOLING
TOLL
TOLLAGE
TOLLAGES
TOLLBAR
TOLLBARS
TOLLBOOTH
TOLLBOOTHS
TOLLED
TOLLER
TOLLERS
TOLLGATE
TOLLGATED
TOLLGATES
TOLLGATING
TOLLHOUSE
TOLLHOUSES

TOLLING
TOLLINGS
TOLLMAN
TOLLMEN
TOLLS
TOLLWAY
TOLLWAYS
TOLT
TOLTS
TOLU
TOLUATE
TOLUATES
TOLUENE
TOLUENES
TOLUIC
TOLUID
TOLUIDE
TOLUIDES
TOLUIDIDE
TOLUIDIDES
TOLUIDIN
TOLUIDINE
TOLUIDINES
TOLUIDINS
TOLUIDS
TOLUOL
TOLUOLE
TOLUOLES
TOLUOLS
TOLUS
TOLUYL
TOLUYLS
TOLYL
TOLYLS
TOM
TOMAHAWK
TOMAHAWKED
TOMAHAWKING
TOMAHAWKS
TOMALLEY
TOMALLEYS
TOMAN
TOMANS
TOMATILLO
TOMATILLOES
TOMATILLOS
TOMATO
TOMATOES
TOMATOEY
TOMB
TOMBAC
TOMBACK
TOMBACKS
TOMBACS
TOMBAK
TOMBAKS
TOMBAL
TOMBED
TOMBING
TOMBLESS
TOMBLIKE
TOMBOLA
TOMBOLAS
TOMBOLO
TOMBOLOS
TOMBOY
TOMBOYISH
TOMBOYISHNESS
TOMBOYISHNESSES
TOMBOYS
TOMBS
TOMBSTONE
TOMBSTONES
TOMCAT
TOMCATS
TOMCATTED
TOMCATTING
TOMCOD
TOMCODS
TOME
TOMENTA
TOMENTOSE
TOMENTUM
TOMES
TOMFOOL
TOMFOOLERIES
TOMFOOLERY
TOMFOOLS
TOMMED
TOMMIES
TOMMING
TOMMY
TOMMYCOD
TOMMYCODS
TOMMYROT
TOMMYROTS
TOMOGRAM
TOMOGRAMS
TOMOGRAPH
TOMOGRAPHIC
TOMOGRAPHIES
TOMOGRAPHS
TOMOGRAPHY
TOMORROW
TOMORROWS
TOMPION
TOMPIONS
TOMS
TOMTIT
TOMTITS
TON
TONAL
TONALITIES
TONALITY
TONALLY
TONDI
TONDO
TONDOS
TONE
TONEARM
TONEARMS
TONED
TONELESS
TONELESSLY
TONELESSNESS
TONELESSNESSES
TONEME
TONEMES
TONEMIC
TONER
TONERS
TONES
TONETIC
TONETICALLY
TONETICS
TONETTE
TONETTES
TONEY
TONG
TONGA
TONGAS
TONGED
TONGER
TONGERS
TONGING
TONGMAN
TONGMEN
TONGS
TONGUE
TONGUED
TONGUELESS
TONGUELIKE
TONGUES
TONGUING
TONGUINGS
TONIC
TONICALLY
TONICITIES
TONICITY
TONICS
TONIER
TONIEST
TONIFIED
TONIFIES
TONIFY
TONIFYING
TONIGHT
TONIGHTS
TONING
TONISH
TONISHLY
TONLET
TONLETS
TONNAGE
TONNAGES
TONNE
TONNEAU
TONNEAUS
TONNEAUX
TONNER
TONNERS
TONNES
TONNISH
TONOMETER
TONOMETERS
TONOMETRIES
TONOMETRY
TONOPLAST
TONOPLASTS
TONS
TONSIL
TONSILAR
TONSILLAR
TONSILLECTOMIES
TONSILLECTOMY
TONSILLITIDES
TONSILLITIS
TONSILLITISES
TONSILS
TONSORIAL
TONSURE
TONSURED
TONSURES
TONSURING
TONTINE
TONTINES
TONUS
TONUSES
TONY
TOO
TOODLE
TOODLED
TOODLES
TOODLING
TOOK
TOOL
TOOLBAR
TOOLBARS
TOOLBOX
TOOLBOXES
TOOLED
TOOLER
TOOLERS
TOOLHEAD
TOOLHEADS
TOOLHOLDER
TOOLHOLDERS
TOOLHOUSE
TOOLHOUSES
TOOLING
TOOLINGS
TOOLLESS
TOOLMAKER
TOOLMAKERS
TOOLMAKING
TOOLMAKINGS
TOOLPUSH
TOOLPUSHES
TOOLROOM
TOOLROOMS
TOOLS
TOOLSET
TOOLSETS
TOOLSHED
TOOLSHEDS
TOOM
TOON
TOONIE
TOONIES
TOONS
TOOT
TOOTED
TOOTER
TOOTERS
TOOTH
TOOTHACHE
TOOTHACHES
TOOTHBRUSH
TOOTHBRUSHED
TOOTHBRUSHES
TOOTHBRUSHING
TOOTHBRUSHINGS
TOOTHED
TOOTHIER
TOOTHIEST

OTHILY
OTHING
OTHLESS
OTHLIKE
OTHPASTE
OTHPASTES
OTHPICK
OTHPICKS
OTHS
OTHSOME
OTHSOMELY
OTHSOMENESS
OTHSOMENESSES
OTHWORT
OTHWORTS
OTHY
OTING
OTLE
OTLED
OTLER
OTLERS
OTLES
OTLING
OTS
OTSES
OTSIE
OTSIES
OTSY
P
PAZ
AZES
AZINE
PCOAT
PCOATS
PCROSS
PCROSSES
PDRESSING
PDRESSINGS
E
ED
EE
EES
ER
ERS
ES
FLIGHT
FUL
FULL
GALLANT
GALLANTS
H
HE
HES
TOPHI
TOPHS
TOPHUS
TOPI
TOPIARIES
TOPIARY
TOPIC
TOPICAL
TOPICALITIES
TOPICALITY
TOPICALLY
TOPICALS
TOPICS
TOPING
TOPIS
TOPKICK
TOPKICKS
TOPKNOT
TOPKNOTS
TOPLESS
TOPLESSNESS
TOPLESSNESSES
TOPLINE
TOPLINES
TOPLOFTICAL
TOPLOFTIER
TOPLOFTIEST
TOPLOFTILY
TOPLOFTINESS
TOPLOFTINESSES
TOPLOFTY
TOPMAST
TOPMASTS
TOPMINNOW
TOPMINNOWS
TOPMOST
TOPNOTCH
TOPNOTCHER
TOPNOTCHERS
TOPO
TOPOCENTRIC
TOPOGRAPH
TOPOGRAPHER
TOPOGRAPHERS
TOPOGRAPHIC
TOPOGRAPHICAL
TOPOGRAPHICALLY
TOPOGRAPHIES
TOPOGRAPHS
TOPOGRAPHY
TOPOI
TOPOISOMERASE
TOPOISOMERASES
TOPOLOGIC
TOPOLOGICAL
TOPOLOGICALLY
TOPOLOGIES
TOPOLOGIST
TOPOLOGISTS
TOPOLOGY
TOPONYM
TOPONYMIC
TOPONYMICAL
TOPONYMIES
TOPONYMIST
TOPONYMISTS
TOPONYMS
TOPONYMY
TOPOS
TOPOTYPE
TOPOTYPES
TOPPED
TOPPER
TOPPERS
TOPPING
TOPPINGS
TOPPLE
TOPPLED
TOPPLES
TOPPLING
TOPS
TOPSAIL
TOPSAILS
TOPSIDE
TOPSIDER
TOPSIDERS
TOPSIDES
TOPSOIL
TOPSOILED
TOPSOILING
TOPSOILS
TOPSPIN
TOPSPINS
TOPSTITCH
TOPSTITCHED
TOPSTITCHES
TOPSTITCHING
TOPSTONE
TOPSTONES
TOPWATER
TOPWORK
TOPWORKED
TOPWORKING
TOPWORKS
TOQUE
TOQUES
TOQUET
TOQUETS
TOQUILLA
TOQUILLAS
TOR
TORA
TORAH
TORAHS
TORAS
TORC
TORCH
TORCHABLE
TORCHBEARER
TORCHBEARERS
TORCHED
TORCHERE
TORCHERES
TORCHES
TORCHIER
TORCHIERE
TORCHIERES
TORCHIERS
TORCHIEST
TORCHING
TORCHLIGHT
TORCHLIGHTS
TORCHLIKE
TORCHLIT
TORCHON
TORCHONS
TORCHWOOD
TORCHWOODS
TORCHY
TORCS
TORE
TOREADOR
TOREADORS
TORERO
TOREROS
TORES
TOREUTIC
TOREUTICS
TORI
TORIC
TORICS
TORIES
TORII
TORMENT
TORMENTED
TORMENTER
TORMENTERS
TORMENTIL
TORMENTILS
TORMENTING
TORMENTOR
TORMENTORS
TORMENTS
TORN
TORNADIC
TORNADO
TORNADOES
TORNADOS
TORNILLO
TORNILLOS
TORO
TOROID
TOROIDAL
TOROIDALLY
TOROIDS
TOROS
TOROSE
TOROSITIES
TOROSITY
TOROT
TOROTH
TOROUS
TORPEDO
TORPEDOED
TORPEDOES
TORPEDOING
TORPEDOS
TORPEFIED
TORPEFIES
TORPEFY
TORPEFYING
TORPID
TORPIDITIES
TORPIDITY
TORPIDLY
TORPIDS
TORPOR
TORPORS
TORQUATE
TORQUE
TORQUED
TORQUER
TORQUERS
TORQUES
TORQUESES
TORQUEY
TORQUIER
TORQUIEST
TORQUING
TORR
TORREFIED
TORREFIES

TORREFY
TORREFYING
TORRENT
TORRENTIAL
TORRENTIALLY
TORRENTS
TORRID
TORRIDER
TORRIDEST
TORRIDITIES
TORRIDITY
TORRIDLY
TORRIDNESS
TORRIDNESSES
TORRIFIED
TORRIFIES
TORRIFY
TORRIFYING
TORRS
TORS
TORSADE
TORSADES
TORSE
TORSES
TORSI
TORSION
TORSIONAL
TORSIONALLY
TORSIONS
TORSK
TORSKS
TORSO
TORSOS
TORT
TORTA
TORTAS
TORTE
TORTELLI
TORTELLINI
TORTELLINIS
TORTELLIS
TORTEN
TORTES
TORTICOLLIS
TORTICOLLISES
TORTILE
TORTILLA
TORTILLAS
TORTIOUS
TORTIOUSLY
TORTOISE
TORTOISES
TORTOISESHELL
TORTOISESHELLS
TORTONI
TORTONIS
TORTRICES
TORTRICID
TORTRICIDS
TORTRIX
TORTRIXES
TORTS
TORTUOSITIES
TORTUOSITY
TORTUOUS
TORTUOUSLY
TORTUOUSNESS
TORTUOUSNESSES
TORTURE
TORTURED
TORTURER
TORTURERS
TORTURES
TORTURING
TORTUROUS
TORTUROUSLY
TORULA
TORULAE
TORULAS
TORUS
TORUSES
TORY
TOSA
TOSAS
TOSH
TOSHES
TOSS
TOSSED
TOSSER
TOSSERS
TOSSES
TOSSING
TOSSPOT
TOSSPOTS
TOSSUP
TOSSUPS
TOST
TOSTADA
TOSTADAS
TOSTADO
TOSTADOS
TOSTONE
TOSTONES
TOT
TOTABLE
TOTAL
TOTALED
TOTALING
TOTALISATOR
TOTALISATORS
TOTALISE
TOTALISED
TOTALISES
TOTALISING
TOTALISM
TOTALISMS
TOTALIST
TOTALISTIC
TOTALISTS
TOTALITARIAN
TOTALITARIANISM
TOTALITARIANIZE
TOTALITARIANS
TOTALITIES
TOTALITY
TOTALIZATOR
TOTALIZATORS
TOTALIZE
TOTALIZED
TOTALIZER
TOTALIZERS
TOTALIZES
TOTALIZING
TOTALLED
TOTALLING
TOTALLY
TOTALS
TOTAQUINE
TOTAQUINES
TOTE
TOTEABLE
TOTED
TOTEM
TOTEMIC
TOTEMISM
TOTEMISMS
TOTEMIST
TOTEMISTIC
TOTEMISTS
TOTEMITE
TOTEMITES
TOTEMS
TOTER
TOTERS
TOTES
TOTHER
TOTING
TOTIPOTENCIES
TOTIPOTENCY
TOTIPOTENT
TOTS
TOTTED
TOTTER
TOTTERED
TOTTERER
TOTTERERS
TOTTERING
TOTTERINGLY
TOTTERS
TOTTERY
TOTTIES
TOTTING
TOTTY
TOUCAN
TOUCANS
TOUCH
TOUCHABLE
TOUCHBACK
TOUCHBACKS
TOUCHDOWN
TOUCHDOWNS
TOUCHE
TOUCHED
TOUCHER
TOUCHERS
TOUCHES
TOUCHHOLE
TOUCHHOLES
TOUCHIER
TOUCHIEST
TOUCHILY
TOUCHINESS
TOUCHINESSES
TOUCHING
TOUCHINGLY
TOUCHLINE
TOUCHLINES
TOUCHMARK
TOUCHMARKS
TOUCHPAD
TOUCHPADS
TOUCHSTONE
TOUCHSTONES
TOUCHTONE
TOUCHTONES
TOUCHUP
TOUCHUPS
TOUCHWOOD
TOUCHWOODS
TOUCHY
TOUGH
TOUGHED
TOUGHEN
TOUGHENED
TOUGHENER
TOUGHENERS
TOUGHENING
TOUGHENS
TOUGHER
TOUGHEST
TOUGHIE
TOUGHIES
TOUGHING
TOUGHISH
TOUGHLY
TOUGHNESS
TOUGHNESSES
TOUGHS
TOUGHY
TOUPEE
TOUPEES
TOUPIE
TOUPIES
TOUR
TOURACO
TOURACOS
TOURBILLION
TOURBILLIONS
TOURBILLON
TOURBILLONS
TOURED
TOURER
TOURERS
TOURING
TOURINGS
TOURISM
TOURISMS
TOURIST
TOURISTA
TOURISTAS
TOURISTED
TOURISTIC
TOURISTICALLY
TOURISTS
TOURISTY
TOURMALINE
TOURMALINES
TOURNAMENT
TOURNAMENTS
TOURNEDOS
TOURNEY
TOURNEYED
TOURNEYING
TOURNEYS
TOURNIQUET

URNIQUETS
URS
USE
USED
USES
USING
USLE
USLED
USLES
USLING
UT
UTED
UTER
UTERS
UTING
UTON
UTONS
UTS
ZLE
ZLED
ZLES
ZLING
ARICH
ARICHES
ARISH
ARISHES
V
VABLE
VAGE
VAGES
VARD
VARDLINESS
VARDLINESSES
VARDLY
VARDS
VAWAY
VAWAYS
VBOAT
VBOATS
VED
VEL
VELED
ELETTE
ELETTES
ELING
ELINGS
ELLED
ELLING
ELLINGS
ELS
ER
ERED
ERIER

TOWERIEST
TOWERING
TOWERINGLY
TOWERLIKE
TOWERS
TOWERY
TOWHEAD
TOWHEADED
TOWHEADS
TOWHEE
TOWHEES
TOWIE
TOWIES
TOWING
TOWLINE
TOWLINES
TOWMOND
TOWMONDS
TOWMONT
TOWMONTS
TOWN
TOWNEE
TOWNEES
TOWNFOLK
TOWNHOME
TOWNHOMES
TOWNHOUSE
TOWNHOUSES
TOWNIE
TOWNIES
TOWNISH
TOWNLESS
TOWNLET
TOWNLETS
TOWNS
TOWNSCAPE
TOWNSCAPES
TOWNSFOLK
TOWNSHIP
TOWNSHIPS
TOWNSITE
TOWNSITES
TOWNSMAN
TOWNSMEN
TOWNSPEOPLE
TOWNSWOMAN
TOWNSWOMEN
TOWNWARD
TOWNWEAR
TOWNY
TOWPATH
TOWPATHS
TOWPLANE

TOWPLANES
TOWROPE
TOWROPES
TOWS
TOWSACK
TOWSACKS
TOWY
TOXAEMIA
TOXAEMIAS
TOXAEMIC
TOXAPHENE
TOXAPHENES
TOXEMIA
TOXEMIAS
TOXEMIC
TOXIC
TOXICAL
TOXICALLY
TOXICANT
TOXICANTS
TOXICITIES
TOXICITY
TOXICOLOGIC
TOXICOLOGICAL
TOXICOLOGICALLY
TOXICOLOGIES
TOXICOLOGIST
TOXICOLOGISTS
TOXICOLOGY
TOXICOSES
TOXICOSIS
TOXICS
TOXIGENIC
TOXIGENICITIES
TOXIGENICITY
TOXIN
TOXINE
TOXINES
TOXINS
TOXOID
TOXOIDS
TOXOPHILIES
TOXOPHILITE
TOXOPHILITES
TOXOPHILY
TOXOPLASMA
TOXOPLASMAS
TOXOPLASMIC
TOXOPLASMOSES
TOXOPLASMOSIS
TOY
TOYED
TOYER

TOYERS
TOYING
TOYISH
TOYLAND
TOYLANDS
TOYLESS
TOYLIKE
TOYO
TOYON
TOYONS
TOYOS
TOYS
TOYSHOP
TOYSHOPS
TOYTOWN
TOYTOWNS
TRABEATE
TRABEATED
TRABEATION
TRABEATIONS
TRABECULA
TRABECULAE
TRABECULAR
TRABECULAS
TRABECULATE
TRACE
TRACEABILITIES
TRACEABILITY
TRACEABLE
TRACEABLY
TRACED
TRACELESS
TRACER
TRACERIED
TRACERIES
TRACERS
TRACERY
TRACES
TRACHEA
TRACHEAE
TRACHEAL
TRACHEARY
TRACHEAS
TRACHEATE
TRACHEATED
TRACHEATES
TRACHEID
TRACHEIDS
TRACHEITIDES
TRACHEITIS
TRACHEITISES
TRACHEOLAR
TRACHEOLE

TRACHEOLES
TRACHEOPHYTE
TRACHEOPHYTES
TRACHEOSTOMIES
TRACHEOSTOMY
TRACHEOTOMIES
TRACHEOTOMY
TRACHLE
TRACHLED
TRACHLES
TRACHLING
TRACHOMA
TRACHOMAS
TRACHYTE
TRACHYTES
TRACHYTIC
TRACING
TRACINGS
TRACK
TRACKABLE
TRACKAGE
TRACKAGES
TRACKBALL
TRACKBALLS
TRACKBED
TRACKBEDS
TRACKED
TRACKER
TRACKERS
TRACKING
TRACKINGS
TRACKLAYER
TRACKLAYERS
TRACKLAYING
TRACKLAYINGS
TRACKLESS
TRACKMAN
TRACKMEN
TRACKPAD
TRACKPADS
TRACKS
TRACKSIDE
TRACKSIDES
TRACKSUIT
TRACKSUITS
TRACKWALKER
TRACKWALKERS
TRACKWAY
TRACKWAYS
TRACT
TRACTABILITIES
TRACTABILITY
TRACTABLE

TRACTABLENESS
TRACTABLENESSES
TRACTABLY
TRACTATE
TRACTATES
TRACTILE
TRACTION
TRACTIONAL
TRACTIONS
TRACTIVE
TRACTOR
TRACTORS
TRACTRICES
TRACTRIX
TRACTS
TRAD
TRADABLE
TRADE
TRADEABLE
TRADECRAFT
TRADECRAFTS
TRADED
TRADEMARK
TRADEMARKED
TRADEMARKING
TRADEMARKS
TRADEOFF
TRADEOFFS
TRADER
TRADERS
TRADES
TRADESCANTIA
TRADESCANTIAS
TRADESMAN
TRADESMEN
TRADESPEOPLE
TRADING
TRADINGS
TRADITION
TRADITIONAL
TRADITIONALISM
TRADITIONALISMS
TRADITIONALIST
TRADITIONALISTS
TRADITIONALIZE
TRADITIONALIZED
TRADITIONALIZES
TRADITIONALLY
TRADITIONARY
TRADITIONLESS
TRADITIONS
TRADITIVE
TRADITOR
TRADITORES
TRADS
TRADUCE
TRADUCED
TRADUCEMENT
TRADUCEMENTS
TRADUCER
TRADUCERS
TRADUCES
TRADUCING
TRAFFIC
TRAFFICABILITY
TRAFFICABLE
TRAFFICKED
TRAFFICKER
TRAFFICKERS
TRAFFICKING
TRAFFICS
TRAGACANTH
TRAGACANTHS
TRAGEDIAN
TRAGEDIANS
TRAGEDIENNE
TRAGEDIENNES
TRAGEDIES
TRAGEDY
TRAGI
TRAGIC
TRAGICAL
TRAGICALLY
TRAGICOMEDIES
TRAGICOMEDY
TRAGICOMIC
TRAGICOMICAL
TRAGICS
TRAGOPAN
TRAGOPANS
TRAGUS
TRAIK
TRAIKED
TRAIKING
TRAIKS
TRAIL
TRAILBLAZER
TRAILBLAZERS
TRAILBLAZING
TRAILBREAKER
TRAILBREAKERS
TRAILED
TRAILER
TRAILERABLE
TRAILERED
TRAILERING
TRAILERINGS
TRAILERIST
TRAILERISTS
TRAILERITE
TRAILERITES
TRAILERS
TRAILHEAD
TRAILHEADS
TRAILING
TRAILLESS
TRAILS
TRAILSIDE
TRAIN
TRAINABILITIES
TRAINABILITY
TRAINABLE
TRAINBAND
TRAINBANDS
TRAINBEARER
TRAINBEARERS
TRAINED
TRAINEE
TRAINEES
TRAINEESHIP
TRAINEESHIPS
TRAINER
TRAINERS
TRAINFUL
TRAINFULS
TRAINING
TRAININGS
TRAINLOAD
TRAINLOADS
TRAINMAN
TRAINMEN
TRAINS
TRAINSPOTTER
TRAINSPOTTERS
TRAINSPOTTING
TRAINWAY
TRAINWAYS
TRAIPSE
TRAIPSED
TRAIPSES
TRAIPSING
TRAIT
TRAITOR
TRAITORESS
TRAITORESSES
TRAITOROUS
TRAITOROUSLY
TRAITORS
TRAITRESS
TRAITRESSES
TRAITS
TRAJECT
TRAJECTED
TRAJECTING
TRAJECTION
TRAJECTIONS
TRAJECTORIES
TRAJECTORY
TRAJECTS
TRAM
TRAMCAR
TRAMCARS
TRAMEL
TRAMELED
TRAMELING
TRAMELL
TRAMELLED
TRAMELLING
TRAMELLS
TRAMELS
TRAMLESS
TRAMLINE
TRAMLINES
TRAMMED
TRAMMEL
TRAMMELED
TRAMMELER
TRAMMELERS
TRAMMELING
TRAMMELLED
TRAMMELLING
TRAMMELS
TRAMMING
TRAMONTANE
TRAMONTANES
TRAMP
TRAMPED
TRAMPER
TRAMPERS
TRAMPIER
TRAMPIEST
TRAMPING
TRAMPISH
TRAMPLE
TRAMPLED
TRAMPLER
TRAMPLERS
TRAMPLES
TRAMPLING
TRAMPOLINE
TRAMPOLINER
TRAMPOLINERS
TRAMPOLINES
TRAMPOLINING
TRAMPOLININGS
TRAMPOLINIST
TRAMPOLINISTS
TRAMPS
TRAMPY
TRAMROAD
TRAMROADS
TRAMS
TRAMWAY
TRAMWAYS
TRANCE
TRANCED
TRANCELIKE
TRANCES
TRANCHE
TRANCHES
TRANCING
TRANGAM
TRANGAMS
TRANK
TRANKED
TRANKING
TRANKS
TRANNIE
TRANNIES
TRANNY
TRANQ
TRANQS
TRANQUIL
TRANQUILER
TRANQUILEST
TRANQUILITIES
TRANQUILITY
TRANQUILIZE
TRANQUILIZED
TRANQUILIZER
TRANQUILIZERS
TRANQUILIZES
TRANQUILIZING
TRANQUILLER
TRANQUILLEST
TRANQUILLISE
TRANQUILLISED
TRANQUILLISER
TRANQUILLISERS
TRANQUILLISES
TRANQUILLISING
TRANQUILLITIES
TRANQUILLITY
TRANQUILLIZE
TRANQUILLIZED

ANQUILLIZER
ANQUILLIZERS
ANQUILLIZES
ANQUILLIZING
ANQUILLY
ANQUILNESS
ANQUILNESSES
ANS
ANSACT
ANSACTED
ANSACTING
ANSACTINIDE
ANSACTION
NSACTIONAL
NSACTIONS
NSACTOR
NSACTORS
NSACTS
NSALPINE
NSAMINASE
NSAMINASES
NSAMINATION
NSAMINATIONS
NSATLANTIC
NSAXLE
NSAXLES
NSBORDER
NSCEIVER
NSCEIVERS
NSCEND
NSCENDED
NSCENDENCE
NSCENDENCES
NSCENDENCIES
NSCENDENCY
NSCENDENT
NSCENDENTAL
NSCENDENTLY
NSCENDING
NSCENDS
NSCRIBE
NSCRIBED
NSCRIBER
NSCRIBERS
NSCRIBES
NSCRIBING
NSCRIPT
SCRIPTASE
NSCRIPTASES
NSCRIPTION
NSCRIPTIONAL
NSCRIPTIONS
NSCRIPTS

TRANSCULTURAL
TRANSCUTANEOUS
TRANSDERMAL
TRANSDERMALLY
TRANSDUCE
TRANSDUCED
TRANSDUCER
TRANSDUCERS
TRANSDUCES
TRANSDUCING
TRANSDUCTANT
TRANSDUCTANTS
TRANSDUCTION
TRANSDUCTIONAL
TRANSDUCTIONS
TRANSECT
TRANSECTED
TRANSECTING
TRANSECTION
TRANSECTIONS
TRANSECTS
TRANSEPT
TRANSEPTAL
TRANSEPTS
TRANSEUNT
TRANSEXUAL
TRANSEXUALISM
TRANSEXUALISMS
TRANSEXUALITIES
TRANSEXUALITY
TRANSEXUALS
TRANSFECT
TRANSFECTED
TRANSFECTING
TRANSFECTION
TRANSFECTIONS
TRANSFECTS
TRANSFER
TRANSFERABILITY
TRANSFERABLE
TRANSFERAL
TRANSFERALS
TRANSFERASE
TRANSFERASES
TRANSFEREE
TRANSFEREES
TRANSFERENCE
TRANSFERENCES
TRANSFERENTIAL
TRANSFEROR
TRANSFERORS
TRANSFERRABLE
TRANSFERRED

TRANSFERRER
TRANSFERRERS
TRANSFERRIN
TRANSFERRING
TRANSFERRINS
TRANSFERS
TRANSFIGURATION
TRANSFIGURE
TRANSFIGURED
TRANSFIGURES
TRANSFIGURING
TRANSFINITE
TRANSFIX
TRANSFIXED
TRANSFIXES
TRANSFIXING
TRANSFIXION
TRANSFIXIONS
TRANSFIXT
TRANSFORM
TRANSFORMABLE
TRANSFORMATION
TRANSFORMATIONS
TRANSFORMATIVE
TRANSFORMED
TRANSFORMER
TRANSFORMERS
TRANSFORMING
TRANSFORMS
TRANSFUSABLE
TRANSFUSE
TRANSFUSED
TRANSFUSES
TRANSFUSIBLE
TRANSFUSING
TRANSFUSION
TRANSFUSIONAL
TRANSFUSIONS
TRANSGENDER
TRANSGENDERED
TRANSGENDERISM
TRANSGENDERISMS
TRANSGENE
TRANSGENES
TRANSGENIC
TRANSGRESS
TRANSGRESSED
TRANSGRESSES
TRANSGRESSING
TRANSGRESSION
TRANSGRESSIONS
TRANSGRESSIVE
TRANSGRESSOR

TRANSGRESSORS
TRANSHIP
TRANSHIPMENT
TRANSHIPMENTS
TRANSHIPPED
TRANSHIPPING
TRANSHIPS
TRANSHISTORICAL
TRANSHUMANCE
TRANSHUMANCES
TRANSHUMANT
TRANSHUMANTS
TRANSIENCE
TRANSIENCES
TRANSIENCIES
TRANSIENCY
TRANSIENT
TRANSIENTLY
TRANSIENTS
TRANSILLUMINATE
TRANSISTOR
TRANSISTORISE
TRANSISTORISED
TRANSISTORISES
TRANSISTORISING
TRANSISTORIZE
TRANSISTORIZED
TRANSISTORIZES
TRANSISTORIZING
TRANSISTORS
TRANSIT
TRANSITED
TRANSITING
TRANSITION
TRANSITIONAL
TRANSITIONALLY
TRANSITIONED
TRANSITIONING
TRANSITIONS
TRANSITIVE
TRANSITIVELY
TRANSITIVENESS
TRANSITIVITIES
TRANSITIVITY
TRANSITORILY
TRANSITORINESS
TRANSITORY
TRANSITS
TRANSLATABILITY
TRANSLATABLE
TRANSLATE
TRANSLATED
TRANSLATES

TRANSLATING
TRANSLATION
TRANSLATIONAL
TRANSLATIONS
TRANSLATIVE
TRANSLATOR
TRANSLATORS
TRANSLATORY
TRANSLITERATE
TRANSLITERATED
TRANSLITERATES
TRANSLITERATING
TRANSLITERATION
TRANSLOCATE
TRANSLOCATED
TRANSLOCATES
TRANSLOCATING
TRANSLOCATION
TRANSLOCATIONS
TRANSLUCENCE
TRANSLUCENCES
TRANSLUCENCIES
TRANSLUCENCY
TRANSLUCENT
TRANSLUCENTLY
TRANSMARINE
TRANSMEMBRANE
TRANSMIGRATE
TRANSMIGRATED
TRANSMIGRATES
TRANSMIGRATING
TRANSMIGRATION
TRANSMIGRATIONS
TRANSMIGRATOR
TRANSMIGRATORS
TRANSMIGRATORY
TRANSMISSIBLE
TRANSMISSION
TRANSMISSIONS
TRANSMISSIVE
TRANSMISSIVITY
TRANSMISSOMETER
TRANSMIT
TRANSMITS
TRANSMITTABLE
TRANSMITTAL
TRANSMITTALS
TRANSMITTANCE
TRANSMITTANCES
TRANSMITTED
TRANSMITTER
TRANSMITTERS
TRANSMITTING

TRANSMOGRIFIED
TRANSMOGRIFIES
TRANSMOGRIFY
TRANSMOGRIFYING
TRANSMONTANE
TRANSMOUNTAIN
TRANSMUTABLE
TRANSMUTATION
TRANSMUTATIONS
TRANSMUTATIVE
TRANSMUTE
TRANSMUTED
TRANSMUTES
TRANSMUTING
TRANSNATIONAL
TRANSNATURAL
TRANSOCEANIC
TRANSOM
TRANSOMED
TRANSOMS
TRANSONIC
TRANSPACIFIC
TRANSPARENCE
TRANSPARENCES
TRANSPARENCIES
TRANSPARENCY
TRANSPARENT
TRANSPARENTIZE
TRANSPARENTIZED
TRANSPARENTIZES
TRANSPARENTLY
TRANSPARENTNESS
TRANSPERSONAL
TRANSPICUOUS
TRANSPIERCE
TRANSPIERCED
TRANSPIERCES
TRANSPIERCING
TRANSPIRATION
TRANSPIRATIONAL
TRANSPIRATIONS
TRANSPIRE
TRANSPIRED
TRANSPIRES
TRANSPIRING
TRANSPLACENTAL
TRANSPLANT
TRANSPLANTABLE
TRANSPLANTATION
TRANSPLANTED
TRANSPLANTER
TRANSPLANTERS
TRANSPLANTING
TRANSPLANTS
TRANSPOLAR
TRANSPONDER
TRANSPONDERS
TRANSPONTINE
TRANSPORT
TRANSPORTABLE
TRANSPORTATION
TRANSPORTATIONS
TRANSPORTED
TRANSPORTER
TRANSPORTERS
TRANSPORTING
TRANSPORTS
TRANSPOSABLE
TRANSPOSE
TRANSPOSED
TRANSPOSES
TRANSPOSING
TRANSPOSITION
TRANSPOSITIONAL
TRANSPOSITIONS
TRANSPOSON
TRANSPOSONS
TRANSRACIAL
TRANSSEXUAL
TRANSSEXUALISM
TRANSSEXUALISMS
TRANSSEXUALITY
TRANSSEXUALS
TRANSSHAPE
TRANSSHAPED
TRANSSHAPES
TRANSSHAPING
TRANSSHIP
TRANSSHIPMENT
TRANSSHIPMENTS
TRANSSHIPPED
TRANSSHIPPING
TRANSSHIPS
TRANSSONIC
TRANSTHORACIC
TRANSUBSTANTIAL
TRANSUDATE
TRANSUDATES
TRANSUDATION
TRANSUDATIONS
TRANSUDE
TRANSUDED
TRANSUDES
TRANSUDING
TRANSURANIC
TRANSURANICS
TRANSURANIUM
TRANSURETHRAL
TRANSVALUATE
TRANSVALUATED
TRANSVALUATES
TRANSVALUATING
TRANSVALUATION
TRANSVALUATIONS
TRANSVALUE
TRANSVALUED
TRANSVALUES
TRANSVALUING
TRANSVERSAL
TRANSVERSALS
TRANSVERSE
TRANSVERSELY
TRANSVERSES
TRANSVESTISM
TRANSVESTISMS
TRANSVESTITE
TRANSVESTITES
TRANSVESTITISM
TRANSVESTITISMS
TRAP
TRAPAN
TRAPANNED
TRAPANNING
TRAPANS
TRAPBALL
TRAPBALLS
TRAPDOOR
TRAPDOORS
TRAPES
TRAPESED
TRAPESES
TRAPESING
TRAPEZE
TRAPEZES
TRAPEZIA
TRAPEZIAL
TRAPEZII
TRAPEZIST
TRAPEZISTS
TRAPEZIUM
TRAPEZIUMS
TRAPEZIUS
TRAPEZIUSES
TRAPEZOHEDRA
TRAPEZOHEDRON
TRAPEZOHEDRONS
TRAPEZOID
TRAPEZOIDAL
TRAPEZOIDS
TRAPLIKE
TRAPLINE
TRAPLINES
TRAPNEST
TRAPNESTED
TRAPNESTING
TRAPNESTS
TRAPPEAN
TRAPPED
TRAPPER
TRAPPERS
TRAPPING
TRAPPINGS
TRAPPOSE
TRAPPOUS
TRAPROCK
TRAPROCKS
TRAPS
TRAPSHOOTER
TRAPSHOOTERS
TRAPSHOOTING
TRAPSHOOTINGS
TRAPT
TRAPUNTO
TRAPUNTOS
TRASH
TRASHED
TRASHER
TRASHERS
TRASHES
TRASHIER
TRASHIEST
TRASHILY
TRASHINESS
TRASHINESSES
TRASHING
TRASHMAN
TRASHMEN
TRASHY
TRASS
TRASSES
TRATTORIA
TRATTORIAS
TRATTORIE
TRAUCHLE
TRAUCHLED
TRAUCHLES
TRAUCHLING
TRAUMA
TRAUMAS
TRAUMATA
TRAUMATIC
TRAUMATICALLY
TRAUMATISE
TRAUMATISED
TRAUMATISES
TRAUMATISING
TRAUMATISM
TRAUMATISMS
TRAUMATIZATION
TRAUMATIZATIONS
TRAUMATIZE
TRAUMATIZED
TRAUMATIZES
TRAUMATIZING
TRAVAIL
TRAVAILED
TRAVAILING
TRAVAILS
TRAVE
TRAVEL
TRAVELED
TRAVELER
TRAVELERS
TRAVELING
TRAVELLED
TRAVELLER
TRAVELLERS
TRAVELLING
TRAVELOG
TRAVELOGS
TRAVELOGUE
TRAVELOGUES
TRAVELS
TRAVERSABLE
TRAVERSAL
TRAVERSALS
TRAVERSE
TRAVERSED
TRAVERSER
TRAVERSERS
TRAVERSES
TRAVERSING
TRAVERTINE
TRAVERTINES
TRAVES
TRAVESTIED
TRAVESTIES
TRAVESTY
TRAVESTYING
TRAVOIS
TRAVOISE
TRAVOISES
TRAWL
TRAWLED
TRAWLER

AWLERMAN
AWLERMEN
AWLERS
AWLEY
AWLEYS
AWLING
AWLNET
AWLNETS
AWLS
AY
AYF
AYFUL
AYFULS
AYS
AZODONE
AZODONES
EACHERIES
EACHEROUS
EACHEROUSLY
EACHEROUSNESS
EACHERY
ACLE
ACLES
ACLIER
ACLIEST
ACLY
AD
ADED
ADER
ADERS
ADING
ADLE
ADLED
ADLER
ADLERS
ADLES
ADLESS
ADLING
ADMILL
ADMILLS
ADS
ASON
ASONABLE
ASONABLY
ASONOUS
ASONS
ASURABLE
ASURE
ASURED
ASURER
ASURERS
ASURERSHIP
ASURERSHIPS

TREASURES
TREASURIES
TREASURING
TREASURY
TREAT
TREATABILITIES
TREATABILITY
TREATABLE
TREATED
TREATER
TREATERS
TREATIES
TREATING
TREATINGS
TREATISE
TREATISES
TREATMENT
TREATMENTS
TREATS
TREATY
TREBBIANO
TREBBIANOS
TREBLE
TREBLED
TREBLES
TREBLING
TREBLY
TREBUCHET
TREBUCHETS
TREBUCKET
TREBUCKETS
TRECENTO
TRECENTOS
TREDDLE
TREDDLED
TREDDLES
TREDDLING
TREDECILLION
TREDECILLIONS
TREE
TREED
TREEHOPPER
TREEHOPPERS
TREEHOUSE
TREEHOUSES
TREEING
TREELAWN
TREELAWNS
TREELESS
TREELIKE
TREELINE
TREELINES
TREEN

TREENAIL
TREENAILS
TREENS
TREENWARE
TREENWARES
TREES
TREETOP
TREETOPS
TREF
TREFA
TREFAH
TREFOIL
TREFOILED
TREFOILS
TREHALA
TREHALAS
TREHALOSE
TREHALOSES
TREILLAGE
TREILLAGES
TREK
TREKKED
TREKKER
TREKKERS
TREKKING
TREKS
TRELLIS
TRELLISED
TRELLISES
TRELLISING
TRELLISWORK
TRELLISWORKS
TREM
TREMATODE
TREMATODES
TREMBLE
TREMBLED
TREMBLER
TREMBLERS
TREMBLES
TREMBLIER
TREMBLIEST
TREMBLING
TREMBLOR
TREMBLORS
TREMBLY
TREMENDOUS
TREMENDOUSLY
TREMENDOUSNESS
TREMOLITE
TREMOLITES
TREMOLITIC
TREMOLO

TREMOLOS
TREMOR
TREMORED
TREMORING
TREMOROUS
TREMORS
TREMS
TREMULANT
TREMULOUS
TREMULOUSLY
TREMULOUSNESS
TREMULOUSNESSES
TRENAIL
TRENAILS
TRENCH
TRENCHANCIES
TRENCHANCY
TRENCHANT
TRENCHANTLY
TRENCHED
TRENCHER
TRENCHERMAN
TRENCHERMEN
TRENCHERS
TRENCHES
TRENCHING
TREND
TRENDED
TRENDIER
TRENDIES
TRENDIEST
TRENDIFIED
TRENDIFIES
TRENDIFY
TRENDIFYING
TRENDILY
TRENDINESS
TRENDINESSES
TRENDING
TRENDOID
TRENDOIDS
TRENDS
TRENDSETTER
TRENDSETTERS
TRENDSETTING
TRENDY
TREPAN
TREPANATION
TREPANATIONS
TREPANG
TREPANGS
TREPANNED
TREPANNER

TREPANNERS
TREPANNING
TREPANS
TREPHINATION
TREPHINATIONS
TREPHINE
TREPHINED
TREPHINES
TREPHINING
TREPID
TREPIDACIOUS
TREPIDANT
TREPIDATION
TREPIDATIONS
TREPIDATIOUS
TREPIDATIOUSLY
TREPONEMA
TREPONEMAL
TREPONEMAS
TREPONEMATA
TREPONEMATOSES
TREPONEMATOSIS
TREPONEME
TREPONEMES
TRES
TRESPASS
TRESPASSED
TRESPASSER
TRESPASSERS
TRESPASSES
TRESPASSING
TRESS
TRESSED
TRESSEL
TRESSELS
TRESSES
TRESSIER
TRESSIEST
TRESSING
TRESSOUR
TRESSOURS
TRESSURE
TRESSURES
TRESSY
TRESTLE
TRESTLES
TRESTLEWORK
TRESTLEWORKS
TRET
TRETINOIN
TRETINOINS
TRETS
TREVALLIES

TREVALLY
TREVALLYS
TREVET
TREVETS
TREWS
TREY
TREYF
TREYFA
TREYS
TRIABLE
TRIAC
TRIACETATE
TRIACETATES
TRIACID
TRIACIDS
TRIACS
TRIACTOR
TRIACTORS
TRIAD
TRIADIC
TRIADICALLY
TRIADICS
TRIADISM
TRIADISMS
TRIADS
TRIAGE
TRIAGED
TRIAGES
TRIAGING
TRIAL
TRIALED
TRIALING
TRIALIST
TRIALISTS
TRIALLED
TRIALLING
TRIALOGUE
TRIALOGUES
TRIALS
TRIAMCINOLONE
TRIAMCINOLONES
TRIANGLE
TRIANGLED
TRIANGLES
TRIANGULAR
TRIANGULARITIES
TRIANGULARITY
TRIANGULARLY
TRIANGULATE
TRIANGULATED
TRIANGULATES
TRIANGULATING
TRIANGULATION
TRIANGULATIONS
TRIARCHIES
TRIARCHY
TRIASSIC
TRIATHLETE
TRIATHLETES
TRIATHLON
TRIATHLONS
TRIATOMIC
TRIAXIAL
TRIAXIALITIES
TRIAXIALITY
TRIAZIN
TRIAZINE
TRIAZINES
TRIAZINS
TRIAZOLE
TRIAZOLES
TRIBADE
TRIBADES
TRIBADIC
TRIBADISM
TRIBADISMS
TRIBAL
TRIBALISM
TRIBALISMS
TRIBALIST
TRIBALISTS
TRIBALLY
TRIBALS
TRIBASIC
TRIBE
TRIBES
TRIBESMAN
TRIBESMEN
TRIBESPEOPLE
TRIBESWOMAN
TRIBESWOMEN
TRIBOELECTRIC
TRIBOLOGICAL
TRIBOLOGIES
TRIBOLOGIST
TRIBOLOGISTS
TRIBOLOGY
TRIBRACH
TRIBRACHIC
TRIBRACHS
TRIBULATE
TRIBULATED
TRIBULATES
TRIBULATING
TRIBULATION
TRIBULATIONS
TRIBUNAL
TRIBUNALS
TRIBUNARY
TRIBUNATE
TRIBUNATES
TRIBUNE
TRIBUNES
TRIBUNESHIP
TRIBUNESHIPS
TRIBUTARIES
TRIBUTARY
TRIBUTE
TRIBUTES
TRIBUTYLTIN
TRIBUTYLTINS
TRICARBOXYLIC
TRICE
TRICED
TRICEP
TRICEPS
TRICEPSES
TRICERATOPS
TRICERATOPSES
TRICES
TRICHIASES
TRICHIASIS
TRICHINA
TRICHINAE
TRICHINAL
TRICHINAS
TRICHINIZE
TRICHINIZED
TRICHINIZES
TRICHINIZING
TRICHINOSES
TRICHINOSIS
TRICHINOUS
TRICHITE
TRICHITES
TRICHLORFON
TRICHLORFONS
TRICHLORPHON
TRICHLORPHONS
TRICHOCYST
TRICHOCYSTS
TRICHOGYNE
TRICHOGYNES
TRICHOID
TRICHOLOGIES
TRICHOLOGIST
TRICHOLOGISTS
TRICHOLOGY
TRICHOME
TRICHOMES
TRICHOMIC
TRICHOMONACIDAL
TRICHOMONACIDE
TRICHOMONACIDES
TRICHOMONAD
TRICHOMONADS
TRICHOMONAL
TRICHOMONAS
TRICHOMONIASES
TRICHOMONIASIS
TRICHOPTERAN
TRICHOPTERANS
TRICHOSES
TRICHOSIS
TRICHOTHECENE
TRICHOTHECENES
TRICHOTOMIES
TRICHOTOMOUS
TRICHOTOMOUSLY
TRICHOTOMY
TRICHROIC
TRICHROMAT
TRICHROMATIC
TRICHROMATISM
TRICHROMATISMS
TRICHROMATS
TRICHROME
TRICING
TRICITIES
TRICITY
TRICK
TRICKED
TRICKER
TRICKERIES
TRICKERS
TRICKERY
TRICKIE
TRICKIER
TRICKIEST
TRICKILY
TRICKINESS
TRICKINESSES
TRICKING
TRICKISH
TRICKISHLY
TRICKISHNESS
TRICKISHNESSES
TRICKLE
TRICKLED
TRICKLES
TRICKLIER
TRICKLIEST
TRICKLING
TRICKLY
TRICKS
TRICKSIER
TRICKSIEST
TRICKSINESS
TRICKSINESSES
TRICKSTER
TRICKSTERS
TRICKSY
TRICKY
TRICLAD
TRICLADS
TRICLINIA
TRICLINIC
TRICLINIUM
TRICLOSAN
TRICLOSANS
TRICOLETTE
TRICOLETTES
TRICOLOR
TRICOLORED
TRICOLORS
TRICOLOUR
TRICOLOURED
TRICOLOURS
TRICORN
TRICORNE
TRICORNERED
TRICORNES
TRICORNS
TRICOT
TRICOTINE
TRICOTINES
TRICOTS
TRICROTIC
TRICTRAC
TRICTRACS
TRICUSPID
TRICUSPIDS
TRICYCLE
TRICYCLED
TRICYCLES
TRICYCLIC
TRICYCLICS
TRICYCLING
TRICYCLINGS
TRIDACTYL
TRIDENT
TRIDENTAL
TRIDENTS
TRIDIMENSIONAL
TRIDUUM

DUUMS
ED
ENE
ENES
ENNIA
ENNIAL
ENNIALLY
ENNIALS
ENNIUM
ENNIUMS
ENS
ENTES
ER
ERARCH
ERARCHIES
ERARCHS
ERARCHY
ERS
ES
ETHYL
FACIAL
FACIALS
FECTA
FECTAS
FFID
FFIDS
ID
LE
LED
LER
LERS
LES
LING
LINGS
LUOPERAZINE
LURALIN
LURALINS
OCAL
OCALS
OLD
OLIATE
OLIOLATE
OLIUM
OLIUMS
ORIA
ORIUM
ORM
ORMED
URCATE
URCATED
URCATES
URCATING
URCATION

TRIFURCATIONS
TRIG
TRIGAMIES
TRIGAMY
TRIGEMINAL
TRIGEMINALS
TRIGGED
TRIGGER
TRIGGERED
TRIGGERFISH
TRIGGERFISHES
TRIGGERING
TRIGGERMAN
TRIGGERMEN
TRIGGERS
TRIGGEST
TRIGGING
TRIGLY
TRIGLYCERIDE
TRIGLYCERIDES
TRIGLYPH
TRIGLYPHIC
TRIGLYPHICAL
TRIGLYPHS
TRIGNESS
TRIGNESSES
TRIGO
TRIGON
TRIGONAL
TRIGONALLY
TRIGONOMETRIC
TRIGONOMETRICAL
TRIGONOMETRIES
TRIGONOMETRY
TRIGONOUS
TRIGONS
TRIGOS
TRIGRAM
TRIGRAMS
TRIGRAPH
TRIGRAPHIC
TRIGRAPHS
TRIGS
TRIHALOMETHANE
TRIHALOMETHANES
TRIHEDRA
TRIHEDRAL
TRIHEDRALS
TRIHEDRON
TRIHEDRONS
TRIHYBRID
TRIHYBRIDS
TRIHYDROXY

TRIJET
TRIJETS
TRIJUGATE
TRIJUGOUS
TRIKE
TRIKES
TRILATERAL
TRILBIED
TRILBIES
TRILBY
TRILINEAR
TRILINGUAL
TRILINGUALLY
TRILITERAL
TRILITERALISM
TRILITERALISMS
TRILITERALS
TRILITH
TRILITHON
TRILITHONS
TRILITHS
TRILL
TRILLED
TRILLER
TRILLERS
TRILLING
TRILLION
TRILLIONS
TRILLIONTH
TRILLIONTHS
TRILLIUM
TRILLIUMS
TRILLS
TRILOBAL
TRILOBATE
TRILOBED
TRILOBITE
TRILOBITES
TRILOGIES
TRILOGY
TRIM
TRIMARAN
TRIMARANS
TRIMER
TRIMERIC
TRIMERISM
TRIMERISMS
TRIMEROUS
TRIMERS
TRIMESTER
TRIMESTERS
TRIMETER
TRIMETERS

TRIMETHOPRIM
TRIMETHOPRIMS
TRIMETRIC
TRIMETROGON
TRIMETROGONS
TRIMLY
TRIMMED
TRIMMER
TRIMMERS
TRIMMEST
TRIMMING
TRIMMINGS
TRIMNESS
TRIMNESSES
TRIMONTHLY
TRIMORPH
TRIMORPHIC
TRIMORPHS
TRIMOTOR
TRIMOTORS
TRIMPOT
TRIMPOTS
TRIMS
TRINAL
TRINARY
TRINDLE
TRINDLED
TRINDLES
TRINDLING
TRINE
TRINED
TRINES
TRINING
TRINITARIAN
TRINITARIANS
TRINITIES
TRINITROTOLUENE
TRINITY
TRINKET
TRINKETED
TRINKETER
TRINKETERS
TRINKETING
TRINKETRIES
TRINKETRY
TRINKETS
TRINKUMS
TRINOCULAR
TRINODAL
TRINOMIAL
TRINOMIALS
TRINUCLEOTIDE
TRINUCLEOTIDES

TRIO
TRIODE
TRIODES
TRIOL
TRIOLET
TRIOLETS
TRIOLS
TRIOS
TRIOSE
TRIOSES
TRIOXID
TRIOXIDE
TRIOXIDES
TRIOXIDS
TRIP
TRIPACK
TRIPACKS
TRIPART
TRIPARTITE
TRIPE
TRIPEDAL
TRIPES
TRIPHASE
TRIPHOSPHATE
TRIPHOSPHATES
TRIPHTHONG
TRIPHTHONGAL
TRIPHTHONGS
TRIPINNATE
TRIPINNATELY
TRIPLANE
TRIPLANES
TRIPLE
TRIPLED
TRIPLES
TRIPLET
TRIPLETAIL
TRIPLETAILS
TRIPLETS
TRIPLEX
TRIPLEXED
TRIPLEXES
TRIPLEXING
TRIPLICATE
TRIPLICATED
TRIPLICATES
TRIPLICATING
TRIPLICATION
TRIPLICATIONS
TRIPLICITIES
TRIPLICITY
TRIPLING
TRIPLITE

TRIPLITES
TRIPLOBLASTIC
TRIPLOID
TRIPLOIDIES
TRIPLOIDS
TRIPLOIDY
TRIPLY
TRIPMAN
TRIPMEN
TRIPOD
TRIPODAL
TRIPODIC
TRIPODIES
TRIPODS
TRIPODY
TRIPOLI
TRIPOLIS
TRIPOS
TRIPOSES
TRIPPANT
TRIPPED
TRIPPER
TRIPPERS
TRIPPET
TRIPPETS
TRIPPIER
TRIPPIEST
TRIPPING
TRIPPINGLY
TRIPPINGS
TRIPPY
TRIPS
TRIPTAN
TRIPTANE
TRIPTANES
TRIPTANS
TRIPTYCA
TRIPTYCAS
TRIPTYCH
TRIPTYCHS
TRIPWIRE
TRIPWIRES
TRIQUETROUS
TRIRADIATE
TRIREME
TRIREMES
TRISACCHARIDE
TRISACCHARIDES
TRISCELE
TRISCELES
TRISECT
TRISECTED
TRISECTING
TRISECTION
TRISECTIONS
TRISECTOR
TRISECTORS
TRISECTS
TRISEME
TRISEMES
TRISEMIC
TRISHAW
TRISHAWS
TRISKELE
TRISKELES
TRISKELIA
TRISKELION
TRISKELIONS
TRISMIC
TRISMUS
TRISMUSES
TRISOCTAHEDRA
TRISOCTAHEDRON
TRISOCTAHEDRONS
TRISODIUM
TRISOME
TRISOMES
TRISOMIC
TRISOMICS
TRISOMIES
TRISOMY
TRISTATE
TRISTE
TRISTEARIN
TRISTEARINS
TRISTEZA
TRISTEZAS
TRISTFUL
TRISTFULLY
TRISTFULNESS
TRISTFULNESSES
TRISTICH
TRISTICHS
TRISTIMULUS
TRISUBSTITUTED
TRISULFIDE
TRISULFIDES
TRISYLLABIC
TRISYLLABLE
TRISYLLABLES
TRITE
TRITELY
TRITENESS
TRITENESSES
TRITER
TRITEST
TRITHEISM
TRITHEISMS
TRITHEIST
TRITHEISTIC
TRITHEISTICAL
TRITHEISTS
TRITHING
TRITHINGS
TRITIATED
TRITICALE
TRITICALES
TRITICUM
TRITICUMS
TRITIUM
TRITIUMS
TRITOMA
TRITOMAS
TRITON
TRITONE
TRITONES
TRITONS
TRITURABLE
TRITURATE
TRITURATED
TRITURATES
TRITURATING
TRITURATION
TRITURATIONS
TRITURATOR
TRITURATORS
TRIUMPH
TRIUMPHAL
TRIUMPHALISM
TRIUMPHALISMS
TRIUMPHALIST
TRIUMPHALISTS
TRIUMPHANT
TRIUMPHANTLY
TRIUMPHED
TRIUMPHING
TRIUMPHS
TRIUMVIR
TRIUMVIRATE
TRIUMVIRATES
TRIUMVIRI
TRIUMVIRS
TRIUNE
TRIUNES
TRIUNITIES
TRIUNITY
TRIVALENT
TRIVALVE
TRIVALVES
TRIVET
TRIVETS
TRIVIA
TRIVIAL
TRIVIALISATION
TRIVIALISATIONS
TRIVIALISE
TRIVIALISED
TRIVIALISES
TRIVIALISING
TRIVIALIST
TRIVIALISTS
TRIVIALITIES
TRIVIALITY
TRIVIALIZATION
TRIVIALIZATIONS
TRIVIALIZE
TRIVIALIZED
TRIVIALIZES
TRIVIALIZING
TRIVIALLY
TRIVIUM
TRIVIUMS
TRIWEEKLIES
TRIWEEKLY
TROAK
TROAKED
TROAKING
TROAKS
TROCAR
TROCARS
TROCHAIC
TROCHAICS
TROCHAL
TROCHANTER
TROCHANTERAL
TROCHANTERIC
TROCHANTERS
TROCHAR
TROCHARS
TROCHE
TROCHEE
TROCHEES
TROCHES
TROCHIL
TROCHILI
TROCHILS
TROCHILUS
TROCHLEA
TROCHLEAE
TROCHLEAR
TROCHLEARS
TROCHLEAS
TROCHOID
TROCHOIDAL
TROCHOIDS
TROCHOPHORE
TROCHOPHORES
TROCK
TROCKED
TROCKING
TROCKS
TROD
TRODDEN
TRODE
TROFFER
TROFFERS
TROG
TROGLODYTE
TROGLODYTES
TROGLODYTIC
TROGON
TROGONS
TROGS
TROIKA
TROIKAS
TROILISM
TROILISMS
TROILITE
TROILITES
TROILUS
TROILUSES
TROIS
TROKE
TROKED
TROKES
TROKING
TROLAND
TROLANDS
TROLL
TROLLED
TROLLER
TROLLERS
TROLLEY
TROLLEYBUS
TROLLEYBUSES
TROLLEYBUSSES
TROLLEYED
TROLLEYING
TROLLEYS
TROLLIED
TROLLIES
TROLLING
TROLLINGS
TROLLISH
TROLLOP

OLLOPS
OLLOPY
OLLS
OLLY
OLLYING
OMBONE
OMBONES
OMBONIST
OMBONISTS
OMMEL
OMMELS
OMP
OMPE
OMPED
OMPES
OMPING
OMPS
ONA
ONAS
ONE
ONES
OOP
OOPED
OOPER
OOPERS
OOPIAL
OOPIALS
OOPING
OOPS
OOPSHIP
OOPSHIPS
OOSTITE
OOSTITES
OOZ
P
PAEOLA
PAEOLUM
PAEOLUMS
PE
PEOLIN
PEOLINS
PES
PHALLAXES
PHALLAXIS
PHIC
PHICALLY
PHIED
PHIES
PHOBLAST
PHOBLASTIC
PHOBLASTS
PHOZOITE
PHOZOITES

TROPHY
TROPHYING
TROPIC
TROPICAL
TROPICALIZE
TROPICALIZED
TROPICALIZES
TROPICALIZING
TROPICALLY
TROPICALS
TROPICS
TROPIN
TROPINE
TROPINES
TROPINS
TROPISM
TROPISMS
TROPISTIC
TROPOCOLLAGEN
TROPOCOLLAGENS
TROPOLOGIC
TROPOLOGICAL
TROPOLOGICALLY
TROPOLOGIES
TROPOLOGY
TROPOMYOSIN
TROPOMYOSINS
TROPONIN
TROPONINS
TROPOPAUSE
TROPOPAUSES
TROPOSPHERE
TROPOSPHERES
TROPOSPHERIC
TROPOTAXES
TROPOTAXIS
TROPPO
TROT
TROTH
TROTHED
TROTHING
TROTHPLIGHT
TROTHPLIGHTED
TROTHPLIGHTING
TROTHPLIGHTS
TROTHS
TROTLINE
TROTLINES
TROTS
TROTTED
TROTTER
TROTTERS
TROTTING

TROTTINGS
TROTYL
TROTYLS
TROU
TROUBADOUR
TROUBADOURS
TROUBLE
TROUBLED
TROUBLEMAKER
TROUBLEMAKERS
TROUBLEMAKING
TROUBLEMAKINGS
TROUBLER
TROUBLERS
TROUBLES
TROUBLESHOOT
TROUBLESHOOTER
TROUBLESHOOTERS
TROUBLESHOOTING
TROUBLESHOOTS
TROUBLESHOT
TROUBLESOME
TROUBLESOMELY
TROUBLESOMENESS
TROUBLING
TROUBLOUS
TROUBLOUSLY
TROUBLOUSNESS
TROUBLOUSNESSES
TROUGH
TROUGHS
TROUNCE
TROUNCED
TROUNCER
TROUNCERS
TROUNCES
TROUNCING
TROUPE
TROUPED
TROUPER
TROUPERS
TROUPES
TROUPIAL
TROUPIALS
TROUPING
TROUSER
TROUSERED
TROUSERS
TROUSSEAU
TROUSSEAUS
TROUSSEAUX
TROUT
TROUTIER

TROUTIEST
TROUTING
TROUTINGS
TROUTS
TROUTY
TROUVERE
TROUVERES
TROUVEUR
TROUVEURS
TROVE
TROVER
TROVERS
TROVES
TROW
TROWED
TROWEL
TROWELED
TROWELER
TROWELERS
TROWELING
TROWELLED
TROWELLER
TROWELLERS
TROWELLING
TROWELS
TROWING
TROWS
TROWSERS
TROWTH
TROWTHS
TROY
TROYS
TRUANCIES
TRUANCY
TRUANT
TRUANTED
TRUANTING
TRUANTLY
TRUANTRIES
TRUANTRY
TRUANTS
TRUCE
TRUCED
TRUCELESS
TRUCES
TRUCING
TRUCK
TRUCKABLE
TRUCKAGE
TRUCKAGES
TRUCKED
TRUCKER
TRUCKERS

TRUCKFUL
TRUCKFULS
TRUCKING
TRUCKINGS
TRUCKLE
TRUCKLED
TRUCKLER
TRUCKLERS
TRUCKLES
TRUCKLINE
TRUCKLINES
TRUCKLING
TRUCKLOAD
TRUCKLOADS
TRUCKMAN
TRUCKMASTER
TRUCKMASTERS
TRUCKMEN
TRUCKS
TRUCULENCE
TRUCULENCES
TRUCULENCIES
TRUCULENCY
TRUCULENT
TRUCULENTLY
TRUDGE
TRUDGED
TRUDGEN
TRUDGENS
TRUDGEON
TRUDGEONS
TRUDGER
TRUDGERS
TRUDGES
TRUDGING
TRUE
TRUEBLUE
TRUEBLUES
TRUEBORN
TRUEBRED
TRUED
TRUEHEARTED
TRUEHEARTEDNESS
TRUEING
TRUELOVE
TRUELOVES
TRUENESS
TRUENESSES
TRUEPENNIES
TRUEPENNY
TRUER
TRUES
TRUEST

TRUFFE
TRUFFES
TRUFFLE
TRUFFLED
TRUFFLES
TRUFFLING
TRUFFLINGS
TRUG
TRUGS
TRUING
TRUISM
TRUISMS
TRUISTIC
TRULL
TRULLS
TRULY
TRUMEAU
TRUMEAUX
TRUMP
TRUMPED
TRUMPERIES
TRUMPERY
TRUMPET
TRUMPETED
TRUMPETER
TRUMPETERS
TRUMPETING
TRUMPETLIKE
TRUMPETS
TRUMPING
TRUMPS
TRUNCAL
TRUNCATE
TRUNCATED
TRUNCATES
TRUNCATING
TRUNCATION
TRUNCATIONS
TRUNCHEON
TRUNCHEONED
TRUNCHEONING
TRUNCHEONS
TRUNDLE
TRUNDLED
TRUNDLER
TRUNDLERS
TRUNDLES
TRUNDLING
TRUNK
TRUNKED
TRUNKFISH
TRUNKFISHES
TRUNKFUL
TRUNKFULS
TRUNKING
TRUNKINGS
TRUNKS
TRUNNEL
TRUNNELS
TRUNNION
TRUNNIONS
TRUSS
TRUSSED
TRUSSER
TRUSSERS
TRUSSES
TRUSSING
TRUSSINGS
TRUST
TRUSTABILITIES
TRUSTABILITY
TRUSTABLE
TRUSTBUSTER
TRUSTBUSTERS
TRUSTED
TRUSTEE
TRUSTEED
TRUSTEEING
TRUSTEES
TRUSTEESHIP
TRUSTEESHIPS
TRUSTER
TRUSTERS
TRUSTFUL
TRUSTFULLY
TRUSTFULNESS
TRUSTFULNESSES
TRUSTIER
TRUSTIES
TRUSTIEST
TRUSTILY
TRUSTINESS
TRUSTINESSES
TRUSTING
TRUSTINGLY
TRUSTINGNESS
TRUSTINGNESSES
TRUSTLESS
TRUSTOR
TRUSTORS
TRUSTS
TRUSTWORTHIER
TRUSTWORTHIEST
TRUSTWORTHILY
TRUSTWORTHINESS
TRUSTWORTHY
TRUSTY
TRUTH
TRUTHFUL
TRUTHFULLY
TRUTHFULNESS
TRUTHFULNESSES
TRUTHLESS
TRUTHS
TRY
TRYING
TRYINGLY
TRYMA
TRYMATA
TRYOUT
TRYOUTS
TRYPANOSOME
TRYPANOSOMES
TRYPANOSOMIASES
TRYPANOSOMIASIS
TRYPSIN
TRYPSINOGEN
TRYPSINOGENS
TRYPSINS
TRYPTAMINE
TRYPTAMINES
TRYPTIC
TRYPTOPHAN
TRYPTOPHANE
TRYPTOPHANES
TRYPTOPHANS
TRYSAIL
TRYSAILS
TRYST
TRYSTE
TRYSTED
TRYSTER
TRYSTERS
TRYSTES
TRYSTING
TRYSTS
TRYWORKS
TSADDIK
TSADDIKIM
TSADE
TSADES
TSADI
TSADIS
TSAR
TSARDOM
TSARDOMS
TSAREVITCH
TSAREVITCHES
TSAREVNA
TSAREVNAS
TSARINA
TSARINAS
TSARISM
TSARISMS
TSARIST
TSARISTS
TSARITZA
TSARITZAS
TSARS
TSATSKE
TSATSKES
TSETSE
TSETSES
TSIMMES
TSK
TSKED
TSKING
TSKS
TSKTSK
TSKTSKED
TSKTSKING
TSKTSKS
TSOORIS
TSORES
TSORIS
TSORRISS
TSOTSI
TSOTSIS
TSOURIS
TSUBA
TSUBAS
TSUBO
TSUBOS
TSUNAMI
TSUNAMIC
TSUNAMIS
TSURIS
TSURISES
TSUTSUGAMUSHI
TSUTSUGAMUSHIS
TUATARA
TUATARAS
TUATERA
TUATERAS
TUB
TUBA
TUBAE
TUBAIST
TUBAISTS
TUBAL
TUBAS
TUBATE
TUBBABLE
TUBBED
TUBBER
TUBBERS
TUBBIER
TUBBIEST
TUBBINESS
TUBBINESSES
TUBBING
TUBBY
TUBE
TUBED
TUBELESS
TUBELIKE
TUBENOSE
TUBENOSES
TUBER
TUBERCLE
TUBERCLES
TUBERCULAR
TUBERCULARS
TUBERCULATE
TUBERCULATED
TUBERCULIN
TUBERCULINS
TUBERCULOID
TUBERCULOSES
TUBERCULOSIS
TUBERCULOUS
TUBEROID
TUBEROSE
TUBEROSES
TUBEROSITIES
TUBEROSITY
TUBEROUS
TUBERS
TUBES
TUBEWELL
TUBEWELLS
TUBEWORK
TUBEWORKS
TUBEWORM
TUBEWORMS
TUBFUL
TUBFULS
TUBIFEX
TUBIFEXES
TUBIFICID
TUBIFICIDS
TUBIFORM
TUBING
TUBINGS
TUBIST

BISTS
BLIKE
BOCURARINE
BOCURARINES
BS
BULAR
BULARLY
BULARS
BULATE
BULATED
BULATES
BULATING
BULATOR
BULATORS
BULE
BULES
BULIN
BULINS
BULOSE
BULOUS
BULURE
BULURES
CHIS
CHISES
CHUN
CHUNS
CHUS
CHUSES
CK
CKAHOE
CKAHOES
CKED
CKER
CKERED
CKERING
CKERS
CKET
CKETS
KING
KINGS
KS
KSHOP
KSHOPS
A
ACEOUS
AS
F
FACEOUS
FET
FETS
FS
OLI
T

TUFTED
TUFTER
TUFTERS
TUFTIER
TUFTIEST
TUFTILY
TUFTING
TUFTINGS
TUFTS
TUFTY
TUG
TUGBOAT
TUGBOATS
TUGGED
TUGGER
TUGGERS
TUGGING
TUGHRIK
TUGHRIKS
TUGLESS
TUGRIK
TUGRIKS
TUGS
TUI
TUILE
TUILES
TUILLE
TUILLES
TUIS
TUITION
TUITIONAL
TUITIONS
TULADI
TULADIS
TULAREMIA
TULAREMIAS
TULAREMIC
TULE
TULES
TULIP
TULIPLIKE
TULIPS
TULIPWOOD
TULIPWOODS
TULLE
TULLES
TULLIBEE
TULLIBEES
TULSI
TULSIS
TUM
TUMBLE
TUMBLEBUG

TUMBLEBUGS
TUMBLED
TUMBLEDOWN
TUMBLER
TUMBLERFUL
TUMBLERFULS
TUMBLERS
TUMBLERSFUL
TUMBLES
TUMBLESET
TUMBLESETS
TUMBLEWEED
TUMBLEWEEDS
TUMBLING
TUMBLINGS
TUMBREL
TUMBRELS
TUMBRIL
TUMBRILS
TUMEFACTION
TUMEFACTIONS
TUMEFIED
TUMEFIES
TUMEFY
TUMEFYING
TUMESCE
TUMESCED
TUMESCENCE
TUMESCENCES
TUMESCENT
TUMESCES
TUMESCING
TUMID
TUMIDITIES
TUMIDITY
TUMIDLY
TUMIDNESS
TUMIDNESSES
TUMMIES
TUMMLER
TUMMLERS
TUMMY
TUMOR
TUMORAL
TUMORIGENESES
TUMORIGENESIS
TUMORIGENIC
TUMORIGENICITY
TUMORLIKE
TUMOROUS
TUMORS
TUMOUR
TUMOURS

TUMP
TUMPED
TUMPING
TUMPLINE
TUMPLINES
TUMPS
TUMS
TUMULAR
TUMULI
TUMULOSE
TUMULOUS
TUMULT
TUMULTS
TUMULTUARY
TUMULTUOUS
TUMULTUOUSLY
TUMULTUOUSNESS
TUMULUS
TUMULUSES
TUN
TUNA
TUNABILITIES
TUNABILITY
TUNABLE
TUNABLENESS
TUNABLENESSES
TUNABLY
TUNAS
TUNDISH
TUNDISHES
TUNDRA
TUNDRAS
TUNE
TUNEABLE
TUNEABLY
TUNED
TUNEFUL
TUNEFULLY
TUNEFULNESS
TUNEFULNESSES
TUNELESS
TUNELESSLY
TUNELESSNESS
TUNELESSNESSES
TUNER
TUNERS
TUNES
TUNESMITH
TUNESMITHS
TUNEUP
TUNEUPS
TUNG
TUNGS

TUNGSTATE
TUNGSTATES
TUNGSTEN
TUNGSTENS
TUNGSTIC
TUNGSTITE
TUNGSTITES
TUNIC
TUNICA
TUNICAE
TUNICATE
TUNICATED
TUNICATES
TUNICLE
TUNICLES
TUNICS
TUNING
TUNINGS
TUNKET
TUNKETS
TUNNAGE
TUNNAGES
TUNNED
TUNNEL
TUNNELED
TUNNELER
TUNNELERS
TUNNELING
TUNNELINGS
TUNNELLED
TUNNELLER
TUNNELLERS
TUNNELLIKE
TUNNELLING
TUNNELS
TUNNIES
TUNNING
TUNNY
TUNS
TUP
TUPELO
TUPELOS
TUPIK
TUPIKS
TUPPED
TUPPENCE
TUPPENCES
TUPPENNY
TUPPING
TUPPINGS
TUPS
TUQUE
TUQUES

TURACO
TURACOS
TURACOU
TURACOUS
TURBAN
TURBANED
TURBANNED
TURBANS
TURBARIES
TURBARY
TURBELLARIAN
TURBELLARIANS
TURBETH
TURBETHS
TURBID
TURBIDIMETER
TURBIDIMETERS
TURBIDIMETRIC
TURBIDIMETRIES
TURBIDIMETRY
TURBIDITE
TURBIDITES
TURBIDITIES
TURBIDITY
TURBIDLY
TURBIDNESS
TURBIDNESSES
TURBINAL
TURBINALS
TURBINATE
TURBINATED
TURBINATES
TURBINE
TURBINES
TURBIT
TURBITH
TURBITHS
TURBITS
TURBO
TURBOCAR
TURBOCARS
TURBOCHARGED
TURBOCHARGER
TURBOCHARGERS
TURBOELECTRIC
TURBOFAN
TURBOFANS
TURBOGENERATOR
TURBOGENERATORS
TURBOJET
TURBOJETS
TURBOMACHINERY
TURBOPROP
TURBOPROPS
TURBOS
TURBOSHAFT
TURBOSHAFTS
TURBOT
TURBOTS
TURBULENCE
TURBULENCES
TURBULENCIES
TURBULENCY
TURBULENT
TURBULENTLY
TURD
TURDINE
TURDS
TURDUCKEN
TURDUCKENS
TUREEN
TUREENS
TURF
TURFED
TURFGRASS
TURFGRASSES
TURFIER
TURFIEST
TURFING
TURFLESS
TURFLIKE
TURFMAN
TURFMEN
TURFS
TURFSKI
TURFSKIING
TURFSKIINGS
TURFSKIS
TURFY
TURGENCIES
TURGENCY
TURGENT
TURGESCENCE
TURGESCENCES
TURGESCENT
TURGID
TURGIDITIES
TURGIDITY
TURGIDLY
TURGIDNESS
TURGIDNESSES
TURGITE
TURGITES
TURGOR
TURGORS
TURION
TURIONS
TURISTA
TURISTAS
TURK
TURKEY
TURKEYS
TURKOIS
TURKOISES
TURKS
TURMERIC
TURMERICS
TURMOIL
TURMOILED
TURMOILING
TURMOILS
TURN
TURNABLE
TURNABOUT
TURNABOUTS
TURNAROUND
TURNAROUNDS
TURNBUCKLE
TURNBUCKLES
TURNCOAT
TURNCOATS
TURNCOCK
TURNCOCKS
TURNDOWN
TURNDOWNS
TURNED
TURNER
TURNERIES
TURNERS
TURNERY
TURNHALL
TURNHALLS
TURNING
TURNINGS
TURNIP
TURNIPIER
TURNIPIEST
TURNIPS
TURNIPY
TURNKEY
TURNKEYS
TURNOFF
TURNOFFS
TURNON
TURNONS
TURNOUT
TURNOUTS
TURNOVER
TURNOVERS
TURNPIKE
TURNPIKES
TURNROUND
TURNROUNDS
TURNS
TURNSOLE
TURNSOLES
TURNSPIT
TURNSPITS
TURNSTILE
TURNSTILES
TURNSTONE
TURNSTONES
TURNTABLE
TURNTABLES
TURNUP
TURNUPS
TURNVEREIN
TURNVEREINS
TUROPHILE
TUROPHILES
TURPENTINE
TURPENTINED
TURPENTINES
TURPENTINING
TURPETH
TURPETHS
TURPITUDE
TURPITUDES
TURPS
TURPSES
TURQUOIS
TURQUOISE
TURQUOISES
TURR
TURRET
TURRETED
TURRETS
TURRICAL
TURRS
TURTLE
TURTLEBACK
TURTLEBACKS
TURTLED
TURTLEDOVE
TURTLEDOVES
TURTLEHEAD
TURTLEHEADS
TURTLENECK
TURTLENECKED
TURTLENECKS
TURTLER
TURTLERS
TURTLES
TURTLING
TURTLINGS
TURVES
TUSCHE
TUSCHES
TUSH
TUSHED
TUSHERIES
TUSHERY
TUSHES
TUSHIE
TUSHIES
TUSHING
TUSHY
TUSK
TUSKED
TUSKER
TUSKERS
TUSKIER
TUSKIEST
TUSKING
TUSKLESS
TUSKLIKE
TUSKS
TUSKY
TUSSAH
TUSSAHS
TUSSAL
TUSSAR
TUSSARS
TUSSEH
TUSSEHS
TUSSER
TUSSERS
TUSSES
TUSSIS
TUSSISES
TUSSIVE
TUSSLE
TUSSLED
TUSSLES
TUSSLING
TUSSOCK
TUSSOCKED
TUSSOCKS
TUSSOCKY
TUSSOR
TUSSORE
TUSSORES
TUSSORS
TUSSUCK
TUSSUCKS

SSUR
SSURS
T
TEE
TEES
TELAGE
TELAGES
TELAR
TELARIES
TELARS
TELARY
TOR
TORAGE
TORAGES
TORED
TORESS
TORESSES
TORIAL
TORIALS
TORING
TORS
TORSHIP
TORSHIPS
TOYED
TOYER
TOYERED
TOYERING
TOYERS
TS
TTED
TI
TTIES
TTING
TTIS
TTY
TU
TUED
TUS
KEDO
KEDOED
KEDOES
KEDOS
KES
ER
ERE
ERES
ERS
ADDLE
ADDLED
ADDLER
ADDLERS

TWADDLES
TWADDLING
TWAE
TWAES
TWAIN
TWAINS
TWANG
TWANGED
TWANGER
TWANGERS
TWANGIER
TWANGIEST
TWANGING
TWANGLE
TWANGLED
TWANGLER
TWANGLERS
TWANGLES
TWANGLING
TWANGS
TWANGY
TWANKIES
TWANKY
TWAS
TWASOME
TWASOMES
TWAT
TWATS
TWATTLE
TWATTLED
TWATTLES
TWATTLING
TWAYBLADE
TWAYBLADES
TWEAK
TWEAKED
TWEAKIER
TWEAKIEST
TWEAKING
TWEAKS
TWEAKY
TWEE
TWEED
TWEEDIER
TWEEDIEST
TWEEDILY
TWEEDINESS
TWEEDINESSES
TWEEDLE
TWEEDLED
TWEEDLES
TWEEDLING
TWEEDS

TWEEDY
TWEEN
TWEENER
TWEENERS
TWEENESS
TWEENESSES
TWEENIE
TWEENIES
TWEENS
TWEENY
TWEEP
TWEEPS
TWEER
TWEEST
TWEET
TWEETED
TWEETER
TWEETERS
TWEETING
TWEETS
TWEEZE
TWEEZED
TWEEZER
TWEEZERS
TWEEZES
TWEEZING
TWELFTH
TWELFTHS
TWELVE
TWELVEMO
TWELVEMONTH
TWELVEMONTHS
TWELVEMOS
TWELVES
TWENTIES
TWENTIETH
TWENTIETHS
TWENTY
TWENTYSOMETHING
TWERP
TWERPIER
TWERPIEST
TWERPS
TWERPY
TWIBIL
TWIBILL
TWIBILLS
TWIBILS
TWICE
TWIDDLE
TWIDDLED
TWIDDLER
TWIDDLERS

TWIDDLES
TWIDDLIER
TWIDDLIEST
TWIDDLING
TWIDDLY
TWIER
TWIERS
TWIG
TWIGGED
TWIGGEN
TWIGGIER
TWIGGIEST
TWIGGING
TWIGGY
TWIGLESS
TWIGLIKE
TWIGS
TWILIGHT
TWILIGHTS
TWILIT
TWILL
TWILLED
TWILLING
TWILLINGS
TWILLS
TWIN
TWINBERRIES
TWINBERRY
TWINBORN
TWINE
TWINED
TWINER
TWINERS
TWINES
TWINFLOWER
TWINFLOWERS
TWINGE
TWINGED
TWINGEING
TWINGES
TWINGING
TWINIER
TWINIEST
TWINIGHT
TWINING
TWINJET
TWINJETS
TWINK
TWINKIE
TWINKIES
TWINKLE
TWINKLED
TWINKLER

TWINKLERS
TWINKLES
TWINKLIER
TWINKLIEST
TWINKLING
TWINKLINGS
TWINKLY
TWINKS
TWINKY
TWINNED
TWINNING
TWINNINGS
TWINS
TWINSET
TWINSETS
TWINSHIP
TWINSHIPS
TWINY
TWIRL
TWIRLED
TWIRLER
TWIRLERS
TWIRLIER
TWIRLIEST
TWIRLING
TWIRLS
TWIRLY
TWIRP
TWIRPS
TWIST
TWISTABLE
TWISTED
TWISTER
TWISTERS
TWISTIER
TWISTIEST
TWISTING
TWISTINGS
TWISTOR
TWISTORS
TWISTS
TWISTY
TWIT
TWITCH
TWITCHED
TWITCHER
TWITCHERS
TWITCHES
TWITCHIER
TWITCHIEST
TWITCHILY
TWITCHING
TWITCHY

TWITS
TWITTED
TWITTER
TWITTERED
TWITTERER
TWITTERERS
TWITTERING
TWITTERS
TWITTERY
TWITTING
TWITTISH
TWIXT
TWIZZLE
TWIZZLES
TWO
TWOFER
TWOFERS
TWOFOLD
TWOFOLDS
TWONESS
TWONESSES
TWOONIE
TWOONIES
TWOPENCE
TWOPENCES
TWOPENNY
TWOS
TWOSOME
TWOSOMES
TWYER
TWYERS
TYCHISM
TYCHISMS
TYCOON
TYCOONS
TYE
TYEE
TYEES
TYER
TYERS
TYES
TYIN
TYING
TYIYN
TYKE
TYKES
TYLOSIN
TYLOSINS
TYMBAL
TYMBALS
TYMPAN
TYMPANA
TYMPANAL
TYMPANI
TYMPANIC
TYMPANIES
TYMPANIST
TYMPANISTS
TYMPANITES
TYMPANITESES
TYMPANITIC
TYMPANO
TYMPANS
TYMPANUM
TYMPANUMS
TYMPANY
TYNE
TYNED
TYNES
TYNING
TYPABLE
TYPAL
TYPE
TYPEABLE
TYPEBAR
TYPEBARS
TYPECASE
TYPECASES
TYPECAST
TYPECASTING
TYPECASTS
TYPED
TYPEFACE
TYPEFACES
TYPEFOUNDER
TYPEFOUNDERS
TYPEFOUNDING
TYPEFOUNDINGS
TYPES
TYPESCRIPT
TYPESCRIPTS
TYPESET
TYPESETS
TYPESETTER
TYPESETTERS
TYPESETTING
TYPESETTINGS
TYPESTYLE
TYPESTYLES
TYPEWRITE
TYPEWRITER
TYPEWRITERS
TYPEWRITES
TYPEWRITING
TYPEWRITINGS
TYPEWRITTEN
TYPEWROTE
TYPEY
TYPHLITIC
TYPHLITIS
TYPHLITISES
TYPHLOSOLE
TYPHLOSOLES
TYPHOID
TYPHOIDAL
TYPHOIDS
TYPHON
TYPHONIC
TYPHONS
TYPHOON
TYPHOONS
TYPHOSE
TYPHOUS
TYPHUS
TYPHUSES
TYPIC
TYPICAL
TYPICALITIES
TYPICALITY
TYPICALLY
TYPICALNESS
TYPICALNESSES
TYPIER
TYPIEST
TYPIFICATION
TYPIFICATIONS
TYPIFIED
TYPIFIER
TYPIFIERS
TYPIFIES
TYPIFY
TYPIFYING
TYPING
TYPINGS
TYPIST
TYPISTS
TYPO
TYPOGRAPH
TYPOGRAPHED
TYPOGRAPHER
TYPOGRAPHERS
TYPOGRAPHIC
TYPOGRAPHICAL
TYPOGRAPHICALLY
TYPOGRAPHIES
TYPOGRAPHING
TYPOGRAPHS
TYPOGRAPHY
TYPOLOGIC
TYPOLOGICAL
TYPOLOGICALLY
TYPOLOGIES
TYPOLOGIST
TYPOLOGISTS
TYPOLOGY
TYPOS
TYPP
TYPPS
TYPY
TYRAMINE
TYRAMINES
TYRANNIC
TYRANNICAL
TYRANNICALLY
TYRANNICALNESS
TYRANNICIDE
TYRANNICIDES
TYRANNIES
TYRANNISE
TYRANNISED
TYRANNISES
TYRANNISING
TYRANNIZE
TYRANNIZED
TYRANNIZER
TYRANNIZERS
TYRANNIZES
TYRANNIZING
TYRANNOSAUR
TYRANNOSAURID
TYRANNOSAURIDS
TYRANNOSAURS
TYRANNOSAURUS
TYRANNOSAURUSES
TYRANNOUS
TYRANNOUSLY
TYRANNY
TYRANT
TYRANTS
TYRE
TYRED
TYRES
TYRING
TYRO
TYROCIDIN
TYROCIDINE
TYROCIDINES
TYROCIDINS
TYRONIC
TYROPITA
TYROPITAS
TYROS
TYROSINASE
TYROSINASES
TYROSINE
TYROSINES
TYROTHRICIN
TYROTHRICINS
TYTHE
TYTHED
TYTHES
TYTHING
TZADDIK
TZADDIKIM
TZAR
TZARDOM
TZARDOMS
TZAREVITCH
TZAREVITCHES
TZAREVNA
TZAREVNAS
TZARINA
TZARINAS
TZARISM
TZARISMS
TZARIST
TZARISTS
TZARITZA
TZARITZAS
TZARS
TZATZIKI
TZATZIKIS
TZEDAKAH
TZEDAKAHS
TZETZE
TZETZES
TZIGANE
TZIGANES
TZIMMES
TZITZIS
TZITZIT
TZITZITH
TZURIS
TZURISES

U

KARI
KARIS
IETIES
IETY
IQUE
IQUINONE
IQUINONES
IQUITIES
IQUITOUS
IQUITOUSLY
IQUITOUSNESS
IQUITY
DER
DERED
DERS
O
OMETER
OMETERS
OMETRIES
OMETRY
ON
ONS
OS
OLOGICAL
OLOGIES
OLOGIST
OLOGISTS
OLOGY
H
HS
LIER
LIES
LIEST
LIFICATION
LIFICATIONS
LIFIED
LIFIER
LIFIERS
LIFIES
LIFY
LIFYING
LILY
LINESS
LINESSES
LY
SOME
LAN
LANS
TAHITE
TAHITES
TAITE

UINTAITES
UITLANDER
UITLANDERS
UKASE
UKASES
UKE
UKELELE
UKELELES
UKES
UKULELE
UKULELES
ULAMA
ULAMAS
ULAN
ULANS
ULCER
ULCERATE
ULCERATED
ULCERATES
ULCERATING
ULCERATION
ULCERATIONS
ULCERATIVE
ULCERED
ULCERING
ULCEROGENIC
ULCEROUS
ULCERS
ULEMA
ULEMAS
ULEXITE
ULEXITES
ULLAGE
ULLAGED
ULLAGES
ULNA
ULNAD
ULNAE
ULNAR
ULNAS
ULPAN
ULPANIM
ULSTER
ULSTERS
ULTERIOR
ULTERIORLY
ULTIMA
ULTIMACIES
ULTIMACY
ULTIMAS
ULTIMATA
ULTIMATE

ULTIMATED
ULTIMATELY
ULTIMATENESS
ULTIMATENESSES
ULTIMATES
ULTIMATING
ULTIMATUM
ULTIMATUMS
ULTIMO
ULTIMOGENITURE
ULTIMOGENITURES
ULTISOL
ULTISOLS
ULTRA
ULTRABASIC
ULTRABASICS
ULTRABRIGHT
ULTRACAREFUL
ULTRACASUAL
ULTRACAUTIOUS
ULTRACENTRIFUGE
ULTRACHEAP
ULTRACHIC
ULTRACIVILIZED
ULTRACLEAN
ULTRACOLD
ULTRACOMMERCIAL
ULTRACOMPACT
ULTRACOMPETENT
ULTRACONVENIENT
ULTRACOOL
ULTRACRITICAL
ULTRADEMOCRATIC
ULTRADENSE
ULTRADISTANCE
ULTRADISTANT
ULTRADRY
ULTRAEFFICIENT
ULTRAENERGETIC
ULTRAEXCLUSIVE
ULTRAEXPENSIVE
ULTRAFAMILIAR
ULTRAFAST
ULTRAFASTIDIOUS
ULTRAFEMININE
ULTRAFICHE
ULTRAFICHES
ULTRAFILTRATE
ULTRAFILTRATES
ULTRAFILTRATION
ULTRAFINE
ULTRAGLAMOROUS

ULTRAHAZARDOUS
ULTRAHEAT
ULTRAHEATED
ULTRAHEATING
ULTRAHEATS
ULTRAHEAVY
ULTRAHIGH
ULTRAHIP
ULTRAHOT
ULTRAHUMAN
ULTRAISM
ULTRAISMS
ULTRAIST
ULTRAISTIC
ULTRAISTS
ULTRALEFT
ULTRALEFTISM
ULTRALEFTISMS
ULTRALEFTIST
ULTRALEFTISTS
ULTRALIBERAL
ULTRALIBERALISM
ULTRALIBERALS
ULTRALIGHT
ULTRALIGHTS
ULTRALOW
ULTRALUMINOUS
ULTRAMAFIC
ULTRAMARATHON
ULTRAMARATHONER
ULTRAMARATHONS
ULTRAMARINE
ULTRAMARINES
ULTRAMASCULINE
ULTRAMICRO
ULTRAMICROSCOPE
ULTRAMICROTOME
ULTRAMICROTOMES
ULTRAMICROTOMY
ULTRAMILITANT
ULTRAMILITANTS
ULTRAMINIATURE
ULTRAMODERN
ULTRAMODERNIST
ULTRAMODERNISTS
ULTRAMONTANE
ULTRAMONTANES
ULTRAMONTANISM
ULTRAMONTANISMS
ULTRAORTHODOX
ULTRAPATRIOTIC
ULTRAPHYSICAL

ULTRAPOSH
ULTRAPOWERFUL
ULTRAPRACTICAL
ULTRAPRECISE
ULTRAPRECISION
ULTRAPURE
ULTRAQUIET
ULTRARADICAL
ULTRARADICALS
ULTRARAPID
ULTRARARE
ULTRARAREFIED
ULTRARATIONAL
ULTRAREALISM
ULTRAREALISMS
ULTRAREALIST
ULTRAREALISTIC
ULTRAREALISTS
ULTRARED
ULTRAREDS
ULTRAREFINED
ULTRARELIABLE
ULTRARELIGIOUS
ULTRARICH
ULTRARIGHT
ULTRARIGHTIST
ULTRARIGHTISTS
ULTRAROMANTIC
ULTRAROMANTICS
ULTRAROYALIST
ULTRAROYALISTS
ULTRAS
ULTRASAFE
ULTRASECRET
ULTRASENSITIVE
ULTRASERIOUS
ULTRASHARP
ULTRASHORT
ULTRASIMPLE
ULTRASLICK
ULTRASLOW
ULTRASMALL
ULTRASMART
ULTRASMOOTH
ULTRASOFT
ULTRASONIC
ULTRASONICALLY
ULTRASONICS
ULTRASONOGRAPHY
ULTRASOUND
ULTRASOUNDS
ULTRASTRUCTURAL

ULTRASTRUCTURE
ULTRASTRUCTURES
ULTRATHIN
ULTRATINY
ULTRAVACUA
ULTRAVACUUM
ULTRAVACUUMS
ULTRAVIOLENCE
ULTRAVIOLENCES
ULTRAVIOLENT
ULTRAVIOLET
ULTRAVIOLETS
ULTRAVIRILE
ULTRAVIRILITIES
ULTRAVIRILITY
ULTRAWIDE
ULU
ULULANT
ULULATE
ULULATED
ULULATES
ULULATING
ULULATION
ULULATIONS
ULUS
ULVA
ULVAS
UM
UMAMI
UMAMIS
UMANGITE
UMANGITES
UMBEL
UMBELED
UMBELLAR
UMBELLATE
UMBELLED
UMBELLET
UMBELLETS
UMBELLIFER
UMBELLIFEROUS
UMBELLIFERS
UMBELLULE
UMBELLULES
UMBELS
UMBELULE
UMBELULES
UMBER
UMBERED
UMBERING
UMBERS
UMBILICAL
UMBILICALS

UMBILICATE
UMBILICATED
UMBILICATION
UMBILICATIONS
UMBILICI
UMBILICUS
UMBILICUSES
UMBLES
UMBO
UMBONAL
UMBONATE
UMBONES
UMBONIC
UMBOS
UMBRA
UMBRAE
UMBRAGE
UMBRAGEOUS
UMBRAGEOUSLY
UMBRAGEOUSNESS
UMBRAGES
UMBRAL
UMBRAS
UMBRELLA
UMBRELLAED
UMBRELLAING
UMBRELLAS
UMBRETTE
UMBRETTES
UMIAC
UMIACK
UMIACKS
UMIACS
UMIAK
UMIAKS
UMIAQ
UMIAQS
UMLAUT
UMLAUTED
UMLAUTING
UMLAUTS
UMM
UMMA
UMMAH
UMMAHS
UMMAS
UMMED
UMMING
UMP
UMPED
UMPH
UMPHS
UMPING

UMPIRAGE
UMPIRAGES
UMPIRE
UMPIRED
UMPIRES
UMPIRING
UMPS
UMPTEEN
UMPTEENTH
UMPTIER
UMPTIEST
UMPTY
UMS
UMTEENTH
UN
UNABASHED
UNABASHEDLY
UNABATED
UNABATEDLY
UNABATING
UNABETTED
UNABIDING
UNABJURED
UNABLE
UNABORTED
UNABRADED
UNABRIDGED
UNABSORBED
UNABSORBENT
UNABUSED
UNABUSIVE
UNACADEMIC
UNACADEMICALLY
UNACCENTED
UNACCEPTABILITY
UNACCEPTABLE
UNACCEPTABLY
UNACCEPTED
UNACCLIMATED
UNACCLIMATIZED
UNACCOMMODATED
UNACCOMMODATING
UNACCOMPANIED
UNACCOUNTABLE
UNACCOUNTABLY
UNACCOUNTED
UNACCREDITED
UNACCRUED
UNACCULTURATED
UNACCUSTOMED
UNACCUSTOMEDLY
UNACERBIC
UNACHIEVED

UNACIDIC
UNACKNOWLEDGED
UNACQUAINTED
UNACTABLE
UNACTED
UNACTORISH
UNADAPTABLE
UNADAPTED
UNADDED
UNADDRESSED
UNADEPT
UNADEPTLY
UNADJUDICATED
UNADJUSTED
UNADMIRED
UNADMITTED
UNADOPTABLE
UNADOPTED
UNADORNED
UNADULT
UNADULTERATED
UNADULTERATEDLY
UNADVENTUROUS
UNADVERTISED
UNADVISED
UNADVISEDLY
UNAESTHETIC
UNAFFECTED
UNAFFECTEDLY
UNAFFECTEDNESS
UNAFFECTING
UNAFFECTIONATE
UNAFFILIATED
UNAFFLUENT
UNAFFORDABLE
UNAFRAID
UNAGED
UNAGEING
UNAGGRESSIVE
UNAGILE
UNAGING
UNAGREED
UNAI
UNAIDED
UNAIDEDLY
UNAIMED
UNAIRED
UNAIS
UNAKIN
UNAKITE
UNAKITES
UNALARMED
UNALERTED

UNALIENABLE
UNALIENATED
UNALIGNED
UNALIKE
UNALLAYED
UNALLEGED
UNALLEVIATED
UNALLIED
UNALLOCATED
UNALLOWED
UNALLOYED
UNALLURING
UNALTERABILITY
UNALTERABLE
UNALTERABLENESS
UNALTERABLY
UNALTERED
UNAMASSED
UNAMAZED
UNAMBIGUOUS
UNAMBIGUOUSLY
UNAMBITIOUS
UNAMBIVALENT
UNAMBIVALENTLY
UNAMENABLE
UNAMENDED
UNAMIABLE
UNAMORTIZED
UNAMPLIFIED
UNAMUSED
UNAMUSING
UNANALYZABLE
UNANALYZED
UNANCHOR
UNANCHORED
UNANCHORING
UNANCHORS
UNANELED
UNANESTHETIZED
UNANIMITIES
UNANIMITY
UNANIMOUS
UNANIMOUSLY
UNANNEXED
UNANNOTATED
UNANNOUNCED
UNANNOYED
UNANSWERABILITY
UNANSWERABLE
UNANSWERABLY
UNANSWERED
UNANTICIPATED
UNANTICIPATEDLY

APOLOGETIC
APOLOGIZING
APPARENT
APPEALABLE
APPEALING
APPEALINGLY
APPEASABLE
APPEASABLY
APPEASED
APPETISING
APPETIZING
APPETIZINGLY
APPLIED
APPRECIATED
APPRECIATION
APPRECIATIONS
APPRECIATIVE
APPROACHABLE
APPROACHABLY
APPROPRIATED
APPROVED
APT
APTLY
APTNESS
APTNESSES
ARCHED
ARGUABLE
ARGUABLY
ARGUED
ARM
ARMED
ARMING
ARMORED
ARMS
AROUSED
ARRAYED
ARROGANT
ARTFUL
ARTICULATED
ARTISTIC
ARY
ASHAMED
ASHAMEDLY
ASKED
ASPIRATED
ASSAILABILITY
ASSAILABLE
ASSAILABLY
ASSAILED
ASSAYED
ASSEMBLED
ASSERTIVE
ASSERTIVELY
UNASSIGNED
UNASSIMILABLE
UNASSIMILATED
UNASSISTED
UNASSOCIATED
UNASSUAGEABLE
UNASSUAGED
UNASSUMING
UNASSUMINGLY
UNASSUMINGNESS
UNASSURED
UNATHLETIC
UNATONED
UNATTACHED
UNATTAINABLE
UNATTENDED
UNATTENUATED
UNATTESTED
UNATTIRED
UNATTRACTIVE
UNATTRACTIVELY
UNATTRIBUTABLE
UNATTRIBUTED
UNATTUNED
UNAU
UNAUDITED
UNAUS
UNAUTHENTIC
UNAUTHORISED
UNAUTHORIZED
UNAUTOMATED
UNAVAILABILITY
UNAVAILABLE
UNAVAILING
UNAVAILINGLY
UNAVAILINGNESS
UNAVENGED
UNAVERAGE
UNAVERTED
UNAVOIDABLE
UNAVOIDABLY
UNAVOWED
UNAWAKE
UNAWAKED
UNAWAKENED
UNAWARDED
UNAWARE
UNAWARELY
UNAWARENESS
UNAWARENESSES
UNAWARES
UNAWED
UNAWESOME
UNAXED
UNBACKED
UNBAKED
UNBALANCE
UNBALANCED
UNBALANCES
UNBALANCING
UNBALE
UNBALED
UNBALES
UNBALING
UNBALLASTED
UNBAN
UNBANDAGE
UNBANDAGED
UNBANDAGES
UNBANDAGING
UNBANDED
UNBANNED
UNBANNING
UNBANS
UNBAPTIZED
UNBAR
UNBARBED
UNBARBERED
UNBARRED
UNBARRICADED
UNBARRING
UNBARS
UNBASED
UNBASTED
UNBATED
UNBATHED
UNBE
UNBEAR
UNBEARABLE
UNBEARABLY
UNBEARDED
UNBEARED
UNBEARING
UNBEARS
UNBEATABLE
UNBEATABLY
UNBEATEN
UNBEAUTIFUL
UNBEAUTIFULLY
UNBECOMING
UNBECOMINGLY
UNBECOMINGNESS
UNBEHOLDEN
UNBEING
UNBEKNOWN
UNBEKNOWNST
UNBELIEF
UNBELIEFS
UNBELIEVABLE
UNBELIEVABLY
UNBELIEVER
UNBELIEVERS
UNBELIEVING
UNBELIEVINGLY
UNBELLIGERENT
UNBELOVED
UNBELT
UNBELTED
UNBELTING
UNBELTS
UNBEMUSED
UNBEND
UNBENDABLE
UNBENDED
UNBENDING
UNBENDINGS
UNBENDS
UNBENIGN
UNBENT
UNBESEEMING
UNBIASED
UNBIASEDNESS
UNBIASEDNESSES
UNBIASSED
UNBIBLICAL
UNBID
UNBIDDEN
UNBIGOTED
UNBILLED
UNBIND
UNBINDING
UNBINDS
UNBITTED
UNBITTEN
UNBITTER
UNBLAMED
UNBLEACHED
UNBLEMISHED
UNBLENCHED
UNBLENDED
UNBLESSED
UNBLEST
UNBLIND
UNBLINDED
UNBLINDING
UNBLINDS
UNBLINKERED
UNBLINKING
UNBLINKINGLY
UNBLOCK
UNBLOCKED
UNBLOCKING
UNBLOCKS
UNBLOODED
UNBLOODY
UNBLURRED
UNBLUSHING
UNBLUSHINGLY
UNBOARDED
UNBOBBED
UNBODIED
UNBOILED
UNBOLT
UNBOLTED
UNBOLTING
UNBOLTS
UNBONDED
UNBONED
UNBONNET
UNBONNETED
UNBONNETING
UNBONNETS
UNBOOKISH
UNBOOTED
UNBORN
UNBOSOM
UNBOSOMED
UNBOSOMER
UNBOSOMERS
UNBOSOMING
UNBOSOMS
UNBOTTLE
UNBOTTLED
UNBOTTLES
UNBOTTLING
UNBOUGHT
UNBOUNCY
UNBOUND
UNBOUNDED
UNBOUNDEDNESS
UNBOUNDEDNESSES
UNBOWDLERIZED
UNBOWED
UNBOWING
UNBOX
UNBOXED
UNBOXES
UNBOXING
UNBRACE
UNBRACED
UNBRACES
UNBRACING

UNBRACKETED
UNBRAID
UNBRAIDED
UNBRAIDING
UNBRAIDS
UNBRAKE
UNBRAKED
UNBRAKES
UNBRAKING
UNBRANCHED
UNBRANDED
UNBREACHABLE
UNBREAKABLE
UNBREAKABLES
UNBREATHABLE
UNBRED
UNBREECH
UNBREECHED
UNBREECHES
UNBREECHING
UNBRIDGEABLE
UNBRIDGED
UNBRIDLE
UNBRIDLED
UNBRIDLES
UNBRIDLING
UNBRIEFED
UNBRIGHT
UNBRILLIANT
UNBROILED
UNBROKE
UNBROKEN
UNBROWNED
UNBRUISED
UNBRUSHED
UNBUCKLE
UNBUCKLED
UNBUCKLES
UNBUCKLING
UNBUDGEABLE
UNBUDGEABLY
UNBUDGETED
UNBUDGING
UNBUDGINGLY
UNBUFFERED
UNBUILD
UNBUILDABLE
UNBUILDING
UNBUILDS
UNBUILT
UNBULKY
UNBUNDLE
UNBUNDLED
UNBUNDLES
UNBUNDLING
UNBURDEN
UNBURDENED
UNBURDENING
UNBURDENS
UNBUREAUCRATIC
UNBURIED
UNBURIES
UNBURNABLE
UNBURNED
UNBURNT
UNBURY
UNBURYING
UNBUSINESSLIKE
UNBUSTED
UNBUSY
UNBUTTERED
UNBUTTON
UNBUTTONED
UNBUTTONING
UNBUTTONS
UNCAGE
UNCAGED
UNCAGES
UNCAGING
UNCAKE
UNCAKED
UNCAKES
UNCAKING
UNCALCIFIED
UNCALCINED
UNCALCULATED
UNCALCULATING
UNCALIBRATED
UNCALLED
UNCALLOUSED
UNCANCELED
UNCANDID
UNCANDIDLY
UNCANDLED
UNCANNED
UNCANNIER
UNCANNIEST
UNCANNILY
UNCANNINESS
UNCANNINESSES
UNCANNY
UNCANONICAL
UNCAP
UNCAPABLE
UNCAPITALIZED
UNCAPPED
UNCAPPING
UNCAPS
UNCAPTIONED
UNCAPTURABLE
UNCARDED
UNCARED
UNCARING
UNCARPETED
UNCARTED
UNCARVED
UNCASE
UNCASED
UNCASES
UNCASHED
UNCASING
UNCASKED
UNCAST
UNCASTRATED
UNCATALOGED
UNCATCHABLE
UNCATCHABLES
UNCATCHY
UNCATEGORIZABLE
UNCATERED
UNCAUGHT
UNCAUSED
UNCEASING
UNCEASINGLY
UNCEDED
UNCELEBRATED
UNCENSORED
UNCENSORIOUS
UNCENSURED
UNCEREMONIOUS
UNCEREMONIOUSLY
UNCERTAIN
UNCERTAINLY
UNCERTAINNESS
UNCERTAINNESSES
UNCERTAINTIES
UNCERTAINTY
UNCERTIFIED
UNCHAIN
UNCHAINED
UNCHAINING
UNCHAINS
UNCHAIR
UNCHAIRED
UNCHAIRING
UNCHAIRS
UNCHALLENGEABLE
UNCHALLENGED
UNCHALLENGING
UNCHANCY
UNCHANGEABILITY
UNCHANGEABLE
UNCHANGEABLY
UNCHANGED
UNCHANGING
UNCHANGINGLY
UNCHANGINGNESS
UNCHANNELED
UNCHAPERONED
UNCHARGE
UNCHARGED
UNCHARGES
UNCHARGING
UNCHARISMATIC
UNCHARITABLE
UNCHARITABLY
UNCHARMING
UNCHARRED
UNCHARTED
UNCHARTERED
UNCHARY
UNCHASTE
UNCHASTELY
UNCHASTENESS
UNCHASTENESSES
UNCHASTER
UNCHASTEST
UNCHASTITIES
UNCHASTITY
UNCHAUVINISTIC
UNCHECKABLE
UNCHECKED
UNCHEWABLE
UNCHEWED
UNCHIC
UNCHICLY
UNCHILDLIKE
UNCHILLED
UNCHIVALROUS
UNCHIVALROUSLY
UNCHLORINATED
UNCHOKE
UNCHOKED
UNCHOKES
UNCHOKING
UNCHOREOGRAPHED
UNCHOSEN
UNCHRISTENED
UNCHRISTIAN
UNCHRONICLED
UNCHRONOLOGICAL
UNCHURCH
UNCHURCHED
UNCHURCHES
UNCHURCHING
UNCHURCHLY
UNCI
UNCIA
UNCIAE
UNCIAL
UNCIALLY
UNCIALS
UNCIFORM
UNCIFORMS
UNCILIATED
UNCINAL
UNCINARIA
UNCINARIAS
UNCINARIASES
UNCINARIASIS
UNCINATE
UNCINEMATIC
UNCINI
UNCINUS
UNCIRCULATED
UNCIRCUMCISED
UNCIRCUMCISION
UNCIRCUMCISIONS
UNCIVIL
UNCIVILISED
UNCIVILIZED
UNCIVILLY
UNCLAD
UNCLAIMED
UNCLAMP
UNCLAMPED
UNCLAMPING
UNCLAMPS
UNCLARIFIED
UNCLARITIES
UNCLARITY
UNCLASP
UNCLASPED
UNCLASPING
UNCLASPS
UNCLASSICAL
UNCLASSIFIABLE
UNCLASSIFIED
UNCLASSY
UNCLAWED
UNCLE
UNCLEAN
UNCLEANED
UNCLEANER
UNCLEANEST

NCLEANLIER
NCLEANLIEST
NCLEANLINESS
NCLEANLINESSES
NCLEANLY
NCLEANNESS
NCLEANNESSES
NCLEAR
NCLEARED
NCLEARER
NCLEAREST
NCLEARLY
NCLEFT
NCLENCH
NCLENCHED
NCLENCHES
NCLENCHING
NCLES
NCLICHED
NCLIMBABLE
NCLIMBABLENESS
NCLINCH
NCLINCHED
NCLINCHES
NCLINCHING
NCLIP
NCLIPPED
NCLIPPING
NCLIPS
NCLOAK
NCLOAKED
NCLOAKING
NCLOAKS
NCLOG
NCLOGGED
NCLOGGING
NCLOGS
NCLOSE
NCLOSED
NCLOSES
NCLOSING
NCLOTHE
NCLOTHED
NCLOTHES
NCLOTHING
NCLOUD
NCLOUDED
NCLOUDEDLY
NCLOUDING
NCLOUDS
NCLOUDY
NCLOYED
NCLOYING

UNCLUBBABLE
UNCLUTTER
UNCLUTTERED
UNCLUTTERING
UNCLUTTERS
UNCO
UNCOALESCE
UNCOALESCED
UNCOALESCES
UNCOALESCING
UNCOATED
UNCOATING
UNCOATINGS
UNCOBBLED
UNCOCK
UNCOCKED
UNCOCKING
UNCOCKS
UNCODED
UNCODIFIED
UNCOERCED
UNCOERCIVE
UNCOERCIVELY
UNCOFFIN
UNCOFFINED
UNCOFFINING
UNCOFFINS
UNCOIL
UNCOILED
UNCOILING
UNCOILS
UNCOINED
UNCOLLECTED
UNCOLLECTIBLE
UNCOLLECTIBLES
UNCOLORED
UNCOMBATIVE
UNCOMBED
UNCOMBINED
UNCOMELY
UNCOMFORTABLE
UNCOMFORTABLY
UNCOMIC
UNCOMMERCIAL
UNCOMMITTED
UNCOMMON
UNCOMMONER
UNCOMMONEST
UNCOMMONLY
UNCOMMONNESS
UNCOMMONNESSES
UNCOMMUNICABLE
UNCOMMUNICATIVE

UNCOMPASSIONATE
UNCOMPELLING
UNCOMPENSATED
UNCOMPETITIVE
UNCOMPLACENT
UNCOMPLAINING
UNCOMPLAININGLY
UNCOMPLETED
UNCOMPLICATED
UNCOMPLIMENTARY
UNCOMPOUNDED
UNCOMPREHENDED
UNCOMPREHENDING
UNCOMPRESSED
UNCOMPROMISABLE
UNCOMPROMISING
UNCOMPUTERIZED
UNCONCEALED
UNCONCEIVABLE
UNCONCERN
UNCONCERNED
UNCONCERNEDLY
UNCONCERNEDNESS
UNCONCERNS
UNCONDITIONAL
UNCONDITIONALLY
UNCONDITIONED
UNCONFESSED
UNCONFINED
UNCONFIRMED
UNCONFORMABLE
UNCONFORMABLY
UNCONFORMITIES
UNCONFORMITY
UNCONFOUNDED
UNCONFUSE
UNCONFUSED
UNCONFUSES
UNCONFUSING
UNCONGENIAL
UNCONGENIALITY
UNCONJUGATED
UNCONNECTED
UNCONQUERABLE
UNCONQUERABLES
UNCONQUERABLY
UNCONQUERED
UNCONSCIONABLE
UNCONSCIONABLY
UNCONSCIOUS
UNCONSCIOUSES
UNCONSCIOUSLY
UNCONSCIOUSNESS

UNCONSECRATED
UNCONSIDERED
UNCONSOLIDATED
UNCONSTRAINED
UNCONSTRAINT
UNCONSTRAINTS
UNCONSTRICTED
UNCONSTRUCTED
UNCONSTRUCTIVE
UNCONSUMED
UNCONSUMMATED
UNCONTAINABLE
UNCONTAMINATED
UNCONTEMPLATED
UNCONTEMPORARY
UNCONTENTIOUS
UNCONTESTED
UNCONTRACTED
UNCONTRADICTED
UNCONTRIVED
UNCONTROLLABLE
UNCONTROLLABLY
UNCONTROLLED
UNCONTROVERSIAL
UNCONVENTIONAL
UNCONVENTIONALS
UNCONVERTED
UNCONVINCED
UNCONVINCING
UNCONVINCINGLY
UNCONVOYED
UNCOOKED
UNCOOL
UNCOOLED
UNCOOPERATIVE
UNCOORDINATED
UNCOPYRIGHTABLE
UNCORK
UNCORKED
UNCORKING
UNCORKS
UNCORRECTABLE
UNCORRECTED
UNCORRELATED
UNCORROBORATED
UNCORRUPT
UNCORSETED
UNCOS
UNCOUNTABLE
UNCOUNTED
UNCOUPLE
UNCOUPLED
UNCOUPLER

UNCOUPLERS
UNCOUPLES
UNCOUPLING
UNCOURAGEOUS
UNCOUTH
UNCOUTHLY
UNCOUTHNESS
UNCOUTHNESSES
UNCOVENANTED
UNCOVER
UNCOVERED
UNCOVERING
UNCOVERS
UNCOY
UNCRACKED
UNCRATE
UNCRATED
UNCRATES
UNCRATING
UNCRAZY
UNCREATE
UNCREATED
UNCREATES
UNCREATING
UNCREATIVE
UNCREDENTIALED
UNCREDITED
UNCREWED
UNCRIPPLED
UNCRITICAL
UNCRITICALLY
UNCROPPED
UNCROSS
UNCROSSABLE
UNCROSSED
UNCROSSES
UNCROSSING
UNCROWDED
UNCROWN
UNCROWNED
UNCROWNING
UNCROWNS
UNCRUMPLE
UNCRUMPLED
UNCRUMPLES
UNCRUMPLING
UNCRUSHABLE
UNCRUSHED
UNCRYSTALLIZED
UNCTION
UNCTIONS
UNCTUOUS
UNCTUOUSLY

UNCTUOUSNESS
UNCTUOUSNESSES
UNCUFF
UNCUFFED
UNCUFFING
UNCUFFS
UNCULTIVABLE
UNCULTIVATED
UNCULTURED
UNCURABLE
UNCURABLY
UNCURB
UNCURBED
UNCURBING
UNCURBS
UNCURED
UNCURIOUS
UNCURL
UNCURLED
UNCURLING
UNCURLS
UNCURRENT
UNCURSED
UNCURTAINED
UNCUS
UNCUSTOMARILY
UNCUSTOMARY
UNCUT
UNCUTE
UNCYNICAL
UNCYNICALLY
UNDAMAGED
UNDAMPED
UNDANCEABLE
UNDARING
UNDATABLE
UNDATED
UNDAUNTABLE
UNDAUNTED
UNDAUNTEDLY
UNDE
UNDEAD
UNDEBATABLE
UNDEBATABLY
UNDEBATED
UNDECADENT
UNDECAYED
UNDECEIVE
UNDECEIVED
UNDECEIVES
UNDECEIVING
UNDECIDABILITY
UNDECIDABLE
UNDECIDED
UNDECIDEDS
UNDECILLION
UNDECILLIONS
UNDECIPHERABLE
UNDECIPHERED
UNDECKED
UNDECLARED
UNDECOMPOSED
UNDECORATED
UNDEDICATED
UNDEE
UNDEFACED
UNDEFEATED
UNDEFENDED
UNDEFILED
UNDEFINABLE
UNDEFINED
UNDEFOLIATED
UNDEFORMED
UNDELEGATED
UNDELETE
UNDELETED
UNDELETES
UNDELETING
UNDELIVERABLE
UNDELIVERED
UNDELUDED
UNDEMANDING
UNDEMOCRATIC
UNDEMONSTRATIVE
UNDENIABLE
UNDENIABLENESS
UNDENIABLY
UNDENIED
UNDENTED
UNDEPENDABLE
UNDER
UNDERACHIEVE
UNDERACHIEVED
UNDERACHIEVER
UNDERACHIEVERS
UNDERACHIEVES
UNDERACHIEVING
UNDERACT
UNDERACTED
UNDERACTING
UNDERACTIVE
UNDERACTIVITIES
UNDERACTIVITY
UNDERACTS
UNDERAGE
UNDERAGED
UNDERAGES
UNDERARM
UNDERARMS
UNDERATE
UNDERBAKE
UNDERBAKED
UNDERBAKES
UNDERBAKING
UNDERBELLIES
UNDERBELLY
UNDERBID
UNDERBIDDER
UNDERBIDDERS
UNDERBIDDING
UNDERBIDS
UNDERBITE
UNDERBITES
UNDERBODIES
UNDERBODY
UNDERBOSS
UNDERBOSSES
UNDERBOUGHT
UNDERBRED
UNDERBRIM
UNDERBRIMS
UNDERBRUSH
UNDERBRUSHES
UNDERBUD
UNDERBUDDED
UNDERBUDDING
UNDERBUDGETED
UNDERBUDS
UNDERBUY
UNDERBUYING
UNDERBUYS
UNDERCARD
UNDERCARDS
UNDERCARRIAGE
UNDERCARRIAGES
UNDERCHARGE
UNDERCHARGED
UNDERCHARGES
UNDERCHARGING
UNDERCLAD
UNDERCLASS
UNDERCLASSES
UNDERCLASSMAN
UNDERCLASSMEN
UNDERCLAY
UNDERCLAYS
UNDERCLOTHES
UNDERCLOTHING
UNDERCLOTHINGS
UNDERCOAT
UNDERCOATED
UNDERCOATING
UNDERCOATINGS
UNDERCOATS
UNDERCOOK
UNDERCOOKED
UNDERCOOKING
UNDERCOOKS
UNDERCOOL
UNDERCOOLED
UNDERCOOLING
UNDERCOOLS
UNDERCOUNT
UNDERCOUNTED
UNDERCOUNTING
UNDERCOUNTS
UNDERCOVER
UNDERCROFT
UNDERCROFTS
UNDERCURRENT
UNDERCURRENTS
UNDERCUT
UNDERCUTS
UNDERCUTTING
UNDERDEVELOPED
UNDERDIAGNOSE
UNDERDIAGNOSED
UNDERDIAGNOSES
UNDERDIAGNOSING
UNDERDIAGNOSIS
UNDERDID
UNDERDO
UNDERDOES
UNDERDOG
UNDERDOGS
UNDERDOING
UNDERDONE
UNDERDOSE
UNDERDOSED
UNDERDOSES
UNDERDOSING
UNDERDRAWERS
UNDERDRAWING
UNDERDRESS
UNDERDRESSED
UNDEREAT
UNDEREATEN
UNDEREATING
UNDEREATS
UNDEREDUCATED
UNDEREMPHASES
UNDEREMPHASIS
UNDEREMPHASIZE
UNDEREMPHASIZED
UNDEREMPHASIZES
UNDEREMPLOYED
UNDEREMPLOYMENT
UNDERESTIMATE
UNDERESTIMATED
UNDERESTIMATES
UNDERESTIMATING
UNDERESTIMATION
UNDEREXPLOITED
UNDEREXPOSE
UNDEREXPOSED
UNDEREXPOSES
UNDEREXPOSING
UNDEREXPOSURE
UNDEREXPOSURES
UNDERFED
UNDERFEED
UNDERFEEDING
UNDERFEEDS
UNDERFINANCED
UNDERFLOW
UNDERFLOWS
UNDERFOOT
UNDERFUND
UNDERFUNDED
UNDERFUNDING
UNDERFUNDS
UNDERFUR
UNDERFURS
UNDERGARMENT
UNDERGARMENTS
UNDERGIRD
UNDERGIRDED
UNDERGIRDING
UNDERGIRDS
UNDERGIRT
UNDERGLAZE
UNDERGLAZES
UNDERGO
UNDERGOD
UNDERGODS
UNDERGOER
UNDERGOERS
UNDERGOES
UNDERGOING
UNDERGONE
UNDERGRAD
UNDERGRADS
UNDERGRADUATE
UNDERGRADUATES
UNDERGROUND

NDERGROUNDER
NDERGROUNDERS
NDERGROUNDS
NDERGROWTH
NDERGROWTHS
NDERHAIR
NDERHAIRS
NDERHAND
NDERHANDED
NDERHANDEDLY
NDERHANDEDNESS
NDERHANDS
NDERHEAT
NDERHEATED
NDERHEATING
NDERHEATS
NDERHUNG
NDERINFLATED
NDERINFLATION
NDERINFLATIONS
NDERINSURED
NDERINVESTMENT
NDERIVED
NDERJAW
NDERJAWS
NDERKILL
NDERKILLS
NDERLAID
NDERLAIN
NDERLAP
NDERLAPPED
NDERLAPPING
NDERLAPS
NDERLAY
NDERLAYING
NDERLAYMENT
NDERLAYMENTS
NDERLAYS
NDERLET
NDERLETS
NDERLETTING
NDERLIE
NDERLIES
NDERLINE
NDERLINED
NDERLINES
NDERLING
NDERLINGS
NDERLINING
NDERLIP
NDERLIPS
NDERLIT
NDERLOAD
UNDERLOADED
UNDERLOADING
UNDERLOADS
UNDERLYING
UNDERLYINGLY
UNDERMAN
UNDERMANNED
UNDERMANNING
UNDERMANS
UNDERMINE
UNDERMINED
UNDERMINES
UNDERMINING
UNDERMOST
UNDERNEATH
UNDERNOURISHED
UNDERNUTRITION
UNDERNUTRITIONS
UNDERPAD
UNDERPADS
UNDERPAID
UNDERPAINTING
UNDERPAINTINGS
UNDERPANTS
UNDERPART
UNDERPARTS
UNDERPASS
UNDERPASSES
UNDERPAY
UNDERPAYING
UNDERPAYMENT
UNDERPAYMENTS
UNDERPAYS
UNDERPERFORM
UNDERPERFORMED
UNDERPERFORMER
UNDERPERFORMERS
UNDERPERFORMING
UNDERPERFORMS
UNDERPIN
UNDERPINNED
UNDERPINNING
UNDERPINNINGS
UNDERPINS
UNDERPLANT
UNDERPLANTED
UNDERPLANTING
UNDERPLANTS
UNDERPLAY
UNDERPLAYED
UNDERPLAYING
UNDERPLAYS
UNDERPLOT
UNDERPLOTS
UNDERPOPULATED
UNDERPOWERED
UNDERPREPARED
UNDERPRICE
UNDERPRICED
UNDERPRICES
UNDERPRICING
UNDERPRIVILEGED
UNDERPRODUCTION
UNDERPROOF
UNDERPROP
UNDERPROPPED
UNDERPROPPING
UNDERPROPS
UNDERPUBLICIZED
UNDERRAN
UNDERRATE
UNDERRATED
UNDERRATES
UNDERRATING
UNDERREACT
UNDERREACTED
UNDERREACTING
UNDERREACTS
UNDERREPORT
UNDERREPORTED
UNDERREPORTING
UNDERREPORTS
UNDERRIPE
UNDERRUN
UNDERRUNNING
UNDERRUNS
UNDERSATURATED
UNDERSCORE
UNDERSCORED
UNDERSCORES
UNDERSCORING
UNDERSEA
UNDERSEAS
UNDERSECRETARY
UNDERSELL
UNDERSELLING
UNDERSELLS
UNDERSERVED
UNDERSET
UNDERSETS
UNDERSETTING
UNDERSEXED
UNDERSHIRT
UNDERSHIRTED
UNDERSHIRTS
UNDERSHOOT
UNDERSHOOTING
UNDERSHOOTS
UNDERSHORTS
UNDERSHOT
UNDERSHRUB
UNDERSHRUBS
UNDERSIDE
UNDERSIDES
UNDERSIGN
UNDERSIGNED
UNDERSIGNING
UNDERSIGNS
UNDERSIZE
UNDERSIZED
UNDERSKIRT
UNDERSKIRTS
UNDERSLUNG
UNDERSOIL
UNDERSOILS
UNDERSOLD
UNDERSONG
UNDERSONGS
UNDERSOW
UNDERSOWED
UNDERSOWING
UNDERSOWN
UNDERSOWS
UNDERSPIN
UNDERSPINS
UNDERSTAFFED
UNDERSTAFFING
UNDERSTAFFINGS
UNDERSTAND
UNDERSTANDABLE
UNDERSTANDABLY
UNDERSTANDING
UNDERSTANDINGLY
UNDERSTANDINGS
UNDERSTANDS
UNDERSTATE
UNDERSTATED
UNDERSTATEDLY
UNDERSTATEMENT
UNDERSTATEMENTS
UNDERSTATES
UNDERSTATING
UNDERSTEER
UNDERSTEERED
UNDERSTEERING
UNDERSTEERS
UNDERSTOOD
UNDERSTORIES
UNDERSTORY
UNDERSTRAPPER
UNDERSTRAPPERS
UNDERSTRENGTH
UNDERSTUDIED
UNDERSTUDIES
UNDERSTUDY
UNDERSTUDYING
UNDERSUPPLIES
UNDERSUPPLY
UNDERSURFACE
UNDERSURFACES
UNDERTAKE
UNDERTAKEN
UNDERTAKER
UNDERTAKERS
UNDERTAKES
UNDERTAKING
UNDERTAKINGS
UNDERTAX
UNDERTAXED
UNDERTAXES
UNDERTAXING
UNDERTENANT
UNDERTENANTS
UNDERTHREW
UNDERTHROW
UNDERTHROWING
UNDERTHROWS
UNDERTHRUST
UNDERTHRUSTED
UNDERTHRUSTING
UNDERTHRUSTS
UNDERTINT
UNDERTINTS
UNDERTONE
UNDERTONES
UNDERTOOK
UNDERTOW
UNDERTOWS
UNDERTREAT
UNDERTREATED
UNDERTREATING
UNDERTREATS
UNDERTRICK
UNDERTRICKS
UNDERUSE
UNDERUSED
UNDERUSES
UNDERUSING
UNDERUTILIZE
UNDERUTILIZED
UNDERUTILIZES
UNDERUTILIZING

UNDERVALUATION
UNDERVALUATIONS
UNDERVALUE
UNDERVALUED
UNDERVALUES
UNDERVALUING
UNDERVEST
UNDERVESTS
UNDERVOTE
UNDERVOTES
UNDERWATER
UNDERWAY
UNDERWEAR
UNDERWEARS
UNDERWEIGHT
UNDERWEIGHTS
UNDERWENT
UNDERWHELM
UNDERWHELMED
UNDERWHELMING
UNDERWHELMS
UNDERWING
UNDERWINGS
UNDERWIRE
UNDERWIRED
UNDERWIRES
UNDERWOOD
UNDERWOODS
UNDERWOOL
UNDERWOOLS
UNDERWORK
UNDERWORKED
UNDERWORKING
UNDERWORKS
UNDERWORLD
UNDERWORLDS
UNDERWRITE
UNDERWRITER
UNDERWRITERS
UNDERWRITES
UNDERWRITING
UNDERWRITTEN
UNDERWROTE
UNDESCENDED
UNDESCRIBABLE
UNDESERVED
UNDESERVING
UNDESIGNATED
UNDESIGNING
UNDESIRABILITY
UNDESIRABLE
UNDESIRABLENESS
UNDESIRABLES
UNDESIRABLY
UNDESIRED
UNDETECTABLE
UNDETECTED
UNDETERMINABLE
UNDETERMINED
UNDETERRED
UNDEVELOPED
UNDEVIATING
UNDEVIATINGLY
UNDEVOUT
UNDIAGNOSABLE
UNDIAGNOSED
UNDIALECTICAL
UNDID
UNDIDACTIC
UNDIES
UNDIGESTED
UNDIGESTIBLE
UNDIGNIFIED
UNDILUTED
UNDIMINISHED
UNDIMMED
UNDINE
UNDINES
UNDIPLOMATIC
UNDIRECTED
UNDISCHARGED
UNDISCIPLINED
UNDISCLOSED
UNDISCOURAGED
UNDISCOVERABLE
UNDISCOVERED
UNDISCUSSED
UNDISGUISED
UNDISGUISEDLY
UNDISMAYED
UNDISPUTABLE
UNDISPUTED
UNDISSOCIATED
UNDISSOLVED
UNDISTINGUISHED
UNDISTORTED
UNDISTRACTED
UNDISTRIBUTED
UNDISTURBED
UNDIVIDED
UNDO
UNDOABLE
UNDOCILE
UNDOCK
UNDOCKED
UNDOCKING
UNDOCKS
UNDOCTORED
UNDOCTRINAIRE
UNDOCUMENTED
UNDOER
UNDOERS
UNDOES
UNDOGMATIC
UNDOGMATICALLY
UNDOING
UNDOINGS
UNDOMESTIC
UNDOMESTICATED
UNDONE
UNDOS
UNDOTTED
UNDOUBLE
UNDOUBLED
UNDOUBLES
UNDOUBLING
UNDOUBTABLE
UNDOUBTED
UNDOUBTEDLY
UNDOUBTING
UNDRAINED
UNDRAMATIC
UNDRAMATICALLY
UNDRAMATIZED
UNDRAPE
UNDRAPED
UNDRAPES
UNDRAPING
UNDRAW
UNDRAWING
UNDRAWN
UNDRAWS
UNDREAMED
UNDREAMT
UNDRESS
UNDRESSED
UNDRESSES
UNDRESSING
UNDREST
UNDREW
UNDRIED
UNDRILLED
UNDRINKABLE
UNDRINKABLES
UNDRUNK
UNDUBBED
UNDUE
UNDULANCE
UNDULANCES
UNDULANT
UNDULAR
UNDULATE
UNDULATED
UNDULATES
UNDULATING
UNDULATION
UNDULATIONS
UNDULATOR
UNDULATORS
UNDULATORY
UNDULLED
UNDULOUS
UNDULY
UNDUPLICATED
UNDUTIFUL
UNDUTIFULLY
UNDUTIFULNESS
UNDUTIFULNESSES
UNDY
UNDYED
UNDYING
UNDYINGLY
UNDYNAMIC
UNEAGER
UNEAGERLY
UNEARMARKED
UNEARNED
UNEARTH
UNEARTHED
UNEARTHING
UNEARTHLIER
UNEARTHLIEST
UNEARTHLINESS
UNEARTHLINESSES
UNEARTHLY
UNEARTHS
UNEASE
UNEASES
UNEASIER
UNEASIEST
UNEASILY
UNEASINESS
UNEASINESSES
UNEASY
UNEATABLE
UNEATEN
UNECCENTRIC
UNECOLOGICAL
UNECONOMIC
UNECONOMICAL
UNEDIBLE
UNEDIFYING
UNEDITED
UNEDUCABLE
UNEDUCATED
UNEFFACED
UNELABORATE
UNELECTABLE
UNELECTED
UNELECTRIFIED
UNEMBARRASSED
UNEMBELLISHED
UNEMBITTERED
UNEMOTIONAL
UNEMOTIONALLY
UNEMPHATIC
UNEMPHATICALLY
UNEMPIRICAL
UNEMPLOYABILITY
UNEMPLOYABLE
UNEMPLOYABLES
UNEMPLOYED
UNEMPLOYEDS
UNEMPLOYMENT
UNEMPLOYMENTS
UNENCHANTED
UNENCLOSED
UNENCOURAGING
UNENCUMBERED
UNENDEARING
UNENDED
UNENDING
UNENDINGLY
UNENDOWED
UNENDURABLE
UNENDURABLENESS
UNENDURABLY
UNENFORCEABLE
UNENFORCED
UNENGAGED
UNENJOYED
UNENLARGED
UNENLIGHTENED
UNENLIGHTENING
UNENRICHED
UNENSURED
UNENTERED
UNENTERPRISING
UNENTHUSIASTIC
UNENVIABLE
UNENVIED
UNENVIOUS
UNEQUAL
UNEQUALED
UNEQUALLED

NEQUALLY
NEQUALS
NEQUIVOCABLY
NEQUIVOCAL
NEQUIVOCALLY
NERASED
NEROTIC
NERRING
NERRINGLY
NESCAPABLE
NESCORTED
NESSAYED
NESSENTIAL
NESSENTIALS
NESTABLISHED
NETHICAL
NETHICALLY
NEVADED
NEVALUATED
NEVEN
NEVENER
NEVENEST
NEVENLY
NEVENNESS
NEVENNESSES
NEVENTFUL
NEVENTFULLY
NEVENTFULNESS
NEVOLVED
NEXALTED
NEXAMINED
NEXAMPLED
NEXCELLED
NEXCEPTIONABLE
NEXCEPTIONABLY
NEXCEPTIONAL
NEXCITABLE
EXCITED
NEXCITING
NEXCUSED
NEXERCISED
NEXOTIC
NEXPECTED
NEXPECTEDLY
NEXPECTEDNESS
NEXPENDED
NEXPERT
NEXPIRED
EXPLAINABLE
NEXPLAINED
EXPLODED
EXPLOITED
EXPLORED

UNEXPOSED
UNEXPRESSED
UNEXPRESSIVE
UNEXPURGATED
UNEXTRAORDINARY
UNFADED
UNFADING
UNFADINGLY
UNFAILING
UNFAILINGLY
UNFAIR
UNFAIRER
UNFAIREST
UNFAIRLY
UNFAIRNESS
UNFAIRNESSES
UNFAITH
UNFAITHFUL
UNFAITHFULLY
UNFAITHFULNESS
UNFAITHS
UNFAKED
UNFALLEN
UNFALSIFIABLE
UNFALTERING
UNFALTERINGLY
UNFAMILIAR
UNFAMILIARITIES
UNFAMILIARITY
UNFAMILIARLY
UNFAMILIARS
UNFAMOUS
UNFANCY
UNFASHIONABLE
UNFASHIONABLES
UNFASHIONABLY
UNFASTEN
UNFASTENED
UNFASTENING
UNFASTENS
UNFASTIDIOUS
UNFATHERED
UNFATHOMABLE
UNFATHOMABLY
UNFAVORABLE
UNFAVORABLENESS
UNFAVORABLY
UNFAVORED
UNFAVORITE
UNFAVOURABLE
UNFAVOURABLY
UNFAZED
UNFEARED

UNFEARFUL
UNFEARING
UNFEASIBLE
UNFED
UNFEELING
UNFEELINGLY
UNFEELINGNESS
UNFEELINGNESSES
UNFEIGNED
UNFEIGNEDLY
UNFELT
UNFELTED
UNFEMININE
UNFENCE
UNFENCED
UNFENCES
UNFENCING
UNFERMENTED
UNFERTILE
UNFERTILIZED
UNFETTER
UNFETTERED
UNFETTERING
UNFETTERS
UNFILIAL
UNFILIALLY
UNFILLED
UNFILMABLE
UNFILMED
UNFILTERED
UNFINDABLE
UNFINISHED
UNFIRED
UNFISHED
UNFIT
UNFITLY
UNFITNESS
UNFITNESSES
UNFITS
UNFITTED
UNFITTING
UNFIX
UNFIXED
UNFIXES
UNFIXING
UNFIXT
UNFLAGGING
UNFLAGGINGLY
UNFLAMBOYANT
UNFLAPPABILITY
UNFLAPPABLE
UNFLAPPABLY
UNFLAPPED

UNFLASHY
UNFLATTERING
UNFLATTERINGLY
UNFLAWED
UNFLEDGED
UNFLEXED
UNFLINCHING
UNFLINCHINGLY
UNFLUTED
UNFLYABLE
UNFOCUSED
UNFOCUSSED
UNFOILED
UNFOLD
UNFOLDED
UNFOLDER
UNFOLDERS
UNFOLDING
UNFOLDMENT
UNFOLDMENTS
UNFOLDS
UNFOND
UNFORCED
UNFORESEEABLE
UNFORESEEN
UNFORESTED
UNFORGED
UNFORGETTABLE
UNFORGETTABLY
UNFORGIVABLE
UNFORGIVABLY
UNFORGIVING
UNFORGIVINGNESS
UNFORGOT
UNFORKED
UNFORMED
UNFORMULATED
UNFORTHCOMING
UNFORTIFIED
UNFORTUNATE
UNFORTUNATELY
UNFORTUNATES
UNFOSSILIFEROUS
UNFOUGHT
UNFOUND
UNFOUNDED
UNFRAMED
UNFREE
UNFREED
UNFREEDOM
UNFREEDOMS
UNFREEING
UNFREES

UNFREEZE
UNFREEZES
UNFREEZING
UNFREQUENTED
UNFRIEND
UNFRIENDED
UNFRIENDING
UNFRIENDLIER
UNFRIENDLINESS
UNFRIENDLY
UNFRIENDS
UNFRIVOLOUS
UNFROCK
UNFROCKED
UNFROCKING
UNFROCKS
UNFROZE
UNFROZEN
UNFRUITFUL
UNFRUITFULLY
UNFRUITFULNESS
UNFULFILLABLE
UNFULFILLED
UNFULFILLING
UNFUNDED
UNFUNNIER
UNFUNNIEST
UNFUNNY
UNFURL
UNFURLED
UNFURLING
UNFURLS
UNFURNISHED
UNFUSED
UNFUSSIER
UNFUSSIEST
UNFUSSILY
UNFUSSY
UNGAINLIER
UNGAINLIEST
UNGAINLINESS
UNGAINLINESSES
UNGAINLY
UNGALLANT
UNGALLANTLY
UNGALLED
UNGARBED
UNGARNISHED
UNGATED
UNGAZING
UNGELDED
UNGENEROSITIES
UNGENEROSITY

UNGENEROUS
UNGENEROUSLY
UNGENIAL
UNGENTEEL
UNGENTLE
UNGENTLEMANLY
UNGENTLY
UNGENTRIFIED
UNGENUINE
UNGERMINATED
UNGIFTED
UNGIMMICKY
UNGIRD
UNGIRDED
UNGIRDING
UNGIRDS
UNGIRT
UNGIVING
UNGLAMORIZED
UNGLAMOROUS
UNGLAZED
UNGLOSSED
UNGLOVE
UNGLOVED
UNGLOVES
UNGLOVING
UNGLUE
UNGLUED
UNGLUES
UNGLUING
UNGODLIER
UNGODLIEST
UNGODLINESS
UNGODLINESSES
UNGODLY
UNGOT
UNGOTTEN
UNGOVERNABLE
UNGOWNED
UNGRACED
UNGRACEFUL
UNGRACEFULLY
UNGRACIOUS
UNGRACIOUSLY
UNGRACIOUSNESS
UNGRADED
UNGRAMMATICAL
UNGRASPABLE
UNGRATEFUL
UNGRATEFULLY
UNGRATEFULNESS
UNGREASED
UNGREEDY
UNGREEN
UNGREENER
UNGREENEST
UNGROOMED
UNGROUND
UNGROUNDED
UNGROUP
UNGROUPED
UNGROUPING
UNGROUPS
UNGRUDGING
UNGRUDGINGLY
UNGUAL
UNGUARD
UNGUARDED
UNGUARDEDLY
UNGUARDEDNESS
UNGUARDEDNESSES
UNGUARDING
UNGUARDS
UNGUENT
UNGUENTA
UNGUENTS
UNGUENTUM
UNGUES
UNGUESSABLE
UNGUIDED
UNGUINOUS
UNGUIS
UNGULA
UNGULAE
UNGULAR
UNGULATE
UNGULATES
UNGULED
UNHACKNEYED
UNHAILED
UNHAIR
UNHAIRED
UNHAIRER
UNHAIRERS
UNHAIRING
UNHAIRS
UNHALLOW
UNHALLOWED
UNHALLOWING
UNHALLOWS
UNHALVED
UNHAMPERED
UNHAND
UNHANDED
UNHANDIER
UNHANDIEST
UNHANDILY
UNHANDINESS
UNHANDINESSES
UNHANDING
UNHANDLED
UNHANDS
UNHANDSOME
UNHANDSOMELY
UNHANDY
UNHANG
UNHANGED
UNHANGING
UNHANGS
UNHAPPEN
UNHAPPENED
UNHAPPENING
UNHAPPENINGS
UNHAPPENS
UNHAPPIER
UNHAPPIEST
UNHAPPILY
UNHAPPINESS
UNHAPPINESSES
UNHAPPY
UNHARMED
UNHARMFUL
UNHARNESS
UNHARNESSED
UNHARNESSES
UNHARNESSING
UNHARRIED
UNHARVESTED
UNHASP
UNHASPED
UNHASPING
UNHASPS
UNHASTY
UNHAT
UNHATCHED
UNHATS
UNHATTED
UNHATTING
UNHEALED
UNHEALTH
UNHEALTHFUL
UNHEALTHIER
UNHEALTHIEST
UNHEALTHILY
UNHEALTHINESS
UNHEALTHINESSES
UNHEALTHS
UNHEALTHY
UNHEARD
UNHEATED
UNHEDGED
UNHEEDED
UNHEEDFUL
UNHEEDING
UNHELM
UNHELMED
UNHELMING
UNHELMS
UNHELPED
UNHELPFUL
UNHELPFULLY
UNHELPFULNESS
UNHELPFULNESSES
UNHERALDED
UNHEROIC
UNHESITATING
UNHESITATINGLY
UNHEWN
UNHINDERED
UNHINGE
UNHINGED
UNHINGES
UNHINGING
UNHIP
UNHIPPER
UNHIPPEST
UNHIRABLE
UNHIRED
UNHISTORICAL
UNHITCH
UNHITCHED
UNHITCHES
UNHITCHING
UNHOLIER
UNHOLIEST
UNHOLILY
UNHOLINESS
UNHOLINESSES
UNHOLY
UNHOMOGENIZED
UNHONORED
UNHOOD
UNHOODED
UNHOODING
UNHOODS
UNHOOK
UNHOOKED
UNHOOKING
UNHOOKS
UNHOPED
UNHOPEFUL
UNHORSE
UNHORSED
UNHORSES
UNHORSING
UNHOSTILE
UNHOUSE
UNHOUSED
UNHOUSELED
UNHOUSES
UNHOUSING
UNHUMAN
UNHUMANLY
UNHUMBLED
UNHUMOROUS
UNHUNG
UNHURRIED
UNHURRIEDLY
UNHURT
UNHUSK
UNHUSKED
UNHUSKING
UNHUSKS
UNHYDROLYZED
UNHYGIENIC
UNHYPHENATED
UNHYSTERICAL
UNHYSTERICALLY
UNI
UNIALGAL
UNIAXIAL
UNIBODIES
UNIBODY
UNIBROW
UNIBROWS
UNICA
UNICAMERAL
UNICAMERALLY
UNICED
UNICELLULAR
UNICOLOR
UNICOM
UNICOMS
UNICORN
UNICORNS
UNICUM
UNICYCLE
UNICYCLED
UNICYCLES
UNICYCLING
UNICYCLIST
UNICYCLISTS
UNIDEAED
UNIDEAL
UNIDENTIFIABLE

NIDENTIFIED
NIDEOLOGICAL
NIDIMENSIONAL
NIDIOMATIC
NIDIRECTIONAL
NIFACE
NIFACES
NIFIABLE
NIFIC
NIFICATION
NIFICATIONS
NIFIED
NIFIER
NIFIERS
NIFIES
NIFILAR
NIFOLIATE
NIFOLIOLATE
NIFORM
NIFORMED
NIFORMER
NIFORMEST
NIFORMING
NIFORMITARIAN
NIFORMITARIANS
NIFORMITIES
NIFORMITY
NIFORMLY
NIFORMNESS
NIFORMNESSES
NIFORMS
NIFY
NIFYING
NIGNORABLE
NIJUGATE
NILATERAL
NILATERALISM
NILATERALISMS
NILATERALIST
NILATERALISTS
NILATERALLY
NILINEAL
NILINEAR
NILINGUAL
NILLUMINATING
NILLUSIONED
NILOBED
NILOCULAR
NIMAGINABLE
NIMAGINABLY
NIMAGINATIVE
NIMAGINATIVELY
NIMAGINED

UNIMBUED
UNIMMUNIZED
UNIMODAL
UNIMPAIRED
UNIMPASSIONED
UNIMPEACHABLE
UNIMPEACHABLY
UNIMPEDED
UNIMPORTANCE
UNIMPORTANCES
UNIMPORTANT
UNIMPOSING
UNIMPRESSED
UNIMPRESSIVE
UNIMPROVED
UNINCORPORATED
UNINDEXED
UNINDICTED
UNINFECTED
UNINFLATED
UNINFLECTED
UNINFLUENCED
UNINFORMATIVE
UNINFORMATIVELY
UNINFORMED
UNINGRATIATING
UNINHABITABLE
UNINHABITABLES
UNINHABITED
UNINHABITEDS
UNINHIBITED
UNINHIBITEDLY
UNINHIBITEDNESS
UNINITIATE
UNINITIATED
UNINITIATES
UNINJURED
UNINOCULATED
UNINSPECTED
UNINSPIRED
UNINSPIRING
UNINSTAL
UNINSTALL
UNINSTALLED
UNINSTALLING
UNINSTALLS
UNINSTALS
UNINSTRUCTED
UNINSTRUCTIVE
UNINSULATED
UNINSURABLE
UNINSURED
UNINSUREDS

UNINTEGRATED
UNINTELLECTUAL
UNINTELLECTUALS
UNINTELLIGENT
UNINTELLIGENTLY
UNINTELLIGIBLE
UNINTELLIGIBLY
UNINTENDED
UNINTENTIONAL
UNINTENTIONALLY
UNINTEREST
UNINTERESTED
UNINTERESTING
UNINTERESTS
UNINTERPRETABLE
UNINTERRUPTED
UNINTERRUPTEDLY
UNINTIMIDATED
UNINUCLEATE
UNINVENTIVE
UNINVITED
UNINVITING
UNINVOKED
UNINVOLVED
UNION
UNIONISATION
UNIONISATIONS
UNIONISE
UNIONISED
UNIONISES
UNIONISING
UNIONISM
UNIONISMS
UNIONIST
UNIONISTS
UNIONIZATION
UNIONIZATIONS
UNIONIZE
UNIONIZED
UNIONIZER
UNIONIZERS
UNIONIZES
UNIONIZING
UNIONS
UNIPARENTAL
UNIPARENTALLY
UNIPAROUS
UNIPLANAR
UNIPOD
UNIPODS
UNIPOLAR
UNIPOTENT
UNIQUE

UNIQUELY
UNIQUENESS
UNIQUENESSES
UNIQUER
UNIQUES
UNIQUEST
UNIRAMOUS
UNIRONED
UNIRONIC
UNIRONICALLY
UNIRRADIATED
UNIRRIGATED
UNIS
UNISEX
UNISEXES
UNISEXUAL
UNISEXUALITIES
UNISEXUALITY
UNISIZE
UNISON
UNISONAL
UNISONANT
UNISONOUS
UNISONS
UNISSUED
UNIT
UNITAGE
UNITAGES
UNITARD
UNITARDS
UNITARIAN
UNITARIANISM
UNITARIANISMS
UNITARIANS
UNITARILY
UNITARY
UNITE
UNITED
UNITEDLY
UNITER
UNITERS
UNITES
UNITIES
UNITING
UNITIVE
UNITIVELY
UNITIZATION
UNITIZATIONS
UNITIZE
UNITIZED
UNITIZER
UNITIZERS
UNITIZES

UNITIZING
UNITRUST
UNITRUSTS
UNITS
UNITY
UNIVALENT
UNIVALENTS
UNIVALVE
UNIVALVED
UNIVALVES
UNIVARIATE
UNIVERSAL
UNIVERSALISM
UNIVERSALISMS
UNIVERSALIST
UNIVERSALISTIC
UNIVERSALISTS
UNIVERSALITIES
UNIVERSALITY
UNIVERSALIZE
UNIVERSALIZED
UNIVERSALIZES
UNIVERSALIZING
UNIVERSALLY
UNIVERSALNESS
UNIVERSALNESSES
UNIVERSALS
UNIVERSE
UNIVERSES
UNIVERSITIES
UNIVERSITY
UNIVOCAL
UNIVOCALLY
UNIVOCALS
UNJADED
UNJAM
UNJAMMED
UNJAMMING
UNJAMS
UNJOINED
UNJOINT
UNJOINTED
UNJOINTING
UNJOINTS
UNJOYFUL
UNJUDGED
UNJUST
UNJUSTIFIABLE
UNJUSTIFIABLY
UNJUSTIFIED
UNJUSTLY
UNJUSTNESS
UNJUSTNESSES

UNKEELED
UNKEMPT
UNKEND
UNKENNED
UNKENNEL
UNKENNELED
UNKENNELING
UNKENNELLED
UNKENNELLING
UNKENNELS
UNKENT
UNKEPT
UNKILLABLE
UNKILLABLES
UNKIND
UNKINDER
UNKINDEST
UNKINDLED
UNKINDLIER
UNKINDLIEST
UNKINDLINESS
UNKINDLINESSES
UNKINDLY
UNKINDNESS
UNKINDNESSES
UNKINGLY
UNKINK
UNKINKED
UNKINKING
UNKINKS
UNKISSED
UNKNIT
UNKNITS
UNKNITTED
UNKNITTING
UNKNOT
UNKNOTS
UNKNOTTED
UNKNOTTING
UNKNOWABILITIES
UNKNOWABILITY
UNKNOWABLE
UNKNOWING
UNKNOWINGLY
UNKNOWINGS
UNKNOWLEDGEABLE
UNKNOWN
UNKNOWNS
UNKOSHER
UNLABELED
UNLABORED
UNLACE
UNLACED
UNLACES
UNLACING
UNLADE
UNLADED
UNLADEN
UNLADES
UNLADING
UNLADYLIKE
UNLAID
UNLAMENTED
UNLASH
UNLASHED
UNLASHES
UNLASHING
UNLATCH
UNLATCHED
UNLATCHES
UNLATCHING
UNLAUNDERED
UNLAWFUL
UNLAWFULLY
UNLAWFULNESS
UNLAWFULNESSES
UNLAY
UNLAYING
UNLAYS
UNLEAD
UNLEADED
UNLEADEDS
UNLEADING
UNLEADS
UNLEARN
UNLEARNABLE
UNLEARNED
UNLEARNING
UNLEARNS
UNLEARNT
UNLEASED
UNLEASH
UNLEASHED
UNLEASHES
UNLEASHING
UNLEAVENED
UNLED
UNLESS
UNLET
UNLETHAL
UNLETTED
UNLETTERED
UNLEVEL
UNLEVELED
UNLEVELING
UNLEVELLED
UNLEVELLING
UNLEVELS
UNLEVIED
UNLIBERATED
UNLICENSED
UNLICKED
UNLIGHTED
UNLIKABLE
UNLIKE
UNLIKEABLE
UNLIKED
UNLIKELIER
UNLIKELIEST
UNLIKELIHOOD
UNLIKELIHOODS
UNLIKELINESS
UNLIKELINESSES
UNLIKELY
UNLIKENESS
UNLIKENESSES
UNLIMBER
UNLIMBERED
UNLIMBERING
UNLIMBERS
UNLIMITED
UNLIMITEDLY
UNLINED
UNLINK
UNLINKED
UNLINKING
UNLINKS
UNLISTED
UNLISTENABLE
UNLIT
UNLITERARY
UNLIVABLE
UNLIVE
UNLIVED
UNLIVELY
UNLIVES
UNLIVING
UNLOAD
UNLOADED
UNLOADER
UNLOADERS
UNLOADING
UNLOADS
UNLOBED
UNLOCALIZED
UNLOCATED
UNLOCK
UNLOCKED
UNLOCKING
UNLOCKS
UNLOOSE
UNLOOSED
UNLOOSEN
UNLOOSENED
UNLOOSENING
UNLOOSENS
UNLOOSES
UNLOOSING
UNLOVABLE
UNLOVED
UNLOVELIER
UNLOVELIEST
UNLOVELINESS
UNLOVELINESSES
UNLOVELY
UNLOVING
UNLUCKIER
UNLUCKIEST
UNLUCKILY
UNLUCKINESS
UNLUCKINESSES
UNLUCKY
UNLYRICAL
UNMACHO
UNMADE
UNMAGNIFIED
UNMAILED
UNMAKE
UNMAKER
UNMAKERS
UNMAKES
UNMAKING
UNMALICIOUS
UNMALICIOUSLY
UNMAN
UNMANAGEABLE
UNMANAGEABLY
UNMANAGED
UNMANFUL
UNMANIPULATED
UNMANLIER
UNMANLIEST
UNMANLINESS
UNMANLINESSES
UNMANLY
UNMANNED
UNMANNERED
UNMANNEREDLY
UNMANNERLINESS
UNMANNERLY
UNMANNING
UNMANNISH
UNMANS
UNMAPPED
UNMARKED
UNMARKETABLE
UNMARRED
UNMARRIED
UNMARRIEDS
UNMASCULINE
UNMASK
UNMASKED
UNMASKER
UNMASKERS
UNMASKING
UNMASKS
UNMATCHABLE
UNMATCHED
UNMATED
UNMATTED
UNMATURED
UNMEANING
UNMEANT
UNMEASURABLE
UNMEASURED
UNMECHANIZED
UNMEDIATED
UNMEDICATED
UNMEET
UNMEETLY
UNMELLOW
UNMELODIOUS
UNMELODIOUSNESS
UNMELTED
UNMEMORABLE
UNMEMORABLY
UNMENDED
UNMENTIONABLE
UNMENTIONABLES
UNMENTIONED
UNMERCIFUL
UNMERCIFULLY
UNMERITED
UNMERRY
UNMESH
UNMESHED
UNMESHES
UNMESHING
UNMET
UNMETABOLIZED
UNMEW
UNMEWED
UNMEWING
UNMEWS
UNMILITARY

MILLED
MINDFUL
MINED
MINGLE
MINGLED
MINGLES
MINGLING
MISSABLE
MISTAKABLE
MISTAKABLY
MITER
MITERED
MITERING
MITERS
MITIGATED
MITIGATEDLY
MITIGATEDNESS
MITRE
MITRED
MITRES
MITRING
MIX
MIXABLE
MIXED
MIXEDLY
MIXES
MIXING
MIXT
MODERNIZED
MODIFIED
MODISH
MODULATED
MOLD
MOLDED
MOLDING
MOLDS
MOLESTED
MOLTEN
MONITORED
MOOR
MOORED
MOORING
MOORS
MORAL
MORALITIES
MORALITY
MORALLY
MORTISE
MORTISED
MORTISES
MORTISING
MOTIVATED
MOULD
UNMOULDED
UNMOULDING
UNMOULDS
UNMOUNTED
UNMOURNED
UNMOVABLE
UNMOVED
UNMOVING
UNMOWN
UNMUFFLE
UNMUFFLED
UNMUFFLES
UNMUFFLING
UNMUSICAL
UNMUZZLE
UNMUZZLED
UNMUZZLES
UNMUZZLING
UNMYELINATED
UNNAIL
UNNAILED
UNNAILING
UNNAILS
UNNAMABLE
UNNAMEABLE
UNNAMED
UNNATURAL
UNNATURALLY
UNNATURALNESS
UNNATURALNESSES
UNNECESSARILY
UNNECESSARY
UNNEEDED
UNNEEDFUL
UNNEGOTIABLE
UNNERVE
UNNERVED
UNNERVES
UNNERVING
UNNERVINGLY
UNNEUROTIC
UNNEWSWORTHY
UNNILHEXIUM
UNNILHEXIUMS
UNNILPENTIUM
UNNILPENTIUMS
UNNILQUADIUM
UNNILQUADIUMS
UNNOISY
UNNOTED
UNNOTICEABLE
UNNOTICED
UNNOURISHING
UNNUANCED
UNNUMBERED
UNOAKED
UNOBJECTIONABLE
UNOBSERVABLE
UNOBSERVED
UNOBSTRUCTED
UNOBTAINABLE
UNOBTRUSIVE
UNOBTRUSIVELY
UNOBTRUSIVENESS
UNOCCUPIED
UNOFFERED
UNOFFICIAL
UNOFFICIALLY
UNOILED
UNOPEN
UNOPENABLE
UNOPENED
UNOPPOSED
UNORDERED
UNORDERLY
UNORGANISED
UNORGANIZED
UNORIGINAL
UNORIGINALITIES
UNORIGINALITY
UNORIGINALS
UNORNAMENTED
UNORNATE
UNORTHODOX
UNORTHODOXES
UNORTHODOXIES
UNORTHODOXLY
UNORTHODOXY
UNOSTENTATIOUS
UNOWNED
UNOXYGENATED
UNPACK
UNPACKED
UNPACKER
UNPACKERS
UNPACKING
UNPACKS
UNPADDED
UNPAGED
UNPAID
UNPAINFUL
UNPAINTED
UNPAIRED
UNPALATABILITY
UNPALATABLE
UNPARALLELED
UNPARASITIZED
UNPARDONABLE
UNPARLIAMENTARY
UNPARTED
UNPASSABLE
UNPASTEURIZED
UNPASTORAL
UNPATCHED
UNPATENTABLE
UNPATRIOTIC
UNPAVED
UNPAYING
UNPEDANTIC
UNPEELED
UNPEG
UNPEGGED
UNPEGGING
UNPEGS
UNPEN
UNPENNED
UNPENNING
UNPENS
UNPENT
UNPEOPLE
UNPEOPLED
UNPEOPLES
UNPEOPLING
UNPERCEIVED
UNPERCEPTIVE
UNPERFECT
UNPERFORMABLE
UNPERFORMED
UNPERSON
UNPERSONS
UNPERSUADED
UNPERSUASIVE
UNPERSUASIVELY
UNPERTURBED
UNPICK
UNPICKED
UNPICKING
UNPICKS
UNPICTURESQUE
UNPIERCED
UNPILE
UNPILED
UNPILES
UNPILING
UNPIN
UNPINNED
UNPINNING
UNPINS
UNPITIED
UNPITTED
UNPITYING
UNPLACEABLE
UNPLACED
UNPLAIT
UNPLAITED
UNPLAITING
UNPLAITS
UNPLANNED
UNPLANTED
UNPLAUSIBLE
UNPLAYABLE
UNPLAYED
UNPLEASANT
UNPLEASANTLY
UNPLEASANTNESS
UNPLEASED
UNPLEASING
UNPLEDGED
UNPLIABLE
UNPLIANT
UNPLOWED
UNPLUCKED
UNPLUG
UNPLUGGED
UNPLUGGING
UNPLUGS
UNPLUMBED
UNPOETIC
UNPOINTED
UNPOISED
UNPOLARIZED
UNPOLICED
UNPOLISHED
UNPOLITE
UNPOLITIC
UNPOLITICAL
UNPOLLED
UNPOLLUTED
UNPOPULAR
UNPOPULARITIES
UNPOPULARITY
UNPOPULARLY
UNPOSED
UNPOSTED
UNPOTTED
UNPRACTICAL
UNPRECEDENTED
UNPRECEDENTEDLY
UNPREDICTABLE
UNPREDICTABLES
UNPREDICTABLY
UNPREGNANT

UNPREJUDICED
UNPREMEDITATED
UNPREPARED
UNPREPAREDNESS
UNPREPOSSESSING
UNPRESSED
UNPRESSURED
UNPRESSURIZED
UNPRETENDING
UNPRETENTIOUS
UNPRETENTIOUSLY
UNPRETTY
UNPRICED
UNPRIMED
UNPRINCIPLED
UNPRINTABLE
UNPRINTED
UNPRIVILEGED
UNPRIZED
UNPROBED
UNPROBLEMATIC
UNPROCESSED
UNPRODUCED
UNPRODUCTIVE
UNPRODUCTIVELY
UNPROFESSED
UNPROFESSIONAL
UNPROFESSIONALS
UNPROFITABLE
UNPROFITABLY
UNPROGRAMMABLE
UNPROGRAMMED
UNPROGRESSIVE
UNPROGRESSIVES
UNPROMISING
UNPROMISINGLY
UNPROMPTED
UNPRONOUNCEABLE
UNPRONOUNCED
UNPROPITIOUS
UNPROSPEROUS
UNPROTECTED
UNPROVABLE
UNPROVED
UNPROVEN
UNPROVOKED
UNPRUNED
UNPUBLICIZED
UNPUBLISHABLE
UNPUBLISHED
UNPUCKER
UNPUCKERED
UNPUCKERING
UNPUCKERS
UNPUNCTUAL
UNPUNCTUALITIES
UNPUNCTUALITY
UNPUNCTUATED
UNPUNISHED
UNPURE
UNPURELY
UNPURGED
UNPUTDOWNABLE
UNPUZZLE
UNPUZZLED
UNPUZZLES
UNPUZZLING
UNQUAKING
UNQUALIFIED
UNQUALIFIEDLY
UNQUANTIFIABLE
UNQUELLED
UNQUENCHABLE
UNQUESTIONABLE
UNQUESTIONABLY
UNQUESTIONED
UNQUESTIONING
UNQUESTIONINGLY
UNQUIET
UNQUIETER
UNQUIETEST
UNQUIETLY
UNQUIETNESS
UNQUIETNESSES
UNQUIETS
UNQUOTE
UNQUOTED
UNQUOTES
UNQUOTING
UNRAISED
UNRAKED
UNRANKED
UNRATED
UNRAVAGED
UNRAVEL
UNRAVELED
UNRAVELING
UNRAVELLED
UNRAVELLING
UNRAVELS
UNRAVISHED
UNRAZED
UNREACHABLE
UNREACHED
UNREAD
UNREADABLE
UNREADIER
UNREADIEST
UNREADILY
UNREADINESS
UNREADINESSES
UNREADY
UNREAL
UNREALISTIC
UNREALISTICALLY
UNREALITIES
UNREALITY
UNREALIZABLE
UNREALIZED
UNREALLY
UNREASON
UNREASONABLE
UNREASONABLY
UNREASONED
UNREASONING
UNREASONINGLY
UNREASONS
UNREBUKED
UNRECEPTIVE
UNRECLAIMABLE
UNRECLAIMED
UNRECOGNISABLE
UNRECOGNIZABLE
UNRECOGNIZABLY
UNRECOGNIZED
UNRECONCILABLE
UNRECONCILED
UNRECONSTRUCTED
UNRECORDED
UNRECOVERABLE
UNRECOVERED
UNRECYCLABLE
UNRECYCLABLES
UNREDEEMABLE
UNREDEEMED
UNREDRESSED
UNREEL
UNREELED
UNREELER
UNREELERS
UNREELING
UNREELS
UNREEVE
UNREEVED
UNREEVES
UNREEVING
UNREFINED
UNREFLECTIVE
UNREFORMED
UNREFRIGERATED
UNREGENERATE
UNREGENERATELY
UNREGISTERED
UNREGULATED
UNREHEARSED
UNREINFORCED
UNRELATED
UNRELAXED
UNRELENTING
UNRELENTINGLY
UNRELIABILITIES
UNRELIABILITY
UNRELIABLE
UNRELIABLY
UNRELIEVED
UNRELIEVEDLY
UNRELUCTANT
UNREMARKABLE
UNREMARKABLY
UNREMARKED
UNREMEMBERED
UNREMINISCENT
UNREMITTING
UNREMITTINGLY
UNREMOVABLE
UNRENEWED
UNRENT
UNRENTED
UNREPAID
UNREPAIR
UNREPAIRS
UNREPEATABLE
UNREPENTANT
UNREPENTANTLY
UNREPORTED
UNREPRESENTED
UNREPRESSED
UNREQUITED
UNRESERVE
UNRESERVED
UNRESERVEDLY
UNRESERVEDNESS
UNRESERVES
UNRESISTANT
UNRESOLVABLE
UNRESOLVED
UNRESPECTABLE
UNRESPECTABLES
UNRESPONSIVE
UNRESPONSIVELY
UNREST
UNRESTED
UNRESTFUL
UNRESTING
UNRESTORED
UNRESTRAINED
UNRESTRAINEDLY
UNRESTRAINT
UNRESTRAINTS
UNRESTRICTED
UNRESTS
UNRETIRE
UNRETIRED
UNRETIRES
UNRETIRING
UNRETOUCHED
UNRETURNABLE
UNRETURNABLES
UNREVEALED
UNREVIEWABLE
UNREVIEWED
UNREVISED
UNREVOKED
UNREVOLUTIONARY
UNREWARDED
UNREWARDING
UNRHETORICAL
UNRHYMED
UNRHYTHMIC
UNRIBBED
UNRIDABLE
UNRIDDEN
UNRIDDLE
UNRIDDLED
UNRIDDLER
UNRIDDLERS
UNRIDDLES
UNRIDDLING
UNRIFLED
UNRIG
UNRIGGED
UNRIGGING
UNRIGHTEOUS
UNRIGHTEOUSLY
UNRIGHTEOUSNES
UNRIGS
UNRIMED
UNRINSED
UNRIP
UNRIPE
UNRIPELY
UNRIPENED
UNRIPENESS
UNRIPENESSES
UNRIPER

RIPEST
RIPPED
RIPPING
RIPS
RISEN
RIVALED
RIVALLED
RIVET
RIVETED
RIVETING
RIVETS
RIVETTED
RIVETTING
ROASTED
ROBE
ROBED
ROBES
ROBING
ROLL
ROLLED
ROLLING
ROLLS
ROMANTIC
ROMANTICALLY
ROMANTICIZED
OOF
OOFED
OOFING
OOFS
OOT
OOTED
OOTING
OOTS
OPE
OPED
OPES
OPING
OUGH
OUND
OUNDED
OUNDING
OUNDS
OVE
OVEN
UFFLED
ULED
ULIER
ULIEST
ULINESS
ULINESSES
ULY
UMPLED
USHED
UNRUSTED
UNS
UNSADDLE
UNSADDLED
UNSADDLES
UNSADDLING
UNSAFE
UNSAFELY
UNSAFER
UNSAFEST
UNSAFETIES
UNSAFETY
UNSAID
UNSAINTLY
UNSALABLE
UNSALABLY
UNSALARIED
UNSALTED
UNSALVAGEABLE
UNSAMPLED
UNSANCTIONED
UNSANITARY
UNSATED
UNSATISFACTORY
UNSATISFIED
UNSATISFYING
UNSATURATE
UNSATURATED
UNSATURATES
UNSAVED
UNSAVORY
UNSAVOURY
UNSAWED
UNSAWN
UNSAY
UNSAYABLE
UNSAYABLES
UNSAYING
UNSAYS
UNSCALABLE
UNSCALED
UNSCANNED
UNSCARRED
UNSCATHED
UNSCENTED
UNSCHEDULED
UNSCHOLARLY
UNSCHOOLED
UNSCIENTIFIC
UNSCRAMBLE
UNSCRAMBLED
UNSCRAMBLER
UNSCRAMBLERS
UNSCRAMBLES
UNSCRAMBLING
UNSCREENED
UNSCREW
UNSCREWED
UNSCREWING
UNSCREWS
UNSCRIPTED
UNSCRIPTURAL
UNSCRUPULOUS
UNSCRUPULOUSLY
UNSEAL
UNSEALED
UNSEALING
UNSEALS
UNSEAM
UNSEAMED
UNSEAMING
UNSEAMS
UNSEARCHABLE
UNSEARCHABLY
UNSEARED
UNSEASONABLE
UNSEASONABLY
UNSEASONED
UNSEAT
UNSEATED
UNSEATING
UNSEATS
UNSEAWORTHY
UNSECURED
UNSEEABLE
UNSEEDED
UNSEEING
UNSEEMLIER
UNSEEMLIEST
UNSEEMLINESS
UNSEEMLINESSES
UNSEEMLY
UNSEEN
UNSEGMENTED
UNSEGREGATED
UNSEIZED
UNSELECTED
UNSELECTIVE
UNSELECTIVELY
UNSELFCONSCIOUS
UNSELFISH
UNSELFISHLY
UNSELFISHNESS
UNSELFISHNESSES
UNSELL
UNSELLABLE
UNSELLING
UNSELLS
UNSENSATIONAL
UNSENSITIZED
UNSENT
UNSENTIMENTAL
UNSEPARATED
UNSERIOUS
UNSERIOUSNESS
UNSERIOUSNESSES
UNSERVED
UNSERVICEABLE
UNSET
UNSETS
UNSETTING
UNSETTLE
UNSETTLED
UNSETTLEDNESS
UNSETTLEDNESSES
UNSETTLEMENT
UNSETTLEMENTS
UNSETTLES
UNSETTLING
UNSETTLINGLY
UNSEW
UNSEWED
UNSEWING
UNSEWN
UNSEWS
UNSEX
UNSEXED
UNSEXES
UNSEXIER
UNSEXIEST
UNSEXING
UNSEXUAL
UNSEXY
UNSHACKLE
UNSHACKLED
UNSHACKLES
UNSHACKLING
UNSHADED
UNSHAKABLE
UNSHAKABLY
UNSHAKEABLE
UNSHAKEN
UNSHAMED
UNSHAPED
UNSHAPELY
UNSHAPEN
UNSHARED
UNSHARP
UNSHAVED
UNSHAVEN
UNSHEATHE
UNSHEATHED
UNSHEATHES
UNSHEATHING
UNSHED
UNSHELL
UNSHELLED
UNSHELLING
UNSHELLS
UNSHIFT
UNSHIFTED
UNSHIFTING
UNSHIFTS
UNSHIP
UNSHIPPED
UNSHIPPING
UNSHIPS
UNSHIRTED
UNSHOCKABLE
UNSHOD
UNSHORN
UNSHOWY
UNSHRUNK
UNSHUT
UNSICKER
UNSIFTED
UNSIGHT
UNSIGHTED
UNSIGHTING
UNSIGHTLIER
UNSIGHTLIEST
UNSIGHTLINESS
UNSIGHTLINESSES
UNSIGHTLY
UNSIGHTS
UNSIGNED
UNSILENT
UNSIMILAR
UNSINFUL
UNSINKABLE
UNSIZED
UNSKILFUL
UNSKILLED
UNSKILLFUL
UNSKILLFULLY
UNSKILLFULNESS
UNSLAKABLE
UNSLAKED
UNSLICED
UNSLICK
UNSLING
UNSLINGING

UNSLINGS
UNSLUNG
UNSMART
UNSMILING
UNSMOKED
UNSMOOTHED
UNSNAG
UNSNAGGED
UNSNAGGING
UNSNAGS
UNSNAP
UNSNAPPED
UNSNAPPING
UNSNAPS
UNSNARL
UNSNARLED
UNSNARLING
UNSNARLS
UNSOAKED
UNSOBER
UNSOBERLY
UNSOCIABILITIES
UNSOCIABILITY
UNSOCIABLE
UNSOCIABLENESS
UNSOCIABLY
UNSOCIAL
UNSOCIALLY
UNSOILED
UNSOLD
UNSOLDER
UNSOLDERED
UNSOLDERING
UNSOLDERS
UNSOLDIERLY
UNSOLICITED
UNSOLID
UNSOLVABLE
UNSOLVED
UNSONCY
UNSONSIE
UNSONSY
UNSOOTHED
UNSOPHISTICATED
UNSORTED
UNSOUGHT
UNSOUND
UNSOUNDED
UNSOUNDER
UNSOUNDEST
UNSOUNDLY
UNSOUNDNESS
UNSOUNDNESSES
UNSOURCED
UNSOURED
UNSOWED
UNSOWN
UNSPARING
UNSPARINGLY
UNSPEAK
UNSPEAKABLE
UNSPEAKABLY
UNSPEAKING
UNSPEAKS
UNSPECIALIZED
UNSPECIFIABLE
UNSPECIFIC
UNSPECIFIED
UNSPECTACULAR
UNSPENT
UNSPHERE
UNSPHERED
UNSPHERES
UNSPHERING
UNSPILLED
UNSPILT
UNSPIRITUAL
UNSPLIT
UNSPOILED
UNSPOILT
UNSPOKE
UNSPOKEN
UNSPOOL
UNSPOOLED
UNSPOOLING
UNSPOOLS
UNSPORTING
UNSPORTSMANLIKE
UNSPOTTED
UNSPRAYED
UNSPRUNG
UNSPUN
UNSQUARED
UNSTABLE
UNSTABLENESS
UNSTABLENESSES
UNSTABLER
UNSTABLEST
UNSTABLY
UNSTACK
UNSTACKED
UNSTACKING
UNSTACKS
UNSTAINED
UNSTALKED
UNSTAMPED
UNSTANDARDIZED
UNSTARRED
UNSTARTLING
UNSTATE
UNSTATED
UNSTATES
UNSTATING
UNSTAYED
UNSTEADIED
UNSTEADIER
UNSTEADIES
UNSTEADIEST
UNSTEADILY
UNSTEADINESS
UNSTEADINESSES
UNSTEADY
UNSTEADYING
UNSTEEL
UNSTEELED
UNSTEELING
UNSTEELS
UNSTEMMED
UNSTEP
UNSTEPPED
UNSTEPPING
UNSTEPS
UNSTERILE
UNSTERILIZED
UNSTICK
UNSTICKING
UNSTICKS
UNSTINTED
UNSTINTING
UNSTINTINGLY
UNSTITCH
UNSTITCHED
UNSTITCHES
UNSTITCHING
UNSTOCKED
UNSTONED
UNSTOP
UNSTOPPABLE
UNSTOPPABLY
UNSTOPPED
UNSTOPPER
UNSTOPPERED
UNSTOPPERING
UNSTOPPERS
UNSTOPPING
UNSTOPS
UNSTRAINED
UNSTRAP
UNSTRAPPED
UNSTRAPPING
UNSTRAPS
UNSTRATIFIED
UNSTRESS
UNSTRESSED
UNSTRESSES
UNSTRING
UNSTRINGING
UNSTRINGS
UNSTRIPED
UNSTRUCTURED
UNSTRUNG
UNSTUCK
UNSTUDIED
UNSTUFFED
UNSTUFFIER
UNSTUFFIEST
UNSTUFFY
UNSTUNG
UNSTYLISH
UNSUBDUED
UNSUBSIDIZED
UNSUBSTANTIAL
UNSUBSTANTIALLY
UNSUBSTANTIATED
UNSUBTLE
UNSUBTLY
UNSUCCESS
UNSUCCESSES
UNSUCCESSFUL
UNSUCCESSFULLY
UNSUITABILITIES
UNSUITABILITY
UNSUITABLE
UNSUITABLY
UNSUITED
UNSULFURED
UNSULLIED
UNSUNG
UNSUNK
UNSUPERVISED
UNSUPPORTABLE
UNSUPPORTED
UNSURE
UNSURELY
UNSURPASSABLE
UNSURPASSED
UNSURPRISED
UNSURPRISING
UNSURPRISINGLY
UNSUSCEPTIBLE
UNSUSPECTED
UNSUSPECTING
UNSUSPICIOUS
UNSUSTAINABLE
UNSWATHE
UNSWATHED
UNSWATHES
UNSWATHING
UNSWAYED
UNSWEAR
UNSWEARING
UNSWEARS
UNSWEETENED
UNSWEPT
UNSWERVING
UNSWOLLEN
UNSWORE
UNSWORN
UNSYMMETRICAL
UNSYMMETRICALLY
UNSYMPATHETIC
UNSYNCHRONIZED
UNSYSTEMATIC
UNSYSTEMATIZED
UNTACK
UNTACKED
UNTACKING
UNTACKS
UNTACTFUL
UNTAGGED
UNTAINTED
UNTAKEN
UNTALENTED
UNTAMABLE
UNTAME
UNTAMED
UNTANGLE
UNTANGLED
UNTANGLES
UNTANGLING
UNTANNED
UNTAPPED
UNTARNISHED
UNTASTED
UNTAUGHT
UNTAXED
UNTEACH
UNTEACHABLE
UNTEACHES
UNTEACHING
UNTECHNICAL
UNTEMPERED
UNTENABILITIES
UNTENABILITY
UNTENABLE

TENABLY
TENANTED
TENDED
TENTED
TENURED
TESTABLE
TESTED
TETHER
TETHERED
TETHERING
TETHERS
THANKED
THAW
THAWED
THAWING
THAWS
THEORETICAL
THINK
THINKABILITY
THINKABLE
THINKABLY
THINKING
THINKINGLY
THINKS
THOUGHT
THREAD
THREADED
THREADING
THREADS
HREATENING
HRIFTY
HRONE
HRONED
HRONES
HRONING
IDIED
IDIER
IDIES
IDIEST
IDILY
IDINESS
IDINESSES
DY
DYING
E
ED
EING
ES
L
LLABLE
LLED
LTED
MED

UNTIMELIER
UNTIMELIEST
UNTIMELINESS
UNTIMELINESSES
UNTIMELY
UNTIMEOUS
UNTINGED
UNTIPPED
UNTIRED
UNTIRING
UNTIRINGLY
UNTITLED
UNTO
UNTOGETHER
UNTOLD
UNTONED
UNTORN
UNTOUCHABILITY
UNTOUCHABLE
UNTOUCHABLES
UNTOUCHED
UNTOWARD
UNTOWARDLY
UNTOWARDNESS
UNTOWARDNESSES
UNTRACEABLE
UNTRACED
UNTRACK
UNTRACKED
UNTRACKING
UNTRACKS
UNTRADITIONAL
UNTRADITIONALLY
UNTRAINED
UNTRAMMELED
UNTRAMMELLED
UNTRANSFORMED
UNTRANSLATABLE
UNTRANSLATED
UNTRAPPED
UNTRAVELED
UNTRAVERSED
UNTREAD
UNTREADED
UNTREADING
UNTREADS
UNTREATABLE
UNTREATED
UNTRENDIER
UNTRENDIEST
UNTRENDY
UNTRIED
UNTRIM

UNTRIMMED
UNTRIMMING
UNTRIMS
UNTROD
UNTRODDEN
UNTROUBLED
UNTRUE
UNTRUER
UNTRUEST
UNTRULY
UNTRUSS
UNTRUSSED
UNTRUSSES
UNTRUSSING
UNTRUSTING
UNTRUSTWORTHY
UNTRUSTY
UNTRUTH
UNTRUTHFUL
UNTRUTHFULLY
UNTRUTHFULNESS
UNTRUTHS
UNTUCK
UNTUCKED
UNTUCKING
UNTUCKS
UNTUFTED
UNTUNABLE
UNTUNE
UNTUNED
UNTUNEFUL
UNTUNES
UNTUNING
UNTURNED
UNTUTORED
UNTWILLED
UNTWINE
UNTWINED
UNTWINES
UNTWINING
UNTWIST
UNTWISTED
UNTWISTING
UNTWISTS
UNTYING
UNTYPICAL
UNTYPICALLY
UNUNBIUM
UNUNBIUMS
UNUNITED
UNUNUNIUM
UNUNUNIUMS
UNURGED

UNUSABLE
UNUSED
UNUSUAL
UNUSUALLY
UNUSUALNESS
UNUSUALNESSES
UNUTILIZED
UNUTTERABLE
UNUTTERABLY
UNUTTERED
UNVACCINATED
UNVALUED
UNVARIED
UNVARNISHED
UNVARYING
UNVEIL
UNVEILED
UNVEILING
UNVEILINGS
UNVEILS
UNVEINED
UNVENTILATED
UNVERBALIZED
UNVERIFIABLE
UNVERSED
UNVESTED
UNVEXED
UNVEXT
UNVIABLE
UNVISITED
UNVOCAL
UNVOICE
UNVOICED
UNVOICES
UNVOICING
UNWAGED
UNWAKENED
UNWALLED
UNWANING
UNWANTED
UNWARIER
UNWARIEST
UNWARILY
UNWARINESS
UNWARINESSES
UNWARLIKE
UNWARMED
UNWARNED
UNWARPED
UNWARRANTABLE
UNWARRANTABLY
UNWARRANTED
UNWARY

UNWASHED
UNWASHEDNESS
UNWASHEDNESSES
UNWASHEDS
UNWASTED
UNWATCHABLE
UNWATCHED
UNWATERED
UNWAVERING
UNWAVERINGLY
UNWAXED
UNWEANED
UNWEARABLE
UNWEARABLES
UNWEARIED
UNWEARIEDLY
UNWEARY
UNWEARYING
UNWEATHERED
UNWEAVE
UNWEAVES
UNWEAVING
UNWED
UNWEDDED
UNWEEDED
UNWEETING
UNWEETINGLY
UNWEIGHED
UNWEIGHT
UNWEIGHTED
UNWEIGHTING
UNWEIGHTS
UNWELCOME
UNWELCOMING
UNWELDED
UNWELL
UNWEPT
UNWET
UNWETTED
UNWHIPPED
UNWHITE
UNWHOLESOME
UNWHOLESOMELY
UNWIELDIER
UNWIELDIEST
UNWIELDILY
UNWIELDINESS
UNWIELDINESSES
UNWIELDY
UNWIFELY
UNWILLED
UNWILLING
UNWILLINGLY

UNWILLINGNESS
UNWILLINGNESSES
UNWIND
UNWINDER
UNWINDERS
UNWINDING
UNWINDS
UNWINKING
UNWINNABLE
UNWISDOM
UNWISDOMS
UNWISE
UNWISELY
UNWISER
UNWISEST
UNWISH
UNWISHED
UNWISHES
UNWISHING
UNWIT
UNWITS
UNWITTED
UNWITTING
UNWITTINGLY
UNWOMANLY
UNWON
UNWONTED
UNWONTEDLY
UNWONTEDNESS
UNWONTEDNESSES
UNWOODED
UNWOOED
UNWORKABILITIES
UNWORKABILITY
UNWORKABLE
UNWORKED
UNWORLDLIER
UNWORLDLIEST
UNWORLDLINESS
UNWORLDLINESSES
UNWORLDLY
UNWORN
UNWORRIED
UNWORTHIER
UNWORTHIES
UNWORTHIEST
UNWORTHILY
UNWORTHINESS
UNWORTHINESSES
UNWORTHY
UNWOUND
UNWOUNDED
UNWOVE
UNWOVEN
UNWRAP
UNWRAPPED
UNWRAPPING
UNWRAPS
UNWREATHE
UNWREATHED
UNWREATHES
UNWREATHING
UNWRINKLE
UNWRINKLED
UNWRINKLES
UNWRINKLING
UNWRITTEN
UNWROUGHT
UNWRUNG
UNYEANED
UNYIELDING
UNYIELDINGLY
UNYOKE
UNYOKED
UNYOKES
UNYOKING
UNYOUNG
UNZEALOUS
UNZIP
UNZIPPED
UNZIPPING
UNZIPS
UNZONED
UP
UPALONG
UPALONGS
UPAS
UPASES
UPBEAR
UPBEARER
UPBEARERS
UPBEARING
UPBEARS
UPBEAT
UPBEATS
UPBIND
UPBINDING
UPBINDS
UPBOIL
UPBOILED
UPBOILING
UPBOILS
UPBORE
UPBORNE
UPBOUND
UPBOW
UPBOWS
UPBRAID
UPBRAIDED
UPBRAIDER
UPBRAIDERS
UPBRAIDING
UPBRAIDS
UPBRINGING
UPBRINGINGS
UPBUILD
UPBUILDER
UPBUILDERS
UPBUILDING
UPBUILDS
UPBUILT
UPBY
UPBYE
UPCAST
UPCASTING
UPCASTS
UPCHUCK
UPCHUCKED
UPCHUCKING
UPCHUCKS
UPCLIMB
UPCLIMBED
UPCLIMBING
UPCLIMBS
UPCOAST
UPCOIL
UPCOILED
UPCOILING
UPCOILS
UPCOMING
UPCOUNTRIES
UPCOUNTRY
UPCOURT
UPCURL
UPCURLED
UPCURLING
UPCURLS
UPCURVE
UPCURVED
UPCURVES
UPCURVING
UPDART
UPDARTED
UPDARTING
UPDARTS
UPDATE
UPDATED
UPDATER
UPDATERS
UPDATES
UPDATING
UPDIVE
UPDIVED
UPDIVES
UPDIVING
UPDO
UPDOMING
UPDOMINGS
UPDOS
UPDOVE
UPDRAFT
UPDRAFTS
UPDRIED
UPDRIES
UPDRY
UPDRYING
UPEND
UPENDED
UPENDING
UPENDS
UPFIELD
UPFLING
UPFLINGING
UPFLINGS
UPFLOW
UPFLOWED
UPFLOWING
UPFLOWS
UPFLUNG
UPFOLD
UPFOLDED
UPFOLDING
UPFOLDS
UPFRONT
UPGATHER
UPGATHERED
UPGATHERING
UPGATHERS
UPGAZE
UPGAZED
UPGAZES
UPGAZING
UPGIRD
UPGIRDED
UPGIRDING
UPGIRDS
UPGIRT
UPGOING
UPGRADABILITIES
UPGRADABILITY
UPGRADABLE
UPGRADE
UPGRADEABILITY
UPGRADEABLE
UPGRADED
UPGRADER
UPGRADERS
UPGRADES
UPGRADING
UPGREW
UPGROW
UPGROWING
UPGROWN
UPGROWS
UPGROWTH
UPGROWTHS
UPHEAP
UPHEAPED
UPHEAPING
UPHEAPS
UPHEAVAL
UPHEAVALS
UPHEAVE
UPHEAVED
UPHEAVER
UPHEAVERS
UPHEAVES
UPHEAVING
UPHELD
UPHILL
UPHILLS
UPHOARD
UPHOARDED
UPHOARDING
UPHOARDS
UPHOLD
UPHOLDER
UPHOLDERS
UPHOLDING
UPHOLDS
UPHOLSTER
UPHOLSTERED
UPHOLSTERER
UPHOLSTERERS
UPHOLSTERIES
UPHOLSTERING
UPHOLSTERS
UPHOLSTERY
UPHOVE
UPHROE
UPHROES
UPKEEP
UPKEEPS
UPLAND
UPLANDER

LANDERS
LANDS
LEAP
LEAPED
LEAPING
LEAPS
LEAPT
LIFT
LIFTED
LIFTER
LIFTERS
LIFTING
LIFTS
IGHT
IGHTED
IGHTING
IGHTINGS
IGHTS
INK
INKED
INKING
INKS
IT
OAD
OADED
OADING
OADS
ANSHIP
ANSHIPS
ARKET
OST
N
ED
ER
ERCASE
ERCASED
ERCASES
ERCASING
ERCLASSMAN
ERCLASSMEN
ERCUT
ERCUTS
ERCUTTING
ERMOST
ERPART
ERPARTS
ERS
LE
LED
LES
LING
NG

UPPINGS
UPPISH
UPPISHLY
UPPISHNESS
UPPISHNESSES
UPPITINESS
UPPITINESSES
UPPITY
UPPITYNESS
UPPITYNESSES
UPPROP
UPPROPPED
UPPROPPING
UPPROPS
UPRAISE
UPRAISED
UPRAISER
UPRAISERS
UPRAISES
UPRAISING
UPRATE
UPRATED
UPRATES
UPRATING
UPREACH
UPREACHED
UPREACHES
UPREACHING
UPREAR
UPREARED
UPREARING
UPREARS
UPRIGHT
UPRIGHTED
UPRIGHTING
UPRIGHTLY
UPRIGHTNESS
UPRIGHTNESSES
UPRIGHTS
UPRISE
UPRISEN
UPRISER
UPRISERS
UPRISES
UPRISING
UPRISINGS
UPRIVER
UPRIVERS
UPROAR
UPROARIOUS
UPROARIOUSLY
UPROARIOUSNESS
UPROARS

UPROOT
UPROOTAL
UPROOTALS
UPROOTED
UPROOTEDNESS
UPROOTEDNESSES
UPROOTER
UPROOTERS
UPROOTING
UPROOTS
UPROSE
UPROUSE
UPROUSED
UPROUSES
UPROUSING
UPRUSH
UPRUSHED
UPRUSHES
UPRUSHING
UPS
UPSADAISY
UPSCALE
UPSCALED
UPSCALES
UPSCALING
UPSELL
UPSELLING
UPSELLS
UPSEND
UPSENDING
UPSENDS
UPSENT
UPSET
UPSETS
UPSETTER
UPSETTERS
UPSETTING
UPSHIFT
UPSHIFTED
UPSHIFTING
UPSHIFTS
UPSHOOT
UPSHOOTING
UPSHOOTS
UPSHOT
UPSHOTS
UPSIDE
UPSIDES
UPSILON
UPSILONS
UPSIZE
UPSIZED
UPSIZES

UPSIZING
UPSKILL
UPSKILLED
UPSKILLING
UPSKILLS
UPSLOPE
UPSLOPES
UPSOAR
UPSOARED
UPSOARING
UPSOARS
UPSOLD
UPSPRANG
UPSPRING
UPSPRINGING
UPSPRINGS
UPSPRUNG
UPSTAGE
UPSTAGED
UPSTAGER
UPSTAGERS
UPSTAGES
UPSTAGING
UPSTAIR
UPSTAIRS
UPSTAND
UPSTANDING
UPSTANDINGNESS
UPSTANDS
UPSTARE
UPSTARED
UPSTARES
UPSTARING
UPSTART
UPSTARTED
UPSTARTING
UPSTARTS
UPSTATE
UPSTATER
UPSTATERS
UPSTATES
UPSTEP
UPSTEPPED
UPSTEPPING
UPSTEPS
UPSTIR
UPSTIRRED
UPSTIRRING
UPSTIRS
UPSTOOD
UPSTREAM
UPSTROKE
UPSTROKES

UPSURGE
UPSURGED
UPSURGES
UPSURGING
UPSWEEP
UPSWEEPING
UPSWEEPS
UPSWELL
UPSWELLED
UPSWELLING
UPSWELLS
UPSWEPT
UPSWING
UPSWINGING
UPSWINGS
UPSWOLLEN
UPSWUNG
UPTAKE
UPTAKES
UPTALK
UPTALKED
UPTALKING
UPTALKS
UPTEAR
UPTEARING
UPTEARS
UPTEMPO
UPTEMPOS
UPTHREW
UPTHROW
UPTHROWING
UPTHROWN
UPTHROWS
UPTHRUST
UPTHRUSTED
UPTHRUSTING
UPTHRUSTS
UPTICK
UPTICKS
UPTIGHT
UPTIGHTNESS
UPTIGHTNESSES
UPTILT
UPTILTED
UPTILTING
UPTILTS
UPTIME
UPTIMES
UPTORE
UPTORN
UPTOSS
UPTOSSED
UPTOSSES

UPTOSSING
UPTOWN
UPTOWNER
UPTOWNERS
UPTOWNS
UPTREND
UPTRENDS
UPTURN
UPTURNED
UPTURNING
UPTURNS
UPWAFT
UPWAFTED
UPWAFTING
UPWAFTS
UPWARD
UPWARDLY
UPWARDNESS
UPWARDNESSES
UPWARDS
UPWELL
UPWELLED
UPWELLING
UPWELLINGS
UPWELLS
UPWIND
UPWINDS
URACIL
URACILS
URAEI
URAEMIA
URAEMIAS
URAEMIC
URAEUS
URAEUSES
URALITE
URALITES
URALITIC
URANIA
URANIAS
URANIC
URANIDE
URANIDES
URANINITE
URANINITES
URANISM
URANISMS
URANITE
URANITES
URANITIC
URANIUM
URANIUMS
URANOGRAPHIES
URANOGRAPHY
URANOLOGIES
URANOLOGY
URANOUS
URANYL
URANYLIC
URANYLS
URARE
URARES
URARI
URARIS
URASE
URASES
URATE
URATES
URATIC
URB
URBAN
URBANE
URBANELY
URBANER
URBANEST
URBANISATION
URBANISATIONS
URBANISE
URBANISED
URBANISES
URBANISING
URBANISM
URBANISMS
URBANIST
URBANISTIC
URBANISTICALLY
URBANISTS
URBANITE
URBANITES
URBANITIES
URBANITY
URBANIZATION
URBANIZATIONS
URBANIZE
URBANIZED
URBANIZES
URBANIZING
URBANOLOGIES
URBANOLOGIST
URBANOLOGISTS
URBANOLOGY
URBIA
URBIAS
URBS
URCEOLATE
URCHIN
URCHINS
URD
URDS
UREA
UREAL
UREAS
UREASE
UREASES
UREDIA
UREDIAL
UREDINIA
UREDINIAL
UREDINIOSPORE
UREDINIOSPORES
UREDINIUM
UREDINIUMS
UREDIOSPORE
UREDIOSPORES
UREDIUM
UREDO
UREDOS
UREDOSPORE
UREDOSPORES
UREIC
UREIDE
UREIDES
UREMIA
UREMIAS
UREMIC
UREOTELIC
UREOTELISM
UREOTELISMS
URETER
URETERAL
URETERIC
URETERS
URETHAN
URETHANE
URETHANED
URETHANES
URETHANING
URETHANS
URETHRA
URETHRAE
URETHRAL
URETHRAS
URETHRITIDES
URETHRITIS
URETHRITISES
URETHROSCOPE
URETHROSCOPES
URETIC
URGE
URGED
URGENCIES
URGENCY
URGENT
URGENTLY
URGER
URGERS
URGES
URGING
URGINGLY
URGINGS
URIAL
URIALS
URIC
URICOSURIC
URICOTELIC
URICOTELICS
URICOTELISM
URICOTELISMS
URIDINE
URIDINES
URINAL
URINALS
URINALYSES
URINALYSIS
URINARIES
URINARY
URINATE
URINATED
URINATES
URINATING
URINATION
URINATIONS
URINATIVE
URINATOR
URINATORS
URINE
URINEMIA
URINEMIAS
URINEMIC
URINES
URINOGENITAL
URINOMETER
URINOMETERS
URINOSE
URINOUS
URN
URNLIKE
URNS
UROBORIC
UROBOROS
UROBOROSES
UROCHORD
UROCHORDATE
UROCHORDATES
UROCHORDS
UROCHROME
UROCHROMES
URODELE
URODELES
UROGENITAL
UROGENITALS
UROGENOUS
UROGRAM
UROGRAMS
UROGYNECOLOGIE
UROGYNECOLOGIS
UROGYNECOLOGY
UROKINASE
UROKINASES
UROLITH
UROLITHIASES
UROLITHIASIS
UROLITHIC
UROLITHS
UROLOGIC
UROLOGICAL
UROLOGIES
UROLOGIST
UROLOGISTS
UROLOGY
UROPOD
UROPODAL
UROPODOUS
UROPODS
UROPYGIA
UROPYGIAL
UROPYGIUM
UROPYGIUMS
UROSCOPIC
UROSCOPIES
UROSCOPY
UROSTYLE
UROSTYLES
URP
URPED
URPING
URPS
URSA
URSAE
URSID
URSIDS
URSIFORM
URSINE
URTEXT
URTEXTE

TEXTS
TICANT
TICANTS
TICARIA
TICARIAL
TICARIAS
TICATE
TICATED
TICATES
TICATING
TICATION
TICATIONS
US
USES
USHIOL
USHIOLS

ABILITIES
BILITY
BLE
BLENESS
BLENESSES
BLY
GE
GES
NCE
NCES
UNCE
UNCES

ABLE
ABLY
D
FUL
FULLY
FULNESS
FULNESSES

USELESS
USELESSLY
USELESSNESS
USELESSNESSES
USER
USERNAME
USERNAMES
USERS
USES
USHER
USHERED
USHERETTE
USHERETTES
USHERING
USHERS
USING
USNEA
USNEAS
USQUABAE
USQUABAES
USQUE
USQUEBAE
USQUEBAES
USQUEBAUGH
USQUEBAUGHS
USQUES
USTULATE
USUAL
USUALLY
USUALNESS
USUALNESSES
USUALS
USUFRUCT
USUFRUCTS
USUFRUCTUARIES
USUFRUCTUARY
USURER

USURERS
USURIES
USURIOUS
USURIOUSLY
USURIOUSNESS
USURIOUSNESSES
USURP
USURPATION
USURPATIONS
USURPED
USURPER
USURPERS
USURPING
USURPS
USURY
UT
UTA
UTAS
UTE
UTENSIL
UTENSILS
UTERI
UTERINE
UTERUS
UTERUSES
UTES
UTILE
UTILES
UTILIDOR
UTILIDORS
UTILISATION
UTILISATIONS
UTILISE
UTILISED
UTILISER
UTILISERS
UTILISES

UTILISING
UTILITARIAN
UTILITARIANISM
UTILITARIANISMS
UTILITARIANS
UTILITIES
UTILITY
UTILIZABLE
UTILIZATION
UTILIZATIONS
UTILIZE
UTILIZED
UTILIZER
UTILIZERS
UTILIZES
UTILIZING
UTMOST
UTMOSTS
UTOPIA
UTOPIAN
UTOPIANISM
UTOPIANISMS
UTOPIANS
UTOPIAS
UTOPISM
UTOPISMS
UTOPIST
UTOPISTIC
UTOPISTS
UTRICLE
UTRICLES
UTRICULAR
UTRICULI
UTRICULUS
UTS
UTTER
UTTERABLE

UTTERANCE
UTTERANCES
UTTERED
UTTERER
UTTERERS
UTTERING
UTTERLY
UTTERMOST
UTTERMOSTS
UTTERNESS
UTTERNESSES
UTTERS
UVAROVITE
UVAROVITES
UVEA
UVEAL
UVEAS
UVEITIC
UVEITIS
UVEITISES
UVEOUS
UVULA
UVULAE
UVULAR
UVULARLY
UVULARS
UVULAS
UVULITIS
UVULITISES
UXORIAL
UXORIALLY
UXORICIDE
UXORICIDES
UXORIOUS
UXORIOUSLY
UXORIOUSNESS
UXORIOUSNESSES

V

NCIES
NCY
NT
NTLY
NTNESS

VACANTNESSES
VACATABLE
VACATE
VACATED
VACATES
VACATING

VACATION
VACATIONED
VACATIONER
VACATIONERS
VACATIONING
VACATIONIST

VACATIONISTS
VACATIONLAND
VACATIONLANDS
VACATIONS
VACCINA
VACCINAL

VACCINAS
VACCINATE
VACCINATED
VACCINATES
VACCINATING
VACCINATION

VACCINATIONS
VACCINATOR
VACCINATORS
VACCINE
VACCINEE
VACCINEES
VACCINES
VACCINIA
VACCINIAL
VACCINIAS
VACILLANT
VACILLATE
VACILLATED
VACILLATES
VACILLATING
VACILLATINGLY
VACILLATION
VACILLATIONS
VACILLATOR
VACILLATORS
VACS
VACUA
VACUITIES
VACUITY
VACUOLAR
VACUOLATE
VACUOLATED
VACUOLATION
VACUOLATIONS
VACUOLE
VACUOLES
VACUOUS
VACUOUSLY
VACUOUSNESS
VACUOUSNESSES
VACUUM
VACUUMED
VACUUMING
VACUUMS
VADOSE
VAGABOND
VAGABONDAGE
VAGABONDAGES
VAGABONDED
VAGABONDING
VAGABONDISH
VAGABONDISM
VAGABONDISMS
VAGABONDS
VAGAL
VAGALLY
VAGARIES
VAGARIOUS
VAGARIOUSLY
VAGARY
VAGI
VAGILE
VAGILITIES
VAGILITY
VAGINA
VAGINAE
VAGINAL
VAGINALLY
VAGINAS
VAGINATE
VAGINATED
VAGINISMUS
VAGINISMUSES
VAGINITIDES
VAGINITIS
VAGINITISES
VAGINOSES
VAGINOSIS
VAGOTOMIES
VAGOTOMY
VAGOTONIA
VAGOTONIAS
VAGOTONIC
VAGRANCIES
VAGRANCY
VAGRANT
VAGRANTLY
VAGRANTS
VAGROM
VAGUE
VAGUELY
VAGUENESS
VAGUENESSES
VAGUER
VAGUEST
VAGUISH
VAGUS
VAHINE
VAHINES
VAIL
VAILED
VAILING
VAILS
VAIN
VAINER
VAINEST
VAINGLORIES
VAINGLORIOUS
VAINGLORIOUSLY
VAINGLORY
VAINLY
VAINNESS
VAINNESSES
VAIR
VAIRS
VAKEEL
VAKEELS
VAKIL
VAKILS
VALANCE
VALANCED
VALANCES
VALANCING
VALE
VALEDICTION
VALEDICTIONS
VALEDICTORIAN
VALEDICTORIANS
VALEDICTORIES
VALEDICTORY
VALENCE
VALENCES
VALENCIA
VALENCIAS
VALENCIES
VALENCY
VALENTINE
VALENTINES
VALERATE
VALERATES
VALERIAN
VALERIANS
VALERIC
VALES
VALET
VALETED
VALETING
VALETS
VALETUDINARIAN
VALETUDINARIANS
VALETUDINARIES
VALETUDINARY
VALGOID
VALGUS
VALGUSES
VALIANCE
VALIANCES
VALIANCIES
VALIANCY
VALIANT
VALIANTLY
VALIANTNESS
VALIANTNESSES
VALIANTS
VALID
VALIDATE
VALIDATED
VALIDATES
VALIDATING
VALIDATION
VALIDATIONS
VALIDITIES
VALIDITY
VALIDLY
VALIDNESS
VALIDNESSES
VALINE
VALINES
VALISE
VALISES
VALKYR
VALKYRIE
VALKYRIES
VALKYRS
VALLATE
VALLATION
VALLATIONS
VALLECULA
VALLECULAE
VALLECULAR
VALLECULAS
VALLEY
VALLEYED
VALLEYS
VALLUM
VALLUMS
VALONIA
VALONIAS
VALOR
VALORISE
VALORISED
VALORISES
VALORISING
VALORIZATION
VALORIZATIONS
VALORIZE
VALORIZED
VALORIZES
VALORIZING
VALOROUS
VALOROUSLY
VALORS
VALOUR
VALOURS
VALPOLICELLA
VALPOLICELLAS
VALSE
VALSES
VALUABLE
VALUABLENESS
VALUABLENESSES
VALUABLES
VALUABLY
VALUATE
VALUATED
VALUATES
VALUATING
VALUATION
VALUATIONAL
VALUATIONALLY
VALUATIONS
VALUATOR
VALUATORS
VALUE
VALUED
VALUELESS
VALUELESSNESS
VALUELESSNESSES
VALUER
VALUERS
VALUES
VALUING
VALUTA
VALUTAS
VALVAL
VALVAR
VALVATE
VALVE
VALVED
VALVELESS
VALVELET
VALVELETS
VALVELIKE
VALVES
VALVING
VALVULA
VALVULAE
VALVULAR
VALVULE
VALVULES
VALVULITIS
VALVULITISES
VAMBRACE
VAMBRACED
VAMBRACES
VAMOOSE
VAMOOSED
VAMOOSES
VAMOOSING
VAMOSE

MOSED
MOSES
MOSING
MP
MPED
MPER
MPERS
MPIER
MPIEST
MPING
MPIRE
MPIRES
MPIRIC
MPIRISH
MPIRISM
MPIRISMS
MPISH
MPISHLY
PLATE
PLATES
PS
PY

ADATE
ADATES
ADIATE
ADIATES
ADIC
ADIUM
ADIUMS
ADOUS
ASPATI
ASPATIS
COMYCIN
COMYCINS
DA
DAL
DALIC
DALISE
DALISED
DALISES
DALISH
ALISING
ALISM
ALISMS
ALISTIC
ALIZATION
ALIZATIONS
ALIZE
ALIZED
ALIZES
ALIZING
ALS

VANDAS
VANDYKE
VANDYKED
VANDYKES
VANE
VANED
VANES
VANG
VANGS
VANGUARD
VANGUARDISM
VANGUARDISMS
VANGUARDIST
VANGUARDISTS
VANGUARDS
VANILLA
VANILLAS
VANILLIC
VANILLIN
VANILLINS
VANISH
VANISHED
VANISHER
VANISHERS
VANISHES
VANISHING
VANISHINGLY
VANITAS
VANITASES
VANITIED
VANITIES
VANITORIES
VANITORY
VANITY
VANLOAD
VANLOADS
VANMAN
VANMEN
VANNED
VANNER
VANNERS
VANNING
VANPOOL
VANPOOLING
VANPOOLINGS
VANPOOLS
VANQUISH
VANQUISHABLE
VANQUISHED
VANQUISHER
VANQUISHERS
VANQUISHES
VANQUISHING

VANS
VANTAGE
VANTAGES
VANWARD
VAPID
VAPIDITIES
VAPIDITY
VAPIDLY
VAPIDNESS
VAPIDNESSES
VAPOR
VAPORABLE
VAPORED
VAPORER
VAPORERS
VAPORETTI
VAPORETTO
VAPORETTOS
VAPORIFIC
VAPORING
VAPORINGS
VAPORISATION
VAPORISATIONS
VAPORISE
VAPORISED
VAPORISER
VAPORISERS
VAPORISES
VAPORISH
VAPORISHNESS
VAPORISHNESSES
VAPORISING
VAPORIZABLE
VAPORIZATION
VAPORIZATIONS
VAPORIZE
VAPORIZED
VAPORIZER
VAPORIZERS
VAPORIZES
VAPORIZING
VAPORLESS
VAPORLIKE
VAPOROUS
VAPOROUSLY
VAPOROUSNESS
VAPOROUSNESSES
VAPORS
VAPORWARE
VAPORWARES
VAPORY
VAPOUR
VAPOURED

VAPOURER
VAPOURERS
VAPOURING
VAPOURS
VAPOURY
VAQUERO
VAQUEROS
VAR
VARA
VARACTOR
VARACTORS
VARAS
VAREC
VARECS
VARENYKY
VARIA
VARIABILITIES
VARIABILITY
VARIABLE
VARIABLENESS
VARIABLENESSES
VARIABLES
VARIABLY
VARIANCE
VARIANCES
VARIANT
VARIANTS
VARIAS
VARIATE
VARIATED
VARIATES
VARIATING
VARIATION
VARIATIONAL
VARIATIONALLY
VARIATIONS
VARICEAL
VARICELLA
VARICELLAS
VARICES
VARICOCELE
VARICOCELES
VARICOLORED
VARICOSE
VARICOSED
VARICOSES
VARICOSIS
VARICOSITIES
VARICOSITY
VARIED
VARIEDLY
VARIEGATE
VARIEGATED

VARIEGATES
VARIEGATING
VARIEGATION
VARIEGATIONS
VARIEGATOR
VARIEGATORS
VARIER
VARIERS
VARIES
VARIETAL
VARIETALS
VARIETIES
VARIETY
VARIFORM
VARIOLA
VARIOLAR
VARIOLAS
VARIOLATE
VARIOLATED
VARIOLATES
VARIOLATING
VARIOLE
VARIOLES
VARIOLITE
VARIOLITES
VARIOLOID
VARIOLOIDS
VARIOLOUS
VARIOMETER
VARIOMETERS
VARIORUM
VARIORUMS
VARIOUS
VARIOUSLY
VARIOUSNESS
VARIOUSNESSES
VARISIZED
VARISTOR
VARISTORS
VARIX
VARLET
VARLETRIES
VARLETRY
VARLETS
VARMENT
VARMENTS
VARMINT
VARMINTS
VARNA
VARNAS
VARNISH
VARNISHED
VARNISHER

VARNISHERS
VARNISHES
VARNISHING
VARNISHY
VAROOM
VAROOMED
VAROOMING
VAROOMS
VARROA
VARROAS
VARS
VARSITIES
VARSITY
VARUS
VARUSES
VARVE
VARVED
VARVES
VARY
VARYING
VARYINGLY
VAS
VASA
VASAL
VASCULA
VASCULAR
VASCULARITIES
VASCULARITY
VASCULARIZATION
VASCULATURE
VASCULATURES
VASCULITIDES
VASCULITIS
VASCULUM
VASCULUMS
VASE
VASECTOMIES
VASECTOMIZE
VASECTOMIZED
VASECTOMIZES
VASECTOMIZING
VASECTOMY
VASEFUL
VASEFULS
VASELIKE
VASELINE
VASELINED
VASELINES
VASELINING
VASES
VASIFORM
VASOACTIVE
VASOACTIVITIES
VASOACTIVITY
VASOCONSTRICTOR
VASODILATATION
VASODILATATIONS
VASODILATION
VASODILATIONS
VASODILATOR
VASODILATORS
VASOMOTOR
VASOPRESSIN
VASOPRESSINS
VASOPRESSOR
VASOPRESSORS
VASOSPASM
VASOSPASMS
VASOSPASTIC
VASOTOCIN
VASOTOCINS
VASOTOMIES
VASOTOMY
VASOVAGAL
VASSAL
VASSALAGE
VASSALAGES
VASSALS
VAST
VASTER
VASTEST
VASTIER
VASTIEST
VASTITIES
VASTITUDE
VASTITUDES
VASTITY
VASTLY
VASTNESS
VASTNESSES
VASTS
VASTY
VAT
VATFUL
VATFULS
VATIC
VATICAL
VATICIDE
VATICIDES
VATICINAL
VATICINATE
VATICINATED
VATICINATES
VATICINATING
VATICINATION
VATICINATIONS
VATICINATOR
VATICINATORS
VATS
VATTED
VATTING
VATU
VATUS
VAU
VAUDEVILLE
VAUDEVILLES
VAUDEVILLIAN
VAUDEVILLIANS
VAULT
VAULTED
VAULTER
VAULTERS
VAULTIER
VAULTIEST
VAULTING
VAULTINGLY
VAULTINGS
VAULTS
VAULTY
VAUNT
VAUNTED
VAUNTER
VAUNTERS
VAUNTFUL
VAUNTIE
VAUNTING
VAUNTINGLY
VAUNTS
VAUNTY
VAUS
VAV
VAVASOR
VAVASORIES
VAVASORS
VAVASORY
VAVASOUR
VAVASOURS
VAVASSOR
VAVASSORS
VAVS
VAW
VAWARD
VAWARDS
VAWNTIE
VAWS
VEAL
VEALED
VEALER
VEALERS
VEALIER
VEALIEST
VEALING
VEALS
VEALY
VECTOR
VECTORED
VECTORIAL
VECTORIALLY
VECTORING
VECTORS
VEDALIA
VEDALIAS
VEDETTE
VEDETTES
VEE
VEEJAY
VEEJAYS
VEENA
VEENAS
VEEP
VEEPEE
VEEPEES
VEEPS
VEER
VEERED
VEERIES
VEERING
VEERINGLY
VEERS
VEERY
VEES
VEG
VEGA
VEGAN
VEGANISM
VEGANISMS
VEGANS
VEGAS
VEGES
VEGETABLE
VEGETABLES
VEGETABLY
VEGETAL
VEGETALLY
VEGETANT
VEGETARIAN
VEGETARIANISM
VEGETARIANISMS
VEGETARIANS
VEGETATE
VEGETATED
VEGETATES
VEGETATING
VEGETATION
VEGETATIONAL
VEGETATIONS
VEGETATIVE
VEGETATIVELY
VEGETATIVENESS
VEGETE
VEGETIST
VEGETISTS
VEGETIVE
VEGGED
VEGGES
VEGGIE
VEGGIES
VEGGING
VEGIE
VEGIES
VEHEMENCE
VEHEMENCES
VEHEMENCIES
VEHEMENCY
VEHEMENT
VEHEMENTLY
VEHICLE
VEHICLES
VEHICULAR
VEIL
VEILED
VEILEDLY
VEILER
VEILERS
VEILING
VEILINGS
VEILLESS
VEILLIKE
VEILS
VEIN
VEINAL
VEINED
VEINER
VEINERS
VEINIER
VEINIEST
VEINING
VEININGS
VEINLESS
VEINLET
VEINLETS
VEINLIKE
VEINOUS
VEINS
VEINSTONE

NSTONES
NULE
NULES
NULET
NULETS
NY
A
AMEN
AMINA
AR
ARIA
ARIUM
ARIZATION
ARIZATIONS
ARIZE
ARIZED
ARIZES
ARIZING
ARS
ATE
CRO
CROS
D
DS
DT
DTS
GER
GERS
TES
EITIES
EITY
ICATE
ICATED
ICATES
ICATING
UM
UMS
CE
CIMETER
CIMETERS
CIPEDE
CIPEDES
CIRAPTOR
CIRAPTORS
CITIES
CITY
DROME
DROMES
UR
URS
UTE
UTES
M

VELURE
VELURED
VELURES
VELURING
VELVERET
VELVERETS
VELVET
VELVETED
VELVETEEN
VELVETEENS
VELVETIER
VELVETIEST
VELVETLIKE
VELVETS
VELVETY
VENA
VENAE
VENAL
VENALITIES
VENALITY
VENALLY
VENATIC
VENATICAL
VENATION
VENATIONS
VEND
VENDABLE
VENDABLES
VENDACE
VENDACES
VENDED
VENDEE
VENDEES
VENDER
VENDERS
VENDETTA
VENDETTAS
VENDEUSE
VENDEUSES
VENDIBILITIES
VENDIBILITY
VENDIBLE
VENDIBLES
VENDIBLY
VENDING
VENDITION
VENDITIONS
VENDOR
VENDORS
VENDS
VENDU
VENDUE
VENDUES

VENDUS
VENEER
VENEERED
VENEERER
VENEERERS
VENEERING
VENEERINGS
VENEERS
VENENATE
VENENATED
VENENATES
VENENATING
VENENE
VENENES
VENENOSE
VENERABILITIES
VENERABILITY
VENERABLE
VENERABLENESS
VENERABLENESSES
VENERABLES
VENERABLY
VENERATE
VENERATED
VENERATES
VENERATING
VENERATION
VENERATIONS
VENERATOR
VENERATORS
VENEREAL
VENEREALLY
VENERIES
VENERY
VENESECTION
VENESECTIONS
VENETIAN
VENETIANS
VENGE
VENGEANCE
VENGEANCES
VENGED
VENGEFUL
VENGEFULLY
VENGEFULNESS
VENGEFULNESSES
VENGES
VENGING
VENIAL
VENIALITIES
VENIALITY
VENIALLY
VENIALNESS

VENIALNESSES
VENIN
VENINE
VENINES
VENINS
VENIPUNCTURE
VENIPUNCTURES
VENIRE
VENIREMAN
VENIREMEN
VENIRES
VENISON
VENISONS
VENOGRAM
VENOGRAMS
VENOGRAPHIES
VENOGRAPHY
VENOLOGIES
VENOLOGY
VENOM
VENOMED
VENOMER
VENOMERS
VENOMING
VENOMOUS
VENOMOUSLY
VENOMOUSNESS
VENOMOUSNESSES
VENOMS
VENOSE
VENOSITIES
VENOSITY
VENOUS
VENOUSLY
VENT
VENTAGE
VENTAGES
VENTAIL
VENTAILS
VENTED
VENTER
VENTERS
VENTIFACT
VENTIFACTS
VENTILATE
VENTILATED
VENTILATES
VENTILATING
VENTILATION
VENTILATIONS
VENTILATOR
VENTILATORS
VENTILATORY

VENTING
VENTLESS
VENTRAL
VENTRALLY
VENTRALS
VENTRICLE
VENTRICLES
VENTRICOSE
VENTRICULAR
VENTRICULI
VENTRICULUS
VENTRILOQUIAL
VENTRILOQUIALLY
VENTRILOQUIES
VENTRILOQUISM
VENTRILOQUISMS
VENTRILOQUIST
VENTRILOQUISTIC
VENTRILOQUISTS
VENTRILOQUIZE
VENTRILOQUIZED
VENTRILOQUIZES
VENTRILOQUIZING
VENTRILOQUY
VENTROLATERAL
VENTROMEDIAL
VENTS
VENTURE
VENTURED
VENTURER
VENTURERS
VENTURES
VENTURESOME
VENTURESOMELY
VENTURESOMENESS
VENTURI
VENTURING
VENTURIS
VENTUROUS
VENTUROUSLY
VENTUROUSNESS
VENTUROUSNESSES
VENUE
VENUES
VENULAR
VENULE
VENULES
VENULOSE
VENULOUS
VENUS
VENUSES
VERA
VERACIOUS

VERACIOUSLY
VERACIOUSNESS
VERACIOUSNESSES
VERACITIES
VERACITY
VERANDA
VERANDAED
VERANDAH
VERANDAHED
VERANDAHS
VERANDAS
VERAPAMIL
VERAPAMILS
VERATRIA
VERATRIAS
VERATRIDINE
VERATRIDINES
VERATRIN
VERATRINE
VERATRINES
VERATRINS
VERATRUM
VERATRUMS
VERB
VERBAL
VERBALISE
VERBALISED
VERBALISES
VERBALISING
VERBALISM
VERBALISMS
VERBALIST
VERBALISTIC
VERBALISTS
VERBALIZATION
VERBALIZATIONS
VERBALIZE
VERBALIZED
VERBALIZER
VERBALIZERS
VERBALIZES
VERBALIZING
VERBALLY
VERBALS
VERBATIM
VERBENA
VERBENAS
VERBIAGE
VERBIAGES
VERBICIDE
VERBICIDES
VERBID
VERBIDS
VERBIFIED
VERBIFIES
VERBIFY
VERBIFYING
VERBIGERATION
VERBIGERATIONS
VERBILE
VERBILES
VERBLESS
VERBOSE
VERBOSELY
VERBOSENESS
VERBOSENESSES
VERBOSITIES
VERBOSITY
VERBOTEN
VERBS
VERDANCIES
VERDANCY
VERDANT
VERDANTLY
VERDERER
VERDERERS
VERDEROR
VERDERORS
VERDICT
VERDICTS
VERDIGRIS
VERDIGRISES
VERDIN
VERDINS
VERDITER
VERDITERS
VERDURE
VERDURED
VERDURES
VERDUROUS
VERECUND
VERGE
VERGED
VERGENCE
VERGENCES
VERGER
VERGERS
VERGES
VERGING
VERGLAS
VERGLASES
VERIDIC
VERIDICAL
VERIDICALITIES
VERIDICALITY
VERIDICALLY
VERIER
VERIEST
VERIFIABILITIES
VERIFIABILITY
VERIFIABLE
VERIFIABLENESS
VERIFICATION
VERIFICATIONS
VERIFIED
VERIFIER
VERIFIERS
VERIFIES
VERIFY
VERIFYING
VERILY
VERISIMILAR
VERISIMILARLY
VERISIMILITUDE
VERISIMILITUDES
VERISM
VERISMO
VERISMOS
VERISMS
VERIST
VERISTIC
VERISTS
VERITABLE
VERITABLENESS
VERITABLENESSES
VERITABLY
VERITAS
VERITATES
VERITE
VERITES
VERITIES
VERITY
VERJUICE
VERJUICES
VERJUS
VERJUSES
VERMEIL
VERMEILS
VERMES
VERMIAN
VERMICELLI
VERMICELLIS
VERMICIDE
VERMICIDES
VERMICULAR
VERMICULATE
VERMICULATED
VERMICULATION
VERMICULATIONS
VERMICULITE
VERMICULITES
VERMICULTURE
VERMICULTURES
VERMIFORM
VERMIFUGE
VERMIFUGES
VERMILION
VERMILIONED
VERMILIONING
VERMILIONS
VERMILLION
VERMILLIONS
VERMIN
VERMINOUS
VERMINS
VERMIS
VERMOULU
VERMOUTH
VERMOUTHS
VERMUTH
VERMUTHS
VERNACLE
VERNACLES
VERNACULAR
VERNACULARISM
VERNACULARISMS
VERNACULARLY
VERNACULARS
VERNAL
VERNALIZATION
VERNALIZATIONS
VERNALIZE
VERNALIZED
VERNALIZES
VERNALIZING
VERNALLY
VERNATION
VERNATIONS
VERNICLE
VERNICLES
VERNIER
VERNIERS
VERNISSAGE
VERNISSAGES
VERNIX
VERNIXES
VERONAL
VERONALS
VERONICA
VERONICAS
VERRUCA
VERRUCAE
VERRUCAS
VERRUCOSE
VERRUCOUS
VERSAL
VERSALS
VERSANT
VERSANTS
VERSATILE
VERSATILELY
VERSATILENESS
VERSATILENESSES
VERSATILITIES
VERSATILITY
VERSE
VERSED
VERSELET
VERSELETS
VERSEMAN
VERSEMEN
VERSER
VERSERS
VERSES
VERSET
VERSETS
VERSICLE
VERSICLES
VERSICULAR
VERSIFICATION
VERSIFICATIONS
VERSIFIED
VERSIFIER
VERSIFIERS
VERSIFIES
VERSIFY
VERSIFYING
VERSIN
VERSINE
VERSINES
VERSING
VERSINS
VERSION
VERSIONAL
VERSIONED
VERSIONING
VERSIONINGS
VERSIONS
VERSO
VERSOS
VERST
VERSTE
VERSTES
VERSTS
VERSUS

RT
RTEBRA
RTEBRAE
RTEBRAL
RTEBRAS
RTEBRATE
RTEBRATES
RTEX
RTEXES
RTICAL
RTICALITIES
RTICALITY
RTICALLY
RTICALNESS
RTICALNESSES
RTICALS
RTICES
RTICIL
RTICILLATE
RTICILS
RTIGINES
RTIGINOUS
RTIGINOUSLY
RTIGO
RTIGOES
RTIGOS
RTISOL
RTISOLS
TS
TU
TUS
VAIN
VAINS
VE
VES
VET
VETS
Y
CA
CAE
CAL
CANT
CANTS
CAS
CATE
CATED
CATES
CATING
CLE
CLES
CULA
CULAE
CULAR

VESICULARITIES
VESICULARITY
VESICULATE
VESICULATED
VESICULATES
VESICULATING
VESICULATION
VESICULATIONS
VESPER
VESPERAL
VESPERALS
VESPERS
VESPERTILIAN
VESPERTINE
VESPIARIES
VESPIARY
VESPID
VESPIDS
VESPINE
VESSEL
VESSELED
VESSELS
VEST
VESTA
VESTAL
VESTALLY
VESTALS
VESTAS
VESTED
VESTEE
VESTEES
VESTIARIES
VESTIARY
VESTIBULAR
VESTIBULE
VESTIBULED
VESTIBULES
VESTIBULING
VESTIGE
VESTIGES
VESTIGIA
VESTIGIAL
VESTIGIALLY
VESTIGIUM
VESTIMENTIFERAN
VESTING
VESTINGS
VESTLESS
VESTLIKE
VESTMENT
VESTMENTAL
VESTMENTS
VESTRAL

VESTRIES
VESTRY
VESTRYMAN
VESTRYMEN
VESTS
VESTURAL
VESTURE
VESTURED
VESTURES
VESTURING
VESUVIAN
VESUVIANITE
VESUVIANITES
VESUVIANS
VET
VETCH
VETCHES
VETCHLING
VETCHLINGS
VETERAN
VETERANS
VETERINARIAN
VETERINARIANS
VETERINARIES
VETERINARY
VETIVER
VETIVERS
VETIVERT
VETIVERTS
VETO
VETOED
VETOER
VETOERS
VETOES
VETOING
VETS
VETTED
VETTER
VETTERS
VETTING
VEX
VEXATION
VEXATIONS
VEXATIOUS
VEXATIOUSLY
VEXATIOUSNESS
VEXATIOUSNESSES
VEXED
VEXEDLY
VEXEDNESS
VEXEDNESSES
VEXER
VEXERS

VEXES
VEXIL
VEXILLA
VEXILLAR
VEXILLARIES
VEXILLARY
VEXILLATE
VEXILLOLOGIC
VEXILLOLOGICAL
VEXILLOLOGIES
VEXILLOLOGIST
VEXILLOLOGISTS
VEXILLOLOGY
VEXILLUM
VEXILS
VEXING
VEXINGLY
VEXT
VIA
VIABILITIES
VIABILITY
VIABLE
VIABLY
VIADUCT
VIADUCTS
VIAL
VIALED
VIALING
VIALLED
VIALLING
VIALS
VIAND
VIANDS
VIATIC
VIATICA
VIATICAL
VIATICALS
VIATICUM
VIATICUMS
VIATOR
VIATORES
VIATORS
VIBE
VIBES
VIBIST
VIBISTS
VIBRACULA
VIBRACULUM
VIBRAHARP
VIBRAHARPIST
VIBRAHARPISTS
VIBRAHARPS
VIBRANCE

VIBRANCES
VIBRANCIES
VIBRANCY
VIBRANT
VIBRANTLY
VIBRANTS
VIBRAPHONE
VIBRAPHONES
VIBRAPHONIST
VIBRAPHONISTS
VIBRATE
VIBRATED
VIBRATES
VIBRATILE
VIBRATING
VIBRATION
VIBRATIONAL
VIBRATIONLESS
VIBRATIONS
VIBRATIVE
VIBRATO
VIBRATOLESS
VIBRATOR
VIBRATORS
VIBRATORY
VIBRATOS
VIBRIO
VIBRIOID
VIBRION
VIBRIONIC
VIBRIONS
VIBRIOS
VIBRIOSES
VIBRIOSIS
VIBRISSA
VIBRISSAE
VIBRISSAL
VIBRONIC
VIBURNUM
VIBURNUMS
VICAR
VICARAGE
VICARAGES
VICARATE
VICARATES
VICARIAL
VICARIANCE
VICARIANCES
VICARIANT
VICARIANTS
VICARIATE
VICARIATES
VICARIOUS

VICARIOUSLY
VICARIOUSNESS
VICARIOUSNESSES
VICARLY
VICARS
VICARSHIP
VICARSHIPS
VICE
VICED
VICEGERAL
VICEGERENCIES
VICEGERENCY
VICEGERENT
VICEGERENTS
VICELESS
VICELIKE
VICENARY
VICENNIAL
VICEREGAL
VICEREGALLY
VICEREINE
VICEREINES
VICEROY
VICEROYALTIES
VICEROYALTY
VICEROYS
VICEROYSHIP
VICEROYSHIPS
VICES
VICHIES
VICHY
VICHYSSOISE
VICHYSSOISES
VICINAGE
VICINAGES
VICINAL
VICING
VICINITIES
VICINITY
VICIOUS
VICIOUSLY
VICIOUSNESS
VICIOUSNESSES
VICISSITUDE
VICISSITUDES
VICISSITUDINOUS
VICOMTE
VICOMTES
VICTIM
VICTIMHOOD
VICTIMHOODS
VICTIMISATION
VICTIMISATIONS
VICTIMISE
VICTIMISED
VICTIMISES
VICTIMISING
VICTIMIZATION
VICTIMIZATIONS
VICTIMIZE
VICTIMIZED
VICTIMIZER
VICTIMIZERS
VICTIMIZES
VICTIMIZING
VICTIMLESS
VICTIMOLOGIES
VICTIMOLOGIST
VICTIMOLOGISTS
VICTIMOLOGY
VICTIMS
VICTOR
VICTORIA
VICTORIAS
VICTORIES
VICTORIOUS
VICTORIOUSLY
VICTORIOUSNESS
VICTORS
VICTORY
VICTRESS
VICTRESSES
VICTUAL
VICTUALED
VICTUALER
VICTUALERS
VICTUALING
VICTUALLED
VICTUALLER
VICTUALLERS
VICTUALLING
VICTUALS
VICUGNA
VICUGNAS
VICUNA
VICUNAS
VID
VIDALIA
VIDALIAS
VIDE
VIDELICET
VIDEO
VIDEOCAM
VIDEOCAMS
VIDEOCASSETTE
VIDEOCASSETTES
VIDEOCONFERENCE
VIDEODISC
VIDEODISCS
VIDEODISK
VIDEODISKS
VIDEOED
VIDEOGENIC
VIDEOGRAPHER
VIDEOGRAPHERS
VIDEOGRAPHIES
VIDEOGRAPHY
VIDEOING
VIDEOLAND
VIDEOLANDS
VIDEOPHILE
VIDEOPHILES
VIDEOPHONE
VIDEOPHONES
VIDEOS
VIDEOTAPE
VIDEOTAPED
VIDEOTAPES
VIDEOTAPING
VIDEOTEX
VIDEOTEXES
VIDEOTEXT
VIDEOTEXTS
VIDETTE
VIDETTES
VIDICON
VIDICONS
VIDIOT
VIDIOTS
VIDS
VIDUITIES
VIDUITY
VIE
VIED
VIELLE
VIELLES
VIER
VIERS
VIES
VIEW
VIEWABLE
VIEWBOOK
VIEWBOOKS
VIEWDATA
VIEWED
VIEWER
VIEWERS
VIEWERSHIP
VIEWERSHIPS
VIEWFINDER
VIEWFINDERS
VIEWIER
VIEWIEST
VIEWING
VIEWINGS
VIEWLESS
VIEWLESSLY
VIEWPOINT
VIEWPOINTS
VIEWPORT
VIEWPORTS
VIEWS
VIEWSHED
VIEWSHEDS
VIEWY
VIFF
VIFFED
VIFFING
VIFFS
VIG
VIGA
VIGAS
VIGESIMAL
VIGIA
VIGIAS
VIGIL
VIGILANCE
VIGILANCES
VIGILANT
VIGILANTE
VIGILANTES
VIGILANTISM
VIGILANTISMS
VIGILANTLY
VIGILS
VIGINTILLION
VIGINTILLIONS
VIGNERON
VIGNERONS
VIGNETTE
VIGNETTED
VIGNETTER
VIGNETTERS
VIGNETTES
VIGNETTING
VIGNETTIST
VIGNETTISTS
VIGOR
VIGORISH
VIGORISHES
VIGOROSO
VIGOROUS
VIGOROUSLY
VIGOROUSNESS
VIGOROUSNESSES
VIGORS
VIGOUR
VIGOURS
VIGS
VIHUELA
VIHUELAS
VIKING
VIKINGS
VILAYET
VILAYETS
VILE
VILELY
VILENESS
VILENESSES
VILER
VILEST
VILIFICATION
VILIFICATIONS
VILIFIED
VILIFIER
VILIFIERS
VILIFIES
VILIFY
VILIFYING
VILIPEND
VILIPENDED
VILIPENDING
VILIPENDS
VILL
VILLA
VILLADOM
VILLADOMS
VILLAE
VILLAGE
VILLAGER
VILLAGERIES
VILLAGERS
VILLAGERY
VILLAGES
VILLAGEY
VILLAGIER
VILLAGIEST
VILLAIN
VILLAINESS
VILLAINESSES
VILLAINIES
VILLAINOUS
VILLAINOUSLY
VILLAINOUSNESS
VILLAINS

LAINY
LANELLA
LANELLAS
LANELLE
LANELLES
LAS
LATIC
LEIN
LEINS
LENAGE
LENAGES
LI
LIFORM
LOSE
LOSITIES
LOSITY
LOUS
LOUSLY
LS
LUS
EN
NA
INAL
NEOUS
S
A
ACEOUS
AIGRETTE
AIGRETTES
AL
ALS
AS
ASSE
ASSES
BLASTINE
BLASTINES
CA
CAS
CIBLE
CIBLY
CRISTINE
CRISTINES
CULA
CULAR
CULUM
CULUMS
DALOO
ALOOS
ICABLE
ICATE
ICATED

VINDICATES
VINDICATING
VINDICATION
VINDICATIONS
VINDICATIVE
VINDICATOR
VINDICATORS
VINDICATORY
VINDICTIVE
VINDICTIVELY
VINDICTIVENESS
VINE
VINEAL
VINED
VINEDRESSER
VINEDRESSERS
VINEGAR
VINEGARED
VINEGARIER
VINEGARIEST
VINEGARISH
VINEGARS
VINEGARY
VINERIES
VINERY
VINES
VINEYARD
VINEYARDIST
VINEYARDISTS
VINEYARDS
VINIC
VINICULTURE
VINICULTURES
VINIER
VINIEST
VINIFERA
VINIFERAS
VINIFICATION
VINIFICATIONS
VINIFIED
VINIFIES
VINIFY
VINIFYING
VINING
VINO
VINOS
VINOSITIES
VINOSITY
VINOUS
VINOUSLY
VINS
VINTAGE
VINTAGER

VINTAGERS
VINTAGES
VINTNER
VINTNERS
VINY
VINYL
VINYLIC
VINYLIDENE
VINYLIDENES
VINYLS
VIOL
VIOLA
VIOLABILITIES
VIOLABILITY
VIOLABLE
VIOLABLENESS
VIOLABLENESSES
VIOLABLY
VIOLACEOUS
VIOLAS
VIOLATE
VIOLATED
VIOLATER
VIOLATERS
VIOLATES
VIOLATING
VIOLATION
VIOLATIONS
VIOLATIVE
VIOLATOR
VIOLATORS
VIOLENCE
VIOLENCES
VIOLENT
VIOLENTLY
VIOLET
VIOLETS
VIOLIN
VIOLINIST
VIOLINISTIC
VIOLINISTS
VIOLINS
VIOLIST
VIOLISTS
VIOLONCELLI
VIOLONCELLIST
VIOLONCELLISTS
VIOLONCELLO
VIOLONCELLOS
VIOLONE
VIOLONES
VIOLS
VIOMYCIN

VIOMYCINS
VIOSTEROL
VIOSTEROLS
VIPER
VIPERFISH
VIPERFISHES
VIPERINE
VIPERISH
VIPEROUS
VIPEROUSLY
VIPERS
VIRAEMIA
VIRAEMIAS
VIRAEMIC
VIRAGINOUS
VIRAGO
VIRAGOES
VIRAGOS
VIRAL
VIRALLY
VIRELAI
VIRELAIS
VIRELAY
VIRELAYS
VIREMIA
VIREMIAS
VIREMIC
VIREO
VIREONINE
VIREONINES
VIREOS
VIRES
VIRESCENCE
VIRESCENCES
VIRESCENT
VIRGA
VIRGAE
VIRGAS
VIRGATE
VIRGATES
VIRGER
VIRGERS
VIRGIN
VIRGINAL
VIRGINALIST
VIRGINALISTS
VIRGINALLY
VIRGINALS
VIRGINITIES
VIRGINITY
VIRGINS
VIRGULATE
VIRGULE

VIRGULES
VIRICIDAL
VIRICIDE
VIRICIDES
VIRID
VIRIDESCENT
VIRIDIAN
VIRIDIANS
VIRIDITIES
VIRIDITY
VIRILE
VIRILELY
VIRILISE
VIRILISED
VIRILISES
VIRILISING
VIRILISM
VIRILISMS
VIRILITIES
VIRILITY
VIRILIZE
VIRILIZED
VIRILIZES
VIRILIZING
VIRILOCAL
VIRION
VIRIONS
VIRL
VIRLS
VIROID
VIROIDS
VIROLOGIC
VIROLOGICAL
VIROLOGICALLY
VIROLOGIES
VIROLOGIST
VIROLOGISTS
VIROLOGY
VIROSES
VIROSIS
VIRTU
VIRTUAL
VIRTUALITIES
VIRTUALITY
VIRTUALLY
VIRTUE
VIRTUELESS
VIRTUES
VIRTUOSA
VIRTUOSAS
VIRTUOSE
VIRTUOSI
VIRTUOSIC

VIRTUOSITIES
VIRTUOSITY
VIRTUOSO
VIRTUOSOS
VIRTUOUS
VIRTUOUSLY
VIRTUOUSNESS
VIRTUOUSNESSES
VIRTUS
VIRUCIDAL
VIRUCIDE
VIRUCIDES
VIRULENCE
VIRULENCES
VIRULENCIES
VIRULENCY
VIRULENT
VIRULENTLY
VIRULIFEROUS
VIRUS
VIRUSES
VIRUSLIKE
VIRUSOID
VIRUSOIDS
VIS
VISA
VISAED
VISAGE
VISAGED
VISAGES
VISAING
VISARD
VISARDS
VISAS
VISCACHA
VISCACHAS
VISCERA
VISCERAL
VISCERALLY
VISCID
VISCIDITIES
VISCIDITY
VISCIDLY
VISCOELASTIC
VISCOELASTICITY
VISCOID
VISCOIDAL
VISCOMETER
VISCOMETERS
VISCOMETRIC
VISCOMETRIES
VISCOMETRY
VISCOSE
VISCOSES
VISCOSIMETER
VISCOSIMETERS
VISCOSIMETRIC
VISCOSITIES
VISCOSITY
VISCOUNT
VISCOUNTCIES
VISCOUNTCY
VISCOUNTESS
VISCOUNTESSES
VISCOUNTIES
VISCOUNTS
VISCOUNTY
VISCOUS
VISCOUSLY
VISCOUSNESS
VISCOUSNESSES
VISCUS
VISE
VISED
VISEED
VISEING
VISELIKE
VISES
VISIBILITIES
VISIBILITY
VISIBLE
VISIBLENESS
VISIBLENESSES
VISIBLY
VISING
VISION
VISIONAL
VISIONALLY
VISIONARIES
VISIONARINESS
VISIONARINESSES
VISIONARY
VISIONED
VISIONING
VISIONINGS
VISIONLESS
VISIONS
VISIT
VISITABLE
VISITANT
VISITANTS
VISITATION
VISITATIONS
VISITATORIAL
VISITED
VISITER
VISITERS
VISITING
VISITINGS
VISITOR
VISITORS
VISITS
VISIVE
VISOR
VISORED
VISORING
VISORLESS
VISORS
VISTA
VISTAED
VISTALESS
VISTAS
VISUAL
VISUALISATION
VISUALISATIONS
VISUALISE
VISUALISED
VISUALISER
VISUALISERS
VISUALISES
VISUALISING
VISUALIST
VISUALISTS
VISUALITIES
VISUALITY
VISUALIZATION
VISUALIZATIONS
VISUALIZE
VISUALIZED
VISUALIZER
VISUALIZERS
VISUALIZES
VISUALIZING
VISUALLY
VISUALS
VISUOSPATIAL
VITA
VITAE
VITAL
VITALISE
VITALISED
VITALISES
VITALISING
VITALISM
VITALISMS
VITALIST
VITALISTIC
VITALISTS
VITALITIES
VITALITY
VITALIZATION
VITALIZATIONS
VITALIZE
VITALIZED
VITALIZER
VITALIZERS
VITALIZES
VITALIZING
VITALLY
VITALNESS
VITALNESSES
VITALS
VITAMER
VITAMERS
VITAMIN
VITAMINE
VITAMINES
VITAMINIC
VITAMINS
VITELLI
VITELLIN
VITELLINE
VITELLINES
VITELLINS
VITELLOGENESES
VITELLOGENESIS
VITELLOGENIN
VITELLOGENINS
VITELLUS
VITELLUSES
VITESSE
VITESSES
VITIABLE
VITIATE
VITIATED
VITIATES
VITIATING
VITIATION
VITIATIONS
VITIATOR
VITIATORS
VITICULTURAL
VITICULTURALLY
VITICULTURE
VITICULTURES
VITICULTURIST
VITICULTURISTS
VITILIGO
VITILIGOS
VITRAIN
VITRAINS
VITRECTOMIES
VITRECTOMY
VITREOUS
VITREOUSES
VITRIC
VITRICS
VITRIFIABLE
VITRIFICATION
VITRIFICATIONS
VITRIFIED
VITRIFIES
VITRIFORM
VITRIFY
VITRIFYING
VITRINE
VITRINES
VITRIOL
VITRIOLED
VITRIOLIC
VITRIOLING
VITRIOLLED
VITRIOLLING
VITRIOLS
VITTA
VITTAE
VITTATE
VITTLE
VITTLED
VITTLES
VITTLING
VITULINE
VITUPERATE
VITUPERATED
VITUPERATES
VITUPERATING
VITUPERATION
VITUPERATIONS
VITUPERATIVE
VITUPERATIVELY
VITUPERATOR
VITUPERATORS
VITUPERATORY
VIVA
VIVACE
VIVACES
VIVACIOUS
VIVACIOUSLY
VIVACIOUSNESS
VIVACIOUSNESSES
VIVACITIES
VIVACITY
VIVANDIERE
VIVANDIERES
VIVARIA

ARIES
ARIUM
ARIUMS
ARY
AS
AT
ATS
E
ERID
ERIDS
ERRID
ERRIDS
ERRINE
ERRINES
ERS
ID
IDER
IDEST
IDLY
IDNESS
IDNESSES
IFIC
IFICATION
IFICATIONS
IFIED
IFIER
IFIERS
IFIES
IFY
IFYING
PARA
PARITIES
PARITY
PAROUS
PAROUSLY
SECT
SECTED
SECTING
SECTION
SECTIONAL
SECTIONIST
SECTIONISTS
SECTIONS
SECTOR
SECTORS
SECTS
EN
ENISH
ENLY
ENS
RD
RDED
RDS
VIZCACHA
VIZCACHAS
VIZIER
VIZIERATE
VIZIERATES
VIZIERIAL
VIZIERS
VIZIERSHIP
VIZIERSHIPS
VIZIR
VIZIRATE
VIZIRATES
VIZIRIAL
VIZIRS
VIZOR
VIZORED
VIZORING
VIZORS
VIZSLA
VIZSLAS
VLEI
VLEIS
VLOG
VLOGGED
VLOGGER
VLOGGERS
VLOGGING
VLOGS
VOCAB
VOCABLE
VOCABLES
VOCABLY
VOCABS
VOCABULAR
VOCABULARIES
VOCABULARY
VOCAL
VOCALESE
VOCALESES
VOCALIC
VOCALICALLY
VOCALICS
VOCALISATION
VOCALISATIONS
VOCALISE
VOCALISED
VOCALISES
VOCALISING
VOCALISM
VOCALISMS
VOCALIST
VOCALISTS
VOCALITIES
VOCALITY
VOCALIZATION
VOCALIZATIONS
VOCALIZE
VOCALIZED
VOCALIZER
VOCALIZERS
VOCALIZES
VOCALIZING
VOCALLY
VOCALNESS
VOCALNESSES
VOCALS
VOCATION
VOCATIONAL
VOCATIONALISM
VOCATIONALISMS
VOCATIONALIST
VOCATIONALISTS
VOCATIONALLY
VOCATIONS
VOCATIVE
VOCATIVELY
VOCATIVES
VOCES
VOCIFERANT
VOCIFERATE
VOCIFERATED
VOCIFERATES
VOCIFERATING
VOCIFERATION
VOCIFERATIONS
VOCIFERATOR
VOCIFERATORS
VOCIFEROUS
VOCIFEROUSLY
VOCIFEROUSNESS
VOCODER
VOCODERS
VODCAST
VODCASTED
VODCASTING
VODCASTS
VODKA
VODKAS
VODOU
VODOUN
VODOUNS
VODOUS
VODUN
VODUNS
VOE
VOES
VOG
VOGIE
VOGS
VOGUE
VOGUED
VOGUEING
VOGUEINGS
VOGUER
VOGUERS
VOGUES
VOGUING
VOGUINGS
VOGUISH
VOGUISHLY
VOGUISHNESS
VOGUISHNESSES
VOICE
VOICED
VOICEFUL
VOICEFULNESS
VOICEFULNESSES
VOICELESS
VOICELESSLY
VOICELESSNESS
VOICELESSNESSES
VOICEMAIL
VOICEMAILS
VOICEOVER
VOICEOVERS
VOICEPRINT
VOICEPRINTS
VOICER
VOICERS
VOICES
VOICING
VOICINGS
VOID
VOIDABLE
VOIDABLENESS
VOIDABLENESSES
VOIDANCE
VOIDANCES
VOIDED
VOIDER
VOIDERS
VOIDING
VOIDNESS
VOIDNESSES
VOIDS
VOILA
VOILE
VOILES
VOLANT
VOLANTE
VOLAR
VOLATILE
VOLATILENESS
VOLATILENESSES
VOLATILES
VOLATILISE
VOLATILISED
VOLATILISES
VOLATILISING
VOLATILITIES
VOLATILITY
VOLATILIZABLE
VOLATILIZATION
VOLATILIZATIONS
VOLATILIZE
VOLATILIZED
VOLATILIZES
VOLATILIZING
VOLCANIC
VOLCANICALLY
VOLCANICITIES
VOLCANICITY
VOLCANICS
VOLCANISM
VOLCANISMS
VOLCANIZE
VOLCANIZED
VOLCANIZES
VOLCANIZING
VOLCANO
VOLCANOES
VOLCANOLOGIC
VOLCANOLOGICAL
VOLCANOLOGIES
VOLCANOLOGIST
VOLCANOLOGISTS
VOLCANOLOGY
VOLCANOS
VOLE
VOLED
VOLERIES
VOLERY
VOLES
VOLING
VOLITANT
VOLITION
VOLITIONAL
VOLITIONS
VOLITIVE
VOLK
VOLKS
VOLKSLIED

VOLKSLIEDER
VOLLEY
VOLLEYBALL
VOLLEYBALLS
VOLLEYED
VOLLEYER
VOLLEYERS
VOLLEYING
VOLLEYS
VOLOST
VOLOSTS
VOLPLANE
VOLPLANED
VOLPLANES
VOLPLANING
VOLT
VOLTA
VOLTAGE
VOLTAGES
VOLTAIC
VOLTAISM
VOLTAISMS
VOLTE
VOLTED
VOLTES
VOLTI
VOLTING
VOLTMETER
VOLTMETERS
VOLTS
VOLUBILITIES
VOLUBILITY
VOLUBLE
VOLUBLENESS
VOLUBLENESSES
VOLUBLY
VOLUME
VOLUMED
VOLUMES
VOLUMETER
VOLUMETERS
VOLUMETRIC
VOLUMETRICALLY
VOLUMING
VOLUMINOSITIES
VOLUMINOSITY
VOLUMINOUS
VOLUMINOUSLY
VOLUMINOUSNESS
VOLUMISE
VOLUMISED
VOLUMISES
VOLUMISING
VOLUMIZE
VOLUMIZED
VOLUMIZES
VOLUMIZING
VOLUNTARIES
VOLUNTARILY
VOLUNTARINESS
VOLUNTARINESSES
VOLUNTARISM
VOLUNTARISMS
VOLUNTARIST
VOLUNTARISTIC
VOLUNTARISTS
VOLUNTARY
VOLUNTARYISM
VOLUNTARYISMS
VOLUNTARYIST
VOLUNTARYISTS
VOLUNTEER
VOLUNTEERED
VOLUNTEERING
VOLUNTEERISM
VOLUNTEERISMS
VOLUNTEERS
VOLUNTOURISM
VOLUNTOURISMS
VOLUNTOURIST
VOLUNTOURISTS
VOLUPTUARIES
VOLUPTUARY
VOLUPTUOUS
VOLUPTUOUSLY
VOLUPTUOUSNESS
VOLUTE
VOLUTED
VOLUTES
VOLUTIN
VOLUTINS
VOLUTION
VOLUTIONS
VOLVA
VOLVAS
VOLVATE
VOLVOX
VOLVOXES
VOLVULI
VOLVULUS
VOLVULUSES
VOMER
VOMERINE
VOMERS
VOMICA
VOMICAE
VOMIT
VOMITED
VOMITER
VOMITERS
VOMITIER
VOMITIEST
VOMITING
VOMITIVE
VOMITIVES
VOMITO
VOMITORIES
VOMITORY
VOMITOS
VOMITOUS
VOMITS
VOMITUS
VOMITUSES
VOMITY
VOODOO
VOODOOED
VOODOOING
VOODOOISM
VOODOOISMS
VOODOOIST
VOODOOISTIC
VOODOOISTS
VOODOOS
VORACIOUS
VORACIOUSLY
VORACIOUSNESS
VORACIOUSNESSES
VORACITIES
VORACITY
VORLAGE
VORLAGES
VORTEX
VORTEXES
VORTICAL
VORTICALLY
VORTICELLA
VORTICELLAE
VORTICELLAS
VORTICES
VORTICISM
VORTICISMS
VORTICIST
VORTICISTS
VORTICITIES
VORTICITY
VORTICOSE
VOTABLE
VOTARESS
VOTARESSES
VOTARIES
VOTARIST
VOTARISTS
VOTARY
VOTE
VOTEABLE
VOTED
VOTELESS
VOTER
VOTERS
VOTES
VOTING
VOTIVE
VOTIVELY
VOTIVENESS
VOTIVENESSES
VOTIVES
VOTRESS
VOTRESSES
VOUCH
VOUCHED
VOUCHEE
VOUCHEES
VOUCHER
VOUCHERED
VOUCHERING
VOUCHERS
VOUCHES
VOUCHING
VOUCHSAFE
VOUCHSAFED
VOUCHSAFEMENT
VOUCHSAFEMENTS
VOUCHSAFES
VOUCHSAFING
VOUDON
VOUDONS
VOUDOUN
VOUDOUNS
VOUSSOIR
VOUSSOIRS
VOUVRAY
VOUVRAYS
VOW
VOWED
VOWEL
VOWELED
VOWELIZE
VOWELIZED
VOWELIZES
VOWELIZING
VOWELLED
VOWELS
VOWER
VOWERS
VOWING
VOWLESS
VOWS
VOX
VOXEL
VOXELS
VOYAGE
VOYAGED
VOYAGER
VOYAGERS
VOYAGES
VOYAGEUR
VOYAGEURS
VOYAGING
VOYAGINGS
VOYEUR
VOYEURISM
VOYEURISMS
VOYEURISTIC
VOYEURISTICALLY
VOYEURS
VROOM
VROOMED
VROOMING
VROOMS
VROUW
VROUWS
VROW
VROWS
VUG
VUGG
VUGGIER
VUGGIEST
VUGGS
VUGGY
VUGH
VUGHS
VUGS
VUGULAR
VULCANIAN
VULCANIC
VULCANICITIES
VULCANICITY
VULCANISATE
VULCANISATES
VULCANISATION
VULCANISATIONS
VULCANISE
VULCANISED
VULCANISES
VULCANISING

LCANISM
LCANISMS
LCANITE
LCANITES
LCANIZATE
LCANIZATES
LCANIZATION
LCANIZATIONS
LCANIZE
LCANIZED
LCANIZER
LCANIZERS
LCANIZES
LCANIZING
LCANOLOGIES
LCANOLOGIST
VULCANOLOGISTS
VULCANOLOGY
VULGAR
VULGARER
VULGAREST
VULGARIAN
VULGARIANS
VULGARISATION
VULGARISATIONS
VULGARISE
VULGARISED
VULGARISES
VULGARISING
VULGARISM
VULGARISMS
VULGARITIES
VULGARITY
VULGARIZATION
VULGARIZATIONS
VULGARIZE
VULGARIZED
VULGARIZER
VULGARIZERS
VULGARIZES
VULGARIZING
VULGARLY
VULGARS
VULGATE
VULGATES
VULGO
VULGUS
VULGUSES
VULN
VULNED
VULNERABILITIES
VULNERABILITY
VULNERABLE
VULNERABLENESS
VULNERABLY
VULNERARIES
VULNERARY
VULNING
VULNS
VULPINE
VULTURE
VULTURES
VULTURINE
VULTURISH
VULTUROUS
VULVA
VULVAE
VULVAL
VULVAR
VULVAS
VULVATE
VULVIFORM
VULVITIS
VULVITISES
VULVOVAGINITIS
VUM
VYING
VYINGLY

W

AH
B
BBLE
BBLED
BBLER
BBLERS
BBLES
BBLIER
BBLIEST
BBLINESS
BBLINESSES
BBLING
BBLY
BS
CK
CKE
CKED
CKER
CKES
CKEST
CKIER
CKIEST
CKILY
CKINESS
CKINESSES
CKO
CKOES
WACKOS
WACKS
WACKY
WAD
WADABLE
WADDED
WADDER
WADDERS
WADDIE
WADDIED
WADDIES
WADDING
WADDINGS
WADDLE
WADDLED
WADDLER
WADDLERS
WADDLES
WADDLING
WADDLY
WADDY
WADDYING
WADE
WADEABLE
WADED
WADER
WADERS
WADES
WADI
WADIES
WADING
WADIS
WADMAAL
WADMAALS
WADMAL
WADMALS
WADMEL
WADMELS
WADMOL
WADMOLL
WADMOLLS
WADMOLS
WADS
WADSET
WADSETS
WADSETTED
WADSETTING
WADY
WAE
WAEFUL
WAENESS
WAENESSES
WAES
WAESUCK
WAESUCKS
WAFER
WAFERED
WAFERING
WAFERS
WAFERY
WAFF
WAFFED
WAFFIE
WAFFIES
WAFFING
WAFFLE
WAFFLED
WAFFLER
WAFFLERS
WAFFLES
WAFFLESTOMPER
WAFFLESTOMPERS
WAFFLIER
WAFFLIEST
WAFFLING
WAFFLINGS
WAFFLY
WAFFS
WAFT
WAFTAGE
WAFTAGES
WAFTED
WAFTER
WAFTERS
WAFTING
WAFTS
WAFTURE
WAFTURES
WAG
WAGE
WAGED
WAGELESS
WAGER
WAGERED
WAGERER
WAGERERS
WAGERING
WAGERINGS
WAGERS
WAGES
WAGEWORKER
WAGEWORKERS
WAGGED
WAGGER
WAGGERIES
WAGGERS
WAGGERY
WAGGING

WAGGISH
WAGGISHLY
WAGGISHNESS
WAGGISHNESSES
WAGGLE
WAGGLED
WAGGLES
WAGGLIER
WAGGLIEST
WAGGLING
WAGGLY
WAGGON
WAGGONED
WAGGONER
WAGGONERS
WAGGONING
WAGGONS
WAGING
WAGON
WAGONAGE
WAGONAGES
WAGONED
WAGONER
WAGONERS
WAGONETTE
WAGONETTES
WAGONING
WAGONLOAD
WAGONLOADS
WAGONS
WAGS
WAGSOME
WAGTAIL
WAGTAILS
WAHCONDA
WAHCONDAS
WAHINE
WAHINES
WAHOO
WAHOOS
WAIF
WAIFED
WAIFING
WAIFISH
WAIFLIKE
WAIFS
WAIL
WAILED
WAILER
WAILERS
WAILFUL
WAILFULLY
WAILING
WAILINGLY
WAILS
WAILSOME
WAIN
WAINS
WAINSCOT
WAINSCOTED
WAINSCOTING
WAINSCOTINGS
WAINSCOTS
WAINSCOTTED
WAINSCOTTING
WAINSCOTTINGS
WAINWRIGHT
WAINWRIGHTS
WAIR
WAIRED
WAIRING
WAIRS
WAIST
WAISTBAND
WAISTBANDS
WAISTCOAT
WAISTCOATED
WAISTCOATS
WAISTED
WAISTER
WAISTERS
WAISTING
WAISTINGS
WAISTLESS
WAISTLINE
WAISTLINES
WAISTS
WAIT
WAITED
WAITER
WAITERED
WAITERING
WAITERS
WAITING
WAITINGS
WAITLIST
WAITLISTED
WAITLISTING
WAITLISTS
WAITPERSON
WAITPERSONS
WAITRESS
WAITRESSED
WAITRESSES
WAITRESSING
WAITRESSINGS
WAITRON
WAITRONS
WAITS
WAITSTAFF
WAITSTAFFS
WAIVE
WAIVED
WAIVER
WAIVERS
WAIVES
WAIVING
WAKAME
WAKAMES
WAKANDA
WAKANDAS
WAKE
WAKEBOARD
WAKEBOARDER
WAKEBOARDERS
WAKEBOARDING
WAKEBOARDINGS
WAKEBOARDS
WAKED
WAKEFUL
WAKEFULLY
WAKEFULNESS
WAKEFULNESSES
WAKELESS
WAKEN
WAKENED
WAKENER
WAKENERS
WAKENING
WAKENINGS
WAKENS
WAKER
WAKERIFE
WAKERS
WAKES
WAKIKI
WAKIKIS
WAKING
WAKINGS
WALE
WALED
WALER
WALERS
WALES
WALI
WALIES
WALING
WALIS
WALK
WALKABLE
WALKABOUT
WALKABOUTS
WALKATHON
WALKATHONS
WALKAWAY
WALKAWAYS
WALKED
WALKER
WALKERS
WALKIES
WALKING
WALKINGS
WALKINGSTICK
WALKINGSTICKS
WALKOUT
WALKOUTS
WALKOVER
WALKOVERS
WALKS
WALKUP
WALKUPS
WALKWAY
WALKWAYS
WALKYRIE
WALKYRIES
WALL
WALLA
WALLABIES
WALLABY
WALLAH
WALLAHS
WALLAROO
WALLAROOS
WALLAS
WALLBOARD
WALLBOARDS
WALLED
WALLET
WALLETS
WALLEY
WALLEYE
WALLEYED
WALLEYES
WALLEYS
WALLFLOWER
WALLFLOWERS
WALLIE
WALLIES
WALLING
WALLOP
WALLOPED
WALLOPER
WALLOPERS
WALLOPING
WALLOPINGS
WALLOPS
WALLOW
WALLOWED
WALLOWER
WALLOWERS
WALLOWING
WALLOWS
WALLPAPER
WALLPAPERED
WALLPAPERING
WALLPAPERS
WALLS
WALLY
WALLYBALL
WALLYBALLS
WALLYDRAG
WALLYDRAGS
WALLYDRAIGLE
WALLYDRAIGLES
WALNUT
WALNUTS
WALRUS
WALRUSES
WALTZ
WALTZED
WALTZER
WALTZERS
WALTZES
WALTZING
WALY
WAMBLE
WAMBLED
WAMBLES
WAMBLIER
WAMBLIEST
WAMBLING
WAMBLY
WAME
WAMEFOU
WAMEFOUS
WAMEFUL
WAMEFULS
WAMES
WAMMUS
WAMMUSES
WAMPISH
WAMPISHED
WAMPISHES
WAMPISHING
WAMPUM

MPUMPEAG
MPUMPEAGS
MPUMS
MPUS
MPUSES
MUS
MUSES
N
ND
NDER
NDERED
NDERER
NDERERS
NDERING
NDERINGS
NDERLUST
NDERLUSTS
NDEROO
NDEROOS
NDERS
NDLE
NDS
NE
NED
NES
NEY
NGAN
NGANS
NGLE
NGLED
NGLER
NGLERS
NGLES
NGLING
NGUN
NGUNS
NIER
NIEST
NIGAN
NIGANS
NING
NION
NIONS
NK
NKED
NKER
NKERS
NKING
NKS
NLY
NNABE
NNABEE
NNABEES

WANNABES
WANNED
WANNER
WANNESS
WANNESSES
WANNEST
WANNIGAN
WANNIGANS
WANNING
WANS
WANT
WANTAGE
WANTAGES
WANTED
WANTER
WANTERS
WANTING
WANTON
WANTONED
WANTONER
WANTONERS
WANTONEST
WANTONING
WANTONLY
WANTONNESS
WANTONNESSES
WANTONS
WANTS
WANY
WAP
WAPENTAKE
WAPENTAKES
WAPITI
WAPITIS
WAPPED
WAPPENSCHAWING
WAPPENSCHAWINGS
WAPPING
WAPS
WAR
WARBIRD
WARBIRDS
WARBLE
WARBLED
WARBLER
WARBLERS
WARBLES
WARBLIER
WARBLIEST
WARBLING
WARBLY
WARBONNET
WARBONNETS

WARCRAFT
WARCRAFTS
WARD
WARDED
WARDEN
WARDENRIES
WARDENRY
WARDENS
WARDENSHIP
WARDENSHIPS
WARDER
WARDERS
WARDING
WARDLESS
WARDRESS
WARDRESSES
WARDROBE
WARDROBED
WARDROBES
WARDROBING
WARDROOM
WARDROOMS
WARDS
WARDSHIP
WARDSHIPS
WARE
WARED
WAREHOUSE
WAREHOUSED
WAREHOUSEMAN
WAREHOUSEMEN
WAREHOUSER
WAREHOUSERS
WAREHOUSES
WAREHOUSING
WAREROOM
WAREROOMS
WARES
WAREZ
WAREZES
WARFARE
WARFARES
WARFARIN
WARFARINS
WARGAME
WARGAMED
WARGAMER
WARGAMERS
WARGAMES
WARGAMING
WARGAMINGS
WARHEAD
WARHEADS

WARHORSE
WARHORSES
WARIER
WARIEST
WARILY
WARINESS
WARINESSES
WARING
WARISON
WARISONS
WARK
WARKED
WARKING
WARKS
WARLESS
WARLIKE
WARLOCK
WARLOCKS
WARLORD
WARLORDISM
WARLORDISMS
WARLORDS
WARM
WARMAKER
WARMAKERS
WARMED
WARMER
WARMERS
WARMEST
WARMHEARTED
WARMHEARTEDNESS
WARMING
WARMINGS
WARMISH
WARMLY
WARMNESS
WARMNESSES
WARMONGER
WARMONGERING
WARMONGERINGS
WARMONGERS
WARMOUTH
WARMOUTHS
WARMS
WARMTH
WARMTHS
WARMUP
WARMUPS
WARN
WARNED
WARNER
WARNERS
WARNING

WARNINGLY
WARNINGS
WARNS
WARP
WARPAGE
WARPAGES
WARPAINT
WARPAINTS
WARPATH
WARPATHS
WARPED
WARPER
WARPERS
WARPING
WARPLANE
WARPLANES
WARPOWER
WARPOWERS
WARPS
WARPWISE
WARRAGAL
WARRAGALS
WARRANT
WARRANTABLE
WARRANTABLENESS
WARRANTABLY
WARRANTED
WARRANTEE
WARRANTEES
WARRANTER
WARRANTERS
WARRANTIED
WARRANTIES
WARRANTING
WARRANTLESS
WARRANTOR
WARRANTORS
WARRANTS
WARRANTY
WARRANTYING
WARRED
WARREN
WARRENER
WARRENERS
WARRENS
WARRIGAL
WARRIGALS
WARRING
WARRIOR
WARRIORS
WARS
WARSAW
WARSAWS

WARSHIP
WARSHIPS
WARSLE
WARSLED
WARSLER
WARSLERS
WARSLES
WARSLING
WARSTLE
WARSTLED
WARSTLER
WARSTLERS
WARSTLES
WARSTLING
WART
WARTED
WARTHOG
WARTHOGS
WARTIER
WARTIEST
WARTIME
WARTIMES
WARTLESS
WARTLIKE
WARTS
WARTY
WARWORK
WARWORKS
WARWORN
WARY
WAS
WASABI
WASABIS
WASH
WASHABILITIES
WASHABILITY
WASHABLE
WASHABLES
WASHATERIA
WASHATERIAS
WASHBAG
WASHBAGS
WASHBASIN
WASHBASINS
WASHBOARD
WASHBOARDS
WASHBOWL
WASHBOWLS
WASHCLOTH
WASHCLOTHS
WASHDAY
WASHDAYS
WASHED
WASHER
WASHERMAN
WASHERMEN
WASHERS
WASHERWOMAN
WASHERWOMEN
WASHES
WASHETERIA
WASHETERIAS
WASHHOUSE
WASHHOUSES
WASHIER
WASHIEST
WASHINESS
WASHINESSES
WASHING
WASHINGS
WASHOUT
WASHOUTS
WASHRAG
WASHRAGS
WASHROOM
WASHROOMS
WASHSTAND
WASHSTANDS
WASHTUB
WASHTUBS
WASHUP
WASHUPS
WASHWOMAN
WASHWOMEN
WASHY
WASP
WASPIER
WASPIEST
WASPILY
WASPINESS
WASPINESSES
WASPISH
WASPISHLY
WASPISHNESS
WASPISHNESSES
WASPLIKE
WASPS
WASPY
WASSAIL
WASSAILED
WASSAILER
WASSAILERS
WASSAILING
WASSAILS
WAST
WASTABLE
WASTAGE
WASTAGES
WASTE
WASTEBASKET
WASTEBASKETS
WASTED
WASTEFUL
WASTEFULLY
WASTEFULNESS
WASTEFULNESSES
WASTELAND
WASTELANDS
WASTELOT
WASTELOTS
WASTEPAPER
WASTEPAPERS
WASTER
WASTERIE
WASTERIES
WASTERS
WASTERY
WASTES
WASTEWATER
WASTEWATERS
WASTEWAY
WASTEWAYS
WASTING
WASTINGLY
WASTREL
WASTRELS
WASTRIE
WASTRIES
WASTRY
WASTS
WAT
WATAP
WATAPE
WATAPES
WATAPS
WATCH
WATCHA
WATCHABLE
WATCHABLES
WATCHBAND
WATCHBANDS
WATCHCASE
WATCHCASES
WATCHCRIES
WATCHCRY
WATCHDOG
WATCHDOGGED
WATCHDOGGING
WATCHDOGS
WATCHED
WATCHER
WATCHERS
WATCHES
WATCHEYE
WATCHEYES
WATCHFUL
WATCHFULLY
WATCHFULNESS
WATCHFULNESSES
WATCHING
WATCHMAKER
WATCHMAKERS
WATCHMAKING
WATCHMAKINGS
WATCHMAN
WATCHMEN
WATCHOUT
WATCHOUTS
WATCHTOWER
WATCHTOWERS
WATCHWORD
WATCHWORDS
WATER
WATERAGE
WATERAGES
WATERBED
WATERBEDS
WATERBIRD
WATERBIRDS
WATERBOARDING
WATERBOARDINGS
WATERBORNE
WATERBUCK
WATERBUCKS
WATERBUS
WATERBUSES
WATERBUSSES
WATERCOLOR
WATERCOLORIST
WATERCOLORISTS
WATERCOLORS
WATERCOLOUR
WATERCOLOURIST
WATERCOLOURISTS
WATERCOLOURS
WATERCOOLER
WATERCOOLERS
WATERCOURSE
WATERCOURSES
WATERCRAFT
WATERCRAFTS
WATERCRESS
WATERCRESSES
WATERDOG
WATERDOGS
WATERED
WATERER
WATERERS
WATERFALL
WATERFALLS
WATERFLOOD
WATERFLOODED
WATERFLOODING
WATERFLOODS
WATERFOWL
WATERFOWLER
WATERFOWLERS
WATERFOWLING
WATERFOWLINGS
WATERFOWLS
WATERFRONT
WATERFRONTS
WATERHEAD
WATERHEADS
WATERHEN
WATERHENS
WATERIER
WATERIEST
WATERILY
WATERINESS
WATERINESSES
WATERING
WATERINGS
WATERISH
WATERISHNESS
WATERISHNESSES
WATERJET
WATERJETS
WATERLEAF
WATERLEAFS
WATERLESS
WATERLESSNESS
WATERLESSNESSES
WATERLILIES
WATERLILY
WATERLINE
WATERLINES
WATERLOG
WATERLOGGED
WATERLOGGING
WATERLOGS
WATERLOO
WATERLOOS
WATERMAN
WATERMANSHIP

ATERMANSHIPS
ATERMARK
ATERMARKED
ATERMARKING
ATERMARKS
ATERMELON
ATERMELONS
ATERMEN
ATERPOWER
ATERPOWERS
ATERPROOF
ATERPROOFED
ATERPROOFER
ATERPROOFERS
ATERPROOFING
ATERPROOFINGS
ATERPROOFNESS
ATERPROOFS
ATERS
ATERSCAPE
ATERSCAPES
ATERSHED
ATERSHEDS
ATERSIDE
ATERSIDES
ATERSKI
ATERSKIING
ATERSKIINGS
ATERSKIS
ATERSLIDE
ATERSLIDES
ATERSPOUT
ATERSPOUTS
ATERTHRUSH
ATERTHRUSHES
ATERTIGHT
ATERTIGHTNESS
ATERWAY
ATERWAYS
ATERWEED
ATERWEEDS
ATERWHEEL
ATERWHEELS
ATERWORK
ATERWORKS
ATERWORN
ATERY
ATERZOOI
ATERZOOIS
ATS
TT
TTAGE
TTAGES

WATTAPE
WATTAPES
WATTER
WATTEST
WATTHOUR
WATTHOURS
WATTLE
WATTLEBIRD
WATTLEBIRDS
WATTLED
WATTLES
WATTLESS
WATTLING
WATTMETER
WATTMETERS
WATTS
WAUCHT
WAUCHTED
WAUCHTING
WAUCHTS
WAUGH
WAUGHT
WAUGHTED
WAUGHTING
WAUGHTS
WAUK
WAUKED
WAUKING
WAUKS
WAUL
WAULED
WAULING
WAULS
WAUR
WAVE
WAVEBAND
WAVEBANDS
WAVED
WAVEFORM
WAVEFORMS
WAVEGUIDE
WAVEGUIDES
WAVELENGTH
WAVELENGTHS
WAVELESS
WAVELESSLY
WAVELET
WAVELETS
WAVELIKE
WAVELLITE
WAVELLITES
WAVEOFF
WAVEOFFS

WAVER
WAVERED
WAVERER
WAVERERS
WAVERIER
WAVERIEST
WAVERING
WAVERINGLY
WAVERS
WAVERY
WAVES
WAVESHAPE
WAVESHAPES
WAVEY
WAVEYS
WAVICLE
WAVICLES
WAVIER
WAVIES
WAVIEST
WAVILY
WAVINESS
WAVINESSES
WAVING
WAVY
WAW
WAWL
WAWLED
WAWLING
WAWLS
WAWS
WAX
WAXABLE
WAXBERRIES
WAXBERRY
WAXBILL
WAXBILLS
WAXED
WAXEN
WAXER
WAXERS
WAXES
WAXIER
WAXIEST
WAXILY
WAXINESS
WAXINESSES
WAXING
WAXINGS
WAXLIKE
WAXPLANT
WAXPLANTS
WAXWEED

WAXWEEDS
WAXWING
WAXWINGS
WAXWORK
WAXWORKER
WAXWORKERS
WAXWORKS
WAXWORM
WAXWORMS
WAXY
WAY
WAYANG
WAYANGS
WAYBILL
WAYBILLS
WAYFARER
WAYFARERS
WAYFARING
WAYFARINGS
WAYGOING
WAYGOINGS
WAYLAID
WAYLAY
WAYLAYER
WAYLAYERS
WAYLAYING
WAYLAYS
WAYLESS
WAYMARK
WAYMARKS
WAYPOINT
WAYPOINTS
WAYS
WAYSIDE
WAYSIDES
WAYWARD
WAYWARDLY
WAYWARDNESS
WAYWARDNESSES
WAYWORN
WAZOO
WAZOOS
WE
WEAK
WEAKEN
WEAKENED
WEAKENER
WEAKENERS
WEAKENING
WEAKENS
WEAKER
WEAKEST
WEAKFISH

WEAKFISHES
WEAKHEARTED
WEAKISH
WEAKISHLY
WEAKLIER
WEAKLIEST
WEAKLINESS
WEAKLINESSES
WEAKLING
WEAKLINGS
WEAKLY
WEAKNESS
WEAKNESSES
WEAKON
WEAKONS
WEAKSIDE
WEAKSIDES
WEAL
WEALD
WEALDS
WEALS
WEALTH
WEALTHIER
WEALTHIEST
WEALTHILY
WEALTHINESS
WEALTHINESSES
WEALTHS
WEALTHY
WEAN
WEANED
WEANER
WEANERS
WEANING
WEANLING
WEANLINGS
WEANS
WEAPON
WEAPONED
WEAPONEER
WEAPONEERED
WEAPONEERING
WEAPONEERS
WEAPONING
WEAPONIZATION
WEAPONIZATIONS
WEAPONIZE
WEAPONIZED
WEAPONIZES
WEAPONIZING
WEAPONLESS
WEAPONRIES
WEAPONRY

WEAPONS
WEAR
WEARABILITIES
WEARABILITY
WEARABLE
WEARABLES
WEARER
WEARERS
WEARIED
WEARIER
WEARIES
WEARIEST
WEARIFUL
WEARIFULLY
WEARIFULNESS
WEARIFULNESSES
WEARILESS
WEARILESSLY
WEARILY
WEARINESS
WEARINESSES
WEARING
WEARINGLY
WEARISH
WEARISOME
WEARISOMELY
WEARISOMENESS
WEARISOMENESSES
WEARPROOF
WEARS
WEARY
WEARYING
WEARYINGLY
WEASAND
WEASANDS
WEASEL
WEASELED
WEASELING
WEASELLED
WEASELLING
WEASELLY
WEASELS
WEASELY
WEASON
WEASONS
WEATHER
WEATHERABILITY
WEATHERBOARD
WEATHERBOARDED
WEATHERBOARDING
WEATHERBOARDS
WEATHERCAST
WEATHERCASTER
WEATHERCASTERS
WEATHERCASTS
WEATHERCOCK
WEATHERCOCKS
WEATHERED
WEATHERGLASS
WEATHERGLASSES
WEATHERING
WEATHERINGS
WEATHERIZATION
WEATHERIZATIONS
WEATHERIZE
WEATHERIZED
WEATHERIZES
WEATHERIZING
WEATHERLY
WEATHERMAN
WEATHERMEN
WEATHERPERSON
WEATHERPERSONS
WEATHERPROOF
WEATHERPROOFED
WEATHERPROOFING
WEATHERPROOFS
WEATHERS
WEATHERWORN
WEAVE
WEAVED
WEAVER
WEAVERBIRD
WEAVERBIRDS
WEAVERS
WEAVES
WEAVING
WEAVINGS
WEAZAND
WEAZANDS
WEB
WEBBED
WEBBIER
WEBBIEST
WEBBING
WEBBINGS
WEBBY
WEBCAM
WEBCAMS
WEBCAST
WEBCASTED
WEBCASTER
WEBCASTERS
WEBCASTING
WEBCASTINGS
WEBCASTS
WEBER
WEBERS
WEBFED
WEBFEET
WEBFOOT
WEBINAR
WEBINARS
WEBISODE
WEBISODES
WEBLESS
WEBLIKE
WEBLOG
WEBLOGGING
WEBLOGGINGS
WEBLOGS
WEBMASTER
WEBMASTERS
WEBPAGE
WEBPAGES
WEBS
WEBSITE
WEBSITES
WEBSTER
WEBSTERS
WEBWORK
WEBWORKS
WEBWORM
WEBWORMS
WEBZINE
WEBZINES
WECHT
WECHTS
WED
WEDDED
WEDDER
WEDDERS
WEDDING
WEDDINGS
WEDEL
WEDELED
WEDELING
WEDELN
WEDELNS
WEDELS
WEDGE
WEDGED
WEDGELIKE
WEDGES
WEDGIE
WEDGIER
WEDGIES
WEDGIEST
WEDGING
WEDGY
WEDLOCK
WEDLOCKS
WEDS
WEE
WEED
WEEDBED
WEEDBEDS
WEEDED
WEEDER
WEEDERS
WEEDIER
WEEDIEST
WEEDILY
WEEDINESS
WEEDINESSES
WEEDING
WEEDLESS
WEEDLIKE
WEEDLINE
WEEDLINES
WEEDS
WEEDY
WEEING
WEEJUNS
WEEK
WEEKDAY
WEEKDAYS
WEEKEND
WEEKENDED
WEEKENDER
WEEKENDERS
WEEKENDING
WEEKENDS
WEEKLIES
WEEKLONG
WEEKLY
WEEKNIGHT
WEEKNIGHTS
WEEKS
WEEL
WEEN
WEENED
WEENIE
WEENIER
WEENIES
WEENIEST
WEENING
WEENS
WEENSIER
WEENSIEST
WEENSY
WEENY
WEEP
WEEPER
WEEPERS
WEEPIE
WEEPIER
WEEPIES
WEEPIEST
WEEPILY
WEEPINESS
WEEPINESSES
WEEPING
WEEPINGLY
WEEPINGS
WEEPS
WEEPY
WEER
WEES
WEEST
WEET
WEETED
WEETING
WEETS
WEEVER
WEEVERS
WEEVIL
WEEVILED
WEEVILLY
WEEVILS
WEEVILY
WEEWEE
WEEWEED
WEEWEEING
WEEWEES
WEFT
WEFTS
WEFTWISE
WEIGELA
WEIGELAS
WEIGELIA
WEIGELIAS
WEIGH
WEIGHABLE
WEIGHED
WEIGHER
WEIGHERS
WEIGHING
WEIGHMAN
WEIGHMEN
WEIGHS
WEIGHT
WEIGHTED
WEIGHTER
WEIGHTERS

EIGHTIER
EIGHTIEST
EIGHTILY
EIGHTINESS
EIGHTINESSES
EIGHTING
EIGHTINGS
EIGHTLESS
EIGHTLESSLY
EIGHTLESSNESS
EIGHTS
EIGHTY
EIMARANER
EIMARANERS
EINER
EINERS
EIR
EIRD
EIRDED
EIRDER
EIRDEST
EIRDIE
EIRDIES
EIRDING
EIRDLY
EIRDNESS
EIRDNESSES
EIRDO
EIRDOES
EIRDOS
EIRDS
EIRDY
EIRS
EISENHEIMER
EISENHEIMERS
EKA
EKAS
ELCH
ELCHED
ELCHER
ELCHERS
ELCHES
ELCHING
ELCOME
ELCOMED
ELCOMELY
ELCOMENESS
ELCOMENESSES
ELCOMER
ELCOMERS
ELCOMES
ELCOMING
ELD

WELDABLE
WELDED
WELDER
WELDERS
WELDING
WELDLESS
WELDMENT
WELDMENTS
WELDOR
WELDORS
WELDS
WELFARE
WELFARES
WELFARISM
WELFARISMS
WELFARIST
WELFARISTS
WELKIN
WELKINS
WELL
WELLADAY
WELLADAYS
WELLAWAY
WELLAWAYS
WELLBORN
WELLCURB
WELLCURBS
WELLDOER
WELLDOERS
WELLED
WELLHEAD
WELLHEADS
WELLHOLE
WELLHOLES
WELLHOUSE
WELLHOUSES
WELLIE
WELLIES
WELLING
WELLNESS
WELLNESSES
WELLS
WELLSITE
WELLSITES
WELLSPRING
WELLSPRINGS
WELLY
WELSH
WELSHED
WELSHER
WELSHERS
WELSHES
WELSHING

WELT
WELTANSCHAUUNG
WELTANSCHAUUNGS
WELTED
WELTER
WELTERED
WELTERING
WELTERS
WELTERWEIGHT
WELTERWEIGHTS
WELTING
WELTINGS
WELTS
WELTSCHMERZ
WELTSCHMERZES
WEN
WENCH
WENCHED
WENCHER
WENCHERS
WENCHES
WENCHING
WEND
WENDED
WENDIGO
WENDIGOES
WENDIGOS
WENDING
WENDS
WENNIER
WENNIEST
WENNISH
WENNY
WENS
WENT
WENTLETRAP
WENTLETRAPS
WEPT
WERE
WEREGILD
WEREGILDS
WEREWOLF
WEREWOLVES
WERGELD
WERGELDS
WERGELT
WERGELTS
WERGILD
WERGILDS
WERNERITE
WERNERITES
WERT
WERWOLF

WERWOLVES
WESKIT
WESKITS
WESSAND
WESSANDS
WEST
WESTBOUND
WESTER
WESTERED
WESTERING
WESTERLIES
WESTERLY
WESTERN
WESTERNER
WESTERNERS
WESTERNISATION
WESTERNISATIONS
WESTERNISE
WESTERNISED
WESTERNISES
WESTERNISING
WESTERNIZATION
WESTERNIZATIONS
WESTERNIZE
WESTERNIZED
WESTERNIZER
WESTERNIZERS
WESTERNIZES
WESTERNIZING
WESTERNMOST
WESTERNS
WESTERS
WESTING
WESTINGS
WESTMOST
WESTS
WESTWARD
WESTWARDS
WET
WETA
WETAS
WETBACK
WETBACKS
WETHER
WETHERS
WETLAND
WETLANDS
WETLY
WETNESS
WETNESSES
WETPROOF
WETS
WETSUIT

WETSUITS
WETTABILITIES
WETTABILITY
WETTABLE
WETTED
WETTER
WETTERS
WETTEST
WETTING
WETTINGS
WETTISH
WETWARE
WETWARES
WHA
WHACK
WHACKED
WHACKER
WHACKERS
WHACKIER
WHACKIEST
WHACKING
WHACKINGS
WHACKO
WHACKOES
WHACKOS
WHACKS
WHACKY
WHALE
WHALEBACK
WHALEBACKS
WHALEBOAT
WHALEBOATS
WHALEBONE
WHALEBONES
WHALED
WHALELIKE
WHALEMAN
WHALEMEN
WHALER
WHALERS
WHALES
WHALING
WHALINGS
WHAM
WHAMMED
WHAMMIES
WHAMMING
WHAMMO
WHAMMY
WHAMO
WHAMS
WHANG
WHANGED

WHANGEE
WHANGEES
WHANGING
WHANGS
WHAP
WHAPPED
WHAPPER
WHAPPERS
WHAPPING
WHAPS
WHARF
WHARFAGE
WHARFAGES
WHARFED
WHARFING
WHARFINGER
WHARFINGERS
WHARFMASTER
WHARFMASTERS
WHARFS
WHARVE
WHARVES
WHAT
WHATCHA
WHATCHAMACALLIT
WHATEVER
WHATNESS
WHATNESSES
WHATNOT
WHATNOTS
WHATS
WHATSIS
WHATSISES
WHATSIT
WHATSITS
WHATSO
WHATSOEVER
WHAUP
WHAUPS
WHEAL
WHEALS
WHEAT
WHEATEAR
WHEATEARS
WHEATEN
WHEATENS
WHEATGRASS
WHEATGRASSES
WHEATLAND
WHEATLANDS
WHEATLESS
WHEATS
WHEATWORM
WHEATWORMS
WHEE
WHEEDLE
WHEEDLED
WHEEDLER
WHEEDLERS
WHEEDLES
WHEEDLING
WHEEL
WHEELBARROW
WHEELBARROWED
WHEELBARROWING
WHEELBARROWS
WHEELBASE
WHEELBASES
WHEELCHAIR
WHEELCHAIRS
WHEELED
WHEELER
WHEELERS
WHEELHORSE
WHEELHORSES
WHEELHOUSE
WHEELHOUSES
WHEELIE
WHEELIES
WHEELING
WHEELINGS
WHEELLESS
WHEELMAN
WHEELMEN
WHEELS
WHEELSMAN
WHEELSMEN
WHEELWORK
WHEELWORKS
WHEELWRIGHT
WHEELWRIGHTS
WHEEN
WHEENS
WHEEP
WHEEPED
WHEEPING
WHEEPLE
WHEEPLED
WHEEPLES
WHEEPLING
WHEEPS
WHEEZE
WHEEZED
WHEEZER
WHEEZERS
WHEEZES
WHEEZIER
WHEEZIEST
WHEEZILY
WHEEZINESS
WHEEZINESSES
WHEEZING
WHEEZY
WHELK
WHELKIER
WHELKIEST
WHELKS
WHELKY
WHELM
WHELMED
WHELMING
WHELMS
WHELP
WHELPED
WHELPING
WHELPLESS
WHELPS
WHEN
WHENAS
WHENCE
WHENCESOEVER
WHENEVER
WHENS
WHENSOEVER
WHERE
WHEREABOUT
WHEREABOUTS
WHEREAS
WHEREASES
WHEREAT
WHEREBY
WHEREFORE
WHEREFORES
WHEREFROM
WHEREIN
WHEREINTO
WHEREOF
WHEREON
WHERES
WHERESOEVER
WHERETHROUGH
WHERETO
WHEREUNTO
WHEREUPON
WHEREVER
WHEREWITH
WHEREWITHAL
WHEREWITHALS
WHEREWITHS
WHERRIED
WHERRIES
WHERRY
WHERRYING
WHERVE
WHERVES
WHET
WHETHER
WHETS
WHETSTONE
WHETSTONES
WHETTED
WHETTER
WHETTERS
WHETTING
WHEW
WHEWS
WHEY
WHEYEY
WHEYFACE
WHEYFACED
WHEYFACES
WHEYISH
WHEYLIKE
WHEYS
WHICH
WHICHEVER
WHICHSOEVER
WHICKER
WHICKERED
WHICKERING
WHICKERS
WHID
WHIDAH
WHIDAHS
WHIDDED
WHIDDING
WHIDS
WHIFF
WHIFFED
WHIFFER
WHIFFERS
WHIFFET
WHIFFETS
WHIFFIER
WHIFFIEST
WHIFFING
WHIFFLE
WHIFFLED
WHIFFLER
WHIFFLERS
WHIFFLES
WHIFFLETREE
WHIFFLETREES
WHIFFLING
WHIFFS
WHIFFY
WHIG
WHIGMALEERIE
WHIGMALEERIES
WHIGS
WHILE
WHILED
WHILES
WHILING
WHILOM
WHILST
WHIM
WHIMBREL
WHIMBRELS
WHIMPER
WHIMPERED
WHIMPERER
WHIMPERERS
WHIMPERING
WHIMPERS
WHIMS
WHIMSEY
WHIMSEYS
WHIMSICAL
WHIMSICALITIES
WHIMSICALITY
WHIMSICALLY
WHIMSICALNESS
WHIMSICALNESSES
WHIMSIED
WHIMSIES
WHIMSY
WHIN
WHINCHAT
WHINCHATS
WHINE
WHINED
WHINER
WHINERS
WHINES
WHINEY
WHINGDING
WHINGDINGS
WHINGE
WHINGED
WHINGEING
WHINGER
WHINGERS
WHINGES
WHINGIER

HINGIEST
HINGING
HINGY
HINIER
HINIEST
HININESS
HININESSES
HINING
HININGLY
HINNIED
HINNIER
HINNIES
HINNIEST
HINNY
HINNYING
HINS
HINSTONE
HINSTONES
HINY
HIP
HIPCORD
HIPCORDS
HIPLASH
HIPLASHED
HIPLASHES
HIPLASHING
HIPLESS
HIPLIKE
HIPPED
HIPPER
HIPPERS
HIPPERSNAPPER
HIPPERSNAPPERS
HIPPET
HIPPETS
HIPPIER
HIPPIEST
HIPPING
HIPPINGS
HIPPIT
HIPPITS
HIPPLETREE
HIPPLETREES
HIPPOORWILL
HIPPOORWILLS
HIPPY
HIPRAY
HIPRAYS
HIPS
HIPSAW
HIPSAWED
HIPSAWING
HIPSAWN
WHIPSAWS
WHIPSNAKE
WHIPSNAKES
WHIPSTALL
WHIPSTALLS
WHIPSTITCH
WHIPSTITCHED
WHIPSTITCHES
WHIPSTITCHING
WHIPSTOCK
WHIPSTOCKS
WHIPT
WHIPTAIL
WHIPTAILS
WHIPWORM
WHIPWORMS
WHIR
WHIRL
WHIRLED
WHIRLER
WHIRLERS
WHIRLIER
WHIRLIES
WHIRLIEST
WHIRLIGIG
WHIRLIGIGS
WHIRLING
WHIRLPOOL
WHIRLPOOLS
WHIRLS
WHIRLWIND
WHIRLWINDS
WHIRLY
WHIRLYBIRD
WHIRLYBIRDS
WHIRR
WHIRRED
WHIRRIED
WHIRRIES
WHIRRING
WHIRRS
WHIRRY
WHIRRYING
WHIRS
WHISH
WHISHED
WHISHES
WHISHING
WHISHT
WHISHTED
WHISHTING
WHISHTS
WHISK
WHISKED
WHISKER
WHISKERED
WHISKERS
WHISKERY
WHISKEY
WHISKEYS
WHISKIES
WHISKING
WHISKS
WHISKY
WHISPER
WHISPERED
WHISPERER
WHISPERERS
WHISPERING
WHISPERINGLY
WHISPERINGS
WHISPERS
WHISPERY
WHIST
WHISTED
WHISTING
WHISTLE
WHISTLEABLE
WHISTLED
WHISTLER
WHISTLERS
WHISTLES
WHISTLING
WHISTLINGS
WHISTS
WHIT
WHITE
WHITEBAIT
WHITEBAITS
WHITEBEARD
WHITEBEARDS
WHITEBOARD
WHITEBOARDS
WHITECAP
WHITECAPS
WHITECOMB
WHITECOMBS
WHITED
WHITEFACE
WHITEFACES
WHITEFISH
WHITEFISHES
WHITEFLIES
WHITEFLY
WHITEHEAD
WHITEHEADS
WHITELY
WHITEN
WHITENED
WHITENER
WHITENERS
WHITENESS
WHITENESSES
WHITENING
WHITENINGS
WHITENS
WHITEOUT
WHITEOUTS
WHITER
WHITES
WHITESMITH
WHITESMITHS
WHITEST
WHITETAIL
WHITETAILS
WHITETHROAT
WHITETHROATS
WHITEWALL
WHITEWALLS
WHITEWASH
WHITEWASHED
WHITEWASHER
WHITEWASHERS
WHITEWASHES
WHITEWASHING
WHITEWASHINGS
WHITEWATER
WHITEWING
WHITEWINGS
WHITEWOOD
WHITEWOODS
WHITEY
WHITEYS
WHITHER
WHITHERSOEVER
WHITHERWARD
WHITIER
WHITIES
WHITIEST
WHITING
WHITINGS
WHITISH
WHITLOW
WHITLOWS
WHITRACK
WHITRACKS
WHITS
WHITTER
WHITTERS
WHITTLE
WHITTLED
WHITTLER
WHITTLERS
WHITTLES
WHITTLING
WHITTLINGS
WHITTRET
WHITTRETS
WHITY
WHIZ
WHIZBANG
WHIZBANGS
WHIZZ
WHIZZBANG
WHIZZBANGS
WHIZZED
WHIZZER
WHIZZERS
WHIZZES
WHIZZIER
WHIZZIEST
WHIZZING
WHIZZY
WHO
WHOA
WHODUNIT
WHODUNITS
WHODUNNIT
WHODUNNITS
WHOEVER
WHOLE
WHOLEHEARTED
WHOLEHEARTEDLY
WHOLEMEAL
WHOLENESS
WHOLENESSES
WHOLES
WHOLESALE
WHOLESALED
WHOLESALER
WHOLESALERS
WHOLESALES
WHOLESALING
WHOLESOME
WHOLESOMELY
WHOLESOMENESS
WHOLESOMENESSES
WHOLESOMER
WHOLESOMEST
WHOLISM
WHOLISMS
WHOLISTIC

WHOLLY
WHOM
WHOMEVER
WHOMP
WHOMPED
WHOMPING
WHOMPS
WHOMSO
WHOMSOEVER
WHOOF
WHOOFED
WHOOFING
WHOOFS
WHOOMP
WHOOMPH
WHOOMPHS
WHOOMPS
WHOOP
WHOOPED
WHOOPEE
WHOOPEES
WHOOPER
WHOOPERS
WHOOPIE
WHOOPIES
WHOOPING
WHOOPLA
WHOOPLAS
WHOOPS
WHOOSH
WHOOSHED
WHOOSHES
WHOOSHING
WHOOSIS
WHOOSISES
WHOP
WHOPPED
WHOPPER
WHOPPERS
WHOPPING
WHOPS
WHORE
WHORED
WHOREDOM
WHOREDOMS
WHOREHOUSE
WHOREHOUSES
WHOREMASTER
WHOREMASTERS
WHOREMONGER
WHOREMONGERS
WHORES
WHORESON
WHORESONS
WHORING
WHORINGS
WHORISH
WHORISHLY
WHORL
WHORLED
WHORLING
WHORLS
WHORT
WHORTLE
WHORTLEBERRIES
WHORTLEBERRY
WHORTLES
WHORTS
WHOSE
WHOSESO
WHOSESOEVER
WHOSEVER
WHOSIS
WHOSISES
WHOSIT
WHOSITS
WHOSO
WHOSOEVER
WHUMP
WHUMPED
WHUMPING
WHUMPS
WHUP
WHUPPED
WHUPPING
WHUPS
WHY
WHYDA
WHYDAH
WHYDAHS
WHYDAS
WHYS
WICCA
WICCAN
WICCANS
WICCAS
WICH
WICHES
WICK
WICKAPE
WICKAPES
WICKED
WICKEDER
WICKEDEST
WICKEDLY
WICKEDNESS
WICKEDNESSES
WICKER
WICKERS
WICKERWORK
WICKERWORKS
WICKET
WICKETKEEPER
WICKETKEEPERS
WICKETS
WICKING
WICKINGS
WICKIUP
WICKIUPS
WICKLESS
WICKS
WICKYUP
WICKYUPS
WICOPIES
WICOPY
WIDDER
WIDDERS
WIDDERSHINS
WIDDIE
WIDDIES
WIDDLE
WIDDLED
WIDDLES
WIDDLING
WIDDY
WIDE
WIDEAWAKE
WIDEAWAKES
WIDEBAND
WIDEBODIES
WIDEBODY
WIDELY
WIDEMOUTHED
WIDEN
WIDENED
WIDENER
WIDENERS
WIDENESS
WIDENESSES
WIDENING
WIDENS
WIDEOUT
WIDEOUTS
WIDER
WIDES
WIDESPREAD
WIDEST
WIDGEON
WIDGEONS
WIDGET
WIDGETS
WIDISH
WIDOW
WIDOWBIRD
WIDOWBIRDS
WIDOWED
WIDOWER
WIDOWERED
WIDOWERHOOD
WIDOWERHOODS
WIDOWERS
WIDOWHOOD
WIDOWHOODS
WIDOWING
WIDOWS
WIDTH
WIDTHS
WIDTHWAY
WIDTHWAYS
WIDTHWISE
WIELD
WIELDABLE
WIELDED
WIELDER
WIELDERS
WIELDIER
WIELDIEST
WIELDING
WIELDS
WIELDY
WIENER
WIENERS
WIENERWURST
WIENERWURSTS
WIENIE
WIENIES
WIFE
WIFEBEATER
WIFEBEATERS
WIFED
WIFEDOM
WIFEDOMS
WIFEHOOD
WIFEHOODS
WIFELESS
WIFELIER
WIFELIEST
WIFELIKE
WIFELINESS
WIFELINESSES
WIFELY
WIFES
WIFEY
WIFEYS
WIFING
WIFTIER
WIFTIEST
WIFTY
WIG
WIGAN
WIGANS
WIGEON
WIGEONS
WIGGED
WIGGER
WIGGERIES
WIGGERS
WIGGERY
WIGGIER
WIGGIEST
WIGGING
WIGGINGS
WIGGLE
WIGGLED
WIGGLER
WIGGLERS
WIGGLES
WIGGLIER
WIGGLIEST
WIGGLING
WIGGLY
WIGGY
WIGHT
WIGHTS
WIGLESS
WIGLET
WIGLETS
WIGLIKE
WIGMAKER
WIGMAKERS
WIGS
WIGWAG
WIGWAGGED
WIGWAGGER
WIGWAGGERS
WIGWAGGING
WIGWAGS
WIGWAM
WIGWAMS
WIKI
WIKIS
WIKIUP
WIKIUPS
WILCO
WILD

LDCARD
LDCARDS
LDCAT
LDCATS
LDCATTED
LDCATTER
LDCATTERS
LDCATTING
LDEBEEST
LDEBEESTS
LDED
LDER
LDERED
LDERING
LDERMENT
LDERMENTS
LDERNESS
LDERNESSES
LDERS
LDEST
LDFIRE
LDFIRES
LDFLOWER
LDFLOWERS
LDFOWL
LDFOWLER
LDFOWLERS
LDFOWLING
LDFOWLINGS
LDFOWLS
LDING
LDINGS
LDISH
LDLAND
LDLANDS
LDLIFE
LDLING
LDLINGS
LDLY
LDNESS
LDNESSES
LDS
LDWOOD
LDWOODS
E
ED
ES
FUL
FULLY
IER
IEST
ILY
INESS
WILINESSES
WILING
WILL
WILLABLE
WILLED
WILLEMITE
WILLEMITES
WILLER
WILLERS
WILLET
WILLETS
WILLFUL
WILLFULLY
WILLFULNESS
WILLFULNESSES
WILLIE
WILLIED
WILLIES
WILLING
WILLINGER
WILLINGEST
WILLINGLY
WILLINGNESS
WILLINGNESSES
WILLIWAU
WILLIWAUS
WILLIWAW
WILLIWAWS
WILLOW
WILLOWED
WILLOWER
WILLOWERS
WILLOWIER
WILLOWIEST
WILLOWING
WILLOWLIKE
WILLOWS
WILLOWWARE
WILLOWWARES
WILLOWY
WILLPOWER
WILLPOWERS
WILLS
WILLY
WILLYARD
WILLYART
WILLYING
WILLYWAW
WILLYWAWS
WILT
WILTED
WILTING
WILTS
WILY
WIMBLE
WIMBLED
WIMBLES
WIMBLING
WIMMIN
WIMP
WIMPED
WIMPIER
WIMPIEST
WIMPINESS
WIMPINESSES
WIMPING
WIMPISH
WIMPISHNESS
WIMPISHNESSES
WIMPLE
WIMPLED
WIMPLES
WIMPLING
WIMPS
WIMPY
WIN
WINCE
WINCED
WINCER
WINCERS
WINCES
WINCEY
WINCEYS
WINCH
WINCHED
WINCHER
WINCHERS
WINCHES
WINCHING
WINCING
WIND
WINDABLE
WINDAGE
WINDAGES
WINDBAG
WINDBAGS
WINDBELL
WINDBELLS
WINDBLAST
WINDBLASTS
WINDBLOWN
WINDBREAK
WINDBREAKER
WINDBREAKERS
WINDBREAKS
WINDBURN
WINDBURNED
WINDBURNING
WINDBURNS
WINDBURNT
WINDCHEATER
WINDCHEATERS
WINDCHILL
WINDCHILLS
WINDED
WINDER
WINDERS
WINDFALL
WINDFALLS
WINDFLAW
WINDFLAWS
WINDFLOWER
WINDFLOWERS
WINDGALL
WINDGALLS
WINDHOVER
WINDHOVERS
WINDIER
WINDIEST
WINDIGO
WINDIGOES
WINDIGOS
WINDILY
WINDINESS
WINDINESSES
WINDING
WINDINGLY
WINDINGS
WINDJAMMER
WINDJAMMERS
WINDJAMMING
WINDJAMMINGS
WINDLASS
WINDLASSED
WINDLASSES
WINDLASSING
WINDLE
WINDLED
WINDLES
WINDLESS
WINDLESSLY
WINDLESTRAW
WINDLESTRAWS
WINDLING
WINDLINGS
WINDLOAD
WINDLOADING
WINDLOADINGS
WINDLOADS
WINDMILL
WINDMILLED
WINDMILLING
WINDMILLS
WINDOW
WINDOWED
WINDOWING
WINDOWINGS
WINDOWLESS
WINDOWPANE
WINDOWPANES
WINDOWS
WINDOWSILL
WINDOWSILLS
WINDOWY
WINDPACK
WINDPACKS
WINDPIPE
WINDPIPES
WINDPROOF
WINDROW
WINDROWED
WINDROWER
WINDROWERS
WINDROWING
WINDROWS
WINDS
WINDSAIL
WINDSAILS
WINDSCREEN
WINDSCREENS
WINDSHIELD
WINDSHIELDS
WINDSLAB
WINDSLABS
WINDSOCK
WINDSOCKS
WINDSTORM
WINDSTORMS
WINDSURF
WINDSURFED
WINDSURFER
WINDSURFERS
WINDSURFING
WINDSURFINGS
WINDSURFS
WINDSWEPT
WINDTHROW
WINDTHROWS
WINDUP
WINDUPS
WINDWARD
WINDWARDS

WINDWAY
WINDWAYS
WINDY
WINE
WINED
WINEGLASS
WINEGLASSES
WINEGROWER
WINEGROWERS
WINELESS
WINEMAKER
WINEMAKERS
WINEMAKING
WINEMAKINGS
WINEPRESS
WINEPRESSES
WINERIES
WINERY
WINES
WINESAP
WINESAPS
WINESHOP
WINESHOPS
WINESKIN
WINESKINS
WINESOP
WINESOPS
WINEY
WING
WINGBACK
WINGBACKS
WINGBEAT
WINGBEATS
WINGBOW
WINGBOWS
WINGCHAIR
WINGCHAIRS
WINGDING
WINGDINGS
WINGED
WINGEDLY
WINGER
WINGERS
WINGIER
WINGIEST
WINGING
WINGLESS
WINGLESSNESS
WINGLESSNESSES
WINGLET
WINGLETS
WINGLIKE
WINGMAN
WINGMEN
WINGNUT
WINGNUTS
WINGOVER
WINGOVERS
WINGS
WINGSPAN
WINGSPANS
WINGSPREAD
WINGSPREADS
WINGTIP
WINGTIPS
WINGY
WINIER
WINIEST
WINING
WINISH
WINK
WINKED
WINKER
WINKERS
WINKING
WINKINGLY
WINKLE
WINKLED
WINKLER
WINKLERS
WINKLES
WINKLING
WINKS
WINLESS
WINNABLE
WINNED
WINNER
WINNERS
WINNING
WINNINGEST
WINNINGLY
WINNINGS
WINNOCK
WINNOCKS
WINNOW
WINNOWED
WINNOWER
WINNOWERS
WINNOWING
WINNOWS
WINO
WINOES
WINOS
WINS
WINSOME
WINSOMELY
WINSOMENESS
WINSOMENESSES
WINSOMER
WINSOMEST
WINTER
WINTERBERRIES
WINTERBERRY
WINTERED
WINTERER
WINTERERS
WINTERFED
WINTERFEED
WINTERFEEDING
WINTERFEEDS
WINTERGREEN
WINTERGREENS
WINTERIER
WINTERIEST
WINTERING
WINTERISH
WINTERIZATION
WINTERIZATIONS
WINTERIZE
WINTERIZED
WINTERIZES
WINTERIZING
WINTERKILL
WINTERKILLS
WINTERLY
WINTERS
WINTERTIDE
WINTERTIDES
WINTERTIME
WINTERTIMES
WINTERY
WINTLE
WINTLED
WINTLES
WINTLING
WINTRIER
WINTRIEST
WINTRILY
WINTRINESS
WINTRINESSES
WINTRY
WINY
WINZE
WINZES
WIPE
WIPEABLE
WIPED
WIPEOUT
WIPEOUTS
WIPER
WIPERS
WIPES
WIPING
WIRABLE
WIRE
WIRED
WIREDRAW
WIREDRAWER
WIREDRAWERS
WIREDRAWING
WIREDRAWN
WIREDRAWS
WIREDREW
WIREGRASS
WIREGRASSES
WIREHAIR
WIREHAIRED
WIREHAIRS
WIRELESS
WIRELESSED
WIRELESSES
WIRELESSING
WIRELESSLY
WIRELIKE
WIRELINE
WIRELINES
WIREMAN
WIREMEN
WIREPHOTO
WIREPHOTOS
WIRER
WIRERS
WIRES
WIRETAP
WIRETAPPED
WIRETAPPER
WIRETAPPERS
WIRETAPPING
WIRETAPPINGS
WIRETAPS
WIREWAY
WIREWAYS
WIREWORK
WIREWORKS
WIREWORM
WIREWORMS
WIRIER
WIRIEST
WIRILY
WIRINESS
WIRINESSES
WIRING
WIRINGS
WIRRA
WIRY
WIS
WISDOM
WISDOMS
WISE
WISEACRE
WISEACRES
WISEASS
WISEASSES
WISECRACK
WISECRACKED
WISECRACKER
WISECRACKERS
WISECRACKING
WISECRACKS
WISED
WISEGUY
WISEGUYS
WISELIER
WISELIEST
WISELY
WISENESS
WISENESSES
WISENHEIMER
WISENHEIMERS
WISENT
WISENTS
WISER
WISES
WISEST
WISEWOMAN
WISEWOMEN
WISH
WISHA
WISHBONE
WISHBONES
WISHED
WISHER
WISHERS
WISHES
WISHFUL
WISHFULLY
WISHFULNESS
WISHFULNESSES
WISHING
WISHLESS
WISING
WISP
WISPED
WISPIER
WISPIEST

SPILY
SPINESS
SPINESSES
SPING
SPISH
SPLIKE
SPS
SPY
SS
SSED
SSES
SSING
ST
STARIA
STARIAS
STED
STERIA
STERIAS
STFUL
STFULLY
STFULNESS
STFULNESSES
STING
STS
T
TAN
TANS
TCH
TCHCRAFT
TCHCRAFTS
TCHED
TCHERIES
TCHERY
TCHES
CHGRASS
CHGRASSES
CHHOOD
CHHOODS
CHIER
CHIEST
CHING
CHINGS
CHLIKE
CHWEED
CHWEEDS
CHY
E
ED
ENAGEMOT
ENAGEMOTE
ENAGEMOTES
ENAGEMOTS
ES

WITH
WITHAL
WITHDRAW
WITHDRAWABLE
WITHDRAWAL
WITHDRAWALS
WITHDRAWING
WITHDRAWN
WITHDRAWNNESS
WITHDRAWNNESSES
WITHDRAWS
WITHDREW
WITHE
WITHED
WITHER
WITHERED
WITHERER
WITHERERS
WITHERING
WITHERINGLY
WITHERINGS
WITHERITE
WITHERITES
WITHEROD
WITHERODS
WITHERS
WITHERSHINS
WITHES
WITHHELD
WITHHOLD
WITHHOLDER
WITHHOLDERS
WITHHOLDING
WITHHOLDINGS
WITHHOLDS
WITHIER
WITHIES
WITHIEST
WITHIN
WITHINDOORS
WITHING
WITHINS
WITHOUT
WITHOUTDOORS
WITHOUTS
WITHSTAND
WITHSTANDING
WITHSTANDS
WITHSTOOD
WITHY
WITING
WITLESS
WITLESSLY

WITLESSNESS
WITLESSNESSES
WITLING
WITLINGS
WITLOOF
WITLOOFS
WITNESS
WITNESSED
WITNESSER
WITNESSERS
WITNESSES
WITNESSING
WITNEY
WITNEYS
WITS
WITTED
WITTER
WITTERED
WITTERING
WITTERS
WITTICISM
WITTICISMS
WITTIER
WITTIEST
WITTILY
WITTINESS
WITTINESSES
WITTING
WITTINGLY
WITTINGS
WITTOL
WITTOLS
WITTY
WIVE
WIVED
WIVER
WIVERN
WIVERNS
WIVERS
WIVES
WIVING
WIZ
WIZARD
WIZARDER
WIZARDEST
WIZARDLY
WIZARDRIES
WIZARDRY
WIZARDS
WIZEN
WIZENED
WIZENING
WIZENS

WIZES
WIZZEN
WIZZENS
WIZZES
WO
WOAD
WOADED
WOADS
WOADWAX
WOADWAXEN
WOADWAXENS
WOADWAXES
WOALD
WOALDS
WOBBLE
WOBBLED
WOBBLER
WOBBLERS
WOBBLES
WOBBLIER
WOBBLIES
WOBBLIEST
WOBBLINESS
WOBBLINESSES
WOBBLING
WOBBLY
WOBEGONE
WODGE
WODGES
WOE
WOEBEGONE
WOEBEGONENESS
WOEBEGONENESSES
WOEFUL
WOEFULLER
WOEFULLEST
WOEFULLY
WOEFULNESS
WOEFULNESSES
WOENESS
WOENESSES
WOES
WOESOME
WOFUL
WOFULLER
WOFULLEST
WOFULLY
WOG
WOGGISH
WOGGLE
WOGGLES
WOGS
WOK

WOKE
WOKEN
WOKS
WOLD
WOLDS
WOLF
WOLFBERRIES
WOLFBERRY
WOLFED
WOLFER
WOLFERS
WOLFFISH
WOLFFISHES
WOLFHOUND
WOLFHOUNDS
WOLFING
WOLFISH
WOLFISHLY
WOLFISHNESS
WOLFISHNESSES
WOLFLIKE
WOLFRAM
WOLFRAMITE
WOLFRAMITES
WOLFRAMS
WOLFS
WOLFSBANE
WOLFSBANES
WOLFSKIN
WOLFSKINS
WOLLASTONITE
WOLLASTONITES
WOLVER
WOLVERINE
WOLVERINES
WOLVERS
WOLVES
WOMAN
WOMANED
WOMANHOOD
WOMANHOODS
WOMANING
WOMANISE
WOMANISED
WOMANISER
WOMANISERS
WOMANISES
WOMANISH
WOMANISHLY
WOMANISHNESS
WOMANISHNESSES
WOMANISING
WOMANISM

WOMANISMS
WOMANIST
WOMANISTS
WOMANIZE
WOMANIZED
WOMANIZER
WOMANIZERS
WOMANIZES
WOMANIZING
WOMANKIND
WOMANLESS
WOMANLIER
WOMANLIEST
WOMANLIKE
WOMANLINESS
WOMANLINESSES
WOMANLY
WOMANNED
WOMANNESS
WOMANNESSES
WOMANNING
WOMANPOWER
WOMANPOWERS
WOMANS
WOMB
WOMBAT
WOMBATS
WOMBED
WOMBIER
WOMBIEST
WOMBLIKE
WOMBS
WOMBY
WOMEN
WOMENFOLK
WOMENFOLKS
WOMENKIND
WOMERA
WOMERAS
WOMMERA
WOMMERAS
WOMYN
WON
WONDER
WONDERED
WONDERER
WONDERERS
WONDERFUL
WONDERFULLY
WONDERFULNESS
WONDERFULNESSES
WONDERING
WONDERLAND
WONDERLANDS
WONDERMENT
WONDERMENTS
WONDERS
WONDERWORK
WONDERWORKS
WONDROUS
WONDROUSLY
WONDROUSNESS
WONDROUSNESSES
WONK
WONKERIES
WONKERY
WONKIER
WONKIEST
WONKILY
WONKISH
WONKISHNESS
WONKISHNESSES
WONKS
WONKY
WONNED
WONNER
WONNERS
WONNING
WONS
WONT
WONTED
WONTEDLY
WONTEDNESS
WONTEDNESSES
WONTING
WONTON
WONTONS
WONTS
WOO
WOOABLE
WOOD
WOODBIN
WOODBIND
WOODBINDS
WOODBINE
WOODBINES
WOODBINS
WOODBLOCK
WOODBLOCKS
WOODBORER
WOODBORERS
WOODBOX
WOODBOXES
WOODCHAT
WOODCHATS
WOODCHOPPER
WOODCHOPPERS
WOODCHUCK
WOODCHUCKS
WOODCOCK
WOODCOCKS
WOODCRAFT
WOODCRAFTS
WOODCUT
WOODCUTS
WOODCUTTER
WOODCUTTERS
WOODCUTTING
WOODCUTTINGS
WOODED
WOODEN
WOODENER
WOODENEST
WOODENHEAD
WOODENHEADED
WOODENHEADS
WOODENLY
WOODENNESS
WOODENNESSES
WOODENWARE
WOODENWARES
WOODFERN
WOODFERNS
WOODGRAIN
WOODGRAINS
WOODHEN
WOODHENS
WOODIE
WOODIER
WOODIES
WOODIEST
WOODINESS
WOODINESSES
WOODING
WOODLAND
WOODLANDER
WOODLANDERS
WOODLANDS
WOODLARK
WOODLARKS
WOODLESS
WOODLICE
WOODLORE
WOODLORES
WOODLOT
WOODLOTS
WOODMAN
WOODMEN
WOODMICE
WOODNOTE
WOODNOTES
WOODPECKER
WOODPECKERS
WOODPILE
WOODPILES
WOODRAT
WOODRATS
WOODRUFF
WOODRUFFS
WOODRUSH
WOODRUSHES
WOODS
WOODSHED
WOODSHEDDED
WOODSHEDDING
WOODSHEDS
WOODSIA
WOODSIAS
WOODSIER
WOODSIEST
WOODSMAN
WOODSMEN
WOODSTOVE
WOODSTOVES
WOODSY
WOODTONE
WOODTONES
WOODWASP
WOODWASPS
WOODWAX
WOODWAXEN
WOODWAXENS
WOODWAXES
WOODWIND
WOODWINDS
WOODWORK
WOODWORKER
WOODWORKERS
WOODWORKING
WOODWORKINGS
WOODWORKS
WOODWORM
WOODWORMS
WOODY
WOODYARD
WOODYARDS
WOOED
WOOER
WOOERS
WOOF
WOOFED
WOOFER
WOOFERS
WOOFING
WOOFS
WOOING
WOOINGLY
WOOL
WOOLED
WOOLEN
WOOLENS
WOOLER
WOOLERS
WOOLFELL
WOOLFELLS
WOOLGATHER
WOOLGATHERED
WOOLGATHERER
WOOLGATHERERS
WOOLGATHERING
WOOLGATHERINGS
WOOLGATHERS
WOOLHAT
WOOLHATS
WOOLIE
WOOLIER
WOOLIES
WOOLIEST
WOOLINESS
WOOLINESSES
WOOLLED
WOOLLEN
WOOLLENS
WOOLLIER
WOOLLIES
WOOLLIEST
WOOLLIKE
WOOLLILY
WOOLLINESS
WOOLLINESSES
WOOLLY
WOOLMAN
WOOLMEN
WOOLPACK
WOOLPACKS
WOOLS
WOOLSACK
WOOLSACKS
WOOLSHED
WOOLSHEDS
WOOLSKIN
WOOLSKINS
WOOLWORK
WOOLWORKS
WOOLY

OMERA
OMERAS
ONERF
ONERFS
OPIE
OPIES
OPS
OPSED
OPSES
OPSING
OPY
ORALI
ORALIS
ORARI
ORARIS
OS
OSH
OSHED
OSHES
OSHING
OZIER
OZIEST
OZILY
OZINESS
OZINESSES
OZY
P
PS
RD
RDAGE
RDAGES
RDBOOK
RDBOOKS
RDED
RDIER
RDIEST
RDILY
RDINESS
RDINESSES
RDING
RDINGS
RDLESS
RDLESSLY
RDLESSNESS
RDLESSNESSES
RDMONGER
RDMONGERS
RDPLAY
RDPLAYS
RDS
RDSMITH
DSMITHERIES
DSMITHERY
WORDSMITHS
WORDY
WORE
WORK
WORKABILITIES
WORKABILITY
WORKABLE
WORKABLENESS
WORKABLENESSES
WORKABLY
WORKADAY
WORKAHOLIC
WORKAHOLICS
WORKAHOLISM
WORKAHOLISMS
WORKBAG
WORKBAGS
WORKBASKET
WORKBASKETS
WORKBENCH
WORKBENCHES
WORKBOAT
WORKBOATS
WORKBOOK
WORKBOOKS
WORKBOOT
WORKBOOTS
WORKBOX
WORKBOXES
WORKDAY
WORKDAYS
WORKED
WORKER
WORKERS
WORKFARE
WORKFARES
WORKFLOW
WORKFLOWS
WORKFOLK
WORKFOLKS
WORKFORCE
WORKFORCES
WORKHORSE
WORKHORSES
WORKHOUR
WORKHOURS
WORKHOUSE
WORKHOUSES
WORKING
WORKINGMAN
WORKINGMEN
WORKINGS
WORKINGWOMAN
WORKINGWOMEN
WORKLESS
WORKLESSNESS
WORKLESSNESSES
WORKLOAD
WORKLOADS
WORKMAN
WORKMANLIKE
WORKMANLY
WORKMANSHIP
WORKMANSHIPS
WORKMATE
WORKMATES
WORKMEN
WORKOUT
WORKOUTS
WORKPEOPLE
WORKPIECE
WORKPIECES
WORKPLACE
WORKPLACES
WORKPRINT
WORKPRINTS
WORKROOM
WORKROOMS
WORKS
WORKSHEET
WORKSHEETS
WORKSHOP
WORKSHOPPED
WORKSHOPPING
WORKSHOPS
WORKSITE
WORKSITES
WORKSONG
WORKSONGS
WORKSPACE
WORKSPACES
WORKSTATION
WORKSTATIONS
WORKTABLE
WORKTABLES
WORKTOP
WORKTOPS
WORKUP
WORKUPS
WORKWEAR
WORKWEEK
WORKWEEKS
WORKWOMAN
WORKWOMEN
WORLD
WORLDBEAT
WORLDBEATS
WORLDER
WORLDERS
WORLDLIER
WORLDLIEST
WORLDLINESS
WORLDLINESSES
WORLDLING
WORLDLINGS
WORLDLY
WORLDS
WORLDVIEW
WORLDVIEWS
WORLDWIDE
WORM
WORMCAST
WORMCASTS
WORMED
WORMER
WORMERS
WORMGEAR
WORMGEARS
WORMHOLE
WORMHOLES
WORMIER
WORMIEST
WORMIL
WORMILS
WORMINESS
WORMINESSES
WORMING
WORMISH
WORMLIKE
WORMROOT
WORMROOTS
WORMS
WORMSEED
WORMSEEDS
WORMWOOD
WORMWOODS
WORMY
WORN
WORNNESS
WORNNESSES
WORRIED
WORRIEDLY
WORRIER
WORRIERS
WORRIES
WORRIMENT
WORRIMENTS
WORRISOME
WORRISOMELY
WORRISOMENESS
WORRISOMENESSES
WORRIT
WORRITED
WORRITING
WORRITS
WORRY
WORRYING
WORRYINGLY
WORRYWART
WORRYWARTS
WORSE
WORSEN
WORSENED
WORSENING
WORSENS
WORSER
WORSES
WORSET
WORSETS
WORSHIP
WORSHIPED
WORSHIPER
WORSHIPERS
WORSHIPFUL
WORSHIPFULLY
WORSHIPFULNESS
WORSHIPING
WORSHIPLESS
WORSHIPPED
WORSHIPPER
WORSHIPPERS
WORSHIPPING
WORSHIPS
WORST
WORSTED
WORSTEDS
WORSTING
WORSTS
WORT
WORTH
WORTHED
WORTHFUL
WORTHIER
WORTHIES
WORTHIEST
WORTHILY
WORTHINESS
WORTHINESSES
WORTHING
WORTHLESS
WORTHLESSLY
WORTHLESSNESS

WORTHLESSNESSES
WORTHS
WORTHWHILE
WORTHWHILENESS
WORTHY
WORTS
WOS
WOST
WOT
WOTCHER
WOTS
WOTTED
WOTTING
WOULD
WOULDEST
WOULDST
WOUND
WOUNDED
WOUNDEDLY
WOUNDING
WOUNDLESS
WOUNDS
WOUNDWORT
WOUNDWORTS
WOVE
WOVEN
WOVENS
WOW
WOWED
WOWEE
WOWING
WOWS
WOWSER
WOWSERS
WRACK
WRACKED
WRACKFUL
WRACKING
WRACKS
WRAITH
WRAITHLIKE
WRAITHS
WRANG
WRANGLE
WRANGLED
WRANGLER
WRANGLERS
WRANGLES
WRANGLING
WRANGS
WRAP
WRAPAROUND
WRAPAROUNDS
WRAPPED
WRAPPER
WRAPPERS
WRAPPING
WRAPPINGS
WRAPS
WRAPT
WRASSE
WRASSES
WRASSLE
WRASSLED
WRASSLES
WRASSLING
WRASTLE
WRASTLED
WRASTLES
WRASTLING
WRATH
WRATHED
WRATHFUL
WRATHFULLY
WRATHFULNESS
WRATHFULNESSES
WRATHIER
WRATHIEST
WRATHILY
WRATHING
WRATHS
WRATHY
WREAK
WREAKED
WREAKER
WREAKERS
WREAKING
WREAKS
WREATH
WREATHE
WREATHED
WREATHEN
WREATHER
WREATHERS
WREATHES
WREATHING
WREATHS
WREATHY
WRECK
WRECKAGE
WRECKAGES
WRECKED
WRECKER
WRECKERS
WRECKFUL
WRECKING
WRECKINGS
WRECKS
WREN
WRENCH
WRENCHED
WRENCHER
WRENCHERS
WRENCHES
WRENCHING
WRENCHINGLY
WRENS
WRENTIT
WRENTITS
WREST
WRESTED
WRESTER
WRESTERS
WRESTING
WRESTLE
WRESTLED
WRESTLER
WRESTLERS
WRESTLES
WRESTLING
WRESTLINGS
WRESTS
WRETCH
WRETCHED
WRETCHEDER
WRETCHEDEST
WRETCHEDLY
WRETCHEDNESS
WRETCHEDNESSES
WRETCHES
WRICK
WRICKED
WRICKING
WRICKS
WRIED
WRIER
WRIES
WRIEST
WRIGGLE
WRIGGLED
WRIGGLER
WRIGGLERS
WRIGGLES
WRIGGLIER
WRIGGLIEST
WRIGGLING
WRIGGLY
WRIGHT
WRIGHTS
WRING
WRINGED
WRINGER
WRINGERS
WRINGING
WRINGS
WRINKLE
WRINKLED
WRINKLES
WRINKLIE
WRINKLIER
WRINKLIEST
WRINKLING
WRINKLY
WRIST
WRISTBAND
WRISTBANDS
WRISTED
WRISTER
WRISTERS
WRISTIER
WRISTIEST
WRISTING
WRISTLET
WRISTLETS
WRISTLOCK
WRISTLOCKS
WRISTS
WRISTWATCH
WRISTWATCHES
WRISTY
WRIT
WRITABLE
WRITE
WRITEABLE
WRITEOFF
WRITEOFFS
WRITER
WRITERLY
WRITERS
WRITES
WRITHE
WRITHED
WRITHEN
WRITHER
WRITHERS
WRITHES
WRITHING
WRITING
WRITINGS
WRITS
WRITTEN
WRONG
WRONGDOER
WRONGDOERS
WRONGDOING
WRONGDOINGS
WRONGED
WRONGER
WRONGERS
WRONGEST
WRONGFUL
WRONGFULLY
WRONGFULNESS
WRONGFULNESSES
WRONGHEADED
WRONGHEADEDLY
WRONGHEADEDNE
WRONGING
WRONGLY
WRONGNESS
WRONGNESSES
WRONGS
WROTE
WROTH
WROTHFUL
WROUGHT
WRUNG
WRY
WRYER
WRYEST
WRYING
WRYLY
WRYNECK
WRYNECKS
WRYNESS
WRYNESSES
WUD
WULFENITE
WULFENITES
WUNDERKIND
WUNDERKINDER
WURST
WURSTS
WURTZITE
WURTZITES
WURZEL
WURZELS
WUSHU
WUSHUS
WUSS
WUSSES
WUSSIER
WUSSIES
WUSSIEST
WUSSY

THER
THERED
THERING
THERS
Z
ANDOTTE

WYANDOTTES
WYCH
WYCHES
WYE
WYES
WYLE

WYLED
WYLES
WYLIECOAT
WYLIECOATS
WYLING
WYN

WYND
WYNDS
WYNN
WYNNS
WYNS
WYSIWYG

WYTE
WYTED
WYTES
WYTING
WYVERN
WYVERNS

THAN
THANS
THATE
THATES
THEIN
THEINS
THENE
THENES
THIC
THIN
THINE
THINES
THINS
THOMA
THOMAS
THOMATA
THONE
THONES
THOPHYLL
THOPHYLLS
THOUS
EC
ECS

A
AL
AS
C
BIOTIC
BIOTICS
BLAST
BLASTS

XENOCRYST
XENOCRYSTS
XENODIAGNOSES
XENODIAGNOSIS
XENODIAGNOSTIC
XENOGAMIES
XENOGAMY
XENOGENEIC
XENOGENIC
XENOGENIES
XENOGENY
XENOGRAFT
XENOGRAFTS
XENOLITH
XENOLITHIC
XENOLITHS
XENON
XENONS
XENOPHILE
XENOPHILES
XENOPHOBE
XENOPHOBES
XENOPHOBIA
XENOPHOBIAS
XENOPHOBIC
XENOPHOBICALLY
XENOPUS
XENOPUSES
XENOTIME
XENOTIMES
XENOTRANSPLANT
XENOTRANSPLANTS

XENOTROPIC
XERARCH
XERIC
XERICALLY
XERISCAPE
XERISCAPES
XERODERMA
XERODERMAE
XERODERMAS
XEROGRAPHIC
XEROGRAPHICALLY
XEROGRAPHIES
XEROGRAPHY
XEROPHILE
XEROPHILIES
XEROPHILOUS
XEROPHILY
XEROPHTHALMIA
XEROPHTHALMIAS
XEROPHTHALMIC
XEROPHYTE
XEROPHYTES
XEROPHYTIC
XEROPHYTISM
XEROPHYTISMS
XERORADIOGRAPHY
XEROSERE
XEROSERES
XEROSES
XEROSIS
XEROTHERMIC
XEROTIC

XEROX
XEROXED
XEROXES
XEROXING
XERUS
XERUSES
XI
XIPHISTERNA
XIPHISTERNUM
XIPHOID
XIPHOIDS
XIS
XU
XYLAN
XYLANS
XYLEM
XYLEMS
XYLENE
XYLENES
XYLIDIN
XYLIDINE
XYLIDINES
XYLIDINS
XYLITOL
XYLITOLS
XYLOCARP
XYLOCARPS
XYLOGRAPH
XYLOGRAPHED
XYLOGRAPHER
XYLOGRAPHERS
XYLOGRAPHIC

XYLOGRAPHICAL
XYLOGRAPHIES
XYLOGRAPHING
XYLOGRAPHS
XYLOGRAPHY
XYLOID
XYLOL
XYLOLS
XYLOPHAGE
XYLOPHAGES
XYLOPHAGOUS
XYLOPHONE
XYLOPHONES
XYLOPHONIST
XYLOPHONISTS
XYLOSE
XYLOSES
XYLOTOMIES
XYLOTOMY
XYLYL
XYLYLS
XYST
XYSTER
XYSTERS
XYSTI
XYSTOI
XYSTOS
XYSTS
XYSTUS

YA
YABBER
YABBERED
YABBERING
YABBERS
YABBIE
YABBIES
YABBY
YACHT
YACHTED
YACHTER
YACHTERS
YACHTIE
YACHTIES
YACHTING
YACHTINGS
YACHTMAN
YACHTMEN
YACHTS
YACHTSMAN
YACHTSMEN
YACHTSWOMAN
YACHTSWOMEN
YACK
YACKED
YACKING
YACKS
YAFF
YAFFED
YAFFING
YAFFLE
YAFFLES
YAFFS
YAG
YAGE
YAGER
YAGERS
YAGES
YAGI
YAGIS
YAGS
YAH
YAHOO
YAHOOISM
YAHOOISMS
YAHOOS
YAHRZEIT
YAHRZEITS
YAIRD
YAIRDS
YAK
YAKITORI
YAKITORIS
YAKKED
YAKKER
YAKKERS
YAKKING
YAKS
YAKUZA
YALD
YAM
YAMALKA
YAMALKAS
YAMEN
YAMENS
YAMMER
YAMMERED
YAMMERER
YAMMERERS
YAMMERING
YAMMERS
YAMS
YAMULKA
YAMULKAS
YAMUN
YAMUNS
YANG
YANGS
YANK
YANKED
YANKING
YANKS
YANQUI
YANQUIS
YANTRA
YANTRAS
YAP
YAPOCK
YAPOCKS
YAPOK
YAPOKS
YAPON
YAPONS
YAPPED
YAPPER
YAPPERS
YAPPIER
YAPPIEST
YAPPING
YAPPINGLY
YAPPY
YAPS
YAR
YARAK
YARAKS
YARD
YARDAGE
YARDAGES
YARDARM
YARDARMS
YARDBIRD
YARDBIRDS
YARDED
YARDER
YARDERS
YARDING
YARDLAND
YARDLANDS
YARDMAN
YARDMASTER
YARDMASTERS
YARDMEN
YARDS
YARDSTICK
YARDSTICKS
YARDWAND
YARDWANDS
YARDWORK
YARDWORKS
YARE
YARELY
YARER
YAREST
YARMELKE
YARMELKES
YARMULKA
YARMULKAS
YARMULKE
YARMULKES
YARN
YARNED
YARNER
YARNERS
YARNING
YARNS
YARROW
YARROWS
YAS
YASHMAC
YASHMACS
YASHMAK
YASHMAKS
YASMAK
YASMAKS
YATAGAN
YATAGANS
YATAGHAN
YATAGHANS
YATTER
YATTERED
YATTERING
YATTERS
YAUD
YAUDS
YAULD
YAUP
YAUPED
YAUPER
YAUPERS
YAUPING
YAUPON
YAUPONS
YAUPS
YAUTIA
YAUTIAS
YAW
YAWED
YAWEY
YAWING
YAWL
YAWLED
YAWLING
YAWLS
YAWMETER
YAWMETERS
YAWN
YAWNED
YAWNER
YAWNERS
YAWNING
YAWNINGLY
YAWNS
YAWP
YAWPED
YAWPER
YAWPERS
YAWPING
YAWPINGS
YAWPS
YAWS
YAY
YAYS
YCLAD
YCLEPED
YCLEPT
YE
YEA
YEAH
YEAHS
YEALING
YEALINGS
YEAN
YEANED
YEANING
YEANLING
YEANLINGS
YEANS
YEAR
YEARBOOK
YEARBOOKS
YEAREND
YEARENDS
YEARLIES
YEARLING
YEARLINGS
YEARLONG
YEARLY
YEARN
YEARNED
YEARNER
YEARNERS
YEARNING
YEARNINGLY
YEARNINGS
YEARNS
YEARS
YEAS
YEASAYER
YEASAYERS
YEAST
YEASTED
YEASTIER
YEASTIEST
YEASTILY
YEASTINESS
YEASTINESSES
YEASTING
YEASTLESS
YEASTLIKE
YEASTS
YEASTY
YECCH
YECCHS
YECH
YECHS
YECHY
YEELIN
YEELINS
YEESH
YEGG

GGMAN
GGMEN
GGS
H
LD
LK
LKS
LL
LLED
LLER
LLERS
LLING
LLINGS
LOW
LOWCAKE
LOWCAKES
LOWED
LOWER
LOWEST
LOWFIN
LOWFINS
LOWHAMMER
LOWHAMMERS
LOWING
LOWISH
LOWLEGS
LOWLY
LOWS
LOWTAIL
LOWTAILS
LOWTHROAT
LOWTHROATS
LOWWARE
LOWWARES
LOWWOOD
LOWWOODS
LOWY
LS
PED
PER
PERS
PING
PS
NED
NING
S
TA
TAS
TE
TES
MAN

YEOMANLY
YEOMANRIES
YEOMANRY
YEOMEN
YEOW
YEP
YEPS
YER
YERBA
YERBAS
YERK
YERKED
YERKING
YERKS
YES
YESES
YESHIVA
YESHIVAH
YESHIVAHS
YESHIVAS
YESHIVOT
YESHIVOTH
YESSED
YESSES
YESSING
YESSIR
YESSIREE
YESSUM
YESTER
YESTERDAY
YESTERDAYS
YESTEREVE
YESTEREVES
YESTERN
YESTERNIGHT
YESTERNIGHTS
YESTERYEAR
YESTERYEARS
YESTREEN
YESTREENS
YET
YETI
YETIS
YETT
YETTS
YEUK
YEUKED
YEUKING
YEUKS
YEUKY
YEW
YEWS
YEZ

YID
YIDS
YIELD
YIELDABLE
YIELDED
YIELDER
YIELDERS
YIELDING
YIELDS
YIKES
YILL
YILLS
YIN
YINCE
YINGYANG
YINGYANGS
YINS
YIP
YIPE
YIPES
YIPPED
YIPPEE
YIPPIE
YIPPIES
YIPPING
YIPS
YIRD
YIRDS
YIRR
YIRRED
YIRRING
YIRRS
YIRTH
YIRTHS
YLEM
YLEMS
YO
YOB
YOBBERIES
YOBBERY
YOBBIER
YOBBIEST
YOBBISH
YOBBO
YOBBOES
YOBBOS
YOBBY
YOBS
YOCK
YOCKED
YOCKING
YOCKS
YOCTOSECOND

YOCTOSECONDS
YOD
YODEL
YODELED
YODELER
YODELERS
YODELING
YODELLED
YODELLER
YODELLERS
YODELLING
YODELS
YODH
YODHS
YODLE
YODLED
YODLER
YODLERS
YODLES
YODLING
YODS
YOGA
YOGAS
YOGEE
YOGEES
YOGH
YOGHOURT
YOGHOURTS
YOGHS
YOGHURT
YOGHURTS
YOGI
YOGIC
YOGIN
YOGINI
YOGINIS
YOGINS
YOGIS
YOGISM
YOGISMS
YOGOURT
YOGOURTS
YOGURT
YOGURTS
YOHIMBE
YOHIMBES
YOHIMBINE
YOHIMBINES
YOICKS
YOK
YOKE
YOKED
YOKEFELLOW

YOKEFELLOWS
YOKEL
YOKELESS
YOKELISH
YOKELS
YOKEMATE
YOKEMATES
YOKES
YOKING
YOKOZUNA
YOKOZUNAS
YOKS
YOLK
YOLKED
YOLKIER
YOLKIEST
YOLKLESS
YOLKS
YOLKY
YOM
YOMIM
YOMP
YOMPED
YOMPING
YOMPS
YON
YOND
YONDER
YONDERS
YONI
YONIC
YONIS
YONKER
YONKERS
YONKS
YOOF
YOOFS
YORE
YORES
YOTTABYTE
YOTTABYTES
YOU
YOUNG
YOUNGBERRIES
YOUNGBERRY
YOUNGBLOOD
YOUNGBLOODS
YOUNGER
YOUNGERS
YOUNGEST
YOUNGISH
YOUNGLING
YOUNGLINGS

YOUNGNESS
YOUNGNESSES
YOUNGS
YOUNGSTER
YOUNGSTERS
YOUNKER
YOUNKERS
YOUPON
YOUPONS
YOUR
YOURN
YOURS
YOURSELF
YOURSELVES
YOUS
YOUSE
YOUTH
YOUTHEN
YOUTHENED
YOUTHENING
YOUTHENS
YOUTHFUL
YOUTHFULLY
YOUTHFULNESS
YOUTHFULNESSES
YOUTHQUAKE
YOUTHQUAKES
YOUTHS
YOW
YOWE
YOWED
YOWES
YOWIE
YOWIES
YOWING
YOWL
YOWLED
YOWLER
YOWLERS
YOWLING
YOWLS
YOWS
YPERITE
YPERITES
YTTERBIA
YTTERBIAS
YTTERBIC
YTTERBIUM
YTTERBIUMS
YTTERBOUS
YTTRIA
YTTRIAS
YTTRIC
YTTRIUM
YTTRIUMS
YUAN
YUANS
YUCA
YUCAS
YUCCA
YUCCAS
YUCCH
YUCH
YUCK
YUCKED
YUCKIER
YUCKIEST
YUCKINESS
YUCKINESSES
YUCKING
YUCKS
YUCKY
YUGA
YUGAS
YUK
YUKATA
YUKATAS
YUKKED
YUKKIER
YUKKIEST
YUKKING
YUKKY
YUKS
YULAN
YULANS
YULE
YULES
YULETIDE
YULETIDES
YUM
YUMMIER
YUMMIES
YUMMIEST
YUMMINESS
YUMMINESSES
YUMMY
YUP
YUPON
YUPONS
YUPPIE
YUPPIEDOM
YUPPIEDOMS
YUPPIEISH
YUPPIES
YUPPIFICATION
YUPPIFICATIONS
YUPPIFIED
YUPPIFIES
YUPPIFY
YUPPIFYING
YUPPY
YUPPYDOM
YUPPYDOMS
YUPS
YURT
YURTA
YURTS
YUTZ
YUTZES
YUZU
YUZUS
YWIS

Z

ZA
ZABAGLIONE
ZABAGLIONES
ZABAIONE
ZABAIONES
ZABAJONE
ZABAJONES
ZACATON
ZACATONS
ZADDICK
ZADDIK
ZADDIKIM
ZAFFAR
ZAFFARS
ZAFFER
ZAFFERS
ZAFFIR
ZAFFIRS
ZAFFRE
ZAFFRES
ZAFTIG
ZAG
ZAGGED
ZAGGING
ZAGS
ZAIBATSU
ZAIDA
ZAIDAS
ZAIDEH
ZAIDEHS
ZAIDIES
ZAIDY
ZAIKAI
ZAIKAIS
ZAIRE
ZAIRES
ZAKAT
ZAKATS
ZALCITABINE
ZALCITABINES
ZAMARRA
ZAMARRAS
ZAMARRO
ZAMARROS
ZAMIA
ZAMIAS
ZAMINDAR
ZAMINDARI
ZAMINDARIS
ZAMINDARS
ZANANA
ZANANAS
ZANDER
ZANDERS
ZANIER
ZANIES
ZANIEST
ZANILY
ZANINESS
ZANINESSES
ZANY
ZANYISH
ZANZA
ZANZAS
ZAP
ZAPATEADO
ZAPATEADOS
ZAPATEO
ZAPATEOS
ZAPPED
ZAPPER
ZAPPERS
ZAPPIER
ZAPPIEST
ZAPPING
ZAPPY
ZAPS
ZAPTIAH
ZAPTIAHS
ZAPTIEH
ZAPTIEHS
ZARATITE
ZARATITES
ZAREBA
ZAREBAS
ZAREEBA
ZAREEBAS
ZARF
ZARFS
ZARIBA

RIBAS
RZUELA
RZUELAS
S
STRUGA
STRUGI
K
ES
IN
INS
EN
ENS
L
LOT
LOTRIES
LOTRY
LOTS
LOUS
LOUSLY
LOUSNESS
LOUSNESSES
LS
TIN
TINS
XANTHIN
XANTHINS
EC
ECK
ECKS
ECS
RA
RAFISH
RAFISHES
RAIC
RANO
RANOS
RAS
RASS
RASSES
RAWOOD
RAWOODS
RINE
RINES
OID
S
HIN
HINI
HINO
HINOS
HINS
N
NS

ZED
ZEDA
ZEDAS
ZEDOARIES
ZEDOARY
ZEDS
ZEE
ZEES
ZEIN
ZEINS
ZEITGEBER
ZEITGEBERS
ZEITGEIST
ZEITGEISTS
ZEK
ZEKS
ZELKOVA
ZELKOVAS
ZEMINDAR
ZEMINDARIES
ZEMINDARS
ZEMINDARY
ZEMSTVA
ZEMSTVO
ZEMSTVOS
ZENAIDA
ZENAIDAS
ZENANA
ZENANAS
ZENDO
ZENDOS
ZENITH
ZENITHAL
ZENITHS
ZEOLITE
ZEOLITES
ZEOLITIC
ZEP
ZEPHYR
ZEPHYRS
ZEPPELIN
ZEPPELINS
ZEPPOLE
ZEPPOLES
ZEPPOLI
ZEPS
ZEPTOSECOND
ZEPTOSECONDS
ZERK
ZERKS
ZERO
ZEROED
ZEROES

ZEROING
ZEROS
ZEROTH
ZEST
ZESTED
ZESTER
ZESTERS
ZESTFUL
ZESTFULLY
ZESTFULNESS
ZESTFULNESSES
ZESTIER
ZESTIEST
ZESTILY
ZESTINESS
ZESTINESSES
ZESTING
ZESTLESS
ZESTS
ZESTY
ZETA
ZETAS
ZETETIC
ZETTABYTE
ZETTABYTES
ZEUGMA
ZEUGMAS
ZEUGMATIC
ZIBELINE
ZIBELINES
ZIBELLINE
ZIBELLINES
ZIBET
ZIBETH
ZIBETHS
ZIBETS
ZIDOVUDINE
ZIDOVUDINES
ZIG
ZIGGED
ZIGGING
ZIGGURAT
ZIGGURATS
ZIGS
ZIGZAG
ZIGZAGGED
ZIGZAGGER
ZIGZAGGERS
ZIGZAGGING
ZIGZAGGY
ZIGZAGS
ZIKKURAT
ZIKKURATS

ZIKURAT
ZIKURATS
ZILCH
ZILCHES
ZILL
ZILLAH
ZILLAHS
ZILLION
ZILLIONAIRE
ZILLIONAIRES
ZILLIONS
ZILLIONTH
ZILLS
ZIN
ZINC
ZINCATE
ZINCATES
ZINCED
ZINCIC
ZINCIFIED
ZINCIFIES
ZINCIFY
ZINCIFYING
ZINCING
ZINCITE
ZINCITES
ZINCKED
ZINCKING
ZINCKY
ZINCO
ZINCOID
ZINCOS
ZINCOUS
ZINCS
ZINCY
ZINE
ZINEB
ZINEBS
ZINES
ZINFANDEL
ZINFANDELS
ZING
ZINGANI
ZINGANO
ZINGARA
ZINGARE
ZINGARI
ZINGARO
ZINGED
ZINGER
ZINGERS
ZINGIER
ZINGIEST

ZINGING
ZINGS
ZINGY
ZINKENITE
ZINKENITES
ZINKIFIED
ZINKIFIES
ZINKIFY
ZINKIFYING
ZINKY
ZINNIA
ZINNIAS
ZINS
ZIP
ZIPLESS
ZIPLOCK
ZIPOLA
ZIPOLAS
ZIPPED
ZIPPER
ZIPPERED
ZIPPERING
ZIPPERS
ZIPPIER
ZIPPIEST
ZIPPILY
ZIPPING
ZIPPO
ZIPPOS
ZIPPY
ZIPS
ZIRAM
ZIRAMS
ZIRCALOY
ZIRCALOYS
ZIRCON
ZIRCONIA
ZIRCONIAS
ZIRCONIC
ZIRCONIUM
ZIRCONIUMS
ZIRCONS
ZIT
ZITHER
ZITHERIST
ZITHERISTS
ZITHERN
ZITHERNS
ZITHERS
ZITI
ZITIS
ZITS
ZIZIT

ZIZITH
ZIZZ
ZIZZED
ZIZZES
ZIZZING
ZIZZLE
ZIZZLED
ZIZZLES
ZIZZLING
ZLOTE
ZLOTIES
ZLOTY
ZLOTYCH
ZLOTYS
ZOA
ZOANTHARIAN
ZOANTHARIANS
ZOARIA
ZOARIAL
ZOARIUM
ZOCALO
ZOCALOS
ZODIAC
ZODIACAL
ZODIACS
ZOEA
ZOEAE
ZOEAL
ZOEAS
ZOECIA
ZOECIUM
ZOETROPE
ZOETROPES
ZOFTIG
ZOIC
ZOISITE
ZOISITES
ZOMBI
ZOMBIE
ZOMBIELIKE
ZOMBIES
ZOMBIFICATION
ZOMBIFICATIONS
ZOMBIFIED
ZOMBIFIES
ZOMBIFY
ZOMBIFYING
ZOMBIISM
ZOMBIISMS
ZOMBIS
ZONA
ZONAE
ZONAL
ZONALLY
ZONARY
ZONATE
ZONATED
ZONATION
ZONATIONS
ZONE
ZONED
ZONELESS
ZONER
ZONERS
ZONES
ZONETIME
ZONETIMES
ZONING
ZONINGS
ZONK
ZONKED
ZONKING
ZONKS
ZONULA
ZONULAE
ZONULAR
ZONULAS
ZONULE
ZONULES
ZOO
ZOOCHORE
ZOOCHORES
ZOOECIA
ZOOECIUM
ZOOEY
ZOOGAMETE
ZOOGAMETES
ZOOGENIC
ZOOGENIES
ZOOGENOUS
ZOOGENY
ZOOGEOGRAPHER
ZOOGEOGRAPHERS
ZOOGEOGRAPHIC
ZOOGEOGRAPHICAL
ZOOGEOGRAPHIES
ZOOGEOGRAPHY
ZOOGLEA
ZOOGLEAE
ZOOGLEAL
ZOOGLEAS
ZOOGLOEA
ZOOGLOEAE
ZOOGLOEAL
ZOOGLOEAS
ZOOGLOEIC
ZOOGRAPHIES
ZOOGRAPHY
ZOOID
ZOOIDAL
ZOOIDS
ZOOIER
ZOOIEST
ZOOKEEPER
ZOOKEEPERS
ZOOKS
ZOOLATER
ZOOLATERS
ZOOLATRIES
ZOOLATRY
ZOOLOGIC
ZOOLOGICAL
ZOOLOGICALLY
ZOOLOGIES
ZOOLOGIST
ZOOLOGISTS
ZOOLOGY
ZOOM
ZOOMABLE
ZOOMANIA
ZOOMANIAS
ZOOMED
ZOOMETRIC
ZOOMETRIES
ZOOMETRY
ZOOMING
ZOOMORPH
ZOOMORPHIC
ZOOMORPHS
ZOOMS
ZOON
ZOONAL
ZOONED
ZOONING
ZOONOSES
ZOONOSIS
ZOONOTIC
ZOONS
ZOOPHILE
ZOOPHILES
ZOOPHILIA
ZOOPHILIAS
ZOOPHILIC
ZOOPHILIES
ZOOPHILOUS
ZOOPHILY
ZOOPHOBE
ZOOPHOBES
ZOOPHOBIA
ZOOPHOBIAS
ZOOPHYTE
ZOOPHYTES
ZOOPHYTIC
ZOOPLANKTER
ZOOPLANKTERS
ZOOPLANKTON
ZOOPLANKTONIC
ZOOPLANKTONS
ZOOS
ZOOSPERM
ZOOSPERMS
ZOOSPORANGIA
ZOOSPORANGIUM
ZOOSPORE
ZOOSPORES
ZOOSPORIC
ZOOSTEROL
ZOOSTEROLS
ZOOTECHNICAL
ZOOTECHNICS
ZOOTIER
ZOOTIEST
ZOOTOMIC
ZOOTOMIES
ZOOTOMIST
ZOOTOMISTS
ZOOTOMY
ZOOTY
ZOOXANTHELLA
ZOOXANTHELLAE
ZORI
ZORIL
ZORILLA
ZORILLAS
ZORILLE
ZORILLES
ZORILLO
ZORILLOS
ZORILS
ZORIS
ZOSTER
ZOSTERS
ZOUAVE
ZOUAVES
ZOUK
ZOUKS
ZOUNDS
ZOWEE
ZOWIE
ZOYSIA
ZOYSIAS
ZUCCHETTI
ZUCCHETTO
ZUCCHETTOS
ZUCCHINI
ZUCCHINIS
ZUGZWANG
ZUGZWANGS
ZUPPA
ZUPPAS
ZUZ
ZUZIM
ZWIEBACK
ZWIEBACKS
ZWITTERION
ZWITTERIONIC
ZWITTERIONS
ZYDECO
ZYDECOS
ZYGAPOPHYSES
ZYGAPOPHYSIS
ZYGODACTYL
ZYGODACTYLOUS
ZYGOID
ZYGOMA
ZYGOMAS
ZYGOMATA
ZYGOMATIC
ZYGOMATICS
ZYGOMORPHIC
ZYGOMORPHIES
ZYGOMORPHY
ZYGOSE
ZYGOSES
ZYGOSIS
ZYGOSITIES
ZYGOSITY
ZYGOSPORE
ZYGOSPORES
ZYGOTE
ZYGOTENE
ZYGOTENES
ZYGOTES
ZYGOTIC
ZYMASE
ZYMASES
ZYME
ZYMES
ZYMOGEN
ZYMOGENE
ZYMOGENES
ZYMOGENIC
ZYMOGENS
ZYMOGRAM
ZYMOGRAMS

MOLOGIC
MOLOGIES
MOLOGY
MOLYSES
ZYMOLYSIS
ZYMOLYTIC
ZYMOMETER
ZYMOMETERS
ZYMOSAN
ZYMOSANS
ZYMOSES
ZYMOSIS
ZYMOTIC
ZYMURGIES
ZYMURGY
ZYZZYVA
ZYZZYVAS
ZZZ